T3-BOE-864

THE INTERNATIONAL STANDARD BIBLE ENCYCLOPAEDIA

John L. Nuelsen.

Associate Editor, International Standard Bible Encyclopaedia

THE
INTERNATIONAL STANDARD BIBLE ENCYCLOPAEDIA

JAMES ORR, M.A., D.D., GENERAL EDITOR

JOHN L. NUELSEN, D.D., LL.D.

EDGAR Y. MULLINS, D.D., LL.D.
ASSISTANT EDITORS

MORRIS O. EVANS, D.D., PH.D., MANAGING EDITOR

MELVIN GROVE KYLE, D.D., LL.D., REVISING EDITOR

VOLUME II
CLEMENT—HERESH

WM. B. EERDMANS PUBLISHING CO.
GRAND RAPIDS, MICH.
1949

Printed in the United States of America
by J. J. Little & Ives Company, New York

CLEMENT, klem'ent (**Κλήμης**, *Klēmēs*, "mild"): A fellow-worker with Paul at Philippi, mentioned with especial commendation in Phil **4** 3. The name being common, no inference can be drawn from this statement as to any identity with the author of the Epistle to the Corinthians published under this name, who was also the third bishop of Rome. The truth of this supposition ("it cannot be called a tradition," Donaldson, *The Apostolical Fathers*, 120), although found in Origen, Eusebius, Epiphanius and Jerome, can neither be proved nor disproved. Even Roman Catholic authorities dispute it (art. "Clement," *Cath. Cyclopaedia*, IV, 13). The remoteness between the two in time and place is against it; "a wholly uncritical view" (Cruttwell, *Literary History of Early Christianity*, 31). H. E. JACOBS

CLEOPAS, klē'ō-pas (**Κλεόπας**, *Kleópas*, "renowned father"): One of the two disciples whom Jesus met on the way to Emmaus (Lk **24** 18). The name is a contraction of Cleopatros, not identical with Clopas of Jn **19** 25. See also ALPHAEUS; CLOPAS.

CLEOPATRA, klē-ō-pā'tra (**Κλεοπάτρα**, *Kleopátra*, "from a famous father"): A daughter of Ptolemy VI (Philometor) and of Queen Cleopatra, who was married first to Alexander Balas 150 BC (1 Macc **10** 58; Jos, *Ant*, XIII, iv, 1) and was afterward taken from him by her father and given to Demetrius Nicator on the invasion of Syria by the latter (1 Macc **11** 12; Jos, *Ant*, XIII, iv, 7). Alexander was killed in battle against the joint forces of Ptolemy and Demetrius while Demetrius was in captivity in Parthia. Cleopatra married his brother Antiochus VII (Sidetes), who in the absence of Demetrius had gained possession of the Syrian throne (137 BC). She was probably privy (Appian, *Syr.*, 68) to the murder of Demetrius on his return to Syria 125 BC, but Josephus (*Ant*, XIII, ix, 3) gives a different account of his death. She afterward murdered Seleucus, her eldest son by Nicator, who on his father's death had taken possession of the government without her consent. She attempted unsuccessfully to poison her second son by Nicator, Antiochus VIII (Grypus), for whom she had secured the succession, because he was unwilling to concede to her what she considered her due share of power. She was herself poisoned (120 BC) by the draught which she had prepared for their son (Justin 39). She had also a son by Antiochus VII (Sidetes Antiochus Cyzicenus), who took his name from the place in which he was educated. He was killed in battle 95 BC. The name Cleopatra was borne by many Egyp princesses, the first of whom was daughter of Antiochus III and was married to Ptolemy V (Epiphanes) 193 BC. J. HUTCHISON

CLEOPHAS, klē'ō-fas. See CLOPAS.

CLERK. See TOWN CLERK.

CLIFF, CLIFT. See CLEFT.

CLOAK, klōk, **CLOKE** (מְעִיל, *me'īl*, שִׂמְלָה, *simlāh*, etc; **ἱμάτιον**, *himátion*, **στολή**, *stolḗ*, etc): "Cloke" is retained in ERV, as in AV, instead of mod. "cloak" (ARV). In the OT, *me'īl* (cf NT *himation*) uniformly stands for the ordinary upper garment worn over the coat (*kethōneth*). In Mt **5** 40 both "cloak" and "coat" are mentioned together; cf Lk **6** 29. In size and material the "cloak" differed according to age and sex, class and occupation, but in shape it was like our mantle or shawl. It might be sewed up to have the surplice form of the robe of the Ephod (Ex **39** 23), or be worn loose and open like a Rom toga, the Arab. *Abaa*, or the Geneva gown. This is the "garment" referred to in Gen **39** 12; Ex **22** 26; Dt **24** 13; "the robe" that Jonathan "stripped himself of" and gave to David (1 S **18** 4); "the robe" of Saul, "the robe" in which it is said the "old man" (Samuel) was "covered" (1 S **28** 14); and in the NT "the best robe" put on the returning prodigal (Lk **15** 22). Paul's "cloak" that he left at Troas (2 Tim **4** 13; *phainólēs*, Lat *paenula*, WH *phelonēs*), it has been suggested, "may have been a light mantle like a cashmere dust-cloak, in which the books and parchment were wrapped" (*HDB*, s.v.).

Figuratively: The word lent itself easily and naturally to fig. uses. We find Paul (1 Thess **2** 5) disclaiming using "a cloak of covetousness" (cf 1 Pet **2** 16) and Jesus (Jn **15** 22) saying, "Now they have no excuse ["cloak"] for their sin." Some such usage seems common to all languages; cf Eng. "palliate." See DRESS. GEO. B. EAGER

CLOD: In Job **7** 5 (גִּישׁ, *gīsh*, גּוּשׁ, *gūsh*, "a mass of earth"), "clods of dust," the crust of his sores, formed by the dry, swollen skin—a symptom of leprosy, though not peculiar to it. In Job **21** 33; **38** 38 (רֶגֶב, *reghebh*, "a soft clod," "lump of clay"), "The clods of the valley shall be sweet unto him," "The clods cleave fast together." In Joel **1** 17 (מֶגְרָפָה, *meghrāphāh*, "a furrow," "something thrown off" [by the spade]), "The seeds rot [m "shrivel"] under their clods."

Figurative: "Jacob shall break his clods" (Hos **10** 11), i.e. "must harrow for himself," used fig. of spiritual discipline (cf Isa **28** 24 AV). M. O. EVANS

CLOPAS, klō'pas (**Κλωπᾶς**, *Klōpás*), **CLEOPHAS:** The former in RV, the latter in AV, of Jn **19** 25, for the name of the husband of one of the women who stood by the cross of Christ. Upon the philological ground of a variety in pronunciation of the Heb root, sometimes identified with Alphaeus, the father of James the Less. Said by tradition to have been the brother of Joseph, the husband of Mary; see BRETHREN OF THE LORD. Distinguished from Cleopas, a Gr word, while Clopas is Aram.

CLOSE, vb. klōz; adj. and advb., klōs (כָּסָה, *kāṣāh*, סָגַר, *ṣāghar;* **καμμύω**, *kammúō*): Other words are *ḥārāh*, "to burn"; "Shalt thou reign, because thou closest thyself in cedar?" (Jer **22** 15 AV), RV "strivest to excel in cedar," m "viest with the cedar"; *'āçam*, "to harden"; "Jeh hath closed your eyes" (Isa **29** 10); *gādhar*, "to hedge" or "wall up" (Am **9** 11); *'āçar*, "to restrain" (Gen **20** 18). In Lk **4** 20, *ptússō*, "to fold up." RV has "was closed," m "is opened," for "are open" (Nu **24** 3.15), "closed" for "narrow" or "covered" (Ezk **40** 16; **41** 16.26). To "keep close," *sigáō* (Lk **9** 36), RV "held their peace." We have also "kept close" (RV Nu **5** 13; Heb *ṣāthar*, "to hide"); also Job **28** 21; "kept himself close," RVm "shut up" (1 Ch **12** 1); "close places," *miṣgereth* (2 S **22** 46; Ps **18** 45="castles or holds shut in with high walls"). W. L. WALKER

CLOSET, kloz'et: Is the rendering in AV of (1) חֻפָּה, *ḥuppāh*, and (2) **ταμεῖον**, *tameion*, also *tamieion*. *Ḥuppāh*, derived from *ḥāphāh*, "to cover," was probably originally the name of the tent specially set apart for the bride, and later (Joel **2** 16) used for the bride's chamber. The word *tameion*, originally storeroom (cf Lk **12** 24, AV "storehouse"; RV "storechamber"), but since for safety it was the inner rooms of the Heb house which were used for storage purposes, the word came to mean inner room, as in Mt **6** 6; Lk **12** 3, in both AV "closet" (cf Mt **24** 26, AV "secret chamber"). In all cases RV uses "inner chamber." See also House.

David Foster Estes

CLOTH, kloth, **CLOTHING,** klōth'ing. See Dress.

CLOTHED, klōthd, **UPON** (ἐπενδύω, *ependúō*, "to put on over" another garment): Used only in 2 Cor **5** 2.4. In ver 4 in contrast with unclothed, cf 1 Cor **15** 53 f, in which the idea of putting on, as a garment, is expressed of incorruption and immortality. The meaning here is very subtle and difficult of interpretation. In all probability Paul thinks of a certain enswathement of his physical mortal body even in this life ("in this we groan," i.e. in this present body), hence the force of the prefixed preposition. The body itself was regarded by the philosophers of his day as a covering of the soul, and hence it was to be clothed upon and at the same time transformed by the superimposed heavenly body. *Ependútēs*, an outer garment, is used several times in LXX for *me'īl*, an upper garment or robe (cf Jn **21** 7).

Walter G. Clippinger

CLOTHES, klōthz, **RENDING OF** (קְרִיעַת בְּגָדִים, *k^erī'ath b^eghādhīm*): This term is used to describe an ordinary tear made in a garment. Samuel's skirt was rent when Saul laid hold upon it (1 S **15** 27). Jesus spoke about a rent being made in a garment (Mt **9** 16). The term is also used to describe a Heb custom which indicated deep sorrow. Upon the death of a relative or important personage, or when there was a great calamity, it was customary for the Hebrews to tear their garments. Reuben rent his clothes when he found that Joseph had been taken from the pit (Gen **37** 29). The sons of Jacob rent their clothes when the cup was found in Benjamin's sack (Gen **44** 13). A messenger came to Eli with his clothes rent to tell of the taking of the ark of God and of the death of his two sons (1 S **4** 12). David rent his garments when he heard that Absalom had slain his brothers (2 S **13** 31). See also 2 S **15** 32; 2 K **18** 37; Isa **36** 22; Jer **41** 5. Rending of clothes was also an expression of indignation. The high priest rent his garment when Jesus spoke what he thought was blasphemy (Mt **26** 65). See also Mourning.

A. W. Fortune

CLOUD, kloud (עָנָן, *'ānān*, עָב, *'ābh*; νεφέλη, *nephélē*, νέφος, *néphos*):

I. Clouds in Palestine.—In the Bible few references are found of particular clouds or of clouds in connection with the phenomena of the weather conditions. The weather in Pal is more even and has less variety than that in other lands. It is a long, narrow country with sea on the W. and desert on the E. The wind coming from the W. is always moist and brings clouds with it. If the temperature over the land is low enough the clouds will be condensed and rain will fall, but if the temperature is high, as in the five months of summer, there can be no rain even though clouds are seen. As a whole the winter is cloudy and the summer clear.

1. Rain Clouds

In the autumn rain storms often arise suddenly from the sea, and what seems to be a mere haze, "as small as a man's hand," such as Gehazi saw (1 K **18** 44) over the sea, within a few hours becomes the black storm cloud pouring down torrents of rain (1 K **18** 45). Fog is almost unknown and there is very seldom an overcast, gloomy day. The west and southwest winds bring rain (Lk **12** 54).

2. Disagreeable Clouds

In the months of April, May and September a hot east wind sometimes rises from the desert and brings with it a cloud of dust which fills the air and penetrates everything. In the summer afternoons, esp. in the month of August, on the seacoast there is apt to blow up from the S. a considerable number of low cirro-stratus clouds which seem to fill the air with dampness, making more oppressive the dead heat of summer. These are doubtless the detested "clouds without water" mentioned in Jude ver 12, and "heat by the shade of a cloud" (Isa **25** 5).

II. Figurative Uses.—The metaphoric and symbolic uses of clouds are many, and furnish some of the most powerful figures of Scripture.

1. Jehovah's Presence and Glory

In the OT, Jeh's presence is made manifest and His glory shown forth in a cloud. The cloud is usually spoken of as bright and shining, and it could not be fathomed by man: "Thou hast covered thyself with a cloud, so that no prayer can pass through" (Lam **3** 44). Jeh Himself was present in the cloud (Ex **19** 9; **24** 16; **34** 5) and His glory filled the places where the cloud was (Ex **16** 10; **40** 38; Nu **10** 34); "The cloud filled the house of Jeh" (1 K **8** 10). In the NT we often have "the Son of man coming on" or "with clouds" (Mt **24** 30; **26** 64; Mk **13** 26; **14** 62; Lk **21** 27) and received up by clouds (Acts **1** 9). The glory of the second coming is indicated in Rev **1** 7 for "he cometh with the clouds" and "we that are alive . . . . shall together with them be caught up in the clouds, to meet the Lord" and dwell with Him (1 Thess **4** 17).

2. Pillar of Cloud

The pillar of cloud was a symbol of God's guidance and presence to the children of Israel in their journeys to the promised land. The Lord appeared in a pillar of cloud and forsook them not (Neh **9** 19). They followed the guidance of this cloud (Ex **40** 36; Ps **78** 14).

3. Bow in Cloud

The clouds are spoken of in the OT as the symbol of God's presence and care over His people; and so the "bow in the cloud" (Gen **9** 13) is a sign of God's protection.

4. Clouds Blot Out

As the black cloud covers the sky and blots out the sun from sight, so Jeh promises "to blot out the sins" of Israel (Isa **44** 22); Egypt also shall be conquered, "As for her, a cloud shall cover her" (Ezk **30** 18; cf Lam **2** 1).

5. Transitory

There is usually a wide difference in temperature between day and night in Pal. The days are warm and clouds coming from the sea are often completely dissolved in the warm atmosphere over the land. As the temperature falls, the moisture again condenses into dew and mist over the hills and valleys. As the sun rises the "morning cloud" (Hos **6** 4) is quickly dispelled and disappears entirely. Job compares the passing of his prosperity to the passing clouds (Job **30** 15).

6. God's Omnipotence and Man's Ignorance

God "bindeth up the waters in his thick clouds" (Job **26** 8) and the "clouds are the dust of his feet" (Nah **1** 3). Jeh "commands the clouds that they rain no rain" (Isa **5** 6), but as for man, "who can number the clouds?" (Job **38** 37); "Can any understand the spreadings of the clouds?" (Job **36** 29); "Dost thou know the balancings of the clouds, the wondrous works of him who is perfect in knowledge?" (Job **37** 16). See Balancings. "He that regardeth the clouds shall not reap" (Eccl **11** 4), for it is God who controls the clouds and man cannot fathom His wisdom. "Thick clouds are a covering to him" (Job **22** 14).

Clouds are the central figure in many visions. Ezekiel beheld "a stormy wind . . . . out of the north, a great cloud" (Ezk **1** 4), and John saw "a white cloud; and on the cloud one sitting" (Rev **14** 14). See also Dnl **7** 13; Rev **10** 1; **11** 12.

7. Visions

The cloud is also the symbol of the terrible and of destruction. The day of Jeh's reckoning is called the "day of clouds" (Ezk **30** 3) and a day of "clouds and thick darkness" (Zeph **1** 15). The invader is expected to "come up as clouds" (Jer **4** 13). Joel (**2** 2) foretells the coming of locusts as "a day of clouds and thick darkness" which is both literal and figurative. Misfortune and old age are compared to "the cloudy and dark day" (Ezk **34** 12) and "the clouds returning after rain" (Eccl **12** 2).

8. The Terrible and Unpleasant

Clouds are used in connection with various other figures. Rapidity of motion, "these that fly as a cloud" (Isa **60** 8). As swaddling clothes of the newborn earth (Job **38** 9); indicating great height (Job **20** 6) and fig. in Isa **14** 14, "I will ascend above the heights of the clouds," portraying the self-esteem of Babylon. "A morning without clouds" is the symbol of righteousness and justice (2 S **23** 4); partial knowledge and hidden glory (Lev **16** 2; Acts **1** 9; Rev **1** 7).

9. Various Other Figures

ALFRED H. JOY

CLOUD, PILLAR OF. See CLOUD, II, 2; PILLAR OF CLOUD.

CLOUT, klout: As subst. (הַסְּחָבוֹת, *ha-ṣeḥābhōth*) a patch or piece of cloth, leather, or the like, a rag, a shred, or fragment. Old "cast clouts and old rotten rags" (Jer **38** 11.12 AV). As vb. (טָלָא, *ṭālā'*) "to bandage," "patch," or mend with a clout. "Old shoes and clouted [ARV "patched"] upon their feet" (Josh **9** 5; cf Shakespeare, *Cym.*, IV, 2: "I thought he slept, And put my *clouted* brogues from off my feet"; Milton, *Comus:* "And the dull swain treads on it daily with his *clouted* shoon."

CLOVEN, klō'v'n: In the OT, represented by a participle from שָׁסַע, *shāṣa'*, "to split," and applied to beasts that divide the hoof (Lev **11** 3; Dt **14** 7). Beasts with hoofs completely divided into two parts, that were also ruminant, were allowed the Israelites as food; see CUD; HOOF. In the NT, for διαμεριζόμεναι, *diamerizómenai*, in Acts **2** 3 AV, RV "tongues parting asunder," i.e. "bifurcated flames." Another explanation found in RVm applies the word, not to tongues, but to the multitude, "parting among them," or "distributing themselves among them," settling upon the head of each disciple. H. E. JACOBS

CLUB, klub. See ARMOR, III, 1; SHEPHERD; STAFF.

CLUSTER, klus'tēr:

(1) אֶשְׁכֹּל, *'eshkōl;* cf proper name VALE OF ESHCOL (q.v.), from root meaning "to bind together." A cluster or bunch of grapes (Gen **40** 10; Nu **13** 23; Isa **65** 8; Cant **7** 8; Mic **7** 1, etc); a cluster of henna flowers (Cant **1** 14); a cluster of dates (Cant **7** 7). "Their grapes are grapes of gall, their clusters are bitter" (Dt **32** 32).

(2) βότρυς, *bótrus*, "gather the clusters of the vine of the earth" (Rev **14** 18).

The "cluster of raisins" (*çimmūḳīm*) of 1 S **25** 18; **30** 12, should rather be "raisin cakes" or "dried raisins." E. W. G. MASTERMAN

CNIDUS, nī'dus, knī'dus (**Κνίδος**, *Knídos*, "age"): A city of Caria in the Rom province of Asia, past which, according to Acts **27** 7, Paul sailed. At the S.W. corner of Asia Minor there projects for 90 miles into the sea a long, narrow peninsula, practically dividing the Aegean from the Mediterranean. It now bears the name of Cape Crio. Ships sailing along the southern coast of Asia Minor here turn northward as they round the point. Upon the very end of the peninsula, and also upon a small island off its point was the city of Cnidus. The island which in ancient times was connected with the mainland by a causeway is now joined to it by a sandy bar. Thus were formed two harbors, one of which could be closed by a chain. Though Cnidus was in Caria, it held the rank of a free city. There were Jews here as early as the 2d cent. BC.

The ruins of Cnidus are the only objects of interest on the long peninsula, and as they may be reached by land only with great difficulty, few travelers have visited them; they may, however, be reached more easily by boat. The nearest modern village is Yazi Keui, 6 miles away. The ruins of Cnidus are unusually interesting, for the entire plan of the city may easily be traced. The sea-walls and piers remain. The acropolis was upon the hill in the western portion of the town; upon the terraces below stood the public buildings, among which were two theaters and the odeum still well preserved. The city was esp. noted for its shrine of Venus and for the statue of that goddess by Praxiteles. Here in 1875–78 Sir C. Newton discovered the statue of Demeter, now in the British Museum. See also the Aphrodite of Cnidus in the South Kensington Museum, one of the loveliest statues in the world. From here also came the huge Cnidian lion. The vast necropolis W. of the ruins contains tombs of every size and shape, and from various ages. E. J. BANKS

COAL, kōl (פֶּחָם, *peḥam*, "charcoal"; cf Arab. *faḥm*, "charcoal"; גַּחֶלֶת, *gaḥeleth*, "burning coal" or "hot ember"; cf Arab. *jaḥam*, "to kindle"; שְׁחוֹר, *sheḥōr*, "a black coal" [Lam **4** 8]; cf Arab. *shaḥḥār*, "soot" or "dark-colored sandstone"; רֶצֶף, *reçeph* [1 K **19** 6], and רִצְפָּה, *riçpāh* [=Rizpah] [Isa **6** 6], m "a hot stone"; cf רֶשֶׁף, *resheph*, "a flame" [Cant **8** 6; Hab **3** 5]; **ἄνθραξ**, *ánthrax*, "a live coal" [Rom **12** 20] [=*gaḥeleth* in Prov **25** 22]; **ἀνθρακιά**, *anthrakiá*, "a live coal" [Jn **18** 18; **21** 9]): There is no reference to mineral coal in the Bible. Coal, or more properly lignite, of inferior quality, is found in thin beds (not exceeding 3 ft.) in the sandstone formation (see GEOLOGY, Nubian Sandstone), but there is no evidence of its use in ancient times. Charcoal is manufactured in a primitive fashion which does not permit the conservation of any by-products. A flat, circular place (Arab. *beidar*, same name as for a threshing-floor) 10 or 15 ft. in diameter is prepared in or conveniently near to the forest. On this the wood, to be converted into charcoal, is carefully stacked in a dome-shaped structure, leaving an open space in the middle for fine kindlings. All except the center is first covered with leaves, and then with earth. The kindlings in the center are then fired and afterward covered in the same manner as the rest. While it is burning or smoldering it is carefully watched, and earth is immediately placed upon any holes that may be formed in the covering by the burning of the wood below. In several days, more or less, according to the size of the pile, the wood is converted into charcoal and the heap is opened. The charcoal floor is also called in Arab. *mashḥarah*, from *shaḥḥār*, "soot"; cf Heb *sheḥōr*. The characteristic odor of the *mashḥarah* clings for months to the spot.

In Ps **120** 4, there is mention of "coals of juniper," RVm "broom," *rōthem*. This is doubtless the Arab. *retem*, *Retama roetam*, Forsk., a kind of broom which is abundant in Judaea and Moab. Charcoal from oak wood, especially *Quercus coccifera*, L., Arab. *sindyān*, is much preferred to other kinds, and fetches a higher price.

In most of the passages where Eng. VSS have "coal," the reference is not necessarily to charcoal, but may be to coals of burning wood. *Peḥam* in Prov **26** 21, however, seems to stand for charcoal:

> "As coals are to hot embers, and wood to fire,
> So is a contentious man to inflame strife."

The same may be true of *peḥam* in Isa **44** 12 and **54** 16; also of *shehōr* in Lam **4** 8.

Alfred Ely Day

COAST, kōst (גְּבוּל, *gebhūl*, etc, "boundary"; cf גֶּבֶל, *gebhal*, "mountain," and Arab. *jebel*, "mountain"; חֶבֶל, *ḥebhel*, lit. "a rope"; cf Arab. *ḥabl* [Josh **19** 29 AV; Zeph **2** 5.6.7]; חוֹף, *ḥōph*, lit. "that which is washed"; cf Arab. *ḥăffet* [Josh **9** 1 AV; Ezk **25** 16]; **παράλιος,** *parálios*, lit. "by the sea" [Lk **6** 17]): "Coast" (fr Lat *costa*, "rib" or "side") in the sense of "seacoast," occurs but a few times in the Bible. In nearly all the many passages where AV has "coast," RV correctly has "border," i.e. "boundary," translating *gebhūl*, etc; in Acts **27** 2 ARV, "coast" is the tr of *τόπος*, *tópos*, lit. "place." That the seacoast is but seldom mentioned arises naturally from the fact that, while the promised land extended to the sea, the coast was never effectively occupied by the Israelites.

RVm in a number of places renders *'ī*, EV "isle" or "island" (q.v.), by "coastland," e.g. Isa **11** 11; **23** 6; **24** 15; **59** 18; Jer **25** 22; Ezk **39** 6; Dnl **11** 18; Zeph **2** 11. In Isa **20** 6, AV has "isle," AVm "country," and RV "coast-land." In Jer **47** 4, AV has "country," AVm and RV "isle," and RVm "sea-coast." See Isle.

Alfred Ely Day

COAT, kōt. See Cloak; Dress, etc.

COAT OF MAIL, māl. See Armor, Arms; Brigandine.

COCK, kok (**ἀλέκτωρ,** *alḗktōr;* Lat *gallus*): There is no reference in the OT to domesticated poultry, which was probably first introduced into Judaea after the Rom conquest. See Chicken. The cock is several times mentioned in the NT and always with reference to its habit of crowing in eastern countries with such regularity as to be almost clocklike. The first full salute comes almost to the minute at half-past eleven, the second at half-past one, and the third at dawn. So uniformly do the cocks keep time and proclaim these three periods of night that we find cock-crowing mentioned as a regular division of time: "Watch therefore: for ye know not when the lord of the house cometh, whether at even, or at midnight, or at cockcrowing, or in the morning" (Mk **13** 35). Jesus had these same periods of night in mind when he warned Peter that he would betray Him. Mt **26** 34; Lk **22** 34; Jn **13** 38, give almost identical wording of the warning. But in all his writing Mark was more explicit, more given to exact detail. Remembering the divisions of night as the cocks kept them, his record reads: "And Jesus saith unto him, Verily I say into thee, that thou today, even this night, before the cock crow twice, shalt deny me thrice" (Mk **14** 30). See Chicken. It is hardly necessary to add that the cocks crow at irregular intervals as well as at the times indicated, according to the time of the year and the phase of the moon (being more liable to crow during the night if the moon is at the full), or if a storm threatens, or there is any disturbance in their neighborhood.

Gene Stratton-Porter

COCKATRICE, kok'a-tris, kok'a-trīs (צֶפַע, *çepha';* צִפְעֹנִי, *çiph'ōnī;* LXX, **βασιλίσκος,** *basilískos*, "basilisk" [q.v.], and **ἀσπίς,** *aspís*, "asp" [see Adder; Asp; Serpent]): A fabulous, deadly, monster. The name "cockatrice" appears to be a corruption of Lat *calcatrix*, from *calcare*, "to tread," *calcatrix* being in turn a tr of the Gr *ἰχνεύμων*, *ichneúmōn*, from *ἴχνος*, *íchnos*, "track" or "footstep." *Herpestes ichneumon*, the ichneumon, Pharaoh's rat, or mongoose, a weasel-like animal, is a native of northern Africa and southern Spain. There are also other species, including the Indian mongoose. It preys on rats and snakes, and does not despise poultry and eggs.

Pliny (see *Oxford Dictionary*, s.v. "Cockatrice") relates that the ichneumon darts down the open mouth of the crocodile, and destroys it by gnawing through its belly. In the course of time, as the story underwent changes, the animal was metamorphosed into a water snake, and was confused with the crocodile itself, and also with the basilisk. According to the *Encyclopaedia Britannica*, 11th ed, the cockatrice was believed as late as the 17th cent. to be produced from a cock's egg and hatched by a serpent, and "to possess the most deadly powers, plants withering at its touch, and men and animals being poisoned by its look. It stood in awe however of the cock, the sound of whose crowing killed it. . . . . The weasel alone among animals was unaffected by the glance of its evil eye, and attacked it at all times successfully; for when wounded by the monster's teeth it found a ready remedy in rue, the only plant which the cockatrice could not wither." The real ichneumon does kill the most deadly snakes, and has been supposed to resort to a vegetable antidote when bitten. It actually dies however when bitten by a deadly snake, and does not possess a knowledge of herbs, but its extraordinary agility enables it ordinarily to escape injury. It is interesting to see how the changing tale of this creature with its marvelous powers has made a hodge-podge of ichneumon, weasel, crocodile, and serpent.

The Bib. references (AV Isa **11** 8; **59** 5; Jer **8** 17) are doubtless to a serpent, the word "cockatrice," with its mediaeval implications, having been introduced by the translators of AV. See Serpent.

Alfred Ely Day

COCK-CROWING, kok'krō-ing (**ἀλεκτοροφωνία,** *alektorophōnía*): An indefinite hour of the night between midnight and morning (Mk **13** 35), referred to by all the evangelists in their account of Peter's denial (Mt **26** 34.74; Mk **14** 30; Lk **22** 34; Jn **13** 38). It is derived from the habit of the cock to crow esp. toward morning. See Cock.

COCKER, kok'ẽr (**τιθηνέω,** *tithēnéō*, "to nurse," "coddle," "pamper"): Occurs only in Ecclus **30** 9 with the meaning "to pamper": "Cocker thy child, and he shall make thee afraid"; so Shakespeare, "a cockered silken wanton"; now seldom used; Jean Ingelow, "Poor folks cannot afford to cocker themselves."

COCKLE, kok''l (AVm "stinking weeds," RVm "noisome weeds"; בָּאְשָׁה, *bo'shāh*, from Heb root בָּאַשׁ, *bā'ash*, "to stink"; **βάτος,** *bátos*): "Let thistles grow instead of wheat, and cockle instead of barley" (Job **31** 40). On account of the meaning of the Heb root we should expect that the reference was rather to repulsive, offensive weeds than to the pretty corn cockle. It is very possible that no particular plant is here intended, though the common Palestinian "stinking" arums have been suggested by Hooker.

CODE OF HAMMURABI. See Hammurabi Code of.

COELE-SYRIA, sē-lē-sir'i-a (AV **Celosyria; Κοίλη Συρία,** *Koílē Suria*, "hollow Syria"): So the Greeks after the time of Alexander the Great named the valley lying between the two mountain ranges, Lebanon and Anti-Lebanon. It is referred to in the OT as *Biḳ'ath ha-L^ebhānōn*, "the valley of Lebanon" (Josh **11** 17), a name the echo of which is still heard in *el-Buḳā'*, the designation applied today to the southern part of the valley. This hollow, which extends about 100 miles in length, is the continuation northward of the Jordan valley. The main physical features are described under LEBANON (q.v.). The name, however, did not always indicate the same tract of territory. In Strabo (xvi.2) and Ptolemy (v.15), it covers the fertile land between *Jebel esh-Sharḳy* and the desert presided over by Damascus. In 1 Esd **2** 17; 2 Macc **3** 8, etc, it indicates the country S. and E. of Mt. Lebanon, and along with Phoenicia it contributed the whole of the Seleucid dominions which lay S. of the river Eleutherus. Jos includes in Coele-Syria the country E. of the Jordan, along with Scythopolis (Beisan) which lay on the W., separated by the river from the other members of the Decapolis (*Ant*, XIII, xiii, 2, etc). In XIV, iv, 5, he says that "Pompey committed Coele-Syria as far as the river Euphrates and Egypt to Scaurus." The term is therefore one of some elasticity.

W. EWING

COFFER, kof'ẽr (אַרְגָּז, *'argāz*): A small box such as that in which the Philis placed their golden mice and other offerings in returning the Ark (1 S **6** 8.11.15).

COFFIN, kof'in. See CHEST; BURIAL.

COGITATION, koj-i-tā'shun, רַעְיוֹן, *ra'yōn*, "the act of thinking or reflecting," as in Dnl **7** 28, "my cogitations much troubled me" (RV "my thoughts").

COHORT, kō'hort: In RVm of Mt **27** 27; Mk **15** 16; Jn **18** 3.12; Acts **10** 1; **21** 31; **27** 1, the tr of *speíra* (AV and RV, "band"); the tenth part of a legion; ordinarily about 600 men. In Jn **18** the word seems to be used loosely of a smaller body of soldiers, a detachment, detail. See ARMY; BAND.

COINS, koinz: There were no coins in use in Pal until after the Captivity. It is not quite certain whether gold and silver were before that time divided into pieces of a certain weight for use as money or not, but there can be no question of coinage proper until the Pers period. Darius I is credited with introducing a coinage system into his empire, and his were the first coins that came into use among the Jews, though it seems probable that coins were struck in Lydia in the time of Croesus, the contemporary of Cyrus the Great, and these coins were doubtless the model upon which Darius based his system, and they may have circulated to some extent in Babylonia before the return of the Jews. The only coins mentioned in the OT are the Darics (see DARIC), and these only in the RV, the word "dram" being used in AV (Ezr **2** 69; **8** 27; Neh **7** 70–72). The Jews had no native coins until the time of the Maccabees, who struck coins after gaining their independence about 143–141 BC. These kings struck silver and copper, or the latter, at least (see MONEY), in denominations of shekels and fractions of the shekel, until the dynasty was overthrown by the Romans. Other coins were certainly in circulation during the same period, esp. those of Alexander and his successors, the Ptolemies of Egypt and the Seleucids of Syria, both of whom bore sway over Pal before the rise of the Maccabees. Besides these coins there were the issues of some of the Phoen towns, which were allowed to strike coins by the Persians and the Seleucids. The coins of Tyre and Sidon, both silver and copper, must have circulated largely in Pal on account of the intimate commercial relations between the Jews and Phoenicians (for examples, see under MONEY). After the advent of the Romans the local coinage was restricted chiefly to the series of copper coins, such as the mites mentioned in the NT, the silver denarii being struck mostly at Rome, but circulating wherever the Romans went. The coins of the Herods and the Procurators are abundant, but all of copper, since the Romans did not allow the Jewish rulers to strike either silver or gold coins. At the time of the first revolt (66–70 AD) the Jewish leader, Simon, struck shekels again, or, as some numismatists think, he was the first to do so. But this series was a brief one, lasting between 3 and 4 years only, as Jerus was taken by Titus in 70 AD, and this put an end to the existence of the Jewish state. There was another short period of Jewish coinage during the second revolt, in the reign of Hadrian, when Simon Barcochba struck coins with Heb legends which indicate his independence of Rom rule. They were of both silver and copper, and constitute the last series of strictly Jewish coins (see MONEY). After this the coins struck in Judaea were Rom, as Jerus was made a Rom colony.

H. PORTER

COLA, kō'la. See CHOLA.

COLD, kōld (קֹר, *ḳōr*; ψυχρός, *psuchrós* [adj.], ψῦχος, *psúchos* [noun]): Pal is essentially a land of sunshine and warmth. The extreme cold of northern latitudes is unknown. January is the coldest month; but the degree of cold in a particular place depends largely on the altitude above the sea. On the seacoast and plain the snow never falls; and the temperature reaches freezing-point, perhaps once in thirty years. In Jerus at 2,500 ft. above the sea the mean temperature in January is about 45° F., but the minimum may be as low as 25° F. Snow occasionally falls, but lasts only a short time. On Mt. Hermon and on the Lebanons snow may be found the whole year, and the cold is most intense, even in the summer. In Jericho and around the Dead Sea, 1,292 ft. below sea-level, it is correspondingly hotter, and cold is not known.

1. Temperature in Palestine

Cold is of such short duration that no adequate provision is made by the people to protect themselves against the cold. The sun is always bright and warm, and nearly always shines for part of the day, even in winter. After sunset the people wrap themselves up and go to sleep. They prefer to wrap up their heads rather than their feet in order to keep warm. The only means of heating the houses is the charcoal brazier around which as many as possible gather for a little warmth. It is merely a bed of coals in an iron vessel. Peter was glad to avail himself of the little heat of the coals as late as the beginning of April, when the nights are often chilly in Jerus: "Having made a fire of coals; for it was cold: . . . . and Peter also was with them, standing and warming himself" (Jn **18** 18). There is no attempt made to heat the whole house. In the cold winter months the people of the mountains almost hibernate. They wrap up their heads in shawls and coverings and only the most energetic venture out: "The sluggard will not plow by reason of the winter" (Prov **20** 4, AV "cold"). The peasants and more primitive people of the desert often make a fire in the open or in partial shelter as in Melita where Paul was cast ashore after shipwreck: "The barbarians . . . . kindled a fire . . . . because of the cold" (Acts **28** 2).

2. Provision against Cold

The cold is greatly dreaded because it causes so much actual suffering: "Who can stand before his cold?" (Ps **147** 17). The last degree of degradation is to have "no covering in the cold" (Job **24** 7).

3. Dread of Cold

In the heat of the long summer, the shadow of a rock or the cool of evening is most grateful, and the appreciation of a cup of cold water can easily be understood by anyone who has experienced the burning heat of the Syrian sun: "As cold waters to a thirsty soul, so is good news from a far country" (Prov **25** 25); "cold of snow in the time of harvest" (Prov **25** 13), probably with reference to the use of snow (shaved ice) in the East to cool a beverage.

4. Cold Grateful in Summer

Figurative uses: "The love of the many shall wax cold" (Mt **24** 12); "I know thy works, that thou art neither cold nor hot" (Rev **3** 15).

Alfred H. Joy

COL-HOZEH, kol-hō'ze (כָּל־חֹזֶה, *kol-ḥōzeh,* "all seeing"; LXX omits): A man whose son Shallum rebuilt the fountain gate of Jerus in the days of Nehemiah (Neh **3** 15). The C. of Neh **11** 5 is probably another man.

COLIUS, kō'li-us (**Κώλιος,** ***Kōlios,*** **1** Esd **9** 23). See Calitas.

COLLAR, kol'ar, kol'ẽr:

(1) (נְטִיפָה, *neṭīphāh,* pl. נְטִיפוֹת, *neṭīphōth,* lit. "drops," from נָטַף, *nāṭaph,* "to drop"). Jgs **8** 26 includes *neṭīphōth* among the spoils taken from the Midianites and Ishmaelites; RV "pendants," AV "collars." Ḳimḥi ad loc. suggests "perfume-dropper."

(2) (פֶּה, *peh,* lit. "mouth"). In Job **30** 18 the word is used to indicate the collar band, or hole of a robe, through which the head was inserted. Job, in describing his suffering and writhing, mentions the disfiguring of his garment, and suggests that the whole thing feels as narrow or close-fitting as the neckband, or perhaps that in his fever and pains he feels as if the neckband itself is choking him.

(3) (צִינֹק, *çīnōḳ,* Jer **29** 26, "stocks"; RV "shackles," which see; RVm "collar"). An instrument of torture or punishment.

Nathan Isaacs

COLLECTION, kō-lek'shun:

(1) In the OT (מַשְׂאֵת, *mas'ēth,* "something taken up"), used in 2 Ch **24** 6.9 AV with reference to the tax prescribed in Ex **30** 12.16; RV "tax."

(2) In the NT "collection" is the tr given to λογία, *logia,* found only twice (classical, συλλογή, *sullogē*). It is used with reference to the collection which Paul took up in the gentile churches for the poor Christians in Jerus, as, for some reason, perhaps more severe persecutions, that church was esp. needy (1 Cor **16** 1.2; ver 2 AV "gatherings"). Other words, such as bounty, contribution, blessing, alms, ministration, are used to indicate this same ministry. Paul seems to have ascribed to it great importance. Therefore, he planned it carefully long in advance; urged systematic, weekly savings for it; had delegates carefully chosen to take it to Jerus; and, in spite of dangers, determined himself to accompany them. Evidently he thought it the crowning act of his work in the provinces of Galatia, Asia, Macedonia and Achaia, for as soon as it was finished he purposed to go to Rome and the West (Acts **24** 17; Rom **15** 25.26; 2 Cor **8**, **9**). See also Communion.

G. H. Trever

COLLEGE, kol'ej: This is the rendering of AV for Heb Mishneh (מִשְׁנֶה, *mishneh,* 2 K **22** 14 = 2 Ch **34** 22; cf Zeph **1** 10). It is found in the Tg of Jonathan on 2 K **22** 14 and rests on a faulty combination with Mish, the well-known code of laws of the 2d cent. AD. RV renders "second quarter" (of the city); 2 Ch **34** 22 AVm "the school."

COLLOP, kol'up (פִּימָה, *pīmāh*): A slice of meat or "fat," AV in Job **15** 27, "maketh collops of fat [thick folds of flesh] on his flanks," said of the "wicked man." ARV reads "[hath] gathered fat upon his loins."

COLONY, kol'ō-ni (**κολωνία,** *kolōnia,* Gr transliteration of Lat *colonia,* from √ *col,* "cultivate"): The word occurs but once (Acts **16** 12) in reference to Philippi in Macedonia. Rom colonies were of three kinds and of three periods: (1) Those of the early republic, in which the colonists, established in conquered towns to serve the state as guardians of the frontier, were exempt from ordinary military service. They were distinguished as (*a*) *c. civium Romanorum,* wherein the colonists retained Rom citizenship, also called *c. maritumae,* because situated on the coast, and (*b*) *c. Latinae,* situated inland among the allies (*socii*), wherein the colonists possessed the *ius Latinum,* entitling them to invoke the Rom law of property (*commercium*), but not that of the family (*connubium*), and received Rom citizenship only when elected to magistracies. (2) The colonies of the Gracchan period, established in pursuance of the scheme of agrarian reforms, to provide land for the poorer citizens. (3) After the time of Sulla colonies were founded in Italy by the Republic as a device for granting lands to retiring veterans, who of course retained citizenship. This privilege was appropriated by Caesar and the emperors, who employed it to establish military colonies, chiefly in the provinces, with various rights and internal organizations. To this class belonged Philippi. Partly organized after the great battle of 42 BC, fought in the neighboring plain by Brutus and Cassius, the champions of the fated Republic, and Antonius and Octavian, it was fully established as a colony by Octavian (afterward styled Augustus) after the battle of Actium (31 BC), under the name Colonia Aug. Iul. Philippi or Philippensis. It received the *ius Italicum,* whereby provincial cities acquired the same status as Italian cities, which possessed municipal self-government and exemption from poll and land taxes. See Citizenship; Philippi; Roman.

William Arthur Heidel

COLOR, kul'ẽr, **COLORS,** kul'ẽrz: The word tr[d] "color" in AV is *'ayin,* which lit. means "eye" or "appearance," and has been so tr[d] in RV. In the NT the Gr πρόφασις, *próphasis,* has the meaning of pretense or show (Acts **27** 30; cf Rev **17** 4 AV). The references to Joseph's coat of many colors (Gen **37** 3.23.32) and "garments of divers colors" (2 S **13** 18.19) probably do not mean the color of the garment at all, but the form, as suggested in ARVm, "a long garment with sleeves." In Jgs **5** 30 the word for "dip" or "dye" appears in the original and has been so tr[d] in ARV (see Dye). In 1 Ch **29** 2 רִקְמָה, *riḳmāh,* meaning "variegated," hence "varicolored," is found. In Isa **54** 11, *pūkh* is used. This name was applied to the sulphide of antimony (Arab. *koḥl*) used for painting the eyes. Hence the ARVm rendering "antimony" instead of "fair colors" (see Paint). In Ezk **16** 16 טָלָא, *ṭālā',* is found, meaning "covered with pieces" or "spotted," hence by implication "divers colors."

Although the ancient Hebrews had no specific words for "color," "paint" or "painter," still, as we know, they constantly met with displays of the art of coloring among the Babylonians (Ezk **23** 14) and Egyptians and the inhabitants of Pal. Pottery, glazed bricks, glassware, tomb walls, sarcophagi, wood and fabrics were submitted to the skill of the colorist. This skill probably consisted in bringing out striking effects by the use of a few primary colors, rather than in any attempt at the blending of shades which characterizes modern coloring. That the gaudy show of their heathen neighbors attracted the children of Israel is shown by such passages as Jgs **8** 27; Ezk **23** 12.16.

Two reasons may be given for the indefiniteness of many of the Bib. references to color. (1) The origin of the Heb people: They had been wandering tribes or slaves with no occasion to develop a color language. (2) Their religious laws: These forbade expression in color or form (Ex **20** 4). Yielding to the attractions of gorgeous display was discouraged by such prophets as Ezekiel, who had sickened of the abominations of the Chaldaeans (Ezk **23** 14.15.16); "And I said unto them, Cast ye away every man the abominations of his eyes" (Ezk **20** 7).

Indefiniteness of color language is common to oriental literature, ancient and modern. This does not indicate a want of appreciation of color but a failure to analyze and define color effects. The inhabitants of Syria and Pal today delight in brilliant colors. Bright yellow, crimson, magenta and green are used for adornment with no evident sense of fitness, according to the foreigners' eyes, other than their correspondence with the glaring brightness of the eastern skies. A soapmaker once told the writer that in order to make his wares attractive to the Arabs he colored them a brilliant crimson or yellow. A peasant chooses without hesitation a flaring magenta or yellow or green *zun-nar* (girdle), rather than one of somber hues. The oriental student in the chemical or physical laboratory often finds his inability to distinguish or classify color a real obstacle. His closest definition of a color is usually "lightish" or "darkish." This is not due to color blindness but to a lack of education, and extends to lines other than color distinctions. The colloquial language of Pal today is poor in words denoting color, and an attempt to secure from a native a satisfactory description of some simple color scheme is usually disappointing. The harmonious color effects which have come to us from the Orient have been, in the past, more the result of accident (see Dye) than of deliberate purpose, as witness the clashing of colors where modern artificial dyes have been introduced.

This inability of the peoples of Bible lands to define colors is an inheritance from past ages, a consideration which helps us to appreciate the vagueness of many of the Bib. references.

The following color words occur in the AV or RV: (1) bay, (2) black, (3) blue, (4) brown, (5) crimson, (6) green, (7) grey, (8) hoar, (9) purple, (10) red, (11) scarlet, (12) sorrel, (13) vermilion, (14) white, (15) yellow. In addition there are indefinite words indicating mixtures of light and dark: (*a*) grisled (grizzled), (*b*) ringstraked (ringstreaked), (*c*) speckled, (*d*) spotted.

(1) *Bay* or red is more properly tr[d] "strong" in the RV.

(2) *Black* (blackish): Eight different words have been tr[d] "black." They indicate various meanings such as "dusky like the early dawn," "ashen," "swarthy," "moved with passion." Black is applied to hair (Lev **13** 31; Cant **5** 11; Mt **5** 36); to marble or pavement (Est **1** 6); to mourning (Job **30** 28.30; Jer **14** 2); to passion (Jer **8** 21 AV; Lam **5** 10); to horses (Zec **6** 2.6; Rev **6** 5); to the heavens (1 K **18** 45; Job **3** 5; Prov **7** 9 AV; Jer **4** 28; Mic **3** 6); to the sun (Rev **6** 12); to the skin (racial) (Cant **1** 5.6); to flocks (Gen **30** 32.33.35.40); to brooks because of ice (Job **6** 16).

(3) *Blue* (תְּכֵלֶת, *tᵉkhēleth*, a color from the cerulean mussel): This word was applied only to fabrics dyed with a special blue dye obtained from a shellfish. See Dye. שֵׁשׁ, *shēsh*, in one passage of the AV is tr[d] "blue" (Est **1** 6). It is properly tr[d] in RV "white cloth." "Blueness of a wound" (Prov **20** 30) is correctly rendered in RV "stripes that wound." Blue is applied to the fringes, veil, vestments, embroideries, etc, in the description of the ark and tabernacle (Ex **25** ff; Nu **4** 6 f; **15** 38); to workers in blue (2 Ch **2** 7.14; **3** 14); to palace adornments (Est **1** 6); to royal apparel (Est **8** 15; Jer **10** 9; Ezk **23** 6; **27** 7.24).

(4) *Brown:* The Heb word meaning "sunburnt" or "swarthy" is tr[d] "black" in RV (Gen **30** 32 ff).

(5) *Crimson* (כַּרְמִיל, *karmīl*): This word is probably of Pers origin and applies to the brilliant dye obtained from a bug. A second word תּוֹלַעַת, *tōla'ath*, is also found. Its meaning is the same. See Dye. Crimson is applied to raiment (2 Ch **2** 7.14; **3** 14; Jer **4** 30 AV); to sins (Isa **1** 18).

(6) *Green* (greenish): This word in the tr refers almost without exception to vegetation. The Heb יָרָק, *yārāḳ*, lit. "pale," is considered one of the three definite color words used in the OT (see White; Red). The Gr equivalent is *chlōrós;* cf Eng. "chlorine." This word occurs in the following vs: Gen **1** 30; **9** 3; Ex **10** 15; Lev **2** 14 (AV); **23** 14 (AV); 2 K **19** 26; Ps **37** 2; Isa **15** 6; **37** 27; Job **39** 8; *chlōros*, Mk **6** 39; Rev **8** 7; **9** 4. רַעֲנָן, *ra'ănān*, closely allied in meaning to *yārāḳ*, is used to describe trees in the following passages: Dt **12** 2; 1 K **14** 23; 2 K **16** 4; **17** 10; **19** 26; 2 Ch **28** 4; Job **15** 32; Ps **37** 35; **52** 8; Cant **1** 16; Isa **57** 5; Jer **2** 20; **3** 6; **11** 16; **17** 2.8; Ezk **6** 13; Hos **14** 8. In the remaining vs the Heb equivalents do not denote color, but the condition of being full of sap, fresh or unripe (cf similar uses in Eng.) (Gen **30** 37 [AV]; Jgs **16** 7.8; Ps **23** 2; Cant **2** 13; Job **8** 16; Ezk **17** 24; **20** 47; Lk **23** 31). In Est **1** 6 the Heb word refers to a fiber, probably cotton, as is indicated by ARVm. Greenish is used to describe leprous spots in Lev **13** 49; **14** 37. The same word is tr[d] "yellow" in Ps **68** 13.

(7) *Gray:* The Heb שֵׂיבָה, *sēbhāh*, means old age, hence refers also to the color of the hair in old age (Gen **42** 38; **44** 29; **44** 31; Dt **32** 25; Ps **71** 18; Hos **7** 9). See *Hoar*, next paragraph.

(8) *Hoar* (hoary): The same word which in other vs is tr[d] "gray" is rendered "hoar" or "hoary," applying to the hair in 1 K **2** 6.9; Isa **46** 4; Lev **19** 32; Job **41** 32; Prov **16** 31. Another Heb word is tr[d] "hoar" or "hoary," describing "frost" in Ex **16** 14; Job **38** 29; Ps **147** 16.

(9) *Purple:* The Heb equivalent is אַרְגָּמָן, *'argāmān;* Gr πορφύρα, *porphúra*. The latter word refers to the source of the dye, namely, a shellfish found on the shores of the Mediterranean. See Dye. This color, which varied widely according to the kind of shellfish used and the method of dyeing, was utilized in connection with the adornment of the tabernacle (Ex **25, 26, 27, 28, 35, 36, 38, 39;** Nu **4** 13). There were workers in purple called to assist in beautifying the temple (2 Ch **2** 7.14; **3** 14). Purple was much used for royal raiment and furnishings (Jgs **8** 26; Est **1** 6; **8** 15; Cant **3** 10; Mk **15** 17.20; Jn **19** 2.5). Purple was typical of gorgeous apparel (Prov **31** 22; Jer **10** 9; Cant **7** 5; Ezk **27** 7.16; Lk **16** 19; Acts **16** 14; Rev **17** 4; **18** 12.16).

(10) *Red:* The Heb אָדוֹם, *'ādhōm*, is from דָּם, *dām*, "blood," hence, "bloodlike." This is one of the three distinctive color words mentioned in the OT (see Green; White), and is found in most of the references to red. Four other words are

used: (*a*) הַכְלִילִי, *ḥakhlīlī*, probably "darkened" or "clouded" (Gen **49** 12; Prov **23** 29); (*b*) חָמַר, *ḥāmar*, "to ferment" (Ps **75** 8m; Isa **27** 2 AV); (*c*) בָּהַט, *bāhaṭ*, probably "to glisten" (Est **1** 6); (*d*) πυῤῥός, *purrós*, "firelike" (Mt **16** 2.3; Rev **6** 4; **12** 3). Red is applied to dyed skins (Ex **25** 5; **26** 14; **35** 7.23; **36** 19; **39** 34); to the color of animals (Nu **19** 2; Zec **1** 8; **6** 2; Rev **6** 4; **12** 3); to the human skin (Gen **25** 25; ruddy, 1 S **16** 12; **17** 42; Cant **5** 10; Lam **4** 7); to the eyes (Gen **49** 12; Prov **23** 29); to sores (Lev **13**); to wine (Ps **75** 8m; Prov **23** 31; Isa **27** 2 AV); to water (2 K **3** 22); to pavement (Est **1** 6); to pottage (Gen **25** 30); to apparel (Isa **63** 2); to the sky (Mt **16** 2.3); to sins (Isa **1** 18); to a shield (Nah **2** 3).

(11) *Scarlet:* Scarlet and crimson colors were probably from the same source (see CRIMSON; DYE). תּוֹלַעַת, *tōlaʿath*, or derivatives have been tr[d] by both "scarlet" and "crimson" (Gr *kókkinos*). A Chald word for purple has thrice been tr[d] "scarlet" in AV (Dnl **5** 7.16.29). Scarlet is applied to fabrics or yarn used (*a*) in the equipment of the tabernacle (Ex **25** ff; Nu **4** 8); (*b*) in rites in cleansing lepers (Lev **14**); in ceremony of purification (Nu **19** 6); to royal or gorgeous apparel (2 S **1** 24; Prov **31** 21; Lam **4** 5; Dnl **5** 7.16.29, "purple"; Nah **2** 3; Mt **27** 28; Rev **17** 4; **18** 12.16); to marking thread (Gen **38** 28.30; Josh **2** 18.21); to lips (Cant **4** 3); to sins (Isa **1** 18); to beasts (Rev **17** 3); to wool (He **9** 19).

(12) *Sorrel:* This word occurs once in the RV (Zec **1** 8).

(13) *Vermilion:* This word, שָׁשַׁר, *shāshar*, occurs in two passages (Jer **22** 14; Ezk **23** 14). Vermilion of modern arts is a sulphide of mercury. It is not at all improbable that the paint referred to was an oxide of iron. This oxide is still taken from the ground in Syria and Pal and used for decorative outlining.

(14) *White:* The principal word for denoting whiteness in the Heb was לָבָן, *lābhān*, a distinctive color word. Some of the objects to which it was applied show that it was used as we use the word "white" (Gen **49** 12). Mt. Lebanon was probably named because of its snow-tipped peaks (Jer **18** 14). White is applied to goats (Gen **30** 35); to rods (Gen **30** 37); to teeth (Gen **49** 12); to leprous hairs and spots (Lev **13**; Nu **12** 10); to garments (Eccl **9** 8; Dnl **7** 9); as symbol of purity (Dnl **11** 35; **12** 10; Isa **1** 18); to horses (Zec **1** 8; **6** 3.6); to tree branches (Joel **1** 7); to coriander seed (Ex **16** 31). The corresponding Gr word, λευκός, *leukós*, is used in NT. It is applied to hair (Mt **5** 36; Rev **1** 14); to raiment (Mt **17** 2; **28** 3; Mk **9** 3; **16** 5; Lk **9** 29; Jn **20** 12; Acts **1** 10; Rev **3** 4.5.18; **6** 11; **7** 9.13.14; **19** 14); to horses (Rev **6** 2; **19** 11.14); to a throne (Rev **20** 11); to stone (Rev **2** 17); to a cloud (Rev **14** 14). Besides *lābhān*, four other Heb words have been tr[d] "white": (*a*) חוֹרִי, *ḥōrī*, or חוּר, *ḥūr*, meaning "bleached," applied to bread (Gen **40** 16); to linen (Est **1** 6; **8** 15); (*b*) צַח, *çaḥ*, or צָחוֹר, *çāḥōr*, lit. "dazzling," is applied to asses (Jgs **5** 10); to human appearance (Cant **5** 10); to wool (Ezk **27** 18); (*c*) דַּר, *dar*, probably mother of pearl or alabaster (Est **1** 6); (*d*) רִיר, *rīr*, lit. "saliva," and, from resemblance, "white of egg" (Job **6** 6).

(15) *Yellow:* This word occurs in Est **1** 6 to describe pavement; in Lev **13** to describe leprous hair; in Ps **68** 13 to describe gold.

Mixtures of colors: (*a*) grizzled (grisled), lit. "spotted as with hail," applied to goats (Gen **31** 10.12); to horses (Zec **6** 3.6); (*b*) ringstreaked (ringstraked), lit. "striped with bands," applied to animals (Gen **30** 35 ff; **31** 8 ff); (*c*) speckled, lit. "dotted or spotted," applied to cattle and goats (Gen **30** 32 ff; **31** 8 ff); to a bird (Jer **12** 9); to horses (Zec **1** 8 AV); (*d*) spotted, lit. "covered with patches," applied to cattle and goats (Gen **30** 32 ff). In Jude ver 23 "spotted" means "defiled."

Figurative: For fig. uses, see under separate colors.

LITERATURE.—Perrot and Chipiez, *History of Art in Ancient Egypt, History of Art in Chaldaea and Assyria, History of Art in Phoenicia and its Dependencies;* Wilkinson, *The Ancient Egyptians; Jew Enc; EB;* Delitzsch, *Iris.*

JAMES A. PATCH

COLOSSAE, kō-los′ē (Κολοσσαί, *Kolossaí*, "punishment"; AV **Colosse**): A city of Phrygia on the Lycus River, one of the branches of the Maeander, and 3 miles from Mt. Cadmus, 8,013 ft. high. It stood at the head of a gorge where the two streams unite, and on the great highway traversing the country from Ephesus to the Euphrates valley, 13 miles from Hierapolis and 10 from Laodicea. Its history is chiefly associated with that of these two cities. Early, according to both Herodotus and Xenophon, it was a place of great importance. There Xerxes stopped 481 BC (Herod. vii.30) and Cyrus the Younger marched 401 BC (Xen. *Anab.* i.2.6). From Col **2** 1 it is not likely that Paul visited the place in person; but its Christianization was due to the efforts of Epaphras and Timothy (Col **1** 1.7), and it was the home of Philemon and Epaphras. That a church was established there early is evident from Col **4** 12.13; Rev **1** 11; **3** 14. As the neighboring cities, Hierapolis and Laodicea, increased in importance, Colossae declined. There were many Jews living there, and a chief article of commerce, for which the place was renowned, was the *collossinus*, a peculiar wool, probably of a purple color. In religion the people were specially lax, worshipping angels. Of them, Michael was the chief, and the protecting saint of the city. It is said that once he appeared to the people, saving the city in time of a flood. It was this belief in angels which called forth Paul's epistle (Col **2** 18). During the 7th and 8th cents. the place was overrun by the Saracens; in the 12th cent. the church was destroyed by the Turks and the city disappeared. Its site was explored by Mr. Hamilton. The ruins of the church, the stone foundation of a large theater, and a necropolis with stones of a peculiar shape are still to be seen. During the Middle Ages the place bore the name of Chonae; it is now called Chonas. E. J. BANKS

COLOSSIANS, kō-losh′ans, kō-los′i-anz, **EPISTLE TO THE:** This is one of the group of St. Paul's epistles known as the Captivity Epistles (see PHILEMON, EPISTLE TO, for a discussion of these as a group).

I. Authenticity.—The external evidence for the Epistle to the Colossians, prior to the middle of the 2d cent., is rather indeterminate. In Ignatius and in Polycarp we have here and there phrases and terminology that suggest an acquaintance with Col but not much more (Ignat., *Ephes.*, x 3, and Polyc. x.1; cf with Col **1** 23). The phrase in *Ep Barnabas*, xii, "in him are all things and unto him are all things," may be due to Col **1** 16, but it is quite as possibly a liturgical formula. The references in Justin Martyr's *Dialogue* to Christ as the firstborn (*prōtótokos*) are very probably suggested by Col **1** 15, "the firstborn of all creation" (*Dial.*, 84, 85, 138). The first definite witness is Marcion, who included this epistle in his collection of those written by St. Paul (Tert., *Adv. Marc.*, v.19). A little later the Muratorian Fragment mentions Col among the Epistles of St. Paul (10*b*, l. 21, *Colosensis*). Irenaeus quotes it frequently and by name (*Adv. haer.*, iii.14, 1). It is familiar to the writers

1. External Evidence

of the following cents. (e.g. Tert., *De praescrip.*, 7; Clem. Alex., *Strom.*, I, 1; Orig., *Contra Celsum*, v.8).

2. Internal Evidence

The authenticity was not questioned until the second quarter of the 19th cent. when Mayerhoff claimed on the ground of style, vocabulary, and thought that it was not by the apostle. The Tübingen school claimed, on the basis of a supposed Gnosticism, that the epistle was the work of the 2d cent. and so not Pauline. This position has been thoroughly answered by showing that the teaching is essentially different from the Gnosticism of the 2d cent., esp. in the conception of Christ as prior to and greater than all things created (see V below). The attack in later years has been chiefly on the ground of vocabulary and style, the doctrinal position, esp. the Christology and the teaching about angels, and the relation to the Ephesian epistle. The objection on the ground of vocabulary and style is based, as is so often the case, on the assumption that a man, no matter what he writes about, must use the same words and style. There are thirty-four words in Col which are not in any other NT book. When one removes those that are due to the difference in subject-matter, the total is no greater than that of some of the acknowledged epistles. The omission of familiar Pauline particles, the use of genitives, of "all" (*pás*), and of synonyms, find parallels in other epistles, or are due to a difference of subject, or perhaps to the influence on the language of the apostle of his life in Rome (von Soden). The doctrinal position is not at heart contradictory to St. Paul's earlier teaching (cf Godet, *Intro NT; St. Paul's Epistles*, 440 f). The Christology is in entire harmony with Phil (q.v.) which is generally admitted as Pauline, and is only a development of the teaching in 1 Cor (**8** 6; **15** 24–28), esp. in respect of the emphasis laid on "the cosmical activity of the preincarnate Christ." Finally, the form in which St. Paul puts the Christology is that best calculated to meet the false teaching of the Colossian heretics (cf V below). In recent years H. Holtzmann has advocated that this epistle is an interpolated form of an original Pauline epistle to the Colossians, and the work of the author of the Epistle to the Ephesians (q.v.). A modification of this theory of interpolation has recently been suggested by J. Weiss (*TLZ*, September 29, 1900). Both these theories are too complicated to stand, and even von Soden, who at first followed Holtzmann, has abandoned the position (von Soden, *Einl.*, 12); while Sanday (*DB*[2]) has shown how utterly untenable it is. Sober criticism today has come to realize that it is impossible to deny the Pauline authorship of this epistle. This position is strengthened by the close relationship between Col and Philem, of which Renan says: "Paul alone, so it would seem, could have written this little masterpiece" (Abbott, *ICC*, lviii). If Philem (q.v.) stands as Pauline, as it must, then the authenticity of Col is established beyond controversy.

II. Place and Date.—The Pauline authorship being established, it becomes evident at once that the apostle wrote Col along with the other Captivity Epistles, and that it is best dated from Rome (see PHILEMON, EPISTLE TO), and during the first captivity. This would be about 58 or, if the later chronology is preferred, 63 or 64.

III. Destination.—The epistle was written, on the face of it, to the church at COLOSSAE (q.v.), a town in the Lycus valley where the gospel had been preached most probably by Epaphras (Col **1** 7; **4** 12), and where St. Paul was, himself, unknown personally (**1** 4.8.9; **2** 1.5). From the epistle it is evident that the Colossian Christians were Gentiles (**1** 27) for whom, as such, the apostle feels a responsibility (**2** 1 ff). He sends to them Tychicus (**4** 7), who is accompanied by Onesimus, one of their own community (**4** 9), and urges them to be sure to read another letter which will reach them from Laodicea (**4** 16).

IV. Relation to Other NT Writings.—Beyond the connection with Eph (q.v.) we need notice only the relation between Col and Rev. In the letter to Laodicea (Rev **3** 14–21) we have two expressions: "the beginning of the creation of God," and "I will give to him to sit down with me in my throne," in which we have an echo of Col which "suggests an acquaintance with and recognition of the earlier apostle's teaching on the part of St. John" (Lightfoot, *Col*, 42, n. 5).

V. The Purpose.—The occasion of the epistle was, we may be sure, the information brought by Epaphras that the church in Colossae was subject to the assault of a body of Judaistic Christians who were seeking to overthrow the faith of the Colossians and weaken their regard for St. Paul (Zahn). This "heresy," as it is commonly called, has had many explanations. The Tübingen school taught that it was gnostic, and sought to find in the terms the apostle used evidence for the 2d cent. composition of the epistle. *Plērōma* and *gnôsis* ("fulness" and "knowledge") not only do not require this interpretation, but will not admit it. The very heart of Gnosticism, i.e. the theory of emanation and the dualistic conception which regards matter as evil, finds no place in Col. The use of *plērōma* in this and the sister epistle, Eph, does not imply gnostic views, whether held by the apostle or by the readers of the letters. The significance in Col of this and the other words adopted by Gnosticism in later years is quite distinct from that later meaning. The underlying teaching is equally distinct. The Christ of the Colossians is not the aeon Christ of Gnosticism. In Essenism, on the other hand, Lightfoot and certain Germans seek the origin of this heresy. Essenism has certain affinities with Gnosticism on the one side and Judaism on the other. Two objections are raised against this explanation of the origin of the Colossian heresy. In the first place Essenism, as we know it, is found in the neighborhood of the Dead Sea, and there is no evidence for its establishment in the Lycus valley. In the second place, no references are found in Col to certain distinct Essene teachings, e.g. those about marriage, washings, communism, Sabbath rules, etc.

The Colossian heresy is due to Judaistic influences on the one hand and to native beliefs and superstitions on the other. The Judaistic elements in this teaching are patent, circumcision (**2** 11), the Law (**2** 14.15), and special seasons (**2** 16). But there is more than Judaism in this false teaching. Its teachers look to intermediary spirits, angels whom they worship; and insist on a very strict asceticism. To seek the origin of angel worship in Judaism, as is commonly done, is, as A. L. Williams has shown, to miss the real significance of the attitude of the Jews to angels and to magnify the bitter jeers of Celsus. Apart from phrases used in exorcism and magic he shows us that there is no evidence that the Jew ever worshipped angels (*JTS*, X, 413 f). This element in the Colossian heresy was local, finding its antecedent in the worship of the river spirits, and in later years the same tendency gave the impulse to the worship of St. Michael as the patron saint of Colossae (so too Ramsay, *HDB*, s.v. "Colossae"). The danger of and the falsehood in this teaching were twofold. In the first place it brought the gospel under the bands of the Law once more, not now with the formality of the Galatian opponents, but none the less surely. But as the apostle's readers are Gentiles (**1** 27) St. Paul is not interested in showing the preparatory aspect of the Law. He simply insists to them that they are quite free from all obligations of the Law because Christ, in whom they have been baptized (**2** 12), has blotted out all the Law (**2** 14). The second danger is that their belief in and worship of the heavenly powers, false ideas about Christ and the material world, would develop even further than it had. They, because of their union with Him, need fear no angelic being. Christ has triumphed over them all, leading them as it were captives in His train (**2** 15), as He conquered on the cross. The spiritual powers cease to have any authority over the Christians. It is to set Christ forward, in this way, as Head over all creation as very God, and out of His relation to the church and to the universe to develop the Christian life, that the apostle writes.

VI. Argument.—The argument of the Epistle is as follows:

1 1.2: Salutation.

1 3–8: Thanksgiving for their faith in Christ, their love for the saints, their hope laid up in heaven, which they had in and through the gospel and of which he had heard from Epaphras.

1 9–13: Prayer that they might be filled with the full knowledge of God's will so as to walk worthy of the Lord and to be fruitful in good works, thankful for their inheritance of the kingdom of His Son.

1 14–23: Statement of the Son's position, from whom we have redemption. He is the very image of God, Creator, preëxistent, the Head of the church, preëminent over all, in whom all the fulness (*plērōma*) dwells, the Reconciler of all things, as also of the Colossians, through His death, provided they are faithful to the hope of the gospel.

1 24—**2** 5: By his suffering he is filling up the sufferings of Christ, of whom he is a minister, even to reveal the great mystery of the ages, that Christ is in them, the Gentiles, the hope of glory, the object of the apostle's preaching everywhere. This explains Paul's interest in them, and his care for them, that their hearts may be strengthened in the love and knowledge of Christ.

2 6—**3** 4: He then passes to exhortation against those who are leading them astray, these false teachers of a vain, deceiving philosophy based on worldly wisdom, who ignore the truth of Christ's position, as One in whom all the Divine *plērōma* dwells, and their relation to Him, united by baptism; raised through the faith; quickened and forgiven; who teach the obligation of the observance of various legal practices, strict asceticisms and angel worship. This exhortation is closed with the appeal that as Christ's they will not submit to these regulations of men which are useless, esp. in comparison with Christ's power through the Resurrection.

3 5–17: Practical exhortations follow to real mortification of the flesh with its characteristics, and the substitution of a new life of fellowship, love and peace.

3 18—**4** 1: Exhortation to fulfil social obligations, as wives, husbands, children, parents, slaves and masters.

4 2–6: Exhortation to devout and watchful prayer.

4 7–18: Salutations and greeting.

LITERATURE.—Lightfoot, *St. Paul's Epistles to the Colossians and Philemon;* Abbott, *Ephesians and Colossians, ICC;* Peake, *Colossians, Expositor's Greek Testament;* Maclaren, *Colossians, Expositor's Bible;* Alexander, *Colossians and Ephesians, Bible for Home and School;* Moule, *Colossians, Cambridge Bible;* Haupt, Meyer's *Krit. u. Exeg. Kom.;* von Soden, *Hand-Kom. zum NT.*

C. S. LEWIS

COLT, kōlt (**FOAL**) (עַיִר, *'ayir,* בֵּן, *ben;* **πῶλος,** *pōlos,* **υἱός,** *huiós,* with some word such as ὑποζυγίου, *hupozugíou,* understood; *huios* alone = "son"): The Eng. words "colt" and "foal" are used in the Bible of the ass everywhere except in Gen **32** 15, where the word "colt" is used of the camel in the list of animals destined by Jacob as presents for Esau. In most cases *'ayir* (cf Arab. *'air,* "ass") means "ass's colt," but it may be joined with *ben,* "son," as in Zec **9** 9, where we have: *'al-ḥămōr wᵉ'al-'ayir ben-'ăthōnōth,* lit. "on an ass, and on an ass's colt, the son of the she-asses"; cf Mt **21** 5: ἐπὶ ὄνον καὶ ἐπὶ πῶλον υἱὸν ὑποζυγίου, *epí ónon kaí epí pōlon huión hupozugíou,* "upon an ass, and upon a colt the foal of an ass." In Jn **12** 15 we have ἐπὶ πῶλον ὄνου, *epí pōlon ónou,* and in the previous ver the diminutive, ὀνάριον, *onárion.* The commonest NT word for "colt" is *pōlos,* akin to which is Ger. *Fohle* and Eng. "foal" and "filly." The Lat *pullus* signifies either "foal" or "chicken," and in the latter sense gives rise to Fr. *poulet* and Eng. "pullet."

In view of the fact that horses are but little mentioned in the Bible, and that only in connection with royal equipages and armies, it is not surprising that "colt" does not occur in its ordinary Eng. sense. ALFRED ELY DAY

COME, kum: The tr of many Heb and Gr words. In the phrase "The Spirit of Jeh came mightily upon him" (Jgs **14** 6.19; **15** 14; 1 S **10** 10; **11** 6; **16** 13), the word is *çālēᵃh;* Jgs **14** 6; **15** 14 "came mightily," which is the uniform tr of RV (cf **13** 25 "to move," i.e. to disturb or stir up). In Jgs **6** 34; 1 Ch **12** 18; 2 Ch **24** 20, it is *lābhēsh,* "to clothe"; RVm "The Spirit . . . . clothed itself with Gideon" and . . . . "with Zechariah," "The Spirit clothed Amasai."

Among its many changes, RV has "come forth" for "come" (Mt **2** 6); "gone up" for "come" (**14** 32, a different text); "come all the way" for "come" (Jn **4** 15); "got out upon the" for "come to" (**21** 9); "draw near" for "come" (He **4** 16); "come" for "come and see" (Rev **6** 1); "secure" for "come by" (Acts **27** 16); "attain unto" for "come in" (Eph **4** 13); and "I come" for "I come again" (Jn **14** 28). W. L. WALKER

COMELINESS, kum'li-nes, **COMELY,** kum'li: Cognate with "becoming," viz. what is suitable, graceful, handsome. The servant of Jeh in Isa **53** 2 is without "comeliness" (*hādhār,* "honor"), i.e. there is in his appearance nothing attractive, while he is bowed beneath man's sin. "Praise is comely" (*nā'wāh,* f. of *nā'weh;* Ps **33** 1; **147** 1), i.e. suitable or befitting "for the righteous," and, therefore, an honor and glory; "uncomely parts," *aschēmona* (1 Cor **12** 23), viz. less honorable. See also 1 S **16** 18, "a comely person"; Cant **6** 4, "comely as Jerus," etc.

COMFORT, kum'fẽrt (נָחַם, *nāḥam;* **παρακαλέω,** *parakaléō*): The NT word is variously trᵈ, as "comfort," "exhort," "beseech," the exact tr to be determined by the context. Etymologically, it is "to call alongside of," i.e. to summon for assistance. To comfort is to cheer and encourage. It has a positive force wanting in its synonym "console," as it indicates the dispelling of grief by the impartation of strength. RV has correctly changed the tr of *paramuthéomai* from AV "comfort," to "consolation." So in the OT, "Comfort ye my people" (Isa **40** 1) is much stronger than "console," which affords only the power of calm endurance of affliction, while the brightest hopes of the future and the highest incentives to present activity are the gifts of the Divine grace that is here bestowed.

H. E. JACOBS

COMFORTABLY, kum'fẽr-ta-bli (עַל־לֵב, *'al lēbh,* "to the heart"): "To speak to the heart," i.e. to speak kindly, to console, to comfort, is the ordinary Heb expression for wooing: e.g. Boaz spake "to the heart" of Ruth (Ruth **2** 13m; AV "friendly," RV "kindly"). The beauty of the Heb term is illustrated in Gen **50** 21 where Joseph "spake kindly" unto his brethren, winning them from fear to confidence. Rendered "comfortably" in five passages: thrice of human speaking, and twice of the tenderness of God's address to His people. David was urged to win back the hearts of the people by kind words: "speak comfortably" (2 S **19** 7). Hezekiah in like manner comforted the Levites (2 Ch **30** 22) and encouraged his captains (2 Ch **32** 6). The term has exceptional wealth of meaning in connection with God's message of grace and forgiveness to His redeemed people. The compassionate love that has atoned for their sins speaks *to the heart* ("comfortably") of Jerus, saying "that her iniquity is pardoned" (Isa **40** 2). The same promise of forgiveness is given to the penitent nation by the prophet Hosea (Hos **2** 14); "**comfortable** words" (Zec **1** 13), i.e. words affording comfort. DWIGHT M. PRATT

COMFORTER, kum'fẽr-tẽr: This is a tr of the word παράκλητος, *paráklētos*, in the Johannine writings. In the Gospel it occurs in **14** 16.26; **15** 26; **16** 7, and refers to the Holy Spirit. The word means lit. "called to one's side" for help. The tr "Comforter" covers only a small part of the meaning as shown in the context. The word "Helper" would be a more adequate tr. The Spirit does a great deal for disciples besides comforting them, although to comfort was a part of His work for them. The Spirit guides into truth; indeed, He is called the Spirit of truth. He teaches and quickens the memory of disciples and glorifies Christ in them. He also has a work to do in the hearts of unbelievers, convicting the world of sin, of righteousness, and of judgment (Jn **14–16**). The Comforter remains permanently with disciples after He comes in response to the prayers of Christ. The word *paraklētos* does not occur elsewhere in the Scriptures except in 1 Jn **2** 1. In Job **16** 2 the active form of the word (*paraklētos* is passive) is found in the pl., where Job calls his friends "miserable comforters." The word "Comforter" being an inadequate, and the word "Helper" a too indefinite, tr of the word in the Gospel of John, it would probably be best to transfer the Gr word into Eng. in so far as it relates to the Holy Spirit (see PARACLETE).

In 1 Jn **2** 1 the word *paraklētos* refers to Christ: "If any man sin, we have an Advocate with the Father, Jesus Christ the righteous." Here the tr Advocate is quite correct. As the next ver shows the writer has in mind the intercession of Christ for Christians on the basis of His mediatorial work: "And he is the propitiation for our sins; and not for ours only, but also for the whole world" (1 Jn **2** 2). See ADVOCATE; HOLY SPIRIT; PARACLETE.

E. Y. MULLINS

COMFORTLESS, kum'fẽrt-les (ὀρφανούς, *orphanoús*, "orphans"): The Gr original is found but twice in the NT; rendered "comfortless" in Jn **14** 18, RV "desolate"; "fatherless" in Jas **1** 27 (cf Ps **68** 5). The term signifies *bereft* of a father, parents, guardian, teacher, guide, and indicates what must be the permanent ministry of the Holy Spirit to the disciples of Jesus, in comforting their hearts. In harmony with these parting words Jesus had called the chosen twelve "little children" (Jn **13** 33); without Him they would be "orphans," comfortless, desolate. The coming of the Holy Spirit would make Christ and the Father forever real to them, an abiding spiritual presence. DWIGHT M. PRATT

COMING OF CHRIST. See ADVENT; PAROUSIA.

COMING, SECOND. See PAROUSIA.

COMMANDMENT, kō-mand'ment, **COMMANDMENTS** (מִצְוָה, *miçwāh;* ἐντολή, *entolḗ*): The commandments are, first of all, prescriptions, or directions of God, concerning particular matters, which He wanted observed with reference to circumstances as they arose, in a period when He spake immediately and with greater frequency than afterward. They were numerous, minute, and regarded as coördinate and independent of each other. In the Ten Commandments, or, more properly, Ten Words, EVm (דְּבָרִים, *dᵉbhārīm*), they are reduced to a few all-comprehensive precepts of permanent validity, upon which every duty required of man is based. Certain prescriptions of temporary force, as those of the ceremonial and forensic laws, are applications of these "Words" to transient circumstances, and, for the time for which they were enacted, demanded perfect and unconditional obedience. The Pss, and esp. Ps **119**, show that even under the OT, there was a deep spiritual appreciation of these commandments, and the extent to which obedience was deemed a privilege rather than a mere matter of constrained external compliance with duty. In the NT, Jesus shows in Mt **22** 37.40; Mk **12** 29.31; Lk **10** 27 (cf Rom **13** 8.10) their organic unity. The "Ten" are reduced to two, and these two to one principle, that of love. In love, obedience begins, and works from within outward. Under the NT the commandments are kept when they are written upon the heart (He **10** 16). While in the Synoptics they are referred to in a more abstract and distant way, in both the Gospel and the Epp. of Jn their relation to Jesus is most prominent. They are "my commandments" (Jn **14** 15.21; **15** 10.12); "my Father's" (Jn **10** 18; **15** 10); or, many times throughout the epp., "his [i.e. Christ's] commandments." The new life in Christ enkindles love, and not only makes the commandments the rule of life, but the life itself the free expression of the commandments and of the nature of God, in which the commandments are grounded. Occasionally the word is used in the singular collectively (Ex **24** 12; Ps **119** 96; 1 Cor **14** 37). See TEN COMMANDMENTS, THE. H. E. JACOBS

COMMANDMENT, THE NEW, nū (ἐντολὴ καινή, *entolḗ kainḗ*): The word "commandment" is used in the Eng. VSS of the OT to translate several Heb words, more esp. those meaning "word" (*dābhār*) as the ten words of God (Ex **34** 28) or king's "command" (Est **1** 12); "precept" (*miçwāh*) of God (Dt **4** 2), of a king (2 K **18** 36); "mouth" or "speech" (*peh*) of God (Ex **17** 1), of Pharaoh (2 K **23** 35). They express the theocratic idea of morality wherein the will or law of God is imposed upon men as their law of conduct (2 K **17** 37).

This idea is not repudiated in the NT, but supplemented or modified from within by making love the essence of the command. Jesus

1. Christ and the Old Commandment

Christ, as reported in the Synoptics, came not "to destroy the law or the prophets . . . . but to fulfil" (Mt **5** 17). He taught that "whosoever therefore shall break one of these least commandments, and shall teach men so, shall be called least in the kingdom of heaven" (Mt **5** 19). He condemned the Pharisees for rejecting the commandments of God as given by Moses (Mk **7** 8-13). There is a sense in which it is true that Christ propounded no new commandment, but the new thing in His teaching was the emphasis laid on the old commandment of love, and the extent and intent of its application. The great commandment is "Thou shalt love the Lord thy God, ... [and] thy neighbor as thyself. On these two commandments the whole law hangeth, and the prophets" (Mt **22** 34-40; Mk **12** 28-34; cf Dt **6** 5; Lev **19** 18).

When the law realizes itself as love for God and man in men's hearts, it ceases to bear the aspect of a command. The force of authority and the active resistance or inertia of the subject disappear; the law becomes a principle, a motive, a joyous harmony of man's will with the will of God; and in becoming internal, it becomes universal and transcends all distinctions of race or class. Even this was not an altogether new idea (cf Jer **31** 31–34; Ps **51**); nor did Christ's contemporaries and disciples think it was. The revolutionary factor was the death of Christ wherein the love of God was exemplified and made manifest as the basis and principle of all spiritual life (Jn **13** 34). Paul therefore generalizes all pre-Christian morality as a system of law and commandments, standing in antithesis to the grace and love which are through Jesus Christ (Rom **5**–**7**). Believers in Christ felt their experience and inward life to be so changed and new, that it needed a new term (*agápē*="love") to express their ideal of conduct (see CHARITY). Another change that grew upon the Christian consciousness, following from the resurrection and ascension of Christ, was the idea that He was the permanent source of the principle of life. "Jesus is Lord" (1 Cor **12** 3). Hence in the Johannine writings the principle described by the new term *agapē* is associated with Christ's lordship and solemnly described as His "new commandment." "A new commandment I give unto you, that ye love one another; even as I have loved you, that ye also love one another" (Jn **13** 34). To the Christians of the end of the 1st cent. it was already an old commandment which they had from the beginning of the Christian teaching (1 Jn **2** 7; 2 Jn 5); but it was also a new commandment which ever came with new force to men who were passing from the darkness of hatred to the light of love (1 Jn **2** 8–11). The term in the Gospel we may owe to the evangelist, but it brings into relief an element in the consciousness of Jesus which the author of the Fourth Gospel had appreciated more fully than the Synoptists. Jesus was aware that He was the bearer of a special message from the Father (Jn **12** 49; Mt **11** 27), that He fulfilled His mission in His death of love and self-sacrifice (Jn **10** 18), and that the mission fulfilled gave Him authority over the lives of men, "even as I have loved you, that ye also love one another." The full meaning of Christ's teaching was only realized when men had experienced and recognized the significance of His death as the cause and principle of right conduct. The Synoptists saw Christ's teaching as the development of the prophetic teaching of the OT. Paul and John felt that the love of God in Christ was a new thing: (*a*) new as a revelation of God in Christ, (*b*) new as a principle of life in the church, and (*c*) new as a union of believers with Christ. While it is love, it is also a commandment of Christ, calling forth the joyous obedience of believers. See also BROTHERLY LOVE.

2. Principle instead of Law

3. Christ's Love Fulfilled in Death Becomes the Law of the Church

4. The New Revelation

T. REES

COMMANDMENTS, THE TEN. See COMMANDMENT; TEN COMMANDMENTS.

COMMEND, kŏ-mend':

(1) For **παρατίθημι**, *paratíthēmi* (Lk **23** 46), translating the Heb *pāḳadh* (Ps **31** 5), in the dying words of Jesus: "Into thy hands I commend my spirit." AV in Ps has the more general word "commit." The use of the Gr word in the sense of "deposit what belongs to one into the hands of another" is not uncommon in the classics. So also the derivatives *parathḗkē* (2 Tim **1** 12) and *parakatathḗkē* (1 Tim **6** 20; 2 Tim **1** 14). See DEPOSIT. This sense of the Eng., while slightly archaic, corresponds to the first meaning of the Lat, whence it comes, "to commit for preservation," esp. of the dying; to commend children, parents, etc, to the care of others (for examples, see Harper's *Latin Dictionary*).

(2) For συνίστημι, *sunístēmi*, "to stand together," and then, by standing together, to establish, prove, exhibit, as "righteousness" and "love of God" (Rom **3** 5; **5** 8), and thus to attest (2 Cor **3** 1; **4** 2), and, finally, to certify or to recommend a stranger (Rom **16** 1; 2 Cor **6** 4). The use of *parístēmi* in 1 Cor **8** 8 is equivalent.

(3) "To praise," ἐπαινέω, *epainéō* (Lk **16** 8), and *sunistemi* in 2 Cor **10** 12.18; for the OT, Heb *hillēl*, in Gen **12** 15 AV; Prov **12** 8. H. E. JACOBS

COMMENTARIES, kom'en-ta-riz:

I. THE WORD—GENERAL SCOPE
II. DIFFERENCES IN CHARACTER OF COMMENTARIES
III. RANGE OF COMMENTARIES
  1. Early Commentaries
    (1) Origen, etc
    (2) Chrysostom, etc
  2. Scholastic Period
    Nicolas de Lyra
  3. Reformation and Post-Reformation Periods
    (1) Luther and Calvin
    (2) Beza, Grotius, etc
    (3) Later Writers
  4. 18th Century
    (1) Calmet, M. Henry, etc
    (2) Patrick, Lowth, Scott
    (3) Gill, Doddridge
    (4) Bengel
  5. The Modern Period—Its Characteristics
    (1) Germany
      (*a*) The Liberal School
      (*b*) Believing Tendency
        (α) Conservative
        (β) Critical
        (γ) Mediating
        (δ) Confessional
        (ε) Godet (Swiss)
    (2) Britain and America
      (*a*) Alford, Eadie
      (*b*) Ellicott and Lightfoot
      (*c*) Westcott
      (*d*) Critical Influences—Broad Church Stanley and Jowett
      (*e*) General Commentaries (Series)
  6. Recent Period
    (1) Germany
    (2) Britain and America
LITERATURE

I. The Word—General Scope.—Etymologically, a commentary (from Lat *commentor*) denotes jottings, annotations, memoranda, on a given subject, or perhaps on a series of events; hence its use in the pl. as a designation for a narrative or history, as the *Commentaries* of Caesar. In its application to Scripture, the word designates a work devoted to the explanation, elucidation, illustration, sometimes the homiletic expansion and edifying utilization, of the text of some book or portion of Scripture. The primary function of a good commentary is to furnish an exact interpretation of the meaning of the passage under consideration; it belongs to it also to show the connection of ideas, the steps of argument, the scope and design of the whole, in the writing in question. This can only be successfully accomplished by the help of a knowledge of the original language of the writing, and of the historical setting of the particular passage; by careful study of the context, and of the author's general usages of thought and speech; and by comparison of parallel or related texts. Aid may also be obtained from external sources, as a knowledge of the history, archaeology, topography, chronology, manners and customs, of the lands, peoples and times referred to; or, as in Deissmann's recent discoveries, from the light thrown on peculiarities of language by papyri or other ancient remains (see his *Light from the Ancient East*).

II. Differences in Character.—It is obvious that commentaries will vary greatly in character and value according as they are more *scholarly,* technical, and critical, entering, e.g. into philological discussions, and tabulating and remarking upon the various views held as to the meaning; or again, more *popular,* aiming only at bringing out the general sense, and conveying it to the mind of the reader in attractive and edifying form. When the practical motive predominates, and the treatment is greatly enlarged by illustration, application, and the enforcement of lessons, the work loses the character of commentary proper, and partakes more of the character of homily or discourse.

III. Range of Commentaries.—No book in the world has been made the subject of so much commenting and exposition as the Bible. Theological libraries are full of commentaries of all descriptions and all grades of worth. Some are commentaries on the original Heb or Gr texts; some on the Eng. or other VSS. Modern commentaries are usually accompanied with some measure of introduction to the books commented upon; the more learned works have commonly also some indication of the *data* for the determination of the textual readings (see CRITICISM, TEXTUAL). Few writers are equal to the task of commenting with profit on the Bible as a whole, and, with the growth of knowledge, this task is now seldom attempted. Frequently, however, one writer contributes many valuable works, and sometimes, by coöperation of like-minded scholars, commentaries on the whole Bible are produced. It is manifestly a very slight survey that can be taken in a brief art. of the work of commenting, and of the literature to which it has given rise; the attempt can only be made to follow the lines most helpful to those seeking aid from this class of books. On the use and abuse of commentaries by the preacher, C. H. Spurgeon's racy remarks in his *Commenting and Commentaries* may be consulted.

1. Early Commentaries

Rabbinical interpretations and paraphrases of the OT may here be left out of account (see next art.; also TARGUMS; TALMUD; F. W. Farrar's *History of Interpretation,* Lect II). Commentaries on the NT could not begin till the NT books themselves were written, and had acquired some degree of authority as sacred writings (see BIBLE). The earliest commentaries we hear of are from the heretical circles of the Gnostics. Heracleon, a Valentinian (cir 175 AD), wrote a commentary on the Gospel of John (fragments in Origen), and on parts at least of the Gospel of Luke. Tatian, a disciple of Justin Martyr, about the same time, compiled his *Diatessaron,* or Harmony of the Four Gospels, on which, at a later time, commentaries were written. Ephraem Syrus (4th cent.) wrote such a commentary, of which an Armenian tr has now been recovered. The Church Father Hippolytus (beginning of 3d cent.), wrote several commentaries on the OT (Ex, Pss, Prov, Eccl, Dnl, Zec, etc), and on Mt, Lk and Rev.

(1) *Origen, etc.*—The strongest impulse, however, to the work of commenting and exposition of Holy Scripture undoubtedly proceeded from the school of Alexandria—esp. from Origen (203–54 AD). Clement, Origen's predecessor, had written a treatise called *Hupotupōseis,* or "Outlines," a survey of the contents of Holy Scripture. Origen himself wrote commentaries on all the books of the OT, Ruth, Est and Eccl alone excepted, and on most of the books of the NT (Mk, 1 and 2 Cor, 1 and 2 Pet, 1, 2, and 3 Jn, Jas, Jude, Rev excepted). He furnished besides, *scholia,* or notes on difficult passages, and delivered Homilies, or discourses, the records of which fill three folio volumes. "By his *Tetrapla* and *Hexapla,*" says Farrar, "he became the founder of all textual criticism; by his Homilies he fixed the type of a popular exposition; his *scholia* were the earliest specimens of marginal explanations; his commentaries furnished the church with her first continuous exegesis" (op. cit., 188). Unfortunately the Alexandrian school adopted a principle of allegorical interpretation which led it frequently into the most extravagant fancies. Assuming a threefold sense in Scripture—a literal, a moral, and a spiritual—it gave reins to caprice in foisting imaginary meanings on the simplest historical statements (Farrar, op. cit., 189 ff). Some of Origen's commentaries, however, are much freer from allegory than others, and all possess high value (cf Lightfoot, *Galatians,* 217). The later teachers of the Alexandrian school continued the exegetical works of Origen. Pamphilus of Caesarea, the friend of Eusebius, is said to have written OT commentaries.

(2) *Chrysostom, etc.*—At the opposite pole from the allegorizing Alexandrian school of interpretation was the Antiochian, marked by a sober, literal and grammatical style of exegesis. Its reputed founder was Lucian (martyred 311 AD); but its real heads were Diodorus of Tarsus(379–94 AD) and Theodore of Mopsuestia (393–428 AD); and its most distinguished representative was John Chrysostom (347–407 AD). Chrysostom wrote continuous commentaries on Isa (only **1—8** 10 remaining) and on Gal; but his chief contributions were his *Homilies,* covering almost the whole of the OT and NT. Of these over 600 remain, chiefly on the NT. They are unequal in character, those on Acts being reputed the feeblest; others, as those on Mt, Rom and Cor, are splendid examples of expository teaching. Schaff speaks of Chrysostom as "the prince of commentators among the Fathers" (*Hist.,* Ante-Nicene Per., 816). Thomas Aquinas is reported to have said that he would rather possess Chrysostom's homilies on Mt than be master of all Paris. In the West, Ambrose of Milan (340–97 AD) wrote expositions of OT histories and of Lk (allegorical and typical), and Jerome (346–420 AD) wrote numerous commentaries on OT and NT books, largely, however, compilations from others.

2. Scholastic Period

The mediaeval and scholastic period offers little for our purpose. There was diligence in copying MSS, and producing *catenae* of the opinions of the Fathers; in the case of the schoolmen, in building up elaborate systems of theology; but the Scriptures were thrown into the background.

Nicolas de Lyra.—The 14th cent., however, produced one commentator of real eminence—Nicolas de Lyra (1270–1340). Nicolas was a Franciscan monk, well versed in Heb and rabbinical learning. While recognizing the usual distinctions of the various senses of Scripture, he practically builds on the literal, and exhibits great sobriety and skill in his interpretations. His work, which bears the name *Postillae Perpetuae in Universa Biblia,* was much esteemed by Luther, who acknowledged his indebtedness to it. Hence the jest of his opponents, *Si Lyra non lyrasset, Lutherus non saltasset* (a notice of Lyra may be seen in Farrar, op. cit. 274–78).

3. Reformation and Post-Reformation Periods

The Reformation brought men's minds back to the Scriptures and opened a new era in Bib. exposition and commentary. It became the custom to expound the Scriptures on Sundays and week-days in all the pulpits of the Protestant churches. "Luther's custom was to expound consecutively in a course of sermons the Old and New Testaments" (Köstlin). The Reformation began at Zürich with a series of discourses by Zwingli on the Gospel of Mt. The same was true of Calvin, Beza, Knox and all associated with them. The production of commentaries or expository homilies was the necessary result.

(1) *Luther and Calvin.*—As outstanding examples may be mentioned Luther's *Commentary on Gal*, and the noble commentaries of Calvin. Not all by any means, but very many of the commentaries of Calvin were the fruit of pulpit prelections (e.g. the expositions of Job, the Minor Prophets, Jer, Dnl). Others, as the commentaries on Rom and the Pss (reputed his best), were prepared with great care. Calvin's supreme excellence as a commentator is disputed by no one. From every school and shade of opinion in Christendom could be produced a chorus of testimony to the remarkable gifts of mind and heart displayed in his expositions of Scripture—to his breadth, moderation, fairness and *modernness* of spirit, in exhibiting the sense of inward genius of Holy Writ. The testimony of Arminius is as striking as any: "I exhort my pupils to peruse Calvin's commentaries . . . . for I affirm that he excels beyond comparison in the interpretation of Scripture, and that his commentaries ought to be more highly valued than all that is handed down to us by the library of the Fathers."

(2) *Beza, Grotius, etc.*—Lutheranism had its distinguished exegetes (Brenz, d. 1572), who wrote able commentaries on the OT, and in both the Calvinistic and Arminian branches of the Reformed church the production of commentaries held a chief place. Beza, Calvin's successor, is acknowledged to have possessed many of the best exegetical qualities which characterized his master. Grotius, in Holland (d. 1645), occupies the foremost place among the expositors in this cent. on the Arminian side. His exegetical works, if not marked by much spirituality, show sagacity and learning, and are enriched by parallels from classical literature. The school of Cocceius (d. 1669) developed the doctrine of the covenants, and revelled in typology. Cocceius wrote commentaries on nearly all the books of Scripture. His pupil Vitringa (d. 1716) gained renown by his expositions of Isa and the Apocalypse.

(3) *Later writers.*—Partly fostered by the habit of basing commentary on pulpit exposition, the tendency early set in to undue prolixity in the unfolding of the meaning of Scripture. "In the Lutheran church," says Van Oosterzee, "they began to preach on whole books of the Bible; sometimes in a very prolix manner, as, e.g. in the case of the 220 sermons by one Striegnitz, a preacher at Meissen, on the history of Jonah, of which four are devoted to the consideration of the words 'Unto Jonah'" (*Practical Theol.*, 120). The habit spread. The commentaries of Peter Martyr (Swiss Reformer, d. 1562) on Jgs and Rom occupy a folio each; N. Byfield (Puritan, d. 1622) on Col fills a folio; Caryl (Independent, d. 1673) on Job extends to 2 folios; Durham (d. 1658) on Isa **53** consists of 72 sermons; Venema (Holland, d. 1787) on Jer fills 2 quartos, and on the Pss no less than 6 quartos. These are only samples of a large class. H. Hammond's *A Paraphrase and Annotations on the NT, from an Arminian Standpoint* belong to this period (1675). Another work which long took high rank is M. Poole's elaborate *Synopsis Criticorum Biblicorum* (5 vols, folio, 1669–76)—a summary of the opinions of 150 Bib. critics; with which must be taken his *Eng. Annotations on the Holy Bible*, only completed up to Isa **58** at the time of his death (1679). The work was continued by his friends.

4. 18th Century

(1) *Calmet, M. Henry, etc.*—The 18th cent. is marked by greater sobriety in exegesis. It is prolific in commentaries, but only a few attain to high distinction. Calmet (d. 1757), a learned Benedictine, on the Roman Catholic side, produced his *Commentaire littéral sur tous les livres de l'Ancien et du Nouveau Testament*, in 23 quarto vols —a work of immense erudition, though now necessarily superseded in its information. On the Protestant side, Matthew Henry's celebrated *Exposition of the Old and New Testament* (1708–10) easily holds the first place among devotional commentaries for its blending of good sense, quaintness, original and felicitous remark, and genuine insight into the meaning of the sacred writers. It is, of course, not a critical work in the modern acceptation, and often is unduly diffuse. M. Henry's work extends only to the end of Acts; the remaining books were done by various writers after his death (1714). Le Clerc (d. 1736) may be named as precursor of the critical views now obtaining on the composition and authorship of the Pent. His commentaries began with Gen in 1693 and were not completed till 1731. Other commentators of note of Arminian views were Daniel Whitby (d. 1726; converted to Arianism), and, later, Adam Clarke, Wesleyan (1762–1832), whose work extends into the next cent. Clarke's *Commentary on the Holy Scriptures* (1810–26), still held by many in high esteem, is marred to some extent by eccentricities of opinion.

(2) *Patrick, Lowth, Scott.*—In the Anglican church the names of chief distinction in this cent. are Bishop Patrick, Bishop Lowth, and later, Thomas Scott. Bishop Patrick, usually classed with the Cambridge Platonists (d. 1707), contributed paraphrases and commentaries on the OT from Gen to Cant, while Bishop Lowth (d. 1787) acquired lasting fame by his *Prelections on Heb Poetry*, and *A New Translation, with Notes on Isaiah.* He was among the first to treat the poetical and prophetic writings really as literature. The commentaries of Patrick and Lowth were subsequently combined with those of Whitby and other divines (Arnold, etc) to form a complete *Critical Commentary* (1809), which went through many editions. The well-known commentary of Thomas Scott (1747–1821), representing a moderate Calvinism, is a solid and "judicious" piece of work, inspired by an earnest, believing spirit, though not presenting any marked originality or brilliance. Brilliance is not the characteristic of many commentators of this age.

(3) *Gill, Doddridge.*—Two other Eng. writers deserving notice are Dr. John Gill (d. 1771; Calvinistic Baptist), who wrote *Expositions on the OT* and *the NT* and a separate *Exposition of the Song of Solomon*—learned, but ponderous and controversial; and Dr. Philip Doddridge (d. 1751), whose *Family Expositor*, embracing the entire NT, with a harmony of the Gospels, and paraphrases of the meaning, is marked by excellent judgment, and obtained wide acceptance.

(4) *Bengel.*—Meanwhile a new period had been preluded in Germany by the appearance in 1742 of the *Gnomon Novi Testamenti* of J. A. Bengel (d. 1751), a work following upon his critical edition of the NT issued in 1734. Though belonging to the 18th cent., Bengel's critical and expository labors really herald and anticipate the best work in these departments of the 19th cent. His scholarship was exact, his judgment sound, his critical skill remarkable in a field in which he was a pioneer; his notes on the text, though brief, were pregnant with significance, and were informed by a spirit of warm and living piety.

The modern period, to which Bengel in spirit, if not in date, belongs, is marked by great changes in the style and character of commentaries. The critical temper was now strong; great advances had been made in the textual criticism of both OT and NT (see CRITICISM, TEXTUAL); the work of the higher criticism had begun in the OT; in Germany, the spirit of humanism, inherited from Lessing, Herder and Goethe, had found its way into literature; knowledge of the sciences, of oriental civilizations, of other peoples and religions, was constantly on the increase; scholarship was more precise and thorough; a higher ideal of what commentary meant had taken possession of the mind. Learning, too, had enlarged its borders, and books on all subjects poured from the press in such numbers that it was difficult to cope with them. This applies to commentaries as to other departments of theological study. Commentaries in the 19th cent., and in our own, are legion. Only the most prominent landmarks can be noted.

5. The Modern Period—Its Characteristics

(1) *Germany* (*a*) *The liberal school.*—In Germany, as was to be anticipated, the rise of the critical spirit and the profound influence exercised by it are reflected in most of the commentaries produced in the first half of the cent. On the liberal side, the rationalistic temper is shown in the rejection of miracle, the denial of prediction in prophecy, and the lowering of the idea of inspiration generally. The scholarship, however, is frequently of a very high order. This temper is seen in De Wette (d. 1849), whose commentaries on the NT, written when his views had become more positive, show grace and feeling; in Gesenius (d. 1842), who produced an epoch-making commentary on Isa; in Knobel (d. 1863), pronouncedly rationalistic, but with keen critical sense, as evinced in his commentaries on the Pent and Josh, Eccl, and Isa; in Hupfeld (d. 1866) in his *Commentary on the Pss* (4 vols); in Hitzig (d. 1875), acute but arbitrary, who wrote on the Pss and most of the Prophets; above all, in Ewald (d. 1875), a master in the interpretation of the poetical and prophetical books, but who commented also on the first three Gospels, on the writings of John, and on Paul's epistles. Ewald's influence is felt in the *History of the Jewish Church* by Dean Stanley, in England. *The Exegetical Handbook* (*Kurzgefasstes exegetisches Handbuch*) embraced compendious annotations by Knobel, Hitzig, Bertheau (school of Ewald), etc, but also Olshausen (d. 1839; wrote likewise on the NT), on all the books of the OT.

(*b*) *Believing tendency.*—On the believing side, from a variety of standpoints, evangelical, critical, mediating, confessional, a multitude of commentaries on the OT and NT were produced. The extremely conservative position in criticism was defended by Hengstenberg (d. 1869; on Pss, Eccl, Ezk, Jn, Rev), by Keil (d. 1888) in the well-known Keil and Delitzsch series (Gen to Est, Jer, Ezk, Dnl, Minor Prophets; also NT commentaries), and by Hävernick (d. 1845; Dnl, Ezk). Delitzsch (d. 1890) wrote valued commentaries on Gen, Job, Pss, Prov, Cant, Eccl, Isa; also on He. After the rise of the Wellhausen school, he considerably modified his views in the newer critical direction. His *New Comm. on Gen* (1887) shows this change, but, with his other works, is still written in a strongly believing spirit. On the other hand, the critical position (older, not newer) is frankly represented by A. Dillmann (d. 1894) in his commentaries on the books of the Pent and Josh (*ET of Genesis*, 1897; many also of the above works are tr[d]).

The mediating school, largely penetrated by the influence of Schleiermacher, had many distinguished representatives. Among the most conspicuous may be named Lücke (d. 1855), who wrote on John; Bleek, the OT and NT critical scholar (d. 1859), who has a work on the first three Gospels, and lectures on Eph, Col, Philem, He and Rev (his *Comm. on He* is the best known), and Tholuck (d. 1877), whose expositions and commentaries on Pss, Jn, Rom and He with his *Comm. on the Sermon on the Mount*, are fine pieces of exegetical work.

A special place must be given to two names of high distinction in the present connection. One is J. P. Lange (d. 1884), the projector and editor of the great *Bibelwerk* (theological and homiletical) in 22 vols, to which he himself contributed the commentaries on Gen to Nu, Hag, Zec, Mal, Mt, Mk, Jn, Rom, Rev, with introductions and homiletic hints. The other is H. A. W. Meyer (d. 1873), whose *Critical and Exegetical Comm. on the NT* from Mt to Phil (the remaining books being done by other scholars, Lünemann, Huther, etc) is an essential part of every NT scholar's equipment.

With the more positive and confessional theologians may be ranked E. R. Stier (d. 1862), whose *Words of the Lord Jesus* (ET in 8 vols; Bib., mystical, tendency to prolixity), with commentaries on 70 selected Pss, Prov, 2d Isa, Eph, He, Jas and Jude, found much acceptance. A. von Harless (d. 1879) wrote a *Comm. on Eph*, praised by Tholuck as one of the finest extant. Philippi (d. 1882), of Jewish extraction, best known by his *Comm. on Rom*, was strictly Lutheran. One of the ablest of the Lutheran Confessionalists was Luthardt (d. 1892), whose works include a *Comm. on St. John's Gospel*. Ebrard (d. 1887), as stoutly confessional on the Reformed side, has an esteemed *Comm. on He*. An eminent continental theologian who cannot be overlooked is the Swiss F. L. Godet (d. 1900), whose admirable *Comm. on St. John's Gospel*, and commentaries on Rom and Cor are highly appreciated.

(2) *Britain and America.*—Meanwhile the Eng.-speaking countries were pursuing their own paths in the production of commentaries, either in continuing their old traditions, or in striking out on new lines, under the foreign influences which, from the beginning of the cent., had begun to play upon them. In England Bishop Blomfield (d. 1857) published *Lectures on Jn and Acts*. In the United States there appeared from the pen of Dr. J. A. Alexander, of Princeton (d. 1860), a noteworthy *Comm. on Isa*, fully abreast of the modern learning, but staunchly conservative; also a *Comm. on Pss*. From the same seminary proceeded the massive commentaries of Dr. Charles Hodge (Calvinistic) on Rom, Eph and Cor. Adapted for popular use and greatly in demand for Sunday-school purposes were the *Notes, Critical, Explanatory and Practical* of Albert Barnes (d. 1871; New School Presbyterian). These *Notes*, the fruit of the use of the early morning hours in a busy pastoral life, covered the whole of the NT, with several books of the OT (Job, Pss, Isa, Dnl). Sensible and informatory, rather than original or profound, they proved helpful to many. Over 1,000,000 copies are stated to have been sold. Of similar aim, though less widely known, were the *Notes* of Professor M. W. Jacobus (d. 1876; on the NT, Gen and Ex).

A new era was opened in critical commentary in England by the publication of the *Gr Testament* (1849–61) of Dean Alford (d. 1871), followed by his *NT for Eng. Readers* (1868). Here was presented a thoroughly critical treatment of the texts, with a full display of the critical apparatus, and notes philological and exegetical, accompanied by learned and lucid introductions, on all the books of the NT. About the same time appeared the solid, if more theological and homiletical, commentaries of the Scottish scholar, J. Eadie (d. 1876), on Gal, Eph, Phil, 1 and 2 Thess. Anglican scholarship produced its ripest fruits in this line in the classical *Critical and Grammatical Comms.* of Bishop Ellicott (d. 1905) on Gal, Eph, Phil, Col, Philem, Thess, Pastoral Epistles, and the yet more remarkable series of commentaries of Bishop J. B. Lightfoot (d. 1889), massive in learning, and wider in outlook than Ellicott's, on Gal, Phil, Col and Philem. A large part of the value of Lightfoot's works consists in the special essays or dissertations on important subjects embodied in them (e.g. "St. Paul and the Three", "The Christian Ministry," "The Colossian Heresy," etc). With these names should be associated that of Bishop Westcott, Dr. Lightfoot's successor in the see of Durham (d. 1901), whose commentaries on the Gospel and Epistles of St. John, and on He, take a place among the foremost. Bishop Moule, who, in turn, succeeded Dr. Westcott, has also written commentaries, simpler in character, on Rom, Eph, Phil and Col, in the *Cambridge Bible Series*, and on Rom in the *Expositor's Bible*. In OT exposition mention should be made of Bishop Perowne's valuable work on the *Book of Psalms* (2d ed, revised, 1870), with his contributions to the *Cambridge Bible* (see below).

The critical and theological liberalism of Germany has made its influence felt in England in the rise of a Broad Church party, the best products of which in commentary were Dean Stanley's (d. 1881) graphic and interesting *Comm. on 1 and 2 Cor* (1855) and Dr. B. Jowett's *Epistles of St. Paul to the Thess, Gal, and Rom, with Critical Notes and Dissertations* (1855). The new spirit culminated in the appearance of the famous *Essays and Reviews* (1860), and in the works of Bishop Colenso on the Pent and Josh (1862–79). Bishop Colenso had already published a tr of Rom, with commentary (1861).

Besides works by individual authors, there appeared during this period several general commentaries, to the production of which many writers contributed. The following may be mentioned. *The Speaker's Comm.* (10 vols, 1871–82), under the general editorship of Canon F. C. Cook (d. 1889), was called forth by the agitation over Bishop Colenso. Dr. Cook himself wrote introductions to Ex, Pss and Acts, and contributed the entire commentaries on Job, Hab, Mk, Luke, 1 Pet, with parts of commentaries on Ex, Pss and Mt. The work is of unequal value. A serviceable series is the *Cambridge Bible for Schools and Colleges* (1877 ff), edited by Bishop Perowne, with *Smaller Cambridge Bible for Schools*, and *Cambridge Gr Test. for Schools and Colleges* (still in process). Dr. Perowne (d. 1904) himself contributed to the first-named the commentaries on Ob, Jon, Hag, Zec, Mal and Gal. Many valuable contributions appear in this series, e.g. A. F. Kirkpatrick on 1 and 2 S and Pss, A. B. Davidson on Job and Ezk, Driver on Dnl, G. G. Findlay on Thess, etc. Next, under the editorship of Bishop Ellicott, were produced (1877–84) *A NT Comm. for Eng. Readers* (3 vols), and *An OT Comm. for Eng. Readers* (5 vols), which contained some valuable work (Gen by R. Payne Smith, Ex by Canon G. Rawlinson, etc). Akin to this in character was the *Popular Comm. on the NT* (4 vols, 1879–83), edited by Dr. W. Schaff. This embraced, with other excellent matter, commentaries on Thess by Dr. Marcus Dods, and on 1 and 2 Pet by Dr. S. D. F. Salmond. *The Pulpit Comm.* (49 vols, 1880 ff), edited by J. S. Exell and Canon H. D. M. Spence, has expositions by good scholars, and an abundance of homiletical material by a great variety of authors. The series of *Handbooks for Bible Classes* (T. & T. Clark, Edinburgh) has a number of valuable commentaries, e.g. that of Dr. A. B. Davidson on He.

6. Recent Period

In the most recent period the conspicuous feature has been the production of commentaries in series or by individual writers embodying the results of an advanced OT criticism—in less degree of a radical NT criticism.

(1) *Germany.*—In Germany, in addition to the *Kurzgefasstes exegetisches Handbuch*, of older standing (see above), to which Dillmann contributed, may be mentioned Marti's *Kurzer Hand-Commentar zum AT* (1897 ff) and Nowack's *Handkommentar zum AT;* also Strack and Zöckler's *Kurzgefasster Kommentar* (OT and NT; critical, but moderate). Marti contributes to his *Hand-Commentar* the vols on Isa, Dnl and the Minor Prophets; Nowack contributes to his *Handkommentar* the vols on Jgs and Ruth, 1 and 2 S and the Minor Prophets (of special importance in Nowack's series are the vols on Gen by H. Gunkel, and on Dt and Josh by C. Steuernagel); Strack writes in his own work the vols on Gen to Nu (Oettli contributes Dt, Josh and Jgs). Much more conservative in spirit are the commentaries of H. C. von Orelli (Basel) on Isa, Jer, Ezk and the Minor Prophets. In the NT, Meyer's *Commentary* has been "revised" by later writers, many of them (J. Weiss, W. Bousset, etc) of much more advanced tendency than the original author.

(2) *Britain and America.*—In Britain and America like currents are observable. Professor T. K. Cheyne, who wrote a helpful commentary on the *Prophecies of Isa* (1880–81), and subsequently commentaries on Mic and Hos (*Cambridge Bible*), Jer (*Pulpit Comm.*), and on *The Book of Psalms* (1884), has become more and more extreme in his opinions. Of works in series the most important is *The International Critical Commentary*, edited by Drs. Driver and Plummer in England, and Dr. C. A. Briggs in the United States, of which 16 vols in the OT and the NT have already appeared. It need not be said that the commentaries in this series are always scholarly and able; those on the OT are, however, all built on the Wellhausen foundations (see CRITICISM OF THE BIBLE, III). Dr. Driver himself writes on Dt; Dr. J. Skinner, on Gen; Dr. G. F. Moore, on Jgs; Dr. H. P. Smith, on 1 and 2 S; Dr. Briggs, on Pss; Dr. Toy, on Prov; Dr. W. R. Harper (d. 1906), on Am and Hos; while Mt in the NT is covered by W. C. Allen, Lk by Dr. Plummer, Rom by Drs. Sanday and Headlam, etc. A similar series is the *Westminister Comm.*, recently commenced, to which Dr. Driver contributes the vol on Gen (1904; 7th ed, 1909). Yet another recent popular series is *The Century Bible*, to which again leading critical scholars lend their aid (Dr. W. H. Bennett on Gen; also on "General Epistles"; Dr. A. R. S. Kennedy on 1 and 2 S; Dr. Skinner on 1 and 2 K; Dr. A. S. Peake on Job; also on He; Dr. Driver on a group of the Minor Prophets, etc). A well-planned one-vol *Comm. on the Holy Bible*, by various writers, has recently been edited by J. R. Dummelow (Cambridge). It is prefaced by a general Introduction, with a large number of arts. on the principal subjects with which a reader of the Bible will desire to be acquainted.

It need only be added that very many of the foreign works mentioned above (not simply those specially noted) are now accessible in Eng. tr[s].

LITERATURE.—Works and arts. specially devoted to commentaries are not numerous. Dr. S. Davidson has an art. "Commentary" in Kitto's *Bib. Enc*, Vol I. See also F. W. Farrar's *Hist of Interpretation* (Bampton Lects for 1885). C. H. Spurgeon's popular talks on *Commenting and Commentaries* are accompanied by extensive lists of Commentaries on all parts of the Bible (severely exclusive of works deemed dangerous). Lists of commentaries on the Bible as a whole, on the OT and NT separately, and on the several books, may be seen in most good works on Introduction, or in prolegomena to commentaries on the different books; e.g. in the general Introduction prefixed to Lange's *Comm. on Genesis;* also in the lengthy sections on Jewish, Gr, Lat and Protestant commentators, and again in the "Index of the More Important Expository Works on the Bks of the OT." In Bleek's *Introduction to the OT*, very full information is given up to the author's date. Full bibliographies of modern books, including commentaries on the OT, are furnished in Dr. Driver's *Introduction*. Similar lists are given in other works regarding the NT

For the writers of the commentaries on the special books in the above-noted German and Eng. series, lists may generally be seen attached to each vol of the series.

JAMES ORR

COMMENTARIES, HEBREW, hē'brōō:

1. Philo Judaeus
2. Targum
3. Midrash
4. Talmud
5. Karaites
6. Middle Ages
   (1) Saadia ben Joseph
   (2) Rashi
   (3) Joseph Kara
   (4) Abraham ibn Ezra
   (5) Kimhi
   (6) Maimonides
   (7) Maimunists
   (8) Kabbalists
   (9) The "Zohar"
   (10) Isaac Arama
7. Modern Times
   Abarbanel
8. The Bi'urists
   (1) Mendelssohn
   (2) Zunz, etc
   (3) Malbim, Ehrlich, etc
   (4) Halévy, Hoffmann, Mueller
   (5) Geiger, Graetz, Kohler

LITERATURE

The following outline alludes to the leading Jewish commentators and their works in chronological order. However widely the principles which guided the various Jewish schools of exegesis, or the individual commentators, differ from those of the modern school, the latter will find a certain suggestiveness in the former's interpretation which well merits attention.

1. Philo

Philo Judaeus: A Hellenistic Jew of Alexandria, Egypt. Born about 20 BC; died after 40 AD. By his allegorical method of exegesis (a method he learned from the Stoics), Philo exercised a far-reaching influence not only on Jewish thought, but even more so on the Christian church. We have but to mention his influence on Origen and other Alexandrian Christian writers. His purpose in employing his allegorical method was, mainly, to reconcile Gr philosophy with the OT. See PHILO JUDAEUS.

Josephus cannot be called a Bible commentator in the proper sense of the term. See JOSEPHUS.

2. Targum

Targūm (pl. *Targūmīm*): The Aram. tr of the OT. Lit. the word designates a tr in general; its use, however, has been restricted to the Aram. version of the OT, as contrasted with the Heb text which was called *miḳrā'*. The Tg includes all the books of the OT excepting Dnl and Ezr-Neh, which are written in part in Aram. Its inception dates back to the time of the Second Temple, and it is considered a first approach to a commentary before the time of Jesus. For the Tg is not a mere tr, but rather a combination of a tr with a commentary, resulting in a paraphrase, or an interpretative tr—having its origin in exegesis. The language of this paraphrase is the vernacular tongue of Syria, which began to reassert itself throughout Pal as the language of common intercourse and trade, as soon as a familiar knowledge of the Heb tongue came to be lost. The *Targūmīm* are:

TO THE PENTATEUCH

(1) Targūm *'Onkelōs* or Bab Tg (the accepted and official);

(2) Targūm *yerūshalmī* or Palestinian Tg ("Pseudo-Jonathan"; aside from this [complete] Tg there are fragments of the Palestinian Tg termed "Fragment Targūm").

TO THE PROPHETS

(1) Targūm Jonathan ben Uzziel (being the official one; originated in Pal and was then adapted to the vernacular of Babylonia);

(2) A Palestinian Targūm, called *Targūm yerūshalmī* (Palestinian in origin; ed. Lagarde, "Prophetae Chaldaice").

Other Targūmīm (not officially recognized): (1) To the Psalms and Job; (2) to Proverbs; (3) to the Five Rolls; (4) to Chronicles—all Palestinian. See TARGUM.

3. Midrash

Midhrāsh: Apparently the practice of commenting upon and explaining the meaning of the Scriptures originated in the synagogues (in the time of Ezra), from the necessity of an exposition of the Law to a congregation many of whom did not or might not understand the language in which it was read. Such commentaries, however, were oral and extempore; they were not until much later crystallized into a definite form. When they assumed a definite and, still later, written shape, the name *Midhrāsh* (meaning "investigation," "interpretation," from *dārash*, "to investigate" a scriptural passage) was given. The word occurs in 2 Ch **13** 22 where the RV translates "commentary." From this fact some have drawn the inference that such *Midhrāshīm* were recognized and extant before the time of the Chronicler. They are: *Midhrāsh Rabbā'* on the Pent and the Five Rolls (the one on Gen occupies a first position among the various exegetical *Midhrāshīm*, both on account of its age and importance). Next comes the one on Lam. (Zunz pointed out that the *Midhrāsh Rabbā'* consists of ten entirely different *Midhrāshīm*.) On the same ten books there is a similar collection, called *ha-Midhrāsh ha-gādhōl* (the "Great Midrash"), being a collection of quotations from a good many works including the *Midhrāsh Rabbā'*. Other *Midhrāshīm* are: The *Midhrāsh Tanḥūmā'* on the Pentateuch; the *Mekhiltā'* on *Exodus* (this has been [Leipzig, 1909] trd into German by Winter and Wuensche; the latter also published, under the main title *Bibliotheca Rabbinica*, a collection of the old *Midhrāshīm* in a German tr with introductions and notes). Further, *Ṣiphrā'* on Lev; *Ṣiphrē* on Nu and Dt; *peṣiḳtā'*, which comments on sections taken from the entire range of Scriptures for various festivals. There are also extant separate *Midhrāshīm* on the Pss, Prov, etc.

In this connection we have yet to mention the *Yalḳuṭ Shim'ōnī*, a haggadic compilation attributed to the 11th or, according to Zunz, the 13th cent. The *Yalḳuṭ* extends over the whole of the OT and is arranged according to the sequence of those portions of the Bible to which reference is made. Further, the *Yalḳuṭ ha-Maḳīrī*, a work similar in contents to the *Yalḳuṭ Shim'ōnī*, ed. Greenup. See COMMENTARIES; MIDRASH.

4. Talmud

Talmud (*Talmūdh*): This term is used here to designate the entire body of literature exclusive of the *Midhrāsh*. Ample exegetical material abounds in the Talm as it does in the *Midhrāshīm*. The critical notes on the Bible by some Talmudists are very characteristic of their intellectual temper. Some of them were extremely radical, and expressed freely their opinions on important problems of Bible criticism, such as on the integrity of the text, on doubtful authorship, etc. An *Āmōrā'* of the 3d cent. AD held the opinion that the story of Job is purely fictitious, both as to the name of the hero and as to his fate. The Talmudists also generalized, and set up critical canons. The "*Bāraithā'*, of the Thirty-two Rules" is the oldest work on Bib. hermeneutics (Philo's hermeneutical rules being rather fantastic), and contains exegetical notices valid to this very day. Hermeneutics, of course, is not exegesis proper, but the theory of exegesis; one results from the other, however. This *Bāraithā'* calls attention, for instance, to the fact that words occur in the OT in an abbreviated form—a thing now generally accepted. See TALMUD.

5. Karaites

Karaites: "Followers of the Bible." They are sometimes referred to as the "Protestants of the Jews," professing to follow the OT to the exclusion of the rabbinical tradition. The founder of this Jewish sect was a Bab Jew in the 8th cent., Anan ben David, by name; hence they were first called Ananites. The principal Karaite commentators of the 9th, 10th and 11th cents. are: Benjamin Al-Nahawendi (he was the first to use the term "Karaites," "*Ba'ălē Miḳrā'*"), Solomon ben Jeroham, Sahl ibn Mazliah, Yusuf al-Basir, Yafith ibn Ali (considered the greatest of this period), and Abu al-Faraij Harum. Of a later date we will mention Aaron ben Joseph and Aaron ben Elijah (14th cent.).

The struggle between the Rabbinites and the Karaites undoubtedly gave the impetus to the great exegetical activity among the Jews in Arab.-

speaking countries during the 10th and 11th cents. The extant fragments of Saadia's commentary on the Pent (not less than his polemical writings proper) are full of polemics against the Karaite interpretation. And the same circumstance aroused Karaites to like efforts.

6. Middle Ages

Middle Ages: In the old *Midhrāshīm* as well as elsewhere the consciousness of a simple meaning of a text was never entirely lost. The principal tendencies in exegesis were four; these were afterward designated by the acrostic "PaRDeṢ": i.e. *Peshaṭ* (or the simple philological explanation of words); *Remez* (or the allegorical); *Derash* (or the ethico-homiletical); and *Ṣōdh* (or the mystical). Naturally enough this division could never be strictly carried out; hence variations and combinations are to be found.

Saadia ben Joseph (892–942), the severest antagonist of the Karaites, trd the OT into Arab. with notes. The parts published are: Pent, Isa, Prov and Job.

Moses ha-Darshān (the Preacher) of Narbonne, France, and Tobiah ben Eliezer in Castoria, Bulgaria (11th cent.), are the most prominent representatives of midrashic-symbolic Bible exegesis. The former's work is known only by quotations, and contained Christian theological conceptions; the latter is the author of "*Leḳaḥ Ṭōbh*" or "*Pesiḳtā' Zūṭartā'*" on the Pent and the five *Meghillōth.*

Rashi (Solomon ben Isaac, of Troyes; born 1040, died 1105) wrote a very popular commentary, which extends over the whole of the OT, with the exception of Ch, Ezr-Neh, and the last part of Job. He strives for the *Peshaṭ,* i.e. for a sober, natural and rational interpretation of the Bible. His is still a commentary both for the boy and the man among the Jews. Christian exegetes of the Middle Ages as well as of more modern times made use of his Bible commentary. Nicolas de Lyra (see COMMENTARIES) followed Rashi closely; and it is a known fact that Luther's tr of the Bible is dependent upon Nicolas de Lyra. Rashi's commentary has called forth numerous supercommentaries.

An independent and important exegete was *Joseph Karā'* (about 1100). He edited and partly completed Rashi's commentary, particularly the part on the Pent.

Abraham ibn Ezra's (1092–1168) commentary on the Pent, like Rashi's commentaries, has produced many supercommentaries. His is very scholarly. He was the first to maintain that Isa contains the work of two authors; and his doubts respecting the authenticity of the Pent were noticed by Spinoza.

The grammarians and the lexicographers were not merely exegetical expounders of words, but many of them were likewise authors of actual commentaries. Such were the *Ḳimḥīs,* Joseph (father), Moses and David (his sons); esp. the latter. The Ḳimḥīs were the most brilliant contributors to Bible exegesis and Heb philology (like Ibn Ezra) in mediaeval times.

Maimonides (1135–1204): Philo employed his allegorical method for the purpose of bringing about a reconciliation of Plato with the OT. Maimonides had something similar in view. To him Aristotle was the representative of natural knowledge and the Bible of supernatural—and he sought for a reconciliation between the two in his religious philosophy. Exegesis proper was the one field, however, to which this great genius made no contribution of first-class importance.

The Maimunists, those exegetes of a philosophical turn, are: Joseph ibn Aknin, Samuel ibn Tibbon, his son Moses, and his son-in-law, Jacob ben Abba Mari Anatolio, whose *Malmadh ha-Talmīdhīm* is the most important work of philosophical exegesis of the period.

Joseph ibn Kaṣpī, chiefly known as a philosopher of the Maimunist type, deserves attention. Ibn Kaṣpī is an exegete of the first quality. His exposition of Isa **53** might be the work of the most modern scholar. He refers the prophecy to Israel, not to an individual, and in this his theory is far superior to that of some other famous Jewish expositors who interpret the chapter as referring to Hezekiah.

Through the philosophical homily, which began to be used after the death of Maimonides, Aristotle was popularized from the pulpit. The pulpit changed to a chair of philosophy. Aristotle's concepts—as Matter and Form, the Four Causes, Possibility and Reality—were then something ordinary in the sermon, and were very popular.

The principal commentators with a *Kabbalistic* tendency are: Naḥmanides (1194–1270?) whose great work is his commentary on the Pentateuch; Immanuel of Rome (1270?–1330?) who does, however, not disregard the lit. meaning of the Scriptures; Bahya ben Asher (d. 1340) who formulated the four methods of exegesis of "PaRDeṢ" referred to above; he took Naḥmanides as his model; many supercommentaries were written on his commentary on the Pent; and Gersonides (1288–1334), a maternal grandson of Naḥmanides, who sees symbols in many Bib. passages; on account of some of his heretical ideas expressed in his philosophy, some rabbis forbade the study of his commentaries.

We must not fail to make mention of the *Zōhar* (the "Bible of the Kabbalists"), the book of all others in the Middle Ages that dominated the thinking and feeling of the Jews for almost 500 years, and which was in favor with many Christian scholars. This work is pseudepigraphic, written partly in Aram. and partly in Heb. It first appeared in Spain in the 13th cent., and was made known through Moses de Leon, to whom many historians attribute it.

Mention must also be made of *Isaac Arama* (1430–94), whose *'Ăḳēdhāh,* his commentary on the Pent (homiletical in style), was the standard book for the Jewish pulpit for cents., much esteemed by the Christian world, and is still much read by the Jews, esp. in Russia and Poland.

7. Modern Times

Modern Times: Isaac Abravanel (or Abarbanel; 1437–1508): A statesman and scholar who came nearest to the modern idea of a Bible commentator by considering not only the literary elements of the Bible but the political and social life of the people as well. He wrote a general introduction to each book of the Bible, setting forth its character; and he was the first to make use of Christian commentaries which he quotes without the least prejudice. Moses Alshech (second half of 16th cent.) wrote commentaries, all of which are of a homiletical character. In the main the Jewish exegesis of the 16th and 17th cents. branched out into homiletics.

We will pass over the critical annotations connected with the various editions of the Heb Bible, based upon the comparison of MSS, on grammatical and Massoretic studies, etc, such as those of Elijah Levita, Jacob ben Hayyim of Tunis (afterward a convert to Christianity), etc.

8. The "Bi'urists"

The "Bi'urists" ("Commentators"): A school of exegetes which had its origin with Mendelssohn's (1729–86) lit. German tr of the Bible, at a time when Christian Bib. studies of a modern nature had made some progress, and under whose influence the Bi'urists wrote. They are: Dubno, Wessely, Jaroslav, H. Homberg, J. Euchel, etc. They laid a foundation for a critico-historical study of the

Bible among modern Jews. It bore its fruit in the 19th cent. in the writings of Philippson, Munk, Fuerst, etc. The same cent. produced Zunz's (1794–1886) *Gottesdienstlichen Vortraege der Juden, the* book of "Jewish science." It also produced three Jewish exegetes, Luzzatto in Italy, Malbim and Ehrlich in Russia (the latter since 1878 residing in New York); he published, in Heb, a commentary on the OT, entitled *Miḳrā' ki-Peshûṭāh* (Berlin, 1899–1901, 3 vols), and, in German, *Randglossen z. hebr. Bibel,* two scholarly works written from the conservative standpoint (Leipzig, 1908–). Malbim was highly esteemed by the Christian commentators Franz Delitzsch and Muehlau, who studied under him. Others are Joseph Halévy, a French Jew, a most original Bible investigator, and D. Hoffmann (the last two named are adversaries of "higher criticism") and D. H. Mueller. M. Heilprin wrote a collection of *Bibelkritische Notizen* (Baltimore, 1893), containing comparisons of various passages of the Bible, and *The Historical Poetry of the Ancient Hebrews* (N.Y., 1879–80, 2 vols), and the American rabbi B. Szold, a *Commentary on Job* (Baltimore, 1886), written in classic Heb, and with accurate scholarship and in which full account is taken of the work of the Massorites. A new Heb commentary on the whole of the OT has been since 1903 in progress under the editorship of A. Kahana. This is the first attempt since Mendelssohn's *Bi'ur* to approach the Bible from the Jewish side with the latest philological and archaeological equipment. Among the authors are Kahana on *Genesis* and *Jonah,* Krauss on *Isaiah,* Chajes on *Psalms* and *Amos,* Wynkoop on *Hosea* and *Joel,* and Lambert on *Daniel.* This attempt well deserves attention and commendation.

There is still to be mentioned the work of M. M. Kalisch (1828–85), whose special object was to write a full and critical comm. on the OT. Of his *Historical and Critical Comm. on the OT, with a New Tr,* only the following parts were published: *Exodus,* 1855; *Genesis,* 1858; *Leviticus* (pts 1–2), 1867–72. They contain a résumé of all that Jewish and Christian learning had accumulated on the subject up to the dates of their publication. In his *Lev* he anticipated Wellhausen to a large extent.

We conclude with some names of *the liberals:* Geiger (whose *Urschrift* is extremely radical), Graetz, the great Jewish historian, and Kohler (president of the Hebrew Union College, Cincinnati, O.) whose *Der Segen Jacobs* is one of the earliest essays of "higher criticism" written by a Jew.

Literature.—Steinschneider, *Jewish Literature,* London, 1857; Zunz, *Gottesdienstlichen Vortraege der Juden,* 2d ed, Frankfurt a. M., 1892; *Jew Enc* (arts. by Bacher and Ginzberg); *Catholic Enc* (art. "Commentaries"); Rosenau, *Jewish Biblical Commentators,* Baltimore, 1906 (popular); Winter-Wuensche, *Geschichte der Juedischen Literatur,* Leipzig, 1892–95, 3 vols (the best existing anthology of Jewish literature in a modern language; it contains very valuable introductions); Wogue, *Histoire de la Bible et l'exegèse biblique jusqu'à nos jours,* Paris, 1881.

Adolph S. Oko

COMMENTARY, kom'en-ta-ri (מִדְרָשׁ, *midhrāsh,* "an investigation," from דָּרַשׁ, *dārash,* "to search," "inquire," "explore"; AV **"story"**): "The c. of the prophet Iddo" (2 Ch **13** 22), "the c. of the book of the kings" (**24** 27). In these passages the word is not used exactly in its modern sense. The Heb term means "an imaginative development of a thought or theme suggested by Scripture, esp. a didactic or homiletic exposition, or an edifying religious story" (Driver, *LOT*[5], 497). In the commentaries (*Midhrāshīm*) mentioned by the Chronicler as among his sources, the story of Abijah's reign was presumably related and elaborated with a view to moral instruction rather than historic accuracy. See Chronicles, Books of; Commentaries, Hebrew.

M. O. Evans

COMMERCE, kom'ẽrs (ἐμπορία, *emporía*):

I. OT Times.—There were forces in early Heb life not favorable to the development of commerce.

1. Early Overland Commerce

Intercourse with foreigners was not encouraged by Israel's social and religious customs. From the days of the appearance of the Hebrews in Canaan, however, some commercial contact with the peoples around was inevitable. There were ancient trade routes between the East and the West, as well as between Egypt and the Mesopotamian valley. Pal lay as a bridge between these objective points. There were doubtless traveling merchants from very remote times, interchanging commodities of other lands for those of Pal. Some of the Heb words for "trading" and "merchant" indicate this (cf סָחַר, *ṣāḥar,* "to travel," רָכַל, *rākhal,* "to go about"). In the nomadic period, the people were necessarily dependent upon overland commerce for at least a part of their food supply, such as grain, and doubtless for articles of clothing, too. Frequent local famines would stimulate such trade. Companies or caravans carrying on this overland commerce are seen in Gen **37** 25.28, "Ishmaelites" and "Midianites, merchantmen," on their way to Egypt, with spices, balm and myrrh. Jacob caused his sons to take certain products to Egypt as a present with money to Joseph in return for grain: balsam, spices, honey, myrrh, nuts, almonds (Gen **43** 11 f). The presence of a "Bab mantle" among the spoils of Ai (Josh **7** 21) indicates commerce between Canaan and the East.

2. Sea Traffic

While there are slight indications of a possible sea trade as early as the days of the Judges (Jgs **5** 17; cf Gen **49** 13), we must wait till the days of the monarchy of David and esp. Solomon for the commerce of ships. Land traffic was of course continued and expanded (1 K **10** 15.28.29; 2 Ch **1** 16). Sea trade at this time made large strides forward. The Philis were earlier in possession of the coast. Friendship with Hiram king of Tyre gave Solomon additional advantages seaward (1 K **5**; **9** 26; **10** 19–29; 2 Ch **8** 17; **9** 14), since the Phoenicians were preëminently the Mediterranean traders among all the people of Pal. Later, commerce declined, but Jehoshaphat attempted to revive it (1 K **22** 48; 2 Ch **20** 36), but without success. Tyre and Sidon as great commercial centers, however, long impressed the life of Israel (Isa **23**; Ezk **26–27**). Later, in the Maccabean period, Simon acquired Joppa as a Jewish port (1 Macc **14** 5), and so extended Mediterranean commerce.

3. Land Traffic in the Time of the Kings

During the peaceful reign of Solomon, there came, with internal improvements and foreign friendships, a stimulus to traffic with Egypt and the Far East over the ancient trade routes as well as with Phoenicia on the northwest. He greatly added to his wealth through tariffs levied upon merchantmen (1 K **10** 15). Trade with Syria in the days of Omri and Ahab is indicated by the permission Benhadad gave to Israelites to open streets, or trading quarters, in Damascus, as Syrians had in Samaria (1 K **20** 34). The prophets disclose repeatedly the results of foreign commerce upon the people in the days of Jotham, Ahaz and Hezekiah, and of Jeroboam II, under whom great material prosperity was attained, followed by simple luxury (Isa **2** 6.7.16; Hos **12** 1.7.8; Am **6** 3–6). The people in their greed of gain could not observe Sabbaths and feast days (Am **8** 5); cf Sabbath trading and its punishment in the days of the restoration (Neh **13** 15–22). "Canaanite" became the nickname for traffickers (Zec **14** 21; cf Isa **23** 8).

II. NT Times.—After the conquests of Alexander 333 BC, trade between East and West was greatly stimulated. Colonies of Jews for trade purposes had been established in Egypt and elsewhere. The dispersion of the Jews throughout the Gr and Rom world added to their interest in commerce. The Mediterranean Sea, as a great Rom lake, under Rom protection, became alive with commercial fleets. The Sea of Galilee with its enormous fish industry became the center of a large trading interest to all parts. The toll collected in Galilee must have been considerable. Matthew was called from his collectorship to discipleship (Mt **9** 9); Zaccheus and other publicans became rich collecting taxes from large commercial interests like that of balsam. Jesus frequently used the commerce of the day as illustration (Mt **13** 45; **25** 14–30). Along the Palestinian coast there were several ports where ships touched: Lydda, Joppa, Caesarea; and further north Ptolemais, Tyre, Sidon and Antioch (port Seleucia).

The apostle Paul made use of ships touching at points on the coast of Asia Minor, and the islands along the coast, and also doing coast trade with Greece, Italy and Spain, to carry on his missionary enterprises (Acts **13** 4–13; **16** 11 f; **18** 18; **20** 13–16; **21** 1–8; **27** 1–44; **28** 1–14). The rapidity with which the gospel spread throughout the Rom world in the 1st cent. was due no little to the use of the great Rom highways, built partly as trade routes; as well as to the constant going to and fro of tradesmen of all sorts; some of whom like Aquila and Priscilla (Acts **18** 2.18.26), Lydia, (**16** 14.40) and Paul himself (who was a traveling tent-maker) were active in disseminating the new faith among the Gentiles. In Jas **4** 13 we have a good representation of the life of a large number of Jews of this period, who would "go into such a city, and continue there a year, and buy and sell, and get gain" (AV). See also TRADE.

EDWARD BAGBY POLLARD

COMMIT, kō-mit′: Used in two senses:

(1) "To give in charge" or "entrust": *sīm*, "to put" (Job **5** 8); *gālal*, "to roll" (Ps **37** 5; Prov **16** 3); *pāḳadh*, "to give in charge" (Ps **31** 5 AV; cf Lk **23** 46); *títhēmi*, "committed to us [RVm "placed in us"] the word of reconciliation" (2 Cor **5** 19); *parathḗke*, "that which I have committed unto him" (2 Tim **1** 12; RVm "that which he hath committed unto me," Gr "my deposit"); "that which is committed unto thee" (1 Tim **6** 20, Gr "the deposit"); "that good thing," etc (2 Tim **1** 14, Gr "the good deposit").

(2) "To do or practise [evil]": *prássō*, "commit such things" (Rom **1** 32, RV "practice"; cf **2** 2). In 1 Jn **3** 4.8 "doeth sin" (*poiéō*, AV "committeth sin") shows that it is not committing a single sin that is in view, but sinful practice.

W. L. WALKER

COMMODIOUS, kó-mō′di-us (ἀνεύθετος, *aneúthetos*, "not well placed"): The word occurs only in Acts **27** 12. "As regards wintering, the place was certainly 'not commodious,' but as regards shelter from some winds (including N.W.), it was a good anchorage" (CH, XXIII, 639).

COMMON, kom′un: κοινός, *koinós*, in the classics, and primarily in the NT, means what is public, general, universal, as contrasted with ἴδιος, *idios*, what is peculiar, individual, not shared with others. Thus, "common faith" (Tit **1** 4), "common salvation" (Jude ver 3), refer to that in which the experience of all Christians unites and is identical: "common," because there is but one faith and one salvation (Eph **4** 4–6). From this comes the derived meaning of what is ordinary and, therefore, to be disesteemed, as contrasted with what pertains to a class, and to be prized, because rare. This naturally coincides with OT exclusivism, particularity and separation. Its religion was that of a separated people, with a separated class as its ministers, and with minute directions as to distinctions of meat, drink, times, places, rites, vessels, etc. Whatever was common or ordinary, it avoided. The NT, on the other hand, with its universalism of scope, and its spirituality of sphere, rose above all such externals. The salvation which it brought was directed to the redemption of Nature, as well as of man, sanctifying the creature, and pervading all parts of man's being and all relations of life. The antithesis is forcibly illustrated in Acts **10** 14 f, where Peter says: "I have never eaten anything that is c. and unclean," and the reply is: "What God hath cleansed, make not thou c." H. E. JACOBS

COMMONWEALTH, kom′un-welth (πολιτεία, *politeía*): Spoken of the theocracy (Eph **2** 12). The same word is rendered **"freedom,"** AV; "citizenship" RV. Also in the sense of commonwealth in the Apoc (2 Macc **4** 11; **8** 17; **13** 14); in the sense of citizenship (3 Macc **3** 21.23). See CITIZENSHIP.

COMMUNE, kō-mūn′, **COMMUNICATE,** kō-mūn′i-kāt, **COMMUNICATION,** ko-mū-ni-kā′shun: To commune is to converse confidentially and sympathetically. It is represented in both Heb and Gr by several words lit. signifying to speak (cf Lk **6** 11, διαλαλέω, *dialaléō;* also Lk **22** 4; Acts **24** 26, ὁμιλέω, *homiléō*). To communicate is to impart something to another, so that it becomes common to giver and receiver. In 1 Tim **6** 18, "willing to communicate" (RVm "sympathize"), represents a single word κοινωνικοί, *koinōnikoí*, and refers to the habit of sharing with others either sympathy or property. RV gives "companionships" for *homilíai* in 1 Cor **15** 33 (AV "communications"). See also COMMUNION.

COMMUNION, kō-mūn′yun (**FELLOWSHIP**): The terms "communion" and "fellowship" of the Eng. Bible are varying tr[s] of the words κοινωνία, *koinōnía*, and κοινωνέω, *koinōnéō*, or their cognates. They designate acts of fellowship observed among the early Christians or express the unique sense of unity and fellowship of which these acts were the outward expression. The several passages in which these terms are used fall into two groups: those in which they refer to acts of fellowship, and those in which they refer to fellowship as experienced.

I. Acts of Fellowship.—The acts of fellowship mentioned in the NT are of four kinds.

1. The Lord's Supper

Our information concerning the nature of the fellowship involved in the observance of this sacrament is confined to the single notice in 1 Cor **10** 16.17, "The cup of blessing which we bless, is it not a communion of the blood of Christ? The bread which we break, is it not a communion of the body of Christ?" Owing to the presence of the material elements in the sacrament there is a temptation to limit the word for communion to the sense of partaking. This, however, does not entirely satisfy the requirements of the context. The full significance of the term is to be sought in the light of the argument of the whole section (vs 14–22).

Paul is making a protest against Christians participating in idolatrous feasts on the ground that such feasts are really celebrated in honor of the demons associated with the idols, and that those who participate in them come into fellowship with demons. As a proof of this point the apostle cites the Lord's Supper with which his readers are familiar. By partaking of the cup and the bread the communicants are linked together in unity: "We, who are many, are one bread, one body: for we all partake of the one bread." Thus the communion of the elements is a real communion of the worshippers one with another and with Christ. Unless the communion be understood in this spiritual sense Paul's illustration falls short of the mark. See EUCHARIST.

2. Communism

The term for fellowship as used in Acts **2** 42 is by some interpreted in this sense: "They continued stedfastly in the apostles' teaching and fellowship, in the breaking of bread and the prayers." The fact that the four terms are used in pairs and that three of them refer to specific acts observed by the company of believers suggests that the term for fellowship also refers to some definite act similar to the others. It is very plausible to refer this to the community of goods described in the verses immediately following (see COMMUNITY OF GOODS). The author might, however, with equal propriety have regarded the *interchange of spiritual experiences* as an act of worship in the same class with "the breaking of bread and the prayers."

3. Contributions

Christian fellowship found a natural mode of expression in almsgiving. This is enjoined as a duty in Rom **12** 13; 1 Tim **6** 18; He **13** 16. An example of such giving is the great collection raised among the gentile converts for the poor saints of Jerus (Rom **15** 26; 2 Cor **8** 4; **9** 13). To this collection St. Paul attached so much importance as a witness to the spirit of fellowship which the gospel inspires in all hearts alike, whether Jew or Gentile, that he desired even at the peril of his life to deliver it with his own hand. See COLLECTION.

4. Coöperation

A form of fellowship closely related to almsgiving was that of formal aid or coöperation in Christian work, such as the aid given to St. Paul by the Philippians (Phil **1** 5). A unique form of this coöperation is the formal endorsement by giving the right hand of fellowship as described in Gal **2** 9.

II. Fellowship as Experienced.—From the very beginning the early Christians experienced a peculiar sense of unity. Christ is at once the center of this unity and the origin of every expression of fellowship. Sometimes the fellowship is essentially an experience and as such it is scarcely susceptible of definition. It may rather be regarded as a mystical union in Christ. In other instances the fellowship approaches or includes the idea of intercourse. In some passages it is represented as a participation or partnership. The terms occur most frequently in the writings of Paul with whom the idea of Christian unity was a controlling principle.

In its various relations, fellowship is represented: (1) As a communion between the Son and the Father. The gospel record represents Jesus as enjoying a unique sense of communion and intimacy with the Father. Among many such expressions those of Mt **11** 25–27 (cf Lk **10** 21.22) and Jn **14**–**15** are especially important. (2) As our communion with God, either with the Father or the Son or with the Father through the Son or the Holy Spirit. "Our fellowship is with the Father, and with his Son Jesus Christ" (1 Jn **1** 3; cf also Jn **14** 6.23.26). (3) As our communion one with another. "If we walk in the light, as he is in the light, we have fellowship one with another" (1 Jn **1** 7). Sometimes the idea of communion occurs in relation with abstract ideas or experiences: "Have no fellowship with the unfruitful works of darkness" (Eph **5** 11); "the fellowship of his sufferings" (Phil **3** 10); "the fellowship of thy faith" (Philem ver 6). In three passages the relation of the fellowship is not entirely clear: the "fellowship of the Spirit" (Phil **2** 1); "the communion of the Holy Spirit" (2 Cor **13** 14); and "the fellowship of his Son Jesus Christ" (1 Cor **1** 9). The fellowship is probably to be understood as that prevailing among Christians by virtue of the grace of Christ and the ministry of the Holy Spirit.

It is not to be inferred that the idea of fellowship is limited to the passages in which the specific words for communion are used. Some of the clearest and richest expressions of unity and fellowship are found in the Gospels, though these words do not occur in them. In fact, perhaps, the most familiar and forcible expressions of the idea are those in which they are represented symbolically, as in the parable of the Vine and the Branches (Jn **15** 1 ff) or in the figure of the Body and its Members (Mt **5** 29 ff; Rom **12** 5; 1 Cor **12**).

RUSSELL BENJAMIN MILLER

COMMUNION WITH DEMONS, dē'monz (**DEVILS,** dev''lz):

I. Use of Term.—The actual expression "communion with demons" (κοινωνοὶ τῶν δαιμονίων, *koinōnoí tōn daimoníōn*) occurs but once in Scripture (1 Cor **10** 20) where its **fig.** meaning is evident, but it is implied in the Eng. version of a number of passages by the terms "one who has" or "those who have" "familiar spirits" (Lev **19** 31; **20** 6.27; Dt **18** 11; 1 S **28** 3.7.8.9; 2 K **21** 6; **23** 24; 1 Ch **10** 13; 2 Ch **33** 6; Isa **8** 19; **19** 3; **29** 4). These passages seem to be somewhat incongruous with Paul's statement, but are in reality so intimately related to it as to give and receive light through the connection.

II. Teaching of Scripture.—To begin with, we may safely say, in general, that there is no ground for asserting that the Bible admits the possibility of conscious and voluntary communion with spirits. This is an essential element of popular demonology in all ages, but it is absent from Scripture. Even in the passages mentioned above which refer to necromancers and wizards, while, as we shall see, the words indicate that such practitioners professed to rely upon spirits in their divinations, the Scriptures carefully refrain from sanctioning these claims, and a number of features in the various passages serve to indicate that the true scriptural view is quite the opposite. As this is not a prevalent opinion, we should do well to examine the passages with some little care.

1. The New Testament

(1) We may first deal with the NT. In the Gospels the demoniacs are consistently looked upon and treated as unconscious and helpless victims (see DEMON, DEMONOLOGY). The frequent use of this term "demonized" (*daimonizómenoi*) together with all that is told us of the methods of treating these cases adopted by Our Lord and His apostles (see EXORCISM) indicates the belief of the NT writers that the control of demons over men is obtained outside of or below the region of conscious volition and that the condition of the sufferers is pathological.

(2) The same must be said of the Lydian maiden whose cure by Paul is recorded in Acts **16** 16. This is the one instance in the NT where divination is connected with spirits. The account emphasizes the excitable neurosis of the patient; and the belief on the part of the apostles and of the writer of Acts that the girl was not the conscious accomplice of her masters, but their unfortunate victim through her mysterious malady, is clear. She was treated, as the other cases recorded in the NT, not as a conscious wrongdoer, but as a sick person to be healed.

(1) Turning now to the OT, the instance which requires the most careful treatment, because it holds the key to all the rest, is the narrative of Saul's

visit to the Witch of Endor in 1 S **28** 3–25. The Heb word *'ōbh* which is usually tr[d] "one who has a familiar spirit" (see list of passages at beginning of art.) occurs in this narrative four times (vs 3, 7 twice, 8).

2. The Old Testament

According to the ordinary interpretation it is used in three different senses, two of which occur here. These three senses are (*a*) a person who controls a spirit, (*b*) the spirit controlled, (*c*) the power to control such a spirit. This meaning appears to be altogether too broad. Omitting to translate the word we have: (ver 3) "Saul had put away *'ōbhōth*, and *yidh'ōnīm*"; (ver 7), a woman, a mistress of an *'ōbh;* (ver 8) "Divine unto me . . . . by the *'ōbh.*" It is extremely unlikely that the same word should be used in two senses so far apart as "person who has a spirit" and the "spirit itself" in the same context. In the last passage mentioned (ver 8) there is a double indication that the word *'ōbh* cannot have either signification mentioned. Saul says: "Divine unto me by the *'ōbh* and *bring me up* whomsoever I shall name unto thee." The expression "divine by" clearly points to some magical object used in divination. Control of a spirit through some magical object is familiar enough. The rest of Saul's statement confirms this view. The result of the divination is the calling up of a spirit. A spirit would hardly be used to call up another spirit. This conclusion is confirmed by the etymology. The word *'ōbh* is supposed to mean "one who has a familiar spirit," from its root-significance of *hollow* and its primary meaning of *wineskin.* According to this derivation the word is applied to a necromancer on the supposition that the spirit inhabits his body and speaks from within. The transference to spirit is extremely unlikely and the explanation is not consistent with primitive ideas on spirit manifestation (see *BDB*, **אוב**, end).

(2) We, therefore, hold with H. P. Smith (*ICC*, "Samuel" in loc.), though partly on different grounds, that the word *'ōbh* has the same meaning in all the passages where it occurs, and that it refers to a sacred object or fetish by which spiritistic divination was carried on.

The significance of this conclusion is that the misleading expression "familiar spirit" disappears from the text, for Dr. Driver's interpretation of the companion word *yidh'ōnīm* (see *ICC*, Comm. Dt in loc.) will scarcely be maintained in the face of this new meaning for *'ōbh.* The prohibition contained in the law (Lev **20** 27) against *'ōbhōth*, and those using them, places them in the same catalogue of offence and futility with idol-worship in general.

(3) This opinion is confirmed by two separate items of evidence. (*a*) In the Witch of Endor story Samuel's appearance, according to the idea of the narrator, was due to a *miracle*, not to the magic power of the feeble and cheating old woman to whom Saul had resorted. God speaks through the apparition a stern message of doom. No one was more startled than the woman herself, who for once had a real vision (ver 12). She not only gave a loud cry of astonishment and alarm but she described the figure which she saw as "a god coming up out of the earth." The story is told with fidelity and clearly indicates the opinion that the actual appearance of a spirit is so violently exceptional as to indicate the immediate power and presence of God.

(*b*) In Isa **8** 19 the *'ōbhōth* and *yidh'ōnīm* are spoken of as those who "chirp and mutter." These terms refer to the necromancers themselves (LXX translates *'ōbhōth* by *eggastrómuthoi* = ventriloquists) who practiced ventriloquism in connection with their magical rites. In Isa **29** 4 it is said "Thy voice shall be as an *'ōbh*, out of the ground." Here *'ōbh* is usually interpreted as "ghost," but it is far more probable (see *BDB* sub loc.) that it refers as in **8** 19 to the ventriloquistic tricks of those who utter their oracles in voices intended to represent the spirits which they have evoked. They are stamped in these passages, as in the Witch of Endor narrative, as deceivers practising a fraudulent art. By implication their power to evoke spirits with whom they were in familiar intercourse is denied.

This leaves the way clear for a brief consideration of the words of Paul in 1 Cor **10** 20 in connection with cognate passages in the OT.

3. The Meaning of Idol-Worship

(1) He argues that since idol-worship is really demon-worship, the partaking of heathen sacrifice is a communion with demons and a separation from Christ. It is usually taken for granted that this characterization of heathen worship was simply a part of the Jewish-Christian polemic against idolatry. Our fuller knowledge of the spiritism which conditions the use of images enables us to recognize the fact that from the viewpoint of heathenism itself Paul's idea was strictly correct. The image is venerated because it is supposed to represent or contain an invisible being or spirit, not necessarily a deity in the absolute sense, but a superhuman living being capable of working good or ill to men.

(2) In the AV the term devils is used in four OT passages (Lev **17** 7; Dt **32** 17; 2 Ch **11** 15; Ps **106** 37). In RV "devils" has disappeared from the text—the word *he-goats* appears in Lev **17** 7 and 2 Ch **11** 15, while "demons" appears in Dt **32** 17 and Ps **106** 37. The tr of *s[e]'īrīm* as "he-goats" is literally correct, but conveys an erroneous conception of the meaning. The practice reprobated is the worship of Satyrs (see SATYR) or wood-demons supposed to be like goats in appearance and to inhabit lonely places. The same word is used in Isa **13** 21; **34** 14. The word tr[d] "demons" in RV is *shēdhīm*, a term used only twice and both times in connection with the rites and abominations of heathen worship. It is interesting to note that the word *shîdu* is applied to the beings represented by the bull-colossi of Assyria (Driver, Dt in loc.). *BDB* holds that the word *shēdhīm* is an Assyr loan-word, while Briggs (*ICC*, Ps **106** 37) holds that *shēdhīm* were ancient gods of Canaan. In either case the word belongs to heathenism and is used in Scripture to describe heathen worship in its own terminology. The interpretation of these beings as evil is characteristic of Bib. demonism in general (see DEMON, etc). The worship of idols was the worship of personal beings more than man and less than God, according to Jewish and Christian ideas (see Driver op. cit., 363). LXX translates both the above words by *daimónia.*

4. Conclusion

The term "communion with demons" does not imply any power on the part of men to enter into voluntary relationship with beings of another world, but that, by sinful compliance in wrongdoing, such as idol-worship and magical rites, men may enter into a moral identification with evil powers against which it is their duty to fight.

LITERATURE.—The Dictionaries and Commentaries dealing with the passages quoted above contain discussions of the various aspects of the subject. Jewish superstitions are ably treated by Edersheim, *LTJM* (8th ed), II, 771, 773.

LOUIS MATTHEWS SWEET

COMMUNITY, kō-mū'ni-ti, **OF GOODS** (**ἅπαντα κοινὰ εἶχον**, *hápanta koiná eíchon*, lit. "They had all things [in] common"): In Acts **2** 44, it is said that, in the infant church at Jerus, "all that believed were together, and had all things common," and (**4** 34 f) "as many as were possessors of lands or houses sold them, and brought the prices of the things that were sold, and laid them at the apostles' feet." The inference from this, that there was an absolute disposal of all the property of all the members of the church, and that its proceeds were contributed to a common fund, has been disputed upon the ground that the example of Barnabas in selling "a field" for this purpose (**4** 37) would not have been mentioned, if this had been the universal rule. The thought conveyed is that all believers in that church held their property as a trust from the Lord, for the benefit of the entire brotherhood, and, as there was need, did as Barnabas.

No commandment, of which record has been preserved, prescribed any such course. It came from the spontaneous impulse of the sense of brotherhood in Christ, when the band of disciples was still small, making them in a sense one family, and under the external constraint of extreme want and persecution. So much there was, that they realized, under such conditions they had in common, that they were ready to extend this to all things. It was, in a sense, a continuance of the practice of a common purse in the band of immediate followers of Our Lord during his ministry. The penalty inflicted on Ananias and Sapphira was not for any failure to comply fully with this custom, but because this freedom which they possessed (Acts **5** 4) they falsely professed to have renounced, thus receiving in the estimation of their brethren a credit that was not their due. This custom did not last long. It was possible only within a limited circle, and under very peculiar circumstances. The NT recognizes the right of individual property and makes no effort to remove the differences that exist among believers themselves. The community of goods which it renders possible is spiritual (1 Cor **3** 21 f), and not one of visible and external things. With respect to the latter, it enjoins upon the Christian, as a steward of God, the possession and administration of property for the progress of the kingdom of God, and the highest interests of men. The spirit of Acts **4** 34 is always to pervade the association of believers as a true Christian community. Meyer, on the above passage, has suggested that it is not unlikely that the well-known poverty of the church at Jerus, and its long dependence upon the alms of other churches, may be connected with this early communistic practice, which, however justifiable and commendable at the time, bore its inevitable fruits in a subsequent season of great scarcity and lack of employment. H. E. JACOBS

COMPACT, kom-pakt′, **COMPACTED,** kom-pakt′ed (חָבַר, *ḥābhar*, "to be joined"; **συμβιβάζω,** *sumbibázō*, "to raise up together"): "Compact" appears as tr of *ḥābhar* in Ps **122** 3, "Jerus . . . . a city that is compact together" (well built, its breaches restored, walls complete, and separate from all around it); and "compacted" (*sumbibazō*) occurs in AV Eph **4** 16, "fitly joined together and compacted," RV "fitly framed and knit together." In RV "compacted" is also the tr of *συνίστημι*, *sunístēmi*, "to set together" (2 Pet **3** 5), "an earth compacted out of water and amidst [m, through] water," which suggests the idea of *water* as the primary material (cf Gen **1** 2). W. L. WALKER

COMPANY, kum′pa-ni: The fertility of the original languages in synonyms and varied shades of meaning is seen by the fact that 20 Heb and 12 Gr words are represented by this single term. An analysis of these words shows that "company" is both an indefinite and limitless term, signifying few or many, and all kinds of assemblages of people, e.g.:

(1) Caravan, (*a*) migratory (Isa **21** 13 AV); (*b*) commercial (Gen **37** 25 AV); Job **6** 19, "The companies of Sheba waited [in vain] for them."

(2) Military, *gᵉdhūdh*, "troop," *hāmōn*, 2 Ch **20** 12; *rō'sh*, "head," "detachment"; Jgs **7** 16.20: "three companies"; **9** 34.37.43: "four companies."

(3) Band (*ḥebher*) or "gang," as rendered by Keil and Delitzsch; a gang of murderous priests (Hos **6** 9).

(4) Camp or encampment (Gen **32** 8.21; **50** 9).

(5) Religious body, "company of prophets" (1 S **19** 20).

(6) Assembly, congregation, "company of nations" (Gen **35** 11; Ezk **38** 4.7.13.15).

(7) A tumultuous crowd (2 K **9** 17).

(8) Associate, companion, often with reference to moral affinity (Job **34** 8; Prov **29** 3; Acts **10** 28), *kolláomai*, "to glue or cement together," indicative of the binding power of moral affinity (RV "to join himself"); as a verb, to "company with" or "keep company" (Acts **1** 21; 1 Cor **5** 9.11; 2 Thess **3** 14). In Apoc in the sense of "to cohabit" (Sus **1** 54.57.58).

(9) A host. "Great was the company," etc (Ps **68** 11 RV "The women . . . . are a great host"). In the East it is the women who celebrate victories with song and dance (see 1 S **18** 6.7).

(10) A chorus, dance (*mᵉḥōlāh*). "The company of two armies" (Cant **6** 13 AV; RV "the dance of Mahanaim").

(11) Meal party, *κλισία*, *klisía*, "a reclining company at meals." "Make them sit down [Gr "recline"] in companies" (Lk **9** 14). Cf "companion," from Lat *com*, "together," and *panis*, "bread."

(12) A myriad, a ten-thousand, an indefinite number (*murías;* He **12** 22 [RV "hosts"]).

(13) Companions on a journey, *sunodía*, "a journeying together" (Lk **2** 44).

(14) Signifying kinship of spirit, *ídios*, "one's own." "They came to their own company" (Acts **4** 23).

(15) A mob (Acts **17** 5 [RV "a crowd"]). DWIGHT M. PRATT

COMPARATIVE, kom-par′a-tiv, **RELIGION:**

I. THE SUBJECT IN GENERAL
  1. Universality of Religion
  2. Theories of Its Origin
  3. Evolution
II. RELATION OF CHRISTIANITY TO ETHNIC FAITHS AND THEIR TENETS
  1. *Karma*
  2. God
  3. The *Summum Bonum*
  4. Self-Revelation of God
  5. Incarnation
  6. Salvation
  7. Faith
  8. Approach to God
III. GENERAL CHARACTERISTICS OF ETHNIC FAITHS
  1. Tenets Common to All Religions
  2. Tendency to Degradation
  3. Mythology and Religion
  4. Religion and Morality
IV. SUPPOSED RESEMBLANCES TO REVEALED RELIGION
  1. Rites
  2. Dogmas
  3. Asserted Parallels to Gospel History
  4. Virgin Birth
  5. Heathen Aspirations
  6. Lessons Taught by Comparative Religion
LITERATURE

I. The Subject in General.—The science of comparative religion is perhaps the latest born of all sciences. Largely in consequence of this fact, our knowledge of what it really proves is still far from definite, and men draw most contradictory conclusions on this point. As in the case of all new sciences in the past, not a few people have endeavored under its shelter to attack Christianity and all revealed religion. These assaults already give signs of failure—as in similar cases previously—and a new evidence of Christianity is emerging from the conflict. It is only "a little learning" that is proverbially dangerous. The subject with which the science of comparative religion deals is religion in general and all the facts which can be learnt about all religions ancient and modern, whether professed by savages or prevalent among highly civilized communities, whether to be studied in sacred books or learnt orally from the people.

1. Universality of Religion

In this way we learn first of all that religion is a *universal* phenomenon, found among all nations, in all conditions, though differing immensely in its teachings, ceremonies and effects in different places. It is perhaps the most powerful for good or evil of all the instincts (for it is an instinct) which influence mankind.

2. Theories of Origin and Growth of Religion

To account for the origin and growth of religion various theories have been propounded: (1) "Humanism," which is the revival of the ancient view of Euhēmeros (cir 400 BC) that all religion arose from fear of ghosts, and all the gods were but men who had died; (2) "Animism," which traces religion to early man's fancy that every object in Nature had a personality like his own; (3) the Astral Theory, which supposes that religion originated from worship of the heavenly bodies. It is clear that there are facts to support each of these hypotheses, yet no one of them satisfies all the conditions of the case. To (1) it has been replied that most tribes from the earliest times clearly distinguished between those deities who had been men, and the gods proper, who had never been men and had never died. Regarding (2), it should be observed that it admits that man's consciousness of his own personality and his fancy that it exists in other creatures also does not account for his *worshipping* them, unless we grant the existence of the *sensus numinis* within him: if so, then *this* explains, justifies, and necessitates religion. (3) The Astral Theory is in direct opposition to Euhēmerism or Humanism. It ascribes personality to the heavenly bodies in man's early fancy; but it, too, has to presuppose the *sensus numinis*, without which religion would be impossible, as would be the science of optics if man had not the sense of sight.

3. Evolution

It is often held that religion is due to evolution. If so, then its evolution, resulting *ex hypothesi* in Christianity as its acme, must be the working out of a Divine "Eternal Purpose" (*próthesis tṓn aiṓnōn*, Eph **3** 11), just as has been the evolution of an amoeba into a man on the Evolutionary Theory. This would be an additional proof of the truth of Christianity. But, though doubtless there has been evolution—or gradual progress under Divine guidance—in religion, the *fact of Christ* is sufficient to show that there is a Divine self-revelation too. Hence the claim of Christianity to be the absolute religion. "The pre-Christian religions were the age-long prayer, the Incarnation was the answer" (Illingworth). Christianity as revealed in Christ adds what none of the ethnic faiths could prove their claim to—authority, holiness, revelation.

II. Relation of Christianity to Ethnic Faiths and Their Tenets.—It is very remarkable that Christianity—though clearly not a philosophy but a religion that has arisen under historical circumstances which preclude the possibility of supposing it the product of Eclecticism—yet sums up in itself all that is good in all religions and philosophies, without the bad, the fearful perversions and corruptions of the moral sense, too often found in them. The more the study of comparative religion is carried on the more plainly evident does this become. It also supplements in a wonderful way the half-truths *concealed* rather than revealed in other systems, whether religious or philosophical. We subjoin a few instances of this.

1. Karma

Karma is strongly insisted on in Hindūism and Buddhism. These teach that every deed, good or bad, must have its result, that "its fruit must be eaten" here or hereafter. So does Christianity quite as forcibly (Gal **6** 7.8). But neither Indian faith explains how sin can be forgiven, evil be overruled for good, nor how, by trampling under foot their vices, men may rise higher (Aug., *Sermo* iii, *De Ascensione*). They recognize, in some sense, the existence of evil, and illogically teach that rites and certain ascetic practices help to overcome it. They know of no Atonement, though modern Hindūism endeavors to propitiate the deities by sacrifices, as indeed was done in Vedic times. Conscience they cannot explain. Christianity, while showing the heinousness of sin as no other system does, and so supplementing the others, supplements them still further by the Atonement, showing that God is just, and teaching how His very righteousness can be brought to "justify" the sinner (Rom **3** 26).

2. God

Mahāyāna Buddhism proclaims an immanent but not transcendent being (*Dharma-kāya*), who is "the ultimate reality that underlies all particular phenomena" (Suzuki), who wills and reflects, though not fully personal. He is not the Creator of the world but a kind of *Animus mundi*. He is the sum total of all sentient beings, and they have no individual existence, no "*ego*-soul." The world of matter has no real existence but is his self-manifestation. Christianity supplements and corrects this by teaching the transcendence as well as the immanence (Acts **17** 28) of the Creator, who is *at least* personal, if not something higher, who is the *Source* of reality though not *Himself* the *sole* reality, and of our personality and life, and "who only hath immortality" (1 Tim **6** 16).

3. The "Summum Bonum"

Vedāntism and Ṣūfīism proclaim that ultimate absorption in the impersonal "It" is the *summum bonum*, and the *Chāndogya Upanishad* says, "There is just one thing, without a second" (Book VI, **2** 1, 2). Of this one thing everything is, so to speak, a part: there being no ultimate difference between the human and the Divine. Thus sin is denied and unreality proclaimed (*Māyā*, illusion). The yearning for union with God underlying all this is satisfied in Christianity, which provides reconciliation with God and shows how by new spiritual birth men may become children of God (Jn **1** 12.13) and "partakers of the divine nature" (2 Pet **1** 4), without being swallowed up therein like a raindrop in the ocean: the union being spiritual and not material.

4. Self-Revelation of God

Orthodox (*Sunnī*) Muslim theology declares God to be separated from man by an impassable gulf and hence to be unknowable. Philosophically this leads to Agnosticism, though opposed to Polytheism. Among the Jews the philosophy of Maimonides ends in the same failure to attain to a knowledge of the Divine or to describe God except by negations (*Ṣēpher Ha-maddā'*, **1** 11). The Bible, on the other hand, while speaking of Him as invisible, and unknowable through merely human effort (Job **11** 7.8; Jn **1** 18), yet reveals Him in Christ, who is God and man. Jewish mysticism endeavored to solve the problem of creation by the invention of the *'Ādhām ḳadhmōn* (archetypal man), and earlier by Philo's *Logos* doctrine and the *Mēmrā'* of the Targums. But these abstractions have neither reality nor personality. The Christian *Logos* doctrine presents no theoretical but the actual historical, eternal Christ (cf Jn **1** 1–3; He **1** 2).

5. Incarnation

Heathenism seeks to give some idea of the Invisible by means of idols; Vaishnavism has its doctrine of *avatāras;* Bābīism and

Bahā'ism their dogma of "manifestations" (*maẓhar*) in human beings; the '*Alī-ilāhīs* are so called because they regard '*Alī* as God. Instead of these unworthy theories and deifications, Christianity supplies the holy, sinless, perfect Incarnation in Christ.

6. Salvation

Hindūism offers *mukti* (*mōksha*), "deliverance" from a miserable existence; Christianity in Christ offers pardon, deliverance from sin, and reconciliation with God.

7. Faith

Kṛishṇaism teaches unreasoning "devotion" (*bhakti*) of "mind, body, property" to certain supposed incarnations of Kṛishṇa (Vishṇu), quite regardless of their immoral conduct; Christianity inculcates a manly, reasonable "faith" in Christ, but only after "proving all things."

8. Approach to God

Pilgrimages in Islām and Hindūism indicate but do not satisfy a need for approach to God; Christianity teaches a growth in grace and in likeness to Christ, and so a spiritual drawing near to God.

III. General Characteristics of Ethnic Faiths.—In all religions we find, though in many various forms, certain common beliefs, such as:

1. Tenets Common to All Religions

(1) the existence of some spiritual power or powers, good or bad, superior to man and able to affect his present and future life; (2) that there is a difference between right and wrong, even though not clearly defined; (3) that there is an after-life of some sort, with happiness or misery often regarded as in some measure dependent upon conduct or upon the observance of certain rites here. In the main the fact of the all but universal agreement of religions upon these points proves that they are true in substance. Even such an agnostic philosophy as original Buddhism was, has been constrained by human need to evolve from itself or admit from without deistic or theistic elements, and thus Buddha himself has been deified by the Mahāyāna School. Yet no ethnic faith satisfies the "human soul naturally Christian," as Tertullian calls it (*Liber Apologeticus*, cap. 17), for none of them reveals One God, personal, holy, loving, just, merciful, omniscient and omnipotent. Even Islām fails here. Ethnic religions are either (1) polytheistic, worshipping many gods, all imperfect and some evil, or (2) mystical, evaporating away, as it were, God's Personality, thus rendering Him a mental abstraction, as in the Hindū philosophical systems and in Mahāyāna Buddhism. Christianity as revealed in Christ does just what all other faiths fail to do, reconciling these two tendencies and correcting both.

2. Tendency to Degradation, not to Progress, in Ethnic Faiths

As a general rule, the nearer to their source we can trace religions, the purer we find them. In most cases a tendency to degradation and not to progressive improvement manifests itself as time goes on, and this is sometimes carried to such an extent that, as Lucretius found in Rome and Greece, religion becomes a curse and not a blessing. Thus, for example, regarding ancient Egypt, Professor Renouf says: "The sublimer portions of the Egyp religion are not the comparatively late result of a process of development. The sublimer portions are demonstrably ancient, and the last stage of the Egyp religion was by far the grossest and most corrupt" (*Hibbert Lectures*, 91). Modern Hindūism, again, is incomparably lower in its religious conceptions than the religion of the Vedas. In Polynesia the same rule holds good, as is evident from the myths about Tangaroa. In Samoa he was said to be the son of two beings, the "Cloudless Heaven" and the "Outspread Heaven." He originally existed in open space. He made the sky to dwell in. He then made the earth. Somewhat later he was supposed to be visible in the moon! But a lower depth was reached. In Hawaii, Tangaroa has sunk to an *evil* being, the leader of a rebellion against another god, Tane, and is now condemned to abide in the lowest depths of darkness and be the god of death. In South Africa, Australia and elsewhere, traditions still linger of a Creator of all things, but his worship has been entirely laid aside in favor of lower and more evil deities.

3. Mythology and Religion

Almost everywhere mythology has arisen and perverted religion into something very different from what it once was. The same tendency has more than once manifested itself in the Christian church, thus rendering a return to Christ's teachings necessary. As an instance, compare the modern popular religion of Italy with that of the NT. It is remarkable that no religion but the Christian, however, has shown its capability of reform.

4. Religion and Morality in Ethnic Faiths

For the most part, in ethnic religions, there is no recognized connection between religion and morality. The wide extension of phallic rites and the existence of *hieródoulai* and *hieródouloi* in many lands show that religion has often consecrated gross immorality. Mythology aids in this degradation. Hence Seneca, after mentioning many evil myths related of Jupiter, etc., says: "By which nothing else was effected but the removal from men of their shame at sinning, if they deemed such beings gods" (L. A. Seneca, *De beata vita* cap. 26). With the possibly doubtful exception of the religion of certain savage tribes, in no religion is the holiness of God taught except in Christianity and its initial stage, Judaism. Ethnic deities are mostly born of heaven and earth, if not identified with them in part, and are rarely regarded as creating them. It was otherwise, however, with Ahura Mazda in Zoroastrianism, and with certain Sumerian deities, and there are other exceptions, too. The "religions of Nature" have generally produced gross immorality, encouraged and even insisted upon as a part of their ritual; cf Mylitta-worship in Babylon and that of the "*Mater deûm*," Venus, Anāhita, etc.

IV. Supposed Resemblances to Revealed Religion.—Much attention has been called to real or supposed community of rites and "myths," esp. when any ethnic faith is compared with Christianity. Sacrifice, for instance, is an essential part of every religion. In Christianity none are now offered, *except* the "living sacrifice" of the believer, though that of Christ offered once for all is held to be the substance foreshadowed by Jewish sacrifices. Purificatory bathings are found almost everywhere, and that very naturally, because of the universality of conscience and of some sense of sin.

1. Rites

2. Dogmas

Belief in the fiery end of the world existed among the Stoics, and is found in the Eddas of Scandinavia and the *Purāṇas* of India. Traditions of an age before sin and death came upon mankind occur in many different lands. Many of these traditions may easily be accounted for. But in some cases the supposed resemblance to revealed religion does not exist, or is vastly exaggerated. The Yōga philosophy in India is popularly supposed to aim at union with God, as does Christianity; but (so understood) the Yōga system, as has already been said, implies loss of personality and absorption into the impersonal, unconscious "It" (*Tat*). The doctrine of a Trinity is nowhere found, only Triads of separate deities. Belief in a resurrection is found in only very late parts of the Pers (Zoroastrian) scriptures, composed after cents. of communication with Jews and Christians. In the earlier Avesta only a "restoration" of the world is mentioned (cf Acts **3** 21). Original (*Hīnayāna*) Buddhism teaches "immortality" (*amata*), but by this is meant *Nirvāṇa* ("extinction"). Mithraism has been said to teach the "resurrection of the body," but, according to Eubūlus and Porphyry, it taught rather the transmigration of the soul.

3. Asserted Parallels to Gospel History

The assertion is often made that many of the leading gospel incidents in the life of Our Lord are paralleled in other religions. It is said, for instance, that the resurrection of Adonis, Osiris and Mithra was believed in by their followers. It is true that, in some places, Adonis was said to have come to life the day after he had met his death by the tusk of a boar (the cold of winter); but everywhere it was recognized that he was not a man who had been killed, but the representative of the produce of the soil, slain or dying down in the cold weather and growing again in spring. As to Osiris, his tomb was shown in more than one place in Egypt, and his body was *never* supposed to have come to life again, though his spirit was alive and was ruler of the underworld. Mithra was admitted to be the genius of the sun. He was said to have sprung from a rock (in old Pers and Sanskrit the same word means "sky," "cloud" and "rock"), but not to have been incarnated, nor to have died, much less to have risen from the dead. The modern erroneous fancy that Mithraists believed in his resurrection rests solely on one or at most two passages in *Christian* writers, which really refer to the burial of Osiris and the removal of his body from the tomb by his hostile brother Typhon (Set). The high morality attributed to Mithraism and even to the worship of Isis rests on no better foundation than the wrong rendering of a few passages and the deliberate ignoring of many which contradict the theory.

4. Virgin Birth

Virgin birth, we have been told, is a doctrine of many religions. As a matter of fact, it is found in hardly one ethnic faith. Nothing of the kind was believed regarding Osiris, Adonis, Horus, Mithra, Krishṇa, Zoroaster. Of Buddha it is denied entirely in all the books of the Southern Canon (*Pāli*), and is found expressed only vaguely in one or two late uncanonical works of the Northern (Sanskṛit) School. It was doubtless borrowed from Christianity. Supernatural birth of quite a different (and very repulsive) kind is found in many mythologies, but that is quite another thing.

5. Heathen Aspirations and Unconscious Prophecies

Heathenism contains some vague aspirations and unconscious prophecies, the best example of which is to be found in Vergil's Fourth Eclogue, if that be not rather due to Jewish influence. Any such foregleams of the coming light as are real and not merely imaginary, such, for instance, as the Indian doctrine of the *avatāras* or "descents" of Vishṇu, are to be accounted for as part of the Divine education of the human race. The "false dawn," so well known in the East, is not a proof that the sun is not about to rise, nor can its existence justify anyone in shutting his eyes to and rejecting the daylight when it comes. It is but a harbinger of the real dawn.

6. Lessons Taught by Comparative Religion

Comparative religion teaches us that religion is essential to and distinctive of humanity. The failures of the ethnic faiths no less than their aspirations show how great is man's need of Christ, and how utterly unable imagination has ever proved itself to be even to conceive of such an ideal character as He revealed to us in the full light of history and in the wonder-working effects of His character upon the lives and hearts of those who then and in all ages since have in Him received life and light.

LITERATURE.—Tylor, *Anthropology;* Jordan, *Comparative Religion, Its Genesis and Growth;* Falke, *Zum Kampfe der drei Weltreligionen;* Gould, *Origin and Development of Religious Belief;* Jevons, *Introduction to the History of Religion;* Reville, *Prolegomena to the History of Religions;* Max Müller, *Introduction to the Science of Religion;* Hardwick, *Christ and Other Masters;* Kellogg, *The Light of Asia and the Light of the World;* Farrar, *The Witness of History to Christ;* A. Lang, *Magic and Religion; The Making of Religion;* Johnson, *Oriental Religions and Their Relation to Universal Religion;* Farnell, *The Evolution of Religion;* Howitt, *The Native Tribes of S.E. Australia;* Smith, *Religion of the Semites;* Reinach, *Cultes, mythes et religions;* Dilger, *Erlöschen des Menschen nach Hinduismus und Christentum;* Rhys Davids, *Origin and Growth of Religion;* Kuenen, *National Religions and Universal Religion* (Hibbert Lectures, 1882); Döllinger, *The Gentile and the Jew in the Courts of the Temple of Christ* (1862); Dodson, *Evolution and Its Bearing on Religion;* MacCulloch, *Comparative Theology;* Baumann, *Über Religionen und Religion;* Waitz, *Anthropologie der Naturvölker;* Hastings, *Encyclopaedia of Religion and Ethics;* Frazer, *Adonis, Attis, Osiris;* Dufourcq, *Hist. comparée des rel. païennes et de la religion juive;* Oesterley, *Evolution of Religious Ideas;* Martindale, *Bearing of Comp. Study of Religions on Claims of Christianity;* W. St. Clair Tisdall, *Comparative Religion.*

W. ST. CLAIR TISDALL

COMPARE, kom-pâr' (דָּמָה, *dāmāh*, מָשַׁל, *māshal*, עָרַךְ, *'ārakh;* **παραβάλλω**, *parabállō*, **συγκρίνω**, *sugkrínō*): "Compare" is the tr of דָּמָה, *dāmāh*, "to be like" (Cant **1** 9); of מָשַׁל, *māshal*, "to liken," "compare" (Isa **46** 5); of עָרַךְ, *'ārakh*, "to set in array," "compare" (Ps **89** 6; Isa **40** 18); of שָׁוָה, *shāwāh*, "to be equal" (Prov **3** 15; **8** 11).

In the NT *sugkrinō*, "to judge" or "sift together," is trd "comparing," "comparing spiritual things with spiritual" (1 Cor **2** 13 ERV), ARV "combining" ("adapting the discourse to the subject," Thayer), RVm "interpreting spiritual things to spiritual [men]."

W. L. WALKER

COMPASS, kum'pas, **COMPASSES,** kum'pas-iz: "Compass," noun, is the tr of חוּג, *ḥūgh*, "a circle," "vault" or "arch" ("when he set a compass upon the face of the depth" Prov **8** 27 AV, RV, ARV "circle"; cf Job **26** 10; and see CIRCLE; VAULT OF EARTH); of כַּרְכֹּב, *karkōbh*, "a margin," "border" (Ex **27** 5, "the compass of the altar," RV "the ledge round," so **38** 4); the phrase "to fetch a compass" is the tr of סָבַב, *sābhabh*, "to turn about," "go round about" (Nu **34** 5; Josh **15** 3, RV "turn about," 2 S **5** 23; 2 K **3** 9, RV "make a circuit"); of *periérchomai*, "to go about" (Acts **28** 13, RV "made a circuit"; m "Some ancient authorities read *cast loose*"; see CIRCUIT).

"Compasses" is RV for "compass," מְחוּגָה, *meḥūghāh*, an instrument for describing a circle: "He marketh it out with the compasses" (Isa **44** 13) in making an idol.

The vb. "to compass" occurs frequently in the senses of "to surround" and "to go round about," e.g. Gen **2** 11, "which compasseth the whole land of Havilah," Dt **2** 1, "We compassed [went around] mount Seir many days"; in Jer **31** 22 we have "A new thing on the earth: a woman shall compass a man," RV "encompass"; possibly as a suitor; but more probably as a protector. In those happy days, the protection of women (under God, ver 28) will be sufficient, while the men are at their work; "to encompass" ("The cords of death compassed me," Ps **18** 4; "the waves of death," 2 S **22** 5). "To gird" (Isa **50** 11 RV); "to lie around," "to be laid around" (He **5** 2, "compassed with infirmity" [clothed with it]; **12** 1, "compassed about with so great a cloud of witnesses").

In Apoc we have "compassed about with yawning darkness" (Wisd **19** 17); "compassed the circuit of heaven" (Ecclus **24** 5); "compassed with pomegranates of gold" (**45** 9); "The rainbow compasseth the heaven" (Ecclus **43** 12); the course of the sun (1 Esd **4** 34). W. L. Walker

COMPASSION, kom-pash'un: Compassion is the tr of רָחַם, *rāḥam,* "to love," "pity," "be merciful" (Dt **13** 17; **30** 3); of *raḥămīm,* "mercies" (1 K **8** 50); of חָמַל, *ḥāmal,* "to pity," "spare" (Ex **2** 6; 1 S **23** 21); רַחוּם, *raḥūm* (Ps **78** 38; **86** 15; **111** 4; **112** 4; **145** 8), is rendered by ARV "merciful." We have σπλαγχνίζομαι, *splagchnizomai,* "to have the bowels yearning," in Mt **9** 36; **14** 14, etc; *sumpathéō* (He **10** 34), "to suffer with [another]"; *sumpathḗs* (1 Pet **3** 8, RV "compassionate," m "Gr sympathetic"); *metriopathéō* (He **5** 2, RV "who can bear gently with"); *eleéō,* "to show mildness," "kindness" (Mt **18** 33; Mk **5** 19; Jude ver 22, RV "mercy"); *oikteírō,* "to have pity" or "mercy" (Rom **9** 15 *bis*).

Both *rāḥam* and *splagchnizomai* are examples of the physical origin of spiritual terms, the bowels being regarded as the seat of the warm, tender emotions or feelings. But, while *rāḥam* applied to the lower viscera as well as the higher, *splágchnon* denoted chiefly the higher viscera, the heart, lungs, liver.

RV gives "*compassion*" for "mercy" (Isa **9** 17; **14** 1; **27** 11; **49** 13; Jer **13** 14; **30** 18; Dnl **1** 9 AV "tender love with"; for "bowels of compassion," **1** Jn **3** 17); for "mercy" (He **10** 28); "full of compassion" for "merciful" (ARV "merciful" in all cases) (Ex **34** 6; Neh **9** 17; Ps **103** 8; Joel **2** 13; Jon **4** 2); "compassions" for "mercies" (Isa **63** 15; Phil **2** 1), for "repentings" (Hos **11** 8).

Compassion, lit. a feeling with and for others, is a fundamental and distinctive quality of the Bib. conception of God, and to its prominence the world owes more than words can express. (1) It lay at the foundation of Israel's faith in Jeh. For it was out of His compassion that He, by a marvelous act of power, delivered them from Egyp bondage and called them to be His own people. Nothing, therefore, is more prominent in the OT than the ascription of compassion, pity, mercy, etc, to God; the people may be said to have gloried in it. It is summed up in such sayings as that of the great declaration in Ex **34** 6: "Jehovah—a God full of compassion [ARV merciful] and gracious" (cf Ps **78** 38; **86** 15; **111** 4; **112** 4; **145** 8; Lam **3** 22, "His compassions fail not"). And, because this was the character of their God, the prophets declared that compassion was an essential requirement on the part of members of the community (Hos **6** 6; Mic **6** 8; cf Prov **19** 17). (2) In Jesus Christ, in whom God was "manifest in the flesh," compassion was an outstanding feature (Mt **9** 36; **14** 14, etc) and He taught that it ought to be extended, not to friends and neighbors only, but to all without exception, even to enemies (Mt **5** 43–48; Lk **10** 30–37).

The God of the NT, the Father of men, is most clearly revealed as "a God full of compassion." It extends to the whole human race, for which He effected not merely a temporal, but a spiritual and eternal, deliverance, giving up His own Son to the death of the cross in order to save us from the worst bondage of sin, with its consequences; seeking thereby to gain a new, wider people for Himself, still more devoted, more filled with and expressive of His own Spirit. Therefore all who know the God and Father of Christ, and who call themselves His children, must necessarily cultivate compassion and show mercy, "even as he is merciful." Hence the many apostolic injunctions to that effect (Eph **4** 32; Col **3** 12; Jas **1** 27; 1 Jn **3** 17, etc). Christianity may be said to be distinctively the religion of Compassion. W. L. Walker

COMPEL, kom-pel': Our Eng. word always has in it now the flavor of force, not always, however, physical. It may be strong moral urgency, though "constrain" better expresses this.

There are several words indicative of such strong pressure: (1) אָנַס, *'ānaṣ,* "to press": "none could compel" to drink (Est **1** 8); (2) נָדַח, *nādhaḥ,* "to drive," "force": "compelled Judah thereto" (AV, RVm); "led Judah astray" RV (2 Ch **21** 11). The same word rendered "force," as the adulteress by flattering words her victim (Prov **7** 21); (3) עָבַד, *'ābhadh,* "to serve": not to compel him to serve as a bond servant (Lev **25** 39 AV, RV "make him serve"); (4) פָּרַץ, *pāraç,* "to break forth upon," "urge": "his servants compelled him" (1 S **28** 23 AV, RV "constrained").

1. In the OT

In the NT two words are found: (1) ἀγγαρεύω, *aggareúō*: The word is of Pers origin and means to employ a courier. The *Ággaroi* were public couriers stationed by appointment of the kings of Persia, at fixed localities, with horses ready for use, to transmit speedily from one to another the royal messages. These couriers had authority to press into their service, in case of need, horses, vessels, and even men, they might meet (Jos, *Ant,* XIII, ii, 3); "compel thee to go a mile" (Mt **5** 41 AV; RVm "impress"); "compelled Simon to bear his cross" (Mt **27** 32; Mk **15** 21 AV; RVm "impressed"). (2) ἀναγκάζω, *anagkázō,* "to constrain," whether by force, threats, entreaties, persuasion, etc: "compel them to come in" (Lk **14** 23 AV; RV "constrain"). This has been a favorite text of religious persecutors. As Robertson says in his history of Charles V, "As they could not persuade, they tried to compel men to believe." But it simply means that utmost zeal and moral urgency should be used by Christians to induce sinners to enter the Kingdom of God. Cf Acts **26** 11.

2. In the NT

George Henry Trever

COMPLAINING, kom-plān'ing (צְוָחָה, *çᵉwāḥāh,* "cry," "outcry," שִׂיחַ, *sīaḥ,* "meditation," "complaint"): *çᵉwāḥāh* is trd "complaining" (Ps **144** 14, RV "outcry," "no c. [outcry] in our streets," i.e. "open places" where the people commonly assembled near the gate of the city (cf 2 Ch **32** 6; Neh **8** 1); a picture of peace in the city (cf Isa **24** 11; Jer **14** 2); some render "battlecry"; *sīaḥ* (RV Prov **23** 29, AV "babbling"), of the drunkard.

COMPLETE, kom-plēt': In AV for πληρόω, *plēróō,* the vb. ordinarily used for the coming to pass of what had been predicted. AV translates this "complete" in Col **2** 10; **4** 12 to express the final and entire attainment of what is treated, leaving nothing beyond to be desired or hoped for; otherwise rendered in RV ("made full"). In RV, c. appears once for Gr *ártios,* from *árō,* "to join," in 2 Tim **3** 17, in sense of "accurately fitted for," where AV has "perfect."

COMPOSITION, kom-pō-zish'un (מַתְכֹּנֶת, *mathkōneth,* "measure"); **COMPOUND,** kom'pound (subst.) (רָקַח, *rāḳah,* "to make perfume," רֹקַח, *rōḳaḥ,* "perfume"): Used of the sacred anointing oil (Ex **30** 25.32.33) and of the holy perfume (vs 37.38), which were not to be used for any profane purpose.

COMPREHEND, kom-prē-hend': Used in a twofold sense in both the OT and NT. This double meaning appears in two Heb and two Gr words which signify in turn (1) mental or spiritual *perception*, (2) capacity *to hold* or *contain*, as in a measure or in an all-inclusive principle, e.g.:

(1) יָדַע, *yādha'*, "to see with the eyes or the mind," hence "know," "understand." Job was urged by Elihu to accept as inscrutable the ways of God, inasmuch as His operations in the physical world are so mighty and mysterious that "we cannot comprehend" them (Job **37** 5). Modern science, in unveiling the secrets of Nature, is opening the way for a better understanding of God's creative purpose and plan.

καταλαμβάνω, *katalambánō*, "to lay hold of," hence mentally *to apprehend:* used of the spiritual capacity of the Christian "to comprehend [RV "apprehend"] with all saints" (Eph **3** 18) the measureless love of God; and of the inability of the unrenewed heart to know or perceive the revelation of God made in Christ: "the darkness comprehended it not" (Jn **1** 5 RV "apprehended"; RVm "overcame"; cf **12** 35).

(2) כּוּל, *kūl*, "to measure" or "contain," as grain in a bushel. So God's immeasurable greatness is seen in His being able to hold oceans in the hollow of His hand and "comprehend the dust of the earth in a measure" (Isa **40** 12).

ἀνακεφαλαιόω, *anakephalaióō*, "to sum up under one head," e.g. love includes every other moral principle and process. The entire law on its manward side, says Paul, "is comprehended [RV "summed up"] in this saying, namely, Thou shalt love thy neighbor as thyself" (Rom **13** 9).

Dwight M. Pratt

CONANIAH, kon-a-nī'a (כּוֹנַנְיָהוּ, *kōnanyāhū*, "Jah has founded or sustained"; AV **Cononiah**):

(1) A Levite, appointed with his brother Shimei by Hezekiah, the king, and Azariah, the ruler of the house of God, to be overseer of the oblations and tithes and the dedicated things (2 Ch **31** 12.13).

(2) One of the chiefs of the Levites mentioned in connection with the passover celebration in Josiah's reign (2 Ch **35** 9).

CONCEAL, kon-sēl' (**παρακαλύπτω**, *parakalúptō*): Found but once in the NT (Lk **9** 45). The primary meaning is to cover by hanging something in front of the object hidden. The purpose of the one concealing is made prominent. There is, therefore, a reserve and studied progress in regard to the statement of facts, that is not always a suppression of truth (Prov **12** 16.23). God withholds more than He reveals (Prov **25** 2; cf Ps **97** 2; 1 Tim **6** 16).

CONCEIT, kon-sēt': An idiomatic rendering of a phrase, φρόνιμοι ἐν ἑαυτοῖς, *phrónimoi en heautoís*, in Rom **11** 25; **12** 16; meaning lit. "wise with one's self," i.e. "in one's own opinion," or, as in ‖ OT passages (Prov **26** 5.12 RVm), "in his own eyes" (Heb *'ayin*).

CONCEPTION, kon-sep'shun, **CONCEIVE**, kon-sēv' (הָרָה, *hārāh*, and derivatives; **συλλαμβάνω**, *sullambánō*): Physically, the beginning of a new life in the womb of a mother, "to catch on," used thus some forty times, as in Gen **3** 16; **4** 1; Ps **51** 5. **Metaphorically,** applied to the start and growth within the heart, of thought, purpose, desire, e.g. "c. mischief" (Job **15** 35; Ps **7** 14), "c. chaff" (Isa **33** 11). This figure is carried out in details in Jas **1** 15: "Lust, when it hath conceived, beareth sin."

CONCEPTION, IMMACULATE. See Immaculate Conception.

CONCERNING, kon-sûrn'ing:
RV makes frequent changes, such as "for," "as for," "from," "about," for "concerning"; "concerning" instead of "for," "of," "over," "in," "against," etc. Some of the other changes are, "unto that which is good" for "concerning" (Rom **16** 19), "concerning" instead of "because of" (Jer **23** 9), for "the miracle of" (Mk **6** 52), for "with" (**10** 41), for "of the Lord" (Acts **18** 25), "concerning Jesus" (different text), "by way of disparagement" (2 Cor **11** 21), instead of "concerning reproach"; "Why askest thou me concerning that which is good?" (Mt **19** 17) instead of "Why callest thou me good?" (different text; see RVm).

W. L. Walker

CONCISION, kon-sizh'un (**κατατομή**, *katatomḗ*, "mutilation," "cutting"): A term by which St. Paul contemptuously designates the merely fleshly circumcision upon which the Judaizers insisted as being necessary for gentile converts (Phil **3** 2), as distinguished from *peritomḗ*, the true circumcision (ver 3). Cf Gal **5** 12 and Dt **23** 1, and see Circumcision.

CONCLUDE, kon-klōōd' (**συμβιβάζω**, *sumbibázō*): Used only in Acts **16** 10, where AV has "assuredly gathering," i.e. "inferring." Where AV has "conclude," RV more accurately renders "reckon" (Rom **3** 28); "giving judgment" (Acts **21** 25); "shut up" (Rom **11** 32; Gal **3** 22).

CONCLUSION, kon-klōō'zhun (סוֹף, *ṣōph*): In Eccl **12** 13 AV, where RV has "the end," viz. a summary of the entire argument of the book.

CONCORDANCE, kon-kôr'dans:

1. Nature of Work
2. Classes of Concordances
3. Their Indispensableness
4. Concordances to Latin Vulgate
5. Concordances to the Heb OT
6. Concordances to the LXX
7. Concordances to the Greek NT
8. Concordances to the English Bible

Literature

1. Nature of Work

The object of a concordance of Scripture is to guide the reader to any passage he is in search of by means of an alphabetical arrangement of the words found in Scripture, and the bringing together under each word of all the passages in which that word occurs. Thus, in the ver: "Cast thy burden upon Jeh" (Ps **55** 22), the reader will look in the concordance under the words "cast" or "burden," and there will find a reference to the text. The merit of a concordance is obviously exhaustiveness and clearness of arrangement. There are abridged concordances of the Bible which give only the most important words and passages. These are seldom satisfactory, and a fuller work has in the end frequently to be resorted to.

2. Classes of Concordances

The ordinary reader is naturally most familiar with concordances of the Eng. Bible, but it will be seen that, for scholarly purposes, concordances are just as necessary for the Scriptures in their original tongues, and for versions of the Scriptures other than Eng. There are required concordances of the OT in Heb, of the NT in Gr, of the LXX version (Gr) of the OT, of the Vulg version (Lat) of the NT, as well as of the trs of the Scriptures into German, French and other living languages. There are now, further, required concordances of the RVV of the English OT and NT, as well as of the AV. There are needed, besides, good concordances to the Apoc, alike in its AV and RV forms. Textual criticism leads to modifications of the earlier concordances of the Heb and Gr texts. It is customary in concordances of the Eng. version to facilitate reference by giving not only single words, but also phrases under which several passages are grouped, and to make the work more useful by furnishing lists of Scripture proper names, with their meanings, and, in the larger works, references to the Heb or Gr words for which the Eng. words stand.

3. Their Indispensableness

The indispensableness of a good concordance for the proper study of the Bible is so apparent that it is not surprising that, since the idea was first conceived, much labor has been expended on the preparation of such works. The wonder rather is that the idea did not occur earlier than it did. No single scholar could ever hope to produce a perfect work of the kind by his own efforts. Modern concordances are based upon the labors of previous generations.

4. Concordances to Latin Vulgate

The oldest concordances date from the 13th cent., and are based, as was then natural, upon the Latin Vulgate. A *Concordantiae Morales* is attributed to Antony of Padua (d. 1231). The first concordance of which we have actual knowledge is that of Hugo of St. Caro, Dominican monk and cardinal (d. 1263). It was called *Concordantiae S. Jacobi* from the monastery in which it was compiled. 500 monks are said to have been engaged upon its preparation. Hugo's Concordance became the basis of others into which successive improvements were introduced. The words of passages, at first wanting, were inserted; indeclinable particles were added; alphabetic arrangement was employed. Verse divisions were unknown till the time of Robert Stephens (1555). See BIBLE.

5. Concordances to the Hebrew OT

The earliest Heb concordance seems to have been that of Rabbi Mordecai ben Nathan (1438–48). It went through several editions and was tr[d] into Lat by Reuchlin (1556). Both original and tr contained many errors. It was improved by Calasio, a Franciscan friar (1621), and more thoroughly by John Buxtorf, whose Concordance was published by his son (1632). This latter formed the basis of Dr. Julius Fürst's *Libr. Sacrorum Vet. Test. Concordantive Heb atque Chald;* 1840 (Eng. tr, *Hebrew and Chaldean Concordance*). A later Heb Concordance in Germany is that of Solomon Mandelkern (1896). In England, in 1754, appeared the valuable *Heb Concordance, Adapted to the Eng. Bible*, by Dr. Taylor, of Norwich. With it may be classed *The Englishman's Heb and Chald Concordance* (1843; rev. ed, 1876).

6. Concordances to the LXX

Though earlier attempts are heard of, the first printed concordance of the LXX (the Gr OT) was that of Trommius, published in Amsterdam in 1718, in the author's 84th year. This important work remained the standard till quite lately. It is very complete, giving references not only to the LXX, but to other VSS (Aquila, Symmachus, Theodotion) in which the words occur, and showing by an index at the end the Heb or Chald words to which the Gr words correspond. In 1887 Bagster published *A Handy Concordance of the Sept.* Earlier works are superseded by the recent publication (1892, 1897, 1900) of Hatch and Redpath's scholarly *Concordance to the Sept, and Other Gr VSS of the OT.*

7. Concordances to the Greek NT

Concordances of the Gr NT began with that of Xystus Betulius (his real name was Birck) in 1554. The Concordance (*Tameion*) of Erasmus Schmid (1638) has often been reprinted and reëdited. On it is based the useful abridged Concordance published by Bagster. Recent works are Bruder's (1842; 4th ed, 1888; based on Schmid, with many improvements); in America, Hudson's *Critical Gr and Eng. Concordance*, revised by Ezra Abbot (1870); in England, Moulton and Geden's *Concordance to the Gr Test. according to the Texts of Westcott and Hort, Tischendorf, and the Eng. Revisers* (1897).

8. Concordances to the English Bible

The list of concordances to the Eng. Bible is a long one; it is necessary here to particularize only a few of the chief. The oldest is a *Concordance of the NT*, brought out before 1540 by one Thomas Gybson, though, as appears from the Preface, it was principally the work of the printer John Day (the producer of Foxe's *Book of Martyrs*). The first Concordance to the whole Bible was that of John Marbeck (1550). In the same year was published a tr by Walter Lynne of the *Index Librorum* of Bullinger, Conrad Pelican and others, under the title of *A Briefe and a Compendious Table, in maner of a Concordance, openying the waye to the principall Histories of the whole Bible*, etc. Alex. Cruden, whose own Concordance, the most adequate of all, was published in 1737, enumerates most of his predecessors in the intervening period. Cruden's personal history is a pathetic one. A recurring mental malady overshadowed his career; but his indomitable perseverance and fixity of purpose, joined with a clear idea of what he wished to accomplish, enabled him to overcome all obstacles, and produce a book for which the Christian world is grateful. The work is entitled *A Complete Concordance to the Holy Scriptures of the Old and New Testaments, etc; to which is added, a Concordance to the Books called Apocrypha.* Mr. Spurgeon said regarding it, "Be sure you buy a genuine unabridged Cruden, and none of the modern substitutes, good as they may be at the price. . . . . You need only one; have none but the best." Many editions of this valuable book have been published. It no longer remains, however, the only authority, nor even the most complete and serviceable, though perhaps still the most convenient, for the purpose of the student. In 1873 was published the *Analytical Concordance to the Bible* by Robert Young, LL.D., to which an appendix has since been added. This bulky work contains "every word in alphabetical order, arranged under its Heb or Gr original; with the literal meaning of each and its pronunciation." It marks 30,000 various readings, and gives geographical and antiquarian notes. Yet more comprehensive is *The Exhaustive Concordance of the Bible* by James Strong, LL.D. This includes the new feature of a comparative concordance of the Authorized and Revised (English) VSS. It embraces also condensed Dictionaries of the Heb and Gr words, to which references are made from the Eng. words by figures. It thus differs in plan from Young's, which gives the Heb and Gr words in the body of the concordance at the head of the passages coming under them. Lastly must be noticed the very valuable work published in the same year (1894) in America by J. B. R. Walker, *Comprehensive Concordance, with an Introduction by Marshall Curtiss Hazard.* It is stated to give 50,000 more passages than Cruden.

LITERATURE.—See arts. on "Concordance" in the various Dicts and Encys; arts. by Dr. Beard in *Kitto's Enc* (Vol I); and by Dr. C. R. Gregory in the *New Sch-Herz Enc* (Vol III); Pref to Cruden's complete *Concordance*, and Introduction by Hazard to Walker's *Compreh. Concordance.*

JAMES ORR

CONCOURSE, kon′kōrs (הָמָה, *hāmāh*, "to hum," "to make a noise"; **συστροφή**, *sustrophḗ*, "a turning" or "twisting together"): *Hāmāh*, usually tr[d] by some word signifying "sound" is rendered "concourse" in Prov 1 21 (perhaps from the noise made by people thronging and talking together;

cf 1 K **1** 41, "uproar"), "She [wisdom] crieth in the chief place of concourse," RVm "*Heb* at the head of the noisy [streets]"; *sustrophē* is tr[d] "concourse" (Acts **19** 40), a riotous crowd. Cf Jth **10** 18.

CONCUBINAGE, koṇ-kū'bi-nāj. See FAMILY.

CONCUPISCENCE, kon-kū'pi-sens (**ἐπιθυμία,** *epithumía*): Not used in RV, but in AV, Rom **7** 8; Col **3** 5; 1 Thess **4** 5. The Gr noun, like the vb. from which it comes, meaning "to yearn," "to long," "to have the heart set upon a thing," is determined in its moral quality by the source whence it springs or the object toward which it is directed. Thus Our Lord uses it to express the intensest desire of His soul (Lk **22** 15). As a rule, when the object is not expressed, it refers to longing for that which God has forbidden, viz. lust. It is not limited to sexual desire, but includes all going forth of heart and will toward what God would not have us to have or be, as its use in the LXX of the Ten Commandments clearly shows, for "Thou shalt not covet" (Ex **20** 17). H. E. JACOBS

CONDEMN, kon-dem', **CONDEMNATION,** kon-dem-nā'shun:

1. In the OT

(1) The causative stem of רָשַׁע, *rāsha'*, "to declare [or make] wrong," "to condemn," whether in civil, ethical or religious relations. Taken in this sense the word needs no comment (Ex **22** 9; Dt **25** 1; Job **40** 8); "Who then can condemn?" (Job **34** 29, AV "make trouble").

(2) עָנַשׁ, *'ānash*, "to fine." "Condemned the land" (2 Ch **36** 3 AV; AVm "mulcted"; RV "amerced"; ARV "fined"); "wine of the condemned" (Am **2** 8; RV "fined" [unjustly]).

(3) The active part. of שָׁפַט, *shāphaṭ*, "to judge." "From those that condemn his soul" (Ps **109** 31 AV; RV "that judge his soul").

2. In the NT

The NT usage is much more complicated, both because of the greater number of Gr words rendered "condemn" and "condemnation," and because AV tr[s] the same word in several different ways, apparently with no rule whatever.

(1) The most important word is *κρίνω*, *krínō*, "to judge." From it are a number of derivative vbs. and nouns. RV has rigidly excluded the harsh words "damn" and "damnation," substituting "judge," "condemn," "judgment," "condemnation." This is proper, since the word damn (Lat *damnare*, "to inflict loss" upon a person, "to condemn"), and its derivatives has, in process of time, suffered degradation, so that in modern Eng. it usually refers to eternal punishment. This special application of the word for some cents. ran side by side with the original meaning, but even as late as Wycliffe's version the word "damn" is usually employed in the sense of condemn, as in Job **9** 20, "My mouth shall dampne me." It is even applied to the condemnation of Jesus by the chief priests and scribes (Mk **10** 33). This degeneration of the word is perhaps due, as Bishop Sanderson says, "not so much to good acts as to bad manners." *Krinō* is rendered uniformly "judge" by RV, even where the context compels the thought of condemnation (Jn **3** 17.18; **12** 47; Acts **7** 7; "might be damned," 2 Thess **2** 12 AV; Rom **14** 22; Jas **5** 9).

(2) The more specific sense of condemn, however, is found in *κατακρίνω*, *katakrínō*, "to judge one down" (Mt **12** 41.42; Mk **14** 64): "is damned if he eat" (Rom **14** 23; 1 Cor **11** 32 AV; RV "condemned"). See also Mk **16** 16; 2 Pet **2** 6.

(3) For "condemnation" there is the noun *κρίμα*, *kríma*, or *κρῖμα*, *kríma* (for accent see Thayer's *Lexicon*), in a forensic sense, "the sentence of the judge" (Lk **23** 40; Mt **23** 14, omitted in RV; "condemnation of the devil" **1** Tim **3** 6; **5** 12; Jude ver 4).

(4) Much stronger is *κατάκριμα*, *katákrima*, "condemnation" (Rom **5** 16.18; **8** 1) with reference to the Divine judgment against sin.

(5) *κρίσις*, *krísis*, "the process of judgment," "tribunal" (Jn **3** 19; **5** 24), with reference to "the judgment brought by men upon themselves because of their rejection of Christ."

(6) A stronger word is the adj. *αὐτοκατάκριτος*, *autokatákritos*, "self-condemned" (Tit **3** 11; cf 1 Jn **3** 20.21). G. H. TREVER

CONDESCENSION, kon-dē-sen'shun, **OF CHRIST.** See KENOSIS.

CONDUCT, kon'dukt. See ETHICS.

CONDUIT, kon'dit. See CISTERN.

CONEY, kō'ni (שָׁפָן, *shāphān* [Lev **11** 5; Dt **14** 7; Ps **104** 18; Prov **30** 26]): The word "coney" (formerly pronounced *cooney*) means "rabbit" (from Lat *cuniculus*). *Shāphān* is rendered in all four passages in the LXX *χοιρογρύλλιος*, *choirogrúllios*, or "hedge-hog," but is now universally considered to refer to the Syrian hyrax, *Procavia* (or *Hyrax*) *Syriaca*, which in southern Pal and Sinai is called in Arab. *wabar*, in northern Pal and Syria *ṭabsūn*, and in southern Arabia *shufun*, which is etymologically closely akin to *shāphān*. The word "*hyrax*" (*ὕραξ*, *húrax*) itself means "mouse" or "shrew-mouse" (cf Lat *sorex*), so that it seems to

Group of Conies.

have been hard to find a name peculiar to this animal. In Lev **11** 5 RVm, we find "rock badger," which is a tr of *klip das*, the rather inappropriate name given by the Boers to the Cape hyrax. The Syrian hyrax lives in Syria, Pal and Arabia. A number of other species, including several that are arboreal, live in Africa. They are not found in other parts of the world. In size, teeth and habits the Syrian hyrax somewhat resembles the rabbit, though it is different in color, being reddish brown, and lacks the long hind legs of the rabbit. The similarity in dentition is confined to the large size of the front teeth and the presence of a large space between them and the back teeth. But whereas hares have a pair of front teeth on each jaw, the hyrax has one pair above and two below. These teeth differ also in structure from those of the hare and rabbit, not having the persistent pulp which enables the rabbit's front teeth to grow continually as they are worn away. They do not hide among herbage like hares, nor burrow like rabbits, but live in holes or clefts of the rock, frequently in the faces of steep cliffs. Neither the hyrax nor the hare is a ruminant, as seems to be implied in Lev **11** 5 and Dt **14** 7, but their manner of chewing their food may readily have led them to be thought to chew the cud. The hyrax has four toes in front and three behind (the same number as in the tapir and in some fossil members of the horse family), all furnished with nails that are almost like hoofs, except the inner hind toes, which have claws. The hyraxes constitute a family of ungulates and, in spite of their small size, have points of resemblance to elephants or rhinoceroses, but are not closely allied to these or to any other known animals.

The camel, the coney and the hare are in the list of unclean animals because they "chew the cud but divide not the hoof," but all three of these are eaten by the Arabs.

The illustration is from a photograph of a group of conies in the Syrian Protestant College at Beirût, prepared by Mr. Douglas Carruthers, who collected these specimens in a cliff in the neighborhood of Tyre. Specimens from the Dead Sea are redder than those from Syria.

ALFRED ELY DAY

CONFECTION, kon-fek'shun, **CONFECTIONARY,** kon-fek'shun-ā-ri (רֹקַח, *rōḳah*, "perfume," "spice," רַקָּחָה, *raḳḳāhāh*, fem. "perfumer"):

(1) "Confection" is found in AV only, and but once "a c. after the art of the apothecary" (Ex **30** 35; RV "perfume"); but the RV renders 1 Ch **9** 30, "the c. [AV "ointment"] of the spices." It stands for something "made up," a mixture of perfumes or medicines, but never sweetmeats, as c. means with us.

(2) Likewise a "confectionary" is a perfumer. This word, too, is found but once (1 S **8** 13), "He will take your daughters to be perfumers [AV "confectionaries"], and to be cooks, and to be bakers." See PERFUMES.

GEO. B. EAGER

CONFEDERATE, kon-fed'ẽr-āt, **CONFEDERACY,** kon-fed'ẽr-a-si: "Confederate" as an adj. in the sense of *united* or *leagued* is twice the tr of בְּרִית, *b^erīth*, "covenant," in several instances tr[d] "league" (Gen **14** 13, *ba'al b^erīth*, "lord or master of a covenant," "an ally," "these were c. with Abram"; cf Ps **83** 5; once of נוּחַ, *nūaḥ*, "to rest," "Syria is c. with Ephraim" (Isa **7** 2, RVm "resteth on Ephraim"; also 1 Macc **10** 47).

As a noun "confederate" occurs in 1 Macc **10** 16, *súmmachos*, "confederates" (1 Macc **8** 20.24.31; **14** 40; **15** 17).

Confederacy, as a "league," occurs as the tr of *b^erīth*, "the men of thy c." (Ob ver 7); as a *conspiracy* it occurs in Isa **8** 12 *bis*, as tr of *ḳesher* from *ḳāshar*, "to bind": "Say ye not, a c." Cf 2 S **15** 12; 2 K **12** 20, etc.

W. L. WALKER

CONFER, kon-fûr', **CONFERENCE,** kon'fẽ-ens: The equivalent of three Gr words of different shades of meaning. In Gal **1** 16, προσανατίθημι, *prosanatíthēmi*, had been used in classical writers for resorting to oracles (Lightfoot on Gal **2** 6; Ellicott on Gal **1** 16); hence, "to take counsel with," "to consult." In Acts **4** 15, συμβάλλω, *sumbállō*, "to compare views," "discuss"; and in Acts **25** 12, συλλαλέω, *sullaléō*, "to talk together." Cf the single passage in the OT (1 K **1** 7).

CONFESSION, kon-fesh'un (יָדָה, *yādhāh;* ὁμολογέω, *homologéō*, and their derivatives): The radical meaning is "acknowledgment," "avowal," with the implication of a change of conviction or of course of conduct on the part of the subject. In Eng. "profession" (AV 1 Tim **6** 12; He **3** 1; **4** 14), besides absence of the thought just suggested, emphasizes the publicity of the act. C., like its Gr equivalent, connotes, as its etymology shows (Lat *con*, Gr *homoú*), that the act places one in harmony with others. It is the uniting in a statement that has previously been made by someone else. Of the two Gr words from the same root in the NT, the compound with the Gr preposition *ek* found, among other places, in Mt **3** 6; Acts **19** 18; Rom **14** 11; Phil **2** 11, implies that it has come from an inner impulse, i.e. it is the expression of a conviction of the heart. It is referred anthropopathically to God in Job **40** 14, where Jeh says to the patriarch sarcastically: "Then will I also confess of [unto] thee"; and in Rev **3** 5, where it means "to recognize" or "acknowledge."

When man is said to confess or make confession, the contents of the confession are variously distinguished. All, however, may be grouped under two heads, confession of faith and confession of sin. Confessions of faith are public acknowledgments of fidelity to God, and to the truth through which God is revealed, as 1 K **8** 33. They are declarations of unqualified confidence in Christ, and of surrender to His service; Mt **10** 32: "Every one . . . . who shall confess me before men." In Phil **2** 11, however, c. includes, alongside of willing, also unwilling, acknowledgment of the sovereignty of Jesus. The word c. stands also for everything contained in the Christian religion—"the faith" used in the objective and widest sense, in He **3** 1; **4** 14. In both these passages, the allusion is to the NT. The "High Priest of our c." (He **3** 1) is the High Priest, of whom we learn and with whom we deal in that new revelation, which in that epistle is contrasted with the old.

Confessions of sins are also of various classes: (1) To God alone. Wherever there is true repentance for sin, the penitent freely confesses his guilt to Him, against whom he has sinned. This is described in Ps **32** 3–6; cf 1 Jn **1** 9; Prov **28** 13. Such c. may be made either silently, or, as in Dnl **9** 19, orally; it may be general, as in Ps **51**, or particular, as when some special sin is recognized; it may even extend to what has not been discovered, but which is believed to exist because of recognized inner depravity (Ps **19** 12), and thus include the state as well as the acts of sin (Rom **7** 18). (2) To one's neighbor, when he has been wronged (Lk **17** 4): "If he sin against thee seven times in the day, and seven times turn again to thee, saying, I repent; thou shalt forgive him." It is to this form of c. that James refers (**5** 16): "Confess . . . . your sins one to another"; cf Mt **5** 23 f. (3) To a spiritual adviser or minister of the word, such as the c. of David to Nathan (2 S **12** 13), of the multitudes to John in the wilderness (Mt **3** 6), of the Ephesians to Paul (Acts **19** 18). This c. is a general acknowledgment of sinfulness, and enters into an enumeration of details only when the conscience is particularly burdened. (4) To the entire church, where some crime has created public scandal. As "secret sins are to be rebuked secretly, and public sins publicly," in the apostolic age, where there was genuine penitence for a notorious offence, the acknowledgment was as public as the deed itself. An illustration of this is found in the well-known case at Corinth (cf 1 Cor **5** 3 ff with 2 Cor **2** 6 f).

For auricular c. in the sense of the mediaeval and Rom church, there is no authority in Holy Scripture. It is traceable to the practice of examining those who were about to make a public c. of some notorious offence, and of giving advice concerning how far the circumstances of the sin were to be announced; an expedient that was found advisable, since as much injury could be wrought by injudicious publishing of details in the c. as by the sin itself. The practice once introduced for particular cases was in time extended to all cases; and the private c. of sin was demanded by the church as a condition of the absolution, and made an element of penitence, which was analyzed into contrition, confession and satisfaction. See the *Examen Concilii Tridentini* (1st ed, 1565) of Dr. Martin Chemnitz, superintendent of Brunswick, for a thorough exegetical and historical discussion of this entire subject. On the historical side, see also Henry Charles Lea, *History of Auricular Confession and Indulgences in the Latin Church* (3 vols, Philadelphia, 1896). H. E. JACOBS

CONFIDENCE, kon'fi-dens (בָּטַח, *bāṭaḥ,* and forms, כֶּסֶל, *keṣel;* **παῤῥησία,** *parrhēsía,* **πείθω,** *peithō,* **πεποίθησις,** *pepoíthēsis,* **ὑπόστασις,** *hupóstasis*): The chief Heb word trd "confidence" (*bāṭaḥ,* and its forms) means, perhaps, radically, "to be open," showing thus what originated the idea of "confidence"; where there was nothing hidden a person felt safe; it is very frequently rendered "trust." In Ps **118** 8.9 we have "It is better to take refuge in Jeh than to put *confidence* in princes," and in **65** 5, "O God of our salvation, thou that art the *confidence* [*mibhṭāh*] of all the ends of the earth." *Mibhṭāh* is trd "confidence" in Job **18** 14; **31** 24; Prov **21** 22, etc.

Keṣel ("firmness," "stoutness") is rendered "confidence" in Prov **3** 26, and *kiṣlāh* in Job **4** 6; *peithō* ("to persuade") is trd "confidence" in 2 Cor **2** 3; Gal **5** 10, etc; *pepoithēsis,* in 2 Cor **1** 15; **8** 22, etc; *hupostasis* ("what stands under"), in 2 Cor **11** 17; He **3** 14; 2 Cor **9** 4; *parrhēsia* ("out-spokenness," "boldness") is invariably trd in RV "boldness" (Acts **28** 31; He **3** 6; **4** 16; **10** 35; 1 Jn **2** 28; **3** 21; **5** 14); *tharseō* or *tharrhéō* ("to have good courage") is so trd in RV, "being therefore always of good courage" (2 Cor **5** 6); "I am of good courage concerning you" (2 Cor **7** 16), AV "confident" and "confidence."

RV has "confidence" for "hope" (Job **8** 14); for "assurance" (Isa **32** 17); for "trust" (2 Cor **3** 4); for "same confident boasting" (2 Cor **9** 4); "is confident" for "trusted" (Job **40** 23); "to have confidence" for "thinketh that he hath whereof he might trust" (Phil **3** 4); "confidently" for "constantly" (Acts **12** 15); "confidently affirm" for "affirm" (1 Tim **1** 7); conversely, we have for "his confidence" (Job **18** 14), "wherein he trusteth," for "with confidence" (Ezk **28** 26) "securely therein."

The Bible teaches the value of *confidence* (Isa **30** 15; He **10** 35), but neither in "gold" (Job **31** 24), nor in man, however great (Ps **118** 8.9; Jer **17** 5), nor in self (Prov **14** 16; Phil **3** 3), but in God (Ps **65** 5; Prov **3** 26; **14** 26), as revealed in Christ (Eph **3** 12; 1 Jn **5** 13.14). W. L. WALKER

CONFIRM, kon-fûrm, **CONFIRMATION,** kon-fẽr-mā'shun: In the OT represented by several Heb words, generally with reference to an increase of external strength, as "c. the feeble knees" (Isa **35** 3); "c. the kingdom" (2 K **15** 19); "c. inheritance" (Ps **68** 9). In the NT, this external, objective sense is expressed by *βεβαιόω, bebaióō,* as in Mk **16** 20; Rom **15** 8. The strengthening of mind, purpose, conviction, i.e. the inner or subjective sense (Acts **14** 22; **15** 32.41) corresponds to *ἐπιστηρίζω, epistērízō.* Used also of ratifying or making valid (*κυρόω, kuróō*) a covenant (Gal **3** 15). The noun is used in the second sense (He **6** 16; Phil **1** 7). Confirmation, the rite, in some denominations, of admission to the full communion of the church, which the Rom church has elevated to the place of a sacrament, has only ecclesiastical, but no Scriptural, authority. It is grounded, however, in the Scriptural precedent of the laying on of hands after baptism. See HANDS, IMPOSITION OF. H. E. JACOBS

CONFISCATION, kon-fis-kā'shun. See PUNISHMENTS.

CONFLICT, kon'flikt (**ἀγών,** *agôn,* "contest," "fight"): In Phil **1** 30, "having the same c. which ye saw in me," and Col **2** 1 AV; 1 Thess **2** 2 (AV "contention"); *ἄθλησις, áthlēsis* (lit. "combat in the public games"), in He **10** 32 (AV "fight"). See also AGONY.

CONFORM, kon-fôrm', **CONFORMABLE,** kon-fôrm'a-b'l (**συμμορφόω,** *summorphóō,* "to become or be like," or "of the same form"): Indicating an inner change of nature, working into the outward life (Rom **8** 29; Phil **3** 10.21); while *συσχηματίζω, suschēmatízō,* "fashioned according to" (Rom **12** 21 RV, AV "conformed"), refers to that which is external.

CONFOUND, kon-found': The physical origin of spiritual terms is well illustrated by the principal Heb words for "confounded" (rendered also "ashamed," etc); בּוֹשׁ, *bōsh,* is "to become pale" (2 K **19** 26; Job **6** 20; Ps **83** 17; **129** 5 AV; Isa **19** 9, etc); חָפֵר, *ḥāphēr,* "to become red" (Ps **35** 4; Isa **1** 29; **24** 23, "the moon shall be confounded," Mic **3** 7); יָבֵשׁ, *yābhash,* "to be dried up" (Jer **46** 24 AV; **48** 1 20 AV; **50** 2 AV; Zec **10** 5); כָּלַם, *kālam,* "to blush" (Ps **69** 6 AV; Isa **41** 11, etc). In Gen **11** 7.9, of the confusion of tongues, the word is בָּלַל, *bālal,* "to mix," "mingle." In Jer **1** 17 AV it is חָתַת, *ḥāthath,* "to bring or put down."

In NT, *kataischúnō,* "to put to shame" (1 Cor **1** 27 AV; 1 Pet **2** 6 AV); and *sugchúnō,* "to pour together," "bewilder" (Acts **2** 6; **9** 22). RV frequently gives "ashamed" and "put to shame" instead of "confounded." W. L. WALKER

CONFUSION, kon-fū'zhun (בֹּשֶׁת, *bōsheth,* "shame, paleness," כְּלִמָּה, *kelimmāh,* "blushing," תֹּהוּ, *tōhū;* **ἀκαταστασία,** *akatastasía,* **σύγχυσις,** *súgchusis*): In the OT *bōsheth* (1 S **20** 30; Ps **109** 29 AV) and *kelimmāh* (Ps **44** 15; Isa **30** 3) are the words most frequently trd "confusion"; *tōhū,* "wastiness," "emptiness" is so trd (Isa **24** 10; **34** 11; **41** 29), also *ḳālōn,* "lightness," "contempt" (Job **10** 15 = ignominy, ARV) and *tebhel,* "profanation" (Lev **18** 23; **20** 12); *ra'ash,* "shaking," "trembling," rendered "confused" in Isa **9** 5 AV; cf RV. Gr *akatastasia,* "instability" is trd "confusion" (1 Cor **14** 33; Jas **3** 16); *sugchusis,* "a pouring out together" (Acts **19** 29). In Wisd **14** 26, "changing of kind" (AV) is rendered "confusion of sex." W. L. WALKER

CONFUSION OF TONGUES. See BABEL, TOWER OF; TONGUES, CONFUSION OF.

CONGREGATION, koṇ-grē-gā'shun (קָהָל, *ḳāhāl,* עֵדָה, *'ēdhāh*): These two words rendered by "congregation" or "assembly" are used apparently without any difference of sense. They appear to include an assembly of the whole people or any section that might be present on a given occasion.

1. Terms Employed

Indeed, sometimes the idea appears to correspond closely to that conveyed by "horde," or even by "crowd." *'Ēdhāh* is once used of bees (Jgs **14** 8). It has been sought to distinguish the two words by means of Lev **4** 13, "if the whole *'ēdhāh* of Israel err, and the thing be hid from the eyes of the *ḳāhāl*." The *ḳāhāl* would then be the smaller body representing the whole *'ēdhāh*, but the general usage is not favorable to this view (compare e.g. Ex **12** 19, "cutting off from the *'ēdhāh* of Israel," with Nu **19** 20, "cutting off from the *ḳāhāl*"). The idea denoted by these words is said by Wellhausen to be "foreign to Heb antiquity," though it "runs through the PC from beginning to end" (*Prolegomena*, 78). Yet it is Dt that presents us with laws excluding certain classes from the *ḳāhāl*, and the word is also found in Gen **49** 6; Nu **22** 4 (RV "multitude"); Dt **5** 22; **9** 10; **31** 30; Josh **8** 35; 1 S **17** 47; 1 K **8** 14; Mic **2** 5, and other early passages, while *'ēdhāh* occurs in 1 K **12** 20 (see further, Eerdmans, *Das Buch Exodus*, 80 f). On the other hand taste and euphony appear to be responsible for the choice of one or other of the words in many cases. Thus the Chronicler uses *ḳāhāl* frequently, but *'ēdhāh* only once (2 Ch **5** 6 = 1 K **8** 5).

2. Legal Provisions

Moses provided for the summoning of the congregation by trumpets (Nu **10** 2–8). For the sin offering to be brought if the whole congregation erred, see Lev **4** 13–21. Dt **23** 1–8 (in Heb 2–9) excludes bastards, Ammonites and Moabites from the assembly, even to the tenth generation, while Edomites and Egyptians were admitted in the third. Those who suffer from certain physical defects are also excluded.

3. Other Terms

One other word must be noted, מוֹעֵד, *mō'ēdh*. It occurs often in the phrase *'ōhel mō'ēdh* ("tent of meeting"; see TABERNACLE). But in Nu **16** 2 we find it used of certain princes who were "men of renown called to the assembly."

For עֲצָרֶת, *'ăçereth*, rendered by RV "solemn assembly," see FEASTS. On מִקְרָא, *miḳrā'*, see CONVOCATION. HAROLD M. WIENER

CONGREGATION, MOUNT OF (הַר־מוֹעֵד, *har-mō'ēdh*, Isa **14** 13): The prophet has depicted the excitement caused in Sheol by the descent of the once mighty king of Babylon into the world of shades, and now himself points the contrast between the monarch's former haughty boastings and his present weak and hopeless condition: "Thou saidst in thy heart, I will ascend into heaven, I will exalt my throne above the stars of God; and I will sit upon the mount of congregation, in the uttermost parts of the north." Instead he is brought down "to the uttermost parts of the pit" (ver 15). By the "mount of congregation" (meeting or assembly) is evidently meant the fancied Olympus of the gods on some lofty northern height. The king vaunted that he would make his abode with the gods in heaven; now he is cast down to the depths of Sheol. JAMES ORR

CONIAH, kō-nī'a (כָּנְיָהוּ, *konyāhū*, "Jah is creating"): A form of the name Jehoiachin, found in Jer **22** 24.28; **37** 1. See JEHOIACHIN.

CONONIAH, kon-ō-nī'a. See CONANIAH.

CONQUEROR, koṇ'kẽr-ẽr: Known only in the compound vb. (ὑπερνικῶμεν, *hupernikōmen*, Rom **8** 37): A usual meaning of the preposition in composition is "above all measure"; hence "more than conquerors," RV, AV. The comparison is to the completeness of the victory. Others may place their enemies in subjection; those here mentioned master not only their foes, but themselves. Others destroy their foes and their resources; while those who are "more than conquerors" convert foes into means of still farther promoting the interests for which they struggle (Rom **3** 3–5). Nor is the victory external and transient, but internal and permanent. H. E. JACOBS

CONSCIENCE, kon'shens (ἡ συνείδησις, *hē suneidēsis*):

I. SEQUENT CONSCIENCE
  1. Judicial
  2. Punitive
  3. Predictive
  4. Social
II. ANTECEDENT CONSCIENCE
III. INTUITIONAL AND ASSOCIATIONAL THEORIES
IV. THE EDUCATION OF CONSCIENCE
V. HISTORY AND LITERATURE
  1. Earlier Views
  2. Reformation and After

I. Sequent Conscience.—The aspect of conscience earliest noticed in lit. and most frequently referred to at all times is what is called the Sequent Conscience—that is to say, it follows action.

1. Judicial

This is (1) *judicial*. No sooner is a decision formed than there ensues a judgment favorable or adverse, a sentence of guilty or not guilty. Conscience has often been compared to a court of law, in which there are culprit, judge, witnesses and jury; but these are all in the subject's own breast, and are in fact himself.

2. Punitive

It is (2) *punitive*. In the individual's own breast are not only the figures of justice already mentioned, but the executioner as well; for, on the back of a sentence of condemnation or acquittal, there immediately follows the pain of a wounded or the satisfaction of an approving conscience; and of all human miseries or blisses this is the most poignant. Esp. has the remorse of an evil conscience impressed the human imagination, in such instances as Cain and Judas, Saul and Herod; and the poets, those knowers of human nature, have found their most moving themes in the delineation of this aspect of human experience. The ancient poets represented the terrors of conscience under the guise of the Erinyes or Furies, who, with swift, silent, unswerving footstep, tracked the criminal and pulled him down, while Shakespeare, in such dramas as *Macbeth* and *Richard the Third*, has burned the same lessons into the imagination of all readers of his works. The satisfaction of a good conscience may stamp itself on the habitual serenity of one face, and the accusations of an evil conscience may impart a hunted and sinister expression to another (cf Wisd **17** 11).

3. Predictive

It is (3) *predictive*. There is no instinct in the soul of man more august than the anticipation of something after death—of a tribunal at which the whole of life will be revised and retribution awarded with perfect justice according to the deeds done in the body. It is this which imparts to death its solemnity; we instinctively know that we are going to our account. And such great natural instincts cannot be false.

4. Social

It is (4) *social*. Not only does a man's own conscience pass sentence on his conduct, but the consciences of others pass sentence on it too; and to this may be due a great intensification of the consequent sensations. Thus, a crime may lie hidden in the memory, and the pain of its guilt may be assuaged by the action of time, when suddenly and unexpectedly it is found out and exposed to the knowledge of all; and, only when the force of the public conscience breaks forth on the culprit, driving him from society, does he feel his guilt in all its magnitude. The "Day of Judgment" (q.v.), as it is represented in Scripture, is an application of this principle on a vast scale; for there the character and conduct of everyone will be submitted to the conscience of all. On the other hand, a friend may be to a man a second conscience, by which his own conscience is kept alive and alert; and this approval from without may, in some cases, be, even more than the judgment within, an encouragement to everything that is good or a protection against temptation.

II. Antecedent Conscience.—From the Sequent is distinguished the Antecedent Conscience, which designates a function of this faculty preceding moral decision or action. When the will stands at the parting of the ways, seeing clearly before it the right course and the wrong, conscience commands to strike into the one and forbids to choose the other. This is its imperative; and—to employ the language of Kant—it is a categorical imperative. What conscience commands may be apparently against our interests, and it may be completely contrary to our inclinations; it may be opposed to the advice of friends or to the solicitations of companions; it may contradict the decrees of principalities and powers or the voices of the multitude; yet conscience in no way withdraws or modifies its claim. We may fail to obey, giving way to passion or being overborne by the allurements of temptation; but we know that we ought to obey; it is our duty; and this is a sublime and sacred word. The great crises of life arise when conscience is issuing one command and self-interest or passion or authority another, and the question has to be decided which of the two is to be obeyed. The interpreters of human life have known how to make use of such moments, and many of the most memorable scenes in literature are of this nature; but the actual history of mankind has also been dignified with numerous instances in which confessors and martyrs, standing on the same ground, have faced death rather than contravene the dictates of the authority within; and there never passes an hour in which the eye of the All-seeing does not behold someone on earth putting aside the bribes of self-interest or the menaces of authority and paying tribute to conscience by doing the right and taking the consequences.

III. Intuitional and Associational Theories.—Up to this point there is little difficulty or difference of opinion; but now we come to a point at which very differing views emerge. It was remarked above, that when anyone stands at the parting of the ways, seeing clearly the right course and the wrong, conscience imperatively commands him which to choose and which to avoid; but how does anyone know which of the two alternatives is the right and which the wrong? Does conscience still suffice here, or is he dependent on another faculty? Here the Intuitional and the Associational, or—speaking broadly—the Scotch and the English, the German and the French schools of ethics diverge, those on the one side holding that conscience has still essential guidance to give, while those on the other maintain that the guidance must now be undertaken by other faculties. The Sensational or Experimental school holds that we are dependent on the authority of society or on our own estimate of the consequences of actions, while the opposite school teaches that in the conscience there is a clear revelation of certain moral laws, approving certain principles of action and disapproving others. The strong point of the former view is the diversity which has existed among human beings in different ages and in different latitudes as to what is right and what is wrong. What was virtuous in Athens might be sinful in Jerus; what is admired as heroism in Japan may be despised as foolhardiness in Britain. To this it may be replied, first, that the diversity has been greatly exaggerated; the unanimity of the human conscience under all skies being greater than is allowed by philosophers of this school. "Let any plain, honest man," says Butler, "before he engages in any course of action, ask himself, Is this I am going about right, or is it wrong? Is it good, or is it evil? and I do not in the least doubt but that this question will be answered agreeably to truth and virtue by almost any fair man in almost any circumstances." Then, there are many moral judgments supposed to be immediate verdicts of conscience which are really logical inferences from the utterances of this faculty and are liable to all the fallacies by which reasoning in any department of human affairs is beset. It is only for the major premise, not for the conclusion, that conscience is responsible. The strong point of the Intuitional school, on the other hand, is the power and right of the individual to break away from the habits of society, and, in defiance of the commands of authority or the voices of the multitude, to follow a course of his own. When he does so, is it a logical conclusion as to the consequences of action he is obeying, or a higher intuition? When, for example, Christianity announced the sinfulness of fornication in opposition to the laxity of Greece and Rome, was it an argument about consequences with which she operated successfully, or an instinct of purity which she divined at the back of the actions and opinions of heathendom? The lettering of the moral law may have to be picked out and cleansed from the accumulations of time, but the inscription is there all the same.

IV. The Education of Conscience.—It may be, however, that a more exact analysis of the antecedent conscience is requisite. Between the categorical imperative, which commands to choose the right path and avoid the wrong, and the indicative, which declares that this is the right way and that the wrong, there ought perhaps to be assumed a certainty that one of the alternative ways is right and must be pursued at all hazards, while the other is wrong and must be abandoned at whatever cost. This perception, that moral distinctions exist, separate from each other as heaven and hell, is the peculiarity of conscience; but it does not exclude the necessity for taking time to ascertain, in every instance, which of the alternatives has the one character and which the other, or for employing a great variety of knowledge to make this sure. Those who would limit conscience to the faculty which utters the major premises of moral reasoning are wont to hold that it can never err and does not admit of being educated; but such a use of the term is too remote from common usage, and there must be room left for the conscience to enlighten itself by making acquaintance with such objective standards as the character of God, the example of Christ, and the teaching of Scripture, as well as with the maxims of the wise and the experience of the good.

Another question of great interest about the conscience is, whether it involves an intuition of God. When it is suffering the pain of remorse, who is it that inflicts the punishment? Is it only the conscience itself? Or is man, in such experiences, aware of the existence of a Being outside of and above himself? When the will is about to act, it receives the command to choose the right and refuse the wrong; but who issues this command? Is it only itself, or does the imperative come with a sanction and solemnity betokening a higher origin? Conscience is an intuition of moral law—the reading, so to speak, of a luminous writing, which hangs out there, on the bosom of Nature—but who penned that writing? It used to be thought that the word Conscience implied, in its very structure, a reference to God, meaning lit. "knowledge along with another," the other being God. Though this derivation be uncertain, many think that it exactly expresses the truth. There are few people with an ethical experience of any depth who have not sometimes been overwhelmingly conscious of the approval or disapproval of an unseen Being; and, if there be any trustworthy argument for the existence of a Deity, prior to supernatural revelation, this is where it is to be found.

V. History and Literature.—Only a few indications of history can be given here. The conscience,

1. Earlier Views

at least the sequent conscience, was identified in the ancient world, and the rise of a doctrine on the subject belongs to the period when the human mind, being shut out from public activity through political changes, was thrown back upon itself and began to watch closely its own symptoms. The word has a specially prominent place in the philosophical writings of Cicero. Strange to say, it does not occur in the OT; but, though not the name, the thing appears there frequently enough. On the very first page of revelation, the voice of God is heard calling among the trees of the garden (Gen **3** 8); and, in the very next incident, the blood of Abel cries out to heaven from the ground (Gen **4** 10). In the NT the word occurs with tolerable frequency, esp. in the speeches (Acts **24** 16, etc) and writings of St. Paul (Rom **2** 15; **9** 1; **13** 5; 1 Cor **6** 7-12, etc); and this might have been expected to secure for it a prominent place in the doctrine of the church. But this did not immediately take effect, although Chrysostom already speaks of Conscience and Nature as two books in which the human mind can read of God, previous to supernatural revelation. In the Middle Ages the conscience received from two sources so much stimulation that both thing and name were certain to come into greater prominence in the speculations of the schools. The one of these influences was the rise of Monasticism, which, driving human beings into solitude, made the movements of their own minds the objects of everlasting study to themselves; and the other was the practice of auricular confession, which became, especially to many of the inmates of the houses of religion, the most interesting business of life; because, in order to meet the confessor, they scanned every thought and weighed every scruple, becoming adepts at introspection and self-discipline. Thus it came to pass that ethics took the form of Cases of Conscience, the priest having to train himself, or to be trained by professors and through books, to be able to answer every query submitted to him in the confessional. The ripest fruit of this method appears in the *Summa* of Aquinas, who discusses elaborately the doctrine of conscience, dividing it into two parts—*synderesis* (from συντήρησις, *suntērēsis*) and *conscientia*—the one of which supplies the major premises and cannot err, while the other draws the inferences therefrom and is liable to make mistakes. The Mystics identified the synderesis as the point in the spirit of man at which it can be brought into contact and connection with the Spirit of God.

At the Reformation the conscience was much in the mouths of men, both because the terrors of

2. The Reformation and After

conscience formed a preparation for comprehending justification by faith and because, in appearing before principalities and powers in vindication of their action, the Reformers took their stand on conscience, as Luther did so memorably at the Diet of Worms; and the assertion of the rights of conscience has ever since been a conspicuous testimony of Protestantism; whereas Romanists, especially as represented by the Jesuits, have treated the conscience as a feeble and ignorant thing, requiring to be led by authority—that is, by themselves. The forms of mediaevalism long clung even to Protestant lit. on this subject. It may not be surprising to find a High Churchman like Jeremy Taylor, in his *Ductor Dubitantium*, discussing ethics as a system of cases of conscience, but it is curious to find a Puritan like Baxter (in his *Christian Directory*), and a Scottish Presbyterian like David Dickson (in his *Therapeutica Sacra*) doing the same. Deism in England and the Enlightenment in Germany magnified the conscience, to which they ascribed such a power of revealing God as made any further revelation unnecessary; but the practical effect was a secularization and vulgarization of the general mind; and it was against these rather than the system which had produced them that Butler in England and Kant in Germany had to raise the standard of a spiritual view of life. The former said of the conscience that, if it had power as it had right, it would absolutely govern the world; and Kant's sublime saying is well known, at the close of his great work on *Ethics:* "Two things fill the soul with ever new and growing wonder and reverence, the oftener and the longer reflection continues to occupy itself with them—the starry heavens above and the moral law within." The rise of an Associational and Developmental Philosophy in England, represented by such powerful thinkers as the Mills, father and son, Professor Bain and Herbert Spencer, tended to dissipate the halo surrounding the conscience, by representing it as merely an emotional equivalent for the authority of law and the claims of custom, so stamped on the mind by the experience of generations that, its earthly source forgotten, it came to be attributed to supernatural powers. But this school was antagonized with success by such thinkers as Martineau and T. H. Green. R. Rothe regarded conscience as a term too popular and of too variable signification to be of much use in philosophical speculation; but most of the great succession of writers on Christian ethics who followed him have treated it seriously; Dorner esp. recognizing its importance, and Newman Smyth bestowing on it a thoroughly modern treatment. Among German works on the subject that of Gass, which contains an appendix on the history of the term *synderesis*, is deserving of special attention; that by Kähler is unfinished, as is also the work in Eng. by Robertson; *The Christian Conscience* by Davison is slight and popular. Weighty discussions will be found in two books on Moral Philosophy—the *Handbook* of Calderwood, and the *Ethics* of Mezes. But there is abundance of room for a great monograph on the subject, which would treat conscience in a comprehensive manner as the subjective standard of conduct, formed by progressive familiarity with the objective standards as well as by practice in accordance with its own authority and with the will of God.

JAMES STALKER

CONSECRATE, kon'sē-krāt, **CONSECRATION**, kon-sē-krā'shun: In the OT for several Heb words of different meanings:

(1) חָרַם, *ḥāram:* "I will consecrate [RV "devote"] their gain unto the Lord," i.e. the spoil of

1. In the OT

the nations shall be dedicated to the service of Jeh (Mic **4** 13). See BAN; CURSE.

(2) נָזַר, *nāzar*, נֵזֶר, *nēzer* (Nu **6** 7.9.12; RV "separate"). See NAZIRITE.

(3) קָדַשׁ, *ḳādhēsh:* "to be set apart," or "to be holy": of Aaron and his sons (Ex **28** 3; **30** 30; RV "sanctify"). The silver and gold and brass and iron of the banned city of Jericho are "consecrated"

things (RV "holy") unto the Lord (Josh **6** 19); of the priests (2 Ch **26** 18); of sacrifices (2 Ch **29** 33; **31** 6; Ezr **3** 5). See HOLINESS.

(4) מִלֵּא יָד, *millē' yadh*, lit. "to fill the hand"; and subst. pl. מִלֻּאִים, *millu'īm*, a peculiar idiom used frequently and generally for the installation of a priest into his office; and subst. for the installation offerings which were probably put into the priest's hands to symbolize his admission into office; hence the phrase, "and thou shalt consecrate Aaron and his sons" (Ex **29** 9; so **28** 41; **29** 29.33.35; **32** 29; Lev **8** 33; **16** 32; **21** 10; Nu **3** 3; Jgs **17** 5.12; 2 Ch **29** 31); of Jeroboam's non-Levitical priesthood (1 K **13** 33; 2 Ch **13** 9); of the altar (Ezk **43** 26) and of those who contributed to build the temple (1 Ch **29** 5). Subst. of an act of installation (Lev **7** 37; **8** 33), and of installation offerings (Ex **29** 22.26.27.31; Lev **8** 22.28.29.31).

2. In the NT In the NT τελειόω, *teleióō*, "to make perfect" (He **7** 28; RV "perfected"); ἐγκαινίζω, *egkainízō*, "to make new" (He **10** 20; RV "dedicated"). T. REES

CONSENT, kon-sent': The vb. implies compliance with the guidance and direction of another, and, therefore, a secondary and subordinate relation of approval, sympathy and concurrence on the part of the one who consents. He does not take the initiative, but yields to what the principal proposes. The phrase ἐκ συμφόνου, *ek sumphónou*, "by consent," means "by mutual agreement" (1 Cor **7** 5), both parties concerned being placed on an equality. "With one consent" (Zeph **3** 9, Heb "with one shoulder"; Lk **14** 18) suggests, although it does not necessarily imply, the result of deliberation and consultation; it may have no other force than that of unanimity. H. E. JACOBS

CONSIDER, kon-sid'ẽr: In the NT the force of the word is brought out most vividly in Mt **6** 26 (**καταμανθάνω**, *katamanthánō*), where it means to "examine closely," as though the observer had to bend down for this purpose, and in Lk **12** 27; He **10** 24 (*katanoéō*, to "observe well"), while in He **13** 7 the *anatheōréō*, "look up toward" or "look again at" is consistent with the reverential regard commended in the context. Used in the OT for a variety of Heb terms, signifying inspecting (Prov **31** 16), examining (Lev **13** 13), giving serious thoughts to (Ps **77** 5; Isa **1** 3), it often means little more than "see" or "behold" (Ps **8** 3; **9** 13). H. E. JACOBS

CONSIST, kon-sist' (**συνίστημι,** *sunístēmi*): To stand together, exist, subsist (Col **1** 17, "in him all things consist," i.e. the continuance of the universe is dependent upon His support and administration). In Lk **12** 15, it trs the vb. εἰμί, *eimí*, "to be," to express the thought that wealth is only an accident, not an essential to the highest ideal of life.

CONSOLATION, kon-sō-lā'shun (**παράκλησις,** *paráklēsis*): "Consolation of Israel" (Lk **2** 25), refers to the fulfilment of the promises in Isa **40** 1 ff. See COMFORT. "Son of consolation" (Acts **4** 36 AV and ARVm); see BARNABAS.

CONSORT, kon-sôrt' (**προσκληρόω,** *prosklēróō*, "to allot," Acts **17** 4). The vb. may be either in the middle or passive voice. RV, AV, and Luther's German tr regard it as middle, and render it: "cast their lots with," "associated," "united with." In advocacy of the passive, see Alford's *Greek Testament*, proposing: "were added," as if by lot, the allotment being determined by God who gave them the Holy Spirit directing their choice. The Eng. has the Lat for "lot" as its base.

CONSPIRACY, kon-spir'a-si. See CONFEDERACY.

CONSTANT, kon'stant, **CONSTANTLY,** kon'-stant-li: In 1 Ch **28** (*ḥāzaḳ*) meaning "firm," "strong." In Prov **21** 28 the advb. ("constantly") of AV is replaced in ARV by "shall speak so as to endure," ERV "unchallenged." RV gives "confidently" for AV "constantly" in Acts **12** 15; Tit **3** 8.

CONSTELLATIONS, kon-ste-lā'shuns (כְּסִילִים, *keṣīlīm*, lit. "Orions"). See ASTRONOMY, II, 11.

CONSTRAIN, kon-strān': Generally in the sense of pressing urgently (2 K **4** 8; Lk **24** 29; Acts **16** 15), to impel or carry away (2 Cor **5** 14); sometimes to be compelled of necessity (Job **32** 18; Acts **28** 19; cf Gal **6** 12). See COMPEL.

CONSULT, kon-sult' (שָׁאַל, *shā'al*, מָלַךְ, *mālakh*, יָעַץ, *yā'aç*, יְעַט [Aram.] *ye'aṭ*; **συμβουλεύομαι,** *sumbouleúomai*):

(1) "To ask," "inquire," "seek advice." Ezekiel speaks of the king of Bab consulting the teraphim (Ezk **21** 21), and the Israelites were admonished to have nothing to do with "a consulter with a familiar spirit" (Dt **18** 11). See ASTROLOGY; COMMUNION WITH DEMONS; DIVINATION.

(2) "To take counsel," "devise," "plan." The various officials of Babylon "consulted together to establish a royal statute" (Dnl **6** 7; cf Mt **26** 4).

(3) "To deliberate with one's self," "make up one's mind." Nehemiah consulted with himself as to what might be done for Jerus (Neh **5** 7). Jesus spoke of a king "consulting" (AV) whether he be able to wage a war (Lk **14** 31; RV "take counsel"). A. W. FORTUNE

CONSUME, kon-sūm' (אָכַל, *'ākhal*, כָּלָה, *kālāh*, תָּמַם, *tāmam*; **ἀναλίσκω,** *analískō*): In OT *'ākhal* ("to eat," "devour") occurs very frequently, and is trd "consumed" (Gen **31** 40; Ex **15** 7; Ps **78** 63, etc); *kālāh* ("to finish") is also frequently trd "consume," "consumed" (Gen **41** 30; Ex **32** 10; Ps **59** 13, etc); *tāmam*, "to be perfect," "finished" (Nu **17** 13; Dt **2** 15; Ps **73** 19, etc). There are many other words trd "consume" and "consumed," e.g. *ṣūph*, "to end" (Jer **8** 13; Dnl **2** 44; Zeph **1** 2.3); *bālāh*, "to fade," "wear away" (Job **13** 28; Ps **49** 14); *gāzal*, implying violence (Job **24** 19); *ṣāphāh*, "to end" (Gen **19** 15.17; Isa **7** 20, etc); *'āshēsh*, "to be old" (Ps **6** 7; **31** 9.10 AV); *māḳaḳ*, "to become completed" (Ezk **4** 17; Zec **14** 12 *bis*); *'āsāh kālāh* is rendered "utterly consume" (Neh **9** 31); *analiskō*, "to use up," occurs in Lk **9** 54; Gal **5** 15; 2 Thess **2** 8 (AV); *dapanáō*, "to spend," is trd "consume" in Jas **4** 3 (RV "spend"); *katanalískō*, "to consume utterly," occurs only in He **12** 29; "for our God is a consuming fire."

In RV "devour," "devoured" are several times substituted for "consume," "consumed," e.g. Job **20** 26; Jer **49** 27; Nu **16** 35; "boil well" (Ezk **24** 10); for "be consumed with dying" (Nu **17** 13), "perish all of us"; "consume" is substituted for "corrupt" in Mt **6** 19; "my spirit is consumed," for "my breath is corrupt" (Job **17** 1); instead of "the flame consumeth the chaff" (Isa **5** 24) we have "as the dry grass sinketh down in the flame"; and for "whom the Lord shall consume" (2 Thess **2** 8), RV reads (after a different text) "whom the Lord Jesus shall slay," "consume" in ARVm. W. L. WALKER

CONSUMMATION, kon-su-mā'shun (כִּלָּיוֹן, *killāyōn*, fr כָּלָה, *kālāh*): The word, meaning destruction, completion, or failing (Isa **10** 23; **28** 22; Dnl **9** 27) is trd interchangeably in the AV for another

Heb word referring to a physical disease, and best tr[d] "consumption"; cf Lev **26** 16; Dt **28** 22. Not used in RV. The Heb variously but more accurately tr[d] "full end"; cf Dnl **9** 27; Isa **10** 23; and "destruction"; cf Isa **10** 22; **28** 22. There seems therefore to be an inconsistency on the part of both the Authorized and Revised tr[s].

WALTER G. CLIPPINGER

CONSUMPTION, kon-sump'shun (שַׁחֶפֶת, *shaḥepheth,* "wasting away"): One of the punishments which was to follow neglect or breach of the law. It may mean pulmonary consumption, which occurs frequently in Pal; but from its association with fever in the texts, Lev **26** 16; Dt **28** 22, it is more likely to be the much more common condition of wasting and emaciation from prolonged or often recurring attacks of malarial fever.

CONTAIN, kon-tān'. See CONTINENCY.

CONTEND, kon-tend', **CONTENTION,** kon-ten'shun: The meeting of effort by effort, striving against opposition; sometimes physically, as in battle (Dt **2** 9), or with horses (Jer **12** 5), sometimes orally (Neh **13** 11), sometimes spiritually (Isa **57** 16). In the NT διακρίνειν, *diakrinein,* for the hostile separation of one from another, dispute (Jude ver 9), or ἐπαγωνίζομαι, *epagōnizomai* (Jude ver 3), descriptive of the strain to which a contestant is put. The noun is almost universally used with an unfavorable meaning, and as worthy of condemnation, for an altercation arising from a quarrelsome disposition. "By pride cometh only contention" (Prov **13** 10). The contentions at Corinth (1 Cor **1** 11) called forth the rebukes of Paul. Where used in AV in a good sense (1 Thess **2** 2) RV has "conflict." In Acts **15** 39, the noun has a peculiar force, where EV translates *paroxusmós* (whence Eng. "paroxysm") by "sharp contention." The Gr word refers rather to the inner excitement and irritation than to its outward expression. H. E. JACOBS

CONTENT, kon-tent', **CONTENTMENT,** kon-tent'ment (יַעַל, *ya'al;* ἀρκέω, *arkéō*): To be free from care because of satisfaction with what is already one's own. The Heb means simply "to be pleased." The Gr brings out the full force of the word in 1 Tim **6** 8; He **13** 5. Contentment (1 Tim **6** 6) is more inward than satisfaction; the former is a habit or permanent state of mind, the latter has to do with some particular occurrence or object.

CONTINENCY, kon'ti-nen-si (ἐγκρατεύομαι, *egkrateúomai,* "to have self-control" or "continency" RV, "to contain" AV): Paul, although he would that all men were like himself unmarried, yet advises that they should marry if they cannot control their sexual passions, and hold them in complete subjection to Christian motives (1 Cor **7** 9). The same Gr vb. is used in 1 Cor **9** 25, and tr[d] "is temperate" (AV and ERV) of the athlete who during the period of training abstains from all indulgence in food, drink, and sexual passion. For the general principle as expressed in subst. *egkráteia* (Acts **24** 25; Gal **5** 23; 2 Pet **1** 6) and adj. *egkratḗs* (Tit **1** 8) see TEMPERANCE, TEMPERATE. T. REES

CONTINUAL, kon-tin'ū-al, **CONTINUALLY,** kon-tin'ū-a-li: Without cessation, although there may be intervals between its presence; that which regularly recurs throughout a period, as Lk **24** 53: "[They] were continually in the temple"; "lest . . . . by her continual coming" (Lk **18** 5). In OT for Heb *tādhīr,* "pursue," as one drop of rain follows another in swift succession, but more frequently by *tāmīdh* for offerings repeated at intervals, as Ex **29** 42; occasionally the Heb has the phrase lit. meaning "all the day" (*kol ha-yōm*), as Gen **6** 5. In the NT most frequently for *diá pantós,* "through all" ("always" Mt **18** 10; He **13** 15), "sometimes," *adialeíptōs,* "incessantly" (Rom **9** 2 AV) and *diēnekḗs,* "continuously" (He **7** 3). H. E. JACOBS

CONTINUANCE, kon-tin'ū-ans: Not in RV; in Ps **139** 16 AV, as an interpretation of Heb *yāmīm,* "days," treating of God's prevision, where RV has: "They were all written, even the days that were ordained for me," i.e. all my days were in view, before one of them actually existed. In Isa **64** 5 AV, for *'ōlām,* "of long time," RV; in Rom **2** 7, for *hupomonḗ,* "patience," RV, or still better, "stedfastness," RVm.

CONTRADICTION, kon-tra-dik'shun: AV for ἀντιλογία, *antilogía* (He **7** 7; **12** 3). In the former passage, RV has "without any dispute," i.e. what has been said requires no argument; in the latter "gainsaying," which is scarcely an improvement, the reference being to the oral attacks upon the words and character of Jesus.

CONTRARY, kon'tra-ri (קְרִי, *ḳerī;* ἐναντίος, *enantíos*): In the OT it has the sense of antagonistic, as one person opposed or hostile to the other, esp. in Lev **26** 21.23.24.27.28.40.41, where Jeh declares His attitude toward the people in such phrases as: "If ye will not for all this hearken unto me, but walk c. unto me; then I will walk c. unto you in wrath."

In the NT it has a more varied significance and is applied to both material and human relations as simply opposite, set over against an object or thing. Used of the wind as in Mt **14** 24; Mk **6** 48; Acts **27** 4, where it is spoken of as c. Refers also to conflicting doctrines, customs or beliefs, as 1 Tim **1** 10, "and if there be any other thing c. to the sound doctrine." Several other Gr words are tr[d] with almost an identical meaning. Occasionally a prefix gives a slightly different shade of meaning.

WALTER G. CLIPPINGER

CONTRIBUTION, kon-tri-bū'shun (κοινωνία, *koinōnía,* "communion" or "fellowship," Rom **15** 26; 2 Cor **9** 13): The meaning "contribution" is drawn from the context, rather than from the Gr word. The phrase in the passage cited, lit. rendered, would be "to exercise" or "put fellowship into activity." The *koinōnía* subsisting among believers because of their inner communion with Christ places them and their gifts and possessions at the service of one another (see COMMUNION). They are enjoined not to forget to communicate (He **13** 16). To be "communicative" (*koinōnikoí*) is to be a habit of their lives, the Christian principle being that of the holding of all property as a trust, to be distributed as there is need (Acts **2** 44 f; 2 Cor **8** 14 f). The first occasion for calling this fellowship into activity, by way of "contributions," was within the church at Jerus and for its needy members (see COMMUNITY OF GOODS). The second occasion was repeatedly from the infant gentile churches for the poor within the same church (Acts **11** 29; Rom **15** 26; 2 Cor **8** 1–4; **9** 2); the fellowship thus widening from intra-congregational to general church benevolence. These contributions were gathered weekly (1 Cor **16** 2 f), were proportioned to the means of the givers (Acts **11** 29; 1 Cor **16** 2), were not exacted or prescribed, in a legalistic manner, but were called forth as the free-will offerings of grateful hearts (2 Cor **8** 7), springing from the community spirit, and were sent to their destination by accredited representatives of the congregations (1 Cor **16** 3; Acts **11** 30). H. E. JACOBS

CONTRITE, kon′trīt, **CONTRITION,** kon-trish′un (דַּכָּא, *dakkā′*, "bruise"): Only in OT (Ps **34** 18; Ps **51** 17; Isa **57** 15); נָכֶה, *nākhēh*, "smitten" (Isa **66** 2). Contrite, "crushed," is only the superlative of "broken"; "a contrite heart" is "a heart broken to pieces." In Holy Scripture, the heart is the seat of all feeling, whether joy or sorrow. A contrite heart is one in which the natural pride and self-sufficiency have been completely humbled by the consciousness of guilt. The theological term "contrition" designates more than is found in these passages. It refers to the grief experienced as a consequence of the revelation of sin made by the preaching of the law (Jer **23** 29). The Augsburg Confession (Art. XII) analyzes repentance into two parts: "Contrition and faith," the one the fruit of the preaching of the law, the other of the gospel. While c. has its degrees, and is not equal in all persons, the promise of forgiveness is not dependent upon the degree of contrition, but solely upon the merit of Christ. It is not simply a precondition of faith, but, as hatred of sin, combined with the purpose, by God's aid, to overcome it, grows with faith. H. E. JACOBS

CONTROVERSY, kon′tro-vẽr-si (רִיב, *rībh*, "strife," "contention"; ὁμολογουμένως, *homologouménōs*, "confessedly," "without controversy"): Used frequently of disputes among men (as Dt **17** 8) and then transferred to the justice of God as directed against the sins of men. Thus we read of Jeh's controversy with the nations (Jer **25** 31); with the inhabitants of the land (Hos **4** 1); with His people (Mic **6** 2). "Without controversy" (1 Tim **3** 16), a positive rather than a negative expression, "by common consent," or better, "as unanimously confessed," introducing a quotation from a hymn or rhythmical confession of the early church. H. E. JACOBS

CONVENIENT, kon-vēn′yent: In RV limited to tr of καιρός, *kairós*, "suitable time," "season," and its compounds: "that which is seasonable" or "opportune" (Mk **6** 21; Acts **24** 25). AV is replaced, in Prov **30** 8 RV, by "needful" (Heb *ḥōḳ*), "feed me with the food that is needful for me"; Jer **40** 4, by "right"; Eph **5** 4, by "befitting"; in Rom **1** 28, by "fitting," and in 1 Cor **16** 12, by "opportunity."

CONVENT, kon-vent′: Found in the AVm of Jer **49** 19: "Who will convent me in judgment?" and in Jer **50** 44: "Who will convent me to plead?" The Heb term which is rendered convent is *yā′adh*, and it means to summon to a court, to call on to plead. Convent is obsolete, but it was formerly used, and meant to summon, or to call before a judge. Shakespeare used it several times. In *King Henry VIII*, Act V, he said, "The lords of the council hath commanded that the archbishop be convented to the council board."

CONVERSANT, kon-vûr′sant (הָלַךְ, *hālakh*, "to go on," "to walk"): This word is trd "conversant" in Josh **8** 35 AV (m "walked"), and 1 S **25** 15 AV meaning "going along with them;" ARV "went."

CONVERSATION, kon-vẽr-sā′shun (ἀναστροφή, *anastrophḗ*, ὁμιλία, *homilía*): This word is another illustration of the changes which time makes in a living language. The modern sense of the term is mutual talk, colloquy, but in AV it never means that, but always behavior, conduct. This broader meaning, at a time not much later than the date of AV, began to yield to the special, limited one of today, perhaps, as has been suggested, because speech forms so large a part of conduct. The NT words for "converse" in the modern sense are *homiléō* (Lk **24** 14.15; Acts **20** 11) and *sunomiléō* (Acts **10** 27).

(1) In the OT the word used to indicate conduct is דֶּרֶךְ, *derekh*, "way," the course one travels (AV Ps **37** 14; m **50** 23). It is the common Heb idea of conduct, possibly due, as Hatch thinks, to the fact that in Syria intercourse between village and village was so much on foot, with difficulty on stony tracks over the hills, and this is reflected in the metaphor.

(2) In the NT the idea of deportment is once rendered by *trópos*, "Let your c. be without covetousness" (He **13** 5 AV; RV "be ye free from the love of money"; RVm "let your turn of mind be free"). But the usual Gr word is *anastrophḗ*, "a turning up and down," possibly due to the fact, as Hatch again avers, that life in the bustling streets of Athens and Rome gave rise to the conception of life as quick motion to and fro. "Ye have heard of my c." (Gal **1** 13 AV; RV "manner of life"). So also Eph **4** 22; 1 Tim **4** 12; He **13** 7; "Let him show out of a good c." (Jas **3** 13 AV; RV "by his good life"); "vexed with the filthy c." (2 Pet **2** 7 AV; RV "lascivious life"); "holy c." (2 Pet **3** 11 AV; RV "holy living"); "Our c. is in heaven" (Phil **3** 20 AV; RV "citizenship" [q.v.]). See also in the Apoc (Tob **4** 14; 2 Macc **5** 8).

The trs in the Revisions put a wholesome emphasis upon conduct, and eliminate the danger of much misunderstanding. See further Hatch, *Essays in Biblical Greek*. G. H. TREVER

CONVERSION, kon-vûr′shun:

I. The Words "Conversion," "Convert," in Biblical Usage.—The noun "conversion" (ἐπιστροφή, *epistrophḗ*) occurs in only one passage in the Bible, "They passed through both Phoenicia and Samaria, declaring the conversion of the Gentiles" (Acts **15** 3).

1. In the English Bible

Derived forms of the vb. "convert" are used in the RV in Jas **5** 19, "convert," "converteth" (**5** 20), "converted" (Ps **51** 13, m "return"), "converts" (Isa **1** 27, m "they that return"). In other instances where the AV uses forms of the vb. "convert" the RV employs "turn again" (Isa **6** 10; Lk **22** 32; Acts **3** 19), or "turn" (Isa **60** 5; Mt **13** 15; **18** 3; Mk **4** 12; Jn **12** 40; Acts **28** 27). In Ps **19** 7 the reading of the AV, "The law of the Lord is perfect, converting the soul," has been changed by the revisers into "restoring the soul." The words commonly used in the Eng. Bible as equivalent with the Heb and Gr terms are "turn," "return," "turn back," "turn again" (cf Dt **4** 30; Isa **55** 7; Jer **3** 12 ff; **25** 5; **35** 15; Ezk **18** 21–23; **33** 11; Mal **3** 7). Thus "convert" is synonymous with "turn," and "conversion" with "turning."

2. In the OT

The principal Heb word is שׁוּב, *shūbh;* other words are פָּנָה, *pānāh*, הָפַךְ, *hāphakh*, סָבַב, *ṣābhabh*, in Hiphil. They are used (1) in the lit. sense, for instance, Gen **14** 7; Dt **17** 16; Ps **56** 9; Isa **38** 8. (2) In the later prophetical writings the vb. *shūbh* refers, both in the Qal and Hiphil forms, to the return from the captivity (Isa **1** 27; Jer **29** 14; **30** 3; Ezk **16** 53; Zeph **2** 7). (3) In the fig., ethical or religious sense (*a*) from God (Nu **14** 43; 1 S **15** 11; 1 K **9** 6); (*b*) more frequently to turn back to God (1 S **7** 3; 1 K **8** 33; Isa **19** 22; Joel **2** 12; Am **4** 6 ff; Hos **6** 11; **7** 10).

The words used in the LXX and NT are στρέφειν, *stréphein*, and its compounds, ἀπο, *apostr.*, ἀνα, *anastr.*, ἐπανα, *epanastr.*, ὑπο, *hupostr.*, and esp. ἐπιστρέφειν, *epistréphein*. The latter word occurs

39 times in the NT. It is used (1) in the lit. sense in Mt **9** 22; **10** 13; **24** 18; Acts **9** 40; **15** 36, etc; (2) in the fig. sense, in transitive form (Lk **1** 16 f; Jas **5** 19 f). In Gal **4** 9 and 2 Pet **2** 21 it denotes to turn from the right way to the wrong. The opposite meaning, to turn from the wrong way to the right, we find in Lk **22** 32; Acts **9** 35; **11** 21; **14** 15; **15** 19; **26** 18; 2 Cor **3** 16; 1 Thess **1** 9; 1 Pet **2** 25. In connection with *metanoeín*, "repent," it is used in Acts **3** 19; **26** 20. The root word *strephein* is used in the fig. sense in Mt **18** 3; Jn **12** 40. LXX and *TR* have here *epistrephein.*

3. In the NT

II. The Doctrine.—While the words "conversion" and "convert" do not occur frequently in our Eng. Bible the teaching contained therein is fundamental in Christian doctrine. From the words themselves it is not possible to derive a clearly defined doctrine of conversion; the materials for the construction of the doctrine must be gathered from the tenor of Bib. teaching.

1. Vague Use of the Word

There is a good deal of vagueness in the modern use of the term. By some writers it is used in "a very general way to stand for the whole series of manifestations just preceding, accompanying, and immediately following the apparent sudden changes of character involved" (E. D. Starbuck, *The Psychology of Religion,* 21). "'To be converted,' 'to be regenerated,' 'to receive grace,' 'to experience religion,' 'to gain an assurance,' are so many phrases which denote the process, gradual or sudden, by which a self, hitherto divided and consciously wrong, inferior and unhappy, becomes unified and consciously right, superior and happy in consequence of its hold upon religious realities. This at least is what conversion signifies in general terms" (William James, *The Varieties of Religious Experience,* 189). In this general, vague way the term is used not only by psychologists, but also by theological writers and in common religious parlance. A converted man is a Christian, a believer, a man who has religion, who has experienced regeneration.

2. Specific Meaning

In its more restricted meaning the word denotes the action of man in the initial process of salvation as distinguished from the action of God. Justification and regeneration are purely Divine acts, repentance, faith, conversion are human acts although under the influence and by the power of the Divine agency. Thus conversion denotes the human volition and act by which man in obedience to the Divine summons determines to change the course of his life and turns to God. Arrested by God's call man stops to think, turns about and heads the opposite way. This presupposes that the previous course was not directed toward God but away from Him. The instances of conversion related in the Bible show that the objective point toward which man's life was directed may be either the service of idols (1 Thess **1** 9) or a life of religious indifference, a self-centered life where material things engross the attention and deaden the sense of things spiritual (rich young ruler, Lk **18** 22), or a life of sensuality, of open sin and shame (prodigal son, Lk **15** 13) or even a mistaken way of serving God (Saul, Acts **26** 9). Accordingly in conversion either the religious or the ethical element may predominate. The moral man who turns from self to God or, as Saul did, from an erroneous notion concerning God's will to a clear conception of his relation to God is more conscious of the religious factor. Conversion brings him into vital, conscious fellowship with God through Jesus Christ. The immoral man who is awakened to a realization of the holiness of God, of the demands of His law, and of his own sin and guilt is more conscious of the outward change in his manner of life. The ethical change is the more outstanding fact in his experience, although it can never be separated from the religious experience of the changed relation to God.

3. Mode

The mode of conversion varies greatly according to the former course of life. It may be a sudden crisis in the moral and intellectual life. This is very frequently the case in the experience of heathen who turn from the worship of idols to faith in Jesus Christ. A sudden crisis is frequently witnessed in the case of persons who, having lived a life of flagrant sin, renounce their former life. Conversion to them means a complete revolution in their thoughts, feelings and outward manner of life. In other instances conversion appears to be the climax of a prolonged conflict for supremacy of divergent motives; and, again, it may be the goal of a gradual growth, the consummation of a process of discerning ever more clearly and yielding ever more definitely and thus experiencing ever more vitally truths which have been implanted and nurtured by Christian training. This process results in the conscious acceptance of Jesus Christ as the personal Saviour and in the consecration of life to His service.

Thus conversion may be an instantaneous act, or a process which is more or less prolonged. The latter is more frequently seen in the case of children and young people who have grown up in Christian families and have received the benefit of Christian training. No conversions of this kind are recorded in the NT. This may be explained by the fact that most of our NT writings are addressed to the first generation of Christians, to men and women who were raised in Jewish legalism or heathen idolatry, and who turned to Christ after they had passed the age of adolescence. The religious life of their children as distinguished in its mode and manifestations from that of the adults does not appear to have been a matter of discussion or a source of perplexity so as to call forth specific instruction.

Conversion comprises the characteristics both of repentance and of faith. Repentance is conversion viewed from its starting-point, the turning *from* the former life; faith indicates the objective point of conversion, the turning *to* God.

4. Conversion and Psychology

Of late the psychology of conversion has been carefully studied and elaborately treated by psychologists. Much valuable material has been gathered. It is shown that certain periods of adolescent life are particularly susceptible to religious influences (cf G. Stanley Hall, *Adolescence,* II, ch xiv; E. D. Starbuck, *Psychology of Religion,* etc). Yet conversion cannot be explained as a natural process, conditioned by physiological changes in the adolescent, esp. by approaching puberty. The laws of psychology are certainly God's laws as much as all other laws of Nature, and His Spirit works in harmony with His own laws. But in genuine conversion there is always at work in a direct and immediate manner the Spirit of God to which man, be he adolescent or adult, consciously responds. Any attempt to explain conversion by eliminating the direct working of the Divine Spirit falls short of the mark. See REGENERATION; REPENTANCE.

LITERATURE.—See REGENERATION.

J. L. NUELSEN

CONVICT, kon-vikt′, **CONVICTION,** kon-vik′shun (ἐλέγχω, *elégchō,* and compounds, "to prove guilty"): Usual tr of EV, where AV has **"convince,"** as in Jn **8** 46; Tit **1** 9; Jas **2** 9; once also replacing AV "reprove" (Jn **16** 8), while RV changes AV "convince" into "reprove" in 1 Cor **14** 24. **It**

always implies the presentation of evidence. It is a decision presumed to be based upon a careful and discriminating consideration of all the proofs offered, and has a legal character, the verdict being rendered either in God's judgment (Rom **3** 19), or before men (Jn **8** 46) by an appeal to their consciences in which God's law is written (Rom **2** 15). Since such conviction is addressed to the heart of the guilty, as well as concerning him externally, the word "reprove" is sometimes substituted. To "convict . . . . in respect of righteousness, and of judgment" (Jn **16** 8), refers to the conviction of the inadequacy and perversity of the ordinary, natural standards of righteousness and judgment, and the approval of those found in Christ, by the agency of the Holy Spirit, as the great interpreter and applier of the work of Christ. H. E. Jacobs

CONVINCE, kon-vins′ (ἐλέγχω, *elégchō*): Another form etymologically of "convict," means to bring to a decision concerning the truth or the falsehood of a proposition (Job **32** 12). As usually applied to what is of a more individual and private character, and having reference to what is either good or bad, or what is in itself without moral quality, it has given way in RV to either "convict," "reprove" or "confute." See Convict.

CONVOCATION, kon-vō-kā′shun: A rendering for מִקְרָא, *miḳrā'*, chiefly in the frequent "Holy Convocation"; but the word is sometimes used alone, e.g. Nu **10** 2; Isa **1** 13; **4** 5. On a holy convocation no work could be done. The phrase differs from "solemn assembly," which in the Pent is only applied to the concluding festivals at the end of Passover and Tabernacles, while "Holy Convocation" is used of the Sabbath and all the great holy days of the Mosaic legislation.

CONVULSING, kon-vuls′ing (Mk **1** 26 m [AV **torn**]). See Unclean Spirit.

COOKING, ko͝ok′ing. See Food.

COOL, ko͞ol (רוּחַ, *rūaḥ*, "wind"; καταψύχω, *katapsúchō*, "to cool down"): "Cool of the day" (Gen **3** 8, m "wind"), when the evening breeze has tempered the heat of the day, enabling Orientals to walk abroad. "Cool my tongue" (Lk **16** 24), a phrase reflecting the Jewish notion that Abraham had power to rescue his descendants from the fires of Hades.

COOS, kō′os. See Cos.

COPING, kō′ping. See House.

COPPER, kop′ẽr (נְחשֶׁת, *neḥōsheth*): The word is trd "copper" in only one passage (Ezr **8** 27 AV). In the ARV of this passage, "brass" has been substituted. Neither describes the actual alloy according to present definitions so well as the word "bronze." Copper was one of the earliest metals to be known and utilized in alloy, but copper, as a single metal, was probably little used. The remains of spears, balances, arms, vases, mirrors, statues, cooking utensils, implements of all kinds, etc, from Bible times are principally of an alloy of copper hardened with tin known today as bronze (see Brass). In such passages as Dt **8** 9, where reference is made to the native metal or ores, "copper" should be substituted for "brass" as in the ARV (cf Job **40** 18). This is true also of coins as χαλκός, *chalkós*, in Mt **10** 9.

Our modern Eng. word "copper" is derived from an old name pertaining to the island of Cyprus. Copper was known to the ancients as Cyprian brass, probably because that island was one of the chief sources for this metal. The Sinai peninsula and the mountains of northern Syria also contributed to the ancient world's supply (see Am Tab). No evidences of copper ore in any quantity are found in Pal proper. See Metal; Mine. James A. Patch

COPPERSMITH, kop′ẽr-smith (χαλκεύς, *chalkeús*): The word is found in NT once only, in 2 Tim **4** 14: "Alexander the coppersmith did [m "showed"] me much evil." As the Bible word rendered "copper" (see Ezr **8** 27 AV) is trd "brass" by RV, so the word here rendered "c." should be rendered "brazier," or "worker in brass." See Copper.

COPTIC VERSIONS, kop′tik vûr′shunz:

I. Language and Alphabet.—The Coptic alphabet consists of the Gr uncial letters, plus seven characters taken from the Egyp demotic to express sounds not represented in the Gr. It can be traced back to the 4th cent., as the oldest Coptic MSS belong to the end of the 4th or beginning of the 5th cent. The language still prevailed in Egypt in the 9th cent., but was no longer understood in Middle Egypt in the 12th. Its last speaker died in 1633.

1. Alphabet

There were at least five written dialects and subdialects of Coptic. Of these the most important from a literary point of view was the (1) *Buḥairic*, the dialect of Lower Egypt, often called Coptic *par excellence*, and also (wrongly) Memphitic. It is used as the ecclesiastical language in the services of the Coptic church. The other four dialects are somewhat more closely allied to one another than to Buḥairic, which shows greater traces of Gr influence. These dialects are, (2) the Sahidic (*Ṣa'īdī*, or dialect of upper Egypt), also called Thebaic; (3) the Bashmūric—or rather *Bushmūric*—(for which *Fayyūmic* has been suggested); (4) the Middle Egyp proper (known from MSS found in the monastery of Jeremias near the Theban *Serapeum*), differing but little from (3); and (5) the *Akhmīmic* (*Akhmīm*=the ancient Chemmis). *Akhmīmic* is more primitive and more closely related to ancient Egyp than any other. Only a few fragments in it (of Ex, Ecclus, 2 Macc, the Minor Prophets, and Catholic epp.) have yet been found. The last three dialects are often classed together as "Middle Egyp" and (4) is then called "Lower Sahidic."

2. Dialects

II. Versions.—In all 5 dialects more or less complete versions of the Bible once existed. They were the earliest made after the early Syr. At latest they began in the 3d cent., though some (e.g. Hyvernat) say as early as the 2d. It is thought that the Sahidic version was the earliest, then the Middle Egyp, and finally the Buḥairic. The latter represents an early and comparatively pure Gr text, free from what are generally termed western additions, while the Sahidic, on the other hand, contains most of the peculiar western readings. It sometimes supports codex א, sometimes codex B, sometimes both, but generally it closely agrees with codex D (Bezae), esp. in the Acts. A Coptic (Sahidic) MS, written considerably before 350 AD, and published by the British Museum in April, 1912, contains Dt, Jon, and Acts, and is older than any other Bib. MS (except a few fragments) yet known to exist. It proves that this Sahidic version was made about 200 AD. It in general supports the "Western" text of cod Bezae (D).

Much of the NT esp. still exists in Sahidic, though not Rev. In Buḥairic we have the Pent, Job, Pss, Prov, Isa, Jer, Ezk, Dnl, the 12 Minor Prophets, and fragments of the historical books of the OT, besides the whole NT, though the Book of Rev is later than the rest. In the other dialects much less had been preserved, as far as is known. In Bushmūric we have fragments of Isa, Lam, Ep. Jer, and a good many fragments of the NT. In more than one dialect we have apoc gospels (see *Texts and Studies*, IV, no. 2, 1896) and Gnostic papyri, etc. The OT was tr[d] from the LXX. The Pss seem to have been tr[d] about 303 AD.

III. Chief Editions.—The Buḥairic Pss were first published in 1659. Wilkins published the Buḥairic NT at London in 1716, and the Pent in 1731; Schwartze the Gospels in 1846–47; de Lagarde the Acts and Epp. in 1852. He also edited the Pss (transliterated) in 1875, 151 in number, of which the last celebrates David's victory over Goliath. He added fragments of the Sahidic Psalter and of the Buḥairic Prov. Tattam published the Minor Prophets in 1836 and the Major in 1852, an ed of the Gospels in London in 1847, and of the rest of the NT in 1852 (*SPCK*), with a literal Arab. version. Horner's ed of the Buḥairic NT (4 vols, 1898, etc, Clarendon Press) and of Sahidic Gospels (1910, 3 vols) is the standard ed. Ford published part of the Sahidic NT in 1799. Various edd of parts of OT and NT have since appeared: e.g. Ciasca published fragments of the Sahidic OT (*Sacrorum Bibliorum Fragmenta Copto-Sahidica Musei Borgiani*) at Rome, 1885–89.

LITERATURE.—*Realencyclopädie für prot. Theol. und Kirche*, III; Hyvernat, *Étude sur les versions coptes; Revue biblique*, 1896, 1897; *Zeitschrift für ägypt. Sprache; Journal of Theol. Studies*, I, 3; Nestle, *Text. Crit of Gr NT;* Forbes Robinson, *Texts and Studies*, IV; Oesterley in Murray's *New Bible Dict.*

W. ST. CLAIR TISDALL

COR, kōr (כֹּר, *kōr*): A liquid and dry measure, same as the homer, of about 90 gals. capacity (Ezk **45** 14). See HOMER; WEIGHTS AND MEASURES.

CORAL, kor'ai (רָאמוֹת, *rā'mōth*, פְּנִינִים, *p^enīnīm*): The red coral or precious coral, *Corallium rubrum*, is confined to the Mediterranean and Adriatic seas. It is the calcareous axis of a branching colony of polyps. It does not form reefs, but occurs in small masses from 40 to 100 fathoms below the surface. It differs totally in structure from the white corals which form coral reefs, belonging to the order of Octactinia or Eight-rayed Polyps, while the reef-building corals belong to the Hexactinia or Six-rayed Polyps.

Rā'mōth, apparently from r. *rā'am*, "to be high" (cf *rūm*, "to be high"), occurs in three passages. In Prov **24** 7, EVV have "too high": "Wisdom is too high for a fool." In Job **28** 12–19, where various precious things are compared with wisdom, EV has "coral" (AVm "Ramoth"). It is mentioned here along with *ṣ^eghōr*, "gold" (RVm "treasure"); *kethem*, "gold of Ophir"; *shōham*, "onyx" (RVm "beryl"); *ṣappīr*, "sapphire"; *zāhābh*, "gold"; *z^ekhūkhīth*, "crystal" (RV "glass"); *pāz*, "gold"; *gābhīsh*, "pearls" (RV "crystal"); *p^enīnīm*, "rubies" (RVm "red coral" or "pearls"); *piṭ^edhāh*, "topaz." While the real meaning of some of these terms is doubtful (see STONES, PRECIOUS), they all, including *rā'mōth*, appear to be precious stones or metals. In Ezk **27** 16, *rā'mōth* occurs with *nōphekh*, "emeralds" (RVm "carbuncles"); *'argāmān*, "purple"; *riḳmāh*, "broidered work"; *būç*, "fine linen"; *kadhkōdh*, "agate" (AVm "chrysoprase," RV "rubies"). Here the context does not require a precious stone or metal, and Vulg has *sericum*, i.e. "Chinese material" or "silk." Notwithstanding, therefore, the traditional rendering, "coral," the real meaning of *rā'mōth* must be admitted to be doubtful.

P^enīnīm (from r. *pānan*, "to divide up," "to separate"; cf Arab. *fanan*, "a branch of a tree") occurs in Job **28** 18; Prov **3** 15; **8** 11; **20** 15; **31** 10; Lam **4** 7. In all these passages EV has "rubies" (Job **28** 18, RVm "red coral" or "pearls"; Lam **4** 7, RVm "corals"). Everywhere a precious substance is indicated, but nowhere does the context give any light as to the nature of the substance, except in Lam **4** 7, where we have the statement that the nobles of Jerus "were more ruddy in body" than *p^enīnīm*. This and the etymology favor a branching red substance such as precious coral. The occurrence of *p^enīnīm* and *rā'mōth* together in Job **28** 18 is, if we give the precedence to *p^enīnīm*, a further argument against *rā'mōth* meaning "coral."

ALFRED ELY DAY

COR-ASHAN, kôr-ash'an, kō-rā'shan (ERV, AV **Chor-ashan;** כּוֹר עָשָׁן, *kōr 'āshān*, 1 S **30** 30): The original reading was probably Bor-ashan, "well of Ashan." See ASHAN.

CORBAN, kôr'ban (קָרְבָּן, *ḳorbān;* **δῶρον,** *dōron;* tr[d] "a gift," "a sacrificial offering," lit. "that which is brought near," viz. to the altar): An expression frequently used in the original text of the OT; in the Eng. Bible it occurs in Mk **7** 11; cf also Mt **15** 5. It is the most general term for a sacrifice of any kind. In the course of time it became associated with an objectionable practice. Anything dedicated to the temple by pronouncing the votive word "C." forthwith belonged to the temple, but only ideally; actually it might remain in the possession of him who made the vow. So a son might be justified in not supporting his old parents simply because he designated his property or a part of it as a gift to the temple, that is, as "C." There was no necessity of fulfilling his vow, yet he was actually prohibited from ever using his property for the support of his parents. This shows clearly why Christ singled out this queer regulation in order to demonstrate the sophistry of tradition and to bring out the fact of its possible and actual hostility to the Scripture and its spirit.

WILLIAM BAUR

CORBE, kôr'bē. See CHORBE.

CORD, kôrd (חֶבֶל, *ḥebhel*, יֶתֶר, *yether*, מֵיתָר, *mēthār*, עֲבֹת, *'ăbhōth;* **σχοινίον,** *schoinion*):

(1) The Arab. *ḥab'l* corresponds to the Heb *ḥebhel* and is still the common name for cord or rope throughout the East. Such ropes or cords are made of goat's or camel's hair, first spun into threads and then twisted or plaited into the larger and stronger form. *Hebhel* is tr[d] rather inconsistently in RV by "cord" (Josh **2** 15; Job **36** 8, etc); by "line" (2 S **8** 2; Mic **2** 5; Ps **16** 6; **78** 55; Am **7** 17; Zec **2** 1); by "ropes" (1 K **20** 31), and by "tacklings" (Isa **33** 23).

(2) *Yether* corresponds to the Arab. *wittar*, which means catgut. With a kindred inconsistency it is tr[d] RV by "withes" (Jgs **16** 7 RVm "bowstring"); by "cord" (Job **30** 11), where some think it may mean "bowstring," or possibly "rein" of a bridle, and by "bowstring" (Ps **11** 2), doubtless the true meaning.

(3) *Mēthār* is considered the equivalent of Arab. *aṭnâb*, which means tent ropes, being constantly so used by the Bedouin. They make the thing so called of goat's or camel's hair. It is used of the "cords" of the tabernacle (Jer **10** 20), of the "cords" of the "hangings" and "pillars" of the courts of the tabernacle in Ex and Nu, and **fig.** by Isa (**54** 2), "Lengthen thy cords," etc.

(4) *'Ăbhōth* is thought to have its equivalent in the Arab. *rŭbŭts*, which means a band, or fastening.

See BAND. It is tr[d] by "cords" in Ps **118** 27; **129** 4; by "bands" in Ezk **3** 25; Job **39** 10; Hos **11** 4; by "ropes" in Jgs **15** 13.14, and by "cart rope" in Isa **5** 18. See CART. See also Nu **15** 38 and AMULET. It seems to have the meaning of something twisted or interlaced.

(5) In the NT "cord" is found in Jn **2** 15, translating *schoinion*, but in Acts **27** 32 the same Gr word is rendered "ropes."

Figurative: (1) of affliction (Job **36** 8); (2) of God's laws (Ps **2** 3); (3) of the artifices of the wicked (Ps **129** 4; **140** 5); (4) of sinful habits (Prov **5** 22); (5) of true friendship or companionship (Eccl **4** 12); (6) possibly of the spinal cord (Eccl **12** 6); (7) of falsehood (Isa **5** 18); (8) of the spirit of enterprise and devotion (Isa **54** 2); (9) of God's gentleness. GEO. B. EAGER

CORDS, kôrdz, **SMALL** (**σχοινίον**, *schoiníon*, the diminutive of *schoínos*, "a rush," hence "a rope of rushes"): Tr[d] "small cords" (Jn **2** 15 AV; RV "cords"). The same word is tr[d] "ropes" in Acts **27** 32. See also Job **41** 2 m.

CORE, kō'rē (**Κορέ**, *Koré*): In AV, Jude ver 11, used as a variant for Korah. See KORAH, 3.

CORIANDER, kor-i-an'dẽr (גַּד, *gadh;* **κόριον**, *kórion*): The fruit of the *Coriandrum Sativum* (N.O. *Umbelliferae*), a plant indigenous around the Mediterranean and extensively cultivated. The fruits are aromatic and stomatic-carminative. They are of a grayish-yellow color, ribbed, ovate-globular and in size about twice that of a hemp-seed. "The manna was like coriander seed" (Nu **11** 7; see also Ex **16** 31).

CORINTH, kor'inth (**Κόρινθος**, *Kórinthos*, "ornament"): A celebrated city of the Peloponnesus, capital of Corinthia, which lay N. of Argolis, and with the isthmus joined the peninsula to the mainland. Corinth had three good harbors (Lechaeum, on the Corinthian, and Cenchreae and Schoenus on the Saronic Gulf), and thus commanded the traffic of both the eastern and the western seas. The larger ships could not be hauled across the isthmus (Acts **27** 6.37); smaller vessels were taken over by means of a ship tramway with wooden rails. The Phoenicians, who settled here very early, left many traces of their civilization in the industrial arts, such as dyeing and weaving, as well as in their religion and mythology. The Corinthian cult of Aphrodite, of Melikertes (Melkart) and of Athene Phoenike are of Phoen origin. Poseidon, too, and other sea deities were held in high esteem in the commercial city. Various arts were cultivated and the Corinthians, even in the earliest times, were famous for their cleverness, inventiveness and artistic sense, and they prided themselves on surpassing the other Greeks in the embellishment of their city and in the adornment of their temples. There were many celebrated painters in Corinth, and the city became famous for the Corinthian order of architecture: an order, which, by the way, though held in high esteem by the Romans, was very little used by the Greeks themselves. It was here, too, that the dithyramb (hymn to Dionysus) was first arranged artistically to be sung by a chorus; and the Isthmian games, held every two years, were celebrated just outside the city on the isthmus near the Saronic Gulf. But the commercial and materialistic spirit prevailed later. Not a single Corinthian distinguished himself in lit. Statesmen, however, there were in abundance: Periander, Phidon, Timoleon.

Harbors are few on the Corinthian Gulf. Hence no other city could wrest the commerce of these waters from Corinth. According to Thucydides, the first ships of war were built here in 664 BC. In those early days Corinth held a leading position among the Gr cities; but in consequence of her great material prosperity she would not risk all as Athens did, and win eternal supremacy over men: she had too much to lose to jeopardize her material interests for principle, and she soon sank into the second class. But when Athens, Thebes, Sparta and Argos fell away, Corinth came to the front again as the wealthiest and most important city in Greece; and when it was destroyed by Mummius in 146 BC, the treasures of art carried to Rome were as great as those of Athens. Delos became the commercial center for a time; but when Julius

Ship-Canal at Corinth.

Caesar restored Corinth a cent. later (46 BC), it grew so rapidly that the Rom colony soon became again one of the most prominent centers in Greece. When Paul visited Corinth, he found it the metropolis of the Peloponnesus. Jews flocked to this center of trade (Acts **18** 1–18; Rom **16** 21 ff; 1 Cor **9** 20), the natural site for a great mart, and flourishing under the lavish hand of the Caesars; and this is one reason why Paul remained there so long (Acts **18** 11) instead of sojourning in the old seats of aristocracy, such as Argos, Sparta and Athens. He found a strong Jewish nucleus to begin with; and it was in direct communication with Ephesus. But earthquake, malaria, and the harsh Turkish rule finally swept everything away except seven columns of one old Doric temple, the only object above ground left today to mark the site of the ancient city of wealth and luxury and immorality —the city of vice *par excellence* in the Rom world. Near the temple have been excavated the ruins of the famous fount of Peirene, so celebrated in Gr literature. Directly S. of the city is the high rock (over 1,800 ft.) Acrocorinthus, which formed an impregnable fortress. Traces of the old ship-canal across the isthmus (attempted by Nero in 66–67 AD) were to be seen before excavations were begun for the present canal. At this time the city was thoroughly

Rom. Hence the many Lat names in the NT: Lucius, Tertius, Gaius, Erastus, Quartus (Rom **16** 21–23), Crispus, Titus Justus (Acts **18** 7.8), Fortunatus, Achaicus (1 Cor **16** 17). According to the testimony of Dio Chrysostomus, Corinth had become in the 2d cent. of our era the richest city in Greece. Its monuments and public buildings and art treasures are described in detail by Pausanias.

The church in Corinth consisted principally of non-Jews (1 Cor **12** 2). Paul had no intention at first of making the city a base of operations (Acts **18** 1; **16** 9.10); for he wished to return to Thessalonica (1 Thess **2** 17.18). His plans were changed by a revelation (Acts **18** 9.10). The Lord commanded him to speak boldly, and he did so, remaining in the city eighteen months. Finding strong opposition in the synagogue he left the Jews and went to the Gentiles (Acts **18** 6). Nevertheless, Crispus, the ruler of the synagogue and his household were believers and baptisms were numerous (Acts **18** 8); but no Corinthians were baptized by Paul himself except Crispus, Gaius and some of the household of Stephanas (1 Cor **1** 14.16) "the firstfruits of Achaia" (1 Cor **16** 15). One of these, Gaius, was Paul's host the next time he visited the city (Rom **16** 23). Silas and Timothy, who had been left at Beroea, came on to Corinth about 45 days after Paul's arrival. It was at this time that Paul wrote his first Epistle to the Thessalonians (**3** 6). During Gallio's administration the Jews accused Paul, but the proconsul refused to allow the case to be brought to trial. This decision must have been looked upon with favor by a large majority of the Corinthians, who had a great dislike for the Jews (Acts **18** 17). Paul became acquainted also with Priscilla and Aquila (**18** 18.26; Rom **16** 3; 2 Tim **4** 19), and later they accompanied him to Ephesus. Within a few years after Paul's first visit to Corinth the Christians had increased so rapidly that they made quite a large congregation, but it was composed mainly of the lower classes: they were neither 'learned, influential, nor of noble birth' (1 Cor **1** 26).

Ruins of Ancient Corinth with Acro-Corinthus in Background.

Paul probably left Corinth to attend the celebration of the feast at Jerus (Acts **18** 21). Little is known of the history of the church in Corinth after his departure. Apollos came from Ephesus with a letter of recommendation to the brethren in Achaia (Acts **18** 27; 2 Cor **3** 1); and he exercised a powerful influence (Acts **18** 27.28; 1 Cor **1** 12); and Paul came down later from Macedonia. His first letter to the Corinthians was written from Ephesus. Both Titus and Timothy were sent to Corinth from Ephesus (2 Cor **7** 13.15; 1 Cor **4** 17), and Timothy returned by land, meeting Paul in Macedonia (2 Cor **1** 1), who visited Greece again in 56–57 or 57–58.

LITERATURE.—Leake, *Travels in the Morea*, III, 229–304; *Peloponnesiaca*, 392 ff; Curtius, *Peloponnesos*, II, 514 ff; Clark, *Peloponnesus*, 42–61; Conybeare and Howson, *The Life and Epistles of St. Paul*, ch xii; Ramsay, "Corinth" (in *HDB*); Holm, *History of Greece*, I, 286 ff; II, 142, and 306–16; III, 31–44, and 283; IV, 221, 251, 347 and 410–12.

J. E. HARRY

CORINTHIANS, kō-rin′thi-anz, FIRST EPISTLE TO THE:

I. AUTHENTICITY OF THE TWO EPISTLES
  1. External Evidence
  2. Internal Evidence
  3. Consent of Criticism
  4. Ultra-Radical Attack (Dutch School)
II. TEXT OF 1 AND 2 COR
  Integrity of 1 Cor
III. PAUL'S PREVIOUS RELATIONS WITH CORINTH
  1. Corinth in 55 AD
  2. Founding of the Church
IV. DATE OF THE EPISTLE
V. OCCASION OF THE EPISTLE
  1. A Previous Letter
  2. Letter from Corinth
VI. CONTENTS
  1. General Character
  2. Order and Division
  3. Outline
    (1) Chs **1-6**
    (2) Chs **7-10**
    (3) Chs **11-16**
VII. DISTINGUISHING FEATURES
  1. Party Spirit
  2. Christian Conscience
  3. Power of the Cross
LITERATURE

I. The Authenticity of the Two Epistles.—1 and 2 Cor, Gal and Rom, all belong to the period of Paul's third missionary journey. They are the most remarkable of his writings, and are usually distinguished as the four great or principal epp.; a distinction which not only is a tribute to their high originality and intrinsic worth, but also indicates the extremely favorable opinion which critics of almost all schools have held regarding their authenticity. Throughout the cents. the tradition has remained practically unbroken, that they contain the very *pectus Paulinum*, the mind and heart of the great apostle of the Gentiles, and preserve to the church an impregnable defence of historical Christianity. What has to be said of their genuineness applies almost equally to both.

The two epp. have a conspicuous place in the most ancient lists of Pauline writings. In the Muratorian Fragment (cir 170) they stand at the head of the nine epp. addressed to churches, and are declared to have been written to forbid heretical schism (*primum omnium Corinthiis schisma haeresis interdicens*); and in Marcion's *Apostolicon* (cir 140) they stand second to Gal. They are also clearly attested in the most important writings of the subapostolic age, e.g. by Clement of Rome (cir 95), generally regarded as the friend of the apostle mentioned in Phil **4** 3; Ignatius (*Ad Ephes.*, ch xviii, second decade of 2d cent.); Polycarp (chs ii, vi, xi, first half of 2d cent.), a disciple of John; and Justin Martyr (b. at close of 1st cent.); while the gnostic Ophites (2d cent.) were clearly familiar with both epp. (cf Westcott, *Canon*, *passim*, and Index II; also Charteris, *Canonicity*, 222–24, where most of the original passages are brought together). The witness of Clement is of the highest importance. Ere the close of the 1st cent. he himself wrote a letter to the Corinthians, in which (ch xlvii, Lightfoot's ed, 144) he made a direct appeal to the authority of 1 Cor: "Take up the letter of Paul the blessed apostle; what did he write to you first in the beginning of the gospel?

1. External Evidence

Verily he gave you spiritual direction regarding himself, Cephas, and Apollos, for even then you were dividing yourselves into parties." It would be impossible to desire more explicit external testimony.

2. Internal Evidence

Within themselves both epp. are replete with marks of genuineness. They are palpitating human documents, with the ring of reality from first to last. They admirably harmonize with the independent narrative of Acts; in the words of Schleiermacher (*Einltg.*, 148), "The whole fits together and completes itself perfectly, and yet each of the documents follows its own course, and the data contained in the one cannot be borrowed from those of the other." Complex and difficult as the subjects and circumstances sometimes are, and varying as the moods of the writer are in dealing with them, there is a naturalness that compels assent to his good faith. The very difficulty created for a modern reader by the incomplete and allusive character of some of the references is itself a mark of genuineness rather than the opposite; just what would most likely be the case in a free and intimate correspondence between those who understood one another in the presence of immediate facts which needed no careful particularization; but what would almost as certainly have been avoided in a fictitious composition. Indeed a modicum of literary sense suffices to forbid classification among the pseudepigrapha. To take but a few instances from many, it is impossible to read such passages as those conveying the remonstrance in 1 Cor **9**, the alternations of anxiety and relief in connection with the meeting of Titus in 2 Cor **2** and **7**, or the ever-memorable passage which begins at **11** 24 of the same ep.: "Of the Jews five times received I," etc, without feeling that the hypothesis of fiction becomes an absurdity. No man ever wrote out of the heart if this writer did not. The truth is that the theory of pseudonymity leaves far more difficulties behind it than any it is supposed to solve. The unknown and unnamable literary prodigy of the 2d cent., who in the most daring and artistic manner gloried in the fanciful creation of those minute and life-like details which have imprinted themselves indelibly on the memory and imagination of mankind, cannot be regarded as other than a chimera. No one knows where or when he lived, or in what shape or form. But if the writings are the undoubted rescripts of fact, to whose life and personality do they fit themselves more exquisitely than to those of the man whose name stands at their head, and whose compositions they claim to be? They suit beyond compare the apostle of the missionary journeys, the tender, eager, indomitable "prisoner of the Lord," and no other. No other that has even been suggested is more than the mere shadow of a name, and no two writers have as yet seriously agreed even as to the shadow. The pertinent series of questions with which Godet (*Intro to NT; Studies on the Epp.*, 305) concludes his remarks on the genuineness may well be repeated: "What use was it to explain at length in the 2d cent. a change in a plan of the journey, which, supposing it was real, had interest only for those whom the promised visit of the apostle personally concerned? When the author speaks of five hundred persons who had seen the risen Christ, of whom the most part were still alive at the time when he was writing, is he telling his readers a mere story that would resemble a bad joke? What was the use of discussing at length and giving detailed rules on the exercise of the glossolalia at a time when that gift no longer existed, so to say, in the church? Why make the apostle say: 'We who shall be alive [at the moment of the Parousia]' at a time when everyone knew that he was long dead? In fine, what church would have received without opposition into its archives, as an ep. of the apostle, half a cent. after his death, a letter unknown till then, and filled with reproaches most severe and humiliating to it?"

3. Consent of Criticism

One is not surprised, therefore, that even the radical criticism of the 19th cent. cordially accepted the Corinthian epp. and their companions in the great group. The men who founded that criticism were under no conceivable constraint in such a conclusion, save the constraint of obvious and incontrovertible fact. The Tübingen school, which doubted or denied the authenticity of all the rest of the epp., frankly acknowledged the genuineness of these. This also became the general verdict of the "critical" school which followed that of Tübingen, and which, in many branches, has included the names of the leading German scholars to this day. F. C. Baur's language (*Paul*, I, 246) was: "There has never been the slightest suspicion of unauthenticity cast on these four epp., and they bear so incontestably the character of Pauline originality, that there is no conceivable ground for the assertion of critical doubts in their case." Renan (*St. Paul*, Intro, V) was equally emphatic: "They are incontestable, and uncontested."

4. Ultra-Radical Attack

Reference, however, must be made to the ultra-radical attack which has gathered some adherents, especially among Dutch scholars, during the last 25 years. As early as 1792 Evanson, a retired Eng. clergyman, rejected Rom on the ground that, according to Acts, no church existed in Rome in Paul's day. Bruno Bauer (1850–51–52) made a more sweeping attack, relegating the whole of the four principal epp. to the close of the 2d cent. His views received little attention, until, in 1886 onward, they were taken up and extended by a series of writers in Holland, Pierson and Naber, and Loman, followed rapidly by Steck of Bern, Völter of Amsterdam, and above all by Van Manen of Leyden. According to these writers, with slight modifications of view among themselves, it is very doubtful if Paul or Christ ever really existed; if they did, legend has long since made itself master of their personalities, and in every case what borders on the supernatural is to be taken as the criterion of the legendary. The epp. were written in the 1st quarter of the 2d cent., and as Paul, so far as he was known, was believed to be a reformer of anti-Judaic sympathies, he was chosen as the patron of the movement, and the writings were published in his name. The aim of the whole series was to further the interests of a supposed circle of clever and elevated men, who, partly imbued with Heb ideals, and partly with the speculations of Gr and Alexandrian philosophy, desired the spread of a universalistic Christianity and true Gnosis. For this end they perceived it necessary that Jewish legalism should be neutralized, and that the narrow national element should be expelled from the Messianic idea. Hence the epp. The principles on which the main contentions of the critics are based may be reduced to two: (1) that there are relations in the epp. so difficult to understand that, since we cannot properly understand them, the epp. are not trustworthy; and (2) that the religious and ecclesiastical development is so great that not merely 20 or 30 years, but 70 or 80 more, are required, if we are to be able rationally to conceive it: to accept the situation at an earlier date is simply to accept what cannot possibly have been. It is manifest that on such principles it is possible to establish what one will, and that any historical lit. might be proved untrustworthy, and reshaped according to the subjective idiosyncrasies of the critic. The underlying theory of intellectual development is too rigid, and is quite oblivious of the shocks it receives from actual facts, by the advent in history from time to time of powerful, compelling, and creative personalities, who rather mould their age than are moulded by it. None have poured greater ridicule on this "*pseudo-Kritik*" than the representatives of the advanced school in Germany whom it rather expected to carry with it, and against whom it complains bitterly that they do not take it seriously. On the whole the vagaries of the Dutch school have rather confirmed than shaken belief in these epp.; and one may freely accept Ramsay's view (*HDB*, I, 484) as expressing the modern mind regarding them, namely, that they are "the unimpeached and unassailable nucleus of admitted Pauline writings." (Reference to the following will give a sufficiently adequate idea of the Dutch criticism and the replies that have been made to it: Van Manen, *EB*, art. "Paul," and *Expos T*, IX, 205, 257, 314; Knowling, *Witness of the Epp.;* Clemen, *Einheitlichkeit der p. B.;* Sanday and Headlam, *Romans, ICC;* Godet, Jülicher and Zahn, in their *Introductions;* Schmiedel and Lipsius in the *Hand-Commentar.*)

II. Text of 1 and 2 Cor.—The text of both epp. comes to us in the most ancient VSS, the Syr (Peshito), the Old Lat, and the Egyp, all of which were in very early use, undoubtedly by the 3d cent. It is complete in the great Gr uncials: Sin. (ℵ* and ℵ^a, 4th cent.), Vat. (B, 4th cent.), Alex. (A, 5th cent., minus two vs, 2 Cor **4** 13; **12** 7), and very nearly complete in Ephraemi (C, 5th cent.), and in the Gr-Lat Claromontanus (D, 6th cent.); as well as in numerous cursives. In both cases the original has been well preserved, and no exegetical difficulties of high importance are presented. (Reference should be made to the Intro in Sanday and Headlam's *Romans, ICC* [1896], where §7 gives valuable information concerning the text, not only of Rom, but of the Pauline epp. generally; also to the recent ed [Oxford, 1910], *NT Graecae*, by Souter, where the various readings of the text used in RV [1881] are conveniently exhibited.)

Integrity of 1 Cor

On the whole the text of 1 Cor flows on consistently, only at times, in a characteristic fashion, winding back upon itself, and few serious criticisms are made on its unity, although the case is different in this respect with its companion ep. Some writers, on insufficient grounds, believe that 1 Cor contains relics of a previous ep. (cf **5** 9), e.g. in **7** 17–24; **9** 1—**10** 22; **15** 1–55.

III. Paul's Previous Relations with Corinth.—When, in the course of his 2d missionary journey, Paul left Athens (Acts **18** 1), he sailed westward to Cenchreae, and entered Corinth "in weakness, and in fear, and in much trembling" (1 Cor **2** 3).

1. Corinth in 55 AD

He was doubtless alone, although Silas and Timothy afterward joined him (Acts **18** 5; 2 Cor **1** 19). The ancient city of Corinth had been utterly laid in ruins when Rome subjugated Greece in the middle of the 2d cent. BC. But in the year 46 BC Caesar had caused it to be rebuilt and colonized in the Rom manner, and during the cent. that had elapsed it had prospered and grown enormously. Its population at this time has been estimated at between 600,000 and 700,000, by far the larger portion of whom were slaves. Its magnificent harbors, Cenchreae and Lechaeum, opening to the commerce of East and West, were crowded with ships, and its streets with travelers and merchants from almost every country under heaven. Even in that old pagan world the reputation of the city was bad; it has been compared (Baring-Gould, *Study of St. Paul*, 241) to an amalgam of Newmarket, Chicago and Paris, and probably it contained the worst features of each. At night it was made hideous by the brawls and lewd songs of drunken revelry. In the daytime its markets and squares swarmed with Jewish peddlers, foreign traders, sailors, soldiers, athletes in training, boxers, wrestlers, charioteers, racing-men, betting-men, courtesans, slaves, idlers and parasites of every description. The corrupting worship of Aphrodite, with its hordes of *hieródouloi*, was dominant, and all over the Gr-Rom world, "to behave as a Corinthian" was a proverbial synonym for leading a low, shameless and immoral life. Very naturally such a polluted and idolatrous environment accounts for much that has to be recorded of the semi-pagan and imperfect life of many of the early converts.

2. Founding of the Church

Paul was himself the founder of the church in Corinth (1 Cor **3** 6.10). Entering the city with anxiety, and yet with almost audacious hopefulness, he determined to know nothing among its people save Jesus Christ and Him crucified (**2** 2). Undoubtedly he was conscious that the mission of the Cross here approached its crisis. If it could abide here, it could abide anywhere. At first he confined himself to working quietly at his trade, and cultivating the friendship of Aquila and Priscilla (Acts **18** 2 f); then he opened his campaign in the synagogue where he persuaded both Jews and Greeks, and ultimately, when opposition became violent, carried it on in the house of Titus Justus, a proselyte. He made deep impressions, and gradually gathered round him a number who were received into the faith (Acts **18** 7.8; 1 Cor **1** 14–16). The converts were drawn largely but not entirely from the lower or servile classes (**1** 26; **7** 21); they included Crispus and Sosthenes, rulers of the synagogue, Gaius, and Stephanas with his household, "the firstfruits of Achaia" (**16** 15). He regarded himself joyfully as the father of this community (**4** 14.15), every member of which seemed to him like his own child.

IV. Date of the Epistle.—After a sojourn of eighteen months (Acts **18** 11) in this fruitful field, Paul departed, most probably in the year 52 (cf Turner, art. "Chron. NT," *HDB*, I, 422 ff), and, having visited Jerus and returned to Asia Minor (third journey), established himself for a period of between two and three years (*trietía*, Acts **20** 31) in Ephesus (Acts **18** 18 onward). It was during his stay there that his ep. was written, either in the spring (pre-Pentecost, 1 Cor **16** 8) of the year in which he left, 55; or, if that does not give sufficient interval for a visit and a letter to Corinth, which there is considerable ground for believing intervened between 1 Cor and the departure from Ephesus, then in the spring of the preceding year, 54. This would give ample time for the conjectured events, and there is no insuperable reason against it. Pauline chronology is a subject by itself, but the suggested dates for the departure from Ephesus, and for the writing of 1 Cor, really fluctuate between the years 53 and 57. Harnack (*Gesch. der altchrist. Litt.*, II; *Die Chron.*, I) and McGiffert (*Apos Age*) adopt the earlier date; Ramsay (*St. Paul the Traveller*), 56; Lightfoot (*Bib. Essays*) and Zahn (*Einl.*), 57; Turner (*ut supra*), 55. Many regard 57 as too late, but Robertson (*HDB*, I, 485–86) still adheres to it.

V. Occasion of the Epistle.—After Paul's departure from Corinth, events moved rapidly, and far from satisfactorily. He was quite cognizant of them. The distance from Ephesus was not great—about eight days' journey by sea—and in the constant coming and going between the cities news of what was transpiring must frequently have come to his ears. Members of the household of

1. A Previous Letter

Chloe are distinctly mentioned (**1** 11) as having brought tidings of the contentions that prevailed, and there were no doubt other informants. Paul was so concerned by what he heard that he sent Timothy on a conciliatory mission with many commendations (**4** 17; **16** 10 f), although the present ep. probably reached Corinth first. He had also felt impelled, in a letter (**5** 9) which is now lost, to send earnest warning against companying with the immoral. Moreover, Apollos, after excellent work in Corinth, had come to Ephesus, and was received as a brother by the apostle (**3** 5.6; **16** 12). Equally welcome was a deputation consisting of Stephanas, Fortunatus and Achaicus (**16** 17), from whom the fullest information could be gained, and who were the probable bearers of a letter from the church of Corinth itself (**7** 1), appealing for advice and direction on a number of points. This letter has not been preserved, but it was evidently the immediate occasion of our ep., and its tenor is clearly indicated by the nature of the apostle's reply. (The letter, professing to be this letter to Paul, and its companion, professing to be Paul's own lost letter just referred to, which deal with gnostic heresies, and were for long accepted by the Syrian and Armenian churches, are manifestly apocryphal. [Cf Stanley's *Corinthians*, Appendix; Harnack's *Gesch. der altchrist. Litt.*, I, 37–39, and II, 506–8; Zahn, *Einl.*, I, 183-249; Sanday, *EB*, I, 906–7.] If there be any relic in existence of Paul's previous letter, it is possibly to be found in the passage 2 Cor **6** 14—**7** 1; at all events that passage may be regarded as reminiscent of its style and message.) So that 1 Cor is no bow drawn at a venture. It treats of a fully understood, and, on the whole, of a most unhappy situation. The church had broken into factions, and was distracted by party cries. Some of its members were living openly immoral lives, and discipline was practically in abeyance. Others had quarrels over which they dragged one another into the heathen courts. Great differences of opinion had also arisen with regard to marriage and the social relations generally; with regard to banquets and the eating of food offered to idols; with regard to the behavior of women in the assemblies, to the Lord's Supper and the love-feasts, to the use and value of spiritual gifts, and with regard to the hope of the resurrection. The apostle was filled with grief and indignation, which the too complacent tone of the Corinthians only intensified. They discussed questions in a lofty, intellectual way, without seeming to perceive their real drift, or the life and spirit which lay imperiled at their heart. Resisting the impulse to visit them "with a rod" (**4** 21), the apostle wrote the present ep., and dispatched it, if not by the hands of Stephanas and his comrades, most probably by the hands of Titus.

2. Letter from Corinth

VI. Contents of the Epistle.—In its general character the ep. is a strenuous writing, masterly in its restraint in dealing with opposition, firm in its grasp of ethical and spiritual principles, and wise and faithful in their application. It is calm, full of reasoning, clear and balanced in judgment; very varied in its lights and shadows, in its kindness, its gravity, its irony. It moves with firm tread among the commonest themes, but also rises easily into the loftiest spheres of thought and vision, breaking again and again into passages of glowing and rhythmical eloquence. It rebukes error, exposes and condemns sin, solves doubts, upholds and encourages faith, and all in a spirit of the utmost tenderness and love, full of grace and truth. It is broad in its outlook, penetrating in its insight, unending in its interest and application.

1. General Character

It is also very orderly in its arrangement, so that it is not difficult to follow the writer as he advances from point to point. Weizsäcker (*Apos Age*, I, 324–25) suggestively distinguishes the matter into (1) subjects introduced by the letter from Corinth, and (2) those on which Paul had obtained information otherwise. He includes three main topics in the first class: marriage, meat offered to idols and spiritual gifts (there is a fourth —the *logia* or collection, **16** 1); six in the second class: the factions, the case of incest, the lawsuits, the free customs of the women, the abuse connected with the Supper and the denial of the resurrection. It is useful, however, to adhere to the sequence of the ep. In broadly outlining the subject-matter we may make a threefold division: (1) chs **1–6**; (2) chs **7–10**; and (3) chs **11**–end.

2. Order and Division

(1) Chs **1–6**: After salutation, in which he associates Sosthenes with himself, and thanksgiving for the grace given to the Corinthians (**1** 1–9), Paul immediately begins (**1** 10–13) to refer to the internal divisions among them, and to the unworthy and misguided party cries that had arisen. (Many theories have been formed as to the exact significance of the so-called "Christus-party," a party whose danger becomes more obvious in 2 Cor. Cf Meyer-Heinrici, *Comm.*, 8th ed; Godet, *Intro*, 250 ff; Stanley, *Cor*, 29–30; Farrar, *St. Paul*, ch xxxi; Pfleiderer, *Paulinism*, II, 28–31; Weiss, *Intro*, I, 259–65; Weizsäcker, *Apos Age*, I, 325–33, and 354 ff. Weizsäcker holds that the name indicates exclusive relation to an authority, while Baur and Pfleiderer argue that it was a party watchword [virtually Petrine] taken to bring out the apostolic inferiority of Paul. On the other hand a few scholars maintain that the name does not, strictly speaking, indicate a party at all but rather designates those who were disgusted at the display of all party spirit, and with whom Paul was in hearty sympathy. See McGiffert, *Apos Age*, 295–97.) After denouncing this petty partisanship, Paul offers an elaborate defence of his own ministry, declaring the power and wisdom of God in the gospel of the Cross (**1** 14—**2** 16), returning in ch **3** to the spirit of faction, showing its absurdity and narrowness in face of the fulness of the Christian heritage in "all things" that belong to them as belonging to Christ; and once more defending his ministry in ch **4**, making a touching appeal to his readers as his "beloved children," whom he had begotten through the gospel. In ch **5** he deals with the case of a notorious offender, guilty of incest, whom they unworthily harbor in their midst, and in the name of Christ demands that they should expel him from the church, pointing out at the same time that it is against the countenancing of immorality within the church membership that he specially warns, and had previously warned in his former ep. Ch **6** deals with the shamefulness of Christian brethren haling one another to the heathen courts, and not rather seeking the settlement of their differences within themselves; reverting once more in the closing vs to the subject of unchastity, which irrepressibly haunts him as he thinks of them.

3. Outline

(2) Chs **7–10**: In ch **7** he begins to reply to two of the matters on which the church had expressly consulted him in its ep., and which he usually induces by the phrase *peri de*, "now concerning." The first of these bears (ch **7**) upon celibacy and marriage, including the case of "mixed" marriage. These questions he treats quite frankly, yet with delicacy and circumspection, always careful to distinguish between what he has received as the direct word of the Lord, and what he only delivers as his

own opinion, the utterance of his own sanctified common-sense, yet to which the good spirit within him gives weight. The second matter on which advice was solicited, questions regarding *eidōlóthuta*, meats offered to idols, he discusses in ch **8**, recurring to it again in ch **10** to end. The scruples and casuistries involved he handles with excellent wisdom, and lays down a rule for the Christian conscience of a far-reaching kind, happily expressed: "All things are lawful; but not all things are expedient. All things are lawful; but not all things edify. Let no man seek his own, but each his neighbor's good" (**10** 23.24). By lifting their differences into the purer atmosphere of love and duty, he causes them to dissolve away. Ch **9** contains another notable defence of his apostleship, in which he asserts the principle that the Christian ministry has a claim for its support on those to whom it ministers, although in his own case he deliberately waived his right, that no challenge on such a matter should be possible among them. The earlier portion of ch **10** contains a reference to Jewish idolatry and sacramental abuse, in order that the evils that resulted might point a moral, and act as a solemn warning to Christians in relation to their own rites.

(3) Chs **11–16**: The third section deals with certain errors and defects that had crept into the inner life and observances of the church, also with further matters on which the Corinthians sought guidance, namely, spiritual gifts and the collection for the saints. Ch **11** 1–16 has regard to the deportment of women and their veiling in church, a matter which seems to have occasioned some difficulty, and which Paul deals with in a manner quite his own; passing thereafter to treat of graver and more disorderly affairs, gross abuses in the form of gluttony and drunkenness at the Lord's Supper, which leads him, after severe censure, to make his classic reference to that sacred ordinance (vs 20 to end). Ch **12** sets forth the diversity, yet true unity, of spiritual gifts, and the confusion and jealousy to which a false conception of them inevitably leads, obscuring that "most excellent way," the love which transcends them all, which never faileth, the greatest of the Christian graces, whose praise he chants in language of surpassing beauty (ch **13**). He strives also, in the following chapter, to correct the disorder arising from the abuse of the gift of tongues, many desiring to speak at once, and many speaking only a vain babble which no one could understand, thinking themselves thereby highly gifted. It is not edifying: "I had rather," he declares, "speak five words with my understanding, that I might instruct others also, than ten thousand words in a tongue" (**14** 19). Thereafter follows the immortal chapter on the resurrection, which he had learned that some denied (**15** 12). He anchors the faith to the resurrection of Christ as historic fact, abundantly attested (vs 3–8), shows how all-essential it is to the Christian hope (vs 13–19), and then proceeds by reasoning and analogy to brush aside certain naturalistic objections to the great doctrine, "then they that are Christ's, at his coming" (ver 23), when this mortal shall have put on immortality, and death be swallowed up in victory (ver 54). The closing chapter gives directions as to the collection for the saints in Jerus, on which his heart was deeply set, and in which he hoped the Corinthians would bear a worthy share. He promises to visit them, and even to tarry the winter with them. He then makes a series of tender personal references, and so brings the great ep. to a close.

VII. Distinguishing Features.—It will be seen that there are passages in the ep. of great doctrinal and historical importance, esp. with reference to the Person of Christ, the Holy Spirit, the Eucharist and the Resurrection; also many that illuminate the nature of the religious meetings and services of the early church (cf particularly on these, Weizsäcker, *Apos Age*, II, 246 ff). A lurid light is cast on many of the errors and evils that not unnaturally still clung to those who were just emerging from paganism, and much allowance has to be made for the Corinthian environment. The thoroughness with which the apostle pursues the difficulties raised into their relations and details, and the wide scope of matters which he subjects to Christian scrutiny and criterion, are also significant. Manifestly he regarded the gospel as come to fill, not a part, but the whole, of life; to supply principles that follow the believers to their homes, to the most secluded sanctum there, out again to the world, to the market-place, the place of amusement, of temptation, of service, of trial, of worship and prayer; and all in harmony with knowing nothing "save Jesus Christ, and him crucified." For Paul regards that not as a restriction, but as a large and expansive principle. He sets the cross on an eminence so high that its shadow covers the whole activities of human life.

Three broad outstanding features of a practical kind may be recognized. The first is the earnest warning it conveys against a factious spirit as inimical to the Christian life. The Corinthians were imbued with the party spirit of Gr democracy, and were infected also by the sporting spirit of the great games that entered so largely into their existence. They transferred these things to the church. They listened to their teachers with itching ears, not as men who wished to learn, but as partisans who sought occasion either to applaud or to condemn. Paul recognizes that, though they are not dividing on deep things of the faith, they are giving way to "schisms" of a pettier and perhaps even more perilous kind, that appeal to the lowest elements in human nature, that cause scandal in the eyes of men and inflict grievous wounds on the Body of Christ. In combating this spirit he takes occasion to go below the surface, and to reveal the foundations of true Christian unity. That must simply be "in Christ." And this is true even if the divergence should be on higher and graver things. Any unity in such a case, still possible to cherish, must be a unity in Christ. None can be unchurched who build on Him; none severed from the true and catholic faith, who confess with their lips and testify with their lives that He is Lord.

1. The Party Spirit

The ep. also renders a high ethical service in the rules it lays down for the guidance of the Christian conscience. In matters where the issue is clearly one of the great imperatives, the conflict need never be protracted. An earnest man will see his way. But beyond these, or not easily reducible to them, there are many matters that cause perplexity and doubt. Questions arise regarding things that do not seem to be wrong in themselves, yet whose abuse or the offence they give to others, may well cause debate. Meat offered to idols, and then brought to table, was a stumbling-block to many Corinthian Christians. They said: "If we eat, it is consenting to idolatry; we dare not partake." But there were some who rose to a higher level. They perceived that this was a groundless scruple, for an idol is nothing at all, and the meat is not affected by the superstition. Accordingly their higher and more rational view gave them liberty and left their conscience free. But was this really all that they had to consider? Some say: "Certainly"; and Paul ac-

2. The Christian Conscience

knowledges that this is undoubtedly the law of individual freedom. But it is not the final answer. There has not entered into it a consideration of the mind of Christ. Christian liberty must be willing to subject itself to the law of love. Granted that a neighbor is often short-sighted and over-scrupulous, and that it would be good neither for him nor for others to suffer him to become a moral dictator; yet we are not quite relieved. The brother may be weak, but the very claim of his weakness may be strong. We may not ride over his scruples rough-shod. To do so would be to put ourselves wrong even more seriously. And if the matter is one that is manifestly fraught with peril to him, conscience may be roused to say, as the apostle says: "Wherefore, if meat maketh my brother to stumble, I will eat no flesh for evermore."

3. The Power of the Cross

A third notable feature of the ep. is its exaltation of the cross of Christ as the power and wisdom of God unto salvation. It was the force that began to move and unsettle, to lift and change from its base, the life of that old heathen world. It was neither Paul, nor Apollos, nor Cephas who accomplished that colossal task, but the preaching of the crucified Christ. The Christianity of Corinth and of Europe began with the gospel of Calvary and the open tomb. It can never with impunity draw away from these central facts. The river broadens and deepens as it flows, but it is never possible for it to sever itself from the living fountain from which it springs.

LITERATURE.—The following writers will be found most important and helpful:
1. *On matters of introduction* (both epp.): Holtzmann, Weiss, Hausrath, Harnack, Pfleiderer, Godet, Weizsäcker, Jülicher, Zahn, Salmon, Knowling, McGiffert, J. H. Kennedy, Ramsay, Sabatier, Farrar, Dobschütz, Robertson (*HDB*), Sanday (*EB*), Plummer (*DB*), Ropes (*Enc Brit*, 11th ed).
2. *Commentaries and lectures* (on 1 Cor or both): Meyer-Heinrici, Godet, T. C. Edwards, Hodge, Beet, Ellicott, Schmiedel (*Hand-Comm.*), Evans (*Speakers' Comm.*), Farrar (*Pulpit Comm.*), Lightfoot (chs i–vii in *Bib. Ess.*), Lias (*Cambr. Gr Test.*), McFadyen, F. W. Robertson, Findlay (*Expos. Gr Test.*); and on 2 Cor alone: Klöpper, Waite (*Speakers' Comm.*), Denney (*Expos. Bible*), Bernard (*Expos. Gr Test.*).
3. *For ancient writers and special articles*, the list at close of Plummer's art. in *DB* should be consulted.

R. DYKES SHAW

CORINTHIANS, SECOND EPISTLE TO THE:

I. Text, Authenticity and Date.—Cf what has already been said in the preceding art. In the two important 5th-cent. uncials, A (Alex.) and C (Ephraemi), portions of the text are lacking.

1. Internal Evidence

As to the genuineness internal evidence very vividly attests it. The distinctive elements of Pauline theology and eschatology, expressed in familiar Pauline terms, are manifest throughout. Yet the ep. is not doctrinal or didactic, but an intensely personal document. Its absorbing interest is in events which were profoundly agitating Paul and the Corinthians at the time, straining their relations to the point of rupture, and demanding strong action on Paul's part. Our imperfect knowledge of the circumstances necessarily hinders a complete comprehension, but the references to these events and to others in the personal history of the apostle are so natural, and so manifestly made in good faith, that no doubt rises in the reader's mind but that he is in the sphere of reality, and that the voice he hears is the voice of the man whose heart and nerves were being torn by the experiences through which he was passing. However scholars may differ as to the continuity and integrity of the text, there is no serious divergence among them in the opinion that all parts of the ep. are genuine writings of the apostle.

2. External Evidence

Externally, the testimony of the sub-apostolic age, though not so frequent or precise as in the case of 1 Cor, is still sufficiently clear to establish the existence and use of the ep. in the 2d cent. Clement of Rome is silent when he might rather have been expected to use the ep. (cf Kennedy, *Second and Third Cor*, 142 ff); but it is quoted by Polycarp (*Ad Phil.*, ii.4 and vi.1), and in the Epistle to Diognetus **5** 12, while it is amply attested to by Irenaeus, Athenagoras, Theophilus, Tertullian and Clement of Alexandria.

3. Date

It was written from Macedonia (probably from Philippi) either in the autumn of the same year as that in which 1 Cor was written, 54 or 55 AD, or in the autumn of the succeeding year.

II. Résumé of Events.—Great difficulty exists as to the circumstances in which the ep. was written, and as to the whole situation between 1 and 2 Cor. In 1 Cor Paul had intimated his intention of visiting the Corinthians and wintering with them, coming to them through Macedonia (**16** 5–7; cf also Acts **19** 21). In 2 Cor **1** 15.16 he refers to a somewhat different plan, Corinth–Macedonia–Corinth–Judaea; and describes this return from Macedonia to Corinth as a second or double benefit. But if this plan, on which he and his friends had counted, had not been entirely carried out, it had been for good reason (**1** 17), and not due to mere fickleness or light-hearted change to suit his own convenience. It was because he would "spare" them (**1** 23), and not come to them "again with sorrow" (**2** 1). That is, he had been with them, but there had been such a profound disturbance in their relations that he dared not risk a return meantime; instead, he had written a letter to probe and test them, "out of much affliction and anguish of heart . . . . with many tears" (**2** 4). Thank God, this severe letter had accomplished its mission. It had produced sorrow among them (**2** 2; **7** 8.9), but it had brought their hearts back to him with the old allegiance, with great clearing of themselves, and fear and longing and zeal (**7** 11). There was a period, however, of waiting for knowledge of this issue, which was to him a period of intense anxiety; he had even nervously regretted that he had written as he did (**7** 5–8). Titus, who had gone as his representative to Corinth, was to return with a report of how this severe letter had been received, and when Titus failed to meet him at Troas (**2** 13), he had "no relief for his spirit," but pushed on eagerly to Macedonia to encounter him the sooner. Then came the answer, and the lifting of the intolerable burden from his mind. "He that comforteth the lowly, even God, comforted" him (**7** 6). The Corinthians had been swayed by a godly sorrow and repentance (**7** 8), and the sky had cleared again with almost unhoped-for brightness. One who had offended (**2** 5 and **7** 12)—but whose offence is not distinctly specified—had been disciplined by the church; indeed, in the revulsion of feeling against him, and in sympathy for the apostle, he had been punished so heavily that there was a danger of passing to an extreme, and plunging him into despair (**2** 7). Paul accordingly pleads for leniency and forgiveness, lest further resentment should lead only to a further and sadder wrong (**2** 6–11). But in addition to this offender there were others, probably following in his train, who had carried on a relentless attack against the apostle both in his person and in his doctrine. He earnestly defends himself against their contemptuous charges of fleshliness and cowardice (ch **10**), and crafty venality (**12** 16.17). Another Jesus is preached, a different spirit, a different gospel (**11** 4). They "commend themselves" (**10** 12), but are false apostles, deceitful workers, ministers of Satan, fashioning themselves into ministers of Christ (**11** 13.14). Their attacks are vehemently repelled in an eloquent apologia (chs **11** and **12**), and he declares that when he comes the third time they will not be spared (**13** 2). Titus, accompanied by other well-known brethren, is again to be the representative of the apostle (**8** 6.17 ff). At no great interval Paul himself followed, thus making his third visit (**12** 14; **13** 1), and so far fulfilled his original purpose that he spent the winter peacefully in Corinth (cf Acts **20** 2.3; Rom **15** 25–27 and **16** 23).

III. The New Situation.—It is manifest that we are in the presence of a new and unexpected situation, whose development is not clearly defined, and concerning which we have elsewhere no source of information. To elucidate it, the chief points requiring attention are: (1) The references to the offender in chs **2** and **7**, and to the false teachers, particularly in the later chapters of the ep.; (2) the painful visit implicitly referred to in **2** 1; and (3) the letter described as written in tears and for a time regretted (**2** 4; **7** 8).

1. The Offender

The offender in 1 Cor **5** 1–5 had been guilty of incest, and Paul was grieved that the church of Corinth did not regard with horror a crime which even the pagan world would not have tolerated. His judgment on the case was uncompromising and the severest possible—that, in solemn assembly, in the name and with the power of the Lord Jesus, the church should deliver such a one to Satan for the destruction of the flesh. On the other hand, the offender in 2 Cor **2** 5 ff is one who obviously has transgressed less heinously, and in a way more personal to the apostle. The church, roused by the apostle to show whether they indeed cared for him and stood by him (**2** 9; **13** 7), had, by a majority, brought censure to bear on this man, and Paul now urged that matters should go no farther, lest an excess of discipline should really end in a triumph of Satan. It is not possible to regard such references as applying to the crime dealt with in 1 Cor. Purposely veiled as the statements are, it would yet appear that a personal attack had been made on the apostle; and the "many" in Corinth (**2** 6), having at length espoused his cause, Paul then deals with the matter in the generous spirit he might have been expected to display. Even if the offender were the same person, which is most improbable, for he can scarcely have been retained in the membership, the language is not language that could have been applied to the earlier case. There has been a new offence in new circumstances. The apostle had been grievously wronged in the presence of the church, and the Corinthians had not spontaneously resented the wrong. That is what wounded the apostle most deeply, and it is to secure their change in this respect that is his gravest concern.

2. The False Teachers

Esp. in the later chs of 2 Cor there are, as we have seen, descriptions of an opposition by false teachers that is far beyond anything met with in 1 Cor. There indeed we have a spirit of faction, associated with unworthy partiality toward individual preachers, but nothing to lead us to suspect the presence of deep and radical differences undermining the gospel. The general consensus of opinion is that this opposition was of a Judaizing type, organized and fostered by implacable anti-Pauline emissaries from Pal, who now followed the track of the apostle in Achaia as they did in Galatia. As they arrogated to themselves a peculiar relation to Christ Himself ("Christ's men" and "ministers of Christ," **10** 7; **11** 13), it is possible that the Christus-party of 1 Cor (and possibly the Cephas-party) may have persisted and formed the nucleus round which these newcomers built up their formidable opposition. One man seems to have been conspicuous as their ringleader (**10** 7.11), and to have made himself specially obnoxious to the apostle. In all probability we may take it that he was the offender of chs **2** and **7**. Under his influence the opposition audaciously endeavored to destroy the gospel of grace by personal attacks upon its most distinguished exponent. Paul was denounced as an upstart and self-seeker, destitute of any apostolic authority, and derided for the contemptible appearance he made in person, in contrast with the swelling words and presumptuous claims of his epp. It is clear, therefore, that a profound religious crisis had arisen among the Corinthians, and that there was a danger of their attachment to Paul and his doctrine being destroyed.

3. The Painful Visit

2 Cor **12** 14 and **13** 1.2 speak of a third visit in immediate prospect, and the latter passage also refers to a second visit that had been already accomplished; while **2** 1 distinctly implies that a visit had taken place of a character so painful that the apostle would never venture to endure a similar one. As this cannot possibly refer to the first visit when the church was founded, and cannot easily be regarded as indicating anything previous to 1 Cor which never alludes to such an experience, we must conclude that the reference points to the interval between 1 and 2 Cor. It was then beyond doubt that the visit "with sorrow," which humbled him (**12** 21) and left such deep wounds, had actually taken place. "Any exegesis," says Weizsäcker justly, "that would avoid the conclusion that Paul had already been twice in Corinth is capricious and artificial" (*Apostolic Age*, I, 343). Sabatier (*Apostle Paul*, 172 n.) records his revised opinion: "The reference here (**2** 1) is to a second and quite recent visit, of which he retained a very sorrowful recollection, including it among the most bitter trials of his apostolical career."

4. The Severe Letter

Paul not only speaks of a visit which had ended grievously, but also of a letter which he had written to deal with the painful circumstances, and as a kind of ultimatum to bring the whole matter to an issue (**2** 4; **7** 8). This letter was written because he could not trust himself meantime to another visit. He was so distressed and agitated that he wrote it "with many tears"; after it was written he repented of it; and until he knew its effect he endured torture so keen that he hastened to Macedonia to meet his messenger, Titus, halfway. It is impossible by any stretch of interpretation to refer this language to 1 Cor, which on the whole is dominated by a spirit of didactic calm, and by a consciousness of friendly *rapport* with its recipients. Even though there be in it occasional indications of strong feeling, there is certainly nothing that we can conceive the apostle might have wished to recall. The alternative has generally been to regard this as another case of a lost ep. Just as the writer of Acts appears to have been willing that the deplorable visit itself should drop into oblivion, so doubtless neither Paul nor the Corinthians would be very anxious to preserve an ep. which echoed with the gusts and storms of such a visit. On the other hand a strong tendency has set in to regard this intermediate ep. as at least in part preserved in 2 Cor **10–13,** whose tone, it is universally admitted, differs from that of the preceding chapters in a remarkable way, not easily accounted for. The majority of recent writers seem inclined to favor this view, which will naturally fall to be considered under the head of "Integrity."

IV. Historical Reconstruction.—In view of such an interpretation, we may with considerable probability trace the course of events in the interval between 1 and 2 Cor as follows: After the dispatch of 1 Cor, news reached the apostle of a disquieting character; probably both Titus and Timothy, on returning from Corinth, reported the growing menace of the opposition fostered by the Judaizing party. Paul felt impelled to pay an immediate visit, and found only too sadly that matters had not been overstated. The opposition was strong and full of effrontery, and the whole trend of things was against him. In face of the congregation he was baffled and flouted. He returned to Ephesus, and poured out his indignation in a severe ep., which he sent on by the hands of Titus. Before Titus could return, events took a disastrous form in Ephesus, and Paul was forced to leave that city in peril of his life. He went to Troas, but, unable to wait patiently there for tidings of the issue in Corinth, he crossed to Macedonia, and met Titus, possibly in Philippi. The report was happily reassuring; the majority of the congregation returned to their old attachment, and the heavy cloud of doubt and anxiety was dispelled from the apostle's mind. He then wrote again—the present ep.—and forwarded it by Titus and other brethren, he himself following a little later, and finally wintering in Corinth as he had originally planned. If it be felt that the interval between spring and autumn of the same year is too brief for these events, the two epp. must be separated by a period of nearly 18 months, 1 Cor being referred to the spring of 54 or 55, and 2 Cor to the autumn of 55 or 56 AD. (Reference on the reconstruction should esp. be made to Weizsäcker's *Apostolic Age*, Eng. tr, I; to Sabatier's Note to the Eng. ed [1893] of his *Apostle Paul;* and to Robertson's art. in *HDB*.)

V. Integrity of the Epistle.—Although the genuineness of the various parts of the ep. is scarcely disputed, the homogeneity is much debated. Semler and some later writers, including Clemen (*Einheitlichkeit*), have thought that ch **9** should be eliminated as logically inconsistent with ch **8,** and as evidently forming part of a letter to the converts of Achaia. But the connection with ch **8** is too close to permit of severance, and the logical objection, founded on the phraseology of **9** 1, is generally regarded as hypercritical. There are two sections, however, whose right to remain integral parts of 2 Cor has been more forcibly challenged.

1. Ch 6:14—7:1

The passage **6** 14 to **7** 1 deals with the inconsistency and peril of intimate relations with the heathen, and is felt to be incongruous with the context. No doubt it comes strangely after an appeal to the Corinthians to show the apostle the same frankness and kindness that he is showing them; whereas **7** 2 follows naturally and links itself closely to such an appeal. When we remember that the particular theme of the lost letter referred to in 1 Cor **5** 9 was the relation of the converts to the immoral, it is by no means unlikely that we have here preserved a stray fragment of that ep.

2. Ch 10:1—13:10

It is universally acknowledged that there is a remarkable change in the tone of the section **10** 1—**13** 10, as compared with that of the previous chs. In the earlier chs there is relief at the change which Titus has reported as having taken place in Corinth, and the spirit is one of gladness and content; but from ch **10** onward the hostility to the apostle is unexpectedly represented as still raging, and as demanding the most strenuous treatment. The opening phrase, "Now I Paul" (**10** 1), is regarded as indicating a distinctive break from the previous section with which Timothy is associated (**1** 1), while the concluding vs, **13** 11 to end, seem fittingly to close that section, but to be abruptly out of harmony with the polemic that ends at **13** 10. Accordingly it is suggested that **13 11** should immediately follow **9** 15, and that **10** 1—**13** 10 be regarded as a lengthy insertion from some other ep. Those who, while acknowledging the change of tone, yet maintain the integrity of the ep., do so on the ground that the apostle was a man of many moods, and that it is characteristic of him to make unexpected and even violent transitions; that new reports of a merely scotched antagonism may come in to ruffle and disturb his comparative contentment; and that in any case he might well deem it advisable finally to deliver his whole soul on a matter over which he had brooded and suffered deeply, so that there might be no mistake about the ground being cleared when he arrived in person. The question is still a subject of keen discussion, and is not one on which it is easy to pronounce dogmatically. On the whole, however, it must be acknowledged that the preponderance of recent opinion is in favor of the theory of interpolation. Hausrath (*Der Vier-Capitel-Brief des Paulus an die Korinther*, 1870) gave an immense impetus to the view that this later section really represents the painful letter referred to in chs **2** and **7**. As that earlier letter, however, must have contained references to the personal offender, the present section, which omits all such references, can be regarded as at most only a part of it. This theory is ably and minutely expounded by Schmiedel (*Hand-Kommentar*); and Pfleiderer, Lipsius, Clemen, Krenkel, von Soden, McGiffert, Cone, Plummer, Rendall, Moffatt, Adeney, Peake, and Massie are prominent among its adherents. J. H. Kennedy (*Second and Third Cor*) presents perhaps the ablest and fullest argument for it that has yet appeared in English. On the other hand Sanday (*EB*) declares against it, and Robertson (*HDB*) regards it as decidedly not proven; while critics of such weight as Holtzmann, Beyschlag, Klöpper, Weizsäcker, Sabatier, Godet, Bernard, Denney, Weiss, and Zahn are all to be reckoned as advocates of the integrity of the ep.

VI. Contents of the Epistle.—The order of matter in the ep. is quite clearly defined. There are three main divisions: (1) chs **1–7**; (2) chs **8–9**; and (3) chs **10–13**.

1. Chs 1–7

The first seven chapters as a whole are taken up with a retrospect of the events that have recently transpired, joyful references to the fact that the clouds of grief in connection with them have been dispelled, and that the evangelical ministry as a Divine trust and power is clearly manifested. After a cordial salutation, in which Timothy is associated, Paul starts at once to express his profound gratitude to God for the great comfort that had come to him by the good news from Corinth, rejoicing in it as a spiritual enrichment that will make his ministry still more fruitful to the church (**1** 3–11). He professes his sincerity in all his relations with the Corinthians, and particularly vindicates it in connection with a change in the plan which had originally promised a return ("a second benefit") to Corinth; his sole reason for refraining, and for writing a painful letter instead, being his desire to spare them and to prove them (**1** 12; **2** 4.9). Far from harboring any resentment against the man who had caused so much trouble, he sincerely pleads that his punishment by the majority should go no farther, but that forgiveness should now reign, lest the Adversary should gain an advantage over them (**2** 5–11). It was indeed an agonizing experience until the moment he met Titus, but the relief was all the sweeter and more triumphant when God at length gave it, as he might have been sure He would give it to a faithful and soul-winning servant of Christ (**2** 12–17). He does not indeed wish to enter upon any further apologies or self-commendation. Some believe greatly in letters of commendation, but his living testimonial is in his converts. This he has, not of himself, but entirely through God, who alone has made him an efficient minister of the new and abiding covenant of the Spirit, whose glory naturally excels that of the old dispensation which fadeth because it really cannot bring life. Regarding this glorious ministry he must be bold and frank. It needs no veil as if to conceal its evanescence. Christ presents it unveiled to all who turn to Him, and they themselves, reflecting His glory, are spiritually transformed (**3** 1–18). As for those who by God's mercy have received such a gospel ministry, it is impossible for them to be faint-hearted in its exercise, although the eyes of some may be blinded to it, because the god of this world enslaves them (**4** 4). It is indeed wonderful that ministers of this grace should be creatures so frail, so subject to pressure and affliction, but it is not inexplicable. So much the more obvious is it that all the power and glory of salvation are from God alone (**4** 7.15). Yea, even if one be called to die in this ministry, that is but another light and momentary affliction. It is but passing from a frail earthly tent to abide forever in a heavenly home (**5** 1). Who would not long for it, that this mortal may be swallowed up in immortality? Courage, therefore, is ours to the end, for that end only means the cessation of our separation from Christ, whom it is a joy to serve absent or present. And present we shall all ultimately be before Him on the judgment throne (**5** 10). That itself unspeakably deepens the earnestness with which preachers of the gospel seek to persuade men. It is the love of Christ constraining them (**5** 14) in the ministry of reconciliation, that they should entreat men as ambassadors on Christ's behalf (**5** 20). So sacred and responsible a trust has subdued the apostle's own life, and is indeed the key to its manifold endurance, and to the earnestness with which he has striven to cultivate every grace, and to submit himself to every discipline (**6** 1–10). Would God the Corinthians might open their hearts to him as he does to them! (Let them have no fellowship with iniquity, but perfect holiness in the fear of God [**6** 14—**7** 1].) He has never wronged them; they are enshrined in his heart, living or dying; he glories in them, and is filled with comfort in all his affliction (**6** 11–13; **7** 2–4). For what blessed comfort that was that Titus brought him in Macedonia to dispel his fears, and to show that the things he regretted and grieved to have written had done no harm after all, but had rather wrought in them the joyful change for which he longed! Now both they and he knew how dear he was to them. Titus, too, was overjoyed by the magnanimity of their reception of him. The apostle's cup is full, and "in everything he is of good courage concerning them" (**7** 16).

2. Chs 8–9

In the second section, chs **8–9,** the apostle, now abundantly confident of their good-will, exhorts the Corinthians on the subject of the collection for the poor saints at Jerus. He tells them of the extraordinary liberality of the Macedonian churches, and invites them to emulate it, and by the display of this additional grace to make full proof of their love (**8** 1–8). Nay, they have a higher incentive than the liberality of Macedonia, even the self-sacrifice of Christ Himself (**8** 9). Wherefore let them go on with the good work they were so ready to initiate a year ago, giving out of a willing mind, as God hath enabled them (**8** 10–15). Further to encourage them he sends on Titus and other well-known and accredited brethren, whose interest in them is as great as his own, and he is hopeful that by their aid the matter will be completed, and all will rejoice when he comes, bringing with him probably some of those of Macedonia, to whom he has already been boasting of their zeal (**8** 16—**9** 5). Above all, let them remember that important issues are bound up with this grace of Christian liberality. It is impossible to reap bountifully, if we sow sparingly. Grudging and compulsory benevolence is a contradiction, but God loveth and rewardeth a cheerful giver. This grace blesseth him that gives and him that takes. Many great ends are served by it. The wants of the needy are supplied, men's hearts are drawn affectionately to one another, thanksgivings abound, and God himself is glorified (**9** 6–15).

3. Chs 10–13

The third section, chs **10–13,** as has been pointed out, is a spirited and even passionate polemic, in the course of which the Judaizing party in Corinth is vigorously assailed. The enemies of the apostle have charged him with being very bold and courageous when he is absent, but humble enough when he is present. He hopes the Corinthians will not compel him to show his courage (**10** 2). It is true, being human, he walks in the flesh, but not in the selfish and cowardly way his opponents suggest. The weapons of his warfare are not carnal, yet are they mighty before God to cast down such strongholds as theirs, such vain imaginations and disobedience. Some boast of being "Christ's," but that is no monopoly; he also is Christ's. They think his letters are mere "sound and fury, signifying nothing"; by and by they will discover their mistake. If he should glory in his authority, he is justified, for Corinth was verily part of his God-appointed province, and he at least did not there enter on other men's labors. But it would be well if men who gloried confined themselves to glorying "in the Lord." For after all it is His commendation alone that is of any permanent value (**10** 3–18). Will the Corinthians bear with him in a little of this foolish boasting? Truly he ventures on it out of concern for them (**11** 2). And as they are manifest adepts in toleration, abounding in patience toward those who have come with a different gospel, they may perhaps extend some of their indulgence to him, for though he cannot lay claim to a polished oratory comparable to that of these "super-eminent" apostles, yet at least he is not behind them in knowledge (**11** 4–6). Can it be that he really sinned in preaching the gospel to them without fee or reward? Was it a mark of fleshly cunning when he resolved not to be burdensome to them, while he accepted supplies from Macedonia? Ah! it was not because he did not love them, but because he decided to give no occasion to those who were too ready to blame him—those false apostles, who, like Satan himself, masqueraded as angels of light and ministers of righteousness (**11** 7–15). Come, then, let him to this glorying, this poor folly, which they in their superlative wisdom bear with so gladly in the case of those insolent creatures who now bully and degrade them (**11** 16–21). Hebrews! Israelites! So is he. Ministers of Christ! There he excels them—in labors, in perils, in persecutions; in burdens, anxieties, sympathies; in visions and revelations of the Lord; in infirmities and weaknesses that have made more manifest in him the strength of Christ (**11** 22—**12** 10). Certainly all this is folly, but they are most to blame for it who, through lack of loyalty, have forced him to it. Did he injure them by declining to be burdensome? Is it so sore a point? Let it be forgiven! Yet when he comes again he will take no other course (**12** 11–18). They must not imagine that in all this he is excusing himself to them. He is sincerely and affectionately concerning himself for their edifying. He trembles lest when they meet again they should be disappointed in each other; lest they should be found in unworthy strife and tumults, and lest he should be humbled of God before them, having cause to mourn over some who are hardened and impenitent in their sins (**12** 19–21). For they must meet again—he is coming for the third time—and this time he will not spare. Let them prove themselves whether they be in the faith; for surely they must know whether Christ be in them. He earnestly prays for their goodness and honor; not to the end that no display of his power may be called for, but simply that he will be glad to appear weak if they should appear strong. Could they but believe it, their perfecting is the aim of all his labors (**13** 1–10). And so, with words of grace and tenderness, exhorting them to unity and peace, and pronouncing over them the threefold benediction, he bids them farewell (**13** 11–14).

VII. Value of the Epistle.—The chief element of value in this ep. is the revelation it gives of the apostle himself. Through all its changing moods, Paul, in perfect abandon, shows us his very soul, suffering, rejoicing, enduring, overcoming. It has been truly said that "it enables us, as it were, to lay our hands upon his breast, and feel the very throbbings of his heart." (1) In relation to his converts, it shows us how sensitive he was, how easy it was to touch him on the quick, and to wound his feelings. The apostle was very human, and nowhere are his kindred limitations more obvious than in these present incidents. He would probably be the first to acquiesce, if it were said that even with him the creed was greater than the life. In the hastily written and nervously repented passages of that severe ep.; in the restless wandering, like a perturbed spirit, from Troas to Macedonia, to meet the news and know the issue of his acts, we see a man most lovable indeed, most like ourselves when issues hang in the balance, but a man not already perfect, not yet risen to the measure of the stature of Christ. Yet we see also the intensity with which Paul labored in his ministry—the tenacity with which he held to his mission, and the invincible courage with which he returned to the fight for his imperiled church. He loved those converts as only a great soul in Christ could love them. His keenest sorrow came in the disaster that threatened them, and he flew to their defence. He had not only won them for Christ, he was willing to die that he might keep them for Christ. (2) The ep. is charged with a magnificent consciousness on the apostle's part of his high calling in Christ Jesus. He has been called with a Divine calling to the most glorious work in which a man can engage, to be to this estranged earth an ambassador of heaven. Received as Divine, this vocation is accepted with supreme devotion. It has been a ministry of sorrow, of strain and suffering, of hair-breadth escapes with the bare life; with its thorn in the flesh, its buffeting of Satan. Yet through it all there rings the note of abounding consolation in Christ Jesus, and never was the "power of Christ," resting on frail humanity, more signally manifested.

Literature.—See the references to both epp., and to 2 Cor alone, under this heading in the preceding art. To the list there given should be added Moffatt's *Introduction to the Literature of the NT*, 1911; valuable for its critical presentation of recent views, and for its references to the literature.

R. Dykes Shaw

CORINTHUS, kō-rin'thus: Lat form for Gr *Kórinthos* in the subscription to Rom (AV). See Corinth.

CORMORANT, kôr'mō-rant (שָׁלָךְ, *shālākh;* καταράκτης, *kataráktēs;* Lat *Corvus marinus*): A large sea-fowl belonging to the genus *Phalacrocorax* and well described by the Heb word used to designate it—which means a "plunging bird." The bird appears as large as a goose when in full feather, but plucked, the body is much smaller. The adult birds are glossy black with bronze tints, touched with white on the cheeks and sides as a festal dress at mating season, and adorned with

Cormorant (*Phalacrocorax carbo*).

filamentary feathers on the head, and bright yellow gape. These birds if taken young and carefully trained can be sent into the water from boats and bring to their masters large quantities of good-sized fish: commonly so used in China. The flesh is dark, tough and quite unfit to eat in the elders on account of their diet of fish. The nest is built mostly of seaweed. The eggs are small for the size of the birds, having a rough, thick, but rather soft shell of a bluish white which soon becomes soiled, as well as the nest and its immediate surroundings, from the habits of the birds. The young are leathery black, then covered with soft down of brownish black above and white beneath and taking on the full black of the grown bird at about three years. If taken in the squab state the young are said to be delicious food, resembling baked hare in flavor. The old birds are mentioned among the abominations for food (Lev **11** 13–19; Dt **14** 12–18). Gene Stratton-Porter

CORN, kôrn (דָּגָן, *dāghān;* σῖτος, *sítos*): A word used for cereals generally (Gen **27** 28.37, etc, AV) much as our Eng. word "corn." ARV almost invariably substitutes "grain" for "corn." The latter may be taken to include (1) barley, (2) wheat, (3) fitches (vetches), (4) lentils, (5) beans, (6) millet, (7) rye—the wrong tr for vetches, (8) pulse—for all these see separate articles. Rye and oats are not cultivated in Pal. For many references to corn see Agriculture; Food. "A corn [κόκκος, *kókkos*, RV "grain"] of wheat" is mentioned (Jn **12** 24).

CORNELIUS, kor-nē'li-us (**Κορνήλιος,** *Kornḗlios,* "of a horn"): The story of Cornelius is given in Acts **10** 1—**11** 18. The name is

1. His Family and Station

Rom and belonged to distinguished families in the imperial city, such as the Scipios and Sulla. Thus he was probably an Italian of Rom blood. Julian the Apostate reckons him as one of the few persons of distinction who became a Christian. He was evidently a man of importance in Caesarea and well known to the Jews (Acts **10** 22). He was a centurion in the Italian cohort. To understand this we must note that the Rom army was divided into two broad divisions, the legions and the auxiliary forces. See ARMY, ROMAN.

Legions were never permanently quartered in Pal until the great war which ended in the destruction of Jerus, 70 AD. From the year 6 AD, when Pal was made into a province of the second rank, until 66 AD, it was garrisoned by auxiliary troops recruited amongst the Samaritans and Syrian Greeks. The headquarters were naturally at Caesarea, the residence of the procurator. But it would not have been prudent for a garrison in Pal to be composed wholly of troops locally recruited. Therefore the Rom government mingled with the garrison 600 soldiers, free Italian volunteers. With this cohort Cornelius was connected as centurion.

He is described as devout and God-fearing, i.e. at least, one of those men so numerous in that effete age of decadent heathenism who, dis-

2. His Character

contented with polytheism, yearned for a better faith, embraced, therefore, the monotheism of the Jews, read the Scriptures, and practised more or less of the Jewish rites. He was well reported of by the Jews, and his religion showed itself in prayer at the regular hours, and in alms to the people (of Israel). Even Jewish bigotry was dumb in presence of so noble a man. Moreover, he seems to have made his house a sort of church, for his kinsfolk and friends were in sympathy with him, and among the soldiers who closely attended him were some devout ones (Acts **10** 1.27).

The story of his conversion and admission into the Christian church is told with some minuteness in Acts **10**. Nothing further is known

3. His Admission into the Christian Church

of Cornelius, though one tradition asserts that he founded the church in Caesarea, and another legend that he became the bishop of Scamandros.

The exact importance of the incident depends upon the position of Cornelius before it occurred. Certainly he was not a proselyte of the sanctuary, circumcised, under the law,

4. Significance of the Incident

a member of the Jewish communion. This is abundantly evident from Acts **10** 28.34.45; **11** 3.18; **15** 7.14. But was he not an inferior form of proselyte, later called "proselytes of the gate"? This question has been much debated and is still under discussion. Ramsay (*St. Paul the Traveller,* 43) says that the expression, "God-fearing," applied to him, is always used in Acts with reference to this kind of proselytes. Such were bound to observe certain regulations of purity, probably those, this author thinks, mentioned in Acts **15** 29, and which stand in close relation to the principles laid down in Lev **17–18** for the conduct of strangers dwelling among Israel. Renan, on the other hand, denies that Cornelius was a proselyte at all, but simply a devout Gentile who adopted some of the Jewish ideas and religious customs which did not involve a special profession. The importance of the whole transaction to the development of the church seems to depend on the circumstance that Cornelius was probably not a proselyte at all. Thus we regard Cornelius as lit. the first-fruits of the Gentiles. The step here taken by Peter was therefore one of tremendous importance to the whole development of the church. The significance of the incident consists exactly in this, that under Divine direction, the first Gentile, not at all belonging to the old theocracy, becomes a Spirit-filled Christian, entering through the front door of the Christian church without first going through the narrow gate of Judaism. The incident settled forever the great, fundamental question as to the relations of Jew and Gentile in the church. The difficulties in the way of the complete triumph of Peter's view of the equality of Jews and Gentiles in the Kingdom of Christ were enormous. It would have been indeed little short of miraculous if the multitude of Christian Pharisees had not raised the question again and again. Did they not dog Paul's steps after the Council? Certainly Ramsay is wrong in saying that the case of Cornelius was passed over or condoned as exceptional, for it was used as a precedent by both Peter and James (Acts **15** 7.14).

As for Peter's subsequent conduct at Antioch, no one who knows Peter need be surprised at it. The very accusation that Paul hurled at him was that for the moment he was carried into inconsistency with his principles (*hupókrisis*). Of course, this incident of Cornelius was only the first step in a long development; but the principle was forever settled. The rest in due time and proper order was sure to follow. By this tremendous innovation it was settled that Christianity was to be freed from the swaddling bands of Judaism and that the Christian church was not to be an appendix to the synagogue. The noble character of Cornelius was just fitted to abate, as far as possible, the prejudices of the Jewish Christians against what must have seemed to them a dangerous, if not awful, innovation. G. H. TREVER

CORNER, kôr'nēr (מִקְצוֹעַ, *miḳçōaʿ*, פֵּאָה, *pē'āh,* פִּנָּה, *pinnāh;* **ἀρχή,** *archḗ,* **γωνία,** *gōnía,* **ἀκρογωνιαῖος,** *akrogōniaíos*): In Ex **26** 24; Ezk **41** 22; **46** 21.22, *miḳçōaʿ*, "angle" is tr[d] "corner"; *pē'āh,* "side," "quarter," and *pinnāh,* "corner," "front," "chief," are more frequently so tr[d], e.g. Ex **25** 26; Lev **19** 9; Jer **9** 26; **25** 23; and Ex **27** 2; 1 K **7** 34; Ps **118** 22; Isa **28** 16 ("corner-stone"); Jer **51** 26. Other words are *kānāph,* "wing" (Isa **11** 12; Ezk **7** 2); *kāthēph,* "shoulder" (2 K **11** 11 AV *bis*); *paʿam,* "foot" (Ex **25** 12 AV); *zāwīyōth,* "corner-stones" (Ps **144** 12; Zec **9** 15 [tr[d] "corners"]).

For "corner" RV has "side" (Ex **36** 25), "corner-stone" (Zec **10** 4), also for "stay" (Isa **19** 13); instead of "teacher removed into a corner" (Isa **30** 20), "be hidden," "hide themselves"; for "corners" we have "feet" (Ex **25** 12; 1 K **7** 30); "ribs" (Ex **30** 4; **37** 27); for "divide into corners" (Neh **9** 22), "allot after their portions"; for "into corners" (Dt **32** 26), "afar"; the words to Israel (Isa **41** 9) "called thee from the chief men [*'ăçīlīm*] thereof" are rendered by RV "called thee from the corners thereof" (of the earth).

In the NT we have *gōnia* ("angle," "corner"), "in the corners of the streets" (Mt **6** 5), "the head of the corner" (**21** 42), "the four corners of the earth" (Rev **7** 1; **20** 8); *archē* ("a beginning") (Acts **10** 11; **11** 5); "chief corner stone" (Eph **2** 20; 1 Pet **2** 6), is a tr of *akrogōniaios* ("at the extreme angle"). W. L. WALKER

CORNER GATE, kôr'nēr gāt. See JERUSALEM.

CORNERS OF THE EARTH. See EARTH, CORNERS OF.

CORNER-STONE, kôr'nēr stōn (פִּנָּה, *pinnāh,* זָוִית, *zāwīth;* **ἀκρογωνιαῖος,** *akrogōniaíos*): Part of the public or imposing buildings to which importance has been attached in all ages and in many nations, both on account of its actual service and its figurative meaning. Ordinarily its use in the Bible is **figurative,** or symbolical. No doubt the original meaning was some important stone, which was laid at the foundation of a building.

(1) With the Canaanites, who preceded Israel in the possession of Pal, corner-stone laying seems to have been a most sacred and impressive ceremonial. Under this important stone of temples, or other great structures, bodies of children or older persons would be laid, consecrating the building by such human sacrifice (see FORTIFICATION, II, 1). This was one of many hideous rites and practices which Israel was to extirpate. It may throw light on the curse pronounced upon the rebuilding of Jericho (Josh **6** 26; see *PEFS*, January, 1904, July, 1908). See CANAAN.

(2) *OT references.*—The Heb word *pinnāh*, "corner," is found or implied in every occurrence of this idea. Derived from a root signifying "to turn," it means "turning," and therefore "edge" or "corner." Ordinarily it is used with *'ebhen*, "stone" (Ps **118** 22); or it may occur alone, having acquired for itself through frequent use the whole technical phrase-idea (Zec **10** 4 AV). While all the passages indicate the stone at the corner, there appear to be two conceptions: (*a*) the foundation-stone upon which the structure rested (Job **38** 6; Isa **28** 16; Jer **51** 26); or (*b*) the topmost or cap-stone, which linked the last tier together (Ps **118** 22; Zec **4** 7); in both cases it is an important or key-stone, and figurative of the Messiah, who is "the First and the Last." In Job **38** 6 it beautifully expresses in figures the stability of the earth, which Jeh created. In Zec **10** 4 the leader or ruler in the Messianic age is represented by the corner-stone. The ancient tradition of the one missing stone, when the temple was in building, is reflected in or has been suggested by Ps **118** 22 (Midr quoted by Pusey under Zec **4** 7). It is probable that we should read in Ps **144** 12 not "corner-stones," but "corner-pillars," or supports (cf Gr Caryatides) from a different Heb word, *zāwīth*, *BDB*, s.v.

Figurative Uses

(3) *NT passages.*—Ps **118** 22 is quoted and interpreted as fulfilled in Jesus Christ in a number of passages: Mt **21** 42; Mk **12** 10; Lk **20** 17; Acts **4** 11 and 1 Pet **2** 7; it is also the evident basis for Eph **2** 20. Isa **28** 16 is quoted twice in the NT: Rom **9** 33, from LXX combined with the words of Isa **8** 14, and in 1 Pet **2** 6, which is quoted with some variation from LXX. The OT passages were understood by the rabbis to be Messianic, and were properly so applied by the NT writers. See also HOUSE. EDWARD MACK

CORNET, kôr'net, kor'net. See MUSIC.

CORNFLOOR, kôrn'flōr (גֹּרֶן דָּגָן, *gōren dāghān*): "Thou hast loved a reward upon every cornfloor" (Hos **9** 1 AV, RV "hire upon every grainfloor"). Israel had deserted Jeh for supposed material benefits and regarded bounteous crops as the gift of the heathen gods which they worshipped. Jeh would therefore cause the corn (grain) and wine to fail (ver 2). See also THRESHING-FLOOR.

CORONATION, kor-ŏ-nā'shun (**πρωτοκλισία**, *prōtoklisía*): Occurs in 2 Macc **4** 21 (AV, RV "enthronement") where Apollonius was sent into Egypt for the coronation of Ptolemy Philometor as king. The Gr word *protoklisia* occurs nowhere else, and its meaning is uncertain. The reading in Swete is *prōtoklēsia*, and this means "the first call."

CORPSE, kōrps: This word in the AV is the tr of two Heb words, פֶּגֶר, *pegher*, and גְּוִיָּה, *g^ewīyāh*, while נְבֵלָה, *n^ebhēlāh*, and גּוּפָה, *gūphāh*, which mean the same, are tr^d "body," with which the Eng. word "corpse" (Lat *corpus*) was originally synonymical. Therefore we find the now apparently unnecessary addition of the adj. "dead" in 2 K **19** 35 and Isa **37** 36. The Gr equivalent is *πτῶμα*, *ptôma*, lit. "a fallen body," "a ruin" (from *πίπτω*, *píptō*, "to fall"), in Mk **6** 29; Rev **11** 8.9.

Corpses were considered as unclean and defiling in the OT, so that priests were not to touch dead bodies except those of near kinsfolk (Lev **21** 1–3), the high priest and a Nazirite not even such (Lev **21** 11; Nu **6** 6–8). Nu **19** presents to us the ceremonial of purification from such defilement by the sprinkling with the ashes of a red heifer, cedar wood, hyssop and scarlet.

It was considered a great calamity and disgrace to have one's body left unburied, a "food unto all birds of the heavens, and unto the beasts of the earth" (Dt **28** 26; 2 S **21** 10; Ps **79** 2; Isa **34** 3; Jer **7** 33, etc). Thence is explained the merit of Rizpah (2 S **21** 10), and of the inhabitants of Jabesh-gilead, who protected or recovered and buried the mutilated bodies of Saul and his sons (1 S **31** 11–13; 2 S **2** 4–7; cf 1 Ch **10** 11.12). See BURIAL.

Even the corpses of persons executed by hanging were not to remain on the tree "all night," "for he that is hanged is accursed of God; that thou defile not thy land which Jeh thy God giveth thee for an inheritance" (Dt **21** 23). H. L. E. LUERING

CORRECTION, ko-rek'shun (מוּסָר, *mūsār*, usually rendered "instruction," is tr^d "correction" in several passages): The vb. from which the noun is derived signifies "to instruct" or "chastise." The idea of chastisement was very closely connected in the Heb mind with that of pedagogy. See CHASTISEMENT. RV and ARV have changed "correction" of AV to "instruction" in Jer **7** 28, reversing the order in the margins. שֵׁבֶט, *shēbheṭ*, rendered "rod" in Job **21** 9, is unnecessarily changed to "correction" in **37** 13. In 2 Tim **3** 16, *ἐπανόρθωσις*, *epanórthōsis*, is tr^d "correction." The difference between correction, discipline and instruction was not clearly drawn in the Heb mind. W. W. DAVIES

CORRUPTION, kŏ-rup'shun: The Heb words מִשְׁחָת, *mishḥāth*, מָשְׁחָת, *mashḥāth*, מַשְׁחִית, *mashḥīth*, and their Gr equivalents, **φθορά**, *phthorá*, and **διαφθορά**, *diaphthorá*, with numerous derivatives and cognate vbs., imply primarily physical degeneration and decay (Job **17** 14; Acts **2** 27, etc). The term שַׁחַת, *shaḥath*, which AV translates with "corruption" in Jon **2** 6, ought to be rendered "pit," as in Ps **30** 9; **35** 7 *et passim*, while *shaḥath b^elī* in Isa **38** 17 means the "pit of nothingness," i.e. of destruction.

Figurative: At an early time we find the above-given words in a non-literal sense denoting moral depravity and corruption (Gen **6** 11; Ex **32** 7; Hos **9** 9; Gal **6** 8, etc), which ends in utter moral ruin and hopelessness, the second death. The question has been raised whether the meaning of these words might be extended so as to include the idea of final destruction and annihilation of the spirit. Upon careful examination, however, this question must be denied both from the standpoint of the OT and of the NT. Apart from other considerations we see this from the metaphors used in the Scriptures to illustrate the condition of "corruption," such as the "unquenchable fire," the "worm" which "dieth not" (Mk **9** 43.48; cf Isa

66 24), and "sleep" (Dnl **12** 2), where a careful distinction is made between the blissful state after death of the righteous and the everlasting disgrace of the godless. The later Jewish theology is also fully agreed on this point. The meaning of the words cannot therefore extend beyond the idea of utter moral degradation and depravity.

H. L. E. LUERING

CORRUPTION, MOUNT OF (הַר־הַמַּשְׁחִית, *har ha-mashḥīth;* **τὸ ὄρος τοῦ Μοσοάθ,** *tó óros toú Mosoáth*): The hill on the right hand of which Solomon built high places for Ashtoreth, Chemosh and Milcom (2 K **23** 13). The mountain referred to is no doubt the Mount of Olives. The high places would, therefore, be on the southern height called in later Christian writings the "Mount of Offence," and now, by the Arabs, *Bāṭen el-Hawa. Har ha-mashḥīth* is probably only a perversion of *har ha-mishḥāh*, "Mount of Anointing," a later name of the Mount of Olives. W. EWING

COS, kos (**Κῶς,** *Kṓs*, "summit"; AV **Coos**): An island off the coast of Caria, Asia Minor, one of the Sporades, mountainous in the southern half, with ridges extending to a height of 2,500 ft.; identified with the modern Stanchio. It was famous in antiquity for excellent wine, amphorae, wheat, ointments, silk and other clothing (*Coae vestes*). The capital was also called Cos. It possessed a famous hospital and medical school, and was the birthplace of Hippocrates (the father of medicine), of Ptolemy Philadelphus, and of the celebrated painter Apelles. The large plane tree in the center of the town (over 2,000 years old) is called "the tree of Hippocrates" to this day. The older capital, Astypalaea, was in the western part of the island, the later (since 366 BC) in the eastern part. From almost every point can be seen beautiful landscapes and picturesque views of sea and land and mountain.

Cos was one of the six Dorian colonies. It soon became a flourishing place of commerce and industry; later, like Corinth, it was one of the Jewish centers of the Aegaean, as well as one of the financial centers of the commercial world in the eastern Mediterranean. Among the benefactors of the people of Cos was Herod the Great. It is mentioned in connection with Paul's third missionary journey in Acts **21** 1, and in its relations with the Jews in 1 Macc **15** 23; *Ant*, XIV, vii, 2; x, 15; *BJ*, I, xxi, 11. For a list of works on the island see Paton-Hicks, *Inscriptions of Cos*, ix.

J. E. HARRY

COSAM, kō'sam (**Κωσάμ,** *Kōsám*): An ancestor of Jesus in St. Luke's genealogy in the 5th generation before Zerubbabel (Lk **3** 28).

COSMOGONY, koz-mog'o-ni. See ANTHROPOLOGY; CREATION; EARTH; EVOLUTION; WORLD.

COSMOLOGY, koz-mol'o-ji. See WORLD; PROVIDENCE.

COSTLINESS, kost'li-nes (**τιμιότης,** *timiótēs*, "preciousness," "an abundance of costly things"): Found only in Rev **18** 19, "made rich by reason of her costliness."

COTES, kōts. See SHEEPCOTE.

COTTAGE, kot'āj. See HOUSE.

COTTON, kot''n (כַּרְפַּס, *karpaṣ*, is the better tr, as in RVm, where AV and RV have "green" in Est **1** 6): The Heb *karpaṣ* is from the Pers *kirpās* and the Sanskrit *karpāsa*, "the cotton plant." The derived words originally meant "muslin" or "calico," but in classical times the use of words allied to *karpaṣ*—in Gr and Lat—was extended to include linen. The probability is in favor of "cotton" in Est **1** 6. This is the product of *Gossypium herbaceum*, a plant originally from India but now cultivated in many other lands.

COUCH, kouch (subst.). See BED.

Couch (vb.): רָבַץ, *rābhaç*, "to crouch," "lurk," as a beast in readiness to spring on its prey. "If thou doest not well, sin coucheth at the door" (Gen **4** 7, AV "lieth"), waiting for it to open. Cain is warned to beware of the first temptations to evil, in his case esp. a sullen and jealous disposition (cf Dante, *Inferno*, I, 30). See ABEL; CAIN. The tribe of Judah is compared for its bravery to a recumbent lion or lioness (Gen **49** 9; cf Nu **24** 9 f); and Issachar to "a strong ass, couching down between the sheepfolds" (**49** 14, AV "between two burdens"; cf Jgs **5** 16). "The deep that coucheth beneath" (Dt **33** 13), probably the springs of water, or possibly, as Driver suggests, "the subterranean deep, pictured as a gigantic monster." See ABYSS.

M. O. EVANS

COUCHING-PLACE, kouch'ing-plās (מַרְבֵּץ, *marbēç;* once in EV [Ezk **25** 5]): The same Heb word, however, which means simply "place of lying down" of animals in repose, is used also in Zeph **2** 15 where the tr is "a place . . . . to lie down in." The figure, a common one in Scripture (see besides, Isa **17** 2; **27** 10), suggests desolation.

COULTER, kol'tẽr. See PLOW.

COUNCIL, koun'sil, **COUNCILLOR,** koun'si-lẽr (**συμβούλιον,** *sumboúlion*): An assembly of advisers (Acts **25** 12); a body of those taking counsel (see Schürer's *Jewish People in the Time of Christ*, I (1), 60). Distinguished from *συνέδριον*, *sunédrion*, the supreme court of the Jews, by being of a less formal character, i.e. less of an institution. For "council" in the latter sense, its most frequent use, see SANHEDRIN. A councillor (Gr *bouleutḗs*) was a member of the Sanhedrin. Applied to Joseph of Arimathea (Mk **15** 43; Lk **23** 50). In AV "counsellor."

COUNSEL, koun'sel, **COUNSELLOR,** koun'se-lẽr (**συμβούλιον,** *sumboúlion*): Ordinarily found as object of vb. "to take" or "to give," expressing, beside the idea of a practical end to be reached, that of consultation and deliberation among those united in a common cause (Mt **12** 14; Mk **3** 6). A counsellor (*súmboulos*) is a confidential adviser (Rom **11** 34); often in the OT (Isa **9** 6; Prov **24** 6, etc). Confounded in AV with "councillor" (see above), the latter being an official adviser, which the former does not necessarily mean.

COUNT, kount (סָפַר, *ṣāphar*, מָנָה, *mānāh;* **ψηφίζω,** *psēphízō*): Used of arithmetical computation "to number" (Ps **139** 18; Nu **23** 10); also for כָּתַב, *kāthabh*, "to reckon," to indicate classification among or identification with, "c. for a stranger" (Job **19** 15); "c. for his enemy" (Job **33** 10). In the NT the arithmetical computation is less prominent, except in the sense of "calculate," *psēphizō, sumpsēphízō*, "to reckon with pebbles," each pebble representing a unit (Lk **14** 28; Acts **19** 19); of moral estimate, *hēgéomai* and *logízomai* (Phil **3** 7.13). The noun, fr Heb *kāṣath*, "a count of" (Ex **12** 4), viz. in the arithmetical sense.

H. E. JACOBS

COUNTENANCE, koun'te-nans:

(1) The noun (see also s.v. FACE) is the tr of a variety of Heb and Gr expressions, פָּנִים, *pānīm;* *πρόσωπον*, *prósōpon*, being the most frequent. Be

sides these there are found מַרְאֶה, *mar'eh*, "appearance," "shape," "comeliness," "visage," עַיִן, *'ayin*, "the eye," תֹּאַר, *tō'ar*, "appearance," "figure," etc, and Aram. זִיו, *zīw*. To the Oriental the countenance mirrors, even more than to us, the character and feelings of the heart. The countenance (*mar'eh*) is "fair" (1 S **17** 42; 2 S **14** 27; Dnl **1** 15); in 1 S **16** 12, lit. "fair of eyes"; "comely" (Cant **2** 14); "beautiful" (*tō'ar*, 1 S **25** 3); "cheerful" (*pānīm*, Prov **15** 13); "angry" (Prov **25** 23); "fierce" (Dnl **8** 23); "troubled" (Ezk **27** 35); "sad" (1 S **1** 18; Neh **2** 2.3; Eccl **7** 3). The countenance is "sharpened," i.e. made keen (Prov **27** 17); it "falls," i.e. looks despondent, disappointed (Gen **4** 5.6); is "cast down" (Job **29** 24); "changed" (Job **14** 20; cf "altered" into glory, Lk **9** 29; Dnl **5** 6.9.10; **7** 28, Aram. *zīw*). To settle one's countenance stedfastly upon a person (2 K **8** 11) is synonymous with staring or gazing at a person. Not infrequently we find compound expressions such as "light of countenance," i.e. favor (Job **29** 24; Ps **4** 6; **44** 3; **89** 15; **90** 8); "health of countenance" (Ps **42** 11; **43** 5); "help of countenance" (Ps **42** 5); "rebuke of countenance" (Ps **80** 16); "pride of countenance" (Heb *'aph*, lit. "haughty," "lofty nose," Ps **10** 4).

(2) As vb. (Heb הָדַר, *hādhar*, "to countenance") we find the word in AV of Ex **23** 3, where the Revisers translate "Neither shalt thou favor [AV "countenance"] a poor man in his cause." Here the meaning seems to be that no distinction of persons shall be made by the judge. See Lev **19** 15, where, however, a different word is used. There is therefore no need of the emendation proposed by Knobel and accepted by Kautzsch, who would read גָּדֹל, *gādhōl*, "great," for וְדַל, *w^edhāl*, "and the poor" of the text. The LXX has πένης, *pénēs*, "poor."

H. L. E. LUERING

COUNTER-CHARM, koun'tēr-charm. See AMULET; CHARM.

COUNTERFEIT, koun'tēr-fit (κίβδηλος, *kíbdēlos*, ἀνατυπόω, *anatupóō*, ὁμοιόω, *homoióō*): "C." occurs as the tr of *kibdēlos*, "mixed with dross," "not genuine" (Wisd **15** 9, "to make c. things," RV "mouldeth counterfeits," spurious things, imitations"); **2** 16 RV "base metal" (cf LXX Lev **19** 19; Dt **22** 11, "mingled garment," and 2 Cor **13** 5.6, *adókimos*, "reprobate" [silver]). "Counterfeit" in the older sense of a representation occurs in Wisd **14** 17 (*anatupoō*, "to make a likeness"), "c. of his visage," RV "imagining the likeness from afar," and Ecclus **38** 27 (*homoioō*, "to make like"), "to c. imagery," RV "to preserve likeness in his portraiture."

W. L. WALKER

COUNTERVAIL, koun-tēr-vāl' (שָׁוָה, *shāwāh*, "equalize"): To thwart or overcome by acting against with equal force; thus, "The enemy could not c. the king's damage" or loss (Est **7** 4 ARV reads "The adversary could not have compensated for the king's damage"). "Nothing doth c. [RV "can be taken in exchange for"] a faithful friend" (Ecclus **6** 15).

COUNTRY, kun'tri (אֶרֶץ, *'ereç*, "land," שָׂדֶה, *sādheh*, "field"; ἀγρός, *agrós*, "field," χώρα, *chṓra*, "region"): The foregoing are the principal words rendered "country" in EV, though we find also *'ădhāmāh*, "earth" (Jon **4** 2); *'ī*, "island" (Jer **47** 4 AV); *g^elīlāh*, "circuit" (Ezk **47** 8 AV); *ḥebhel*, "rope" (Dt **3** 14); *māḳōm*, "place" (Gen **29** 26 AV); *nepheth*, "hill" or "height" (Josh **17** 11 AV); *génos*, "race" (Acts **4** 36 AV); γῆ, *gḗ*, "earth" (Mt **9** 31 AV; Acts **7** 3 AV); πατρίς, *patrís*, "native land" (Lk **4** 23; Jn **4** 44; He **11** 14); περίχωρος, *períchōros*, "country [ARV "region"] round about" (Mt **14** 35; Lk **3** 3; **4** 37; **8** 37). In He **11** 14 ff, "heaven" is referred to as a country. Egypt and Assyria were "far countries" (Jer **8** 19 AV; Zec **10** 9). The hill country (cf the numerous Gibeahs [*gibh'āh*, "a hill"]) was the mountainous region to the N. or to the S. of Jerus. The low country, *sh^ephēlāh* (see SHEPHELAH), consisted of the foothills to the west of the hill country. The south country or NEGEB (*neghebh*), q.v., was the dry, extreme southern part of Pal, approximately between Beersheba and Kadesh-barnea.

ALFRED ELY DAY

COUNTRYMAN, kun'tri-man (συμφυλέτης, *sumphulétēs*): "Of the same tribe" (1 Thess **2** 14); also in idiomatic rendering (γένος, *génos*) for those of one's own race or kin (2 Cor **11** 26; Gal **1** 14 AV, "one's own nation"). Cf Mk **6** 4; Rom **9** 3; and see COUSIN; KINSMAN, etc.

COUPLE, kup''l:

(1) Used as a noun, indicates two objects of the same kind that are considered together. Thus we read of a couple of cakes (2 S **13** 6, used loosely), and a couple of asses (2 S **16** 1, Heb *çemedh*).

(2) Used as a vb., it means to join or fasten one thing to another. This term occurs most frequently in the description of the tabernacle (see Ex **26** 6.9.11; **36** 10.13.16). Couple is used in 1 Pet **3** 2 to describe the joining of fear to chaste behavior (Heb *ḥābhar*).

COUPLING, kup'ling: Is the EV rendering of מַחְבֶּרֶת, *maḥbereth*. This Heb word means joining, or the place where one thing is joined to another, as of the curtains of the tabernacle (Ex **26** 4.5), and of the different parts of the ephod (Ex **28** 27; **39** 20).

It is also the EV rendering of מְחַבְּרוֹת, *m^eḥabb^erōth*, and this refers more to the thing that joins the two objects, as beams of wood (2 Ch **34** 11), or hooks of iron (1 Ch **22** 3).

COURAGE, kur'āj: Heb *ḥāzaḳ*, "to show oneself strong" (Nu **13** 20; 2 S **10** 12; 1 Ch **19** 13; 2 Ch **15** 8; Ezr **10** 4; Ps **27** 14; **31** 24; Isa **41** 6); *rūaḥ*, "spirit," "animus" (Josh **2** 11 AV); *'āmaç*, "to be alert" (physically and mentally), "to be agile," "quick," "energetic" (Dt **31** 6.7.23; Josh **1** 6.9.18; **10** 25; 1 Ch **22** 13; **28** 20); *lēbhābh*, "the heart," and **fig.**: "person," "spirit" (Dnl **11** 25); Gr *thársos*, "cheer" (Acts **28** 15). A virtue highly esteemed among all nations, one of the four chief "natural" (cardinal) virtues (Wisd **8** 7), while cowardice ranks as one of the mortal sins (Ecclus **2** 12.13; Rev **21** 8).

COURSE, kōrs (from Lat *cursus*, "a running," "race," "voyage," "way"):

(1) εὐθυδρομέω, *euthudroméō*, "forward or onward movement," as of a ship: "We made a straight c." (Acts **16** 11; cf Acts **21** 1); "We had finished our c." (RV "voyage," Acts **21** 7).

(2) A (prescribed or self-appointed) path, as of the sun: "Swift is the sun in his c." (1 Esd **4** 34); of the stars: "The stars in their courses fought against Sisera" (Jgs **5** 20 AV) (see ASTRONOMY; ASTROLOGY); of a river (or irrigating canal?): "as willows by the watercourses" (Isa **44** 4); of a race (τρέχω, *tréchō*): "that the word of the Lord may have free c." (RV "may run") (2 Thess **3** 1).

(3) A career in such a course (δρόμος, *drómos*): "I have finished my [RV "the"] c." (2 Tim **4** 7); "as John fulfilled [RV "was fulfilling"] his c." (Acts **13** 25); "that I might finish [RV "may accomplish"] my c." (Acts **20** 24).

(4) A way or manner, as of life: "Every one

turned to his c." (Jer **8** 6); "their c. is evil" (Jer **23** 10); "walked according to the c. [αἰών, *aiôn*, RVm "age"] of this world" (Eph **2** 2).

(5) Orderly succession: "sang together by c." (ARV "sang one to another") (Ezr **3** 11); "by c." (RV "in turn") (1 Cor **14** 27); the courses of the priests and Levites (1 Ch **27** 1–15; 1 Ch **28** 1; 2 Ch **5** 11; Lk **1** 5.8). See PRIESTS AND LEVITES.

(6) A row or layer, as of masonry: "All the foundations of the earth are out of c." (RV "are moved"; ARV "are shaken") (Ps **82** 5).

(7) [The tongue] "setteth on fire the c. [RV "wheel"] of nature" (Jas **3** 6). The cycle of generation (*tón trochón tês genéseōs*) here means the physical world as constituted by the round of origin and decay, and typified by the Orphic (legendary) cycle of births and deaths through which the soul passes in metempsychosis. See also GAMES.

WILLIAM ARTHUR HEIDEL

COURSE OF PRIESTS AND LEVITES. See PRIESTS AND LEVITES.

COURT, kōrt. See HOUSE.

COURT OF THE GENTILES. See TEMPLE (HEROD'S).

COURT OF THE SABBATH. See COVERED WAY.

COURT, kōrt, **OF THE SANCTUARY,** saṇk'ṭū-a-ri (**TABERNACLE, TEMPLE**): By "court" (חָצֵר, *ḥāçēr*) is meant a clear space inclosed by curtains or walls, or surrounded by buildings. It was always an uncovered inclosure, but might have within its area one or more edifices.

1. The Tabernacle

The first occurrence of the word is in Ex **27** 9, where it is commanded to "make the court of the tabernacle." The dimensions for this follow in the directions for the length of the linen curtains which were to inclose it. From these we learn that the perimeter of the court was 300 cubits, and that it consisted of two squares, each 75 ft., lying E. and W. of one another. In the westerly square stood the tabernacle, while in that to the E. was the altar of burnt offering. This was the worshipper's square, and every Heb who passed through the entrance gate had immediate access to the altar (cf W. Robertson Smith, note on Ex **20** 26, *OTJC*, 435). The admission to this scene of the national solemnities was by the great east gate described in Ex **27** 13–16 (see EAST GATE).

2. Solomon's Temple

The fundamental conception out of which grew the resolve to build a temple for the worship of Jeh was that the new structure was to be an enlarged duplicate in stone of the tent of meeting (see TEMPLE). The doubling in size of the holy chambers was accompanied by a doubling of the inclosed area upon which the holy house was to stand. Hitherto a rectangular oblong figure of 150 ft. in length and 75 ft. in breadth had sufficed for the needs of the people in their worship. Now an area of 300 ft. in length and 150 ft. in breadth was inclosed within heavy stone walls, making, as before, two squares, each of 150 ft. This was that "court of the priests" spoken of in 2 Ch **4** 9, known to its builders as "the inner court" (1 K **6** 36; cf Jer **36** 10). Its walls consisted of "three courses of hewn stone, and a course of cedar beams" (1 K **6** 36), into which some read the meaning of colonnades. Its two divisions may have been marked by some fence. The innermost division, accessible only to the priests, was the site of the new temple. In the easterly division stood the altar of sacrifice; into this the Heb laity had access for worship at the altar. Later incidental allusions imply the existence of "chambers" in the court, and also the accessibility of the laity (cf Jer **35** 4; **36** 10; Ezk **8** 16).

3. The Great Court

In distinction from this "inner" court a second or "outer" court was built by Solomon, spoken of by the Chronicler as "the great court" (2 Ch **4** 9). Its doors were overlaid with brass (bronze). Wide difference of opinion obtains as to the relation of this outer court to the inner court just described, and to the rest of the Solomonic buildings—particularly to "the great court" of "the house of the forest of Lebanon" of 1 K **7** 9.10. Some identify the two, others separate them. Did this court, with its brass-covered gates, extend still farther to the E. than the temple "inner" court, with, however, the same breadth as the latter? Or was it, as Keil thinks, a much larger inclosure, surrounding the whole temple area, extending perhaps 150 cubits eastward in front of the priests' court (cf Keil, *Bib. Archaeology*, I, 171, ET)? Yet more radical is the view, adopted by many modern authorities, which regards "the great court" as a vast inclosure surrounding the temple and the whole complex of buildings described in 1 K **7** 1–12 (see the plan, after Stade, in G. A. Smith's *Jerusalem*, II, 59). In the absence of conclusive data the question must be left undetermined.

4. Ezekiel's Temple

In Ezekiel's plan of the temple yet to be built, the lines of the temple courts as he had known them in Jerus are followed. Two squares inclosed in stone walling, each of 150 ft., lie N. and S. of one another, and bear the distinctive names, "the inner court" and "the outer court" (Ezk **8** 16; **10** 5).

5. Temple of Herod

In the Herodian temple the old nomenclature gives place to a new set of terms. The extensive inclosure known later as "the court of the Gentiles" does not appear under that name in the NT or in Jos. What we have in the tract *Middōth* of the Mishnah and in Jos is the mention of two courts, the "court of the priests" and "the court of Israel" (*Middōth*, ii.6; v.1; Jos, *BJ*, V, v, 6). The data in regard to both are difficult and conflicting. In *Middōth* they appear as long narrow strips of 11 cubits in breadth extending at right angles to the temple and the altar across the inclosure—the "court of Israel" being railed off from the "court of the priests" on the E.; the latter extending backward as far as the altar, which has a distinct measurement. The design was to prevent the too near approach of the lay Israelite to the altar. Jos makes the 11 cubits of the "court of Israel" extend round the whole "court of the priests," inclusive of altar and temple (see TEMPLE; and cf G. A. Smith, *Jerusalem*, II, 506–9, with the reconstruction of Waterhouse in *Sacred Sites of the Gospels*, 111 ff). For the "women's court," see TREASURY.

Many expressions in the Pss show how great was the attachment of the devout-minded Heb in all ages to those courts of the Lord's house where he was accustomed to worship (e.g. Ps **65** 4; **84** 2; **92** 13; **96** 8; **100** 4; **116** 19). The courts were the scene of many historical events in the OT and NT, and of much of the earthly ministry of Jesus. There was enacted the scene described in the parable of the Pharisee and Publican (Lk **18** 10–14).

W. SHAW CALDECOTT

COURTS, JUDICIAL, jōō-dish'al, jū-dish'al: At the advice of Jethro, Moses appointed judges (שֹׁפְטִים, *shōphᵉṭīm*, Ex **18**). In Egypt

1. Their Organization

it appears that the Hebrews did not have their own judges, which, of course, was a source of many wrongs. Leaving Egypt, Moses took the judicial functions upon himself, but it was impossible that he should be equal to the task of administering justice to two and one-half million people; hence he proceeded to organize a system of jurisprudence. He appointed judges over tens, fifties, hundreds, thousands—in all 78,600 judges. This system was adequate for the occasion, and these courts respectively corresponded practically to our Justices of the Peace, Mayor's Court, District Court, Circuit Court. Finally, there was a Supreme Court under Moses and his successors. These courts, though graded, did not afford an opportunity of appeal. The lower courts turned their difficult cases over to the next higher. If the case was simple, the judge over tens would take it, but if the question was too intricate for him, he would refer it to the next higher court, and so on until it finally reached Moses. There were certain kinds of questions which the tens, fifties, and hundreds would not take at all, and the people understood it and would bring them to the higher courts for original jurisdiction. When any court decided it, that was the end of that case, for it could not be appealed (Ex **18** 25.26). On taking possession in Pal, the judges were to be appointed for every city and vicinity (Dt **16** 18), thus giving to all Israel a speedy and cheap method of adjudication. Though not so prescribed by the constitution, the judges at length were generally chosen from among the Levites, as the learned class. The office was elective. Jos states this plainly, and various passages of the Scriptures express it positively by inference (see Dt **1** 13). Jephthah's election by vote of the people is clearly set forth (Jgs **11** 5–11).

2. Character of the Judges

Among the Hebrews, the law was held very sacred; for God Himself had given it. Hence those who administered the law were God's special representatives, and their person was held correspondingly sacred. These circumstances placed upon them the duty of administering justice without respect to persons (Dt **1** 17; **16** 18). They were to be guided by the inalienable rights granted to every citizen by the Heb constitution: (1) No man was to be deprived of life, liberty or property without due process of law (Nu **35** 9–34). (2) Two or three witnesses were required to convict anyone of crime (Dt **17** 6; **19** 2–13). (3) Punishment for crime was not to be transferred or entailed (Dt **24** 16). (4) A man's home was inviolate (Dt **24** 10.11). (5) One held to bondage but having acquired liberty through his own effort should be protected (Dt **23** 15.16). (6) One's homestead was inalienable (Lev **25** 23–28.34). (7) Slavery could not be made perpetual without the person's own consent (Ex **21** 2–6).

3. Their Work

Gradually a legal profession developed among the Hebrews, the members of which were designated as "Lawyers" or "Scribes," also known as "Doctors of the Law" (Lk **2** 46). Their business was threefold: (1) to study and interpret the law; (2) to instruct the Heb youth in the law; and (3) to decide questions of the law. The first two they did as scholars and teachers; the last either as judges or as advisers in some court, as, for instance, the Senate of Jerus or some inferior tribunal. No code can go into such details as to eliminate the necessity of subsequent legislation, and this usually, to a great extent, takes the form of judicial decisions founded on the code, rather than of separate enactment; and so it was among the Hebrews. The provisions of their code were for the most part quite general, thus affording large scope for casuistic interpretation. Regarding the points not explicitly covered by the written law, a substitute must be found either in the form of established custom or in the form of an inference drawn from the statute. As a result of the industry with which this line of legal development was pursued during the cents. immediately preceding our era, Hebrew law became a most complicated science. For the disputed points, the judgments of the individual lawyers could not be taken as the standard; hence the several disciples of the law must frequently meet for a discussion, and the opinion of the majority then prevailed. These were the meetings of the "Doctors." Whenever a case arose concerning which there had been no clear legal decision, the question was referred to the nearest lawyer; by him, to the nearest company of lawyers, perhaps the Sanhedrin, and the resultant decision was henceforth authority.

Before the destruction of Jerus technical knowledge of the law was not a condition of eligibility to the office of judge. Anyone who could command the confidence of his fellow-citizens might be elected, and many of the rural courts undoubtedly were conducted, as among us, by men of sterling quality, but limited knowledge. Such men would avail themselves of the legal advice of any "doctor" who might be within reach; and in the more dignified courts of a large municipality it was a standing custom to have a company of lawyers present to discuss and decide any new law points that might arise. Of course, frequently these men were themselves elected to the office of judge, so that practically the entire system of jurisprudence was in their hands.

4. Limitations under Roman Rule

Though Judaea at this time was a subject commonwealth, yet the Sanhedrin, which was the body of supreme legislative and judicial authority, exercised autonomous authority to such an extent that it not only administered civil cases in accordance with Jewish law—for without such a right a Jewish court would be impossible—but it also took part to a great extent in the punishment of crime. It exercised an independent police power, hence could send out its own officers to make arrests (Mt **26** 47; Mk **14** 43; Acts **4** 3; **5** 17.18). In cases that did not involve capital punishment, its judgments were final and untrammeled (Acts **4** 2–23; **5** 21–40). Only in capital punishment cases must the consent of the procurator be secured, which is not only clearly stated in Jn **18** 31, but is also evident in the entire course of Christ's trial, as reported by the Synoptic Gospels. In granting or withholding his consent in such cases, the procurator could follow his pleasure absolutely, applying either the Jewish or Rom law, as his guide. In one class of cases the right to inflict capital punishment even on Rom citizens was granted the Sanhedrin, namely, when a non-Jewish person overstepped the bounds and entered the interior holy place of the temple. Even in this case the consent of the procurator must be secured, but it appears that the Rom rulers were inclined to let the law take its course against such wanton outrage of the Jews' feelings. Criminal cases not involving capital punishment need not be referred to the procurator.

5. Time and Place of Sessions

The city in which the Sanhedrin met was Jerus. To determine the particular building, and the spot on which the building stood, is interesting to the archaeologist, not to the student of law. The local courts usually held their sessions on the second and fifth day (Monday and Thursday) of the week, but we do not know whether the same custom was observed by the Great Sanhedrin. On feast days no court was held, much less on the Sabbath. Since the death penalty was not to be pronounced until the day after the trial, such cases were avoided also on the day preceding a Sabbath or other sacred day. The emphasis placed on this observance may be seen from the edicts issued by Augustus, absolving the Jews from the duty of attending court on the Sabbath. See DOCTOR; LAWYER; SANHEDRIN; SCRIBE.

FRANK E. HIRSCH

COUSIN, kuz′′n (**ἀνεψιός**, *anepsiós*): Only in Col **4** 10, where Mark is said to be "cousin" (RV) to Barnabas, and not as in AV, "sister's son." The renderings "cousin" of AV for *συγγενής*, *suggenḗs*, in Lk **1** 36.58 were probably understood at the time of the tr, in the wider, and not in the more restricted, sense of the term, now almost universally prevalent. In view of this the renderings "kinswoman," "kinsfolk" in RV are preferable. As a title of honor and dignity, it occurs in 1 Esd **4** 42, etc. See KINSMAN.

COUTHA, kou′tha, kōō′tha. See CUTHAH.

COVENANT, kuv′e-nant (**IN THE OT**) (**בְּרִית**, *b^erīth*):

I. General Meaning.—The etymological force of the Heb *b^erīth* is not entirely certain. It is probable that the word is the same as the Assyr *birîtu*, which has the common meaning "fetter," but also means "covenant." The significance of the root from which this Assyr word is derived is uncertain. It is probable that it is "to bind," but that is not definitely established. The meaning of *birîtu* as covenant seems to come directly from the root, rather than as a derived meaning from fetter. If this root idea is to bind, the covenant is that which binds together the parties. This, at any rate, is in harmony with the general meaning of the word.

In the OT the word has an ordinary use, when both parties are men, and a distinctly religious use, between God and men. There can be no doubt that the religious use has come from the ordinary, in harmony with the general custom in such cases, and not the reverse. There are also two shades of meaning, somewhat distinct, of the Heb word: one in which it is properly a covenant, i.e. a solemn mutual agreement, the other in which it is more a command, i.e. instead of an obligation voluntarily assumed, it is an obligation imposed by a superior upon an inferior. This latter meaning, however, has clearly been derived from the other. It is easy to see that an agreement, including as the contracting parties those of unequal position, might readily include those agreements which tended to partake of the nature of a command; but the process could not readily be reversed.

II. Among Men.—We consider first a covenant in which both contracting parties are men. In essence a covenant is an agreement, but an agreement of a solemn and binding force. The early Sem idea of a covenant was doubtless that which prevailed among the Arabs (see esp. W. Robertson Smith, *Religion of the Semites*, 2d ed, *passim*). This was primarily blood-brotherhood, in which two men became brothers by drinking each other's blood. Ordinarily this meant that one was adopted into the clan of the other. Hence this act involved the clan of one of the contracting parties, and also brought the other party into relation with

1. Early Idea

the god of this clan, by bringing him into the community life of the clan, which included its god. In this early idea, then, "primarily the covenant is not a special engagement to this or that particular effect, but bond of troth and life-fellowship to all the effects for which kinsmen are permanently bound together" (W. Robertson Smith, op. cit., 315 f). In this early ceremonial the religious idea was necessarily present, because the god was kindred to the clan; and the god had a special interest in the covenant, because he esp. protects the kindred blood, of which the stranger thus becomes a part. This religious side always persisted, although the original idea was much modified. In later usage there were various substitutes for the drinking of each other's blood, viz. drinking together the sacrificial blood, sprinkling it upon the parties, eating together the sacrificial meal, etc; but the same idea found expression in all, the community of life resulting from the covenant.

2. Principal Elements

The covenant in the OT shows considerable modification from the early idea. Yet it will doubtless help in understanding the OT covenant to keep in mind the early idea and form. Combining statements made in different accounts, the following seem to be the principal elements in a covenant between men. Some of the details, it is to be noted, are not explicitly stated in reference to these covenants, but may be inferred from those between God and men. (1) A statement of the terms agreed upon (Gen **26** 29; **31** 50.52). This was a modification of the earlier idea, which has been noted, in which a covenant was all-inclusive. (2) An oath by each party to observe the terms, God being witness of the oath (Gen **26** 31; **31** 48–53). The oath was such a characteristic feature that sometimes the term "oath" is used as the equivalent of covenant (see Ezk **17** 13). (3) A curse invoked by each one upon himself in case of disregard of the agreement. In a sense this may be considered a part of the oath, adding emphasis to it. This curse is not explicitly stated in the case of human covenants, but may be inferred from the covenant with God (Dt **27** 15–26). (4) The *formal* ratification of the covenant by some solemn external act. The different ceremonies for this purpose, such as have already been mentioned, are to be regarded as the later equivalents of the early act of drinking each other's blood. In the OT accounts it is not certain that such formal act is expressly mentioned in relation to covenants between men. It seems probable, however, that the sacrificial meal of Gen **31** 54 included Laban, in which case it was a covenant sacrifice. In any case, both sacrificial meal and sprinkling of blood upon the two parties, the altar representing Jeh, are mentioned in Ex **24** 4–8, with allusions elsewhere, in ratification of the covenant at Sinai between Jeh and Israel. In the covenant of God with Abraham is another ceremony, quite certainly with the same purpose. This is a peculiar observance, viz. the cutting of animals into two parts and passing between the severed portions (Gen **15** 9–18), a custom also referred to in Jer **34** 18. Here it is to be noted that it is a smoking furnace and a flaming torch, representing God, not Abraham, which passed between the pieces. Such an act, it would seem, should be shared by both parties, but in this case it is doubtless to be explained by the fact that the covenant is principally a promise by Jeh. He is the one who binds Himself. Concerning the significance of this act there is difference of opinion. A common view is that it is in effect a formal expression of the curse, imprecating upon oneself the same, i.e. cutting in pieces, if one breaks the terms of the covenant. But, as W. R. Smith has pointed out (op. cit., 481), this does not explain the passing between the pieces, which is the characteristic feature of the ceremony. It seems rather to be a symbol that the two parties "were taken within the mystical life of the victim." (Cf the interpretation of He **9** 15–17 in COVENANT IN THE NT.) It would then be an inheritance from the early times, in which the victim was regarded as kindred with the tribe, and hence also an equivalent of the drinking of each other's blood.

The immutability of a covenant is everywhere assumed, at least theoretically.

Other features beyond those mentioned cannot be considered as fundamental. This is the case with the setting up of a stone, or raising a heap of stones (Gen **31** 45.46). This is doubtless simply an ancient custom, which has no direct connection with the covenant, but comes from the ancient Sem idea of the sacredness of single stones or heaps of stones. Striking hands is a general expression of an agreement made (Ezr **10** 19; Ezk **17** 18, etc).

3. Different Varieties

In observing different varieties of agreements among men, we note that they may be either between individuals or between larger units, such as tribes and nations. In a great majority of cases, however, they are between the larger units. In some cases, also, when an individual acts it is in a representative capacity, as the head of a clan, or as a king. When the covenant is between tribes it is thus a treaty or alliance. The following passages have this use of covenant: Gen **14** 13; **21** 27.32; **26** 28; **31** 44; Ex **23** 32; **34** 12.15; Dt **7** 2; Josh **9** 6.7.11.15.16; Jgs **2** 2; 1 S **11** 1; 1 K **5** 12; **15** 19 ‖ 2 Ch **16** 3; 1 K **20** 34; Ps **83** 5; Isa **33** 8; Ezk **16** 61; **17** 13–19; **30** 5; Dnl **11** 22; Am **1** 9. In other cases it is between a king and his subjects, when it is more a command or ordinance, as 2 S **3** 12.13.21; **5** 3 ‖ 1 Ch **11** 3; Jer **34** 8–18; Dnl **9** 27. In other cases it is between individuals, or between small groups, where it is an agreement or pledge (2 K **11** 4 ‖ 2 Ch **23** 1; Job **31** 1; **41** 4; Hos **10** 4). Between David and Jonathan it is more specifically an alliance of friendship (1 S **18** 3; **20** 8; **23** 18), as also apparently in Ps **55** 20. It means an alliance of marriage in Mal **2** 14, but probably not in Prov **2** 17, where it is better to understand the meaning as being "her covenant with God."

4. Phraseology Used

In all cases of covenants between men, except Jer **34** 10 and Dnl **9** 27, the technical phrase for making a covenant is *kārath b^e^rīth*, in which *kārath* meant originally "to cut." Everything indicates that this vb. is used with reference to the formal ceremony of ratification above mentioned, of cutting animals in pieces.

III. Between God and Men.—As already noted, the idea of covenants between God and men doubtless arose from the idea of covenants between men. Hence the general thought is similar. It cannot in this case, however, be an agreement between contracting parties who stand on an equality, but God, the superior, always takes the initiative. To some extent, however, varying in different cases, it is regarded as a mutual agreement; God with His commands makes certain promises, and men agree to keep the commands, or, at any rate, the promises are conditioned on human obedience. In general, the covenant of God with men is a Divine ordinance, with signs and pledges on God's part, and with promises for human obedience and penalties for disobedience, which ordinance is accepted by men. In one passage (Ps **25** 14), it is used in a more general way of an alliance of friendship between God and man.

1. Essential Idea

A covenant of this general kind is said in the OT to have been made by God with Noah (Gen **9** 9–17 and elsewhere). In this the promise is that there shall be no more deluge. A covenant is made with Abraham, the thought of which includes his descendants. In this the promise of God is to multiply the descendants of Abraham, to give them the land of Canaan, and to make them a blessing to the nations. This is narrated in Gen **15** 18; **17** 2–21, etc. A covenant is made with the nation Israel at Sinai (Horeb) (Ex **19** 5; **24** 7.8; **34** 10.27.28, etc), ratified by a covenant sacrifice and sprinkling of blood (Ex **24** 4–8). This constituted the nation the peculiar people of God, and was accompanied by promises for obedience and penalties for disobedience. This covenant was renewed on the plains of Moab (Dt **29** 1). In these national covenants the individual had a place, but only as a member of the nation. The individual might forfeit his rights under the covenant, however, by deliberate rebellion against Jeh, sinning "with a high hand" (Nu **15** 30 f), and then he was regarded as no longer a member of the nation, he was "cut off from among his people," i.e. put to death. This is the teaching of P, and is also implied elsewhere; in the mercy of God, however, the punishment was not always inflicted. A covenant with the tribe of Levi, by which that became the priestly tribe, is alluded to in Dt **33** 9; Jer **33** 21; Mal **2** 4 ff. The covenant with Phinehas (Nu **25** 12.13) established an everlasting priesthood in his line. The covenant with Joshua and Israel (Josh **24**) was an agreement on their part to serve Jeh only. The covenant with David (2 S **7** ‖ 1 Ch **17**; see also Ps **89** 3.28.34.39; **132** 12; Jer **33** 21) contained a promise that his descendants should have an everlasting kingdom, and should stand to God in the relation of sonship. The covenant with Jehoiada and the people (2 K **11** 17 ‖ 2 Ch **23** 3) was an agreement on their part to be the people of Jeh. The covenant with Hezekiah and the people (2 Ch **29** 10) consisted essentially of an agreement on their part to reform the worship; the covenant with Josiah and the people (2 K **23** 3), of an agreement on their part to obey the Book of the Law. The covenant with Ezra and the people (Ezr **10** 3) was an agreement on their part to put away foreign wives and obey the law. The prophets also speak of a new covenant, most explicitly in Jer, but with references elsewhere, which is connected with the Messianic time (see Isa **42** 6; **49** 8; **55** 3; **59** 21; **61** 8; Jer **31** 31.33; **32** 40; **50** 5; Ezk **16** 60.62; **20** 37; **34** 25; **37** 26; Hos **2** 18).

2. Covenants Recorded in the OT

3. Phraseology Used

Various phrases are used of the making of a covenant between God and men. The vb. ordinarily used of making covenants between men, *kārath*, is often used here as well. The following vbs. are also used: *hēḳīm*, "to establish" or "confirm"; *nāthan*, "to give"; *sīm*, "to place"; *çiwwāh*, "to command"; *'ābhar*, "to pass over," followed by *b^e^*, "into"; *bō'*, "to enter," followed by *b^e^*; and the phrase *nāsā' b^e^rīth 'al pī*, "to take up a covenant upon the mouth of someone."

4. History of Covenant Idea

The history of the covenant idea in Israel, as between God and man, is not altogether easy to trace. This applies esp. to the great covenants between God and Israel, viz. the one with Abraham, and the one made at Sinai. The earliest references to this relation of Israel to Jeh under the term "covenant" are in Hos **6** 7; **8** 1. The interpretation of the former passage is doubtful in details, but the reference to such a covenant seems clear. The latter is considered by many a

later addition, but largely because of this mention of the covenant. No other references to such a covenant are made in the prophets before Jeremiah. Jeremiah and Ezekiel speak of it, and it is implied in Second-Isaiah. It is a curious fact, however, that most of the later prophets do not use the term, which suggests that the omission in the earlier prophets is not very significant concerning a knowledge of the idea in early times.

In this connection it should be noted that there is some variation among the Hexateuchal codes in their treatment of the covenants. Only one point, however, needs special mention. P gives no explicit account of the covenant at Sinai, and puts large emphasis upon the covenant with Abraham. There are, however, apparent allusions to the Sinaitic covenant (Lev **2** 13; **24** 8; **26** 9.15.25.44.45). The facts indicate, therefore, principally a difference of emphasis.

In the light partly of the facts already noted, however, it is held by many that the covenant idea between God and man is comparatively late. This view is that there were no covenants with Abraham and at Sinai, but that in Israel's early conceptions of the relation to Jeh He was their tribal God, bound by *natural* ties, not *ethical* as the covenant implies. This is a larger question than at first appears. Really the whole problem of the relation of Israel to Jeh throughout OT history is involved, in particular the question at what time a comprehensive conception of the ethical character of God was developed. The subject will therefore naturally receive a fuller treatment in other articles. It is perhaps sufficient here to express the conviction that there was a very considerable conception of the ethical character of Jeh in the early history of Israel, and that consequently there is no sufficient reason for doubting the fact of the covenants with Abraham and at Sinai. The statement of W. Robertson Smith expresses the essence of the matter (op. cit., 319): "That Jeh's relation is not natural but ethical is the doctrine of the prophets, and is emphasized, in dependence on their teaching, in the Book of Dt. But the passages cited show that the idea has its foundation in pre-prophetic times; and indeed the prophets, though they give it fresh and powerful application, plainly do not regard the conception as an innovation."

A little further consideration should be given to the **new covenant** of the prophets. The general teaching is that the covenant was broken by the sins of the people which led to the exile. Hence during the exile the people had been cast off, the covenant was no longer in force. This is stated, using other terminology, in Hos **3** 3 f; **1** 9; **2** 2. The prophets speak, however, in anticipation, of the making of a covenant again after the return from the exile. For the most part, in the passages already cited, this covenant is spoken of as if it were the old one renewed. Special emphasis is put, however, upon its being an everlasting covenant, as the old one did not prove to be, implying that it will not be broken as was that one. Jeremiah's teaching, however, has a little different emphasis. He speaks of the old covenant as passed away (**31** 32). Accordingly he speaks of a new covenant (**31** 31.33). This new covenant in its provisions, however, is much like the old. But there is a new emphasis upon individuality in approach to God. In the old covenant, as already noted, it was the nation as a whole that entered into the relation; here it is the individual, and the law is to be written upon the individual heart.

In the later usage the specific covenant idea is sometimes less prominent, so that the term is used practically of the religion as a whole; see Isa **56** 4; Ps **103** 18.

LITERATURE.—Valeton, *ZATW*, XII, XIII (1892–93); Candlish, *Expos T*, 1892, Oct , Nov.; Kraetzschmar, *Die Bundesvorstellung im AT*, Marburg, 1896; arts. "Covenant" in *HDB* and *EB*.

GEORGE RICKER BERRY

COVENANT (IN THE NT): Διαθήκη, *Diathḗkē*, was the word chosen by the LXX translators to render the Heb *b^erīth*, and it appears thus nearly 300 times in the Gr OT in the sense of covenant, while *sunthḗkē* and *entolaí* are each used once only. The choice of this word seems to have been occasioned by a recognition that the covenant which God makes with men is not fully mutual as would be implied in *sunthēkē*, the Gr word commonly used for covenant (although not a NT word), while at the same time the rarity of wills among the Jews made the common sense of *diathēkē* relatively unfamiliar. The Apocryphal writers also frequently use the same word in the same sense and no other.

In the NT *diathēkē* is used some thirty times in a way which makes it plain that its tr must be "covenant." In Gal **3** 15 and He **9** 15–17 it is held by many that the sense of covenant must be set aside in favor of will or testament. But in the former passage it can be taken in the sense of a disposition of affairs or arrangement made by God, a conception in substantial harmony with its regular NT use and with the sense of *b^erīth*. In the passage in He the interpretation is more difficult, but as it is acknowledged on all hands that the passage loses all argumentative force if the meaning testament is accepted, it seems best to retain the meaning covenant if possible. To do this it is only necessary to hold that the death spoken of is the death of the animal sometimes, if not, indeed, commonly slain in connection with the making of a covenant, and that in the mind of the author this death symbolized the death of the contracting parties so far at least as to pledge them that thereafter in the matter involved they would no more change their minds than can the dead. If this view is taken, this passage falls in line with the otherwise invariable use of the word *diathēkē* by Jewish Hellenists. See TESTAMENT.

LITERATURE.—Lightfoot, *Comm. on Gal;* Ramsay, *Comm. on Gal;* Westcott, *Comm. on Hebrews;* art. on He **9** 15–17, *Baptist Review and Expos.*, July, 1904.

DAVID FOSTER ESTES

COVENANT, kuv'e-nant, kuv'ĕ-nant, **ARK OF THE.** See ARK OF THE COVENANT.

COVENANT OF SALT, sôlt (בְּרִית מֶלַח, *b^erīth melaḥ;* **ἅλας,** *hálas*, classical Gr **ἅλς,** *háls*): As salt was regarded as a necessary ingredient of the daily food, and so of all sacrifices offered to Jeh (Lev **2** 13), it became an easy step to the very close connection between salt and covenant-making. When men ate together they became friends. Cf the Arab. expression, "There is salt between us"; "He has eaten of my salt," which means partaking of hospitality which cemented friendship; cf "eat the salt of the palace" (Ezr **4** 14). Covenants were generally confirmed by sacrificial meals and salt was always present. Since, too, salt is a preservative, it would easily become symbolic of an enduring covenant. So offerings to Jeh were to be by a statute for ever, "a covenant of salt for ever before Jeh" (Nu **18** 19). David received his kingdom forever from Jeh by a "covenant of salt" (2 Ch **13** 5). In the light of these conceptions the remark of Our Lord becomes the more significant: "Have salt in yourselves, and be at peace one with another" (Mk **9** 50).

EDWARD BAGBY POLLARD

COVENANT, THE BOOK OF THE (סֵפֶר הַבְּרִית, *ṣēpher ha-b^erīth*):

1. Historical Connection
2. Analysis
3. Critical Theories
4. True, or Biblical Conception
5. Nature of the Laws

LITERATURE

The name given in Ex **24** 7 to a code or collection of laws found in the preceding chapters, **20–23**, as the terms of the covenant made with Jeh, and given for Israel's guidance until a more complete legislation should be provided. In this covenant between Jeh and Israel, Moses served as mediator; animals were sacrificed, the blood thus shed being also called "the blood of the covenant" (*dam hab^e rīth*, Ex **24** 8).

This brief book of laws occupies a fitting and clearly marked place in the Pentateuchal collection.

1. Historical Connection

Examination of the historical context shows that it is put where it belongs and belongs where it is put. A few months after the Exodus (Ex **19** 1) Israel arrived at Sinai. Immediately at the command which Moses had received from Jeh in the Mount, they prepared themselves by a ceremonial of sanctification for entrance into covenant relation with Jeh. When the great day arrived for making this covenant, Moses in the midst of impressive natural phenomena went again to meet Jeh in the top of the mountain. On his return (Ex **19** 25), the words of the law, or the terms of the covenant, were declared to the people, and accepted by them. The first part of these covenant-terms, viz. the Decalogue (Ex **20** 2–17), was spoken by the Divine voice, or its declaration was accompanied by awe-inspiring natural convulsions (Ex **20** 18). Therefore in response to the pleadings of the terrified people Moses went up again into the mountain and received from Jeh for them the rest of the "words" and "ordinances" (**24** 3); and these constitute the so-called Book of the Covenant (**20** 22—**23**). In this direct and unequivocal manner the narrator connected the book with the nation's consecration at Sinai. The prophets regarded the making of the Sinaitic covenant as the marriage of Israel and Jeh, and these laws were the terms mutually agreed upon in the marriage contract.

While it is not possible to arrange the materials of this document into hard-and-fast divisions, the following analysis may be suggestive and serviceable:

2. Analysis

(1) directions concerning worship, specifying prohibition of images and the form of altar for animal sacrifices (**20** 23–26); (2) ordinances for protection of Heb slaves, including betrothal, for a price, of a daughter (**21** 2–11); (3) laws concerning injuries, (*a*) to man by man (vs 12–27), (*b*) to man by beast (vs 28–32), (*c*) to beast by man (vs 33.34), (*d*) to beast by beast (vs 35.36); (4) concerning theft (**22** 1–4); (5) concerning damage to a neighbor's property, including violence to his daughter (vs 5–17); (6) sundry laws against profaning Jeh's name, under which are included proper worship, avoidance of oppression and dutiful offering of first-fruits (vs 18–31); (7) against various forms of injustice and unbrotherliness (**23** 1–9); (8) festal occasions, including the Sabbatical year and the three annual feasts: unleavened bread, first-fruits and ingathering (vs 10–17); (9) warning against certain wrong practices in their sacrifices (vs 18.19); (10) in conclusion, a promise of God's continual presence with them in the person of His Angel, and the consequent triumph over enemies (vs 20–33).

In this legislation are found two forms of laws or deliverances: (1) the ordinances (*mishpāṭīm*), which deal principally with civil and moral matters, are like court decisions, and are introduced by the hypothetical "if"; (2) words, or commands (*d^e bhārīm*), which relate chiefly to religious duties, being introduced by the imperative "thou shalt."

3. Critical Theories

The critical analysis and dismemberment of the books of Moses, if accepted, renders the simple historical explanation of the introduction to this body of laws untrue and impossible. The four chapters are assigned to JE, the Decalogue to E, and the Book of the Covenant to J or E, the repetition of the Decalogue in chs **32–34** being J's account. Ordinarily the Book of the Covenant is held to be earlier than the Decalogue, and is indeed the oldest body of Heb legislation. However, it could not have been given at one time, nor in the wilderness, since the laws are given for those in agricultural life, and seem to be decisions made at various times and finally gathered together. Furthermore, this more primitive code either contradicts the later legislation of D and P or reveals an entirely different point of view. The chief contradictions or divergences are: nature and number of altars, absence of an official priestly class, and simpler conception of the annual feasts as agricultural celebrations. JE came into united form in the 9th or 8th cent., but this body of laws existed much earlier, embodying the earliest legal developments of Heb life in Canaan. It is suggested by some, as Driver, *LOT*, although he does not attempt the analysis, that this code is itself a composite of various layers and ages. See CRITICISM (GRAF-WELLHAUSEN HYPOTHESIS).

But in favor of the simpler interpretation of these laws as the ethical obligations of the new bond between Jeh and Israel some statements deserve to be made.

4. True, or Biblical Conception

If a solemn league and covenant was made at Sinai—and to this all the history, all the prophets and the Psalms give testimony—there must have been some statement of the germinal and fundamental elements of the nation's moral relation to Jeh. Such statement need not be final nor exhaustive, but rather intended to instruct and guide until later and more detailed directions might be given. This is exactly the position and claim of the Book of the Covenant; and that this was the thought of the editor of the Pent, and that this is the first and reasonable impression made by the unsuspecting and connected reading of the record, can hardly be questioned by candid minds. In answer to the criticism that the agricultural flavor of the laws presupposes settlement in Canaan—a criticism rather remarkable for its bland ignorance—it may be suggested: (1) Israel had occupied in Egypt an agricultural section, and must have been able either to form or to receive a body of laws dealing with agricultural pursuits. (2) They were on the march toward a land in which they should have permanent settlement in agricultural life; and not the presence of allusions to such life, but rather their absence, should cause surprise. (3) However, references to settled farm life are not so obtrusively frequent as those seeking signs would have us think. References to the animal life of the flock and herd of a shepherd people, such as the Israelites were at Sinai, are far more frequent (**21** 28.33.35; **22** 1.10; **23** 4, etc). The laws are quite generic in form and conception, enforcing such duties as would devolve upon both temporary nomad and prospective tillers of the soil. R. B. Taylor therefore (art. in one-vol *HDB*) accepts this code as originating in the desert wanderings.

In answer to the view, best presented by Wellhausen in *Proleg.* and W. R. Smith in *OTJC*, that this code is in conflict with later legislation, it may be said that the Book of the Covenant, as an ethical and civil summary, is in its proper place in the narrative of the sojourn at Sinai, and does not preclude the expectancy of more elaborate organization of both ceremonial and civil order. But the whole question relates more properly to discussion of the later legislation or of the particular topics in dispute (q.v.). For a thorough treatment of them consult W. H. Green, *Heb Feasts*.

In the Book of the Covenant the moral elements strongly emphasized are:

5. Nature of the Laws

simplicity, directness and spirituality of worship; a high and equitable standard of right; highest consideration for the weak and the poor; humane treatment of dumb animals; purity in the relations of life; the spirit of brotherhood; and the simple and joyful life. Whatever development in details came with later legislation

did not nullify the simple but lofty standards of the earlier laws.

LITERATURE.—Driver, *LOT*, under "Exodus"; Wellhausen, *PHI; Comp. d. Hex;* W. R. Smith, *OTJC;* W. H. Green, *Heb Feasts; Higher Crit of Pent;* Dillmann, *Comm. Ex-Lev.*

EDWARD MACK

COVENANT, THE NEW (בְּרִית חֲדָשָׁה, *b^e rīth ḥădhāshāh*, Jer **31** 31; ἡ διαθήκη καινή, *hē diathēkē kainē*, He **8** 8.13, etc, or νέα, *néa*, He **12** 24: the former Gr adj. has the sense of the "new" primarily in reference to quality, the latter the sense of "young," the "new," primarily in reference to time):

1. Contrast of "New" and "Old"—The Term "Covenant"
2. Christ's Use at the Last Supper
3. Relation to Ex **24**
4. Use in Ep. to the Hebrews
5. The Mediator of the New Covenant
6. "Inheritance" and "Testament"
7. Relation to Jer **31** 31–34
8. To Ezekiel
9. Contrast of Old and New in 2 Cor **3**

The term "New" Covenant necessarily implies an "Old" Covenant, and we are reminded that God's dealings with His people in the various dispensations of the world's history have been in terms of covenant. The Holy Scriptures by their most familiar title keep this thought before us, the OT and the NT or Covenant; the writings produced within the Jewish "church" being the writings or Scriptures of the Old Covenant, those within the Christian church, the Scriptures of the New Covenant. The alternative name "Testament"—adopted into our Eng. description through the Lat, as the equivalent of the Heb *b^e rīth*, and the Gr *diathēkē*, which both mean a solemn disposition, compact or contract—suggests the disposition of property in a last will or testament, but although the word *diathēkē* may bear that meaning, the Heb *b^e rīth* does not, and as the Gr usage in the NT seems esp. governed by the OT usage and the thought moves in a similar plane, it is better to keep to the term "covenant." The one passage which seems to favor the "testament" idea is He **9** 16.17 (the Revisers who have changed the AV "testament" into "covenant" in every other place have left it in these two vs), but it is questionable whether even here the better rendering would not be "covenant" (see below). Certainly in the immediate context "covenant" is the correct tr and, confessedly, "testament," if allowed to stand, is an application by transition from the original thought of a solemn compact to the secondary one of testamentary disposition. The theological terms "Covenant of Works" and "Covenant of Grace" do not occur in Scripture, though the ideas covered by the terms, esp. the latter, may easily be found there. The "New Covenant" here spoken of is practically equivalent to the Covenant of Grace established between God and His redeemed people, that again resting upon the eternal Covenant of Redemption made between the Father and the Son, which, though not so expressly designated, is not obscurely indicated by many passages of Scripture.

1. Contrast of "New" and "Old"—the Term "Covenant"

Looking at the matter more particularly, we have to note the words of Christ at the institution of the Supper. In all the three Synoptists, as also in Paul's account (Mt **26** 28; Mk **14** 24; Lk **22** 20; 1 Cor **11** 25) "covenant" occurs. Mt and Mk, "my blood of the [new] covenant"; Lk and Paul, "the new covenant in my blood." The Revisers following the critical text, have omitted "new" in Mt and Mk, but even if it does not belong to the original MS, it is implied, and there need be little doubt that Jesus used it. The old covenant was so well known to these Jewish disciples, that to speak of *the* covenant in this emphatic way, referring manifestly to something other than the old Mosaic covenant, was in effect to call it a "new" covenant. The expression, in any case, looks back to the old and points the contrast; but in the contrast there are points of resemblance.

2. Christ's Use at Last Supper

It is most significant that Christ here connects the "new" covenant with His "blood." We at once think, as doubtless the disciples would think, of the transaction described in Ex **24** 7, when Moses "took the book of the covenant, and read in the audience of the people" those "words," indicating God's undertaking on behalf of His people and what He required of them; "and they said, All that Jeh hath spoken will we do, and be obedient," thus taking up their part of the contract. Then comes the ratification. "Moses took the blood [half of which had already been sprinkled on the altar], and sprinkled it on the people, and said, Behold the blood of the covenant, which Jeh hath made with you concerning all these words" (ver 8). The blood was sacrificial blood, the blood of the animals sacrificed as burnt offerings and peace offerings (Ex **24** 5.6). The one half of the blood sprinkled on the altar tells of the sacrifice offered to God, the other half sprinkled on the people, of the virtue of the same sacrifice applied to the people, and so the covenant relation is fully brought about. Christ, by speaking of His blood in this connection, plainly indicates that His death was a sacrifice, and that through that sacrifice His people would be brought into a new covenant relationship with God. His sacrifice is acceptable to God and the virtue of it is to be applied to believers—so all the blessings of the new covenant are secured to them; the blood "is poured out for you" (Lk **22** 20). He specifically mentions one great blessing of the new covenant, the forgiveness of sins—"which is poured out for many unto remission of sins" (Mt **26** 28).

3. Relation to Ex 24

This great thought is taken up in He and fully expounded. The writer draws out fully the contrast between the new covenant and the old by laying stress upon the perfection of Christ's atonement in contrast to the material and typical sacrifices (He **9** 11–23). He was "a high priest of the good things to come," connected with "the greater and more perfect tabernacle." He entered the heavenly holy place "through his own blood," not that of "goats and calves," and by that perfect offering He has secured "eternal redemption" in contrast to the temporal deliverance of the old dispensation. The blood of those typical offerings procured ceremonial cleansing; much more, therefore, shall the blood of Christ avail to cleanse the conscience "from dead works to serve the living God"—that blood which is so superior in value to the blood of the temporal sacrifices, yet resembles it in being sacrificial blood. It is the blood of Him "who, through the eternal Spirit offered himself without blemish unto God." It is the fashion in certain quarters nowadays to say that it is not the blood of Christ, but His spirit of self-sacrifice for others, that invests the cross with its saving power, and this verse is sometimes cited to show that the virtue lies in the surrender of the perfect will, the shedding of the blood being a mere accident. But this is not the view of the NT writers. The blood-shedding is to them a necessity. Of course, it is not the natural, material blood, or the mere act of shedding it, that saves. The blood is the life. The blood is the symbol of life; the blood shed is the symbol of life outpoured—of the penalty borne; and while great emphasis must be laid, as in this verse it is laid, upon Christ's perfect surrender of His holy will to God, yet the essence of the matter is found

4. Use in Ep. to the Hebrews

in the fact that He willingly endured the dread consequences of sin, and as a veritable expiatory sacrifice shed His precious blood for the remission of sins.

5. The Mediator of the New Covenant

On the ground of that shed blood, as the writer goes on to assert, "He is the mediator of a new covenant, that a death having taken place for the redemption of the transgressions that were under the first covenant, they that have been called may receive the promise of the eternal inheritance" (ver 15). Thus Christ fulfils the type in a twofold way: He is the sacrifice upon which the covenant is based, whose blood ratifies it, and He is also, like Moses, the Mediator of the covenant. The death of Christ not only secures the forgiveness of those who are brought under the new covenant, but it was also for the redemption of the transgressions under the first covenant, implying that all the sacrifices gained their value by being types of Christ, and the forgiveness enjoyed by the people of God in former days was bestowed in virtue of the great Sacrifice to be offered in the fulness of time.

6. "Inheritance" and "Testament"

Not only does the blessing of perfect forgiveness come through the new covenant, but also the promise of the "eternal inheritance" in contrast to the earthly inheritance which, under the old covenant, Israel obtained. The mention of the inheritance is held to justify the taking of the word in the next verse as "testament," the writer passing to the thought of a testamentary disposition, which is only of force after the death of the testator. Undoubtedly there is good ground for the analogy, and all the blessings of salvation which come to the believer may be considered as bequeathed by the Saviour in His death, and accruing to us because He has died. It has, in that sense, tacitly to be assumed that the testator lives again to be His own executor and to put us in possession of the blessings. Still, we think there is much to be said in favor of keeping to the sense of "covenant" even here, and taking the clause, which, rendered lit., is: "a covenant is of force [or firm] over the dead," as meaning that the covenant is established on the ground of sacrifice, that sacrifice representing the death of the maker of the covenant. The allusion may be further explained by a reference to Gen **15** 9.10.17, which has generally been considered as illustrating the ancient Sem method of making a covenant: the sacrificial animals being divided, and the parties passing between the pieces, implying that they deserved death if they broke the engagement. The technical Heb phrase for making a covenant is "to cut a covenant."

There is an interesting passage in Herodotus iii.8, concerning an Arabian custom which seems akin to the old Heb practice. "The Arabians observe pledges as religiously as any people; and they make them in the following manner; when any wish to pledge their faith, a third person standing between the two parties makes an incision with a sharp stone in the palm of the hand, nearest the longest fingers of both the contractors; then taking some of the nap from the garments of each, he smears seven stones placed between him and the blood; and as he does this he invokes Bacchus and Urania. When this ceremony is completed, the person who pledges his faith binds his friends as sureties to the stranger, or the citizen, if the contract is made with a citizen, and the friends also hold themselves obliged to observe the engagement"—Cary's tr.

Whatever the particular application of the word in ver 17, the central idea in the passage is that death, blood-shedding, is necessary to the establishment of the covenant, and so he affirms that the first covenant was not dedicated without blood, and in proof quotes the passage already cited from Ex **24**, and concludes that "apart from shedding of blood there is no remission" (ver 22). See COVENANT IN NT.

7. Relation to Jer 31:31–34

This new covenant established by Christ was foretold by the prophet Jeremiah, who uses the very word "new covenant" in describing it, and very likely Christ had that description in mind when He used the term, and meant His disciples to understand that the prophetic interpretation would in Him be realized. There is no doubt that the author of He had the passage in mind, for he has led up to the previous statement by definitely quoting the whole statement of Jer **31** 31–34. He had in ch **7** spoken of the contrast between Christ's priesthood "after the order of Melchizedek" (ver 11) and the imperfect Aaronic priesthood, and he designates Jesus as "the surety of a better covenant" (ver 22). Then in ch **8**, emphasizing the thought of the superiority of Christ's heavenly high-priesthood, he declares that Christ is the "mediator of a better covenant, which hath been enacted upon better promises" (ver 6). The first covenant, he says, was not faultless, otherwise there would have been no need for a second; but the fault was not in the covenant but in the people who failed to keep it, though perhaps there is also the suggestion that the external imposition of laws could not suffice to secure true obedience. "For finding fault with them he saith, Behold the days come, saith the Lord, that I will make a new covenant with the house of Israel and with the house of Judah." The whole passage (chs **8–12**) would repay careful study, but we need only note that not only is there prominence given to the great blessings of the covenant, perfect forgiveness and fulness of knowledge, but, as the very essence of the covenant—that which serves to distinguish it from the old covenant and at once to show its superiority and guarantee its permanence—there is this wonderful provision: "I will put my laws into their mind, and on their heart also will I write them: and I will be to them a God, and they shall be to me a people." This at once shows the spirituality of the new covenant. Its requirements are not simply given in the form of external rules, but the living Spirit possesses the heart; the law becomes an internal dominating principle, and so true obedience is secured.

8. To Ezekiel

Ezekiel had spoken to the same effect, though the word "new covenant" is not used in the passage, ch **36** 27: "I will put my Spirit within you, and cause you to walk in my statutes, and ye shall keep mine ordinances, and do them." In ch **37** Ezekiel again speaks of the great blessings to be enjoyed by the people of God, including cleansing, walking in God's statutes, recognition as God's people, etc, and he distinctly says of this era of blessing: "I will make a covenant of peace with them; it shall be an everlasting covenant with them" (ver 26). Other important foreshadowings of the new covenant are found in Isa **54** 10; **55** 3; **59** 21; **61** 8; Hos **2** 18–23; Mal **3** 1–4. We may well marvel at the spiritual insight of these prophets, and it is impossible to attribute their forecasts to natural genius; they can only be accounted for by Divine inspiration.

The writer to the Hebrews recurs again and again to this theme of the "New Covenant"; in **10** 16.17 he cites the words of Jeremiah already quoted about writing the law on their minds, and remembering their sins no more. In **12** 24, he speaks of "Jesus the mediator of a new covenant," and "the blood of sprinkling," again connecting the "blood" with the "covenant," and finally, in **13** 20, he prays for the perfection of the saints through the "blood of an eternal covenant."

In 2 Cor **3** Paul has an interesting and instructive contrast between the old covenant and the new. He begins it by saying that "our sufficiency is

from God; who also made us sufficient as ministers of a new covenant; not of the letter, but of the spirit: for the letter killeth, but the Spirit giveth life" (vs 5.6). The "letter" is the letter of the law, of the old covenant which could only bring condemnation, but the spirit which characterizes the new covenant gives life, writes the law upon the heart. He goes on to speak of the old as that "ministration of death" which nevertheless "came with glory" (ver 7), and he refers esp. to the law, but the new covenant is "the ministration of the spirit," the "ministration of righteousness" (vs 8.9), and has a far greater glory than the old. The message of this "new covenant" is "the gospel of Christ." The glory of the new covenant is focused in Christ; rays forth from Him. The glory of the old dispensation was reflected upon the face of Moses, but that glory was transitory and so was the physical manifestation (ver 13). The sight of the shining face of Moses awed the people of Israel and they revered him as a leader specially favored of God (vs 7–13). When he had delivered his message he veiled his face and thus the people could not see that the glow did not last; every time that he went into the Divine presence he took off the veil and afresh his face was lit up with the glory, and coming out with the traces of that glory lingering on his countenance he delivered his message to the people and again veiled his face (cf Ex **34** 29–35), and thus the transitoriness and obscurity of the old dispensation were symbolized. In glorious contrast to that symbolical obscurity, the ministers of the gospel, of the new covenant, use great boldness of speech; the veil is done away in Christ (vs 12 ff). The glory which comes through Him is perpetual, and fears no vanishing away.

9. Contrast of Old and New in 2 Cor 3

ARCHIBALD M'CAIG

COVER, kuv'ẽr, **COVERING,** kuv'ẽr-ing: The tr of several Heb words. The covering of the ark (מִכְסֶה, *mikhṣeh*, Gen **8** 13) was possibly the lid of a hatchway (cf Mitchell, *World before Abraham*, 215).

To the sons of Kohath was assigned the task of caring for the furniture of the Tabernacle whenever the camp was moved, a suitable covering (כָּסָה, *kāṣāh*) of sealskin being designated for each of the specially sacred objects, the temple curtains also being used (Nu **4** 8.9.11.12 ff).

Nu **19** 15 (*çāmīdh*) may refer to anything used as a lid or covering; Job **24** 7; **31** 19 (*keṣūth*) refer to clothing or bed-covering.

Figurative: "Abaddon hath no covering" (*keṣūth*) from God (Job **26** 6); "He will destroy . . . . the face of the covering [*ha-lōṭ*] that covereth all peoples" (Isa **25** 7). The removal of the veil, often worn as a token of mourning (cf 2 S **19** 4), signified the destruction of death. W. N. STEARNS

COVERED WAY, kuv'ẽrd wā (מֵיסָךְ, *mēṣākh*, "a covered walk"): Mentioned in 2 K **16** 18 (AV "covert") as a gallery belonging to the temple, concerning the purpose of which opinions differ. Some consider it to have been the place where the king stood or sat during the Sabbath services; others, a public place for teaching; others, the way by which the priest entered the sanctuary on the Sabbath.

COVERING, kuv'ẽr-ing, **FOR THE HEAD** (**περιβόλαιον,** *peribólaion*): Mentioned in the NT only in 1 Cor **11** 15: "For her hair is given her for a covering," lit. "something cast round," probably equivalent to "veil" (q.v.). Read in the light of the context: "Every woman praying or prophesying with her head unveiled dishonoreth her head" (ver 5). The meaning would seem to be that Nature itself, in providing women with a natural veil, has taught the lesson underlying the prevailing custom, that woman should not be unveiled in the public assemblies. GEO. B. EAGER

COVERT, kuv'ẽrt: Now seldom used, except for game, and then generally spelt "cover." "A covered way" (2 K **16** 18 AV); also a shelter of any kind (Isa **4** 6); "a hiding place," "a lair," "a hut" (Job **38** 40); "a place of secrecy," "a secret way" (1 S **25** 20; Job **40** 21; Ps **61** 4; Isa **16** 4; **32** 2); "a den," "a lair" (Jer **25** 38).

COVET, kuv'et (אָוָה, *'āwāh;* ζηλόω, *zēlóō*, "to desire earnestly," "to set the heart and mind upon anything"): Used in two senses: *good*, simply to desire earnestly but legitimately, e.g. AV 1 Cor **12** 31; **14** 39; *bad*, to desire unlawfully, or to secure illegitimately (בָּצַע, *bāça'; ἐπιθυμέω, epithuméō*, Rom **7** 7; **13** 9, etc); hence called "lust" (Mt **5** 28; 1 Cor **10** 6), "concupiscence" (AV Rom **7** 8; Col **3** 5).

COVETOUSNESS, kuv'et-us-nes: Has a variety of shades of meaning determined largely by the nature of the particular word used, or the context, or both. Following are some of the uses: (1) To gain dishonestly (בָּצַע, *bāça'*), e.g. AV Ex **18** 21; Ezk **33** 31. (2) The wish to have more than one possesses, inordinately, of course (πλεονεξία, *pleonexía*), e.g. Lk **12** 15; 1 Thess **2** 5. (3) An inordinate love of money (*φιλάργυρος, philárguros*, AV Lk **16** 14; 2 Tim **3** 2; *philarguría*, 1 Tim **6** 10); negative in He **13** 5 AV.

Covetousness is a very grave sin; indeed, so heinous is it that the Scriptures class it among the very gravest and grossest crimes (Eph **5** 3). In Col **3** 5 it is "idolatry," while in 1 Cor **6** 10 it is set forth as excluding a man from heaven. Its heinousness, doubtless, is accounted for by its being in a very real sense the *root* of so many other forms of sin, e.g. departure from the faith (1 Tim **6** 9.10); lying (2 K **5** 22–25); theft (Josh **7** 21); domestic trouble (Prov **15** 27); murder (Ezk **22** 12); indeed, it leads to "many foolish and hurtful lusts" (1 Tim **6** 9). Covetousness has always been a very serious menace to mankind, whether in the OT or NT period. It was one of the first sins that broke out after Israel had entered into the promised land (Achan, Josh **7**); and also in the early Christian church immediately after its founding (Ananias and Sapphira, Acts **5**); hence so many warnings against it. A careful reading of the OT will reveal the fact that a very great part of the Jewish law—such as its enactments and regulations regarding duties toward the poor, toward servants; concerning gleaning, usury, pledges, gold and silver taken during war—was introduced and intended to counteract the spirit of covetousness.

Eerdmans maintains (*Expos*, July, 1909) that the commandment, "Thou shalt not covet thy neighbor's house" (Ex **20** 17), meant to the Israelite that he should not take anything of his neighbor's possessions that were momentarily unprotected by their owner. Cf Ex **34** 23 ff. Thus, it refers to a category of acts that is not covered by the commandment, "Thou shalt not steal." It is an oriental habit of mind from of old that when anyone sees abandoned goods which he thinks desirable, there is not the least objection to taking them, and Ex **20** 17*b* is probably an explanation of what is to be understood by "house" in ver 17*a*.

Examples of covetousness: Achan (Josh **7**); Saul (1 S **15** 9.19); Judas (Mt **26** 14.15); Ananias and Sapphira (Acts **5** 1–11); Balaam (2 Pet **2** 15 with Jude ver 11). WILLIAM EVANS

COW, kou, **KINE**, kīn (בָּקָר, *bāḳār* [cf Arab. *baḳar*, "cow"]; עֶגְלַת בָּקָר, *'eghlath bāḳār* [Isa **7** 21]; פָּרָה, *pārāh* [cf Arab. *furār*, "young of a sheep, goat, or cow"]; פָּרוֹת עָלוֹת, *pārōth 'ālōth* [1 S **6** 7.10], "milch kine," from עוּל, *'ūl*, "to suckle"; אֲלָפִים, *'eleph*): In Am **4** 1, the term, "kine of Bashan," is applied to the voluptuous women of Samaria. In Gen **41** 1–36 is the narration of Pharaoh's dream of the seven fat and seven lean kine. In Isaiah's vision (Isa **11** 7) we have: "And the cow and the bear shall feed; their young ones shall lie down together." Cows do not seem to have been sacrificed. The sacrifice of the kine that brought the ark back from the Philis (1 S **6** 14) was due to the exceptional circumstances. See CALF; CATTLE.

ALFRED ELY DAY

COZ, koz (קוֹץ, *kōç*, "thorn"): A man of Judah (1 Ch **4** 8). ARV has added the art., making the name Hakkoz without sufficient reason. The name occurs with the art. (*Ha-ḳōç*) in Ezr **2** 61; Neh **3** 4.21; **7** 63, and 1 Ch **24** 10, but not with reference to the same person. Coz was of the tribe of Judah, while Hakkoz belonged to the family of Aaron.

COZBI, koz'bī (כָּזְבִּי, *kozbī*, "deceitful"): A Midianitish woman, distinguished as the daughter of Zur, "head of the people of a fathers' house in Midian." She was slain by Phinehas at Shittim in company with "Zimri, the son of Salu, a prince of a fathers' house among the Simeonites" (Nu **25** 6–18).

COZEBA, ko-zē'ba (1 Ch **4** 22). See ACHZIB.

CRACKNEL, krak'nel: Occurs in 1 K **14** 3, where Jeroboam bids his wife go to Abijah to inquire concerning their son: "And take with thee ten loaves and cracknels" (AVm "cakes," ERV "cracknels," ARV "cakes"). The Heb word is נִקֻּדִים, *nikḳuddīm*, from *nāḳadh*, "to prick" or "mark"; most probably cakes with holes pricked in them like our biscuits.

CRAFT, kraft, **CRAFTINESS**, kraf'ti-nes (πανουργία, *panourgia*), **CRAFTY**, kraf'ti (πανοῦργος, *panoúrgos*): The original meaning is that of "ability to do anything," universally applied in a bad sense to unscrupulous wickedness, that stops short of no measure, however reprehensible, in order to attain its purposes; then, in a modified form, to resourcefulness in wrong, cunning (Dnl **8** 25; 2 Macc **12** 24; RVm "jugglery"). In Lk **20** 23, Jesus perceives "the craftiness" of His adversaries, i.e. the complicated network which they have laid to ensnare Him. The art with which a plot is concealed, and its direction to the ruin of others, are elements that enter into the meaning. Heinrici on 1 Cor **3** 19 illustrates from Plato the distinction between craftiness and wisdom. There is a touch of humor in 2 Cor **12** 16, when Paul speaks of his conduct toward the Corinthians as having been "crafty."

H. E. JACOBS

CRAFTS:

I. SOURCES OF OUR KNOWLEDGE OF THE CRAFTS OF THE BIBLE
  1. Written Records and Discoveries of Craftsmanship
    (1) Jewish
    (2) Canaanitish and Phoenician
    (3) Assyrian and Babylonian
    (4) Egyptian
  2. Post-Biblical Writings
  3. Present Methods in Bible Lands
II. CRAFTS MENTIONED IN THE BIBLE
  1. Brickmaking
  2. Carpentering (Wood-Working)
  3. Carving (Engraving)
  4. Ceramics
  5. Dyeing and Cleansing
  6. Embroidering (Needlework)
  7. Glass-Making
  8. Grinding
  9. Mason Work
  10. Metal-Working (Mining)
  11. Oil-Making
  12. Painting
  13. Paper-Making
  14. Perfume-Making
  15. Plastering
  16. Spinning and Weaving
  17. Tanning
  18. Tent-Making
  19. Wine-Making
III. CRAFTSMEN
LITERATURE

I. Sources of Our Knowledge.—Our knowledge of the arts and crafts of Bible times has come to us through two principal ways. First, from Bib., Assyr, Bab and Egyp written records. Of these the Egyp are the most illuminating. Second, from examples of ancient handicraft which have been buried and preserved through many cents. and brought to light again by modern discoveries.

1. Written Records and Discoveries of Craftsmanship

(1) *Jewish craftsmanship.*—The chief written documents from which we may learn about Heb handicraft are the Bible records. A study of what few references there are leads us to believe that before the Israelites came in contact with the people of Canaan and Phoenicia they had not developed any considerable technical skill (1 K **5** 6; 1 Ch **14** 1; 2 Ch **2** 7.14; Ezr **3** 7). Some of the simpler operations, such as the spinning and weaving of the common fabrics and the shaping of domestic utensils, were performed in the household (Ex **35** 25.26) but the weaving and dyeing of fine fabrics, carving, inlaying, metal-working, etc, was the work of foreigners, or was learned by the Jews after the Exodus, from the dwellers in Pal.

The Jews, however, gradually developed skill in many of these crafts. It is believed that as early as Nehemiah's time, Jewish craftsmen had organized into guilds (Neh **3** 8.31.32). In post-Bib. times the Jews obtained monopolies in some of the industries, as for example, glass-making and dyeing. These trades remained the secrets of certain families for generations. It is because of this secrecy and the mystery that surrounded these trades, and is still maintained in many places, that we know so little as to how they were conducted. Until recently the principal indigo dyers in Damascus were Jews, and the Jews shared with Moslem craftsmen the right to make glass. In some of the Syrian cities Jewish craftsmen are now outnumbering other native workmen in certain trades.

Few examples of Heb handicraft have been discovered by the archaeologists which shed much light upon early Heb work. Aside from the pottery of the Israelitish period, and a few seals and coins, no traces of Heb workmanship remain. It is even doubtful how many of the above objects are really the work of this people.

(2) *Canaanitish and Phoenician craftsmanship.*—It is generally conceded that what technical skill the Hebrews acquired resulted from their contact with the Canaanites and Phoenicians. Frequent mention of the workmanship of these peoples is made in the Bible, but their own records are silent. Ezekiel's account of the glories of Tyre (Ezk **27**) gives some idea of the reputation of that city for craftsmanship: "Thy builders have perfected thy beauty" (ver 4); "Syria was thy merchant . . . . Damascus was thy merchant for the multitude of thy handiworks" (vs 16.18). Adad-nirari III (812–783 BC), the Assyr king, enumerates the tribute which he exacted from the king of Damascus. "Variegated cloth, linen, an ivory bed, a seat of inlaid ivory, a table" were among the captured articles. These were probably Phoen work.

Many examples of Phoen craftsmanship have been discovered. These are characterized, from the standpoint of art, by a crudeness which distinguishes them from the more delicately and artistically wrought work of their teachers, the Babylonians and Egyptians. The credit remains, however, to the Phoenicians of introducing skilled workmanship into Pal. The Phoenicians, too, furnished the means of intercourse between the Babylonians and Egyptians. From the very earliest times there was an interchange of commodities and ideas between the people of the Nile and those of the Tigris and Euphrates.

(3) *Assyrian and Babylonian craftsmanship.*—The Babylonians and Assyrians made few references to their own handicraft in their records, but the explorers of recent years have revealed many examples of the remarkable workmanship of the early inhabitants of Mesopotamia. In referring to a silver vase found in that country (Telloh), dating from the 4th millennium BC, Clay (see "Literature") says "the whole is exceedingly well rendered and indicates remarkable skill, which in no respect is less striking than that of Egyp contemporaries in this handicraft." Jewelry, weapons, votive images, various utensils, tools of many kinds, statues in the hardest stones, delicately wrought, gems, dating from the times of Abraham and earlier, lead us to ask when these people acquired their skill.

(4) *Egyptian craftsmanship.*—The written records of Egypt are doubly important, because they not only refer to the various crafts, but also illustrate the processes by drawings which can leave no doubt as to how the workmen accomplished their ends. The extensive explorations in Egypt have given to the world many priceless relics of craftsmanship, some of them dating from the very dawn of civilization. Among the ruins of early Syrian and Palestinian cities are found numerous objects witnessing to the skill of the Egyptians. These objects and the evidences of the influence of their work on the Phoen arts show the part that the Egyptians played in moulding the ideas of the workmen who were chosen to build the temple at Jerus. In the following brief summary of the crafts mentioned in the Bible, it will be noticeable how well they may be illustrated by the monuments of the Nile country. To confirm the knowledge derived from the above sources, post-Bib. writings and some of the present-day customs in Bible lands are valuable. These will be mentioned in discussing the various crafts.

2. and 3. Egyptian and Post-Biblical Craftsmanship

II. Crafts Directly or Indirectly Mentioned in the Bible.—(For a more detailed treatment of the crafts see under separate arts.) This industry probably originated in Babylonia, but the knowledge of the process was early carried to Egypt, where later the Hebrews, along with other captives, were driven to making the bricks of the Egyp kings. The making of sun-dried bricks called for little skill, but the firing and glazing of bricks required trained workmen. See Brick.

1. Brick-making

Wood was extensively used by ancient builders. With the exception of the Egyp antiquities, little remains but the records to indicate this fact. Numerous references are made to the carpenter work in building the temple and subsequent repairing of this structure (1 K **5** 6; 2 Ch **2** 3; 2 K **12** 11; 2 Ch **24** 12; 2 K **22** 6; Ezr **3** 7; **4** 1). David's house and that of Solomon and his favorite wife were made partly of wood. In the story of the building of the tabernacle, wood-working is mentioned (Ex **25**). The people of Tyre built ships of cypress, with masts of cedar wood and oars of oak (Ezk **27** 5.6). Idols were carved from wood (Dt **29** 17; 2 K **19** 18; Isa **37** 19; **45** 20). The Philis built a wooden cart to carry the ark (1 S **6** 7). Threshing instruments and yokes were made of wood (2 S **24** 22). Ezra read the law from a pulpit of wood (Neh **8** 4). Solomon's chariots were made of wood (Cant **3** 9). Inlaid work, still a favorite form of decoration in Syria, was used by the Phoenicians (Ezk **27** 6). How the ancient carpenters did their work can be assumed from the Egyp monuments. Some of the operations there pictured are still performed in the same ways. See Tools; Carpenter.

2. Carpentering (Wood-Working)

The terms "carving" and "engraving" are used interchangeably in translating OT passages. The first mention made of engraved objects is the signet of Judah (Gen **38** 18). The art of engraving on various hard objects, such as clay, bone, ivory, metals and precious stones, probably came from Mesopotamia. The Hebrews learned engraving from the Canaanites. The nature of this engraving is shown by the Assyr cylinders and Egyp scarabs. It is doubtful how many of the signets found in Pal are Heb work, as the engraved devices are mostly Phoen or Egyp. From the earliest times it has been the custom in the Orient for men of affairs to carry constantly with them their signets. The seal was set in a ring, or, as was the case with Judah, and as the Arabs do today, it was worn on a cord suspended about the neck. One of the present-day sights in a Syrian city street is the engraver of signets, seated at his low bench ready to cut on one of his blank seals the buyer's name or sign.

3. Carving (Engraving)

The second form of carving is suggested by the Decalogue (Ex **20** 4). The commandment explains why sculpturing remained undeveloped among the Jews, as it has to this day among the Moslems. In spite of the commandment, however, cherubim were carved on the wooden fittings of the temple interior (1 K **6** 23).

Among the peoples with whom the Jews came in contact, stone-cutting had reached a high degree of perfection. No stone proved too hard for their tools. In Egyp and Phoen tombs the carving was often done on plastered surfaces. See Carving.

Both the Egyptians and Babylonians were skilled in molding and baking objects of clay. The early Bab records consist of burnt clay tablets. Glazed bricks formed an important decorative feature. In Egypt, idols, scarabs and amulets were often made of fired clay, glazed or unglazed. By far the most important branch of ceramic art was the making of jars for holding water or other liquids. These jars have been used throughout the East from earliest times. The Jews learned what they knew about this art from the Phoenicians. See Pottery.

4. Ceramics

Dyeing is one of the oldest of the crafts. The only references to the act of dyeing in the Bible are (a) in connection with the dyed skins of animals (Ex **25** 5; **26** 14), and (b) Jgs **5** 30. That it was a highly developed trade is implied in the many other references to dyed stuffs both in the Bible and in profane lit. Cleansing was done by the fuller, who was probably a dyer also. See Color; Dye; Fuller.

5. Dyeing and Cleansing

Very little is known of the work of embroidering, further than that it was the working-in of color designs on cloth. In Ezk **27** 7 we learn that it was one of the exports of Egypt. See Embroidering.

6. Embroidering (Needlework)

In Dt **33** 19 "hidden treasures of the sand" is interpreted by some to mean the making of glass objects from the sand. There can be no question about the

Hebrews being acquainted with glass-making, as its history extends back to very early times.

7. Glass-Making The Egyptians and Phoenicians made bottles, glass beads, idols, etc. These objects are among those usually found in the tombs. Glass beads of very early manufacture were found in the mound at Gezer. Some of the pigments used for painting were made of powdered colored glass. In the NT we read of the "sea of glass like unto crystal" (Rev **4** 6). See GLASS.

Grinding was a domestic task and can hardly be classed as one of the crafts. When flour was needed,

8. Grinding the housewife, or more likely the servant, rubbed the wheat or barley between two millstones (see MILLSTONE) or, with a rounded river stone, crushed the wheat on a large flat stone. It is still a common custom in Syria and Pal for two women to work together as indicated in Mt **24** 41 and Lk **17** 35. Grinding of meal was a menial task, considered the employment of a concubine; hence setting Samson to grinding at the mill was intended as a disgrace.

The rhythmic sound of the stone cutter at his work never ceases in the prosperous oriental city. It is

9. Mason Work more common today, however, than in the earlier cents. when only high officials could afford stone houses. Frequently only the temple or shrines or tombs of a city were made of stone. As such buildings were very common, and much attention was paid to every detail of their construction, there was developed an efficient corps of masons, especially in Egypt and Syria. When the Israelites abandoned their nomadic life, among the first things that they planned were permanent places of worship. As these developed into structures more pretentious than mere piles of stones, the builders naturally resorted to the skill of the master builders of the country. A visitor to Jerus may still see the work of the ancient masons. The so-called Solomon's quarries under the city, the great drafted stones of the temple area, belong to an early date. The very shape of the masons' tools may be determined from the marks on the stones. See MASON.

Among the oldest objects that have been preserved are those of silver, gold and bronze. These

10. Metal-Working (Mining) are proof that the ancients understood the various processes of mining, smelting, refining and working of metals. See MINING; METAL-WORKING.

11. Oil-Making The oil referred to in the Bible is olive oil. Pliny mentions many other oils which were extracted in Egypt. The oils were usually extracted by first crushing the fruit and then pressing the crushed mass. At Gezer, *Tell es Ṣâfi* and other ancient ruins old oil presses have been discovered. See OIL.

One who has visited the tombs and temples of Egypt will never forget the use which the ancient

12. Painting Egyp painters made of colors. The otherwise somber effect produced by expansive plain walls was overcome by sculpturing, either in relief or intaglio, on a coating of stucco, and then coloring these engravings in reds, yellows, greens and blues. Architectural details were also painted. The capitals of columns and the columns themselves received special attention from the painter. Colors were similarly used by the Greeks and Phoenicians. In the Sidon tombs, at Palmyra and similar ruins, traces of painting are still evident. See PAINTING.

The word "paper" occurs twice, once in the OT (Isa **19** 7 AV) and once in NT (2 Jn ver 12). In Isa **19** 7 the RV renders "paper reeds," "meadows." PAPYRUS (q.v.) occurs in Isa **18** 2 and RVm of Ex **2** 3. The nearest approach to

13. Paper-Making our paper which the ancients possessed was that made from a species of papyrus. The process consisted in spreading out, side by side, long strips of the inner lining of the papyrus reed, then over these other strips at right angles to the first, afterward soaking with some adhesive material and finally pressing and drying. Sheets made in this way were fastened together with glue into a long scroll. The Gr for papyrus plant is *"biblos,"* from which the Eng. word "Bible" is derived. Parchment, leather and leaves were also used as paper. The natives of Syria and Pal still call a sheet of paper a "leaf" (Arab. *waraḳet*).

The art of perfume-making dates back to the ancient Egyptians. In Ex **30** 35 we have the

14. Perfume-Making first mention of scented anointing oils. The perfumers' (AV "confectioner" or "apothecary") products were used (*a*) for religious rites as offerings and to anoint the idols and (*b*) for personal use on the body or clothes. Some perfumes were powders (incense); others were scented oils or fats (ointments). See PERFUME.

The trade of plastering dates back to the beginning of the history of building. There were two

15. Plastering (AV "Plaistering") reasons for using plastering or stucco: (*a*) to render the buildings more resisting to the weather and (*b*) to make the surfaces more suitable for decoration by engraving or painting. See PLASTER.

The arts of spinning and weaving were early practised in the household (Ex **35** 25). Many

16. Spinning and Weaving different fibers were spun and woven into cloth. Fabrics of wool, cotton, flax, silk, wood fiber have been preserved from Bible times. In the more progressive communities, the weaving of the fabrics was taken over by the weavers who made it their profession. In 1 Ch **4** 21 it is stated that many of the families of the house of Asbea were workers in fine linen. The modern invasion of European manufacturers has not yet driven out the weavers who toil at looms much like those described by the ancient Egyp drawings. See SPINNING; WEAVING.

Although it is known that tanning was practised, the only reference to this trade mentioned in the

17. Tanning Bible is to Simon the tanner (Acts **9** 43; **10** 6.32). Leather girdles are mentioned in 2 K **1** 8; Mt **3** 4. Relics taken from the tombs show that the ancients understood the various methods for preserving skins which are used in present-day practice. See TANNER.

We think of Paul as the tent-maker. The tents which he made however were probably not like

18. Tent-Making those so frequently referred to in the OT. Tents in Paul's time were made from Cilician cloth. Paul's work was probably the sewing together of the proper lengths of cloth and the attaching of ropes and loops. In OT times the tents were made of strips of coarse goat's hair cloth or of the skins of animals. See TENT.

This art. is being written within sound of festivities about the winepresses of Mt. Lebanon

19. Wine-Making where men and women are gathered for the annual production of wine and molasses (Arab. *dibs*). Their process is so like that of Bible times that one is transported in thought to similar festivities that must have attended the wine-making even so far back as the early Egyp kings. That these workers understood the precautions necessary for procuring a desirable product is evidenced by early writings. The choice of proper soil for the vineyards, the adding of preservatives to keep the wine, boiling the juice to kill undesirable ferments, guarding against putting new wine into old bottles, are examples of their knowledge of wine-making. See WINE PRESS.

III. Craftsmen.—Craftsmen were early segregated into groups. A trade usually remained in a family. This is true to some extent in the East today. In such cities as Beirût, Damascus, or Aleppo the shops of the craftsmen of a given trade will be found grouped together. There is a silver and goldsmiths' market (Arab. *sûḳ*), an iron market, a dyeing quarter, etc. Jewish craftsmen in early times sat separately in the synagogues. Some crafts were looked upon with disfavor, esp. those which brought men in contact with women, as for example, the trade of goldsmith, carder, weaver, fuller or tanner. There was a fellow-feeling among craftsmen referred to by Isaiah (Isa **41** 6.7). This same feeling is observed among Syrian workmen today. The Arab has many phrases of encouragement for a man at his work, such as, "Peace to your hands," "May God give you strength." A crowd of men pulling at a pulley rope, for example, shout or sing together as they pull.

LITERATURE.—Perrot and Chipiez, *History of Art in Sardinia, Judaea*, etc; *History of Art in Ancient Egypt; History of Art in Phoenicia and Cyprus;* Wilkinson, *The Ancient Egyptians;* Macalister, *Bible Side-Lights from the Mound of Gezer; Standard Dict. of the Bible;* Bliss, Macalister and Wünsch, *Excavations in Pal;* Hilprecht, *Explorations in Bible Lands during the 19th Cent.;* Harper, *The Bible and Modern Discoveries;* Delitzsch, *Jewish Artisan Life*, etc; Clay, *Light on the OT from Babel; Jew Enc.*

JAMES A. PATCH

CRAG, krag (שֵׁן, *shēn* [1 S **7** 12; **14** 4; Job **39** 28 AV and ERV]): In a mountainous country composed of sedimentary rocks, like the cretaceous rocks of Pal, cliffs are formed on a slope where hard strata are underlaid by softer strata. The soft strata wear away more rapidly, undermining the hard strata above them, which for a time project, but finally break off by vertical joint-planes, the fragments rolling down to form the talus slope at the foot of the cliff. As the breaking off of the undermined hard strata proceeds irregularly, there are left projecting crags, sometimes at the top of the cliff, and sometimes lower down. Two such crags (*shēn ha-ṣela'*, "sharp rock," RV "rocky crag"), which were given particular names, Bozez and Seneh, marked the scene of the exploit of Jonathan described in 1 S **14**. Conder failed to identify the crags, and it has been proposed to alter the text rather extensively to make it read: "wall of rock" instead of "crag" (*EB* s.v. "Michmash"). Such rocks form safe resting-places for birds of prey, as it is said of the eagle in Job **39** 28 ERV:

"She dwelleth on the rock and hath her lodging there,
Upon the crag of the rock, and the stronghold."

ALFRED ELY DAY

CRANE, krān (עָגוּר, *'āghūr;* γέρανος, *géranos;* Lat *Grus cinerea*): A bird of the family *gruidae*. The crane is mentioned twice in the Bible: once on account of its voice (Isa **38** 14: "Like a swallow or a crane, so did I chatter"); again because of the unforgettable picture these birds made in migration (Jer **8** 7): "Yea, the stork in the heavens knoweth her appointed times; and the turtle-dove and the swallow and the crane observe the time of their coming; but my people know not the law of Jeh." Some commentators have adduced reasons for dropping the crane from the ornithology of the Bible, but this never should be permitted. They were close relatives of stork, heron and ibis; almost as numerous as any of these, and residents of Pal, except in migration. The two quotations concerning them fit with their history, and point out the two features that made them as noticeable as any birds of Pal. Next to the ostrich and pelican they were the largest birds, having a wing sweep of 8 ft. from tip to tip and standing 4 ft. in height. In migration such immense flocks passed over Pal as to darken the sky, and when they crossed the Red Sea they appeared to sweep from shore to shore, and so became the most noticeable migratory bird, for which reason, no doubt, they were included in Isaiah's reference to spring migration with the

Crane—*Grus cinerea.*

beloved doves, used in sacrifice and for caged pets, and with the swallows that were held almost sacred because they homed in temples. Not so many of them settled in Pal as of the storks, but large flocks lived in the wilderness S. of Jerus, and a few pairs homed near water as far north as Merom. The grayish-brown cranes were the largest, and there were also a crested, and a white crane. They nested on the ground or in trees and laid two large eggs, differing with species. The eggs of the brown bird were a light drab with brown speckles, and those of the white, rough, pale-blue with brown splotches. They were not so affectionate in pairs or to their young as storks, but were average parents. It is altogether probable that they were the birds intended by Isaiah, because they best suited his purpose, the crane and the swallow being almost incessant talkers among birds. The word "chatter," used in the Bible, exactly suits the notes of a swallow, but is much too feeble to be used in describing the vocalizing of the crane. They migrated in large wedge-shaped companies and cried constantly on wing. They talked incessantly while at the business of living, and even during the watches of the night they scarcely ceased passing along word that all was well, or sending abroad danger signals. The Arabs called the cry of the cranes "bellowing." We usually express it by whooping or trumpeting. Any of these words is sufficiently expressive to denote an unusual voice, used in an unusual manner, so that it appealed to the prophet as suitable for use in a strong comparison. GENE STRATTON-PORTER

CRASHING, krash'ing (שֶׁבֶר, *shebher*): This word, meaning "a breach," **fig.** "destruction," is tr[d] "crashing" in Zeph **1** 10: "a great crashing from the hills," representing the doom to fall on evil-doers in Jerus, as the enemy advanced against the city from the north.

CRATES, krā'tēz (**Κράτης,** *Krátēs*), governor of the Cyprians, left as deputy of Sostratus when the latter, who was governor of Jerus, was summoned to Antioch by Antiochus Epiphanes, in consequence of a dispute with Menelaus (2 Macc **4** 29). As Cyprus was not at the time in the possession of Antiochus, the words have been generally taken to mean Krates "who had formerly been, or afterward was, governor of the Cyprians." The Vulg translates the Gr into "Sostratus autem praelatus est Cypriis."

CREATION, krē-ā'shun (בָּרָא, *bārā'*, "to create"; **κτίσις,** *ktísis,* "that which is created," "creature"):

1. Creation as Abiding
2. Mistaken Ideas
3. True Conception
4. The Genesis Cosmogony
5. Matter not Eternal
6. "Wisdom" in Creation
7. A Free, Personal Act
8. Creation and Evolution
9. Is Creation Eternal?
10. Creation *ex nihilo*
11. From God's Will
12. Error of Pantheism
13. First Cause a Necessary Presupposition
14. The End—the Divine Glory

LITERATURE

Much negative ground has been cleared away for any modern discussion of the doctrine of creation.

1. Creation as Abiding

No idea of creation can now be taken as complete which does not include, besides the world as at first constituted, all that to this day is in and of creation. For God creates not being that can exist independently of Him, His preserving agency being inseparably connected with His creative power. We have long ceased to think of God's creation as a machine left, completely made, to its own automatic working. With such a doctrine of creation, a theistic evolution would be quite incompatible.

Just as little do we think of God's creative agency, as merely that of a First Cause, linked to

2. Mistaken Ideas

the universe from the outside by innumerable sequences of causes and effects. Nature in her entirety is as much His creation today as she ever was. The dynamic ubiquity of God, as efficient energy, is to be affirmed. God is still All and in All, but this in a way sharply distinguished from pantheistic views, whether of the universe as God, or of God as the universe. Of His own freedom He creates, so that gnostic theories of natural and necessary emanation are left far behind. Not only have the "carpenter" and the "gardener" theories—with, of course, the architect or world-builder theory of Plato—been dismissed; not only has the conception of evolution been proved harmonious with creative end, plan, purpose, ordering, guidance; but evolutionary science may itself be said to have given the thought of theistic evolution its best base or grounding. The theistic conception is, that the world—that all cosmic existences, substances, events—depend upon God.

The doctrine of creation—of the origin and persistence, of all finite existences—as the work of God,

3. True Conception

is a necessary postulation of the religious consciousness. Such consciousness is marked by deeper insight than belongs to science. The underlying truth is the anti-patheistic one, that the energy and wisdom—by which that, which was not, *became*—were, in kind, other than its own. For science can but trace the continuity of sequences in all Nature, while in creation, in its primary sense, this law of continuity must be transcended, and the world viewed solely as product of Divine Intelligence, immanent in its evolution. For God is the Absolute Reason, always immanent in the developing universe. Apart from the cosmogonic attempts at the beginning of Genesis, which are clearly religious and ethical in scope and character, the OT furnishes no theoretic account of the manner and order in which creative process is carried on.

The early chs of Genesis were, of course, not given to reveal the truths of physical science, but

4. The Genesis Cosmogony

they recognize creation as marked by order, continuity, law, plastic power of productiveness in the different kingdoms, unity of the world and progressive advance. The Genesis cosmogony teaches a process of becoming, as well as a creation (see EVOLUTION). That cosmogony has been recognized by Haeckel as meritoriously marked by the two great ideas of separation or differentiation, and of progressive development or perfecting of the originally simple matter. The OT presents the conception of time-worlds or successive ages, but its real emphasis is on the energy of the Divine Word, bringing into being things that did not exist.

The OT and the NT, in their doctrine of creation, recognize no eternal matter before creation. We

5. Matter not Eternal

cannot say that the origin of matter is excluded from the Genesis account of creation, and this quite apart from the use of *bārā'*, as admitting of material and means in creation. But it seems unwise to build upon Genesis passages that afford no more than a basis which has proved exegetically insecure. The NT seems to favor the derivation of matter from the non-existent—that is to say, the time-worlds were due to the effluent Divine Word or originative Will, rather than to being built out of God's own invisible essence. So the best exegesis interprets He **11** 3.

In OT books, as the Pss, Prov, and Jer, the creation is expressly declared to be the work of

6. "Wisdom" in Creation

Wisdom—a Wisdom not disjoined from Goodness, as is yet more fully brought out in the Book of Job. The heavens declare the glory of God, the world manifests or reveals Him to our experience, as taken up and interpreted by the religious consciousness. The primary fact of the beginning of the time-worlds—the basal fact that the worlds came into being by the Word of God—is something apprehensible only by the power of religious faith, as the only principle applicable to the case (He **11** 3). Such intuitive faith is really an application of first principles in the highest—and a truly rational one (see LOGOS). In creation, God is but expressing or acting out the conscious Godhood that is in Him. In it the thought of His absolute Wisdom is realized by the action of His perfect Love. It is philosophically necessary to maintain that God, as the Absolute Being, must find the end of creation in Himself. If the end were external to, and independent of, Him, then would He be conditioned thereby.

What the religious consciousness is concerned to maintain is, the absolute freedom of God in the

7. A Free, Personal Act

production of the universe, and the fact that He is so much greater than the universe that existence has been by Him bestowed on all things that do exist. The Scriptures are, from first to last, shot through with this truth. Neither Kant nor Spencer, from data of self-consciousness or sense-perception, can rise to the conception of creation, for they both fail to reach the idea of Divine Personality. The inconceivability of creation has been pressed by Spencer, the idea of a self-existent Creator, through whose agency it has been made, being to him unthinkable. As if it were not a transparent sophism, which Spencer's own scientific practice refuted, that a hypothesis may not have philosophical or scientific value, because it is what we call unthinkable or inconceivable. As if a true and sufficient cause were not enough, or a Divine act of will were not a *vera causa.* Dependent existence inevitably leads thought to demand existence that is not dependent.

8. Creation and Evolution

Creation is certainly not disproved by evolution, which does not explain the origin of the homogeneous stuff itself, and does not account for the beginning of motion within it. Of the original creative action, lying beyond mortal ken or human observation, science—as concerned only with the manner of the process—is obviously in no position to speak. Creation may, in an important sense, be said not to have taken place in time, since time cannot be posited prior to the existence of the world. The difficulties of the ordinary hypothesis of a creation in time can never be surmounted, so long as we continue to make eternity mean simply indefinitely prolonged time. Augustine was, no doubt, right when, from the human standpoint, he declared that the world was not made in time, but with time. Time is itself a creation simultaneous with, and conditioned by, world-creation and movement. To say, in the ordinary fashion, that God created in time, is apt to make time appear independent of God, or God dependent upon time. Yet the time-forms enter into all our psychological experience, and a concrete beginning is unthinkable to us.

9. Is Creation Eternal?

The time-conditions can be transcended only by some deeper intuition than mere logical insight can supply—by such intuitive endeavor, in fact, as is realized in the necessary belief in the self-existent God. If such an eternal Being acts or creates, He may be said to act or create in eternity; and it is legitimate enough, in such wise, to speak of His creative act as eternal. This seems preferable to the position of Origen, who speculatively assumed an eternal or unbeginning activity for God as Creator, because the Divine Nature must be eternally self-determined to create in order to the manifestation of its perfections. Clearly did Aquinas perceive that we cannot affirm an eternal creation impossible, the creative act not falling within our categories of time and space. The question is purely one of God's free volition, in which—and not in "nothing"—the Source of the world is found.

10. Creation "ex nihilo"

This brings us to notice the frequently pressed objection that creation cannot be out of nothing, since out of nothing comes nothing. This would mean that matter is eternal. But the eternity of matter, as something other than God, means its independence of God, and its power to limit or condition Him. We have, of course, no direct knowledge of the origin of matter, and the conception of its necessary self-existence is fraught with hopeless difficulties and absurdities. The axiom, that out of nothing nothing comes, is not contradicted in the case of creation. The universe comes from God; it does not come from nothing. But the axiom does not really apply to the world's creation, but only to the succession of its phenomena. Entity does not spring from non-entity. But there is an opposite and positive truth, that something presupposes something, in this case rather some One—*aliquis* rather than *aliquid.*

11. From God's Will

It is enough to know that God has in Himself the powers and resources adequate for creating, without being able to define the ways in which creation is effected by Him It is a sheer necessity of rational faith or spiritual reason that the something which conditions the world is neither ὕλη, *húlē,* nor elemental matter, but personal Spirit or originative Will. We have no right to suppose the world made out of nothing, and then to identify, as Erigena did, this "nothing" with God's own essence. What we have a right to maintain is, that what God creates or calls into being owes its existence to nothing save His will alone, Ground of all actualities. Pre-existent Personality is the ground and the condition of the world's beginning.

12. Error of Pantheism

In this sense, its beginning may be said to be relative rather than absolute. God is always antecedent to the universe—its *prius,* Cause and Creator. It remains an effect, and sustains a relation of causal dependence upon Him. If we say, like Cousin, that God of necessity creates eternally, we run risk of falling into Spinozistic pantheism, identifying God, in excluding from Him absolute freedom in creation, with the impersonal and unconscious substance of the universe. Or if, with Schelling, we posit in God something which is not God—a dark, irrational background, which original ground is also the ground of the Divine Existence —we may try to find a basis for the matter of the universe, but we are in danger of being merged—by conceptions tinged with corporeity—in that form of pantheism to which God is but the soul of the universe.

The universe, we feel sure, has been caused; its existence must have some ground; even if we held a philosophy so idealistic as to make the scheme of created things one grand illusion, an illusion so vast would still call for some explanatory Cause. Even if we are not content with the conception of a First Cause, acting on the world from without and antecedently in time, we are not yet freed from the necessity of asserting a Cause. An underlying and determining Cause of the universe would still need to be postulated as its Ground.

13. First Cause a Necessary Presupposition

Even a universe held to be eternal would need to be accounted for—we should still have to ask how such a universe came to be. Its endless movement must have direction and character imparted to it from some immanent ground or underlying cause. Such a self-existent and eternal World-Ground or First Cause is, by an inexorable law of thought, the necessary correlate of the finitude, or contingent character of the world. God and the world are not to be taken simply as cause and effect, for modern metaphysical thought is not content with such a mere *ens extra-mundanum* for the Ground of all possible experience. God, self-existent Cause of the ever-present world and its phenomena, is the ultimate Ground of the possibility of all that is.

14. The End—the Divine Glory

Such a Deity, as *causa sui,* creatively bringing forth the world out of His own potence, cannot be allowed to be an arbitrary resting-place, but a truly rational Ground, of thought. Nor can His Creation be allowed to be an aimless and mechanical universe: it is shot through with end or purpose that tends to reflect the glory of the eternal and personal God, who is its Creator in a full and real sense. But the Divine action is not dramatic: of His working we can truly say, with Isa **45** 15, "Verily thou art a God that hidest thyself." As creation becomes progressively disclosed to us, its glory, as revealing God, ought to excite within us an always deeper sense of the sentiment of Ps **8** 1.9, "O Jeh our Lord, how excellent is thy name in all the earth!" See also ANTHROPOLOGY; EARTH; WORLD.

LITERATURE.—James Orr, *Christian View of God and the World,* 1st ed, 1893; J. Iverach, *Christianity and Evolution,* 1894; S. Harris, *God the Creator and Lord of All,* 1897; A. L. Moore, *Science and the Faith,* 1889; B. P. Bowne, *Studies in Theism,* new ed, 1902; G. P. Fisher,

Grounds of Theistic and Christian Belief, new ed, 1902; J. Lindsay, *Recent Advances in Theistic Philosophy of Religion*, 1897; A. Dorner, *Religionsphilosophie*, 1903; J. Lindsay, *Studies in European Philosophy*, 1909; O. Dykes, *The Divine Worker in Creation and Providence*, 1909; J. Lindsay, *The Fundamental Problems of Metaphysics*, 1910.

James Lindsay

CREATOR, krē-ā'tēr (**κτιστής**, *ktistḗs*, 1 Pet **4** 19): The distinctive characteristic of Deity, as the Creator, is that He is the Cause of the existent universe—Cause of its being, not merely of its evolution or present arrangements. The doctrine of His being the Creator implies, that is to say, that He is the real and the exclusive Agent in the production of the world. For, as Herder remarked, the thought of the Creator is the most fruitful of all our ideas. As Creator, He is the Unconditioned, and the All-conditioning, Being. The universe is thus dependent upon Him, as its causative antecedent. He calls it, as Aquinas said, "according to its whole substance," into being, without any presupposed basis. His power, as Creator, is different in kind from finite power. But the creative process is not a case of sheer almightiness, creating something out of nothing, but an expression of God, as the Absolute Reason, under the forms of time and space, causality and finite personality. In all His work, as Creator, there is no incitement from without, but it rather remains an eternal activity of self-manifestation on the part of a God who is Love.

1. God as Creator

God's free creative action is destined to realize archetypal ends and ideals, which are peculiar to Himself. For thought cannot be content with the causal category under which He called the world into being, but must run on to the teleological category, wherein He is assumed to have created with a purpose, which His directive agency will see at last fulfilled. As Creator, He is distinct from the universe, which is the product of the free action of His will. This theistic postulation of His freedom, as Creator, rules out all theories of necessary emanation. His creative action was in no way necessarily eternal—not even necessary to His own blessedness or perfection, which must be held as already complete in Himself. To speak, as Professor James does, of "the stagnant felicity of the Absolute's own perfection" is to misconceive the infinite plenitude of His existence, and to place Him in a position of abject and unworthy dependence upon an eternal activity of world-making.

2. Purpose in Creation

God's action, as Creator, does not lower our conception of His changelessness, for it is a gratuitous assumption to suppose either that the will to create was a sudden or accidental thing, or that He could not will a change, without, in any proper sense, changing His will. Again, grave difficulties cluster around the conception of His creative thought or purpose as externalized in time, the chief source of the trouble being, as is often imperfectly realized, that, in attempting to view things as they were when time began, we are really trying to get out of, and beyond, experience, to the thinking of which time is an indispensable condition. God's work as Creator must have taken place in time, since the world must be held as no necessary element in the Absolute Life.

3. Relation to Time

The self-determined action of the Divine Will, then, is to be taken as the ultimate principle of the cosmos. Not to any causal or metaphysical necessity, but to Divine or Absolute Personality, must the created world be referred. "Of him, and through him, and unto him, are all things" (Rom **11** 36). This creative action of God is mediated by Christ—by whom "were all things created, in the heavens and upon the earth, things visible and things invisible, whether thrones or dominions or principalities or powers; all things have been created through him, and unto him" (Col **1** 16). See Creation.

4. Christ in Creation

James Lindsay

CREATURE, krē'ṭūr: The word "creature," as it occurs in the NT, is the tr and also the exact Eng. equivalent of the Gr *κτίσις*, *ktísis*, or *κτίσμα*, *ktísma*, from *κτίζω*, *ktízō*, "to create." In the OT, on the other hand, it stands for words which have in the original no reference to creation, but which come from other roots. *Nephesh*, "living creature" (lit. "a breathing thing"), occurs in the accounts of the Creation and the Flood and at the close of the lists of clean and unclean animals in Lev **11** 46. *Ḥay*, "living creature" (lit. "a living thing"), occurs 13 times in Ezk **1, 3** and **10** (see Creature, Living). *Shereç*, "moving creature" (lit. "a swarming thing," generally rendered "creeping thing," q.v.), occurs once in Gen **1** 20. *'Ōḥīm*, "doleful creatures," occurs once only in Isa **13** 21. It appears to be an onomatopoetic word referring to the mournful sounds emitted by the animals in question. From the context it is fair to suppose that owls may be the animals referred to. See Owl; Creation.

Alfred Ely Day

CREATURE, LIVING (**חַיָּה**, *ḥayyāh*; **ζῷον**, *zṓon*): "Living creature" (*ḥayyāh*) is the designation of each of the composite figures in Ezekiel's visions (**1** 5.13 ff; **3** 13; **10** 15.17.20) and, RV, of the similar beings in the visions of the Apocalypse, instead of the extremely unfortunate tr of *zōon* in AV by "beasts" (Rev **4** 6 ff; **5** 6 ff; **6** 1 ff; **7** 11; **14** 3; **15** 7; **19** 4), which, however, went back to Wiclif, in whose time the word had not the *low* meaning which "beast," "beastly" have with us; hence he translates **1** Cor **15** 44, "It is sowen a beestli body," meaning simply *animal* (see Trench's *Select Glossary*); in Rev "the beasts of the earth," the "beasts" that came up, the notable "beast" that men worshipped, represent the Gr *thērion*, "a wild beast."

The "living creatures" in Ezekiel's vision (**1** 5 ff) were four in number, "with the general appearance of a man, but each with four faces and four wings, and straight legs with the feet of an ox. Under their wings are human hands, and these wings are so joined that they never require to turn. The front face is that of a man; right and left of this are the faces of a lion and [of] an ox, and behind, that of an eagle . . . . out of the midst of them gleam fire, torches, lightnings, and connected with them are four wheels that can turn in every direction, called whirling wheels (**10** 12.13). Like the creatures, these are alive, covered with eyes, the sign of intelligence; the spirit of the living creatures is in them. They are afterward discovered by the prophet to be *cherubim*" (Schultz, *OT Theology*, II, 233). See Cherubim. In Ezekiel's vision they seem to be the bearers of the throne and glory of God; the bearers of His presence and of His revelation (**9** 3; **10** 3). They also sound forth His praise (**3** 12; **10** 2). (See Schultz as above.)

The four living creatures in Rev (**4** 6) are not *under* the throne but "in the midst of the throne" (ARVm "before"; see **7** 17; cf **5** 6) and "round about the throne." They are also *cherubim*, and seem to represent the four beings that stand at the head of the four divisions of the creation; among the untamed animals the *lion;* among cattle the *calf* or *ox;* among birds the *eagle;* among all created beings the *man*. It gives "a perfect picture of true service, which should be as brave as the lion, patient as the ox, aspiring as the eagle, intelligent as man" (Milligan in loc.). They represent the powers of Nature—of the creation, "full of eyes" as denoting its permeation with the Divine Reason, the wings signifying its constant, ready service, and the unceasing praise the constant doing of God's will. The imagery is founded on Ezekiel as that had been modified in apocalyptic writings and as it was exalted in the mind of the Seer of Patmos.

W. L. WALKER

CREDIT, kred'it (**πιστεύειν,** *pisteúein;* 1 Macc **10** 46 AV, RV "gave no credence"; Wisd **18** 6 AV, RV "trusted"; 1 Macc **1** 30 AV, RV "credence"): In the modern commercial sense the noun "credit" does not occur in the canonical Scriptures or in the Apoc.

CREDITOR, kred'i-tẽr ([*a*] נֹשֶׁה, *nōsheh,* participle of נָשָׁה, *nāshāh:* Ex **22** 24 [ET 25]; 2 K **4** 1; Isa **50** 1; tr[d] "extortioner," Ps **109** 11; "taker of usury," Isa **24** 2 AV; [*b*] מַלְוֶה, *malweh,* participle of לָוָה, *lāwāh,* Isa **24** 2 RV, AV "lender"; [*c*] בַּעַל מַשֵּׁה יָדוֹ, *ba'al mashshēh yādhō:* "lord of the loan of his hand," Dt **15** 2; [*d*] **δανιστής,** *danistḗs:* Lk **7** 41, "creditor" AV, "lender" RV; cf further *danistós,* Sir **29** 28, "lender" AV, "money-lender" RV): In the ideal social system of the OT, debts are incurred only because of poverty, and the law protected the poor debtor from his creditor, who in Ex **22** 25 is forbidden to demand interest, and in Dt **15** 2 to exact payment in view of the nearness of the year of release. 2 K **4** 1 shows that the actual practice was not so considerate, and in consequence the creditor fell into bad repute. In Ps **109** 11 he is the extortioner; in Prov **29** 13 the oppressor is evidently the creditor, though a different word is used; cf also Prov **22** 7. In Sir **29** 28 the importunity of the creditor is one of the hardships of the poor man of understanding. The actual practice of the Jews may be gathered from Neh **5** 1 ff; Jer **34** 8 ff; and Sir **29** 1–11. See also DEBT.

WALTER R. BETTERIDGE

CREED, krēd, **CREEDS:**

By "creed" we understand the systematic statement of religious faith; and by the creeds of the Christian church we mean the formal expression of "the faith which was delivered unto the saints." The word is derived from the first word of the Lat VSS of the Apostles' Creed, and the name is usually applied to those formulae known as the Apostles', the Nicene and the Athanasian creeds.

In this art. we shall first indicate the Scriptural foundation and rudimentary Bib. statements upon which the distinctive dogmas of the church are based; and, secondly, briefly describe the origin and nature of the three most important symbols of belief which have dominated Christian thought.

I. Scriptural Basis.—There are three forms in which the religious instinct naturally expresses itself—in a ritual, a creed and a life. Men first seek to propitiate the Deity by some outward act and express their devotion in some external ceremony. Next they endeavor to explain their worship and to find a rationale of it in certain facts which they formulate into a confession; and lastly, not content with the outward act or the verbal interpretation of it, they attempt to express their religion in life.

Pagan religion first appears in the form of a rite. The worshipper was content with the proper performance of a ceremony and was not, in the earliest stage at least, concerned with an interpretation of his act. The myths, which to some extent were an attempt to rationalize ritual, may be regarded as the earliest approach to a formulated statement of belief. But inasmuch as the myths of early pagan religion are not obligatory upon the reason or the faith of the worshipper, they can scarcely be regarded as creeds. Pagan religion, strictly speaking, has no theology and having no real historical basis of facts does not possess the elements of a creed. In this respect it is distinguished from revealed religion. This latter rests upon facts, the meaning and interpretation of which are felt to be necessary to give to revelation its values and authority.

1. In the OT

Even in the OT there are not wanting the germs of a creed. In the Decalogue we have the beginnings of the formulation of belief, and in the proclamation, "Hear, O Israel: Jeh our God is one Jeh" (Dt **6** 4), we have what may be regarded as the symbol of the OT faith and the earliest attempt to enunciate a doctrine.

2. In the NT—Gospels

It is to the NT, however, we must turn to find the real indications of such a statement of belief as may be designated a creed. We must remember that Christ lived and taught for a time before any attempt was made to portray His life or to record His sayings. The earliest writings are not the Gospels, but some of the Epistles, and it is to them we must look for any definite explanation of the facts which center in the appearance of Christ upon the earth. At the same time in the sequence of events the personality and teaching of Jesus come first, and in the relation to Him of His disciples and converts and in their personal confessions and utterances of faith we have the earliest suggestions of an expression of belief. The confession of Nathanael (Jn **1** 49), "Rabbi, thou art the Son of God," and still more the utterance of St. Peter (Mt **16** 16), "Thou art the Christ, the Son of the living God," and the exclamation of Thomas (Jn **20** 28), contain the germ of a creed. It is to be noted that all these expressions of belief have Christ as their object and give utterance with more or less explicitness to a conviction of His Divine nature and authority.

3. In the Epistles

But while these sayings in the Gospels were no doubt taken up and incorporated in later interpretations, it is to the Epistles that we must first go, for an explanation of the facts of Christ's person and His relation to God and man. Paul's Epistles are really of the nature of a confession and manifesto of Christian belief. Communities of believers already existed when the apostle directed to them his earliest letters. In their oral addresses the apostles must have been accustomed not only to state facts which were familiar to their hearers, but also to draw inferences from them as to the meaning of Christ and the great truths centering in His person—His incarnation, His death and resurrection (as we may see from the recorded sermons of Peter and Paul in Acts). It is to these facts that the Epistles appeal. It was at once natural and necessary that some expression of the faith once delivered to the saints should be formulated for a body whose members were pledged to each other and united for common action, and whose bond of union was the acknowledgment of "one Lord, one faith." Paul recognizes it as vital to the very spirit of religion that some definite profession of belief in Christ should be made: "If thou shalt confess with thy mouth Jesus as Lord, and shalt believe in thy heart that God raised him from the dead, thou shalt be saved" (Rom **10** 9). These words would seem to imply that a confession of the Deity, the atoning death, and resurrection of Jesus was the earliest form of Christian creed.

It must also be observed that from the very first the confession of faith seems to have been connected with the *administration of baptism*. Already in the story of the Ethiopian eunuch (Acts **8** 37 AV) (a passage indeed of doubtful genuineness but attested by Irenaeus and therefore of great antiquity) we find that as a condition of baptism the convert is asked to declare his belief in Jesus Christ as the Son of God. The passage in 1 Tim (**6** 12; cf He **10** 23), "Lay hold on the life eternal, whereunto thou wast called, and didst confess the good confession in the sight of many witnesses," may refer to a confession required only of those who were being ordained: but the context leads us to infer that it was a baptismal vow asked of members not less than of ministers of the church. The probability is that the earliest form of creed reflected little more than Christ's final command to baptize all men "into the name of the Father and of the Son and of the Holy Spirit" (Mt **28** 19), or perhaps simply "into the name of the Lord Jesus" (Acts **19** 5). The ver in **8** 37 AV, though disputed by some, is instructive in this connection. Faith in Jesus Christ was regarded as the cardinal point of the New Revelation and may have been taken to imply a relation to the Father as well as a promise of the Holy Spirit.

It is evident that the creeds that have come down to us are mainly an expression of the doctrine of the Trinity as embodied in the original baptismal formula derived from Our Lord's commission. Already indeed in some places of the OT this doctrine is foreshadowed; but it is first clearly incorporated in the Lord's command just mentioned and in the benediction of St. Paul (2 Cor **13** 14), and subsequently in the Christian doxologies. Some scholars have preferred to find traces in the later writings of the NT of a more definite summary of belief: as in the allusion to the form of sound words (2 Tim **1** 13), the "deposit" or "good deposit" which was to be kept (1 Tim **6** 20 RVm; 2 Tim **1** 14 RVm); also in "the faithful words" enumerated in these epistles (1 Tim **1** 15; **3** 1; **4** 8.9; 2 Tim **2** 11); and in the remarkable passage in the beginning of He **6** in which the elementary doctrines of the Christian religion are enumerated; first on the subjective side, *repentance* and *faith*, and then objectively, the *resurrection* and the *judgment*. There are also brief summaries in several of the Pauline Epistles of what the apostle must have considered to be essential tenets. Thus for example we have the death, burial and resurrection of Christ mentioned in 1 Cor **15** 3 f; Rom **1** 3 f. Such summaries or confessions of personal faith as in 2 Thess **2** 13 f are frequent in Paul's writings and may correspond to statements of truth which the apostle found serviceable for catechetical purposes as he moved from one Christian community to another. See CATECHIST.

It is not indeed till a much later age—the age of Irenaeus and Tertullian (175–200)—that we meet with any definite summary of belief. But it cannot be doubted that these Scriptural passages to which we have referred not only served as the first forms of confession but also contributed the materials out of which the articles of the church's faith were formulated. As soon as Christian preaching and teaching were exercised there would be a felt need for explicit statement of the truths revealed in and through Jesus Christ. It may be said that all the main facts which were subsequently embodied in the creeds have their roots in the NT Scripture and esp. in the Pauline Epistles. The only exception which might be made is in the case of the virgin birth. It does not lie within the scope of this art. to comment upon the silence of the epistles on this subject. This, however, we may say, that the omissions of Paul's reference to it does not prove it untrue. It only proves at most that it was not a part of the ground upon which the Christ was commended to the first acceptance of faith. But though no direct allusion to the virgin birth occurs in Paul's writings the truth which gives spiritual value to the fact of the virgin conception, viz., God's new creation of humanity in Christ, is a vital and fundamental element in the faith both of St. Paul and of the whole early church. The Christian life is essentially a new creation (2 Cor **5** 17; Gal **6** 15; Rom **6** 4) in Jesus Christ, the second Adam (Rom **5** 12–21), who is from heaven (1 Cor **15** 47). Into this spiritual context the facts recorded by Matthew and Luke introduce no alien or incompatible element (cf W. Richmond, *The Creed in the Epistles of Paul;* Orr, *The Virgin Birth of Christ*). And therefore the story of Christ's birth as we have it in the Synoptics finds a natural place in the creed of those who accept the Pauline idea of a new creation in Christ. See VIRGIN BIRTH.

It is beyond the scope of this art. to discuss the evidences of development in the main doctrines of the gospel, but however the later ages may have elaborated them, the leading tenets of the subsequent faith of the church—the doctrine of the Trinity; Our Lord's divinity and real humanity; His atoning death and resurrection; the doctrine of the Holy Spirit and of the catholicity and unity of the church—stand clear and distinct in these earliest Scriptural sources.

II. Historical Forms.—Faith implies a creed as a confession and testimony. Such a confession and testimony answers to a natural impulse of the soul. Hence a profession of faith is at once a personal, a social and a historical testimony. A formal creed witnesses to the universality of faith, binds believers together, and unites the successive ages of the church. It is the spontaneous expression of the life and experience of the Christian society. As the purpose of this art. is chiefly to indicate the Scriptural sources of the creeds rather than to discuss their origin and history, we can only briefly describe the main historical forms which have prevailed in the Christian church.

1. The Apostles' Creed

The Apostles' Creed, anciently called the Roman Creed, though popularly regarded as the earliest, was probably not the first in chronological order. Its origin and growth are involved in considerable obscurity (see separate art., APOSTLES' CREED; and cf Heurtley, *Harmonia Symbolica*).

2. The Nicene Creed

The Nicene Creed, called sometimes "the Creed of the 318" from the number of bishops reputed to have been present, was authorized at the Council of Nice in 325 AD, and completed by the Council of Constantinople in 381, when the clauses which follow the mention of the Holy Ghost were added. The opinions of Arius at the beginning of the 4th cent. created such unrest as to call forth not only the admonition of bishops but also the intervention of the emperor Constantine, who, as a professed Christian, had become the patron of the church. The efforts of the emperor, however, had no effect in allaying the dissensions of the church at Alexandria, which, upon the banishment of Arius, spread throughout eastern Christendom. It was decided, therefore, to convoke a general council of bishops in which the Catholic doctrine should be once and for all formally declared. This, the first œcumenical council, met at Nicaea in Bithynia in 325 AD. There is no detailed record of the proceedings. "We do not know whether it lasted weeks or days" (Stanley, *Lects on East Ch.*). Arius, being only a presbyter, had no seat in the conclave, but was allowed to express his opinions. His chief opponent was Athanasius.

The controversy turned upon the nature of the Son and His relation to the Father. The word *homooúsios* ("of one substance with"), used in the course of the argument with a view of controverting the extreme orthodox position, became the battleground between the parties. The Arians violently condemned. The Sabellians or Semi-Arians to evade its full force contended for the term *homoioúsios* ("of like substance"). But the majority finally adopted the former expression as the term best suited to discriminate their view of the relation of the Father and Son from the Arian view. The assent of the emperor was gained and the words "being of one substance with the Father" were incorporated into the creed. The clauses descriptive of the Holy Spirit were added or confirmed at a later council (382), and were designed to refute the Macedonian heresy which denied His equality with the Father and Son, and reduced the Holy Spirit to a level with the angels.

The phrase "proceedeth from the Father and the Son" is also of historical importance. The last three words are a later addition to the creed by western churches, formally adopted by the Council of Toledo in 589. But when the matter was referred in the 9th cent. to Leo III he pronounced against them as unauthorized. This interpolation, known as the *Filioque*, marks the difference still between the Lat and Gr churches. From the 9th cent. no change has been made in the Nicene Creed. It has remained, without the *Filioque* clause, the œcumenical symbol of the Eastern Church; and with the addition of that word it has taken its place among the three great creeds of the Western Church.

3. The Athanasian Creed

The Athanasian Creed, or the *Symbolum Quicunque*, as it is called, from its opening words, differs entirely in its origin and history from those we have just considered. It is not a gradual growth like the Apostles' Creed, nor is it the outcome of synodical authority like the Nicene Creed. "When the composition appears for the first time as a document of authority it is cited in its completeness and as the work of the Father whose name it has since, in the most part, borne, although it was not brought to light for many cents. after his death" (Lumby, *Hist of the Creeds*). Without going into the full and intricate evidence which has been brought forward by scholars to prove that it is incorrectly attributed to Athanasius, it is sufficient to observe that both authorship and date are uncertain. Dr. Swainson proves in the most conclusive manner that the existence of this creed cannot be traced before the age of Charlemagne, and that its origin may probably be ascribed to the then existing demand for a more detailed exposition of the faith than was to be found in the Apostles' Creed. It is nowhere mentioned at synods before the end of the 8th cent., whose special business it was to discuss the very matters which were afterward embodied within it in such detail.

The question of imposture has been raised with regard to this creed, and it has been maintained by some that it was originally a forgery of the same nature as the "false decretals" and the equally famous "Donation of Constantine" (Swainson). But it may be said that the word "imposture" is incorrectly applied to "a natural and inevitable result of the working of the mind of the Western Church toward a more elaborate and detailed confession of its Trinitarian faith" (Tulloch, *Enc Brit*). The imposture, if there was any, consisted not in the origin of the creed but in the ascription of it to a name and a date with which it had no connection. This was done no doubt to secure for it credit and authority, and was supposed to be justified by its special doctrinal import.

This symbol, though too compendious and elaborate to serve the purposes of a creed, itself standing in need of exposition and explanation, has its value as representing a further stage of doctrinal development. If the Apostles' Creed determined the nature of God and the Nicene Creed defined the character and relation of the Son and the Holy Spirit, the Athanasian Creed may be regarded as establishing the great doctrine of the Trinity. Its distinguishing features are the *monitory* clauses and its uncompromising statement of the value of the Christian faith. The other creeds set forth the mercies of Revelation; this adds the danger of rejecting them. The others declare the faith; this insists also on its necessity. This, also, alone insists upon the necessity of good works (Yonge, *An Exposition of the Apostles' Creed*). The closing warning is based on Christ's own words: "Depart from me," etc (Mt **25** 41.46). If this creed is solemn in its admonitions, we must remember that so also are the Gospels. On the whole it is a comprehensive summary of truth, laying down the rule of faith as a foundation, following out its issues of good or evil. True belief is closely connected with right action.

With the adoption of the "Athanasian" symbol, the creed-making of the early and mediaeval church ceases. Of the three mentioned one only in the broadest sense, the Nicene, is Catholic. Neither the Apostles' nor the Athanasian Creed is known to the Gr or oriental church which remained faithful to the faith settled by the holy Fathers at Nicaea. The two others adopted by the West are really gradual growths or consequences from it, without any definite parentage or synodic authority. But the faith as defined at Nicaea and ratified by subsequent councils is the only true Catholic symbol of the universal church.

4. The Reformation Creeds

With the *Reformation* a new era of creed-formation began. It will not, however, be necessary to do more than mention some of the confessions of the Reformed churches which consist mainly of elaborations of the original creeds with the addition of special arts. designed to emphasize and safeguard the distinctive doctrines and ecclesiastical positions of particular branches of the church. Of this nature are the Confessions of the Lutheran church—the Augsburg Confession of 1530; the Genevese or Calvinistic of 1549 consisting of 26 arts., defining particularly the nature of the Sacraments; confessions of the Dutch church confirmed at the Synod of Dort in 1619 and known as the "Decrees of Dort"; and the famous Heidelberg Catechism. To this series of Protestant confessions must be added the 39 Articles of the Church of England and the Westminster Confession of Faith, which is the doctrinal standard not only of the churches of Scotland, but of the principal Presbyterian churches of Britain and America.

LITERATURE.—Winer, *Doctrines and Confessions of Christendom* (tr Clark, 1873); Lumby, *History of the Creeds;* Swainson, *The Nicene and Apostles' Creeds* (1875); Heurtley, *Harmonia Symbolica* (1858); Zahn, *Apost. Symb.* (1892); Harnack, *Apost. Glaubensbekenntnis;* Swete, *Apostles' Creed;* Hefele, *Councils of the Church;* Schaff, *The Creeds of Christendom.* For exposition, and of a more popular nature, may be mentioned the works of Hooker, Barrow, and Beveridge, and esp. Bishop Pearson; Westcott, *Historic Faith;* Norris, *Rudiments of Theology;* W. W. Harvey, *The Three Creeds;* J. Eyre Yonge, *An Exposition of the Apostles' Creed* (1888); Wilfred Richmond, *The Creed in the Epistles of Paul* (1909).

ARCHIBALD ALEXANDER

CREEK, krēk, colloq. krik (**κόλπος**, *kólpos* [Acts **27** 39], RV "bay"): The spot has been identified as the traditional Bay of St. Paul about 8 miles N.W. of the town of Valetta in the island of Malta. See MELITA.

CREEPING, THING (רֶמֶשׂ, *remes*, שֶׁרֶץ, *shereç;* **ἑρπετόν**, *herpetón*): *Remes* and *shereç*, with the root vbs. *rāmas* and *shāraç*, are used without any sharp distinction for insects and other small creatures. *Rāmas* means clearly "to creep," and is used even of the beasts of the forest (Ps **104**

20), while *shāraç* is rather "to swarm." But in at least one passage (Lev **11** 44), we have the noun, *shereç*, with the vb. *rāmas;* "with any manner of creeping thing that moveth upon the earth." The principal passages where these words occur are the accounts of the Creation and the Flood and the references to unclean animals in Lev and in the vision of Peter. In the last we have the word *herpeton* as the Gr equivalent of the Heb words (Acts **10** 12). Winged creeping things (*shereç hā-'ōph*, Lev **11** 20 ff), as well as the wingless, are unclean, but an exception is made in favor of the locusts, "which have legs above their feet, wherewith to leap upon the earth." See Insects; Locust.

Alfred Ely Day

CREMATION, krē-mā'shun (cf שָׂרַף, *sāraph*, Josh **7** 15, etc, "shall be burnt with fire"; **καίω,** *kaíō*, 1 Cor **13** 3, "If I give my body to be burned," etc): Cremation, while the customary practice of the ancient Greeks, and not unknown among the Romans, was certainly not the ordinary mode of disposing of the dead among the Hebrews or other oriental peoples. Even among the Greeks, bodies were often buried without being burned (Thuc. i. 134.6; Plato *Phaedo* 115 E; Plut. *Lyc.* xxvii). Cicero thought that burial was the more ancient practice, though among the Romans both methods were in use in his day (*De leg.* ii.22.56). Lucian (*De luctu* xxi) expressly says that, while the Greeks burned their dead, the Persians buried them (see Burial, and cf 2 S **21** 12–14). In the case supposed by Amos (**6** 10), when it is predicted that Jeh, in abhorrence of "the excellency of Jacob," shall "deliver up the city," and, "if there remain ten men in one house, that they shall die," and "a man's kinsman [ARVm] shall take him up, *even he that burneth him*," etc, the suggestion seems to be that of pestilence with accompanying infection, and that this, or the special judgment of Jeh, is why burning is preferred. When Paul (1 Cor **13** 3) speaks of giving his body to be burned, he is simply accommodating his language to the customs of Corinth. (But see Plutarch on Zarmanochegas, and C. Beard, *The Universal Christ.*)

How far religious, or sanitary, or practical reasons were influential in deciding between the different methods, it is impossible to say. That bodies were burned in times of pestilence in the Valley of Hinnom at Jerus is without support (see Ezk **39** 11–16). The "very great burning" at the burial of Asa (2 Ch **16** 14) is not a case of cremation, but of burning spices and furniture in the king's honor (cf Jer **34** 5). Nor is 1 K **13** 2 a case in point; it is simply a prophecy of a king who shall take the bones of men previously buried, and the priests of the high places that burn incense in false worship, and cause them to be burned on the defiled altar to further pollute it and render it abominable.

There is in the NT no instance of cremation, Jewish, heathen or Christian, and clearly the early Christians followed the Jewish practice of burying the dead (see Tert., *Apol.*, xlii; Minuc. Felix, *Octav.*, xxxix; Aug., *De civ. Dei*, i.12,13). Indeed, cremation has never been popular among Christians, owing largely, doubtless, to the natural influence of the example of the Jews, the indisputable fact that Christ was buried, the vivid hope of the resurrection and the more or less material views concerning it prevalent here and there at this time or that. While there is nothing anti-Christian in it, and much in sanitary considerations to call for it in an age of science, it is not likely that it will ever become the prevailing practice of Christendom.

Geo. B. Eager

CRESCENS, kres'enz (**Κρήσκης,** *Krēskēs*, "increasing"): An assistant of Paul, mentioned in 2 Tim **4** 10 as having gone to Galatia. That he was one of the Seventy, and that he founded the church in Vienna in Gaul, are traditions without any trustworthy basis.

CRESCENTS, kres'ents (שַׂהֲרֹנִים, *sahărōnīm*): Moon-shaped necklaces (Jgs **8** 21.26; Isa **3** 18).

CRETE, krēt (**Κρήτη,** *Krḗtē*, ethnic **Κρῆτες,** *Krḗtes*, Acts **2** 11; Tit **1** 12): An island bounding the Aegean Sea on the S. It stretches from 34° 50′ to 35° 40′ N. lat. and from 23° 30′ to 26° 20′ E. long. With Cythera on the N.W. and Carpathos and Rhodos on the N.E., it forms a continuous bridge between Greece and Asia Minor. The center of the island is formed by a mountain chain rising to a height of 8,193 ft. in Mt. Ida, and fringed with low valleys beside the coast. There are no considerable rivers; the largest, the Metropole, on the S., is a tiny stream, fordable anywhere. An island of considerable extent (156 miles long, and from 7 to 30 miles broad), in several districts very fertile and possessing one or two good harbors, it seems marked out by its position for an important rôle in the history of the eastern Mediterranean. But never since an age which was already legendary when Gr history began has Crete occupied a dominating position among the powers of the surrounding continents. Internal dissensions, due in ancient times to the diversity of races inhabiting its soil (Eteocretans—the original inhabitants—Pelasgians, Achaeans, Cydonians and Dorians), and in modern times to the fact that a large minority of the population has accepted the Ottoman religion along with Ottoman government, have kept Crete in a position of political inferiority throughout the historical period.

1. Early History

Mt. Ida in Crete was famous in Gr legend as the birthplace of Zeus. The half-legendary, half-historical King Minos was said to be the son of Zeus, and to have derived from his father the wisdom to which, by a type of myth common in Gr lands, the constitution of the Cretan cities was ascribed. Minos was accepted as a historical personage by Thucydides and Aristotle, who say that he was the first dynast in Greece to establish dominion on the sea. One of his exploits was the suppression of piracy in Cretan waters, a feat which had to be repeated by the Rom Pompeius at a later period. Aristotle compares the Cretan institutions with those of Sparta; the island was said to have been colonized by Dorians from Peloponnesus (*Politics* ii.10). The most important cities in Crete were Knossos (whose palace has been excavated with fruitful results by Mr. Arthur Evans), Gortyna, near the Gulf of Messara, and Cydonia, with its river Iardanus. The excavations of Mr. Evans at Knossos and of the Italians at Phaestos (near Fair Havens) prove that Crete was a center of Mediterranean civilization in an early age. In the Homeric poems, Crete is said to have contained an hundred cities; at that period the Cretans were still famed as daring sailors. In the classical age of Gr history they never held a leading position. They are mentioned chiefly as traders and mercenary soldiers, skilled esp. in archery. During the Hellenistic period Crete remained free. Demetrius Nicator made the island his base of operations before his defeat at Azotus in 148.

2. The Jews in Crete

In 141, the Cretan Jews were influential enough to secure the patronage of Rome. They were being oppressed by the people of Gortyna, and appealed to Rome, which granted them protection. In strengthening the position of the Jews, the Romans were copying the Seleucid policy in Asia Minor; both the Seleucids and the Romans found the Jews among their most devoted supporters in their subject states. This interference of Rome in the interest of her future partisans paved the way for her annexation of the island in the following cent. From this date, there was a strong and prosperous body of Jews in Crete, and Cretans are mentioned among the strangers present at the Feast of Pentecost in Acts **2** 11. Its alliance with Mithradates the Great, and the help it gave to the Cilician pirates gave Rome the pretext she desired for making war on Crete, and the island was annexed by Metellus in 67 BC. With Cyrene on the N. coast of Africa, it was formed into a Rom province. When Augustus divided the Empire between the Senate and himself, Crete and Cyrene were sufficiently peaceful to be given to the Senate.

They formed one province till the time of Constantine, who made Crete a separate province.

3. Later History

The Saracens annexed Crete in 823 AD, but it was recaptured for the Byzantine Empire by Nicephorus Phokas in the following cent. From the 13th till the 17th cent. it was held by the Venetian Republic: from this period dates its modern name "Kandia," which the Venetians gave to the Saracen capital Khandax, and afterward to the whole island. After a desperate resistance, lasting from 1645 to 1669 AD, Crete fell into the hands of the Turks, who still exercise a nominal suzerainty over the island.

4. Crete in the OT

In 1 S **30** 14; Ezk **25** 16, and Zeph **2** 5, the Philis are described as Cherethites, which is usually taken to mean Cretans. The name is connected with Caphtor and the Caphtorim (Dt **2** 23; Jer **47** 4; Am **9** 7). The similarity between the river-names Jordan and Iardanos (Homer *Odyssey* iii. 292) "about whose streams the Kydones dwelt," has suggested that Caphtor is to be identified with Cydonia; or possibly it was the name of the whole island. Tacitus believed in an ancient connection between Crete and Pal; the Jews, he said, were fugitives from Crete, and derived their name Iudaei from Mt. Ida (*Hist.* v.2). Crete is mentioned in connection with the campaign of Demetrius Nicator, referred to above, in 1 Macc **10** 67. See Caphtor; Cherethites.

5. Crete in the NT

Crete owes its connection with Pauline history to the accident of a gale which forced the ship carrying Paul to Rome to take shelter on the S. coast of the island. In the harbor of Myra, on the coast of Lycia, the centurion in charge of Paul transferred him from the Adramyttian ship which had brought them from Caesarea, to a ship from Alexandria in Egypt, bound for Ostia with a cargo of grain. The fact that the centurion was in virtual command of the ship (Acts **27** 11) proves that it was one of the vessels in the imperial transport service. Leaving Myra they came opposite Cnidus with difficulty, against a head-wind. The ordinary course from Cnidus in good weather was to steer straight for Cythera, but on this occasion the W. or N.W. winds made this route impracticable, and they sailed under the lee of Crete, whose S. coast would shelter them from a N.W. gale, and afford occasional protection from a W. gale. They passed Salmone, the N.E. corner of Crete, with difficulty, and worked round the coast to Fair Havens, a harbor somewhat to the E. of Cape Matala. The great Feast fell while they were at Fair Havens; in 59 AD it was on October 5, in the middle of the season when the equinoxes made sailing impossible. Paul advised the centurion to winter in Fair Havens, but the captain wished to reach Phoenix, a harbor farther to the W., where ships from Egypt were accustomed to put in during the stormy season. It was decided to follow the captain's advice; but on its way to Phoenix the ship was struck by a N.E. wind called Euraquilo, which rushed down from Mt. Ida. The ship was carried out to sea; it managed to run under the lee of Cauda, an island 23 miles W. of Cape Matala, where the crew hauled in the boat, undergirded the ship, and slackened sail. On the fourteenth night they were driven on the coast of Malta, and wrecked.

The narrative does not state that Paul landed in Crete, but as the ship lay for some time at Fair Havens (Acts **27** 8.9) he had plenty of opportunity to land, but not to travel inland. The centurion gave him permission to land at Sidon. Paul left Titus in Crete (Tit **1** 5); tradition made the latter its first bishop, and patron saint.

6. The Cretans

Cretans were present, as noted above, at the Feast of Pentecost (Acts **2** 11). Paul's estimate of the Cretan character (Tit **1** 10–16) was the one current in antiquity. Paul quotes (**1** 12) a well-known line of the Cretan poet Epimenides (who lived about 600 BC) on the mendacity of the Cretans. The sentiment was repeated by Callimachus (*Hymn to Zeus* 8). Other ancient witnesses to the detestation in which the Cretan character was held are Livy xliv.45, and Plutarch *Aemilius* § 23.

Literature.—Smith, *Voyage and Shipwreck of St. Paul;* Ramsay, *St. Paul the Traveller and Roman Citizen,* 320–30. On Crete in Gr and Rom times, consult e.g. Grote, Holm, and Mommsen. A succinct account of the prehistoric archaeology of the island is given in Burrows, *The Discoveries in Crete,* and Baikie, *The Sea Kings of Crete.*

W. M. Calder

CRIB (אֵבוּס, *'ēbhūṣ*): "Crib" translates the Heb word *'ēbhūṣ* exactly, as it denotes "a barred receptacle for fodder used in cowsheds and foldyards; also in fields, for beasts lying out in the winter." The Heb is from a word meaning to feed (אָבַס, *'ābhaṣ*), and is used in the precise sense of the Eng. word in Job **39** 9 of the "crib" of the wild ox, in Prov **14** 4, "Where no oxen are, the crib is clean," and in Isa **1** 3, "The ox knoweth his owner, and the ass his master's crib."

CRICKET, krik'et (חַרְגֹּל, *ḥargōl*): This occurs in Lev **11** 22 (AV "beetle"), and doubtless refers to some kind of locust or grasshopper. See Beetle; Locust; Insect.

CRIER, krī'ēr (קָרָא, *ḳārā'*; cf βοάω, *boáō*):

(1) Neither is this exact word found in EV, nor a word exactly corresponding to it in the Heb Bible, but the character it stands for appears as "one who cries aloud," i.e., proclaims mandates or gives public messages. In Prov **1** 21 it is said, "She [Wisdom] crieth in the chief place of concourse." John the Baptist calls himself "the voice of one crying in the wilderness" (Jn **1** 23)—like a herald going before the king.

(2) In the East today every village even has its public crier, selected for his loud or penetrating voice, and appointed to give notice of the fresh orders or mandates of the *mudir* ("governor") or other authorities. The *muezzin* of the Moslems, who at the five appointed times of prayer mounts the minaret and calls the faithful to prayer, is another striking example. Something like the ancient "heralds" of the king were the "heralds" of the Middle Ages in Europe who, preceded by trumpeters, made official proclamations.

Geo. B. Eager

CRIME, krīm, **CRIMES**, krīmz: This term is used in Eng. as the equivalent of the Heb מִשְׁפָּט, *mishpāṭ*, "judgment," "verdict" (Ezk **7** 23); זִמָּה, *zimmāh*, "a heinous crime" (Job **31** 11); אָשָׁם, *'āshām*= "a fault," "sin" (Gen **26** 10, EV "guiltiness");

and Gr **αἰτία**, *aitía*, "case," "cause" (Acts **25** 27, RV "charges"). In AV Jn **18** 38; **19** 4.6, the rendition is "fault."

ἔγκλημα, *égklēma*, "indictment," "charge" (Acts **25** 16 AV) is changed in RV to "matter." A crime is a transgression against the public right; serious offence against the law; a base weakness or iniquity, all of which are regarded by the Bible as offences against (1) God, or (2) man, or (3) both. An injury to the creature is regarded as obnoxious to the Creator. Specific forms of crime are the following:

Adultery.—See separate art.

Assassination.—This term does not occur in the EV, but, of course, is included in the more general "to kill," or "to slay" (הָרַג, *hāragh*="to smite with deadly intent," "destroy," "kill," "murder," "put to death"). The law distinguished between unpremeditated and premeditated slaying, pronouncing a curse upon the latter (Dt **27** 25). David expresses the deepest abhorrence of such an act (2 S **4** 9–12). Instances are found recorded in Jgs **3** 15–22; 2 S **3** 27; **4** 5–7; **13** 28.29; **20** 9.10; 2 K **12** 20; **19** 37; Isa **37** 38. See also separate art.

Bestiality.—According to Webster: "unnatural connection with a beast." This form of vice was treated by the Mosaic law as something exceedingly loathsome and abhorrent, calling for extreme language in its description and rigorous measures in its punishment. Both the beast and the guilty human were to be put to death (Ex **22** 19; Lev **18** 23; **20** 15.16; Dt **27** 21), in order, as the Talm says, to obliterate all memory of the crime.

Blasphemy.—See separate art.

Breach of Covenant (פָּרַר אֶת־הַבְּרִית, *pārar 'eth ha-b^e^rīth*).—According to Poucher (*HDB*, art. "Crimes"), this term included: (1) failure to observe the Day of Atonement (Lev **23** 29); work on that day (Lev **23** 28); (2) sacrifice of children to Molech (Lev **20** 3); (3) neglect of circumcision (Gen **17** 14; Ex **4** 26); (4) unauthorized manufacture of the holy oil (Ex **30** 33); (5) anointing an alien therewith (Ex **30** 33); (6) neglect of the Passover (Nu **9** 13). Note also the following: Gen **17** 14; Lev **26** 15–44; Dt **29** 25; **31** 16.20. Paul (Rom **1** 31) speaks of **ἀσύνθετοι**, *asúnthetoi* ="covenant-breakers."

Breach of Ritual.—A term not found in the Scriptures, but designed to cover a number of acts prohibited by the ceremonial law. They have been exhaustively enumerated by Poucher (*HDB*, art. "Crimes"): (1) eating blood, whether of fowl or beast (Lev **7** 27; **17** 14); (2) eating fat of the beast of sacrifice (Lev **7** 25); (3) eating leavened bread during the Passover (Ex **12** 15.19); (4) failure to bring an offering when an animal is slaughtered for food (Lev **17** 4); (5) offering sacrifice while the worshipper is under the ban of uncleanness (Lev **7** 20.21; **22** 3.4.9); (6) making holy ointment for private use (Ex **30** 32.33); (7) using the same for perfume (Ex **30** 38); (8) neglect of purification in general (Nu **19** 13.20); (9) slaughtering an animal for food away from the door of the tabernacle (Lev **17** 4.9); even the alien must comply, so that the introduction of worship at other places might be avoided; (10) touching holy things illegally (Nu **4** 16.20 RV "the sanctuary"). The punishment for the non-observance of these prohibitions was the "cutting off" from the transgressor's people (נִכְרַת מִקֶּרֶב, *nikhrath miḳḳerebh*="cut off from among," i.e. excommunicated).

Breach of Trust.—See Trust, Breach of.

Bribery.—See separate art.

Burglary.—This term does not occur. The corresponding act is defined as "thievery accompanied by breaking," and it places the offender beyond protection from violence (Ex **22** 2). The crime might be committed in various degrees, and to burglarize the "devoted things" was punishable by death (Josh **7** 25), as was also man-stealing (Ex **21** 16; Dt **24** 7).

Debt.—See separate art.

Deception.—See separate art.

Disobedience.—See separate art.

Divination.—See separate art.

Drunkenness.—See separate art.

Evil Speaking (Slander).—See **Speaking Evil.**

Falsehood.—Occurs as the rendition of מַעַל, *ma'al*="treachery," "sin," "trespass" (Job **21** 34); and of שֶׁקֶר, *sheḳer*="a sham," "deceit," "lying" (2 S **18** 13; Ps **7** 14; **119** 118; **144** 8.11; Isa **28** 15; **57** 4; **59** 13; Jer **10** 14; **13** 25; Hos **7** 1; Mic **2** 11). In every case wilful perversion of the truth or preference for the untruth is at least presupposed, hence falsehood always marks an evil disposition, enmity against truth, and hence against God; consequently is criminal in the fullest sense.

False Swearing.—"Swearing to a lie or falsehood" (שֶׁקֶר, *sheḳer*) is mentioned in Lev **6** 3.5; **19** 12; Jer **5** 2; **7** 9; Hos **10** 4; Zec **5** 4. From these passages and their context, it appears that this crime was considered in the twofold sense of a wrong against (1) the neighbor, and (2) against God, for the oath was an appeal to God as a witness to the truthfulness of the statement; hence to swear falsely was to represent God as supporting a false statement.

Fornication.—Heb, זָנָה, *zānāh* = "to commit adultery," esp. of the female, and less frequently of mere fornication, seldom of involuntary ravishment; also used **figuratively** in the sense of idolatry, the Jewish people being regarded as the spouse of Jeh (2 Ch **21** 11; Isa **23** 17; Ezk **16** 26). Once we find the derivative noun תַּזְנוּת, *taznūth* (Ezk **16** 29). In the NT, with both the literal and the **figurative** application, we find **πορνεία**, *porneía*, and **πορνεύω**, *porneúō* (Mt **5** 32; **15** 19; Jn **8** 41; Acts **15** 20; 1 Cor **5** 1; **6** 13.18; **7** 2; **10** 8; 2 Cor **12** 21; Gal **5** 19; Eph **5** 3; Col **3** 5; 1 Thess **4** 3; Rev **2** 14.20.21; **9** 21; **14** 8; **17** 2.4). The intensive **ἐκπορνεύω**, *ekporneúō*="to be utterly unchaste" is found in Jude ver 7. Every form of unchastity is included in the term "fornication."

Forswear.—Found only in Mt **5** 33 in the sense of committing perjury (**ἐπιορκέω**, *epiorkéō*).

Harlotry.—The avocational or at least habitual, notorious practice of unchastity. In most instances the ordinary term for unchaste living, זָנָה, *zānāh*, is employed (Gen **34** 31; **38** 15.24; Lev **21** 14; Josh **2** 1 [Rahab]; Jgs **11** 1; **16** 1; 1 K **3** 16; Prov **7** 10; **29** 3; Jer **5** 7; Am **7** 17). For the publicly known woman of the street and the professional devotee in the pagan temple-worship, the term קְדֵשָׁה, *k^e^dhēshāh*, was employed (Gen **38** 21.22 AV; Hos **4** 14). The Gr **πόρνη**, *pórnē*, occurs in Mt **21** 31 f; Lk **15** 30; 1 Cor **6** 15.16; He **11** 31; Jas **2** 25). **Figurative**: Often used metaphorically of idolatry or any defection from the Divine covenant, and applied particularly to Jerus (Isa **1** 21); the Jewish nation (Jer **2** 20; **3** 1.6 ff; often in Ezk **16** and **23**; Mic **1** 7); Israel (Hos **4** 15); Nineveh (Nah **3** 4); Tyre, with reference to the various arts employed to renew her commerce (Isa **23** 16) and to her restored traffic (ver 17); and to anti-Christian "Babylon" (Rev **17** 5.15; **19** 2). See also **Fornication.**

Homicide="manslayer" (רָצַח, *rāçaḥ*, "to dash in pieces," "to kill," "to murder"; Gr **ἀνδροφόνος**, *androphónos*, with the same meaning): Mentioned in Nu **35** 6.12; 1 Tim **1** 9. The Heb law distinguished between the premeditated and the unpremeditated slaying. See separate art.

Idolatry.—See separate art.

Ill-treatment of Parents (Ex **21** 15.17; Lev **20** 9; Dt **21** 18 ff).—See below.

Injuries to the Person (Ex **21** 18 ff; Lev **24** 19 f; Dt **25** 11).

Irreverence.—Lack of respect for God or His natural representatives, the parents or governmental officers. See also **Parents, Crimes against; Blasphemy.**

Incest.—Designated in Heb by זִמָּה, *zimmāh*, "vice," "wickedness," "refined immorality" (Lev **18** 17; **20** 14); also "unnatural vice," תֶּבֶל, *tebhel*, the same word that is used to designate the unnatural commingling with beasts. Amnon's deed is designated as חֶסֶד, *ḥeṣedh*, indicating the degradation of the tenderness natural between brothers and sisters into a tenderness of an immoral character (2 S **13**). The crime of sexual relation of persons within the degrees of relationship forbidden by the Levitical law, as for instance, that of Lot's daughters with their father (Gen **19** 33); the son with his father's concubines, as for instance, Reuben (Gen **35** 22), and Absalom (2 S **16** 22; cf 1 Cor **5** 1); that of the father-in-law with his daughter-in-law (Gen **38** 15 ff; cf Ezk **22** 11); of the brother with the sister or half-sister, as for instance, Amnon (2 S **13** 14); of the brother-in-law with the sister-in-law (Mt **14** 3); with the wife's mother, or the wife's daughter while living in apparent marriage with the mother (Lev **20** 14; **18** 17). Illicit relation with the brother's widow is designated (Lev **20** 21) as a disgraceful deed, lit. "uncleanness" (excepting the levirate marriage). Such acts were forbidden on the ground that the Jews were to avoid the evil practices of the Canaanites and the Egyptians in regard to marriage within the specified limits, because this would naturally result in breaking down the sanctity of the bonds connecting near relatives, and in throwing open the flood gates of immorality among them. It is the Divine plan that the unions based on mutual choice and love, mingled with carnality, shall become clarified more and more into the purer love of close consanguineal relations; not vice versa. Then, too, such provisions would secure higher results in training and in the production of mentally and physically healthy children, the balancing and evening up of contrasts of Nature, and the production of new and improved types. The principle on which the prohibitions are imposed seems to be this: Marriage is forbidden between any person and a direct ancestor or a direct descendant or any close relative, such as brother or sister of either himself or any of his ancestors or any of his immediate descendants.

Infanticide.—This crime, in the form in which it has been and is prevalent among barbarous nations, seems to have been quite foreign to the minds of the Hebrews, for they had too lofty a conception of the value of human life, and children were considered a blessing; their absence in the home, a curse (cf Ex **1** 17.21; Ps **127, 128**). For this reason, there appeared to be no reason to prohibit it by law, excepting as the Israelites might be influenced to sacrifice their children to Molech when following the religious customs of the Canaanites. See Molech.

Kidnapping (Man-Stealing).—**ἀνδραποδιστής**, *andrapodistēs* = "man-stealer," "slave-dealer" (1 Tim **1** 10). This was a mortal offence; but it seems that it, like some other forms of iniquity, was unknown to the Hebrews, excepting as they came in contact with it through their intercourse with other nations, such as the Romans and the Greeks, whose mythology frequently alludes to such acts.

Lying, Malice, Manslaughter, Murder, Oath.—See separate arts.

Parents, Crimes against.—The law enjoined upon the infant all the reverence toward his parents, esp. the father, that he could bestow on a merely human being. The reason for this lay in the fact that the heads of families were expected to transmit the Divine law to their household, and thus to stand in the place of God. That the mother was to share this reverence practically on equal terms with the father is shown by the fact that each is mentioned separately whenever obedience and reverence are enjoined upon the child (Dt **5** 16). As the specific crime against Jeh consisted in blasphemy and open rebellion against the law, so the crime against parents consisted in deliberate disobedience and stubbornness (Dt **21** 18). And here again both the father and the mother are directed to lay hands upon him and bring him unto the elders for punishment. How greatly such conduct was held in horror is seen in many of the Proverbs, esp. **30** 17. It would be hard to specify all the acts which, in view of the above, would be considered crimes against the parents, but it is evident that everything which would lower their dignity and influence or violate their sense of just recognition must be carefully avoided, as witness the curse visited upon Ham (Gen **9** 20–27).

Perjury.—See **False Swearing; Forswear** above; also art. Oath.

Prophesying, False.—By reason of his position as the recognized mouthpiece of Jeh, the prophet's word was weighty in influence; hence to prophesy falsely was equivalent to practicing fraud publicly. Jeremiah described the condition as "wonderful and horrible," which made such things possible (**5** 30.31). See also Jer **23** 32; **29** 8.9; Ezk **21** 23; Zec **10** 2; Mt **7** 15; **24** 11.24; Mk **13** 22; Lk **6** 26; Acts **13** 6 (Bar-Jesus); 2 Pet **2** 1; 1 Jn **4** 1; Rev **16** 13; **19** 20; **20** 10. See also separate art.

Prostitution.—Heb and Christian morality never condoned this practice, though the Bible recognizes its existence as a fact even among God's people. The Heb father was forbidden (Lev **19** 29) to give his daughter over to a life of shame (חָלַל, *ḥālal*, "to profane a person, place or thing," "to pollute"). See also **Fornication, Harlotry,** and **Whoredom** below.

Rape.—חָזַק, *ḥāzaḳ* = "to seize," "bind," "restrain," "conquer," "force," "ravish." The punishment for this crime was greater when the act was committed against a betrothed woman (Dt **22** 25–29). See also **Seduction.**

Removing Landmarks (Dt **19** 14). See Landmarks.

Reviling (Ex **22** 28). See **Irreverence** above and art. Revile.

Robbery.—גָּזַל, *gāzal* = "to pluck off," "strip," "rob," "take away by force or violence"; forbidden in the law and frequently referred to as despicable (Lev **19** 13; **26** 22; 1 S **23** 1; Prov **22** 22; Isa **10** 2.13; **17** 14; Ezk **33** 15; **39** 10; Mal **3** 8.9).

Sabbath-Breaking.—As the Heb Sabbath was regarded as a day of rest, all acts absolutely unnecessary were considered a violation, a "breaking" of the Sabbath, which appears sufficiently from the commandment (Ex **20** 8–11); and the head of the household was held responsible for the keeping of this commandment on the part of all sojourners under his roof.

No other law gave the sophistical legalists of later Judaism so much opportunity for hair-splitting distinctions as did this. In answer to the question what labors were forbidden, they mentioned 39 specific forms of work, and then proceeded to define what constituted each particular form. But as even these definitions would not cover all possible questions, special precepts were invented. In order that one might not be caught in the midst of unfinished labors, when the Sabbath began (at sunset), certain forms of work must not be undertaken on Friday. Thus it was forbidden to fry meat, onions or eggs, if there was not sufficient time for them to be fully cooked before evening. No bread, no cakes, must be put into the oven, if there was not sufficient time remaining for their surface to brown before night. See SABBATH.

Seduction.—תָּעָה, *tā'āh*, "to dissemble," "seduce," and טָעָה, *ṭā'āh*, with the same meaning; **ἀποπλανάω**, *apoplanáō*, "to lead astray"; **πλανάω**, *planáō*, "to go astray," "deceive," "err," "seduce"; and **γόης**, *góēs*, "a wizard," "an impostor," "seducer." In all the passages in which the idea of seduction is expressed in the Eng. the term is used not in the modern sense of a trespass against a woman's person, but in the more general and **figurative** sense of leading into sin generally (2 K **21** 9; Prov **12** 26 AV; Isa **19** 13 AV; Ezk **13** 10; Mk **13** 22 AV; 2 Tim **3** 13 AV; 1 Jn **2** 26 AV; Rev **2** 20). However, the modern Eng. idea of the word is expressed in the law found in Ex **22** 16.17.

Slander.—See separate art.

Sodomy.—See **Unnatural Vice.**

Speaking Evil="to bring an evil [רַע, *rā'*] name upon" (Dt **19** 15; 1 K **22** 23; Ps **34** 13; **41** 5; **50** 19; **109** 20; **140** 11; Prov **15** 28; **16** 30). Evil speaking is considered a crime because it is simply the expression of the evil intents of the heart. This is brought out more clearly in the NT (Mt **7** 17.18; **12** 34.35; Mk **9** 39; Lk **6** 45). As such, evil speaking (**βλασφημία**, *blasphēmía*) is represented as entirely unworthy a Christian character (Eph **4** 31; 1 Pet **4** 4.14; 2 Pet **2** 2; 10.12; Jas **4** 11; Jude ver 10); and **καταλαλέω**, *katalaléō*="babble against," "gossip." It will be noticed from the above that evil speaking against those in authority is designated with the same word ("blasphemy") as raillery against God, they being considered God's representatives on earth. See also EVIL SPEAKING; SLANDER.

Stealing.—Heb גָּנַב, *gānabh*="to thieve" (lit. or fig.); by implication, "to deceive," "carry away," "secretly bring," "steal away" (Gen **44** 8; Ex **20** 15; **21** 16; **22** 1; Prov **6** 30; Zec **5** 3; Gen **31** 20. 26 f; 2 S **15** 6; **19** 3; Job **27** 20; Prov **9** 17 ["Stolen waters are sweet"; the forbidden is attractive; cf Rom **7** 7]). Gr **κλέπτω**, *kléptō*="to filch," "steal" (Mt **6** 19.20; **19** 18; Jn **10** 10; Rom **2** 21; **13** 9; Eph **4** 28). See **Theft.**

Suicide.—No special law is found against this crime, for it is included in the prohibition against killing. Contrary to the practice and the philosophy of paganism, the act was held in deep abhorrence by the Hebrews because of the high value placed on human life. It was held inexcusable that any but the most degraded and satanic should lay hands on their own lives. Only the remorse of the damned could drive one to it, as witness Saul (1 S **31** 4) and Judas (Mt **27** 5).

Theft.—Heb גְּנֵבָה, *g^enēbhāh* "stealing" (concrete), "something stolen," "theft" (Ex **22** 3.4); mentioned in connection with other wickedness (**κλοπή**, *klopḗ*) in Mt **15** 19; Mk **7** 21; and (**κλέμμα**, *klémma*) in Rev **9** 21. All three words are used abstractly for the act and concretely for the thing stolen. See THIEF.

Unchastity.—No other form of sin is mentioned with disapproval and threats more frequently than the various forms of carnal vice, for no other sin is more natural or widespread. See CHASTITY; LEWDNESS; MARRIAGE.

Unnatural Vice (Sodomy).—Alluded to with delicacy, but positively condemned as an abomination (Gen **13** 13; **19** 5.7; Lev **18** 22; **20** 13). It was the specific form of wickedness through which Sodom became notorious, so that "sodomite" is the regular tr of קָדֵשׁ, *ḳādhēsh*, "a [quasi] sacred person," i.e. (technically) "a [male or female] devotee to licentious idolatry" (Dt **23** 17; 1 K **14** 24; **15** 12; **22** 46; 2 K **23** 7; Job **36** 14m). Though permitted and even encouraged in heathen cult, it was never to be tolerated in the worship of Jeh.

Usury.—See separate art.

Witnessing, False.—The Heb idiom is עֵד שֶׁקֶר, *'ēdh sheḳer*, "witness of a falsehood," "lie" (Ex **20** 16; Dt **19** 16.18; Prov **6** 19; **14** 5.25; **19** 5.9); Gr **ψευδομαρτυρέω**, *pseudomarturéō*, "to bring false testimony"; **-μαρτυρία**, *-marturía*, "bearing of false testimony" (Mk **10** 19; **14** 56.57). It goes without saying that the law was emphatic in its denunciation of this practice, and in order that the innocent might be protected against the lying accuser, a criminal was to be convicted only on the testimony of at least two or three witnesses, testifying to the same facts (Nu **35** 30). If one be found testifying falsely, he was to be punished by suffering the penalty which would have been inflicted on him against whom he testified, had he been convicted (Dt **19** 16–19).

Whoredom.—Heb זָנָה, *zānāh*="to commit adultery," "fornication or illicit incontinence of any kind"; and its derivative תַּזְנוּת, *taznūth*="fornication," "harlotry," "whoredom"; Gr **πορνεύω**, *porneúō* (vb.), and **πορνεία**, *porneía* (noun), of the same meaning. The following passages will reveal the estimate in which such uncleanness was held, and the fact that men and women given to it were held in equal abhorrence and designated by the same terms: Gen **38** 24; Lev **19** 29; Nu **14** 33; **25** 1; Ezk **16**; **23** 3.7.8.11.27.29.43; **43** 7.9; Hos **1** 2; **2** 4; **4** 11.12; **6** 10; Nah **3** 4; Mt **5** 32; Rom **1** 26 f; 1 Cor **5** 1; **7** 2; **10** 8; Jude ver 7; Rev **2** 14.20 f; **18** 9; **19** 2.

Figurative: Because of the infidelity to the life-mate and to right living involved in such acts, the practice became symbolical of infidelity to God and His law, and thus served as a frequent figure of speech for Israel's error and apostasy. See HARLOT.

FRANK E. HIRSCH

CRIMSON, krim'z'n. See COLORS.

CRIPPLE, krip''l (**χωλός**, *chōlós*): Only occurs in Acts **14** 8, denoting the congenitally lame man at Lystra. In AV (1611) the word is spelled "creeple." It originally meant one whose body is bent together as in the attitude of creeping. This was probably a case of infantile paralysis.

CRISPING, kris'ping, **PINS:** Pins for crisping, or curling, the hair. Thus the AV renders Heb חֲרִיטִים, *ḥărīṭīm* (Isa **3** 22; cf Vulg). RV substitutes more correctly "satchels" (so Ḳimḥi [cf 2 K **5** 23]; cf Arab.). Others think of girdles; still others of veils or head-bands.

CRISPUS, kris'pus (**Κρίσπος**, *Kríspos*, "curled"): One of the small number baptized by Paul among the Corinthian Christians (1 Cor **1** 14). He had been ruler of the Jewish synagogue, but he "believed in the Lord with all his house"; and, following Paul, withdrew from the synagogue (Acts **18** 7.8). He seems to have been succeeded by Sosthenes (ver 17). According to tradition he became bishop of Aegina.

CRITICISM AND ARCHAEOLOGY. See ARCHAEOLOGY AND CRITICISM.

CRITICISM, krit'i-siz'm, **OF THE BIBLE:**

II. Lower or Textual Criticism
  1. Origin of the Science
  2. Methods Employed
  3. Causes of Error
  4. Weighing of Authorities
    (1) The OT
      MSS and VSS
    (2) The NT
      (a) MSS and VSS
      (b) The Western Text
      (c) Results
III. Higher Criticism
  1. The OT
    (1) Astruc and Successors
    (2) Hupfeld
    (3) Graf and Wellhausen
    (4) Literary and Historical Grounds of Theory
    (5) The Codes
    (6) Effects on History, etc
    (7) General Results
    (8) Criticism of Theory
  2. The NT
    (1) The School of Baur
    (2) Synoptical Criticism
      (a) Oral, Documentary, and Dependence Theories
      (b) The "Logia"
      (c) Two-Source Theory
      (d) Authorship—Lukan and Johannine Questions
    (3) Modern "Critical-Historical" School
    (4) Remaining Writings of NT
Literature

Criticism in General

So much has been said and written in recent years on "Criticism" that it is desirable that the reader should have an exact idea of what criticism is, of the methods it employs, and of the results it reaches, or believes itself to have reached, in its application to Scripture. Such a survey will show the legitimacy and indispensableness of a truly scientific criticism, at the same time that it warns against the hasty acceptance of speculative and hypothetical constructions. Criticism is more than a description of phenomena; it implies a process of sifting, testing, proving, sometimes with the result of establishing, often with that of modifying or reversing, traditional opinions. Criticism goes wrong when used recklessly, or under the influence of some dominant theory or prepossession. A chief cause of error in its application to the record of a supernatural revelation is the assumption that nothing supernatural can happen. This is the vitiating element in much of the newer criticism, both of the OT and of the NT.

I. Divisions.—Criticism of Scripture ("Bib. criticism") is usually divided into what is called "lower or textual criticism" and "higher criticism"—the latter a phrase round which many misleading associations gather.

1. Lower or Textual Criticism

"Lower criticism" deals strictly with the *text* of Scripture, endeavoring to ascertain what the real text of each book was as it came from the hands of its author; "higher criticism" concerns itself with the resultant problems of age, authorship, sources, simple or composite character, historical worth, relation to period of origin, etc.

2. Higher Criticism

The former—"textual criticism"—has a well-defined field in which it is possible to apply exact canons of judgment: the latter—"higher criticism"—while invaluable as an aid in the domain of Bib. introduction (date, authorship, genuineness, contents, destination, etc), manifestly tends to widen out illimitably into regions where exact science cannot follow it, where, often, the critic's imagination is his only law.

It was only gradually that these two branches of criticism became differentiated. "Textual criticism" for long took the lead, in association with a sober form of Bib. "introduction." The relations now tend to be reversed. "Higher criticism," having largely absorbed "introduction" into itself, extends its operations into the textual field, endeavoring to get behind the text of the existing sources, and to show how this "grew" from simpler beginnings to what it now is. Here, also, there is wide opening for arbitrariness. It would be wrong, however, to deny the legitimate place of "higher criticism," or belittle the great services it is capable of rendering, because of the abuses to which it is frequently liable.

It is now necessary that these two forms of criticism should be looked at more particularly.

II. Lower or Textual Criticism.—We take first lower or textual criticism.

1. Origin of the Science

There has never been a time when criticism of Scripture—lower and higher—has been altogether absent. The Jews applied a certain criticism to their sacred writings, alike in the selection of the books, and in the settlement of the text. Examples are seen in the marginal notes to the Heb Scriptures (Ḳ^{e}rē and K^{e}thībh). The Fathers of the early church compared MSS of the NT books, noting their differences, and judging of the books themselves. The Reformers, it is well known, did not accept blindly the judgments of antiquity, but availed themselves of the best light which the new learning afforded. The materials at the disposal of scholars in that age, however, were scanty, and such as existed were not used with much thoroughness or critical discernment. As aids multiplied with progress of discovery, comparison of MSS and VSS one with another and with patristic quotations, revealed manifold divergencies and it became apparent that, in both OT and NT, the text in current use in the church was far from perfect. "Various readings" accumulated. Not a few of these, indeed, were obvious blunders; many had little or no support in the more ancient authorities; for others, again, authority was fairly equally divided. Some were interpolations which had no right to be in the text at all. How, in these circumstances, was the true text to be ascertained? The work was one of great delicacy, and could only be accomplished by the most painstaking induction of facts, and the strictest application of sound methods. Thus arose a science of textual criticism, which, ramifying in many directions, has attained vast dimensions, and yielded an immense body of secure knowledge in its special department.

2. Methods Employed

The materials with which textual criticism works (*apparatus criticus*) are, as just said, chiefly MSS, VSS (translations into other tongues), quotations and allusions in patristic writings, with lectionaries (church service-books), and similar aids. The first step is the collection and collation of the material, to which fresh discovery is constantly adding; the noting of its peculiarities, and testing of its age and value; the grouping and designation of it for reference. A next important task is the complete collection of the "various readings" and other diversities of text (omissions, interpolations, etc), brought to light through comparison of the material, and the endeavor to assign these to their respective *causes*.

3. Causes of Error

More frequently than not errors in MSS are unintentional, and the causes giving rise to them are sufficiently obvious. Such are the carelessness of scribes, lapses of memory, similarity of sounds (in dictation), or in shape of letters (in copying), wrong dividing of words, omission of a line or clause owing to successive lines or clauses ending with the same word. Intentional changes, again, arise from insertion in the text of marginal notes or glosses, from motives of harmonizing, from the substitution of smoother for harsher or more abrupt expressions—more rarely, from dogmatic reasons.

Mistakes of the above kinds can generally be detected by careful scrutiny of sources, but a large number of cases remain in which the correct reading is still doubtful. These, next, have to be dealt with by the impartial weighing and balancing of authorities; a task involving new and delicate inquiries, and the application of fresh rules. It does not suffice to reckon numbers; MSS and VSS have themselves to be tested as respects reliability and value. Through the presence of peculiarities pointing to a common origin MSS come to be grouped into classes and families, and their individual testimony is correspondingly discounted. Older authorities, naturally, are preferred to younger but the possibility has to be reckoned with that a later MS may preserve a reading which the older MSS have lost. Such rules obtain as that, of two readings, preference is to be given to the more difficult, as less likely to be the result of corruption. But even this has its limits, for a reading may be difficult even to the point of unintelligibility, yet may arise from a simple blunder. As a last resort, in cases of perplexity, conjectural emendation may be admitted; only, however, as yielding probability, not certainty.

4. Weighing of Authorities

In the application of these principles an important distinction has to be made between the OT and the NT, arising from the relative paucity of material for critical purposes in the one case, and the abundance in the other. The subject is treated here generally; for details see arts. on LANGUAGE OF THE OT; LANGUAGE OF THE NT; TEXT AND MSS OF THE NT.

(1) *In the OT*, textual criticism labors under the peculiar disadvantage that, with one minute exception (a papyrus fragment of the 2d cent., giving a version of the Decalogue), all known Heb MSS are late (the oldest not going beyond the 9th cent. AD); further, that the MSS seem all to be based on one single archetype, selected by the rabbis at an early date, and thereafter adhered to by copyists with scrupulous care (cf G. A. Smith, *OTJC*, 69 ff; Driver, *Text of Sam*, xxxvii ff; Strack, however, dissents). The variations which these MSS present, accordingly, are slight and unimportant. For a knowledge of the state of the text prior to the adoption of this standard, criticism is dependent on comparison with the VSS—esp. the SEPTUAGINT (q.v.), with the SAM PENT (q.v.), and with ‖ passages in the OT itself (e.g. in S, K, Ch). Frequent obscurities in the Heb text, with undeniable discrepancies in names and numbers, show that before the fixing of the text extensive corruption had already entered. A simple instance of mistake is in Isa **9** 3, where the AV reads: "Thou hast multiplied the nation, and not increased the joy." The context shows that the "not" is out of place: the RV therefore rightly reads (with the Heb Ḳ^{e}rē: the sounds are similar), "thou hast increased their joy." In the LXX the divergences are often very great in order, arrangement, and readings; there are extensive interpolations and omissions (in Jer, Graf reckons that 2,700 words of the Massoretic text are omitted); evidences, where the alterations are not of design, that the Heb MSS employed by the translators often differed widely from those approved in Pal. The Sam recension likewise exhibits considerable differences.

It does not follow that, where difference exists, these rival texts are to be preferred to the Massoretic. Few, since the exhaustive examination of Gesenius, would affirm the superiority of the Sam to the Heb; even in regard to the LXX the trend of opinion seems increasingly in favor of the text of the Massoretes (cf Skinner, "Genesis," *ICC*, xxxv–xxxvi). There is no need, however, to maintain the general superiority of the above texts to the Massoretic to be convinced that, in many instances, the LXX, in some cases, probably, even the Sam, has retained readings from which the MT has departed. OT criticism has, therefore, a clear field for its labors, and there can be little doubt that, in its cautious application, it has reached many sound results. Less reliance can be placed on the conjectural criticism now so largely in vogue. Dr. G. A. Smith has justly animadverted on the new textual criticism of the poetical and prophetical books, "through which it drives like a great ploughshare, turning up the whole surface, and menacing not only the minor landmarks, but, in the case of the prophets, the main outlines of the field as well" (*Quarterly Rev.*, January, 1907). This, however, trenches on the domain of the *higher* criticism.

(2) *In the NT* the materials of criticism are vastly more abundant than in the OT; but, with the abundance, while a much larger area of certainty is attainable, more intricate and difficult problems also arise. The wealth of MSS of the whole or parts of the Gr NT far exceeds that existing for any other ancient writings (Nestle mentions 3,829: 127 uncials and 3,702 cursives: *Intro to the Textual Criticism of the Gr NT*, ET, 34–35, 81); the MSS of VSS (excluding the Vulg, reckoned by thousands), are likewise very numerous.

(*a*) MSS and VSS: Gr MSS are usually divided into uncials and cursives (or minuscules) from the character of the writing; the oldest uncials go back to the 4th and 5th cents. The five chief, that alone need be named, are the Codex Sinaiticus (א, 4th cent.), the Codex Vaticanus (B, 4th cent.), the Codex Alexandrinus (A, 5th cent.), the Codex Ephraemi (C, 5th cent.), the Codex Bezae (D, Gospels and Acts, Gr and Lat, 6th cent.). These MSS again are grouped according to affinities (Bengel, Griesbach, Lachmann, are here chief precursors; Westcott and Hort, chief modern authority), א and B going together as representing one type of text, in the opinion of WH the best (the so-called "Neutral"); D representing a "Western" text, with marked peculiarities; A and C exhibiting mixed texts. The VSS, in turn, Syr, Old Lat, Egyp (originating with 2d and 3d cents.), present interesting problems in their relations to one another and to the Gr MSS א, B, and D. With the Syr VSS (Sinaitic, Curetonian, Peshitta), Tatian's *Diatessaron*, or Harmony of the Gospels, ought to be mentioned. Formerly the Pesh was taken to be the oldest Syr VS (2d cent.); now, esp. since the discovery of the Lewis (Sinaitic) palimpsest, it tends to be regarded as a later revision of the older Syr texts (probably by Rabula of Edessa, beginning of the 5th cent.). The old Lat, also the old Syr, MSS show marked affinities with the text of D—the "Western" type.

(*b*) The Western text: The question chiefly exercising scholars at the present time is, accordingly, the relation of the WH text based on א and B to the Western text represented by D, but now finding early support from the Old Lat and Syr, as well as from quotations in the 2d and 3d Fathers. The Western text is discounted by WH for its paraphrastic character, and "astonishing freedom" in changing, inserting and omitting (WH, 122 ff); yet, on internal grounds, certain important omissions in this text of the last three chs of Lk are accepted by these authorities as representing the purer text, the rejected readings being termed "non-Western interpolations." A newer school, however, is disposed to accept the Western readings, as, to a much larger extent than was formerly supposed, the more original; while some writers, as Blass, Nestle, in part Zahn (cf Nestle, op. cit., 324 ff), seek a solution of the difference of texts in the theory of two editions (Blass, Lk and Acts; Zahn, Acts alone). This theory has not met with much acceptance, and the problems of the Western text must still be regarded as unsolved. The question is not, indeed, vital, as no important doctrine of the NT is affected; but it touches the genuineness of several passages to which high value is attached. E.g. the words at the Supper, "which is given for you," etc (Lk **22** 19.20, not in D), are excluded by WH as a *non-Western* interpolation; while the passage on the angel and the bloody sweat (Lk **22** 43.44 in both א and D), and the first word on the cross, "Father, forgive them," etc (Lk **23** 34, in א, omitted by D and Sin Syr), are rejected as *Western* interpolations. The RV retains these passages with marginal note.

(*c*) Results: As respects results, it may be said generally that the labors of a long line of scholars have given us a NT text on which, in nearly all essential respects, we can safely rely. Others, it is to be owned, take a less sanguine view (cf Nestle, op. cit., 227 ff). The correct reading seems undeniably settled in a large majority of cases. The RV embodies most of the assured results; doubtful cases are noted in the margin. Among passages long known to be interpolations, now altogether removed, is that on the three witnesses in 1 Jn **5** 8. The two longest passages noted as not belonging to the original text are the last 12 vs of Mk (**16** 9–20), and the story of the woman taken in adultery (Jn **7** 53—**8** 11).

III. Higher Criticism.—The scope of the higher criticism has already been indicated. Many of the inquiries it undertakes were formerly covered by what was called Bib. introduction; the flight of the newer science, however, is bolder, and the problems it seeks to solve are more complicated and far-reaching. An important part of its work is the analysis of books, with the view of determining their component parts (e.g. the J,E,P,D, of the Pent), the age, origin, and characteristics of each, their connection with external conditions and the state of belief and life of the time. The nature of its task will be better understood from a rapid survey of its procedure.

Higher criticism began, mainly, with *the OT*. Already in the 2d cent., Gnostics assailed the OT as the work of an inferior deity (the Demiurge), and heretical Ebionites (*Clementine Recognitions and Homilies*) declared it to be corrupted with false prophecy. In the 17th cent. Spinoza prepared the way in his *Tractatus* (1670) for future rationalistic attacks.

1. The OT

(1) *Astruc and successors.*—The beginning of higher criticism in the stricter sense is commonly associated with the French physician Astruc, who, in his *Conjectures*, in 1753, drew attention to the fact that, in some sections of Gen, the Divine name employed is "Elohim" (God), in others, "Jehovah." This he accounted for by the use of distinct documents by Moses in the composition of the book. Eichhorn (1779), to whom the name "higher criticism" is due, supplemented Astruc's theory by the correct observation that this distinction in the use of the names was accompanied by other literary peculiarities. It soon became further evident that, though the distinction in the names mostly ceased after the revelation of Jeh to Moses (Ex **3** 6), the literary peculiarities extended much farther than Gen, indeed till the end of Josh (Bleek, 1822; Ewald, 1831; Stähelin, 1835). Instead of a "Pentateuch," recognized as of composite authorship, there was now postulated a "Hexateuch" (see Pentateuch; Hexateuch). Meanwhile De Wette (1805–6), on grounds of style and contents, had claimed for Dt an origin not earlier than the reign of Josiah. "Fragmentary" theories, like Vater's, which contributed little to the general development, may be left unnoticed. A conservative school, headed by Hengstenberg (1831) and Hävernick (1837), contested these conclusions of the critics, and contended for the unity and Mosaic authorship of the Pent. Bolder spirits, as Vatke (1835), anticipated the conclusions of the newer critical school in declaring that the Levitical laws were latest of all in origin. Their voices were as yet unheeded.

(2) *Hupfeld.*—A distinct advance on preceding theories was made by Hupfeld (1853; in part anticipated by Ilgen, 1789). Hitherto the prevailing assumption had been that there was one fundamental document—the so-called Elohistic, dated usually in the age of the Judges, or the time of Saul or David—and that the Jehovistic parts were "supplementary" to this (not a separate document). It was the merit of Hupfeld to perceive that not a few of the sections in the "Elohistic" document did not bear the usual literary marks of that writing, but closely resembled the "Jehovistic" sections in everything but the use of the Divine name. These portions he singled out and erected into a document by themselves (though they bear no signs of being such), while the Jehovistic parts were relieved of their "supplementary" character, and regarded as belonging to a distinct document also. There were thus now 3 documents, attributed to as many authors—the original Elohist, the 2d or Younger Elohist and the Jehovist. Dt, as a distinct book, was added to these, making 4 documents in all.

(3) *Graf and Wellhausen.*—Thus matters stood till the appearance of Graf's work, *The Historical Books of the OT*, in 1866, through which something like a revolution in the critical outlook was effected. Following in the track of Vatke, earlier, Reuss, of Strassburg, had taken up the idea that the Levitical legislation could not, as was commonly presumed, be earlier than Dt, but was, on the contrary, later —in fact, a product of the age of the exile. Graf adopted and developed this theory. He still for a time, while putting the laws late, maintained an earlier date for the Elohistic narratives. He was soon led, however, to see that laws and history must go together; so the whole Elohistic writing was removed from its former place, and brought down bodily to the end of the religious development. Graf, at the same time, did not regard it as an independent document. At first the theory was scouted, but gradually, through the able advocacy of Kuenen and Wellhausen—esp. the latter—it secured ascendency, and is now regarded as *the* critical view *par excellence*. Order and nomenclature of the assumed documents were now changed. The Elohist, instead of standing first, was put last under the designation P or PC (Priestly Code). Wellhausen's symbol for this writing was Q. Its date was taken to be post-exilian. The Jehovist becomes J; the Elohist E. These are placed in the 9th or 8th cents. BC (cir 850–750), but are supposed to have been combined a cent. or so later (JE). Dt, identified with the law-book found in the temple in the reign of Josiah (2 K **22**), is thought to have been written shortly before that time. The order is therefore no longer 1st Elohist–Jehovist and 2d Elohist–Dt, but J and E–Dt–P. The whole, it is held, was finally united into the great law-book (Pent) brought by Ezra to Jerus from Babylon (458 BC; Ezr **7** 6–10), and read by him before the people 14 years later (444 BC; Neh **8**).

(4) *Literary and historical grounds of theory.*—A sketch like the above gives, of course, no proper idea of the grounds on which, apart from the distinction in the Divine names, the critical theory just described is based. The grounds are partly *literary*—the discrimination of documents, e.g. resting on differences of style and conception

duplicates, etc (see PENTATEUCH)—but partly also *historical*, in accordance with the critic's conception of the development of religion and institutions in Israel. A main reliance is placed on the fact that the history, with its many sanctuaries up to the time of Dt, is in conflict with the law of that book, which recognizes only one sanctuary as legitimate (ch **12**), and equally with the PC, which throughout assumes this centralizing law. The laws of Dt and PC, therefore, cannot be early. The prophets, it is held, knew nothing of a Levitical legislation, and refused to regard the sacrificial system as Divine (Jer **7** 22 ff).

(5) *The code* under which older Israel lived was that formulated in the Book of the Covenant (Ex **20–23**), which permitted many altars (Ex **20** 24 f). The law of Dt was the product of a centralizing movement on the part of the prophets, issuing in the reformation of Josiah. The PC was the work of fertile brains and pens of post-exilian priests and scribes, incorporating older usage, devising new laws, and throwing the whole into the fictitious form of Mosaic wilderness legislation.

(6) *Effects on history, etc.*—The revolution wrought by these newer constructions, however, is not adequately realized till regard is had to their effects on *the picture given in the OT itself* of Israel's history, religion and literature. It is not too much to say that this picture is nearly completely subverted. By the leaders of the school (Graf, Kuenen, Wellhausen, Duhm, Stade, etc) the supernatural element in the history and religion is totally eliminated; even by those who do not go so far, little is left standing. The history of the Pent—indeed the history down to the time of the kings—is largely given up. Gen is legend, Ex hardly more trustworthy, Josh a romance. The histories of Samuel and David are "written up" by a theocratic narrator. None of the laws—even the Decalogue—are allowed to be certainly Mosaic. Monotheism is believed to have come in with Amos and Hosea; earlier, Jeh was a "tribal" God. Ark, tabernacle, priesthood, feasts, as depicted in the PC, are post-exilic fiction. The treatment accorded to the Pent necessarily reacts on the other historical books; the prophetic lit. suffers in an almost equal degree through disintegration and mutilation. It is not Isaiah alone—where the question has long been mooted of the post-exilian origin of chs **40–66** (see ISAIAH); the critical knife is applied with scarcely less freedom to the remaining prophetical books. Few, if any, of the psalms are allowed to be preëxilic. Dnl is a work of the Maccabean age.

(7) *General results.*—As a general summary of the results of the movement, which it is thought "the future is not likely to reverse," the following may be quoted from Professor A. S. Peake: "The analysis of the Pent into four main documents, the identification of the law on which Josiah's reformation was based with some form of the Deuteronomic Code, the compilation of that code in the reign of Manasseh at the earliest, the fixing of the Priestly Code to a date later than Ezekiel, the highly composite character of some parts of the prophetic lit., esp. the Book of Isa, the post-exilian origin of most of the Pss, and large parts of the Book of Prov, the composition of Job not earlier than the exile and probably later, the Maccabean date of Dnl, and the slightly earlier date of Eccl" ("Present Movement of Biblical Science," in Manchester, *Inaugural Lects*, 32).

(8) *Criticism of theory.*—The criticism of this elaborate theory belongs to the arts. which deal with the several points involved, and is not here attempted at length (cf the present writer's *POT*). The gains that have accrued from it on the literary side in a more exact and scholarly knowledge of the phenomena to be explained (e.g. distinction in the Divine names; distinction of P element in the Pent from that known as JE) are not to be questioned; on the historical and religious sides also much has been done to quicken interest, enlarge knowledge and correct older ideas which have proved untenable—in general, to place the whole facts of the OT in a clearer and more assured light. On the other hand, much even in the literary criticism is subjective, arbitrary and conjectural, while the main hypothesis of the posteriority of the Levitical law to Ezekiel, with the general view taken of the historical and religious development in Israel, is open to the most serious exception. The OT has its own account to give of the origin of its religion in the monotheism of Abraham, the covenants with the patriarchs, the legislation through Moses, which is not thus readily to be set aside in the interests of a theory resting largely on naturalistic presuppositions (see BIBLE). There is not a word in the history in Neh **8** to suggest that the law introduced by Ezra was a new one; it was received without demur by a deeply divided community as the ancient law of Moses. So with the law of Dt in the time of Josiah (2 K **22**). Its genuineness was doubted by no one. The position of the theory, generally, is by no means so secure as many of its adherents suppose. Internally, it is being pushed to extremes which tend to discredit it to sober minds, and otherwise is undergoing extensive modifications. Documents are multiplied, dates lowered, authors are converted into "schools." Archaeologists, in large majority, declare against it. The facts they adduce tend to confirm the history in parts where it had been most impugned. The new Bab school in Germany (that of Winckler) assails it in its foundations. Recently, the successor of Kuenen in Leyden, Professor B. D. Eerdmans, formerly a supporter, has broken with the theory in its entirety, and subjects the documentary hypothesis to a damaging criticism. It is too early yet to forecast results, but the opinion may be hazarded that, as in the case of the Tübingen NT critical school in last cent. referred to below, the prevailing critical theory of the OT will experience fundamental alteration in a direction nearer to older ideas, though it is too much to expect that traditional views will ever be resuscitated in their completeness.

2. The NT

Higher criticism of *the NT* may be said to begin, in a Deistic spirit, with Reimarus (*Fragments*, published by Lessing, 1778), and, on Hegelian lines, with Strauss (*Life of Jesus*, 1835). In the interests of his mythical theory, Strauss subjected every part of the gospel history to a destructive criticism.

(1) *The school of Baur.*—In a more systematic way, F. Baur (1826–60), founder of the famous Tübingen school, likewise proceeding from Hegel, applied a drastic criticism to all the documents of the NT. Strauss started with the Gospels. Baur sought firmer ground in the phenomena of the Apostolic Age. The key to Baur's theory lies in the alleged existence of Pauline and Petrine parties in the early church, in conflict with one another. The true state of matters is mirrored, he holds, not in the Book of Acts, a composition of the 2d cent., written to gloze over the differences between the original apostles and Paul, but in the four contemporary and undoubtedly genuine epistles of Paul, Gal, 1 and 2 Cor, and Rom, and in the Book of Rev. In these documents the church is seen rent by a schism that threatened its very existence. By and by attempts were made at conciliation, the stages of which are reflected in the Gospels and remaining writings of the NT. The Fourth Gospel, about 170 AD, brings up the rear. This theory, which found

influential support in the scholarship of the time (Schwegler, Zeller, etc), could not stand the test of impartial investigation, and is now on all sides discredited. Professor Bacon, in a recent work, pronounces its theory of the Johannine writings to be "as obsolete as the Ptolemaic geography" (*Fourth Gospel*, 20). Its influence on later criticism has, however, been considerable.

(2) *Synoptic criticism.*—Meanwhile more sober scholarship was concerning itself with the intricate problem of the relations of the *Synoptic Gospels.* The problem is a very real one (see GOSPELS). The three gospels of Mt, Mk and Lk are seen on inspection to exhibit an amount of agreement in subject-matter, order, often in language, which cannot be accounted for except on the theory of some common source. Suppose the Gospels divided into sections, in 52 of these the narratives coincide, 12 more are common to Mt and Mk, 5 to Mk and Lk, and 14 to Mt and Lk, while 5 are peculiar to Mt, 2 to Mk and 9 to Lk. The verbal agreement is greater in the recital of the words of others, particularly of words of Jesus, than in the narrative portions.

How is this to be explained? Three forms of theory were early propounded—the *oral*, the *documentary*, and the hypothesis of *dependence* of one gospel upon another. Of these theories, the oldest is the 3d (Augustine already held that Mk was an abridgment of Mt and Lk), and to it, in combination with the 2d, though in reversed order (Mk being put first), it will be seen below that criticism has largely reverted. The oral theory, proposed by Gieseler (1818), has, till recently, been the favorite one in England (Westcott, Alford, etc, with Godet, Pressensé, Ebrard, etc, on the Continent). In it resemblances in the three Gospels are explained by an oral tradition assumed to have attained a relatively fixed form while the apostles were yet teaching together in Jerus. The documentary theory took its origin with Eichhorn (1794), but in the hands of Marsh (1801), finally in Eichhorn's own (1804), received so elaborate a development as completely to discredit it. The dependence theory, in turn, went through every possible shape. Gradually, with sifting, certain combinations were eliminated (those which put Lk first, or Mt last, or made Mk a middle term), till only two remained—Mt, Lk, Mk (Griesbach 1789–90, Baur, etc), and Mk, Mt, Lk (Weisse, 1838, Wilke, 1838, etc). The prestige of the Baur school obtained a temporary ascendency for the former view—that which put Mk last; this, however, has now quite given way in favor of Mk's priority. There remained a division of opinion as to whether the Mk employed by the other evangelists was the canonical Mk (Weisse, Meyer, B. Weiss, etc), or an *ur-Markus* (Holtzmann, Reuss, etc), but the difficulties of the latter hypothesis proved so insurmountable that Holtzmann finally gave it up.

It is obvious, however, that the use of Mk by the other evangelists, even if granted, does not yet completely solve the synoptical problem. There is still to be considered that large mass of matter—chiefly discourses—common to Mt and Lk, not to speak of the material peculiar to Lk itself. For the explanation of these sections it becomes necessary to postulate a *second* source, usually identified with the much-canvassed *Logia* of Papias, and designated by recent scholars (Wellhausen, etc) Q. It is regarded as a collection of discourses, possibly by Matthew, with or without an admixture of narrative matter (B. Weiss, etc). This yields the "two-source" theory at present prevailing in synoptical criticism (for a different view, cf Zahn's *Introduction*). Mt and Lk, on this view, are not independent Gospels, but are drawn up on the basis of (1) Mk and (2) Q=the *Logia*, with original material on the part of Luke (see GOSPELS). A theory which commands the assent of so many scholars has necessarily great weight. It cannot, however, be regarded as finally established. Many grave difficulties remain; there is, besides, a prima facie improbability in a Gospel like Mark's being treated in the manner supposed or included among the "attempts" which Luke's own Gospel was designed to supersede (Lk **1** 1–4; cf Wright, *St. Luke's Gospel in Gr*, xiv, xv).

With criticism of the *sources* of the Gospels there goes, of course, the question of *authorship.* A powerful vindication of the Lucan authorship of the 3d Gospel and the Book of Acts has recently come from the pen of Professor A. Harnack, who maintains that in this, as in most other points regarding early Christian lit., "tradition is right" (cf his *Luke, the Physician*, ET). Outside the Synoptics, the burning question still is the authorship of the Johannine writings. Here also, however, the extreme positions of the Baur school are entirely given up ("It is perfectly apparent," says Professor Bacon, "that Baur mistook the period of *dissemination* for that of *origin*," op. cit., 21), and powerful defences of Johannine authorship have of late appeared (notably Sanday's *Criticism of the Fourth Gospel*, and ex-Principal Drummond's *Character and Authorship of the Fourth Gospel*). See GOSPEL OF JOHN.

(3) *Modern "historical-critical" school.*—On the other hand, a new and intensely aggressive radical school has recently come to the front, the so-called "historical-critical," which treats the text and history of the Gospels generally with a recklessness to which no limits can be put. It is even doubted if Jesus claimed to be the Messiah (Wrede). Sayings are accepted, rejected, or mutilated at pleasure. The latest phase of this school is the "Apocalyptic," which finds the essence of Christ's message in His insistence on the approaching end of the world (cf Schweitzer, *Von Reimarus zu Wrede;* ET *The Quest of the Historical Jesus*). These excesses may be depended on to cure themselves.

(4) *Remaining writings of the NT.*—For the rest of the writings on the NT, the trend of criticism has been in the main in a conservative direction. One by one the Pauline Epistles have been given back to the apostle—doubt chiefly still resting in certain minds on the Pastorals. The Book of Rev is restored by most to the age of Domitian, where tradition places it. Its relation to the Fourth Gospel and to St. John is still in dispute, and some moderns would see in it a groundwork of Jewish apocalypse. These and kindred questions are discussed in the arts. devoted to them.

LITERATURE.—Arts. on Text, MSS, VSS, of OT and NT in Bible Dicts. and Encyclopaedias: works on Introduction to OT and NT.

On the OT.—S. Davidson, *Revision of the English OT;* W. R. Smith, *OT in the Jewish Church;* Wellhausen, *Prol to the Hist of Israel* (ET); Kuenen, *The Hexateuch* (ET); Oxford *Hexateuch according to the RV;* Orr, *Prob of the OT*, and *Bible Under Trial;* H. M. Wiener, *Essays on Pentateuchal Criticism;* W. Möller, *Are the Critics Right?* (ET).

On the NT.—Westcott and Hort, *The NT in Gr*, Intro; F. G. Kenyon, *Handbook to the Textual Criticism of the NT;* Nestle, *Textual Crit of the Gr Test.* (ET); Scrivener, *Intro to the Crit of the NT*, 4th ed; K. Lake, *The Text of the NT;* Ebrard, *Gospel History* (ET); F. C. Burkitt, *The Gospel History and Its Transmission;* Sanday, *The Life of Christ in Recent Research;* Schweitzer, *Von Reimarus zu Wrede* (ET *The Quest of the Historical Jesus*); A. S. Peake, *Crit. Intro to the NT.*

JAMES ORR

CRITICISM (The Graf-Wellhausen Hypothesis):

I. Preliminary.—In Jer **7** 22.23 we read: "For I spake not unto your fathers, nor commanded them in the day that I brought them out of the land of Egypt, concerning burnt-offerings or sacrifices: but this thing I commanded them, saying, Hearken unto my voice, and I will be your God, and ye shall be my people." It is the contention of the present art. that this statement of the prophet is correct (cf II, 5).

1. Thesis

More specifically, it is contended that evidence can be produced from the OT to show that Israel's religion can be seen in a long period of growth; and in this growth a fixed sacrificial law, with a minutely regulated ritual obligatory on all Israelites, the culmination and not the beginning of the process. It is contended, moreover, that this conception of the development of the institutional side of the religion of the OT is attained by the strictest evaluation of *all* the OT evidence and by no a priori considerations.

To be sure, one is met at once in the OT by what seem to be complete denials of this point of view. In the Pentateuch we find statement after statement that a given law was due not to some late author but to Moses himself, and there are numerous passages in the historical books (most notably in Ch) that speak of these laws as in effect from the earliest times. Such evidence must be paid all possible respect and must be overruled only on the most imperative considerations.

2. Historical Perspective

However, if for the moment the books of the OT be viewed only as historical documents, it will be admitted that the possibility of overruling such evidence may well arise. And it may very well arise without calling in question in the slightest degree the good faith of the writers of questioned passages; for an acquisition of historical perspective comes very late in intellectual evolution, particularly—though not only—in the realm of religious history. Even the trained scholar has to be on his guard lest he read back the concepts of his own time into some past generation, while the non-specialist never succeeds in avoiding this error completely. For the uncultured mind, especially for the Oriental, the problem scarcely exists. That which is generally accepted and which is not obviously novel tends to be classified as that which "always has been." A law so old that its actual source is forgotten is referred as a matter of course to some great lawgiver of the past. A custom that in a writer's own day is universally observed by the pious must always have been observed by the pious. Even documentary evidence to the contrary is not convincing to such a writer, for that documents may be wrong is not a modern discovery. To be sure, the older document may be copied mechanically or the discrepancy may not even be noticed. But it is never surprising when we find a writer simply accrediting the pious men of old with the customs of his own day, since even documentary evidence to the contrary he felt *could* not be right. This is not forgery, as we understand the word, nor need there be the faintest moral reproach connected with such conduct. Quite on the contrary, such a writer may well be acting in the only sense that the conscience of any man of his generation could conceive right.

However, the OT is not a mere collection of human documents, and another question arises. Does the acceptance of inspiration compel us to assume that in every case a writer's ordinary historical methods were entirely overruled? The question is a rather broad one and does not relate merely to the correct transmission of historic facts. To be asked, rather, is this: Did God present to His instruments a mechanically accurate set of past facts which would give a conception of history that no one of the sacred writer's generation could understand? Or did He suffer His revelation to find expression in terms of the current conceptions of history, much as we are accustomed to say it found expression in terms of the current conceptions of science? A full discussion of the various theological arguments involved would be quite outside the province of an art. of this Encyclopaedia, but reference must be made to two important Bib. arguments: (1) In a question which thus affects the amount covered by the inspiration of the Bible, quotations from the Bible itself beg the question when adduced to show entire infallibility. So appeals to the NT are hardly helpful. Moreover, they prove too much. In Jude vs 14.15 there is a quotation from the Book of En (**1** 9), which is made in the most formal manner possible. But will anyone maintain that this compels us to believe that our Book of En was actually written by Enoch, the seventh from Adam? Yet if the quotation had been taken from an OT work, precisely this would have been maintained. (2) Far more important is the use of the OT by Christ, for here a quite different authority comes in. But the question must be asked: Just how far did Our Lord's use of a passage involve ratification of all the current ideas about that passage? A good answer is supplied by Acts **1** 6.7. When He is asked, "Dost thou at this time restore the kingdom to Israel?" we know that the pedantically "correct" answer would have been, "The kingdom never will be restored to Israel in any such sense as ye conceive of it." Yet this is precisely what Christ does *not* say. "It is not for you to know times or seasons." No hint was given at all that the kingdom was universal, for the disciples would find that out for themselves in good time. In order that they should be able to do God's work there was no need to bewilder them with a truth as yet altogether revolutionary. And any close student of the "Kingdom of God" passages soon realizes how often Christ uses current terminology without comment, even when it seems almost materialistic. A literal exegesis of Lk **22** 18 would necessitate believing that grapes will grow in the world to come and that Christ will drink wine made from them, and almost certainly the disciples gathered just this idea from the words. But no one today finds them in the least a difficulty. The exact extent of the kingdom and the exact nature of the happiness in it were irrelevant to what the disciples had to *do*. And so it cannot be thought an injustice to treat Christ's use of the OT by exactly the same rules, all the more as nowhere, not even in Mk **12** 36, does the argument turn on the original human author or the date of writing. What Christ Himself, in His inner consciousness, knew on the subject is something beyond our immediate data. But His use of the OT lends no support to a Kenotic theory, not even on the wildest OT critical hypotheses. See Kenosis.

3. Inspiration

II. The Legislation.—As is well known, among the laws of the Pentateuch there exist several well-marked groups, of which the most formal is Dt **12–26**. Another such group is Lev **17–26** or the Holiness Code (H), and still another is Ex **20** 22—**23** 19 or the Covenant Code (CC). With this last is closely connected the Decalogue and the little compend Ex **34** 17–26. Now it will be convenient for

1. Groups

present purposes to designate the remaining mass of Pentateuchal legislation under the non-committal symbol X.

In the first place, attention may be directed to CC as a whole. Whatever it was meant to be, it was not meant as a mere interims-code for the period of the wanderings, either in its civil or its religious prescriptions. One piece of evidence alone is enough to show the contrary: in the laws touching settlements of disputes it is presupposed that Moses himself is not accessible. And the life assumed is agricultural. Men are living in fields with settled boundaries (**22** 5.6). The vine and the olive are both under cultivation (**22** 5.29; **23** 11), under such settled circumstances that the rest of the Sabbatical year can be observed. And of the feasts, Weeks and Tabernacles are connected with the harvests (**23** 16). Of course, Moses may very well have given commands that looked to the future, but the present contention is simply that it was the remote and not the immediate future that is in point on this assumption. The life is Canaan and not the wilderness. But, now, the life is very primitive life. Flocks are of great importance, as is shown by the proportion of space given to laws about them. Rulers are mentioned only in **22** 28 (*nāsī'*), and judges, as settled officers, are not mentioned at all, for the very rare word in **21** 22 (*pālīl*, Dt **32** 31; Job **31** 11 only) should be tr[d] "umpire." Indeed in **23** 1-9 the duties of citizens, witness and judge are so intermingled as to suggest that judgment was administered by a general gathering of the people. It is taken for granted that a master has marital rights over his maidservants (**21** 7-11). Coined money is mentioned only in **21** 32, if there. There is no attempt to define proportions exactly; cf **22** 5 ("best of his own field") and **22** 29 (the amount of the gift—a tenth?—not stated). Similarly there is no precise dating of the feasts of Weeks and Tabernacles in **23** 16, while the exact day in Abib (ver 15) is at least not specified. Now, if this code could be isolated from the rest of the legislation, would not one refer it naturally on the above grounds alone to a time not very far either way from that of Saul?

2. Covenant Code

Now, in what follows, the prescriptions of the various codes will be compared with each other in regard to the various institutions of Israel's religion and also studied in the wider evidence of the historical books. The evidence of Ch, however, will be omitted for the most part, as a separate section is devoted to it (III, 1).

3 The Sanctuary

(1) The firstling is to be with its dam seven days, but on the *eighth* (not later!) it is to be given to God. The offerings from the harvest and from the presses (wine and olives) are to be offered without delay (Ex **22** 29.30). Consequently the place of offering must have been readily accessible. By what has been said above and by the mention of "presses" here, ready accessibility *in Palestine* is presupposed. But this implies a multiplicity of sanctuaries. And in Samuel-Kings this multiplicity of sanctuaries is exactly what is found. Samuel sacrifices in Mizpah (1 S **7** 9), in Ramah (**9** 12 ff), in Gilgal (**11** 15) and in Bethlehem (**16** 5). David's family held a yearly sacrifice in Bethlehem, which David attended regularly (**20** 6). Solomon received a special revelation from God at Gibeon (1 K **3** 4 ff—for the account in Ch see III, 1). Although the heart of Asa was perfect and the way of Jehoshaphat right, yet the many altars were suffered to remain (**15** 14; **22** 43—again for Ch see III, 1). The destruction of the altars of God was to Elijah a terrible calamity (**19** 10). While Amos and Hosea abound in denunciations of sacrifices as substitutes for righteousness, yet they never even intimate a duty to offer sacrifices in some other *place* (Am **1** 2; Hos **3** 5 are irrelevant). Not even do Mic **4** 2 and Isa **2** 2 imply that Jerus was to have the *sole* right to the cultus.

(2) Ezekiel is the first prophet who makes the *place* of sacrifice a matter of paramount importance, and this importance of the place is, in the Pentateuch, emphasized primarily in Dt. It is needless to collect the familiar evidence from Dt, but an illuminating comparison with CC is given by the laws for firstlings. No longer is the firstling given on the eighth day. It must be kept, but not worked or shorn, until the time when "year by year" it may be eaten in the chosen place (Dt **15** 19.20). So now the fruits of the field and the "presses" are not offered "without delay" but again "year by year," with a provision for turning them into money if the way be too long to the sanctuary (**14** 22-27). Dt and CC evidently have distinct conceptions—and again attention may be called to the fact that CC contains laws for Pal, not for the wilderness. H is as explicit as Dt—sacrifice anywhere except at the Tent is a capital offence (Lev **17** 8.9). And the evidence of X need not be collected, but, passing out of the Pentateuch for the moment, Josh **22** 10-34 represents Israel as understanding from the first entrance into Canaan that sacrifice at any altar but the one was the worst of crimes.

(3) How is the offering of sacrifices in various places by such men as Samuel to be explained? That the worship was disorganized and the proper sanctuary could not be reached is hardly an explanation. For no disorganization of the country could be great enough to justify the offering of sacrifices in places not only unauthorized but flatly forbidden in Lev **17** 8.9. On the theory of Mosaic origin for the whole of the Pentateuchal legislation, Samuel knew as much about the clear statements of the Law as does any Jew of today, but it is clearly enough recognized by all Jews that no disorganization of the county or Divine reprobation of the Temple justifies sacrifice in any other place. A key, however, seems to be found in Dt **12** 8-11, where sacrifice in various places is actually authorized until such a time as the land should be pacified and the Divine choice given to a place—a time represented in the history of Israel as about the time of David, or perhaps Solomon. This certainly does explain the situation as it is found in Samuel-Kings. Only, it is in flat contradiction with H and X.

This point is important. Dt **12** 8-11 not only represents sacrifice in various places as permitted until some later time, but it represents Moses and the Israelites as practising the same things in the wilderness—"the things that we do here this day, every man whatsoever is right in his own eyes; for ye are not as yet come," etc; i.e. Dt's conception was that in the wilderness Moses and the Israelites offered sacrifice wherever they thought good. This was to continue until God gave them rest from their enemies round about. *Then* the sacrifices were to be brought to the chosen place and to be offered nowhere else. Now, the conception in H and X is wholly different. On the mount Moses received directions for the building of the Tabernacle, with its altar. From the beginning it was a capital offence to offer sacrifices on any other altar than this (Lev **17** 8.9), which was carried everywhere on the wanderings and brought into Canaan. In the very days of Phinehas, the offering of sacrifices on a different altar was enough to make civil war justifiable (Josh **22** 12). For further discussion see III, 2.

(4) The difficulties of these data are obvious but are completely satisfied by the assumption that

different conceptions of past history are present. Dt belongs to a period when the unity of the sanctuary had become an established fact, but still before the memory of the many altars as comparatively legitimate was extinguished. H and X, however, belong to a considerably later day, when the unity of the sanctuary had been so long taken for granted that no pious Israelite could conceive that anything else had ever existed. The reference of the commands to Moses is altogether in oriental manner.

NOTE.—Ex **20** 24 has not been used in the above argument, but with the evidence presented there seems to be no obstacle to the trs of the EV. The familiar evidence of Jgs is of course merely cumulative.

4. Kinds of Sacrifice

Lev **1–7** contains a list of the various kinds of sacrifices: (*a*) the sin offering and the trespass offering, very elaborately treated and obviously of the highest importance; (*b*) the whole burnt offering and the peace offering; and, standing a little by itself, the meal offering. The latter is of no especial significance for the present discussion and may be neglected. Now a curious fact may be noted. In the prophetic writings before Ezk *there is not one single reference to class* (*a*). This is not simply the argument from silence, for sacrifices with their special names are mentioned freely and sacrificial rites described—invariably of class (*b*), even when presented for penitential purposes. If the offering is not burnt whole, the worshipper eats of it—it is a peace offering. Jer **7** 21 is a particularly significant example, but cf Am **4** 4.5; **5** 22.25; Hos **8** 13; **9** 4; Isa **1** 11; **22** 12–14; **28** 7.8; Jer **6** 20. Turning to Samuel-Kings we find this borne out. The names of the sin and trespass offerings appear in 2 K **12** 16, but it is money that is referred to (the EV should be checked with the Heb here), just as the golden mice appear as a trespass offering in 1 S **6** 3 ff. And in the codes, neither CC nor Dt mentions class (*a*) and even in H they appear only in Lev **19** 21.22; i.e. what in later times appear as the greatest sacrifices of Israel—by Lev **8** Israel's first sacrifice was a sin offering—are found only in X and are mentioned in the prophets for the first time in Ezk **40** 39, while the other classes are mentioned frequently. It seems difficult to escape the inference that class (*a*) appeared relatively late in Israel's history, a point discussed more fully in IV.

5. Sacrifice in General

The problem presented by Jer **7** 22 is a very serious one. Obviously, to say that the command to offer sacrifice was not given on the day of the Exodus but on Sinai, is quite unsatisfactory, for this would make Jeremiah quibble. He denies categorically that a command to offer sacrifice *was part of the Divine Law at all.* Now, if it be noted that the offering of firstlings and first-fruits was altogether distinct from the regular sacrifices, it will be seen that Jer can very well presuppose CC or even Dt, both of which contain only *regulative* prescriptions for sacrifice. (Whether Jer actually *did* conceive CC and Dt as binding is another question.) But by what exegesis of the passage can Jer presuppose X? The natural inference is that the regulations of X became obligatory on Israel *after* Jeremiah's day.

6. Vestments

What follows is in itself an infinitesimal matter but the evidence is significant. The prohibition of steps for the altar in Ex **20** 26 is based on the fact that the ministrants were very scantily clad (cf the light clothing of pilgrims at Mecca). This is corroborated in 2 S **6** 14.20–22, where Michal reproves David for exposing himself. But in X the priests wear rather elaborate vestments, *over linen breeches* (Ex **28** 42). And, to call in Ch for the moment, this is the conception found there of David's religious zeal at the bringing in of the ark. *Besides* the ephod he wears a long linen robe and Michal despises him, not for exposing himself, but only for dancing (1 Ch **15** 27–29).

7. Priests and Levites

(1) CC has no regulations regarding the priesthood, but of course it does not follow that this silence has any significance. However, Samuel-Kings furnish us with certain evidence. Samuel, although an Ephraimite (1 S **1** 1), offers sacrifice repeatedly (see 3, above). In 2 S **20** 25.26 the Hebrew says that Zadok and Abiathar were *kōhănīm,* and also Ira the Jairite was *kōhēn* unto David. Exactly the same word is used for Zadok and Ira in practically the same sentence, and no one without prior conceptions would have dreamed of giving it entirely distinct trs under the circumstances, as do the AV and the RVV texts (not margins). Again in 2 S **8** 18 it is said that David's sons were *kōhănīm* and in 1 K **4** 5 that Zabud was *kōhēn.* Now if *kōhēn* does not mean "priest" in these passages, they are the only cases out of a total of 750 occurrences. That the Chronicler understood the word to mean priest is shown by the fact that in his parallel to 2 S **8** 18 (1 Ch **18** 17) he uses a different word altogether. The natural inference from these passages is that the restriction of priestly ministration to a certain line came about after Solomon's time (cf Jgs **17** 12.13, a Levite is desirable but not essential).

(2) In Dt the priesthood appears as limited to the sons of Levi, but it is at least safe to say that no *explicit* distinction is made within the tribe. In **21** 5 the priests are the "sons of Levi," just as in **17** 9; **18** 1; **24** 8 the term is "the priests the Levites." In **10** 8 the right to bless and in **33** 8–11 the right to offer incense and sacrifice are in no ways said to be restricted to a very small proportion of the tribe. Cf Jer **33** 21.22 (here questions of authenticity are irrelevant). A clear distinction within the tribe of Levi appears in the prophetic writings for the first time in Ezk **44** 10–31, where two kinds of Levites are spoken of, "the priests the Levites, the sons of Zadok" (ver 15) and the Levites, simply (ver 10). No third class is recognized (cf **40** 45.46, where the distinction is between two classes of priests). Now, the distinction between the Zadokian and non-Zadokian Levites is based by Ezekiel on one thing only, in the past the former had been faithful and the latter had not (vs 10–15). *Because* the former had ministered before idols, *therefore* should they not come to execute the office of a priest, but perform only inferior ministrations. Now this can mean only that the non-Zadokians are excluded from priestly privileges that they once possessed. The non-Zadokians, if they had not sinned, would still have been legitimate priests in Ezekiel's eyes, for otherwise the exclusion from the altar would be eviscerated of all meaning as a punishment; i.e. Ezekiel knows of only two kinds of Levites, both kinds originally legitimate priests, but one class now to be forbidden access to the altar because of sin. A third class of Levite, non-Aaronites, who never had had access to the altar, but who, because of their righteousness, had been blessed with the privilege to perform minor ministerial acts, is conspicuous in Ezk by its absence. And this absence, in the face of the immense amount of minute detail contained in Ezk **40–48**, can be explained on no other hypothesis than that Ezk did not know of such a class. When the immense importance of the non-Aaronite Levites in Ch, Ezr, etc, is thought of, what other explanation can be given for their omission in Ezk's elaborate regulations for the cultus? To whom did Ezk consider the more menial work in the Temple would have fallen if the non-Zadokians had not sinned? Probably he never raised the question at all, but there is no objection to supposing that he would have assigned it to the priesthood as a whole.

(3) It is needless to collect the evidence of X. The non-Aaronite Levites appear there as ministers of the greatest importance, elaborately set apart, and with their duties and privileges accurately defined (Nu **8**, esp.). Now, it is submitted that this evidence points in its most natural interpretation to a gradual narrowing of the priestly privileges in Israel through a period of many cents. It is natural, though by no means necessary, to identify the non-Zadokians of Ezk with the non-Aaronites of X. At all events it is argued that in course of time, long after the priesthood had become restricted to Levites only, a considerable proportion of the latter lost their priestly privilege. Ezk stood near enough to the change (that he was the actual innovator is improbable) to state the fact of the degradation and its cause. X regarded the distinction as of such long standing that it must be accredited to Moses himself. It is highly probable that evidence of the change is to be found in Dt **18** 6–8, but this will not be pressed here.

8. Dues

(1) In CC first-fruits are to be offered in Ex **23** 19 and a portion (perhaps a tenth, but not specified as such) of the whole harvest in **22** 29. Nothing is said about their disposition. In Dt, the first-fruits of grain, wine and oil (with fleece) belong to the "priests the Levites" (**18** 4). And the basket of "fruit" in the beautiful rite of **26** 1–11 probably had the

same destination. Of the general harvest the tithe is to be dedicated, as explained at length in **14** 22–29. The worshipper is to eat it himself, but shall take care to see that the Levite receives a portion. Every third year, however, the tithe is to be spent for the benefit of all who need charity, including the Levite. Note that in either case the Levite receives only a *part* of the tithe. In X the first-fruits are again assigned to the clergy (but now specifically to the *priests*—Nu **18** 12.13). But it appears that the tithe is to be given *wholly* to the Levites in Nu **18** 21–24. The contradiction with Dt **14** 22–29 is real. That *two* tithes were to be paid by the worshipper may safely be assumed as impossible, as a tax of one-fifth would have been unendurable. (It may be noted, though, that in later days the very pious took this interpretation—cf Tob **1** 7—but it is certain that no such ruling ever maintained generally.) An alternative explanation offered is that it could be assumed that the Levite would invite the worshipper to join in a feast on the tithe. Frankly, it is difficult to treat this as quite candid. In Dt the worshipper is anything rather than a mere guest at another man's banquet. When the tithe has been brought as money, the worshipper is to spend it on anything that best pleases him, and of the Levite it is said only "thou shalt not forsake him." Moreover, the tithe is to be consumed at the sanctuary and nowhere else (Dt **14** 23; cf **12** 11). In Nu **18**, however, the tithe becomes the exclusive property of the Levite and it is assigned him as his source of income (vs 25–32) and so exclusively is it his that it in turn is tithed. And, far from being turned into a feast at which the worshipper shares, it need not be consumed at the sanctuary at all but may be eaten in "every place," wherever the Levite and his family may happen to live (ver 31). It would be hard to conceive of two rules more mutually exclusive than the tithe directions in Dt and Nu. That the livelihood provided for the Levite in Dt is pitiful is hardly in point and at all events he received more than did the widow and the orphan. But cf IV.

(2) Firstlings in CC must be offered on the eighth day (Ex **22** 30), but in Dt **15** 19–22 they were preserved, without being worked or shorn, until "year by year" they could be taken up to the sanctuary. (Apparently by **14** 23–25 it might be converted into money in case of great distance.) Here the worshipper was to offer it and eat of it (a peace offering). But in Nu **18** 15–18 the firstling becomes the personal property of the priest and *he* receives the flesh of the animal, if it can be sacrificed (i.e. it is *his* peace offering, not the worshipper's). There is no question of giving back a portion to the worshipper, again. Note, moreover, that in Dt **15** 21–23, an animal not fit for sacrifice was eaten at *home* by the worshipper and so did not come in contact with the priest at all; contrast Nu **18** 15.

(3) A minor matter is found in the portion of the peace offering that went to the priest. In Dt **18** 3 it is specified as the shoulder, two cheeks and maw. In X (Ex **29** 26–28, etc) this has become the breast and the right thigh—a considerably more advantageous portion.

(4) In Dt it is laid down that a Levite has no inheritance among his brethren (**10** 9; **12** 12; **18** 1) and hence is recommended as an object of charity, like the widow and the orphan. And, like the widow and the orphan, he lives "within thy gates" (**12** 12, etc), i.e. in the same cities as the rest of the Israelites. Now in X the adjurations to charity disappear, because he receives a fixed income (from the tithe), but it is said that this tithe is given the Levites in lieu of an inheritance, "Among the children of Israel they shall have no inheritance" (Nu **18** 21–24). In another part of X, however, there is still a different conception—the Levites receive no less than forty-eight cities with ample "suburbs," expressly said to be given them "from the inheritance" of Israel (Nu **35** 1–8). So in Lev **25** 32–34 the houses of the Levites are "their possession among the children of Israel," and the fields "their perpetual possession" and inalienable. Is there any natural explanation of these passages except that they represent increasing efforts to provide properly for the Levites as time went on? That the different rules represent advances within Moses' own period cannot be taken seriously, esp. as on this hypothesis the Dt laws would have been the latest. See, in addition, III.

9. Miscellaneous

(1) CC and Dt have little mention of coined money and little attempt to define fractions exactly. Contrast the elaborate regulations of, e.g. Lev **27**. It is not contended that the Israelites could not have had enough culture in Moses' day to calculate so accurately, but attention must be drawn to the extreme contrast.

(2) In CC (Ex **23** 16) the year begins in the fall, in H (Lev **23** 5) and X (Ex **12** 2; Nu **9** 5; **28** 16) it begins in the spring.

(3) Dt (**16** 3) explains the use of unleavened bread at the Passover as due to the haste with which the Israelites left Egypt (as in Ex **12** 39), while Ex **12** 15–20 makes this use depend on the positive command of God *before* the first-born were slain. And note that, in Ex **12**, vs 18–20 are a simple repetition of vs 15–17 with a more precise dating added. For this matter of dating compare the rough statements of CC with the exactness of Lev **23**.

(4) In CC marital rights of the master over his maidservants are taken for granted (Ex **21** 7–11); in Dt (**15** 17) the maidservant has the same privilege of release as the manservant, with the evident assumption that slavery does not confer marital rights on the master. (It is of course gratuitous to assume that two different kinds of maidservants are meant, particularly as in both cases the maidservant is contrasted in general with the manservant in general.) Note, moreover, that in Ex **20** 17 "wife" follows "house" in the prohibition against coveting, while in Dt **5** 21 "wife" precedes "house" and a different vb. is used. The inference is natural that between CC and Dt woman, both as slave and as wife, had risen to a higher position.

(5) In both CC (Ex **21** 6) and Dt (**15** 17) life-long slavery is permitted, if the slave desires it, otherwise the slave is free at the end of the sixth year. In H (Lev **25** 39–43), the slave serves until the Jubilee year and then goes free absolutely.

10. Summary

Now, it is not claimed that all the discrepancies in the above lists are incapable of reconciliation, although the examples chosen are among those where reconciliation is extremely difficult. The claim is made, however, that all of this evidence is cumulative and that each successive item points more and more forcibly toward a single conclusion—that in the legislation of the Pentateuch, esp. when considered in connection with the Prophets and with Samuel-Kings, there have been incorporated laws belonging to very different periods. And, for the most part, a development from the simple to the highly organized can be traced. *And this conclusion explains all the facts.*

11. Additional Note

The above examples have been chosen as those where no changes in the text need be made. Of the other instances, only one need be considered—Lev **17**. On its surface, this ch appears to refer solely to life in the wilderness. But in vs 8.10.12.13.15 it appears that living in the midst of the Israelites are settled non-Israelites. And the "open field" of ver 5 is a contrast to city, not to tent, life. Now in vs 3–5 the question is not at all idolatry but eating of blood at an ordinary meal. An exact commentary is found on this in 1 S **14** 32–35, where the Israelites sin in eating the blood of animals "slain on the ground"; i.e. in both Lev **17** and 1 S **14**, at every slaying of an animal for food, some formal disposition of the blood had to be made. In Lev **17** 4 this is sacrificial, and the appearance of the altar in 1 S **14** 35 points in the same direction. Now this investing of every slaying of an animal with a sacrificial character, explains the permission of Dt **12** 20–25 to eat flesh "after all the desire of thy soul," a permission inexplicable unless there had been an earlier contrary practice. It is to be noted, moreover, that in Dt **12** 16 the blood is to be disposed of by pouring it on the earth, the practice *condemned* in 1 S **14** 32. The conclusion is that before the legislation of Dt the Israelite offered the blood of every slain sacrificial animal at the local sanctuary. Dt's rigid enforcement of the one sanctuary made this impossible, and so permission was given to eat flesh at home, provided the blood was not eaten, *and* provided that it was disposed of in a *non*-sacrificial way. Now in Lev **17** 3–5 it becomes clear what has happened. The passage read originally something like this: 'What man soever there be of the house of Israel, that killeth an ox, or lamb, or goat, and hath not brought it to offer it as an oblation unto Jeh, blood shall be imputed unto that man. . . . .' This offering was to take place at the local sanctuary. But when the passage was incorporated into the whole body of the legislation, the editor was working at a time when the legitimacy of the local sanctuaries had long been forgotten. And so references to the "camp" and "the tent of meeting" were inserted, in accordance with the only laws that the editor conceived could ever have prevailed. The discrepancies with vs 5.8, etc, were probably not observed.

It is to be understood that this passage is not used as presenting a basic argument for the Graf-Wellhausen hypothesis. But it is cited as an example of other passages where the text is to be considered. And, also, because the assertion is made that this particular passage is a death-blow to the "critical" hypothesis. Naturally, it is nothing of the sort.

III. The History.—It may be said at the outset that many of the attacks on the historic value of Ch have been very gravely exaggerated. But, none the less, a close comparison with Samuel-Kings shows that the Chronicler has most certainly read back into history the religious institutions of his own late day—it need not be said, with perfect innocence and sincerity. For instance, in comparing 2 K **11** 4 with 2 Ch **23** 2–6, we find the statement of K that Jehoiada brought captains of the Carites and of the guard into the house of Jeh quite altered. In Ch Jehoiada summons *Levites* and heads of houses, with the express provision that only Levites shall enter into the house of Jeh. So holy a priest as Jehoiada could not have acted as K says he did act. Similarly, the statement in 1 K **15** 14 that Asa did *not* remove the high places is changed into the statement that he *did* remove the high places (2 Ch **14** 3–5), and only those in (northern) Israel were left (**15** 17). So did Jehoshaphat (**17** 6), although in **20** 33 the explicit statement to the contrary is copied (unnoticed?) from 1 K **22** 43. Such righteous kings *must* have enforced the single sanctuary. The almost trivial matter of David's garb when the ark was brought into Jerus (contrast 2 S **6** 20–22 with **1** Ch **15** 27–29) has been noticed already in II, 6. The important matter in Ch, however, is the history of the Tabernacle. In 1 Ch **16** 39–42 the Tabernacle is at Gibeon, with the full ministry surrounding it, with the exception of a detail left before the Ark in Jerus (cf **9** 17–32). And in 2 Ch **5** 5 it is brought up to Jerus, although the disposition made of it is not explained. Otherwise it is mentioned in 1 Ch **6** 48; **21** 29; 2 Ch **1** 3. But the narrative presents some serious difficulties. Why did David build a special tent for the Ark in Jerus (1 Ch **16** 1), if the one Divinely appointed covering for the Ark was still standing—not to be brought

1. Chronicles

to Jerus until its utility was past (2 Ch **5** 5)? That it was too fragile to be moved can hardly be taken seriously. In the first place, this explanation is without the least support in the text. And, in the second place, it is incredible for such a solid structure of wood, silver and brass, however much repair the curtains might have needed. Moreover, this explanation will not do at all for Bezalel's brazen altar, which was still quite usable in 2 Ch **1** 5, making the construction of a new altar (**4** 1) altogether inexplicable. The impression is created at once that the Chronicler has injected the Tabernacle into a narrative that knew nothing of it. This is corroborated by 1 Ch **21** 29.30; the altar at the floor of Ornan is explained by the difficulty of reaching the Tabernacle. But the Ark, the natural means for an inquiry of God, was in Jerus, with an altar by it (**16** 1)—why this *third* altar on the threshing-floor? The inaccessibility of the Tabernacle is invoked here only to solve what was a difficulty to the Chronicler. Now if 2 Ch **1** 3 be compared with 1 K **3** 2–4, the key of the whole is discovered. K not only does not mention the presence of the Tabernacle at Gibeon, but excludes it. Solomon's sacrificing at Gibeon is explained by saying that such was the custom of all Israel, who sacrificed in high places before the Temple was built; Solomon also sacrificed in high-places and Gibeon was a great high-place. This is an *apology* for Solomon's conduct—why should the editor of K have apologized for sacrifice offered at the Divinely appointed Tabernacle? The Chronicler, however, could not believe that God blessed Solomon when offering sacrifice in a way forbidden by the law of Ch's times, and hence he solves the difficulty by bringing in something that is unknown to the narrative in K.

Indeed, K mentions the Tabernacle only in 1 K **8** 4. S mentions the Tabernacle as such only in 1 S **2** 22. Jgs does not mention the Tabernacle at all (**18** 31 is the only possibility and the word there is "house"). Now 1 S **2** 22 is not found in the Vatican LXX, and the description of the Tabernacle as a tent contradicts **1** 9; **3** 15, where it appears as a *temple* or *house*. So it must be dropped as a gloss. Nor will it be denied that 1 K **8** 4 looks suspiciously like a gloss as well, particularly in view of the presence of Levites there, who are practically unmentioned elsewhere in Samuel-Kings. At all events, there are only these two possible mentions of what should have been the center of Israel's worship in *all* of Jgs-Samuel-Kings. This is not the ordinary argument from silence, it is silent about what should have been the most vital matter of all. Dt knows nothing of the Tabernacle, and, as has already been shown in II, states as clearly as language only can that in the wilderness the centralization of worship was *not* observed. The argument from silence alone would be conclusive here, for how could the author of Dt in his passionate advocacy of the single sanctuary fail to appeal to the single sanctuary already established by God's decree, if he knew anything about it? But not only is there no such mention in Dt but a positive exclusion of such a sanctuary in express terms. The case would seem to be complete. The Tabernacle of X and Ch is an ideal structure projected back into the past, just as the temple of Ezk is an ideal structure projected into the future. And it is needless to appeal to the familiar argument that the Tabernacle of Ex **26** would have been blown to pieces by the first storm. It had no provision for tent poles deeply sunk, which alone could resist the blasts of the desert.

2. Kings, etc

It is impossible in the space of the present art. to enter into all the corroborative evidence, but a very few important arguments may be mentioned. Simple people tend most naturally to think of heroes of the past as more and more glorious as time passes. Now Jgs **1** describes the conquest of Canaan as a slow and laborious process after Joshua's death. But in Josh **10** 40–43; **11** 10–23; **21** 43–45—esp. **11** 16–19—Canaan was *completely* swept of its inhabitants by Joshua in a series of annihilatory campaigns, making Jgs **1** quite impossible. Evidently the Josh passages cited belong to a very much later conception of the past history. The fate of Hebron is especially interesting. In Jgs **1** 20 Caleb takes Hebron after Joshua's death. But in Josh **15** Caleb takes Hebron during Joshua's lifetime and at the latter's direction. In Josh **10** 36.37, however, Joshua takes Hebron personally and annihilates its inhabitants. Here are three distinct conceptions of Hebron's fate, again. But still a fourth is found in Josh **21** 11.12: it was not Caleb who received the city but the Levites. This evidently belongs to the time when the Levitical right to cities had become a commonplace, and was therefore referred to the earliest days. The accounts of the annihilation of the Canaanites arose naturally enough. Accordings to Jgs the conquest was gradual and merciful. But the Canaanites seduced Israel to idolatry repeatedly. Therefore they should have been routed out (Dt **20** 16–18). But Joshua was righteous and had all power. Therefore he *must* have rooted them out. How they suddenly reappeared again was a question that was not raised. But perhaps it may be thought a relief to understand that the ruthless campaigns of the Israelites are due to reflection and not to descriptions of what actually happened.

3. The Conquest

Simple people think of God quite naturally and reverently as a greater man. So in Ex **24** 9–11 we read that Moses and many others met God in the mount, they all saw Him, and ate and drank before Him. A slightly more refined point of view is in Ex **33** 11, where Moses (but no one else) sees God face to face, and Nu **12** 8, where again he (alone) sees the form of God. But in Ex **33** 20 no man, not even Moses, can see God face to face. In Dt **4** 11–15 it is laid down that only darkness was seen—"ye saw no form." Perhaps Moses was thought of as an exception, but the contradiction of the concept that conceived over seventy Israelites besides Moses to have seen God is complete.

4. Ideas of God

The reading back of an official priesthood into the time of Moses can be seen in certain passages where Aaron appears predominantly. Contrast, e.g. Ex **8** 20–24; **15** 23–26; **17** 1–7 with **7** 1–19; **16** 9.10; Nu **20** 2–13. Yet despite the importance of Aaron in the latter passages, in Ex **33** 11 the minister of Moses in the Tent is Joshua, who is not a priest at all. Contrast similarly Dt **31** 14.15 with Nu **27** 18–21, noting how Eleazar appears in the latter passage, although the former excludes him. At the time of X it was not thought possible that Moses could have acted without the official mediation of the official priest.

5. Priesthood

Reasons of space preclude a further discussion of the other arguments here, such as the linguistic. As a matter of fact, the sections that contain the more developed concepts contain also a different vocabulary. To be repeated, however, is the fact that the argument is *cumulative* and that a *single* explanation of the differences is offered in the hypothesis of very varying dates for the various portions. Of course an exact analysis of every ver and a rigorous reconstruction of every source is not claimed to be possible. Many scholars have been carried by their enthusiasm for analysis into making preposterous dissections. But the principal lines of division are sufficiently clear. And it may be hoped the reader will not think that the acceptance of them has been dictated by any motive except that of facing the truth—least of all by any motive of a weakened faith in the power of God or a suspicion of the miraculous.

6. Summary

IV. Reconstruction.—Israel came into Canaan, after having received through the mediation of Moses a covenant relation with God and (almost certainly) some accompanying legislation. But this legislation seems not to have prescribed the ritual form that the worship of God was to take. In part, old forms were simply continued and in part new forms were gradually developed or appropriated, the emphasis of the Law at that time being on the moral and the ritual being left quite free. In especial, sacrifices were offered wherever Israelites happened to live, doubtless frequently at former Canaanite sanctuaries, now rededicated to Jeh. The local sanctuary was the center of the life. Men went thither to learn God's will and to give a religious character to what we should call purely secular transactions (contracts, etc). Firstlings were offered there on the eighth day, first-fruits at once, every meal of flesh food was given a sacrificial character (peace offering), and, for more solemn purposes, the whole burnt offering was offered. So the local sanctuary corresponded to our "village church"; it was the religious *home* of the people. Certain of these sanctuaries had an especial dignity, above all Shiloh, where the Ark was. Later, when a united Israel had been realized, David brought the Ark to Jerus that the national capital might become the center of the national religious life as well, and Solomon enshrined the Ark in the Temple. So to Jerus there resorted naturally the best of Israel's religious leaders, and there the worship of God would be found in its purest form, normally speaking.

1. Covenant Code

As time went on, the progress of culture and the freer contact with other nations had bad effects as well as good. New and degrading religious practices flowed into the country and they revived old but equally degrading religious practices that had survived from the Canaanites. The priesthood at Jerus did not escape a taint, but the place where such rites gained the readiest foothold was of course the obscure local sanctuaries. Not the best-minded king or the most zealous prophet could watch all the services at them all, and attempts at purging them of idolatry or idolatrous rites (Elijah, Jehu, etc) could not effect permanent improvement. And it could not have been very long after David's own day that the idea must have begun to grow that complete prohibition of country sacrifices and the rigid centralization of everything at Jerus was the only measure possible. This would soon become a fixed conviction of the better class of the Jerus priesthood and in a few generations would be a tradition. Detailed precepts to carry this tradition into effect arose necessarily and in turn became a tradition and in course of time were regarded as Moses' work and committed to writing. In this way the legislation of Dt took form and at the time of its discovery under Josiah there is not the slightest occasion to attribute fraud to anyone engaged in the transaction. The document agreed fairly well with what was the tradition of Jerus, and no one at that day could distinguish between a writing a cent. old or even less and a writing of Moses' own time. The country priests and the mass of the people were not consulted as to enforcing it, and they would not have known if they had been consulted. On any reading of the history, the reforms proceeded from a very small group, and any general "tradition of the Jews" was nonexistent.

2. Deuteronomy

(1) The reforms added to the theoretical tradition the additional influence of practical experience and the idea of course dominated the minds of the more earnest among the exiles. Ezekiel, in

particular, realized that only at a single sanctuary could the worship of God be kept pure—the single sanctuary was God's will. And Ezekiel's influence was immense. Now it is to be noted that at the return only those came back who had a real enthusiasm for Jerus, as Babylonia was, materially speaking, a far more attractive place than the Pal of that day. That the single sanctuary could have been questioned by any of these Jews or that they could have conceived of Moses as instituting anything of less dignity is impossible.

3. Later

(2) Other reforms also had been at work. Even in Dt the more primitive note of joyousness was maintained in the sacrifices. But joyousness in simple life is often dissipation in cultured life and the peace offering could be made a debauch (Isa **22** 12–14; Prov **7** 14). A sense of *personal* guilt had become far better developed and the incongruity of penitential worship with a festal meal was recognized. A very slight change was made: the portion was to be eaten by the priest instead of the worshipper—and the sin and trespass offerings emerged. The abuses were cut away by this one stroke and the peace offering proper retired into the background. And sacrifices were made the proper center of the official worship. In accord with the growing culture, proportions of gifts, dates of feasts, etc, were specified more and more exactly, the worship was surrounded with a more impressive ritual, and, in particular, the officiating priests substituted vestments suited to the better taste of the time for the old loin-cloth. Traces are left in the OT of difficulties regarding the rights of the various classes of priests to minister but the matter was settled eventually in a manner that satisfied all. Priests formerly guilty of idolatry and their descendants were admitted to share in the worship and the priestly revenues, but the actual offering of sacrifice was restricted to those who had been faithful. The proper support of the clergy so formed required, in accordance with their dignity, more elaborate provisions than had been needed in the simpler times of old, but was accomplished in a manner again entirely satisfactory. The religion of no other nation could have survived the Bab exile intact. But Israel returned, with the elements formerly necessary but now outgrown changed into a form adapted to the new task the nation had before it—the preparation of itself and the world for the advent of Christ.

This growth toward the higher, involving as it did the meeting of all kinds of obstacles, the solving of all kinds of problems, the learning when to abandon elements that had been transcended, is unique in the history of religions. And the explanation of its uniqueness can be found only in the guidance of God. And in the history as reconstructed God is seen truly as the Father, who trained His children little by little, giving them only what they were able to receive but bringing them surely to Himself. And in the documents that contain the precepts for each stage of progress God's hand can be seen no less clearly. To be sure, in the secular science of history (as in physics or astronomy) His revelation was expressed in forms that His people could understand. This alteration—and this alteration only—in our view of what is covered by Bib. inspiration is the sacrifice demanded by the Graf-Wellhausen hypothesis.

4. Evaluation

Literature.—This is overwhelming and reference must be made to the separate arts. The standard analysis is that of *The Oxford Hexateuch* (1900), more briefly in *The Composition of the Hexateuch* by Carpenter and Harford (Battersby) (1902). Merx, *Die Bücher Moses und Josua* (1907), is the best brief introduction. Gunkel's *Genesis* (1910) in the Nowack series, his more popular *Die Urgeschichte und die Patriarchen* (1911), and his "Die israelitische Literatur" in *Die Kultur der Gegenwart*, I, 7 (1906), should on no account be neglected. The best treatment of the inspiration question from the standpoint of pure dogmatics is F. J. Hall's *Authority: Ecclesiastical and Biblical* (1908).

In the above discussion it has been assumed that our text of the OT is at least relatively trustworthy. The reader interested in what can be done by textual reconstruction will find the opposite poles represented in the works of Wiener and of Cheyne.

Burton Scott Easton

[Editorial Note.—The promoters of the *Encyclopaedia* are not to be understood as endorsing all the views set forth in Dr. Easton's art. (see Criticism of the Bible). It was thought right, however, that, in such a work of reference, there should be given a full and adequate presentation of so popular a theory.]

CROCODILE, krok'ō-dīl. See Leviathan; Dragon.

CROCODILE, LAND. See Chameleon.

CROOK-BACKED, kroŏk'bakt (גִּבֵּן, *gibbēn;* **κυρτός,** *kurtós*): A disqualification for the priesthood (Lev **21** 20); was probably an angular curvature of the spine, usually the result of tubercular caries of the vertebrae. It was by no means uncommon in ancient Egypt, where I have found a considerable number of spines affected with this disease. Some Talmudic authorities explain it as meaning "very dark colored," but this is unlikely.

The woman bound by the spirit of infirmity and unable to lift herself (Lk **13** 11–17) was affected with senile kyphosis, a chronic bone disease often found among aged men (and more frequently women) whose lives have been spent in agricultural labor. In these the vertebrae become altered in shape so that it is impossible to straighten the back. Some rabbinical authorities believed all deformities to be due to Satan, and to this Our Lord seems to have alluded in his rebuke to those who caviled at His healing on the Sabbath. I have found this condition in some Egyp skeletons, and have seen it in a Palestinian fellah. A skeleton affected with a similar curvature was found buried under the threshold of a house at Gezer, where she had evidently been offered as a foundation sacrifice.

Alex. Macalister

CROOKED, kroŏk'ed (עָוָה, *'āwāh,* עָקַשׁ, *'āḳash,* עֲקַלְקָל, *'ăḳalḳāl,* עֲקַלָּתוֹן, *'ăḳallāthōn,* פְּתַלְתֹּל, *pᵉthaltōl;* **σκολιός,** *skoliós*): Primarily designates something that is bent, twisted or deformed (Isa **27** 1; **45** 2 AV).

Figurative: (1) It designates a course of action that deviates from rectitude, esp. deceit, guile, hypocrisy (Dt **32** 5; Prov **2** 15; Eccl **1** 15; Lk **3** 5; cf Phil **2** 15); (2) trials (sent by God, Eccl **7** 13; Lam **3** 9); (3) difficulties (removed by God, Isa **42** 16).

CROOKED SERPENT, kroŏk'ed sûr'pent. See Astronomy.

CROP:

(1) As noun the translation of מֻרְאָה, *mur'āh* (Lev **1** 16), which is the craw of a bird, esp. of doves and pigeons, which had to be removed by the priest before he offered the birds as a burnt sacrifice.

(2) As a vb. it is (Ezk **17** 4.22) the tr of קָטַף, *ḳāṭaph,* which has the meaning of "cutting off," "cutting down," "plucking."

CROSS (**σταυρός,** *staurós,* "a cross," "the crucifixion"; **σκόλοψ,** *skólops,* "a stake," "a pole"): The name is not found in the OT. It is derived from the Lat word *crux.* In the Gr language it is *stauros,* but sometimes we find the word *skolops* used as its Gr equivalent. The historical writers, who transferred the events of Rom history into the

Gr language, make use of these two words. No word in human language has become more universally known than this word, and that because all of the history of the world since the death of Christ has been measured by the distance which separates events from it. The symbol and principal content of the Christian religion and of Christian civilization is found in this one word.

1. Forms of the Cross

The cross occurs in at least four different forms: (1) the form usually seen in pictures, the *crux immissa*, in which the upright beam projected above the shorter crosspiece; this is most likely the type of cross on which the Saviour died, as may be inferred from the inscription which was nailed above His head; (2) the *crux commissa*, or St. Anthony's cross, which has the shape of the letter **T**; (3) the Gr cross of later date, in which the pieces are equally long; (4) the *crux decussata*, or St. Andrew's cross, which has the shape of the letter **X**.

2. Discovery of the True Cross

The early church historians Socrates (1,17), Sozomen (2,1), Rufinus (1,7) and Theodoret (1,18) all make mention of this tradition. The most significant thing is that Eusebius (*Vit. Const.*, iii.26–28), who carries more weight than they all together, wholly omits it.

According to it, Helena, the mother of Constantine the Great, in 325 AD, when she was 79 years old, discovered the true cross of Jesus by an excavation she caused to be made on the traditional spot of His grave. With the cross of the Saviour were found the two crosses of the malefactors who were crucified with Him. A miracle of healing, wrought by touching the true cross, revealed its identity. When found it was intact, even the holy nails of the crucifixion being discovered. The main part of the cross was deposited by Helena in a church erected over the spot. Of the remainder, a portion was inserted into the head of the statue of Constantine, and the balance was placed in a new church, specially erected for it at Rome and named after it Santa Croce. Small fragments of the wood of the true cross were sold, encrusted with gold and jewels, and since many among the wealthy believers were desirous of possessing such priceless relics, the miracle of the "multiplication of the cross" was devised, so that the relic suffered no diminution "et quasi intacta maneret" (Paulinus ep 11 *ad Sev*). Fragments of the true cross are thus to be found in many Roman Catholic churches of many countries, all over Christendom. It is said that the East celebrated the *staurosimos hēmera* (Crucifixion Day) on September 14, since the 4th cent. The evidence for this fact is late and untrustworthy. It is certain that the West celebrated the Invention of the Cross, on May 3, since the time of Gregory the Great in the 6th cent. The finding and publication of the apocryphal "Doctrina Addaei" has made it evident that the entire legend of the discovery of the cross by Helena is but a version of the old Edessa legend, which tells of an identical discovery of the cross, under the very same circumstances, by the wife of the emperor Claudius, who had been converted to Christianity by the preaching of Peter.

3. Symbolical Uses of the Cross

(1) *Extra-scriptural*.—The sign of the cross was well known in the symbolics of various ancient nations. Among the Egyptians it is said to have been the symbol of divinity and eternal life, and to have been found in the temple of Serapis. It is known either in the form of the Gr cross or in the form of the letter **T**. The Spaniards found it to be well known, as a symbol, by the Mexicans and Peruvians, perhaps signifying the four elements, or the four seasons, or the four points of the compass.

(2) *Scriptural*.—The suffering implied in crucifixion naturally made the cross a symbol of pain, distress and burden-bearing. Thus Jesus used it Himself (Mt **10** 38; **16** 24). In Paulinic lit. the cross stands for the preaching of the doctrine of the Atonement (1 Cor **1** 18; Gal **6** 14; Phil **3** 18; Col **1** 20). It expresses the bond of unity between the Jew and the Gentile (Eph **2** 16), and between the believer and Christ, and also symbolizes sanctification (Gal **5** 24). The cross is the center and circumference of the preaching of the apostles and of the life of the NT church.

4. Crucifixion

As an instrument of death the cross was detested by the Jews. "Cursed is everyone that hangeth on a tree" (Gal **3** 13; cf Dt **21** 23), hence it became a stumbling-block to them, for how could one accursed of God be their Messiah? Nor was the cross differently considered by the Romans. "Let the very name of the cross be far away not only from the body of a Roman citizen, but even from his thoughts, his eyes, his ears" (Cicero *Pro Rabirio* 5). The earliest mode of crucifixion seems to have been by impalation, the transfixion of the body lengthwise and crosswise by sharpened stakes, a mode of death-punishment still well known among the Mongol race. The usual mode of crucifixion was familiar to the Greeks, the Romans, the Egyptians, Persians and Babylonians (Thuc. 1, 110; Herod. iii.125, 159). Alexander the Great executed two thousand Tyrian captives in this way, after the fall of the city. The Jews received this form of punishment from the Syrians and Romans (*Ant*, XII, v, 4; XX, vi, 2; *BJ*, I, iv, 6). The Rom citizen was exempt from this form of death, it being considered the death of a slave (Cicero *In Verrem* i. 5, 66; Quint. viii.4). The punishment was meted out for such crimes as treason, desertion in the face of the enemy, robbery, piracy, assassination, sedition, etc. It continued in vogue in the Rom empire till the day of Constantine, when it was abolished as an insult to Christianity. Among the Romans crucifixion was preceded by scourging, undoubtedly to hasten impending death. The victim then bore his own cross, or at least the upright beam, to the place of execution. This in itself proves that the structure was less ponderous than is commonly supposed. When he was tied to the cross nothing further was done and he was left to die from starvation. If he was nailed to the cross, at least in Judaea, a stupefying drink was given him to deaden the agony. The number of nails used seems to have been indeterminate. A tablet, on which the feet rested or on which the body was partly supported, seems to have been a part of the cross to keep the wounds from tearing through the transfixed members (Iren., *Adv. haer.*, ii.42). The suffering of death by crucifixion was intense, esp. in hot climates. Severe local inflammation, coupled with an insignificant bleeding of the jagged wounds, produced traumatic fever, which was aggravated by the exposure to the heat of the sun, the strained position of the body and insufferable thirst. The wounds swelled about the rough nails and the torn and lacerated tendons and nerves caused excruciating agony. The arteries of the head and stomach were surcharged with blood and a terrific throbbing headache ensued. The mind was confused and filled with anxiety and dread foreboding. The victim of crucifixion literally died a thousand deaths. Tetanus not rarely supervened and the rigors of the attending convulsions would tear at the wounds and add to the burden of pain, till at last the bodily forces were exhausted and the victim sank to unconsciousness and death. The sufferings were so frightful that "even among the raging passions of war pity was sometimes excited" (*BJ*,

V, xi, 1). The length of this agony was wholly determined by the constitution of the victim, but death rarely ensued before thirty-six hours had elapsed. Instances are on record of victims of the cross who survived their terrible injuries when taken down from the cross after many hours of suspension (Jos, *Vita*, 75). Death was sometimes hastened by breaking the legs of the victims and by a hard blow delivered under the armpit before crucifixion. *Crura fracta* was a well-known Rom term (Cicero *Phil.* xiii.12). The sudden death of Christ evidently was a matter of astonishment (Mk **15** 44). The peculiar symptoms mentioned by John (**19** 34) would seem to point to a rupture of the heart, of which the Saviour died, independent of the cross itself, or perhaps hastened by its agony. See BLOOD AND WATER. HENRY E. DOSKER

CROSSWAY, kros'wā (פֶּרֶק, *pereḳ*, lit. "division"): A forking or dividing of the way. Obadiah warns Edom, "And stand thou not in the crossway, to cut off those of his that escape" (Ob ver 14). In LXX, "a mountain pass."

CROWN, kroun: The word crown in the OT is a tr of five different Heb words, and in the NT of two Gr words. These express the several meanings, and must be examined to ascertain the same.

1. In Hebrew

The five Heb words are as follows: (1) קָדְקֹד, *ḳodhḳōdh*, from קָדַד, *ḳādhadh;* (2) זֵר, *zēr*, from זָרַר, *zārar;* (3) נֵזֶר, *nezer*, or נֶזֶר, *nēzer*, both from נָזַר, *nāzar;* (4) עֲטָרָה, *ʽăṭārāh*, from עָטַר, *ʽāṭar;* (5) כֶּתֶר, *kether*, from כָּתַר, *kāthar*.

(1) *Ḳodhḳōdh* means "the crown of the head," and is also rendered in AV "top of the head," "scalp," "pate." It comes from *ḳādhadh*, meaning "to shrivel up," "contract," or bend the body or neck through courtesy. Both RV and ARV, in Dt **28** 35 and **33** 16, tr it "crown" instead of "top" as in AV. Jacob in his prophecy concerning his sons says: "The blessings of thy father . . . . shall be on the head of Joseph, and on the *crown* of the head of him that is prince among his brethren" (Gen **49** 26 ARVm). Other references are: Dt **33** 20; 2 S **14** 25; Job **2** 7; Isa **3** 17; Jer **2** 16; **48** 45. Tr[d] "scalp" in Ps **68** 21 and "pate" in Ps **7** 16.

(2) *Zēr* means a "chaplet," something spread around the top as a molding about the border, and because of its wreath-like appearance called a crown. "That which presses, binds" (*BDB*). Comes from *zārar*, meaning "to diffuse" or "scatter." It is used in Ex **25** 11.24.25; **30** 3.4; **37** 2.11.12.26.27.

(3) *Nezer* means something "set apart"; i.e. a dedication to the priesthood or the dedication of a Nazarite, hence a chaplet or fillet as a symbol of such consecration. The word in AV is rendered "crown," "consecration," "separation," "hair." Comes from *nāzar*, meaning "to hold aloof" from impurity, even from drink and food, more definitely, "to set apart" for sacred purposes, i.e. "to separate," "devote," "consecrate." It is found in Ex **29** 6; **39** 30; Lev **8** 9; **21** 12; 2 S **1** 10; 2 K **11** 12; 2 Ch **23** 11; Ps **89** 39; **132** 18; Prov **27** 24; Zec **9** 16.

(4) *ʽĂṭārāh* means a crown in the usual sense. Comes from *ʽāṭar*, meaning "to encircle," as in war for offence or defence; also actually and **figuratively** "to crown." Rendered sometimes "to compass." It is used in 2 S **12** 30; 1 Ch **20** 2; Est **8** 15; Job **19** 9; **31** 36; Ps **21** 3; Prov **4** 9; **12** 4; **14** 24; **16** 31; **17** 6; Cant **3** 11; Isa **28** 1.3.5; **62** 3; Jer **13** 18; Lam **5** 16; Ezk **16** 12; **21** 26; **23** 42; Zec **6** 11.14; "crowned," Cant **3** 11; "crownest," Ps **65** 11; "crowneth," Ps **103** 4. RV tr[s] "crowned," of Ps **8** 5 "hast crowned." ARV prefers to tr "crowning," in Isa **23** 8, "the bestower of crowns."

(5) *Kether* means a "circlet" or "a diadem." From *kāthar*, meaning "to inclose": as a friend, "to crown"; as an enemy, "to besiege." Variously tr[d] "beset round," "inclose round," "suffer," "compass about." Found in Est **1** 11; **2** 17; **6** 8; "crowned," in Prov **14** 18.

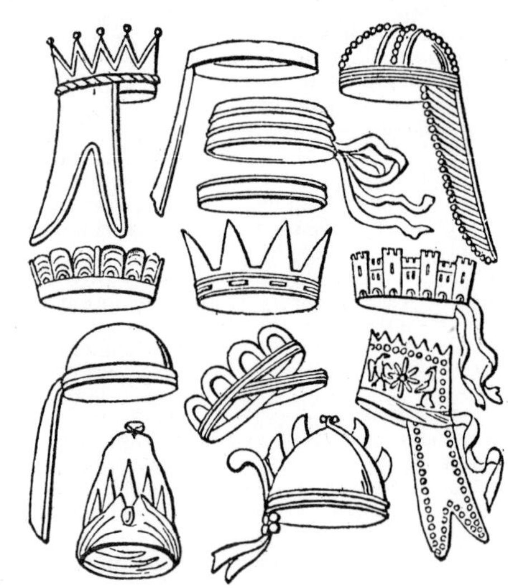

Ancient Asiatic Crowns.

The two Gr words of the NT tr[d] crown are: (1) στέφανος, *stéphanos*, from *stéphō*, and (2) διάδημα, *diádēma*, from *diadéō*, "to bind round."

2. In Greek

(1) *Stephanos* means a chaplet (wreath) made of leaves or leaf-like gold, used for marriage and festive occasions, and expressing public recognition of victory in races, games and war; also **figuratively** as a reward for efficient Christian life and service (see GAMES). This symbol was more noticeable and intricate than the plain fillet. Only in the Rev of John is *stephanos* called "golden." The "crown of thorns" which Jesus wore was a *stephanos* (woven wreath) of thorns; the kind is not known (Mt **27** 29; Mk **15** 17; Jn **19** 2.5). Lk makes no mention of it. Whether intended to represent royalty or victory, it was a caricature crown. *Stephanos* is found in 1 Cor **9** 25; Phil **4** 1; 1 Thess **2** 19; 2 Tim **4** 8; Jas **1** 12; 1 Pet **5** 4; Rev **2** 10; **3** 11; **6** 2; **12** 1; **14** 14; plur. in Rev **4** 4.10; **9** 7; "crowned" in 2 Tim **2** 5; He **2** 9; "crownedst" in He **2** 7.

(2) *Diadēma* is the word for "diadem," from *dia* (about) and *deō* (bound), i.e. something bound about the head. In the three places where it occurs (Rev **12** 3; **13** 1 and **19** 12) both RV and ARV tr it not "crowns" but "diadems," thus making the proper distinction between *stephanos* and *diadēma*, such as is not done either in AV or the LXX (see Trench, *Synonyms of the NT*). According to Thayer the distinction was not observed in Hellenic Gr. "Diadems" are on the dragon (Rev **12** 3), the beast (Rev **13** 1) and on the Rider of the White Horse, "the Faithful and True" (Rev **19** 12). In each case the "diadems" are symbolic of power to rule.

3. Use and Significance

There are five uses of the crown as seen in the Scripture references studied, viz. decoration, consecration, coronation, exaltation, and remuneration.

(1) *Decoration.*—The *zēr* of Ex, as far as it was a crown at all, was for ornamentation, its position not seeming to indicate

any utility purpose. These wavelet, gold moldings, used in the furnishings of the tabernacle of Moses, were placed about (*a*) the table of shewbread (Ex **25** 24; **37** 11); (*b*) the ark of the covenant (Ex **25** 11; **37** 2); (*c*) the altar of incense (Ex **30** 3.4; **37** 26.27). The position of these crowns is a debated question among archaeologists. Their purpose other than decoration is not known. The encircling gold might signify gratitude, purity and enduring worth.

(2) *Consecration.*—The *nezer* had a twofold use as the crown of consecration: (*a*) It was placed as a frontlet on the miter of the high priest, being tied with a blue lace (Ex **39** 30). The priestly crown was a flat piece of pure gold, bearing the inscription, "Holy to Jeh," signifying the consecration of the priest as the representative of the people (Ex **29** 6; Lev **8** 9). (*b*) Likewise the Heb king (2 K **11** 12) was set apart by God in wearing on his head a royal *nezer*, whether of silk or gold we do not know. It was set with jewels (Zec **9** 16) and was light enough to be taken into battle (2 S **1** 10).

(3) *Coronation.*—The ordinary use of the crown. There were three kinds of kingly crowns used in coronation services: (*a*) The *nezer* or consecration crown, above referred to, was the only one used in crowning Heb kings. What seems to be an exception is in the case of Joshua, who represented both priest and king (Zec **6** 11 ARVm). (*b*) The *'ăṭārāh*, and (*c*) the *kether* were used in crowning foreign monarchs. No king but a Heb could wear a *nezer*—a "Holy to Jeh" crown. It is recorded that David presumed to put on his own head the *'ăṭārāh* of King Malcam (2 S **12** 30 ARVm). The *kether* or jeweled turban was the crown of the Pers king and queen (Est **1** 11; **2** 17; **6** 8).

(4) *Exaltation.*—The *'ăṭārāh*, the *stephanos* and the *diadēma* were used as crowns of exaltation. *Stephanos* was the usual crown of exaltation for victors of games, achievement in war and places of honor at feasts. The *'ăṭārāh* was worn at banquets (Cant **3** 11; Isa **28** 1.3), probably taking the form of a wreath of flowers; also as a crown of honor and victory (Ezk **16** 12; **21** 26; **23** 42). *Stephanos* is the crown of exaltation bestowed upon Christ (Rev **6** 2; **14** 14; He **2** 9). "Exaltation was the logical result of Christ's humiliation" (Vincent). The Apocalyptic woman and locusts receive this emblem of exaltation (Rev **12** 1; **9** 7). The symbolic dragon and beast are elevated, wearing *diadēma* (Rev **12** 3; **13** 1). The conquering Christ has "upon his head . . . . many diadems" (Rev **19** 12). See further Tertullian, *De corona.*

(5) *Remuneration.*—Paul, witnessing the races and games, caught the vision of wreath-crowned victors flush with the reward of earnest endeavor. See GAMES. He also saw the persistent, faithful Christian at the end of his hard-won race wearing the symbolic *stephanos* of rejoicing (1 Thess **2** 19 AV), of righteousness (2 Tim **4** 8), of glory (1 Pet **5** 4), of life (Jas **1** 12; Rev **2** 10). Paul's fellow-Christians were his joy and *stephanos* (Phil **4** 1), "of which Paul might justly make his boast" (Ellicott). Long before Paul, his Heb ancestors saw the *'ăṭārāh* of glory (Prov **4** 9) and the *'ăṭārāh* of a good wife, children's children, riches and a peaceful old age (Prov **12** 4; **14** 24; **16** 31; **17** 6). For Apoc references see 1 Macc **10** 29; **11** 35; **13** 39.

WILLIAM EDWARD RAFFETY

CROWN OF THORNS, thôrnz (**ἀκάνθινος στέφανος**, *akánthinos stéphanos*): Three of the four evangelists mention the crown of thorns, wherewith the rude Rom soldiers derided the captive Christ (Mt **27** 29; Mk **15** 17; Jn **19** 2). All speak of the akanthine (Acanthus) crown, but there is no certainty about the peculiar plant, from the branches of which this crown of cruel mockery was plaited. The rabbinical books mention no less than twenty-two words in the Bible signifying thorny plants, and the word *ákantha* in the NT Gr is a generic and not a specific term. And this word or its adj. is used in the three Gospels, quoted above. It is therefore impossible definitely to determine what was the exact plant or tree, whose thorny branches were selected for this purpose. Tobler (*Denkbl.*, 113, 179) inclines to the *Spina Christi*, as did Hasselquist. Its botanical name is *Zizyphus Spina Christi*. It is very common in the East. Its spines are small and sharp, its branches soft, round and pliable, and the leaves look like ivy, with a dark, shiny green color, making them therefore very adaptable to the purpose of the soldiers. Others have designated the *Paliurus aculeatus* or the *Lycium horridum*. Both Geikie (*Life of Christ*, 549) and Farrar (*Life of Christ*, note 625) point to the Nubk (*Zizyphus lotus*). Says the latter, "The Nubk struck me, as it has all travelers in Pal, as being most suitable both for mockery and pain, since its leaves are bright and its thorns singularly strong. But though the Nubk is very common on the shores of Galilee, I saw none of it near Jerus." The settlement of the question is manifestly impossible.

HENRY E. DOSKER

CRUCIFIXION, kroo-si-fik'shun. See CROSS; PUNISHMENTS.

CRUEL, kroo'el, **CRUELTY**, kroo'el-ti (אַכְזָר, *'akhzār*, "harsh," "fierce," חָמָס, *ḥāmāṣ*, "violence"): There are various uses of the word "cruel" in the OT: (*a*) "the cruel [deadly] venom of asps" (Dt **32** 33); (*b*) spoken of men of relentless hate: "They hate me with cruel hatred" (Ps **25** 19; cf Prov **5** 9; **11** 17; **12** 10; Jer **6** 23; **50** 42); (*c*) Job speaks of God's dealings with him as "cruel" and arbitrary: "Thou art turned to be cruel to me" (Job **30** 21); conscious of his virtue, yet holding God to be the author of his sufferings, Job is driven to the conclusion that God has become his enemy and is bent upon destroying him; (*d*) the "day of Jeh"—a prophetic phrase to denote the time of God's manifestation in judgment—is described as coming, "cruel, with wrath and fierce anger" (Isa **13** 9). The word "cruelty" has nearly disappeared from the Bible. In RV it occurs only in Ps **27** 12. AV has it in Gen **49** 5; Ps **74** 20 (RV "violence"); Ezk **34** 4 (פֶּרֶךְ, *perekh*, "crushing," RV "rigor").

The OT records many acts on the part of chosen individuals and the elect nation which are marked by gross cruelty, particularly when measured by the standards of our own age. Some of these acts are sanctioned by Scripture or even presented as commanded by God, as, for example, the sacrifice of Isaac, the extermination of the Canaanites, the authorization of the avenger of blood and of human slavery, and of retaliation for evil. Some of the deeds performed by Divinely appointed leaders of Israel are characterized by inhumanity. Samuel "hewed Agag in pieces" (1 S **15** 33). David massacred the Ammonites with great barbarity (2 S **12** 31). Elijah slew the prophets of Baal (1 K **18** 40; cf 2 K **1** 10; **10** 25). Some of the utterances of the Psalmists breathe the spirit of hate and revenge, as in the so-called imprecatory psalms (Ps **137** 8.9; **139** 21 f). This has often been a matter of great perplexity to the devout student of the Bible. He has found it difficult to reconcile such practices, which bear the stamp of Divine approval, with the highest standards of Christian morality. It is sometimes urged in justification that these deeds are permitted, but not commanded by God. But this answer hardly meets the facts of the case. We shall arrive at a truer answer if we recognize the fact, which Jesus emphasizes, that the OT religion is a self-accommodation to the low moral standard of those whom it was designed to instruct. This He reiterates in the Sermon on the Mount (Mt **5** 22.28.34), and affirms in His reference to the hardness of the ancestral Jewish heart (Mt **19** 8). In the OT we are dealing with the childhood of the world, in which revelation is compelled to limit itself to the comprehension of its subjects. It must speak so that they can understand. It must start with them where it finds them. It must lead them along lines in which they of their own volition can walk, that character may grow step by step. A gradual development of spiritual and ethical ideals may clearly be traced in the sacred records. We must therefore read the OT narratives and interpret their teaching, not according to the standards of our own age, but in the light of the age to which these narratives belong. The spirit of Elijah may not be the spirit of Christ (Lk **9** 55). While many of the acts of cruelty and barbarity recorded in the OT are indicative of an age of a low type of morality, yet we must at the same time recognize the fact, that Israel's religion by emphasizing holy living and righteous conduct created an atmosphere favorable for the growth of high ethical ideals. Wherever this religion is seen at its best, as in the teachings of the prophets, it is the mark of the righteous man to treat human life as sacred and to refrain scrupulously from inflicting unnecessary pain. Even the Gentiles shall be brought to judgment for their barbarities and inhuman practices (Am **1** 2 f; 2 K **25** 7). Among the blessings of the Messianic kingdom, predicted by the prophets, is the cessation of war with all of its attendant cruelties and horrors. The Law of Israel also reflected this tendency toward humanity, and many of its ordinances, while seemingly inhuman, really tended to mitigate prevailing barbarity. Instances of such ordinances are those referring to the maltreatment of slaves (Ex **21** 20), to the Cities of Refuge (Nu **35** 19 ff; cf Josh **20**), to rules of warfare (Dt **20** 10 f), etc. The extermination of the Canaanites is represented as a Divine judgment upon a morally corrupt civilization (Gen **15** 16; Dt **12** 30). It is declared necessary in order to guard the Hebrews from contamination by the sins of the Canaanites (Ex **23** 32). It is not so far back, that many of the practices that are condemned by the most enlightened Christianity of our day, prevailed universally and were not thought incompatible with Christian civilization. Even our own time needs to secure a more widespread practical recognition of the principles of humanity, kindness and justice, which are professedly the law of the Christian life. L. KAISER

CRUMB, krum (ψιχίον, *psichíon*, "a little bit"): Occurs only in the NT, of remnants of food, scraps. Lazarus desired "to be fed with the crumbs that fell from the rich man's table" (Lk **16** 21). "Even the [little] dogs eat of the crumbs" (Mt **15** 27; Mk **7** 28), "possibly the fragments of bread on which the guests wiped their hands (after thrusting them into the common dish), and flung to the dogs" (Farrar, *Life of Christ*, I, 476).

CRUSE, krōōs: A small earthen vessel or flask, usually for holding liquids: צַפַּחַת, *çappaḥath;* as water, 1 S **26** 11.12.16; 1 K **19** 6; it being porous, the liquid is kept cool; also for holding oil, as in 1 K **17** 12.14.16.

In 1 K **14** 3 ("a cruse of honey") the word בַּקְבֻּק, *baḳbūḳ*, would be better rendered "bottle," doubtless deriving its name from the gurgling sound of issuing liquids. In 2 K **2** 20 צְלֹחִית, *ç^elōḥīth*, is not a jar or flask, but a dish, or platter, for salt or other substances.

In the NT a small jar or vial, ἀλάβαστρον, *alábastron*, "alabaster cruse" or flask, for holding ointment; not "box" as in AV (Mt **26** 7; Mk **14** 3; Lk **7** 37; cf 1 S **10** 1; 2 K **9** 1.3, where "box" in AV is used for "vial" RV). EDWARD BAGBY POLLARD

CRY, CRYING, krī'ing (זָעַק, *zā'aḳ*, צָעַק, *çā'aḳ* [and forms], קָרָא, *ḳārā'*, שָׁוַע, *shāwa'*, רִנָּה, *rinnāh;* βοάω, *boáō*, κράζω, *krázō*, φωνέω, *phōnéō*):

Various words are tr^d "cry," "crying," etc, the chief of which are those above given; *zā'aḳ* and *çā'aḳ* denote esp. a cry for help, from pain or distress, and are frequently used for crying to God, e.g. (*zā'aḳ*, Ex **2** 23; Jgs **3** 9.15; Ps **22** 5; **107** 13. 19; Mic **3** 4); (*çā'aḳ*, Ex **8** 12; **15** 25; Ps **34** 17; **77** 1; Isa **19** 20; Lam **2** 18); *ḳārā'* (a mimetic word) has the widest signification, but is often used of appealing to God (frequently tr^d "call," "called," etc, Gen **39** 14.15.18; **41** 43; Dt **15** 9; **24** 15; 1 K **18** 27; Ps **3** 4; **22** 2; **27** 7; Prov **1** 21; Isa **34** 14; Jer **2** 2, etc); *shāwa'*, "to cry aloud" (Job **29** 12; **30** 20.28; Ps **18** 6.41; **88** 13; Jon **2** 2; Hab **1** 2, etc); *rinnāh*, "a shouting," whether for joy or grief (1 K **8** 28; Ps **17** 1; **61** 1; **88** 2; **119** 169; **142** 6; Isa **43** 14 RV "rejoicing," etc). Other Heb words are *'ānaḳ*, "to groan" (Ezk **9** 4; **24** 17 AV; **26** 15 AV); *hāmāh*, "to make a noise" (Ps **55** 17 AV); *rūa'*, "to shout" (Jgs **7** 21 AV; Job **30** 5; Isa **42** 13, etc); *rānan*, "to cry aloud" (Ps **84** 2; Lam **2** 19); *shōa'*, "crying" (Isa **22** 5); *t^eshu'ōth*, "crying," "noise" (Job **39** 7 AV).

In the NT we have *boaō*, "to cry," "shout" (Mt **3** 3; Mk **1** 3; **15** 34; Gal **4** 27, etc); *krazō* (mimetic, the hoarse cry of the raven), "to cry out" (Mt **9** 27; **14** 30; **21** 9; **27** 50; Mk **5** 5; Gal **4** 6; Rev **6** 10; **7** 2, etc); *phōneō*, "to give forth the voice," "sound" (Lk **8** 8; **16** 24; **23** 46; Acts **16** 28; Rev **14** 18 AV); *anaboáō*, "to cry out" (Mt **27** 46; Lk **9** 38); *aphíēmi*, "to let go," "to send away" (Mk **15** 37 AV); *epiboáō*, "to cry about" (anything) (Acts **25** 24); *epiphōnéō*, "to give forth the voice upon" (Lk **23** 21 AV); *kraugázō*, "to make a cry, or outcry, or clamor" (Mt **12** 19; **15** 22; Jn **11** 43; **18** 40; **19** 6.15; Acts **22** 23); *anakrázō*, "to cry out" (Mk **1** 23; Lk **4** 33, etc); *kraugḗ*, "a crying out" (Mt **25** 6; Acts **23** 9 AV; He **5** 7; Rev **21** 4).

For "cry" RV has "sound" (2 Ch **13** 12); "cry because of these things" (Job **30** 24 ERV); "cry out" (Job **31** 38; Isa **42** 14); "call" (Ps **28** 1; **61** 2; **141** 1); "be blind" (Isa **29** 9); "groan" (Ezk **26** 15); "pant" (Joel **1** 20); "cry aloud" (Mt **12** 19); "clamor" (Acts **23** 9). Among the other changes are, "moan" for "cry aloud" (Ps **55** 17); "sound an alarm" (Hos **5** 8); "take your pleasure," m "blind yourselves," for "cry ye out" (Isa **29** 9); "sigh, but not aloud" for "forbear to cry" (Ezk **24** 17); "shoutings" for "crying" (Job **39** 7); "destruction" for "crying" (Prov **19** 18, where we have instead of "let not thy soul spare for his crying," "set not thy heart on his destruction," m, Heb "causing him to die" [*mūth*, "to put to death"]); "went up" for "crying aloud" (Mk **15** 8, different text); "cry" for "voice" (Lk **1** 42); for "had cried" (Lk **23** 46), ARV has "crying."

W. L. WALKER

CRYSTAL, kris'tal: In EV the word is probably intended to signify rock-crystal, crystallized quartz. This the Greeks called κρύσταλλος, *krústallos*, "ice," believing it to have been formed from water by intense cold. Thus in Rev **4** 6; **21** 11; **22** 1, either "crystal" (EV) or "ice" (Gr *krustallos*) suits the context. The word rendered "crystal" in Ezk **1** 22 (קֶרַח, *ḳeraḥ*) is ambiguous in precisely the same way (RVm "ice"). In Job **28** 17 the context favors AV "crystal," rather than RV "glass" (זְכוּכִית, *z^ekhūkhīth*). Finally, in Job **28** 18 RV reads "crystal" for AV "pearls" (Heb *gābhīsh;* the weight of evidence favors RV in spite of the parallelism suggested by AV). See also STONES, PRECIOUS. F. K. FARR

CUB, kub (כּוּב, *kūbh;* AV **Chub**): The word occurs only in Ezk **30** 5. There it is almost certainly a corruption, and we should read, as in LXX, "Lub," i.e. Libya. Libya, in the earlier part of the same ver (AV), is a mistr of "Put," thus correctly rendered in RV.

CUBIT, kū'bit (אַמָּה, *ammāh;* πῆχυς, *pēchus*): The standard for measures of length among the Hebrews. They derived it from the Babylonians, but a similar measure was used in Egypt with which they must have been familiar. The length of the cubit is variously estimated, since there seems to have been a double standard in both countries, and because we have no undisputed example of the cubit remaining to the present time. The original cubit was the length of the forearm, from the elbow to the end of the middle finger, as is implied from the derivation of the word in Heb and in Lat (*cubitum*). It seems to be referred to also in Dt **3** 11: "after the cubit of a man." But this was too indefinite for a scientific standard, and the Babylonians early adopted a more accurate method of measurement which passed to the nations of the West. They had a double standard, the so-called royal cubit and the ordinary one. From the remains of buildings in Assyria and Babylonia, the former is made out to be about 20.6 in., and a cubit of similar length was used in Egypt and must have been known to the Hebrews. This was probably the cubit mentioned by Ezk **40** 5 and perhaps that of Solomon's temple, "cubits after the first measure" (2 Ch **3** 3), i.e. the ancient cubit. The ordinary cubit of commerce was shorter, and has been variously estimated at between 16 and 18 or more inches, but the evidence of the Siloam inscription and of the tombs in Pal seems to indicate 17.6 in. as the average length. See WEIGHTS AND MEASURES. This was the cubit of six palms, while the longer one was of seven (Ezk **40** 5). The cubit mentioned in Jgs **3** 16 is from a different word in Heb (גֹּמֶד, *gōmedh*) and was probably shorter, for Ehud girded it on his thigh under his clothing.

The NT references are Mt **6** 27; Lk **12** 25, "Which of you . . . . can add a c. unto the measure of his life?"; Jn **21** 8, "about two hundred cubits off"; Rev **21** 17, "the wall thereof, a hundred and forty and four cubits." H. PORTER

CUCKOW, kŏŏk'ōō, kuk'ōō (שַׁחַף, *shāḥaph;* λάρος, *láros;* Lat *Cuculus canorus*): The Heb root from which the word *shāḥaph* is derived means "to be lean" and "slender," and in older VSS of the Bible was tr[d] cuckow (cuckoo). It was mentioned twice in the Bible (Lev **11** 16, and practically the same in Dt **14** 15 AV "cuckoo"), in the list of unclean birds. The Lat term by which we designate the bird is very similar to the Arab., and all names for it in different countries are so nearly the same that they prove themselves based on its double cry, "cuck-oo," or the single note "kowk" or "gouk." The bird is as old as history, and interesting because the European species placed its eggs in the nests of other birds, which gave rise to much fiction concerning its habits. The European bird is a brownish gray with white bars underneath, and larger than ours, which are a beautiful olive gray, with tail feathers of irregular length touched with white, knee tufts, black or yellow bill, according to species, and beautiful sleek head and shining eyes. Our birds build their own nests, attend their young with care and are much loved for their beauty. Their food is not repulsive in any species; there never was any reason why they should have been classed among the abominations, and for these reasons scientists in search of a "lean, slender" bird of offensive diet and habit have selected the "sea-mew" (q.v.) which is substituted for cuckoo in the RV with good natural-history reason to sustain the change. GENE STRATTON-PORTER

CUCUMBER, kū'kum-bẽr (קִשֻּׁאִים, *ḳishshu'īm;* σίκυος, *síkuos*): One of the articles of food for which Israel in the wilderness looked back with longing to Egypt (Nu **11** 5). Cucumbers are great favorites with all the people of Pal. Two varieties occur, *Cucumis sativus* (Arab. *Khyār*), originally a product of N.W. India, which is smooth-skinned, whitish and of delicate flavor, and requires much water in its cultivation, and *Cucumis chate* (Arab. *faqqūs*), which is long and slender but less juicy than the former. Probably the Bib. reference is to this latter as it is a plant much grown in Egypt where it is said to attain unusual excellence.

A "garden of cucumbers," or more literally a "place of cucumbers" (*miḳshāh*), is mentioned in Isa **1** 8; Bar **6** 70. "A lodge in a garden of cucumbers" (Isa **1** 8) is the rough wooden booth erected by the owner from which he keeps guard over his ripening vegetables. It is commonly raised upon poles and, when abandoned for the season, it falls into decay and presents a dreary spectacle of tottering poles and dead leaves. E. W. G. MASTERMAN

CUD. See CHEW.

CULTURE, kul'ţūr: Found only in 2 Esd **8** 6 AV and RV, "give . . . . culture to our understanding," i.e. to nourish it as seed in the ground.

CUMBER, kum'bẽr, **CUMBERED** (καταργέω, *katargéō*, "to make idle," περισπάομαι, *perispáomai*, "to be drawn about," in mind "to be distracted"): Spoken of the barren fig tree in the parable: "Cut it down; why doth it also cumber [block up, make unproductive] the ground?" (Lk **13** 7). Cumbered means to be over-occupied with cares or business, distracted: "But Martha was cumbered about much serving" (Lk **10** 40). The word cumbrance occurs only in Dt **1** 12: "How can I myself alone bear your cumbrance?" (טֹרַח, *ṭōraḥ*, "an encumbrance," "a burden"). Cf Isa **1** 14, where RVm has "cumbrance," RV "trouble."

CUMI, kōō'mē, kū'mī. See TALITHA.

CUMMIN, kum'in (כַּמֹּן, *kammōn;* κύμινον, *kúminon*): The seed of the herb *Cuminum cyminum* (N.O. *Umbelliferae*). It has carminative properties and is used for flavoring various dishes, esp. during fasts. In flavor and appearance it resembles caraway, though it is less agreeable to western palates. As an illustration of Jeh's wisdom it is said (Isa **28** 25.27) that cummin is scattered in sowing and beaten out with a rod in threshing. These facts are true in Pal today. The Jews paid tithes of cummin (Mt **23** 23) (see cut on following page).

CUN, kun (כּוּן, *kūn;* A, ἐκ τῶν ἐκλεκτῶν πόλεων, *ek tōn eklektōn póleōn*, "from the chosen cities"): One of the cities of Hadarezer, king of Syria, spoiled by David (1 Ch **18** 8, AV "Chun"). In the ‖ passage (2 S **8** 8) its place is taken by BEROTHAI, which see.

CUNNING, kun'ing (חָכָם, *ḥākhām*, חָשַׁב, *ḥāshabh*): In Bible-English "cunning" means always "wise" or "skilful"; the word does not occur in the bad sense, and it is found in the OT only. The chief Heb words are *ḥākhām*, "wise," "skilful" (2 Ch **2** 7 AV "a man cunning to work in gold"; ver 13; Isa **3** 3 AV, etc); *ḥāshabh*, "to think," "devise," "desire" (Ex **26** 1.31; **28** 6.15 AV, etc). We have also *da'ath*, "knowledge" (1 K **7** 14 AV); *bīn*, "to be intelligent" (1 Ch **25** 7 AV); *maḥăshebheth*, "thought," "device," "design" (Ex **31** 4; **35** 33.35 AV); *'āmān*, "artificer" (Cant **7** 1 AV); *yādha'*, "to know," once trd "cunning" (Dnl **1** 4 AV).

For "cunning" ARV gives "skilful" (Ex **31** 4, etc; Isa **3** 3 "expert"); for "cunning work" the work of the "skilful workman" (Ex **26** 1.31, etc, ERV "cunning workman"); for "curious," "skilfully woven," ERV "cunningly woven" (Ex **28** 8, etc).

W. L. Walker

Cummin.

CUP (most frequently, כּוֹס, *kōṣ;* four other words in one passage each; ποτήριον, *potḗrion*): A vessel for drinking from, of a variety of material (gold, silver, earthenware), patterns (Est **1** 7) and elaboration.

Figurative: By ordinary fig. of speech, put sometimes for the contents of the cup, viz. for that which is drunk (Mt **26** 39). In both OT and NT applied **fig.** to that which is portioned out, and of which one is to partake; most frequently used of what is sorrowful, as God's judgments, His wrath, afflictions, etc (Ps **11** 6; **75** 8; Isa **51** 17; Rev **14** 10). In a similar sense, used by Christ concerning the sufferings endured by Him (Mt **26** 39), and the calamities attending the confession of His name (Mt **20** 23). In the OT applied also to the blessedness and joy of the children of God, and the full provision made for their wants (Ps **16** 5; **23** 5; **116** 13; cf Jer **16** 7; Prov **31** 6). All these passages refer not only to the experience of an allotted joy and sorrow, but to the fact that all others share in this experience. Within a community of those having the same interests or lot, each received his apportioned measure, just as at a feast, each cup is filled for the individual to drain at the same time that his fellow-guests are occupied in the same way.

The Holy Supper is called "the cup of the Lord" (1 Cor **10** 21), since it is the Lord who makes the feast, and tenders the cup, just as "the cup of demons" with which it is contrasted, refers to what they offer and communicate. In 1 Cor **11** 25, the cup is called "the new covenant in my blood," i.e. it is a pledge and seal and means of imparting the blessings of the new covenant (He **10** 16 f)—a covenant established by the shedding of the blood of Christ. The use of the word "cup" for the sacrament shows how prominent was the part which the cup had in the Lord's Supper in apostolic times. Not only were all commanded to drink of the wine (Mt **26** 27), but the very irregularities in the Corinthian church point to its universal use (1 Cor **11** 27). Nor does the Rom church attempt to justify its withholding the cup from the laity (the communion in one form) upon conformity with apostolic practice, or upon direct Scriptural authority. This variation from the original institution is an outgrowth of the doctrines of transubstantiation and sacramental concomitance, of the attempt to transform the sacrament of the Eucharist into the sacrifice of the Mass, and of the wide separation between clergy and laity resulting from raising the ministry to the rank of a sacerdotal order. The practice was condemned by Popes Leo I (d. 461) and Gelasius (d. 496); but gained a firm hold in the 12th cent., and was enacted into a church regulation by the Council of Constance in 1415. See also Blessing, Cup of.

As to the use of cups for divination (Gen **44** 5), the reference is to superstitious practice derived from the Gentiles. For various modes of divining what is unknown by the pouring of water into bowls, and making observations accordingly, see Geikie, *Hours with the Bible*, I, 492 f, and art. Divination.

H. E. Jacobs

CUPBEARER, kup'bâr-ẽr (מַשְׁקֶה, *mashḳeh*, "one giving drink"; οἰνοχόος, *oinochóos*): An officer of high rank at ancient oriental courts, whose duty it was to serve the wine at the king's table. On account of the constant fear of plots and intrigues, a person must be regarded as thoroughly trustworthy to hold this position. He must guard against poison in the king's cup, and was sometimes required to swallow some of the wine before serving it. His confidential relations with the king often endeared him to his sovereign and also gave him a position of great influence. This officer is first mentioned in Scripture in Gen **40** 1 ff, where the Heb word elsewhere trd "cupbearer" is rendered "butler." The phrase "chief of the butlers" (ver 2) accords with the fact that there were often a number of such officials under one as chief (cf Xen. *Hellen.* vii.1, 38). Nehemiah (cf **1** 11) was cupbearer to Artaxerxes Longimanus, and was held in high esteem by him, as the record shows. His financial ability (Neh **5** 8.10.14.17) would indicate that the office was a lucrative one. Cupbearers are mentioned further in 1 K **10** 5; 2 Ch **9** 4, where they, among other evidences of royal splendor, are stated to have impressed the queen of Sheba with Solomon's glory. The title Rabshakeh (Isa **36** 2), once thought to mean "chief of the cupbearers," is now given a different derivation and explained as "chief of the officers," or "princes" (*BDB* s.v.). See further on cupbearers Herod. iii.34; Xen. *Cyrop.* i.3, 8, 9; Jos, *Ant*, XVI, viii, 1; Tob **1** 22.

Benjamin Reno Downer

CUPBOARD, kub'ẽrd (κυλίκιον, *kulíkion*, 1 Macc **15** 32): A kind of sideboard in or on which Simon's gold and silver vessels were displayed, and which, among other evidences of his glory, amazed the Syrian envoy Athenobius. Cf the Rom *abacus*, said to have been introduced into Rome from Asia.

CURDLE, kûr'd'l (קָפָא, *ḳāphā'*, "to congeal," "harden," "curdle"): Occurs in Job **10** 10, "Hast thou not . . . . curdled me like cheese?" i.e. made him take solid form. "The formation of the embryo is a mystery on which the Heb dwells with a deep and reverential awe: cf Ps **139** 13–16." These similes are often met with in the Koran and oriental poetry. See *Speaker's Comm.* in loc.

CURE, kūr, **CURES:** Represents the words גָּהָה, *gāhāh*, מַרְפֵּא, *marpē'*, רָפָה, *rāphāh;* θεραπεύω, *therapeúō*, ἴασις, *íasis*. *Gāhāh* in Prov **17** 22 trd "medicine" means properly the removal of a bandage from a healed wound, and is used **figuratively** in Hos **5** 13; *marpē'*, "healing," is used in the sense of deliverance of the city in Jer **33** 6; with a negative particle in 2 Ch **21** 18 it is used to describe the bowel disease of Jehoram as incurable. The Gr words are used of physical cures (*iasis* in Lk **13** 32) as contradistinguished from the casting out of demons as Mt **17** 16; Lk **7** 21; Jn **5** 10. Cure is only used in the NT in the sense of physical healing; in the OT usually in the sense of spiritual or national deliverance from danger.

ALEX. MACALISTER

CURIOUS, kū'ri-us (מַחֲשֶׁבֶת, *maḥăshebheth;* περίεργος, *periergos*): The above Heb word, meaning "thought," "device," "design," is tr[d] "curious," Ex **35** 32 AV "curious works"; ERV "cunning"; ARV "skilful"; *ḥēshebh* ("device," "devised work"), tr[d] AV "curious girdle," is tr[d] by ERV "cunningly woven band," ARV "skilfully" (Ex **28** 8.27.28; **29** 5; **39** 5.20.21; Lev **8** 7). In Ps **139** 15 *rāḳam*, "embroidered," "variegated" is used **fig.** of a child in the womb, tr[d] "curiously wrought"; "the body or the foetus is described as woven together of so many different-colored threads, like a cunning and beautiful network or tapestry" (Perowne in loc.). See also CURDLE. *Periergos*, "working round about," is used of the "curious arts" of some in Ephesus who brought their books to be burned (Acts **19** 19 ARV "magical"). See ASTROLOGY 14.

W. L. WALKER

CURRENT MONEY. See MONEY, CURRENT.

CURSE, kûrs (אָלָה, *'ālāh* [Nu **5** 21.23.27, etc], מְאֵרָה, *m[e]'ērāh* [Prov **3** 33; Mal **2** 2, etc], קְלָלָה, *k[e]lālāh* [Gen **27** 12.13]; κατάρα, *katára* [Gal **3** 10. 13]): This word as noun and vb. renders different Heb words, some of them being more or less synonymous, differing only in degree of strength. It is often used in contrast with "bless" or "blessing" (Dt **11** 29). When a curse is pronounced against any person, we are not to understand this as a mere wish, however violent, that disaster should overtake the person in question, any more than we are to understand that a corresponding "blessing" conveys simply a wish that prosperity should be the lot of the person on whom the blessing is invoked. A curse was considered to possess an inherent power of carrying itself into effect. Prayer has been defined as a wish referred to God. Curses (or blessings) were imprecations referred to supernatural beings in whose existence and power to do good or inflict harm primitive man believed. The use of magic and spells of all kinds is based on the belief that it is possible to enlist the support of the superhuman beings with whom the universe abounds, and to persuade them to carry out the suppliant's wishes. It has been suggested that spells were written on pieces of parchment and cast to the winds in the belief that they would find their way to their proper destination—that some demoniac being would act as postman and deliver them at the proper address. In Zec (**5** 1–3) the "flying roll," with curses inscribed on it "goeth forth over the face of the whole land." It would find its way into the house of every thief and perjurer. But it was not always possible to commit curses to writing, it was enough to utter them aloud. Generally the name of some deity would be coupled with such imprecations, as Goliath cursed David by his gods (1 S **17** 43). Such curses once uttered possessed the power of self-realization. It was customary for heads of families in their declining years to bless their children, such a blessing being, not simply a paternal wish that their children should prosper in life, but a potent factor in determining their welfare (Gen **9** 25). In this case Jacob seeks his father's blessing, which was more than his father's good wishes for his future career. Such blessings and curses were independent of moral considerations. Before moral distinctions played any part in molding theological conceptions it was not necessary, before a spell could be effectual, that the individual against whom the spell was pronounced should be deserving, on moral grounds, of the fate which was invoked on him. It was sufficient that he should be the foe of the author of the curse. We may assume that such curses signalized the commencement of a battle. But in process of time such indiscriminate imprecations would not satisfy enlightened moral judgment. In the dramatic situation depicted in Dt (**11** 29; **27** 12 f) the curse was placed on Mt. Ebal and the blessing on Mt. Gerizim. But the curse was the penalty for disobedience, as the blessing was the reward for obedience. The Book of Prov (**26** 2) summarily dismisses the traditional belief—"the curse that is causeless alighteth not." "In the discourses of Jesus we find blessings and curses. They are however simply authoritative declarations of the eternal connection between right doing and happiness, wrong doing and misery" (Cheyne).

Whereas curses by ordinary persons were considered more or less efficacious—some god being always only too glad to speed them on their way to their destination—yet special persons—"holy" persons—in virtue of their special relation to Divine beings possessed special powers of pronouncing effectual curses on account of their powers of enlisting supernatural aid. Balaam, according to the narrative in Nu (**22** f), was an expert in the art. Balak was convinced that Balaam's curse would bring about the defeat of the Israelites (see Gray, "Numbers," *ICC*).

The term—and the thing signified—plays an important part in Paul's interpretation of the cross. In the light of the law all men are guilty. There is no acquittal through appeal to a law that commands and never forgives—prohibits and never relents. The violator of the law is under a curse. His doom has been pronounced. Escape is impossible. But on the cross Jesus Christ endured the curse—for "cursed is every one that hangeth on a tree" (Gal **3** 10.13)—and a curse that has overtaken its victim is a spent force. See PUNISHMENTS.

Jesus commands His disciples, "Bless them that curse you" (Lk **6** 28; cf Rom **12** 14). He Himself cursed the fruitless fig tree (Mk **11** 21)—a symbol of the doom of a fruitless people.

Curse as the rendering of חֵרֶם, *ḥērem*, implies a totally different idea (see ACCURSED). T. LEWIS

CURTAIN, kûr't'n, -ten, -tin: The word ordinarily used for curtain is יְרִיעָה, *y[e]rī'āh*. Thus in Ex **26** 1 ff; **36** 8 ff of the curtains of the tabernacle (see TABERNACLE); in 2 S **7** 2; Ps **104** 2; Cant **1** 5; Isa **54** 2; Jer **4** 20; **10** 20; **49** 29; Hab **3** 7.

Figurative: In Isa **40** 22 (like Ps **104** 2, of the heavens), the word used is דֹּק, *dōḳ*, lit. "gauze."

CUSH, kush (כּוּשׁ, *kūsh*):

1. The Ancestor of Many Nations

(1) The first of the sons of Ham, from whom sprang Seba, Havilah, Sabtah, Raamah and Sabtecah. He was also the father of Nimrod, who founded Babel (Babylon) and the other great states of Shinar or Babylonia (Gen **10** 6–8). The meaning of the name is uncertain.

(2) The name of the country around which the Gihon flowed (Gen **2** 13), rendered "Ethiopia" in the AV, but in view of the distance

of that country from the other rivers mentioned, this seems to be an unlikely identification. Fried.

2. A District of the Garden of Eden

Delitzsch has suggested (*Wo lag das Paradies?* 74 ff) that the watercourse in question is the canal *Gu-ḫandê* or *Araḫtu*, which, coming from the S., entered Babylon a little to the E. of the Euphrates, and, flowing alongside the Festival-Street, entered the Euphrates to the N. of Nebuchadrezzar's palace. Koldewey (*Tempel von Babylon und Borsippa*, 38) regards the *Gu-ḫandê* as the section of the Euphrates itself at this point. There is no indication, however, that the district which it inclosed was ever called *Kûšu* or Cush, and the suppression of the final syllable of *Gu-ḫandê* would remain unexplained. Moreover, the identification of Cush with a possible *Caš*, for *Kasdu*, "Chaldea," seems likewise improbable, esp. as that name could only have been applied, in early times, to the district bordering on the Persian Gulf (see CHALDEA). Another theory is, that the Cush of Gen **2** 13 is the *Kusu* of certain Assyr letters, where it seems to designate a district in the neighbor-

3. Probably not in Asia Minor

hood of Cappadocia. This identification apparently leads us back to an ancient tradition at one time current in the East, but later forgotten, which caused the Pyramus river to assume the name of *Jîhûn* (i.e. Gihon). This stream rises in the mountains N.E. of the Gulf of Alexandretta, and, taking a southwesterly course, flows into the Mediterranean near Karatash. Though nearer than the Ethiopian Cush, this is still too far W., and therefore unsatisfactory as an identification—all the streams or waterways of the Garden of Eden ought to flow through the same district.

(3) The well-known country of Cush or Ethiopia, from Syene (Ezk **29** 10) southward—Egyp *Kôš*, Bab *Kûšu*, Assyr *Kûsu*. This

4. The Ethiopian Cush

name sometimes denotes the land (Isa **11** 11; **18** 1; Zeph **3** 10; Ezk **29** 10; Job **28** 19; Est **1** 1; **8** 9); sometimes the people (Isa **20** 4; Jer **46** 9; Ezk **38** 5); but is in many passages uncertain. Notwithstanding that the descendants of Ham are always regarded as non-Semites, the Ethiopians, Ge'ez, as they called themselves, spoke a Sem language of special interest on account of its likeness to Himyaritic, and its illustration of certain forms in Assyro-Babylonian. These Cushites were in all probability migrants from another (more northerly) district, and akin to the Canaanites—like them, dark, but by no means black, and certainly not Negroes. W. Max Müller (*Asien und Europa*, 113 n.) states that it cannot be proved whether the Egyptians had quite black neighbors (on the S.). In earlier times they are represented as brown, and later as brown mingled with black, implying that negroes only came to their knowledge as a distinct and extensive race in comparatively late times. Moses' (first?) wife (Nu **12** 1) was certainly therefore not a Negress, but simply a Cushite woman, probably speaking a Sem language—prehistoric Ge'ez or Ethiopian (see CUSHITE WOMAN). In all probability Sem tribes were classed as Hamitic simply because they acknowledged the supremacy of the Hamitic Egyptians, just as the non-Sem Elamites were set down as Semites (Gen **10** 22) on account of their acknowledging Bab supremacy. It is doubtful whether the Hebrews, in ancient times, knew of the Negro race—they probably became acquainted with them long after the Egyptians.

In the opinion of W. Max Müller (*A. und E.*, 112), the Egyptians, when they became acquainted with the Negroes, having no word to express this race, classed them with the *neḥesē*, which thereafter included the Negroes. If the Heb name Phinehas (*Pī-neḥāṣ*) be really Egyp, and mean "the black," there is still no need to suppose that this meant "the Negro," for no Israelite

5. Negroes Probably not Included

would have borne a name with such a signification. The treasurer of Candace queen of Meroë (Acts **8** 27–39)—the Ethiopian eunuch—was an Abyssinian, not a Negro; and being an educated man, was able to read the Heb Scriptures in the Gr (Sept) version. Cush (*mât Kusi*, pr. *Kushi*) is frequently mentioned in the Assyr inscriptions in company with Meluḫḫa (*Meroḫḫa*) to indicate Ethiopia and Meroë. See EDEN; ETHIOPIA; TABLE OF NATIONS. T. G. PINCHES

CUSH, kush (כּוּשׁ, *kūsh;* LXX Χουσεί, *Chousei*, Ps **7** title): A Benjamite, perhaps he that "was without cause" the "adversary" of David (cf Ps **7** 4). See CUSHI.

CUSHAN, kū'shan: In the Ps of Habakkuk (Hab **3** 7) "the tents of C." are mentioned in an individualizing description of the effects of a theophany. Parallel is the phrase "the curtains of the land of Midian." LXX renders C., כּוּשָׁן, *kūshān*, by Αἰθιόπων, *Aithiópōn*, reading perhaps כּוּשִׁים, *kūshīm*, or כּוּשִׁין, *kūshīn* (כּוּשִׁן, *kūshin*). The context indicates that the same land or people is intended as the OT elsewhere calls Cush, yet vaguely and not in any strict geographical usage that would limit it to Africa.

CUSHAN-RISHATHAIM, kū'shan-rish-a-thā'im (כּוּשַׁן רִשְׁעָתַיִם, *kūshan rish'āthayim*, tr[d], or rather interpreted, as "man from Cush, he of the twofold crime"; LXX Χουσαρσαθάιμ, *Chousarsatháim*, AV **Chushan-rishathaim**): Mentioned in Jgs **3** 8–10 as a king of Mesopotamia who was chosen by God as his tool to chastise the Israelites for their idolatry. After Joshua's death the children of Israel soon began to affiliate themselves with the heathen peoples among whom they dwelt. This was the fertile source of all their troubles. God delivered ("sold") them into the hands of the heathen. C.-r. is the first whose name is given in this connection. Barring this short passage in Jgs nothing is known of the man. Eight years the Israelites were under his dominion, when the Lord raised up a deliverer to them, Othniel, the son of Kenaz, Caleb's younger brother—the first of the judges. See KIRIATH-SEPHER. WILLIAM BAUR

CUSHI, kū'shī: This name represents כּוּשִׁי, *kūshī*, in the original (LXX Χουσεί, *Chousei*, Χουσί, *Chousi*), either with or without the art. With the art. (so in 2 S **18** 21-32 seven out of eight times, all readings supported by LXX) it simply indicates that the person so designated was of the Cushite people, as in Jer **38** 7 ff. Its use without the art. has doubtless developed out of the foregoing according to a familiar process. For the Cush of Ps **7**, title read "Cushi" with LXX.

(1) The messenger (RV "the Cushite") sent by Joab to acquaint David with the victory over Absalom. That this man was in fact a foreigner is indicated by his ignorance of a shorter path which Ahimaaz took, by his being unrecognized by the watchman who recognizes Ahimaaz, and by his ignorance, as compared with Ahimaaz, of the sentiments of David, whom he knows only as a king and not as a man. 2 S **18** 21 (twice, the second time without the art.), 22.23.31 (twice), 32 (twice).

(2) The great-grandfather of Jehudi, a contemporary of Jeremiah (Jer **36** 14). The name Jehudi itself ("a man of Judah") is sufficient refutation of the opinion that the use of C. as or in lieu of a proper

name "seems to show that there were but few Cushites among the Israelites."

(3) The father of Zephaniah the prophet (Zeph **1** 1). J. Oscar Boyd

CUSHION, ko͝osh'un (**προσκεφάλαιον,** *proskephálaion*): In NT, only in Mk **4** 38 RV. The word means lit. a cushion for the head (AV "pillow") but was also used of one for sitting or reclining upon, e.g. of a rower's cushion. The art. used with it in this passage suggests that it was one of the customary furnishings of the boat, and it was probably similar to the cushion placed for the comfort of passengers in the stern of modern boats on the Sea of Galilee. "Silken cushions" of Am **3** 12 RV is a rendering of the Heb *d*ᵉ*meshek̦* from its supposed connection with *damask*. These cushions formed the divan, often the only article of furniture in an oriental reception room. "Cushions" occurs further in the somewhat doubtful RVm rendering of Prov **7** 16; **31** 22. Benjamin Reno Downer

CUSHITE, kush'īt: Whereas כּוּשִׁי, *kūshī*, is elsewhere rendered Ethiopian, in 2 S **18** 21–32 it is rendered Cushite in the RV (see Cushi and cf Cushite Woman). Its pl., which occurs in Zeph, Dnl and 2 Ch, also in the form כֻּשִׁיִּים, *kushīyīm*, in Am, is uniformly trd Ethiopians, following LXX. The other OT books use simply כּוּשׁ, *kūsh*, for people as well as land.

CUSHITE, kush'īt **(ETHIOPIAN) WOMAN:** In Nu **12** 1 Moses is condemned by his sister Miriam and his brother Aaron "because of the Cushite woman [הָאִשָּׁה הַכֻּשִׁית, *hā-'ishshāh ha-kushīth*] whom he had married"; and the narrator immediately adds by way of needed explanation, "for he had married a Cushite woman" (אִשָּׁה כֻשִׁית, *'ishshāh khushīth*). Views regarding this person have been of two general classes: (1) She is to be identified with Zipporah (Ex **2** 21 and elsewhere), Moses' Midianitish wife, who is here called "the Cushite," either in scorn of her dark complexion (cf Jer **13** 23) and foreign origin (so most older exegetes), or as a consequence of an erroneous notion of the late age when this apocryphal addition, "because of the Cushite," etc, was inserted in the narrative (so Wellhausen). (2) She is a woman whom Moses took to wife after the death of Zipporah, really a Cushite (Ethiopian) by race, whether the princess of Meroë of whom Jos (*Ant*, II, x, 2) romances (so *Targum of Jonathan*), or one of the "mixed multitude" (Ex **12** 38; cf Nu **11** 4) that accompanied the Hebrews on their wanderings (so Ewald and most). Dillmann suggests a compromise between the two classes of views, viz. that this woman is a mere "variation in the saga" from the wife elsewhere represented as Midianitish, yet because of this variation she was understood by the author as distinct from Zipporah. The implication of the passage, in any case, is clearly that this connection of Moses tended to injure his prestige in the eyes of race-proud Hebrews, and, equally, that in the author's opinion such a view of the matter was obnoxious to God. J. Oscar Boyd

CUSTODY, kus'tō-di (יָד, *yādh*, פְּקֻדָּה, *p*ᵉ*k̦uddāh*): In Est **2** 3.8 *bis*.14, *yādh*, "the hand," is trd "custody"; *p*ᵉ*k̦uddāh*, "numbering," "charge"; occurs in Nu **3** 36 RV "the appointed charge," m, Heb, "the office of the charge."

CUSTOM, kus'tum (tax): (*a*) הֲלָךְ, *hălākh*, Ezr **4** 13.20; **7** 24 AV; (*b*) בְּלוֹ, *b*ᵉ*lō*, Ezr **4** 13, etc; (*c*) *τελώνιον*, *telōnion*, Mt **9** 9; Mk **2** 14; Lk **5** 27, "receipt of custom" AV, RV "place of toll," the collectors' office; (*d*) *τέλος*, *télos*, Mt **17** 25 (RV "toll"); Rom **13** 7; 1 Macc **11** 35 (RV "tolls"; cf 1 Macc **10** 31). The tax designated by *hălākh* in Ezr **4** 13, etc, is usually taken to mean a road tax, a toll, from root *hălākh*, but cf *AOF*, II, 463, which derives from root *ilku*, a command, a decree, hence an imposed tax. *B*ᵉ*lō* from root *yābhal* is supposed to be a tax on merchandise or produce (as distinguished from "tribute," or the tax on houses, lands and persons), usually paid in kind and levied for the support of the native or provincial government. See Ryle, *Cambridge Bible*, Ezr-Neh, loc. cit. *Telos* in NT and Macc is an indirect tax farmed out to the publicans.

Walter R. Betteridge

CUSTOM, kus'tum (usage): In the OT, except Gen **31** 35 where RV renders, better, "manner" (דֶּרֶךְ, *derekh*, "way"), the words trd "custom" are *ḥōk̦*, *ḥuk̦k̦āh*, "statute," and *mishpāṭ*, "judgment." Such passages as Jgs **11** 39; Jer **32** 11, and esp. Ezr **3** 4 (AV "custom," RV "ordinance"), illustrate the difficulty of deciding upon the proper tr in cases where "custom" might become "statute," "usage" establish itself as "law." In Lev **18** 30; Jer **10** 3 the reference is to heathen religious practices.

In the NT Lk **1** 9; **2** 42; Acts **6** 14; **15** 1 (AV "manner"); **16** 21; **21** 21; **26** 3; **28** 17 (*ἔθος*, *éthos*), and Lk **2** 27 from the same Gr root, refer likewise to definitely established *religious* practices; in every case except Acts **16** 21, those of the Jewish law. The RV makes the tr of *ethos* uniform, reading "custom" in Lk **22** 39 (AV "wont") and in Jn **19** 40; Acts **25** 16; He **10** 25 (AV "manner"). Gr *εἰωθός*, *eiōthós*, from the same root, is rendered "custom" in Lk **4** 16 by EV, and by RV also in Acts **17** 2, its only other occurrence in the NT. In Jn **18** 39; 1 Cor **11** 16 "custom" is the tr of Gr *sunḗtheia*, in the sense of "usage" rather than of "law." F. K. Farr

CUT, CUTTING (כָּרַת, *kārath*, גָּדַע, *gādha'*, כָּחַד, *kāḥadh*, נָתַח, *nāthaḥ*; **ἀποκόπτω,** *apokóptō*, **ἐκκόπτω,** *ekkóptō*): Many Heb words are trd "cut." Of these *kārath*, "to cut down, out, off," is the most frequent. As "cut off" it is used in the sense of laying or destroying (Gen **9** 11; Dt **12** 29; 1 K **11** 16; Ps **101** 8, etc), also for cutting off transgressors from the community of Jeh, which meant probably separation, or exclusion, rather than death or destruction (Gen **17** 14; Ex **12** 15. 19). Other words are *dāmam*, "to be silent," "cease" (Jer **25** 37 AV; **48** 2); *çāmath*, "to destroy" (Ps **54** 5 AV; **94** 23, etc); *gādhadh*, "to cut one's self," is used of the cutting of one's flesh before heathen gods and in mourning for the dead, which was forbidden to the Israelites (Dt **14** 1; 1 K **18** 28; Jer **16** 6; **41** 5; **47** 5); *sereṭ*, *sāreṭeth*, "incision," are also used of those "cuttings of the flesh" (Lev **19** 28; cf **21** 5). See Cuttings in the Flesh. The cutting of the hair of head and beard in mourning for the dead is referred to in Isa **15** 2; "Every beard is cut off" (*gādha'*), and Jer **7** 29, *gazaz*, "Cut off thy hair [RVm "thy crown"], O Jerusalem" (cf Isa **22** 12; Jer **16** 6; Ezk **7** 18; Am **8** 10). This early and widespread practice was also forbidden to the Israelites as being unworthy of them in their relation to Jeh (Lev **19** 27; Dt **14** 1).

Ḥărōsheth, "carving," "engraving," is used for the "cutting of stones" (Ex **31** 5; **35** 33).

In the NT we have *apokoptō*, "to cut away" (Mk **9** 43.45; Gal **5** 12 AV; see Concision); *diapríō*, "to saw through" (Acts **5** 33, "they were cut to the heart"); *dichotoméō*, "to cut in two" (Mt **24** 51); *suntémnō*, "to cut together" (Rom **9** 28), "finishing it and cutting it short," i.e. "making it conclusive and brief."

Among the changes of RV are "brought to silence" for "cut down" (Jer **25** 37), also for "cut off" (Jer **49** 26; **50** 30); "sore wounded" for "cut in pieces" (Zec **12** 3); for "cut off," "pass through" (Job **11** 10), "gone" (Ps **90** 10); "rolled up" (Isa **38** 12); "cut off" for "destroy" (Ps **18** 40; **69** 4; **118** 10.11.12); for "cut them in the head" (Am **9** 1), "break them in pieces on the head of"; for "in the cutting off of my days" (Isa **38 10**; Heb $d^emī$, "silence," "rest"), "noontide," m "Or, tranquillity" (Gesenius, Delitzsch, etc, "in the quiet of my days"); instead of, "I would that they were even cut off which trouble you" (Gal **5** 12), ERV has "cut themselves off," m "mutilate themselves," ARV "go beyond circumcision," m "Gr mutilate themselves."

W. L. WALKER

CUTH, kuth, **CUTHAH,** kū'tha (כּוּת, *kūth,* כּוּתָה, *kūthāh;* **Χουά,** *Chouá,* **Χουνθά,** *Chounthá*): The longer writing is the better of the two, and gives the Heb form of the name of one of the cities from which Sargon of Assyria brought colonists to fill the places of the Israelites which he deported from Samaria in 772 BC (2 K **17** 24.30). Probably in consequence of their predominating numbers, the inhabitants of Samaria in general were then called *kūthīyīm,* or Cutheans.

From contract-tablets found at *Tel-Ibrahîm* by the late Hormuzd Rassam, on which the ancient name of the place is given as *Gudua* or *Kutû,* it would seem that that is the site which has to be identified with the Bib. Cuthah. It lies to the N.E. of Babylon, and was one of the most important cities of the Bab empire. The explorer describes the ruins as being about 3,000 ft. in circumference and 280 ft. high, and adjoining them on the W. lies a smaller mound, crowned with a sanctuary dedicated to Ibrahîm (Abraham). From the nature of the ruins, Rassam came to the conclusion that the city was much more densely populated after the fall of Babylon than in earlier times. A portion of the ruins were in a very perfect state, and suggested an unfinished building.

1. The Ruins of Cuthah

The great temple of the city was called *Ê-meš-lam,* and was dedicated to Nergal (cf 2 K **17** 30), one of whose names was Meŝlam-ta-êa. Both city and temple would seem to have been old Sumerian foundations, as the name *Gudua* and its later Sem form, *Kutû,* imply.

2. The Temple

LITERATURE.—See Rassam, *Asshur and the Land of Nimrod,* 396, 409, and, for details of the worship of Nergal, *PSBA,* December, 1906, 203–18.

T. G. PINCHES

CUTHA, kū'tha (**Κουθά,** *Kouthá;* 1 Esd **5** 32, AV **Coutha**): Head of a family of temple servants who returned with Zerubbabel from Babylon; not mentioned in the canonical lists.

CUTHAH. See CUTH, CUTHAH.

CUTHEAN, kū-thē'an, **CUTHITE,** kuth'īt. See CUTH; SAMARITANS.

CUTTING ASUNDER. See ASUNDER; PUNISHMENTS.

CUTTING OFF. See CONCISION; PUNISHMENTS.

CUTTINGS IN THE FLESH (שֶׂרֶט, *sereṭ,* שָׂרֶטֶת, *sāreṭeth*): For relatives or friends to cut or beat themselves even to free blood-flowing, especially in the violence of grief in mourning for their dead (see BURIAL; MOURNING), was a widely prevalent custom among ancient peoples, and is well-nigh universal among uncivilized races today (see Spencer, *Prin. of Soc.,* 3d ed, I, 163 ff). The fact is abundantly attested for most of the nations of antiquity, but there are two notable exceptions, the Egyptians (Herod. ii.61, 85; Wilk., *Anc. Egyp,* II, 374), and the Hebrews (Dt **14** 1; Lev **21** 5). According to Plutarch (*Sol.* 21) Solon forbade the women of Athens to beat themselves to the effusion of blood, and the laws of the Twelve Tables, quoted by Cic. (*De leg.* ii.23) contained a like injunction. Among the ancient Arabs the forbidden practice was associated, as among the Hebrews, with the cutting off of the hair (Wellhausen, *Skizzen,* III, 160 f).

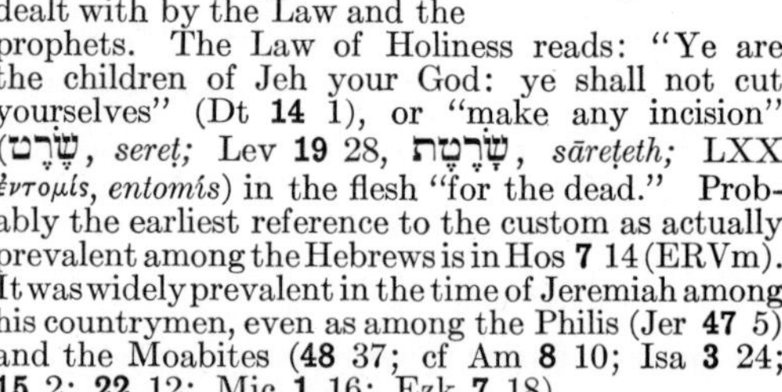
Cutting the Flesh.

That the prohibition among the Hebrews was urgently called for is made clear by the way it is dealt with by the Law and the prophets. The Law of Holiness reads: "Ye are the children of Jeh your God: ye shall not cut yourselves" (Dt **14** 1), or "make any incision" (שֶׂרֶט, *sereṭ;* Lev **19** 28, שָׂרֶטֶת, *sāreṭeth;* LXX ἐντομίς, *entomís*) in the flesh "for the dead." Probably the earliest reference to the custom as actually prevalent among the Hebrews is in Hos **7** 14 (ERVm). It was widely prevalent in the time of Jeremiah among his countrymen, even as among the Philis (Jer **47** 5) and the Moabites (**48** 37; cf Am **8** 10; Isa **3** 24; **15** 2; **22** 12; Mic **1** 16; Ezk **7** 18).

In seeking for the reason or purpose underlying all such prohibitions, we may note, first, that the "cuttings" and "baldness" forbidden are alike said to be "for the dead." Not less explicitly are they said to be incompatible with Israel's unique relation to Jeh—a relation at once of sonship (Dt **14** 1) and of consecration (**14** 2). Moreover such mutilations of the body are always dealt with as forming part of the religious rites of the heathen (as of the Canaanitish Baal [1 K **18** 28] note "after their manner," see art. in *HDB,* s.v.). Both such shedding of blood and the dedication of the hair are found in almost all countries of that day in intimate connection with the rituals of burial and the prevailing belief in the necessity of propitiating the spirit of the deceased. The conclusion, then, seems clearly warranted that such tokens of grief were prohibited because they carried with them inevitably ideas and associations distinctly heathen in character and so incompatible with the pure religion of Jeh, and unworthy of those who had attained to the dignity of the sons ("children") of Jeh. See also MARK; STIGMATA.

LITERATURE.—Benzinger, *Heb Arch.,* §23; Nowack, *Heb Arch.,* I, 33 f; Tylor, *Prim. Cult.;* W. R. Smith, *Rel Sem,* Lect IX; and Comm., Knobel-Dillmann, *Ex-Lev* on Lev **19** 28; Driver, *Dt* on **14** 1; and Lightfoot, *Gal* on **6** 17.

GEO. B. EAGER

CYAMON, sī'a-mon (**Κυαμών,** *Kuamōn,* Jth **7** 3): Probably identical with JOKNEAM (q.v.).

CYMBAL, sim'bal. See MUSIC.

CYPRESS, sī'pres. See HOLM TREE.

CYPRIANS, sip'ri-ans (**Κύπριοι,** *Kúprioi*): Occurs in 2 Macc **4** 29. Menelaus who was high priest at Jerus, and Sostratus who was governor of the citadel, were summoned by King Antiochus to appear before him. "Menelaus left his own brother Lysimachus for his deputy in the high-priesthood; and Sostratus left Crates, who was over the Cyprians." The Cyprians were the inhabitants of the island of Cyprus. Barnabas, who was Paul's associate on his first missionary journey, was a Cyprian (*Kuprios;* see Acts **4** 36). RV designates him as a man of Cyprus. The governor of the island was called a Cypriarch (see 2 Macc **12** 2, and cf ASIARCH). A. W. FORTUNE

CYPRUS, sī'prus (**Κύπρος,** *Kúpros*): An island situated near the N.E. corner of the Levant, in an angle formed by the coasts of Cilicia and Syria. In the OT it is called **Kittim,** after the name of its Phoen capital Kition. The identification is expressly made by Jos (*Ant,* I, vi, 1) and by the Cyprian bishop Epiphanius (*Haer.,* xxx.25). In the tablets from Tell el-Amarna it is referred to as Alashia (E. Meyer, *Gesch. des Alterthums,* I², §499), in Egyp records as Asi, while in the Assyr cuneiform inscriptions it is named Yavnan.

1. Name

2. Geography

The island is the largest in the Mediterranean with the exception of Sardinia and Sicily, its area being about 3,584 sq. miles. It lies in 34° 30′–35° 41′ N. latitude and 32° 15′–34° 36′ E. longitude, only 46 miles distant from the nearest point of the Cilician coast and 60 miles from the Syrian. Thus from the northern shore of the island the mainland of Asia Minor is clearly visible and Mt. Lebanon can be seen from Eastern Cyprus. This close proximity to the Cilician and Syrian coasts, as well as its position on the route between Asia Minor and Egypt, proved of great importance for the history and civilization of the island. Its greatest length, including the N.E. promontory, is about 140 miles, its greatest breadth 60 miles. The S.W. portion of Cyprus is formed by a mountain complex, culminating in the peaks of Troödos (6,406 ft.), Mádhari (5,305 ft.), Papoûtsa (5,124 ft.) and Máchaira (4,674 ft.). To the N.E. of this lies the great plain of the Mesoréa, nearly 60 miles in length and 10 to 20 in breadth, in which lies the modern capital Nicosia (Lefkosia). It is watered chiefly by the Pediaeus (mod. *Pediás*), and is bounded on the N. by a mountain range, which is continued to the E.N.E. in the long, narrow promontory of the Karpass, terminating in Cape Andrea, the ancient Dinaretum. Its highest peaks are Buffavénto (3,135 ft.) and Hagios Elías (3,106 ft.). The shore-plain to the N. of these hills is narrow, but remarkably fertile.

3. Products

Cyprus is richly endowed by nature. Its fruits and flowers were famous in antiquity. Strabo, writing under Augustus, speaks of it as producing wine and oil in abundance and corn sufficient for the needs of its inhabitants (XIV, 684). The elder Pliny refers to Cyprian salt, alum, gypsum, mica, unguents, laudanum, storax, resin and precious stones, including agate, jasper, amethyst, lapis lazuli and several species of rock-crystal. His list includes the diamond (xxxvii.58) and the emerald (xxxvii.6, 66), but there is reason to believe that under these names a variety of rock-crystal and the beryl are intended. The chief source of the island's wealth, however, lay in its mines and forests. Silver is mentioned by Strabo (loc. cit.) among its products; copper, which was called by the Greeks after the name of the island, was extensively mined there from the earliest period down to the Middle Ages; iron too was found in considerable quantities from the 9th cent. until Rom times. Scarcely less important were the forests, which at an early date are said to have covered almost the whole island. The cypress seems to have been the principal tree, but Pliny tells of a giant cedar, 130 Rom feet in height, felled in Cyprus (xvi.203), and the island supplied timber for shipbuilding to many successive powers.

4. Early History

The original inhabitants of Cyprus appear to have been a race akin to the peoples of Asia Minor. Its vast resources in copper and timber gained for it a considerable importance and wide commercial relations at a very remote period. Its wealth attracted the attention of Babylonia and Egypt, and there is reason to believe that it was conquered by Sargon I, king of Accad, and about a millennium later by Thothmes III, of the XVIIIth Egyptian Dynasty (1501–1447 BC). But the influences which molded its civilization came from other quarters also. Excavation has shown that in Cyprus were several seats of the Minoan culture, and there can be little doubt that it was deeply influenced by Crete. The Minoan writing may well be the source of the curious Cyprian syllabic script, which continued in use for the representation of the Gr language down to the 4th cent. BC (A. J. Evans, *Scripta Minoa,* I). But the Minoan origin of the Cyprian syllabary is still doubtful, for it may have been derived from the Hittite hieroglyphs. Phoen influences too were at work, and the Phoen settlements—Citium, Amathus, Paphos and others—go back to a very early date. The break-up of the Minoan civilization was followed by a "Dark Age," but later the island received a number of Gr settlers from Arcadia and other Hellenic states, as we judge not only from Gr tradition but from the evidence of the Cyprian dialect, which is closely akin to the Arcadian. In 709 BC Sargon II of Assyria made himself master of Cyprus, and tribute was paid by its seven princes to him and to his grandson, Esarhaddon (681–667 BC). The overthrow of the Assyr Empire probably brought with it the independence of Cyprus, but it was conquered afresh by Aahmes (Amasis) of Egypt (Herod. ii. 182) who retained it till his death in 526 BC; but in the following year the defeat of his son and successor Psamtek III (Psammenitus) by Cambyses brought the island under Pers dominion (Herod. iii.19, 91).

5. Cyprus and the Greeks

In 501 the Gr inhabitants led by Onesilus, brother of the reigning prince of Salamis, rose in revolt against the Persians, but were decisively beaten (Herod. v.104 ff), and in 480 we find 150 Cyprian ships in the navy with which Xerxes attacked Greece (Herod. vii.90). The attempts of Pausanias and of Cimon to win Cyprus for the Hellenic cause met with but poor success, and the withdrawal of the Athenian forces from the Levant after their great naval victory off Salamis in 449 was followed by a strong anti-Hellenic movement throughout the island led by Abdemon, prince of Citium. In 411 Euagoras ascended the throne of Salamis and set to work to assert Hellenic influence and to champion Hellenic civilization. He joined with Pharnabazus the Pers satrap and Conon the Athenian to overthrow the naval power of Sparta at the battle of Cnidus in 394, and in 387 revolted from the Persians. He was followed by his son Nicocles, to whom Isocrates addressed the famous panegyric of Euagoras and who formed the subject of an enthusiastic eulogy by the same writer. Cyprus seems later to have fallen once again under Pers rule, but after the battle of Issus (333 BC) it voluntarily gave in its submission to Alexander the Great and rendered him valuable aid at the siege of Tyre. On his death (323) it fell to the share of Ptolemy of Egypt. It was, however, seized by Demetrius Poliorcetes, who defeated Ptolemy in a hotly contested battle off Salamis in 306. But eleven years later it came into the hands of the Ptolemies and remained a province of Egypt or a separate but dependent kingdom until the intervention of Rome (cf 2 Macc **10** 13). We hear of a body of Cyprians, under the command of a certain Crates, serving among the troops of Antiochus Epiphanes of Syria and forming part of the garrison of Jerus about 172 BC (2 Macc **4** 29). This interpretation of the passage seems preferable to that according to which Crates had been governor of Cyprus under the Ptolemies before entering the service of Antiochus.

6. Cyprus and Rome

In 58 BC the Romans resolved to incorporate Cyprus in their empire and Marcus Porcius Cato was intrusted with the task of its annexation. The reigning prince, a brother of Ptolemy Auletes of Egypt, received the offer of an honorable retirement as high priest of Aphrodite at Paphos, but he preferred to end his life by poison, and treasures amounting to some 7,000 talents passed into Rom hands, together with the island, which was attached to the province of Cilicia. In the partition of the Rom empire between Senate and Emperor, Cyprus was at first (27–22 BC) an imperial province (Dio Cassius liii.12), administered by a *legatus Augusti pro praetore* or by the imperial legate of Cilicia. In 22 BC, however, it was handed over to the Senate together with southern Gaul in exchange for Dalmatia (Dio Cassius liii.12; liv.4) and was subsequently governed by ex-praetors bearing the honorary title of proconsul and residing at Paphos. The names of about a score of these governors are known to us from ancient authors, inscriptions and coins and will be found in D. G. Hogarth, *Devia Cypria*, App. Among them is Sergius Paulus, who was proconsul at the time of Paul's visit to Paphos in 46 or 47 AD, and we may notice that the title applied to him by the writer of the Acts (**13** 7) is strictly accurate.

Coin of Cyprus under Emperor Claudius.

The proximity of Cyprus to the Syrian coast rendered it easy of access from Pal, and Jews had probably begun to settle there even before the time of Alexander the Great. Certainly the number of Jewish residents under the Ptolemies was considerable (1 Macc **15** 23; 2 Macc **12** 2) and it must have been increased later when the copper mines of the island were farmed to Herod the Great (Jos, *Ant*, XVI, iv, 5; XIX, xxvi, 28; cf *CIG*, 2628). We shall not be surprised, therefore, to find that at Salamis there was more than one synagogue at the time of Paul's visit (Acts **13** 5). In 116 AD the Jews of Cyprus rose in revolt and massacred no fewer than 240,000 Gentiles. Hadrian crushed the rising with great severity and drove all the Jews from the island. Henceforth no Jew might set foot upon it, even under stress of shipwreck, on pain of death (Dio Cassius lxviii.32).

7. Cyprus and the Jews

In the life of the early church Cyprus played an important part. Among the Christians who fled from Judaea in consequence of the persecution which followed Stephen's death were some who "travelled as far as Phoenicia, and Cyprus" (Acts **11** 19) preaching to the Jews only. Certain natives of Cyprus and Cyrene took a further momentous step in preaching at Antioch to the Greeks also (Acts **11** 20). Even before this time Joseph Barnabas, a Levite born in Cyprus (Acts **4** 36), was prominent in the early Christian community at Jerus, and it was in his native island that he and Paul, accompanied by Barnabas' nephew, John Mark, began their first missionary journey (Acts **13** 4). After landing at Salamis they passed "through the whole island" to Paphos (Acts **13** 6), probably visiting the Jewish synagogues in its cities. The Peutinger Table tells us of two roads from Salamis to Paphos in Rom times, one of which ran inland by way of Tremithus, Tamassus and Soli, a journey of about 4 days, while the other and easier route, occupying some 3 days, ran along the south coast by way of Citium, Amathus and Curium. Whether the "early disciple," Mnason of Cyprus, was one of the converts made at this time or had previously embraced Christianity we cannot determine (Acts **21** 16). Barnabas and Mark revisited Cyprus later (Acts **15** 39), but Paul did not again land on the island, though he sighted it when, on his last journey to Jerus, he sailed south of it on his way from Patara in Lycia to Tyre (Acts **21** 3), and again when on his journey to Rome he sailed "under the lee of Cyprus," that is, along its northern coast, on the way from Sidon to Myra in Lycia (Acts **27** 4). In 401 AD the Council of Cyprus was convened, chiefly in consequence of the efforts of Theophilus of Alexandria, the inveterate opponent of Origenism, and took measures to check the reading of Origen's works. The island, which was divided into 13 bishoprics, was declared autonomous in the 5th cent., after the alleged discovery of Matthew's Gospel in the tomb of Barnabas at Salamis. The bishop of Salamis was made metropolitan by the emperor Zeno with the title "archbishop of all Cyprus," and his successor, who now occupies the see of Nicosia, still enjoys the privilege of signing his name in red ink and is primate over the three other bishops of the island, those of Paphos, Kition and Kyrenia, all of whom are of metropolitan rank.

8. The Church in Cyprus

Cyprus remained in the possession of the Rom and then of the Byzantine emperors, though twice overrun and temporarily occupied by the Saracens, until 1184, when its ruler, Isaac Comnenus, broke away from Constantinople and declared himself an independent emperor. From him it was wrested in 1191 by the Crusaders under Richard I of England, who bestowed it on Guy de Lusignan, the titular king of Jerus, and his descendants. In 1489 it was ceded to the Venetians by Catherine Cornaro, widow of James II, the last of the Lusignan kings, and remained in their hands until it was captured by the Ottoman Turks under Sultan Selim II, who invaded and subjugated the island in 1570 and laid siege to Famagústa, which, after a heroic defence, capitulated on August 1, 1571. Since that time Cyprus has formed part of the Turkish empire, in spite of serious revolts in 1764 and 1823; since 1878, however, it has been occupied and administered by the British government, subject to an annual payment to the Sublime Porte of £92,800 and a large quantity of salt. The High Commissioner, who resides at Nicosia, is assisted by a Legislative Council of 18 members. The estimated population in 1907 was 249,250, of whom rather more than a fifth were Moslems and the remainder chiefly members of the Gr Orthodox church.

9. Later History

Literature.—An exhaustive bibliography will be found in C. D. Cobham, *An Attempt at a Bibliography of Cyprus*, Nicosia, 4th ed, 1900. The following works may be specially mentioned: E. Oberhummer, *Aus Cypern*, Berlin, 1890–92; *Studien zur alten Geographie von Kypros*, Munich, 1891; A. Sakellarios, *Τὰ Κυπριακά*, Athens, 1890–91. References in ancient sources are collected in J. Meursius, *Cyprus*, Amsterdam, 1675, and W. Engel, *Kypros*, Berlin, 1841. For Cyprian archaeology see P. Gardner, *New Chapters in Gr History*, ch vi, London, 1892; J. L. Myres and M. Ohnefalsch-Richter, *Catalogue of the Cyprus Museum*, Oxford, 1899; M. O. Richter, *Kypros, die Bibel und Homer*, Berlin, 1893; D. G. Hogarth, *Devia Cypria*, London, 1889; and J. L. Myres' art. on "Cypriote Archaeology" in *Enc Brit*, 11th ed, VII, 697 ff. For excavations, *Journal of Hellenic Studies*, IX, XI, XII, XVII, and *Excavations in Cyprus*, London (British Museum), 1900; for art, G. Perrot and C. Chipiez, *Art in Phoenicia and Cyprus*, ET, London, 1885; for coins, B. V. Head, *Historia Numorum*, Oxford, 1911; for inscriptions, *Sammlung der griech. Dialekt-Inschriften*, I, Göttingen, 1883; for the Cyprian church, J. Hackett, *History of the Orthodox Church of Cyprus*, London, 1901; for authorities on mediaeval and modern history, C. D. Cobham, *Enc Brit*, 11th ed, VII, 701.

Marcus N. Tod

CYRAMA, si-rā′ma, sir′a-ma. See Kirama.

CYRÉNE, sī-rē′nē (**Κυρήνη**, *Kurḗnē*, "wall"): Cyrene was a city of Libya in North Africa, lat. 32° 40′ N., long. 22° 15′ E. It lay W. of ancient Egypt, from which it was separated by a portion of the Libyan desert, and occupied the territory now belonging to Barca and Tripoli. It was situated upon an elevated plateau about 2,000 ft. above the sea, from which it was distant some 10 miles. A high range of mountains lies to the S., about 90 miles inland. This shelters the coast land from the scorching

1. Location

heat of the Sahara. The range drops down toward the N. in a series of terrace-like elevations, thus giving to the region a great variety of climate and vegetation. The soil is fertile.

Cyrene was originally a Gr colony founded by Battus in 630 BC. Because of the fertility of the

2. History soil, the great variety in climate and vegetation, together with its commercial advantages in location, the city soon rose to great wealth and importance. Greater fame, however, came to it through its distinguished citizens. It was the home of Callimachus the poet, Carneacles the founder of the New Academy at Athens, and Eratosthenes the mathematician. To these must be added, from later times, the elegant ancient Christian writer Synesius. So important did this Gr colony become that, in little more than half a century, Amasis II of Egypt formed an alliance with Cyrene, marrying a Gr lady of noble, perhaps royal, birth (Herod. ii.181). Ptolemy III (Euergetes I), 231 BC, incorporated Cyrene with Egypt. The city continued, though with much restlessness, a part of the Egyp empire until Apion, the last of the Ptolemies, willed it to Rome. It henceforth belonged to a Rom province.

In the middle of the 7th cent., the conquering Saracens took possession of Cyrene, and from that time to this it has been the habitation of wandering tribes of Arabs.

Cyrene comes into importance in Bib. history through the dispersion of the Jews. Ptolemy I,

3. Biblical Importance son of Lagus, transported Jews to this and other cities of Libya (Jos, *CAp*, II, 4) and from this time on Jews were very numerous there. By the return of the Jews of the Dispersion to the feasts at Jerus, Cyrenians came to have a conspicuous place in the NT history. "A man of Cyrene, Simon by name," was caught by the Rom soldiers and compelled to bear the cross of Jesus (Mt **27** 32; cf Mk **15** 21; Lk **23** 26). See CYRENIAN. Jews from Cyrene were among those present on the day of Pentecost. Their city appears as one of the important points in the wide circle of the Dispersion described by Peter in his sermon on that occasion (Acts **2** 10). Cyrenian Jews were of sufficient importance in those days to have their name associated with a synagogue at Jerus (**6** 9). And when the persecution arose about Stephen, some of these Jews of Cyrene who had been converted at Jerus, were scattered abroad and came with others to Antioch and preached the word "unto the Jews only" (**11** 19.20 AV), and one of them, Lucius, became a prophet in the early church there. In this case, as in so many others, the wise providence of God in the dispersion of the Jews in preparation for the spread of the gospel of the Messiah is seen.

Coin of Cyrene.

In the ruins of Cyrene are to be seen the remains of some beautiful buildings, and a few sculptures

4. Archaeology have been removed. The most interesting remains of the wondrous civilization of this Gr colony are in a great system of tombs, some built, but the finest cut in the solid rock of the cliff. Doric architecture and brilliant decorative painting adorn these tombs.

LITERATURE.—Herod. ii; Jos, *CAp;* Thrige, *Res Cyrenensium.*

M. G. KYLE

CYRENIAN, sī-rē′ni-an, **CYRENIANS** (**Κυρηναῖος**, *Kurēnaíos*, "a native or inhabitant of Cyrene"): Two Jews of Cyrene are mentioned in the NT, viz. Simon (Mk **15** 21 and Lk **23** 26 AV) who was impressed to bear the Lord's cross (Mk **15** 21 RVm), and Lucius, a Christian teacher at Antioch (Acts **13** 1). See CYRENE; LUCIUS; SIMON. For **Cyrenians** see CYRENE.

CYRENIUS, sī-rē′ni-us (**Κυρήνιος**, *Kurḗnios*, "of Cyrene"). See QUIRINIUS.

CYRIA, sir′i-a (**Κυρία**, *Kuría*): The word means "lady," feminine of lord, and it is so tr[d] in AV and the text of RV (2 Jn ver 5 RVm). But it is possible that the word is a proper name, and this possibility is recognized by placing *Cyria*, the usual transliteration of the word, in the margin by RV.

CYRUS, sī′rus (כּוֹרֶשׁ, *kōresh;* Old Pers *Kuruš;* Bab *Kur[r]aš*, *Kur[r]ašu;* Gr **Κῦρος**, *Kúros*, 2 Ch **36** 22, etc):

1. Genealogy of Cyrus
2. His Country, Anšan or Anzan
3. His Origin (Herodotus)
4. " " (Xenophon)
5. " " (Nicolaus of Damascus)
6. " " (Ctesias)
7. Babylonian Records of His Reign—the Cylinder of Nabonidus
8. The Babylonian Chronicle
9. " " " —The Capture of Babylon
10. The Cylinder of Cyrus
11. Cyrus' History from Greek Sources
12. The Massagetae
13. The Sacae, Berbices, etc
14. Doubt as to the Manner of His Death
15. Cyrus' Reputation
16. Why Did the Babylonians Accept Him?
17. Cyrus and the Jews
18. Cyrus in Persia—His Bas-relief

The son of the earlier Cambyses, of the royal race of the Achemenians. His genealogy, as given by

1. Genealogy of Cyrus himself, is as follows: "I am Cyrus, king of the host, the great king, the mighty king, king of Tindir [Babylon], king of the land of Šumeru and Akkadū, king of the four regions, son of Cambyses, the great king, king of the city Anšan, grandson of Cyrus, the great king, king of the city Anšan, great-grandson of Šišpiš [*Teispes*], the great king, king of the city Anšan, the all-enduring royal seed whose sovereignty Bel and Nebo love," etc (*WAI*, V, pl. 35, 20–22).

As, in the Bab inscriptions, Aššan (Anšan, Anzan) is explained as Elam—the city was, in fact,

2. His Country, Anšan or Anzan the capital of that country—it is probable that Cyrus' name was Elamite; but the meaning is doubtful. The old Gr etymology connecting it with *khor*, "the sun," in Persian, may therefore be rejected. According to Strabo, he was at first called Agradatēs, the name by which he was universally known being taken from that of the river Cyrus. This, however, is more likely to have been the reason why his grandfather (after whom he was probably named) was called Cyrus.

Several versions of his birth and rise to power are recorded. Herodotus (i.95) mentions three. In

3. His Origin (Herodotus) that which he quotes (i.107 ff), it is said that Mandane was the daughter of the Median king Astyages, who, in consequence of a dream which he had had, foretelling the ultimate triumph of her son over his dynasty, gave her in marriage to a Persian named Cambyses, who was not one of his peers. A second dream caused him to watch for her expected offspring, and when Cyrus came into the world Astyages delivered the child to his relative, Harpagus, with orders to destroy it. Being unwilling to do this, he handed the infant to a shepherd named Mitradates, who, his wife having brought forth a still-born child, consented to spare the life of the infant Cyrus. Later on, in consequence of his imperious acts, Cyrus was recognized by Astyages, who came to learn the whole story, and spared him because, having once been made king by his companions in play, the Magians held the predictions concerning his ultimate royal state to have been fulfilled. The vengeance taken by Astyages upon Harpagus for his apparent disobedience to orders is well known: his son was slain, and a portion, disguised, given him to eat. Though filled with grief, Harpagus concealed his feelings, and departed with the remains of his son's body; and Cyrus, in due course, was sent to stay with his parents, Cambyses and Mandane. Later on, Harpagus persuaded Cyrus to induce the Persians to revolt, and Astyages having blindly appointed Harpagus commander-in-chief of the Median army, the last-named went over to the side of Cyrus. The result was an easy victory for the latter, but Astyages took care to impale the Magians who had advised him to spare his grandson. Having gathered another, but smaller, army, he took the field in person, but was defeated and captured. Cyrus, however, who became king of Media as well as of Persia, treated him honorably and well.

According to Xenophon, *Cyropaedia* i. §2, Cambyses, the father of Cyrus, was king of Persia.[1]

4. His Origin (Xenophon)

Until his 12th year, Cyrus was educated in Persia, when he was sent for, with his mother, by Astyages, to whom he at once manifested much affection. Astyages is said to have been succeeded by his son Cyaxares, and Cyrus then became his commander-in-chief, subduing, among others, the Lydians. He twice defeated the Assyrians (= Babylonians), his final conquest of the country being while the Median king was still alive. As, however, the *Cyropaedia* is a romance, the historical details are not of any great value.

Nicolaus of Damascus describes Cyrus as the son of a Mardian bandit named Atradates, his mother's name being Argostē. While

5. Nicolaus of Damascus

in service in the palace of Astyages, he was adopted by Artembarēs, a cupbearer, and thus obtained prominence. Cyrus now made his bandit-father satrap of Persia, and, with base ingratitude, plotted against his king and benefactor. The preparations for a revolt having been made, he and his general Oibaras were victorious at Hyrba, but were defeated at Parsagadae, where his father Atradates was captured and later on died. Cyrus now took refuge in his mountain home, but the taunts of the women sent him and his helpers forth again, this time to victory and dominion.

Ctesias also states that there was no relationship between Cyrus and Astyages (Astyigas), who, when Cyrus conquered Media, fled to

6. His Origin (Ctesias)

Ecbatana, and was there hidden by his daughter Amytis, and Spitamas her husband. Had not Astyages yielded, Cyrus, it is said, would have tortured them, with their children. Cyrus afterward liberated Astyages, and married his daughter Amytis, whose husband he had put to death for telling a falsehood. The Bactrians are said to have been so satisfied at the reconciliation of Cyrus with Astyages and his daughter, that they voluntarily submitted. Cyrus is said by Ctesias to have been taken prisoner by the Sacae, but he was ransomed. He died from a wound received in battle with the Derbices, assisted by the Indians.

In the midst of so much uncertainty, it is a relief to turn to the contemporary documents of the Babylonians, which, though they do not

7. Babylonian Records of His Reign—the Cylinder of Nabonidus

speak of Cyrus' youth in detail, and refer only to other periods of his career in which they were more immediately interested, may nevertheless, being contemporary, be held to have an altogether special authority. According to the inscriptions, the conflict with Astyages took place in 549 BC. From the cylinder of Nabonidus we learn that the Medes had been very successful in their warlike operations, and had gone even as far afield as Haran, which they had besieged. The Babylonian King Nabonidus desired to carry out the instructions of Merodach, revealed in a dream, to restore the temple of Sin, the Moon-god, in that city. This, however, in consequence of the siege, he could not do, and it was revealed to him in a dream that the power of Astyages would be overthrown at the end of three years, which happened as predicted. "They [the gods Sin and Merodach] then caused Cyrus, king of Anzan, his [Merodach's] young servant, with his little army, to rise up against him [the Median]; he destroyed the wide-spreading Umman-manda [Medes], Ištuwegu [Astyages], king of the Medes, he captured, and took [him] prisoner to his [own] land." The account of this engagement in the Babylonian Chronicle (which is, perhaps, Cyrus' own), is as follows: "[Astyages] gathered his army, and went against Cyrus, king of Anšan, to

8. The Babylonian Chronicle

capture him, and [as for] Astyages, his army revolted against him and took him, and gave him to Cyrus. Cyrus went to the land of Ecbatana, his royal city. He carried off from Ecbatana silver, gold, furniture, merchandise, and took to the land of Anšan the furniture and merchandise which he had captured."

The above is the entry for the 6th year of Nabonidus, which corresponds with 549 BC; and it will be noticed that he is here called "king of Anšan." The next reference to Cyrus in the Bab Chronicle is the entry for Nabonidus' 9th year (546 BC), where it is stated that "Cyrus, king of the land of Parsu [Persia], gathered his army, and crossed the Tigris below Arbela," and in the following month (Iyyar) entered the land of Iš- . . . . , where someone seems to have taken a bribe, garrisoned the place, and afterward a king ruled there. The passage, however, is imperfect, and therefore obscure, but we may, perhaps, see therein some preparatory move on the part of Cyrus to obtain possession of the tract over which Nabonidus claimed dominion.

The next year (545 BC) there seems to have been another move on the part of the Persians, for the Elamite governor (?) is referred to, and had apparently some dealings with the governor of Erech. All this time things seem to have been the same in Babylonia, the king's son (he is not named, but apparently Belshazzar is meant) and the soldiers remaining in Akkad (possibly used in the old sense of the word, to indicate the district around Sippar), where it was seemingly expected that the main attack would be delivered. The reference to the governor of Erech might imply that some conspiracy was on foot more to the south—a movement of which the native authorities possibly remained in ignorance.

After a gap which leaves four years unaccounted for, we have traces of four lines which mention the goddess Ištar of Erech, and the gods of the land

[1] He may have added Persia to his dominion, but according to Cyrus himself, he was king of Anšan or Elam.

of Par . . . . (?Persia) are referred to. After this comes the long entry, which, though the date is broken away, must refer to the 17th year of Nabonidus. A royal visit to a temple is referred to, and there is mention of a revolt. Certain religious ceremonies were then performed, and others omitted. In the month Tammuz, Cyrus seems to have fought a battle in Opis, and succeeded in attacking the army of Akkad situated on the Tigris. On the 14th of the month, Sippar was taken without fighting, and Nabonidus fled. On the 16th Ugbaru (Gobryas) governor of Media, entered Babylon, with the army of Cyrus, without fighting, and there Nabonidus was captured with his followers. At this time Ê-saggil and the temples of the land seem to have been closed, possibly to prevent the followers of Nabonidus from taking sanctuary there, or else to prevent plotters from coming forth; and on the 3d of Marcheswan (October), Cyrus entered Babylon. "Crowds collected before him, proposing peace for the city; Cyrus, command the peace of Babylon, all of it." Gobryas, his vice-regent, then appointed governors in Babylon, and the gods whom Nabonidus had taken down to Babylon, were returned to their shrines. On the night of the 11th of Marcheswan, Ugbaru went against (some part of Babylon), and the son of the king died; and there was mourning for him from the 27th of Adar to the 3d of Nisan (six days). There is some doubt as to whether the text speaks of the king or the son of the king, but as there is a record that Nabonidus was exiled to Carmania, it would seem most likely that the death of Belshazzar "in the night" is here referred to. The day after the completion of the mourning (the 4th of Nisan), Cambyses, son of Cyrus, performed ceremonies in the temple Ê-nig-ḫad-kalamma, probably in connection with the new year's festival, for which Cyrus had probably timed his arrival at Babylon. According to Herodotus (i.191), Babylón was taken during a festival, agreeing with Dnl **5 1** ff.

9. The Chronicle—the Capture of Babylon

The other inscription of Cyrus, discovered by Mr. H. Rassam at Babylon, is a kind of proclamation justifying his seizure of the crown. He states that the gods (of the various cities of Babylonia) forsook their dwellings in anger that he (Nabonidus) had made them enter within Šu-anna (Babylon). Merodach, the chief divinity of Babylon, sought also a just king, the desire of his heart, whose hand he might hold—Cyrus, king of Anšan, he called his title—to all the kingdoms together (his) name was proclaimed.

10. The Cylinder of Cyrus

The glory of Cyrus' conquests probably appealed to the Babylonians, for Cyrus next states that Merodach placed the whole of the troops of Qutû (Media) under his feet, and the whole of the troops of the Manda (barbarians and mercenaries). He also caused his hands to hold the people of the dark head (Asiatics, including the Babylonians)—in righteousness and justice he cared for them. He commanded that he should go to his city Babylon, and walked by his side like a friend and a companion—without fighting and battle Merodach caused him to enter Šu-anna. By his high command, the kings of every region from the upper sea to the lower sea (the Mediterranean to the Persian Gulf), the kings of the Amorites, and the dwellers in tents, brought their valuable tribute and kissed his feet within Šu-anna (Babylon). From Nineveh(?), the city Aššur, Susa, Agadé, the land of Ešnunnak, Zamban, Mê-Ṭurnu, and Dêru, to the borders of Media, the gods inhabiting them were returned to their shrines, and all the people were collected and sent back to their dwellings. He finishes by soliciting the prayers of the gods to Bel and Nebo for length of days and happiness, asking them also to appeal to Merodach on behalf of Cyrus "his worshipper," and his son Cambyses.

It was probably between the defeat of Astyages and the capture of Babylon that Cyrus defeated Croesus and conquered Lydia. After preparing to attack the Gr cities of Asia Minor, he returned to Ecbatana, taking Croesus with him. The states which had formed the Lydian empire, however, at once revolted, and had again to be reduced to submission, this time by Harpagus, his faithful general, after a determined resistance. It was at this period that Cyrus subdued the nations of Upper Asia, his next objective being Babylonia (§ 9 and the two preceding paragraphs). In this connection it is noteworthy that, in the Bab official account, there is no mention of his engineering works preparatory to the taking of Babylon—the turning of the waters of the Gyndes into a number of channels in order to cross (Herod. i.189); the siege of Babylon, long and difficult, and the final capture of the city by changing the course of the Euphrates, enabling his army to enter by the bed of the river (Herod. i.190–91). There may be some foundation for this statement, but if so, the king did not boast of it—perhaps because it did not entail any real labor, for the irrigation works already in existence may have been nearly sufficient for the purpose. It seems likely that the conquest of Babylon opened the way for other military exploits. Herodotus states that he next attacked the Massagetae, who were located beyond the Araxes. One-third of their army was defeated, and the son of Tomyris, the queen, captured by a stratagem; but on being freed from his bonds, he committed suicide. In another exceedingly fierce battle which followed, the Pers army was destroyed, and Cyrus himself brought his life to an end there, after a reign of 29 years. (He had ruled over Media for 11, and over Babylonia [and Assyria] for 9 years.) According to the Bab contract-tablets, Cambyses, his son, was associated with him on the throne during the first portion of his 1st year of rule in Babylon.

11. Cyrus' History from Greek Sources

12. The Massagetae

According to Ctesias, Cyrus made war with the Bactrians and the Sacae, but was taken prisoner by the latter, and was afterward ransomed. He died from a wound received in battle with the Berbices. Diodorus agrees, in the main, with Herodotus, but relates that Cyrus was captured by the Scythian queen (apparently Tomyris), who crucified or impaled him.

13. The Sacae, Berbices, etc

It is strange that, in the case of such a celebrated ruler as Cyrus, nothing certain is known as to the manner of his death. The accounts which have come down to us seem to make it certain that he was killed in battle with some enemy, but the statements concerning his end are conflicting. This absence of any account of his death from a trustworthy source implies that Herodotus is right in indicating a terrible disaster to the Pers arms, and it is therefore probable that he fell on the field of battle—perhaps in conflict with the Massagetae, as Herodotus states. Supposing that only a few of the Pers army escaped, it may be that not one of those who saw him fall lived to tell the tale, and the world was dependent on the more or less trustworthy statements which the Massagetae made.

14. Doubt as to the Manner of His Death

That he was considered to be a personage of noble character is clear from all that has come down to us concerning him, the most noteworthy being Xenophon's *Cyropaedia* and *Institution of Cyrus*. The

Bab inscriptions do not reproduce Bab opinion, but the fact that on the occasion of the siege of Babylon the people trusted to his honor and came forth asking peace for the city (apparently with every confidence that their request would be granted); and that the Babylonians, as a whole, were contented under his rule, may be regarded as tacit confirmation. Nabonidus, before the invasion of his territory by the Pers forces, was evidently well disposed toward him, and looked upon him, as we have seen, as "the young servant of Merodach," the patron deity of Babylon. It is not altogether clear, however, why the Babylonians submitted to him with so little resistance—their inscriptions contain no indication that they had real reason to be dissatisfied with the rule of Nabonidus—he seems to have been simply regarded as somewhat unorthodox in his worship of the gods; but could they expect an alien, of a different religion, to be better in that respect? Dissatisfaction on the part of the Babylonian priesthood was undoubtedly at the bottom of their discontent, however, and may be held to supply a sufficient reason, though it does not redound to the credit of Bab patriotism. It has been said that the success of Cyrus was in part due to the aid given him by the Jews, who, recognizing him as a monotheist like themselves, gave him more than mere sympathy; but it is probable that he could never have conquered Babylonia had not the priests, as indicated by their own records, spread discontent among the people. It is doubtful whether we may attribute a higher motive to the priesthood, though that is not altogether impossible. The inner teaching of the Bab polytheistic faith was, as is now well known, monotheistic, and there may have been, among the priests, a desire to have a ruler holding that to be the true faith, and also not so inclined as Nabonidus to run counter to the people's (and the priests') prejudices. Jewish influence would, in some measure, account for this.

15. Cyrus' Reputation

16. Why Did the Babylonians Accept Him?

If the Jews thought that they would be more sympathetically treated under Cyrus' rule, they were not disappointed. It was he who gave orders for the rebuilding of the Temple at Jerus (2 Ch **36** 23; Ezr **1** 2; **5** 13; **6** 3), restored the vessels of the House of the Lord which Nebuchadnezzar had taken away (Ezr **1** 7), and provided funds to bring cedar trees from Lebanon (**3** 7). But he also restored the temples of the Babylonians, and brought back the images of the gods to their shrines. Nevertheless the Jews evidently felt that the favors he granted them showed sympathy for them, and this it probably was which caused Isaiah (**44** 28) to see in him a "shepherd" of the Lord, and an anointed king (Messiah, τῷ χριστῷ μου, *tô Christô mou*, Isa **45** 1)—a title suggesting to later writers that he was a type of Christ (Hieron., *Comm.* on Isa **44** 1).

17. Cyrus and the Jews

From Persia we do not get any help as to his character, nor as to the estimation in which he was held. His only inscription extant is above his idealized bas-relief at Murghâb, where he simply writes: "I am Cyrus, the Achemenian." The stone shows Cyrus standing, looking to the right, draped in a fringed garment resembling those worn by the ancient Babylonians, reaching to the feet. His hair is combed back in the Pers style, and upon his head is an elaborate Egyp crown, two horns extending to front and back, with a uraeus serpent rising from each end, and between the serpents three vase-like objects, with discs at their bases and summits, and serrated leaves between. There is no doubt that this crown is symbolical of his dominion over Egypt, the three vase-like objects being modifications of the triple helmet-crown of the Egyp deities. The king is represented as four-winged in the Assyro-Babylonian style, probably as a claim to divinity in their hierarchy as well as to dominion in the lands of Merodach and Aššur. In his right hand, which is raised to the level of his shoulder, he holds a kind of scepter seemingly terminating in a bird's head—in all probability also a symbol of Bab dominion, though the emblem of the Bab cities of the South was most commonly a bird with wings displayed.

18. Cyrus in Persia—His Bas-relief

T. G. Pinches

D

DABAREH, dab′a-re. See Daberath.

DABBESHETH, dab′e-sheth, (דַּבֶּשֶׁת, *dabbesheth;* **Δαβασθαί,** *Dabasthaí;* AV **Dabbasheth,** dab′a-sheth): A town on the western boundary of Zebulun (Josh **19** 11). It is probably identical with the modern *Dabsheh,* a ruined site to the E. of Acre.

DABERATH, dab′ē-rath (הַדָּבְרַת, *ha-dābhᵉrath,* "pasture"; **Δαβειρώθ,** *Dabeirôth*): A city in the territory of Issachar, on the boundary between that tribe and Zebulun (Josh **19** 12). It was assigned to the Gershonite Levites (Josh **21** 28; 1 Ch **6** 72). The most probable identification is with *Dabūriyeh,* a village on the lower western slopes of Tabor.

DABRIA, dā′bri-a: One of the five who wrote down the visions of Esdras, described (2 Esd **14** 24) as "ready to write swiftly."

DACUBI, da-kū′bī, AV **Dacobi,** dā-kō′bī: Head of a family of gate-keepers (1 Esd **5** 28). See Akkub; Dakubi.

DADDEUS, da-dē′us, RV LODDEUS (**Λοδδαῖος,** *Loddaíos*), which see.

DAGGER, dag′ẽr. See Armor, Arms.

DAGON, dā′gon (דָּגוֹן, *dāghōn;* apparently derived from דָּג, *dāgh,* "fish"): Name of the god of the Philis (according to Jerome on Isa **46** 1 of the Philis generally); in the Bible Dagon is associated with Gaza (Jgs **16**) but elsewhere with Ashdod (cf 1 S **5** and 1 Macc **10** 83 f; **11** 4); in 1 Ch **10** 10 there is probably an error (cf the ∥ passage 1 S **31** 10). The god had his temple ("the house of Dagon") and his priests. When the ark was captured by the Philis, it was conducted to Ashdod where it was placed in the house of Dagon by the side of the idol. But on the morrow it was found that the idol lay prostrate before the ark of the Lord. It was restored to its place; but on the following day Dagon again lay on the ground before the ark, this time with the head and both hands severed from the body and lying upon the *miphtān* (the word is commonly interpreted to mean "threshold"; according to Winckler, it means "pedestal"); the body alone

Dagon.

remained intact. The Heb says: "Dagon alone remained." Whether we resort to an emendation (דָּגוֹ, *dāghō*, "his fish-part") or not, commentators appear to be right in inferring that the idol was half man, half fish. Classic authors give this form to Derceto. The sacred writer adds that from that time on the priests of Dagon and all those that entered the house of Dagon refrained from stepping upon the *miphtān* of Dagon. See 1 S **5** 1–5. The prophet Zephaniah (**1** 9) speaks of an idolatrous practice which consisted in leaping over the *miphtān*. The Septuagint in 1 S indeed adds the clause: "but they were wont to leap." Leaping over the threshold was probably a feature of the Phili ritual which the Hebrews explained in their way. A god Dagon seems to have been worshipped by the Canaanites; see BETH-DAGON, BETH-SHEAN.

LITERATURE.—Commentaries on Jgs and 1 S; Winckler, *Altoriental. Forschungen*, III, 383.

MAX L. MARGOLIS

DAILY, dā'li: This word, coming as it does from the Heb יוֹם, *yōm*, "day," and the Gr ἡμέρα, *hēmĕra*, suggests either day by day (Ex **5** 13), that which is prepared for one daily (Neh **5** 18), as e.g. our "daily bread," meaning bread sufficient for that day (Mt **6** 11); or day by day continuously, one day after another in succession, as "the daily burnt offering" (Nu **29** 6 AV), "daily ministration" (Acts **6** 1), and "daily in the temple" (Acts **5** 42 AV). The meaning of the word "daily" as used in the Lord's Prayer (Mt **6** 11) seems to indicate sufficient for our need, whether we consider that need as a day at a time, or day after day as we are permitted to live. "Give us bread sufficient for our sustenance." WILLIAM EVANS

DAILY OFFERING, or **SACRIFICE.** See SACRIFICE.

DAINTIES, dān'tis, **DAINTY (MEATS)** (מַטְעַמּוֹת, *maṭʻammōth*, "things full of taste," מַנְעַמִּים, *manʻammīm*, מַעֲדָן, *maʻădhān*; λιπαρός, *liparós*, "fat," "shining"): Jacob is represented as predicting of Asher, "He shall yield royal d." (Gen **49** 20; cf ‖ clause, "His bread shall be fat," and Dt **33** 24, "Let him dip his foot in oil"). David, praying to be delivered from the ways of "men that work inquity," cries, "Let me not eat of their d." (Ps **141** 4). The man who sitteth "to eat with a ruler" (Prov **23** 1–3) is counseled, "If thou be a man given to appetite, be not desirous of his d.; seeing they are deceitful food" (cf John's words in the woes upon Babylon [Rev **18** 14], "All things that were d. and sumptuous are perished from thee," and Homer's *Iliad* [Pope], xviii.456). "Dainties," then, are luxuries, costly, delicate and rare. This idea is common to all the words thus rendered; naturally associated with kings' tables, and with the lives of those who are lovers of pleasure and luxury. By their associations and their softening effects they are to be abstained from or indulged in moderately as "deceitful food" by those who would live the simple and righteous life which wisdom sanctions. They are also "offered not from genuine hospitality, but with some by-ends." He should also shun the dainties of the niggard (Prov **23** 6), who counts the cost (ver 7 RVm) of every morsel that his guest eats. See DELICATE; FOOD, etc.

GEO. B. EAGER

DAISAN, dā'san, dā'i-san (Δαισάν, *Daisán*): Head of a family of temple servants (1 Esd **5** 31) called Rezin in Ezr **2** 48; Neh **7** 50, the interchange of *D* and *R* in Heb being not uncommon.

DAKUBI, da-kū'bi, da-kōō'bi (Δακούβ, *Dakoúb*, Δακουβί, *Dakoubí;* AV **Dacobi**): Head of a family of gate-keepers (1 Esd **5** 28) called "Akkub" in the canonical lists.

DALAIAH, da-lā'a, da-lā-ī'a. See DELAIAH.

DALAN, dā'lan (Δαλάν, *Dalán;* AV **Ladan**): Head of a family that returned to Jerus, but which "could shew neither their families, nor their stock, how they were of Israel" (1 Esd **5** 37); corresponds to Delaiah (Ezr **2** 60). Another reading is "Asan."

DALE, dāl, **KING'S** (עֵמֶק הַמֶּלֶךְ, *'ēmeḳ ha-melekh*):

(1) "Absalom in his lifetime had taken and reared up for himself the pillar, which is in the king's dale" (2 S **18** 18). According to Jos (*Ant*, VII, x, 3) this was a marble pillar, which he calls "Absalom's hand" and it was two furlongs from Jerus. Warren suggests that this dale was identical with the KING'S GARDEN (q.v.), which he places at the open valley formed at the junction of the Tyropœon with the Kidron (see JERUSALEM). The so-called Absalom's Pillar, which the Jews still pelt with stones in reprobation of Absalom's disobedience, and which a comparatively recent tradition associates with 2 S **18** 18, is a very much later structure, belonging to the Graeco-Rom period, but showing Egyp influence.

(2) **King's Vale** (Gen **14** 17; AV **dale**). See KING'S VALE; VALE. E. W. G. MASTERMAN

DALETH, dä'leth (ד, ד): The 4th letter of the Heb alphabet, and as such used in Ps **119** to designate the 4th section; transliterated in this Encyclopaedia with the *dagesh* as *d*, and, without, as *dh* (=*th* in *the*). It came also to be used for the number four (4), and with the dieresis for 4,000. With the apostrophe it is sometimes used as abbreviation for the tetragrammaton. For name, etc, see ALPHABET.

DALLY, dal'i: Occurs in Wisd **12** 26: "But they that would not be reformed by that correction wherein he *dallied* with them" (παιγνίοις ἐπιτιμήσεως, *paigníois epitimēseōs*, "child play of correction"), the reference being to the earlier and lighter plagues of Egypt; RV renders "by a mocking correction as of children," "by a correction which was as children's play," Gr (as above). He first tried them by those lighter inflictions before sending on them the heavier. In later usage "dally" implies *delay*.

DALMANUTHA, dal-ma-nū'tha. See MAGADAN. Cf Mk **8** 10; Mt **15** 39.

DALMATIA, dal-mā'shi-a (Δαλματία, *Dalmatía*, "deceitful"): A district of the Rom empire lying on the eastern shore of the Adriatic. Writing from Rome to Timothy during his second imprisonment (in 66 or 67 AD, according to Ramsay's chronology), Paul records the departure of Titus to Dalmatia (2 Tim **4** 10). No mention is made of his special mission, and we cannot tell whether his object was to traverse regions hitherto unevangelized or to visit churches already formed. Nor can we determine with certainty the meaning of the word Dalmatia as here used. Originally it denoted the land of the barbarous Dalmatae or Delmatae, a warlike Illyrian tribe subjugated by the Romans after a long and stubborn resistance; it was then applied to the southern portion of the Rom province of Illyricum, lying between the river Titius (mod. *Kerka*) and the Macedonian frontier; later the name was extended to the entire province. On the whole it seems most probable that the apostle uses it in this last sense. See further s.v. ILLYRICUM.

MARCUS N. TOD

DALPHON, dal'fon (דַּלְפוֹן, *dalphōn*, "crafty"): The second of the ten sons of Haman, slain by the Jews (Est **9** 7).

DAM (אֵם, *'ēm*, ordinary Heb word for "mother"): Heb law prohibited the destruction of the "dam" and the young of birds at the same time, commanding that if the young be taken from a nest the dam be allowed to escape (Dt **22** 6.7). In the same spirit it enjoined the taking of an animal for slaughter before it had been seven days with its "dam" (Ex **22** 30; Lev **22** 27; cf Ex **23** 19).

DAMAGE, dam'āj (חֲבָלָא, *ḥăbhālā'*): This word expresses any inflicted loss of value or permanent injury to persons or things. "Why should damage grow to the hurt of the kings?" (Ezr **4** 22). In Prov **26** 6 "damage" means "wrong," "injury" (Heb חָמָס, *ḥāmāṣ*). The tr of Est **7** 4 is doubtful: "Although the adversary could not have compensated for the king's damage" (RVm "For our affliction is not to be compared with the king's damage"; AV "could not countervail the king's damage"); but Heb נֵזֶק, *nēzeḳ* (Est **7** 4) and Aram. נָזִק, *nāziḳ* (Dnl **6** 2) have the meaning of "molestation" or "annoyance" (see Ges.-Buhl *Dict.* [15th ed] 489, 806, 908). We therefore ought to read 'for that oppression would not have been worthy of the molestation of the king' (Est **7** 4) and 'that the king should have no molestation' (Dnl **6** 2). The Gr ζημία, *zēmía*, "loss" and ζημιόω, *zēmióō*, "to cause loss"; RV therefore translates Acts **27** 10 "will be with injury and much loss" (AV 'damage"), and 2 Cor **7** 9 "that ye might suffer loss by us in nothing" (AV "damage"). A. L. BRESLICH

DAMARIS, dam'a-ris (Δάμαρις, *Dámaris*, possibly a corruption of δάμαλις, *dámalis*, "a heifer"): The name of a female Christian of Athens, converted by Paul's preaching (Acts **17** 34). The fact that she is mentioned in this passage together with Dionysius the Areopagite has led some, most probably in error, to regard her as his wife. The singling out of her name with that of Dionysius may indicate some personal or social distinction. Cf Acts **17** 12.

DAMASCENES, dam-a-sēnz', dam'a-sēnz (τὴν πόλιν Δαμασκηνῶν, *tḗn pólin Damaskēnṓn*, "the city of the Damascenes"): The inhabitants of Damascus under Aretas the Arabian are so called (2 Cor **11** 32).

DAMASCUS, da-mas'kus:

1. Name
2. Situation and Natural Features
3. The City Itself
4. Its History
   (1) The Early Period (to cir 950 BC)
   (2) The Aramaean Kingdom (cir 950–732 BC)
   (3) The Middle Period (732 BC–650 AD)
   (4) Under Islam

The Eng. name is the same as the Gr Δαμασκός, *Damaskós*. The Heb name is דַּמֶּשֶׂק, *Dammeseḳ*, but the Aram. form דַּרְמֶשֶׂק, *Darmeseḳ*, occurs in 1 Ch **18** 5; 2 Ch **28** 5. The name appears in Egyp inscriptions as *Ti-mas-ku* (16th cent. BC), and *Sa-ra-mas-ki* (13th cent. BC), which W. M. Müller, *Asien u. Europa*, 227, regards as representing *Ti-ra-mas-ki*, concluding from the *"ra"* in this form that Damascus had by that time passed under Aram. influence. In the Am Tab the forms *Ti-ma-aš-gi* and *Di-maš-ka* occur. The Arab. name is *Dimashk esh-Sham* ("Damascus of Syria") usually contrasted to *Esh-Sham* simply. The meaning of the name Damascus is unknown. *Esh-Sham* (Syria) means "the left," in contrast to the *Yemen* (Arabia) = "the right."

1. Name

Damascus is situated (33° 30′ N. lat., 36° 18′ E. long.) in the N.W. corner of the Ghuta, a fertile plain about 2,300 ft. above sea level, W. of Mt. Hermon. The part of the Ghuta E. of the city is called *el-Merj*, the "meadow-land" of Damascus.

2. Situation and Natural Features

The river Barada (see ABANA) flows through Damascus and waters the plain, through which the *Nahr el-Awaj* (see PHARPAR) also flows, a few miles S. of the city. Surrounded on three sides by bare hills, and bordered on the E., its open side, by the desert, its well-watered and fertile Ghuta, with its streams and fountains, its fields and orchards, makes a vivid impression on the Arab of the desert. Arab. lit. is rich in praises of Damascus, which is described as an earthly paradise. The European or American traveler is apt to feel that these praises are exaggerated, and it is perhaps only in early summer that the beauty of the innumerable fruit trees—apricots, pomegranates, walnuts and many others—justifies enthusiasm. To see Damascus as the Arab sees it, we must approach it, as he does, from the desert. The Barada (Abana) is the life blood of Damascus. Confined in a narrow gorge until close to the city, where it spreads itself in many channels over the plain, only to lose itself a few miles away in the marshes that fringe the desert, its whole strength is expended in making a small area between the hills and the desert really fertile. That is why a city on this site is inevitable and permanent. Damascus, almost defenceless from a military point of view, is the natural mart and factory of inland Syria. In the course of its long history it has more than once enjoyed and lost political supremacy, but in all the vicissitudes of political fortune it has remained the natural harbor of the Syrian desert.

Damascus lies along the main stream of the Barada, almost entirely on its south bank. The city is about a mile long (E. to W.) and about half a mile broad (N. to S.). On the south side a long suburb, consisting for the most part of a single street, called the *Meidan*, stretches for a mile beyond the line of the city wall, terminating at the *Bawwabet Allah*, the "Gate of God," the starting-point of the *Haj*, the annual pilgrimage to Mecca. The city has thus roughly the shape of a broad-headed spoon, of which the *Meidan* is the handle. In the Gr period, a long, colonnaded street ran through the city, doubtless the "street which is called Straight" (Acts **9** 11). This street, along the course of which remains of columns have been discovered, runs westward from the *Babesh-Sherki*, the "East Gate." Part of it is still called *Derb el-Mustakim* ("Straight Street"), but it is not certain that it has borne the name through all the intervening cents. It runs between the Jewish and Christian quarters (on the left and right, respectively, going west), and terminates in the *Suk el-Midhatiyeh*, a bazaar built by Midhat Pasha, on the north of which is the main Moslem quarter, in which are the citadel and the Great Mosque. The houses are flat-roofed, and are usually built round a courtyard, in which is a fountain. The streets, with the exception of Straight Street, are mostly narrow and tortuous, but on the west side of the city there are some good covered bazaars. Damascus is not rich in antiquities. The Omayyad Mosque, or Great Mosque, replaced a Christian church, which in its time had taken the place of a pagan temple. The site was doubtless occupied from time immemorial by the chief religious edifice of the city. A small part of the ancient Christian church is still extant. Part of the city wall has been preserved, with a foundation going back to Rom times, surmounted by Arab work. The traditional site of Paul's escape (Acts **9** 25;

3. The City Itself

2 Cor **11** 33) and of the House of Naaman (2 K **5**) are pointed out to the traveler, but the traditions are valueless. The charm of Damascus lies in the life of the bazaars, in the variety of types which may be seen there—the Druse, the Kurd, the Bedouin and many others—and in its historical associations. It has always been a manufacturing city. Our word "damask" bears witness to the fame of its textile industry, and the "Damascus blades" of the Crusading period were equally famous; and though Timur (Tamerlane) destroyed the trade in arms in 1399 by carrying away the armorers to Samarcand, Damascus is still a city of busy craftsmen in cloth and wood. Its antiquity casts a spell of romance upon it. After a traceable history of thirty-five cents. it is still a populous and flourishing city, and, in spite of the advent of the railway and even the electric street car, it still preserves the flavor of the East.

ABANA RIVER.

4. Its History

(1) *The early period* (*to cir 950 BC*).—The origin of Damascus is unknown. Mention has already been made (§ 1) of the references to the city in Egyp inscriptions and in the Am Tab. It appears once—possibly twice—in the history of Abraham. In Gen **14** 15 we read that Abraham pursued the four kings as far as Hobah, "which is on the left hand [i.e. the north] of Damascus." But this is simply a geographical note which shows only that Damascus was well known at the time when Gen **14** was written. Greater interest attaches to Gen **15** 2, where Abraham complains that he is childless and that his heir is "Dammesek Eliezer" (ERV), for which the Syr version reads "Eliezer the Damaschul." The clause, however, is hopelessly obscure, and it is doubtful whether it contains any reference to Damascus at all. In the time of David Damascus was an Aramaean city, which assisted the neighboring Aramaean states in their unsuccessful wars against David (2 S **8** 5 f). These campaigns resulted indirectly in the establishment of a powerful Aramaean kingdom in Damascus. Rezon, son of Eliada, an officer in the army of Hadadezer, king of Zobah, escaped in the hour of defeat, and became a captain of banditti. Later he established himself in Damascus, and became its king (1 K **11** 23 ff). He cherished a not unnatural animosity against Israel, and the rise of a powerful and hostile kingdom in the Israelitish frontier was a constant source of anxiety to Solomon (1 K **11** 25).

(2) *The Aramaean kingdom* (*cir 950–732 BC*).—Whether Rezon was himself the founder of a dynasty is not clear. He has been identified with Hezion, father of Tab-rimmon, and grandfather of Ben-hadad (1 K **15** 18), but the identification, though a natural one, is insecure. Ben-hadad (Bir-idri) is the first king of Damascus, after Rezon, of whom we have any detailed knowledge. The disruption of the Heb kingdom afforded the Aramaeans an opportunity of playing off the rival Heb states against each other, and of bestowing their favors now on one, and now on the other. Ben-hadad was induced by Asa of Judah to accept a large bribe, or tribute, from the Temple treasures, and relieve Asa by attacking the Northern Kingdom (1 K **15** 18 ff). Some years later (cir 880 BC) Ben-hadad (or his successor?) defeated Omri of Israel, annexed several Israelitish cities, and secured the right of having Syrian "streets" (i.e. probably a bazaar for Syrian merchants) in Samaria (1 K **20** 34). Ben-hadad II (according to Winckler the two Ben-hadads are really identical, but this view, though just possible chronologically, conflicts with 1 K **20** 34) was the great antagonist of Ahab. His campaigns against Israel are narrated in 1 K **20** 22. At first successful, he was subsequently twice defeated by Ahab, and after the rout at Aphek was at the mercy of the conqueror, who treated him with generous leniency, claiming only the restoration of the lost Israelitish towns, and the right of establishing an Israelitish bazaar in Damascus. On the renewal of hostilities three years later Ahab

fell before Ramoth-gilead, and his death relieved Ben-hadad of the only neighboring monarch who could ever challenge the superiority of Damascus. Further light is thrown upon the history of Damascus at this time by the Assyrian inscriptions. In 854 BC the Assyrians defeated a coalition of Syrian and Palestine states (including Israel) under the leadership of Ben-hadad at Karkar. In 849 and 846 BC renewed attacks were made upon Damascus by the Assyrians, who, however, did not effect any considerable conquest. From this date until the fall of the city in 732 BC the power of the Aramaean kingdom depended upon the activity or quiescence of Assyria. Hazael, who murdered Ben-hadad and usurped his throne cir 844 BC, was attacked in 842 and 839, but during the next thirty years Assyria made no further advance westward. Hazael was able to devote all his energies to his western neighbors, and Israel suffered severely at his hands. In 803 Mari' of Damascus, who is probably identical with the Ben-hadad of 2 K **13** 3, Hazael's son, was made tributary to Ramman-nirari III of Assyria. This blow weakened Aram, and afforded Jeroboam II of Israel an opportunity of avenging the defeats inflicted upon his country by Hazael. In 773 Assyria again invaded the territory of Damascus. Tiglath-pileser III (745–727 BC) pushed vigorously westward, and in 738 Rezin of Damascus paid tribute. A year or two later he revolted, and attempted in concert with Pekah of Israel, to coerce Judah into joining an anti-Assyrian league (2 K **15** 37; **16** 5; Isa **7**). His punishment was swift and decisive. In 734 the Assyrians advanced and laid siege to Damascus, which fell in 732. Rezin was executed, his kingdom was overthrown, and the city suffered the fate which a few years later befell Samaria.

(4) *The middle period (cir 732 BC–650 AD).*—Damascus had now lost its political importance, and for more than two cents. we have only one or two inconsiderable references to it. It is mentioned in an inscription of Sargon (722–705 BC) as having taken part in an unsuccessful insurrection along with Hamath and Arpad. There are incidental references to it in Jer **49** 23 ff and Ezk **27** 18; **47** 16 ff. In the Pers period Damascus, if not politically of great importance, was a prosperous city. The overthrow of the Pers empire by Alexander was soon followed (301 BC) by the establishment of the Seleucid kingdom of Syria, with Antioch as its capital, and Damascus lost its position as the chief city of Syria. The center of gravity was moved toward the sea, and the maritime commerce of the Levant became more important than the trade of Damascus with the interior. In 111 BC the Syrian kingdom was divided, and Antiochus Cyzicenus became king of Coele-Syria, with Damascus as his capital. His successors, Demetrius Eucaerus and Antiochus Dionysus, had troubled careers, being involved in domestic conflicts and in wars with the Parthians, with Alexander Jannaeus of Judaea, and with Aretas the Nabataean, who obtained possession of Damascus in 85 BC. Tigranes, being of Armenia, held Syria for some years after this date, but was defeated by the Romans, and in 64 BC Pompey finally annexed the country. The position of Damascus during the first cent. and a half of Rom rule in Syria is obscure. For a time it was in Rom hands, and from 31 BC–33 AD its coins bear the names of Augustus or Tiberius. Subsequently it was again in the hands of the Nabataeans, and was ruled by an ethnarch, or governor, appointed by Aretas, the Nabataean king. This ethnarch adopted a hostile attitude to Paul (2 Cor **11** 32 f). Later, in the time of Nero, it again became a Rom city. In the early history of Christianity Damascus, as compared with Antioch, played a very minor part. But it is memorable in Christian history on account of its associations with Paul's conversion, and as the scene of his earliest Christian preaching (Acts **9** 1–25). All the NT references to the city relate to this event (Acts **9** 1–25; **22** 5–11; **26** 12.20; 2 Cor **11** 32 f; Gal **1** 17).

Traditional House of Ananias.

Afterward, under the early Byzantine emperor, Damascus, though important as an outpost of civilization on the edge of the desert, continued to be second to Antioch both politically and ecclesiastically. It was not until the Arabian conquest (634 AD when it passed out of Christian hands, and reverted to the desert, that it once more became a true capital.

(4) *Under Islam.*—Damascus has now been a Moslem city, or rather a city under Moslem rule, for nearly thirteen centuries. For about a cent. after 650 AD it was the seat of the Omayyad caliphs, and enjoyed a position of preëminence in the Moslem world. Later it was supplanted by Bagdad, and in the 10th cent. it came under the rule of the Fatimites of Egypt. Toward the close of the 11th cent. the Seljuk Turks entered Syria and captured Damascus. In the period of the Crusades the city, though never of decisive importance, played a considerable part, and was for a time the headquarters of Saladin. In 1300 it was plundered by the Tartars, and in 1399 Timur exacted an enormous ransom from it, and carried off its famous armorers, thus robbing it of one of its most important industries. Finally, in 1516 AD, the Osmanli Turks under Sultan Selim conquered Syria, and Damascus became, and still is, the capital of a province of the Ottoman Empire.

C. H. Thomson

DAMMESEK ELIEZER (Gen **15** 2 ERV). See Eliezer (1).

DAMN, dam, **DAMNATION,** dam-nā'shun, **DAMNABLE,** dam'na-b'l: These words have undergone a change of meaning since the AV was made. They are derived from Lat *damnare*="to inflict a loss," "to condemn," and that was their original meaning in Eng. Now they denote exclusively the idea of everlasting punishment in hell. It is often difficult to determine which meaning was intended by the translators in AV. They have been excluded altogether from RV. The words for which they stand in AV are:

(1) ἀπώλεια, *apōleia*, "destruction," tr[d] "damnable" and "damnation" only in 2 Pet **21** 3 (RV "destructive," "destruction"). False prophets taught doctrines calculated to destroy others, and themselves incurred the sentence of destruction such as overtook the fallen angels, the world in the Deluge, and the cities of the Plain. *Apōleia* occurs otherwise 16 times in the NT, and is always tr[d] in AV and RV by either "perdition" or "destruction": twice of waste of treasure (Mt **26** 8=Mk **14** 4); twice of the beast that comes out of the abyss and goes into perdition (Rev **17** 8.11). In all other cases, it refers to men, and defines the destiny that befalls them as the result of sin: Judas is the "son of perdition" (Jn **17** 12). Peter consigns Simon Magus and his money to perdition (Acts **8** 20).

Some men are "vessels of wrath fitted unto destruction" (Rom **9** 22), and others, their "end is perdition" (Phil **3** 19). It is the antithesis of salvation (He **10** 39; Phil **1** 28). Of the two ways of life, one leads to destruction (Mt **7** 13). Whether it is utter, final and irretrievable destruction is not stated.

(2) κρίνω, *krinō*, trd "damned" only in AV of 2 Thess **2** 12 (RV "judged") means "to judge" in the widest sense, "to form an opinion" (Lk **7** 43), and forensically "to test and try" an accused person. It can only acquire the sense of "judging guilty" or "condemning" from the context.

(3) κατακρίνω, *katakrinō*, trd "damned" only in AV of Mk **16** 16; Rom **14** 23 ("condemned" in RV), means properly "to give judgment against" or "to condemn" and is so trd 17 t in AV and always in RV.

(4) κρίσις, *krisis*, trd "damnation" in AV of Mt **23** 33; Mk **3** 29; Jn **5** 29 (RV "judgment," but in Mk **3** 29, "sin" for ἁμάρτημα, *hamártēma*), means (*a*) judgment in general like *krinō*, and is so used about 17 t, besides 14 t in the phrase "day of judgment"; (*b*) "condemnation," like *katakrinō*, about 14 t.

(5) κρίμα, *kríma*, trd in AV "damnation" 7 t (Mt **23** 14=Mk **12** 40=Lk **20** 47; Rom **3** 8; **13** 2; 1 Cor **11** 29; 1 Tim **5** 12), "condemnation" 6 t, "judgment" 13 t, "law" and "avenged" once each; in RV "condemnation" 9 t (Mt **23** 14 only inserted in m), "judgment" 17 t, and once in m, "lawsuit" and "sentence" once each. "Judgment" may be neutral, an impartial act of the judge weighing the evidence (so in Mt **7** 2; Acts **24** 25; Rom **11** 33; He **6** 2; 1 Pet **4** 17; Rev **20** 4) and "lawsuit" (1 Cor **6** 7); or it may be inferred from the context that judgment is unto condemnation (so in Rom **2** 2.3; **5** 16; Gal **5** 10; 2 Pet **2** 3; Rev **17** 1; **18** 20, and RV Rom **13** 2; 1 Cor **11** 29). In places where *krima* and *krisis* are rightly trd "condemnation," and where "judgment" regarded as an accomplished fact involves a sentence of guilt, they together with *katakrinō* define the relation of a person to the supreme authority, as that of a criminal, found and held guilty, and liable to punishment. So the Rom empire regarded Jesus Christ, and the thief on the cross (Lk **23** 40; **24** 20). But generally these words refer to man as a sinner against God, judged guilty by Him, and liable to the just penalty of sin. They imply nothing further as to the nature of the penalty or the state of man undergoing it, nor as to its duration. Nor does the word "eternal" (αἰών, αἰώνιος, *aiōn*, *aiōnios*, often wrongly trd "everlasting" in AV) when added to them, determine the question of duration. Condemnation is an act in the moral universe, which cannot be determined under categories of time.

These terms define the action of God in relation to man's conduct, as that of the Supreme Judge, but they express only one aspect of that relation which is only fully conceived, when coördinated with the more fundamental idea of God's Fatherhood. See ESCHATOLOGY; JUDGMENT.

LITERATURE.—Salmond, *Christian Doctrine of Immortality;* Charles, *Eschatology.*

T. REES

DAMSEL, dam'zel: A young, unmarried woman; a girl (lass); maiden (cf Fr. *demoiselle*). RV in Mt **26** 69; Jn **18** 17; Acts **12** 13; **16** 16 gives "maid" for παιδίσκη, *paidiskē*, "a girl," i.e. (spec.) a maidservant or young female slave (AV "damsel"), and "child" for παιδίον, *paidíon*, "a half-grown boy or girl," in Mk **5** 39.40 *bis*.41.

DAN (דָּן, *dān*, "judge"; Δάν, *Dán*): The fifth of Jacob's sons, the first borne to him by Bilhah, the maid of Rachel, to whom, as the child of her slave, he legally belonged. At his birth Rachel, whose barrenness had been a sore trial to her, exclaimed "God hath judged me . . . . and hath given me a son," so she called his name Dan, i.e. "judge" (Gen **30** 6). He was full brother of Naphtali. In Jacob's Blessing there is an echo of Rachel's words, "Dan shall judge his people" (Gen **49** 16). Of the patriarch Dan almost nothing is recorded. Of his sons at the settlement in Egypt only one, Hushim, is mentioned (Gen **46** 23). The name in Nu **26** 42 is Shuham.

1. Name

The tribe however stands second in point of numbers on leaving Egypt, furnishing 62,700 men of war (Nu **1** 39); and at the second census they were 64,400 strong (**26** 43). The standard of the camp of Dan in the desert march, with which were Asher and Naphtali, was on the north side of the tabernacle (Nu **2** 25; **10** 25; cf Josh **6** 9 AVm "gathering host"). The prince of the tribe was Ahiezer (Nu **1** 12). Among the spies Dan was represented by Ammiel the son of Gemalli (**13** 12). Of the tribe of Dan was Oholiab (AV "Aholiab") one of the wise-hearted artificers engaged in the construction of the tabernacle (Ex **31** 6). One who was stoned for blasphemy was the son of a Danite woman (Lev **24** 10 f). At the ceremony of blessing and cursing, Dan and Naphtali stood on Mount Ebal, while the other Rachel tribes were on Gerizim (Dt **27** 13). The prince of Dan at the division of the land was Bukki the son of Jogli (Nu **34** 22).

2. The Tribe

The portion assigned to Dan adjoined those of Ephraim, Benjamin and Judah, and lay on the western slopes of the mountain. The reference in Jgs **5** 17: "And Dan, why did he remain in ships?" seems to mean that on the W. Dan had reached the sea. But the passage is one of difficulty. We are told that the Amorites forced the children of Dan into the mountain (Jgs **1** 34), so they did not enjoy the richest part of their ideal portion, the fertile plain between the mountain and the sea. The strong hand of the house of Joseph kept the Amorites tributary, but did not drive them out. Later we find Dan oppressed by the Philis, against whom the heroic exploits of Samson were performed (Jgs **14** ff).

3. Territory

The expedition of the Danites recorded in Jgs **18** is referred to in Josh **19** 47 ff. The story affords a priceless glimpse of the conditions prevailing in those days. Desiring an extension of territory, the Danites sent out spies, who recommended an attack upon Laish, a city at the north end of the Jordan valley. The people, possibly a colony from Sidon, were careless in their fancied security. The land was large, and there was "no want of anything that was in the earth." The expedition of the 600, their dealings with Micah and his priest, their capture of Laish, and their founding of an idol shrine with priestly attendant, illustrate the strange mingling of lawlessness and superstition which was characteristic of the time. The town rebuilt on the site of Laish they called Dan—see following art. Perhaps 2 Ch **2** 14 may be taken to indicate that the Danites intermarried with the Phoenicians. Divided between its ancient seat in the S. and the new territory in the N. the tribe retained its place in Israel for a time (1 Ch **12** 35; **27** 22), but it played no part of importance in the subsequent history. The name disappears from the genealogical lists of Ch; and it is not mentioned among the tribes in Rev **7** 5 ff (Albright, *Annual Amer. Schools*, 1926, 17).

4. The Danite Raid

Samson was the one great man produced by Dan, and he seems to have embodied the leading characteristics of the tribe: unsteady, unscrupulous, violent, possessed of a certain grim humor; stealthy in tactics—"a serpent in the way, an adder in the path" (Gen **49** 17)—but swift and strong in striking—"a lion's whelp, that leapeth forth from Bashan" (Dt **33** 22). Along with Abel, Dan ranked as a city in which the true customs of old Israel were preserved (2 S **20** 18 LXX). W. Ewing

DAN: A city familiar as marking the northern limit of the land of Israel in the common phrase "from Dan even to Beer-sheba" (Jgs **20** 1; 1 S **3** 20, etc). Its ancient name was Laish or Leshem (Jgs **18** 7, etc). It was probably an outlying settlement of Tyre or Sidon. Its inhabitants, pursuing the ends of peaceful traders, were defenceless against the onset of the Danite raiders. Having captured the city the Danites gave it the name of their own tribal ancestor (Jgs **18**). It lay in the valley near Beth-rehob (ver 28). Jos places it near Mt. Lebanon and the fountain of the lesser Jordan, a day's journey from Sidon (*Ant*, V, iii, 1; VIII, viii, 4; *BJ*, IV, i, 1). *Onom* says it lay 4 Rom miles from Paneas on the way to Tyre, at the source of the Jordan. This points decisively to *Tell el-Ḳāḍy*, in the plain W. of Banias. The mound of this name—*Ḳāḍy* is the exact Arab. equivalent of the Heb *Dan*—rises from among the bushes and reeds to a height varying from 40 to 80 ft. The largest of all the springs of the Jordan rises on the west side. The waters join with those of a smaller spring on the other side to form *Nahr el-Leddān* which flows southward to meet the streams from *Bāniās* and *Ḥasbeiyeh*. The mound, which is the crater of an extinct volcano, has certain ancient remains on the south side, while the tomb of *Sheikh Marzuk* is sheltered by two holy trees. The sanctuary and ritual established by the Danites persisted as long as the house of God was in Shiloh, and the priesthood in this idolatrous shrine remained in the family of Jonathan till the conquest of Tiglath-pileser (Jgs **18** 30; 2 K **15** 29). Here Jeroboam I set up the golden calf. The ancient sanctity of the place would tend to promote the success of his scheme (1 K **12** 28 f, etc). The calf, according to a Jewish tradition, was taken away by Tiglath-pileser. Dan fell before Benhadad, king of Syria (1 K **15** 20; 2 Ch **16** 4). It was regained by Jeroboam II (2 K **14** 25). It shared the country's fate at the hands of Tiglath-pileser (2 K **15** 29).

It was to this district that Abraham pursued the army of Chedorlaomer (Gen **14** 14). For Dr. G. A. Smith's suggestion that Dan may have been at *Bāniās* see *HGHL*[1], 473, 480 f. W. Ewing

DAN (Ezk **27** 19 AV). See Vedan.

DANCING, dan'sing. See Games.

DANDLE, dan'd'l (שֳׁעֳשַׁע, *shā'ŏsha'*, a Pulpal form, from root שָׁעַע, *shā'a'*, with sense of to "be caressed"). Occurs in Isa **66** 12, "shall be dandled upon the knees."

DANGER, dān'jẽr: Danger does not express a state of reality but a possibility. In Mt **5** 21 f, however, and also AV Mk **3** 29 (RV "but is guilty of an eternal sin") the expression "danger" refers to a certainty, for the danger spoken of is in one case judgment which one brings upon himself, and in the other the committing of an unpardonable sin. Both are the necessary consequences of a man's conduct. The reason for translating the Gr ἔνοχος, *énochos* (lit. "to be held in anything so one cannot escape") by "is in danger," instead of "guilty" or "liable," may be due to the translator's conception of these passages as a warning against such an act rather than as a statement of the judgment which stands pronounced over every man who commits the sin. A. L. Breslich

DANIEL, dan'yel (דָּנִיֵּאל, *dānīyē'l*, דָּנִאֵל, *dāni'ēl*, "God is my judge"; Δανιήλ, *Daniḗl*):

(1) One of the sons of David (1 Ch **3** 1).

(2) A Levite of the family of Ithamar (Ezr **8** 2; Neh **10** 6).

(3) A prophet of the time of Nebuchadnezzar and Cyrus, the hero and author of the Book of Dnl.

1. Early Life

We know nothing of the early life of Daniel, except what is recorded in the book bearing his name. Here it is said that he was one of the youths of royal or noble seed, who were carried captive by Nebuchadnezzar in the third year of Jehoiakim, king of Judah. These youths were without blemish, well-favored, skilful in all wisdom, endued with knowledge, and understanding science, and such as had ability to stand in the king's palace. The king commanded to teach them the knowledge and tongue of the Chaldaeans; and appointed for them a daily portion of the king's food and of the wine which he drank. After having been thus nourished for three years, they were to stand before the king. Ashpenaz, the master or chief of the eunuchs, into whose hands they had been intrusted, following a custom of the time, gave to each of these youths a new and Bab name. To Daniel, he gave the name Belteshazzar. In Bab this name was probably Belu-lita-sharri-usur, which means "O Bel, protect thou the hostage of the king," a most appropriate name for one in the place which Daniel occupied as a hostage of Jehoiakim at the court of the king of Babylon. The youths were probably from 12 to 15 years of age at the time when they were carried captive. (For changes of names, cf Joseph changed to Zaphenath-paneah [Gen **41** 45]; Eliakim, to Jehoiakim [2 K **23** 34]; Mattaniah, to Zedekiah [2 K **24** 17]; and the two names of the high priest Johanan's brother in the Sachau Papyri, i.e. Ostan and Anani.)

Having purposed in his heart that he would not defile himself with the food and drink of the king, Daniel requested of Ashpenaz permission to eat vegetables and drink water. Through the favor of God, this request was granted, notwithstanding the fear of Ashpenaz that his head would be endangered to the king on account of the probably resulting poor appearance of the youths living upon this blood-diluting diet, in comparison with the expected healthy appearance of the others of their class. However, ten days' trial having been first granted, and at the end of that time their countenances having been found fairer and their flesh fatter than the other youths', the permission was made permanent; and God gave to Daniel and his companions knowledge and skill in all learning and wisdom, and to Daniel understanding in all visions and dreams; so that at the end of the three years when the king communed with them, he found them much superior to all the magicians and enchanters in every matter of wisdom and understanding.

Daniel's public activities were in harmony with his education. His first appearance was as an interpreter of the dream recorded in Dnl **2**.

2. Dream-Interpreter

Nebuchadnezzar having seen in his dream a vision of a great image, excellent in brightness and terrible in appearance, its head of fine gold, its breast and its arms of silver, its belly and its thighs of brass, its legs of iron, its feet part of iron and part of clay, beheld a stone cut out without hands smiting the image and breaking it in pieces, until it became like chaff and was carried away by the wind; while the stone that smote the image became a great mountain and filled the whole earth. When the king awoke from his troubled sleep, he forgot, or feigned that he had forgotten, the dream, and summoned the wise men of Babylon both to tell him the dream and

SOURCES OF THE JORDAN AT DAN

to give the interpretation thereof. The wise men having said that they could not tell the dream, nor interpret it as long as it was untold, the king threatened them with death. Daniel, who seems not to have been present when the other wise men were before the king, when he was informed of the threat of the king, and that preparations were being made to slay all of the wise men of Babylon, himself and his three companions included, boldly went in to the king and requested that he would appoint a time for him to appear to show the interpretation. Then he went to his house, and he and his companions prayed, and the dream and its interpretation were made known unto Daniel. At the appointed time, the dream was explained and the four Hebrews were loaded with wealth and given high positions in the service of the king. In the 4th chapter, we have recorded Daniel's interpretation of the dream of Nebuchadnezzar about the great tree that was hewn at the command of an angel, thus prefiguring the insanity of the king.

3. Interpreter of Signs

Daniel's third great appearance in the book is in ch **5**, where he is called upon to explain the extraordinary writing upon the wall of Belshazzar's palace, which foretold the end of the Bab empire and the incoming of the Medes and Persians. For this service Daniel was clothed with purple, a chain of gold put around his neck, and he was made the third ruler in the kingdom.

4. Seer of Visions

Daniel, however, was not merely an interpreter of other men's visions. In the last six chapters we have recorded four or five of his own visions, all of which are taken up with revelations concerning the future history of the great world empires, esp. in their relation to the people of God, and predictions of the final triumph of the Messiah's kingdom.

5. Official of the Kings

In addition to his duties as seer and as interpreter of signs and dreams, Daniel also stood high in the governmental service of Nebuchadnezzar, Belshazzar, and Darius the Mede, and perhaps also of Cyrus. The Book of Dnl, our only reliable source of information on this subject, does not tell us much about his civil duties and performances. It does say, however, that he was chief of the wise men, that he was in the gate of the king, and that he was governor over the whole province of Babylon under Nebuchadnezzar; that Belshazzar made him the third ruler in his kingdom; and that Darius made him one of the three presidents to whom his hundred and twenty satraps were to give account; and that he even thought to set him over his whole kingdom. In all of these positions he seems to have conducted himself with faithfulness and judgment. While in the service of Darius the Mede, he aroused the antipathy of the other presidents and of the satraps. Unable to find any fault with his official acts, they induced the king to make a decree, apparently general in form and purpose, but really aimed at Daniel alone. They saw that they could find no valid accusation against him, unless they found it in connection with something concerning the law of his God. They therefore caused the king to make a decree that no one should make a request of anyone for the space of thirty days, save of the king. Daniel, having publicly prayed three times a day as he was in the habit of doing, was caught in the act, accused, and on account of the irrevocability of a law of the Medes and Persians, was condemned in accordance with the decree to be cast into a den of lions. The king was much troubled at this, but was unable to withhold the punishment. However, he expressed to Daniel his belief that his God in whom he trusted continually would deliver him; and so indeed it came to pass. For in the morning, when the king drew near to the mouth of the den, and called to him, Daniel said that God had sent His angel and shut the mouths of the lions. So Daniel was taken up unharmed, and at the command of the king his accusers, having been cast into the den, were destroyed before they reached the bottom.

LITERATURE.—Besides the commentaries and other works mentioned in the art. on the Book of Dnl, valuable information may be found in Jos and in Payne Smith's *Lectures on Daniel.*

R. DICK WILSON

DANIEL, dan'yel, BOOK OF:

I. Name.—The Book of Dnl is rightly so called, whether we consider Daniel as the author of it, or as the principal person mentioned in it.

II. Place in the Canon.—In the Eng. Bible, Dnl is placed among the Major Prophets, immediately after Ezk, thus following the order of the Sept and of the Lat Vulg. In the Heb Bible, however, it is placed in the third division of the Canon, called the Kethuvim or writings, by the Hebrews, and the hagiographa, or holy writings, by the Seventy. It has been claimed, that Dnl was placed by the Jews in the third part of the Canon, either because they thought the inspiration of its author to be of a lower kind than was that of the other prophets, or because the book was written after the second or prophetical part of the Canon had been closed. It is more probable, that the book was placed in this part of the Heb Canon, because Daniel is not called a *nābhī'* ("prophet"), but was rather a *ḥōzeh* ("seer") and a *ḥākhām* ("wise man"). None but the works of the *n^{e}bhī'īm* were put in the second part of the Jewish Canon, the third being reserved for the heterogeneous works of seers, wise men, and priests, or for those that do not mention the name or work of a prophet, or that are poetical in form. A confusion has arisen, because the Gr word prophet is used to render the two Heb words *nābhī'* and *ḥōzeh.* In the Scriptures, God is said to speak to the former, whereas the latter see visions and dream dreams. Some have attempted to explain the position of Daniel by assuming that he had the prophetic gift without holding the prophetic office. It must be kept in mind that all reasons given to account for the order and place of many of the books in the Canon are purely conjectural, since we have no historical evidence bearing upon the subject earlier than the time of Jesus ben Sirach, who wrote probably about 180 BC.

III. Divisions of the Book.—According to its subject-matter, the book falls naturally into two great divisions, each consisting of six chapters, the first portion containing the historical sections, and the second the apocalyptic, or predictive, portions; though the former is not devoid of predictions, nor the latter of historical statements. More specifically, the first chapter is introductory to the whole book; chs **2–6** describe some marvelous events in the history of Daniel and his three companions in their relations with the rulers of Babylon; and chs **7–12** narrate some visions of Daniel concerning the great world-empires, esp. in relation to the kingdom of God.

According to the languages in which the book is written, it may be divided into the Aram. portion, extending from **2** 4*b* to the end of ch **7,** and a Heb portion embracing the rest of the book.

IV. Languages.—The language of the book is partly Heb and partly a dialect of Aram., which has been called Chaldee, or Bib. Aram. This Aram. is almost exactly the same as that which is found in portions of Ezr. On account of the large number of Bab and Pers words characteristic of this Aram. and of that of the papyri recently found in Egypt, as well as on account of the general similarity of the nominal, verbal and other forms, and of the syntactical construction, the Aram. of this period might properly be called the Bab-Pers Aram. With the exception of the sign used to denote the sound *dh,* and of the use of *ḳōph* in a few cases where Dnl has *'ayin,* the spelling in the papyri is the same in general as that in the Bib. books. Whether the change of spelling was made at a later time in the MSS of Dnl, or whether it was a peculiarity of the Bab Aram. as distinguished from the Egyp, or whether it was due to the unifying, scientific genius of Daniel himself, we have no means at present to determine. In view of the fact that the Elephantine Papyri frequently employ the *d* sign to express the *dh* sound, and that it is always employed in Ezr to express it; in view further of the fact that the *z* sign is found as late as the earliest Nabatean inscription, that of 70 BC (see Euting, 349: 1, 2, 4) to express the *dh* sound, it seems fatuous to insist on the ground of the writing of these two sounds in the Book of Dnl, that it cannot have been written in the Pers period. As to the use of *ḳōph* and *'ayin* for the Aram. sound which corresponds to the Heb *çadhē* when equivalent to an Arab. *dad,* any hasty conclusion is debarred by the fact that the Aram. papyri of the 5th cent. BC, the MSS of the Sam Tg and the Mandaic MSS written from 600 to 900 AD all employ the two letters to express the one sound. The writing of *'āleph* and *hē* without any proper discrimination occurs in the papyri as well as in Dnl. The only serious objection to the early date of Dnl upon the ground of its spelling is that which is based upon the use of a final *n* in the pronominal suffix of the second and third persons masc. pl. instead of the *m* of the Aram. papyri and of the Zakir and Sendschirli inscriptions. It is possible that Dnl was influenced in this by the corresponding forms of the Bab language. The Syr and Mandaic dialects of the Aram. agree with the Bab in the formation of the pronominal suffixes of the second and third persons masc. pl., as against the Heb, Arab., Minaean, Sabaean and Ethiopic. It is possible that the occurrence of *m* in some west Aram. documents may have arisen through the influence of the Heb and Phoen, and that pure Aram. always had *n* just as we find it in Assyr and Bab, and in all east Aram. documents thus far discovered.

The supposition that the use of *y* in Dnl as a preformative of the third person masculine of the imperfect proves a Palestinian provenience has been shown to be untenable by the discovery that the earliest east Syr also used *y.* (See M. Pognon, *Inscriptions sémitiques,* première partie, 17.)

This inscription is dated 73 AD. This proof that in the earlier stages of its history the east Aram. was in this respect the same as that found in Dnl is confirmed by the fact that the forms of the 3d person of the imperfect found in the proper names on the Aram. dockets of the Assyr inscriptions also have the preformative *y.* (See *CIS,* II, 47.)

V. Purpose of the Book.—The book is not intended to give an account of the life of Daniel. It gives neither his lineage, nor his age, and recounts but a few of the events of his long career. Nor is it meant to give a record of the history of Israel during the exile, nor even of the captivity in Babylon. Its purpose is to show how by His providential guidance, His miraculous interventions, His foreknowledge and almighty power, the God of heaven controls and directs the forces of Nature and the history of nations, the lives of Heb captives and of the mightiest of the kings of the earth, for the accomplishment of His Divine and beneficent plans for His servants and people.

VI. Unity.—The unity of the book was first denied by Spinoza, who suggested that the first part was taken from the chronological works of the Chaldaeans, basing his supposition upon the difference of language between the former and latter parts. Newton followed Spinoza in suggesting two parts, but began his second division with ch **7,** where the narrative passes over from the 3d to the 1st person. Köhler follows Newton, claiming, however, that the visions were written by the Daniel of the exile, but that the first 6 chapters were composed by a later writer who also redacted the whole work. Von Orelli holds that certain prophecies of Daniel were enlarged and interpolated by a Jew living in the time of Antiochus Epiphanes, in order to show his contemporaries the bearing of the predictions of the book upon those times of oppression. Zöckler and Lange hold to the unity of the book in general; but the former thought that **11** 5–45 is an interpolation; and the latter, that **10** 1—**11** 44 and **12** 5–13 have been inserted in the original work. Meinhold holds that the Aram. portions existed as early as the times of Alexander the Great—a view to which Strack also inclines. Eichhorn held that the book consisted of ten different original sections, which are bound together merely by the circumstance that they are all concerned with Daniel and his three friends. Finally, De Lagarde, believing that the fourth kingdom was the Rom, held that ch **7** was written about 69 AD. (For the best discussion of the controversies about the unity of Dnl, see Eichhorn, *Einleitung,* §§ 612–19, and Buhl in *RE,* IV, 449–51.)

VII. Genuineness.—With the exception of the neo-Platonist Porphyry, a Gr non-Christian philosopher of the 3d cent. AD, the genuineness of the Book of Dnl was denied by no one until the rise of the deistic movement in the 17th cent. The attacks upon the genuineness of the book have been based upon (1) the predictions, (2) the miracles, (3) the text, (4) the language, (5) the historical statements.

1. The Predictions

The assailants of the genuineness of Dnl on the ground of the predictions found therein, may be divided into two classes—those who deny prediction in general, and those who claim that the apocalyptic character of the predictions of Dnl is a sufficient proof of their lack of genuineness. The first of these two classes includes properly those only who deny not merely Christianity, but theism; and the answering of them may safely be left to those who defend the doctrines of theism, and particularly of revelation. The second class of assailants is, however, of a different character, since it consists of those who are sincere believers in Christianity and predictive prophecy. They claim, however, that certain characteristics of definiteness and detail, distinguishing the predictive portions of the Book of Dnl from other predictions of the OT, bring the genuineness of Dnl into question.

The kind of prediction found here, ordinarily called apocalyptic, is said to have arisen first in the 2d cent. BC, when parts of the Book of En and of the Sibylline Oracles were written; and a main characteristic of an apocalypse is said to be that it records past events as if they were still future, throwing the speaker back into some distant past time, for the purpose of producing on the reader the impression that the book contains real predictions, thus gaining credence for the statements of the writer and giving consolation to those who are thus led to believe in the providential foresight of God for those who trust in Him.

Since those who believe that God has spoken unto man by His Son and through the prophets will not be able to set limits to the extent and definiteness of the revelations which He may have seen fit to make through them, nor to prescribe the method, style, time and character of the revelations, this attack on the genuineness of Dnl may safely be left to the defenders of the possibility and the fact of a revelation. One who believes in these may logically believe in the genuineness of Dnl, as far as this objection goes. That there are spurious apocalypses no more proves that all are spurious than that there are spurious gospels or epistles proves that there are no genuine ones. The spurious epp. of Philaris do not prove that Cicero's Letters are not genuine; nor do the false statements of 2 Macc, nor the many spurious Acts of the Apostles, prove that 1 Macc or Luke's Acts of the Apostles is not genuine. Nor does the fact that the oldest portions of the spurious apocalypses which have been preserved to our time are thought to have been written in the 2d cent. BC, prove that no apocalypses, either genuine or spurious, were written before that time. There must have been a beginning, a first apocalypse, at some time, if ever. Besides, if we admit that the earliest parts of the Book of En and of the Sibylline Oracles were written about the middle of the 2d cent. BC, whereas the Book of Esd was written about 300 AD, 450 years later, we can see no good literary reason why Dnl may not have antedated En by 350 years. The period between 500 BC and 150 BC is so almost entirely devoid of all known Heb literary productions as to render it exceedingly precarious for anyone to express an opinion as to what works may have characterized that long space of time.

2. The Miracles

Secondly, as to the objections made against the Book of Dnl on the ground of the number or character of the miracles recorded, we shall only say that they affect the whole Christian system, which is full of the miraculous from beginning to end. If we begin to reject the books of the Bible because miraculous events are recorded in them, where indeed shall we stop?

3. The Text

Thirdly, a more serious objection, as far as Dnl itself is concerned, is the claim of Eichhorn that the original text of the Aram. portion has been so thoroughly tampered with and changed, that we can no longer get at the genuine original composition. We ourselves can see no objection to the belief that these Aram. portions were written first of all in Heb, or even, if you will, in Bab; nor to the supposition that some Gr translators modified the meaning in their version either intentionally, or through a misunderstanding of the original. We claim, however, that the composite Aram. of Dnl agrees in almost every particular of orthography, etymology and syntax, with the Aram. of the North Sem inscriptions of the 9th, 8th and 7th cents. BC and of the Egyp papyri of the 5th cent. BC, and that the vocabulary of Dnl has an admixture of Heb, Bab and Pers words similar to that of the papyri of the 5th cent. BC; whereas, it differs in composition from the Aram. of the Nabateans, which is devoid of Pers, Heb, and Bab words, and is full of Arabisms, and also from that of the Palmyrenes, which is full of Gr words, while having but one or two Pers words, and no Heb or Bab.

As to different recensions, we meet with a similar difficulty in Jeremiah without anyone's impugning on that account the genuineness of the work as a whole. As to interpolations of verses or sections, they are found in the Sam recension of the Heb text and in the Sam and other Tgs, as also in certain places in the text of the NT, Jos and many other ancient literary works, without causing us to disbelieve in the genuineness of the rest of their works, or of the works as a whole.

4. The Language

Fourthly, the objections to the genuineness of Dnl based on the presence in it of three Gr names of musical instruments and of a number of Pers words do not seem nearly as weighty today as they did a hundred years ago. The Gr inscriptions at Abu Simbal in Upper Egypt dating from the time of Psamtek II in the early part of the 6th cent. BC, the discovery of the Minoan inscriptions and ruins in Crete, the revelations of the wide commercial relations of the Phoenicians in the early part of the 1st millennium BC, the lately published inscriptions of Sennacherib about his campaigns in Cilicia against the Gr seafarers to which Alexander Polyhistor and Abydenus had referred, telling about his having carried many Greeks captive to Nineveh about 700 BC, the confirmation of the wealth and expensive ceremonies of Nebuchadnezzar made by his own building and other inscriptions, all assure us of the possibility of the use of Gr musical instruments at Babylon in the 6th cent. BC. This, taken along with the well-known fact that names of articles of commerce and esp. of musical instruments go with the thing, leave no room to doubt that a writer of the 6th cent. BC may have known and used borrowed Gr terms. The Aramaeans being the great commercial middlemen between Egypt and Greece on the one hand and Babylon and the Orient on the other, and being in addition a subject people, would naturally adopt many foreign words into their vocabulary.

As to the presence of the so-called Pers words in Dnl, it must be remembered that many words which were formerly considered to be such have been found to be Bab. As to the others, perhaps all of them may be Median rather than Pers; and if so, the children of Israel who were carried captive to the cities of the Medes in the middle of the 8th cent. BC, and the Aramaeans, many of whom were subject to the Medes, at least from the time of the fall of Nineveh about 607 BC, may well have adopted many words into their vocabulary from the language of their rulers. Daniel was not writing merely for the Jews who had been carried captive by Nebuchadnezzar, but for all Israelites throughout the world. Hence, he would properly use a language which his scattered readers would understand rather than the purer idiom of Judaea. Most of his foreign terms are names of officials, legal terms, and articles of clothing, for which there were no suitable terms existing in the earlier Heb or Aram. There was nothing for a writer to do but to invent new terms, or to transfer the current foreign words into his native language. The latter was the preferable method and the one which he adopted.

5. Historical Statements

Fifthly, objections to the genuineness of the Book of Dnl are made on the ground of the historical misstatements which are said to be found in it. These may be classed as (1) chronological, (2) geographical, and (3) various.

(1) *Chronological objections.*—The first chronological objection is derived from Dnl **1** 1, where it is said that Nebuchadnezzar made an expedition against Jerus in the 3d year of Jehoiakim, whereas Jeremiah seems to imply that the expedition was made in the 4th year of that king. As Daniel was writing primarily for the Jews of Babylon, he would naturally use the system of dating that was

employed there; and this system differed in its method of denoting the 1st year of a reign from that used by the Egyptians and by the Jews of Jerus for whom Jeremiah wrote.

The second objection is derived from the fact that Daniel is said (Dnl **1** 21) to have lived unto the 1st year of Cyrus the king, whereas in **10** 1 he is said to have seen a vision in the 3d year of Cyrus, king of Persia. These statements are easily reconciled by supposing that in the former case it is the 1st year of Cyrus as king of Babylon, and in the second, the 3d year of Cyrus as king of Persia.

The third chronological objection is based on **6** 28, where it is said that Daniel prospered in the kingdom of Darius and in the kingdom of Cyrus the Persian. This statement is harmonized with the facts revealed by the monuments and with the statements of the book itself by supposing that Darius reigned synchronously with Cyrus, but as sub-king under him.

The fourth objection is based on **8** 1, where Daniel is said to have seen a vision in the third year of Belshazzar the king. If we suppose that Belshazzar was king of the Chaldaeans while his father was king of Babylon, just as Cambyses was king of Babylon while his father, Cyrus, was king of the lands, or as Nabonidus II seems to have been king of Harran while his father, Nabonidus I, was king of Babylon, this statement will harmonize with the other statements made with regard to Belshazzar.

(2) *Geographical objections.*—As to the geographical objections, three only need be considered as important. The first is, that Shushan seems to be spoken of in **7** 2 as subject to Babylon, whereas it is supposed by some to have been at that time subject to Media. Here we can safely rest upon the opinion of Winckler, that at the division of the Assyr dominions among the allied Medes and Babylonians, Elam became subject to Babylon rather than to Media. If, however, this opinion could be shown not to be true, we must remember that Daniel is said to have been at Shushan in a vision.

The second geographical objection is based on the supposition that Nebuchadnezzar would not have gone against Jerus, leaving an Egyp garrison at Carchemish in his rear, thus endangering his line of communication and a possible retreat to Babylon. This objection has no weight, now that the position of Carchemish has been shown to be, not at Circesium, as formerly conjectured, but at Jirabis, 150 miles farther up the Euphrates. Carchemish would have cut off a retreat to Nineveh, but was far removed from the direct line of communication with Babylon.

The third geographical objection is derived from the statement that Darius placed 120 satraps in, or over, all his kingdom. The objection rests upon a false conception of the meaning of satrap and of the extent of a satrapy, there being no reason why a sub-king under Darius may not have had as many satraps under him as Sargon of Assyria had governors and deputies under him; and the latter king mentions 117 peoples and countries over which he appointed his deputies to rule in his place.

(3) *Other objections.*—Various other objections to the genuineness of Dnl have been made, the principal being those derived from the supposed non-existence of Kings Darius the Mede and Belshazzar the Chaldaean, from the use of the word Chaldaean to denote the wise men of Babylon, and from the silence of other historical sources as to many of the events recorded in Dnl. The discussion of the existence of Belshazzar and Darius the Mede will be found under BELSHAZZAR and DARIUS. As to the argument from silence in general, it may be said that it reduces itself in fact to the absence of all reference to Daniel on the monuments, in the Book of Ecclus, and in the post-exilic lit. As to the latter books it proves too much; for Hag, Zec, and Mal, as well as Ezr, Neh, and Est, refer to so few of the older canonical books and earlier historical persons and events, that it is not fair to expect them to refer to Daniel—at least, to use their not referring to him or his book as an argument against the existence of either before the time when they were written. As to Ecclus, we might have expected him to mention Daniel or the Three Children; but who knows what reasons Ben Sira may have had for not placing them in his list of Heb heroes? Perhaps, since he held the views which later characterized the Sadducees, he may have passed Daniel by because of his views on the resurrection and on angels. Perhaps he failed to mention any of the four companions because none of their deeds had been wrought in Pal; or because their deeds exalted too highly the heathen monarchies to which the Jews were subject. Or, more likely, the book may have been unknown to him, since very few copies at best of the whole OT can have existed in his time, and the Book of Dnl may not have gained general currency in Pal before it was made so preëminent by the fulfilment of its predictions in the Maccabean times.

It is not satisfactory to say that Ben Sira did not mention Daniel and his companions, because the stories concerning them had not yet been imbedded in a canonical book, inasmuch as he does place Simon, the high priest, among the greatest of Israel's great men, although he is not mentioned in any canonical book. In conclusion, it may be said, that while it is impossible for us to determine why Ben Sira does not mention Daniel and his three companions among his worthies, if their deeds were known to him, it is even more impossible to understand how these stories concerning them cannot merely have arisen but have been accepted as true, between 180 BC, when Ecclus is thought to have been written, and 169 BC, when, according to 1 Macc, Matthias, the first of the Asmoneans, exhorted his brethren to follow the example of the fortitude of Ananias and his friends.

As to the absence of all mention of Daniel on the contemporary historical documents of Babylon and Persia, such mention is not to be expected, inasmuch as those documents give the names of none who occupied positions such as, or similar to, those which Daniel is said to have filled.

VIII. Interpretation.—Questions of the interpretation of particular passages may be looked for in the commentaries and special works. As to the general question of the kind of prophecy found in the Book of Dnl, it has already been discussed above under the caption of "Genuineness." As to the interpretation of the world monarchies which precede the monarchy of the Messiah Prince, it may be said, however, that the latest discoveries, ruling out as they do a separate Median empire that included Babylon, support the view that the four monarchies are the Bab, the Pers, the Gr, and the Rom. According to this view, Darius the Mede was only a sub-king under Cyrus the Pers. Other interpretations have been made by selecting the four empires from those of Assyria, Babylonia, Media, Persia, Medo-Persia, Alexander, the Seleucids, the Romans, and the Mohammedans. The first and the last of these have generally been excluded from serious consideration. The main dispute is as to whether the 4th empire was that of the Seleucids, or that of the Romans, the former view being held commonly by those who hold to the composition of Dnl in the 2d cent. BC, and the latter by those who hold to the traditional view that it was written in the 6th cent. BC.

IX. Doctrines.—It is universally admitted that the teachings of Daniel with regard to angels and the resurrection are more explicit than those found elsewhere in the OT. As to angels, Daniel attributes to them names, ranks, and functions not mentioned by others. It has become common in certain quarters to assert that these peculiarities of Daniel are due to Pers influences. The Bab monuments, however, have revealed the fact that the Babylonians believed in both good and evil spirits with names, ranks, and different functions. These spirits correspond in several respects to the Heb angels, and may well have afforded Daniel the background for his visions. Yet, in all such matters, it must be remembered that Daniel purports to give us a vision, or revelation; and a revelation cannot be bound by the ordinary laws of time and human influence.

As to the doctrine of the resurrection, it is generally admitted that Daniel adds some new and distinct features to that which is taught in the other canonical books of the Old Testament. But it will be noted that he does not dwell upon this doctrine, since he mentions it only in **12** 2. The materials for his doctrine are to be found in Isa **26** 14.21 and **66** 24; Ezk **37** 1–14, and in Job **14** 12; **19** 25; Hos **6** 2; 1 K **17**; 2 K **4**, and **8** 1–5, as well as in the use of the words for sleep and awakening from sleep, or from the dust, for everlasting life or everlasting contempt in Isa **26** 19; Ps **76** 6; **13** 3; **127** 2; Dt **31** 16; 2 S **7** 12; 1 K **1** 21; Job **7** 21, and Jer **20** 11; **23** 40. The essential ideas and phraseology of Daniel's teachings are found in Isa, Jer, and Ezk. The first two parts of the books of En and 2 Macc make much of the resurrection; but on the other hand, Eccl seems to believe not even in the immortality of the soul, and Wisd and 1 Macc do not mention a resurrection of the body.

That the post-exilic prophets do not mention a resurrection does not prove that they knew nothing about Dnl any more than it proves that they knew nothing about Isa, Jer, and Ezk.

There are resemblances, it is true, between the teachings of Daniel with regard to the resurrection and those of the Avesta. But so are there between his doctrines and the ideas of the Egyptians, which had existed for millenniums before his time. Besides there is no proof of any derivation of doctrines from the Persians by the writers of the canonical books of the Jews; and, as we have seen above, both the ideas and verbiage of Daniel are to be found in the acknowledgedly early Heb literature. And finally, this attempt to find a natural origin for all Bib. ideas leaves out of sight the fact that the Scriptures contain revelations from God, which transcend the ordinary course of human development. To a Christian, therefore, there can be no reason for believing that the doctrines of Dnl may not have been promulgated in the 6th cent. BC.

Commentaries and Introductions

The best commentaries on Dnl from a conservative point of view are those by Calvin, Moses Stuart, Keil, Zöckler, Strong in Lange's *Bibelwerk*, Fuller in the *Speaker's Commentary*, Thomson in the *Pulpit Commentary*, and Wright, *Daniel and His Critics*. The best defences of Daniel's authenticity and genuineness are Hengstenberg, *Authenticity of the Book of Daniel*, Tregelles, *Defense of the Authenticity*, Auberlen, *The Prophecies of Daniel*, Fuller, *Essay on the Authenticity of Daniel*, Pusey, *Daniel the Prophet* (still the best of all), C. H. H. Wright, *Daniel and His Critics*, Kennedy, *The Book of Daniel from the Christian Standpoint*, Joseph Wilson, *Daniel*, and Sir Robert Anderson, *Daniel in the Critics' Den*. One should consult also Pinches, *The Old Testament in the Light of the Historical Records of Assyria and Babylonia*, Clay, *Light on the Old Testament from Babel*, and Orr, *The Problem of the OT*. For Eng. readers, the radical school is best represented by Driver in his *Lit. of the OT* and in his *Daniel;* by Bevan, *The Book of Daniel;* by Prince, *Commentary on Daniel*, and by Cornill in his *Intro to the OT*.

X. Apocryphal Additions.—In the Gr translations of Dnl three or four pieces are added which are not found in the original Heb or Aram. text as it has come down to us. These are The Prayer of Azarias, The Song of the Three Holy Children, Susanna, and Bel and the Dragon. These additions have all been rejected from the Canon by the Protestant churches because they are not contained in the Heb Canon. In the Church of England they are "read for example of life and instruction of manners." The Three was "ordered in the rubric of the first Prayer Book of Edward VI (AD 1549) to be used in Lent as a responsory to the OT Lesson at the Morning Prayer." It contains the Prayer of Azarias from the midst of the fiery furnace, and the song of praise by the three children for their deliverance; the latter being couched largely in phrases borrowed from Ps **148**. Sus presents to us the story of a virtuous woman who resisted the seductive attempts of two judges of the elders of the people, whose machinations were exposed through the wisdom of Daniel who convicted them of false witness by the evidence of their own mouth, so that they were put to death according to the law of Moses; and from that day forth Daniel was held in great reputation in the sight of the people. Bel contains three stories. The first relates how Daniel destroyed the image of Bel which Nebuchadnezzar worshipped, by showing by means of ashes strewn on the floor of the temple that the offerings to Bel were devoured by the priests who came secretly into the temple by night. The second tells how Daniel killed the Dragon by throwing lumps of mingled pitch, fat and hair into his mouth, so causing the Dragon to burst asunder. The third gives a detailed account of the lions' den, stating that there were seven lions and that Daniel lived in the den six days, being sustained by broken bread and pottage which a prophet named Habakkuk brought to him through the air, an angel of the Lord having taken him by the arm and borne him by the hair of his head and through the vehemency of his spirit set him in Babylon over the den, into which he dropped the food for Daniel's use.

Literature.—For commentaries on the additions to the Book of Dnl, see the works on Dnl cited above, and also *The Apocrypha* by Churton and others; the volume on the Apocrypha in Lange's *Commentary* by Bissell; "The Apocrypha" by Wace in the *Speaker's Commentary*, and Schürer, *History of the Jewish People*.

R. Dick Wilson

DANITES, dan′īts (הַדָּנִי, *ha-dānī*): Occurs as describing those belonging to Dan in Jgs **13** 2; **18** 1.11; 1 Ch **12** 35.

DAN-JAAN, dan-jā′an (דָּן יַעַן, *dān ya'an;* B, Δὰν Εἰδὰν καὶ Οὐδάν, *Dán Eidán kaí Oudán*): A place visited by Joab and his officers when taking the census (2 S **24** 6). It is mentioned between Gilead and Sidon. Some would identify it with *Khān Dāniān*, a ruined site N. of Achzib. The text is probably corrupt. Klostermann would read "toward Dan and Ijon" (cf 1 K **15** 20).

DANNAH, dan′a (דַּנָּה, *dannāh*): One of the cities in the hill country of Judah (Josh **15** 49) between Socoh and Kiriath-sannah (Debir), probably Idhna—the Iedna of the *Onom*—8 miles W. of Hebron. See *PEF*, III, 305, 330.

DAPHNE, daf′nē (Δάφνη, *Dáphnē*, "bay-tree"): A suburb of Antioch on the Orontes, according to Strabo and the Jerus itinerary, about 40 furlongs, or 5 miles distant. It is identified with *Beit el-Mā'* on the left bank of the river, to the S.W. of the city. Here were the famous grove and sanctuary of Apollo. The grove and shrine owed their origin to Seleucus Nicator. It was a place of great natural beauty, and the Seleucid kings spared no outlay in adding to its attractions. The precincts enjoyed the right of asylum. Hither fled Onias the high priest (171 BC) from the wrath of Menelaus whom he had offended by plain speech. To the disgust and indignation of Jew and Gentile alike, he was lured from the sanctuary by Andronicus and basely put to death (2 Macc **4** 33–38). It sheltered fugitives dyed with villainy of every shade. It was the great pleasure resort of the citizens of Antioch; and it gained an evil repute for immorality, as witnessed by the proverbial *Daphnici mores*. *In Tiberim defluxit Orontes*, says Juvenal (iii.62), indicating one main source of the corruption that demoralized the imperial city. The decline of Daphne dates from the days of Christian ascendency in the reign of Julian. The place is still musical with fountains and luxuriant with wild vegetation; but nothing now remains to suggest its former splendor. See ANTIOCH; Gibbon, *Decline and Fall*, ch xxiii.

W. EWING

DARA, dâr′a (דָּרַע, *dāra‘*). See DARDA.

DARDA, där′da (דַּרְדַּע, *darda‘*, "pearl of wisdom"): One of the wise men to whom Solomon is compared (1 K **4** 31). He was either a son of Mahol (ibid) or a son of Zerah, son of Judah (1 Ch **2** 6, where the corresponding name in the same list is given as DARA). In rabbinic lore the name has been interpreted as *dōr dē^{a}‘*, "the generation of knowledge"—the generation of the wilderness.

DARE, dâr: The expression "to dare" in the Scriptures never has the meaning of "to defy," "to challenge," or "to terrify." It is always found as the tr of τολμάω, *tolmáō*, "to manifest courage." This is particularly evident from 2 Cor **10** 12, "for we are not bold to number or compare ourselves" (AV "for we dare not make ourselves of the number").

DARIC, dar′ik (דַּרְכְּמוֹן, *dark^{e}mōn*, and אֲדַרְכּוֹן, *'adharkōn;* δαρεικός, *dareikós*): A Pers gold coin about a guinea or five dollars in value. The first form of the word occurs in 1 Ch **29** 7; Ezr **2** 69, and Neh **7** 70–72; the second in Ezr **8** 27 and is rendered "dram" in AV and "daric" in RV. In the passage in Ch, it must refer to a weight, since at the time of David there were no coins, but in the days of Ezra and Nehemiah the Pers darics were current. See MONEY.

DARIUS, da-rī′us: The name of three or four kings mentioned in the OT. In the original Pers it is spelled "Darayavaush"; in Bab, usually "Dariamush"; in Susian(?), "Tariyamaush"; in Egyp, "Antaryuash"; on Aram. inscriptions, דריוהוש or דריווהוש; in Heb, דָּרְיָוֶשׁ, *dār^{e}yāwesh;* in Gr, Δαρεῖος, *Dareíos;* in Lat, "Darius." In meaning it is probably connected with the new Pers word *Dara*, "king." Herodotus says it means in Gr, 'Ερξείης, *Erxeiēs, coercitor*, "restrainer," "compeller," "commander."

(1) Darius the Mede (Dnl **6** 1; **11** 1) was the son of Ahasuerus (Xerxes) of the seed of the Medes (Dnl **9** 1). He received the government of Belshazzar the Chaldaean upon the death of that prince (Dnl **5** 30.31; **6** 1), and was made king over the kingdom of the Chaldaeans.

From Dnl **6** 28 we may infer that Darius was king contemporaneously with Cyrus. Outside of the Book of Dnl there is no mention of Darius the Mede by name, though there are good reasons for identifying him with Gubaru, or Ugbaru, the governor of Gutium, who is said in the Nabunaid-Cyrus Chronicle to have been appointed by Cyrus as his governor of Babylon after its capture from the Chaldaeans. Some reasons for this identification are as follows:

(*a*) Gubaru is possibly a tr of Darius. The same radical letters in Arab. mean "king," "compeller," "restrainer." In Heb, derivations of the root mean "lord," "mistress," "queen"; in Aram., "mighty," "almighty."

(*b*) Gutium was the designation of the country N. of Babylon and was in all possibility in the time of Cyrus a part of the province of Media.

(*c*) But even if Gutium were not a part of Media at that time, it was the custom of Pers kings to appoint Medes as well as Persians to satrapies and to the command of armies. Hence Darius-Gubaru may have been a Mede, even if Gutium were not a part of Media proper.

(*d*) Since Daniel never calls Darius the Mede king of Media, or king of Persia, it is immaterial what his title or position may have been before he was made king over the realm of the Chaldaeans. Since the realm of the Chaldaeans never included either Media or Persia, there is absolutely no evidence in the Book of Dnl that its author ever meant to imply that Darius the Mede ever ruled over either Media or Persia.

(*e*) That Gubaru is called governor (*pihatu*), and Darius the Mede, king, is no objection to this identification; for in ancient as well as modern oriental empires the governors of provinces and cities were often called kings. Moreover, in the Aram. language, no more appropriate word than "king" can be found to designate the ruler of a sub-kingdom, or province of the empire.

(*f*) That Darius is said to have had 120 satraps under him does not conflict with this; for the Pers word "satrap" is indefinite as to the extent of his rule, just like the Eng. word "governor." Besides, Gubaru is said to have appointed *pihatus* under himself. If the kingdom of the Chaldaeans which he received was as large as that of Sargon he may easily have appointed 120 of these sub-rulers; for Sargon names 117 subject cities and countries over which he appointed his prefects and governors.

(*g*) The peoples, nations and tongues of ch **6** are no objection to this identification; for Babylonia itself at this time was inhabited by Babylonians, Chaldaeans, Arabians, Aramaeans and Jews, and the kingdom of the Chaldaeans embraced also Assyrians, Elamites, Phoenicians and others within its limits.

(*h*) This identification is supported further by the fact that there is no other person known to history that can well be meant. Some, indeed, have thought that Darius the Mede was a reflection into the past of Darius Hystaspis; but this is rendered impossible inasmuch as the character, deeds and empire of Darius Hystaspis, which are well known to us from his own monuments and from the Gr historians, do not resemble what Daniel says of Darius the Mede.

(2) Darius, the fourth king of Persia, called Hystaspes because he was the son of a Pers king named Hystaspis, is mentioned in Ezr (**4** 5, et al.), Hag (**1** 1) and Zec (**1** 1). Upon the death of Cambyses, son and successor to Cyrus, Smerdis the Magian usurped the kingdom and was dethroned by seven Pers nobles from among whom Darius was selected to be king. After many rebellions and wars he succeeded in establishing himself firmly upon the throne (*Ant*, XI, i). He reorganized and enlarged the Pers empire. He is best known to general history from his conflict with Greece culminating at Marathon, and for his re-digging of the Suez Canal. In sacred history he stands forth as the king who enabled the Jews under Jeshua and Zerubbabel to rebuild the temple at Jerus.

(3) Darius, called by the Greeks Nothus, was called Ochus before he became king. He reigned from 424 to 404 BC. In the Scriptures he is mentioned only in Neh **12** 22, where he is called Darius the Pers, probably to distinguish him from Darius the Mede. It is not necessary to suppose that

Darius Codomannus who reigned from 336 to 330 BC, is meant by the author of Neh **12**, because he mentions Jaddua; for (*a*) Johanan, the father of this Jaddua, was high priest about 408 BC, as is clear from the Aram. papyrus from Elephantine lately published by Professor Sachau of Berlin, and Jaddua may well have succeeded him in those troublous times before the death of Darius Nothus in 404 BC. And (*b*) that a high priest named Jaddua met Alexander in 332 BC, is attested only by Jos (*Ant*, XI, viii, 5). It is not fair to take the testimony of Jos as to Jaddua without taking his testimony as to the meeting with Alexander and as to the appeal of Jaddua to the predictions of the Book of Dnl. But even if Jos be right, there may have been two Jadduas, one high priest in 404 BC, and the other in 332 BC; or the one who was alive and exercising his functions in 404 BC may still have been high priest in 332 BC. He need not have exceeded 90 years of age. According to the Eshki Harran inscription, which purports to have been written by himself, the priest of the temple in that city had served for 104 years. In our own time how many men have been vigorous in mind and body at the age of 90, or thereabouts; Bismarck and Gladstone, for example? R. DICK WILSON

DARK, därk, **DARKNESS,** därk'nes (חֹשֶׁךְ, *ḥōshekh;* **σκότος,** *skótos*): The day and night, light and darkness, are notable antitheses in Pal. There the day does not slowly fade away into the night after a period of twilight, but before sunset there is the brightness of day, and when the sun has disappeared everything has changed and night is at hand. From sunset until the darkness of night is less than an hour.

1. Darkness and Light in Palestine

In the Bible the main use of darkness is in contrast to light. Light is the symbol of God's purity, wisdom and glory. Darkness is the opposite. Miraculous occurrence of darkness in the land of Egypt for three days is recorded in Ex **10** 21.22, and at the death of Christ (Mt **27** 45). See PLAGUES; ECLIPSE.

2. Symbolic Uses

The **fig.** uses of darkness are many and various. It is used as a symbol (*a*) of moral depravity and its punishment. The wicked walk and work in darkness (Ps **82** 5; Prov **2** 13; Jn **3** 19; Rom **13** 12), and their reward is to "sit in darkness" (Ps **107** 10) or to be "cast forth into the outer darkness" (Mt **8** 12); (*b*) of things mysterious or inexplicable (1 K **8** 12; Ps **97** 2); (*c*) of trouble and affliction (2 S **22** 29; Job **5** 14; Prov **20** 20; Isa **9** 2; cf Gen **15** 12); (*d*) of punishment (Lam **3** 2; Ezk **32** 8; Zeph **1** 15); (*e*) of death (1 S **2** 9; Job **10** 21 f; Eccl **11** 8); (*f*) of nothingness (Job **3** 4–6); (*g*) of human ignorance (Job **19** 8; 1 Jn **2** 11).

"A dark [RVm "squalid"] place" (2 Pet **1** 19) refers esp. to the state of things described in ch **2**. ALFRED H. JOY

DARKLY, därk'li: The word occurs in 1 Cor **13** 12, "For now we see in a mirror, darkly," in tr of the words *ἐν αἰνίγματι, en ainigmati,* RVm "in a riddle." The contrast is with the "face to face" vision of Divine things in eternity. Earth's best knowledge is partial, obscure, enigmatic, a broken reflection of the complete truth ("broken lights of Thee").

DARKON, där'kon (דַּרְקוֹן, *darḳōn,* "carrier"): Ancestor of a subdivision of "Solomon's servants," so called, in post-exilic times (Ezr **2** 56; Neh **7** 58; Lozon, 1 Esd **5** 33).

DARK SAYINGS (Prov **1** 6; Ps **78** 2; sing., Ps **49** 4[5]; חִידוֹת, *ḥīdhōth,* sing. חִידָה, *ḥīdhāh,* elsewhere rendered "riddle," "proverb"): In the heading to the canonical Book of Prov, the general term "proverbs" is made to include "a proverb [מָשָׁל, *māshāl*], and a figure [or, an interpretation, מְלִיצָה, *m^elīçāh*], the words [sing. דָּבָר, *dābhār*] of the wise, and their dark sayings [or, riddles]." The "proverb" is either a saying current among the people (cf 1 S **10** 12; "the proverb of the ancients" **24** 13[14]), or a sentence of ethical wisdom composed by the order of wise men (חֲכָמִים, *ḥăkhāmīm*). Of the latter kind are the sententious maxims of the Wisdom lit. (chiefly Prov, but also Job, Eccl, and among the uncanonical writings Ecclus). They are characterized by a secular touch; wisdom, moreover, flourished among the neighbors of Israel as well; so in Edom and elsewhere. Whatever the date of the collection known as the "Proverbs of Solomon," the wise men existed in Israel at a very early period; the prophets allude to them. But the Heb *māshāl* is sometimes of a more elaborate character corresponding to our "parables"; frequently a vein of taunt runs through them, and they played an important part in compositions directed against other nations (cf Nu **21** 27). The prophets are fond of employing this genre of literary production; in their hands the *māshāl* becomes a **fig.** or allegorical discourse (cf Ezk **21** 5 ff [8 ff]). The *māshāl* in the sense of a didactic poem occurs also in the Psalms (Pss **49** and **78**). Hence it is that "proverb" and "figure," or "proverb" and "dark saying" are interchangeable terms. The "dark saying" is the popular "riddle" (cf Jgs **14**) raised to the dignity of elaborate production. It is in short an allegorical sentence requiring interpretation. Both prophets and psalmists avail themselves thereof. The word of God comes to the prophet in the form of a vision (cf the visions of Amos or Jeremiah), i.e. the truth presents itself to them in the form of a simile. To the perfect prophet of the type of Moses the revelation comes direct in the shape of the naked truth without the mediation of figures of speech or obscure utterances requiring elucidation (cf Nu **12**). In the same way St. Paul (1 Cor **13**) distinguishes between the childish manner of speaking of things spiritual and the manner of a man: "For now we see in a mirror, darkly [Gr "in a riddle"]; but then face to face." The rabbis say that, whereas all the other prophets saw God and things Divine in a dim mirror, Moses saw them in a polished, clear mirror. Both St. Paul and the rabbis feel the difference between mediate and immediate vision, the revelation which requires dark fig. language as a vehicle and the clear perception which is the direct truth. MAX L. MARGOLIS

DARLING, där'ling (יְחִידָה, *yāḥīdh,* "only," AVm "only one"; ARVm "*dear* life"): Used poetically for the life or soul (Ps **22** 20; **35** 17).

DART, därt (חֵץ, *ḥēç;* **βέλος,** *bélos*): A pointed missile weapon, as an arrow or light spear (2 S **18** 14; Job **41** 26). See ARMOR, ARMS, III, 4; ARROW.

Figurative: (1) Of the penalty of sin (Prov **7** 23 AV); (2) of strong suggestions and fierce temptations to evil (Eph **6** 16; cf 1 Macc **5** 51).

DART-SNAKE, därt'snake (Isa **34** 15). See ARROWSNAKE.

DASH: The idea of "to throw violently" or "to strike" with purpose of causing destruction is usually connected with the word "to dash." There is perhaps but one exception to this: Ps **91** 12 and the quotations of this passage in the NT (Mt **4** 6; Lk **4** 11, *προσκόπτω, proskóptō*), have the meaning "to strike against accidentally" and not intentionally. Nah **2** 1, "he that dasheth in pieces" is doubtful,

"He that scatters" would be in better harmony with the Heb מְפִיץ, *mēphīç*, and the following description of destruction. In all other cases "to dash" is connected with the idea of destruction, esp. the infliction of punishment which is usually expressed by רָטַשׁ, *rāṭash*, "to dash to the ground" (2 K **8** 12; Isa **13** 16 ff, et al., "to dash in pieces," AV simply "to dash"), but also by נָפַץ, *nāphaç*, "to break to pieces" (Ps **2** 9; **137** 9, et al.). See also PUNISHMENTS. A. L. BRESLICH

DATES, dāts (דְּבַשׁ, *d^ebhash*): Arab. *dibbs* (2 Ch **31** 5 AVm); EV HONEY (q.v.). See also PALM TREE.

DATHAN, dā'than (דָּתָן, *dāthān*, meaning and derivation unknown, though the name is found in Assyr, in the records of Shalmanezer II): The son of Eliab the son of Pallu the son of Reuben (Nu **26** 5 ff; Dt **11** 6; Ps **106** 17). He and his brother Abiram, with others, followed Korah the Levite in disputing the authority of Moses and Aaron in the wilderness (Nu **16**-**17**, **26**; Dt **11** 6; Ps **106** 17). Other followers of Korah perished by fire before the tent of meeting, but Dathan and Abiram were swallowed up by the earth, with their families and their goods, at their tents. See KORAH.

WILLIS J. BEECHER

DATHEMA, dath'ē-ma (**Δάθεμα**, *Dáthema*): A stronghold (1 Macc **5** 29) in Gilead to which the Jews fled for refuge from the heathen (ver 9). They were delivered by Judas and Jonathan his brother. It was within a night's march from Bosora. It may possibly be identical with *'Athamān* which lies E. of *el-Muzērīb*.

DAUB, dôb: "To daub" always has the meaning "to cover," "to smear with" in the Scriptures. Ezk compares the flatteries of the false prophets to a slight wall covered with whitewash (lit. "spittle"). See Ezk **13** 10 ff; **22** 28. In Ex **2** 3 "daubed it with slime and with pitch" (Heb וַתַּחְמְרָה, *wattaḥm^erāh*, denom. of חֵמָר, *ḥēmār*, "bitumen" or "asphalt"), "to daub" has the same meaning as in the Ezk passage.

DAUGHTER, dô'tēr (בַּת, *bath*; **θυγάτηρ**, *thugátēr*): Used in Scriptures in several more or less distinct senses: (*a*) for daughter in the ordinary, literal sense (Gen **46** 25; Ex **1** 16); (*b*) daughter-in-law (Ruth **2** 2); (*c*) granddaughter or other female descendant (Ex **21**; Lk **1** 5; **13** 16); (*d*) the women of a country, or of a place, taken collectively (Lk **23** 28), of a particular religion (Mal **2** 11); (*e*) all the population of a place, taken collectively, esp. in Prophets and poetic books (Ps **9** 14; Isa **23** 10; Jer **46** 24; Mt **21** 5); (*f*) used in familiar address, "Daughter, be of good comfort" (Mt **9** 22 AV; Mk **5** 34; Lk **8** 48); (*g*) women in general (Prov **31** 29); (*h*) the personification of towns or cities, as of the female sex (Isa **47** 1; Ezk **16** 44.46; cf Nah **3** 4.7), esp. of dependent towns and villages (Ps **48** 11; Nu **21** 25 m; Jgs **1** 27 m); (*i*) in Heb idiom for person or thing belonging to or having the characteristics of that with which it is joined, as "daughter of ninety years," of Sarah, ninety years old (Gen **17** 17); "daughters of music," singing birds, or singing women (Eccl **12** 4); daughters of a tree, i.e. branches; daughter of the eye, i.e. the pupil.

Daughters were not so highly prized as sons, not being usually mentioned by name. A father might sometimes sell his daughter as bondwoman (Ex **21** 7); though not to a foreigner (ver 8); daughters might sometimes inherit as did sons, but could not take the inheritance outside of the tribe (Nu **36** 1-12). EDWARD BAGBY POLLARD

DAUGHTER-IN-LAW. See RELATIONSHIPS, FAMILY.

DAVID

I. Name.—David, dā'vid (דָּוִד, *dāwīdh*, "beloved"; also written fully דָּוִיד *dāwīdh* 1 K **3** 14; **11** 4, 36; Ezk **34** 23); possibly a shortened form of *Dōdavahu* (דּוֹדָוָהוּ 2 Ch **20** 37) "beloved of Jeh" or *Dōdō* (דּוֹדוֹ 2 S **23** 24) "his beloved." The form *Dūdū* occurs in the Tel el-Amarna tablets. LXX **Δαυίδ**, *dâ vid* (Cod Vat **Δαυειδ**), NT **Δαβίδ**, *dâ bid*. The name is given to no one in the OT except the great king of Israel.

II. Genealogy.—David was the son of Jesse the Bethlehemite, and the youngest of eight brothers (1 S **16** 1, 10-11, 13). His genealogy is given in Ruth **4** 18-22 as running back ten generations through Jesse, Obed, Boaz, Salmon, Nahshon, Amminadab, Ram, and Hezron to Perez; who, according to Gen **38**, was the son of Judah by Tamar. David was the youngest of a family of eight sons; yet, in the registry of the tribe of Judah in 1 Ch **2** 13-15 only seven of these sons of Jesse are named; probably, because one died without issue. In his ancestral line were Nahshon "the prince of the children of Judah" (Nu **2** 3; 1 Ch **2** 10) and brother-in-law of Aaron (Ex **6** 23); and Ruth, a Moabitess, was his great-grandmother. Foreign blood thus flowed in his veins. Nothing is known concerning his mother: the references in Ps **86** 16 and **116** 16 to David himself as "the son of thy handmaid" are too uncertain of identification to postulate for her the virtue of "godliness." Dean Stanley suggests that David's mother may have been the wife or concubine of Nahash, and then married Jesse. This, he thinks, will agree with the difference of age between David and his sisters. The later rabbis represent him as born in adultery (cf Ps **51** 5). On the other hand, in the earlier rabbis we have an attempt at "immaculate conception." They make Nahash —"the serpent"—to be another name of Jesse, because he had no sin, except that which he contracted from the original serpent; and thus David inherited none (cf Jerome on 2 S **17** 25)! She also may have been a Moabitess, as was Ruth, inasmuch as, when driven out of his own land by Saul, David placed both her and his father under the protection of the king of Moab till he knew "what God would do for him" (1 S **22** 3-4).

III. The Shepherd boy of Bethlehem.—Concerning the details of David's life, we know more than of any other OT character. In his case, as in that of St. Paul we have not only a detailed narrative of his life, but certain writings which were beyond question products of his own composition. These we can compare, and from them reconstruct his biography. He appears under a great variety of circumstances—as shepherd, musician, soldier, king, and poet. To the prophets of later times he became the nation's ideal (Mic **5** 2 ff; Jer **33** 15). His life may be divided into three portions: first, as a shepherd-boy; second, in exile driven by Saul from place to place; and third, as king of Israel.

David evidently loved his native town of Bethlehem. One of the most touching incidents in his soldier-life is when, in the war with the Philistines, he longed for a drink of the water of the well of Bethlehem (2 S **23** 15; 1 Ch **11** 17)! To Chimham David gave a portion of his own inherited Bethlehem patrimony, apparently, as a reward for the kindness of his aged father Barzillai to him when exiled by Absalom (2 S **19** 37–38; Jer **41** 17).

1. First Appearance

The first time David appears in Biblical history is in connection with an annual feast in Bethlehem, to which, at Jeh's command, the prophet Samuel repaired with a heifer for sacrifice. The apparent moral obliquity contained in 1 S **16** 2–3 can be explained by supposing, with Davidson, that "the historian's object is to show how *God* guided the history, not to tell how men's minds moved or co-operated." Jesse, the sheikh of the village, seems to have presided (1 S **20** 6). Samuel's heifer was killed and all was ready for the sacrificial feast, when Samuel announced his official mission. All the older brothers of David were passed by, and he was chosen and annointed by Samuel as king, to take the place of Saul. He was bright-eyed, ruddy (i.e., auburn-haired; as Esau, Gen **25** 25), courageous, swift of foot, and contemplative (1 S **16** 12 18; **17** 42). Samuel's choice of him doubtless had a most inspiriting influence upon his subsequent life. But his consecration by Samuel did not require him to abandon at once his shepherd vocation. As Sayce puts it, "Saul still reigned, notwithstanding the mystic power, conferred by the consecration, had passed to another."

The pastures for grazing about Bethlehem were celebrated in ancient times as they are today. The "Tower of the Flock" (Gen **35** 21) was there; and there it was the angel found shepherds abiding still with their flocks by night (Lk **2** 8). As a shepherd boy, David carried a club and a sling (1 S **17** 40, 43), and a scrip or wallet round his neck, to receive anything that might be needed by him in his shepherd life (1 S **17** 40). During the long hours of his pastoral care, day after day, he practiced slinging until he acquired marvelous accuracy of aim. He also cultivated his genius for music, playing his harp, or crude *rūbaba*, such as the Bedouin shepherd plays today—an instrument having often but a single string, seldom more than two! He played it with his hand (1 S **16** 23), perhaps using a quill. Josephus describes David's genius in manufacturing instruments of music thus: "He made instruments of music, and taught the Levites to sing hymns to God. The viol was an instrument of ten strings, it was played upon with a bow; the psaltery had twelve musical notes, and was played upon by the fingers; the cymbals were broad and large instruments, and were made of brass" (*Ant* vii. 12. 3). The prophet Amos also long centuries before alluded to David's cleverness in inventing instruments of music (**6** 5). In fact David was "the Hebrew Orpheus, in whose music birds and mountains joined."

He composed lyrics also, doubtless improvising songs of both secular and sacred character, as do the God-fearing shepherds of Palestine in modern times. It can hardly be mere imagination on the part of all those who harbored and have handed down the tradition that David was not only musical but composed songs and hymns (cf 2 S **22** 1; **23** 1; 1 Ch **23** 5–6; Acts **2** 25; **4** 25). His elegies on Saul and Jonathan (2 S **1** 19–27), and Abner (**3** 33–34), though brief are witnesses to his poetic skill! It is certainly probable—highly probable—yea, more than probable—that at least some of the seventy-three psalms which are ascribed to David by the editors of the Hebrew psalter were actually composed by him. Nature poems such as Ps **8**, **19**, and **29**, and a Shepherd-guest Psalm, like the **23**rd, seem most certainly to have been born out of his early pastoral experience; the Great Shepherd speaks to a shepherd's heart! To David, Nature was vocal!

Such was the character of his outer life, when, as a later OT psalmist says, "Jeh chose David also his servant, and took him from the sheepfolds; from following the ewes that have their young he brought him to be the shepherd of Jacob his people, and Israel his inheritance. So he was their shepherd according to the integrity of his heart, and guided them by the skilfulness of his hands" (Ps **78** 70–72). God thus promoted him, and he never forgot how he had been exalted from the humble station of caring for the sheepcote (2 S **23** 1; **7** 8; Ps **89** 19).

2. At Court

While still shepherd of his father's flocks, David was invited to visit the palace of the king to sooth with music his troubled spirit. This was David's first meeting with Saul. For a while all went well. Saul loved David and made him his armor-bearer, or personal adjutant. According to Seneca, Pythagoras quieted the troubles of his own mind with a harp. Elisha, too, once called for a minstrel 2 K **3** 15). But music can only temporarily alleviate spiritual malady. "Vain are all merely worldly prescriptions for the sin-burdened soul."

3. David and Goliath

David's first visit to the court of Saul was only temporary. It is explicitly stated in 1 S **17** 15 that he "went to and fro from Saul to feed his father's sheep at Bethlehem." In due time the battle between Israel and the Philistines at Ephes-dammim in the Shephelah, or foot hills of Judah, took place. In the valley of Elah, Saul's army is encamped on one side of the Wādy, and the Philistines on the other. A Philistine of gigantic stature, and covered with armor challenges the timid Israelites to a duel. Goliath is said in 1 S **17** 4 to have been "six cubits and a span" in height, or about 9 ft. 4 in (A Dutchman, named Jan van Albert, who lived in Port Arthur, Ont., Canada, was reported in 1921 as 9 ft. 5 in. in height). No one dares to respond. At this juncture David appears on the scene, having been sent by his father with ten loaves and ten cheeses to his three eldest brothers who were with Saul (1 S **17** 13). As he approaches the camp he hears the repeated challenge of the Philistine monster. He is told of the reward which the king has promised to the soldier who vanquishes the Philistine, and he volunteers to enter the combat. Saul's armor is too cumbersome; but with his sling David is well acquainted. The story is familiar. The diminutive shepherd-boy, who was at first scorned by the Giant and contemned also by his brothers and the Israelites, returns from the valley-bed with the Giant's head and sword. David's victory over Goliath was the turning-point of his career. On the one side was a huge monster of "impregnable panoply," and on the other, an agile youth armed with a shepherd's staff, a sling, and five smooth stones, but full of the spirit of faith in God. In the encounter, the youth stunned the boaster, stood over his insensible antagonist, decapitated him, and returned bringing with him the trophies which all Israel coveted. The result was that the terror which had paralyzed the Israelites now passed over to the other side; and from that day forward the Philistines at least regarded David as "the king of the land" (1 S **21** 11). But Saul was reluctant to give his daughter to the young shepherd of Bethlehem. Thrice over he inquired, "Whose son is this youth?" (1 S **17** 55–56, 58). One wonders that the king did not recognize his favorite harpist! But during the indefinitely long period between his first visit to the court of Saul and his defeat of the Philistine champion, he probably passed out of youth into early manhood. And so, this would account, in part at least, for Saul's non-recognition of him (1 S **17** 55–58).

This is one of the many critical difficulties of the record. But note that Saul inquires not merely who David is, but "*whose son* is this youth?" Saul knew that he was from Bethlehem and that he was the son of Jesse (1 S **16** 18), but what he wished to know was further information concerning David's family, into which his daughter was now to marry!

David's heroic victory over the champion of Gath brought him unprecedented glory.

Michelangelo's masterpiece is a colossal statue of David. It is to be seen in Florence. According to the story, it was fashioned from a block of marble which a blundering sculptor had ruined by chipping a great slice from its side. For a century it lay at Florence, mere useless rubbish, until the eye of the master perceived its possibilities. He hewed out of it the shepherd-lad just as he had launched the stone from the sling, adapting the great cleft to the curving poise of the lithe figure.

"To what extent David's shepherd life actually produced any of the existing psalms ascribed to him may be questioned. But it can hardly be doubted that it suggested some of their most beautiful imagery"; so wrote Dean Stanley. The **23**rd Psalm at least seems to be the echo of a shepherd's life. David's dumb sheep had taught him that Jeh was his shepherd! Ps **144,** though its contents were probably much later, is ascribed in the Septuagint to David when he fought "against Goliath." And there is also a psalm preserved in both the Greek and the Syriac, which in these versions stands at the end of the Psalter, and sums up this early period of David's life. It is also associated with the duel fought by David with Goliath. It reads as follows:

1. "I was small amongst my brethren,
   And the youngest in my father's house.
2. I used to feed my father's sheep,
   And I found a lion and a wolf, and I slew them and rent them.
3. My hands made a harp.
   And my fingers fashioned a psaltery.
4. And who shall tell it to my Lord?
   He is the Lord, He heareth.
5. He sent his angel and took me from my father's flocks,
   And anointed me with the oil of His anointing.
6. My brethren were handsome and tall
   But in them the Lord had no pleasure.
7. I, it was, who went out to meet the Philistine,
   And he cursed me by his idols.
8. But I drew his own sword and beheaded him,
   And took away the reproach from Israel."

A further critical difficulty arises in the story of David's killing Goliath, when we turn to 2 S **21** 19 in which it is stated that "Elhanan the son of Jaare-oregim, the Bethlehemite slew Goliath the Gittite, the staff of whose spear was like a weaver's beam" (cf. 1 S **17** 7). Various explanations have been given: one, that the Giant killed by David being usually spoken of anonymously (cf 1 S **17** 4 and **21** 9), the name of Elhanan's antagonist was transferred to the giant killed by David (Ewald); another, that Elhanan was the same as David (Jerome). But the best solution is to regard Elhanan's encounter as subsequent to David's: "there was *again* war with the Philistines" (2 S **21** 19).

IV. Saul's Jealousy of David.—Saul's disposition was of such a nature that he often opposed others. For example, his wilful disobedience in sparing Agag, the king of the Amalekites, and the sheep and oxen captured for sacrifice, caused schism between himself and Samuel (1 S **15** 35). Because of his repeated acts of disobedience Jeh rejected him from being king over Israel. At a later period in a fit of jealousy he broke with the priesthood also, ordering the execution of all the sacerdotal order at Nob (1 S **22** 17–19). He never knew what obedience really meant.

In his foreign wars, he won distinction both for himself and for his country. A general summary of his triumphs recorded in 1 S **14** 47 ascribes to him victories over Ammon, Moab, and Edom in the East and Southeast, over the Philistines and Amalekites, in the South, and over the kings of Zobah in the distant North, beyond Damascus. But at home the course of events was less happy for him. The manner in which he enviously eyed David is even more pathetic. His madness had shown itself long before David became his rival or was even well known to him (1 S **16** 14–23).

1. David's Popularity

But David's sudden leap into popularity after killing the giant Goliath excited more grivously the king's jealousy. His jealousy, in fact, soon developed into hate. The women used to sing antiphonally one to another as they played:

"Saul hath slain his thousands,
And David his ten thousands" (1 S **18** 7).

The king brooded over these words, until, as Sayce puts it, in his moments of insanity they overpowered all prudence and restraint. Still, being in honor bound by his promise to reward the vanquisher of the Philistine giant, the king brought David to his court, made him general over a thousand, and gave him on conditions difficult to fulfil (1 S **18** 25) his daughter Michal to wife, whom he maliciously hoped to make a snare to him. Through months and even long years, the unwelcome boastings of the women which made him inferior to David still sounded in his ears, and his feigned friendship toward his son-in-law concealed murder in his heart.

2. David and Jonathan

Jonathan, the unselfish, generous son of the king, though he never forgot his filial obligations to his father, became growingly fond of David. "The soul of Jonathan was knit with the soul of David" (1 S **18** 1). Even Saul in his better moments never lost his strong affection for David. But the friendship between David and Jonathan is of the purest type in all literature. Michal, Saul's daughter, had married him. Nevertheless, by rapid steps Saul drove David into involuntary exile. Neither the unselfish love of Jonathan nor the loyalty of Michal, who by means of a household image deceived the ruffians that surrounded her house, and enabled her husband to escape successfully, was sufficient to allay the feelings of discouragement which at times overwhelmed David's spirit. He knew that Saul had avowed his purpose to slay him. Open schism followed.

First, and naturally, David fled to Samuel at Ramah, taking refuge in the sacred inclosure of the Naioth, or monastery (1 S **19** 18), i.e., student-apartments! From Ramah he was impelled to betake himself to Ahimelech at Nob. But neither Samuel, the prophet, nor Ahimelech, the priest, was able to furnish him assured protection. Samuel was doubtless suspected by Saul of plotting against the throne, while Ahimelech was probably afraid of Saul. Even Jonathan was powerless to shield him; for, as Cornill puts it, "Saul probably suspected that David had entered with Jonathan into a conspiracy against him to depose him and put Jonathan in his place." But one course, therefore, remained open, namely, to put himself outside the reach of Saul's pursuers. Accordingly, he fled to Achish, king of Gath, hazardously throwing himself upon the mercy of his enemies the Philistines. There, at least, Saul could not pursue him (1 S **19** 11) (cf the title to Ps **59,** which associates this Psalm with David's wedding night).

David's resort to Achish of Gath was short-sighted being due to a lack of faith. He soon found that he was unwelcome among his enemies, and so his stay at the court of Achish was brief. The presence of the sword of Goliath, too, which he had with him (1 S **21** 9) may have revived the national enmity of the Philistines against their former conqueror. He only escaped by feigning madness, and gesticulating violently, hammering on the gates of the city, letting his beard grow and foaming at the mouth (1 S **21** 13 LXX). The **56**th and **34**th psalms are both referred by their titles to this event, and they add that the Philistines had imprisoned him and that Achish set him free.

Accordingly, as an independent outlaw, he betook himself to the Cave of Adullam—a large cavern not far southwest of Bethlehem, best identified with a place called in Arabic ʿ*Aid el-Ma*. Thither resorted his relatives, through fear of Saul, and a beggarly rabble of four hundred men whom distress, debt, and discontent had driven to flight. These were the unconscious materials out of which a new world was to be formed. Among those who joined themselves to David at this time were Gad the seer and Abiathar the priest. Probably, also, some of the aboriginal Canaanites of the land gathered about him.

But the tragedy of Saul's pursuit of David was only begun. It is noteworthy that in the desultory warfare which for several years ensued between the king and David, the latter never employed any weapon but flight; for, David chose to flee his country rather than raise his hand against the king. What the effect of such a life was upon his spiritual nature is obvious from the story of his subsequent career, and from the psalms of deliverance which are ascribed to him (cf 1 S **22,** Ps **34** and **27**). As Alexander Maclaren has well expressed it: "It deepened his unconditional dependence on God. By the alternations of heat and cold, fear and hope, danger and safety, it tempered his soul and made it flexible, tough and bright as steel. It evolved the qualities of a leader of men: teaching him command and forbearance, promptitude and patience, valor and gentleness. And it gathered round him a force of men devoted to him by the enthusiastic attachment bred from long years of common danger and hardship."

3. Persecution

For the sake of their greater security, David abandoned the Cave of Adullam, in order to remove his aged parents from Bethlehem to Mizpeh in Moab (1 S **22** 3–4; cf Ruth **4** 18–22). There under the protection of the king of Moab his father and mother abode all the while that David was in the stronghold. Rabbinical tradition says that David's father, mother, and brothers were slain by the Moabites while sojourning in the land as their guests. Quite possibly the "stronghold" is to be identified with Masada, a high fastness in the neighborhood of En-gedi on the west shore of the Dead Sea. At the advice of the prophet Gad, he repaired to the forest of Hereth (1 S **22** 5), located somewhere to the east or south of Hebron. There he hid until the Philistines made an attack upon Keilah, a town in southwestern Judah. By divine direction, David and his men, whose numbers had now increased to six hundred, went down and delivered Keilah out of the hands of the Philistines. It was quite probably at this time that the three chivalrous heroes of David's men broke through the host of the Philistines who were then garrisoned in Bethlehem and brought David a drink of water from the well of Bethlehem (2 S **23** 15–16). It seems to have been the greater part of his business at that time to defend the lives and property of his fellow-countrymen from unscrupulous robbers. David took possession of Keilah and would have abode there indefinitely had not Saul speedily dispatched an army to besiege the fortress of Keilah and entrap him. But before Saul's forces reached Keilah, David had consulted the ephod of Abiathar, the priest, and had been divinely warned not to intrust himself to the inhabitants of the city, but to flee. He did so, his 600 men scattering in various directions (1 S **23** 1–13).

The text of 1 S from this point on becomes difficult to follow. The question arises in reference to certain passages, such as 1 S **24** and **26,** whether the two narratives relate to two different occasions, or whether they are not rather merely different versions of the same occurrence. There are remarkable resemblances between the two accounts; but though there are differences of detail, these are hardly greater, as Driver allows, than might have grown up in a story current among the people.

David next repaired to the wilderness of Ziph, southeast of Hebron. There he received a farewell visit from his loyal friend Jonathan. They parted in Covenant love. 1 S **23** 17 contains one of the noblest and most unselfish utterances ever made by human lips: "And he [Jonathan] said unto him, Fear not; for the hand of Saul my father shall not find thee; and thou shalt be king over Israel, and I shall be next unto thee; and that also Saul my father knoweth. When the Ziphites treacherously offered to betray David into Saul's hands, he escaped to the wilderness of Maon, a little farther to the southeast. Saul persisted in his pursuit, hunting him like a partridge (1 S **23** 14; **22** 23). He had almost succeeded in effecting his capture, when a messenger brought the king the timely news that the Philistines were making another invasion of his territory, and he and his men were thrown into a panic (1 S **23** 24–27). This was the first of two (or three) occasions on which the pursuer and the pursued presumably caught sight of each other (1 S **23** 26).

David next betook himself to the fastness of En-gedi on the western shore of the Dead Sea. Saul renewed his search for him, assisted by 3,000 men (1 S **24** 1–2). The pursuer and the pursued on this occasion actually sighted each other. David came near enough to Saul to cut off the skirt of his long robe while he was covering his feet (1 S **24** 3). Then ensued the pathetic scene of remonstrance and forgiveness (1 S **24** 8–22). Before they parted, Saul confessed his sin and besought of David, when he succeeded to the throne, not to destroy his house. Ps **7** and **57** are thought by some to find a historical basis in the experiences of David at the cave near En-gedi, where he cut off Saul's skirt.

Samuel died about this time and the house of Ramah became extinct. He was especially missed, as no successor arose of Samuel's type to admonish the self-willed king. At En-gedi, Saul had expressed sorrow for having rewarded David evil for good. But David dared not trust himself to one so mercurial and spasmodic as Saul. He, accordingly, arose and went down into the wilderness of Paran, south of Judah. Henceforth, David no longer appears as a solitary fugitive, but as "a powerful freebooter." He and his 600 followers constituted themselves a kind of bodyguard, and voluntarily protected the flocks of many a herdsman from the predatory Bedouins. Nabal a wealthy sheep master of the clan of Caleb, who lived near Carmel in southern Judah, was one of those who were greatly indebted to David (1 S **25** 21). The annual sheep-shearing season came. David politely requested of Nabal, through ten of his own young men, that the aristocratic sheep-farmer give him and his 600 attachées some food supplies. But Nabal was a man of niggardly disposition and selfish character. "His wealth had not endowed him with common sense." David's messengers were met with a stern gruff refusal which was reported by them to their master. David's anger was kindled; and he determined at once to take vengeance on the "rich fool" (as his name "Nabal" implied). Such a

4. Exile

purpose was morally unjustifiable, of course, but it was in keeping with the customs of the Orient in David's time. Meanwhile, Abigail, Nabal's prudent wife, hearing what was about to occur, prepared a present, and went to meet David with due apology. Her act was timely; for David was already on his way to exterminate Nabal's entire household. Abigail threw herself at his feet, and presented her petition so effectively that David's conscience was touched, and he retracted his vow. Ten days later Nabal died; David in due time married his beautiful and gracious widow, and the wealth of Nabal passed into his hands (1 S **25** 14–42). In this section of the record there is valuable instruction on reprisals and the moral right to take vengeance (1 S **25** 30–31)! Vengeance belongs to Jeh (cf Dt **32** 35; Rom **12** 19). But David was a child of Old Testament times. David also married Ahinoam of Jezreel (1 S **25** 43); perhaps prior to his marriage with Abigail, but in the same general neighborhood (cf Jos **15** 55–56).

The Ziphites seem to have betrayed David a second time; for Saul, with 3,000 men and Abner, the captain of his host, made a final attempt to capture the king's imagined enemy. Weary, the king and his men lay down to rest within a barricade of wagons in the midst of the camp. While they slept, David, with his nephew Abishai, stole the king's spear and a cruse of water; David might have taken at the same time the king's life, but he would not. Going, however, over to the top of a high mountain across the valley, David taunted Abner for not having defended the king more faithfully; and as he spoke, Saul recognized David, and said, "Is this thy voice, my son David? Return, for I will no more do thee harm." But David went his way, and Saul returned to his place. This was David's last interview with Saul!

David's exile-life was drawing near to an end. And well it was, for he was evidently becoming weary of the life of an outlaw. In desperation he again threw himself upon the mercy of his hereditary enemy, Achish the king of Gath. This time David came to Achish not as a fugitive but as the chief of a powerful band. His 600 men had now grown into an organized community, having with them their wives and families (1 S **27** 3–4). To secure his friendship, Achish gave David Ziklag, a city on the southwest borders of Judah, which was perhaps at that time uninhabited, which David accepted and dwelt therein with his two wives, remaining sixteen months. But, by going over to the Philistines, he involved himself in a long course of cruelty and deceit. During this period, according to the Chronicler, David was reinforced by many mighty men of Israel who came over to his side (1 Ch **12**). But what is especially noteworthy, during this period David succeeded in making Achish believe that in the forays which he made from time to time, he was fighting against the enemies of the Philistines, whereas he was primarily paving the way for his own rule as king by exterminating Israel's foes. In all this, it is to be feared David was guilty of much clever cunning (1 S **27** 8–12). He fought Judah's enemies all the time, pretending to Achish that he was fighting against Judah; and to keep the matter secret he took no prisoners. Nevertheless, Achish continued to trust him blindly; and when he prepared himself for a formidable assault upon Saul, which culminated at Gilboa, he invited David to accompany him. But the lords of the Philistines did not share their king's credulity. For, they protested against David as an ally, and forced him to return. "And David probably never thanked his God more ardently than when he was sent home" (Cornill).

V. The Tribal King of Judah.—Saul's career ended in tragedy. The Philistines had again broken into Israelite territory and occupied the eastern end of the Plain of Esdraelon. The Israelites with Saul as their leader took up a position in the region of Mount Gilboa. Some time before, Saul, in a fit of religious enthusiasm, had put away all those who had familiar spirits out of the land, yet, on the night before his fatal conflict, he yielded to the superstitious side of his character and secretly circumvented the Philistine encampment in order to consult a witch in Endor. The story is a sad one. Saul was discouraged. As Davidson describes the struggle which went on in his soul: "In his last extremity he sought Samuel, the friend of his early rule. His mind was coming back to old times. But, alas! it was in vain!" Having lost confidence in both himself and his God, when he returned to the battlefield, he saw that the contest was hopeless, and so, leaning heavily upon his spear, he died (1 S **31** 1–6).

David was one of his sincerest mourners. The noble elegy contained in 2 S **1** 19–27, which has been extracted by the sacred historian from the ancient *Book of Jashar*, is an immortal witness to his personal grief. The poem is known as the "Song of the Bow," and is considered one of the gems of Hebrew poetry. It is probably a genuine composition of David, himself. It may have been originally designed as a memorial to Jonathan, as he was an archer who was particularly fond of the bow, but David was its author, and it unveils so perfectly the magnanimous spirit of David, "the exile," toward his pursuer that it may fittingly be called a lamentation over king Saul. In it David does not dissociate his dead enemy from his dead friend, but, grouping them both together, he sings:

1. Mourns for Saul

"Saul and Jonathan were lovely
And pleasant in their lives,
And in their death they were not divided:
They were swifter than eagles,
They were stronger than lions.
How are the mighty fallen,
And the weapons of war perished!"

David thus found an outlet for his sorrow over the tragic death of a great man; who, though he had been his deadly enemy for years, he was wholly ready to forgive. The poem has been called, "the dirge of a man of God over his dead enemy and his dead friend," and is pronounced "one of the most beautiful anticipations to be found in the Old Testament of Christ's command to love one's enemies" (G. A. Smith). The lyric grandeur of this beautiful poem has been expressed in music, in the famous Dead March in "Saul," which is frequently used when great men are carried to their sepulchres.

Fortunately, for many reasons, David was not allowed to fight with the Philistines against Saul. Having been dismissed by Achish, because he was an objectionable mercenary to the Philistine lords, he returned to Ziglag, only to find that it had been looted and burned by a band of marauding Amalekites, and that his two wives had been taken captive (1 S **29** and **30**). David lost no time in pursuing the offenders. When he succeeded in overtaking them, and had recovered his wives and property, with characteristic foresight he sent portions of the spoil to the elders of Judah who had befriended him in the days of his involuntary exile. "But," as Sayce says, "the pretext was more than transparent. A crown was already within measurable distance of the Jewish chieftain; all that was needed was the goodwill of the elders."

David's reign falls into two unequal periods: "seven years reigned he in Hebron, and thirty and three years reigned he in Jerusalem" (1 K **2** 11). Saul and Jonathan being both now dead, and having been himself assured by Jeh of his right to the throne, with confidence, therefore, David marched to Hebron, accompanied by his "armed veterans and devoted adherents," and there offered himself to the Jewish elders as king of Judah. Tribal feeling was sufficiently powerful to lead Judah to act independently of the rest of the nation. And so, without opposition, and possibly with the promise of Philistine protection, David was anointed king over the tribe of Judah at Hebron; a city which, on account of its holy associations and central location, was best adapted, temporarily at least, to become David's capital. Thus the son of Jesse was permitted to reap the fruit of his "judicious courtesies and prudent marriage alliances."

David's first public act after his coronation was to send an embassy to the men of Jabesh-gilead to commend them for their nobility in caring for the bodies of Saul and his three sons. But at the same time, he took care to communicate to them the news that the elders of Judah had made him king over their tribe. The men of Jabesh, however, made no response (2 S **2** 5–7). Meanwhile, upon the death of Saul, Abner, Saul's cousin and commander-in-chief, had taken Ishbosheth (or Eshbaal, as in 1 Ch **8** 33), the youngest son of Saul, and proclaimed him king at Mahanaim, east of the Jordan. "There out of the ruins of Saul's dominions," as Cornill observes, "he hoped to establish a kingdom; Ishbosheth also probably being under Philistine suzerainty." Ishbosheth however, was never more than the shadow of a king. "Whether he was a minor or an imbecile it is impossible to say with certainty: most probably he was but a child" (Sayce). On the other hand, compare 2 S **2** 10, in which we are informed that Ishbosheth was "forty years old when he began to reign over Israel, and he reigned two years." Abner was the real king; He drove the Philistines out of Ashur (or Geshur), from Jezreel, and Ephraim, and Benjamin, and from all Israel (2 S **2** 8–9). But when he attempted to subject Judah also, war ensued. The contest at first took the form of a duel, which was fought at Gibeon between two companies of twelve men each. But later, a fierce battle was fought, in which Abner and his men were put to flight by Joab, David's nephew, who now appears in the record for the first time. Joab lost 20 men in the battle; Abner, 360.

2. War with Israel

When Abner saw that, in the contest between the house of David and the house of Saul, he was on the losing side, he forsook Ishbosheth and came over to the side of David. The deed was an act of treachery. The pretext arose out of Abner's having married Rizpah, Saul's concubine; an act which Ishbosheth naturally interpreted, in keeping with eastern views, as equivalent to claiming the throne. In a fit of temper, Ishbosheth rebuked Abner for marrying the wife of his dead father; whereupon, Abner became indignant, and openly declared his purpose to desert him and go over to the side of David. He immediately despatched messengers to David, offering him his sword, and giving assurances that he could bring with him all Israel from Dan to Beersheba. David, however, did not permit himself to manifest undue eagerness in the matter; but stipulated, in order probably to test his loyalty, that Abner should fetch, in particular, Michal, David's former wife, whom Saul had wrenched from him. For David saw that, when recognized "as the acknowledged son-in-law of Saul, he would stand before the Israelites as the rightful heir of their former king" (Kent). Abner complied with the king's command, and tore Michal from her sorrowing husband. Meanwhile, David, like an oriental despot, had added four other new wives to his harem from the neighboring principalities (2 S **3** 2–5). When, however, Joab heard of what David and Abner had done, he was bitterly offended, and sharply rebuked the king for his simplicity in extending a welcome to the cunning diplomatist. And because Abner had slain his brother Asahel, Joab treacherously sent for Abner, took him aside, and slew him in cold blood. No act, of course, could have been more calculated to defeat David's desire to secure the friendship of Abner's constituency; and had not the king severely rebuked Joab, and put on sackcloth, and proclaimed a public mourning for Abner, he would probably have failed utterly in winning the loyalty of the northern tribes.

One foul deed rapidly followed another. Two Gibeonite captains of Benjamin assassinated Ishbosheth and this atrocious act brought the long struggle between the house of David and the house of Saul to a crisis. The covenant made with the Gibeonites, centuries before in the days of Joshua, had been violated by Saul, who "had put to death the Gibeonites" (2 S **21** 1), and these two Gibeonite captains had determined now to avenge themselves. Though their treachery must be recorded as another heinous crime in the annals of Israel, it nevertheless furthered mightily the cause of David. The story is tragic. Entering Ishbosheth's bedchamber one summer afternoon while he was taking his *siesta*, they slew him on his bed. Cutting off his head, they hastened with it to David, expecting to receive a handsome reward. But David was no enemy of Saul's house; he was rather its champion. He therefore rewarded them as he had previously done the Amalekite who claimed to have slain Saul (2 S **1** 1–16). By David's order, accordingly, the royal guards struck them down. Ishbosheth's head was then respectfully buried, at David's direction, in the grave of Abner at Hebron (2 S **4**).

With the death of Ishbosheth, the house of Saul became so weakened that all hope on the part of northern Israel to maintain a separate independence completely vanished. No other rival now stood in David's path except the crippled twelve-year-old son of Jonathan, named Mephibosheth, or more correctly "Merib-baal" (1 Ch **8** 34). But he laid no claims to the throne. Toward him David showed the utmost kindness. The other surviving descendants of Saul were either too young or too weak to offer resistance. Later, as the record shows, seven of them were executed, because of a famine which was supposed to have been caused by Saul's violation of the covenant between Israel and Gibeon (2 S **21** 1–9). Yet, Mephibosheth was spared. But the throne, so long waiting for David, was now vacant, and the united voice of the whole people at once called him to occupy it.

VI. King of all Israel.—The northern tribes of Israel soon made it known that they, too, desired David to rule over them. Coming together in a great national assembly at Hebron, they reminded him that he and they belonged to a common ancestry; and there they then anointed him king over all Israel, sealing their covenant to be his loyal subjects with an oath (2 S **5** 1–3). A feast of three days' duration followed (1 Ch **12** 39). But in accepting Israel's offer of fealty, David practically renounced the vassalage to the Philistines. At any rate, in their eyes he was guilty of revolt, and they determined to destroy his kingdom in the bud. Even before David had time to gather his forces, they invaded Judah, seized Bethlehem, and forced him to take refuge in his former stronghold, either the Cave of Adullam, or the newly captured stronghold of Zion. For a considerable time, David and the Philistines carried on a guerilla warfare. More and more, however, the Israelites gained in power, until at length, at a place near Gibeon called Baal-perazim, the Philistines were completely routed and forever driven from Israel's territory. In their flight, they left the images of their gods behind them.

1. David's Capital

David showed rare military genius also in capturing Jerusalem from the Jebusites and in establishing there his new capital. The fortress of this ancient citadel had always been considered impregnable. With singular prescience David fixed on it as his future capital. When he ventured to assail it, the taunt was returned that even the lame and the blind could easily defend it against him (2 S **5** 6). Nevertheless, by one sudden assault the stronghold of Jebus was taken and David made it his capital; and, thereafter, it became known as "the city of David" (2 S **5** 9; 2 Ch **11** 7). Probably, also, about this time men began to call it Jerusalem and Zion. The importance of this event cannot be overestimated. Jerusalem's central location, its natural defense, "difficult to capture and easy to defend"; its situation on neutral ground between Judah and Benjamin, and its ancient associations with the priest-king Melchizedek, made this the wisest selection possible as a capital for the reunited kingdom; and it is one of the best illustrations of David's foresight and executive ability. Of all the cities of Palestine, Jerusalem has vindicated by its long permanence the choice of its founder. The importance of the capture was marked at the time. The reward bestowed on Joab, who successfully scaled "the watercourse," was the highest place in the army, as captain of the host (1 Ch **11** 6).

2. Distinguishing Qualities

Now, among the many qualities which distinguished David, prior to his coronation as king of all Israel, were (1) his courage in slaying Goliath; (2) his passive submission to Saul's cruel hate; (3) his diplomacy in winning to himself both the sympathy of his own countrymen and the friendship of his enemies, the Philistines; (4) his forbearance with the house of Saul, when he was the divinely designated successor to the throne, as announced by Samuel at his sacrifice in Bethlehem; (4) his wise statesmanship in the choice of Jerusalem as the new capital of reunited Israel; and (6) above all, his unswerving trust in the Providence of God. From this point in his life on, we shall discover how well he stood the strain of his new and exalted position, and what on the other hand, were some of his weaknesses.

VII. Jerusalem Made a Religious Center.—David, in contrast with Saul, was not content to have a capital without a shrine. The ark of the covenant, which for almost seventy years had been in the possession of an Israelite at Kiriath-jearim, David determined to bring up and deposit within his new citadel. Uzzah's rashness, however, in handling the sacred chest, thwarted the king's first attempt, and consequently it was left to abide in the house of Obed-edom, the Gittite, who greatly prospered through its presence. But after three months the king renewed his purpose (the ark being borne this time upon men's shoulders, 2 S **6** 13), and brought it with pomp and joy and music and dancing into the new tent which David had prepared for it (2 Ch **1** 3–4). It was the ark's presence which made Jerusalem "the Holy City." That was the greatest day in David's life, and marked a turning-point in Israel's history. Only one incident marred its glory. Michal, who apparently never became weaned from her teraphim (1 S **19** 13), showed her utter lack of sympathy with the devotional side of David's nature by pouring forth a torrent of venomous sarcasm. David replied to his unsympathetic, half-pagan wife in volleys similar. "Taunts provoke taunts." As a result, Michal and David seem to have parted forever (2 S **6**).

The event of bringing the ark to Jerusalem has been celebrated by the Psalmist in the **24**th Psalm; concerning which Cornill penetratingly remarks, "If anything in the Psalms was really composed by David, it is the words of the twenty-fourth psalm, which may well have been sung on the occasion of that great celebration." Its splendor appears when read antiphonally. It should be noted that the portals of the heathen city are fancied by David as too low for the "King of Glory" to enter; Other psalms are also, by some, associated with the festival of bringing up the ark (Ps **15, 29, 30, 101, 68,** and **132.**

But David was not satisfied that the ark of God should dwell "within curtains." He wished to build Jehovah a permanent house. At first, Nathan the prophet bade him to "do all that was in his heart," but subsequently God gave him answer to the contrary. So, Nathan finally commanded: "Thou shalt not build Jehovah a house. But Jehovah will build you a house; that is, He will build for you a throne, a dynasty, and a kingdom, which will culminate implicitly in the Messiah"; hence, permanent and perpetual (2 S **7** 13). The Chronicler gives the reason why David was not permitted to construct a permanent sanctuary: "Thou shalt not build a house for my name, because thou art a man of war, and hast shed blood" (1 Ch **28** 3). This means more than merely that David was too busy fighting to build a permanent sanctuary for the ark (cf 1 Ch **22** 8)!

VIII. David's Marvelous Victories.—David was a great warrior. As in his warfare with the house of Saul, he is said to have "waxed stronger and stronger," so in his conflicts with foreign nations, he won victories far and near; for example:

(1) *Over the Philistines.* Though already incorporated into David's kingdom, by renewed hostilities with them he entirely broke their spirit, and took forever from them whatever supremacy they had in times past enjoyed. As Sayce interprets 2 S **8** 1, "Instead of his being their vassal, they became vassals to him, paying him tribute." Likewise, (2) *Over Moab.* According to a Jewish tradition, the king of Moab had put to death David's aged parents. But whatever was the cause of the war between Moab and Israel, whether revenge or greed, David was completely successful, exterminating two-thirds of the nation, and reducing the remainder to slavery (2 S **8** 2; cf **23** 30). In the same manner also, he humbled (3) *Hadadezer, King of Zobah.* Assyria and Babylonia were at that time powerless. Hadadezer of Syria seized the chance to establish his empire on the ruins of the empire of the Hittites. David accordingly warred a long time with him and his allies, but in the end came off conqueror having taken rich booty. The result was that the whole region about Damascus was added to David's possessions; even Toi, the king of Hamath, sending David valuable presents (2 S **8** 3–12). And (4) *Over the Edomites*, also, he was supremely victorious. The text in 2 S **8** 13–14 which reads "Syrians," as having been vanquished, is corrected in the parallel account by the Chronicler (1 Ch **18** 12) to read "Edomites." While David, as it appears, was occupied in the extreme north, the Edomites invaded Judah from the south, and Joab responded for David, defeating them at the south end of the Dead Sea, so that they became tributaries to Israel. Another victory recorded in the history, is that (5) *Over the Ammonites.* The insult which Hanun insolently returned David's ambassadors who had been sent to congratulate him was received by David as a declaration of war, and the war was a protracted one. The Ammonites found it feasible to hire their neighbors, the Arameans, as mercenaries. A double attack was planned, Abishai assisted Joab. Both were victorious, and after a longe seige, even Rabbah, the capital of the Ammonites fell (2 S **10**). (6) *Amalek, too, was conquered* (2 S **8** 12). In short, "Jehovah gave victory to David whithersoever he

went" (2 S **8** 6, 14). Thus, under David's leadership, and because of his military prowess, Israel, in a few years, became the dominant and most important people in western Asia; "and yet," as Cornill has remarked, "it cannot be claimed that David began a single one of these wars." In the sequence, David dealt justly and righteously with all his defeated subjects. His success and popularity were obviously due to what is related in 2 S **8** 15, "David executed justice and righteousness unto all his people." Associated with these wars are such Psalms as **110, 60** 6–12 (repeated in Ps **108** 7–13), **68,** 18 (cf 2 S **22**), **20** and **21.**

IX. The Calamities of David's Maturer Years.—The greatest tragedy of David's life is recorded in 2 S **11** and **12.** For, just when he reached the zenith of his power, he fell; having conquered all the nations round about him, he failed to conquer himself. He committed a double crime—one which sowed seeds of evil for the remainder of his life. It is the great blemish of his otherwise successful career. To understand the heinousness of the transgression, it is necessary to remember the exalted loftiness of his regal position. He was at the head of one of the most conspicuous world-powers of the ancient world. He had an army of 280,000 soldiers. Joab was his celebrated commander-in-chief; under him there were more than thirty heroes or officers, who had distinguished themselves for their valor during the Philistine wars (cf 2 S **23**; 1 Ch **11**). He also had a personal body guard of 600 hired mercenaries known as Pelethites, Cherethites, and Gittites (2 S **8** 18). Besides, David was a great organizer. He instituted courts of justice, developed commerce, appointed superintendents of agriculture (1 Ch **27** 25), and organized the Levites and the singers of the tabernacle In fact, as of Augustus it was said that "he found Rome brick and left it marble," so it may be said of David he found the nation in chaos and organized it.

Yet David fell. He committed adultery and then attempted to cover his transgression with murder.

1. Bathsheba

He was fully fifty years of age at the time, and ought to have known better. But "in every good man there are still two natures striving for the mastery." It should be noted, that David was tempted when enjoying prosperity and during a period of idleness: Joab had gone out with the army to battle, but "David tarried at Jerusalem" (2 S **11** 1). His sin was, of course, but the natural climax to a long life of polygamy; one common to oriental despots (cf 2 S **3** 2–5). But no apology can excuse him. "Passion had dethroned conscience"! A whole year passed before his sin was made public and confessed. The prophet Nathan brought it about. As the agent of God, Nathan, by means of the exquisite parable of the "Ewe Lamb" (which is incomparably the finest thing of its kind in the Old Testament), brought the king to himself. David received with meekness the prophet's solemn indictment, "Thou art the man," and acknowledged freely that he had sinned against Jeh. Few kings would have made such frank confession. Two psalms are presumably to be associated with his double crime, of adultery with Bathsheba and his virtual murder of Uriah, namely, Ps **51** and **32.** The former is a psalm of confession; the latter, one of forgiveness. Both are solemnly beautiful!

The other great calamity which overtook David in maturer years was the rebellion of Absalom, his

2. Rebellion of Absalom

usurpation of the throne, and David's flight to save his life. This happened perchance ten years after his double crime against Uriah and Bathsheba. "Though the repentance of the king was deep and sincere," as Ottley says, "the long train of miseries which resulted from David's evil example forms a kind of divine commentary on the heinous character of his crime." Other tragedies happened in his polygamous household; Amnon defiled his half-sister Tamar and then turned her away dishonored from his door (2 S **13** 1–19). Absalom, Tamar's brother, waited subtly for two years and then revengefully slew Amnon. Strictly, Absalom, in killing Amnon, had only done what David was required by law to do. For three years in Geshur, whither he had fled for refuge, and for two more in Jerusalem, during which "he saw not the king's face," David and Absalom became estranged (2 S **14**). About this time David seems to have fallen sick (cf Ps **41** 8; **39** 4, 13). Absalom took advantage of the situation and planned to seize his father's throne. For four years he systematically courted popularity with the people, and apparently succeeded. David's treatment of Absalom had alienated him, and his indifference to the people seems also to have alienated them. Disaffection spread rapidly. Even Ahithophel, the aged grandfather of Bathsheba (2 S **11** 3; **23** 34), and David's faithful counselor, deserted him and went over to Absalom.

David was forced to abdicate, and seek involuntary exile. He fled to Mahanaim, far away on the east of the Jordan, leaving ten of his concubines behind to look after the house (2 S **15** 16). Many of his nearest friends and servants, among whom were his two cousins, Joab and Abishai, his bodyguard also, and the Levites accompanied him. But David refused to allow the ark to be carried with him. Indeed, Zadok and Abiathar, the priests, were commissioned to remain and report to him any information they might gather concerning Absalom's designs. Hushai, the Archite, was officially deputed to return from following the king in order to thwart the counsel of Ahithophel. Absalom with his retinue entered Jerusalem almost immediately after David's departure. His first act was to take public possession of the palace and of his father's harem. This from the oriental point of view made future reconciliation between him and his father impossible. Ahithophel then advised that Absalom and his men pursue the king at once. But Hushai advised, rather, the mustering of an army first. The latter's advice carried. Ahithophel's pride was humbled and he killed himself—the first case of deliberate and premeditated suicide recorded in the Scriptures!

With the suicide of Ahithophel, the plot to thwart Absalom's plans of pursuit reaches its climax. Absalom recognizes the scheme, and without further delay he and his army pass over the Jordan. David meanwhile divided his own forces into three companies under Joab, Abishai, and Ittai, respectively. The fatal battle between them and Absalom took place in the "forest of Ephraim," somewhere near Mahanaim. David was too old, as well as too valuable, to enter the contest in person. But his parting advice to his officers was to spare his son's life. Joab, however, knew that the death of Absalom meant victory for the king. When, therefore, Absalom got caught by the head (Josephus says, "hair") in a terebinth, Joab thrust him through with three darts. David's extreme sorrow over his rebellious son was natural but indefensible. As Sayce says, "He allowed the passion of his emotion to sweep him away, and he wept as a woman and not as a man." As a matter of fact, his unrestrained and oriental feeling, though a proof of his genuine affection for his son, almost cost him his kingdom. His followers began to forsake him in disgust. Joab's harsh rebuke, however, brought him to his senses. Nevertheless, David never fully forgave Joab for his rough speech (2 S **19** 5–7; cf 1 K **2** 5–6).

The war over, all the tribes of Israel, except Judah, invited David to return to Jerusalem. The elders of Judah waited until the king shamed them into requesting his return. Just here David lost his wonted discretion. He made the vital mistake of allowing Judah alone to escort him in triumphal procession back to his capital. The result was Israel became jealous; and not long after, Sheba, a Benjamite, led a movement, which two generations later, culminated in permanent schism between Israel and Judah. The king appointed Amasa to quell Sheba's rebellion. This was an insult to Joab, which he fully recognized, and so he murdered Amasa in cold blood, as he had aforetime Abner. Joab then went forward with the royal army, and drove Sheba into the extreme north of the country to Abel, near Dan, where eventually the rebel was beheaded.

X. The Closing Years of David's Life.—The last ten years of David's life seem to have been passed in undisturbed repose. "Israel was at peace with her neighbors, and there was no Absalom to steal away the hearts of the people by his winsomeness of manner" (Sayce). Assyria, Babylonia, and Egypt were all weak during David's period; while the smaller kingdoms of Syria, Ammon, Moab, Edom, and Phoenicia were either wholly subdued by David or in alliance with him. Saul's house was completely fallen, and David's dynasty was apparently secure. But, still, David suffered one more great calamity. This was the three days' pestilence which visited Jerusalem at the warning of the prophet Gad. David had insisted on numbering the children of Israel and Judah; not, however, with a view to the levying of taxes, but in order to ascertain the number of fighting men in the nation. But to take a census was not oriental. Such a royal conscription was not only displeasing to God, but unpopular with the people (2 S **24** 3). The Orientals still have strong prejudices against a census of any kind. David's own heart smote him for having done it (2 S **24** 10), and he was punished. But the divine chastisement issued in his purchase of the threshing-floor of Araunah, the Jebusite, as a place on which to build an altar (2 S **24** 16–18). It afterward became the site of Solomon's temple (2 Ch **3** 1).

More and more David became enfeebled in mind and body. The hardships and privations of his early years and the self-indulgence of his polygamous life in maturer manhood had weakened his constitution, and he slowly sank into his grave. He was approaching seventy years of age. Two of his sons became rivals for the throne: Adonijah, his oldest son, and therefore the natural heir, and Solomon, the son of the ambitious Bathsheba. Joab and Abiathar favored Adonijah, Nathan the prophet and Zadok the priest supported Solomon. The conspiracy was formidable. Adonijah proceeded to usurp the power while the king was still alive, but the plot was soon stifled and Solomon's inauguration took place. The dying king, through Bathsheba's intercession, formally recognizing Solomon as the rightful successor to the throne (1 K **1**), David died soon after. Ps. **2** is thought by some to relate to this period. His "last words" are embodied in 2 S **23** 1–7, a poetical passage in which we have a striking epitome of the ideals which, as a just ruler, he had always placed before himself, and an account of the difficulties which he had felt in realizing them. But, his final mandate to his successor upon the throne is of an entirely different character. After charging Solomon to be strong and to show himself a man, and to keep the law of Moses in order that he might prosper (1 K **2** 1–4), he warns him against Joab and Shimei charging him not to forget their crimes, but to bring their hoar heads down to Sheol in blood (1 K **2** 5–9). The sons of Barzillai, the Gileadite, on the other hand, who showed kindness to David during his exile in Mahanaim, when he fled from Absalom, he charges Solomon to remember, and to let them be of those that eat at the royal table (1 K **2** 7).

David died, according to Josephus, at the age of seventy (*Ant* viii. 15. 2), and "was buried in the city of David" (cf Neh **3** 16). Peter on the day of Pentecost alludes to his sepulchre as "with us unto this day" (Acts **2** 29). Josephus states that Solomon buried vast treasure in it, and that one of its chambers was broken open by Hyrcanus, and another by Herod the Great (*Ant* vii. 15. 3; xiii. 8. 4; xvi. 7. 1). Today archaeologists are seeking to discover it.

XI. An Estimate of David.—In estimating the character of David, it is generally allowed that he is the most gifted and versatile personage in Israelitish history; that he is surpassed in ethical greatness and general historical importance only by Moses; that he completed what Moses began; that he created out of Israel a nation and raised it to its highest eminence; and that in spite of all his human frailties he was a genuinely pious man, an ideal ruler, a lover of righteousness and peace, and the only man of his age who appreciated Israel's religious destiny. According to Dean Stanley, there is no other character of the OT to be compared to David's in the complexity of its elements, passion, tenderness, generosity, and fierceness; David was soldier, shepherd, poet, statesman, priest, prophet, king, the romantic friend, the chivalrous leader, and the devoted father, all in one; Jacob's comes nearest in the variety of elements included in it. "And so," as Cornill suggests, "we can easily understand how the eyes of Israel rested in grateful reverence upon his figure, and how a Second David became the dream of Israel's future."

He founded a dynasty. He established the principle of monarchy. He was patriotic, generous, and kind; a man of strong impulses and firm faith; brave, politic, and forgiving; yet a child of his time. Above everything else David placed religion. He fostered a simple trust in God; he was a heinous sinner, but a correspondingly sincere penitent. He was "the sweet psalmist of Israel" (2 S **23** 1); there is really no reason why many of the 73 Psalms ascribed in their titles to him should not belong to his period, and therefore be the work of David himself. According to some, Ps **18**, which is a duplicate of 2 S **22**, is the only poem of the entire collection which was really composed by him. But as Murray, in his monograph on the *Origin and Growth of the Psalms* (1898) has well said: However "the historian may settle David's character, whether he be a just ruler, great in his own right, or an astute usurper who has snatched the laurels of another, his authentic writings will hand him down to all future time as the world's greatest master of lyric song. He has entered closest to the heart of nature; he has caught, as none other, its ever manifold expression; he has soared nearest heaven, and lifted mankind toward divinity." In short, the least that can be said in praise of David is that he freed his country from its enemies, unified the nation, gave them Jerusalem as their capital, established religion and gave it a home, and as a just and patriotic ruler became an ideal of succeeding generations, and a type of the Messiah. According to 1 S **13** 14, he was "a man after God's own heart" (cf Acts **13** 22); this made him one of the most lovable characters in the OT, and "the most luminous figure and the most gifted personage in the history of Israel" (Cornill).

Among the many virtues which David possessed, the one which stands out above all others is his poetical genius. Other shepherd-boys had harps but David alone could so play as to make his harp work cures of mind! He was the only musician in all Israel who had an ear for music and put his heart into his song. For it was David's heart that made his music cheer others' hearts: it was the divine nature in him that made him a divine musician.

But there were times when his harp was laid aside; for David was a sinner like other men. He was the prodigal son of the Old Testament! After his double crime against Uriah and Bathsheba, David lived for a year, or more, without a word of confession. So far as we know, no penitential psalms were composed during that year. Not until Nathan, indeed, ventured to go to King David and rebuke him for his sins, did he publish the hypocrisy which had quietly slumbered in his soul. The 51st Ps is a confession of his guilt. How he could have lived those twelve months "soaked to the eyes in adultery and murder and not go mad, is simply inconceivable" to one of his friendly biographers. Later, when he realized that God had accepted of his confession, he wrote the song of deliverance which is found in Ps 32. It is a hymn of forgiveness, beginning with the blessedness of forgiveness, and closing with the joy of being forgiven. Augustine inscribed it on the wall of his chamber near his bed.

David wrote another psalm which demonstrates that he was a true theist, and really believed in God. In this psalm he courts twice over the microscopic examination of the all-seeing eye (Ps **139** 23–24). One expositor speaks of David as the "author" of this psalm and of Jesus as its "finisher"! It was psalms like this one, and the 23d, that Mary taught her little son in Nazareth, and which in maturer years became, so to speak, his prayer-book! In due time the language of Jesus became saturated with that of David's psalms (cf Ps **22** 1 and Mt **27** 46).

David's gratitude also furnished him with a great poetic theme. Isaac Walton once remarked: "Though the prophet David was guilty of murder and adultery, and many others of the most deadly sins, yet he was said to be a man after God's own heart, because he abounded more and more with thankfulness than any other that is mentioned in Holy Scripture." He was always ready to yield his own will to God's will. Recall the Scottish version of Ps **103** 1:

"Bless, O my soul, the Lord thy God,
And not forgetful be
Of all his gracious benefits
He hath bestowed on thee."

David's greatest service, we think, was the composition of his psalms. Some 73 are ascribed to him; if, of these he actually wrote only the half, his chief work was not war, nor statescraft, but religious song.

It is possible for the New Testament Christian still to pray in David's own language:

"O Lord, our Lord, how excellent is thy name in all the earth (**8** 1). We call upon our souls and all that is within us to bless his holy name (**103** 1). The lines have fallen unto us in pleasant places (**16** 6). The Lord hath not dealt with us after our sins, nor rewarded us after our iniquities (**103** 10). Against thee, thee only, have I sinned, and done that which is evil in thy sight. Have mercy upon us, O God, according to thy loving-kindness; according to the multitude of thy tender mercies blot out our transgressions. Create also, in us clean hearts, O God, and renew right spirits within us (**51** 4, 1, 10).

And now, Lord, what wait we for? Our hope is in thee (**39** 7). With thee is the fountain of life. In thy light shall we see light (**36** 9). Lift thou up the light of thy countenance upon us (**4** 6). We commit our way unto thee (**37** 5); we cast our burdens upon thee (**55** 22). Keep us as the apple of thine eye. Hide us under the shadow of thy wings (**17** 8). Make us to know our end, and the measure of our days, what it is, that we may know how frail we are (**39** 4). Into thy hand we commend our spirits; redeem us, O thou God of truth (**31** 5).

Blessed be the Lord God, the God of Israel, who only doeth wondrous things; and blessed be his glorious name forever. And let the whole earth be filled with his glory. Amen and Amen (**72** 18, 19)."

The Psalms, being primarily devotional, lead the worshiper up to God. Accordingly, they "will live as long as men are moved by the impulse to praise and to pray." The Rabbins were wont to say: "Though all offerings cease in the future, the offering of praise alone shall not cease; though all prayers cease, thanksgiving alone shall not cease." At the same time, the Psalms, alone, are insufficient to express Christian praise, and for the same reason that the Old Testament is insufficient as a rule of faith. The Church needs not only the song of Moses, but also of the Lamb!

LITERATURE.—Beside the many commentaries on the Psalms by Delitzsch, (5th ed., 1894), Perowne (6th ed., 1886), Cheyne (1888), Maclaren (1890–92), Kirkpatrick (1893–95), Briggs (1906), King (1898–1905), and *The New Century Bible*, there are the various histories of Israel and Judah, and biographies of David, to which special attention should be given: e.g., Ottley, *A Short History of the Hebrews* (1901); Cornill, *History of the People of Israel* (1898); Wade, *OT History* (1903); Sayce, *The Early History of the Hebrews* (1897); Stanley, *Lectures on the History of the Jewish Church* (1893); Whyte, *Bible Characters* (1900); Matheson, *Representative Men of the Bible* (1903); Geikie, *OT Characters* (1884); Willett, *The Moral Leaders of Israel* (1916); Peritz, *OT History* (1915); Sarson and Phillip, *The History of the People of Israel* (1912); Foakes-Jackson, *The Biblical History of the Hebrews to the Christian Era* (1922); Sanders, *History of the Hebrews* (1914); Blackwood, *Bible History* (1928); Kittel, *History of the Hebrews* (1895–96).

GEORGE L. ROBINSON

DAVID, CITY OF. See ZION.

DAVID, ROOT, rōōt, **OF** (**ἡ ῥίζα Δαυείδ,** *hē rhíza Daueíd,* Rev **5** 5; **22** 16): Root here means stock, family, descendant, hence "the Root of David" is that which descended from David, not that from which David descended. Jesus Christ in His human nature and family connections was a descendant of David, a member of his family.

DAVID, TOWER, tou'ẽr, **OF.** See JERUSALEM.

DAWN, dôn, **DAWNING:** The word means the approach of the morning light, the breaking of the day. There are several words in the Bible that indicate this. נֶשֶׁף, *nesheph,* "twilight" of the morning (Job **7** 4; Ps **119** 147). The same word is used for evening twilight (1 S **30** 17; 2 K **7** 5.7); פְּנוֹת הַבֹּקֶר, *penōth ha-bōḳer,* "the turning" of the morning, the change from darkness to light, approach of the morning (Jgs **19** 26); עַפְעַפֵּי שַׁחַר, *'aph'appē shaḥar,* "the eyelids" of the morning (Job **3** 9; **41** 18 [10]); עֲלוֹת הַשַּׁחַר, *'ălōth ha-shaḥar,* "the ascent" or "rise" of the morning (Josh **6** 15); ἐπιφώσκω, *epiphōskō,* "to grow light," the approach of the dawn (Mt **28** 1; Lk **23** 54 m); διαυγάζω, *diaugázō,* "to grow bright," "lustrous" (2 Pet **1** 19), "until the day dawn"; **fig.** of the Second Coming of Christ (cf ver 16).

H. PORTER

DAY, dā (**יוֹם**, *yōm;* **ἡμέρα,** *hēméra*): This common word has caused some trouble to plain readers, because they have not noticed that the word is used in several different senses in the Eng. Bible. When the different uses of the word are understood the difficulty of interpretation vanishes. We note several different uses of the word:

(1) It sometimes means the time from daylight till dark. This popular meaning is easily discovered by the context, e.g. Gen **1** 5; **8** 22, etc. The marked periods of this daytime were morning, noon and night, as with us. See Ps **55** 17. The early hours were sometimes called "the cool of the day" (Gen **3** 8). After the exile the day or daytime was divided into twelve hours and the night into twelve (see Mt **20** 1–12; Jn **11** 9; Acts **23** 23); 6 AM would correspond to the first hour, 9 AM to the third; 12 M to the sixth, etc. The hours were longer during the longer days and shorter during the shorter days, as they always counted 12 hours between sunrise and sunset.

(2) Day also means a period of 24 hours, or the

time from sunset to sunset. In Bible usage the day begins with sunset (see Lev **23** 32; Ex **12** 15–20; 2 Cor **11** 25, where night is put before day). See DAY AND NIGHT.

(3) The word "day" is also used of an indefinite period, e.g. "the day" or "day that" means in general "that time" (see Gen **2** 4; Lev **14** 2); "day of trouble" (Ps **20** 1); "day of his wrath" (Job **20** 28); "day of Jehovah" (Isa **2** 12); "day of the Lord" (1 Cor **5** 5; 1 Thess **5** 2; 2 Pet **3** 10); "day of salvation" (2 Cor **6** 2); "day of Jesus Christ" (Phil **1** 6).

(4) It is used **figuratively** also in Jn **9** 4, where "while it is day" means "while I have opportunity to work, as daytime is the time for work." In 1 Thess **5** 5.8, "sons of the day" means spiritually enlightened ones.

(5) We must also bear in mind that with God time is not reckoned as with us (see Ps **90** 4; 2 Pet **3** 8).

(6) The apocalyptic use of the word "day" in Dnl **12** 11; Rev **2** 10, etc, is difficult to define. It evidently does not mean a natural day. See APOCALYPSE.

(7) On the meaning of "day" in the story of Creation we note (*a*) the word "day" is used of the whole period of creation (Gen **2** 4); (*b*) these days are days of God, with whom one day is as a thousand years; the whole age or period of salvation is called "the day of salvation"; see above. So we believe that in harmony with Bible usage we may understand the creative days as creative periods. See also ASTRONOMY; CREATION; EVOLUTION.

G. H. GERBERDING

Figurative: The word "day" is used fig. in many senses, some of which are here given.

(1) *The span of human life.*—Gen **5** 4: "And the days of Adam . . . . were eight hundred years." "And if thou wilt walk . . . . then I will lengthen thy days" (1 K **3** 14; cf Ps **90** 12; Isa **38** 5).

(2) *An indefinite time.*—Existence in general: Gen **3** 14: "All the days of thy life" (cf Gen **21** 34; Nu **9** 19; Josh **22** 3; Lk **1** 24; Acts **21** 10).

(3) *A set time.*—Gen **25** 24: "And when her days . . . . were fulfilled"; Dnl **12** 13: "Thou shalt stand in thy lot, at the end of the days" (cf Lev **12** 6; Dnl **2** 44).

(4) *A historic period.*—Gen **6** 4: "The Nephilim were in the earth in those days"; Jgs **17** 6: "In those days there was no king in Israel" (cf 1 S **3** 1; 1 Ch **5** 17; Hos **2** 13).

(5) *Past time.*—Ps **18** 18: "the day of my calamity"; Ps **77** 5: "I have considered the days of old" (cf Mic **7** 20; Mal **3** 7; Mt **23** 30).

(6) *Future time.*—Dt **31** 14: "Thy days approach that thou must die"; Ps **72** 7: "In his days shall . . . ." (cf Ezk **22** 14; Joel **2** 29; Mt **24** 19; 2 Pet **3** 3; Rev **9** 6).

(7) *The eternal.*—In Dnl **7** 9.13, where God is called "the ancient of days."

(8) *A season of opportunity.*—Jn **9** 4: "We must work the works of him that sent me, while it is day: the night cometh, when no man can work" (cf Rom **13** 12.13; 1 Thess **5** 5–8). See DAY (4), above.

(9) *Time of salvation.*—Specially referring to the hopes and prospects of the *parousia* (see ESCHATOLOGY OF NT). Rom **13** 12: "The night is far spent, and the day is at hand."

HENRY E. DOSKER

DAY AND NIGHT: "Day," יוֹם, *yōm;* ordinarily, the Heb "day" lasted from dawn to the coming forth of the stars (Neh **4** 21). The context usually makes it clear whether the term "day" refers to the period of twenty-four hours or to daytime; when there was a possibility of confusion, the term לַיְלָה, *laylāh,* "night," was added (Gen **7** 4.12; **31** 39). The "day" is reckoned from evening to evening, in accordance with the order noted in the account of Creation, viz. "And there was evening and there was morning, one day" (Gen **1** 5); Lev **23** 32 and Dnl **8** 14 reflect the same mode of reckoning the day. The phrase עֶרֶב בֹּקֶר, *'erebh bōḳer,* "evening-morning," used in this last passage, is simply a variation of *yōm* and *laylāh,* "day" and "night"; it is the equivalent of the Gr νυχθήμερον, *nuchthēmeron* (2 Cor **11** 25). That the custom of reckoning the day as beginning in the evening and lasting until the following evening was probably of late origin is shown by the phrase "tarry all night" (Jgs **19** 6–9); the context shows that the day is regarded as beginning in the morning; in the evening the day "declined," and until the new day (morning) arrived it was necessary to "tarry all night" (cf also Nu **11** 32).

The transition of day to night begins before sunset and lasts till after sunset; the change of night to day begins before sunrise and continues until after sunrise. In both cases, neither *'erebh,* "evening," nor *bōḳer,* "morning," indicate an exact space of time (cf Gen **8** 11; Ex **10** 13; Dt **16** 6). The term נֶשֶׁף, *nesheph,* is used for both evening twilight and morning dawn (cf 1 S **30** 17; 2 K **7** 5.7; Job **7** 4). As there were no definite measurements of the time of day, the various periods were indicated by the natural changes of the day; thus "midday" was the time of the day when the sun mounted its highest (צָהֳרַיִם, *çohŏrayim*); afternoon was that part of the day when the sun declined (נְטוֹת הַיּוֹם, *n^eṭōth ha-yōm*); and evening was the time of the going down of the sun (עֶרֶב, *'erebh*). "Between the evenings" (בֵּין הָעַרְבַּיִם, *bēn hā-'arbayim*) was the interval between sunset and darkness. The day was not divided into hours until a late period. שָׁעָה, *shā'āh*=Aram. (Dnl **3** 6), is common in Syr and in later Heb; it denoted, originally, any short space of time, and only later came to be equivalent to our "hour" (Driver). The threefold division of the day into watches continued into post-exilic Rom times; but the Rom method of four divisions was also known (Mk **13** 35), where all four divisions are referred to: "at even" (ὀψέ, *opsé*), "midnight" (μεσονύκτιον, *mesonúktion*), "at cock crowing" (ἀλεκτοροφωνία, *alektorophōnía*), "in the morning" (πρωί, *prōí*). These last extended from six to six o'clock (cf also Mt **14** 25; Mk **13** 35). Acts **12** 4 speaks of four parties of four Rom soldiers (quaternions), each of whom had to keep guard during one watch of the night. In *B^erākhōth* **3***b*, Rabbi Nathan (2d cent.) knows of only three night-watches; but the patriarch, Rabbi Judah, knows four. See also DAY.

HORACE J. WOLF

DAY BEFORE THE SABBATH (ἡ παρασκευή, *hē paraskeuḗ,* "preparation"): Considered as a day of preparation, in accordance with Ex **16** 23, both before the regular Sabbath and before a feast Sabbath (Mt **27** 62; Mk **15** 42; Lk **23** 54; Jn **19** 14.31.42). At 3 PM, the Hebrews began to prepare their food for the next day, and to perform all labors which were forbidden to be done on the Sabbath and yet must be done. They bathed and purified themselves, dressed in festive apparel, set their tables, and lighted their lamps. On the day before Easter, the Hebrews of the later period made it their chief business to remove all leaven from the house (1 Cor **5** 7). This custom of converting at least a portion of the day before the Sabbath into a holy day was recognized by the Romans to such an extent that, according to a rescript of Augustus, Jews need not appear in court after 3 PM on such days. Criminal cases were not brought before court on this day, and journeys exceeding 12 Rom miles were prohibited. The signal for the preparations was given by the priests by means of trumpets blown six times at intervals.

FRANK E. HIRSCH

DAY, BREAK OF. See BREAK OF DAY.

DAY, JOSHUA'S LONG. See BETH-HORON, BATTLE OF.

DAY, LAST (ἡ ἐσχάτη ἡμέρα, *hē eschátē hēméra*): Repeatedly used by Jesus in Jn (**6** 39.40.44.54; **11** 24; **12** 48) for the day of resurrection and judgment (see ESCHATOLOGY OF THE NT). Cf the usage in the OT (Isa **2** 2; Mic **4** 1) and the NT (Acts **2** 17; 2 Tim **3** 1; 2 Pet **3** 3; 1 Jn **2** 18; Jude ver 18) of "last days" and "last time" to denote the Messianic age. See LATTER DAYS; LAST DAYS; LAST TIME.

In Jn **7** 37, "the last day, the great day of the feast" refers to the eighth day of the feast of Tabernacles. This closing day was observed as a Sabbath (Lev **23** 36). On it the libation of water made on other days was not made; hence the allusion of Jesus to Himself as the Giver of the living water.

JAMES ORR

DAY, LORD'S. See LORD'S DAY.

DAY OF ATONEMENT. See ATONEMENT, DAY OF.

DAY OF CHRIST. See DAY OF THE LORD.

DAY OF JEHOVAH. See DAY OF THE LORD.

DAY OF JUDGMENT. See JUDGMENT, LAST.

DAY OF THE LORD (JEHOVAH) (יוֹם יְהוָֹה, *yōm YHWH;* ἡ ἡμέρα τοῦ Κυρίου, *hē hēméra toú Kuríou*): The idea is a common OT one. It denotes the consummation of the kingdom of God and the absolute cessation of all attacks upon it (Isa **2** 12; **13** 6.9; **34** 8; Ezk **13** 5; **30** 3; Joel **1** 15; **2** 11; Am **5** 18; Zeph **1** 14; Zec **14** 1). It is a "day of visitation" (Isa **10** 3), a day "of the wrath of Jeh" (Ezk **7** 19), a "great day of Jeh" (Zeph **1** 14). The entire conception in the OT is dark and foreboding.

On the other hand the NT idea is pervaded with the elements of hope and joy and victory. In the NT it is eminently the day of Christ, the day of His coming in the glory of His father. The very conception of Him as the "Son of Man" points to this day (E. Kuehl, *Das Selbstbewusstsein Jesu*, 68). Jn **5** 27: "And he gave him authority to execute judgment, because he is a son of man" (cf Mt **24** 27.30; Lk **12** 8). It is true in the NT there is a dark background to the bright picture, for it still remains a "day of wrath" (Rom **2** 5.6), a "great day" (Rev **6** 17; Jude ver 6), a "day of God" (2 Pet **3** 12), a "day of judgment" (Mt **10** 15; 2 Pet **3** 7; Rom **2** 16). Sometimes it is called "that day" (Mt **7** 22; 1 Thess **5** 4; 2 Tim **4** 8), and again it is called "the day" without any qualification whatever, as if it were the only day worth counting in all the history of the world and of the race (1 Cor **3** 13). To the unbeliever, the NT depicts it as a day of terror; to the believer, as a day of joy. For on that day Christ will raise the dead, esp. His own dead, the bodies of those that believed in Him—"that of all that which he hath given me I should lose nothing, but should raise it up at the last day" (Jn **6** 39). In that day He comes to His own (Mt **16** 27), and therefore it is called "the day of our Lord Jesus" (2 Cor **1** 14), "the day of Jesus Christ" or "of Christ" (Phil **1** 6.10), the day when there "shall appear the sign of the Son of man in heaven" (Mt **24** 30). All Paulinic lit. is esp. suffused with this longing for the "*parousia*," the day of Christ's glorious manifestation. The entire conception of that day centers therefore in Christ and points to the everlasting establishment of the kingdom of heaven, from which sin will be forever eliminated, and in which the antithesis between Nature and grace will be changed into an everlasting synthesis. See also ESCHATOLOGY (OF OT AND NT).

HENRY E. DOSKER

DAY'S JOURNEY, jûr'ni (דֶּרֶךְ יוֹם, *derekh yōm*, Gen **30** 36; Nu **10** 33; **11** 31; ἡμέρας ὁδός, *hēméras hodós*, Lk **2** 44): The common way of estimating distances in the East is by hours and days. This is natural in a country where roads are mere bridle paths or non-existent, as in the desert. The distance traveled must of course differ largely according to the difficulties of the way, and it is more important to know where night will overtake the traveler than the actual distance accomplished. A day's journey is now commonly reckoned at about 3 miles per hour, the distance usually covered by a loaded mule, the number of hours being about 8. Hence a day's journey is about 24 miles, and this may be taken as a fair estimate for Bible times.

H. PORTER

DAYS, LAST. See LAST DAYS.

DAYSMAN, dāz'man (יָכַח, *yākhaḥ*, "to argue, decide, convince," RV UMPIRE): The use of this word appears to have been more common in the 16th cent. than at the later date of the tr of AV, when its adoption was infrequent. The oldest instance of the term given in the *Oxford English Dictionary* is *Plumpton Corresp.* (1489), p. 82: "Sir, the dayesmen cannot agre us." It appears also in the 1551 ed of the OT in 1 S **2** 25, where the EV "judge" is tr[d] "dayes-man." Tindale's tr has for Ex **21** 22, "He shall paye as the dayesmen appoynte him" (EV as the "judges determine"). See also Edmund Spenser's *Faerie Queene*, ii, c. 8, published in 1590. As used in AV (Job **9** 33) the word means an arbitrator, umpire, referee; one who stands in a judicial capacity between two parties, and decides upon the merits of their arguments or case at law. "Neither is there any daysman [RV "umpire"] betwixt us, that might lay his hand upon us both" (cf Gen **31** 37). It was the eastern custom for a judge to lay his hands upon the heads of the two parties in disagreement, thus emphasizing his adjudicatory capacity and his desire to render an unbiased verdict. Job might consider a human judge as capable of acting as an umpire upon his own claims, but no man was worthy to question the purposes of Jeh, or **metaphorically**, to "lay his hands upon" Him.

In the NT (1 Cor **4** 3, ἀνθρωπίνη, *anthrōpínē*, ἡμέρα, *hēméra*) "man's judgment" is lit. "man's day," in the sense of a day fixed for the trial of a case. Both Tindale and Coverdale so translate. See also 1 Tim **2** 5, where the Saviour is termed the "one mediator . . . . between God and men." Here the word understands a pleader, an advocate before an umpire, rather than the adjudicator himself (see Job **19** 25–27).

ARTHUR WALWYN EVANS

DAYSPRING, dā'spring: This beautiful Eng. word, in current use in the time of the AV, is found in the OT as the tr of שַׁחַר, *shaḥar*, "Hast thou . . . . caused the dayspring to know his place?" (Job **38** 12 AV). This is no doubt intended lit. for the dawn. The "place" of the dayspring is the particular point of the horizon at which the sun comes up on any given day. This slowly changes day by day through the year, moving northward from midwinter till midsummer, and back again southward from midsummer to midwinter. See ASTRONOMY, I, 2. Also once in the NT for ἀνατολή, *anatolḗ*, "a rising."

"The dayspring from on high hath visited us" (AV; RV "shall visit us," Lk **1** 78). Also in Apoc, "At the dayspring pray unto thee" (AV; RV "plead with thee at the dawning of the light," Wisd **16** 28). Both the Heb and Gr words, however, are of frequent occurrence, but variously rendered, "dawn," "break of day," "morning," "sunrise," "east." Note esp. "the spring of the day" (1 S **9** 26), "the day began to spring" (Jgs **19** 25). Used with *hēlíou*, "sun," for rising of the sun (Rev **7** 2; **16** 12). In LXX the same Gr word is used for Heb *çemaḥ*, "branch," to designate the Messiah (Jer **23** 5; Zec **6** 12). But this sense of the word is wholly unknown in profane Gr. The word is also employed in LXX to express the rising of a heavenly body, as the moon (Isa **60** 19). This is good Gr. See the kindred vb. *anatéllō*, "to rise" (LXX, Isa **60** 1; Mal **4** 2).

What is the meaning of *anatolē* in Lk **1** 78? Certainly not branch; that does not fit any of the facts, unless it be rendered "branch of light" (see Reynolds, *John the Baptist*, 115). It occurs in Zacharias' hymn over the birth of his son. The ode consists of two parts, "The glory and security of the Messiah's kingdom," and "The glory of the Forerunner." The expression before us is in the latter part. It naturally refers, therefore, not to the Messiah himself, but to John. He is the dayspring from on high who hath visited the people who sat in darkness and the shadow of death. With Godet we believe that the picture is borrowed from the caravan which has missed its way in the desert. The unfortunate pilgrims, overtaken by the night, are sitting down expecting death, when suddenly a star brightly beams above them. They take courage at the sight. The whole caravan leaps to its feet. It is the herald of the coming day and soon they see the great orb himself filling the east with orient pearl and gold. Is not one tempted to go a little farther and see here the morning star, herald of the coming sun to be obliterated by his rising? 'He must wax, but I must wane' (Jn **3** 30). What was John's work but, by his own testimony, to guide the benighted pilgrims into the way of peace, that is, to Him who was the Prince of Peace? If, however, as by most commentators, it be taken to refer to the Messiah, it probably implies prophetic knowledge that the conception of Jesus had already taken place, and that the Messianic era was at hand, when the Jewish world should be filled with spiritual splendor. See DAY-STAR. G. H. TREVER

DAY-STAR (הֵילֵל בֶּן־שָׁחַר, *hēlēl ben-shaḥar*, Isa **14** 12; **φωσφόρος**, *phōsphóros*, 2 Pet **1** 19): The OT passage is rendered in AV "Lucifer, son of the morning," in AVm and RV "day-star," i.e. the morning star. The reference is to the king of Babylon (ver 4). In 2 Pet **1** 19, "Until . . . . the day-star arise in your hearts," the word is lit. "light-bringer." It is applicable, therefore, not only to the planet Venus, seen as a morning star, herald of the dawn, but to the sun itself, and is used here as a title of Our Lord. See ASTRONOMY, I, 6.

DAY, THAT (THE). See DAY OF THE LORD.

DEACON, dē'k'n, **DEACONESS,** dē'k'n-es: The term διάκονος, *diákonos*, and its cognates occur many times in the NT, as do its synonyms ὑπηρέτης, *hupērétēs*, and δοῦλος, *doúlos*, with their respective cognates. It may be said in general that the terms denote the service or ministration of the bondservant (*doulos*), underling (*hupēretēs*) or helper (*diakonos*), in all shades and gradations of meaning both literal and metaphorical. It would serve no useful purpose to list and discuss all the passages in detail. Christianity has from the beginning stood for filial service to God and His kingdom and for brotherly helpfulness to man, and hence terms expressive of these functions abound in the NT. It behooves us to inquire whether and where they occur in a technical sense sufficiently defined to denote the institution of a special ecclesiastical office, from which the historical diaconate may confidently be said to be derived.

Many have sought the origin of the diaconate in the institution of the Seven at Jerus (Acts **6**), and this view was countenanced by many of the church Fathers. The Seven were appointed to "serve tables" (*diakoneín trapézais*), in order to permit the Twelve to "continue stedfastly in prayer, and in the ministry [*diakonía*] of the word." They are not called deacons (*diakonoi*), and the qualifications required are not the same as those prescribed by Paul in 1 Tim **3** 8–12; furthermore, Stephen appears in Acts preëminently as a preacher, and Philip as an evangelist. Paul clearly recognizes women as deaconesses, but will not permit a woman to teach (1 Tim **2** 12). The obvious conclusion is that the Seven may be called the first deacons only in the sense that they were the earliest recorded helpers of the Twelve as directors of the church, and that they served in the capacity, among others, of specially appointed ministrants to the poor.

Paul says, "I commend unto you Phoebe our sister, who is a servant [RVm "or, deaconess"] of the church that is at Cenchreae" (Rom **16** 1). This is by many taken as referring to an officially appointed deaconess; but the fact that there is in the earlier group of Paul's epistles no clear evidence of the institution of the diaconate, makes against this interpretation. Phoebe was clearly an honored helper in the church closely associated with that at Corinth, where likewise evidence of special ecclesiastical organization is wanting.

In Phil **1** 1 Paul and Timothy send greetings "to all the saints . . . . at Philippi, with the bishops and deacons." Here then we find mention of "deacons" in a way to suggest a formal diaconate; but the want of definition as to their qualifications and duties renders it impossible to affirm with certainty the existence of the office.

In 1 Tim **3** 8–12, after prescribing the qualifications and the method of appointment of a bishop or overseer, Paul continues: "Deacons in like manner must be grave, not double-tongued, not given to much wine, not greedy of filthy lucre; holding the mystery of the faith in a pure conscience. And let these also first be proved; then let them serve as deacons, if they be blameless. Women in like manner must be grave, not slanderers, temperate, faithful in all things. Let deacons be husbands of one wife, ruling their children and their own houses well." Deacons and deaconesses are here provided for, and the character of their qualifications makes it clear that they were to be appointed as dispensers of alms, who should come into close personal relations with the poor.

We conclude, therefore, that the Seven and Phoebe did not exercise the diaconate in a technical sense, which appears first certainly in 1 Tim **3**, although it is not improbably recognized in Phil **1** 1, and was foreshadowed in the various agencies for the dispensing of alms and the care of the poor of the church instituted in various churches at an earlier date. See also BISHOP; CHURCH; CHURCH GOVERNMENT. WILLIAM ARTHUR HEIDEL

DEAD, ded (מוּת, *mūth*; **νεκρός**, *nekrós*): Used in several senses: (1) as a substantive, denoting the body deprived of life, as when Abraham speaks of burying his dead (Gen **23**); (2) as a collective noun including all those that have passed away from life (as Rev **20** 12). In several passages *dead* in this sense is used in contrast to the quick or living (as Nu **16** 48). This collective mode of expression is used when resurrection is described as "rising from the dead"; (3) as an adj., coupled with body, carcase or man, as Dt **14** 8 AV; (4) most frequently it is used as a complement of the vb. "to be," referring to the condition of being deceased or the period of death, e.g. 2 S **12** 19; Mk **5** 35; (5) in the sense of being liable to death it occurs in Gen **20** 3; Ex **12** 33; 2 S **16** 9; (6) as an intensive adj. it is used in the phrase "dead sleep," to mean profound sleep simulating death (Ps **76** 6); (7) **figuratively** "dead" is used to express the spiritual condition of those who are unable to attain to the life of faith. They are dead in trespasses, as in Eph **2** 1, or conversely, those who by the New Birth are delivered from sin, are said to be dead to the Law (as Col **2** 20, etc). A faith which does not show its life in the practical virtues of Christianity is called *dead* (Jas **2** 17); (8) in Rom **4** 19; He **11** 12, "dead" signifies the senile condition of loss of vigor and virility.

The passage in Job (**26** 5), wherein in AV "dead things" seem to mean things that never had life, is more accurately tr[d] in RV as "they that are deceased," i.e. the shades of the dead.

There are few references to the physical accompaniments of the act of dying. Deborah has a poetical account of the death of Sisera (Jgs **5** 24 ff), and in Eccl **12**, where the failure of the bodily faculties in old age culminates in death, it is pictorially compared to the breaking of a lamp extinguishing the flame ("golden" being probably used of "oil," as it is in Zec **4** 12), and the loosing of the silver *ḥebhel* or chain by which the lamp is suspended in the tent of the Arab.

The dead body defiled those who touched it (Lev **11** 31) and therefore sepulture took place speedily, as in the case of Lazarus (Jn **11** 17–39) and Ananias and Sapphira (Acts **5** 6–10). This practice is still followed by the fellahin.

The uselessness of the dead is the subject of a proverb (Eccl **9** 4) and the phrase "dead dog" is used as a contemptuous epithet as of a person utterly worthless (1 S **24** 14; 2 S **9** 8; **16** 9).

ALEX. MACALISTER

DEAD, BAPTISM FOR THE. See BAPTISM FOR THE DEAD.

DEAD BODY. See CORPSE.

DEADLY, ded'li: In the OT two words are used in the sense of a "mortal [Heb *nephesh*, "hateful," "foul"] enemy" (Ps **17** 9), and in the sense of "fatal disease," the destructiveness of which causes a general panic (Heb *māweth*, "death," 1 S **5** 11).

In the NT we have in Rev **13** 3.12 the expression "deadly wound" (Gr *thánatos*), better "death-stroke," as in RV, and the phrases "deadly thing," i.e. poison (*thanásimón ti*, Mk **16** 18), and "full of deadly poison" (*mestḗ ioú thanatēphórou*, Jas **3** 8), said of an unruly tongue. Both Gr words convey the idea of "causing or bringing death" and occur in classical lit. in a variety of uses in combination with the bite of venomous reptiles, deadly potions, mortal wounds and fatal contagion.

H. L. E. LUERING

DEAD SEA, THE:

The name given by Gr and Lat writers to the remarkable inland lake occupying the deepest part of the depression of the ARABAH (q.v.). In the Bible it is called the Salt Sea (Gen **14** 3; Dt **3** 17); the Sea of the Plain (*'Ărābhāh*) (Josh **3** 16); and the (East) Eastern Sea (Ezk **47** 18; Joel **2** 20). Among the Arabs it is still called *Bahr Lût* (Sea of Lot). By Jos it was called Lake Asphaltites (*Ant*, I, ix) from the quantities of bitumen or asphalt occasionally washed upon its shores and found in some of the tributary wadies.

I. Present Area.—The length of the lake from N. to S. is 47 miles; its greatest width 10 miles narrowing down to less than 2 miles opposite Point Molyneux on *el-Lisân*. Its area is approximately 300 sq. miles. From various levelings its surface is found to be 1,292 ft. below that of the Mediterranean, while its greatest depth, near the eastern shore 10 miles S. of the mouth of the Jordan is 1,278 ft. But the level varies from 10 to 15 ft. semiannually, and more at longer intervals; and we are not sure from which one of these levels the above figures have been derived. Throughout the northern half of the lake on the E. side the descent to the extreme depth is very rapid; while from the western side the depth increases more gradually, esp. at the extreme northern end, where the lake has been filled in by the delta of the Jordan.

Jebel Usdum from the South, Looking over the Mud Flat (Vale of Siddim) Covered by the Sea in High Water. (Photo. by Libbey.)

About two-thirds of the distance to the southern end, the peninsula, *el-Lisân* ("the Tongue"), projects from the E. more than half-way across the lake, being in the shape, however, of a boot rather than a tongue, with the toe to the N., forming a bay between it and the eastern mainland. The head of this bay has been largely filled in by the débris brought down by *Wady Kerak*, and *Wady Ben Hamid*, and shoals very gradually down to the greatest depths to the N. The toe of this peninsula is named Point Costigan, and the heel, Point Molyneux, after two travelers who lost their lives about the middle of the 19th cent. in pioneer attempts to explore the lake. Over the entire area S. of Point Molyneux, the water is shallow, being nowhere more than 15 ft. deep, and for the most part not over 10 ft., and in some places less than 6 ft. In high water the lake extends a mile or more beyond low-water mark, over the Mud Flat (*Sebkah*) at the south end.

From the history of the crossing of the Jordan by Joshua and the expedition of Chedorlaomer when Lot was captured, it is evident that the outlines of the sea were essentially the same 3,500 years ago as they are now, showing that there has been no radical change in climatic conditions since then.

II. Former Enlargement.—But if we go back a few thousand years into prehistoric times the evidence is abundant that the valley has witnessed remarkable climatic changes (see ARABAH). At *Ain Abu Werideh*, about 40 miles beyond the south end of the lake, Hull in 1883 discovered deposits of an abandoned shore line 1,400 ft. above its level (see ARABAH). A pronounced abandoned shore line at the 650 ft. level had been observed first by Tristram, and noted afterward by many travelers. But from the more detailed examination made by Professor Ellsworth Huntington in 1909 (see *Pal and Its Transformation*) five abandoned shore lines of marked size have been determined,

Remnant of the 650-ft. Abandoned Shore Line at S. W. Corner of Dead Sea, Surmounted by Crusaders' Castle and in Places Excavated to Furnish Places of Shelter. (Photo. by F. B. Wright.)

surrounding the valley at the following approximate heights above the present level of the lake: 1,430, 640, 430, 300 and 250 ft. He writes that "at its greatest extent the sea stretched at least 30 miles south of its present termination, while northward it probably covered the Sea of Galilee and the Waters of Merom, and sent an arm into the Vale of Jezreel. . . . . Lacustrine deposits exist in the Jordan valley shortly south of the Sea of Galilee. A mile north of *Jisr el-Mujamiyeh*, as the modern railroad bridge is called, a tilted series of clays, apparently lacustrine, lies under some untilted whitish clays, also apparently lacustrine. The elevation here is about 840 ft. below that of the Mediterranean Sea, or 450 above the Dead Sea. . . . . So far as can be detected by the aneroid the highest deposits [about the Dead Sea] lie at the same elevation on all sides of the lake."

There are also numerous minor strands below the 250 ft. major strand. These are estimated by Huntington as 210, 170, 145, 115, 90, 70, 56, 40, 30 and 12 ft. above the lake successively. It is noted, also, that the lower beaches all show less erosion than those above them. This certainly points to a gradual diminution of the water in the basin during the prehistoric period, while on the other hand there is much evidence that there has been a considerable rise in the water within the historic period. Date palms and tamarisks are seen standing out from the water in numerous places some little distance from the present shore where the water is several feet deep. These are of such size as to show that for many years the soil in which they grew was not subject to overflow. As long ago as 1876 Merrill noticed such trees standing in the water 40 ft. from the shore, near the N.E. corner of the lake (*East of the Jordan*, 224). Numerous trunks of date palms and tamarisks can now be seen submerged to a similar extent along the western shore. In 1818 Irby and Mangles (*Travels*, 454) saw a company of Arabs ford the lake from Point Molyneux to the west side, and noted that the line of the ford was marked by branches of trees which had been stuck into the bottom. In 1838 Robinson found the water at such a stage that the ford was impracticable and so it has been reported by all travelers since that time. But Mr. A. Forder, having recently examined the evidence for the Pal Exploration Fund, learns from the older Arabs that formerly there was a well-known causeway leading from *el-Lisân* opposite *Wady Kerak* to *Wady Umm Baghek*, across which sheep, goats and men could pass, while camels and mules could be driven across anywhere in the water. Moreover the Arab guide said that the channel "was so narrow that the people of his tribe used to sit on the edge of the *Lisân* and parley with Arabs from the west as to the return of cattle that had been stolen by one or other of the parties." (See *PEFS* [April, 1910], 112.)

III. Level of, in Early Historic Times.—Numerous general considerations indicate that in the early historic period the level of the water was so much lower than now that much of the bay S. of Point Molyneux was dry land. In Josh **15** 2.5 f the south border of Judah is said to extend from "the bay [tongue, *Lisân*] that looketh southward"; while the "border of the north quarter was from the bay [tongue, *Lisân*] of the sea at the end of the Jordan; and the border went up to *Beth-hoglah*, and passed along by the north of *Beth-arabah*." If the limits of the north end of the Dead Sea were the same then as now the boundary must have turned down to the mouth of the Jordan by a sharp angle. But according to the description it runs almost exactly E. and W. from beyond Jerus to *Beth-hoglah*, and nothing is said about any change in direction, while elsewhere, any such abrupt change in direction as is here supposed is carefully noted. Furthermore, in detailing the boundary of Benjamin (Josh **18** 19) we are told that "the border passed along to the side of Beth-hoglah northward; and the goings out of the border were at the north bay [tongue, *Lisân*] of the Salt Sea, at the south end of the Jordan: this was the south border." This can hardly have any other meaning than that the north end of the Dead Sea was at *Beth-hoglah*. From these data Mr. Clermont-Ganneau (see *Recueil d'archéologie orientale*, V [1902], 267–80) inferred that in the time of Joshua the level of the sea was

Beach at Low Water at the North End of the Dead Sea, Bordering the Plain of Jericho. (Photo. by Libbey.)

so much higher than now that a tongue-like extension reached the vicinity of *Beth-hoglah*, while the underlying topography was essentially the same as now. On the contrary, our present knowledge of the geologic forces in operation would indicate that at that time the Dead Sea was considerably lower than now, and that its rise to its present level has been partly caused by the silting up of a bay which formerly extended to *Beth-hoglah*.

VIEW FROM MOUNT OF OLIVES, OVERLOOKING THE DEAD SEA

The geological evidence concerning this point is so interesting, and of so much importance in its bearing upon our interpretation of various historical statements concerning the region, that it is worth while to present it somewhat in detail. As already stated (see ARABAH), the present level of the Dead Sea is determined by the equilibrium established between the evaporation (estimated at 20,000,000 cubic ft. per diem) over the area and the amount of the extent to which these encroachments have tended to narrow the limits of the original lake. The sediment deposited by the Jordan, at the north end of the Dead Sea, is practically all derived from the portion of the drainage basin between it and the Sea of Galilee—the latter serving as a catch-basin to retain the sediment brought down from the upper part of the valley. The *Zôr*, or narrow channel which the Jordan has eroded in the sedimentary

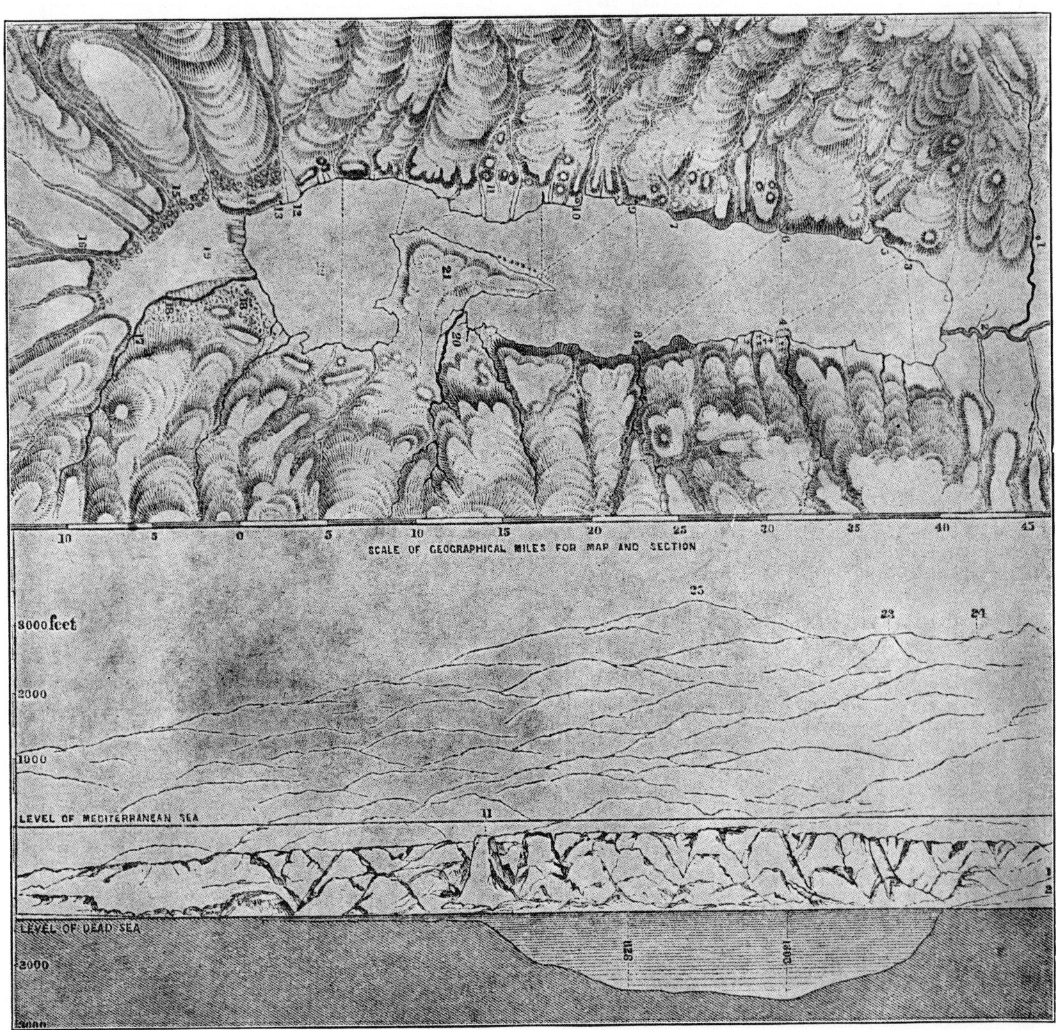

MAP AND LONGITUDINAL SECTION (FROM NORTH TO SOUTH) OF THE DEAD SEA, FROM THE OBSERVATIONS, SURVEYS AND SOUNDINGS OF LYNCH, ROBINSON, DE SAULCY, VAN DE VELDE AND OTHERS.

1. Jericho. 2. Ford of Jordan. 3. Wady Kumran. 4. Wady Zerka Ma'ain. 5. Râs Feshkah. 6. Ain Terâbeh. 7. Râs Mersed. 8. Wady Mojib. 9. Ain Jidy. 10. Birket el-Khulil. 11. Sebbeh. 12. Wady Zuweirah. 13. Um Zoghal. 14. Jebel Usdum. 15. Wady el-Fikri. 16. Wady el-Jeib. 17. Wady Tufileh. 18. Ghor es Safieh. 19. Plain es Sebkah. 20. Wady ed Dra'ah. 21. The Peninsula. 22. The Lagoon. 23. The Frank Mountain. 24. Bethlehem. 25. Hebron. (The dotted lines show the place of the transverse sections shown in the following illustration.)

water brought into the valley by the tributary streams. The present area of the sea is, in round numbers, 300 sq. miles. The historical evidence shows that this evaporating surface has not varied appreciably since the time of Abraham. But the encroachments of the delta of the Jordan upon this area, as well as of the deltas of several other streams, must have been very great since that period. The effect of this would be to limit the evaporating surface, which would cause the water to rise until it overflowed enough of the low land at the south end to restore the equilibrium.

It is easy to make an approximate calculation of plain through which it flows (see JORDAN, VALLEY OF), is approximately half a mile wide, 100 feet deep, and 60 miles long. All the sediment which formerly filled this has been swept into the head of the sea, while the *Jarmuk*, the *Jabbok*, and a score of smaller tributaries descending rapidly from the bordering heights of Gilead, three or four thousand ft. above the valley, bring an abnormal amount of débris into the river, as do a large number of shorter tributaries which descend an equal amount from the mountains of Galilee, Samaria, and Judah. The entire area thus contributing to this part of the Jordan is not less than 3,000 sq. miles.

All writers are impressed by the evidence of the torrential floods which fill these water courses after severe storms. The descent being so rapid, permits the water after each rainfall to run off without delay, and so intensifies its eroding power. The well-known figure of Our Lord (Mt **7** 26 ff) in describing the destruction of the house which is built upon the sand, when the rains descend and the winds beat upon it, is drawn from Nature. The delta terraces at the mouths of such mountain streams where they debouch on the lowlands are formed and re-formed with extreme rapidity, each succeeding storm tending to wash the previous delta down to lower levels and carry away whatever was built upon it.

The storms which descend upon the plains of Gilead, as well as those upon the Judaean hills, are exceedingly destructive. For though the rainfall at Jerus, according to the observations of Chaplin (see J. Glaisher, "On the Fall of Rain at Jerus," *PEFS* [January, 1894], 39) averages but 20 inches annually, ranging from 32.21 inches in 1878 to 13.39 inches in 1870, nearly all occurs in the three winter months, and therefore in quantities to be most effective in erosive capacity. And this is effective upon both sides of the Jordan valley, in which the rainfall is very slight. "Day after day," Tristram remarks, "we have seen the clouds, after pouring their fatness on Samaria and Judaea, pass over the valley, and then descend in torrents on the hills of Gilead and Moab," a phenomenon naturally resulting from the rising column of heated air coming up from the torrid conditions of the depressed Jordan valley.

Tristram (*The Land of Moab*, 23, 24) gives a vivid description of the effect of a storm near Jerus. As his party was encamped during the night the whole slope upon which they pitched became a shallow stream, while "the deep ravines of the wilderness of Judah [were] covered with torrents, and tiny cascades rolling down from every rock. . . . . So easily disintegrated is the soft limestone of these wadies, that the rain of a few hours . . . . did more to deepen and widen the channels than the storms of several years could effect on a Northumbrian hillside. No geologist could watch the effect of this storm without being convinced that in calculating the progress of denudation, other factors than that of time must be taken into account, and that denudation may proceed most rapidly where rains are most uncertain."

Lieutenant Lynch writes that while ascending the Kerak "there came a shout of thunder from the dense cloud which had gathered at the summit of the gorge, followed by a rain, compared to which the gentle showers of our more favoured clime are as dew drops to the overflowing cistern. . . . . The black and threatening cloud soon enveloped the mountain tops, the lightning playing across it in incessant flashes, while the loud thunder reverberated from side to side of the appalling chasm. Between the peals we soon heard a roaring and continuous sound. It was the torrent from the rain cloud, sweeping in a long line of foam down the steep declivity, bearing along huge fragments of rocks, which, striking against each other, sounded like mimic thunder."

I can bear similar testimony from observations when traveling in Turkestan where the annual rainfall is only about 4 inches. At one time a storm was seen raging upon the mountains 20 miles away, where it spent its entire force without shedding a drop upon the plain. Upon skirting the base of the mountain the next day, however, the railroad track was covered for a long distance 2 or 3 ft. deep with débris which had been washed down by the cloudburst. No one can have any proper comprehension of the erosive power of the showers of Pal without duly taking into account the extent and the steepness of the descent from the highlands on either side, and the irregularity of the rainfall. These form what in the Rocky Mountains would be called

1. From Ain Feshkhah to E. shore.

West East

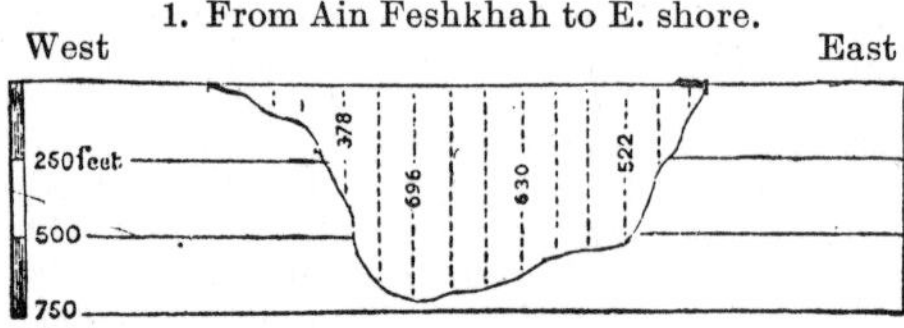

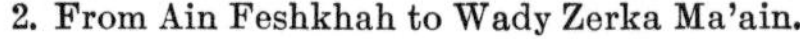
2. From Ain Feshkhah to Wady Zerka Ma'ain.

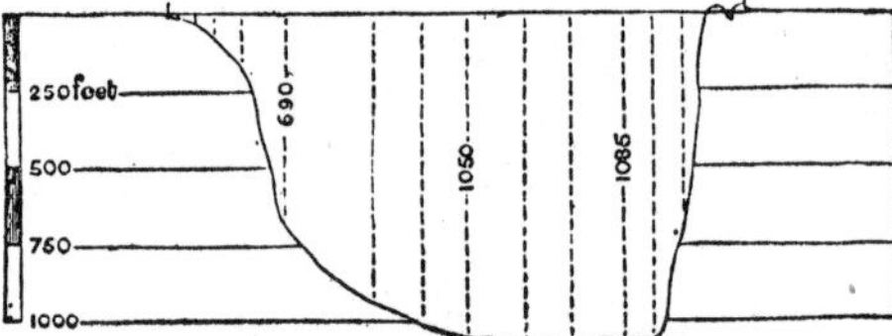

3. From Ain Terâbeh to Wady Zerka.

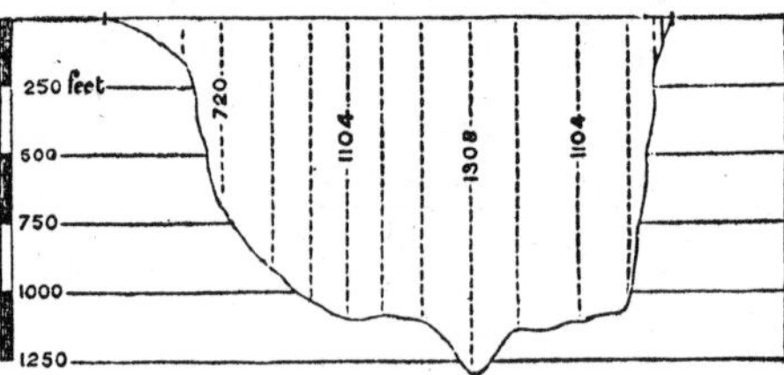

4. From Ain Terâbeh to Wady Mojib.

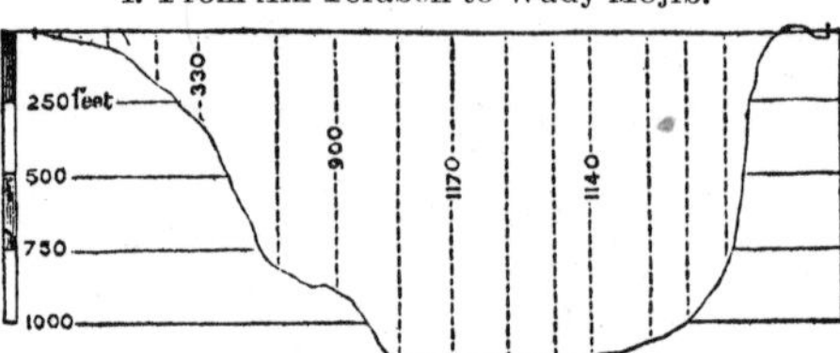

5. From Ain Jidy to Wady Mojib.

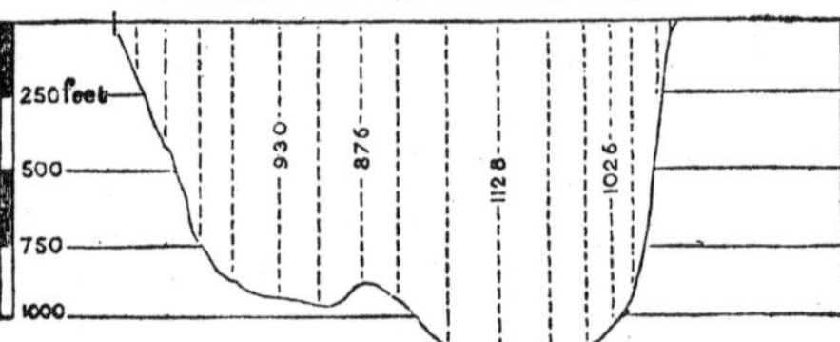

6. From Ain Jidy to the N. point of Peninsula.

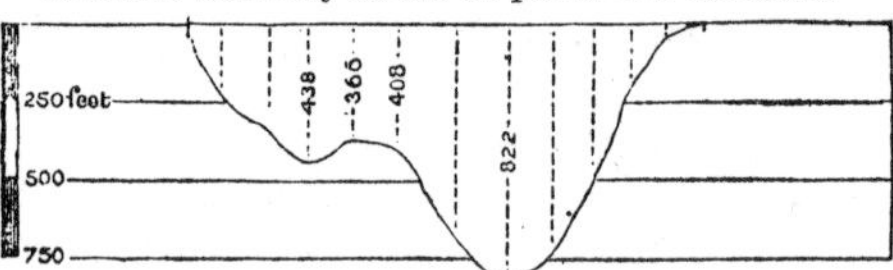

7. From the W. shore to the N. point of Peninsula.

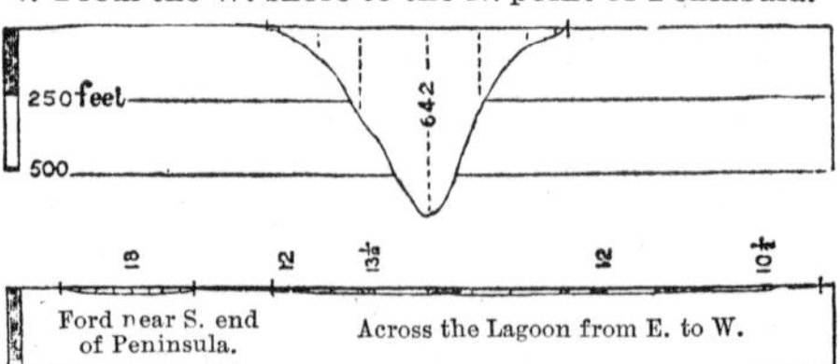

Transverse Section (from West to East) of the Dead Sea; Plotted from the Soundings Given by Lynch, 1849.

arroyos. After the débris has been brought into the Jordan by these torrents, and the rise of water makes it "overflow all its banks," the sediment is then swept on to the Dead Sea with great rapidity.

All these considerations indicate that the deltas of the streams coming into the valley of the Jordan and the Dead Sea must be increasing at an unusually rapid rate. It will be profitable, therefore, to compare it with other deltas upon which direct observations have been made. The Mississippi River is sweeping into the Gulf of Mexico sediment at a rate which represents one foot of surface soil over the whole drainage basin, extending from the Rocky Mountains to the Alleghenies, in a little less than 5,000 years. The Hoang-Ho is lowering its drainage basin a foot in 1,464 years, while the river Po is reducing its level a foot in 729 years. So rapidly has the river Po filled up its valley that the city of Adria, which was a seaport 2,000 years ago, is now 14 miles from the mouth of the river. The Tigris and Euphrates rivers have silted up the head of the Persian Gulf nearly 100 miles. (See Croll, *Climate and Time*, 332, 333; Darwin, *Formation of Vegetable Mould through the Action of Worms*, 233.) From these considerations it is a conservative estimate that the tributaries of the Jordan valley between the Lake of Galilee and the Dead Sea bring down sediment enough to lower the basin one foot in 2,000 years, so that since the time of Abraham 167,-270,400,000 cubic feet of solid matter have been added to its delta. This would cover 25 sq. miles 250 ft. deep. Taking into consideration the probable depth of water at the north end of the sea, it is, therefore, not an extravagant supposition that the Jordan delta has encroached upon the sea to the extent of 15 or 20 sq. miles, limiting the evaporating surface to that extent and causing the level of the water to rise, and extend an equal amount over the low lands at the south end.

At the same time the other streams coming directly into the lake have been contributing deltas to narrow its margin at various points. The *Kerak*, the *Arnon* and the *Zerka Ma'ain* bring in an immense amount of sediment from the E.; *el-Hessi*, *el-Jeib* and *el-Fikri* from the S.; and *Wady el-Muhauwât*, *el-Areyeh* and the Kedron, with numerous smaller intermediate streams, from the W. A detailed examination of these deposits will serve the double purpose of establishing the point in question and of giving a vivid conception of the sea and its surroundings.

Throughout the lower part of its course the river Jordan flows as has been already said, through a narrow gorge called the *Zôr*, which the river has eroded in the soft sedimentary deposits which cover the bottom of the valley (or *Ghôr*) from side to side. Opposite Jericho the *Ghôr* is about 15 miles wide. The *Zôr*, however, does not average more than one-half mile in width and is about 100 ft. lower than the general level of the *Ghôr*. But at "the Jews' Castle," about 8 miles from the mouth of the Jordan, the *Zôr* begins to enlarge and merge into a true delta. The embankment of the *Zôr* slopes away in a S.W. direction till it reaches the Judaean mountains at *Khurbet Kumran*, 10 miles distant, leaving a triangle of low land between it and the Dead Sea averaging fully one mile in width and being nearly 3 miles wide opposite the mouth of the Jordan. The face of the embankment separating the *Zôr* from the *Ghôr* has in several places been deeply cut into by the small wadies which come down from the western mountains, and the wash from these wadies as well as that from more temporary streams after every shower has considerably raised the western border of the *Zôr* throughout this distance. But it can safely be estimated that the original boundary of the Dead Sea has here been encroached upon to the extent of 10 or 15 sq. miles. Again, upon the eastern side of the Jordan the other limb of the delta, though smaller, is equally in evidence. Merrill (*East of the Jordan*, 223, 224), in describing his survey of the region, says he was compelled to walk for some hours along the shore and then north to reach his horses, which evidently had been coming over the harder and more elevated surface of the *Ghôr*. "The plain," he says, "for many sq. miles north of the sea is like ashes in which we often sank over shoe."

Returning to the N.W. corner of the lake we find the delta deposit which we left at *Khurbet Kumran* extending 2 miles farther south with an average width of one-half mile to *Râs Feshkah*, which rises abruptly from the water's edge, and renders it impossible for travelers to follow along the shore. But just beyond *Râs Feshkah* a delta half a mile or more in length and width is projected into the sea at the mouth of *Wady en Nâr*, which comes down from Jerus and is known in its upper portions as Kedron. This is the wady which passes the convent of *Mar Saba* and is referred to in such a striking manner in Ezk **47**. Like most of the other wadies coming into the Dead Sea, this courses the most of its way through inaccessible defiles and has built up a delta at its mouth covered with "fragments of rock or boulders swept along by the torrent in its periodical overflows" (De Saulcy, I, 137, 138).

From *Râs Feshkah* to *Râs Mersid*, a distance of 15 miles, the shore is bordered with a deposit of sand and gravel averaging a half a mile in width, while opposite *Wady ed Derajeh* and *Wady Hŭsâsa* (which descend from Bethlehem and the wilderness of Tekoah) the width is fully one mile. At the mouth of one of the smaller gorges De Saulcy noted what geologists call a "cone of dejection" where "the gravel washed down from the heights was heaped up to the extent of nearly 250 yards" (I, 44).

Râs Mersid, again, obstructs the passage along the shore almost as effectually as did *Râs Feshkah*, but farther south there is no other obstruction. The plain of **En-gedi,** connected in such an interesting manner with the history of David and with numerous other events of national importance, is described by the Pal Exploration Fund as "about half a mile broad and a mile in length." This consists of material brought down for the most part by *Wady el-'Areijeh*, which descends from the vicinity of Hebron with one branch passing through Tekoah. The principal path leading from the west side of the Dead Sea to the hills of Judaea follows the direction of this wady.

Between *En-gedi* and *Sebbeh* (*Masada*), a distance of 10 miles, the limestone cliffs retreat till they are fully 2 miles from the shore. Across this space numerous wadies course their way bringing down an immense amount of débris and depositing it as deltas at the water's edge. These projecting deltas were noticed by Robinson as he looked southward from the height above *En-gedi*, but their significance was not understood.

"One feature of the sea," he says, "struck us immediately, which was unexpected to us, viz. the number of shoal-like points and peninsulas which run into its southern part, appearing at first sight like flat sand-banks or islands. Below us on the S. were two such projecting banks on the western shore, composed probably of pebbles and gravel, extending out into the sea for a considerable distance. The larger and more important of these is on the S. of the spot called *Birket el-Khŭlîl*, a little bay or indentation in the western precipice, where the water, flowing into shallow basins when it is high, evaporates, and deposits salt. This spot is just S. of the mouth of *Wady el-Khŭbarah*" (*BR*, I, 501). One of these deltas is described by De Saulcy as 500 yds. in breadth and another as indefinitely larger.

Photograph of the Channel of Wady Muhauwât, as It Enters the Dead Sea, at the North End of Jebel Usdum Which Appears on the Right, Masada and the Western Cliffs on the Left. Note the Size of the Bowlders Rolled Along by the Torrent of Water. (Photo. by Libbey.)

Six miles S. of *Masada*, probably at the mouth of *Wady Umm Baghek*, Lynch notes a delta extending "half a mile out into the sea." Still farther S. the combined delta of the *Wady Zuweirah* and *Wady Muhauwât* covers an area of 2 or 3 sq. miles, and is dotted with bowlders and fragments of rock a foot or more in diameter, which have been washed over the area by the torrential floods. Beyond *Jebel Usdum*, *Wady el-Fikreh*, draining an area of 200 or 300 sq. miles, has deposited an immense amount of coarse sediment on the W. side of the *Sebkah* (a mud flat which was formerly occupied, probably by a projection of the Dead Sea). Into the S. end of the depression, extending from the *Sebkah* to the Ascent of **Akrabbim,** deltas of *Wady el-Jeib*, *Wady el-Khanzireh* and *Wady Tufileh* have in connection with *Wady Fikreh* encroached upon the valley to the extent of 12 or 15 sq. miles. Altogether these wadies drain an area of more than 3,000 sq. miles, and the granitic formations over which they pass have been so disintegrated by atmospheric influences that an excessive amount of coarse sediment is carried along by them (see Hull, *Mount Seir*, etc, 104–6). In ascending them, one encounters every indication of occasional destructive floods.

Following up the eastern shore, *Wady el-Hessi* coming down from the mountains of Edom has built up the plain of *Safieh* which pushes out into the neck of the *Sebkah* and covers an area of 3 or 4 sq. miles. Farther N., *Wady Kerak* and *Wady Beni Hamid* have with their deltas encroached to the extent of 2 or 3 sq. miles upon the head of the bay, projecting into the *Lisân* east of Point Costigan. Still farther N., *Wady Mojib* (the *Arnon*) and *Wady Zerka Ma'ain* (coming down from the hot springs of Callirrhoe) have built up less pronounced deltas because of the greater depth of the water on the E. side, but even so they are by no means inconsiderable, in each case projecting a half-mile or more into the lake.

Putting all these items together, there can be little doubt that the area of the Dead Sea has been encroached upon to the extent of 25 or 30 sq. miles since the time of Abraham and that this has resulted in a rise of the general level of the water sufficient to overflow a considerable portion of the lagoon at the S. end, thus keeping the evaporating area constant. The only escape from this conclusion is the supposition that the rainfall of the region is less than it was at the dawn of history, and so the smaller evaporating area would be sufficient to maintain the former level. But of this we have no adequate evidence. On the contrary there is abundant evidence that the climatic conditions connected with the production of the Glacial Period had passed away long before the conquest of the Vale of Siddim by Amraphel and his confederates (Gen **14**).

The consequences of this rise of water are various and significant. It lends credibility to the persistent tradition that the sites of Sodom and Gomorrah are covered by the shallow water at the S. end of the sea, and also to the statement of Scripture that the region about these cities (on the supposition that they were at the S. end of the sea) was like the garden of the Lord; for that plain was then much larger than it is now, and was well watered, and possessed greater elements of fertility than are now apparent. Furthermore, this supposed lower level of the lake in early times may have greatly facilitated the passage of armies and caravans from one end to the other, thus rendering it more easy to understand the historical statements relating to the earliest periods of occupation. Even now the road at the base of *Jebel Usdum* which is open at low water is impassable at high water. On the last of December, 1883, Professor Hull (*Mount Seir*, etc, 133) traversed the shore at the base of the salt cliffs along a gravel terrace 100 ft. wide, which "abruptly terminated in a descent of about 5 ft. to the line of driftwood which marked the upper limit of the waters." On the 1st of January, 1901, the water along the base of the salt cliffs was so deep that it was impossible for my party to pass along the shore. It is easy to believe that the level might have been lowered sufficiently to expose a margin of shore which could be traversed on the W. side from one end to the other.

IV. Constitution of the Water.—As in the case of all inclosed basins, the waters of the Dead Sea are impregnated to an excessive degree with saline matter. "The salt which they contain," however, "is not wholly or even principally common salt, but is mostly the chloride and bromide of magnesium and calcium, so that they are not merely a strong brine, but rather resemble the mother liquors of a salt-pan left after the common salt has crystallized out" (Dawson, *Egypt and Syria*, 123). The following analysis is given by Booth and Muckle of water brought by Commander Lynch and taken by him May 5 from 195 fathoms deep opposite the mouth of *Wady Zerka Ma'ain*. Other analyses vary from this more or less, owing doubtless to the different localities and depths from which the specimens had been obtained.

Specific gravity at 60°	1.22742
Chloride of magnesium	145.8971
Chloride of calcium	31.0746
Chloride of sodium	78.5537
Chloride of potassium	6.5860
Bromide of potassium	1.3741
Sulphate of lime	0.7012
	264.1867
Water	735.8133
	1000.0000
Total amount of solid matter found by direct experiment	264.0000

What is here labeled bromide of potassium, however, is called by most other analysts bromide of magnesium, it being difficult to separate and distinguish these elements in composition. The large percentage of bromide, of which but a trace is found in the ocean, is supposed to have been derived from volcanic emanations. As compared with sea water, it is worthy of note that that of the Dead Sea yields 26 lbs. of salts to 100 lbs. of water, whereas that of the Atlantic yields only 6 lbs. in the same quantity. Lake Urumiah is as salt as the Dead Sea.

As results of this salinity the water is excessively buoyant and is destructive of all forms of animal life. Lynch found that his metal boats sank an inch deeper in the Jordan when equally heavily laden than they did in the Dead Sea. All travelers who bathe in it relate that when they throw themselves upon their backs their bodies will be half out of the water. Jos (*BJ*, IV, viii, 4) relates that the emperor Vespasian caused certain men who could

Bathing at the North End of the Dead Sea, the Mountains of Moab in the Background. (Photo. by F. B. Wright.)

not swim to be thrown into the water with their hands tied behind them, and they floated on the surface. Dead fish and various shells are indeed often found upon the shore, but they have evidently been brought in by the tributary fresh-water streams, or belong to species which live in the brackish pools of the bordering lagoons, which are abundantly supplied with fresh water. The report extensively circulated in earlier times that birds did not fly over the lake has no foundation in fact, as some species of birds are known even to light upon the surface and sport upon the waters. The whole depression is subject to frequent storms of wind blowing through its length. These produce waves whose force is very destructive of boats encountering them owing to the high specific gravity of the water; but for the same reason the waves rapidly subside after a storm, so that the general appearance of the lake is placid in the extreme.

Salt Cliffs on the East Side of Jebel Usdum, Washed by the Waters of the Lake. Pillar of Salt Ready to Fall. (Photo. by F. B. Wright.)

The source from which these saline matters have been derived has been a subject of much speculation —some having supposed that it was derived from the dissolution of the salt cliffs in *Jebel Usdum.* But this theory is disproved by the fact that common salt forms but a small portion of the material held in solution by the water. It is more correct to regard this salt mountain as a deposit precipitated from the saturated brine which had accumulated, as we have supposed, during the Cretaceous age. Probably salt is now being deposited at the bottom of the lake from the present saturated solution to appear in some future age in the wreck of progressive geological changes. The salts of the Dead Sea, like those in all similarly inclosed basins, have been brought in by the streams of water from all over the drainage basin. Such streams always contain more or less solid matter in solution, which becomes concentrated through the evaporation which takes place over inclosed basins. The ocean is the great reservoir of such deposits, but is too large to be affected to the extent noticeable in smaller basins. The extreme salinity of the Dead Sea water shows both the long continuance of the isolation of the basin and the abundance of soluble matter contained in the rocks of the inscribed area. The great extent of recent volcanic rocks, esp. in the region E. of the Jordan, accounts for the large relative proportion of some of the ingredients.

V. Climate.—Owing to the great depression below sea level, the climate is excessively warm, so that palms and other tropical trees flourish on the borders of the rivers wherever fresh water finds soil on which to spread itself. Snow never falls upon the lake, though it frequently covers the hills of Judaea and the plateau of Moab. As already explained the rainfall in the Jordan valley is less than on the bordering mountains. During the winter season the Arab tribes go down to the valley with their flocks of sheep and goats and camp upon the surrounding plains. But the excessive heat of the summer, rising sometimes to 130° F., drives them back to the hills again.

VI. Roads.—Except at the N. end the approaches to the Dead Sea are few and very difficult to travel. On the W. side the nearest approach is at *En-gedi,* and this down a winding descent of 2,000 ft. where a few men at the top of the cliff could hold an army at bay below. The path up *Wady Zuweirah* from the N. end of *Jebel Usdum* is scarcely better. Upon the S. end the path leads up *Wady Fikreh* for a considerable distance on the W. side of the Mud Flat, and then crosses over to the *Wady el-Jeib,* up whose torrential bed during the dry season caravans can find their way through the *Arabah* to *Akabah.* More difficult paths lead up from the E. of the Mud Flat into the *Arabah,* and through the mountains of Moab to Petra into the plains beyond and the Pilgrim route from Damascus to Mecca. From the *Lisân* a difficult path leads up *Wady Kerak* to the fortress of the same name 20 miles distant and 5,000 ft. above the lake. Another path a little farther north leads up the *Wady Beni Hamid* to Ar of Moab. From the Arnon to the N. end of the Dead Sea the mountains are so precipitous that travel along the shore is now practically impossible. But there are, according to Tristram (*The Land of Moab,* 355), remnants of an "old and well-engineered road of ancient times" extending as far S. at least as the *Zerka Ma'ain.*

VII. Miscellaneous Items.—There are numerous points about the border of the lake of special interest.

1. The Plain of the Jordan

When Lot and Abraham looked down from the heights of Bethel (Gen **13** 10 ff) they are said to have beheld "all the Plain of the Jordan, that it was well watered every where, before Jeh destroyed Sodom and Gomorrah, like the garden of Jeh, like the land of Egypt, as thou goest unto Zoar. So Lot chose him all the Plain of the Jordan; and Lot journeyed east: . . . . and Lot dwelt in the cities of the Plain, and moved his tent as far as Sodom." The word here tr[d] "Plain" is *kikkār* (Ciccar), meaning "circle," and indicating the appearance from Bethel of the Jordan valley surrounding the N. end of the Dead Sea. From this fact, many recent writers have located Sodom and Gomorrah at that end of the sea (see Cities of the Plain). But it is by no means certain that it is necessary thus to narrow down the meaning of the phrase. Though the S. end of the Dead Sea is not visible from the heights of Bethel, it is so connected with the general depression that it may well have been in the minds of Abraham and Lot as they were dividing the country between them, one choosing the plain, a part of which was visible, the other remaining on the bordering mountainous area, so different in all its natural resources and conditions. The extent of the region chosen by Lot may therefore be left to be determined by other considerations.

2. Ain Jidi (En-gedi)

Ain Jidi, "fountain of the kid" (?) (see En-gedi) is an oasis at the base of the western cliffs about half-way between the N. and the S. ends of the lake, fed by springs of warm water which burst from beneath the overhanging cliffs. The 650 ft. shore line composed of shingle and calcareous marl is here prominent, and, as already remarked, there is an extensive gravel terrace at the present water level. Palms and vines formerly flourished here (Cant **1** 14), but now only a few bushes of acacia and tamarisk are to be found. From time immemorial, however, it has been the terminus of the principal trail which zig-zags up the cliffs to the plateau, across which paths lead to Hebron and Bethlehem.

The Fortress of Masada was the last stronghold held by the fanatical Jews (Zealots) after the destruction of Jerus by the Romans, and offers a bird's-eye view of the Dead Sea, which is as instructive as it is interesting. It is situated half-way between *Jebel Usdum* and *En-gedi,* directly opposite the northern promontory of *el-Lisân.* Here on a precipitous height, 2,000 ft. above the sea, is a plateau about 700 yds. long, and 200 wide, adorned with ruins of dwellings, palaces and temples of the Herodian age. Standing upon this height one sees the outlines of the Rom camp, near the shore of the sea, and those of another camp in a depression several hundred yards to the W., from which the final attack of the besiegers was made over a pathway constructed along a sloping ridge.

3. The Fortress of Masada

View from *Ain Jidi*, Looking South
(From a drawing by W. Tipping, Esq., 1842.)

Here many miles away from their base of supplies the Romans slowly but irresistibly drew in their besieging lines to the final tragic consummation when the last remnant of the defenders committed suicide (*BJ*, VII, ix, 1). The view gives one a profound impression of the difficulties attending military campaigns in all that region. Upon lifting up one's eyes to take in the broader view, he sees the Dead Sea in its whole length with the low ridge of *Jebel Usdum,* the Valley of Salt, the Ascent of *Akrabbim,* the depression of the *Arabah,* and Mt. Hor, to the S., while across the whole horizon to the E. is the long wall of Moab dissected by *Wady Kerak* and the river Arnon, leading up to the strongholds of *Ker, Aroer* and *Dibon,* of Moab; while immediately in the front are the white cliffs of *el-Lisân,* and to the N., near by, the green oasis of *En-gedi,* and, dimmed by distance, the plains of Jericho, and the cluster of peaks surrounding Mt. Pisgah; while the sea itself sparkles like a gem of brilliant azure in the midst of its desolate surroundings, giving no token of the deadly elements which permeate its water.

4. Jebel Usdum

Jebel Usdum (Mount of Sodom) is a salt mountain extending 7 or 8 miles along the S.W. shore of the lake and on the W. side of the Valley of Salt to its southern boundary. Its name is derived from the traditional belief that Sodom was located at the S. end of the sea; but, on the other hand, it is not unlikely that the name would become attached to it because of its seeming to contain the pillar of salt, which, according to the ordinary tr, marked the place where Lot's wife was overwhelmed. The mountain rises 600 ft. above the lake, and has a general level surface except where streams have worn furrows and gullies in it. The eastern face presents a precipitous wall of rock salt, which, as said above, at the time of my visit (January, 1901), was washed by the waves of the lake making it impossible to pass along its base. At other times when the water is low, travelers can pass along the whole length of the shore. This wall of salt presents much the appearance of a glacier, the salt being as transparent as ice, while the action of the waves has hollowed out extensive and picturesque caverns and left isolated towers and connected pinnacles of salt often resembling a Gothic cathedral. These towers and pinnacles are, of course, being displaced from time to time, while others are formed to continue the illusion. Any pillar of salt known to the ancients must be entirely different from those which meet the eye of the modern traveler. It follows also as a matter of course that the gradual dissolution of this salt must partly account for the excessive salinity of the Dead Sea.

It is uncertain how deep the deposit extends below the surface. It rises upward 200 or 300 ft., where it is capped by consolidated strata of sedimentary material, consisting of sand and loam, which most geologists think was deposited at the time of the formation of the 650 ft. terrace already described, and which they connect with the climatic conditions of the Glacial period.

This view is presented as follows by Professor B.K. Emerson: "In the earlier portion of the post-glacial stadium, a final sinking of a fraction of the bottom of the trough, near the S. end of the lake, dissected the low salt plateau, sinking its central parts beneath the salt waters, while fragments remain buttressed against the great walls of the trench forming the plains of *Jebel Usdum* and the peninsula *el-Lisân* with the swampy *Sebkah* between. . . . . It exposed the wonderful eastern wall of *Jebel Usdum:* 7 miles long, with 30–45 m. of clear blue salt at the base, capped by 125–140 m. of gypsum-bearing marls impregnated with sulphur, and conglomerates at times cemented by bitumen" ("Geological Myths," *Proc. Am. Assoc. for Adv. of Sci.* [1896], 110, 111). If this was the case there has been a depression of the S. end of the Dead Sea to the extent of several hundred feet within a comparatively few thousand years, in which case the traditional view that Sodom and Gomorrah were overwhelmed by Dead Sea water at the time of their destruction would refer to an occurrence exactly in line with movements that have been practically continuous during Tertiary, Glacial, and post-Glacial times.

With more reason, Lartet contends that this salt is a Cretaceous or Tertiary deposit covered with late Tertiary strata, in which case the sinking of the block between *Jebel Usdum* and *el-Lisân*, for the most part, took place at a much earlier date than the formation of the 650 ft. terrace. A striking corollary of this supposition would be that the climatic conditions have been practically the same during all of the post-Carboniferous times, there having been cycles of moist and dry climate in that region succeeding each other during all these geological periods.

The Vale of Siddim (Gen **14** 3.8.10) is probably the same as the Valley of Salt (2 K **14** 7; 1 Ch **18** 12; 2 Ch **25** 11). This is in all probability the plain extending from the southern end of the Dead Sea to the "Ascent of Akrabbim" which crosses the valley from side to side, and forms the southern margin of the *Ghôr*. At present the area of the vale is about 50 sq. miles; but if our theory concerning the lower level of the Dead Sea in the time of Abraham is correct, it may then have included a considerable portion of the lagoon S. of *el-Lisân* and so have been a third larger than now. In Gen **14** 10 the vale is said to have been full of slime (that is, of bitumen or asphalt) pits. In modern times masses of asphalt are occasionally found floating in the southern part of the Dead Sea. After the earthquake of 1834 a large quantity was cast upon the shore near the S.W. corner of the lake, 3 tons of which were brought to market by the Arab natives. After the earthquake of January, 1837, a mass of asphaltum was driven aground on the W. side not far from *Jebel Usdum*. The neighboring Arabs swam off to it, cut it up with axes and carried it to market by the camel load, and sold it to the value of several thousand dollars. At earlier times such occurrences seem to have been still more frequent. Jos affirms that "the sea in many places sends up black masses of asphaltum having the form and size of headless oxen"; while Diodorus Siculus relates that the bitumen (asphaltum) was thrown up in masses covering sometimes two or three acres and having the appearance of islands (Jos, *BJ*, IV, viii, 4; Diod. Sic. ii.48; Pliny, *NH*, vii.13; Tac. *Hist.* v.6; Dioscor., *De re Med.*, i.99).

5. Vale of Siddim

VIEW FROM THE HEIGHTS BEHIND MASADA, SHOWING THE WIDE BEACH ON THE WESTERN SIDE OF THE LAKE, AND THE TONGUE-SHAPED PENINSULA.
(From a drawing by W. Tipping, Esq.)

Since asphalt is a product of petroleum from which the volatile elements have been evaporated, the ultimate source of these masses is doubtless to be found in the extensive beds of bituminous limestone which appear in numerous places on both sides of the Dead Sea. An outcrop of it can be observed at *Neby Mousa*, on the road from Jerus to Jericho, which Dawson describes as resembling dry chalk saturated with coal tar. When long weathered this becomes white and chalky at the surface, so that a mass of it, quite white externally, reveals an intense blackness when broken. It is this that the people of Bethlehem call "Dead Sea stone," and which they carve into various ornamental articles and expose for sale. Some specimens of it are sufficiently bituminous to burn with flame like cannel-coal. These beds are still more abundant about the S. end of the lake and doubtless underlie the whole region, and for all time must have been exuding bituminous and gaseous matter, but much more abundantly in former times than now.

In these accumulations of bitumen at the S. end of the *Ghôr* we probably have the incentive which led the Babylonians under Amraphel and Chedorlaomer to make such long expeditions for the sake of conquering the region and holding it under their power. Bitumen was much in demand in Babylonia.

6. El-Lisân

El-Lisân (the Tongue), which projects half-way across the lake from the mouth of *Wady Kerak*, is, like *Jebel Usdum*, a promontory of white calcareous sediment containing beds of salt and gypsum, and breaking off on its western side in a cliff 300 ft. high. Its upper surface rises in terraces to the 600 ft. level on the E., as *Jebel Usdum* does on the W. The length of the promontory from N. to S. is 9 miles. This corresponds so closely in general structure and appearance to *Jebel Usdum* on the opposite side of the lake that we find it difficult to doubt the theory of Professor Emerson, stated above, that the formation originally extended across and that a block of the original bottom of the lake has dropped down, leaving these remnants upon the sides. Frequent occurrences similar to this are noted by the United States geologists in the Rocky Mountain region.

VIII. History.—Difficulty of access has prevented the Dead Sea from playing any important part in history except as an obstruction both to commerce and to military movements. Boats have never been used upon it to any considerable extent. From earliest times salt has been gathered on its western shores and carried up to market over the difficult paths leading to Jerus. A similar commerce has been carried on in bitumen; that from the Dead Sea being specially prized in Egypt, while as already remarked, it is by no means improbable that the pits of bitumen which abounded in the "Vale of Siddim" were the chief attraction leading the kings of Babylonia to undertake long expeditions for the conquest of the region. Productive as may have been the plain at the S. end of the sea, it was too far outside the caravan route leading through Petra to the S. end of the *Arabah* and the mines of the Sinaitic Peninsula to divert the course of travel. Still the settlements on the eastern border of the Vale of Siddim were of sufficient importance in mediaeval times to induce the Crusaders to visit the region and leave their marks upon it. The Arabian town of *Zoghar*, probably the Bib. Zoar, appears at one time to have been a most important place, and was the center of considerable commercial activity. Indigo was grown there, and the oasis was noted for its fine species of dates. The country round about abounded in springs and there was much arable land (see Le Strange, *Pal under the Moslems*, 286 ff). The hot springs upon the eastern shore of the Dead Sea at Callirrhoe some distance up the *Wady Zerka Ma'ain* were much resorted to for their medicinal properties. Here Herod came as a last resort, to secure relief from his loathsome malady, but failed of help. The fortress of Machaerus, where John the Baptist was imprisoned, is situated but a few miles S. of the *Zerka Ma'ain*, but access to this region is possible only through a difficult road leading over the mountains a few miles E. of the sea.

On four occasions important military expeditions were conducted along the narrow defiles which border the S.W. end of the Dead Sea: (1) That of Amraphel and his confederates from Babylonia, who seem first to have opened the way past Petra to the mines of the Sinaitic Peninsula, and then to have swept northward through the land of the Amalekites and Amorites and come down to the Dead Sea at *En-gedi*, and then to have turned to subdue the Cities of the Plain, where Lot was dwelling. This accomplished, they probably retreated along the west shore of the lake, which very likely afforded at that time a complete passage-way to the valley of the Jordan. Or they may have gone on eastward to the line of the present pilgrim route from Damascus to Mecca and followed it northward. (2) In the early part of the reign of Jehoshaphat (2 Ch **20**), the Moabites, Ammonites and some other tribes joined together, forming a large army, and, following around the S. end of the Dead Sea, marched along the W. shore to *En-gedi*, and having ascended the zigzag path leading up the precipitous heights to the wilderness of Tekoa, were there thrown into confusion and utterly annihilated. (3) Not many years later Jehoram and Jehoshaphat "fetched a compass [RV "made a circuit"] of seven days' journey" (2 K **3** 9) around the S. end of the Dead Sea and attacked the Moabites in their own country, but returned without completing the conquest. The particulars of this expedition are given in 2 K **3** and in the inscription on the Moabite Stone. (4) The Romans shortly after the destruction of Jerus conducted a long siege of the fortress of Masada, of which an account has already been given in a previous section (VII, 3). All their supplies must have come down the tortuous path to *En-gedi* and thence been brought along the western shore to the camp, the remains of which are still to be seen at the base of the fortress.

For many cents., indeed for well-nigh 1,800 years, the Dead Sea remained a mystery, and its geology and physical characteristics were practically unknown. The first intimation of the depression of the lake below sea level was furnished in 1837 by Moore and Beke, who made some imperfect experiments with boiling water from which they inferred a depression of 500 ft. In 1841 Lieutenant Simmons of the British navy, by trigonometrical observations, estimated the depression to be 1,312 ft. In 1835 Costigan, and again in 1847 Lieutenant Molyneux ventured upon the sea in boats; but the early death of both, consequent upon their exposures, prevented their making any full reports. Appropriately, however, their names have been attached to prominent points on the *Lisân*. In 1848 Lieutenant Lynch, of the United States navy, was dispatched to explore the Jordan and the Dead Sea. The results of this expedition were most important. Soundings of the depths were carefully and systematically conducted, and levels were run from the Dead Sea by Jerus to the Mediterranean, giving the depression at the surface of the Dead Sea as 1,316.7 ft., and its greatest depth 1,278 ft. More recently Sir C. W. Wilson in connection with the Ordinance Survey of Pal carried levels over the same route with the result of reducing the depression to 1,292 ft., which is now generally accepted to be correct. But as already stated the stage of water in the lake is not given, and that is known to vary at least 15 ft. annually, and still more at longer intervals. See CITIES OF THE PLAIN.

LITERATURE.—Hull, *Mount Seir, Sinai and Western Pal*, 1889; Huntington, *Pal and Its Transformation*, 1911; Lartet, *Voyage d'exploration de la Mer Morte*, 1880; Lynch, *Report of U.S. Expedition to the Jordan and Dead Sea*, 1852; Robinson, *BR*, 1841; De Saulcy, *Voyage dans la Syrie*, 1853; Tristram, *Land of Israel*, 2d ed, 1872, *The*

Land of Moab, 1873; G. A. Smith, *HGHL; Wright, Scientific Confirmations of OT Hist*, 1906, and *Journal of Bib. Lit.*, 1911.

George Frederick Wright

DEAD, STATE OF THE. See Hades.

DEAF, def (חֵרֵשׁ, *ḥērēsh;* κωφός, *kōphós*): Used either in the physical sense, or **figuratively** as expressing unwillingness to hear the Divine message (Ps **58** 4), or incapacity to understand it for want of spirituality (Ps **38** 13). The prophetic utterances were sufficiently forcible to compel even such to hear (Isa **42** 18; **43** 8) and thereby to receive the Divine mercy (Isa **29** 18; **35** 5).

The expression "deaf adder that stoppeth her ear" (Ps **58** 4) alludes to a curious notion that the adder, to avoid hearing the voice of the charmer, laid its head with one ear on the ground and stopped the other with the tip of its tail (*Diary of John Manninghan*, 1602). The adder is called deaf by Shakespeare (*2 Hen VI*, iii, 2, 76; *Troilus and Cressida*, ii, 2, 172). The erroneous idea probably arose from the absence of external ears.

Physical deafness was regarded as a judgment from God (Ex **4** 11; Mic **7** 16), and it was consequently impious to curse the deaf (Lev **19** 14). In NT times deafness and kindred defects were attributed to evil spirits (Mk **9** 18 ff). See Dumb.

Alex. Macalister

DEAL, dēl: The noun "deal" is not found in RV. The AV tr of עִשָּׂרוֹן, *'issārōn*, "the tenth deal" (Ex **29** 40; Lev **14** 10, et al.) is rendered uniformly "the tenth part" in RV (see Weights and Measures). The vb. "to deal" often means "to apportion," "to distribute" (cf 2 S **6** 19; 1 Ch **16** 3; Isa **58** 7; Rom **12** 3), but more frequently it is used in the sense of "to act," "to do," "to have transaction of any kind with." In the Pss "to deal" always means "to confer benefit," "to deal bountifully," with the exception of Ps **105** 25, where it means "to deal subtly with." The expression "to deal," i.e. "to be engaged in," is not found in the Scriptures. The tr of συγχράομαι, *sugchráomai*, in Jn **4** 9, "Jews have no dealings with Samaritans," conveys the idea that they have nothing in common.

A. L. Breslich

DEAR, dēr, **DEARLY**, dēr′li ("held at a great price," "highly valued"): In Acts **20** 24, Paul does not hold his life "dear" (τίμιος, *tímios*, "at a price"); cf 1 Cor **3** 12, "costly stones"; 1 Pet **1** 19, "precious blood." Lk **7** 2, the servant was "dear" to the centurion (ἔντιμος, *éntimos*, "highly prized"; cf Phil **2** 29; 1 Pet **2** 6). 1 Thess **2** 8, "very dear to us" (ἀγαπητός, *agapētós*, "beloved"). In RV, *agapētos* is generally trd "beloved." "Dearly" before "beloved" of AV is omitted in all passages in RV. The word "dear" occurs but once in the OT, viz. Jer **31** 20. RV correctly changes "dear Son" of AV (Col **1** 13) into "the Son of his love."

H. E. Jacobs

DEARTH, dûrth. See Famine.

DEATH (מָוֶת, *māweth;* θάνατος, *thánatos*):

Physiological and Figurative View

The word **"Death"** is used in the sense of (1) the process of dying (Gen **21** 16); (2) the period of decease (Gen **27** 7); (3) as a possible synonym for poison (2 K **4** 40); (4) as descriptive of person in danger of perishing (Jgs **15** 18; "in deaths oft" 2 Cor **11** 23). In this sense the shadow of death is a familiar expression in Job, the Psalms and the Prophets; (5) death is personified in 1 Cor **15** 55 and Rev **20** 14. Deliverance from this catastrophe is called the "issues from death" (Ps **68** 20 AV; trd "escape" in RV). Judicial execution, "putting to death," is mentioned 39 times in the Levitical Law.

Figuratively: Death is the loss of spiritual life as in Rom **8** 6; and the final state of the unregenerate is called the "second death" in Rev **20** 14.

Alex. Macalister

Theological View

1. Conception of Sin and Death

According to Gen **2** 17, God gave to man, created in His own image, the command not to eat of the tree of knowledge of good and evil, and added thereto the warning, "in the day that thou eatest thereof, thou shalt surely die." Though not exclusively, reference is certainly made here in the first place to bodily death. Yet because death by no means came upon Adam and Eve on the day of their transgression, but took place hundreds of years later, the expression, "in the day that," must be conceived in a wider sense, or the delay of death must be attributed to the entering-in of mercy (Gen **3** 15). However this may be, Gen **2** 17 places a close connection between man's death and his transgression of God's commandment, thereby attaching to death a religious and ethical significance, and on the other hand makes the life of man dependent on his obedience to God. This religious-ethical nature of life and death is not only decidedly and clearly expressed in Gen **2**, but it is the fundamental thought of the whole of Scripture and forms an essential element in the revelations of salvation. The theologians of early and more recent times, who have denied the spiritual significance of death and have separated the connection between ethical and physical life, usually endeavor to trace back their opinions to Scripture; and those passages which undoubtedly see in death a punishment for sin (Gen **2** 17; Jn **8** 44; Rom **5** 12; **6** 23; 1 Cor **15** 21), they take as individual opinions, which form no part of the organism of revelation. But this endeavor shuts out the organic character of the revelation of salvation. It is true that death in Holy Scripture is often measured by the weakness and frailty of human nature (Gen **3** 19; Job **14** 1.12; Ps **39** 5.6; **90** 5; **103** 14.15; Eccl **3** 20, etc). Death is seldom connected with the transgression of the first man either in the OT or the NT, or mentioned as a specified punishment for sin (Jn **8** 44; Rom **5** 12; **6** 23; 1 Cor **15** 21; Jas **1** 15); for the most part it is portrayed as something natural (Gen **5** 5; **9** 29; **15** 15; **25** 8, etc), a long life being presented as a blessing in contrast to death in the midst of days as a disaster and a judgment (Ps **102** 23 f; Isa **65** 20). But all this is not contrary to the idea that death is a consequence of, and a punishment for, sin. Daily, everyone who agrees with Scripture that death is held out as a punishment for sin, speaks in the same way. Death, though come into the world through sin, is nevertheless at the same time a consequence of man's physical and frail existence now; it could therefore be threatened as a punishment to man, because he was taken out of the ground and was made a living soul, of the earth earthy (Gen **2** 7; 1 Cor **15** 45.47). If he had remained obedient, he would not have returned to dust (Gen **3** 19), but have pressed forward on the path of spiritual development (1 Cor **15** 46.51); his return to dust was possible simply because he was made from dust (see Adam in the NT). Thus, although death is in this way a consequence of sin, yet a long life is felt to be a blessing and death a disaster and a judgment, above all when man is taken away in the bloom of his youth or the strength of his years. There is nothing strange, therefore, in the manner in which Scripture speaks about death; we all express ourselves daily in the same way, though we at the same time consider it as the wages of sin. Beneath the ordinary, everyday expressions about death lies the deep consciousness that it is unnatural and contrary to our innermost being.

This is decidedly expressed in Scripture, much more so even than among ourselves. For we are influenced always more or less by the Greek, Platonic idea, that the body dies, yet the soul is immortal. Such an idea is utterly contrary to the Israelite consciousness, and is nowhere found in the OT. The *whole* man dies, when in death the spirit (Ps **146** 4; Eccl **12** 7), or soul (Gen **35** 18; 2 S **1** 9; 1 K **17** 21; Jon **4** 3), goes out of a man. Not only his body, but his soul also returns to a state of death and belongs to the nether-world; therefore the OT can speak of a death of one's soul (Gen **37** 21 [Heb]; Nu **23** 10m; Dt **22** 21; Jgs **16** 30; Job **36** 14; Ps **78** 50), and of defilement by coming in contact with a dead body (Lev **19** 28; **21** 11; **22** 4; Nu **5** 2; **6** 6; **9** 6; **19** 10ff; Dt **14** 1; Hag **2** 13). This death of man is not annihilation, however, but a deprivation of all that makes for life on earth. The Sheol (*$sh^{e'}$ōl*) is in contrast with the land of the living in every respect (Job **28** 13; Prov **15** 24; Ezk **26** 20; **32** 23); it is an abode of darkness and the shadow of death (Job **10** 21.22; Ps **88** 12; **143** 3), a place of destruction, yea destruction itself (Job **26** 6; **28** 22; **31** 12; Ps **88** 11; Prov **27** 20), without any order (Job **10** 22), a land of rest, of silence, of oblivion (Job **3** 13.17.18; Ps **94** 17; **115** 17), where God and man are no longer to be seen (Isa **38** 11), God no longer praised or thanked (Ps **6** 5; **115** 17), His perfections no more acknowledged (Ps **88** 10–13; Isa **38** 18.19), His wonders not contemplated (Ps **88** 12), where the dead are unconscious, do no more work, take no account of anything, possess no knowledge nor wisdom, neither have any more a portion in anything that is done under the sun (Eccl **9** 5.6.10). The dead ("the Shades" RVm; cf art. DECEASED) are asleep (Job **26** 5; Prov **2** 18; **9** 18; **21** 6; Ps **88** 11; Isa **14** 9), weakened (Isa **14** 10) and without strength (Ps **88** 4).

2. The Meaning of Death

The dread of death was felt much more deeply therefore by the Israelites than by ourselves. Death to them was separation from all that they loved, from God, from His service, from His law, from His people, from His land, from all the rich companionship in which they lived. But now in this darkness appears the light of the revelation of salvation from on high. The God of Israel is the living God and the fountain of all life (Dt **5** 26; Josh **3** 10; Ps **36** 9). He is the Creator of heaven and earth, whose power knows no bounds and whose dominion extends over life and death (Dt **32** 39; 1 S **2** 6; Ps **90** 3). He gave life to man (Gen **1** 26; **2** 7), and creates and sustains every man still (Job **32** 8; **33** 4; **34** 14; Ps **104** 29; Eccl **12** 7). He connects life with the keeping of His law and appoints death for the transgression of it (Gen **2** 17; Lev **18** 5; Dt **30** 20; **32** 47). He lives in heaven, but is present also by His spirit in Sheol (Ps **139** 7.8). Sheol and Abaddon are open to Him even as the hearts of the children of men (Job **26** 6; **38** 17; Prov **15** 11). He kills and makes alive, brings down into Sheol and raises from thence again (Dt **32** 39; 1 S **2** 6; 2 K **5** 7). He lengthens life for those who keep His commandments (Ex **20** 12; Job **5** 26), gives escape from death, can deliver when death menaces (Ps **68** 20; Isa **38** 5; Jer **15** 20; Dnl **3** 26), can take Enoch and Elijah to Himself without dying (Gen **5** 24; 2 K **2** 11), can restore the dead to life (1 K **17** 22; 2 K **4** 34; **13** 21). He can even bring death wholly to nothing and completely triumph over its power by rising from the dead (Job **14** 13–15; **19** 25–27; Hos **6** 2; **13** 14; Isa **25** 8; **26** 19; Ezk **37** 11.12; Dnl **12** 2).

3. Light in the Darkness

This revelation by degrees rejects the old contrast between life on earth and the disconsolate existence after death, in the dark place of Sheol, and puts another in its place. The physical contrast between life and death gradually makes way for the moral and spiritual difference between a life spent in the fear of the Lord, and a life in the service of sin. The man who serves God is alive (Gen **2** 17); life is involved in the keeping of His commandments (Lev **18** 5; Dt **30** 20); His word is life (Dt **8** 3; **32** 47). Life is still for the most part understood to mean length of days (Prov **2** 18; **3** 16; **10** 30; Isa **65** 20). Nevertheless it is remarkable that Prov often mentions death and Sheol in connection with the godless (**2** 18; **5** 5; **7** 27; **9** 18), and on the other hand only speaks of life in connection with the righteous. Wisdom, righteousness, the fear of the Lord is the way of life (**8** 35.36; **11** 19; **12** 28; **13** 14; **14** 27; **19** 23). The wicked is driven away in his wickedness, but the righteous hath hope in his death (**14** 32). Blessed is he who has the Lord for his God (Dt **33** 29; Ps **1** 1.2; **2** 12; **32** 1.2; **33** 12; **34** 9, etc); he is comforted in the greatest adversity (Ps **73** 25–28; Hab **3** 17–19), and sees a light arise for him behind physical death (Gen **49** 18; Job **14** 13–15; **16** 16–21; **19** 25–27; Ps **73** 23–26). The godless on the contrary, although enjoying for a time much prosperity, perish and come to an end (Ps **1** 4–6; **73** 18–20; Isa **48** 22; Mal **4** 3, etc).

4. Spiritual Significance

The righteous of the OT truly are continually occupied with the problem that the lot of man on earth often corresponds so little to his spiritual worth, but he strengthens himself with the conviction that for the righteous it will be well, and for the wicked, ill (Eccl **8** 12.13; Isa **3** 10.11). If they do not realize it in the present, they look forward to the future and hope for the day in which God's justice will extend salvation to the righteous, and His anger will be visited on the wicked in judgment. So in the OT the revelation of the new covenant is prepared wherein Christ by His appearance hath abolished death and hath brought life and immortality to light through the gospel (2 Tim **1** 10). See ABOLISH. This everlasting life is already here on earth presented to man by faith, and it is his portion also in the hour of death (Jn **3** 36; **11** 25.26). On the other hand, he who lives in sin and is disobedient to the Son of God, is in his living dead (Mt **8** 22; Lk **15** 32; Jn **3** 36; **8** 24; Eph **2** 1; Col **2** 13); he shall never see life, but shall pass by bodily death into the second death (Rev **2** 11; **20** 6.14; **21** 8).

5. Death in Non-Christian Religions and in Science

This view of Scripture upon death goes much deeper than that which is found in other religions, but it nevertheless receives support from the unanimous witness of humanity with regard to its unnaturalness and dread. The so-called nature-peoples even feel that death is much more of an enigma than life; Tiele (*Inleiding tot de goddienst-artenschap*, II [1900], 202, referring to Andrew Lang, *Modern Mythology*, ch xiii) says rightly, that all peoples have the conviction that man by nature is immortal, that immortality wants no proof, but that death is a mystery and must be explained. Touching complaints arise in the hearts of all men on the frailty and vanity of life, and the whole of mankind fears death as a mysterious power. Man finds comfort in death only when he hopes it will be an end to a still more miserable life. Seneca may be taken as interpreter of some philosophers when he says: *Stultitia est timore mortis mori* ("It is stupid to die through the fear of death") and some may be able, like a Socrates or a Cato, to face death calmly and courageously; what have these few to say to the millions, who through fear of death are all their lifetime subject to bondage (He **2** 15)? Such a mystery has death remained up to the present day. It may be said with Kassowitz, Verworm and others that the "cell" is the beginning, and the old, gray man is the natural end of an uninterrupted life-development, or with Metschnikoff, that science will one day so lengthen life that it will fade away like a rose at last and death lose all its dread; death still is no less a riddle, and one which swallows up all the strength of life. When one considers, besides, that a number of creatures, plants, trees, animals, reach a much higher age than man; that the larger half of mankind dies before or shortly after birth; that another large percentage dies in the bloom of youth or in the prime of life; that the law of the survival of the fittest is true only when the fact of the survival is taken as a proof of their fitness; that the graybeards, who, spent and decrepit, go down to the grave, form a very small number; then the enigma of death increases more and more in mysteriousness. The endeavors to bring death into connection with certain activities of the organism and to explain it by increasing weight, by growth or by fertility, have all led to shipwreck. When Weismann took refuge in the immortality of the "*einzellige Protozoën*," he raised a hypothesis which not only found many opponents, but which also left mortality of the "*Körperplasma*" an insoluble mystery (Beth, "*Ueber Ursache und Zweck des Todes, Glauben und Wissen* [1909], 285–304, 335–48). Thus science certainly does not compel us to review Scripture on this point, but rather furnishes a strong proof of the mysterious majesty of death. When Pelagius, Socinus, Schleiermacher, Ritschl and a number of other theologians and philosophers separate death from its connection with sin, they are not compelled to do so by science, but are led by a defective insight into the relation between *éthos* and *phúsis*. Misery and death are not absolutely always consequences and punishment of a great personal transgression (Lk **13** 2; Jn **9** 3); but that they are connected with sin, we learn from the experience of every day. Who can number the victims of mammonism, alcoholism and licentiousness? Even spiritual sins exercise their influence on corporal life; envy is a rottenness of the bones (Prov **14** 30). This connection is taught us in a great measure by Scripture, when it placed the not yet fallen man in a Paradise, where death had not yet entered, and eternal life was not yet possessed and enjoyed; when it sends fallen man, who, however, is destined for redemption, into a world full of misery and death; and at last assigns to the wholly renewed man a new heaven and a new earth, where death, sorrow, crying or pain shall no longer exist (Rev **21** 4).

Finally, Scripture is not the book of death, but of life, of everlasting life through Jesus Christ Our Lord. It tells us, in oft-repeated and unmistakable terms, of the dreaded reality of death, but it proclaims to us still more loudly the wonderful power of the life which is in Christ Jesus. See also DECEASE.

HERMAN BAVINCK

DEATH, BODY OF. See BODY OF DEATH.

DEATH, SECOND (ὁ δεύτερος θάνατος, *ho deúteros thánatos*): An expression, peculiar to the Book of Rev (**2** 11; **20** 6.14; **21** 8) in Scripture, denoting the final penalty of the unrighteous; parallel with another expression likewise peculiar, "the lake of fire," in **20** 14; **21** 8. See ESCHATOLOGY OF THE NT.

DEBATE, dē-bāt′: This word is used only once in RV (Prov **25** 9). It evidently refers to the settling of a difficulty with a neighbor, and anticipates Mt **18** 15. It argues for and shows the advantage of private, peaceable settlement of difficulties. Cf Ecclus **28** 9, and see MAKEBATES.

DEBIR, dē′bēr (דְּבִיר, *debhīr*, or דְּבִר, *debhir*, "oracle"): King of Eglon, one of the five Amorite kings whose confederation against Israel was overcome and who were killed by Joshua (Josh **10** 3).

DEBIR, dē′bēr (דְּבִיר, *debhīr;* Δαβείρ, *Dabeír*): "And Joshua returned, and all Israel with him, to Debir, and fought against it: and he took it, and the king thereof, and all the cities thereof; and they smote them with the edge of the sword . . . . he left none remaining" (Josh **10** 38.39). In Josh **15** 15–17 and Jgs **1** 11–13 is an account of how Othniel captured Debir, which "beforetime was *Kiriath-sepher*," and won thereby the hand of Achsah, Caleb's daughter. In Josh **15** 49 Debir is called *Kiriath-sannah*. It had once been inhabited by the Anakim (Josh **11** 21). It was a Levitical city (Josh **21** 15; 1 Ch **6** 58). See KIRIATH-SEPHER.

1. The Meaning of the Name

(1) *Debir* is usually accepted as meaning "back," but this is doubtful; the word *debhīr* is used to denote the "holy of holies" (1 K **6** 5). According to Sayce (*HDB*), "the city must have been a sacred one with a well-known temple." *Kiriath-sepher* is tr[d] "town of books," and Sayce and others consider that in all probability there was a great storehouse of clay tablets here; perhaps the name may have been *ḳiryath ṣōphēr*, "town of scribes." *Kiriath-sannah* (Josh **15** 49) is probably a corruption of *Kiriath-sepher;* the LXX has here as in references to the latter πόλις γραμμάτων, *pólis grammátōn*, "town of books."

2. The Site

Unfortunately this site, important even if the speculations about the books are doubtful, is still a matter of uncertainty. *Edh-Dháherīyeh*, some 11 miles S.W. of Hebron, has a good deal of support. It was unquestionably a site of importance in ancient times as the meeting-place of several roads; it is in the Negeb (cf Jgs **1** 15), in the neighborhood of the probable site of Anab (Josh **11** 21; **15** 50); it is a dry site, but there are "upper" and "lower" springs about 6½ miles to the N. A more thorough examination of the site than has as yet been undertaken might produce added proofs in favor of this identification. No other suggestion has any great probability. See *PEF*, III, 402; *PEFS*, 1875.

(2) *Debir*, on the border between Judah and Benjamin (Josh **15** 7), must have been somewhere E. of Jerus not far from the modern Jericho road. *Thoghgret ed Debr*, "the pass of the rear," half a mile S.W. of the *Tal'at ed Dumm* (see ADUMMIN), close to the so-called, "Inn of the Good Samaritan," may be an echo of the name which has lingered in the neighborhood. Many authorities consider that there is no place-name in this reference at all, the text being corrupt.

(3) *Debir* RVm, *Lidebir* (Josh **13** 26), a town on the border of Gad, near Mahanaim; Ibdar, S. of the Yarmuk has been suggested. May be identical with Lo-debar (2 S **9** 4).

E. W. G. MASTERMAN

DEBORAH, deb′ō-ra (דְּבוֹרָה, *debhōrāh*, signifying "bee"):

(1) Rebekah's nurse, who died near Bethel and was buried under "the oak of weeping" (Gen **35** 8 m).

(2) A prophetess, fourth in the order of the "judges." In aftertimes a palm tree, known as the "palm tree of Deborah," was shown between Ramah and Bethel, beneath which the prophetess was wont to administer justice. Like the rest of the "judges" she became a leader of her people in

times of national distress. This time the oppressor was Jabin, king of Hazor, whose general was Sisera. Deborah summoned Barak of Kedesh-naphtali and delivered to him the Divine message to meet Sisera in battle by the brook Kishon. Barak induced Deborah to accompany him; they were joined by 10,000 men of Zebulun and Naphtali. The battle took place by the brook Kishon, and Sisera's army was thoroughly routed. While Barak pursued the fleeing army, Sisera escaped and sought refuge with Jael the wife of Heber the Kenite, near Kedesh. The brave woman, the prototype of Judith, put the Canaanite general to sleep by offering him a draft of milk and then slew him by driving a peg into his temple. Thus runs the story in Jgs **4**. It is on the whole substantiated by the ode in ch **5** which is ascribed jointly to Deborah and Barak. It is possible that the editor mistook the archaic form קַמְתִּי, *ḳamtī*, in ver 7 which should be rendered "thou arosedst" instead of "I arose." Certainly the ode was composed by a person who, if not a contemporary of the event, was very near it in point of time. The song is spoken of as one of the oldest pieces of Heb lit. Great difficulties meet the exegete. Nevertheless the general substance is clear. The Lord is described as having come from Sinai near the "field of Edom" to take part in the battle; 'for from heaven they fought, the very stars from their courses fought against Sisera' (ver 20). The nation was in a sad plight, oppressed by a mighty king, and the tribes loth to submerge their separatist tendencies. Some, like Reuben, Gilead, Dan and Asher remained away. A community by the name of Meroz is singled out for blame, 'because they came not to the help of Jeh, to the help of Jeh among the mighty' (ver 23; cf RVm). Ephraim, Issachar, Machir, Benjamin were among the followers of Barak; "Zebulun . . . . jeoparded their lives unto the death, and Naphtali, upon the high places of the field" (ver 18). According to the song, the battle was fought at Taanach by the waters of Megiddo; Sisera's host was swept away by "that ancient river, the river Kishon" (ver 21). Jael, the wife of Heber the Kenite, receives here due meed of praise for her heroic act. The paean vividly paints the waiting of Sisera's mother for the home-coming of the general; the delay is ascribed to the great booty which the conqueror is distributing among his Canaanite host. "So let all thine enemies perish," concludes the song; "O Jeh: but let them that love him be as the sun when he goeth forth in his might." It is a song in praise of the "righteous acts" of the Lord, His work of victory which Israel's leaders, 'the long-haired princes,' wrought, giving their lives freely to the nation's cause. And the nation was sore bestead because it had become faithless to the Lord and chosen new gods. Out of the conflict came, for the time being, victory and moral purification; and the inspiring genius of it all was a woman in Israel, the prophetess Deborah.

(3) Tobit's grandmother (AV "Debora," Tob **1** 8). MAX L. MARGOLIS

DEBT, det, **DEBTOR,** det′ẽr: It is difficult nowadays to think of debt without associating with it the idea of interest, and even usury. Certain it is that this idea is associated with the OT idea of the word, at least in the later period of OT history. This is true of the NT entire. The Heb word (נְשִׁי, *n^e^shī*) always carries with it the idea of "biting interest" (cf 2 K **4** 7). The Gr words δάνειον, *dáneion* (Mt **18** 27), and ὀφειλή, *opheilḗ* (Mt **18** 32), may point only to the fact of indebtedness; the idea of interest, however, is clearly taught in the NT (cf Mt **25** 27).

Quite extensive legislation is provided in the OT governing the matter of debt and debtors. Indebtedness and loaning had not, however, the commercial aspect among the Jews so characteristic of the nations surrounding Pal. Indeed the Mosaic legislation was seemingly intended to guard against just such commercialism. It was looked upon as a misfortune to be in debt; it indicated poverty brought on probably by blighted harvests; consequently those in debt were to be looked upon with pity and dealt with in leniency. There must be no oppression of the poor under such circumstances (Ex **22** 25; Dt **23** 19.20; Ezk **18** 18). Even where a pledge is given and received, certain restrictions are thrown around it, e.g. the creditor must not take a mill, nor a necessary garment, nor a widow's ox, etc, in pledge (Ex **22** 25–27; Dt **24** 6.10–13; Job **22** 6; Am **2** 8). And further, the pledge is to be restored in some instances "before the sun goeth down" (Ex **22** 26.27), and in all cases full redemption in the seventh and jubilee years (Neh **10** 31, etc). The Jews were strictly exhorted to take no interest at all from their own nation (Ex **22** 25; Dt **23** 19.20). Strangers, however, might be charged interest (ibid). A devout Jew would not lend money to another Jew on interest.

It would seem that as Israel came into contact with the surrounding nations, debt became increasingly a commercial matter. The Mosaic laws regarding clemency toward the poor who were compelled for the time being to become debtors were utterly disregarded, and the poor were oppressed by the rich. An illustration of the severity with which debtors came to be dealt with is to be found in 2 K **4** 1–7, in which, because of the inability of a widow to pay a small debt contracted by her dead husband, the woman complains to the prophet that the creditors have come to sell her two children in order that the debt might be paid. Strangely the prophet, while helping the widow by miraculously multiplying the oil in order that the debt might be paid, says nothing by way of condemnation of such conduct on the part of the creditors. Are we to understand by this that commercialism had already so powerful a grip upon Israel that even to a prophet the practice had come to seem proper, or at least expected? The debtor himself or his family might be sold for debt, or the debtor might become a slave for a certain length of time until the debt was paid (Lev **25** 39.47; Isa **50** 1). So oppressive had the commercial system in Israel become that the debtor cursed the creditor and the creditor the debtor (Jer **15** 10). Sometimes debtors were outlawed, as in the case of the men who came to David in the cave of Adullam (1 S **22** 2). That the matter of borrowing and lending had assumed very grievous proportions is evident from the very sharp warnings concerning the matter in the Book of Prov (**6** 1; **11** 15; **20** 16, etc).

The teaching of the NT on this subject is confined very largely to the parables of Our Lord. Some think that the expression, "Owe no man anything" (Rom **13** 8), is an absolute warning against indebtedness. Quite a noticeable advance in the matter of debts and debtors is noticed as we enter the time of the NT. We read of bankers, exchangers, money-changers, interest, investments, usury (Mt **25** 16–27; Jn **2** 13–17). The taking of interest does not seem to be explicitly condemned in the NT. The person of the debtor, as well as his family and lands, could be seized for non-payment of debt (Mt **18** 21–26). Indeed, the debtor was often cast into prison and tormented because of non-payment (Mt **18** 30.34). That compassion and leniency should be exercised toward those in debt is the clear teaching of Christ in the parables of the Unmerciful Servant (Mt **18** 23–35) and the Two Debtors (Lk **7** 41–43).

Figurative: Debt and debtor are used in a moral

sense also as indicating the obligation of a righteous life which we owe to God. To fall short in righteous living is to become a debtor. For this reason we pray, "Forgive us our debts" (Mt **6** 12). Those who are ministered to in spiritual things are said to be debtors to those who minister to them (Rom **15** 27). To make a vow to God is to put one's self in debt in a moral sense (Mt **23** 16–18; RVm "bound by his oath"). In a deeply spiritual sense the apostle Paul professed to be in debt to all men in that he owed them the opportunity to do them good (Rom **1** 14).

The parables of Jesus as above named are rich with comforting truth. How beautiful is the willingness of God, the great and Divine Creditor, to release us from our indebtedness! Just so ought we to be imitators of the Father in heaven who is merciful. WILLIAM EVANS

DECALOGUE, dek'a-log. See TEN COMMANDMENTS.

DECAPOLIS, dē-kap'ō-lis (**Δεκάπολις**, *Dekápolis*): The name given to the region occupied by a league of "ten cities" (Mt **4** 25; Mk **5** 20; **7** 31), which Eusebius defines (*Onom*) as "lying in the Peraea, round Hippos, Pella and Gadara." Such combinations of Gr cities arose as Rome assumed dominion in the East, to promote their common interests in trade and commerce, and for mutual protection against the peoples surrounding them. This particular league seems to have been constituted about the time of Pompey's campaign in Syria, 65 BC, by which several cities in Decapolis dated their eras. They were independent of the local tetrarchy, and answerable directly to the governor of Syria. They enjoyed the rights of association and asylum; they struck their own coinage, paid imperial taxes and were liable to military service (*Ant*, XIV, iv, 4; *BJ*, I, vii, 7; II, xviii, 3; III, ix, 7; *Vita*, 65, 74). Of the ten cities, Scythopolis, the ancient Bethshean, alone, the capital of the league, was on the W. side of Jordan. The names given by Pliny (*NH*, v.18) are Scythopolis (*Beisān*), Hippos (*Susiyeh*), Gadara (*Umm Ḳeis*), Pella (*Fahil*), Philadelphia (*'Ammān*), Gerasa (*Jerash*), Dion (*Adūn?*), Canatha (*Ḳanawāt*), Damascus and Raphana. The last named is not identified, and Dion is uncertain. Other cities joined the league, and Ptolemy, who omits Raphana, gives a list of 18. The Gr inhabitants were never on good terms with the Jews; and the herd of swine (Mk **5** 11 ff) indicates contempt for what was probably regarded as Jewish prejudice. The ruins still seen at Gadara, but esp. at *Ḳanawāt* (see KENATH) and Jerash, of temples, theaters and other public buildings, attest the splendor of these cities in their day. W. EWING

DECAY, dē-kā': Although this word is still in good use in both its lit. sense, of the putrefaction of either animal or vegetable matter, and its derived sense, denoting any deterioration, decline or gradual failure, the RV has replaced it by other expressions in Lev **25** 35; Eccl **10** 18; Isa **44** 26; He **8** 13; in some of these cases with a gain in accuracy of tr. In Neh **4** 10 (כָּשַׁל, *kāshal*, "to be feeble," "stumble") RV retains "is decayed"; in Job **14** 11 (חָרֵב, *ḥārēbh*, "to be dried up") ARV substitutes "wasteth," and in Jn **11** 39 ARV has "the body decayeth" instead of the more literal tr offensive to modern ears (*ὄζει*, *ózei*, "emits a smell"). F. K. FARR

DECEASE, IN OT AND APOC (רָפָא, *rāphā'*, pl. *r*ᵉ*phā'īm*, "ghosts," "shades," is trᵈ by "dead," "dead body," and "deceased" in both AV and RV): The word seems to mean "soft," "inert," but its etymology is uncertain (see REPHAIM). The various writers of the OT present, as is to be expected on such a subject, different conceptions of the condition of the deceased. In the beginning probably a vague idea of the continuation of existence was held, without the activities (Isa **59** 10) and the joys of the present life (Ps **49** 17). They dwell in the "land of forgetfulness" (Job **14** 21; Ps **88** 5; cf Isa **26** 14), they "tremble" of cold (Job **26** 5), they totter and "stumble at noonday as in the twilight" (Isa **59** 10), their voice is described as low and muttering or chirping (Isa **8** 19; **29** 4), which may refer to the peculiar pitch of the voice of the spirit medium when a spirit speaks through him. (The calling up of the dead, which was strictly forbidden to Israel [Lev **19** 31; **20** 27] is referred to in 1 S **28** 13 and perhaps in Isa **14** 9.) The deceased are separated from their friends; love and hatred have both ceased with them (Eccl **9** 5.6); "There is no work, nor device, nor knowledge, nor wisdom, in Sheol" (Eccl **9** 10). The deceased are unable to praise Jeh (Ps **6** 5; **88** 10–12; Isa **38** 18; Bar **2** 17; Sir **17** 27.28). Nor does there seem to have been at first an anticipation of reward or punishment after death (Ps **88** 10; Sir **41** 4), probably because the shades were supposed to be lacking the organs by which either reward or punishment could be perceived; nevertheless they are still in the realm of God's power (1 S **2** 6; Ps **86** 13; **139** 8; Prov **15** 11; Isa **7** 11; Hos **13** 14; Am **9** 2; Tob **13** 2).

Gradually the possibility of a return of the departed was conceived (Gen **5** 24; 2 K **13** 21; Ps **49** 15; **73** 24; **86** 13; Hos **13** 14; Wisd **3** 1–7; **4** 13.14; **6** 18.19; **10** 14). Even here it is often more the idea of the immortality of the soul than that of the resurrection of the body, and some of these passages may be interpreted as allegorical expressions for a temporal rescue from great disaster (e.g. 1 S **2** 6); nevertheless this interpretation presupposes the existence of a deliverance from the shadows of Sheol to a better life in the presence of Jeh. Some passages refer clearly to such an escape at the end of the age (Dnl **12** 2; Isa **26** 19). Only very few of the OT believers reached the sublime faith of Job (**19** 25.26) and none the blessed expectation taught in the NT, for none but Christ has "brought life and immortality to light" (2 Tim **1** 10; Jn **5** 28.29).

The opinion that the dead or at least the newly buried could partake of the food which was placed in graves, a custom which recent excavations have clearly shown to have been almost universal in Pal, and which is referred to in Dt **26** 14 and Tob **4** 17, was soon doubted (Sir **30** 18), and food and drink prepared for the funeral was henceforth intended as the "bread of comfort" and the "cup of consolation" for the mourners (Jer **16** 7; 2 S **3** 35; Ezk **24** 17). Similarly the offering and burning of incense, originally an homage to the deceased, became a relief for the mourner (2 Ch **16** 14; **21** 19; Jer **34** 5). See also Wisd **3** 2; **7** 6; Sir **38** 23, and arts. on CORPSE; DEATH; HADES; SHEOL.

H. L. E. LUERING

DECEASE, dē-sēs', **IN NT** (**τελευτάω**, *teleutáō*, "to come to an end," "married and deceased" [Mt **22** 25]): With *θανάτῳ*, *thanátō*, "death," "die the death" (Mt **15** 4; Mk **7** 10, RVm "surely die"). Elsewhere the word is trᵈ "die" (Mt **2** 19; **9** 18; Mk **9** 48 and often; He **11** 22, RV "end was nigh").

Also the subst., *ἔξοδος*, *éxodos*, "exodus," "exit," "departure," "his decease which he was about to accomplish" (Lk **9** 31, RVm "departure"); "after my decease" (2 Pet **1** 15, RVm "departure").

DECEIT, dē-sēt' (מִרְמָה, *mirmāh;* **δόλος**, *dólos*): The intentional misleading or beguiling of another:

in Scripture represented as a companion of many other forms of wickedness, as cursing (Ps **10** 7), hatred (Prov **26** 24), theft, covetousness, adultery, murder (Mk **7** 22; Rom **1** 29). The RV introduces the word in Prov **14** 25; 2 Thess **2** 10; but in such passages as Ps **55** 11; Prov **20** 17; **26** 26; 1 Thess **2** 3, renders a variety of words, more accurately than the AV, by "oppression," "falsehood," "guile," "error."

DECEIVABLENESS, dē-sēv′a-b'l-nes, **DECEIVE,** dē-sēv′ (נָשָׁא, *nāshā'*, "to lead astray"): "The pride of thy heart hath deceived thee" (Jer **49** 16), i.e. "Thy stern mountain fastnesses have persuaded thee that thou art impregnable." In Jer **20** 7, "O Lord, thou hast deceived me, and I was deceived," פָּתָה, *pāthāh*, signifies "to be enticed," "persuaded," as in ARV and RVm.

In the OT most often, and in the NT regularly, the various words rendered in AV "deceive" denote some deliberate misleading in the moral or spiritual realm. False prophets (Jer **29** 8), false teachers (Eph **5** 6) and Satan himself (Rev **12** 9) are deceivers in this sense. In the gospels, AV "deceive" (πλανάω, *planáō*, 9 t, Mt **24** 4.5 ‖ Mk **13** 5.6 ‖ Lk **21** 8; Mt **24** 11.24; Jn **7** 12.47) becomes in RV "lead astray"; the same change is made in 1 Jn **2** 26; **3** 7; but elsewhere (13 t) both AV and RV render *planaō* by "deceive."

"Deceivableness" (ἀπάτη, *apátē*), only in 2 Thess **2** 10, signifies power to deceive, not liability to deception; RV "deceit." F. K. Farr

DECENTLY, dē′sent-li (εὐσχημόνως, *euschēmónōs*): Only once is this word found in our Eng. Bible (1 Cor **14** 40). It is in the last verse of that remarkable chapter on the proper use of spiritual gifts in the church and the proper conduct of public worship. It does not refer here to absence of impurity or obscenity. It rather refers to good order in the conduct of public worship. All things that are done and said in public worship are to be in harmony with that becoming and reverent spirit and tone that befit the true worshippers of God.

DECISION, dē-sizh′un: Has several different shades of meaning. It expresses the formation of a judgment on a matter under consideration. It expresses the quality of being firm or positive in one's actions. It expresses the termination of a contest or question in favor of one side or the other, as the decision of the battle, or the decision of the judge.

Until recent times the decision of disputed points between nations was determined by force of arms.

1. National Decisions

Thus the questions of dispute were decided between Israel and the surrounding tribes, between Israel and Assyria, between Israel and Egypt, and later between Judaea and Rome.

In the earliest times the questions of dispute between individuals were decided by the patriarch who was the head of the family.

2. Judicial Decisions

When Israel became a nation men were appointed to decide the difficulties between the people. At first this was one of the most important duties of Moses, but when the task became too great he appointed judges to assist him (see Ex **18** 13–26). One important function of those who are called judges was to decide the difficulties between the people (see Jgs **4** 4.5). The kings also decided questions of dispute between individuals (see 2 S **15** 1–6; 1 K **3** 16–28). As the people developed in their national ideals the decisions in judicial matters were rendered by councils appointed for that purpose.

Perplexing questions were many times decided by the casting of lots. The people believed that God would in this way direct them to the right decision (Prov **16** 33; Josh **7** 10–21; **14** 2; 1 S **10** 20 f).

3. Methods of Forming Decisions

Casting lots must have been a common method of deciding perplexing questions (see 1 S **14** 41.42; Jon **1** 7). It was resorted to by the apostles to decide which of the two men they had selected should take the place of Judas (Acts **1** 21–26). The custom gradually lost in favor, and decisions, even of perplexing questions, were formed by considering all the facts. See Augury IV, 3; Lots. A. W. Fortune

DECISION, VALLEY OF. See Jehoshaphat, Valley of.

DECLARATION, dek-la-rā′shun, **DECLARE,** dē-klâr′: "Declare" is the tr of a variety of Heb and Gr words in the OT and NT, appearing to bear uniformly the meaning "to make known," "set forth," rather than (the older meaning) "to explain" (Dt **1** 5). **Declaration** (Est **10** 2 AV, RV "full account"; Job **13** 17; Ecclus **43** 6; Lk **1** 1 AV, RV "narrative"; 2 Cor **8** 19 AV, RV "to show") has the like meaning.

DECLINE, dē-klīn′ (סוּר, *ṣūr*, or שׂוּר, *sūr*, נָטָה, *nāṭāh*): In AV this word occurs 9 t in its original sense (now obsolete) of "turn aside." RV substitutes "turn aside" in Ex **23** 2; Dt **17** 11; 2 Ch **34** 2; Job **23** 11. In Ps **102** 11; **109** 23, the lengthening shadows of afternoon are said to "decline," and RV introduces the word in the same general sense in Jgs **19** 8; 2 K **20** 10; Jer **6** 4. See Afternoon.

DEDAN, dē′dan, **DEDANITES,** dē′dan-īts (AV **Dedanim,** ded′a-nim; דְּדָן, *dᵉdhān*, "low," דְּדָנִים, *dᵉdhānīm*): An Arabian people named in Gen **10** 7 as descended from Cush; in Gen **25** 3 as descended from Keturah. Evidently they were, like the related Sheba (Sabaeans), of mixed race (cf Gen **10** 7.28). In Isa **21** 13 allusion is made to the "caravans of Dedanites" in the wilds of Arabia, and Ezk mentions them as supplying Tyre with precious things (Ezk **27** 20; in ver 15, "Dedan" should probably be read as in LXX, "Rodan," i.e. Rhodians). The name seems still to linger in the island of Dadan, on the border of the Pers Gulf. It is found also in Min. and Sab. inscriptions (Glazer, II, 392 ff). James Orr

DEDICATE, ded′i-kāt, **DEDICATION,** ded-i-kā′shun (חֲנֻכָּה, *ḥănukkāh*, "initiation," "consecration"; קָדֵשׁ, *ḳādhēsh*, "to be clean," "sanctify"; חֵרֶם, *ḥērem*, "a thing devoted [to God]"): Often used in Heb of the consecration of persons, but usually in the EV of the setting apart of things to a sacred use, as of the altar (Nu **7** 10f.84.88; cf Dnl **3** 2.3, "the d. of the image"), of silver and gold (2 S **8** 11; 2 K **12** 4), of the Temple (1 K **8** 63; Ezr **6** 16 f; cf Ex **29** 44), of the wall of Jerus (Neh **12** 27), of private dwellings (Dt **20** 5). RV substitutes "devoted" for "dedicated" in Ezk **44** 29. See Consecration; Sanctification.

DEDICATION, ded-i-kā′shun, **FEAST OF** (**τὰ ἐγκαίνια,** *tá egkaínia*, Jn **10** 22): A feast held by the Jews throughout the country for eight days, commencing on the 25th Kiṣlev (December), in commemoration of the cleansing of the temple and dedication of the altar by Judas Maccabaeus after their desecration by Antiochus Epiphanes (1 Macc **4** 56.59). The feast was to be kept "with mirth and gladness." 2 Macc **10** 6.7 says it was kept like the Feast of the Tabernacles, with the carrying of palm and other branches, and the singing of psalms. Jos calls it "Lights," from the joy which accompanied it (*Ant*, XII, vii, 7). At this winter feast Jesus delivered in the temple the discourse recorded in Jn **10** 24 ff, at Jerus. JAMES ORR

DEED, dēd: Used in its ordinary modern sense in EV. In the OT it is used to tr five Heb words: *g^emūlāh*, lit. "recompense" (Isa **59** 18); *dābhār*, lit. "word," "thing" (2 Ch **35** 27 AV, RV "acts"; Est **1** 17.18; Jer **5** 28); *ma'ăseh* (Gen **20** 9; **44** 15; Ezr **9** 13); *'ălīlāh* (1 Ch **16** 8 AV, RV "doings"; Ps **105** 1 AV, RV "doings"); *pō'al* (Ps **28** 4 AV, RV "work"; Jer **25** 14). In the NT "deed" very frequently translates ἔργον, *érgon* (same root as Eng. "work"; cf "energy"), which is still more frequently (esp. in RV) rendered "work." In Lk **23** 51; Acts **19** 18; Rom **8** 13; Col **3** 9 AV, RV "doings," it stands for Gr πρᾶξις, *práxis* (lit. "a doing," "transaction"), each time in a bad sense, equivalent to wicked deed, crime, a meaning which is frequently associated with the pl. of *praxis* (cf Eng. "practices" in the sense of trickery; so often in Polybius; Deissmann maintains that *praxis* was a technical term in magic), although in Mt **16** 27 (AV "works") and Rom **12** 4 the same Gr word has a neutral meaning. In Jas **1** 25 AV "deed" is the tr of Gr ποίησις, *poíēsis*, more correctly rendered "doing" in RV. D. MIALL EDWARDS

DEEP (תְּהוֹם, *t^ehōm;* **ἄβυσσος,** *ábussos*, Lk **8** 31 AV; Rom **10** 7 AV; **βάθος,** *báthos*, Lk **5** 4; **βυθός,** *buthós*, 2 Cor **11** 25): The Heb word ("water in commotion") is used (1) of the primeval watery waste (Gen **1** 2), where some suggest a connection with Bab Tiamat in the creation-epic; (2) of the sea (Isa **51** 10 and commonly); (3) of the subterranean reservoir of water (Gen **7** 11; **8** 2; **49** 25; Dt **33** 13; Ezk **31** 4, etc). In the RV the Gr word first noted is rendered, lit., "abyss." See ABYSS; also ASTRONOMY, III, 7.

DEEP SLEEP. See SLEEP, DEEP.

DEER, dēr (אַיָּל, *'ayyāl*, fem. אַיָּלָה, *'ayyālāh*, and אַיֶּלֶת, *'ayyeleth* [cf Arab. *'ayyāl* and *'iyāl*, "deer" and אַיִל, *'ayil*, "ram," and Lat *caper* and *capra*, "goat," *caprea*, *capreolus*, "wild goat," "chamois," or "roe deer"]; יַחְמוּר, *yaḥmūr* [cf Arab. *yaḥmūr*, "deer"]; יַעֲלָה, *ya'ălāh*, fem. of יָעֵל, *yā'ēl* [cf Arab. *wa'l*, "Pers wild goat"]; צְבִי, *ç^ebhī*, and fem. צְבִיָּה, *ç^ebhīyāh* [cf Arab. *ẓabi* and fem. *ẓabīyah*, "gazelle"]; עֹפֶר, *'ōpher* [cf Arab. *ghafr* and *ghufr*, "young of the mountain goat"]):

Of the words in the preceding list, the writer believes that only the first two, i.e. *'ayyāl* (with its fem. forms) and *yaḥmūr* should be trd "deer," *'ayyāl* for the roe deer and *yaḥmūr* for the fallow deer. Further, he believes that *yā'ēl* (incl. *ya'ălāh*) should be trd "ibex," and *ç^ebhī*, "gazelle." *'Ōpher* is the young of a roe deer or of a gazelle.

'Ayyāl and its fem. forms are regularly in EV rendered "hart" and "hind," terms which are more commonly applied to the male and female of the red deer, *Cervus elaphus*, which inhabits Great Britain, the continent of Europe, the Caucasus and Asia Minor, but which has never been reported as far south as Syria or Pal. The roe deer, *Capreolus caprea*, however, which inhabits the British Isles, the greater part of Europe, the Caucasus and Persia, is certainly found in Pal. The museum of the Syrian Protestant College at *Beirût* possesses the skeleton of a roe deer which was shot in the mountains near Tyre. As late as 1890 it was fairly common in southern Lebanon and Carmel, but has now (1912) become very scarce. The fallow deer, *Cervus dama*, is a native of Northern Africa and countries about the Mediterranean. It is found in central Europe and Great Britain, where it has been introduced from its more southern habitat. A variety of the fallow deer, sometimes counted as a separate species under the name of *Cervus Mesopotamicus*, inhabits northeastern Mesopotamia and Persia. It may in former times have been found in Pal, and Tristram reports having seen the fallow deer in Galilee (*Fauna and Flora of Pal*), but while Tristram was a remarkably acute observer, he appears sometimes to have been too readily satisfied, and his observations, when unaccompanied, as in this case, by specimens, are to be accepted with caution. Now *'ayyāl* (and its fem. forms) occurs in the Bible 22 t, while *yaḥmūr* occurs only twice, i.e. in the list of clean animals in Dt **14** 5, and in 1 K **4** 23, in the list of animals provided for Solomon's table. In both places AV has "fallow deer" and RV "roebuck." In view of the fact that the roe deer has within recent years been common in Pal, while the occurrence of the fallow deer must be considered doubtful, it seems fair to render *'ayyāl* "roe deer" or "roebuck," leaving *yaḥmūr* for fallow deer.

The Arabs call the roe deer both *'ayyāl* and *wa'l*. *Wa'l* is the proper name of the Pers wild goat, *Capra aegagrus*, and is also often used for the Arab. or Sin ibex, *Capra beden*, though only by those who do not live within its range. Where the ibex is at home it is always called *beden*. This looseness of nomenclature must be taken into account, and we have no reason to suppose that the Hebrews were more exact than are the Arabs. There are many examples of this in Eng., e.g. panther, coney, rabbit (in America), locust, adder and many others.

Yā'ēl (incl. *ya'ălāh*) occurs 4 t. In Job **39** 1; Ps **104** 18; 1 S **24** 2, EV renders *yā'ēl* by "wild goat." For *ya'ălāh* in Prov **5** 19, AV has "roe," while RV has "doe," which is non-committal, since the name, "doe," may be applied to the female of a deer or of an ibex. Since the Arab. *wa'l*, which is etymologically closely akin to *yā'ēl*, means the Pers wild goat, it might be supposed that that animal was meant, were it not that it inhabits the plains of the Syrian desert, and not the mountains of Southern Pal, where the ibex lives. At least two of the passages clearly indicate the latter locality, i.e. Ps **104** 18: "The high mountains are for the wild goats," and 1 S **24** 2: "Saul . . . . went to seek David and his men upon the rocks of the wild goats." The conclusion then seems irresistible that *yā'ēl*, and consequently *ya'ălāh*, is the ibex.

Ç^ebhī (incl. *ç^ebhīyāh*) is uniformly rendered "roe" or "roebuck" in AV, while RV, either in the text or in the margin, has in most cases "gazelle." In two places "roe" is retained in RV without comment, i.e. 2 S **2** 18: "Asahel was as light of foot as a wild roe," and 1 Ch **12** 8: "were as swift as the roes upon the mountains." *'Ayyāl* and *ç^ebhī* occur together in Dt **12** 15.22; **14** 5; **15** 22; 1 K **4** 23; Cant **2** 9.17, i.e. in 7 of the 16 passages in which we find *ç^ebhī*. If therefore it be accepted that *'ayyāl* is the roe deer, it follows that *ç^ebhī* must be something else. Now the gazelle is common in Pal and satisfies perfectly every passage in which we find *ç^ebhī*. Further, one of the Arab. names of the gazelle is *ẓabi*, a word which is etymologically much nearer to *ç^ebhī* than appears in this transliteration.

'Ōpher is akin to *'āphār*, "dust," and has reference to the color of the young of the deer or gazelle, to both of which it is applied. In Cant **2** 9.17 and **8** 14, we have *'ōpher hā-'ayyālīm*, EV "young hart," lit. "fawn of the roe deer." In Cant **4** 5 and **7** 3, we have *'ŏphārīm t^e'ōmē ç^ebhīyāh*, AV "young roes that are twins," RV "fawns that are twins of a roe,"

RVm "gazelle" (for "roe"). For further reference to these questions, see ZOÖLOGY.

With the exception of mere lists of animals, as in Dt **14** and 1 K **4**, the treatment of these animals is highly poetical, and shows much appreciation of their grace and beauty. ALFRED ELY DAY

DEFAME, dē-fām′, **DEFAMING,** dē-fām′ing: These words occur but twice in AV, and are translations of דִּבָּה, *dibbāh*, "slander," from *dābhath*, "to slander," or spread an evil report, and βλασφημέω, *blasphēmĕō*, "to speak injuriously" of anyone (Jer **20** 10; 1 Cor **4** 13). "To defame" differs from "to revile" in that the former refers to *public* slander, the latter to *personal* abuse.

DEFECT, dē-fekt′, **DEFECTIVE,** dē-fekt′iv (ἥττημα, *hēttēma*, "loss," "a defect"): Occurs in 1 Cor **6** 7: "Nay, already it is altogether a defect in you [AV "there is utterly a fault among you"], that ye have lawsuits one with another." "Defect" means "want or absence of something necessary for completeness" (RVm "a loss to you"). The meaning of the passage in RV is that when Christians have lawsuits one with another it produces a lack of something which brings them short of completeness, they suffer a spiritual loss or defeat, and perhaps defect is not quite strong enough fully to express that idea.

Defective: Sir **49** 4 AV, RV "committed trespass." A. W. FORTUNE

DEFENCE, dē-fens′. See COURTS, JUDICIAL.

DEFENCED. See FORTIFICATION.

DEFER, dē-fûr′ (אָחַר, *'āḥar* [in Hiphil], אָרַךְ, *'ārakh* [in Hiphil], מָשַׁךְ, *māshakh* [in Niphal], "to postpone," more or less definitely; "delay"): In OT passages such as Isa **48** 9; Ezk **12** 25.28; Dnl **9** 19, the idea of indefinite postponement agrees with the Heb and with the context. In the only NT occurrence of the word (ἀναβάλλω, *anabállō*, in the middle voice, Acts **24** 22) a definite postponement is implied.

DEFILE, dē-fīl′, **DEFILEMENT,** dē-fīl′ment (AS *āfȳlau*, etc; ME *defoulen*, "make foul," "pollute," render [AV] 9 Heb roots [RV six]: גָּאַל, *gā'al*, "defile"; חָלַל, *ḥālal*, "defile" [from "untie, loosen, open," i.e. "make common," hence "profane"]; חָנֵף, *ḥānēph*, "incline away" [from right or religion], hence "profane," "defile" [Jer **3** 9, ARV "pollute"]; טָמֵא, *ṭāmē'*, the principal root, over 250 t, tr[d] "defile" 74 t, "to become, or render, unclean"; טָנַף, *ṭānaph*, "to soil" [Cant **5** 3]; עָלַל, *'ālal*, "deal severely, or decidedly, with," "roll" [Job **16** 15, AV, ARVm]; עָנָה, *'ānāh*, "humble" [Gen **34** 2 AV, ARV "humble"]; קָדַשׁ, *ḳādhash*, "separate," "sanctify," "devote to religious use," hence "forfeit" [Dt **22** 9 AV, ARV "forfeit," m "consecrated"]. They also render 6 [AV] Gr roots [ARV, 4]: κοινός, *koinós*, etc, "common" or "unclean," because appertaining to the outside world and not to the people of God, opposite of *katharós*, "clean," used 13 t; μιαίνω, *miaínō*, μίασμα, *miasma*, μιασμός, *miasmós*, "stain," "tinge," "dye": "In their dreamings d. the flesh," Jude ver 8; μολύνω, *molúnō*, "stain," "contaminate": "not d. their garments" [Rev **3** 4]; σπιλόω, *spilóō*, "spot," "stain": "d. the whole body" [Jas **3** 6]; φθείρω, *phtheírō*, "corrupt," "destroy": the temple of God [1 Cor **3** 17 AV, ARV "destroyeth"]; ἀρσενοκοίτης, *arsenokoítēs*: "d. themselves with men" [1 Tim **1** 10 AV, ARV "abusers of"]):

Defilement in the OT was physical, sexual, ethical, ceremonial, religious, the last four, esp., overlapping.

1. Defilement in the OT

(1) **Physical:** "I have washed my feet; how shall I d. them?" (Cant **5** 3). (2) **Sexual:** which might be ceremonial or moral; of individuals by illicit intercourse (Lev **18** 20), or by intercourse at forbidden times (**15** 24; 1 S **21** 5); of the land by adultery: "Shall not that land be greatly defiled?" (Jer **3** 1 ARV "polluted," usually substituted where the moral or religious predominates over the ceremonial). (3) **Ethical:** "Your hands are defiled with blood" (Isa **59** 3); "Neither shall they d. themselves any more with .... any of their transgressions" (Ezk **37** 23). (4) **Ceremonial:** to render ceremonially unclean, i.e. disqualified for religious service or worship, and capable of communicating the disqualification. (*a*) Persons were defiled by contact with carcases of unclean animals (Lev **11** 24); or with any carcase (**17** 15); by eating a carcase (**22** 8); by contact with issues from the body, one's own or another's, e.g. abnormal issues from the genitals, male or female (**15** 2.25); menstruation (Lev **15** 19); by contact with anyone thus unclean (**15** 24); copulation (**15** 16–18); uncleanness after childbirth (**12** 2–5); by contact with unclean persons (**5** 3), or unclean things (**22** 6), or with leprosy (esp. defiling; **13** 14), or with the dead (Nu **6** 12), or with one unclean by such contact (**19** 22), or by funeral rites (Lev **21** 1); by contact with creeping things (**22** 5), or with unclean animals (**11** 26). (*b*) Holy objects were ceremonially defiled by the contact, entrance or approach of the defiled (**15** 31; Nu **19** 13); by the presence of dead bodies, or any remains of the dead (Ezk **9** 7; 2 K **23** 16: Josiah's defilement of heathen altars by the ashes of the priests); by the entrance of foreigners (Ps **79** 1; see Acts **21** 28); by forbidden treatment, as the altar by being tooled (Ex **20** 25); objects in general by contact with the unclean. Ceremonial defilement, strictly considered, implied, not sin, but ritual unfitness. (5) **Religious:** not always easily distinguished or entirely distinguishable from the ceremonial, still less from the ethical, but in which the central attitude and relationship to Jeh as covenant God and God of righteousness, was more fully in question. The land might be defiled by bloodshed (Nu **35** 33), esp. of the just or innocent; by adultery (Jer **3** 1); by idolatry and idolatrous practices, like sacrificing children to idols, etc (Lev **20** 3; Ps **106** 39); the temple or altar by disrespect (Mal **1** 7.12); by offering the unclean (Hag **2** 14); by any sort of unrighteousness (Ezk **36** 17); by the presence of idols or idolatrous paraphernalia (Jer **7** 30).

The scope of defilement in its various degrees (direct, or primary, as from the person or thing defiled; indirect, or secondary, tertiary, or even further, by contact with the defiled) had been greatly widened by rabbinism into a complex and immensely burdensome system whose shadow falls over the whole NT life. Specific mentions are comparatively few. Physical d. is not mentioned.

2. Defilement in NT

Sexual d. appears, in a **figurative** sense: "These are they that were not defiled with women" (Rev **14** 4). Ceremonial d. is found in, but not approved by, the NT. Examples are: by eating with unwashed, "common," not ceremonially cleansed, hands (Mk **7** 2); by eating unclean, "common," food (Acts **10** 14; Peter's vision); by intimate association with Gentiles, such as eating with them (not expressly forbidden in Mosaic law; Acts **11** 3), or entering into their houses (Jn **18** 28; the Pharisees refusing to enter the Praetorium); by the presence of Gentiles in the Temple (Acts **21**

28). But with Christ's decisive and revolutionary dictum (Mk **7** 19): "This he said, making all meats clean," etc, and with the command in Peter's vision: "What God hath cleansed, make not thou common" (Acts **10** 15), and with Paul's bold and consistent teaching: "All things indeed are clean" (Rom **14** 20, etc), the idea of ceremonial or ritual d., having accomplished its educative purpose, passed. Defilement in the NT teaching, therefore, is uniformly ethical or spiritual, the two constantly merging. The ethical is found more predominantly in: "The things which proceed out of the mouth come forth out of the heart; and they defile the man" (Mt **15** 18); "that did not defile their garments" (Rev **3** 4); "defileth the whole body" (Jas **3** 6). The spiritual seems to predominate in: "defiled and unbelieving" (Tit **1** 15); "conscience being weak is defiled" (by concession to idolatry) (1 Cor **8** 7); "lest any root of bitterness springing up trouble you, and thereby the many be defiled" (He **12** 15). For the supposed origins of the idea and details of defilement, as from hygienic or aesthetic causes, "natural aversions," "taboo," "totemism," associations with ideas of death, or evil life, religious symbolism, etc, see POLLUTION; PURIFICATION; UNCLEAN. Whatever use God may have made of ideas and feelings common among many nations in some form, the Divine purpose was clearly to impress deeply and indelibly on the Israelites the ideas of holiness and sacredness in general, and of Jeh's holiness, and their own required holiness and separateness in particular, thus preparing for the deep NT teachings of sin, and of spiritual consecration and sanctification.

PHILIP WENDELL CRANNELL

DEFY, dē-fī′ (חָרַף, *ḥāraph*, זָעַם, *zā'am*): In 1 S **17** 10.25.26.36.45 (the story of David and Goliath) and kindred passages, this word is used in its most familiar sense—"to taunt," "challenge to combat" (Heb *ḥāraph*). In Nu **23** 7.8 "denounce" would be a better tr than "defy" (Heb *zā'am*).

DEGENERATE, dē-jen′ẽr-āt: Only in Jer **2** 21, where Judah is compared to a "noble vine" which it "turned into the degenerate branches of a foreign vine." It represents Heb *ṣūrīm* = "stray" or "degenerate (shoots)," from *ṣūr* = "to turn aside," esp. to turn aside from the right path (Gr *pikria*, lit. "bitterness").

DEGREE, dē-grē′ (מַעֲלָה, *ma'ălāh*, "a going up" or "ascent," hence a staircase or flight of steps; "rank": **ταπεινός**, *tapeinós*, "low"): By derivation it should mean "a step down" (Lat, *de*, down, *gradus*, step). It is used, however, of any step, up or down; then of grade or rank, whether high or low. (1) In its literal sense of step (as of a stair), it is used in the pl. to translate Heb *ma'ălōth* ("steps"), in the ‖ passages 2 K **20** 9–11 AV (5 t); Isa **38** 8 AV (3 t), where we read of the "degrees" (RV "steps") on the "dial of Ahaz" (Heb "steps of Ahaz"). See DIAL OF AHAZ. It seems to mean steps or progressive movements of the body toward a certain place in the phrase "A Song of Degrees" (RV "Ascents"), which forms the title of each of the Pss **120–34**, probably because they were sung on the way up to the great feasts at Jerus. See PSALMS. (2) The secondary (but now the more usual) sense of rank, order, grade is found in the following passages: (*a*) 1 Ch **15** 18, "their brethren of the second (degree)," lit. "of the seconds" (Heb *mishnīm;* cf 2 Ch **28** 7, "Elkanah that was next to the king," Heb, "the king's second," i.e. in rank); (*b*) 1 Ch **17** 17, "a man of high degree" (Heb *ma'ălāh*, "step"); (*c*) Ps **62** 9, "men of low degree . . . . men of high degree," a paraphrase of Heb "sons of man . . . . sons of man," the first "man" being Heb *'ādhām* ("common humanity"; cf Gr *ánthrōpos*, Lat *homo*, Welsh *dyn*), and the second Heb *'īsh* (man in a superior sense; cf Gr *anḗr*, Lat *vir*, Welsh *gwr*); (*d*) "of low degree" for Gr *tapeinos* in Sir **11** 1; Lk **1** 52; Jas **1** 9; (*e*) In 1 Tim **3** 13 AV "a good degree" (Gr *bathmós kalós*, RV "a good standing") is assured to those who have "served well as deacons." Some take this to mean promotion to a higher official position in the church; but it probably means simply a position of moral weight and influence in the church gained by faithfulness in service (so Hort).

D. MIALL EDWARDS

DEGREES, SONGS OF (שִׁיר הַמַּעֲלוֹת, *shīr ha-ma'ălōth;* LXX **ᾠδὴ τῶν ἀναβαθμῶν**, *ōdḗ tōn anabathmṓn;* Vulg *canticum graduum*, RV "a song of ascents"): The title prefixed to 15 psalms (Pss **120–34**) as to the significance of which there are four views: (1) The Jewish interpretation. According to the Mish, *Middōth* **2** 5, *Ṣukkāh* 51*b*, there was in the temple a semicircular flight of stairs with 15 steps which led from the court of the men of Israel down to the court of the women. Upon these stairs the Levites played on musical instruments on the evening of the first day of Tabernacles. Later Jewish writers say that the 15 psalms derived their title from the 15 steps. (2) Gesenius, Delitzsch and others affirm that these psalms derive their name from the step-like progressive rhythm of their thoughts. They are called Songs of Degrees because they move forward climactically by means of the resumption of the immediately preceding word. But this characteristic is not found in several of the group. (3) Theodoret and other Fathers explain these 15 hymns as traveling songs of the returning exiles. In Ezr **7** 9 the return from exile is called "the going up [*ha-ma'ălāh*] from Babylon." Several of the group suit this situation quite well, but others presuppose the temple and its stated services. (4) The most probable view is that the hymns were sung by pilgrim bands on their way to the three great festivals of the Jewish year. The journey to Jerus was called a "going up," whether the worshipper came from north or south, east or west. All of the songs are suitable for use on such occasions. Hence the title Pilgrim Psalms is preferred by many scholars. See DIAL OF AHAZ.

JOHN RICHARD SAMPEY

DEHAITES, dē-hā′tēz (דֶּהָוֵא, *dehāwē';* AV **Dehavites**): A people enumerated in Ezr **4** 9 with Elamites, etc, as among those settled by the Assyr king Osnappar (Assurbanipal) in Samaria. The identification is uncertain.

DEHORT, dē-hôrt′ (ἀποστρέφω, *apostréphō;* RV DISSUADE): Not found in the Eng. Bible; once only in Apoc (1 Macc **9** 9). An obsolete Eng. word; the opposite of "exhort." It means "to dissuade," "to forbid," "to restrain from."

DEKAR, dē′kär (דֶּקֶר, *deḳer*, "lancer"): Father of one of Solomon's commissaries (1 K **4** 9 AV). See BEN-DEKER.

DELAIAH, dē-lā′ya (דְּלָיָה, *dlāyāh*, "God has raised"):

(1) A descendant of David (1 Ch **3** 24; AV "Dalaiah").

(2) One of David's priests and leader of the 23d course (1 Ch **24** 18).

(3) One of the princes who pleaded with Jehoiakim not to destroy the roll containing the prophecies of Jeremiah (Jer **36** 12.25).

(4) The ancestor of a post-exilic family whose genealogy was lost (Ezr **2** 60; Neh **7** 62; 1 Esd **5** 37 m). See DALAN.

(5) The father of timorous Shemaiah (Neh **6** 10)

DELAY, dē-lā′: The noun "delay" (Acts **25** 17, "I made no delay"; AV "without any delay") means "procrastination." The vb. "to delay" (Ex **22** 29; אָחַר, *'āḥar*) involves the idea "to stop for a time," the people being admonished not to discontinue a custom. The Pil. pf. of בּוֹשׁ, *bōsh* (Ex **32** 1), "Moses delayed to come," expresses not only the fact that he tarried, but also the disappointment on the part of the people, being under the impression that he possibly was put to shame and had failed in his mission, which also better explains the consequent action of the people. "To delay" (χρονίζω, *chronízō*) is used transitively in Mt **24** 48 (RV "My lord tarrieth") and in Lk **12** 45. The meaning here is "to prolong," "to defer."

A. L. BRESLICH

DELECTABLE, dē-lek′ta-b'l (חָמַד, *ḥāmadh*, "to desire"): Found only in Isa **44** 9 AV: "Their delectable things shall not profit," AVm "desirable." ARV translates: "the things that they delight in." The reference is to idols or images. Delitzsch renders the phrase: "Their *darlings* are good for nothing." The word may be traced back to the Lat *delectabilis*, "pleasant," or "delightful."

DELICACY, del′i-ka-si (τὸ στρῆνος, *tó strēnos*): Found only in Rev **18** 3 AV: "The merchants of the earth are waxed rich through the abundance of her delicacies." RV has very properly changed delicacies to "wantonness," and "luxury" in the margin, which is much nearer to the original.

DELICATE, del′i-kāt, **DELICATELY,** del′i-kāt-li (עֵדֶן, *'ēdhen*, עָנֹג, *'ānōgh*; ἐν τρυφῇ, *en truphḗ*): "Delicate" usually an adj., but once a subst. (Jer **51** 34 AV), "He hath filled his belly [RV "maw"] with my **delicates**." RV retains the word, but ARV very properly has replaced it with "delicacies." In Sir **30** 18, RV *agathá*, "good things." The adj. seems to have two meanings, though not easily distinguished: (1) tenderly reared, and (2) wanton or voluptuous. In Dt **28** 54.56; Isa **47** 1; Jer **6** 2, "luxurious" or "daintily bred" would certainly be nearer the original than "delicate." "Delicate children" of Mic **1** 16 AV is changed by RV to "children of thy delight," i.e. beloved children, rather than children begotten in passion. The advb. "delicately" is employed in the same sense as the adj. (Lam **4** 5; Lk **7** 25). In the old Eng. writers "delicate" is often used for voluptuous: "Dives for his delicate life to the devil went" (Piers Plowman). The meaning of "delicately" (*ma'ădhān*) in 1 Sam **15** 32 (AV) is a real puzzle. The AV reads, "And Agag came unto him delicately," with a possible suggestion of weakness or fear. ARV and RVm substitute "cheerfully." Others, by metathesis or change of consonants in the Heb word, tr "in bonds" or "fetters."

W. W. DAVIES

DELICIOUSLY, dē-lish′us-li (στρηνιάω, *strēniáō*, "to live hard or wantonly"): "She [Babylon] . . . . lived deliciously" (Rev **18** 7.9 AV, RV "wantonly," RVm "luxuriously").

DELIGHT, dē-līt′ (vb., חָפֵץ, *ḥāphēç*, רָצָה, *rāçāh*, שָׁעַע, *shā'a'*; συνήδομαι, *sunēdomai*): "To delight" is most frequently expressed by *ḥāphēç*, which means originally "to bend" (cf Job **40** 17, "He moveth his tail"), hence, "to incline to," "take pleasure in." It is used of God's pleasure in His people (Nu **14** 8; 2 S **22** 20; Ps **18** 19, etc), and in righteousness, etc (Isa **66** 4; Jer **9** 24; Mic **7** 18, etc), also of man's delight in God and His will (Ps **40** 8; **73** 25; AV and RV, "There is none upon earth that I *desire* besides thee"), and in other objects (Gen **34** 19; 1 S **18** 22; Est **2** 14; Isa **66** 3); *shā'a'*, "to stroke," "caress," "be fond of," occurs in Ps **94** 19, "Thy comforts delight my soul"; **119** 16.47.70, "I will delight myself in thy statutes." Similarly, St. Paul says (Rom **7** 22), "I delight [*sunēdomai*] in [m, RV "Gr with"] the law of God after the inward man." This is the only occurrence of the word in the NT.

"To delight one's self" (in the Lord) is represented chiefly by *'ānagh* (Job **22** 26; **27** 10; Ps **37** 4.11; Isa **58** 14).

Delight (noun), chiefly *ḥēpheç* (1 S **15** 22; Ps **1** 2; **16** 3), *rāçōn* (Prov **11** 1.20; **12** 22; **15** 8), *sha'ăshū'īm* (Ps **119** 24.77.92.143.174; Prov **8** 30. 31). RV has "delight" for "desire" (Neh **1** 11; Ps **22** 8; **51** 16), for "observe," different reading (Prov **23** 26), "no delight in" for "smell in" (Am **5** 21), "delightest in me" for "favorest me" (Ps **41** 11), "his delight shall be in" (m "Heb 'scent' ") for "of quick understanding" (Isa **11** 3).

The element of joy, of delight in God and His law and will, in the Heb religion is noteworthy as being something which we are apt to fall beneath even in the clearer light of Christianity.

W. L. WALKER

DELIGHTSOME, dē-līt′sum: חֵפֶץ, *ḥēpheç*, is rendered "delightsome": Mal **3** 12, "Ye shall be a delightsome land," lit. "a land of delight."

DELILAH, dē-lī′la (דְּלִילָה, *d^elīlāh*, "dainty one," perhaps; LXX Δαλειδά, *Daleidá*, Δαλιδά, *Dalidá*): The woman who betrayed Samson to the Philis (Jgs **16**). She was presumably a Phili, though that is not expressly stated. She is not spoken of as Samson's wife, though many have understood the account in that way. The Philis paid her a tremendously high price for her services. The account indicates that for beauty, personal charm, mental ability, self-command, nerve, she was quite a wonderful woman, a woman to be admired for some qualities which she exhibits, even while she is to be utterly disapproved. See SAMSON.

WILLIS J. BEECHER

DELIVER, dē-liv′ẽr (נָצַל, *nāçal*, נָתַן, *nāthan*; ῥύομαι, *rhúomai*, παραδίδωμι, *paradidōmi*): Occurs very frequently in the OT and represents various Heb terms. The Eng. word is used in two senses, (1) "to set free," etc, (2) "to give up or over."

(1) The word most often tr^d "deliver" in the first sense is *nāçal*, meaning originally, perhaps, "to draw out." It is used of all kinds of deliverance (Gen **32** 11; Ps **25** 20; **143** 9, etc; Jer **7** 10; Ezk **3** 19, etc; Zeph **1** 18, etc). The Aram. *n^eçal* occurs in Dnl **3** 29; **6** 14; **8** 4.7; *yāsha'*, "to save," in Jgs **3** 9.31 AV, etc; *mālaṭ*, "to let or cause to escape," in Isa **46** 2, "recover," etc. In the NT *rhuomai*, "to rescue," is most frequently tr^d "deliver" in this sense (Mt **6** 13 AV, "Deliver us from evil"); *katargéō*, "to make useless" or "without effect" (Rom **7** 6 RV, "discharged"). In the NT "save" takes largely the place of "deliver" in the OT, and the idea is raised to the spiritual and eternal.

(2) For "deliver" in the sense of "give over, up," etc, the most frequent word is *nāthan*, the common word for "to give" (Gen **32** 16; **40** 13 AV; Ex **5** 18). Other words are *māghan* (Hos **11** 8, AV and ERV "How shall I deliver thee Israel?" i.e. "How shall I give thee up?" as in the first clause of the verse, with a different word [*nāthan*], ARV "How shall I cast thee off?"), *y^ehabh*, Aram. (Ezr. **5** 14). In the NT *paradidōmi*, "to give over to," is most frequent (Mt **5** 25; **11** 27, "All things have been delivered [given or made over] unto me of my Father"; Mk **7** 13; Lk **1** 2; 1 Tim **1** 20, etc); *charízomai*, "to grant as a favor" (Acts **25** 11. 16 AV).

(3) *Yāladh*, "to bring forth," is also rendered "deliver" in the sense of childbirth (Gen **25** 24; Ex **1** 19, etc). In the NT this sense is borne by τίκτω, *tíktō* (Lk **1** 57; **2** 6; Rev **12** 2.4), and γεννάω, *gennáō* (Jn **16** 21).

In RV there are many changes, such as, for "deliver," "restore" (Gen **37** 22; **40** 13; Ex **22** 26; Dt **24** 13); for "delivered," "defended" (1 Ch **11** 14); for "cannot deliver thee," "neither . . . turn thee aside" (Job **36** 18); for "betray," "betrayed" we have "deliver," "delivered up," etc (Mt **10** 4 m; Mk **13** 12; **14** 10f; Lk **21** 16); for "delivered into chains," "committed to pits" (2 Pet **2** 4, m "some ancient authorities read *chains*"; cf Wisd **17** 17); "Deliver us from evil," omitted in Lk **11** 4, m "Many ancient authorities add *but deliver us from the evil* one (or, *from evil*)."

W. L. Walker

DELOS, dē'los (Δῆλος, *Dēlos*): An island, now deserted, one of the Cyclades in the Aegaean Sea, about 3 miles long and 1 mile broad, with a rocky mountain (Cynthus) several hundred feet high in the center. In antiquity Delos enjoyed great prosperity. According to Gr legend the island once floated on the surface of the water, until Poseidon fastened it on four diamond pillars for the wandering Leto, who, like Io, was pursued by the vengeful Hera. It was here that Apollo and Artemis were born; hence the island was sacred, and became one of the chief seats of worship of the two deities. Numerous temples embellished Delos. The most magnificent was that of Apollo, which contained a colossal statue of the god, a dedicatory offering of the Naxians. This temple was a sanctuary visited by all the Greeks, who came from far and near to worship at the deity's shrine. There was a Dorian peripteral temple in Delos from the beginning of the 4th cent. BC. To the N. was a remarkable altar composed entirely of ox-horns. The various Ionian cities sent sacred embassies (*theōríai*) with rich offerings. There was also a celebrated oracle in Delos which was accounted one of the most trustworthy in the world. Every five years the famous Delian festival was celebrated with prophecies, athletic contests and games of every kind. All the nations of Greece participated.

The earliest inhabitants of Delos were Carians; but about 1000 BC the island was occupied by Ionians. For a long time it enjoyed independence. In 478 Delos was chosen as the place for the convention of the representatives of the Gr states for deliberation about means for defence against Persia. The treasury of the Athenian Confederacy was kept here after 476. The island became independent of Athens in 454. During the 2d and 1st cents. BC it became one of the chief ports of the Aegaean. This was partly due to its location, and partly to the fact that the Romans, after 190 BC, favored the island as a rival to the sea-power of Rhodes. In 166 Delos was given to Athens; the inhabitants fled to Achaea, and the island was colonized by Athenians, together with Romans.

The ruins of the city of Delos, which became a flourishing commercial port, are to the N. of the temple. It became the center of trade between Alexandria and the Black Sea, and was for a long time one of the chief slave markets of the Gr world. But Delos received a severe blow, from which it never recovered, in the war between Rome and Mithridates. The latter's general landed in 88 BC and massacred many, and sold the remainder of the defenceless people, and sacked and destroyed the city together with the temple and its countless treasures. At the conclusion of peace (84) Delos came into the possession of the Romans, who later gave it back to Athens. Under the Empire the island lost its importance entirely.

Delos was one of the states to which Rome addressed letters in behalf of the Jews (138–137 BC; see 1 Macc **15** 16–23). Among those who came to Delos from the East must have been many of this nation. Jos cites in full a decree passed in Delos which confirmed the Jewish exemption from military service (*Ant*, XIV, x, 4).

The excavations of the French have laid bare 8 temples within the sacred inclosure (Apollo, Artemis, Dionysus). Numerous statues, dating from the earliest times of Gr art down to the latest, have been discovered; also 2,000 inscriptions, among which was an inventory of the temple treasure.

By the side of Delos, across a very narrow strait, lies Rheneia, another island which was the burying-ground of Delos; for on the sacred isle neither births, deaths nor burials were permitted. In 426 BC Delos was "purified" by the Athenians—by the removal of the bodies that had been interred there previously.

Literature.—Lebègue, *Recherches sur Délos* (Paris, 1876); V. v. Schöffer, *De Deli Insulae rebus*, *Berliner Studien für klass. Phil.* (Berlin, 1889); Homolle, S. Reinach and others, in the *Bulletin de corresp. Hellén.* (VI, 1–167; VII, 103–25, 329–73; VIII, 75–158; XIV, 389–511; XV, 113–68); Homolle, *Archives de l'intendance sacrée à Délos*; Jebb, *Journal of Hellenic Studies* (1880), 7–62.

J. E. Harry

DELUGE, del'ūj, **OF NOAH, THE:**

1. The Biblical Account
2. "Noah's Log Book"
3. The Egyptian Tradition
4. The Indian "
5. The Chinese "
6. The Greek "
7. The British "
8. The American Indian Traditions
9. The Babylonian Tradition
10. Cuneiform Tablets
11. Was the Flood Universal?

1. The Biblical Account

The means described in Gen **6–8** by which the Lord destroyed, on account of their wickedness, all the members of the human race except Noah and his family. According to the account, Noah was warned of the event 120 years before (Gen **6** 3; 1 Pet **3** 20; 2 Pet **2** 5). During all this time he is said to have been a "preacher of righteousness" "while the ark was a preparing," when we may well suppose (according to the theory to be presently propounded) the physical events leading up to the final catastrophe may have given point to his preaching. When the catastrophe came, the physical means employed were twofold, namely, the breaking up of the "fountains of the great deep" and the opening of "the windows of heaven" (Gen **7** 11). But the rain is spoken of as continuing as a main cause only 40 days, while the waters continued to prevail for 150 days (ver 24), when (**8** 2.3) "the fountains also of the deep and the windows of heaven were stopped, and the rain from heaven was restrained; and the waters returned from off the earth continually," so that after 10 months the ark rested upon "the mountains of Ararat" (not the peak of Mount Ararat, but the highlands of Armenia in the upper part of the valley of the Euphrates and Tigris; see Ararat). Here it rested 40 days before the water subsided sufficiently to suggest disembarking, when a raven (which could easily find its food on the carcases of the animals which had been destroyed) was sent forth, and did not return (ver 7); but a dove sent out at the same time found no rest and returned empty to the ark (ver 9). After 7 days, however, it was sent out again and returned with a fresh olive leaf (ver 11). After 7 days more the dove was sent forth again and did not return. After 56 days more of waiting Noah and his family departed from the ark. The following are the leading points in the story which has been appropriately styled by Sir William Dawson "Noah's log book" (see S. E. Bishop's art. in *Bib. Sac.* [1906], 510–17, and Rev. Joseph B. Davidson in the author's *Scientific Confirmations of OT History*, 180–84).

2. "Noah's Log Book"

"Noah's Log Book"

Month	Day		Number of Days
2	17	All enter the ark; God shuts the door. Rains fall. Floods pour in from sea. Ark floats. Ark sails swiftly.	40
3	27	Rain stops. Floods keep pouring in and water rising	110
7	17	Ark touches bottom on top of high mountains and stays there. Waters stop rising. Water stationary......	40
8	27	Waters begin to settle. Settle fifteen cubits in..........................	34
10	1	Ark left on dry land. Waters continue to settle. Noah waits.............	40
11	11	Noah sends out a raven. It returns not. Waters settle. Noah waits....	7
11	18	Noah sends out a dove. It returns. Waters settle. Noah waits........	7
11	25	Noah sends out dove again. Dove brings an olive leaf just grown. Waters settle. Noah waits	7
12	2	Noah sends out dove again. It returns not. Waters settle. Noah waits...	29
1	1	Noah removes covering, looks all around. No water can be seen. Ground dries up. Noah waits....................	56
2	27	God opens the door, and says, "Go forth." Total time of flood........	370

It will thus be seen that there is no need of supposing any duplication and overlapping of accounts in the Bib. story. There is continual progress in the account from beginning to end, with only such repetitions for literary effect as we are familiar with in oriental writings. In Gen **6** 5—**7** 13 the wickedness of the world is assigned as the reason which prevailed in the Divine counsels for bringing about the contemplated catastrophe. While emphasizing the righteousness of Noah which led to his preservation, **6** 13–21 contains the direction for the making of the ark and of the preparations to bring into it a certain number of animals. This preparation having been made, the order was given (**7** 1–4) for the embarkation which (ver 5) was duly accomplished. We are then told that Noah and his family, and beasts both clean and unclean, were shut up in the ark during the prevalence of the water and its final subsidence. Altogether the account is most graphic and impressive (see W. H. Green, *Unity of the Book of Genesis*, 83 ff).

Compared with other traditions of the Deluge, the Bib. account appears in a most favorable light, while the general prevalence of such traditions strongly confirms the reality of the Bib. story.

3. The Egyptian Tradition

An Egyp legend of the Deluge is referred to in Plato's *Timaeus*, where the gods are said to have purified the earth by a great flood of water from which only a few shepherds escaped by climbing to the summit of a high mountain. In the Egyp documents themselves, however, we find only that Ra' the creator, on account of the insolence of man, proceeded to exterminate him by a deluge of blood which flowed up to Heliopolis, the home of the gods; but the heinousness of the deed so affected him that he repented and swore never more to destroy mankind.

4. The Indian Tradition

In Indian mythology there is no reference to the Flood in the *Rig Veda*, but in the laws of Manu we are told that a fish said to Manu, "A deluge will sweep all creatures away. . . . . Build a vessel and worship me. When the waters rise enter the vessel and I will save thee. . . . . When the Deluge came, he had entered the vessel. . . . . Manu fastened the cable of the ship to the horn of the fish, by which means the latter made it pass over the mountains of the North. The fish said: 'I have saved thee; fasten the vessel to a tree that the water may not sweep it away while thou art in the mountain; and in proportion as the waters decrease, thou shalt descend.' Manu descended with the waters, and this is what is called the Descent of Manu on the mountains of the North. The Deluge had carried away all creatures, and Manu remained alone" (tr[d] by Max Müller).

5. The Chinese Tradition

The Chinese tradition is embodied in sublime language in their book of *Li-Ki*: "And now the pillars of heaven were broken, the earth shook to its very foundation; the sun and the stars changed their motions; the earth fell to pieces, and the waters enclosed within its bosom burst forth with violence, and overflowed. Man having rebelled against heaven, the system of the universe was totally disordered, and the grand harmony of nature destroyed. All these evils arose from man's despising the supreme power of the universe. He fixed his looks upon terrestrial objects and loved them to excess, until gradually he became transformed into the objects which he loved, and celestial reason entirely abandoned him."

6. The Greek Tradition

The Greeks, according to Plutarch, had five different traditions of the Deluge, that of Deucalion being the most important. According to this, Prometheus warned his son Deucalion of the flood which Zeus had resolved to bring upon the earth by reason of its wickedness. Accordingly Deucalion constructed an ark and took refuge in it, but with his vessel was stranded on Mount Parnassus in Thessaly, whereupon they disembarked and repeopled the earth by the fantastic process revealed to them by the goddess Themis of throwing stones about them, those which Deucalion threw becoming men and those which Pyrrha threw becoming women. Lucian's form of the legend, however, is less fantastic and more nearly in line with Sem tradition. In the Gr legend as in the Sem, a dove is sent forth which returns both a first and a second time, its feet being tinged with mud the second time, intimating the abatement of the flood. But neither Homer nor Hesiod have this tradition. Probably it was borrowed from the Semites or the Hindus.

7. The British Tradition

In Britain there is a Druid legend that on account of the profligacy of mankind, the Supreme Being sent a flood upon the earth when "the waves of the sea lifted themselves on high round the border of Britain. The rain poured down from heaven and the waters covered the earth." But the patriarch, distinguished for his integrity, had been shut up with a select company in a strong ship which bore them safely upon the summit of the waters (Ed. Davies in his *Mythology and Rites of British Druids*). From these the world was again repeopled. There are various forms of this legend but they all agree in substance.

8. American Indian Traditions

Among the American Indians traditions of the Deluge were found by travelers to be widely disseminated. Mr. Catlin says, "Among the 120 different tribes which I visited in North, South, and Central America, not a tribe exists that has not related to me distinct or vague traditions of such a calamity, in which one, or three, or eight persons were saved above the waters upon the top of a high mountain" (quoted by Wm. Restelle in *Bib. Sac.* [January, 1907], 157). While many, perhaps most, of these traditions bear the stamp of

Christian influence through the early missionaries, the Mexican legend bears evident marks of originality. According to it the 4th age was one of water, when all men were turned into fishes except Tezpi and his wife Hochiquetzal and their children, who with many animals took refuge in a ship which sailed safely over the tumultuous waters which overwhelmed the earth. When the flood subsided the ship stranded on Mount Cohuacan, whereupon he sent forth a vulture which did not return, and then a humming bird which returned with some leaves in its beak. The Peruvian story differs from this in many particulars. According to it a single man and woman took refuge in a box and floated hundreds of miles from Cuzco to an unknown land where they made clay images of all races, and animated them.

The Moravian missionary Cranz, in his *History of Greenland*, says that "the first missionaries among the Greenlanders found a tolerably distinct tradition of the Deluge" to the effect that "the earth was once tilted over and all men were drowned" except one "who smote afterward upon the ground with a stick and thence came out a woman with whom he peopled the earth again." Moreover, the Greenlanders point to the remains of fishes and bones of a whale on high mountains where men never could have dwelt, as proof that the earth was once flooded. Among the North American Indians generally legends of the Deluge are so embellished that they become extremely fantastic, but in many of them there are peculiarities which point unquestionably to a common origin of extreme antiquity.

The unprejudiced reader cannot rise from the study of the subject without agreeing in general with François Lenormant, who writes: "As the case now stands, we do not hesitate to declare that, far from being a myth, the Bib. Deluge is a real and historical fact, having, to say the least, left its impress on the ancestors of three races—Aryan, or Indo-European, Sem, or Syrio-Arabian, Chamitic, or Kushite—that is to say on the three great civilized races of the ancient world, those which constitute the higher humanity—before the ancestors of these races had as yet separated, and in the part of Asia together inhabited" (*Contemporary Review*, November, 1879).

9. The Babylonian Tradition

The most instructive of these traditions are those which have come down to us from Babylonia, which until recently were known to us only through the Gr historian Berosus of the 4th cent. BC, who narrates that a great deluge happened at some indefinite time in the past during the reign of Xisuthrus, son of Ardates. Xisuthrus was warned beforehand by the deity Cronos, and told to build a ship and take with him his friends and relations and all the different animals with all necessary food and trust himself fearlessly to the deep, whereupon he built "a vessel 5 stadia [3,000 ft.] long and 2 stadia [1,200 ft.] broad." After the flood subsided Xisuthrus, like Noah, sent out birds which returned to him again. After waiting some days and sending them out a second time, they returned with their feet tinged with mud. Upon the third trial they returned no more, whereupon they disembarked and Xisuthrus with his wife, daughter and pilot offered sacrifice to the gods and were translated to live with the gods. It was found that the place where they were was "the land of Armenia," but they were told to return to Babylon. Berosus concluded his account by saying that "the vessel being thus stranded in Armenia, some part of it yet remains in the Corcyraean mountains."

An earlier and far more important tradition was found inscribed on cuneiform tablets in Babylonia dating from 3000 BC. These were discovered by George Smith in 1870 and filled as many as 180 lines. The human hero of the account, corresponding to Noah of the Bible and Xisuthrus of Berosus, is Gilgamesh, who lived in Shurippak, a city full of violence, on the banks of the Euphrates.

10. Cuneiform Tablets

He was warned of an approaching flood and exhorted to pull down his house and build a ship and cause "seed of life of every sort to go up into it." The ship, he says, was to be "exact in its dimensions, equal in its breadth and its length. . . . . Its sides were 140 cubits high, the border of its top equaled 140 cubits. . . . . I constructed it in 6 stories, dividing it into 7 compartments. Its floors I divided into 9 chambers. . . . . I chose a mast (or rudder pole), and supplied what was necessary. Six sars of bitumen I poured over the outside; three sars of bitumen over the inside." After embarking, the storm broke with fearful violence and the steering of the ship was handed over to Bezur-Bel, the ship man. But amidst the roll of thunder and the march of mountain waves the helm was wrenched from the pilot's hands and the pouring rain and the lightning flashes dismayed all hearts. "Like a battle charge upon mankind" the water rushed so that the gods even were dismayed at the flood and cowered like dogs, taking refuge in the heaven of Anu while Ishtar screamed like a woman in travail, and repenting of her anger, resolved to save a few and "to give birth to my people" till like "the fry of fishes they fill the sea." The ship was therefore turned to the country of Nizir (Armenia).

It is worthy of notice that the cuneiform tablet exhibits as much variety of style as does the Bib. account. Plain narrative and rhetorical prose are intermingled in both accounts, a fact which effectually disposes of the critical theory which regards the Bib. account as a clumsy combination made in later times by piecing together two or more independent traditions. Evidently the piecing together, if there was any, had been accomplished early in Bab history. See BABYLONIA AND ASSYRIA.

On comparing the Bib. account with that of the cuneiform tablets, the following similarities and contrasts are brought to light:

(1) That the cuneiform inscription is from start to finish polytheistic (ll. 3–17), whereas the narrative in Gen is monotheistic.

(2) The cuneiform agrees with the Bib. narrative in making the Deluge a Divine punishment for the wickedness of the world (ll. 5, 6).

(3) The names differ to a degree that is irreconcilable with our present knowledge.

(4) The dimensions of the ark as given in Gen (**6** 15) are reasonable, while those of Berosus and the cuneiform tablets are unreasonable. According to Gen, the ark was 300 cubits (562½ ft.) long, 50 cubits (93¾ ft.) wide, and 30 cubits (56¼ ft.) deep, which are the natural proportions for a ship of that size, being in fact very close to those of the great steamers which are now constructed to cross the Atlantic. The "Celtic" of the White Star line, built in 1901, is 700 ft. long, 75 ft. wide and 49⅓ ft. deep. The dimensions of the "Great Eastern," built in 1858 (692 ft. long, 83 ft. broad, and 58 ft. deep), are still closer to those of the ark. The cuneiform tablets represent the length, width and depth each as 140 cubits (262 ft.) (ll. 22, 23, 38–41), the dimensions of an entirely unseaworthy structure. According to Berosus, it was 5 stadia (3,000 ft.) and 2 stadia (1,200 ft.) broad; while Origen (*Against Celsus*, 4.41), represented it to be 135,000 ft. (25 miles) long, and 3,750 ft. (¾ mile) wide.

(5) In the Bib. account, nothing is introduced conflicting with the sublime conception of holiness

and the peculiar combination of justice and mercy ascribed to God throughout the Bible, and illustrated in the general scheme of providential government manifest in the order of Nature and in history; while, in the cuneiform tablets, the Deluge is occasioned by a quarrel among the gods, and the few survivors escape, not by reason of a merciful plan, but by a mistake which aroused the anger of Bel (ll. 146–50).

(6) In all the accounts, the ark is represented as floating up stream. According to Gen, it was not, as is usually tr[d], on "Mount Ararat" (**8** 4), but in the "mountains of Ararat," designating an indefinite region in Armenia upon which the ark rested; according to the inscriptions, it was in Nizir (ll. 115–20), a region which is watered by the Zab and the Tornadus; while, according to Berosus, it was on the Corcyraean Mountains, included in the same indefinite area. In all three cases, its resting-place is in the direction of the headwaters of the Euphrates valley, while the scene of the building is clearly laid in the lower part of the valley.

(7) Again, in the Bib. narrative, the spread of the water floating the ark is represented to have been occasioned, not so much by the rain which fell, as by the breaking-up of "all the fountains of the great deep" (**7** 11), which very naturally describes phenomena connected with one of the extensive downward movements of the earth's crust with which geology has made us familiar. The sinking of the land below the level of the ocean is equivalent, in its effects, to the rising of the water above it, and is accurately expressed by the phrases used in the sacred narrative. This appears, not only in the language concerning the breaking-up of the great deep which describes the coming-on of the Flood, but also in the description of its termination, in which it is said, that the "fountains also of the deep . . . . were stopped, ... and the waters returned from off the earth continually" (**8** 2.3). Nothing is said of this in the other accounts.

(8) The cuneiform tablets agree in general with the two other accounts respecting the collecting of the animals for preservation, but differ from Gen in not mentioning the sevens of clean animals and in including others beside the family of the builder (ll. 66–69).

(9) The cuneiform inscription is peculiar in providing the structure with a mast, and putting it in charge of a pilot (ll. 45, 70, 71).

(10) The accounts differ decidedly in the duration of the Flood. According to the ordinary interpretation of the Bib. account, the Deluge continued a year and 17 days; whereas, according to the cuneiform tablets, it lasted only 14 days (ll. 103–7, 117–22).

(11) All accounts agree in sending out birds; but, according to Gen (**8** 8) a raven was first sent out, and then in succession two doves (**8** 8–12); while the cuneiform inscription mentions the dove and the raven in reverse order from Gen, and adds a swallow (ll. 121–30).

(12) All accounts agree in the building of an altar and offering a sacrifice after leaving the ark. But the cuneiform inscription is overlaid with a polytheistic coloring: "The gods like flies swarmed about the sacrifices" (ll. 132–43).

(13) According to the Bib. account, Noah survived the Flood for a long time; whereas Nûh-napishtim and his wife were at once deified and taken to heaven (ll. 177–80).

(14) Both accounts agree in saying that the human race is not again to be destroyed by a flood (Gen **9** 11; ll. 162–69).

Close inspection of these peculiarities makes it evident that the narrative in Gen carries upon its face an appearance of reality not found in the other accounts. It is scarcely possible that the reasonable dimensions of the ark, its floating up stream, and the references to the breaking-up of the fountains of the great deep should have been hit upon by accident. It is in the highest degree improbable that correct statements of such unobvious facts should be due to the accident of legendary guesswork. At the same time, the duration of the Deluge, according to Gen, affords opportunity for a gradual progress of events which best accords with scientific conceptions of geological movements. If, as the most probable interpretation would imply, the water began to recede after 150 days from the beginning of the Flood and fell 15 cubits in 74 days, that would only be $3\frac{2}{3}$ inches per day—a rate which would be imperceptible to an ordinary observer Nor is it necessary to suppose that the entire flooded area was uncovered when Noah disembarked. The emergence of the land may have continued for an indefinite period, permitting the prevailing water to modify the climate of all western and central Asia for many cents. Evidence that this was the case will be found in a later paragraph.

11. Was the Flood Universal?

In considering the credibility of the Bib. story we encounter at the outset the question whether the narrative compels us to believe the Flood to have been universal. In answer, it is sufficient to suggest that since the purpose of the judgment was the destruction of the human race, all the universality which it is necessary to infer from the language would be only such as was sufficient to accomplish that object. If man was at that time limited to the Euphrates valley, the submergence of that area would meet all the necessary conditions. Such a limitation is more easily accepted from the fact that general phrases like "Everybody knows," "The whole country was aroused," are never in literature literally interpreted. When it is said (Gen **41** 54–57) that the famine was "in all lands," and over "all the face of the earth," and that "all countries came into Egypt . . . . to buy grain," no one supposes that it is intended to imply that the irrigated plains of Babylonia, from which the patriarchs had emigrated, were suffering from drought like Pal. (For other examples of the familiar use of this hyperbole, see Dt **2** 25; Job **37** 3; Acts **2** 25; Rom **1** 8.)

As to the extent to which the human race was spread over the earth at the time of the Flood, two suppositions are possible. First, that of Hugh Miller (*Testimony of the Rocks*) that, owing to the shortness of the antediluvian chronology, and the violence and moral corruption of the people, population had not spread beyond the boundary of western Asia. An insuperable objection to this theory is that the later discoveries have brought to light remains of prehistoric man from all over the northern hemisphere, showing that long before the time of the Flood he had become widely scattered.

Another theory, supported by much evidence, is that, in connection with the enormous physical changes in the earth's surface during the closing scenes of the Glacial epoch, man had perished from off the face of the earth except in the valley of the Euphrates, and that the Noachian Deluge is the final catastrophe in that series of destructive events (see ANTEDILUVIANS). The facts concerning the Glacial epoch naturally lead up to this conclusion. For during the entire epoch, and esp. at its close, the conditions affecting the level of the land surfaces of the northern hemisphere were extremely abnormal, and continued so until some time after man had appeared on the earth.

The Glacial epoch followed upon, and probably was a consequence of, an extensive elevation of all the land surfaces of the northern hemisphere at the close of the Tertiary period. This elevation was certainly as much as 2,000 ft. over the northern part of the United States, and over Canada and Northern Europe. Snow accumulated over this high land until the ice formed by it was certainly a mile thick, and some of the best authorities say 2, or even 3 miles. The surface over which this was spread amounted to 2,000,000 sq. miles in Europe and 4,000,000 in North America. The total amount of the accumulation would therefore be 6,000,000 cubic miles at the lowest calculation, or twice or three times that amount if the largest estimates are accepted. (For detailed evidence see Wright, *Ice Age in North America*, 5th ed.) But in either case the transference of so much weight from the ocean beds to the land surfaces of the northern hemisphere brings into the problem a physical force sufficient to produce incalculable effects. The weight of 6,000,000 cubic miles of ice would be twenty-four thousand million million (24,000,000,000,000,000) tons, which is equal to that of the entire North American continent above sea level. Furthermore this weight was first removed from the ocean beds, thus disturbing still more the balance of forces which secure the stability of the land. The geological evidence is abundant that in connection with the overloading of the land surfaces in the Northern Hemisphere, and probably by reason of it, the glaciated area and a considerable margin outside of it sank down until it was depressed far below the present level. The post-Glacial depression in North America was certainly 600 ft. below sea level at Montreal, and several hundred feet lower farther north. In Sweden the post-Glacial sea beaches show a depression of the land 1,000 ft. below the sea.

The evidences of a long-continued post-Glacial subsidence of the Aral-Caspian basin and much of the surrounding area is equally conclusive. At Trebizond, on the Black Sea, there is an extensive recent sea beach clinging to the precipitous volcanic mountain back of the city 750 ft. above the present water level. The gravel in this beach is so fresh as to compel a belief in its recent origin, while it certainly has been deposited by a body of water standing at that elevation after the rock erosion of the region had been almost entirely effected. The deposit is about 100 ft. thick, and extends along the precipitous face of the mountain for a half-mile or more. So extensive is it that it furnishes an attractive building place for a monastery. When the water was high enough to build up this shore line, it would cover all the plains of southern Russia, of Western Siberia and of the Aral-Caspian depression in Turkestan. Similar terraces of corresponding height are reported by competent authorities on the south shore of the Crimea and at Baku, on the Caspian Sea.

Further and most interesting evidence of this post-Glacial land depression is found in the existence of Arctic seal 2,000 miles from the Arctic Ocean in bodies of water as widely separated as the Caspian Sea, the Aral Sea and Lake Baikal. Lake Baikal is now 1,500 ft. above sea level. It is evident, therefore, that there must have been a recent depression of the whole area to admit the migration of this species to that distant locality. There are also clear indications of a smaller depression around the eastern shores of the Mediterranean Sea, where there are abandoned sea beaches from 200 to 300 ft. above tide, which abound in species of shells identical with those now living nearby.

These are found in Egypt, in the valley of the Red Sea, and in the vicinity of Joppa and Beirût. During their formation Asia and Africa must have been separated by a wide stretch of water connecting the Mediterranean with the Red Sea. The effect of such lingering wide expanses of water upon the climate of Western Asia must have been profound, and would naturally provide those conditions which would favor the early development of the human race in Armenia (where even now at an elevation of 5,000 ft. the vine is indigenous), from which the second distribution of mankind is said to have taken place.

Furthermore there is indubitable evidence that the rainfall in central Asia was, at a comparatively recent time, immensely greater than it has been in the historic period, indicating that gradual passage from the conditions connected with the Deluge to those of the present time, at which we have hinted above. At the present time the evaporation over the Aral Sea is so great that two rivers (the ancient Oxus and the Jaxartes), coming down from the heights of central Asia, each with a volume as great as that of Niagara, do not suffice to cause an overflow into the Caspian Sea. But the existence of such an overflow during the prehistoric period is so plain that it has been proposed to utilize its channel (which is a mile wide and as distinctly marked as that of any living stream) for a canal.

Owing to the comparatively brief duration of the Noachian Deluge proper, we cannot expect to find many positive indications of its occurrence. Nevertheless, Professor Prestwich (than whom there has been no higher geological authority in England during the last cent.) adduces an array of facts relating to Western Europe and the Mediterranean basin which cannot be ignored (see *Phil. Trans. of the Royal Soc. of Lond.*, CXXIV [1893], 903–84; *SCOT*, 238–82). Among these evidences one of the most convincing is to be found in the cave of San Ciro at the base of the mountains surrounding the plain of Palermo in Sicily. In this cave there was found an immense mass of the bones of hippopotami of all ages down to the foetus, mingled with a few of the deer, ox and elephant. These were so fresh when discovered that they were cut into ornaments and polished and still retained a considerable amount of their nitrogenous matter. Twenty tons of these bones were shipped for commercial purposes in the first six months after their discovery. Evidently the animals furnishing these bones had taken refuge in this cave to escape the rising water which had driven them in from the surrounding plains and cooped them up in the amphitheater of mountains during a gradual depression of the land. Similar collections of bones are found in various ossiferous fissures, in England and Western Europe, notably in the Rock of Gibraltar and at Santenay, a few miles S. of Chalons in central France, where there is an accumulation of bones in fissures 1,000 ft. above the sea, similar in many respects to that in the cave described at San Ciro, though the bones of hippopotami did not appear in these places; but the bones of wolves. bears, horses and oxen, none of which had been gnawed by carnivora, were indiscriminately commingled as though swept in by all-pervading currents of water. Still further evidence is adduced in the deposits connected with what is called the rubble drift on both sides of the English Channel and on the Jersey Islands. Here in various localities, notably at Brighton, England, and near Calais, France, elephant bones and human implements occur beneath deep deposits of unassorted drift, which is not glacial nor the product of limited and local streams of water, but can be accounted for only by general waves of translation produced when the land was being reëlevated from beneath the water by a series of such sudden earthquake shocks as cause the tidal waves which are often so destructive.

Thus, while we cannot appeal to geology for direct proof of the Noachian Deluge, recent geological discoveries do show that such a catastrophe is perfectly credible from a scientific point of view; and the supposition that there was a universal destruction of the human race, in the northern hemisphere at least, in connection with the floods accompanying the melting off of the glacial ice is supported by a great amount of evidence. There was certainly an extensive destruction of animal species associated with man during that period. In Europe the great Irish elk, the *machairodus*, the cave lion, the rhinoceros, the hippopotamus and the elephant disappeared with prehistoric man, amid the floods at the close of the Glacial epoch. In North America equally large felines, together with horses, tapirs, llamas, great mastodons and elephants and the huge megalonyx went to destruction in connection with the same floods that destroyed so large a part of the human race during the dramatic closing scenes of the period. It is, therefore, by no means difficult for an all-round geologist to believe in a final catastrophe such as is described in Gen. If we disbelieve in the Bib. Deluge it is not because we know too much geology, but too little. GEORGE FREDERICK WRIGHT

DELUSION, dē-lū'zhun: (1) Isa **66** 4, "I also will choose their delusions" (RVm "mockings"), Heb *ta'ălūlīm,* which occurs only here and Isa **3** 4 (where it is tr[d] "babes," RVm "childishness"). Its meaning is somewhat ambiguous. The best tr seems to be "wantonness," "caprice." "Their wanton dealing, i.e. that inflicted on them" (*BDB*). Other tr[s] suggested are "insults" (Skinner), "freaks of fortune" (Cheyne), "follies" (Whitehouse). LXX has *empaígmata,* "mockings," Vulg *illusiones.* (2) 2 Thess **2** 11 AV, "God shall send them strong delusion" (RV "God sendeth them a working of error"), πλάνη, *plánē,* "a wandering," "a roaming about," in the NT "error," either of opinion or of conduct. D. MIALL EDWARDS

DEMAND, dē-mand': The peremptory, imperative sense is absent from this word in its occurrences in AV, where it means no more than "ask," "inquire" (cf Fr. *demander*) one or the other of which RV substitutes in 2 S **11** 7; Mt **2** 4; Lk **3** 14; **17** 20; Acts **21** 33. RV retains "demand" in Ex **5** 14; Job **38** 3; **40** 7; **42** 4; Dnl **2** 27; and inserts it (AV "require") in Neh **5** 18.

DEMAS, dē'mas (Δημᾶς, *Dēmás,* "popular"): According to Col **4** 14; 2 Tim **4** 10; Philem ver 24, one who was for a time a "fellow-worker" with Paul at Rome (Col, Philem), but at last, "having loved this present world," forsook the apostle and betook himself to Thessalonica (2 Tim). No other particulars are given concerning him. See APOSTASY; DEMETRIUS.

DEMETRIUS, dē-mē'tri-us (Δημήτριος, *Dēmḗtrios,* "of" or "belonging to Demeter," an ordinary name in Greece):

(1) **Demetrius I,** surnamed Σωτήρ, *Sōtḗr* ("saviour"), was the son of Seleucus IV (Philopator). He was sent as a boy to Rome, by his father, to serve as a hostage, and remained there quietly during his father's life. He was detained also during the reign of his uncle, ANTIOCHUS EPIPHANES (q.v.) from 175 to 164 BC; but when Antiochus died Demetrius, who was now a young man of 23 (Polyb. xxxi.12), chafed at a longer detention, particularly as his cousin, Antiochus Eupator, a boy of 9, succeeded to the kingdom with Lysias as his guardian. The Rom Senate, however, refused to listen to his plea for the restoration to Syria, because, as Polybius says, they felt surer of their power over Syria with a mere boy as king.

In the meantime, a quarrel had arisen between Ptolemy Philometor and Euergetes Physkon (Livy *Epit.* 46; Diod. Sic. fr xi), and Gnaeus Octavius, who had been sent to quell the disorder, was assassinated in Syria, while plundering the country. Demetrius, taking advantage of the troubled condition of affairs, consulted with his friend Polybius as to the advisability of attempting to seize the throne of Syria (op. cit. xxxi.19). The historian advised him not to stumble twice on the same stone, but to venture something worthy of a king, so after a second unsuccessful appeal to the Senate, Demetrius escaped to Tripolis, and from there advanced to Antioch where he was proclaimed king (162 BC). His first act was to put to death young Antiochus, his cousin, and his minister Lysias (Appian, *Syr.,* c. 47; *Ant,* XII, x, 1; 1 Macc **7** 1–4; 2 Macc **14** 1.2).

As soon as he was established in power, Demetrius made an attempt to placate the Romans by sending them valuable gifts as well as the assassin of Gn. Octavius (Polyb. xxi.23); and he then tried to secure the Hellenizing party by sending his friend BACCHIDES (q.v.) to make the wicked Alcimus high priest. After a violent struggle and much treachery on the part of Bacchides (*Ant,* XII, x, 2), the latter left the country, having charged all the people to obey Alcimus, who was protected by an army.

The Jews under Judas resented his presence, and Judas inflicted severe punishment on all who had gone over to Alcimus (1 Macc **7** 24). Alcimus, in fear, sent a message for aid to Demetrius, who sent to his assistance Nicanor, the best disposed and most faithful of his friends, who had accompanied him in his flight from Rome (*Ant,* XII, x, 4). On his arrival in Judaea, he attempted to win by guile, but Judas saw through his treachery, and Nicanor was forced to fight openly, suffering two signal defeats, the first at Capharsalama (1 Macc **7** 31.32), and the second (in which Nicanor himself was killed), at Adasa (**7** 39 ff; 2 Macc **15** 26 ff).

In a short while, however, Demetrius, hearing of the death of Nicanor, sent Bacchides and Alcimus into Judaea again (1 Macc **9** 1). Judas arose against them with an army of 3,000 men, but when these saw that 20,000 opposed them, the greater part of them deserted, and Judas, with an army of 800, lost his life, like another Leonidas, on the field of battle (1 Macc **9** 4.6.18). Then Bacchides took the wicked men and made them lords of the country (1 Macc **9** 25); while Jonathan, who was appointed successor to Judas, fled with his friends (1 Macc **9** 29 ff).

During the next seven years, Demetrius succeeded in alienating both the Romans (Polyb. xxxii.20) and his own people, and ALEXANDER BALAS (q.v.) was put forward as a claimant to the throne, his supporters maintaining that he was the son of Antiochus Epiphanes (1 Macc **10** 1–21; *Ant,* XIII, ii, 1–3). Both Alexander and Demetrius made bids for the support of the Jews, the former offering the high-priesthood and the title of King's Friend (1 Macc **10** 20), and the latter freedom from taxes, tributes and customs (**10** 28 ff). Alexander's bait proved more alluring, since the Jews "gave no credence" to the words of Demetrius, and with the aid of the Maccabees, he vied with Demetrius for the space of two years for the complete sovereignty of Syria. At the end of this time, a decisive battle took place, in which Demetrius was slain, and Alexander became king of Syria (150 BC) (**10** 48–50; *Ant,* XIII, ii, 4; Polyb. iii.5; see also MACCABEES).

(2) **Demetrius II,** surnamed Νικάτωρ, *Nikátōr* ("conqueror"), was the son of Demetrius Soter. When Balas was warring with Demetrius I, he sent his son to a place of safety in Crete. Three years after his father's death (147 BC), the unpopularity of Alexander gave the young man an opportunity

to return and seize the government. He landed in Cilicia with Cretan mercenaries and secured the support of all Syria with the exception of Judaea (1 Macc **10** 67 ff). Apollonius, his general, the governor of Coele-Syria, who essayed the conquest of the Jews, was defeated at Azotus with great loss.

Ptolemy Philometor, whose daughter was the wife of Alexander Balas, now entered into the struggle, and taking Cleopatra, his daughter, from Alexander, he gave her to Demetrius (**11** 12). He then joined Demetrius' army and the combined forces inflicted a defeat on Balas (145 BC), and from this Demetrius received his surname *Nikator* (*Ant*, XIII, iv, 8; 1 Macc **11** 14 ff).

Jonathan now concluded a favorable treaty with Demetrius, whereby three Samaritan provinces were added to Judaea and the whole country was made exempt from tax (1 Macc **11** 20–37; *Ant*, XIII, iv, 9). Demetrius then dismissed his army except the foreigners, thinking himself safe with the loyalty of the Jews assured. In the meantime, Tryphon, one of Balas' generals, set up the son of Alexander, Antiochus, as a claimant to the throne, and secured the assistance of the discarded army of Demetrius. Jonathan's aid was sought and he quelled the rebellion, on condition that the Syrian garrison be removed from Jerus (1 Macc **11** 41–52; *Ant*, XIII, v, 2–3).

The king, however, falsified all that he had said, and kept none of his promises, so the Jews, deserting him, took sides with Tryphon and supported the claims of the boy Antiochus (1 Macc **11** 53–59; *Ant*, XIII, v, 5–11). Demetrius' generals then entered Syria but were defeated by Jonathan at Hazor (1 Macc **11** 63–74), and by skilful generalship he made futile a second attempt at invasion (**12** 24 ff).

Tryphon, who was now master of Syria, broke faith with Jonathan (**12** 40) and essayed the conquest of Judaea. Jonathan was killed by treachery, and Simon, his successor, made proposals of peace to Demetrius, who agreed to let bygones be bygones (1 Macc **13** 36–40; *Ant*, XIII, vi, 7). Demetrius then left Simon to carry on the war, and set out to Parthia, ostensibly to secure the assistance of the king, Mithridates, against Tryphon (1 Macc **14** 1). Here he was captured and imprisoned (**14** 3; *Ant*, XIII, v, 11; Jos, however, puts this event in 140 rather than 138 BC).

After an imprisonment of ten years, he was released and resumed the sovereignty 128 BC, but becoming involved in a quarrel with Ptolemy Physkon, he was defeated in battle at Damascus. From this place, he fled to Tyre, where he was murdered in 125 BC, according to some, at the instigation of Cleopatra, his wife (Jos, *Ant*, XIII, ix, 3).

(3) **Demetrius III,** Εὔκαιρος, *Eúkairos* ("the fortunate"), was the son of Antiochus Grypus, and grandson of Demetrius Nikator. When his father died, civil war arose, in which his two elder brothers lost their lives, while Philip, the third brother, secured part of Syria as his domain. Demetrius then took up his abode in Coele-Syria with Damascus as his capital (*Ant*, XIII, xiii, 4; *BJ*, I, iv, 4).

War now broke out in Judaea between Alexander Jannaeus and his Pharisee subjects, who invited Demetrius to aid them. Thinking this a good opportunity to extend his realm, he joined the insurgent Jews and together they defeated Jannaeus near Shechem (*Ant*, XIII, xiv, 1; *BJ*, I, iv, 5).

The Jews then deserted Demetrius, and he withdrew to Beroea, which was in the possession of his brother Philip. Demetrius besieged him, and Philip summoned the Parthians to his assistance. The tables were turned, and Demetrius, besieged in his camp and starved into submission, was taken prisoner and sent to Arsaces, who held him captive until his death (*Ant*, XIII, xiv, 3). The dates of his reign are not certain. Arthur J. Kinsella

DEMETRIUS, dē-mē′tri-us (Δημήτριος, *Dēmḗtrios*, "belonging to Ceres"): The name of two persons:

(1) A Christian disciple praised by St. John (3 Jn ver 12).

(2) A silversmith of Ephesus who manufactured the little silver shrines of the goddess Diana to sell to the visiting pilgrims (Acts **19** 23 ff). Because the teachings of Paul were injuring the trade of the silversmiths, there arose a riot of which Demetrius was the chief. Upon an inscription which Mr. Wood discovered among the ruins of the city, there appeared the name Demetrius, a warden of the Ephesian temple for the year 57 AD, and some authors believe the temple warden to be identical with the ringleader of the rebellion. The name, however, has been most common among the Greeks of every age. Because of its frequent use it cannot be supposed that Demetrius, the disciple of 3 Jn ver 12, was the silversmith of Ephesus, nor that Demas of 2 Tim **4** 10, who bore the name in a contracted form, may be identified with him.

E. J. Banks

DEMON, dē′mon, **DEMONIAC,** dē-mō′ni-ak, **DEMONOLOGY,** dē-mon-ol′-ō-ji (Δαιμόνιον, *daimónion*, earlier form δαίμων, *daímōn* = πνεῦμα ἀκάθαρτον, πονηρόν, *pneúma akátharton, ponērón*, "demon," "unclean or evil spirit," incorrectly rendered **devil** in AV):

I. Definition.—The word *daimōn* or *daimonion* seems originally to have had two closely related meanings; a deity, and a spirit, superhuman but not supernatural. In the former sense the term occurs in the LXX tr of Dt **32** 17; Ps **106** 37; Acts **17** 18. The second of these meanings, which involves a general reference to vaguely conceived personal beings akin to men and yet belonging to the unseen realm, leads to the application of the term to the peculiar and restricted class of beings designated "demons" in the NT.

II. The Origin of Biblical Demonology.—An interesting scheme of development has been suggested (by Baudissin and others) in which Bib. demonism is brought through polytheism into connection with primitive animism.

A simple criticism of this theory, which is now in the ascendant, will serve fittingly to introduce what should be said specifically concerning Bib. demonology.

1. The Evolutionary Theory

(1) Animism, which is one branch of that general primitive view of things which is designated as spiritism, is the theory that all Nature is alive (see Ladd, *Phil. Rel.*, I, 89 f) and that all natural processes are due to the operation of living wills. (2) Polytheism is supposed to be the outcome of animism. The vaguely conceived spirits of the earlier conception are advanced to the position of deities with names, fixed characters and specific functions, organized into a pantheon. (3) Bib. demonology is supposed to be due to the solvent of monotheism upon contemporary polytheism. The Hebrews were brought into contact with surrounding nations, esp. during the Pers, Bab and Gr periods, and monotheism made room for heathenism by reducing its deities to the dimension of demons. They are not denied all objective reality but are denied the dignity and prerogatives of deity.

The objections to this ingenious theory are too many and too serious to be overcome.

2. Objections to the Theory

(1) The genetic connection between animism and polytheism is not clear. In fact, the specific religious character of animism is altogether problematical. It belongs to the category of primitive philosophy rather than of religion. It is difficult

to trace the process by which spirits unnamed and with characteristics of the vaguest become deities —esp. is it difficult to understand how certain spirits only are advanced to the standing of deities. More serious still, polytheism and animism have coexisted without close combination or real assimilation (see Sayce, *Babylonia and Assyria*, 232; Rogers, *Religion of Babylonia and Assyria*, 75 f) for a long course of history. It looks as if animism and polytheism had a different *raison d'être*, origin and development. It is, at least, unsafe to construct a theory on the basis of so insecure a connection. (2) The interpretation of heathen deities as demons by no means indicates that polytheism is the source of Bib. demonology. On general principles, it seems far more likely that the category of demons was already familiar, and that connection with polytheism brought about an extension of its application. A glance at the OT will show how comparatively slight and unimportant has been the bearing of heathen polytheism upon Bib. thought. The demonology of the OT is confined to the following passages: Lev **16** 21.22; **17** 7; Isa **13** 21; **34** 13; Dt **32** 17; Ps **106** 37 (elsewhere commented upon; see COMMUNION WITH DEMONS). Gesenius well says of Lev **16** 21 that it is "vexed with the numerous conjectures of interpreters." If the prevalent modern view is accepted we find in it an actual meeting-point of popular superstition and the religion of Jeh (see AZAZEL). According to Driver (*HDB*, I, 207), this item in the Levitical ritual "was intended as a symbolical declaration that the land and the people are now purged from guilt, their sins being handed over to the evil spirit to whom they are held to belong, and whose home is in the desolate wilderness remote from human habitations (ver 22, into a land cut off)." A more striking instance could scarcely be sought of the way in which the religion of Jeh kept the popular spiritism at a safe distance. Lev **17** 7 (see COMMUNION WITH DEMONS) refers to participation in the rites of heathen worship. The two passages—Isa **13** 20.21; **34** 13.14—are poetical and really imply nothing as to the writer's own belief. Creatures both seen and unseen supposed to inhabit places deserted of man are used, as any poet might use them, to furnish the details for a vivid word-picture of uninhabited solitude. There is no direct evidence that the narrative of the Fall (Gen **3** 1–19) has any connection with demonology (see *HDB*, I, 590 n.), and the suggestion of Whitehouse that the mention of satyrs and night-monsters of current mythology with such creatures as jackals, etc, implies "that demons were held to reside more or less in all these animal denizens of the ruined solitude" is clearly fanciful. It is almost startling to find that all that can possibly be affirmed of demonology in the OT is confined to a small group of passages which are either legal or poetical and which all furnish examples of the inhibiting power of high religious conceptions upon the minds of a naturally superstitious and imaginative people. Even if we add all the passages in which a real existence seems to be granted to heathen deities (e.g. Nu **21** 29; Isa **19** 1, etc) and interpret them in the extreme sense, we are still compelled to affirm that evidence is lacking to prove the influence of polytheism in the formation of the Bib. doctrine of demons. (3) This theory breaks down in another still more vital particular. The demonology of the Bible is not of kin either with primitive animism or popular Sem demonism. In what follows we shall address ourselves to NT demonology—that of the OT being a negligible quantity.

III. NT Demonology.—The most marked and significant fact of NT demonology is that it provides no materials for a discussion of the nature and characteristics of demons. Whitehouse says (*HDB*, I, 593) that NT demonology "is in all its broad characteristics the demonology of the contemporary Judaism stripped of its cruder and exaggerated features." How much short of the whole truth this statement comes will appear later, but as it stands it defines the specific direction of inquiry into the NT treatment of demons; namely, to explain its freedom from the crude and exaggerated features of popular demonism. The presence among NT writers of an influence curbing curiosity and restraining the imagination is of all things the most important for us to discover and emphasize. In four of its most vital features the NT attitude on this subject differs from all popular conceptions: (*a*) in the absence of all imaginative details concerning demons; (*b*) in the emphasis placed upon the moral character of demons and their connection with the ethical disorders of the human race; (*c*) in the absence of confidence in magical methods of any kind in dealing with demons; (*d*) in its intense restrictions of the sphere of demoniacal operations.

A brief treatment under each of these heads will serve to present an ordered statement of the most important facts.

(*a*) In the NT we are told practically nothing about the origin, nature, characteristics or habits of demons. In a highly **figurative** passage (Mt **12** 43) Our Lord speaks of demons as passing through "waterless places," and in the story of the Gadarene demoniac (Lk **8** 31) the "abyss" is mentioned as the place of their ultimate detention. The method of their control over human beings is represented in two contrasted ways (cf Mk **1** 23 ff; Lk **4** 33 ff), indicating that there was no fixed mode of regarding it. With these three scant items our direct information ceases. We are compelled to infer from the effects given in the limited number of specific instances narrated. And it is worthy of more than passing mention that no theoretical discussion of demons occurs. The center of interest in the Gospels is the person of Jesus, the sufferers and the cures. Interest in the demons as such is absent. Certain passages seem to indicate that the demons were able to speak (see Mk **1** 24.26.34; Lk **4** 41, etc), but comparing these statements with others (cf Mk **1** 23; Lk **8** 28) it is seen that no distinction is drawn between the cries of the tormented in the paroxysms of their complaint and the cries attributed to the demons themselves. In other particulars the representation is consistent. The demons belong to the unseen world, they are incapable of manifestation except in the disorders which they cause—there are no materializations, no grotesque narratives of appearances and disappearances, no morbid dealing with repulsive details, no license of speculation in the narratives. In contrast with this reticence is not merely the demonology of primitive people, but also that of the non-canonical Jewish books. In the Book of En demons are said to be fallen angels, while Jos holds that they are the spirits of the wicked dead. In the rabbinical writings speculation has run riot in discussing the origin, nature and habits of demons. They are represented as the offspring of Adam and Eve in conjunction with male and female spirits, as being themselves sexed and capable of reproduction as well as performing all other physical functions. Details are given of their numbers, haunts and habits, of times and places where they are esp. dangerous, and of ways and methods of breaking their power (see EXORCISM). Full sweep is also given to the imagination in descriptive narratives, oftentimes of the most morbid and unwholesome character, of their doings among men. After reading some of these narratives one can agree with

Edersheim when he says, "Greater contrast could scarcely be conceived than between what we read in the NT and the views and practices mentioned in Rabbinic writings" (*LTJM*, II, 776).

(*b*) It is also clearly to be noted that while in its original application the term *daimonion* is morally indifferent, in NT usage the demon is invariably an ethically evil being. This differentiates the NT treatment from extra-canonical Jewish writings. In the NT demons belong to the kingdom of Satan whose power it is the mission of Christ to destroy. It deepens and intensifies its representations of the earnestness of human life and its moral issues by extending the sphere of moral struggle to the invisible world. It clearly teaches that the power of Christ extends to the world of evil spirits and that faith in Him is adequate protection against any evils to which men may be exposed. (For significance of this point see Plummer, *St. Luke* [*ICC*], 132–33.)

(*c*) The NT demonology differs from all others by its negation of the power of magic rites to deliver from the affliction. Magic which is clearly separable from religion at that specific point (see Gwatkin, *Knowledge of God*, I, 249) rests upon and is dependent upon spiritism. The ancient Bab incantation texts, forming a surprisingly large proportion of the extant documents, are addressed directly to the supposed activities and powers of demons. These beings, who are not trusted and prayed to in the sense in which deities are, command confidence and call forth prayer, are dealt with by magic rites and formulas (see Rogers, op. cit., 144). Even the Jewish non-canonical writings contain numerous forms of words and ceremonies for the expulsion of demons. In the NT there is no magic. The deliverance from a demon is a spiritual and ethical process (see EXORCISM).

(*d*) In the NT the range of activities attributed to demons is greatly restricted. According to Bab ideas: "These demons were everywhere; they lurked in every corner, watching for their prey. The city streets knew their malevolent presence, the rivers, the seas, the tops of mountains; they appeared sometimes as serpents gliding noiselessly upon their victims, as birds horrid of mien flying resistlessly to destroy or afflict, as beings in human forms, grotesque, malformed, awe-inspiring through their hideousness. To these demons all sorts of misfortune were ascribed—a toothache, a headache, a broken bone, a raging fever, an outburst of anger, of jealousy, of incomprehensible disease" (Rogers, op. cit., 145). In the extra-canonical Jewish sources the same exuberance of fancy appears in attributing all kinds of ills of mind and body to innumerable, swarming hosts of demons lying in wait for men and besieging them with attacks and ills of all descriptions. Of this affluence of morbid fancy there is no hint in the NT. A careful analysis of the instances will show the importance of this fact. There are, taking repetitions and all, about 80 references to demons in the NT. In 11 instances the distinction between demon-possession and diseases ordinarily caused is clearly made (Mt **4** 24; **8** 16; **10** 8; Mk **1** 32.34; **6** 13; **16** 17.18; Lk **4** 40.41; **9** 1; **13** 32; Acts **19** 12). The results of demon-possession are not exclusively mental or nervous (Mt **9** 32.33; **12** 22). They are distinctly and peculiarly mental in two instances only (Gadarene maniac, Mt **8** 28 and parallels, and Acts **19** 13 f). Epilepsy is specified in one case only (Mt **17** 15). There is distinction made between demonized and epileptic, and demonized and lunatic (Mt **4** 24). There is distinction made between diseases caused by demons and the same disease not so caused (cf Mt **12** 22; **15** 30). In most of the instances no specific symptoms are mentioned. In an equally large proportion, however, there are occasional fits of mental excitement often due to the presence and teaching of Christ.

Conclusions

A summary of the entire material leads to the conclusion that, in the NT cases of demon-possession, we have a specific type of disturbance, physical or mental, distinguishable not so much by its symptoms which were often of the most general character, as by its *accompaniments*. The *aura*, so to say, which surrounded the patient, served to distinguish his symptoms and to point out the special cause to which his suffering was attributed. Another unique feature of NT demonology should be emphasized. While this group of disorders is attributed to demons, the victims are treated as sick folk and are healed. The whole atmosphere surrounding the narrative of these incidents is calm, lofty and pervaded with the spirit of Christ. When one remembers the manifold cruelties inspired by the unreasoning fear of demons, which make the annals of savage medicine a nightmare of unimaginable horrors, we cannot but feel the world-wide difference between the Bib. narratives and all others, both of ancient and modern times, with which we are acquainted. Every feature of the NT narratives points to the conclusion that in them we have trustworthy reports of actual cures. This is more important for NT faith than any other conclusion could possibly be.

It is also evident that Jesus treated these cases of invaded personality, of bondage, of depression, of helpless fear, as due to a real superhuman cause, to meet and overcome which He addressed Himself. The most distinctive and important words we have upon this obscure and difficult subject, upon which we know far too little to speak with any assurance or authority, are these: "This kind can come out by nothing, save by prayer" (Mk **9** 29).

LITERATURE.—(1) The most accessible statement of Baudissin's theory is in Whitehouse's art. "Demons," etc, in *HDB*. (2) For extra-canonical Jewish ideas use Lange, *Apocrypha*, 118. 134; Edersheim, *LTJM*, Appendices XIII, XVI. (3) For spirit-lore in general see Ladd, *Phil. Rel.*, index s.v., and standard books on Anthropology and Philosophy of Religion under Spiritism. (4) For Bab demonology see summary in Rogers, *Religion of Babylonia and Assyria*, 144 ff.

LOUIS MATTHEWS SWEET

DEMOPHON, dem'ō-fon (**Δημοφῶν**, *Dēmophōn*): A Syrian general in Pal under Antiochus V (Eupator) who continued to harass the Jews after covenants had been made between Lysias and Judas Maccabaeus (2 Macc **12** 2).

DEN (מָעוֹן, *mā'ōn*, מְעוֹנָה, *me'ōnāh*, "habitation"; מְעָרָה, *me'ārāh*, and **σπήλαιον**, *spēlaion*, "cave"; מְאוּרָה, *me'ūrāh* [Isa **11** 8], "a light-hole," fr אוֹר, *'ōr*, "light," perhaps for *me'ārāh;* סֹךְ, *ṣōkh* [Ps **10** 9 AV], and סֻכָּה, *ṣukkāh* [Job **38** 40], "a covert," elsewhere "booth"; אֶרֶב, *'erebh*[Job **37** 8], "covert," as in RV; גֹּב, *gōbh;* cf Arab. *jubb*, "pit" [Dnl **6** 7]; מִנְהָרוֹת, *minhārōth*, "fissure" or "cleft" [Jgs **6** 2]): In the limestone mountains of Pal, caves, large and small, are abundant, the calcium carbonate, of which the rock is mainly composed, being dissolved by the water as it trickles over them or through their crevices. Even on the plains, by a similar process, pits or "lime sinks" are formed, which are sometimes used by the Arabs for storing straw or grain. Of this sort may have been the pit, *bōr*, into which Joseph was cast by his brethren (Gen **37** 20). Caves and crevices and sometimes spaces among piled-up bowlders at the foot of a cliff or in a stream bed are used as dens by jackals, wolves and other wild animals. Even the people, for longer or shorter periods, have lived as troglodytes. Cf Jgs **6** 2: "Because of Midian the children of Israel made them the dens [*minhārōth*] which are in the mountains, and the caves [*me'ārāh*], and the strongholds [*meçādh*]." The precipitous sides of the valleys contain many caves converted by a little labor into human habitations. Notable instances are the valley of the Kidron near *Mār-Sāba*, and *Wādi-ul-Ḥamām* near the Sea of Tiberias. See CAVE.

ALFRED ELY DAY

DENARIUS, dē-nā'ri-us (**δηνάριον,** *dēnárion*): A Rom silver coin, 25 of which went to the *aureus*, the standard gold coin of the empire in the time of Augustus, which was equal in value to about one guinea or $5.25; more exactly £1.0.6=$5.00, the £=$4.866. Hence the value of the denarius

Denarius of Tiberius.

would be about 20 cents and this was the ordinary wage of a soldier and a day laborer. The word is uniformly rendered "penny" in the AV and "shilling" in the ARV, except in Mt **22** 19; Mk **12** 15 and Lk **20** 24, where the Lat word is used, since in these passsages it refers to the coin in which tribute was paid to the Rom government. See MONEY.

H. PORTER

DENOUNCE, dē-nouns': Occurs in Dt **30** 18: "I denounce unto you this day, that ye shall surely perish." It is used here in the obsolete sense of "to declare," to make known in a solemn manner. It is not found in the Bible with the regular meaning of "to censure," "arraign," etc.

DENY, dē-nī': This word is characteristic of the NT rather than the OT, although it translates three different Heb originals, viz. כָּחַשׁ, *kāḥash*, "to lie," "disown" (Gen **18** 15; Josh **24** 27; Job **8** 18; **31** 28; Prov **30** 9); מָנַע, *māna'*, "to withhold," "keep back" (1 K **20** 7; Prov **30** 7); שׁוּב, *shūbh*, "to turn back," "say no" (1 K **2** 16).

In the NT, ἀντιλέγω, *antilégō*, is once trd "deny," in the case of the Sadducees who denied the resurrection (Lk **20** 27 AV), and where it carries the sense of speaking against the doctrine. But the word commonly is ἀρνέομαι, *arnéomai*, with or without the prefix *ap*. In the absence of the prefix the sense is "to disown," but when it is added it means "to disown totally" or to the fullest extent. In the milder sense it is found in Mt **10** 33; **26** 70. 72; of Simon Peter, Mk **14** 68.70 (Acts **3** 13.14; 2 Tim **2** 12.13; 2 Pet **2** 1; 1 Jn **2** 22.23; Jude ver 4; Rev **2** 13; **3** 8). But it is significant that the sterner meaning is associated with Mt **16** 24 and its parallels, where Christ calls upon him who would be His disciple to deny himself and take up his cross and follow Him. See also PETER, SIMON.

JAMES M. GRAY

DEPOSIT, dē-poz'it (**παραθήκη,** *parathḗkē*, 1 Tim **6** 20; 2 Tim **1** 12.14 RVm, paraphrased in both AV and RV into "that which is committed" [see COMMEND]): The noun was used in the classical Gr, just as its Eng. equivalents, for "that which is placed with another for safe keeping," a charge committed to another's hands, consisting often of money or property; cf Ex **22** 7; Lev **6** 2. This practice was common in days when there were no banks. (1) In 1 Tim **6** 20; also 2 Tim **1** 14, the reference is to a deposit which God makes with man, and for which man is to give a reckoning. The context shows that this deposit is the Christian faith, "the pattern of sound words" (2 Tim **1** 13), that which is contrasted with the "oppositions of the knowledge which is falsely so called" (1 Tim **6** 20). "Keep the talent of the Christian faith safe and undiminished" (Vincentius Lirenensis). (2) In 2 Tim **1** 12, the deposit is one which man makes with God. The key to the meaning of this expression is found probably in Ps **31** 5: "Into thy hand I commend my spirit: Thou hast redeemed me," i.e. "All that I am, with all my interests, have been intrusted to Thy safe keeping, and, therefore, I have no anxieties with respect to the future. The day of reckoning, 'that day,' will show how faithful are the hands that hold this trust."

H. E. JACOBS

DEPTH. See ABYSS.

DEPUTY, dep'ū-ti: This is the correct rendering of נִצָּב, *niççābh* (1 K **22** 47). In Est **8** 9 and **9** 3 the term improperly represents סָגָן, *çāghān*, in AV, and is corrected to "governor" in RV. In the NT "deputy" represents ἀνθύπατος, *anthúpatos* (Acts **13** 7.8.12; **18** 12; **19** 38), which RV correctly renders "proconsul" (q.v.). The Rom proconsuls were officers invested with consular power over a district outside the city, usually for one year. Originally they were retiring consuls, but after Augustus the title was given to governors of senatorial provinces, whether they had held the office of consul or not. The proconsul exercised judicial as well as military power in his province, and his authority was absolute, except as he might be held accountable at the expiration of his office. See GOVERNMENT.

WILLIAM ARTHUR HEIDEL

DERBE, dûr'bē (**Δέρβη,** *Dérbē*, Acts **14** 20.21; **16** 1; **Δερβαῖος,** *Derbaíos*, **20** 4; **Δερβήτης,** *Derbḗtēs*, Strabo, Cicero): A city in the extreme S.E. corner of the Lycaonian plain is mentioned twice as having been visited by Paul (on his first and second missionary journeys respectively), and it may now be regarded as highly probable that he passed through it on his third journey (to the churches of Galatia). The view that these churches were in South Galatia is now accepted by the majority of Eng. and Am. scholars, and a traveler passing through the Cilician Gates to Southern Galatia must have traversed the territory of Derbe.

1. History

Derbe is first mentioned as the seat of Antipater, who entertained Cicero, the Rom orator and governor of Cilicia. When the kingdom of Amyntas passed, at his death in 25 BC, to the Romans, it was made into a province and called Galatia (see GALATIA). This province included Laranda as well as Derbe on the extreme S.E., and for a time Laranda was the frontier city looking toward Cappadocia and Cilicia and Syria via the Cilician Gates. But between 37 and 41 AD Laranda was transferred to the "protected" kingdom of Antiochus, and Derbe became the frontier city. It was the last city on distinctively Rom territory, on the road leading from Southern Galatia to the E.; it was here that commerce entering the province had to pay the customs dues. Strabo records this fact when he calls Derbe a *limēn*, or "customs station." It owed its importance (and consequently its visit from Paul on his first journey) to this fact, and to its position on a great Rom road leading from Antioch, the capital of Southern Galatia, to Iconium, Laranda, Heracleia-Cybistra, and the Cilician Gates. Rom milestones have been found along the line of this road, one at a point 15 miles N.W. of Derbe. It was one of those Lycaonian cities honored with the title "Claudian" by the emperor Claudius; its coins bear the legend "Claudio-Derbe." This implied considerable importance and prosperity as well as strong pro-Rom feeling;

yet we do not find Derbe standing aloof, like the Rom *coloniae* Iconium and Lystra, from the Common Council of Lycaonian cities (*Koinon Lykaonias*).

Derbe remained in the province Galatia till about 135 AD, when it passed to the jurisdiction of the triple province Cilicia-Isauria-Lycaonia. It continued in this division till 295 AD, and was then included in the newly formed province Isauria. This arrangement lasted till about 372 AD, when Lycaonia, including Derbe, was formed into a separate province. The statement of Stephanus of Byzantium that Derbe was "a fortress of Isauria" originated in the arrangement which existed from 295 to 372 AD. Coins of the city represent Heracles, Fortuna and a winged Victory writing on a shield (after the pattern of the Venus of Melos, in the Louvre, Paris). Derbe is mentioned several times in the records of the church councils. A bishop, Daphnus of Derbe, was present at the Council of Constantinople in 381.

2. Situation

The site of Derbe was approximately fixed by the American explorer Sterrett, and more accurately by Sir W. M. Ramsay, who, after carefully examining all the ruins in the neighborhood, placed it at Gudelisin. Up to 1911, certain epigraphic evidence fixing the site had not been found, but Ramsay's identification meets all the conditions, and cannot be far wrong. On the E., Derbe was conterminous with Laranda, on the N.E. with Barata in the Kara Dagh. It bordered on the territory of Iconium on the N.W., and on Isauria on the W. Its territory touched the foothills of Taurus on the S., and the site commands a fine view of the great mountain called *Hadji Baba* or the Pilgrim Father. The Greeks of the district say that the name is a reminiscence of St. Paul, "over whose travels" the mountain "stood as a silent witness."

The remains are mostly of the late Rom and Byzantine periods, but pottery of an earlier date has been found on the site. An inscription of a village on the territory of Derbe records the erection of a building by two architects from Lystra. A line of boundary stones, separating the territory of Derbe from that of Barata, is still standing. It probably belongs to an early delimitation of the territory of the frontier town of Galatia (Ramsay).

3. Paul at Derbe

In Acts **14** 20.21, it is narrated that Paul and Barnabas, after being driven out of Lystra, departed to Derbe, where they "preached the gospel . . . . and made many disciples." But they did not go farther. Paul's mission included only the centers of Graeco-Rom civilization; it was no part of his plan to pass over the frontier of the province into non-Rom territory. This aspect of his purpose is illustrated by the reference to Derbe on his second journey (Acts **16** 1). Paul started from Antioch and "went through Syria and Cilicia, confirming the churches" (**15** 41). "Then he came to Derbe and Lystra" (**16** 1 AV). The unwarned reader might forget that in going from Cilicia to Derbe, Paul must have passed through a considerable part of Antiochus' territory, and visited the important cities of Heracleia-Cybistra and Laranda. But his work ends with the Rom Cilicia and begins again with the Rom Galatia; to him, the intervening country is a blank. Concentration of effort, and utilization only of the most fully prepared material were the characteristics of Paul's missionary journeys in Asia Minor. That Paul was successful in Derbe may be gathered (as Ramsay points out) from the fact that he does not mention Derbe among the places where he had suffered persecution (2 Tim **3** 11). Gaius of Derbe (among others) accompanied Paul to Jerus, in charge of the donations of the churches to the poor in that city (Acts **20** 4).

LITERATURE.—The only complete account of Derbe is that given in Sir W. M. Ramsay's *Cities of St. Paul*, 385–404. On Paul's mission there, see the same author's *St. Paul the Traveller and Rom Citizen*, 119, 178. Many inscriptions of the later Rom period are collected in Sterrett, *Wolfe Expedition to Asia Minor*, Nos. 18–52. The principal ancient authorities, besides Acts, are Cicero *Ad Fam*. xiii.73; Strabo xxx.569; Ptolemaeus, v.6, 17; Steph. Byz., *Hierocl*., 675; *Notit. Episcop*., I, 404, and the *Acta Conciliorum*.

W. M. CALDER

DERISION, dē̆-rizh'un: Three vbs. are so tr^d: לוּץ, *lūç*, "scorn" (Ps **119** 51); לָעַג, *lā'agh*, "mock" (**2** 4; **59** 8; Ezk **23** 32); and שָׂחַק, *sāhak*, "laugh at" (Job **30** 1; Ex **32** 25 m, "a whispering"; cf Wisd **5** 3). This word is found almost exclusively in the Psalms and Prophets; Jeremiah is fond of it. It is used both as a subst. and a vb., the latter in the phrase "to have in derision."

DESCEND, dē̆-send' (יָרַד, *yāradh;* **καταβαίνω**, *katabainō*, "go down"); **DESCENT**, dē̆-sent' (**κατάβασις**, *katábasis*): Of Jeh (Ex **34** 5); of the Spirit (Mt **3** 16); of angels (Gen **28** 12; Mt **28** 2; Jn **1** 51); of Christ (1 Thess **4** 16; Eph **4** 9). "He also descended into the lower parts of the earth" is variously interpreted, the two chief interpretations being the one of the incarnation, and the other of the "descent into hell" (1 Pet **3** 19). The former regards the clause "of the earth," an appositive genitive, as when we speak of "the city of Rome," viz., "the lower parts, i.e. the earth." The other regards the genitive as possessive, or, with Meyer, as governed by the comparative, i.e. "parts lower than the earth." For the former view, see full discussion in Eadie; for the latter, Ellicott and esp. Meyer, in commentaries on Eph. H. E. JACOBS

DESCENT, dē̆-sent', **OF JESUS**. See APOCRYPHAL GOSPELS.

DESCRIBE, dē̆-skrīb': This vb., now obsolete, in the sense used in Josh **18** 4.6.8.9 and Jgs **8** 14, is a tr of כָּתַב, *kāthabh*, usually rendered "to write" or "inscribe." But in the above passages it has the OE meaning of dividing into parts or into lots, as for example: "Walk through the land, and describe it according to their inheritance" (Josh **18** 4); that is, describe in writing the location and size of the several parcels of land thus portioned out. In Jgs **8** 14 "described" should be tr^d "wrote down a list of." "Describe" occurs twice in the AV of the NT (Rom **4** 6 and **10** 5), where λέγω, *légō*, and γράφω, *gráphō*, are both rendered "describeth." RV corrects both, and substitutes "pronounceth" in the first and "writeth" in the second passage.

Description = "list" (1 Esd **5** 39).

W. W. DAVIES

DESCRY, dē̆-skrī': This word like "describe" came into the Eng. through the Fr. *descrire* (Lat *describere);* it occurs only in the AV of Jgs **1** 23: "And the house of Joseph sent to descry Bethel." תּוּר, *tūr*, the vb. thus tr^d, signifies "to explore" or "examine," and RV correctly renders "sent to spy out."

DESERT, dez'ẽrt (מִדְבָּר, *midhbār*, חָרְבָּה, *ḥorbāh*, יְשִׁימוֹן, *y^eshīmōn*, עֲרָבָה, *'ărābhāh*, צִיָּה, *çīyāh*, תֹּהוּ, *tōhū;* **ἔρημος**, *érēmos*, **ἐρημία** *erēmía*): *Midhbār*, the commonest word for "desert," more often rendered "wilderness," is perhaps from r. *dābhar*, in the sense of "to drive," i.e. a place for driving or pasturing flocks. *Y^eshīmōn* is from *yāsham*, "to be empty"; *ḥorbāh* (cf Arab. *kharib*, "to lie waste"; *khirbah*, "a ruin"; *kharāb*, "devastation"), from *ḥārabh*, "to be dry"; cf also *'ārabh*, "to be dry," and *'ărābhāh*, "a desert" or "the Arabah" (see CHAMPAIGN). For *'ereç çīyāh* (Ps **63** 1; Isa **41** 18), "a dry land," cf *çīyīm*, "wild beasts of the desert" (Isa **13** 21, etc). *Tōhū*, variously rendered "without form" (Gen **1** 2 AV), "empty space," AV "empty place" (Job **26** 7), "waste," AV "nothing" (Job **6** 18), "confusion," RVm "wasteness" (Isa **24** 10 ERV), may be compared with Arab. *tāh*, "to go astray," *at-Tīh*, "the desert of the wandering." In the NT we find *erēmos* and *erēmia:* "The child [John] . . . . was in the deserts till the day of his showing unto Israel" (Lk **1** 80); "Our fathers did eat manna in the desert" (Jn **6** 31 AV).

In the Desert of Edom.

The desert as known to the Israelites was not a waste of sand, as those are apt to imagine who have in mind the pictures of the Sahara. Great expanses of sand, it is true, are found in Arabia, but the nearest one, *an-Nufūd*, was several days' journey distant from the farthest southeast reached by the Israelites in their wanderings. Most of the desert of Sinai and of Pal is land that needs only water to make it fruitful. E. of the Jordan, the line between "the desert" and "the sown" lies about along the line of the *Ḥijāz* railway. To the W. there is barely enough water to support the crops of wheat; to the E. there is too little. Near the line of demarkation, the yield of wheat depends strictly upon the rainfall. A few inches more or less of rain in the year determines whether the grain can reach maturity or not. The latent fertility of the desert lands is demonstrated by the season of scant rains, when they become carpeted with herbage and flowers. It is marvelous, too, how the camels, sheep and goats, even in the dry season, will find something to crop where the traveler sees nothing but absolute barrenness. The long wandering of the Israelites in "the desert" was made possible by the existence of food for their flocks and herds. Cf Ps **65** 11.12:

"Thou crownest the year with thy goodness;
And thy paths drop fatness.
They drop upon the pastures of the wilderness,
And the hills are girded with joy";

and also Joel **2** 22: "The pastures of the wilderness do spring."

"The desert" or "the wilderness" (*ha-midhbār*) usually signifies the desert of the wandering, or the northern part of the Sinaitic Peninsula. Cf Ex **3** 1 AV: "Moses . . . . led the flock [of Jethro] to the backside of the desert"; Ex **5** 3 AV: "Let us go . . . . three days' journey into the desert"; Ex **19** 2 AV: "They . . . . were come to the desert of Sinai"; Ex **23** 31 AV: "I will set thy bounds from the Red Sea even unto the sea of the Philistines, and from the desert unto the river" (Euphrates). Other uncultivated or pasture regions are known as Wilderness of Beersheba (Gen **21** 14), W. of Judah (Jgs **1** 16), W. of En-gedi (1 S **24** 1), W. of Gibeon (2 S **2** 24), W. of Maon (1 S **23** 24), W. of Damascus; cf Arab. *Bādiyet-ush-Shām* (1 K **19** 15), etc. *Midhbar yām*, "the wilderness of the sea" (Isa **21** 1), may perhaps be that part of Arabia bordering upon the Pers Gulf.

Aside from the towns and fields, practically all the land was *midhbār* or "desert," for this term included mountain, plain and valley. The terms, "desert of En-gedi," "desert of Maon," etc, do not indicate circumscribed areas, but are applied in a general way to the lands about these places. To obtain water, the shepherds with their flocks traverse long distances to the wells, springs or streams, usually arranging to reach the water about the middle of the day and rest about it for an hour or so, taking shelter from the sun in the shadows of the rocks, perhaps under some overhanging ledge.

Alfred Ely Day

DESIRE, dē-zīr': The vb. "to desire" in the Scriptures usually means "to long for," "to ask for," "to demand," and may be used in a good or bad sense (cf Dt **7** 25 AV). RV frequently renders the more literal meaning of the Heb. Cf Job **20** 20, "delight"; Prov **21** 20, "precious"; Ps **40** 6, "delight"; αἰτέω, *aitéō* (except Col **1** 9), and ἐρωτάω, *erōtáō* (except Lk **7** 36) are rendered "to ask" and ζητέω, *zētéō*, "to seek" (cf Lk **9** 9 et al.). The Heb כָּסַף, *kāṣaph*, lit. "to lose in value," is tr[d] (Zeph **2** 1) by "hath no shame" (RVm "longing," AV "not desired"). The literal tr "to lose in value," "to degenerate," would be more in harmony with the context than the translations offered. The Heb חֶמְדָּה, *ḥemdāh* (2 Ch **21** 20, "without being desired"), means according to the Arab. "to praise," "to give thanks." The context brings in contrast the burial of the king Jehoram with that of his fathers. In the latter case there was "burning," i.e. recognition and praise, but when Jehoram died, there was no *ḥemdāh*, i.e. there was no praise for his services rendered to the kingdom. For "desire" in Eccl **12** 5, see Caperberry. A. L. Breslich

DESIRE OF ALL NATIONS: This phrase occurs only in Hag **2** 7 (AV, ERV "desirable things," ARVm "things desired"), and is commonly applied to the Messiah.

At the erection of the temple in Ezra's time, the older men who had seen the more magnificent house of Solomon were disappointed and distressed at the comparison. The prophet, therefore, is directed to encourage them by the assurance that Jeh is with them nevertheless, and in a little while will shake the heavens, the earth, the sea, the dry land and the nations, and "the desire of all nations" shall come, and the house shall be filled with glory, so that "the later glory of this house shall be greater than the former."

(1) Many expositors refer the prophecy to the first advent of Christ. The shaking of the heavens, the earth, the sea and the dry land is the figurative setting of the shaking of the nations, while this latter expression refers to those changes of earthly dominion coincident with the overthrow of the Persians by the Greeks, the Greeks by the Romans, and so on down to the beginning of our era. The house then in process of construction was filled with glory by the later presence of the Messiah, which glory was greater than the Shekinah of Solomon's time. Objections are presented to this view as follows: First, there is the element of time. Five cents., more or less, elapsed between the building of Ezra's temple and the first advent of Christ, and the men of Ezra's time needed comfort for the present. Then there is the difficulty of associating the physical phenomena with any shaking of the nations occurring at the first advent. Furthermore, in what sense, it is asked, could Christ, when He came, be said to be the desire of all nations? And finally, what comfort would a Jew find in this magnifying of the Gentiles?

(2) These difficulties, though not insuperable, lead others to apply the prophecy to the second advent of Christ. The Jews are to be restored to Jerus, and another temple is to be built (Ezk **40**–**48**). The shaking of the nations and the physical

phenomena find their fulfilment in the "Great Tribulation" so often spoken of in the OT and Rev, and which is followed by the coming of Christ in glory to set up His kingdom (Mal **3** 1; Mt **24** 29. 30 and other places). Some of the difficulties spoken of in the first instance apply here also, but not all of them, while others are common to both interpretations. One such common difficulty is that Ezra's temple can hardly be identified with that of the time of Herod and Christ, and certainly not with that of Ezekiel; which is met, however, by saying that all the temples, including Solomon's, are treated as but one "house"—the house of the Lord, in the religious sense, at least, if not architecturally. Another such difficulty touches the question of time, which, whether it includes five centuries or twenty, is met by the principle that to the prophets, "ascending in heart to God and the eternity of God, all times and all things of this world are only a mere point." When the precise time of particular events is not revealed, they sometimes describe them as continuous, and sometimes blend two events together, having a near or partial, and also a remote or complete fulfilment. "They saw the future in space rather than in time, or the perspective rather than the actual distance." It is noted that the Lord Jesus so blends together the destruction of Jerus by Titus, AD 70, and the days of the anti-Christ at the end of this age, that it is difficult to separate them, and to say which belongs exclusively to either (Mt **24**). That the words may have an ultimate fulfilment in the second advent of Christ receives strength from a comparison of vs 21 and 22 of the same chapter (ch **2**) of Hag with He **12** 26.27. The writer of that epistle condenses the two passages in Hag **2** 6.7 and 21. 22, implying that it was one and the same shaking, of which the former vs denote the beginning, and the latter the end. The shaking, in other words, began introductory to the first advent and will be finished at the second. Concerning the former, cf Mt **3** 17; **27** 51; **28** 2; Acts **2** 2; **4** 31, and concerning the latter, Mt **24** 7; Rev **16** 20; **20** 11 (Bengel, quoted by Canon Faussett).

(3) Other expositors seek to cut the Gordian knot by altogether denying the application to the Messiah, and translating "the desire of all nations" by "the beauty," or "the desirable things of all nations," i.e. their precious gifts (see Isa **60** 5.11; **61** 6). This application is defended in the following way: (*a*) The Heb word means the *quality* and not the *thing* desired; (*b*) the Messiah was not desired by all the nations when He came; (*c*) the vb. "shall come" is pl., which requires the noun to be understood in the pl., whereas if the Messiah be intended, the noun is singular; (*d*) "The silver is mine," etc (Hag **2** 8) accords with the tr "the desirable things of all nations"; (*e*) the agreement of the Sept and Syr VSS with such rendering.

All these arguments, however, can be fairly met by counter-arguments, leaving the reader still in doubt. (*a*) An abstract noun is often put for the concrete; (*b*) the result shows that while the Jews rejected Christ, the Gentiles received and hence desired Him; (*c*) where two nouns stand together after the manner of "the desire" and "nations," the vb. agrees in number sometimes with the latter, even though the former be its nominative; (*d*) the 8th ver of the prophecy can be harmonized about as easily with one view as the other; (*e*) the AV is sustained by the Vulg and early Jewish rabbis.

James M. Gray

DESOLATE, des'ō-lāt (very frequently in the OT for שָׁמֵם, *shāmēm*, and its derivatives; less frequently, חָרֵב, *ḥārēbh*, and its derivatives, and other words. In the NT it stands for ἔρημος, *érēmos* [Mt **23** 38; Acts **1** 20; Gal **4** 27], *erēmóō* [Rev **17** 16], and *monóō* [1 Tim **5** 5]): From Lat *de*, intens., *solus*, alone. Several shades of meaning can be distinguished: (1) Its primary sense is "left lonely," "forlorn," e.g. Ps **25** 16, "Have mercy upon me; for I am desolate" (Heb *yāḥīdh*, "alone"); 1 Tim **5** 5, "she that is a widow indeed, and desolate" (Gr *memonōménē*, "left alone"). (2) In the sense of "laid waste," "destitute of inhabitants," e.g. Jer **4** 7, "to make thy land desolate, that thy cities be laid waste, without inhabitant." (3) With the meaning "comfortless," "afflicted," e.g. Ps **143** 4, "My heart within me is desolate." (4) In the sense of "barren," "childless," "unfruitful," e.g. Job **15** 34; Isa **49** 21 (Heb *galmūdh*).

D. Miall Edwards

DESOLATION, ABOMINATION OF. See Abomination of Desolation.

DESPAIR, dē-spâr': The subst. only in 2 Cor **4** 8, "perplexed, but not in [RV "yet not unto"] despair," lit. "being at a loss, but not utterly at a loss." "Unto despair" here conveys the force of the Gr prefix *ex* ("utterly," "out and out"). **Desperate,** in Job **6** 26; Isa **17** 11. In the latter instance, the Heb adj. is derived from a vb. = "to be sick," and the lit. rendering would be "incurable" (cf Job **34** 6, "my wound is incurable"). **Desperately** in Jer **17** 9 AV, where the heart is said to be "desperately [i.e. incurably] wicked" or "sick."

DESPITE, dē-spīt', **DESPITEFUL,** dē-spīt'fool: "Despite" is from Lat *despectus*, "a looking down upon." As a noun (= "contempt") it is now generally used in its shortened form, "spite," while the longer form is used as a prep. (= "in spite of"). In EV it is always a noun. In the OT it translates Heb *shᵉ'āṭ*, in Ezk **25** 6, and in RV Ezk **25** 15; **36** 5 ("with despite of soul"). In He **10** 29 ("hath done despite unto the Spirit of grace") it stands for Gr *enubrízō*, "to treat with contempt." The adj. "despiteful" occurs in AV Ezk **25** 15; **36** 5; Sir **31** 31 ("despiteful words," RV "a word of reproach"); Rom **1** 30 (RV "insolent" = Gr *hubrís-tēs*, fr *hupér*, "above"; cf Eng. "uppish").

D. Miall Edwards

DESSAU, des'ô, des'a-ū (**Δεσσαού**, *Dessaoú* [2 Macc **14** 16]): RV LESSAU (which see).

DESTINY, des'ti-ni (**MENI**): A god of Good Luck, possibly the Pleiades. See Astrology, 10; Meni.

DESTROYER, dē-stroi'ẽr: In several passages the word designates a supernatural agent of destruction, or destroying angel, executing Divine judgment. (1) In Ex **12** 23, of the "destroyer" who smote the first-born in Egypt, again referred to under the same title in He **11** 28 RV (AV "he that destroyed"). (2) In Job **33** 22, "the destroyers" (lit. "they that cause to die") = the angels of death that are ready to take away a man's life during severe illness. No exact ‖ to this is found in the OT. The nearest approach is "the angel that destroyed the people" by pestilence (2 S **24** 16.17 ‖ 1 Ch **21** 15.16); the angel that smote the Assyrians (2 K **19** 35 = Isa **37** 36 ‖ 2 Ch **32** 21); "angels of evil" (Ps **78** 49). (3) In the Apoc, "the destroyer" is once referred to as "the minister of punishment" (RV; lit. "him who was punishing"), who brought death into the world (Wisd **18** 22–25). (4) In 1 Cor **10** 10, "the destroyer" is the angelic agent to whose instrumentality Paul attributes the plague of Nu **16** 46–49.

In later Jewish theology (the Tgs and Midr), the "destroyer" or "angel of death" appears under the name Sammael (i.e. the poison of God), who was once an archangel before the throne of God, and who caused the serpent to tempt Eve. According to Weber, he is not to be distinguished from Satan. The chief distinction between the "destroyer" of early thought and the Sammael of later Judaism is that the former was regarded as the emissary of Jeh, and subservient to His will, and sometimes was not clearly distinguished from Jeh Himself, whereas the latter was regarded as a perfectly distinct individuality, acting in independence or semi-independence, and from purely malicious and evil motives. The change was largely due to the influence of Pers dualism, which made good and evil to be independent powers.

D. Miall Edwards

DESTRUCTION, dḗ-struk′shun: In AV this word translates over 30 Heb words in the OT, and 4 words in the NT. Of these the most interesting, as having a technical sense, is *'ăbhaddōn* (from vb. *'ābhadh,* "to be lost," "to perish"). It is found 6 t in the Wisdom Literature, and nowhere else in the OT; cf Rev **9** 11. See Abaddon.

DESTRUCTION, CITY OF (Isa **19** 18; **HELIOPOLIS OR CITY OF THE SUN**). See Astronomy, I, 2; Ir-ha-heres; On.

DETERMINATE, dḗ-tûr′mi-nāt (ὡρισμένος, *hōrisménos,* "determined," "fixed"): Only in Acts **2** 23, "by the determinate counsel and foreknowledge of God," Gr *hōrismenos,* fr *horízō,* "to set boundaries," "determine," "settle" (cf Eng. word "horizon"—lit. "that which bounds"). It is remarkable that Peter in one and the same sentence speaks of the death of Christ from two quite distinct points of view. (1) From the historical standpoint, it was a crime perpetrated by men who were morally responsible for their deed ("him . . . . ye by the hand of lawless men did crucify and slay"). (2) From the standpoint of Divine teleology, it was part of an eternal plan ("by the determinate," etc). No effort is made to demonstrate the logical consistency of the two ideas. They represent two aspects of the one fact. The same Gr word is used in Lk **22** 22, where Christ speaks of His betrayal as taking place "as it was [RV "hath been"] determined" (*katá tó hōrisménon*). Cf Lk **24** 26.

D. Miall Edwards

DETERMINE, dḗ-tûr′min:

(1) "To resolve," "decide." This is the primary meaning of the word and it is also the one that is the most common. In the NT the Gr word κρίνω, *krínō,* is tr[d] "determine," and it has the above meaning (Acts **20** 16; **25** 25; 1 Cor **2** 2). The word occurs frequently in the OT with this meaning (see Ex **21** 22; 1 S **20** 7.9.33).

(2) "To decree," "ordain," "mark out." The Gr word that is rendered "determine" with this meaning is *horízō.* See Determinate.

The Heb term *ḥāraç* is tr[d] "determine" with the above meaning; as "his days are determined" (Job **14** 5); "a destruction is determined" (Isa **10** 22); "desolations are determined" (Dnl **9** 26). The Heb term *mishpāṭ,* which means "judgment" or "sentence," is tr[d] "determination" in Zeph **3** 8.

A. W. Fortune

DETESTABLE, dḗ-tes′ta-b'l, **THINGS** (שִׁקּוּץ, *shiḳḳūç;* שֶׁקֶץ, *sheḳeç,* synonymous with תּוֹעֵבָה, *tō'ēbhāh,* "abomination," "abominable thing"): The tr of *shiḳḳuçīm* in Jer **16** 18; Ezk **5** 11; **7** 20; **11** 18.21; **37** 23; a term always applied to idol-worship or to objects connected with idolatry; often also tr[d] "abomination," as in 1 K **11** 5.7 (*bis*); Jer **4** 1; Ezk **20** 7.8.30. *Sheḳeç,* tr[d] "abomination," is applied in the Scriptures to that which is ceremonially unclean (Lev **7** 21), creatures forbidden as food, as water animals without fins or scales (**11** 10–12), birds of prey and the like (ver 18), winged creeping things (vs 20.23), creeping vermin (vs 41 f). Cf also Isa **66** 17. By partaking of the food of the animals in question one makes himself detestable (Lev **11** 43; **20** 25). Similarly the idolatrous appurtenances are to be held in detestation; nothing of the kind should be appropriated for private use (Dt **7** 26). See Abomination.

Max L. Margolis

DEUEL, dū′el, dḗ-ū′el (דְּעוּאֵל, *de'ū'ēl,* "knowledge of God"): A Gadite, the father of Eliasaph, the representative of the tribe of Gad in the census-taking (Nu **1** 14), in making the offering of the tribe at the dedication of the altar (**7** 42.47), and as leader of the host of the tribe of the children of Gad in the wilderness (**10** 20). Called **Reuel** in Nu **2** 14, ד (*d*) being confused with ר (*r*).

DEUTERO-CANONICAL, dū-tēr-ō-ka-non′i-kal, **BOOKS:** A term sometimes used to designate certain books, which by the Council of Trent were included in the OT, but which the Protestant churches designated as apocryphal (see Apocrypha), and also certain books of the NT which for a long time were not accepted by the whole church as Scripture. Webster says the term pertains to "a second Canon or ecclesiastical writing of inferior authority," and the history of these books shows that they were all at times regarded by a part of the church as being inferior to the others and some of them are so regarded today. This second Canon includes Tob, Jth, Wisd, Ecclus, 2 Esd, 1 Macc and 2 Macc of the OT, and He, Jas, 2 Pet, 2 Jn, 3 Jn, Jude and Rev of the NT.

1. The OT Books

The OT books under consideration were not in the Heb Canon and they were originally designated as apocryphal. The LXX contained many of the apoc books, and among these were most of those which we have designated deutero-canonical. The LXX was perhaps the Gr Bible of NT times and it continued to be the OT of the early church, and hence these books were widely distributed. It seems, however, that they did not continue to hold their place along with the other books, for Athanasius, bishop of Alex, in his *Festal Epistle* in 367 gave a list of the books of the Bible which were to be read, and at the close of this list he said: "There are also other books besides these, not canonized, yet set by the Fathers to be read to those who have just come up and who wish to be informed as to the word of godliness: Wisd, Sir, Est, Jth, Tob, the so-called Teaching of the Apos, and the Shepherd of Hermas." Jerome also made a distinction between the apoc books and the others. In his Preface, after enumerating the books contained in the Heb Canon, he adds: "This prologue I write as a preface to the books to be translated by us from the Heb into Lat, that we may know that all the books which are not of this number are apoc; therefore Wisd, which is commonly ascribed to Solomon as its author, and the book of Jesus the son of Sir, Jth, Tob and the Shep are not in the Canon." Rufinus made the same distinction as did Jerome. He declared that "these books are not canonical, but have been called by our forefathers ecclesiastical." Augustine included these books in his list which he published in 397. He begins the list thus: "The entire canon of Scripture is comprised in these books." Then follows a list of the books which includes Tob, Jth, 1 Macc, 2 Macc, 2 Esd, Wisd and Ecclus, and it closes with these words: "In these 44 books is comprised all the authority of the OT." Inasmuch as these books were regarded by the church at large as ecclesiastical and helpful, and Augustine had given them canonical sanction, they rapidly gained in favor and most of them are found in the great MSS. See Canon of the OT.

It is not probable that there was any general council of the church in those early centuries that set apart the various books of the NT and canonized them as Scripture for the whole church. There was no single historical event which brought together the NT books which were everywhere to be regarded as Scripture. These books did not make the same progress in the various provinces and churches. A careful study of conditions reveals the fact that there was no uniform NT canon in the church during at least the first 3 cents. The Ethiopic church, for example, had 35 books in its NT, while the Syrian church had only 22 books.

2. The NT Books

From an early date the churches were practically agreed on those books which are sometimes designated as the protocanonical, and which Eusebius designated as the homologoumena. They differed, however, in regard to the 7 disputed books which form a part of the so-called deutero-canon, and which Eusebius designated as the **antilegomena**. They also differed in regard to other ecclesiastical writings, for there was no fixed line between canonical and non-canonical books. While there was perhaps no council of the church that had passed on the books and declared them canonical, it is undoubtedly true that before the close of the 2d cent. all the books that are in our NT, with the exception of those under consideration, had become recognized as Scripture in all orthodox churches.

The history of these seven books reveals the fact that although some of them were early used by the Fathers, they afterward fell into disfavor. That is esp. true of He and Rev. Generally speaking, it can be said that at the close of the 2d cent. the 7 books under consideration had failed to receive any such general recognition as had the rest; however, all, with perhaps the exception of 2 Pet, had been used by some of the Fathers. He was freely attested by Clement of Rome and Justin Martyr; Jas by Hermas and probably by Clem of Rome; 2 Jn, 3 Jn and Jude by the Muratorian Fragment; Rev by Hermas and Justin Martyr who names John as its author. See Canon of the NT.

Jerome, who prepared the Vulg in the closing years of the 4th cent., accepted all 7 of the doubtful books, yet he held that 2 Jn and 3 Jn were written by the Presbyter, and he intimated that 2 Pet and Jude were still rejected by some, and he said the Latins did not receive He among the canonical Scriptures, neither did the Gr churches receive Rev. **Augustine,** who was one of the great leaders during the last part of the 4th cent. and the first part of the 5th, accepted without question the 7 disputed books. These books had gradually gained in favor and the position of Jerome and Augustine practically settled their canonicity for the orthodox churches. The Council of Carthage, held in 397, adopted the catalogue of Augustine. This catalogue contained all the disputed books both of the NT and the OT.

Since the Reformation.—The Canon of Augustine became the Canon of the majority of the churches and the OT books which he accepted were added to the Vulg, but there were some who still held to the Canon of Jerome. The awakening of the Reformation inevitably led to a reinvestigation of the Canon, since the Bible was made the source of authority, and some of the disputed books of the NT were again questioned by the Reformers. The position given the Bible by the Reformers led the Rom church to reaffirm its sanction and definitely to fix the books that should be accepted. Accordingly the Council of Trent, which convened in 1546, made the Canon of Augustine, which included the 7 apoc books of the OT, and the 7 disputed books of the NT, the Canon of the church, and it pronounced a curse upon those who did not receive these books. The Protestants at first followed the example of Rome and adopted these books which had long had the sanction of usage as their Bible. Gradually, however, the questioned books of the OT were separated from the others. That was true in Coverdale's tr, and in Matthew's Bible they were not only separated from the others but they were prefaced with the words, "the volume of the book called Hagiographa." In Cranmer's Bible, Hagiographa was changed into Apoc, and this passed through the succeeding ed into the AV. A. W. Fortune

DEUTERONOMY, dū-tẽr-on'ō-mi:

1. Name
2. What Dt Is
3. Analysis
4. Ruling Ideas
5. Unity
6. Authorship
7. Dt Spoken Twice
8. Dt's Influence in Israel's History
9. The Critical Theory

Literature

1. Name

In Heb אֵלֶּה הַדְּבָרִים, *'ēlleh hă-debhārīm,* "these are the words"; in Gr, Δευτερονόμιον, *Deuteronómion,* "second law"; whence the Lat *deuteronomii,* and the Eng. Deuteronomy. The Gr title is due to a mistranslation by the Sept of the clause in Dt **17** 18 rendered, "and he shall write for himself this *repetition* of the law." The Heb really means "and he shall write out for himself a *copy* of this law." However, the error on which the Eng. title rests is not serious, as Dt is in a very true sense a *repetition* of the law.

2. What Dt Is

Dt is the last of the five books of the Pent, or "five-fifths of the Law." It possesses an individuality and impressiveness of its own. In Ex-Nu Jeh is represented as speaking unto Moses, whereas in Dt, Moses is represented as speaking at Jeh's command to Israel (**1** 1-4; **5** 1; **29** 1). It is a hortatory recapitulation of various addresses delivered at various times and places in the desert wanderings—a sort of homily on the constitution, the essence or gist of Moses' instructions to Israel during the forty years of their desert experience. It is "a Book of Reviews"; a tr of Israel's redemptive history into living principles; not so much a history as a commentary. There is much of retrospect in it, but its main outlook is forward. The rabbins speak of it as "the Book of Reproofs." It is the text of all prophecy; a manual of evangelical oratory; possessing "all the warmth of a St. Bernard, the flaming zeal of a Savonarola, and the tender, gracious sympathy of a St. Francis of Assisi." The author's interest is entirely moral. His one supreme purpose is to arouse Israel's loyalty to Jeh and to His revealed law. Taken as a whole the book is an exposition of the great commandment, "Thou shalt love Jeh thy God with all thy heart, and with all thy soul, and with all thy might." It was from Dt Jesus summarized the whole of the Old Covenant in a single sentence (Mt **22** 37; cf Dt **6** 5), and from it He drew His weapons with which to vanquish the tempter (Mt **4** 4.7.10; cf Dt **8** 3; **6** 16.13).

3. Analysis

Dt is composed of three discourses, followed by three short appendices: (1) **1** 1—**4** 43, historical; a review of God's dealings with Israel, specifying in great detail where and when delivered (**1** 1-5), recounting in broad oratorical outlines the chief events in the nation's experience from Horeb to Moab (**1** 6—**3** 29), on which the author bases an earnest appeal to the people to be faithful and obedient, and in particular to keep clear of all possible idolatry (**4** 1-40). Appended to this first discourse is a brief note (vs 41-43) concerning Moses' appointment of three cities of refuge on the E. side of the Jordan. (2) **4** 44—**26** 19, hortatory and legal; introduced by a superscription (**4** 44-49), and consisting of a résumé of Israel's moral and civil statutes, testimonies and judgments. Analyzed in greater detail, this second discourse is composed of two main sections: (*a*) chs **5-11,** an extended exposition of the Ten Commandments on which the theocracy was based;

(*b*) chs **12–26**, a code of special statutes concerning worship, purity, tithes, the three annual feasts, the administration of justice, kings, priests, prophets, war, and the private and social life of the people. The spirit of this discourse is most ethical and religious. The tone is that of a father no less than that of a legislator. A spirit of humanity pervades the entire discourse. Holiness is its ideal. (3) **27** 1—**31** 30, predictive and minatory; the subject of this third discourse being "the blessings of obedience and the curses of disobedience." This section begins with directions to inscribe these laws on plastered stones to be set up on Mt. Ebal (**27** 1–10), to be ratified by an antiphonal ritual of blessings and cursings from the two adjacent mountains, Gerizim and Ebal (vs 11–26). These are followed by solemn warnings against disobedience (**28** 1—**29** 1), and fresh exhortations to accept the terms of the new covenant made in Moab, and to choose between life and death (**29** 2—**30** 20). Moses' farewell charge to Israel and his formal commission of Joshua close the discourse (ch **31**). The section is filled with predictions, which were woefully verified in Israel's later history. The three appendices, spoken of above, close the book: (*a*) Moses' Song (ch **32**), which the great Lawgiver taught the people (the Law was given to the *priests*, **31** 24–27); (*b*) Moses' Blessing (ch **33**), which forecast the future for the various tribes (Simeon only being omitted); (*c*) a brief account of Moses' death and burial (ch **34**) with a noble panegyric on him as the greatest prophet Israel ever had. Thus closes this majestic and marvelously interesting and practical book. Its keyword is "possess"; its central thought is "Jeh has chosen Israel, let Israel choose Jeh."

4. Ruling Ideas

The great central thought of Dt is the unique relation which Jeh as a unique God sustains to Israel as a unique people. "Hear O Israel; Jeh our God is one Jeh." The monotheism of Dt is very explicit. Following from this, as a necessary corollary almost, is the other great teaching of the book, the unity of the sanctuary. The motto of the book might be said to be, "One God, one sanctuary."

(1) *Jehovah, a unique god.*—Jeh is the only God, "There is none else besides him" (**4** 35.39; **6** 4; **32** 39), "He is God of gods, and Lord of lords" (**10** 17), "the living God" (**5** 26), "the faithful God, who keepeth covenant and lovingkindness with them that love him and keep his commandments" (**7** 9), who abominates graven images and every species of idolatry (**7** 25.26; **12** 31; **13** 14; **18** 12; **20** 18; **27** 15), to whom belong the heavens and the earth (**10** 14), who rules over all the nations (**7** 19), whose relation to Israel is near and personal (**28** 58), even that of a Father (**32** 6), whose being is spiritual (**4** 12.15), and whose name is "Rock" (**32** 4.15.18.30.31). Being such a God, He is jealous of all rivals (**7** 4; **29** 24–26; **31** 16.17), and hence all temptations to idolatry must be utterly removed from the land, the Canaanites must be completely exterminated and all their altars, pillars, Asherim and images destroyed (**7** 1–5.16; **20** 16–18; **12** 2.3).

(2) *Israel, a unique people.*—The *old* Israel had become unique through the covenant which Jeh made with them at Horeb, creating out of them "a kingdom of priests, and a holy nation" (Ex **19** 6). The *new* Israel who had been born in the desert were to inherit the blessings vouchsafed to their fathers, through the covenant just now being made in Moab (Dt **26** 16–19; **27** 9; **29** 1; **5** 2.3). By means of it they became the heirs of all the promises given unto their fathers the patriarchs (**4** 31; **7** 12; **8** 18; **29** 13); they too became holy and peculiar, and especially beloved of Jeh (**7** 6; **14** 2.21; **26** 18.19; **28** 9; **4** 37), disciplined, indeed, but for their own good (**8** 2.3.5.16), to be established as a people, as Jeh's peculiar lot and inheritance (**32** 6.9; **4** 7).

(3) *The relation between Jehovah and Israel a unique relation.*—Other nations feared their deities; Israel was expected not only to fear Jeh but to love Him and cleave to Him (**4** 10; **5** 29; **6** 5; **10** 12.20; **11** 1.13.22; **13** 3.4; **17** 19; **19** 9; **28** 58; **30** 6.16.20; **31** 12.13). The highest privileges are theirs because they are partakers of the covenant blessings; all others are strangers and foreigners, except they be admitted into Israel by special permission (**23** 1–8).

5. Unity

The essential unity of the great kernel of Dt (chs **5–26**) is recognized and freely allowed by nearly everyone (e.g. Kautzsch, Kuenen, Dillmann, Driver). Some would even defend the unity of the whole of chs **1–26** (Knobel, Graf, Kosters, Colenso, Kleinert). No other book of the OT, unless it be the prophecies of Ezekiel, bears such unmistakable signs of unity in aim, language and thought. "The literary style of Dt," says Driver, "is very marked and individual; in his command of a chaste, yet warm and persuasive eloquence, the author of Dt stands unique among the writers of the OT" (*Dt*, lxxvii, lxxxviii). Many striking expressions characterize the style of this wonderful book of oratory: e.g. "cause to inherit"; "Hear O Israel"; the oft-repeated root, meaning in the Ḳal vb.-species "learn," and in the Piel vb.-species "teach"; "be willing"; "so shalt thou exterminate the evil from thy midst"; "as at this day"; "that it may be well with thee"; "the land whither thou goest in to possess it"; "with all thy heart and with all thy soul"; and many others, all of which occur frequently in Dt and rarely elsewhere in the OT, thus binding, so far as style can, the different sections of the book into one solid unit. Barring various titles and editorial additions (**1** 1–5; **4** 44–49; **29** 1; **33** 1.7.9.22; **34** 1) and a few archaeological notes such as **2** 10–12.20–23; **3** 9.11.14; **10** 6–9, and of course the last chapter, which gives an account of Moses' death, there is every reason necessary for supposing that the book is a unit. Few writings in the entire field of literature have so clear a unity of purpose or so uniform a style of address.

6. Authorship

There is one passage bearing upon the authorship of Dt wherein it is stated most explicitly that Moses wrote "this law." It reads, "And Moses wrote this law, and delivered it unto the priests the sons of Levi. . . . . And it came to pass, when Moses had made an end of writing the words of this law in a book, until they were finished [i.e. to the end], that Moses commanded the Levites, that bare the ark of the covenant of Jeh, saying, Take this book of the law, and put it by the side of the ark of the covenant of Jeh your God, that it may be there for a witness against thee" (Dt **31** 9.24–27). This passage is of more than traditional value, and should not be ignored as is so often done (e.g. by Ryle, art. "Dt," *HDB*). It is not enough to say that Moses was the great fountain-head of Heb law, that he gave oral but not written statutes, or, that Moses was only the traditional source of these statutes. For it is distinctly and emphatically stated that "Moses wrote this law." And it is further declared (**31** 22) that "Moses wrote this song," contained in ch **32**. Now, these statements are either true, or they are false. There is no escape. The authorship of no other book in the OT is so explicitly emphasized. The present writer believes that Moses actually wrote the great body of Dt, and for the following general reasons:

(1) *Dt as a whole is eminently appropriate to what we know of Moses' times.*—It closes most fittingly

the formative period of Israel's history. The historical situation from first to last is that of Moses. The references to foreign neighbors—Egypt, Canaan, Amalek, Ammon, Moab, Edom—are in every case to those who flourished in Moses' own times. As a law book its teaching is based upon the Ten Commandments. If Moses gave the Ten Commandments, then surely he may have written the Book of Dt also. Besides, the Code of Ḥammurabi, which antedates Moses by at least 700 years, makes it possible certainly that Moses also left laws in codified or written form.

(2) *Dt is represented as emanating from Moses.*—The language is language put into Moses' mouth. Nearly forty times his name occurs, and in the majority of instances as the authoritative author of the subject-matter. The first person is used predominatingly throughout: "I commanded Joshua at that time" (**3** 21); and "I charged your judges at that time" (**1** 16); "And I commanded you at that time" (ver 18); "I have led you forty years in the wilderness" (**29** 5). "The language surely purports to come from Moses; and if it was not actually used by him, it is a most remarkable case of impersonation, if not of literary forgery, for the writer represents himself as reproducing, not what Moses might have said. but the exact words of Moses" (Zerbe, *The Antiquity of Heb Writing and Lit.*, 1911, 261).

(3) *Dt is a military law book, a code of conquest, a book of exhortation.*—It was intended primarily neither for Israel in the desert nor for Israel settled in Canaan, but for Israel on the borderland, eager for conquest. It is expressly stated that Moses taught Israel these statutes and judgments in order that they should obey them in the land which they were about to enter (**4** 5.14; **5** 31). They must expel the aborigines (**7** 1; **9** 1–3; **20** 17; **31** 3), but in their warfare they must observe certain laws in keeping with the theocracy (**20** 1–20; **23** 9–14; **21** 10–14; **31** 6.7), and, when they have finally dispossessed their enemies, they must settle down to agricultural life and live no longer as nomads but as citizens of a civilized land (**19** 14; **22** 8–10; **24** 19–21). All these laws are regulations which should become binding in the future only (cf Kittel, *History of the Hebrews*, I, 32). Coupled with them are prophetic exhortations which seem to be genuine, and to have had their birth in Moses' soul. Indeed the great outstanding feature of Dt is its parenetic or hortatory character. Its exhortations have not only a military ring as though written on the eve of battle, but again and again warn Israel against allowing themselves to be conquered in religion through the seductions of idolatry. The book in short is the message of one who is interested in Israel's political and religious *future*. There is a paternal vein running throughout it which marks it with a genuine Mosaic, not a merely fictitious or artificial, stamp. It is these general features, so characteristic of the entire book, which compel one to believe in its Mosaic authorship.

7. Dt Spoken Twice

Certain literary features exist in Dt which lead the present writer to think that *the bulk of the book was spoken twice;* once, to the first generation between Horeb and Kadesh-barnea in the 2d year of the Exodus wanderings, and a second time to the new generation, in the plains of Moab in the 40th year. Several considerations point in this direction:

(1) *The names of the widely separated geographical places mentioned in the title* (***1*** *1.2*).—"These are the words which Moses spake unto all Israel beyond the Jordan in the wilderness, in the Arabah over against Suph, between Paran, and Tophel, and Laban, and Hazeroth, and Di-zahab"; to which is added, "It is eleven days' journey from Horeb by the way of Mount Seir unto Kadesh-barnea." If these statements have any relevancy whatever to the contents of the book which they introduce, they point to a wide area, from Horeb to Moab, as the historico-geographical background of the book. In other words, Dt, in part at least, seems to have been spoken first on the way between Horeb and Kadesh-barnea, and later again when Israel were encamped on the plains of Moab. And, indeed, what would be more natural than for Moses when marching northward from Horeb expecting to enter Canaan *from the south,* to exhort the Israel of that day in terms of chs **5–26**? Being baffled, however, by the adverse report of the spies and the faithlessness of the people, and being forced to wait and wander for 38 years, what would be more natural than for Moses in Moab, when about to resign his position as leader, to repeat the exhortations of chs **5–26,** adapting them to the needs of the new desert-trained generation and prefacing the whole by a historical introduction such as that found in chs **1–4**?

(2) *The double allusion to the cities of refuge* (***4*** *41–43;* ***19*** *1–13*).—On the supposition that chs **5–26** were spoken first between Horeb and Kadesh-barnea, in the 2d year of the Exodus, it could not be expected that in this section the names of the three cities chosen E. of the Jordan should be given, and in fact they are not (**19** 1–13); the territory of Sihon and Og had not yet been conquered and the cities of refuge, accordingly, had not yet been designated (cf Nu **35** 2 14). But in **4** 41–43, on the contrary, which forms a part of the historical introduction, which *ex hypothesi* was delivered just at the end of the 39 years' wanderings, after Sihon and Og had been subdued and their territory divided, the three cities of refuge E. of the Jordan are actually named, just as might be expected.

(3) *The section* ***4*** *44–49,* which, in its original form, very probably introduced chs **5–26** before these chapters were adapted to the new situation in Moab.

(4) *The phrase "began Moses to declare this law"* (***1*** *5*), suggesting that the great lawgiver found it necessary to expound what he had delivered at some previous time. The Heb word tr[d] "to declare" is found elsewhere in the OT only in Dt **27** 8 and in Hab **2** 2, and signifies "to make plain."

(5) *The author's evident attempt to identify the new generation in Moab with the patriarchs.*—"Jeh made not this covenant with our fathers, but with us, even us, who are all of us here alive this day," i.e. with us who have survived the desert discipline (Dt **5** 3). In view of these facts, we conclude that the book in its present form (barring the exceptions above mentioned) is the product of the whole 39 years of desert experience from Horeb on, adapted, however, to meet the exigencies of the Israelites as they stood between the victories already won on the E. of the Jordan and those anticipated on the W. The impression given throughout is that the aged lawgiver's work is done, and that a new era in the people's history is about to begin.

8. Dt's Influence in Israel's History

The influence of Dt began to be felt from the very beginning of Israel's career in Canaan. Though the references to Dt in Josh, Jgs, S and K are comparatively few, yet they are sufficient to show that not only the principles of Dt were known and observed but that they were known in written form as codified statutes. For example, when Jericho was taken, the city and its spoil were "devoted" (Josh **6** 17.18) in keeping with Dt **13** 15 ff (cf Josh **10** 40; **11** 12.15 with Dt **7** 2; **20** 16.17). Achan trespassed and he and his household were stoned, and afterward burned with fire (Josh **7** 25; cf Dt **13** 10; **17** 5). The fact that his sons and his daughters were put to death with him seems at first sight to contradict Dt **24** 16, but there is no proof that they suffered *for their father's sin* (see ACHAN; ACHOR); besides the Hebrews recognized the unity of the household, even that of Rahab the harlot (Josh **6** 17). Again when Ai was taken, "only the cattle and the spoil" did Israel take for a prey unto themselves (Josh **8** 27), in keeping with Dt **20** 14; also, the body of the king of Ai was taken down before nightfall from the tree on which he had been hanged (Josh **8** 29), which was in keeping with Dt **21** 23 (cf Josh **10** 26.27). As in warfare, so in worship. For instance, Joshua built an altar on Mt. Ebal (Josh **8** 30.31), "as Moses the servant of Jeh commanded" (Dt **27** 4–6), and he wrote on them a copy of the law (Josh **8** 32), as Moses had also enjoined (Dt **27** 3.8). Moreover, the elders and officers and judges stood on either side of the ark of the covenant between Ebal and Gerizim (Josh **8** 33), as directed in Dt **11** 29; **27** 12.13, and Joshua read to all the congregation of Israel all the words of the law, the blessings and the cursings (Josh **8** 34.35), in strict accord with Dt **31** 11.12.

But the passage of paramount importance is the story of the two and a half tribes who, on their return to their home on the E. side of the Jordan, erected a memorial at the Jordan, and, when accused by their fellow-tribesmen of plurality of sanctuary, emphatically disavowed it (Josh **22** 29; cf Dt **12** 5). Obviously, therefore, Dt was known in the days of Joshua. A very few instances in the history of the Judges point in the same direction: e.g. the utter destruction of Zephath (Jgs **1** 17; cf Dt **7** 2; **20** 16 f); Gideon's elimination of the fearful and faint-hearted from his army (Jgs **7** 1–7; cf Dt **20** 1–9); the author's studied concern to justify Gideon and Manoah for sacrificing at altars other than at Shiloh on the ground that they acted in obedience to Jeh's direct commands (Jgs **6** 25–27; **13** 16); esp. the case of Micah, who congratulated himself that Jeh would do him good seeing he had a Levite for a priest, is clear evidence that Dt was known in the days of the Judges (Jgs **17** 13; cf Dt **10** 8; **18** 1–8; **33** 8–11). In 1 S **1** 1–9.21.24 the pious Elkanah is pictured as going yearly to worship Jeh at Shiloh, the central sanctuary at that time. After the destruction of Shiloh, when the ark of the covenant had been captured by the Philis, Samuel indeed sacrificed at Mizpah, Ramah and Bethlehem (1 S **7** 7–9.17; **16** 5), but in doing so he only took advantage of the elasticity of the Deuteronomic law: "*When* . . . . he giveth you rest from all your enemies round about, so that ye dwell in safety; *then* it shall come to pass that to the place which Jeh your God shall choose, to cause his name to dwell there, thither shall ye bring all that I command you: your burnt-offerings, and your sacrifices" (Dt **12** 10.11). It was not until Solomon's time that Israel's enemies were all subdued, and even then Solomon did not observe strictly the teachings of Dt; "His wives turned away his heart," so that he did not faithfully keep Jeh's "covenant" and "statutes" (1 K **11** 3.11). Political disruption followed, and religion necessarily suffered. Yet Jehoiada the priest gave the youthful Joash "the crown" and "the testimony" (2 K **11** 12; cf Dt **17** 18). King Amaziah did not slay the children of the murderers who slew his father, in conscious obedience apparently to the law of Dt (2 K **14** 6; cf Dt **24** 16). Later on, Hezekiah, the cultured king of Judah, reformed the cultus of his day by removing the high places, breaking down the pillars, cutting down the Asherahs, and even breaking in pieces the brazen serpent which Moses had made (2 K **18** 4.22). Hezekiah's reforms were unquestionably carried through under the influence of Dt.

It is equally certain that the prophets of the 8th cent. were not ignorant of this book. For example, Hosea complains of Israel's sacrificing upon the tops of the mountains and burning incense upon the hills, and warns Judah not to follow Israel's example in coming up to worship at Gilgal and Beth-aven (Hos **4** 13.15). He also alludes to striving with priests (Hos **4** 4; cf Dt **17** 12), removing landmarks (Hos **5** 10; cf Dt **19** 14), returning to Egypt (Hos **8** 13; **9** 3; cf Dt **28** 68), and of Jeh's tender dealing with Ephraim (Hos **11** 3; cf Dt **1** 31; **32** 10). The courage of Amos, the shepherd-prophet of Tekoa, can best be explained, also, on the basis of a written law such as that of Dt with which he and his hearers were already more or less familiar (Am **3** 2; cf Dt **7** 6; **4** 7.8). He condemns Israel's inhumanity and adultery in the name of religion, and complains of their retaining over-night pledges wrested from the poor, which was distinctly forbidden in Dt (Am **2** 6–8; cf Dt **24** 12–15; **23** 17). Likewise, in the prophecies of Isaiah there are conscious reflections of Dt's thought and teaching. Zion is constantly pictured as the center of the nation's religion and as Jeh's secure dwelling-place (Isa **2** 2–4; **8** 18; **28** 16; **29** 1.2; cf Mic **4** 1–4). In short, no one of the four great prophets of the 8th cent. BC—Isaiah, Micah, Amos, Hosea—ever recognized "high places" as legitimate centers of worship.

Over against the Bib. view, certain modern critics since De Wette (1805) advocate a late origin of Dt, claiming that it was first published in 621 BC, when Hilkiah found "the book of the law" in the temple in the 18th year of King Josiah (2 K **22** 8 ff).

9. The Critical Theory

The kernel of Dt and "the book of the law" discovered by Hilkiah are said to be identical. Thus, Dr. G. A. Smith claims that "a code like the Book of Dt was not brought forth at a stroke, but was the expression of the gradual results of the age-long working of the Spirit of the Living God in the hearts of His people" (*Jerusalem*, II, 115). According to Dr. Driver, "Dt may be described as the prophetic reformulation and adaptation to new needs, of an older legislation. It is probable that there was a tradition, if not a written record, of a final legislative address delivered by Moses in the steppes of Moab: the plan followed by the author would rest upon a more obvious motive, if he thus worked upon a traditional basis. But be that as it may, the bulk of the laws contained in Dt is undoubtedly far more ancient than the author himself. . . . . What is essentially new in Dt is not the *matter*, but the *form*. . . . . The new element in Dt is thus not the laws, but their parenetic setting" (*Dt*, lxi, lvi). This refined presentation of the matter would not be so very objectionable, were Drs. Smith and Driver's theory not linked up with certain other claims and allegations to the effect that Moses in the 15th cent. BC could not possibly have promulgated such a lofty monotheism, that in theological teaching "the author of Dt is the spiritual heir of Hosea," that there are discrepancies between it and other parts of the Pent, that in the early history of Israel down to the 8th cent. plurality of sanctuaries was legally permissible, that there are no traces of the influence of the principal teachings of a *written* Dt discoverable in Heb lit. until the time of Jeremiah, and that the book as we possess it was originally composed as a program of reform, not by Moses but in the name of Moses as a forgery or pseudepigraph. For example, F. H. Woods says, "Although not a *necessary* result of accepting the later date, the majority of critics believe this book of the law to have been the result of a pious fraud promulgated by Hilkiah and Shaphan with the intention of deceiving Josiah into the belief that the reforms which they desired were the express command of God revealed to Moses" (*HDB*, II, 368). Some are unwilling to go so far. But in any case, it is claimed that the law book discovered and published by Hilkiah, which brought about the reformation by Josiah in 621 BC, was no other than some portion of the Book of Dt, and of Dt alone. But there are several considerations which are opposed to this theory: (1) Dt emphasizes centralization of worship at one sanctuary (**12** 5); Josiah's reformation was directed rather against idolatry in general (2 K **23** 4 ff). (2) In Dt **18** 6–8, a Levite coming from the country to Jerus was allowed to minister and share in the priestly perquisites; but in 2 K **23** 9, "the priests of the high places came not up to the altar of Jeh in Jerus, but they did eat unleavened bread among their brethren." And according to the critical theory, "Levites" and "priests" are interchangeable terms. (3) The following passages in Ex might almost equally with Dt account for Josiah's reformation: **20** 3; **22** 18.20; **23** 13.24.32.33; **34** 13.14–17. (4) The law book discovered by Hilkiah was recognized at once as an *ancient* code which the fathers had disobeyed (2 K **22** 13). Were they all deceived? Even Jeremiah (cf Jer **11** 3.4)? "There were many persons in Judah who had powerful motives for exposing this forgery if it was one" (Raven, *OT Introduction*, 112). (5) One wonders why so many archaic and, in Josiah's time, apparently obsolete laws should have been incorporated in a code whose express motive was to reform an otherwise hopeless age: e.g. the command to exterminate the Canaanites, who had long since ceased to exist (Dt **7** 18.22), and to blot out Amalek (Dt **25** 17–19), the last remnants of whom were completely destroyed in Hezekiah's time (1 Ch **4** 41–43). Esp. is this true of the score and more of laws *peculiar to Dt*, concerning building battlements on the roofs of houses (Dt **22** 8), robbing birds' nests (vs 6.7), the sexes exchanging garments (ver 5), going out to war (**20** 1 ff), etc. (6) Esp. remarkable is it that if Dt were written, as alleged, shortly before the reign of Josiah, there should be no anachronisms in it betraying a post-Mosaic origin. There are no allusions to the schism between Judah and Israel, no hint of Assyr oppression through the exaction of tribute, nor any threats of Israel's exile either to Assyria or Babylonia, but rather to Egypt (Dt **28** 68). "Jerusalem" is never mentioned. From a literary point of view, it is psychologically and historically well-nigh impossible for a writer to conceal all traces of his age and circumstances. On the other hand, no Egyptologist has ever discovered any anachronisms in Dt touching Egyp matters. From first to last the author depicts the actual situation of the times of Moses. It is consequently hard to believe, as is alleged, that a later writer is studying to give "an imaginative revivification of the past."

(7) The chief argument in favor of Dt's late origin is its alleged teaching concerning the unity of the sanctuary. Wellhausen lays special emphasis upon this point. Prior to Josiah's reformation, it is claimed, plurality of sanctuaries was allowed. But in opposition to this, it is possible to point victoriously to Hezekiah's reformation (2 K **18** 4. 22), as a movement in the direction of unity; and especially to Ex **20** 24, which is so frequently misinterpreted as allowing a multiplicity of sanctuaries. This classical passage when correctly interpreted allows only that altars shall be erected in every place *where Jeh records His name*, "which presumably during the wanderings and the time of the judges would mean *wherever the Tabernacle was*" (Mackay, *Intro to OT*, 110). This interpretation of this passage is confirmed and made practically certain, indeed, by the command in Ex **23** 14–19 that Israel shall repair three times each year *to the house of Jeh* and there present their offering. On the other hand, Dt's emphasis upon unity of sanctuary is often exaggerated. *The Book of Dt requires unity only after Israel's enemies are all overcome* (Dt **12** 10.11). "When" Jeh giveth them rest, "then" they shall repair for worship to the place which "God shall choose." As Davidson remarks: "It is not a law that is to come into effect on their entry into Canaan; it is to be observed from the time that Jeh shall have given them rest from all their enemies round about; that is, from the times of David, or more particularly, Solomon; for only when the temple was built did that place become known which Jeh had chosen to place His name there" (*OT Theology*, 361). Besides, it should not be forgotten that in Dt itself the command is given to build an altar in Mt. Ebal (**27** 5–7). As a matter of fact, the unity of sanctuary follows as a necessary consequence of monotheism; and if Moses taught monotheism, he probably also enjoined unity of worship. If, on the other hand, monotheism was first evolved by the prophets of the 8th cent., then, of course, unity of sanctuary was of 8th-cent. origin also.

(8) Another argument advanced in favor of the later origin of Dt is the contradiction between the laws of Dt and those of Lev-Nu concerning the priests and Levites. In Nu **16** 10.35.40, a sharp distinction is drawn, it is alleged, between the priests and common Levites, whereas in Dt **18** 1–8, all priests are Levites and all Levites are priests. But as a matter of fact, the passage in Dt does not invest a Levite with *priestly* but with Levitical functions (cf **18** 7). "The point insisted upon is that all Levites shall receive full recognition at the sanctuary and be accorded their prerogatives. It goes without saying that if the Levite be a priest he shall serve and fare like his brethren the priests; if he be not a priest, he shall enjoy the privileges that belong to his brethren who are Levites, but not priests" (J. D. Davis, art. "Dt," in *DB*, 117). The Book of Dt teaches not that *all* the tribe, but *only* the tribe of Levi may exercise priestly functions, thus restricting the exercise of priestly prerogatives to one and only one tribe. This was in perfect harmony with Lev-Nu and also in keeping with the style of popular discourse.

(9) Recently Professor Ed. Naville, the Egyptologist, has propounded a theory of the origin of "the Book of the Law" discovered by Hilkiah, which is not without some value. On the analogy of the Egyp custom of burying texts of portions of "the Book of the Dead" at the foot of statues of gods and within foundations of temple walls, as at Hermopolis, he concludes that Solomon, when he constructed the Temple, probably deposited this "Book of the Law" in the foundations, and that when Josiah's workmen were about their tasks of repairing the edifice, the long-forgotten document came to light and was given to Hilkiah the priest. Hilkiah, however, upon examination of the document found it difficult to read, and so, calling for Shaphan the scribe, who was more expert in deciphering antique letters than himself, he gave the sacred roll to him, and he in turn read it to both Hilkiah and the king. The MS may indeed have been written in cuneiform. Thus, according to Naville, "the Book of the Law," which he identifies with Dt, must be pushed back as far as the age of Solomon at the very latest. Geden shares a similar view as to its date: "some time during the prosperous period of David and the United Monarchy" (*Intro to the Heb Bible*, 1909, 330).

But why not ascribe the book to the traditional author? Surely there can be no philosophical objection to doing so, in view of the now-known Code of Ḥammurabi, which antedates Moses by so many hundreds of years! No other age accounts so well for its origin as that of the great lawgiver who claims to have written the bulk of it. And the history of the disintegration of the book only shows to what extremes a false method may lead; for example, Steuernagel separates the "Thou" and "Ye" sections from each other and assigns them to different authors of late date: Kennett, on the other hand, assigns the earliest strata to the period of the Exile (*Jour. of Theol. Studies*, 1904). On the whole, no theory is so satisfactory as that which, in keeping with Dt **31** 22.24, ascribes to Moses the great bulk of the book. See also CRITICISM; PENTATEUCH.

LITERATURE.—On the conservative side: James Orr, *The Problem of the OT*, The Bross Prize, 1906; art. "Dt," *Illustrated Bible Dict.*, 1908; James Robertson, *The Early Religion of Israel*, 1892; art. "Dt," *The Temple Bible Dict.*, 1910; John D. Davis, art. "Dt," Davis' *Dict. of the Bible*, 1911; John H. Raven, *OT Intro*, 1906; A. S. Geden, *Intro to the Heb Bible*, 1909; W. Möller, *Are the Critics Right?* 1903; R. B. Girdlestone, *The Student's Dt*, 1899; Hugh Pope, *The Date of the Composition of Dt*, 1911; A. S. Zerbe, *The Antiquity of Heb Writing and Lit.*, 1911; Ed. Naville, *The Discovery of the Book of the Law under King Josiah*, 1911; E. C. Bissell, *The Pent: Its Origin and Structure*, 1885; G. L. Robinson, *The Expositor*, "The Genesis of Dt," October and November, 1898, February, March, May, 1899; W. H. Green, *Moses and the Prophets*, 1891; *The Higher Criticism of the Pent*, 1895; A. M. Mackay, *The Churchman's Intro to the OT*, 1901; J. W. Beardslee, *Outlines of an Intro to the OT*, 1903; G. Vos, *The Mosaic Origin of the Pentateuchal Codes*, 1886.

On the other side: S. R. Driver, *A Crit. and Exeg. Comm. on Dt*, 1895; *The Hexateuch*, by J. Estlin Carpenter and G. Harford-Battersby, I, II, 1900; G. A. Smith, *Jerus*, II, 1908; W. Robertson Smith, *The OT in the Jewish Church*, 1895; A. Kuenen, *The Hexateuch*, 1886; H. E. Ryle, art. "Dt," *HDB*, 1898; G. F. Moore, art. "Dt," *Enc Bibl.*, 1899; J. A. Paterson, art. "Dt," *Enc Brit*, VIII, 1910.

In German: De Wette, *Dissert. crit-exeget.*, 1805; Kleinert, *Das Dt u. d. Deuteronomiker*, 1872; Wellhausen, *Die Comp. des Hex. u. d. hist. Bücher des AT*, 1889; *Gesch. Israels*, 1895; Steuernagel, *Der Rahmen des Dt*, 1894; *Entsteh. des dt. Gesetzes*, 1896.

GEORGE L. ROBINSON

DEVICE, dē̆-vīs′: "A scheme," "invention," "plot." In the OT it stands for six Heb words, of which the most common is *maḥăshebheth* (from *ḥāshabh*, "to think," "contrive"). In the NT it occurs only twice, once for Gr *enthúmēsis* (Acts **17** 29), and once for *nóēma* (2 Cor **2** 11). Sometimes the word means simply that which is planned or invented, without any evil implication, as in 2 Ch **2** 14; Acts **17** 29 (of artistic work or invention), and Eccl **9** 10 (in the general sense of reasoning or contriving). But more frequently it is used in an evil sense, of a wicked purpose or plot, "Let us devise devices against Jeremiah" (Jer **18** 18); "For we are not ignorant of his [i.e. Satan's] devices" (2 Cor **2** 11), etc. D. MIALL EDWARDS

DEVIL, dev′'l. See DEMON; SATAN.

DEVOTED, dē̆-vōt′ed, **THINGS** (חֵרֶם, *ḥērem*). See CURSE; DEDICATE.

DEVOTION, dē̆-vō′shun, **DEVOTIONS** (σεβάσματα, *sebásmata*): For AV "your devotions" (Acts **17** 23), RV has "the objects of your worship," which is probably the intended meaning of AV. RV reads "devotion" for AV "prayer" in Job **15** 4 (RVm "meditation," Heb *sīaḥ*).

DEVOUT, dē̆-vout′ (εὐλαβής, *eulabḗs*, εὐσεβής, *eusebḗs*, σέβομαι, *sébomai*, "pious," "dutiful," "reverential"): The word is peculiar to St. Luke. Applied to Simeon (Lk **2** 25), Cornelius (Acts **10** 2.7), Ananias (**22** 12). "Devout proselytes" (**13** 43, AV "religious proselytes"), with possible reference to the proselytes of righteousness as distinguished from the proselytes of the gate (see PROSELYTE). "Devout women of honorable estate" (**13** 50), proselytes to Judaism and wives of the men in high position among the heathen (see Jos, *BJ*, II, xx, 2). "Devout Greeks" (**17** 4), probably, though not necessarily, proselytes of the gate, heathen by birth, who attended the synagogue services and worshipped God. "Devout persons" (ver 17), proselytes of the gate. M. O. EVANS

DEW, dū (טַל, *ṭal;* δρόσος, *drósos*): Two things are necessary for the formation of dew, moisture and cold. In moist countries there is less dew because the change in temperature between day and night is too small. In the deserts where the change in temperature between day and night is sometimes as much as 40° F., there is seldom dew because of lack of moisture in the atmosphere. Pal is fortunate in being near the sea, so that there is always a large percentage of water vapor in the air. The skies are clear, and hence there is rapid radiation beginning immediately after sunset, which cools the land and the air until the moisture is condensed and settles on cool objects. Air at a low temperature is not capable of holding as much water vapor in suspension as warm air. The ice pitcher furnishes an example of the formation of dew. Just as the drops of water form on the cool pitcher, so dew forms on rocks, grass and trees.

1. Formation of Dew

In Pal it does not rain from April to October, and were it not for the dew in summer all vegetation would perish. Dew and rain are equally important. If there is no rain the winter grass and harvests fail; if no dew, the late crops dry up and there is no fruit. Failure of either of these gifts of Nature would cause great want and hardship, but the failure of both would cause famine and death. Even on the edge of the great Syrian desert in Anti-Lebanon, beyond Jordan and in Sinai, a considerable vegetation of a certain kind flourishes in the summer, although there is not a drop of rain for six months. The dews are so heavy that the plants and trees are literally soaked with water at night, and they absorb sufficient moisture to more than supply the loss due to evaporation in the day. It is more surprising to one who has not seen it before to find a flourishing vineyard practically in the desert itself. Some of the small animals of the desert, such as the jerboa, seem to have no water supply except the dew. The dew forms most heavily on good conductors of heat, such as metals and stones, because they radiate their heat faster and cool the air around them. The wetting of Gideon's fleece (Jgs **6** 38) is an indication of the amount of dew formed, and the same phenomenon might be observed any clear night in summer in Pal.

2. Value of Dew in Palestine

Dew was a present necessity to the people of Israel as it is today to the people of the same lands, so Jeh says, "I will be as the dew unto Israel" (Hos **14** 5). Dew and rain are of equal importance and are spoken of together in 1 K **17** 1. It was esp. valued by the children of Israel in the desert, for it supplied the manna for their sustenance (Ex **16** 13; Nu **11** 9).

3. Importance to Israel

Isaac in blessing Jacob asked that the "dew of heaven" (Gen **27** 28) may be granted to him; that these things which make for fertility and prosperity may be his portion. "The remnant of Jacob shall be in the midst of many peoples as dew from Jeh" (Mic **5** 7), as a means of blessing to the nations. "Blessed of Jeh for . . . . dew" (Dt **33** 13).

4. Symbol of Blessing

5. Symbol of Refreshment

Dew is the means of refreshing and reinvigorating all vegetation. Many Scripture references carry out this idea. The song of Moses says, "My speech shall distil as the dew" (Dt **32** 2). "A cloud of dew" (Isa **18** 4) refreshes the harvesters. "My head is filled with dew" (Cant **5** 2). "Like the dew of Hermon" (Ps **133** 3). "Thou hast the dew of thy youth" (Ps **110** 3). "Thy dew is as the dew of herbs" (Isa **26** 19). Job said of the time of his prosperity, "The dew lieth all night upon my branch" (Job **29** 19).

Other **figures** use dew as the symbol of stealth, of that which comes up unawares (2 S **17** 12), and of inconstancy (Hos **6** 4; **13** 3). God's knowledge covers the whole realm of the phenomena of Nature which are mysteries to man (Job **38** 28; Prov **3** 20). ALFRED H. JOY

DIADEM, dī'a-dem: There are seven Bible references to the diadem, four in the OT and three in the NT. The Heb words do not mark any clear distinctions.

(1) צָנִיף, *çānīph*, צָנוֹף, *çānōph*, צְנִיפָה, *çānīphāh* (all from צָנַף, *çānaph*, primarily "to wrap," "dress," "roll") mean a headdress in the nature of a turban or piece of cloth wrapped or twisted about the head. The word is also rendered "hood," "mitre." Job **29** 14: "My justice was as a robe and a diadem" (RVm, "turban"); Isa **62** 3: "a royal diadem in the hand of thy God."

(2) צְפִירָה, *çᵉphīrāh*, means "a crown," "diadem," i.e. something round about the head; Isa **28** 5: "a diadem of beauty, unto the residue of his people."

(3) מִצְנֶפֶת, *miçnepheth*, means an official turban or tiara of priest or king, trd also "mitre." Ezk **21** 26: "Remove the mitre, and take off the crown."

(4) διάδημα, *diádēma*, the Gr word in the NT for "diadem," means "something bound about the head." Found 3 t, all in Rev—**12** 3: "a great red dragon . . . . and upon his heads seven diadems" (AV "crowns"); **13** 1: "a beast . . . . and on his horns ten diadems"; **19** 11.12: "a white horse . . . . and upon his head are many diadems." See CROWN. WILLIAM EDWARD RAFFETY

DIAL, dī'al, OF AHAZ, ā'haz, THE:

1. Hezekiah's Sickness and the Sign
2. The Sign a Real Miracle
3. The "Dial" a Staircase
4. Time of Day of the Miracle
5. Hezekiah's Choice of the Sign
6. Meaning of the Sign
7. The Fifteen "Songs of Degrees"

1. Hezekiah's Sickness and the Sign

One of the most striking instances recorded in Holy Scripture of the interruption, or rather reversal, of the working of a natural law is the going back of the shadow on the dial of Ahaz at the time of Hezekiah's recovery from his illness. The record of the incident is as follows. Isaiah was sent to Hezekiah in his sickness, to say:

"Thus saith Jehovah, the God of David thy father, I have heard thy prayer, I have seen thy tears: behold, I will heal thee; on the third day thou shalt go up unto the house of Jehovah. . . . . And Hezekiah said unto Isaiah, What shall be the sign that Jehovah will heal me, and that I shall go up unto the house of Jehovah the third day? And Isaiah said, This shall be the sign unto thee from Jehovah, that Jehovah will do the thing that he hath spoken: shall the shadow go forward ten steps, or go back ten steps? And Hezekiah answered, It is a light thing for the shadow to decline ten steps: nay, but let the shadow return backward ten steps. And Isaiah the prophet cried unto Jehovah; and he brought the shadow ten steps backward, by which it had gone down on the dial of Ahaz" (2 K **20** 5–11). And in Isa **38** 8, it is said, "Behold, I will cause the shadow on the steps, which is gone down on the dial of Ahaz with the sun, to return backward ten steps. So the sun returned ten steps on the dial whereon it was gone down."

2. The Sign a Real Miracle

The first and essential point to be noted is that this was no ordinary astronomical phenomenon, nor was it the result of ordinary astronomical laws then unknown. It was peculiar to that particular place, and to that particular time; otherwise we should not read of "the ambassadors of the princes of Babylon, who sent . . . . to inquire of the wonder that was done in the land" (2 Ch **32** 31). It is impossible, therefore, to accept the suggestion that the dial of Ahaz may have been improperly constructed, so as to produce a reversal of the motion of the shadow at certain times. For such a maladjustment would have occasioned the repetition of the phenomenon every time the sun returned to the same position with respect to the dial. The narrative, in fact, informs us that the occurrence was not due to any natural law, known or unknown, since Hezekiah was given the choice and exercised it of his own free will, as to whether a shadow should move in a particular direction or in the opposite. But there are no alternative results in the working of a natural law. "If a state of things is repeated in every detail, it must lead to exactly the same consequences." The same natural law cannot indifferently produce one result, or its opposite. The movement of the shadow on the dial of Ahaz was, therefore, a miracle in the strict sense of the term. It cannot be explained by the working of any astronomical law, known or unknown. We have no information as to the astronomical conditions at the time; we can only inquire into the setting of the miracle.

3. The "Dial" a Staircase

It is unfortunate that one important word in the narrative has been rendered in both AV and RV by a term which describes a recognized astronomical instrument. The word "dial" (*ma'ălōth*) is usually trd "degrees," "steps," or "stairs," and indeed is thus rendered in the same verse. There is no evidence that the structure referred to had been designed to serve as a dial or was anything other than a staircase, "the staircase of Ahaz." It was probably connected with that "covered way for the sabbath that they had built in the house, and the king's entry without," which Ahaz turned "round the house of Jeh, because of the king of Assyria" (2 K **16** 18 RVm). This staircase, called after Ahaz because the alteration was due to him, may have been substituted for David's "causeway that goeth up," which was "westward, by the gate of Shallecheth" (1 Ch **26** 16), or more probably for Solomon's "ascent by which he went up unto the house of Jehovah" which so impressed the queen of Sheba (2 Ch **9** 4). At certain times of the day the shadow of some object fell upon this staircase, and we learn

4. Time of Day of the Miracle

from both 2 K and Isa that this shadow had already gone down ten steps, while from Isa we learn in addition that the sun also was going down. The miracle therefore took place in the afternoon, when the sun moves on its downward course, and when all shadows are thrown in an easterly direction. We are not told what was the object that cast the shadow, but it must have stood to the west of the staircase, and the top of the staircase must have passed into the shadow first, and the foot of the staircase have remained longest in the light. The royal palace is understood to have been placed southeast of the Temple, and it is therefore probable that it was some part of the Temple buildings that had cast its shadow down the stairway in full view of the dying king, as he lay in his chamber. If the afternoon were well advanced the sun would be moving rapidly in altitude, and but little in azimuth; or, in other words, the shadow would be advancing down the steps at its quickest rate, but be moving only slowly toward the left of those who were mounting them. It may well have been the case, therefore, that the time had come when the priests from Ophel, and the officials and courtiers from the palace, were going up the ascent into the house of the Lord to be present at the evening sacrifice; passing from the bright sunshine at the foot of the stairs into the shadow that had already fallen upon the upper steps. The sun would be going straight down behind the buildings and the steps already in shadow would sink into deeper shadow, not to emerge again into the light until a new day's sun had arisen upon the earth.

5. Hezekiah's Choice of the Sign

We can therefore understand the nature of the choice of the sign that was offered by the prophet to the dying king. Would he choose that ten more steps should be straightway engulfed in the shadow, or that ten steps already shadowed should be brought back into the light? Either might serve as a sign that he should arise on the third day and go up in renewed life to the house of the Lord; but the one sign would be in accordance with the natural progress of events, and the other would be directly opposed to it. It would be a light thing, as Hezekiah said, for the shadow to go forward ten steps; a bank of cloud rising behind the Temple would effect that change. But no disposition of cloud could bring the shadow back from that part of the staircase which had already passed into it, and restore it to the sunshine. The first change was, in human estimation, easily possible, "a light thing"; the second change seemed impossible. Hezekiah chose the seemingly impossible, and the Lord gave the sign and answered his prayer. We need not ask whether the king showed more or less faith in choosing the "impossible" rather than the "possible" sign. His father Ahaz had shown his want of faith by refusing to put the Lord to the test, by refusing to ask a sign, whether in the heaven above or in the earth beneath. The faith of Hezekiah was shown in asking a sign, which was at once in the heaven above and in the earth beneath, in accepting the choice offered to him, and so putting the Lord to the test. And the sign chosen was most fitting. Hezekiah lay dying, whether of plague or of cancer we do not know, but his disease was mortal and beyond cure; he was already entering into the shadow of death. The word of the Lord was sure to him; on "the third day" he would rise and go up in new life to the house of God. But what of the sign? Should the shadow

6. Meaning of the Sign

of death swallow him up; should his life be swiftly cut off in darkness, and be hidden until a new day should dawn, and the light of a new life, a life of resurrection, arise? (Cf Jn **11** 24.) Or should the shadow be drawn back swiftly, and new years be added to his life before death could come upon him? Swift death was in the natural progress of events; restoration to health was of the impossible. He chose the restoration to health, and the Lord answered his faith and his prayer.

We are not able to go farther into particulars. The first temple, the royal palace, and the staircase of Ahaz were all destroyed in the destruction of Jerus by Nebuchadnezzar, and we have no means of ascertaining the exact position of the staircase with respect to Temple or palace, or the number of the steps that it contained, or the time of the day, or the season of the year when the sign was given. It is possible that if we knew any or all of these, a yet greater significance, both spiritual and astronomical, might attach to the narrative.

7. The Fifteen "Songs of Degrees"

Fifteen years were added to the life of Hezekiah. In the restoration of the second temple by Herod fifteen steps led from the Court of the Women to the Court of Israel, and on these steps the Levites during the Feast of Tabernacles were accustomed to stand in order to sing the fifteen "songs of degrees" (Pss **120**-**34**). At the head of these same steps in the gateway, lepers who had been cleansed from their disease presented themselves to the priests. It has been suggested that Hezekiah himself was the compiler of these fifteen "songs of the steps," in thankfulness for his fifteen years of added life. Five of them are ascribed to David or as written for Solomon, but the remaining ten bear no author's name. Their subjects are, however, most appropriate to the great crises and desires of Hezekiah's life. His great Passover, to which all the tribes were invited, and so many Israelites came; the blasphemy of Rabshakeh and of Sennacherib's threatening letter; the danger of the Assyr invasion and the deliverance from it; Hezekiah's sickness unto death and his miraculous restoration to health; and the fact that at that time he would seem to have had no son to follow him on the throne—all these subjects seem to find fitting expression in the fifteen Psalms of the Steps.

E. W. Maunder

DIAMOND, dī'a-mund. See Stones, Precious.

DIANA, dī-an'a (**ARTEMIS**) (Ἄρτεμις, *Artemis*, "prompt," "safe"): A deity of Asiatic origin, the mother goddess of the earth, whose seat of worship was the temple in Ephesus, the capital of the Rom province of Asia. Diana is but the Latinized form of the Gr word Artemis, yet the Artemis of Ephesus should not be confused with the Gr goddess of that name.

She may, however, be identified with the Cybele of the Phrygians whose name she also bore, and with several other deities who were worshipped under different names in various parts of the Orient. In Cappadocia she was known as Ma; to the Syrians as Atargatis or Mylitta; among the Phoenicians as Astarte, a name which appears among the Assyrians as Ishtar; the modern name Esther is derived from it. The same goddess seems to have been worshipped by the Hittites, for a female deity is sculptured on the rocks at Yazili Kaya, near the Hittite city of Boghazkeui. It may be shown ultimately that the various goddesses of Syria and Asia Minor all owe their origin to the earlier Assyrian or Babylonian Ishtar, the goddess of love, whose chief attributes they possessed. The several forms and names under which she appears are due to the varying developments in different regions.

Tradition says that Diana was born in the woods near Ephesus, where her temple was built, when her image of wood (possibly ebony; Pliny, *NH*, xvi. 40; Acts **19** 35) fell from the sky (see also Astronomy, I, 8 [2]). Also according to tradition the city which was later called Ephesus was founded by the Amazons, and Diana or Cybele was the deity of those half-mythical people. Later when Ephesus fell into the possession of the Greeks, Gr civilization partly supplanted the Asiatic, and in that city the two civilizations were blended together. The Gr name of Artemis was given to the Asiatic goddess, and many of the Gr colonists represented her on their coins as Greek. Her images and forms of worship remained more Asiatic than Gr. Her earliest statues were figures crudely carved in wood. Later when she was represented in stone and metals, she bore upon her head a mural headdress, representing a fortified city wall; from it, drapery hung upon each side of her face to her shoulders. The upper part of her body was completely covered with rows of breasts to signify that she was the mother of all life. The lower arms were extended. The lower part of the body resembled a rough block, as if her legs had been wrapped up in cloth like those of an Egyp mummy. In later times her Gr followers represented her with stags or lions standing at her sides. The most renowned of her statues stood on the platform before the entrance to her temple in Ephesus. As the statues indicate, she impersonated the reproductive powers of men and of animals and of all other life.

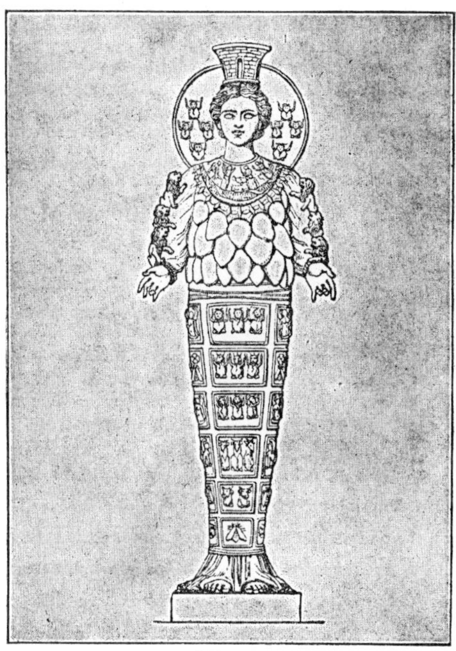

Diana.

At the head of her cult was a chief priest, originally a eunuch who bore the name and later the title Megabyzos. Under him were priests known as Essenes, appointed, perhaps from the city officials, for but a single year; it was their duty to offer the sacrifices to the goddess in behalf of the city. Other subordinate classes of priests known as *Kourētes*, *Krouatai* and *Hilroi* performed duties which are now obscure. The priestesses were even more numerous, and, probably from their great numbers, they were called *Melissai* or bees; the Ephesian symbol therefore which appears commonly upon the coins struck in the city, is a bee. The *Melissai*, which in the early times were all virgins, were of three classes; it is no longer known just what the special duties of each class were. The ritual of the temple services consisted of sacrifices and of ceremonial prostitution, a practice which was common to many of the religions of the ancient Orient, and which still exists among some of the obscure tribes of Asia Minor.

The temple of Diana was not properly the home of the goddess; it was but a shrine, the chief one, devoted to her service. She lived in Nature; she was everywhere wherever there was life, the mother of all living things; all offerings of every possible nature were therefore acceptable to her; hence the vast wealth which poured into her temple. Not only was she worshipped in her temple, but in the minute shrines or *naoi* which were sometimes modeled after the temple. More frequently the shrines were exceedingly crude objects, either of silver or stone or wood or clay. They were made at Ephesus by dependents of the temple, and carried by the pilgrims throughout the world. Before them Diana might also be worshipped anywhere, just as now from the soil of the sacred Mesopotamian city of Kerbela, where the sons of Ali were martyred, little blocks are formed and are carried away by the Shiah Moslems that they may pray upon sacred ground wherever they may be. The makers of the shrines of Diana formed an exceedingly large class among whom, in Paul's time, was Demetrius (Acts **19** 24). None of the silver shrines have been discovered, but those of marble and of clay have appeared among the ruins of Ephesus. They are exceedingly crude; in a little shell-like bit of clay, a crude clay female figure sits, sometimes with a tambourine in one hand and a cup in the other, or with a lion at her side or beneath her foot. Though the shrines were sold as sacred dwelling-places of the goddess, that the pilgrims who carried them to their distant homes, or buried them in the graves with their dead, might be assured of her constant presence, their real purpose was to increase the temple revenues by their sale at a price which was many times their cost. With the shrines of Diana may be compared the household gods of clay found in abundance among the ruins of the earlier Bab cities, esp. those cities in which temples to the goddess Ishtar stood. E. J. BANKS

DIASPORA, dī-as′pō-ra. See DISPERSION.

DIBLAH, dib′la (דִּבְלָה, *dibhlāh*, "circle"; **Δεβλάθα,** *Deblátha*): The name occurs only in Ezk **6** 14 (AV "Diblath"), and the place has not been identified. If the reading is correct it may possibly be represented by *Dibl*, a village in Upper Galilee, S. of *Tibnīn*. But more likely it is a scribal error for **Riblah.**

DIBLAIM, dib′lā-im, dib-lā′im (דִּבְלַיִם, *dibhlayim*, "two cakes"): A native of Northern Israel and father of Gomer, the wife of Hosea (Hos **1** 3).

DIBLATH, dib′lath. See DIBLAH.

DIBLATHAIM, dib-la-thā′im. See ALMON-DIBLATHAIM.

DIBON, dī′bon, **DIBON-GAD** (דִּיבוֹן, *dībhōn*, "washing"; **Δαιβών,** *Daibōn*):

(1) A city of Moab captured by the Amorites (Nu **21** 30), and held by them at the invasion by Israel. It was taken and given to the tribe of Gad, whence it is called **Dibon-gad** (Nu **32** 34; **33** 45). In Josh **13** 17 it is reckoned to Reuben. Along with other cities in the territory N. of the Arnon, Dibon changed hands several times between Moab and Israel. Mesha claims it (MS), and in Jer **48** 18.22 it is named among the cities of Moab. The form of the name, Dimon, in Isa **15** 9, may have been given to make it resemble the Heb *dām*, "blood," to support the play upon words in the verse (*HDB*, s.v.). It is represented by the modern *Dhībān*, about 4 miles N. of Aroer (*'Arā'ir*), on the line of the old Rom road. The ruins that spread over two adjacent knolls are of no importance: walls, a tower, cistern, etc. Near Dibon the famous Moabite Stone was found.

(2) A town in Judah, occupied after the exile (Neh **11** 25). It may be the same as **Dimonah** (Josh **15** 22); unidentified. W. EWING

DIBRI, dib′rī (דִּבְרִי, *dibhrī*, "eloquent" [?]): A Danite, whose daughter Shelomith married an Egyptian. Their son was "cut off" (stoned) for blasphemy (Lev **24** 11).

DICE-PLAYING. See GAMES.

DICTIONARIES, dik′shun-a-riz: A dictionary is a word-book or a list of words arranged in some fixed order, generally alphabetical, for ready reference, and usually with definitions or longer treatises. The vocabulary or glossary is a mere list of words, often without definitions; the Lexicon or dictionary of language (words or concepts) has bare definitions, and the alphabetical encyclopaedia or dictionary of knowledge or information (objects, things, subjects, topics, etc) has longer treatises, but they are all dictionaries: the alphabetical order being the main essential in modern use. There is, however, historically no good reason why the dictionary should not be logical or chronological. The earliest use of the word as quoted by Murray's *Dictionary* (Joh. de Garlandia, cir 1225) was of a collection of words classified and not alphabetical. So, too, almost the earliest use in Eng. (J. Withal's *Dictionarie*, 1556) was of a book of words classified by subjects. A book like Roget's *Thesaurus*, which is a list of classified words without definition, or a systematic encyclopaedia of treatises like Coleridge's unfortunate experiment, the *Encyclopedia Metropolitana*, is a dictionary in the historic sense. The earliest books usually quoted in the lists of Bib. dictionaries were also in fact classified or chronological, and not alphabetical (Eusebius' *Onomasticon;* Jerome's *De viris illustribus*). Classified word lists, syllabaries, etc, of pre-alphabetic times, as well as in Chinese and other non-alphabetic languages of today, are of course also non-alphabetic, but strictly dictionaries.

In pre-alphabetic times the dictionaries include, besides the syllabaries of which there were many examples in Assyria, Babylonia, Egypt, Cyprus, etc, and the word lists proper, chronological lists of kings and various classified lists of tribute, and of astronomical or other objects. They include, in short, all the many lists where the material is grouped round a series of catchwords.

The alphabetical dictionary began with the alphabet itself, for this is a list of names of objects. The earlier alphabetical dictionaries were sometimes called alphabets. In a sense the alphabetical acrostics are dictionaries rather than acrostics, and Ps **119,** where considerable material is grouped under each letter of the alphabet, comes rather close to the dictionary idea.

So long as the quantity of literary material remained small, there was very little need for the development of the alphabetical dictionary, and the examples are rather few, the *Lexicon* of Suidas being perhaps the most noteworthy. With the immense increase in literary material there was a rapidly growing appreciation of the advantage of alphabetical arrangement, over the chronological or the systematic, in all cases where the object is to refer to a specific topic, rather than to read a book through or survey many topics with reference to their relation to one another. The number of alphabetical dictionaries of knowledge increased rapidly with the growth of learning from the 13th cent.; now it has become legion and there are few subjects so narrow that they cannot boast their dictionary of information.

1. Bible Dictionaries

The earliest Bible dictionary is usually counted the *Onom* of Eusebius, a geographical encyclopaedia; then came Jerome's *De nominibus hebraicis*, and his *De viris illustribus* (chronological). The more noteworthy steps in the history of Bible dictionaries are represented by the names of Alsted, Calmet, Winer, Kitto, William Smith, Fairbairn, Schenkel. The best recent dictionaries among the larger works are the *Encyclopaedia Biblica*, standing for the extreme higher critical wing; Hastings, representing the slightly less radical; and this present *International Standard Bible Encyclopaedia,* which represents a growing distrust of the extreme positions of the 19th cent. higher critics. All of these are on a large scale and stand for the latest and best scholarship, and the same quality is reflected in at least two of the recent single-volume dictionaries, *A Standard Bible Dictionary* (M. W. Jacobus), and the single-volume Hastings' dictionary. Both of these in tendency stand between Cheyne's *Encyclopaedia Biblica* and this dictionary, Hastings facing rather toward Cheyne, and Jacobus toward this present work.

2. Bibliography

The John Crerar Library list of encyclopaedias forms an excellent guide to the lit. of general encyclopaedias within its scope, which includes chiefly technology and physical and social sciences, but includes among its reference books very admirably chosen first-reference dictionaries to language, history, fine arts, and even philosophy and religion.

Kroeger, Alice B. *Guide to the Study and Use of Reference Books*, 2d ed, Boston, 1908, is an admirable introduction. Its select lists and bibliographical references supplemented by the John Crerar and other reference library lists will give complete orientation.

Following is a list of previous dictionaries:

BIBLICAL DICTIONARIES

Ayre, J. *Treasury of Bible Knowledge*. London, 1866.

Barnum, Samuel W. *A Comprehensive Dictionary of the Bible*. New York: Appleton, 1867.

Barr, John. *A Complete Index and Concise Dictionary of the Holy Bible*. New York: Methodist Book Concern, 1852.

Bastow, J. A. *Biblical Dictionary*. London, 1848, 3 vols; condensed ed, London, 1859; 4th ed, 1877.

Beck, J. C. *Vollständ. bibl. Wörterbuch*. Basel, 1770, 2 vols.

Besser, H. *Bibl. Wörterbuch*. Gotha, 1866.

Bible Cyclopaedia, The. London: Parker, 1841.

Bost, J. A. *Dictionnaire de la Bible*. Paris, 1865.

Bourazan, F. A. *Sacred Dictionary*. London: Nisbet, 1890.

Brown, John. *A Dictionary of the Holy Bible*. Edinburgh, 1768, 4th ed; London: Murray, 1797; American ed, from the 12th Edinburgh ed, New York: Harper, 1846.

Calmet, A. *Dict. historique, critique, chronologique, géographique et littéral de la Bible*. Paris, 1719.

Calmet, Augustine. *Dictionary of the Holy Bible*. 5th ed, revised and enlarged, 5 vols, London: Holdsworth, 1829; new ed, London: Bohn, 1847; abridged by Buckley, new ed, London: Routledge, 1862.

Cassell's *Bible Dictionary*. Illustrated with nearly 600 engravings; London and New York, 2 vols: Cassell, 1866; new ed, 1869.

Cheyne, T. K. and Black, J. S. *Encyclopaedia Biblica*. London, 1899–1903, 4 vols.

Conder, F. R. and C. R. *A Handbook to the Bible*. London: Longmans, 1879; 2d ed, 1880, New York: Randolph, n.d. [1880].

Dalmasius, J. A. *Dictionarium manuale biblicum*. Aug. Vind., 1776, 2 vols.

Davis, J. D. *Dictionary of the Bible*. Philadelphia, 1898; new ed, 1903.

Eadie, John. *A Biblical Cyclopaedia*. London: Rel. Tr. Soc., 1848; 14th ed, London: Griffin, 1873.

Easton, M. G. *Illustrated Bible Dictionary*. London: Nelson; New York: Methodist Book Concern, 1893.

Fairbairn, Patrick. *The Imperial Bible Dictionary*. London: Blackie, 1866, 2 vols.

Farrar, John. *A Biblical and Theological Dictionary*. London: Mason, 1852; new ed, London: Wesl. Conf. Off., 1889.

Faussett, A. R. *The Englishman's Bible Encyclopaedia*. London: Hodder, 1878. Republished with title. *Bible Cyclopaedia, Critical and Expository*. New York: Funk, 1891.

Gardner, J. *Christian Encyclopaedia*. Edinburgh, n.d.

Gebhardt, G. L. *Biblisches Wörterb*. Lemgo, 1793–96, 3 vols.

Goodhue, W. and Taylor, W. C. *Pictorial Dictionary of the Holy Bible*. London, 1843, 2 vols.

Granbery, John C. *Bible Dictionary*. Nashville: So. Meth. Pub. Soc., 1883.

Green, S. *Biblical and Theol. Dictionary*. London, 1840, 1860.

Guthe, H. *Kurzes Bibelwörterbuch*. 1903.

Hagen. *Lexicon biblicum*. Paris, 1905–, 4 vols (Roman Catholic).

Hamburger. *Realencyklopädie für Bibel und Talmud*. New ed, 1896–97; 2 vols and 4 sup. vols (Jewish point of view).

Hamburger, J. *Biblisch-talmudisches Wörterbuch*. Strelitz, 1866.

Hastings. *Dictionary of the Bible*. Edinburgh and New York, 1898–1902, 4 vols and sup. vol, 1904. 1-vol ed, 1909.

Hastings, James, and others. *Dictionary of Christ and the Gospels*. New York: Scribner; Edinburgh: Clark, 1906–8, 2 vols.

Haupt, C. G. *Bibl. Real-Encyklopädie*. Quedlinb., 1820–27, 3 vols.

Hezel, W. F. *Biblisches Real-Lexikon*. Leipzig, 1783–85, 3 vols.

Hoffmann, A. C. *Allgem. Volks-Bibellexikon*. Leipzig 1842.

Hunter, R. *Concise Bible Dict.* London: Cassell, 1894.
Inglis, James. *Bible Text Cyclopaedia.* London: Houlston, 1861; new ed, Rel. Tr. Soc., 1865, Philadelphia: Lippincott, 1877.
Jacobus, M. W. *A Standard Bible Dictionary.* New York: Funk, 1909.
Jones, William. *The Biblical Cyclopaedia; or Dictionary of the Holy Scriptures.* London: Wightman, 1840; new ed, Tegg, 1847; revised, 1873.
Kitto, John. *Cyclopaedia of Biblical Literature.* 3d ed, ed Alexander, Edinburgh, 1862–65, 3 vols (best ed of Kitto), and after.
Krehl. *Neutestamentl. Handwörterbuch.* Göttingen, 1857.
Lawson, J. P. *Bible Cyclopaedia.* London, 1849, 3 vols.
Leun, F. G. *Bibl. Encyklopädie.* Gotha, 1793–98, 4 vols.
Macbean, A. *Dictionary of the Bible.* London, 1779.
Macpherson, John. *The Universal Bible Dictionary.* London: Hodder, 1892.
Malcom, Howard. *New Bible Dictionary.* Boston: Gould; New York: Sheldon, 1852.
Malcom, H. *Dictionary of the Bible.* London, 1854.
Oetinger, F. C. *Biblisches Wörterb.* Stuttgart, 1849.
Oliver, P. *Scripture Lexicon.* Birmingham, 1784; London, 1843.
Otho, J. H. *Lex. Rabbinico-philologicum.* Geneva, 1675.
Rand, W. W. *A Dictionary of the Holy Bible.* New York: Am. Tr. Soc., n.d. [1859]; rev. ed, 1886.
Ravanel, P. *Bibliotheca Sacra.* Geneva, 1660.
Rawson, A. L. *The Bible Handbook, for Sunday Schools.* 4th ed, New York: Thompson, 1870.
Rechenbergius, A. *Hierolexicon reale collectum.* Leipzig und Frankfort, 1714, 2 vols.
Rice, Edwin W. *People's Dictionary of the Bible.* Philadelphia: Am. S.S. U., 1893.
Riehm and Bäthgen. *Handwörterbuch des biblischen Altertums.* Bielefeld, 1893–94, 2 vols.
Roberts, Francis. *Clavis Bibliorum.* 1675.
Robinson, E. *Dictionary of the Bible.* New York: Worthington, 1879.
Schaff, Philip. *A Dictionary of the Bible.* Philadelphia: Am. S S. U., 1880; 5th ed, 1890.
Schenkel. *Bibel Lexikon.* 1869–75, 5 vols.
Schneider, M. C. F. *Wörterb. üb. d. Bibel.* Leipzig, 1795–1817, 4 vols.
Simon, Richard. *Grand dictionnaire de la Bible.* Lyons, 1693.
Smith, W. *Dictionary of the Bible.* London, 1860–63, 3 vols; 2d ed, Smith and Fuller, 1893.
Smith, W. *Dictionary of the Bible.* Boston, n.d., 4 vols.
Smith, W. *Bible Dictionary.* Acme ed, New York: Alden, 1885.
Vigouroux. *Dictionnaire de la Bible contenant tous les noms de personnes, de lieux . . . . mentionnés dans les s. Ecritures.* Paris, 1895–.
Vollbeding, J. C. *Bibl. Wörterb.* Berlin, 1800–1805, 3 vols.
Watson, R. *Biblical and Theol. Dictionary.* London, 1831; New York, also Nashville.
Wahl, C. A. *Bibl. Handwörterb.* Leipzig, 1828, 2 vols.
Walbrecht, C. L. *Biblisch. Wörterbuch.* Göttingen, 1837.
Westcott, A., and Watt, J. *Concise Bible Dictionary.* London: Isbister, 1893.
Wilson, T. *Complete Christian Dictionary.* London, 1661.
Winer, G. B. *Biblisches Realwörterb.* 3d ed, 1847–48, 2 vols (still useful).
Zeller, H. *Biblisches Wörterb.* Stuttgart, 1855–58, 2 vols.

Other recent one-vol. dictionaries are: Angus (1907), Bevis (1900), Gamble (1906), Ewing (1910), Hyamson (1907), Piercy (1908).

3. General Religious Encyclopaedias

Next in importance for Bible students to the Bible dictionaries are the general dictionaries of religious knowledge. Many of the more recent of these, such as the Hauck ed of *RE*, the new Sch-Herz, *Jew Enc*, the *Catholic Encyclopaedia*, and in general all the larger and some of the smaller recent ones have arts. of real importance for Bible study, often better than some of the specific Bible dictionaries.

GENERAL THEOLOGICAL DICTIONARIES

Abbott, Lyman. *A Dictionary of Religious Knowledge.* New York: Harper, 1875.
Addis, William E. *A Catholic Dictionary.* New York: Cath. Pub. Soc. Co., 1884; 4th ed, revised, London: Paul, 1893.
Aschbach. *Kirchenlexikon.* n.p. 1846–51, 4 vols.
Benham, William. *Dictionary of Religion.* London and New York: Cassell, 1887.
Buchberger. *Kirchliches Handlexikon.* München, 1907 (short but comprehensive).
Buck, Charles. *A Theological Dictionary.* Enlarged by Dr. Henderson. London: Tegg, 1847; Am. ed, revised and enlarged by George Bush; Philadelphia: Desilver, n.d.
Ceccaroni, A. *Dizionaro ecclesiastico illustrato.* Milano.
Dwight, H. O., Tupper, H. O., Jr. and Bliss, E. M. *The Encyclopaedia of Missions.* New York, 1904.
Eadie, J. *The Ecclesiastical Encyclopaedia.* London: Griffin, 1847; new ed, 1875.
Eden, Robert. *The Churchman's Theological Dictionary.* 2d ed, London: Parker, 1846; new ed, 1859.
Encyclopaedia of Religious Knowledge, The; or, Dictionary of the Bible. Rev. ed, Philadelphia: Claxton, 1870.
Farrar, John. *An Ecclesiastical Dictionary.* London: Mason, 1853, revised, 1871.
Gardner, James. *The Christian Encyclopaedia.* London: Groombridge, 1854; new ed, 1858.
Glaire, J. B. *Dictionnaire universel des sciences ecclésiastiques.* Paris, 1868, 2 vols.
Herbermann, Pace, Pellen, Shahan and Wynne. *Catholic Encyclopaedia.* New York, 1906–, 15 vols.
Herzog. *Realencyclopädie für protestantische Theologie u. Kirche.* 1853–68, 21 vols; 3d ed, ed Hauck, 1896–1908, 21 vols, tr New York, 1908– (best of all ecclesiastical dictionaries).
Herzog, J. J. *A Protestant, Theological, and Ecclesiastical Encyclopaedia.* Vols I and II. Philadelphia: Lindsay, 1858–60.
Holtzmann and Zöpffel. *Lexikon für Theologie und Kirchenwesen.* 2d ed, Brunswick, 1888 (Prot).
Jackson, Samuel Macauley. *Concise Dictionary of Religious Knowledge and Gazetteer.* New York: Christian Lit. Co., 1890, 1891; 3d ed, New York: Maynard, 1893.
Jackson, S. M. *The New Schaff-Herzog.* New York: Funk, 1908, sq. (good and modern).
Jewish Encyclopedia. New York, 1901–6, 12 vols (most scholarly).
Lichtenberger, F. *Dict. des sci. eccl.* Paris, 1877–82, 15 vols (French Protestant).
McClintock, John and Strong, James. *Cyclopaedia of Biblical, Theological, and Ecclesiastical Literature.* 10 vols. New York: Harper, 1867–81. With sup. in 2 vols, 1890.
Marsden, J. B. *A Dictionary of Christian Churches and Sects.* London: Bentley, 1857.
Migne. *Encycl. théologique.* Paris, 1844–75 (over 100 special lexicons).
Moroni. *Dizionario di erudizione storico-ecclesiastica.* Venice, 1840–79, 103 vols, and Index, 6 vols.

Among the older ones the huge encyclopaedia of Migne, which is a classified series of alphabetical dictionaries, and the Moroni, with its 109 vols, are still of great usefulness to the scholar on out-of-the-way topics, not so much for Bib. topics but at least for Bib. related matters.

Perthes. *Handlexikon für evangelische Theol.* Gotha, 1890–1901, 3 vols.
Robinson, John. *Theological, Biblical and Ecclesiastical Dictionary.* London: Whittaker, 1815; 4th ed, 1835.
Schaff, Philip and Jackson, Samuel Macauley. *A Religious Encyclopaedia.* New York: Christian Lit. Co., 1882; 3d ed, New York: Funk, 1891. Together with an *Encyclopaedia of Living Divines*, etc.
Schaffer. *Handlexikon der kath. Theologie.* Ratisbon, 1881–91, 3 vols.
Schiele. *Die Religion in Geschichte und Gegenwart.* Tübingen, 1909–, 5 vols.
Shipley, Orby. *A Glossary of Ecclesiastical Forms.* London: Rivingtons, 1871.
Staunton, William. *An Ecclesiastical Dictionary,* New York: Prot. Ep. S.S. U., 1861.
Vacant and Mangenot. *Dictionnaire de théologie catholique.* Paris, 1903–.
Wetzer and Welte. *Kirchenlexicon.* Freiburg, 1847–60; 2d ed, 1880–91, 13 vols, and index, 1903 (Roman Catholic scientific best).

4. Dictionaries of Comparative Religion

The monumental dictionary in this class supersеding all others is Hastings' *Encyclopaedia of Religion and Ethics*, but Forlong has served a useful purpose and some of the special dictionaries like Röscher are quite in the same class with Hastings.

COMPARATIVE RELIGION

Balfour, E. *Cyclopaedia of India, and of E. and So. Asia.* 3d ed, London, 1885, 3 vols.
Beale, Th. W. *Oriental Biographical Dictionary.* Calcutta, 1881; London, 1894.
Brewer, E. C. *Dictionary of Phrase and Fable.* London 1905.
Encyclopaedia of Islam. London: Luzac.
Forlong, J. G. R. *Faiths of Man; a Cyclopaedia of Religions.* London, 1906, 3 vols.
Hastings, James. *Encyclopaedia of Religion and Ethics.* Edinburgh, Clark; New York. Scribner, 1908–.
Hazlitt, W. C. *Faiths and Folklore; a Dictionary of National Beliefs.* London, 1905.
Hughes, T. P. *Dictionary of Islam.* London, 1885.

The admirable Jewish and Catholic encyclopaedias mentioned above, like the Methodist M'Clintock and Strong, belong rather to general than denominational encyclopaedias, but the Catholic dictionaries of Addis and of Thien are denominational in the same sense as those of the Episcopal, Lutheran, etc, churches, mentioned below, among which perhaps the best executed example is the *Lutheran Encyclopaedia* of Jacobs.

5. Denominational Dictionaries

DICTIONARIES OF DENOMINATIONS

Addis, W. E. *A Catholic Dictionary*, 3d ed, New York, 1884.
Benton, A. A. *The Church Cyclopaedia.* Philadelphia, 1884.
Burgess, G. A. *Free Baptist Cyclopaedia.* Chicago: Free Bapt. Cyclop. Co., 1889.
Cathcart, Wm. *The Baptist Encyclopaedia.* Philadelphia, 1881, 2 vols.
Catholic Encyclopaedia. New York, 1907 sq. See General Religious Encyclopaedias.
Hook, Walter F. *A Church Dictionary.* Philadelphia: Butler, 1853; 7th ed, Tibbals, 1875.
Jacobs, H. E. and Haas, J. A. W. *The Lutheran Cyclopedia.* New York, 1905.
Jewish Encyclopedia. See General Theological Encyclopaedias.
Nevin, A. *Encyclopaedia of the Presbyterian Church in the United States of America.* Philadelphia, 1884.
Simpson, M. *Cyclopaedia of Methodism.* Philadelphia, 1878.
Thein, J. *Ecclesiastical Dictionary.* New York, 1900 (Roman Catholic).

SPECIAL DICTIONARIES: ANCIENT AND MEDIAEVAL HISTORY

Blunt, J. H. *Dictionary of Sects, Heresies*, etc. London, 1892.
Blunt, J. H. *Dictionary of Doctrinal and Historical Theology.* Philadelphia, 1870.
Brewer, E. C. *A Dictionary of Miracles.* Philadelphia, 1884.
Brodrick, M. *Concise Dictionary of Egyptian Archaeol.* London, 1902.
Cabrol. *Dictionnaire d'archéologie chrétienne et de liturgie.* Paris, 1907–.
Chevalier, Ul. *Répertoire des sources hist. du moyen-age.* Bio-bibliog. Paris, 1905-7.
——— *Répertoire des sources historiques du moyen-age.* Topo-bibliog. Montbéliard, 1894–1903, 2 vols.
Fabricius, J. A. *Bibliotheca latina mediae et infimae aetatis.* Patavii, 1754, 6 vols in 3.
Julian, J. ed. *A Dictionary of Hymnology.* New York, 1892.
Kraus. *Real-Encyklopädie der christlichen Alterthümer.* Freiburg i. Br., 1882–86, 2 vols.
Lee, F. G. *A Glossary of Liturgical and Ecclesiastical Terms.* London, 1877.
Martigny. *Dictionnaire des antiquités chrétiennes.* 2d ed, Paris, 1877.
Pauly. *Realencyk. der klass. Altertumswissenschaft.* Stuttgart, 1842-66, 6 vols; ed Wissowa, 1894 and later.
Roscher, W. H. *Lexikon der griechischen und römischen Mythologie.* Leipzig, 1884–1902, 5 vols.
Smith, Wm. *Dictionary of Greek and Roman Biography and Mythology.* Boston, 1849, 3 vols.
Smith, Wm. *Dictionary of Greek and Roman Geography.* Boston, 1854–57, 2 vols.
Smith, Sir William, Wayte, William, and Marindin, G. E. *Dictionary of Greek and Roman Antiquities.* 3d ed, enl. London: Murray; Boston: Little, 1890–91, 2 vols.
Smith, W. and Cheetham. *A Dictionary of Christian Antiquities.* Boston, 1875–1880, 2 vols.
Smith, W. and Wace, H. *A Dictionary of Christian Biography.* Boston, 1877–87, 4 vols; abridged ed by Wace and Piercy, 1911.
Stadler and Heim. *Heiligenlexikon.* 1858–82, 5 vols.
Wolcott, Mackenzie E. C. *Sacred Archaeology.* London: Reeve, 1868.

What has been said of general religious encyclopaedias applies almost equally to Bib. articles in the good general encyclopaedias. Among these the *Encyclopaedia Britannica*, of which a new ed appeared in 1911, is easily first, and has maintained through its many edd a high standard. The previous ed was edited by Professor Robertson Smith, who gave a peculiarly high quality of scholarship to its Bib. articles, while at the same time rather tingeing them with extreme views. Among the British encyclopaedias, Chambers' is still kept up to a high standard. The recent American edd include the *New International*, the Nelson, and the *Americana*, the former, perhaps, contributing most on Bible matters. The annual supplement to the *International* gives a useful résumé of the progress of Bib. archaeology during each year.

6. Universal Encyclopaedias

UNIVERSAL ENCYCLOPAEDIAS

America and England

Adams, Charles Kendall. *Universal Cyclopaedia and Atlas.* New York: Appleton, 1905, 12 vols.
American Cyclopaedia. New York, 1858–63, 16 vols; new ed, 1873–76 ("Appleton's encyclopaedia").
Chambers, Ephraim. *Cyclopaedia.* London, 1728.
Chambers' Encyclopaedia. London, 1860–68, 10 vols; new ed, 1901.
Colby, Frank Moore. *Nelson's Encyclopaedia.* (c 1905-6), 12 vols.
Encyclopaedia Americana. New York: The Americana Co. (c 1903–4), 16 vols.
Encyclopaedia Britannica. 1771; 9th ed, 1875–89, 29 vols and Index, sup., 11 vols, Index and atlas, 1902–3; 11th ed, Cambridge, England, 1910–11, 28 vols.
Gilman, D. C. *New International Encyclopaedia.* New York: Dodd, 1907 (c 1902–7), 20 vols.
Hunter. *Encyclopaedic Dictionary.* London, New York, 1879–88, 7 vols.
Johnson's New Universal Encyc. New York, 1874–78, 4 vols; new ed, 1893–95, 8 vols.
Knight. *English Cyclopedia.* London, 1854–73, 27 vols, 4 sup.
New International Year Book. New York: Dodd, 1908–.
Rees. *New Encyclopaedia.* London, 1802–20. 45 vols.
Schem. *Deutsch-amerikanisches Konversations-Lex.* New York, 1870–74.
Smedley (Coleridge?). *Encyclopaedia Metropolitana.* 1818–45, 30 vols (classed with some alphabetical sections).

France

Bayle. *Dict. historique et critique.* Rotterdam, 1695–97 (very widely circulated).
Berthelot, Derenbourg and others. *La grande encyclopédie.* See below.
Corneille, Thomas. [*Dict.*] Paris, 1694.
Dictionnaire de la conversation et de la lecture. 1851–58, 16 vols.
Diderot and D'Alembert. *Encyclopédie.* Paris, 1751–52, 28 vols; 5 sup. vols, Amsterdam, 1776–77; 2 vols Index, Paris, 1780.
(Also Voltaire, Rousseau, etc. This is in the history of dictionary encyclopaedias "the encyclopaedia" par excellence and epoch-making in the history of "free thought." Many edd; 1st ed, 30,000 copies.)
Encyclopédie des gens du monde. 1833–45, 22 vols.
Encyclopédie du XIXe siècle. 1837–59, 75 vols; 3d ed, 1867–72. Continues as *Annuaire encyc.*
Encyclopédie moderne. 1846–51; new ed, 1856–72, 30 vols, 12 sup. vols, atlas, 2 vols.
Furetière. [*Dict.*] Rotterdam, 1690.
Grande encyclopédie. Paris: Lamirault, 1885–1903, 31 vols (known as Lamirault's).
Larousse. *Dict. univ.*, 1865–90, 17 vols; new ed, 1895.
———. *Dict. complet illustré.* 129th ed, 1903.
Moérin. *Grand dict. historique.* Lyons, 1674.
Nouveau Larousse illustré. Paris, 1898–1904, 8 vols.
Panckoucke and Agasse. *Encyclopédie méthodique.* Paris, 1782–1832, 166 vols, text, 51 vols, illus. (classed-alphabetic method like Migne).

Germany

Allgemeine Realencyklopädie für das katholische Deutschland. 1846–49, 13 vols; 4th ed, 1880–90.
Brockhaus. *Konversationslexikon.* 14th ed, 1901 (B. and Meyer are the standard German encyclopaedias).
Ersch and Gruber. *Allgemeine encyklopädie.* 1813–90, 99 +43 +25 vols (scholarly and exhaustive; many arts. are complete treatises).
Herder. *Konversationslexikon.* Freiburg, 1853–57, 5 vols; 3d ed, 1901–8, 8 vols (Roman Catholic; high grade).
Hübner. *Reales-, Staats-, Zeitungs- und Konversations-Lexikon;* 31st ed, Leipzig, 1824–28.
Jablonski. *Lexikon. . . .* Leipzig, 1721.
Köster and Roos. [*Encyc.*] Frankfort, 1778–1804, 23 vols (stops at "Kinol").
Krünitz [and others]. *Oekonomisch-technolog. Encykl.* Berlin, 1773–1858, 242 vols.
Ludewig, Y. J. von. *Grosses, vollständiges, Universal-Lexikon.* Leipzig, 1731–54, 68 vols ("Zedler," which was publisher's name; most admirable and still useful: on account of the vast number of topics it often serves when all other sources fail).
Meyer. *Konversations-lexikon.* Leipzig, 1840–52, 37 vols; 6th ed, 1902, 20 vols; 7th ed, abridged, 1907, 6 vols (Meyer and Brockhaus are the standard German encyclopaedias).
Pierer. *Universallexikon.* 7th ed, 1888–93, 12 vols.

Spamer. *Illustriertes Konversationslexikon.* 1869–79, 5 vols, sup. vols, 1879–82; 2d ed, 1884–91.
Zedler. *Universal-Lexikon.* See Ludewig above.

Italy

Berri. *Enciclopedia popolare economica.* Milan, 1871.
Coronelli. *Biblioteca universale.* Venice, 1701, 7 vols (incomplete).
Lessona and Valle. *Dizionario universale.* Milan, 1874–83.
Nuova encic. popolare italiana. Turin, 1841–51, 14 vols; 6th ed, 1875–89, 25 vols, sup., 1889–99.
Piccola enciclopedia Hoepli. Milan, 1891.

Netherlands

De algemeene Nederlandsche Encyclopedie. Zütphen, 1865–68, 15 vols.
Löbel. [*Encyc.*] Amsterdam, 1796–1810 ("first enc according to modern ideas").
Mollerup. *Nordisk Konversationsleksikon.* 3d ed, Copenhagen, 1883–94.
Nieuwenhuis Woordenboek. Leyden, 1851–68.
Sijthoff. *Woordenboek voor Kennis en Kunst.* Leyden, 1891.
Winkler Prins. *Geïllustreerde Encyclopedie.* Amsterdam, 1905, sq. 3d ed.

Russia and Poland

Meijer. *Konversationsleksikon.* 1889–94.
Brockhaus and Efron. *Entciklopedicheskij Slovai.* St. Petersburg, 1890–1902, 35 vols.
Jushakow. *Boljšaja Enciklopedija.* St. Petersburg, 1899.
Sikoroski, Warsaw, 1890.
Orgelbrand. *Encjklopedya Powszechna.* Warsaw, 1859–68, 28 vols.

Scandinavia

Blangstrup. *Store Illustererede Konversationsleksikon.* Copenhagen, 1891–1901, 12 vols.
Johnsen, *Norsk Haandbog.* 1879–88.
Nordisk Familjsbok; Konversationslexikon. Stockholm, 1876–99, 20 vols.
Salmonsen. *Store Illustrerede Konversationsleksikon.* Kjöbenhavn, 1893–1907, 18 vols.

Spain and Portugal

Diccionario Popular Hist. Geogr. Mytholog. Biograph. Lisbon, 1876–90, 16 vols.
Enciclopedia Universal Illustrada Europeo-Americana. Barcelona, 1907– (Catholic).
Costa. *Diccionario Universal Portuguez.*
Lemos. *Enciclopedia Portugueza Illustrada.* 254 nos. to 1903.
Mellados. *Enciclopedia moderna.* Madrid, 1848–51, 34 vols; 3 vols of charts.
Montaner y Simon. *Diccionario Encic Hispano-Americano.* Barcelona, 1887–99, 25 vols.

Other

Arabian Encyc. Discontinued when it reached the 9th vol, Beirut, 1876–87.
Enciclop. Romănă. Herrmannstadt, 1896–1903, 3 vols (Rumanian).
Kober. *Slovník Naučný.* Prague, 1860–87, 12 vols.
Otto. *Ottův Slovník Naučný.* Prague, 1888–1901, 17 vols.
Pallas Nagy Lexikona. Budapest, 1893–97, 16 vols; sup. 1900.

7. Dictionaries of Philosophy

The dictionaries of philosophy often bear on Bible study almost as much as the religious dictionaries. Baldwin's *Dictionary of Philosophy and Psychology,* which is the most comprehensive work, is also very full in its bibliographical reference, and has in vols III and IV a colossal bibliography of philosophy continued and kept up to date in the *Psychological Index.* The dictionary of Eisler is on the historical principle and of very great importance in interpreting the doctrines of Bib. theology.

DICTIONARIES OF PHILOSOPHY

Baldwin, J. M. *Dictionary of Philosophy and Psychology,* New York, 1901 sq.
Eisler, R. *Philosophisches Wörterbuch.* Berlin, 1904. 2 vols; new ed, 3 vols.
Frank. *Dictionnaire des sciences philosophiques.* 3d ed. 1885.

The dictionaries of architecture often treat of Egyp, Bab, and sometimes Palestinian matters The dictionaries of painting, engraving, music, etc, have less direct matter but are important and necessary in view of the fact that so large a part of the best work is on Bib. themes.

8. Dictionaries of Art and Music

ART

Architectural Publication Society. *Dictionary of Architecture.* London, 1852–92, 6 vols.
Bryan, Michael. *Bryan's Dictionary of Painters and Engravers.* New ed. London: Bell, 1903–5, 5 vols.
Champlin, John Denison, Jr. *Cyclopedia of Painters and Painting.* New York: Scribner, 1892 (c 1885–87), 4 vols.
Clement, Mrs. Clara Erskine. *Handbook of Christian Symbols.*
Gwilt, Joseph. *Encyclopaedia of Architecture.* New ed. London: Longmans, 1888.
James, Ralph N. *Painters and Their Works.* London, 1896.
Müller, Hermann Alexander. *Allgemeines Künstlerlexicon.* 3d ed. Frankfurt a. M., 1895–1901, 5 vols.
Nagler, G. K. *Neues allgemeines Künstlerlexikon.* 2. Aufl. Linz., 1904–7, vols 1–10.
Seubert. *Allgemeines Künstlerlex.* Frankfurt, 1879, 3 vols.
Sturgis, Russell. *Dictionary of Architecture and Building.* New York: Macmillan, 1901, 3 vols.
Thieme, Ulrich, and Becker, Felix. *Allgemeines Lexikon der bildenden Künstler.* Leipzig, 1907.
Viollet-le-Duc, Eugène Emmanuel. *Dictionnaire raisonné de l'architecture.* Paris, 1868, 10 vols.

MUSIC

Baker, Theodore. *Biographical Dictionary of Musicians.* New York: Schirmer, 1900.
Champlin, John Denison, Jr. *Cyclopedia of Music and Musicians.* New York: Scribner, 1893.
Eitner, R. *Biog-bibliog. Lexikon d. Musiker.* Leipzig, 1900–4, 10 vols.
Fétis, François Joseph. *Biographie universelle des musiciens.* 2d ed. Paris, 1860–66, 8 vols; 2d sup. 1875–81.
Grove, George. *Dictionary of Music.* London: 1878–89, 4 vols and sup. 2d ed by J. A. Fuller Maitland. 1905.
Kornmüller. *Lexikon der kirchlichen Tonkunst.* 2d ed. Ratisbon, 1891–95, 2 vols.
Mendel and Reissmann. *Musikalisches Konversationslexikon.* Berlin, 1870–83, 12 vols and sup.
Riemann, Hugo. *Musik-Lexikon.* 4th ed, 1894.
———. *Dictionary of Music.* London [1899].

Many of these bear occasionally or indirectly on Bib. topics.

9. Dictionaries of Social Science

SOCIAL SCIENCES

Birkmeyer. *Encykl. der Rechtswissenschaft.* Berlin, 1901.
Bliss, William Dwight Porter. *New Encyclopedia of Social Reform.* New York: Funk, 1908.
Bluntschli. *Deutsches Staatswörterbuch.* 1857–70, 2 vols; new ed, 1869–74, 3 vols.
Bruder. *Staats-Lexikon of the Görres Society.* Freiburg i. Br., 1889–97, 5 vols; 4th ed, ed Bachem, 1908– (Roman Catholic).
Buisson, F. *Dictionnaire de pédagogie.* Paris, 1882, 4 vols.
Conrad, J. *Handwörterbuch der Staatswissenschaften.* Jena, 1898 sq. 3d ed to Vol XVIII (1911).
Conrad, Elster, Lexis and Loening. *Handwörterbuch der Staatswissenschaften.* 1889–98, 6 vols; 2 sup. vols.
Cyclopaedia of Temperance and Prohibition. New York: Funk, 1891.
Elster. *Wörterbuch der Volkswirtschaft,* 1808, 2 vols; 2d ed, 1907–.
Fay and Chailley. *Nouveau dict. d'économie politique.* Paris: 1891–92, 2 vols.
Holtzendorff, F. von. *Encyk. der Rechtswissenschaft.* 6th ed, 1903–.
Lalor, J. J. *Cyclopaedia of Political Science.* New York, 1889–90, 3 vols.
Palgrave, R. H. I. *Dictionary of Political Economy.* London, 1894–96, 3 vols.
Reichesberg. *Handwörterbuch der schweizer Volkswirtschaft.* 1901.
Rotteck and Welcker. *Staatslex.* Altona, 1835–44, 15 vols; 3d ed, 1856–66, 14 vols.
Schmid, K. A. *Encyclopädie d. Erziehungswesens.* Gotha.
Sonnenschein, W. S. *Cyclopaedia of Education,* arr. and ed. by A. W. Fletcher, Syracuse, 1899.
Wagener, H. *Staats- und Gesellschafts-Lex.* Berlin, 1859–68, 26 vols.

The modern gazetteers are indispensable for identifications.

MODERN GAZETTEERS

Chisholm, George Goudie. *Longmans' Gazetteer of the World.* London, 1902.

10. Dictionaries of Geography

Hunter, W. W. *Imperial Gazetteer of India.* London, 1881, 9 vols.
Lippincott's New Gazetteer. Philadelphia: Lippincott, 1906.
Ritter's geographisch-statistisches Lexikon. 9. umgearb. Aufl. Leipzig, 1905–6. 2 vols.
Vivien de Saint Martin, Louis. *Nouveau dictionnaire de géographie universelle.* Paris, 1879–95, 7 vols.

The great modern biographical dictionaries, although of little use for Scripture names, are of much value to the Bib. student for the writings on Bib. subjects, and in the case of ancient biography, of much value for contemporary persons in other lands.

11. Biographical Dictionaries

MODERN BIOGRAPHY

Aa, Anton Jacobus van der. *Biographisch Woordenboek der Nederlander.* Haarlem, 1876–78, 21 vols.
Académie royale de Belgique. *Biographie nationale.* Bruxelles. 1866–1907, vols 1–19.
Allgemeine deutsche Biographie. Leipzig, 1875–1906, 52 vols.
Allgemeine deutsche Biographie. Leipzig: Duncker, 1875–1900, 45 vols.
Allibone, S. A. *A Critical Dictionary of English Literature.* Philadelphia, 1870–72, 3 vols; 1891, 2 vols.
Appleton's Cyclopaedia of American Biography,. ed. by J. G. Wilson. New York: Appleton, 1888–1900, 7 vols.
Biografiskt Lexikon öfver namnkunnige svenske Män. Stockholm, 1874, 23 vols.
Biographisches Jahrbuch und deutscher Nekrolog. Berlin, 1897–1906, 9 vols.
Bricka, Carl Frederik. *Dansk biografisk Lexikon.* 1887–1905, 19 vols.
Century Cyclopedia of Names, ed. by B. E. Smith. New York: Century Co. (c 1894).
Dictionary of National Biography, ed. by Leslie Stephen. London: Smith; New York: Macmillan, 1885–1900, 63 vols.
Feller, F. X. de. *Biographie universelle ou dictionnaire historique.* Paris, 1847–50, 8 vols in 4.
Giles, Herbert Allen. *A Chinese Biographical Dictionary.* London: Quaritch, 1898.
Glasius, B. *Godeleerd Nederland.* 1851–56, 3 vols.
Hoefer, Ferdinand. *Nouvelle biographie universelle.* Paris: Didot, 1852–66, 46 vols.
Hofberg, Herman. *Svenskt biografiskt Handlexikon.* Stockholm, 1906, vols 1–2.
Joecher, C. G. *Allgemeines Gelehrten-Lexikon.* Leipzig, 1750–51.
Lamb's Biographical Dictionary of the United States. Boston, 1900–1903, 7 vols.
Michaud, Joseph François. *Biographie universelle.* Paris, 1842–65, 45 vols.
National Cyclopaedia of American Biography. New York: White, 1892–1906, 13 vols.
Schaff and Jackson. *Encyclopedia of Living Divines and Christian Workers.* New York, 1887.
Vapereau, L. G. *Dictionnaire universel des littérateurs.* Paris, 1876.
Vapereau. *Dictionnaire des contemporains.* Paris, 1858; 6th ed, 1893; sup. 1895.
———. *Dictionnaire des littérateurs.* 1876; 2d ed, 1884.
Wurzbach, C. von. *Biographisches Lexikon Oesterreichs.* 1856–91, 60 vols.
———. *Biographisches Lexikon des Kaiserthums Oesterreichs.* Wien: Zamarski, 1856–91, 60 vols.

The lexicons of the Bib. languages and versions are treated under the head of the respective languages. The chief dictionaries in Eng. are the great *Murray* and the encyclopaedic *Century.* The best one-vol dictionaries are perhaps the *Standard* and the last ed of Webster.

12. Dictionaries of Language

DICTIONARIES OF LANGUAGE

Brown, F., Driver, S. R., Briggs, C. A. *A Hebrew and English Lexicon of the OT.* Boston, 1906.
Thayer, J. H. *A Greek-English Lexicon of the NT.* New York, 1887; corrected ed, 1889.
Century-Dictionary, an Encyclopedic Lexicon. New York: Century Co. (c 1889–1901), 6 vols.
Murray, James Augustus Henry. *New English Dictionary on Historical Principles.* Oxford: Clarendon Press, 1888–.
Standard Dictionary of the English Language. New York: Funk.
Stormonth's Dictionary of the English Language. New York: Scribner, 1899.
Webster, Noah. *International Dictionary of the English Language.* Springfield (Mass.), 1891 (c 1864–90); new ed, 1909.
Worcester, Joseph Emerson. *Dictionary of the English Language.* New ed, enl. Philadelphia: Lippincott, 1891.

The art. "Dictionary" in the new *Enc Brit* (11th ed) covers the whole matter of dictionaries of language with extraordinary fulness.

E. C. RICHARDSON

DIDACHE, did'a-kē. See LITERATURE, SUB-APOSTOLIC.

DIDRACHMA, dī-drak'ma: Two drachmas. See DRACHMA, DRAM.

DIDYMUS, did'i-mus (**Δίδυμος,** *Dídumos,* i.e. "twin"): The surname of THOMAS (q.v.).

DIE (מוּת, *mūth,* גָּוַע, *gāwa'*; **ἀποθνήσκω,** *apothnēskō,* **τελευτάω,** *teleutáō*): "To die," etc, is of very frequent occurrence, and in the OT is generally the tr of *mūth,* meaning perhaps originally, "to be stretched out" or "prostrate." "To die," should be the consequence of eating the forbidden fruit (Gen **2** 17; cf **20** 7; 2 K **1** 4.6). "Die" is commonly used of *natural death* (Gen **5** 8; **25** 8). It is used also of *violent death* (Gen **26** 9.11; Ex **21** 20); *punitive* (Ex **19** 12; **21** 12.14; **28** 43; Nu **4** 15; Ezk **3** 1 8 ff); *as the result of wilfulness or indifference* (Prov **10** 21; **15** 10; **19** 16). To die *"the death of the righteous"* is something to be desired (Nu **23** 10).

In the NT the word for "to die," etc, is generally *apothnēskō,* "to die off or away," used of dying in all forms: of *natural death* (Mt **22** 24); of *violent death* (Jn **11** 50.51; **19** 7; Acts **25** 11); of *the death of Christ* (Jn **12** 33); of death as *the consequence of sin* (Jn **8** 21.24; Rom **8** 13); *teleutaō,* "to end [life]," also occurs several times (Mt **15** 4); *thnēsko,* "to die," occurs once (Jn **11** 21), and *apóllumi,* "to destroy" (Jn **18** 14); in Acts **25** 16 (*TR*) we have *eis apōleian,* "to destruction."

The **figurative** use of "to die" is not frequent, if indeed it ever occurs. In 1 S **25** 37 it may be equivalent to "faint," "His heart died within him, and he became as a stone," but this may be meant literally. In Am **2** 2 it is said that Moab "shall die," i.e. perish as a nation. Paul describes the condition of the apostles of Christ as "dying, and behold, we live" (2 Cor **6** 9), and says, "I die daily" (1 Cor **15** 31), but the references may be to exposure to death. When in Rom **7** 9 he says, "When the commandment came . . . . I died," he may mean that it rendered him liable to death. In Rom **6** 2 we have "we who died to sin," i.e. in Christ, and in our acceptance of His death as representing ours; similarly we read in 2 Cor **5** 14, "One died for all, therefore all died" (RV), i.e. *representatively,* and in Col **2** 20 "if ye died with Christ"; **3** 3, "for ye died," RV (in Christ). Cf 2 Tim **2** 11; 1 Pet **2** 24.

Figurative Use

Of the changes in RV may be mentioned "abode" for "died" (Gen **25** 18, m "or settled, Heb fell"); "he that is to die" for "worthy of death" (Dt **17** 6); "died" for "are dead" (Jn **6** 49.58, and ARV **8** 52.53); "though he die" for "were dead" (Jn **11** 25); "many died" for "were dead" (Rom **5** 15); "died for nought" for "in vain" (Gal **2** 21); "when his end was nigh" for "died" (He **11** 22). Of special importance are the changes from "be, are, were, dead" in Rom **6** 2.7.8; 2 Cor **5** 14; Col **2** 20; **3** 3; 2 Tim **2** 11, and "having died" for "being dead" in 1 Pet **2** 24, as bringing out the truth that in the sight of God all men died in Christ. See also DEATH.

W. L. WALKER

DIET, dī'et (אֲרֻחָה, *'ăruḥāh,* "prescribed"): A daily allowance or portion of food, as that given by King Evil-merodach to Jehoiachin, king of Judah (Jer **52** 34 AV; cf 2 K **25** 30).

DIG (קוּר, *ḳūr*, "to dig", חָתַר, *ḥāthar*; διορύσσω, *diorússō*, "to dig through"): "I have digged and drunk strange waters" (2 K **19** 24). In his campaigns on foreign soil, where the enemy had stopped up the watersprings, Sennacherib would at once dig fresh wells for his armies. "They dig through houses" (Job **24** 16; cf Mt **6** 19.20 m). Walls of eastern houses are often made of mud or clay, and frequently have no windows; and as the threshold of a Syrian house is sacred, the thief breaks in through the wall (see Trumbull, *The Threshold Covenant*).

M. O. Evans

DIGNITIES, dig'ni-tiz, **DIGNITY,** dig'ni-ti (Heb *mārōm*, *sᵉ'ēth*, *gᵉdhullāh*): Rank or position, not nobility or austerity of personal character or bearing, is denoted by this word in its OT occurrences (Gen **49** 3; Est **6** 3; Eccl **10** 6; Hab **1** 7). In 2 Pet **2** 10; Jude ver 8, "dignities" (δόξαι, *dóxai*) are angels, lofty spiritual beings, possible objects of blasphemy; cf the context in both passages.

DIKE, dī'kē (δίκη, *díkē*, "justice"): The avenging justice of God personified as a goddess (Acts **28** 4). See Justice.

DIKLAH, dik'lä (דִּקְלָה, *diḳlāh*, "place of palms"): One of the "sons" of Joktan (Gen **10** 27; 1 Ch **1** 21). Perhaps a south-Arabian tribal or place-name connected with a palm-bearing district.

DILEAN, dil'ē-an (דִּלְעָן, *dil'ān*, "cucumber"): A town in the Shephelah of Judah named with Migdal-gad and Mizpeh (Josh **15** 38, ERV "Dilan"), which lay probably on the N. of Lachish and Eglon. It has not been identified.

DILIGENCE, dil'i-jens, **DILIGENT, DILIGENTLY,** dil'i-jent-li: This word is used in various senses in our Eng. Bible.

1. In the OT

In Ezr **5** 8, "with diligence" means "with care"; in Ezr **6** 12; **7** 17, "with speed," "speedily"; in Prov **4** 23 "watchfulness"; in Dt **4** 9; **6** 17; **19** 18; Ps **77** 6; Prov **27** 23; Isa **55** 2; Mic **7** 3, "with care," "scrupulously," "earnestly." Sometimes it means "early," "with haste" (Job **8** 5; Prov **8** 17). It may mean "industrious," "exacting" (Prov **10** 4; **12** 27; **22** 29).

2. In the NT

The American revisers have rendered "diligence" for various words in AV, e.g. for "business" in Rom **12** 11; "giving diligence" for "endeavoring" (Eph **4** 3); "give diligence" for "study" (2 Tim **2** 15), for "labor" (He **4** 11); "diligently" for "carefully" (Phil **2** 28; He **12** 17); "be diligent in" for "meditate upon" (1 Tim **4** 15). It is well also to remember that the Old Eng. meaning of diligence is "with love," from *diligo*, "to love."

G. H. Geberding

DILL. See Anise.

DIMINISH, di-min'ish: RV has retained nearly all passages of AV where "to diminish" is used. Some of these uses have become obsolete: Dt **4** 2, "neither shall ye diminish from it." "Diminish" generally means "to reduce," "to lessen." In this sense it is employed in Ezk **5** 11 from the Heb גָּרַע, *gāra'*, lit. "to shear." The picture of shearing the beard, expressing degradation and loss of manhood, may underlie this passage.

DIMNAH, dim'nä (דִּמְנָה, *dimnāh*, "dung"; Δαμνά, *Damná*): A city of the Merarite Levites in the territory of Zebulun (Josh **21** 35). The name is probably a clerical error for Rimmon.

DIMON, dī'mon, **DIMONAH,** di-mō'na. See Dibon.

DINAH, dī'na (דִּינָה, *dīnāh*, "justice"): The daughter of Jacob and Leah, whose violation by Shechem, son of Hamor, caused her brothers, esp. Simeon and Levi, to slay the inhabitants of Shechem, although they had induced the Shechemites to believe, if they would submit to circumcision, Shechem, the most honored of all the house of his father, would be permitted to have the maiden to whom his soul clave for wife (Gen **34** 1–31). The political elements of the story (cf vs 21–23 and 30) suggest a tribal rather than a personal significance for the narrative.

Nathan Isaacs

DINAITES, dī'na-īts (דִּינָיֵא, *dīnāyē'*): A people mentioned in Ezr **4** 9, as settled in the city of Samaria by Osnappar (Assurbanipal). The identification is uncertain.

DINHABAH, din'ha-bä, din-hā'ba (דִּנְהָבָה, *dinhābhāh*): The royal city of Bela, son of Beor, king of Edom (Gen **36** 32; 1 Ch **1** 43). There may be a resemblance in the name of *Hodbat et-Teneib*, about 8 miles E. of Heshbon; but this is in the land of Moab, and probably much too far to the N. No satisfactory identification has been proposed.

DINNER, din'ẽr (ἄριστον, *áriston;* Mt **22** 4; Lk **11** 38 [RVm "breakfast"]; **14** 12; cf Ruth **2** 14; Jn **21** 13): In oriental as in classical lands it was customary, anciently, as now, to have but two meals in the day, and the evidence, including that of Jos, goes to show that the second or evening meal was the principal one. The "morning morsel," as the Talm calls it, was in no sense a "meal." The peasant or artisan, before beginning work, might "break [his] fast" (Jn **21** 12.15) by taking a bit of barley bread with some simple relish, but to "eat [a full meal] in the morning" was a reproach (Eccl **10** 16). The full meal was not to be taken until a little before or after sunset, when the laborers had come in from their work (Lk **17** 7; cf the "supper time" of **14** 17). The noon meal, taken at an hour when climatic conditions called for rest from exertion (the *ariston* of the Greeks, rendered "dinner" in EV, Mt **22** 4; Lk **11** 38, RVm "breakfast"), was generally very simple, of bread soaked in light wine with a handful of parched corn (Ruth **2** 14), or of "pottage and bread broken into a bowl" (Bel 33), or of bread and broiled fish (Jn **21** 13). Many, when on a journey especially, are content with one meal a day, taken after sunset. In general, eating at other times is casual and informal; evening is the time for the formal meal, or feast. See Meals.

Geo. B. Eager

DIONYSIA, dī-ō-nish'i-a (Διονύσια, *Dionúsia*, "festivals of Dionysus" [Bacchus]): The rural (vintage) Dionysia were celebrated in the month of Poseideon (19th day), which is roughly our December. The celebration consisted of feasts, processions, songs and (sometimes) scenic performances. The Ascolia formed one of the most prominent features. After sacrificing a goat to the god, they filled the wine-skin with wine, made it slippery on the outside with oil, and then tried to hop on it with one leg. Whoever fell down furnished great sport for the spectators, but if anyone succeeded in maintaining an upright position to the end, he was declared victor. The demarch conducted the festival, the expenses of which were paid by the deme.

The Lenaea were celebrated on the 12th of Gamelion (January) in Athens, and later in Ionia in Asia Minor. At this festival also the new wine was tasted. A procession was formed and they marched through the city, indulging in all sorts of jesting and buffoonery, to attend the pantomimic performances.

The Anthesteria (Flower-Feast) came in the month of Anthesterion (February), when the first flowers appeared. This festival resembled somewhat our Christmas. On the first day (11th of the month) the wine-cask was opened; on the second was the feast of pitchers. Wine was drunk, and contests in trumpet-playing were held. At the drinking contest everybody was permitted to make as much merriment as he pleased. There was also a mystic marriage of the king archon's wife to Dionysus (compare the marriage of the Doges of Venice to the sea). On the third day they offered pots filled with vegetables to Hermes, Conductor of the Dead. This day was sacred to the gods of the nether world and to the spirits of the departed (All Souls' Day); and the people celebrated Persephone's resurrection and reunion with the god.

The Greater, or City Dionysia, were held in Elaphebolion (March) as a spring festival. This is the most important of all the Dionysia (for us), since practically all the great tragedies of Aeschylus, Sophocles and Euripides were performed in conjunction with this festival. All the demes took part. They accompanied the ancient image of Dionysus Eleutherios (from Eleutherae in Boeotia, one of the first places in which the worship of the god was established in Greece), as it was carried in solemn procession from the Lenaeon (the original center of his cult in Athens) to a small temple in the Ceramicus in the northwestern part of the city, while choruses of men and boys sang the *dithúrambos* (the ancient hymn to Dionysus). Crowned with the vine and dressed in unusual costumes, they greeted the god with loud shouts of joy.

The festival was revived with great pomp by the Pisistratidae. In the theater of Dionysus all the people beheld an imposing rehearsal of their great achievements. Even the poorest and humblest were given an opportunity to see and hear the contests between the professional rhapsodists, who recited Homer, between choruses specially trained to sing the dithyrambs, and between poets, whose great dramatic productions were presented for the first time. The state set aside a special fund for the purchase of tickets for those who were too poor to buy for themselves. Comedies, tragedies and satyr dramas were presented after elaborate preparation and at a great expenditure of money. The prize, a bronze tripod, was erected with an appropriate inscription on the Street of Tripods. The awarding of prizes to the victors concluded the festival.

The quinquennial festival at Brauron in Attica was also celebrated with extraordinary license and merriment. The city of Athens sent delegates regularly to attend the festival.

There were also Dionysiac clubs in Athens at the time of the Peloponnesian War. These had peculiar doctrines and observances. They had their foundation in Orphic mysticism. The members refrained from eating the flesh of animals. They possessed holy scriptures and had peculiar propitiatory rites. The Dionysiac religious observance continued as a state cult down to 366 AD. See BACCHUS.

J. E. HARRY

DIONYSIUS, dī-ŏ-nish′i-us (**Διονύσιος**, *Dionúsios*, surnamed "the Areopagite"): One of the few Athenians converted by Paul (Acts **17** 34). We know nothing further about him (see AREOPAGUS). According to one account he was the first bishop of the church at Athens; according to another he suffered martyrdom in that city under Domitian. We are even told that he migrated to Rome and was sent to Paris, where he was beheaded on Montmartre (Mount of the Martyr). The patron saint of France is St. Denys; cf the French "Denys d'Halicarnasse" (Dionysius of Halicarnassus). The mystical writings which were circulated in the Middle Ages and are still extant, are pronounced by the best authorities to be forgeries, and date from a period not earlier than the 5th cent.

J. E. HARRY

DIONYSUS, dī-ŏ-nī′sus (**BACCHUS**) (**Διόνυσος**, *Diónusos*): The youngest of the Gr gods. In Homer he is not associated with the vine. In later Gr legend he is represented as coming from India, as traversing Asia in a triumphal march, accompanied by woodland beings, with pointed ears, snub noses and goat-tails. These creatures were called satyrs. The vine was cultivated among European-Aryans first in Thrace, and here Dionysus is said to have established his worship first in Europe. Then the cult of Dionysus passed down through the Balkan peninsula to Thebes; and in the localized form of the myth the deity was born here—son of Zeus and Semele.

"Offspring of Zeus on high
. . . .
Thou that carest for all
Who on Bacchus in Italy call
And in Deo's sheltered plain
Of Eleusis lord dost reign,
Whither worshippers repair!
O Bacchus that dwellest in Thebes,
On whose broad and fertile glebes
Fierce warriors from the dragon's teeth rose,
Where Ismenus softly flows,
The city that Semele bare!"
—Sophocles, *Antigone*.

Among all the Gr deities none appealed more vividly to the imagination than Dionysus. Gr tragedy is a form of worship, the ritual cult of the god of wine, who makes the initiate wise and the ungodly mad. Dionysus speaks most strongly to the sense and to the spirit at the same time. There is nothing monotonous in the Dionysiac legend; it is replete with both joy and sorrow—in some aspects it is a "passion," in others a triumph. All the passion plays of the world (even the Oberammergau *Schauspiel*) are in the ancient spirit. One Dionysus after another has been substituted, but from the first there has been a desire on the part of the devotee to realize his god vividly with thrilling nearness, to partake of his joys and sorrows and triumphs in his manifold adventures. In the early myths Dionysus was one of the lesser gods; he is mentioned only twice in the *Iliad* and twice in the *Odyssey;* but he is always represented as being more nearly akin to man than the great august deities of Olympus. He is a man-god, or god-man. To the inhabitants of the vine-clad slopes of Attica, to which his cult had been brought from Phrygia through Thracian Boeotia, he was particularly dear. At their vintage feasts last year's cask of wine was opened; and when the new year brought life again to the vines, the bountiful god was greeted with songs of joyful praise. The burial of the wine in the dark tomb of the jars through the winter, and the opening of these jars at the spring festival symbolized the great awakening of man himself, the resurrection of the god's worshippers to a fuller and more joyous life. The vine was not the only manifestation of the god—oil and wheat were also his; he was the god of ecstasy, the giver of physical joy and excitement, the god of life, the god of certain laws of Nature, germination and extinction, the external coming into being and the dying away of all things that are, fructification in its widest aspect whether in the bursting of the seed-grain that lies intreasured in the earth, or in the generation of living creatures. Hence the prominence given to the phallus in the solemn processions in honor of the god.

Nicanor (2 Macc **14** 33) and Antiochus Epiphanes (2 Macc **6** 7) thought that the cult of Dionysus would not be objectionable to the Jews. Ptolemy Philopator branded the Jews with an ivy-leaf (3 Macc **2** 29), which was sacred to Dionysus. See also BACCHUS.

J. E. HARRY

DIOSCORINTHIUS, dī-os-kŏ-rin′thi-us: A certain (unidentified) month (2 Macc **11** 21). See CALENDAR; TIME.

DIOSCURI, dī-os'kū-rī (Διόσκουροι, *Dióscouroi;* in Acts **28** 11, AV **Castor and Pollux,** RV THE TWIN BROTHERS; in m, "Dioscuri"): The sign of the ship on which Paul sailed from Melita to Syracuse and Rhegium. The Dioscuri (i.e. sons of Zeus), Castor and Pollux, are the two chief stars in the constellation of the Twins. Some 4,000 years BC they served as pointers to mark the beginning of the new year by setting together with the first new moon of springtime. The constellation of the Twins was supposed to be esp. favorable to sailors, hence ships were often placed under the protection of the twin gods. E. W. MAUNDER

DIOTREPHES, dī-ot're-fēz (Διοτρέφης, *Diotrephēs*): A person mentioned in 3 Jn vs 9.10 as contentiously resisting the writer's authority and forbidding others from exercising the Christian hospitality which he himself refused to show. The words "who loveth to have the preëminence, among them" may indicate that he was a church official, abusing his position.

DIP: Priests when offering a sin offering were required to dip a finger into the blood of the sacrificed bullock and "to sprinkle of the blood seven times before Jeh" (cf Lev **4** 6, et al.). See also the law referring to the cleansing of infected houses (Lev **14** 51) and the cleansing of a leper (Lev **14** 16). In all such cases "to dip" is "to moisten," "to besprinkle," "to dip in," the Heb טָבַל, *ṭābhal,* or the Gr βάπτω, *báptō.* See also ASHER. In Ps **68** 23 "dipping" is not tr[d] from the Heb, but merely employed for a better understanding of the passage: "Thou mayest crush them, dipping thy foot in blood" (AV "that thy foot may be dipped in the blood"). Rev **19** 13 is a very doubtful passage. AV reads: "a vesture dipped in blood" (from *baptō,* "to dip"); RV following another reading (either *rhaínō,* or *rhantízō,* both "to sprinkle"), translates "a garment sprinkled with blood." RVm gives "dipped in." See also SOP. A. L. BRESLICH

DIPHATH, dī'fath (דִּיפַת, *dīphath*): A son of Gomer, son of Japheth, son of Noah (1 Ch **1** 6), called RIPHATH (q.v.) in the corresponding genealogy in Gen **10** 3.

DISALLOW, dis-a-lou': "To disallow" as used in the Scriptures means either "to oppose," "not permit" (Heb *nō',* Nu **30** 5.8.11), or "to reject" (Gr *apodokimázō,* lit. "to consider useless," 1 Pet **2** 4.7 AV, RV "rejected").

DISANNUL, dis-a-nul'. See ANNUL.

DISAPPOINT, dis-a-point': "To disappoint" may be used transitively or intransitively. In the former case it naturally has a more forceful meaning. Therefore RV changes the tr of AV wherever "disappoint" is used with an object: Job **5** 12, "frustrateth"; Ps **17** 13, "confront him," RVm "forestall"; Jth **16** 6, "brought them to nought"; but RV retains "disappoint" where the person who disappoints is not expressed. Cf Prov **15** 22.

DISCERN, di-zûrn': Five Heb words are thus tr[d]: *bīn, yādha', nākhar, rā'āh* and *shāma'.* It may simply mean "observe" (*bīn*), "I discerned among the youths" (Prov **7** 7); or discriminating knowlege, "A wise man's heart discerneth time and judgment" (Eccl **8** 5, *yādha'*); "He discerned him not, because his hands," etc (Gen **27** 23, *nākhar*); "Then shall ye return and discern between the righteous and the wicked" (Mal **3** 18, *rā'āh*); "So is my lord the king to discern good," etc (2 S **14** 17, *shāma'*). In the NT the words *anakrínō, diakrínō* and *dokimázō* are thus tr[d], expressing close and distinct acquaintance with or a critical knowledge of things. Used in 1 Cor **2** 14 AV of "the things of the spirit of God"; in 1 Cor **11** 29 of "the [Lord's] body" in the sacrament; in Mt **16** 3 of "the face of the heaven"; in He **5** 14 of a clear knowledge of good and evil as the prerogative of a full-grown man. See also next art. HENRY E. DOSKER

DISCERNINGS, di-zûrn'inz, **OF SPIRITS** (διακρίσεις πνευμάτων, *diakríseis pneumátōn,* "judicial estimation," "through judgment or separation"): Occurs in 1 Cor **12** 10 as being one of the gifts of the Spirit. The Gr word occurs in He **5** 14; and Rom **14** 1: "But him that is weak in faith receive ye, yet not for decision of scruples." This tr scarcely expresses the meaning, which Thayer has freely rendered, "not for the purpose of passing judgment on opinions, as to which one is to be preferred as the more correct." Taking these three passages together it is evident that the Gr term which is rendered "discerning" means a distinguishing or discriminating between things that are under consideration; hence the one who possessed the gift of "discernings of spirits" was able to make distinction between the one who spoke by the Spirit of God and the one who was moved by a false spirit. This gift seems to have been exercised chiefly upon those who assumed the rôle of teachers, and it was esp. important in those days, because there were many false teachers abroad (see 2 Jn ver 7; Acts **20** 29.30). See also SPIRITUAL GIFTS. A. W. FORTUNE

DISCIPLE, di-sī'p'l:

(1) Usually a subst. (μαθητής, *mathētēs,* "a learner," from *manthánō,* "to learn"; Lat *discipulus,* "a scholar"): The word is found in the Bible only in the Gospels and Acts. But it is good Greek, in use from Herodotus down, and always means the pupil of someone, in contrast to the master or teacher (διδάσκαλος, *didáskalos*). See Mt **10** 24; Lk **6** 40. In all cases it implies that the person not only accepts the views of the teacher, but that he is also in practice an adherent. The word has several applications. In the widest sense it refers to those who accept the teachings of anyone, not only in belief but in life. Thus the disciples of John the Baptist (Mt **9** 14; Lk **7** 18; Jn **3** 25); also of the Pharisees (Mt **22** 16; Mk **2** 18; Lk **5** 33); of Moses (Jn **9** 28). But its most common use is to designate the adherents of Jesus. (*a*) In the widest sense (Mt **10** 42; Lk **6** 17; Jn **6** 66, and often). It is the only name for Christ's followers in the Gospels. But (*b*) esp. the Twelve Apostles, even when they are called simply the disciples (Mt **10** 1; **11** 1; **12** 1, et al.). In the Acts, after the death and ascension of Jesus, disciples are those who confess Him as the Messiah, Christians (Acts **6** 1.2.7; **9** 36 [fem., *mathētria*]; **11** 26, "The disciples were called Christians"). Even half-instructed believers who had been baptized only with the baptism of John are disciples (Acts **19** 1–4).

(2) We have also the vb., μαθητεύω, *mathēteúō,* "Jesus' disciple" (lit. "was discipled to Jesus," Mt **27** 57); "Make disciples of all the nations" (AV "teach," Mt **28** 19); "had made many disciples" (AV "taught many," Acts **14** 21); "every scribe who hath been made a disciple to the kingdom of heaven" (AV "instructed," Mt **13** 52). The disciple of Christ today may be described in the words of Farrar, as "one who believes His doctrines, rests upon His sacrifice, imbibes His spirit, and imitates His example."

The OT has neither the term nor the exact idea, though there is a difference between teacher and scholar among David's singers (1 Ch **25** 8), and among the prophetic guilds the distinction between the rank and file and the leader (1 S **19** 20; 2 K **6** 5). G. H. Trever

DISCIPLINE, dis'i-plin (מוּסָר, *mūṣār*): In AV only in Job **36** 10, where it refers to moral discipline, the strenuous cultivation of the righteous life; RV "instruction." RV in 2 Tim **1** 7 has "discipline" for a Gr word (*sōphronismós*) meaning "sobering"; in 2 Tim **3** 16 m, for Gr *paideía*, "instruction." In classic Gr *paideia* means "education," mental culture. Through the influence of the LXX, which translates the Heb *mūṣār* by *paideía*, the meaning of "chastisement" accompanies *paideia* in the NT. Cf He **12** 5.7.8.11. See Chastisement; and for ecclesiastical discipline see Church.

DISCOMFIT, dis-kum'fit, **DISCOMFITURE,** dis-kum'fi-tūr (הוּם, *hūm*, מְהוּמָה, *m^ehūmāh*): These words are now obsolete or at least obsolescent and are confined in Bib. lit. wholly to the OT. The meaning in general is "to annoy," "harass," "confuse," "rout" and "destroy." The most common usage is that based upon the root meaning, "to trouble" or "annoy," sometimes to the point of destruction (Josh **10** 10; Jgs **4** 15; 1 S **7** 10; 2 S **22** 15).

The AV errs in the tr in Isa **31** 8, where the meaning is obviously "to become subject to task work" or "to place a burden upon one." There seems also to be an unwarranted use of the word in Nu **14** 45, where it means rather "to bruise" or "strike." The purest use is perhaps in 1 S **14** 20, where the statement is made that "every man's sword was against his fellow, and there was a very great discomfiture." Walter G. Clippinger

DISCOURSE, dis-kōrs': In RV of Acts **20** 7.9, the tr of Gr *dialégomai* (AV "preach"), elsewhere rendered, according to the implications of the context, "reason" or "dispute," as Acts **17** 2; **19** 9 (AV "disputing," RV "reasoning"); Jude ver 9.

DISCOVER, dis-kuv'ẽr: In modern usage the word "discover" signifies "to get first sight or knowledge of," "to ascertain," or "to explore." Such usage appears in 1 S **22** 6 of the discovery of David's hiding-place, where the Heb uses יָדַע, *yādha'*. In AV the word "discover" often occurs in a sense now archaic or even obsolete. (Note in the cases cited below the Heb word is גָּלָה, *gālāh*, except Jer **13** 26 [חָשַׂף, *ḥāshaph*, "to make bare"] and Hab **3** 13 [עָרַר, *'ārar*, "to make naked"].) (1) "To exhibit," "uncover" (or "betray"), in which examples ERV also reads with AV "discover"; ARV "uncover" (Ex **20** 26; Job **12** 22; Isa **57** 8 ["discovered thyself" AV and ERV]; Jer **13** 26; Lam **2** 14; Hos **7** 1; Nah **3** 5). (2) "To cause to be no longer a covering," "to lay bare" (2 S **22** 16 AV). (3) "To bring to light," "disclose" (1 S **14** 8.11 [ERV with AV "discover"]). (4) "To unmask" or "reveal oneself" (Prov **18** 2 AV). (5) "To take away the covering of" (Isa **22** 8 AV). (6) "To lay bare" (Hab **3** 13). In Ps **29** 9, AV reads: "The voice of the Lord . . . . discovereth the forests," where RV reads, "strippeth the forests bare," i.e. "strippeth the forests of their leaves" (Perowne, *The Psalms*, I, 248); "strippeth bare the forests" (Briggs, *Psalms*, I, 251, 253).

In the NT (AV), the word "discover" occurs as a tr of the Gr *anaphánantes* in Acts **21** 3, and for *katenóoun* in Acts **27** 39, where RV reads in the first instance "had come in sight of," and in the latter case "perceived." W. N. Stearns

DISCREPANCIES, dis-krep'an-siz, **BIBLICAL,** bib'li-kal: By this term should be understood substantial disagreements in the statements of Bib. writers. Such disagreements might subsist between the statements of different writers or between the several statements of a single writer. Contradictions of Bib. views from extra-Bib. sources as history, natural science, philosophy, do not fall within the scope of our subject.

1. Definition

Observant Bible readers in every age have noted, with various degrees of insight, that the Scriptures exhibit manifold interior differences and contrasts. Differences of literary form and method have ever seemed, except to those who maintained a mechanical theory of inspiration, wholly natural and fitting. Moreover, that there was progress in the Bib. revelation, esp. that the NT of Jesus Christ signifies a vastly richer revelation of God than the OT, has been universally recognized. In fulfilling the law and the prophets Christ put a marked distance between Himself and them, yet He certainly affirmed rather than denied them. The Christian church has ever held to the essential unity of the Divine library of the Holy Scriptures. Moreover, the evangelical churches have recognized the Bible as "the only and sufficient rule of both faith and practice." Indeed, in the generation following the Reformation, the strictest and most literal theory of inspiration and inerrancy found general acceptance. Over against such a body of presuppositions, criticism, some generations later, began to allege certain errors and discrepancies in the Bible. Of course the orthodox sought to repel all these claims; for they felt that the Bible, whatever the appearances might seem to indicate, *must* be free from error, else it could not be the word of God. So there came with criticism a long period of sturdy defence of the strictest doctrine of Bib. inerrancy. Criticism, however, kept on its way. It has forced the church to find a deeper and surer ground of confidence in the authority of the Bible as the witness to God's self-revelation to man. In our day the church has for the most part overcome the notion that the certainty of the saving grace of God in Christ stands or falls with the absolute inerrancy of each several statement contained in the Bible. Still there remains, and doubtless ever must remain, a need of a clear understanding of the issue involved in the allegation—along with other "human limitations"—of Bib. discrepancies.

2. Criticism v. Doctrine of Inerrancy

Alleged discrepancies pertain (1) to statements of specific, concrete facts, and (2) to the utterance of principles and doctrines. Under the first head fall disagreements respecting numbers, dates, the form and order of historical events, records of spoken words, geography, natural history, etc. Under the second head fall disagreements respecting moral and religious truths, the "superhistorical" realities and values. Our inquiry resolves itself into three parts: (1) to determine whether there be discrepancies, of either or both sorts, in the Bible; (2) to obtain at least a general understanding of the conditions and causes that may have given rise to the discrepancies, real or apparent; (3) to determine their significance for faith.

3. Synopsis of the Argument

As to the first point, it should be observed that apparent inconsistencies may not be real ones; as so often in the past, so again it may come about that the discovery of further data may resolve many an apparent contradiction. On the other hand, the affirmation a priori that there can be and are no *real* discrepancies in the Bible is not only an outrage upon the human understanding, but it stands also in contradiction to the spirit of freedom that is of faith. Besides, it should not be overlooked that the discoveries of modern historical and archaeological research, which have tended to confirm so many Bib. statements, seem just as surely to reveal discrepancies. In any event we must bow to reality, and we may do this with fearless confidence in "the God of things as they are." But are there real discrepancies in the Bible? It is no part of the present plan to attempt the impossible and at all events useless task of exhibiting definite statistics of all the alleged discrepancies, or even of all the principal ones. Passing by the childish folly that would find a "discrepancy" in mere rhetorical antitheses, such as that in Prov **26** 4.5 ("Answer not a fool," and "Answer a fool according to his folly"), or instances of merely formal contrariety of expression, where the things intended are manifestly congruous (e.g. Mt **12** 30; Lk **11** 23 contrasted with Mk **9** 40; Lk **9** 50: "He that is not with me is against me," "He that is not against us is for us"), it will serve our purpose to notice a few representative examples of real or apparent discrepancy. The chronologies of K and Ch are inconsistent (cf CHRONOLOGY OF OT). The genealogies in Gen **46**; Nu **26**; 1 Ch **2–7** show considerable variations. The two lists of exiles who returned with Zerubbabel (Ezr **2**; Neh **7** 6 ff) show many discrepancies, including a marked difference in the enumeration. The accounts of the creation in Gen **1** and **2** (cf CREATION)—to take an example dependent upon the results of modern criticism—are mutually independent and in important particulars diverse. But the center of interest in our inquiry is the gospel history. Since Tatian and his *Diatessaron* in the 2d cent., the variations and contrasts in the Gospels have not only been noted and felt, but many have striven to "harmonize" them. After all, however, there remain some irreducible differences. The Gospels, generally speaking, do not give us *ipsissima verba* of Jesus; in reporting His discourses they show many variations. In so far as the essential meaning is the same in all, no one speaks of discrepancies; but where the variation clearly involves a difference of meaning (e.g. Mt **12** 39.40 and Lk **11** 29.30), one may say that at least a technical discrepancy exists. In recording sayings or events the evangelists manifestly do not always observe the same chronological order; Lk, e.g. records in wholly different connections sayings which Mt includes as parts of the Sermon on the Mount (e.g. the Lord's Prayer, Mt **6** 9 ff; Lk **11** 1–4; cf JESUS CHRIST; CHRONOLOGY OF NT). We have two distinct genealogies of Jesus (Mt **1** 1–16; Lk **3** 23 ff; cf GENEALOGY). We may even note that Pilate's superscription over the cross of Jesus is given in four distinct forms. Here, however, the discrepancy is not real except in the most technical sense, and is worth mentioning only to show that the evangelists' interest does not lie in a mere objective accuracy. That a perfect agreement as to the significance of an event exists where there are undeniable discrepancies in external details may be illustrated by the two accounts of the healing of the centurion's servant (Mt **8** 5 ff; Lk **7** 1 ff). Of enormously greater interest are the various accounts of the appearances of the risen Christ. If a complete certainty as to the form and order of these events is necessary to faith, the case is not a happy one, for the harmonists have been unable to render a perfect account of these matters (cf JESUS CHRIST; RESURRECTION). Turning from the Gospels to apostolic history, we meet some real problems, e g. how to relate Paul's autobiographical notes in Gal **1** with the accounts in Acts.

4. Alleged Discrepancies Pertaining to Facts

The discrepancies thus far noted pertain to historical matters, and not one of them involves the contradiction of a fact in which faith is interested. But are there also real or apparent discrepancies in matters of doctrine? Many scholars maintain, for instance, that the ideal of the prophets and that of the priestly class stand in a relative (not absolute) opposition to each other (cf, e.g. Isa **1** 11; Mic **6** 8 with the ritualism of Lev and Dt). Or, to turn to the NT, some would assert—among them Luther—that James stands in opposition to Paul in respect to faith and works (cf Jas **2** 17 ff in contrast with Gal **2** 16 and many other passages in Paul). But particular interest attaches to the problem of Christ's attitude toward the OT law. His "but I say unto you" (Mt **5** 22 and *passim*) has been interpreted by many as a distinct contradiction of the OT. Another question of acute interest is the agreement of the Johannine picture of Jesus with that of the Synoptists.

5. Alleged Discrepancies Pertaining to Doctrine

It can scarcely require proof that some of these alleged discrepancies are not such at all. For example, Jesus' attitude toward the OT was one of profound reverence and affirmation. He was perfectly conscious that the OT law represented a stage in the Divine education of mankind. His "but I say unto you" was not a denying of the degree of advancement represented by the OT law, but a carrying out of the principle of the law to its full expression (cf LAW; FULFILMENT). Of course, the Divine education of Israel did not mean the mere inculcation of the truth in a fallow and hitherto unoccupied soil. There was much superstition and error to be overcome. If then one should insist that the errors, which revelation was destined to overcome, still manifest themselves here and there in the OT, it may be replied that at all events the one grand tendency of Divine revelation is unmistakably clear. An idea is not "Scriptural" simply by virtue of its having been incidentally expressed by a Biblical writer, but because it essentially and inseparably belongs to the organic whole of the Biblical testimony. In the case of James v. Paul the antithesis is one of emphasis, not of contradiction of a first principle. And as for the variations in the gospel history, these do not deserve to be called real discrepancies so long as the Gospels unite in giving one harmonious picture and testimony concerning the personal life and the work and teaching of Jesus. Even from this point of view, John, though so much more theological, preaches the same Christ as the Synoptists.

6. Causes of Discrepancies

It is most important to note the real nature of discrepancies as things which do not sound together. Two notes on the piano may not sound together, but a musician adds a third and makes sweet harmony. One thing needed had been lacking. So, two witnesses from very different standpoints give account of an event; their account shows discrepancies, because something is omitted which appeared only from another standpoint on the circle. A distinguished lawyer was asked what he would think of two witnesses who told exactly the same story in all details and aspects. He replied that he would think they had fixed up that story. The various evangelists give every indication of being independent witnesses without collusion. If there were no discrepancies, their witness would show manifest collusion.

Faith, however, has no interest in explaining away the human limitations in God's chosen witnesses. It is God's way to place the heavenly "treasure in earthen vessels" (2 Cor **4** 7). It seems that God has purposely led the church to see, through the necessity of recognizing the human limitations of the Bible, just where her faith is grounded. God has made Himself known through His Son. The Scriptures of the NT, and of the OT in preparation for Him, give us a clear and sufficient testimony to the Christ of God. The clearness and persuasive power of that testimony make all questions of verbal and other formal agreement essentially irrelevant. The certainty that God has spoken unto us in His Son and that we have this knowledge through the Scripture testimony lifts us above all anxious concern for the possible errors of the witnesses in matters evidently nonessential.

7. Their Significance for Faith

LITERATURE.—Besides the lit. noted under REVELATION and INSPIRATION, J. W. Haley, *An Examination of the Alleged Discrepancies of the Bible*, Andover, 1873; M. S. Terry, *Bib. Hermeneutics*, New York, 1883; Kähler, *Zur Bibelfrage*, Leipzig, 1907.

REVISED BY M. G. K. J. R. VAN PELT

DISCUS, dis'kus (**δίσκος,** *dískos*, "the summons of the discus," 2 Macc **4** 14 m, "to the game of the discus," AV "the game of discus"): The *discus* was a round stone slab or metal plate of considerable weight (a kind of quoit), the contest of throwing which to the greatest distance was one of the exercises in the Gr *gymnasia*, being included in the *pentathlon*. It was introduced into Jerus by Jason the high priest in the time of Antiochus Epiphanes, 175–164 BC, in the Palaestra he had formed there in imitation of the Gr games. His conduct led to his being described in 2 Macc **4** 13.14 as that "ungodly man" through whom even the priests forsook their duties to play at the *discus*. A statue of a *discobolos* (discus-thrower) is in the British Museum. From *discus* we have the words "disc," "dish," "desk." See GAMES. W. L. WALKER

DISEASE, di-zēz', **DISEASES,** di-zēz'iz (חָלָה, *ḥālāh*, חֳלִי, *ḥŏlī*; **νόσος,** *nósos*): Palestine, from its position and physical conditions, ought to be a healthy country. That it is not so depends on the unsanitary conditions in which the people live and the absence of any attempts to check the introduction or development of zymotic diseases. The number of marshes or pools is fairly small, and the use of active measures to destroy the larvae of mosquitos might easily diminish or abolish the malarial fevers which now prevail all over the country. The freeing of Ismâilieh and Port Said from these pests is an object-lesson in sanitation. When one examines the conditions of life in towns and villages all over the country, the evidences of the ravages of these fevers and their sequelae appear on every hand as they affect all ages from infancy to middle age, and one meets but few individuals of extreme old age. The absence of any adequate system of drainage and the pollution of the water supplies are also factors of great importance in preserving this unhealthiness.

In ancient times it was regarded as healthier than Egypt, as it well might be, hence the diseases of Egypt are referred to as being worse than those of Pal (Dt **7** 15; **28** 60; Am **4** 10). The sanitary regulations and restrictions of the PC would doubtless have raised the standard of public health, but it is unlikely that these were ever observed over any large area.

The types of disease which are referred to in the Bible are those that still prevail. Fevers of several kinds, dysentery, leprosy, intestinal worms, plague, nervous diseases such as paralysis and epilepsy, insanity, ophthalmia and skin diseases are among the commonest and will be described under their several names. Methods of treatment are described under MEDICINE; PHYSICIAN. The word "disease" or "diseases" in AV is changed to "sickness" in RV in 2 K **1** 2; **8** 8; Mt **9** 35, and left out in Jn **5** 4; while in Mt **8** 17 "sicknesses" is replaced by "diseases." RV also changes "infirmity" in Lk **7** 21 to "diseases," and in Ps **38** 7 "a loathsome disease" is changed to "burning."

ALEX. MACALISTER

DISEASES OF THE EYE. See EYES, DISEASES OF.

DISH: The rendering in EV in some connections of three Heb and one Gr word. The *ḳeʿārāh* of Ex **25** 29; **37** 16; Nu **4** 7 was apparently a kind of salver, in this case of gold, for holding the loaves of the "presence bread." The same word represents

Slave Bearing Covered Dishes.

the silver "platters" (Nu **7** 13 ff) brought by the princes as a dedication gift. The *ṣēphel* of Jgs **5** 25 was a large bowl, so trd in Jgs **6** 38. "Lordly dish" is lit. "*bowl of* [fit for] *nobles*." The *çallaḥath* of 2 K **21** 13; Prov **19** 24; **26** 15 (last two AV "bosom" after LXX) refers probably to the wide, deep dish in which the principal part of the meal was served. Of somewhat similar form may have been the *trúblion* (LXX for *ḳeʿārāh*) mentioned in connection with the Passover meal (Mt **26** 23; Mk **14** 20). BENJAMIN RENO DOWNER

DISHAN, dī'shan, **DISHON,** dī'shon (דִּישָׁן, *dīshān*, דִּישׁוֹן, *dīshōn*, "antelope," "pygarg"): A Horite clan, mentioned as the youngest "son" and elsewhere as the "grandson" of Seir. The form **Dishon** occurs several times in the list of Horite clans, together with many other totem names (Gen **36** *passim;* 1 Ch **1** 38.41). See Gray, *HPN*, 89.

DISHONESTY, dis-on'es-ti: Only in 2 Cor **4** 2, the AV rendering of Gr *aischúnē;* AV elsewhere and RV uniformly, "shame."

DISOBEDIENCE, dis-ō-bē'di-ens, **DISOBEDIENT** (מָרָה, *mārāh;* **ἀπειθέω,** *apeithéō*, **παρακούω,** *parakoúō*): The word used chiefly in the NT has the general meaning of a lack of regard for authority or rulership. The stronger meaning of actual stubbornness or violence is perhaps conveyed in the OT (1 K **13** 26; Neh **9** 26; cf 1 K **13** 21).

In the NT there seem to be two rather clearly defined uses of the word, one objective and practical, the other ethical and psychological. The first refers more to conduct, the second to belief and one's mental attitude toward the object of disobedience. To the first belong such passages as refer to the overt act of disobedience to one's parents (Rom **1** 30; 2 Tim **3** 2). Illustrating this more fully, the tr according to the AV of 1 Tim **1** 9 is given as "unruly" in the RV. By far the greater emphasis, however, is placed upon the distinctly ethical quality in which disobedience is really an attitude of the mind and finds its essence in a heart of unbelief and unfaithfulness (1 Pet **2** 7.8; Eph **2** 2; **5** 6; Col **3** 6). In the latter three references "children [sons] of disobedience" are mentioned, as if one should become the very offspring of such an unhappy and unholy state of mind. The classic phrase of NT lit. (Acts **26** 19) contains both the practical and the ethical aspects. Paul's convictions were changed by the vision and his conduct was made to conform immediately to it. WALTER G. CLIPPINGER

DISORDERLY, dis-ôr'dẽr-li (ἄτακτος, *átaktos*): The word is found four times in the Epp. to the Thess (1 Thess **5** 14; 2 Thess **3** 6.7.11), "Withdraw yourselves from every brother that walketh d."; "We behaved not ourselves d."; "We hear of some that walk among you d." The word is a military term and has reference to the soldier who does not keep the ranks (*inordinatus*, Liv). Then it refers to people who refuse to obey the civil laws, and thus it gets its meaning, "disorderly." It points to members in the early church, who, by their lives, became a reproach to the gospel of Christ (cf 1 Thess **4** 11.12). HENRY E. DOSKER

DISPATCH, dis-pach': Occurs Tob **7** 8 in the sense of dispatch of business, "Let this business be dispatched" (RV "finished"); 2 Macc **12** 18, "before he had dispatched anything" (RV "without accomplishing"); Wisd **11** 19 [20] in the sense of finishing, destroying, "dispatch them at once" (RV "consume"); 2 Macc **9** 4 "dispatch the journey" (*katanúein*), which may mean "finish it quickly." RV spells "despatch."

DISPENSATION, dis-pen-sā'shun: The Gr word (*oikonomía*) so tr[d] signifies primarily, a stewardship, the management or disposition of affairs intrusted to one. Thus 1 Cor **9** 17, AV "A dispensation of the gospel is committed unto me," RV "I have a stewardship intrusted to me." The idea is similar in Eph **3** 2 ‖ Col **1** 25 (RVm "stewardship"). In Eph **1** 10 God's own working is spoken of as a "dispensation."

DISPERSION, dis-pûr'shun, **THE** (διασπορά, *diasporá*):

1. Golah and Dispersion
2. Purpose of "
3. Causes of "
4. Extent of "
5. The Eastern "
6. The Egyptian "
7. Testimony of Aramaic Papyri
8. Jewish Temple at Syene
9. Theories of the Syene Settlement
10. Importance of the Discovery
11. A New Chapter of OT History
12. Alexandrian Judaism
13. The Jews and Hellenism
14. The Septuagint
15. Early Evidence of a Jewish Community
16. The Dispersion in Syria
17. In Arabia
18. In Asia Minor
19. Among Greeks Proper
20. The Roman Dispersion
21. Jews and Pompey
22. Jews and the First Caesars
23. Influence of Jews in the Early Roman Empire
24. Jews in Italy, Gaul, Spain and N. Africa.
25. The Numbers of the Dispersion
26. Jewish Proselytism
27. Internal Organization
28. Unity of the Jewish People
29. Dispersion Influenced by Greek Thought
30. The Dispersion a Preparation for the Advent of Christ
31. The Dispersion an Auxiliary to the Spread of the Gospel

The Dispersion is the comprehensive designation applied to Jews living outside of Pal and maintaining their religious observances and customs among the Gentiles.

1. Golah and Diaspora

They were known as the *Gōlāh* (Aram. *Gālūthā'*), the captivity—an expression describing them in relation to their own land; and the *Diaspora*, the Dispersion, an expression describing them in relation to the nations among whom they were scattered. On a notable occasion Jesus said, "Ye shall seek me, and shall not find me: and where I am, ye cannot come. The Jews therefore said among themselves, Whither will this man go that we shall not find him? Will he go unto the Dispersion among the Greeks, and teach the Greeks?" (Jn **7** 34.35).

2. Purpose of the Dispersion

In 2 Macc certain priests of Jerus are represented as praying to God: "Gather together our Dispersion, set at liberty them that are in bondage among the heathen" (2 Macc **1** 27; cf 2 Esd **2** 7; Jas **1** 1; 1 Pet **1** 1). The thought of such a Dispersion as a punishment for the disobedience of the people finds frequent expression in the Prophets: Hosea (**9** 3), Jeremiah (**8** 3; **16** 15, etc), Ezekiel (**4** 13), and Zechariah (**10** 9). And it appears also in the Deuteronomic Law (Dt **28** 25; **30** 1). That the Dispersion of the Jews was for the benefit of the Gentiles is a conception to which expression is given in utterances of psalmists and prophets (Ps **67**; Mic **5** 7, etc). It is found also in the Apoc Bar, a work belonging to the 1st cent. AD: "I will scatter this people among the Gentiles, that they may do good to the Gentiles" (**1** 7).

3. Causes of the Dispersion

The causes of the Dispersion most obvious to the student of OT history were the Assyr and Bab captivities, when the king of Assyria carried Israel away into his own land and placed them in Halah, and in Habor by the river of Gozan, and in the cities of the Medes (2 K **17** 5 ff); and when in the reign of Nebuchadrezzar, king of Babylon, Judah was carried away into Babylonia (2 K **24** 14). See CAPTIVITY. But there were other captivities which helped to scatter the children of Abraham. Ptolemy I of Egypt (322–285 BC) by his expeditions to Pal and his capture of Jerus added largely to the Jewish population of Alexandria. Antiochus the Great of Syria (223–187 BC) removed from the Jewish communities in Mesopotamia and Babylon 2,000 families and settled them in Phrygia and Lydia (Jos, *Ant*, XII, iii, 4). Pompey after his capture of Jerus in 63 BC carried off hundreds of Jews to Rome, where they were sold as slaves, but, afterward, many of them obtained their freedom and civic rights.

4. Extent of the Dispersion

There was, besides, a voluntary emigration of Jewish settlers for purposes of trade and commerce into the neighboring countries, and esp. into the chief cities of the civilized world. The successors of Alexander, and their successors in turn, encouraged immigration into their territories and the mingling of nationalities. They needed colonists for the settlements and cities which they established, and with the offer of citizenship and facilities for trade and commerce they attracted many of the Jewish people.

"In this way," says Philo, "Jerus became the capital, not only of Judaea, but of many other lands, on account of the colonies which it sent out from time to time into the bordering districts of Egypt, Phoenicia, Syria, Coele-Syria, and into the more distant regions of Pamphylia, Cilicia, the greater part of Asia Minor as far as Bithynia, and the remotest corners of Pontus. And in like manner into Europe: into Thessaly, and Boeotia, and Macedonia, and Aetolia, and Attica and Argos, and Corinth, and into the most fertile and fairest parts of the Peloponnesus. And not only is the continent full of Jewish colonists, but also the most important islands, such as Euboea, Cyprus, and Crete. I say nothing of the countries beyond the Euphrates. All of them except a very small portion, and Babylon, and all the satrapies which contain fruitful land, have Jewish inhabitants" (Philo, *Leg ad Caium*, 36).

About the middle of the 2d cent. BC the Sibylline Oracles could say of the Jewish people: "Every land and every sea is full of thee" (**3** 271). About the same period the Rom Senate, being anxious to extend protection to the Jews, had a circular letter written in their favor to the kings of Egypt, Syria, Pergamum, Cappadocia and Parthia, and to a great number of provinces, cities and islands of the Mediterranean, where presumably there was a larger or smaller number of Jews (1 Macc **15** 15 ff). It is no surprise, therefore, to read that for the Feast of Pentecost at Jerus, there were present after the ascension of Jesus: "Parthians and Medes and Elamites, and the dwellers in Mesopotamia, in Judaea and Cappadocia, in Pontus and Asia, in Phrygia and Pamphylia, in Egypt and the parts of Libya about Cyrene, and sojourners from Rome, both Jews and proselytes, Cretans and Arabians" (Acts **2** 9–12).

The Eastern Dispersion, caused by the Assyrian and Babylonian captivities, seems to have increased and multiplied, and to have enjoyed a considerable measure of liberty, and of prosperity. When the return from the captivity took place under Zerubbabel, it was only a small proportion of the exiles who sought a home again in the land of their fathers. Nor did the numbers who accompanied Ezra from Babylon greatly diminish the exiles who remained behind. In the time of Christ, Jos could speak of the Jews in Babylonia by "innumerable myriads" (*Ant*, XI, v, 2). He also tells us of the 2,000 Jewish families whom Antiochus transferred from Babylon and Mesopotamia to Phrygia and Syria. Of the peculiarities of the Jews as a people living apart and observing their own customs and arousing the ill-will of the neighbors, we have a glimpse in the Pers period in the Book of Est (**3** 8). Babylonia remained a focus of eastern Judaism for centuries, and from the discussions in rabbinical schools there were elaborated the Talm of Jerus in the 5th cent. of our era, and the Talm of Babylon a cent. later. The two chief centers of Mesopotamian Judaism were Nehardea, a town on the Euphrates, and Nisibis on the Mygdonius, an affluent of the Chaboras, which were also centers of Syrian Christianity.

5. The Eastern Dispersion

The Egyp Dispersion is of special interest and importance, and recent discoveries have thrown unexpected light upon it. As far back as the days of Sheshenq, the founder of the 22d Dynasty, the Shishak of 1 K **14** 25 f; 2 Ch **12** 2 f, who invaded Pal in the 10th cent. BC, and engraved on the S. wall of the great Temple of Karnak the names of many districts and cities he had captured, prisoners of war and hostages may have been carried off to Egypt by the conqueror. At a later time Jewish mercenaries are said to have fought in the expedition of Psammetichus II against Ethiopia, to which expedition belong the famous inscriptions of Abu Simbel (594–589 BC). So we learn from the well-known Letter of Aristeas. But the clearest and best-known example of a settlement of Jews in Egypt is that connected with the prophet Jeremiah. When Gedaliah, the governor of Judaea, after the destruction of Jerus in 586 BC, had been treacherously murdered, the depressed and dispirited remnant under Johanan, the son of Kareah, resolved to take flight into Egypt, against the counsel of Jeremiah. A host of fugitives, including Jeremiah and his friend Baruch, accordingly set out thither, and settled at Migdol and Tahpanhes and Noph (Memphis), and in the country of Pathros in upper Egypt (Jer **43, 44**). It was in Egypt with those fugitives that Jeremiah ended his life. Many of the fugitives were taken prisoners by Nebuchadrezzar on one of his latest expeditions to the west, and were transported to Babylon (Jos, *Ant*, X, ix, 7; cf Jer **43** 8 f).

6. The Egyptian Dispersion

Of this colony of Jews it is natural to see a strong confirmation in the recent discovery of Aram. papyri at Assouan, the Syene of the ancients. The papyri were the contents of a deed box of a member of a Jewish colony in upper Egypt, and the deeds refer to house property in which Jews are concerned. Here then at Assouan, about 470 BC is a colony of Jews who have acquired houses and other property, and have become bankers and money lenders, within a cent. of the death of Jeremiah. In the papyri there is evidence of the existence of a tribunal of the Hebrews, a court where cases could be decided, as fully recognized by law as any of the other courts, Egyp or Pers, for Egypt, "the basest of kingdoms," was then subject to a Pers suzerain. Most significant of all, Jeh is acknowledged as the God of the Jews, and the existence of a chapel and even of an altar of sacrifice is beyond all doubt. Evidently these Jews in Egypt did not consider that an altar of Jeh could not stand anywhere else than at Jerus, or that outside Jerus the worship of the synagogue was the only worship of the God of their fathers. These facts are rendered still more striking when we regard them as a fulfilment of Isaiah's prophecy: "In that day there shall be five cities in the land of Egypt that speak the language of Canaan, and swear to Jehovah of hosts; one shall be called the city of destruction. In that day there shall be an altar to Jehovah in the midst of the land of Egypt, and a pillar at the border thereof to Jehovah" (Isa **19** 18.19). These papyri give information similar to that which the clay tablets discovered at Nippur give regarding the house of Murashu Sons (see CAPTIVITY) about the same time—the time when Ezra was setting out from Babylon to restore at Jerus the worship of the temple which Zerubbabel had rebuilt. It was just about a cent. from the time that Jeremiah had gone down to Egypt that we have the first of these deeds, and it was the grandfathers, or great-grandfathers, of the persons concerned whom he had accompanied thither so much against his will.

7. Testimony of Aramaic Papyri

These papyri were discovered in 1904, and a year or two later, additional papyri were discovered in a mound which stands on the site of the ancient Elephantiné or Yeb, an island in the Nile, on the frontier also. One of these papyri contains a petition from the Jewish colony in Elephantiné addressed to Bagohi (called Bagoas by Jos, *Ant*, XI, vii, 7), the Pers governor of Judah, about 408 BC. They ask for assistance to enable them to rebuild the temple of Jeh in Elephantiné, which had been destroyed at the instigation of the priests of the ram-headed Egyp god Khnub, who had a temple in the fortress of Yeb or Elephantiné. This Jewish temple had been erected to Jeh at least 120 years before and had been spared by Cambyses in 525 BC when he destroyed all the temples erected to the gods of Egypt. The destruction of the temple at Yeb occurred in the 14th year of Darius, 411 BC. It contained an altar for burnt sacrifice, and there were gold and silver vessels in which the blood of sacrifice was collected. The head of the college of priests presenting this petition is Jedoniah, a name found in an abbreviated form in Jadon (Neh **3** 7).

8. Jewish Temple at Syene

An attempt has been made to show that the bearers of these Heb names were descended from the captivity of the Northern Kingdom. It is suggested that they had come into Egypt with the Pers army under Cambyses from their adopted homes in Assyria and the cities of the Medes and had obtained possessions on the southern frontier of Egypt. Names believed to point to the Northern Kingdom, like Hosea and Menahem, occur very frequently, but this is too narrow a foundation for such a theory, and the Israelitish origin of the Syene colonists is not established (*JQR* [1907], 441 ff). There is more to be said in favor of the view that they were the descendants of a Jewish military colony. That Jewish mercenaries fought in the campaigns of the Pharaohs we have already seen. And that Elephantiné was an important garrison town on the frontier is also certain. Jos (*Ant*, XIV, vi, 2) mentions a Jewish military colony holding a post at Pelusium in the cent. before Christ, and this might be a similar garrison stationed at the opposite extremity of the land in the 5th cent. Such a garrison would attract Jews engaged in business and in the occupations of civil life, and so a distinct Jewish community would be formed. It has even been suggested that the tidings of the destruction of the temple at Jerus furnished the motive to these Egyp Jews to build the temple and rear the altar of burnt offering which the heathen priests of Khnub had destroyed.

9. Theories of the Syene Settlement

While the petition to the religious authorities at Jerus indicates that the priests of Elephantiné regarded their temple as dependent upon the temple at Jerus, it is significant that they were also, as is shown in their letter, in communication with Delaiah and Shelemiah the sons of Sanballat, the governor of Samaria. That this was Nehemiah's enemy (Neh **4** 1; **6** 1, etc) is impossible, for he lived nearly a cent. earlier. But the association with descendants of his, themselves Samaritans, gives a schismatical appearance to the position of the Elephantiné temple. The existence of this temple with its priesthood, its altar of sacrifice, and its offerings, from 500 years BC, is an important fact in the history of the Dispersion. It was meant to keep those Jewish exiles true to the religion of their fathers and in religious fellowship with their brethren in Pal. For a like purpose the Temple of Onias at Leontopolis was erected in the early years of the Maccabean struggle. Onias had to flee from Jerus with a number of priests and Levites, and for the aid he rendered to Ptolemy Philometor, the king of Egypt, he received a gift of land upon which he built a

10. Importance of the Discovery

temple like to the Temple at Jerus. Professor Flinders Petrie believes he has discovered this temple of Onias IV at Tel el-Yehudiyeh (*Hyksos and Israelite Cities*, 31). The discovery confirms the account given of the temple by Jos, who is our only authority for its erection (*Ant*, XIII, iii, 2; XIV, viii, 2).

11. A New Chapter of OT History

The Elephantiné-Syene papyri have added a new and valuable chapter to OT history. We know now of a Jewish temple in Egypt which certainly reaches 400 years farther into antiquity than the temple of Onias IV at Leontopolis, and we obtain important information as to the relations of its priesthood with the leaders of the Jerus Jews and the Samaritans. We know now from unbiased authorities that the Jewish settlements in the Valley of the Nile are much older than has hitherto been believed. We have valuable confirmation not only of the notices in the Book of Jer, but also of the statements in the later Hellenistic lit. Moreover, it is now shown that the skepticism which has prevailed in some quarters as to the very existence of any considerable Egyp Dispersion before the time of Alexander the Great is unwarranted (Peters, *Die jüdische Gemeinde von Elephantiné-Syene*, 50 f; Schürer, *GJV*[4], III, 19 f).

12. Alexandrian Judaism

What exactly were the fortunes of this Jewish community at a later time, no record has yet been found to tell. Possibly it decayed in course of time, for Herodotus who visited Egypt about 450 BC makes no mention of it and found no Jews in sufficient numbers to attract his attention. It was undoubtedly with the founding of Alexandria in 332 BC that the flourishing period of Judaism in Egypt commenced. Alexander the Great had hastened from the field of victory at Issus 333 BC, through Syria by way of Tyre, the siege of which occupied him some months, showing clemency to the inhabitants of Jerus and severity to the recalcitrant inhabitants of Gaza till by its eastern gate he entered Egypt and took possession of the land of the Pharaohs. The Jews appear to have been friendly to Macedonian conquest, and in Alexander's new city they received the rights of citizenship and two quarters all to themselves. That they were restricted to their own quarters does not appear, and in the time of Philo, at the commencement of the Christian era, they had synagogues and places of prayer in all parts of the city. Alexander died in 323 BC but the favor which he had accorded to the Jews was continued by the Ptolemies who succeeded to his Egyp empire. The first Ptolemy, Lagi or Soter (322–285 BC), increased the Jewish population of Alexandria by raids into Pal on which he brought back a large number of captives, both Jews and Samaritans. Other Jews, hearing of his liberality and of the prosperity of their coreligionists, were attracted to Egypt and settled in Alexandria of their own accord (Jos, *Ant*, XII, i, 1). Under their own ethnarch they enjoyed great prosperity and had full religious liberty. The principal synagogue of the city was on a scale of great magnificence. In the reign of Ptolemy Philometor (182–146 BC) they were allowed to set up the temple at Leontopolis, as we have already noticed. In the time of Philo the Jewish colony in Egypt was considered to number a million.

13. The Jews and Hellenism

It was in Alexandria that the Jews first came so powerfully under the influence of Hellenism, and here that the peculiar Graeco-Jewish philosophy sprang up of which Philo was the most notable representative. The same soil was eminently favorable to early Christianity which had from the end of the 2d cent. onward its greatest teachers and their learned catechetical school. See ALEXANDRIA.

14. The Septuagint

The great monument of Hellenistic Judaism, which had its chief seat in Alexandria, is the LXX tr of the OT, which became such a powerful *praeparatio evangelica*, and was the Bible of the Apostles and the first Christians even of the Lord Jesus Christ Himself. It is ascribed in the *Letter of Aristeas* to the interest of Ptolemy II Philadelphus (285–247 BC) in a proposal to secure a copy of the Jewish Law in an accessible tr for the famous Royal Library. It is more likely that as familiarity with their Heb tongue diminished in their new surroundings, the need of an intelligible version of the Law to begin with was felt, and Jewish hands were set to work to produce it. In course of time the rest followed, but from the tradition of its being the work of 70 or 72 translators it is known as the LXX. See SEPTUAGINT.

15. Early Evidence of a Jewish Community

The question has been raised whether too much has not been made of a Jewish community in Alexandria so early, and it has been asserted that we can scarcely speak of a Jewish Dispersion anywhere before the Maccabean period in the second half of the 2d cent. BC. The evidence as we have seen points to the existence of Jewish communities continuously from the days of Jeremiah. Papyri prove the presence of Jews in Egypt, not only in the towns but in country districts from a comparatively early period. A remarkable inscription has recently come to light showing that at Schedia, some 20 miles from Alexandria, there existed a Jewish community which had built a synagogue and dedicated it to the honor of Ptolemy III Euergetes (247–222 BC) and his queen Berenice. If such a community was organized in the little town of Schedia at that date, we can well believe the cosmopolitan city of Alexandria to have had a considerable Jewish community at a still earlier date.

16. Dispersion in Syria

When we turn to Syria, we find large numbers of Jews, notwithstanding the hatred of Greeks and Syrians. Jos (*BJ*, VII, iii, 3) says that it is the country which has the largest percentage of Jewish inhabitants, and Antioch among the towns of Syria had the preëminence. In Damascus, which seems to have had a Jewish quarter or Jewish bazaars in the days of Ahab (1 K **20** 34 and Burney's note ad loc.), the Jewish population was numbered by thousands. From Galilee and Gilead and the region of the Hauran, Judas Maccabaeus and his brother Jonathan brought bodies of Jews, who were settlers among a pagan population, for safety to Judaea (1 Macc **5**).

17. In Arabia

Even in Arabia Judaism had considerable footing. Edward Glaser, who prosecuted valuable archaeological researches in Arabia (see Hilprecht, *Recent Researches in Bible Lands*, 131 ff), professes to have found Himyaritic inscriptions of the 4th and 5th cents. of our era which are monotheistic and therefore Jewish, but there is still uncertainty as to this. In the beginning of the 6th cent. a Jewish king actually reigned in Arabia, and because of his persecution of the Christians he was attacked and overthrown by the Christian king of Abyssinia.

18. In Asia Minor

Of the widespread distribution of the Dispersion in Asia Minor there is abundant testimony, not only in the texts of the apostles, but in classical and early Christian lit. and in the epigraphic lit. which has been accumulating for the last 30 years. At Pergamum, in Lydia, in Karia, at Magnesia, at Tralles, at Miletum, in Cappadocia, Bithynia, and Pontus, considerable Jewish communities existed at the beginning of the Christian era. At Smyrna the Jews played a prominent part in the death of Polycarp 155 AD, being esp. zealous in heaping up fagots upon the fire that consumed the martyr. In his *Cities and Bishoprics of Phrygia* Sir William Ramsay mentions numerous indications found on inscriptions of Jewish settlers, and his chapter on "The Jews in Phrygia" focuses the results of his inquiries (op. cit., 667 ff; cf 649 ff). He has also made it extremely probable that long before St. Paul's day there was a strong body of Jews in Tarsus of Cilicia, and he holds that a Jewish colony was settled there as early as 171 BC. "The Seleucid kings," he says, like the Ptolemies, "used the Jews as an element of the colonies which they founded to strengthen their hold on Phrygia and other countries." But it is difficult to trace out the profound influence they exerted in the development of their country from the fact that they adopted to such an extent Gr and Rom names and manners, and were thus almost indistinguishable. At Laodicea and Hierapolis there have been found many evidences of their presence: for example, at the latter place an inscription on a gravestone tells how the deceased Publius Aelius Glycon mortified a sum of money to provide for the decoration of his tomb every year at the Feast of Unleavened Bread.

19. Among Greeks Proper

The Dispersion among the Greeks proper had attained to considerable dimensions in the time of Christ. Philo, as noticed above, mentions Thessaly, Boeotia, Macedonia, Aetolia, Attica, Argos, Corinth and the fairest and most fertile parts of the Peloponnesus as having Jewish inhabitants. Inscriptions recovered from Delphi and elsewhere relating to the manumission of slaves in the 2d cent. BC contain the names of Jews (Deissmann, *Light from the Ancient East*, 325 f). In Sparta and Sicyon, Jews lived in the days of the Maccabees (1 Macc **15** 23). At Philippi we know from Acts **16** 16 there was a *proseuchē*, or place of of prayer, and at Thessalonica, Berea, Athens, Corinth there were synagogues in St. Paul's time. On the islands of the Greek archipelago and the Mediterranean there were Jews. Cyprus, the home of Barnabas, had a large Jewish population; and Euboea and Crete are named by Philo as Jewish centers. Rhodes has the distinction of having produced two opponents of Judaism in the first half of the 1st cent. BC. Clearchus of Soli, a disciple of Aristotle, introduces in one of his dialogues a Jew from Coele-Syria, Hellenic not in speech only but in mind, representing him as having come in his travels to Asia Minor and there conversed with Aristotle. Such an experience may have been rare so early; the incident may not be fact, but fiction; yet such as it is it tells a tale of the spread of Judaism.

20. The Roman Dispersion

The relations of Rome with the Jewish people lend special interest to the Dispersion there. Jews do not appear to have been settled in Rome before the Maccabean period. There is a certain pathos in the appeal made to the Rom state by Judas Maccabaeus, amid the difficulties that were gathering round his position, for "a league of amity and confederacy" with the Rom people (1 Macc **8** 17–32). His brother and successor, Jonathan, followed this up later (**12** 1–4.16). And in 140 BC Simon sent a delegation which concluded a treaty, offensive and defensive, with Rome, which was duly intimated by the Senate to their allies in various countries, esp. of the East. During the stay of the mission at Rome its members seem to have made attempts at religious propagandism, and the praetor Hispalus compelled them to return to their homes for attempting to corrupt Rom morals by introducing the worship of Jupiter Sabazius which is no doubt the Rom interpretation of the Lord of Hosts (Jehovah Sabaoth). But ere long in Rome, as in Alexandria, they formed a colony by themselves, occupying Trastevere, the Transtiberine portion of the city, together with an island in the Tiber. Their prosperity grew with their numbers. When Cicero in 59 BC was defending Flaccus he speaks of gold being sent out of Italy, and all the provinces, to Jerus, and there was present among his listeners a large body of Jews interested in the case.

21. Jews and Pompey

When Pompey had captured Jerus in 63 BC, he brought back with him to Rome a number of Jewish captives. They were sold as slaves, but many of them received their freedom and rights to citizenship. When Julius Caesar, who was a great patron and protector of the Jews, was assassinated, they wept over him for nights on end.

22. Jews and the First Caesars

Augustus protected and encouraged them. Tiberius, however, adopted repressive measures toward them, and 4,000 Jews were deported by him to Sardinia while others were driven out of the city. With the downfall of Sejanus, the unworthy favorite of Tiberius, this repressive policy was reversed and they were allowed to return to Rome. Claudius again devised measures against them (c 50 AD), and they were banished from the city.

23. Influence of Jews in the Early Roman Empire

They had, however, so multiplied and they had attained such influence that it was impossible to get rid of them altogether. Their customs and religious observances brought down upon them the scorn of Juvenal and others, while their faith and worship had attractions for the thoughtful and the superstitious.

"The Jews from the time of the first Caesar," says Sir Samuel Dill, "have worked their way into every class of society. A Jewish prince had inspired Caligula with an oriental ideal of monarchy. There were adherents of Judaism in the household of the great freedmen of Claudius, and their growing influence and turbulence compelled that emperor to expel the race from his capital. The worldly, pleasure-loving Poppaea had, perhaps, yielded to the mysterious charms of the religion of Moses. But it was under the Flavians, who had such close associations with Judaea, that Jewish influences made themselves most felt. And in the reign of Domitian, two members of the imperial house, along with many others, suffered for following the Jewish mode of life" (*Roman Society from Nero to Marcus Aurelius*, 84).

In recent excavations, which have laid bare much of subterranean Rome, many Jewish tombs have been examined and have yielded much additional knowledge of the conditions of Jewish life in the capital of the Caesars. Probably Jews gracing Pompey's triumph after his Syrian campaign, 61 BC, made the first Rom catacombs similar to those on Jewish hillsides and esp. round Jerus; and in these Jewish catacombs pagans and Christians were never laid.

24. Jews in Italy, Gaul, Spain and North Africa

In Italy, apart from Rom and Southern Italy, where they were widely spread, the number of Jews at the beginning of our era was not large. In Southern Gaul they were numerous and in Spain they were numerous and powerful. In North Africa there were Jewish communities in many centers, and Cyrene was the home of a large and flourishing Jewish population.

25. Numbers of the Dispersion

It is not easy to form a trustworthy estimate of the Jewish population of the world in the times of Christ. Harnack reckons up four or four and a half millions (*Expansion of Christianity*, I, 10) within the Rom Empire. The Judaism of the Dispersion would at least be several times more numerous than the Judaism of Pal.

26. Jewish Proselytism

The question has been discussed how far the Jews of the Dispersion recruited their ranks by proselytism. That they should maintain a propaganda on behalf of their ancestral faith would only be in keeping with the character of their religion as a religion of revelation. Although they had to live within "the hedge of the Law" to protect them against the corruptions and idolatries of the Gentiles, there was nevertheless at the heart of Judaism a missionary purpose, as we see from the universalism of the Pss and the Prophets. Judaism was burdened with a message which concerned all men, to the effect that there was one God, holy and spiritual, Creator of heaven and earth, who had committed to the family of Abraham in trust for the world His Law. To witness for the Living God, and to proclaim His Law, was the chief element of the Jewish propaganda in the Rom empire, and their system of proselytism enabled them to gain adherents in numbers. In this the OT Scriptures and the observance of the Sabbath were important factors, and enabled them to win the adherence of intelligent and educated people.

27. Internal Organization

That the Jews of the Dispersion had an internal organization with courts of their own, having considerable jurisdiction, not only in spiritual but in civil affairs, there is no doubt. This would only be in accordance with the analogy of their constitution as seen in the NT, and of their commercial organization in many lands to this day.

28. Unity of the Jewish People

In all the lands of their Dispersion the Jews never lost touch with the land of their fathers, or Jerus, the city of the Great King. The bond of unity was maintained by the pilgrimages they made from all the countries where they were scattered to their three great national feasts; by the payment of the half-shekel toward the services of the Temple as long as it stood; and by their voluntary submission, so long as they had a national polity, to the decrees of the great Sanhedrin.

29. Dispersion Influenced by Greek Thought

That Judaism was influenced in its Dispersion by contact of the larger world of life and thought in which the Jews had their place outside of Pal we can see by the example of Alexandria. It was there that it felt most powerfully the penetrating and pervasive influence of Gr thought, and the large apocryphal and apocalyptic lit. which sprang up there is one of the most notable results. "The Alexandrian Jew was in reality both a Jew and a Greek; he held the faith of Jeh and sincerely worshipped the God of his fathers, but he spoke the Gr language, had received a Gr education, and had contracted many Gr ideas and habits. Still those in his position were Jews first, and Greeks afterward, and on all 'the fundamentals' were in thorough sympathy with their Palestinian brethren" (Fairweather, *From the Exile to the Advent*, 109 f).

30. The Dispersion a Preparation for the Advent of Christ

The Jewish people thus widely distributed over the Rom world with their monotheism, with their Scriptures, and with their Messianic hopes, did much to prepare the way for the advent of the Redeemer who was to be the fulfilment of Jewish expectation and hope. It was due to the strange and unique influence of Judaism and to the circulation of the glowing visions of Israel's prophets among the nations, that there was so widespread an expectation, mentioned by Tacitus, by Suetonius and by Jos, that from Judaea would arise a Ruler whose dominion would be over all. It is now believed that Virgil's conception of the Better Age which was to be inaugurated by the birth of a child was derived from Isaiah's prophecies. And not only did the Jewish Dispersion thus prepare the way for the world's Redeemer in the fulness of the time, but when He had come and suffered and died and risen and ascended, it furnished a valuable auxiliary to the proclamation of the gospel. Wherever the apostles and the first preachers traveled with the good news, they found Jewish communities to whom they offered first the great salvation.

31. An Auxiliary to the Spread of the Gospel

The synagogue services lent themselves most effectively to the ministry of St. Paul and his colleagues, and it was to the synagogue that they first repaired in every city they visited. Even to this day this preservation of "the dispersed of Israel" is one of the marvels of the Divine government of the world, proving the truth of the word of God by one of the earliest prophets: "I will sift the house of Israel among all the nations, like as grain is sifted in a sieve, yet shall not the least kernel fall upon the earth" (Am **9** 9).

LITERATURE.—Schürer, *GJV*[4], III, 1 ff; Harnack, *Expansion of Christianity*, I, 1–40; Fairweather, *Background of the Gospel* and *From the Exile to the Advent; Jew Enc*, art. "Diaspora"; Sayce and Cowley, *Aram. Papyri Discovered at Assuan;* Oesterley and Box, *Religion and Worship of the Synagogue.*

T. NICOL

DISPERSION OF NATIONS. See BABEL; DISPERSION; TABLE OF NATIONS.

DISPOSITION, dis-pō-zish′un (**διαταγαί**, *diatagaí*): Only in Acts **7** 53, "received the law by the disposition of angels," where it bears the meaning of "administration"; RV "as it was ordained by angels."

DISPUTATION, dis-pū-tā′shun: In Acts **15** 2, RV reads "questioning" for AV "disputation" (Gr *suzḗtēsis*). In Rom **14** 1, AV "doubtful disputations" becomes in RV "decision of scruples" (Gr *diakríseis dialogismṓn*, lit. "discussions of doubts"). The Gr in neither case implies what the word "dispute" has come to mean in modern Eng., but rather "to discuss" or "argue."

DISTAFF, dis′taf (פֶּלֶךְ, *pelekh*): This word occurs once in Prov **31** 19; "spindle" is found in the same passage. In RV the meanings of the two words have been exchanged. See SPINNING.

DISTIL, dis-til′: Only found twice in the Eng. Bible (Dt **32** 2; Job **36** 27), in both cases in its original meaning of "to fall in drops," as dew or rain (derived through Fr. from Lat *de*, "down," *stillo*, "to drop"). It does not occur in its later technical sense, for the process we call distillation was not known in ancient times.

DISTINCTLY, dis-tiṅkt′li: Only Neh **8** 8, "They read in the book, in the law of God, *distinctly*." Probably the better rendering is RVm "with an interpretation," i.e. translating into Aram. The Heb word is a part. of vb. *pārash* = "to make distinct." The corresponding Aram. word occurs in Ezr **4** 18 = "plainly" AV and RV, better "translated" RVm.

DITCH, dich: The word is used indiscriminately in AV to represent at least three different ideas: a conduit or trench (2 K **3** 16); a reservoir or cistern; or simply a pit or hole in the ground. In RV this distinction is observed more carefully. Cf Job **9** 31; Ps **7** 15 ("pit"), and Isa **22** 11 ("reservoir"), the former meaning a pit or any similar place of destruction or corruption; the latter a reservoir or cistern of water. The NT usage (Mt **15** 14 AV) corresponds somewhat with the former See also 2 K **3** 16 ("trenches").

DIVERS, dī′vẽrz, **DIVERSE,** dī-vûrs′, **DIVERSITIES,** dī-vûr′si-tiz: "Divers" meaning "various," "different in kind," is now obsolete and used only as a synonym of "several," i.e. more than one. The distinction between "divers" and "diverse" in AV seems to be that the former is the wider term, the latter being restricted to the meaning of "different in kind," while "divers" is also used to express difference of number. RV retains "diverse" in all instances but changes "divers" nearly everywhere, except where it has the meaning "several." Cf Mt **24** 7; Lk **21** 11; He **9** 10, et al. It is hard to understand why RV retains "divers" as a tr of ποικίλος, *poikílos*, in Mt **4** 24; Mk **1** 34, et al., because *poikilos* certainly cannot have the meaning "several" but "different in kind," and the idea expressed in these passages is not that some of the people had several diseases but that different people had different kinds of diseases. The same is true in He **13** 9 where "divers" does not refer to number but to various kinds of teaching. He **2** 4 and Jas **1** 2 rightly change the reading of AV "divers" to "manifold."

In other passages RV changes "divers" to "diverse," and thus renders the idea of the original text "different in kind." Cf Dt **25** 13 f; Prov **20** 10.23. Other passages are changed the better to render the original text: Dt **22** 9, "two kinds of seed"; Jgs **5** 30, "dyed"; 2 Ch **30** 11, "certain men"; Mk **8** 3 and Acts **19** 9, "some." AV reads in all these passages "divers." RV changes AV He **1** 1 "at sundry times and in divers manners," an expression often found in Old Eng., to "by divers portions and in divers manners."

"Diversities" is found twice as tr of διαίρεσις, *diaíresis*, lit. "distribution" (1 Cor **12** 4 ff), but RV changes AV, 1 Cor **12** 28, "diversities" to "divers kinds," as tr of γένη, *génē*, "kinds."

A. L. Breslich

DIVES, dī'vēz. See Lazarus.

DIVIDE, di-vīd': It is difficult to decide whether רָגַע, *rāgha'* (Job **26** 12; Isa **51** 15; Jer **31** 35) should be rendered "to stir up" or "to still." The Heb has both meanings. Some render "He causes the sea to tremble." RV reads "to stir" in text and "to still" in margin, while AV has "to divide" in all three cases. 2 Ch **35** 13, "carried them quickly" (AV "divided them speedily"). Since חָלַק, *ḥālak*, may mean either "to distribute" or "to be smooth," Hos **10** 2 reads "their heart is divided" in the text, but offers "smooth" in margin (AV "divided"). The Gr ὀρθοτομέω, *orthotoméō*, means "to cut straight," hence the more lit. tr of 2 Tim **2** 15, "handling aright the word of truth" (note "holding a straight course in the way of truth" or "rightly dividing the word of truth"; AV "rightly dividing").

A. L. Breslich

DIVINATION, div-i-nā'shun:

1. Definition

Divination is the act of obtaining secret knowledge, esp. that which relates to the future, by means within the reach almost exclusively of special classes of men.

2. Kinds of Divination

Of this there are two main species: (1) artificial, (2) inspirational, or, as it was called in ancient times (Cicero, Lord Bacon, etc), natural divination. Artificial divination depends on the skill of the agent in reading and in interpreting certain signs called omens. See Augury. In inspirational or natural divination the agent is professedly under the immediate influence of some spirit or god who enables the diviner to see the future, etc, and to utter oracles embodying what he sees. Among the Romans artificial divination prevailed almost exclusively, the other having vogue largely among the Greeks, a proof surely of the more spiritual trend of the Gr mind. Yet that great Roman, Cicero, in his memorable treatise on *Divination*, says he agrees with those who take cognizance of these two distinct kinds of divination. As examples of inspirational divination he instances men dreaming or in a state of ecstasy (*De Divinatione*, i. 18). But though Cicero arranges diviners according to their pretentions, he does not believe in any superhuman communication. Thus he explains dreams on psychological principles much as modern psychologists would (op. cit. ii.63 ff). As a matter of fact Cicero was an atheist, or at least an agnostic.

The Lat word *divinatio* was confined almost exclusively to divination by outward signs, though its etymology (*deus*, "god") suggests that it denoted originally the other kind—that due to the inspiration of superhuman beings. Chrysippus (d. at Athens 207 BC), though himself a Gr philosopher, defines the word in a way which would have commanded the approval of nearly every Rom, including Cicero himself who gives it. "Divination," Cicero makes him say (op. cit. ii.63), is "a power in man which foresees and explains those signs which the gods throw in his way." The Greeks were, on the other hand, a more imaginative and emotional people, and with them inspirational divination held much the larger place. The Gr *mántis* (μάντις) bears a close resemblance to the OT prophet, for both claimed to be inspired from without and to be superhumanly informed. The Gr term for divination (*hē*) *mantikḗ* (=*hē mantikḗ téchnē*) has reference to the work of the *mantis*, and it hardly ever means divination of the lower sort—that by means of signs.

3. Fundamental Assumption in Divination

Underlying all methods of divination there lay the belief that certain superhuman spiritual beings (gods, spirits) possess the secret knowledge desired by men, and that, on certain conditions, they are willing to impart it.

(1) The word "divination" itself, from *deus*, "god," or *divus*, "pertaining to god," carries with it the notion that the information obtained came from deity. Similarly the Gr *mantikē* implies that the message comes to the *mantis* from gods or spirits by way of inspiration.

(2) **Astrology,** or astromancy, is but one form of divination and it rests upon the ultimate belief that the heavenly bodies are deities controlling the destinies of men and revealing the future to those who have eyes to see. According to the *Weltanschauung* or conception of the universe advocated by Hugo Winckler, Alfred Jeremias (see *The OT in the Light of the East*) and others, terrestrial events are but shadows of the celestial realities (cf Plato's doctrine of ideas). These latter represented the mind of the gods (see Astrology secs. 1,2).

(3) On **hepatoscopy,** or divining from the liver, see below, **6**, (2), (*c*).

(4) It can be proved that among the ancient peoples (Babylonians, Egyptians, Greeks, Romans, etc) the view prevailed that not only oracles but also omens of all kinds are given to men by the gods and express the minds of these gods.

4. Legitimate and Illegitimate Divination

Among the ancient Babylonians, Egyptians, Greeks and Romans the diviner stood in the service of the state and was officially consulted before wars and other great enterprises were undertaken. But among these and other ancient peoples certain classes of diviners were prohibited by the government from exercising their calling, probably because they were supposed to be in league with the gods of other and hostile nations. The gods of a people were in the beliefs of the time the protectors of their people and therefore the foes of the foes of their protégés. It is on this account that **witchcraft** has been so largely condemned and punished (see WITCHCRAFT). **Necromancy** is uniformly forbidden in the OT (see Lev **19** 31; Dt **18** 11; Isa **8** 19; **19** 3), probably on account of its connection with ancestor worship. But among other ancient peoples it was allowed and largely practised. Note that the Heb words tr[d] (Dt **18** 11) "consulter with a familiar spirit" and "wizards" denote alike such persons as seek oracles from the spirits of the dead (see the present writer's *Magic, Divination, and Demonology among the Hebrews*, 85 ff). The early Fathers believed that in the divination of heathenism we have the work of Satan who wished to discredit the true religion by producing phenomena among pagan races very similar to the prophetical marvels of the chosen people. This of course rests on a view of the OT prophet which makes him a "predicter" and little if anything more. See PROPHECY.

5. The Bible and Divination

The attitude of the Bible toward divination is on the whole distinctly hostile and is fairly represented by Dt **18** 10 f, where the prophet of Yahweh is contrasted with diviners of all kinds as the only authorized medium of supernatural revelation. Yet note the following:

(1) Balaam (Nu **22–24**) was a heathen diviner whose words of blessing and of cursing were believed to have magical force, and when his services are enlisted in the cause of Yahwism, so that, instead of cursing he blessed Israel, there is not a syllable of disapproval in the narrative.

(2) In Isa **3** 2 diviners are ranked with judges, warriors and prophets as pillars of the state. They are associated with prophets and seers in Jer **27** 9; **29** 8; Ezk **22** 28 (cf **13** 6–9; **12** 24). It is true that the prophets and diviners mentioned in these passages use utter falsehoods, saying peace where there is none; all the same the men called prophets and diviners are classed together as similar functionaries.

Pure Yahwism in its very basal principle is and must ever have been antagonistic to divination of every kind, though inspirational divination has resemblances to prophetism and even affinities with it. Why then does the Bible appear to speak with two voices, generally prohibiting but at times countenancing various forms of divination? In the actual religion of the OT we have a syncretism in which, though Yahwism forms the substructure, there are constituents from the religions of the native aborigines and the nations around. The underlying thought in all forms of divination is that by employing certain means men are able to obtain knowledge otherwise beyond their reach. The religion of Israel made Yahweh the source of that knowledge and the prophet the medium through which it came to men. We have an analogous example of syncretism resulting in the union of opposite elements in ancient Zarathustraism (Zoroastrianism) which, though in its central principle inconsistent with divination by omens, yet took on from the native Turanian cults of Persia certain forms of divination, esp. that by lot (see Lenormant, *La Divination*, 22 ff). Nor should it be forgotten that the Bible is a library and not a book, and where so many writers, living at widely separated times, have been at work it is natural to look for diversity of teaching, though no one can deny that in fundamental matters Bible authors are wonderfully consistent.

For modes of divination in vogue among the ancient Babylonians, Egyptians, Greeks, Romans, etc, see the relevant works and dictionary articles.

6. Modes of Divination Mentioned in the Bible

The species of divination spoken of in the Bible may be arranged under two heads: (1) those apparently sanctioned, and (2) those condemned in the Bible.

(1) *Methods of divination tacitly or expressly sanctioned in the Bible.*—(*a*) The following are instances of inspirational divination:

(α) The case of Balaam has already been cited. He was a Moabite and therefore a heathen soothsayer. His word of blessing or of curse is so potent that whether he blesses or curses his word secures its own realization. So far is his vocation from being censured that it is actually called into the service of Yahweh (see Nu **22–24**).

(β) To **dreams** the Bible assigns an important place as a legitimate means of revealing the future. Such dreams are of two kinds:

(i) Involuntary or such as come unsought. Even these are regarded as sent for guidance in human affairs. The bulk of the dreams spoken of in the Bible belong to this class: see Gen **20** 3.6 (Abimelech); **28** 2 f; **31** 10–14 (Jacob); **37** 5–9 (Joseph; see ASTRONOMY, II, 6); **40** 5–21 (Pharaoh's butler and baker); **41** 1–35 (Pharaoh); Jgs **7** 9–14 (Gideon and an unnamed man); Dnl **1** 17 (Daniel had understanding of dreams); Dnl **2** 1–49 (Nebuchadnezzar's dream and its interpretation by Daniel); Mt **1** 20; **2** 13 f.19 f (Joseph, husband of Mary the virgin); **27** 19; see also Jer **23** 25 ff, where the lawfulness of prophetic dreams is assumed (cf ver 32, where "lying dreams" imply genuine ones). In the document usually ascribed by modern critics to the Elohist (E), dreams bulk largely as the above examples serve to show. Among the Babylonians belief in the significance of dreams gave rise to a science (oneiromancy) so elaborate that only special interpreters called seers (sing. *baru*) were considered able to explain them (see Lenormant, op. cit., 143, for examples).

(ii) The other species of dreams consists of such as are induced by what is called "incubation," i.e. by sleeping in a sacred place where the god of the place is believed to reveal his secrets to the sleeper. Herodotus (iv.172) says that the Nasamonians, an Egyp tribe, used to practise divination by sleeping in the graves of their ancestors. The dreams which then came to them were understood to be revelations of their deified ancestors. See Herod. i.181 for another instance of incubation in Nineveh. We have a reference to this custom in Isa **65** 4 ("that sit among the graves"), where Yahweh enters into judgment with the Jews for their sin in yielding to this superstition. Solomon's dream (1 K **3** 5–15) came to him at the high place of Gibeon. See also DREAM, DREAMER.

(*b*) But the Bible appears in some places to give its approval to some kinds of artificial or (as it may be called) ominal divination.

(α) **Sortilege** or divination by lot. The use of the lot as a means of ascertaining the will of Deity is referred to at least without expressed censure, and, as the present writer thinks, with tacit approval, in many parts of the Bible. It was by lot that Aaron decided which of the two goats was to be for Yahweh and which for Azazel (Lev **16** 7–10). It was by lot that the land of Canaan was divided after the conquest (Nu **26** 56 ff; Josh **18, 19**). For other Bib. instances see Josh **7** 14 (Achan found out by lot); 1 Ch **6** 54 ff; **24** 5 ff; **25** 8 f; **26** 13 f; Est **3** 7 ("They cast Pur, that is, the lot"; see *Century Bible* in loc.); Neh **10** 34; **11** 1; Jon **1** 7 ("The lot fell upon Jonah"); Mt **27** 35; Acts **1** 26. In the URIM AND THUMMIM (q.v.), as explained by modern scholars, the same principle is applied, for these two words, though etymologically still obscure, stand for two objects (pebbles?), one denoting *yes* or its equivalent, and the other *no*. Whichever the high priest took from his ephod was believed to be the answer to the question asked. In all cases it is taken for granted that the lot cast was an expression and indication of the Divine will. See AUGURY, IV, 3.

(*β*) **Hydromancy,** or divination by water. In Gen **44** 5 Joseph is represented as practising this kind of divination and not a word of disapproval is expressed. See AUGURY, IV, 2.

(*γ*) We read in the OT of other signs or omens which are implicitly approved of, thus Jgs **6** 36–40 (Gideon's fleece); 1 S **14** 8–13 (Jonathan decides whether or not he is to attack the Philis by the words which he may happen to hear them speak).

(2) *Modes of divination condemned.*—The following methods of divination are explicitly or implicitly condemned in the OT:

(*a*) **Astromancy** (=Astrology). See ASTROLOGY.

(*b*) **Rhabdomancy,** or the use of the divining rod, referred to apparently in Hos **4** 12 (which may be paraphrased: "My people ask counsel of a bit of wood, and the rod made thereof answers their questions"); Ezk **8** 17 ("They put a rod [EV "the branch"] to their nose").

(*c*) By an examination of the liver of animals; see Ezk **21** 21. This mode of divining, **hepatoscopy,** as it is has been called, was very widespread among the Babylonians, Greeks, Romans, etc, of the ancient world, and it is still in vogue in Borneo, Burmah and Uganda. We have no evidence that it was practised among the Israelites, for in the above passage it is the king of Babylon (Nebuchadnezzar) who is said to have "looked in the liver."

Opinions differ as to how the state of the liver could act as an omen. Jastrow says the liver was considered to be the seat of life, and that where the liver of the animal sacrificed (generally a sheep) was accepted, it took on the character of the deity to whom it was offered. The soul of the animal as seen in the liver became then a reflector of the soul of the god (see *EB*, XX, 102 f). On the other hand, Alfred Jeremias says that in the view of the ancient Babylonians the lines and forms of the sheep's liver were regarded as reflecting the universe and its history (*The OT in the Light of the Ancient East*, I, 61). Neither of these explanations is made probable by its advocates.

(*d*) By **teraphim** (cf TERAPHIM); see 1 S **15** 23; Ezk **21** 21; Zec **10** 2.

(*e*) **Necromancy,** or consulting the dead; see Lev **19** 31; **20** 6; Dt **18** 11; Isa **8** 19; **19** 3; see above.

(*f*) Divination through the **sacrifice of children** by burning (see Dt **18** 10). The context makes it almost certain that the words tr[d] "that maketh his son or his daughter to pass through the fire" (EV; but read and render "that burns his son or his daughter in the fire") refer to a mode of obtaining an oracle (cf 2 K **3** 27). The Phoenicians and Carthaginians sacrificed their children to Kronos in times of grave national danger or calamity (Porphyry *Apud Euseb. Praep. Ev.* iv.64,4; Diod. Sic. xx.14).

These are examined in detail in T. Witton Davies' *Magic, Divination, and Demonology among the Hebrews and Their Neighbors.* See also the art. "Divination" in *EB* by the same writer. The following brief notes must suffice here.

7. Terms Used in the OT in Connection with Divination

(1) קֶסֶם, *ḳeṣem*, generally rendered "divination," is a general term for divination of all kinds. In Ezk **21** 21 [26] it stands for divination by arrows while in 1 S **28** 8 it is used of divination through the medium of an *'ōbh* ("familiar spirit"). On the derivation of the word see *EB*, art. "Magic," § 3.

(2) מְעוֹנֵן, *meʿōnēn*, probably from a Sem root (cf Arab. *ʿanna*) which denotes to emit a hoarse nasal sound such as was customary in reciting the prescribed formula (see CHARM). For "oak of the *meʿōnīm*" see AUGUR'S OAK. Some say the word means one who divines from the clouds, deriving from עָנָן, *ʿānān*, "a cloud," though nothing in the context suggests this sense, and the same remark applies to the meaning "one who smites with the evil eye," making the term a denominative from *ʿayin*, "eye." The usual rendering in AV is pl "observers of times" and in RV "them that practise augury" (Dt **18** 10.14).

(3) The vb. נִחֵשׁ, *niḥēsh*, of which לִחֵשׁ, *liḥēsh*, is but a variant, is probably a denominative from נָחָשׁ, *nāḥāsh*, "a serpent" (*l* and *n* interchange in Heb), denoting "to hiss," "to whisper" (like a serpent), then "to utter divinatory formulae." As it is used for so many kinds of divination, W. R. Smith concludes that it came to be a general term for divine. The part. of this vb. is tr[d] "enchanter" in Dt **18** 10, the cognate vb., "to use enchantments" in Lev **19** 26; 2 K **21** 6; 2 Ch **33** 6, and the corresponding noun "enchantment" in Nu **23** 23; **24** 1.

(4) גָּזְרִין, *gāzᵉrīn*, lit. "cutters," i.e. such as kill (in Arab. the cognate vb.="to slaughter") for the purpose of examining the liver or entrails as omens. Perhaps the etymology implies "sacrifice," animals being sacrificed as an appeal to deity. The word occurs only in Dnl (**2** 27; **4** 7 [4]; **5** 7.11), and is tr[d] "soothsayers." Some think they were "astrologers," the etymology in that case referring to the dividing of the heavens with a view, by casting the horoscope, to forecasting the future.

(5) אַשָּׁף, *'ashshāph* (AV "astrologer," RV "enchanter"), occurs only in Dnl in the Heb (**1** 20; **2** 2) and in the Aram. (**2** 10; **4** 4 [7], etc) parts of the book. The term is probably taken from the Bab and denotes a magician and esp. an exorcist rather than a diviner.

(6) כַּשְׂדָּאִים, *kasdā'īm*, the same word as the Gr *Chaldaíoi* (Χαλδαῖοι) (EV "Chaldeans"), denotes in Dnl (**1** 4, etc) where alone it occurs, not the people so designated but a class of astrologers. This usage (common in classical writers) arose after the fall of the Bab empire, when the only Chaldaeans known were astrologers and soothsayers. See further, MAGIC. For "spirit of divination" (Acts **16** 16) see PYTHON; PHILIPPI.

Inspirational divination and OT prophecy have much in common. Both imply the following conditions:

8. Divination and Prophecy

(1) the primitive instinct that craves for secret knowledge, esp. that relating to the future; (2) the belief that such knowledge is possessed by certain spiritual beings who are willing on certain terms to impart it; (3) such secret knowledge is imparted generally to special classes of men (rarely women) called diviners or (Bab) seers and prophets.

Many anthropologists (Tylor, Frazer, etc) and OT scholars (Wellhausen, W. Robertson Smith, etc) consider prophecy to be but an outgrowth and higher form of divination. The older theologians almost to a man, and a goodly number of moderns, take precisely the opposite view, that divination is a corruption of prophecy. Probably neither view is strictly true. Sometimes in human life we find evidences of progress from lower to higher. Sometimes the process is the very reverse. It is important to take notice of the differences as well as the resemblances between the diviner and the prophet.

(1) The OT prophet believes in a personal God whose spokesman he considers himself to be. When he spoke or wrote it was because he was, at least professedly, inspired and informed by Yahweh. "Thus says Yahweh," was the usual formula with

which he introduced his oracles. The Gr and Rom *mantis*, on the other hand, worked himself up to the necessary ecstatic state by music, drugs (intoxicants, etc), sacrificial smoke and the like. Sometimes it has been thought a sufficient means of divination to swallow the vital portions of birds and beasts of omen. It was believed that by eating the hearts of crows, or moles, or of hawks, men took into their bodies the presaging soul of the creature (Frazer, *Golden Bough*², II, 355).

(2) The *mantis* practised his art as a remunerative occupation, charging high fees and refusing in most cases to ply his calling without adequate remuneration. The local oracle shrines (Delphi, Clavis, etc) were worked for personal and political ends. The OT prophet, on the other hand, claimed to speak as he was bidden by his God. It was with him a matter of conviction as to what lives men ought to live, what state of heart they should cultivate. So far from furthering his own material interests, as he could by saying what kings and other dignitaries wished to hear, he boldly denounced the sins of the time, even when, as often, he had to condemn the conduct of kings and the policy of governments. Look, for example, at Isaiah's fearless condemnation of the conduct of Ahaz in summoning the aid of Assyria (Isa **7** ff), and at the scathing words with which Jeremiah censured the doings of the nation's leaders in his day (Jer **2** 36, etc), though both these noble prophets suffered severely for their courage, esp. Jeremiah, who stands out as perhaps the finest recorded example of what, in the face of formidable opposition, the religious teacher ought ever to be. Of Micaiah ben Imlah, King Ahab of Israel said, "I hate him; for he doth not prophesy good concerning me, but evil." What reward did this prophet have for his fidelity to his conscience and his God? Imprisonment (1 K **22** 1–35). Had he pleased the king by predicting a happy, prosperous future that was never to be, he would have been clothed in gorgeous robes and lodged in a very palace.

LITERATURE.—In addition to the references above and the full bibliography prefixed to the present writer's book named above (*Magic*, etc), note the following: Bouché-Leclercq, *Histoire de la divination dans l'antiquité;* E. B. Tylor, *Primitive Culture*³, I, 78–81; 117–33; II, 155; J. G. Frazer, *Golden Bough*², I, 346; II, 355; III, 342, *et passim*, and the arts. in the principal Bible dictionaries.

T. WITTON DAVIES

DIVINE, di-vīn′, **DIVINER**, di-vīn′ẽr. See AUGURY; ASTROLOGY; DIVINATION.

DIVINE NAMES. See GOD, NAMES OF.

DIVINE VISITATION. See PUNISHMENTS.

DIVISION, di-vizh′un: Used in EV in the following senses:

(1) A separate body of people (*a*) of the tribal divisions of Israel (Josh **11** 23; **12** 7; **18** 10); (*b*) of sections of a tribe, "the divisions of Reuben" (Jgs **5** 15.16 AV; but RV rightly substitutes "the watercourses of Reuben"; in Job **20** 17 the same word is rendered "rivers"); (*c*) of the (late) organization of priests and Levites into classes or families who ministered in the temple in rotation; tr[d] "courses" generally in AV, and always in RV (1 Ch **24** 1; **26** 1.12.19; Neh **11** 36; cf 2 Ch **35** 5). Much prominence is given by the Chronicler to the 24 classes of priests, singers, and doorkeepers, who served in turns in the temple (cf Lk **1** 5.8).

(2) Separation, distinction: "I will put a division [RVm "sign of deliverance"] between my people and thy people" (Ex **8** 23). The Heb word here is $p^e dh\bar{u}th$="ransom," "redemption" (cf Ps **111** 9), but the reading is doubtful. AV and RV follow LXX, Syr and Vulg, which render "set a distinction," perhaps on the basis of a different reading from that of our Heb text.

(3) In the NT, dissension, disunion, schism (Lk **12** 51; Rom **16** 17; 1 Cor **3** 3 AV, omitted in RV; 1 Cor **1** 10; **11** 18; Gal **5** 20).

D. MIALL EDWARDS

DIVORCE, di-vōrs′, **IN OT:** Woman, among the Hebrews, as among most nations of antiquity, occupied a subordinate position. Though the Heb wife and mother was treated with more consideration than her sister in other lands, even in other Sem countries, her position nevertheless was one of inferiority and subjection. The marriage relation from the standpoint of Heb legislation was looked upon very largely as a business affair, a mere question of property. A wife, nevertheless, was, indeed, in most homes in Israel, the husband's "most valued possession." And yet while this is true, the husband was unconditionally and unreservedly the head of the family in all domestic relations. His rights and prerogatives were manifest on every side. Nowhere is this more evident than in the matter of divorce. According to the laws of Moses a husband, under certain circumstances, might divorce his wife; on the other hand, if at all possible, it was certainly very difficult for a wife to put away her husband. Unfortunately a double standard of morality in matters pertaining to the sexes is, at least, as old as Moses (see Ex **21** 7–11).

1. Subordinate Position of Woman

The OT law concerning divorce, apparently quite clear, is recorded most fully in Dt **24** 1 ff. A perusal of the commentaries will, nevertheless, convince anyone that there are difficulties of interpretation. The careful reader will notice that the renderings of the AV and RV differ materially. AV reads in the second part of ver 1: "*then let him* write a bill," etc, RV has "*that he shall* write," etc, while the Heb original has neither "then" nor "that," but the simple conjunction "and." There is certainly no command in the words of Moses, but, on the other hand, a clear purpose to render the proceeding more difficult in the case of the husband. Moses' aim was "to regulate and thus to mitigate an evil which he could not extirpate." The evident purpose was, as far as possible, to favor the wife, and to protect her against an unceremonious expulsion from her home and children.

2. Law of Divorce: Dt 24:1–4

As already suggested, marriage among the Hebrews, as among most Orientals, was more a legal contract than the result of love or affection. It would be, however, a great mistake to assume that deep love was not often present, for at all times the domestic relations of the Heb married couple have compared most favorably with those of any other people, ancient or modern. In its last analysis it was, nevertheless, a business transaction. The husband or his family had, as a rule, to pay a certain dowry to the parents or guardians of the betrothed before the marriage was consummated. A wife thus acquired could easily be regarded as a piece of property, which, without great difficulty, could be disposed of in case the husband, for any reason, were disposed to rid himself of an uncongenial companion and willing to forfeit the *mōhar* which he had paid for his wife. The advantage was always with the husband, and yet a wife was not utterly helpless, for she, too, though practically without legal rights, could make herself so intolerably burdensome and hateful in the home that almost any husband would gladly avail himself of his prerogatives and write her a bill of divorcement. Thus, though a wife could not divorce her husband, she could force him to divorce her.

3. Marriage a Legal Contract

The following words of Professor Israel Abrahams, Cambridge, England, before "the Divorce Commission" (London, November 21, 1910), are to the point: "In all such cases where the wife was concerned as the moving party she could only demand that her husband should divorce her. The divorce was always from first to last, in Jewish law, the husband's act."

4. Divorce Applicable Only to Wives

The common term used in the Bible for divorce is שִׁלּוּחַ אִשָּׁה, *shillūaḥ 'ishshāh,* "the sending away of a wife" (Dt **22** 19.29). We never read of "the sending away of a husband." The fem. part., גְּרוּשָׁה, *gerūshāh,* "the woman thrust out," is the term applied to a divorced woman. The masc. form is not found.

5. Process and Exceptions

The Mosaic law apparently, on the side of the husband, made it as difficult as possible for him to secure a divorce. No man could unceremoniously and capriciously dismiss his wife without the semblance of a trial. In case one became dissatisfied with his wife, (1) he had to write her a Bill of Divorce (q.v.) drawn up by some constituted legal authority and in due legal form. In the very nature of the case, such a tribunal would use moral suasion to induce an adjustment; and, failing in this, would see to it that the law in the case, whatever it might be, would be upheld. (2) Such a bill or decree must be placed in the hand of the divorced wife. (3) She must be forced to leave the premises of her former husband. Divorce was denied two classes of husbands: (1) The man who had falsely accused his wife of antenuptial infidelity (Dt **22** 13 ff), and (2) a person who had seduced a virgin (Dt **22** 28 f). In addition, a heavy penalty had to be paid to the father of such damsels.

It is probable that a divorced wife who had not contracted a second marriage or had been guilty of adultery might be reunited to her husband. But in case she had married the second time she was forever barred from returning to her first husband, even if the second husband had divorced her or had died (Dt **24** 3 f). Such a law would serve as an obstacle to hasty divorces.

Divorces from the earliest times were common among the Hebrews. All rabbis agree that a separation, though not desirable, was quite lawful. The only source of dispute among them was as to what constituted a valid reason or just cause.

6. Grounds of Divorce (Doubtful Meaning of Dt 24:1)

The language in Dt **24** 1 ff has always been in dispute. The Heb words, עֶרְוַת דָּבָר, *'erwath dābhār,* on which a correct interpretation depends, are not easy of solution, though many exegetes, influenced possibly by some preconceived notion, pass over them quite flippantly. The phrase troubled the Jewish rabbis of olden times, as it does Jewish and Christian commentators and translators in our day. AV renders the two words, "some uncleanness," and in the margin, "matter of nakedness." The latter, though a literal tr of the Heb, is quite unintelligible. RV and ARV both have: "some unseemly thing." Professor Driver translates the same words "some indecency." The Ger. RV (Kautzsch) has "*etwas Widerwärtiges*" ("something repulsive"). We know of no modern version which makes *'erwath dābhār* the equivalent of fornication or adultery. And, indeed, in the very nature of the case, we are forced to make the words apply to a minor fault or crime, for, by the Mosaic law, the penalty for adultery was death (Dt **22** 20 ff). It is, however, a question whether the extreme penalty was ever enforced. It is well known that at, and some time before, the time of our Saviour, there were two schools among the Jewish rabbis, that of Shammai and that of Hillel. Shammai and his followers maintained that *'erwath dābhār* signified nothing less than unchastity or adultery, and argued that only this crime justified a man in divorcing his wife. Hillel and his disciples went to the other extreme. They placed great stress upon the words, "if she find no favor in his eyes" immediately preceding *'erwath dābhār* (Dt **24** 1), and contended that divorce should be granted for the flimsiest reason: such as the spoiling of a dish either by burning or careless seasoning. Some of the rabbis boldly taught that a man had a perfect right to dismiss his wife, if he found another woman whom he liked better, or who was more beautiful (Mish, *Giṭṭīn,* **14** 10). Here are some other specifications taken from the same book: "The following women may be divorced: She who violates the Law of Moses, e.g. causes her husband to eat food which has not been tithed. . . . . She who vows, but does not keep her vows. . . . . She who goes out on the street with her hair loose, or spins in the street, or converses [flirts] with any man, or is a noisy woman. What is a noisy woman? It is one who speaks in her own house so loud that the neighbors may hear her." It would be easy to extend the list, for the Mish and rabbinic writings are full of such laws.

From what has been said, it is clear that adultery was not the only valid reason for divorce. Besides, the word adultery had a peculiar significance in Jewish law, which recognized polygamy and concubinage as legitimate. Thus a Hebrew might have two or more wives or concubines, and might have intercourse with a slave or bondwoman, even if married, without being guilty of the crime of adultery (Lev **19** 20), for adultery, according to Jewish law, was possible only when a man dishonored the "free wife" of a Hebrew (**20** 10 ff).

Divorcement, Bill of: This expression, found in Dt **24** 1.3; Isa **50** 1; Jer **3** 8 is the tr of the Heb סֵפֶר כְּרִיתֻת, *sēpher kerīthuth.* The two words, lit. rendered, signify a document or book of cutting off, i.e. a certificate of divorce given by a husband to a wife, so as to afford her the opportunity or privilege of marrying another man. The Heb term is rendered by the LXX *βιβλίον ἀποστασίου, biblion apostasion.* This is also found in the NT (Mk **10** 4). Mt **5** 31 has "writing of divorcement" in EV, but Mt **19** 7 AV has "writing," while RV and ARV have "bill." The certificate of divorce is called גֵּט, *gēṭ,* pl. גִּטִּין, *giṭṭīn,* in the Talm. There is an entire chapter devoted to the subjects in the Mish. It is not positively known when the custom of writing bills of divorcement commenced, but there are references to such documents in the earliest Heb legislation. The fact that Joseph had in mind the putting away of his espoused wife, Mary, without the formality of a bill or at least of a public procedure proves that a decree was not regarded as absolutely necessary (Mt **1** 19). The following was the usual form of a decree:

"On the —— day of the week —— in the month —— in the year —— from the beginning of the world, according to the common computation in the province of —— I —— the son of —— by whatever name I may be known, of the town of —— with entire consent of mind, and without any constraint, have divorced, dismissed and expelled thee —— daughter of —— by whatever name thou art called, of the town —— who hast been my wife hitherto; But now I have dismissed thee —— the daughter of —— by whatever name thou art called, of the town of —— so as to be free at thy own disposal, to marry whomsoever thou pleasest, without hindrance from anyone, from this day for ever. Thou art therefore free for anyone [who would marry thee]. Let this be thy bill of divorce from me, a writing of separation and expulsion, according to the law of Moses and Israel.

——, the son of ——, witness
——, the son of ——, witness

Spiritual application.—The Heb prophets regarded Jeh not only as the father and king of the chosen people, and thus entitled to perfect obedience and loyalty on their part, but they conceived of Him as a husband married to Israel. Isaiah, speaking to his nation, says: "For thy Maker is thy husband; Jehovah of hosts is his name" (**54** 5). Jeremiah too makes use of similar language in the following: "Return, O backsliding children, saith Jehovah; for I am a husband unto you" (**3** 14). It is perfectly natural that NT writers should have regarded Christ's relation to His church under the same figure. Paul in 2 Cor says: "I am jealous over you with a godly jealousy: for I espoused you to one husband, that I might present you as a pure virgin to Christ" (**11** 2); see also Mt **9** 15; Jn **3** 29; Rev **19** 7. Any unfaithfulness or sin on the part of Israel was regarded as spiritual adultery, which necessarily broke off the spiritual ties, and divorced the nation from God (Isa **1** 21; Ezk **16** 22; Rev **2** 22). See also MARRIAGE.

LITERATURE.—Amram, *Jewish Law of Divorce according to the Bible and Talmud*, London, 1897; Abrahams, *Jewish Life in the Middle Ages*, London, 1896; Mackie, *Bible Manners and Customs*, London, 1898; *The Mishna*, *Tr^d into Eng.*, De Sola and Raphall, London, 1843; Benzinger, *Hebräische Archäologie*, Freiburg, 1894; Nowack, *Lehrbuch der hebräischen Archäologie*, 1894

W. W. DAVIES

DIVORCE IN NT (**τὸ ἀποστάσιον**, *tó apostásiou*): The Scripture doctrine of divorce is very simple. It is contained in Mt **19** 3–12.

We are not called upon to treat of divorce in the Mosaic legislation (Dt **24** 1–4). That was passed upon by Jesus in the above discussion and by Him ruled out of existence in His system of religion. After Jesus had spoken as above, the Mosaic permission of divorce became a dead letter. There could not be practice under it among His disciples. So such OT divorce is now a mere matter of antiquarian curiosity.

It may be of interest in passing to note that the drift of the Mosaic legislation was restrictive of a freedom of divorce that had been practised before its enactment. It put in legal proceedings to bar the personal will of one of the parties. It recognized marriage as a social institution which should not be disrupted without reference to the rights of society in it. In this restrictive character "the law is become our tutor to bring us unto Christ" (Gal **3** 24). But here, as in numerous other instances, Christ went behind the enactments to primitive original principles whose recognition would make the law of none effect, because no practice was to be permitted under it. Thus the OT is disposed of.

Of course what Jesus said will dominate the New. In fact, Jesus is the only author in the NT who has treated of divorce. It has been thought that Paul had the subject in hand. But we shall find on examination, farther along, that he did not. We need then look nowhere but to this 19th ch of Mt for the Scripture doctrine of divorce.

True, we have other reports of what Jesus said (Mk **10** 2–12; Lk **16** 18). But in Mt **19** we have the fullest report, containing everything that is reported elsewhere and one or two important observations that the other writers have not included. Lk has but one ver where Mt has ten. Lk's ver is in no necessary connection with context. It seems to be a mere memorandum among others of the spiritual or ethical teachings of Christ. Luke however caught the gist of the whole teaching about divorce in recording the prohibition to put away one wife and marry another. The records in Mt **19** and Mk **10** cover one and the same occasion. But there is nothing in Mk that is not in Mt; and the latter contains nearly a third more of text than the former. There is nothing, however, essential in Mt that is not in Mk, save the clause "except for fornication." That exception will be treated farther along. We seem to be justified then in saying that the total doctrine of the Scripture pertaining to divorce is contained in Mt **19**.

Attention must be called to the fact that, in the Sermon on the Mount (Mt **5** 27–32), Jesus treated of divorce, and that in every essential particular it agrees with the elaboration in ch **19**. Jesus there as plainly as in the argument with the Pharisees put Moses' permission of divorce under ban; as plainly there declared the putting away of one partner to marry another person to be adultery. This may also be noticed, that the exception to the absolute prohibition is in the text of the Sermon on the Mount.

We have then a summary of the NT doctrine of divorce stated by Christ Himself as follows: "Whosoever shall put away his wife, except for fornication, and shall marry another, committeth adultery" (Mt **19** 9). This puts Him in line with the ideal of the monogamic, indissoluble family which pervades the whole of the OT.

It may be well here to treat of the exception which Christ made in His rule to the indissolubility of marriage.

1. The Family

It is very widely maintained in the Christian church that there should be no divorce for any cause whatever. This position is in plain contradiction to Christ's teaching in Mt **5** and **19**. One of the grounds adduced for this denial of divorce in case a partner is guilty of adultery is that Lk and Mk do not record the exception. It is a difficult matter to invade the psychology of writers who lived nearly two thousand years ago and tell why they did not include something in their text which someone else did in his. Neither Luke nor Mark were personal disciples of the Lord. They wrote at second hand. Matthew was a personal disciple of Christ and has twice recorded the exception. It will be a new position in regard to judgment on human evidence when we put the silence of absentees in rank above the twice expressed report of one in all probability present—one known to be a close personal attendant.

This may be said: Matthew's record stands in ancient MS authority, Greek and also the Versions. And on this point let it be noted that the testimony of the MSS was up before the English and American Revisers, and they have deliberately reaffirmed the text of 1611 and given us the exception in Christ's rule in each place (Mt **5** 32; **19** 9). This makes the matter as nearly *rēs adjudicata* as can be done by human wisdom.

Let us consider the rationality of the exception. That feature has had scant attention from theologians and publicists, yet it will bear the closest scrutiny. In fact it is a key to much that is explanatory of the basic principle of the family. To begin with, the exception is not on its face an afterthought of some transcriber, but was called out by the very terms of the question of the Pharisees: "Is it lawful for a man to put away his wife for *every cause?*" This plainly called for a specification from Jesus of exceptions which he would allow to the rule against divorce. It is fortunate that the Pharisees asked the question in the form they did, for that put on Jesus the necessity of enumerating such exceptions as he would allow. He mentioned one, and but one in reply. That puts the matter of exceptions under the rule in logic: *Expressio unius exclusio alterius.* All other pretences for divorce were deliberately swept aside by Christ—a fact that should be remembered when other causes are sought to be foisted in alongside this one allowed by Christ. The question may come up, Whose insight is likely to be truest?

Why, then, will reason stand by this exception? Because adultery is *per se* destructive of monogamic family life. Whoever, married, is guilty of adultery has taken another person into family relation. Children may be born to that relation—are born to it. Not to allow divorce in such case is to force an innocent party in marriage to live in a polygamous state. There is the issue stated so plainly that "the wayfaring man need not err therein," and "he who runs may read," and "he who reads may run."

It is the hand of an unerring Master that has made fornication a ground for divorce from the bond of matrimony and limited divorce to that single cause. Whichever way we depart from strict practice under the Saviour's direction we land in polygamy. The society that allows by its statutes divorce for any other cause than the one that breaks the monogamic bond, is simply acting in aid of polygamy, consecutive if not contemporaneous.

Advocates of the freedom of divorce speak of the

above view as "the ecclesiastical." That is an attempt to use the argument *ad invidiam.* The church of Christ held and holds its views, not because ecclesiastics taught it, but because Christ taught it, and that in His teaching we have a statement out from the righteousness, wisdom, insight and rationality of the all-wise God.

2. Paul

Paul is the only other NT author besides Christ who has been supposed to treat of divorce. But a careful examination of Paul's writing will disclose the fact that he has nowhere discussed the question—for what cause or causes a man might put away his wife, or a woman her husband, with liberty of marriage to another person. If Paul has treated of divorce at all it is in 1 Cor **7**. But even a careless reading of that chapter will disclose the fact that Paul is not discussing the question for what causes marriage might be disrupted, but the question of manners and morals *in* the relation. Paul has not modified Christ in any respect. It has been supposed that in ver 15 Paul has allowed divorce to a believing partner who has been deserted by one unbelieving, and so he has been sometimes understood as adding desertion to the exception Christ made as cause for divorce.

But Paul has not said in that verse or anywhere else that a Christian partner deserted by a heathen may be married to someone else. All he said is: "If the unbelieving departeth, let him depart: the brother or the sister is not under bondage [*dedoúlōtai*] in such cases: but God hath called us in peace." To say that a deserted partner *"hath not been enslaved"* is not to say that he or she may be *remarried.* What is meant is easily inferred from the spirit that dominates the whole chapter, and that is that everyone shall accept the situation in which God has called him just as he is. "Be quiet" is a direction that hovers over every situation. If you are married, so remain. If unmarried, so remain. If an unbelieving partner deserts, let him or her desert. So remain. "God hath called us in peace." Nothing can be more beautiful in the morals of the marriage relation than the direction given by Paul in this chapter for the conduct of all parties in marriage in all trials.

Many reasons might be given why Paul could not have given liberty of remarriage, besides the one that he did not in his text; but attention should be called to the fact that such an assumption of authority in divorce would soon have brought him into conflict with the Rom government. Paul's claim that he was a Rom citizen was of some value to himself. Would not some Rom citizen have claimed to scrutinize pretty closely Paul's right to issue a decree of divorce against him because he had "departed" from a wife who had become a Christian? There would be two sides to such divorces. Would not Paul, careful, shrewd, politic as he was, have known that, and have avoided an open rupture with a government that did not tolerate much interference with its laws? That neither Paul nor anyone else ever put such construction upon his language, is evidenced by the fact that there is no record in history of a single case where it was attempted for 400 years after Paul was in his grave, and the Rom Empire had for a century been Christian. Then we wait 400 years more before we find the suggestion repeated. That no use was ever made of such construction of Paul in the whole era of the adjustment of Christianity with heathenism is good evidence that it was never there to begin with. So we shall pass Paul as having in no respect modified the doctrine of divorce laid down by Christ in Mt **19**.

3. Remedies for Marriage Ills

In all civilized countries the machinery of legislation and law can always be open for removal or relief of troubles in marriage without proceeding to its annulment. If a father is cruel to his children, we do not abolish the parental relation, but punish the father for his cruelty. If he deserts his children, we need not assist him to rear other children whom he can desert in turn, but we can punish him for his desertion. What can be done by law in case of parent and child can be done in case of husband and wife. By putting in absolute divorce (frequently for guilty and innocent alike) we invite the very evils we seek to cure. We make it the interest of a dissatisfied party to create a situation that a court will regard as intolerable, and so he or she may go free.

Then by affording an easy way out of the troubles of married life we are inviting carelessness about entering marriage. We say by divorce statutes to a young woman: "If your husband deserts you, you may have another. If he is cruel, you may have another. If he fails to support you, you may have another. If he is drunken, you may have another. If he is incompatible or makes you unhappy, you may have another"—and yet others beyond these. When an easy road is thus made out of marriage, will there be proper caution about entering into marriage? By just as much as a crevice for relief of the miseries of married life is opened by divorce, by so much the flood gates are opened into those miseries. The more solemnly society is impressed that the door of marriage does not swing outward as well as inward the more of happiness and blessing will it find in the institution. See Family.

C. Caverno

DI-ZAHAB, dī′za-hab, diz′a-hab (דִּי־זָהָב, *dī-zā-hābh;* LXX **Καταχρύσεα,** *Katachrúsea,* lit. "abounding in gold"): The name occurs in a list apparently intended to fix definitely the situation of the camp of Israel in the plains of Moab (Dt **1** 1). No place in the region has been found with a name suggesting this; and there is no other clue to its identification. Some names in the list are like those of stations earlier in the wanderings. Thinking that one of these may be intended Burckhardt suggested *Mina edh-Dhahab,* a boat harbor between *Ras Mohammad* and *'Aqaba.* Cheyne gets over the difficulty by accepting a suggestion of Sayce that Di-zahab corresponds to Me-zahab (Gen **36** 39); this latter he then transforms into Mitzraim, and identifies it with the North Arabian *Muṣri* (*EB* s.v.). The changes, however, seem greater than can be justified.

W. Ewing

DOCTOR, dok′tẽr: In Lk **2** 46 (**διδάσκαλος,** *didáskalos*) "doctor" is equivalent to "teacher," which latter is the tr of RV. So in Lk **5** 17; Acts **5** 34, AV and RV "doctors," "doctor," of the law (*nomodidáskalos*). See Education; Rabbi; Scribe.

DOCTRINE, dok′trin: Lat *doctrina,* from *doceo,* "to teach," denotes both the act of teaching and that which is taught; now used exclusively in the latter sense.

(1) In the OT for (*a*) *leḳah* "what is received," hence "the matter taught" (Dt **32** 2; Job **11** 4; Prov **4** 2; Isa **29** 24, ARV "instruction"); (*b*) *shemū'āh,* "what is heard" (Isa **28** 9, RV "message," RVm "report"); (*c*) *mūṣār,* "discipline" (Jer **10** 8 m, "The stock is a doctrine [RV "instruction"] of vanities," i.e. "The discipline of unreal gods is wood (is like themselves, destitute of true moral force)" (*BDB*).

(2) In the NT for (i) *didaskalia* = (*a*) "the act of teaching" (1 Tim **4** 13.16; **5** 17; 2 Tim **3** 10.16), all in RV "teaching"; (*b*) "what is taught" (Mt **15** 9; 2 Tim **4** 3). In some passages the meaning is ambiguous as between (*a*) and (*b*). (ii)

didachē, always tr[d] "teaching" in RV, except in Rom **16** 17, where "doctrine" is retained in the text and "teaching" inserted in m = (*a*) the act

1. Meaning of Terms

of teaching (Mk **4** 2; Acts **2** 42, AV "doctrine"); (*b*) what is taught (Jn **7** 16.17; Rev **2** 14.15.24, AV "doctrine"). In some places the meaning is ambiguous as between (*a*) and (*b*) and in Mt **7** 28; Mk **1** 22; Acts **13** 12, the manner, rather than the act or matter of teaching is denoted, namely, with authority and power.

The meaning of these words in the NT varied as the church developed the content of its experience into a system of thought, and came to

2. Christ's Teaching Informal

regard such a system as an integral part of saving faith (cf the development of the meaning of the term "faith"): (1) The doctrines of the Pharisees were a fairly compact and definite body of teaching, a fixed tradition handed down from one generation of teachers to another (Mt **16** 12, AV "doctrine"; cf Mt **15** 9; Mk **7** 7). (2) In contrast with the Pharisaic system, the teaching of Jesus was unconventional and occasional, discursive and unsystematic; it derived its power from His personality, character and works, more than from His words, so that His contemporaries were astonished at it and recognized it as a new teaching (Mt **7** 28; **22** 33; Mk **1** 22.27; Lk **4** 32). So we find it in the Synoptic Gospels, and the more systematic form given to it in the Johannine discourses is undoubtedly the work of the evangelist, who wrote rather to interpret Christ than to record His *ipsissima verba* (Jn **20** 31).

The earliest teaching of the apostles consisted essentially of three propositions: (*a*) that Jesus was the Christ (Acts **3** 18); (*b*) that He

3. Apostolic Doctrines

was risen from the dead (Acts **1** 22; **2** 24.32); and (*c*) that salvation was by faith in His name (Acts **2** 38; **3** 16). While proclaiming these truths, it was necessary to coördinate them with Heb faith, as based upon OT revelation. The method of the earliest reconstruction may be gathered from the speeches of Peter and Stephen (Acts **2** 14–36; **5** 29–32; **7** 2–53). A more thorough reconstruction of the coördination of the Christian facts, not only with Heb history, but with universal history, and with a view of the world as a whole, was undertaken by Paul. Both types of doctrine are found in his speeches in Acts, the former type in that delivered at Antioch (**13** 16–41), and the latter in the speeches delivered at Lystra (**14** 15–17) and at Athens (**17** 22–31). The ideas given in outline in these speeches are more fully developed into a doctrinal system, with its center removed from the resurrection to the death of Christ, in the epistles, esp. in Gal, Rom, Eph, Phil and Col. But as yet it is the theological system of one teacher, and there is no sign of any attempt to impose it by authority on the church as a whole. As a matter of fact the Pauline system never was generally accepted by the church. Cf James and the Apostolic Fathers.

In the Pastoral and General Epistles a new state of things appears. The repeated emphasis on "sound" or "healthy doctrine" (1 Tim

4. Beginnings of Dogma

1 10; **6** 3; 2 Tim **1** 13; **4** 3; Tit **1** 9; **2** 1), "good doctrine" (1 Tim **4** 6) implies that a body of teaching had now emerged which was generally accepted, and which should serve as a standard of orthodoxy. The faith has become a body of truth "once for all delivered unto the saints" (Jude ver 3). The content of this "sound doctrine" is nowhere formally given, but it is a probable inference that it corresponded very nearly to the Rom formula that became known as the Apostles' Creed. See DOGMA.

T. REES

DOCUS, dō′kus. See DOK.

DODAI, dō′dī, dō′dā-ī (1 Ch **27** 4). See DODO.

DODANIM, dō′da-nim (דֹּדָנִים, *dōdhānīm*, "leaders"): In Gen **10** 4, the son of Javan, the son of Japheth. This would place the Dodanim among the Ionians. The ‖ passage 1 Ch **1** 7, with the LXX and S, has, however, "Rodanim," which is probably the true reading. This identifies the people with the Rhodians (cf on Ezk **27** 15 under DEDAN).

DODAVAHU, dō-dav′a-hū (דּוֹדָוָהוּ, *dōdhāwāhū*, "loved of God"; AV **Dodavah**): Father of Eliezer of Mareshah, a prophet in the days of Jehoshaphat (2 Ch **20** 37).

DODO, dō′dō, **DODAI** (דּוֹדוֹ, *dōdhō*, דּוֹדַי, *dōdhay*, "beloved"):

(1) The grandfather of Tola of the tribe of Issachar, one of the judges (Jgs **10** 1).

(2) "The Ahohite," father of Eleazar, one of David's heroes, and (2 S **23** 9; 1 Ch **11** 12) himself the commander of one of the divisions of the army (1 Ch **27** 4).

(3) The Bethlehemite, father of Elhanan, one of David's mighty men (2 S **23** 24; 1 Ch **11** 26).

DOE, dō. See DEER.

DOEG, dō′eg (דּוֹאֵג, דֹּאֵג, *dō′ēgh*, "anxious," "cared for"): "The Edomite," a servant of Saul, who watched David's intercourse with the priest Ahimelech, then denounced the priest to the king, and later executed his command to slay the priests at Nob. The position he held is described as that of "the mightiest" of S.'s herdsmen (1 S **21** 7 m). LXX reads: "tending the mules." Rabbinical legends speak of him as the greatest scholar of his time. The traditional title of Ps **52** associates the composition of that Ps with the events that led to the slaying of the priests (1 S **21** 7; **22** 9.18.22).

NATHAN ISAACS

DOG (כֶּלֶב, *kelebh;* [cf Arab. *kelb*, "dog"]; **κύων**, *kúōn;* and dimin. **κυνάριον**, *kunárion*): References to the dog, both in the OT and in the NT, are usually of a contemptuous character. A dog, and esp. a dead dog, is used as a figure of insignificance. Goliath says to David (1 S **17** 43): "Am I a dog, that

Pariah Dog at Beirût.

thou comest to me with staves?" David says to Saul (1 S **24** 14): "After whom dost thou pursue? after a dead dog, after a flea." Mephibosheth says to David (2 S **9** 8): "What is thy servant, that thou shouldest look upon such a dead dog as I am?" The same figure is found in the words of Hazael to Elisha (2 K **8** 13). The meaning, which is obscure in AV, is brought out well in RV: "But what is thy servant, who is but a dog, that he should do this great thing?" The characteristically oriental interrogative form of these expressions should be noted.

Other passages express by inference the low esteem in which dogs are held. Nothing worse could happen to a person than that his body should be devoured by dogs (1 K **14** 11; **16** 4; **21** 19.23, etc). Job **30** 1 says of the youth who deride him that he disdained to set their fathers with the dogs of his flock In Phil **3** 2 and Rev **22** 15, dogs are coupled with evil-workers, sorcerers, etc. In Mt **7** 6 we read: "Give not that which is holy unto the dogs, neither cast your pearls before the swine."

Job **30** 1 (cited above) refers to the use of dogs to guard flocks; and the comparison of inefficient watchmen with dumb dogs (Isa **56** 10) implies that at least some dogs are useful. In the apocryphal Book of Tob, Tobias' dog is his companion on his travels (Tob **5** 16; **11** 4; on this see *Expos T*, XI, 258; *HDB*, IV, 989; Geiger, *Civilization of E. Iranians*, I, 85 ff).

There is further the reference to the greyhound (Prov **30** 31 EV) as one of the four things which are "stately in their going." But the rendering, "greyhound," rests solely upon inference, and is contrary to the LXX and Vulg, which have respectively *aléktōr* and *gallus*, i.e. "cock," AVm "horse." The Heb has *zarzīr mothnayim*, which AVm renders "girt in the loins." RVm has "war-horse," Heb "well girt [or, well knit] in the loins." In support of the meaning, "girt," for *zarzīr*, there is the word *zēr*, which, with *zarzīr*, is assigned to the obs root *zārar* and the Arab. *zirr*, "button," from *zarr*, "to button," "to compress." Further, to render *zarzīr* by "cock" logically requires a change in the text, for *mothnayim*, "loins," becomes superlative and inappropriate (see *EB*, s.v. "Cock"). On the other hand, the Arab. *zarzūr* is a starling (cf Arab. *zarzar*, "to utter cries," said of birds; *ṣarṣar*, "to cry out"; *ṣarṣūr*, "cockroach," or "*cricket*"). Also, according to *EB* (s.v. "Cock"), "the Talmudic *zarzīr* . . . . means some bird (a kind of raven)." If the text stands, there appears to be no better rendering than "girt in the loins," which might fairly be taken to refer to a war horse or to a greyhound. The Pers greyhound would in that case be understood, a hairy race, which, according to the *Royal Natural History*, is less fleet than the Eng. breed and is used in coursing gazelles and in hunting the wild ass, and which according to Doughty (*Arabia Deserta*) is kept by the Bedawin. "These dogs are said to be sometimes girdled by their owners to prevent them from over-eating and becoming fat" (L. Fletcher, *British Museum* [Natural History]).

Domestic dogs have probably been derived from various species of wolves and jackals. In this connection, it is noteworthy that the dogs of certain regions greatly resemble the wolves of those regions. The pariah dogs of Syria and Pal resemble the jackals, esp. in color and in the tail, differing in their greater size and in the shape of muzzle and ears. It is fair to assume that they are much the same as existed in Bible times. They are in general meek and harmless creatures, and are valuable as scavengers, but disturb the night with their barking. Each quarter of the city has its own pack of dogs, which vigorously resents any invasion of its territory. A dog which for any reason finds itself in foreign territory gets home as quickly as possible, and is lucky if it does not have to run the gauntlet of a pack of vicious foes. The pariah dog is sometimes brought up to be a sheep dog, but the best shepherd dogs are great wolfish creatures, which are usually obtained from Kurdistan.

ALFRED ELY DAY

DOGMA, dog'ma (**δόγμα,** *dógma*, from **δοκέω,** *dokéō*, "that which seems," "an opinion," particularly the opinion of a philosopher): In

1. As Law and Ordinance

the decadent period of Gr philosophy, the opinion, or *ipse dixit*, of the master of a philosophical school came to be quoted as authoritative truth; also, the opinion of a sovereign imposed as law upon his subjects: a decree or ordinance of the civil authority. The word never appears in EV, although it is used 5 t in the Gr NT, but with the one exception of Acts **16** 4, in a sense widely different from that which ecclesiastical usage has given to it from the 2d cent. downward. "Dogma" is used in the NT, (1) of Rom laws: "a decree [Gr *dogma*] from Caesar Augustus" (Lk **2** 1); "the decrees of Caesar" (Acts **17** 7) = the whole body of Rom law; (2) of ordinances of religious law: "the law of commandments contained in ordinances" (Eph **2** 15); "the bond written in ordinances" (Col **2** 14) = the Mosaic ordinances as expressing the moral law which condemned the sinner, and whose enmity Christ abolished by His death. It is a significant revelation of the spirit of Gr theology that all the Gr commentators understood by ordinances in these two places, the gospel as a body of dogmas which had removed the commandment or bond that was against us (see Lightfoot, *Col*, ad loc.); (3) of the decrees of the Council of Jerus (Acts **15** 20), which Paul and his companions delivered to the gentile churches (Acts **16** 4). Here we have one element that entered into the later ecclesiastical meaning of the word. These dogmas were decisions on religious matters, imposed by a more or less authoritative council of the church as a condition of admission to its membership.

There is however one important difference. These decrees relate to moral and ceremonial matters, but from the 2d cent. downward, dog-

2. As Formulated Teaching

ma means esp. a theological doctrine. In Gr theology "doctrine" and "dogma" meant the same thing. Each had its origin in the opinion of some great teacher; each rested upon revelation and claimed its authority; each meant an exposition of a particular truth of the gospel, and of the whole Christian truth, which the church adopted as the only right exposition. Each word might be used for the teaching of a philosopher, or of a heretic, although for the latter, "heresy" became the regular term. On the one side stood the doctrines or dogmas of the majority or the "Catholic" church, and on the other side, those of the heretics. So long as the "Catholic" ideal of orthodoxy and uniformity of belief held the field, there was no room for the distinction now made between "doctrine," as a scientific and systematic expression of the truth of the Christian religion, and "dogma," as those truths "authoritatively ratified as expressing the belief of the church." This distinction could only arise when men began to think that various expressions of Christian truth could coexist in the church, and is therefore quite modern and even recent. Dogma in this sense denotes the ancient conception of theology as an authoritative system of orthodoxy, and doctrine, the modern conception, outside the dogmatic churches, where theology is regarded as a scientific exposition of truth.

LITERATURE.—Harnack, *History of Dogma*, I, ch i; Drummond, *Studies in Christian Doctrine*, 1–7.

T. REES

DOK, dōk (**Δώκ,** *Dṓk*, **Δαγών,** *Dagṓn*): A small fortress, "little stronghold" near Jericho (1 Macc **16** 15), built by Ptolemy, son of Abubus, where he entertained and murdered his father-in-law Simon Maccabaeus and his two sons. Jos (*Ant*, XIII, viii, 1; *BJ*, I, ii, 3) calls the place Dagon and places it above Jericho. The name persists in *Ain Duk* with its copious springs of excellent water about 4 miles N.W. of Jericho. Some ancient foundations in the neighborhood are possibly those of Ptolemy's fortress, but more probably of a Templars' station which is known to have stood there as late as the end of the 13th cent. For its importance in earlier Jewish history, see Smith, *HGHL*, 250, 251

J. HUTCHISON

DOLEFUL, dōl'fo͝ol (אֹחַ, *'ōaḥ*, "howling"): The "doleful creatures" referred to in Isa **13** 21 are probably "jackals," although some have suggested "leopard," or "hyaena." The older EV gives "great owls." The word rendered "doleful lamentation" in Mic **2** 4 (*nihᵉyāh*) is simply a form of the word ordinarily tr[d] "wailing" (*nᵉhī*). Cf AVm.

DOLPHIN, dol'fin. See BADGER.

DOMINION, dō-min'yun: In Eph **1** 21; Col **1** 16 the word so tr[d] (**κυριότης,** *kuriótēs*) appears to denote a rank or order of angels. The same word is probably to be so interpreted in Jude ver 8 (AV and RV "dominion"), and in 2 Pet **2** 10 (AV "government," RV "dominion"). See ANGEL.

DOOM, dōōm: Occurs only once in AV (2 Esd **7** 43), "The day of doom shall be the end of this time" (RV "the day of judgement"); but RV gives it as the rendering of צְפִירָה, *çᵉphīrāh*, in Ezk **7** 7. 10 (AV "the morning," RVm "the turn" or "the crowning time"; but the meaning is not yet quite certain); and in 1 Cor **4** 9 (*ἐπιθανάτιος, epithanátios*, "as men doomed to death," AV "appointed [originally "approved"] unto death"). Our word "doom" is connected with the word "deem," and signifies either the act of judging or (far more often) the sentence itself or the condition resulting therefrom (cf "Deemster" of Isle of Man and Jersey). Generally, but not always, an unfavorable judgment is implied. Cf Dryden, *Coronation of Charles II*, i, 127:

"Two kingdoms wait your doom, and, as you choose,
This must receive a crown, or that must lose."

J. R. VAN PELT

DOOR, dōr: Most commonly the rendering of Heb *pethah*, "doorway," *deleth*, "door" proper (the two distinguished in Gen **19** 6), or of Gr *θύρα, thúra*, which represents both meanings. The door proper was usually of wood, frequently sheeted with metal, sometimes of one slab of stone, as shown in excavations in the Hauran. It turned on pivots (the "hinges" of Prov **26** 14) working in sockets above and below, and was provided with a bolt (2 S **13** 17) or with lock and key (Jgs **3** 23). The doorway was inclosed by the stone threshold (1 K **14** 17), the two doorposts on either side, and the lintel above (Ex **12** 7). Doors were frequently two-leaved, and folding ones are mentioned in connection with the temple (1 K **6** 34). Where "door" is used in connection with city gates (Neh **3** 1 ff) it refers to the door proper which swings on its hinges as distinguished from the whole structure. The custom of fastening to the doorposts small cases containing a parchment inscribed with the words of Dt **6** 4–9; **11** 13–21 had its origin in the command there given. See also GATE; HOUSE.

Figurative: (1) Christ is "the door" into the gospel ministry (Jn **10** 1.2.7); ministers must receive their authority from Him, and exercise it in His spirit. (2) 'Through faith in Him also both shepherds and sheep enter into the kingdom of God (ver 9), and find all their spiritual needs supplied.' (3) The fig. in Rev **3** 20 is expressive of Christ's patient, persistent and affectionate appeal to men. (4) Elsewhere also of opportunity (Mt **25** 10; Acts **14** 27; 1 Cor **16** 9; 2 Cor **2** 12; Rev **3** 8). (5) Of freedom and power (Col **4** 3). See also ACHOR; SHEPHERD. BENJAMIN RENO DOWNER

DOORKEEPER, dōr'kēp-ēr (שׁוֹעֵר, *shō'ēr*): The gates of an oriental city and of the temple courts so closely resembled the door of a house that the same Heb word was used for doorkeeper and gatekeeper. It is often tr[d] by the less definite word "porter" (q.v.).

In the preëxilic writings (2 S **18** 26; 2 K **7** 10. 11) reference is made to porters at the gates of the cities Mahanaim and Samaria. In these early writings there is also mention of a small number of "keepers of the threshold" of the temple, whose duties included the gathering of money from the people for temple purposes, and the care of the sacred vessels (2 K **12** 9; **22** 4; **23** 4). They held an honorable position (2 K **25** 18), and occupied chambers in the temple (Jer **35** 4). The same term is used to describe officers in the household of the king of Persia (Est **2** 21; **6** 2).

Differing from these "keepers of the threshold" in some respects are the doorkeepers or porters mentioned in Ch, Ezr and Neh. These formed a numerous sacred order (1 Ch **9** 22; **23** 5) from the time of David. Their duties and the words describing them in two passages, "keepers of the thresholds" (1 Ch **9** 19) and "porters of the thresholds" (2 Ch **23** 4), connect them in some measure with the "keeper of the threshold" referred to above. They guarded the gates of the house of Jeh (1 Ch **9** 23), closing and opening them at the proper times (ver 27) and preventing the unclean from entering the sacred inclosure (2 Ch **23** 19); they had charge of the sacred vessels and of the free-will offerings (2 Ch **31** 14), and dwelt in the chambers about the temple (1 Ch **9** 27). They were Levites, and came in from the Levitical villages every seventh day for service in their turn (1 Ch **9** 25). Their office was honorable, ranking with the singers, after the priests and Levites (Ezr **2** 42; 1 Ch **15** 18).

In Ps **84** 10, "I had rather be a d. in the house of my God," the word is not used in its technical sense. RVm gives "stand [AVm "sit"] at the threshold," to an eastern mind a situation of deep humility (cf title of the Ps and 1 Ch **9** 19).

In the NT the order of temple doorkeepers is not referred to. But a doorkeeper (*θυρωρός, thurōrós*) is mentioned in connection with a private house (Mk **13** 34), with the high priest's house (Jn **18** 16.17), and with sheep-folds (Jn **10** 3), a maid serving as doorkeeper in some cases (Acts **12** 13).

GEORGE RICE HOVEY

DOORPOST, dōr'pōst. See HOUSE.

DOPHKAH, dof'ka (דָּפְקָה, *dophkāh*, "drover"): A desert camp of the Israelites, the first after leaving the wilderness of Sin (Nu **33** 12.13). See WANDERINGS OF ISRAEL.

DOR, dôr, **DORA,** dō'ra (דֹּאר, *dō'r*, דּוֹר, *dōr*, "habitation," "circle"; **Δώρ,** *Dṓr;* Jos, **Δῶρα,** *Dṓra;* mod. *Ṭanṭūrah*): A town of the coast of Pal, S. of Carmel (*CAp*, II, 10; *Vita*, 8), about 8 miles N. of Caesarea. It was occupied in the earliest times by the Canaanites and probably belonged to Phoenicia, tradition saying that it was a Sidonian colony. It furnished an abundance of the shell-fish so valuable for the manufacture of the Tyrian purple, and this would have led the Phoenicians to occupy the site. In the 12th cent. BC, the region was occupied by the northern people who raided the whole Syrian coast and Egypt. They were driven back by the Egyptians, but renewed the attack, and the weakness of Egypt in the middle of the cent. enabled them to settle in the coast region S. of Carmel; a tribe of them occupied Dor, and others the territory to the limits of the desert of Sinai, and became the Phili people so well known by their contests with the Hebrews. Naphoth-dor, "the heights of Dor," may be the slopes of Carmel inland from *Ṭanṭūrah*. Dor fell within the territory assigned to Manasseh (Josh **17** 11; cf *Ant*, V, i, 22). It was the seat of a king who possessed other towns on the heights back of the coast. He was one of the allies of Jabin of Hazor in the conflict with Joshua (Josh **11** 2) and was conquered by him (**12** 23), but Dor was not occupied by the Israelites (**17** 11; Jgs **1** 27).

The inhabitants of Dor were at enmity with the

Phoen towns and it would seem that the Sidonians seized it to obtain its rich supplies of shell-fish, and this probably caused the war of retaliation waged by the Philis, under the lead of Ashkelon, against Sidon in the middle of the 11th cent. Sidon was besieged by land, and the inhabitants were compelled to flee to Tyre. Dor seems to have been occupied by Solomon since he placed one of his purveyors in the town (1 K **4** 11), and Tiglath-pileser III reduced it and set a governor over it (Rawl., *Phoen.*, 84). Here Tryphon was besieged by Antiochus, but escaped to Apamea (1 Macc **15** 11.13.25; *Ant*, XIII, vii, 2). It was made free by Pompey, and joined to the province of Syria (XIV, iv, 4). The youths of the place set up a statue of Tiberius in the Jewish synagogue, an outrage that was reported to Publius Petronius by Agrippa, and reparation was made (XIX, vi, 3). It does not seem to have been of much importance in later times, though the fortifications still remaining on the ruined site, from the period of the Middle Ages, show that it was then occupied. It is now only a miserable village nestled in the ruins. H. PORTER

DORCAS, dôr′kas (**Δορκάς**, *Dorkás*, the Gr equivalent of Aram. *tabītha*, "a gazelle"): The name was borne by a Christian woman of Joppa. She is called a disciple (*mathḗtria:* Acts **9** 36, the only place in the NT where the fem. form is used). She seems to have had some means and also to have been a leader in the Christian community. Dorcas was beloved for the manner in which she used her position and means, for she "was full of good works, and almsdeeds which she did." Among her charities was the clothing of the poor with garments she herself made (ver 39), and by following her example, numerous "Dorcas societies" in the Christian church perpetuate her memory. There is a local memorial in the "Tabitha School" in Jaffa devoted to the care and education of poor girls.

Her restoration to life by Peter is recorded. At the time of her death Peter was in Lydda where he had healed Aeneas. Being sent for, he went to Joppa, and, by the exercise of the supernatural powers granted to him, "he presented her alive" to the mourning community. In consequence of this miracle "many believed on the Lord" (ver 42). S. F. HUNTER

DORYMENES, dō-rim′e-nēz (**Δορυμένης**, *Doruménēs*): Father of Ptolemy Macron (1 Macc **3** 38; 2 Macc **4** 45); probably the same man who fought against Antiochus the Great (Polyb. v.61).

DOSITHEUS, dō-sith′ē-us (**Δοσίθεος**, *Dosítheos*): (1) A captain of Judas Maccabaeus (2 Macc **12** 19–25); along with Sosipater he captured Timotheus after the battle of Carnion, but granted him his life and freedom on the representation that "he had in his power the parents of many of them and the brethren of some," who, if they put him to death, should "be disregarded."

(2) A soldier in the army of Judas Maccabaeus (2 Macc **12** 35); he made a special attack upon Gorgias, governor of Idumaea, the opposing general, and would have taken the "accursed man" prisoner but for the interference of a Thracian horseman.

(3) A Jew, son of Drimylus (3 Macc **1** 3) who rescued Ptolemy Philopator from a plot of Theodotus. He afterward proved an apostate from Judaism.

(4) A Levite priest who "in the 4th year of the reign of Ptolemy and Cleopatra" carried the tr of the Book of Est to Alexandria (Ad Est **11** 1). J. HUTCHISON

DOTAEA, dō-tē′a (AV, incorrectly, **Judea**; **Δωταία**, *Dōtaía*): Another form of the name DOTHAN (q.v.).

DOTE, dōt: "To dote" means either "to be weakminded" or "to be foolishly fond." In the latter sense it is employed in Ezk **23** 5 ff; in the former, in Jer **50** 36 AV (RV "shall become fools"); AV Sir **25** 2 (RV "lacking understanding"), and AV 1 Tim **6** 4 (RVm "to be sick"; AVm "a fool").

DOTHAIM, dō′thā-im: Mentioned in Jth **4** 6 and frequently in connection with the invasion of Holofernes. See next art.

DOTHAN, dō′than (דֹּתַיְן, *dōthayin*, דֹּתָן, *dōthān*, "two wells," "double feast"; **Δωθάειμ**, *Dōtháeim*): A place to the N. of Shechem whither Jacob's sons went for pasture for the flocks; where Joseph who followed them was sold to the Ishmaelites, after having been imprisoned in a "pit" (Gen **37** 17 ff).

Dothan.

Here in later days the eyes of Elisha's servant were opened to see the mountain "full of horses and chariots of fire," guarding his master from the encircling Syrians (2 K **6** 13 ff). This is certainly to be identified with *Tell Dōthān*, which lies on the E. of the ancient road leading from Gilead across Esdraelon to the seacoast, and thence to Egypt. It is about 5 miles to the S.W. of *Jenīn*. There are some traces of old buildings, two cisterns—*Dōthayin* or *Dōthayim*="two cisterns" or "pits"—and one copious spring. Excellent pasture is found in the surrounding plain, and on the adjoining slopes. W. EWING

DOUBLE, dub′'l (שָׁנָה, *shānāh*, "to repeat," as in counting; כָּפַל, *kāphal*, "to fold over," or "double," as a cloth): A word used quite frequently in the OT. Jacob ordered his sons to take double money in their hands, i.e. twice the necessary amount (Gen **43** 12.15). If a thief be caught with a living animal he was to restore double (Ex **22** 4); if property be stolen out of the house of one to whom it is intrusted he was to restore double (Ex **22** 7.9). The firstborn was to receive a double portion of the inheritance (Dt **21** 17). Likewise also by a beautiful symbol Elisha asked for a double portion of Elijah's spirit to fall upon him (2 K **2** 9). Degrees of punishment or sufferings were also expressed by the idea of a doubling (Isa **61** 7; Jer **16** 18; **17** 18; Zec **9** 12). The use of the second Heb form in Job **11** 6 and **41** 13 seems quite confusing in its tr. AV translates it simply "double," but RV gives it its expanded and derived meaning, "manifold in understanding," and "who shall come within his jaws," respectively, "manifold" in the first instance meaning multiplied, and "jaws" doubtless meaning the double row of teeth. The classic phrases in the NT are those used by James to represent instability and a wavering disposition, *δίψυχος*, *dípsuchos*, lit. "doubleminded" (Jas **1** 8; **4** 8). WALTER G. CLIPPINGER

DOUBT, dout: This word, found only a score of times in the Bible, translates nevertheless about half as many different Heb and Gr originals with a corresponding variety of meanings.

In Gen **37** 33 "without doubt" is to be taken in the common sense of "certainly"; in Job **12** 2 in the sarcastic sense of "indeed!" In Dnl **5** 12.16, it is used as a difficult problem or mystery to be explained, and these are the only cases of its employment in the OT.

In the NT it is about equally used to translate διαπορέω, *diaporéō*, and διακρίνω, *diakrínō*, and their cognates. The first means "to be without resource," "utterly at a loss," "nonplussed"; and the second, "to judge diversely." For the first, see Jn **13** 22; Acts **2** 12 AV; **5** 24 AV; **10** 17 AV; **25** 20 AV; and Gal **4** 20 AV. For the second see Mt **21** 21; Mk **11** 23; Acts **10** 20; Rom **14** 23. The last-named is deserving of particular attention. "He that doubteth is condemned [AV "damned"] if he eat," means that in a case of uncertainty as to one's Christian liberty, it were better to err on the side of restraint. In Lk **12** 29 "to be of doubtful mind" (μετεωρίζω, *meteōrízō*, lit. "to suspend"; vide Thayer, s.v.), means "to be driven by gusts," or "to fluctuate in mid-air."

Here, as in Mt **14** 31, "doubt" does not indicate a lack of faith, but rather "a state of *qualified* faith": its weakness, but not its absence.

In Jn **10** 24 "doubt" translates αἴρω ψυχήν, *aírō psuchḗn*, which lit. means "to lift up the soul," or "to keep one in suspense"; so RV. See also DISPUTATION. JAMES M. GRAY

DOUGH, dō. See BREAD.

DOVE, duv (תּוֹר, *tōr*, יוֹנָה, *yōnāh;* περιστερά, *peristerá;* Lat *Zenaedura carolinensis*): A bird of the family *Columbidae*. Doves and pigeons are so closely related as to be spoken and written of as synonymous, yet there is a distinction recognized from the beginning of time. It was esp. marked in Pal, because doves migrated, but pigeons remained in their chosen haunts all the year. Yet doves were the wild birds and were only confined singly or in pairs as caged pets, or in order to be available for sacrifice. Pigeons, without question, were the first domesticated birds, the record of their conquest by man extending if anything farther back than ducks, geese and swans. These two were the best known and the most loved of all the myriads of birds of Pal. Doves were given preference because they remained wild and were more elusive. The thing that escapes us is usually a little more attractive than the thing we have. Their loving natures had been noted, their sleek beautiful plumage, their plump bodies. They were the most precious of anything offered for sacrifice. Their use is always specified in preference to pigeons if only one bird was used; if both, the dove is frequently mentioned first. Because of their docility when caged, their use in sacrifice, and the religious superstition concerning them, they were allowed to nest unmolested and, according to species, flocked all over Pal. The turtle-dove nested in gardens and vineyards, and was almost as tame as the pigeons. The palm turtle-dove took its name from its love of homing in palm trees, and sought these afield, and in cities, even building near the temple in Jerus. It also selected thorn and other trees. It has a small body, about ten inches in length, covered with bright chestnut-colored feathers, the neck dappled with dark, lustrous feathers. The rock dove swarmed over, through, and among the cliffs of mountains and the fissures of caves and ravines. The collared turtle-dove was the largest of the species. It remained permanently and homed in the forests of Tabor and Gilead, around the Dead Sea, and along the Jordan valley. This bird was darker than the others and took its name from a clearly outlined collar of dark feathers encircling the neck, and was esp. sought for caged pets on account of its size and beauty.

In all, the dove is mentioned about fifty times in the Bible. Many of these references are concerning its use in sacrifice and need not all be mentioned. The others are quoted and explained from a scientific standpoint and in accordance with the characteristics and habits of the birds. The first reference to the dove occurs in Gen **8** 8–12, in the history of the flood; then follows its specified use in sacrifice; note of its migratory habits is made, and then in poetry, prophecy, comparison, simile and song, it appears over and over throughout the Bible.

In Gen **8** 8–12, we read, "And he sent forth a dove from him, to see if the waters were abated." Noah first sent out a raven, because it was a strong, aggressive bird and would return to its mate. But the raven only flew over the water and returned to perch on the ark. This was not satisfactory, so Noah in looking for a bird better suited to his purpose, bethought him of the most loving and tender bird he knew—the dove. It not only would return to the ark, but would enter and go to the cage of its mate, and if it found green food it would regurgitate a portion for her or its young, or if not nesting he could tell by its droppings if greenery had been eaten and so decide if the waters were going down. And this is precisely what happened. The dove came back, and the watching Noah saw it feed its mate little green olive leaves, for the dove never carries food in the beak, but swallows and then regurgitates it to mate and young. This first reference to birds was made on account of the loving, tender characteristics of the species; the next, because they were the most loved by the people, and therefore chosen as most suitable to offer as sacrifice (Gen **15** 9). In Lev **1** 14 f, doves are mentioned as sacrifice: "And the priest shall bring it unto the altar, and wring off its head, and burn it on the altar; and the blood thereof shall be drained out on the side of the altar." In Lev **5** 7 the proper preparation of the sacrifice is prescribed. For method of handling sacrifice see vs 8.9.10. In Lev **12** 6 the law for a sacrifice for a mother is given, and ver 8 of same ch provides that if she be too poor to offer a lamb, doves or pigeons will suffice. In Lev **14** 4–8 the reference for the sacrifice of a leper is merely to "birds," because it is understood that they are pigeons and doves, and it contains the specification that if the victim is too poor to afford so elaborate a sacrifice, a smaller one will suffice. The birds are named in ver 22: "Two turtle-doves, or two young pigeons, such as he is able to get; and the one shall be a sin-offering, and the other a burnt-offering" (cf Lev **15** 14.29; Nu **6** 10). When David prayed for the destruction of the treacherous, he used the dove in comparison, and because he says he would "lodge in the wilderness" he indicates that he was thinking of the palm turtle.

> "And I said, Oh that I had wings like a dove!
> Then would I fly away, and be at rest" (Ps **55** 6).

In chanting a song of triumph, David used an exquisite thought.

> "When ye lie among the sheepfolds,
> It is as the wings of a dove covered with silver,
> And her pinions with yellow gold" (Ps **68** 13).

He referred to the rock dove because the metallic luster on its neck would gleam like gold in sunshine, and the soft grayish-white feathers beneath the wings as he would see the bird above him in flight would appear silver-like. By this quotation David meant that in times of peace, when men slept contentedly at home among their folds, their life was as rich with love and as free in peace as the silver wing of the dove that had the gold feathers and was unmolested among the inaccessible caves and cliffs. In Ps **74** 19 the term "turtle-dove" is used to indicate people whom the Almighty is implored to protect: "Oh deliver not the soul of thy turtle-dove unto the wild beast: forget not the life of thy poor for ever."

Solomon uses the dove repeatedly in comparison or as a term of endearment. In Cant **1** 15; **4** 1; **5** 12, he compares the eyes of his bride full, tender, beautiful, with those of a dove. In **2** 12 he uses

Turtle-Dove (*Turtur auritus*).

the voice of the dove as an indication of spring. In **2** 14 he addresses the bride as a rock dove. In **5** 2 is another term of endearment, this time used in the dream of the bride (cf **6** 9). Isa **38** 14 has reference to the wailing, mournful dove note from which the commonest species take the name "mourning dove." The reference in Isa **60** 8 proves that the prophet was not so good an observer, or so correct in his natural history as David, who may have learned from the open. As a boy, David guarded the flocks of his father and watched the creatures around him. When exulting over the glory of the church in the numerous accessions of Gentiles, Isaiah cried, "Who are these that fly as a cloud, and as the doves to their windows?" This proves that he confounded pigeons and doves. Doves were wild, mostly migratory, and had no "windows." But the clay cotes of pigeons molded in squares so that one large cote sheltered many pairs in separate homes had the appearance of latticed windows and were used as a basis in estimating a man's wealth. This reference should be changed to read, "and as pigeons to their windows." In Jer **8** 7 the fact is pointed out that doves were migratory; and in **48** 28 people are advised to go live in solitary places and be peaceable, loving and faithful, like the rock doves. See also Ezk **7** 16: "But those of them that escape shall escape, and shall be on the mountains like doves of the valleys, all of them moaning, every one in his iniquity." This merely means that people should be driven to hide among the caves and valleys where the rock doves lived, and that the sound of their mourning would resemble the cry of the birds. It does not mean, however, that the doves were mourning, for when doves coo and moan and to our ears grow most pitiful in their cries, they are the happiest in the mating season. The veneration cherished for doves in these days is inborn, and no bird is so loved and protected as the dove—hence it is unusually secure and happy and its mournful cry is the product of our imagination only. The dove is the happiest of birds. Hos **7** 11 and **11** 11 each compares people with doves; the first, because the birds at times appear foolishly trusting; the second, because, while no bird is more confiding, none is more easily frightened. "And Ephraim is like a silly dove, without understanding: they call unto Egypt, they go to Assyria" (**7** 11). "They shall come trembling as a bird out of Egypt, and as a dove out of the land of Assyria; and I will make them to dwell in their houses, saith Jeh" (**11** 11). The reference in Nah **2** 7 is to the voice of the birds.

NT references will be found in a description of the baptism of Jesus (Mt **3** 16). People are admonished to be "harmless as doves" (**10** 16). "And Jesus entered into the temple of God, and cast out all them that sold and bought in the temple, and overthrew the tables of the money-changers, and the seats of them that sold the doves" (Mt **21** 12). This proves that these birds were a common article of commerce, probably the most used for caged pets, and those customarily employed for sacrifice.

Dove's Dung (חֲרֵי יוֹנִים, *ḥărī yōnīm*, K^e^thībh for דִּבְיוֹנִים, *dibhyōnīm*): 2 K **6** 25: "And there was a great famine in Samaria: and, behold, they besieged it, until an ass's head was sold for fourscore pieces of silver, and the fourth part of a kab of dove's dung for five pieces of silver." This seems so repulsive that some commentators have tried to prove the name applied to the edible root of a plant, but the history of sieges records other cases where matter quite as offensive was used to sustain life. The text is probably correct as it stands.

GENE STRATTON-PORTER

DOWRY, dou'ri: In all Heb marriages, the dowry held an important place. The dowry sealed the betrothal. It took several forms. The bridegroom presented gifts to the bride. There was the מֹהַר, *mōhar*, "dowry" as distinguished from מַתָּן, *mattān*, "gifts to the members of the family" (cf Gen **24** 22.53; Gen **34** 12). The price paid to the father or brothers of the bride was probably a survival of the early custom of purchasing wives (Gen **34** 12; Ex **22** 17; 1 S **18** 25; cf Ruth **4** 10; Hos **3** 2). There was frequently much negotiation and bargaining as to size of dowry (Gen **34** 12). The dowry would generally be according to the wealth and standing of the bride (cf 1 S **18** 23). It might consist of money, jewelry or other valuable effects; sometimes, of service rendered, as in the case of Jacob (Gen **29** 18); deeds of valor might be accepted in place of dowry (Josh **15** 16; 1 S **18** 25; Jgs **1** 12). Occasionally a bride received a dowry from her father; sometimes in the shape of land (Jgs **1** 15), and of cities (1 K **9** 16). In later Jewish history a written marriage contract definitely arranged for the nature and size of the dowry.

EDWARD BAGBY POLLARD

DOXOLOGY, dok-sol'ō-ji (**δοξολογία,** *doxología*, "a praising," "giving glory"): A hymn or liturgical formula expressive of praise to God, as the *Gloria in Excelsis* (an expansion of Lk **2** 14), sometimes called the Greater Doxology, and the *Gloria Patri* ("Glory be to the Father, and to the Son, and to the Holy Ghost, world without end, Amen") also known as the Lesser Doxology.

The clause, "as it was in the beginning, is now, and ever shall be," was probably added to the original simple formula to emphasize the church's dissent from the Arian conception of Christ.

The term is applied in particular to the concluding paragraph of the Lord's Prayer (Mt **6** 13 m, "For thine is the kingdom," etc; cf 1 Ch **29** 11, and see LORD'S PRAYER).

To the same general class belong Ps **41** 13; **72** 18 f; **89** 52; Rom **16** 27; Eph **2** 20; 1 Tim **1** 17; Jude ver 25; Rev **5** 13 f; **19** 1-3, and the modern stanza beginning "Praise God, from whom all blessings flow."

M. O. EVANS

DRACHMA, drak'ma, **DRAM** (**δραχμή,** *drachmḗ*): The word is used in the LXX as the rendering of

בֶּקַע, *beḳa'*, "half-shekel," which must refer to the light standard for the shekel, as its weight was about 62 grains. In the NT the word occurs only in Lk **15** 8.9, where it is rendered "a piece of silver" (m "drachma"). It was commonly taken as equivalent to the Rom denarius, though not strictly so.

DRAGON, drag′un (תַּנִּין, *tannīn*, pl. תַּנִּים, *tannīm*, תַּנּוֹת, *tannōth;* **δράκων,** *drákōn*):

Tannīn and the pl. *tannīnīm* occur 14 t, and in EV are variously rendered "dragon," "whale," "serpent" or "sea-monster"; but Lam **4** 3, AV "sea-monster," AVm "sea calves," RV "jackals." *Tannīm* occurs 12 t, and is rendered "dragons," RV "jackals," except in Ezk **29** 3, where AV has "dragon" (ARV "monster"), and in Ezk **32** 2, where AV has "whale" and ERV and AVm "dragon" (ARV "monster"). *Tannōth* occurs once, in Mal **1** 3, where it is rendered "dragons," RV "jackals." *Drakōn* occurs 12 t in Rev **12, 13, 16,** and **20,** where it is uniformly rendered "dragon." (Cf Arab. *tinnīn*, the constellation, Draco.) *Tannōth* (LXX δώματα *dṓmata*, "dwellings") is a fem. pl. form as if from *tannāh*, but it suits the context to give it the same meaning as *tannīm*.

In Ex **7** 9.10.12, *tannīn* is used of the serpents which were produced from Aaron's rod and the rods of the Egyp magicians, whereas in Ex **4** 3 and **7** 15, for the serpent produced from Aaron's rod, we find *nāḥāsh*, the ordinary word for serpent. In two passages we find "whale," RV "sea-monster"; Gen **1** 21: "And God created the great sea-monsters, and every living creature that moveth"; Job **7** 12: "Am I a sea, or a sea-monster, that thou settest a watch over me?" Other passages (ERV and AV) are Dt **32** 33: "Their wine is the poison of dragons [ARV "serpents"], and the cruel venom of asps"; Neh **2** 13: "And I went out by night by the valley gate, even toward the dragon's [ARV "jackal's"] well" (AV "dragon well"); Ps **91** 13: "Thou shalt tread upon the lion and adder: the young lion and the serpent [AV "dragon"] shalt thou trample under foot"; Ps **148** 7: "Praise Jeh from the earth, ye sea-monsters [AV "dragons"], and all deeps"; Jer **51** 34: "Nebuchadrezzar the king of Babylon hath devoured me, ... like a monster" (AV "dragon"). Here also two *tannīm* passages; Ezk **29** 3: "Thus saith the Lord Jeh: Behold, I am against thee, Pharaoh king of Egypt, the great monster [AV "dragon"] that lieth in the midst of his rivers, that hath said, My river is mine own, and I have made it for myself"; and Ezk **32** 2: "Son of man, take up a lamentation over Pharaoh king of Egypt, and say unto him, Thou wast likened unto a young lion of the nations: yet art thou as a monster [ERV "dragon," AV "whale"] in the seas; and thou didst break forth with thy rivers, and troubledst the waters with thy feet, and fouledst their rivers."

The foregoing passages offer no especial difficulties in the interpretation of the word *tannīn*. All may fairly be understood to refer to a serpent or sea-monster or some imaginary creature, without invoking any ancient myths for their elucidation. The same may be said of the passages in Rev. A dragon is taken as the personification of Satan, as of Pharaoh in the passages in Ezk. It is of course true that ancient myths may more or less distantly underlie some of these dragon and serpent references, and such myths may be demonstrated to throw additional light in certain cases, but at least the passages in question are intelligible without recourse to the myths. This however is not equally true of all the *tannīn* passages. In Ps **74** 12 we read: "Yet God is my King of old, working salvation in the midst of the earth. Thou didst divide the sea by thy strength: thou brakest the heads of the sea-monsters [AV "dragons"] in the waters." Cf Isa **27** 1; **51** 9 f.

The three passages just cited seem to denote each some particular act, and are referred by Canon Cheyne (*EB* s.v. "Dragon") to the old Bab myth of the conflict of Marduk and Tiāmat in the Assyr creation-legend (thus Gunkel, etc). Indeed he refers to that myth not only these passages, but also Jer **51** 34; Ezk **29** 3–6; **32** 2–8 and Job **7** 12, which have been cited above. In translating the last two passages, Canon Cheyne uses the definite article, "*the* dragon," instead of "*a*" as in RV, which makes a great difference in the meaning. In Ps **87** 4, it is clear that Rahab is a country, i.e. Egypt. Isa **30** 7 is to the same point. In Isa **51** 9.10, "that didst cut Rahab in pieces" and "that didst pierce the monster" (AV "dragon"), are two coördinate expressions of one idea, which is apparently the defeat of the Egyptians, as appears in the reference to the passage of the Red Sea. In Isa **27** 1, "leviathan the swift serpent" and "leviathan the crooked serpent" and "the monster [AV and ERV "dragon"] that is in the sea" have been identified with Babylon, Persia and Egypt (*EB* s.v. "Dragon," 4). It is more probable that the first two expressions are coördinate, and amount to "leviathan the swift and crooked serpent," and that the verse may therefore refer to Babylonia and Egypt. Ps **74** 12–15 is more in line with the idea of the art. in *EB*, but it is nevertheless susceptible of an explanation similar to that of the other two passages.

Tannīm, "dragons" (RV "jackals") occurs in Job **30** 29; Ps **44** 19; Isa **13** 22; **34** 13; **35** 7; **43** 20; Jer **9** 11; **10** 22; **14** 6; **49** 33; **51** 37; *tannōth*, "dragons" (RV "jackals") is found in Mal **1** 3. In all these passages, "jackal" suits the context better than "dragon," "sea-monster" or "serpent." An exception to the rendering of "dragon" or "serpent" or "sea-monster" for *tannīn* is found in Lam **4** 3: "Even the jackals draw out the breast, they give suck to their young ones." AV has "sea-monster," AVm "sea calves." A mammal is indicated, and RV apparently assumes that *tannīn* is an error for *tannīm*. Two other exceptions are in Ezk **29** 3 and **32** 2, where EV renders *tannīm* by "dragon," since in these two passages "jackal" obviously will not suit. See JACKAL.

On the constellational dragons or snakes, see ASTRONOMY, II, 1–5.

ALFRED ELY DAY

DRAGON, BEL AND THE. See BEL AND THE DRAGON.

DRAGON, RED. See REVELATION, BOOK OF.

DRAGON WELL (Neh **2** 13 AV). See JACKAL'S WELL.

DRAM. See DRACHMA; MONEY.

DRAMA MIMIC, drä′ma mim′ik. See GAMES.

DRAUGHT, draft (**ἀφεδρών,** *aphedrṓn;* Mt **15** 17; Mk **7** 19): "Closet," "sink" or "privy" (Rheims), lit. "place for sitting apart" (cf 2 K **10** 27, "draught-house," and Mish "water-house"). According to the Mish Jehu turned the temple of Baal in Samaria into public *latrines*, "water-houses." Mk adds here (**7** 19) that by this saying Jesus cleansed all articles of food, i.e., declared them to be clean.

DRAWER, drô′ēr, **OF WATER** (שֹׁאֵב מַיִם, *shō'ēbh mayim*, from שָׁאַב, *shā'abh*, "to bale up" water): In Syria and Pal, outside of Mt. Lebanon and the Anti-Lebanon, the springs of water are scarce and the inhabitants of these less favored places have always depended upon wells and cisterns for their water supply. This necessitates some device for drawing the water. In the case of a cistern or shallow well, an earthenware water jar or a bucket made of tanned goats' skin is lowered into the water by a rope and then raised by pulling up the rope hand over hand (probably the ancient method), or by running the rope over a crude pulley fixed directly over the cistern or well. In the case of deep wells, the rope, attached to a larger bucket, is run over a pulley so that the water may be raised by the drawers walking away from the well as they pull the rope. Frequently animals are hitched to the rope to do the pulling.

In some districts where the water level is not too deep, a flight of steps leading down to the water's edge is constructed in addition to the opening vertically above the water. Such a well is pointed out near Haran in Mesopotamia as the one from which Rebekah drew water for Abraham's servant. In Gen **24** 16 we read that Rebekah "went down to the fountain, and filled her pitcher, and came up."

The deep grooves in their curbs, worn by the ropes as the water was being raised, attest to the antiquity of many of the wells of Pal and Syria. Any one of the hundreds of grooves around a single well was many years in being formed. The fact that the present method of drawing water from these wells is not making these grooves, shows that they are the work of former times.

St. Mary's Well at Nazareth.

The drawing of water was considered the work of women or of men unfit for other service (Gen **24** 11.13.43; 1 S **9** 11; Jn **4** 7). In Syria, today, a girl servant willingly goes to draw the daily supply of water, but seldom is it possible to persuade a boy or man to perform this service. When the well or fountain is at a distance, or much water is needed, tanned skins or earthen jars are filled and transported on the backs of men or donkeys.

Water drawing was usually done at evening time (Gen **24** 11), and this custom has remained unchanged. There is no sight more interesting than the daily concourse at a Syrian water source. It is bound to remind one of the Bible stories where the setting is a wellside (Gen **24**; Jn **4**).

The service of water drawing was associated, in early times, with that of hewer of wood (Dt **29** 11). Joshua made the Gibeonites hewers of wood and drawers of water in exchange for their lives (Josh **9** 21.23.27). The inhabitants of Nineveh were exhorted to draw water and fill the cisterns of their fortresses in preparation for a siege (Nah **3** 14).

Figurative: Water drawing is mentioned in the metaphor of Isa **12** 3, "Ye draw water out of the wells of salvation." JAMES A. PATCH

DREAM, drēm, **DREAMER,** drēm'ẽr (חֲלוֹם, *ḥălōm*, חֵלֶם, *ḥēlem*; ὄναρ, *ónar*): In all time dreams and their interpretation have been the occasion of much curious and speculative inquiry. Because of the mystery by which they have been enshrouded, and growing out of a natural curiosity to know the future, much significance has been attached to them by people esp. of the lower stages of culture. Even the cultured are not without a superstitious awe and dread of dreams, attaching to them different interpretations according to local color and custom.

Naturally enough, as with all other normal and natural phenomena for which men could assign no scientific and rational explanation, they would be looked upon with a certain degree of superstitious fear.

> "Dreams,
> Which are the children of an idle brain,
> Begot of nothing but vain fantasy,
> Which is as thin of substance as the air
> And more inconstant than the wind."
> —*Shakespeare.*

1. Physiological and Psychological Ground

While a fully satisfactory theory of dreams has not yet been established and while it is hardly possible that there will ever be a satisfactory explanation for each individual dream, yet through the rapid discoveries of physiological psychology in the recent decade or more, much new light is thrown on the subject. With the contribution modern psychology has made to our knowledge of the association of ideas through the connected relation of certain cortical centers and areas, it has come to be pretty well established that the excitation of certain bodily organs or surfaces will stimulate certain brain areas. Conversely the stimulation of certain cortical areas will produce a response in certain bodily regions over which these centers or areas preside. Connecting thought processes are therefore dependent upon the proper correlation of ideas through what are known physiologically as the association centers. If then it comes to pass that, as occurs in dreams, only fragmentary ideas or loosely connected trains of thought occur and if, as frequently happens, there is momentary connection, but little connection with normal waking experience, it will easily be seen that the excitation of certain centers will awaken certain trains of thought which are but poorly related to the balance of one's thinking processes. Much is being said about the dissociation of ideas and the disturbance of personality of which dreams are one of several forms. Others are hallucinations, trances, visions, etc. Dreams are abnormal and sometimes pathological. Sleep is a normal experience. Perfect and natural sleep should be without dreams of any conscious occurrence. Perhaps psychologically there can be no such thing as perfectly dreamless sleep. Such a condition would probably be death itself. Nature doubtless has her silent vigils, keeping watch in the chambers of the soul during the deepest sleep. The only difference is that they do not come to the threshold of consciousness. Thus, dreams are to the sleeping state what visions and hallucinations are to the waking state, and like them have their ground in a distorted image-making function. While the source of the materials and the excitant may not be the same in each case, yet functionally they are the same.

The stimuli of dreams may be of two kinds. First, they may be physical and objective, or they may be due to suggestions and the association of ideas. They may be due to some physical disorder, such as imperfect digestion or circulation, improper ventilation or heating, or an uncomfortable position. Since by the very nature of the case dreams do not occur in a conscious state, the real cause cannot easily be discoverable and then only after the subject is entirely awakened through the effects of it. They may also be due to the association of ideas. Suggestion plays a large part. The vividness and recency of a conscious impression during the waking state may be thrown up from the subconscious region during the sleeping hours. The usual distorted aspect of dreams is doubtless due to the uncoupling of groups of ideas through the uncoupling of the cortical association areas, some of them being less susceptible than others to the existing stimulus.

The materials of dreams need not be recent; they may have been furnished by the conscious processes a long time before, but are brought to the threshold only by means of some train of ideas during a semi-conscious state. It is interesting to note that while time and space seem quite real in dreams, the amount covered in a single dream may occupy but a moment of time for the dreamer.

2. History of Belief in Dreams

Dreams have always played an important part in the lit. and religion of all peoples. They have furnished mythologies; they have been the sources of systems of necromancy; they have become both the source and the explanation of otherwise inexplicable acts of Providence. Growing out of them we have a theory of nightmares and demonology. They have become the working material of the prophet both Bib. and pagan. Mediaeval civilization is not without its lasting effects of dreams, and modern civilization still clings with something of reverence to the unsolved mystery of certain dreams. While we have almost emerged from anything like a slavish adherence to a superstitious belief in dreams, we must still admit the possibility of the profound significance of dreams in the impressions they make upon the subject.

3. Dreams in the OT

The Bible, contrary to a notion perhaps too commonly held, attaches relatively little religious significance to dreams. Occasionally, however, reference is made to communications from God through dreams (Gen **20** 6; 1 K **3** 5; Mt **1** 20; **2** 12.13.19.22). It recognizes their human relations more frequently. In the OT lit. dreams play but little part except in the books of Gen and Dnl, in which there are abundant references to them. For their moral bearings the most important ones perhaps are those referred to in Gen **37** 5–10. An uncritical attitude will give to them a lifeless and mechanical interpretation. A sympathetic and rational explanation gives them beauty, naturalness and significance. Joseph was the youngest and most beloved son of Jacob. He was just in the prime of adolescence, the very period of day dreaming. He was perhaps inordinately ambitious. This was doubtless heightened by the attentions of a doting father. The most natural dream would be that suggested by his usual waking state, which was one of ambition and perhaps unhealthy rivalry (see Astronomy, II, 6). The source of Pharaoh's dreams and his solicitude are likewise capable of interpretation on somewhat natural grounds (Gen **41** 7–32). The significance of them was given by Joseph.

Another illustration of the psychological exposition preceding is the dream of Solomon (1 K **3** 5.11–15). In this narrative, after Solomon had done what pleased Jeh and had offered a most humble prayer on an occasion which to him was a great crisis and at the same time a moment of great ecstasy in his life, he doubtless experiences a feeling of sweet peace in consequence of it. His sleep would naturally be somewhat disturbed by the excitement of the day. The dream was suggested by the associations and naturally enough was the approving voice of Jeh.

Dreaming and the prophetic function seem to have been closely associated (Dt **13** 1.3.5). Whether from a coldly mechanical and superstitious, a miraculous, or a perfectly natural point of view, this relation is consistent. The prophet must be a seer, a man of visions and ideals. As such he would be subject, as in his waking states, so in his sleeping states, to extraordinary experiences. The remarkable dreams of Nebuchadnezzar, who stands out as an exceptional example, afford an illustration of what may be styled a disturbed personality (Dnl **2** 3–45; **4** 5–19). The effort made by the magicians, the enchanters, the Chaldaeans, and the soothsayers, according to the best skill of the Orientals, was unavailing. Daniel, whether by extraordinary intellectual insight or by Divine communication, was able by his interpretation and its moral to set before the king a powerful lesson.

The NT gives still less place and importance to dreams than the OT. There are only six references and one citation to dreams or dreamers. It is significant that all these references are by Mt, and still more significant that Jesus nowhere refers to dreams, evidently attaching little if any importance to them. The references in Mt are confined entirely to warnings and announcements (Mt **1** 20; **2** 12.13.19.22; **27** 19). Once a citation (Acts **2** 17) is used for illustrative purposes (cf Joel **2** 28). See also Augury, IV, 5; Divination, VI, 1, 1(*b*); Magic; Revelation.

Whether God communicates directly or indirectly by dreams is still unsettled. With our present knowledge of spirit communication it would not seem unreasonable to assume that He may reveal Himself directly; and yet on the other hand the safest and perhaps surest explanation for our own day and experience is that in dream states the mind is more impressionable and responsive to natural causes through which God speaks and operates. That dreams have been and are valuable means of shaping men's thoughts and careers cannot be denied, and as such, have played an important part in the social and moral life of individuals and of society. A valuable modern illustration of this is the dream of Adoniram Judson Gordon (see *How Christ Came to Church*), through the influence of which his entire religious life and that of his church were completely transformed.

Literature.—Judd, *Psychology;* Cutten, *The Psychological Phenomena of Christianity;* Ladd, *Philosophy of Knowledge;* Baldwin, *Dictionary of Philosophy and Psychology;* Ellis, *The World of Dreams* (Houghton, Mifflin Co.).

Walter G. Clippinger

DREDGE, drej: A mixture of oats and barley (Job **24** 6 AVm; AV "corn"; RV "provender"). The Heb word is בְּלִיל, *b^e^līl*, usually "mixed grain," *ZDMG*, XLVIII, 236: grain not ground and boiled in water. Cf Job **6** 5; Isa **30** 24.

DREGS, dregs: The "sediments," "lees," "grounds of liquor"; only in pl. In AV it stands for: (1) Heb *ḳubba'ath*, "bowl," "chalice," found only in Isa **51** 17.22: "the dregs of the cup of trembling"; "the dregs of the cup of my fury." RV correctly changes "dregs" into "bowl." (2) Heb *sh^e^mārīm*, "sediments" or "dregs," esp. lees of wine. "The dregs thereof, all the wicked of the earth shall wring [ARV "drain"] them out and drink them" (Ps **75** 8), i.e. God gives to the wicked the cup of wrathful judgment, which they must drink to the last drop.

DRESS: In the Heb and Gr there is a wonderful wealth of terminology having to do with the general subject of dress among the ancient Orientals. This is reflected in the numerous synonyms for "dress" to be found in EV, "apparel," "attire," "clothes," "raiment," "garments," etc. But the words used in the originals are often greatly obscured through the inconsistent variations of the translators. Besides there are few indications even in the original Heb or Gr of the exact shape or specific materials of the various articles of dress named, and so their identification is made doubly difficult. In dealing with the subject, therefore, the most reliable sources of information, apart from the meaning of the terms used in characterization, are certain well-known facts about the costumes and dress-customs of the orthodox Jews, and others about the forms of dress worn today by the people of simple life and primitive habits in modern Pal. Thanks to the ultra-conservatism and unchanging usages of the nearer

East, this is no mean help. In the endeavor to discover, distinguish and deal with the various oriental garments, then, we will consider: 1. The Meaning

A Native of Jericho.

of Terms; 2. The Materials; 3. The Outer Garments; 4. The Inner Garments; 5. The Headdress; 6. The Foot-gear; 7. The Dress of Jesus and His Disciples.

There was originally a sharp distinction between classical and oriental costume, but this was palpably lessened under the cosmopolitanism of the Rom Empire. This of course had its effect both in the modification of the fashions of the day and upon the words used for articles of clothing in the NT.

1. Meaning of Terms

(1) The terms most used for clothes in general were, in the OT, *ṣādhīn, simlāh, salmāh,* and in the NT *himátion* (Mt **21** 7; **24** 18; **26** 65; Lk **8** 27) and *énduma* (Mt **22** 11 f; cf **7** 15), pl., though the oldest and most widely distributed article of human apparel was probably the "loin-cloth" (Heb *'ēzōr*), entirely different from "girdle" (Gr *zōnē*). Bib. references for clothes are nearly all to the costume of the males, owing doubtless to the fact that the garments ordinarily used indoors were worn alike by men and women.

(2) The three normal body garments, the ones most mentioned in the Scriptures, are *ṣādhīn*, a rather long "under garment" provided with sleeves; *k^ethōneth* (Gr *chitôn*), a long-sleeved tunic worn over the *ṣādhīn*, likewise a shirt with sleeves (see Masterman, *DCG*, art. "Dress"); and *simlāh* (Gr *himation*), the cloak of AV and RV, used in the pl. for "garments" in general; and the "girdle" (Gr *zōnē;* Arab. *zunnar*). The "headdress" (two types are now in use, the "turban" and the "*kufiyeh*") is never definitely named in the Bible, though we know it was the universal custom among ancient Orientals to cover the head.

(3) The *simlāh* (Gr *himation*) signifies an "outer garment" (see below), a "mantle," or "cloak" (see lexicons). A kindred word in the Gr *himatismós*, (tr^d "raiment" in Lk **9** 29, "garments" in Mt **27** 35, and "vesture" in Jn **19** 24) stands in antithesis to *himation*. The Gr *chitōn*, Heb *k^ethōneth*, the "under garment," is tr^d "coat" in Mt **5** 40, "clothes" in Mk **14** 63. The Heb word *m^e'īl*, Gr *stolē*, Lat *stola*, stands for a variety of garment used only by men of rank or of the priestly order, rendered RV "robe." It stands for the long garments of the scribes rendered "long robes" (Mk **12** 38; Lk **20** 46) and "best robe" in the story of the Prodigal Son (Lk **15** 22). (For difference between *m^e'īl* and *simlāh*, see Kennedy, one-vol *HDB*, 197.) Oriental influences led to the adoption of the long tunic in Rome, and in Cicero's time it was a mark of effeminacy. It came to be known in its white form as *tunica alba*, or "white tunic," afterward in English "*alb*."

Other NT terms are *πορφύραν*, *porphúran*, the "purple" (Lk **16** 19); the purple robe of Jesus is called *himation* in Jn **19** 2; *léntion*, "the towel" with which Jesus girded himself (**13** 4.5); then *othónion*, "linen cloth" (Lk **24** 12; Jn **19** 40); *sindōn*, "linen cloth" (Mt **27** 59); and *bússos*, "fine linen" (Lk **16** 19).

The primitive "aprons" of Gen **3** 7, made of "sewed fig-leaves," were quite different from the "aprons" brought to the apostles in Acts **19** 12. The latter were of a species known among the Romans as *semicinctium*, a short "waist-cloth" worn esp. by slaves (Rich, *Dict. of Rom and Gr Antiq.*).

2. The Materials

Anthropology, Scripture and archaeology all witness to the use by primitive man of *skins of animals* as dress material (Gen **3** 21, "coats of skin"; cf He **11** 37, "went about in sheepskins, in goatskins").

Even today the traveler will occasionally see in Pal a shepherd clad in "a coat of skin." Then, as now, *goat's hair* and *camel's hair* supplied the materials for the coarser fabrics of the poor. John the Baptist had his raiment, *enduma*, of camel's hair (lit. "of camel's hairs," Mt **3** 4). This was a coarse cloth made by weaving camel's hairs. There is no evidence that coats of camel's skin, like those made of goat's skin or sheep's skin have ever been worn in the East, as imagined by

A Shepherd of Bethany (with Sheepskin Coat).

painters (see Meyer, Bleek, Weiss and Broadus; but cf *HDB*, art. "Camel"). The favorite materials, however, in Pal, as throughout the Orient, in ancient times, were *wool* (see Prov **27** 26, "The lambs are for thy clothing") and *flax* (see Prov **31**

13, where it is said of the ideal woman of King Lemuel, "She seeketh wool and flax, and worketh willingly with her hands"). The finest quality of ancient "linen" seems to have been the product of

Sculpture on Behistun Rock.

Egypt (see LINEN). The "silk" of Prov **31** 22 AV is really "fine linen," as in RV. The first certain mention of "silk" in the Bible, it is now conceded, is in Rev **18** 12, as the word rendered "silk" in Ezk **16** 10.13 is of doubtful meaning.

3. The Outer Garments

(1) We may well begin here with the familiar saying of Jesus for a basal distinction: "If any man would go to law with thee, and take away thy coat [Gr *chitōn*], let him have thy cloak [*himation*] also" (Mt **5** 40). Here the "coat" (Heb *k^ethōneth*) was the ordinary "inner garment" worn by the Jew of the day, in which he did the work of the day (see Mt **24** 18; Mk **13** 16). It resembled the Roman "tunic," corresponding most nearly to our "long shirt," reaching below the knees always, and, in case it was designed for dress occasions, reaching almost to the ground. Sometimes "two coats" were worn (Lk **3** 11; cf Mt **10** 10; Mk **6** 9), but in general only one. It was this garment of Jesus that is said by John (**19** 23) to have been "without seam, woven from the top throughout."

(2) The word *himation*, here rendered "cloak," denotes the well-known "outer garment" of the Jews (see Mt **9** 20.21; **14** 36; **21** 7.8; but cf also **9** 16; **17** 2; **24** 18; **26** 65; **27** 31.35). It appears in some cases to have been a loose robe, but in most others, certainly, it was a large square piece of cloth, like a modern shawl, which could be wrapped around the person, with more or less taste and comfort. Now these two, with the "girdle" (a necessary and almost universal article of oriental dress), were commonly all the garments worn by the ordinary man of the Orient. The "outer garment" was frequently used by the poor and by the traveler as his only covering at night, just as shawls are used among us now.

(3) The common Heb name for this "outer garment" in the OT is as above, *simlāh* or *salmāh*. In most cases it was of "wool," though sometimes of "linen," and was as a rule certainly the counterpart of the *himation* of the Gr (this is its name throughout the NT). It answered, too, to the *pallium* of the Romans. It belonged, like them, not to the

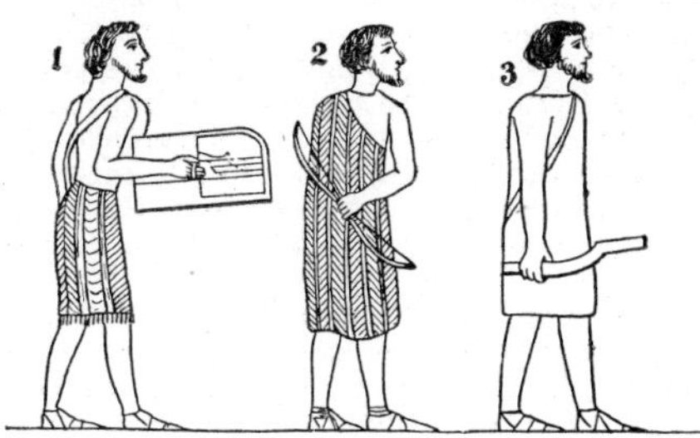

Painting at Beni Hassan.
1. Fringed Skirt; 2 and 3. Tunics.

endúmata, or garments "put on," but to the *peribl̆ēmata*, or garments "wrapped around" the body. It was concerning this "cloak" that the Law of Moses provided that, if it were taken in pawn, it should be returned before sunset—"for that is his only covering, it is his raiment for his skin: wherein shall he sleep? . . . . for I am gracious" (Ex **22** 27). The Jewish tribunals would naturally, therefore, allow the "inner garment" to be taken by legal process, rather than the outer one (Mt **5** 40; Lk **6** 29); but Jesus virtually teaches that rather than have difficulty or indulge animosity one would better yield one's rights in this, as in other matters; cf 1 Cor **6** 7.

Some identify the *simlāh* of the ancient Hebrews with modern *aba*, the coarse blouse or overcoat worn today by the Syrian peasant (Nowack, Benzinger, Mackie in *HDB*); but the distinction between these two garments of the Jews, so clearly made in the NT, seems to confirm the conclusion otherwise reached, that this Jewish "outer garment" closely resembled, if it was not identical with, the *himation* of the Greeks (see *Jew Enc*, art. "Cloke"

Woman's Headdress and Veil (Modern).

and 1-vol *HDB*, "Dress," 197; but cf Masterman, *DCG*, art. "Dress," 499, and Dearmer, *DCG*, art. "Cloke"). In no respect has the variety of renderings in our EV done more to conceal from Eng. readers the meaning of the original than in the case of this word *simlāh*. For instance it is the "garment" with which Noah's nakedness was covered (Gen **9** 23); the "clothes" in which the Hebrews bound up their kneading-troughs (Ex **12** 34); the "garment" of Gideon in Jgs **8** 25; the "raiment" of Ruth (**3** 3); just as the *himation* of the NT is the "cloak" of Mt **5** 40, the "clothes" of Mt **24** 18 AV (RV "cloak"), the "garment" (Mk **13** 16 AV, RV "cloak").

4. The Under Garments

(1) In considering the under garments, contrary to the impression made by EV, we must begin with the "loin-cloth" (Heb *'ēzōr*), which unlike the "girdle" (see GIRDLE), was always worn next to the skin. The figurative use made of it in Isa **11** 5, and Jer **13** 11, e.g. will be lost unless this is remembered. Often it was the only "undergarment," as with certain of the prophets (Elijah, 2 K **1** 8; cf John the Baptist, Mt **3** 4; Isaiah, **20** 2, and Jeremiah, **13** 1 ff). In later times it was displaced among the Hebrews by the "shirt" or

"tunic" (see TUNIC). The universal "sign of mourning" was the girding of the waist with an *'ēzōr* or "hair-cloth" (EV "sack-cloth"). A "loin-cloth" of "linen" was worn by the priests of early times and bore the special name of *'ēphōdh* (1 S **2** 18; cf 2 S **6** 14 ff).

(2) The ordinary "under garment," later worn by all classes—certain special occasions and individuals being exceptions—was the "shirt" (Heb *kethōneth*) which, as we have seen, reappears as *chitōn* in Gr, and *tunica* in Lat. It is uniformly rendered "coat" in EV, except that RVm has "tunic" in Jn **19** 23. The well-known piece of Assyr sculpture, representing the siege and capture of Lachish by Sennacherib, shows the Jewish captives, male and female, dressed in a moderately tight garment, fitting close to the neck (cf Job **30** 18) and reaching almost to the ankles; which must represent the *kethōneth*, or *kuttōneth* of the period, as worn in towns at least. Probably the *kuttōneth* of the peasantry was both looser and shorter, resembling more the modern *kamis* of the Syrian *fellah* (cf Lat *camisa*, and Eng. "chemise").

(3) As regards *sleeves*, they are not expressly mentioned in the OT, but the Lachish tunics mentioned above have short sleeves, reaching half-way to the elbows. This probably represents the prevailing type of sleeve among the Hebrews of the earlier period. An early Egyp picture of a group of Sem traders (c 2000 BC) shows a colored tunic without sleeves, which, fastened on the left shoulder, left the right bare. Another variety of sleeves, restricted to the upper and wealthy classes, had long and wide sleeves reaching to the ground. This was the tunic worn by Tamar, the royal princess (2 S **13** 18, "A garment of divers colors upon her; for with such robes were the king's daughters that were virgins apparelled"), "the tunic of [i.e. reaching to] palms and soles" worn by Joseph, familiarly known as the "coat of many colors" (Gen **37** 3), a rendering which represents now an abandoned tradition (cf Kennedy, *HDB*). The long white linen tunic, which was the chief garment of the ordinary Jewish priest of the later period, had sleeves, which, for special reasons, were tied to the arms (cf Jos, *Ant*, III, vii, 2).

(4) Ultimately it became usual, even with the people of the lower ranks, to wear an under "tunic," or "real shirt" (Jos, *Ant*, XVII, vi, 7; Mish, *passim*, where it is called *ḥālūḳ*). In this case the upper tunic, the *kuttōneth* proper, would be removed at night (cf Cant **5** 3, "I have put off my garment").

The *material* for the tunic might be either (1) woven on the loom in two pieces, and afterward put together without cutting (cf *Dict. of Rom and Gr Antiq.*, art. "Tunica"), or (2) the garment might be woven whole on a special loom, "without seam," i.e. so as to require no sewing, as we know from the description given in Jn **19** 23, and from other sources, was the *chitōn* worn by Our Lord just before His crucifixion. The garments intended by the Heb (Dnl **3** 21–27), rendered "coats" AV, have not been certainly made out. The AVm has "mantles," the ERV "hosen," ARV "breeches" (see HOSEN). For "coat of mail" (1 S **17** 5) see ARMOR.

When the Hebrews first emerged into view, they seem to have had no covering for the head except on special demand, as in case of war, when a *leather-helmet* was worn (see ARMOR). Ordinarily, as with the fellah of Pal today, a rope or cord served as a fillet (cf 1 K **20** 32, and Virgil, *Aeneid* [Dryden], iv.213: "A golden fillet binds his awful brows"). Such "fillets" may be seen surviving in the representation of Syrians on the monuments of Egypt. Naturally, in the course of time, exposure to the Syrian sun in the tropical summer time would compel recourse to some such covering as the modern *kufiyeh*, which lets in the breeze, but protects in a graceful, easy way, the head, the neck and the shoulders. The head-gear of Ben-hadad's tribute-carriers (see above) resembles the Phrygian cap.

5. The Headdress

Modern Druse Headdress.

The head covering, however, which is best attested, at least for the upper ranks of both sexes, is the *turban* (Heb *çānīph*, from a root meaning to "wind round"). It is the ladies' "hood" of Isa **3** 23, RV "turban"; the "royal diadem" of Isa **62** 3, and the "mitre" of Zec **3** 5, RVm "turban" or "diadem." Ezekiel's description of a lady's headdress: "I bound thee with attire of fine linen" (Ezk **16** 10 m), points to a turban. For the egg-shaped turban of the priests see BONNET (RV "head-tires"). The *hats* of Dnl **3** 21 (RV "mantles") are thought by some to have been the conical Bab headdress seen on the monuments. According to 2 Macc **4** 12 RV the young Jewish nobles were compelled by Antiochus Epiphanes to wear the *pétasos*, the low, broad-brimmed hat associated with Hermes. Other forms of headdress were in use in NT times, as we learn from the Mish, as well as from the NT, e.g. the *suddar* (σουδάριον, *soudárion*) from Lat *sudarium* (a cloth for wiping off perspiration, *sudor*) which is probably the "napkin" of Jn **11** 44; **20** 7, although there it appears as a kerchief, or covering, for the head. The female captives from Lachish (see above) wear over their tunics an upper garment, which covers the forehead and falls down over the shoulders to the ankles. Whether this is the garment intended by the Heb in Ruth **3** 15, rendered "vail" by AV and "mantle" by RV, and "kerchiefs for the head" (Ezk **13** 18 RV), we cannot say. The "veil" with which Rebekah and Tamar "covered themselves" (Gen **24** 65; **38** 14) was most likely a large "mantle" in which the whole body could be wrapped, like the *ṣādhīn* (see above). But is seems impossible to draw a clear distinction between "mantle" and "veil" in the OT (Kennedy). The case of Moses (Ex **34** 33) gives us the only express mention of a "face-veil."

6. Footgear

The ancient Hebrews, like Orientals in general, went barefoot within doors. Out of doors they usually wore sandals, less frequently shoes. The simplest form of sandal then, as now, consisted of a sole of untanned leather, bound to the foot by a leather thong, the shoe-latchet of Gen **14** 23 and the

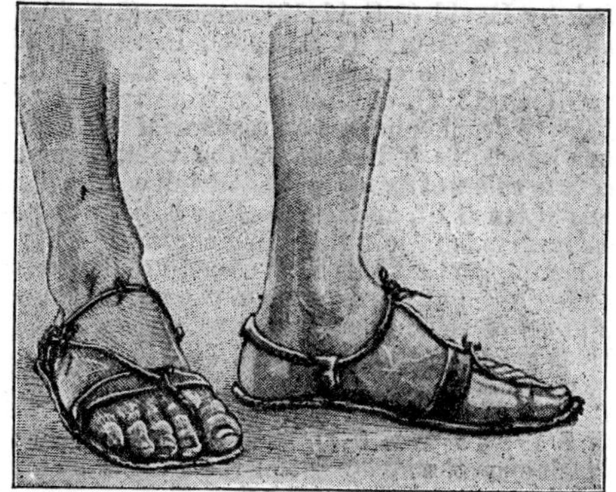

Sandals.

latchet of Mk **1** 7, etc. In the obelisk of Shalmanezer, however, Jehu's attendants are distinguished by shoes completely covering the feet, from the Assyrians, who are represented as wearing sandals fitted with a heel-cap. Ladies of Ezekiel's day wore shoes of "sealskin" (Ezk **16** 10 RV). The soldiers' "laced boot" may be intended in Isa **9** 5 (RVm). Then, as now, on entering the house of a friend, or a sacred precinct (Ex **3** 5; Josh **5** 15), or in case of mourning (2 S **15** 30), the sandals, or shoes, were removed. The priests performed their offices in the Temple in bare feet (cf the modern requirement on entering a mosque).

7. The Dress of Jesus and His Disciples

In general we may say that the clothes worn by Christ and His disciples were of the simplest and least sumptuous kinds. A special interest must attach even to the clothes that Jesus wore. These consisted, it seems quite certain, not of just five separate articles (see Edersheim, *LTJM*, I, 625), but of six. In His day it had become customary to wear a linen shirt (*ḥālūḳ*) beneath the tunic (see above). That Our Lord wore such a "shirt" seems clear from the mention of the laying aside of the upper garments (*himátia*, pl.), i.e. the "mantle" and the "tunic," before washing His disciples' feet (Jn **13** 4). The tunic proper worn by Him, as we have seen, was "woven without seam" throughout, and was of the kind, therefore, that fitted closely about the neck, and had short sleeves. Above the tunic would naturally be the linen girdle, wound several times about the waist. On His feet were leather sandals (Mt **3** 11). His upper garment was of the customary sort and shape, probably of white woolen cloth, as is suggested by the details of the account of the Transfiguration (Mk **9** 3), with the four prescribed "tassels" at the corners. As to His headdress, we have no description of it, but we may set it down as certain that no Jewish teacher of that day would appear in public with the head uncovered. He probably wore the customary white linen "napkin" (*sudarium*), wound round the head as a *turban*, with the ends of it falling down over the neck. The dress of His disciples was, probably, not materially different.

In conclusion it may be said that, although the dress of even orthodox Jews today is as various as their lands of residence and their languages, yet there are two garments worn by them the world over, the *ṭallīth* and the *'arba' kanᵉphōth* (see *DCG*, art. "Dress," col. 1). Jews who affect special sanctity, esp. those living in the Holy Land, still wear the *ṭallīth* all day, as was the common custom in Christ's time. As the earliest mention of the *'arba' kanᵉphōth* is in 1350 AD, it is clear that it cannot have existed in NT times.

Literature.—Nowack's and Benzinger's *Heb Archäologie;* Tristram, *Eastern Customs in Bible Lands;* Rich, *Dict. of Rom and Gr Antiq.;* Edersheim, *Life and Times of Jesus the Messiah*, 625, and elsewhere; arts. on "Dress," "Clothing," "Costumes," etc, *HDB, DCG, Jew Enc* (by Nöldeke) in *EB* (by Abrahams and Cook); Masterman, "Dress and Personal Adornment in Mod. Pal," in *Bib. World*, 1902, etc.

Geo. B. Eager

DRINK. See Food; Drink, Strong.

DRINK OFFERING. See Sacrifice in OT and NT.

DRINK, STRONG (שֵׁכָר, *shēkhār;* σίκερα, *síkera;* from שָׁכַר, *shākhar*, "to be or become drunk"; probably from the same root as *sugar, saccharine*): With the exception of Nu **28** 7, "strong drink" is always coupled with "wine." The two terms are commonly used as mutually exclusive, and as together exhaustive of all kinds of intoxicants.

Originally *shēkhār* seems to have been a general term for intoxicating drinks of all kinds, without reference to the material out of which they were made; and in that sense, it would include wine. Reminiscences of this older usage may be found in Nu **28** 7 (where *shēkhār* is clearly equivalent to wine, as may be seen by comparing it with ver 14, and with Ex **29** 40, where the material of the drink offering is expressly designated "wine").

When the Hebrews were living a nomadic life, before their settlement in Canaan, the grape-wine was practically unknown to them, and there would be no need of a special term to describe it. But when they settled down to an agricultural life, and came to cultivate the vine, it would become necessary to distinguish it from the older kinds of intoxicants; hence the borrowed word *yayin* ("wine") was applied to the former, while the latter would be classed together under the old term *shēkhār*, which would then come to mean all intoxicating beverages *other than* wine (Lev **10** 9; Nu **6** 3; Dt **14** 26; Prov **20** 1; Isa **24** 9). The exact nature of these drinks is not clearly indicated in the Bible itself. The only fermented beverage other than grape-wine specifically named is pomegranate-wine (Cant **8** 2: "the juice of my pomegranate," RVm "sweet wine of my pomegranate"); but we may infer that other kinds of *shēkhār* besides that obtained from pomegranates were in use, such as drinks made from dates, honey, raisins, barley, apples, etc. Probably Jerome (c 400 AD) was near the mark when he wrote, "Sikera in the Heb tongue means every kind of drink which can intoxicate, whether made from grain or from the juice of apples, or when honeycombs are boiled down into a sweet and strange drink, or the fruit of palm oppressed into liquor, and when water is coloured and thickened from boiled herbs" (*Ep. ad Nepotianum*). Thus *shēkhār* is a comprehensive term for all kinds of fermented drinks, excluding wine.

Probably the most common sort of *shēkhār* used in Bib. times was palm- or date-wine. This is not actually mentioned in the Bible, and we do not meet with its Heb name *yēn temārīm* ("wine of dates") until the Talmudic period. But it is frequently referred to in the Assyr-Bab contract tablets (cuneiform), and from this and other evidence we infer that it was very well known among the ancient Sem peoples. Moreover, it is known that the palm tree flourished abundantly in Bib. lands, and the presumption is therefore very strong that wine made of the juice of dates was a common beverage. It must not be supposed, however, that the term *shēkhār* refers exclusively to date-wine. It rather designates all intoxicating liquors other than grape-wine, while in a few cases it probably includes even wine.

There can be no doubt that *shēkhār* was intoxicating. This is proved (1) from the etymology of the word, it being derived from *shākhar*, "to be or become drunk" (Gen **9** 21; Isa **29** 9; Jer **25** 27, etc); cf the word for drunkard (*shikkār*), and for drunkenness (*shikkārōn*) from the same root; (2) from descriptions of its effects: e.g. Isaiah graphically describes the stupefying effect of *shēkhār* on those who drink it excessively (**28** 7.8). Hannah defended herself against the charge of being drunk by saying, "I have drunk neither wine nor strong drink," i.e. neither wine nor any other intoxicating liquor (1 S **1** 15). The attempt made to prove that it was simply the unfermented juice of certain fruits is quite without foundation. Its immoderate use is strongly condemned (Isa **5** 11.12; Prov **20** 1; see DRUNKENNESS). It was forbidden to ministering priests (Lev **10** 9), and to Nazirites (Nu **6** 3; Jgs **13** 4.7.14; cf Lk **1** 15), but was used in the sacrificial meal as drink offering (Nu **28** 7), and could be bought with the tithe-money and consumed by the worshipper in the temple (Dt **14** 26). It is commended to the weak and perishing as a means of deadening their pain; but not to princes, lest it might lead them to pervert justice (Prov **31** 4–7). D. MIALL EDWARDS

DROMEDARY, drum'ē-dā-ri, drom'ē-dā-ri. See CAMEL.

DROP, DROPPING: "To drop" expresses a "distilling" or "dripping" of a fluid (Jgs **5** 4; Prov **3** 20; Cant **5** 5.13; Joel **3** 18; Am **9** 13; cf 1 S **14** 26, "the honey dropped" [m "a stream of honey"]); Job **29** 22 and Isa **45** 8 read "distil" (AV "drop"). The continuous "droppings" of rain through a leaking roof (roofs were usually made of clay in Pal, and always liable to cracks and leakage) on a "very rainy day" is compared to a contentious wife (Prov **19** 13; **27** 15); "What is described is the irritating, unceasing, sound of the fall, drop after drop, of water through the chinks in the roof" (Plumptre loc. cit.); cf also AV Eccl **10** 18 (RV "leaketh").

DROPSY, drop'si (ὑδρωπικός, *hudrōpikós*, "a man afflicted with *húdrōps* or dropsy"): Both forms of this disease occur in Pal, that in which the limbs and body are distended with water called *anasarca*, depending generally on cardiac or renal disease, and the form confined to the abdomen, usually the result of liver affection. The latter is the commoner, as liver disease is a frequent result of recurrent attacks of malarial fever. The man was evidently able to move about, as he had entered into the Pharisee's house (Lk **14** 2).

DROSS, dros (סִיג, *ṣīgh*): The refuse of smelting of precious metal (Prov **25** 4; **26** 23); used **figuratively** of what is base or worthless (Isa **1** 22.25; Ezk **22** 18.19; Ps **119** 119).

DROUGHT, drout. See FAMINE.

DROVE, drōv. See CATTLE.

DROWNING, droun'ing. See PUNISHMENTS.

DRUM, drum (τύμπανον, *túmpanon*): This was the Heb *tōph*, "tabret" or "timbrel," a hand-drum, consisting of a ring of wood or metal covered with a tightly drawn skin, with small pieces of metal hung around the rim, like a tambourine. It was raised in the one hand and struck with the other, usually by women, but sometimes also by men, at festivities and on occasions of rejoicing. See 1 Macc **9** 39, RV "timbrels."

DRUNKENNESS, drunk''n-nes (רָוֶה, *rāweh*, שִׁכָּרוֹן, *shikkārōn*, שְׁתִי, *sh*ᵉ*thī*; μέθη, *méthē*):

I. Its Prevalence.—The Bible affords ample proof that excessive drinking of intoxicants was a common vice among the Hebrews, as among other ancient peoples. This is evident not only from individual cases of intoxication, as Noah (Gen **9** 21), Lot (Gen **19** 33.35), Nabal (1 S **25** 36), Uriah made drunk by David (2 S **11** 13), Amnon (2 S **13** 28), Elah, king of Israel (1 K **16** 9), Benhadad, king of Syria, and his confederates (1 K **20** 16), Holofernes (Jth **13** 2), etc, but also from frequent references to drunkenness as a great social evil. Thus, Amos proclaims judgment on the voluptuous and dissolute rulers of Samaria "that drink wine in [large] bowls" (Am **6** 6), and the wealthy ladies who press their husbands to join them in a carousal (**4** 1); he also complains that this form of self-indulgence was practised even at the expense of the poor and under the guise of religion, at the sacrificial meals (**2** 8; see also Isa **5** 11.12.22; **28** 1–8; **56** 11 f). Its prevalence is also reflected in many passages in the NT (e.g. Mt **24** 49; Lk **21** 34; Acts **2** 13.15; Eph **5** 18; 1 Thess **5** 7). Paul complains that at Corinth even the love-feast of the Christian church which immediately preceded the celebration of the Eucharist, was sometimes the scene of excessive drinking (1 Cor **11** 21). It must, however, be noted that it is almost invariably the well-to-do who are charged with this vice in the Bible. There is no evidence to prove that it prevailed to any considerable extent among the common people. Intoxicants were then an expensive luxury, beyond the reach of the poorer classes. See DRINK, STRONG.

II. Its Symptoms and Effects.—These are most vividly portrayed: (1) some of its physical symptoms (Job **12** 25; Ps **107** 27; Prov **23** 29; Isa **19** 14; **28** 8; **29** 9; Jer **25** 16); (2) its mental effects: exhilaration (Gen **43** 34), jollity and mirth (1 Esd **3** 20), forgetfulness (1 Esd **3** 20), loss of understanding and balance of judgment (Isa **28** 7; Hos **4** 11); (3) its effects on man's happiness and prosperity: its immediate effect is to make one oblivious of his misery; but ultimately it "biteth like a serpent, and stingeth like an adder," and leads to woe and sorrow (Prov **23** 29–32) and to poverty (Prov **23** 21; cf **21** 17; Ecclus **19** 1); hence wine is called a "mocker" deceiving the unwise (Prov **20** 1); (4) its moral and spiritual effects: it leads to a maladministration of justice (Prov **31** 5; Isa **5** 23), provokes anger and a contentious, brawling spirit (Prov **20** 1; **23** 29; 1 Esd **3** 22; Ecclus **31** 26.29 f), and conduces to a profligate life (Eph **5** 18; "riot," lit. profligacy). It is allied with gambling and licentiousness (Joel **3** 3), and indecency (Gen **9** 21 f). Above all, it deadens the spiritual sensibilities, produces a callous indifference to religious influences and destroys all serious thought (Isa **5** 12).

III. Attitude of the Bible to the Drink Question.—Intemperance is condemned in uncompromising terms by the OT and the NT, as well as by the semi-canonical writings. While total abstinence is not prescribed as a formal and universal rule, broad principles are laid down, esp. in the NT, which point in that direction.

1. In the OT

In the OT, intemperance is most repugnant to the stern ethical rigorism of the prophets, as well as to the more utilitarian sense of propriety of the "wisdom" writers. As might be expected, the national conscience was but gradually quickened to the evil of immoderate drinking. In the narratives of primitive times, excessive indulgence, or at least indulgence to the point of exhilaration, is mentioned without censure as a natural thing, esp. on festive occasions (as in Gen **43** 34 RVm). But a conscience more sensitive to the sinfulness of over-indulgence was gradually developed, and is reflected in the denunciations of the prophets and the warning of the wise men (cf references under I and II, esp. Isa **5** 11 f.22; **28** 1–8; Prov **23** 29–33). Nowhere is the principle of total abstinence inculcated as a rule applicable to all. In particular cases it was recognized as a duty. Priests while on duty in the sanctuary were to abstain from wine and strong drink (Lev **10** 9; cf Ezk **44** 21). Nazirites were to abstain from all intoxicants during the period of their vows (Nu **6** 3 f; cf Amos **2** 12), yet not on account of the intoxicating qualities of wine, but because they represented the simplicity of the older pastoral life, as against the Canaanite civilization which the vine symbolized (W. R. Smith, *Prophets of Israel*, 84 f). So also the Rechabites abstained from wine (Jer **35** 6.8.14) and social conveniences, because they regarded the nomadic life as more conducive to Jeh-worship than agricultural and town life, with its temptations to Baal-worship. In Daniel and his comrades we have another instance of voluntary abstinence (Dnl **1** 8–16). These, however, are isolated instances. Throughout the OT the use of wine appears as practically universal, and its value is recognized as a cheering beverage (Jgs **9** 13; Ps **104** 15; Prov **31** 7), which enables the sick to forget their pains (Prov **31** 6). Moderation, however, is strongly inculcated and there are frequent warnings against the temptation and perils of the cup.

2. Deutero- and Extra-Canonical Writings

In Apoc, we have the attitude of prudence and common sense, but the prophetic note of stern denunciation is wanting. The path of wisdom is the golden mean. "Wine is as good as life to men, if thou drink it in its measure; . . . . wine drunk in season and to satisfy is joy of heart, and gladness of soul: wine drunk largely is bitterness of soul, with provocation and conflict" (Ecclus **31** 27–30 RV). A vivid picture of the effects of wine-drinking is given in 1 Esd **3** 18–24. Stronger teaching on the subject is given in the Testament of the Twelve Patriarchs. The use of wine is permitted to him who can use it temperately, but abstinence is enjoined as the wiser course (XII P, Jud **16** 3).

3. In the NT

In the NT, intemperance is treated as a grave sin. Only once, indeed, does Our Lord explicitly condemn drunkenness (Lk **21** 34), though it is implicitly condemned in other passages (Mt **24** 49=Lk **12** 45). The meagerness of the references in Our Lord's teaching is probably due to the fact already mentioned, that it was chiefly prevalent among the wealthy, and not among the poorer classes to whom Our Lord mainly ministered. The references in Paul's writings are very numerous (Gal **5** 21; Eph **5** 18, et al.). Temperance and sobriety in all things are everywhere insisted on (e.g. Acts **24** 25; Gal **5** 23; 2 Pet **1** 6). A bishop and those holding honorable position in the church should not be addicted to wine (1 Tim **3** 2 f; Tit **1** 7 f; **2** 2 f). Yet Jesus and His apostles were not ascetics, and the NT gives no rough-and-ready prohibition of strong drink on principle. In contrast with John the Baptist, who was a Nazirite from birth (Lk **1** 15), Jesus was called by His enemies a "wine-bibber" (Mt **11** 19). He took part in festivities in which wine was drunk (Jn **2** 10). There are indications that He regarded wine as a source of innocent enjoyment (Lk **5** 38 f; **17** 8). To insist on a distinction between intoxicating and unfermented wine is a case of unjustifiable special pleading. It must be borne in mind that the drink question is far more complex and acute in modern than in Bib. times, and that the conditions of the modern world have given rise to problems which were not within the horizon of NT writers. The habit of excessive drinking has spread enormously among the common people, owing largely to the cheapening of alcoholic drinks. The fact that the evil exists today in greater proportions may call for a drastic remedy and a special crusade. But rather than defend total abstinence by a false or forced exegesis, it were better to admit that the principle is not formally laid down in the NT, while maintaining that there are broad principles enunciated, which in view of modern conditions should lead to voluntary abstinence from all intoxicants. Such principles may be found, e.g. in Our Lord's teaching in Mt **16** 24 f; Mk **9** 42 f, and in the great Pauline passages—Rom **14** 13–21; 1 Cor **8** 8–13.

IV. Drunkenness in Metaphor.—Drunkenness very frequently supplies Bib. writers with striking metaphors and similes. Thus, it symbolizes intellectual or spiritual perplexity (Job **12** 25; Isa **19** 14; Jer **23** 9), bewilderment and helplessness under calamity (Jer **13** 13; Ezk **23** 33). It furnishes a figure for the movements of sailors on board ship in a storm (Ps **107** 27), and for the convulsions of the earth on the day of Jeh (Isa **24** 20). Jeh's "cup of staggering" is a symbol of affliction, the fury of the Lord causing stupor and confusion (Isa **51** 17–23; cf Isa **63** 6; Jer **25** 15 ff; Ezk **23** 33; Ps **75** 8). The sword and the arrow are said to be sodden with drink like a drunkard with wine (Dt **32** 42; Jer **46** 10). In the Apocalypse, Babylon (i.e. Rome) is portrayed under the figure of a "great harlot" who makes kings "drunken with the wine of her fornication"; and who is herself "drunken with the blood of the saints, and . . . . of the martyrs of Jesus" (Rev **17** 2.6).

D. Miall Edwards

DRUSILLA, drōō-sil'a (**Δρούσιλλα**, *Droúsilla*, or **Δρουσίλλα**, *Drousílla*): Wife of Felix, a Jewess, who along with her husband "heard [Paul] concerning the faith in Christ Jesus" during Paul's detention in Caesarea (Acts **24** 24). **β** text gives the rendering "Drusilla the wife of Felix, a Jewess, asked to see Paul and to hear the word." The fact that Drusilla was a Jewess explains her curiosity, but Paul, who was probably acquainted with the past history of her and Felix, refused to satisfy their request in the way they desired, and preached to them instead concerning righteousness and self-restraint and the final judgment. At this "Felix was terrified" (Acts **24** 25). **β** text states that Paul's being left in bonds on the retirement of Felix was due to the desire of the latter to please Drusilla (cf Acts **24** 27). Probably this explanation, besides that of the accepted text, was true also, as Drusilla, who was a member of the ruling house, saw in Paul an enemy of its power, and hated him for his condemnation of her own private sins.

The chief other source of information regarding Drusilla is Jos. Drusilla was the youngest of the three daughters of Agrippa I, her sisters being Bernice and Mariamne. She was born about 36 AD and was married when 14 years old to Azizus, king of Emeza. Shortly afterward she was induced to desert her husband by Felix, who employed a Cyprian sorcerer, Simon by name, to carry out his purpose. She was also influenced to take this step by the cruelty of Azizus and the hatred of Bernice who was jealous of her beauty. Her marriage with Felix took place about 54 AD and by him she had one son, Agrippa, who perished under Titus in an eruption of Mt. Vesuvius. The mention by Jos of "the woman" who perished along with Agrippa (*Ant*, XX, vii, 2) refers probably not to his mother Drusilla but to his wife.

C. M. Kerr

DUALISM, dū'al-iz'm. See Philosophy.

DUE, dū. See DUTY.

DUKE, dūk: The rendering in AV in Gen **36** 15 ff; Ex **15** 15, and 1 Ch **1** 51 ff of אַלּוּף, *'allūph* (ARV and ERVm "chief"), and in Josh **13** 21 of *n^eṣīkhīm* ("dukes," RV "princes"). It occurs also, as the rendering of *stratēgós*, in 1 Macc **10** 65 (RV "captain"). Elsewhere *n^eṣīkhīm* is tr^d "princes" or "principal men." The fact that with two exceptions the term is applied in EV only to the chiefs of Edom has led to the impression that in the family of Esau the chiefs bore a special and hereditary title. But *'allūph* was a general term for tribal chief or prince (cf Zec **9** 7; **12** 5.6; RV "chieftains," AV "governors").

Moreover, at the time the AV was made the word "duke" was not used as a title in England: the term had the same general force as *dux*, the word employed in the Vulg. So Sir T. Elyot (d. 1546) speaks of "Hannibal, duke of Carthage" (*The Governour*, II, 233); Shakespeare, *Henry V*, III, 2, 20, "Be merciful, great duke, to men of mould" (cf *Midsummer Night's Dream*, I, 1, 21); Sylvester (1591) *Du Bartas*, "The great Duke, that (in dreadful aw) | Upon Mt. Horeb learn'd th' eternall law." In a still earlier age Wiclif uses the word of the Messiah (Mt **2** 6); and in *Select Works*, III, 137, "Jesus Christ, duke of oure batel."

Yet in all probability the Heb word was more specific than "chief" or "duke" in the broad sense. For if *'allūph* is derived from *'eleph*, "thousand," "tribe," the term would mean the leader of a clan, a "chiliarch" (cf LXX, Zec **9** 7; **12** 5.6). ARV has eliminated the word "duke." See CHIEF.

J. R. VAN PELT

DULCIMER, dul'si-mẽr. See MUSIC under *Nebhel* and *Sumphonia*.

DUMAH, dū'ma (דּוּמָה, *dūmāh*, "silence"): This word occurs in the OT with the following significations: (1) the land of silence or death, the grave (Ps **94** 17; **115** 17); (2) a town in the highlands of Judah between Hebron and Beersheba, now *ed-Daume* (Josh **15** 52); (3) an emblematical designation of Edom in the obscure oracle (Isa **21** 11.12); (4) an Ishmaelite tribe in Arabia (Gen **25** 14; 1 Ch **1** 30). According to the Arab. geographies this son of Ishmael founded the town of Dūmat-el-Jandal, the stone-built Dūmah, so called to distinguish it from another D. near the Euphrates. The former now bears the name of the *Jauf* ("belly"), being a depression situated half-way between the head of the Persian Gulf and the head of the gulf of Akaba. Its people in the time of Mohammed were Christians of the tribe of Kelb. It contained a great well from which the palms and crops were irrigated. It has often been visited by European travelers in recent times. See *Jour. Royal Geog. Soc.*, XXIV (1854), 138–58; W. G. Palgrave, *Central and Eastern Arabia*, ch ii. It is possible that the oracle in Isa (no. 3 above) concerns this place.

THOMAS HUNTER WEIR

DUMB, dum (אִלֵּם, *'ālam*, אִלֵּם, *'illēm*, lit. "tied in the tongue"; κωφός, *kōphós*): Used either as expressing the physical condition of speechlessness, generally associated with deafness, or **figuratively** as meaning the silence produced by the weight of God's judgments (Ps **39** 2–9; Dnl **10** 15) or the oppression of external calamity (Ps **38** 13). As an adj. it is used to characterize inefficient teachers destitute of spirituality ("dumb dogs," Isa **56** 10). The speechlessness of Saul's companions (Acts **9** 7) was due to fright; that of the man without the wedding garment was because he had no excuse to give (Mt **22** 12). Idols are called dumb, because helpless and voiceless (Hab **2** 18.19; 1 Cor **12** 2). The dumbness of the sheep before the shearer is a token of submission (Isa **53** 7; Acts **8** 32).

Temporary dumbness was inflicted as a sign upon Ezekiel (**3** 26; **24** 27; **33** 22) and as a punishment for unbelief upon Zacharias (Lk **1** 22). There are several cases recorded of Our Lord's healing the dumb (Mt **15** 30; Mk **7** 37; Lk **11** 14, etc). Dumbness is often associated with imbecility and was therefore regarded as due to demoniac possession (Mt **9** 32; **12** 22). The evangelists therefore describe the healing of these as effected by the casting out of demons. This is esp. noted in the case of the epileptic boy (Mk **9** 17). The deaf man with the impediment in his speech (Mk **7** 32) is said to have been cured by loosening the string of his tongue. This does not necessarily mean that he was tongue-tied, which is a condition causing lisping, not stammering; he was probably one of those deaf persons who produce babbling, incoherent and meaningless sounds. I saw in the asylum in Jerus a child born blind and deaf, who though dumb, produced inarticulate noises.

In an old 14th-cent. psalter "dumb" is used as a vb. in Ps **39**: "I doumbed and meked and was ful stille."

ALEX. MACALISTER

DUNG, dung, **DUNG GATE** (אַשְׁפּוֹת, *'ashpōth*, דֹּמֶן, *dōmen*, פֶּרֶשׁ, *peresh*; σκύβαλον, *skúbalon*, etc): Nine different words occurring in the Heb have been tr^d "dung" in the OT. The word used to designate one of the gates of Jerus (*'ashpōth*, Neh **2** 13; **3** 14) is more general than the others and may mean any kind of refuse. The gate was probably so named because outside it was the general dump heap of the city. Visitors in recent years riding outside the city walls of Jerus, on their way to the Mt. of Olives or Jericho, may have witnessed such a dump against the wall, which has existed for generations.

The first mention made of dung is in connection with sacrificial rites. The sacred law required that the dung, along with what parts of the animal were not burned on the altar, should be burned outside the camp (Ex **29** 14; Lev **4** 11; **8** 17; **16** 27; Nu **19** 5).

The fertilizing value of dung was appreciated by the cultivator, as is indicated by Lk **13** 8 and possibly Ps **83** 10 and Isa **25** 10.

Dung was also used as a fuel. Ezk **4** 12.15 will be understood when it is known that the dung of animals is a common fuel throughout Pal and Syria, where other fuel is scarce. During the summer, villagers gather the manure of their cattle, horses or camels, mix it with straw, make it into cakes and dry it for use as fuel for cooking, esp. in the winter when wood or charcoal or straw are not procurable. It burns slowly like peat and meets the needs of the kitchen. In Mesopotamia the writer saw it being used with forced draft to fire a steam boiler. There was no idea of uncleanness in Ezekiel's mind, associated with the use of animal dung as fuel (Ezk **4** 15).

Figuratively: Dung was frequently used **figuratively** to express the idea (*a*) of worthlessness, esp. a perishable article for which no one cares (1 K **14** 10; 2 K **6** 25; **9** 37; Job **20** 7; Ps **83** 10; Jer **8** 2; **9** 22; **16** 4; **25** 33; Zeph **1** 17; Phil **3** 8 [ARV "refuse"]). Dunghill was used in the same way (1 S **2** 8; Ezr **6** 11; Ps **113** 7; Isa **25** 10; Dnl **2** 5; **3** 29; Lk **14** 35; Lam **4** 5); (*b*) as an expression of disgust (2 K **18** 27; Isa **36** 12); (*c*) of rebuke (Mal **2** 3).

JAMES A. PATCH

DUNGEON, dun'jun. See PRISON.

DUNGHILL, dung'hil (אַשְׁפֹּת, *'ashpōth*, 1 S **2** 8, מַדְמֵנָה, *madhmēnāh*, etc, with other words; κοπρία, *kopría*, Lk **14** 35): Dung heap, or place of refuse. To sit upon a dunghill (1 S **2** 8; Ps **113** 7; Lam **4** 5) is significant of the lowest and most wretched condition. To turn a house into a dunghill (Dnl

2 5; **3** 29), or be flung upon a dunghill (Lk **14** 35), marks the extreme of ignominy. See also DUNG.

DURA, dū'ra (דּוּרָא, *dūrā'*): The name of the plain on which Nebuchadnezzar, king of Babylon, set up the great golden image which all his subjects were ordered to worship (Dnl **3** 1). Oppert placed it to the S.E. of Babylon, near a small river and mounds bearing the name of *Douair* or *Dûair*, where, also, was what seemed to be the base of a great statue (*Expéd. scientifique en Mésopotamie*, I, 238 f). Others have believed that name to indicate a portion of the actual site of Babylon within the great wall (*dûru*) of the city—perhaps the rampart designated *dûr Šu-anna*, "the rampart [of the city] Lofty-defense," a name of Babylon. The fact that the plain was within the city of Babylon precludes an identification with the city *Dûru*, which seems to have lain in the neighborhood of Erech (Hommel, *Grundriss*, 264, n. 5). It is noteworthy that the LXX substitutes Δεειρά, *Deeirá*, for Dura, suggesting that the Gr translators identified it with the Bab *Dêru*, a city which apparently lay toward the Elamite border. It seems to have been called also *Dûr-îli*, "god's rampart." That it was at some distance is supported by the list *WAI*, IV, 36 [38], where *Dûru*, *Tutul* and *Gudua* (Cuthah), intervene between *Dêru* or *Dûr-îli* and *Tindir* (Babylon). "The plain of the *dûr*" or "rampart" within Babylon would therefore seem to be the best rendering.

T. G. PINCHES

DURE, dūr (πρόσκαιρος, *próskairos*): Used for "endure" (q.v.), AV Mt **13** 21 (RV "endureth").

DUST, dust (עָפָר, *'āphār*; κονιορτός, *koniortós*, χοῦς, *choûs*): Small particles of earth. The word has several **figurative** and symbolic meanings: (1) Dust being the material out of which God is said to have formed man (Gen **2** 7), it became a symbol of man's frailty (Ps **103** 14, "For he knoweth our frame; he remembereth that we are dust"; cf Gen **18** 27; Job **4** 19, etc), and of his mortality (Gen **3** 19, "Dust thou art, and unto dust shalt thou return"; cf Job **34** 15; Ps **104** 29; Eccl **3** 20; **12** 7, etc) Hence it is used **figuratively** for the grave (Ps **22** 15.29; **30** 9; Dnl **12** 2). (2) Such actions as to lie in the dust, to lick the dust, to sprinkle dust on the head, are symbols expressive of deep humiliation, abasement or lamentation (e.g. Job **2** 12; **42** 6, Ps **72** 9; Isa **2** 10; **47** 1; **49** 23; Lam **2** 10; **3** 29; Ezk **27** 30; Mic **7** 17; Rev **18** 19). Hence such expressions as "He raiseth up the poor out of the dust," i.e. out of their state of lowliness (1 S **2** 8; Ps **113** 7). (3) Throwing dust was an act expressive of execration. Thus Shimei "cursed" David and "threw stones at him, and cast dust," lit. "dusted [him] with dust" (2 S **16** 13). So the crowd which Paul addressed at Jerus manifested their wrath against him by tossing about their garments and casting dust into the air (Acts **22** 23). (4) Shaking the dust off one's feet against anyone (Mt **10** 14; Mk **6** 11; Lk **9** 5; **10** 11; Acts **13** 51) is symbolic of renunciation, as we would say "washing one's hands of him," an intimation that all further intercourse was at an end. It was practised by the Pharisees on passing from gentile to Jewish soil, it being a rabbinical doctrine that the dust of a heathen land defiles. (5) It is also used **fig.** for an innumerable multitude (e.g. Gen **13** 16; **28** 14; Job **27** 16; Ps **78** 27). (6) The expression "Jeh will make the rain of thy land powder and dust" (Dt **28** 24) means the dust in consequence of the drought shall fall down instead of rain on the dry ground. In Judaea and vicinity during a sirocco, the air becomes filled with sand and dust, which are blown down by the wind with great violence.

D. MIALL EDWARDS

DUTY, dū'ti (דָּבָר, *dābhār*; ὀφείλω, *opheílō*): The word d. occurs only three times in the OT and twice in the NT. In the OT it is the tr of *dābhār*, which, meaning originally "speech," or "word," came to denote any particular "matter" that had to be attended to. In the two places where it is rendered "duty" (2 Ch **8** 14; Ezr **3** 4) the reference is to the performance of the Temple services—praise and sacrifice—and it is probably from these passages that the phrase "taking duty" in church services is derived. In other passages we have different words employed to denote the priests' *dues:* AV Lev **10** 13.14, *ḥōḳ* ("statutory portion"); Dt **18** 3, *mishpāṭ* ("judgment"). In Prov **3** 27, we have a reference to d. in the moral sense, "Withhold not good from them to whom it is due," *ba'al* (i.e. as in AVm, "from the *owners* thereof"). In Ex **21** 10 we have the "duty of marriage" (*'ōnāh*), that which was due to the wife.

In the NT "duty" is expressed by *opheilō*, "to owe," "to be due." In Lk **17** 10, we have "Say, ... we have done that which it was our duty to do," and in Rom **15** 27 AV, it is said of the Gentiles with reference to the Jewish Christians, "Their duty is also to minister unto them in carnal things," ARV "they owe it." In Mt **18** 34 we have "till he should pay all that was due" (*opheilō*, "owing"), and in 1 Cor **7** 3 AV, "Render unto the wife due [*opheilḗ*] benevolence," ARV "her due." See also ETHICS.

W. L. WALKER

DWARF, dwôrf: The rendering in EV of Heb דַּק, *daḳ*, "thin," "small," in Lev **21** 20, where a list is given of physical failings which forbade a man of the seed of Aaron to officiate at the altar, though he might partake of the sacrificial gifts. The precise meaning of the Heb word here is uncertain; elsewhere it is used of the lean kine (Gen **41** 3) and blasted ears (ver 23) of Pharaoh's dream; of the grains of manna (Ex **16** 14), of the still, small voice (1 K **19** 12), of dust (Isa **29** 5), etc. LXX and Vulg suggest defective eyes; but "withered" would perhaps best express the meaning. See PRIESTS AND LEVITES.

F. K. FARR

DWELL, dwel:

(1) In the OT "dwell" trs 9 words, of which by far the most frequent is יָשַׁב, *yāshabh*, "to sit down," trd "dwell" over 400 times (Gen **4** 20; Josh **20** 4; 1 Ch **17** 1.4.5, etc); also very frequently "sit," and sometimes "abide," "inhabit," "remain." Another word often rendered "dwell" is שָׁכַן or שָׁכֵן, *shākhan* or *shākhēn* ("to settle down"), from which is derived the rabbinic word שְׁכִינָה, *shekhīnāh* (lit. "that which dwells"), the light on the mercy-seat which symbolized the Divine presence (Ex **25** 8, etc). In order to avoid appearing to localize the Divine Being, wherever God is said to "dwell" in a place, the Tg renders that He "causes His Shekinah to dwell" there.

(2) In the NT "dwell" most frequently stands for οἰκέω, *oikéō*, or one of its compounds; also σκηνόω, *skēnóō*, and (chiefly in the Johannine writings) μένω, *ménō*, which, however, is always trd "abide" in RV, and generally in AV. Mention may be made of the mystical significance of the word in some NT passages, of the indwelling of the Father or of the Godhead in Christ (Jn **14** 10; Col **1** 19; **2** 9), of the believer in Christ (Jn **6** 56 AV; Eph **3** 17), and in God (1 Jn **4** 15 AV; cf Ps **90** 1; **91** 1), and of the Holy Spirit or God in the believer (Jn **14** 17; AV 1 Jn **3** 24; **4** 15 f).

D. MIALL EDWARDS

DYE, dī, **DYEING,** dī'ing (מְאָדָּם, *me'oddām*, חָמוּץ, *ḥāmūç*, טְבוּל, *ṭebhūl*, צֶבַע, *çebha'*): Four different Heb words have been trd "dyed": AV (*a*) *m^e'oddām*, found in Ex **25** 5; **26** 14; **35** 7; **36** 19; **39** 34; (*b*) *ḥāmūç* (RVm "crimsoned") (Isa **63** 1); (*c*) *ṭ^ebhūl* (Ezk **23** 15). *Ṭ^ebhūl* is probably more correctly rendered "flowing turban" as in the RV of the above vs (*BDB*); (*d*) *çebha'*, "dyed" is so tr[d] in ARV of Jgs **5** 30 (*BDB*); cf Arab. *sabagh*. The above references and other color words mentioned elsewhere (see COLOR) indicate that the Israelites were acquainted with dyed stuffs, even if they themselves did not do the dyeing. An analysis of the various Bib. references shows but four colors which were produced on cloth by dyeing, namely, purple, blue (violet), crimson and scarlet. Of these, purple is the one best known because of the many historical references to it. It was the symbol of royalty and luxury. Because of its high price, due to the expensive method of obtaining it, only royalty and the rich could afford purple attire. One writer tells us that the dyestuff was worth its weight in silver. Probably it was because of its scarcity, and because it was one of the very limited number of dyes known, rather than for any remarkable beauty of color, that the purple was so much sought after. If Pliny's estimate is to be accredited, then "in the dye the smell of it was offensive and the color itself was harsh, of a greenish hue and strongly resembling that of the sea when in a tempestuous state."

1. Purple and Blue

The purple and blue dyes were extracted from shellfish. The exact process used by the ancients is still a question in spite of the attempts of early writers to describe it. Tyre and Sidon were noted as the suppliers of these colors, hence the name "Tyrian purple." The inhabitants of these cities were at first simply dealers in the purple (Ezk **27** 7.24), but they afterward became the manufacturers, as the heaps of the emptied shells of the *Murex trunculus*, which still exist in the vicinity of these cities, testify. The pigment was secreted by a gland in the lining of the stomach. The shell was punctured and the fish removed in order to secure the dye. The juice, at first whitish, changed on exposure to yellowish or greenish and finally to red, amethyst or purple, according to the treatment. A modified color was obtained by first dipping the textile in a cochineal bath and then in the purple. Tyrian purple was considered most valuable when it was "exactly the color of clotted blood and of a blackish hue" (Pliny). See also LYDIA; THYATIRA. Besides the shellfish above mentioned, several other species are noted by different writers, namely, *Murex branderis*, *Murex erinaceus*, *Murex buccinum* (*purpura haemastoma*). This latter species is still used by the dwellers on the shores where it is found. Various species of the *murex* are found today at Haifa (Syria), about the Gr isles and on the N. coast of Africa. The purple color has been produced from them by modern chemists, but it is of historical interest only, in the light of the discovery of modern artificial dyes with which it could not compete commercially.

Two words have been used in the Heb Bible to describe the colors from shellfish: (*a*) *'argāmān* (Gr *porphúra*). This has been tr[d] "purple"; (*b*) *t^ekhēleth* which was probably a shade of violet, but has been tr[d] "blue" in both AV and RV.

2. Crimson and Scarlet

As indicated elsewhere (see COLORS), three Heb words have been rendered crimson or scarlet: (*a*) *karmīl* (cf Arab. *ḳirmiz* and Eng. "carmine"), (*b*) *tōla'*, and (*c*) *shānī*. We know nothing further about the method of producing these colors than that they were both obtained from the kermes insect which feeds on a species of live oak growing in Southern Europe and Turkey in Asia. The modern dyer can obtain several shades from the cochineal insect by varying the mordants or assistants used with the dye. Pliny mentions the same fact as being known by the ancient Egyptians. Some of the Syrian dyers still use the kermes, commonly called *dûd* ("worms"), although most of them have resorted to the artificial European dyes which they indiscriminately call *dûd frangy* ("foreign worms").

The "rams' skins dyed red" mentioned in Ex **25** are still made in Syria. After the ram's skin has been tanned in sumac, it is laid out on a table and a solution of the dye, made by boiling *dûd* in water, is rubbed on. After the dye is dry, the skin is rubbed with oil and finally polished. No native product is more characteristic of the country than the slippers, Beduin shoes, and other leather articles made from "rams' skins dyed red" (see TANNER).

3. Other Dyes Probably Known

Other dyes probably known were:

(1) *Madder*.—In Jgs **10** 1, we read that "after Abimelech there arose to save Israel Tola the son of Puah." These were probably names of clans. In the Heb they are also color words. *Tōlā'* is the scarlet dye and *pū'āh*, if, as is probable, it is the same as the Arab. *fûwah*, means "madder." This would add another dyestuff. Until the discovery of alizarin, which is artificial madder, the growing of *fûwah* was one of the industries of Cyprus and Syria. It was exported to Europe and was also used locally for producing "Turkey red" on cotton and for dyeing dull reds on wools for rug making (see THYATIRA). It was the custom near Damascus for a father to plant a new madder field for each son that was born. The field began to yield in time to support the boy and later become his inheritance. Madder is mentioned in the Talm and by early Lat writers. A Saracenic helmet and a shield of similar origin, in the possession of the writer, are lined with madder-dyed cotton.

(2) *Indigo*.—Another dye has been discovered among the Egyp mummy cloths, namely, indigo. Indigo blue was used in weaving to form the borders of the cloths. This pigment was probably imported from India.

(3) Yellows and browns of doubtful origin have also been found in the Egyp tombs.

The Jews acquired from the Phoenicians the secret of dyeing, and later held the monopoly in this trade in some districts. A Jewish guild of purple dyers is mentioned on a tombstone in Hieropolis. In the 12th cent. AD Jews were still dyers and glass workers at Tyre. Akhissar, a Jewish stronghold in Asia Minor, was famous as a dyeing city. See also ATTIRE, DYED.

LITERATURE.—See "Crafts" esp. in Wilkinson, Perrot and Chipiez, *Jew Enc*, and *HDB*.

JAMES A. PATCH

DYSENTERY, dis'en-ter-i (**δυσεντερία**, *dusentería*): In Acts **28** 8 RV uses this word in place of the phrase "bloody flux" of AV to describe the disease by which the father of Publius was affected in Malta at the time of St. Paul's shipwreck. The acute form of this disease is often attended with a high temperature, hence Luke speaks of it as "fever and dysentery" (*puretoís kaí dusentería*). The disease is still occasionally epidemic in Malta where there have been several bad outbreaks among the garrison in the last cent., and it has proved to be an intractable and fatal disease there. It is due to a parasitic microbe, the *Bacillus dysenteriae*. In 2 Ch **21** 19 there is reference to an epidemic of a similar nature in the days of Jehoram. The malady, as predicted by Elisha, attacked the king and assumed a chronic form in the course of which portions of the intestine sloughed. This condition sometimes occurs in the amoebic form of dysentery, cases of which sometimes last over two years.

ALEX. MACALISTER

E

EAGLE, ē′g'l (נֶשֶׁר, *nesher;* ἀετός, *aetós;* Lat *aquila*): A bird of the genus *aquila* of the family *falconidae*. The Heb *nesher*, meaning "to tear with the beak," is almost invariably tr[d] "eagle," throughout the Bible; yet many of the most important references compel the admission that the bird to which they applied was a vulture. There were many large birds and carrion eaters flocking over Pal, attracted by the offal from animals slaughtered for tribal feasts and continuous sacrifice. The eagle family could not be separated from the vultures by their habit of feeding, for they ate the offal

Short-toed Eagle (*Circaëtus gallicus*).

from slaughter as well as the vultures. One distinction always holds good. Eagles never flock. They select the tallest trees of the forest, the topmost crag of the mountain, and pairs live in solitude, hunting and feeding singly, whenever possible carrying their prey to the nest so that the young may gain strength and experience by tearing at it and feeding themselves. The vultures are friendly, and collect and feed in flocks. So whereever it is recorded that a "flock came down on a carcase," there may have been an eagle or two in it, but the body of it were vultures. Because they came in such close contact with birds of prey, the natives came nearer dividing them into families than any birds. Of perhaps a half-dozen, they recognized three eagles, they knew three vultures, four or five falcons, and several kites; but almost every Bib. reference is tr[d] "eagle," no matter how evident the text makes it that the bird was a vulture. For example, Mic **1** 16: "Make thee bald, and cut off thy hair for the children of thy delight: enlarge thy baldness as the eagle[m "vulture"]; for they are gone into captivity from thee." This is a reference to the custom of shaving the head when in mourning, but as Pal knew no bald eagle, the text could refer only to the bare head and neck of the griffon vulture. The eagles were, when hunger-driven, birds of prey; the vultures, carrion feeders only. There was a golden eagle (the osprey of AV), not very common, distinguished by its tan-colored head; the imperial eagle, more numerous and easily identified by a dark head and white shoulders; a spotted eagle; a tawny eagle, much more common and readily distinguished by its plumage; and the short-toed eagle, most common of all and especially a bird of prey, as also a small hooded eagle so similar to a vulture that it was easily mistaken for one, save that it was very bold about taking its own food.

The first Bib. reference to the eagle referred to the right bird. Ex **19** 4: "Ye have seen what I did unto the Egyptians, and how I bare you on eagles' wings, and brought you unto myself." This "bare you on eagles' wings" must not be interpreted to mean that an eagle ever carried anything on its back. It merely means that by strength of powerful wing it could carry quite a load with its feet and frequently was seen doing this. Vultures never carried anything; they feasted and regurgitated what they had eaten to their young. The second reference is found in Lev **11** 13 and repeated in Dt **14** 12, the lists of abominations. It would seem peculiar that Moses would find it necessary to include eagles in this list until it is known that Arab mountaineers were eating these birds at that time. The next falls in Dt **28** 49: "Jeh will bring a nation against thee from far, from the end of the earth, as the eagle flieth; a nation whose tongue thou shalt not understand." This also refers to the true eagle and points out that its power of sustained flight, and the speed it could attain when hastening to its hunger-clamoring young, had been observed. The next reference is in Dt **32** 11:

> "As an eagle that stirreth up her nest,
> That fluttereth over her young,
> He spread abroad his wings, he took them,
> He bare them on his pinions."

This is good natural history at last. Former VSS made these lines read as if the eagle carried its young on its wings, a thing wholly incompatible with flight in any bird. Samuel's record of the lamentation of David over Saul and Jonathan is a wonderful poetic outburst and contains reference to this homing flight of the eagle (2 S **1** 23). In Job **9** 26 the arrow-like downward plunge of the hunger-driven eagle is used in comparison with the flight of time. In Job **39**, which contains more good natural history than any other chapter of the Bible, will be found everything concerning the eagle anyone need know:

> "Is it at thy command that the eagle mounteth up,
> And maketh her nest on high?
> On the cliff she dwelleth, and maketh her home,
> Upon the point of the cliff, and the stronghold.
> From thence she spieth out the prey;
> Her eyes behold it afar off.
> Her young ones also suck up blood:
> And where the slain are, there is she" (vs 27–30).

Ps **103** 5 is a reference to the long life of the eagle. The bird has been known to live to an astonishing age in captivity; under natural conditions, the age it attains can only be guessed.

> "Who satisfieth thy desire with good things,
> So that thy youth is renewed like the eagle."

Prov **23** 5 compares the flight of wealth with that of an eagle; **30** 17 touches on the fact that the eye of prey is the first place attacked in eating, probably because it is the most vulnerable point and so is frequently fed to the young.

Ver 19:

> "The way of an eagle in the air;
> The way of a serpent upon a rock;
> The way of a ship in the midst of the sea;
> And the way of a man with a maiden."

This reference to the eagle is to that wonderful power of flight that enables a bird to hang as if frozen in the sky, for long periods appearing to our sight immovable, or to sail and soar directly into the eye of the sun, seeming to rejoice in its strength of flight and to exult in the security and freedom of the upper air.

The word "way" is here improperly translated. To the average mind it always means a road, a path. In this instance it should be translated:

> The characteristics of an eagle in the air;
> The habit of a serpent upon the rock;
> The path of a ship in the midst of the sea;
> And the manner of a man with a maid.

Each of these lines stood a separate marvel to Agur, and had no connection with the others (but cf Wisd **5** 10.11, and see WAY).

Isa **40** 31 is another flight reference. Jer **49** 16 refers to the inaccessible heights at which the eagle loves to build and rear its young. Ver 22 refers to the eagle's power of flight. Ezk **1** 10 recounts a vision of the prophet in which strange living creatures had faces resembling eagles. The same book (**17** 3) contains the parable of the eagle: "Thus saith the Lord Jeh: A great eagle with great wings and long pinions, full of feathers, which had divers colors, came unto Lebanon, and took the top of the cedar." Hos **8** 1 is another flight reference. Ob ver 4 is almost identical with Jer **49** 16. The next reference is that of Micah, and really refers to the griffon vulture (Mic **1** 16). In Hab **1** 8 the reference is to swift flight. Mt **24** 28 undoubtedly refers to vultures. In Rev **4** 7 the eagle is used as a symbol of strength. In Rev **8** 13 the bird is represented as speaking: "And I saw, and I heard an eagle [AV "angel"], flying in mid heaven, saying with a great voice, Woe, woe, woe, for them that dwell on the earth, by reason of the other voices of the trumpet of the three angels, who are yet to sound." The eagle makes its last appearance in the vision of the woman and the dragon (Rev **12** 14).

GENE STRATTON-PORTER

EANES, ē'a-nēz (1 Esd **9** 21): RV MANES (q.v.), RVm "Harim."

EAR, ēr (אֹזֶן, *'ōzen;* **οὖς**, *oús*, **ὠτίον**, *ōtíon*, the latter word [lit. "earlet"] in all the Gospels only used of the ear of the high priest's servant, which was cut off by St. Peter: Mt **26** 51; Mk **14** 47; Lk **22** 51 [not **22** 50]; Jn **18** 10.26):

(1) The physical organ of hearing which was considered of peculiar importance as the chief instrument by which man receives information and commandments. For this reason the ear of the priest had to be specially sanctified, the tip of the right ear being touched with sacrificial blood at the consecration (Lev **8** 23). Similarly the ear of the cleansed leper had to be rededicated to the service of God by blood and oil (Lev **14** 14.17.25.28). The ear-lobe of a servant, who preferred to remain with the family of his master rather than become free in the seventh year, was to be publicly bored or pierced with an awl in token of perpetual servitude (Ex **21** 6). It has been suggested that Ps **40** 6 should be interpreted in this sense, but this is not probable (see below). The cutting off of the ears and noses of captives was an atrocious custom of war frequently alluded to in oriental lit. (Ezk **23** 25). The phrase "to open the ear," which originally means the uncovering of the ear by partially removing the turban, so as to permit a clearer hearing, is used in the sense of revealing a secret or of giving important (private) information (1 S **9** 15; **20** 2.12.13; 2 S **7** 27; 1 Ch **17** 25; also Ps **40** 6), and the NT promises similarly that "things which eye saw not, and ear heard not" are to be revealed by the reconciled God to the heart that in gladsome surrender has come to Him to be taught by His spirit (1 Cor **2** 9).

(2) The inner ear, the organ of spiritual perception. If the ear listens, the heart willingly submits, but often the spiritual ear is "hardened" (Isa **6** 10; Zec **7** 11; Mt **13** 15; Acts **28** 27), or "heavy" (Isa **6** 10; also Dt **29** 4), either by self-seeking obstinacy or by the judgment of an insulted God. Such unwilling hearers are compared to the "deaf adder . . . . which hearkeneth not to the voice of charmers, charming never so wisely" (Ps **58** 4.5; cf also Prov **21** 13; **28** 9; Acts **7** 57). The expression "He that hath ears to hear let him hear" is frequent in the Synoptic Gospels, occurring 7 or 8 times: Mt **11** 15; **13** 9.43; Mk **4** 9.23 (**7** 16 RV omits); Lk **8** 8; **14** 35, and while not found in the Fourth Gospel, it occurs seven times in Rev **2** and **3**. "Itching ears," on the other hand, are those that have become tired of the sound of oft-repeated truth and that long for new though deceitful teaching (2 Tim **4** 3). Ears may "tingle" at startling news, esp. of disaster (1 S **3** 11; 2 K **21** 12; Jer **19** 3).

(3) God's ears are often mentioned in the anthropopathic style of Scripture, signifying the ability of God to receive the petitions of His people, for "He that planted the ear, shall he not hear?" (Ps **94** 9; also Ps **10** 17; **34** 15; **130** 2; Isa **59** 1; 1 Pet **3** 12). But God also hears the murmurings of the wicked against Him (Nu **11** 1; 2 K **19** 28; Wisd **1** 10; Jas **5** 4); still it lies in His power to refuse to hear (Ezk **8** 18; Lam **3** 8; cf also ver 56).

H. L. E. LUERING

EARING, ēr'ing (חָרִישׁ, *ḥārīsh*): The Heb word is twice trd "earing" in AV (Gen **45** 6; Ex **34** 21). The RV rendering is "plowing": "There shall be neither plowing nor harvest." See also Dt **21** 4; 1 S **8** 12; Isa **30** 24.

EARLY, ûr'li (**ὄρθρος**, *órthros*, and related words; **πρωΐ**, *prōî*): The word generally refers to the day, and means the hour of dawn or soon after (Gen **19** 2; 2 Ch **36** 15; Hos **6** 4; Lk **24** 22). Sometimes it refers to the beginning of the season, e.g. the early rain (Ps **84** 6; Jas **5** 7; see RAIN). It may also have the sense of "speedily" (Ps **46** 5). The early morning is frequently commended as the hour for prayer. See examples of Jesus (Mk **1** 35; Lk **21** 38; Jn **8** 2); also Abraham (Gen **19** 27), Jacob (Gen **28** 18), Gideon (Jgs **6** 38), Samuel (1 S **15** 12), David (1 S **17** 20).

G. H. GERBERDING

EARNEST, ûr'nest (**ἀρραβών**, *arrhabōn*): Found three times in the NT: The "earnest of our inheritance" (Eph **1** 14); "the earnest of the Spirit" (2 Cor **1** 22; **5** 5). It has an equivalent in Heb *'ērābhōn* (found in Gen **38** 17.18.20), in Lat *arrabo*, Fr. *arrhes* and the OE *arles*. The term is mercantile and comes originally from the Phoenicians. Its general meaning is that of a pledge or token given as the assurance of the fulfilment of a bargain or promise. It also carries with it the idea of forfeit, such as is now common in land deals, only from the obverse side. In other words, the one promising to convey property, wages or blessing binds the promise with an advance gift or pledge partaking of the quality of the benefit to be bestowed. If the agreement be about wages, then a part of the wages is advanced; if it be about land, then a clod given to the purchaser or beneficiary may stand as the pledge of final and complete conveyance of the property.

Figurative: In the spiritual sense, as used in the passages above named, the reference is to the work of the Spirit of God in our hearts being a token and pledge of a perfect redemption and a heavenly inheritance. There is more than the idea of security in the word as used, for it clearly implies the continuity and identity of the blessing.

C. E. SCHENK

EARRING, ēr′ring: An ornamental pendant of some kind hanging from the ears has been worn by both sexes in oriental lands from the earliest times. Among the Greeks and Romans, as with western peoples in general, its use was confined to females. The ears in the statue of the Medicean Venus are pierced and probably were originally ornamented with earrings. It is clear, however, that among the Hebrews and related oriental peoples earrings were worn by both sexes. Abraham's servant "put the earring upon [Rebekah's] face, and the bracelets upon her hands" (Gen **24** 47 AV), in accordance with custom, evidently, but it is implied that it was customary for men also to wear earrings, in that the relatives and friends of Job "every one [gave him] an earring of gold" (Job **42** 11 AV). Such ornaments were usually made of gold, finely wrought, and often set with precious stones, as archaeology has shown. Such jewels were worn in ancient times for protective as well as for decorative purposes. RV renders "amulets" for AV "earrings" in Isa **3** 20, the Heb word (*l^eḥāshīm*) being elsewhere associated with serpent-charming; but the earrings of Gen **35** 4, also, were more than mere ornaments, so the AV and RV may both be right in their renderings here (Kennedy). The influence of Egypt, where amulets of various kinds were worn by men and gods, by the living and the dead, is shown by recent excavations at Gezer, Taanach and Megiddo. See AMULET; ORNAMENT.

GEO. B. EAGER

EARTH, ûrth (אֲדָמָה, *'ădhāmāh*, אֶרֶץ, *'ereç*, עָפָר, *'āphār*; γῆ, *gḗ*, οἰκουμένη, *oikouménē*): In a hilly limestone country like Pal, the small amount of iron oxide in the rocks tends to be oxidized, and thereby to give a prevailing reddish color to the soil. This is esp. the case on relatively barren hills where there is little organic matter present to prevent reddening and give a more blackish tinge.

'Ădhāmāh (cf *'ādhām*, "a man," and Adam) is from *'ādham*, "to be red," and is used in the senses: "earth" (Ex **20** 24), "land" (Ps **105** 35), a "land" or country (Isa **14** 2), "ground" (Gen **4** 11), "the earth" (Gen **7** 4).

The word most in use is *'ereç*, undoubtedly from a most ancient root occurring in many languages, as Eng. "earth," Ger. *Erde*, Arab. *'arḍ*. It is used in most of the senses of *'ădhāmāh*, but less as "soil" and more as "the earth" as a part of the universe; frequently with *shāmayim*, "heavens," as in Gen **1** 1: "In the beginning God created the heavens and the earth."

'Āphār and its root word and derivatives are closely paralleled in the Arab., and refer mainly to "dust" or "dry earth" (cf Arab. *'afir*, "to be of the color of dust"; *'afar*, "dust"; *ya'fūr*, "a gazelle"; Heb *'ōpher*, "a gazelle"). Cf Gen **2** 7: "Jehovah God formed man of the dust of the ground"; Job **2** 12: ". . . . sprinkled dust upon their heads"; Ps **104** 29: ". . . . they die, and return to their dust"; Gen **18** 27: "dust and ashes."

In the LXX and NT, *gē* is used in nearly all cases, *oikoumenē* being used a few times for the "habitable earth," as in Lk **21** 26 AV. See further ANTHROPOLOGY; ASTRONOMY; EVOLUTION; WORLD.

ALFRED ELY DAY

EARTH, CIRCLE OF THE. See ASTRONOMY, III, 1, 3.

EARTH, CORNERS OF THE: The "corners" or "ends" of the earth are its "wings" (*kan^ephōth hā-'āreç*), i.e. its borders or extremities. The word in general means a wing, because the wing of a bird is used as a covering for its young, and from this meaning it acquires that of the extremity of anything stretched out. It is thus used in Dt **22** 12: "Thou shalt make thee fringes upon the four borders [wings] of thy vesture, wherewith thou coverest thyself." It thus also means the coasts or boundaries of the land surface of the earth; its extremities. It is tr^d "corners" in Isa **11** 12; "ends" in Job **37** 3 and **38** 13. The "four corners" of the earth (Isa **11** 12) or "land" (Ezk **7** 2) are therefore simply the extremities of the land in the four cardinal directions. See also ASTRONOMY, III, 3.

E. W. MAUNDER

EARTH, ENDS OF THE. See EARTH, CORNERS OF THE.

EARTH, PILLARS OF THE. See ASTRONOMY, III, 2.

EARTH, THE NEW. See ESCHATOLOGY OF THE NT, IX; HEAVENS (NEW).

EARTH, VAULT, vôlt, **OF THE:** In one passage God is said to have "founded his vault [*'ăghuddāh*] upon the earth" (Am **9** 6). It is not quite certain whether this dome or vault refers to the earth itself, or to the heavens arched above it. The latter is the usual interpretation, but in either case the reference is rather to the strength of the structure than to its form; the word implying something that is firmly bound together and hence an arch or dome because of its stability. See also ASTRONOMY, III, 2.

EARTHEN, ûrth′'n, **VESSELS** (חֶרֶשׂ, *ḥeres*, יֵצֶר, *yeçer*; ὀστράκινος, *ostrákinos*): These vessels were heat-resisting and were used for cooking and for boiling clothes (Lev **6** 28; **11** 33; **14** 5.50). They were probably non-porous and took the place of the *ḳidri* or *ma'ajin* used in Syria today. A traveler in the interior of Pal may still meet with the hospitality showed to David (2 S **17** 28). The generous natives brought not only gifts of food but the necessary vessels in which to cook it. An earthen vessel was used to preserve a land deed (Jer **32** 14).

Figurative: In Jer **19** 1 breaking of an earthen vessel was symbolical of the destruction of Jerus. These vessels were also used to symbolize the commonness (Lam **4** 2) and frailness of our bodies (2 Cor **4** 7). See POTTERY. JAMES A. PATCH

EARTHLY, ûrth′li (ἐπίγειος, *epígeios*, "existing upon the earth," "terrestrial," from ἐπί, *epí*, "upon" and γῆ, *gē*, "earth"; Vulg *terrenus*): Of or pertaining to the earth, or to the present state of existence. The word *epigeios* is not found in LXX, but occurs in classical Gr from Plato down. In Plutarch *Mor.* 566 D, it occurs in the remarkable phrase, "that which is earthly of the soul." Its meaning is primarily merely local ("being on the earth"). The word *gē* ("earth") has not in itself an ethical significance, and does not carry a suggestion of moral taint, such as the word *kósmos* ("world") has, esp. in the Johannine writings, and *sárx* ("flesh"), esp. in Paul. It does, however, suggest a certain limitation or frailty; and in some passages, the context gives the adj. *epigeios* an ethical color, though in the NT the purely local meaning is never lost sight of. It is tr^d "earthly" in the following passages: (1) Jn **3** 12, "if I told you earthly things," i.e. things which are realized *on earth*, things within the circle of human observation, truths of subjective experience (e.g. the new birth); in contrast to "heavenly things," the objective truths which, as not directly realizable in human experience, must be revealed from above (the mysteries of the Divine purpose and plans). Clearly "earthly" here implies no *moral* contrast to the heavenly or spiritual. (2) 2 Cor **5** 1, "the earthly house of our tabernacle," i.e. the body with which we are clothed *on earth*, in contrast to the spiritual resurrection-body, "which is from heaven" (ver 2). Here again the word has a merely local, not an ethical, significance. (3) Phil **3** 19, "whose glory is in their shame, who mind earthly things," i.e. whose thoughts rest on earth, on the pleasures of life here below. (4) Jas **3** 15, "This wisdom is not a wisdom that cometh down from above, but is earthly," i.e. it is on the plane of life on earth, merely human, incapable of ascending to the level of Divine wisdom. In the last two passages, the literal local meaning is still evident, but the word shades off into the moral and suggests that which is opposed to the spiritual in character. The same word is tr[d] "terrestrial" in 1 Cor **15** 40, and "things in [RV "on"] earth" in Phil **2** 10. AV has "earthly" in Jn **3** 31, where it translates *ek tḗs gḗs*=lit. "out of the earth," the reference being to the character and mission of the Baptist as partaking of the limitations of his earthly (human) origin, in contrast to the Messiah "that cometh from heaven." The AV rendering is somewhat misleading, for it introduces a confusion with the "earthly" of ver 12 (vide Westcott in loc.). RV rightly renders "of the earth."

"Earthly" is to be distinguished from "earthy" =made of earth or clay (*choikós*, from *choús*, "earth dug out," 1 Cor **15** 47 ff). D. MIALL EDWARDS

EARTHQUAKE, ûrth'kwāk (רַעַשׁ, *ra'ash*; **σεισμός**, *seismós*): The last earthquake which worked any damage in Pal and Syria occurred in 1837, and destroyed the village of *Safed*, near Mt. Hermon, and was felt even to Hebron. Since that time a few feeble shocks have been felt but no damage was done. The region is just on the edge of the great earthquake circle whose center is in Armenia, and is liable to earthquakes. The large number of references in the Bible to earthquakes, and the evident fear in the minds of the people of those times, would seem to indicate that they were more frequent in Bible times than recently.

1. Earthquakes in Palestine

There are three main causes of earthquakes:

(1) *Earthslips.*—In the slow process of cooling, the crust of the earth tends to wrinkle and fold as it contracts. This causes a stress to be set up in the strata composing the crust. If the strata are too rigid to bend there must come after a time a break or fault. The shock caused by the break, which is usually several miles below the surface of the earth, is an earthquake, and it spreads in the form of earth waves from the break as center. Seismographs in all parts of the world are now adjusted to receive the waves even though the origin is on the opposite side of the earth.

2. Causes of Earthquakes

(2) *Explosion of steam or gases under the surface.*—Some earthquakes, especially those underneath the sea, are thought to be caused by water seeping through the soil and rocks and finding its way to the heated masses below. Steam is formed and if there is no escape for it, an explosion takes place whose force is felt on the surface.

(3) *Volcanic.*—As earthquakes are of common occurrence in volcanic regions it seems likely that there is some connection between the two, but the relation has not been fully traced. It may be that the second cause is the origin of both the volcano and earthquake. See further, DELUGE OF NOAH.

Many destructive earthquakes have been recorded in the history of Syria, but they have been mostly in the north, in the region of Aleppo. Jerus itself has seldom been affected by earthquakes. The *Hauran* beyond the Jordan is covered with volcanic remains and signs of violent shocks, and the cities on the coast have suffered much, but Jerus on the higher ground between has usually escaped with little destruction.

3. Earthquakes in Jerusalem

A number of earthquakes are mentioned in the Scriptures: (1) At Mount Sinai (Ex **19** 18); (2) Korah and companions destroyed in fissure and sinking ground (Nu **16** 31; *Ant*, IV, iii, 3); (3) in the Phili camp in the days of Saul (1 S **14** 15); (4) after Elijah's flight (1 K **19** 11); (5) in the reign of Uzziah, between 790 and 740 BC (Am **1** 1); Zec **14** 5 probably refers to the same (*Ant*, IX, x, 4); (6) at Christ's death (Mt **27** 51–54); (7) at Christ's resurrection (Mt **28** 2); (8) at Philippi when Paul and Silas were freed from prison (Acts **16** 26). Most of these shocks seem to have been slight and caused little loss of life. Jos mentions one in the reign of Herod, "such as had not happened at any other time, which was very destructive to men and cattle" (*Ant*, XV, v, 2). Professor G. A. Smith in his recent work on *Jerusalem* is of the opinion that earthquakes were sufficiently frequent and strong to account for the appearance and disappearance of Nehemiah's Fountain (*Jerus*, I, 74). The Heb *ra'ash* is commonly used to mean a great noise. Large earthquakes are sometimes accompanied by a rumbling noise, but as a rule they come silently and without warning.

4. Earthquakes in Scripture

In the Scriptures earthquakes are mentioned as tokens of God's power (Job **9** 6) and of His presence and anger (Ps **68** 8; **18** 7; Isa **13** 13): "She shall be visited of Jeh of hosts . . . . with earthquake, and great noise" (Isa **29** 6); also as a sign of Christ's "coming, and of the end of the world" (Mt **24** 3-7). See also Rev **11** 13.19; **16** 18.

5. Symbolic Use

LITERATURE.—Milne, *Earthquakes* (Inter. Scient. ser.); Plumptre, *Bib. Studies*, 136; Dutton, *Earthquakes*.

ALFRED H. JOY

EASE, ēz (שַׁאֲנָן, *sha'ănān*, שַׁלְאֲנָן, *shal'ănān*, chiefly, "at ease"): Used 19 t in the OT and once in the NT, most frequently meaning tranquillity, security or comfort of mind; in an ethical sense, indicating carelessness or indifference with reference to one's moral or religious interests. The prophet Jeremiah used the phrase as an indication of national or tribal indifference: "Moab hath been at e. from his youth" (Jer **48** 11); "I am very sore displeased with the nations that are at e." (Zec **1** 15). Frequent allusions are made also by various prophets to individuals or groups of individuals, as "Woe to them that are at e. in Zion" (Am **6** 1); "Rise up, ye women that are at e." (Isa **32** 9), and "Tremble, ye women that are at e." (ver 11).

The word in another form is used also in a verbal sense and to apply to physical ease and comfort, as "My couch shall e. my complaint" (Job **7** 13; cf esp. 2 Ch **10** 4.9). Simple mental tranquillity or peace of mind is also expressed by it (Jer **46** 27).

The single instance of its use in the NT is illustrative of its **figurative** but most common usage in the OT, where it refers to moral indifference in the parable of the Rich Fool: "Soul . . . . take thine e., eat, drink, be merry" (Lk **12** 19).

WALTER G. CLIPPINGER

EAST, ēst, **CHILDREN OF THE** (מִזְרָח, *mizrāḥ*, קֶדֶם, *ḳedhem*, קֵדֶם, *ḳēdhem*, and other derivatives of the same root; **ἀνατολή**, *anatolḗ*): *Mizrāḥ* is the equivalent of the Arab. *meshriḳ*, "the orient" or "place of sunrise." In the same way *ma'ărābh*, "west," corresponds to the Arab. *maghrib*, and both *mizrāḥ* and *ma'ărābh* occur in Ps **103** 12: "As far as the east is from the west, so far hath he removed our transgressions from us." *Ḳādham*, "to precede" (whence *ḳedhem*, "east"), and its derivatives correspond closely to the Arab. *ḳadham*, except that the Arab. derivatives do not include the signification "east." In the majority of cases "east" and other words of direction require no explanation, but the expressions "the children of the east" (*b'nē* *ḳedhem*), "the land of the children of the east" (*'ereç b^e nē ḳedhem*), and "the east country" (*'ereç ḳedhem*), belong to a different category. In the story of Gideon (Jgs **6** 3.33; **7** 12; **8** 10), we find several times the expression "the Midianites and the Amalekites and the children of the east." In Jgs **8** 24 it is said of the same host: "For they had golden earrings, because they were Ishmaelites." In Jer **49** 28.29: "Go up to Kedar, and destroy the children of the east. Their tents and their flocks shall they take." In Gen **25** 6: "But unto the sons of the concubines, that Abraham had, Abraham gave gifts; and he sent them away from Isaac his son, while he yet lived, eastward, unto the east country." Now Ishmael is the son of Abraham and Hagar, Midian of Abraham and Keturah, Kedar the son of Ishmael, and Amalek the grandson of Esau, dwelling in Edom. It is evident that we have to do with the Syrian desert and in a general way with Arabia, esp. its northern part, and with peoples like the modern Bedawin who kept camels and dwelt in tents, "houses of hair" (*buyūt sha'r*), as they are called by the Arabs of today.

A striking passage is Gen **29** 1: "Then Jacob went on his journey, and came to the land of the children of the east." As one journeys eastward through the country E. of the Jordan he traverses first a region of towns and villages with fields of grain, and then the wide desert where the Bedawin wander with their herds. The line is a sharp one. Within a very few hours he passes from the settled part where the rain, though scanty, is sufficient to bring the grain to maturity, to the bare desert.

Job was "the greatest of all the children of the east" (Job **1** 3). These desert people had a name for wisdom as we see from 1 K **4** 30, "Solomon's wisdom excelled the wisdom of all the children of the east, and all the wisdom of Egypt"; and from Mt **2** 1: "Now when Jesus was born . . . . Wise-men from the east came." ALFRED ELY DAY

EAST COUNTRY, kun'tri (אֶרֶץ מִזְרָח, *'ereç mizrāḥ*): Lit. "country of the sunrise" over against the "country of the sunset" (Zec **8** 7). The two together form a poetical expression indicating the whole earth.

EAST GATE. See GATE, THE EAST.

EAST (EASTERN, ēs'tẽrn) **SEA** (Zec **14** 8). See DEAD SEA.

EAST WIND. See WIND.

EASTER, ēs'tẽr (πάσχα, *páscha*, fr Aram. פַּסְחָא, *paṣḥā'*, and Heb פֶּסַח, *peṣaḥ*, the Passover festival): The Eng. word comes from the AS *Eastre* or *Estera*, a Teutonic goddess to whom sacrifice was offered in April, so the name was transferred to the paschal feast. The word does not properly occur in Scripture, although AV has it in Acts **12** 4 where it stands for Passover, as it is rightly rendered in RV. There is no trace of Easter celebration in the NT, though some would see an intimation of it in 1 Cor **5** 7. The Jewish Christians in the early church continued to celebrate the Passover, regarding Christ as the true paschal lamb, and this naturally passed over into a commemoration of the death and resurrection of Our Lord, or an Easter feast. This was preceded by a fast, which was considered by one party as ending at the hour of the crucifixion, i.e. at 3 o'clock on Friday, by another as continuing until the hour of the resurrection before dawn on Easter morning. Differences arose as to the time of the Easter celebration, the Jewish Christians naturally fixing it at the time of the Passover feast which was regulated by the paschal moon. According to this reckoning it began on the evening of the 14th day of the moon of the month of *Nīṣān* without regard to the day of the week, while the gentile Christians identified it with the first day of the week, i.e. the Sunday of the resurrection, irrespective of the day of the month. This latter practice finally prevailed in the church, and those who followed the other reckoning were stigmatized as heretics. But differences arose as to the proper Sunday for the Easter celebration which led to long and bitter controversies. The Council of Nice, 325 AD, decreed that it should be on Sunday, but did not fix the particular Sunday. It was left to the bishop of Alexandria to determine, since that city was regarded as the authority in astronomical matters and he was to communicate the result of his determination to the other bishops. But this was not satisfactory, esp. to the western churches, and a definite rule for the determination of Easter was needed. By some it was kept as early as March 21, and by others as late as April 25, and others followed dates between. The rule was finally adopted, in the 7th cent., to celebrate Easter on the Sunday following the 14th day of the calendar moon which comes on, or after, the vernal equinox which was fixed for March 21. This is not always the astronomical moon, but near enough for practical purposes, and is determined without astronomical calculation by certain intricate rules adopted by ecclesiastical authority. These rules involve the Dominical Letters, or the first seven of the alphabet, representing the days of the week, A standing for the first day of the year and the one on which Sunday falls being called the Dominical for that year. There are also involved the Golden Numbers and the Epacts, the first being the numbers from 1 to 19, the cycle of the moon when its phases recur on the same days of the year, the first of the cycle being that in which the new moon falls on January 1. The Epacts indicate the moon's age at the beginning of each year. Easter was thus fixed by these rules, but another difficulty arose when the Gregorian calendar was adopted in 1582, the difference between it and the Julian being then 10 days. This of course affected the determination of Easter, and its celebration by the Gr church, which has never admitted the Gregorian calendar, occurs usually at a different time from that followed by the western churches. This difference may be as much as five weeks and it may occur as late as April 30, while in the West it cannot occur later than April 25 nor earlier than March 22. Occasionally the two come together but this is rare, since the difference between the two calendars is now 13 days. The Easter feast has been and still is regarded as the greatest in the Christian church, since it commemorates the most important event in the life of its Founder. H. PORTER

EBAL, ē'bal (עֵיבָל, *'ēbhāl*, "bare") or **OBAL** (עוֹבָל, *'ōbhāl*):

(1) A people and region of Joktanite, Arabia. See Dillmann, *Gen*, and Glaser, *Skizze*, II, 426. The latter form of the name is that given in Gen **10** 28, the former in 1 Ch **1** 22 and in the Sam text of Gen **10** 28.

(2) A son of Shobal, son of Seir, the Horite (Gen **36** 23; 1 Ch **1** 40).

EBAL, ē'bal, **MOUNT** (הַר עֵיבָל, *har 'ēbhāl*; Γαιβάλ, *Gaibál*): Rises N. of the vale of Shechem, over against Mt. Gerizim on the S. The mountain (Arab. *el-Iṣlamīyeh*) reaches a height of 1,402 ft. above the floor of the valley, and 3,077 ft. above the level of the Mediterranean. The Samaritans feign that Gerizim is the higher; but it is more than 200 ft. lower than Ebal. These two mountains overhang the pass through which runs the main artery of intercourse between E. and W., the city of Nāblus lying in the throat of the valley to the W. The ancient Shechem probably stood farther to the E. The lower slopes of Ebal as one ascends from Nāblus are covered with gardens and orchards, the copious streams from the fountains under Gerizim washing its foot, and spreading fertility and beauty. The vine, the fig and the olive grow luxuriantly. Higher up we scramble over rough rocky terraces, where grow only the ubiquitous thistles and prickly shrubs.

Mount Ebal.

From the broad summit a view of surpassing interest and beauty rewards the climber's toil. Westward beyond the hills and the plain of Sharon with its coast line of yellow sand running from Jaffa to Carmel, stretch the blue waters of the Mediterranean. From Carmel to Gilboa, Little Hermon and Tabor, roll the fruitful breadths of Esdraelon: the uplands of Galilee, with Nazareth showing on the brow above the plain, rise away to the buttresses of Lebanon in the N. From the snowy peak of Hermon the eye ranges over the Jaulān and Mount Gilead to the Mountain of Bashan in the E., with the steep eastern wall of the Jordan valley in the foreground. The land of Moab is visible beyond the Dead Sea; and the heights around Jerus close the view on the S.

Round this splendid mountain, seen from afar on all sides, religious associations have gathered from old time. The Moslem Weley on the top—the usual white-domed sanctuary—where it is said the head of the Baptist is buried, is doubtless the modern representative of some ancient seat of worship. The ruins of a church show that Christians also came under the spell of the hill.

The slopes of Ebal toward Gerizim played their part in that memorable scene, when, having conquered the central region of Pal, Joshua led the people hither, erected an altar of unhewn stones, wrote upon the stones—either engraving on the stone itself, or impressing on plaster placed there for the purpose—a copy of the law, and then, as Moses the servant of the Lord had commanded, placed half the tribes on the slope of Gerizim, and half on those of Ebal, and the ark with the priests and Levites in the center. Then with dramatic responses from the two divisions of the people, the blessings and the cursings of the law were read (Josh **8** 30 ff; cf Dt **27** 11 ff). In all the future, therefore, this mountain, towering aloft in the very heart of the land, would remind beholders far and near of their people's covenant with God. It has sometimes been questioned if the reading of the law could be heard by the people in the way described. The formation of the sides of the valley at the narrowest part, and the acoustics, which have been tested more than once, leave no reasonable doubt as to the possibility.

The importance of the mountain from a military point of view is illustrated by the ruins of a massive fortress found on the summit. W. Ewing

EBED, ē'bed (עֶבֶד, *'ebhedh,* "servant"):

(1) Father of Gaal, who rebelled against Abimelech (Jgs **9** 26–35).

(2) A companion of Ezra in his return (Ezr **8** 6) =Obeth (1 Esd **8** 32).

EBED-MELECH, ē-bed-mē'lek, eb-ed-mē'lek (עֶבֶד־מֶלֶךְ, *'ebhedh-melekh,* "servant of the king" or "of [god] Melek"): An Ethiopian eunuch in the service of King Zedekiah, who interceded with the king for the prophet Jeremiah and rescued him from the dungeon into which he had been cast to die (Jer **38** 7–13). For this, the word of Jeh through Jeremiah promised Ebed-melech that his life should be spared in the fall of Jerus (Jer **39** 15–18).

EBEN-BOHAN. See Bohan.

EBEN-EZEL. See Ezel.

EBEN-EZER, eb-en-ē'zēr (אֶבֶן הָעֵזֶר, *'ebhen hā-'ezer,* "stone of the help"; **'Αβενέζερ,** *Abenézer*):

(1) Here Israel was defeated by the Philis, 4,000 men falling in the battle (1 S **4** 1 ff). It appears also to have been the scene of the disaster when the ark of God was captured (vs 3 ff). The place is not identified. It was over against Aphek; but this site is also unknown (cf Josh **12** 18). *Onom* places it between Jerus and Ascalon, in the neighborhood of Beth-shemesh. Conder suggests *Deir Abān,* fully 2 miles E. of *'Ain Shems* (*PEF,* III, 24).

(2) A stone set up by Samuel to perpetuate the memory of the signal victory granted to Israel over the Philis in answer to his prayer (1 S **7** 12). It stood between Mizpeh and Shen. The latter is probably identical with *'Ain Sinia,* N. of Bethel. This defines the district in which it may be found; but no identification is yet possible. W. Ewing

EBER, ē'bēr (עֵבֶר, *'ēbher;* **Ἔβερ,** *Éber,* in Gen; **'Ωβήδ,** *Ōbēd,* in Ch):

(1) Occurs in the genealogies (Gen **10** 21.25; **11** 14 ff) as the great-grandson of Shem and father of Peleg and Joktan. The word means "the other side," "across," and the form "Hebrew," which is derived from it, is intended to denote the people or tribe who came "from the other side of the river" (i.e. the Euphrates), from Haran (Gen **11** 31), whence Abraham and his dependents migrated to Canaan.

(2) A Gadite (1 Ch **5** 13).

(3) (4) Two Benjamites (1 Ch **8** 12.22).

(5) The head of a priestly family (Neh **12** 20).

A. C. Grant

EBEZ, ē'bez (אֶבֶץ, *'ebheç,* meaning unknown; **'Ρέβες,** *Rhébes;* AV **Abez**): One of the 16 cities in Issachar (Josh **19** 20). The name seems to be cognate to that of the judge Ibzan (Jgs **12** 8–10). All else concerning it is conjecture.

EBIASAPH, ē-bī'a-saf: A descendant of Kohath the son of Levi (1 Ch **6** 37). See Abiasaph.

EBIONISM, ē'bi-ō-niz'm, **EBIONITES,** ē'bi-ō-nīts (**'Εβιωναῖοι,** *Ebiōnaíoi,* from אֶבְיוֹנִים, *'ebhyōnīm,* "poor people"):

General Statement
I. Origin of the Name
1. The Poor Ones
2. Origin of the Name

General Statement

The Ebionites were a sect of heretics frequently mentioned by the early Fathers. In regard to their opinions, as in regard to those of most early heretical sects, there is the difficulty that to a large extent we are dependent for our information on their opponents. These opponents were not generally very careful to apprehend exactly the views of those whose opinions they undertook to refute. It adds to the difficulty in the present case that there is a dubiety as to the persons designated by the title. Sometimes, it is admitted, the name was used to designate all Jewish Christians irrespective of their opinions; at other times it denotes a sect akin to the Gnostics, who ascribed a purely human origin to Our Lord. There are, however, certain works, the Clementine writings, which from statements of the Fathers may be assumed to represent the views of this sect, but as these represent views to some extent divergent, it is difficult to decide which is the truly Ebionitic. There are also certain apocalyptic books which present affinities with Ebionism. The quotations from the Gospel according to the Hebrews—the only gospel the Ebionites received—likewise afford means of appreciating their views. This gospel has come down to us only in isolated quotations, for the accuracy of which we have no guarantee. Finally, it has to be borne in mind that no sect can persist through centuries of changing circumstances, and not in turn undergo change.

I. Origin of the Name.—Tertullian and Epiphanius assume the sect to have received its name from a certain Ebion or Hebion. Others of the Fathers, without affirming it, use language which seems to imply the belief in a person called Ebion. This, however, is generally now regarded as a mistake. No trace of the existence of such a person is to be found. The sect in question seems to have assumed the name Ebionites, "the poor ones," from the first Beatitude (Mt **5** 3), claiming to be the continuation into the new dispensation of the "poor and needy" of the Pss, e.g. **69** 33; **70** 5; **74** 21.

1. The Poor Ones

It has been mooted that the sect may have had a leader who assumed the title "the poor man." Besides that we have no trace of his existence, the name would almost certainly have been treated as an Aram. word and put in the *status emphaticus* as *Ebiona*, which in Gr would have become *Ebionas*.

2. Origin of the Name

The ordinary view of the origin of the name has the advantage of analogy in its favor. The pre-Reformation Protestants of the 12th and 13th cents. in France called themselves "the poor men" (of Lyons). The fact that the apostle James in his Epistle implies a natural union between poverty and piety (**2** 5), "Did not God choose them that are poor as to the world to be rich in faith . . . . ?" would confirm the Jewish Christians in their use of the name.

Some have been inclined to press unduly a play on the name in which some of the Fathers indulge, as if the poor views of this sect as to the person of Christ had led to their receiving this name from without.

II. Authorities for the Opinions of the Ebionites.—As indicated above, the main authorities for these are Irenaeus, Tertullian and Hippolytus.

1. Irenaeus, Tertullian and Hippolytus

The characteristics of the Ebionites noted by them were, *first*, the negative one that they did not, like the other Gnostics, distinguish between the Supreme God and the Creator of the world—the demiurge—who was identified with the God of the Jews. With them Jeh was the Supreme God—the God of Israel and the Creator of the heavens and the earth. The *second* characteristic, also negative, was that they denied the supernatural birth of Our Lord. He was the son of Joseph and Mary in the ordinary sense of the word. The *third* was that they, along with the Cerinthians and Carpocratians, affirmed that a Divine power came down on Jesus at His baptism—the reward of His perfect holiness. According to one form of the theory, the Holy Ghost was the eternal Son of God. Another view was that the power which descended upon Him was the Divine wisdom, the Logos. By the influence of this Divine power He performed miracles and taught with superhuman wisdom. But this Divine influence deserted Jesus on the Cross, hence the cry of being forsaken (Mt **27** 46). The Divine power, however, raised Him from the dead and caused Him to ascend on high. Hippolytus brings the Ebionites into close connection with the Elkasaites and with a certain Alcibiades, whose views he had to combat in Rome. The last claimed to found his views on a work of Elkasai.

2. Origen and Jerome

From two other sources we derive further information: Origen and Jerome both notify the fact that the Ebionites tr^d *'almāh* "young woman" (it is rendered "virgin" in our AV and RV). This tr, so far as the mere word is concerned, is indubitably correct. There is another point in which both afford us information. The first says (*Contra Celsum*, v.61) that there are two classes of Ebionites, one of which denies the miraculous conception and birth of Our Lord, the other of which affirms it. Jerome, in his letter to Augustine, not only asserts the same thing but calls the one class, those affirming the miraculous birth, Nazareans, and the other Ebionites. Origen in his second book against Celsus speaks as if the only distinction between the Ebionites and other Christians was their obedience to the Mosaic law, and by their example rebuts the assertion that the Jews in becoming Christians deserted the law of their fathers. Another feature of Ebionism presented to us by Jerome (*In Jesaiam*, lxvi.24) is their chiliastic view—the personal reign of Our Lord for 1,000 years as the Jewish Messiah.

3. Epiphanius' Description

The writer who gives the most voluminous account of the Ebionites—"Ebionaeans" as he calls them—is Epiphanius. With him it is at once heresy No. X and heresy No. XXX. Before discussing the Ebionites he takes up the closely related sect of the Nazareans as heresy No. XXIX. He had already in a more compendious way considered a similarly named sect, numbering it No. XVIII. It, however, is Jewish while this is Christian. The Jewish sect is distinguished by eating no animal food and offering no sacrifices. They have thus an affinity with the Essenes. They have a peculiarity that, while they honored the patriarchs, they rejected the Pent which related their history. These Nazareans dwelt E. of the Jordan in Gilead and Bashan. Heresy No. XXIX is the Christian Nazareans. This name had been at first applied to all Christians. Epiphanius identifies them with the Essenes and declares their distinguishing peculiarity to be the retention of circumcision and the ceremonial law. They use the Gospel of Mt but without the genealogies. As Heresy No. XXX he proceeds to consider the Ebionites. Ebion, Epiphanius assumes to have been a man, and calls him a "polymorphic portent," and asserts that he was connected with the Samaritans, the Essenes, the Cerinthians and Carpocratians, yet desired to be regarded a Christian. The heresy originated after the flight of the church to Pella. They denied the miraculous birth of Our Lord, but maintained that a Divine influence came down upon Him at His baptism. This Divine wisdom had inspired, and in a sense dwelt, in all the patriarchs. In some sense the body of Jesus was regarded as that of Adam revived. This body was crucified and rose again. They receive only the Gospel of Mt in the form the Cerinthians use it, i.e. the Gospel according to the Hebrews. Epiphanius gives some account of this gospel and its defects. They use also other books; one which he esp. describes, The Journeyings of Peter, appears to be in the main identical with the Clementine Homilies. He connects the Ebionites, as does Hippolytus, with Elkasai; from him they learned that the heavenly Christ was 96 miles high and 24 broad, and that the Holy Ghost had a female form of similar dimensions, only invisible. Although he connects the Ebionites with the Essenes he mentions that, unlike the Essenes of Jos and Philo, the Ebionites not only permitted but enjoined matrimony on young men. Epiphanius adds as an especial enormity that the Ebionites permit second, third and even seventh marriages. Although they enjoin marriage they have a low opinion of women, crediting Eve with originating heathenism, in this agreeing with the Essenian opinion of the sex. Mysteriously Epiphanius represents the Ebionites as not only rejecting the prophets in a body but deriding them. He also mentions the rejection of St. Paul by the Ebionites. It is exceedingly difficult to form a clear, self-consistent view of the doctrines of the Ebionites from the statements of Epiphanius, yet there are points in which his information is of value.

4. Justin Martyr

Though Justin Martyr does not name the Ebionites in his dialogue with Trypho the Jew (47), he mentions two classes of Jewish Christians: (*a*) those who not only themselves observe the law but would compel the gentile believers also to be circumcised and keep the whole law, and will hold no communion with those who refuse to become Jews; (*b*) those who, observing the Mosaic law themselves, enter into communion with uncircumcised gentile believers. The former appear to be an early form of Ebionites. It is to be noted that Justin does not ascribe to them any doctrinal divergence from the orthodox views. In the following ch he mentions some that denied the divinity of Our Lord, but these were Gentiles (*hēmetérou génous*) "of our race."

III. Literature of the Ebionites.—One thing of importance we do owe to Epiphanius—the indication of the lit. produced by the Ebionites, from which we may get their views at first hand. This includes the Gospel according to the Hebrews, the Clementines (*Homilies and Recognitions*); to which we would add the Ascension of Isaiah and the Odes of Solomon. It may be remarked that this lit. appears to represent the opinion of different classes of the Ebionites. We shall merely consider here the bearing these works have on the Ebionites.

1. The Gospel According to the Hebrews

The Gospel according to the Hebrews we know only through quotations. We can have no certainty that these quotations are accurate. The quotations may have been interpolated, and further the book from which the quotations have been made has probably passed through several recensions. The discussion of the question of the relation of this book to the canonical Gospel of Mt is considered elsewhere (see APOCRYPHAL GOSPELS). One thing is clear, there were at least two recensions of this gospel, one nearer and the other farther from the canonical Gospel; the former, the Nazarean, differed only by omitting the genealogy from the First Gospel of the Canon. The other was more strictly Ebionite and omitted all mention of the miraculous birth. The Ebionite recension began, as Epiphanius tells us, abruptly with the calling of the Apostles. The assertion of Epiphanius that the Ebionites rejected the prophets is supported by a quotation from the Gospel according to the Hebrews in Jerome (*Adv. Pelag.*, iii.2): "In the prophets, after they were anointed by the Spirit, sin was found." The change from *akrídas* ("locusts") to *egkrídas* (lit. "cakes of honey and oil"; cf Ex **16** 31; Nu **11** 8) in the account of the food of John may be due to the avoidance of animal food attributed to this sect. One passage, which appears to be a denunciation of wealth in itself, is an addition of a second rich man to the story of the young ruler of the synagogue. A singular verse, quoted from this gospel both by Origen and Jerome, deserves special notice for several reasons: "My mother, the Holy Ghost, took me by one of my hairs and bore me to the great mountain Tabor." The designation of the Holy Ghost as "my mother" is unexampled. It implies a materialistic view of the doctrine of the Trinity after the form of a human family. It is a note of geographical ignorance to call Tabor a "great" mountain. It is only some 2,000 ft. high and behind it are the mountains of the hill country of Galilee rising up to 4,000 ft. in Jebel Jermuk, and behind that the white top of Hermon, 10,000 ft. It is difficult to understand anyone resident in Pal calling Tabor a "great" mountain. Rising from the plain of Esdraelon it is prominent, but with the higher mountains behind it, it could not even seem great. In a quotation by Jerome (*Adv. Pelag.*, iii.2) Our Lord declares Himself unwilling to be baptized by John as unconscious of sin. This suits the representation of Ebionite views which we find in Irenaeus that it was His sinlessness that made Jesus capable of receiving the Holy Ghost.

2. The Clementines

The Clementine lit. attributed by Epiphanius to the Ebionites is a more important source of information for their opinions. It has come down to us complete in three or four forms, the *Homilies*, the *Recognitions*, and two Epitomes which, however, differ less than the two larger works. They all seem to be recensions of an earlier work which has disappeared. The foundation of all of these is a species of religious novel on which are grafted sermons of Peter and his discussions with Simon Magus. Clement, a young Roman orphan of rank in search of a religion, meets Barnabas, who tells him of Christ, describing Him as the "Son of God," and says that He had appeared in Judaea. To learn more about Jesus, Clement proceeds to Caesarea, where he meets Peter. He thereafter accompanies Peter to the various places whither the apostle pursues Simon Magus, and in course of his journeyings he meets and recognizes his father, his brother and his mother; hence the title *Recognitions*. It is in the discourses of Peter that the Ebionism appears. Its theology is fundamentally Jewish and Essenian. That it is Judaizing is evidenced by the covert hostility to the apostle Paul. There are elements that are not those of orthodox Judaism. The Messiah is coequal, or nearly so, with the devil; in other words, the position is a modification of Parseeism (*Hom.*, III, 5). If the discourse of Barnabas is excluded, Our Lord is always called the "prophet" (*Hom.*), the "Teacher" (*Recog.*). He is never asserted nor assumed to be Divine. Nothing is said of His miraculous birth. At the same time in the *Recognitions* He is regarded as not merely man. It is said He "assumed a Jewish body" (*Recog.*, I, 60). This agrees with what Epiphanius says of the Ebionite idea that it was as the body of Adam that the Christ appeared. The apostle Peter, who is represented as the model Christian, eats only herbs and practises frequent ablutions, quite in the manner of the Essenes. In his discourses Peter declares that the true prophet "quenches the fire of altars and represses war." These are Essenian peculiarities, but he "sanctions marriage," against Essenism as we find it in Philo and Jos. The phrase implies an opposition to some who not only did not sanction, but forbade, marriage (*Hom.*, III, 26).

3. Apocalyptic Literature

If the ignoring of the work and apostleship of St. Paul be regarded as the criterion of the Judaizers, that is to say, the Ebionites, then in apocalyptic lit. we find works from which we can draw information as to views. The Ascension of Isaiah was one of the earliest of these books to be recovered in modern times. The writer refers to the martyrdom of Peter in Rome, but makes no mention of Paul (IV, 3). The description of elders and shepherds hating one another (III, 29), "lawless elders and unjust shepherds who will ravage their sheep" (III, 24), seems a view of the church's state as it appeared to a Judaizer when the Pauline view was prevailing. Notwithstanding this not only is the Divine dignity maintained, but the doctrine of the Trinity, "They all glorified the Father of all and His beloved Son and the Holy Spirit" (VIII, 18), is affirmed. As to the person of Christ, He descended through the successive heavens to the earth to be born (IX, 13; X, 8–31). The virginity of Mary is affirmed (X, 12), and the child is born without pain, miraculously (XI, 8–14). A similar view of the birth of Christ is to be found in the Odes of Solomon (XIX, 7).

IV. History of Ebionism.—All authorities combine in asserting a close connection between the Ebionites and the Essenes. At first sight there are serious points of difference, principally these, the Ebionites enjoined marriage, while the Essenes, if we may believe Philo and Jos, forbade it. This forbiddal, however, appears to have been true only of the coenobites of Engedi. Moreover, some of the Judaizers, that is Ebionites, are charged with forbidding to marry (1 Tim **4** 3). The Essenes in all their varieties seem to have come over to Christianity on the fall of the Jewish state and the retreat of the church to Pella. When they joined the believers in their exile the Parsee elements began a ferment in the church and Ebionism was one of the products. This probably is the meaning of the statement that Ebion began to teach his doctrines at Pella. If we may judge from the statements of Scripture and from the earliest of the non-canonical apocalypses, the Ebionites were not at first heretical in their Christology. Only they maintained the universal obligation of the ceremonial law, holding that believers of gentile descent could be received into the church only if they were first circumcised. The keen dialectic of Paul forced them from this position. The abrogation of the Law was closely connected in Paul's reasonings with the Divinity of Our Lord; consequently some of them may have felt that they could maintain their views more easily by denying His supreme Divinity and the reality of the incarnation. The phenomena of His life rendered it impossible for anyone to declare Him to be merely man. Hence the complex notion of a Divine influence—an aeon, coming down upon Him. If, however, His birth were miraculous, then the supreme greatness of Moses would be impugned, consequently they were led to deny the virgin birth.

1. Ebionites and Essenes

Not till Theodotus appeared was the purely humanitarian view of Our Lord's person maintained. All the Heb Christians, however, did not pursue the above course. A large section remained at each general stage, and to the end one portion, the Nazareans, maintained their orthodox doctrinal position, and at the same time obeyed the requirements of the Law. The dualism which is found in the Clementines is an endeavor to explain the power of evil in the world and the function of Satan. The Clementines confirm the statement of the Fathers that the Ebionites used only the Gospel of Mt, for there are more quotations from Mt than from all the other books of the NT put together: These quotations are, however, all from chapters after the 3d. There are, it is to be noted, several unmistakable quotations from the Fourth Gospel. In the Clementines as noticed above there is an avoidance of attributing Divinity to Our Lord. He is the Teacher, the Prophet; only in the discourse ascribed to Barnabas is He called the Son of God. This, we are aware, is the reverse of the ordinarily received idea of the historic succession of beliefs. It is thought that, beginning with the belief in the purely ordinary nature of Our Lord's birth, these Jewish believers gradually added feature after feature until He was regarded as a Divine person, the Divine Logos made flesh by miraculous conception and birth. The abstract possibility of such being the course of events is not denied, but we do say that what evidence we have tends in the direction we have taken. There are elements kindred to Ebionism in the Epistle of Jas, the prominence given to the poor, the little prominence given to the Divinity of Our Lord or to the doctrines of grace all tend in that direction. Yet there is no developed Ebionism; the Divinity of Christ, if not stated in terms, is implied. Schwegler, followed in more recent times by Dr. Campbell of Dundee, finds a strong Ebionite bias in the Gospel of Lk, in which certainly there is no lessening of Our Lord's supreme Divinity. All that it amounts to is a prominence given to the poor. The identification of the poor with the righteous has not come down to us as a tenet of the Ebionites; it has been ascribed to them from their name. As already stated in the Ascension of Isaiah, the Divinity of the Messiah is strongly asserted. The farther down the stream of history we go more and more clearly do the Ebionite features appear, till by the time when Alcibiades, the follower of Elkasai, appeared in Rome, we have something widely removed from the Ebionism of the Clementines, far as that is from the simple position occupied by the Nazareans.

The Jewish Christians appear to have formed an organization of their own, separate from the church Catholic. The places where they assembled they did not call *ekklēsíai*, "churches," but *sunagōgaí*, "synagogues." If we may believe the Clementine Homilies they had evolved a complete episcopal system for themselves. We, however, must not think that every variation of faith had a separate organization for itself. Strict Jewish ceremonial allowed no Jew to eat with any other not a Jew. The "love-feasts" of the early church implied this eating in common. If gentile Christians were present the Ebionites could not join, hence the need of a separate church. All Jewish Christians who reverenced the law could meet together and partake of the "love-feast," whatever their belief as to the person of Christ. In short, Ebionism was a thing of individuals, whose opinion ran through the whole gamut of faith, from the Nazareans, who differed from the orthodox simply in remaining Jews, to those whose Judaism alone prevented them from becoming followers of Theodotus of Byzantium, and who therefore sank back into pure Judaism.

2. Organization of Ebionites

V. Evidence from Ebionism for the Doctrine of the Primitive Church.—In dealing with this branch of our subject we have to consider that the tendency of those who in the early days wrote against heresy was to exaggerate the difference between the heretics and the orthodox. On the other hand we have to consider the psychological difficulty involved in a person recognizing that anyone whom he daily met, whom he saw eating and sleeping like other men, was more than man, was Divine. This difficulty, great to all, was doubly so to the Jew. Yet again we have to consider what the origin of Christian theology was. It was an attempt to give a reasoned and systematic explanation of the phenomenon of Jesus Christ. Christ's character, His deeds and His claims had to be explained. The orthodox explanation which gradually became more definite as time rolled on was that He was the second person of the Trinity become incarnate, and the purpose of this incarnation that He might save many from their sins. This purpose He accomplished by dying on the cross and rising again. The primitive church owed its theology to Paul and John. Repugnant as much of this was to the Jews, yet the Ebionites, earnest, prejudiced Jews as they were, could not affirm in the presence of the facts of His career that Jesus was merely a man. They had to imagine a Divine influence coming down upon Him at His baptism, setting Him apart from all others. We have no trace of this at first: it stands at the end of a process of degradation of the ideal concerning the person of Christ. It was only when the effect of His personality had somewhat faded that men began to doubt His Divinity. The division of the personality seems to emerge at the same time. The earlier Ebionites, like the rest of the 1st-cent. believers, regarded Christ as one person; only later do they reach the notion of a heavenly aeon separate from Jesus. The Ebionites seem to have held under varying forms a

1. Christology of the Early Church

doctrine of the Trinity, and their holding it is an evidence that the church at large held it, not of course in that definiteness it assumed later, but essentially.

To some extent the same may be said in regard to the Pauline doctrine of redemption. It is to be observed that both writers, he of the *Homilies* as well as the writer of the *Recognitions*, dislike and ignore Paul, even if they do not attempt to pillory him under the image of Simon Magus, as many have thought that they do. What, however, is also to be observed, is that they do not venture to denounce him by name. Paul and his teachings must have been, in the early part of the 2d cent., held in such deep reverence that no one could hope to destroy them by direct assault; the only hope was a flank attack. This reverence for Paul implies the reception of all he taught. All the specially Pauline doctrines of original sin, of redemption through the sacrificial death of Christ, and all the cognate ideas must have been held strongly by the early church or the Ebionites would have denounced Paul in the Clementines by name. Schwegler would argue that Justin Martyr was an Ebionite because he neither mentions nor quotes Paul. To this it may be answered that as the emperors to whom he addressed his apologies were heathens, and Trypho, with whom he had his dialogue, was a Jew, he naturally did not name one whose authority would be valueless to those he was addressing. He is equally silent as to Peter, James and John. If he does not quote Paul there are several indubitable echoes of his phrases and his thoughts.

2. Paulinism of the Early Church

In the face of the recent discoveries made in Egypt one cannot despair of MSS turning up which may throw needed light on this heresy. Were the Gospel according to the Hebrews to be found, or a MS of Hegesippus, we should be in a better position to decide a number of questions.

Literature.—Contemporary writers on Ebionites: Irenaeus; Tertullian; Hippolytus; Origen; Eusebius, III, 27; Epiphanius; Jerome; Justin Martyr (*Trypho*, 47, 48) refers to the Ebionites without naming them.

Ebionite writings: Clementine Homilies; Clementine Recognitions; Clementine Epitomes; Asc Isa; Odes of Solomon.

Modern church historians: Neander, *General History of the Christian Religion and Church;* Schröck, *Kirchengeschichte;* Walch, *Historie der Ketzereien*, I, 95–124; Baur, *Kirchengeschichte*, I, 172–74, and *Dogmengeschichte*, 140–61, and *Christliche Gnosis;* Schwegler, *Nachapostolisches Zeitalter*, 17–198; Ritschl, *Altkatholische Kirche*, 107–271; Matter, *Gnosticisme*, III, 11–28; Harnack, *History of Dogma*, 1–89 ff; Reuss, *Hist. de la Théologie*, I, 115–25; Donaldson, *Christian Literature and Doctrine from the Death of the Apostles to the Nicene Council*, I, 39 ff; Mansel, *Gnostic Heresies*, 123–26; Helgenfeld, *Ketzergeschichte*, 421–46, and *Clementines*.

Articles in theological dictionaries: Smith and Wace; *RE*, 1st, 2d and 3d eds; *Jew Enc;* Holtzman u. Zöpffel; Lightfoot, *Galatians*, Disc. III; Colin Campbell, *Studies in St. Luke.*

J. E. H. Thomson

EBIONITES, GOSPEL OF THE. See Apocryphal Gospels; Ebionism.

EBONY, eb'o-ni (הָבְנִים, *hobhnīm* [pl. only], vocalization uncertain; cf Arab. *ābnūs*): Mentioned (Ezk **27** 15) along with ivory as merchandise of Tyre brought by the men of Dedan. This is the heavy, black, heart-wood of various species of *Diospyros*, natives of Southern India and Ceylon; the best kind is obtained from *D. ebenum*. The sap-wood, being white and valueless, is cut away, but the trunks are sufficiently large to leave blocks of heart-wood 2 ft. in diameter and 10 or more ft. long. Ebony was used by the ancient Egyptians, Greeks and Romans, as well as the Phoenicians, for various purposes; it was frequently inlaid with ivory. In Europe it has been a favorite for cabinet-making down to recent times.

E. W. G. Masterman

EBRON, ē'brun (עֶבְרֹן, *'ebhrōn;* AV wrongly, **Hebron**): A town in the territory of Asher (Josh **19** 28). Probably we should read here **Abdon**, as in Josh **21** 30; 1 Ch **6** 74, the substitution of ר for ד being a common copyist's error. See Abdon.

EBRONAH, ĕ-brō'na: In AV (Nu **33** 34.35) for Abronah, which see.

ECANUS, ĕ-kā'nus: RV Ethanus (q.v).

ECBATANA, ek-bat'a-na (Ezr **6** 2 m). See Achmetha.

Ebony.

ECCE HOMO, ek'sē hō'mō (Ἰδοὺ ὁ ἄνθρωπος, *idoú ho ánthrōpos*, "Behold, the man!" Jn **19** 5): Pilate's statement regarding Jesus during His trial. While the significance of this statement is somewhat debatable, yet there is little doubt, as judged from his attitude and statement immediately following, that Pilate was endeavoring to appeal to the accusers' sympathies and to point out to them the manly qualities of Jesus. The ordinary punctuation which places an exclamation point after "Behold" and a period after "the man" is evidently incorrect if the grammatical structure in the Gr is to be observed, which gives to the second and third words the nominative form, and which therefore admits of a mild exclamation, and therefore of the emphasis upon "the man." Some, however, hold the contrary view and maintain that the utterance was made in a spirit of contempt and ridicule, as much as to say, "Behold here a mere man." See esp. on this view Marcus Dods in *Expositor's Gr Test.* It would seem, however, that the former of the two views would be sustained by the chief facts in the case.

Walter G. Clippinger

ECCLESIASTES, e-klē-zi-as'tēz, or **THE PREACHER** (קֹהֶלֶת, *ḳōheleth;* Ἐκκλησιαστής, *Ekklēsiastḗs*, perhaps "member of assembly"; see below):

Reading this book one soon becomes aware that it is a discussion of certain difficult problems of human life. It begins with a title (**1** 1), followed by a preface (vs 2–11). It has a formal conclusion (**12** 8–13). Between the preface and the conclusion the body of the book is made up of materials of two kinds—first a series of "I" sections, sections uttered in the 1st per. sing., a record of a personal experience; and second, an alternating series of gnomic sections, sections made up of proverbs (say **4** 5.6.9–12; **5** 1–12; **7** 1–14.16–22; **8** 1–8; **9** 7–10; **10** 1–4; **10** 8—**12** 7). These may be called the "thou" sections, as most of them have the pronoun of the 2d per. sing. The idea of the vanity of all things characterizes the record of experience, but it also appears in the "thou" sections (e.g. **9** 9). On the other hand the proverb element is not wholly lacking in the "I" sections (e.g. **4** 1–3).

1. Structure of the Book

In the preface the speaker lays down the proposition that all things are unreal, and that the results of human effort are illusive (**1** 2.3). Human generations, day and night, the wind, the streams, are alike the repetition of an unending round (vs 4–7). The same holds in regard to all human study and thinking (vs 8–11). The speaker shows familiarity with the phenomena which we think of as those of natural law, of the persistence of force, but he thinks of them in the main as monotonously limiting human experience. Nothing is new. All effort of Nature or of man is the doing again of something which has already been done.

2. The Contents

After the preface the speaker introduces himself, and recounts his experiences. At the outset he had a noble ambition for wisdom and discipline, but all he attained to was unreality and perplexity of mind (vs 12–18). This is equally the meaning of the text, whether we translate "vanity and vexation of spirit" or "vanity and a striving after wind," ("emptiness, and struggling for breath"), though the first of these two tr[s] is the better grounded.

Finding no adequate satisfaction in the pursuits of the scholar and thinker, taken by themselves, he seeks to combine these with the pursuit of agreeable sensations—alike those which come from luxury and those which come from activity and enterprise and achievement (**2** 1–12). No one could be in better shape than he for making this experiment, but again he only attains to unreality and perplexity of spirit. He says to himself that at least it is in itself profitable to be a wise man rather than a fool, but his comfort is impaired by the fact that both alike are mortal (vs 13–17). He finds little reassurance in the idea of laboring for the benefit of posterity; posterity is often not worthy (vs 18–21). One may toil unremittingly, but what is the use (vs 22.23)?

He does not find himself helped by bringing God into the problem. 'It is no good for a man that he should eat and drink and make his soul see good in his toil' (vs 24–26, as most naturally translated), even if he thinks of it as the gift of God; for how can one be sure that the gift of God is anything but luck? He sees, however, that it is not just to dismiss thus lightly the idea of God as a factor in the problem. It is true that there is a time for everything, and that everything is "beautiful in its time." It is also true that ideas of infinity are in men's minds, ideas which they can neither get rid of nor fully comprehend (**3** 1–18). Here are tokens of God, who has established an infinite order. If we understood His ways better, that might unravel our perplexities. And if God is, immortality may be, and the solution of our problems may lie in that direction. For a moment it looks as if the speaker were coming out into the light, but doubt resumes its hold upon him. He asks himself, "Who knoweth?" and he settles back into the darkness. He has previously decided that for a man to "eat and drink, and make his soul enjoy good" is not worth while; and now he reaches the conclusion that, unsatisfactory as this is, there is nothing better (vs 19–22).

And so the record of experiences continues, hopeful passages alternating with pessimistic passages. After a while the agnosticism and pessimism recede somewhat, and the hopeful passages become more positive. Even though "the poor man's wisdom is despised," the speaker says, "the words of the wise heard in quiet are better than the cry of him that ruleth among fools" (**9** 17). He says "Surely I know that it shall be well with them that fear God" (**8** 12), no matter how strongly appearances may indicate the contrary.

The gnomic sections are mostly free from agnosticism and pessimism. The book as a whole sums itself up in the conclusion, "Fear God, and keep his commandments" (**12** 13).

Of course the agnostic and pessimistic utterances in Eccl are to be regarded as the presentation of one side of an argument. Disconnect them and they are no part of the moral and religious teaching of the book, except in an indirect way. At no point should we be justified in thinking of the author as really doubting in regard to God or moral obligation. He delineates for us a soul in the toils of mental and spiritual conflict. It is a delineation which may serve for warning, and which is in other ways wholesomely instructive; and in the outcome of it, it is full of encouragement.

In some passages the speaker in Eccl has in mind the solution of the problems of life which we are accustomed to call Epicurean (e.g. **5** 18–20; **7** 16. 17; **8** 15; but not **2** 24)—the solution which consists in avoiding extremes, and in getting from life as many agreeable sensations as possible; but it is not correct to say that he advocates this philosophy. He rather presents it as an alternative.

His conclusion is the important part of his reasoning. All things are vanity. Everything passes away. Yet (he says) it is better to read and use good words than bad words. Therefore because the Great Teacher is wise, he ever teaches the people knowledge, and in so doing he ever seeks *good words*, acceptable words, upright words, words of truth. "The words of the wise are as goads; and as nails well fastened" ("clinched at the back") (**12** 11). Such are the words of all the great masters. So (he ends) my son, be warned! There are many books in this world. Choose good ones. And his conclusion is: Reverence the Mighty Spirit. Keep to good principles. That is the whole duty of man. For everything at last becomes clear; and "good" stands out clearly from "evil."

We have noticed that our book has "I" sections and "thou" sections. Certainly these are structural marks, but as such they are capable of being interpreted in various ways. Partitional hypotheses can easily be formed, and perhaps there is no great objection to them; but there are no phenomena which cannot be accounted for by the hypothesis that we have here just the work of one author, who sometimes quotes proverbial utterances, either his own or those of other men. As proving the integrity of the book three points present themselves. First, in some cases (e.g. **7** 14*b*–16) the experience matter and the gnomic matter are closely combined in sense and in grammatical construction. Second, it is possible to interpret all the gnomic sections as a part of the continuous argument. Third, if we so interpret them the book is a unit, the argument moving forward con-

3. Composite Authorship?

tinuously out of the speculative into the practical, and out of the darkness into the light.

The speaker in Eccl calls himself *Ḳōheleth* (**1** 1.2.12 and other places), rendered "the Preacher" in the EV. The word does not occur elsewhere, although it is from a stem that is in common use. Apparently it has been coined for a purpose by the author of Eccl. In form it is a fem. participle, though it denotes a man. This is best explained as a case of the using of an abstract expression for a concrete, as when in Eng. we say "Your Honor," "Your Majesty." The other words of the stem are used of people gathering in assemblies, and the current explanation is to the effect that Koheleth is a person who draws an audience whom he may address. To this there are two objections: First, the participle is intransitive; its natural implication is that of a person who participates in an assembly, not of one who causes the participants to assemble. Second, the assembly distinctively indicated by the words of this stem is the official assembly for the transaction of public business. Worked out on this basis Koheleth seems to mean citizenship, or concretely, a citizen—a citizen of such respectability that he is entitled to participate in public assemblies. It is in the character of citizen-king that the speaker in Eccl relates his experiences and presents his ideas.

4. Koheleth

This word for "assembly" and its cognates are in the Gr often tr[d] by *ekklēsia* and its cognates (e.g. Dt **4** 10; **9** 10; Jgs **20** 2; **21** 5.8). So we are not surprised to find *Ḳōheleth* rendered by the Gr *Ekklēsiastēs*, and this Latinized into Ecclesiastes.

The speaker in Eccl speaks not only in the character of Koheleth, but in that of "the son of David, king in Jerus" (**1** 1). So far as this clause is concerned the king in question might be either Solomon or any other king of the dynasty, or might be a composite or an ideal king. He is represented (**1** 12—**2** 11) as "king over Israel," and as distinguished for wisdom, for his luxuries, for his great enterprises in building and in business. These marks fit Solomon better than any other king of the dynasty, unless possibly Uzziah. Possibly it is not absurd to apply to Solomon even the phrase "all that were before me over Jerus," or "in Jerus" (**1** 16; **2** 7.9; cf 1 Ch **29** 25; 1 K **3** 12; 2 Ch **1** 12). It is safer, however, to use an alternative statement. The speaker in Eccl is either Solomon or some other actual or composite or ideal king of the dynasty of David.

5. "King in Jerusalem"

If it were agreed that Solomon is the citizen king who, in Eccl, is represented as speaking, that would not be the same thing as agreeing that Solomon is the author of the book. No one thinks that Sir Galahad is the author of Tennyson's poem of that name. Koheleth the king is the character into whose mouth the author of Ecclesiastes puts the utterances which he wishes to present, but it does not follow that the author is himself Koheleth.

6. Date and Authorship

The statement is often made that Jewish tradition attributes the writing of Eccl to Solomon; but can anyone cite any relatively early tradition to this effect? Is this alleged tradition anything else than the confusing of the author with the character whom he has sketched? The well-known classic tradition in *Bābhā' Bathrā'* attributes Eccl to "Hezekiah and his company," not to Solomon. And the tradition which is represented by the order in which the books occur in the Heb Bibles seems to place it still later. Concerning this tradition two facts are to be noted: First, it classes Eccl with the 5 miscellaneous books (Cant, Ruth, Lam, Eccl, Est) known as the five *m^eghillōth*, the five Rolls. Second, in the count of books which makes the number 22 or 24 it classes Eccl as one of the last 5 books (Eccl, Est, Dan, Ezr-Neh, 1 and 2 Ch). That the men who made this arrangement regarded the books of this group as the latest in the Bible is a natural inference.

This agrees with the internal marks which constitute the principal evidence we have on this point. The grammatical character and the vocabulary of Eccl are exceptionally peculiar, and they strongly indicate that the book was written in the same literary period with these other latest books of the OT. The true date is not much earlier or later than 400 BC (see CHRONICLES), though many place it a cent. or a cent. and a half later. Details concerning these phenomena may be found in Driver's *Introduction* or other Introductions, or in commentaries. Only a few of the points will be given here, with barely enough illustrative instances to render the points intelligible.

7. Linguistic Peculiarities

In Eccl the syntax of the vb. is peculiar. The imperfect with *waw* consecutive, the ordinary Heb narrative tense, occurs—for example, "And I applied my heart" (**1** 17)—but it is rare. The narrator habitually uses the perfect with *waw* (e.g. **1** 13; **2** 11.12.14.15 *bis*. 17). In any Eng. book we should find it very noticeable if the author were in the habit of using the progressive form of the vb. instead of the ordinary form—if instead of saying "And I applied my heart" he should say "And I was applying my heart," "And I was looking on all the works," "And I was turning" (**1** 13; **2** 11.12), and so on. Another marked peculiarity is the frequent repeating of the pronoun along with the vb.: 'I said in my heart, even I'; 'And I was hating, even I, all my labor' (**2** 1.18 and continually). The use of the pronoun as copula is abnormally common in Eccl as compared with other parts of the Heb Bible (e.g. **4** 2). The abbreviated form of the relative pronoun is much used instead of the full form, and in both forms the pronoun is used disproportionately often as a conjunction. In these and many similar phenomena the Heb of Eccl is affiliated with that of the later times.

The vocabulary presents phenomena that have the same bearing. Words of the stem *tāḳan* appear in Eccl (**1** 15; **7** 13; **12** 9) and in the Aram. of Dnl (**4** 36), and not elsewhere in the Bible; they are frequent in the Talm. Words of the stem *zāman* (**3** 1) are used only in Eccl, Ezr, Neh, Dnl, Est. Words of the stem *shālaṭ*, the stem whence comes our word "sultan," are frequent in Eccl—words which are used elsewhere only in the avowedly post-exilian books and in Gen **42** 6, though a different word of this stem appears in the history of the time of David. Only in Eccl and Est are found the vb. *kāshēr*, "to be correct" (whence the modern Jewish *kosher*) and its derivative *kishrōn*. The Pers word *pardēṣ*, "park" (**2** 5), occurs elsewhere only in Neh and Cant, and the Pers word *pithgām*, "official decision" or "record" (**8** 11), only in Est **1** 20, and in the Aram. parts of Ezr and Dnl. Eccl also abounds in late words formed from earlier stems—for example, *ṣekhel* and *ṣikh^elūth*, "folly" (**10** 6; **2** 3, et al.); or *m^edhīnāh*, "province" (**5** 8), frequent in the latest books, but elsewhere found only in one passage in 1 K (**20** 14.15.17.19). Esp. common are new derivatives that end in *n*, for example, *yithrōn*, "profit"; *'inyān*, "travail"; *ḥeṣrōn*, "that which is missing"; *ra'yōn*, "vexation" (**1** 3.13.15.17 and often). To these add instances of old words used in new meanings, and the various other groups of phenomena that are usual in such cases. No parts of the book are free from them.

The arguments for a later date than that which has been assigned are inconclusive. The Heb of

Eccl is more like the language of the Talmuds than is that of the Chronicler or Dnl or even Est; but if one infer that Eccl is therefore later than the others the inference will prove to be in various ways embarrassing. The differences are better accounted for by the fact that Eccl belongs to a different type of lit. from the others.

8. Certain Inconclusive Arguments

Various passages have local color (e.g. **11** 1), or make the impression of being allusions to specific events (e.g. **4** 13–16; **6** 2.3; **9** 13–18), but the difficulty lies in locating the events. Dr. Kleinert argues plausibly for the writing of the book in Egypt in the time of the Ptolemies, but other equally probable hypotheses might be devised.

It is alleged that Eccl copies from Ecclus, but it is more probable that the latter copied from the former. It is alleged that the Wisd controverts Eccl; if it does, that does not prove that the two are contemporary. It is alleged that the writer is familiar with the philosophy of Epicurus, and therefore must have lived later than Epicurus, who died 270 BC, or even later than Lucretius of the 1st cent. BC. If there were proof that this was a case of borrowing, Epicurus or Lucretius might have been the borrowers; but there is no such proof; the selfishness which constitutes the nucleus of Epicureanism has exhibited itself in human lit. from the beginning. The strong resemblances between Eccl and Omar Khayyám have no weight to prove that the Heb author was later than the Pers. Eccl presents a perfectly distinct doctrine of immortality, whether it affirms the doctrine or not; but that proves a relatively early date for the doctrine, rather than a late date for Eccl. At every point the marks of Eccl are those of the Pers period, not of the Gr.

9. Canonicity

In the early Christian cents., as in all the cents. since, there have been disputes concerning the canonicity of Eccl. It was not questioned that Eccl belonged to the canon as traditionally handed down. No question of admitting it to the canon was raised. But it was challenged because of the agnostic quality of some of its contents, and, every time, on close examination, the challenge was decided in its favor.

Literature.—There are volumes on Eccl in all the great commentaries, and treatments of it in the volumes on Introduction. A few of the many separate commentaries are those of Moses Stuart, Andover, 1864; H. Grätz, Leipzig, 1871; G. Wildeboer, Tübingen, 1898; E. H. Plumptre, Cambridge, 1881. Other works are those of J. F. Genung, *Eccl*, and *Omar Khayyám*, 1901, *Words of Koheleth*, 1904, and *The Hebrew Lit. of Wisdom in the Light of Today*, 1906; C. H. H. Wright, *Book of Koheleth*, 1883; S. Schiffer, *Das Buch Coheleth nach Talmud und Midrasch*, 1885; A. H. McNeile, *Intro to Eccl*, New York, 1904.

Willis J. Beecher

ECCLESIASTICUS, e-klē-zi-as′ti-kus. See Sirach.

ECLIPSE, ĕ-klips′. See Astronomy.

ED (עֵד, *ʿēdh*, "witness"): The name of the altar erected by the trans-Jordanic tribes upon finally taking possession of Gilead (Josh **22** 10.11.34); probably E. of the Jordan opposite Jericho. But neither the MT nor the LXX contained the word. Both the AV and RV, however, insert the word on the authority of a few MSS. It has been suggested that it is the final *ʿēdh* in *Galʿēdh*, the name given by Laban and Jacob to the memorial heap of stones erected by them in the vicinity (Gen **31** 47.48). According to the MT, the name of the altar is the entire sentence: "It is a witness between us that Jeh is God." The opposition of the ten tribes to the erection of this altar was on the score that it was built after the pattern of the great altar of burnt offering (Josh **22** 11.29), which was a horned altar forbidden in ordinary lay sacrifice. There is in it, therefore, no indication of a general opposition to lay sacrifices on altars of earth or unhewn stone (see Wiener, *EPC*, 198).

George Frederick Wright

EDAR, ē′där. See Eder.

EDDIAS, ed-ī′as. See Ieddias.

EDDINUS, ed′i-nus (B, **Ἐδδεινοῦς**, *Eddeinoús*, A, **Ἐδδινοῦς**, *Eddinoús*): One of the "holy singers" at Josiah's Passover (1 Esd **1** 15). AV reads here **Jeduthun**, the corresponding name in the ‖ passage (2 Ch **35** 15).

EDEN, ē′d'n (עֵדֶן, *ʿēdhen*, "delight"; **Ἐδέμ**, *Édem*):

(1) The land in which "Jeh God planted a garden," where upon his creation "he put the man whom he had formed" (Gen **2** 8). In the Assyr inscriptions *ìdinu* (Accadian *êdin*) means "plain" and it is from this that the Bib. word is probably derived. Following are the references to Eden in the Bible, aside from those in Gen **2** and **3**: Gen **4** 16; Isa **51** 3; Ezk **28** 13; **31** 9.16.18; **36** 35; Joel **2** 3. The Garden of Eden is said to be "eastward, in Eden" (Gen **2** 8); where the vegetation was luxurious (**2** 9) and the fig tree indigenous (**3** 7), and where it was watered by irrigation. All kinds of animals, including cattle, beasts of the field and birds, were found there (**2** 19.20). Moreover the climate was such that clothing was not needed for warmth. It is not surprising, therefore, that the pl. of the word has the meaning "delights," and that Eden has been supposed to mean the land of delights, and that the word became a synonym for Paradise.

The location of Eden is in part to be determined from the description already given. It must be where there is a climate adapted to the production of fruit trees and of animals capable of domestication, and in general to the existence of man in his primitive condition. In particular, its location is supposed to be determined by the statements regarding the rivers coursing through it and surrounding it. There is a river (*nāhār*) (Gen **2** 10) which was parted and became four heads (*roʾshīm*), a word which (Jgs **8** 16; Job **1** 17) designates main detachments into which an army is divided, and therefore would more properly signify branches than heads, permitting Jos and others to interpret the river as referring to the ocean, which by the Greeks was spoken of as the river (*ōkeanós*) surrounding the world. According to Jos, the Ganges, the Tigris, the Euphrates and the Nile are the four rivers, being but branches of this one river. Moreover it is contended by some, with much show of reason, that the word *perāth* trd Euphrates is a more general term, signifying "the broad" or "deep" river, and so may here refer to some other stream than the Euphrates, possibly to a river in some other region whose name is perpetuated in the present Euphrates, as "the Thames" of New England perpetuates the memory of the Thames of Old England. In ancient times there was a river Phrath in Persia, and perhaps two. It is doubtful whether the phrase "eastward, in Eden" refers to the position with reference to the writer or simply with reference to Eden itself. So far as that phrase is concerned, therefore, speculation is left free to range over the whole earth, and this it has done.

1. Central Asia

Columbus when passing the mouth of the Orinoco surmised that its waters came down from the Garden of Eden. It is fair to say, however, that he supposed himself to be upon the E. coast of Asia. The traditions of its location somewhere in Central Asia are numerous and persistent. Naturalists have, with Quatrefages, pretty generally fixed upon the portion of Central Asia stretching E. from the Pamir, often referred to as the roof of the world, and from which flow four great rivers—the Indus, the Tarim, the Sur Daria (Jaxartes), and the Amu Daria (Oxus)—as the original cradle of mankind. This conclusion has been arrived at from the fact that at the present time the three fundamental types of the races of mankind are grouped about this region. The Negro races are, indeed, in general far removed from the location, but still fragments of them both pure and mixed are found in various localities both in the interior and on the seashore and adjacent islands where they would naturally radiate from this center, while the yellow and the white races here meet at the present time in close contact. In the words of Quatrefages, "No other region of the globe presents a similar union of extreme human types distributed round a common center" (*The Human Species*, 176).

Philology, also, points to this same conclusion. On the E. are the monosyllabic languages, on the N. the polysyllabic or agglutinative languages, and on the W. and S. the inflectional or Aryan languages, of which the Sanskrit is an example, being closely allied to nearly all the languages of Europe. Moreover, it is to this center that we trace the origin of nearly all our domesticated plants and animals. Naturally, therefore, the same high authority writes, "There we are inclined to say the first human beings appeared and multiplied till the populations overflowed as from a bowl and spread themselves in waves in every direction" (ib, 177). With this conclusion, as already said, a large number of most eminent authorities agree. But it should be noted that if, as we believe, there was a universal destruction of antediluvian man, the center of dispersion had in view by these naturalists and archaeologists would be that from the time of Noah, and so would not refer to the Eden from which Adam and Eve were driven. The same may be said of Haeckel's theory that man originated in a submerged continent within the area of the Indian Ocean.

Dr. William F. Warren has with prodigious learning attempted to show that the original Eden was at the North Pole, a theory which has too many considerations in its support to be cast aside unceremoniously, for it certainly is true that in preglacial times a warm climate surrounded the North Pole in all the lands which have been explored. In Northern Greenland and in Spitzbergen abundant remains of fossil plants show that during the middle of the Tertiary period the whole circumpolar region was characterized by a climate similar to that prevailing at the present time in Southern Europe, Japan, and the southern United States (see Asa Gray's lectures on "Forest Geography and Archaeology" in the *American Journal of Science*, CXVI, 85–94, 183–96, and Wright, *Ice Age in North America*, 5th ed, ch xvii). But as the latest discoveries have shown that there is no land within several hundred miles of the North Pole, Dr. Warren's theory, if maintained at all, will have to be modified so as to place Eden at a considerable distance from the actual pole. Furthermore, his theory would involve the existence of "Tertiary man," and thus extend his chronology to an incredible extent, even though with Professor Green (see ANTEDILUVIANS) we are permitted to consider the genealogical table of Gen **5** as sufficiently elastic to accommodate itself to any facts which may be discovered.

2. The North Pole

Much also can be said in favor of identifying Eden with Armenia, for it is here that the Tigris and Euphrates have their origin, while two others, the Aras (Araxes) emptying into the Caspian Sea and the Choruk (thought by some to be the Phasis) emptying into the Black Sea, would represent the Gihon and the Pishon. Havilah would then be identified with Colchis, famous for its golden sands. But Cush is difficult to find in that region; while these four rivers could by no possibility be regarded as branches of one parent stream.

3. Armenia

Two theories locate Eden in the Euphrates valley. Of these the first would place it near the head of the Pers Gulf where the Tigris and Euphrates after their junction form the *Shatt el-'Arab* which bifurcates into the eastern and the western arm before reaching the Gulf. Calvin considered the Pishon to be the eastern arm and the Gihon the western arm. Other more recent authorities modify the theory by supposing that Gihon and Pishon are represented by the Karum and the Kerkhah rivers which come into the *Shatt el-'Arab* from the east. The most plausible objection to this theory is that the Bib. account represents all these branches as down stream from the main river, whereas this theory supposes that two of them at least are up stream. This objection has been ingeniously met by calling attention to the fact that 2,000 years before Christ the Pers Gulf extended up as far as Eridu, 100 miles above the present mouth of the river, and that the Tigris and the Euphrates then entered the head of the Gulf through separate channels, the enormous amount of silt brought down by the streams having converted so much of the valley into dry land. In consequence of the tides which extend up to the head of the Gulf, the current of all these streams would be turned up stream periodically, and so account for the Bib. statement. In this case the river (*nāhār*) would be represented by the Pers Gulf itself, which was indeed called by the Babylonians *nar marratum*, "the bitter river." This theory is further supported by the fact that according to the cuneiform inscriptions Eridu was reputed to have in its neighborhood a garden, "a holy place," in which there grew a sacred palm tree. This "tree of life" appears frequently upon the inscriptions with two guardian spirits standing on either side.

4. Babylonia

The other theory, advocated with great ability by Friedrich Delitzsch, places Eden just above the site of ancient Babylon, where the Tigris and Euphrates approach to within a short distance of one another and where the country is intersected by numerous irrigating streams which put off from the Euphrates and flow into the Tigris, whose level is here considerably lower than that of the Euphrates —the situation being somewhat such as it is at New Orleans where the Mississippi River puts off numerous streams which empty into Lake Pontchartrain. Delitzsch supposes the *Shatt el-Nil*, which flows eastward into the Tigris, to be the Gihon, and the Pallacopas, flowing on the W. side of the Euphrates through a region producing gold, to be the Pishon. The chief difficulties attending this theory pertain to the identification of the Pishon with the Pallacopas, and the location of Havilah on its banks. There is difficulty, also, in all these theories in the identification of Cush (Ethiopia), later associated with the country from which the Nile emerges, thus giving countenance to the belief of Jos and many others that that river represented the Gihon. If we are compelled to choose between these theories it would seem that the one which locates Eden near the head of the Pers Gulf combines the greater number of probabilities of every kind.

(2) A Levite of the time of Hezekiah (2 Ch **29** 12; **31** 15).

LITERATURE.—Dawson, *Modern Science in Bible Lands*; Friedrich Delitzsch, *Wo lag das Paradies?* (1881); Sayce, *HCM*, 95 ff; Hommel, *Anc. Heb Tradition*, 314; William F. Warren, *Paradise Found*, 1885.

GEORGE FREDERICK WRIGHT

EDEN, CHILDREN OF. See CHILDREN OF EDEN.

EDEN, HOUSE OF. See AVEN; BETH-EDEN; CHILDREN OF EDEN.

EDER, ē'dēr (עֵדֶר, *'ēdher*, "flock"):

(1) One of the "uttermost cities" of Judah in the Negeb ("South") near the border of Edom (Josh **15** 21), possibly *Kh. el 'Adar*, 5 miles S. of Gaza, but probably this is too far west.

(2) *Eder* (AV **Edar**) or better Migdal Eder, מִגְדַּל־עֵדֶר, *mighdal 'ēdher*, "the tower of the flock"; Γάδερ, *Gáder*. After Rachel died and was buried "in the way to Ephrath (the same is Bethlehem) . . . . Israel journeyed, and spread his tent beyond the tower of Eder" (Gen **35** 19.21). In ver 27 he is described as proceeding to Hebron. This "tower of the flock," which may have been only a tower and no town, must therefore be looked for between Bethlehem and Hebron. Jerome says that it was one Rom mile from Bethlehem. In the LXX, however, vs 16 and 21 are transposed, which suggests that there may have been a tradition that Migdal Eder was between Bethel and Bethlehem. There must have been many such towers for guarding flocks against robbers. Cf "tower of the watchman" (2 K **18** 8, etc). The phrase "Migdal Eder" occurs in Mic **4** 8 where Jerus is compared to such a tower. E. W. G. MASTERMAN

EDER, ē'dēr (עֵדֶר, *'ēdher*, "flock")

(1) A Merarite Levite in the days of David (1 Ch **23** 23; **24** 30); son of Mushi.

(2) A Benjamite (1 Ch **8** 15, AV "Ader").

EDES, ē'dēz: RV EDOS (q.v.).

EDGE, ej: Very frequently occurs in the phrase "the edge of the sword" (Josh **10** 28, et al.) from the Heb פֶּה, *peh*, "lip," or שָׂפָה, *sāphāh*, "lip." Ex **28** 7 and **39** 4 read "ends," from קָצָה, *ḳāçāh*, "end" (AV "edge"), and Josh **13** 27 has "uttermost part" for the same Heb word (AV "edge"). In Jer **31** 29 and Ezk **18** 2, "The children's teeth are *set on edge*" (קָהָה, *ḳāhāh*, "to be blunt"), i.e. set hard one against another.

EDIFICATION, ed-i-fi-kā'shun, **EDIFY,** ed'i-fī: The Gr words οἰκοδομέω, *oikodoméō*, "to build," οἰκοδομή, *oikodomḗ*, "the act of building," are used both lit. and fig. in the NT; "edify," "edifying," "edification," are the tr of AV in some 20 passages, all in the **fig.** sense of the promotion of growth in Christian character. RV in 2 Cor **10** 8; **13** 10; Eph **4** 12.16; 1 Thess **5** 11 renders "build up," "building up," making the force of the figure clearer to the Eng. reader. In 1 Tim **1** 4 the Gr text followed by RV has οἰκονομία, *oikonomía*, "dispensation," instead of οἰκοδομία, *oikodomía*, "edifying" (AV). F. K. FARR

EDNA, ed'na (Ἔδνα, *Édna*): Wife of Raguel and mother of Sarah who married Tobias (Tob **7** 2, etc; **10** 12; **11** 1). E. in Heb means "pleasure" and corresponds to Lat *Anna*.

EDOM, ē'dum, **EDOMITES,** ē'dum-īts (אֱדֹם, *'ĕdhōm*, "red"; **Ἐδώμ**, *Edṓm*): The boundaries of Edom may be traced with some approach to accuracy. On the E. of the 'Arabah the northern border ran from the Dead Sea, and was marked by *Wādy el-Ḳurāḥī*, or *Wādy el-Ḥasā*. On the E. it marched with the desert. The southern border ran by Elath and Ezion-geber (Dt **2** 8). On the W. of the 'Arabah the north boundary of Edom is determined by the south border of Israel, as indicated in Nu **34** 3 f: a line running from the Salt Sea southward of the Ascent of Akrabbim to Zin and Kadesh-barnea. This last, we are told, lay in the "uttermost" of the border of Edom (Nu **20** 16). The line may be generally indicated by the course of *Wādy el-Fiḳrah*. How much of the uplands W. of the 'Arabah southward to the Gulf of 'Aḳaba was included in Edom it is impossible to say.

1. Boundaries

The land thus indicated varies greatly in character and features. S. of the Dead Sea in the bottom of the valley we have first the stretch of salt marsh land called *es-Sebkha;* then, beyond the line of white cliffs that crosses the valley diagonally from N.W. to S.E., a broad depression strewn with stones and sandhills, the débris of an old sea bottom, rises gradually, and 60 miles to the S. reaches a height of about 700 ft. above the level of the Red Sea, 2,000 ft. above that of the Dead Sea. From this point it sinks until it reaches the shore of the Gulf of 'Aḳaba, 45 miles farther S. The whole depression is known today as *Wādy el-'Arabah* (cf Heb *hā-'ărābhāh*, Dt **2** 8 RV, etc). On either side the mountains rise steeply from the valley, their edges carved into many fantastic shapes by the deep wadys that break down from the interior (see ARABAH). The northern part of the plateau on the W. forms the spacious grazing ground of the *'Azāzimeh* Arabs. The mountains rise to a height of from about 1,500 ft. to a little over 2,000 ft. This district was traversed by the ancient caravan road to South Pal; and along the eastern side traces of the former civilization are still to be seen. The desert region to the S. is higher, reaching to as much as 2,600 ft. The mountain range E. of the 'Arabah is generally higher in the S. than in the N. *Jebel Harūn*, beside Petra, is 4,780 ft. above sea-level; while E. of 'Aḳaba, *Jebel el-Ḥismā* may be as much as 5,900 ft. in height. Limestone, porphyry and Nubian sandstone are the prevailing formation; but volcanic rocks are also found. The range consists mainly of rough rocky heights with many almost inaccessible peaks separated by deep gorges. But there are also breadths of fertile land where wheat, grapes, figs, pomegranates and olives are grown to advantage. The northern district is known today by the name *el-Jebāl*, corresponding to the ancient Gebal. Seir is the name applied to the eastern range in Gen **36** 8; Dt **2** 1.5; 2 Ch **20** 23. It is also called Edom, and the Mount of Esau (Ob vs 8 f). Seir, however, is used for the western highlands in Dt **33** 2. This seems to be its meaning also in Jgs **5** 4, where it appears as the equivalent of "the field of Edom." With this same phrase, however, in Gen **32** 3 it may more fitly apply to the eastern range. See illustration under DESERT.

2. Character and Features

The name Edom, "red," may have been derived from the red sandstone cliffs characteristic of the country. It was applied to Esau because of the color of his skin (Gen **25** 25), or from the color of the pottage for which he sold his birthright (ver 30). In Gen **36** 8 Esau is equated with Edom as dwelling in Mt. Seir; and he is described as the father of Edom (ver 9, Heb). The name however is probably much older. It may be traced in the records of the Twelfth Dynasty in Egypt. In the Am Tab (Brit Mus No. 64) Udumu, or Edom, is named; and in Assyr inscriptions the name Udumu occurs of a city and of a country. Egyp records, Pharaoh of the Exodus, contain request of Edomites to pasture their flocks in Succoth (Papyrus Anastasia; Mueller, *Asien und Europa*, 136).

3. Origin of Name

The children of Esau are said to have "destroyed" the Horites who dwelt in Seir before them (Gen **14**

6; Dt **2** 22). This only means that the Horites were subdued. Esau married the daughter of Anah, a Horite (Gen **36** 20—in ver 2 he is called a Hivite); and the lists in this chapter show that the races intermingled. The Horite government was in the hands of "dukes" (Gen **36** 29 f, RV "chiefs"). They were succeeded by dukes of the house of Esau (vs 40 ff). This form of government gave way to that of an elective monarchy (vs 31 ff); and this had existed some time before Israel left the wilderness. The then reigning king would not permit Israel to pass through the land (Nu **20** 14 ff; **21** 4). Israel was forbidden to "abhor an Edomite," on the ground that he was a brother; and children of the third generation might enter the assembly of the Lord (Dt **23** 7 f). War with Edom was out of the question.

4. History

Some thirty years after the Exodus, Ramses III "smote the people of Seir." The Israelites could not have been far off. We first hear of war between Israel and Edom under Saul (1 S **14** 47). David prosecuted the war with terrific energy, slaying 18,000 Edomites (so read instead of "Syrians") in the Valley of Salt (2 S **8** 13 f); Joab remaining for six months in the country, which was garrisoned by Israelites, "until he had cut off every male in Edom" (1 K **11** 15 f). Hadad of the blood royal of Edom escaped to Egypt, and later became a source of trouble to Solomon (vs 14 ff.25). The conquest of Edom opened to Israel the ports of the Red Sea, whence the expeditions of Solomon and Jehoshaphat set out. In Jehoshaphat's time the king is called a "deputy" (**22** 47). Its king acknowledged the supremacy of Judah (2 K **3** 9, etc). Under Jehoram son of Jehoshaphat, Edom revolted. Jehoram defeated them at Zair, but was unable to quell the rebellion (**8** 20 ff). Amaziah invaded the country, slew 10,000 in the Valley of Salt, and took Sela which he named Joktheel (**14** 7). Uzziah restored the Edomite port of Elath (**14** 22). In the Syrian war Rezin regained Elath for Syria, and cast out the Jews. It was then permanently occupied by Syrians—here also probably we should read Edomites (**16** 6). From the cuneiform inscriptions we learn that when Tiglath-pileser subdued Rezin, among the kings from whom he received homage at Damascus was Qaus-malaka of Edom (736 BC). Later Malik-ram paid homage to Sennacherib. To Ezarhaddon also they were compelled to render service. They gave what help they could to Nebuchadnezzar, and exulted in the destruction of Jerus, stirring the bitterest indignation in the hearts of the Jews (Lam **4** 21; Ezk **25** 12; **35** 3 ff; Ob vs 10 ff). The Edomites pressed into the now empty lands in the S. of Judah. In 300 BC Mt. Seir with its capital Petra fell into the hands of the Nabataeans. West of the 'Arabah the country they occupied came to be known by the Gr name Idumaea, and the people as Idumaeans. Hebron, their chief city, was taken by Judas Maccabaeus in 165 BC (1 Macc **4** 29.61; **5** 65). In 126 BC the country was subdued by John Hyrcanus, who compelled the people to become Jews and to submit to circumcision. Antipater, governor of Idumaea, was made procurator of Judaea, Samaria and Galilee by Julius Caesar. He paved the way to the throne for his son Herod the Great. With the fall of Judah under the Romans, Idumaea disappears from history.

5. Idumaea and the Idumaeans

The names of several Edomite deities are known: Hadad, Qaus, Kozé, and, possibly, Edom; but of the religion of Edom we are without information. The language differed little from Heb.

W. Ewing

EDOS, ē′dos (Ἠδαΐς, *Ēdaïs;* AV **Edes**): One who agreed to put away his foreign wife (1 Esd **9** 35); called Iddo, AV "Jadan," in Ezr **10** 43.

EDREI, ed′rē-ī (אֶדְרֶעִי, *'edhre'ī;* Ἐδράειν, *Edráein*):

(1) One of the cities of Og, not far from Ashtaroth, where the power of his kingdom received its deathblow from the invading Israelites (Josh **12** 4; Nu **21** 33 ff, etc). It seems to mark the western limit of Bashan as against Salecah on the E. (Dt **3** 10). It was given to Machir, son of Manasseh (Josh **13** 31). *Onom* places it 24 Rom miles from Bostra. The most probable identification is with *Der'ah,* a town of between 4,000 and 5,000 inhabitants, on the southern lip of *Wādy Zeideh,* about 29 miles as the crow flies E. of the Sea of Galilee. It is the center of an exceedingly fruitful district. The accumulated rubbish in the town covers many remains of antiquity. It is, however, chiefly remarkable for the extraordinary subterranean city, as yet only partially explored, cut in the rock under the town. This is certainly very ancient, and was doubtless used by the inhabitants as a refuge in times of stress and peril. For a description see Schumacher, *Across the Jordan,* 121 ff.

(2) A place not identified, between Kedesh and En-hazor (Josh **19** 37). W. Ewing

EDUCATION, ed-ū-kā′shun:

I. Education Defined.—By education we understand the sum total of those processes whereby society transmits from one generation to the next its accumulated social, intellectual and religious experience and heritage. In part these processes are informal and incidental, arising from participation in certain forms of social life and activity which exist on their own account and not for the sake of their educative influence upon the rising generation. The more formal educative processes are designed (1) to give the immature members of society a mastery over the symbols and technique of civilization, including language (reading and writing), the arts, the sciences, and religion, and (2) to enlarge the fund of individual and community knowledge beyond the measure furnished by the direct activities of the immediate environment (cf Dewey, art. on "Education" in Monroe's *CE;* cf Butler, *ME*).

Religious education among ancient and modern peoples alike reveals clearly this twofold aspect of all education. On its informal side it consists in the transmission of religious ideas and experience by means of the reciprocal processes of imitation and example; each generation, by actually participating in the religious activities and ceremonies of the social group, imbibing as it were the spirit and ideals of the preceding generation as these are modified by the particular economic and industrial conditions under which the entire process takes place. Formal religious education begins with the conscious and systematic effort on the part of the mature members of a social group (tribe, nation, or religious fellowship) to initiate the immature members by means of solemn rites and ceremonies, or patient training, or both, into the mysteries and high privileges of their own religious fellowship and experience. As regards both the content and form of this instruction, these will in every case be determined by the type and stage of civilization reflected in the life, occupations, habits and customs of the people. Among primitive races educational method is simpler and the content of formal instruction less differentiated than on higher culture levels (Ames, *PRE*). All education is at first religious in the sense that religious motives and ideas predominate in the educational efforts of all primitive peoples. The degree to which religion continues preëminent in the educational system of a progressive nation depends upon the vitality of its religion and upon the measure of efficiency and success with which from the first that religion is instilled into the very bone and sinew of each succeeding generation. Here lies the explanation of the religious-educational character of Heb national life, and here, too, the secret of Israel's incomparable influence upon the religious and educational development of the world. The religion of Israel was a vital religion and it was a teaching religion (Kent, *GTJC*).

II. Education in Early Israel (from Patriarchal Times to the Exile).—In their social and national development the Hebrews passed through several clearly marked cultural stages which it is important to note in connection with their educational history. At the earliest point at which the OT gives us any knowledge of them, they, like their ancestors, were nomads and shepherds. Their chief interest centered in the flocks and herds from which they gained a livelihood, and in the simple, useful arts that seem gradually to have become hereditary in certain families. With the settlement of the Heb tribes in Pal and their closer contact with Canaanitish culture, a more established agricultural life with resulting changes in social and religious institutions gradually superseded the nomadic stage of culture. A permanent dwelling-place made possible, as the continual warfare of gradual conquest made necessary, a closer federation of the tribes, which ultimately resulted in the establishment of the monarchy under David (W. R. Smith, *RS;* Davidson, *HE*).

1. Nomadic and Agricultural Periods

In these earliest cultural periods, both the nomadic and the agricultural, there was no distinct separation between the spheres of religion and ordinary life. The relation of the people to Yahweh was conceived by them in simple fashion as involving on their part the obligation of filial obedience and loyalty, and on Yahweh's part reciprocal parental care over them as His people. The family was the social unit and its head the person in whom centered also religious authority and leadership. The tribal head or patriarch in turn combined in himself the functions which later were differentiated into those of priest and prophet and king. Education was a matter of purely domestic interest and concern. The home was the only school and the parents the only teachers. But there was real instruction, all of which, moreover, was given in a spirit of devout religious earnestness and of reverence for the common religious ceremonies and beliefs, no matter whether the subject of instruction was the simple task of husbandry or of some useful art, or whether it was the sacred history and traditions of the tribe, or the actual performance of its religious rites. According to Jos (*Ant*, IV, viii, 12) Moses himself had commanded, "All boys shall learn the most important parts of the law since such knowledge is most valuable and the source of happiness"; and again he commanded (*Apion*, II, 25) to teach them the rudiments of learning (reading and writing) together with the laws and deeds of the ancestors, in order that they might not transgress or seem ignorant of the laws of their ancestors, but rather emulate their example. Certain it is that the earliest legislation, including the Decalogue, emphasized parental authority and their claim on the reverence of their children: "Honor thy father and thy mother, that thy days may be long in the land which Jeh thy God giveth thee" (Ex **20** 12); "And he that smiteth his father, or his mother, shall be surely put to death. And he that curseth his father or his mother, shall surely be put to death" (Ex **21** 15.17); while every father was exhorted to explain to his son the origin and significance of the great Passover ceremony with its feast of unleavened bread: "And thou shalt tell thy son in that day, saying, It is because of that which Jeh did for me when I came forth out of Egypt" (Ex **13** 8).

2. The Monarchical Period

The period of conquest and settlement developed leaders who not only led the allied tribes in battle, but served as judges between their people, and were active in the maintenance of the ancestral religion. In time, sufficient coöperation was obtained to make possible the organization of strong intertribal leagues and, finally, the kingship. "This increasing political unification," says Ames, "was accompanied by a religious consciousness which became ultimately the most remarkable product of the national development" (Ames, *PRE*, 174 f). The establishment of the kingdom and the beginnings of city and commercial life were accompanied by more radical cultural changes, including the differentiation of religious from other social institutions, the organization of the priesthood, and the rise and development of prophecy. Elijah, the Tishbite, Amos, the herdsman from Tekoa, Isaiah, the son of Amoz, were all champions of a simple faith and ancient religious ideals as over against the worldly-wise diplomacy and sensuous idolatry of the surrounding nations. Under the monarchy also a new religious symbolism developed. Yahweh was thought of as a king in whose hands actually lay the supreme guidance of the state: "Accordingly the organization of the state included provision for consulting His will and obtaining His direction in all weighty matters" (W. R. Smith, *RS*, 30). Under the teaching of the prophets the ideal of personal and civic righteousness was moved to the very forefront of Heb religious thought, while the prophetic ideal of the future was that of a time when "the earth shall be full of the knowledge of Jeh, as the waters cover the sea" (Isa **11** 9), when all "from the least of them unto the greatest of them" shall know him (Jer **31** 34). Concerning the so-called "schools of the prophets" which, in the days of Elijah, existed at Bethel, Jericho and Gilgal (2 K **2** 3.5; **4** 38 f), and probably in other places, it should be noted that these were associations or brotherhoods established for the purpose of mutual edification rather than education. The Bible does not use the word "schools" to designate these fraternities. Nevertheless we cannot conceive of the element of religious training as being entirely absent.

3. Deuteronomic Legislation

Shortly before the Bab captivity King Josiah gave official recognition and sanction to the teachings of the prophets, while the Deuteronomic legislation of the same period strongly emphasized the responsibility of parents for the religious and moral instruction and training of their children. Concerning the words of the law Israel is admonished: "Thou shalt teach them diligently unto thy children, and shalt talk of them when thou sittest in thy house, and when thou walkest by the way, and when thou liest down, and when thou risest up" (Dt **6** 7; **11** 19). For the benefit of children as well as adults the law was to be written "upon the door-posts" and "gates" (**6** 9; **11** 20), and "very plainly" upon "great stones" set up for this purpose upon the hilltops and beside the altars (Dt **27** 1-8). From the Deuteronomic period forward, religious training to the Jew became the synonym of education, while the word *Tōrāh*, which originally denoted simply "Law" (Ex **24** 12; Lev **7** 1; **26** 46), came to mean "religious instruction or teaching," in which sense it is used in Dt **4** 44; **5** 1, "This is the law which Moses set before the children of Israel: . . . . Hear, O Israel, the statutes and the ordinances which I speak in your ears this day, that ye may learn them, and observe to do them"; and in Prov **6** 23,

> "For the commandment is a lamp; and the law is light;
> And reproofs of instruction are the way of life."

(Cf Ps **19** 8; Prov **3** 1; **4** 2.)

4. Reading and Writing

With the development and reorganization of the ritual, priests and Levites, as the guardians of the law, were the principal instructors of the people, while parents remained in charge of the training of the children. In families of the aristocracy the place of the parents was sometimes taken by tutors, as appears from the case of the infant Solomon, whose training seems to have been intrusted to the prophet Nathan (2 S **12** 25). There is no way of determining to what extent the common people were able to read and write. Our judgment that these rudiments of formal education in the modern sense were not restricted to the higher classes is based upon such passages as Isa **29** 11.12, which distinguishes between the man who "is learned" (lit. "knoweth letters") and the one who is "not learned," and Isa **10** 19, referring to the ability of a child "to write," taken together with such facts as that the literary prophets Amos and Micah sprang from the ranks of the common people, and that "the workman who excavated the tunnel from the Virgin's Spring to the Pool of Siloam carved in the rock the manner of their work" (Kennedy in *HDB*). It should be added that the later Jewish tradition reflected in the Talm, Tg and Midr, and which represents both public, elementary and college education as highly developed even in patriarchal times, is generally regarded as altogether untrustworthy.

III. Education in Later Israel (from the Exile to the Birth of Christ).—The national disaster that befell the Heb people in the downfall of Jerus and the Bab captivity was not without its compensating, purifying and stimulating influence upon the religious and educational development of the nation. Under the pressure of adverse external circumstances the only source of comfort for the exiled people was in the law and covenant of Yahweh, while the shattering of all hope of immediate national greatness turned the thought and attention of the religious leaders away from the present toward the future. Two types of Messianic expectation characterized the religious development of the exilic period. The first is the priestly, material hope of return and restoration reflected in the prophecies of Ezekiel. The exiled tribes are to return again to Jerus; the temple is to be restored, its ritual and worship purified and exalted, the priestly ordinance and service elaborated. The second is the spiritualized and idealized Messianic expectation of the Second Isaiah, based on teachings of the earlier prophets. For the greatest of Heb prophets Yahweh is the only God, and the God of all nations as well as of Israel. For him Israel is Yahweh's servant, His instrument for revealing Himself to other nations, who, when they witness the redemption of Yahweh's suffering Servant, will bow down to Yahweh and acknowledge His rule. "Thus the trials of the nation lead to a comprehensive universalism within which the suffering Israel gains an elevated and ennobling explanation" (Ames, *PRE*, 185). In the prophetic vision of Ezekiel we must seek the inspiration for the later development of Jewish ritual, as well as the basis of those eschatological hopes and expectations which find their fuller expression in the apocalypse of Dnl and the kindred lit. of the later cents. The prophecies of the Isaiahs and the Messianic hope which these kindled in the hearts of the faithful prepared the way for the teachings of Jesus concerning a Divine spiritual kingdom, based upon the personal, ethical character of the individual and the mutual, spiritual fellowship of believers.

1. Educational Significance of the Prophets

The educational significance of the prophetic writings of this as of the preceding periods is that the prophets themselves were the real religious leaders and representative men (*Kulturträger*) of the nation. In advance of their age they were the heralds of Divine truth; the watchmen on the mountain tops whose clear insight into the future detected the significant elements in the social and religious conditions and tendencies about them, and whose keen intellect and lofty faith grasped the eternal principles which are the basis of all individual and national integrity and worth. These truths and principles they impressed upon the consciousness of their own and succeeding generations, thereby giving to future teachers of their race the essence of their message, and preparing the way for the larger and fuller interpretation of religion and life contained in the teachings of Jesus. The immediate influence of their teaching is explained in part by the variety and effectiveness of their teaching method, their marvelous simplicity and directness of speech, their dramatic emphasis upon essentials and their intelligent appreciation of social conditions and problems about them.

2. The Book of the Law

The immediate bond of union, as well as the textbook and program of religious instruction, during the period of the captivity and subsequently, was the Book of the Law, which the exiles carried with them to Babylon. When in 458 BC a company of exiles returned to Pal, they, along with their poorer brethren who had not been carried away, restored the Jewish community at Jerus, and under the suzerainty of Persia, founded a new nationalism, based, even more than had been the earlier monarchy, upon the theocratic conception of Israel's relation to Yahweh. During this period it was that writings of poets, lawgivers, prophets and sages were brought together into one sacred collection of scrolls, known later as the OT canon, of which the Torah (the law) was educationally the most significant. The recognized teachers of this period included, in addition to the priests and Levites, the "wise men," or "sages" and the "scribes" or *ṣōphᵉrīm* (lit. "those learned in Scriptures").

3. Wise Men or Sages

Whether or not the sages and scribes of the later post-exilic times are to be regarded as one and the same class, as an increasing number of scholars are inclined to believe, or thought of as distinct classes, the wise men clearly antedate, not only the *ṣōphᵉrīm*, but in all probability all forms of book learning as well. Suggestions of their existence and function are met with in earliest times both in Israel and among other nations of the East. As illustrations of their appearance in preëxilic OT history may be cited the references in 2 S **14** 1–20; 1 K **4** 32; Isa **29** 10. It is no lesser personage than King Solomon who, both by his contemporaries and later generations as well, was regarded as the greatest representative of this earlier group of teachers who uttered their wisdom in the form of clever, epigrammatic proverbs and shrewd sayings. The climax of Wisdom-teaching belongs, however, to the later post-exilic period. Of the wise men of this later day an excellent description is preserved for us in the Book of Ecclus (**39** 3.4.8.10; cf **1** 1–11):

"He seeks out the hidden meaning of proverbs,
And is conversant with the subtilties of parables,
He serves among great men,
And appears before him who rules;
He travels through the land of strange nations;
For he hath tried good things and evil among men.
. . . .
He shows forth the instruction which he has been taught,
And glories in the law of the covenant of the Lord.
. . . .
Nations shall declare his wisdom,
And the congregation shall tell out his praise."

Of the pedagogic experience, wisdom and learning of these sages, the Book of Prov forms the Bib. repository. Aside from the Torah it is thus the oldest handbook of education. The wise men conceive of life itself as a discipline. Parents are the natural instructors of their children:

4. The Book of Proverbs

"My son, hear the instruction of thy father,
And forsake not the law of thy mother."
—Prov **1** 8.

(Cf **4** 1–4 ff; **6** 20; **13** 1.) The substance of such parental teaching is to be the 'fear of Yahweh' which "is the beginning of wisdom"; and fidelity in the performance of this parental obligation has the promise of success:

"Train up a child in the way he should go,
And even when he is old he will not depart from it."
—Prov **22** 6.

In their training of children, parents are to observe sternness, not hesitating to apply the rod of correction, when needed (cf **23** 13.14), yet doing so with discretion, since wise reproof is better than "a hundred stripes" (**17** 10). Following the home training there is provision for further instruction at the hands of professional teachers for all who would really obtain unto "wisdom" and who can afford the time and expense of such special training. The teachers are none other than the wise men or sages whose words "heard in quiet" (Eccl **9** 17) are "as goads, and as nails well fastened" (**12** 11). Their precepts teach diligence (Prov **6** 6–11), chastity (**7** 5), charity (**14** 21), truthfulness (**17** 7) and temperance (**21** 17; **23** 20.21.29–35); for the aim of all Wisdom-teaching is none other than

"To give prudence to the simple,
To the young man knowledge and discretion:
That the wise man may hear, and increase in learning;
And that the man of understanding may attain unto sound counsels."—Prov **1** 4.5.

5. Scribes and Levites

The *ṣōpherīm* or "men of book learning" were editors and interpreters as well as scribes or copyists of ancient and current writings. As a class they did not become prominent until the wise men, as such, stepped into the background, nor until the exigencies of the situation demanded more teachers and teaching than the ranks of priests and Levites, charged with increasing ritualistic duties, could supply. Ezra was both a priest and a *ṣōphēr* (Ezr **7** 11; Neh **8** 1 f), concerning whom we read that he "set his heart to seek the law of Jeh, and to do it, and to teach in Israel statutes and ordinances" (Ezr **7** 10). Likewise the Levites often appear as teachers of the law, and we must think of the development of sopherism (scribism) as a distinct profession as proceeding very gradually. The same is true of the characteristic Jewish religious-educational institution, the synagogue, the origin and development of which fell within this same general period (cf SYNAGOGUE). The pupils of the *ṣōpherīm* were the Pharisees (*perūshīm* or "separatists") who during the Maccabean period came to be distinguished from the priestly party or Sadducees.

6. Greek and Roman Influences

The conquest of Persia by Alexander (332 BC) marks the rise of Gr influence in Pal. Alexander himself visited Pal and perhaps Jerus (Jos, *Ant*, X, i, 8), befriended the Jews and granted to them the privilege of self-government, and the maintenance of their own social and religious customs, both at home and in Alexandria, the new center of Gr learning, in the founding of which many Jews participated (see ALEXANDRIA). During the succeeding dynasty of the Ptolemies, Gr ideas and Gr culture penetrated to the very heart of Judaism at Jerus, and threatened the overthrow of Jewish social and religious institutions. The Maccabean revolt under Antiochus Epiphanes (174–164 BC) and the reëstablishment of a purified temple ritual during the early part of the Maccabean period (161–63 BC) were the natural reaction against the attempt of the Seleucidae forcibly to substitute the Gr gymnasium and theater for the Jewish synagogue and temple (Felten, *NZ*, I, 83 f; cf 1 Macc **1, 3, 9, 13** and 2 Macc **4–10**). The end of the Maccabean period found Phariseeism and strict Jewish orthodoxy in the ascendency with such Hellenic tendencies as had found permanent lodgment in Judaism reflected in the agnosticism of the aristocratic Sadducees. The establishment of Rom authority in Pal (63 BC) introduced a new determining element into the environmental conditions under which Judaism was to attain its final distinguishing characteristics. The genius of the Romans was practical, legalistic and institutional. As organizers and administrators they were preeminent. But their religion never inspired to any exalted view of life, and education to them meant always merely a preparation for life's practical duties. Hence the influence of Rom authority upon Judaism was favorable to the development of a narrow individualistic Phariseeism, rather than to the fostering of Gr idealism and universalism. With the destruction of Jerus by the Romans a little more than a cent. later (70 AD) and the cessation of the temple worship, the Sadducees as a class disappeared from Judaism, which has ever since been represented by the Pharisees devoted to the study of the law. Outside of Jerus and Pal, meanwhile, the Jewish communities at Alexandria and elsewhere were much more hospitable to Gr culture and learning, at the same time exerting a reciprocal, modifying influence upon Gr thought. It was, however, through its influence upon early Christian theology and education that the Hellenistic philosophy of the Alexandrian school left its deeper impress upon the substance and method of later Christian education.

IV. Education in New Testament Times (from the birth of Christ to the end of the 1st cent.).—Elementary schools: Jewish education in the time of Christ was of the orthodox traditional type and in the hands of scribes, Pharisees and learned rabbis. The home was still the chief institution for the dispensation of elementary instruction, although synagogues, with attached schools for the young, were to be found in every important Jewish community. Public elementary schools, other than those connected with the synagogues, were of slower growth and do not seem to have been common until, some time after Joshua ben Gamala, high priest from 63–65 AD, ordered that teachers be appointed in every province and city to instruct children having attained the age of 6–7 years. In the synagogue schools the *ḥazzān*, or attendant, not infrequently served as schoolmaster (cf SCHOOL; SCHOOLMASTER).

1. Subject-Matter of Instruction

As in earlier times the Torah, connoting now the sacred OT writings as a whole, though with emphasis still upon the law, furnished the subject-matter of instruction. To this were added, in the secondary schools (colleges) of the rabbis, the illustrative and parabolical rabbinical interpretation of the law (the *haggādhāh*) and its application to daily life in the form of concise precept or rule of conduct (the *halākhāh*). Together the *haggādhāh* and *halākhāh* furnish the content of the Talm (or Talmuds), as the voluminous collections of orthodox Jewish teachings of later cents. came to be known.

2. Method and Aims

As regards teaching method the scribes and rabbis of NT times did not improve much upon the practice of the *ṣōpherīm* and sages of earlier cents. Memorization, the exact reproduction by the pupil of the master's teaching, rather than general knowledge or culture, was the main objective. Since the voice of prophecy had become silent and the canon of revealed truth was considered closed, the intellectual mastery and interpretation of this sacred revelation of the past was the only aim that education on its intellectual side could have. On its practical side it sought, as formerly, the inculcation of habits of strict ritualistic observance, obedience to the letter of the law as a condition of association and fellowship with the selected company of true Israelites to which scribes and Pharisees considered themselves to belong. The success with which the teachings of the scribes and rabbis were accompanied is an evidence of their devotion to their work, and more still of the psychological insight manifested by them in utilizing every subtle means and method for securing and holding the attention of their pupils, and making their memories the trained and obedient servants of an educational ideal. The defects in their work were largely the defects in that ideal. Their theory and philosophy of education were narrow. "Their eyes were turned too much to the past rather than the present and future." They failed to distinguish clearly the gold from the dross in their inherited teachings, or to adapt these to the vital urgent needs of the common people. In its struggle against foreign cults and foreign culture, Judaism had incased itself in a shell of stereotyped orthodoxy, the attempt to adapt which to new conditions and to a constantly changing social order resulted in an insincere and shallow casuistry of which the fantastic conglomerate mass of Talmudic wisdom of the 4th and 6th cents. is the lasting memorial.

3. Valuable Results of Jewish Education

Nevertheless, "Jewish education, though defective both in matter and in method, and tending to fetter rather than to free the mind, achieved four valuable results: (1) it developed a taste for close, critical study; (2) it sharpened the wits, even to the point of perversity; (3) it encouraged a reverence for law and produced desirable social conduct; and (4) it formed a powerful bond of union among the Jewish people." To these four points of excellence enumerated by Davidson (*HE*, 80) must be added a fifth which, briefly stated, is this: (5) Jewish education by its consistent teaching of lofty monotheism, and its emphasis, sometimes incidental and sometimes outstanding, upon righteousness and holiness of life as a condition of participation in a future Messianic kingdom, prepared the way for the Christian view of God and the world, set forth in its original distinctness of outline and incomparable simplicity in the teachings of Jesus.

4. The Pre-eminence of Jesus as a Teacher

Jesus was more than a teacher; but He was a teacher first. To His contemporaries he appeared as a Jewish rabbi of exceptional influence and popularity. He used the teaching methods of the rabbis; gathered about Him, as did they, a group of chosen disciples (learners) whom He trained and taught more explicitly with a view to perpetuating through them His own influence and work. His followers called Him Rabbi and Master, and the scribes and Pharisees conceded His popularity and power. He taught, as did the rabbis of His time, in the temple courts, in the synagogue, in private, and on the public highway as the exigencies of the case demanded. His textbook, so far as He used any, was the same as theirs; His form of speech (parable and connected discourse), manner of life and methods of instruction were theirs. Yet into His message and method He put a new note of authority that challenged attention and inspired confidence. Breaking with the traditions of the past He substituted for devotion to the letter of the law an interest in men, with boundless sympathy for their misfortune, abiding faith in their worth and high destiny and earnest solicitude for their regeneration and perfection. To say that Jesus was the world's greatest and foremost example as a teacher is to state a fact borne out by every inquiry, test and comparison that modern educational science can apply to the work and influence of its great creative geniuses of the past. Where His contemporaries and even His own followers saw only "as in a glass, darkly," He saw clearly; and His view of God and the world, of human life and human destiny, has come down through the ages as a Divine revelation vouchsafed the world in Him. Viewed from the intellectual side, it was the life philosophy of Jesus that made His teachings imperishable; esthetically it was the compassionate tenderness and solicitude of His message that drew the multitudes to Him; judged from the standpoint of will, it was the example of His life, its purpose, its purity, its helpfulness, that caused men to follow Him; and tested by its immediate and lasting social influence, it was the doctrine, the ideal and example of the human brotherliness and Divine sonship, that made Jesus the pattern of the great teachers of mankind in every age and generation. With a keen, penetrating insight into the ultimate meaning of life, He reached out, as it were, over the conflicting opinions of men and the mingling social and cultural currents of His time backward to the fundamental truths uttered by the ancient prophets of His race and forward to the ultimate goal of the race. Then with simple directness of speech He addressed Himself to the consciences and wills of men, setting before them the ideal of the higher life, and with infinite patience sought to lift them to the plane of fellowship with Himself in thought and action.

5. Educational Work of the Early Disciples

It remained for the disciples of Jesus to perpetuate His teaching ministry and to organize the new forces making for human betterment. In this work, which was distinctly religious-educational in character, some found a field of labor among their own Jewish kinsmen, and others, like Paul, among the needy Gentiles (Gal **1** 16; **2** 7; 1 Tim **2** 7). As regards a division of labor in the apostolic church, we read of apostles, prophets, evangelists, pastors and teachers (1 Cor **12** 28; Eph **4** 11). The apostles were the itinerant leaders and missionaries of the entire church. Their work was largely that of teaching, Paul insisting on calling himself a teacher as well as an apostle (2 Tim **1** 11; 1 Cor **4** 17). The prophets were men with a special message like that of Agabus (Acts **21** 10.11). The evangelists were itinerant preachers, as was Philip (**8** 40), while the pastors, also called bishops, had permanent charge of individual churches. The professional teachers included both laymen and those ordained by the laying on of hands. Their work was regarded with highest honor in the church and community. In contrast with the itinerant church officers, apostles and evangelists, they, like the pastors, resided permanently in local communities. With this class the author of the Epistle of Jas identifies himself, and there can be little doubt that the epistle which he wrote reflects both the content and form of the instruction which these earliest Christian teachers gave to their pupils. Before the close of the 1st cent. the religious educational work of the church had been organized into a more systematic form, out of which there developed gradually the catechumenate of the early post-apostolic period (see CATECHIST). In the *Did*, or Teachings of the Apostles, there has been reserved for us a textbook of religious instruction from this earlier period (Kent, *GTJC*). Necessarily, the entire missionary and evangelistic work of the apostolic church was educational in character, and throughout this earliest period of church history we must think of the work of apostles, evangelists and pastors, as well as that of professional teachers, as including a certain amount of systematic religious instruction. See further PEDAGOGY; SCHOOL; TEACHER; TUTOR.

LITERATURE.—Ames, *Psychology of Religious Experience*, ch x; Box, art. "Education," in *EB;* Butler, *The Meaning of Education;* Davidson, *History of Education;* Dewey, art. "Education," in Monroe's *Cyclopedia of Education;* Edersheim, "The Upbringing of Jewish Children," in *SJSL*, and *Life and Times of Jesus*, I, 225 f; Fairweather, *Background of the Gospels;* Felten, "Schriftgelehrten, Synagogen u. Schulen," in *Neutestamentliche Zeitgeschichte*, I; Ginsburg, art. "Education," in Kitto's *Biblical Cyclopedia;* Hiegemoser u. Bock, *Quellenbuch u. Überblick d. Geschichte d. Pädagogik;* Katzer, arts. "Jesus als Lehrer" and "Judenchristentum," in Rein's *Encyklopädisches Handbuch d. Pädagogik;* Kennedy, art. "Education," in *HDB*, I; Kohler and Gudemann, art. "Education" in *Jew Enc*, V; Kent, *Great Teachers of Judaism and Christianity* and *Makers and Teachers of Judaism;* Laurie, *Historical Survey of Pre-Christian Education;* Lewit, *Darstellung d. theoretischen u. praktischen Pädagogik im jüd. Altertume;* Oehler, art. "Pädagogik d. Alten Testaments," in Schmid's *Encyclopädie d. Gesammten Erziehungs- u. Unterrichtswesen;* Schürer, "Schriftgelehrsamkeit, Schule u. Synagoge," in *Geschichte d. jüd. Volkes* (ed 1907); W. R. Smith, *Religion of the Semites;* Straussburger, *Geschichte d. Unterrichts bei d. Israeliten;* von Rohden, art. "Katechetik" in Rein's *EHP*.

H. H. MEYER

EDUTH, ē'duth (עֵדוּת, *'ēdhūth*, "testimony," a technical term for the Ten Commandments or for the Law): In Ps **60** title, "set to Shushan Eduth" (lit. "a lily [is] the testimony"); **80** title, "set to Shoshannim Eduth" (lit. "lilies [is] the testimony"). The Heb words appear to be intended to designate a melody by the first few words ordinarily associated with it. See PSALMS.

EFFECT, ē-fekt', **EFFECTUAL,** ē-fek'tū-al: In the OT, RV renders "fulfilment" for "effect" in Ezk **12** 23 (Heb *dābhār*, "matter"); and in Jer **48** 30 "His boastings have wrought nothing" for the vaguer "His lies shall not so effect" of AV. In AV of the NT, "make of none effect" occurs repeatedly: as the tr of Gr *akuróō*, "render void" (Mt **15** 6; Mk **7** 13); of *katargéō*, "annul" (Rom **3** 3 [AV "make without effect"]; **4** 14; Gal **3** 17); and of *kenóō*, "make empty" (1 Cor **1** 17). RV renders "make of none effect" in Rom **3** 3; Gal **3** 17; "make void" in the other cases, with no apparent reason for the lack of uniformity. Gr *energéō* is the opposite in meaning of *katargeō* above. Its derivative *energḗs*, "effective," is rendered "effectual" by EV in 1 Cor **16** 9; Philem ver 6. RV dispenses with "effectual," "effectually," in the other cases where AV has used these words as auxiliary in the tr of *energeō* or of *enérgeia*, "working" (2 Cor **1** 6; Gal **2** 8; Eph **3** 7; **4** 16; 1 Thess **2** 13; Jas **5** 16).

F. K. FARR

EGG (בֵּיצָה, *bēçāh;* ᾠόν, *ōón;* Lat *ovum*): An oval or spheroid body produced by birds, fishes and reptiles, from which their young emerge when incubated or naturally developed. The fertile egg of a bird consists of the yolk, a small disk from which the embryo develops, the albuminous white, and a calcareous shell. The most ancient records prove that eggs have been used as an article of diet ever since the use of the flesh of fowl began. Chickens were unknown in Pal in the days of Job, so that his query concerning the taste of the white of an egg might have referred to those of pigeons, ducks, eggs taken from the nests of geese or swans, game birds or ostriches. "Can that which hath no savor be eaten without salt? Or is there any taste in **the white of an egg?"** (Job **6** 6, RVm "the juice of purslain"). In Lk **11** 12 there is every possibility that the egg of our common domestic fowl is referred to, as "chickens" (q.v.) had been imported and were numerous in Pal at that time. "Or if he shall ask an egg, will he give him a scorpion?" The reference in Isa **59** 5 is to the egg of a serpent, and is **figurative** of the schemes of evil men: "They hatch adders' eggs, and weave the spider's web: he that eateth of their eggs dieth; and that which is crushed breaketh out into a viper."

GENE STRATTON-PORTER

EGLAH, eg'la (עֶגְלָה, *'eghlāh*, "heifer"): Wife of David and mother of Ithream (2 S **3** 5 ‖ 1 Ch **3** 3).

EGLAIM, eg'lā-im (אֶגְלַיִם, *'eghlayim;* Ἀγαλείμ, *Agaleím*): A place named in Isa **15** 8, possibly in the S. of Moab. *Onom* identifies it with Agallim, a village 8 Rom miles S. of Areopolis. It cannot now be identified.

EGLATH-SHELISHIYAH, eg'lath-shel-i-shī'ya (עֶגְלַת שְׁלִשִׁיָּה, *'eghlath shᵉlīshīyāh*): Found in Isa **15** 5; Jer **48** 34 (Heb) in oracles against Moab. AV trˢ "an heifer of three years old"; RV takes it as the name of a place, but ARVm has "a heifer three years old," acc. to LXX. In the former case strong and unconquered cities, Zoar and Horonaim, are compared to the heifer not yet broken to the yoke. Such use of "heifer" is not infrequent (cf Jer **46** 20; Hos **10** 11, etc). The majority of scholars, however, take it as a place-name. Some would read "the third Eglath," as if there were three towns of that name. No probable identification has been suggested.

W. EWING

EGLON, eg'lon (עֶגְלוֹן, *'eghlōn*, "circle"): A king of Moab in the period of the Judges who, in alliance with Ammon and Amalek, overcame Israel and made Jericho his capital, presumably driven across the Jordan by the turmoil in his own kingdom which at that time was probably being used as a battle ground by Edom and the desert tribes (cf Gen **36** 35). After 18 years of servitude the children of Israel were delivered by Ehud the Benjamite, who like so many other Benjamites (cf Jgs **20** 16) was left-handed. Under the pretext of carrying a present to the tyrant, he secured a private interview and assassinated him with a two-edged sword which he had carried concealed on his right side (Jgs **3** 19–22). Ehud made his escape, rallied the children of Israel about him and returned to conquer the Moabites (Jgs **3** 30). ELLA DAVIS ISAACS

EGLON, eg′lon (עֶגְלוֹן, *ʽeghlōn;* **Ὀδολλάμ,** *Odollám*): A royal Canaanite city whose king joined the league headed by Adonizedek of Jerus against the Gibeonites, which suffered overwhelming defeat at the hands of Joshua (Josh **10**). Joshua passed from Libnah to Lachish, and from Lachish to Eglon on his way to Hebron (vs 31 ff). It was in the Shephelah of Judah (**15** 39). The name seems to be preserved in that of *Khirbet ʽAjlān,* about 10 miles W. of *Beit Jibrīn.* Professor Petrie, however, thinks that the site of *Tell Nejīleh* better suits the requirements. While *Khirbet ʽAjlān* is a comparatively modern site, the city at *Tell Nejīleh* must have been contemporary with that at *Tell el-Ḥesy* (Lachish). It lies fully three miles S.E. of *Tell el-Ḥesy.* W. EWING

EGYPT, ē′jipt:

I. THE COUNTRY
  1. The Basis of the Land
  2. The Nile Valley
  3. Earliest Human Remains
  4. Climate
  5. Conditions of Life
  6. The Nile
  7. The Fauna
  8. The Flora
  9. The Prehistoric Races
II. THE HISTORY
  1. 1st and 2d Ages: Prehistoric
  2. 3d Age: Ist and IId Dynasties
  3. 4th Age: IIId–VIth Dynasties
  4. 5th Age: VIIth–XIVth Dynasties
  5. 6th Age: XVth–XXIVth Dynasties
  6. 7th Age: XXVth Dynasty to Roman Times
  7. 8th Age: Arabic
  8. Early Foreign Connections
III. THE OT CONNECTIONS
  1. Semitic Connections
  2. Abramic Times
  3. Circumcision
  4. Joseph
  5. Descent into Egypt
  6. The Oppression
  7. The Historic Position
  8. The Plagues
  9. Date of the Exodus
  10. Route of the Exodus
  11. Numbers of the Exodus
  12. Israel in Canaan
  13. Hadad
  14. Pharaoh's Daughter
  15. Shishak
  16. Zerakh
  17. The Ethiopians
  18. Tahpanhes
  19. Hophra
  20. The Jews of Syene
  21. The New Jerusalem of Oniah
  22. The Egyptian Jew
  23. Cities and Places Alphabetically
IV. THE CIVILIZATION
  1. Language
  2. Writing
  3. Literature
  4. Four Views of Future Life
  5. Four Groups of Gods
  6. Foreign Gods
  7. Laws
  8. Character
LITERATURE

Egypt (מִצְרַיִם, *miçrayim;* **ἡ Αἴγυπτος,** *hē Aíguptos*): Usually supposed to represent the dual of *Misr,* referring to "the two lands," as the Egyptians called their country. This dualism, however, has been denied by some.

I. The Country.—Though Egypt is one of the earliest countries in recorded history, and as regards its continuous civilization, yet it is a late country in its geological history and in its occupation by a settled population.

1. The Basis of the Land

The whole land up to Silsileh is a thick mass of Eocene limestone, with later marls over that in the lower districts. It has been elevated on the E., up to the mountains of igneous rocks many thousand ft. high toward the Red Sea. It has been depressed on the W., down to the Fayum and the oases below sea-level. This strain resulted in a deep fault from N. to S. for some hundreds of miles up from the Mediterranean. This fault left its eastern side about 200 ft. above its western, and into it the drainage of the plateau poured, widening it out so as to form the Nile valley, as the permanent drain of Northeast Africa. The access of water to the rift seems to have caused the basalt outflows, which are seen as black columnar basalt S. of the Fayum, and brown massive basalt at Khankah, N. of Cairo.

2. The Nile Valley

The gouging out of the Nile valley by rainfall must have continued when the land was 300 ft. higher than at present, as is shown by the immense falls of strata into collapsed caverns which were far below the present Nile level. Then, after the excavations of the valley, it has been submerged to 500 ft. lower than at present, as is shown by the rolled gravel beds and deposits on the tops of the water-worn cliffs, and the filling up of the tributary valleys—as at Thebes—by deep deposits, through which the subsequent stream beds have been scoured out. The land still had the Nile source 30 ft. higher than it is now within the human period, as seen by the worked flints in high gravel beds above the Nile plain. The distribution of land and water was very different from that at present when the land was only 100 ft. lower than now. Such a change would make the valley an estuary up to S. of the Fayum, would submerge much of the western desert, and would unite the Gulf of Suez and the Mediterranean. Such differences would entirely alter the conditions of animal life by sea and land. And as the human period began when the water was considerably higher, the conditions of climate and of life must have greatly changed in the earlier ages of man's occupation.

3. Earliest Human Remains

The earliest human remains belonging to the present condition of the country are large palaeolithic flints found in the side valleys at the present level of the Nile. As these are perfectly fresh, and not rolled or altered, they show that palaeolithic man lived in Egypt under the present conditions. The close of this palaeolithic age of hunters, and the beginning of a settled population of cultivators, cannot have been before the drying up of the climate, which by depriving the Nile of tributary streams enfeebled it so that its mud was deposited and formed a basis for agriculture. From the known rate of deposit, and depth of mud soil, this change took place about 10,000 years ago. As the recorded history of the country extends 7,500 years, and we know of two prehistoric ages before that, it is pretty well fixed that the disappearance of palaeolithic man, and the beginning of the continuous civilization must have been about 9,000 to 10,000 years ago. For the continuation of this subject see the section on "History" below.

4. The Climate

The climate of Egypt is unique in the world. So far as solar heat determines it, the condition is tropical; for, though just N. of the tropic which lies at the boundary of Egypt and Nubia, the cloudless condition fully compensates for higher latitude. So far as temperature of the air is concerned, the climate is temperate, the mean heat of the winter months being 52° and of the summer about 80°, much the same as Italy. This is due to the steady prevalence of north winds, which maintain fit conditions for active, strenuous work. The rainlessness and dry air give the same facility of living that is found in deserts, where shelter is only needed for temperature and not for wet; while the inundation provides abundant moisture for the richest crops.

5. Conditions of Life

The primitive condition—only recently changed—of the crops being all raised during five cool months from November to April, and the inundation covering the land during all the hot weather, left the population free from labor during the enervating season, and only required their energies when work was possible under favorable conditions. At the same time it gave a great opportunity for monumental work, as any amount of labor could be drawn upon without the smallest reduction in the produce of the country. The great structures which covered the land gave training and organization to the people, without being any drain upon the welfare of the country. The inundation covering the plain also provided the easiest transport for great masses from the quarries at the time when labor was abundant. Thus the climatic conditions were all in favor of a great civilization, and aided its production of monuments. The whole mass of the country being of limestone, and much of it of the finest quality, provided material for construction at every point. In the south, sandstone and granite were also at hand upon the great waterway.

6. The Nile

The Nile is the great factor which makes life possible in Northeast Africa, and without it Egypt would only be a desolate corner of the Sahara. The union of two essentially different streams takes place at Khartum. The White or light Nile comes from the great plains of the Sudan, while the Blue or dark Nile descends from the mountains of Abyssinia. The Sudan Nile from Gondokoro is filtered by the lakes and the *sudd* vegetation, so that it carries little mud; the Abyssinian Nile, by its rapid course, brings down all the soil which is deposited in Egypt, and which forms the basis for cultivation. The Sudan

First Cataract of the Nile.

Nile rises only 6 ft. from April to November; while the Abyssinian Nile rises 26 ft. from April to August. The latter makes the rise of the inundation, while the Sudan Nile maintains the level into the winter. In Egypt itself the unchecked Nile at Aswan rises 25 ft. from the end of May to the beginning of September; while at Cairo, where modified by the irrigation system, it rises 16 ft. from May to the end of September. It was usually drained off the land by the beginning of November, and cultivation was begun. The whole cultivable land of Egypt is but the dried-up bed of the great river, which fills its ancient limits during a third of the year. The time taken by a flush of water to come down the Nile is about 15 days from 400 miles above Khartum to Aswan, and about 6 days from Aswan to Cairo, or 80 to 90 miles a day, which shows a flow of 3 to 3½ miles an hour when in flood.

7. The Fauna

The fauna has undergone great changes during the human period. At the close of the prehistoric age there are represented the giraffe, elephant, wild ox, lion, leopard, stag, long-necked gazelle and great dogs, none of which are found in the historic period. During historic times various kinds of antelopes have been exterminated, the hippopotamus was driven out of the Delta during Rom times, and the crocodile was cleared out of Upper Egypt and Nubia in the last century. Cranes and other birds shown on early sculptures are now unknown in the country. The animals still surviving are the wolf, jackal, hyaena, dogs, ichneumon, jerboa, rats, mice, lizards (up to 4 ft. long) and snakes, besides a great variety of birds, admirably figured by Whymper, *Birds of Egypt.* Of tamed animals, the ox, sheep, goat and donkey are ancient; the cat and horse were brought in about 2000 BC, the camel was not commonly known till 200 AD, and the buffalo was brought to Egypt and Italy in the Middle Ages.

8. The Flora

The cultivated plants of Egypt were numerous. In ancient times we find the maize (*durrah*), wheat, barley and lentil; the vine, currant, date palm, dum palm, fig, olive and pomegranate; the onion, garlic, cucumber, melon and radish; the *sont* acacia, sycamore and tamarisk; the flax, henna and clover; and for ornament, the lotus, convolvulus and many others. The extension of commerce brought in by the Gr period, the bean, pea, sesame, lupin, helbeh, colocasia and sugar-cane; also the peach, walnut, castor-oil and pear. In the Rom and Arab. ages came in the chick pea, oats, rice, cotton, orange and lemon. In recent times have come the cactus, aloe, tomato, Indian corn, lebbek acacia and beetroot. Many European flowering and ornamental plants were also used in Egypt by the Greeks, and brought in later by the Arabs.

9. The Prehistoric Races

The original race in Egypt seems to have been of the steatopygous type now only found in South Africa. Figures of this race are known in the caves of France, in Malta, and later in Somaliland. As this race was still known in Egypt at the beginning of the neolithic civilization, and is there represented only by female figures in the graves, it seems that it was being exterminated by the newcomers and only the women were kept as slaves.

The neolithic race of Egypt was apparently of the Libyan stock. There seems to have been a single type of the Amorites in Syria, the prehistoric Egyptians and the Libyans; this race had a high, well-filled head, long nose slightly aquiline, and short beard; the profile was upright and not prognathous, the hair was wavy brown. It was a better type than the present south Europeans, of a very capable and intelligent appearance. From the objects found, and the religious legends, it seems that this race was subdued by an eastern, and probably Arabian race, in the prehistoric age.

II. The History.—The founders of the dynastic history were very different, having a profile with nose and forehead in one straight line, and rather thick, but well-formed lips. Historically the indications point to their coming from about Somaliland by water, and crossing into Egypt by the Koptos road from the Red Sea. The IId Dynasty gave place to some new blood, probably of Sudany origin. In the VIth and VIIth Dynasties foreigners poured in apparently from the N., perhaps from Crete, judging by their foreign products. The XVth and XVIth Dynasties were Hyksos, or Sem "princes of the desert" from the E. The XVIIth and XVIIIth

Dynasties were Berber in origin. The XIXth Dynasty was largely Sem from Syria. The XXIId Dynasty was headed by an eastern adventurer Sheshenq, or Shusinak, "the man of Susa." The XXVth Dynasty was Ethiopian. The XXVIth Dynasty was Libyan. The Greeks then poured into the Delta and the Fayum, and Hellenized Egypt. The Roman made but little change in the population; but during his rule the Arab began to enter the eastern side, and by 641 AD the Arab conquest swept the land, and brought in a large part—perhaps the majority—of the ancestors of the present inhabitants. After 3 cents. the Tunisians—the old Libyans—conquered Egypt again. The later administrations by Syrians, Circassians, Turks and others probably made no change in the general population. The economic changes of the past cent. have brought in Greeks, Italians and other foreigners to the large towns; but all these only amount to an eightieth of the population. The Copts are the descendants of the very mixed Egyptians of Rom age, kept separate from the Arab invaders by their Christianity. They are mainly in Upper Egypt, where some villages are entirely Coptic, and are distinguished by their superior cleanliness, regularity, and the freedom of the women from unwholesome seclusion. The Copts, though only a fifteenth of the population, have always had a large share of official posts, owing to their intelligence and ability being above that of the Muslim.

In dealing with the history, we here follow the dating which was believed and followed by the Egyptians themselves. All the monumental remains agree with this, so far as they can check it; and the various arbitrary reductions that have been made on some periods are solely due to some critics preferring their internal sense to all the external facts. For the details involved in the chronology, see *Historical Studies*, II (British School of Archaeology in Egypt). The general outline of the periods is given here, and the detailed view of the connection with OT history is treated in later sections.

1. 1st and 2d Ages: Prehistoric

1st Age.—The prehistoric age begins probably about 8000 BC, as soon as there was a sufficient amount of Nile deposit to attract a settled population. The desert river valley of Egypt was probably one of the latest haunts of steatopygous palaeolithic man of the Bushman type. So soon as there was an opening for a pastoral or agricultural people, he was forced away by settlers from Libya. These settlers were clad in goatskins, and made a small amount of pottery by hand; they knew also of small quantities of copper, but mainly used flint, of which they gradually developed the finest working known in any age. They rapidly advanced in civilization. Their pottery of red polished ware was decorated with white clay patterns, exactly like the pottery still made in the mountains of Algeria. The forms of it were very varied and exquisitely regular, although made without the wheel. Their hardstone vases are finer than any of those of the historic ages. They adopted spinning, weaving and woodwork.

2d Age.—Upon these people came in others probably from the E., who brought in the use of the Arab face-veil, the belief in amulets, and the Pers lapis lazuli. Most of the previous forms of pottery disappear, and nearly all the productions are greatly altered. Copper became common, while gold, silver and lead were also known. Heliopolis was probably a center of rule.

3d Age.—About 5900 BC a new people came in with the elements of the art of writing, and a strong political ability of organization. Before 5800 BC they had established kings at Abydos in Upper Egypt, and for 3 cents. they gradually increased their power. On the carved slates which they have left, the standards of the allied tribes are represented; the earliest in style shows the standard of Koptos, the next has a standard as far N. as Hermopolis, and the latest bears the standard of Letopolis, and shows the conquest of the Fayum, or perhaps one of the coast lakes. This last is of the first king of the Ist Dynasty, Mena.

2. 3d Age: Ist and IId Dynasties

The conquest of all Egypt is marked by the beginning of the series of numbered dynasties beginning with Mena, at about 5550 BC. The civilization rapidly advanced. The art was at its best under the third king, Zer, and thence steadily declined. Writing was still ideographic under Mena, but became more syllabic and phonetic toward the end of the dynasty. The work in hardstone was at its height in the vases of the early part of the Ist Dynasty, when an immense variety of beautiful stones appear. It greatly fell off on reaching the IId Dynasty. The tombs were all of timber, built in large pits in the ground.

3. 4th Age: IIId–VIth Dynasties

4th Age.—The IId Dynasty fell about 5000 BC, and a new power rapidly raised the art from an almost barbarous state to its highest triumphs by about 4750 BC, when the pyramid building was started. Khufu, the builder of the Great Pyramid in the IVth Dynasty, was one of the greatest rulers of Egypt. He organized the administration on lines which lasted for ages. He reformed the religious system, abolishing the endowments, and substituting models for the sacrifice of animals. He trained the largest body of skilled labor that ever appeared, for the building of his pyramid, the greatest and most accurate structure that the world has ever seen. The statuary of this age is more lifelike than that of any later age. The later reigns show steady decay in the character of work, with less dignity and more superficiality in the art.

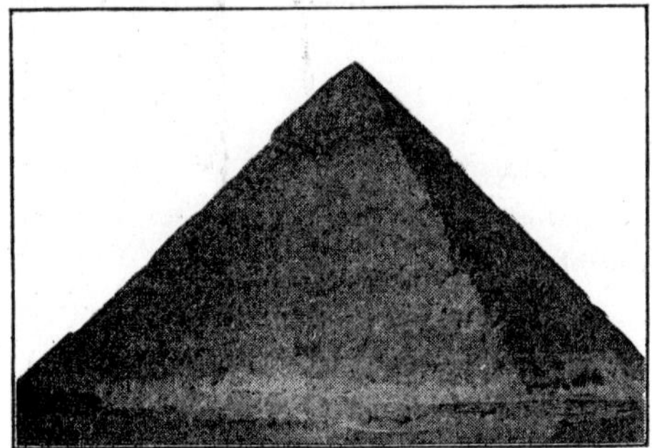

Great Pyramid of Khufu.

4. 5th Age: VIIth–XIVth Dynasties

5th Age.—By about 4050 BC, the decline of Egypt allowed of fresh people pressing in from the N., probably connected with Crete. There are few traces of these invaders; a curious class of barbaric buttons used as seals are their commonest remains. Probably the so-called "Hyksos sphinxes" and statues are of these people, and belong to the time of their attaining power in Egypt. By 3600 BC, the art developed into the great ages of the XIth to the XIIth Dynasties which lasted about 2 cents. The work is more scholastic and less natural than before; but it is very beautiful and of splendid accuracy. The exquisite jewelry of Dahshur is of this age. After some centuries of decay this civilization passed away.

6th Age.—The Sem tribes had long been filtering into Egypt, and Bab Semites even ruled the land until the great migration of the Hyksos took place about 2700 BC. These tribes were ruled by kings entitled "princes of the desert," like the Sem Absha, or Abishai, shown in the tomb of Beni-hasan, as coming to settle in Egypt. By 1700 BC the Berbers who had adopted the Egyp civilization pressed down from the S., and ejected the Hyksos rule. This opened the most flourishing period of Egyp history, the XVIIIth Dynasty, 1587–1328 BC. The profusion of painted tombs at Thebes, which were copied and popularized by Gardner Wilkinson, has made the life of this period very familiar to us. The immense temples of Karnak and of Luqsor, and the finest of the Tombs of the Kings have impressed us with the royal magnificence of this age. The names of

5. 6th Age: XVth–XXIVth Dynasties

Sheshenq I (Shishak) in 952 BC, the founder of the XXIId Dynasty. His successors gradually decayed till the fall of the XXIIId Dynasty in 721 BC. The Ethiopian XXVIth Dynasty then held Egypt as a province of Ethiopia, down to 664 BC.

7th Age.—It is hard to say when the next age began—perhaps with the Ethiopians; but it rose to importance with the XXVIth Dynasty under Psamtek (Psammitichos I), 664–610 BC, and continued under the well-known names of Necoh, Hophra and Amasis until overthrown by the Persians in 525 BC. From 405 to 342 the Egyptians were independent; then the Persians again crushed them, and in 332 they fell into the hands of the Macedonians by the conquest of Alexander.

6. 7th Age: XXVth Dynasty–Roman Times

Obelisk of Thothmes I.

Thothmes I and III, of the great queen Hatshepsut, of the magnificent Amenhotep III, and of the monotheist reformer Akhenaton are among those best known in the history. Their foreign connections we shall notice later.

The XIXth and XXth Dynasties were a period of continual degradation from the XVIIIth. Even in the best work of the 6th Age there is hardly ever the real solidity and perfection which is seen in that of the 4th or 5th Ages. But under the Ramessides cheap effects and showy imitations were the regular system. The great Rameses II was a great advertiser, but inferior in power to half a dozen kings of the previous dynasty. In the XXth Dynasty one of the royal daughters married the high priest of Amen at Thebes; and on the unexpected death of the young Rameses V, the throne reverted to his uncle Rameses VI, whose daughter then became the heiress, and her descendants, the high priests of Amen, became the rightful rulers. This priestly rule at Thebes, beginning in 1102 BC, was balanced by a purely secular rule of the north at Tanis (Zoan). These lasted until the rise of

The Macedonian Age of the Ptolemies was one of the richest and most brilliant at its start, but soon faded under bad rulers till it fell hopelessly to pieces and succumbed to the Rom subjection in 30 BC. From that time Egypt was ground by taxation, and steadily impoverished. By 300 AD it was too poor to keep even a copper currency in circulation, and barter became general. Public monuments entirely ceased to be erected, and Decius in 250 AD is the last ruler whose name was written in the old hieroglyphs, which were thenceforward totally forgotten. After three more cents. of increasing degradation and misery, the Arab invasion burst upon the land, and a few thousand men rode through it and cleared out the remaining effete garrisons of the empire in 641 AD.

8th Age.—The Arab invasion found the country exhausted and helpless; repeated waves of tribes poured in, and for a generation or two there was no chance of a settlement. Gradually the majority of the inhabitants were pressed into Islam, and by about 800 AD a strong government was established

7. 8th Age: Arabic

from Bagdad, and Egypt rapidly advanced. In place of being the most impoverished country it became the richest land of the Mediterranean. The great period of mediaeval Egypt was under the guidance of the Mesopotamian civilization, 800–969 AD. The Tunisian dominion of the Fatimites, 969–1171, was less successful. Occasionally strong rulers arose, such as Salah-ed-Dîn (Saladin), but the age of the Mamalukes, 1250–1577, was one of steady decline. Under the Turkish dominion, 1517, Egypt was split up into many half-independent counties, whose rulers began by yielding tribute, but relapsed into ignoring the Caliphate and living in continual internal feuds. In 1771 Aly Bey, a slave, succeeded in conquering Syria. The French and British quarrel left Muhamed Aly to rise supreme, and to guide Egypt for over 40 years. Again Egypt conquered Syria, 1831–39, but was compelled by Europe to retreat. The opening of the Suez Canal (1869) necessarily led to the subjection of Egypt to European direction.

8. Early Foreign Connections

The foreign connections of Egypt have been brought to light only during the last 20 years. In place of supposing that Egypt was isolated until the Gr conquest, we now see that it was in the closest commercial relation with the rest of the world throughout its history. We have already noted the influences which entered by conquest. During the periods of high civilization in Egypt, foreign connections came into notice by exploration and by trade. The lazuli of Persia was imported in the prehistoric age, as well as the emery of Smyrna. In the Ist Dynasty, Egypt conquered and held Sinai for the sake of the turquoise mines. In the IIId Dynasty, large fleets of ships were built, some as much as 160 ft. long; and the presence of much pottery imported from Crete and the north, even before this, points to a Mediterranean trade. In the Vth Dynasty, King Unas had relations with Syria. From the XIIth Dynasty comes the detailed account of the life of an Egyptian in Pal (Sanehat); and Cretan pottery of this age is found traded into Egypt.

III. Old Testament Connections.—The Hyksos invasion unified the rule of Syria and Egypt, and

1. Semitic Connections

Syrian pottery is often found in Egypt of this age. The return of the wave, when Egypt drove out the Hyksos, and conquered Syria out to the Euphrates, was the greatest expansion of Egypt. Tahutmes I set up his statue on the Euphrates, and all Syria was in his hands. Tahutmes III repeatedly raided Syria, bringing back plunder and captives year by year throughout most of his reign. The number of Syrian artists and of Syrian women brought into Egypt largely changed the style of art and the standard of beauty. Amenhotep III held all Syria in peace, and recorded his triumphs at the Euphrates on the walls of the temple of Soleb far up in Nubia. His monotheist son, Amenhotep IV, took the name of Akhenaton, "the glory of the sun's disc," and established the worship of the radiant sun as the Aton, or Adon of Syria. The cuneiform letters from Tell el-Amarna place all this age before us in detail. There are some from the kings of the Amorites and Hittites, from Naharain and even Babylonia, to the great suzerain Amenhotep III. There is also the long series describing the gradual loss of Syria under Akhenaton, as written by the governors and chiefs, of the various towns. The main letters are summarized in the *Students' History of Egypt*, II, and full abstracts of all the letters are in *Syria and Egypt*, arranged in historical order.

Pal was reconquered by Seti I and his son Rameses II, but they only held about a third of the extent which formerly belonged to Amenhotep III. Merenptah, son of Rameses, also raided Southern Pal. After that, it was left alone till the raid of Shesheng in 933 BC. The only considerable assertion of Egyp power was in Necoh's two raids up to the Euphrates, in 609 and 605 BC. But Egypt generally held the desert and a few minor points along the south border of Pal. The Ptolemies seldom possessed more than that, their aspirations in Syria not lasting as permanent conquests. They were more successful in holding Cyprus.

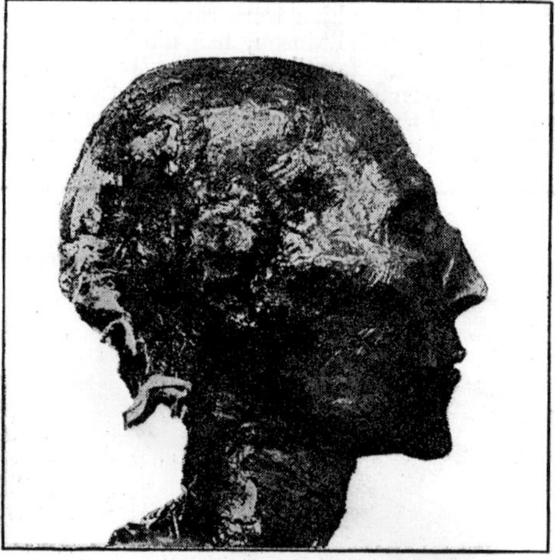

Seti I.

2. Abramic Times

We now come to the specific connections of Egypt with the OT. The movement of the family of Abram from Ur in the south of Mesopotamia up to Haran in the north (Gen **11** 31) and thence down Syria into Egypt (Gen **12** 5.10) was like that of the earlier Sem "princes of the desert," when they entered Egypt as the Hyksos kings about 2600 BC. Their earlier dominion was the XVth Dynasty of Egypt, and that was followed by another movement, the XVIth Dynasty, about 2250 BC, which was the date of the migration of Terah from Ur. Thus the Abramic family took part in the second Hyksos movement. The cause of these tribal movements has been partly explained by Mr. Huntington's researches on the recurrence of dry periods in Asia (Royal Geogr. Soc., May 26, 1910: *The Pulse of Asia*). Such lack of rain forces the desert peoples on to the cultivated lands, and then later famines are recorded. The dry age which pushed the Arab tribes on to the Mediterranean in 640 AD was succeeded by famines in Egypt during 6 cents. So as soon as Abram moved into Syria a famine pushed him on to Egypt (Gen **12** 10). To this succeeded other famines in Canaan (Gen **26** 1), and later in both Canaan and Egypt (Gen **41** 56; **43** 1; **47** 13). The migration of Abram was thus conditioned by the general dry period, which forced the second Hyksos movement of which it was a part. The culture of the Hyksos was entirely nomadic, and agrees in all that we can trace with the patriarchal culture pictured in Gen.

3. Circumcision

Circumcision was a very ancient mutilation in Egypt, and is still kept up there by both Muslim and Christian. It was first adopted by Abram for Ishmael, the son of the Egyp Hagar (Gen **16** 3; **17** 23), before Isaac was promised. Hagar married Ishmael to an Egyptian (Gen **21** 21), so that the Ishmaelites, or Hagarenes, of Gilead and Moab were three-quarters Egyptian.

At Gerar, in the south of Pal, Egyptian was the prevailing race and language, as the general of

Abimelech was Phichol, the Egyp name Pa-khal, "the Syrian," showing that the Gerarites were not Syrians.

4. Joseph

The history of Joseph rising to importance as a capable slave is perfectly natural in Egypt at that time, and equally so in later periods down to our own days. That this occurred during the Hyksos period is shown by the title given to Joseph—*Abrekh*, (*'abhrēkh*) (Gen **41** 43) which is *Abarakhu*, the high Bab title. The names Zaphnath-paaneah, Asenath, and Potipherah have been variously equated in Egyptian, Naville seeing forms of the XVIIIth Dynasty in them, but Spiegelberg, with more probability, seeing types of names of the XXIId Dynasty or later. The names are most likely an expansion of the original document; but there is not a single feature or incident in the relations of Joseph to the Egyptians which is at all improbable from the history and civilization that we know. See Joseph.

5. Descent into Egypt

The descent into Egypt and sojourn there are what might be expected of any Sem tribe at this time. The allocation in Goshen (Gen **47** 27) was the most suitable, as that was on the eastern border of the Delta, at the mouth of the Wady Tumilat, and was a district isolated from the general Egyp population. The whole of Goshen is not more than 100 sq. miles, being bounded by the deserts, and by the large Egyp city of Budastis on the W. The accounts of the embalming for 40 days and mourning for 70 days (Gen **50** 3), and putting in a coffin (Gen **50** 26) are exact. The 70 days' mourning existed both in the Ist Dynasty and in the XXth.

6. The Oppression

The oppression in Egypt began with a new king that knew not Joseph. This can hardly be other than the rise of the Berber conquerors who took the Delta from the Hyksos at the beginning of the XVIIIth Dynasty, 1582 BC, and expelled the Hyksos into Syria. It could not be later than this, as the period of oppression in Egypt is stated at 4 cents. (Gen **15** 13; Acts **7** 6), and the Exodus cannot be later than about 1220 BC, which leaves 360 years for the oppression. Also this length of oppression bars any much earlier date for the Exodus. The 360 years of oppression from 430 of the total sojourn in Egypt, leaves 70 years of freedom there. As Joseph died at 110 (Gen **50** 26), this implies that he was over 40 when his family came into Egypt, which would be quite consistent with the history.

Statue of Rameses II at Luqsor.

7. The Historic Position

The store cities Pithom and Raamses are the sites *Tell el-Maskhuta* and *Tell Rotāb* in the Wady Tumilat, both built by Rameses II as frontier defences. It is evident then that the serving with rigor was under that king, probably in the earlier part of his long reign of 67 years (1300–1234 BC), when he was actively campaigning in Pal. This is shown in the narrative, for Moses was not yet born when the rigor began (Ex **1**; **2** 2), and he grew up, slew an Egyptian, and then lived long in Midian before the king of Egypt died (Ex **2** 23), perhaps 40 or 50 years after the rigorous servitude began, for he is represented as being 80 at the time of the Exodus (Dt **34** 7). These numbers are probably not precise, but as a whole they agree well enough with Egyp history. After the king died, Moses returned to Egypt, and began moving to get his kin away to the eastern deserts, with which he had been well acquainted in his exile from Egypt. A harsher servitude ensues, which might be expected from the more vigorous reign of Merenptah, after the slackness of the old age of Rameses. The campaign of Merenptah against Israel and other people in Pal would not make him any less severe in his treatment of Semites in Egypt.

8. The Plagues

The plagues are in the order of usual seasonal troubles in Egypt, from the red unwholesome Nile in June, through the frogs, insects, hail and rain, locusts, and sandstorms in March. The death of the firstborn was in April at the Passover.

9. Date of the Exodus

The date of the Exodus is indicated as being about 1200 BC, by the 4 cents. of oppression, and by the names of the land and the city of Rameses (Gen **47** 4; cf Ex **1** 11). The historical limit is that the Egyptians were incessantly raiding Pal down to 1194 BC, and then abandoned it till the invasion of Shishak. As there is no trace of these Egyp invasions during all the ups and downs of the age of the Judges, it seems impossible to suppose the Israelites entered Canaan till after 1194 BC. The setting back of the Exodus much earlier has arisen from taking three simultaneous histories of the Judges as consecutive, as we shall notice farther on. The facts stated above, and the length of all three lines of the priestly genealogies, agree completely with the Egyp history in putting the Exodus at about 1220 BC, and the entry into Canaan about 1180 BC.

10. Route of the Exodus

The route of the Exodus was first a concentration at Raamses or *Tell Rotāb*, in the Wady Tumilat, followed by a march to Succoth, a general name for the region of Bedawy booths; from there to Etham in the edge of the wilderness, about the modern *Nefisheh*. Thence they turned and encamped before Pi-hahiroth, the Egyp Pa-qaheret, a Serapeum. Thus turning S. to the W. of the Red Sea (which then extended up to *Tell el-Maskhuta*), they had a Migdol tower behind them and Baal-zephon opposite to them. They were thus "entangled in the land." Then the strong east wind bared the shallows, and made it possible to cross the gulf and reach the opposite shore. They then went "three days in the wilderness," the three days' route without water to Marah, the bitter spring of Hawara, and immediately beyond reached Elim, which accords entirely with the Wady Gharandel. Thence they encamped by the Red Sea. All of this account exactly agrees with the traditional route down the W. of the Sinaitic peninsula; it will not agree with any other route, and there is no reason to look for any different location of the march. See Exodus, I.

11. Numbers of the Exodus

The numbers of the Israelites have long been a difficulty. On the one hand are the census lists (Nu **1**, **2** and **26**), with their summaries of 600,000 men besides children and a mixed multitude (Ex **12** 37.38; **38** 26; Nu **1** 46; **11** 21). On the other hand there are the exact statements of there being 22,273 firstborn, that is, fathers of families (Nu **3** 43), and that 40,000 armed men entered Canaan with Joshua (Josh **4** 13), also the 35,000 who fought at Ai (Josh **8** 3.12), and the 32,000 who fought against Midian (Jgs **7** 3). Besides these, there are the general considerations that only 5,000 to 10,000 people could live in Goshen, that the Amalekites with whom the Israelites were equally matched (Ex **17** 11) could not have exceeded about 5,000 in Sinai, that Moses judged all disputes, and that two midwives attended all the Israelite births, which would be 140 a day on a population of 600,000. Evidently the statements of numbers are contradictory, and the external evidence is all in accord with lesser numbers. Proposals to reduce arbitrarily the larger numbers have been frequent; but there is one likely line of misunderstanding that may have originated the increase. In the census lists of the tribes, most of the hundreds in the numbers are 400 or 500, others are near those, and there are none whatever on 000, 100, 800 or 900. Evidently the hundreds are independent of the thousands. Now in

King Merenptah.

writing the statements, such as "Reuben, 46,500," the original list would be 46 *'eleph*, 5 hundred people, and *'eleph* means either "thousands" or else "groups" or "families." Hence a census of 46 tents, 500 people, would be ambiguous, and a later compiler might well take it as 46,500. In this way the whole census of 598 tents, 5,550 people, would be misread as 603,550 people. The checks on this are, that the number per tent should be reasonable in all cases, that the hundreds should not fluctuate more than the tents between the first and last census, and that the total should correspond to the known populations of Goshen and of Sinai; these requirements all agree with this reading of the lists. The ulterior details beyond the Egyptian period are dealt with in *Egypt and Israel*, 45, 55. See EXODUS, IV.

12. Israel in Canaan

Two points need notice here as incidentally bearing on the Egyp connections: (1) the Israelites in Pal before the Exodus, indicated by Merenptah triumphing over them there before 1230 BC, and the raids during the Egyp residence (1 Ch **7** 21); (2) the triple history of the Judges, west, north, and east, each totaling to 120 years, in accord with the length of the four priestly genealogies (1 Ch **6** 4–8.22–28.33–35.39–43.44–47), and showing that the dates are about 1220 BC the Exodus, 1180 BC the entry to Canaan, 1150 BC the beginning of Judges, 1030 BC Saul (*Egypt and Israel*, 52–58).

13. Hadad

The connections with the monarchy soon begin. David and Joab attacked Edom (2 S **8** 14), and Hadad, the young king, was carried off by his servants to Egypt for safety. The Pharaoh who received and supported him must have been Siamen, the king of Zoan, which city was then an independent capital apart from the priest kings of Thebes (1 K **11** 15–22). Hadad was married to the Egyp queen's sister when he grew up, probably in the reign of Pasebkhanu II.

14. Pharaoh's Daughter

The Pharaoh whose daughter was married to Solomon must have been the same Pasebkhanu; he reigned from 987–952 BC, and the marriage was about 970 in the middle of the reign. Another daughter of Pasebkhanu was Karamat, who was the wife of Shishak. Thus Solomon and Shishak married two sisters, and their aunt was queen of Edom. This throws light on the politics of the kingdoms. Probably Solomon had some child by Pharaoh's daughter, and the Egyptians would expect that to be the heir. Shishak's invasion, on the death of Solomon, was perhaps based upon the right of a nephew to the throne of Judah.

15. Shishak

The invasion of Shishak (Egyp, Sheshenq) took place probably at the end of his reign. His troops were Lubim (Libyans), Sukkim (men of Succoth, the east border) and Kushim (Ethiopians). The account of the war is on the side of the great fore-court at Karnak, which shows long lists of places in Judah, agreeing with the subjugation recorded in 1 K **14** 25.26, and 2 Ch **12** 2–4. He also subjugated places in Israel.

16. Zerakh

Zerakh, or Usarkon, was the next king of Egypt, the son of Karamat, Solomon's sister-in-law. He invaded Judah unsuccessfully in 903 BC (2 Ch **14** 9) with an army of Libyans and Sudanis (2 Ch **16** 8). A statue of the Nile, dedicated by him, and naming his descent from Karamat and Pasebkhanu, is in the British Museum.

17. The Ethiopians

After a couple of cents. the Ethiopian kings intervened. Shabaka was appointed viceroy of Egypt by his father Piankhy, and is described by the Assyrians as Sibe, commander-in-chief of Muzri, and by the Hebrews as Sua or So, king of Egypt (2 K **17** 4). Tirhakah next appears as a viceroy, and Hezekiah was warned against trusting to him (2 K **19** 9). These two kings touch on Jewish history during their viceroyalties, before their full reigns began. Necho next touches on Judah in his raid to Carchemish in 609 BC, when he slew Josiah for opposing him (2 K **23** 29.30; 2 Ch **35** 20–24).

18. Tahpanhes

After the taking of Jerus, for fear of vengeance for the insurrection of Ishmael (2 K **25** 25.26; Jer **40, 41, 42**), the remnant of the Jews fled to the frontier fortress of Egypt, Tahpanhes, Tehaphnehes, Gr Daphnae, mod. *Defenneh*, about 10 miles W. of the present Suez Canal (Jer **43** 7–13). The brick pavement in front of the entrance to the fortress there, in which Jeremiah hid the stones, has been uncovered and the fortress completely planned. It was occupied by Greeks, who there brought Gr words and things into contact with the traveling Jews for a couple of generations before the fall of Jerus.

19. Hophra

The prophecy that Hophra would be delivered to them that sought his life (Jer **44** 30) was fulfilled, as he was kept captive by his successor, Amasis, for 3 years, and after a brief attempt at liberty, he was strangled.

20. The Jews at Syene

The account of the Jews settled in Egypt (Jer **44**) is singularly illustrated by the Aram. Jewish papyri found at Syene (Aswan). These show the use of Aram. and of oaths by Yahu, as stated of 5 cities in Egypt (Isa **19** 18). The colony at Syene was well-to-do, though not rich; they were householders who possessed all their property by regular title-deeds, who executed marriage settlements, and were fully used to litigation, having in deeds of sale a clause that no other deed could be valid. The temple of Yahu filled the space between two roads, and faced upon 3 houses, implying a building about 60 or 70 ft. wide. It was built of hewn stone, with stone columns, 7 gates, and a cedar roof. It was destroyed in 410, after lasting from before Cambyses in 525 BC, and a petition for rebuilding it was granted in 407.

21. The New Jerusalem of Oniah

The most flourishing period of the Jews in Egypt was when Oniah IV, the son of the rightful high priest Oniah, was driven from Jerus by the abolition of Jewish worship and ordinances under Antiochus. In 170 BC he fled to Egypt, and there established a new Jerus with a temple and sacrifices as being the only way to maintain the Jewish worship. Oniah IV was a valiant man, general to queen Cleopatra I; and he offered to form the Jewish community into a frontier guard on the E. of Egypt, hating the Syrians to the uttermost, if the Jews might form their own community. They so dominated the eastern Delta that troops of Caesar could not pass from Syria to Alexandria without their assent. The new Jerus was 20 miles N. of Cairo, a site now known as *Tell el-Yehudiyeh.* The great mound of the temple still remains there, with the Passover ovens beneath it, and part of the massive stone fortifications on the front of it. This remained a stronghold of free Judaism until after Titus took Jerus; and it was only when the Zealots tried to make it a center of insurrection, that at last it was closed and fell into decay. Jos is the original authority for this history (see *Egypt and Israel*, 97–110).

22. The Egyptian Jew

The Jew in Egypt followed a very different development from the Bab Jew, and this Egyp type largely influenced Christianity. In the colony at Syene a woman named "Trust Yahveh" had no objection to swearing by the Egyp goddess Seti when making an Egyp contract; and in Jer **44** 15–19, the Jews boasted of their heathen worship in Egypt. Oniah had no scruple in establishing a temple and sacrifices apart from Jerus, without any of the particularism of the Maccabean zealots. Philo at Alexandria labored all his life for the union of Jewish thought with Gr philosophy. The Hermetic books show how, from 500 to 200 BC, religious thought was developing under eclectic influence of Egyp, Jewish, Pers, Indian and Gr beliefs, and producing the tenets about the second God, the Eternal Son, who was the Logos, and the types of Conversion, as the Divine Ray, the New Birth, and the Baptism. Later the Wisdom lit. of Alexandria, 200–100 BC, provided the basis of thought and simile on which the Pauline Epp. were built. The great wrench in the history of the church came when it escaped from the Bab-Jewish formalism of the Captivity, which ruled at Jerus, and grew into the wider range of ideas of the Alexandrian Jews. These ideas had been preserved in Egypt from the days of the monarchy, and had developed a great body of religious thought and phraseology from their eclectic connections. The relations of Christianity with Egypt are outside our scope, but some of them will be found in *Egypt and Israel*, 124–41.

23. Cities and Places Alphabetically

The Egyp cities, places and peoples named in the OT may briefly be noted. Aven (Ezk **30** 17) or On (Gen **41** 45) is the *'An* of Egyptian, the Gr Heliopolis, now *Matarieh,* 7 miles N. of Cairo. It was the seat of prehistoric government, the royal emblems were kept there as the sacred relics of the temple, and its high priest was "the great seer," one of the greatest of the religious officials. The schools of Heliopolis were celebrated, and it seems to have always been a center of learning. The site is now marked by the great inclosure of the temple, and one obelisk of Senusert (XIIth Dynasty). It was here that the Egyp kings had at their installation to come and bathe in the lake in which the sun bathes daily, the *'Ainesh-Shems,* or "Lake of the Sun" of the Arabs, connected with the fresh spring here which Christian tradition attributes to the visit of the Virgin and Child. The great sycamore tree here is the successor of that under which the Virgin is said to have rested.

Baal-zephon was a shrine on the eastern site of the head of the Red Sea, a few miles S. of Ismailiyeh; no trace is now known of it (Ex **14** 2).

Cushim or Ethiopians were a part of the Egyp army of Shishak and of Usarkon (2 Ch **12** 3; **16** 8). The army was in 4 brigades, that of Ptah of Memphis, central Egypt; that of Amen of Thebes, Southern Egypt and Ethiopia; that of Set of the eastern frontier (Sukkim); and that of Ra, Heliopolis and the Delta.

Goshen was a fertile district at the west end of the Wady Tumilat, 40 to 50 miles N.E. of Cairo. It was bounded by the deserts on the N. and S.E., and by the Egyp city of Bubastis on the W. Its area was not over 100 sq. miles; it formerly supported 4,000 Bedawin and now about 12,000 cultivators.

Lubim, the Libyans who formed part of the Egyp army as light-armed archers, from very early times.

Migdol is the name of any tower, familiar also as Magdala. It was applied to some watchtower on the W. of the Red Sea, probably on the high land above the Serapeum.

No is Thebes, in Assyr *Nia,* from the Egyp Nu, "the city." This was the capital of the XIIth Dynasty, and of the XVIIth–XXIst Dynasties. Owing to the buildings being of sandstone, which is not of much use for reworking, they have largely remained since the desolation of the city under Ptolemy X. The principal divisions of the site are: (1) Karnak, with the temple of the XIIth Dynasty, built over by all the successive kings of the XVIIIth Dynasty, and enlarged by Seti I and Rameses II, and by Shishak, Tirhakah, and the Ptolemies. The whole temple of Amon and its subsidiary temples form the largest mass of ruins that is known. (2) Luqsor, the temple to commemorate the divine birth of Amenhotep III (1440 BC), added to by Rameses II. (3) The funerary temples, bordering the western shore, of the kings of the XVIIIth to XXth Dynasties. These have mostly been destroyed, by the unscrupulous quarrying done by each king on the work of his predecessors; the only temple in fair condition is that of Rameses III, which is left because no later king required its material for building. (4) The great cemetery, ranging from the splendid rock halls of the Tombs of the Kings, covered with paintings, down to the humblest graves. For any detailed account see either Baedeker's or Murray's *Guides*, or Weigall's *Guide to Antiquities.*

Noph, the Egyp Men-nofer, Gr Memphis, now *Mitraheny,* 12 miles S. of Cairo. This was the capital from the foundation at the beginning of the dynasties. Thebes and Alexandria shared its importance, but it was the seat of government down to the Arab invasion. In Rom times it was as large as London N. of the Thames. The outlying parts are now all buried by the rise of the soil, but more than a mile length of ruins yet remains, which are now being regularly worked over by the British School. The heart of the city is the great metropolitan temple of Ptah, nearly all of which is now under 10 feet of soil, and under water most of the year. This is being excavated in sections, as it is all private property. At the north end of the ruins is the palace mound, on which has been cleared the palace of Apries (Hophra). Other temples have been located, as well as the foreign quarter containing early Gr pottery and the temple of Proteus named by Herodotus (see *Memphis*, I, II, III).

PATHROS is the usual name for Upper Egypt in the prophets. It is the Egyp Pa-ta-res, "the south land."

PIBESETH is the Egyp Pa-Bast, Gr Bubastis, at the eastern side of the Delta, the city of the cat-headed goddess Bast. The ruins are still large, and the temple site has been excavated, producing sculptures from the IVth Dynasty onward.

PITHOM is the Egyp Pa-Tum, the city of the Sun-god Tum or Atmu, who was worshipped on the E. of the Delta. The site has remains of the fortress of Rameses II, built by the Israelites, and is now known as *Tell el-Maskhuta*, 11 miles W. of Ismailia.

RAAMSES is the other city built by the Israelites, now *Tell Rotāb*, 20 miles W. of Ismailia. A walled camp existed here from early times, and the temple of Rameses was built on the top of the older ruins. A large part of the temple front is now at Philadelphia, excavated by the British School.

SIN is the Gr Pelusium, Assyr *Siinu*, Arab. *Tineh*, now some desolate mounds at the extreme E. coast of Egypt.

SUCCOTH was the district of "booths," the eastern part of the Wady Tumilat. It was written in Egyp Thuku and abbreviated to Thu in which form it appears as a Rom name. The people of Succoth were Sukkim, named in the army of Shishak (2 Ch **12** 3).

SYENE, Heb *Sᵉwēnēh*, mod. *Aswan*, the southern border town of Egypt at the Cataract. The greater part of the old town was on the island of Elephantine. There the Jewish papyri were found, and that was probably the Jewish settlement with the temple of Yahu. The town on the eastern bank—the present *Aswan*—was of less importance.

TAHPANHES, TEHAPHNEHES, Gr Daphnae, Arab. *Tell Defeneh.* This was the first station on the Syrian road which touched the Nile canals, about 10 miles W. of Kantara on the Suez Canal. It seems to have been founded by Psammetichus about 664 BC, to hold his Gr mercenaries. The fort, built by him, abounded in Gr pottery, and was finally desolated about 566 BC, as described by Herodotus. The fort and camp have been excavated; and the pavement described by Jeremiah (ch **43**), as opposite to the entrance, has been identified.

ZOAN, Gr Tanis, Arab. *San*, is about 26 miles from the Suez Canal, and slightly more from the coast. The ruins of the temple are surrounded by the wall of Pasebkhanu, 80 ft. thick of brickwork, and a ring of town ruins rises high around it. The temple was built in the VIth Dynasty, adorned with many statues in the XIIth and XIIIth Dynasties, and under Rameses II had many large granite obelisks and statues, esp. one colossus of the king in red granite about 90 ft. high. It is probable that the Pharaoh lived here at the time of the Exodus.

IV. The Civilization.—We now turn to some outline of the civilization of the Egyptians. The language had primitive relations with the Sem and the Libyan. Perhaps one common stock has separated into three languages—Sem, Egyp and Libyan. But though some basal words and grammar are in common, all the bulk of the words of daily life were entirely different in the three, and no one could be said to be derived from the other. Egyp, so far as we can see, is a separate language without any connection as close as that between the Indo-European group. From its proximity to Syria, Sem loan words were often introduced, and became common in the XVIIIth Dynasty and fashionable in the XIXth. The language continually altered, and decayed in the later periods until Coptic is as different from it as Italian is from Latin.

1. Language

2. Writing

The writing was at first ideographic, using a symbol for each word. Gradually, signs were used phonetically; but the symbol, or some emblem of the idea of the word, continued to be added to it, now called a determinative. From syllabic signs purely alphabetic signs were produced by clipping and decay, so that by 1000 to 500 BC the writing was almost alphabetic. After that it became modified by the influence of the short Gr alphabet, until by 200 AD it was expressed in Gr letters with a few extra signs. The actual signs used were elaborate pictures of the objects in the early times, and even down to the later periods very detailed signs were carved for monumental purposes. But as early as the Ist Dynasty a very much simplified current hand had been started, and during the pyramid period this became hardly recognizable from the original forms. Later on this current hand, or *hieratic*, is a study by itself and was written much more fully than the hieroglyphs on monuments, as its forms were so corrupt that an ample spelling was needed to identify the word. By about 800 BC begins a much shortened set of signs, still more remote from their origins, known as *demotic*, which continued as the popular writing till Rom times. On public decrees the hieroglyphic and demotic are both given, showing that a knowledge of one was useless for reading the other, and that they were separate studies.

3. Literature

The literature begins during the pyramid period, before 4000 BC, with biographies and collections of maxims for conduct; these show well-regulated society, and would benefit any modern community in which they were followed. In the XIIth Dynasty tales appear, occupied with magic and foreign travel and wonders. A long poem in praise of the king shows very regular versification and system, of the type of Ps **136**, the refrain differing in each stanza and being probably repeated in chorus, while the independent lines were sung by the leader. In the XVIIIth Dynasty, tales of character begin to develop and show much skill, long annals were recorded, and in the XIXth Dynasty there is an elaborate battle poem describing the valor of Rameses II. At about 700 BC there is a considerable tale which describes the quarrels of the rival chiefs, and the great fight regulated like a tournament by which the differences were settled. Such are the principal literary works apart from business documents.

4. Four Views of Future Life

The religion of Egypt is an enormous subject, and that by which Egypt is perhaps most known. Here we can only give an outline of the growth and subdivisions of it. There never was any one religion in Egypt during historic times. There were at least four religions, all incompatible, and all believed in at once in varying degrees. The different religions can best be seen apart by their incongruity regarding the future life.

(1) The dead wandered about the cemetery seeking food, and were partly fed by the goddess in the sycamore tree. They therefore needed to have plates of food and jars of water in the tomb, and provided perpetually by their descendants in front of the doorway to the grave. The deceased is represented as looking out over this doorway in one case. Here came in the great principle of substitution. For the food, substitute its image which cannot decay, and the carved table of offerings results. For the farmstead of animals, substitute its carved image on the walls and the animal sculptures result. For the life of the family, substitute their carved figures doing all that was wanted, sacrificing and serving, and the family sculptures result. For the house, substitute a model upon the grave, and the pottery soul-houses appear with their

ANCIENT EGYPTIAN PAINTINGS ON CLOTH

furniture and provisions. For the servants, put their figures doing household work, and their service is eternal. For the master himself, put the most lifelike image that can be made, and his soul will occupy that as a restful home fitted for it. This principle is still believed in. Funeral offerings of food are still put even in Muslim graves, and a woman will visit a grave, and, removing a tile, will talk through a hole to her dead husband.

(2) The dead went to the kingdom of Osiris, to which only the good were admitted, while the evil were rejected, and consumed either by monsters or by fire. This heavenly kingdom was a complete duplicate of the earthly life. They planted and reaped, sported and played. And as the Egyp felicity consisted in making others work for them, so each man was provided with a retinue of serfs to cultivate the land for him. These *ushabti* figures in later times usually number 400, and often 1 in 10 of them is clad as an overseer. A special chapter of the Book of the Dead is to be recited to animate them, and this, more or less abbreviated, is often inscribed upon the figures.

(3) The dead joined the company of the immortal gods, who float on the heavenly ocean in the boat of the sun. With them they have to face the terrors of the hours of the night when the sun goes through the underworld. Long charms and directions are needed for safety in this passage, and these form a large part of the funerary tests, esp. on the Tombs of the Kings in the XVIIIth–XXIst Dynasties. To reach the boat of the sun a boat must be provided in the tomb, with its sailors and sails and oars. Such are frequent from the VIth–XIIIth Dynasties.

(4) The dead were carried off by the Hathor cow, or a bull, to wait for a bodily resurrection. In order to preserve the body for some life after the present age, each part must be protected by an appropriate amulet; hence dozens of different amulets were placed on the body, esp. from about 600–400 BC.

Now it will be seen that each of these beliefs contradicts the other three, and they represent, therefore, different religious origins.

5. Four Groups of Gods

The mythology is similarly diverse, and was unified by uniting analogous gods. Hence when we see the compounds such as Ptah-Sokar-Osiris, or Amen-Ra or Osiris-Khentamenti, it is clear that each god of the compound belongs to a different religion, like Pallas-Athene or Zeus-Labrandeus, in Gr compounds. So far as we can at present see, the gods linked with each of the beliefs about the soul are as follows:

(1) *The soul in the tombs and cemetery.*—With this belief belong the animal gods, which form the earliest stratum of the religion; also Sokar the god of "Silence," and Mert Sokar, the "Lover of Silence," as the gods of the dead. With this was allied a belief in the soul sometimes going to the west, and hence Khent-amenti, a jackal-headed god, "he who is in the west," became the god of the dead.

(2) *The soul in the heavenly kingdom.*—Osiris is the lord of this kingdom, Isis his sister-wife, Horus their son, Nebhat (Nephthys) the sister of Isis, and Set her husband. Set also was regarded as coequal with Horus. This whole mythology results probably from the fusion of tribes who were originally monotheistic, and who each worshipped one of these deities. It is certain that the later parts of this mythology are tribal history, regarded as the victories and defeats of the gods whom the tribes worshipped.

(3) *The soul in the sun-boat.*—Ra was the Sun-god, and in other forms worshipped as Khepera and Atmu. The other cosmic gods of the same group are Nut, the heaven, and her husband Geb, the earth; Shu, space, and his sister Tefnut. Anher the Sky-god belongs to Upper Egypt.

(4) *The mummy with amulets, preserved for a future life.*—Probably to this group belong the gods of principles, Hathor the female principle; Min the male principle; Ptah the architect and creator of the universe; his spouse Maat, abstract truth and justice.

6. Foreign Gods

Foreign gods frequently appear also in Egypt, mostly from Syria. Two importations were of great effect. Aton the radiant energy of the sun, the Adon or "lord," Adonai, Adonis, was introduced as a sole deity by Akhenaton 1380 BC, and all other gods were proscribed. This was a strictly rational and scientific religion, attributing all life and power to the action of the sun's rays; but it only lasted 20 years in Egypt, and then vanished. The other important worship was that of Zeus Sarapis. The Zeus statue is said to have been imported from Sinope by Ptolemy I, but the Sarapis was the god of Memphis, Osarhapi, the Osiris form of the Hapi bull. The Egyptian worshipped his old gods; the Greek was satisfied with Zeus; and both nations united in adoring Zeus Sarapis. The temples and ritual are too wide a subject to touch in our present space; but the essential principle was that of providing a banquet for the god, and feasting in his temple, not that of an expiatory sacrifice or burnt offering, which is Semitic.

7. Laws

The laws are but little known until the late Gr accounts. Marriage was usual with a sister, but this may have been with a half-sister, as among the Greeks and early Hebrews. Polygamy was unusual, but was legal, as many as six wives being represented in one instance. Kings of course had unlimited *harēms*. Divorce was unusual, but was probably easy. In Coptic times a marriage contract provides for divorce by either party, on paying six times the marriage gift. Property was strictly guarded.

8. Character

The national character was easygoing, kindly, never delighting in torture like the Assyrians and Romans, but liable to be too slack and careless—as at present. Firmness, decision and fortitude were held up as the leading virtues. The structure of society, the arts and the industries are outside of the scope of this article.

[For differing views on chronology and sites, see arts. EXODUS; WANDERINGS; PITHOM; RAAMSES, etc, and on individual kings, etc, arts. under their names, and EGYPTIAN KINGS.]

LITERATURE.—Works in Eng., that are the most accessible, are stated in preference to foreign works, the references to which will be seen in the books stated below. P = Petrie.

The Country: Baedeker's *Egypt;* on the flora, P, *Hawara, Biahmu, and Arsinoe.*

The History: Prehistoric: P, *Diospolis Parva,* etc; de Morgan, *Recherches;* Maspero, *The Dawn of Civilization, The Struggle of the Nations, The Passing of the Empires;* P, *Student's History of Egypt;* Breasted, *A History of Egypt,* etc. On the Ist–IId Dynasties, P, *Royal Tombs.* On the IIId–VIth Dynasties, P, *The Pyramids and Temples of Gizeh;* Murray, *Saqqara Mastabas I.* On the VIIth–XIVth Dynasties, P, *Gizeh and Rifeh;* de Morgan, *Dahchour,* I, II. On the XVth–XXIVth Dynasties, Weigall, *Guide to Antiquities;* Baedeker on Thebes; P, *Six Temples at Thebes.* On the XXVth Dynasty to Roman times, P, *Temple of Apries;* Mahaffy, *The Empires of the Ptolemies;* Milne, *History of Egypt under Roman Rule.* On the early foreign connections, P, *Methods and Aims in Archaeology.*

On the Sem connections: P, *Syria and Egypt from the Tell el-Amarna Tablets.*

On the OT connections: P, *Egypt and Israel.*

On the language: Murray, *Elementary Grammar.*

On the writing and lit.: Erman, *Life in Ancient Egypt;* P, *Egyptian Tales,* I, II.

On the religion: Wiedemann, *Religion of the Ancient Egyptians.*

On the customs: Wilkinson, *Manners and Customs of the Ancient Egyptians.*

On the arts: P, *The Arts and Crafts of Ancient Egypt.*

W. M. FLINDERS PETRIE

EGYPT, RECENT DISCOVERIES (Supplement 1929)

I. Heliopolis
II. Beth-shean
III. Gerar and Kiriath-sepher

I. Heliopolis.—In addition to the admirable article on Egypt by Sir Flinders Petrie some things of special interest to Bible students may now be presented, as well as some account of more recent discoveries by Sir Flinders and others. The very remarkable story of Joseph, the Prime Minister, one of the most romantic, as well as providential, careers on record either in the Bible or outside of it, is of very special interest to all who love the Word and more especially as these later years of discovery in Egypt and Palestine have but served to make the story of the Prime Minister, one of many Prime Ministers in Egypt, stand out in greater relief.

The excavations of Petrie at Heliopolis in 1912 cut the great Hyksos wall surrounding the temple area within which Joseph, who married a daughter of "The Priest of On" (Heliopolis), almost certainly resided and from which he ruled the greatest empire of that age (Gen **39**–**41**). The strange providence which surrounded and followed the Palestine peasant lad, the young slave of Midianite merchants in an Ishmaelite caravan going down into Egypt (Gen **37** 28–36) the servant of an officer of the Pharaoh, a prisoner who was the devout guide of his fellow-prisoners, the slave suddenly elevated to the Court and the Premiership of the greatest empire of the time, then the wise and adroit brother and son, and above all the remarkable illustration, if not the express type, of the Saviour of the world—all this sets before us the providential working of Him who "makes even the wrath of man to praise Him." Sir Flinders has graphically set before us the picture as it appears in Egyp history. The Hyksos princes, friendly to the Palestinian people, were on the throne. They were surrounded for the most part by their own henchmen as is shown by the explanation concerning one of them, that he was "an Egyptian" (Gen **39** 1). Thus the political conditions fit into God's providence exactly, or shall we not say that God, as always, is able to use the machinations of men even to "make the wrath of men to praise Him." We can trace the footsteps of the King of Kings in that history as well as the footsteps of the heads of earthly dynasties. It is even so with political conditions as with the material remains of the events of Biblical history; the reality as dug up out of the ground or discovered in ancient history exactly corroborates the Biblical narrative. The rather sensational reports of the discovery of Joseph's tomb near Jacob's well in Palestine have not been fully realized, though there can be no doubt concerning the immediate neighborhood of the tomb. Few places in Palestine are more certain than Jacob's well.

II. Beth-shean.—The discoveries at *Beisan*, the ancient Beth-shean, have contributed additional valuable information concerning the place in Egyp history to which the Exodus must be assigned and much also on the general history of Egypt as reflected in the article above on Egypt. It is well known that, among Biblical scholars, and to a less extent among Egyptologists, there is a wide division of opinion concerning the period in Egyp history at which the Exodus took place. These opinions vary all the way from 1450 BC down to 1150 BC. Here are 300 years of possible error which must be distributed all through the history of the patriarchs and the years of the national life of Israel in the promised land from the Conquest to the Exile.

The view generally received by Egyptologists, and by many Biblical scholars, is that which is presented in the article on Egypt. It places the Exodus at the close of the reign of Rameses II and the beginning of the reign of Merenptah, both of the XIXth Dynasty. Those who advocate the earlier date for the Exodus put the oppression under Thothmes III and the Exodus in the time, most probably, of Amenophis III or IV all of the XVIIIth Dynasty some 300 years earlier (i.e. 1450 BC according to the theory). The discoveries by Naville at Pithom (see Pithom) seemed to establish beyond question that Rameses II was the Pharaoh of the Oppression. Despite this seeming, some have sharply called in question Naville's conclusions, if not his discoveries, and have stoutly claimed that whatever building, if any, Rameses did at Pithom was rebuilding, and that the work of the Hebrews at this place had been done a long time before, in fact under Thothmes III.

Now, however, at Beth-shean in Palestine, which as indicated in the Biblical narrative (1 S **31**), was in

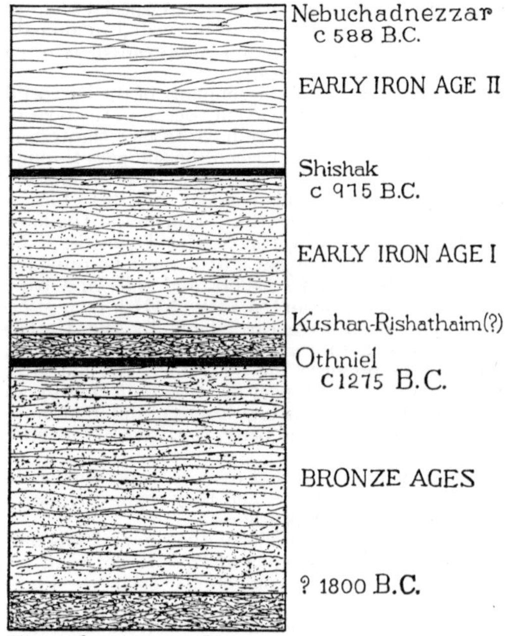

Stratification, Kiriath-sepher (Fig. 1)

Philistine hands down until after the disastrous battle of Gilboa, the Philistines hung up the trophies of Saul and Jonathan in the temple of Ashtaroth (1 S **21** 10) and their bodies on the walls of Beth-shean (*id* 12). The Philistines themselves were at the same time, in some way, the exact extent of which we do not know, under Egyp control. And here is found not only the very Philistine temple of Ashtaroth, but a stele of Rameses II, who, among other things, declares that he had built the other store city, Raamses, and that he built it with Semitic Asiatic slaves (see Beth-shean). This statement also received confirmation at Pithom, as I found in a personal re-examination of Naville's work there (see Pithom, Supplement 1929), for the work at that place on the store chambers was in the well-known big brick of Rameses II, showing that the work done there by the Israelite slaves was done in the time of Rameses II. Thus the place which Petrie gives to the Exodus in the article on Egypt is still abreast of the latest discoveries (See also Chronology, Supplement 1929).

III. Gerar and Kiriath-sepher.—This corroboration of patriarchal history and its synchronization with Egyp history has now received additional and, may we not say, final confirmation through the work of excavation at the old Philistine city of Gerar 1928 by Sir Flinders Petrie and the excavations at Kiriath-sepher 1926–28 by Xenia Theological Seminary in coöperation with the American School of Oriental Research at Jerusalem. At the latter place (see KIRIATH-SEPHER) there was found inside the great chariot gate on the east on unusually thick layer of ashes betokening a great burning of the city. This layer of ashes divided exactly between the Canaanite period, as indicated by all the finds below the ashes, and the Israelite period as conclusively shown by all the remains above the ashes. The break was sharp and final both below and above the ashes. These ashes, also equally and as decisively, divided between the Bronze Age and the Iron Age above (Fig. **1**). This layer of ashes determined three things beyond question: that there was a conquest of the city in which it was burned, that Israelites were the conquerors who continued to hold the city ever afterward to the end of their national history, and that this event occurred exactly at the transition period from the Bronze Age to the Iron Age. The ashes exactly separated the two.

Now at the same time (1928) Petrie in his work at Gerar, Fig **2** (see GERAR), discovered the smelting

Region of Gerar (Fig. 2).

furnaces of the Philistines where they smelted iron. It was the establishment of furnaces for smelting iron ore which made iron abundant and cheap, and so able quickly to drive out the more expensive bronze, and thus ushered in the Iron Age in Palestine. We need not be surprised to find that the Philistines, the most alert people of that ancient world, sought to secure a monopoly of the iron business. This is clearly indicated (1 S **13** 19–21). Even as late as the time of Saul no smithy was permitted to the Israelites by the Philistines, but every man must take his tools and his implements to the Philistine smith-shops to be sharpened. Thus not only was a monopoly held in the iron business, but the Israelites were prevented from making iron weapons for themselves. The introduction of the Iron Age in Palestine was thus not only contemporaneous with the Conquest by Israel, but equally contemporaneous with the great ascendency of the Philistines in the land and the introduction of iron furnaces and the "chariots of iron." To put the Conquest back to the middle of the 15th cent. BC, as the early date for the Exodus proposes to do, in the time of Amenophis III or IV in Egypt, would thrust the Iron Age back almost to the middle of the Bronze Age. Moreover, it would make the Conquest identical with the Ḥabiri invasion, an utterly discredited theory. However similar to the events of the Conquest the invasion of the Ḥabiri as told in the Tell el-Amarna tablets may be made to appear by artful translation and transliteration, and the frequent occurrence of names common in the Orient, the Ḥabiri are now well known as northern allies of the Hittites (Sayce, *Jour. Theological Studies*, 1929).

On the other hand, the Philistine power, as indicated unmistakably by the Philistine pottery, came at the end of the Late Bronze Age and the beginning of the Iron Age (1300–1250 BC). This exactly accords with the place in Egyp history given to the Exodus by Petrie's article on Egypt, the end of the reign of Rameses II and the beginning of the reign of Merenptah.

If further evidence be desired, it is to be found in the synchronizing of Egyp history on the Israel tablet of Merenptah and Biblical history in the record of the turning back at Kadesh Barnea. In 1906, Prof. Petrie found the Israel tablet at the Ramesseum in upper Egypt (Petrie, *Six Temples of Egypt*). The inscription (see EXODUS) has been by some interpreted as denoting a time when the Israelites were already in Palestine, but best accords both with the hieroglyphic inscription and with the Biblical history, when taken as a poetic jeer at the failure of the Israelites to enter KHAR (Palestine by way of Dead Sea) because their "seed" was not, the boy babies having been destroyed in an effort to make the people a nation of women and so easily kept in slavery. This inscription is of the fifth year of Merenptah, the Pharaoh of the Exodus according to the article on Egypt by Petrie. Moses was sent back at the death of those who sought to slay him, thus the death of Rameses II. A year must be allowed in the Orient for his return. The conflict with Pharaoh as indicated by the Plagues occupied a full year. Two years more elapsed before the Israelites turned back at Kadesh Barnea. The turning back would thus be at the fifth year of Moses. So the fifth year of Merenptah, in which his inscription is dated, would be the fifth year of Moses.

Still further corroboration of the date of the beginning of the Iron Age in Palestine, as given above, is furnished by a recent discovery in Egypt. The Egyptian government has been slowly completing the work at the tomb of Tut-ankh-amon the discovery of which made such a sensation a few years ago. In an annex to the tomb was found a mixed lot of articles much destroyed by tomb robbers, before the final robbers came to take everything away. Among these various articles was found a wooden box. It proved to be about the last thing to be expected in a tomb, a tool-box. It contained quite a collection of tools made of small pieces of iron fitted into wood. They are believed to have been models of rools. As tools they are instructive, but their great value is of a different kind. They mark the earliest point for the introduction of the Iron Age in Egypt and from the frugal way in which the iron is used, almost as a precious metal, they denote the beginning of the use of iron, when it was like aluminum some years ago, or as radium still is in the modern world. Iron had been discovered, the smelting of iron invented, but as yet the new metal was too scarce and expensive to mark the beginning of a real Iron Age.

Now Tut-ankh-amon lived about 125 years before the Exodus. Even if the full introduction of the Iron Age in Egypt and also Palestine were marked by this discovery, it would still be fatal to the early date for the Exodus in the time of Amenophis IV a century and a half before. The real Iron Age, when iron become abundant and cheap and completely drove out the bronze for ordinary purposes, must have come after this sparing use of iron.

The wideness of God's providence, so manifest in all this portion of Israel's history, is nowhere more clearly manifest than in the history of Egypt leading up to the Exodus and subsequent to that event as delineated in the article on Egypt.

M. G. KYLE

EGYPT, BROOK (RIVER, STREAM) OF. See BROOK OF EGYPT.

EGYPTIAN KINGS (LATER). See PHARAOH HOPHRA; NECOH; SHISHAK; EGYPT, III.

EGYPTIAN, ē-jip′shan, **THE** (ὁ **Αἰγύπτιος,** *ho Aigúptios*): Mentioned in Acts **21** 38, by Claudius Lysias as having "before these days stirred up to sedition and led out into the wilderness the four thousand men of the ASSASSINS" (q.v.). Reference to this Egyptian and to the suppression of his rebellion by the procurator Felix is likewise found in Jos (*Ant,* XX, viii, 6; *BJ,* II, xiii, 5).

EGYPTIAN VERSIONS, vûr′shuns. See COPTIC VERSIONS.

EGYPTIANS, GOSPEL ACCORDING TO THE. See APOCRYPHAL GOSPELS.

EHI, ē′hī (אֵחִי, *'ēḥī*): Apparently a contracted form (Gen **46** 21). See AHIRAM.

EHUD, ē′hud (אֵהוּד, *'ēhūdh,* "united," "strong"): A Benjamite, son of Gera, deliverer of Israel from oppression by Moab (Jgs **3** 15–30). Gaining access alone to the presence of King Eglon under pretence of a secret errand connected with the payment of Israel's tribute, Ehud, a left-handed man, drew the sword he had concealed upon his right side, and thrust the king through. He locked the doors of the upper chamber after him, made his escape, and with the Israelites overcame Moab at the fords of the Jordan, slaying some 10,000. Ehud's name occurs again in the Benjamite genealogy (1 Ch **7** 10). F. K. FARR

EITHER, ē′thẽr, ī′thẽr: Often in the sense still common, "one or the other" (1 Ch **21** 21; Mt **6** 24, etc), but also in the obs sense of "both" or "each" (Lev **10** 1; 1 K **7** 15; Jn **19** 18; Rev **22** 2), or in place of (RV) "or" (Lk **6** 42; **15** 8; Phil **3** 12; Jas **3** 12).

EKER, ē′kẽr (עֵקֶר, *'ēḳer,* "root"): A Jerahmeelite (1 Ch **2** 27).

EKREBEL, ek′rē-bel (**Ἐκρεβήλ,** *Ekrebḗl*): Appears only in Jth **7** 18. It lay on the brook Mochmur, S. of Dothan. It is identical with Akrabbein, of which *Onom* speaks as the capital of the district of Akrabattine. It corresponds to the mod. *'Akrabeh,* 8 miles S.E. of Nāblus.

EKRON, ek′ron, **EKRONITE,** ek′ron-īt (עֶקְרוֹן, *'eḳrōn,* "migration," "rooting out"; **Ἀκκαρών,** *Akkarṓn*): The most northerly of the chief cities of the Philis. It was not subdued by Joshua (**13** 3) but was allotted, in the division of the land, first to Judah and then to Dan (**15** 11.45.46; **19** 43). It was taken by Judah (Jgs **1** 18). The people of E. are prominent in the story of the ark in the land of the Philis. It was they who proposed to have it sent back to Israel (1 S **5** 10; **6** 16.17). After the defeat of the Philis, when David killed Goliath, the Israelites pursued them to the gates of E., which was evidently the nearest walled town in which the fugitives could take refuge (**17** 52). It was the seat of the worship of the god Baalzebub, as appears in the account of the sickness and death of Ahaziah (2 K **1** 2.3.6.16). It is included among other cities in the denunciations of Amos (**1** 8) and of Jeremiah (**25** 20). Zephaniah declares that it shall be rooted up (**2** 4), and Zechariah speaks of its consternation at the fall of Tyre (**9** 5.7). From the Assyr records we learn that it revolted against Sennacherib and expelled Padi, the governor he had placed over it, and sent him to Hezekiah, at Jerus, for safe keeping. Sennacherib marched against it and E. called in the aid of the king of Mutsri, formerly supposed to be Egypt but now regarded by some scholars as a district of Northwestern Arabia. Sennacherib raised the siege of E. to defeat this army, which he did at Eltekeh, and then returned and took the city by storm and put to death the leaders of the revolt and carried their adherents into captivity. He then compelled Hezekiah to restore Padi, who was once more made governor. This affair led to the famous attack of Sennacherib on Hezekiah and Jerus (Rawl., *Anc. Mon.,* II, 159). E. is mentioned in 1 Macc **10** 89 as being given by Alexander Balas to Jonathan Maccabaeus, and it appears in the accounts of the first Crusade.

Ekronite: An inhabitant of Ekron, used in pl. in Josh **13** 3 and 1 S **5** 10. H. PORTER

EL. See GOD, NAMES OF.

ELA, ē′la (**Ἠλά,** *Ēlá,* 1 Esd **9** 27):
(1) Same as Elam (Ezr **10** 26).
(2) Father of Shimei (1 K **4** 18, AV "Elah"). See ELAH, 2.

ELADAH, el′a-da. See ELEADAH.

ELAH, ē′la (אֵלָה, *'ēlāh,* "oak" or "terebinth"):
(1) A "duke" or "sheik" (head of a clan, RV "chief") of Edom (Gen **36** 41).
(2) Shimei-ben-Elah, Solomon's commissary in Benjamin (1 K **4** 18 AV).
(3) A son of Caleb the son of Jephunneh (1 Ch **4** 15).
(4) Father of Hoshea, last king of Israel (2 K **15** 30; **17** 1).
(5) A Benjamite, son of Uzzi, one of the chiefs of the tribes when the country was settled (1 Ch **9** 8).
(6) King of Israel. See next article.

ELAH, ē′la. Son of Baasha, fourth king of Israel (1 K **16** 6–14). He reigned two years, 888–887 BC. The statement that he came to the throne in the 26th year of Asa, reigned two years, and died in the 27th year of Asa, illustrates the Heb method of synchronizing the reigns of the kings of Israel and Judah (cf 1 K **15** 33; **16** 8). Elah appears to have been a debauchee. While he was drinking himself drunk in the house of Azra, his chamberlain, Zimri, one of his military leaders, conspired against him and murdered him. According to Jos (VIII, xii, 4) he took advantage of the absence of the army, which was at Gibbethon, to kill Elah. The extirpation of the royal family followed the murder of the king. Baasha's dynasty had its origin in a murder and it ended in a murder. The government had no stability. These revolutions illustrate the truth that "they who take the sword shall perish with the sword." S. K. MOSIMAN

ELAH, VALE OF (עֵמֶק הָאֵלָה, *'ēmeḳ hā-'ēlāh,* "valley of the terebinth"; **ἡ κοιλὰς Ἠλά,** *hē koilás Ēlá;* A, **τῆς δρυός,** *tḗs druós*): The scene of the events of 1 S **17** 2 ff, referred to also in 1 S **21** 9. There can be no doubt that this is the *Wady eṣ Ṣunṭ* ("valley of the terebinth"), or part of it. This is the southernmost of the great valleys which cut through the Shephelah. Commencing near Hebron, close to *Beit Sûr,* it descends under the name *Wady es Sûr* in a more or less northerly direction until near *Beit Nettîf* where it turns abruptly west and receives the name *Wady eṣ Ṣunṭ.* Here it is joined by the *Wady en Najil,* coming from the N., and from the E. by the *Wady el-Jindy,* down which descends an ancient road from Bethlehem. Where all these valleys coalesce the *Wady eṣ Ṣunṭ* expands into a wide and level bottom, half a mile across. On a steep hill to the southern side and a little S.E. of the wide expanse is *Kh. esh-Shuweikeh*, the site of Socoh. That the great events of 1 S **17** 2 ff took place here there can be no doubt: the Philis ranged themselves upon the southern hills; the Israelites to the N. or N.E. Upon the wide level valley the contest with Goliath occurred. The exact position of Saul's forces may be a matter of speculation, but the late Principal Miller of Madras, who made a special study of the locality (*Least of All Lands*, ch v), considered that the little valley ascending N.E. from *Wady eṣ Ṣunṭ* to *Beit Nettîf* was probably the actual Vale of Elah and that here the Israelites had their fortifications. His elucidation of the whole story is most convincing.

E. W. G. Masterman

ELAM, ē'lam (עֵילָם, *'ēlām*):

(1) A son of Shem (Gen **10** 22; 1 Ch **1** 17; see Elamites).

(2) A Benjamite (1 Ch **8** 24).

(3) A Korahite (1 Ch **26** 3).

(4) Heads of families in the return (Ezr **2** 7 ‖ Neh **7** 12; Ezr **2** 31 ‖ Neh **7** 34; Ezr **8** 7; **10** 2.26).

(5) A chief of the people (Neh **10** 14).

(6) A priest (Neh **12** 42).

ELAM, ē'lam, **ELAMITES,** ē'lam-īts (עֵילָם, *'ēlām;* **Αἰλάμ,** *Ailám;* Jer **49** 36. **א*** reads **'Ελάμ,** *Elám*):

1. Geographical Position and Names
2. Surface Configuration
3. Mountain Ranges
4. Rivers
5. Climate
6. Vegetation
7. Fauna
8. The Population
9. The Principal Cities
10. Apirti and the "Bandit Nations"
11. The Languages of Elam
12. History
    - (1) The Earliest Period
    - (2) Sargon of Agadé and His Successors
    - (3) The Suzerainty of the Kings of Ur
    - (4) Elam Becomes Predominant 2280 Years BC
    - (5) The Extension of Elamite Authority Westward
    - (6) Babylonia Again Supreme
    - (7) Ḫurbatila's Challenge to Kuri-galzu
    - (8) Elam Again Supreme
    - (9) Elam Again Defeated, but Recovers
    - (10) The Conflict between Elam and Assyria
    - (11) Sennacherib against Chaldaea and Elam
    - (12) Assyrian Friendship and Elamite Ingratitude
    - (13) Te-umman and the Elamite Seed-royal. Assyria's Triumph
    - (14) Elamite Ingratitude and Treachery
    - (15) Elam's Further Changes of Rulers
    - (16) King Tammaritu's Treachery
    - (17) Dominion Passes from Assyria
    - (18) The Later State of Elam
13. Elamite Religion
14. Elam's Importance. Her Literature
15. Art during the 1st and 2d Prehistoric Periods
16. Art in the Archaic Period, That of the Viceroys, and That of the Kings
17. Temperament of the Inhabitants of Elam

Literature

1. Geographical Position and Names A well-known tract, partly mountainous, whose western boundary, starting on the N.E. side of the Pers Gulf, practically followed the course of the lower Tigris. It was bounded on the N. by Media, on the E. by Persia and on the W. by Babylonia. The Assyro-Babylonians called the tract *Êlamtu*, expressed ideographically by the Sumerian characters for *Nimma* or *Numma*, which seems to have been its name in that language. As *Numma* or Elam apparently means "height," or the like, these names were probably applied to it on account of its mountainous nature. Another name by which it was known in early times was *Ashshan*, for *Anshan* or *Anzan* (*Anzhan*), one of its ancient cities. The great capital of the tract, however, was Susa (Shushan), whence its Gr name of Susiana, interchanging with Elymais, from the Sem Elam.

2. Surface Configuration Elam consisted of a plain occupying a depression in the mountains of Iran or Persia. Of this the smaller part—which, however, was also the most ancient historically—lay between the Pusht-e-Kuh on the W., the Lur mountains on the N., the Bakhtiari heights to the E. and S.E., and the hills of Ahwaz to the S. The larger plain has as its northern boundary these same Ahwaz hills, and reaches to the sea on the S.

3. Mountain Ranges The Pusht-e-Kuh mountains are a series of very high parallel ranges described as "a veritable wall" between Mesopotamia and the elevated depression of the Kerkha. Its principal peak is in the Kebir-Kuh (2,500 meters=8,200 ft.)—a difficult range of surprising regularity. The valleys on the S.W. slope belong properly to Babylonia, and could be invaded on that side with ease, but N.E. of the Kebir-Kuh the country is well protected not only against Mesopotamia, on the W., but also against Persia on the E. The nomad Lurs of the present day are practically independent of Persia. The mountain ranges of Luristan increase in height as one approaches the Pers plain, the loftiest summits of the principal range attaining a height of 5,000 meters (=16,400 ft.).

4. Rivers From these mountain ranges descend large rivers which flow through Elam to the sea. The Kerkha (*Gamas-âb*) rises in the Pers plain near Nehâvend, and is practically a torrent until it reaches Susa, below which it becomes less rapid, and loses itself in the Hawizeh marshes. The Ab-e-Diz, a river with a greater volume of water, is formed by the uniting of two streams above Dizful. It is so violent that it carries down boulders and even tree-trunks from the mountains, and after a winding course joins the Kârun at Kut-e-Bende-Kir. The Belâd-Rud, between the Ab-e-Diz and the Kerkha, rises in the mountains of Luristan, and varies greatly as to its volume, being sometimes a mere brook, and at others a large river. The Kârun, with which a number of small streams unite, rises in the Bakhtiari mountains. After receiving the Ab-e-Diz and the Belâd-Rud at Kut-e-Bende-Kir, it becomes an important waterway, navigable as far as Shuster. This is identified with the Bib. Ulai (Assyr *Ulâa*, classical *Eulaeus*). Anciently emptying itself into the Pers Gulf, which in past cents. extended much farther inland than now, it at present joins the Shatt-el-Arab at Mohammerah.

5. Climate The climate is a variable one. Between November 1 and 15 the rains begin, with S.E. and S. winds, and the mountains are covered with snow. In January and February there are violent storms, and the night brings 8° or 10° of frost. Spring begins at the end of February, and vegetation advances so rapidly that harvest takes place about the end of April. The wind then turns S. and S.W., bringing with it a heat rising sometimes to 140° F., destroying all the verdure of the country. Notwithstanding the rigors of the climate, however, it was anciently a well-populated district, and exceedingly fruitful, as now. That the district of Arabistan is poor and barren is due to the carelessness and improvidence of the people, who, like the people of the Turkish province of Bagdad, have neglected the ancient irrigation canals which fertilized the land.

The vegetation of Susiana is said not to be very varied. On the river banks are to be found willows, tamarisks and many kinds of acacias. Apparently there are no forests—the sacred groves referred to by Aššur-bani-âpli are thought by De Morgan to have been artificial plantations. Oranges and lemons, which are at present cultivated there, are late importations. The date palm has been brought from the banks of the Shatt-el-Arab, and the pomegranate and other fruit trees from the Iranian plain. Wheat and barley, sown in October and November, are harvested in April. Sorghum remains in the ground all through the dry season, and is watered artificially until October, and cut in November. Castor beans, indigo, lentils, haricots, etc, are less cultivated.

6. Vegetation

The fauna is said at present to be less numerous than formerly. It contains species both of central Asia, Europe, and, to a certain extent, Africa. The elephant, wild ass, wild ox and ostrich are no longer to be found on the Chaldeo-Elamite plain, but a few examples of the lion still exist there. Bears, panthers, wild boars, wolves, wild cats, foxes, jackals, and several species of wild dogs, however, still exist. Numbers of porcupines inhabit the brushwood by the rivers and marshes. Among the birds which do not leave the country are the eagle, vulture, falcon, raven, francolin, martin, sparrow, tomtit, wagtail, etc. The winter birds of passage are the pelican, stork, crane, cormorant, sea gull, many species of wild duck, the wild goose, bustard, woodcock, snipe, pigeon, turtledove, and numerous brilliantly colored waders. The water-courses are full of fish, among them being the barbel, silurus, carp (sometimes of great size), and gurnards similar to those of the Nile. Some of the rivers being salt, sea fish are also to be found, and it is not rare to see sharks at Shuster, and eels in the lower Kârun.

7. Fauna

The population is naturally not homogeneous. Arab tribes, who are in reality Semites, occupy the plains, while Iranians inhabit the cities and dwell at the mountain bases. According to De Morgan, the original population was mainly negritic, and has mingled with the Arab stock to such an extent that mulattoes among them are not rare. He regards this type as being represented among the soldiers as well as among the people conquered by Naram-Sin about 3000 BC. Nevertheless pure Semites had settled in the country at a very early date, and it is probably on account of this that Elam is called (Gen **10** 22) a son of Shem—indeed, the many Sem inscriptions found by the Fr. explorers at Susa show how strong their influence was. It was to all appearance during the 2d millennium BC that certain Kassites overran W. Mesopotamia, and settled in the northern part of Elam, which was thereafter called by the Assyrians *mât Kaššî*, "the land of the Cossaeans." As these people seem to have spoken an Aryan language, there was apparently no really new race introduced in consequence of their invasion.

8. The Population

The two principal cities were Susa or Shushan, called Susun in the native texts, and regarded as the old capital, situated on the Ulai (Kârkha); and Anzan (*Ashshan, Anshan*), more to the S.W. This latter was the capital of Cyrus the Great and his immediate predecessors, the tract having been conquered apparently by Šišpiš (*Teispes*), his ancestor, at the end of the 6th cent. BC. Susa, an important commercial center in the 3d millennium BC, became again one of the three capitals of the Pers empire during the rule of the Achaemenians.

9. The Principal Cities

From the inscriptions of Mal-Amir, to the E., we learn that that was the place of another kingdom called Apirti, the land of the Apharsites of Ezr **4** 9. In the 2d (so-called Median or Scythian) version of the late Pers inscriptions this name is given as *Ḫapirti, Ḫalpirti*, and *Ḫaltupirti*, and appears as the equivalent of the Bab *Elammat* (*Elamtu*) or Elam without the nominative ending. In the Pers version this appears as (*H*)*uwaja* or (*H*)*uwazha*, whence the modern *Hûz* or *Khuzistan*. This implies that the kings of Apirti at one time held dominion over Susa, and perhaps the whole of Elam. Strabo (xi.13.3,6), quoting Nearchus, speaks of "four bandit nations" who occupied the mountains E. of the Euphrates—the Amardians or Mardians on the Pers border, the Uxians, and Elymeans on the borders of Persia and Susa, and the Cossaeans (Kassites) by the Medes. The Amardians would seem to have been the Apirti (*Ḫapirti*), the Uxians were probably from (H)uwaja, while the Elymeans (cf 1 Macc **6** 1) were the Elamites. Among the tribes who made the history of the country, therefore, were probably the Uxians, who seem not to be mentioned in the early inscriptions.

10. Apirti and the "Bandit Nations"

The dialects of Susa, the second Achaemenian VSS, and of Apirti, differ but slightly from each other. They are variants of an agglutinative tongue, and are apparently not related to any other known language. The statement in Gen **10** 22, therefore, applies only to the Sem section of the population, as it is unlikely that the people speaking Apirtian could be described as "sons of Shem."

11. The Languages of Elam

(1) *The earliest period.*—Beginning with the semi-mythical period, we have the story of the fight of the Bab hero Gilgameš with the Elamite tyrant Ḫumbaba, who was defeated by the hero and his helper Enki-du, and beheaded. The earliest really historical reference to the Elamites as the foes of Babylonia, however, is apparently that contained in a letter from the priest Lu-enna to the priest En-e-tarzi announcing that the Elamites had invaded Lagaš and carried off considerable booty. The writer, however, had attacked the Elamites, and taken plunder from them in his turn. As there seems to be a reference to division of spoil, this is an excellent parallel to the Elamite expedition, made in alliance with the Babylonians, against the cities of the plain (Gen **14**).

12. History

(2) *Sargon of Agadé and his successors.*—Sargon of Agadé, early in his reign, attacked the Elamites, but apparently Elam only fell under the dominion of the Babylonians during the time of Narâm-Sin, his son, who is seemingly shown leading his troops in that region on the splendid stele bearing his name that was found at Susa. Elam apparently regained its independence, however, during the time of Uruwuš, king of Kiš, who invaded the country, and brought back considerable spoil. One of the chiefs of Susa about this time was Šimbi-išḫak. Chaldaean domination, however, did not last long, for Dungi, king of Ur of the Chaldees, about 2500 BC, invaded the country, accompanied by his vassal Gudea, viceroy of Lagaš. Dungi has left evidences of his conquests in the buildings which he erected at Susa, but the principal buildings of this period were constructed by Ba-ša-Šušinak, son of Šimbi-išḫak, viceroy of Susa and potentate in Elam. He built a temple to the god Šugu, reservoirs, the gate of Šušinak, and dug the Sidur canal. He was evidently one of the great rulers of the land.

(3) *The suzerainty of the kings of Ur.*—Somewhat later came Idadu I, his son Kal-Ruḫuratir, and his grandson Idadu II, who in turn occupied the throne during the time of Bûr-Sin, king of Ur. Elam

was at this time still under Bab suzerainty, which continued under his successor, Gimil-Sin, who also built at Susa, his vassal being Ebarti-kin-Daddu, viceroy of Susa. Gimil-Sin was succeeded by his son Ibi-Sin as overlord in Elam, who invaded and devastated the country, probably to suppress a a revolt. There was apparently no ill-will between the two nations, however, for the viceroy of Susa is said to have married a daughter of Ibi-Sin. Another and possibly later viceroy seems to have married Mekubi, daughter of Billama, viceroy of Ašnunnak, who, as Elamite princess, erected buildings at Susa.

Naram-Sin.

(4) *Elam becomes predominant 2280 BC.*—It was probably shortly after this that Kudur-Naḫḫunte threw off the Sem yoke, and, invading Babylonia, brought back much spoil to Elam. The date indicated for this ruler by the inscriptions of Aššur-bani-âpli is 2280 BC. The positions of the rulers of Elam and Babylonia were now changed, and the kings of Babylon had to acknowledge Elamite suzerainty. As Elamite and Bab sovereign, Kudur-Naḫḫunte intrusted Susa to a feudatory ruler, and among the viceroys who governed Elam may be mentioned Širukdu', who constructed at Susa, and Temti-Agun, his sister's son, who built in that city the temple to Išme-karab, "for the health of Kutir-Naḫḫunte and his family." After passing to other rulers, the government of Susa fell to Ebari, father of Šilḫaḫa, during whose reign Simti-Šilḫak ruled in Babylonia. Nûr-Addi and Rîm-Anum, kings of Larsa (Elassar), were his vassals.

(5) *The extension of Elamite authority westward.*—Attapakšu (or Attaḫušu), Šilḫaḫa's sister's son, then became "shepherd of Susa." Among the temples which he built was one dedicated to the goddess Narute, and he erected a bridge near his residence. Kudur-mabuk, son of Simti-Šilḫak, was at this time *adda* ("father," probably meaning protector) of Emutbālu and the W.—Amurrū, the land of the Amorites, whither marched Chedorlaomer and Amraphel, with their allies, in the time of Abraham (Gen **14**). Kudur-mabuk of Larsa was succeeded by his son Eri-Aku (probably the Iri-Agun of Larsa of the Elamite texts), and if he be really, as seems probable, the Arioch of Gen **14** 1.9, then this is also the period when Chedorlaomer ruled in Elam. The strange thing, however, is, that the name of this last does not occur in any recognizable form, unless it be the Kudurlaḫgumal of certain half-legendary inscriptions (see CHEDORLAOMER). The Elamite line in Larsa was continued after the death of Eri-Aku by Rîm-Sin, his brother, who succeeded him.

(6) *Babylonia again supreme.*—What the history of Elam during this period was remains to be discovered, but Ḫammurabi, who is identified with the Amraphel of Gen **14** 1.9, seems to have invaded the country in his 30th year. In his 31st he defeated Rîm-Sin of Larsa, following this up, in his 32d, by overthrowing the army of Ašnunnak. All these successes in Elam and its dependencies probably made the kingdom of Babylon supreme in the land. But more details bearing upon this period are needed. It is thought probable that the Elamite king Sadi(?) or Taki (?) came into conflict with, and was defeated by, Ammi-ṣaduga, the 4th in descent from Ḫammurabi, who reigned about 1890 BC. Apparently the Elamite ruler had tried to regain his independence, but failed.

(7) *Ḫurbatila's challenge to Kuri-galzu.*—Omitting the names of rulers concerning whom but little or nothing is known, we come to the reign of Untaš-Gal, patron of the arts. Numerous temples were built by him, and sanctuaries at Susa dedicated. He has left a magnificent bronze statue representing his queen Napir-Asu. He seems to have been overthrown by Untaḫaš-Gal, of a more legitimate line, who was likewise a builder of temples. After the apparently short reign of Kidin-Ḫutran came that of Ḫurpatila (Ḫurbatila), who, desiring to throw off the Babylonian yoke, challenged Kuri-galzu, king of Babylon, to battle at Dûr-Dungi. The challenge was accepted, with disastrous results, for Ḫurbatila was captured by the Bab king at the place named. This, however, did not put an end to the strife, and in the end Kidin-Ḫutrudaš was victorious over Bêl-nadin-šum, king of Babylon, about 1180 BC.

(8) *Elam again supreme.*—Later came the military exploits of Šutruk-Naḫḫunte, who invaded Babylonia, slew the king Zagaga-šum-iddina, and helped by his son Kutir-Naḫḫunte, destroyed Sippar, and took away the stele of Naram-Sin, the code of Ḫammurabi, and several other monuments, which were carefully preserved at Susa. He also defeated the king of Ašnunnak. It is this collection of spoils which has contributed to make the success of the Fr. excavations at Susa what it is.

(9) *Elam again defeated, but recovers.*—The war between Babylonia and Elam recorded for the reign of Nebuchadrezzar I (c 1020 BC) probably took place, according to Scheil, during the reign of Silḫina-ḫamru-Laqamar. The Elamite king was defeated on the banks of the Ulai, Elam was ravaged, and much spoil taken. The principality called Namar was detached from Susian territory and reunited to the domain of Babylonia. Apparently the Elamites now turned their attention to regaining their military prestige, the result being that an Elamite king occupied the Bab throne from 939 to 934 BC. The history of this period has still to be discovered, but the Babylonians apparently soon shook off the Elamite yoke. It is about this time, however, that another power—Assyria—appeared on the scene, and took the field—not only against Babylon, but also on the borders of Elam. An Elamite contemporary of Nabonassar of Babylon was Ḫumbanigaš, 742 BC.

(10) *The conflict between Elam and Assyria.*—At this time, however, the Assyrians became dominant in Babylonia (see TIGLATH-PILESER and

Shalmaneser), but it was probably not until the reign of Sargon of Assyria (see Sargon) that Elam came into conflict with Assyria. Merodach-baladan, a pretendant to the throne of Babylon, made common cause with Ḫumbanigaš, who fought with the Assyr army at Dêr. Naturally the Assyrians claim the victory, but the Babylonians say that they were defeated. After the death of Ḫumbanigaš, his successor, Šutur-Naḫḫundi or Ištar-ḫundu (Bab), still befriended Merodach-baladan, and advanced to his help. Sargon first attacked the Chaldaeans and defeated them at Dûr-Atḫara, and, entering Elam, stormed and captured the cities of the land. The Elamite king took refuge in the mountains, and Merodach-baladan had to resist the Assyrians unaided.

The Installation of Ummanigaš.

(11) *Sennacherib against Chaldaea and Elam.*—As Sargon had his attention fully occupied elsewhere, he made no attempt to follow up his success, and it seems not to have been until the reign of Sennacherib that any serious invasion of the country on the part of the Assyrians was made. In 697 BC that king marched again against Merodach-baladan, who had taken refuge at Nagîtu and other places on the Elamite side of the then elongated Pers Gulf. Here the Chaldaeans, with their Elamite allies, were defeated, and the Elamite cities plundered and destroyed. Ḫallušu, king of Elam, on the retirement of the Assyr troops, invaded Babylonia as being part of the territories of the Assyr king, and having captured Aššur-nadin-šum, Sennacherib's son, who had ruled in Babylon 6 years, carried him off to Elam, setting Nergal-ušêzib on the throne of Babylonia. On the arrival of the Assyr avenging host in Babylonia, Nergal-ušêzib fled to Elam, but was captured near Niffer. The Elamites were evidently very dissatisfied with their king—possibly owing to his policy—and killed him in a revolt after a reign of six years. This action on the part of the Elamites, however. did not save the people from Assyr vengeance, for Sennacherib invaded and ravaged the country from Râŝ to Bît-Burnaki. Apparently the Elamites had expected their new ruler, Kudurru (Kudur-Naḫḫunte), to save them from the reprisals of the Assyrians, but as he had failed to do this, he, in his turn, was deposed and killed after a reign of 10 months. The new king of Elam was Umman-Menanu, who espoused the cause of Mušêzib-Marduk, the new king of Babylon, and gathering a force of Babylonians and Elamites at Ḫalulê, fought a battle there, in which the Babylonians record success for the allies. Sennacherib, however, himself claims the victory, and describes with great wealth of detail the horrors of the fight. Next year (689 BC) Sennacherib marched into Babylonia to complete the work, and Mušêzib-Marduk, having been captured, was sent prisoner to Assyria. Umman-Menanu died at the end of the year, after a 4 years' reign, and was succeeded by Ḫumba-ḫaldâšu I (689–682 BC), of whom nothing is known. In 682 BC Ḫumba-ḫaldâšu II mounted the throne. The death of Sennacherib and the troubles attending the accession of Esarhaddon encouraged Nabû-zêr-napišti-lîšir, son of Merodach-baladan, again to raise the standard of revolt. Defeat was the result, and he fled to Elam, there to be captured by Ḫumba-ḫaldâšu and put to death.

(12) *Assyrian friendship and Elamite ingratitude.*—Friendship with Assyria was a complete reversal of Elamite policy, and to all appearance peace, though probably unpopular, persisted between the two countries for several years. Ḫumba-ḫaldâšu's two brothers revolted against him and assassinated him, and Urtaku, one of the murderers, took the Elamite throne. Not daring to be openly hostile to Assyria, however, he sent his brother Te-umman to intrigue in Chaldaea in favor of a man named Nabûušallim, but the Chaldaean chiefs answered that Na'id-Marduk, their lord, lived, and they were the servants of the king of Assyria. Also, during a

famine in Elam, certain Elamite tribes migrated into Assyria to escape the scarcity, and were kindly treated by Aššur-bani-âpli, who had succeeded his father on the Assyr throne. Notwithstanding this, however, Urtaku invaded Babylonia as ally of certain Chaldaean tribes. Overtaken by the Assyr army, he fought with them near his own border, but was defeated and fled. He died prematurely (by his own hand) the same year, and was succeeded by his brother Te-umman (Tepti-Ḫumban).

(13) *Te-umman and the Elamite seed-royal; Assyria's triumph.*—This king, who is described by Aššur-bani-âpli as being in the likeness of an evil spirit, immediately set to work to secure the death of all the sons of Urtaku and Umman-aldāše (Ḫumba-Ḫaldašu II), his brother; and these princes, five ir number, with 60 of the royal seed of Elam, fled and sought refuge with the Assyr king. Te-umman immediately sent two messengers to Aššur-bani-âpli demanding the surrender of the fugitives. This was refused, and war broke out between the two countries immediately after. The Assyrians came up with the Elamites at Dêr, but Te-umman feared to join issue there, and retreating, took up a strong position near his capital, Susa, with his front protected by the river Ulai. Defections from his army now so weakened the forces of Te-umman that he endeavored to treat with Aššur-bani-âpli, who naturally refused to iisten to terms, and ordered his troops to attack. The defeat of the Elamites was a foregone conclusion, and Te-umman perished, with his son, in the thick of the battle, as is dramatically depicted by the sculptors of Aššur-bani-âpli in the bas-reliefs which adorned the walls of his palace. An Assyr general was now sent to Susa with Umman-igaš, the prince chosen to succeed Te-umman, and he was proclaimed while the bodies of the fallen Elamites covered the battlefield, and the waters of the Ulai carried others down to the place of its outflow. Tammaritu, the new king's youngest brother, was at the same time made king of Ḫidalu, in the mountain region. In the triumphal procession at Nineveh which took place on the Assyr army's return, the head of Te-umman and his son Tamritu figured, the former hanging from the neck of Dunanu, king of Gambulu, and the latter from the neck of Samgunu, Dunanu's brother.

Last Stand of Te-umman.

(14) *Elamite ingratitude and treachery.*—For a time there was peace in Elam, but soon the discontent of Šamaš-šum-ukîn, king of Babylon, Aššur-bani-âpli's brother, sought to break it. Urged by him, Umman-igaš forgot the benefits which he had received at the hands of Aššur-bani-âpli, and sent an army into Babylonia under the command of Undasi, son of Te-umman, telling him to avenge upon Assyria the killing of his father. Notwithstanding the great strength of the allied army, they did not succeed in making headway against the Assyrians. Tammaritu, nephew of Umman-igaš, after the defeat of the Elamite forces in Chaldaea, revolted against him, and having defeated him, cut off his head, and took the crown. Šamaš-šum-ukîn immediately turned his attention to the new ruler, and induced him by fresh presents to come likewise to his aid.

Presentation of Umman-igaš to His Subjects by the Assyrian General.

Tammaritu therefore marched at the head of an army into Babylonia, but in his absence Indabigaš, one of his servants, headed a revolt against him, and proclaimed himself king in Susa. In the battle which ensued between the two pretenders, Tammaritu was defeated, and fled to the seacoast with a part of the Elamite royal family. He ultimately embarked in a ship on the Pers Gulf with the intention of escaping, but was wrecked, and gave himself up to an Assyr officer, who sent him to Assyria.

(15) *Elam's further changes of rulers.*—Indabigaš, the new Elamite king, now sent an embassy to make peace with Aššur-bani-âpli, who at once demanded the surrender of Nabû-bêl-šumāti, son of Merodach-baladan, and the Assyrians whom he had enticed and taken with him. Before this demand could reach Indabigaš, however, his people had revolted against him and put him to death, and Umman-aldāsu, son of Attametu, sat on the throne, after defeating Indabigaš on the banks of the Ḫutḫut. The same demand was made to Umman-aldāsu as had been made to Indabigaš, but Nabû-bêl-šumāti, not wishing to fall into the hands of the Assyrians, called on his armor-bearer to dispatch him, and the two ran each other through with their swords.

(16) *King Tammaritu's treachery.*—Nevertheless Aššur-bani-âpli decided to replace Tammaritu, the former Elamite king, on the throne, and to this end invaded Elam. The Assyrians were, as usual, successful, and on learning this, Umman-aldās fled to the mountains. Entering Susa, Tammaritu was once more proclaimed king of Elam, he, in return, promising to regard Aššur-bani-âpli as his lord, and to pay tribute. No sooner had the Assyr army departed, than the new king of Elam began to plot against the power which had raised him. To all appearance his intentions to revolt were reported to the Assyr king, who at once sent an army and plundered the country, and Tammaritu again fell into Aššur-bani-âpli's hands. Umman-aldās now returned and resumed the government. Unwilling to regard his former efforts as fruitless, the Assyr king decided to finally subdue the land, and to this end invaded it, the pretext being that the Elamites refused to deliver up the image of the goddess Nanâ, which had been carried off from Erech 1,635 years before, in the time of Kudur-Naḫḫunte (see [4] above). The two armies faced each other on the

banks of the Itite, and after an attack in which the Assyrians were at a disadvantage, the Elamites gave way, and Umman-aldās fled to the mountains. According to the Assyr king's record, an enormous booty was taken, including many sacred and ancient royal statues preserved at Susa. The image of Nanâ was restored to its shrine at Erech with great rejoicing. In the triumphal celebrations at Nineveh, Tammaritu was one of the captive kings who drew the Assyr king's chariot to the temple of Ištar, when he rendered the goddess thanks for his victories.

(17) *Dominion passes from Assyria.*—To all appearance Elam now became a province of the Assyr empire, though not for long, as this collapsed in the year 606 BC, and the center of government was shifted to Babylon, under Nabopolassar, who became its ruler. Nebuchadrezzar (604), Evil-Merodach (561), Neriglissar (559), and Nabonidus (555–538 BC), were successively masters of Elam. The mention of the kings of Elam in Jer **25** 25, however, suggests that the old states of the country had practically resumed their independence; though **49** 35–39 prophesies the dismemberment of the country, and the destruction of its king and princes. This is thought to refer to the annexation of the country by Teispes, and its passing, through his line—Cyrus, Cambyses, and Cyrus the Great, who were all kings of Anzan—to Darius Hystaspis. In Isa **21** 2 it is apparently the later Cyrus who is referred to when Elam, with Media, is called upon "to go up" to the siege of Babylon.

(18) *The later state of Elam.*—After Cyrus, the history of Elam was that of Persia, of which it henceforth formed a part. In all probability, however, the Elamites were as warlike and as intractable as ever. During the reign of the little-known Kharacenian king, Aspāsinē, they made incursions into Babylonia, one of the opponents of this king's generals being Pittit, "the enemy, the Elamite"—a phrase of old standing, apparently. Elam, to its whole extent, was smitten with the sword, and Pittit [was slain or captured]. One of the cities which they attacked was Apameia, probably that on the Sellas river. Acts **2** 9 implies that the old language of Elam was still in use, and the Elamites were still recognized as a nationality, as late as the 1st cent. of our era.

13. Elamite Religion

Owing to the many Semites in Elam, and the nearness of the Bab states, Bab deities—Anu and Anatu, Enlil and Ninlil, Merodach and Zēr-panîtu, Šamaš and Aa, Tammuz and Ištar, Ninip, Nergal, Hadad or Rimmon, etc—were largely worshipped (see Babel, Babylon). The chief deity of the non-Semitic pantheon seems to have been In-šušinak, the patron-deity of Susa, identified with Ninip, the son of Enlil, by the Babylonians, who quote also other names applied to him—Laḫuratil Simeš, Adaene, Šušinak, and Dagbak. Merodach seems to have been represented by the Sumerian character *Gal*, "great," and Zēr-panîtu was apparently called Nin-siš in Elam. Ištar was known as Usan. Lagamar, Laqamar, or Lagamal, was apparently identified with the Bab Lagamal, one of the gods of Dailem near Babylon—his name is generally regarded as forming part of the name Chedorlaomer (q.v.). Naḫḫunte, Na'ḫunte, or (Bab) Nanḫundi was the Bab sun-god Šamas; Kunzibami was the W. Šem. Hadad, also known by his Mitannian (Hittite) name of Tešup. Ḫumban, Ḫuman, or Umman (Assyr), "the god of gods," "the king," was possibly regarded as the Bab Merodach. The currency of Bab myths in Elam is suggested by the name of the goddess Belala, possibly the Bab Belili, sister of Tammuz. The word for "god" in Elamite was *nap*, explained by the Babylonians as one of the names of Enlil, implying that the Elamites regarded him as "the god" by divine right. Of their deities, six (one of them being Lagamar) were worshipped only by Elamite kings. Elam had temples and temple-towers similar to those in Babylonia, as well as sacred groves, wherein no stranger penetrated. (See *ERE*, s.v. "Elamites.")

14. Elam's Importance; Her Literature

The rediscovery of the history of Elam is one of the most noteworthy things of modern research. It has revealed to us the wonderful development which that kingdom had made at an exceedingly early date, and shows that it was politically just as important as the Bab states 4,000 years BC, though probably hardly so advanced in art and lit. Nevertheless, the country had adopted the cuneiform method of writing, and possessed also another script, seemingly of more ancient date. As both Sem Bab and Susian (Anzanite) were spoken in the country, numerous documents in both languages have been found, mostly historical, or of the nature of dedications, some of which are inscribed on objects presented to temples. There are also a number of archaic tablets of the nature of accounts, written in a peculiar cuneiform character. The cylinder-seals are either inscribed with dedications, or with the name of the owner, his father, and the god whom he worshipped, as in Babylonia. Of other lit. there are but mere traces—an exorcism against mosquitos shows the desire of the people to rid themselves of the discomforts of this life. Contracts testify to the existence of laws, but the laws themselves have yet to be discovered. The stele of Ḫammurabi, which was found at Susa, did not belong to Elamitic lit., but to that of Babylonia.

15. Art during the 1st and 2d Prehistoric Periods

Elamite art during the first period was naturally rude, and it is doubtful whether metals were then used, as no traces of them were found. There were also no inscribed monuments. The pottery, however, was of extreme delicacy, and very elegant. The second period is described as being less artistic than the first. The pottery is more ordinary, and also more roughly made, though better ware also exists. Painted ornamentation is found. Vessels of white

The Spinning-Woman (from Susa).

or pink limestone, some of them very large, occur, but alabaster is exceedingly rare. There is no indication of writing at this period, but rudely engraved seals, with animal forms, are found. The buildings were of crude brick or piled-up earth, though baked brick was sometimes used. A change seems to have taken place in the conditions of life at the end of this period, implying invasion by a more civilized race.

The indications of invasion during the second prehistoric period are confirmed, according to M. Jéquier, by what is found in the layer of the archaic period, which succeeded it. This is accentuated by the numerous inscribed clay tablets, some of which have impressions of quite remarkable cylinder-seals. The pottery is scanty and not characteristic, but the working of alabaster into vases had developed considerably, and some of the smaller forms (ointment or scent-bottles) are good and varied. Some have the form of the duck, the wild boar, and other animals. During the period of the *iššakē* or viceroys, fine sculptures in low relief occur—the scorpion-man and the sacred tree, military prisoners with their guard, siege-operations and the dead on the battlefield; and as examples of work in the round, ivory and alabaster statuettes. Later on, during the time of the kings of Elam and Susa, the objects of art increase in number, though large objects in the round are rare. Noteworthy are the statuettes and statues in bronze, the former being very numerous. The largest production of this kind is the almost life-size statue of queen Napir-Asu, consort of Untaš-Gal, which, however, is unfortunately headless. It is a remarkable piece of work, and has great artistic merit.

16. Art in the Archaic Period, That of the Viceroys, and That of the Kings

In all probability Elam was much hindered in her material and intellectual development by the intractable and warlike nature of her people—indeed, the history of the country, as far as it is known, is a record of strife and conflict, and the temperament indicated by the ancient records seems to have been inherited by the wild tribes which occupy the more inaccessible districts. What conduced to quarrels and conflicts in ancient times was the law of succession, for the Elamite kings were not generally succeeded by their eldest sons, but by their brothers (see Ellasar). The inhabitants of the towns at the present time in all probability do not differ in any essential respect from those of Persia in general, and among them there is probably no great amount of ancient Elamite blood, though the Elamite type is met with, and probably occurs, in consequence of ancient mingling, in various parts of modern Persia.

17. Temperament of the Inhabitants of Elam

Literature.—For the most complete account of the discoveries in Elam, see *Mémoires de la délégation en Perse*, I ff, *Mission scientifique en Perse*, I ff, and *Histoire et travaux de la délégation en Perse*, all under the editorship of J. de Morgan, and written by De Morgan, V. Scheil, G. Lampré, G. Jéquier, etc; also W. K. Loftus, *Chaldea and Susiana*, 1857.

T. G. Pinches

ELASA, el′a-sa (**Ἀλασά**, *Alasá;* AV **Eleasa**, el-ē-ā′sa): The place where Judas pitched his camp before the battle in which he was overwhelmed and slain (1 Macc **9** 5). It probably corresponds to the modern *Khirbet il'asā*, between the two Beth-horons.

ELASAH, el′a-sa (אֶלְעָשָׂה, *'el'āsāh*, "God has made"):

(1) An Israelite who had married a foreign wife (Ezr **10** 22).

(2) A son of Shaphan, by whom, with Gemariah, King Zedekiah sent a message to Babylon (Jer **29** 3). See Eleasah.

ELATH, ē′lath, or **ELOTH**, ē′loth (אֵילוֹת, *'ēlōth*, אֵילַת, *'ēlath;* **Αἰλών**, *Ailōn* [Dt **2** 8], **Αἰλάθ**, *Ailáth* [2 K **16** 6]): A seaport on the Red Sea in the territory of Edom. It is named along with Ezion-geber in the account of Israel's journey round the land of Edom (Dt **2** 8). It appears as Ailath, and Ailōn in the LXX, and in Jos as Ilanis (*Ant*, VIII, vi, 4), while *Onom* has Αἰλά, *Ailá*. From this we may gather that the Aram. *Ilān* or *Ilānā* was in use as well as the Heb *'ēlath* or *'ēlōth*. The name, "grove," was doubtless derived from the presence of certain sacred trees. It may be identical with El-paran of Gen **14** 6, and Elah of Gen **36** 41. When David conquered Edom, Elath passed into the hands of Israel (2 S **8** 14). It was a position of great importance in connection with the trade with South Arabia. Here the merchant fleets of Solomon and Jehoshaphat were fitted out, and hence they sailed (1 K **9** 26; 2 Ch **8** 17; 1 K **22** 48). In the reign of Jehoram, son of Jehoshaphat, Edom shook off the hand of Judah (2 K **8** 20), but under Amaziah and Uzziah it was again subdued (**14** 7.10.22). Finally it was taken from Ahaz by Rezin, king of Syria. The Jews were driven out and the Syrians (Edomites?) took permanent possession (**16** 6). It is identical with the modern *'Aḳaba*, at the head of the gulf of that name.

W. Ewing

ELBERITH, el-bē′rith (Jgs **9** 46). See Baal-berith.

EL-BETH-EL, el-beth′el (אֵל בֵּית־אֵל, *'ēl bēth-'ēl*, "God of Bethel"; **Βαιθήλ**, *Baithḗl*): By this name Jacob called the scene of his vision at Luz, when he returned from Paddan-aram (Gen **35** 7).

ELCIA, el′shi-a, RV ELKIAH (q.v.).

ELDAAH, el-dā′a (אֶלְדָּעָה, *'eldā'āh*, "God has called"?): A son of Midian (Gen **25** 4; 1 Ch **1** 33).

ELDAD, el′dad (אֶלְדָּד, *'eldādh*, "God has loved"): One of the 70 elders chosen by Moses at the command of Jeh to share "the burden of the people" (Nu **11** 16–25). Eldad and his companion Medad were not present with the rest at the tent of meeting, yet the Spirit rested also upon them and they prophesied in the camp (vs 26–29).

ELDAD, el′dad, **AND MODAD**, mō′dad, **BOOK OF:** In the LXX they are called Eldad and Modad. In the AV the names are given as Eldad and Medad; meaning "God has loved" ("God loves") and "object of love" (?). They were two of the seventy elders chosen by Moses (Nu **11** 26), and while the others obeyed the summons and went to the tabernacle, these two remained in the camp and prophesied (Nu **11** 26). The nature of their prophecy is not recorded, and this naturally became a good subject for the play of the imagination. It furnished the basis for a lost work which was quoted by Hermas (*Vis* **2** 3): "The Lord is near to them who return unto him, as it is written in Eldad and Modad, who prophesied to the people in the wilderness." The Pal Tgs also filled in the subject of the prophecy of Eldad and Modad, and, as they have it, it related to the coming of Gog and Magog against Israel at the end of the days. One of the Tgs has the expression, "The Lord is near to them that are in the hour of tribulation." The authors of the Tgs were either dependent upon that work or upon a similar tradition; and the former of these views is the more probable. Lightfoot and Holtzman think the lengthy quotation in 1 Clem **23** and 2 Clem **11** is from the Book of Eldad and Modad. The work is found in the Stichometry of Nicephorus and consists of 400 stichoi, which would make it about twice the length of the Cant.

A. W. Fortune

ELDER, el′-dẽr, **IN THE OT** (זָקֵן, *zāḳēn*): Among primitive peoples authority seems naturally to be invested in those who by virtue of greater age and, consequently, experience are best fitted to govern: thus *Iliad* iii.149. Later the idea of age became merged in that of dignity (*Il.* ii.404, ii.570; *Odyssey* ii.14). In like manner the word *patres* came to be used among the Romans (Cic. *Rep.* 2.8. 14). So also among the Germans authority was intrusted to those who were older; cf Tacitus *Agricola*. The same is true among the Arabians to the present day, the sheik being always a man of age as well as of authority.

From the first the Hebrews held this view of government, although the term "elder" came later to be used of the idea of the authority for which, at first, age was regarded necessary. Thus the office appears in both J (9th cent. BC) (Ex **3** 16; **12** 21; **24** 1, of the elders of the Hebrews; and of the Egyptians, Gen **50** 7); and E (8th cent. BC) (Ex **17** 5; **18** 12; **19** 7 [D_2]; Josh **24** 31, elders of Israel, or of the people. Cf the principle of selection of heads of tens, fifties, etc, Ex **18** 13 ff, seventy being selected from a previous body of elders); cf *JE* (Nu **11** 16.24). Seventy are also mentioned in Ex **24** 1, while in Jgs **8** 14 seventy-seven are mentioned, although this might be taken to include seven princes. Probably the number was not uniform.

Elder as a title continues to have place down through the times of the Judges (Jgs **8** 16; **2** 7[D]; cf Ruth **4** 2 ff) into the kingdom. Saul asked to be honored before the elders (1 S **15** 30); the elders of Bethlehem appeared before Samuel (**16** 4); the elders appeared before David in Hebron (2 S **17** 15; 1 Ch **11** 3); elders took part in the temple procession of Solomon (1 K **8** 3; 2 Ch **5** 4). They continued through the Pers period (Ezr **5** 5.9; **6** 7.14; **10** 8.14; Joel **1** 14m) and the Maccabean period (Jth **6** 16; **7** 23; **8** 10; **10** 6; **13** 12; 1 Macc **12** 35), while the NT (πρεσβύτερος, *presbúteros*, Mt **16** 21; **26** 47.57; Mk **8** 31; Lk **9** 22; Acts **4** 5.23) makes frequent mention of the office.

The elders served as local magistrates, in bringing murderers to trial (Dt **19** 12; **21** 1 ff; Josh **20** 4), punishing a disobedient son (Dt **21** 19), inflicting penalty for slander (**22** 15), for noncompliance with the Levirate marriage law (**25** 7 ff), enforcing the Law (**27** 1), conducting the service in expiation of unwitting violation of the Law (Lev **4** 13 ff).

In certain passages different classes of officers are mentioned as "judges and officers" (Dt **16** 18), "elders" and "officers" (**31** 28), "heads, tribes, elders, officers" (**29** 10 [Heb 9]). It is probable that both classes were selected from among the elders, and that to one class was assigned the work of judging, and that the "officers" exercised executive functions (Schürer). In entirely Jewish communities the same men would be both officers of the community and elders of the synagogue. In this case the same men would have jurisdiction over civil and religious matters.

LITERATURE.—Schürer, *GJV*³, § 23, esp. 175 ff (Eng. ed, II, i, 149 ff; Benzinger, *HA*², 51; Deissmann, *Bibelstudien*, 153 ff (s.v. πρεσβύτερος); *BDB*, 278 (זָקֵן); Preuschen, *Griechisch-Deutsches Handwörterbuch*, s.v., 958 f.

W. N. STEARNS

ELDER IN THE NT (πρεσβύτερος, *presbúteros*):

(1) The word is used adjectivally to denote seniority (Lk **15** 25; 1 Tim **5** 2).

(2) Referring to the Jewish elders of the synagogue, usually associated with the scribes and Pharisees, and NT passages cited in the previous article.

(3) It denotes certain persons appointed to hold office in the Christian church, and to exercise spiritual oversight over the flock intrusted to them. From the references in Acts (**14** 23; **20** 17) it may be inferred that the churches generally had elders appointed over them. That "elders" and "bishops" were in apostolic and sub-apostolic times the same, is now almost universally admitted; in all NT references their functions are identical. The most probable explanation of the difference of names is that "elder" refers mainly to the person, and "bishop" to the office; the name "elder" emphasizes what he is, while "bishop," that is "overseer," emphasizes what the elder or presbyter does. See BISHOP; CHURCH GOVERNMENT; MINISTRY.

A. C. GRANT

ELEAD, el′ē-ad (אֶלְעָד, *'el'ādh*, "God has testified"): An Ephraimite, slain while making a raid, by the men of Gath (1 Ch **7** 21).

ELEADAH, el-ē-ā′da, **ELADAH** (AV) (אֶלְעָדָה, *'el'ādhāh*, "God has adorned"): An Ephraimite (1 Ch **7** 20).

ELEALEH, ē-lē-ā′le (אֶלְעָלֵה, *'el'ālēh*, "God has ascended"): Lay in the country taken from Sihon and within the lot given to Reuben (Nu **32** 3.37 f). "Their names being changed" seems to apply to all the towns mentioned. There is no indication of the other names. Elealeh is noticed with Heshbon in the oracles against Moab in Isa **15** 4; **16** 9; Jer **48** 34. *Onom* locates it one Rom mile from Heshbon. It is represented today by *el'Āl*, a mound crowned with ruins, about a mile N. of *Ḥesbān*.

ELEASA, el-ē-ā′sa. See ELASA.

ELEASAH, el-ē-ā′sa (in Heb identical with ELASAH, which see):

(1) A descendant of Judah (1 Ch **2** 39.40).

(2) A Benjamite, a descendant of Saul (1 Ch **8** 37; **9** 43).

ELEAZAR, el-ē-ā′zar, ē-lē-ā′zar (אֶלְעָזָר, *'el'āzār*; Ἐλεάζαρ, *Eleázar*, "God is helper"):

(1) The 3d son of Aaron by Elisheba (Ex **6** 23; Nu **3** 2). He married one of the daughters of Putiel, who bore him Phinehas (Ex **6** 25). With his father and 3 brothers he was consecrated to the priest's office (Ex **28** 1). After the destruction of Nadab and Abihu, he occupied a more important position, and he and Ithamar "ministered in the priest's office in the presence of Aaron their father" (Lev **10** 6 f; Nu **3** 4; 1 Ch **24** 2 ff). He was given the oversight of the Levites and had charge of the tabernacle and all within it (Nu **3** 32; **4** 16). To Eleazar fell the duty of beating out for an altar covering the censers of Korah and his fellow-conspirators who had attempted to seize the priesthood (Nu **16** 37.39). On the death of Aaron, Eleazar succeeded him (Nu **20** 25 ff). He assisted Moses with the census after the plague in the plains of Moab (Nu **26** 1 ff), and with Moses and the elders heard the petition of the daughters of Zelophehad who wished to be served as heirs to their father (Nu **27** 1 ff). After the entrance into Canaan, Eleazar and Joshua gave effect to the decision arrived at by giving the daughters of Zelophehad a share in the land of Manasseh (Josh **17** 4). He was priest and adviser to Joshua, the successor of Moses (Nu **27** 19; **31** 12 ff), whom he also assisted in partitioning Canaan among the tribes (Nu **34** 17; Josh **14** 1; **19** 51; **21** 1). He was buried in the hill (RVm "Gibeah") of Phinehas his son in the hill country of Ephraim (Josh **24** 33). For some reason unknown the descendants of Ithamar seem to have held the chief position among the priests from Eli till the accession of Solomon, when Abiathar was sent into retirement, and Zadok, the descendant of Eleazar, was appointed in his place (1 K **2** 26 ff). Ezra was a descendant of Zadok

(Ezr **7** 1 ff); and the high priest's office was in the family of Zadok till the time of the Maccabees.

(2) The son of Abinadab, sanctified to keep the ark of Jeh, when it was brought from Beth-shemesh to Kiriath-jearim after being sent back by the Philis (1 S **7** 1).

(3) The son of Dodai, one of David's three mighty men. A famous feat of arms with David at Ephes-dammim is recorded (2 S **23** 9 f; 1 Ch **11** 12 f where he is named the son of Dodo).

(4) A Levite, a son of Mahli, a Merarite. It is recorded that he had no sons, but daughters only, who were married to their cousins (1 Ch **23** 21.22; **24** 28).

(5) A priest who accompanied Ezra from Babylon (Ezr **8** 33); the son of Phinehas. (5) and (6) may be identical.

(6) A priest who took part in the dedication of the wall of Jerus (Neh **12** 42).

(7) A son of Mattathias and brother of Judas Maccabaeus (1 Macc **2** 5; **6** 43 f; 2 Macc **8** 23). See ASMONEANS; MACCABEES.

(8, 9) Two others are mentioned in 1 Macc **8** 17; 2 Macc **6** 18 ff.

(10) An ancestor of Jesus, 3 generations before Joseph (Mt **1** 15). S. F. HUNTER

ELEAZURUS, el-ē-a-zū'rus, RV ELIASIBUS (q.v.).

ELECT, ē-lekt': That is, "chosen," "selected." In the OT the word represents derivatives of בָּחַר, *bāḥar, elegit;* in the NT ἐκλεκτός, *eklektós*. It means properly an object or objects of selection. This primary meaning sometimes passes into that of "eminent," "valuable," "choice"; often thus as a fact, in places where AV uses "chosen" (or "elect") to translate the original (e.g. Isa **42** 1; 1 Pet **2** 6). In AV "elect" (or "chosen") is used of Israel as the race selected for special favor and to be the special vehicle of Divine purposes (so 4 t in Apoc, Tob and Ecclus); of the great Servant of Jeh (cf Lk **23** 35; the "Christ of God, his chosen"); cf eminent saints as Jacob, Moses, Rufus (Rom **16** 13); "the lady," and her "sister" of 2 Jn; of the holy angels (1 Tim **5** 21), with a possible suggestion of the lapse of other angels. Otherwise, and prevalently in the NT, it denotes a human community, also described as believers, saints, the Israel of God; regarded as in some sense selected by Him from among men, objects of His special favor, and correspondingly called to special holiness and service. See further under ELECTION. In the Eng. VSS "elect" is not used as a vb.: "to choose" is preferred; e.g. Mk **13** 20; Eph **1** 4. HANDLEY DUNELM

ELECT LADY, ē-lekt' lā'di (ἐκλεκτῇ κυρίᾳ, *eklektē kuria;* 2 Jn ver 1): In accordance with strict grammatical usage these words of address may be tr[d] in three ways: "to an elect lady" (which as an address is too indefinite); or, both words being taken as proper names, "to *Eklektē Kuria*" (an improbable combination of two very rare names); or "to *Eklektē*, lady" = *anglice*, "to the lady [or 'Madam'] *Eklektē*." The other translations which have been given—"to the elect lady" or "to the elect Kuria"—are open to objection on account of the omission of the article; but this violation of rule is perhaps not without parallel (cf 1 Pet **1** 1). The translation adopted will partly depend upon whether we regard the epistle as addressed to an individual or to a community. Dr. Rendel Harris believes this question to be settled by the discovery in the papyri of numerous instances which prove that *kurios* and *kuria* were used by ancient letter-writers as terms of familiar endearment, applicable to brother, sister, son, wife, or intimate friend of either sex (*Expositor*, March, 1901; see also Findlay, *Fellowship in the Life Eternal*, ch iii). In the light of this suggestion we should naturally translate, "to my [dear] lady Eklektē." Grammatically, this is strongly supported by 1 Tim **1** 2 and 2 Tim **1** 2 (Τιμοθέῳ γνησίῳ . . . . ἀγαπητῷ . . . . τέκνῳ, *Timothéō gnēsiō . . . . agapētō . . . . téknō* = "to Timothy my true . . . . beloved . . . . child"); and the fact that the name *Eklektē* has not yet been discovered, though *Eklektós* has, offers no grave objection. This is the tr favored by Clement of Alexandria, who says of the epistle: *scripta vero est ad quandam Babyloniam nomine Electam, significat autem electionem ecclesiae sanctae* ("It is written to a certain Babylonian, Electa by name; but it signifies the further election of the holy church"). It seems doubtful whether he means by the last clause that Electa is simply a personification of the church, or a real person whose name was derived from the Christian idea of election. Either way the rendering, "to the lady Electa," is suitable, and upon the whole it seems the best. *Eklektē* is not an adj. but a noun. If a person is intended, it is "the lady Electa"; if a church, it is designated, not "the elect Lady," but "the lady Elect." The mention of "thy elect sister" in 2 Jn ver 13 does not hinder either supposition. See further CYRIA; JOHN, THE EPISTLES OF. ROBERT LAW

ELECTION, ē-lek'shun (ἐκλογή, *eklogḗ*, "choice," "selection"):

I. THE WORD IN SCRIPTURE
II. THE MYSTERIOUS ELEMENT
III. INCIDENCE UPON COMMUNITY AND INDIVIDUAL
IV. COGNATE AND ILLUSTRATIVE BIBLICAL LANGUAGE
V. LIMITATIONS OF INQUIRY HERE. SCOPE OF ELECTION
VI. PERSEVERANCE
VII. CONSIDERATIONS IN RELIEF OF THOUGHT
1. Antinomies
2. Fatalism Another Thing
3. The Moral Aspects
4. "We know in Part"
5. The Unknown Future

I. The Word in Scripture.—The word is absent from the OT, where the related Heb vb. (בָּחַר, *bāḥar*) is frequent. In the NT it occurs 6 t (Rom **9** 11; **11** 5.7.28; 1 Thess **1** 4; 2 Pet **1** 10). In all these places it appears to denote an act of Divine selection taking effect upon human objects so as to bring them into special and saving relations with God: a selection such as to be at once a mysterious thing, transcending human analysis of its motives (so eminently in Rom **9** 11), and such as to be knowable by its objects, who are (2 Pet) exhorted to "make it sure," certain, a fact to consciousness. It is always (with one exception, Rom **9** 11; see below) related to a community, and thus has close affinity with the OT teachings upon the privileged position of Israel as the chosen, selected race (see under ELECT). The objects of election in the NT are, in effect, the Israel of God, the new, regenerate race called to special privilege and special service. From one point of view, that of the external marks of Christianity, they may thus be described as the Christian community in its widest sense, the sense in which the sacramental position and the real are *prima facie* assumed to coincide. But from 2 Pet it is manifest that much more than this has to be said if the incidence of the word present to the writer's mind is to be rightly felt. It is assumed there that the Christian, baptized and a worshipper, may yet need to make "sure" his "calling and election" as a fact to his consciousness. This implies conditions in the "election" which far transcend the tests of sacred rite and external fellowship.

II. The Mysterious Element.—Such impressions of depth and mystery in the word are confirmed by the other passages. In Rom **9** 11 the context is charged with the most urgent and even staggering challenges to submission and silence in the presence of the inscrutable. To illustrate large assertions as to the liberty and sovereignty of the Divine dealings with man, the apostle brings in Esau and Jacob, individuals, twins as yet unborn, and points to the inscrutable difference of the Divine action toward them as such. Somehow, as a matter of fact, the Eternal appears as appointing to unborn Esau a future of comparative disfavor and to Jacob of favor; a future announced to the still pregnant mother. Such discrimination was made and announced, says the apostle, "that the purpose of God according to election might stand." In the whole passage the gravest stress is laid upon the isolation of the "election" from the merit or demerit of its objects.

III. Incidence upon Community and Individual.—It is observable that the same characteristic, the inscrutable, the sovereign, is attached in the OT to the "election" of a favored and privileged *nation.* Israel is repeatedly reminded (see e.g. Dt **7**) that the Divine call and choice of them to be the people of God has no relation to their virtues, or to their strength. The reason lies out of sight, in the Divine mind. So too "the Israel of God" (Gal **6** 16) in the NT, the Christian community, "the new, peculiar race," holds its great privileges by quite unmerited favor (e.g. Tit **3** 5). And the nature of the case here leads, as it does not in the case of the natural Israel, to the thought of a Divine election of the individual, similarly inscrutable and sovereign. For the *idea* of the New Israel involves the thought that in every genuine member of it the provisions of the New Covenant (Jer **31** 31 f) are being fulfilled: the sins are remembered no more, and the law is written in the heart. The bearer of the Christian name, but not of the Christian spiritual standing and character, having "not the Spirit of Christ, is none of his" (Rom **8** 9). The chosen community accordingly, not as it seems *ab extra*, but as it is in its essence, is a fellowship of individuals each of whom is an object of unmerited Divine favor, taking effect in the new life. And this involves the exercise of electing mercy. Cf e.g. 1 Pet **1** 3. And consider Rom **11** 4-7 (where observe the exceptional use of "the election," meaning "the company of the elect").

IV. Cognate and Illustrative Biblical Language.—It is obvious that the aspects of mystery which gather round the word "election" are not confined to it alone. An important class of words, such as "calling," "predestination," "foreknowledge," "purpose," "gift," bears this same character; asserting or connoting, in appropriate contexts, the element of the inscrutable and sovereign in the action of the Divine will upon man, and particularly upon man's will and affection toward God. And it will be felt by careful students of the Bible in its larger and more general teachings that one deep characteristic of the Book, which with all its boundless multiplicity is yet one, is to emphasize on the side of man everything that can humble, convict, reduce to worshipping silence (see for typical passages Job **40** 3.4; Rom **3** 19), and on the side of God everything which can bring home to man the transcendence and sovereign claims of his almighty Maker. Not as unrelated utterances, but as part of a vast whole of view and teaching, occur such passages as Eph **2** 8.9 and Rom **11** 33-36, and even the stern, or rather awestruck, phrases of Rom **9** 20.21, where the potter and the clay are used in illustration.

V. Limitations of Inquiry Here. Scope of Election.—We have sought thus in the simplest outline to note first the word "election" and then some related Scriptural words and principles, weighing the witness they bear to a profound mystery in the action of the Divine will upon man, in the spiritual sphere. What we have thus seen leaves still unstated what, according to Scripture, is the goal and issue of the elective act. In this art., remembering that it is part of a *Bible* Encyclopaedia, we attempt no account of the history of thought upon election, in the successive Christian cents., nor again any discussion of the relation of election in Scripture to extra-Scriptural philosophies, to theories of necessity, determination, fatalism. We attempt only to see the matter as it lies before us in the Bible. Studying it so, we find that this mysterious action of God on man has relation, in the Christian revelation, to nothing short of the salvation of the individual (and of the community of such individuals) from sin and condemnation, and the preservation of the saved to life eternal. We find this not so much in any single passage as in the main stream of Bib. language and tone on the subject of the Divine selective action. But it is remarkable that in the recorded thought of Our Lord Himself we find assertions in this direction which could hardly be more explicit. See Jn **6** 37. 44.45; **10** 27-29. To the writer the best summary of the Scriptural evidence, at once definite and restrained, is the language of the 17th Anglican art.: "They which be endued with so excellent a benefit of God be called according to God's purpose by His Spirit working in due season; they through grace obey the calling; they be justified freely; they be made sons of God by adoption; they be made like the image of His only begotten Son Jesus Christ; they walk religiously in good works, and at length, by God's mercy, they attain to everlasting felicity."

VI. Perseverance.—The anxious problem of PERSEVERANCE will be treated under that word. It may be enough here to say that alike what we are permitted to read as revealed, and what we may humbly apprehend as the reason of the case, tend to the reverent belief that a perseverance (rather of the Lord than of the saints) is both taught and implied. But when we ponder the nature of the subject we are amply prepared for the large range of Scriptures which on the other hand condemn and preclude, for the humble disciple, so gross a misuse of the doctrine as would let it justify one moment's presumption upon Divine mercy in the heart which is at the same time sinning against the Divine love and holiness.

VII. Considerations in Relief of Thought.—We close, in view of this last remark, with some detached notes in relief, well remembering the unspeakable trial which to many devout minds the word before us has always brought.

1. Antinomies

First in place and importance is the thought that a spiritual fact like election, which belongs to the innermost purpose and work of the Eternal, necessarily leads us to a region where *comprehension* is impossible, and where we can only reverently *apprehend.* The doctrine passes upward to the sphere where antinomies live and move, where we must be content to hear what sound to us contradictions, but which are really various aspects of infinite truth. Let us be content to know that the Divine choice is sovereign; and also that "his tender mercies are over all his works," that 'He willeth not the death of a sinner,' that "God is love." Let us relieve the tension of such submissive reliance by reverently noting how the supreme antinomy meets one type of human need with its one side, and with its other another. To the "fearful saint" the Divine sovereignty of love is a sacred cordial. To the seeking penitent the Divine comprehensiveness of love opens the door of peace. To the deluded theorist who does not love and obey, the warnings of a fall and ruin which are possible, humanly, from any spiritual height, are a merciful beacon on the rocks.

2. Fatalism Another Thing

Further, we remember that election, in Scripture, is as different as possible from the fatal necessity of, e.g. the Stoics. It never appears as mechanical, or as a blind destiny. It has to do with the will of a God who has given us otherwise supreme proofs that He is all-good and all-kind. And it is related to man not as a helpless and innocent being but as a sinner. It is never presented as an arbitrary *force majeure*. Even in Rom **9** the "silence" called for is not as if to say, "You are hopelessly passive in the grasp of infinite power," but, "You, the creature, cannot judge *your Maker*, who must know infinitely more of cause and reason than his handiwork can know." The mystery, we may be sure, had behind it supreme right and reason, but in a region which at present at least we cannot penetrate. Again, election never appears as a violation of human will. For never in the Bible is man treated as irresponsible. In the Bible the relation of the human and Divine wills is inscrutable; the reality of both is assured.

3. The Moral Aspects

Never is the doctrine presented apart from a moral context. It is intended manifestly to deepen man's submission to—not force, but—mystery, where such submission means faith. In the practical experience of the soul its designed effect is to emphasize in the believer the consciousness (itself native to the true state of grace) that *the whole* of his salvation is due to the Divine mercy, no part of it to his merit, to his virtue, to his wisdom. In the sanctified soul, which alone, assuredly, can make full use of the mysterious truth, is it designed to generate, together and in harmony, awe, thanksgiving and repose.

4. "We Know in Part"

A necessary caution in view of the whole subject is that here, if anywhere in the regions of spiritual study, we inevitably "know in part," and in a very limited part. The treatment of election has at times in Christian history been carried on as if, less by the light of revelation than by logical processes, we could tabulate or map the whole subject. Where this has been done, and where at the same time, under a sort of mental rather than spiritual fascination, election has been placed in the foreground of the system of religious thought, and allowed to dominate the rest, the truth has (to say the least) too often been distorted into an error. The Divine character has been beclouded in its beauty. Sovereignty has been divorced from love, and so defaced into an arbitrary *fiat*, which has for its only reason the assertion of omnipotence. Thus the grievous wrong has been done of *αἰσχρόν τι λέγειν περὶ τοῦ Θείου*, "defamation of God." For example, the revelation of a positive Divine selection has been made by inference to teach a corresponding rejection ruthless and terrible, as if the Eternal Love could ever by any possibility reject or crush even the faintest aspiration of the created spirit toward God. For such a thought not even the dark words of Rom **9** 18 give Scriptural excuse. The case there in hand, Pharaoh's, is anything but one of arbitrary power trampling on a human will looking toward God and right. Once more, the subject is one as to which we must on principle be content with knowledge so fragmentary that its parts may seem contradictory in our present imperfect light. The one thing we may be sure of behind the veil is, that nothing can be hidden there which will really contradict the supreme and ruling truth that God is love.

5. The Unknown Future

Finally, let us from another side remember that here, as always in the things of the Spirit, "we know in part." The chosen multitude are sovereignly "called, ... justified, ... glorified" (Rom **8** 29.30). But for what purposes? Certainly not for an end terminating in themselves. They are saved, and kept, and raised to the perfect state, for the service of their Lord. And not till the cloud is lifted from the unseen life can we possibly know what that service under eternal conditions will include, what ministries of love and good in the whole universe of being. HANDLEY DUNELM

ELECTRUM, ė-lek'trum: The RVm rendering of חַשְׁמַל, *ḥashmal*, of Ezk **1** 4.27; **8** 2 (LXX **ἤλεκτρον,** *ēlektron*, Vulg *electrum*). Both AV and ERV have "amber" while the ARV has "glowing metal." Gesenius says electrum must not be understood as being here used for amber, but for a kind of metal remarkable for brightness, compounded of gold and silver. "Amber" is undoubtedly a poor rendering, as the Heb term means "polished brass." ARV has the more correct rendering. Amber, however, may well have been known to Ezekiel (*EB* s.v.). See also STONES, PRECIOUS; BUYING, IV.

A. W. FORTUNE

EL-ELOHE-ISRAEL, el-ė-lō'hė-iz'rȧ-el, el-el'ō-he-iz'rȧ-el (אֵל אֱלֹהֵי יִשְׂרָאֵל, *'ēl 'ĕlōhē yisrā'ēl*, tr[d] "God, the God of Israel" in ARVm and AVm): Found only in Gen **33** 20 as the name given to the altar erected at Shechem by Jacob, henceforth known as Israel, on the parcel of ground purchased by him from the inhabitants of Shechem, his first encampment of length and importance since the return to Pal from Paddan-aram and the eventful night at Peniel (Gen **32** 30). This unusual combination of names has given occasion for much speculation and for various text emendations. Already the LXX sought to meet the difficulty by reading *wa-yiḳrā' 'el 'ĕlōhē yisrā'ēl*, "and he called *upon* the God of Israel," instead of the *wa-yiḳrā' lō 'ēl* of MT, "and he called it El" etc. Wellhausen, followed by Dillmann, Driver and others, changes "altar" to "pillar," because the Heb verb, *hiççībh*, is used with *maççēbhāh*, "pillar," in Gen **35** 14.20, so making this religious act a parallel to that at Bethel. But Delitzsch, *New Comm. on Gen*, properly rejects this purely fanciful change, and understands the compound name as the altar's inscription. Dillmann well suggests that "altar" (or "pillar") be supplied, reading thus: "called it *the altar of El*, the God of Israel." The peculiar phrase is best and most readily understood in its close connection with the struggle at Peniel, recorded in Gen **32**. Being victorious in that struggle, Jacob received the new name "Israel"; and to his first altar in Pal he gave that name of God which appeared in his own new name, further explaining it by the appositive phrase "Elohe-Israel." Thus his altar was called, or dedicated to, "El, the God of Israel." EDWARD MACK

EL ELYON, el ė-lī'on. See GOD, NAMES OF.

ELEMENT, el'ė-ment, **ELEMENTS** (**τὰ στοιχεῖα,** *tá stoicheia*, "the letters of the alphabet," "the elements out of which all things are formed," "the heavenly bodies," "the fundamental principles of any art or science"):

(1) In 2 Pet **3** 10, the constituent parts of the physical universe ("elements shall be dissolved with fervent heat," ARVm "the heavenly bodies").

(2) In Gal **4** 3.9, RV has "rudiments," as in AVm, and in Col **2** 8.20, where the reference is to imperfect Jewish ordinances. See RUDIMENTS.

ELEPH, e'lef (הָאֶלֶף, *hā-'eleph*, "the ox"): A place

in the lot of Benjamin not far from Jerus (Josh **18** 28). The name is omitted by LXX, unless, indeed, it is combined with that of Zelah. It may be identical with *Lifta*, a village W. of Jerus (Conder, ***HDB***, s.v.). Others identify *Lifta* with Nephtoah.

ELEPHANT, el'ē-fant (Job **40** 15 AVm [ARVm "hippopotamus," RV "ivory"]; 1 K **10** 22 AVm; 2 Ch **9** 21 AVm; 1 Macc **3** 34; **6** 28 ff; **8** 6): Possibly in Job it is the extinct mammoth. See Behemoth; Ivory.

ELEPHANTINE, el-ē-fan-tī'nē. See Seveneh.

ELEUTHERUS, ē-lū'thēr-us (**'Ελεύθερος,** *Eleútheros;* 1 Macc **11** 7; **12** 30): A river separating Syria and Phoenicia.

ELEVEN, ē-lev'n, **STARS.** See Astronomy.

ELEVEN, ē-lev'n, **THE** (**οἱ ἕνδεκα,** *hoi héndeka*): The eleven apostles remaining after the death of Judas. The definite art. used serves to designate them as a distinct and definite group whose integrity was not destroyed by the loss of one of the twelve. The college of "the Twelve" had come to be so well recognized that the gospel writers all used on occasions the word with the definite art. to represent the Twelve Apostles chosen by Jesus. This custom still remained and the numeral merely changed, as, "Afterward he was manifested unto the eleven" (Mk **16** 14; cf Lk **24** 9.33; Acts **2** 14). On the other hand, however, the subst. is also sometimes used, as "The eleven disciples went into Galilee" (Mt **28** 16; cf also Acts **1** 26). As an illustration of the fixedness of usage, Paul refers to the eleven as "the twelve" when he recounts the appearances of Jesus after His resurrection: "And that he appeared to Cephas; then to the twelve" (1 Cor **15** 5). Walter G. Clippinger

ELHANAN, el-hā'nan (אֶלְחָנָן, *'elḥānān,* "whom God gave"):

(1) A great warrior in the army of David who slew a Phili giant. There is a discrepancy between 2 S **21** 19 and 1 Ch **20** 5. In the former passage we read, "And there was again war with the Philis at Gob; and Elhanan, the son of Jaare-oregim the Beth-lehemite, slew Goliath the Gittite, the staff of whose spear was like a weaver's beam"; while in the latter we are told, "And there was again war with the Philis; and Elhanan the son of Jair slew Lahmi the brother of Goliath the Gittite, the staff of whose spear was like a weaver's beam." Most modern critics prefer as the original text of the latter part of the two discrepant statements the following: "and Elhanan the son of Jair the Beth-lehemite slew Goliath the Gittite, the staff of whose spear was like a weaver's beam." It is contended that the Chronicler slightly modified the text before him, in order to bring it into harmony with 1 S **17,** where David is said to have slain a Phili giant Goliath. There is almost unanimous agreement that "Jaare-oregim" is a corrupt reading, and the "Jair" in 1 Ch is to be preferred. From Jerome to the present some scholars identify Elhanan with David, and thus remove the discrepancy. Ewald (*Hist,* III, 70) argued that the name "Goliath" was inserted in 1 S **17** and **21** by the narrators whose compositions are embodied in Samuel, Elhanan being the real victor over Goliath, while David's antagonist was simply called "the Philistine."

(2) The son of Dodo of Bethlehem, one of David's mighty men (2 S **23** 24; 1 Ch **11** 26). Some moderns think that there was only one Elhanan, and that he was the son of Dodo of the clan of Jair. John Richard Sampey

ELI, ē'lī (עֵלִי, *'ēlī*): A descendant of Ithamar, the fourth son of Aaron, who exercised the office of high priest in Shiloh at the time of the birth of Samuel. For the first time in Israel, Eli combined in his own person the functions of high priest and judge, judging Israel for 40 years (1 S **4** 18). The incidents in Eli's life are few; indeed, the main interest of the narrative is in the other characters who are associated with him. The chief interest centers in Samuel. In Eli's first interview with Hannah (1 S **1** 12 ff), she is the central figure; in the second interview (1 S **1** 24 ff), it is the child Samuel. When Eli next appears, it is as the father of Hophni and Phinehas, whose worthless and licentious lives had profaned their priestly office, and earned for them the title "men of Belial" (or "worthlessness"). Eli administered no stern rebuke to his sons, but only a gentle chiding of their greed and immorality. Thereafter he was warned by a nameless prophet of the downfall of his house, and of the death of his two sons in one day (1 S **2** 27–36), a message later confirmed by Samuel, who had received this word directly from Jeh Himself (1 S **3** 11 ff). The prophecy was not long in fulfilment. During the next invasion by the Philis, the Israelites were utterly routed, the ark of God was captured, and Hophni and Phinehas were both slain. When the news reached Eli, he was so overcome that he "fell from off his seat backward by the side of the gate; and his neck brake, and he died" (1 S **4** 18). The character of Eli, while sincere and devout, seems to have been entirely lacking in firmness. He appears from the history to have been a good man, full of humility and gentleness, but weak and indulgent. His is not a strong personality; he is always overshadowed by some more commanding or interesting figure.
A. C. Grant

ELI, ē'lī or ā'lē, **ELI, LAMA,** lä'mä, **SABACHTHANI,** sa-bak'tha-nī. See Eloi, Eloi, etc.

ELIAB, ē-lī'ab (אֱלִיאָב, *'ĕlī'ābh,* "God is father"):

(1) Prince of the tribe of Zebulun in the Exodus (Nu **1** 9; **2** 7; **7** 24.29; **10** 16).

(2) A Reubenite, father of Dathan and Abiram (Nu **16** 11.12; **26** 8 f; Dt **11** 6).

(3) Eldest son of Jesse and brother of David (1 S **16** 6), once called Elihu (1 Ch **27** 18). He was of commanding appearance (1 S **16** 6), and when serving with Saul's army at the time when it was confronting the Philis and Goliath, was inclined to lord it over his brother David (**17** 28 f). His daughter Abihail became a wife of Rehoboam (2 Ch **11** 18).

(4) An Ephraimite, an ancestor of Samuel (1 Ch **6** 27); called Eliel in ver 34, and Elihu in 1 S **1** 1.

(5) A Gadite warrior with David (1 Ch **12** 9), one of 11 mighty men (vs 8.14).

(6) A Levite musician (1 Ch **15** 18.20; **16** 5).

(7) An ancestor of Judith (Jth **8** 1; cf **9** 2).
F. K. Farr

ELIADA, ē-lī'a-da, **ELIADAH** (אֶלְיָדָע, *'elyādhā',* "God is knowing." Cf *HPN,* 219, 266, 301; **'Επιδαέ** *Epidaé,* or **'Ελιδαέ,** *Elidaé*):

(1) One of the sons of David (2 S **5** 16; 1 Ch **3** 8; called Beeliada, 1 Ch **14** 7 [q.v.]).

(2) A descendant of Benjamin and a captain in the army of Jehoshaphat, commander of 200,000 men (2 Ch **17** 17).

(3) Father of Rezon, an "adversary" of Solomon (1 K **11** 23, AV "Eliadah").

ELIADAS, ē-lī'a-das (**'Ελιαδάς,** *Eliadás*): A son of Zamoth who had married a strange wife (1 Esd **9** 28); called Elioenai in Ezr **10** 27.

ELIADUN, ē-lī'a-dun, RV ILIADUN (q.v.).

ELIAH, ḗ-lī′a. See ELIJAH.

ELIAHBA, ḗ-lī′a-ba, ē-lī-ä′ba (אֶלְיַחְבָּא, *'elyaḥbā'*, "God hides"): One of David's 30 mighty men (2 S **23** 32; 1 Ch **11** 33).

ELIAKIM, ḗ-lī′a-kim (אֶלְיָקִים, *'elyāḳīm;* **'Ελιακείμ,** *Eliakeím*, "God sets up"):

(1) The son of Hilkiah who succeeded Shebna as governor of the palace and "grand vizier" under Hezekiah (Isa **22** 20). The functions of his office are seen from the oracle of Isaiah in which Shebna is deposed and Eliakim set in his place (Isa **22** 15 ff). He is the "treasurer" (RVm "steward"), and is "over the house" (ver 15). At his installation he is clothed with a robe and girdle, the insignia of his office, and, having the government committed into his hand, is the "father to the inhabitants of Jerus, and to the house of Judah" (ver 21). The key of the house of David is laid on his shoulder, and he alone has power to open and shut, this being symbolic of his absolute authority as the king's representative (ver 22).

One of Solomon's officials is the first mentioned as occupying this position (1 K **4** 6), and this office was continued in both the Northern and Southern Kingdom (1 K **16** 9; **18** 3; 2 K **10** 5; **15** 5). Its importance is seen from the fact that after Azariah was smitten with leprosy, Jotham his heir "was over the household, judging the people of the land" (2 K **15** 5).

When Sennacherib sent an army against Jerus in 701, Eliakim was one of these Jewish princes who held on behalf of Hezekiah a parley with the Assyr officers (2 K **18** 18.26.37; Isa **36** 3.11.22). As a result of the invader's threats, he was sent by Hezekiah in sackcloth to Isaiah, entreating his prayers to Jeh on behalf of Jerus (2 K **19** 2; Isa **37** 2).

(2) The original name of Jehoiakim, the son of Josiah, whom Pharaoh-necoh made king of Judah (2 K **23** 34; 2 Ch **36** 4).

(3) A priest who assisted at the dedication of the wall of Jerus, rebuilt after his return from Babylon (Neh **12** 41).

(4) A grandson of Zerubbabel and ancestor of Jesus (Mt **1** 13).

(5) An ancestor of Jesus (Lk **3** 30).

S. F. HUNTER

ELIALI, ḗ-lī′a-lī (**'Ελιαλεί,** *Elialeí*): 1 Esd **9** 34; possibly corresponds to "Binnui" in Ezr **10** 38.

ELIAM, ḗ-lī′am (אֱלִיעָם, *'ělī'ām*, "people's God"?):

(1) Father of Bathsheba (2 S **11** 3); in 1 Ch **3** 5 called Ammiel.

(2) One of David's "thirty," son of Ahithophel the Gilonite (2 S **23** 34).

ELIAONIAS, ḗ-lī-a-ō-nī′as (**'Ελιαλωνίας,** *Elialōnías*): A descendant of Phaath Moab (1 Esd **8** 31); called "Eliehoenai" in Ezr **8** 4.

ELIAS, ḗ-lī′as. See ELIJAH.

ELIASAPH, ḗ-lī′a-saf (אֶלְיָסָף, *'elyāṣāph*, "God has added"):

(1) Son of Deuel; prince of the tribe of Gad in the Exodus (Nu **1** 14; **2** 14; **7** 42.47; **10** 20).

(2) Son of Lael; prince of the Gershonites (Nu **3** 24).

ELIASHIB, ḗ-lī′a-shib (אֶלְיָשִׁיב, *'elyāshībh*, "God restores"):

(1) A descendant of David (1 Ch **3** 24).

(2) Head of the eleventh course of priests (1 Ch **24** 12).

(3) The high priest in the time of Nehemiah. He, with his brethren the priests, helped in the rebuilding of the wall (Neh **3** 1). But later he was "allied unto Tobiah" the Ammonite (**13** 4) and allowed that enemy of Nehemiah the use of a great chamber in the temple (ver 5); and one of his grandsons, a son of Joiada, married a daughter of Sanballat the Horonite and was for this expelled from the community by Nehemiah (ver 28). See SANBALLAT.

(4, 5, 6) Three Israelites, one a "singer," who had married foreign wives (Ezr **10** 24.27.36).

(7) Father of Jehohanan (Ezr **10** 6); probably identical with (3) above. Called Eliasib in 1 Esd **9** 1.

F. K. FARR

ELIASIB, ḗ-lī′a-sib. See ELIASHIB.

ELIASIBUS, ē-li-as′i-bus (**'Ελιάσιβος,** *Eliásibos*, AV **Eleazurus**): One of the holy singers who had married a foreign wife (1 Esd **9** 24); called "Eliashib" in Ezr **10** 27.

ELIASIMUS, ē-li-as′i-mus (**'Ελιάσιμος,** *Eliásimos;* AV **Elisimus**): One who had married a foreign wife (1 Esd **9** 28).

ELIASIS, ḗ-lī′a-sis (**'Ελιάσις,** *Eliásis*): One who had married a foreign wife (1 Esd **9** 34); corresponds to "Jaasu" in Ezr **10** 37.

ELIATHAH, ḗ-lī′a-tha (אֱלִיאָתָה, *'ělī'āthāh*, "God has come"): A Hemanite, head of the twentieth division of the temple musicians (1 Ch **25** 4.27).

ELIDAD, ḗ-lī′dad (אֱלִידָד, *'ělīdhādh*, "God has loved"): Prince of Benjamin in the division of the land (Nu **34** 21); perhaps the same as ELDAD (q.v.).

ELIEHOENAI, ḗ-lī-ḗ-hō′ḗ-nī (אֶלְיְהוֹעֵינַי, *'elyᵉhō'ēnay*, "to Jeh are mine eyes"):

(1) (AV Elioenai) a Korahite doorkeeper (1 Ch **26** 3).

(2) (AV Elihoenai) Head of a family in the Return (Ezr **8** 4).

ELIEL, ḗ-lī′el, el′i-el (אֱלִיאֵל, *'ělī'ēl*, "El is God," or "my God is God"):

(1, 2, 3) Mighty men of David (1 Ch **11** 46.47; **12** 11).

(4) A chief of Manasseh, east of the Jordan (1 Ch **5** 24).

(5, 6) Two chiefs of Benjamin (1 Ch **8** 20.22).

(7) A chief Levite from Hebron (1 Ch **15** 9.11).

(8) A Kohathite in the line of Elkanah, Samuel and Heman (1 Ch **6** 34); see ELIAB (4).

(9) A Levite of the time of Hezekiah (2 Ch **31** 13).

ELIENAI, el-i-ē′nā-i (אֱלִיעֵינַי, *'ělī'ēnay*): A Benjamite chief (1 Ch **8** 20).

ELIEZER, el-i-ē′zēr, ē-lī-ē′zēr (אֱלִיעֶזֶר, *'ělī'ezer;* **'Ελιέζερ,** *Eliézer*, "God is help"):

(1) The chief servant of Abram (Gen **15** 2); ARV "Eliezer of Damascus," ERV "Dammesek Eliezer." The Heb is peculiar: lit. "And the son of the possession [*meshek*] of my house is *Dammasek* [of] Eliezer." A possible but unlikely meaning is that his property would become the possession of Damascus, the city of Eliezer. Tg Syr (RVm) read "Eliezer the Damascene": this supposes a reading, "Eliezer *ha-dammaskī*" or "*mid-dammesek*." The text may be corrupt: the assonance between *meshek* and Dammesek is suspicious. Abram calls Eliezer "one born in my house," i.e. a dependant, a member of his household, and so regards him as his

heir, Lot having gone from him (Gen **13**). Eliezer is probably the servant, "the elder of his house, that ruled over all that he had," of Gen **24**.

(2) The 2d son of Moses and Zipporah, called thus for "the God of my father was my help, and delivered me from the sword of Pharaoh" (Ex **18** 4; 1 Ch **23** 15 ff).

(3) A son of Becher, one of the sons of Benjamin (1 Ch **7** 8).

(4) A priest who assisted in bringing up the ark from the house of Obed-edom to Jerus (1 Ch **15** 24).

(5) The son of Zichri, ruler over the Reubenites in the time of David (1 Ch **27** 16).

(6) The son of Dodavahu of Mareshah who prophesied the destruction of the ships which Jehoshaphat, king of Judah, built, because he had done so in coöperation with Ahaziah, king of Israel (2 Ch **20** 35 ff).

(7) One of the messengers whom Ezra sent to Iddo, the chief at Casiphia, with the request for ministers for the Temple (Ezr **8** 16 ff).

(8, 9, 10) A priest, a Levite, and one of the sons of Harim who had married non-Israelitish women (Ezr **10** 18.23.31).

(11) An ancestor of Jesus in the genealogy given by St. Luke (Lk **3** 29). S. F. Hunter

ELIHABA, ē-lī'ha-ba. See Eliahba.

ELIHOENAI, el-i-hō-ē'nā-ī. See Eliehoenai.

ELIHOREPH, el-i-hō'ref (אֱלִיחֹרֶף, *'ĕlīḥōreph,* "God of autumn"?): A scribe of Solomon and son of Shisha (1 K **4** 3).

ELIHU, ē-lī'hū (אֱלִיהוּ, *'ĕlīhū;* **Ἠλείου,** *Ēleíou,* "He is [my] God," or "my God is He"):

(1) An ancestor of Samuel (1 S **1** 1), called Eliel in 1 Ch **6** 34 and Eliab in 1 Ch **6** 27 (see Eliab).

(2) Found in 1 Ch **27** 18 for Eliab, David's eldest brother (1 S **16** 6); called "one of the brethren of D."

(3) A Manassite who joined David at Ziklag (1 Ch **12** 20).

(4) A Korahite porter (1 Ch **26** 7).

(5) A friend of Job. See next art.

(6) An ancestor of Judith (Jth **8** 1).

ELIHU (אֱלִיהוּ, *'ĕlīhū,* אֱלִיהוּא, *'ĕlīhū',* "He is [my] God"; **Ἐλιοῦς,** *Elioús*): One of the disputants in the Book of Job; a young man who, having listened in silence to the arguments of Job and his friends, is moved to prolong the discussion and from his juster views of truth set both parties right. He is of the tribe of Buz (cf Gen **22** 21), a brother-tribe to that of Uz, and of the family of Ram, or Aram, that is, an Aramaean. He is not mentioned as one of the characters of the story until ch **32;** and then, as the friends are silenced and Job's words are ended, Elihu has the whole field to himself, until the theophany of the whirlwind proves too portentous for him to bear. His four speeches take up chs **32**–**37**. Some critics have considered that the Elihu portion of the Book of Job was added by a later hand, and urge obscurities and prolixities, as well as a different style, to prove that it was the work of an inferior writer. This estimate seems, however, to take into account only the part it plays in a didactic treatise, or a theological debate. It looks quite different when we read it as a real dramatic element in a story; in other words, when we realize that the prevailing interest of the Book of Job is not dialectic but narrative. Thus viewed, the Elihu episode is a skilfully managed agency in preparing the *dénouement.* Consider the situation at the end of Job's words (**31** 40). Job has vindicated his integrity and stands ready to present his cause to God (**31** 35–37). The friends, however, have exhausted their resources, and through three discourses have been silent, as it were, snuffed out of existence. It is at this point, then, that Elihu is introduced, to renew their contention with young constructive blood, and represent their cause (as he deems) better than they can themselves. He is essentially at one with them in condemning Job (**34** 34–37); his only quarrel with them is on the score of the inconclusiveness of their arguments (**32** 3.5). His self-portrayal is conceived in a decided spirit of satire on the part of the writer, not unmingled with a sardonic humor. He is very egotistic, very sure of the value of his ideas; much of his alleged prolixity is due to that voluble self-deprecation which betrays an inordinate opinion of oneself (cf **32** 6–22). This, whether inferior composition or not, admirably adapts his words to his character. For substance of discourse he adds materially to what the friends have said, but in a more rationalistic vein; speaks edifyingly, as the friends have not done, of the disciplinary value of affliction, and of God's means of revelation by dreams and visions and the interpreting of an intercessory friend (**33** 13–28). Very evidently, however, his ego is the center of his system; it is he who sets up as Job's mediator (**33** 5–7; cf **9** 32–35), and his sage remarks on God's power and wisdom in Nature are full of self-importance. All this seems designed to accentuate the almost ludicrous humiliation of his collapse when from a natural phenomenon the oncoming tempest shows unusual and supernatural signs. His words become disjointed and incoherent, and cease with a kind of attempt to recant his pretensions. And the verdict from the whirlwind is: "darkeneth counsel by words without knowledge." Elihu thus has a real function in the story, as honorable as overweening self-confidence is apt to be. John Franklin Genung

ELIJAH, ē-lī'ja (אֵלִיָּהוּ *'ēlīyāhū* or [4 t] אֵלִיָּה *'ēlīyāh,* "Jah is God"; LXX **Ἠλειού,** *Ēleioú,* NT **Ἠλείας,** *Ēleías,* AV of NT Elias):

I. The Works of Elijah
 1. The Judgment of Drought
 2. The Ordeal by Prayer
 3. At Horeb
 4. The Case of Naboth
 5. Elijah and Ahaziah
 6. Elijah Translated
 7. The Letter to Jehoram
II. The Work of Elijah
III. Character of the Prophet
IV. Miracles in the Elijah Narratives
V. Elijah in the NT
Literature

(1) The great prophet of the times of Ahab, king of Israel. E. is identified at his first appearance (1 K **17** 1) as "E. the Tishbite, who was of the sojourners of Gilead." Thus his native place must have been called Tishbeh. A Tishbeh (Thisbe) in the territory of Naphtali is known from Tob **1** 2; but if (with most modern commentators) the reading of the LXX in 1 K is followed, the word tr[d] "sojourners" is itself "Tishbeh," locating the place in Gilead and making the prophet a native of that mountain region and not merely a "sojourner" there.

I. The Works of Elijah.—In 1 K **16** 29–34 we read of the impieties of Ahab, culminating in his patronage of the worship of the Tyrian Baal, god of his Tyrian queen Jezebel (ver 31). Ver 34 mentions as another instance of the little weight attached in Ahab's time to ancient prophetic threatenings, the rebuilding by Hiel the Bethelite of the banned city of Jericho, "with the loss" of Hiel's eldest and youngest sons. This is the situation which calls for a judgment of Jeh, announced beforehand, as is often the case, by a faithful prophet of Jeh.

Whether E. was already a familiar figure at the court of Ahab, the narrative beginning with 1 K **17** 1 does not state. His garb and manner identified him as a prophet, in any case (2 K **1** 8; cf Zec **13** 4). E. declared in few words that Jeh, true and only rightful God of Israel, whose messenger he was, was even at the very time sending a drought which should continue until the prophet himself declared it at an end. The term is to be fixed, indeed, not by E. but by Jeh; it is not to be short ("these years"), and it is to end only when the chastisement is seen to be sufficient. Guided, as true prophets were continually, by the "word of Jeh," E. then hid himself in one of the ravines east of ("before") the Jordan, where the brook Cherith afforded him water, and ravens brought him abundant food ("bread and flesh" twice daily), 1 K **17** 2–6. As the drought advanced the brook dried up. E. was then directed, by the "word of Jeh," as constantly, to betake himself beyond the western limit of Ahab's kingdom to the Phoen village of Zarephath, near Sidon. There the widow to whom Jeh sent him was found gathering a few sticks from the ground at the city gate, to prepare a last meal for herself and her son. She yielded to the prophet's command that he himself should be first fed from her scanty store; and in return enjoyed the fulfilment of his promise, uttered in the name of Jeh, that neither barrel of meal nor cruse of oil should be exhausted before the breaking of the drought. (Jos, *Ant*, VIII, xiii, 2, states on the authority of Menander that the drought extended to Phoenicia and continued there for a full year.) But when the widow's son fell sick and died, the mother regarded it as a Divine judgment upon her sins, a judgment which had been drawn upon her by the presence of the man of God. At the prayer of E., life returned to the child (vs 17–24).

1. The Judgment of Drought

"In the third year," 1 K **18** 1 (Lk **4** 25; Jas **5** 17 give three years and six months as the length of the drought), E. was directed to show himself to Ahab as the herald of rain from Jeh. How sorely both man and beast in Israel were pressed by drought and the resulting famine, is shown by the fact that King Ahab and his chief steward Obadiah were in person searching through the land for any patches of green grass that might serve to keep alive some of the king's own horses and mules (vs 5.6). The words of Obadiah upon meeting with E. show the impression which had been produced by the prophet's long absence. It was believed that the Spirit of God had carried E. away to some unknown, inaccessible, mysterious region (vs 10.12). Obadiah feared that such would again be the case, and, while he entreated the prophet not to make him the bearer of a message to Ahab, appealed to his own well-known piety and zeal, as shown in his sheltering and feeding, during Jezebel's persecution, a hundred prophets of Jeh. E. reassured the steward by a solemn oath that he would show himself to Ahab (ver 15). The king greeted the prophet with the haughty words, "Is it thou, thou troubler of Israel?" E.'s reply, answering scorn with scorn, is what we should expect from a prophet; the woes of Israel are not to be charged to the prophet who declared the doom, but to the kings who made the nation deserve it (vs 17.18).

2. The Ordeal by Prayer

Elijah went on to challenge a test of the false god's power. Among the pensioners of Jezebel were 450 prophets of Baal and 400 prophets of the Asherah—still fed by the royal bounty in spite of the famine. Accepting E.'s proposal, Ahab called all these and all the people to Mt. Carmel (vs 19.20). E.'s first word to the assembly implied the folly of their thinking that the allegiance of a people could successfully be divided between two deities: "How long go ye limping between the two sides?" (possibly "leaping over two thresholds," in ironical allusion to the custom of leaping over the threshold of an idol temple, to avoid a stumble, which would be unpropitious; cf 1 S **5** 1–5). Taking the people's silence as an indication that they admitted the force of his first words, E. went on to propose his conditions for the test: a bullock was to be offered to Baal, a bullock to Jeh, but no fire put under; "The God that answereth by fire, let him be God." The voice of the people approved the proposal as fair (vs 22–24). Throughout a day of blazing sunshine the prophets of Baal called in frenzy upon their god, while E. mocked them with merciless sarcasm (vs 25–29). About the time for the regular offering of the evening sacrifice in the temple of Jeh at Jerus, E. assumed control. Rebuilding an ancient altar thrown down perhaps in Jezebel's persecution, using in the rebuilding twelve stones, symbolizing an undivided Israel such as was promised to the patriarch Jacob of old; drenching sacrifice and wood with water from some perennial spring under the slopes of Carmel, until even a trench about the altar, deep and wide enough to have a two-*ṣ^e'āh* (half-bushel) measure set in it, was filled—the prophet called in few and earnest words upon the God of the fathers of the nation (vs 30–37). The answer of Jeh by fire, consuming bullock, wood, altar and the very dust, struck the people with awe and fear. Convinced that Jeh was God alone for them, they readily carried out the prophet's stern sentence of death for the prophets of the idol god (vs 38–40). Next the prophet bade Ahab make haste with the meal, probably a sacrificial feast for the multitude, which had been made ready; because rain was at hand. On the mountain top E. bowed in prayer, sending his servant seven times to look out across the sea for the coming storm. At last the appearance of a rising cloud "as small as a man's hand" was reported; and before the hurrying chariot of the king could cross the plain to Jezreel it was overtaken by "a great rain" from heavens black with clouds and wind after three rainless years. With strength above nature, E. ran like a courier before Ahab to the very gate of Jezreel (vs 41–46).

3. At Horeb

The same night a messenger from Jezebel found E. The message ran, "As surely as thou art E. and I am Jezebel" (so the LXX), "so let the gods do to me, and more also" (i.e. may I be cut in pieces like a sacrificed animal if I break my vow; cf Gen **15** 8–11.17.18; Jer **34** 18.19), "if I make not thy life as the life of one of" the slain prophets of Baal "by to-morrow about this time." Explain E.'s action how we may—and all the possible explanations of it have found defenders—he sought safety in instant flight. At Beersheba, the southernmost town of Judah, he left his "servant," whom the narrative does not elsewhere mention. Going onward into the southern wilderness, he sat down under the scanty shade of a desert broom-bush and prayed that he might share the common fate of mankind in death (**19** 1–4). After sleep he was refreshed with food brought by an angel. Again he slept and was fed. In the strength of that food he then wandered on for forty days and nights, until he found himself at Horeb, the mountain sacred because there Jeh had revealed Himself to Moses (vs 5–8). The repetition of identical words by E. in vs 10 and 14 represents a difficulty. Unless we are to suppose an accidental repetition by a very early copyist (early, since it appears already in the LXX), we may see in it an indication that E.'s despondency was not easily removed, or that he sought at Horeb an especial manifestation of Jeh for his encouragement, or both. The prophet was bidden to take his stand upon the sacred mount; and Jeh passed by, heralded by tempest, earthquake and thunderstorm (vs 9–12). These were Jeh's forerunners only; Jeh was not in them, but in the "still small voice," such as the prophets were accustomed to hear within their souls. When E. heard the not unfamiliar inner voice, he recognized Jeh present to hear and answer him. E. seems to be seeking to justify his own retreat to the wilderness by the plea that he had been "very jealous," had done in Jeh's cause all that mortal prophet could do, before he fled, yet all in vain! The same people who had forsaken the law and "covenant" of Jeh, thrown down His altars and slain His prophets, would have allowed the slaughter of E. himself at the command of Jezebel; and in him would have perished the last true servant of Jeh in all the land of Israel (vs 13.14).

Divine compassion passed by E.'s complaint in order to give him directions for further work in Jeh's cause. E. must anoint Hazael to seize the throne of Syria, Israel's worst enemy among the neighboring powers; Jehu, in like manner, he must anoint to put an end to the dynasty of Ahab and assume the throne of Israel; and Elisha, to be his own successor in the prophetic office. These three, Hazael and his Syrians, Jehu and his followers, even Elisha himself, are to execute further judgments upon the idolaters and the scorners in Israel. Jeh will leave Himself 7,000 (a round number, a limited but not an excessively small one, conveying a doctrine, like the doctrine of later prophets, of the salvation of a righteous remnant) in Israel, men proof against the judgment because they did not share the sin. If E. was rebuked at all, it was only in the contrast between the 7,000 faithful and the one, himself, which he believed to number all the righteous left alive in Israel (vs 15–18).

The anointing of Hazael and of Jehu seems to have been left to E.'s successor; indeed, we read of no anointing of Hazael, but only of a significant interview between that worthy and Elisha (2 K **8** 7–15). E. next appears in the narrative as rebuker of Ahab for the judicial murder of Naboth. In the very piece of ground which the king had coveted and seized, the prophet appeared, unexpected and unwelcome, to declare upon Ahab, Jezebel and all their house the doom of a shameful death (1 K **21**). There was present at this scene, in attendance upon the king, a captain named Jehu, the very man already chosen as the supplanter of Ahab, and he never forgot what he then saw and heard (2 K **9** 25.26).

4. The Case of Naboth

Ahab's penitence (1 K **21** 28.29) averted from himself some measure of the doom. His son Ahaziah pulled it down upon his own head. Sick unto death from injuries received in a fall, Ahaziah sent to ask an oracle concerning his recovery at the shrine of Baal-zebub in Ekron. E. met the messengers and turned them back with a prediction, not from Baal-zebub but from Jeh, of impending death. Ahaziah recognized by the messengers' description the ancient "enemy" of his house. A captain and fifty soldiers sent to arrest the prophet were consumed by fire from heaven at E.'s word. A second captain with another fifty met the same fate. A third besought the prophet to spare his life, and E. went with him to the king, but only to repeat the words of doom (2 K **1**).

5. Elijah and Ahaziah

A foreboding, shared by the "sons of the prophets" at Beth-el and Jericho, warned E. that the closing scene of his earthly life was at hand. He desired to meet the end, come in what form it might, alone. Elisha, however, bound himself by an oath not to leave his master. E. divided Jordan with the stroke of his mantle, that the two might pass over toward the wilderness on the east. Elisha asked that he might receive a firstborn's portion of the spirit which rested upon his master. "A chariot of fire, and horses of fire" appeared, and parted the two asunder; "and E. went up by a whirlwind into heaven" (2 K **2** 1–11).

6. Elijah Translated

In 2 Ch **21** 12–15 we read of a "writing" from E. to Jehoram, son of Jehoshaphat, king of Judah. The statements of 2 K **3** 11.12 admit of no other interpretation than that the succession of Elisha to independent prophetic work had already occurred in the lifetime of Jehoshaphat. It has been pointed out that the difficult verse, 2 K **8** 16, appears to mean that Jehoram began to reign at some time before the death of his father; it is also conceivable that E. left a message, reduced to writing either before or after his departure, for the future king of Judah who should depart from the true faith.

7. The Letter to Jehoram

II. The Work of Elijah.—One's estimate of the importance of the work of E. depends upon one's conception of the condition of things which the prophet confronted in Northern Israel. While it is true that the reign of Ahab was outwardly prosperous, and the king himself not without a measure of political sagacity together with personal courage, his religious policy at best involved such tolerance of false faiths as could lead only to disaster. Ever since the time of Joshua, the religion of Jeh had been waging its combat with the old Canaanite worship of the powers of Nature, a worship rendered to local deities, the "Baalim" or "lords" of this and that neighborhood, whose ancient altars stood "upon the high mountains, and upon the hills, and under every green tree" (Dt **12** 2). The god imported from Phoenicia by Jezebel bore also the title Baal; but his character and his worship were worse and more debasing than anything that had before been known. Resistance offered by the servants of Jeh to the claims of the queen's favored god led to persecution, rightly ascribed by the historian to Jezebel (1 K **18** 4). In the face of this danger, the differences between the worship of Jeh as carried on in the Northern Kingdom and the same worship as practised at Jerus sank out of sight. The one effort of E. was to recall the people from the Tyrian Baal to Jeh, the God of their fathers. The vitality of the true religion in the crisis is shown by the fidelity of such a man as Obadiah (1 K **18** 3 f), or by the perseverance of a righteous remnant of 7,000, in spite of all that had happened of persecution (**19** 18). The work begun by E. was finished, not without blood, by Jehu; we hear no more of the worship of the Tyrian Baal in Israel after that anointed usurper's time (2 K **9, 10**). To say that E. at Horeb "learns the gentleness of God" (Strachan in *HDB*) is to contradict the immediate text of the narrative and the history of the times. The direction given E. was that he should anoint one man to seize the throne of Syria, another to seize that of Israel, and a prophet to continue his own work; with the promise and prediction that these three forces should unite in executing upon guilty Israel the judgment still due for its apostasy from Jeh and its worship of a false god. E. was not a reformer of peace; the very vision of peace was hidden from his eyes, reserved for later prophets for whom he could but prepare the way. It was his mission to destroy at whatever cost the heathen worship which else would have destroyed Israel itself, with consequences whose evil we cannot estimate. Amos and Hosea would have had no standing-ground had it not been for the work of E. and the influences which at Divine direction he put in operation.

III. Character of the Prophet.—It is obvious that the Scripture historian does not intend to furnish us with a character-study of the prophet E. Does he furnish even the material upon which such a study may profitably be attempted? The characterization found in Jas **5** 17, "E. was a man of like passions [m "nature"] with us," is brief indeed; but examination of the books which have been written upon the life of E. leads to the conclusion that it is possible to err by attaching to events meanings which those events were never intended to bear, as well as by introducing into one's study too much of sheer imagination. It is easy, for example, to observe that E. is introduced *to the reader* with suddenness, and that his appearances and disappearances *in the narrative* seem abrupt; but is one warranted in arguing from this a like abruptness in the prophet's character? Is not the sufficient explanation to be reached by observing that the historian's purpose was not to give a complete biography of any individual, whether prophet or king, but to display the working of Jeh upon and with the kingdoms of Israel and Judah through the prophets? Few personal details are therefore to be found recorded concerning even such a prophet as E.; and none at all, unless they have a direct bearing upon his message. The imagination of some has discerned a "training of E." in the experiences of the prophet; but to admit that there must have been such a training does not oblige us to discover traces of it in the scenes and incidents which are recorded.

Distrusting, for the reasons above suggested, any attempt at a detailed representation of the prophet's inner life, one may seek, and prize, what seems to lie upon the surface of the narrative: faith in Jeh as God of Nature and as covenant God of the patriarchs and their descendants; consuming "zeal" against the false religion which would displace Jeh from the place which must be His alone; keen vision to perceive hypocrisy and falsehood, and sharp wit to lash them, with the same boldness and disregard of self that must needs mark the true prophet in any age.

IV. Miracles in the Elijah Narratives.—The miraculous element must be admitted to be prominent in the experiences and works of E. It cannot be estimated apart from the general position which the student finds it possible to hold concerning miracles recorded in the OT. The effort to explain away one or another item in a rationalistic way is wholly unprofitable. E.'s "ravens" may indeed be converted by a change of vowel-points into "Arabians"; but, in spite of the fact that Orientals would bring offerings of food to a holy hermit, the whole tenor of the narrative favors no other supposition than that its writer meant "ravens," and saw in the event another such exercise of the power of Jeh over all things as was to be seen in the supply of meal and oil for the prophet and the widow of Zarephath, the fire from heaven, the parting of the Jordan, or the ascension of the prophet by a whirlwind into heaven. Some modern critics recognize a different and later source in the narrative of 2 K **1**; but here again no real difficulty, if any difficulty there be, is removed. The stern prophet who would order the slaughter of the 450 Baal prophets might well call down fire to consume the soldiers of an apostate and a hostile king. The purpose and meaning of the E. chapters is to be grasped by those who accept their author's conception of Jeh, of His power, and of His work in Nature and with men, rather than by those who seek to replace that conception by another.

V. Elijah in the NT.—Malachi (**4** 5) names E. as the forerunner of "the great and terrible day of Jeh," and the expectation founded upon this passage is alluded to in Mk **6** 15 ‖ Lk **9** 8; Mt **16** 14 ‖ Mk **8** 28 ‖ Lk **9** 19; Mt **27** 47–49 ‖ Mk **15** 35.36. The interpretation of Malachi's prophecy foreshadowed in the angelic annunciation to Zacharias (Lk **1** 17), that John the Baptist should do the work of another Elijah, is given on the authority of Jesus Himself (Mt **11** 14). The appearance of E., with Moses, on the Mt. of Transfiguration, is recorded in Mt **17** 1–13 ‖ Mk **9** 2–13 ‖ Lk **9** 28–36, and in Mt **11** 14 ‖ Mk **9** 13 Jesus again identifies the E. of Malachi with John the Baptist. The fate of the soldiers of Ahaziah (2 K **1**) is in the mind of James and John on one occasion (Lk **9** 54). Jesus Himself alludes to E. and his sojourn in the land of Sidon (Lk **4** 25.26). Paul makes use of the prophet's experience at Horeb (Rom **11** 2–4). In Jas **5** 17.18 the work of E. affords an instance of the powerful supplication of a righteous man.

(2) A "head of a father's house" of the tribe of Benjamin (1 Ch **8** 27, AV "Eliah").

(3) A man of priestly rank who had married a foreign wife (Ezr **10** 21).

(4) A layman who had married a foreign wife (Ezr **10** 26).

LITERATURE.—The histories of Israel and commentaries on Kings are many. Those which tend to rationalizing tend also to decrease the importance of E. to the history. F. W. Robertson, *Sermons*, 2d ser., V; Maurice, *Prophets and Kings of the OT*, Sermon VIII; Milligan, *Elijah* ("Men of the Bible" ser.); W. M. Taylor, *Elijah the Prophet*.

F. K. FARR

ELIKA, ē-lī'ka (אֱלִיקָא, *'ĕlīḳā'*, "God is rejector[?]"): The Harodite (Uradite), one of David's guard, the "thirty" (2 S **23** 25). Omitted from 1 Ch **11** 27.

ELIM, ē'lim (אֵילִם, *'ēlīm*, "terēbinths"; Αἰλείμ, *Aileím*): The second encampment of the Israelites after crossing the Red Sea. It was a contrast to the previous camp called "Marah" because of the bitterness of the waters, for there "were twelve springs of water, and threescore and ten palm trees" (Ex **15** 27; **16** 1; Nu **33** 9 f). The traditional site is an oasis in *Wādy Ghurundel*, cir 63 miles from Suez. See EXODUS; WANDERINGS OF ISRAEL.

ELIMELECH, ē-lim'e-lek (אֱלִימֶלֶךְ, *'ĕlīmelekh*, "my God is king"; Ἀβειμέλεχ, *Abeimélech*, Ἀλιμέλεκ, *Alimélek*): Elimelech was a member of the tribe of Judah, a native of Bethlehem Judah, a man of wealth and probably head of a family or clan (Ruth **1** 2.3; **2** 1.3). He lived during the period of the Judges, had a hereditary possession near Bethlehem, and is chiefly known as the husband of Naomi, the mother-in-law of Ruth and ancestress of David the king. Because of a severe famine in Judaea, he emigrated to the land of Moab with his wife and his sons, Mahlon and Chilion. Not long afterward he died, and his two sons married Moabitish women, Ruth and Orpah. Ten years in all were spent in Moab, when the two sons died, and the three widows were left. Soon afterward Naomi decided to return to Judah, and the sequel is told in the Book of Ruth. See RUTH; NAOMI.

J. J. REEVE

ELIOENAI, ē-lī-ō-ē'nā-i. See ELIEHOENAI.

ELIONAS, el-i-ō'nas (Ἐλιωνάς, *Eliōnás*, Ἐλιωναΐς, *Eliōnaís*): The name of two men who had married foreign wives (1 Esd **9** 22.23), corresponding respectively to "Elioenai" and "Eliezer" in Ezr **10** 22.31.

ELIPHAL, ē-lī'fal, el'i-fal (אֱלִיפַל, *'ĕlīphāl*, "God has judged"): Son of Ur, one of the mighty men of David's armies (1 Ch **11** 35). RV in a footnote identifies him with Eliphelet, son of Ahasbai, the son of the Maachathite (2 S **23** 34; cf Davis, *Dict. of the Bible*, s.v. "Ur"). See also 1 Ch **14** 5.7.

ELIPHALAT, ē-lif′a-lat (Ἐλιφαλέτ, *Eliphalét;* 1 Esd **8** 39; **9** 33): Called "Eliphelet" in Ezr **8** 13; **10** 33.

ELIPHAZ, el′i-faz, ē-lī′faz (אֱלִיפַז, *'ĕlīphaz,* "God is fine gold" [?]):

(1) Son of Esau by Adah, and father of Teman, Kenaz and Amalek (Gen **36** 4.10; 1 Ch **1** 35 f). See also Edom.

(2) See next article.

ELIPHAZ: The first and most prominent of the three friends of Job (Job **2** 11), who come from distant places to condole with and comfort him, when they hear of his affliction. That he is to be regarded as their leader and spokesman is shown by the greater weight and originality of his speeches (contained in chs **4, 5, 15, 22**), the speeches of the other friends being in fact largely echoes and emotional enforcements of his thoughts, and by the fact that he is taken as their representative (Job **42** 7) when, after the address from the whirlwind, Jeh appoints their expiation for the wrong done to Job and to the truth. He is represented as a venerable and benignant sage from Teman in Idumaea, a place noted for its wisdom (cf Jer **49** 7), as was also the whole land of Edom (cf Ob ver 8); and doubtless it is the writer's design to make his words typical of the best wisdom of the world. This wisdom is the result of ages of thought and experience (cf Job **15** 17–19), of long and ripened study (cf **5** 27), and claims the authority of revelation, though only revelation of a secondary kind (cf Eliphaz' vision, **4** 12 ff, and his challenge to Job to obtain the like, **5** 1). In his first speech he deduces Job's affliction from the natural sequence of effect from cause (**4** 7–11), which cause he makes broad enough to include innate impurity and depravity (**4** 17–19); evinces a quietism which deprecates Job's self-destroying ebullitions of wrath (**5** 2.3; cf Job's answer, **6** 2.3 and **30** 24); and promises restoration as the result of penitence and submission. In his second speech he is irritated because Job's blasphemous words are calculated to hinder devotion (**15** 4), attributes them to iniquity (vs 5.6), reiterates his depravity doctrine (vs 14–16), and initiates the lurid descriptions of the wicked man's fate, in which the friends go on to overstate their case (**15** 20–35). In the third speech he is moved by the exigencies of his theory to impute actual frauds and crimes to Job, iniquities indulged in because God was too far away to see (**22** 5–15); but as a close holds open to him still the way of penitence, abjuring of iniquity, and restoration to health and wealth (**22** 21–30). His utterances are well composed and judicial (*too* coldly academic, Job thinks, **16** 4.5), full of good religious counsel abstractly considered. Their error is in their inveterate presupposition of Job's wickedness, their unsympathetic clinging to theory in the face of fact, and the suppressing of the human promptings of friendship.

John Franklin Genung

ELIPHELEHU, ē-lif′e-lē-hū (אֱלִיפְלֵהוּ, *'ĕlīphᵉlēhū,* "May God distinguish him," AV **Elipheleh**): The eleventh of the fourteen doorkeepers mentioned as "brethren of the second degree" and as appointed in connection with the bringing up of the ark to Jerus by David (1 Ch **15** 18).

ELIPHELET, ē-lif′e-let. See Eliphalat; Eliphal.

ELISABETH, ē-liz′a-beth (Ἐλισάβετ, *Elisábet,* WH Ἐλεισάβετ, *Eleisábet,* from Heb *'ĕlīshebha'* [Elisheba], "God is [my] oath," i.e. a worshipper of God): Wife of Zacharias the priest and mother of John the Baptist (Lk **1** 5 ff). E. herself was of priestly lineage and a "kinswoman" (AV Cousin, q.v.) of the Virgin Mary (ver 36), of whose visit to E. a remarkable account is given in vs 39–56. See Zacharias.

ELISEUS, el-i-sē′us. See Elisha.

ELISHA, ē-lī′sha (אֱלִישָׁע, *'ĕlīshā',* "God is salvation"; LXX Ἐλεισαῖε, *Eleisaíe;* NT Ἐλισαῖος, *Elisaíos,* Eliseus [Lk **4** 27 AV]):

A prophet, the disciple and successor of Elijah. He was the northern end of the son of Shaphat, lived at Abel-meholah, at the northern end of the Jordan valley and a little S. of the Sea of Galilee. Nothing is told of his parents but the father's name, though he must have been a man of some wealth and doubtless of earnest piety. No hint is given of Elisha's age or birthplace, and it is almost certain that he was born and reared at Abel-meholah, and was a comparatively young man when we first hear of him. His early life thus was spent on his father's estate, in a god-fearing family, conditions which have produced so many of God's prophets. His moral and religious nature was highly developed in such surroundings, and from his work on his father's farm he was called to his training as a prophet and successor of Elijah.

I. His Call and Preparation.—The first mention of him occurs in 1 K **19** 16. Elijah was at Horeb, learning perhaps the greatest lesson of his life; and one of the three duties with which he was charged was to anoint Elisha, the son of Shaphat of Abel-meholah, as prophet in his stead.

Elijah soon went northward and as he passed the lands of Shaphat he saw Elisha plowing in the rich level field of his father's farm. Twelve yoke of oxen were at work, Elisha himself plowing with the twelfth yoke.

1. His Call

Crossing over to him Elijah threw his mantle upon the young man (1 K **19** 19). Elisha seemed to understand the meaning of the symbolic act, and was for a moment overwhelmed with its significance. It meant his adoption as the son and successor of Elijah in the prophetic office. Naturally he would hesitate a moment before making such an important decision. As Elijah strode on, Elisha felt the irresistible force of the call of God and ran after the great prophet, announcing that he was ready to follow, only he wished to give a parting kiss to his father and mother (**19** 20). Elijah seemed to realize what it meant to the young man, and bade him "Go back again; for what have I done to thee?" The call was not such an urgent one as Elisha seemed to think, and the response had better be deliberate and voluntary. But Elisha had fully made up his mind, slew the yoke of oxen with which he was plowing, boiled their flesh with the wood of the implements he was using, and made a farewell feast for his friends. He then followed Elijah, making a full renunciation of home ties, comforts and privileges. He became Elijah's servant; and we have but one statement describing their relationship (2 K **3** 11): he "poured water on the hands of Elijah."

2. His Preparation

They seem to have spent several years together (1 K **22** 1; 2 K **1** 17), for Elisha became well known among the various schools of the prophets. While ministering to the needs of his master, Elisha learned many deep and important lessons, imbibed much of his spirit, and developed his own religious nature and efficiency until he was ready for the prophetic service himself. It seems almost certain that they lived among the schools of the prophets, and not in the mountains and hills as Elijah had previously done. During these years the tie between the two men became very deep and strong. They were years of great significance to the young prophet and of careful teaching on the part of the older. The lesson learned at Horeb was not forgotten and its meaning would be profoundly impressed upon the younger man, whose whole after-life shows that he had deeply imbibed the teaching.

3. The Parting Gift of Elijah

The final scene shows the strong and tender affection he cherished toward his master. Aware that the end was near, he determined to be with him until the last. Nothing could persuade him to leave Elijah. When asked what should be done for him, before his master was taken away, he asks for the elder son's portion, a double portion, of his master's spirit (2 K **2** 9). He has no thought of equality; he would be Elijah's firstborn son. The request shows how deeply he had imbibed of his master's spirit already. His great teacher disappears in a whirlwind, and, awestruck by the wonderful sight, Elisha rends his clothes, takes up the garment of Elijah, retraces his steps to the Jordan, smites the waters to test whether the spirit of Elijah had really fallen upon him, and as the water parts, he passes over dry shod. The sons of the prophets who have been watching the proceedings from the hills, at once observe that the spirit of Elijah rested upon Elisha, and they bowed before him in reverence and submission (2 K **2** 12–15). Elisha now begins his prophetic career which must have lasted 50 years, for it extended over the reign of Jehoram, Jehu, Jehoahaz and Joash. The change in him is now so manifest that he is universally recognized as Elijah's successor and the religious leader of the prophetic schools. The skepticism of the young prophets regarding the translation of Elijah found little sympathy with Elisha, but he is conciliatory and humors them (2 K **2** 16–18).

II. His Prophetic Career.—As we study the life of Elisha we look first at the record of his career.

1. Record of His Career

The compiler of these records has followed no strict chronological order. Like other Scripture writers he has followed the system of grouping his materials. The records in 2 K **2** 19—**5** 27 are probably in the order of their occurrence. The events in chs **6**-**9** cannot be chronologically arranged, as the name of the king of Israel is not mentioned. In **6** 23 we are told that the Syrians came no more into the land of Israel, and ver 24 proceeds to give an account of Ben-hadad's invasion and the terrible siege of Samaria. In ch **5** Gehazi is smitten with leprosy, while in ch **8** he is in friendly converse with the king. In ch **13** the death of Joash is recorded, and this is followed by the record of his last interview with Elisha (2 K **13** 14–19) which event occurred some years previously.

2. His Ministry in a Private Capacity

When he began his career of service he carried the mantle of Elijah, but we read no more of that mantle; he is arrayed as a private citizen (2 K **2** 12) in common garments (*beghādhīm*). He carries the walking-staff of ordinary citizens, using it for working miracles (2 K **4** 29). He seems to have lived in different cities, sojourning at Bethel or Jericho with the sons of the prophets, or dwelling in his own home in Dothan or Samaria (2 K **6** 24.32). He passed Shunem so frequently on foot that a prophet's chamber was built for his special use (**4** 8–11).

(1) Elijah's ministry began by shutting up the heavens for three and a half years; Elisha's began by healing a spring of water near Jericho (**2** 21). One of these possessed certain noxious qualities, and complaint is made to Elisha that it is unfit for drinking and injurious to the land (**2** 19). He takes salt in a new vessel, casts it into the spring and the waters are healed so that there was not "from thence any more death or miscarrying" (**2** 21).

(2) Leaving Jericho, 'a pleasant situation,' he passes up to the highlands of Ephraim, doubtless by the Wady Suweinit, and approaches Bethel, a seat of Baal worship and headquarters of idolatry. The bald head, or perhaps closely cropped head, of Elisha, in contrast with that of Elijah, provoked the ridicule of some "young lads out of the city," who called after him "Go up, thou baldhead," their taunt manifesting the most blatant profanity and utter disregard of God or anything sacred. Elisha, justly angered, turned and cursed them in the name of Jeh. Two bears soon break forth from the woods of that wild region and make fearful havoc among the boys. Elisha may have shown severity and a vindictiveness in this, but he was in no way to blame for the punishment which overtook the boys. He had nothing to do with the bears and was in no way responsible for the fate of the lads. The Sept adds that they threw stones, and the rabbis tell how E. was himself punished, but these attempts to tone down the affair are uncalled for and useless (**2** 23.24).

(3) From Bethel E. passed on to Mt. Carmel, the home of a school of the prophets, spent some time there and returned to Samaria the capital (**2** 25). His next deed of mercy was to relieve the pressing needs of a widow of one of the prophets. The name of the place is not given (**4** 1–7)

(4) On his many journeys up and down the country, he frequently passed by the little village of Shunem, on the slopes of "Little Hermon." The modern name is *Sôlam*. It was about three miles from Jezreel. Accustomed to accept hospitality of one of the women of the place, he so impressed her with his sanctity that she appealed to her husband to build a chamber for the "holy man of God, that passeth by us continually." This was done, and in return for this hospitality a son was born to the woman, who suddenly dies in early boyhood and is restored to life by the prophet (**4** 8–37).

(5) E. is next at Gilgal, residing with the sons of the prophets. It is a time of famine and they are subsisting on what they can find. One of them finds some wild gourds (*paḳḳu'ōth*), shreds them into the pot and they are cooked. The men have no sooner begun to eat than they taste the poison and cry to Elisha, "O man of God, there is death in the pot." Throwing in some meal, E. at once renders the dish harmless and wholesome (**4** 38–41).

(6) Probably at about the same time and place and during the same famine, a man from Baal-shalishah brought provisions as a present to Elisha—twenty loaves of fresh barley bread and fresh ears of grain. Unselfishly E. commands that it be given to the people to eat. The servant declared it was altogether insufficient for a hundred men, but E. predicts that there will be enough and to spare (**4** 42–44). This miracle closely resembles the two miracles of Jesus.

(7) The next incident is the healing of Naaman, the leprous commander of the Syrian army (**5** 1–19). He is afflicted with the white leprosy, the most malignant kind (ver 27). A Jewish maiden, captured in one of their numerous invasions of Eastern Pal, and sold into slavery with a multitude of others, tells her mistress, the wife of Naaman, about the wonder-working Elisha. The maiden tells her mistress that Elisha can heal the leprosy, and Naaman resolves to visit him. Through the king he obtains permission to visit E. with a great train and rich presents. The prophet sends his servant to tell him to dip seven times in the Jordan and he will be healed. Naaman is angered at the lack of deference on the part of Elisha and turns away in a rage to go home. Better counsels prevail, and he obeys the prophet and is cured. E. absolutely refuses the rich presents Naaman offers, and permits the Syrian to take some earth from Jeh's land, that he

may build an altar in Syria and worship Jeh there. The idea was that a God was localized and could be worshipped only on his own land. E. grants Naaman permission apparently to worship Rimmon while avowedly he is a worshipper of Jeh. The prophet appreciates the difficulties in Naaman's path, believes in his sincerity, and by this concession in no way proves that he believes in the actual existence of a god named Rimmon, or that Jeh was confined to his own land, or in any way sanctions idolatrous worship. He is conciliatory and tolerant, making the best of the situation.

(8) An act of severity on the part of Elisha follows, but it was richly deserved. Gehazi's true character now manifests itself. He covets the rich presents brought by Naaman, runs after him, and by a clever story secures a rich present from the general. E. divines his trick and dooms him and his family to be afflicted with Naaman's leprosy forever (**5** 20–27).

(9) A group of the sons of the prophets, probably at Jericho, finding their quarters too small, determine to build new quarters near the Jordan. While felling the timber the ax-head of one, a borrowed tool, fell into the water and disappeared. It would have been useless to have attempted to search for it in that swift and muddy stream, so he cries in distress to the prophet. E. breaks off a stick, casts it in the spot where the ax fell, and makes the iron swim on the surface (**6** 1–7).

Elisha's services to his king and country were numerous and significant.

3. His Ministry in a Public and National Capacity

(1) The first one recorded took place during the attempt of Jehoram to resubjugate Moab which had revolted under King Mesha. In company with Jehoshaphat and the king of Edom, his southern allies, the combined hosts found themselves without water in the wilderness of Edom. The situation is desperate. Jehoram appeals to Jehoshaphat, and on discovering that Elisha was in the camp all three kings appeal to him in their extremity. He refuses any help to Jehoram, bidding him appeal to the prophets of his father Ahab and his mother Jezebel. For Jehoshaphat's sake he will help, calls for a minstrel, and under the spell of the music receives his message. He orders them to dig many trenches to hold the water which shall surely come on the morrow from the land of Edom and without rain. He moreover predicted that Moab would be utterly defeated. These predictions are fulfilled, Mesha is shut up in his capital, and in desperation sacrifices his firstborn son and heir on the walls in sight of all Israel. In great horror the Israelites withdraw, leaving Mesha in possession (**3** 4–27).

(2) His next services occurred at Samaria. The king of Syria finds that his most secret plans are divulged in some mysterious way, and he fails more than once to take the king of Israel. He suspects treachery in his army, but is told of Elisha's divining powers. Elisha is living at Dothan; and thither the king of Syria sends a large army to capture him. Surrounded by night, E. is in no way terrified as his servant is, but prays that the young man's eyes may be opened to see the mountains full of the chariots and horses of Jeh. Going forth to meet the Syrians as they close in, E. prays that they may be stricken with blindness. The word *ṣanwērīm* is used only here and in Gen **19** 11 and probably means mental blindness, or bewilderment, a confusion of mind amounting to illusion. He now tells them that they have come to the wrong place, but he will lead them to the right place. They follow him into the very heart of Samaria and into the power of the king. The latter would have smitten them, but is rebuked by E. who counseled that they be fed and sent away (2 K **6** 8–23). Impressed by such mysterious power and strange clemency the Syrians ceased their marauding attacks.

(3) The next incident must have occurred some time previous, or some time after these events. Samaria is besieged, the Israelites are encouraged to defend their capital to the last, famine prices prevail, and mothers begin to cook their children and eat them. The king in horror and rage will wreak vengeance on Elisha. The latter divines his purpose, anticipates any action on the king's part, and predicts that there will be abundance of food on the morrow. That night a panic seized the Syrian host. They imagined they heard the Hittites coming against them, and fled in headlong rout toward the Jordan. Four lepers discover the deserted camp and report the fact to the king. He suspects an ambuscade, but is persuaded to send a few men to reconnoitre. They find the camp deserted and treasures strewing the path right to the Jordan. The Samaritans lose no time in plundering the camp and Elisha's predictions are fulfilled to the letter (**6** 24—**7**).

(4) The prophet's next act was one of great significance. It was the carrying out of the first order given to Elijah at Horeb, and the time seemed ripe for it. He proceeds north to Damascus and finds Benhadad sick. Hearing of his presence the king sends a rich present by the hands of his chief captain Hazael and inquires whether he will recover. Elisha gives a double answer. He will recover, the disease will not be fatal, yet he will die. Fixing his eyes on Hazael, E. sees a fierce and ruthless successor to Benhadad who will be a terrible scourge to Israel. The man of God weeps, the fierce captain is ashamed, and when told of what he shall do, represents himself as a dog and not able to do such things. But the prospect is too enticing; he tells Benhadad he will recover, and on the morrow smothers him and succeeds to the throne (**8** 7–15).

(5) The next move of E. was even more significant. It is the fulfilling of the second order given Elijah at Mt. Horeb. The Israelites are fighting the Syrians in defense of Ramoth-gilead. The king, Jehoram, is wounded and returns home to Jezreel to recover. E. seizes on the opportune moment to have the house of Ahab avenged for its many sins. He despatches one of the young prophets with a vial of oil to Ramoth-gilead with orders to anoint Jehu, one of the captains of the army, as king over Israel. The young prophet obeys, delivers his message and flees. Jehu tries to conceal the real nature of the interview, but is forced to tell, and is at once proclaimed king. He leaps into his chariot, drives furiously to Jezreel, meets the king by the vineyard of Naboth, sends an arrow through his heart, tramples to death the queen Jezebel, butchers the king's sons and exterminates the royal family. He then treacherously murders the priests of Baal and the revolution is complete; the house of Ahab is destroyed, Baal worship overthrown and an able king is upon the throne (chs **9, 10**).

(6) Elisha retains his fervent and patriotic spirit until the last. His final act is in keeping with his long life of generous deeds and faithful patriotic service. He is on his death bed, having witnessed the fearful oppressions of Israel by Hazael who made Israelites as dust under his feet. The young king Joash visits him, weeps over him, calling him, "My father, the chariots of Israel and the horsemen thereof." The dying prophet bids him take his bow and arrow and shoot eastward, an act symbolic of his victory over Syria. Being then commanded to smite upon the ground, he smites three times and stops. The prophet is angry, tells him he should have smitten many times, then he would have smitten

Syria many times, but now he shall smite her only thrice (**13** 14–19).

(7) The last wonder in connection with Elisha occurs after this death. His bones were reported to have vitalizing power (**13** 20–21). Tradition says that the man thus restored to life lived but an hour; but the story illustrates something of the reverence held for E.

4. Characteristics of His Ministry

(1) *In comparison with Elijah.*—In many respects Elisha is a contrast to his great predecessor. Instead of a few remarkable appearances and striking events, his was a steady lifelong ministry; instead of the rugged hills his home was in the quiet valley and on the farm; instead of solitariness he loved the social life and the home. There were no sudden appearances and disappearances, people always knew where to find him. There were no long seasons of hiding or retirement, he was constantly moving about among the people or the prophetic schools. There were no spectacular revolutions, only the effect of a long steady ministry. His career resembled the latter portion of Elijah's more than the earlier. Elijah had learned well his lesson at Horeb. God is not so much in the tempest, the fire and the earthquake, as in the "still small voice" (1 K **19** 12). Elijah was a prophet of fire, Elisha more of a pastor. The former called down fire out of heaven to consume those sent to take him; Elisha anticipates the king when he comes to take him (2 K **6** 32.33) and gives promises of relief. He merely asks for blindness to come upon the army which surrounded him at Dothan, and spares them when the king would have smitten them (**6** 21–23). Elijah was austere and terrible, but Elisha was so companionable that the woman at Shunem built him a chamber. His prophetic insight could be helped more by the strains of music than by the mountain solitude (**3** 15). Some of his miracles resemble Elijah's. The multiplication of the oil and the cruse is much like the continued supply of meal and oil to the widow of Zarephath (1 K **17** 10–16), and the raising of the Shunammite's son like the raising of the widow's son at Zarephath (**17** 17–24).

(2) *General features of his ministry.*—His services as a pastor-prophet were more remarkable than his miracles. He could be very severe in the presence of deliberate wrongdoing, stern and unflinching when the occasion required. He could weep before Hazael, knowing what he would do to Israel, yet he anointed him king of Syria (2 K **8** 11–15). When the time was ripe and the occasion opportune, he could instigate a revolution that wiped out a dynasty, exterminated a family, and caused the massacre of the priests of Baal (chs **8, 9**). He possessed the confidence of kings so fully that they addressed him as father and themselves as sons (**6** 21; **13** 14). He accompanied an army of invasion and three kings consult him in extremity (**3** 11–19). The king of Syria consults him in sickness (**8** 7.8). The king of Israel seems to blame him for the awful conditions of the siege and would have wreaked vengeance on him (**6** 31). He was something of a military strategist and many times saved the king's army (**6** 10). The king of Israel goes to him for his parting counsel (**13** 14–19). His advice or command seemed to be always taken unhesitatingly. His contribution to the religious life of Israel was not his least service. Under Jehu he secured the destruction of the Baal worship in its organized form. Under Hazael the nation was trodden down and almost annihilated for its apostasy. By his own ministry many were saved from bowing the knee to Baal. His personal influence among the schools of the prophets was widespread and beneficial. He that escaped the sword of Hazael was slain by Jehu, and he that escaped Jehu was slain by Elisha. Elisha finished the great work of putting down Baal worship begun by Elijah. His work was not so much to add anything to religion, as to cleanse the religion already possessed. He did not ultimately save the nation, but he did save a large remnant. The corruptions were not all eradicated, the sins of Jeroboam the son of Nebat were never fully overcome. He passed through a bitter and distressing national humiliation, but emerged with hope. He eagerly watched every turn of events and his counsels were more frequently adopted than those perhaps of any other prophet. He was "the chariots of Israel and the horsemen thereof" (**13** 14). No condemnation of calf-worship at Dan and Bethel is recorded, but that does not prove that he fully sanctioned it. His was a contest between Jeh worship and Baal worship. The corrupted form of Jeh worship was a problem which Amos and Hosea had to face nearly a cent. later.

III. General Estimate.—His character was largely molded by his home life. He was friend and benefactor of foreigner as well as of Israelite. He was large-hearted and generous, tolerant to a remarkable degree, courageous and shrewd when the occasion required, a diplomat as well as a statesman, severe and stern only in the presence of evil and when the occasion demanded. He is accused of being vindictive and of employing falsehood with his enemies. His faults, however, were the faults of his age, and these were but little manifested in his long career. His was a strenuous pastor's life. A home-loving and social man, his real work was that of teaching and helping, rather than working of miracles. He continually went about doing good. He was resourceful and ready and was gifted with a sense of humor. Known as "the man of God," he proved his right to the title by his zeal for God and loving service to man.

LITERATURE.—Driver, *LOT*, 185 f; W. R. Smith, *Prophets of Israel*, 85 ff; Cornill, *Isr. Prophets*, 14 f, 33 ff; Farrar, *Books of Kings;* Kuenen, *Religions of Israel*, I, 360 ff; Montefiore, *Hibbert Lectures*, 94 f; Maurice, *Prophets and Kings*, 142; Liddon, *Sermons on OT Subjects*, 195–334.

J. J. REEVE

ELISHAH, ē-lī′sha (אֱלִישָׁה, *'ĕlīshāh*, "God saves"; **'Ελισά,** *Elisá*, **'Ελεισαί,** *Eleisaí*): Mentioned in Gen **10** 4 as the eldest son of Javan, and in Ezk **27** 7 as the source from which the Tyrians obtained their purple dyes. On the ground of this latter statement attempts have been made to identify it with Southern Italy or the north of Africa. Jos (*Ant*, I, vi, 1) identified Elishah with the Aeolians. The Tg on Ezk gives "the province of Italy." Other suggestions include Hellas, Elis, and Alsa; the last-named is a kingdom mentioned in the Am Tab, but its precise location is unknown. It is impossible as yet to claim certainty for any of these conjectures.

A. C. GRANT

ELISHAMA, ē-lish′a-ma (אֱלִישָׁמָע, *'ĕlīshāmā'*, "God has heard"):

(1) Grandfather of Joshua and son of Ammihud; prince of the tribe of Ephraim in the Exodus (Nu **1** 10; **7** 48.53; 1 Ch **7** 26).

(2) A son of David, born in Jerus (2 S **5** 16; 1 Ch **3** 8).

(3) By textual corruption in 1 Ch **3** 6 for Elishua, another of David's sons; cf 2 S **5** 15.

(4) A scribe of Jehoiakim (Jer **36** 12.20.21).

(5) One "of the seed royal," grandfather of Ishmael, the slayer of Gedaliah (2 K **25** 25; Jer **41** 1).

(6) A man of the tribe of Judah (1 Ch **2** 41).

(7) One of the priests appointed by Jehoshaphat to teach the law (2 Ch **17** 8).

F. K. FARR

ELISHAPHAT, ē-lish′a-fat (אֱלִישָׁפָט, *'ĕlīshāphāṭ*, "God is judge"): This man figures in the Levitical conspiracy against Athaliah, to make Joash king. He was one of the "captains of hundreds" employed in the enterprise by Jehoiada the priest (2 Ch **23** 1).

ELISHEBA, ē-lish′ē-ba (אֱלִישֶׁבַע, *'ĕlīshebha'*, "God swears," "God is an oath"): Daughter of Amminadab, sister of Nashon, wife of Aaron, mother of Nadab, Abihu, Eleazar and Ithamar, the foundress, therefore, of the entire Levitical priesthood (Ex **6** 23).

ELISHUA, el-i-shū'a, ē-lish'ū-a (אֱלִישׁוּעַ, *'ĕlīshūa'*, "'God is rich," "God is salvation"): Son of David (2 S **5** 15; 1 Ch **14** 5); apparently called Elishama (1 Ch **3** 6). In the latter locus we have most probably a misreading by the copyist of the name Elishua.

ELISIMUS, ē-lis'i-mus, RV ELIASIMUS (q.v.).

ELIU, ē-lī'ū (**'Ηλιού,** *Ēlioú;* RV ELIHU): One of the ancestors of Judith (Jth **8** 1), and therefore of the tribe of Simeon.

ELIUD, ē-lī'ud (**'Ελιούδ,** *Elioúd,* "God my praise"): An ancestor of Jesus, four generations before Joseph (Mt **1** 15).

ELIZAPHAN, el-i-zā'fan, ē-liz'a-fan (אֱלִיצָפָן, *'ĕlīçāphān;* LXX **'Ελεισαφάν,** *Eleisaphán,* **'Ελισαφάν,** *Elisaphán,* **'Ελισαφά,** *Elisaphá,* **'Ελισαφάτ,** *Elisaphát,* "God has protected"; cf צְפַנְיָה, *çephanyāh,* Zephaniah, "Yah has protected," and Phoen צפנבעל, "Baal has protected"):

(1) The son of Uzziel, the son of Kohath, and so a prince of the Levitical class of the Kohathites (Nu **3** 30; 1 Ch **15** 8; 2 Ch **29** 13). But in 1 Ch **15** 8; 2 Ch **39** 13 his class seems to be coordinate with that of the Kohathites. He is called Elzaphan in Ex **6** 22; Lev **10** 4.

(2) A "prince" or chief of Zebulun, who represented that tribe in the division of the land (Nu **34** 25). WALTER R. BETTERIDGE

ELIZUR, ē-lī'zur (אֱלִיצוּר, *'ĕlīçūr;* LXX **'Ελειούρ,** *Eleioúr,* **'Ελισούρ,** *Elisoúr,* "My God is a rock"; cf Zuriel "my rock is God" [Nu **3** 35]): A chief or prince of the tribe of Reuben (Nu **1** 5; **2** 10; **7** 30.35; **10** 18).

ELKANAH, el-kā'na (אֶלְקָנָה, *'elkānāh,* "God has possessed"):

(1) An Ephraimite, the father of Samuel (1 S **1** 1–28; **2** 11–20). Of his two wives, Hannah, the childless, was best beloved. At Shiloh she received through Eli the promise of a son. Elkanah, with Hannah, took the young Samuel to Shiloh when he was weaned, and left him with Eli as their offering to Jeh. They were blessed with three other sons and two daughters.

(2) The second son of Korah (Ex **6** 24), who escaped the fate of Korah, Dathan and Abiram (Nu **26** 11).

(3) One "next to the king" in Jerus in the time of Ahaz; slain by one Zichri of Ephraim in war with Pekah (2 Ch **28** 7).

(4) One of the Korahites among David's "mighty men" (1 Ch **12** 1.6).

(5) A Levite, possibly the same as (2) above (1 Ch **6** 23.25.36).

(6) Another Levite of the same line (1 Ch **6** 26.35).

(7) Another Levite, ancestor of Berechiah (1 Ch **9** 16).

(8) Another Levite (if not the same as [4] above), one of the "doorkeepers for the ark" (1 Ch **15** 23). F. K. FARR

ELKIAH, el-kī'a (**'Ελκία,** *Elkía;* AV **Elcia**): An ancestor of Judith (Jth **8** 1).

ELKOSHITE, el'kosh-īt (הָאֶלְקֹשִׁי, *hā-'elkōshī;* LXX **'Ελκεσαίου,** *Elkesaíou,* **'Ελκαισέου,** *Elkaiséou,* **'Ελκεσέου,** *Elkeséou*): Used with the art. "the Elkoshite" (Nah **1** 1). Probably a gentilic adj. giving the home of the prophet; not definitely identified. Three traditions may be noted: (1) The Nestorians venerate the supposed tomb of the prophet in the village of *Alkush* not far from the east bank of the Tigris, about two days' journey almost directly north of *Mosul.* (2) Jerome states in the prologue to his commentary on Nah that the village of Helkesei in Galilee was pointed out to him as Elkosh. This Helkesei is probably *El-Kauzeh* between *Ramieh* and *Bint Jebeil.* (3) The treatise *De Vitis Prophetarum* of the Pseudo-Epiphanius says that Nahum came from "Elkesei beyond Jordan towards Begabor and was of the tribe of Simeon." Nestle has shown that the words "beyond Jordan" are probably a gloss, and that for Begabor should be read Betogabra, the modern *Beit Jibrin* in Southern Pal. In favor of this identification may be urged the following facts: (*a*) that parallels to the name Elkosh, such as Eltekeh and Eltekon, are found in the southern country; (*b*) that the word probably contains the name of the Edomite god Kaush, whose name appears in the names of Edomite kings in the Assyr inscriptions of the 8th and 7th cents. BC, such as Kaush-malaka and the like, and (*c*) that the internal evidence of the prophecy makes the Judaean origin of the prophet almost certain.

LITERATURE.—Davidson, "Nah," "Hab," "Zeph," in *Cambridge Bible,* 9–13; G. A. Smith, "Book of the Twelve," in *Expositor's Bible, Comm.* on Nah; Billerbeck and Jeremias, *Beitraege zur Assyriologie,* III, 91 ff; Peiser, *ZATW,* 1897, 349; Nestle, *PEFS,* 1879, 136.

WALTER R. BETTERIDGE

ELLASAR, el-ā'sär (אֶלָּסָר, *'ellāsār*): The city over which Arioch (*Eri-Aku*) and other Bab kings ruled (Gen **14** 1). The Sem-Bab form of its name is (*âl*) *Larsa,* "the city Larsa," a form which implies that the Heb has interchanged *r* and *s,* and transposed the final vowel. Its Sumerian name is given as *Ararwa,* apparently for *Araurutwa,* "light-abode," which, in fact, is the meaning of the ideographic group with which it is written. The ruins of this ancient site are now known as *Senqāra,* and lie on the E. bank of the Euphrates, about midway between *Warka* (Erech) and *Muqayyar* (Ur of the Chaldees). In addition to the name Larsa, it seems also to have been called *Ašte-azaga,* "the holy [bright, pure] seat" (or throne), and both its names were apparently due to its having been one of the great Bab centers of sun-god worship.

1. The Name and Its Etymology

Like most of the principal cities of Babylonia, it had a great temple-tower, called *Ê-dur-an-ki,* "house of the bond of heaven and earth." The temple of the city bore the same name as that at Sippar, i.e. *Ê-babbar,* "House of Light," where the sun-god Šamaš was worshipped. This fane was restored by Ur-Engur, Ḫammurabi (Amraphel), Burnaburiaš, Nebuchadrezzar and Nabonidus. Among the tablets found on this site by Loftus was that which gives measures of length and square and cube roots, pointing to the place as one of the great centers of Bab learning. Besides the remains of these temples, there are traces of the walls, and the remains of houses of the citizens. The city was at first governed by its own kings, but became a part of the Bab empire some time after the reign of Ḫammurabi.

2. Its Holy Places

LITERATURE.—Loftus, *Chaldea and Susiana;* Delitzsch, *Wo lag das Paradies?;* Zehnpfund, *Babylonien in seinen wichtigsten Ruinenstätten,* 53–54.

T. G. PINCHES

ELM, elm: Hos **4** 13 AV, but in RV TEREBINTH (q.v.).

ELMADAM, el-mā'dam (WH **'Ελμαδάμ,** *Elmadám; TR* **'Ελμωδάμ,** *Elmōdám;* AV **Elmodam**): An ancestor of Jesus, according to St. Luke's genealogy, in the 6th generation before Zerubbabel (Lk **3** 28).

ELNAAM, el-nā'am (אֶלְנַעַם, *'elna'am,* "God is delightfulness"; cf Phoen "Gadnaam"): According to MT the father of two of David's warriors (1 Ch **11** 46); according to LXX himself one of the warriors.

ELNATHAN, el-nā'than (אֶלְנָתָן, *'elnāthān,* "God has given"):

(1) The grandfather of Jehoiachin (2 K **24** 8).

(2) A courtier of Jehoiakim; he was one of those sent to Egypt to bring back the prophet Uriah (Jer **26** 22), and one of those who heard the reading of Jeremiah's roll and entreated Jehoiakim not to burn the roll (Jer **36** 12.25)—possibly the same person as (1) above.

(3, 4, 5) The name of two "chief men"—unless textual corruption has introduced the name at its second occurrence—and of one "teacher" sent for by Ezra from the camp at the river Ahava (Ezr **8** 16). F. K. Farr

ELOHIM, e-lō'him, el'o-hēm. See God, Names of.

ELOI, ē'loi, ē-lō'ī. See God, Names of.

ELOI, ē'loi, ē-lō'ī, **ELOI, LAMA,** lä'mä, **SABACHTHANI,** sa-bakh'tha-ni, or **ELI, ELI, LAMA SABACHTHANI** (Ἐλωί, ἐλωί, λαμὰ σαβαχθανεί, *Elōí, elōí, lamá sabachthaneí*): The forms of the first word as tr[d] vary in the two narratives, being in Mk as first above and in Mt as in second reading. With some perversions of form probably from Ps **22** 1 (אֵלִי אֵלִי לָמָה עֲזַבְתָּנִי, *'ēlī 'ēlī lāmāh 'ăzabhtānī*). A statement uttered by Jesus on the cross just before his death, tr[d], "My God, my God, why hast thou forsaken me?" (Mt **27** 46; Mk **15** 34).

There is an interesting but difficult problem in connection with the interpretation of this passage. There seems to be a mixture of Aram. and Heb. The first two words, whether in Heb or Aram., have sufficient similarity to each other and each sufficient similarity to the name itself to warrant the jeer that Jesus was calling upon Elias, or the sincere supposition of those who might not fully understand the language, that he was actually calling on Elias. The forms *lema* and *lama* used in Mt and Mk respectively (WH ed) represent the various possible forms, the first the Aram., and the second the Heb. The various readings and tr[s] of the latter word, *sabachthani,* only add confusion to an effort at ultimate explanation of the real statement. Certainly the influence of the Aram. played a great part in the tr and transmission of the original. The spirit revealed by Jesus in this utterance seems to be very much like that displayed in the Garden when He cried out to have the cup removed from Him.

Walter G. Clippinger

ELON, ē'lon (אֵילוֹן, אֵילֹן, אֵלוֹן, *'ēlōn,* "terebinth"):

(1) A Zebulunite, who judged Israel ten years, and was buried in Aijalon (Jgs **12** 11.12).

(2) A son of Zebulun (Gen **46** 14; Nu **26** 26).

(3) A Hittite whose daughter Esau wedded (Gen **26** 34; **36** 2).

ELON, ē'lon (אֵילוֹן, *'ēlōn,* a "terebinth"; Αἰλών, *Ailōn*): An unidentified town in the territory of Dan named between Ithlah and Timnah (Josh **19** 43). It is possibly identical with Elon-beth-Hanan which, along with Shaalbim and Bethshemesh, formed one of Solomon's commissariat districts (1 K **4** 9). Conder has suggested *Beit 'Anān,* about 4 miles N.W. of *Neby Samwīl:* it is quite uncertain.

ELON-BETH-HANAN, ē-lon-beth-hā'nan. See Elon.

ELONITES, ē'lon-īts: Descendants of Elon (q.v. [2]) (Nu **26** 26).

ELOQUENT, el'ō-kwent: "Moses said . . . . I am not eloquent" (אִישׁ דְּבָרִים, *'īsh d[e]bhārīm,* "a man of words" [Ex **4** 10]); but Aaron could "speak well." In Isa **3** 3 RV בִּין, *bīn,* "intelligent," is rendered "skilful [enchanter]," AV "eloquent [orator]." Apollos was "an eloquent man" (λόγιος, *lógios,* "full of words" [Acts **18** 24, AVm "a learned man"]).

ELOTH, ē'loth. See Elath.

ELPAAL, el-pā'al (אֶלְפַּעַל, *'elpa'al,* "God has wrought" [cf אֶלְעָשָׂה, *'el'āsāh,* Jer **29** 3]): The name of a descendant of Benjamin (1 Ch **8** 11.12. 18).

ELPALET, el-pā'let (RV ELPELET): The name of a son of David (1 Ch **14** 5). See Eliphalat.

EL-PARAN, el-pā'ran. See Paran.

ELPELET, el'pe-let. See Eliphalat.

EL ROI (Gen **16** 13 m). See God, Names of.

EL SHADDAI, el shad'ā-ī, el shad'ī. See God, Names of.

ELTEKE, el'tē-kē, **ELTEKEH** (אֶלְתְּקֵה, *'elt[e]ḳēh* [Josh **19** 44], אֶלְתְּקֵא, *'elt[e]ḳē'* [**21** 23]; B, Ἀλκαθά, *Alkathá;* A, Ἐλκεθώ, *Elkethō*): A place in the territory of Dan named between Ekron and Gibbethon (Josh **19** 44), and again between Beth-horon and Gibbethon, as given to the Kohathite Levites (**21** 23). It is probably identical with the Assyr *Altaḳu,* where Sennacherib (*Hexagon prism inscrip.*) claims to have defeated the allied armies of the Philis and the Egyptians. It should probably be sought somewhere E. of Ekron. *Beit Likia,* the place marked *Eltekeh* on the *PEF* map, seems a position for such an encounter. It is about 2½ miles S.W. of Beth-horon the Upper. W. Ewing

ELTEKON, el'tē-kon (אֶלְתְּקֹן, *'elt[e]ḳōn,* "founded by God"): A city in the hill country of Judah (Josh **15** 59) near Bethanoth (q.v.) to be looked for, therefore, a little N. of Hebron. Site unknown.

ELTOLAD, el-tō'lad (אֶלְתּוֹלַד, *'eltōladh,* "kindred of God"): A city of Judah in the Negeb near Edom (Josh **15** 30); in Josh **19** 4 ascribed to Simeon. Probably the same as Tolad (1 Ch **4** 29), the Arab. art. *el* being omitted. Site unknown.

ELUL, ē'lul, e-lōōl' (אֱלוּל, *'ĕlūl,* Neh **6** 15; Ἐλούλ, *Eloúl,* 1 Macc **14** 27): The 6th month of the Heb year, corresponding to August-September. The derivation is uncertain. See Time.

ELUZAI, ē-lū'zā-ī (אֶלְעוּזַי, *'el'ūzai,* "God is my strength"; cf Uzziel): One of David's heroes (1 Ch **12** 5).

ELYMAEANS, el-i-mē'ans. See Elamites.

ELYMAIS, el-i-mā'is (Ἐλύμαις, *Elúmais*): This name, representing the OT Elam (see Elam), was given to a district of Persia lying S. of Media and N. of Susiana. In 1 Macc **6** 1 the common reading, which is adopted by AV, refers to Elymais as a rich city in Persia. No other reference, however, to such a city is found except in Jos (*Ant.* XII. ix, 1) who simply follows 1 Macc. The text should therefore be corrected to read as in RV, "in Elymais in Persia there was a city."

ELYMAS, el'i-mas (**Ἐλύμας,** *Elúmas,* "wise"; Acts **13** 8). See BAR-JESUS.

ELYON, ē-lī'on. See EL-ELYON; GOD, NAMES OF.

ELZABAD, el-zā'bad (אֶלְזָבָד, *'elzābhādh,* "God has given"; cf ZABDIEL and ZEBADIAH):

(1) The ninth of David's Gadite heroes (1 Ch **12** 12).

(2) A Korahite doorkeeper (1 Ch **26** 7).

ELZAPHAN, el-zā'fan. See ELIZAPHAN.

EMADABUN, ē-mā'da-bun (**Ἠμαδαβούν,** *Ēmadaboún;* AV **Madiabun** [1 Esd **5** 58]): The head of a family of Levites who superintended the repair of the temple; not named in Ezr **3** 9.

EMATHEIS, ē-ma-thē'is (**Ἀμαθίας,** *Amathías;* Emeus; B, **Ἐμαθθίς,** *Emaththís;* A, **Ἐμαθείς,** *Ematheís;* AV **Amatheis**): One of the sons of Bebai (1 Esd **9** 29), called "Athlai" in Ezr **10** 28.

EMBALMING, em-bäm'ing (חָנַט, *ḥānaṭ,* "to spice"): E. is mentioned in Scripture only in the cases of Jacob and Joseph (Gen **50** 2 f.26). It was a distinctly Egyp invention and method of preserving the bodies of men and animals. Examples of it reach back to over 3,000 years ago. It prevailed to some extent among the peoples of Asia, and at a later period among the Greeks and Romans, but was in origin and use distinctly non-Israelitish. See BURIAL.

EMBRACE, em-brās': The word has two distinct meanings in the OT: (1) to clasp and hold fondly in the arms, pointing to a common custom (Gen **29** 13; **33** 4; **48** 10; 2 K **4** 16; Cant **2** 6; **8** 3; cf Acts **20** 10), and (2) to have sexual intercourse (Prov **4** 8; **5** 20; Eccl **3** 5). It seems to have acquired this technical sense in later Jewish usage.

EMBROIDERY, em-broid'ēr-i (רִקְמָה, *riḳmāh;* AV **Needlework**):

Riḳmāh was applied to any kind of cloth which showed designs in variegated colors. The method of manufacture is unknown. The designs may have been woven into cloth or drawn in by a needle or hook (Jgs **5** 30; Ps **45** 14; Ezk **16** 10.13.18; **26** 16; **27** 7.16.24).

Ma'ăseh rāḳām is tr[d] "the work of the embroiderer" in RV instead of "needlework" (Ex **26** 36; **27** 16; **28** 39; **36** 37; **38** 18; **39** 29; Jgs **5** 30; Ps **45** 14).

Rāḳām, "embroiderer," occurs in Ex **35** 35; **38** 23. The fact that this word is used instead of *'āragh,* "weaver," would lead us to suppose that the embroiderers' work was either different from that of the weaver or that a "*rāḳām*" was esp. skilled in fine weaving. Another word, *ḥōshēbh,* is used to describe a skilful weaver. "Cunning work" in AV of Ex **26** 1.31; **28** 6.15; **35** 33.35; **36** 8.35; **39** 3.8 is rendered in ARV "work of the skilful workmen." The passage has been freely rendered "designers."

In RV of Ex **28** 39 *shābhaç* is tr[d] "weave."

In Ex **28** 4 occurs the word *tashbēç,* which is tr[d] "broidered" in AV and "checker work" in RV. If this kind of work is what it is supposed to be, it is more truly "needlework" than the embroidery. This work is still done in some of the Syrian cities and towns, esp. in Damascus. Small caps for men to wear under their ordinary headdress and loose outer garments or dressing-gowns are the forms in which it is commonly seen. The checker-work effect is obtained by sewing in a cotton string between two pieces of cloth, so as to form designs. The patterns usually run to straight lines such as zigzags or squares. The effect is striking, and we can well imagine would have made an impressive priest's robe, esp. if costly materials were used. See also CRAFTS. JAMES A. PATCH

EMEK-KEZIZ, ē-mek-kē'ziz (עֵמֶק קְצִיץ, *'ēmeḳ ḳēçīç;* AV **Valley of Keziz** [Josh **18** 21]): A town in Benjamin named between Beth-hoglah and Beth-arabah, and therefore to be sought in the plain, probably S. of Jericho. The name has not been recovered.

EMERALD, em'ēr-ald. See STONES, PRECIOUS.

EMERODS, em'ēr-odz (עֳפָלִים, *'ŏphālīm,* טְחֹרִים, *ṭḥōrīm*): These words are used in the account of the plague which broke out among the Philis while the captive Ark of the Covenant was in their land. *'Ŏphālīm* lit. means rounded eminences or swellings, and in RV is tr[d] "tumors" (1 S **5** 6–12). In the Heb text of this passage Ḳrē substitutes for it the word *ṭḥōrīm,* a term which occurs in the next chapter in the description of the golden models of these swellings that were made as votive offerings (**6** 11–17). The swellings were symptoms of a plague, and the history is precisely that of the outbreak of an epidemic of bubonic plague. The older writers supposed by comparison of the account in 1 S with Ps **78** 66 that they were hemorrhoids (or piles), and the older Eng. term in AV is a 16th-cent. form of that Gr word, which occurs in several medical treatises of the 16th and 17th cents. There is, however, no evidence that this identification is correct. In the light of the modern research which has proved that the rat-flea (*Pulex cheopis*) is the most active agent in conveying the virus of plague to the human subject, it is worthy of note that the plague of tumors was accompanied by an invasion of mice (*'akhbōr*) or rats. The rat is not specifically mentioned in the Bible, although it was as common in Can. and Israelite times as it is today, a fact demonstrated by the frequency with which their bones occur in all strata of the old Palestinian cities, so it is probable that the term used was a generic one for both rodents.

The coincidence of destructive epidemics and invasions of mice is also recorded by Herodotus (ii.141), who preserves a legend that the army of Sennacherib which entered Egypt was destroyed by the agency of mice. He states that a statue of Ptah, commemorating the event, was extant in his day. The god held a mouse in his hand, and bore the inscription: "Whosoever sees me, let him reverence the gods." This may have been a reminiscence of the story in Isa **37** 36. For other references see PLAGUE. ALEX. MACALISTER

EMIM, ē'mim (אֵימִים, *'ēmīm;* **Ὀμμαείν,** *Ommaeín,* **Ὀμμείν,** *Ommeín,* or **Ὀμμιείν,** *Ommieín*): Stated to have been the earlier inhabitants of Moab (Dt **2** 10.11), and to have been of tall stature, and hence "accounted Rephaim [or giants] as the Anakim" or the Zamzummim of Ammon (ver 20). As the name was given to them by the Moabites, it may not have been that by which they called themselves. A tall race, known to the Israelites as REPHAIM (q.v.), once existed in Southern Pal as well as on the E. side of the Jordan, but its exact relationship is unknown. In the time of Abraham the Emim were living in the Moabite district of Shaveh-kiriathaim, identified with the modern *Kureiyat* (Gen **14** 5). A. H. SAYCE

EMINENT, em'i-nent: In AV (only in Ezk **16** 24.31.39; **17** 22) refers lit. to physical elevation; RV in the last passage renders "lofty" (Heb *tālūl*, "uplifted," "heaped up") and in the others "vaulted place" (Heb *gabh*, "rounded place," "mound," ERVm "a vaulted chamber").

EMMANUEL, ē-man'ū-el. See IMMANUEL.

EMMAUS, ē-mā'us, em'ā-us (**Ἐμμαούς**, *Emmaoús*, derivation uncertain, but probably from חַמַּת, *ḥammath*, "a hot spring"): Jos (*BJ*, IV, i, 3) says: "Now Emmaus, if it be interpreted, may be rendered 'a warm bath' for therein is a spring of warm water useful for healing." Here he is referring to the hot springs near Tiberias. Possibly the same Gr name may not always have been derived from the same Heb, and as Cheyne suggests (2) may have come from הַמֹּצָה, *ha-mōçāh* (see below).

1. Emmaus of the Apocrypha

(1) A place where Judas Maccabaeus defeated Gorgias (1 Macc **4**); it was "in the plain" (1 Macc **3** 40); it was subsequently fortified by Bacchides (1 Macc **9** 50). It is frequently mentioned by Jos (*Ant*, XIV, xi, 2; *BJ*, I, xi, 2; II, v, 1; xx, 4; IV, viii, 1; V, i, 6), and also in the Talm and Midr. It is now the modern mud-village of *'Amwas*, 20 miles along, and a little N. of, the main road from Jerus to Jaffa. In the 3d cent. it was called Nicopolis and was an episcopal see; in early Christian times it was famous for a spring of reputed healing qualities.

(2) The Emmaus of Lk **24** 13, a village 60 furlongs (stadia) from Jerus.

2. Emmaus of St. Luke

Early Christian tradition appears to have identified it with (1) and hence, to harmonize the distance, some MSS have 160 furlongs. Eusebius and Jerome place this Emmaus at *'Amwas;* but in the first place (1) was a city and not a village (*kṓmē*), and secondly (2) the distance, 40 miles there and back, is an almost impossible one for the narrative. In Crusading times this difficulty appears to have been realized, and on what grounds is not known, *Kubeibeh* at just over 60 stadia, N.W. of Jerus, was selected as the site of Emmaus. There a fine church was built which has in recent years been rebuilt and today a Franciscan hospice and school, attached to the church, and a newer German R. C. hospice, combine with the considerable picturesqueness of the place itself to fortify the tradition.

A much more probable site is *Ḳuloniyeh*, a village about 35 stadia from Jerus, on the road to Jaffa. Jos narrates (*BJ*, VII, vi, 6) that Vespasian "assigned a place for 800 men only whom he had dismissed from his army which he gave them for their habitation; it is called Emmaus and is distant from Jerus 60 furlongs." This is almost certainly the Emmaus of Lk; it is highly probable that the name *ḳuloniyeh* is derived from the fact of its being this *Colonia*. Close to this place is a ruin known as *Bēt Mizza*, which is probably the Mozah (הַמֹּצָה, *ha-mōçāh*) of Josh **18** 26 which in the Talm (*Ṣukk.* **4** 5) is also described as a *colonia*. Today it is a "colony" of Jews who have revived and always use the old name *Mōçāh* for their settlement.

Other suggestions for this Emmaus are (*a*) *el Khamsa*, considerably over 60 stadia S.W. of Jerus (Conder); (*b*) *Koriet el 'enab*, some 10 stadia farther along the Jerus-Jaffa road than *Kuloniyeh* (*LB*, etc); and (*c*) *'Artas*, S. of Bethlehem, where remains of Rom baths have been found (Mrs. Finn). In not one of the places suggested are there any hot springs.

E. W. G. MASTERMAN

EMMER, em'ẽr (**Ἐμμήρ**, *Emmḗr*): Head of a family, some of whom had married foreign wives (1 Esd **9** 21); called "Immer" in Ezr **10** 20.

EMMERUTH, em'ẽr-uth (**Ἐμμηρούθ**, *Emmēroúth;* AV **Meruth;** 1 Esd **5** 24): Corresponding to "Immer" in Ezr **2** 37.

EMMOR, em'or: Transliterated from the Gr Ἐμμώρ, *Emmṓr*, the tr of Heb חֲמוֹר, *ḥămōr*, "ass" (Acts **7** 16 AV; RV "Hamor", q.v.).

EMPEROR, emp'ẽr-ẽr (**ὁ σεβαστός**, *ho sebastós;* Lat *augustus:* The title of the Rom emperors; Acts **25** 21.25). See AUGUSTUS; CAESAR.

EMPTY, emp'ti, **EMPTIER,** emp'ti-ẽr (**κενός**, *kenós*): "Empty," adj. meaning void, etc, as the tr of רֵק, *rēḳ*, רִיק, *rīḳ*, רֵיקָם, *rēḳām*, etc, occurs in the literal sense of "with nothing" (Gen **31** 42; Job **22** 9); in 2 S **1** 22, it is equivalent to "in vain," "hungry" (Isa **29** 8); in some instances the meaning is comparative only; בָּקַק, *bāḳaḳ*, "to gush out," "to pour out," "to empty" is used adjectivally (Hos **10** 1, "Israel is an empty vine"; but RV takes the Heb word in its original sense of "pouring out," rendering "Israel is a *luxuriant* vine"); *tōhū*, "emptiness" (Job **26** 7); *kenos*, "empty" is so tr[d] (Mk **12** 3); in Mt **12** 44, the Gr word is *scholázō*, "to be free," "unoccupied"; "to empty" (vb.) is the tr of *bāḳaḳ* (Nah **2** 2), of *dālal*, "to become poor," etc (Isa **19** 6, ERV "minished," ARV "diminished"). RV has "empty" for "vain" (Eph **5** 6), "emptied himself" for "made himself of no reputation" (Phil **2** 7), "emptied out" for "gathered" (2 K **22** 9; 2 Ch **34** 17, m "poured out"). W. L. WALKER

EMULATION, em-ū-lā'shun (**ζῆλος**, *zēlos*, **παραζηλόω**, *parazēlóō*): Occurs twice in the NT, once in a bad and once in a good sense.

(1) In Gal **5** 20 AV it is the tr of *zēlos* ("zeal," "earnestness," "enthusiasm") where it is classed among "the works of the flesh" and signifies the stirring up of jealousy or envy in others, because of what we are, or have, or profess. The Gr word is used in this sense in Acts **13** 45; Rom **13** 13; 1 Cor **3** 3; Jas **3** 14.16; 2 Cor **12** 20; Gal **5** 20; RV tr[d] by "jealousy." It denotes a work of the flesh or lower nature, which Christians often fail sufficiently to guard against; it pleases "the flesh" to excite such a feeling in others.

(2) In Rom **11** 14 AV "emulation" is the tr of *parazēloō* ("to make one zealous or jealous"), and is there used in a good sense. "If by any means I may provoke to emulation [RV jealousy] them that are my flesh" (cf Rom **10** 19, quoted from Dt **32** 21). It is well to "provoke to emulation" in this sense, those who are slow or indifferent, by the example of earnestness and zeal on our part. This is not to please "the flesh," but to serve "the Spirit." W. L. WALKER

EN- (עַיִן, *'ayin* [cf Arab. *'Ain*]): The Heb word for "spring" or "fountain" (Gen **16** 7; Nu **33** 9; Neh **2** 14; Prov **8** 28 [fem. pl.]). It occurs in numerous compound words, as EN-GEDI, EN-HADDAH, EN-HAKKORE, EN-HAZOR, EN-RIMMON, EN-ROGEL, EN-SHEMESH (q.v.). In the same way the word *'Ain* is a very common component of Arab. names of places throughout Pal and Syria at the present day. Places with names compounded with *En-* were almost certainly located near a spring. See FOUNTAIN; WELL.

ENABLE, en-ā'b'l: Only in 1 Tim **1** 12 (AV and RV) in the sense of "strengthen" (Gr *endunamóō*, "endue with strength").

ENAIM, ē-nā'im (עֵינַיִם, *'ēnayim*, "place of a fountain"; **Αἰνάν**, *Ainán;* Gen **38** 14 [AV "in an open place"; ver 21 AV "openly"]): A place which lay between Adullam and Timnath; probably the same as Enam (Josh **15** 34). Also mentioned in close connection with Adullam. It was in the

Shephelah of Judah. The Talm (*Pesik. Rab.* **23**) mentions a Kephar Enaim. Conder proposes *Khurbet Wady 'Alîn*, which is an ancient site, evidently of great strength and importance, lying between *Kh. 'Ain Shems* and the village of *Deir Aban*. The ruins crown a lofty and almost isolated hill; the greatest objection to the identification is that there is no fountain at all in the immediate neighborhood. There may have been one in earlier times. See *PEF*, III, 128. E. W. G. Masterman

ENAM, ē'nam. See preceding article.

ENAN, ē'nan (עֵינָן, *'ēnān*, "having fountains," or "eyes," i.e. "keen-eyed"; in LXX **Αἰνάν,** *Ainán*): The father of Ahira, and prince of Naphtali at the first census of Israel (Nu **1** 15; **2** 29; **7** 78.83; **10** 27).

ENASIBUS, ē-nas'-i-bus (**'Ενάσιβος,** *Enásibos*, 1 Esd **9** 34): Corresponding to "Eliashib" in Ezr **10** 36.

ENCAMPMENT, en-kamp'ment. See War.

ENCAMPMENT BY THE RED SEA: According to the version of the wanderings of Israel given in Nu **33**, they "encamped by the Red Sea" (ver 10) after leaving Elim and before entering the Wilderness of Sin. See Wanderings of Israel.

ENCHANTMENT, en-chant'ment: The occult arts, either supposedly or pretentiously supernatural, were common to all oriental races. They included enchantment, sorcery, witchcraft, soothsaying, augury, necromancy, divination in numberless forms, and all kinds of magic art. Nine varieties are mentioned in one single passage in the Pent (Dt **18** 10.11); other varieties in many passages both in the OT and NT, e.g. Lev **19** 26.31; Isa **2** 6; **57** 3; Jer **27** 9; Mic **5** 12; Acts **8** 9.11; **13** 6.8; Gal **5** 20; Rev **9** 21. The extent of the magic arts (forbidden under Judaism and Christianity) may incidentally be seen from the fact that the Scriptures alone refer to their being practised in Chaldaea (Dnl **5** 11), Babylon (Ezk **21** 21), Assyria (2 K **17** 17), Egypt (Ex **7** 11), Canaan (Lev **18** 3.21; **19** 26.31), Asia (Ephesus, Acts **19** 13. 19), Greece (Acts **16** 16), Arabia also, as "customs from the East," etc (Isa **2** 6) indicates. These secret arts were prohibited by the laws of Moses (Dt **18** 9–12), inasmuch as they constituted a peculiar temptation to Israel to apostatize. They were a constant incentive to idolatry, clouded the mind with superstition, tended and were closely allied to imposture (Mt **24** 24). The term "enchantment" is found only in the OT and its Heb originals indicate its varieties.

(1) לָטִים, *lāṭīm*, and לְהָטִים, *lᵉhāṭīm*, "to wrap up," "muffle," "cover," hence "clandestine," "secret." It was this hidden element that enabled the magicians of Egypt to impose on the credulity of Pharaoh in imitating or reproducing the miracles of Moses and Aaron; "They. . . . did in like manner with their enchantments" (Ex **7** 11.22). Their inability to perform a genuine miracle is shown by Ex **8** 18.

(2) נָחַשׁ, *nāḥash*, "to hiss," "whisper," referring to the mutterings of sorcerers in their incantations. Used as a derivative noun this Heb word means "a serpent." This involves the idea of cunning and subtlety. Although employed in the wider sense of augury or prognostication, its fundamental meaning is divination by serpents. This was the form of enchantment sought by Balaam (Nu **24** 1). Its impotence against the people of God is shown by Nu **23** 23 m. Shalmaneser forced this forbidden art upon the Israelites whom he carried captive to Assyria (2 K **17** 17). It was also one of the heathen practices introduced during the apostasy under Ahab, against which Elijah protested (cf 1 K **21** 20).

(3) לָחַשׁ, *lāḥash*, "to whisper," "mutter," an onomatopoetic word, like the above, in imitation of the hiss of serpents. It is used of the offensive practice of serpent charming referred to in Eccl **10** 11, and as Delitzsch says, in loc., "signifies the whispering of formulas of charming." See also Isa **3** 3, "skilful enchanter"; Jer **8** 17, "serpents, cockatrices [RV "adders"] . . . . which will not be charmed"; Ps **58** 4.5, "the voice of charmers [RVm "enchanters"], charming never so wisely." Ophiomancy, the art of charming serpents, is still practised in the East.

(4) חֶבֶר, *ḥebher*, "spell," from חָבַר, *ḥābhar*, "to bind," hence "to bind with spells," "fascinate," "charm," descriptive of a species of magic practised by binding knots. That this method of imposture, e.g. the use of the magic knot for exorcism and other purposes, was common, is indicated by the monuments of the East. The moral mischief and uselessness of this and other forms of enchantment are clearly shown in Isa **47** 9.12. This word is also used of the charming of serpents (Dt **18** 11; Ps **58** 5).

(5) עָנַן, *'ānan*, "to cover," "to cloud," hence "to use covert arts." This form of divination was esp. associated with idolatry (so Gesenius, *Heb Lex.*). Delitzsch, however, in a note on this word (Isa **2** 6), doubts the meaning "conceal" and thinks that it signifies rather "to gather auguries from the clouds." He translates it "cloud-interpretive" (Mic **5** 12). This view is not generally supported. Rendered "enchanters" (Jer **27** 9, RV "soothsayers"; so also in Isa **2** 6). Often trd in RV "practice augury," as in Lev **19** 26; Dt **18** 10.14; 2 K **21** 6; 2 Ch **33** 6; a form of magical art corresponding in many respects to that of the Gr *mántis*, who uttered oracles in a state of divine frenzy. LXX κληδονίζομαι, *klēdonízomai*, i.e. augury through the reading or acceptance of a sign or omen. A kindred form of enchantment is mentioned in the NT (2 Tim **3** 13; Gr γόητες, *góētes*, "enchanters," "jugglers," the original indicating that the incantations were uttered in a kind of howl; rendered "seducers" AV, "impostors" RV; cf Rev **19** 20). The NT records the names of several magicians who belonged to this class of conscious impostors: Simon Magus (Acts **8** 9); Bar-Jesus and Elymas (Acts **13** 6.8); the slave girl with the spirit of Python ("divination," Acts **16** 16); "vagabond [RV "strolling"] Jews, exorcists" (Acts **19** 13; cf Lk **11** 19); also the magicians of Moses' day, named Jannes and Jambres (2 Tim **3** 8).

All these forms of enchantment claimed access through supernatural insight or aid, to the will of the gods and the secrets of the spirit world. In turning away faith and expectation from the living God, they struck a deadly blow at the heart of true religion. From the enchanters of the ancient Orient to the medicine-men of today, all exponents of the "black art" exercise a cruel tyranny over the benighted people, and multitudes of innocent victims perish in body and soul under their subtle impostures. In no respect is the exalted nature of the Heb and Christian faiths more clearly seen than in their power to emancipate the human mind and spirit from the mental and moral darkness, the superstition and fear, and the benighting effect of these occult and deadly arts. For more detailed study see Divination; Astrology.

Dwight M. Pratt

END (קֵץ, *ķēç*, אֶפֶס, *'epheṣ*, כָּלָה, *kālāh;* **τέλος**, *télos*, **συντελέω**, *sunteléō*): The end of anything is its *termination*, hence also, *final object* or *purpose*. It is the tr of several Heb and Gr words, chiefly in the OT of *ķēç* (properly, "a cutting off") and other words from the same root (Gen **6** 13, "The end of all flesh is come before me"); *'aḥărīth*, "hinder part," is also frequently trd "end" (Dt **11** 12; Ps **37** 37. 38, ARV "There is a happy end to the man of peace . . . . The end of the wicked shall be cut off"; ERV "latter end" [ver 37], m "reward" or "future posterity"; **73** 17; Jer **5** 31); *ṣōph* (from *ṣūph* "to come to an end") is several times trd "end" (2 Ch **20** 16; Eccl **3** 11; **7** 2). "End" in the sense of *purpose* is the tr of *lemaʻan*, "to the intent" (Ex **8** 22, "to the end thou mayest know"), and of *dibhrāh* (from *dābhar*, "to speak"); Eccl **7** 14, "to the end that man should find nothing after him" (RV "should not find out anything [that shall be] after him"). "Ends of the earth" is the tr of *'epheṣ*, "extremities" (Dt **33** 17; Ps **22** 27), also of *kānāph*, "wing" (Job **37** 3; **38** 13). Other words are *neçaḥ*, "utmost" (Job **34** 36), *teķūphāh*, "circuit," "revolution" (Ex **34** 22; 2 Ch **24** 23, RVm "revolution"), etc. The vb. occurs almost invariably in the phrase "to make an end," as the tr of *kālāh*, "to finish," "complete" (Gen **27** 30; Dt **20** 9; Jer **26** 8, etc); also of *nālāh*, "to complete" (Isa **33** 1), and *shālam*, "to finish" (**38** 12.13).

In Dnl **9** 24, the Heb text has חָתַם, *ḥātham*, "to seal up" ("to complete or finish"), but the margin, followed by AV, RV, Driver and most moderns, has חָתֵם, *ḥāthēm*, "to finish," "end," "complete," a difference of one letter, but practically none in the sense, "to bring to an end"; cf "to finish the transgression," which precedes.

In the NT the common word for "end" is *telos* "an end," "completion," "termination" (Mt **10** 22; **24** 6; Jn **13** 1, RVm "to the uttermost"; Rom **6** 21, "The end of those things is death"; **6** 22, "the end eternal life"; **10** 4, "Christ is the end of the law unto righteousness"; Rev **21** 6; **22** 13, etc); *ékbasis*, "outgoing" (He **13** 7, RV "issue"); *suntéleia*, "full end," is used of "the end of the world" (Mt **13** 39; He **9** 26); *péras*, "extremity," "the ends of the world" (Rom **10** 18); *ákros*, "a point, end" (Mt **24** 31, "from one end of heaven to the other"). "End" as *purpose* is the tr of *eis tó*, "with a view to" (Acts **7** 19; Rom **1** 11; **4** 16; 1 Thess **3** 13); of *eis toúto*, "unto this" (Jn **18** 37; Rom **14** 9; 2 Cor **2** 9); of *prós tó*, "toward this" (Lk **18** 1). "To end" (vb.) is *plēróō*, "to fill up" (Lk **7** 1; Acts **19** 21); once *ginomai*, "to become" (Jn **13** 2, "supper being ended," which RV corrects, giving, "during supper").

For "end" RV has "uttermost part" (Josh **15** 8, etc), "latter end" (Ps **73** 17; ERV Ps **37** 38; Prov **5** 4); "issue" (Dnl **12** 8, m "latter end"; He **13** 7); "side" (Ezk **41** 12). Conversely it has "end" for "uttermost part" (Josh **15** 5); for "side" (Dt **4** 32); for "conclusion" (Eccl **12** 13); for "an end" (Prov **23** 18); "a reward," m "sequel" or "future," Heb "latter end"; "final" (He **6** 16); for "an end of" (Job **18** 2), "snares for" (ARV "hunt for"); for "at one end" (Jer **51** 31), "on every quarter"; for "until the day and night come to an end" (Job **26** 10), "unto the confines of light and darkness"; for "have an end" (Lk **22** 37), "hath fulfilment," m "Gr 'end'"; for "to the end for" (1 Pet **1** 13), "perfectly on"; "at the end of" for "in these last days" (He **1** 2); "His end was nigh" for "He died" (He **11** 22); "its own end," instead of "for himself" (Prov **16** 4, m "his own purpose"); "neither is there any end to" instead of "for thine iniquities are infinite" (Job **22** 5); "to this end" for "therefore" (Mk **1** 38; 1 Tim **4** 10); for "for this cause," "to this end" (Jn **18** 37 *bis*), "unto this end" (1 Pet **4** 6); "to this end" for "for this purpose" (Acts **26** 16; 1 Jn **3** 8); "to which end" for "wherefore" (2 Thess **1** 11); "to the end" is inserted in Gen **18** 19 *bis*, and several other passages. For "ends of the earth" see Astronomy, III, 2. W. L. Walker

END OF THE WORLD. See Eschatology; World, End of the.

ENDAMAGE, en-dam'āj: Archaic for "damage"; Ezr **4** 13 AV: "Thou shalt endamage the revenue of the kings," RV "It will be hurtful unto the kings" (Aram. נְזִק, *nezaķ*); cf 1 Esd **6** 33.

ENDEAVOR, en-dev'ẽr: The sense of this word has suffered weakening since the time of AV. Then it implied utmost exertion and success; now rather forlorn hope and possible failure. Thus RV reads "giving diligence," "give diligence," for AV "endeavoring," "endeavor," in Eph **4** 3; 2 Pet **1** 15, respectively; but "endeavored" is suffered to remain in 1 Thess **2** 17 (σπουδάζω, *spoudázō*, "hasten," "exert oneself"). Cf also Acts **16** 10, AV "endeavored," RV "sought" (Gr *zētéō*, "seek").

ENDIRONS, end'ī-urnz (שְׁפַתַּיִם, *shephattayim*): Used once (Ezk **40** 43 AV) in the m only. In text, both AV and RV, "hooks," denoting stalls or places for the fastening of victims for sacrifice, or perhaps the two hearthstones. The term is a corruption from another word similar in form and identity of usage. This word, "andiron," from Middle Eng., has assumed many peculiar forms, as "anderne," "aundirne," from which the form is doubtless derived, though this is not the original and has no relation to it. ARVm reads, "According to Vulg and Syr, *ledges*."

ENDLESS, end'les (**ἀκατάλυτος**, *akatálutos* [He **7** 16], **ἀπέραντος**, *apérantos* [1 Tim **1** 4]): This Eng. word occurs twice in the NT, and is there represented by the two Gr words above noted.

(1) In He **7** 16 Jesus is said to be a priest "after the power of an endless life." The word means lit., as in RVm, "indissoluble." It is not simply that Christ's priesthood was eternal. The priesthood was based upon His possession, by nature, of a life which in time and eternity death could not touch. This distinguished Him essentially from priests under the law.

(2) In 1 Tim **1** 4, Paul warns Timothy against giving heed in his ministry to "fables [*múthoi*] and endless [limitless] genealogies." The allusion seems to be to the series of emanations (aeons) in gnostic speculation, to which no limit could be set.

Distinct from the above are the words denoting "everlasting," "eternal," which see. James Orr

EN-DOR, en'dor (עֵין דֹּר, *'ēn dōr*, Josh **17** 11; עֵין דּוֹר, *'ēn dōr*, 1 S **28** 7; עֵין דֹּאר, *'ēn dō'r*, Ps **83** 10; A, **Νηνδώρ**, *Nēndōr;* B, **'Αελδώρ**, *Aeldōr*): A town in the lot of Issachar assigned to Manasseh (Josh **17** 11). Here dwelt the woman who had a familiar spirit, whom Saul consulted on the night before the battle of Gilboa (1 S **28** 7). Here also, according to Ps **83** 10, perished fugitives of Sisera's army, after their defeat at the Kishon. The place was therefore not far from the Kishon and Tabor. It is generally identified with the modern *Endūr*, a small village on the northern slope of *Jebel ed-Duḥy*, with several ancient caves. It is not far from Nain and Shunem, and looks across the valley along which the broken ranks of Sisera may have attempted to make their way eastward to the open uplands, and thence to their native North. Coming hither from Gilboa, eluding the Phili outposts under cover of the darkness, Saul would cross the Vale of Jezreel, and pass round the eastern base of the mountain, the Philis being on the west. W. EWING

En-dor.

EN-DOR, WITCH, wich, **OF:** In 1 S **28** 3–25, it is narrated how Saul, in despair of mind because Jeh had forsaken him, on the eve of the fatal battle of Gilboa, resorted in disguise to "a woman that had a familiar spirit" (*'ōbh:* see DIVINATION; NECROMANCY), at En-dor, and besought the woman to divine for him, and bring him up from the dead whom he should name. On the woman reminding him how Saul had cut off from the land those who practised these arts—a proof of the existence and operation of the laws against divination, witchcraft, necromancy, etc (Lev **19** 31; Dt **18** 9–14)—the king assured her of immunity, and bade her call up Samuel. The incidents that followed have been the subject of much discussion and of varied interpretation. It seems assumed in the narrative that the woman did see an appearance, which the king, on her describing it, recognized to be that of Samuel. This, however, need be only the narrator's interpretation of the events. It is not to be credited that the saintly Samuel was actually summoned from his rest by the spells of a professional diviner. Some have thought that Samuel, by God's permission, did indeed appear, as much to the woman's dismay as to the king's; and urge in favor of this the woman's evident surprise and terror at his appearance (vs 12 ff), and the true prophecy of Saul's fate (vs 16–19). It may conceivably have been so, but the more reasonable view is that the whole transaction was a piece of feigning on the part of the woman. The LXX uses the word *eggastrímuthos* ("a ventriloquist") to describe the woman and those who exercised kindred arts (ver 9). Though pretending ignorance (ver 12), the woman doubtless recognizes Saul from the first. It was she who saw Samuel, and reported his words; the king himself saw and heard nothing. It required no great skill in a practised diviner to forecast the general issue of the battle about to take place, and the disaster that would overtake Saul and his sons; while if the forecast had proved untrue, the narrative of the witch of En-dor would never have been written. Saul, in fact, was not slain, but killed himself. The incident, therefore, may best be ranked in the same category as the feats of modern mediumship.

JAMES ORR

ENDOW, en-dou', **ENDUE,** en-dū': "Endow" meant originally "to provide with a dowry"; "indue" took the meaning "clothe"; the likeness between the lit. meanings has confused the metaphorical use of the words in spite of their difference in origin. Thus we find in Gen **30** 20, AV "endued me with a good dowry," RV "endowed" (זָבַד, *zābhadh,* "bestow upon," "endow"); Ex **22** 16, AV "endow her to be his wife," RV "pay a dowry for her" (מָהַר, *māhar,* "purchase," "endow"); cf Dt **22** 29; 2 Ch **2** 12.13, AV and RV "endued" with understanding (from יָדַע, *yādha',* "know"); and Lk **24** 49, AV "endued with power," RV "clothed" (ἐνδύω, *endúō,* "clothe"). F. K. FARR

ENDS OF THE EARTH. See ASTRONOMY, III, 2.

ENDURE, en-dūr': Used in the Bible (1) in the sense of "continue," "last," as in Ps **9** 7, "The Lord shall endure for ever" (ARV "Jeh sitteth as king for ever"); **30** 5, "Weeping may endure for a night" (RV "tarry," m "may come in to lodge at even"); Jn **6** 27, "the meat which endureth," AV, RV "the food which abideth"; (2) in the sense of "bear" (He **12** 20): "bear up under" hardship, persecution, etc (2 Tim **3** 11; 1 Pet **2** 19); "to remain under" (He **10** 32; **12** 2; Jas **1** 12; **5** 11); "to be strong, firm" (He **11** 27); "to persevere" beneath a heavy burden (Mt **10** 22).

EN-EGLAIM, en-eg'lā-im, en-eg-lā'im (עֵין עֶגְלַיִם, *'ēn 'eghlayim,* "fountain of calves"?): In Ezekiel's vision of the waters it is one of the two points between which "fishers shall stand" (Ezk **47** 10). The situation must be near the entrance of the Jordan into the Dead Sea (see EN-GEDI). Tristram (*Bible Places,* 93) identifies it with *'Ain Hajlah* (cf BETH-HOGLAH); Robinson (*BRP,* II, 489), with *'Ain Feshkah.*

ENEMESSAR, en-ē-mes'ar (**Ἐνεμεσσάρ,** *Enemessár,* **Ἐνεμέσσαρος,** *Eneméssaros*): Generally allowed, since Grotius, to be a corruption, though occasionally defended as an alternative form, of Shalmaneser (Tob **1** 2.15, etc) who carried Israel captive to Nineveh, as related in 2 K. Among the captives was Tobit, taken from Thisbe in Gilead, where the prophet Elijah was born and for a time lived. The writer of Tob makes Sennacherib the son (**1** 15), as well as the successor of Enemessar, whereas, according to the Assyr inscriptions, Sennacherib was the son of Sargon. This is only one of several serious historical difficulties in the narrative of Tob. The corruption of the name is variously explained. Rawlinson supposes the first syllable of the word *Shal* to have been dropped, comparing the Bupalussor of Abydenus for Nabopolassar. Dr. Pinches takes Enemessar for Senemessar, the *sh* being changed to *s* and then to the smooth breathing, though the rough breathing more commonly takes the place of a dropped *s;* both scholars admit the easy transposition of the liquids *m* and *n.* *Shalman-asharid* is the Assyr form of Shalmaneser.

J. HUTCHISON

ENEMY, en'e-mi (אֹיֵב, *'ōyēbh,* צַר, *çar,* צָר, *çār;* **ἐχθρός,** *echthrós*): "Enemy," "enemies," are frequent words in the OT. The Heb word most often so tr[d] is *'ōyēbh,* meaning perhaps lit. "one who hates"; very frequent in the Pss, e.g. **3** 7; **6** 10; **7** 5; **8** 2; **9** 3.6; **13** 2, where the cry is often for deliverance from enemies. Another word for "enemy," found chiefly in the poetical books, is *çār,* or *çar,* "distresser," "straitener" (Nu **10** 9; Job **16** 9; Ps **27** 2.12, RV "adversary," etc); also *çārar* (Est **3** 10; Ps **8** 2; **10** 5 AV, etc). Other words are *'ār,* "one awake" (1 S **28** 16 AV; Dnl **4** 19 AV), *sānē',* perhaps, "to be sharp or bite" (Ex **1** 10; Prov **25** 21; **27** 6); *shārar,* "to watch" (Ps **5** 8; **27** 11), and *ḳūm,* "to stand up," or "withstand" (Ex **32** 25).

In the NT *echthros,* "enemy," "opponent," is the only word tr[d] "enemy" (Mt **5** 43.44; Mk **12** 36; Lk **1** 71.74, etc; Rom **5** 10; **11** 28, etc), once with *ánthrōpos* ("a man"), joined to *echthros* (Mt **13** 28).

In RV "adversary" is frequently substituted for "enemy" (Nu **24** 8; Dt **32** 41; Ps **6** 7; **7** 6; **44** 10, etc); for "O thou enemy," etc (Ps **9** 6) we have "The enemy are come to an end"; instead of "When the enemy shall come in like a flood, the Spirit of the Lord shall lift up a standard against him" (Isa **59** 19) we have "For he will come as a rushing stream, which the breath of Jeh driveth" (with the text of AV in m); for "The fire of thine enemies shall devour them" (**26** 11), "Fire shall devour thine adversaries" (text of AV in m).

The frequent reference to enemies in the OT is what we should expect to see in these early times on the part of a people settling in a land that had been occupied by other tribes, worshipping other gods. The spirit of their law was that expressed by Our Lord in His Sermon on the Mount, "Thou shalt love thy neighbor, and hate thine enemy." This He changed: "but I say unto you, Love your enemies." An approach toward this spirit had been made in the later prophets by their inclusion of the whole world under one God, who had a gracious purpose toward all, but the near statement of it we only find in Prov **25** 21 (quoted by St. Paul, Rom **12** 20). See also Ex **23** 4, and cf 2 K **6** 22; 2 Ch **28** 15.

W. L. Walker

ENENEUS, ĕ-nē′nē-us, en-e-nē′us (**Ἐνήνιος**, *Enḗnios;* AV **Enenius**, RVm "Enenis"): Occurring only in Apoc. According to 1 Esd **5** 8, E. was one of the 12 leaders over the returning exiles from Babylon under Zerubbabel. Ezr **2** contains the parallel list of the returning leaders but omits E., giving only 11; but E. corresponds to Nahamani (Neh **7** 7).

ENFLAME. See Inflame.

EN-GADDI, en-gad′ī (Sir **24** 14 RV, "on the sea shore"). See En-gedi.

ENGAGE, en-gāj′: From עָרַב, *‛ārabh*, "to pledge," Jer **30** 21, AV "Who is this that engaged his heart?"; RV "he that hath had boldness?"; RVm Heb "hath been surety for his heart?"

EN-GANNIM, en-gan′im (עֵין גַּנִּים, *‛ēn gannīm*, "spring of gardens"):

(1) A town in the territory of Judah, named with Zanoah and Eshtaol (Josh **15** 34). It is probably identical with the modern *Umm Jīna*, S. of *Wādy eṣ-Ṣarār*, not far from Zanoah (*Zanū‛a*).

(2) A town in the lot of Issachar (Josh **19** 21), assigned to the Gershonite Levites (**21** 29). In 1 Ch **6** 73 it is replaced by Anem. It probably corresponds to the Ginnea of Jos (*Ant*, XX, vi, 1; *BJ*, III, iii, 4), and may certainly be identified with the modern *Jenīn*, a prosperous village on the southern edge of the plain of Esdraelon, with beautiful gardens, fruitful orchards and plentiful supplies of water from the local springs.

W. Ewing

EN-GEDI, en′ge-dī, en-gē′dī (עֵין גֶּדִי, *‛ēn gedhī*, "fountain of the kid"): Identical with the present *Ain Jidi.* According to 2 Ch **20** 2 it is the same as Hazazon-tamar, mentioned in Gen **14** 7 as occupied by the Amorites and as having been attacked by Chedorlaomer after leaving Kadesh and El Paran on his way to the Vale of Siddim. The place is situated upon the W. shore of the Dead Sea about midway between the N. and the S. ends, and was included in the territory of Judah (Josh **15** 62). The spot is rendered attractive by the verdure clothing it by reason of immense fountains of warm water, 80° F., which pour out from beneath the limestone cliffs. In the time of Solomon (Cant **1** 14) palms and vines were cultivated here. Jos also mentions its beautiful palm groves. In the time of Eusebius it was still a place of importance, but since the Middle Ages it has been almost deserted, being occupied now only by a few Arabs. The oasis occupies a small area a few hundred feet above the Dead Sea marked by the 650 ft. sedimentary terrace heretofore described (see Dead Sea). The limestone borders rise so abruptly to a height of 2,000 ft. immediately on the W., that the place can be approached only by a rock-cut path. Two

En-gedi.

streams, *Wady Sugeir* and *Wady el-Areyeh*, descend on either side through precipitous rocky gorges from the uninhabitable wilderness separating it from Bethlehem and Hebron. It was in the caves opening out from the sides of these gorges that David took refuge from Saul (1 S **24** 1). During the reign of Jehoshaphat (2 Ch **20** 2), the children of Ammon, Moab and Mt. Seir attempted to invade Judah by way of En-gedi, but were easily defeated as they came up from the gorges to occupy the advantageous field of battle chosen by Jehoshaphat.

George Frederick Wright

ENGINE, en′jin (2 Ch **26** 15; Ezk **26** 9; 1 Macc **6** 51; **13** 43 f). See Siege.

ENGLISH, iṇ′glish, **VERSIONS**, vûr′shunz:

1. Introductory
2. The Bible in Anglo-Saxon and Norman Times
3. John Wycliffe
4. How Far Was the 14th-Century Version Wycliffe's Work?
5. From Wycliffe to Tyndale
6. William Tyndale
7. Miles Coverdale
8. Matthew's Bible
9. Richard Taverner
10. The Great Bible (Cranmer's Bible)
11. Reaction, 1541–57
12. Edward VI
13. Mary
14. The Geneva Bible (the "Breeches Bible")
15. The Bishops' Bible
16. Rheims and Douai Version
17. The Authorized Version
18. The Apocrypha
19. Further Revisions
20. English Revised Version
21. American Revised Version
22. Has the RV Displaced the AV?

Literature

English Versions of the Scriptures.—The battle for vernacular Scripture, the right of a nation to have the sacred writings in its own tongue, was fought and won in England. Ancient VSS, such as the Syr and the Gothic, were produced to meet obvious requirements of the teacher or the missionary, and met with no opposition from any quarter. The same was the case with the efforts of the Anglo-Saxon church to provide portions of Scripture for the use of the people. Even in later times the Lat church seems to have followed no consistent policy in permitting or forbidding the tr of the Scriptures. In one country the practice was forbidden, in another it was regarded with forbearance or permitted under authority (Addis and Arnold, *Catholic Dictionary*, London, 1884, art. "Bible"); and so it came about that the different nations of Europe came by the inestimable boon of an open Bible in different ways. Germany, for example, after the attempts of numerous translators who seem to have been quite untram-

1. Introductory

meled in their work owed, under Providence, to the faith, the intrepidity and the genius of Luther the national version which satisfied it for more than three centuries, and, after a recent and essentially conservative revision, satisfies it still. In England, as related below, things took a different course. In the Reformation period the struggle turned mainly on the question of the tr of the Bible.

2. The Bible in Anglo-Saxon and Norman Times

The clergy and learned men had always of course access to the Scriptures in the Vulg, a tr of the original Scriptures into Lat completed by Jerome at the very beginning of the 5th cent.; and from this version—the Vulg—practically all further tr[s] were made till the days of Luther. Within a century or little more after the landing of Augustine in England and his settlement at Canterbury (597 AD) **Caedmon**, a monk of Whitby, produced (670) his metrical version of the Bible, hardly indeed to be reckoned a version of the Scriptures in the ordinary sense, though it paved the way for such. **Bede** of Jarrow (672-735) tr[d] the Creed and the Lord's Prayer and, according to the beautiful letter of his pupil, Cuthbert, breathed his last on the completion of his tr of the Gospel of John into the language of the people. **Aldhelm,** bishop of Sherborne in the county of Dorset (d. 709), tr[d] the Psalter in another tr with which the name of **King Alfred** is associated; and the other efforts of that ruler to spread the knowledge of the Scriptures among his people are well known. Notice, too, should be taken of the glosses. "The gloss," says Eadie (*English Bible*, I, 14, n.), "was neither a free nor yet a literal tr, but the interlinear insertion of the vernacular, word against word of the original, so that the order of the former was really irrespective of idiom and usage." The finest example of these is seen in the Lindisfarne Gospels, which were written in Lat about the year 700, and provided with an interlinear tr about 950 by **Aldred,** the priest. These with a version of a considerable section of the OT by **Ælfric,** archbishop of Canterbury about the year 990, comprise the main efforts at Bible tr into Eng. before the Norman Conquest. In Anglo-Saxon there is no proof of the existence of any tr of the complete Bible, or even of the complete NT. The sectional VSS, moreover, cannot be shown to have had any influence upon succeeding VSS. For nearly three centuries after the Conquest the interrelations of the different sections of the people and the conditions of the language prevented any real literary progress. The period, however, was marked by the appearance of fragmentary tr[s] of Scripture into Norman French. From some Augustinian monastery, too, in the north of the East Midland district of England, about the year 1200, appeared **the Ormulum,** a curious metrical work of some 20,000 lines, consisting of a paraphrase of the Gospel of the day and an explanatory homily for 32 days of the year. Like the work of Caedmon the monk, it was not exactly Bible tr, but it doubtless prepared the way for such. Three VSS of the Psalter, naturally always a favorite portion of Scripture with the translator, are assigned to the first half of Wycliffe's century. The reformer himself in one of his tracts urges a tr of the Bible to suit the humbler classes of society, on the plea that the upper classes already have their version in French. It was only in the long and splendid reign of Edward III (1327-77), when the two races that had existed in the country since the Conquest were perfectly united, that the predominance of English asserted itself, and the growth of the power and of the mental activity of the people instinctively demanded a new form of expression. The century of Wycliffe, it is to be remembered, was also that of Langland, Gower and Chaucer.

3. John Wycliffe

Born in Yorkshire about the year 1320, Wycliffe was educated at Balliol College, Oxford, of which he soon became a Fellow and was for a short time Master, resigning the latter position in the year 1361 on his presentation to a living in Lincolnshire. He died at Lutterworth in Leicestershire in 1384. It was during the last quarter of his life that he came forward as a friend of the people and as a prolific writer on their behalf. Notwithstanding the external glory of the reign of Edward III, there was much in the ecclesiastical and social circumstances of the time to justify popular discontent. The Pope derived from England alone a revenue larger than that of any prince in Christendom. The nobles resented the extortion and pretensions of the higher clergy; and, according to Green, "the enthusiasm of the Friars, who in the preceding century had preached in praise of poverty, had utterly died away and left a crowd of impudent mendicants behind it." The Black Death, "the most terrible plague the world ever witnessed," fell in the middle of the century and did much further to embitter the already bitter condition of the poor. In France things were no better than in England, and the Turk had settled permanently in Europe. It is not wonderful that Wycliffe began, as is said, his version of the NT with the Book of Rev. With his social teaching the present art. is not specially concerned. It probably involved no more than the inculcation of the inherently democratic and leveling doctrines of Christianity, though some of the Lollards, like the Munster peasants in the German Reformation, associated it with dangerous socialistic practice. In any case the application of Christianity to the solution of social problems is not in any age easy to effect in practice. His tracts show (Eadie, I, 59 ff) that it was from what Wycliffe had felt the Bible to be to himself that there sprang his strong desire to make the reading of it possible for his countrymen. To this was due the first Eng. version of the Bible. To this also was likewise due the institution of the order of "poor priests" to spread the knowledge of the Bible as widely as possible throughout the country.

4. How far Was the Translation Wycliffe's Work?

There is some uncertainty as to the exact share which Wycliffe had in the production of the 14th cent. version. The tr of the NT was finished about the year 1380 and in 1382 the tr of the entire Bible was completed, the greater part of the OT being the work of **Nicholas Hereford,** one of the reformer's most ardent supporters at Oxford. The work was revised on thoroughly sound principles of criticism and interpretation, as these are explained in the prologue to the new edition, by John Purvey, one of Wycliffe's most intimate friends during the latter part of his life, and finished in 1388. "Other scholars," says Mr. F. G. Kenyon, of the British Museum, "assisted him in his work, and we have no certain means of knowing how much of the tr was actually done by himself. The NT is attributed to him, but we cannot say with certainty that it was entirely his own work" (*Our Bible and the Ancient Manuscripts*, 200, 3d ed, London, 1898). This entirely corresponds with the position taken up by Forshall and Madden, the editors of the great Oxford edition of Wycliffe's version issued in 4 large quarto vols in 1850. That work was undertaken to honor Wycliffe and in some measure to repay England's indebtedness to the reformer. The editors were men of the first literary rank; they spent 22 years upon this work; and it is recognized as a credit at once to the scholarship and research of Oxford and of England. Its honest and straightforward Introduction answers by anticipation by far the greater part of the criticisms and claims put forth by Dr. Gasquet (*Our Old English Bible and Other Essays*, London, 1898; 2d ed, 1908). The claim is made that the work published in Oxford in 1850 is really not Wycliffe's at all but that of his bitterest opponents, the bishops of the English church who represented the party of Rome. Gasquet's work on this subject is mainly worthy of notice on account of his meritorious research in other departments of the English Reformation. His arguments and statements are met by Kenyon (op. cit., 204-8). The controversy is further noticed in *The Age of Wycliffe*, by G. M. Trevelyan (2d ed, London, 1908), a work which cannot be too highly praised for its deep research, its interesting exposition and its cordial appreciation of the reformer and his works. "Nothing," says Trevelyan (Appendix, 361), "can be more damning than the licenses to particular people to have Eng. Bibles, for they distinctly show that without such licenses it was thought wrong to have them." The age of printing, it is to be remembered, was not yet.

The Wycliffe Bible was issued and circulated in copies each of which was written by the hand. About 170 copies of this manuscript Bible are still in existence. They form a striking proof of what England and the world owe to the faith, the courage and the labor of John Wycliffe and his "poor priests."

5. From Wycliffe to Tyndale

It is a remarkable fact that before the year 1500 most of the countries of Europe had been supplied with a version of the Scriptures printed in the vernacular tongue, while England had nothing but the scattered copies of the Wycliffe MS version. Even Caxton, eager as was his search for works to translate and to print, while he supplied priests with service-books, preachers with sermons, and the clerk with the "Golden Legende," left the Scriptures severely alone. Nor was there a printed Eng. version, even of the NT, for close on half a century after Caxton's death, a circumstance largely due to the energy of the Tudor dictatorship and the severity of the Arundelian Constitutions enacted by Convocation at Oxford in the year 1408 against Wycliffe and his work. These enactments forbade "upon pain of the greater excommunication the unauthorised tr of any text of the Scriptures into English or any other tongue by way of a book, pamphlet, treatise or the reading of such." Meanwhile the study of the new learning, including that of the original languages of Scripture, though generally resisted by the clergy, was greatly promoted by the invention of printing.

6. William Tyndale

Erasmus, perhaps the chief representative name of the new age in the domain of learning, was professor of Greek at Cambridge from 1509 to 1524, and in the 2d year of his professorship William Tyndale, an Oxford student in the 26th year of his age, migrated to Cambridge to study Greek. Ten years later Tyndale returned to his native county—Gloucestershire—to take up a private tutorship and there formed the determination which became the one fixed aim of his life—to put an ET, not of the Vulg but of the original Gr and Heb Scriptures, into the hands of his countrymen. "If God spared him life," he said, "ere many years he would cause a boy that driveth a plough to know more of the Scriptures than the Pope did." Erasmus at Cambridge had uttered a similar aspiration. "He boldly avows his wish for a Bible open and intelligible to all. . . . . 'I long for the day when the husbandman shall sing to himself portions of the Scriptures as he follows the plough, when the weaver shall hum them to the time of his shuttle, when the traveller shall while away with their stories the weariness of his journey'" (Green, *History of the English People*, 1st ed, 308). In 1522 Tyndale went to London to try to find a patron for his work in Tunstall, bishop of London, who had studied Gr with Latimer at Padua and was one of the most noted humanists of the day. To show himself capable for the work, Tyndale took with him to London a version of a speech of Isocrates. But the Bishop of London's service was full; and after spending a year with a friendly alderman in London, "at last," he says in the Preface to his *Five Books of Moses*, "I understood not only that there was no room in my Lord of London's palace to translate the NT, but also that there was no place to do it in all England." He left the country and never returned to it. He spent the remaining twelve years of his life in exile and for the most part in great hardship, sustained by steady labor and by the one hope of his life—the giving to his countrymen of a reliable version of the Holy Scriptures in their own tongue. He went first to Hamburg, and there, as it seems, issued in the year 1524 versions of Mt and Mk separately, with marginal notes. Next year he removed to Cologne, and arranged for the printing of the complete NT, the tr of which he accomplished alone, from the study of the Gr text of Erasmus in its original and revised editions and by a comparison of these with the Vulg and several European vernacular VSS which, as already stated, had anticipated that of England. The story of the interruption by Cochlaeus of the actual work of printing, and of his warning the King and Wolsey of the impending invasion of England by Lutheranism, reads like a romance. His interference resulted in the prohibition by the city authorities of the printing of the work and in the sudden flight of Tyndale and his assistant, Joye, who sailed up the Rhine with the precious sheets already printed of their 3,000 quarto edition to Worms, the city of the famous Diet in which Luther four years before had borne his testimony before the Emperor. The place was now Lutheran, and here the work of printing could be carried out in security and at leisure. To baffle his enemies, as it seems, a small octavo edition was first printed without glosses; then the quarto edition was completed. The "pernicious literature" of both editions, without name of the translator, was shipped to England early in 1526; and by 1530 six editions of the NT in English (three surreptitiously) were distributed, numbering, it is computed, 15,000 copies. The unfavorable reception of Tyndale's work by the King and the church authorities may in some measure be accounted for by the excesses which at the moment were associated with the Reformation in Germany, and by the memories of Lollardism in connection with the work of Wycliffe. So vehement was the opposition at any rate to Tyndale's work, and so determined the zeal in buying up and burning the book, that of the six editions above mentioned there "remains of the first edition one fragment only; . . . . of the second one copy, wanting the title-page, and another very imperfect; and of the others, two or three copies which are not however satisfactorily identified" (Westcott, *History of the English Bible*, 45, London, 1868). Meanwhile Tyndale took to working on the OT. Much discussion has taken place on the question whether he knew Heb (see Eadie, I, 209 ff). Tyndale's own distinct avowal is that it was from the Heb direct that such tr of the OT as he accomplished was made. Very early in 1531 he published separately VSS of Gen and Dt, and in the following year the whole of the Pent in one volume, with a preface and marginal glosses. In 1534 appeared the Book of Jon, with a prologue; and in the same year a new version of the NT to counteract one made by Joye from the Vulg. This has been described by Westcott (op. cit., 185) as "altogether

Tyndale's noblest monument," mainly on account of its short and pregnant glosses. "Bengel himself is not more terse or pointed." A beautifully illuminated copy of this edition was struck off on vellum and presented to Queen Anne Boleyn; and an edition of his revised NT was printed in London—"The first volume of Holy Scripture printed in England"—in 1536, the year of the Queen's death. Tyndale had for some time lived at Antwerp, enjoying a "considerable yearly exhibition" from the English merchants there; but his enemies in England were numerous, powerful and watchful. In 1534 he was betrayed and arrested; and after an imprisonment of nearly a year and a half at the castle of Vilorde, about 18 miles from Brussels, he was strangled and then burned in 1536, the same year as that of the death of the Queen. The last days of the hero and martyr may have been cheered by the news of the printing of his revised edition of the NT in England.

7. Miles Coverdale

Miles Coverdale, who first gave England a complete and authorized version of the Bible, was a younger contemporary of Tyndale. Tyndale was a year younger than Luther, who was born in 1483, and Coverdale was four years younger than Tyndale. Born in the North Riding of Yorkshire, he found his way to Cambridge at the time when Erasmus was professor of Gr, and appears at an early date—how is not known—to have got into the good graces of Crumwell, the "malleus monachorum," factotum and secretary to Wolsey, and later on the King's principal abettor in his efforts to render the Church of England thoroughly national, if not to an equal extent Protestant. Adopting the liberal party in the church, he held Lutheran or evangelical views of religion, cast off his monastic habit, and, as Bale says, gave himself up wholly to the preaching of the gospel. He is found in 1527 in intimate connection with More and Crumwell and probably from them he received encouragement to proceed with a tr of the Bible. In 1528 he was blamed before Tunstall, bishop of London, as having caused some to desert the mass, the confessional and the worship of images; and seeking safety, he left England for the Continent. He is said by Foxe to have met Tyndale at Hamburg in 1529, and to have given him some help in the tr of the Pent. An uncertainty hangs over Coverdale's movements from 1529 to 1535, a period during which much was happening that could not fail to be powerfully changing opinion in England. The result of the Assembly held at Westminster by Warham in May, 1530, and of the Convocation held under his successor, Cranmer, in December, 1534, was that in the latter it was petitioned that "his Majesty would vouchsafe to decree that the sacred Scriptures should be tr[d] into the Eng. tongue by certain honest and learned men, named for that purpose by his Majesty, and should be delivered to the people according to their learning." Crumwell, meanwhile, who had a shrewd forecast of the trend of affairs, seems to have arranged with Coverdale for the printing of his tr. However this may be, by the year 1534 "he was ready, as he was desired, to set forth" (i.e. to print) his tr; and the work was finished in 1535. And thus, "as the harvest springs from the seed which germinates in darkness, so the entire Eng. Bible, tr[d] no one knows where, presented itself, unheralded and unanticipated, at once to national notice in 1535" (Eadie, I, 266). It is declared on the title-page to be "faithfully and truly translated out of Douche and Latyn into Englishe: MDXXXV." Coverdale's own statements about his work leave the impression that he was a conspicuously honest man. Unlike Tyndale who regarded himself as, in a way, a prophet, with his work as a necessity Divinely laid upon him, Coverdale describes that he had no particular desire to undertake the work—and how he wrought, as it were, in the language of these days, under a committee from whom he took his instructions and who "required him to use the Douche [i.e. the German] and the Latyn." He claims further to have done the work entirely himself, and he certainly produced a new version of the OT and a revised version of the NT. He used, he says, five sundry interpreters of the original languages. These interpreters were, in all probability, the Vulg, Luther's version, the Zurich or Swiss-German Bible, the Lat version of Pagninus, and he certainly consulted Tyndale on the Pent and the NT. He successfully studied musical effect in his sentences and many of the finest phrases in the AV are directly traced to Coverdale. His version of the Pss is that which is retained and is still in daily use in the ritual of the Church of England. Two new editions of Coverdale's version were issued in 1537 "with the King's most gracious license," and after this the Eng. Bible was allowed to circulate freely. Certain changes in the title-page, prefaces and other details are discussed in the works mentioned at the end of this article.

8. Matthew's Bible

Convocation meanwhile was not satisfied with Coverdale's tr, and Coverdale himself in his honest modesty had expressed the hope that an improved tr should follow his own. Accordingly in 1537—probably at the suggestion of, and with some support from, Crumwell and certainly to his satisfaction—a large folio Bible appeared, as edited and dedicated to the King, by Thomas Matthew. This name has, since the days of Foxe, been held to be a pseudonym for John Rogers, the protomartyr of the Marian persecution, a Cambridge graduate who had for some years lived in intimacy with Tyndale at Antwerp, and who became the possessor of his MS at his death. Besides the NT, Tyndale, as above mentioned, had published tr[s] of the Pent, the Book of Jon, and portions of the Apoc, and had left a MS version of Josh to 2 Ch. Rogers, apparently taking all he could find of the work of Tyndale, supplemented this by the work of Coverdale and issued the composite volume with the title, "The Bible, which is all the Holy Scriptures, in which are contayned the Olde and Newe Testaments, truely and purely translated into English by Thomas Matthew. Esaye I, Hearken to, ye heavens, and thou earth, geave eare: for the Lord speaketh. MDXXXVII." After the banning and burning of Tyndale's NT on its arrival in England 11 years before, it is not easy to account for the royal sanction with which the tr appeared. It was probably granted to the united efforts of Cranmer and Crumwell, aided perhaps by the King's desire to show action independent of the church. The royal sanction, it will be noted, was given in the same year in which it was given to Coverdale's second edition. That version became the basis of our present Bible. It was on Matthew's version that for 75 years thereafter all other versions were based

9. Richard Taverner

Matthew's first edition of 1,500 copies was soon exhausted, and a new edition was issued with some revision by Richard Taverner, a cultivated young layman and lawyer who had in his early years been selected by Wolsey for his college at Oxford. He was imprisoned in its cellar for reading Tyndale's NT; but he was soon released for his singular musical accomplishments. He was an excellent Grecian, of good literary taste and of personal dignity. For the OT curiously enough he made, good Grecian as he was, no use of the Sept; but throughout aimed successfully at idiomatic expression, as also at compression and vividness. Some of his changes are kept in the AV, such as "parables" for "similitudes," and in Mt **24** 12, "The love of the many shall wax cold," and others. He also does greater justice to the Gr article. His dedication to the king is manly and dignified and compares most favorably with the dedications of other translators, including that of the AV. The book appeared in two editions, folio and quarto, in 1539, and in the same year two editions, folio and quarto, of the NT. The Bible and the NT were each reprinted once, and his OT was adopted in a Bible of 1551. But with these exceptions Taverner's version was practically outside of influence on later tr[s].

The next Bible to appear was named from its size. Its pages are fully 15 in. long and over 9 in. broad.

10. The Great Bible

It was meant to be in a way a state edition, and is known as the Great Bible. As sufficiently good type, paper and other requisites could not be found in England, it was resolved that it should be printed in Paris. Coverdale and Grafton, the printer, went to Paris to superintend the printing; but the French church authorities interfered and the presses, types and workmen had to be transferred to London where the work was finished. It was the outcome of the Protestant zeal of Crumwell who wished to improve upon the merely composite volume of Tyndale and Coverdale. Its origin is not very accurately known, and authorities such as Hume, Burnet and Froude have ventured upon statements regarding it, for which there is really no proof (Eadie, I, 356 ff). The duty of editor or reviser was by Crumwell assigned to Coverdale who, as a pliant man and really interested in the improvement of the Eng. version, was quite willing to undertake a work that might supersede his own. The rapidity with which the work was executed and the proofs of the minute care devoted to it by Coverdale may appear remarkable to those who are acquainted with the deliberate and leisurely methods of the large committee that produced the AV in the reign of King James or the RV in the reign of Queen Victoria. Of course Coverdale had been over all the work before and knew the points at which improvements were to be applied; and a zealous and expert individual can accomplish more than a committee. Luther tr[d] the NT and, after revising his work with Melanchthon, had it printed and published in less than a year. The printing of the Great Bible began in May, 1538, and was completed in April, 1539, a handsome folio, printed in black letter, with the title, "The Byble in Englyshe, that is to say, the contents of all the holy scripture, bothe of the olde and newe testament, truly translated after the veryte of the Hebrue and Greke textes, by the dylygent studye of dyverse excellent learned men, expert in the forsayde tongues. Prynted by Rychard Grafton and Edward Whitchurch. *Cum privilegio ad imprimendum solum* 1539." The elaborate notes for which asterisks and various other marks are provided were never supplied; but the actual tr shows devoted attention to the work and much fine appreciation of the original languages and of English. In the NT the version derived assistance from the Lat version of Erasmus, and in the OT from Munster and Pagninus. Variations in the text could of course be got from the Complutensian Polyglot. The Great Bible shows considerable improvement upon Tyndale in the NT, and upon Coverdale in the OT. "So careful," says Eadie (I, 370), "had been Coverdale's revision and so little attachment had he to his own previous version, that in the 53rd chapter of Isaiah the Bible of 1539 differs in nearly forty places from his version of 1535." The clergy of course had no love for Crumwell and still less for his work, though to avert clerical prejudices, Coverdale had made concessions in his tr. The work was cordially welcomed by the people, and a copy was ordered to be printed for every parish church, the cost to be paid half by the parson and half by the parishioners. A further revision of this version was carried out by Coverdale for a second edition which appeared in April, 1540, and is known as Cranmer's Bible, mainly from the judicious and earnest preface which the archbishop wrote for it. "It exhibits a text formed on the same principles as that of 1539, but after a fuller and more thorough revision" (Westcott, 254). Two other editions followed in the same year and three more in the year following (1541).

After the publication of the Great Bible (1539–41) no further advance took place for many years.

11. Reaction, 1541–57

The later years of Henry VIII indeed were marked by serious reaction. In 1542 Convocation with the royal consent made an attempt, fortunately thwarted by Cranmer, to Latinize the Eng. version and to make it in reality what the Romish version of Rheims subsequently became. In the following year Parliament, which then practically meant the King and two or three members of the Privy Council, restricted the use of the Eng. Bible to certain social classes that excluded nine-tenths of the population; and three years later it prohibited the use of everything but the Great Bible. It was probably at this time that there took place the great destruction of all previous work on the Eng. Bible which has rendered examples of that work so scarce. Even Tunstall and Heath were anxious to escape from their responsibility in lending their names to the Great Bible. In the midst of this reaction Henry VIII died, January 28, 1547.

No new work marked the reign of Edward VI, but great activity prevailed in the printing of previous VSS.

12. Edward VI

Thirty-five New Testaments and thirteen Bibles were published during his reign of six years and a half; and injunctions were issued urging every person to read "the very lively Word of God" and for a copy of the Great Bible with the Eng. paraphrase of Erasmus to be set up in every church. By royal order a NT was to be sold for 22*d*., a sum representing as many shillings of present value.

Less repressive work regarding the tr and diffusion of Scripture than might have been expected occurred in the reign of Mary, though

13. Mary

in other directions the reaction was severe enough. According to Lord Burghley, during the three years and nine months of Mary's reign, the number of 400 persons perished —men, women, maidens and children—by imprisonment, torment, famine and fire. Among the martyrs were Cranmer and Rogers; Coverdale escaped martyrdom only by exile and the powerful intervention of the king of Denmark. The copies of the Bibles in the churches were of course burned; and—though individual tr[s] were not specified—proclamations were issued against certain books and authors. Still the books were not, as formerly, bought up and confiscated; and so the activity of Edward's reign in the production of Bibles left copies widely distributed throughout the country at the close of Mary's reign. At this time a NT was printed at Geneva which had great influence upon future VSS of the Bible.

This NT was issued in 1557 and was most probably the work of W. Whittingham, an English exile

14. The Geneva Bible

who had married Calvin's sister. It was tr[d] from the Gr and compared carefully with other VSS. It had also a marginal commentary which was more complete than anything similar that had yet appeared in England; and it was the first tr that was printed in roman letter and in which chapters were divided into verses. Calvin wrote for it an introductory epistle, and it had also an address by the reviser himself. A few months after its publication the more serious task of the revision of the whole Bible was begun and continued for the space of two years and more, the translators working at it "day and night." Who the translators were is not said; but Whittingham, probably with Gilby and Sampson, stayed at Geneva for a year and a half after Elizabeth came to the throne, and saw the work through. It was finished in 1560, and in a dignified preface was dedicated to Elizabeth. The cost was met by members of the Congregation at Geneva, among whom was John Bodley, father of the founder of the great library at Oxford. Its handy form—a modest quarto—along with its vigorously expressed commentary, made it popular even with people who objected to its source and the occasional Calvinistic tinge of its doctrines. It became and remained the popular edition for nearly three-quarters of a century. The causes of its popularity are explained in Westcott, 125 f. Bodley had received the patent for its publication; and upon his asking for an extension of the patent for twelve years, the request was generously granted by Archbishop Parker and Grindly, bishop of London, though the Bishops' Bible was already begun.

The "Breeches Bible."—The Geneva version is often called the "Breeches Bible" from its tr of Gen **3** 7: "They sewed figleaves together, and made themselves breeches." This tr, however, is not peculiar to the Genevan version. It is the tr of *perizômata* in both the Wycliffe VSS; it is also found in Caxton's version of the "Golden Legende."

15. The Bishops' Bible

Queen Elizabeth, the beginning of whose reign was beset with great difficulties, restored the arrangements of Edward VI. A copy of the Great Bible was required to be provided in every church, and every encouragement was given to the reading of the Scriptures. The defects of the Great Bible were admitted, and were the not unnatural result of the haste with which—notwithstanding its two revisions—it had been produced. These became more apparent when set beside the Geneva version, which, however, the archbishop and clergy could hardly be expected to receive with enthusiasm, as they had had nothing to do with its origin and had no control over its renderings and marginal notes. Archbishop Parker, moreover, who had an inclination to Bib. studies, had at the same time a passion for uniformity; and probably to this combination of circumstances may be traced the origin of the Bishops' Bible. Parker superintended the work, which was begun in 1563-64; he was aided by eight bishops—from whom the version received its name—and other scholars. It appeared in a magnificent volume in 1568, without a word of flattery, but with a preface in which the revisers express a lofty consciousness of the importance of their work. It was published in 1568 *cum privilegio regiae Majestatis*. A revised and in many places corrected edition was issued in 1572, and another in 1575, the year of the archbishop's death. The general aim of the version is a quaint literality, but along with this is found the use of not a few explanatory words and phrases not found in the original text. More exact notice also than in previous VSS is taken of the use of the Gr art. and of the particles and conjunctions. It bears marks, however, of the hand of the individual translators by whom the work was done; and of the want of the revision of each translator's work by the rest, and of some general revision of the whole. The Genevan version was the work of collegiate labor, to which much of its superiority is due. Though Parker did not object to the circulation of the Genevan version, Convocation after his death made some unsuccessful attempts to popularize the Bishops' Bible; but the Genevan tr was not easily thrust aside. "It grew," says Eadie (II, 35), "to be in greater demand than the Bishops' or Cranmer's. Ninety editions of it were published in the reign of Elizabeth, as against forty of all the other VSS. Of Bibles, as distinct from New Testaments, there were twenty-five editions of Cranmer's and the Bishops', but sixty of the Genevan."

16. Rheims and Douai Version

The production of an official version of the sacred Scriptures for Eng. Roman Catholics was probably due more to rivalry with the Reformers than to any great zeal of the authorities of the Roman church for the spread of vernacular Scripture; though, according to the Arundelian Constitution above mentioned, it was only to the printing and reading of unauthorized tr[s] that objection was then taken by the Rom authorities. But if there was to be a special version for Catholics, it was clearly reasonable that the work should be done by Catholics and accompanied by Catholic explanations. This was undertaken by some Eng. Catholic scholars who, on the success of the Reformation in England, had left the country and settled at Douai in the N.E. of France, with a short transference of their seminary to Rheims. The version was probably produced under the influence of (Cardinal) Allen and an Oxford scholar, Gregory Martin. It was made from the Vulg, the Bible of Jerome and Augustine, and not, like the Protestant VSS, from the Heb and Gr originals. The NT was issued from Rheims in 1582 and the OT from Douai in 1609. The main objection to the version is the too close adherence of the translators to the words of the original and the too great Latinizing of the Eng., so that their tr "needs," as Fuller said, "to be tr[d]." Still they have a few words which along with a few Latinisms were adopted by the translators of the AV, such as "upbraideth not," "bridleth his tongue," "at his own charges," and others; and they have the special merit of preserving uniformity of rendering. The tr met with no great success and the circulation was not large.

17. The Authorized Version

The AV owed its origin to a chance remark regarding mistranslations in the existing VSS made at the Hampton Court Conference, a meeting of bishops and Puritan clergy held (1604) in the interest of religious toleration before James was actually crowned. The meeting was ineffectual in all points raised by the Puritans, but it led to the production of the Eng. Bible. Dr. Reynolds, president of Corpus Christi College, Oxford, probably with some reference to the rivalry between the Bishops' Bible and the Genevan version, remarked on the imperfections of the current Bibles. The remark was not very enthusiastically received except by the King, who caught eagerly at the suggestion of a fresh version, "professing that he could never yet see a Bible well translated in English," and blaming specially the Genevan version, probably on account of the pointed character of its marginal notes. Probably with the aid of the universities, the King without delay nominated the revisers to the number of fifty-four from among the best Heb and Gr scholars of the day. Only 47 actually took part in the work which, however—officially at least—they were in no hurry to begin; for, although named in 1604 and with all the preliminaries arranged before the end of that year, they did not begin their work till 1607. Their remuneration was to be by church preferment, for which the archbishop was to take measures. The immediate expenses, the King suggested, should be supplied by the bishops and chapters who, however, did not respond. "King James' version never cost King James a farthing," says Eadie (II, 153 f), who here gives some interesting information on this aspect of the revision. They wrought in six companies of which two met respectively in Westminster, Cambridge and Oxford. Elaborate rules, given in full in most histories of the Bible, were laid down for the revisers' guidance, the King being particularly insistent upon Rule 9, which provided for the revision of the work of each Company by the rest. When any Company had finished the revision of a book, it was to be sent to all the rest for their criticism and suggestions, ultimate differences of opinion to be settled at a general meeting of each Company. Learned men outside the board of revisers were to be invited to give their opinions in cases of special difficulty.

18. The Apocrypha

One of the Cambridge Companies was specially appointed to revise the Apoc, in which considerable license was taken, as the seven members composing the Company had probably no very firm belief in the inspiration of its books. The marginal notes, too, are freer in character than those of the OT. By the early translators, Tyndale and Coverdale, the Apoc was simply accepted as part of the heritage of the church; it had a place likewise in the Great Bible, the Bishops' Bible and most even of the Genevan copies. But by the middle of the 17th cent. opinion even in the Church of England had changed regarding it, and it was about this time that Bibles began to be printed having the canonical books only. The Apoc is now hardly at all printed otherwise than separately (note also should be taken of the treatment of the Apoc in the RV, as stated below).

Impressed with the importance of their task, the revisers worked strenuously at it for two years; and nine months more were devoted to revision by a special committee consisting of two members from each center, and in 1611 the result of the work appeared. It is not wonderful that the work was described by a contemporary entitled to give a judgment on it (Selden, *Table Talk*) as "the best tr in the world"—a verdict that later opinion has abundantly ratified. It was the copestone of a work on which 90 years of solid labor had by different hands been expended, and it was done by half a hundred of the foremost scholars of the day who knew Heb and Gr, and who also knew Eng. For three centuries it has grown in popular esteem, and it is justly regarded as one of the best possessions and one of the most unifying influences of the widely scattered English-speaking race.

On the title-page as issued in 1611 the version is described as "newly translated out of the original tongues" and as "appointed to be read in churches," two statements not easy to reconcile with the actual facts. The first rule for the revisers' guidance provided that the work was to consist in a revision of the Bishops' Bible: it was not said that it was to be a new tr. There is, further, no sanction of the version by King, Parliament, Convocation or Privy Council. Like Jerome's version twelve centuries before, it was left to find acceptance as best it might by its own intrinsic merit.

19. Further Revisions

Already in the days of the Commonwealth proposals were made for a new version; but though several meetings were held of a committee appointed by Parliament for the purpose in 1657, nothing came of the movement (Lewis, *History of Translations*, 354). For nearly half a century the chief rival of the AV was the Geneva Bible which was in wide private use. Formal revision was not undertaken again till the reign of Queen Victoria. But between 1611 and the date of the recent revision not a few small alterations had been silently introduced into the AV, as was indeed only to be expected if the changes in the orthography of the language were to be correctly represented on the printed page. Advancing literary criticism, too, and minute linguistic study showed that since the days of the revisers many words had changed their meaning, and that verbal inaccuracies and a few less venial errors could be proved in the revisers' work. But what probably weighed most with scholars in inducing them to enter upon a new version was the extraordinary increase that since the last revision had taken place in our knowledge of the Heb text and more especially of the Gr text of Scripture. Important MSS had been brought to light of which the 17th-cent. revisers knew nothing, and scholars had with minute care examined and compared all the early copies of the Scripture studies which, without altering the main import of the gospel story, were shown to have considerable importance on the actual words and sometimes on the meaning of the text. After much discussion of the subject in special volumes and in the leading magazines and reviews of Britain and America, there was a general agreement among scholars that a fresh version was advisable.

20. English Revised Version

The history of the Eng. revision is given at length in the preface to the ERV of the NT. It originated with the Convocation of Canterbury of the Church of England in the year 1870, when a committee of 16 members was appointed with power to add to its numbers. By this committee invitations to join it were issued to the outstanding Heb and Gr scholars of the country, irrespective of religious denomination, and eventually two Companies were formed, one for the OT and one for the NT, consisting each of 27 members, in which all the churches of the country were represented, the Roman Catholics alone excepted, and Dr. Newman had been invited to join the NT committee. The churches of America were also invited to coöperate, and this they did by forming two Companies corresponding to the British with due provision for the mutual comparison of results and suggestions. Where the suggestions from America were not accepted by the British revisers, they were recorded in an appendix to the published volume. The names of the revisers and the rules and principles laid down for the procedure of both Companies will be found in Eadie (II, 481 ff). The NT was published in May, 1881; the work occupied the Company for about 40 days in each year for 10 years. The OT revision occupied the Company for 792 days in a period of 14 years. The entire Bible was published in May, 1885. It did not include the Apoc, a revision of which was issued separately in 1895. This was undertaken, not by Convocation, but by the University Presses, a special Company being formed for the purpose from the OT and NT Companies.

21. American Revised Version

For American Revised Version see separate article. On Revised Version see also Bible.

22. Has the RV Displaced the AV?

The RV has been before the English-speaking world for a quarter of a century and it can hardly be said with safety that it has as yet made any progress in displacing the AV in public esteem. Of course as much could be said for the AV in its day. It was very slow in gaining acceptance with the people: and yet unreasoning affection for its very words and phraseology is now one of the main obstacles to the acceptance of an admittedly more scientifically based original text and a more correct and not displeasing rendering of the same. A large number of the changes are certainly not such as appeal strongly to popular sympathy. "The Gr text of the NT of 1881 has been estimated to differ from that of 1611 in no less than 5,788 readings, of which about a quarter are held notably to modify the subject-matter; though even of these only a small proportion can be considered as of first-rate importance" (Kenyon, 239). On the other hand Heb, and esp. the cognate Semitic languages, are now a great deal better known than before 1611, and considerable improvement is noticeable in the bringing out of the meaning in the poetical and prophetical books. The RV contains the best results of the scholarship of the Victorian age and cannot fail to be regarded as of the greatest utility to the reader and student of the AV. In the religious life the mind is essentially conservative, and nothing but time will show whether the undoubted merits of the RV are such as to outweigh the claims of sentiment and affection with which the AV is held. See further AMERICAN REVISED VERSION.

LITERATURE.—Perhaps the most complete work on the subject in all its aspects is that by Dr. John Eadie, *The English Bible: an External and Critical History of the Various English Trs of Scripture*, 1876. Eadie was himself one of the revisers of 1870, and some of his concluding chapters contain "Remarks on the Need of Revision of the English NT." He is also highly appreciative but judiciously critical of his predecessors in the same field, e.g. of Lewis, *Complete History of Several Trs of the Holy Bible and NT into Eng.*, 1731, 1818; and Christopher Anderson, *The Annals of the English Bible*, 2 vols, 1845, 1 vol rev. ed, 1862. An earlier and also very good book is Westcott's *General View of the History of the English Bible*, 1868. Westcott was also one of the revisers of 1870 and criticizes the work of the various translators as well as narrates the succession of the trs. A good discussion of the internal history of the text will also be found in the *History of the English Bible* by Dr. Moulton, another of the revisers. Kenyon, *Our Bible and Ancient MSS*, 1895, considers specially the text on which the successive Eng. VSS were based. He writes judiciously also on the Wycliffe period and on the RV. The Wycliffe period should also be studied in Forshall and Madden, 4 vols, 4to, Oxford, 1850; *England in the Age of Wycliffe*, by G. M. Trevelyan; Dr. Gasquet's *Our Old English Bible and Other Essays*, 1908; and Lechler's *John Wycliffe and His English Precursors*, trd and edited by Lorimer. For the Reformation period generally Foxe's *History of the Acts and Monuments of the Church* still deserves to be studied. "Foxe's story is doubtless substantially true, although disfigured by credulity and bitter prejudice." For Tyndale's special work see *William Tyndale, a Biography*, by R. Demaus, new ed by Lovett, 1886; and Fry's *Bibliographical Descriptions of the Editions of the NT, Tyndale's Version in Eng.* Fry has also written special works on the Great Bible, Cranmer's Bible and the Genevan Version. The AV is very fully described in the works above mentioned, and in this connection notice is due to Scrivener, *The Authorised Edition of the English Bible*, 1884, and more esp. to his careful and thorough "Introduction" to the *Quarto Paragraph Bible*, 1873. More popular histories of the Bible are those of Stoughton, Pattison, 1874, and Professor Milligan of Glasgow, 1895. General histories of England and of Eng. literature may also be profitably consulted on the history of the Bible and its tr into the vernacular, such as those of Hume, Burnet, Hallam, Froude, Green and Gardiner. The revision of the AV called forth a large literature, either in the way of preparation for it or of criticism of it when carried through. To this literature many of the revisers themselves contributed, among whom may be mentioned Eadie, Ellicott, Westcott, Humphry, Newth and Kennedy; nor should the important contributions of Archbishop Trench and Dean Alford, though of a slightly earlier generation, be overlooked. The American revisers also republished a series of Essays written by some of their number on *Biblical Revision: Its Necessity and Purpose*, 1879; and account should be taken also of the *Documentary History of the American Committee on Revision* prepared by that committee for the use of its members.

J. HUTCHISON

ENGRAFT, en-graft' (Jas **1** 21 AV, RV IMPLANT [q.v.]).

ENGRAVING, en-grāv'ing. See CARVING; CRAFTS.

EN-HADDAH, en-had'a (עֵין חַדָּה, *'ēn ḥaddāh*, "swift fountain"): A town in the lot of Issachar mentioned along with En-gannim (Josh **19** 21). It is probably identical with *Kefr Adān*, a village some 3 miles W. of *Jenīn*.

EN-HAKKORE, en-hak'ō-rē, en-hak-ō'rē (עֵין הַקּוֹרֵא, *'ēn ha-ḳōrē'*, "spring of the partridge"): Interpreted (Jgs **15** 19) as meaning "the spring of him that called." So LXX: πηγὴ τοῦ ἐπικαλουμένου, *pēgē toú epikalouménou*. The spring was in Lehi but the site is unknown.

EN-HAZOR, en-hā'zor (עֵין חָצוֹר, *'ēn ḥāçōr;* πηγὴ 'Ασόρ, *pēgē Asór*): A city in the territory of Naphtali mentioned along with Kedesh, Edrei and Iron (Josh **19** 37). The ancient name probably survives in that of *Hazīreh*, on the slopes W. of Kedesh. "En" however points to a fountain. and no fountain has been found here.

ENIGMA, ē-nig'ma. See GAMES.

ENJOIN, en-join': Its usual sense is "to impose something," as a command, a charge or a direction. In this last sense it is used in Job **36** 23, i.e. "Who hath directed?" In Est **9** 31 it means "to command"; in Philem ver 8, "to order" or "direct."

ENLARGE, en-lärj', **ENLARGEMENT**, en-lärj'ment: "To enlarge" is very frequently used **fig.**: "God enlarge Japheth" (Gen **9** 27), i.e. "make him a great nation"; or "Thou hast enlarged my steps under me" (2 S **22** 37), i.e. "Thou hast given me success." A very peculiar use of "enlarge" is found in AV Ps **4** 1: "Thou hast enlarged me" (RV "set me at large"), i.e. "Thou hast given me freedom, deliverance from distress." "Our heart is enlarged" (πλατύνω, *platúnō;* 2 Cor **6** 11), and "Be ye also enlarged" (ver 13), express great love of one party to another. See also 1 S **2** 1, "My mouth is enlarged," i.e. "full of praise." Ezk **41** 7, "were broader" (AV "an enlarging").

Enlargement, AV Est **4** 14 from רֶוַח, *rāwaḥ*, "to enlarge," "to respite," is rendered "relief" by RV in better harmony with "deliverance" with which the word is paired. A. L. BRESLICH

ENLIGHTEN, en-līt''n:

(1) אוֹר, *'ōr*, "illumination" in every sense, used in the ordinary sense of giving natural light (Ps **97** 4 AV; see also Ezr **9** 8) or as a sign of health and vigor (1 S **14** 27.29). "His eyes were enlightened," lit. "became bright." He had become weary and faint with the day's exertions and anxieties, and now recovers (see Job **33** 30 and cf Ps **13** 3). Thus in sickness and grief, the eyes are dull and heavy; dying eyes are glazed; but health and joy render them bright and sparkling, as with a light from within.

(2) In Ps **18** 28 AV, the word נָגַהּ, *nāghah*, **fig.** describes the believer's deliverance from the gloom of adversity and the restoration of joy in the knowledge of God.

(3) Most frequently the terms so trd mean the giving of spiritual light to the soul (Ps **19** 8; Eph **1** 18, φωτίζω, *phōtízō;* He **6** 4; **10** 32). This spiritual enlightening the Spirit of God brings about through the Divine word (Ps **119** 130; 2 Tim **3** 15; 2 Pet **1** 19). Sin mars the intellectual discernment; "but he that is spiritual discerneth all things" (1 Cor **2** 15 AVm). M. O. EVANS

EN-MISHPAT, en-mish'pat. See KADESH.

ENMITY, en'mi-ti (אֵיבָה, *'ēbhāh;* ἔχθρα, *échthra*): "Enmity" (hate) occurs as the tr of *'ēbhāh* in Gen **3** 15, "I will put enmity between thee and the woman, and between thy seed and her seed," and in Nu **35** 21.22, where the absence of enmity on the part of the man-slayer modifies the judgment to be passed on him.

In the NT "enmity" is the tr of *echthra:* Lk **23** 12; Rom **8** 7, "The mind of the flesh is enmity against God." Jas **4** 4, "The friendship of the world is enmity with God" (because "the world" is preferred to God); in Eph **2** 15.16, Christ is said to have "abolished in his flesh the enmity," by His cross to have "slain the enmity," that is, the opposition between Jew and Gentile, creating in Himself "one new man, [so] making peace." See also ABOLISH; HATE. W. L. WALKER

ENNATAN, en'a-tan (**Ἐνναtάν**, *Ennatán;* AV Eunatan [a misprint]): One of Ezra's messengers to fetch Levites for the temple service (1 Esd **8** 44); called "Elnathan" in Ezr **8** 16.

ENOCH, ē'nok (חֲנוֹךְ, *ḥănōkh,* "initiated"; **Ἐνώχ**, *Henōch*):

(1) The eldest son of Cain (Gen **4** 17.18).

(2) The son of Jared and father of Methuselah, seventh in descent from Adam in the line of Seth (Jude ver 14). He is said (Gen **5** 23) to have lived 365 years, but the brief record of his life is comprised in the words, "Enoch walked with God: and he was not; for God took him" (Gen **5** 24). The expression "walked with God" denotes a devout life, lived in close communion with God, while the reference to his end has always been understood, as by the writer of He, to mean, "By faith Enoch was translated that he should not see death; and he was not found, because God translated him" (He **11** 5). See further, APOCALYPTIC LITERATURE, II, i, 1. A. C. GRANT

ENOCH (CITY): In Gen **4** 17 it is narrated that Cain, who had taken up his abode in the land of Nod, E. of Eden (ver 16), built there a city, and called it after the name of his firstborn son Enoch. It is impossible to fix more definitely the locality of this first of cities, recorded, as Delitzsch says (*Genesis,* in loc.), as registering an advance in civilization. The "city" would be a very simple affair, a place of protection for himself, wife and household, perhaps connected with the fear spoken of in **4** 14.

ENOCH, ETHIOPIC, ē-thi-op'ik, **BOOK OF.** See APOCALYPTIC LITERATURE.

ENOCH, SLAVONIC, sla-von'ik, **BOOK OF.** See APOCALYPTIC LITERATURE.

ENOCH, THE BOOK OF THE SECRETS OF. See APOCALYPTIC LITERATURE.

ENORMITY, e-nôr'mi-ti: The marginal rendering in AV of Hos **6** 9 for "lewdness," and in RV of Lev **18** 17; **19** 29; **20** 14 for "wickedness." In each case it is the tr of זִמָּה, *zimmāh,* meaning originally, "thought" or "plot," mostly in a bad sense, lewdness, wickedness; in Lev it is unnatural wickedness—incest.

ENOS, ē'nos, **ENOSH,** ē'nosh (אֱנוֹשׁ, *'ĕnōsh,* "mortal"; **Ἐνώς**, *Enōs*): In the NT (RV and AV) and the OT (AV except 1 Ch **1** 1), the form is Enos; in the OT (RV and 1 Ch **1** 1 AV), the form is Enosh. The son of Seth and grandson of Adam (Gen **4** 26; **5** 6 ff; 1 Ch **1** 1; Lk **3** 38). *Enosh* denotes man as frail and mortal. With Enosh a new religious development began, for "then began men to call upon the name of Jeh" (Gen **4** 26). There seems to be an implied contrast to Gen **4** 17 ff which records a development in another department of life, represented by Enoch the son of Cain. S. F. HUNTER

ENQUIRE, en-kwīr': This is an OE word now obsolescent. It is common in AV. In ARV it is nearly always replaced by the more modern "inquire," a few times by "seek" and "ask," once by "salute" (1 Ch **18** 10). With this one exception in the OT the change does not affect the meaning. In Acts **23** 15, "enquire something more perfectly" is substituted by "judge more exactly." In Mt **10** 11, "search out" replaces it. In Mt **2** 7.16, "learned exactly" replaces "inquired diligently." See INQUIRE.

EN-RIMMON, en-rim'on (עֵין־רִמּוֹן, *'ēn-rimmōn,* "the fountain of Rimmon" [see RIMMON], or perhaps "the spring of the pomegranate"; **Ἐρωμώθ**, *Erōmōth,* **Ῥεμμών**, *Rhemmōn*): A city of Judah (Josh **15** 32), "Ain and Rimmon"; ascribed to Simeon (Josh **19** 7; 1 Ch **4** 32, "Ain, Rimmon"). In Neh **11** 29 mentioned as reinhabited after the Captivity. Zec **14** 10, runs: "All the land shall be made like the Arabah, from Geba to Rimmon, south of Jerus." It must have been a very southerly place. In the *Onom* ("Erimmon") it is described as a "very large village 16 miles S. of Eleutheropolis." *Kh. Umm er Rumāmīn,* 9 miles N. of Beersheba is the usually accepted site. See *PEF,* 398; Sh XXIV. E. W. G. MASTERMAN

EN-ROGEL, en-rō'gel (עֵין רֹגֵל, *'ēn rōghēl;* **πηγὴ Ῥωγήλ**, *pēgē Rhōgēl;* meaning uncertain, but interpreted by some to mean "the spring of the fuller"):

No argument from this meaning can be valid because (1) it is a very doubtful rendering and (2) "fulling" vats are common in the neighborhood of most town springs and are today plentiful at both the proposed sites. G. A. Smith thinks "spring of the current," or "stream," from Syr *rogûlo,* more probable.

(1) En-rogel was an important landmark on the boundary between Judah and Benjamin (Josh **15** 7; **18** 16). Here David's spies, Jonathan and Ahimaaz, hid themselves (2 S **17** 17), and here (1 K **1** 9) "Adonijah slew sheep and oxen and fatlings by the stone of Zoheleth, which is beside En-rogel," when he anticipated his father's death and caused himself rebelliously to be proclaimed king.

(2) The identification of this important landmark is of first-class importance in Jerus topography. Two sites have been proposed:

(*a*) The older view identifies En-rogel with the spring known variously as "the Virgin's Fount," *'Ain sitti Miriam* and *'Ain Umm el deraj,* an intermittent source of water which rises in a cave on the W. side of the Kedron valley opposite Siloam (see GIHON). The arguments that this is the one Jerus spring and that this must have been a very important landmark are inconclusive. The strongest argument for this view is that put forward by M. Clermont-Ganneau, who found that a rough rock surface on the mountain slope opposite, an ascent to the village of *Silwân,* is known as *es Zehweleh,* a word in which there certainly appears to linger an echo of Zoheleth. The argument is, however, not as convincing as it seems. Firstly, Zoheleth was a stone; this is a natural rock scarp; such a stone might probably have been transferred from place to place. Secondly, it is quite common for a name to be transferred some miles; instances are numerous. Thirdly, the writer, after frequent inquiries of the *fellahîn* of *Silwân,* is satisfied that the name is by no means confined to the rock scarp near the spring, but to the whole ridge running along from here to, or almost to, *Bîr Eyyûb* itself. The strongest argument against this identification is, however, that there are so much stronger reasons for identifying the "Virgin's Fount" with Gihon (see GIHON), and that the two springs En-rogel and Gihon cannot be at one site, as is clear from the narrative in 1 K **1**.

(*b*) The view which places En-rogel at *Bîr Eyyûb* in every way harmonizes with the Bible data. It has been objected that the latter is not a spring but a well. It is today a well, 125 ft. deep, but one with an inexhaustible supply—there must be a true spring at the bottom. Probably one reason it only overflows today after periods of heavy rain is that such enormous quantities of débris have now covered the original valley bed that the water cannot rise to the surface; much of it flows away down the valley deep under the present surface. The water is brackish and is impregnated with sewage, which is not extraordinary when we remember that a large part of the rock strata from which the water comes is overlaid by land constantly irrigated with the city's sewage.

Although the well may itself be of considerable antiquity, there is no need to insist that this is the *exact position* of the original spring En-rogel. The source may in olden times have arisen at some spot in the valley bottom which is now deeply buried under the rubbish, perhaps under the southernmost of the irrigated gardens of the *fellahîn* of *Silwân*. The neighborhood, at the junction of two deep valleys—not to count the small *el wâd*, the ancient Tyropœon—is a natural place for a spring. There would appear to have been considerable disturbance here. An enormous amount of débris from various destructions of the city has collected here, but, besides this, Jos records a tradition which appears to belong to this neighborhood. He says (*Ant*, IX, x, 4) that an earthquake took place once at Eroge—which appears to be En-rogel—when "half of the mountain broke off from the remainder on the W., and rolling 4 furlongs, came to stand on the eastern mountain till the roads, as well as the king's gardens, were blocked." It is sufficient that En-rogel is to be located either at *Bîr Eyyûb* or in its immediate neighborhood; for practical purposes the former will do. En-rogel was an important point on the boundary line between Judah and Benjamin. The line passed down the lower end of the Kidron valley, past En-rogel (*Bîr Eyyûb*) and then up the Valley of Hinnom (*Wady er Rabābi*)—a boundary well adapted to the natural conditions.

With regard to David's spies (2 S **17** 17), whereas the Virgin's Fount—the great source of the city's water supply (see GIHON)—just below the city walls (see ZION) was an impossible place of hiding, this lower source, out of sight of almost the whole city and removed a considerable distance from its nearest point, was at least a possible place. Further, the facts that it was off the main road, that it afforded a supply of one of the main necessities of life—water—and that there were, as there are today, many natural caves in the neighborhood, greatly added to its suitability.

Here too was a most appropriate place for Adonijah's plot (1 K **1** 9). He and his confederates dared not go to Gihon, the original sacred spring, but had to content themselves with a spot more secluded, though doubtless still sacred. It is recorded (1 K **1** 40.41) that the adherents of Solomon saluted him at Gihon (the Virgin's Fount) and the people "rejoiced with great joy, so that the earth rent with the sound of them. And Adonijah and all the guests that were with him [at En-rogel] heard it as they had made an end of eating." The relative positions of these two springs allow of a vivid reconstruction of the narrative as do no other proposed identifications. The two spots are out of sight the one of the other, but not so far that the shout of a multitude at the one could not be carried to the other. E. W. G. MASTERMAN

ENROLMENT, en-rōl'ment. See QUIRINIUS; TAX.

ENSAMPLE, en-sam'p'l. See EXAMPLE.

EN-SHEMESH, en-shē'mesh (עֵין־שֶׁמֶשׁ, *'ēn shemesh*, "spring of the sun"): An important landmark on the boundary line between Judah and Benjamin (Josh **15** 7; **18** 17). The little spring *'Ain el ḥaud*, E. of Bethany, the last spring on the road descending to Jericho, seems to suit the conditions. *'Ain el ḥaud* is usually called the "Apostles' Fountain" by Christians, on account of a tradition dating from the 15th cent. that the apostles drank there.

ENSIGN, en'sīn. See BANNER.

ENSUE, en-sū': Synonymous with "to pursue," "ensue" is found in 1 Pet **3** 11 AV as a tr of διώκω, *diōkō*, "to follow after," "to pursue." Also in Jth **9** 5, "such as ensued after" (τὰ μετέπειτα, *tá metépeita*, "the things that follow").

ENTANGLE, en-taṇ'g'l: Found but 5 t in the Scriptures (AV), once in the OT, yet most significant as illustrating the process of mental, moral and spiritual confusion and enslavement.

(1) Used of *physical* entanglement, as in the mazes of a labyrinth (בּוּךְ, *būkh*, "to involve," "be perplexed"). At Moses' command the children of Israel, before crossing the Red Sea, took the wrong way in order to give Pharaoh the impression that they were lost in the wilderness and cause him to say "They are entangled in the land" (Ex **14** 3).

(2) *Mental:* παγιδεύω, *pagideúō*, "to entrap," "ensnare," with words, as birds are caught in a snare; cf Eccl **9** 12. The Pharisees sought to "entangle" (RV "ensnare") Jesus in His talk (Mt **22** 15).

(3) *Moral:* ἐμπλέκω, *emplékō*, "to inweave," hence intertwine and involve. "A good soldier of Jesus Christ," says Paul, does not "entangle himself," i.e. become involved, "in the affairs of this life" (2 Tim **2** 4). Having "escaped the defilements of the world," Christians are not to be "again entangled therein" (2 Pet **2** 20).

(4) *Spiritual:* ἐνέχω, *enéchō*, "to hold in," hence to hold captive, as a slave in fetters or under a burden. Having experienced spiritual emancipation, freedom, through Christ from bondage to sin and false religion (Gal **5** 1; cf **4** 8), the Gentiles were not to become "entangled again in a yoke of bondage" by submission to mere legal requirements, as the external rite of circumcision.

With reference to the thoroughness and irresistibleness of God's judgments, we read in Nah **1** 10, "For entangled like thorns" (AV "while they be folden together as thorns"), damp, closely packed and intertwined, "they are consumed utterly as dry stubble" (AV "devoured as stubble fully dry").

DWIGHT M. PRATT

EN-TAPPUAH, en-tap'ū-ä, en-ta-pū'a (עֵין תַּפּוּחַ, *'ēn tappūaḥ*; πηγὴ Θαφθώθ, *pēgḗ Thaphthōth*, "apple spring"): Probably in the land of Tappuah which belonged to Manasseh, although Tappuah, on the border of Manasseh, belonged to Ephraim (Josh **17** 7 f). It lay on the border of Ephraim which ran southward E. of Shechem, and is probably to be identified with the spring at *Yāsūf*, about 3 miles N. of Lebonah.

ENTREAT, en-trēt'. See INTREAT.

ENVY, en'vi (קִנְאָה, *ḳin'āh;* **ζῆλος,** *zḗlos,* **φθόνος,** *phthónos*): "Envy," from Lat *in,* "against," and *video,* "to look," "to look with ill-will," etc, toward another, is an evil strongly condemned in both the OT and the NT. It is to be distinguished from jealousy. "We are *jealous* of our own; we are *envious* of another man's possessions. *Jealousy* fears to lose what it has; *envy* is pained at seeing another have" (Crabb's *Eng. Synonyms*). In the OT it is the tr of *ḳin'āh* from *ḳānā',* "to redden," "to glow" (Job **5** 2, RV "jealousy," m "indignation"; in Isa **26** 11 RV renders "see thy zeal for the people"; Prov **27** 4, etc); the vb. occurs in Gen **26** 14, etc; Nu **11** 29 AV; Ps **106** 16; Prov **3** 31, etc; in the NT it is the tr of *phthonos,* "envy" (Mt **27** 18; Rom **1** 29; Gal **5** 21, "envyings," etc); of *zēlos,* "zeal," "jealousy," "envy" (Acts **13** 45), trd "envying," RV "jealousy" (Rom **13** 13; 1 Cor **3** 3; 2 Cor **12** 20; Jas **3** 14.16); the vb. *phthonéō* occurs in Gal **5** 26; *zēlóō* in Acts **7** 9; **17** 5, RV "moved with jealousy"; 1 Cor **13** 4, "charity [RV "love"] envieth not."

The power of envy is stated in Prov **27** 4: "Who is able to stand before envy?" (RV "jealousy"); its evil effects are depicted in Job **5** 2 (RV "jealousy"), in Prov **14** 30 (RVm "jealousy"); it led to the crucifixion of Christ (Mt **27** 18; Mk **15** 10); it is one of "the works of the flesh" (Gal **5** 21; cf Rom **1** 29; 1 Tim **6** 4); Christian believers are earnestly warned against it (Rom **13** 13 AV; 1 Cor **3** 3 AV; Gal **5** 26; 1 Pet **2** 1). In Jas **4** 5 "envy" is used in a good sense, akin to the *jealousy* ascribed to God. Where AV has "The *spirit* that dwelleth in us lusteth to envy," RV reads "Doth the spirit which he made to dwell in us long unto envying?"; ARVm "The spirit which he made to dwell in us he yearneth for even unto jealous envy"; cf Jer **3** 14; Hos **2** 19f; or ERVm "That spirit which he made to dwell in us yearneth [for us] even unto jealous envy." This last seems to give the sense; cf "Ye adulteresses" (ver 4), ARVm "*That is,* who break your marriage vow to God." W. L. WALKER

EPAENETUS, ep-ē'ne-tus (**Ἐπαίνετος,** *Epaínetos,* "praised"): One of the Christians at Rome to whom greetings are sent by Paul (Rom **16** 5). All that is known of him is told here. Paul describes him as (1) "my beloved," (2) "who is the firstfruits of Asia unto Christ." *TR* has "firstfruits of Achaia" but this wrong reading is due to 1 Cor **16** 15. He was one of the first Christians in the Rom province of Asia.

This salutation brings up the question of the destination of vs 3–16, for it is argued that they are addressed to the church in Ephesus owing to the fact that Prisca and Aquila and Epaenetus are known to have dwelt in Asia. On the other hand, there are more than 20 others in this list who are not known to have spent any time in Asia. Prisca and Aquila had once dwelt in Rome (Acts **18** 2), and there is nothing unusual in an Ephesian dwelling in the capital of the empire. An interesting discovery was made in Rome of an inscription in which was the name of Epaenetus, an Ephesian.
S. F. HUNTER

EPAPHRAS, ep'a-fras (**Ἐπαφρᾶς,** *Epaphrás*): A contracted form of Epaphroditus. He must not, however, be confounded with the messenger of the Philippian community. He was with Paul during a part of his 1st Rom imprisonment, joining in Paul's greetings to Philemon (Philem ver 23). Epaphras was the missionary by whose instrumentality the Colossians had been converted to Christianity (Col **1** 7), and probably the other churches of the Lycus had been founded by him. In sending his salutation to the Colossians Paul testified, "He hath much labor for you, and for them in Laodicea, and for them in Hierapolis" (Col **4** 13). Epaphras had brought to Paul good news of the progress of the gospel, of their "faith in Christ Jesus" and of their love toward all the saints (Col **1** 4). Paul's regard for him is shown by his designating him "our beloved fellow-servant," "a faithful minister of Christ" (Col **1** 7), and "a bondservant of Christ Jesus" (Col **4** 12 m). The last designation Paul uses several times of himself, but only once of another besides Epaphras (Phil **1** 1). S. F. HUNTER

EPAPHRODITUS, ē-paf-rō-dī'tus (**Ἐπαφρόδιτος,** *Epaphróditos,* "lovely"): Mentioned only in Phil **2** 25; **4** 18. The name corresponds to the Lat Venustus (=handsome), and was very common in the Rom period. "The name occurs very frequently in inscriptions both Gr and Lat, whether at full length Epaphroditus, or in its contracted form Epaphras" (Lightfoot, *Philippians,* 123). Epaphroditus was the delegate of the Christian community at Philippi, sent with their gift to Paul during his first Rom imprisonment. Paul calls him "my brother and fellow-worker and fellow-soldier." "The three words are arranged in an ascending scale: common sympathy, common work, common danger and toil and suffering" (Lightfoot, l.c.). On his arrival at Rome, Epaphroditus devoted himself to "the work of Christ," both as Paul's attendant and as his assistant in missionary work. So assiduously did he labor that he lost his health, and "was sick nigh unto death." He recovered, however, and Paul sent him back to Philippi with this letter to quiet the alarm of his friends, who had heard of his serious illness. Paul besought for him that the church should receive him with joy and hold him in honor.
S. F. HUNTER

EPHAH, ē'fa (עֵיפָה, *'ēphāh,* "darkness"; **Γεφάρ,** *Gephár* [Gen **25** 4], **Γαιφά,** *Gaiphá* [Isa **60** 6]): The name of three persons in the OT, both masc. and fem.

(1) The son of Midian, descended from Abraham by his wife Keturah (Gen **25** 4=1 Ch **1** 33), mentioned again in Isa **60** 6 as a transporter of gold and frankincense from Sheba, who shall thus bring enlargement to Judah and praise to Jeh. According to Fried. Delitzsch, Schrader, and Hommel, *'Ēphāh* is an abbreviation of *'Ayappa,* the Khayappa Arabs of the time of Tiglath-pileser III and Sargon. See treatment of this view in Dillmann's *Comm. on Gen* (**25** 4).

(2) A concubine of Caleb (1 Ch **2** 46).

(3) The son of Jahdai, a descendant of Judah (1 Ch **2** 47). CHARLES B. WILLIAMS

EPHAH, ē'fa (אֵיפָה, *'ēphāh*): A dry measure of about one bushel capacity. It corresponds to the bath in liquid measure and was the standard for measuring grain and similar articles since it is classed with balances and weights (Lev **19** 36; Am **8** 5) in the injunctions regarding just dealing in trade. In Zec **5** 6–10 it is used for the utensil itself (see WEIGHTS AND MEASURES).

EPHAI, ē'fī, ē'fā-ī (עֵיפַי, *'ēphay,* in Ḳerē, עוֹפַי, *'ōphai,* in Kethībh; **Ἰωφέ,** *Iōphé,* **Ὠφέ,** *Ōphé,* "gloomy," "obscuring," in LXX): "The Netophathite," whose sons were numbered among "the captains of the forces" left in Judah after the carrying away to Babylon (Jer **40** [LXX 47] 8). His sons assembled at Mizpah with Gedaliah, governor of the scattered Jews, and with him were slain by Ishmael, the son of Nethaniah (Jer **41** 3).

EPHER, ē'fẽr (עֵפֶר, *'ēpher,* "calf," "young deer"; **Ἄφερ,** *Ápher,* **Ὄφερ,** *Ópher*):

(1) The second son of Midian, descended from

Abraham by his wife Keturah (Gen **25** 4; 1 Ch **1** 33). See further Dillmann's *Comm. on Gen* (**25** 4).

(2) The third son of Ezra, descended from the tribe of Judah (1 Ch **4** 17).

(3) The first of five heads of their fathers' houses, "mighty men of valor, famous men," in the half-tribe of Manasseh, who dwelt between Bashan and Mt. Hermon (1 Ch **5** 23.24).

EPHES-DAMMIM, ē-fes-dam′im (אֶפֶס דַּמִּים, *'epheṣ dammīm*): Some spot between Socoh and Azekah (1 S **17** 1) where the Philis were encamped; called in 1 Ch **11** 13, "Pas-dammin." Ephes = "end of" or "boundary" and the whole word may mean the "boundary of blood." The deep red color of the newly ploughed earth in this situation is noticeable and may have given origin to the idea of "blood" (cf Adammim). Cheyne suggests that from אֲדֻמִּים, *'ădhummīn*, to דַּמִּים, *dammīm*, is an easy step, and that the former, meaning "red brown earth," may have been the original. No other satisfactory locality has been found to explain the name or fix the site. E. W. G. Masterman

EPHESIAN, e-fē′zhan (Ἐφέσιος, *Ephésios*), **EPHESIANS**, e-fē′zhanz: A term which, as in Acts **19** 28.34.35 and **21** 29, was applied to those natives or residents of the city of Ephesus who were adherents of the cult of the goddess Diana. A Jew or a Christian, though a native of Ephesus, would probably have been designated as such, rather than as an Ephesian.

EPHESIANS, EPISTLE TO THE:

I. Authenticity.—None of the epistles which are ascribed to St. Paul have a stronger chain of evidence to their early and continued use than that which we know as the Epistle to the Ephesians. Leaving for the moment the question of the relation of Eph to other NT writings, we find that it not only colors the phraseology of the Apostolic Fathers, but is actually quoted. In Clement of Rome (c 95 AD) the connection with Eph might be due to some common liturgical form in xlvi.6 (cf Eph **4** 6); though the resemblance is so close that we must feel that our epistle was known to Clement both here and in lxiv (cf Eph **1** 3-4); xxxviii (cf **5** 21); xxxvi (cf **4** 18); lix (cf **1** 18; **4** 18). Ignatius (d. 115) shows numerous points of contact with Eph, esp. in his Epistle to the Ephesians. In cap. xii we read: "Ye are associates and fellow students of the mysteries with Paul, who in every letter makes mention of you in Christ Jesus." It is difficult to decide the exact meaning of the phrase "every letter," but in spite of the opinion of many scholars that it must be rendered "in all his epistle," i.e. in every part of his epistle, it is safer to take it as an exaggeration, "in all his epistles," justified to some extent in the fact that besides Eph St. Paul does mention the Ephesian Christians in Rom (**16** 5); 1 Cor (**15** 32; **16** 8.19); 2 Cor (**1** 8 f); 1 Tim (**1** 3) and 2 Tim (**1** 18). In the opening address the connection with Eph **1** 3-6 is too close to be accidental. There are echoes of our epistle in cap. i (**6** 1); ix (**2** 20-22); xviii (*oikonomia*, **1** 10); xx (**2** 18; **4** 24); and in *Ignat. ad Polyc.* v we have close identity with Eph **5** 25 and less certain connection with Eph **4** 2, and in vi with Eph **6** 13-17. The Epistle of Polycarp in two passages shows verbal agreement with Eph: in cap. i with Eph **1** **8**, and in xii with Eph **4** 26, where we have (the Gr is missing here) *ut his scripturis dictum est.* Hermas speaks of the grief of the Holy Spirit in such a way as to suggest Eph (*Mand.* X, ii; cf Eph **4** 30). Sim. IX, xiii, shows a knowledge of Eph **4** 3-6, and possibly of **5** 26 and **1** 13. In the *Did* (4) we find a ‖ to Eph **6** 5: "Servants submit yourselves to your masters." In Barnabas there are two or three turns of phrase that are possibly due to Eph. There is a slightly stronger connection between II Clement and Eph, esp. in cap. xiv, where we have the Ephesian figure of the church as the body of Christ, and the relation between them referred to in terms of husband and wife.

1. External Evidence

This early evidence, slight though it is, is strengthened by the part Eph played in the 2d cent. where, as we learn from Hippolytus, it was used by the Ophites and Basilides and Valentinus. The latter (according to Hip., *Phil.*, VI, 29) quoted Eph **3** 16-18, saying, "This is what has been written in Scripture," while his disciple Ptolemais is said by Irenaeus (*Adv. Haer*, i.8, 5) to have attributed Eph **5** 13 to St. Paul by name. According to the addenda to the eighth book of the *Stromateis* of Clement of Alexandria, Theodotus, a contemporary of Valentinus, quoted Eph **4** 10 and 30 with the words: "The apostle says," and attributes Eph **4** 24 to St. Paul. Marcion knew Eph as Tertullian tells us, identifying it with the epistle referred to in Col **4** 16 as *ad Laodicenos*. We find it in the Muratorian Fragment (10*b*, l. 20) as the second of the epistles which "Paul wrote following the example of his predecessor John." It is used in the letter from the church of Lyons and Vienne and by Irenaeus, Tertullian, Clement of Alexandria, Origen and later writers. We can well accept the dictum of Dr. Hort that it "is all but certain on this evidence that the Epistle was in existence by 95 AD; quite certain that it was in existence by about fifteen years later or conceivably a little more" (Hort, *Judaistic Christianity*, 118).

2. Internal Evidence

To this very strong chain of external evidence, reaching back to the very beginning of the 2d cent., if not into the end of the 1st, showing Eph as part of the original Pauline collection which no doubt Ignatius and Polycarp used, we must add the evidence of the epistle itself, testing it to see if there be any reason why the letter thus early attested should not be accredited to the apostle.

(1) That it claims to be written by St. Paul is seen not only in the greeting, "Paul, an apostle of Christ Jesus through the will of God, to the saints that are at Ephesus," but also in **3** 1, where we read: "For this cause I Paul, the prisoner of Christ Jesus in behalf of you Gentiles," a phrase which is continued in **4** 1: "I therefore, the prisoner in the Lord." This claim is substantiated by the general character of the epistle which is written after the Pauline norm, with greeting and thanksgiving, leading on to and serving as the introduction of the special doctrinal teaching of the epistle. This is the first great division of the Pauline epistles and is regularly followed by an application of the teaching to practical matters, which in turn yields to personal greetings, or salutations, and the final benediction, commonly written by the apostle's own hand. In only one particular does Eph fail to answer completely to this outline. The absence of the personal greetings has always been marked

as a striking peculiarity of our letter. The explanation of this peculiarity will meet us when we consider the destination of the epistle (see III below).

(2) Further evidence for the Pauline authorship is found in the general style and language of the letter. We may agree with von Soden (*Early Christ. Lit.*, 294) that "every sentence contains verbal echoes of Pauline epistles, indeed except when ideas peculiar to the Epistle come to expression it is simply a mosaic of Pauline phraseology," without accepting his conclusion that St. Paul did not write it. We feel, as we read, that we have in our hands the work of one with whom the other epistles have made us familiar. Yet we are conscious none the less of certain subtle differences which give occasion for the various arguments that critics have brought against the claim that St. Paul is the actual author. This is not questioned until the beginning of the last century, but has been since Schleiermacher and his disciple Usteri, though the latter published his doubts before his master did his. The Tübingen scholars attacked the epistle mainly on the ground of supposed traces of Gnostic or Montanist influences, akin to those ascribed to the Colossians. Later writers have given over this claim to put forward others based on differences of style (De Wette, followed by Holtzmann, von Soden and others); dependence on Colossians (Hitzig, Holtzmann); the attitude to the Apostles (von Soden); doctrinal differences, esp. those that concern Christology and the Parousia, the conception of the church (Klöpper, Wrede and others). The tendency, however, seems to be backward toward a saner view of the questions involved; and most of those who do not accept the Pauline authorship would probably agree with Jülicher (*EB*), who ascribes it to a "Pauline Christian intimately familiar with the Pauline epistles, esp. with Col, writing about 90," who sought in Eph "to put in a plea for the true catholicism in the meaning of Paul and in his name."

(3) Certain of these positions require that we should examine the doctrinal objections. (*a*) First of these is the claim that Eph has a different conception of the person and work of Christ from the acknowledged epistles of St. Paul. Not only have we the exaltation of Christ which we find in Col **1** 16 ff, but the still further statement that it was God's purpose from the beginning to "sum up all things in Christ, the things in the heavens, and the things upon the earth" (Eph **1** 10). This is no more than the natural expansion of the term, "all things," which are attributed to Christ in 1 Cor **8** 6, and is an idea which has at least its foreshadowing in Rom **8** 19 20 and 2 Cor **5** 18.19. The relation between Christ and the church as given in **1** 22 and **5** 23 is in entire agreement with St. Paul's teaching in Rom **12** and 1 Cor **12**. It is still the Pauline figure of the church as the body of Christ, in spite of the fact that Christ is not thought of as the head of that body. The argument in the epistle does not deal with the doctrine of the cross from the standpoint of the earlier epistles, but the teaching is exactly the same. There is redemption (**1** 7.14; **4** 30); reconciliation (**2** 14–16); forgiveness (**1** 7; **4** 32). The blood of Christ shed on the cross redeems us from our sin and restores us to God. In like manner it is said that the Parousia is treated (**2** 7) as something far off. But St. Paul has long since given up the idea that it is immediately; even in 2 Thess **2** he shows that an indeterminate interval must intervene, and in Rom **11** 25 he sees a period of time yet unfulfilled before the end. (*b*) The doctrine of the church is the most striking contrast to the earlier epistles. We have already dealt with the relation of Christ to the church. The conception of the church universal is in advance of the earlier epistles, but it is the natural climax of the development of the apostle's conception of the church as shown in the earlier epistles. Writing from Rome with the idea of the empire set before him, it was natural that Paul should see the church as a great whole, and should use the word *ecclesia* absolutely as signifying the oneness of the Christian brotherhood. As a matter of fact the word is used in this absolute sense in 1 Cor **12** 28 before the Captivity Epistles (cf 1 Cor **1** 2; **10** 32). The emphasis here on the unity of Jew and Gentile in the church finds its counterpart in the argument of the Epistle to the Rom, though in Eph this is "urged on the basis of God's purpose and Christian faith, rather than on the Law and the Promises." Neither is it true that in Eph the Law is spoken of slightingly, as some say, by the reference to circumcision (**2** 11). In no case is the doctrinal portion of the epistle counter to that of the acknowledged Pauline epistles, though in the matter of the church, and of Christ's relationship to it and to the universe, there is evidence of progress in the apostle's conception of the underlying truths, which none the less find echoes in the earlier writings. "New doctrinal ideas, or a new proportion of these ideas, is no evidence of different authorship." (*c*) In the matter of organization the position of Eph is not in any essential different from what we have in 1 Cor.

(4) The linguistic argument is a technical matter of the use of Gr words that cannot well be discussed here. The general differences of style, the longer "turgid" sentences, the repetitions on the one hand; the lack of argument, the full, swelling periods on the other, find their counterpart in portions of Rom. The minute differences which show themselves in new or strange words will be much reduced in number when we take from the list those that are due to subjects which the author does not discuss elsewhere (e.g. those in the list of armor in **6** 13 ff). Holtzmann (*Einl*, 25) gives us a list of these *hápax legómena* (76 in all). But there are none of these which, as Lock says, St. Paul could not have used, though there are certain which he does not use elsewhere and others which are only found in his accepted writings and here. The following stand out as affording special ground for objection. The phrase "heavenly places" (*tá epouránía*, **1** 3.20; **2** 6; **3** 10; **6** 12) is peculiar to this epistle. The phrase finds a partial ∥ in 1 Cor **15** 49 and the thought is found in Phil **3** 20. The devil (*ho diábolos*, **4** 27; **6** 11) is used in place of the more usual Satan (*satanás*). But in Acts St. Paul is quoted as using *diabolos* in **13** 10 and *satanas* in **26** 18. It is at least natural that he would have used the Gr term when writing from Rome to a Gr-speaking community. The objection to the expression "holy" (*hagíois*) apostles (**3** 5) falls to the ground when we remember that the expression "holy" (*hágios*) is St. Paul's common word for Christian and that he uses it of himself in this very epistle (**3** 8). In like manner "mystery" (*mustḗrion*), "dispensation" (*oikonomia*) are found in other epistles in the same sense that we find them in here.

The attack on the epistle fails, whether it is made from the point of teaching or language; and there is no ground whatever for questioning the truth of Christian tradition that St. Paul wrote the letter which we know as the Epistle to the Ephesians.

II. Place and Date of Writing.—The time and place of his writing Eph turn on the larger question of the chronology of St. Paul's life (see PAUL) and the relation of the Captivity Epistles to each other; and the second question whether they were written from Caesarea or Rome (for this see PHILEMON, EPISTLE TO). Suffice it here to say that the place was undoubtedly Rome, and that they were written during the latter part of the two years' captivity which we find recorded in Acts **28** 30. The date will then be, following the later chronology, 63 or 64 AD; following the earlier, which is, in many ways, to be preferred, about 58 AD.

III. Destination.—To whom was this letter written? The title says to the Ephesians. With this

1. Title

the witness of the early church almost universally agrees. It is distinctly stated in the Muratorian Fragment (10*b*, l. 20); and the epistle is quoted as to the

Ephesians by Irenaeus (*Adv. Haer.*, v.14, 3; 24, 3); Tertullian (*Adv. Marc.*, v.11, 17; *De Praesc.*, 36; *De Monag.*, v); Clement of Alexandria (*Strom.*, iv.65; *Paed.*, i.18) and Origen (*Contra Celsum*, iii.20). To these must be added the evidence of the extant MSS and VSS, which unite in ascribing the epistle to the Ephesians. The only exception to the universal evidence is Tertullian's account of Marcion (cir 150 AD) who reads *Ad Laodicenos* (*Adv. Marc.*, v.11: "I say nothing here about another epistle which we have with the heading 'to the Ephesians,' but the heretics 'to the Laodiceans' . . . . [v.17]: According to the true belief of the church we hold this epistle to have been dispatched to the Ephesians, not to the Laodiceans; but Marcion had to falsify its title, wishing to make himself out a very diligent investigator").

This almost universal evidence for Ephesus as the destination of our epistle is shattered when we turn to the reading of the first verse.

2. The Inscription

Here according to *TR* we read "Paul unto the saints which are at Ephesus [*en Ephésō*] and to the faithful in Christ Jesus." When we look at the evidence for this reading we find that the two words *en Ephesō* are lacking in Codex Sinaiticus and Codex Vaticanus, and that the corrector of the cursive known as 67 has struck them out of his copy. Besides these a recently described MS, Cod. Laura 184, giving us a text which is so closely akin to that used by Origen that the scribe suggests that it was compiled from Origen's writings, omits these words (Robinson, *Ephesians*, 293). To this strong manuscript evidence against the inclusion of these two words in the inscription we must add the evidence of Origen and Basil. Origen, as quoted in Cramer's *Catena* ad loc., writes: "In the Ephesians alone we found the expression 'to the saints which are,' and we ask, unless the phrase 'which are' is redundant, what it can mean. May it not be that as in Exodus He who speaks to Moses declares His name to be the Absolute One, so also those who are partakers of the Absolute become existent when they are called, as it were, from non-being into being?" Origen evidently knows nothing here of any reading *en Ephesō*, but takes the words "which are" in an absolute, metaphysical sense. Basil, a century and a half later, probably refers to this comment of Origen (*Contra Eun.*, ii.19) saying: "But moreover, when writing to the Ephesians, as to men who are truly united with the Absolute One through clear knowledge, he names them as existent ones in a peculiar phrase, saying 'to the saints which are and faithful in Christ Jesus.' For so those who were before us have handed it down, and we also have found [this reading] in old copies." In Jerome's note on this verse there is perhaps a reference to this comment on Origen, but the passage is too indefinitely expressed for us to be sure what its bearing on the reading really is. The later writers quoted by Lightfoot (*Bib. Essays*, 384 f) cannot, as Robinson shows (*Eph*, 293), be used as witnesses against the Textus Receptus. We may therefore conclude that the reading *en Ephesō* was wanting in many early MSS, and that there is good ground for questioning its place in the original autograph.

But the explanations suggested for the passage, as it stands without the words, offend Pauline usage so completely that we cannot accept them. To take "which are" in the phrase "the saints which are" (*toís oúsin*) as absolute, as Origen did; or as meaning "truly," is impossible. It is possible to take the words with what follows, "and faithful" (*kaí pistoís*), and interpret this latter expression (*pistoís*) either in the NT sense of "believers" or in the classical sense of "steadfast." The clause would then read either "to the saints who are also believers," or "to the saints who are also faithful," i.e. steadfast. Neither of these is wholly in accord with St. Paul's normal usage, but they are at least possible.

The determining factor in the question of the destination of the epistle lies in the epistle itself. We must not forget that, save perhaps Corinth, there was no church with which Paul was so closely associated as that in Ephesus.

3. The Evidence of the Letter Itself

His long residence there, of which we read in Acts (chs **19, 20**), finds no echo in our epistle. There is no greeting to anyone of the Christian community, many of whom were probably intimate friends. The close personal ties, that the scene of Acts **20** 17–38 shows us existed between him and his converts in Ephesus, are not even hinted at. The epistle is a calm discussion, untouched with the warmth of personal allusion beyond the bare statement that the writer is a prisoner (**3** 1; **4** 1), and his commendation of Tychicus (**6** 21.22), who was to tell them about St. Paul's condition in Rome. This lack of personal touch is intensified by the assumption underlying chs **3** and **4** that the readers do not know his knowledge of the mysteries of Christ. In **3** 2 and **4** 21.22 there is a particle (*eíge*, "if indeed") which suggests at least some question as to how far St. Paul himself was the missionary through whom they believed. All through the epistle there is a lack of those elements which are so constant in the other epistles, which mark the close personal fellowship and acquaintance between the apostle and those to whom he is writing.

This element in the epistle, coupled with the strange fact of Marcion's attributing it to the Laodiceans, and the expression in Col **4** 16 that points to a letter coming from Laodicea to Colosse, has led most writers of the present day to accept Ussher's suggestion that the epistle is really a circular letter to the churches either in Asia, or, perhaps better, in that part of Phrygia which lies near Colosse.

4. Conclusion

The readers were evidently Gentiles (**2** 1; **3** 1.2) and from the mission of Tychicus doubtless of a definite locality, though for the reasons given above this could not well be Ephesus alone. It is barely possible that the cities to whom St. John was bidden to write the Revelation (Rev **1–3**) are the same as those to whom St. Paul wrote this epistle, or it may be that they were the churches of the Lycus valley and its immediate neighborhood. The exact location cannot be determined. But from the fact that Marcion attributed the epistle to Laodicea, possibly because it was so written in the first verse, and from the connection with Colossians, it is at least probable that two of these churches were at Colosse and Laodicea. On this theory the letter would seem to have been written from Rome to churches in the neighborhood of, or accessible to, Colosse, dealing with the problem of Christian unity and fellowship and the relations between Christ and the church and sent to them by the hands of Tychicus. The inscription was to be filled in by the bearer, or copies were to be made with the name of the local church written in, and then sent to or left with the different churches. It was from Ephesus, as the chief city of Asia in all probability, that copies of this circular letter reached the church in the world, and from this fact the letter came to be known in the church at large as that from Ephesus, and the title was written "to the Ephesians," and the first verse was made to read to the "saints which are in Ephesus."

IV. Relation to Other New Testament Writings.—Eph raises a still further question by the close resemblances that can be traced between it and various other NT writings.

The connection between Eph and 1 Pet is not beyond question. In spite of the disclaimer of as careful a writer as Dr. Bigg (*ICC*) it is impossible to follow up the references given by Holtzmann and others and not feel that St. Peter either knew Eph or at the very least had discussed these subjects with its author. For, as Dr. Hort tells us, the similarity is one of thought and structure rather than of phrase. The following are the more striking passages with their parallels in 1 Pet: Eph **1** 3 (1 Pet **1** 3); **1** 18–20 (1 Pet **1** 3–5); **2** 18–22 (1 Pet **2** 4–6); **1** 20–22 (1 Pet **3** 22); **3** 9 (1 Pet **1** 20); **3** 20 (1 Pet **1** 12); **4** 19 (1 Pet **1** 14). The explanations that 1 Pet and Eph are both from the pen of the same writer, or that Eph is based on 1 Pet, are overthrown, among other reasons, by the close relation between Eph and Col.

1. 1 Peter

The connection with the Apocalypse is based on Eph **2** 20 as compared with Rev **21** 14; Eph **3** 5 and Rev **10** 7; Eph **5** 11 and Rev **18** 4, and the figure of the bride of the Lamb (Rev **19** 7; cf Eph **5** 25). Holtzmann adds various minor similarities, but none of these are sufficient to prove any real knowledge of, let alone dependence on Eph. The contact with the Fourth Gospel is more positive. Love (*agápē*) and knowledge (*gnṓsis*) are used in the same sense in both Eph and the Gospel. The application of the Messianic title, the Beloved (Eph **1** 6), to Christ does not appear in the Gospel (it is found in Mt **3** 17), but the statement of the Father's love for Him constantly recurs. The reference to the going up and coming down of Christ (Eph **4** 9) is closely akin to Jn **3** 13 ("No man hath ascended into heaven, but he," etc). So, too, Eph **5** 11.13 finds echo in Jn **3** 19.20; Eph **4** 4.7 in Jn **3** 34; Eph **5** 6 in Jn **3** 36. Eph **5** 8 f is akin to 1 Jn **1** 6 and Eph **2** 3 to 1 Jn **3** 10.

2. Johannine Writings

When we turn to Col we find a situation that is without parallel in the NT. Out of 155 verses in Eph, 78 are found in Col in varying degrees of identity. Among them are these: Eph **1** 6 ‖ Col **1** 13; Eph **1** 16 ff ‖ Col **1** 9; Eph **1** 21 ff ‖ Col **1** 16 ff; Eph **2** 16 ‖ Col **2** 20; Eph **4** 2 ‖ Col **3** 12; Eph **4** 15 ‖ Col **2** 19; Eph **4** 22 ‖ Col **3** 9; Eph **4** 32 ‖ Col **3** 12 ff; Eph **5** 5 ‖ Col **3** 5; Eph **5** 19 ff ‖ Col **3** 16 ff; Eph **6** 4 ‖ Col **3** 21; Eph **6** 5–9 ‖ Col **3** 22—**4** 1. For a fuller list see Abbott (*ICC*, xxiii). Not only is this so, but there is an identity of treatment, a similarity in argument so great that Bishop Barry (*NT Comm. for Eng. Readers*, Ellicott) can make a ‖ analysis showing the divergence and similarity by the simple device of different type. To this we must add that there are at least a dozen Gr words common to these two epistles not found elsewhere. Over against this similarity is to be set the dissimilarity. The general subject of the epistles is not approached from the same standpoint. In one it is Christ as the head of all creation, and our duty in consequence. In the other it is the church as the fulness of Christ and our duty—put constantly in the same words—in consequence thereof. In Eph we have a number of OT references, in Col only one. In Eph we have unique phrases, of which "the heavenly spheres" (*ta epourania*) is most striking, and the whole treatment of the relation of Jew and Gentile in the church, and the marriage tie as exemplified in the relation between Christ and the church. In Col we have in like manner distinct passages which have no ‖ in Eph, esp. the controversial section in ch **2**, and the salutations. In truth, as Davies (*Ep. St. Paul to Eph, Col, and Phil*) well says: "It is difficult indeed to say, concerning the patent coincidences of expression in the two epistles, whether the points of likeness or of unlikeness between them are the more remarkable." This situation has given rise to various theories. The most complicated is that of H. Holtzmann, who holds that some passages point to a priority of Col, others to that of Eph; and as a result he believes that Col, as we have it, is a composite, based on an original epistle of St. Paul which was expanded by the author of Eph—who was not St. Paul—after he had written this epistle. So Holtzmann would give us the original Col (Pauline), Eph (based on it), and the present Col (not Pauline) expanded from the former through the latter. The theory falls to the ground on its fundamental hypothesis, that Col as it stands is interpolated. The most reasonable explanation is that both Col and Eph are the work of St. Paul, written at practically the same time, and that in writing on the same subjects, to different people, there would be just the differences and similarity which we have in these epistles. The objection that St. Paul could not repeat himself and yet differ as these two letters do is purely imaginary. Zahn shows us that men do just this very thing, giving an account of Bismarck's speaking on a certain subject to a group of officers and later to a large body of men, and yet using quite different language. Moreover, St. Paul is not averse to repeating himself (cf Rom and Gal and 1 Tim and 2 Tim) when to do so will serve his purpose. "Simultaneous authorship by one writer," and that writer St. Paul, is the only explanation that will satisfy all the facts in the case and give them due proportion.

3. Colossians

V. The Purpose.—If our interpretation of the circumstances, composition and destination of Eph be right, we are now in a position to look beneath the surface and ask why the apostle wrote it. To understand its central theme we must remember that St. Paul, the prisoner of the Lord, is writing in the calm of his imprisonment, far from the noise and turmoil, the conflict and strife, that marked his earlier life. He is now able to look out on the church and get a view of it in its wholeness, to see the part it is to play in God's scheme for the restoration of the human race, to see God's purpose in it and for it and its relation to Him. With this standpoint he can write to the churches about Ephesus on the occasion of Tychicus' return to Colosse, not to correct false views on some special point, but to emphasize the great central truth which he had put in the very forefront of his letter. God's eternal purpose is to gather into one the whole created universe, to restore harmony among His creatures and between them and Himself. The apostle's whole prayer is for this end, his whole effort and desire is toward this goal: that they may have full, clear knowledge of this purpose of God which He is working out through Christ Jesus, who is the head of the church, the very fulness of Him who is being fulfilled all over the world. Everything, for the apostle, as he looks forth upon the empire, centers in the purpose of God. The discord between the elements in the church, the distinction between Jew and Gentile, all these must yield to that greater purpose. The vision is of a great oneness in Christ and through Him in God, a oneness of birth and faith and life and love, as men, touched with the fire of that Divine purpose, seek to fulfil, each in himself, the part that God has given him to play in the world, and, fighting against the foes of God, to overcome at last.

It is a noble purpose to set before men this great mystery of the church as God's means by which, in Christ, He may restore all men to union with Himself. It is an impossible vision except to one who, as St. Paul was at the time, is in a situation where the strife and turmoil of outside life can enter but little, but a situation where he can look out with a calm vision and, in the midst of the world's discord, discern what God is accomplishing among men.

VI. Argument.—The Argument of Eph is as follows:

1 1.2: Greeting.

1 3-10: Hymn of praise to God for the manifestation of His purpose for men in Christ Jesus, chosen from the beginning to a holy life in love, predestined to adoption as sons through Jesus Christ, in whom as the Beloved He has given us grace (vs 3-6). Redeemed by the blood of Christ by whom we have forgiveness of sins through His grace abounding in us and making us know the mystery of His purpose, viz. to unite all in one, even the entire universe (vs 7-10).

1 11-14: For this Israel has served as a preparation, and to this the Gentiles are come, sealed unto salvation by the Holy Spirit of power.

1 15.16*a*: Thanksgiving for their faith.

1 16*b*-21: Prayer that they may, by the spirit of wisdom and revelation, know their destiny and the power of God to fulfil it.

1 22—**2** 10: Summary of what God has done in Christ. Christ's sovereignty (vs 22.23), and headship in the church (vs 22.23); His work for men, quickening us from a death of sin into which man has sunk, and exalting us to fellowship with Christ by His grace, who has created us for good works as part of His eternal purpose (**2** 1-10).

2 11-13: The contrast between the former estate of the Gentiles, as strangers and aliens, and their present one, "near" by the blood of Christ.

2 14-18: Christ, who is our peace, uniting Jew and Gentile and reconciling man to God through the cross; by whom we all have access to the Father.

2 19-22: This is theirs who as fellow-citizens of the saints, built up on the foundation of the apostles and prophets, become a sanctuary of God in the Spirit.

3 1-21: A digression on the "mystery," i.e. the revelation to St. Paul, together with a prayer that men may grasp it. The "mystery" is that all men, Jews and Gentiles, are partakers of the promise. Of this St. Paul is a minister, to whom has been given the stewardship of that mystery, unfolding to all creatures God's wisdom, in accord with His eternal purpose (vs 1-13). Prayer that they may live up to their opportunities (vs 14-19). Doxology (vs 20.21).

4 1-6: The outcome of this privilege, the fulfilment of the Divine purpose, must show itself in unity of life in the Christian fellowship.

4 7-16: The different gifts which the Christians have are for the upbuilding of the church into that perfect unity which is found in Christ.

4 17-24: The spiritual darkness and corruption of the old gentile life set over against the enlightenment and purity and holiness of the new life in Christ.

4 25—**6** 9: Special features of the Christian life, arising out of the union of Christians with Christ and making for the fellowship in the church. On the side of the individual: sins in word (**4** 25-30); of temper (vs 31.32); self-sacrifice as opposed to self-indulgence (**5** 1-8); the contrast of the present and the past repeated (vs 9-14); general behavior (vs 15-20); on the side of social relations: husband and wife exemplified in the relation of Christ and the church (vs 23-33); children and parents (**6** 1-4); servants and masters (vs 5-9).

6 10-20: The Christian warfare, its foes and armor and weapons.

6 21-24: Conclusion.

VII. Teaching.—The keynote to the doctrinal basis of the epistle is struck at the very outset. The hymn of praise centers in the thought of God, the Father of Our Lord Jesus Christ. It is to Him that the blessing is due, to Him, who had chosen us from the beginning, in whom there is redemption (**1** 3-7). God as the very heart and soul of everything, "is over all, and through all, and in all" (**4** 6). He is the Father from whom all revelation comes (**1** 17), and from whom every human family derives its distinctive characteristics (**3** 15). But He is not only Father in relation to the universe: He is in a peculiar sense the Father of Our Lord Jesus Christ (**1** 3). The eternity of Our Lord is distinctly asserted (vs 4.5) as of one existing before the foundation of the world, in whom everything heavenly as well as earthly is united, summed up (ver 10; cf **2** 12; **4** 18). He is the Messiah (the Beloved [**1** 6] is clearly a Messianic term, as the voice from heaven at Christ's baptism, "This is my beloved Son, in whom I am well pleased," shows [Mt **3** 17]). In Him we are quickened (**2** 5). He is made flesh (ver 15). He died on the cross (ver 16), and by His blood (**1** 7) we have redemption (**4** 30), and reconciliation with God (**2** 16). He whom God raised from the dead (**1** 20), now is in heaven (**1** 20; **4** 8) from which place He comes (**4** 8), bringing gifts to men. (This interpretation makes the descent follow the ascent, and the passage teaches the return of Christ through His gifts of the Spirit which He gave to the church.) He who is in heaven fills all things (ver 10); and, from a wealth which is unsearchable (**3** 8), as the Head of the church (**1** 22), pours out His grace to free us from the power of sin (**2** 1). To this end He endues us with His Spirit (**3** 16). This teaching about God, Father, Son and Holy Spirit, is no abstract theorizing. It is all intensely practical, having at its heart the purpose of God from the ages, which, as we saw above, is to restore again the unity of all things in Him (**1** 9.10); to heal the breach between man and God (**2** 16.17); to break down the separation between Jew and Gentile, and to abolish the enmity not only between them, but between them and God. This purpose of God is to be accomplished in a visible society, the one church, built upon the foundation of the apostles and prophets (ver 20), of which Jesus Christ is the head of the corner, into which men are to be admitted by holy baptism, where they own one Lord, hold to one faith, in one God and Father of all who is above all and through all (**4** 4-7).

The teaching as to the church is one of the most striking elements of the epistle. In the first place we have the absolute use of the term, which has been already discussed. The apostle sees the whole Christian community throughout the world bound together into a unity, one fellowship, one body. He has risen to a higher vision than man had ever had before. But there is a further teaching in the epistle. Not only is the church throughout the world one body, but it is the body of Christ who is its Head (**1** 21 f). He has, as Lightfoot suggests, the same relation to the church which in ver 10 He has to the universe. He is its Head, "the inspiring, ruling, guiding, combining, sustaining power, the mainspring of its activity, the center of its unity, and the seat of its life." But the relation is still closer. If, as the evidence adduced would necessitate, one accepts J. Armitage Robinson's explanation of *plērōma*, as that without which a thing is incomplete (*Eph*, 255 f), then the church, in some wonderful mystery, is the complement of Christ, apart from which He Himself, as the Christ, lacks fulness. We are needed by Him, that so He may become all in all. He, the Head of restored humanity, the Second Adam, needs His church, to fulfil the unity which He came upon earth to accomplish (cf Stone, *Christian Church*, 85, 86). Still further, we find in this epistle the two figures of the church as the Temple of the Spirit (**2** 21 ff), and the Bride of Christ (**5** 23 ff). Under the latter figure we find the marriage relation of the Lord to Israel, which runs through the OT (Hos **3** 16, et al.), applied to the union between Christ and the church. The significance is the close tie that binds them, the self-sacrificing love of Christ, and the self-surrender of obedience on the part of the church; and the object of this is that so the church may be free from any blemish, holy and spotless. In the figure of the Temple, which is an expansion of the earlier figure in 1 Cor **3** 16; 2 Cor **6** 16, we see the thought of a spiritual building, a sanctuary, into which all the diverse elements of the churches grow into a compact unity. These figures sum up the apostle's thought of that in which the Divine purpose finds its fulfilment. The progress forward to that fulfilment is due to the combined effort of God and man. "The church, the society of Christian men . . . . is built and yet it grows. Human endeavor and Divine energy coöperate in its development" (Westcott). Out of this doctrinal development the apostle works out the practical life by which this Divine purpose can find its fulfilment. Admitted into the fellowship of the church by baptism, we become members one of another (**4** 25). It is on this basis that he urges honesty and patience and truth in our intercourse with each other, and pleads for gentleness and a forgiving spirit (vs 25–32). As followers of God we are to keep free from the sins that spring from pride and self-indulgence and any fellowship with the spirit of evil (**5** 1–14). Our life is to be lived as seeking the fulfilment of God's purpose in all the relationships of life (**5** 15—**6** 9). All is to be done with the full armor of the Christian soldier, as is fitting for those who fight spiritual enemies (**6** 10 ff). The epistle is preëminently practical, bringing the significance of the great revelation of God's will to the everyday duties of life, and lifting all things up to a higher level which finds its ideal in the indwelling of Christ in our hearts, out of which we may be filled with all the fulness of God (**3** 17–19).

LITERATURE.—J. Armitage Robinson, *St. Paul's Epistle to the Eph;* Westcott, *Epistle to the Eph;* Abbott, "Eph and Col," *ICC;* Moule, "Eph," *Cambridge Bible;* Salmond, "Eph," *Expositor's Gr Testament;* Macpherson, *Comm. on Eph;* Findlay, "Epistle to the Eph," *Expositor's Bible;* Alexander, "Col and Eph," *Bible for Home and School;* Haupt, *Meyer's Exeget. und krit. Kommentar;* von Soden, *Handcommentar;* Hort, *Prolegomena to the Epistles to the Rom and Eph;* Dale, *Lectures on the Eph.*

CHARLES SMITH LEWIS

EPHESUS, ef′ē-sus (Ἔφεσος, *Éphesos*, "desirable"): A city of the Rom province of Asia, near the mouth of the Cayster river, 3 miles from the western coast of Asia Minor, and opposite the island of Samos. With an artificial harbor accessible to the largest ships, and rivaling the harbor at Miletus, standing at the entrance of the valley which reaches far into the interior of Asia Minor, and connected by highways with the chief cities of the province, Ephesus was the most easily accessible city in Asia, both by land and sea. Its location, therefore, favored its religious, political and commercial development, and presented a most advantageous field for the missionary labors of Paul. The city stood upon the sloping sides and at the base of two hills, Prion and Coressus, commanding a beautiful view; its climate was exceptionally fine, and the soil of the valley was unusually fertile.

Tradition says that in early times near the place where the mother goddess of the earth was born, the Amazons built a city and a temple in which they might worship. This little city of the Amazons, bearing at different times the names of Samorna, Trachea, Ortygia and Ptelea, flourished until in the early Gr days it aroused the cupidity of Androclus, a prince of Athens. He captured it and made it a Gr city. Still another tradition says that Androclus was its founder. However, under Gr rule the Gr civilization gradually supplanted that of the Orientals, the Gr language was spoken in place of the Asiatic; and the Asiatic goddess of the temple assumed more or less the character of the Gr Artemis. Ephesus, therefore, and all that pertained to it, was a mixture of oriental and Gr. Though the early history of the city is obscure, it seems that at different times it was in the hands of the Carians, the Leleges and Ionians; in the early historical period it was one of a league of twelve Ionian cities. In 560 BC it came into the possession of the Lydians; 3 years later, in 557, it was taken by the Persians; and during the following years the Greeks and Persians were constantly disputing for its possession. Finally, Alexander the Great took it; and at his death it fell to Lysimachus, who gave it the name of Arsinoe, from his second wife. Upon the death of Attalus II (Philadelphus), king of Pergamos, it was bequeathed to the Rom Empire; and in 190, when the Rom province of Asia was formed, it became a part of it. Ephesus and Pergamos, the capital of Asia, were the two great rival cities of the province. Though Pergamos was the center of the Rom religion and of the government, Ephesus was the more accessible, the commercial center and the home of the native goddess Diana; and because of its wealth and situation it gradually became the chief city of the province.

Coin Showing Image of Diana.

It is to the temple of Diana, however, that its great wealth and prominence are largely due. Like the city, it dates from the time of the Amazons, yet what the early temple was like we now have no means of knowing, and of its history we know little excepting that it was seven times destroyed by fire and rebuilt, each time on a scale larger and grander than before. The wealthy king Croesus supplied it with many of its stone columns, and the pilgrims from all the oriental world brought it of their wealth. In time the temple possessed valuable lands; it controlled the fisheries; its priests were the bankers of its enormous revenues. Because of its strength the people stored there their money for safe-keeping; and it became to the ancient world practically all that the Bank of England is to the modern world.

In 356 BC, on the very night when Alexander the Great was born, it was burned; and when he grew to manhood he offered to rebuild it at his own expense if his name might be inscribed upon its portals. This the priests of Ephesus were unwilling to permit, and they politely rejected his offer by saying that it was not fitting for one god to build a temple to another. The wealthy Ephesians themselves undertook its reconstruction, and 220 years passed before its final completion.

Not only was the temple of Diana a place of worship, and a treasure-house, but it was also a museum in which the best statuary and most beautiful paintings were preserved. Among the paintings was one by the famous Apelles, a native of Ephesus, representing Alexander the Great hurling a thunderbolt. It was also a sanctuary for the criminal, a kind of city of refuge, for none might be arrested for any crime whatever when within a bowshot of its walls. There sprang up, therefore, about the temple a village in which the thieves and murderers and other criminals made their homes. Not only did the temple bring vast numbers of pilgrims to the city, as does the Kaaba at Mecca at the present time, but it employed hosts of people apart from the priests and priestesses; among them were the large number of artisans who manufactured images of the goddess Diana, or shrines to sell to the visiting strangers.

Such was Ephesus when Paul on his 2d missionary journey (Acts **18** 19–21) first visited the city, and when, on his 3d journey (**19** 8–10; **20** 31), he remained there for two years preaching in the synagogue (**19** 8.10), in the school of Tyrannus (**19** 9) and in private houses (**20** 20). Though Paul was probably not the first to bring Christianity to Ephesus, for Jews had long lived there (**2** 9; **6** 9), he was the first to make progress against the worship of Diana. As the fame of his teachings was carried by the pilgrims to their distant homes, his influence extended to every part of Asia Minor. In time the pilgrims, with decreasing faith in Diana, came in fewer numbers; the sales of the shrines of the goddess fell off; Diana of the Ephesians was no longer great; a Christian church was founded there and flourished, and one of its first leaders was the apostle John. Finally in 262 AD, when the temple of Diana was again burned, its influence had so far departed that it was never again rebuilt. Diana was dead. Ephesus became a Christian city, and in 341 AD a council of the Christian church was held there. The city itself soon lost its importance and decreased in population. The sculptured stones of its great buildings, which were no longer in use and were falling to ruins, were carried away to Italy, and esp. to Constantinople for the great church of Saint Sophia. In 1308 the Turks took possession of the little that remained of the city, and deported or murdered its inhabitants. The Cayster river, overflowing its banks, gradually covered with its muddy deposit the spot where the temple of Diana had once stood, and at last its very site was forgotten.

The small village of *Ayasaluk*, 36 miles from Smyrna on the Aidin R.R., does not mark the site of the ancient city of Ephesus, yet it stands nearest to its ruins. The name *Ayasaluk* is the corruption of three Gr words meaning "the Holy Word of God." Passing beyond the village one comes to the ruins of the old aqueduct, the fallen city walls, the so-called church of St. John or the baths, the Turkish fort which is sometimes called Paul's prison, the huge theater which was the scene of the riot of Paul's time, but which now, with its marble torn away, presents but a hole in the side of the hill Prion. In 1863 Mr. J. T. Wood, for the British Museum, obtained permission from the Turkish government to search for the site of the lost temple of Diana. During the eleven years of his excavations at Ephesus, $80,000 were spent, and few cities of antiquity have been more thoroughly explored. The city wall of Lysimachus was found to be 36,000 ft. in length, inclosing an area of 1,027 acres. It was 10½ ft. thick, and strengthened by towers at intervals of 100 ft. The six gates which pierced the wall are now marked by mounds of rubbish. The sites and dimensions of the various public buildings, the streets, the harbor, and the foundations of many of the private houses were ascertained, and numerous inscriptions and sculptures and coins were discovered. Search, however, did not reveal the site of the temple until January 1, 1870, after six years of faithful work. Almost by accident it was then found in the valley without the city walls, several feet below the present surface. Its foundation, which alone remained, enabled Mr. Wood to reconstruct the entire temple plan. The temple was built upon a foundation which was reached by a flight of ten steps. The building itself was 425 ft. long and 220 ft. wide; each of its 127 pillars which supported the roof of its colonnade was 60 ft. high; like the temples of Greece, its interior was open to the sky. For a further description of the temple, see Mr. Wood's excellent book, *Discoveries at Ephesus*. E. J. Banks

EPHLAL, ef'lal (אֶפְלָל, *'ephlāl*, "judgment"): A descendant of Judah (1 Ch **2** 37).

EPHOD, ef'od (אֵפוֹד [28 t], אֵפֹד [20 t], *'ēphōdh;* LXX **ἐπωμίς,** *epōmis,* **ἐφώθ,** *ephṓth,* **ἐφώδ,** *ephṓd,* **ἐφούδ,** *ephoúd,* **στολὴ ἔξαλλος,** *stolḗ éxallos,* **στολὴ βυσσίνη,** *stolḗ bussínē*):

(1) A sacred vestment originally designed for the high priest (Ex **28** 4 ff; **39** 2 ff), and made "of gold, blue, and purple, and scarlet, and fine twined linen," held together by two shoulderpieces and a skilfully woven band which served as a girdle for the ephod. On the shoulderpieces were two onyx stones on which were engraved the names of the twelve tribes of Israel. It is not known whether the ephod extended below the hips or only to the waist. Attached to the ephod by chains of pure gold was a breastplate containing twelve precious stones in four rows. Underneath the ephod was the blue robe of the ephod extending to the feet of the priest. The robe of the ephod was thus a garment comprising, in addition to the long robe proper, the ephod with its shoulderpieces and the breastplate of judgment.

(2) From the historical books we learn that ephods were worn by persons other than the high priest. Thus the boy Samuel was girded with a linen ephod while assisting the aged high priest (1 S **2** 18); the priests at Nob, 85 in number, are described as men wearing a linen ephod (**22** 18); and David was girded with a linen ephod when he danced in the procession that brought the ark into Jerus (2 S **6** 14). The ephod was considered appropriate for the king on this solemn and happy occasion; but it would be reading into the narrative more than it contains to infer that lay worshippers were regularly clothed with the ephod; nor are we to suppose that priests other than the high priest were accustomed to wear ephods as rich and elaborate as that of the high priest. Abiathar, who became high priest after the assassination of his father by Doeg, probably brought to the camp of David the ephod worn by the high priest in his ministrations at Nob (1 S **23** 6), and through this ephod David sought in certain crises to learn Jeh's will (**23** 9; **30** 7). Some have argued that the ephod, which Abiathar brought in his hand, was an image rather than a priestly garment, but there seems no sufficient reason for regarding it as other than a vestment for the high priest. The ephod behind which the sword of Goliath was kept wrapped in a cloth may well have been a garment suspended from the wall or itself wrapped in a protecting cloth (**21** 9).

(3) The ephod mentioned in Jgs **17** 5; **18** 14 f; Hos **3** 4 is associated with teraphim and other idolatrous images. We may frankly confess that we do not know the shape, size and use of the ephod in these cases, though even here also the ephod may well have been a priestly garment. The same remark holds good of the ephod made by Gideon, and which became an object of idolatrous worship in Israel (Jgs **8** 27). It has been argued that a vestment would not cost seventeen hundred shekels of gold. Possibly Gideon set up an apparatus of worship containing other articles, just as the mother of Micah began with the promise to make a graven image and a molten image, and afterward added an ephod and teraphim (**17** 1–5). Moreover, if gems and brilliants were put on Gideon's ephod, who can say that it did not cost seventeen hundred shekels?

Literature.—Braun, *De vestitu sacerdotum* (1698), 462 ff; Ugolini, *Thesaurus antiquitatum sacrarum* (1744–69), XII, 785 f; Ancessi, *Annales de philos. chrétienne*, 1872; König, *Rel. Hist. of Israel*, 107 ff; Van Hoonacker, *Le sacerdoce lévitique* (1899), 370 ff; Foote, *The Ephod*, in "Johns Hopkins University Circulars," 1900.

John Richard Sampey

EPHOD, ē'fod (אֵפֹד, *'ēphōdh*): Father of Hanniel, prince of Manasseh (Nu **34** 23).

EPHPHATHA, ef'a-tha, ef-ă'tha (**'Εφφαθά,** *Ephphathá*): Aram. word used by Christ (Mk **7** 34), the 'Ethpa'al imper. of Aram. *pethaḥ* (Heb *pāthaḥ*), translated, "Be [thou] opened"; cf Isa **35** 5. The Aram. was the sole popular language of Pal (*HJP*, II*g*, 9) and its use shows that we have here the graphic report of an eyewitness, upon whom the dialectic form employed made a deep impression. This and the corresponding act of the touch with the moistened finger is the foundation of a corresponding ceremony in the Roman Catholic formula for baptism.

EPHRAIM, ē′fra-im, ē′frā-im (אֶפְרַיִם, *'ephrayim*, "double fruit"): The younger of the two sons of Joseph and Asenath, born in Egypt.

1. The Patriarch

He and his brother Manasseh were adopted by Jacob, and ranked as his own sons, each becoming the ancestor of a tribe in Israel. In blessing his grandchildren, despite their father's protest, Jacob preferred the younger, foreshadowing the future eminence of his descendants (Gen **41** 50 ff; **48** 20 ff). In the Blessing of Jacob, however, the two are included under the name of Joseph (**49** 22 f).

2. The Tribe

At the first census on leaving Egypt, Ephraim's men of war numbered 40,500; and at the second census they are given as 32,500 (Nu **1** 33; **26** 37). See, however, art. NUMBERS. The head of the tribe at the Exodus was Elishama, son of Ammihud (**1** 10). With the standard of the tribe of Ephraim on the W. of the tabernacle in the desert march were Manasseh and Benjamin (**2** 18 ff). The Ephraimite among the spies was Hoshea (i.e. Joshua), the son of Nun (**13** 8). At the division of the land Ephraim was represented by prince Kemuel, son of Shiphtan (**34** 24). The future power of this tribe is again foreshadowed in the Blessing of Moses (Dt **33** 17). When Moses died, a member of the tribe, Joshua, whose faith and courage had distinguished him among the spies, succeeded to the chief place in Israel. It was natural that the scene of national assemblies, and the center of the nation's worship, should be chosen within the land occupied by the children of Joseph, at Shechem and Shiloh respectively. The leadership of Ephraim was further emphasized by the rule of Samuel. From the beginning of life in Pal they enjoyed a certain prestige, and were very sensitive on the point of honor (Jgs **7** 24; **8** 1; **12** 1 ff). Their acceptance of and loyalty to Saul, the first king chosen over Israel, may be explained by his belonging to a Rachel tribe, and by the close and tender relations existing between Joseph and Benjamin. But they were never reconciled to the passing of the scepter to Judah in the person of David (2 S **2** 8 f). That Israel would have submitted to the sovereignty of Absalom, any more than to that of David, is not to be believed; but his revolt furnished an opportunity to deal a shrewd blow at the power of the southern tribe (**15** 13). Solomon's unwisdom and the crass folly of Rehoboam in the management of the northern tribes fanned the smoldering discontent into a fierce flame. This made easy the work of the rebel Jeroboam; and from the day of the disruption till the fall of the Northern Kingdom there was none to dispute the supremacy of Ephraim, the names Ephraim and Israel being synonymous. The most distinguished of Ephraim's sons were Joshua, Samuel and Jeroboam I.

3. The Territory

The central part of Western Pal fell to the children of Joseph; and, while the boundaries of the territory allotted to Ephraim and Manasseh respectively are given in Josh **16**; **17** 1 ff, it seems to have been held by them in common for some time (**17** 14). The Canaanites in certain cities of both divisions were not driven out. It was probably thought more profitable to enslave them (**16** 10; **17** 13). The boundaries of Ephraim cannot be followed with accuracy, but roughly, they were as follows: The southern boundary, agreeing with the northern border of Benjamin, started from Bethel, and passed down westward by nether Beth-horon and Gezer toward the sea (**16** 3; in ver 5 it stops at upper Beth-horon); it turned northward to the southern bank of the brook Kanah (*Wādy Kānāh*) along which it ran eastward (**17** 10) to Michmethath (the plain of *Mukhneh*); thence it went northward along the western edge of the plain to Shechem. It then bent eastward and southward past Taanath-shiloh (*Ta'ana*), Janoah (*Yanūn*) to Ataroth and Naarah (unidentified) and the Jordan (**16** 7). From Ataroth, which probably corresponds to Ataroth-addar (ver 5), possibly identical with the modern *et-Trūneh*, the southern border passed up to Bethel. Along the eastern front of the land thus defined there is a steep descent into the Jordan valley. It is torn by many gorges, and is rocky and unfruitful. The long slopes to the westward, however, furnish much of the finest land in Pal. Well watered as it is, the valleys are beautiful in season with cornfields, vineyards, olives and other fruit trees. The uplands are accessible at many points from the maritime plain; but the great avenue of entrance to the country runs up *Wādy esh-Sha'īr* to Nāblus, whence, threading the pass between Gerizim and Ebal, it descends to the Jordan valley. In this favored region the people must have lived in the main a prosperous and happy life. How appropriate are the prophetic allusions to these conditions in the days of Ephraim's moral decay (Isa **28** 1.4; Jer **31** 18; Hos **9** 13; **10** 11, etc)! W. EWING

EPHRAIM:

(1) A position apparently of some importance, since the position of Baal-hazor (probably = *Tell 'Asūr*), where Abraham's sheep-farm was located, is determined by relation to it (2 S **13** 23). That it lay N. of Jerus seems to be indicated in ver 34. It may be identical with the Ephraim of *Onom*, 20 Rom miles N. of Jerus, and therefore to be sought somewhere in the neighborhood of *Sinjil* and *el-Lubbān*. Connected with this may have been the name Aphaerema, a district in Samaria mentioned in 1 Macc **11** 34; *Ant*, XIII, iv, 9.

(2) The town near the wilderness to which Jesus retired after the raising of Lazarus (Jn **11** 54). This probably corresponds to Ephrem of *Onom* (s.v. "Afra") 5 Rom miles E. of Bethel. This may be the place named along with Bethel by Jos (*BJ*, IV, ix, 9). It probably answers to *eṭ-Ṭaiyebeh*, a large village about 4 miles N. of *Beitīn*. The antiquity of the site is attested by the cisterns and rock tombs. It stands on a high hill with a wide outlook including the plains of Jericho and the Dead Sea. See EPHRON. W. EWING

EPHRAIM, FOREST OF (יַעַר אֶפְרָיִם, *ya'ar 'ephrayim*): The word *ya'ar* (Heb) probably agrees in meaning with the Arab. *wa'r*, which indicates a rough country, abounding in rocks, stones and scrub, with occasional trees; not a "forest," as we understand the term. Here Absalom was defeated and slain (2 S **18** 6 ff, AV "wood of Ephraim"). It must be sought, therefore, E. of the Jordan, in the neighborhood of Mahanaim; but no identification is yet possible.

EPHRAIM, GATE OF. See JERUSALEM.

EPHRAIM, MOUNT (הַר אֶפְרָיִם, *har 'ephrayim*): Means that part of the mountain which fell to Ephraim (Josh **19** 50, etc). The natives speak today of *Jebel Nāblus*, *Jebel Ṣafed*, etc, meaning that section of the central range which is subject to each city. It is better therefore to retain the rendering of AV, and not to read with RV "hill-country of Ephraim."

EPHRAIM, WOOD OF. See EPHRAIM, FOREST OF.

EPHRAIMITE, ē′fra-im-īt (אֶפְרַיִם, *'ephrayim*; sing. אֶפְרָתִי, *'ephrāthī*): A member of the tribe of Ephraim (Josh **16** 10, etc). See also EPHRATHITE.

EPHRAIN, ē′fra-in (2 Ch **13** 19), RV EPHRON, which see.

EPHRATH, ef′rath, ē′frath (אֶפְרָת, *'ephrāth;* **'Εφράθα,** *Ephrátha;* Gen **35** 16; **48** 7); **EPHRATHAH,** ef′ra-tha, ef-rä′tha (אֶפְרָתָה, *'ephrāthāh,* in the other references: Josh **15** 59 [in added ver of LXX only]; Ruth **4** 11; 1 Ch **2** 19.24.50; Ps **132** 6; Mic **5** 2, AV "Ephratah"): The name either of Bethlehem itself or of a district in which Bethlehem was situated. A man of this place was called an **Ephrathite** (Ruth **1** 2; 1 S **17** 12). It is held by many authorities that the Ephrath where Rachel was buried (Gen **35** 16; **48** 7) was a different place, the words "the same is Bethlehem" being a gloss. The reading in Ps **132** 6 is doubtful; RVm has "Ephraim." E. W. G. MASTERMAN

EPHRATHITE, ef′rath-īt, ē′frath-īt. See EPHRATH.

EPHRON, ē′fron (עֶפְרוֹן, *'ephrōn,* "fawnlike"): The Hittite of whom Abraham bought the field and cave of Machpelah (Gen **23** 8 ff; **25** 9; **49** 30). The transaction was conducted in true oriental fashion, with excessive courtesy; but the large sum of 400 shekels' weight of silver was in the end required (cf **33** 19; 1 K **16** 24). See also MONEY; MONEY, CURRENT.

EPHRON, ē′fron (עֶפְרוֹן, *'ephrōn;* **'Εφρών,** *Ephrōn*):

(1) 2 Ch **13** 19: "And Abijah pursued after Jeroboam, and took cities from him, Beth-el with the towns thereof, and Jeshanah with the towns thereof, and Ephron with the towns thereof." Another reading is "Ephraim" (RVm). This is thought by many to be identical with Ophrah (עָפְרָה, *'ophrāh,* Josh **18** 23) and perhaps with Ephraim (אֶפְרַיִם, *'ephrayim,* 2 S **13** 23) which both have been localized at the lofty town of *eṭ Ṭaiyibeh.*

(2) A city E. of the Jordan between Carnion (Ashteroth-karnain) and Scythopolis (Beisan): "Then Judas gathered together all the Israelites that were in the country. . . . . Now when they came unto Ephron (this was a great city in the way as they should go, very well fortified) they could not turn from it either on the right hand or on the left, but they must needs pass through the midst of it" (1 Macc **5** 45.46 AV; *Ant,* XII, viii, 5; also 2 Macc **12** 27). Buhl and Schumacher propose *Ḳaṣr Wady el Ghafr,* a ruined tower which completely commands the deep *Wady el Ghafr,* but the ruins appear to be scanty.

(3) Mt. Ephron: The border of Judah is described (Josh **15** 9): "It went out to the cities of Mount Ephron." The position will depend on that of Nephtoah and of Kiriath-jearim.

E. W. G. MASTERMAN

EPICUREANS, ep-i-kū-rē′anz (**'Επικούρειοι,** *Epikoúreioi*):

1. Social and Political Causes
2. Egoistic Hedonism
3. Back to Nature
4. Ataraxy
5. Pleasure Is the Absence of Pain
6. Social Contract
7. Atomic Theory
8. Materialism
9. Theory of Ideas
10. Epicurean Gods
11. *Consensus Gentium*
12. Causes of Success
13. Complete Antithesis of Paul's Teaching

LITERATURE

The Epicureans with the STOICS (q.v.) encountered Paul in Athens (Acts **17** 18). They were the followers of Epicurus, a philosopher who was born in Samos in 341 BC, and who taught first in Asia Minor and afterward in Athens till his death in 270 BC. His system, unlike most philosophies, maintained its original form, with little development or dissent, to the end of its course. The views of Paul's opponents of this school may therefore be gathered from the teaching of Epicurus.

The conditions for the rise of Epicureanism and Stoicism were political and social rather than intellectual.

1. Social and Political Causes

Speculative thought had reached its zenith in the great constructive ideals of Plato, and the encyclopaedic system of Aristotle. Criticism of these would necessarily drive men back upon themselves to probe deeper into the meaning of experience, as Kant did in later times. But the conditions were not propitious to pure speculation. The breaking up of the Gr city-states and the loss of Gr independence had filled men's minds with a sense of insecurity. The institutions, laws and customs of society, which had hitherto sheltered the individual, now gave way; and men demanded from philosophy a haven of rest for their homeless and weary souls. Philosophy, therefore, became a theory of conduct and an art of living.

Epicurus deprecated the pursuit of knowledge for its own sake, whether as philosophy or science, and directed his inquiries to the two practical questions: What is the aim of life? and How to attain to it? Philosophy he defined as "a daily business of speech and thought to secure a happy life."

His *ethical teaching* is therefore the central and governing factor of Epicurus' philosophy.

2. Egoistic Hedonism

It belongs to the type generally described as Egoistic Hedonism. The same general principles had been taught by Aristippus and his school, the Cyrenaics, a century earlier, and they were again revived in the 17th cent. in England by Thomas Hobbes.

The aim and end of life for every man is his own happiness, and happiness is primarily defined as pleasure. "Wherefore we call pleasure the Alpha and Omega of a blessed life. Pleasure is our first and kindred good. It is the starting-point of every choice and of every aversion, and to it we come back, inasmuch as we make feeling the rule by which to judge every good thing" (Epicurus, *Letter to Menœceus*). So far Epicurus might seem to be simply repeating the view of the Cyrenaics. But there are important differences. Aristippus held the pleasure of the moment to be the end of action; but Epicurus taught that life should be so lived as to secure the greatest amount of pleasure during its whole course. And in this larger outlook, the pleasures of the mind came to occupy a larger place than the pleasures of the body. For happiness consists not so much in the satisfaction of desires, as in the suppression of wants, and in arriving at a state of independence of all circumstances, which secures a peace of mind that the privations and changes of life cannot disturb. Man's desires are of various kinds: "Some are natural, some are groundless; of the natural, some are necessary as well as natural, and some are natural only. And of the necessary desires, some are necessary if we are to be happy, some if the body is to be rid of uneasiness, some if we are even to live." Man's aim should be to suppress all desires that are unnecessary, and esp. such as are artificially produced. Learning, culture, civilization and the distractions of social and political life are proscribed, much as they were in the opposite school of the Cynics, because they produce many desires difficult to satisfy, and so disturb the peace of the mind. This teaching has been compared to that of Rousseau and even of Buddha. Like the former, Epicurus enjoins the withdrawal of life from the complexities and perplexities of civilization, to the bare necessities of Nature, but he stops short of the doctrine of Nirvana, for life and the desire to live he regards as good things. He even rises above Naturalism to a view that has some kinship with modern Spiritualism, in his affirmation of the mastery of mind over adverse circumstances. "Though he is being tortured on the rack, the wise man is still happy."

3. Back to Nature

Epicurus' definition of the end of life and of the way to it bears a superficial resemblance to that of his opponents, the Stoics. The end sought by both is *ataraxia*, "imperturbability," a peace of mind that transcends all circumstances, and the way to it is the life according to Nature. But Nature for Epicurus is purely physical and material, and the utmost happiness attainable is the complete absence of pain.

4. Ataraxy

He justly protests against the representation of his teaching as gross and immoral. "When we say, then, that pleasure is the end and aim, we do not mean the pleasures of the prodigal, or the pleasures of sensuality, as we are understood to do by some, through ignorance, prejudice or wilful misrepresentation. By pleasure we mean the absence of pain in the body and trouble in the soul" (*Letter to Menœceus*). His own life was marked by a simplicity verging on asceticism, and by kindly consideration for his friends. But the theory was capable of serving the purposes of worse men to justify license and selfishness.

5. Pleasure Is the Absence of Pain

Justice and ordinary morality were recognized in the system as issuing from an original social compact, such as Hobbes and Rousseau supposed, and resting upon the self-interest and happiness of individuals who entered into the compact the better to gain those ends. Ordinary morality has therefore no stronger sanction than the individual's desire to secure his own happiness. Against public violations of the moral code, the sanction finds its agent in the social order and the penalties it inflicts; but the only deterrent from secret immorality is the fear of being found out, and the necessarily disturbing character of that fear itself. Friendship, the supreme virtue of Epicureanism, is based upon the same calculating selfishness, and is to be cultivated for the happiness it begets to its owners. The fundamental defect of the system is its extreme individualism, which issues in a studied selfishness that denies any value of their own to the social virtues, and in the negation of the larger activities of life.

6. Social Contract

Epicurus had no interest in knowledge for its own sake, whether of the external world, or of any ultimate or supreme reality. But he found men's minds full of ideas about the world, immortality and the gods, which disturbed their peace and filled them with vain desires and fears. It was therefore necessary for the practical ends of his philosophy to find a theory of the things outside of man that would give him tranquillity and serenity of mind.

For this purpose Epicurus fell back upon Democritus' atomic theory of the world. The original constituents of the universe, of which no account could be given, were atoms, the void, and motion. By a fixed law or fate, the atoms moved through the void, so as to form the world as we know it. The same uniform necessity maintains and determines the abiding condition of all that exists. Epicurus modified this system so far as to admit an initial freedom to the atoms, which enabled them to divert slightly from their uniform straight course as they fell like rain through space, and so to impinge, combine and set up rotatory motions by which the worlds, and all that is in them, came into being. He did not follow the idea of freedom in Nature and man beyond the exigencies of his theory, and the thoroughly materialistic nature of his universe precluded him from deducing a moral realm. By this theory he gets rid of the causes of fear and anxiety that disturb the human mind. Teleology, providence, a moral order of the universe, the arbitrary action of the gods, blind fate, immortality, hell, reward and punishment after death, are all excluded from a universe where atoms moving through space do everything. The soul, like the body, is made of atoms, but of a smaller or finer texture. In death, the one like the other dissolves and comes to its end.

7. Atomic Theory

8. Materialism

From the same premises one would expect the complete denial of any Divine beings. But it is a curiosity of the system that a grossly materialistic theory of knowledge should require the affirmation of the existence of the gods. Men's ideas are derived from thin material *films* that pass from the objects around them into the kindred matter of their minds. It follows that every idea must have been produced by a corresponding object. Men generally possess ideas of gods. Therefore, gods must exist to produce those ideas, which come to men in sleep and dreams. But they are not such gods as men generally believe to exist. They are constituted of the same atomic matter as men, but of a still finer texture. They dwell in the *intermundia*, the interspaces outside the worlds, where earthly cares and the dissolution of death cannot approach them. They are immortal and completely blessed. They cannot therefore know anything of the world, with its pain and its troubles, nor can they be in any way concerned with it. They are apotheoses of the Epicurean sage, entirely withdrawn from the world's turmoil, enjoying a life of calm repose, and satisfied with the bounty that Nature provides for them. "For the nature of the gods must ever in itself of necessity enjoy immortality with supreme repose, far removed and withdrawn from our concerns; since exempt from every pain, exempt from all dangers, strong in its own resources, not wanting aught of us, it is neither gained by favors nor moved by anger" (Lucretius). All religion is banned, though the gods are retained. Epicurus' failure to carry the logic of his system to the denial of the gods lies deeper than his theory of ideas. He was impressed by the fact that "a steadfast unanimity continues to prevail among all men without exception" that gods exist. "A consciousness of godhead does not allow him to deny the existence of God altogether. Hence his attempt to explain the fact so as not to interfere with his general theory" (Wallace, *Epicureanism*, 209).

9. Theory of Ideas

10. Epicurean Gods

11. "Consensus Gentium"

During his lifetime, Epicurus attracted a large following to his creed, and it continued to flourish far down into the Christian era. It was presented to the Rom world by the poet Lucretius in his poem *De natura rerum*, which is still the chief source for the knowledge of it. One OT writer, the author of Eccl, may have been influenced by its spirit, though he did not adopt all its ideas.

The personal charm and engaging character of Epicurus himself drew men to him, and elevated him into the kind of ideal sage who personified the teaching of the school, as was the custom of all schools of philosophy. The system was clear-cut and easily understood by ordinary men, and it offered a plausible theory of life to such as could not follow the profounder and more difficult speculations of other schools. Its moral teaching found a ready response in all that was worldly, commonplace and self-seeking in men that had lost their high ideals and great enthusiasms. Above all it delivered men from the terrors of a dark superstition that had taken the place of religion. It is a remarkable revelation of the inadequacy of Gr religion that Epicurus should have relegated the gods from the visible world, without any sense of loss, but only the relief of a great deliverance.

12. Causes of Success

It was inevitable that the teaching of Paul should have brought this school up against him. He came to Athens teaching a God who had become man, who had suffered and died to accomplish the utmost self-sacrifice, who had risen from the dead and returned to live among men to guide and fashion their lives, and who at last would judge all men, and according to their deeds reward or punish them in a future world. To the Epicurean this was the revival of all the ancient and hated superstitions. It was

13. Complete Antithesis of Paul's Teaching

not only folly but impiety; for Epicurus had taught that "not the man who denies the gods worshipped by the multitude, but he who affirms of the gods what the multitude believe about them, is truly impious."

LITERATURE.—Hicks, *Stoic and Epicurean* (whose translations are adopted in all quotations in this art.); Zeller, *Stoics, Epicureans and Sceptics;* Wallace, *Epicureanism;* Lucretius, *De natura rerum.*

T. REES

EPILEPSY, ep'i-lep-si. See LUNATIC.

EPIPHANES, ē-pif'a-nēz. See ANTIOCHUS IV.

EPIPHI, ep'i-fī (Ἐπιφί, *Epiphí*): Name of a month mentioned in connection with Pachon in 3 Macc **6** 38. See TIME.

EPISTLE, ē-pis''l (ἐπιστολή, *epistolḗ*, "a letter," "epistle"; from ἐπιστέλλω, *epistéllō*, "to send to"):

1. NT Epistles
2. Distinctive Characteristics
3. Letter-Writing in Antiquity
4. Letters in the OT
5. Letters in the Apocrypha
6. Epistolary Writings in the NT
7. Epistles as Distinguished from Letters
8. Patristic Epistles
9. Apocryphal Epistles

A written communication; a term inclusive of all forms of written correspondence, personal and official, in vogue from an early antiquity.

1. NT Epistles

As applied to the twenty-one letters, which constitute well-nigh one-half of the NT, the word "epistle" has come to have chiefly a technical and exclusive meaning. It refers, in common usage, to the communications addressed by five (possibly six) NT writers to individual or collective churches, or to single persons or groups of Christian disciples. Thirteen of these letters were written by St. Paul; three by St. John; two by St. Peter; one each by St. James and St. Jude; one — the epistle to the Hebrews—by an unknown writer.

As a whole the Epistles are classified as Pauline, and Catholic, i.e. general; the Pauline being divided into two classes:

2. Distinctive Characteristics

those written to churches and to individuals, the latter being known as Pastoral (1 and 2 Tim, and Tit; some also including Philem; see Lange on *Romans*, Am. ed, 16). The fact that the NT is so largely composed of letters distinguishes it, most uniquely, from all the sacred writings of the world. The Scriptures of other oriental religions—the Vedas, the Zend Avesta, the Tripitaka, the Koran, the writings of Confucius—lack the direct and personal address altogether. The Epistles of the NT are specifically the product of a new spiritual life and era. They deal, not with truth in the abstract, but in the concrete. They have to do with the soul's inner experiences and processes. They are the burning and heart-throbbing messages of the apostles and their confrères to the fellow-Christians of their own day. The chosen disciples who witnessed the events following the resurrection of Jesus and received the power (Acts **1** 8) bestowed by the Holy Spirit on, and subsequent to, the Day of Pentecost, were spiritually a new order of men. The only approach to them in the spiritual history of mankind is the ancient Heb prophets. Consequently the Epistles, penned by men who had experienced a great redemption and the marvelous intellectual emancipation and quickening that came with it, were an altogether new type of literature. Their object is personal. They relate the vital truths of the resurrection era, and the fundamental principles of the new teaching, to the individual and collective life of all believers. This specific aim accounts for the form in which the apostolic letters were written. The logic of this practical aim appears conspicuously in the orderly Epistles of St. Paul who, after the opening salutation in each letter, lays down with marvelous clearness the doctrinal basis on which he builds the practical duties of daily Christian life. Following these, as each case may require, are the personal messages and affectionate greetings and directions, suited to this familiar form of address.

The Epistles consequently have a charm, a directness, a vitality and power unknown to the other sacred writings of the world. Nowhere are they equaled or surpassed except in the personal instructions that fell from the lips of Jesus. Devoted exclusively to experimental and practical religion they have, with the teachings of Christ, become the textbook of the spiritual life for the Christian church in all subsequent time. For this reason "they are of more real value to the church than all the systems of theology, from Origen to Schleiermacher" (Schaff on St. Paul's Epistles, *Hist of Christian Church*, 741). No writings in history so unfold the nature and processes of the redemptive experience. In St. Paul and St. John, esp., the pastoral instinct is ever supreme. Their letters are too human, too personal, too vital to be formal treatises or arguments. They throb with passion for truth and love for souls. Their directness and affectionate intensity convert their authors into prophets of truth, preachers of grace, lovers of men and missionaries of the cross. Hence their value as spiritual biographies of the writers is immeasurable. As letters are the most spontaneous and the freest form of writing, the NT Epistles are the very life-blood of Christianity. They present theology, doctrine, truth, appeal, in terms of life, and pulsate with a vitality that will be fresh and re-creative till the end of time. (For detailed study of their chronology, contents and distinguishing characteristics, see arts. on the separate epistles.)

While the NT Epistles, in style and quality, are distinct from and superior to all other lit. of this class,

3. Letter-Writing in Antiquity

they nevertheless belong to a form of personal and written address common to all ages. The earliest known writings were epistolary, unless we except some of the chronologies and inscriptions of the ancient Bab and Assyr kings. Some of these royal inscriptions carry the art of writing back to 3800 BC, possibly to a period still earlier (see Goodspeed, *Kent's Historical Series*, 42–43, secs. 40–41), and excavations have brought to light "an immense mass of letters from officials to the court—correspondence between royal personages or between minor officials," as early as the reign of Khammurabi of Babylon, about 2275 BC (ib, 33). The civilized world was astonished at the extent of this international correspondence as revealed in the Am Tab (1480 BC), discovered in Egypt in 1887, among the ruins of the palace of Amenophis IV. This mass of political correspondence is thus approximately synchronous with the Heb exodus and the invasion of Canaan under Joshua.

As might be expected, then, the OT abounds with evidences of extensive epistolary correspondence in and between the oriental nations.

4. Letters in the OT

That a postal service was in existence in the time of Job (Job **9** 25) is evident from the Heb term רָצִים, *rāçīm*, signifying "runners," and used of the mounted couriers of the Persians who carried the royal edicts to the provinces. The most striking illustration of this courier service in the OT occurs in Est **3** 13.15; **8** 10.14 where King Ahasuerus, in the days of Queen Esther, twice sends royal letters to the Jews and satraps of his entire realm from India to Ethiopia, on the swiftest horses. According to Herodotus, these were usually stationed, for the sake of the greatest speed, four parasangs apart. Hezekiah's letters to Ephraim and Manasseh were sent in the same way (2 Ch **30** 1.6.10). Other instances of epistolary messages or communications in the OT are David's letter to Joab concerning Uriah and sent by him (2 S **11** 14.15); Jezebel's, to the elders and nobles of Jezreel, sent in Ahab's name, regarding Naboth (1 K **21** 8.9); the letter of Ben-hadad, king of Syria, to Jehoram, king of Israel, by the hand of Naaman (2 K **5** 5–7); Jehu's letters to the rulers of Jezreel, in Samaria (2 K **10** 1.2.6.7); Sennacherib's letter to Hezekiah (2 K **19** 14; Isa **37** 14; 2 Ch **32** 17), and also that of Merodach-baladan, accompanied with a gift (2 K **20** 12; Isa **39** 1). Approximating the NT epistle in purpose and spirit is the letter of earnest and loving counsel sent by Jeremiah to the exiles in Babylon. It is both apostolic and pastoral in its prophetic fervor, and is recorded in full (Jer **29** 1.4–32) with its reference to the bitterly hostile and jealous letter of Shemaiah, the false prophet, in reply.

As many writers have well indicated, the Bab captivity must have been a great stimulus to letter-writing on the part of the separated Hebrews, and between the far East and Pal. Evidences of this appear in the histories of Ezra and Nehemiah, e.g. the correspondence, back and forth, between the enemies of the Jews at Jerus and Artaxerxes, king of Persia, written in the Syrian language (Ezr **4** 7–23); also the letter of Tattenai (AV "Tatnai") the governor to King Darius (Ezr **5** 6–17); that of Artaxerxes to Ezra (Ezr **7** 11 ff), and to Asaph, keeper of the royal forest (Neh **2** 8); finally the interchange of letters between the nobles of Judah and Tobiah; and those of the latter to Nehemiah (Neh **6** 17.19; so Sanballat ver 5).

The OT Apoc contains choice specimens of personal and official letters, approximating in literary form the epistles of the NT. In each case they begin, like the latter, in true epistolary form with a salutation: "greeting," or "sendeth greeting" (1 Macc **11** 30.32; **12** 6.20; **15** 2.16), and in two instances closing with the customary "Fare ye well" or "Farewell" (2 Macc **11** 27–33. 34–38; cf 2 Cor **13** 11), so universally characteristic of letter-writing in the Hellenistic era.

5. Letters in the Apocrypha

The most felicitous and perfect example of official correspondence in the NT is Claudius Lysias' letter to Felix regarding St. Paul (Acts **23** 25–30). Equally complete in form is the letter, sent, evidently in duplicate, by the apostles and elders to their gentile brethren in the provinces of Asia (Acts **15** 23–29). In these two letters we have the first, and with Jas **1** 1, the only, instance of the Gr form of salutation in the NT (χαίρειν, *chaírein*). The latter is by many scholars regarded as probably the oldest letter in epistolary form in the NT, being in purport and substance a Pastoral Letter issued by the Apostolic Council of Jerus to the churches of Antioch, Syria and Cilicia. It contained instructions as to the basis of Christian fellowship, similar to those of the great apostle to the churches under his care.

6. Epistolary Writings in the NT

The letters of the high priest at Jerus commending Saul of Tarsus to the synagogues of Damascus are samples of the customary letters of introduction (Acts **9** 2; **22** 5; cf **28** 21; also **18** 27). As a Christian apostle St. Paul refers to this common use of "epistles of commendation" (2 Cor **3** 1; 1 Cor **16** 3) and himself made happy use of the same (Rom **16** 1 ff); he also mentions receiving letters, in turn, from the churches (1 Cor **7** 1).

Worthy of classification as veritable epistles are the letters, under the special guidance of the Holy Spirit, to the seven churches of Asia (Rev **2** 1—**3** 22). In fact, the entire Book of Rev is markedly epistolary in form, beginning with the benedictory salutation of personal and apostolic address, and closing with the benediction common to the Pauline epistles. This again distinguishes the NT lit. in spirit and form from all other sacred writings, being almost exclusively direct and personal, whether in vocal or written address. In this respect the gospels, histories and epistles are alike the product and exponent of a new spiritual era in the life of mankind.

This survey of epistolary writing in the far East, and esp. in the OT and NT periods, is not intended to obscure the distinction between the *letter* and the *epistle*. A clear line of demarkation separates them, owing not merely to differences in form and substance, but to the exalted spiritual mission and character of the apostolic letters. The characterization of a letter as more distinctly personal, confidential and spontaneous, and the epistle as more general in aim and more suited to or intended for publication, accounts only in part for the classification. Even when addressed to churches Paul's epistles were as spontaneous and intimately and affectionately personal as the ordinary correspondence. While intended for general circulation it is doubtful if any of the epistolary writers of the NT ever anticipated such extensive and permanent use of their letters as is made possible in the modern world of printing. The epistles of the NT are lifted into a distinct category by their spiritual eminence and power, and have given the word *epistle* a meaning and quality that will forever distinguish it from *letter*. In this distinction appears that Divine element usually defined as *inspiration:* a vitality and spiritual enduement which keeps the writings of the apostles permanently "living and powerful," where those of their successors pass into disuse and obscurity.

7. Epistles as Distinguished from Letters

Such was the influence of the NT Epistles on the lit. of early Christianity that the patristic and pseudepigraphic writings of the next century assumed chiefly the epistolary form. In letters to churches and individuals the apostolic Fathers, as far as possible, reproduced their spirit, quality and style. See Literature, Sub-apostolic.

8. Patristic Epistles

Pseudo-epistles extensively appeared after the patristic era, many of them written and circulated in the name of the apostles and apostolic Fathers. See Apocryphal Epistles. This early tendency to hide ambitious or possibly heretical writings under apostolic authority and Scriptural guise may have accounted for the anathema pronounced by St. John against all who should attempt to add to or detract from the inspired revelation (Rev **22** 18.19). It is hardly to be supposed that all the apostolic letters and writings have escaped destruction. St. Paul in his epistles refers a number of times to letters of his that do not now exist and that evidently were written quite frequently to the churches under his care (1 Cor **5** 9; 2 Cor **10** 9.10; Eph **3** 3); "in every epistle" (2 Thess **3** 17) indicates not merely the apostle's uniform method of subscription but an extensive correspondence. Col **4** 16 speaks of an "epistle from Laodicea," now lost, doubtless written by St. Paul himself to the church at Laodicea, and to be returned by it in exchange for his epistle to the church at Colosse.

9. Apocryphal Epistles

Dwight M. Pratt

EPISTLES, CAPTIVITY. See Philemon, Epistle to.

EPISTLES, THE PASTORAL. See Pastoral Epistles.

EPISTLES, SPURIOUS, spū'ri-us. See Apocryphal Epistles.

EQUAL, ē'kwal (ἴσος, *ísos*): In Ezk (**18** 25.29; **33** 17.20), "The way of the Lord is not equal" translates Heb *yittākhēn* for *tākhan*, "to weigh," and means "is not adjusted to any fixed standard," "arbitrary," "fitful," and, therefore, "not equitable, fair, or impartial" (LXX "is not set straight"). Cf same Heb word in 1 S **2** 3, where the Lord is said to 'weigh actions.' "Equal," therefore, is what will bear the closest investigation and strictest judgment. In Mt **20** 12, "made them equal" means "put them upon the same footing," i.e. regarded their brief service as though it were the very same as our long hours of toil. In Lk **20** 36 the context restricts the equality to a particular relation. The precise meaning of *isos* in Jn **5** 18, "making himself equal with God," is clearly defined by the preceding clause, for Our Lord's opponents say that He has "called God his own Father" (Gr *ídion patéra*, i.e. His Father in a peculiar and exclusive sense; cf *idíou huioú* of Rom **8** 32, applying the same adj. to the Son in His relation to the Father, i.e. His Son in a sense in which no one else can claim the title). They correctly interpreted the language of Jesus as declaring that He was the Son of God in a way that put Him on an equality with God. The charge against Him is not that He said that He was "like" (*hómoios*), but that He was "equal" (*isos*), i.e. of the very same rank and authority.

H. E. Jacobs

EQUALITY, ē-kwol'i-ti (ἰσότης, *isótēs*): In 2 Cor **8** 14, lit. "out of equality," i.e. "in equal proportion" or "that there may be equality." In Phil **2** 6, it occurs in a paraphrase of Gr *tó eínai ísa theṓ*, "the being on an equality with God." In this much-discussed passage, *isa*, according to a not unusual Attic idiom, is construed adverbially (see Meyer on passage), meaning, therefore, not 'the being equal' (AV), which would require *íson*, but "the having equal prerogatives and privileges." The personal equality is one thing; the equality of attributes is another, and it is the latter which is here expressed (Lightfoot). The "being on an equality" and the "having equal prerogatives" are both deductions from the possession of "the form of God." The thought is that if He who had "the form of God" had under all circumstances exercised His Divine attributes, He would have been employing only what belonged to Him, and would in no way have derogated from what belongs only to God. We regard this as referring to the incarnate Son in His historical manifestation.

H. E. Jacobs

EQUITY, ek'wi-ti: Is synonymous with "uprightness," which is found in Prov **17** 26; Isa **59** 14; Mal **2** 6 in place of AV "equity." Eccl **2** 21 has "skilfulness" and RVm "success" for AV "equity." The context favors this tr of כִּשְׁרוֹן, *kishrōn*, which is derived from כָּשֵׁר, *kāshēr*, "to succeed."

Equity is the spirit of the law behind the letter; justice is the application of the spirit of equity; honesty is the general everyday use of justice or fairness, equity being the interior or abstract ideal. The Court of Equity overrides the Court of Common Law, deciding not upon terms, but the spirit of the deed.

M. O. Evans

ER, ûr (עֵר, *'ēr*, "watcher"; Ἤρ, *Ḗr*):

(1) The eldest son of Judah, the son of Jacob, by Shua the Canaanite. Judah took for him a wife named Tamar. It is recorded that Er "was wicked in the sight of Jeh; and Jeh slew him" (Gen **38** 3.6.7; **46** 12).

(2) "Er the father of Lecah" is mentioned among "the sons of Shelah the son of Judah" (1 Ch **4** 21).

(3) An ancestor of Jesus in St. Luke's genealogy in the 7th generation before Zerubbabel (Lk **3** 28).

ERA, ē'ra: We find no definite era in use in OT times, and such usage does not appear until we reach the period of the Maccabees. There are some references to important events that might have served as eras had they been generally accepted and constantly employed. Such was the Exodus; and this is referred to as the starting-point in fixing the date of the building of Solomon's temple (1 K **6** 1), and also for the date of Aaron's death (Nu **33** 38). An earthquake is referred to by Amos (**1** 1) as a well-known event by which to date the beginning of his prophetic career; and Ezekiel in two passages refers to the captivity of Judah as a date for marking certain events in his life. Of these the Exodus would have been the most appropriate event to use as an era, since it marked the birth of the Heb nation; but the universal custom of antiquity was to date from the regnal years of the kings, as we see in the history of Egypt and Babylonia and Assyria; this custom was followed by the Israelites as soon as the kingdom was established, and was continued down to the Captivity. After the return of the Jews they naturally adopted the regnal years of the Pers kings, under whose rule they were, until the overthrow of the kingdom by Alexander. After this event, the era that prevailed most widely in Syria was that of the Seleucid kingdom, which began in 312 BC, and must have been familiar to the Jews, and we have evidence that they made use of it. When Simon the Maccabee secured the independence of the Jews from the Seleucid king, Demetrius II, in 141–140, they began to date their instruments and contracts from this event as is stated in 1 Macc **13** 41.42; and we find that the year of their independence is fixed by reference to the Seleucid era, the first year of Simon being the 170th of that era (see Jos, *Ant*, XIII, vi, 7). After this they used the era of Simon, dating by his regnal years; but whether they used this as a permanent era during the Asmonean Dynasty or dated simply from the accession of each king, we do not know. There is no doubt that the Seleucid era continued to be used throughout the country for several centuries after the downfall of the Seleucid kingdom, as we have abundant evidence from inscriptions. When the Romans took possession of Syria and Pal, their era was of course employed by Rom officials, but this did not prevail among the people. The dynasty of the Herods sometimes employed their own regnal years and sometimes those of the emperors, as appears from their coins. The Jews must have been familiar with the eras employed by some of the Phoen towns, such as Tyre and Sidon. Tyre had a local era which began in 126 BC, and Sidon one beginning in 112 BC; and most of the towns on the coast used the era of Alexander, dating from the battle of Issus, until the establishment of the Seleucid era. The Jews would be familiar with these from their commercial connections with the coast towns, but we do not know that they used them. They did not adopt the era of the Creation until after the time of Christ. It was fixed at 4,000 years before the destruction of the later temple, or 3760 BC.

H. Porter

ERAN, ē'ran (עֵרָן, *'ērān*, "watcher," "watchful"; Ἐδέν, *Edén*): The son of Ephraim's oldest son Shuthelah (Nu **26** 36). **Eranites,** the descendants of Eran (ib).

ERASTUS, ē-ras'tus (Ἔραστος, *Érastos*, "beloved"): The name occurs three times, each time denoting a companion of Paul.

(1) Erastus was sent with Timothy from Ephesus into Macedonia while Paul remained in Asia for a while. They are designated "two of them that ministered unto him" (Acts **19** 22).

(2) "Erastus the treasurer of the city" sent greetings to the Christians in Rome (Rom **16** 23). He was apparently an important person in the Corinthian community, and with Gaius probably represented that church in these fraternal relations with the Rom community.

(3) Erastus is one who, in 2 Tim **4** 20, "remained at Corinth."

We have no means of discovering whether one or more than one person is meant in these references. A. C. Headlam (*HDB*, s.v.) thinks it improbable that one who held an office implying residence in one locality should have been one of Paul's companions in travel. On the other hand Paul may be designating Erastus (Rom **16** 23) by an office he once held, but which he gave up to engage in mission work. S. F. Hunter

ERECH, ē'rek, er'ek (אֶרֶךְ, *'erekh*; Ὀρέχ, *Orech*): The second of the cities founded by Nimrod, the others being Babel, Accad and Calneh (Gen **10** 10). The derivation of the name is well known, Erech being the Sem-Bab *Uruk*, from the Sumerian *Unug*, a word meaning "seat," probably in the sense of "residential city." The character with which it is written enters into the composition of the Bab names of Larsa and Ur of the Chaldees.

1. Etymology of the Name

Its identification with *Warka*, on the left bank of the Euphrates, half-way between *Hillah* (Babylon) and *Korna*, is beyond a doubt. It is thought that the Euphrates must have flowed nearer to the city in ancient times, as the Gilgameš legend relates that that hero and his companion Enkidu washed their hands in the stream after having killed the divine bull sent by the goddess Ištar to destroy them. The shape of the ruin is irregular, the course of the walls of the N.E. having been seemingly determined by that of the Nile canal (*Shatt-en-Nil*), which flowed on that side. The extreme length of the site from N. to S. is over 3,000 yds., and its width about 2,800 yds. This space is very full of remains of buildings; and the foundations of the walls, with their various windings, gateways and defences, are traceable even now.

2. Position and Nature of the Ruins

Two great deities, Ištar and Nanaa, were worshipped in this city, the temple of the former being Ê-anna, "the house of heaven" (or "of Anu," in which case it is probable that the god of the heavens, Anu, was also one of the patrons of the city). The shrine dedicated to Ištar is apparently now represented by the ruin known as *Buwārīyya* or "reed-mats," and so called on account of the layers of matting at intervals of 4 or 5 ft. This is the great temple-tower (*ziqqurat*) of the place, called *Ê-gipar-imina*, "the house of 7 enclosures." The remains are situated in a large courtyard measuring 350 ft. by 270 ft. As in the case of other Bab erections, the corners are directed toward the cardinal points, and its height is about 100 ft. above the desert-plain.

3. Its Patron-Deities and Their Temples

As Erech is mentioned with Babylon, Niffer (Calneh) and Eridu, as one of the cities created by Merodach (Nimrod), it is clear that it was classed with the oldest foundations in Babylonia. It was the city of Gilgameš, the half-mythical king of the earliest period, who seems to have restored the walls and temples. Its earliest known ruler of historical times was Enšag-kuš-anna, about 4,000 BC. The celebrated shrine of Ištar was already in existence in the time of Lugal-zaggi-si, who came somewhat later. King Dungi (2600 BC) restored Ê-anna and built its great wall. This was in the time of the great Ur Dynasty, but later the city seems to have come under the dominion of the kings of Isin, Libit-Ištar having apparently restored the sanctuary of Ištar on Ê-gipara. Another great ruler of the early period was Sin-gašid, king of Erech, who was a patron of Ê-anna; and when he restored this shrine, he endowed it with grain, wool, oil and 1 shekel of gold. There seems also to have been a shrine to Nergal, god of war, which was restored by King Sin-gamil. About 2280 BC Kudur-Nanḫunde, the Elamite king, plundered the city, and carried off the statue of the goddess Nanaa, which was only restored to its place by Aššur-bani-âpli, the Assyr king, about 635 BC. Samsu-iluna seems to have surpassed his father Ḫammurabi (Amraphel) in the restoration of the city's temples, and other rulers who did not forget Erech were Nebuchadrezzar and Nabonidus.

4. History of the City's Temples, etc

Many tablets have been found on the site, and give promise of interesting discoveries still to come.

Having been the capital of the hero-king Gilgameš, who saw the wonders of the wide world, spoke with the Bab Noah face to face, and almost attained immortality as a living man, it was always a place of romance. Poetical compositions concerning it exist, one of the most interesting being a lamentation possibly written after the invasion of Kudur-Nanḫundi, when famine was rife in the city, blood flowed like water in Ê-ulbar, the house of Ištar's oracle, and the enemy heaped up fire in all the goddess' lands as one heaps up embers.

5. Literature Referring to Erech

The consideration in which the city was held is made plain by the geographical lists, from which it would seem that it had no less than 11 names, among them being *Illab* or *Illag*, *Tir-anna*, "the heavenly grove"; *Ub-imina*, "the 7 regions"; *Uru-gipara-imina*, "the city of the 7 enclosures"; and *Uruk-supuri*, "Erech of the folds" (the name which it always bears in the Gilgameš legend), given to it either on account of its being a center where pastoral tribes gathered, or because of the flocks kept for sacrifice to its deities.

6. The City's Numerous Names

Besides the inscriptions of the kings already mentioned, tablets of the reigns of Nabopolassar, Nebuchadrezzar, Nabonidus, Cyrus, Darius and some of the Seleucids have been found on the site. In the ruins of the town and the country around, numerous glazed earthenware (slipper-shaped) coffins and other receptacles, used for and in connection with the burial of the dead, occur. These are mostly of the Parthian period, but they imply that the place was regarded as a necropolis, possibly owing to the sanctity attached to the site.

7. Tablets and Tombs of Late Date

Literature.—Schrader, *KAT*; Loftus, *Chaldæa and Susiana*, 162 ff; Fried. Delitzsch, *Wo lag das Paradies?* 221 f; Zehnpfund, *Babylonien in seinen wichtigsten Ruinenstätten*, 48 ff.

T. G. Pinches

ERI, ē'rī, **ERITES**, ē'rīts (עֵרִי, *'ērī*, "watcher"): The fifth of the seven sons of Gad (Gen **46** 16; Nu **26** 16). Patronymic, **Erites** (ib), a clan of Gad.

ERI-AKU, er-i-a-kōō', ē-ri-ā-kū': This is the probable Sumerian reading of the well-known Bab name written with the characters for "servant" (Sem *wardu* or *ârdu*) and the group standing for the Moon-god Sin (written *En-zu*= *Zu-en*), otherwise Aku, the whole meaning "servant of the Moon-god." This ruler, who was king of Larsa (ELLASSAR—cf that art.), is generally identified with the ARIOCH (q.v.) of Gen **14** 9. Several Assyriologists read the name with the Sem Bab pronunciation of *Warad-Sin;* and, if this be correct, there would be a certain amount of doubt as to the generally received identification; though this, on the other hand, might simply prove that the ancient Hebrews obtained their transcription from a Sumerian source.

1. The Name and Its Etymology

In addition to a number of contract-tablets, the following inscriptions mentioning Eri-Aku or Warad-Sin are known:

2. Inscriptions Mentioning Eri-Aku

(1) A dedication, by Kudur-mabuk, "father of Martu" (*Amurrū*, the land of the Amorites), son of Simti-Šilḫak, of some sacred object to the Moon-god Nannar, for his own life and that of Eri-Aku, his son, the king of Larsa.

(2) A dedication, by Eri-Aku, to Ištar of Ḫallabu, for his own life and that of his father and begetter Kudur-mabuk. The text records the restoration of Ištar's sanctuary.

(3) A dedication, by Eri-Aku, to the god Nannar, for the preservation of his own life and that of his father, Kudur-mabuk. The restoration of several temples is referred to.

(4) An inscription of Eri-Aku, "the powerful man," "the nourisher of Ur [of the Chaldees], the king of Larsa, the king of Šumer and Akkad; son of Kudur-mabuk, the father of Êmutbāla." The text records that he raised the wall of Ur, called "Nannar is the consolidator of the foundations of the land," high like a mountain.

(5) A dedication by Eri-Aku to Nin-insina (titles as above). It records the building of the temple Ê-u-namtila, for his own life, and the life of Kudur-mabuk, the father his begetter.

These inscriptions and others show that Eri-Aku belonged to an Elamite family which held the throne of Larsa, a state which, in common with Babylonia itself, acknowledged the suzerainty of Elam. Kudur-mabuk would seem, from motives of policy, to have given his sons Sumerian and Sem Bab names; and it is noteworthy that he did not retain the rule of Larsa for himself, but delegated it to his offspring, keeping for himself the dominion of Êmutbāla and, as his own inscription shows, the land of the Amorites. With regard to these it may be noted, that the expression *adda*, "father," probably means simply "administrator."

3. The Nationality of His Family

Eri-Aku seems to have died while his father was still alive, and was succeeded by Rîm-Sin, who, as François Thureau-Dangin points out, must have been his brother. As in the case of Eri-Aku, Kudur-mabuk inaugurated the reign of Rîm-Sin by a dedication; but there seems to be no inscription in which Rîm-Sin makes a dedication for the life of his father, implying that Kudur-mabuk died soon after his second son came to the throne.

4. Eri-Aku and Rîm-Sin

And here the question of the identification of Eri-Aku with Eri-Eaku (var. -Ekua) claims consideration. This name occurs on certain tablets of late date from Babylonia, and is coupled with a name which may be read Kudur-laḫgumal (for *Kudur-laḫgomar*, i.e. Chedorlaomer), and Tud-ḫul,[1] the Bib. Tidal. These inscriptions are very mutilated, but from the smaller one it would seem that Eri-[E]aku had a son named Durmah-îlāni, who ravaged some district, and there were floods at Babylon. [But] his son slaughtered him like a lamb, and old man and child [were slain] with the sword. Similar things seem to be said of Tudḫul or Tidal. The larger fragment gives further details of the life of Durmaḫ-îlāni, who had usurped royal power and had been killed with the sword. If the events recorded belong to this period, they must have taken place after the death of Eri-Aku (-Eaku, -Ekua), but before that of Kudur-laḫgumal. It is to be noted that, in accordance with Elamite usage, the crown did not pass to the eldest son after a king's death, but to the king's eldest brother. In Elam this led to endless conflicts, and the same probably took place in Larsa until incorporated with the states of Babylonia.

5. Is Eri-Aku to Be Identified with Eri-Eaku?

The fact that the history of Kudur-laḫgumal (?) forms the subject of a poetical legend suggests that the texts mentioning these kings may have belonged to a kind of historical romance, of which Chedorlaomer (Amraphel), Arioch, and Tidal were the heroes—and, in truth, this is implied by their style. That they are utterly apocryphal, however, remains to be proved.

6. A Historical Romance

LITERATURE.—See "Inscriptions and Records Referring to Babylonia and Elam," etc, *Journal of the Victoria Institute*, 1895–96 (also separately); and the arts. CHEDORLAOMER and ELAM, sec. 12 (5).

T. G. PINCHES

[1] Written *Tudḫula*, but the syllabaries indicate the final *a* as silent.

ERR, ûr, **ERROR**, er'ẽr:

To err is in the OT the tr of שָׁגָה, *shāghāh*, and תָּעָה, *tā'āh*, both of which mean lit. "to wander," "to go astray." We have *shāghāh* in 1 S **26** 21, "I have played the fool, and have erred"; Job **19** 4, "Mine error remaineth with myself," i.e. "is my own concern," or, perhaps, "only injures myself"; Ps **119** 118; Isa **28** 7 AV (thrice); *tā'āh*, Ps **95** 10; Prov **14** 22; Isa **35** 8. It means also "to cause to err" (Isa **3** 12; **30** 28, "a bridle that causeth to err"; Jer **23** 13.32; "Their lies [i.e. the unreal deities, creatures of their own imagination] have caused them to err," Am **2** 4).

In the NT the word is generally πλανάομαι, *planáomai*, "to wander" (Mk **12** 24.27; He **3** 10; Jas **5** 19); *astochéō*, "to miss the mark," "to swerve," occurs twice (1 Tim **6** 21; 2 Tim **2** 18).

Error in the OT represents various words: *sheghāghāh*, "mistake," "oversight" (Eccl **5** 6; cf Prov **20** 25 and see INQUIRY); *meshūghāh*, with the same meaning, "wandering" (Job **19** 4; cf Ps **19** 12); *shal*, "rashness," "mistake" (2 S **6** 7, "God smote him there for his error," RVm "rashness"); *shālū*, Aram. "mistake" (Dnl **6** 4); *tō'āh*, "injury" (Isa **32** 6).

In the NT we have *plánē*, "wandering" (Rom **1** 27; Jas **5** 20; 1 Jn **4** 6; Jude ver 11, "the error of Balaam"); *agnóēma*, "ignorance" (He **9 7**, m Gr "ignorances"). For "is deceived" (Prov **20** 1) RV has "erreth," m "or reeleth"; for "them that are out of the way" (He **5** 2), "the ignorant and erring"; for "deceit" (1 Thess **2** 3), "error."

The Eng. word "error" has the same original meaning as the Heb and Gr main words, being derived from *erro*, "to wander." "To err is human," but there are errors of the heart as well as of the head. The familiar phrase just quoted seems to have its equivalent in the marginal rendering of Gen **6** 3, "in their going astray they are flesh." Errors through ignorance are in the Bible distinguished from errors of the heart and wilful errors (Lev **5** 18; Nu **15** 22; Ezk **45** 20).

W. L. WALKER

ESAIAS, ē-zā'yas. See ISAIAH.

ESARHADDON, ē-sar-had′on (אֵסַר־חַדּוֹן, *'ēṣar-ḥaddōn;* Assyr *Ašur-aḫ-iddina,* "Ashur hath given a brother"): During his lifetime, Sennacherib, king of Assyria, made his favorite son, Esarhaddon (680-668 BC), the viceroy of Babylon; and although he was not the eldest son, he decreed that he should become the legal heir to the throne of Assyria. Sennacherib, having been slain in 681, apparently by two of his sons, who are called in the OT Adrammelech and Sharezer (2 K **19** 37), Esarhaddon proceeded to Nineveh, where the rebellion which followed the death of his father collapsed, having existed for about a month and a half. The OT informs us that the murderers of his father fled to Armenia. This is corroborated by the inscriptions which say that at Melid, in the land of Hanirabbat, which can be said to be in Armenia, Esarhaddon fought the rebels and defeated them; whereupon he was proclaimed king. His father had been so displeased with Babylon that he had attempted to annihilate the city by making it a swamp. Esarhaddon, however, having been infatuated with the ancient culture of the Babylonians, adopted a conciliatory attitude toward the people. Immediately he planned to restore the city on magnificent proportions. The foundations of his work were laid with impressive ceremonies, and in every way he endeavored to ameliorate the inhabitants by his gracious deeds. Even at Nippur evidences of his work in restoring the ancient shrine of Ellil are seen. The kings of the West who became his vassals, among them being Manasseh of Judah, were required to furnish building materials for his operations in Babylonia. His work in that land explains why the Judaean king was incarcerated at Babylon (2 Ch **33** 11) instead of Assyria.

Esarhaddon was first compelled to defend the kingdom against the inroads of the hordes from the North. The Gimirrá (perhaps referring to Gomer of the OT), who were called Manda, seemed to pour into the land. A decisive victory was finally gained over them, and they were driven back into their own country. Afterward, the Medes and the Chaldaeans were also subjugated. He then directed his attentions toward the West. Sidon having revolted against Assyria, Esarhaddon laid siege to the city, which after three years was finally captured and destroyed. He built another city upon the same site, which he called Kar-Esarhaddon, and endeavored to revive its commerce. And, as is mentioned in Ezr **4** 2; cf 10, he repeopled the city (Samaria) with captives from Elam and Babylonia.

The capture of Tyre was also attempted, but, the city being differently situated, a siege from the land was insufficient to bring about submission, as it was impossible to cut off the commerce by sea. The siege, after several years, seems to have been lifted. Although on a great monolith Esarhaddon depicts Ba'al, the king of Tyre, kneeling before him with a ring through his lips, there is nothing in the inscriptions to bear this out.

His work in Canaan was preparatory to his conquest of Egypt. Tirhakah, the Ethiopian king of Egypt, was attacked on the borders, but no victory was gained. Several years later he crossed the borders and gained a decisive victory at Iskhupri. He then proceeded to lay siege to Memphis, which soon capitulated; and Egypt, to the confines of Nubia, surrendered to Assyria. Esarhaddon reorganized the government, and even changed the names of the cities. Necoh was placed over the 22 princes of the land. In 668, Egypt revolted and Esarhaddon, while on his way to put down the revolt, died. He had arranged that the kingdom be divided between two of his sons: Ashurbanipal was to be king of Assyria, and Shamash-shum-ukin was to reign over Babylonia. The nobles decreed, however, that the empire should not be divided, but Shamash-shum-ukin was made viceroy of Babylonia.

A. T. Clay

ESAU, ē′sô (עֵשָׂו, *'ēsāw,* "hairy"; Ἠσαύ, *Ēsaú*): Son of Isaac, twin brother of Jacob. The name was given on account of the hairy covering on his body at birth: "all over like a hairy garment" (Gen **25** 25). There was a prenatal foreshadowing of the relation his descendants were to sustain to those of his younger brother, Jacob (ver 23). The moment of his birth also was signalized by a circumstance that betokened the same destiny (ver 26).

The young E. was fond of the strenuous, daring life of the chase—he became a skilful hunter, "a man of the field" (*'īsh sādheh*). His father warmed toward him rather than toward Jacob, because E.'s hunting expeditions resulted in meats that appealed to the old man's taste (ver 28). Returning hungry from one of these expeditions, however, E. exhibited a characteristic that marked him for the inferior position which had been foretokened at the time of his birth. Enticed by the pottage which Jacob had boiled, he could not deny himself, but must, at once, gratify his appetite, though the calm and calculating Jacob should demand the birthright of the firstborn as the price (vs 30–34). Impulsively he snatched an immediate and sensual gratification at the forfeit of a future glory. Thus he lost the headship of the people through whom God's redemptive purpose was to be wrought out in the world, no less than the mere secular advantage of the firstborn son's chief share in the father's temporal possessions. Though E. had so recklessly disposed of his birthright, he afterward would have secured from Isaac the blessing that appertained, had not the cunning of Rebekah provided for Jacob. Jacob, to be sure, had some misgiving about the plan of his mother (Gen **27** 12), but she reassured him; the deception was successful and he secured the blessing. Now, too late, E. bitterly realized somewhat, at least, of his loss, though he blamed Jacob altogether, and himself not at all (vs 34.36). Hating his brother on account of the grievance thus held against him, he determined upon fratricide as soon as his father should pass away (ver 41); but the watchful Rebekah sent Jacob to Haran, there to abide with her kindred till E.'s wrath should subside (vs 42–45).

E., at the age of forty, had taken two Hittite wives, and had thus displeased his parents. Rebekah had shrewdly used this fact to induce Isaac to fall in with her plan to send Jacob to Mesopotamia; and E., seeing this, seems to have thought he might please both Isaac and Rebekah by a marriage of a sort different from those already contracted with Canaanitish women. Accordingly, he married a kinswoman in the person of a daughter of Ishmael (Gen **28** 6.9). Connected thus with the "land of Seir," and by the fitness of that land for one who was to live by the sword, E. was dwelling there when Jacob returned from Mesopotamia. While Jacob dreaded meeting him, and took great pains to propitiate him, and made careful preparations against a possible hostile meeting, very earnestly seeking Divine help, E., at the head of four hundred men, graciously received the brother against whom his anger had so hotly burned. Though E. had thus cordially received Jacob, the latter was still doubtful about him, and, by a sort of duplicity, managed to become separated from him, E. returning to Seir (Gen **33** 12–17). E. met his brother again at the death of their father, about twenty years later (Gen **35** 29). Of the after years of his life we know nothing.

E. was also called Edom ("red"), because he said to Jacob: "Feed me, I pray thee, with that same red pottage" (Gen **25** 30). The land in which he established himself was "the land of Seir," so called from Seir, ancestor of the Horites whom E. found there; and called also Edom from E.'s surname, and, it may be, too, from the red sandstone of the country (Sayce).

"Esau" is sometimes found in the sense of the descendants of E., and of the land in which they dwelt (Dt **2** 5; Ob vs 6. 8.18.19).

E. J. FORRESTER

ESAY, ē'sā (Ἠσαΐας, *Ēsaías*): AV for Isaiah (2 Esd **2** 18; Ecclus **48** 22).

ESCHATOLOGY, es-ka-tol'ō-ji, OF THE OLD TESTAMENT:

A) Scope of Article
B) Dr. Charles's Work
Individual Religion in Israel
I. FUNDAMENTAL IDEAS
1. Idea of God
2. Idea of Man
Body, Soul and Spirit
3. Sin and Death
II. CONCEPTIONS OF THE FUTURE LIFE—SHEOL
Had Israel No Belief in a Future Life?
1. Reserve on This Subject: Hopes and Promises Largely Temporal
2. A Future State not Therefore Denied
Belief Non-Mythological
3. Survival of Soul, or Conscious Part
4. The Hebrew Sheol
III. THE RELIGIOUS HOPE—LIFE AND RESURRECTION
a) Nature and Grace—Moral Distinctions
b) Religious Hope of Immortality
1. Sheol, Like Death, Connected with Sin
2. Religious Root of Hope of Immortality Not Necessarily Late
3. Hope of Resurrection
(1) Not a Late or Foreign Doctrine
(2) The Psalms
(3) The Book of Job
(4) The Prophets
(5) Daniel—Resurrection of Wicked
IV. THE IDEA OF JUDGMENT—THE DAY OF JEHOVAH
Judgment a Present Reality
1. Day of Jehovah
(1) Relation to Israel
(2) To the Nations
2. Judgment beyond Death
(1) Incompleteness of Moral Administration
(2) Prosperity of Wicked
(3) Suffering of Righteous with Wicked
3. Retribution beyond Death
V. LATER JEWISH CONCEPTIONS—APOCRYPHAL, APOCALYPTIC, RABBINICAL
1. Sources
(1) Apocrypha
(2) Apocalyptic Literature
(3) Rabbinical Writings
2. Description of Views
(1) Less Definite Conceptions
(2) Ideas of Sheol
(3) The Fallen Angels
(4) Resurrection
(5) Judgment
The Messiah
(6) The Messianic Age and the Gentiles
(7) Rabbinical Ideas
LITERATURE

Eschatology of the OT (with Apocryphal and Apocalyptic Writings).—By "eschatology," or doctrine of the last things, is meant the ideas entertained at any period on the future life, the end of the world (resurrection, judgment; in the NT, the Parousia), and the eternal destinies of mankind. In this art. it is attempted to exhibit the beliefs on these matters contained in the OT, with those in the Jewish apocryphal and apocalyptic writings that fill up the interval between the OT and the NT.

***A*) Scope of Article**

The subject here treated has been dealt with by many writers (see "Literature" below); by none more learnedly or ably than by Dr. R. H. Charles in his work on Heb, Jewish and Christian eschatology (*A Critical History of the Doctrine of a Future Life in Israel, in Judaism, and in Christianity*). The present writer is, however, unable to follow Dr. Charles in many of his very radical critical positions, which affect so seriously the view taken of the literary evidence, and of the development of Israel's religion; is unable, therefore, to follow him in his interpretation of the religion itself. The subject, accordingly, is discussed in these pages from a different point of view from his.

***B*) Dr. Charles's Work**

Individual religion in Israel.—One special point in which the writer is unable to follow Dr. Charles in his treatment, which may be noticed at the outset, is in his idea—now so generally favored—that till near the time of the Exile religion was not *individual*—that Jeh was thought of as concerned with the well-being of the people as a whole, and not with that of its individual members. "The individual was not the religious unit, but the family or tribe" (op. cit., 58). How anyone can entertain this idea in face of the plain indications of the OT itself to the contrary is to the present writer a mystery. There is, indeed, throughout the OT, a solidarity of the individual with his family and tribe, but not at any period to the exclusion of a personal relation to Jeh, or of individual moral and religious responsibility. The pictures of piety in the Book of Gen are nearly all individual, and the narratives containing them are, even on the critical view, older than the 9th cent. Adam, Noah, Abraham, Jacob, Joseph, are all of them, to the writers of the history, individuals; Moses, Joshua, Caleb, are individuals; the deeds of individuals are counted to them for righteousness; the sins of others slay them. If there had been ten righteous persons in Sodom, it would have been spared (Gen **18** 32). It was as an individual that David sinned; as an individual he repented and was forgiven. Kings are judged or condemned according to their individual character. It is necessary to lay stress on this at the beginning; otherwise the whole series of the OT conceptions is distorted.

I. Fundamental Ideas.—The eschatology of the OT, as Dr. Charles also recognizes, is dependent on, and molded by, certain fundamental ideas in regard to God, man, the soul and the state after death, in which lies the peculiarity of Israel's religion. Only, these ideas are differently apprehended here from what they are in this writer's learned work.

1. Idea of God

In the view of Dr. Charles, Yahwè (Jehovah), who under Moses became the God of the Heb tribes, was, till the time of the prophets, simply a national God, bound up with the land and with this single people; therefore, "possessing neither interest nor jurisdiction in the life of the individual beyond the grave. . . . . Hence, since early Yahwism possessed no eschatology of its own, the individual Israelite was left to his hereditary heathen beliefs. These beliefs we found were elements of Ancestor Worship" (op. cit., 52; cf 35). The view taken here, on the contrary, is, that there is no period known to the OT in which Jeh—whether the name was older than Moses or not need not be discussed—was not recognized as the God of the whole earth, the Creator of the world and man, and Judge of all nations. He is, in both Gen **1** and **2,** the Creator of the first pair from whom the whole race springs; He judged the whole world in the Flood; He chose Abraham to be a blessing to the families of the earth (Gen **12** 3); His universal rule is acknowledged (Gen **18** 25); in infinite grace, displaying His power over Egypt, He chose Israel to be a people to Himself (Ex **19** 3–6). The ground for denying jurisdiction over the world of the dead thus falls The word of Jesus to the Sadducees is applicable here: "Have ye not read . . . . I am the God of Abraham, and the God of Isaac, and the God of Jacob? God is not the God of the dead, but of the living" (Mt **22** 31.32). The OT instances of resurrection in answer to prayer point in the same direction (1 K **17** 21 ff; 2 K **4** 34 ff; cf Ps **16** 10; **49** 15, etc; see further, below).

2. Idea of Man

According to Dr. Charles, the OT has two contradictory representations of the constitution of man, and of the effects of death. The older or pre-prophetic view distinguishes between soul and body in man (pp. 37 ff, 45 ff), and regards the soul as surviving death (this is not easily reconcilable with the other proposition [p. 37] that the "soul or *nephesh* is identical with the blood"), and as retaining a certain self-consciousness, and the power of speech and movement in Sheol (pp. 39 ff). This view is in many respects identical with that of ancestor worship, which is held to be the primitive belief in Israel (p. 41). The other and later view, which is thought to follow logically from the account in Gen **2** 7, supposes the soul to perish at death (pp. 41 ff). We read there that "Jehovah God formed man of the dust of the ground, and breathed into his nostrils the breath of life; and man became a living soul." The "breath of life" (*nishmath ḥayyīm*) is identified with the "spirit of life" (*rūaḥ ḥayyīm*) of Gen **6** 17, and is taken to mean that the soul has no independent existence, but is "really a function of the material body when quickened by the [impersonal] spirit" (p. 42). "According to this view the annihilation of the soul ensues inevitably at death, that is, when the spirit is withdrawn" (p. 43). This view is held to be the parent of Sadduceeism, and is actually affirmed to be the view of Paul (pp. 43–44, 409)—the apostle who repudiated Sadduceeism in this very article (Acts **23** 6–9).

Body, soul and spirit.—The above view of man's nature is here rejected, and the consistency of the OT doctrine affirmed. The Bib. view has nothing to do with ancestor worship (cf the writer's *POT*, 135–36). In Gen **1** 26.27 man is created in God's image, and in the more anthropomorphic narrative of Gen **2** 7, he becomes "a living soul" through a unique act of Divine inbreathing. The soul (*nephesh*) in man originates in a Divine inspiration (cf Job **32** 8; **33** 4; Isa **42** 5), and is at once the animating principle of the body (the blood being its vehicle, Lev **17** 11), with its appetites and desires, and the seat of the self-conscious personality, and source of rational and spiritual activities. It is these higher activities of the soul which, in the OT, are specially called "spirit" (*rūaḥ*). Dr. Charles expresses this correctly in what he says of the supposed earlier view ("the *rūaḥ* had become the seat of the highest spiritual functions in man," p. 46; see more fully the writer's *God's Image in Man*, 47 ff). There is no ground for deducing "annihilation" from Gen **2** 7. Everywhere in Gen man is regarded as formed for living fellowship with God, and capable of knowing, worshipping and serving Him. See SOUL; SPIRIT.

3. Sin and Death

It follows from the above account that man is regarded in the OT as a compound being, a union of body and soul (embracing spirit), both being elements in his one personality. His destiny was not to death, but to life—not life, however, in separation of the soul from the body (disembodied existence), but continued embodied life, with, perhaps, as its sequel, change and translation to higher existence (thus Enoch, Elijah; the saints at the Parousia). This is the true original idea of immortality for man (see IMMORTALITY). Death, accordingly, is not, as it appears in Dr. Charles, a natural event, but an abnormal event—a mutilation, separation of two sides of man's being never intended to be separated—due, as the Scripture represents it, to the entrance of sin (Gen **2** 17; **3** 19.22; Rom **5** 12; 1 Cor **15** 21.22). It is objected that nothing further is said in the OT of a "Fall," and a subjection of man to death as the result of sin. In truth, however, the whole picture of mankind in the OT, as in the NT, is that of a world turned aside from God, and under His displeasure, and death and all natural evils are ever to be considered in relation to that fact (cf Dillmann, *Alttest. Theol.*, 368, 376 ff; *God's Image in Man*, 198 ff, 249 ff). This alone explains the light in which death is regarded by holy men; their longing for deliverance from it (see below); the hope of resurrection; the place which resurrection—"the redemption of our body" (Rom **8** 23)—after the pattern of Christ's resurrection (Phil **3** 21), has in the Christian conception of immortality.

II. Conceptions of the Future Life—Sheol.—It is usual to find it contended that the Israelites, in contrast with other peoples, had not the conception of a future life till near the time of the Exile; that then, through the teaching of the prophets and the discipline of experience, ideas of individual immortality and of judgment to come first arose. There is, however, a good deal of ambiguity of language, if not confusion of thought, in such statements. It is true there is development in the teaching on a future life; true also that in the OT "life" and "immortality" are words of pregnant meaning, to which bare survival of the soul, and gloomy existence in Sheol, do not apply. But in the ordinary sense of the expression "future life," it is certain that the Israelites were no more without that notion than any of their neighbors, or than most of the peoples and races of the world to whom the belief is credited.

Had Israel No Belief in a Future Life?

1. Reserve on This Subject: Hopes and Promises Largely Temporal

Israel, certainly, had not a developed mythology of the future life such as was found in Egypt. There, life in the other world almost overshadowed the life that now is; in contrast with this, perhaps because of it, Israel was trained to a severer reserve in regard to the future, and the hopes and promises to the nation—the rewards of righteousness and penalties of transgression—were chiefly temporal. The sense of individual responsibility, as was shown at the commencement, there certainly was—an individual relation to God. But the feeling of corporate existence—the sense of connection between the individual and his descendants—was strong, and the hopes held out to the faithful had respect rather to multiplication of seed, to outward prosperity, and to a happy state of existence (never without piety as its basis) on earth, than to a life beyond death. The reason of this and the qualifications needing to be made to the statement will afterward appear; but that the broad facts are as stated every reader of the OT will perceive for himself. Abraham is promised that his seed shall be multiplied as the stars of heaven, and that the land of Canaan shall be given them to dwell in (Gen **12** 1–3; **15**); Israel is encouraged by abundant promises of temporal blessing (Dt **11** 8 ff; **28** 1–14), and warned by the most terrible temporal curses (**28** 15 ff); David has pledged to him the sure succession of his house as the reward of obedience (2 S **7** 11 ff). So in the Book of Job, the patriarch's fidelity is rewarded with return of his prosperity (ch **42**). Temporal promises abound in the Prophets (Hos **2** 14 ff; **14**; Isa **1** 19.26; **35**, etc); the Book of Prov likewise is full of such promises (**3** 13 ff, etc).

All this, however, in no way implies that the Israelites had no conceptions of, or beliefs in, a state of being beyond death, or believed the death of the body to be the extinction of existence. This was very far from being the case. A *hope* of a future life it would be wrong to call it; for there was nothing to suggest hope, joy or life in the good sense, in the ideas they entertained of death or the hereafter. In this they resembled most peoples whose ideas are still primitive, but to whom it is not customary to deny belief in a future state. They stand as yet, though with differences to be afterward pointed out, on the general level of Sem peoples in their conceptions of what the future state was. This is also the view taken by Dr. Charles. He recognizes that early Israelitish thought attributed a "comparatively large measure of life, movement, knowledge and likewise power [?] to the departed in Sheol" (op. cit., 41). A people that does this is hardly destitute of all notions of a future state. This question of Sheol now demands more careful consideration. Here again our differences from Dr. Charles will reveal themselves.

2. A Future State not Therefore Denied

Belief non-mythological.—It would, indeed, have been amazing had the Israelites, who dwelt so long in Egypt, where everything reminded of a future life, been wholly destitute of ideas on that subject. What is clear is that, as already observed, they did not adopt any of the Egyp notions into their religion. The simplicity of their belief in the God of their fathers kept them then and ever after from the importation of mythological elements into their faith. The Egyp Amenti may be said, indeed, to answer broadly to the Heb Sheol; but there is nothing in Israelitish thought to correspond to Osiris and his assessors, the trial in the hall of judgment, and the adventures and perils of the soul thereafter. What, then, was the Heb idea of Sheol, and how did it stand related to beliefs elsewhere?

3. Survival of Soul, or Conscious Part

That the soul, or some conscious part of man for which the name may be allowed to stand, does not perish at death, but passes into another state of existence, commonly conceived of as shadowy and inert, is a belief found, not only among the lower, so-called nature-peoples, but in all ancient religions, even the most highly developed. The Egyp belief in Amenti, or abode of the dead, ruled over by Osiris, is alluded to above; the Bab Arallu (some find the word "Sualu"$=sh^{e}$'*ōl*), the land of death, from which there is no return; the Gr Hades, gloomy abode of the shades of the departed, are outstanding witnesses to this conception (the various ideas may be seen, among other works, in Salmond, *Christian Doctrine of Immortality*, I [ideas of lower races, Indian, Egyp, Bab, Pers and Gr beliefs]; in Sayce, Hibbert Lectures, *Religion of Ancient Babylonians*, and Gifford Lectures, *Religions of Ancient Egypt and Babylonia;* Dr. Charles, *Eschatology*, ch iii, on Gr conceptions). The Heb conception of Sheol, the gathering-place of the dead, is not in essentials dissimilar. "The resemblance," says Dr. Salmond, "between the Heb Sheol, the Homeric Hades, and Bab Arallu is unmistakable" (op. cit., 3d ed, 173). As to its origin, Dr. Charles would derive the belief from ancestor worship. He supposes that "in all probability Sheol was originally conceived as a combination of the graves of the clan or nation, and as thus its final abode" (op. cit., 33). It is far from proved, however, that ancestor worship had the rôle he assigns to it in early religion; and, in any case, the explanation inverts cause and effect. The survival of the soul or shade is already assumed before there can be worship of ancestors. Far simpler is the explanation that man is conscious from the first of a thinking, active principle within him which disappears when death ensues, and he naturally thinks of this as surviving somewhere else, if only in a ghost-like and weakened condition (cf Max Müller, *Anthropological Religion*, 195, 281, 337–38). Whatever the explanation, it is the case that, by a sure instinct, peoples of low and high culture alike all but universally think of the conscious part of their dead as surviving. On natural grounds, the Hebrews did the same. Only, in the Scriptural point of view, this form of survival is too poor to be dignified with the high name of "immortality."

4. The Hebrew Sheol

It is not necessary to do more than sketch the main features of the Heb sh^{e}'*ōl* (see SHEOL). The word, the etymology of which is doubtful (the commonest derivations are from roots meaning "to ask" or "to be hollow," *shā'al*), is frequently, but erroneously, tr[d] in RV "grave" or "hell." It denotes really, as already said, the place or abode of the dead, and is conceived of as situated in the depths of the earth (Ps **63** 9; **86** 13; Ezk **26** 20; **31** 14; **32** 18.24; cf Nu **16** 30; Dt **32** 22). The dead are there gathered in companies; hence the frequently recurring expression, "gathered unto his people" (Gen **25** 8; **35** 29; **49** 33; Nu **20** 24, etc), the phrase denoting, as the context shows, something quite distinct from burial. Jacob, e.g. was "gathered unto his people"; afterward his body was embalmed, and, much later, buried (Gen **50** 2 ff). Poetical descriptions of Sheol are not intended to be taken with literalness; hence it is a mistake, with Dr. Charles, to press such details as "bars" and "gates" (Job **17** 16; **38** 17; Ps **9** 14; Isa **38** 10, etc). In the general conception, Sheol is a place of darkness (Job **10** 21.22; Ps **143** 3), of silence (Ps **94** 17; **115** 17), of forgetfulness (Ps **88** 12; Eccl **9** 5.6.10). It is without remembrance or praise of God (Ps **6** 5), or knowledge of what transpires on earth (Job **14** 21). Even this language is not to be pressed too literally. Part of it is the expression of a depressed or despairing (cf Isa **38** 10 ff) or temporarily skeptical (thus in Eccl; cf **12** 7.13.14) mood; all of it is relative, emphasizing the contrast with the brightness, joy and activity of the earthly life (cf Job **10** 22, "where the light is as midnight"—comparative). Elsewhere it is recognized that consciousness remains; in Isa **14** 9 ff the shades (r^{e}*phā'īm*) of once mighty kings are stirred up to meet the descending king of Babylon (cf Ezk **32** 21). If Sheol is sometimes described as "destruction" (Job **26** 6 m; **28** 22; Prov **15** 11 m) and "the pit" (Ps **30** 9; **55** 23), at other times, in contrast with the weariness and trouble of life, it is figured and longed for as a place of "rest" and "sleep" (Job **3** 17 ff; **14** 12.13). Always, however, as with other peoples, existence in Sheol is represented as feeble, inert, shadowy, devoid of living interests and aims, a true state of the *dead* (on Egyp, Bab and Gr analogies, cf Salmond, op. cit., 54–55, 73–74, 99 ff, 173–74). The idea of Dr. Charles, already commented on, that Sheol is outside the jurisdiction of Jeh, is contradicted by many passages (Dt **32** 22; Job **26** 6; Prov **15** 11; Ps **139** 8; Am **9** 2, etc; cf above).

III. The Religious Hope—Life and Resurrection.—Such is Sheol, regarded from the standpoint of nature; a somewhat different aspect is presented when it is looked at from the point of view of grace. As yet no trace is discernible between righteous and wicked in Sheol; the element of retribution seems absent. Reward and punishment are in this world; not in the state beyond. Yet one must beware of drawing too sweeping conclusions even here. The state, indeed, of weakened consciousness and slumbrous inaction of Sheol does not admit of much distinction, and the thought of exchanging the joys of life for drear existence in that gloomy underworld may well have appalled the stoutest hearts, and provoked sore and bitter complainings. Even the Christian can bewail a life brought to a sudden and untimely close.

a) Nature and Grace—Moral Distinctions

But even on natural grounds it is hardly credible that the pious Israelite thought of the state of the godly gathered in peace to their people as quite the same as those who perished under the ban of God's anger, and went down to Sheol bearing their iniquity. There is a pregnancy not to be overlooked in such expressions as, "The wicked shall be turned back unto Sheol" (Ps **9** 17), a "lowest Sheol" unto which God's anger burns (Dt **32** 22), "uttermost parts of the pit" (Isa **14** 15; Ezk **32** 23) to which the proud and haughty in this life are consigned. Dr. Charles goes so far as to find a "penal character of Sheol" in Pss **49** and **73** (op. cit., 74). Consolation breathes in such utterances as, "Mark the perfect man, and behold the upright; for there is a happy end to the man of peace" (Ps **37** 37), or (with reference to the being taken from the evil to come), "He entereth into peace; they rest in their beds, each one that walketh in his uprightness" (Isa **57** 2; cf ver 21: "There is no peace, saith my God, to the wicked"). Even Balaam's fervent wish, "Let me die the death of the righteous, and let my last end be like his" (Nu **23** 10), seems weakened when interpreted only of the desire for a green and blessed old age. It is possible to read too much into OT expressions; the tendency at the present time would seem to be to read a great deal too little (P. Fairbairn, *Typology of Scripture*, I, 173 ff, 422 ff, may profitably be consulted).

b) Religious Hope of Immortality

To get at the true source and nature of the hope of immortality in the OT, however, it is necessary to go much farther than the idea of any happier condition in Sheol. This dismal region is never there connected with ideas of "life" or "immortality" in any form. Writers who suppose that the hopes which find utterance in passages of Pss and Prophets have any connection with existence in Sheol are on an altogether wrong track. It is not the expectation of a happier condition in Sheol, but the hope of deliverance from Sheol, and of restored life and fellowship with God, which occupies the mind. How much this implies deserves careful consideration.

1. Sheol, Like Death, Connected with Sin

It has already been seen that, in the OT, Sheol, like death, is not the natural fate of man. A connection with sin and judgment is implied in it. Whatever Sheol might be to the popular, unthinking mind, to the reflecting spirit, that really grasped the fundamental ideas of the religion of Jeh, it was a state wholly contrary to man's true destiny. It was, as seen, man's dignity in distinction from the animal, that he was not created under the law of death. Disembodied existence, which is of necessity enfeebled, partial, imperfect existence, was no part of the Divine plan for man. His immortality was to be *in* the body, not out of it. Separation of soul and body, an after-existence of the soul in Sheol, belong to the doom of sin. Dr. Salmond fully recognizes this in his discussion of the subject. "The penal sense of death colours all that the OT says of man's end. It is in its thoughts where it is not in its words" (op. cit., 159; see the whole passage; cf also Oehler, *Theol. of the OT*, I, 242 ff, ET; A. B. Davidson, *Theol. of the OT*, 432 ff, 439 ff). The true type of immortality is therefore to be seen in cases like those of Enoch (Gen **5** 24; cf He **11** 5) and Elijah (2 K **2** 11); of a bare "immortality of the soul," Scripture has nothing to say.

2. Religious Root of Hope of Immortality

It is on all hands conceded that, so far as the hope of immortality, in any full or real sense, is found in the OT, it is connected with religious faith and hope. It has not a natural, but a religious, root. It springs from the believer's trust and confidence in the living God; from his conviction that God—his God—who has bound him to Himself in the bonds of an unchanging covenant, whose everlasting arms are underneath him (Dt **33** 27; cf Ps **90** 1), will not desert him even in Sheol—will be with him there, and will give him victory over its terrors (cf A. B. Davidson, *Comm. on Job*, 293–95; Salmond, op. cit., 175). Life is not bare existence; it consists in God's favor and fellowship (Ps **16** 11; **30** 5; **63** 3). The relevant passages in Pss and Prophets will be considered after. Only, it is contended by the newer school, this hope of immortality belongs to a late stage of Israel's religion—to a period when, through the development of the monotheistic idea, the growth of the sense of individuality, the acute feeling of the contradictions of life, this great "venture" of faith first became possible. One asks, however, Was it so? Was this hope so entirely a matter of "intuitous ventures, and forecasts of devout souls in moments of deepest experience or keenest conflict," as this way of considering the matter represents?

Not necessarily late.—That the hope of immortality could only exist for strong faith is self-evident. But did strong faith come into existence only in the days of the prophets or the Exile? Exception has already been taken to the assumption that monotheism was a late growth, and that individual faith in God was not found in early times. It is not to be granted without demur that, as now commonly alleged, the Pss and the Book of Job, which express this hope, are post-exilian products. If, however, faith in a covenant-keeping God is of earlier date—if it is present in patriarchal and Mosaic days—the question is not, Why should it not give rise to similar hopes? but rather, How should it be prevented from doing so? If a patriarch like Abraham truly walked with God, and received His promises, could he, any more than later saints, be wholly distrustful of God's power to keep and deliver him in and from Sheol? It is hard to credit it. It is replied, there is no evidence of such hope. Certainly these ancient saints did not write psalms or speak with the tongues of prophets. But is there nothing in their quiet and trustful walk, in their tranquil deaths, in their sense of uncompleted promises, in their pervading confidence in God in all the vicissitudes of life, to suggest that they, too, were able to commit themselves into the hands of God in death, and to trust Him to see that it was, or would ultimately be, well with them in the future? Thus at least Jesus understood it (Mt **22** 32); thus NT writers believed (He **11** 13.14). Faith might falter, but in principle, this hope must have been bound up with faith from the beginning.

3. Hope of Resurrection

This raises now the crucial question, What shape did this hope of immortality assume? It was not, as already seen, an immortality enjoyed in Sheol; it could only then be a hope connected with deliverance from the power of Sheol—in essence, whether precisely formulated or not, a hope of resurrection. It is, we believe, because this has been overlooked, that writers on the subject have gone so often astray in their discussions on immortality in the OT. They have thought of a blessedness in the future life of the *soul* (thus Charles, op. cit., 76–77); whereas the redemption the Bible speaks of invariably embraces the whole personality of man, body and soul together. Jesus, it may be remembered, thus interprets the words, "I am the God of Abraham," etc (Mt **22** 32), as a pledge not simply of continued existence, but of resurrection. This accords with what has been seen of the connection of death with sin and its abnormality in the case of man. The immortality man would have enjoyed, had he not sinned, would have been an immortality of his whole person. It will be seen immediately that this is borne out by all the passages in which the hope of immortality is expressed in the OT. These never contemplate a mere immortality of the soul, but always imply resurrection.

(1) *Not a late or foreign doctrine.*—If the above is correct, it follows that it is a mistake to place the belief in resurrection so late as is often done, still more to derive it from Zoroastrianism (thus Cheyne, *Origin of Psalter*, lect viii) or other foreign sources. It was a genuine corollary from the fundamental Israelitish beliefs about God, man, the soul, sin, death and redemption. Professor Gunkel emphasizes "the immeasurable significance" of this doctrine, and speaks of it as "one of the greatest things found anywhere in the history of religion," but thinks "it cannot be derived from within Judaism itself, but must take its origin from a ruling belief in the Orient of the later time" (*Zum religionsgeschichtlichen Verständniss des NT*, 32–33; for criticism of Gunkel's positions see the writer's *Resurrection of Jesus*, 255 ff). To make good his theory, however, he has to discount all the evidences for the belief furnished by the earlier OT writings, and this, it is believed, cannot be done successfully. It was before noted that cases of resurrection appear in the historical books (1 K **17** 21 ff; 2 K **4** 34 ff). It is not impossible that the reverent care of the patriarchs for their dead was, as with the Egyptians, inspired by some hope of this kind (Gen **23**; **50** 5.25; Ex **13** 19; cf He **11** 22). In any case an impartial survey of the evidence proves that the thought of resurrection colors all the later expressions of the hope of immortality (see IMMORTALITY; cf also the writer's appendix on the subject in *Christian View of God*, 200 ff).

(2) *The Psalms.*—The passages in the Pss in which faith rises to the hope of immortality are principally Ps **16** 8–11; **17** 15; **49** 14.15; **73** 24. There are a few others, but these are the chief, and so far as they are allowed to express a hope of immortality at all, they do so in a form which implies resurrection. Dr. Cheyne, believing them to be influenced by Zoroastrianism, formerly granted this (*Origin of Psalter*, lect viii); now he reads the passages differently. There is no good reason for putting these psalms in post-exilian times, and, taken in their most natural sense, their testimony seems explicit. Ps **16** 8–11 (cited in Acts **2** 24–31 as a prophecy of the resurrection of Christ) reads "My flesh also shall dwell in safety [or confidently, m]. For thou wilt not leave my soul to Sheol; neither wilt thou suffer thy holy one to see corruption [or the pit, m]. Thou wilt show me the path of life," etc. In Ps **17** 15, the Psalmist, after describing the apparent prosperity of the wicked, says, "As for me, I shall behold thy face in righteousness; I shall be satisfied, when I awake, with beholding thy form" (AV, ERV, "with thy likeness"). Cheyne (op. cit., 406) refers this to the resurrection (cf Delitzsch, Perowne, etc). Yet more explicit is Ps **49** 14.15, "They [the wicked] are appointed as a flock for Sheol .... and the upright shall have dominion over them in the morning. .... But God will redeem my soul from the power [hand, m] of Sheol; for he will receive me." The last clause, lit. "He will take me," has, as Perowne, Delitzsch, Cheyne (formerly), even Duhm, allow, allusion to cases like those of Enoch and Elijah. It cannot, however, contemplate actual bodily translation; it must therefore refer to resurrection. Similar in strain is Ps **73** 24, "Thou wilt guide me with thy counsel, and afterward receive me to glory." Dr. Charles grants that, in Pss **49** and **73**, "God takes the righteous to Himself" in heaven (pp. 76–77), but fails to connect this with the doctrine of resurrection which he finds appearing about the same time (p. 78).

(3) *The Book of Job.*—Before looking at the prophets, a glance should be taken at the Book of Job, which, irrespective of date (it is quite unwarrantably made post-exilian), reflects patriarchal conditions. Ch **14** raises the question, "If a man die, shall he live again?" (ver 14), and it is to be remarked that the form in which it does it, is the possibility of bodily revival. The appearances hostile to man's living again are enumerated (vs 7–12), then faith, reasserting itself, flings itself on God to accomplish the apparently impossible: "Oh that thou wouldest hide me in Sheol, that thou wouldest keep me secret, until thy wrath be past, that thou wouldest appoint me a set time and remember me. .... Thou wouldest call and I would answer thee: thou wouldest have a desire to the work of thy hands" (vs 13–15; m reads "Thou shalt call," etc). Dr. A. B. Davidson says, "To his mind this involves a complete return to life again of the whole man" (Cambridge *Comm. on Job*, in loc.). With this must be taken the splendid outburst in **19** 25–27, "I know that my Redeemer liveth," etc, which, whatever doubts may attach to the precise rendering of certain clauses, undoubtedly expresses a hope not inferior in strength to that in the verse just quoted.

(4) *The Prophets.*—The presence of the idea of resurrection in the Prophets is not doubted, but the passages are put down to exilic or preëxilic times, and are explained of "spiritual" or "national," not of individual, resurrection (cf Charles, op. cit., 128–29). It seems plain, however, that, before the figure of resurrection could be applied to the nation, the idea of resurrection must have been there; and it is by no means clear that in certain of the passages the resurrection of individuals is not included. Cheyne granted this regarding the passages in Isa (**25** 6–8; **26** 19): "This prospect concerns not merely the church-nation, but all of its believing members, and indeed all, whether Jews or not, who submit to the true king, Jeh" (op. cit., 402). There is no call for putting the remarkable passages in Hos—"After two days will he revive us: on the third day he will raise us up, and we shall live before him" (**6** 2); "I will ransom them from the power of Sheol: I will redeem them from death: O death, where are thy plagues? O Sheol, where is thy destruction?" (**13** 14)—later than the time of that prophet. In them the idea of resurrection is already fully present; as truly as in the picture in Ezk **37** 1–10 of the valley of dry bones. The climax is, however, reached in Isa **25** 6–8; **26** 19, above referred to, from which the individual element cannot be excluded (cf Salmond, op. cit., 211–12: "The theme of this great passage, **26** 19, therefore, is a personal, not a corporate resurrection").

(5) *Daniel—resurrection of wicked.*—Finally, in the OT we have the striking statement in Dnl **12** 2, "And many of them that sleep in the dust .... shall awake, some to everlasting life, and some to shame and everlasting contempt. And they that are wise shall shine as the brightness of the firmament," etc. The peculiarity of this passage is, that in it, for the first time, is announced a resurrection of the wicked as well as of the righteous (cf in the NT Jn **5** 28.29; Acts **24** 15; Rev **20** 12 ff). The word "many" is not to be understood in contrast with "all," though probably only Israel is in view. The event is connected with a "time of trouble" (ver 1) following upon the overthrow of Antiochus, here representative of Antichrist. The really difficult problem is, How did this conception of the resurrection of the wicked come about? The resurrection of the righteous, it has been seen, is a corollary from the covenant-faithfulness of Jeh.

But this does not apply to the wicked. Whence then does the idea come? It is given as a revelation, but even revelation connects itself with existing ideas and experiences. The resurrection of the wicked, certainly, does not arise, like that of the righteous, from the consciousness of an indissoluble union with God, but it may well arise from the opposite conviction of the *judgment* of God. As the sense of individuality grew strong—and it is granted that the teaching of the prophets did much to strengthen that feeling—and the certainty of moral retribution developed, it was inevitable that this should react on the conception of the future, in making it as certain that the wicked should be punished, as that the good should be rewarded, in the world to come. Naturally too, as the counterpart of the other belief, this shaped itself into the form of a resurrection to judgment. We are thus brought, as a last step, to consider the idea of judgment and its effects as found in the prophetic teaching.

IV. The Idea of Judgment—the Day of Jehovah.—It was seen that, under Mosaism, the promises and threatenings of God were mainly confined to the present life, and that the sense of distinctions in Sheol, though not absent, was vague and wavering. Through temporal dispensations men were trained to faith in the reality of moral retribution. Under the prophets, while the judgments of God on nations and individuals were still primarily viewed as pertaining to this life, there gradually shaped itself a further idea—that of an approaching consummation of history, or Day of Jehovah, when God's enemies would be completely overthrown, His righteousness fully vindicated and His kingdom established in triumph throughout the earth. The developments of this idea may now briefly be exhibited. In this relation, it need only be stated that the writer does not follow the extraordinary mangling of the prophetic texts by certain critics, accepted, though with some misgiving, by Dr. Charles.

Judgment a Present Reality

The "Day of Jehovah," in the prophetic writings, is conceived of, sometimes more generally, as denoting any great manifestation of God's power in judgment or salvation (e.g. the locusts in Joel **2**), sometimes more eschatologically, of the final crisis in the history of God's kingdom, involving the overthrow of all opposition, and the complete triumph of righteousness (e.g. Isa **2** 2–5; Joel **3**; Am **9** 11 ff; Zec **14**, etc). The two things are not unconnected; the one is the prelude, or anticipatory stage, of the other. That feature of prophetic vision sometimes spoken of as the absence of perspective is very conspicuous in the fact that chronology is largely disregarded, and the "Day of Jehovah" is seen looming up as the immediate background of every great crisis in which the nation may for the time be involved (Assyr invasions; Bab captivity; Maccabean persecution). The one thing ever certain to the prophet's mind is that the "Day" is surely coming—it is the one great, dread, yet for God's people joyful, event of the future—but the steps by which the goal is to be reached are only gradually revealed in the actual march of God's providence.

1. Day of Jehovah

(1) *Relation to Israel.*—The "Day" is in its primary aspect a day of judgment (Isa **2** 12); not, however, to be thought of as a day of vengeance only on the adversaries of Israel (Am **5** 18 ff). Israel itself would be the first to experience the strokes of the Divine chastisement: "You only have I known of all the families of the earth: therefore I will visit upon you all your iniquities" (Am **3** 2). God's judgments on Israel, while retributive, were also purifying and sifting; a "remnant" would remain, who would be the seed of a holier community (Isa **6** 13; Am **9** 9; Zeph **3** 13.20, etc). The Book of Hos beautifully exhibits this aspect of the Divine dealings.

(2) *To the nations.*—Of wider scope is the relation of the "Day" to the gentile world. The nations are used as the instruments of God's judgments on Israel (Assyrians, Chaldaeans, Persians), but they, too, would in turn be judged by Jeh (cf the prophecies against the nations in Isa, Jer, Ezk, Nah, Hab, etc). The end would be, although this does not fully appear in every prophet, that a remnant of the heathen also would turn to Jeh, and be rescued from the judgment (Zec **14** 16). More generally, an extension of the kingdom of God would take place till the earth was filled with God's glory (e.g. Isa **2** 2–5, with Mic **4** 1–5; Isa **42** 4; **60**; **66** 3–6; Jer **12** 14–16; **16** 19–21; Ezk **16** 53.55. 61, God will turn the captivity of Sodom and her daughters; Am **9** 11; Hab **2** 14; cf Ps **22** 27–31; **65** 2.5; **86** 9; **87**). These events, in prophetic speech, belong to "the latter days" (Isa **2** 2; Jer **48** 47; Ezk **38** 16; Hos **3** 5; Mic **4** 1). In Daniel's great prophecy of the four kingdoms, these are represented as broken in pieces by the kingdom of heaven, symbolized by a stone cut out of the mountain without hands (Dnl **2** 44.45; cf **7** 27). The kingdom is given by the Ancient of Days to one "like unto a son of man" (**7** 13). Haggai and Zechariah, the post-exilian prophets, share in these glowing hopes (Hag **2** 6.7; Zec **2** 10; **8** 20–23; **14** 16). In Mal is found one of the noblest of all the prophetic utterances: "From the rising of the sun even unto the going down of the same my name shall be great among the Gentiles," etc (**1** 11); and prophecy closes with the announcement of Him, Jeh's messenger, by whom this "great and terrible day of Jeh" is to be brought in (Mal **4**).

2. Judgment beyond Death

The purview, in what is said of the "Day of Jehovah," is thus seen to be confined to earth, though the references to resurrection, and the passages in the close of Isa (**65** 17; **66** 22) about "new heavens and a new earth" imply a further vista. The hope of immortality—of resurrection life—in the case of the righteous has already been considered. But what of judgment after death in the case of the wicked? Only dim premonitions of retribution, it was seen, are found in the earlier doctrine of Sheol. There are frequent references to "judgment" in the Pss, sometimes on the world (e.g. **96** 13; **98** 9; cf **50**), sometimes on individuals (e.g. **1** 5), but it is doubtful if any of them look beyond earth. Yet many things combined to force this problem on the attention.

(1) *Incompleteness of moral administration.*—There was the sharpening of the sense of individual responsibility in the prophetic age (Jer **31** 29.30; Ezk **18** 2 ff), and the obvious fact of the incompleteness of the Divine moral administration in the present life, as respects the individual. The working of moral laws could be discerned, but this fell far short of exact individual retribution. Life was full of moral anomalies and perplexities (cf Job, Book of).

(2) *Prosperity of wicked.*—There was the special difficulty that the wicked did not always seem to meet with the punishment due to their misdeeds in time. On the contrary they often seemed to flourish, to have success in their schemes, to triumph over the godly, who were afflicted and oppressed. This was the enigma that so painfully exercised the minds of the psalmists (Pss **10**, **17**, **37**, **49**, **73**, etc). The solution they found was that the prosperity of the wicked did not endure. It came to a sudden end (Ps **37** 35.36; **73** 18–20), while the

righteous had a sure compensation in the future (Ps **17** 15; **49** 15; **73** 24, etc). It was not, however, always the case that the wicked were thus visibly cut off. Besides, a sudden end hardly seemed an adequate punishment for a long career of triumphant iniquity, and, if the righteous were recompensed hereafter, the thought lay near that the wicked might be, and should be, also.

(3) *Suffering of righteous with wicked.*—There was the kindred fact that, in the calamities that overtook the wicked, the righteous were often the involuntary sharers. The wicked did not suffer by themselves; the godly were involved in the storm of judgment (war, captivity, plagues) that broke upon them. Here was something else calling for redress at the hands of a God of righteousness.

3. Retribution beyond Death

From these causes the thought almost necessarily presented itself of the extension of retribution for the wicked into the state beyond death. Hence, as before seen, Sheol did come in the later age to assume something of a penal character for the unrighteous. There was a wrath of God that burned to the lowest Sheol (Dt **32** 22; cf Charles, op. cit., 74). But this abode of the shades was not, for the evil any more than for the good, a fitting sphere for moral recompense. If, for the complete reward of the righteous, a resurrection-state was necessary, did not the same hold true for the wicked? It is questioned whether the very definite announcements of an individual judgment in Eccl **11** 9; **12** 14 refer to the state beyond death—it is probable that they do (cf Salmond, op. cit., 216–17). The first clear intimation of a resurrection of the wicked, however, is found, as already said, in Dnl **12** 2, which likewise implies judgment. Perhaps a hint of the same idea is given in Isa **66** 24: "They shall go forth [the prophet is speaking of the times of the new heavens and the new earth, ver 22], and look upon the dead bodies of the men that have transgressed against me: for their worm shall not die, neither shall their fire be quenched; and they shall be an abhorring unto all flesh." Dr. Charles connects this with the idea of Gehenna as "a place of punishment for rebellious and apostate Jews," which he thinks also to be implied in Isa **50** 11 (op. cit., 158). It is the same word "abhorrence" (*dērā'ōn*), found in the above passage, which is rendered in Dnl **12** 2 "contempt," and Dr. Charles says "the reference in both is to Gehenna," and the punishment "is conceived of as eternal" (pp. 158–59).

It is hardly possible to carry the subject farther within the limits of the OT. Further developments belong to the later Judaism.

V. Later Jewish Conceptions—Apocryphal, Apocalyptic, Rabbinical.—The sources of our knowledge of the eschatological conceptions among the Jews in the immediately pre-Christian period are:

1. Sources

(1) *Apocrypha.*—The books of the OT Apoc (see Apocrypha), taken over, with the exception of 2 Esd, from the LXX. 2 Esd, better known as 4 Esd, is more properly classed with the apocalyptic writings. The original work consists only of chs **3–14,** with a passage in ch **7** not found in the ordinary version. The book is post-Christian (c 80–96 AD).

(2) *Apocalyptic literature* (see art. under that head, II, i, 1; II, ii).—The remains of this lit. consist of the Sib Or (oldest parts, Book III, from 2d cent. BC), the Book En (see below), the Ps Sol (70–40 BC), with the Apoc Bar (50–100 AD), the Book of Jub, and XII P (see below), the Asm M (early 1st cent. AD), and the Asc Isa (before 50 AD). A good deal turns on the dating of some of these books. Several (Apoc Bar, Asm M, Asc Isa, with 4 Esd) are post-Christian. The Book of Jub and XII P have also usually been regarded as such, but Dr. Charles argues for dates going back to the close of the 2d cent. BC for both. Late Jewish and Christian additions are recognized in the latter. Formerly Dr. Charles dated Jub "before 10 AD." The chief dispute relates to chs **37–70** (the "Similitudes") of the Book of En. These important sections are held by some (Dr. Stanton, etc) to be post-Christian (end of 1st cent. AD)—a view to which we incline; Dr. Charles and others place them in the 1st cent. BC. Most of the remaining portions of the book are assigned to dates in the 2d cent. BC. To the above should be added the notices of Jewish opinions in Jos.

(3) *Rabbinical writings.*—For rabbinical ideas, we are chiefly dependent on the Talmudic writings and the Tgs—sources whose late character makes their witness often doubtful (see Talmud; Targums).

2. Description of Views

It is only possible to summarize very briefly the varying and frequently conflicting conceptions on eschatological subjects to be gleaned from this extensive lit. The representations are often wildly imaginative, and, so far as they are not genuine developments from OT ideas, have value only as they may be supposed to throw light on the teachings of the NT. With one or two exceptions, little is to be gathered from the apocryphal books, and it will be best to treat the subject under headings.

(1) *Less definite conceptions.*—In the apocryphal Ecclus (Wisdom of the Son of Sirach) we remain still on the old ground of Sheol as a place in which there is no remembrance, thanksgiving or retribution (**17** 27.28; **41** 3.4, etc; a somewhat different note is heard in **21** 10). It is the same in Bar (**2** 17) and Tob (**3** 6). In 1 Macc we have simply the OT phrases, "gathered to his fathers" (**2** 69), "gathered to his people" (**14** 30). In the Book of Wisd, the influence of Gr ideas is seen in a doctrine of the immortality of the *soul* only (**2** 23; **3** 1–4; **4** 13.14; **15** 3; not a resurrection), possibly of preëxistence (**8** 20). The wicked suffer punishment in Sheol (**3** 1–10; **5** 1–14, etc).

(2) *Ideas of Sheol.*—Generally, however, in the apocalyptic books, a marked change is seen in the ideas of Sheol. It is still the place of the dead, but is regarded more as a state intermediate between death and the resurrection for such as shall be raised; in which righteous and wicked are separated; in which the wicked suffer punishment. The Book of En distinguishes four abodes for the departed—two for the righteous, and two for the wicked (**21** 1–13). One class of the wicked (those already punished in this life) remain there forever, while the others are raised, and pass to the torment of Gehenna (**17** 2). The righteous are in Paradise—"the garden of life" (**61** 12), "the garden of righteousness" (**67** 3). This character of Sheol as a place of punishment (intermediate or final) is met with frequently (Book of Jub **7** 29; **22** 22; 2 Macc **6** 23; Ps Sol **14** 6; **15** 11; **16** 2, etc). In certain places, Dr. Charles says, "Sheol has become an abode of fire, and therefore synonymous so far with Gehenna. . . . . In several passages in the Similitudes, and throughout En **91–104,** Sheol and Gehenna are practically identical" (op. cit., 237). Similar ideas are found in the Slavonic version of En (ib, 261 ff).

(3) *The fallen angels.*—Much prominence in the Book of En is given to the fallen angels (those who sinned with women, Gen **6** 2). They are consigned in the judgment to ever-burning fire (En **21** 1–6; **90** 20–25).

(4) *Resurrection.*—Ideas of the resurrection vary. In En **22,** the righteous and one class of the wicked

are raised; elsewhere all the righteous are raised and none of the wicked (En **61** 5; **90** 33; Ps Sol **3** 16); sometimes there is to be a resurrection of all, just and unjust (En **51** 1.2). 2 Macc dwells much on the resurrection, which seems to embrace all Israel (**3** 16; **13** 9; **7** 9.14.23, etc). For the Gentiles there is no resurrection (**7** 14.36). In En **90** 38, the bodies of the righteous are described as "transformed" in the resurrection (cf in the "Similitudes," **39** 7; **51** 4; **62** 15). The doctrine of the resurrection (universal) is taught in the Apoc Bar **30** 2–5; **50, 51,** and in 4 Esd **7** 32–37. In Jos the Pharisees are said to have believed in the resurrection of the righteous only (*Ant*, XVIII, i, 3). This does not coincide with Paul's statement in Acts **24** 15.

(5) *Judgment.*—The reality of a final judgment, supervening upon the intermediate judgment in Sheol, is strongly affirmed in most of the apocalyptic books. The Book of En speaks much of this final judgment. It describes it as "the great day," "the righteous judgment," "the great day of judgment," "the last judgment," "the judgment of all eternity" (**10** 6.12; **16** 1; **19** 1; **22** 4.11; **25** 4; **90** 26.27, etc). Wicked angels and men are judged, and sentenced to Gehenna—a doom without end.

The Messiah: An interesting point is the relation of the Messiah to this judgment. With the exception of 4 Esd, the apocryphal books are silent on the Messiah. In the apocalyptic books the Messiah does appear, but not always in the same light. In the Sib Or (**3**), Ps of Sol (**17, 18**), Apoc Bar (**39, 40**) and in 4 Esd (**13** 32 ff) the appearance of Messiah is associated with the overthrow and judgment of the ungodly worldly powers; in the older portions of En (**90** 16–25) God Himself executes this judgment, and holds the great assize—the Messiah does not appear till after. In the sec. of En, chs **37–70,** on the other hand, the Messiah appears definitely as the judge of the world, and titles resembling those in the NT, "the Righteous One" (**38** 2; **53** 6), "the Elect One" (**40** 5; **45** 3. 4, etc), above all, "the Son of Man" (**46** 2–4; **48** 2, etc), are given Him. It is these passages which suggest Christian influence, especially as the conception is not found elsewhere in pre-Christian Apocalypse, and the Book of Jub, which refers otherwise to En, makes no mention of these passages. Yet another idea appears in later Apocalypse, that, viz. of a *limited* reign of Messiah, *after* which take place the resurrection and judgment. 4 Esd has the extraordinary notion that, after a reign of 400 years, the Messiah dies (**7** 28.29). God in this case is the judge.

(6) *The Messianic age and the Gentiles.*—The Messianic age, when conceived of as *following* the judgment (the older view), is unlimited in duration, has Jerus for its center, and includes in the scope of its blessing the converted Gentiles (Sib Or **3** 698–726; En **90** 30.37; cf **48** 5; **53** 1; Ps Sol **17** 32–35). The righteous dead of Israel are raised to participate in the kingdom. Already in En **90** 28.29 is found the idea that the new Jerus is not the earthly city, but a city that comes down from heaven, where, as in 4 Esd, the Messianic reign is limited, the blessed life after resurrection is transferred to heaven.

(7) *Rabbinical ideas.*—Little is to be added from the rabbinical conceptions, which, besides being difficult to ascertain precisely, are exceedingly confused and contradictory. Most of the ideas above mentioned appear in rabbinical teaching. With the destruction of the hostile world-powers is connected in later rabbinism the appearance of "Armilus"—an Antichrist. The reign of Messiah is generally viewed as limited in duration—400 years (as in 4 Esd), and 1,000 years being mentioned (cf Schürer, *Hist of Jewish People*, Div II, Vol II, 179, ET). At its close takes place a renovation of the world, resurrection (for Israelites only, certain classes being excluded), judgment, and eternal heavenly happiness for the righteous. The punishments of the wicked appear mostly to be regarded as eternal, but the view is also met with of a limited duration of punishment (see authorities in Schürer, op. cit., 183; Edersheim, *Jesus the Messiah*, app. XIX, and other works noted in "Literature" below).

LITERATURE.—R. H. Charles, D.D., *A Crit. Hist of the Doct of a Future Life* (1899); apocalyptic works trd and edited by same writer (*Book of En, Apoc Bar, Book of Jub, Test. of 12 Patriarchs*, etc; V. H. Stanton, *The Jewish and the Christian Messiah* (1886); S. D. F. Salmond, *Christian Doct of Immortality* (4th ed, 1901); A. Edersheim, *Life and Times of Jesus the Messiah*, ed 1906 (esp. app. XIX); E. Schürer, *Hist of the Jewish People in the Time of Jesus Christ* (Div II, Vol II, ET). OT Theologies: Oehler, A. B. Davidson, etc; arts. in Dictionaries: Hastings, *EB*, etc. For fuller lists, see Charles.

JAMES ORR

ESCHATOLOGY, es-ka-tol'ō-ji, OF THE NEW TESTAMENT:

I. Doctrinal and Religious Significance.—The subject of eschatology plays a prominent part in NT teaching and religion. Christianity in its very origin bears an eschatological character. It means the appearance of the Messiah and the inauguration of His work; and from the OT point of view these form part of eschatology. It is true in Jewish theology the days of the Messiah were not always included in the eschatological age proper, but often regarded as introductory to it (cf Weber, *Jüdische Theol.*², 371 ff). And in the NT also this point of view is to some extent represented, inasmuch as, owing to the appearance of the Messiah and the only partial fulfilment of the prophecies for the present, that which the OT depicted as one synchronous movement is now seen to divide into two stages, viz. the present Messianic age and the consummate state of the future. Even so, however, the NT draws the Messianic period into much closer connection with the strictly eschatological process than Judaism. The distinction in Judaism rested on a consciousness of difference in quality between the two stages, the content of the Messianic age being far less spiritually and transcendentally conceived than that of the final state. The NT, by spiritualizing the entire Messianic circle of ideas, becomes keenly alive to its affinity to the content of the highest eternal hope, and consequently tends to identify the two, to find the age to come anticipated in the present. In some cases this assumes explicit shape in the belief that great eschatological transactions have already begun to take place, and that believers have already attained to at least partial enjoyment of eschatological privileges. Thus the present kingdom in Our Lord's teaching is one in essence with the final kingdom; according to the discourses in John eternal life is in principle realized here; with Paul there has been a prelude to the last judgment and resurrection in the death and resurrection of Christ, and the life in the Spirit is the first-fruits of the heavenly state to come. The strong sense of this may even express itself in the paradoxical form that the eschatological state has arrived and the one great incision in history has already been made (He **2** 3.5; **9** 11; **10** 1; **12** 22–24). Still, even where this extreme consciousness is reached, it nowhere supersedes the other more common representation, according to which the present state continues to lie this side of the eschatological crisis, and, while directly leading up to the latter, yet remains to all intents a part of the old age and world-order. Believers live in the "last days," upon them "the ends of the ages are come," but "the last day," "the consummation of the age," still lies in the future (Mt **13** 39.40.49; **24** 3; **28** 20; Jn **6** 39.44.54; **12** 48; 1 Cor **10** 11; 2 Tim **3** 1; He **1** 2; **9** 26; Jas **5** 3; 1 Pet **1** 5.20; 2 Pet **3** 3; 1 Jn **2** 18; Jude ver 18).

The eschatological interest of early believers was no mere fringe to their religious experience, but the very heart of its inspiration. It expressed and embodied the profound supernaturalism and soteriological character of the NT faith. The coming world was not to be the product of natural development but of a Divine interposition arresting the process of history. And the deepest motive of the longing for this world was a conviction of the abnormal character of the present world, a strong sense of sin and evil. This explains why the NT doctrine of salvation has grown up to a large extent in the closest interaction with its eschatological teaching. The present experience was interpreted in the light of the future. It is necessary to keep this in mind for a proper appreciation of the generally prevailing hope that the return of the Lord might come in the near future. Apocalyptic calculation had less to do with this than the practical experience that the earnest of the supernatural realities of the life to come was present in the church, and that therefore it seemed unnatural for the full fruition of these to be long delayed. The subsequent receding of this acute eschatological state has something to do with the gradual disappearance of the miraculous phenomena of the apostolic age.

II. General Structure.—NT eschatology attaches itself to the OT and to Jewish belief as developed on the basis of ancient revelation. It creates on the whole no new system or new terminology, but incorporates much that was current, yet so as to reveal by selection and distribution of emphasis the essential newness of its spirit. In Judaism there existed at that time two distinct types of eschatological outlook. There was the ancient national hope which revolved around the destiny of Israel. Alongside of it existed a transcendental form of eschatology with cosmical perspective, which had in view the destiny of the universe and of the human race. The former of these represents the original form of OT eschatology, and therefore occupies a legitimate place in the beginnings of the NT development, notably in the revelations accompanying the birth of Christ and in the earlier (synoptical) preaching of John the Baptist. There entered, however, into it, as held by the Jews, a considerable element of individual and collective eudaemonism, and it had become identified with a literalistic interpretation of prophecy, which did not sufficiently take into account the typical import and poetical character of the latter. The other scheme, while to some extent the product of subsequent theological development, lies prefigured in certain later prophecies, esp. in Dnl, and, far from being an importation from Bab, or ultimately Pers, sources, as some at present maintain, represents in reality the true development of the inner principles of OT prophetic revelation. To it the structure of NT eschatology closely conforms itself. In doing this, however, it discards the impure motives and elements by which even this relatively higher type of Jewish eschatology was contaminated. In certain of the apocalyptic writings a compromise is attempted between these two schemes after this manner, that the carrying out of the one is merely to follow that of the other, the national hope first receiving its fulfilment in a provisional Messianic kingdom of limited duration (400 or 1,000 years), to be superseded at the end by the eternal state. The NT does not follow the Jewish theology along this path. Even though it regards the present work of Christ as preliminary to the consummate order of things, it does not separate the two in essence or quality, it does not exclude the Messiah from a supreme place in the coming world, and does not expect a temporal Messianic kingdom in the future as distinguished from Christ's present spiritual reign, and as preceding the state of eternity. In fact the figure of the Messiah becomes central in the entire eschatological process, far more so than is the case in Judaism. All the stages in this process, the resurrection, the judgment, the life eternal, even the intermediate state, receive the impress of the absolute significance which Christian faith ascribes to Jesus as the Christ. Through this Christocentric character NT eschatology acquires also far greater unity and simplicity than can be predicated of the Jewish schemes. Everything is practically reduced to the great ideas of the resurrection and the judgment as consequent upon the Parousia of Christ. Much apocalyptic embroidery to which no spiritual significance attached is eliminated. While the overheated phantasy tends to multiply and elaborate, the religious interest tends toward concentration and simplification.

III. Course of Development.—In NT eschatological teaching a general development in a well-defined direction is traceable. The starting-point is the historico-dramatic conception of the two successive ages. These two ages are distinguished as *hoútos ho aiṓn, ho nún aiṓn, ho enestṓs aiṓn*, "this age," "the present age" (Mt **12** 32; **13** 22; Lk **16** 8; Rom **12** 2; 1 Cor **1** 20; **2** 6.8; **3** 18; 2 Cor **4** 4; Gal **1** 4; Eph **1** 21; **2** 2; **6** 12; 1 Tim **6** 17; 2 Tim **4** 10; Tit **2** 12), and *ho aiṓn ekeínos, ho aiṓn méllōn, ho aiṓn erchómenos*, "that age," "the future age" (Mt **12** 32; Lk **18** 30; **20** 35; Eph **2** 7; He **6** 5). In Jewish lit. before the NT, no instances of the developed antithesis between these two ages seem to be found, but from the way in which it occurs in the teaching of Jesus and Paul it appears to have been current at that time. (The oldest undisputed occurrence is a saying of Joḥanan ben Zakkay, about 80 AD.) The contrast between these two ages is (esp. with Paul) that between the evil and transitory, and the perfect and abiding. Thus to each age belongs its own characteristic order of things, and so the distinction passes over into that of two "worlds" in the sense of two systems (in Heb and Aram. the same word *'ōlām, 'ālam*, does service for both, in Gr *aiṓn* usually renders the meaning "age," occasionally "world" [He **1** 2; **11** 3], *kósmos* meaning "world"; the latter, however, is never used of the future world). Cf Dalman, *Die Worte Jesu*, I, 132–46. Broadly speaking, the development of NT eschatology consists in this, that the two ages are increasingly recognized as answering to two spheres of being which coexist from of old, so that the coming of the new age assumes the character of a revelation and extension of the supernal order of things, rather than that of its first entrance into existence. Inasmuch as the coming world stood for the perfect and eternal, and in the realm of heaven such a perfect, eternal order of things already existed, the reflection inevitably arose that these two were in some sense identical. But the new significance which the antithesis assumes does not supersede the older historico-dramatic form. The higher world so interposes in the course of the lower as to bring the conflict to a crisis. The passing over of the one contrast into the other, therefore, does not mark, as has frequently been asserted, a recession of the eschatological wave, as if the interest had been shifted from the future to the present life. Esp. in the Fourth Gospel this "deëschatologizing" process has been found, but without real warrant. The apparent basis for such a conclusion is that the realities of the future life are so vividly and itensely felt to be existent in heaven and from there operative in the believer's life, that the distinction between what is now and what will be hereafter enjoyed becomes less sharp. Instead of the supersedure of the eschatological, this means the very opposite, viz. its most real anticipation. It should further be observed that the development in question is intimately connected and keeps equal pace with the disclosure of the preëxistence of Christ, because this fact and the descent of Christ from heaven furnished the clearest witness to the reality of the heavenly order of things. Hence it is esp. observable, not in the earlier epistles of Paul, where the structure of eschatological thought is still in the main historico-dramatic, but in the epistles of the first captivity (Eph **1** 3.20–22; **2** 6; **3** 9.10; **4** 9.10; **6** 12; Phil **2** 5–11; **3** 20; Col **1** 15.17; **3** 2; further, in He **1** 2.3; **2** 5; **3** 4; **6** 5.11; **7** 13.16; **9** 14; **11** 10.16; **12** 22.23). The Fourth Gospel marks the culmination of this line of teaching, and it is unnecessary to point out how here the contrast between heaven and earth in its christological consequences determines the entire structure of thought. But here it also appears how the last outcome of the NT progress of doctrine had been anticipated in the highest teaching of Our Lord. This can be accounted for by the inherent fitness that the supreme disclosures which touch the personal life of the Saviour should come not through any third person, but from His own lips.

IV. General and Individual Eschatology.—In the OT the destiny of the nation of Israel to such an extent overshadows that of the individual, that only the first rudiments of an individual eschatology are found. The individualism of the later prophets, esp. Jeremiah and Ezekiel, bore fruit in the thought of the intermediate period. In the apocalyptic writings considerable concern is shown for the ultimate destiny of the individual. But not until the NT thoroughly spiritualized the conceptions of the last things could these two aspects be perfectly harmonized. Through the centering of the eschatological hope in the Messiah, and the suspending of the individual's share in it on his personal relation to the Messiah, an individual significance is necessarily imparted to the great final crisis. This also tends to give greater prominence to the intermediate state. Here, also, apocalyptic thought had pointed the way. None the less the OT point of view continues to assert itself in that even in the NT the main interest still attaches to the collective, historical development of events. Many questions in regard to the intermediate period are passed by in silence. The OT prophetic foreshortening of the perspective, immediately connecting each present crisis with the ultimate goal, is reproduced in NT eschatology on an individual scale in so far as the believer's life here is linked, not so much with his state after death, but rather with the consummate state after the final judgment. The present life in the body and the future life in the body are the two outstanding illumined heights between which the disembodied state remains largely in the shadow. But the same foreshortening of the perspective is also carried over from the OT into the NT delineation of general eschatology. The NT method of depicting the future is not chronological. Things lying widely apart to our chronologically informed experience are by it drawn closely together. This law is adhered to doubtless not from mere limitation of subjective human knowledge, but by reason of adjustment to the general method of prophetic revelation in OT and NT alike.

V. The Parousia.—The word denotes "coming," "arrival."

1. Definition

It is never applied to the incarnation of Christ, and could be applied to His second coming only, partly because it had already become a fixed Messianic term, partly because there was a point of view from which the future appearance of Jesus appeared the sole adequate expression of His Messianic dignity and glory. The explicit distinction between "first advent" and "second advent" is not found in the NT. It occurs in Test. XII P, Test. Abr. **92** 16. In the NT it is approached in He **9** 28 and in the use of *epipháneia* for both the past appearance of Christ and His future manifestation (2 Thess **2** 8; 1 Tim **6** 14; 2 Tim **1** 10; **4** 1; Tit **2** 11.13). The Christian use of the word "parousia" is more or less colored by the consciousness of the present bodily absence of Jesus from His own, and consequently suggests the thought of His future abiding presence, without, however, formally coming to mean the state of the Saviour's presence with believers (1 Thess **4** 17). Parousia occurs in Mt **24** 3.37 .39; 1 Cor **15** 23; 1 Thess **2** 19; **3** 13; **4** 15; **5** 23; 2 Thess **2** 1.8; Jas **5** 7.8; 2 Pet **1** 16; **3** 4.12; 1 Jn **2** 28. A synonymous term is *apokálupsis*, "revelation," probably also of pre-Christian origin, presupposing the preëxistence of the Messiah in hidden form previous to His manifestation, either in heaven or on earth (cf Apoc Bar **29** 3; **30** 1; 4 Ezr (2 Esd) **7** 28; Test. XII P, Test. Levi **18**; Jn **7** 27; 1 Pet **1** 20). It could be adopted by Christians because Christ had been withdrawn into heaven and would be publicly demonstrated the Christ on His return, hence used with special reference to enemies and unbelievers (Lk **17** 30; Acts **3** 21; 1 Cor **1** 7; 2 Thess **1** 7.8; 1 Pet **1** 13.20; **5** 4). Another synonymous term is "the day of the [Our] Lord," "the day," "that day," "the day of Jesus Christ." This is the rendering of the well-known OT phrase. Though there is no reason in any particular passage why "the Lord" should not be Christ, the possibility exists that in some cases it may refer to God (cf "day of God" in 2 Pet **3** 12). On the other hand, what the OT with the use of this phrase predicates of God is sometimes in the NT purposely transferred to Christ. "Day," while employed of the parousia generally, is, as in the OT, mostly associated with the judgment, so as to become a synonym for judgment (cf Acts **19** 38; 1 Cor **4** 3). The phrase is found in Mt **7** 22; **24** 36; Mk **13** 32; Lk **10** 12; **17** 24; **21** 34; Acts **2** 20; Rom **13** 12; 1 Cor **1** 8; **3** 13; **5** 5; 2 Cor **1** 14; Phil **1** 6; **2** 16; 1 Thess **5** 2.4 (cf vs 5.8); 2 Thess **2** 2; 2 Tim **1** 12.18; **4** 8; He **10** 25; 2 Pet **3** 10.

The parousia is preceded by certain **signs** heralding its approach.

2. Signs Preceding the Parousia

Judaism, on the basis of the OT, had worked out the doctrine of "the woes of the Messiah," *ḥebhᵉlē ha-māshīªḥ*, the calamities and afflictions attendant upon the close of the present and the beginning of the coming age being interpreted as birth pains of the latter. This is transferred in the NT to the parousia of Christ. The phrase occurs only in Mt **24** 8; Mk **13** 8, the idea, in Rom **8** 22, and allusions to it occur probably in 1 Cor **7** 26; 1 Thess **3** 3; **5** 3.

Besides these general "woes," and also in accord with Jewish doctrine, the appearance of the Antichrist is made to precede the final crisis. Without Jewish precedent, the NT links with the parousia as preparatory to it, the pouring out of the Spirit, the destruction of Jerus and the temple, the conversion of Israel and the preaching of the gospel to all the nations. The problem of the sequence and interrelation of these several precursors of the end is a most difficult and complicated one and, as would seem, at the present not ripe for solution. The "woes" which in Our Lord's eschatological discourse (Mt **24**; Mk **13**; Lk **21**) are mentioned in more or less close accord with Jewish teaching are: (1) wars, earthquakes and famines, "the beginning of travail"; (2) the great tribulation; (3) commotions among the heavenly bodies; cf Rev **6** 2–17. For Jewish parallels to these, cf Charles, *Eschatology*, 326, 327. Because of this element which the discourse has in common with Jewish apocalypses, it has been assumed by Colani, Weiffenbach, Weizsäcker, Wendt, et al., that here two sources have been welded together, an actual prophecy of Jesus, and a Jewish or Jewish-Christian apocalypse from the time of the Jewish War 68–70 (*HE*, III, 5, 3). In the text of Mk this so-called "small apocalypse" is believed to consist of vs 7.8.14–20.24–27.30.31. But this hypothesis mainly springs from the disinclination to ascribe to Jesus realistic eschatological expectations, and the entirely unwarranted assumption that He must have spoken of the end in purely ethical and religious terms only. That the typically Jewish "woes" bear no direct relation to the disciples and their faith is not a sufficient reason for declaring the prediction of them unworthy of Jesus. A contradiction is pointed out between the two representations, that the parousia will come suddenly, unexpectedly, and that it will come heralded by these signs. Esp. in Mk **13** 30.32 the contradiction is said to be pointed. To this it may be replied that even after the removal of the assumed apocalypse the same twofold representation remains present in what is recognized as genuine discourse of Jesus, viz. in Mk **13** 28.29 as compared with vs 32.33–37 and other similar admonitions to watchfulness. A real contradiction between ver 30 and ver 32 does not exist. Our Lord could consistently affirm both: "This generation shall not pass away, until all these things be accomplished," and "of that day or that hour knoweth no one." To be sure, the solution should not be sought by understanding "this generation" of the Jewish race or of the human race. It must mean, according to ordinary usage, the then living generation. Nor does it help matters to distinguish between the prediction of the parousia within certain wide limits and the denial of knowledge as to the precise day and hour. In point of fact the two statements do not refer to the same matter at all. "That day or that hour" in ver 32 does not have "these things" of ver 30 for its antecedent. Both by the demonstrative pronoun "that" and by "but" it is marked as an absolute self-explanatory conception. It simply signifies as elsewhere the day of the Lord, the day of judgment. Of "these things," the exact meaning of which phrase must be determined from the foregoing, Jesus declares that they will come to pass within that generation; but concerning the parousia, "that [great] day," He declares that no one but God knows the time of its occurrence. The correctness of this view is confirmed by the preceding parable, Mk vs 28.29, where in precisely the same way "these things" and the parousia are distinguished. The question remains how much "these things" (ver 29; Lk ver 31), "all these things" (Mt vs 33.34, Mk ver 30), "all things" (Lk ver 32) is intended to cover of what is described in the preceding discourse. The answer will depend on what is there represented as belonging to the precursors of the end, and what as strictly constituting part of the end itself; and on the other question whether Jesus predicts one end with its premonitory signs, or refers to two crises each of which will be heralded by its own series of signs. Here two views deserve consideration. According to the one (advocated by Zahn in his *Comm. on Mt*, 652–66) the signs cover only Mt **24** 4–14. What is related afterward, viz. "the abomination of desolation," great tribulation, false prophets and Christs, commotions in the heavens, the sign of the Son of Man, all this belongs to "the end" itself, in the absolute sense, and is therefore comprehended in the parousia and excepted from the prediction that it will happen in that generation, while included in the declaration that only God knows the time of its coming. The destruction of the temple and the holy city, though not explicitly mentioned in vs 4–14, would be included in what is there said of wars and tribulation. The prediction thus interpreted would have been literally fulfilled. The objections to this view are: (1) It is unnatural thus to subsume what is related in vs 15–29 under "the end." From a formal point of view it does not differ from the phenomena of vs 4–14 which are "signs." (2) It creates the difficulty, that the existence of the temple and the temple-worship in Jerus are presupposed in the last days immediately before the parousia. The "abomination of desolation" taken from Dnl **8** 13; **9** 27; **11** 31; **12** 11; cf Sir **49** 2—according to some, the destruction of the city and temple, better a desecration of the temple-site by the setting up of something idolatrous, as a result of which it becomes desolate—and the flight from Judaea, are put among events which, together with the parousia, constitute the end of the world. This would seem to involve chiliasm of a very pronounced sort. The difficulty recurs in the strictly eschatological interpretation of 2 Thess **2** 3.4, where "the man of sin" (see SIN, MAN OF) is represented as sitting in "the temple of God," and in Rev **11** 1.2, where "the temple of God" and "the altar," and "the court which is without the temple" and "the holy city" figure in an episode inserted between the sounding of the trumpet of the sixth angel and that of the seventh. On the other hand it ought to be remembered that eschatological prophecy makes use of ancient traditional imagery and stereotyped formulas, which, precisely because they are fixed and applied to all situations, cannot always bear a literal sense, but must be subject to a certain degree of symbolical and spiritualizing interpretation. In the present case the profanation of the temple by Antiochus Epiphanes may have furnished the imagery in which, by Jesus, Paul and John, anti-Christian developments are described of a nature which has nothing to do with Israel, Jerus or the temple, lit. understood. (3) It is not easy to conceive of the preaching of the gospel to all the nations as falling within the lifetime of that generation. It is true Rom **1** 13; **10** 18; **15** 19–24; Col **1** 6; 1 Tim **3** 16; 2 Tim **4** 17 might be quoted in support of such a view. In the statement of Jesus, however, it is definitely predicted that the preaching of the gospel to all the nations not only must happen before the end, but that it straightway precedes the end: "Then shall the end come" (Mt **24** 14). To distinguish between the preaching of the gospel to all the nations and the completion of the gentile mission, as Zahn proposes, is artificial. As over against these objections, however, it must be admitted that the grouping of all these later phenomena before the end proper avoids the difficulty arising from "immediately" in Mt **24** 29 and from "in those days" in Mk **13** 24.

The other view has been most lucidly set forth

by Briggs, *Messiah of the Gospels*, 132–65. It makes Jesus' discourse relate to two things: (1) *the destruction of Jerus and the temple;* (2) *the end of the world.* He further assumes that the disciples are informed with respect to two points: (1) *the time;* (2) *the signs.* In the answer to the *time*, however, the two things are not sharply distinguished, but united into one prophetic perspective, the parousia standing out more conspicuously. The definition of the time of this complex development is: (*a*) negative (Mk **13** 5–8); (*b*) positive (vs 9–13). On the other hand in describing the *signs* Jesus discriminates between (*a*) the signs of the destruction of Jerus and the temple (vs 14–20); (*b*) the signs of the parousia (vs 24–27). This view has in its favor that the destruction of the temple and the city, which in the question of the disciples figured as an eschatological *event*, is recognized as such in the answer of Jesus, and not alluded to after a mere incidental fashion, as among the *signs*. Esp. the version of Lk **21** 20–24 proves that it figures as an *event*. This view also renders easier the restriction of Mk **13** 30 to the first event and its signs. It places "the abomination of desolation" in the period preceding the national catastrophe. The view that the two events are successively discussed is further favored by the movement of thought in vs 32 ff. Here, after the Apocalypse has been brought to a close, the application to the disciples is made, and, in the same order as was observed in the prophecy, *first*, the true attitude toward the national crisis is defined in the parable of the Fig Tree and the solemn assurance appended that it will happen in this generation (vs 28–31); *secondly*, the true attitude toward the parousia is defined (vs 32–37). The only serious objection that may be urged against this view arises from the close concatenation of the section relating to the national crisis with the section relating to the parousia (Mt **24** 29: "immediately after . . . . those days"; Mk **13** 24: "in those days"). The question is whether this mode of speaking can be explained on the principle of the well-known foreshortening of the perspective of prophecy. It cannot be a priori denied that this peculiarity of prophetic vision may have here characterized also the outlook of Jesus into the future which, as ver 32 shows, was the prophetic outlook of His human nature, as distinct from the Divine omniscience. The possibility of misinterpreting this feature and confounding sequence in perspective with chronological succession is in the present case guarded against by the statement that the gospel must first be preached to all the nations (cf Acts **3** 19.25.26; Rom **11** 25; Rev **6** 2) before the end can come, that no one knows the time of the parousia except God, that there must be a period of desolation after the city shall have been destroyed, and that the final coming of Jesus to the people of Israel will be a coming not of judgment, but one in which they shall hail Him as blessed (Mt **23** 38.39; Lk **13** 34.35), which presupposes an interval to account for this changed attitude (cf Lk **21** 24: "until the times of the Gentiles be fulfilled"). It is not necessary to carry the distinction between the two crises joined together here into the question as put by the disciples in Mt **24** 3, as if "when shall these things be?" related to the destruction of the temple exclusively, as the other half of the question speaks of the coming of Jesus and the end of the world. Evidently here not the two events, but *the events* (complexly considered) and *the signs* are distinguished. "These things" has its antecedent not exclusively in ver 2, but even more in **23** 38.39. The disciples desired to know not so much when the calamitous national catastrophe would come, but rather when that subsequent coming of the Lord would take place, which would put a limit to the distressing results of this catastrophe, and bring with it the re-acceptance of Israel into favor. This explains also why Jesus does not begin His discourse with the national crisis, but first takes up the question of the parousia, to define negatively and positively the time of the latter, and that for the purpose of warning the disciples who in their eagerness for the ultimate issue were inclined to foreshorten the preceding calamitous developments. That Jesus could actually join together the national and the cosmical crises appears from other passages, such as Mt **10** 23, where His interposition for the deliverance of the fugitive disciples is called a "coming" of the Son of Man (Mt **16** 28; Mk **9** 1; Lk **9** 27, where a coming of the Son of Man in His kingdom [Mt], or a coming of the kingdom of God with power [Mk], or a seeing of the kingdom of God [Lk] is promised to some of that generation). It is true these passages are frequently referred to the parousia, because in the immediately preceding context the latter is spoken of. The connection of thought, however, is not that the parousia and this promised coming are identical. The proximate coming is referred to as an encouragement toward faithfulness and self-sacrifice, just as the reward at the parousia is mentioned for the same purpose. The conception of an earlier coming also receives light from the confession of Jesus at His trial (Mt **26** 64; where the "henceforth" refers equally to the coming on the clouds of heaven and to the sitting at the right hand of God; cf Mk **14** 62; Lk **22** 69). The point of the declaration is, that He who now is condemned will in the near future appear in theophany for judgment upon His judges. The closing discourses of Jn also have the conception of the coming of Jesus to His disciples in the near future for an abiding presence, although here this is associated with the advent of the Spirit (Jn **14** 18.19.21.23; **16** 16. 19.22.23). Finally the same idea recurs in Rev, where it is equally clear that a preliminary visitation of Christ and not the parousia for final judgment can be meant (**2** 5.16; **3** 3.20; cf also the pl. "one of the days of the Son of man" in Lk **17** 22).

3. Events Preceding the Parousia

To the events preceding the parousia belongs, according to the uniform teaching of Jesus, Peter and Paul, *the conversion of Israel* (Mt **23** 39; Lk **13** 35; Acts **1** 6.7; **3** 19. 21; where the arrival of "seasons of refreshing" and "the times of restoration of all things" is made dependent on the [eschatological] sending of the Christ to Israel), and this again is said to depend on the repentance and conversion and the blotting out of the sins of Israel; Rom **11**, where the problem of the unbelief of Israel is solved by the twofold proposition: (1) that there is even now among Israel an election according to grace; (2) that in the future there will be a comprehensive conversion of Israel (vs 5.25–32).

Among the precursors of the parousia appears further the *Antichrist*. The word is found in the NT in 1 Jn **2** 18.22; **4** 3; 2 Jn ver 7 only, but the conception occurs also in the Synoptics, in Paul and in Rev. There is no instance of its earlier occurrence in Jewish lit. *Anti* may mean "in place of" and "against"; the former includes the latter. In Jn it is not clear that the heretical tendencies or hostile powers connected with the anti-Christian movement make false claim to the Messianic dignity. In the Synoptics the coming of false Christs and false prophets is predicted, and that not merely as among the nearer signs (Mk **13** 6), but also in the remote eschatological period (ver 22). With Paul, who does not employ the word, the conception is clearly the developed one of the counter-Christ. Paul ascribes to him an *apokálupsis* as he does to

Christ (2 Thess **2** 6.8); his manner of working and its pernicious effect are set over against the manner in which the gospel of the true Christ works (vs 9–12). Paul does not treat the idea as a new one; it must have come down from the OT and Jewish eschatology and have been more fully developed by NT prophecy; cf in Dnl **7** 8.20; **8** 10.11 the supernaturally magnified figure of the great enemy. According to Gunkel (*Schöpfung und Chaos*, 1895) and Bousset (*Der Antichrist in der Überlieferung des Judenthums, des NT und der alten Kirche*, 1875) the origin of the conception of a final struggle between God and the supreme enemy must be sought in the ancient myth of Chaos conquered by Marduk; what had happened at the beginning of the world was transferred to the end. Then this was anthropomorphized, first in the form of a false Messiah, later in that of a political tyrant or oppressor. But there is no need to assume any other source for the idea of a last enemy than OT eschatological prophecy (Ezk and Dnl and Zec). And no evidence has so far been adduced that the Pauline idea of a counter-Messiah is of pre-Christian origin. This can only be maintained by carrying back into the older period the Antichrist tradition as found later among Jews and Christians. It is reasonable to assume in the present state of the evidence that the combination of the two ideas, that of the great eschatological enemy and that of the counter-Messiah, is a product of Christian prophecy. In fact even the conception of a *single* last enemy does not occur in pre-Christian Jewish lit.; it is found for the first time in Apoc Bar **40** 1.2, which changes the general conception of 4 Ezr to this effect. Even in the eschatological discourse of Jesus the idea is not yet unified, for false Christs and false prophets in the plural are spoken of, and the instigator of "the abomination of desolation," if any is presupposed, remains in the background. In the Epistle of Jn the same plural representation occurs (1 Jn **2** 18.22; 2 Jn ver 7), although the idea of a personal Antichrist in whom the movement culminates is not only familiar to the author and the reader (1 Jn **2** 18, "as ye heard that antichrist cometh"), but is also accepted by the writer (**4** 3, "This is the spirit of the antichrist, whereof ye have heard that it cometh; and now it is in the world already"; cf 2 Thess **2** 7, "The mystery of lawlessness doth already work").

Various views have been proposed to explain the concrete features of the Pauline representation in 2 Thess **2** and that of Rev **13** and **17**. According to Schneckenburger, *JDT*, 1859, and Weiss, *SK*, 1869, Paul has in mind the person whom the Jews will acclaim as their Messiah. The idea would then be the precipitate of Paul's experience of hostility and persecution from the part of the Jews. He expected that this Jewish Messianic pretender would, helped by Satanic influence, overthrow the Rom power. The continuance of the Rom power is "that which restraineth," or as embodied in the emperor, "one that restraineth now" (2 Thess **2** 6.7). (For an interesting view in which the rôles played by these two powers are reversed, cf Warfield in *Expos*, 3d ser., IV, 30–44.) The objection to this is that "the lawless one," not merely from Paul's or the Christian point of view, but in his own avowed intent, opposes and exalts himself against all that is called God or worshipped. This no Jewish pretender to the Messiahship could possibly do: his very Messianic position would preclude it. And the conception of a counter-Christ does not necessarily point to a Jewish environment, for the idea of Messiahship had in Paul's mind been raised far above its original national plane and assumed a universalistic character (cf Zahn, *Einleitung in das NT*[1], I, 171). Nor does the feature that according to ver 4, "the lawless one" will take his seat in the temple favor the view in question, for the desecration of the temple by Antiochus Epiphanes and later similar experiences may well have contributed to the figure of the great enemy the attribute of desecrator of the temple. It is not necessary to assume that by Paul this was understood literally; it need mean no more than that the Antichrist will usurp for himself Divine honor and worship. Patristic and later writers gave to this feature a chiliastic interpretation, referring it to the temple which was to be rebuilt in the future. Also the allegorical exegesis which understands "the temple" of the Christian church has found advocates. But the terms in which "the lawless one" is described exclude his voluntary identification with the Christian church. According to a second view the figure is not a Jewish but a pagan one. Kern, Baur, Hilgenfeld and many others, assuming that 2 Thess is post-Pauline, connect the prophecy with the at-one-time current expectation that Nero, the great persecutor, would return from the East or from the dead, and, with the help of Satan, set up an anti-Christian kingdom. The same expectation is assumed to underlie Rev **13** 3.12.14 (one of the heads of the beast smitten unto death and his death stroke healed); **17** 8.10.11 (the beast that was, and is not, and is about to come up out of the abyss; the eighth king, who is one of the seven preceding kings). As to Paul's description, there is nothing in it to make us think of a Nero reappearing or redivivus. The parousia predicated of the lawless one does not imply it, for parousia as an eschatological term means not "return" but "advent." The Antichrist is not depicted as a persecutor, and Nero was the persecutor *par excellence*. Nor does what is said about the "hindering" or the "hinderer" suit the case of Nero, for the later Rom emperors could not be said to hold back Nero's reappearance. As to Rev, it must be admitted that the rôle here ascribed to the beast would be more in keeping with the character of Nero. But, as Zahn has well pointed out (*Einleitung in das NT*[1], II, 617–26), this interpretation is incompatible with the date of Rev. This book must have been written at a date when the earlier form of the expectation that Nero would reappear still prevailed, viz. that he would return from the East to which he had fled. Only when too long an interval had elapsed to permit of further belief in Nero's still being alive, was this changed into the superstition that he would return from the dead. But this change in the form of the belief did not take place until after Rev must have been written. Consequently, if the returning Nero did figure in Rev, it would have to be in the form of one reappearing from the East. As a matter of fact, however, the beast or the king in which Nero is found is said by Rev **13** 1; **17** 8 to have been smitten unto death and healed of the death stroke, to come up out of the sea or the abyss, which would only suit the later form of the expectation. It is therefore necessary to dissociate the description of the beast and its heads and horns entirely from the details of the succession of the Rom empire; the prophecy is more grandly staged; the description of the beast as partaking of several animal forms in **13** 2 refers back to Dnl, and here as there must be understood of the one world-power in its successive national manifestations, which already excludes the possibility that a mere succession of kings in one and the same empire can be thought of. The one of the heads smitten unto death and the death stroke healed must refer to the world-power to be made powerless in one of its phases, but afterward to revive in a new phase. Hence here already the healing of the death stroke is predicated, not merely of one of the heads, but also of the beast itself (cf **13** 3 with **13**

12). And the same interpretation seems to be required by the mysterious statements of ch **17**, where the woman sitting upon the beast is the metropolis of the world-power, changing its seat together with the latter, yet so as to retain, like the latter in all its transformations, the same character whence she bears the same name of Babylon (ver 5). Here as in ch **13** the beast has seven heads, i.e. passes through seven phases, which idea is also expressed by the representation that these seven heads are seven kings (ver 10), for, as in Dnl **7**, the kings stand not for individual rulers, but for kingdoms, phases of the world-power. This explains why in ver 11 the beast is identified with one of the kings. When here the further explanation, going beyond ch **13**, is added, that the beast was and is not and is about to come up out of the abyss (ver 8), and in vs 10.11 that of the seven kings five are fallen, one is, the other is not yet come, and when he comes must continue a little while, to be followed by the eighth, who is identical with the beast that was and is not, and with one of the seven, the only way to reconcile these statements lies in assuming that "the beast," while in one sense a comprehensive figure for the world-power in all its phases, can also in another sense designate the supreme embodiment and most typical manifestation of the world-power in the past; in respect to this acute phase the beast was and is not and is to appear again, and this acute phase was one of seven successive forms of manifestation, and in its reappearance will add to this number the eighth. Although a certain double sense in the employment of the figures thus results, this is no greater than when on the other view Nero is depicted both as "the beast" and as one of the heads of "the beast." Which concrete monarchies are meant by these seven phases is a matter of minor importance. For a suggestion cf Zahn, op. cit., II, 624: (1) Egypt; (2) Assyria; (3) Babylon; (4) the Medo-Pers power; (5) the Graeco-Alexandrian power; (6) the Rom power; (7) a short-lived empire to succeed Rome; (8) the eighth and last phase, which will reproduce in its acute character the fifth, and will bring on the scene the Antichrist, the counterpart and, as it were, reincarnation of Antiochus Epiphanes. The seer evidently has his present in the Rom phase of the power of the beast, and this renders it possible for him to give in **17** 9 another turn to the figure of the seven heads, interpreting it of the seven mountains on which the woman sits, but this apocalyptic looseness of handling of the imagery can furnish no objection to the view just outlined, since on any view the two incongruous explanations of the seven heads as seven mountains and seven kings stand side by side in vs 9 and 10. Nor should the mysterious number of 666 in **13** 18 be appealed to in favor of the reference of the beast to Nero, for on the one hand quite a number of other equally plausible or implausible solutions of this riddle have been proposed, and on the other hand the interpretation of Nero is open to the serious objection, that in order to make out the required number from the letters of Nero's name this name has to be written in Heb characters and that with *scriptio defectiva* of *Ḳesar* (*Nerōn Ḳēsar*) instead of *Ḳeisar*, the former of which two peculiarities is out of keeping with the usage of the book elsewhere (cf Zahn, op. cit., II, 622, 624, 625, where the chief proposed explanations of the number 666 are recorded). Under the circumstances the interpretation of the figure of the beast and its heads must be allowed to pursue its course independently of the mystery of the number 666 in regard to which no certain conclusion appears attainable.

The following indicates the degree of definiteness to which, in the opinion of the writer, it is possible to go in the interpretation of the prophecy. The terms in which Paul speaks remind of Daniel's description of the "little horn." Similarly Rev attaches itself to the imagery of the beasts in Dnl. Both Paul and Rev also seem to allude to the self-deification of rulers in the Hellenistic and Rom world (cf *ZNTW*, 1904, 335 ff). Both, therefore, appear to have in mind a politically organized world-power under a supreme head. Still in both cases this power is not viewed as the climax of enmity against God on account of its political activity as such, but distinctly on account of its self-assertion in the religious sphere, so that the whole conception is lifted to a higher plane, purely spiritual standards being applied in the judgment expressed. Paul so thoroughly applies this principle that in his picture the seductive, deceptive aspect of the movement in the sphere of false teaching is directly connected with the person of "the lawless one" himself (2 Thess **2** 9–12), and not with a separate organ of false prophecy, as in Rev **13** 11–17 (the second beast). In Rev, as shown above, the final and acute phase of anti-Christian hostility is clearly distinguished from its embodiment in the Rom empire and separated from the latter by an intermediate stage. In Paul, who stands at a somewhat earlier point in the development of NT prophecy, this is not so clearly apparent. Paul teaches that the "mystery of lawlessness" is already at work in his day, but this does not necessarily involve that the person of "the lawless one," subsequently to appear, must be connected with the same phase of the world-power, with which Paul associates this mystery already at work, since the succeeding phases being continuous, this will also insure the continuity between the general principle and its personal representative, even though the latter should appear at a later stage. It is impossible to determine how far Paul consciously looked beyond the power of the Rom empire to a later organization as the vehicle for the last anti-Christian effort. On the other hand, that Paul must have thought of "the lawless one" as already in existence at that time cannot be proven. It does not follow from the parallelism between his "revelation" and the parousia of Christ, for this "revelation" has for its correlate simply a previous hidden presence for some time somewhere, not an existence necessarily extending to Paul's time or the time of the Rom empire, far less a preëxistence, like unto Christ's, in the supernatural world. Nor is present existence implied in what Paul says of "the hindering power." This, to be sure, is represented as asserting itself at that very time, but the restraint is not exerted directly upon "the lawless one"; it relates to the power of which he will be the ultimate exponent; when this power, through the removal of the restraint, develops freely, his revelation follows. According to ver 9 his "parousia is according to the working of Satan," but whether this puts a supernatural aspect upon the initial act of his appearance or relates more to his subsequent presence and activity in the world, which will be attended with all powers and signs and lying wonders, cannot be determined with certainty. But the element of the supernatural is certainly there, although it is evidently erroneous to conceive of "the lawless one" as an incarnation of Satan, literally speaking. The phrase "according to the working of Satan" excludes this, and "the lawless one" is a true human figure, "the man of sin" (or "the man of lawlessness," according to another reading; cf the distinction between Satan and "the beast" in Rev **20** 10), ver 3. The "power" and "signs" and "wonders" are not merely "seeming"; the genitive *pseúdous* is not intended to take them out of the category of the supernatural, but simply means that what they are intended to accredit is a lie, viz. the Divine dignity of "the lawless one." Most difficult of all is the determination of what Paul means by the hindering power or the hinderer in ver 7. The most common view refers this to the Rom authority as the basis of civil order and protection, but there are serious objections to this. If Paul at all associated the Antichrist in any way with the Rom power, he cannot very well have sought the opposite principle in the same quarter. And not only the hindering power but also the hindering person seems to be a unit, which latter does not apply to the Rom empire, which had a succession of rulers. It is further difficult to dismiss the thought that the hindering principle or person must be more or less supernatural, since the supernatural factor in the work of "the lawless one" is so prominent. For this reason there is something attractive in the old view of von Hofmann, who assumed that Paul borrowed from Dnl, besides other features, also this feature that the historical conflict on earth has a supernatural background in the world of spirits (cf Dnl **10**). A more precise definition, however, is impossible. Finally it should be noticed that, as in the eschatological discourse of Jesus "the abomination of desolation" appears connected with an apostasy within the church through false teaching (Mk **13** 22.23), so Paul joins to the appearance of "the lawless one" the destructive effect of error among many that are lost (2 Thess **2** 9–12). The idea of the Antichrist in general and that of the apostasy in particular reminds us that we may not expect an uninterrupted progress of the Christianization of the world until the parousia. As the reign of the truth will be extended, so the forces of evil will gather strength, esp. toward the end. The universal sway of the kingdom of God cannot be expected from missionary effort alone; it requires the eschatological interposition of God.

4. The Manner of the Parousia

In regard to the manner and attending circumstances of the parousia we learn that it will be widely visible, like the lightning (Mt **24** 27; Lk **17** 24; the point of comparison does not lie in the suddenness); to the unbelieving it will come unexpectedly (Mt **24** 37–42; Lk **17** 26–32; 1 Thess **5** 2.3). A sign will precede, "the sign of the Son of Man," in regard to the nature of which nothing can be determined. Christ will come "on the clouds," "in clouds," "in a cloud," "with great power and glory" (Mt **24** 30; Mk **13** 26; Lk **21** 27); attended by angels (Mt **24** 31 [cf **13** 41; **16** 27; Mk **8** 38; Lk **9** 26]; Mk **13** 27; 2 Thess **1** 7).

VI. The Resurrection.—The resurrection coincides with the parousia and the arrival of the future aeon (Lk **20** 35; Jn **6** 40; 1 Thess **4** 16). From 1 Thess **3** 13; **4** 16 it has been inferred that the dead rise before the descent of Christ from heaven is completed; the sounds described in the later passage are then interpreted as sounds accompanying the descent (cf Ex **19** 16; Isa **27** 13; Mt **24** 31; 1 Cor **15** 52; He **12** 19; Rev **10** 7; **11** 15; "the trump of God" = the great eschatological trumpet). The two words for the resurrection are *egeírein*, "to wake," and *anistánai*, "to raise," the latter less common in the active than in the intransitive sense.

1. Its Universality

The NT teaches in some passages with sufficient clearness that all the dead will be raised, but the emphasis rests to such an extent on the soteriological aspect of the event, esp. in Paul, where it is closely connected with the doctrine of the Spirit, that its reference to non-believers receives little notice. This was already partly so in the OT (Isa **26** 19; Dnl **12** 2). In the intervening Jewish lit. the doctrine varies; sometimes a resurrection of the martyrs alone is taught (En **90**); sometimes of all the righteous dead of Israel (Ps Sol **3** 10 ff; En **91–94**); sometimes of all the righteous and of some wicked Israelites (En **1–36**); sometimes of all the righteous and all the wicked (4 Ezr [2 Esd] **5** 45; **7** 32; Apoc Bar **42** 8; **50** 2). Jos ascribes to the Pharisees the doctrine that only the righteous will share in the resurrection. It ought to be noticed that these apocalyptic writings which affirm the universality of the resurrection present the same phenomena as the NT, viz. that they contain passages which so exclusively reflect upon the resurrection in its bearing upon the destiny of the righteous as to create the appearance that no other resurrection was believed in. Among the Pharisees probably a diversity of opinion prevailed on this question, which Jos will have obliterated. Our Lord in His argument with the Sadducees proves only the resurrection of the pious, but does not exclude the other (Mk **12** 26.27); "the resurrection of the just" in Lk **14** 14 may suggest a twofold resurrection. It has been held that the phrase, *hē anástasis hē ek nekrôn* (Lk **20** 35; Acts **4** 2), always describes the resurrection of a limited number from among the dead, whereas *hē anástasis tôn nekrôn* would be descriptive of a universal resurrection (Plummer, *Comm.* on Lk **20** 35), but such a distinction breaks down before an examination of the passages.

The inference to the universality of the resurrection sometimes drawn from the universality of the judgment is scarcely valid, since the idea of a judgment of disembodied spirits is not inconceivable and actually occurs. On the other hand the punishment of the judged is explicitly affirmed to include the body (Mt **10** 28). It cannot be proven that the term "resurrection" is ever in the NT eschatologically employed without reference to the body, of the quickening of the spirit simply (against, Fries, in *ZNTW*, 1900, 291 ff). The sense of Our Lord's argument with the Sadducees does not require that the patriarchs were at the time of Moses in possession of the resurrection, but only that they were enjoying the covenant-life, which would in due time inevitably issue in the resurrection of their bodies. The resemblance (or "equality") to the angels (Mk **12** 25) does not consist in the disembodied state, but in the absence of marriage and propagation. It has been suggested that Hebrews contains no direct evidence for a bodily resurrection (Charles, *Eschatology*, 361), but cf **11** 22.35; **12** 2; **13** 20. The spiritualism of the epistle points, in connection with its Pauline type of teaching, to the conception of a pneumatic heavenly body, rather than to a disembodied state.

2. The Millennium

The NT confines the event of the resurrection to a single epoch, and nowhere teaches, as chiliasm assumes, a resurrection in two stages, one, at the parousia, of saints or martyrs, and a second one at the close of the millennium. Although the doctrine of a temporary Messianic kingdom, preceding the consummation of the world, is of pre-Christian Jewish origin, it had not been developed in Judaism to the extent of assuming a repeated resurrection; the entire resurrection is always placed at the end. The passages to which this doctrine of a double resurrection appeals are chiefly Acts **3** 19–21; 1 Cor **15** 23–28; Phil **3** 9–11; 1 Thess **4** 13–18; 2 Thess **1** 5–12; Rev **20** 1–6. In the first-named passage Peter promises "seasons of refreshing," when Israel shall have repented and turned to God. The arrival of these coincides with the sending of the Christ to the Jews, i.e. with the parousia. It is argued that Peter in ver 21, "whom the heavens *must* [present tense] receive until the times of restoration of all things," places after this coming of

Jesus to His people a renewed withdrawal of the Lord into heaven, to be followed in turn, after a certain interval, by the restoration of all things. The "seasons of refreshing" would then constitute the millennium with Christ present among His people. While this interpretation is not grammatically impossible, there is no room for it in the general scheme of the Petrine eschatology, for the parousia of Christ is elsewhere represented as bringing not a provisional presence, but as bringing in the day of the Lord, the day of judgment (Acts **2** 17-21). The correct view is that "the seasons of refreshing" and "the times of restoration of all things" are identical; the latter phrase relates to the prospects of Israel as well as the former, and should not be understood in the later technical sense. The present tense in ver 21, "must receive," does not indicate that the reception of Christ into heaven still lies in the future, but formulates a fixed eschatological principle, viz. that after His first appearance the Christ must be withdrawn into heaven till the hour for the parousia has come.

In 1 Cor **15** 23-28 two *tágmata*, "orders," of the resurrection are distinguished, and it is urged that these consist of "believers" and "non-believers." But there is no reflection here upon non-believers at all, the two "orders" are Christ, and they that are Christ's. "The end" in ver 24 is not the final stage in the resurrection, i.e. the resurrection of non-believers, but the end of the series of eschatological events. The kingdom of Christ which comes to a close with the end is not a kingdom beginning with the parousia, but dates from the exaltation of Christ; it is to Paul not future but already in operation.

In 1 Thess **4** 13-18 the presupposition is not that the readers had worried about a possible exclusion of their dead from the provisional reign of Christ and from a first resurrection, but that they had sorrowed even as the Gentiles who have no hope whatever, i.e. they had doubted the fact of the resurrection as such. Paul accordingly gives them in ver 14 the general assurance that in the resurrection of Jesus that of believers is guaranteed. The vb. "precede" in ver 15 does not imply that there was thought of precedence in the enjoyment of glory, but is only an emphatic way of affirming that the dead will not be one moment behind in inheriting with the living the blessedness of the parousia. In ver 17, "so shall we *ever* be with the Lord," the word "ever" excludes the conception of a provisional kingdom. 2 Thess **1** 5-12 contains merely the general thought that sufferings and glory, persecution and the inheritance of the kingdom are linked together. There is nothing to show that this glory and kingdom are aught else but the final state, the kingdom of God (ver 5).

In Phil **3** 9-11, it is claimed, Paul represents attainment to the resurrection as dependent on special effort on his part, therefore as something not in store for all believers. Since the general resurrection pertains to all, a special grace of resurrection must be meant, i.e. inclusion in the number of those to be raised at the parousia, at the opening of the millennial kingdom. The answer to this is, that it was quite possible to Paul to make the resurrection *as such* depend on the believer's progress in grace and conformity to Christ, seeing that it is not an event out of all relation to his spiritual development, but the climax of an organic process of transformation begun in this life. And in ver 20 the resurrection of all is joined to the parousia (cf for the Pauline passages Vos, "The Pauline Eschatology and Chiliasm," *PTR*, 1911, 26-60).

The passage Rev **20** 1-6 at first sight much favors the conception of a millennial reign of Christ, participated in by the martyrs, brought to life in a first resurrection, and marked by a suspension of the activity of Satan. And it is urged that the sequence of visions places this millennium after the parousia of Christ narrated in ch **19**. The question of historic sequence, however, is in Rev difficult to decide. In other parts of the book the principle of "recapitulation," i.e. of cotemporaneousness of things successively depicted, seems to underlie the visions, and numbers are elsewhere in the book meant symbolically. These facts leave open the possibility that the thousand years are synchronous with the earlier developments recorded, and symbolically describe the state of glorified life enjoyed with Christ in heaven by the martyrs during the intermediate period preceding the parousia. The terms employed do not suggest an anticipated bodily resurrection. The seer speaks of "souls" which "lived" and "reigned," and finds in this the first resurrection. The scene of this life and reign is in heaven, where also the "souls" of the martyrs are beheld (**6** 9). The words "this is the **first resurrection"** may be a pointed disavowal of a more realistic (chiliastic) interpretation of the same phrase. The symbolism of the thousand years consists in this, that it contrasts the glorious state of the martyrs on the one hand with the brief season of tribulation passed here on earth, and on the other hand with the eternal life of the consummation. The binding of Satan for this period marks the first eschatological conquest of Christ over the powers of evil, as distinguished from the renewed activity to be displayed by Satan toward the end in bringing up against the church still other forces not hitherto introduced into the conflict. In regard to a book so enigmatical, it were presumptuous to speak with any degree of dogmatism, but the uniform absence of the idea of the millennium from the eschatological teaching of the NT elsewhere ought to render the exegete cautious before affirming its presence here (cf Warfield, "The Millennium and the Apocalypse," *PTR*, 1904, 599-617).

3. The Resurrection of Believers

The resurrection of believers bears a twofold aspect. On the one hand it belongs to the forensic side of salvation. On the other hand it belongs to the pneumatic transforming side of the saving process. Of the former, traces appear only in the teaching of Jesus (Mt **5** 9; **22** 29-32; Lk **20** 35.36). Paul clearly ascribes to the believer's resurrection a somewhat similar forensic significance as to that of Christ (Rom **8** 10.23; 1 Cor **15** 30-32.55-58). Far more prominent with him is, however, the other, the pneumatic interpretation. Both the origin of the resurrection life and the continuance of the resurrection state are dependent on the Spirit (Rom **8** 10.11; 1 Cor **15** 45-49; Gal **6** 8). The resurrection is the climax of the believer's transformation (Rom **8** 11; Gal **6** 8). This part ascribed to the Spirit in the resurrection is not to be explained from what the OT teaches about the Spirit as the source of physical life, for to this the NT hardly ever refers; it is rather to be explained as the correlate of the general Pauline principle that the Spirit is the determining factor of the heavenly state in the coming aeon. This pneumatic character of the resurrection also links together the resurrection of Christ and that of the believer. This idea is not yet found in the Synoptics; it finds expression in Jn **5** 22-29; **11** 25; **14** 6.19. In early apostolic teaching a trace of it may be found in Acts **4** 2. With Paul it appears from the beginning as a well-established principle. The continuity between the working of the Spirit here and His part in the resurrection does not, however, lie in the body. The resurrection is not the culmination of a pneumatic change which the body in this life undergoes. There is no preformation of the spiritual body on earth. Rom **8** 10.11; 1 Cor

15 49; 2 Cor **5** 1.2; Phil **3** 12 positively exclude this, and 2 Cor **3** 18; **4** 7–18 do not require it. The glory into which believers are transformed through the beholding (or reflecting) of the glory of Christ as in a mirror is not a bodily but inward glory, produced by illumination of the gospel. And the manifestation of the life of Jesus in the body or in the mortal flesh refers to the preservation of bodily life in the midst of deadly perils. Equally without support is the view that at one time Paul placed the investiture with the new body immediately after death. It has been assumed that this, together with the view just criticized, marks the last stage in a protracted development of Paul's eschatological belief. The initial stage of this process is found in 1 Thess: the resurrection is that of an *earthly* body. The next stage is represented by 1 Cor: the future body is pneumatic in character, although not to be received until the parousia. The third stage removes the inconsistency implied in the preceding position between the character of the body and the time of its reception, by placing the latter at the moment of death (2 Cor, Rom, Col), and by an extreme flight of faith the view is even approached that the resurrection body is in process of development now (Teichmann, Charles). This scheme has no real basis of fact. 1 Thess does not teach an unpneumatic eschatology (cf **4** 14.16). The second stage given is the only truly Pauline one, nor can it be shown that the apostle ever abandoned it. For the third position named finds no support in 2 Cor **5** 1–10; Rom **8** 19; Col **3** 4. The exegesis of 2 Cor **5** 1–10 is difficult and cannot here be given in detail. Our understanding of the main drift of the passage, put into paraphrase, is as follows: we feel assured of the eternal weight of glory (**4** 17), because we know that we shall receive, after our earthly tent-body shall have been dissolved (aor. subj.), a new body, a supernatural house for our spirit, to be possessed eternally in the heavens. A sure proof of this lies in the heightened form which our desire for this future state assumes. For it is not mere desire to obtain a new body, but specifically to obtain it as soon as possible, without an intervening period of nakedness, i.e. of a disembodied state of the spirit. Such would be possible, if it were given us to survive till the parousia, in which case we would be *clothed upon* with our habitation from heaven (=supernatural body), the old body not having to be put off first before the new can be put on, but the new body being superimposed upon the old, so that no "unclothing" would have to take place first, what is mortal simply being swallowed up of life (**5** 2.4). And we are justified in cherishing this supreme aspiration, since the ultimate goal set for us in any case, even if we should have to die first and to unclothe and then to put on the new body over the naked spirit, since the ultimate goal, I say, excludes under all circumstances a state of nakedness at the moment of the parousia (ver 3). Since, then, such a new embodied state is our destiny in any event, we justly long for that mode of reaching it which involves least delay and least distress and avoids intermediate nakedness. (This on the reading in ver 3 of *eí ge kaí endusámenoi ou gumnoí heurethēsómetha.* If the reading *ei ge kai ekdusamenoi* be adopted the rendering of ver 3 will have to be: "If so be that also having put off [i.e. having died], we shall not at the end be found naked." If *eiper kai ekdusamenoi* be chosen it will be: "Although even having put off [i.e. having died] we shall not at the end be found naked." These other readings do not materially alter the sense.) The understanding of the passage will be seen to rest on the pointed distinction between being "clothed upon," change at the parousia without death (vs 2.4), to be "unclothed," loss of the body in death with nakedness resulting (ver 4), and "being clothed," putting on of the new body after a state of nakedness (ver 3). Interpreted as above, the passage expresses indeed the hope of an instantaneous endowment with the spiritual body immediately after this life, but only on the supposition that the end of this life will be at the parousia, not for the case that death should intervene before, which latter possibility is distinctly left open. In Rom **8** 19 what will happen at the end to believers is called a "revealing of the sons of God," not because their new body existed previously, but because their status as sons of God existed before, and this status will be revealed through the bestowal upon them of the glorious body. Col **3** 3.4 speaks of a "life . . . . hid with Christ in God," and of the "manifestation" of believers with Christ in glory at the parousia, but "life" does not imply bodily existence, and while the "manifestation" at the parousia presupposes the body, it does not imply that this body must have been acquired long before, as is the case with Christ's body. In conclusion it should be noted that there is ample evidence in the later epistles that Paul continued to expect the resurrection body at the parousia (2 Cor **5** 10; Phil **3** 20.21).

4. The Resurrection Body

The main passage informing us as to the *nature* of the resurrection body is 1 Cor **15** 35–58. The difficulty Paul here seeks to relieve does not concern the substance of the future body, but its kind (cf ver 35 "With *what manner* of body do they come?"). Not until ver 50 is the deeper question of difference in substance touched upon. The point of the figure of "sowing" is not that of identity of substance, but rather this, that the impossibility of forming a concrete conception of the resurrection body is no proof of its impossibility, because in all vegetable growth there appears a body totally unlike that which is sown, a body the nature and appearance of which are determined by the will of God. We have no right to press the figure in other directions, to solicit from it answers to other questions. That there is to be a real connection between the present and the future body is implied rather than directly affirmed. Ver 36 shows that the distinction between the earthly body and a germ of life in it, to be intrusted with it to the grave and then quickened at the last day, does not lie in the apostle's mind, for what is sown is the body; it dies and is quickened in its entirety. Esp. the turn given to the figure in ver 37—that of a naked grain putting on the plant as a garment—proves that it is neither intended nor adapted to give information on the degree of identity or link of continuity between the two bodies. The "bare grain" is the body, not the spirit, as some would have it (Teichmann), for it is said of the seed that it dies; which does not apply to the Pneuma (cf also ver 44). The fact is that in this entire discussion the subjective spirit of the believer remains entirely out of consideration; the matter is treated entirely from the standpoint of the body. So far as the Pneuma enters into it, it is the objective Spirit, the Spirit of Christ. As to the time of the sowing, some writers take the view that this corresponds to the entire earthly life, not to the moment of burial only (so already Calvin, recently Teichmann and Charles). In vs 42.43 there are points of contact for this, inasmuch as esp. the three last predicates "in dishonor," "in weakness," "a natural body," seem more applicable to the living than to the dead body. At any rate, if the conception is thus widened, the act of burial is certainly included in the sowing. The objection arising from the difficulty of forming a conception of the resurrection body is further met in vs 39–41, where Paul argues from the multitude of bodily forms God has at His disposal. This thought is illustrated from the animal world (ver 39); from the difference between the heavenly and the earthly bodies (ver 40); from the difference existing among the heavenly bodies themselves (ver 41). The structure of the argument is indicated by the interchange of two words for "other," *állos* and *héteros*, the former designating difference of species within the genus, the latter difference of genus, a distinction lost in the Eng. version. In all this the reasoning revolves not around the substance of the bodies but around their kind, quality, appearance (*sárx* in ver 39 = *sôma*, "body," not = "flesh"). The conclusion drawn is that the resurrection body will differ greatly in kind from the present body. It will be *héteros*, not merely *állos*. The points of difference are enumerated in vs 42.43. Four contrasts are named; the first three in each case appear to be the result of the fourth. The dominating antithesis is that between the *sôma psuchikón* and the *sôma pneumatikón*. Still Paul can scarcely mean to teach that "corruption," "dishonor," "weakness" are in the same sense necessary and natural results of the "psychical" character of the earthly body, as the corresponding opposites are necessary and natural concomitants of the pneumatic character of the resurrection body. The sequel shows that the "psychical body" was given man at creation, and according to ver 53 corruption and death go together, whereas death is not the result of creation but of the entrance of sin according to Paul's uniform teaching elsewhere. Hence also the predicate *sarkikós* is avoided in vs 46.47, where the reference is to creation, for this word is always associated in Paul with sin. The connection, therefore, between the "natural [psychical, m] body" and the abnormal attributes conjoined with it, will have to be so conceived, that in virtue of the former character, the body, though it need not of itself, yet will fall a prey to the latter when sin enters. In this lies also the explanation of the term "psychical body." This means a body in which the *psychē*, the natural soul, is the vitalizing principle, sufficient to support life, but not sufficient to that supernatural, heavenly plane, where it is forever immune to death and corruption. The question must be asked, however, why Paul goes back to the original state of man's body and does not content himself with contrasting the body in the state of sin and in the state of eternal life. The answer is found in the exigency of the argument. Paul wished to add to the argument for the possibility of a different body drawn from analogy, an argument drawn from the typical character of the original creation-body. The body of creation, on the principle of prefiguration, pointed already forward to a higher body to be received in the second stage of the world-process: 'if there exists a psychical body, there exists also a pneumatic body' (ver 44). The proof lies in Gen **2** 7. Some think that Paul here adopts the Philonic doctrine of the creation of two men, and means ver 45*b* as a quotation from Gen **1** 27. But the sequence is against this, for Paul's spiritual man appears on the scene last, not first, as in Philo. Nor can the statement have been meant as a correction of Philo's sequence, for Paul cannot have overlooked that, once a double creation were found in Gen **1** and **2**, then Philo's sequence was the only possible one, to correct which would have amounted to correcting Scripture. If Paul *does* here correct Philo, it must be in the sense that he rejects the entire Philonic exegesis, which found in Gen a twofold creation (cf 1 Cor **11** 7). Evidently for Paul, Gen **2** 7 taken by itself contains the proof of his proposition, that there is both a psychical and a pneumatic body. Paul regarded the creation of the first Adam in a typical light. The first creation gave only the provisional form in which God's purpose with reference to man was embodied, and in so far looked forward to a higher embodiment of the same idea on a higher pneumatic plane (cf Rom **5** 14): "The first man is of the earth, earthy: the second man is of heaven" (1 Cor **15** 47); "of" or "from heaven" does not designate heavenly material, for even here, by not giving the opposite to *choïkós*, "earthly," Paul avoided the question of substantiality. A "pneumatic" body is not, as many assume, a body made out of *pneúma* as a higher substance, for in that case Paul would have had *pneumatikón* ready at hand as the contrast to *choïkón*. Only negatively the question of substance is touched upon in ver 50: "Flesh and blood cannot inherit the kingdom of God," but the apostle does not say what will take their place. Cf further, for the non-substantial meaning of *pneumatikós*, Rom **15** 27; 1 Cor **9** 11; **10** 3.4; Eph **1** 3; **5** 19; **6** 12; Col **1** 9. The only positive thing which we learn in this direction is formal, viz. that the resurrection body of the believer will be the image of that of Christ (ver 49).

VII. The Change of Those Living at the Parousia.—This is confined to believers. Of a change in the body of non-believers found living or raised at the parousia the NT nowhere speaks. The passages referring to this subject are 1 Cor **15** 51–53; 2 Cor **5** 1–5; Phil **3** 20.21. The second of these has already been discussed: it represents the change under the figure of a putting-on of the heavenly body over the earthly body, in result of which what is mortal is swallowed up so as to disappear by life. This representation starts with the new body by which the old body is absorbed. In 1 Cor **15** and Phil **3**, on the other hand, the point of departure is from the old body which is changed into a new. The difference between the resurrection and the charge of the living is brought out in 2 Cor **5** 1–5 in the two figures of "putting on" and "putting on over," *endúsasthai* and *ependúsasthai*. Some exegetes find in 1 Cor **15** 51–53 the description of a process kept in such general terms as to be equally applicable to those raised and to those transformed alive. If this be adopted it yields new evidence for the continuity between the present body and the resurrection body. Others, however, find here the expectation that Paul and his readers will "all" survive until the parousia, and be changed alive, in which case no light is thrown on the resurrection-process. The more plausible exegesis is that which joins the negative to "all" instead of to the vb., and makes Paul affirm that "not all" will die, but that all, whether dead or surviving, will be changed at the parousia; the difficulty of the exegesis is reflected in the early attempts to change the reading. In Phil **3** 20.21 there are no data to decide whether the apostle conceives of himself and his readers as living at the moment of the parousia or speaks generally so as to cover both possibilities.

VIII. The Judgment.—The judgment takes place on a "day" (Mt **7** 22; **10** 15; **24** 36; Lk **10** 12; **21** 34; 1 Cor **1** 8; **3** 13; 2 Tim **4** 8; Rev **6** 17), but this rests on the OT conception of "the day of Jehovah," and is not to be taken literally, whence also "hour" interchanges with "day" (Mk **13** 32; Rev **14** 7). While not confined to an astronomical day the judgment is plainly represented as a definitely circumscribed transaction, not as an indefinite process. It coincides with its parousia. Of a judgment immediately after death, the NT nowhere speaks, not even in He **9** 27.28. Its locality is the earth, as would seem to follow from its dependence on the parousia (Mt **13** 41.42; Mk **13** 26.27), although some infer from 1 Thess **4** 17 that, so far as believers are concerned, it will take place in the air. But this passage does not speak of the judgment, only of the parousia and the meeting of believers with Christ. The judge is God

(Mt **6** 4.6.14.18; **10** 28.32 ff=Lk **12** 8 ff; **21** 36; Acts **10** 42; **17** 30.31; Rom **2** 2.3.5.16; **14** 10; 1 Cor **4** 3–5; **5** 13; He **12** 25; **13** 4; 1 Pet **1** 17; **2** 23; Rev **6** 10; **14** 7), but also Christ, not only in the great scene depicted in Mt **25** 31–46, but also in Mk **8** 38; **13** 26 ff; Mt **7** 22=Lk **13** 25–27; Acts **17** 31; 2 Cor **5** 10; Rev **19** 11, whence also the OT conception of "the day of Jehovah" is changed into "the day of the Lord" (1 Cor **5** 5; 2 Cor **1** 14; 1 Thess **5** 2; 2 Pet **3** 10). In the sense of the final assize the judgment does not in earlier Jewish eschatology belong to the functions of the Messiah, except in En **51** 3; **55** 4; **61** 8 ff; **62** 1 ff; **63**. Only in the later apocalypses the Messiah appears as judge (4 Ezr [2 Esd] **13**; Apoc Bar **72** 2 [cf Sib Or **3** 286]). In the more realistic, less forensic, sense of an act of destruction, the judgment forms part of the Messiah's work from the outset, and is already assigned to Him by the Baptist and still more by Paul (Mt **3** 10.11.12=Lk **3** 16.17; 2 Thess **2** 8.10.12). The one representation passes over into the other. Jesus always claims for Himself the judgment in the strictly forensic sense. Already in His present state He exercises the right to forgive sin (Mk **2** 5.10). In the Fourth Gospel, it is true, He denies that His present activity involves the task of judging (Jn **8** 15; **12** 47). That this, however, does not exclude His eschatological judgeship appears from **5** 22.27 (notice the article in ver 22 "the whole judgment," which proves the reference to the last day). But even for the present, though not directly, yet indirectly by His appearance and message, Christ according to Jn effects a judgment among men (**8** 16; **9** 39), which culminates in His passion and death, the judgment of the world and the Prince of the world (**12** 31; **14** 30; **16** 11). A share of the judgment is assigned to angels and to the saints (Mt **13** 39. 41.49; **16** 27; **24** 31; **25** 31; 1 Thess **3** 13; 2 Thess **1** 7; Jude vs 14 f). In regard to the angels this is purely ministerial; of believers it is affirmed only in 1 Cor **6** 1–3 that they will have something to do with the act of judgment itself; passages like Mt **19** 28; **20** 23; Lk **22** 30; Rev **3** 21 do not refer to the judgment proper, but to judging in the sense of "reigning," and promise certain saints a preëminent position in the kingdom of glory. The judgment extends to all men, Tyre, Sidon, Sodom, as well as the Galilean cities (Mt **11** 22.24); all nations (**25** 32; Jn **5** 29; Acts **17** 30.31; Rom **2** 6.16; 2 Cor **5** 10). It also includes the evil spirits (1 Cor **6** 3; 2 Pet **2** 4; Jude ver 6). It is a judgment according to works, and that not only in the case of non-believers; of believers also the works will come under consideration (Mt **25** 34 ff; 1 Cor **4** 5; 2 Cor **5** 10; Rev **22** 12). Side by side with this, however, it is taught already in the Synoptics that the decisive factor will be the acknowledgment of individuals by Jesus, which in turn depends upon the attitude assumed by them toward Jesus here, directly or indirectly (Mt **7** 23; **19** 28; **25** 35–45; Mk **8** 38). By Paul the principle of judgment according to works is upheld, not merely hypothetically as a principle preceding and underlying every soteriological treatment of man by God (Rom **2**), and therefore applying to non-Christians for whose judgment no other standard is available, but also as remaining in force for Christians, who have already, under the soteriological régime of grace, received absolute, eternal acquittal in justification. This raises a twofold problem: (*a*) why justification does not render a last judgment superfluous; (*b*) why the last judgment in case of Christians saved by grace should be based on works. In regard to (*a*) it ought to be remembered that the last judgment differs from justification in that it is not a private transaction *in foro conscientiae*, but public, *in foro mundi*. Hence Paul emphasizes this element of publicity (Rom **2** 16; 1 Cor **3** 13; 2 Cor **5** 10). It is in accordance with this that God the Father is always the author of justification, whereas as a rule Christ is represented as presiding at the assize of the last day. As to (*b*), because the last judgment is not a mere private but a public transaction, something more must be taken into account than that on which the individual eternal destiny may hinge. There can be disapproval of works and yet salvation (1 Cor **3** 15). But the trial of works is necessary for the sake of the vindication of God. In order to be a true theodicy the judgment must publicly exhibit and announce the complete overthrow of sin in man, and the complete working out in him of the idea of righteousness, including not merely his acquittal from the guilt, but also his deliverance from the power, of sin, not merely his imputed righteousness, but also his righteousness of life. In order to demonstrate this comprehensively, the judgment will have to take into account three things: faith (Gal **5** 5), works done in the Christian state, sanctification. Besides this the works of the Christian appear as the measure of gracious reward (Mt **5** 12.46; **6** 1; **10** 41.42; **19** 28; **20** 1–16; **25** 14–45; Mk **9** 41; Lk **6** 23.35; 1 Cor **3** 8.14; **9** 17.18; Col **2** 18; **3** 24; He **10** 35). These works, however, are not mechanically or commercially appraised, as in Judaism, for Paul speaks by preference of "work" in the singular (Rom **2** 7.15; 1 Cor **3** 13; **9** 1; Gal **6** 4; Eph **4** 12; Phil **1** 6.22; 1 Thess **1** 3; 2 Thess **1** 11). And this one organic product of "work" is traced back to the root of faith (1 Thess **1** 3; 2 Thess **1** 11, where the gen. *písteōs* is a gen. of origin), and Paul speaks as a rule not of *poieîn* but of *prássein*, i.e. of the practice, the systematic doing, of that which is good.

The judgment assigns to each individual his eternal destiny, which is absolute in its character either of blessedness or of punishment, though admittedly of degrees within these two states. Only two groups are recognized, those of the condemned and of the saved (Mt **25** 33.34; Jn **5** 29); no intermediate group with as yet undetermined destiny anywhere appears. The degree of guilt is fixed according to the knowledge of the Divine will possessed in life (Mt **10** 15; **11** 20–24; Lk **10** 12–15; **12** 47.48; Jn **15** 22.24; Rom **2** 12; 2 Pet **2** 20–22). The uniform representation is that the judgment has reference to what has been done in the embodied state of this life; nowhere is there any reflection upon the conduct or product of the intermediate state as contributing to the decision (2 Cor **5** 10). The state assigned is of endless duration, hence described as *aiōnios*, "eternal." While this adjective etymologically need mean no more than "what extends through a certain aeon or period of time," yet its eschatological usage correlates it everywhere with the "coming age," and, this age being endless in duration, every state or destiny connected with it partakes of the same character. It is therefore exegetically impossible to give a relative sense to such phrases as *púr aiōnion*, "eternal fire" (Mt **18** 8; **25** 41; Jude ver 7), *kólasis aiōnios*, "eternal punishment" (Mt **25** 46), *ólethros aiōnios*, "eternal destruction" (2 Thess **1** 9), *krísis aiōnios* or *kríma aiōnion*, "eternal judgment" (Mk **3** 29; He **6** 2). This is also shown by the figurative representations which unfold the import of the adj.: the "unquenchable fire" (Mt **3** 12), "the never-dying worm" (Mk **9** 43–48), "The smoke of their torment goeth up for ever and ever" (Rev **14** 11), "tormented day and night forever and ever" (Rev **20** 10). The endless duration of the state of punishment is also required by the absolute eternity of its counterpart, *zōē aiōnios*, "eternal life" (Mt **25** 46).

In support of the doctrine of conditional immortality it has been urged that other terms descriptive of the fate of the condemned, such as *apôleia*, "perdition," *phthorá*, "corruption," *ólethros*, "destruction," *thánatos*, "death," point rather to a cessation of being. This, however, rests on an unscriptural interpretation of these terms, which everywhere in the OT and the NT designate a state of existence with an undesirable content, never the pure negation of existence, just as "life" in Scripture describes a positive mode of being, never mere existence as such. Perdition, corruption, destruction, death, are predicated in all such cases of the welfare or the ethical spiritual character of man, without implying the annihilation of his physical existence. No more support can be found in the NT for the hypothesis of an *apokatástasis pánton*, "restoration of all things," i.e. absolute universalism implying the ultimate salvation of all men. The phrase occurs only in Acts **3** 21, where, however, it has no cosmical reference but relates to the fulfilment of the promises to Israel. Jos uses it of the restoration of the Jews to their land after the Captivity, Philo of the restoration of inheritances in the year of jubilee (cf Mal **4** 6; Mt **17** 11; Mk **9** 12; Acts **1** 6). Absolute universalism has been found in Rom **5** 18; 1 Cor **15** 22.28; Eph **1** 10; Col **1** 20, but in all these passages only a cosmical or national universalism can be found, not the doctrine of the salvation of all individuals, which latter would bring the statements in question in direct contradiction to the most explicit deliverances of Paul elsewhere on the principle of predestination and the eternity of the destiny of the wicked.

IX. The Consummate State.—Side by side with "the future age," and characterizing it from a less formal point of view, the phrase "kingdom of God" designates the consummate state, as it will exist for believers after the judgment. Jesus, while making the kingdom a present reality, yet continues to speak of it in accordance with its original eschatological usage as "the kingdom" which lies in the future (Mt **13** 43; **25** 34; **26** 29; Mk **9** 47; Lk **12** 32; **13** 28.29; **21** 31). With Paul the phrase bears preponderatingly an eschatological sense, although occasionally he uses it of the present state of believers (Rom **14** 17; 1 Cor **4** 20; **6** 9.10; **15** 24. 50; Gal **5** 21; Eph **5** 5; Col **1** 13; **4** 11; 1 Thess **2** 12; 2 Thess **1** 5; 2 Tim **4** 1.18). Elsewhere in the NT the eschatological use occurs in He **12** 28; Jas **2** 5; 2 Pet **1** 11; Rev **11** 15. The idea is universalistic, unpolitical, which does not exclude that certain privileges are spoken of with special reference to Israel. Although the eschatological kingdom differs from the present kingdom largely in the fact that it will receive an external, visible embodiment, yet this does not hinder that even in it the core is constituted by those spiritual realities and relations which make the present kingdom. Still it will have its outward form as the doctrine of the resurrection and the regenerated earth plainly show. Hence the figures in which Jesus speaks of it, such as eating, drinking, reclining at table, while not to be taken sensually, should not on the other hand be interpreted allegorically, as if they stood for wholly internal spiritual processes: they evidently point to, or at least include, outward states and activities, of which our life in the senses offers some analogy, but on a higher plane of which it is at present impossible to form any concrete conception or to speak otherwise than in figurative language. Equivalent to "the kingdom" is "life." But, unlike the kingdom, "life" remains in the Synoptics an exclusively eschatological conception. It is objectively conceived: the state of blessedness the saints will exist in; not subjectively as a potency in man or a process of development (Mt **7** 14; **18** 8.9; **19** 16.29; **25** 46; Mk **10** 30). In Jn "life" becomes a present state, and in connection with this the idea is subjectivized, it becomes a process of growth and expansion. Points of contact for this in the Synoptics may be found in Mt **8** 22 (=Lk **9** 60); Lk **15** 24; **20** 38. When this eschatological life is characterized as *aiônios*, "eternal," the reference is not exclusively to its eternal duration, but the word has, in addition to this, a qualitative connotation; it describes the kind of life that belongs to the consummate state (cf the use of the adj. with other nouns in this sense: 2 Cor **5** 1; 2 Tim **2** 10; He **5** 9; **9** 12. 15; 2 Pet **1** 11, and the unfolding of the content of the idea in 1 Pet **1** 4). With Paul "life" has sometimes the same eschatological sense (Rom **2** 7; **5** 17; Tit **1** 2; **3** 7), but most often it is conceived as already given in the present state, owing to the close association with the Spirit (Rom **6** 11; **7** 4.8. 11; **8** 2.6; Gal **2** 19; **6** 8; Eph **4** 18). In its ultimate analysis the Pauline conception of "life," as well as that of Jesus, is that of something dependent on communion with God (Mt **22** 32=Mk **12** 27=Lk **20** 38; Rom **8** 6.7; Eph **4** 18). Another Pauline conception associated with the consummate state is that of *dóxa*, "glory." This glory is everywhere conceived as a reflection of the glory of God, and it is this that to the mind of Paul gives it religious value, not the external radiance in which it may manifest itself as such. Hence the element of "honor" conjoined to it (Rom **1** 23; **2** 7; **8** 21; **9** 23; 1 Cor **15** 43). It is not confined to the physical sphere (2 Cor **3** 18; **4** 16.17). The outward *doxa* is prized by Paul as a vehicle of revelation, an exponent of the inward state of acceptance with God. In general Paul conceives of the final state after a highly theocentric fashion (1 Cor **15** 28); it is the state of immediate vision of and perfect communion with God and Christ; the future life alone can bring the perfected sonship (Rom **6** 10; **8** 23.29; cf Lk **20** 36; 2 Cor **4** 4; **5** 6.7.8; **13** 4; Phil **1** 23; Col **2** 13; **3** 3.4; 1 Thess **4** 17).

The scene of the consummate state is the new heaven and the new earth, which are called into being by the eschatological palingenesia "regeneration" (Mt **5** 18; **19** 28; **24** 35; 1 Cor **7** 31; He **1** 12; **12** 26.27; 2 Pet **3** 10; 1 Jn **2** 17; Rev **21** 1, in which last passage, however, some exegetes understand the city to be a symbol of the church, the people of God). An annihilation of the substance of the present world is not taught (cf the comparison of the future world-conflagration with the Deluge in 2 Pet **3** 6). The central abode of the redeemed will be in heaven, although the renewed earth will remain accessible to them and a part of the inheritance (Mt **5** 5; Jn **14** 2.3; Rom **8** 18–22; and the closing visions of the Apocalypse).

X. The Intermediate State.—In regard to the state of the dead, previously to the parousia and the resurrection, the NT is far less explicit than in its treatment of what belongs to general eschatology. The following points may here briefly be noted:

(1) The state of death is frequently represented as a "sleeping," just as the act of dying as a "falling asleep" (Mt **9** 24; Jn **9** 4; **11** 11; 1 Cor **7** 39; **11** 30; **15** 6.18.20.51; 1 Thess **4** 13.15; 2 Pet **3** 4). This usage, while also purely Gr, rests on the OT. There is this difference, that in the NT (already in the apocryphal and pseudepigraphical books) the conception is chiefly used with reference to the righteous dead, and has associated with it the thought of their blessed awaking in the resurrection, whereas in the OT it is indiscriminately applied to all the dead and without such connotation. With Paul the word always occurs of believers. The

representation applies not to the "soul" or "spirit," so that a state of unconsciousness until the resurrection would be implied. It is predicated of the person, and the point of comparison is that as one who sleeps is not alive to his surroundings, so the dead are no longer *en rapport* with this earthly life. Whatever may have been the original implications of the word, it plainly had become long before the NT period a figurative mode of speech, just as *egeírein*, "to wake," was felt to be a figurative designation of the act of the resurrection. Because the dead are asleep to our earthly life, which is mediated through the body, it does not follow that they are asleep in every other relation, asleep to the life of the other world, that their spirits are unconscious. Against the unconsciousness of the dead cf Lk **16** 23; **23** 43; Jn **11** 25.26; Acts **7** 59; 1 Cor **15** 8; Phil **1** 23; Rev **6** 9–11; **7** 9. Some have held that the sleep was for Paul a euphemism employed in order to avoid the terms "death" and "to die," which the apostle restricted to Christ. 1 Thess **4** 16 shows that this is unfounded.

(2) The NT speaks of the departed after an anthropomorphic fashion as though they were still possessed of bodily organs (Lk **16** 23.24; Rev **6** 11; **7** 9). That no inference can be drawn from this in favor of the hypothesis of an intermediate body appears from the fact that God and angels are spoken of in the same manner, and also from passages which more precisely refer to the dead as "souls," "spirits" (Lk **23** 46; Acts **7** 59; He **12** 23; 1 Pet **3** 19; Rev **6** 9; **20** 4).

(3) The NT nowhere encourages the living to seek converse with the dead. Its representation of the dead as "sleeping" with reference to the earthly life distinctly implies that such converse would be abnormal and in so far discountenances it, without explicitly affirming its absolute impossibility. Not even the possibility of the dead for their part taking knowledge of our earthly life is affirmed anywhere. He **12** 1 does not necessarily represent the OT saints as "witnesses" of our race of faith in the sense of spectators in the literal sense, but perhaps in the figurative sense, that we ought to feel, having in memory their example, as if the ages of the past and their historic figures were looking down upon us (Lk **16** 29; Acts **8** 9; **13** 6 ff; **19** 13 ff).

(4) As to the departed saints themselves, it is intimated that they have mutual knowledge of one another in the intermediate state, together with memory of facts and conditions of the earthly life (Lk **16** 9.19–31). Nowhere, however, is it intimated that this interest of the departed saints in our earthly affairs normally expresses itself in any act of intercession, not even of intercession spontaneously proffered on their part.

(5) The NT does not teach that there is any possibility of a fundamental change in moral or spiritual character in the intermediate state. The doctrine of a so-called "second probation" finds in it no real support. The only passages that can with some semblance of warrant be appealed to in this connection are 1 Pet **3** 19–21 and **4** 6. For the exegesis of the former passage, which is difficult and much disputed, cf SPIRITS IN PRISON. Here it may simply be noted that the context is not favorable to the view that an extension of the opportunity of conversion beyond death is implied; the purport of the whole passage points in the opposite direction, the salvation of the exceedingly small number of eight of the generation of Noah being emphasized (**3** 20). Besides this it would be difficult to understand why this exceptional opportunity should have been granted to this peculiar group of the dead, since the contemporaries of Noah figure in Scripture as examples of extreme wickedness. Even if the idea of a gospel-preaching with soteriological purpose were actually found here, it would not furnish an adequate basis for building upon it the broad hypothesis of a second probation for all the dead in general or for those who have not heard the gospel in this life. This latter view the passage is esp. ill fitted to support, because the generation of Noah had had the gospel preached to them before death. There is no intimation that the transaction spoken of was repeated or continued indefinitely. As to the second passage (1 Pet **4** 6), this must be taken by itself and in connection with its own context. The assumption that the sentence "the gospel [was] preached even to the dead" must have its meaning determined by the earlier passage in **3** 19–21, has exercised an unfortunate influence upon the exegesis. Possibly the two passages had no connection in the mind of the author. For explaining the reference to "the dead" the connection with the preceding verse is fully sufficient. It is there stated that Christ is "ready to judge the living and the dead." "The living and the dead" are those who will be *alive* and *dead* at the parousia. To both the gospel was preached, that Christ might be the judge of both. But that the gospel was preached to the latter in the state of death is in no way indicated. On the contrary the telic clause, "that they might be judged according to men in the flesh," shows that they heard the gospel during their lifetime, for the judgment according to men in the flesh that has befallen them is the judgment of physical death. If a close connection between the passage in ch **3** and that in ch **4** did exist, this could only serve to commend the exegesis which finds in the earlier passage a gospel-preaching to the contemporaries of Noah during their lifetime, since, on that view, it becomes natural to identify the judgment in the flesh with the Deluge.

(6) The NT, while representing the state of the dead before the parousia as definitely fixed, nevertheless does not identify it, either in degree of blessedness or punishment, with the final state which follows upon the resurrection. Although there is no warrant for affirming that the state of death is regarded as for believers a positively painful condition, as has been mistakenly inferred from 1 Cor **11** 30; 1 Thess **4** 13, nevertheless Paul shrinks from it as from a relatively undesirable state, since it involves "nakedness" for the soul, which condition, however, does not exclude a relatively high degree of blessedness in fellowship with Christ (2 Cor **5** 2–4.6.8; Phil **1** 23). In the same manner a difference in the degree or mode of punishment between the intermediate state and the age to come is plainly taught. For on the one hand the eternal punishment is related to persons in the body (Mt **10** 28), and on the other hand it is assigned to a distinct place, *Gehenna*, which is never named in connection with the torment of the intermediate state. This term occurs in Mt **5** 22.29.30; **10** 28=Lk **12** 5; **18** 9; **23** 33; Mk **9** 43.45.47; Jas **3** 6. Its opposite is the eschatological kingdom of God (Mk **9** 47). The term *ábussos* differs from it in that it is associated with the torment of evil spirits (Lk **8** 31; Rom **10** 7; Rev **9** 1.2; **11** 7; **20** 1), and in regard to it no such clear distinction between a preliminary and final punishment seems to be drawn (cf also the vb. *tartaroún*, "to bind in Tartarus"; of evil spirits in 2 Pet **2** 4). Where the sphere of the intermediate state is locally conceived, this is done by means of the term *Hades*, which is the equivalent of the OT *She'ōl*. The passages where this occurs are Mt **11** 23; **16** 18; Lk **16** 23; Acts **2** 27.31; 1 Cor **15** 55 (where others read "death"); Rev **1** 18; **6** 8; **20** 13.14). These passages should not be interpreted on the basis of the Gr classical usage, but in the light of the OT

doctrine about *Sheʼōl*. Some of them plainly employ the word in the non-local sense of the state of death (Mt **16** 18; possibly Acts **2** 27.31; 1 Cor **15** 55 [personified]; Rev **1** 18; **6** 8 [personified]; **20** 13 [personified]). The only passage where the conception is local is Lk **16** 23, and this occurs in a parable, where aside from the central point in comparison, no purpose to impart topographical knowledge concerning the world beyond death can be assumed, but the imagery is simply that which was popularly current. But, even if the doctrine of Hades as a place distinct from Gehenna should be found here, the terms in which it is spoken of, as a place of torment for Dives, prove that the conception is not that of a general abode of neutral character, where without blessedness or pain the dead as a joint-company await the last judgment, which would first assign them to their separate eternal habitations. The parable plainly teaches, whether Hades be local and distinct from Gehenna or not, that the differentiation between blessedness and punishment in its absolute character (ver 26) is begun in it and does not first originate at the judgment (see further, HADES).

LITERATURE.—Besides the arts. on the several topics in the Bible Dictionaries and in Cremer's *Lexicon of NT Gr*, and the corresponding chs in the handbooks on NT Theology, the following works and arts. may be consulted: Bousset, *Die Religion des Judenthums*[2], 1906, esp. 233–346; id, *Der Antichrist in der Ueberlieferung des Judenthums, des NT und der alten Kirche*, 1895; Bruston, *La vie future d'après St. Paul*, 1895; Charles, *Eschatology Heb, Jewish and Christian: A Critical History of the Doctrine of a Future Life*, 1899; Cremer, *Ueber den Zustand nach dem Tode*[3], 1892; Grimm, "Ueber die Stelle 1 Kor **15** 20–28," *ZWT*, 1873; Haupt, *Die eschatologischen Aussagen Jesu in den synoptischen Evangelien*, 1895; Kabisch, *Eschatologie des Paulus in ihren Zusammenhängen mit dem Gesamtbegriff des Paulinismus*, 1893; Kennedy, *St. Paul's Conceptions of the Last Things*, 1904; Kliefoth, *Christliche Eschatologie*, 1886; Klöpper, "Zur Paulinischen Lehre von der Auferstehung: Auslegung von 2 Kor **5** 1–6," *JDT*, 1862 (the author modified his views in his comm. on 2 Cor); Köstlin, "Die Lehre des Apostels Paulus von der Auferstehung," *JDT*, 1877; Luthardt, *Lehre von den letzten Dingen*[3], 1885; Muirhead, *The Eschatology of Jesus*, 1904; Oesterley, *The Doctrine of the Last Things*, 1908; Philippi, *Die biblische und kirchliche Lehre vom Antichrist*, 1877; Rinck, *Vom Zustande nach dem Tode*, 1885; Salmond, *The Christian Doctrine of Immortality*[5], 1901; Schwally, *Das Leben nach dem Tode*, 1892; Sharman, *The Teaching of Jesus about the Future According to the Synoptic Gospels*, 1909; Stähelin, "Zur Paulinischen Eschatologie," *JDT*, 1874; Teichmann, *Die Paulinischen Vorstellungen von Auferstehung und Gericht*, 1896; Volz, *Jüdische Eschatologie von Daniel bis Akiba*, 1903; Waitz, "Ueber 2 Kor **5** 1–4," *JPT*, 1882; Wetzel, "Ueber 2 Kor **5** 1–4," *SK*, 1886; Wendt, *Die Begriffe Fleisch und Geist im biblischen Sprachgebrauch*, 1878.

GEERHARDUS VOS

ESCHEW, es-chōō′ (סוּר, *ṣūr*; **ἐκκλίνω**, *ekklínō*): Only 4 t in AV (Job **1** 1.8; **2** 3; 1 Pet **3** 11), in all of which ARV renders by the appropriate form of "turn away from."

ESDRAELON, es-drā-ē′lon, **PLAIN OF** (יִזְרְעֶאל, *yizreʻe'l*; in Apoc the name varies: **Ἐσδρηλών**, *Esdrēlôn*, **Ἐσδραηλών**, *Esdraēlôn*, **Ἐσδρηλώμ**, *Esdrēlôm*, **Ἐσρηλών**, *Esrēlôn*, **Ἐσρηχών**, *Esrēchôn*):

1. The Name

The Gr name of the great plain in Central Pal (Jth **3** 9; **7** 3, etc). It is known in Scripture by the Heb name "valley of Jezreel" (Josh **17** 16; Jgs **6** 33, etc). It is called *ʻēmeḳ* in Jgs **5** 15, which properly denotes "a depression," or "deepening," and is used more commonly of the vale running eastward between Gilboa and Little Hermon. *Biḳʻāh* is the term usually employed (2 Ch **35** 22, etc), which accurately describes it, "an opening," a level space surrounded by hills. The modern name is *Merj*

2. Position and Description

ibn ʻĀmr, "meadow of the son of Amr." It lies between Gilboa and Little Hermon on the E., and Mt. Carmel on the W. It is inclosed by irregular lines drawn from the latter along the base of the foothills of Nazareth to Tabor; from Tabor, skirting Little Hermon and Gilboa to *Jenīn*, and from *Jenīn* along the N. edge of the Samaritan uplands to Carmel. These sides of the triangle are, respectively, about 15, 15 and 20 miles in length. N. of *Jenīn* a bay of the plain sweeps eastward, hugging the foot of Mt. Gilboa. An offshoot passes down to the Jordan valley between Gilboa and Little Hermon; and another cuts off the latter hill from Tabor. The average elevation of the plain is 200 ft. above the level of the Mediterranean. The Vale of Jezreel between *Zerʻīn* and *Beisān*, a distance of about 12 miles, descends nearly 600 ft., and then sinks suddenly to the level of the Jordan valley. The chief springs supplying water for the plain are those at *Jenīn* and at Megiddo. The former are the most copious, and are used to create a "paradise" on the edge of the plain. Those at Megiddo drive mills and serve for irrigation, besides forming extensive marshes. The springs near *Zerʻīn*, three in number, *ʻAin Jalūd*, possibly identical with the well of Harod, being the most copious, send their waters down the vale to the Jordan. The streams from the surrounding heights are gathered in the bed of the Kishon, a great trench which zigzags through the plain, carrying the water through the gorge at Carmel to the sea. For the most of its course this sluggish stream is too low to be available for irrigation. The deep, rich soil, however, retains the moisture from the winter rains until far on in the year, the surface only, where uncovered by crops, being baked to brick in the sun. When winter sets in it quickly absorbs the rain, great breadths being turned to soft mud. This probably happened in the battle with Sisera: the northern cavalry, floundering in the morass, would be an easy prey to the active, lightly armed foot-soldiers. The fertility of the plain is extraordinary: hardly anywhere can the toil of the husbandman find a greater reward. The present writer has ridden through crops of grain there, when from his seat on the saddle he could no more than see over the tops of the stalks. Trees do not flourish in the plain itself, but on its borders, e.g. at *Jenīn*, the palm, the olive and other fruit trees prosper. The oak covers the slopes of the hills N. of Carmel.

"Gideon's Fountain" in the Plain of Esdraelon.

This wide opening among the mountains played a great part in the history of the land. This was

3. Part Played in History

due to the important avenues of communication between N. and S. that lay across its ample breadths. The narrow pass between the promontory of Carmel and the sea was not suitable for the transport of great armies: the safer roads over the plain were usually followed. So it happened that here opposing hosts often met in deadly strife. Hardly an equal area of earth can so often have been drenched with the blood of men. No doubt many conflicts were waged here in far-off times of which no record remains. The first battle fought in the plain known to history was that in which Sisera's host was overthrown (Jgs **5** 20). The children of the East were surprised and routed by Gideon's 300 chosen men in the stretches N. of *Zer'īn* (Jgs **7**). Near the same place the great battle with the Philis was fought in which Saul and his sons, worsted in the plain, retired to perish on the heights of Gilboa (1 S **31**). In the bed of the Kishon at the foot of Carmel Elijah slaughtered the servants of Baal (1 K **18** 40). Dark memories of the destruction of Ahab's house by the furiously driving Jehu linger round Jezreel. Ahaziah, fleeing from the avenger across the plain, was overtaken and cut down at Megiddo (2 K **9**). In the vale by Megiddo Josiah sought to stay the northward march of Pharaoh-necoh, and himself fell wounded to death (2 K **23** 30; 2 Ch **35** 20 ff). The army of Holofernes is represented as spreading out over all the southern reaches of the plain (Jth **7** 18.19). Much of the fighting during the wars of the Jews transpired within the circle of these hills. It is not unnatural that the inspired seer should place the scene of war in "the great day of God" in the region so often colored crimson in the history of his people—the place called in the Heb tongue "Har-Magedon" (Rev **16** 14.16).

Esdraelon lay within the lot of Issachar (Josh **19** 17). The Canaanite inhabitants were formidable with their chariots of iron (**17** 16.18). The tribe does not appear to have prosecuted the conquest with vigor. Issachar seems to have resumed the tent life (Dt **33** 18), and ignobly to have secured enjoyment of the good things in the land by stooping to "taskwork" (Gen **49** 14 f).

4. Arab Raids

Through many centuries the plain was subject to raids by the Arabs from the E. of the Jordan. The approach was open and easy, and the rich breadths of pasture irresistibly attracted these great flock masters. The Romans introduced some order and security; but with the passing of the eastern empire the old conditions resumed sway, and until comparatively recent times the alarm of an Arab invasion was by no means infrequent.

The railway connecting Haifa with Damascus and Mecca crosses the plain, and enters the Jordan valley near *Beisān*. W. Ewing

ESDRAS, ez′dras, es′dras, THE FIRST BOOK OF:

1. Name
2. Contents
3. Relation to Ch, Ezr, Neh
4. Versions
5. Date and Authorship

Literature

1. Name

In some of the Gr uncials (B, etc) of the LXX the book is called Ἔσδρας Α, *Ésdras A* (or Πρῶτον, *Prōton*); so in the editions of Fritzsche, Tischendorf, Nestle and Swete. It is absent from Cod Sin (א) and in A its name is Ὁ Ἱερεύς, *Ho Hiereús* = The Priest, i.e. Ezra, who is emphatically *the* priest. It is also called 1 Esd in the old Lat and Syr VSS, as well as in the Eng., Welsh and other modern tr^s. In the Eng. and other Protestant Bibles which generally print the Apoc apart, this book stands first in the Apoc under the influence partly of its name, and in part on account of its contents, as it seemed a suitable link between the canonical and the apocryphal writings. The Eng. 2 Esd is the apocalyptic Esd and stands immediately after the Eng. and Gr 1 Esd. The Vulg, following Jerome's version, gave the names 1, 2 and 3 Esd to our Ezr, Neh, and 1 Esd, respectively, and in editions of the Vulg down to that of Pope Sixtus (d. 1590) these three books appear in that order. The name 3 Esd is, therefore, that current in the Roman church, and it has the sanction of the 6th article of the Anglican Creed and of Miles Coverdale who in his tr follows the Vulg in naming the canonical Ezr, Neh and the apocryphal 1 Esd, 1, 2 and 3 Esd, respectively. Other reformers adhered to these titles. In Fritzsche's commentary on the Apoc 3 Esd is preferred and he treats this book first. In Kautzsch's Ger. ed of the Apoc and in most recent Ger. works the Lat designation 3 is revived. The Eng. commentators Bissell (Lange) and Wace (*Speaker's Comm.*) follow the custom of the Bible and speak of 1 Esd, placing the book first in the collection, and this is the prevailing custom among Eng. Protestant theologians. The name 2 Esd has also been given to this book, the canonical Ezr and Neh being then counted as one—1 Esd. See Origen quoted by *HE*, V, 25; Zunz, *Der Gottesdienst, Vorträge* Berlin, 1832, 15.

2. Contents

With the exception of **3** 1—**5** 6—the incident of the royal banquet and the contest for a prize of the three young men—the present books agree in everything essential, down to the minutest details, with the canonical Ezr and part of 2 Ch and Neh. Before discussing the relation between 1 Esd and the Bib. books named (see next section), it will be advantageous to give an outline of the book now specially under consideration, with reference to the ‖ passages in the corresponding parts of the Canon. It will be seen that practically the whole of Ezr is concerned, and for explanations of the parts common to this book and to Neh reference may be made to the *Century Bible Commentary* on Ezr, Neh, and Est.

1. Ch **1** = 2 Ch **35** 1—**36** 21 and may be analyzed thus:
   1 1–20 = 2 Ch **35** 1–19: Josiah's great Passover.
   1 21 f has no exact parallel.
   1 23–31 = 2 Ch **35** 20–27: The death of Josiah. This took place on the battlefield at Megiddo according to 2 K **23** 29, but 1 Esd **1** 31 and 2 Ch **35** 24 say he died at Jerus.
   1 32–58 = 2 Ch **36** 1–21, closing years of the monarchy followed by the exile in Babylon.
2. **2** 1–15 = Ezr **1** 1–11: The return from Babylon through the edict of Cyrus.
3. **2** 16–26 = Ezr **4** 7–24. Certain Pers officials in Samaria induced King Artaxerxes I (d. 424 BC) to stop the work of rebuilding the temple, which is not resumed until the second year of the reign of Darius Hystaspis (519 BC).
4. **3** 1—**5** 6 has no ‖ in any part of the OT.

King Darius (Hystaspis?) makes a great feast, after which he returns to his bedchamber but finds sleeping very difficult. Three young men belonging to his bodyguard resolve each to make a sentence to be written down and placed under the king's pillow, so that upon rising from his bed he might hear the three sayings read to him. The question which each one seeks to answer is, What in this world is strongest? The first says it is "wine," the second, that it is "the king." The reply of the third is "woman, though strongest of all is truth" (from this arose the Lat saying *Magna est veritas et prevalebit*). The third is declared the best, and as a reward the king offers him whatever he might wish. This young man happened to be Zerubbabel (Zorobabel), and the request that he makes is that King Darius might perform the vow which he made on coming to the throne to rebuild Jerus and its temple and to restore the sacred vessels removed to Babylon. This request is at once granted, and there follows an account of the home-coming of Jews exiled in Babylon and the protection accorded them by the Pers government similar to what we read of in ch **1** as taking place in the reign of Cyrus. But many things in this narrative are striking and indeed odd. Zerubbabel is called a young man. Among those mentioned in **5** 5 Zerubbabel is not named, though his son Joakim is. In the very next verse (**5** 6) this Joakim is identified with the young man (Zerubbabel) who won the king's prize for writing the wisest sentence, though the sense is not quite clear; perhaps Zerubbabel is meant in ver 6. Fritzsche argues that Joakim can alone be meant. This whole episode stands in no organic connection with the rest of 1 Esd, and if it is omitted the narrative is continuous. Besides this the account given of the return from Babylon contradicts what is said in ch **1** and the corresponding part of Ezr. We must regard **3** 1—**5** 6 as a Jewish haggada which at an early time was written in the margin as supplying illustrative matter and then got incorporated into the text. Nevertheless from a literary point of view this part of the book is the gem of the whole.

5. **5** 7–73 = Ezr **2**—**4** 1–5: The names of those who returned with number of animals (horses, etc) (**5** 7–43); altar of burnt offering erected (ver 48); sacrifices offered on it (ver 50). Foundation of the temple laid (vs 56 f). The Jews refuse the offer of the Sam party to help in the rebuilding of the temple, with the result that this party had the work stopped (vs 66–73). Ezr **4** 6–24 finds its ‖ in 1 Esd **2** 16–30 (see above). 1 Esd **2** 30 and **5** 73 are evidently duplicates.

6. **6** 1—**7** 15 = Ezr **5** 1—**6** 22: Building of the temple resumed through the preaching of Haggai and Zechariah (**6** 1 f). Pers officials unsuccessfully oppose the work (vs 3–34) which is soon completed, the temple being then dedicated (**7** 1–11). Observance of the Passover (vs 12–15).

   Between chs **7** and **8** there is an interval of some 60 years, for ch **8** begins with the arrival of Ezra (458 BC).

7. **8** 1–67 = Ezr **7** 1—**8** 36: Journey of Ezra and his party from Babylon to Jerus bearing letters of authority from King Artaxerxes I (d. 424 BC) (**8** 1–27); list of those who return (vs 28–40); gathering together of the party by the river Ahava; incidents of the journey; the arrival (ver 41).

8. **8** 68–90 = Ezr **9**: Ezra's grief on hearing of the marriage of some Jews with foreign wives (vs 68–73). His confession and prayer (vs 74–90).

9. **8** 91—**9** 36 = Ezr **10**: The means used to end the mixed marriages; lists of the men (priests and others) who had married strange wives.

10. **9** 37–55 = Neh **7** 73*b*—**8** 12: The reforms of Ezra. In the Canonical Scriptures Neh **7** 73*b*—**10** gives the history of Ezra, not that of Nehemiah—the two never labored or lived together at Jerus. (The name Nehemiah in Neh **8** 9 and **10** 1 is an evident interpolation.) In 1 Esd Nehemiah is not once mentioned in this section. In **9** 49 (‖ Neh **8** 9) "Attharates" is the word used, and as a proper name (see 1 Esd **5** 40, "Nehemiah and Attharates"). The majority of modern scholars assign this section to Ezra, adding it to Ezr **10**, or incorporating it into the Ezra narrative. So Ewald, Wellhausen, Schrader, Klostermann, Baudissin, Budde and Ryssel. The present writer defends this view in the *Century Bible* in Ezr-Neh-Est, 242 f. In this case 1 Esd borrows from Ch and Ezr alone and not from Neh. It should be remembered however that Ezr-Neh formed originally but one book. Some will say that Ch preceded Ezr-Neh as a single book, but for this there is no evidence (see *Century Bible*, 4). The last verse of 1 Esd in all MSS ends in the middle of a sentence: "And they assembled . . . ." showing that the closing part of the book has been lost. The present writer suggests that the missing part is Neh **8** 13—**10**, which begins, "And on the second day were gathered together [assembled] the heads of fathers' houses," etc, the same verb being used in the LXX Gr of both passages with a very slight difference (ἐπισυνήχθησαν, *episunēchthēsan*, and συνήχθησαν, *sunēchthēsan*, in Ezr and Esd respectively).

Since Neh **7** 73*b*—**8** 12 belongs to the Book of Ezr (see above) describing the work of Ezra, not that of Nehemiah, the contents of 1 Esd are ‖ with those of Ezra alone with the exception of ch **1** which agrees with 2 Ch **35** 1—**36** 21.

3. The Relation Between 1 Esd and Ch, Ezr, Neh

Various explanations have been offered, the following being the principal: (1) that 1 Esd is a compilation based on the LXX of Ch, Ezr and Neh: so Keil, Bissell and formerly Schürer (*GJV*, II, ii, 179 f; Herzog[2], I, 496); the arguments for this opinion are well marshaled by Bissell in his *Comm. on the Apoc* (Lange); (2) that 1 Esd is an independent Gr tr from a now lost Heb (or Aram.) origin in many respects superior to our MT: so Whiston, Pohlmann, Herzfeld, Fritzsche, Ginsburg, Cheyne, Thackeray, Nestle, Howarth, Torrey and Bertholet. Most of these writers hold that the original 1 Esd included the whole of Ch, Ezr and Neh; (3) the bulk of those who support view 2 argue that the original 1 Esd formed the real LXX version of Ch, Ezr and Neh, what exists in our present LXX being another Gr tr, probably by Theodotion (fl. about 150 AD), just as we now know that what up to 1772 (the date of the publication in Rome of the Codex Chisianus) was considered as the LXX of Dnl is really Theodotion's version. Howarth (see arts. in the *Academy*, 1893; *PSBA*, XXIX, etc), and Torrey (*Ezra Studies*) stoutly champion this view. The evidence offered is of two kinds, external and internal:

(1) *External evidence.*—(*a*) Jos uses this version as his source for the period, though for other OT books he follows the LXX. (*b*) In the foreword to the Syr version of 1 Esd in Walton's *Polyglot* it is said that this version follows the LXX, which surely counts for nothing since copies of the LXX known to us contain both 1 Esd and the Gr tr reckoned up to recently as the true LXX. (*c*) Howarth maintains, but without proof, that in Origen's *Hexapla*, 1 Esd takes the place of our LXX version, and that the same is true of the *Vitus Itala*.

(2) *Internal evidence.*—(*a*) It is said by Dr. Gwyn, Thackeray and Howarth that the Gr of the true LXX of Dnl and that of 1 Esd are very similar in character, which however only goes to prove that one man tr[d] both. (*b*) Howarth holds that the Gr of Dnl and Ezr in the orthodox LXX version is very literal, as was all Theodotion's tr work. But such statements have to be received with very great caution, as in judging of style so much depends on the personal equation. The present writer has compared carefully parts ascribed with confidence to Theodotion and the LXX without reaching the above conclusions. At the most the matter has not been set at rest by any facts or reasoning as yet supplied. It must be admitted that 1 Esd and Jos preserve the true sequence of the events chronicled in Neh **7** 73*b*—**10**, the MT and the Gr version based on it having gone wrong at this point, probably through the mixing of Heb skins or leaves. Those who see in 1 Esd the true LXX agree almost to a man that 1 Esd **3** 1—**5** 6 is a late interpretation, never having had a Heb original. This may account in a large degree for the vigor and elegance of the Gr. Howarth, however, parts company with his friends Torrey, Bertholet, etc, by arguing strenuously for this part. (See more fully in *Century Bible*, Ezr, etc, 27 ff.)

1 Esd exists in the following ancient VSS in addition to the Gr text which may or may not be a tr (see 3 above):

4. Versions

(1) *Latin:* (*a*) Jerome; (*b*) Vulgate. (2) *Syriac:* (*a*) The Pesh, given in Walton's *Polyglot* and with a critically revised text by Lagarde (*Libri Veteris Testamenti Apocrypha Syriace*, 1861); (*b*) The Hexaplar Syr version. For details of MSS, etc, see "Literature" below.

Nothing is known or can be conjectured as to the author or translator of 1 Esd, nor can anything be positively affirmed as to the date.

5. Date and Authorship

If the work be the genuine LXX text this would give it an earlier origin than the view which makes it depend on the LXX. But this is to say but little. As Jos (d. 95 AD) used this book it must have been written some years before he wrote his history (say 67 AD). We must assume that it existed some time before the beginning of our era. Ewald, on account of some resemblances to the earliest of the Sibylline Books, dates 1 Esd about 190 BC. But admitting dependence in this matter—which is doubtful—it is impossible to say which is dependent and which is independent in such cases.

LITERATURE.—The most important books have been named at the end of the general art. on APROCRYPHA (q.v.). Recent contributions by Howarth and Torrey have been mentioned in the course of the foregoing article.

T. WITTON DAVIES

ESDRAS, FOURTH BOOK OF. See APOCALYPTIC LITERATURE, II, i, 5.

ESDRAS, SECOND BOOK OF. See APOCALYPTIC LITERATURE, II, i, 5.

ESDRAS, THE SECOND (FOURTH) BOOK OF, or The Apocalyptic Esdras:

1. Name
2. Contents
3. Language
4. Versions
5. Origin of the Book
6. Date

LITERATURE

This book was not received by the Council of Trent as canonical, nor has it ever been acknowledged as such by the Anglican church.

1. Name

The book is not found in the LXX and no complete copy of the Gr text is known, though at one time it did exist. The oldest extant name is "The Prophet Ezra" ("Εσδρας ὁ προφήτης, *Ésdras ho prophḗtēs;* see Clem. Alex., *Strom.*, iii.16): It has been often called the Lat Esd because it exists more completely in that language; cf the name Gr Esd for 1 Esd.

3 Esd is the designation in old editions of the Vulg, 1 Esd being Ezr and Neh, 2 Esd denoting what in Eng. is called 1 Esd. But in editions of the Vulg later than the Council of Trent, and also in Walton's *Polyglot*, Ezr is called 1 Esd, Neh 2 Esd, 1 Esd = 3 Esd, the present book (the Lat Esd) being known as 4 Esd. In authorized copies of the Vulg, i.e. in those commonly used, this book is lacking. On account of its contents, Westcott, following the example of Anastasius Sinaita (bishop of Antioch from 559 AD), called the book the "Apocalypse of Esdras." But as Tischendorf in 1866 edited a later and inferior work with this title the present writer suggests the name "The Apocalyptic Esdras." Of all the Jewish apocalypses this is the sublimest and most pleading; see APOCALYPTIC LITERATURE, II, i, 5.

2. Contents

The original work consists of chs **3–14**, chs **1** f and **15** f being late additions. The entire book of 16 chapters exists in the Lat version only, the other VSS containing chs **3–14** only. The real 2d (apocalyptic) Esd, consisting of chs **3–14**, is made up of 7 visions given to Ezra in exile 30 years after the destruction of Jerus by the Babylonians. The drift of these visions is, How can a just and loving God allow His own people to suffer so much? The problem thus raised is fully and beautifully dealt with. For lack of space the present writer must refer for a fuller analysis to the art. APOCALYPTIC LITERATURE, I, 5, and the lit. there cited. For chs **1** ff and **15** ff see under ESDRAS 5 AND 6.

3. Original Language

Though no complete text even of chs **3–14** has survived, a careful examination of the Lat shows that it has been made from a Gr original. (1) Some fragments of the Gr can be traced, as **5** 35 in Clement of Alexandria and **8** 23 in the Apos Const. (2) The order of the twelve prophets in **1** 39 f follows that in the LXX. (3) The Lat version bears throughout clear traces of Gr idiom. Thus the gen. is used with the comparative (**5** 3; **11** 29); we have the gen. (not abl.) absolute in **10** 9, the double negative and the use of *de* (Gr ἀπό) and *ex* (Gr ἐκ) with the gen. in various parts. But there are cogent reasons for concluding that the Gr version implied in the Lat itself implies a Heb original, and the proof is similar to that of a Gr version as the basis of the Lat. In the Gr there are idioms which are Heb, not Gr, not even in their frequency Hellenistic Gr. The participle used to strengthen the finite vb. is the regular Heb idiom of the absolute with the finite vb.: see **4** 2 (*excedens excessit*); **5** 30 (*odiens odisti*). For other examples see Gunkel (in Kautzsch, *Die Apokryphen u. Pseud. des AT*, 332 f); R. H. Charles (*Enc Brit*, X, 106). Ewald was the first to defend a Heb original, but in 1866 he was followed by his distinguished pupil Wellhausen and also by R. H. Charles (*Apoc Bar*, lxxii).

4. Versions

(1) *Latin.*—The Latin version is far the most important and on it the EV depends. But all published editions of the Lat text (those of Fabricius, Hilgenfeld, Fritzsche, etc) go back to one and the same MS, the so-called Codex Sangermanensis (date 822), which omits a large part of the text between **7** 36 and **7** 37. Any reader of the Eng. text can see the lack of continuity between these verses. In 1875 Bensly published the missing fragment with an Intro and critical notes. In 1895 Bensly and James published a critical edition of *The Fourth Book of Ezra* in Lat, restoring the missing fragment and correcting with the aid of the best-known MSS.

(2) *Other versions.*—There are Syr (Pesh), Ethiopic, Arab., Armenian and yet other VSS, but all depend on the lost Gr except one of the two extant Arab. trs. The number and variety of VSS show that 2 Esd was widely circulated. By the Gr and Lat Fathers it was quoted as a genuine prophetical work. Its importance in the estimation of the mediaeval Roman church is vouched for by the fact that it has reached us in a number of well-known MSS of the Scriptures, and that it was added to the authorized Vulg as an appendix.

5. Origin of the Book

Two main views may briefly be noted: (1) That of Kabisch (*Das vierte Buch Esra*, 1889) who holds that the editor of the book freely used a goodly number of sources, subtracting, adding and altering to suit his purpose. He gives a list of probable sources. R. H. Charles (*Enc Brit*, X, 107) is inclined to adopt this analysis. (2) Gunkel (loc. cit.) maintains and tries to prove that the book is the production of a single writer. Yet he admits that the book contains a large number of inconsistencies which he explains by assuming that the editor made free use of oral and written traditions. The two views do not therefore stand very far apart, for both take for granted that several sources have been used. It is simply a question of more or less.

Wellhausen is probably right in saying that the author of 2 (4) Esd had before him the Apoc of Bar, written under the impression awakened by the destruction of Jerus in 71 AD.

6. Date

The opinion of the best modern scholars is that the book was written somewhere in the East in the last decade of the 1st cent. of our era. This conclusion rests mainly on the most likely interpretation of the vision of the Eagle and the Lion in **11** 1—**12** 51; but also on the fact that Clement of Alexandria (d. 217 AD) quotes the Gr of **5** 35.

LITERATURE.—Besides the lit. referred to above see Schürer, *A Hist of the Jewish People in the Time of Jesus Christ*, II, iii, 93 ff (Ger. ed⁴, III, 315 ff); the arts. in *HDB* (Thackeray) and *EB* (James); the New Sch-Herz s.v. "Pseudepigrapha, Old Testament" (G. Beer), and in the present work under APOCRYPHA and APOCALYPTIC LITERATURE.

T. WITTON DAVIES

ESDRAS (or 4 Ezr) **5 AND 6:** These names have been applied respectively to the first two and the last two chs of 2 (4) Esd in the Lat Bible of 1462. In matter these chapters, which are of Christian origin, agree in the main with the genuine parts of 2 (4) Esd. See foregoing article.

ESDRIS, ez′dris, es′dris (**Ἔσδρις,** *Ésdris*): A leader mentioned in 2 Macc **12** 36 in best texts and adopted in RV for **Gorgias** of AV. Grotius conjectured "men of Ephron" from ver 27.

ESEBON, es′ē-bon (Jth **5** 15) = HESHBON (RV), the chief city of the Ammonites.

ESEBRIAS, es-ē-brī′as, ē-sē′bri-as. See ESEREBIAS; SHEREBIAH.

ESEK, ē'sek (עֵשֶׂק, *'ēseḳ;* LXX **'Αδικία,** *Adikía*): The name given by Isaac to a well dug by his servants, for the use of which the herdmen of Gerar strove with them—"contention" (Gen **26** 20). It lay in the neighborhood of Rehoboth and Gerar: but the site is not identified.

ESEREBIAS, es-er-ē-bī'as (**'Εσερεβίας,** *Eserebías*): One of the chiefs of the priests (1 Esd **8** 54).

ESHAN, ē'shan (אֶשְׁעָן, *'esh'ān;* **'Εσάν,** *Esán;* AV **Eshean**): A town of Judah in the uplands of Hebron (Josh **15** 52). No satisfactory identification has yet been suggested. Some think the name may be a corruption of Beersheba (*EB* s.v.).

ESHBAAL, esh'bā-al. See Ishbosheth.

ESHBAN, esh'ban (אֶשְׁבָּן, *'eshbān;* perhaps "thoughtful," "intelligent"; **'Ασβάν,** *Asbán*): Name of a chief of the Horites (Gen **36** 26; 1 Ch **1** 41).

ESHCOL, esh'kol (אֶשְׁכֹּל, *'eshkōl,* "cluster"; **'Εσχώλ,** *Eschōl*): The brother of Mamre and Aner, the Amorite allies of Abraham who took part with him in the pursuit and defeat of Chedorlaomer's forces (Gen **14** 13.24). He lived in the neighborhood of Hebron (**13** 18), and may have given his name to the valley of Eshcol, which lay a little N. of Hebron (Nu **13** 23).

ESHCOL, esh'kol (אֶשְׁכֹּל, *'eshkōl;* **Φάραγξ βότρυος,** *Pháragx bótruos,* "a cluster of grapes"): The spies came to Hebron "and they came unto the valley of Eshcol, and cut down from thence a branch with one cluster of grapes" (Nu **13** 23.24; **32** 9; Dt **1** 24). It was a valley near Hebron rich in vineyards. Fruitful vineyards are still the most characteristic feature of the environs of Hebron, esp. on the N. No particular valley can be identified, though popular tradition favors the wide and fertile valley, near the traditional site of "Abraham's oak," a little to the W. of the carriage road just before it enters the outskirts of Hebron. E. W. G. Masterman

ESHEAN, esh'ē-an, ē'shē-an. See Eshan.

ESHEK, ē'shek (עֵשֶׁק, *'ēsheḳ,* "oppressor"): A descendant of Jonathan, son of Saul, first king of Israel (1 Ch **8** 39).

ESHKALONITE, esh'ka-lon-īt. See Askelonite.

ESHTAOL, esh'tā-ol (אֶשְׁתָּאוֹל, *'eshtā'ōl;* **'Ασταώλ,** *Astaōl*): A town in the Shephelah of Judah named next to Zorah (Josh **15** 33; **19** 41). Between these two cities lay Mahaneh-dan (the camp of Dan) where the Spirit of the Lord began to move Samson (Jgs **13** 25), and where he was buried (**16** 31). A contingent from Eshtaol formed part of the 600 Danites who captured Laish (**18** 2.11). It is probably represented by the modern *Ashū'a,* about a mile and a half E. of Zorah, the modern *Ṣar'ah.*

ESHTAOLITES, esh'tā-ol-īts (הָאֶשְׁתָּאֻלִי, *hā-'eshtā'ulī,* lit. "the Eshtaolite"; AV **Eshtaulites,** esh-ta-ū'līts): Inhabitants of Eshtaol, named among the descendants of Shobal, the son of Caleb (1 Ch **2** 53).

ESHTEMOA, esh-tē-mō'a, esh'tē-mō-a (אֶשְׁתְּמוֹעַ, *'eshtemōa'*): A Levitical city in the hill country of Judah (Josh **21** 14; 1 Ch **6** 57); **Eshtemoh** (אֶשְׁתְּמֹה, *'eshtemōh,* Josh **15** 50). In 1 Ch **4** 17.19, Eshtemoa is said to be a Maacathite and "son" of Ishbah. David after routing the Amalekites sent a present to his friends in (among other places) Eshtemoa (1 S **30** 28). It is now *es-Semū'a,* a considerable village of evident antiquity some 8 miles S. of Hebron.

ESHTEMOH, esh'tē-mō. See Eshtemoa.

ESHTON, esh'ton (אֶשְׁתּוֹן, *'eshtōn,* "uxorious"): A name found in the genealogical table of Judah (1 Ch **4** 12).

ESLI, es'lī (**'Εσλεί,** *Esleí,* **'Εσλί,** *Eslí;* probably for Heb אֲצַלְיָהוּ, *'ăçalyāhū*): An ancestor of Jesus in St. Luke's genealogy, the 10th before Joseph, the husband of Mary (Lk **3** 25).

ESORA, ē-sō'ra. See Aesora.

ESPOUSAL, es-pouz'al, **ESPOUSE,** es-pouz': In AV these words, following Eng. usage of an earlier day, are used to signify either marriage or betrothal, while the ARV discriminates, and uses them only for marriage. For example, in 2 S **3** 14, "I espoused to me" (Heb *'ērastī lī*) becomes "I betrothed to me." So also, in Mt **1** 18; Lk **1** 27; **2** 5 which refer to the relation between Joseph and Mary before the birth of Jesus, "espoused" (*μνηστεύω, mnēsteúō*) becomes "betrothed." On the other hand, "espoused" is retained in Cant **3** 11 ("the day of his espousals"—that is, day of marriage); in Jer **2** 2 ("the love of thine espousals"—that is, the love of married state); and in 2 Cor **11** 2 ("I espoused [*ἡρμοσάμην, hērmosámēn*] you to one husband"). E. J. Forrester

ESPY, es-pī': "Espy" in modern Eng. means "to catch sight of," rather than "to explore secretly." RV therefore retains it in Gen **42** 27, "He espied his money" (Heb רָאָה, *rā'āh,* "see"), while in Josh **14** 7 "espy out the land" (AV) becomes "spy out the land." RV substitutes "watch" for "espy" in Jer **48** 19, and "searched out" for "espied" in Ezk **20** 6, with a gain in accuracy of rendering (cf the context).

ESRIL, es'ril, ez'ril: RV Ezril (which see).

ESROM, es'rom, ez'rom (**'Εσρώμ,** *Esrōm*): AV, the Gr form of Hezron (thus RV) (Mt **1** 3; Lk **3** 33).

ESSENES, es-sēnz', **THE** (**'Εσσηνοί,** *Essēnoí,* **'Εσσαῖοι,** *Essaíoi*):

I. The Name
 Forms It Assumes—Etymology
II. Authorities
 1. Philo
  (1) Description from *Quod Omnis Probus Liber*
  (2) Description from Quotation in Eusebius, *Prep. Evang.*
  (3) Description of Therapeutae from *De Vita Contemplativa*
 2. Josephus
  (1) Description from *Antiquities of the Jews,* XVIII, i, 5
  (2) Description from *Wars of the Jews,* II, viii, 2–13
  (3) Incidental Notices
 3. Pliny
 4. Hegesippus
 5. Porphyry
 6. Hippolytus—Uses Josephus, but to Some Extent Independent
 7. Epiphanius—Confused Account
III. Deductions and Combinations
 1. Government
 2. Doctrines
IV. History and Origin
 1. Essenes and Ḥasidhīm
 2. Position of Essenes in Josephus
 3. Doctrinal Affinities
 4. Essenes and Pythagoras
 5. Buddhism and Essenism
 6. Parseeism and Essenism
 7. Essenism Mainly Jewish

When Jos describes the sects of the Jews, he devotes most of his time and attention to the third of these sects, the Essenes. Strangely enough, although there are frequent references in the NT to the other two sects, the Sadducees and Pharisees, no reference has been found to the Essenes. Notwithstanding this silence of the Gospels, the prominence of this third sect is undeniable. Even in Egypt they are known. Philo, the Jewish philosopher, gives an account of these Essenes in terms that, while in the main resembling those used in Jos, yet differ enough to prove him clearly an independent witness. Another contemporary, Pliny the Naturalist, also mentions these Essenes. Approximately a century later we have a long account of the habits and tenets of these sectaries in Hippolytus' *Refutation of All Heresies*. A century and a half later still Epiphanius describes these under various titles. Despite the fact that no reference to the Essenes can be found in the Gospels or the Acts, at all events under that name, there can be no doubt of their existence. Would one understand the Pal in which Our Lord's ministry was carried on, he must comprehend the place occupied by the Essenes.

I. The Name.—This assumes several forms in different authors—indeed sometimes two forms appear in the same author. Jos uses most frequently the form of the name which stands at the head of this art., but sometimes he speaks of individuals as "Essaeans" (*BJ*, II, vii, 3; viii, 4). This latter form is that preferred by Philo, a form that is adopted by Hegesippus as quoted by Eusebius, IV, 22. Pliny in his *Natural History*, v.15 writes "Essaeans." Hippolytus also has "Essenus." Epiphanius has mixed his information so that this sect appears with him under several names as "Ossaei" and "Jessaei."

Forms It Assumes—Etymology, Origin

It is clear that the name is not primarily Gr—it has passed into Gr from another tongue, since none of the forms has any easy derivation in Gr. Notwithstanding, there have been attempts to derive it from some Gr root, but all are preposterous as etymologies. The etymology must be sought either in Heb or its cognate, Aram. The usage in regard to the tr of proper names is our only guide. Reasoning from the practice as seen in the Gr tr of the Scriptures and in Jos, we can deduce that the first letter of the original word must have been one of the gutturals עחהא. That the second letter was a sibilant is certain, and the last was probably יא, for the final *n* in the common form of the name is due to the desire to render the word suitable for Gr accidence. We may say that to us the two most likely derivations are עשׂיא, '*ăsīyā*', "doers" or אסיא, '*ăsīyā*', "healers." Our preference is for the latter, as one of the characteristics of the Essenes dwelt upon by Jos is the fact that they were healers by means of herbs and incantations (*BJ*, II, viii, 6). This view is held by the great mass of investigators, as Bellerman, Gfrörer, Hamburger, Herzfeld, Dähm, etc. The name "Therapeutae" given by Philo to the kindred sect in Egypt supports this etymology, as it would be in one of its senses a tr of it. Lightfoot's objection that it is improbable that the ordinary name of the sect "should have been derived from a pursuit which was merely secondary and incidental" does not follow analogy. The term "Methodist" was derived from a purely temporary characteristic of the society that gathered round Wesley. The extreme probability, from the fact that the name is not found in the NT, is that it was the nature of a nickname, like "Quakers" applied to the Society of Friends. The multitude that followed Our Lord affords evidence of the influence that a reputation for healing gave to one.

II. The Authorities for the Tenets of the Essenes.—Philo and Jos, as contemporaries and Jews, are necessarily our principal sources of information. Next is Pliny, though a contemporary of the sect, yet as a Roman, of necessity receiving his information second-hand. There is next in point of date Hippolytus in his work *Refutation of All Heresies*, written more than a century after the fall of the Jewish state and the disappearance of the Essenes. One point in his favor as an authority is his habit of quoting from sources that would be reckoned good even now. He seems to have founded to some extent on Jos, but he appears to have made use of some other source or sources as well. Slightly later is Porphyry. He avowedly draws all his information from Jos. The latest of the ancients who may be reckoned as authorities is Epiphanius. Writing in the 4th cent., and naturally of a somewhat confused intellect, any statement of his unsupported by other authority is to be received with caution.

1. Philo

In estimating the evidence that Philo gives concerning the Essenes, we must remember that he was living in Alexandria, not shut up in a Ghetto, but mingling to some extent with the scholars and philosophers of that city. The Jewish community there appears to have been more completely Hellenized than any other assemblage of Jews. The object of Philo's numerous works seems to have been the twofold one of commending Jewish religious thought to the Gr philosophic society in which he mingled, and of commending Gr philosophy to his Jewish kinsmen. The geographic distance from Pal may be to some degree neglected from the frequent communications between it and Egypt. The work in which Philo devotes most attention to the Essenes is his early work, *Quod Omnis Probus Liber*, "that every good man is free." This treatise is intended for a gentile audience—the "Lawgiver of the Jews" is introduced casually first, and then more emphatically, till he is named. The Essenes are brought forward as the very flower and perfection of Mosaism.

(1) *Description of Essenes from "Quod Omnis Probus Liber."*—"There is a portion of that people called Essenes—over four thousand in my opinion. They are above all servants [*therapeutaí*] of God. They do not sacrifice animals but study to preserve the sanctity of life. They live in villages, avoiding all cities on account of the lawlessness of those that inhabit them. Some of these men cultivate the soil, others live by peaceful arts and so benefit themselves and all their neighbors. They do not lay up treasures of gold or silver for themselves, judging contentment and frugality the great riches. With them are no makers of arms or of military engines and no one is occupied with anything connected with war. They all avoid commerce and navigation, thinking that these employments make for covetousness. They possess no slaves, holding all men to be free and all are expected to aid one another as real [*gnēsíois*] brethren. They devote their attention to the moral part of philosophy—to the neglect of logic—using, as instructors, the laws of their country which it would have been impossible for the human mind to devise save by Divine inspiration. They abstain from all work on the seventh day, which they look on as sacred. On it they assemble in sacred buildings which are called synagogues and, seated in order according to age, they hear the Scriptures [*tás bíblous*] read and expounded. They are thus taught to choose what is right and to avoid what is wrong. They use a threefold criterion—love of God, love of virtue, love of man. They carefully avoid oaths and falsehood—they regard God as the author of all good. They all dwell in companies, so that no one has a dwelling absolutely his own. They have everything in common, their expenses, their garments, their food. When they work for wages they do not retain these for themselves, but bring it into the common stock. The sick are not neglected when they are unable to contribute to the common store. They respect their seniors as if they were their parents. Such men never can be enslaved. As a proof of this none of the many oppressors of their land were able to bring any accusation against the Holy Essenes."

The above is a very much condensed summary of the passage on the Essenes in Philo, *QOPL*. No one can fail to be struck with the resemblance all this has in the first place to the teaching of the Sermon on the Mount and the practice of the early church. Although celibacy is not mentioned it is implied in the picture here presented of the Essenes.

There is another account in a passage quoted from Philo by Eusebius, *Preparatio Evangelica*, VIII, 11:

(2) *Philo's Account.*—"Our lawgiver trained [*ēleipsen*, "anointed"] ten thousands of his followers and formed

them into a community called Essenes from their holiness. They dwell as numerous communities in many cities and villages of Judaea." It will be observed that this contradicts the statement above that there were only 4,000 Essenes and that they avoided cities. "This sect is not hereditary. There are no children nor youths among the Essenes as such persons are unstable. No one among them has property of his own. They regard all possessions as part of a common stock. They all dwell in the same place, forming themselves into clubs and societies. They do everything for the benefit of the whole society, but different members take up different employments, laboring ceaselessly despite cold or heat. Before sunrise they go to their work and do not quit it till sunset. Some are tillers of the soil, some shepherds, some tend bees, some are artisans. These men when they have received their wages give them up to the general manager who purchases what is necessary. Those who live together eat at the same table day after day. Their dress also is common. In winter they have thick cloaks, in summer light mantles. Each takes what he wants. When anyone falls sick he is cured from their common resources. Old men, even if they happen to be childless, are as if they had a numerous offspring of affectionate children. They repudiate marriage because they look on woman as a selfish creature and specially addicted to jealousy and hypocrisy, thus likely to dissolve their brotherhood. A man bound to a woman is hampered by his affection, is no longer a free man but a slave" (cf 1 Cor 7 1. St. Paul mentions the same difficulties in regard to wedlock).

(3) *Philo on the "Therapeutae."*—In his Treatise *De Vita Contemplativa* Philo, commencing with a reference to the Essenes, passes on to describe a similar class of coenobites who have their settlements near the Moerotic Lake. These he calls *Therapeutae*, or in the fem., *Therapeutrides*, a title which he interprets as "healers." While there are many points of resemblance, there are also not a few features of difference. We shall give as full an extract as in the previous instances.

It is related that they have separate houses and only come together for worship or for feasts. They have parallel societies for men and for women. As in the case of the Essenes there is a reading of ancient sacred books and an exposition of the passage read. The name *Therapeutae*, with the explanation of the name given by Philo, affords a link, as said above, with the Essenes, if the etymology of their name which we have seen reason to prefer be the true one. There seems also to be some connection between these Jewish monks and the Christian monks of some three centuries later. It ought to be remarked that many suspicions have been thrown on the authenticity of *De Vita Contemplativa*. Although critical names of authority may be named on that side, yet it may be doubted whether the reasons are sufficient. Lucius, who is the main opponent, does so mainly to invalidate the existence of the *Therapeutae*. He thinks *De Vita Contemplativa* was composed by a Christian to give an antiquity to the Christian monks. To prove a practice to have been Jewish would be far from commending it to Christians. But more, the resemblance to the Christian monks, although close on some points, in others of importance the difference is equally prominent. While the common feast suggests the Agapae of the early church, we must remember that this was not a monastic peculiarity. The fact that a female community existed alongside of the male and joined with them in worship is out of harmony with what we know of early monasticism. The feast of the 50th day has no parallel in Christianity.

2. Josephus

Like Philo, Jos wrote for a non-Jewish audience. In Rome the philosophic ideas held in the Hellenic world were prevalent, so he, as much as Philo, had a temptation to be silent on any subject which might shock the sensibilities or provoke the ridicule of his masters. In particular, in describing the habits and tenets of the Essenes, for whom he professed so high an admiration, he would need to be specially careful to avoid causes of offence, as in such a case he would be liable to be involved in their condemnation. In dealing with the notices he gives of the Essenes we would consider the descriptions at length first, and then the incidental notices of individual Essenes.

The description which comes earliest in history—not, however, the earliest written—is in *Antiquities of the Jews*, XVIII, in connection with the census and survey under Quirinius (Cyrenius) and the resistance to it by Judas of Gamala.

He there (*Ant*, XVIII, i, 5) begins by referring to their theological position, that they believed in the most absolute preordination. They teach the immortality of souls and a state of rewards and punishments. Although they dedicated gifts to the temple they offered no sacrifices, presumably bloody sacrifices, as they have offerings of their own. A singular statement is made that "they are on this account excluded from the common court" (*koinoú temenísmatos*). They occupy themselves with husbandry. "They excel in justice all other men." They have all things in common. They neither marry wives nor keep slaves. He says, as does Philo, that they number over four thousand men. They appoint "good men priests who should receive the fruits of their labor for the sake of corn and food."

A much fuller account is found in the earlier written treatise on the *Wars of the Jews*, II, viii, 3. In this work he emphasizes the ascetic side of Essenism.

"The Essenes," he says, "reject pleasures as vice. They despise marriage though they do not absolutely repudiate it, but are suspicious of women. They despise riches and have all things in common. They think oil a defilement. They wear white garments. They elect overseers (*epimelētaí*) to manage their common affairs, much as the Christian bishops did those of the churches under them. They have no one city but many of them dwell in every city." It may be observed that this statement is a contradiction of Philo's statement and that of Jos himself above, that they were only 4,000. "When any of them go from one city to another they find the houses of those of their sect open to them as if they were their own." It is probable that as the apostles, when sent out by Our Lord to preach, were on entering a city to ask who in it was worthy, the traveling Essenes would inquire who in it were Essenes. Like the apostles they took nothing with them when they traveled save weapons for defence against robbers, just as the apostles had at the time of the Last Supper two swords with which they had likely provided themselves for similar reasons. "They get up before sunrise and offer up prayers which they have received from their ancestors. They are then dismissed to their several employments to the fifth hour, they bathe in cold water, put on white linen garments and enter the refectory as if into a temple. Food is set before each." Much like the Christian grace before meat, a priest offers up prayer. Again, as grace after meat, when the meal is finished the priest again prays. "Both before and after their refection they sing praise to God. As Christ commanded His disciples and said, 'Swear not at all,' they avoid oaths, indeed esteem them worse than perjury. New members were admitted to the society by baptism, and oaths were laid upon them that they were to be submissive to those in authority in the society. They were to keep the doctrines of the sect secret. They kept the Sabbath with greater strictness than did any other section of the Jews. Heinous sins were punished by expulsion from the order which, as they felt their oaths still binding on them, amounted to death. Judicial sentences are arrived at with the utmost care; decisions are come to by an assembly of not less than a hundred who are chosen to be judges. When once the sentence has been pronounced it stands fixed. They regard the bodies as corruptible but the souls are immortal. They believe in a Paradise resembling the Islands of the Blest." One thing is to be observed: "they are bound by oath to preserve the sacred books of their sect, *tá hairéseōs autôn bíblia*, and the names of the angels." They utter predictions by means of their sacred books, which predictions are generally fulfilled. There is, however, another sort of Essenes who do not avoid marriage.

The philosopher Porphyry mentions that Jos had an account of the Essenes in the second book against the Gentiles. If this means *Contra Apionem*, no such passage is to be found in that work now. It may, however, be some work of Jos which has not come down to us, which Porphyry has misnamed, though this is unlikely.

This is not, however, the whole of the information concerning the Essenes which we can gather from Jos. The earliest of these incidental notices occurs under the reign of Jonathan (*Ant*, XIII, v, 9), when the historian mentions the three sects of the Jews, when the only peculiarity he assigns to the Essenes is that they believe that everything happens according to fate. Next, in relating the fate of Antigonus, he tells how Judas, an Essene teaching in the temple, when he saw Antigonus, declared that he was proved a false prophet, as he had foretold that Antigonus was to die that day at Strato's tower (Caesarea), and he was now six hundred furlongs off from there. Here the statement that the Essenes were excluded from the temple seems directly contradicted. In the days of Herod (XV, x, 4.5) Josephus relates that while Herod demanded oaths of submission from others he excused the Essenes, from the favor he had to them on account of one Menahem, a member of this sect, who foretold his reign. This Essene seems to have been about the court and to have nothing of the coenobitic agriculturist about him. The Essenian fame for prediction and the interpretation of dreams is related in regard to Archelaus, the son of Herod (*BJ*, II, vii, 3). Archelaus had a dream, and applied to an Essene, Simon or Simeon, who foretold the end of his reign. In singular contrast to what had been said by Philo of the objection the Essenes had in regard to everything connected with war, one of the leading generals of the Jews when they rebelled against the Romans was John the Essene, who was made governor of certain toparchies in the North (*BJ*, II, xx, 4). He was killed in the battle near Ascalon with which the war began, which ended in the capture of Jerus by Titus (*BJ*, III, ii, 1). There is also mention of a gate of the Essenes in Jerus, which seems to imply that a number of them permanently resided there.

3. Pliny

Pliny speaks of the Essenes in his *Natural History* (v.17) in somewhat rhetorical terms. They dwell on the west side of the Dead Sea—"a wonderful race without women, without money, associates of the palms." They are recruited by those wearied of life, broken in fortunes. "Thus a race is eternal through thousands of ages [*seculorum*] in which no one is born; so fruitful to them is repentance of life in others." He refers to the fertility of Engedi and adds, "now burned up."

4. Hegesippus

There is an enigmatical passage quoted by Eusebius from Hegesippus in which the Essaeans (Essenes), the Galileans, Hemerobaptists, Masbotheans, Samaritans and Pharisees are declared to hold different opinions about circumcision among the sons of Israel "against the tribe of Judah and of Christ" (*katá tēs phúlēs Ioúda kaí Christoú*).

5. Porphyry

Porphyry's note regarding the Essenes is simply taken from Jos.

6. Hippolytus

In the great work of the mysterious bishop, Hippolytus, discovered some sixty years ago, there is a description of the Essenes. Although the work is a *Refutation of All Heresies*, implying that the opinions maintained were erroneous and required to be refuted, the author does nothing to exhibit the erroneousness of the Essene tenets or habits. In regard to the gnostic heresies Hippolytus endeavored to reach original sources; presumably he did so in the present case. Although there is no doubt of his indebtedness to Jos, yet for the features where he differs from Jos, or supplements him, we may assume that he has behind his statements some authority which he regarded as valid. In some cases there may be a suspicion that in his eagerness to show that certain heresies were derived from this or that heathen philosophical system he has modified the heresy to suit the derivation he has supposed. This, however, does not apply to the Essenes.

In the ninth book of his *Refutation of All Heresies*, Hippolytus takes up Jewish sects (*haíreseis*) which, following Jos, he reckons as three. The first he discusses is the Essenes. They are very devotional and temperate and eschew matrimony. They despise wealth, and from sharing with the destitute they do not turn away (cf Mt **5** 42; the vb. used is the same). Anyone joining the sect must sell all that he has (cf Mt **19** 21; the same words are used in Acts **4** 32.37). Overseers (*epimelētai*) are chosen by show of hands (*cheirotoneín*) (Acts **14** 23). They do not stay in one city but many settle in every city. They dress always in white, but do not own two cloaks or two pairs of shoes, much as Our Lord's instructions to His apostles when He sent them out two and two (Mt **10** 10). Their daily course of conduct is described very much in the same terms as those used by Jos. Before dawn they begin their day by prayer and singing a hymn. They return from their work before midday, at the fifth hour, and bathe themselves in cold water and clothe themselves in garments of white linen. After that they repair into the common apartment. They seat themselves in silence; the cook places food before each individual. The priest prays and pronounces a blessing on the food. At the end of the meal the priest again prays, and those who have partaken join in singing a hymn of thanksgiving. They lay aside their white linen garments, and resume their ordinary clothing and betake themselves again to their occupations. Supper at sunset is conducted in a similar manner. All obey the president (*proestōs*) in whatever he enjoins. No one amongst them is in the habit of swearing. They are careful to read the law and the prophets. Other works of faithful men they also study. All that join the sect are put on probation. The entrant receives a white robe and a linen girdle, and is supplied with an axe for the purposes mentioned in Dt **23** 13. He has to take solemn oaths to worship God, to be just, not to hate anyone who injures him, but to pray for him (cf Mt **5** 44). He promises also to show respect to all in authority, as all authority is from God (1 Pet **2** 13). He is not to divulge the secret doctrines of the society. There follows a description of the fate of those expelled from the society and the mode of conducting trials, borrowed from Jos. Hippolytus proceeds to give an account of four different subsects of the Essenes, all seeming of more than even the wonted fanaticism of the Essenes. One sect would not use coins because of the image of the Emperor on them, inasmuch as this was of the nature of idolatry. Others were prepared to enforce circumcision at the point of the sword. According to Hippolytus the Zealots were Essenes. Later he mentions the class that were freer and did not abjure marriage. A very marked point of difference between the tenets of the Essenes, as described by Philo and Jos, and those attributed to them by Hippolytus, is in regard to the doctrine of the resurrection. Hippolytus affirms that they did believe in the resurrection of the body. The others, while not in terms denying that they did believe in it, ignore it in such a way as might lead the reader, as indeed it did Bishop Lightfoot, to think that they denied it altogether. The treatment Paul received at Athens when he preached the resurrection showed how incongruous this doctrine seemed to the Greeks. Philo and Jos wrote for Gr audiences—for the Romans, so far as culture went, were Greeks—and had to consider their taste. Another point held in abeyance by both those writers was the Messianic hopes that we know from the NT were so prevalent. Hippolytus says "all sections look for the Messiah," but held that He was to be merely man born in the ordinary way. The reason of Philo's silence and that of Jos is easily understood. They had commended the Essenes so highly; if they mentioned that they had treasonable hopes of a Messiah who should rule the world, their own personal loyalty would become doubtful. For our part we should regard all the positive elements in Hippolytus' description as worthy of acceptance.

7. Epiphanius

The last authority to whom we would refer is Epiphanius. In his anxiety to make up the number of heresies, the Essenes figure repeatedly under different names. He declares the Essenes to be a sect of the Samaritans closely associated with the Sebuans and Gortheni. Among the Jews he has three sects whom he calls Hemerobaptistae, Nazaraei and Osseni. Besides he has a sect called Sampseans, evidently also Essenes, which he mixes up with the followers of Elkaisa. He does not seem to have any clear idea about their tenets or habits. The Samaritan sects differ about the three Jewish feasts, but he does not make it clear in what they differ. The Sebuans seem to have reversed the order of the Jewish feasts, but whether the Essenes and Gortheni did so likewise is not clear. That the Essenes whom we are considering were not Samaritans appears to be as certain as anything about this enigmatic sect can be. The obscure sentence quoted by Eusebius from Hegesippus might be interpreted as supporting this statement of Epiphanius, but it is too enigmatic to be pressed. As to the three Jewish sects the first named—*Hemerobaptistae*—suits the daily washings of the Essenes, but he asserts that they agree with the Sadducees in denying the resurrection. The Nazareans or Nazarenes are not to be confounded with a Christian sect of nearly the same name. They resided in the district E. of Jordan. They held with the Jews in all their customs, believing in the patriarchs, but did not receive the Pent, though they acknowledged Moses. The Osseni are the likest to the Essenes, as they are said to dwell near the Dead Sea, only it is on the side opposite to Engedi. Epiphanius leaves them to denounce Elxai and his brother Jexais, of which latter nothing further is known.

III. Deductions and Combinations.—From the characteristics so many, so confusing, indeed, in some respects so contradictory, it is difficult to get a consistent picture. They are said to be only four thousand, yet they are many ten thousands. They reside in Engedi, a company of coenobites. They dwell in villages and avoid towns, yet they dwell many in every city and in populous communities. They avoid everything connected with war, yet one of their number is one of the trusted generals of the Jews in their rebellion against the Romans. They keep away from the Temple, yet one of them, Judas, is teaching in the Temple when he sees Antigonus, whose death he had foretold. The only way in which any consistency can be brought into these accounts is by taking advantage of what Jos and Hippolytus say about the subsections into which the Essenes were distinguished.

A parallel the present writer has elsewhere used of the Methodists is illuminative. While the most prominent body of Methodists are Arminians, there are the Calvinistic Methodists. While Wesleyan Methodists do not allow women to preach, the Primitive Methodists do. This is so far confirmed by the fact that while the abjuring of marriage is a marked feature in the representation of Philo, yet the latter says that one class of the Essenes not only do not themselves oppose matrimony but regard those that do oppose it as enemies of the human race. The residents in Engedi formed but a small proportion of the Essenes. It is probable that of them the statement, found alike in Philo and Jos, that they were 4,000, applies. All the features of the picture of the daily common meals, rising before sunrise, joint devotions, may be true in their fulness only of the community by the Dead Sea. What Philo says (quoted by Eusebius, *Prep. Evan.*, VIII, 11), that among the Essenes "there are no youths or persons just entering on manhood, only men already declining towards old age," would indicate that the settlement at Engedi was an asylum for those who, having borne the burden and heat of the day, now retired to enjoy repose.

1. Government

They had communities apparently all over Pal, if not also beyond its bounds, over each of which there was a president appointed (Hip., IX, 15). This would mean that in towns of any size they would have a synagogue. They appear to have had houses of call, though it may have been that every member of the Essene community kept open house for all members of their sect who might be traveling. The traveler, when he came to a city, would inquire for any that were Essenes, as the apostles were commanded by their Lord, in similar circumstances, to inquire ("search out") who in a city were "worthy." The common meals might to some extent be observed in these different scattered communities, probably at intervals, not daily as at Engedi. At these the secret sacred books, read and studied with so great regularity at Engedi, would also be read. In this synagogue not only would the canonical books be preserved but also those other books which gave them the names of the angels, as now in the synagogues of Pal the library preserved in the synagogue may be used by those connected with it throughout the week. The head of the community at Engedi might have some suzerainty over all the different communities, but in regard to this we have no information. One external feature which would at once make the Essenes known to each other was the fact that they always dressed in white linen. They had priests probably in every one of their communities. The Jewish exorcists in Ephesus, in whom Bishop Lightfoot (*Col*, 93) recognizes Essenes, were the sons of one Sceva, a high priest (*archiereús*, Acts **19** 14). The high-priesthood was evidently not connected with the temple at Jerus, for no such name appears in the list of high priests. It thus most probably was an Essenian high-priesthood.

2. Doctrines

In regard to their tenets, their belief in the absolute preordination by God of everything appears the feature in the doctrinal position which most appealed to Jos. Hippolytus affirms in terms their belief in the resurrection of the body. This point, as above noted, Philo and Jos ignore. The passage in Hippolytus is the more striking from the fact that the latter portion so closely resembles the ‖ passage in Jos. Jos, as we have suggested above, avoided crediting the Essenes with belief in resurrection because of the ridicule to which it would expose not only the Essenes, his protégés, but also himself. Hippolytus, writing with information other than what might be got from Jos or Philo and as, writing for Christian readers, without the fear of ridicule, in regard to the resurrection of the body, boldly and in terms ascribes that doctrine to them. The silence of our two main witnesses as to the Essenes cherishing any Messianic hopes cannot be pressed, as their silence may be explained as above mentioned by fear of the suspicions of Rome in regard to any such hopes. The statement of Hippolytus that all the Jews had these expectations may be said to cover this case. The abjuring of marriage and the shunning of everything connected with war seem to be prominent opinions in some sections of the Essenes, but not held by others.

IV. History and Origin.—There is much in Essenism that is difficult to understand. We have seen contradictory features assigned to the Essenes by different authorities; but even in the case of those features concerning which there is least dubiety the new difficulty emerges as to how it appeared as a characteristic of a Jewish sect. This is esp. the case in regard to abstinence from marriage. Easterners always have an earnest desire to have sons to keep their memory green, for on a death many of them had and still have ceremonies which only the son of the dead can perform. Yet despite this they avoided marriage. The Jews with their Messianic hopes desired children, as no one knew but that his child might prove the child of promise, the Christ of God.

The earliest note of the existence of the Essenes as of the Pharisees and Sadducees, is under the pontificate of Jonathan, the successor of Judas Maccabaeus (*Ant*, XIII, v, 9). Jos says "at this time there were three sects of the Jews," and proceeds to name them. If this, however, were precisely true, it is singular that there is no mention of any of these sects in either of the books of the Maccabees. The only sect named is the Hasidaeans (*ḥăṣīdhīm*) who are called (1 Macc **2** 42) "mighty men of Israel, every one that offered himself willingly for the law" (AV "voluntarily devoted himself to the law"; Gr *hekousiazómenos*). These again are not mentioned by Jos. The meaning of the word is "saints," and in this sense it appears frequently in the Pss. A parallel in modern history to their warlike activity and their claim to saintliness may be found in the Cameronians of "society folk" in Scotland toward the end of the 17th cent. They were Peden's "praying folk," yet they fought and won battles. When William of Orange came they formed the Cameronian regiment which helped to quell the clans and checked their advance after Killiecrankie. Some have identified these Hasidaeans with the Pharisees (as W. Robertson Smith, art. "Assidaeans," *EB*, and others). Hitzig would regard their successors as the Essenes. The great resemblance there was between the Pharisees and the Essenes renders it not improbable that originally they were really one sect and split off. If Jos is to be trusted this division must have occurred, if not before the Maccabean struggle, at least early during its continuance. The Sadducean authors of 1 Macc may have grouped them together. According to Jos, John Hyrcanus was a Pharisee, from which it may be presumed that Judas Maccabaeus and his brethren belonged to the same sect of the Jews. The Assidaeans deserted Maccabaeus, so that it would seem at least possible that by that time the separation had become complete, so that the Hasidaeans are now to be regarded as Essenes. It would seem as if they deserted the Maccabeans when they—the Maccabeans—made alliances with heathen powers like Rome. Then they objected to the high-priestly family being passed over for the Hasmoneans, hence their foolish surrender to Bacchides because Alcimus (called by Jos Jacimus =*Jehoiakim*) was with him, a descendant of the race of the high priests. All this is utterly unlike the quiet contemplative lives of the coenobites in Engedi. It would seem that the thousand who died in the wilderness themselves, their wives, their children and their cattle (1 Macc **1** 29–38), were more like the inhabitants of Engedi. Before leaving the Hasidaeans it must be said that the representation of the connection of the Hasidaeans with Judas Maccabaeus put in the mouth of Alcimus by the writer of 2 Macc (**14** 6) is not trustworthy. After this desertion of the Maccabeans the more religious of them retired to Engedi, while the rest of the party were scattered over the country in the various cities and villages.

1. Essenes and Ḥassidim

As above mentioned the earliest mention of Essenes is by Jos (*Ant*, XIII, v, 9) while Jonathan was high priest. The next is the story of Judas the Essene seated in the Temple surrounded by his scholars "who attended him [*parémenon*] in order to learn the art of foretelling," thinking that the appearance of Antigonus in the Temple courts proved his prophecy false that he was that day to die in Strato's tower (Caesarea). Judas is evidently a resident in Jerus and meets his pupils in the Temple courts. This would imply that he had no horror of the Temple nor was debarred from its courts. He had no repugnance for residence in cities. Menahem, the next figure that presents itself, shows a man who is mingling in court circles. He inflicts on Herod, the son of the favorite counsellor of the high priest, a playful domestic chastisement and prophesies his future greatness. Herod, as we are told, always favored the Essenes in consequence. Later Archelaus consults Simon or Simeon, an Essene, as to the interpretation of a dream. He is at all events resident in Jerus and known in the court circles. He may have been Simeon of Lk **2** 25–35. It must, however, be observed that the name is one of the commonest among the Jews at that time. After this they disappear, unless Hippolytus' identification of the Zealots with a section of the Essenes is admitted. Those in Engedi were aside from the course of the war, though if Pliny's representation is to be taken as accurate the vines and palm trees of Engedi had been burned and the settlement had been rendered desolate. They may have betaken themselves to Pella like the Christians, so as not to be involved in the destruction of the city and the Temple. The communities of the sect in Asia Minor disappear also. To all appearance they are absorbed in the church.

2. Position of Essenes in Josephus

Owing to the fact that so many of the doctrines and practices attributed to the Essenes have no resemblance to anything else in Judaism the question of origin has a special meaning in regard to them. Although like all Easterners the Jews have a desire for progeny—indeed the man who has no child occupies a secondary place in social esteem—yet the Essenes, or at all events some of them, shunned marriage. Despite the elaborate system of animal sacrifices that claimed to originate with Moses whom they venerated, they abjured bloody sacrifices. Although the seed of Aaron were anointed priests, they set up priests of their own. Their habit of morning and evening prayer, timed by the rising and setting of the sun, suggested sun-worship. The external resemblance of these tenets of the Essenes to those of the Pythagoreans impressed Jos, and was emphasized by him all the more readily, since thus he brought himself and his nation into line with Gr thought. This suggestion of Jos has led some, e.g. Zeller, to the deduction that they were Jewish neo-Pythagoreans. The features of resemblance are formidable when drawn out in catalogue. He shows (*Philos. der Griechen*, I. Theil, II, 239–92) that like the Pythagoreans the Essenes regarded asceticism a means of holiness. Both abstained from animal food and bloody sacrifices, admired celibacy and, dressing in white linen garments, had frequent washings. Both prohibited oaths; both formed a corporate body into which admission was had by act of initiation and after probation. Community of goods was the custom in both. Both believed in transmigration of souls. The value of this formidable list is lessened by the fact that there is something of uncertainty on both sides as to the precise views and customs. Philo and Jos unquestionably Hellenized the views of the Essenes when they presented them before readers educated in Gr culture; further the views of Pythagoras have come down to us in a confused shape. As to the assertion that the Pythagoreans dressed in white linen, Diogenes Laertius says that linen was not yet invented. Zeller has no sufficient evidence that the Essenes avoided the flesh of animals as food, and Diogenes Laertius expressly says that Pythagoras ate fish, though rarely (VIII, 18). While there seems no doubt as to the Pythagorean belief in the transmigration of souls, it seems certain that this was not a doctrine of the Essenes. Neither Philo nor Jos attribute this view to them. This is the more striking that, immediately after dealing with the Essenes, Jos proceeds to take up the doctrines of the Pharisees to whom he does attribute that view. Moreover

3. Doctrinal Affinities

4. Essenes and Pythagoras

the distinctive views of the Pythagoreans as to numbers and music have no sign of being held by the Essenes. On the other hand the fact that Pythagoras had a wife seems to throw doubt on their alleged preference for celibacy. Another chronological difficulty has to be met. The Pythagoreans as a society were put down in the 5th cent. before Christ. They may be regarded as having disappeared, till in the 2d cent. AD they reappear as prominent neo-Pythagoreans. It is true that Cicero and Seneca mention Pythagoreans, but only as individuals who would claim to be the followers of Pythagoras, and not as members of a sect: they were without influence even in Italy.

5. Buddhism and Essenism

Chronology is equally against the view favored by Hilgenfeld that the influence of Buddhism may be traced in Essenism. As late as the end of the 2d cent. AD, Clement of Alexandria, although acquainted with the name Buddha, is ignorant of his tenets and of divisions of his followers. The Alexandria which Hilgenfeld identified with Alexandria of Egypt, in which there was a Buddhist settlement, was really to be found in Bactria, where a Buddhist settlement was likely.

6. Parseeism and Essenism

There is more to be alleged in favor of Parsee influence being traceable. Neither geography nor chronology protests against this influence. The Jews were for centuries under the domination of the Persians, who were followers of Zoroaster. They seem on the whole to have been favored by the Pers rulers, a state of matters that would make the Jews all the more ready to view with sympathy the opinions and religion of these masters. Moreover the Pers worship had spread away to the west, far beyond Syria. At the same time it is easy to exaggerate the points of resemblance. The dualism alleged to be a leading feature in Essenism is more a matter of deduction than of distinct statement. Indeed the proofs alleged by Zeller are almost ludicrous in their insufficiency, since Philo says that the Essenes shun marriage because women are selfish (*phílautos*), and Jos, that they do so because women are addicted to excess (*asélgeia*); that therefore they regard the female generally as under the dominion of the evil principle, the fact being that this is really a part of the Hellenizing which the Essene views underwent at the hands of Philo and Jos. The alleged sun-worship is scarcely more worthy of credit: it is a deduction not even plausible. When carefully looked at the evidence points the other way. Their first prayer is offered not at sunrise but before it (*BJ*, II, viii, 5); in other words, they work while it is day. Their evening orisons are offered after the sun has set. At the same time their elaborate angelology seems to be due to the influence of the Zend-Avesta, but in this the Essenes merely shared with the rest of the Jews. We know that the Jews brought the names of the angels with them from Babylon.

7. Essenism Mainly Jewish

The most singular feature in Essenism is really a feature of Judaism emphasized out of proportion. It was unlike the Jews to shun marriage, yet in seasons when special holiness was required intercourse between the sexes was forbidden (Ex **19** 15; 1 S **21** 5). The whole act of sexual intercourse was regarded as unclean (Lev **15** 16–18). In the Pauline Epistles *uncleanness* is used as equivalent to fornication (Rom **1** 24; **6** 19, etc). So also in 2 Pet **2** 10. Such a view naturally led to the idea which soon became regnant in Christianity that the state of virginity was one of special sanctity (Rev **14** 4). The respect they gave to the unmarried state may be exaggerated. If Philo's representation (quoted in Euseb., *Prep. Evan.*, VIII, 11) be correct, men were not admitted until maturity was attained and passed, when, therefore, such desires had begun to die down. Their avoidance of marriage is a matter of less importance. Their extreme reverence for the Sabbath is of a piece with their celibacy. Their avoidance of the Temple sacrifices, so far as they did so, may well be due to something of more than contempt for the religion of the Sadducean high-priestly party. Moreover the long residence of Israel in Babylon, when the Temple worship had to be in abeyance, and the consequent prevalence of synagogue worship, tended to lessen the importance of the sacrifices of the Temple. Thus it would seem that the Essenes were really a Jewish sect that had retained more of the Zoroastrian elements than had the rest of the Jews.

V. Relation to the Apocalyptic Books.—Among the features of Essenism which seem to have impressed Jos most was the fact that they had sacred books of their sect which they preserved, as also the names of the angels, thus bringing the Essenian special books into connection with angelology. These books their proselytes were bound by oath to preserve (*BJ*, II, viii, 7). Concerning the kindred sect of the *Therapeutae*, Philo says, "They have also writings of ancient men" (*De Vita Contemp.*, III). On the other hand we have a mass of writings the same in character, dependent on one another, all apparently proceeding from one school of Jewish thought. Of the three sects of the Jews from which alone they could have proceeded the Sadducees are excluded because, while the apocalyptic books are full of angels, they believe neither in angel nor spirit (Acts **23** 8). While doctrinally the Pharisees might suit, the fact that practically there is no reference to any of these books in the Talm, which proceeded from the Pharisaic school, renders them unlikely to have been the authors. The Essenes seem to us to have been the school from which these apocalyptic works proceeded.

1. Reasons for Holding the Essenes to Be the Writers of the Apocalypses

The sect, at the fall of the Jewish state, disappeared in Christianity, and in the Christian church these books are preserved. The section of the Essenes who dwelt as coenobites beside the Dead Sea were in circumstances specially liable to see visions and to have distorted views of morality, so that the composition of pseudonymous writings, literary forgeries, might seem right. As seen in the study of the apocalyptic books there is the undue prominence given to sexual sin—a prominence that seems to be symptomatic of the unhealthy mental state engendered by celibacy. These writings are the product of a school that professed to have secret sacred books. In 2 (4) Esd **14** 45.46 we have an account of how, while 24 of the sacred books were published to the multitude, 70 were retained for the "worthy," that is, for some inner circle, some brotherhood like the Essenes. In the Asm M, Joshua is commanded to place the revelations given him "in certain vessels and anoint them with oil of cedar." Such an order would be held as explaining at once the disappearance of the book for the years succeeding Moses and its opportune reappearance. On the one hand we have a sect that professes to have secret sacred books, and on the other we have sacred books that have been composed by a school that must have had many features which we recognize as Essenian. Further the Essenes disappeared in the Christian church, and in the Christian church and not among the Jews are these books preserved.

The main objection to this ascription is the prominence of the Messianic hope in the apocalyptic books, and the absence of any notice in Jos and Philo that the Essenes had this hope. But from neither of these writers could be discovered that any of the Jews cherished this hope. Yet from the NT we know that this hope was a prominent feature in national aspirations. Philo, associating perpetually with Greeks, would be sensitive to the ridicule to which such views would expose him, and how it would undo much of his laborious efforts to commend Judaism to the Greeks as a higher philosophy. Jos had not only that motive, but the more serious one of personal safety. To have enlarged on Messianic hopes and declared these hopes to have been cherished by these Essenes whom he had praised so much would be liable to bring him under suspicion of disloyalty to Rome. The silence of these two writers proves nothing because it proves too much; and further we have easy explanation of this silence. The assumption of Dr. Charles that the Essenian ideal was ethical and individualistic is pure assumption. There is another objection that while the doctrine of resurrection is recognized in these books we know nothing of the Essenes holding it. That the Greeks and their scholars in philosophy, the Romans, looked at the idea of resurrection from the dead as a subject for ridicule would be reason sufficient for Philo and Jos to suppress such a feature in their description of the Essenes. From them it could not be learned that the Pharisees ever had any such belief. It is also objected that while the Essenes held the preëxistence of souls, there is no trace of this belief in the apocalyptic books. Jos, however, does not really assert that they believed in the prior existence of individual souls, but rather in a soul-stuff from which individual souls were separated. Thus both positively and negatively we think there is a strong case for the Essenes being regarded as the authors of the apocalyptic books. Further objections are brought forward by Dr. Charles as applicable to the Asm M specially. One is the interest manifested in the Temple by the writer while, so says Dr. Charles, "the Essene was excluded from its courts," and refers to Jos, *Ant*, XVIII, i, 5. He must have forgotten, while penning this sentence, *Ant*, XIII, xi, 2, in which Judas, the Essene, is represented as teaching in the Temple. His objection that Jos credits the Essenes with a belief in a paradise beyond the ocean like the Gr Islands of the Blest, appears to us to lay too much stress on what is in both cases **fig.** language. Moreover, in En the description of Paradise (chs **24**–**26**) would almost seem to be the original from which Jos (*BJ*, II, viii, 11) drew his picture. He seems to regard our ignorance of how far the Essenes agreed with the rest of their countrymen in considering the enemies of Israel "the wicked," as evidence that they disagreed with them on that point.

2. Objections Answered

VI. The Essenes and Christianity.—That there were many points of resemblance between the Essenes and the church in its earliest form cannot be denied. The Essenes, we are told, maintained a community of goods and required anyone who joined their society to sell all he had and present it to the community (Hippolytus, *Adv. Heret.*, ix; x; Jos, *BJ*, II, viii, 3), just as so many of the primitive Christians did in Jerus (Acts **4** 37). Another peculiarity of the Essenes—noted by Jos (*BJ*, II, viii, 4)—that they moved about from city to city, and wherever they went found accommodation with members of their order, although perfect strangers, may be compared with Our Lord's instructions to His disciples when He sent them forth (Mt **10** 11): "Into whatsoever city or village ye shall enter, search out who in it is worthy." When one thinks of who those worthy persons could be, and what was the evidence by which their worthiness was expected to be established, one is almost obliged to suppose that it was some specially easily recognized class that was so designated. If the worthiness in question was the moral quality, there are so many ideas of moral worth that when the apostles inquired, on entering a city, who was worthy, before they could act on the answer they would need to discover what was the criterion of worthiness in the mind of him from whom they had inquired. If, however, this term was the private designation of the members of a sect, one by which they, in speaking of each other, indicated that they were co-members, as the "Quakers" speak of each other as "Friends," the inquiry for those who were worthy would be simple enough. If the Essenes were "the worthy," then identification would be complete, but we cannot assume that. The majority of the points in which the Essenes resembled the primitive Christians are noted above in connection with each feature as it appears in the passage or passages of the authorities that record it, and to these we refer our readers.

1. Resemblances between Essenism and Christianity

At the same time, although there are thus many points of likeness, it is not to be denied that there are also many features in Essenism which are at variance with the practice of the early church and the teaching of Our Lord and His apostles. The most prominent of these is the difference of attitude toward marriage and the female sex. Our Lord sanctified marriage by His presence at the marriage at Cana of Galilee, although He himself never married. He used the festivities of marriage again and again as illustrations. He drew women to Him and had none of the contempt of the sex which Jos and Philo attribute to the Essenes. The apostles assume the marriage relationship as one into which Christians may be expected in due course to enter, and give exhortations suited to husbands and wives (1 Pet **3** 1–7; Eph **5** 22–33; Col **3** 18.19). The apostle Paul uses the relation of husband and wife as the symbol of the relation of Christ to His church (Eph **5** 32). The writer of the Epistle to the He declares, "Marriage is honourable in all" (He **13** 4 AV).

2. Points of Difference

Another point in which the Essenes differed from the practice of Our Lord and His disciples was the exaggerated reverence the former gave to the Sabbath, not even moving a vessel from one place to another on the seventh day. Our Lord's declaration, "The sabbath was made for man, and not man for the sabbath" (Mk **2** 27), cuts at the feet of that whole attitude. The point of His conflict with the Pharisees was His disregard of the Sabbath as fenced by their traditions. The Essenes shrank from contact with oil, which Our Lord certainly did not do. On the contrary He rebuked the Pharisee for his neglect (Lk **7** 46). He was twice anointed by women, and in both cases commended the deed. The purely external and material bulked largely in the opinions of the Essenes. Our Lord emphasized the internal and spiritual. Many have held and do hold that Our Lord was an Essene. If at the beginning of His career He belonged to this sect He must have broken with it long before the end of His ministry.

Why Our Lord never meets the Essenes.—There are some phenomena which, irrespective of these resemblances and differences, have a bearing on the relation between Essenism and Christianity. The first is the fact that Our Lord, who met so many different classes of the inhabitants of Pal—Pharisees and Sadducees, Zealots and Herodians, publicans, Samaritans, Greeks—never is recorded to have met an Essene. The common answer, which satisfied even Bishop Lightfoot, is that they were so few and lived so retired that it was no marvel that He never encountered any of them. They had little or no effect on the national life. This mistaken answer is due to forgetting that though both Jos and Philo say the Essenes were 4,000 they also declare that they were "many in every city," that there were "ten thousands of them." Our Lord must have met them; but if the name "Essene" was a designation given from without like "Quakers," then they may appear in the Gospels under another name. There is a class of persons three times referred to—those "that waited for the consolation of Israel" (Lk **2** 25 AV), "looking for the redemption" (**2** 38), "waited for the kingdom of God" (Mk **15** 43 AV; Lk **23** 51 AV). There are thus Simeon and Anna at the beginning of His earthly life, and Joseph of Arimathea at the end, connected with this sect. If, then, this sect were the Essenes under another name, the difficulty would be removed. If, further, in any sense Our Lord belonged, or had belonged, to the Essenes, then as He would be perpetually meeting and associating with them, these meetings would not be chronicled. A man cannot meet himself. If they are the authors of the apocalyptic books, as we contend, then the title "waiters for the kingdom of God" would be most suitable, full as these books are of Messianic hopes. If this opinion is correct Our Lord's assumption of the title "Son of Man" is significant, taken in connection with the prominence given to that title in the Enoch books.

3. Disappearance of Essenism in Christianity

Another significant phenomenon is the disappearance of Essenism in Christianity. Bishop Lightfoot, in his dissertation on the Colossian Heresy (*Comm. on Col*, 21–111), proves that it was Essenism. These Essenes must have been baptized into Christ, or they could not have got entry into the Christian communities which had been drawn to Christ from heathenism. But that is not the only heresy that is connected with the Essenes. The Ebionites seem to have been Essenes who had passed over into Christianity. In the Apos Const the Ebionites and Essenes are brought into very close connection. Epiphanius, in his confused way, mixes up the various names under which the Essenes appear in his works with a certain Elkaisa, a connection also to be found in Hippolytus, an earlier and better authority. But Elkaisa claimed to be a Christian. His leading follower, Alcibiades, appeared in Rome and was resisted by Hippolytus. The Clementine Homilies, a religious novel of which St. Peter is the hero, has many Essenian features. It is assumed to be Ebionite, but that only makes the evidence that the Essenes had become Christians all the more convincing. The Ebionites were Christians, if defective in their views, and the presence of Essenian features in a work proceeding from them emphasizes the identity. See EBIONISM.

4. Monachism

There is another phenomenon, more extensive and important than those we have considered above—the presence of Monachism in the church. Notwithstanding that Our Lord prayed "not that" the disciples be taken "out of the world," but that they be kept "from the evil" (Jn **17** 15), implying that they were not to retire into solitude, and that the apostle Paul regards it as demonstrating the falsity of our possible interpretation of an exhortation of his that it would imply that the disciples "must needs go out of the world" (1 Cor **5** 10); yet the monks did retire from the world and regarded themselves as all the holier for so doing, and were regarded so by others. The apostle Paul declares the "forbidding to marry" one of "the doctrines of demons," yet very soon asceticism set in and virginity was regarded as far holier than the married state. Retirement from the world and asceticism were the two cardinal characteristics of Monachism. Despite that these were in antagonism to the teachings of Christ and His apostles, within little more than a century after Our Lord's ascension Monachism began to appear, and prevailed more and more and continues to this day. These characteristics, retirement from the world and asceticism, esp. forbidding to marry, were marked features of Essenism. The wholesale entrance of the Essene sect into the church would explain this. On the other hand this wholesale passing over into Christianity of so intensely Jewish a sect implies a historic connection or affinity. It is true that the catechetic school of Alexandria praises the contemplative life, so admired by their contemporaries, the neo-Platonists, and that philosophy which had been looked at askance by the church was, so to say, taken under their protection by the Alexandrian school, and the retirement of solitaries into the deserts or the formation of monasteries served to promote this contemplation. This led to all the extravagances of the monks being regarded as heights of philosophy. Such views were a cause, but as certainly were they also effects. The cause of these effects as it seems to us was to some extent the admiration extended by Philo, the Alexandrian, to the Essenes and *Therapeutae*, and the influence of Philo on his Christian successors in Alexandria.

LITERATURE.—Sources: Philo, Jos, Pliny, Hegesippus, Porphyry, Hippolytus, Epiphanius.

Secondary literature: Besides works specially on the Essenes, the following are mentioned: Frankel, *Die Essäer;* Lucius, *Der Essenismus;* Ginsburg, *Essenes;* and portions of books, as Delaunay, *Moines et Sibylles*, 1–88; Thomson, *Books Which Influenced Our Lord*, 74–122; Ritschl, *Die Entstehung der alt-katholischen Kirche*, 179–203; Lightfoot, *Comm. on Col*, 7–111, 347–417.

There are in histories of the Jews discussions of the questions in order. Of these may be noted: Ewald, *Hist of Israel*, V, 370–71; Grätz, *Geschichte der Juden*, III, 657–63; Schürer, *The Jewish People in the Time of Jesus Christ*, II, ii, 188–218, tr. This opens with a fairly full account of the lit. up to the date of the 2d German ed; Zeller, *Geschichte der Philos. der Griechen*, III, ii, 2, pp. 235–93. There are also arts. in various Bible and theological dictionaries, as Smith and Wace, *Dict. of Eccles Biography;* Smith and Fuller, *Dict. of the Bible; HDB; Jew Enc; RE;* Schenkel, *Bibel-Lexikon;* M'Clintock, *Theological Dict.*

At the same time, while submitting these as a sample, and only as a sample, of the vast lit. of the subject, we agree in the advice given by F. C. Conybeare—in *HDB*, s.v.: "The student may be advised to study for himself the very limited documentary sources relating to the Essenes and then to draw his own conclusions." We feel the importance of this advice all the more that perusal has shown us that most of these secondary writers have considered exclusively the coenobite community at Engedi to the neglect of the wider society. After the student has formed opinions from a careful study of the sources he may benefit by those secondary works.

J. E. H. THOMSON

ESTATE, es-tāt′: While AV uses both "estate" and "state" with the meaning of "condition," ARV distinguishes, using "state" for the idea of condition, "estate" for position; and replaces "estate" of AV by more definite expressions in many cases. Cf Col **4** 7 AV, "All my state shall Tychicus declare unto you," but ver 8, AV "might know your estate," RV "may know our state"; Lk **1** 48 AV and RV "the low estate" (of the Lord's handmaiden); Mk **6** 21, AV "chief estates," RV "chief men"; Dnl **11** 7.20.21.38, AV "his estate," RV "his place," both with m "his office."

F. K. FARR

ESTEEM, es-tēm′ (חָשַׁב, *ḥāshabh;* ἡγέομαι, *hēgéomai*): "To esteem" means sometimes simply "to think" or "reckon"; in other connections it means "to regard as honorable" or "valuable." We have examples of both senses in the Bible. The word oftenest so tr[d] in the OT is *ḥāshabh*, meaning perhaps originally, "to bind," hence "combine," "think," "reckon" (Job **41** 27 AV; Isa **29** 16.17; **53** 4; Lam **4** 2). In Isa **53** 3 we have the word in the higher sense, "We esteemed him not." This sense is expressed also by *'ārakh*, "to set in array," "in order" (Job **36** 19, AV "Will he esteem thy riches?" ERV "Will thy riches suffice?" m "Will thy cry avail?" which ARV adopts as the text); also by *çāphan*, "to hide," "to conceal" (Job **23** 12, AV "I have esteemed the words of his mouth," RV "treasured up"); *ḳālāh*, "to be light," is tr[d] "lightly esteemed" (1 S **18** 23, "I am a poor man, and lightly esteemed"), also *ḳālal*, same meaning (1 S **2** 30, "They that despise me shall be lightly esteemed"). In the NT, *hēgeomai*, "to lead out," is used in the sense of "counting honorable," etc (Phil **2** 3, RV "counting"; 1 Thess **5** 13; perhaps He **11** 26, but RV has simply "accounting"); *krínō*, "to judge," is used in the sense of "to reckon" (Rom **14** 5 *bis*); also *logízomai*, "to reckon" (Rom **14** 14, RV "accounteth"); *hupsēlós*, "high," "exalted," is rendered "highly esteemed" in Lk **16** 15 AV, but in RV "exalted"; *exoutheneō*, "to think nothing of," is tr[d] "least esteemed" (1 Cor **6** 4 AV, RV "of no account").

The following changes in RV are of interest: for "*He that* is despised and hath a servant, is better than he that honoreth himself and lacketh bread" (Prov **12** 9), "Better is he that is lightly esteemed"; for "Better *is he* than both they, which hath not yet been" (Eccl **4** 3), "Better than them both *did I esteem* him," m "Better than they both is he"; for "Surely your turning of things upside down shall be esteemed as the potter's clay" (Isa **29** 16), "Ye turn things upside down!" (m "Oh your perversity!"), "Shall the potter be esteemed [ERV "counted"] as clay," etc—in this connection a forcible assertion of the necessary possession of knowledge by the Creator of man. W. L. WALKER

ESTHER, es'tẽr (אֶסְתֵּר, *'eṣtēr*, akin to the Zend *çtara*, the Sanskrit *stṛi*, the Gr **ἀστήρ**, *astḗr*, "a star," **Ἐσθήρ**, *Esthḗr*): Esther was a Jewish orphan, who became the queen of Xerxes, in some respects the greatest of the Pers kings. She was brought up at Susa by her cousin Mordecai, who seems to have held a position among the lower officials of the royal palace. Vashti, Xerxes' former queen, was divorced; and the most beautiful virgins from all the provinces of the empire were brought to the palace of Susa that the king might select her successor. The choice fell upon the Jewish maiden. Soon after her accession a great crisis occurred in the history of the Jews. The entire people was threatened with destruction. The name of Esther is forever bound up with the record of their deliverance. By a course of action which gives her a distinguished place among the women of the Bible, the great enemy of the Jews was destroyed, and her people were delivered. Nothing more is known of her than is recorded in the book which Jewish gratitude has made to bear her name.

Change of Name

The change in the queen's name from Hadassah (הֲדַסָּה), "a myrtle," to Esther, "a star," may possibly indicate the style of beauty for which the Pers queen was famous. The narrative displays her as a woman of clear judgment, of magnificent self-control, and capable of the noblest self-sacrifice. See ESTHER, BOOK OF. JOHN URQUHART

ESTHER, BOOK OF:

1. The Canonicity of Esther
2. Its Authorship
3. Its Date
4. Its Contents
5. The Greek Additions
6. The Attacks upon the Book
7. Some of the Objections
8. Confirmations of the Book

This book completes the historical books of the OT. The conjunction ו, "and," with which it begins, is significant. It shows that the book was designed for a place in a series, the ו linking it on to a book immediately preceding, and that the present arrangement of the Heb Bible differs widely from what must have been the original order. At present Est follows Eccl, with which it has no connection whatever; and this tell-tale "and," like a body-mark on a lost child, proves that the book has been wrenched away from its original connection. There is no reason to doubt that the order in the Sept follows that of the Heb Bible of the 3d or the 4th cent. BC, and this is the order of the Vulg, of the Eng. Bible, and other VSS. The initial ו is absent from Gen, Dt, 1 Ch and Neh. The historical books are consequently arranged, by the insertion and the omission of ו, into these four divisions: Gen to Nu; Dt to 2 K; 1 Ch to Ezr; Neh and Est.

1. The Canonicity of Esther

Of the canonicity of the book there is no question. That there was a distinct guardianship of the Canon by the Jewish priesthood has figured less in recent discussions than it should. Jos shows that there was a Temple copy which was carried among the Temple spoils in the triumph of Vespasian. The peculiarities of the Heb text also prove that all our MSS are representatives of one standard copy. In the Jewish Canon Est had not only a recognized, but also a distinguished, place. The statement of Junilius in the 6th cent. AD that the canonicity of Est was doubted by some in his time has no bearing on the question. The high estimation of the book current among the ancient Jews is evident from its titles. It is usually headed "M[e]gillath Esther" (the volume of Est), and sometimes "M[e]gillāh" (the volume). Maimonides says that the wise men among the Jews affirm that the book was dictated by the Holy Spirit, and adds: "All the books of the Prophets, and all the Hagiographa shall cease in the days of the Messiah, except the volume of Est; and, lo, that shall be as stable as the Pent, and as the constitutions of the oral law which shall never cease."

2. Its Authorship

By whom was the book written? This is a point in regard to which no help is afforded us either by the contents of the book or by any reliable tradition. Mordecai, whose claims have been strongly urged by some, is excluded by the closing words (**10** 3), which sum up his life work and the blessings of which he had been the recipient. The words imply that when the book was written, that great Israelite had passed away.

3. Its Date

Light is thrown upon the date of the book by the closing references to Ahasuerus (**10** 2): "And all the acts of his power and of his might, ... are they not written in the book of the chronicles of the kings of Media and Persia?" The entire history, therefore, of Xerxes was to be found in the state records when the book was written. In other words, Xerxes had passed away before it saw the light. That monarch was assassinated by Artabanus in 465 BC. This gives us, say 460 BC, as the highest possible date. The lowest possible date is the overthrow of the Pers empire by Alexander in 332 BC; for the royal records of the Median and Pers kings are plainly in existence and accessible, which they would not have been had the empire been overthrown. The book must have been written, therefore, some time within this interval of 128 years. There is another fact which narrows that interval. The initial *waw* shows that Est was written after Neh, that is, after 430 BC. The interval is consequently reduced to 98 years; and, seeing that the Pers dominion was plainly in its pristine vigor when Est was written, we cannot be far wrong if we regard its date as about 400 BC.

4. Its Contents

The book is characterized by supreme dramatic power. The scene is "Shushan the palace," that portion of the ancient Elamitic capital which formed the fortified residence of the Pers kings. The book opens with the description of a high festival. All the notabilities of the kingdom are present, together with their retainers, both small and great. To grace the occasion, Vashti is summoned to appear before the king's guests; and, to the dismay of the great assembly, the queen refuses to obey. A council is immediately summoned. Vashti is degraded; and a decree is issued that every man bear rule in his own house (ch **1**). To find a successor to Vashti, the fairest damsels in the empire are brought to Shushan; and Hadassah, the cousin and adopted daughter of Mordecai, is of the number. The chapter (**2**) closes with a notice of two incidents: (1) the coronation of Hadassah (now and henceforth named "Esther") as queen; (2) Mordecai's discovery of a palace plot to assassinate the king. Ch **3** introduces another leading personage, Haman, the son of Hammedatha, whose seat the king had set "above all the princes that were with him." All the king's servants who are at the king's gates prostrate themselves before the powerful favorite. Mordecai, who is not a trained courtier but a God-fearing Jew, refrains. Though expostulated with, he will not conform. The matter is brought to Haman's notice for whose offended dignity Mordecai is too small a sacrifice. The whole Jewish people must perish. Lots are cast to find a lucky day for their extermination. The king's consent is obtained, and the royal decree is sent into all the provinces fixing the slaughter for the 13th day of the 12th month.

The publication of the decree is followed by universal mourning among the Jews (ch **4**). News of Mordecai's mourning is brought to Esther, who, through the messengers she sends to him, is informed of her own and her people's danger. She is urged to save herself and them. She eventually decides to seek the king's presence at the risk of her life. She presents herself (ch **5**) before the king and is graciously received. Here we breathe the atmosphere of the place and time. Everything depends upon the decision of one will—the king's. Esther does not attempt too much at first: she invites the king and Haman to a banquet. Here the king asks Esther what her petition is, assuring her that it shall be granted. In reply she requests his and Haman's presence at a banquet the following day. Haman goes forth in high elation. On his way home he passes Mordecai, who "stood not up nor moved for him." Haman passes on filled with rage, and unbosoms himself to his wife and all his friends. They advise that a stake, fifty cubits high, be prepared for Mordecai's impalement; that on the morrow he obtain the royal permission for Mordecai's execution; and that he then proceed with a merry heart to banquet with the queen. The stake is made ready.

But (ch **6**) that night Xerxes cannot sleep. The chronicles of the kingdom are read before him. The reader has come to Mordecai's discovery of the plot, when the king asks what reward was given him. He is informed that the service had received no acknowledgment. It is now early morn, and Haman is waiting in the court for an audience to request Mordecai's life. He is summoned to the king's presence and asked what should be done to the man whom the king desires to honor. Believing that the king can be thinking only of him, he suggests that royal honors be paid him. He is appalled by the command to do so to Mordecai. Hurrying home from his lowly attendance upon the hated Jew, he has hardly time to tell the mournful story to his wife and friends when he is summoned to Esther's banquet. There, at the king's renewed request to be told her desire, she begs life for herself and for her people (ch **7**). The king asks in astonishment, who he is, and where he is, who dared to injure her and them. The reply is that Haman is the adversary. Xerxes, filled with indignation, rises from the banquet and passes into the palace garden. He returns and discovers that Haman, in the madness of his fear, has thrown himself on the queen's couch, begging for his life. That act seals his doom. He is led away to be impaled upon the very stake he had prepared for the Jew. The seal of the kingdom is transferred to Mordecai (ch **8**). Measures are immediately taken to avert the consequence of Haman's plot (chs **9–10**). The result is deliverance and honor for the Jews. These resolve that the festival of Purim should be instituted and be ever after observed by Jews and proselytes. The decision was confirmed by letters from Esther and Mordecai.

5. The Greek Additions

The Sept, as we now have it, makes large additions to the original text. Jerome, keeping to the Heb text in his own tr, has added these at the end. They amount to nearly seven chapters. There is nothing in them to reward perusal. Their age has been assigned to 100 BC, and their only value consists in the indication they afford of the antiquity of the book. That had been long enough in existence to perplex the Heb mind with the absence of the name of God and the omissions of any reference to Divine worship. Full amends are made in the additions.

6. The Attacks upon the Book

The opponents of the Book of Est may undoubtedly boast that Martin Luther headed the attack. In his *Table-Talk* he declared that he was so hostile "to the Book of Est that I would it did not exist; for it Judaizes too much, and has in it a great deal of heathenish naughtiness." His remark in his reply to Erasmus shows that this was his deliberate judgment. Referring to Est, he says that, though the Jews have it in their Canon, "it is more worthy than all" the apocryphal books "of being excluded from the Canon." That repudiation was founded, however, on no historical or critical grounds. It rested solely upon an entirely mistaken judgment as to the tone and the intention of the book. Luther's judgment has been carried farther by Ewald, who says: "We fall here as if from heaven to earth; and, looking among the new forms surrounding us, we seem to behold the Jews, or indeed the small men of the present day in general, acting just as they now do." Nothing of all this, however, touches the historicity of Est.

The modern attack has quite another objective. Semler, who is its real *fons et origo*, believed Est to be a work of pure imagination, and as establishing little more than the pride and arrogance of the Jews. DeWette says: "It violates all historical probability, and contains striking difficulties and many errors with regard to Pers manners, as well as just references to them." Dr. Driver modifies that judgment. "The writer," he says, "shows himself well informed on Pers manners and institutions; he does not commit anachronisms such as occur in Tob or Jth; and the character of Xerxes as drawn by him is in agreement with history." The controversy shows, however, no sign of approaching settlement. Th. Nöldeke (*EB*) is more violent than De Wette. "The story," he writes, "is in fact a tissue of improbabilities and impossibilities." We shall look first of all at the main objections urged by him and others and then at the recent confirmations of the historicity of Esther.

(1) "There is something fantastic, but not altogether unskilful," says Nöldeke, "in the touch whereby Mordecai and Haman are made to inherit

an ancient feud, the former being a member of the family of King Saul, the latter a descendant of Agag, king of Amalek." It is surely unworthy of a scholar to make the book responsible for a Jewish fable. There is absolutely no mention in it of either King Saul or Agag, king of Amalek, and not the most distant allusion to any inherited feud. "Kish, a Benjamite" is certainly mentioned (**2** 5) as the great-grandfather of Mordecai; but if this was also the father of Saul, then the first of the Israelitish kings was a sharer in the experiences of the Bab captivity, a conception which is certainly fantastic enough. One might ask also how an Amalekite came to be described as an Agagite; and how a childless king, who was cut in pieces, became the founder of a tribe. But any semblance of a foundation which that rabbinic conceit ever had was swept away years ago by Oppert's discovery of "Agag" in one of Sargon's inscriptions as the name of a district in the Pers empire. "Haman the son of Hammedatha the Agagite" means simply that Haman or his father had come from the district of Agag. (2) The statement that **2** 5.6 represents Mordecai as having been carried away with Jeconiah from Jerus, and as being therefore of an impossible age, is unworthy of notice. The relative "who" (**2** 6) refers to Kish, his great-grandfather. (3) "Between the 7th and the 12th years of his reign, Xerxes' queen was Amestris, a superstitious and cruel woman (Hero l. vii.114; ix.112), who cannot be identified with Esther, and who leaves no place for Esther beside her" (Driver). Scaliger long ago identified Esther with Amestris, an identification which Prideaux rejected on account of the cruelty which Herodotus has attributed to that queen. Dr. Driver has failed to take full account of one thing—the striking fact that critics have leveled this very charge of cruelty against the heroine of our book. It is quite possible that Esther, moving in a world of merciless intrigue, may have had to take measures which would form a foundation for the tales recorded by the Gr historian. (4) The aim of the book is said to be the glorification of the Jews. But, on the contrary, it is merely a record of their being saved from a skilfully planned extirpation. (5) The description of the Jews (**3** 8) as "dispersed among the peoples in all the provinces of" the kingdom is said to be inapplicable to the Pers period. That argument is based upon an ignorance of the ancient world which investigation is daily correcting. We now know that before the time of Est Jews were settled both in Eastern and in Southern Egypt, that is, in the extreme west of the Pers empire. In the troubles at the end of the 7th and of the 6th cents. BC, multitudes must have been dispersed, and when, at the latter period, the ties of the fatherland were dissolved, Jewish migrations must have vastly increased. (6) The Heb of the book is said to belong to a much later period than that of Xerxes. But it is admitted that it is earlier than the Heb of Ch; and recent discoveries have shown decisively that the book belongs to the Pers period. (7) The suggestion is made (Driver) "that the danger which threatened the Jews was a local one," and consequently, that the book, though possessed of a historical basis, is a romance. But against that are the facts that the observance of the feast has from the first been universal, and that it has not been observed more fully or more enthusiastically in any one place than in the others. (8) There is no reference to it, it is urged, by Ch, Ezr or Ben Sira (Ecclus). But Ch ends with the proclamation of Cyrus, granting permission to the Jews to return and to rebuild the Temple. There is little to be wondered at that it contains no reference to events which happened 60 years afterward. In Ezr, which certainly covers the period of Esther, reference to the events with which she was connected is excluded by the plan of the work. It gives the history of the return, the first part under Zerubbabel in 536 BC, the second under Ezra himself, 458 BC. The events in Est (which were embraced within a period of a few months) fell in the interval and were connected with neither the first return nor the second. Here again the objector is singularly oblivious of the purpose of the book to which he refers. There is quite as little force in the citation of Ecclus. In dealing with this time Ben Sira's eye is upon Jerus. He magnifies Zerubbabel, "Jesus the son of Josedek," and Nehemiah (**49** 11–13). Even Ezra, to whom Jerus and the new Jewish state owed so much, finds no mention. Why, then, should Esther and Mordecai be named who seem to have had no part whatever in rebuilding the sacred city? (9) The book is said to display ignorance of the Pers empire in the statement that it was divided into 127 provinces, whereas Herodotus tells us that it was partitioned into 20 satrapies. But there was no such finality in the number, even of these great divisions of the empire. Darius in his Behistun inscriptions gives the number as 21, afterward as 23, and in a third enumeration as 29. Herodotus himself, quoting from a document of the time of Xerxes, shows that there were then about 60 nations under the dominion of Persia. The objector has also omitted to notice that the *mᵉdhīnāh* ("province") mentioned in Est (**1** 1) is not a satrapy but a subdivision of it. Judaea is called a *mᵉdhīnāh* in Ezr **2** 1, and that was only a small portion of the 5th satrapy, that, namely, of Syria. But the time is past for objections of this character. Recent discoveries have proved the marvelous accuracy of the book. "We find in the Book of Esther," says Lenormant (*Ancient Hist of the East*, II, 113), "a most animated picture of the court of the Pers kings, which enables us, better than anything contained in the classical writers, to penetrate the internal life and the details of the organization of the central government established by Darius."

7. Some of the Objections

These discoveries have removed the discussion to quite another plane—or rather they have ended it. Since Grotefend in 1802 read the name of Xerxes in a Pers inscription and found it to be, letter for letter, the Ahasuerus of Est, research has heaped up confirmation of the historical character of the book. It has proved, to begin with, that the late date suggested for the book cannot be maintained. The language belongs to the time of the Pers dominion. It is marked by the presence of old Pers words, the knowledge of which had passed away by the 2d cent. BC, and has been recovered only through the decipherment of the Pers monuments. The Sept translators were unacquainted with them, and consequently made blunders which have been repeated in our own AV and in other trˢ. We read (Est **1** 5.6 AV) that "in the court of the garden of the king's palace," "were white, green, and blue hangings, fastened with cords of fine linen and purple," etc. As seen in the ruins of Persepolis, a marked feature in the Pers palace of the period was a large space occupied by pillars which were covered with awnings. It may be noted in passing that these were situated, as the book says, in the court of the palace garden. But our knowledge of the recovered Pers compels us now to read: "where was an awning of fine white cotton and violet, fastened with cords of fine white linen and purple." White and blue (or violet) were the royal Pers colors. In accord with this we are told that Mordecai (**8** 15) "went forth from the presence of the king in royal apparel of blue and

8. Confirmations of the Book

white." The highly organized postal system, the king's scribes, the keeping of the chronicles of the kingdom, the rigid and elaborate court customs, are all characteristic of the Persia of the period. We are told of the decree obtained by Haman that "in the name of King Ahasuerus was it written, and sealed with the king's ring" (or signet). It was not signed but sealed. That was the Pers custom. The seal of Darius, Xerxes' father, has been found, and is now in the British Museum. It bears the figure of the king shooting arrows at a lion, and is accompanied by an inscription in Pers, Susian and Assyr: "I, Darius, Great King." The identification of Ahasuerus, made by Grotefend and which subsequent discoveries amply confirmed, placed the book in an entirely new light. As soon as that identification was assured, previous objections were changed into confirmations. In the alleged extravagances of the monarch, scholars saw then the Xerxes of history. The gathering of the nobles of the empire in "the third year of his reign" (**1** 3) was plainly the historical assembly in which the Grecian campaign was discussed; and "the seventh year," in which Esther was made queen, was that of his return from Greece. The book implies that Susa was the residence of the Pers kings, and this was so. The proper form of the name as shown by the inscriptions was "Shushan"; "Shushan the Palace" indicates that there were two Susas, which was the fact, and *bīrāh* ("palace") is a Pers word meaning fortress. The surprisingly rigid etiquette of the palace, to which we have referred, and the danger of entering unbidden the presence of the king have been urged as proof that the book is a romance. The contrary, however, is the truth. "The palace among the Persians," says Lenormant, "was quite inaccessible to the multitude. A most rigid etiquette guarded all access to the king, and made it very difficult to approach him. . . . . He who entered the presence of the king, without having previously obtained permission, was punished with death" (*Ancient Hist of the East*, II, 113–14; cf Herodotus i.99). But a further, and peculiarly conclusive, testimony to the historical character of the book is afforded by the recovery of the palace of Xerxes and Esther. An inscription of Artaxerxes Mnemon found at Susa tells us that it was destroyed by fire in the days of Artaxerxes Longimanus, the son and successor of Xerxes. Within some 30 years, therefore, from the time of Esther, that palace passed from the knowledge of men. Nevertheless, the references in the book are in perfect accord with the plan of the great structure as laid bare by the recent Fr. excavations. We read (ch **4**) that Mordecai, clad in sackcloth, walked in "the broad palace of the city, which was before the king's gate." The ruins show that the House of the Women was on the E. side of the palace next to the city, and that a gate led from it into "the street of the city." In **5** 1, we read that Esther "stood in the inner court of the king's house, over against the king's house." "The king," we also read, "sat upon his royal throne in the royal house, over against the entrance of the house," and that from the throne he "saw Esther the queen standing in the court." Every detail is exact. A corridor led from the House of the Women to the inner court; and at the side of the court opposite to the corridor was the hall, or throne-room of the palace. Exactly in the center of the farther wall the throne was placed and from that lofty seat the king, overlooking an intervening screen, saw the queen waiting for an audience. Other details, such as that of the king's passing from the queen's banqueting-house into the garden, show a similarly exact acquaintance with the palace as it then was. That is a confirmation the force of which it is hard to overestimate. It shows that the writer was well informed and that his work is characterized by minute exactitude.

The utter absence of the Divine name in Est has formed a difficulty even where it has not been urged as an objection. But that is plainly part of some Divine design. The same silence is strictly maintained throughout in regard to prayer, praise and every approach toward God. That silence was an offence to the early Jews; for, in the Sept additions to the book, there is profuse acknowledgment of God both in prayer and in praise. But it must have struck the Jews of the time and the official custodians of the canonical books quite as painfully; and we can only explain the admission of Est by the latter on the ground that there was overwhelming evidence of its Divine origin and authority. Can this rigid suppression be explained? In the original arrangement of the OT canonical books (the present Heb arrangement is post-Christian), Est is joined to Neh. In 1895 I made a suggestion which I still think worthy of consideration: More than 60 years had passed since Cyrus had given the Jews permission to return. The vast majority of the people remained, nevertheless, where they were. Some, like Nehemiah, were restrained by official and other ties. The rest were indifferent or declined to make the necessary sacrifices of property and of rest. With such as these last the history of God's work in the earth can never be associated. In His providence He will watch over and deliver them: but their names and His will not be bound together in the record of the labor and the waiting for the earth's salvation. JOHN URQUHART

ESTHER, THE REST OF:

1. Name
2. Contents
3. Original language
4. Versions
5. Date

LITERATURE

Introductory.—The Book of Est in the oldest MSS of the LXX (B,A,N, etc) contains 107 verses more than in the Heb Bible. These additions are scattered throughout the book where they were originally inserted in order to supply the religious element apparently lacking in the Heb text. In Jerome's version and in the Vulg, which is based on it, the longest and most important of these additions are taken out of their context and put together at the end of the canonical book, thus making them to a large extent unintelligible. In Eng., Welsh and other Protestant VSS of the Scriptures the whole of the additions appear in the Apoc.

In the EV the full title is "The Rest of the Chapters of the Book of Esther, which are found neither in the Hebrew, nor in the Chaldee."

1. Name Since in the LXX, including the editions by Fritzsche, Tischendorf and Swete, these chapters appear in their original context, they bear no separate title. The same is true of Brereton's Eng. tr of the LXX; but in Thompson's tr the whole of the Apoc is omitted, so that it is not strictly a tr of the whole LXX.

In Swete's edition of the LXX the interpretations constituting "the Rest of Esther" (sometimes given as "Additions to Esther") are

2. Contents designated by the capital letters of the alphabet, and in the following enumeration this will be followed. The several places in the Gr Bible are indicated in each case.

A (Lat, Eng., **11** 2—**12** 6): Mordecai's dream; how he came to honor. Precedes Est **1** 1.

B (Lat, Eng., **13** 1-7): Letter of Artaxerxes. Follows Est **3** 13.

C (Lat, Eng., **13** 8—**14** 19): The prayers of Mordecai and Esther. Follows Est **4** 17.

D (Lat, **15** 4-19; Eng., **16** 1-16): Esther visits

the king and wins his favor. Follows C, preceding immediately Est **5**.

E (Lat, Eng., **16** 1–24): Another letter of Artaxerxes. Follows Est **8** 12.

F (Lat, Eng., **10** 4—**11**): Epilogue describing the origin of the Feast Purim. Follows Est **10** 3.

But besides the lengthy interpolations noticed above there are also in the LXX small additions omitted from the Lat and therefore from the Eng., Welsh, etc, Apoc. These short additions are nearly all explanatory glosses.

In the *Century Bible* (Ezr, Neh, Est) the exact places where the insertions occur in the LXX are indicated and described in the notes dealing with the relevant passages of the canonical text. With the help thus given any Eng. reader is able to read the additions in their original setting. Unless they are read in this way they are pointless and even in most cases senseless.

3. Original Language

All scholars agree that "The Rest of Esther" was written originally in Gr. Both external and internal evidence bears this out. But the Gr text has come down to us in two recensions which differ considerably.

(1) The commonly received text supported by the MSS B,A,N, and by Jos (*Ant*, XI, i).

(2) A revision of (1) contained in the MSS 19, 93*a* and 108*b*. In the last two MSS both recensions occur. This revised text has been ascribed by many recent scholars (Lagarde, Schürer, R. H. Charles) to Lucian. In his *Libr. Vet. Test. Canon. Graece, Pars Prior, 1833* (all published), Lagarde gives on ‖ pages both recensions with critical notes on both. The two Gr texts are also given

4. Versions

by Fritzsche (1871) and Swete (1891) in their editions of the LXX, and also by Scholz in his Ger. *Comm. on the Book of Est* (1892). For the ancient VSS see "Esther Versions."

5. Date

Practically all modern scholars agree in holding that "The Rest of Esther" is some decades later than the canonical book. In his comm. on Est (*Century Bible*) the present writer has given reasons for dating the canonical Est about 130 BC. One could not go far astray in fixing the date of the original Gr of the Ad Est at about 100 BC. It is evident that we owe these interpolations to a Jewish zealot who wished to give the Book of Est a religious character. In his later years John Hyrcanus (135–103 BC) identified himself with the Sadducean or rationalistic party, thus breaking with the Pharisee or orthodox party to which the Maccabeans had hitherto belonged. Perhaps we owe these additions to the zeal aroused among orthodox Jews by the rationalizing temper prevailing in court circles. R. H. Charles (*Enc Brit*, XI, 797*b*) favors a date during the early (?) Maccabean period; but this would give the Ad Est an earlier date than can be ascribed to the canonical Est.

LITERATURE.—See the lit. cited above, and in addition note the following: Fritzsche, *Exegetisches Handbuch zu den Apokryphen* (1851), 67–108; Schürer, *History of the Jewish People*, II, iii, 181 ff (Ger. ed[4], III, 449 ff); Ryssel (in Kautzsch, *Apoc*, 193 ff); Swete, *Intro to the OT in Gr*, 257 ff; the arts. in the principal Bible Dictionaries, including *Jew Enc* and *Enc Brit*. See also under ESTHER.

T. WITTON DAVIES

ESTIMATE, es′ti-māt, **ESTIMATION,** es-ti-mā′shun (עָרַךְ, *ʽārakh*, עֵרֶךְ, *ʽērekh*): These words, meaning "to set in order," "valuation," are used in connection with the priestly services in Lev **5** 15. 18; **6** 6; **27** 14, and frequently; Nu **18** 16.

ESYELUS, ē-sī-ē′lus (Ἠσυήλ, *Ēsuḗl*, Ἠσύηλος, *Ēsúēlos;* AV **Syelus**): One of the governors of the Temple in the time of Josiah (1 Esd **1** 8); called "Jehiel" in 2 Ch **35** 8.

ETAM, ē′tam (עֵיטָם, *ʽēṭām;* A, Ἀπάν, *Apán*, B, Αἰτάν, *Aitán*):

(1) Mentioned in LXX along with Tekoa, Bethlehem and Phagor (Josh **15** 59). In 2 Ch **11** 6 it occurs, between Bethlehem and Tekoa, as one of the cities built "for defence in Judah" by Rehoboam. Jos writes that "there was a certain place, about 50 furlongs distant from Jerus which is called Ethan, very pleasant it is in fine gardens and abounding in rivulets of water; whither he [Solomon] used to go out in the morning" (*Ant*, VIII, vii, 3). Mention of *ʽAin ʽAitān*, which is described as the most elevated place in Pal, occurs in the Talm (*Zebhāḥīm* **54***b*), and in the Jer. Talm (*Yōmā'* **3** fol 41) it is mentioned that a conduit ran from *ʽAṭān* to the Temple.

The evidence all points to *ʽAin ʽAṭān*, the lowest of the springs supplying the aqueduct running to Solomon's pools. The gardens of Solomon may very well—by tradition, at any rate—have been in the fertile valley below *ʽUrṭas*. The site of the ancient town Etam is rather to be looked for on an isolated hill, with ancient remains, a little to the E. of *ʽAin ʽAṭān*. 1 Ch **4** 3 may also have reference to this Etam.

(2) A town assigned to Simeon (1 Ch **4** 32). Mentioned with EN-RIMMON (q.v.), identified by Conder with *Khurbet ʽAiṭūn* in the hills N.W. of Beersheba.

(3) The **rock of Etam,** where Samson took up his dwelling after smiting the Philis "hip and thigh with a great slaughter" (Jgs **15** 8.11), was in Judah but apparently in the low hill country (ib). The rocky hill on which lies the village of *Beit ʽAṭab*, near *Surʽah* (Zorah), was suggested by Conder, but unless (3) is really identical with (1), which is quite possible, the cavern known as *ʽArak Ismaʽin*, described by Hanauer (*PEFS*, 1886, 25), suits the requirements of the story better. The cavern, high up on the northern cliffs of the *Wady Ismaʽin*, is a noticeable object from the railway as the train enters the gorge.

E. W. G. MASTERMAN

ETERNAL, ē-tûr′nal (עוֹלָם, *ʽōlām;* αἰώνιος, *aiōnios*, from αἰών, *aiōn*): The word "eternal" is of very varying import, both in the Scriptures and out of them.

1. ʽŌlām

In the OT, the Heb word *ʽōlām* is used for "eternity," sometimes in the sense of unlimited duration, sometimes in the sense of a cycle or an age, and sometimes, in later Heb, in the signification of world. The Heb *ʽōlām* has, for its proper NT equivalent, *aiōn*, as signifying either time of particular duration, or the unending duration of time in general. Only, the Heb term primarily signified unlimited time, and only in a secondary sense represented a definite or specific period. Both the Heb and the Gr terms signify the world itself, as it moves in time.

2. Aiōn, Aiōnios

In the NT, *aiōn* and *aiōnios* are often used with the meaning "eternal," in the predominant sense of futurity. The word *aiōn* primarily signifies time, in the sense of age or generation; it also comes to denote all that exists under time-conditions; and, finally, superimposed upon the temporal is an ethical use, relative to the world's course. Thus *aiōn* may be said to mean the subtle informing spirit of the world or cosmos—the totality of things. By Plato, in his *Timaeus*, *aiōn* was used of the eternal Being, whose counterpart, in the sense-world, is Time. To Aristotle, in speaking of the world, *aiōn* is the ultimate principle which, in itself, sums up all existence. In the NT, *aiōn* is found combined with prepositions in nearly three score and ten instances, where the idea of unlimited duration appears to be meant. This is the usual method of expressing eternity in the LXX also. The *aiōnios* of 2 Cor **4** 18 must be eternal, in a temporal use or reference, else the antithesis would be gone.

In Rom **1** 20 the word *aïdios* is used of Divine action and rendered in AV "eternal" (RV "everlasting"), the only other place in the NT where the word occurs being Jude ver 6, where the rendering is

3. Aídios

"everlasting," which accords with classical usage. But the presence of the idea of eternal in these passages does not impair the fact that *aiōn* and *aiōnios* are, in their natural and obvious connotation, the usual NT words for expressing the idea of eternal, and this holds strikingly true of the LXX usage also. For, from the idea of aeonian life, there is no reason to suppose the notion of duration excluded. The word *aiōnios* is sometimes used in the futurist signification, but often also, in the NT, it is concerned rather with the quality, than with the quantity or duration, of life. By the continual attachment of *aiōnios* to life, in this conception of the spiritual or Divine life in man, the aeonian conception was saved from becoming sterile.

4. Enlargement of Idea

In the use of *aiōn* and *aiōnios* there is evidenced a certain enlarging or advancing import till they come so to express the high and complex fact of the Divine life in man. In Gr, *aiōnes* signifies ages, or periods or dispensations. The *aiōnes* of He **1** 2, and **11** 3, is, however, to be taken as used in the concrete sense of "the worlds," and not "the ages," the world so taken meaning the totality of things in their course or flow.

5. Eternal Life

Our Lord decisively set the element of time in abeyance, and took His stand upon the fact and quality of life—life endless by its own nature. Of that eternal life He is Himself the guarantee—"Because I live, ye shall live also" (Jn **14** 19). Therefore said Augustine, "Join thyself to the eternal God, and thou wilt be eternal." See Eternity.

James Lindsay

ETERNITY, ē-tûr′ni-ti (עוֹלָם, *'ōlām;* Gr equivalent, **αἰών**, *aiōn*):

1. Contrast with Time
2. In the OT
3. In the NT
4. The Eternal "Now"
5. Defect of This View
6. Philosophic Views
7. Time Conceptions Inadequate
8. All Succession Present in One Act to Divine Consciousness
9. Yet Connection between Eternity and Time
10. The Religious Attitude to Eternity

Literature

1. Contrast with Time

Eternity is best conceived, not in the merely negative form of the non-temporal, or immeasurable time, but positively, as the mode of the timeless self-existence of the Absolute Ground of the universe. The flux of time grows first intelligible to us, only when we take in the thought of God as eternal—exalted above time. Timeless existence—being or entity without change—is what we here mean by eternity, and not mere everlastingness or permanence through time. God, in His internal being, is raised above time; in His eternal absoluteness, He is throned above temporal development, and knows, as the Scriptures say, no changeableness. The conception of eternity, as without beginning or ending, leaves us with but a negation badly in need of filling out with reality. Eternity is not a mere negative idea; to make of eternity merely a blank and irrelevant negation of temporality would not satisfy any proper theory of being; it functions as the positive relation to time of that eternal God, who is King of all the aeons.

2. In the OT

In the OT, God's eternity is only negatively expressed, as implying merely indefinitely extended time (Gen **21** 33; Dt **33** 27), though Isa **40** 28 takes more absolute form. Better is the view of eternity, objectively considered, as a mode of being of God in relation to Himself. For He was eternal, while as yet the world and time were not. But

3. In the NT

even in the NT, the negative form of expression prevails. Time, with its succession of events, helps to fill out such idea as we can form of the eternal, conceived as an endless progress. But, as finite beings, we can form no positive idea of eternity. Time is less contradictory of eternity, than helpful in revealing what we know of it. Plato, in his *Timaeus*, says that time is the "moving image of eternity," and we may allow that it is its type or revelation. Not as the annulment of time, though it might be held to be in itself exclusive of time, is eternity to be taken, but rather as the ground of its reality.

4. The Eternal "Now"

Eternity might, no doubt, be taken as just time no longer measured by the succession of events, as in the finite universe. But, on a strict view, there is something absurd in an eternity that includes time, and an eternity apart from time is a vain and impossible conception. Eternity, as a discharge from all time limits, is purely negative, though not without importance. Eternity, absolutely taken, must be pronounced incommensurable with time; as Aquinas said, *non sunt mensurae unius generis*. Eternity, that is to say, would lose its character as eternal in the very entering into relations with the changeful or becoming. Eternity, as in God, has, since the time of Augustine and the Middle Ages, been frequently conceived as an eternal Now. The Schoolmen were wont to adopt as a maxim that "in eternity is one only instant always present and persistent." This is but a way of describing eternity in a manner characteristic of succession in time; but eternal Deity, rather than an eternal Now, is a conception far more full of meaning for us.

5. Defect of This View

To speak of God's eternity as an eternal Now—a present in the time-sense—involves a contradiction. For the eternal existence is no more described by the notion of a present than by a past or a future. Such a Now or present presupposes a not-now, and raises afresh the old time-troubles, in relation to eternity. Time is certainly not the form of God's life, His eternity meaning freedom from time. Hence it was extremely troublesome to the theology of the Middle Ages to have a God who was not in time at all, supposed to create the world at a particular moment in time.

6. Philosophical Views

Spinoza, in later times, made the eternity of God consist in His infinite—which, to Spinoza, meant His necessary—existence. For contingent or durational existence would not, in Spinoza's view, be eternal, though it lasted always. The illusoriness or unreality of time, in respect of man's spiritual life, is not always very firmly grasped. This wavering or uncertain hold of the illusiveness of time, or of higher reality as timeless, is still very prevalent; even so strong-souled a poet as Browning projects the shadow of time into eternity, with rarely a definite conception of the higher life as an eternal and timeless essence; and although Kant, Hegel and Schopenhauer may have held to such a timeless view, it has by no means become a generally adopted doctrine so far, either of theologians or of philosophers. If time be so taken as unreal, then eternity must not be thought of as future, as is done by Dr. Ellis McTaggart and some other metaphysicians today. For nothing could, in that case, be properly future, and eternity could not be said to begin, as is often done in everyday life.

The importance of the eternity conception is seen in the fact that neo-Kantian and neo-Hegelian thinkers alike have shown a general tendency to regard time-conceptions as unfit, in metaphysics, for the ultimate explanation of the universe.

7. Time-Conceptions Inadequate

Eternity, one may surely hold, must span or include, for God's eternal consciousness, the whole of what happens in time, with all of past, present or future, that lies within the temporal succession. But we are by no means entitled to say, as does Royce, that such wholeness or totality of the temporal constitutes the eternal, for the eternal belongs to quite another order, that, namely, of timeless reality. Eternity is not to be defined in terms of time at all. For God is to us the supra-temporal *ens perfectissimum*, but One whose timeless self-sufficiency and impassable aloofness are not such as to keep Him from being strength and helper of our temporal striving. Our metaphysical convictions must not here be of barren and unfruitful sort for ethical results and purposes.

8. All Succession Present in One Act to Divine Consciousness

Eternity is, in our view, the form of an eternal existence, to which, in the unity of a single insight, the infinite series of varying aspects or processes are, together-wise, as a *totum simul*, present. But this, as we have already shown, does not imply that the eternal order is nowise different, essentially, from the temporal; time is not to be treated as a segment of eternity, nor eternity regarded as interminable duration; the eternal cannot pass over into the temporal; for, an eternal Being, who should think all things as present, and yet view the time-series as a succession, must be a rather self-contradictory conception. For the Absolute Consciousness, time does not exist; the future cannot, for it, be thought of as beginning to be, nor the past as having ceased to be.

9. Yet Connection Between Eternity and Time

After all that has been said, however, eternity and time are not to be thought of as without connection. For the temporal presupposes the eternal, which is, in fact, its positive ground and its perpetual possibility. These things are so, if only for the reason that the Divine mode of existence does not contradict or exclude the human mode of existence. The continuity of the latter—of the temporal—has its guaranty in the eternal. The unconditioned eternity of God brings into harmony with itself the limitations and conditions of the temporal. For time is purely relative, which eternity is not. No distinctions of before and after are admissible in the eternity conception, hence we have no right to speak of time as a portion of eternity. Thus, while we maintain the essential difference between eternity and time, we at the same time affirm what may perhaps be called the affinity between them. The metaphysics of eternity and its time-relations continue to be matter of proverbial difficulty, and both orders—the eternal and the temporal—had better be treated as concrete, and not left merely to abstract reflection. Our idea of the eternal will best be developed, in this concrete fashion, by the growth of our God-idea, as we more completely apprehend God, as actualized for us in His incarnate Son.

10. Religious Attitude to Eternity

Thus, then, it is eternity, not as immeasurable time, but rather as a mode of being of the immutable God, who is yet progressively revealing Himself in time, which we have here set forth. This is not to say that the religious consciousness has not its own need of the conception of God as being "from everlasting to everlasting," as in Ps **90** 2, and of His kingdom as "an everlasting kingdom" (Dnl **4** 3). Nor is it to make us suppose that the absolute and self-existent God, who so transcends all time-dependence, is thereby removed far from us, while, on the contrary, His very greatness makes Him the more able to draw near unto us, in all the plenitude of His being. Hence it is so truly spoken in Isa **57** 15, "Thus saith the high and lofty One that inhabiteth eternity, whose name is Holy: I dwell in the high and holy place, with him also that is of a contrite and humble spirit, to revive the spirit of the humble, and to revive the heart of the contrite." Hence also the profound truthfulness of sayings like that in Acts **17** 27.28, "He is not far from each one of us: for in him we live, and move, and have our being." After all that has been said, our best knowledge of eternity, as it exists in God, is not developed in any metaphysical fashion, but after the positive and timeless modes of the spiritual life—the modes of trust and love.

LITERATURE.—H. Cremer, *Lexicon of NT Gr*, Eng. ed, 1880; G. B. Winer, *Grammar of NT Gr*, 3d ed, 1882; R. C. French, *Synonyms of the NT*, 9th ed, 1880; E. H. Plumptre, *The Spirits in Prison*, 3d ed, 1885; J. Orr, *Christian View of God and the World*, 1st ed, 1893; I. A. Dorner, *System of Christian Doctrine*, Eng. ed, 1885; J. H. Stirling, *Philosophy and Theology*, 1890; J. Lindsay, *Studies in European Philosophy*, 1909; *The Fundamental Problems of Metaphysics*, 1910.

JAMES LINDSAY

ETHAM, ē'tham (אֵתָם, *'ēthām*; Ὀθώμ, *Othōm*, Ex **13** 20; Βουθάν, *Bouthán*, Nu **33** 6.7; in **33** 8 the LXX has a different reading, "in their wilderness," showing another pointing for the word): The name used to be explained as the Coptic *Atium*, "border of the Sea" (Gesenius, *Lex.*, s.v.) which would agree with the Heb (Nu **33** 8) where the "wilderness of Etham" is noticed instead of that of Shur (Ex **15** 22) E. of the Red Sea (see SHUR). At Etham (Ex **13** 20), the Hebrews camped in the "edge," or at "the end," of the desert W. of the sea that they were to cross (see EXODUS). This camp was probably near the N. end of the Bitter Lakes, a march from Succoth. Brugsch (*Hist. Egypt*, II, 359) would compare Etham with the Egyp *Khetam* ("fort"), but the Heb word has no guttural. The word *Khetam* is not the name of a place (see Pierret, *Vocab. hiéroglyph.*, 453), and more than one such "fort" seems to be noticed (see PITHOM). In the reign of Seti II a scribe's report mentions the pursuit of two servants, apparently from Zoan, to the fortress of *I-k-u* southward, reaching *Khetam* on the 3d day; but if this was the "Khetam of Rameses II," or even that "of Minepthah," it would not apparently suit the position of Etham. See MIGDOL.

C. R. CONDER

ETHAN, ē'than (אֵיתָן, *'ēthān*, "firm," "enduring"; Γαιθάν, *Gaithán*):

(1) A wise man with whom Solomon is compared (1 K **4** 31). Called there "Ethan the Ezrahite," to whom the title of Ps **89** ascribes the authorship of that poem.

(2) A "son of Kishi," or "Kishaiah," of the Merari branch of the Levites, and, along with Heman and Asaph, placed by David over the service of song (1 Ch **6** 44; **15** 17.19). See JEDUTHUN.

(3) An ancestor of Asaph of the Gershomite branch of the Levites (1 Ch **6** 42).

ETHANIM, eth'a-nim (אֵתָנִים, *'ēthānīm*): The seventh month of the Jewish year (1 K **8** 2). The word is of Phoen origin and signifies "perennial," referring to living streams. It corresponds to September-October. See CALENDAR; TIME.

ETHANUS, ē-thā'nus, AV Ecanus (Apoc): One of the scribes who wrote for forty days at the dictation of Ezra (2 Esd **14** 24).

ETHBAAL, eth-bā'al, eth'bā-al (אֶתְבַּעַל, *'eth-ba'al*, "with Baal"): "King of the Sidonians," and father of Jezebel, whom Ahab king of Israel took to wife (1 K **16** 31).

ETHER, ē'thẽr (עֶתֶר, *'ether;* 'Αθέρ, *Athér*): A town in Judah (Josh **15** 42), near Libnah, assigned to Simeon (**19** 7). *Kh. el 'Atr* (identical in spelling with Ether) is possibly the site. It is near *Beit Jibrîn* and is described as "an ancient site: cisterns, foundations, quarried rock and terraces" (*PEF*, III, 261, 279).

ETHICS, eth'iks:

In this article, which proposes to be of a general and introductory character, we shall first deal with the *nature and function* of ethics generally, showing its difference from and relation to other cognate branches of inquiry. Secondly, we shall sketch briefly the *history of ethics* in so far as the various stages of its development bear upon and prepare the way for Christian ethics, indicating also the subsequent course of ethical speculation. Thirdly, we shall give some account of *Biblical ethics;* treating first of the main moral ideas contained in the OT, and enumerating, secondly, the general principles and leading characteristics which underlie the ethical teaching of the NT.

I. Nature and Function of Ethics.—Ethics is that branch of philosophy which is concerned with human character and conduct. It deals with man, not so much as a subject of knowledge, as a source of action. It has to do with life or personality in its inward dispositions, outward manifestations and social relations. It was Aristotle who first gave to this study its name and systematic form. According to the Gr signification of the term, it is the science of customs (ἠθικά, *ēthiká*, from ἦθος, *ēthos*, "custom," "habit," "disposition"). But inasmuch as the words "custom" and "habit" seem to refer only to outward manners or usages, the mere etymology would limit the nature of the inquiry. The same limitation exists in the Lat designation, "moral," since *mores* concerns primarily manners.

Men live before they reflect, and act before they examine the grounds of action. So long as there is a congruity between the habits of an individual or a people and the practical requirements of life, ethical questions do not occur. It is only when difficulties arise and new problems appear as to right and duty in which the existing customs of life offer no solution, that doubt awakes, and with doubt reflection upon the actual morality which governs life. It is when men begin to call in question their past usages and institutions and to readjust their attitude to old traditions and new interests that ethics appears. Ethics is not morality but reflection upon morality. When, therefore, Aristotle, following Socrates and Plato, employed the term, he had in view not merely a description of the outward life of man, but rather the sources of action and the objects as ends which ought to guide him in the proper conduct of life. According to the best usage the names Moral Philosophy and Ethics are equivalent and mean generally the rational explanation of our nature, actions and relations as moral and responsible beings. Ethics therefore may be defined as the systematic study of human character, and its function is to show how human life must be fashioned to realize its end or purpose.

1. Rise of Ethics

But accepting this general definition, how, it may be asked, can we speak of a science of conduct at all? Has not science to do with necessary truths, to trace effects from causes, to formulate general laws according to which these causes act, and to draw inevitable and necessary consequences? But is not character just that concerning which no definite conclusions can be predicted? Is not conduct, dependent as it is on the human will, just that which cannot be explained as the resultant of calculable forces? If the will is free then you cannot decide beforehand what line it will take, or predict what shape character must assume. The whole conception of a science of ethics, it is contended, must fall to the ground if we admit an invariable and calculable element in conduct. But this objection is based partly upon a misconception of the function of science and partly upon a too narrow classification of the sciences. Science has not only to do with cause and effect and the laws according to which phenomena actually occur. Science seeks to deal systematically with all truths that are presented to us; and there is a large class of truths not belonging indeed to the realm of

2. Ethics as a Science

natural and physical events which, however, may be studied and correlated. Ethics is not indeed concerned with conduct, as a natural fact, as something done here and now following from certain causes in the past and succeeded by certain results in the future. It is concerned with *judgments* upon conduct—the judgment that such conduct is right or wrong as measured by a certain standard or end. Hence a distinction has been made between the physical sciences and what are called normative sciences.

3. A Normative Science

The natural or physical sciences are concerned simply with phenomena of Nature or mind, actual occurrences which have to be analyzed and classified. The normative sciences, on the other hand, have to do not with mere facts in time or space, but with *judgments* about these facts, with certain standards or ends (norms, from *norma*, "a rule") in accordance with which the facts are to be valued. Man cannot be explained by natural law. He is not simply a part of the world, a link in the chain of causality. When we reflect upon his life and his relation to the world we find that he is conscious of himself as an end and that he is capable of forming purposes, of proposing new ends and of directing his thoughts and actions with a view to the attainment of these ends, and making things subservient to him. Such an end or purpose thus forms a *norm* for the regulation of life; and the laws which must be observed for the attainment of such an end form the subjects of a normal or normative science. Ethics therefore has to do with the norm or standard of right or wrong, and is concerned primarily with the laws which regulate our judgments and guide our actions.

4. Relation to Cognate Sciences

Man is of course a unity, but it is possible to view his self-consciousness in three different aspects, and to regard his personality as constituted of an intellectual, sentient and volitional element. Roughly corresponding to these three aspects, one in reality but separable in thought, there arise three distinct though interdependent mental sciences: *metaphysics*, which has to do with man's relation to the universe of which he forms a part; *psychology*, which deals with the nature, constitution and evolution of his faculties and feelings as a psychical being; and *ethics*, which treats of him as a volitional being, possessing will or determining activity.

(1) *Ethics and metaphysics.*—Ethics, though distinct from, is closely connected with metaphysics on the one hand, and psychology on the other. If we take metaphysics in its widest sense as including natural theology and as positing some ultimate end to the realization of which the whole process of the world is somehow a means, we may easily see how it is a necessary presupposition or basis of ethical inquiry. The world as made and governed by and for an intelligent purpose, and man as a part of it, having his place and function in a great teleological cosmos, are postulates of the moral life and must be accepted as a basis of all ethical study. The distinction between ethics and metaphysics did not arise at once. In early Gr philosophy they were closely united. Even now the two subjects cannot be completely dissociated. Ethics invariably runs back into metaphysics, or at least into theology, and in every philosophical system in which the universe is regarded as having an ultimate end or good, the good of human beings is conceived as identical with or included in the universal good (see Ziegler, *Gesch. der christlichen Ethik;* also Sidgwick, *History of Ethics*).

(2) *Ethics and psychology.*—On the other hand ethics is closely associated with, though distinguishable from, *psychology*. Questions of conduct inevitably lead to inquiries as to certain states of the agent's mind, for we cannot pronounce an action morally good or bad until we have investigated the qualities of intention, purpose, motive and disposition which lie at the root of the action. Hence all students of ethics are agreed that the main object of their investigation must belong to the psychical side of human life, whether they hold that man's ultimate end is to be found in the sphere of pleasure or they maintain that his well-being lies in the realization of virtue. Questions as to existence, evolution and adequacy of a moral faculty (see CONSCIENCE); as to the relation of pleasure and desire; as to the meaning of validity of voluntary action; as to the historical evolution of moral customs and ideals, and man's relation at each stage of his being to the social, political and religious institutions, belong indeed to a science of ethics, but they have their roots in psychology as a study of the human soul.

The very existence of a science of ethics depends upon the answers which psychology gives to such questions. If, for example, we decide that there is no such faculty in man as conscience and that the moral sense is but a natural manifestation which has gradually evolved with the physical and social evolution of man (Darwin, Spencer); or if we deny the self-determining power of human beings and assume that the freedom of the will is a delusion, or in the last resort a negligible element, and treat man as one of the many phenomena of a physical universe, then indeed we may continue to speak of a science of the moral life as some naturalistic writers do, but such a science would not be a science of ethics as we understand it. Whatever be our explanation of conscience and freedom, no theory as to these powers must depersonalize man, and we may be justly suspicious of any system of psychology which undermines the authority of the moral sense or paves the way for a complete irresponsibility.

The "ought."—Ethics is based on the assumption that man is a person possessing rights and having duties—responsible therefore for his intentions as well as his actions. The idea of personality involves not only a sense of accountability but carries with it also the conception of a law to which man is to conform, an ideal at which he is to aim. The end of life with all its implications forms the subject of ethics. It is concerned not simply with what a man is or does, but more particularly with what he should be and do. Hence the word "ought" is the most distinctive term of ethics. The "ought" of life constitutes at once the end or ideal and the law of man. It comprises *end, rule* and *motive* of action. Thus the problem of ethics comes to be regarded as the highest good of man, the τὸ ἀγαθόν, *tó agathón*, of the Greeks, the *summum bonum* of Lat philosophy.

5. Relation of Christian Ethics to Moral Philosophy

If ethics generally is based upon the postulates of philosophy and psychology, and at each stage of human consciousness grounds its principles of life upon the view of the world and of man to which it has attained, Christian ethics presupposes *the Christian view* of life as revealed by Christ, and its definition must be in harmony with the Christian ideal. Christian ethics is the science of morals conditioned by Christianity, and the problems which it discusses are the nature, laws and duties of the moral life as dominated by the Supreme Good which Christians believe to have been revealed in and through the life and teaching of Jesus Christ. Christian ethics is thus a branch or particular application of general ethics. So far from being opposed to moral philosophy it is the inevitable outcome of the evolution of thought. For if the revelation of God through Christ is true, then it is a factor, and the greatest in life and destiny, which must condition man's entire outlook and give a new value to his aims and duties.

(1) *Not an opposition.*—In Christianity we are confronted with the motive power of a great Personality entering into the current of human history, and by His preëminent spiritual force giving a direction to the moral life of man. This means that the moral life can only be understood by reference to the creative power of this Personality. If there is any place at all for a distinct science of Christian ethics, that place can be indicated only by starting from the ethical ideal embodied in Christ, and working out from that point a code of morality for the practical guidance of the Christian life. But while this truth gives to Christian ethics its distinctive character and preëminent worth, it neither throws discredit upon philosophical ethics nor separates the two sciences by any hard-and-fast lines. They have much in common. A large domain of conduct is covered by both. The so-called pagan virtues have their worth for Christian character and are in the line of Christian virtues. Man even in his natural state is constituted for the moral life and is not without some knowledge of right and wrong (Rom **1** 20). The moral attainments of the ancients are not simply "splendid vices." Duty may differ in content, but it is of the same kind under every system. Purity is purity, and benevolence benevolence, and both are excellences, whether manifested in a heathen or a Christian. While therefore Christian ethics takes its point of departure from the revelation of God and the manifestation of man's possibilities in Christ, it accepts and uses the results of moral philosophy in so far as they throw light upon the fundamental facts of human nature. As a system of morals Christianity claims to be inclusive. It takes cognizance of all the data of consciousness, and assumes all ascertained truth as its own. It completes what is lacking in other systems in so far as their conclusions are based on an incomplete survey of facts. Christian morals, in short, deal with personality in its highest ranges of moral power and spiritual consciousness, and seek to interpret life by its greatest possibilities and loftiest attainments as they have been revealed in Christ.

(2) *Philosophical postulates.*—As illustrating what has just been said two distinctive features of Christian morals may be noted, of which philosophical ethics takes little or no account:

(*a*) Christian ethics assumes *a latent spirituality in man* awaiting the Spirit of God to call it forth. "Human nature," says Newman Smyth, "has its existence in an ethical sphere and for moral ends of being." There is a natural capacity for ethical life to which man's whole constitution points. Matter itself may be said to exist ultimately for spirit, and the spirit of man for the Holy Spirit (cf Rothe, *Theologische Ethik*, I, 459). No theory of man's physical beginning can interfere with the assumption that man stands upon a moral plane and is capable of a life which shapes itself to spiritual ends. Whatever be man's history and evolution, he has from the beginning been made in God's image, and he bears the Divine impress in all the lineaments of his body and soul. His degradation cannot wholly obliterate his nobility, and his actual corruption bears witness to his possible holiness. Christian morality is therefore nothing else than the morality prepared from all eternity, and is but the highest realization of that which heathen virtue was striving after. This is the Pauline view of human nature. Jesus Christ, according to the apostle, is the end and consummation of the whole creation. Everywhere there is a capacity for Christ. Man is not simply what he now is, but all that he is yet to be (1 Cor **15** 47–49).

(*b*) Connected with this peculiarity is another which further differentiates Christian ethics from philosophical—the problem of *the re-creation of character*. Speculative systems do not advance beyond the formation of moral requirements; they prescribe what ought ideally to be done or avoided. Christianity, on the other hand, is primarily concerned with the question, By what power can I achieve the right and the good? (cf Ottley, *Christian Ideas and Ideals*, 22). It regards human nature as in need of renewal and recovery. It points to a process by which character can be restored and transformed. It claims to be the power of God unto salvation to everyone that believeth (Rom **1** 16). Christian ethics thus makes the twofold assumption, and in this its contrast to philosophical ethics is disclosed, that the ideal of humanity has been revealed in Jesus Christ and that in Him also there is supplied a power by which man may become his true self, all that his natural life gives promise of and potentially is.

(3) *Method.*—Passing from a consideration of the data of Christian ethics to its *method*, we find that here again there is much that is common to philosophy and Christian morals. The method in both is the rational method. The Christian ideal, though given in Christ, has to be examined, analyzed and applied by the very same faculties as man employs in regard to speculative problems. All science must be furnished with facts, and its task is to give a consistent explanation of them. While the speculative thinker finds his facts in the constitution of the moral world at large, the Christian discovers his in Scripture, and more particularly in the teachings of Christ. But it is sufficient to point out that while the NT is largely occupied with ethical matters, there is no attempt at a scientific formulation of them. The materials of systematic treatment are there, but the task of coordinating and classifying principles is the work of the expositor. The data are supplied but these data require to be interpreted, unified and applied so as to form a system of ethics. Consequently in dealing with his facts, the same method must be employed by the Christian expositor as by the student of science. That is the method of rational inquiry and inductive procedure—the method imposed upon all mental problems by the essential nature of the mind itself. The authority to which Christian ethics appeals is not an external oracle which imposes its dictates in a mechanical way. It is an authority embodied in intelligible forms and appealing to the reasoning faculties of man. Christian ethics is not a cut-and-dried, ready-made code. It has to be thought out by man and brought to bear, through the instrumentality of his thinking powers, upon all the relationships of life. According to the Protestant view, at least, ethics is no stereotyped compendium of rules which the Bible or the church supplies to save a man from the trouble of thinking. It is a complete misapprehension of the nature of Scripture and of the purpose of Christ's example and teaching to assume that they afford a mechanical standard which must be copied or obeyed in a slavish way. Christ appeals to the rational nature of man, and His words are life and spirit only as they are apprehended in an intelligent way and become by inner conviction and personal appropriation the principles of thought and action.

6. Relation of Christian Ethics to Dogmatics

Within the domain of theology the two main constituents of Christian teaching are dogmatics and ethics, or doctrine and morals. Though it is convenient to treat these separately, they really form a whole, and are but two sides of one subject. It is difficult to define their limits, and to say where dogmatics ends and ethics begins.

The distinction has sometimes been expressed by saying that dogmatics is a theoretic, while ethics is a practical science. It is true that ethics stands nearer to everyday life and deals with methods of practical conduct, while dogmatics is concerned with beliefs and treats of their origin and elucidation. But on the other hand ethics discusses thoughts as well as actions, and is interested in inner judgments not less than outward achievements. There is a practical side to all doctrine; and there is a theoretic side of all morals. In proportion as dogmatic theology becomes divorced from practical interest there is a danger that it may become mere pedantry. Even the most theoretic of sciences, metaphysics, while, as Novalis said, it bakes no bread, has its justification in its bearing upon life. On the other hand, ethics would lose all scientific value and would sink into a mere enumeration of duties if it had no dogmatic basis and did not draw its motives from beliefs. The common statement that dogmatics shows what we should believe and ethics what we should do is only approximately true and is inadequate. For moral laws and precepts are also objects of faith, and what we should believe involves a moral requirement and has a moral character.

(1) *The connection.*—Schleiermacher has been frequently charged with ignoring the differences between the two disciplines, but with scant justice; for while he regards the two studies as but different branches of Christian doctrine and while emphasizing their intimate connection, he by no means neglects their differences (cf Schleiermacher, *Christliche Lehre,* 1–24). Recent Christian moralists (Dorner, Martensen, Wuttke, Haering, Lemme) tend to accentuate the distinction and claim for them a separate discussion. The ultimate connection cannot indeed be overlooked without loss to both. It leads only to confusion to talk of a creedless morality, and the attempt to deal with moral questions without reference to their dogmatic implication will not only rob Christian ethics of its distinctive character and justification, but will reduce the exposition to a mere system of emotionalism. Dogmatics and ethics may be regarded as interdependent and mutually serviceable. On the one hand, ethics saves dogmatics from evaporating into unsubstantial speculation, and, by affording the test of life and workableness, keeps it upon the solid foundation of fact. On the other hand, dogmatics supplies ethics with its formative principles and normative standards, and preserves the moral life from degenerating into the vagaries of fanaticism or the apathy of fatalism.

(2) *The distinction.*—While both sciences form the complementary sides of theology, and stand in the relation of mutual service, ethics presupposes dogmatics and is based upon its postulates. Dogmatics presents the essence, contents and object of the religious consciousness; ethics presents this consciousness as a power determining the human will (Wuttke). In the one, the Christian life is regarded from the standpoint of dependence on God; in the other, from the standpoint of human freedom. Dogmatics deals with faith in relation to God, and as the receptive organ of Divine grace; ethics considers it rather in its relation to man as a human activity, and as the organ of conduct (cf Lemme, *Christliche Ethik,* I, 15). Doctrine shows us how our adoption into the kingdom of God is the work of Divine love; ethics shows us how this knowledge of salvation manifests itself in love to God and our neighbor and must be worked out through all the relationships of life (cf Haering).

(3) *Theological postulates.*—From this point of view we may see how dogmatics supplies to ethics certain postulates which may briefly be enumerated.

(*a*) Ethics assumes *the Christian idea of God.* God is not merely a force or even a creator as He is presented in philosophy. Divine power must be qualified by what we term the moral attributes of God. We do not deny His omnipotence, but we look beyond it to "the love that tops the power, the Christ in God." Moreover we recognize a gradation in God's moral qualities: (*a*) *benevolence* or kindness; (*b*) more deeply ethical and in seeming contrast to His benevolence, *Divine justice*—not mere blind benevolence but a kindness which is wise and discriminating (cf Butler); (*c*) highest in the scale of Divine attributes, uniting in one comprehensive quality kindness and justice, stands *Divine love* or *grace.* The God whom dogmatics postulates to ethics is God in Christ.

(*b*) Ethics again presupposes the *Christian doctrine of sin.* It is not the province of ethics to discuss the origin of evil or propound a theory of sin. But it must see to it that the view it takes is consistent with the truths of revelation and in harmony with the facts of life. A false or inadequate conception of sin is as detrimental for ethics as it is for dogmatics, and upon our doctrine of evil depends very largely our view of life as to its difficulties and purposes, its trials and triumphs. Three views of sin have been held. According to some (e.g. the ancient Greeks) sin is simply a *defect* or shortcoming, a missing of the mark (ἁμαρτία, *hamartía,* the active principle, or ἁμάρτημα, *hamártēma,* the result); according to others, it is a disease, a thing latent in the constitution or at least an infirmity or limitation inherent in the flesh and resulting from heredity and environment (see EVOLUTION).

While there is truth in both of these views, by themselves, each separately, or both in combination, is defective. They do not sufficiently take account of the personal self-determinative element in all sin. It is a misfortune, a fate from which the notion of guilt is absent. The Christian view implies these conceptions, but it adds its own distinctive note which gives to them their value. Sin is not merely a negative thing, it is something *positive,* an inward dominating force. It is not merely an imperfection, or want; it is an excess, a trespass. It is not simply an inherited and inherent malady; it is a self-chosen perversion. It is not inherent in the flesh or animal impulses and physical passions: it belongs rather to the mind and will. Its essence lies in selfishness. It is the deliberate choice of self in preference to God. It is personal and wilful rebellion. It is to be overcome, therefore, not by the suppression of the body or the excision of the passions, but by the acceptance of a new principle of life and a transformation of the whole man. There are of course degrees and stages of wrongdoing, and there are compensating circumstances which must be taken into account in estimating the significance of evil; but in its last resort Christian ethics postulates the fact of sin and regards it as personal rebellion against the holiness of God, as the deliberate choice of self and the wilful perversion of all the powers of man into instruments of unrighteousness.

(*c*) A third postulate arises as a consequence from the Christian view of God and the Christian view of sin, viz. *the responsibility of man.* Christian ethics treats every man as accountable for his thoughts and actions, and therefore capable of choosing the good as revealed in Christ. While not denying the sovereignty of God or minimizing the mystery of evil and clearly recognizing the universality of sin, Christianity firmly maintains the doctrine of human freedom and accountability. An ethic would be impossible if, on the one side, grace were absolutely irresistible, and if, on the other, sin were necessitated, if at any single point wrongdoing were inevitable. Whatever be our doctrine on these subjects, ethics demands that freedom of the will be safeguarded.

At this point an interesting question emerges as to the possibility, apart from a knowledge of Christ, of choosing the good. Difficult as this question is, and though it was answered by Augustine and many of the early Fathers in the negative, the modern, and probably the more just, view is that we cannot hold mankind responsible unless we accord to all men the larger freedom. If non-Christians are fated to do evil, then no guilt can be imputed. History shows that a love for goodness has sometimes existed, and that many isolated acts of purity and kindness have been done, among people who have known nothing of the historical Christ. The NT recognizes degrees of depravity in nations and individuals and a measure of noble aspiration and earnest effort in ordinary human nature. St. Paul plainly assumes some knowledge and performance on the part of the heathen, and though he denounces their immorality in unsparing terms he does not affirm that pagan society was so utterly corrupt that it had lost all knowledge of moral good.

II. Historical Sketch of Ethics.—A comprehensive treatment of our subject would naturally include a history of ethics from the earliest times to the present. For ethics as a branch of philosophical inquiry partakes of the historical development of all thought, and the problems which it presents to our day can be rightly appreciated only in the light of certain categories and concepts—such as end, good, virtue, duty, pleasure, egoism and altruism —which have been evolved through the successive stages of the movement of ethical thoughts. All we can attempt here, however, is the baldest outline of the different epochs of ethical inquiry as indicating the preparatory stages which lead up to and find their solution in the ethics of Christianity.

1. Greek Philosophy

(1) *The Sophists.*—All the great religions of the world—of India, Persia and Egypt—have had their ethical implicates, but these have consisted for the most part of loosely connected moral precepts or adages. Before the golden age of Gr philosophy there were no ethics in the strict sense. The moral consciousness of the Greeks takes its rise with the Sophists, and particularly with Socrates, who were the first to protest against the long-established customs and traditions of their land. The so-called "wise men" were in part moralists, but their sayings are but isolated maxims presenting no unity or connection. Philosophy proper occupied itself primarily with purely metaphysical or ontological questions as to the nature of being, the form and origin and primal elements of the world. It was only when Gr religion and poetry had lost their hold upon the cultured and the beliefs of the past had come to be doubted, that questions as to the meaning of life and conduct arose.

(2) *Socrates.*—Already the Sophists had drawn attention to the vagueness and inconsistency of common opinion, and had begun to teach the art of conduct, but it was Socrates who, as it was said, first brought philosophy down from heaven to the sphere of the earth and directed men's minds from merely natural things to human life. He was indeed the first moral philosopher, inasmuch as, while the Sophists talked about justice and law and temperance, they could not tell, when pressed, what these things were. The first task of Socrates, therefore, was to expose human ignorance. All our confusion and disputes about good arise, says Socrates, from want of clear knowledge. He aimed, therefore, at producing knowledge, not merely for its own sake, but because he believed it to be the ground of all right conduct. Nobody does wrong willingly. Let a man know what is good, that is, what is truly beneficial, and he will do it. Hence the famous Socratic dictum, "Virtue is knowledge and vice is ignorance." With all his intellectualism Socrates was really a hedonist, believing that pleasure was the ultimate end of life. For it must not be imagined that he conceived of knowledge of virtue as distinct from interest. Everyone naturally seeks the good because the good is really identified with his happiness. The wise man is necessarily the happy man, and hence "to know one's self" is to learn the secret of well-being.

(3) *Plato.*—While Socrates was the first to direct attention to the nature of virtue, his one-sided and fragmentary conception of it received a more systematic treatment from Plato, who attempted to define the nature and end of man by his place in the cosmos. Plato thus brought ethics into intimate connection with metaphysics. He conceived an ideal world in which everything earthly and human had its prototype. The human soul is derived from the world-soul and, like it, is a mixture of two elements. On the one side, in virtue of reason, it participates in the world of ideas, or the life of God; and on the other, by virtue of its animal impulses, it partakes of the world of decay, the corporeal world. These two dissimilar parts are connected by an intermediate element, which Plato calls θυμός, *thumós*, embracing courage, the love of honor and the affections of the heart—a term which may be translated by the will. The constitution of the inner man is manifested in his outward organization. The head is the seat of reason, the breast of the heart and the affections, and the lower part of the body of the organs of animal desire. If we ask, Who is the just man? Plato answers, The man in whom the three elements just mentioned harmonize. We thus arrive at the scheme of the so-called "cardinal virtues" which have persisted through all ages and have given direction to all ethical discussion —*wisdom, courage, temperance* which, in combination, give us *justice*. It will thus be observed that virtue is no longer simply identified with knowledge; but another form of bad conduct besides ignorance is assumed, viz. the internal disorder and conflict of the soul, in which the lower impulses war with the higher. This, it will be seen, is a distinct advance on the one-sided position of Socrates, but in his attempt to reconcile the two movements in the conflict of life, Plato does not succeed in overcoming the duality. The inner impulses are ever dragging man down, and man's true well-being lies in the attainment of the life of reason. But though there are gleams of a higher solution in Plato, as a rule he falls back upon the idea that virtue is to be attained only by the suppression of the animal passions and the mortifying of the lower life. Plato affords us also the primal elements of social ethics. Morality as conceived by him is not something belonging merely to the individual, but has its full realization in the state. Man is indeed but a type of the larger cosmos, and it is not as an individual but as a citizen that he is capable of realizing his true life.

(4) *Aristotle.*—The ethics of Aristotle, while it completes, does not essentially differ from that of Plato. He is the first to treat of the subject formally as a science, which assumes in his hands a division of politics. For, as he says, man is really "a social animal"; and, even more decisively than Plato, he treats of man as a part of society. Aristotle begins his great work on ethics with the discussion of the *chief good*, which he declares to be happiness or well-being. Happiness does not consist, however, in sensual pleasure, or even in the pursuit of honor, but in a life of well-ordered contemplation, "an activity of the soul in accordance with reason" (*Nic. Eth.*, I, ch v). But to reach the goal of right

thinking and right doing, both favorable surroundings and proper instruction are required. Virtue is not virtue until it is a habit, and the only way to become virtuous is to practise virtue. It will thus be seen that Aristotle balances the one-sided emphasis of Socrates and Plato upon knowledge by the insistence upon habit. Activity must be combined with reason. The past and the present, environment and knowledge, must both be acknowledged as elements in the making of life. The virtues are thus habits, but habits of deliberate choice. Virtue is therefore an activity which at every point seeks to strike the *mean* between two opposite excesses. Plato's list of virtues had the merit of simplicity, but Aristotle's, though fuller, lacks system and consists generally of right actions which are determined in reference to two extremes. One defect which strikes a modern is that among the virtues benevolence is not recognized except obscurely as a form of liberality; and in general the gentler self-sacrificing virtues so prominent in Christianity have no place. The virtues are chiefly aristocratic and are impossible for a slave. Again while Aristotle did well, in opposition to previous philosophy, to recognize the function of habit, it must be pointed out that habit of itself cannot make a man virtuous. Mere habit may be a hindrance and not a help to higher attainment. You cannot reduce morality to a succession of customary acts. But the main defect of Aristotle's treatment of virtue is that he regards the passions as wholly irrational and immoral. He does not see that passion in this sense can have no mean. If you may have too much of a good thing, you cannot have even a little of a bad thing. In man the desires and impulses are never purely irrational. Reason enters into all his appetites and gives to the body and all the physical powers an ethical value and a moral use. We do not become virtuous by curbing the passions but by transfiguring them into the vehicle of good. Aristotle, not less than Plato, is affected by the Gr duality which makes an antithesis between reason and impulse, and imparts to the former an external supremacy.

(5) *Stoics and Epicureans.*—The two conflicting elements of reason and impulse which neither Plato nor Aristotle succeeded in harmonizing ultimately gave rise to two opposite interpretations of the moral life. The Stoics selected the rational nature as the true guide to an ethical system, but they gave to it a supremacy so rigid as to threaten the extinction of the affections. The Epicureans, on the other hand, seizing the doctrine that happiness is the chief good, so accentuated the emotional side of nature as to open the door for all manner of sensual enjoyment. Both agree in determining the happiness of the individual as the final goal of moral conduct. It is not necessary to dwell upon the particular tenets of Epicurus and his followers. For though both Epicureanism and Stoicism, as representing the chief tendencies of ethical inquiry, have exercised incalculable influence upon speculation and practical morals of later ages, it is the doctrines of Stoicism which have more specially come into contact with Christianity.

(6) *Stoicism.*—Without dwelling upon the stoic conception of the world, according to which the universe was a whole, interpenetrated and controlled by an inherent spirit, and the consequent view of life as proceeding from God and being in all its parts equally Divine, we may note that the Stoics, like Plato and Aristotle, regarded the realization of man's natural purpose as the true well-being or highest good. This idea they formulated into a principle: "Life according to Nature." The wise man is he who strives to live in agreement with his rational nature in all the circumstances of life. The law of Nature is to avoid what is hurtful and strive for what is appropriate; and pleasure arises as an accompaniment when a being obtains that which is fitting. Pleasure and pain are, however, to be regarded as mere accidents or incidents of life and to be met by the wise man with indifference. He alone is free, the master of himself and the world, who acknowledges the absolute supremacy of reason and makes himself independent of earthly desires. This life of freedom is open to all, for all men are equal, members of one great body. The slave may be as free as the consul and each can make the world his servant by living in harmony with it.

There is a certain sublimity in the ethics of Stoicism. It was a philosophy which appealed to noble minds and "it inspired nearly all the great characters of the early Rom empire and nerved every attempt to maintain the dignity and freedom of the human soul" (Lecky, *History of European Morals*, I, ch ii). We cannot, however, be blind to its defects. With all their talk of Divine immanence and providence, it was nothing but an impersonal destiny which the Stoics recognized as governing the universe. "Harmony with Nature" was simply a sense of proud self-sufficiency. Stoicism is the glorification of reason, even to the extent of suppressing all emotion. It has no real sense of sin. Sin is un-reason, and salvation lies in the external control of the passions, in indifference and apathy begotten of the atrophy of desire. The great merit of the Stoics is that they emphasized inner moral integrity as the one condition of all right action and true happiness, and in an age of degeneracy insisted on the necessity of virtue. In its preference for the joys of the inner life and its scorn of the delights of sense; in its emphasis upon duty and its advocacy of a common humanity, together with its belief in the direct relation of each human soul to God, Stoicism, as revealed in the writings of a Seneca, a Marcus Aurelius and an Epictetus, not only showed how high paganism at its best could reach, but proved in a measure a preparation for Christianity with whose practical tenets, in spite of its imperfections, it had much in common.

(7) *Stoicism and St. Paul.*—That there are remarkable affinities between Stoicism and Pauline ethics has frequently been pointed out. The similarity both in language and sentiment can scarcely be accounted for by mere coincidence. There were elements in Stoic philosophy which St. Paul would not have dreamt of assimilating, and features with which he could have no sympathy. The pantheistic view of God and the material conception of the world, the self-conscious pride, the absence of all sense of sin and need of pardon, the temper of apathy and the unnatural suppression of feelings—these were features which could not but rouse in the apostle's mind strong antagonism. But on the other hand there were certain well-known characteristics of a nobler order in Stoic morality which we may believe Paul found ready to his hand, ideas which he did not hesitate to incorporate in his teaching and employ in the service of the gospel. Without enlarging upon this line of thought (cf Alexander, *Ethics of St. Paul*), of these we may mention the *immanence of God* as the pervading cause of all life and activity; the *idea of wisdom* or knowledge as the ideal of man; the *conception of freedom* as the prerogative of the individual; and the *notion of brotherhood* as the goal of humanity.

2. Scholasticism

It will be possible only to sketch in a few rapid strokes the subsequent development of ethical thought. After the varied life of the early centuries had passed, Christian ethic (so prominent in the Gospels and Epistles), like Christian theology, fell under the blight of Gnosticism (Alexandrian philosophy; cf Hatch, *Hibbert Lectures*) and latterly, of Scholasticism. Christian truth stiffened into a cumbrous catalogue of ecclesiastical observances. In the early Fathers (Barnabas, Clement, Origen, Gregory), dogmatic and ethical teaching were hardly distinguished. Cyprian discussed moral questions from the standpoint of church discipline.

The first real attempt at a Christian ethic was made by Ambrose, whose treatise on the *Duties* is an imitation of Cicero's work of the same title. Even Augustine, notwithstanding his profound insight into the nature of sin, treats of moral questions incidentally. Perhaps the only writers among the schoolmen, excepting Alcuin (*Virtues and Vices*), who afford anything like elaborate moral treatises, are Abelard (*Ethica*, or *Scito te Ipsum*), Peter Lombard (*Sentences*), and, above all, Thomas Aquinas (*Summa*, II).

3. Reformation

Emancipation from a legal dogmatism first came with the *Reformation* which was in essence a moral revival. The relation of God and man came to be re-stated under the inspiration of Bib. truth, and the value and rights of man as man, so long obscured, were disclosed. The conscience was liberated and Luther became the champion of individual liberty.

Descartes and Spinoza.—The philosophical writers who most fully express in the domain of pure thought the protestant spirit are Descartes and Spinoza, with whom speculation with regard to man's distinctive nature and obligations took a new departure. Without following the fortunes of philosophy on the continent of Europe, which took a pantheistic form in Germany and a materialistic tone in France (though Rousseau directed the thought of Europe to the constitution of man), we may remark that in England thought assumed a practical complexion, and on the basis of the inquiries of Locke, Berkeley and Hume into the nature and limits of the human understanding, the questions as to the source of moral obligation and the faculty of moral judgment came to the front.

4. English Moralists

British moralists may be classified mainly according to their views on this subject. Beginning with Hobbes, who maintained that man was naturally selfish and that all his actions were self-regarding, Cudworth, More, Wallaston, Shaftesbury, Hutchison, Adam Smith and others discussed the problem, with varying success, of the relation of individual and social virtues, agreeing generally that the right balance between the two is due to a *moral sense* which, like taste or perception of beauty, guides us in things moral. All these intuitional writers fall back upon a native selfish instinct. Selfishness, disguise it as we may, or, as it came to be called, *utility*, is really the spring and standard of action. Butler in his contention for the supremacy and uniqueness of conscience took an independent but scarcely more logical attitude. Both he and all the later British moralists, Paley, Bentham, Mill, suffer from a narrow, artificial psychology which conceives of the various faculties as separate and independent elements lying in man.

5. Utilitarianism

Utilitarianism is a scheme of consequences which finds the moral quality of conduct in the effects and feelings created in the subject. With all their differences of detail the representatives of the theory are at one in regarding the chief end of man as happiness. Bentham and Mill made the attempt to deduce benevolence from the egoistic starting-point. "No reason can be given," says Mill (*Utilitarianism*, ch iv), "why the general happiness is desirable except that each person . . . . desires his own happiness . . . . and the general happiness therefore is a good to the aggregate of all persons." Late utilitarians, dissatisfied with this *non-sequitur* and renouncing the dogma of personal pleasure, maintain that we ought to derive universal happiness because reason bids us (cf Sidgwick, *Methods of Ethics*, III, xiii). But what, we may ask, is this reason, and why should I listen to her voice?

6. Evolutionary Ethics

The intuitional theory has more recently allied itself with the hypothesis of organic evolution. "These feelings of self-love and benevolence are really," says Spencer, "the products of development. The natural instincts and impulses to social good, though existent in a rudimentary animal form, have been evolved through environment, heredity and social institutions to which man through his long history has been subject." But this theory only carries the problem farther back, for, as Green well says (*Proleg. to Ethics*), "that countless generations should have passed during which a transmitted organism was progressively modified by reaction on its surroundings till an eternal consciousness could realize itself . . . . might add to the wonder, but it could not alter the results."

7. Kant

The great rival of the pleasure-philosophy is that which has been styled "duty for duty's sake." This position was first taken by Kant whose principle of the "Categorical Imperative" utterly broke down the theory of "pleasure for pleasure's sake." For Kant, conscience is simply practical reason; and its laws by him are reduced to unity. Reason, though limited in its knowledge of objects to phenomena of the senses, in the region of practice transcends the phenomenal and attains the real. The autonomy of the will carries us beyond the phenomenal into the supersensible world. Here the "Categorical Imperative" or moral law utters its "thou shalt" and prescribes a principle of conduct irrespective of desire or ulterior end. In accordance with the nature of the Categorical Imperative, the formula of all morality is, "Act from a maxim at all times fit for law universal" (*Kritik d. praktischen Vernunft* and *Grundlage zur Metaphysik der Sitten*).

This principle is, however, defective. For while it determines the subjective or formal side of duty, it tells us nothing of the objective side, of the content of duty. We may learn from Kant the grandeur of duty in the abstract and the need of obedience to it, but we do not learn what duty is. Kant's law remains formal, abstract and contentless, without relation to the matter of practical life.

8. German Idealists

To overcome this abstraction, to give content to the law of reason and find its realization in the institutions and relationships of life and society, has been the aim of the later idealistic philosophy which starts from Kant.

(1) *Hegel.*—Following Fichte, for whom morality is action according to the ideas of reason—self-consciousness finding itself in and through a world of deeds—Hegel starts with the Idea as the source of all reality, and develops the conception of Conscious Personality which, by overcoming the antithesis of impulse and thought, gradually attains to the full unity and realization of self in the consciousness of the world and of God. The law of Right or of all ethical ideal is, "Be a person and respect others as persons" (Hegel, *Philosophie des Rechtes*, sec. 31). These views have been worked out in recent British and American works of speculative ethics by Green, Bradley, Caird, McTaggart, Harris, Royce, Dewey, Watson.

Man as a self is rooted in an infinite self or personality. Our individual self-consciousness is derived from and maintained by an infinite eternal and universal self-consciousness. Knowledge is, therefore, but the gradual discovery of mind in things, the progressive realization of the world as the self-manifestation of an infinite Personality with whom the finite intelligence of man is one. Hence morality is the gradual unfolding of an eternal purpose whose whole is the perfection of man.

(2) *Watchwords: Pleasure and Duty.*—We have thus seen that in the history of ethics two great rival watchwords have been sounded—*pleasure* and *duty*, or, to put it another way, egoism and altruism. Both have their justification, yet each taken separately is abstract and one-sided. The problem of ethics is how to harmonize without suppressing these two extremes, how to unite social duty and individual right in a higher unity. We have seen that philosophical ethics has sought a synthesis of these conflicting moments in the higher and more adequate conception of human personality—a personality whose ideals and activities are identified with the eternal and universal personality of God. Christianity also recognizes the truth contained in the several types of ethical philosophy which we have passed under review, but it adds something which is distinctively its own, and thereby gives a new meaning to happiness and to duty, to self and to others.

Christian synthesis: Christianity also emphasizes the realization of personality with all that it implies as the true goal of man; but while Christ bids man "be perfect as God is perfect," He shows us that we only find ourselves as we find ourselves in others; only by dying do we live; and only through profound self-surrender and sacrifice do we become ourselves and achieve the highest good.

III. Principles and Characteristics of Biblical Ethics.—The sketch of the history of ethics just offered, brief as it necessarily is, may serve to indicate the ideas which have shaped modern thought and helped toward the interpretation of the Christian view of life which claims to be the fulfilment of all human attempts to explain the highest good. We now enter upon the third division of our subject which embraces a discussion generally of Bib. ethics, dealing first with the ethics of the OT and next with the leading ideas of the NT.

1. Ethics of the OT

The gospel of Christ stands in the closest relation with Heb religion, and revelation in the NT fulfils and completes the promise given in the OT. We have seen that the thinkers of Greece and Rome have contributed much to Christendom, and have helped to interpret Bible teaching with regard to truth and duty; but there is no such inward relation between them as that which connects Christian ethics with OT morality. Christ himself, and still more the apostle Paul, assumed as a substratum of his teaching the revelation which had been granted to the Jews. The moral and religious doctrines which were comprehended under the designation of "the Law" formed for them, as Paul said (Gal **3** 24.25), a παιδαγωγός, *paidagōgós*, or servant whose function it was to lead them to the school of Christ. In estimating the special character of OT ethics, we are not concerned with questions as to authenticity and dates of the various books, nor with the manifold problems raised by modern Bib. criticism. While not forgetting the very long period which these books cover, involving changes of belief and life and embracing successive stages of political society, it is possible to regard the OT simply as a body of writings which represent the successive ethical ideas of the Hebrews as a people.

(1) *Religious character of Hebrew ethics.*—At the outset we are impressed by the fact that the moral ideal of Judaism was distinctly religious. The moral obligations were conceived as Divine commands and the moral law as a revelation of the Divine will. The religion was monotheistic. At first Jeh may have been regarded merely as a tribal Deity, but gradually this restricted view gave place to a wider conception of God as the God of all men; and as such He was presented by the later prophets. God was for the Jew the supreme source and author of the moral law, and throughout his history duty was embodied in the Divine will. Early in the Pent the note of law is struck, and the fundamental elements of Jewish morality are embedded in the story of Eden and the Fall. God's commandment is the criterion and measure of man's obedience. Evil which has its source and head in a hostile though subsidiary power consists in violation of Jeh's will.

(*a*) The Decalogue: First among the various stages of OT ethic must be mentioned the *Mosaic legislation* centering in the *Decalogue* (Ex **20**; Dt **5**). Whether the Ten Commandments issue from the time of Moses, or are a later summary of duty, they hold a supreme and formative place in the moral teaching of the OT. All, including even the 4th, are purely moral enactments. But they are largely negative, only the 5th rising to positive duty. They are also chiefly external, regulative of outward conduct, forbidding acts but not taking note of intent and desire. The 6th and 7th commandments protect the rights of persons, while the 8th guards outward property. Though these laws may be shown to have their roots and sanctions in the moral consciousness of mankind and as such are applicable to all times and all men, it is clear that they were at first conceived by the Israelites to be restricted in their scope and practice to their own tribes.

(*b*) Civil laws: A further factor in the ethical education of Israel arose from the civil laws of the land. The Book of the Covenant (Ex **20**-**23**), as revealing a certain advance in political legislation and jurisprudence, may be regarded as of this kind. Still the hard legal law of retaliation—"an eye for an eye and a tooth for a tooth"—discloses a barbarous conception of right. But along with the more primitive enactments of revenge and stern justice there are not wanting provisions of a kindlier nature, such as the law of release, the protection of the fugitive, the arrangements for the gleaner and the institution of the Year of Jubilee.

(*c*) Ceremonial laws: Closely connected with the civil laws must be mentioned the ceremonial laws as an element in the moral life of Israel. If the civil laws had reference to the relation of man to his fellows, the ceremonial laws referred rather to the relation of man to God. The prevailing idea with regard to God, next to that of sovereign might, was holiness or separateness. The so-called Priestly Code, consisting of a number of ceremonial enactments, gradually took its place alongside of the Mosaic law, and was established to guard the being of God and the persons of the worshippers from profanation. These had to do (*a*) with *sacrifices* and offerings and forms of ritual which, while they typified and preshadowed the ideas of spiritual sanctity, often degenerated into superstitious practices (cf Am **5** 25.26; Hos **6** 6; Isa **1** 11-13); (*b*) *commands and prohibitions* with regard to personal deportment—"meats and drinks and divers washings." Some of these had a sanitary significance; others guarded the habits of daily life from heathen defilement.

(*d*) Prophecy: The dominant factor of OT ethics lay in *the influence of the prophets.* They and not the priests were the great moralists of Israel. They are the champions of righteousness and integrity in political life, not less than of purity in the individual. They are the witnesses for God and the ruthless denouncers of all idolatry and defection from Him. They comment upon the social vices to which a more developed people is liable. They preach a social gospel and condemn wrongs done by man to man. Government and people are summoned to instant amendment and before the nation is held up a lofty ideal. The prophets are not only the preachers, but also the philosophers of the people, and they direct men's minds to the spiritual and ideal side of things, inveighing against worldliness and materialism.

Under their reflection, theories as to the origin and nature of evil begin to emerge, and the solemnity and worth of life are emphasized. While on the one hand the sense of individual responsibility is dwelt upon, on the other the idea of a hereditary taint of soul is developed, and it is shown that the consequences of sin may affect even the innocent. A man may inherit suffering and incur penalties, not apparently through any fault of his own, but simply by reason of his place in the solidarity of the race. Problems like these awaken deep perplexity which finds a voice not only in the Prophets but also in the Book of Job and in many of the Pss. The solution is sought in the thought that God works through evil, and by its effects evolves man's highest good. These conceptions reach their climax in the Second Isa, and particularly in ch **53**. God is constantly represented as longing to pardon and reinstate man in His favor; and the inadequacy of mere ceremonial as well as the failure of all material means of intercourse with Jeh are repeatedly dwelt upon as preparing the way for the doctrine of salvation. In the Book of Pss—the devotional manual of the people reflecting the moral and religious life of the nation at various stages of its development—the same exalted character of God as a God of righteousness and holiness, hating evil and jealous for devotion, the same profound scorn of sin and the same high vocation of man are prevalent.

(*e*) Books of Wisdom: Without dwelling at length on the ethical ideas of the other writings of the OT—the Books of Wisd, Prov, Job, Eccl—we may remark that the teaching is addressed more to individuals than prophecy is; while not being particularly lofty it is healthy and practical, shrewd, homely common sense. While the motives appealed to are not always the highest and have regard frequently to earthly prosperity and worldly policy, it must not be overlooked that moral practice is also frequently allied with the fear of God, and the right choice of wisdom is represented as the dictate of piety not less than of prudence.

It is to the sapiential books (canonical and apocryphal) that we owe the most significant ethical figures of the OT—*the wise man* and *the fool.* The wise man is he who orders his life in accordance with the laws of God. The fool is the self-willed man, whose life, lacking principle, fails of success. The nature of wisdom lies not in intellectual knowledge so much as in the control of passion and the prudent regulation of desire. The idea of human wisdom is connected in these books with the sublime conception of Divine wisdom which colors both them and the Pss. In some of the finest passages, Wisdom is personified as the counsellor of God in the creation of the world (Prov **8**; Wisd **10**; Job **28**), or the guide which guards the destinies of man (Wisd **10** 15 ff).

If the sapiential books are utilitarian in tone the Book of Eccl is pessimistic. The writer is impressed with the futility of life. Neither pursuit of knowledge nor indulgence in pleasure affords satisfaction. All is vanity. Yet there is an element of submission in this book which only escapes despair by a grim and stolid inculcation of obedience to Divine command.

(*f*) Apocryphal books: In an art. on the Ethics of the Bible some allusion ought to be made to the spirit of the apocryphal books, reflecting as they do the ideas of a considerable period of Jewish history immediately before and contemporaneous with the advent of Christ. While in general there is a distinct recognition of true moral life and a high regard for the moral law, there is no system of ethics nor even a prevailing ethical principle in these books. The collection presents the ideas of no one man or party, or even of one period or locality. The moral ideas of each book require to be considered separately (see special arts.), and they ought to be studied in connection with the philosophy of Philo and generally with the speculation of Alexandria, upon which they exercised considerable influence. The Wisdom of Solomon is supposed by Pfleiderer and others to have affected the Hellenic complexion of Paul's thought and also to have colored the stoic philosophy.

The apocryphal books as a whole do not give prominence to the idea of an ancient covenant and are not dominated by the notion of a redemptive climax to which the other OT books bear witness. As a consequence their moral teaching lacks the spirituality of the OT; and there is an insistence upon outward works rather than inward disposition as essential to righteousness. While wisdom and justice are commended, there is a certain self-satisfaction and pride in one's own virtue, together with, on the part of the few select spirits which attain to virtue, a corresponding disparagement of and even contempt for the folly of the many. In Sir esp. this tone of self-righteous complacency is observable. There is a manifest lack of humility and sense of sin, while the attainment of happiness is represented as the direct result of personal virtue (Sir **14** 14 ff).

The Book of Wisd shows traces of neo-Platonic influences and recognizes the four Platonic virtues (**8** 7), and while admitting the corruption of all men (**9** 12 ff) attributes the causes of evil to other sources than the will, maintaining the Gr dualism of body and soul and the inherent evil of the physical nature of man. The Book of Jth presents in narrative form a highly questionable morality. On the whole it must be recognized that the moral teaching of the Apoc is much below the best teaching of the OT. While Sir gives expression to a true piety, it manifests its want of depth in its treatment of sin and in the inculcation of merely prudential motives to goodness. In general the essence of love is unknown, and the moral temper is far inferior to the ethics of Jesus. It is a mundane morality that is preached. Hope is absent and righteousness is rewarded by long life and prosperity (Tob). Legalism is the chief characteristic (Bar), and Pharisaic ceremonialism on the one hand, and Sadducaic rationalism on the other are the natural and historical consequences of apocryphal teachings.

(2) *Limitations of OT ethics.*—In estimating the ethics of the OT as a whole the fact must not be forgotten that it was preparatory, a stage in the progressive revelation of God's will. We are not surprised, therefore, that, judged by the absolute standard of the NT, the morality of the OT comes short in some particulars. Both in *intent* and *extent,* in spirit and in scope, it is lacking.

(*a*) As to intent: The tendency to dwell upon *the sufficiency of external acts* rather than the necessity of inward disposition, may be remarked; though as time went on, particularly in the later Prophets and some of the Pss, the need of inward purity is insisted upon. While the ideal both for the nation and the individual is an exalted one—"Be ye holy for I am holy"—the aspect in which the character of God is represented is sometimes stern if not repellent (Ex **24**; Nu **14** 18; Gen **18**; 2 S **24** 17). But at the same time there are not wanting more tender features (Isa **1** 17; Mic **6** 8), and the Divine Fatherhood finds frequent expression. Even though the penal code is severe and the ceremonial law stern, a gentler spirit shines through many of its provisions, and protection is afforded to the wage-earner, the poor and the dependent, while the regulations regarding slaves and foreigners and even lower animals are merciful (Dt **24** 14.15; Jer **22** 13.17; Mal **3** 5; Dt **25** 4).

Material motives: Again we have already remarked that the motives to which the OT appeals are often mercenary and material. Material prosperity plays an important part as an inducement to moral conduct, and the good which the pious patriarch contemplates is earthly plenty, something which will enrich himself and his family. At the same time we must not forget that the revelation of God's purpose is progressive, and His dealing with men educative. There is naturally therefore a certain accommodation of the Divine law to the various stages of moral apprehension of the Jewish people, and on the human side a growing sense of the meaning of life as well as an advancing appreciation of the nature of righteousness. Gradually the nation is being carried forward by the promise of material benefits to the spiritual blessings which they enshrine. If even in the messages of the prophets there is not wanting some measure of threats and penalties, we must remember the character of the people they were dealing with—a people wayward and stubborn, whose imaginations could scarcely rise above the material and the temporal. We must judge prophecy by its best, and we shall see that these penalties and rewards which undoubtedly occupy a prominent place in OT ethics were but goads to spur the apathetic. They were not ends in themselves, nor mere arbitrary promises or threats, but instruments subservient to higher ideals.

(*b*) As to extent: With regard to the extent or application of the Heb ideal it must be acknowledged that here also OT ethics is imperfect as compared with the universality of Christianity. God is represented as the God of Israel and not as the God of all men. It is true that a prominent commandment given to Israel is that which Our Lord indorsed: "Thou shalt love thy neighbor as thyself" (Lev **19** 18). The extent of the obligation, however, would seem to be restricted in the language immediately preceding it: "Thou shalt not take vengeance, nor bear any grudge against the children of thy people." It has been pointed out that the term רֵעַ, *rē'a'* is of wider signification than the Eng. word "neighbor," and expresses the idea of friend, and is applied to any person. The wider rendering is enforced by the fact that in vs 33.34 the word "stranger" or "foreigner" is substituted for neighbor. The stranger is thus regarded as the special client of God and is commended to look to Him for protection. However this may be, in practice at least the Jews were not faithful to the humanitarianism of their law, and generally, in keeping with other races of antiquity, showed a tendency to restrict Divine favor within the limits of their own land and to maintain an attitude throughout their history of aloofness and repellent isolation toward foreigners. At the same time the obligation of hospitality was regarded as sacred and was practised in early Heb life (Gen **18** 1-9). Nor must we forget that whatever may have been the Jewish custom the promise enshrined in their revelation implies the unity of mankind (Gen **12** 3), while several of the prophecies and Pss look forward to a world-wide blessing (Isa **61**; Ps **22** 27; **48** 2.10; **87**). In Isa **54** we even read, "God of the whole earth shall he be called." "Everything," it has been said, "is definitely stated except the equality of all men in God's love." The morality of bare justice is also in some measure transcended. The universal Fatherhood of God, if not clearly stated, is implied in many passages, and in Second Isa and Hos there are most tender revelations of Divine mercy though it is mercy to Israel only. But we know that the apostle Paul drew the inference from God's treatment of Israel that His mercy and salvation would extend to all.

We are now prepared to indicate briefly the distinctive features of the ethics of Christianity. As this art. is, however, professedly introductory, and as the ethics of Jesus forms the subject of a separate treatment (see ETHICS OF JESUS), it will not be necessary to offer an elaborate statement of the subject. It will be sufficient to suggest the formative principles and main characteristics. What we have to say may conveniently be divided under three heads: (1) the Christian ideal; (2) the dynamic power; (3) the virtues, duties and spheres of Christian activity.

2. Outline of NT Ethics

(1) *Ethics of Jesus and St. Paul.*—Before, however, entering upon these details, a few words may fittingly be said upon *the relation of the ethics of Jesus to those of St. Paul.* It has been recently alleged that a marked contrast is perceptible between the teaching of Jesus and that of Paul, and that there is a great gulf fixed between the Gospels and the Epistles. Jesus is a moralist, Paul a theologian. The Master is concerned with the conditions of life and conduct; the disciple is occupied with the elaboration of dogma. This view seems to us to be greatly exaggerated. No one can read the Epistles without perceiving the ethical character of a large portion of their teaching and noticing how even the great theological principles which Paul enunciates have a profound moral import. Nor does it seem to us that there is any radical difference in the ethical teaching of Christ and that of the Apostle.

(2) *Character.*—Both lay emphasis on character, and the great words of Christ are the great words of Paul. The inmost spring of the new life of love is the same for both. The great object of the Pauline dialectic is to place man emptied of self in a condition of receptiveness before God. But this idea, fundamental in Paul, is fundamental also in the teaching of Jesus. It is the very first law of the kingdom. With it the Sermon on the Mount begins: "Blessed are the poor in spirit." If we analyze this great saying it surely yields the whole principle of the Pauline argument and the living heart of the Pauline religion. In perfect agreement with this is the fundamental importance assigned both by Jesus and Paul to faith. With both it is something more than mental assent or even implicit confidence in providence. It is the spiritual vision in man of the ideal, the inspiration of life, the principle of conduct.

(3) *Inwardness of motive.*—Again the distinctive note of Christ's ethic is the inwardness of the moral law as distinguished from the externality of the ceremonial law. Almost in identical terms Paul insists upon the need of inward purity, the purity of the inner man of the heart. Once more both lay emphasis upon the fulfilment of our duties to our fellow-men, and both are at one in declaring that man owes to others an even greater debt than duty. Christ's princ ple is, "Thou shalt *love* thy neighbor as thyself"; Paul's injunction is "Owe no man anything but to love one another." Christ transforms morality from a routine into a life; and with Paul also goodness ceases to be a thing of outward rule and becomes the spontaneous energy of the soul. For both all virtues are but the various expressions of a single vital principle. "Love is the fulfilling of the law." The dynamic of devotion according to Christ is, "God's love toward us"; according to Paul, "The love of Christ constraineth us."

Ideal of life: And if we turn from the motive and spring of service to the purpose of life, again we find substantial agreement: "Be ye perfect as your Father in heaven is perfect" is the standard of Christ; to attain to the perfect life—"the prize of the high calling of God in Christ"—is the aim of Paul.

(4) *Ultimate end.*—Nor do they differ in their conception of the ultimate good of the world. Christ's ethical ideal, which He worked for as the realization of the object of His mission, was a redeemed humanity, a reëstablishment of human society, which He designated "the kingdom of God." Paul with his splendid conception of humanity sees that kingdom typified and realized in the Risen Life of his Lord. It is by growing up in all things unto Him who is the Head that the whole body will be perfected in the perfection of its members. And this is what Paul means when he sums up the goal and ideal of all human faith and endeavor—"till we all attain . . . . unto a fullgrown man, unto . . . . the fulness of Christ" (Eph **4** 13). Paul everywhere acknowledges himself to be a pupil of the Master and a teacher of His ways (1 Cor **4** 17). Without pursuing this subject there can be no doubt that in their hidden depths and in their practical life the precepts of the apostle are in essential agreement with those of the Sermon on the Mount, and have a common purpose—the presenting of every man perfect before God (cf Alexander, *Ethics of St. Paul*).

3. The Ethical Ideal

The ethical ideal of the NT is thus indicated. The chief business of ethics is to answer the question, What is man's supreme good? For what should a man live? What, in short, is the ideal of life? A careful study of the NT discloses three main statements implied in what Christ designates "the kingdom of God": man's highest good consists generally in doing God's will and more particularly in the attainment of likeness to Christ and in the realization of human brotherhood—a relation to God, to Christ and to man. The first is the pure white light of the ideal; the second is the ideal realized in the one perfect life which is viewed as standard or norm; the third is the progressive realization of the ideal in the life of humanity which is the sphere of the new life.

(1) *Holiness* as the fulfilment of the Divine will is, as we have seen, Christ's own ideal—Be ye perfect as your Father; and it is Paul's—This also we wish, even your perfection (2 Cor **13** 11). The ideas of righteousness and holiness as the attributes of God are the features of the kingdom of God or of heaven, the realization of which Jesus continually set forth as the highest aim of man; and running through all the epistles of Paul the constant refrain is that ye might *walk worthy of God* who hath called you unto His kingdom and glory. To walk worthy of God, to fulfil His will in all sincerity and purity, is for the Christian as for the Jew the end of all morality. Life has a supreme worth and sacredness because God is its end. To be a man is to fulfil in his own person God's idea of humanity. Before every man, just because he is man with the touch of the Divine hand upon him and his Maker's end to serve, lies this ultimate goal of existence—the realization of the perfect life according to the idea of God.

(2) *Christlikeness.*—If Godlikeness or holiness is the end, Christlikeness is the *norm* or standard in which that end is presented in the Gospel. In Christianity God is revealed to us through Jesus Christ, and the abstract impersonal ideas of holiness and righteousness are transmuted into the features of a living personality whose spirit is to be reproduced in the lives of men. In two different ways Christ is presented in the NT as ideal. He is at once the Pattern and the Principle or Power of the new life.

(*a*) He is the *Pattern* of goodness which is to be reproduced in human lives. It would lead us to trench on the succeeding art. if we were to attempt here a portrayal of the character of Jesus as it is revealed in the Gospels. We only note that it is characteristic of the NT writers that they do not content themselves with imaginative descriptions of goodness, but present a living ideal in the historical person of Jesus Christ.

(*b*) He is also *Principle* of the new life—not example only, but power—the inspiration and cause of life to all who believe (Eph **1** 19.20). Paul says not, "Be like Christ," but "Have the mind in you which was also in Christ." The literal imitation of an example has but a limited reign. To be a Christian is not the mechanical work of a copyist. Kant goes the length of saying that "imitation finds no place in all morality" (*Metaphysics of Ethics*, sec. ii). Certainly the imitation of Christ as a test of conduct covers a quite inadequate conception of the intimate and vital relation Christ bears to humanity. "It is not to copy after Him," says Schultz (*Grundriss d. evangelischen Ethik*, 5), "but to let His life take form in us, to receive His spirit and make it effective, which is the moral task of the Christian." It is as its motive and creative power that Paul presents Him. "Let Christ be born in you." We could not even imitate Christ if He were not already within us. He is our example only because He is something more, the principle of the new life, the higher and diviner self of every man. "He is our life"; "Christ in us the hope of glory."

(3) *Brotherhood and unity of man.*—The emphasis hitherto has been laid on the perfection of the individual. But both Christ and His apostles imply that the individual is not to be perfected alone. No man finds himself till he finds his duties. The single soul is completed only in the brotherhood of the race. The social element is implied in Christ's idea of the Kingdom, and many of the apostolic precepts refer not to individuals but to humanity as an organic whole. The church is Christ's body of which individuals are the members, necessary to one another and deriving their life from the head. The gospel is social as well as individual, and the goal is the kingdom of God, the brotherhood of man. Paul proclaims the unity and equality before God of Greek and Roman, bond and free.

4. The Dynamic Power of the New Life

In the dynamic power of the new life we reach the central and distinguishing feature of Christian ethics. Imposing as was the ethic of Greece, it simply hangs in the air. Plato's ideal state remains a theory only. Aristotle's "virtuous man" exists only in the mind of his creator. Nor was the Stoic more successful in making his philosophy a thing of actuality. Beautiful as these old-time ideals were, they lacked impelling force, the power to change dreams into realities. The problems which baffled Gr philosophy it is the glory of Christianity to have solved. Christian ethics is not a theory. The good has been manifested in a life. The Word was made flesh. It was a new creative force—a spirit given and received, to be worked out and realized in the actual life of common men.

(1) *The dynamic on its Divine side.*—The problem with Paul was, How can man achieve that good which has been embodied in the life and example of Jesus Christ? Without entering into the details of this question it may be said at once that the originality of the gospel lies in this, that it not only reveals the good but discloses the power which makes the good possible in the hitherto unattempted

derivation of the new life from a new birth under the influence of the Spirit of God. Following his Master, when Paul speaks of the new ethical state of believers he represents it as a renewal or rebirth of the Holy Spirit. It is an act of Divine creative power.

Without following out the Pauline argument we may say he connects the working of the Holy Spirit with two facts in the life of Christ, for him the most important in history—the *death* and *resurrection* of Our Lord. Here we are in the region of dogmatics, and it does not concern us to present a theory of the atonement. All we have to do with is the fact that between man and the new life lies *sin*, which must be overcome and removed, both in the form of guilt and power, before reconciliation with God can be effected. The deed which alone meets the case is the *sacrifice of Christ*. In virtue of what Christ has achieved by His death a fundamentally new relationship exists. God and man are now in full moral accord and vital union.

But not less important as a factor in creating the new life is the *resurrection*. It is the seal and crown of the sacrifice. It was the certainty that He had risen that gave to Christ's death its sacrificial value. "If Christ be not risen ye are yet in your sins." The new creature is the work of Christ. But His creative power is not an external influence. It is an inner spirit of life. All that makes life life indeed—an exalted, harmonious and completed existence—is derived from the Holy Spirit through the working of the crucified risen Christ.

(2) *The dynamic on its human side.*—Possession of power implies obligation to use it. The force is given; it has to be appropriated. The spirit of Christ is not offered to free a man from the duties and endeavors of the moral life. Man is not simply the passive recipient of the Divine energy. He has to make it his own and work it out by an act of free resolution. When we inquire what constitutes the subjective or human element, we find in the NT two actions which belong to the soul entering upon the new world in Christ—*repentance* and *faith*. These are complementary and constitute what is commonly called conversion. *Repentance* in the NT is a turning away in sorrow and contrition from a life of sin and a breaking with evil under the influence of Christ. If repentance looks back and forsakes, *faith* looks forward and accepts. In general it is the outgoing of the whole man toward his Lord, the human power or energy by which the individual receives and makes his own the life in Christ. It is not merely intellectual acceptance or moral trust; it is above all appropriating energy. It is the power of a new obedience. As the principle of moral appropriation it has its root in personal trust and its fruit in Christian service. Faith, in short, is the characteristic attitude and action of the whole Christian personality in its relation to the spiritual good offered to it in Christ.

It but remains to indicate how this new power manifests itself in character and in practical conduct. Character is expressed in *virtue*, and duty is conditioned by station and relationships.

5. Virtues, Duties and Spheres of the New Life

(1) *The virtues.*—The systematic enumeration of the virtues is one of the most difficult tasks of ethics. Neither in ancient nor in modern times has complete success attended attempts at classification. Plato's list is too meager. Aristotle's lacks system and is marred by omission. Nowhere in Scripture is there offered a complete description of all the virtues that flow from faith. But by bringing Christ's words and the apostolic precepts together we have a rich and suggestive cluster (Mt **5**, **6**; Gal **5** 22.23; Col **3** 12.13; Phil **4** 8; 1 Pet **2** 18.19; **4** 7.8; 2 Pet **1** 5–8; 1 Jn **3**; Jude). We may make a threefold classification:

(*a*) The *heroic virtues*, sometimes called the cardinal, handed down from antiquity—wisdom, fortitude, temperance, justice. While these were accepted and dwelt upon, Christianity profoundly modified their character so that they became largely new creations. "The old moral currency was still kept in circulation, but it was gradually minted anew" (Strong).

(*b*) The *amiable virtues*, which are not merely added on to the pagan, but being incorporated with them, give an entirely new meaning to those already in vogue. While Plato lays stress on the intellectual or heroic features of character, Christianity brings to the foreground the gentler virtues. Two reasons may have induced the Christian writers to dwell more on the self-effacing side of character: partly as a protest against the spirit of militarism and the worship of material power prevalent in the ancient world; and chiefly because the gentler self-sacrificing virtues more truly expressed the spirit of Christ. The one element in character which makes it beautiful and effective and Christlike is *love*—the element of sacrifice. Love evinces itself in *humility* which lays low all vaunting ambition and proud self-sufficiency. Closely allied to humility are *meekness* and its sister, long-suffering—the attitude of the Christian in the presence of trial and wrong. With these again are connected *contentment* and *patience* and *forbearance*, gentle and kindly consideration for others. Lastly there is the virtue of *forgiveness*. For it is not enough to be humble and meek; we have a duty toward wrongdoers. We must be ready to forget and forgive (Rom **12** 20). "Be ye kind one to another, tenderhearted, forgiving each other, even as God also in Christ forgave you" (Eph **4** 32).

(*c*) The *theological virtues* or Christian graces—*faith, hope, charity*. Some have been content to see in these three graces the summary of Christian excellence. They are fundamental in Christ's teaching and the apostolic combination of them may have had its basis in some lost word of the Master (Harnack). These graces cannot be separated. They are all of a piece. He who has faith has also love, and he who has faith and love cannot be devoid of hope. *Love* is the first and last word of apostolic Christianity. No term is more expressive of the spirit of Christ. Love was practically unknown in the ancient world. Pre-Christian philosophy exalted the intellect but left the heart cold. Love in the highest sense is the discovery and creation of the gospel, and it was reserved for the followers of Jesus to teach men the meaning of charity and to find in it the law of freedom. It is indispensable to true Christian character. Without it no profession of faith or practice of good deeds has any value (1 Cor **13**). It is the fruitful source of all else that is beautiful in conduct. *Faith* itself works through love and finds in its activity its outlet and exercise. If character is formed by faith it lives in love. And the same may be said of *hope*. It is a particular form of faith which looks forward to a life that is to be perfectly developed and completed in the future. Hope is faith turned to the future—a vision inspired and sustained by love.

(2) *The duties.*—Of the duties of the Christian life it is enough to say that they find their activity in the threefold relationship of the Christian to self, to his fellow-men and to God. This distinction is not of course quite logical. The one involves the other. Self-love implies love of others, and all duty may be regarded as duty to God. The individual and society are so inextricably bound together in the kingdom of love that neither can reach its goal without the other.

(*a*) *Duties toward self* are, however, plainly recognized in the NT. Our Lord's commandment, "Thou shalt love thy neighbor as thyself," makes a rightly conceived self-love the measure of love to one's neighbor. But the duties of self-regard are only lightly touched upon, and while the truth that the soul has an inalienable worth is insisted upon, to be constantly occupied with the thought of oneself is a symptom of morbid egoism and not a sign of healthy personality. But the chief reason why the NT does not enlarge upon the duty of self-culture is that according to the spirit of the gospel the true realization of self is identical with self-sacrifice. Only as a man loses his life does he find it. Not by anxiously standing guard over one's soul but by dedicating it freely to the good of others does one realize one's true self.

At the same time several self-respecting duties are recognized, of which mention may be made: (i) *stability* of purpose or singleness of aim; (ii) *independence* of other's opinion; (iii) *supremacy of conscience* and a proper self-estimate. In this connection may be noticed also the Christian's proper regard for the body which, as the temple of God, is not to be despised but presented as a living sacrifice; his attitude to worldly goods; his obligation to work; his right to recreation; and his contentment with his station—all of which duties are to be interpreted by the apostolic principle, "Use the world as not abusing it." The Christian ideal is not asceticism or denial for its own sake. Each must make the best of himself and the most of life's trust. All the faculties, possessions, pursuits and joys of life are to be used as vehicles of spiritual service, instruments which make a man a fit subject of the kingdom of God to which he belongs.

(*b*) *Duties in relation to others*, or brotherly love, are defined as to their extent and limit by the Christian's relation to Christ. Their chief manifestations are: (i) *justice*, involving (α) respect for others, negatively refraining from injury and positively yielding deference and honor, (β) truthfulness, in word and deed, "speaking the truth in love," (γ) just judgment, avoiding censoriousness and intolerance; (ii) *kindness* or goodness, embracing (α) sympathy, (β) service and (γ) practical beneficence which provides for physical need, administers comfort and gives, by example and direct instruction, edification; (iii) *patience*, comprising (α) forbearance, (β) peaceableness.

(*c*) *Duties in relation to God:* Here morality runs up into religion and duty passes into love. Love rests on knowledge of God as revealed in Christ, and expresses itself in devotion. Love to God is expressed generally in (i) thankfulness, (ii) humility, (iii) trustfulness; and particularly in worship (sacraments and prayers), and in witness-bearing—adorning the doctrine by beauty of life.

(3) *Spheres and relationships.*—Of the various spheres and relationships in which the Christian finds opportunity for the exercise and cultivation of his spiritual life we can only name, without enlarging upon them, the *family*, the *state* and the *church*. Each of these spheres demands its own special duties and involves its own peculiar discipline. While parents owe to their children care and godly nurture, children owe their parents obedience. The attitude of the individual to the state and of the state to the individual are inferences which may be legitimately drawn from NT teaching. It is the function of the state not merely to administer justice but to create and foster those agencies and institutions which work for the amelioration of the lot and the development of the weal of its citizens, securing for each full liberty to make the best of his life. On the other hand it is the duty of the individual to realize his civic obligations as a member of the social organism. The state makes its will dominant through the voice of the people, and as the individuals are so the commonwealth will be.

6. Conclusion

Absoluteness, inwardness and universality.—In closing we may say that the three dominant notes of Christian ethics are, its *absoluteness*, its *inwardness* and its *universality*. The gospel claims to be supreme in life and morals. For the Christian no incident of experience is secular and no duty insignificant, because all things belong to God and all life is dominated by the Spirit of Christ. The uniqueness and originality of the ethics of Christianity are to be sought, however, not so much in the range of its practical application as in the unfolding of an ideal which is at once the power and pattern of the new life. That ideal is Christ in whom the perfect life is disclosed and through whom the power for its realization is communicated. Life is a force, and character is a growth which takes its rise in and expands from a hidden seed. Hence in Christian ethics all apathy, passivity and inaction, which occupy an important place in the moral systems of Buddhism, Stoicism, and even mediaeval Catholicism, play no part. On the contrary all is life, energy and unceasing endeavor.

There are many details of modern social life with which the NT does not deal: problems of present-day ethics and economics which cannot be decided by a direct reference to chapter and verse, either of the Gospels or Epistles. But St. Paul's great principles of human solidarity; of equality in Christ; of freedom of service and love; his teachings concerning the church and the kingdom of God, the family and the state; his precepts with regard to personal purity, the use of wealth and the duty of work, contained the germs of the subsequent renewal of Europe and still contain the potency of social and political transformation.

LITERATURE.—General works on Ethics: Lotze, Paulsen, Wundt, Green, Sidgwick, Stephen, Dewey and Tufts, Palmer, Bowne, Mezer; Harris, *Moral Evolution;* Dubois; Randall, *Theory of Good and Evil;* Calderwood, *Handbook of Moral Philosophy;* Muirhead, *Elementary Ethics;* Sutherland, *Origin and Growth of Moral Instinct;* Simmel, *Einleitung in die Moralwissenschaft;* Givycky, *Moralphilosophie;* Guyot, *La morale;* Janet, *Theory of Morals* (tr); Mackenzie, *Manual of Ethics;* Eucken, works generally; Hensel, *Hauptproblem der Ethik;* Lipps, *Die ethischen Grundfragen;* Natorp, *Socialpädagogik;* Schuppe, *Grundzüge der Ethik u. Rechtsphilosophie;* Schwarz, *Das sittliche Leben;* Wentscher, *Ethik.*

General History: See Histories of Philosophy; Zeller, Erdmann, Windelband, Maurice, Turner, Weber, Rogers, Alexander; Jodl, *Geschichte der Ethik in der neueren Philosophie.*

Works on theological or Christian Ethics—OT: Dillmann, Baudissin, Bertmann, *Geschichte der christlichen Sitte;* König, *Hauptprobleme der AT Religions-Geschichte;* Delitzsch, Riehm, Kuenen; Mozley, *Ruling Ideas in Early Ages;* Hessey, *Moral Difficulties in the Bible;* Moore, in *Lux mundi;* Ladd, *Doctrine of Sacred Scripture;* Robertson, *Early Religion of Israel;* Caillard, *Progressive Revelation;* Schultz, *OT Theology* (ET); Bruce, *Ethics of the OT;* N. Smyth, *Christian Ethics;* Stanton; Strong.

NT and Christianity: Martinsen, Wuttke, Schleiermacher, Rothe, Dorner, H. Weiss, Harlen, Hofmann, Frank, Luthardt, Beck, Kübel, Kähler, Pfleiderer, Schultz, Köstlin; Herrmann, *Faith and Morals; Communion of the Christian with God;* Thomas, Jacoby, Lemme, Strong, Knight, N. Smyth; Ottley in *Lux mundi* and *Christian Ideas and Ideals;* W. L. Davidson, *Christian Ethics*, Guild Series; W. T. Davidson, *Christian Interpretation of Life* and *Christian Conscience;* Mackintosh; Murray, *Handbook of Christian Ethics;* Maurice, *Social Morality;* Nash, *Ethics and Revelation;* Dobschütz, *Christian Life in the Primitive Church;* Clark, *Christian Method of Ethics;* Mathews, *The Church and the Changing Order;* Freemantle, *The World as the Subject of Redemption; The Gospel in Secular Life;* Sladden, *Applied Christianity;* Leckie, *Life and Religion;* Rauschenbusch, *Christianity and the Social Order;* Peile, *The Reproach of the Gospel;* Coe, *Education in Religion and Morals;* Haering, *The Ethics of the Christian Life* (ET); Tymms, *Ancient Faith in Modern Light;* Harris, *God, the Creator;* Bovon, *Morale chrétienne;* Wace, *Christianity and Morality;* Kidd, *Morality and Religion;* Drummond, *Via, Veritas, Vita;* Hatch, *Greek Ideas and the Christian Church;* Matheson, *Landmarks of NT Morality.*

Works on NT Theology; also contain section on Ethics; Weiss, Holtzmann, Beyschlag; Harnack, *Das Wesen, or What Is Christianity?*; Stevens; Wernle, *The Beginnings of Christianity;* Adeney, Gould, Gardner, Bosworth, Briggs; Caird, *Evolution of Religion.*

Works on the Teaching of Jesus: esp. Wendt, Bruce, Stevens, Horton, Jackson, Swete, Latham, *Pastor Pastorum;* Tolstoy; Jülicher. See next art. for the works on the Ethics of Jesus.

Special works on Apostolic Ethics: Ernesti, *Ethik des Apostels Paulus;* A. Alexander, *The Ethics of St. Paul;* Weinel, *Paul;* Baur, *Paulinismus;* Joh. Weiss, *Paul and Jesus.*

History of Christian Ethics: Wuttke, Sidgwick, Ziegler, Luthardt, Thomas; Martineau, *Types of Ethical Theory;* Gass; Scharling, *Christliche Sittenlehre;* Lecky, *History of European Morals;* Pfleiderer.

ARCHIBALD ALEXANDER

ETHICS, eth′iks, OF JESUS:

I. In the Synoptic Gospels.—If, following the custom prevalent at present, we adopt, as the general name for the teaching of Jesus in the Synoptists, the Kingdom of God, then the divisions of His ethical teaching will be (1) the Blessings of the Kingdom, (2) the Character of the Subjects, (3) the Commandments of the King.

1. The Blessings of the Kingdom

(1) *Nature of the kingdom.*—"The Kingdom of God" was not a phrase invented by Jesus. It was used before Him by the Baptist. Its proximate source, for both Jesus and John, was the prophet Daniel, who uses it in very striking passages (**2** 44.45; **7** 13.14). The idea of a kingdom of God goes back to the very commencement of the monarchy in Israel, when the prophet Samuel told those who demanded a king that Jeh was their king, and that they should desire no other. Through all the subsequent history of the monarchy, which was, on the whole, so disappointing to patriotic and pious minds, the conviction lingered that, if God Himself were king, all would be well; and, when at length the Heb state was destroyed and the people were carried into captivity, the prophets still believed that for their country there was a future and a hope, if only Jeh would take to Himself His great power and reign. In the period between the OT and the NT such sentiments so greatly prevailed that Schürer has compiled, from the apocryphal literature, a kind of Messianic creed, embracing no fewer than eleven articles, which he supposes to have prevailed before the Advent. It may be doubtful how far such beliefs had taken possession of the general mind. Many of the Sadducees were too satisfied with things as they were to concern themselves about such dreams. But the Pharisees undoubtedly gave a large place in their minds to Messianic expectations, and for these the Zealots were ready to fight. It is, however, to the *prosdechómenoi,* as they are called, because they were "waiting for the consolation of Israel," that we must look for the purest expression of this heritage derived from the piety of the past. In the hymns at the beginning of the Gospels of Mt and Lk, with which the birth of Jesus was greeted, we encounter an intense and lofty conception of the kingdom of God; and, as the earthly home in which Jesus grew up belonged to this select section of the population, there is little doubt that it was here He imbibed both His Messianic ideas and the phraseology in which these were expressed. His use of the term, the kingdom of God, has sometimes been spoken of as an accommodation to the beliefs and language of His fellow-countrymen. But it was native to Himself; and it is not unlikely that the very commonness of it in the circle in which He grew up rendered Him unconscious of the difference between His own conception and that which prevailed outside of this circle. For, as soon as He began to preach and to make known the sentiments which He included within this phrase, it became manifest that He and His contemporaries, under a common name, were thinking of entirely different things. They emphasized the first half of the phrase—"the kingdom"; He the second—"of God." They were thinking of the external attributes of a kingdom—political emancipation, an army, a court, subject provinces; He of the doing of God's will on earth as it is done in heaven. Even He had felt, at one stage, the glamor of their point of view, as is manifest from the account of the Temptation in the Wilderness; but He had decisively rejected it, resolving not to commence with an external framework on a large scale, to be subsequently filled with character, but to begin with the individual, and trust to time and Providence for visible success. The triumphal entry into Jerus proves that He never abandoned the claim to be the fulfiller of all the OT predictions about the kingdom of God; but His enemies not unnaturally interpreted the failure of that attempt as a final demonstration that their own view had been the correct one all along. Still, God was not mocked, and Jesus was not mocked. When, at the end of a generation, the Jewish state sank into ruin and the city by which Jesus was martyred had been destroyed, there were springing up, all over the world, communities the members of which were bound more closely to one another than the members of any other kingdom, obeyed the same laws and enjoyed the same benefits, which they traced up to a King ruling in the heavens, who would appear again on the great white throne, to be the Judge of quick and dead.

(2) *Blessedness of the kingdom.*—The enemies of Jesus may be said to have carried out to the bitter end their conception of the kingdom of God, when they nailed Him to a tree; but, in the face of opposition, He carried out His own conception of it too, and He never abandoned the practice of employing this phrase as a comprehensive term for all the blessings brought by Him to mankind. He used, however, other nomenclature for the same objects, such as Gospel, Peace, Rest, Life, Eternal Life, Blessedness. His exposition of the last of these, at the commencement of the Sermon on the Mount, is highly instructive. Seldom, indeed, has the structure of the Beatitudes been clearly understood. Each of them is an equation, in which "blessed" stands on the one side and on the other two magnitudes—the one contained in the subject of the sentence, such as "the poor in spirit," "the meek," and so on; and the other contained in a qualifying clause introduced by "for." Sometimes one of these magnitudes may be a minus quantity,

as in "they that mourn"; but the other is so large a positive magnitude that the two together represent a handsome plus, which thoroughly justifies the predicate "blessed." It is remarkable that the first and the eighth of the reasons introduced by "for" are the same: "for theirs is the kingdom of heaven," justifying the statement that this is Christ's own name for the blessedness brought by Him to the world; and the sentences between these, introduced in the same way, may be looked upon as epexegetic of this great phrase. They embrace such great conceptions as comfort, mercy, the inheritance of the earth, the vision of God and sonship, which are all certainly blessings of the kingdom; and the list does not finish without mentioning a great reward in heaven—an immortal hope, which is the greatest blessing of all.

(3) *Righteousness—its contrasts.*—If the preacher of the Sermon on the Mount was to expound at length any one of these bright conceptions, it might have been expected to be the kingdom of God itself; and this we should have desired. But the one to which this honor fell has still to be mentioned. It is "righteousness." In one of the Beatitudes the speaker had promised that to be filled with this should be part of the blessedness which He was expounding; and, when He had finished the Beatitudes, He turned back to this conception and devoted the rest of His discourse to its interpretation. Nowhere else, in the reports of His preaching which have come down to us, is there to be found an exposition so sustained and thorough. There is no better way of describing a new thing, with which those who listen are unfamiliar, than to contrast it with something with which they are perfectly acquainted; and this was the method adopted by Jesus. He contrasted the righteousness with which the subjects of the kingdom were to be blessed with the figure of the righteous man familiar to them, first, in the discourses of the scribes, to which they were wont to listen in the synagogue, and secondly, in the example of the Pharisees, to whom they were wont to look up as the patterns of righteousness. It is well known what ample opportunities He found, by means of this felicitous disposition, for probing to the very depths of morality, as well as for covering His opponents with ridicule and exploding the honor in which they stood with the masses. The whole of this scheme is, however, exhausted long before the Sermon comes to a close; and the question is, whether, in the latter half of the Sermon, He still keeps up the exposition of righteousness by contrasting it with the ordinary course of the world. I am inclined to think that this is the case, and that the key to the latter half of the discourse is the contrast between righteousness and worldliness. The doctrine, at all events, which issues from the whole discussion is that the righteousness promised is distinguished by three characteristics—inwardness, as distinguished from the externality of those who believed morality to extend to outward words and deeds alone, and not to the secret thoughts of the heart; secrecy, as distinguished from the ostentation of those who blew a trumpet before them when they were doing their alms; and naturalness, like that of the flower or the fruit, which grows spontaneously from a healthy root, without forcing. See SERMON ON THE MOUNT.

(4) *Apocalyptic theories.*—This substitution of righteousness for the kingdom in the greatest public discourse which has come down to us is a significant indication of the direction in which the mind of Jesus was tending, as He drew away from the notions and hopes of contemporary Judaism. It is evident that He was filling the idea of the kingdom more and more with religious and moral contents, and emptying it of political and material elements. There are scholars, indeed, at the present day, who maintain that His conception of the kingdom was futuristic, and that He was waiting all the time for an apocalyptic manifestation, which never came. He was, they think, expecting the heavens to open and the kingdom to descend ready made to the earth, like the New Jerusalem in the Apocalypse. But this is to assume toward Jesus exactly the attitude taken up toward Him in His own day by Pharisees and high priests, and it degrades Him to the level of an apocalyptic dreamer. It ignores many sayings of His, of which the parable of the Mustard Seed may be taken as an example, which prove that He anticipated for Christianity a long development such as it has actually passed through; and it fails to do justice to many passages in His teaching where He speaks of the kingdom as already come. Of the latter the most remarkable is where He says, "The kingdom of God is within you"—a statement preceded by a distinct rejection of the notion of an apocalyptic manifestation; for the word "observation," which He employs in describing the way in which the kingdom is not to come, is an astronomical term, describing precisely such a phenomenon as He is supposed by such scholars as John Weiss and Schweitzer to have been expecting. The more it became evident that He was not to command the homage of the nation, the more did He devote Himself to the education of the Twelve, that they might form the nucleus of His kingdom upon earth; and it was certainly not with apocalyptic visions that He fed their receptive minds.

2. The Character of the Subjects of the Kingdom

(1) *Conditions of entrance.*—The righteousness described so comprehensively in the Sermon on the Mount is not infrequently spoken of as the condition of entrance to the kingdom of God; but this is altogether to misunderstand the mind of Jesus. The righteousness described by Him is the gift of God to those who are already inside the kingdom; for it is the supreme blessing for the sake of which the kingdom is to be sought; and the condition imposed on those who are outside is not the possession of righteousness, but rather a bottomless sense of the want of it. The more utterly they feel their own lack of righteousness, the more ready are they for entrance into the kingdom. They must "hunger and thirst after righteousness." It has been remarked already that the description, in the Beatitudes, of the character of the candidates for the kingdom is sometimes of a negative character; and indeed, this is the account in the teaching of Jesus generally of those whom He attracts to Himself. They are drawn by a sense of boundless need in themselves and by the apprehension of an equivalent fulness in Him; He calls those "that labor and are heavy laden," that He may give them rest.

(2) *Christ's attitude to sin.*—The first word of the prophetic message in the OT was always the denunciation of sin; and only after this had done its work did the vision of a good time coming rise on the horizon. The same was repeated in the message of John the Baptist; and it did not fail to reappear in the teaching of Jesus, though His mode of treating the subject was entirely His own. He did not, like the prophets, take up much time with convicting gross and open sinners. Perhaps He thought that this had been sufficiently done by His predecessors; or, perhaps He refrained because He understood the art of getting sinners to convict themselves. Yet, in the parable of the Prodigal Son, He showed how profoundly He understood the nature and the course of the commonest sins. If, however, He thus spared transgressors who had no covering for their wickedness, He made up for this leniency by the vigor and even violence with which

He attacked those who hid their sins under a cloak of hypocrisy. Never was there a prophetic indignation like that with which He assailed such sinners in Mt **23**; and He shaped the same charges into an unforgettable picture in the parable of the Pharisee and the Publican. He never named the Sadducees in the same unreserved manner as He thus designated their antagonists; but in more parables than one it is possible that He had them in view. The Unjust Judge was probably a Sadducee; and so was the Rich Man at whose gate the beggar Lazarus was wont to sit. The sin of the Sadducees, at all events, did not escape His prophetic animadversion. In Lk esp. He alludes with great frequency to worldliness and the love of money as cankers by which the life of the human soul is eaten out and its destiny destroyed. Thus did Jesus exercise the prophetic office of denouncing all the sins of His time; and He showed what, in this respect, He thought of mankind in general when He began a sentence with, "If ye then, being evil" (Lk **11** 13), and when He gave the dreadful description of the heart of man which begins, "Out of the heart come forth evil thoughts" (Mt **15** 19).

(3) *Attainment of righteousness.*—To all serious students of the Sermon on the Mount it is well known that the popular notion of it, as containing a simple religion and an easy-going morality, is utterly mistaken; on the contrary, the righteousness sketched by the Preacher is far loftier than that ever conceived by any other religious teacher whatever. Not only, however, does He thus propose to conduct human beings to a platform of attainment higher than any attempted before, but He, at the same time, recognizes that He must begin with men lower than almost any others have allowed. It is here that the ethics of Jesus differ from those of the philosophers. He takes the task much more seriously; and, as the ascent from the one extreme to the other is much longer, so the means of reaching the goal are much more difficult. Philosophers, assuming that man is equal to his own destiny, lay the demands of the moral law before him at once, taking it for granted that he is able to fulfil them; but the path adopted by Jesus is more remote and humbling. There are in it steps or stages which, in His teaching, it is easy to discern.

(*a*) Repentance: The first of these is repentance. This was a watchword of all the prophets: after sin had been denounced, penitence was called for; and no hope of improvement was held out until this had been experienced. In the message of John the Baptist it held the same place; and, in one of the Gospels, it is expressly stated that Jesus began His ministry by repeating this watchword of His predecessor. Not a few of the most touching scenes of His earthly ministry exhibit penitents at His feet, the most moving of them all being that of the woman who was "a sinner"; and, in the parable of the Prodigal Son, we have a full-length picture of the process of repentance.

(*b*) Faith: The second step is faith—a word of constant recurrence in the teaching of Jesus. In many cases it is connected with His healing ministry; but this was a parable of a more interior ministry for the soul. In many cases it formed a school of preparation for the other, as in the case of the man borne of four, who was brought to Christ for the healing of his body, but was presented, in addition, with the gift of the forgiveness of his sins. In healing him Jesus expressly claimed the power of forgiving sins; and, in His great saying at the institution of the Lord's Supper, He showed the connection which this was to have with His own death.

(*c*) Imitation of Christ—Service: Instead of speaking of faith and of believing, Jesus frequently spoke of "coming" to Himself; and then followed the invitation to "follow" Him, which, accordingly, is the third stage. Following Him meant, in many cases, lit. leaving home and occupation, in order to accompany Him from place to place, as He journeyed through the land; and, as this involved sacrifice and self-denial, He frequently combined with "following" the invitation to take up "the cross." But by degrees this literal meaning dropped away from the invitation, or at least became secondary to that of imitation, which must be the only meaning when St. Paul, adopting the language of his Master, calls upon men and women to be "followers" of him, as he was of Christ. It is seldom that Jesus, in so many words, calls upon others to imitate Himself; indeed, He does so less frequently than St. Paul; but it is implied in following Him, if not lit. expressed; and it was a direct consequence of keeping company with Him and coming under the influence of His example. It is highly characteristic that, in the only place where He directly calls upon others to "learn" from Him, the virtue to which He draws attention is meekness—"Learn of me; for I am meek and lowly in heart." The same quality was often emphasized by Him, when He was describing the character which He wished to see exhibited by others, "For every one that exalteth himself shall be humbled; and he that humbleth himself shall be exalted" (Lk **14** 11). In spite, however, of the importance thus attached by Him to humility, He not only combined with it, as has been pointed out by Bushnell, in his famous chapter on the character of Christ in *Nature and the Supernatural*, the most stupendous personal claims, but also attributed to His followers a position of personal distinction among men, and called upon them to perform services far beyond the reach of ordinary mortals, saying to them, "Ye are the salt of the earth," "Ye are the light of the world," and ordering them to make disciples of all nations. The principle by which this apparent contradiction is bridged over is another favorite idea of His teaching, namely, Service. He who is able to serve others on a large scale is, in a sense, superior to those he serves, because he is furnished with the resources of which they stand in need; yet he places himself beneath them and forgets his own claims in ministering to their necessities. There are few of the utterances of Jesus in which the very genius of His ethical system is more fully expressed than that in which He contrasts greatness as it is conceived among men of the world with greatness as He conceives it and His followers must learn to conceive it: "Ye know that the princes of the Gentiles exercise dominion over them, and they that are great exercise authority upon them. But it shall not be so among you: but whosoever will be great among you, let him be your minister; and whosoever will be chief among you, let him be your servant." Of this difficult rule, He was able to add, He Himself had given, and was still to give, the most perfect illustration; for "even the Son of man came not to be ministered unto, but to minister, and to give his life a ransom for many" (Mt **20** 25 ff AV).

This reminds us that, while the character of the subjects of the kingdom is to be learned from the words of Jesus, it may be also derived from His example. That which He demanded from others He fulfilled in His own conduct; and thus the dry precepts of the moral law were invested with the charm of a living personality. Brief as the records of His life are, they are wonderfully rich in instruction of this kind; and it is possible, by going through them with study and care, to form a clear image of how He bore Himself in all the departments of human life—in the home, in the state, in the church, as a friend, in society, as a man of prayer, as a student of Scripture, as a worker, as a sufferer, as a philanthropist, as a winner of souls, as a preacher, as a teacher, as a controversialist, and so on. This is the modern imitation of Christ—that of the details of His earthly existence—the *Imitation* of à Kempis was an imitation of the cosmical history of the Son of God, as He moves on His Divine mission from heaven to the cross and back to the throne of the universe. See the writer's *Imago Christi.*

3. The Commandments of the King

The great commandments.—In accordance with Scriptural usage, Jesus called by the name of "commandments" those actions which we call "duties"; and He has made this part of our subject easy by reducing the commandments to two: "Thou shalt love the Lord thy God with all thy heart, and with all thy soul, and with all thy mind. This is the great and first commandment. And a second like unto it is this, Thou shalt love thy neighbor as thyself" (Mt **22** 37–39). He did not invent either of these commandments; for both occur in the OT (Dt **6** 5; Lev **19** 18). There, however, they lie far apart and are buried out of sight. The second of them was still more deeply buried under a misinterpretation of the scribes, to which reference is made in the Sermon on the Mount. Jesus rescued them from oblivion; He showed the vital and indissoluble connection between the sentiments which they enforce—love of God and love of man—which had been long and violently separated; and He lifted them up into the firmament of ethics, to shine forever as the sun and moon of duty.

(*a*) Love to God: It has been denied by some writers on Christian ethics that there can be any such thing as duties to God, and by writers on philosophical ethics love to God is not generally regarded as coming within the scope of their science. But the duty of man is concerned with all the objects, and esp. all the beings, he is related to; and to Jesus the outflow of man's heart toward Him who is the author of his being and the source of all his blessings seemed the most natural of actions. "I love Jeh" was a sentiment to which mankind had risen even in the OT (Ps **116** 1), where it corresponds with not a few expressions of the Divine love equally fervent; and it is not a figure of speech at all when Jesus demands love for His Father from heart and soul, strength and mind.

Love to God involves, however, love to what may be called the Things of God, toward which Jesus always manifested tenderness and honor. Those who are not themselves ecclesiastically minded have, indeed, taken it for granted that Jesus was indifferent, if not hostile, to the objects and actions by which the Almighty is honored; and it is often said that the only service of God which mattered in His eyes was the service of man. But, although, like the prophets before Him, Jesus exposed with withering rebuke the hypocrisy of those who put ritual in the place of righteousness, it requires no more than a glance at His sayings, and the other records of His life, to perceive that His mind was occupied no less with duties to God than with duties to men; indeed, the former bulk more largely in His teaching. The only arrangement of religion with which He seems out of sympathy is the Sabbath; but this was due to a peculiarity of the times; and it is quite conceivable that in other circumstances He might have been a strenuous supporter of Sabbath observance. If there had been in His day a Sadducean attempt to rob the people of the day of rest, He would have opposed it as strenuously as He did the Pharisaic attempt to make it a burden and a weariness to the common man. By declaring the Sabbath to have been made for man (Mk **2** 27) He recognized that it was instituted at the beginning and intended for the entire course of man's existence upon earth. With the other things of God, such as His House, His Word, and His Worship, He manifested sympathy equally by word and deed; He frequented both the Temple and the synagogue; so imbued was His mind with the lit. of the OT that He spoke habitually in its spirit and phraseology, having its figures and incidents perfectly at command; and by both precept and example He taught others to pray.

Nothing is commoner than the statement that Jesus had nothing to do with the founding of the church or the arrangement of its polity; but this is a subjective prejudice, blind to the facts of the case. Jesus realized that the worship of the OT was passing away, but He was Himself to replace it by a better order. He did not merely breathe into the air a spirit of sweetness and light; if this had been all He did, Christianity would soon have vanished from the earth; but He provided channels in which, after His departure, His influence should flow to subsequent generations. Not only did He found the church, but He appointed the most important details of its organization, such as preaching and the sacraments; and He left the Twelve behind Him not only as teachers, but as those who were able to instruct other teachers also. There may be ecclesiastical arrangements which are worked in a spirit far removed from the love of God; and such are of course contrary to the mind of Christ; but the love of God, if it is strong, inevitably overflows into the things of God, and cannot, in fact, permanently exist without them.

(*b*) Duty to man: As has been hinted above, the sayings of Our Lord about the details of duty to man are less numerous than might have been expected, but what may be lacking in numbers is made up for in originality and comprehensiveness. Many single sayings, like the Golden Rule (Mt **7** 12) and the lovely word about a cup of cold water given in the name of Christ (**10** 42), are revolutionary in the ethical experience of mankind; and so are such parables as the Good Samaritan, the Prodigal Son and the Unmerciful Servant. The commandment to love enemies and to forgive injuries (**5** 43–48), if not entirely novel, received a prominence it had never possessed before. The spirit of all such sayings of Jesus is the same: He seeks to redeem men from selfishness and worldliness and to produce in them a godlike passion for the welfare of their fellow-creatures. These they may bless with gifts of money, where such may be required, still more with sympathy and helpfulness, but most of all with the gospel.

Besides such directions as to the behavior of man to man, there are also among the words of Jesus memorable maxims about the conduct of life in the family, in the state, and in society; and here again He taught even more by example than by precept. As son, brother and friend, He fulfilled all righteousness; but He also, as teacher, determined what righteousness was. Thus He opposed the laxity as to divorce prevalent in His time, pointing back to the pure ideal of Paradise. His conception of womanhood and His tenderness toward childhood have altered entirely the conceptions of men about these two conditions. He was a patriot, glorying in the beauty of His native Galilee and weeping over Jerus; and though, from birth to death, He was exposed to constant persecution from the constituted authorities, He not only obeyed these Himself but commanded all others to do the same. Nothing moved Him more than the sight of talents unused, and, therefore, it lay deep in His system of thought to call upon everyone to contribute his part to the service of the body politic; but no less did He recognize the right of those who have done their part of the general task to share in the fruits of industry; "for the laborer is worthy of his hire" (Lk **10** 7).

Priceless, however, as are the commandments of Jesus in regard to the things of man, as well as in regard to the things of God, it is not in these that we have to seek His ethical originality, but in the new motive brought into play by Him for doing the Divine will, when once it has been ascertained. As He made it easy to love God by revealing God's love, so did He make it easy to love man by revealing the greatness of man, as an immortal creature, who has come from God and is going to God. Whatever is done to man, good or evil, Jesus esteems as done to Himself; for the great saying to this effect, in the account of the Last Judgment in Mt **25**, though applicable in the first place to Christians, may be extended to men in general. The corollary of the fatherhood of God is the brotherhood of men; and the second great commandment stands under the protection of the first.

II. In the Fourth Gospel.—In the Fourth Gospel Eternal Life takes the same place as the kingdom of God in the other three. The author is not, indeed, unaware that Jesus employed the latter phrase for the sum of the blessings brought by Him to the world; and it has already been remarked that the Synoptists occasionally employ "life" as an equivalent for the phrase they usually make use of. The reason of John's preference for his own phrase may have lain in some personal idiosyncrasy, or it may have been due to the gentile environment in which he wrote. But the phrase is one suggestive and instructive in itself in the highest degree. It had already entered deeply into the language of religion before the time of Christ; indeed, in every part of Holy Writ the idea is common that separation from God is death, but that union with Him is life.

1. Eternal Life

In the teaching of Jesus, as this is found in Jn, the world lies in death, because it has become separated from God, and the children of men are in danger of perishing everlastingly as the punishment of their sin; but "God so loved the world, that he gave his only begotten Son, that whosoever believeth on him should not perish, but have eternal life" (**3** 16).

2. Its Source in God

This life is, first, in God, who abides in everlasting blessedness; but it is not, even in Him, at rest, but agitated with an impulse to communicate itself. Then, it is in the Son—"For as the Father hath life in himself, even so gave he to the Son also to have life in himself" (**5** 26); not, however, for Himself alone, but for the purpose of being communicated to those destitute of it. For this reason He was made flesh and dwelt among us; and He communicated it through His words, which were "words of eternal life." The words of Jesus, as thus bringing life, are the "light" of the world; and they are the "truth"—two favorite expressions of this Gospel—or He of whom they speak is Himself the light and the truth; He said Himself, "I am the way, and the truth, and the life." He is in His word in such a way that, when it is received in the right spirit, He enters the soul personally—"ye in me, and I in you" (**14** 20). As food is taken into the body, to sustain life, so does He become the life of the soul; He is the "bread of life" and the "water of life" (**6** 35). As, however, bread has to be broken, before it is eaten, and water to be poured out, when it is drunk, so does the virtue which is in the Son of God only become available through His death—"I am the living bread which came down out of heaven: if any man eat of this bread, he shall live for ever: yea and the bread which I will give is my flesh, for the life of the world" (**6** 51).

3. Through the Son

The world lying dead in sin, a new birth is required for those who are to enter into life; and this is necessary even for so fine a character as Nicodemus (**3** 3.5.7). Without this change, the children of men are insensible to Divine revelations; and even the children of privilege, who had enjoyed the OT revelation, were indifferent to eternal life, when it came near to them in the person of Christ. Hence there was required a special drawing on the part of God to awaken the sleeping soul—"No man can come to me, except the Father that sent me draw him" (**6** 44); and, where this influence was not responded to, there might be the most violent and persistent opposition to Christ on the part of those who believed themselves to be the favorites of heaven. The new birth is accompanied with spiritual vision—"seeing the kingdom of God" (**3** 3)—and, throughout the Fourth Gospel, remarkable stress is laid on the virtue of such seeing or knowing. It leads so directly to faith that to "know" and to "believe" are virtually the same act (**10** 38). Faith is the reception into the soul of the life eternal, or of Him who has been discerned by the spiritual vision and who is Himself the life. It is the eating of the bread of life, the drinking of the water of life, and it makes and keeps alive.

4. Need of New Birth

Since faith is thus the means whereby the eternal life becomes a personal possession, it is the one thing needful and the sum of all the commandments—"This is the work of God, that ye believe on him whom he hath sent" (**6** 29). It is the unique commandment, comprehending all the commandments, and it "worketh by love" toward the fulfilment of them all. What these are is, however, less brought out in detail in this Gospel than in the others, for it is a peculiarity of the mind of Jesus, as recorded by John, to deal with central principles and to assume that the consequences will follow as a matter of course. Of the organization, for example, of the community which was to perpetuate His influence, after He had left the world, He says much less in this Gospel than even in the Synoptists; yet He characterizes the very essence of the new body in such words as this, "I in them, and thou in me, that they may be perfected into one; that the world may know that thou didst send me, and lovedst them, even as thou lovedst me" (**17** 23). In the last half of this saying there is a hint of the influence to be exerted on the outside world by the display of Christian character, with the result of producing belief; but this aim was to be sought more directly through testimony (**15** 27) and the "word" of the disciples (**17** 20). Thus would even the distant, "which are not of this fold," be brought in, so that there might be "one flock" and "one shepherd" (**10** 16). Inside the fold it is the greatest privilege and honor, as well as responsibility, to feed the "sheep" and to feed the "lambs" (**21** 15.16.17).

5. Nature of Faith

Character and conduct are, even for the disciples of Christ, "commandments," as, indeed, Jesus does not disdain to speak of the various parts of His own vocation by the same humble name, implying the necessity of moral effort and the temptation to failure (**15** 10). Therefore, they are also proper subjects for prayer. He prayed for the disciples, both that they might be kept from the evil in the world and that they might be sanctified through the truth (**17** 15.17), and doubtless He expected them to ask the same things for themselves, as theirs was to be a life of prayer (**16** 24). But, in the last resort, they are the fruits of union with Himself, and eternal life is not merely a gift of the future, to be given at the death of the body, but is enjoyed even now by those who abide in the vine.

6. Fruits of Union with Christ

Literature.—Monographs on the ethics of Jesus in Ger. by Grimm and in Eng. by King; compare also Peabody, *Jesus Christ and the Social Question*, and *Jesus Christ and the Christian Character;* relevant portions in works of larger scope, such as Jacoby, *NT Ethik*, Wendt, *The Teaching of Jesus*, and the handbooks of NT theology by Weiss, Holtzmann, Schlatter, Feine, Weinel, Stevens. Very ample references to lit. in Stalker, *The Ethic of Jesus*.

James Stalker

ETHIOPIA, ē-thi-ō′pi-a (כּוּשׁ, *kūsh;* **Αἰθιοπία**, *Aithiopía*):

1. Location, Extent and Population

Critically speaking E. may refer only to the Nile valley above the First Cataract, but in ancient as in modern times the term was often used not only to include what is now known as Nubia and the Sūdān (Soudan), but all the unknown country farther W. and S., and also at times Northern, if not Southern, Abyssinia. While E. was so indefinitely large, yet the narrow river valley, which from the First to the Fifth Cataract represented the main agricultural resources of the country, was actually a territory smaller than Egypt and, excluding deserts, smaller than Belgium (W. Max Müller). The settled population was also small, since in ancient as in modern times Egypt naturally drew away most of the able-bodied and energetic youth as servants, police and soldiers. The prehistoric population of Northern Nubia was probably Egyp, but this was displaced in early historic time by a black race, and the thick lips and woolly hair of the typical African are as well marked in the oldest Egyp paintings as in the latest. But by the side of these natives of *K'sh*, the artist also represents various reddish-brown varieties; for from the beginning of historic time the pure Negro stock has been mixed with the fellaheen of Egypt and with the Sem population of the Arabian coast. The rulers of E. were generally of foreign blood. The Negroes, though brave and frugal, were slow in thought, and although controlled for centuries by cultivated neighbors, under whom they attained at times high official prominence, yet the body of the people remained uninfluenced by this civilization. The country which we now know as Abyssinia was largely controlled, from the earliest known date, by a Caucasian people who had crossed the Red Sea from Arabia. The true Abyssinians, as Professor Littmann shows, contain no Negro blood and no Negro qualities. In general they are "well formed and handsome, with straight and regular features, lively eyes, hair long and straight or somewhat curled and in color dark olive approaching brown." Modern discoveries prove their close racial and linguistic connection with Southern Arabia and particularly with the kingdom of Sheba (the Sabaeans), that most powerful people whose extensive architectural and literary remains have recently come to light. The Sabaean inscriptions found in Abyssinia go back some 2,600 years and give a new value to the Bible references as well as to the constant claim of Jos that the queen of Sheba was a "queen of E." The Falashas are a Jewish community living near Lake Tsana, of the same physical type and probably of the same race as other Abyssinians. Their religion is a "pure Mosaism" based upon the Ethiopic version of the Pent, but modified by the fact that they are ignorant of the Heb language (*Jew Enc*). It is uncertain when they became Jews. The older scholars thought of them as dating back to the Solomonic era, or at least to the Bab captivity. Since the researches of Joseph Halévy (1868), some date within the Christian era has seemed preferable, notwithstanding their ignorance of Talmudic rules. However, the newly discovered fact that a strong Jewish community was flourishing at Syene in the 6th cent. BC makes it clear that Jewish influence may have been felt in E. at least that early. Although Abyssinians are noted for their strict adherence to ancient custom, Jewish characteristics are prominent all over the entire country. The opening formula of the king in every official letter—"The Lion of the Tribe of Judah has Conquered!"—is no more Jewish than scores of ordinary phrases and customs. Although it is barely possible that some rites, like circumcision and observance of the Sabbath, may have been received from the ancient Egyptians or Christian Copts (*New Sch-Herz Enc*) yet a strong Heb influence cannot be denied. All travelers speak of the "industry" of the Falashas and of the "kindliness and grave courtesy" of the Abyssinians. Besides those named above there are many communities of mixed races in E., but the ancient basis is invariably Negro, Sem or Egyp.

2. History

The ancient Gr writers are full of fantastic and fabulous stories about E. Sometimes they become so puzzled in their geography as to speak of E. as extending as far as India; their notes concerning the miraculous fauna and flora are equally Munchausian. Homer praises the Ethiopians as the "blameless race," and other writers rank them first among all men for their religious knowledge. This latter notion may have had its origin from a priestly desire to consider the Ethiopian reverence for the priesthood—which had the power of life and death over the kings—as the Divinely ordained primitive custom, or it may have sprung from the fact that the Egyp "Land of the Gods" was partly situated in Southern Abyssinia. It is suggestive that the Heb prophets never fell into these common errors but invariably "gave a very good idea of geographical and political conditions" (W. Max Müller). The oldest important historic document referring to E. is from the IVth Dynasty of Egypt when Sneferu laid waste the land, capturing 7,000 slaves and 100,000 cattle.

In the VIth Dynasty the Egyptians reached as far S. as the Second Cataract and brought back some dwarfs, but did not establish any permanent control. In the XIIth Dynasty Egypt's real occupation of E. began. Usertesen III records his contempt by saying: "The Negro obeys as soon as the lips are opened. They are not valiant, they are miserable, both tails and bodies!" Notwithstanding this satiric reference, these naked Ethiopians clad in skins and tails of wild animals, compelled the Pharaoh to make several campaigns before he could establish a frontier at the Second Cataract beyond which no Negro could come without a permit. That the natives were not cowardly may be seen from the songs of triumph over their subjection and from the fact that every later Pharaoh encouraged them to enlist in his army, until finally the very hieroglyphic for archer became a Nubian. The XVIIIth Dynasty pushed the frontier beyond the Third Cataract into the splendid Dongola district and often boasts of the rich tribute from E., in one case 2,667 "manloads" of ivory, ebony, perfumes, gold and ostrich feathers besides cattle, wild beasts and slaves. The chairs of ivory and the jewelry sometimes shown seem barbaric in style but excellent in workmanship. Copper and bronze factories and great iron foundries date also to a very early time in E. (*PSBA*, XXXIII, 96). The Ethiopian gold mines where hundreds of criminals toiled, with ears and noses mutilated, made gold in Egypt in the 15th cent. BC as "common as dust." The choicest son of the Pharaoh, next to him in power, was proud to be called "Prince of Kush." Amenhotep IV (1370 BC), the religious reformer, built his second greatest temple (the only one of his works now existent) in Nubia. The XIXth Dynasty sought to colonize E., and some of the most magnificent temples ever built by man can be seen as far S. as the Fourth

Cataract. For over five cents. Egyp rule was maintained, until about 1000 BC a war for independence began which was so successful that the victorious Ethiopian kings finally carried their armies against Thebes and Memphis and for a century (763–663) ruled all Egypt from Napata—which in religious architecture became the Southern Thebes—and for another century (and even at times during the Ptolemaic era) controlled upper Egypt. While the leaders of this revolution were doubtless descendants of exiled priests from Thebes, yet the mixture of Ethiopian blood is plainly discernible and is perhaps also shown in their "Puritan morals" (Petrie, III, 276) and spirit of clemency, so different from the legitimate Pharaohs. Shabaka = So (715–707) and Taharka = Tirhaḳah (693–667), both mentioned in the Bible, were the last great kings of E. When Tanutamen, son of Shabaka and nephew of Taharka (667–664), was forced by Ashurbanipal to give up his claim to Egypt and retire to the S., the influence of E. ceased. Cambyses (525–521) made E. tributary clear to the Third Cataract (cf Ezk **30** 4), while King Ergamenes, near the close of the 3d cent. BC, broke forever the power of the Egyptian priesthood. Though the Romans held a nominal protectorate over E., it was of so little importance as to be scarcely ever mentioned. After being expelled from Egypt the Ethiopians still continued to honor the gods of Thebes, but, as foreign influence ceased, the representations of this worship became more and more African and barbaric. Even after Christianity had triumphed everywhere else, the Nubians, as late as the 5th cent. AD, were still coming to Philae to give honor to the statue of Isis (Erman). In the 6th cent. AD a native king, Silko, established a Christian kingdom in the Northern Sūdān with Dongola as its capital. This raised somewhat the culture of the land. In the next century the Arabs made Nubia tributary, though it took an immense army to do it. For six centuries thereafter Islam demanded a tribute of 360 slaves annually, and other treasure, though innumerable campaigns were necessary to collect it. The Nubian kings refused all overtures to become Moslems, and Christian churches multiplied along the banks of the Nile. In the 8th cent. Egypt was invaded by 100,000 Nubians to repay an insult given to the Coptic patriarch and to the sacred pictures in the Egyp Christian churches. In the 13th cent., David, king of Nubia, not only withheld tribute but invaded Egypt. He was terribly punished, however, by the Arabs, who sacked churches and tortured Christians clear to the Fourth Cataract. This was the beginning of the end. By the close of the 15th cent. almost every Christian altar was desolate and every church destroyed.

Photograph by the University of Chicago Expedition.

Temple of Tirhaḳah at Napata

3. Bible References

Winckler long ago proved that the Assyrians designated a district in Northern Arabia by the same name which they ordinarily applied to E. Skinner (*Genesis*, 1910, 208) thinks the Hebrews also made this distinction and were therefore entirely right when they spoke of Nimrod as "son of Cush," since the earliest Bab dynasty had as a matter of fact a Sem origin. There may be other references to an Arabian district, but undoubtedly the African *Kush* must be the one generally designated. This is referred to once in the NT and over 40 times in the OT. Many secular monuments speak of the high honor paid to women in E., and Candace (Acts **8** 27) seems certainly to have been an official or dynastic name for a number of Ethiopian queens. One of the pyramids of Meröe was Candace's—her picture can still be seen at Kaga—and to her belonged the wonderful treasure of jewelry found in 1834 by Ferlini and now in the Berlin museum. Petronius (24 BC) raided E. for Rome and stormed the capital, but Candace sent ambassadors to Rome and obtained peace. The "eunuch" who may have been the treasurer of this very queen was probably "no black proselyte but a Jew who had placed the business ability of his race at the service of the Nubian woman" (W. Max Müller). In the OT E. is spoken of with great respect, and several Bible characters are named Cushi (2 S **18** 21 AV; Jer **36** 14; Zeph **1** 1); even Moses married an Ethiopian wife (Nu **12** 1), and Ebed-melek the Ethiopian is helper to Jeremiah (Jer **38** 7). It is a great land situated beyond the frontiers of the civilized world (Ezk **29** 10), yet with Jews in its farthest district (Zeph **3** 10). It is very rich (Job **28** 19; Isa **43** 3); is engaged in trade with Arabia (**45** 14), and its citizens are proud of their nationality (Ps **87** 4). Again and again the relation of Cush with Sheba is mentioned (Gen **10** 7.28; Isa **43** 3, etc), which latter statement is strangely corroborated by the recently discovered Sabaean inscriptions throughout Abyssinia. Its typical inhabitants have a color as unchangeable as the leopard's spots (Jer **13** 23), are careless (Ezk **30** 9), but very warlike (Ezk **38** 5; Jer **46** 9), giving "infinite" strength to Nineveh (Nah **3** 9), but who can be resisted by Israel because of Jeh's favor (2 Ch **16** 8; Isa **20** 5; **36** 6). Jeh is interested in the history of E. as well as Egypt (Isa **20** 3), loves the children of E. as the children of Israel (Am **9** 7), and the time is coming when E. shall yet stretch out her hands to Jeh (Ps **68** 31). Cush and Mizraim are correctly mentioned as a political unit (Isa **20** 4 f), and several kings of E. are mentioned by name—Zerah (2 Ch **14** 9), So (2 K **17** 4) and Tirhaḳah (2 K **19** 9; Isa **37** 9). The statements concerning these kings have been pronounced incorrect because it seemed that Zerah could not possibly be an equivalent for Usarkon or So for Shabaka—the known kings of Egypt at those periods—and also because the reigns of Shabaka and Tirhaḳah did not begin until after the dates at which in the Heb records they were called "kings of E."

Recent, information, however, makes it clear that both Shabaka and Tirhaḳah exercised royal authority in the Delta before they were given it farther south, and that the Heb transcription of names was very easy and natural. (See W. M. Flinders Petrie, *Hist of Egypt*, III, 280–309; *Egypt and Israel* [1911], 76–78.)

4. The Church in Abyssinia

Sem influence entered Abyssinia at least as early as the 7th or 8th cent. BC (see above), and the kings of Axum claimed descent from Menelek, son of Solomon, but the first certain information concerning the kingdom of Axum comes from the middle of the 1st cent. AD, at which time Axum was a rich capital, and its ancient sacredness was so great that from that period clear down to the 19th cent. the kings of Abyssinia would travel there to be crowned. There is no reason to doubt that Frumentius (cir 330 AD) was the first to introduce Christianity. Merope of Tyre, according to the often-told story, when returning from India with his two nephews, was captured and killed off the Ethiopian coast, but the two boys were carried to the Abyssinian king; and although one perished the other, Frumentius, succeeded in converting the king and his people to Christianity, and later was himself consecrated by St. Athanasius of Alexandria as the first Metropolitan of E., taking as his title *Abu Salama* ("Father of Peace"). From that time until now, with but one single interruption, the *Abuna* ("Father") has always been appointed by the Patriarch of Alexandria and, since the 13th cent., has been by legal necessity not a native Abyssinian, but a Copt.

After the Council of Chalcedon (450 AD) condemned all as heretics who did not accept the "double nature" of Christ, both the Egyp and Abyssinian churches separated themselves from Rome, believing so thoroughly in the Deity of Christ as to refuse to accept His humanity as essential "nature." In the 5th cent. a great company of monks entered Abyssinia, since which time the monastic tendency has been strongly marked. About 525, Caleb, king of Axum, attacked the Homeritae across the Red Sea—either for their persecution of Christians or their interference with his trade—and for some half a century controlled a large district of Arabia. At this time Abyssinian trade was extensive. Gr influence was also felt, and the Christian cathedral at Axum was a magnificent work of architectural art. The early churches were protected by heavy surrounding walls and strong towers. The invasion of Africa by Islam in the 7th cent. required 300 years of battle for the preservation of Abyssinian liberty and Christian faith. It alone of all the African states succeeded in preserving both—but its civilization was destroyed, and for 1,000 years it was completely hidden from the eyes of its fellow-Christians in Europe. Occasionally during those centuries a rumor would reach Europe of a "Prester John" somewhere in the Far East who was king of a Christian people, yet it was a thrilling surprise to Christendom when Pedro de Cavilham in the 15th cent. discovered this lost Christian kingdom of Abyssinia completely surrounded by infidel pagans and bigoted Mohammedans. When, early in the 16th cent., the Negus of Abyssinia sent an envoy to the king of Portugal asking his help against the Moslems, the appeal was met with favor. In 1520 the Portuguese fleet arrived in the Red Sea and its chaplain, Father Francisco Alvarez, 20 years later stirred the Christian world by his curious narratives. Not long afterward, when the Arabs actually invaded the country, another Portuguese fleet was sent with a body of military, commanded by Christopher de Gama. These 450 musketeers and the six little pieces of artillery gave substantial aid to the endangered state. Father Lobo tells the story. The Abyssinian king must have been grateful for such help, yet presently the strenuous efforts of the Portuguese clergy to convert him and his people to the Roman Catholic faith became so offensive that Bermudez, the most zealous missionary, was compelled to leave the country and the Jesuits who remained were mistreated. Other efforts to win the Abyssinian Christians to renounce the Monophysitic heresy and accept the doctrine and control of Rome were somewhat more successful. Early in the 17th cent. Father Pedro Paez, an ecclesiastic of much tact, won the king fully to his faith, and under his direction many churches were erected and advantageous government works carried on. However, his successor Mendez lacked his conciliatory ability and, although a punishment of seven years' chastisement was proclaimed against recalcitrants, the opposition became so violent and universal that the Negus Sysenius finally abdicated in favor of his son Fasilidas, who in 1633 sent all Jesuits out of the country and resumed official relations with the Egyp church. Since then, although many efforts have been made, no controlling influence has ever been obtained by Rome. Once more, for over a century, Abyssinia became completely hidden from the eyes of the outside world until James Bruce, the explorer, visited the country, 1770–72, and made such a report as to arouse again the interest of Christendom. The tr of the Bible, which was made by his Abyssinian guide, was adopted and published by the British and Foreign Bible Society, and in 1829 the Church Missionary Society sent out Gobat and Kugler as the first Protestant missionaries to Abyssinia, who were followed shortly after by some Roman Catholics. Owing chiefly to the opposition of native priests the Protestants were expelled in 1838 and the expulsion of the Roman missionaries followed in 1854. In 1858 a Copt who had been influenced as a youth by a Protestant school, became *Abuna*, and Protestant missionaries were again admitted, but succeeded in doing little permanent work owing to the political disturbances while King Kesa (Theodore)—the Napoleon of Africa—was attempting to consolidate native resources and build up an African empire. At this period the influence of Great Britain began to be felt in Abyssinia. After the suicide of Theodore (1868) and esp. after Menelek II had succeeded in making himself emperor (1899), this influence became great. During the 20th cent. missionaries have been able to work in Abyssinia without much danger, but the Moslem influence is so preponderating that little has been attempted and little done. The religion of the Crescent seems now almost completely victorious over the strange land which for so many centuries, alone and unhelped, held aloft in Africa the religion of the Cross. (See esp. *The Mohammedan World of Today*, by Zwemer, Wherry, and Barton, 1907; *Missionary World*, 1910–11.)

5. Beliefs and Practices

In creed, ritual, and practice, the Abyssinian church agrees generally with the Coptic. There are seven sacraments and prayers for the dead, high honor is paid to the Virgin Mary and to the saints; fasts and pilgrimages are in much favor; adults are baptized by immersion and infants by affusion. A blue cord is placed about the neck at baptism.

An extract from one of the Gospels, a silver ring, an ear pick and a small cross, often very artistic, are also worn about the neck. No charms or beads or crucifixes ("graven images") are worn. The Jewish as well as the Christian Sabbath is kept sacred, and on an average every other day during the year is a religious holiday. The people are ignorant and superstitious, yet impress observers with their grave kindliness and seem at times eager to learn. The clergy can marry before but not after ordination. Priests must be able to read and recite the Nicene Creed (the "Apostles' Creed" is not known), but do not understand the Geʿez language in which the liturgies are written. They conduct many and long services and attend to the ceremonial purifications. Deacons must also be able to read; they prepare the bread for the Holy Sacrament and in general help the priests. The monastic clergy have chief care of the education of the young—though this consists mainly in Scripture reading—and their head, the *Etshege*, ranks next to the *Abuna*.

The ancient churches were often basilican, but modern native churches are quadrangular or circular. The Holy of Holies always stands in the center, and is supposed to contain an ark. Tradition declares that the ark in the cathedral at Axum is the original ark from Solomon's temple. An outer court surrounds the body of the church, which is freely used by laymen and as a place of entertainment for travelers. Very crude pictures are common. These show both Egyp and European influence, and are probably not merely decorations but have a relation, as in Egyp thought, to spiritual advancement in this life or the next (cf Budge, Intro to *Lives of Mabâ' Sĕyôn* and *Gabra Krĕstôs*, 1898). The services consist of chanting psalms, reading Scriptures and reciting liturgies.

6. Abyssinian Literature

The Abyssinian canon (*Semanya Ahadu*) consists of 46 OT and 35 NT books. Besides the usually accepted books, they count Shepherd of Hermas, Synodos (Canons), Epistles of Clement, Macc, Tob, Jth, Wisd, Ecclus, Bar, 4 Ezr, Asc Isa, Book of Adam, Joseph ben Gorion, En and Jub. The Ethiopic texts of the two latter give these books in the most ancient form, and their discovery has led to much valuable discussion. The use of the Geʿez language in which these are written dates back to a time shortly before the introduction of Christianity. From the 5th to 7th cents. AD, the lit. is almost exclusively tr[d] from Gr writers or adaptations of such writings. Quotations abound from Basil, Gregory, Ignatius, Athanasius, Epiphanus, Cyril, Dioscurus, etc. The second literary period begins 1268, when the old "Solomonic" Dynasty regained its place and continues to the present; it consists mainly of tr[s] from the Arabic. In both periods the topics are few: liturgies, hymns, sermons, the heroic deeds of the saints and their orthodoxy. Each saint uses the four Holy Gospels, as David his four stones, to kill every heretical Goliath (cf Goodspeed and Crum, *Patrologia Orientalis*, IV, 1908). A large place is given to miracles and magic prayers and secret names (cf Budge, *Miracles of the Virgin Mary*, 1900, and "Magic Book of Disciples," *JAOS*, 1904). The legends or histories are occasionally well written, as the famous "Magda Queen of Sheba" (ET by Mrs. J. Van Vorst, 1907), but usually are as inferior in style as in thought (cf Littmann, *Bibliotheca-Abessinica*, 1904). A few specimens of "popular literature" and many Abyssinian "proverbs" are extant (*JAOS*, XXIII, 51–53; XXV, 1–48; *Jour. asiatique*, IV, 487–95).

7. Nubian Literature

The modern Nubian does not write, and his ancient predecessors wrote but little. Even in the days of the Pharaohs the hieroglyphics in most Nubian temples were written so poorly as to be almost unintelligible, and in later pre-Christian monuments put up by native rulers the usual tablets accompanying the Divine tableaux are often left blank. Some cents. before our era the necessary monumental inscriptions began to be composed in the Nubian language, though still written in hieroglyphics. Shortly after the beginning of the Christian era a native cursive writing begins to be used on the monuments, closely resembling the Egyp demotic, from which undoubtedly its alphabet was derived (F. L. Griffith in *Areika*). Finally, after Nubia became Christian (6th cent.), another native system appears written in Gr and Coptic letters. Lepsius found two such inscriptions on the Blue Nile and numbers have since been discovered, but until 1906 these were as unreadable as the other two forms of Nubian writing. In that year Dr. Karl Schmidt found in Cairo two precious fragments of parchment which had been owned by some Nubian Christians of probably the 8th or 9th cent. One of these contained a selection of passages from the NT—as was ascertained by comparing it with the Gr and Coptic Scriptures. By the aid of bilingual cartouches several proper names were soon deciphered. New inscriptions are now being brought to light every few months, and undoubtedly the tr of this important tongue, which contains the "history of an African Negro dialect for some 2,000 years" and also the religious history of the long-lost Christian church of the Sūdān, will soon be accomplished. The other fragment found by Schmidt was a curious Hymn of the Cross, well representing the ancient Ethiopian hymnology:

"The cross is the hope of Christians;
The cross is the resurrection of the dead;
The cross is the physician of the sick;
The cross is the liberator of the slave," etc.

—James H. Breasted in *BW*, December, 1908; *Nation*, June 2, 1910.

8. Exploration

Scientific observation of Nubia began with Burckhardt (1813), Cailliaud, and Waddington (1821), and esp. with Lepsius (1844), but excavation in the proper sense was begun by the University of Chicago (1905–7), followed (1907–10) by expeditions sent out by the Royal Academy of Berlin, University of Pennsylvania, University of Liverpool, and Oxford University.

Literature.—Besides the works quoted above, among recent Encyclopaedias, see esp. *Enc Brit* (11th ed) and *New Sch-Herz;* and among the more recent books: James T. Bent, *The Sacred City of the Ethiopians* (1893); Glaser, *Die Abessinier in Arabien und Afrika* (1895); A. B. Wylde, *Modern Abyssinia* (1901); R. P. Skinner, *Abyssinia of Today* (1906); Th. Noeldeke, *Die äthiopische Litteratur* (1906); Louis J. Morié, *Les civilisations africaines* (1904); Littmann, *Geschichte der äthiopischen Litteratur* (1907); W. Max Müller, *Aethiopien* (1904); Petrie, *Hist of Egypt* (1895–1901); J. H. Breasted, *Temples of Lower Nubia* (1906); *Monuments of Sudanese Nubia* (1908); A. E. Weigall, *Report of Antiquities of Lower Nubia* (1906); E. A. W. Budge, *The Egyptian Sudan* (1907); Kromrei, *Glaubenslehre und Gebräuche der älteren abessinischen Kirche* (1895); M. Fowler, *Christian Egypt* (1901); Dowling, *Abyssinian Church* (1909); "*Meroe,*" *the City of the Ethiopians*, by Liverpool University Expedition (1909–10); University of Pennsylvania Publications, Egyp Dept., Eckley B. Coxe, Jr., *Expedition to Nubia*, I–IV (1909–11); *Archeological Survey of Nubia;* and Egyp government reports.

Camden M. Cobern

ETHIOPIAN EUNUCH, ē-thi-ō′pi-an ū′nuk (**εὐνοῦχος,** *eunoúchos*): A man who occupied a leading position as treasurer at the court of Candace, queen of the Ethiopians, and who was converted and baptized by Philip the deacon (Acts **8** 27–39). Being a eunuch, he was not in the full Jewish communion (cf Dt **23** 1), but had gone up to Jerus to worship, probably as a proselyte at the gate. During his return journey he spent the time in studying Isaiah, the text which he used being that of the LXX

ANCIENT EGYPTIAN TEMPLE—PHILAE

(cf Professor Margoliouth, art. "Ethiopian Eunuch" in *HDB*). On meeting with Philip the deacon, who was on his way to Gaza, he besought of him to shed light upon the difficulties of the Scripture he was reading, and through this was converted. The place of his baptism, according to Jerome and Eusebius, was Bethsura: by some modern authorities, e.g. G. A. Smith, it has been located at or near Gaza. The verse containing the confession of the eunuch, "I believe that Jesus Christ is the Son of God," is omitted either in whole or in part by some texts, but Hilgenfeld, Knowling, etc, regard it as quite in keeping with the context. Tischendorf, WH, RV text, etc, uphold the omission. The verse occurs in the body of AV, but is given only as a footnote in RV and ARV. The diligence with which the eunuch pursued his reading, the earnestness with which he inquired of Philip, and the promptness with which he asked for baptism—all testify to the lofty nature of his character. C. M. Kerr

ETHIOPIAN WOMAN. See Cushite Woman.

ETHIOPIC LANGUAGE, ē-thi-op'ik laṇ'gwāj: The language commonly called Ethiopic is the language in which the inscriptions of the kings of the ancient Aksumitic (Axumite) empire and most of the lit. of Christian Abyssinia are written. It is called *lesāna Ge'ez*, "the tongue of Ge'ez," by the Abyssinians themselves, most probably because it was originally the dialect of the Ge'ez tribe, who in antiquity must have dwelt in or near Aksum (Axum).

The names Ethiopia and Ethiopians have been used in many different meanings by various peoples. To the Greeks, Ethiopia was a country S. of Egypt, and in this sense the word is generally used in the histories of Egypt. The Ethiopian kings came from that country which is now called Nubia in the Anglo-Egyp Sudan. In Hellenistic times the term received a wider meaning, and Ethiopia was the name of all the land between the Red Sea and the Nile, south of Egypt proper. Sometimes "Indian" and "Ethiopian" were synonymous, or Ethiopia was even considered to stretch as far as to the Atlantic Ocean in the W. But of these countries the Greeks and Romans had very little exact geographical knowledge. See Ethiopia.

The fact that Ethiopia at some time meant the country between the Red Sea and the Nile prompted the pagan kings of Aksum in northern Abyssinia to adopt this name for their own country and to give it a narrower sense than the one which it had at that time. Therefore in the bilingual inscription of King Αειζανας, *Aeizanas* (*'Ēzānā*), the word Αἰθιοπία, *Aithiopía*, is a rendering of the Sem *Ḥabashat* ("Abyssinia," but here more specially referring to Northern Abyssinia). Under this same king, about 350 AD, Abyssinia became Christian; and after the Bible had been tr^d into the Ge'ez language, the Abyssinians found that Ethiopia was mentioned there several times. Their national pride was flattered by the thought that their country should be referred to in the Holy Scriptures, and for this reason they were all the more ready to apply the name in question to their own country. Up to the present day they call it Ethiopia (*'Itīōpiyā*), and themselves Ethiopians; their legends speak even of an ancestor Ītīōpīs.

We may then, if we choose to do so, speak of a Nubian and an Abyssinian Ethiopia, but the term "Ethiopic language" has come into general usage as an equivalent of *lesāna Ge'ez*, and should therefore be applied only to the ancient literary language of Abyssinia.

This language is closely allied to the languages of Southern Arabia: it represents the southwestern branch of the southern division of the Sem languages. The most important branch of this division is, of course, the Arab. language, and with this Ethiopic has a great deal in common. On the other hand there are many words and forms in Ethiopic which are not found in Arab., but in Heb or even in Bab and Assyr. It has been held that the home of the Semites was in Africa; and if that were the case, the people who spoke the Ethiopic language may never have migrated very much. But the majority of scholars who have expressed their opinion upon the subject believe that Asia was the home of the Semites; this is the opinion of the writer of this art. also. Then the Sem inhabitants of Abyssinia must have come from across the Red Sea. Their migration must have begun many centuries BC. It has hardly ever stopped, since Arabs in smaller, and sometimes in larger, numbers have been drifting into Abyssinia at all periods.

The Sem conquerors of Abyssinia found peoples of two different races in the country where they settled: (1) African aborigines and (2) Kushites, a branch of the Hamitic family. Their languages were different from each other and, of course, different from that of the Semites also; some of them are spoken up to the present day. When the Semites first came and formed their literary language, they did not allow the languages of the country to influence their own speech very much; but gradually this influence grew stronger and stronger, and it is very evident in the modern Sem languages of Abyssinia. An outline of the history of the Ethiopic language is as follows: Its oldest monument known so far is the Sem part of the bilingual inscription of King 'Ēzānā, which dates from the first half of the 4th cent. AD. Before that time Ethiopic must have been spoken, without doubt, but it was not written: Gr and Sabaean were written instead. At the time of King 'Ēzānā the knowledge of the Sabaean language seems to have been very little; but Sabaean script was still used. The Sem part of the inscription just mentioned is in the Ethiopic language, but carved once in Sabaean script and a second time in the native Ethiopic script which had been derived from the Sabaean. In the first of these two "editions" two or three Sabaean words are used instead of their Ethiopic equivalents. A few other ancient inscriptions found in the Aksumitic empire may also be dated from the same period.

Possibly in the same 4th cent. the tr of the Bible into Ethiopic was begun; and this fact marks the beginning of a real Ethiopic lit. Perhaps the Pss and the Gospels were tr^d first, being most needed in the service of the Christian church. The different books of the Scriptures were tr^d by different men, some of whom rendered literally, some more according to the sense, some having a good, some only a poor, knowledge of the language from which, and the language into which, they translated. Both Testaments were tr^d from the Gr by men whose mother-tongue was probably Aramaic. This is proved by the presence of Gr and Aram. words and by the forms in which the Heb names appear in Ethiopic transliteration. The oldest influences which the Ethiopic language experienced were therefore: (1) Sabaean; a number of technical terms may have been adopted by the ancient Aksumites from the Sabaean at the time when this was their literary language; (2) African, i.e. Kushite and native African; the Sem conquerors found a great many new animals and trees or plants, which they did not know, in their new country, and in many cases they adopted their African names; (3) Aramaic, i.e. Jewish and Christian; these are mostly words referring to religious or theological matters; (4) Gr; some of the Gr words found in Ethiopic refer to religious matters in the same way as the Aram., others denote objects or ideas which the ancient Abyssinians received from the civilized world, others again are mere transliterations of Gr words in the

Bible and other religious books, which the translators did not understand.

The time of the Aksumitic empire was the time when the Ethiopic language flourished. This empire was overthrown probably in the 7th or 8th cent. AD; and we know very little indeed of the history of Abyssinia from about 700 until about 1300 AD. In 1270 the so-called Solomonic Dynasty came to the throne again; the seat of the empire, however, was no longer Aksum but Gondar, N. of Lake Tsānā. Meanwhile the literary language had become a dead language; new dialects had sprung up and taken its place in everyday conversation. But Geʻez continued to be the sacred language; it was the language of the Bible and of the church, and when in the 14th and 15th cents. a revival of Abyssinian lit. came about, the literary language was Geʻez. But it was influenced by the new dialects, esp. by the Amharic, the language of Amhara, where Gondar was situated and where most of the books were written or tr[d]. This influence affected in particular the spelling of Geʻez in those books which dealt with religious matters and which therefore had to be written in pure Geʻez. In historical books a great many words were taken from the Amharic; and this language, called *lesāna tārīk*, "the tongue of the chronicles," has often the appearance of a mixed language.

In the 16th and 17th cents. European missionaries came to Abyssinia and tried to convert the monophysite Abyssinian Christians to Romanism. In order to come into close contact with the common people they used Amharic as a literary language, so that everybody, not only the learned, might understand their books. Their example was followed by the defenders of the native church; and since that time Amharic has become a recognized literary language in Abyssinia, although Geʻez is still considered the real language of the church.

Amharic was derived from a sister language of the Ethiopic; the direct descendant of the Ethiopic language is modern Tigriña; a language derived from a dialect very closely related to Geʻez is modern Tigrē.

LITERATURE.—Ludolf, *Historia Aethiopica*, 1681; id, *Commentarius ad suam historiam Aethiopicam*, 1691; Dillmann, *Grammatik der äthiopischen Sprache* (tr[d] into Eng. by Crichton) 1907, Intro; Littmann, *Geschichte der äthiopischen Litteratur*, 1907.

ENNO LITTMANN

ETHIOPIC VERSIONS, ē-thi-op'ik vûr'shuns: Christianity was introduced into Abyssinia by Tyrian missionaries, who probably spoke Gr, about the time of Constantine the Great. The Bible was tr[d] into Ethiopic, or, to use the native name, *Lesāna Geʻez*, the OT being from the LXX, between the 4th and 5th cents., by various hands, though the work was popularly ascribed to Frumentius, the first bishop. The fact of the Scriptures having been tr[d] into Ethiopic was known to Chrysostom (*Hom.* II, *in Joannem*). The versions thus made were revised some time about the 14th cent., and corrected by means of the MT. The Ethiopic Scriptures contain the books found in the Alexandrine recension with the exception of the Books of Macc; but their importance lies in their pseudepigraphic writings, the Asc Isa, the Book of En and the Book of Jub. The 1st ed of the NT appeared at Rome in 1548–49 (reprinted in Walton), but a critical edition has yet to be made; one issued by the British and Foreign Bible Society in 1830 contains many errors. The OT canonical books and Apoc have been edited by Dillmann (the Octoteuch and 1–4 Kings and Apoc), Bachmann (d. 1894) (Isa, Lam, Ob and Mal), and Ludolph (Pss). The Psalter has been often printed from 1513 on. The Book of En was first tr[d] by Richard Laurence and published at Oxford in 1821, but the standard editions are those of Dillmann (Leipzig, 1853) and R. H. Charles (Oxford, 1893). The importance of this work lies in the fact that "the influence of En on the NT has been greater than that of all the other apocryphal and pseudepigraphal books taken together" (Charles, 41). Not only the phraseology and ideas, but the doctrines of the NT are greatly influenced by it. Of the canonical books and Apoc the MSS are too poor and too late to be of any value for the criticism of the Gr text.

THOMAS HUNTER WEIR

ETH-KAZIN, eth-kā'zin (עִתָּה קָצִין, *ʻittāh ḳāçīn;* AV **Ittah Kazin**): A town on the eastern border of Zebulun, mentioned between Gath-hepher and Rimmon (Josh **19** 13). The site is not identified. "Ittah" of AV is due to misunderstanding of the ה locale.

ETHMA, eth'ma (**Ἐθμά** *Ethmá*), RV NOOMA (q.v.).

ETHNAN, eth'nan (אֶתְנָן, *'ethnan*, "gift" or "hire"; **Ἐθναδί**, *Ethnadí*): A Judahite (1 Ch **4** 7).

ETHNARCH, eth'närk (2 Cor **11** 32 m). See GOVERNOR.

ETHNI, eth'nī (אֶתְנִי, *'ethnī*, "gift"): An ancestor of Asaph, of the Gershom branch of the Levites (1 Ch **6** 41).

ETHNOGRAPHY, eth-nog'ra-fi, **ETHNOLOGY**, eth-nol'ō-ji. See TABLE OF NATIONS.

EUBULUS, ū-bū'lus (**Εὔβουλος**, *Eúboulos*, lit. "of good counsel," 2 Tim **4** 21): One of the members of the church in Rome at the time of Paul's second imprisonment in that city.

The apostle mentions how, at his first answer to the charges brought against him at the emperor's tribunal, the Rom Christians as a whole proved disloyal to him—"no one took my part, but all forsook me" (ver 16). In these circumstances when the desertion of Paul by the Christians in Rome was so disheartening, it is pleasing to find that there were some among them who were true, and Eubulus was one of these. Paul therefore in writing the last of all his epistles sends to Timothy a greeting from Eubulus.

Nothing more is known in regard to Eubulus. As his name is Gr, he was probably a Gentile by birth.

JOHN RUTHERFURD

EUCHARIST, ū'ka-rist. See LORD'S SUPPER.

EUMENES II, ū'me-nēz (**Εὐμένης**, *Euménēs*, "well-disposed"): King of Pergamus, son and successor of Attalus I (197 BC). He is mentioned in the Apoc (1 Macc **8** 8) in connection with the league which Judas Maccabaeus made with the Romans. As their ally in the war against Antiochus the Great and in recognition of his signal service at the decisive battle of Magnesia (190 BC), E. was rewarded with such extensive tracts of country as raised him at once from comparative insignificance to be the sovereign of a great state. The statement in the Apoc describing his extension of territory differs from those of Livy, Polybius and Appian, and cannot be correct. The Romans are said to have taken "India, and Media and Lydia" from Antiochus and to have given them to E. Antiochus never had any possessions in India nor had any earlier king of Syria. He was obliged to give up only the countries on the side of Taurus toward Rome. No suggestion for the reading "India" in the narrative has met with acceptance (it may possibly have been a copyist's error for "Ionia"; see Livy xxxvii.44). E. cultivated the Roman alliance carefully but became suspected in connection with the affairs of Perseus, the last king of Macedonia.

He never came to an open rupture with the Romans, and died in 159 BC, after a reign of 39 years.

J. HUTCHISON

EUNATAN, ū-nā′tan. See ENNATAN.

EUNICE, ū-nī′sē, ū′nis (**Εὐνίκη,** *Euníkē,* is the correct reading, and not **Εὐνείκη,** *Euneikē,* which is read by the *TR* of Stephen, three syllables: *Eu-ní-kē,* lit. "conquering well"; 2 Tim **1** 5): The mother of Timothy. Her name is Gr and this might lead to the inference that she was a Gentile by birth, but such a conclusion would be wrong, for we read in Acts **16** 1 that she was a Jewess. Her husband however was a heathen Gr. She was in all probability a daughter of Lois, the grandmother of Timothy, for both of those Christian women are spoken of, in one breath, by Paul, and this in high terms of commendation.

1. Eunice's Home

Timothy had not been circumcised in childhood, probably because of his father's being a Gentile; but the mother and the grandmother did all that lay in their power to train Timothy in the fear of God and in the knowledge of the Scriptures of the OT. "From a child" Eunice had taught her boy to "know the holy scriptures" (2 Tim **3** 15 AV). It is right therefore to connect this home training of Timothy in the fear of God, with his and his mother's conversion to the gospel. His name Timothy—chosen evidently not by the father, but by Eunice—signifies "one who fears God." The "wisdom" of the Hebrews consisted not in worldly prudence or in speculative philosophy, but in the fear of the Lord, as is shown in such passages as Ps **111** 10, and in Job **28,** and in Prov throughout. His name, as well as his careful home training, shows how he was prepared to give a welcome both to Paul and to the gospel proclaimed by him, when the apostle in his first great missionary journey came to Lystra, one of the cities of Lycaonia or Southern (?) Galatia, where Eunice and her family lived. This is implied in the account of Paul's second missionary journey (Acts **16** 1), where we read that he came to Lystra, and found there a certain disciple named Timotheus, the son of a certain woman who was a Jewess, who believed.

2. How She Trained Her Son

It is therefore certain that Eunice and Timothy were not brought to a knowledge of the gospel at this time, but that they were already Christians; she, "a believer"; he, "a disciple." This evidently means that Eunice, Lois and Timothy had been converted on Paul's former visit to Lystra. This conclusion is confirmed in 2 Tim **3** 11, where Paul recalls to Timothy the fact that he had fully known the persecutions and afflictions which came to him at Lystra. The apostle repeats it, that Timothy knew what persecutions he then endured. Now this persecution occurred on Paul's first visit to that city. Eunice was therefore one of those who on that occasion became "disciples." And her faith in Christ, and her son's faith too, were genuine, and stood the test of the "much tribulation" of which Paul warned them (Acts **14** 22 AV); and on Paul's next visit to Lystra, Eunice had the great joy and satisfaction of seeing how the apostle made choice of her son to be his companion in his missionary work. Eunice is not afterward mentioned in the NT; though it is a possible thing that there may be reference to her in what is said about widows and the children of widows in 1 Tim **5** 4.5.

3. Her Conversion to Christ

JOHN RUTHERFURD

EUNUCH, ū′nuk (סָרִיס, *ṣārīṣ;* **σπάδων,** *spádōn;* **εὐνοῦχος,** *eunoúchos*): Primarily and lit. a eunuch is an emasculated man (Dt **23** 1). The Heb word *ṣārīṣ* seems, however, to have acquired a figurative meaning, which is reflected in EV where "officer" and "chamberlain" are found as renderings (cf Gen **37** 36; **39** 1, where *ṣ.* is applied to married men; Est **4** 4). The barbarous practice of self-mutilation and the mutilation of others in this way was prevalent throughout the Orient. The religious disabilities under which men thus deformed labored under the Mosaic law had the effect of making the practice abominable to the Jews as a people (Dt **23** 1; Lev **22** 23–25). The law excluded eunuchs from public worship, partly because self-mutilation was often performed in honor of a heathen god, and partly because a maimed creature of any sort was deemed unfit for the service of Jeh (Lev **21** 16 ff; **22** 24). That ban, however, was later removed (Isa **56** 4.5). On the other hand, the kings of Israel and Judah followed their royal neighbors in employing eunuchs (1) as guardians of the harem (2 K **9** 32; Jer **41** 16), and (2) in military and other official posts (1 S **8** 15 m; 1 K **22** 9 m; 2 K **8** 6 m; **23** 11 AVm; **24** 12.13 m; **25** 19 m; 1 Ch **28** 1 m; 2 Ch **18** 8 m; Jer **29** 2; **34** 19; **38** 7; cf Gen **37** 36; **40** 2.7; Acts **8** 27). Jos informs us that eunuchs were a normal feature of the courts of the Herods (*Ant,* XV, vii, 4; XVI, viii, 1). From the single reference to the practice in the Gospels (Mt **19** 12), we infer that the existence and purpose of eunuchs as a class were known to the Jews of Jesus' time. There is no question with Jesus as to the law of Nature: the married life is the norm of man's condition, and the union thereby effected transcends every other natural bond, even that of filial affection (Mt **19** 5.6). But He would have His hearers recognize that there are exceptional cases where the rule does not hold. In speaking of the three classes of eunuchs (ver 12), He made a distinction which was evidently well known to those whom He addressed, as was the metaphorical use of the word in application to the third class well understood by them (cf Lightfoot, *Horae Heb et Talm;* Schöttgen, *Horae Heb,* in loc.).

How Origen misunderstood and abused the teaching of this passage is well known (Euseb., *HE,* VI, 8), and his own pathetic comment on the passage shows that later he regretted having taken it thus lit. and acted on it. His is not the only example of such a perverted interpretation (see Talm, *Shabbāth* 152*a,* and cf Midr on Eccl **10** 7). The Council of Nicaea, therefore, felt called on to deal with the danger as did the 2d Council of Aries and the *Apos Canons* (cir 21). (Cf Bingham's *Ant,* IV, 9.)

It is significant that Jesus expresses no condemnation of this horrible practice. It was in keeping with His far-reaching plan of instilling principles rather than dealing in denunciations (Jn **3** 17; **8** 11). It was by His positive teaching concerning purity that we are shown the lines along which we must move to reach the goal. There is a more excellent way of achieving mastery of the sexual passion. It is possible for men to attain as complete control of this strong instinct as if they were physically sexless, and the resultant victory is of infinitely more value than the negative, unmoral condition produced by self-emasculation. These "make themselves eunuchs" with a high and holy purpose, "for the kingdom of heaven's sake"; and the interests created by that purpose are so absorbing that neither time nor opportunity is afforded to the "fleshly lusts, which war against the soul" (1 Pet **2** 11). They voluntarily forego marriage even, undertake virtual "eunuchism" because they are completely immersed in and engrossed by "the kingdom of heaven" (cf Jn **17** 4; 1 Cor **7** 29.33 f; **9** 5 and see Bengel, *Gnomon Novi Test.* in loc. and Clem. Alex., *Strom.,* iii.1 ff). See MARRIAGE.

LITERATURE.—Driver, "Deuteronomy," *ICC,* Dt **23** 1; *Comm. on Mt,* in loc. by Morison and Broadus; Neander *Ch. Hist,* II, 493; Wendt, *The Teaching of Jesus,* II, 72 ff; *Expos,* IV, vii (1893), 294 ff; *Enc Brit,* art. "Eunuch."

GEO. B. EAGER

EUODIA, ū-ō'di-a (**Εὐοδία,** *Euodía,* lit. "prosperous journey." The *TR* of Stephen reads **Εὐωδία,** *Euōdía,* which means "fragrant," Phil **4** 2. AV has transformed *Euodia* into *Euodias,* which is a man's name. The mistake is rectified in RV): A Christian woman, one of the members of the church in Philippi.

1. Women Prominent in Church at Philippi

She and Syntyche, who is named in the same verse, were evidently persons of note, prominent in the work of the church there. At Philippi the gospel was first preached to women (Acts **16** 13), and the church was first formed among women—evidently in the house of Lydia (vs 15.40). Paul here makes a request of Euodia and Syntyche. He requests—the word is never used of prayer from us to God—he asks, he beseeches Euodia, and then he repeats the word, he beseeches Syntyche, to be of the same mind in the Lord. Possibly, as Lightfoot suggests, they may have been deaconesses in the Philippian church, but whatever their position in this respect may have been, differences had arisen between them on some subject, we know not what. But whatever the subject in dispute was, it had become so serious that, instead of the breach being healed, matters had become chronic; and news regarding this lack of forbearance between Euodia and Syntyche had been carried to Paul in his captivity in Rome.

2. The Difference Which Arose

The state of Christian life in the church at Philippi gave Paul almost unmingled satisfaction. He regarded with joy their faith and steadfastness and liberality. There was no false teaching, no division, among them. The only thing which could cause him any uneasiness was the want of harmony between Euodia and Syntyche. He beseeches them to give up their differences, and to live at peace in the Lord. Such is the motive which he puts before them with a view to bring about their reconciliation; to live in dispute and enmity is not worthy of those who are "in the Lord," who have been redeemed by the Lord, and whose whole life should be an endeavor to please Him.

3. Paul Entreats Them

Paul proceeds to ask a certain person, unnamed, but whom he terms "true yokefellow" to assist them, that is, to assist Euodia and Syntyche; for each of them, he says, "labored with me in the gospel." It is uncertain what is meant by "true yokefellow." He may refer to Epaphroditus, who carried the epistle from Rome to Philippi. Other names have been suggested—Luke, Silas, Timothy. It has been thought by some that Paul here refers to his own wife, or to Lydia. But such a suggestion is untenable, inasmuch as we know from his own words (1 Cor **7** 8) that he was either unmarried or a widower. And the idea that the "true yokefellow" is Lydia, is equally wrong, because the word "true" is in the Gr masc. Another suggestion is that "yokefellow" is really a proper name—Syzygus. If so, then the apostle addresses Syzygus; or if this is not so, then he speaks to the unnamed "true yokefellow"; and what he says is that he asks him to help Euodia and Syntyche, inasmuch as their work in the gospel was no new thing. Far from this, when Paul brought the gospel to Philippi at the first, these two Christian women had been his loyal and earnest helpers in spreading the knowledge of Christ. How very sad then that any difference should exist between them; how sad that it should last so long! He asks Clement also, and all the other Christians at Philippi, his fellow-laborers, whose names, though not mentioned by the apostle, are nevertheless in the book of life, to assist Euodia and Syntyche; he asks them all to aid in this work of reconciliation. Doubtless he did not plead in vain. See SYNTYCHE; YOKEFELLOW.

4. The True Yokefellow

5. The Plea for Reconciliation

JOHN RUTHERFURD

EUPATOR, ū'pa-tor (**Εὐπάτωρ,** *Eupátōr,* "of noble father"): The name given to Antiochus V who had succeeded his father Antiochus IV (Epiphanes), 164 BC, while still a child under the guardianship of Lysias (1 Macc **3** 32; **6** 17). In the absence of Philip, a friend and foster-brother of the child's father, whom on his deathbed he had appointed guardian for his son, Lysias continued his duty as guardian, set the king upon the throne and named him Eupator. Shortly after his accession he collected a large army and marched against Jerus, accompanied by Lysias, for the relief of a Syrian garrison that was hard pressed by Judas Maccabaeus (**6** 19 ff). Judas was repulsed at Bethzacharias and after a severe struggle Bethsura was captured (vs 31–50). The Jewish force in the temple was hard pressed and indeed reduced to the last extremity (ver 53), when Lysias, hearing that his rival Philip had returned from Persia and had made himself master of Antioch (Jos, *Ant,* XII, ix, 5 f), made a hasty peace and returned to meet Philip, whom he easily overpowered. In the following year (162 BC) Antiochus and Lysias were put to death by Demetrius Soter, son of Seleucus, in requital of wrongs inflicted upon himself by Antiochus Epiphanes (1 Macc **7** 2–4; 2 Macc **14** 1.2; Jos, *Ant,* XII, x, 1). J. HUTCHISON

EUPHRATES, ū-frā'tēz (פְּרָת, *perāth;* **Εὐφράτης,** *Euphrátēs,* "the good and abounding river"): The longest (1,780 miles) and most important stream of Western Asia, generally spoken of in the OT as "the river" (Ex **23** 31; Dt **11** 24). Its description naturally falls into 3 divisions—the upper, middle and lower. The upper division traverses the mountainous plateau of Armenia, and is formed by the junction of 2 branches, the Frat and the Murad. The Frat rises 25 miles N.E. of Erzerum, and only 60 miles from the Black Sea. The Murad, which, though the shorter, is the larger of the two, rises in the vicinity of Mt. Ararat. After running respectively 400 and 270 miles in a westerly direction, they unite near Keban Maaden, whence in a tortuous channel of about 300 miles, bearing still in a southwesterly direction, the current descends in a succession of rapids and cataracts to the Syrian plain, some distance above the ancient city of Carchemish, where it is only about 200 miles from the N.E. corner of the Mediterranean. In its course through the Armenian plateau, the stream has gathered the sediment which gives fertility to the soil in the lower part of the valley. It is the melting snows from this region which produce the annual floods from April to June.

The middle division, extending for about 700 miles to the bitumen wells of Hit, runs S.E. "through a valley of a few miles in width, which it has eroded in the rocky surface, and which, being more or less covered with alluvial soil, is pretty generally cultivated by artificial irrigation. . . . . Beyond the rocky banks on both sides is the open desert, covered in spring with a luxuriant verdure, and dotted here and there with the black tent of the Bedouin" (Sir Henry Rawlinson). Throughout this portion the river formed the ancient boundary between the Assyrians and Hittites whose capital was at Carchemish, where there are the remains of an old bridge. The ruins of another ancient bridge occur 200 miles lower down at the ancient Thapsacus, where the Greeks forded it under Cyrus the younger. Throughout the middle section the stream is too rapid to permit of successful navigation except by small boats going downstream, and has few and insignificant tributaries. It here has, however, its greatest width (400 yds.) and depth. Lower down the water is drawn off by irrigating canals and into lagoons.

The fertile plain of Babylonia begins at Hit, about 100 miles above Babylon; 50 miles below Hit the Tigris and Euphrates approach to within 25 miles of each other, and together have in a late geological period deposited the plain of Shinar or of Chaldaea, more definitely referred to as Babylonia. This plain is about 250 miles long, and in its broadest place 100 miles wide. From Hit an artificial canal conducts water along the western edge of the alluvial plain to the Pers Gulf, a distance of about 500 miles. But the main irrigating canals put off from the E. side of the Euphrates, and can be traced all over the plain past the ruins of Accad, Babylon, Nippur, Bismya, Telloh, Erech, Ur and numerous other ancient cities.

Originally the Euphrates and Tigris entered into the Pers Gulf by separate channels. At that time the Gulf extended up as far as Ur, the home of Abraham, and it was a seaport. The sediment from these rivers has filled up the head of the Pers Gulf for nearly 100 miles since the earliest monumental records. Loftus estimates that since the Christian era the encroachment has proceeded at the rate of 1 mile in 70 years. In early times Babylonia was rendered fertile by immense irrigating schemes which diverted the water from the Euphrates, which at Babylon is running at a higher level than the Tigris. A large canal left the Euphrates just above Babylon and ran due E. to the Tigris, irrigating all the intervening region and sending a branch down as far S. as Nippur. Lower down a canal crosses the plain in an opposite direction. This ancient system of irrigation can be traced along the lines of the principal canals "by the winding curves of layers of alluvium in the bed," while the lateral channels "are hedged in by high banks of mud, heaped up during centuries of dredging. Not a hundredth part of the old irrigation system is now in working order. A few of the mouths of the smaller canals are kept open so as to receive a limited supply of water at the rise of the river in May, which then distributes itself over the lower lying lands in the interior, almost without labor on the part of the cultivators, giving birth in such localities to the most abundant crops; but by far the larger portion of the region between the rivers is at present an arid, howling wilderness, strewed in the most part with broken pottery, the evidence of former human habitation, and bearing nothing but the camel thorn, the wild caper, the colocynth-apple, wormwood and the other weeds of the desert" (Rawlinson). According to Sir W. Willcocks, the eminent Eng. engineer, the whole region is capable of being restored to its original productiveness by simply reproducing the ancient system of irrigation. There are, however, in the lower part of the region, vast marshes overgrown with reeds, which have continued since the time of Alexander who came near losing his army in passing through them. These areas are probably too much depressed to be capable of drainage. Below the junction of the Euphrates and the Tigris, the stream is called *Shat el Arab*, and is deep enough to float war vessels.

LITERATURE.—Fried. Delitzsch, *Wo lag das Paradies?* 169 f; Chesney, *Narrative of the Euphrates Exped.*, I; Loftus, *Travels, etc, in Chaldæa and Susiana;* Layard, *Nineveh and Babylon*, chs xxi, xxii; Rawlinson, *Herodotus*, I, essay ix; Ellsworth Huntington, "Valley of the Upper Euphrates River," *Bull. Amer. Geog. Soc.*, XXXIV, 1902.

GEORGE FREDERICK WRIGHT

EUPOLEMUS, ū-pol′ē-mus (**Εὐπόλεμος**, *Eupólemos*): Son of John, the son of Accos=Hakkoz (**'Ακκώς**, *Akkṓs;* Neh **3** 4.21, etc); was one of the two deputies sent by Judas Maccabaeus (1 Macc **8** 17; 2 Macc **4** 11) to Rome cir 161 BC to ask the help of the Romans against Demetrius. A critical estimate of the narrative (1 Macc **8** and Jos, *Ant*, XII, x, 6) of the first meeting of the representatives of the Jewish nation and the Romans will be found in Stanley, *Lectures on the History of the Jewish Church*, III, 350 ff, where it is admitted that "inaccuracies of detail only confirm the general faithfulness of the impression." Keil (*Comm.*, 14) further remarks on this point: "that the author of 1 Macc wrote from twenty to twenty-five years after the destruction of Corinth (146 BC) by the Romans; and that the Jews of Pal were not accurately informed concerning the wars of the Romans with the Greeks." E. has been identified with the historian of the same name quoted by Eusebius (*Praep. Ev.*, IX, 17 ff); but there is no evidence that the historian was of Jewish origin. J. HUTCHISON

EURAQUILO, ū-rak′wi-lō (RV **εὐρακύλων**, *eurakúlōn;* AV **εὐροκλύδων**, *euroklúdōn;* AV **Euroclydon**, ū-rok′li-don): The east or northeast wind which drove Paul's ship to shipwreck at Melita (Acts **27** 14). The term seems to have been the sailor's term for that particular wind, and Paul uses the word which was used by them on that occasion. The difference in the text is explained by the fact that the term was not in general use and was therefore subject to being changed. The precise name is doubtful, but the Euraquilo is more easily explained as a compound of Gr *eúros*, "east wind," and Lat *aquilo*, "northeast wind," hence *euraquilo*, "east northeast wind." This agrees with the experience of navigators in those waters. For a summary of the various readings see Sanday, *Appendices ad NT*, 140. Full discussion of the circumstances are given in the Lives of Paul by various writers.

ALFRED H. JOY

EUTYCHUS, ū′ti-kus (**Εὔτυχος**, *Eútuchos*, "fortunate"): The story of Eutychus occurs in the "we" section of Acts, and is therefore related by an eyewitness of the incidents (Acts **20** 7–12). On the first day of the week the Christians of Troas had met for an evening service in an upper chamber, and were joined by Paul and his company. As he was to leave in the morning, Paul "prolonged his speech until midnight." A youth named Eutychus, who was sitting at the open window, became borne down with sleep owing to the lateness of the hour, and ultimately fell through the opening from the third story. He "was taken up dead." This direct statement is evaded by De Wette and Olshausen, who translate "for dead." Meyer says this expresses the judgment of those who took him up. However, Luke, the physician, is giving his verdict, and he plainly believes that a miracle was wrought by Paul in restoring a corpse to life. The intention of Luke in relating this incident is to relate a miracle. Paul went down and embraced the youth while comforting the lamenting crowd, "Make ye no ado; for his life is in him." The interrupted meeting was resumed, the bread was broken, and the conversation continued till break of day. "And they brought the lad alive, and were not a little comforted." S. F. HUNTER

EVANGELIST, ē-van′jel-ist: This is a form of the word ordinarily tr^d "gospel" (εὐαγγέλιον, *euaggélion*), except that here it designates one who *announces* that gospel to others (εὐαγγελιστής, *euaggelistḗs*, "a bringer of good tidings"), lit. God Himself is an evangelist, for He "preached the gospel beforehand unto Abraham" (Gal **3** 8); Jesus Christ was an evangelist, for He also "preached the gospel" (Lk **20** 1); Paul was an evangelist as well as an apostle (Rom **1** 15); Philip the deacon was an evangelist (Acts **21** 8); and Timothy, the pastor (2 Tim **4** 5); and indeed all the early disciples who, on being driven out of Jerus, "went everywhere preaching the word" (Acts **8** 4 AV).

But Eph **4** **11** teaches that one particular order of the ministry, distinguished from every other, is singled out by the Head of the church for this work in a distinctive sense. All may possess the gift of an evangelist in a measure, and be obligated to exercise its privilege and duty, but some are specially endued with it. "He gave some to be apostles; and some, prophets; and some, evangelists; and some, pastors and teachers."

It will be seen that as an order in the ministry, the evangelist precedes that of the pastor and teacher, a fact which harmonizes with the character of the work each is still recognized as doing. The evangelist has no fixed place of residence, but moves about in different localities, preaching the gospel to those ignorant of it before. As these are converted and united to Jesus Christ by faith, the work of the pastor and teacher begins, to instruct them further in the things of Christ and build them up in the faith.

At a later time, the name of "evangelist" was given the writers of the four Gospels because they tell the story of the gospel and because the effect of their promulgation at the beginning was very much like the work of the preaching evangelist. In character, the Gospels bear something of the same relation to the Epistles as evangelists bear to pastors and teachers. James M. Gray

EVE, ēv, **IN THE OT** (חַוָּה, *ḥawwāh*, "life"; **Εὕα,** *Eúa;* the name given, as the Scripture writer says, Gen **3** 20 [**Ζωή,** *Zōḗ*], from her unique function as "the mother of all living"): The first created woman; created secondarily from Adam (or man) as a "help meet for him" (**2** 18–22), and later named and designated as the mother of the human race.

For the literary type and object of the story of Eve, see under Adam, I, 2.

1. The Names Given to Her

Two names are given to her, both bestowed by the man, her mate. The first, אִשָּׁה, *'ishshāh*, "woman" (lit. "man-ess"), is not strictly a name but a generic designation, referring to her relation to the man; a relation she was created to fulfil in default of any true companionship between man and the beasts, and represented as intimate and sacred beyond that between child and parents (**2** 18–24). The second, Eve, or "life," given after the transgression and its prophesied results, refers to her function and destiny in the spiritual history or evolution of which she is the beginning (**3** 16.20). While the names are represented as bestowed by the man, the remarks in **2** 24 and **3** 20*b* may be read as the interpretative addition of the writer, suited to the exposition which it is the object of his story to make.

2. Her Relation to Man

As mentioned in the art. Adam, the distinction of male and female, which the human species has in common with the animals, is given in the first general account of creation (**1** 27); and then, in the more particularized account (Gen **2**) of the creation of man, the human being is described at a point before the distinction of sex existed. This second account may have a different origin, but it has also a different object, which does not conflict with but rather supplements the other. It aims to give the spiritual meanings that inhere in man's being; and in this the relation of sex plays an elemental part. As spiritually related to the man-nature, the woman-nature is described as derivative, the helper rather than the initiator, yet equal, and supplying perfectly the man's social and affectional needs. It is the writer's conception of the essential meaning of mating and marriage. To bring out its spiritual values more clearly he takes the pair before they are aware of the species meanings of sex or family, while they are "naked" yet "not ashamed" (**2** 25), and portrays them purely as companions, individual in traits and tendencies, yet answering to each other. She is the helpmeet for him (*'ēzer k^eneghdō*, "a help answering to him").

3. Her Part in the Change of Condition

True to her nature as the being relatively acted upon rather than acting, she is quicker than the man to respond to the suggestion initiated by the serpent and to follow it out to its desirable results. There is eagerness of desire in her act of taking the fruit quite different from the quasi matter-of-course attitude of the man. To her the venture presents itself wholly from the alluring side, while to him it is more like taking a desperate risk, as he detaches himself even from the will of God in order to cleave to her. All this is delicately true to the distinctive feminine and masculine natures. A part of her penalty is henceforth to be the subordinated one of the pair (**3** 16), as if for her the values of life were to be mediated through him. At the same time it is accorded to her seed to perpetuate the mortal antipathy to the serpent, and finally to bruise the serpent's head (ver 15).

4. In Subsequent History

After these opening chapters of Gen, Eve is not once mentioned, nor even specifically alluded to, in the canonical books of the OT. It was not in the natural scope of OT history and doctrine, which were concerned with Abraham's descendants, to go back to so remote origins as are narrated in the story of the first pair. The name Eve occurs once in the Apoc, in the prayer of Tobit (Tob **8** 6): "Thou madest Adam, and gavest him Eve his wife for a helper and a stay; of them came the seed of men"; the text then going on to quote Gen **2** 18. In 1 Esd **4** 20.21 there is a free quotation, or rather paraphrase, of Gen **2** 24. But not even in the somber complaints of 2 Esd concerning the woe that Adam's transgression brought upon the race (see under Adam in OT, III, 2) is there any hint of Eve's part in the matter.

John Franklin Genung

EVE IN THE NT (**Εὕα,** *Eúa;* WH, **Εὑα,** *Heúa*): "Eve" occurs twice in the NT and both references are in the Pauline writings. In 1 Tim **2** 12–14 woman's place in teaching is the subject of discussion, and the writer declares that she is a learner and not a teacher, that she is to be in quietness and not to have dominion over a man. Paul elsewhere expressed this same idea (see 1 Cor **14** 34.35). Having stated his position in regard to woman's place, he used the Gen account of the relation of the first woman to man to substantiate his teaching. Paul used this account to illustrate woman's inferiority to man, and he undoubtedly accepted it at its face value without any question as to its historicity. He argued that woman is inferior in position, for "Adam was first formed, then Eve." She is inferior in character, for "Adam was not beguiled, but the woman being beguiled hath fallen into transgression." See Child-Bearing. In 2 Cor **11** 3, Paul is urging loyalty to Christ, and he uses the temptation of Eve to illustrate the ease with which one is corrupted. Paul seems to have had no thought but that the account of the serpent's beguiling Eve should be taken literally.

A. W. Fortune

EVE, GOSPEL OF: A gnostic doctrinal treatise mentioned by Epiphanius (*Haer.*, xxvi.2 ff) in which Jesus is represented as saying in a loud voice,

"I am thou, and thou art I, and wherever thou art there am I, and in all things I am sown. And from whencesoever thou gatherest me, in gathering me thou gatherest thyself." See Logia; and cf Ropes, *Die Sprüche Jesu*, 56.

EVEN, ē'v'n, **EVENING,** ēv'ning, **EVENTIDE,** ēv-'n-tīd' ("even," "evening," עֶרֶב, *'erebh;* **ὀψία,** *opsía,* **ὀψέ,** *opsé;* vide Thayer s.v.): The words are used in slightly different meanings: (1) The time of sunset, the beginning of the Heb day, as in Lev **15,** where directions are given for the removal of uncleanness, which took place at sunset. (2) Twilight, the time of approaching darkness when lamps are lighted; Ex **30** 8 (lit. "between the two evenings"); Jer **6** 4 ("the *shadows* of the evening"). (3) The early part of the night (Prov **7** 9; Ezk **12** 7). The Gr *opse* is lit. "late" (Mk **11** 19). The Gr *ἑσπέρα, hespéra,* refers evidently to sunset, in Lk **24** 29. "Eventide," עֵת עֶרֶב, *'ēth 'erebh,* "time of evening" (2 S **11** 2; Isa **17** 14). "Evening," used in connection with wolves (Jer **5** 6; Zeph **3** 3), is from the Heb עֲרָבָה, *'ărābhāh,* which may mean "darkness" or "dark cloud," but more probably "plain" or "desert."

H. Porter

EVENINGS, BETWEEN THE: The time of day (RV reads "at even," m "between the two evenings") when the Passover lamb was slain (Ex **12** 6; Nu **9** 3), or the offering made of the evening portion of the continual burnt offering (Nu **28** 4). See preceding article.

EVENT, ē-vent': In Eccl **2** 14; **9** 2.3, the tr of מִקְרֶה, *miḳreh,* "what happens," "lot," "fate." The Eng. word bore this sense at the time of AV. The meaning of "result," "outcome" (*ἐκβάσεις, ekbáseis*), attaches to it in Wisd **8** 8, "events of seasons," RV "issues."

EVERLASTING, ev-ēr-last'ing (עוֹלָם, *'ōlām,* עַד, *'adh;* **ἀΐδιος,** *aḯdios,* **αἰώνιος,** *aiṓnios*): "Everlasting," in strictness, is that which endures forever; either that which has no beginning and will have no end (in which sense it is applicable to God only), or that which, having a beginning, will have no end, but henceforth will exist forever (thus of beings created for immortality; see Immortality). **Figuratively** also the term is applied to objects of impressive stability and long duration, as mountains, hills (e.g. Gen **49** 26; Hab **3** 6).

Of the terms indicated as rendered by this word, *'ōlām* in the OT and *aiōnios* in the NT, lit. "age-long," generally bear the full sense of "eternal" (always as applied to God, His mercy, His covenant, His kingdom and to the eternal life of believers). Hence in RV the rendering "everlasting" in AV is, in the NT, uniformly changed to "eternal" (e.g. Mt **18** 8; **25** 41.46; Lk **16** 9; **18** 30; Jn **3** 16.36, etc; Acts **13** 46; Rom **6** 22; **16** 26; Gal **6** 8; He **13** 20). In the OT the rendering "everlasting" is usually retained in RV, and sometimes takes the place of other words or phrases, as "lasting" (Dt **33** 15), "ever," "forever" (1 Ch **16** 36; Neh **9** 5), "perpetual" (Hab **3** 6; Jer **50** 5), "of old" (Hab **3** 6 m). In Ps **100** 5; **119** 144, on the other hand, RV changes the word to "for ever." In much the larger number of places *'ōlām* is tr[d] "ever" or "for ever."

The word *'adh,* in the two cases in which it is tr[d] "everlasting" in AV (more frequently "for ever"), is in RV, in Isa **9** 6, retained, with m, "Father of Eternity," and in Hab **3** 6 is changed into "eternal." Another word, *ḳedhem,* with the meaning "ancient time," is rendered "everlasting" in Hab **1** 12 ("Art not thou from everlasting?"). With the same meaning it occurs in Dt **33** 27, "The eternal God is thy dwelling-place."

The word which strictly answers to "everlasting" in the NT is *aïdios* (Rom **1** 20; Jude ver 6), rendered by AV in the former passages "eternal," but correctly by RV in both passages, "everlasting." The sense of the word "everlasting," in application to future punishment, is considered in art. Punishment, Everlasting.

The term "everlasting" or "eternal," applied to God, describes Him as filling, or enduring through, all the "ages" of time. It is only thus that we can symbolically represent eternity. In reality, however, the eternity of God is not simply His filling of ever-flowing "ages," but rather that aspect of His being in which He is above time; for which time (the succession-form of existence) does not exist; to which the terms past, present and future do not apply. Yet, while God is not in time (rather holds time in Himself), time-sequence, as the form of existence of the world, is a reality for God. See Eternal; Eternity.

James Orr

EVI, ē'vī (אֱוִי, *'ĕwī,* "desire"; **Εὐεί,** *Eueí*): One of the five kings, or chiefs of the Midianites, slain by Israel during their sojourn in the plains of Moab (Nu **31** 8; Josh **13** 21).

EVIDENCE, ev'i-dens, **EVIDENT, EVIDENTLY,** ev'i-dent-li (סֵפֶר, *ṣēpher;* **ἔλεγχος,** *élegchos,* **φανερῶς,** *phanerōs*): In Jer **32** 10.11.12.14.16.44, *ṣēpher,* "a writing," is tr[d] (AV) "evidence" (of the purchase of the field in Anathoth), RV "deed"; "evidence" is also the tr of *elegchos,* "conviction," in AV of He **11** 1, "Now faith is . . . . the evidence of things not seen," ERV "proving," m "or test," better, as ARV, "conviction," m "or test." The Gr word denotes "putting to the test," examining for the purpose of proof, bringing to conviction (Dr. W. F. Moulton). Thus if "test" or "proving" be adopted, a firm *conviction* of the reality of things not seen is implied as the result of putting to the proof. Trench remarks (*NT Synonyms*), "in juristic Gr *elégchein* is not merely to reply to, but to refute, an opponent." Hence the Vulg tr *argumentum,* followed by Wyclif and Rheims version; Tyndale and Cranmer have "certayntie." (The sense of "conviction" appears in Jn **8** 46, "Which of you convinceth [*elegchei,* RV "convicteth"] me of sin?"; **3** 20, "reproved," RVm "convicted"; **16** 8 AV "He will reprove the world of sin," RV "convict." Cf 1 Cor **14** 24.) "Evident" is the tr of *'al pānīm* ("on the face") in Job **6** 28, AV "Look upon me; for it is evident unto you if I lie," m "Heb before your face," RV "to your face," m "And it will be evident unto you if I lie," which is, perhaps, to be preferred to the text; *dēlos,* "manifest," is tr[d] "evident" (Gal **3** 11); *katádēlos,* "very manifest," is in He **7** 15, AV "far more evident," RV "more abundantly evident"; *pródēlos,* "manifest before-hand" (**7** 14), "evident." "Evidently" occurs only in Acts **10** 3, as the tr of *phanerōs,* "openly," "manifestly," RV "openly."

It is important to note the true nature of faith according to the correct tr of He **11** 1, as being the well-grounded and assured *conviction* of things not seen.

W. L. Walker

EVIL, ēv''l, ē'vil (רַע, *ra';* **πονηρός,** *ponērós,* **κακός,** *kakós,* **κακόν,** *kakón*): In the Bible it is represented as moral and physical. We choose to discuss the subject under these heads. Many of the evils that come upon men have not been intended by those who suffer for them. Disease, individual and national calamity, drouth, scarcity of food, may not always be charged to the account of intentional wrong. Many times the innocent suffer with, and even for, the guilty. In such cases, only physical evil is apparent. Even when the suffering has been occasioned by sin or dereliction of duty, whether the wrong is active or passive, many, perhaps the majority of those who are injured, are not accountable in any way for the ills which come upon them. Neither is God the author of moral evil. "God cannot be tempted with evil, and he himself tempteth no man" (Jas **1** 13). See TEMPTATION.

1. Moral Evil

By this term we refer to wrongs done to our fellowman, where the actor is responsible for the action. The immorality may be present when the action is not possible. "But if that evil servant shall say in his heart" (Mt **24** 48.49), whether he shall smite his fellow-servants or not, the moral evil is present. See SIN. "All these evil things proceed from within, and defile the man" (Mk **7** 21–23). The last six commandments of the Decalogue apply here (Ex **20** 12–17). To dishonor one's parents, to kill, to commit adultery, to steal, to bear false witness and to covet are moral evils. The spiritual import of these commandments will be found in Mt **5** 21. 22.27.28. "But if thine eye be evil, thy whole body shall be full of darkness" (**6** 23). Words and deeds are coined in the heart before the world sees or hears them (**12** 34.35). The word *ought* or its equal may be found in all languages; hence it is in the mind of all people as well as in our laws that for the deeds and words we do and speak, we are responsible. "Break off thy sins by righteousness" (Dnl **4** 27) shows that, in God's thought, it was man's duty, and therefore within his power, to keep the commandment. "Wash you, make you clean; put away the evil of your doings from before mine eyes; cease to do evil; learn to do well" (Isa **1** 16 f). We cannot think of God commanding men to do what He knew they had no ability to do! God has a standing offer of pardon to all men who turn from their evil ways and do that which is right (Ezk **33** 11–14 f). Evil begins in the least objectionable things. In Rom **1** 18–23, we have Paul's view of the falling away of the Gentiles. "Knowing God" (ver 21), they were "without excuse" (ver 20), but "glorified him not as God, neither gave thanks; but became vain in their reasonings, and their senseless heart was darkened" (ver 21). "Professing themselves to be wise, they became fools" (ver 22). This led the way into idolatry, and that was followed by all the corruption and wrongdoing to be instigated by a heart turned away from all purity, and practised in all the iniquity to be suggested by lust without control. Paul gives fifteen steps in the ladder on which men descend into darkness and ruin (Gal **5** 19–21). When men become evil in themselves, they necessarily become evil in thought and deed toward others. This they bring upon themselves, or give way to, till God shall give "them up unto a reprobate mind, to do those things which are not fitting" (Rom **1** 28). Those thus fallen into habits of error, we should in meekness correct, that "they may recover themselves out of the snare of the devil, having been taken captive by him unto his will" (2 Tim **2** 25.26).

2. Physical Evil

Usually, in the OT the Heb word *ra'* is employed to denote that which is bad. Many times the *bad* is physical; it may have been occasioned by the sins for which the people of the nation were responsible, or it may have come, not as a retribution, but from accident or mismanagement or causes unknown. Very many times the evil is a corrective, to cause men to forsake the wrong and accept the right. The flood was sent upon the earth because "all flesh had corrupted their way" (Gen **6** 12). This evil was to serve as a warning to those who were to live after. The ground had already been cursed for the good of Cain (**4** 12). Two purposes seemed to direct the treatment: (1) to leave in the minds of Cain and his descendants the knowledge that sin brings punishment, and (2) to increase the toil that would make them a better people. God overthrew Sodom, Gomorrah, Admah and Zeboim, cities of the plain, making them "an example unto those that should live ungodly" (2 Pet **2** 6). In the Book of Isa the prophet, we find a number of "burdens": the burden of Babylon (**13** 1–22); the burden of Moab (**15** 1–9); the burden of Damascus (**17** 1–14); the burden of Egypt (**19** 1–17); the burden of the Wilderness of the Sea (**21** 1–10); the burden of Dumah (vs 11.12); the burden upon Arabia (vs 13–17); the burden of the Valley of Vision (**22** 1–25); the burden of Tyre (**23** 1–18); the burden of the Beasts of the South (**30** 6–14); the burden of the Weary Beast (**46** 1.2). These may serve as an introduction to the story of wrongdoing and physical suffering threatened and executed. Isa contains many denunciations against Israel: against the Ten Tribes for following the sin introduced by Jeroboam the son of Nebat; and the threatening against Judah and Benjamin for not heeding the warnings. Jeremiah saw the woes that were sure to come upon Judah; for declaring them, he was shut up in prison, and yet they came, and the people were carried away into Babylon. These were the evils or afflictions brought upon the nations for their persistence in sin. "I form the light, and create darkness; I make peace, and create evil; I am Jeh, that doeth all these things" (Isa **45** 7). These chastisements seemed grievous, and yet they yielded peaceable fruit unto them that were exercised thereby (He **12** 11).

DAVID ROBERTS DUNGAN

EVIL-DOERS, ē-v'l-dōō'ērz (מְרֵעִים, *m^erē'īm;* from רָעַע, *rā'a';* κακοποιός, *kakopoiós*, always pl.): Malefactors or offenders of God's law. Used generally of the ungodly, as, "Fret not thyself because of e." (Ps **37** 1). Sometimes also of personal offenders: "He hath delivered the soul of the needy from the hand of e." (Jer **20** 13).

EVIL EYE (רַע עַיִן, *ra' 'ayin*, "evil of eye"; ὀφθαλμὸς πονηρός, *ophthalmós ponērós*): The superstition of the influence of the "evil eye," so widely spread over the earth, has had a mighty influence on life and language in Pal, though direct references to it are not frequent in the Scriptures (Dt **15** 9; **28** 54.56; Prov **23** 6; **28** 22; Mt **20** 15 [cf Mt **6** 23; Lk **11** 34]; Mk **7** 22). In the Bible the expression is synonymous with envy, jealousy and some forms of covetousness. In comparing Rom **1** 29 with Mk **7** 22 we find that *ophthalmos poneros* corresponds to *φθόνος, phthónos*. See Trench, *NT Synonyms*, s.v. The eye of the envious (as also the tongue of the invidious by an apparently appreciative word, which, however, only disguises the strong desire of possessing the object of comment or of destroying it for its rightful owner) was supposed to have a baneful influence upon the well-being of others, esp. of children. Therefore mothers bestowed constant care against the frustration of such fancied designs by means of innumerable sorts of charms. They often allowed their darlings to appear as unlovely as possible, through uncleanliness or rags, so as to spare them the harmful rising of envy in the hearts of others. Lane, *Manners and Customs of the Modern Egyptians*, gives perhaps the most accessible account of this superstition as held at the present day in Egypt, and Thomson, *The Land and the Book*, does the same for Pal, while an equal amount of evidence might be collected from every other oriental country. Instances of the same superstition, though possibly slightly disguised, are by no means wanting among ourselves. Cf the expression, "green-eyed jealousy" (*Othello*, III, iii; *Merchant of Venice*, III, ii), etc.

For certain Bib. phrases referring to the "evil eye" see ENVY; EYE.

LITERATURE.—F. T. Elworthy, *The Evil Eye*, London, 1895.

H. L. E. LUERING

EVIL-FAVOREDNESS, ē-v'l-fā'vērd-nes: The word is the tr of the Heb דָּבָר רַע, *dābhār ra'*, lit. "evil thing," and refers to the ritual unfitness for sacrifice of any animal which, though included in the class of clean beasts, yet possesses a blemish (see the word), or otherwise lacks beauty of symmetry, or is lean-fleshed (Dt **17** 1 AV; cf "ill blemish," Dt **15** 21). We find these conditions combined in Gen **41** 3.4.19.20.21.27, where the seven "ill-favored and lean-fleshed" kine of Pharaoh's dream are mentioned.

EVIL-MERODACH, ē-vil-me-rō'dak; -mer'ō-dak (אֱוִיל מְרֹדַךְ, *'ĕwīl m^erōdhakh;* LXX **Εὐειαλμαρωδέκ**, *Eueialmarōdék;* so B in K, but B in Jer, and A and Q in both places much corrupted): The name of the son and immediate successor of Nebuchadnezzar II, king of Babylon. The Bab form of the name is *Amelu-Marduk,* that is, "man of Marduk." About 30 contract tablets dated in this reign have been found. They show that Evil-merodach reigned for two years and about five months. He is said by Berosus to have conducted his government in an illegal and improper manner, and to have been slain by his sister's brother, Nergal-shar-uṣur, who then reigned in his stead. Evil-merodach is said in 2 K **25** 27–30 and in the ∥ passage in Jer **52** 31–34 to have taken Jehoiachin, king of Judah, from his prison in Babylon, where he seems to have been confined for 37 years, to have clothed him with new garments, to have given him a seat above all the other kings, and to have allowed him to eat at the king's table all the days of his life. It is an undesigned coincidence, that may be worthy of mention, that the first dated tablet from this reign was written on the 26th of Elul, and Jer **52** 31 says that Jehoiachin was freed from prison on the 25th of the same month. R. DICK WILSON

EVIL ONE (**ὁ πονηρός**, *ho ponērós*): Nearly all peoples who have expressed their religious thought and feeling believe in a spirit that presides over the destinies of men for their good. They believe that there is also a spirit, a person, whose work it is to lead men into temptation: a spirit of light and a spirit of darkness. Feelings and preferences may have much to do with the conclusions. In Mt **5** 37.39.45; **6** 13, AV gives "evil," RV "the evil *one,*" m "evil," the personal form referring to the enemy of the race known by various terms: Satan, "the adversary" or "the accuser," occurs 50 t; Beelzebub is found 7 t; devil, 35 t; it means "accuser," "calumniator." See SATAN.

DAVID ROBERTS DUNGAN

EVIL-SPEAKING, ē-v'l-spēk'ing: Occurs twice in EV: (1) 1 Pet **2** 1 it is the tr of *καταλαλιά, katalaliá,* "a speaking against," rendered "backbiting" in 2 Cor **12** 20; cf *katálalos,* "backbiter" (Rom **1** 30); the vb. *katalaléō* is rendered to "speak against" (1 Pet **2** 12; Jas **4** 11; 1 Pet **3** 16); (2) of *βλασφημία, blasphēmía,* "what is hurtful to the good name of anyone," "detraction," "slander" (Eph **4** 31 RV, "railing"; cf 1 Tim **6** 4; Jude ver 9; Col **3** 8); the vb. *blasphemeō* is rendered to "speak evil of" (Rom **14** 16; 1 Cor **10** 30; Tit **3** 2, etc); to "speak evil" occurs in Mk **9** 39 as the tr of *kakologéō,* "lightly [RV "quickly"] speak evil of me"; Acts **19** 9 AV "spake evil of that way." In Ps **140** 11, we have "evil-speaker" as the tr of *'īsh lāshōn,* "a man of tongue"; so RV. The wrong thing condemned as evil-speaking seems to be essentially *detraction,* what is hurtful to the reputation, and it is often too lightly regarded even among Christians. See BLASPHEMY; RAILING; SLANDER.

W. L. WALKER

EVIL SPIRIT. See DEMON; DEMONIAC; COMMUNION WITH DEMONS; SATAN.

EVIL THING (**τὸ κακόν**, *tó kakón,* pl. in Lk **16** 25): An evil thing or evil things may be the thoughts of evil men, their plans or their deeds; or the things men suffer for their own wrongs; or the evils consequent upon the errors of others. In the dark picture of fallen men in Rom **1** 30, "inventors of evil things" appear. "The evil man out of his evil treasure bringeth forth evil [*ponērós*] things" (Mt **12** 35). Men should not lust after evil (*kakós*) things (1 Cor **10** 6). This fixing the mind upon, with desire, leads to increased wrong. "The mouth of the wicked poureth out evil [*ra'*] things" (Prov **15** 28). The rich man had good things in his life, but did not use them to the glory of God or the good of men. The poor man had evil things: sickness, nakedness, hunger. The scene changes after death (Lk **16** 25).

DAVID ROBERTS DUNGAN

EVOLUTION, ev-ō-lū'shun: Evolution is a scientific and philosophical theory designed to explain the origin and course of all things in the universe. By origin, however, is not understood the production or emergence of the substance and of the cause or causes of things, but that of the forms in which they appear to the observer. Sometimes the term is vaguely used to cover absolute origin in the sense just excluded. A moment's reflection will make it clear that such a view can never secure a place in the realm of pure science. The problem of ultimate origin is not one that science can solve. If it is solved at all, it must be by purely philosophical as distinguished from scientific or scientific-philosophical methods. Evolution, therefore, must be viewed in science purely and strictly as a process of orderly change in the form of things. As such it assumes the existence of substance or substances and of a force or forces working its successive transformations.[1]

1. The Idea of Evolution

As an orderly change of the form of things, evolution may be viewed as operative in the field of inorganic matter, or in that of life. In the first, it is known and called cosmic evolution; in the second, organic evolution. Of cosmic evolution again there appear two aspects, according as the process, or law of transformation, is observed to operate in the realm of the lower units of matter (atoms and molecules), or is studied in the region of the great. In the first sphere, it is made to account for the emergence in Nature of the qualities and powers of different kinds of matter called elements. In the second, it explains the grouping together, the movements and transformations of the solar and of stellar systems. Similarly, of organic evolution there appear to be two varieties. The first occurs in the world of life including the vegetable and animal kingdoms. Evolution here accounts for the various forms of living beings building their bodies and passing from one stage to another in their existence as individuals, and for the course of the history of all life as it differentiates into species and genera. The second variety of evolution operates in the higher realm of intelligence, morality, social activity and religion.

The idea of a law of orderly change governing all things is not a new one. Historians of science find

[1] This position is apparently contradicted in the title of Henri Bergson's *L'évolution créatrice.* But an examination of Bergson's system shows that the contradiction is only apparent. Bergson's evolution is neither substance nor efficient cause or principle. The latter is given in his vital impetus (*élan vital*); the former in his concept of duration.

it in some form or other embodied in the philosophies of Heraclitus, Democritus, Lucretius and Aristotle. There are those who find it also in the system of Gautama (Buddha). But in none of these was there a sufficiently wide basis of fact inductively brought together, or a thorough enough digestion and assimilation of the material to give the view as presented by them a firm standing. Hegel's idealistic theory of Development is kindred to the evolution theory in its essence; but it too antedates the working out of the system upon the basis of the scientific induction of the phenomena of Nature.

2. Recent Origin of Notion

Until the time of Herbert Spencer, the scientific use of the word evolution was limited to the narrow department of embryology. By him, the term was made synonymous with all orderly change in Nature. The notion that such change is the result of chance, however, was not a part of Spencer's teaching. On the contrary, that philosopher held that chance is but the expression of laws undiscerned by the human mind. Yet these laws are just as definite and rigid as those already discovered and formulated.

Since the appearance of the inductive method in scientific research, and the rise of the science of biology in particular, the idea of evolution has been elaborated into a great systematic generalization, and proposed as the philosophy of all perceptible phenomena. Beginning as a working hypothesis in a special narrow department, that of biology, it has been extended into all the sciences until all come under its dominance, and it is viewed no longer as a mere working hypothesis, but as a demonstrated philosophy with the force and certainty of fact.

3. Evolution and Biblical Truth

It was natural that such an important proposition as the explanation of the present form of the whole universe by the theory of evolution should in its course have occasioned much controversy. On one side extravagant claims were bound to be put forth in its behalf, combined with a misconception of its field. On the other a stubborn denial of its sufficiency as an explanation, even in the narrow sphere where it first made its appearance, was destined to confront it. This challenge, too, was the result of the misconception of it as an all-sufficient theory of the universe as distinguished from a law or method of the operation of a cause ulterior and superior to itself. The period of this warfare is now nearly, if not altogether, over. The task which remains to be accomplished is to recognize the bearings of the theory on forms of thought arrived at apart from the light thrown on the world by itself.

Since such forms of thought are given in the Bible, certain problems arise which must be solved, if possible, in the light of evolution. These problems concern mainly the following topics: (1) The belief in a personal God, such as the Christian Scriptures present as an object of revelation; (2) The origin of the different species of living beings as portrayed in the Book of Gen; (3) The particular origin of the human species (the descent [ascent] of man); (4) The origin of morality and religion, and (5) The essential doctrines of the Christian faith, such as supernatural revelation, the idea of sin, the person of Christ, regeneration and immortality. Beyond the answers to these primary questions, it will be neither possible nor profitable to enter within the brief compass of the present article.

4. Evolution and Creation

The relation of creation to evolution has been already suggested in the introductory explanation of the nature of evolution. If creation be the act of bringing into existence material or substance which did not previously exist, evolution does not touch the problem. It has nothing to say of a First Cause. The idea of a first cause may be regarded as material for metaphysics or the ground of religious belief. It may be speculated about, or it may be assumed by faith. The theory of evolution begins with matter or substance already in existence. A fairly representative statement of this aspect of it is illustrated by Huxley's dictum, "The whole world living and not living is the result of the mutual attraction according to definite laws of the powers possessed by the molecules of which the primitive nebulosity of the universe was composed" (*Life of Darwin*, II, 210). This statement leaves two things unaccounted for, namely, molecules in the form of a "primitive nebulosity" and "powers possessed by these molecules." How did primitive nebulosity come to exist? How did it come to be composed of molecules possessed of certain powers, and how did there come to be definite laws governing these molecules? The agnostic answers, "We do not know, we shall not know" (*ignoramus, ignorabimus*, DuBois-Reymond). The pantheist says, "They are the substance and attributes of the Ultimate Being." The theist posits "an uncaused Cause who is greater than they, and possesses all the potentialities exhibited in them, together with much more (therefore at least a personal being), has brought them into existence by the power of His will" (cf EPICUREANS).

Thus the believer in evolution may be an agnostic, a pantheist or a theist, according to his attitude toward, and answer to, the question of beginnings. He is an evolutionist because he believes in evolution as the method of the transformation of molecules under the control of the powers possessed by them. Conversely the theist (and by implication the Christian) may be an evolutionist. As an evolutionist he may be thoroughgoing. He may accept evolution either as a working hypothesis or as a well-established generalization, even in the form in which it is defined by Herbert Spencer: the integration of matter out of an indefinite incoherent homogeneity into definite coherent heterogeneity with concomitant dissipation of energy. (For the exact definition in its full length, see *First Principles*, 367.) In this definition, as in every other form of it, evolution is the name of a process of transformation, not a theory of absolute causation or creation *ex nihilo*. The human mind may leave the problem of initial creation uninvestigated; it may assume that there is no problem by regarding matter and energy as uncaused and ultimate realities or phases of one reality; or it may trace these back to a First Cause which has at least the powers and characteristics perceptible in the universe and particularly in itself as mind (i.e. individuality, intelligence and freedom), or in other words, to a personal God. In any of these contingencies it may hold to the theory of evolution.

5. Evolution and the Origin of Species

Evolution is strongest in the realm of life. It is here that it first achieved its most signal conquests; and it is here that it was first antagonized most forcibly by the champions of religious faith. Here it proved irresistibly fascinating because it broke down the barriers supposed to exist between different species (whether minor or major) of life. It showed the unity and solidarity of the entire living universe with all its infinite variety. It reduced the life-process to one general law and movement. It traced back all present different forms, whether recognized as individuals, varieties, species, genera, families or kingdoms, to a single starting-point. In this realm the adjective "organic" has been prefixed to it, because the characteristic result is secured through organization. One of its most enthusiastic supporters defines it as "progressive change according to certain laws and by means of resident forces" (LeConte).

The proof for organic evolution is manifold. It cannot be given here at any length. Its main lines, however, may be indicated as follows: (1) The existence of gradations of structure in living forms beginning with the simplest (the amoeba usually furnishes the best illustration) and reaching to some of the most complex organisms (the human body). (2) The succession of living forms in time. This means that, according to the evidence furnished by geology, the simpler organisms appeared earlier on the face of the earth than the more complex, and that the progress of forms has been in general from the simpler to the more complex. (3) The parallelism between the order thus discovered in the history of life upon earth and the order observed in the transformations of the embryo of the highest living forms from their first individual appearance to their full development. (4) The existence of rudimentary members and organs in the higher forms.

The most striking of these proofs of evolution are the two commonly designated the paleontological and the ontogenetic. The first is based on the fact that in the strata of the earth the simpler forms have been deposited in the earlier, and the more complex in the later. This fact points to the growth in the history of the earth of the later, more complex forms of life, from earlier simpler ones. The second consists in the observation that each individual of complexly constructed species of organisms begins its life in the embryonic stage as the simplest of all living forms, a single cell (constituted in some cases out of parts of two preëxisting cells). From this beginning it advances to its later stages of growth as an embryo, assuming successively the typical forms of higher organisms until it attains the full form of its own species, and thus begins its individual post-embryonic life. It thus recapitulates in its individual history the history of its species as read in the paleontological records. This consideration shows that whatever the truth may be as to the species as a whole (for instance of man), each individual of the species (each man) has been evolved in his prenatal life, if not exactly from definitely known and identifiable species (anthropoid individuals perfectly formed), at least from foetal organisms apparently of the same type as those of anthropoids.

But assuming organic evolution to be true upon these grounds, and upon others of the same character, equally convincing to the scientific man, it must not be left out of account that it is to be distinguished quite sharply from cosmic evolution. These two phases of the law are identical at their basis, but become very different in their application according to the nature of the field in which they operate. Cosmic evolution works altogether through reactions. These are invariable in their cause and effect. Given material elements and conditions, they always issue in the same results. Their operations are grouped together under the sciences of chemistry and physics. Organic evolution works through processes to which the term "vital" is applied. Whether these are identical with the chemico-physical processes in the ultimate analysis is an open question among scientists. In the field of purely descriptive science, however, which limits itself to the observation of facts, it can scarcely emerge as a question, since the true nature of vitality is beyond the reach of observation. And upon the whole, the theory that there is an inner difference between vitality and physico-chemical attractions and affinities is supported by certain obvious considerations. But even if vitality should prove to be nothing more than a series of reactions of a chemical and physical nature, the type of evolution to which it yields is differentiated by broad characteristics that distinguish it from merely molecular attractions and affinities.

(1) Vital processes cannot be correlated with the chemico-physical ones. Heat, light, electricity, magnetism, gravitation, chemical affinity, are interchangeable and interchanged among themselves. But none of these can be converted into life as far as now known. (2) All life is from preëxisting life (*omne vivum e vivo*). Biogenesis still holds the field as far as experimental science has anything to say about it, and abiogenesis is at the most an attractive hypothesis. (3) The vital processes overcome and reverse the chemical and physical ones. When a living organism is constituted, and as long as it subsists in life, it breaks up and reconstitutes forms of matter into new forms. Carbon, nitrogen, hydrogen and oxygen, in combination with other elements, are separated from one another and reunited in new combinations in the tissues of the plant and the animal. On the other hand, the moment the vital process ceases, the chemical and physical resume their course. The organism in which the vital process has been annihilated is immediately put under the operation of chemical affinities, and reduced into its first elements. So long as the vital process is on, there seems to be a ruling or directive principle modifying and counteracting the normal and natural course of the so-called chemical and physical forces. (4) The vital process is characterized by the manifestation in matter of certain peculiarities that never show themselves apart from it. These are irritability, assimilation of non-living matter in the process of growth, differentiation or the power in each kind of living organism to develop in its growth regularly recurring characteristics, and (5) reproduction. The result of the vital process is the tendency in the organic product of it to maintain itself as a unity, and become more and more diversified in the course of its life.

These features of organic evolution make it necessary to account not only for the origin of the matter and the energy which are assumed in the cosmic form of evolution, but also for the origin and nature of the unknown something (or combination of things) which is called life in the organism, whether this be a unitary and distinct force or a group of forces. (It is interesting to notice the return to the notion of life as primal energy in the philosophy of Bergson [*élan vital*]; cf *Creative Evolution*. The same view is advocated by Sir Oliver Lodge, *Life and Matter*.)

Furthermore, care must be taken not to confuse any special variety of evolutionary theory in the organic realm with the generic theory itself. Evolutionists hold and propound different hypotheses as to the application of the principle. The Lamarckian, the Darwinian, the Weismannian, the De Vriesian views of evolution are quite different from, and at certain points contradictory of, one another. They assume the law to be real and aim to explain subordinate features or specific applications of it as seen in certain given series of facts. They differ from one another in insisting on details which may be real or unreal without affecting the truth of the main law. Lamarckian evolution, for instance (revived recently under the name neo-Lamarckian), makes much of the alleged transmissibility through heredity of acquired traits. Darwinian evolution is based largely on the principle of accidental variations worked over by natural selection and the slow insensible accumulation of traits fitting individuals to survive in the struggle for life. Weismannian evolution posits an astonishingly complex germinal starting-point. DeVriesian evolution is built on the sudden appearance of mutations ("sports") which are perpetuated, leading to new species. It is unscientific to array any of these against the other in the effort to undermine the generic theory of evolution, or to take their differences as indicating the collapse of the theory and a return to the idea of creation by *fiat*. The differences between them are insignificant as compared with the gulf which separates them all from the conception of a separate creative beginning for each species at the first appearance of life upon earth. (On some differences between the primitive form of Darwinian and later theories of the same general type, see Rudolph Otto, in *Naturalism and Religion* [ET].)

With these limitations, the law of organic evolution may be taken into the Bib. account of creation as given in Gen, chs **1** and **2**. The question raised at once is one of the relation of the doctrine to the Bib. account. If the evolutionary conception is true, it naturally follows that the Bib. account cannot be accepted in its literal interpretation. For the one of these accounts pictures the different species and general types as coming into existence gradually out of preëxisting ones, whereas the other (lit. interpreted) represents them as created by a Divine fiat. This difference it is true may be artificially exaggerated. Nowhere does the Bib. account explicitly ascribe the creation of each species to the fiat of God. The word "created" (*bārā'*), as used in Gen, does not necessarily exclude preëxisting matter and form. On the other hand, expressions such as "Let the earth bring forth" (**1** 11 AV) indicate a certain mediation of secondary powers in the elements ("resident forces," LeConte) through which organisms came into being. "After their kind" suggests the principle of heredity. "Abundantly" suggests the law of rapid and ample reproduction leading to the "struggle for life," "natural selection" and "survival of the fittest." But all efforts to harmonize Gen with science upon this basis lead at the best to the negative conclusion that these two are so far different in their purpose and scope as not to involve radical contradiction. A positive agreement between them cannot be claimed.

The difficulty vanishes in its entirety when it is borne in mind that the two accounts are controlled by different interests, treat primarily of different matters and, where they appear to cover the same ground, do so each in an incidental way. This means that their statements outside of the sphere of their primary interests are popularly conceived and expressed, and cannot be set over against each other as rivals in scientific presentation. Upon this basis the Gen account is the vehicle of religious instruction (not, however, an allegory); its cosmogonic accounts are not intended to be scientifically correct, but popularly adequate. For all that science is concerned, they may be traditional conceptions, handed down in the form of folklore, and purged of the grotesque, purely mythological element so apt to luxuriate in folklore. Between such accounts and the dicta of pure science, it would be absurd either to assume or to seek for harmony or discord. They are parallel pictures; in the one the foreground is occupied by the actual unfolding of the facts, the religious element is concealed deep by the figures in the foreground. In the other the background of haze and cloud is the domain of fact, the foreground of definite figures consists of the religious ideas and teachings. The evolutionary notion of the origin of living forms on the earth can thus in no way be assumed as in contradiction either to the letter or the spirit of the teaching of Gen.

6. The Descent (Ascent) of Man

A still more important problem arises when the evolutionary theory touches the origin of man upon earth. Here, too, not simply the Bib. account of the creation of Adam and Eve, and their primitive life in the Garden of Eden as recorded in Gen **2** is affected, but all that is said of man as a child of God, clothed with peculiar dignity and eternal worth.

(1) The difference between the Bib. and evolutionary records of the creation of man may easily be resolved if the Bib. account (Gen **2**) is not viewed as a literal statement of actual occurrences, but as the vehicle of certain determinative thoughts designed to affiliate man in his proper relation to God. This means that what is essential in the Bib. account is that man as a distinctive and different being in the world came into existence as the result of a special act of will on the part of God, that he was created as the golden summit of the whole upward movement of life. He is not a mere creature of Nature, but the offspring of the Divine will, with power to know his Maker, to hold fellowship with Him and to carry in him the rational and moral image of the Creator of all. Against this view of the origin of man, evolutionary science has nothing to set over. It is concerned with the process through which the emergence of such a being as man was accomplished, and the time and circumstances in which it took place. These points it finds as it finds similar points affecting other living beings.

It would be easy of course to take materialistic forms of the evolutionary theory, such as that advocated by Haeckel, Guyeau, Ray Lankester, and establish an irreconcilable discord between them and the Bib. account; but such varieties of the theory are distinguished, not by the occurrence of the idea of evolution in them, but rather by the materialistic metaphysics underlying them; when, for instance, Haeckel defines the notion of evolution by excluding from it intelligence or purpose, and by obliterating differences between the lower animal creation and man, he does so not as an evolutionist in science, but as a materialist (Monist of the materialistic type) in metaphysics. The moment the evolutionist determines to limit himself to the scientific side of his task, and the interpreter of the Bib. account to the religious side of his task, the assumed discord in Gen **2** and the evolutionary theory totally vanishes.

(2) The more important point of contact between the theory of evolution and the Bib. conception of man, however, is that of the notion of the dignity and worth of man. The very existence of a Bible is based on the idea that man is of some consequence to the Creator. And through the Bible this idea not only appears early (Gen **1** 26), "Let us make man in our image, after our likeness," followed by the statement, "And God created man in his own image, in the image of God created he him; male and female created he them," but is interwoven with every fundamental teaching.

It is contended that a representation like this is not compatible with the evolutionary conception of the origin of man from simian ancestors. The contention would be well supported if the evolutionary theory actually obliterated the line of distinction between man and the lower creation; and in any form of it in which such line is ignored, and man is regarded as a being of the same order (neither more or less) as those from which he sprang, it is not capable of being harmonized with the Bib. doctrine. But as a matter of fact, the whole drift and tendency of evolutionary thought ought to be and is the very opposite of belittling man. For according to it, man is the culmination and summit of a process whose very length and complexity simply demonstrate his worth and dignity as its final product. Accordingly, some of the most radical evolutionists, such as John Fiske (*Through Nature to God*) have extended and strengthened the argument for the immortality of man by an appeal to his evolutionary origin.

7. The Origin and Nature of Religion

Kindred to the problem of the origin of man, and, in some aspects of it, a part of that problem, is the further problem of the origin and nature of religion. First of all, according to evolution, religion cannot be an exception to the general law of the emergence of the more complex from simpler antecedents. Accordingly, it must be supposed to have evolved from non-religious or pre-religious elements. But the very statement of the case in this form necessitates the clear conception of the idea of religion. If religion is the sense in the human soul of an infinite and eternal being, or beings, issuing in influences upon life, then it is coeval with man and inseparable from the human soul. There never was a time when man was not religious. The very emergence of this sense in the mind of a prehuman ancestor of man would change the brute into the man.

We may speak of the states of the prehuman brute's mind as "materials for the making of religion," but not as religion. Their transformation into religion is therefore just as unique as the creation of the man himself. Whatever the mental condition of the brute before the emergence of the sense of an eternal reality and the dependence of itself upon that reality, it was not a religious being. Whatever the form of this sense, and whatever its first content and results, after the emergence of man it became religion. What caused it to appear at that particular moment and stage in the course of the onward movement? This is a question of causes, and its answer eludes the search of science, both pure and philosophical, and if undertaken by pure philosophy, leads to the same diversity of hypotheses as has been found to control the solution of the problem of beginnings in general (Agnosticism, Pantheism, Theism).

For the rest, that the general features hold true in the field of religion is obvious at a glance. Religious thought, religious practices, religious institutions, have undergone the same type of changes as are observed in the material universe and in the realm of life.

What is true of religion as an inner sense of a reality or realities transcending the outward world is equally, and even more clearly, true of the moral life which in one aspect of it is the outward counterpart of religion. To speak of the evolution of the conscience from non-ethical instincts is either to extend the meaning and character of the ethical into a region where they can have no possible significance, or to deny that something different has come into being when the sense of obligation, of duty, of virtue, and the idea of the supreme good have appeared.

8. The Moral Nature

In other particulars, the development of the moral nature of man, both in the individual and in the community, manifestly follows the process discerned in the material universe at large, and in the realm of organized life in particular. As an observed fact of history, the gradual growth of moral ideas and the mutual play of the inner controlling principle of the sense of oughtness ("the voice of God") and of social conditions and necessities, arising from the nature of man as a social being, are so manifest that they could neither be denied nor better explained in any other way than in accordance with the evolutionary view.

But the rise of the evolutionary theory calls for a new consideration not only of the questions of the origin and nature of religion and morality, but also of that of the content of the Gospel.

9. Christianity and Christian Doctrine

(1) At the basis of Christianity lies the idea of revelation. The God whom Jesus presented to men is supremely concerned in men. He communicates to them His interest in and His wishes concerning them. This fact the followers of Jesus have in general called "revelation." Some have insisted and still do insist that such revelation must be supernatural. Setting aside the consideration that the term "supernatural" does not occur in Bib. phraseology, and that the notion is deduced by a process of interpretation which leaves a large flexibility to it, i.e. a possibility of conceiving it in a variety of ways, revelation itself is not necessarily bound up with any special method of the communication of the Divine will (cf REVELATION). Analogies drawn from human life furnish many different ways of making known to the minds of intelligent fellow-beings the thought of one's own mind. These include, first, the pragmatic resort to some act or attitude of a physical nature, as, for instance, the touch of the whip or the point of the spur on the horse; the frown or the smile for the higher class of understanding of the human type. Secondly, the linguistic, wherein by conventional, articulate, highly complex sounds, one tells in words what lies in his own consciousness. All such expression is necessarily partial, indirect and symbolic. Thirdly, the telepathic and mysterious method (whose reality some still doubt) by which communication takes place without the mediation of either language or action. The evolutionary view does not exclude the possibility of any of these methods conceived as ethical and psychological processes. It does exclude any and all of them if understood as magical or preternatural phenomena. There is nothing, however, in a proper interpretation of the facts of Christian revelation to force the magical interpretation of the coming of the Divine message.

On the contrary, there is everything in the gradual and progressive method of the formation of the Christian Scriptures to suggest that the law of evolution was not violated here. One of the latest writers in Scripture plainly represents the whole method of revelation from the Divine point of view as a cumulative delivery of knowledge in different and successive parts and aspects (He **1** 1). Both at its inception and in the course of its history, the gospel shows conformity to this fundamental law.

(2) Evolution and incarnation: One of the strongest objections to the idea of an all-comprehensive generalization of the law of evolution has been said to be that such a law would destroy the uniqueness of the personality of Jesus Christ. This is, however, due to a confusion of thought. In reality it is no more a denial of uniqueness to say that the Son of God entered the world in accordance with the laws of the world as ordered by the Father, than to say that He was subject to those laws after He entered the world; for instance, that He hungered and thirsted, was weary and needed rest and sleep, that His hands and feet bled when they were pierced and that He ceased to breathe when His heart failed to beat. It is a denial of uniqueness as to the method of entrance into the world, but not a denial of uniqueness of character, of nature, even of essence in the Nicene sense. It behooved Him, in bringing many sons to perfection, "to make the captain of their salvation perfect through suffering." The question of the Virgin Birth of Jesus is definitely excluded from the discussion because it is one of historical evidence chiefly, and, in whatever way the evidence may solve it, the theory of evolution will have no difficulty to set over against the solution. See VIRGIN BIRTH.

From the evolutionist's point of view, the incarnation is the climax and culmination of the controlling process of the universe (see INCARNATION). Evolution demands such a consummation as the appearance of a new type of person, and particularly the type which appeared in Jesus Christ. This is not saying that other men can be or have been of the same nature and essence as the incarnate Saviour. It is saying simply that through the incarnation God brings into perfection the ideal embodied and unfolded in previous generations partially, and held in view as the goal through the whole process of previous struggle and attainment. In other words, the New Adam, in Jesus Christ, emerges in the course of the upward ascent of man as the Adam of Gen emerged in the upward ascent from the lower creation. Theology from the point of view of revelation must necessarily explain this as the voluntary entrance of the Son of God into humanity for purposes of redemption. In doing so it does not contradict the evolutionary view, but simply presents another aspect of the subject.

Assuming, as is done throughout, that the evolution theory concerns not causes and principles, but the processes of transformation of life, the idea of the world is not complete with the creation of man in the image of God. That image must be brought into perfection through the incoming of eternal life. But eternal life is the life of God lived in the species of time and space. It could only come in a personal form through fellowship with God. The bringing of it must therefore be the necessary goal to which all the age-long ascent pointed.

The Incarnation fulfils the conditions of the evolutionary process in that it inserts into the world by a variation the new type governed by the principle of self-sacrifice for others. This is a new principle with Christ, although it is constituted out of preexisting motives and antecedents, such as the "struggle for others" (cf Drummond, *The Ascent of Man*) and "altruism" (in its noble instances in human history). It is a new principle, first, because in its pre-Christian and extra-Christian antecedents it is not real self-sacrifice, not being consciously consummated as the result of the outplay of the motive given in eternal life, and secondly, because it reverses the main stream of antecedent motive. It enthrones love by revealing God's supreme character and motive to be love. Thus viewed the Incarnation is the real entrance into the stream of cosmic movement of the Superman. Nietzsche's Superman would be exactly the contrary of this, i.e. the reversion of man to the beast, the denial of the supremacy of love, and the assertion of the supremacy of might.

(3) Another difficulty met by the harmonist of the Christian system with the evolutionary theory is that of the problem of sin. The method of the origin of sin in the human race, as well as its nature, are given in the Bib. account in apparently plain words. The first man was sinless. He became sinful by an act of his own.

As compared with this, according to one common conception of the law of evolution, all the bad tendencies and propensities in man are the survival of his animal ancestry. Cruelty, lust, deceitfulness and the like are but the "tiger and the ape" still lingering in his spiritual constitution, just as the vermiform appendix and the coccyx remain in the physical, mere rudiments of former useful organs; and just like the latter, they are apt to interfere with the welfare of the species later developed. Here, as in every previous stage of our survey, the difficulty arises from the failure to distinguish between that which appears in man as man, and the propensities in animals which lead to acts similar in appearance, but different in their place and function in the respective lives of those animals. As a matter of fact, the tendencies to cruelty, greed, lust and cunning in the brute are not sinful. They are the wholesome and natural impulses through which the individual and the race are preserved from extinction. They are sinful in man because of the dawn in the soul of a knowledge that his Maker is showing him a better way to the preservation of the individual and the race in the human form. Until the sense of the obligation to follow the better way has arisen, there can be no sin. But when it has come, the first act performed in violation of that sense must be regarded as sinful. As the apostle Paul puts it, "I had not known sin, except through the law." "I was alive apart from the law once: but when the commandment came, sin revived [was made to live] and I died" (Rom **7** 7.9).

Instead of militating against the idea of a primitive fall, the discovery of the law of evolution confirms it by showing that at some time, as the moral sense in man arose, in the very earliest stage of his existence as man, by an act of his own will, he set aside the new and better principle of conduct presented to him in his inner consciousness (disobeyed the voice of God), and fell back to the prehuman nonmoral rule of his life. If this is not the doctrine of the Fall expressed in the terms of present-day science, it would be hard to conceive how that doctrine could be formulated in modern words. (F. J. Hall, *Evolution and the Fall;* cf FALL, THE.)

According to this theory, it was possible for man as he first began his career upon the earth to have passed at once into the condition of perfect fellowship with God. Development might have been sinless. But it was not likely. And it was not desirable that it should be (see ADAM IN OT AND APOC). For moral character apart from struggle and victory is weak and only negatively perfect. The elimination of sin was to be accomplished by a process which according to the evolutionary philosophy everywhere and always produces higher and stronger types. It is only as progress is achieved by regeneration following degeneration that the best results are secured. Thus "where sin abounded," it was 'in order that grace might superabound' (Rom **5** 20). Yet neither is sin the less sinful nor grace the less supernatural. It would be reading an unwarrantable doctrine into Scripture to say that upon the whole an unfallen race would have been superior to a fallen and redeemed race. The world as it is is not a mistake but the wisest thought of God.

The mystery of evil in the world is thus left neither more nor less difficult to understand under the evolutionary conception than under any other. The difficulty of an unbroken continuity between the lower and the higher forms of life, culminating in the free will of man, with the necessary possibility of conflict with the will of God, is not treated by the evolutionary philosophy, even though it may not be materially relieved. To this extent, however, it is relieved, that the Divine action is here understood to be analogous and consistent with itself throughout, even though transcending in scope and extent the human intelligence.

(4) In the light of what has already been made clear, it will be easy to dismiss the correlative doctrine of salvation from sin as fully compatible with the idea of evolution. The Christian doctrine of salvation falls into two general parts: the objective mediatorial work of the Redeemer, commonly called the Atonement, and the subjective transforming work of the Holy Spirit, begun in regeneration and continued in sanctification.

The idea of the Atonement lies somewhat remote from the region where the law of evolution is most clearly seen to operate. At first sight it may be supposed to sustain no special relation to evolution either as offering difficulties to it or harmonizing with it and corroborating it. Yet in a system whose parts are vitally interrelated, it would be strange if the acceptance of the evolutionary theory did not in some way and to some extent affect the conception. It does so by fixing attention on the following particulars: (*a*) That with the emergence of man as a personality, the relation of the creature to the Creator comes to be personal. If that personal relation is disturbed, it can be restored to its normal state in accordance with the laws observed in the relations of persons to one another. The Atonement is such a restoration of personal relations between God and man. (*b*) In achieving the goal of perfect fellowship with Himself on the part of creatures bearing His own image, the Creator must in a sense sacrifice Himself. This Divine self-sacrifice is symbolized and represented in the Cross. Yet the meaning of the Cross is not exhausted in mere external influence upon the sinful creature whose return to the holy Father is thereby aimed at. (*c*) Since the alienation of the creature by sin represents an offence to the person of the Creator, there is necessity that this offence should be removed; and this is done through the sacrifice of the Incarnate Son identifying Himself with, and taking the place of, the sinful creature.

The correlative doctrine of Regeneration stands

much nearer the center of the thought of evolution. It has always been conceived and expressed in biological phraseology. The condition of sin postulated by this doctrine is one of death. Into this condition a new life is inserted, an act which is called the New Birth. Whatever life may be in its essence, it overcomes, reverses and directs the lower forces to other results than they are observed to achieve apart from its presence. In analogy to this course of life in the process of regeneration, a new direction is given to the energies of the new-born soul. But the analogy goes farther. Regeneration is from above as life is always from above. It is God's Spirit through the word and work of Christ that begets the new Christian life, nurtures, trains and develops it to its full maturity revealed in the image and stature of Christ Himself (see REGENERATION).

10. Conclusion

If the above considerations are valid, the evolutionary and the Christian views of the world cannot logically be placed against each other as mutually exclusive and contradictory. They must be conceived as supplementing one another, and fulfilling each the promise and possibility of the other. Evolution is a scientific generalization which, kept within the limits of science, commends itself as a satisfactory explanation of the great law controlling all the movements of matter, life and mind. Christianity, so far as it enters into the intellectual life, is interested in the idea of God and of man's relation to God. It may confidently leave the facts in the lower world of processes of transformation to be schematized under the scientific generalization of evolution.

LITERATURE.—The lit. of the subject is vast. At the basis of the discussion stand the works of Darwin, Huxley, Wallace, Spencer, Weismann, Haeckel, Romanes and others. For a clear statement of the theory, see Metcalf, *An Outline of the Theory of Organic Evolution*, 1905; Saleeby, *Evolution the Master-Key*, 1907; Osborn, *From the Greeks to Darwin* (historical), 1908. On its relation to religion and Christianity, B. F. Tefft, *Evolution and Christianity*, 1885; E. Caird, *The Evolution of Religion*, 1893; Le Conte, *Evolution; Its Nature, Its Evidences and Its Religious Thought*, 1888; McCosh, *The Religious Aspect of Evolution*, 1888; Iverach, *Christianity and Evolution*, 1894. On its bearing on the ideas of man, sin and redemption, Griffith-Jones, *The Ascent through Christ*, 1900; H. Drummond, *The Ascent of Man*, 12th ed, 1901; Tyler, *The Whence and Whither of Man;* Orr, *The Image of God in Man*, 1907; *Sin as a Problem of Today*, 1910; Hall, *Evolution and the Fall*, 1910; Murray, *Christian Faith and the New Psychology*, 1911; T. A. Palm, *The Faith of an Evolutionist*, 1911.

ANDREW C. ZENOS

[EDITORIAL NOTE.—It will be understood, that while Professor Zenos has been asked and permitted to state his views on this question unreservedly, neither the publishers nor the editors are to be held as committed to all the opinions expressed.]

EVOLUTION. THE THEORY DISPROVED:

I. General Viewpoint.—Evolution is so vast a subject that limitation both as to viewpoint and aspects of the general theme to be emphasized is vital. An entire article might well be devoted to so-called inorganic Ev. Or, if the field of thought is restricted to organic Ev., then also selection must be rigidly made. If Darwin's theories are the basis of consideration, then Mendel's epoch-making discoveries and the work of De Vries are seen at once largely to negative them. If Lamarck's ideas are followed, then we must take up also Weismann's differing views.

1. Limitation Vital

2. Disagreement among Evolutionists

As over against the stubborn subservience to the rigid Ev. doctrine by such contemporary men as Osborn, Conklin, Newman, Kellogg, and others, we may put the increasing doubt and uncertainty about the doctrine, and even in some cases the open rejection of it, either *in toto* or in some of its branches, by such men as Bateson, Morgan, Price, Lotsy, Scott, Fairhurst, and Wright. The assertion, therefore, that Ev. is now "accepted" by all enlightened people and all real scientists is very wide of the mark. There is a general acceptance in the philosophical field of some sort of principle of development or unfoldment which is fully as compatible with creationism as with evolutionism, but any universal acceptance of Ev., in the strict, technical, scientific sense, either in whole or in any of its branches, has simply not come about. Real scientific facts have never yet been brought together sufficient to prove the theories of organic Ev. in even a single one of its many branches, let alone the main theory that all matter and life have so come up.

3. A Bankrupt Theory

So true is it that the general theories of Ev. are not proving true in either the biological or geological field, that one scientific observer has aptly remarked that the present vogue of these theories in the popular and pseudo-scientific mind may be likened to the continued, though dwindling, activities of a central commercial "trust," whose supporting subsidiary companies had all gone into bankruptcy. Furthermore, it is highly significant that many who at first are fascinated by the plausible generalizations of Ev. turn from it after further examination of its proffered evidences and more mature consideration of its claims.

Disillusionment came to the present writer when he discovered that Ev. is not a fact of science, but a dogma of philosophy; that both its history and its essential nature prove that it belongs primarily to the realm of subjective speculation and not to the field of objective fact.

II. Evolution Is Unchristian.—It is significant that the idea of Ev. originated in heathen and pagan minds and was not a native product of the Christian intellect. Traces of these ideas are discernible in early Indian thought, while Thales, Anaximander, Empedocles, Heraclitus, Anaxagoras, Lucretius, Aristotle, and other Greeks speculated on the origin of the world in a fire-mist, the natural development of animal forms, etc.

1. In Its Origin

Aristotle, for example, argued that the different parts of the body have resulted from merely accidental relationships, and, as he expressed it, were "preserved, having been appropriately constituted by an internal spontaneity; and whatsoever things were not thus constituted, perished and still perish" (*Physicae Auscultationes*, lib. ii, cap. 8, S. 2). Thus Aristotle clearly conceived the idea of evolution through "an internal spontaneity"; or as Le Conte and others later put it, through "resident forces," long before the speculations of Darwin, Wallace, Lamarck, and Spencer. All of these theories, of course, were entirely heathen or pagan and quite apart from any faith in a living God.

2. In Its Definitions

The general run of modern definitions of Ev. are also not only completely independent of any thought of a living God, but for the most part are either directly antagonistic to that thought or practically irreconcilable with it. Le Conte, for example, has given perhaps as concise and yet comprehensive a definition of real Ev. as can be given. He says that Ev. is "continuous, progressive change; according to certain [fixed] laws; by means of resident forces" (*Evolution and Religious Thought*). Though Le Conte was a religious man, and the effect of his early training lingered with him throughout life, nevertheless, there is in this definition not only no living God, but there is no place for God. According to this definition of Ev., its operation is uninterrupted—"continuous"; and is ever upward—"progressive"; and consequently never reaches any climax, but is ever in a state of "change." All of this, too, is "according to certain laws"—that is, laws that are fixed and, of necessity, unchangeable. And the forces that bring about this continuous, progressive change, according to these fixed laws, are "resident forces"—that is, they are *entirely within*. If God, therefore, be proclaimed as the "resident force," it has to be admitted that such a God is merely a "force," and that He is locked up in nature. In other words, as we shall later see, there is no possible God that can be fitted into the definitions of real Ev. except the impersonal god of Pantheism—not God at all, but a mere blind "force," or non-sentient "principle," which comes to self-consciousness only in man. A God who is transcendent to nature, as well as immanent in nature, is, therefore, of necessity, excluded by thoroughgoing Ev.

The standard definitions of Ev. which are given by real evolutionists are, therefore, consistently and completely in line with these anti-God theories.

The *Century Dict. and Enc.* defines Ev. as: "The doctrine of the derivation or descent with modification of all existing species, genera, orders, classes, etc., of animals and plants from a few simple forms of life, if not from one. In this sense, Ev. is *opposed to creationism*." Huxley, in his *American Addresses* (p. 10), said: "The hypothesis of Ev. supposes that in all this vast progression there would be no breach of continuity (that is, no Divine intervention), no point at which we could say: This is a natural process and this is not a natural process." And he specifically declared further: "It is clear that the doctrine of Ev. is directly antagonistic to that of creation. As applied to the creation of the world as a whole, it is opposed to that of direct creative volition. Ev., if consistently accepted, makes it impossible to believe the Bible." In his article on Ev. in the *Enc Brit*, Prof. James Sulley defines Ev. as a "*natural* history of the cosmos, including organic beings, expressed in *physical* terms as a *mechanical* process"; and the article further says: "In the modern doctrine of Ev., the cosmic system appears as a natural product of elementary matter and its laws. The various grades of life on our planet are the natural consequences of certain physical processes involved in the gradual transformations of the earth."

There is here no God, and no need for God.

Lamarck argued that all change in the organic, as well as in the inorganic, world was the result of law and not of miraculous interposition, that is, of Divine power; and Charles Darwin followed after Lamarck and amplified these theories in his notable scientific works. The very terms that he employed, "natural selection," etc., rule out the thought of creation or anything beyond the operation of blind force. Though again and again Darwin admitted certain gaps in his theory, and acknowledged its difficulties, he nevertheless believed and taught, to use his own words, "that the more complex organs and instincts have been perfected, not by means superior to, though analogous with, human reason (that is, not by God), but by the accumulation of innumerable slight variations, each good for the individual possessor," that is, through purely natural and mechanical means by resident forces (*Origin of Species*, p. 499).

Herbert Spencer, the leading and most influential exponent of the philosophy of Ev., explicitly set the idea of Ev. through resident forces over against the doctrine of creation and the providential preservation of all things by a living God. His thought of God got no higher than "The Eternal Energy," an impersonal thing, and this he called "The Unknowable." This, of course, is a complete denial of revelation and is practically atheism! So Spencer's definition of Ev. as "the integration of matter out of an indefinite, incoherent homogeneity into definite, coherent heterogeneity with a concomitant dissipation of energy" is purely mechanical and anti-supernatural. More recent evolutionists, even those who try to maintain belief in some sort of God, nevertheless see no real God behind creation. Dr. Osborn, for example, in his notable book, *The Origin and Evolution of Life* (p. 2), can see nothing except dead matter, blind force, chemico-electrical agencies, as the first cause.

Ernest Haeckel, the most logical, consistent and thoroughgoing of modern evolutionists, the only legitimate successor to Darwin's place and greatness, argued that Ev. could completely dispense with the supernatural in any form and with any sort of personal interposition. He says: "It entirely excludes supernatural process, every prearranged and conscious act of a personal character. Nothing will make the full meaning of the theory of descent clearer than calling it the non-miraculous theory of creation" (*History of Creation*, pp. 397, 422). But Haeckel went farther still. He explicitly ruled out the idea of a living God or Creator. He said: "This notion [of a personal God or Creator] is rendered quite untenable by the advancements of monistic science. It is already antiquated, and is destined before the present century is ended to drop out of currency throughout the entire domain of purely scientific philosophy." Another frank evolutionist, Carl Vogt, says: "Ev. turns the Creator out of doors."

These definitions, therefore, of necessity have to substitute blind force and mere chance for the creative power of a living God. Those who try to reconcile these theories with the Christian system of truth assert that such is not the case, yet the definitions given, and many others that might be given, prove that God is of necessity ruled out, and that in favor of chance.

3. In Its Teachings

Ev. is also unchristian, of necessity, in its teachings. Rightly viewed, it must be seen to be diametrically opposed to the Christian system of thought at all essential points.

(1) *Excludes a transcendent God.*—As already shown, it excludes the idea of a living God, transcendent to nature, as well as immanent in nature. Thus it leads inevitably to Pantheism instead of to Theism.

The late Prof. George Burman Foster, while a professor of the University of Chicago, said: "A God outside the cosmos is dead," and he then proceeded to reduce God to "the omnipresent *principle* of the order of nature—the world of space—and the supreme *law* of the good in history" (*The Finality of the Christian Religion*). Dr. Faunce, President of Brown University, defined God for a group of inquiring Chinese students by saying: "His [God's] eternal spirit *sleeps* in matter(!), wakes in mind, and finds its highest expression in Jesus of Nazareth" (Booklet issued by Unitarian Laymen's League of Boston). This loss of faith in a living God, which comes from these theories, carries naturally with it the harmful religious and ethical results of Pantheism in any or all of its forms; namely, nature-worship, idolatry, and the final deification of man himself.

Prof. Clifford says: "The allegiance of man may not be diverted from man by any divinity. . . . A helper of man outside of humanity, the truth will not permit us to see. . . . The dim and shadowy outline of the superhuman deity fades slowly away from before us, and as the mist of His presence floats aside, we perceive with greater and greater clearness the shape of a yet greater and nobler figure of Him who made all gods, and shall unmake them (namely man). From the dim dawn of history and from the inmost depth of every soul, the face of our father Man looks out upon us with the fire of eternal youth in his eyes and says: 'Before Jehovah was, I am.'" The result of this teaching is an ever-growing wave of unbelief, especially among college professors and students. (See startling statistics showing this in Prof. Leuba's book, *Belief in God and Immortality*.)

(2) *Nullifies idea of creation.*—The Christian idea of creation by a living God (Gen **1** 1; Jn **1** 1–4) is also of necessity ruled out. The first sublime statement of Genesis, "In the beginning God created the heav-

ens and the earth," gives information which the human mind not only craves, but imperatively demands for its satisfaction and peace.

Accepted as a revelation of truth, this statement tells us first that there was a beginning—which is in line with the conclusions of science concerning the finiteness of the present world; second, that in that beginning, before there was any material universe, God was; which brings us to the tremendous truth that the universe is primarily a spiritual sovereignty and not a mere material machine; and third, that in that beginning the pre-existent spiritual God created the heavens and the earth. Some light is shed on the possible lines of God's creative activity by the recent discoveries of science that matter is not composed of minute particles of solid substance, called atoms—"Those foundation stones of the universe, unbroken and unworn," as Clerk Maxwell called them in 1875—but that the atom is made up of "electrons," which are simply centers of electrical energy. Under this conception, matter is only a manifestation of force, and creation by God is simply a question of readjusting forces so that they emerge out of invisibility and intangibility into solid form, as for example, steam—an invisible force—emerges into fog, a visible substance, when brought into contact with the cold air.

As over against these tremendous and satisfying affirmations, upon which religion, organized states, homes, and educational systems may be builded, Ev. can give us nothing save hypotheses, speculations, theories, and guesses: "the Nebular Hypothesis," "the Planetesimal Theory," "the Assumption of Spontaneous Generation," etc. Darwin himself said positively, "The beginning of the universe is an *unsolvable* mystery." Scientific Ev., having no revelation and no possible means of ascertaining the true facts, can merely *assume* the existence of matter, force, etc., in the beginning, which leaves the entire question of the origin of both the earth and man in a state of complete and permanent uncertainty. The only logical result of Ev., therefore, in the religious realm, is agnosticism at best, with its dire pessimism (Spencer's "The Unknowable"—not merely the unknown, but the *unknowable*), and, as we saw from the definitions, bald atheism at the worst.

As to the creation of man, the Bible, when the Hebrew is taken as it is, and is allowed to say what it is trying to say, clearly teaches the direct creation of man through the will and power of God acting immediately, instead of through process of intermediate law or "resident forces," involving vast ages of time. The agency by which God effects creation is the Logos or Word, manifesting Himself in the making of man perhaps as "The Angel of the Lord," as in the OT miracles.

Man is revealed in the Bible as a trinity—"spirit, soul and body" (1 Thess **5** 23). In accordance with this teaching, there are three significant Hebrew words used in the Old Testament in relation to the origin of man. It is written: (1) "God created (*bara*) man" (Gen **1** 27); (2) "God said, let us make (*asah*) man" (Gen **1** 26), and (3) "The Lord God formed (*yatzar*) man" (Gen **2** 7). In Isa **43** 7 these three expressive words are all brought together in one declarative statement, namely, "I have created him for my glory; I have formed him, yea, I have made him." The word translated "formed" conveys the idea of a potter forming or fashioning clay as he shapes it into a vessel. It evidently refers to man's body, which was given distinctive existence as it was shaped from the dust. The words translated "made" and "created" related to the inbreathing by Deity of the animal existence—the soul—into the body thus formed, and the impartation of *spirit*, which made man the crown of the creation and gave him the likeness of God and the capacity for fellowship with God. The theory of Ev. cannot possibly be made to fit in with the root meaning of these words, as they do not, by any stretching of etymology, have in view any slow process of development from dust stretching over illimitable periods of time and bringing about effects through "natural forces." *And as to woman, the Bible teaching is so clear that she was created directly by God and from a part of man, that it cannot possibly be reconciled with any sort of Ev.*

An all-powerful God could have made the world and created man and woman by evolutionary processes if He had so desired and willed; but the Bible revelation tells us that He did not so make the world, man and woman, and we may stand upon that revelation with full assurance. There is ample ground, therefore, for the emphatic conclusion of such scholarly and discriminating recent writers as Prof. Mullins, Prof. Machen, Dr. Conrad, and others, that acceptance of Ev. leads not merely to a type of religion (?) that is radically different from Christianity, but diametrically opposed to real Christianity.

(3) *Degrades man.*—This teaching, by destroying the Christian doctrine of the direct Divine origin of man, thereby imperils the dignity and potential value of man. The Bible account is that man was made "in the image" and "after the likeness" of God, and was blessed of God and commissioned to replenish the earth and subdue it and have dominion. All of this is beautiful, inspiring, and ennobling, as it pictures man as the child of God, destined to an eternal fellowship with the heavenly and the Divine.

Such evolutionists as Darwin (*The Descent of Man*), Prof. Edward Clodd (*The Making of a Man*, p. 126), and Prof. Morris (*The Destiny of Man*, p. 55) describe the degraded monkey beast, from which man is supposed to have descended, as follows: "The arms were long and lank, the back being much curved, the chest flat and narrow, the abdomen protruding, the legs rather short and bowed, the walk a waddling motion somewhat like that of the gibbon. It had deep-set eyes, greatly protruding mouth with gaping lips, huge ears, and general 'ape-like' aspect" (Morris).

Thus, it was a beast that was "the image of God" and to which God imparted His spirit, if we are to believe the "theistic evolutionists." This strange creature was the Adam of "theistic Ev." And this creature, described by Darwin, Clodd, Morris, and others, is the one who, according to "theistic Ev.," fell. A thing has to be at some elevation before it can fall; but how did this awful creature, who had had no elevation, fall? This, too, is the creature which, according to "theistic Ev.," is a type of Christ, who is "the second Adam," and through whom Christ's lineage is traced back to God Himself!

(4) *Invalidates Bible authority.*—The authority of the Bible as a real revelation from the living God is of necessity completely overthrown if Ev. is accepted as true.

With commendable frankness, Huxley, as quoted, declared truly that it was impossible to believe the Bible if Ev. is true. Darwin said, explicitly, in his *Life and Letters:* "For myself, I do not believe that there ever has been any revelation."

As the only possible god of Ev. is a mere pantheistic "principle" or "force" locked up in nature, there is no living God who could reveal Himself, and so the Bible is regarded as itself an Ev. through natural forces and takes its place along with the other so-called sacred books of the ethnic religions. This, of course, completely destroys its authority as a supernatural, moral, and spiritual guide. The Bible miracles, etc., are all impossible under evolutionary conceptions, as such conceptions rule out the supernatural in all its forms. In Ev. there is not only no miracle, but there is no One to work a miracle. The Virgin Birth, as taught in the Bible, for example, is utterly incompatible with evolutionary theories. The effort to reconcile such an event with Ev. through "resident forces" is manifestly impossible, idle, and even absurd. The Scripture statement is that the Holy Ghost "came upon" Mary and the power of the Highest overshadowed her, and she conceived by direct outside Divine intervention and not through "resident forces."

If the effort be made to evade the issue of the Virgin Birth by saying that it is only a question of the record, it must be replied that the record, the Bible, is the only means we have of knowing anything whatsoever about the matter, and if the reliability of the record is overthrown by a contrary theory, then the truth itself is lost This remark applies to all the other doctrines. Christianity is a religion founded on definite historical facts. Those facts—including the creation of the world, the creation, fall, and salvation of man, the Virgin Birth, the Resurrection, and other facts in the life of Christ—are all recorded in the Bible. If, therefore, the Bible is rejected as untruthful or unreliable, then Christianity itself is rejected.

(5) *Denies truth of Christ.*—Ev. denies the truth of Christ: (*a*) As we have already seen, as to His incarnation and Virgin Birth, and hence as to His full deity. It puts Him in the same category as other men, only He is regarded as being a little farther up the scale. It is a difference in degree, however, and not in kind.

The following words from a so-called "theistic evolutionist" show just where Ev. really leads to: "Granted the greatness and goodness of Jesus, how do you account for Him? What is the relation to Him of this theory of Ev.? Do you mean to include Him and His work in the general scheme? Can it be done? And the answer is: Yes; if Ev. fails at one point, it fails utterly. We have then a case of that special intervention by a non-resident Deity, which we have repeatedly repudiated. Ev. must include Jesus, or we must abandon the theory. There is no break or flaw or chasm. The process is one, from fire-mist to soul; from the soul to its highest expression. Jesus is as much the product of the laws and forces in nature and in society as Shakespeare or Napoleon" (Marion D. Shutter in *Applied Evolution*).

The effort to fit into Ev. the supernatural facts of Christianity is manifestly either the result of delusion, or else it is a mere subterfuge which has of necessity to deny the very essentials.

(*b*) As to Christ's resurrection and second coming —it is simply inconceivable that one who had died, in whom all animate forces and functions had ceased, should from within (by "resident forces") reverse that state and come back to life in a resurrection. Therefore, so-called theistic or Christian evolutionists have to reduce the resurrection to a mere "spiritual resurrection," which is a misnomer, because the spirit does not die and therefore cannot be resurrected. With the literal resurrection, the literal second coming is also thrown out, because it is entirely contrary to evolutionary principles of progress by resident forces, etc.

(6) *Denies fall of man.*—Ev. denies the fall of man and thereby vitiates the atonement. If Ev. is true, then there has been no fall, but a constant rise, through "resident forces." Hence there is no need for an atonement, and the whole scheme of Christian salvation, therefore, falls to the ground.

The effort to make a place for a "fall" in the evolutionary philosophy by saying that the fall consisted in a relapse of man into his previous beasthood is not only entirely unbiblical, but it is puerile, because that would mean that man after his relapse was no longer man. With such a "fall," it was a beast, not a man, that God is supposed to have driven from the Garden of Eden! Real scientific evolutionists scorn any such weak and evasive efforts to fit the "fall" into Ev., as that would reverse the evolutionary processes. Sir Oliver Lodge, for example, says: "Taught by science, we learn that there has been no fall of man; there has been a rise. Through an ape-like ancestry, back to a tadpole and fish-like ancestry, away to the early beginnings of life, the origin of man is being traced" (*Ideals of Science and Faith*).

(7) *Destroys doctrine of sin.*—The Christian doctrine of sin is also destroyed by Ev. The God of the Bible is revealed to us as a moral Ruler who has given righteous laws and eternal ethical principles for the guidance of the human race. The Bible, therefore, teaches that "sin is the transgression of the law." It is guilt, and not error; fault, not misfortune. But Ev. changes all of this. Prof. John Fiske, who perhaps exerted a wider influence upon the American student body than any other man of his age, says this: "Theology has much to say about original sin. This original sin is neither more nor less than the brute inheritance that every man carries with him."

Dr. Shailer Mathews, therefore, follows the evolutionary philosophy to its logical and necessary end when he says: "But for men who think of God as dynamically immanent, in an infinite universe, who think of man's relation to Him as determined not by statutory, but cosmic law, who regard sin and righteousness alike as the working out of the fundamental forces of life itself, the conception of God as King and of man as condemned or acquitted subject is but a figure of speech" (*The Church and the Changing Order*, p. 16).

Such a doctrine as this absolutely and forever destroys man's responsibility for sin; for if sin is what Dr. Mathews suggests it is—"the working out of the fundamental forces of life itself"—then it is inherent. The logic of Ev. likewise destroys the doctrine of the holiness of God, for it makes God the author of sin.

Le Conte says: "If Ev. be true, and especially if man be indeed a product of Ev., then what we call evil is not a unique phenomenon confined to man and the result of an accident (the fall), but must be a great fact pervading all nature and a part of its very constitution."

Who can escape such a conclusion? If Ev. in any form is a fact, then the thing the Bible calls sin was either somehow imbedded, by a competent and responsible Creator, in man's very constitution as a necessary process in his Ev., or else it slipped into the race through the bungling of God, and neither man himself nor the devil can be held responsible for it.

(8) *Negatives regeneration.*—The Christian doctrine of regeneration—taught in the Bible and verified in human experience—is also negatived by Ev. It is inconceivable that there should come about in Ev. by "resident forces" and "fixed laws" an automatic reversal of process which changes the whole nature of the one in whom it occurs. Since regeneration is a known fact, it must come about by outside forces ("born of the spirit," "born from above"), and therefore this fact in itself disproves Ev.

(9) *Contrary to Christian ethics.*—Ev. is contrary to Christian ethics. Its teaching of progress, "the survival of the fittest" through selfish struggle and striving against others, is the exact antithesis of the Christian teaching of love, service, and growth through self-sacrifice. We have seen in modern times, through the moral wreck and ruin which came to Germany, just what these theories will do to an entire nation when they are accepted in thorough-going fashion and really put into practice. The glorification of the flesh over the spirit, of animalism over idealism, through the brute philosophy of Ev., is the real key to the moral decay of our times.

To argue that the Christian can accept Ev. by admitting that the Bible is not to be taken "literally," and by thinking of the incarnation, the atonement, and other great Christian doctrines in terms that are not at all in line with the teaching of the Bible on these great themes, is really to sacrifice Christianity before its foes. An apologetic which gives the entire case away is of necessity both a foolish and a false apologetic. There is no reason in fact, either, why the great truths of revealed religion should be warped and twisted in the effort to make them fit in with unchristian and unbiblical theories, which are themselves entirely unproved. The knowledge which comes to us by faith and through our intuitions is really more dependable than that which comes by reason and logical processes because if premises are wrong, then the entire logical building falls to the ground, despite the beauty of the rationalizing processes which may have erected it!

III. Evolution Is Untrue.—The conclusions reached by those who hold to Ev. are so varied, diverse, and even contradictory as to cause immediate doubt concerning the reliability of the data upon which these conclusions are grounded in any part of the field.

1. Unreliable Data

Tyndal says that the world began in a fire-mist that contracted as it became cold, but Spencer says it was a "cold cloud" which became heated as it contracted. The age of man is estimated all the way from "millions of years" by Myers and others, to 10,000 as a minimum by Le Conte, and 6,000 as a minimum by Prof. Townsend. And as to the probable age of the earth, the estimates run all the way from that of Prof. Ramsay:

"10,000 million years," to that of Prof. Tait (*Recent Advancements in Physical Science*), which he puts as "at almost ten million years." Here, then, is a variation of 9,990 *millions* of years between the highest and one of the lowest estimates!

The plea is made that the scientists are merely estimating about these things and therefore should be given leeway for their estimates, *but the real point is the flimsiness and unreliability of data that can lend itself to such diverse conclusions!*

2. The Argument from Morphology

It is found that there is a general similarity of plan between the lower animals and man. It is argued, therefore, that all of these forms of life have come from some remote common ancestor. This argument, put into simple language, may be stated as follows: Man and monkey are so much alike that man must have come from some sort of remote monkey ancestor. Thus, the argument from resemblance is to the effect that similarity in structure and organic function argues oneness of original parentage and is proof of common descent. But this is neither sound logic nor sound science. Granting that such resemblances do exist, do they really prove the astounding conclusions that are founded upon them? Emphatically, they do not. Resemblance proves nothing but resemblance. Similarity proves nothing but similarity. Resemblance and similarity run through all of nature and life. They are illustrated in the leaves of the trees, and in all other directions, and in things that evidently have no connection one with the other.

(1) *Physical similarities.*—Indeed, if the fact of an intelligent Creator behind all nature and life be accepted, then we would expect a degree of similarity on all sides, even in a world of infinite variety. This resemblance of parts is just what we should expect in things originating from one intelligent operator, whether Creator or manufacturer. It is found in every factory. The wheel is the same in the wheelbarrow, the cart, the carriage, and the locomotive. In fact, uniformity of plan proves unity in the cause, and not the diversity which chance Ev. would necessitate. The Bible teaches that God made the lower animals before He made man. We may regard them, in a way, as understudies. The mere fact that all forms of animals have to breathe air and exist on the same sort of food largely necessitates more or less similarity between them. It necessitates hearts, lungs, circulatory systems, etc.; and the mere fact of external similarities, therefore, would also be naturally expected. But the profound dissimilarities between man and the lower animals—not only in body, but especially in brain—prove that they are not *vitally* related. Virchow said: "The differences between man and monkey are so wide that almost any fragment is sufficient to diagnose them" (*Smithsonian Report* [1889], p. 566). If such considerations were not conclusive, however, it would still be true that the facts of similarity between man and the lower animals would argue the descent of the beasts from man by a process of degeneration, just as strongly as they would argue the opposite. Some ground might be found, also, for this argument in the warnings of the Bible against any cohabiting between man and the beasts.

(2) *Rudimentary and vestigial organs.*—So, also, as to rudimentary, unused, or "useless" organs that are found in man and lower animals alike. They really prove nothing but resemblance, and no one can say with justification that they are not useful. Prof. Arthur Keith, in his address as President of the Anthropological Sec. of the Brit. Asso., meeting at Bournemouth (*Smithsonian Report* [1919], p. 448) said: "We have hitherto regarded the pineal gland, little bigger than a wheat grain and buried deeply in the brain, as a mere useless vestige of a median or parietal eye, derived from some distant human ancestor in whom that eye was functional, but on the clinical and experimental evidence now rapidly accumulating we must assign to it a place in the machinery which controls the growth of the body." Of the thyroid gland, whose removal entails myxœdema, Huxley said: "The recent discovery of the important part played by the thyroid gland should be a warning to all speculators about 'useless' organs."

3. Genetics

Darwin and other evolutionists argue that plants and animals have within themselves a tendency to vary in many and all directions and to an *unlimited degree.* Upon this idea, Darwin founded his other ideas of natural selection, the inheritance of acquired characters, and concluded that thus species originated. All of this now, however, has been swept away by further investigations. Mendel's experiments proved conclusively that plants and animals, even under man's selective skill in breeding, do not tend to vary in all directions and to an unlimited degree, but that the variations are within strict limits and work according to fixed laws producing unvarying results. Furthermore, the theory of inheritance of acquired characters has failed of proof. The forms of vegetable and animal life that man succeeds in improving by human selection revert rapidly to type as soon as man's directing skill is withdrawn. This undeniable fact makes very reasonable the inference that there are certain established types and species which can be extended —quite widely, it may be admitted—within the limits of the species, but that no change into a new species can come about either by natural or artificial selection. The iron law of sterility (each "after its kind" and according to its "seed," Gen **1** 21 and **1** 11) stands on guard at the far frontiers of the species.

There is a certain potency of development which seems to be implanted in all things, but these potential powers are led out into actual development and improvement, not through "resident forces," but only through *outside* intervention and help. Man can develop the wild rose into the American beauty, or the wild pony into the Kentucky thoroughbred, by selection, better environment, breeding, etc.; but it is most significant that these improvements do not continue to increase, or even persist, when things are left to themselves. On the other hand, as remarked, the rose will revert to its original wild state, and the horse begins to go back to type the very moment man's skill and power are omitted. This leads to the inevitable conclusion that whatever unfoldment or development has occurred among either animals or plants in all the past has come about only through God's guidance and directing care *from the outside!* The Bible teaching as to the creation of man in the beginning, and the later variation of the original stock into the various races of mankind, is exactly in line with all of this.

All arguments from analogy, such as the development of the automobile or of the flying machine, as proofs of Ev. completely break down in the light of this truth. The gradual development and perfecting of machines, etc., is not Ev., but simply development under outside skill and power. No scientist has ever been able to bring forth a new species, or to demonstrate that acquired characters are hereditary. Dr. D. T. MacDougal, Gen. Sec. of the Amer. Asso. for the Advancement of Science, and Dir. of the Laboratory for Plant Physiology of the Carnegie Inst., declared at the last meeting of the Asso. that the inheritance of acquired characters had not been established (*New York Times*, Jan. 20, 1924). Herbert Spencer himself frankly said: "Close contemplation of the facts impresses me more strongly than ever with the two alternatives—either there has been inheritance of acquired characters, or there has been no Ev." (*Contemp. Review*, Feb.-March, 1893). Since, then, the latest declaration of the scientists is that there has been no such inheritance, therefore the conclusion holds that there has been no Ev. John Burroughs, the great naturalist, before his recent death, said of Darwin (August, 1920, *Atlantic Monthly*): "He has already been as completely shorn of his selection doctrines as Samson was shorn of his locks."

If now there is no "natural selection," then we are driven, of necessity, back to *supernatural* selection. The teachings of the Bible—written long before our "scientific age"—as to the nature of life, the blood, differences in animal flesh, increase "after their kind" and according to their "seed," etc., have all been verified by the progressive discoveries of science in a most amazing manner. These now known facts, founded upon experiment and exact observation, all point to the direct supernatural and creative power of God, and prove the Bible to be an inspired and therefore true Revelation.

4. Embryology

The arguments for Ev. from embryology have broken down as completely as those from natural selection, the "survival of the fittest," etc. It was found that embryos of different forms of life are somewhat alike. Therefore, it was argued that they all came from some original common ancestor. It is also known that the human embryo passes through several distinct stages in its development, and it is claimed that these stages recapitulate the steps in the alleged evolutionary journey of the race upward from the original simple life-cell to man. Haeckel confidently asserted these claims. He and his fellow-scientists even named this process the "biogenetic law." But the idea that man has evolved from lower forms of life because the human embryo passes through a series of stages which are supposed to reflect the several stages in Ev. is not consistent with the accepted principles of the evolutionary hypothesis. For one thing, as to the rate of development, Ev. presupposes a slow and tedious process, covering, as the evolutionists say, "millions and millions of years." But the human embryo passes through its stages of development with tremendous rapidity, and in the case of the embryos of some other forms of life, the progress is so rapid that it seems almost miraculous. The evolutionary hypothesis, therefore, which scorns miracles in other fields, cannot invoke a sustaining miracle in its own behalf and to prove its own claim in this field.

Furthermore, it is now known that there are radical differences between the embryos of vertebrates and invertebrates, which we would not have a right to expect if it were true that both have come from common ancestors. So far as the human embryo is concerned, it is now admitted that the entire first half of the supposed evolutionary progression is not repeated at all. The author of the article on Embryology in the *Enc Brit*, Oskar Heurtwig, Erich Wasmann, and other embryologists have completely shattered the "fish-like gill slits" of the human embryo, and other similar false inductions in the field of embryology. The arguments from the alleged "little tail of man," etc., and the similarity between the embryos of different forms of life, have all been exploded by Prof. Wilford Hall (*The Problem of Human Life*, p. 374), Prof. Fairhurst (*Scientific Evolution Considered*), and other such writers.

So eager have some of the scientists been to make good on these theories that Haeckel was caught by his fellow-scientists falsifying certain plates and pictures of embryos, etc., and forced to admit his guilt (see "Haeckel's Frauds and Forgeries" by Assmuth and Hull, *Examiner Press*, Bombay); while just recently American scientists, connected with one of our great museums, were exposed by Sir E. Ray Lancaster in connection with distorting a dead gorilla's foot (and altering pictures of it) to make it look more like the foot of a man. (For this entire *exposé*, with pictures and diagrams, see *Nature* for Jan. 5, 1924, and March 29, 1924.)

We would naturally expect some similarity between the embryos of all forms of life, since all start from a single life-germ or combination of two germs. Of necessity, the embryos of different animals would run along together in appearance for a certain time, just as the tracks of different railway systems run parallel as they leave the union depot and pass through a city—to separate later, however, and find their termini in widely different parts of the country. The argument from embryology has been considered one of the very strongest arguments for Ev., and yet in the face of the *real facts* it breaks down completely!

5. Geology and Paleontology

(1) *The strongest argument.*—The very Gibraltar of Ev., however, has been the argument from Geology and Paleontology—the rocks and the fossils. Prof. T. H. Morgan, of Columbia University, rests his faith in the theory of Ev. largely on this argument. He says: "The direct evidence furnished by fossil remains is by all odds the strongest evidence we have in favor of organic Ev." (*Critique*, p. 24). If, then, the theory fails of proof at this point, it may confidently be dismissed as untrue.

(2) *Fragmentary and inadequate evidence.*—As we turn to this argument, we find on the very threshold that the scientists themselves have to admit that the fossil remains and the general evidences of alleged evolution are extremely fragmentary and obscure. (See admissions in Darwin's *Origin of Species*, pp. 184, 334, etc.; Osborn's *Hall of the Age of Man*, Leaflet No. 52, p. 3, etc.) It is now known that the fossil beds are of quite limited extent, varying from a few square yards or a few acres each to a few hundred square miles in area at most. The old "onion coat" theory of the building up of the strata—the only logical theory, if Ev. were really true—has been smashed to pieces and given up by scientists, and it seems that the dependence for argument upon these fragmentary beds will have also to be given up. The so-called "ape-men"—the alleged "missing links"—replicas of which are to be found in museums, have only the skimpiest and the most unstable foundation in real fact. They are about one-tenth fact and nine-tenths fiction.

The "Piltdown man," for example, was no "man" at all. All that was found in the gravel pit in Sussex, England, near Piltdown Common, were two or three bits of skull-bone, a piece of jaw-bone, and a canine tooth. And these few fragments were not found all together and at one time by the same person. They were scattered widely in the gravel pit, some of them were found by one person, and others by another person, and some of them were found in one year, and others in another year. With these few little scraps, that a juggler could conceal in the palm of one hand, and found under these loose conditions, the scientists "reconstructed" the "Piltdown man" and proclaimed it as a new genus, which they called Eoanthropus or "Dawn-man," and they named the species "Dawsoni" in honor of Mr. Dawson, the English scientist. But after the first reconstruction by Dawson and Dr. A. Smith Woodward, Prof. Arthur Keith, Curator of the Royal College of Surgeons of London, took up these fragments of bone and made a reconstructed man much higher than the ape-like creature that Dawson and Woodward had produced. Prof. Keith declared that the capacity of the Piltdown skull was nearer 1,500 c.c. than 1,070 as Dawson and Woodward had made it. And the climax was capped when Prof. Hrdlicka reached the conclusion that the Piltdown jaw and tooth did not belong with the fragments of skull at all, but really "belonged to a fossil chimpanzee."

(3) *Imaginary "ape-men" as "missing links."*—The case is even worse for the "Java Ape-man." There are only three fragments of this specimen. There is a part of a skull, a part of a femur bone, and one molar tooth. The bones were not found at the same time or all together in one place. The femur bone was found a year after the bit of skull was picked up. The bones were scattered far apart in a gravel pit on the bank of a rushing stream. The femur bone was 50 feet from where the skull was found. When Dr. Dubois discovered these pitiful bits of bones he announced his belief that they belonged to a being between the man-apes and men. Other scientists, however, who examined these bones asserted that the fragments did not belong to the same individual at all. Dana took the position that the bones, if they belonged to the same individual, belonged to a low-grade man or to an *idiot*. Virchow rejected them, and finally, another authority of the first rank, Prof. Klaatsch, of Heidelberg University, declared that the creature was no "missing link" at all. The other so-called ape-men are worse still!

(4) *Artificiality of the geological scheme.*—Not only is the alleged evidence utterly fragmentary and entirely inadequate, but it has now been demon-

strated, as a result of recent research in the field of geology, that *the whole arrangement of the rocks in the old geological scheme, upon which depends the value of the time element in the so-called ape-men's remains, is altogether artificial, contrary to now known facts, and therefore that it must be repudiated entirely.* Such discriminating scientists as Dana and Sir William Dawson, in their generation, warned against the delusions of Lyell's theories and other similar ideas that were hypnotizing the minds of Darwin and his followers by the evolutionary obsession which seemed to blind them to obvious facts.

The various kinds of fossils which were so long thought to be found only in the same relative order, all over the globe wherever they occur, are now known to occur in practically every conceivable order of rock stratification. Scientific investigators are coming, therefore, in increasing numbers to see that the arrangement of the different strata of rocks by the older geologists is not only a purely artificial and arbitrary scheme, but that the facts which have been discovered since that artificial arrangement of the rocks was worked out really overthrow the entire scheme. Instead of the "older" rocks being found at the bottom and the "younger" rocks on the top, etc., as would be the case if Ev. were true, it is now found that often the so-called "oldest" rocks are at the top of mountains while the so-called "youngest" rocks are found at the very bottom of the mountain, and *all in perfect order! This reverse order is found in stretches of territory in Europe and America, some of them 1,800 miles long, containing as much as 20,000 square miles of territory. It is now seen that such vast extent makes the thought of an "overthrust" impossible.* In the light of these real facts, Prof. George McCready Price, the well-known scientist, in his great book, *The New Geology*—a work on which he labored in gathering data, etc., in all parts of the world for over twenty years—formulates "the great law of conformable stratigraphic sequence," which he says may be stated as follows: "Any kind of fossiliferous bed whatever, 'young' or 'old,' may be found occurring conformably on any other fossiliferous beds, 'older' or 'younger.'" Then he adds: "This law forever puts an end to all evolutionary speculations about the order in which the various plants and animals have developed, in the minds of those who are correctly informed regarding these facts. This law alone is quite sufficient to relegate the whole theory of organic Ev. to the lumber room of science, there to become the amusement of the future students of the history of cosmological speculations" (p. 638). These, then, are the conclusions of up-to-date scientists, in the light of well-authenticated and most recent facts.

IV. More Rational Ways of Accounting for All the Phenomena than by Evolution.—It may be said with confidence, that "Creation" is a far more valid and rational way of accounting for the phenomena of nature and life than is Ev.

1. Creation versus Evolution

(1) *Dissipation of energy.*—Such phenomena as dissipation of energy and disintegration of particles within matter (as radium, etc.) prove that such processes could not have been in continuance from an eternal past, and therefore that matter is not eternal, but that it had a beginning.

(2) *The finiteness of matter.*—Since, then, it is admitted by scientists that matter is finite in duration and had a beginning, it is irrational to think that there was no cause for its beginning. It is an absurdity of thought to say that nothing (which was in the beginning) made something out of nothing!

(3) *A first cause indispensable.*—Therefore adequate power and creative design are prima facie necessities to logical thought concerning these issues. The thought of mere chance operating in a matterless vacuum "in the beginning" is an impossible thought. But accept God, an omnipotent, eternal, spiritual Personality, "in the beginning," and all becomes immediately rational, entirely consistent, and clear.

(4) *"Spontaneous generation"* of life may be dismissed as a begging of the question, and as an admitted absurdity of thought (so say Darwin, Wallace, et al.). Since, then, "spontaneous generation" of life is confessedly impossible and therefore did not occur, we are driven back to accept the only other alternative, namely, the creative activity of a living God. Since "resident forces" are impossible to account for the emergence of life, then non-resident forces, namely God, must be accepted.

(5) *No Evolution without power of reproduction.*—Furthermore, it is self-evident there could be no Ev. without the power of reproduction in living things. Since, then, reproduction is a prior condition to Ev., it, therefore, cannot be the product of Ev. Hence, we face the logical necessity for direct creation as a *start* for all developing life. Again, the power of reproduction is not in the embryo, but only in the mature parent. An egg cannot produce an egg. It is also true that an egg is not improvable. Improvement can come only in the matured form. Therefore, a parent-form of life must have been created in the beginning to have produced the egg from which offspring alone can come.

2. The Cataclysm of the Deluge

To accept the fact of a universal deluge, as the Bible teaches it, and science confirms, will enable us to account for the fossils and other such phenomena in a far more rational and satisfying way than any which Ev. offers.

The fact that simple fossil forms are sometimes found alone in certain strata of rocks while more complex forms are found in other strata may be easily accounted for because of the well-known fact that lower forms of life live for the most part in shallow water or at the edge of the sea, while the vertebrates, the fish, and the great sea-monsters, live in the deep water. If, therefore, the animal life in one section of the sea, with its shore, were to be now changed into fossils, and these fossils should be discovered in some after-age, the discoverers would find the remains of the simple forms of life in one place and the remains of higher forms—fish and sea-monsters—in another part. Furthermore, just as we see around us today different forms of life, from the simplest one-cell animal up to and including all the other animals and human forms, living side by side, so, in the absence of any real facts proving the contrary, it is entirely logical to conclude that the simplest forms of animals and human beings lived side by side in the ages that are gone. There is absolutely not one scintilla of proof from real facts that the lower forms of life came first on this earth, or the higher forms evolved out of the lower.

It is also now known that much of the life that was destroyed in former ages leaving fossil forms behind it, could only have been destroyed by some tremendous catastrophe, and that the strata which entombed it were laid down *suddenly* by a deluge instead of slowly by sedimentation, which is supposed to have taken "millions of years" to gather.

Whole schools of fish, for example, covering large fields have been found with every indication that violent death fell instantly, not on a few individuals, but on entire tribes. These fish are found not in a relaxed and placid state, but often with their heads twisted around to their tails and with every fin extended, the position in which a fish always dies when overtaken by an enemy or some natural catastrophe. In the extensive fields of fossilized and frozen mammoths in the Arctic regions—where multitudes of these giant creatures have been found—some have been discovered with their stomachs filled with undigested food, and in some instances with their mouths also full of the food which they were eating, showing that the animals were destroyed suddenly while they were quietly feeding, when the crisis fell upon them.

The conclusion of open-minded investigators, therefore, seems well grounded that the phenomena which we find in connection with fossils in the earth can be accounted for most rationally on the ground that there was a universal deluge, brought about perhaps because of a change in the inclination of the earth's axis to the plane of its orbit, which change caused torrential rains and suddenly sent great floods of water, tidal waves, sweeping in from the sea, recurring periodically every few weeks for months, overwhelming all forms of life and piling mud and sediment upon them, which, in the course of time, changed into the coal beds, rock strata, etc., as we find them today. Such a cataclysm would also account for the change of climate in the Arctic regions from tropical conditions in which such animals as the mammoth alone could have flourished. Investigators, therefore, are forced back by such facts to the Bible teaching concerning the deluge, and they find an amazing verification of the Bible's statements as to the methods by which the flood was brought about, including the breaking up of the "fountains of the great deep," the time covered by the waxing and waning of the flood, etc.

3. Devolution versus Evolution

A final and conclusive consideration in this whole problem of alleged Ev. is that there is evidence on all sides going to prove that *the whole world and all that is in it is running down, degenerating, and moving toward some climax of judgment and re-creation, even as the Bible says, instead of ever evolving upward into higher and better forms.*

(1) *Chemistry discloses no upward urge.*—It is most significant that in the science of chemistry, through which we come closest to the deeper facts and forces of both inanimate matter and life, there is no evidence of any resident "urge" upward. Not only is it true that the laws of chemical affinity seem to be static and unchangeable as to their operations, but it is now known that there is a disintegrating tendency downward instead of upward that seems characteristic of all matter. The tendency for atoms of high atomic weight to break up into other atoms of lower atomic weight seems to be a universal tendency of matter. Uranium disintegrates into radium, and radium disintegrates into lead, and so the old song seems justified: "Change and decay in all around I see." The universe, and the matter that makes it up, seems rather more like a clock that is running down than a machine that is automatically advancing from forces within!

(2) *The vegetable kingdom.*—The science of botany and an observation of the whole vegetable kingdom disclose the same startling and significant fact. It is a commonplace of knowledge that the trees and vegetation of former ages were far greater and more beautiful than those of today. The "big trees" of California are but so many grim proofs that the glory of the vegetable kingdom is fading.

(3) *In the animal kingdom*, the same is true. The remains of former forms of life upon this planet prove that animals were once much greater and more beautiful than now. The mammoth was more magnificent than our elephants, the woolly rhinoceros, the saber-tooth tiger, and all other living things had their golden age in the past, and their descendants of today are but degenerate pigmies in comparison with them.

(4) *Man himself degenerating.*—There are good grounds for saying the same thing about man himself. Instead of coming steadily upward, there are reliable evidences that the human race is a degeneration from nobler and higher forms. The Cro-Magnon race proves this. Stanton Coblentz, in a book just off the press on *The Decline of Man*, says in his final summary (p. 236): "The human race, we found, is to be regarded as senile rather than youthful, wizened and decrepit rather than rosy-cheeked and adolescent."

(5) *Downward tendency in religion.*—Even in the field of religion, to which the social evolutionists at first turned with such confidence to find the proof of progress and Ev. upward, it is now known that the tendencies have been downward rather than the reverse. Such students of comparative religion as Max Mueller, Le Page Renouf, Emmanuel Rougé, Dr. F. Hommell, Frederick De Litzsch, Schlegel, Johann Warneck, and others agree in the final verdict that the history of religions proves not that they have come up through animism to polytheism, and from polytheism to crude monotheism, and from that to a high and spiritual monotheism, but rather the reverse. These masters in the field of comparative religion tell us that the earliest forms of religion among primitive peoples such as the Africans, the Battaks of Sumatra, the ancient Indians, Persians, Egyptians, Greeks, and other people of the past were not crude and degraded, but that they were pure and high, and that in each case there was a degeneration into grosser and lower forms. In Greece, for example, Max Mueller and others have made clear that there was a pure monotheism long before the later polytheism. W. St. Clair Tisdale gives a very adequate summary of such teachings in his *Christianity and Other Faiths* when he says: "It follows that monotheism historically preceded polytheism and that the latter is a corruption of the former. It is impossible to explain the facts away. Taken together, they show that, as the Bible asserts, man at the very beginning of history knew the one true God. This implies a revelation of some sort, and traces of that revelation are still found in many ancient faiths."

4. Conclusion

It may be remarked in conclusion that faith and intuition are trustworthy as messengers to bring in truth, and there are many things in the realm of ethics and philosophy which are just as sure, understandable, and dependable as anything which biology or geology may seek to bring us. It is admissible also to remark that if half the time, thought, and labor which have been employed in the effort to prove the theories of Ev. had been used in assembling and ordering the scientific, historical, and psychological facts behind the truth of the creation and providential care of all things by a living God, that truth would be overwhelmingly demonstrated and fully acceptable to the rational mind of man, even apart from the faith element.

If God did make all things by the methods which evolutionists allege, then we must not only give up the Bible as a true record and a real revelation, but we must also completely change our ideas of *the kind of being God really is*. It is impossible for any balanced and rational mind to think that an all-wise, all-powerful, all-*good* God would have resorted to a cruel and merciless process for producing His creatures. And it is especially revolting to think that a good and loving God would have produced man—the crown of His creation—by a long-drawn-out ordeal of selfish struggle, cruelty, vindictiveness, and callous disregard of the rights, feelings, and desires of other creatures, which had to be trampled down in order that man might rise. All of this is not only contrary to right conceptions of God, but also to the deeper facts observable on all sides. We close, therefore, our consideration of this theme by pointing out that the fundamental fallacy of Ev. is the idea that strife and struggle are the way of life.

It is not true that the brute struggle for existence and the "survival of the fittest" are the profoundest facts of nature and life. There is another higher and greater truth, a more universal principle than the principle of conflict, competition and war, and that is the fact of co-operation, helpfulness, and sacrifice in service. The fact stands that the forces which make for union and harmony have always been greater than the forces which make for disunion and strife. *The fundamental fact that the universe is a cosmos instead of a chaos proves that.* The cohesive forces are stronger than the disruptive forces; the centripetal forces are greater than the centrifugal forces. So the struggle for life is not the greatest factor, nor is it the factor that should be most stressed. The struggle for the life of others is of far greater prominence in nature, when we but see the truth deeply enough. The little bird will battle more fiercely for its young than for its own food or life, and everywhere self-sacrifice for others is seen. Nature is not *prevailingly*, therefore, "red in tooth and claw." Much is made by the evolutionists of the struggle for food as a determinative factor in the alleged Ev. This, however, overlooks the profound truth that the *purpose* of food is not merely to sustain individual life, but to make possible *the procreation of other life.* Nutrition is accompanied by reproduction in order that life may continue; and the sacrifices of fatherhood and motherhood throughout all of nature are, in themselves, eloquent of the truth that unselfishness and concern for others are infinitely greater, as well as more beautiful and more important, than the selfish struggle for the "survival of the fittest." All of which is but proof of the cheering prophecy that at last "the meek shall inherit the earth, and shall delight themselves in the abundance of peace."

There is a great tenderness at the heart of the world, and this expresses itself in the highest truth known to man, namely, that "God is love." The supreme expression of that love in human history was the cross that stood on the place called Golgotha; and the One who was nailed to the cross has taught us that God is not a heartless force, but a heavenly Father, who, because of His infinite love, gave His own Son to die that we might be saved from sin and enter into everlasting life. It is the philosophy of the cross, with its great teaching of self-sacrifice in service, which is needed today, and not the philosophy of the brute struggle for survival—the philosophy of the shambles, which is the apotheosis of self and the mother of all wars, immoralities, hatreds, and wrongs. The great need of the time is not self-assertiveness and arrogant pride, but rather humility, gentleness, and self-sacrifice in service.

It is not true that we came up from the slime and the beasts through the jungle, and that we pass out into a night of oblivion unlighted by a single star. It *is* true that "in the beginning God created the heavens and the earth" and that He made "man in His own image." It *is* true that we came from God through the Garden, and that we are destined by obedience to Him to an eternity of joy in a land that is "fairer than day," where we will meet again our loved ones who went before, and upon whose blissful shore there falls no shadow and rests no stain!

LITERATURE.—In addition to the standard works listed by Prof. Zenos in the preceding article, and the books cited in the body of this article, see V. L. Kellogg, *Evolution, the Way of Man;* H. H. Newman, *Readings in Evolution, Genetics, and Eugenics;* W. B. Scott, *The Theory of Evolution;* St. G. Mivart, *The Genesis of Species;* A. Weismann, *Studies in the Theory of Descent;* G. Paulin, *No Struggle for Existence, No Natural Selection;* William Bateson, *Mendel's Principles of Heredity;* T. B. Bishop, *Evolution Criticised;* Hugo De Vries, *The Mutations Theory;* J. P. Lotsy, *Evolution by Means of Hybridization;* Thomas Hunt Morgan, *The Mechanism of Mendelian Heredity;* Sir H. H. Howarth, *The Mammoth and the Flood* and *The Glacial Nightmare and the Flood;* Percy E. Davidson, *The Recapitulation Theory;* Alfred Fairhurst, *Organic Evolution Considered;* George McCready Price, *The New Geology* and *The Phantom of Organic Evolution;* Th. Graebner, *Evolution—An Investigation and a Criticism;* Doran, Publishers, *The Straton-Potter Debates;* Philip Mauro, *Evolution at the Bar;* Alexander Patterson, *The Other Side of Evolution;* John Roach Straton, *The Case against Evolution.*

JOHN ROACH STRATON

EWE, ū (רָחֵל, *rāḥēl,* עוּל, *'ūl,* שֶׂה, *seh,* "a female sheep"): *Rāḥēl* (cf pr. n. Rachel, and Arab. *raḥala,* "to migrate") is the ordinary Heb word for ewe, but is tr^d "sheep," though with clear indication of sex in context, in Isa **53** 7 and Cant **6** 6 (RV "ewes"). *'Ālōth,* part. of *'ūl,* "to suckle" (cf. Arab. *ghāl*) is found in Ps **78** 71 and Isa **40** 11 (AV "are with young," ERV "that give suck," ARV "have their young"). In 1 S **6** 7.10 occurs *pārōth 'ālōth,* "milch kine." *Seh,* in Lev **22** 28, while tr^d "ewe," might from the context be "ewe" or "she-goat" and indeed seems to be used here as a term applying equally to either, being used elsewhere for one of a flock of sheep or goats. See SHEEP.

ALFRED ELY DAY

EXACT, eg-zakt':

(1) נָגַשׂ, *nāghas* (Dt **15** 2.3; 2 K **23** 35; Isa **58** 3), to secure by force or pressure interest or money for tribute, and perhaps, in Isa **58** 3, labor or toil; but cf RVm "oppress all your laborers"; probably better with a slight change of text, "exact money lent on pledges" (reading for עֲבֹט בְּיֶדְכֶם, *'ăbhōṭ b^eyedh^ekhem,* עַצְּבֵיכֶם, *'aççe^bhēkhem*).

(2) נָשָׁא, *nāshā',* or נָשָׁה, *nāshāh* (Neh **5** 7.10 [AV not RV].11; Job **11** 6 [but see below]; Ps **89** 22), to demand interest, to be a harsh and importunate creditor, a practice which Nehemiah asks the Jews to forego. Job **11** 6 better with RVm for "exact," "causeth to be forgotten."

(3) יוֹצֵא, *yōçē'* (2 K **15** 20 [if text is correct]). Menahem secured the tribute which the king of Assyria demanded by levying a tax on the chief men of his kingdom.

(4) πράσσειν, *prássein* (Lk **3** 13 AV [cf Dnl **11** 20 LXX]; 1 Macc **10** 35 RV), to demand money or tribute or taxes of anyone.

WALTER R. BETTERIDGE

EXACTION, eg-zak'shun: (1) מַשָּׁא, *mashshā'* (Neh **10** 31), a demand for money lent on pledge, which the Jews agreed to forego in the seventh year; (2) גְּרוּשָׁה, *g^erūshāh* (Ezk **45** 9, "your exactions," RVm "expulsions"), eviction from house and home.

EXACTORS, eg-zak'tẽrs (נֹגְשַׂיִךְ, *nōgh^esayikh* [Isa **60** 17, RVm "taskmasters"; cf Ex **1** 11; **3** 7]): Righteousness personified is in Zion to take the place of the officials who oppress the people. In Isa **14** 4 ARVm, Babylon is called an "exactress of gold."

EXALT, *eg-zôlt'* (רוּם, *rūm,* גָּבַהּ, *gābhah* [*mappīḳ hē*], נָשָׂא, *nāsā';* ὑψόω, *hupsóō*): The Heb word most often tr^d "exalt," "exalted," is *rūm,* "to lift up," "to be or become high." It is used with reference to both God and man, e.g., Ex **15** 2, "My father's God, and I will exalt him"; Ps **99** 5.9, "Exalt ye Jeh our God"; cf **107** 32; **118** 28; 1 S **2** 10, "Exalt the horn of his anointed"; Job **17** 4, "Therefore shalt thou not exalt them"; cf Isa **13** 2 AV; **14** 13; *gābhah,* "to be high," **fig.** "to be exalted," occurs in Job **36** 7; Prov **17** 19 AV; Isa **5** 16, etc; *nāsā',* "to lift up," occurs in Nu **24** 7; 1 Ch **29** 11, etc; other words are *ṣālal,* "to raise up" (Ex **9** 17; Prov **4** 8), *sāghabh* (Job **5** 11; **36** 22 AV; Isa **2** 11.17; **12** 4; **33** 5), *rāmam,* "to be high" (Job **24** 24; Ps **118** 16).

In the NT "exalt" is the tr of *hupsóō,* "to elevate" (not used with reference to God) (Mt **11** 23; **23** 12; Acts **2** 33; 2 Cor **11** 7; 1 Pet **5** 6, etc); also (twice) of *epaírō,* "to lift up, upon or against" (2 Cor **10** 5; **11** 20), once of *huperaírō,* "to lift up above" (2 Thess **2** 4); in 2 Cor **12** 7 *bis,* this word is tr^d "exalted above measure," RV "exalted overmuch"; *huperupsóō,* "to lift up above" (Phil **2** 9), is tr^d "highly exalted"; *húpsos,* "elevation," is tr^d "exalted" (Jas **1** 9, RV "high estate").

For "it increaseth" (Job **10** 16), RV gives "and if my head exalt itself"; instead of "God exalteth by His power" (**36** 22), "God doeth loftily in his power"; for "though thou exalt thyself as the eagle" (Ob ver 4), "mount on high"; for "highly esteemed" (Lk **16** 15), "exalted"; for "exalteth itself" (2 Cor **10** 5), "is exalted"; for "He shall lift you up" (Jas **4** 10), "He shall exalt you."

Self-exaltation is strongly condemned, esp. by Christ; humbleness is the way to true exaltation (Mt **23** 12; Lk **14** 11; **18** 14; cf Jas **4** 10; 1 Pet **5** 6); the supreme example is that of Christ Himself (Phil **2** 5–11). W. L. WALKER

EXALTATION OF CHRIST, THE. See CHRIST, THE EXALTATION OF.

EXAMINE, eg-zam'in, **EXAMINATION,** eg-zam-i-nā'shun: דָּרַשׁ, *dārash,* "to follow," "inquire," "make inquisition" (Ezr **10** 16); and בָּחַן, *bāhan*, "to test," "investigate," "prove," "tempt" (Ps **26** 2). The former was the judicial term. ἀνακρίνω, *anakrínō*, "scrutinize," "investigate," "interrogate" (in court), "judge," "search" (Lk **23** 14; Acts **4** 9; **12** 19; **28** 18; 1 Cor **9** 3); and ἀνετάζω, *anetázō*, "to investigate" (judicially), "examine" (Acts **22** 24.29). Also δοκιμάζω, *dokimázō*, "to test," "examine," "try" (1 Cor **11** 28 AV); and πειράζω, *peirázō*, "scrutinize," "discipline" (2 Cor **13** 5 AV). The noun ἀνάκρισις, *anákrisis*, "examination," "investigation," occurs in Acts **25** 26. See also Courts, Judicial. Frank E. Hirsch

EXAMPLE, eg-zam′p'l (**τύπος**, *túpos*, "a pattern," **ὑπόδειγμα**, *hupódeigma*, "copy," "representation," **ὑπογραμμός**, *hupogrammós*, "a writing-copy," "example"): A typical, representative, or illustrative case; a pattern or model for imitation (*hupodeigma*, Jn **13** 15; He **8** 5 AV; Jas **5** 10; *hupogrammos*, 1 Pet **2** 21; *tupos*, 1 Tim **4** 12 AV) or warning (δεῖγμα, *deígma*, "a sample," "exhibition," Jude ver 7; cf 2 Pet **2** 6; *hupodeigma*, He **4** 11; *tupos*, 1 Cor **10** 6.11).

"Ensample" (*tupos*, 2 Macc **6** 28.31; Phil **3** 17; 1 Thess **1** 7; 2 Thess **3** 9; 1 Tim **4** 12; 1 Pet **5** 3) and "example" have the same meaning, but the former is always suggestive of goodness.

EXCEED, ek-sēd′, **EXCEEDING, EXCEEDINGLY:** The vb. is found in other than its present sense in Job **36** 9 AV, "They have exceeded" (RV "behaved themselves proudly"); 1 S **20** 41, "They . . . . wept . . . . until David exceeded" (AV and RV). In both these passages the idea is that of going too far, beyond proper bounds (Heb, respectively, *gābhar*, "be strong" [in Hithp.]; *gādhal*, "be great" [in Hiph.]. "Exceeding" (as an advb. with adjs. and rarely as an adj.) and "exceedingly" occur often as representing various expressions for the superlative in Heb and Gr.

EXCELLENCY, ek′se-len-si (גָּאוֹן, *gā'ōn*, גַּאֲוָה, *ga'ăwāh;* **ὑπερβολή**, *huperbolḗ*): "Excellency" in the OT is chiefly the tr of *gā'ōn*, "mounting," "swelling" (Ex **15** 7; Job **37** 4 AV; Ps **47** 4 AV; Isa **13** 19 AV, etc); *ga'ăwāh*, "rising," is thrice so rendered (Dt **33** 26.29; Ps **68** 34); *se'ēth*, "rising" (twice) (Job **13** 11 AV; Ps **62** 4 AV); *yether*, "superabundance" (twice) (Gen **49** 3 AV; Job **4** 21 AV), and *hādhār*, "honor," "beauty," "majesty" (twice) (Isa **35** 2); *gōbhah*, "uplifted" (Job **40** 10); *yithrōn*, "advantage" (Eccl **7** 12); *sī'*, "elevation" (Job **20** 6, RV "height"). In the NT *huperbolē*, "surpassing," "a casting beyond," occurs (2 Cor **4** 7, "that the excellency of the power may be of God," RV "exceeding greatness"); *huperochḗ*, "a holding over" or "beyond," is trd "excellency" (1 Cor **2** 1), and *tó huperéchon*, "the preëminence" (Phil **3** 8), "the excellency of the knowledge of Christ."

Instead of "excellency" RV has "pride" (Isa **13** 19; Ezk **24** 21), "majesty" (Job **37** 4 and ARV **13** 11; **31** 23), ARV has "preëminence" (Gen **49** 3.4), "glory" (Ps **47** 4), "dignity" (Ps **62** 4); for "the fat of lambs" (Ps **37** 20), ERV has "the excellency of the pastures," with m "the fat of lambs"; ARV retains the AV rendering with ERV in m; instead of "Doth not their excellency which is in them go away?" (Job **4** 21), RV has "Is not their tent-cord plucked up within them?" m "Is not their excellency which is in them removed?"
W. L. Walker

EXCELLENT, ek′se-lent (אַדִּיר, *'addīr*, יַתִּיר, *yattīr* [Aram.]; **διαφορώτερος**, *diaphorṓteros*, **κράτιστος**, *krátistos*): The tr of various Heb words, chiefly of *'addīr*, "great," "honorable" (Ps **8** 1.9; **16** 3; **76** 4); *yattīr*, "surpassing," is Aram., occurring in Dnl **2** 31; **4** 36; **5** 12.14; **6** 3. Other words are *bāhar*, "to glow," "try," "choose" (Cant **5** 15); *gā'ōn*, "mounting," "swelling" (Isa **4** 2; see Excellency); *gādhal*, "to make or become great" (Isa **28** 29), and other words occurring singly.

In the NT we have *diaphorṓteros*, "greater," "better" (He **1** 4; **8** 6); *kratistos*, "most excellent," "most noble" (Lk **1** 3; Acts **23** 26); *tá diaphéronta*, "things that differ," "are preëminent" (Rom **2** 18; Phil **1** 10); *megaloprepḗs*, "becoming to the great" (2 Pet **1** 17, AV "a voice to him from the excellent glory," ARV and ERVm "the Majestic Glory"); *kath' huperbolḗn* "very surpassing" (1 Cor **12** 31, "Yet I show unto you a more excellent way," RV "most excellent"); *pleíōn*, "greater," "fuller" (He **11** 4; see Abel). W. L. Walker

EXCHANGE, eks-chānj′, **EXCHANGER**, eks-chān′jẽr. See Bank, Banking.

EXCOMMUNICATION, eks-ko-mū-ni-kā′shun: Exclusion from church fellowship as a means of personal discipline, or church purification, or both. Its germs have been found in (1) the Mosaic "ban" or "curse" (חֵרֶם, *hērem*, "devoted"), given over entirely to God's use or to destruction (Lev **27** 29); (2) the "cutting off," usually by death, stoning of certain offenders, breakers of the Sabbath (Ex **31** 14) and others (Lev **17** 4; Ex **30** 22–38); (3) the exclusion of the leprous from the camp (Lev **13** 46; Nu **12** 14). At the restoration (Ezr **10** 7.8), the penalty of disobedience to Ezra's reforming movements was that "all his substance should be forfeited [*hērem*], and himself separated from the assembly of the captivity." Nehemiah's similar dealing with the husbands of heathen women helped to fix the principle. The NT finds a well-developed synagogal system of excommunication, in two, possibly three, varieties or stages. נִדּוּי, *niddūy*, for the first offence, forbade the bath, the razor, the convivial table, and restricted social intercourse and the frequenting of the temple. It lasted thirty, sixty, or ninety days. If the offender still remained obstinate, the "curse," *hērem*, was formally pronounced upon him by a council of ten, and he was shut out from the intellectual, religious and social life of the community, completely severed from the congregation. שַׁמְּתָא, *shammāthā'*, supposed by some to be a third and final stage, is probably a general term applied to both *niddūy* and *hērem*. We meet the system in Jn **9** 22: "If any man should confess him to be Christ, he should be put out of the synagogue" (ἀποσυναγωγός, *aposunagōgós*); Jn **12** 42: "did not confess . . . . lest they should be put out of the s."; and Jn **16** 2: "put you out of the s." In Lk **6** 22 Christ may refer to the three stages: "separate you from their company [ἀφορίσωσιν, *aphorísōsin*], and reproach you [ὀνειδίσωσιν, *oneidísōsin*=*hērem*, "malediction"], and cast out your name as evil [ἐκβάλωσιν, *ekbálōsin*]."

It is doubtful whether an express prescription of excommunication is found in Our Lord's words (Mt **18** 15–19). The offence and the penalty also seem purely personal: "And if he refuse to hear the church also, let him be unto *thee* as the Gentile and the publican," out of the pale of association and converse. Yet the next verse might imply that the church also is to act: "Verily I say unto you, What things soever ye shall bind on earth shall be bound in heaven," etc. But this latter, like Mt **16** 19, seems to refer to the general enunciations of principles and policies rather than to specific ecclesiastical enactments. On the whole, Jesus seems here to be laying down the principle of dignified personal avoidance of the obstinate offender, rather than prescribing ecclesiastical action. Still, personal avoidance may logically correspond in proper cases to excommunication by the church. 2 Thess **3** 14: "Note that man, that ye have no company with him"; Tit **3** 10: "A factious man . . . . avoid" (ARVm); 2 Jn ver 10: "Receive him not into your house," etc, all inculcate discreet and faithful avoidance but not necessarily excommunication, though that might come to be the logical result. Paul's "anathemas" are not to be understood as excommunications, since the first is for an offence no ecclesiastical tribunal could well investigate: 1 Cor **16** 22, "If any man loveth not the Lord, let him be anathema"; the second touches Paul's deep relationship to his Lord: Rom **9** 3, "I myself . . . . anathema from Christ"; while the third would subject the apostle or an angel to ecclesiastical censure: Gal **1** 8.9, "Though we, or an angel . . . . let him be anathema."

Clear, specific instances of excommunication or directions regarding it, however, are found in the Pauline and Johannine writings. In the case of the incestuous man (1 Cor **5** 1–12), at the instance of the apostle ("I verily, being absent in body but present in spirit"), the church, in a formal meeting ("In the name of our Lord Jesus, ye being gathered together"), carrying out the apostle's desire and will ("and my spirit"), and using the power and authority conferred by Christ ("and with the power of our Lord Jesus"), formally cut off the offender from its fellowship, consigning (relinquishing?) him to the power of the prince of this world ("to deliver such a one unto Satan"). Further, such action is enjoined in other cases: "Put away the wicked man from among yourselves." 2 Cor **2** 5–11 probably refers to the same case, terminated by the repentance and restoration of the offender. 'Delivering over to Satan' must also include some physical ill, perhaps culminating in death; as with Simon Magus (Acts **8** 20), Elymas (Acts **13** 11), Ananias (Acts **5** 5). 1 Tim **1** 20: "Hymenaeus and Alexander . . . . that they might be taught not to blaspheme," is a similar case of excommunication accompanied by judicial and disciplinary physical ill. In 3 Jn vs 9.10 we have a case of excommunication by a faction in control: "Diotrephes . . . . neither doth he himself receive . . . . and them that would he . . . . casteth out of the church."

Excommunication in the NT church was not a fully developed system. The NT does not clearly define its causes, methods, scope or duration. It seems to have been incurred by heretical teaching (1 Tim **1** 20) or by factiousness (Tit **3** 10 [?]); but the most of the clear undoubted cases in the NT are for immoral or un-Christian conduct (1 Cor **5** 1.11.13; perhaps also 1 Tim **1** 20). It separated from church fellowship but not necessarily from the love and care of the church (2 Thess **3** 15 [?]). It excluded from church privileges, and often, perhaps usually, perhaps always, from social intercourse (1 Cor **5** 11). When pronounced by the apostle it might be accompanied by miraculous and punitive or disciplinary physical consequences (1 Cor **5** 5; 1 Tim **1** 20). It was the act of the local church, either with (1 Cor **5** 4) or without (1 Cor **5** 13; 3 Jn ver 10) the concurrence of an apostle. It might possibly be pronounced by an apostle alone (1 Tim **1** 20), but perhaps not without the concurrence and as the mouthpiece of the church. Its purpose was the amendment of the offender: "That the spirit may be saved in the day of the Lord Jesus" (1 Cor **5** 5); and the preservative purification of the church: "Purge out the old leaven, that ye may be a new lump, even as ye are unleavened" (1 Cor **5** 7). It might, as appears, be terminated by repentance and restoration (2 Cor **2** 5–11). It was not a complex and rigid ecclesiastical engine, held *in terrorem* over the soul, but the last resort of faithful love, over which hope and prayer still hovered.

LITERATURE.—Arts. in *HDB*, *DB*, *Jew Enc*, *DCG*; Martensen, *Christian Ethics*, III, 330 ff; Nowack, Benzinger, *Heb Archaeol.*; Comms. in loc.

PHILIP WENDELL CRANNELL

EXECUTE, ek'sē-kūt, **EXECUTIONER,** ek-sē-kū'shun-ēr (עָשָׂה, *'āsāh*, "to do," דִּין, *dīn*, "to judge," "decide"; **ποιέω**, *poiéō*, "to do"; **σπεκουλάτωρ**, *spekoulátōr*, Lat *speculator*, "an attendant"): "Execute" in the sense of "executing judgment," "vengeance," etc, is often found in the OT (Ex **12** 12; Dt **10** 18; Ps **149** 7; Jer **22** 3; Ezk **25** 11; Mic **5** 15; cf Jer **21** 12, "Execute justice in the morning") and a few times in the NT (Jn **5** 27; Rom **13** 4 AV; Jude ver 15). In the sense of punishing capitally, by legal process, it is not found. "Executioner" is found only in Mk **6** 27 AV, where Herod, the king, is said to have "sent an executioner" (*spekoulatōr*) to behead John the Baptist, but RV and ARV have instead, according to the stricter meaning of the text, "The king sent forth a soldier of his guard." The office of executioner, however, was a recognized office in all the great nations of antiquity.

GEO. B. EAGER

EXEGESIS, ek-sē-jē'sis. See INTERPRETATION.

EXERCISE, ek'sēr-sīz (עָשָׂה, *'āsāh*; **γυμνάζω**, *gumnázō*, **ποιέω**, *poiéō*): "Exercise" (meaning originally, "to drive or thrust out") has different shades of meaning: It means (1) "to do," "to put into action" (Jer **9** 24, *'āsāh*, "to do," "Jeh who exerciseth lovingkindness"; Rev **13** 12, *poieō*, "to do," "He exerciseth all the authority of the first"; Tob **12** 9, RV "do"); (2) with violence implied, *gāzal*, "to take away violently," "have exercised robbery" (Ezk **22** 29); "to act habitually" (Ps **131** 1, *hālakh*, "to walk," "Neither do I exercise myself in great matters," RVm "walk"; Acts **24** 16, *askéō*, "to work up"; cf 2 Esd **15** 8; Ecclus **50** 28); (3) "to train" or "discipline," *gumnazō*, "to use exercise," "to train up" (1 Tim **4** 7, "Exercise thyself unto godliness"; He **5** 14; **12** 11; 2 Pet **2** 14; cf 1 Macc **6** 30; 2 Macc **15** 12); (4) "to afflict (Eccl **1** 13; **3** 10, *'ānāh*, "to be afflicted," "exercised therewith," "exercised in it"); in Mt **20** 25; Mk **10** 42, *katakurieúō*, "to lord it over," and *katexousiázō*, "to exercise authority," are trd respectively "exercise dominion" and "exercise authority," ERV "lord it over" and "exercise authority"; in Lk **22** 25, the Gr words are *kurieúō*, "to be lord over" and *exousiázō*, "to have power or authority over," RV "have lordship," "have authority." In 1 Tim **4** 8 the noun, *gumnasía*, meaning gymnastic exercise, occurs (*sōmatikḗ gumnasía*), trd "bodily exercise," contrasted with "exercise unto godliness," RV "For bodily exercise is profitable for a little [m "for little"]; but godliness is profitable for all things," a saying to which the youth of all times would do well to give heed. In 2 Macc **4** 9, Jason is said to have set up "a place of exercise" (*gumnásion*) in Jerus. In 1 Pet **5** 2 RV, "exercising the oversight" is substituted for "taking the oversight."

W. L. WALKER

EXHORTATION, ek-sor-tā'shun (**παράκλησις**, *paráklēsis*): The Gr word trd "exhortation" (*paraklēsis*) signifies, originally, "a calling near or for" (as an advocate or helper who should appeal on one's behalf), and carries the twofold sense of "exhortation" and "consolation" (which see). In the LXX of the OT it is used in the sense of "consolation"; but in 2 Macc **7** 24, it is trd "exhort," RV "appeal." The vb. *parakaléō* is also trd "exhortation" (1 Macc **13** 3 AV) and "exhort" (2 Macc **9** 26).

In the NT *paraklēsis* is trd "exhortation" (Acts **13** 15; Rom **12** 8, RV "exhorting"; 1 Cor **14** 3, ERV "comfort," ARVm "or comfort"; 2 Cor **8** 17; 1 Thess **2** 3; 1 Tim **4** 13; He **12** 5; **13** 22). ARV has also "exhortation," instead of "consolation" in Phil **2** 1. In Lk **3** 18, *parakaleō*, "to call near or for," is trd exhortation," "and many other things in his exhortation," RV "with many other exhortations," and in Acts **20** 2, *parakaléō lógō pollṓ* is rendered (AV and RV), "had given them much exhortation."

W. L. Walker

EXILE, ek'sīl, eg'zīl (גָּלָה, *gālāh*, צָעָה, *çā'āh*): Occurs twice only in AV (2 S **15** 19 [*gālāh*, "to remove"]; Isa **51** 14 [*çā'āh*, "to be bowed down"]). In RV "exile" is substituted for "captivity" (Ezr **8** 35 [*shebhī*], and Ezk **12** 4 [*gōlāh*]); "go into exile," for "remove and go" (Ezk **12** 11); "exiles of Ethiopia" for "Ethiopians captives" (Isa **20** 4); "He shall let my exiles go free" for "He shall let go my captives" (**45** 13); "an exile" for "a captive" (**49** 21). "The exile" is in AV and RV "the captivity" (q.v.).

EXODUS, ek'sō-dus, **THE:**

I. The Route.—On the 14th Abib (early in April) the Hebrews were gathered at Rameses (Ex **12** 37; Nu **33** 5) where apparently the hostile Pharaoh was also living (Ex **12** 31). From Ps **78** 12.43 it appears that the wonders preceding the Exodus occurred in the "field of Zoan," where the starting-point may be placed (see Raamses; Zoan). Dr. Naville has suggested that the court was at Bubastis, not at Zoan, and that the route lay from near *Zagazig* down *Wâdy Tumeilât*—a line well fitted for a people driving flocks and herds. On the other hand, in favor of the starting-point having been at Zoan, we read that the "way of the land of the Philis" was "near" (Ex **13** 17). This route, which was not taken lest the people should be discouraged by defeat at Gaza where the Egyptians always had troops, reached Egypt at Migdol (see Migdol, 2), and ran thence to Daphnai—some 15 miles—and to Zoan by a second march of the same length. The route from Bubastis to Daphnai (some 50 miles) is less likely to have been described as "near." Although an Arab will march 30 miles in a day on foot, yet when moving camp with camels, who travel only about 2 miles an hour, with women and children and herds, he only covers about 12 or 15 miles a day. We cannot suppose the Heb cattle to have covered more than this distance without water on any single march.

1. The Starting-Point

We are not told how many days were occupied on the way from Rameses to Succoth (q.v.), though the general impression is that the stages mentioned (Nu **33**) represent a day's journey each. Measuring back from the first camp after crossing the Red Sea, we find that Succoth probably lay in the lower part of *Wâdy Tumeilât*, where there was plenty of water and herbage. The direct route from Zoan leads to Phakousa (*Tell Faḳûs*) by a march of 15 miles through well-watered lands. A second march, across the desert to Heroopolis and down the valley to Succoth, would be of the same length. The Hebrews departed "in haste," and no doubt made as long marches as they could. If the whole of the people were not in Rameses, but scattered over Goshen, it is possible that some came down the valley from near Bubastis, and that the whole force concentrated at Succoth.

2. Rameses to Succoth

The next march (Ex **13** 20; Nu **33** 6) led Israel to Etham, on the "edge of the wilderness" which lies W. of the Bitter Lakes, not far from where the Nile water then entered them, and no doubt made them sweet. The intention of Moses probably was to reach the desert of Shur by rounding the head of this stretch of water; but we are told (Ex **14** 2f) that he was commanded to "turn"—evidently to the S.—and to encamp before "the mouth of the lakes" (see Pi-Hahiroth), in order that Pharaoh might conclude that the Hebrews were "entangled in the land," and shut in between the lakes on their left and the desert mountains on their right. This camp would seem to have been W. of the lakes, and some 10 miles N. of Suez. It was perhaps two days' journey from Etham, since the lakes are 30 miles long; or, if Etham was farther S. than the head of the lakes, the distance may have been covered by one forced march of 20 to 25 miles, the beasts being watered from the lakes if they were then filled with fresh water, as they would be when having an outlet to a tideless sea.

3. Succoth to Etham

The sea which Israel crossed is not named in the actual account of the journey, but in the Song of Moses (Ex **15** 4) it is called the "Red Sea" in the EV, following the LXX, the Heb name being *Yam Ṣūph*, or "weedy sea," a term which applied not only to the Gulf of Suez (Nu **33** 10), but also to the Gulf of 'Aḳabah (Dt **2** 8; 1 K **9** 26). We are also told that the route chosen was "the way of the wilderness by the Red Sea" (Ex **13** 18). It is generally supposed that the head of the Gulf of Suez at the time of the Exodus was farther N. than at present; and, as the Bitter Lakes were then probably filled by the Nile waters flowing down *Wâdy Tumeilât*, they would no doubt have carried the Nile mud into this gulf, which mud had gradually filled up this Nile branch before 600 BC. The probable point of passage was the narrow channel (about 2 miles across) by which the lakes discharged into the sea, and was thus about 10 miles N. of Suez. We are told that the water was driven back by "a strong east [or "contrary"] wind" in the night (Ex **14** 21), and the sea (or "lake," as the word *yam* often means in the OT; see Gesenius, *Lexicon*, s.v.) was thus "divided," a shoal being formed and the waters being heaped up (Ex **15** 8), so that when the wind ceased they rushed back; whereas, during the passage, they were a "wall" or "defence" (**14** 22) against any flank attacks by the Egyptians (cf 1 S **25** 16, where David's men are said to have been a "wall" when defending Nabal's shepherds). The effect of the wind on shallow waters can be seen at the mouth of the Kishon, where a shoal exists which is dry with a west wind, but under water and impassable when the wind blows down the river. In 1882, Sir Alexander Tulloch saw the waters of Lake Menzaleh driven back more than a mile by the east wind. Thus, however opportune the occurrence,

4. Passage of the Sea

the drying up of the sea, as described in the Bible, was a perfectly natural phenomenon. The Hebrews crossed in the morning, and a march of 15 miles would bring them to the springs from which Suez is supplied, called *'Ain Nâba'* and *'Ayyûn Mûsa* ("the gushing spring" and "the spring of Moses"), from which point their wanderings in the desert of Shur would begin (see WANDERINGS OF ISRAEL).

5. Other Views of the Route

This view of the Exodus route is practically the same as advocated by Dr. Robinson, by Dr. E. Naville, by Sir S. Warren, by Sir W. Dawson, and by others who have visited the region in question. The view advocated by Brugsch, according to which the sea crossed was a lagoon near Pelusium, has found no supporters, because it directly conflicts with the statement that Israel did not follow the shore road to Philistia, but went by the wilderness of the Red Sea. Another theory (see SINAI), according to which the "Red Sea" always means the Gulf of 'Aḳabah, is equally discarded by most writers of experience, because the distance from Egypt to Elath on this gulf is 200 miles, and the Israelites could not have traversed that distance in four marches, especially as the route has hardly any water along it in springtime. As detailed above, the route offers no difficulties that would discredit the historical character of the narrative.

II. The Date.—The actual statements of the Books of K, giving ‖ reigns from the time of Solomon's death down to the fixed date of the fall of Samaria in 722 BC, place the foundation of the Temple within a few years of 1000 BC. It is true that this interval is reduced, by about 30 years, by scholars who accept the very doubtful identification of Ahabu of Sir-lai with Ahab of Israel; but this theory conflicts with the fact that Jehu was contemporary with Shalmaneser II of Assyria; and, since we have no historical account of the chronology of Heb kings other than that of the OT, for this period, and no monumental notice of Israel in Egypt, or of the Exodus, we must either adopt OT chronology or regard the dates in question as being unknown.

1. OT Chronology Adopted

2. Date of Conquest of Palestine

We have several statements which show that the Heb writers believed the conquest of Pal by Joshua to have occurred early in the 15th cent. BC, and this date fully agrees with the most recent results of monumental study of the history of the XVIIIth (or Theban) Dynasty in Egypt, as about to be shown, and with the fact that Israel is noticed as being already in Pal in the 5th year of Minepthah, the successor of Rameses II. In 1 K **6** 1 we read that the Temple was founded "in the 480th year after the children of Israel were come out of the land of Egypt," this referring to the Conquest and not to the Exodus, as appears from other notices. The LXX reads "440 years," but the details show that the Heb text is preferable. In Jgs **11** 26 the first victory of Jephthah is said to have occurred 300 years after Joshua's conquest. The details given for this interval, in other passages of the same book, amount to 326 years; but the periods of "rest" may be given in round numbers, and thus account for this minor discrepancy. Samuel ruled apparently for 20 years (1 S **7** 2), and Saul (the length of whose reign is not stated in our present text of this same book) very probably ruled for 20 years also, as Jos (*Ant*, VI, xiv, 9) states. Thus 175 years elapsed between Jephthah's victory and the foundation of the Temple—a total of 475 years, or rather more, from Joshua's conquest.

3. Date of Exodus

The popular belief that many of the judges were contemporary does not agree with these facts, and is indeed in conflict with ten definite statements in Jgs. In Acts **13** 19.20 we read that after the Conquest there were judges about the space of 450 years, and this rough estimate (including the rule of Samuel) agrees pretty nearly with the 415, or 420, years of the various passages in the OT. According to the Pent and later accounts (Am **5** 25; Acts **7** 30), Israel abode in the desert 40 years. We therefore find that Joshua's conquest is placed about 1480 BC, and the Exodus about 1520 BC. According to the revised chronology of the XVIIIth Dynasty of Egypt (see HITTITES), which rests on the notices of contemporary Kassite kings in Babylon, it thus appears that the Pharaoh of the oppression was Thothmes III—a great enemy of the Asiatics—and the Pharaoh of the Exodus would be Amenophis II or Thothmes IV. If Moses was 80 at the time of the Exodus, he must have been born when Thothmes III was an infant, and when his famous sister Hatasu (according to the more probable rendering of her name by Fr. scholars) was regent, and bore the title Ma-ka-Ra. She therefore might be the "daughter of Pharaoh" (Ex **2** 5) who adopted Moses—no king being mentioned in this passage, but appearing (ver 15) only when Moses was "grown"; for her regency lasted more than 20 years, till Thothmes III came of age.

4. Other Views

As regards this date, it should be remarked that the theory of Lepsius, which has been adopted by Brugsch and by many writers who accept his authority, is not accepted by every scholar. E. de Bunsen supposed that the Exodus occurred early in the times of the XVIIIth Dynasty; Sir Peter le Page Renouf said that "no materials have yet been discovered for fixing historical dates in periods of Egyp history as far back as the Heb Exodus"—which was true when he wrote. Professor J. Lieblein supposes the Exodus to have occurred late in the time of Amenophis III—also of the XVIIIth Dynasty (see *Proc. Bib. Arch. Soc.*, 1890, 157–60; 1892, 60–62; 1898, 277; 1899, 53; 1907, 214). Dr. Hommel has also recently declared in favor of the view that the Exodus took place under the XVIIIth Dynasty (*Expos T*, February, 1899). Lepsius asserted that the Exodus occurred in 1314 BC, being the 15th year of Minepthah; but this is generally regarded as at least half a century too early for the year in question, and Israel was not in Egypt even ten years earlier in his reign.

5. Astronomical Calculations

The approximate dates given by Brugsch for the XVIIIth and XIXth Dynasties are very close to those which can be deduced from notices of contemporary kings of Babylon (*Hist Egypt*, II, 314). The later dates which Mahler based on certain astronomical calculations of the Fr. astronomer Biot (*Académie des inscriptions*, March 30, 1831, 597, 602–4) are not accepted by other Egyptologists. Brugsch says that on this question, "scientific criticism has not yet spoken its last word" (*Hist Egypt*, I, 36). Renouf (*Proc. Bib. Arch. Soc.*, December, 1892, 62) more definitely states that "unfortunately there is *nothing* on Egyp documents which have as yet come down to us which can, by astronomical calculations, be made to result in a date." This judgment appears to be justified by recent discoveries, since Mahler's dates are about a century too late, as shown by the known history of the Kassites of Babylon. Biot's calculations were based on recorded observations of the rising of Sirius just before the sun, in certain years of certain Egyp kings. But Sirius is not in the plane of the earth's orbit, and its rising is not constant in retardation. The "heliacal" rising is now about 2½ min. later each year, but about the date in question the retardation was about 12 min., so that a cycle of 1,461 years cannot be used by simple addition. Biot also assumed that the Egyp observations were as accurate as those made by a modern astronomer with a telescope, whereas, when using the naked eye, the Egyp observer may well have been a day wrong, which would make a difference of 120 years in the date, or even more. The Bab chronology thus gives a far safer basis than do these doubtful observations. On the basis of Biot's calculations the Exodus has been placed in 1214 BC, or even (by Dr. Flinders Petrie) in 1192 BC (*Proc. Bib. Arch. Soc.*, December, 1896, 248). He thus cuts off more than three centuries in the period of the Judges, many of whom he regards as contemporary. Lepsius in like manner, in order to establish his date, accepted the chronology of the Talm, which is notoriously 166 years too late for the known date of the fall of Samaria, and he endeavored (while rejecting the OT statement as to the 480 years) to base himself on the number of generations before the Exodus, whereas it is well known that the Heb genealogies often give only the better-known names and skip several links.

As regards the relation between the earlier date for the Exodus (about 1520 BC) and the chronology of the Heb patriarchs, the Heb text

6. Relation between Date of Exodus and Date of Patriarchs

gives an interval of 645 years, and the Gr text of 430 years between the Exodus and the call of Abraham; and the call would thus be dated about 2165 BC or 1950 BC. Abraham is very generally held to have been contemporary with Ḥammurabi of Babylon (Amraphel), whose accession dates (according to Dr. F. Peiser) in 2139 BC. Dr. Hommel and Mr. King prefer a later date, about 1950 BC, though Nabunahid (the last king of Babylon) places Ḥammurabi about 2140 BC. The longer reckoning is reconcilable with the Heb text, and the shorter with the Gr text, of Gen, without disturbing the approximate date for the Exodus which has been advocated above.

There is in fact no discrepancy between the actual results of monumental study and the chronology of the OT. If the Exodus occurred under

7. Agreement between Monuments and OT Chronology

Thothmes IV, it would have been useless for Israel to attempt the entrance into Pal by the "way of the land of the Philis," because at Gaza, Ashkelon and in other cities, the road was still held by forces of Egyp chariots, which had been established by Thothmes III. But about 40 years later the rebellion of the Amorites against Egypt began, in the time of the Egyp general Yankhamu, and general chaos resulted in Southern Pal. The Egyp garrison at Jerus (*Amarna Tablets*, Berlin, No. 102) was withdrawn in his time—about 1480 BC—and it is then (nos. 102–3–4–6, 199) that a fierce people coming from Seir, and called the *'Abiri* or *Ḥabiri*, are noticed by the Amorite king of Jerus as "destroying all the rulers" of the country. They are not named in any of the other Amarna letters (the term *gum-gaz*, or "man of war," though once applying probably to them, being used of other warriors as well); and the name is geographical for they are called (no. 199) "people of the land of the *'Abiri*." The first sign has the guttural sounds *'A* and *Ḥ*, and has not the sound *K*, which has been wrongly attributed to it, making the word to mean *Kabiri*, "or great ones." Nor can it be rendered "allies," for it is the name of a people, and quite another word is used for "allies" in this correspondence. The date agrees with that mentioned in the OT for the Heb conquest of Pal, and the only objection to the identification of the *'Abiri* (who attacked Ajalon, Lachish, Ashkelon and other cities) with the Hebrews is, that it upsets the theory of Lepsius, and the popular views as to the date of the Exodus which he maintained.

Nor is this the only evidence which destroys his theory; for Dr. Flinders Petrie (*Contemporary Review*, May, 1896) has published an

8. A Text of Minepthah

equally important text of the 5th year of Minepthah, from Thebes. A slab of black syenite, bearing this text, was reused from a temple of Amenophis III. In it Minepthah boasts of his conquest of the invaders who—as elsewhere stated—attacked the Delta, and penetrated to Belbeis and Heliopolis. He says that "Sutekh [the Hittite god] has turned his back on their chief"; "the Hittites are quieted, Pa-Kan'ana is ravaged with all violence"—this town being otherwise known to have been near Tyre—"the people of Israel is spoiled, it has no seed"; "Ruten has become as the widows of the land of Egypt." Thus, so far from the Exodus having occurred in the 15th year of Minepthah, Israel is noticed 10 years earlier in connection with a place near Tyre with Hittites yet farther N. Even if the Hebrews had only just arrived, they must have left Egypt 40 years before—in the reign of Rameses II—if we attach any value to OT statements; and all the dates variously given by followers of Lepsius are quite upset; whereas the notice of the *'Abiri*, two centuries before Minepthah's accession, is quite in accord with this allusion to Israel, as well as with OT chronology.

III. The Theory of Lepsius.—The reasons which influenced Lepsius require, however, to be stated, and the objections to a date for the Heb Conquest about 1480 BC (or a little later) to be considered, since the theory that Rameses II was the Pharaoh of the oppression, and Minepthah the Pharaoh of the Exodus is often said to be a secure result of monumental studies, whereas it is really not so, because the only monumental allusions to Israel and the Hebrews are those just mentioned.

The arguments adduced in favor of the later date are as follows: In the first place, Lepsius (*Letters from Egypt*, 1842–44) held that no city

1. 1st Argument: City Rameses

called Rameses could have been so named, or built by the Hebrews, before the reign of Rameses II, and he placed the site at Heroopolis. This was a very doubtful assumption (see Raamses), and his identification of the city is now abandoned. The theory always was vitiated by an objection which he seems to have overlooked: for the "land of Rameses" is noticed in the time of Jacob (Gen **47** 11), and since it is impossible to suppose that Jacob lived in the time of Rameses II, the followers of Lepsius are obliged to regard this notice as an anachronism, which destroys their case, as it might equally be an anachronism in the account of the Exodus, though it is probably correct.

The second argument is based on the account by Manetho of the expulsion of leprous and unclean tribes from Egypt. Manetho was an

2. 2d Argument: Manetho's Statements

Egyp priest who wrote about 268 BC, and who evidently hated the Jews. His account only reaches us secondhand through Jos (*CAp*, I, 14, 15, 26–31), this Heb author rejecting it as fabulous. Manetho apparently said that, after the Hyksos kings had ruled for 511 years, and had fortified Avaris (see Zoan), they agreed with King Thummosis to leave Egypt, and went through the desert to Jerus, being afraid of the Assyrians (who had no power in Pal at this time). He continued to relate that, after Armesses Miamon (Rameses II) had ruled 66 years, he was succeeded by an Amenophis whom Jos calls a "fictitious king"—and rightly so since the name does not occur in the XIXth Dynasty. Apparently Minepthah was meant—

though perhaps confused with Amenophis II—and he is said by Manetho to have sent the leprous people to quarries E. of the Nile, but to have allowed them later to live in Avaris where the shepherds had been. They were induced by Osarsiph, a priest of Heliopolis, to renounce the Egyp gods, and this Osarsiph Manetho identified with Moses. They then induced the shepherds who had been expelled by Thummosis to return from Jerus to Avaris, and Amenophis fled to Memphis and Ethiopia. His son Rhampses (apparently Rameses III is meant) was sent later to expel the shepherd and polluted people, whom he met at Pelusium and pursued into Syria. This story Jos discredits, remarking: "I think therefore that I have made it sufficiently evident that Manetho, while he followed his ancient records, did not much mistake the truth of the history, but that, when he had recourse to fabulous stories without any certain author, he either forged them himself without any probability, or else gave credit to some men who spoke so out of their ill will to us"—a criticism sounder than that of Lepsius, who prefers the libelous account of a prejudiced Egyp priest of the 3d cent. BC, identifying Moses with a renegade priest of Heliopolis named Osarsiph, to the ancient Heb records in the Bible.

A thread of truth underlay Manetho's stories, but it has nothing to do with the Exodus, and the details to be found on Egyp monuments do not agree with Manetho's tale. The Hyksos rulers were not expelled by any Thothmes, but by Aahmes who took Avaris about 1700 BC, and who reopened the quarries of the Arabian chain. Minepthah, about 1265 BC, was attacked in Egypt by Aryan tribes from the N., who had nothing to do with Hyksos chiefs, being Lycians, Sardians and Cilicians. He repelled them, but they again attacked Rameses III (about 1200 BC), and were again driven to the N. No mention of Israel occurs in connection with any of these events.

3. Relation of Manetho's Stories to the Exodus

The story of the leprous Jews was, however, repeated by other Gr writers. Cheremon (see *CAp*, I, 32) says that Rameses, the son of Amenophis, defeated and expelled a diseased people led against him, at Pelusium, by Tisithen and Petesiph, whom he identified with Moses and Joseph. Lysimachus said that a scabby people were led by Moses through the desert by Judaea and Jerus in the time of Bocchoris (735 BC). Diodorus Siculus (*Fr. of Bk*, 34) repeats the tale, about 8 BC, saying that lepers were driven out of Egypt, and were led by Moses who founded Jerus, and "established by law all their wicked customs and practices," and again (*Fr. of Bk*, 40) that strangers in Egypt caused a plague by their impurity, and being driven out were led by Moses. Tacitus, about 100 AD (*Hist*, v.ii), believed the Jews to have fled from Crete to Libya and, being expelled from Egypt, to have been led by their "Captains Jerusalem and Judah." Again he says (v. iii) that under Bocchoris (735 BC) there was sickness in Egypt, and that the infected being driven out were led by Moses, and reached the site of their temple on the 7th day.

4. Greek and Latin Writers

No true critic of the present time is likely to prefer these distorted accounts of the Exodus, or any of the Gr and Rom calumnies leveled against the hated Jews, to the simple narration of the Exodus in the Bible. The historic conditions in the 5th year of Minepthah were very different from those at the time of Moses. The invaders of Egypt reached Belbeis and Heliopolis (see Brugsch, *Hist Egypt*, II, 117), and Minepthah states, in his text on the wall of the temple of Amon at Thebes, that he had to defend Heliopolis and Memphis against his foes from the E. The region was then "not cultivated but was left as pasture for cattle, on account of the foreigners. It lay waste from the time of our forefathers." The kings of upper Egypt remained in their entrenchments, and the kings of lower Egypt were besieged in their cities by warriors, and had no mercenaries to oppose them. But Israel, as Minepthah himself has told us now, was in Pal, not in Egypt, in this year of his reign; and, far from desiring to expel Asiatic pastoral peoples, the same Pharaoh encouraged their immigration into the region of Goshen (see PITHOM) laid waste by the Aryan raid.

5. Condition of Egypt under Minepthah

Objections to the view that the Exodus occurred two centuries and a half before the reign of Minepthah began, and attempts to explain away the statements on his monuments require some notice.

6. Explanations of Minepthah's Statements

(1) *Pithom was Heroopolis.*—The first of these objections is due to the belief that Pithom was Heroopolis, and was a city founded by Rameses II; but this (see PITHOM) is too hazardous a conclusion to suffice for the entire neglect of OT chronology which it involves, since the site of this city is still very doubtful.

(2) *Rameses II not named in Judges.*—A second objection is made, that the OT shows complete ignorance of Egyp history if it makes Rameses II contemporary with Jgs because he is not named in that book. But OT references to foreign history are always very slight, while on the other hand it is quite probable that there are allusions, in this book, to the events which took place in the reigns of Rameses II, and of Minepthah. The Hebrews were then confined to the mountains (Jgs **1** 19) and the Egyptians to the plains. No Pharaoh is mentioned by name in the OT till the time of Rehoboam. In his 8th year Rameses II took various towns in Galilee including Salem (N. of Taanach), Merom, Beth-Anath, Anem and Dapur (Daberath at the foot of Tabor). The revolt of Barak probably occurred about the 25th year of Rameses II, and began at Tabor. In the Song of Deborah (Jgs **5** 2), the first words (*bi-ph^{e}rō^{a}ʿ p^{e}rāʿoth*), rendered by the LXX (Alex MS) "when the rulers ruled," may be more definitely tr^d "when the Pharaohs were powerful," esp. as Sisera—who commanded the Can. forces—bears a name probably Egyp (*ses-Ra*, or "servant of Ra"), and may have been an Egyp resident at the court of Jabin. So again when, about 1265 BC, Minepthah says that "Israel is ruined, it has no seed," the date suggests the time of Gideon when wild tribes swarmed over the plains, "and destroyed the increase of the earth, till thou come unto Gaza, and left no sustenance in Israel" (Jgs **6** 4). The Midianites and Amalekites may have then joined the tribes from Asia Minor who, in the 5th year of Minepthah, ruined the Hittites and invaded the Delta.

(3) *Some Hebrews were never in Egypt.*—But another explanation of the presence of Israel in this year on the line of Minepthah's pursuit of these tribes after their defeat has been suggested, namely, that some of the Hebrews never went to Egypt at all. This of course contradicts the account in the Pent (Ex **1** 1–5; **12** 41) where we read that all Jacob's family (70 men) went down to Goshen, and that "all the hosts of the Lord" left Egypt at the Exodus; but it is supposed to be supported by a passage (1 Ch **7** 21) where we read of one of the sons of Ephraim "whom the men of Gath born in the land slew, because they came down to take away their cattle." Ephraim however was born in Egypt (Gen **41** 52), and his sons and "children of the third generation" (**50** 23) remained there. The

meaning no doubt is that men of Gath raided Goshen; and there were probably many such raids by the inhabitants of Philistia during the times of the Hyksos kings, similar to those which occurred in the time of Minepthah and of Rameses III. The objections made to the OT date for the Exodus early in the reign of Amenophis III, or in that of his predecessor Thothmes IV, thus appear to have little force; and the condition of Egypt before the 5th year of Minepthah was unlike that which would have existed at the time of the Exodus. The theory of Lepsius was a purely literary conjecture, and not based on any monumental records. It has been falsified by the evidence of monuments found during the last 20 years, and these are fully in accord with the history and chronology of the OT.

IV. The Numbers.—The historic difficulty with respect to the Exodus does not lie in the account of plagues natural to Egypt even now, nor in the crossing of the Red Sea, but in a single statement as to the numbers of Israel (Ex **12** 37), 'about 600,000 footmen—strong men—with many children, and also many wanderers.' The women are not mentioned, and it has been supposed that this represents a host of 2,000,000 emigrants at least. The objection was urged by Voltaire, and the consequences were elaborately calculated by Colenso. Even if 600,000 means the total population, the "heroes," or "strong men on foot" would, it is urged, have been as numerous as the largest Assyr army (120,000 men) employed in the conquest of Syria. With an army of more than half a million Moses would have held control over Egypt and Pal alike; and the emigrants, even in close column of companies, would have stretched for 20 miles; the births would occur every ten minutes; and the assembly before Sinai would have been impossible.

1. Colenso's Criticism of Large Number

It is also difficult to suppose, on ordinary calculations of the increase of population, that in 430 years (Ex **12** 40), or in 215 years as given in the LXX, a tribe of 70 males (Gen **46** 26 f; Ex **1** 5; **6** 14) could have increased to 600,000, or even 100,000 men. But on the other hand we are specially told (Ex **1** 7-20) that the children of Israel "increased abundantly," and the comments of Dr Orr (*Problem of the OT*, 1906, 363-65) on this question should be studied. A young and vigorous nation might multiply much faster than is now usual in the East. Dr. Flinders Petrie has suggested that for "thousand" we should read "families"; but, though the word (*'eleph*) sometimes has that meaning (Jgs **6** 15; 1 S **10** 19; **23** 23), it is in the sing., and not in the pl., in the passage in question (Ex **12** 37).

2. Increase of Population

It should not be forgotten that variations in numbers are very commonly found in various texts, VSS, and ‖ passages of the OT. Thus for instance (1 S **13** 5) the Syr version reads 3,000 for the 30,000 chariots mentioned in the Heb and Gr; and the LXX (1 K **5** 11) gives 20,000 for the 20 measures of oil noticed in the Heb text. The probable reason for these discrepancies may be found in the fact that the original documents may have used numeral signs—as did the Egyptians, Assyrians, Hittites and Phoenicians—instead of writing the words in full as they appear in the NT. These numeral signs—esp. in cuneiform—were apt to be misread, and the sign for "unity" could easily be confused with those denoting "sixty" (the Bab unit) and "an hundred"—if, in the latter case, a short stroke was added. In the opinion of the present writer the difficulty is due to a corruption of the original statement, which occurred during the course of some fifteen centuries, or more, of continued recopying; but the reader will no doubt form his own conclusions as to this question.

3. Number a Corruption of Original Statement

The general questions of the credibility of that history of the Exodus which is given us in the Pent, and of the approximate date of the event, have been treated above in the light of the most recent monumental information. No reference has yet been found in Egyp records to the presence of Israel in the Delta, though the Hebrews are noticed as present in Pal before the 5th year of Minepthah. The Pharaohs as a rule—like other kings—only recorded their victories, and no doubt reckoned Israel only as a tribe of those "hostile Shasu" (or "nomads") whom the Theban kings of the XVIIIth Dynasty drove back into Asia. It would be natural that a disaster at the Red Sea should not be noticed in their proud records still extant on the temple walls in Egypt. See also WANDERINGS OF ISRAEL.

4. Review

C. R. CONDER

EXODUS: DATE AND NUMBERS (Alternative view).

An early and a late date for the Exodus claim acceptance. It is rather disconcerting to note that they differ by as much as 300 years.

I. Date.—There are difficulties concerning the date of the Exodus no matter at what place in history it may be thought to belong. Those who think to determine absolutely that date and believe all difficulties met have simply ignored the difficulties presented by the alternative date. The wise course is to determine upon some principle for deciding the question and then follow its lead.

1. Difficulties

The principle of determination now to be followed is that every case dependent upon human testimony, as are all historical questions, turns upon hinges like a door. A door may bind in one place and leave an opening in another, may squeak not a little when moved; nevertheless it turns upon its hinges. So in this, and every case, of historical controversy. Turning aside from the difficulties attendant upon alternative dates for the Exodus, it is proposed to seek and to point out clearly the hinges upon which this case turns.

2. Hinges, Principle

(1) The account in Ex (**1** 11) unmistakably ascribes the building of the Store Cities, Pithom and Raamses, to the Israelite slaves on the order of Pharaoh, but gives no indication of the name of the king. For Pharaoh (Egyp *Per-aa*, "Great House," like the "*Sublime Porte*" or the "Crown") is but the appellation of the government. These Store Cities were for long a mystery and variously located by different Etyptologists (see PITHOM) and no definite information was obtained until Naville uncovered the ruins at *Tell Maskhûtah*. At that place every phase of the story was illustrated and certified, except the location of the land of Succoth This was later corroborated by the discovery of the tombstone of a priest of that region of *Thuku*, Egyp equivalent of Succoth. A visit to the ruins

and a careful examination of Naville's work in 1908 found every part of his much disputed report exactly confirmed. On the gateway was an inscription in which Rameses II states categorically, "I built Pithom." It has been urged that Rameses was a great plagiarist, and so he was. But this inscription was an original one, has never been tampered with. No one before Rameses would put it here, and certainly no one after Rameses, unless the inscription stated the truth. Moreover, the bricks are the well-known bricks of Rameses II, and yet the whole Israelite story of the building of Pithom is told in them. At Beth-shean also a tablet was found in which Rameses II states that he built Raamses, the other Store City, and that too with Asiatic Semitic slaves (see BETH-SHEAN). Here then at Pithom and Beth-shean is one hinge on which the case for the date of the Exodus turns. Israel built Pithom; Rameses II built Pithom; hence Rameses was the final oppressor immediately before the Exodus.

(2) Mariette in his excavations at Zoan uncovered a tablet erected by Rameses II to the memory of his father Seti (some think in honor of the god Set), on which is an epochal date. The most important thing in the inscription is this date, perhaps the only epochal date in early Egyp history. The tablet is dated in the 400th year of king Nubti. The exact date of Nubti is not known, but he was a little before, or immediately after, Apophis who, on the authority of Syncellus, was the Pharaoh of Joseph. To Abram it was said "Know of a surety that thy seed shall be a stranger in a land that is not theirs and shall serve them; and they shall afflict them 400 years" (Gen **15** 13). In Ex (**12** 40) the time in Egypt is said to have been exactly 430 years. Thus the 400 years of the prophecy from Joseph to Moses and the 400 years of the tablet from Nubti to Rameses II makes the deadly parallel from which there seems to be no escape. This is another hinge upon which the case turns.

(3) The Israel tablet found by Petrie at the Rameseum in 1906 has been the subject of much controversy and is by some interpreted to mean that Israel was already in Palestine, thus bolstering up the early date of the Exodus. If some think it may be so, there are others who, on certainly equally good ground, believe it, when correctly interpreted, to be in support of the late date of the Exodus. The name "Israel" occurs between Ashkelon and Khar in this inscription. Now Khar is the name for Canaan by the way of the Dead Sea. And Israel named between Ashkelon and Khar seems to put it between them, i.e., in the region of Kadesh Barnea. Every name in the list has the determinatives for a "people" and an "own land," except Israel. Then Khar which follows Israel has again both determinatives. This is exactly in accord with the condition of Israel wandering in the wilderness, a "people," without "an own country," and it is not at all in accord with the idea that Israel was settled in the promised land where she would have an "own country." It is also said in the inscription "there seed is not." It has been urged that "seed" must be translated "crops." But two inscriptions, one of Hatshepsut and one of Rameses II, use the same word to mean unmistakably "child" or "children." The inscription of Hatshepsut represents the god Amon addressing the queen as his daughter with this Egyp word and the appellation "holy," "holy *pert*." Imagine a father addressing his child as "holy crops"! So the word in Merenptah's inscription may well mean children and the inscription become a jeering boast that the children of Israel had not entered the promised land because they were characteristically a nation of women, despoiled of their "seed" by the destruction of the boy babies. And then, last of all, the poet adds, "Khar has become like the widows of Egypt," meaning that Palestine was mourning for the Israelites that did not come, as a widow mourning for her husband. Now this inscription is dated as of the 5th year of Merenptah. Moses received the call, when the king had died who desired his life. One year must be allowed in the Orient for his return. Two years more, before they left Sinai, and thus the turning back at Kadesh Barnea would be at the beginning of the 5th year. And so the 5th year of Moses becomes the 5th year of Merenptah. Thus another hinge.

(4) Palestine has been called the Bridge of Nations, because over it in the ancient world every army and every traveler must pass between the countries of Africa and Asia and Europe. They did not cross the sea, only skirted the shore; they could not cross the desert. The Bridge is only 40 miles wide on the average and narrows to a few rods at the pass of Megiddo. This Bridge of Nations was more important in the ancient world of the Orient than the Bosphorus and the Dardanelles now in the modern western world.

Yet the books of Jos, Jgs, and 1 S and 2 S recite the history of Israel during that period without a single molestation by either of the great nations of the south, of the north, or of the east. Only the petty nations around about disturbed their peace for practically 500 years. The great nations left them during this period in absolute possession of the Bridge of Nations. Thus Israel grew great. If the Exodus took place at the early date, then these books of the Bible would not be history at all. For during the centuries subsequent to that early day the great Pharaohs, Amenophis III, Seti I, and Rameses II ravaged and pillaged that land again and again, and the booty they carried off and described on their monuments (Muller, *Egyptological Researches*) could not be duplicated from all the museums of the world today; and yet there is not a word of these invasions in the Biblical history of that time. Such a lack in the record is incredible. On the other hand, if the Exodus took place at the end of the reign of Rameses II, from that date Egypt went down, down, down 500 years, until Shishak, the Ethiopian came up and sacked the temple 25 years after it was built. Merenptah and Rameses III did make Palestinian excursions along the seashore which Israel *did not hold*, but not through the part of the land occupied by Israel. At the beginning of the same 500-year period the old Babylonian kingdom had gone down, been supplanted by Assyria, but it took Assyria 500 years to grow great and begin her meteoric career. So here again is the 500-year period in Assyria *as well as* in Egypt. Another hinge.

(5) Last of all and strongest of all, at Kiriath-sepher in the excavations by Xenia Seminary in cooperation with the American School of Oriental Research at Jerusalem, 1926–28, there was found an exact cultural date for the Conquest and so for the Exodus. A great layer of ashes, charcoal, and lime from the burned limestone of the walls was found inside the east gate showing that the city had been burned. Everything below that level was Canaanite of the Bronze Age, all the pottery, all weapons and tools. Everything above that level was Israelite of the Iron Age, all the pottery, all the weapons and tools. Manifestly Israel came in exactly at the change of the Bronze Age to the Iron Age. This took place quite suddenly, when the Philistines established their smelting furnaces for iron at Gerar (Petrie, *Gerar*). Iron became abundant and cheap, and at once drove out the bronze. Will anyone say that the power of the Philistines was 300 years earlier, in the reign of Amenophis III, or that the Iron Age was introduced in Palestine at the close of the reign of Thothmes III? The Iron Age came in,

according to Père Vincent, about 1275 BC. Thus certainly a cultural date for the Exodus is established at Kiriath-sepher; it was at the beginning of the Iron Age. And so another hinge. On these five hinges the case turns. In time all difficulties will be resolved.

II. Number of the People.—The scant evidence concerning the number of the people is both direct and inferential.

1. Fear

There is the fear of the Israelites manifest by the Egyptians in their frantic efforts to keep down the increase of the male population (Ex **1**) and the panic created among the people of Canaan at the prospect of an Israelite invasion. It is incredible that the great Egyp Empire with a standing army and many mercenaries should have been afraid of the Israelites, if they were *only a small company,* as has been computed by some investigators. And the fear of the Canaanites is equally ridiculous, if the Israelites were only a *few tribes of desert people.*

2. A Large Army

A large army is clearly indicated by the specific numbers of males in the various tribes and this again is most positively corroborated in the character of the fortresses taken in Palestine by the Israelites. It is said that "All Israel" (Jos **10** 38) went to take Kiriath-sepher. And the sight of the great walls and gates of that fortress, walls more than 40 feet high and 10 to 14 feet thick with every known device for defense confirms it. Not only would the whole army be needed for the siege of such a place, but also it must have been a large army to stand the wearing down of hand fighting by which only could a city be taken, the defenders being reduced to a few, while the attacking force continued in strength.

3. The 600,000

The significance of the 600,000 when carefully scrutinized is very illuminating, "600,000 on foot, men beside children." The word translated "men" is *gibbōrīm* which corresponds, not to the latin word *homo,* but to *vir.* Moreover, these *gibbōrīm* are described as "on foot," i.e., "marchers," "600,000 strong ones who marched, beside the children. Here again the word is not the ordinary word for children, but a playful word, as we would say a nursery word, *tappīm,* an onomatopoetic word imitating the sound of little feet, "tap, tap, tap," "little patter-foots," who, in contrast with those who walked, had to be carried. Nothing specifically is said about women. They must be included among the "strong ones" who are described as going "on foot." The ratio in which these "strong ones" were divided between men and women can only be estimated. We know that the Egyptians tried to disturb the equilibrium between the sexes in order to make the people characteristically a nation of women and so unable to make an insurrection. To what extent they carried out this dastardly design we do not know. Certainly a reduction of one-sixth in the number of males would be a reasonable estimate. Thus the 600,000 would represent 400,000 women and 200,000 men. Slave women, especially in the Orient, have many children. If we count only two little ones to each woman, there would be 800,000 children. The "mixed multitude" is still more vague in number, but, if we reckon them at 100,000, there would be in all about 1,500,000. The number cannot have been more, it may have been much less. But this is a reasonable estimate.

4. Compatibility Facts

The problem of the date of the Exodus and the number of the people presents many conflicting elements, but whatever is, is possible and compatible, however antagonistic it may seem. However many difficulties there may be in the way of our understanding of the facts of this history, they all existed and there was room for them. The necessity for a large group of Israelites to account for the fear of the Egyp and the Canaanites is matched by the hardship of the desert journey and especially by the fewness of the springs; but the narrative demands both. The difficulties of constructing a chronology of the Patriarchal period from Abraham to the Exodus with its seeming demand for a long period of time and the insistance of many (based especially upon the authority of Jos who apparently makes the Exodus of the Hebrews to be identical with the expulsion of the lepers from Egypt), that the Exodus took place about 1450 BC is set over against the indubitable fact now known from the excavations at Kiriath-sepher that the Conquest was at the beginning of the Iron Age in Palestine nearly 200 years later. These difficulties are antagonistic, but it will not do to argue that they are impossible. We need to learn all the facts. When all have been obtained, and properly correlated, they will be found to be entirely compatible. M. G. KYLE

EXODUS, ek'sō-dus, THE BOOK OF:

[NOTE.—For the signs J (Jahwist), E (Elohist), P or PC (Priest Codex), R (Redactor) cf art. GENESIS.]

I. In General.—

1. Name

The second book of the Pent bears in the LXX the name of Ἔξοδος, *Exodus,* in the Vulg accordingly Ex, on the basis of the chief contents of the first half, dealing with the departure of the children of Israel out of Egypt. The Jews named the book after the first words: וְאֵלֶּה שְׁמוֹת, *w^e-'ēlleh sh^emōth* ("and these are the names"), or sometimes after the first noun שְׁמוֹת ("names"), a designation already known to Origen in the form of Οὐαλεσμώθ, *Oualesmōth.*

2. Contents in General

In seven parts, after the Introduction (**1** 1–7), which furnishes the connection of the contents with Gen, the book treats of (1) the sufferings of Israel in Egypt, for which mere human help is insufficient (**1** 8—**7** 7), while Divine help through human mediatorship is promised; (2) the power of Jeh, which, after a preparatory miracle, is glorified through the ten plagues inflicted on Pharaoh and which thus forces the exodus (**7** 8—**13** 16); (3) the love of Jeh for Israel, which exhibits itself in a most brilliant manner, in the guidance of the Israelites to Mt. Sinai, even when the people murmur (**13** 17—**18** 27); (4) making the Covenant at Mt. Sinai together with the revelation of the Ten Words (**20** 1 ff) and of the legal ordinances (**21** 1 ff) as the condition of making the Covenant (**19** 1—**24** 18); (5) the directions for the building of the Tabernacle, in which Jeh is to dwell in the midst of His people (**24** 18—**31** 18); (6) the renewal of the Covenant on the basis of new demands after Israel's great apostasy in the worship of the Golden Calf, which seemed for the time being to make doubtful the realization of the promises mentioned in (5) above

(**32** 1—**35** 3); (7) the building and erection of the Tabernacle of Revelation (or Tent of Meeting) and its dedication by the entrance of Jeh (**35** 4—**40** 38). As clearly as these seven parts are separated from one another, so clearly again are they most closely connected and constitute a certain progressive whole.

In the case of the last four, the separation is almost self-evident. The first three as separate parts are justified by the ten plagues standing between them, which naturally belong together and cause a division between that which precedes and that which follows. Thus in the first part we already find predicted the hardening of the heart of Pharaoh, the miracles of Jeh and the demonstrations of His power down to the slaying of the firstborn, found in the 2d part (cf **2** 23—**7** 7).

In part 3, the infatuation of Pharaoh and the demonstration of the power of Jeh are further unfolded in the narrative of the catastrophe in the Red Sea (**14** 4.17). Further the directions given with reference to the Tabernacle (chs **25**–**31** taken from P) presuppose the Decalogue (from E); cf e.g. **25** 16.21; **31** 18; as again the 6th section (chs **32** ff) presupposes the 5th part, which had promised the continuous presence of God (cf **32** 34 J; **33** 3.5.7 ff JE; vs 12.14–17 J; **34** 9 J, with **25** 8; **29** 45 f P; cf also the forty days in **34** 28 J with those in **24** 18 P) as in **34** 1.28 J and vs 11–27 J refers back to the 4th part, viz. **20** 1 ff E; **21** 1 ff E; **24** 7 JE (Decalogue; Books of the Covenant; Making the Covenant). In the same way the last section presupposes the third, since the cloud in **40** 34 ff P is regarded as something well known (cf **13** 21 f JE; **14** 19 E and J, 24 J). The entire contents of the Book of Ex are summarized in an excellent way in the word of God to Israel spoken through Moses concerning the making of the covenant: "Ye have seen what I did unto the Egyptians, and how I bare you on eagles' wings, and brought you unto myself. Now therefore, if ye will obey my voice indeed, and keep my covenant, then ye shall be mine own possession from among all peoples: for all the earth is mine: and ye shall be unto me a kingdom of priests, and a holy nation" (Ex **19** 4–6). Here reference is made to the powerful deeds of God done to the Egyptians, to His deeds of lovingkindness done to Israel in the history of how He led them to Sinai, to the selection of Israel, and to the conditions attached to the making of the covenant, to God's love, which condescended to meet the people, and to His holiness, which demands the observance of His commandments; but there is also pointed out here the punishment for their transgression. The whole book is built on one word in the preface to the ten commandments: "I am Jeh thy God, who brought thee out of the land of Egypt, out of the house of bondage" (**20** 2 E; cf **29** 45 f P).

3. Connection with the Other Books of the Pentateuch

The events which are described in the Book of Ex show a certain contrast to those in Gen. In the first eleven chapters of this latter book we have the history of mankind; then beginning with **11** 27, a history of families, those of Abraham, Isaac and Jacob. In Ex we have following this the beginning of the history of the chosen people. Then there is also a long period of time intervening between the two books. If Israel was 430 years in Egypt (cf **12** 40 f P; also Gen **15** 13 J; see III, 4 below), and if the oppression began during the long reign of the predecessors of the Pharaoh, during whose reign Israel left the country (**2** 23; **1** 8), then, too, several centuries must have elapsed between the real beginning of the book (**1** 8 ff), and the conclusion of Gen. Notwithstanding these differences, there yet exists the closest connection between the two books. Ex **1** 1–7 connects the history of the people as found in Ex with the family history of Gen, by narrating how the seventy descendants of Jacob that had migrated to Egypt (cf Ex **1** 5; Gen **46** 27) had come to be the people of Israel, and that God, who offers Himself as a liberator to Moses and the people, is also the God of those fathers, of whom Gen spoke (cf Ex **3** 6 JE, vs 13 E, 15 f R; **4** 5 J; **6** 3 P). Indeed, His covenant with the fathers and His promises to them are the reasons why He at all cares for Israel (**2** 24 P; **6** 8 P; **33** 1 JE), and when Moses intercedes for the sinful people, his most effective motive over against God is found in the promises made to the patriarchs (**32** 13 JE).

As is the case with Gen, Ex stands in the closest connection also with the succeeding books of the Pent. Israel is certainly not to remain at Sinai, but is to come into the promised land (**3** 17 JE; **6** 8 P; **23** 20 ff JE; **32** 34 J; **33** 1 ff JE; vs 12 ff J; **34** 9 ff J and D; cf also the many ordinances of the Books of the Covenant, **21** 1 ff E; **34** 11 ff D and J). In this way the narratives of the following books, which begin again in Nu **10** 11 ff P and JE with the story of the departure from Sinai, continue the history in Ex. But the legislation in Lev also is a necessary continuation and supplement of the Book of Ex, and is prepared for and pointed to in the latter. The erection of the burnt-offering altar (**27** 1 ff; **38** 1 ff), as well as the mention made of the different kinds of sacrifices, such as the burnt sacrifices and the sin offering (**29** 18.14) and of the heave offering (**29** 28), point to the promulgation of a law of sacrifices such as we find in Lev **1**–**7**. The directions given in regard to the consecration of the priests (Ex **29**) are carried out in Lev **8** f. The indefinite commands of **30** 10 in reference to the atonement on the horn of the incense altar once every year renders necessary the special ritual of the Day of Atonement in Lev **16** as its supplement. The more complete enlargement in reference to the shewbread mentioned in **25** 30 is found in Lev **24** 5–9; and even the repetitions in references to the candlesticks (Ex **25** 31 ff; Lev **24** 1–4; Nu **8** 1–4), as also the *tāmīdh* ("continuous") sacrifices (cf Nu **28** 3–8 with Ex **29** 38–42), point to a certain connection between Ex and the following books. How close the connection between Dt and Ex is, both in regard to the historical narratives and also to their legal portions (cf the Decalogue and the Books of the Covenant), can only be mentioned at this place.

4. Significance of These Events for Israel

When we remember the importance which the exodus out of Egypt and the making of the covenant had for the people of Israel, and that these events signalized the birth of the chosen people and the establishment of the theocracy, then we shall understand why the echo of the events recorded in Ex is found throughout later lit., viz. in the historical books, in the preaching of the prophets and in the Pss, as the greatest events in the history of the people, and at the same time as the promising type of future and greater deliverances. But as in the beginning of the family history the importance of this family for the whole earth is clearly announced (Gen **12** 1–3), the same is the case here too at the beginning of the history of the nation, perhaps already in the expression "kingdom of priests" (Ex **19** 6), since the idea of a priesthood includes that of the transmission of salvation to others; and certainly in the conception 'first-born son of Jeh' (**4** 22), since this presupposes other nations as children born later.

The passages quoted above are already links connecting this book with Christianity, in the ideas of a general priesthood, of election and of sonship of God. We here make mention of a few specially significant features from among the mass of such relationships to Chris-

5. Connecting Links with Christianity

tianity. How great a significance the Decalogue, in which the law is not so intimately connected with what is specifically Jewish and national, as e.g. in the injunctions of the Priest Codex, according to the interpretation of Christ in Mt **5**, has attained in the history of mankind! But in Mt **5** 17 ff Jesus has vindicated for the law in all its parts an everlasting authority and significance and has emphasized the eternal kernel, which accordingly is to be assigned to each of these legal behests; while Paul, on the other hand, esp. in Rom, Gal and Col, emphasizes the transitory character of the law, and discusses in detail the relation of the Mosaic period to that of the patriarchs and of the works of the law to faith, while in 2 Cor **3** he lauds the glory of the service in the spirit over that of the letter (cf Ex **34**)—an idea which in reference to the individual legal institutions is also carried out in the Ep. to the He. Cf on this subject also the arts. LEVITICUS and DAY OF ATONEMENT. Then too the Passover lamb was a type of Jesus Christ (cf e.g. 1 Cor **5** 7; Jn **19** 36; 1 Pet **1** 19). In Ex **12** the Passover rite and the establishment of the covenant (**24** 3–8) are found most closely connected also with the Lord's Supper and the establishment of the New Covenant. In the permanent dwelling of God in the midst of His people in the pillar of fire and in the Tabernacle there is typified His dwelling among mankind in Christ Jesus (Jn **1** 14) and also the indwelling of the Holy Ghost in the Christian congregation (1 Pet **2** 5; Eph **4** 12) and in the individual Christian (1 Cor **3** 16; **6** 19; 2 Cor **6** 16; Jn **14** 23). The Apocalypse particularly is rich in thought suggested by the exodus out of Egypt. Unique thoughts in reference to the OT are found in the conceptions that the law was given through angels (Acts **7** 53; Gal **3** 19; He **2** 2); further that the rock mentioned in Ex **17** 6 followed, and was Christ (1 Cor **10** 4); and that in He **9** 4 the real connection of the altar of incense with the Holy of Holies appears as changed into a local connection (Ex **40** 26.27), while the idea found in He **9** 4 that the manna was originally in the Ark of the Covenant, is perhaps not altogether excluded by Ex **16** 33; and the number 430 years, found in Gal **3** 17, probably agrees with Ex **12** 40.41, in so far as the whole of the patriarchal period could be regarded as a unit (cf on the reading of the LXX in Ex **12** 40.41, III, 4 below).

II. Structure of the Book according to the Scriptures and according to Modern Analyses.—In the following section (*a*) serves for the understanding of the Bib. text; (*b*) is devoted to the discussion and criticism of the separation into sources.

1. In General

(*a*) The conviction must have been awakened already by the general account of the contents given in I, 2 above, that in the Book of Ex we are dealing with a rounded-off structure, since in seven mutually separated yet intimately connected sections, one uniform fundamental thought is progressively carried through. This conviction will only be confirmed when the details of these sections are studied, the sections being themselves again organically connected by one leading thought. Since, in addition, the Book of Gen is clearly divided into ten parts by the ten *tōl^edhōth* ("generations") (cf also the division made by typical numbers in arts. LEVITICUS and DAY OF ATONEMENT), thus too the number seven, as itself dividing the Book of Ex into seven parts, is probably not accidental; and this all the less, as in the subordinate parts too, a division is to be found according to typical numbers, this in many cases appearing as a matter of course, and in other cases traced without difficulty, and sometimes lying on the surface (cf 10 plagues, 10 commandments). Yet in all of the following investigations, as is the case in the arts. GENESIS, LEVITICUS and DAY OF ATONEMENT, the demonstration of the fundamental thought must be the main thing for us. The division according to typical numbers is to be regarded merely as an additional confirmation of the literary unity of the book. We refer here first of all to a number of cases, where certain numbers independently of the separate chief parts combine the Bib. text into a unity. In Nu **14** 22 R, Jeh states that Israel had now tempted Him and been disobedient to Him ten times: cf Ex **14** 11 ff JE (?) (Red Sea); **15** 23 f JE (Marah); **16** 2.3 P; ver 20 JE; vs 27.28 R (Manna); **17** 1 ff JE (Massah and Meribah); **32** 1 ff JE (Golden Calf); Nu **11** 1 ff JE (Taberah); vs 4 ff JE (Graves of Lust); **14** 2 ff P and JE (Spies). Most of these cases are accordingly reported in the Book of Ex, but in such manner that in this particular a clearly marked progress can be noticed, as Jeh does not begin to punish until Ex **32**; but from here on He does so with constantly increasing severity, while down to Ex **32** grace alone prevails, and in this particular, previous to Ex **32**, there is found nothing but a warning (**16** 27). Ten times it is further stated of Pharaoh, in a great variety of forms of expression, that he hardened his own heart (**7** 13 P; ver 14 JE; ver 22 P; **8** 15 P; ver 32 JE; **9** 7.34.35 JE; **13** 15 D); ten times the hardening is ascribed to God (**4** 21 JE; **7** 3 P; **9** 12 P; **10** 1 R; ver 20 JE; ver 27 E; **11** 10 R; **14** 4.8 P; 17 P ?). Here already we must note that within the narrative of the miracles and the plagues at first there is mention made only of the hardening by Pharaoh himself (**7** 13 P; ver 14 JE; ver 22 P; **8** 11 ff; **8** 15 P; ver 28 JE; **9** 7 JE, i.e. seven times) before a single word is said that God begins the hardening; and this latter kind of hardening thereupon alone concludes the whole tragedy (**14** 4.8 P; 17 P ?). Ten months cover the time from the arrival at Sinai (**19** 1 P) to the erection of the sacred dwelling-place of God (**40** 17 P). Since, further, exactly three months of this time are employed in **19** 10.16 JE; **24** 3 ff JE; ver 16 P (ten days); **24** 18 P (40 days); **34** 28 J (40 days), there remain for the building of the tabernacle exactly seven months.

(*b*) What has been said does anything but speak in favor of the customary division of Ex into different sources. It is generally accepted that the three sources found in Gen are also to be found in this book; in addition to which a fourth source is found in Ex **13** 3–16, of a Deuteronomistic character. It is true and is acknowledged that the advocates of this hypothesis have more difficulties to overcome in Ex than in Gen, in which latter book too, however, there are insufficient grounds for accepting this view, as is shown in the art. GENESIS. Beginning with Ex **6** the chief marks of such a separation of sources falls away as far as P and J are concerned, namely, the different uses of the names of God, Elohim and Jeh. For, according to the protagonists of the documentary theory, P also makes use of the name Jeh from this chapter on; E, too, does the same from Ex **3** 13 ff on, only that, for a reason not understood, occasionally the word Elohim is still used by this source later on, e.g. **13** 17 ff; **18** 1 ff. But as a number of passages using the name Elohim are unhesitatingly ascribed by the critics to J, this difference in the use of the name of God utterly fails to establish a difference of sources. To this is to be added, that J and E are at this place closely interwoven; that, while the attempt is constantly being made to separate these two sources, no generally accepted results have been reached and many openly acknowledge the impossibility of such a separation, or admit that it can be effected only to a very limited extent. Peculiarities which are regarded as characteristic of the different sources, such as the sin of Aaron in J, the staff of Moses in E, Sinai in J and P, Horeb in E, the dwelling of the Israelites in Goshen in J, but according to E their living in the midst of the Egyptians, and others, come to nought in view of the uniform text in the passages considered. This has been proved most clearly, e.g. by Eerdmans in his *Alttestamentliche Studien*, III ("Das Buch Exodus") in regard to many of these passages. Narratives of a similar character, like the two stories in which Moses is described as striking the rock to produce water (Ex **17** 1; Nu **20** 1 ff), are not duplicates, but are different events. Cf the different localities in Ex **17** 7 and Nu **20** 1, as also the improbability that

Israel would without cause in the first passage have put into permanent form the story of its shame, and then in the latter there would have been an uncertainty as to the importance of this locality for the career of Moses; and finally, we must notice the distinction expressly made by the additional statement, "waters of Meribah of Kadesh in the wilderness of Zin," in Nu **27** 12–14; Dt **32** 51 (cf Ezk **47** 19; **48** 28). Then, too, these occurrences, if we accept the division into J and E at this place, are not reduced to a single event, since both sources would share in both narratives. The same condition of affairs is found in Ex **16** in so far as JE comes into consideration, and in Ex **18** in comparison with Nu **11**. In the case of Nu **11** there is express reference made to a former narrative by the word "again," and in the second case all the details in their differences point to different occurrences. Concerning other so-called duplicates in Ex, see later in this article. But the acceptance of P in contradistinction to the text of JE does also not lead to tangible results, notwithstanding that there exists a general agreement with regard to the portions credited to P. Not taking into consideration certain that are peculiar, the following sections are attributed to this source: **1** 1–7.13–15; **2** 23*b*–25; **6** 2—**7** 13 (**6** 28–30 R); **7** 19.20*a*.21*b*.22; **8** 1–3.11*b*–15; **9** 8–12; **12** 1–20.28.37*a*.40–50; **13** 1–2.20; **14** 1–4. 8–10.15–18?.21*aa*.22–23.29; **16** 1–3.9–14.15*b*–18.21–26.31–32.34*a*.35; **17** 1*a*; **19** 1.2*a*; **24** 15—**31** 17; **34** 29—**40** 38. It is claimed that in the Book of Gen these sources constitute the backbone of the whole work; but this is not claimed for Ex. The sections ascribed to P constitute in this place, too, anything but an unbroken story. In both language and substance they are, to a certain extent, most closely connected with the parts ascribed to JE, and in part they are indispensable for the connection whence they have been taken (cf for details below). It is absolutely impossible to separate on purely philological grounds in the purely narrative portions in Ex the portions belonging to P. That genealogies like **6** 14 ff, or chronological notices like **12** 40.41.51; **16** 1; **19** 1, or directions for the cultus like **12; 25** ff have their own peculiar forms, is justified by self-evident reasons; but this does not justify the acceptance of separate authors. It is the result of the peculiar matter found in each case. We must yet note that the passages attributed to P would in part contain views which could not be harmonized with the theological ideas ascribed to this source, which are said to include an extreme transcendental conception of God; thus in **16** 10 the majesty of Jeh suddenly appears to the congregation, and in **40** 34 ff this majesty takes possession of the newly erected dwelling. In **8** 19 mention is made of the finger of God, and in **7** 1 Moses is to be as God to Pharaoh. In Ex **12** 12 the existence of the Egyp gods is presupposed and the heathen sorcerers are able to act in competition with Moses and Aaron for a while; **7** 11.12.22; **8** 3. P also describes the Passover, which on account of the handling of the blood in **12** 7 cannot be regarded in any other light than as a sacrifice in the house, and in Nu **9** 7.13, this act is expressly called a *ḳorban* Jahwe ('sacrifice of Jeh'). Cf also the commands in Ex **12** 10.43.48. But more than anything else, what has been said under (*a*) above goes to show that all these sources have been united in a way that characterizes the work of a systematic writer, and declares against any view that would maintain that these sources have been mechanically placed side by side and interwoven into each other. What has here been outlined for the whole book in general must now be applied to the different parts in particular.

(1) **1** 8—**7** 7: (*a*) Everything that is narrated in this section, which in so worthy a manner introduces the whole book, is written from a standpoint of the Egyp oppression, from which human help could give no deliverance, but from which the mighty power of Jeh, working through human agency, offered this deliverance. It is a situation which demands faith (**4** 31). This section naturally falls into ten pericopes, of which in each instance two are still more closely connected.

2. In the Separate Pericopes

Nos. 1+2 (**1** 8–14.15–22), namely, the oppression through forced labor and the threat to take the life of the newly born males of the Israelites; and in contrast to this, the Divine blessing in the increase of the people in general and of the midwives in particular; nos. 3+4 (**2** 1–10.11–22), namely, the birth and youth of Moses stand in contrast. The child seems to be doomed, but God provides for its deliverance. Moses, when grown to manhood, tries to render vigorous assistance to his people through his own strength, but he is compelled to flee into a far-off country. Nos. 5+6 (**2** 23—**4** 17; **4** 18–31) report the fact that also in the reign of a new Pharaoh the oppression does not cease, and that this causes God to interfere, which in **2** 23–25 is expressed in strong terms and repeatedly, and this again leads to the revelation in the burning bush (**3** 1 ff). And at the same time the narrative shows how little self-confidence Moses still had (three signs, a heavy tongue, direct refusal). The sixth pericope and also the beginning of the last four, describe, from an external viewpoint, the return of Moses to Midian, and his journey from there to Egypt. Here, too, mention is made of the troubles caused by Pharaoh, which God must remove through His power. This deliverance is not at all deserved by Israel, since not even any son in a family had up to this time been circumcised. On the other hand, everything here is what can be expected. Those who sought the life of Moses had died; the meeting with Aaron at the Mount of the Lord; in Egypt the faith of the people. In an effective way the conclusion (**4** 31) returns to the point where the two companion narratives (**2** 24 f) begin. After this point, constituting the center and the chief point in the introductory section, nos. 7+8 (**5** 1—**6** 1; **6** 2–12), everything seems to have become doubtful. Pharaoh refuses to receive Moses and Aaron; the oppression increases; dissatisfaction in Israel appears; Moses despairs; even the new revelations of God, with fair emphasis on fidelity to the Covenant which is to unfold Jeh's name in full, are not able to overcome the lack of courage on the part of the people and of Moses. Nos. 9+10, introduced by **6** 13 (**6** 14–27 and **6** 28—**7** 7), show that after Moses and Aaron have already been mentioned together in **4** 14.27 ff; **5** 1 ff, and after it has become clear how little they are able of themselves to accomplish anything, they are now here, as it were, for the first time, before the curtain is raised, introduced as those who in the following drama are to be the mediators of God's will (cf the concluding verses of both pericopes, **6** 27; **7** 7), and they receive directions for their common mission, just at that moment when, humanly speaking, everything is as unfavorable as possible.

(*b*) The unity of thought here demonstrated is in this case too the protecting wall against the flood-tide of the documentary theory. For this theory involves many difficulties. In **1** 13 f there would be an account of the oppression by P, but the motive for this can be found only in the preceding verses, which are ascribed to JE; **2** 24 speaks of the Covenant of God with Isaac, concerning which P is said to have reported nothing in the Book of Gen, as in the latter book a reference to this matter is found only in **26** 2–5 R; **26** 24 J. In **6** 2 ff Moses and Aaron are mentioned; but as the text of P reads we know absolutely nothing from this source as to who these men are. According to **7** 1 ff Aaron is to be the speaker for Moses before Pharaoh. But according to P neither

Moses nor Aaron speaks a single word. The omissions that are found by critics in documents J and E—which, if they are separated, have lines of demarkation claimed for the separation that are very unsettled—we here pass over in silence.

On the critical theory, the narratives of P, in the Book of Ex, as also in Gen, would have discarded many of the stereotyped formulas characteristic of this source (cf **2** 23 ff; **6** 2 ff; **7** 1 ff), and in both form and contents would be made very similar to the rest of the text **1** 9.10.12 JE; **1** 20 E; **7** 1 P; and to a great extent expressions similar to these are here found and in part refer to these. The same must be said concerning **3** 7 JE in its relation to **2** 23 ff P; **6** 6 ff (*sibhlōth*) P in its relation to **1** 11 JE; **2** 11 E; **5** 4.5 JE (in contrast **1** 13.14; **2** 23). JE, in **4** 9 for "dry land," makes use of the term *ha-yabbāshāh*, which in Gen **1** 9 f and Ex **14** 16 is ascribed to P, and a different expression is used for this thought by J in Gen **7** 22. In reference to **7** 1 P cf **4** 14 E (?). In reference to the hardening of Pharaoh, which is found in all the sources (**7** 3 P), see above under 1*a;* in reference to the miracles, and their purpose of making Yahweh known to the Egyptians (**7** 3–5 P) see the following paragraph. The four generations mentioned in **7** 14 ff P find their ‖ in Gen **15** 16 J (cf **46** 8 ff); and the sons of Aaron mentioned in **6** 23 P, Nadab and Abihu, are mentioned also in the text of **24** 1 9, ascribed to JE although, except in Lev **10** P, their names are not found elsewhere in the Pent. In reference to the repetitions, it must be said that **1** 13 P is either the continuation (in so far as the Israelites instead of being compulsory laborers became slaves), or is a concluding summary, such as is found frequently. The new revelation of God in Ex **6** P, according to ch **3** JE, finds its psychological and historical motive in the account of the failure described in **5** 1 ff JE, and in the discouragement of the Israelites and of Moses resulting therefrom. In the same way the renewed mention by Moses of his difficulties of speech (**6** 12 P; cf with **4** 10 ff J+E (?)) is very characteristic of human ways, and this again necessitates the twice repeated consideration of this matter by God (**6** 30 R; **4** 10 ff J+E (?); concerning the names of God, see GENESIS; GOD, NAMES OF).

One difficulty, which is also not made clear by the proposed division of sources, is found in the name of the father-in-law of Moses; since according to **2** 18 J, this name is Reuel, and according to **3** 1; **18** 1 JE, it is Jethro (**4** 18 E in the form "Jether"); in Nu **10** 29 JE is called Hobab and a son of Reuel (AV "Raguel") for all of these passages are ascribed to J or E. It is probable that the name Jethro is a title ("Excellency"); and as for the rest, in Nu **10** 29 *hōthēn* probably does not mean father-in-law but brother-in-law (Jgs **1** 16; **4** 11); or in **2** 18 we find father and in **2** 21 daughter in the place of grandfather and granddaughter; otherwise we should be compelled to accept different traditions, by which view, however, the Mosaic authorship of Ex would be made impossible (cf IV, below).

(2) **7** 8—**13** 16: (*a*) This section is separated as a matter of course from the rest by the typical number of ten plagues. It is introduced by the transformation of the rod into a serpent in the presence of Pharaoh (**7** 8–13). To explain the fact that there were ten plagues on the ground of the accidental combination of sources, is from the very outset a precarious undertaking. To this must be added the following reasons that indicate a literary editing of the material. All of the plagues are introduced by the same formula (**7** 12 JE; **8** 1 J; ver 12 P; ver 16 JE; ver 20 JE; **9** 1 JE; ver 8 P; ver 13 JE; **10** 1.12 JE; ver 21 E; **11** 1 E), and in connection with each plague the hardening of the heart of Pharaoh is mentioned (cf [1*a*] above); cf **7** 22 P; **8** 11 J; ver 15 P; ver 28 JE; **9** 7 JE; ver 12 P; ver 34 JE; ver 35 JE; **10** 1 R; ver 20 JE; ver 27 E; **11** 10 R; **13** 15 D. As is the case in the first section, we find here too in each instance two plagues more closely connected, viz. nos. 1+2 already externally united by the double address of Jeh (cf **7** 14 JE; ver 19 P and **7** 26 J; **8** 1 P), but also by the methods of punishment that are related to each other (water changed to blood and frogs); and, finally, by the extension of the plague (the Nile and beyond the river). In 3+4 we have to deal with insects (stinging flies and dung flies); in 5+6 with a kind of pest (pest among cattle, and boils); 7+8 are again formally joined by the repeated command of Jeh to Moses in **9** 13.22 JE and **10** 1.12 JE, as also by the fulness of the account the two show and their similarity, in both also use being made of the staff (**9** 23 f JE; **10** 13 f JE), in the repetition of the emphasis put on the remarkable character of the plague (**9** 18.24; **10** 6.14 JE). By both plagues vegetation is destroyed; and in the plague of locusts special reference is made also to the hail (cf **10** 5.12.15). In the case of 9+10, the darkness constitutes a connecting link (cf **10** 21 E; **11** 4 J; **12** 12 P; **12** 30.31 JE). By the side of the occasional rhythm formed of two members there is also one formed of three members (after the manner of a triole in a measure of two beats). In the case of each group of three plagues, two are announced beforehand (thus 1 JEP+2 JP; 4 JE+5 JE; 7 JE+8 JE; 10 EJ over against 3 P, 6 P and 9 E); the first of each group of three plagues, as 1, 4+7, is to be announced by Moses on the following morning to Pharaoh (**7** 15; **8** 20; **9** 13 JE). Also in regard to the impression caused by the plagues a distinct progress can be noticed, in this too, that the Egyp sorcerers are active only down to the third plague. Naturally, too, over against these facts, further peculiarities can be pointed out in the separate plagues, e.g. the fact that Goshen, or rather that Israel, is spared in the 4th, 5th, 7th–10th plagues (**8** 22; **9** 6.26 JE; **10** 23 E; **11** 7 J); and in the mention made of the intercession in the 2d, 4th, 7th, 8th (**8** 8 J; ver 12; **9** 28.33; **10** 17 f JE) without thereby destroying the artistic construction of the whole that has been described above, or that in each such case of individuality of presenting the matter there is to be found a reason for claiming a separate source.

(*b*) In the same way, too, it is not a permissible conclusion, that in the first miracle and in the first three plagues mention is made of the fact that Aaron performed this miracle with his staff (**7** 8 ff.19; **8** 5–20 ff P). At any rate, in the parts ascribed to P, no absolute uniformity is to be found, since plagues 1 to 3 are commanded to Moses, while the 6th is commanded to Moses and Aaron (**7** 19; **8** 1.20 over against **9** 8); and since, further, in the 6th plague (**9** 8) it is Moses, and in the 10th (**12** 12) it is God Himself who really carries out the command, and not Aaron, as was the case in the introductory miracles and in the first three plagues. Further, according to JE (**4** 30), it appears that the presupposition is that we are to consider all of the addresses and actions in general as taking place through Aaron, even in those cases where this is not esp. mentioned.

Only the 1st plague (**7** 14 ff) furnishes an apparent reason for the acceptance of two sources. In this case mention is made at times of the waters of the Nile only, and then of all other waters being changed into blood; and a separation from this point of view at least could be carried through. But this possibility disappears at once in the case of the 2d plague (frogs), where the passage **8** 1–3, ascribed to P, which verses contain the consummation of the plague announced in **7** 26–29 J (Heb), is altogether necessary for this connection; as otherwise the impression made upon Pharaoh by this plague, which is not mentioned in P at all, would be a torso. The similarity in the construction of the 2d and the 1st plague, however (cf under [*a*] above), and the same difference in the mention made of the Nile and of the other waters in the 2d plague, make it possible and even advisable in the case of the first plague, too, to discard the hypothesis of a difference in sources, because in the 2d plague this difference cannot be carried out. Then, too, there would be other omissions found in P. According to the customary separation of sources, P would not contain the fulfilment of the threatened tenth plague announced in **12** 12 at all. In the same way the statement in **12** 28 refers to the carrying out of a command, the announcement of which to Israel in **12** 21 ff would be found in another source. Further in **12** 37*a* we would have P, as when the parts belonging to P have been eliminated, the other sources too would contain omissions in **12** 21 ff, mostly JE; ver 37*b* E; **13** 3 ff D. In the same way the announcement of a large number of miracles (**7** 3 P; **11** 9 R) is too comprehensive, if these verses refer only to the narratives found in P. In addition, there is a remarkable similarity found in all of the narratives of P with those parts which are ascribed to JE; cf the first miracle in **7** 8 ff with **4** 2 ff J; ver 17 E. In P, too, as is the case with JE, it is stated that the purpose of the miracle is, that Pharaoh, or the Egyptians, or Israel, are to recognize that Jeh is God and the Lord of the earth, or something to this effect (**7** 5 P; ver 17 JE; **8** 10 R; ver 22; **9** 14. 29.30 JE; **10** 2 R; **11** 7 J; cf from the next section, **14** 4 P; ver 18 P, which at the same time is also the fundamental thought that forms the connecting link of the whole section). The position of **11** 1–3 E between **10** 28.29 E and **11** 8 J constitutes a difficulty, because in the last-mentioned passages Moses is represented as standing continuously before Pharaoh. The announcement made by Jeh to Moses, that one more plague is to come, and that the Israelites should borrow articles of value from the Egyptians, must in reality have been made before, but for good reasons it is mentioned for the first time at this place, in order to explain the confident utterance of Moses, that he would not again appear before Pharaoh (**10** 29). But the fact that according to **12** 31 JE Pharaoh does in reality once more cause Moses and Aaron to be called, can readily be explained on the ground of the events that happened in the meantime.

The structure of chs **12** f contains nothing that could not have been written by one and the same author. Only Moses naturally did not at once communicate (**12** 21 ff) to the leading men of Israel the command given in **12** 15 ff concerning the unleavened bread, which command had been given for later generations; and not until **13** 3 ff is this command mentioned in connection with the order given to the people in the meantime concerning the firstborn (**13** 1 f). The further fact, that the story of the exodus reaches a preliminary conclusion in **12** 42 before the details of the Passover (vs 3 ff) have been given, is in itself justifiable. As far as contents are concerned, everything in chs **12** f, namely, the exodus, the festival of unleavened bread, the firstborn, and orders pertaining thereto, that the month of the exodus is to be regarded as the first month, etc, are closely connected with the Passover and the 10th plague. Because the latter had to be described more fully than the other plagues, we find already in **11** 9.10, after the announcement of this plague and its results, a comprehensive notice concerning all the miracles through which Jeh demonstrated how He, amid great manifestations of power (**7** 4 P) and with a mighty hand (**6** 1 JE), has led His people forth.

(3) **13** 17—**18** 27: (*a*) This section finds its connecting thought in the emphasis placed on the love of Jeh, on His readiness to help, and His long-suffering in the leading of His at times murmuring people on the road to and as far as Sinai. This section covers two months. What is narrated, beginning with ch **16** 1, transpires even within a single two weeks (cf ch **19** 1). No. 1 (**13** 17–22), describes the journey to Etham (out of love God does not lead the people the direct way, since He fears that they will become unfaithful in the event of a battle; Joseph's bones are taken along, since God now really is taking care of His people [cf Gen **50** 24.26]; Jeh's friendly presence is shown in the pillar of fire). No. 2 (**14** 1–31) contains the passage through the Red Sea (Jeh the helper; cf vs 10.15. 13.14.30.21.24.26 f.31, notwithstanding the murmuring of Israel, vs 11 f). No. 3 (**15** 1 ff) contains the thanksgiving hymn of Moses for Jeh's help, with which fact each one of the four strophes begins (vs 1 ff.6 ff.11.16*b* ff). No. 4 (**15** 20 f) contains Miriam's responsorium. No. 5 (**15** 22–27) treats of Marah and Elim (Jeh proves Himself to be Israel's helper and physician [vs 25 f] notwithstanding the murmuring of Israel [ver 24]). No. 6 introduces the last five pericopes, with a designation of the time (**16** 1–36), and describes the miraculous feeding with manna and quails. (The murmuring is particularly emphasized in vs 2.7–9.12. Israel also gathers more than they have been directed to do [vs 16 f]; reserves some for the following day [vs 19 f]; collects some on the Sabbath [ver 27]; Jeh, who in vs 6–12 alone is mentioned in rapid succession no fewer than ten times, at first does not even utter a word of reproach, and when the Sabbath has been violated He does nothing more than reprove.) No. 7 (**17** 1–7) reports the help of Jeh (ver 4) at the Waters of Contention (Strife). He even appears on the rock (ver 6), notwithstanding the murmuring (vs 2–4.7). No. 8 (**17** 8–16) describes the victory over the Amalekites, which furnished the occasion for the erection of the memorial altar, called 'Jeh-my-Banner.' Possibly in this connection Joshua ("Jeh helps") was changed from Hosea (Nu **13** 16). Cf Hengstenberg, *Authenthic. des Pentateuches*, II, 395 f. No. 9 (**18** 1–12) shows in a constantly changing variety of expressions that emphasis is laid on the impression which the deeds of God in connection with Israel make on Jethro, the father-in-law of Moses, while he was visiting the latter (vs 1.8–12). Effective in this connection is also the mention made of the symbolical names of the sons of Moses (Gershom, "I have been a sojourner in a foreign land"; and Eliezer, "The God of my father was my help, and delivered me from the sword of Pharaoh" [vs 3 f]). Further, the name Mount of God (ver 5; cf ver 12) probably is a reminder of the fulfilment of **3** 12. No. 10 (**18** 13–17) shows how God helps Moses (cf ver 19) through the advice of Jethro to appoint judges. In this part, too, **13** 17—**18** 27, we have ten sections, which can easily be arranged in groups of two and two. Thus nos. 1+2 are connected by their analogous beginnings (**13** 17.18 RE; **14** 1.2 P) and by the cloud of fire (**13** 21 f JE; **14** 19.24 J); nos. 3+4 by the responsive hymn; nos. 5+6, which already by the feeling of hunger and thirst are connected in thought, by their reference to the ordinances of Jeh (**15** 25 D; **16** 4 JE ?; ver 28 R); nos. 7+8 by the use made of Moses' staff (**17** 5.9 JE); nos. 9+10 by Jethro's person, and the close connection of their contents in point of time (**18** 13). Further, the Bib. text of this place is clearly presupposed in the list of stations, expressly stated to have been prepared at the command of Moses (Nu **33**). This list, as is acknowledged on all sides, has the characteristics of P; and it takes into consideration not only the portions ascribed to this source, but also the text of JE. Cf **33** 9 (Marah and Elim) with Ex **15** 22–27, and Nu **33** 14 (lack of water in Rephidim) with Ex **17** 1 ff.

(*b*) Over against the analysis into different sources the following data in detail can also be advanced. In P the last demonstration of the power of Jeh over Pharaoh would be indeed endangered in **14** 4.15 ff.21*a*, but afterward would not be related. In ch **16** 1 we cannot find in P, unless we bring in also **15** 27 from JE, how Israel came to be in Elim. On the other hand, in **16** 4 ff (JE?) the promise of bread from heaven is groundless without the preceding verses, which are attributed to P; and without **17** 1 P, we do not know to what the word "there" in ver 3 belonging to JE refers, and how in ver 8 JE the Israelites had come to Rephidim.

How entirely data taken from the language utterly fail here in establishing the separation of sources we see from the fact that in Ex the distribution of the different portions and verses between P and E becomes a matter of doubt, and also in Ex **16** a harmony of view has not been gained as to whether only P, or in addition also J, E or JE have contributed to the text. The hymn found in Ex **15** 1 ff, which certainly is an old composition, presupposes passages which are assigned to different sources, and in this way speaks for the unity of the text. Cf **15** 2 with **14** 30 J; ver 13 JE (?); **15** 3 with **14** 14 JE (?); ver 25 J; ver 4*a* with **14** 9 P; ver 4*b* with **14** 7 JE; ver 8 with **14** 22 EP; ver 29 P; with **14** 9.

On the other hand, **14** 19*a* and *b* cannot be utilized in favor of a division of sources E and J; but rather the analogous structure of this passage presupposes the same author, and there is only indicated what elsewhere is always a presupposition, namely, that God Himself has taken His abode somewhere in the cloud of fire (**13** 21.22 JE; **14** 24 J; cf **40** 34 ff P). Just as little are the two commands found in **14** 16 to be divided between P and E and J, one stating what Moses does, and the other what Jeh does, since both rather belong together (cf **9** 22 f with ver 33; **10** 13). At first glance **16** 6 ff does not appear to be in its proper place, as Moses and Aaron in vs 6.7 have already told Israel what only in vs 9 ff is revealed through the appearance of Jeh and His injunction to Moses. But these very verses are in harmony with the character of the whole section (cf under *a* above), since it is here stated that under all circumstances Israel is to be convinced of this, that Jeh has proven Himself to be Jeh, and has heard their murmuring. In addition, the appearance of Jeh in ver 10 is clearly announced by ver 7. Accordingly, vs 9 ff serve only to confirm and strengthen what is found in vs 6 ff. The fact that not until in **18** 2 JE Jethro brings the wife and the sons of Moses, while the latter himself according to **4** 20 J had taken them along when he joined Israel, finds a satisfactory explanation in **18** 2*b*. He sent them back doubtless because of the conduct of Zipporah on the occasion of the circumcision of her son (**4** 25 J). The fact that Jethro comes to Moses at the Mount of God (**18** 5 JE), while the latter does not arrive at Mt. Sinai until **19** 1 ff according to P and J, is no contradiction; for by the Mount of God is meant the whole chain of Horeb, which Moses has already reached according to **17** 6 JE; but Mt. Sinai is a single mountain. The special legal ordinances and decisions mentioned in **18** 20 JE before the giving of the law (**19** ff E+JE) are in perfect harmony with **15** 25 D; **16** 4 JE (?); ver **28** R.

(4) **19** 1—**24** 18*a*: (*a*) This fourth section contains the conclusion of the covenant at Mt. Sinai (cf **19** 5 R at beginning; **24** 7.8 JE toward the end). The contents cover a period of ten days (cf **19** 10.11.16; **24** 3.4 JE; ver 16 P). The text of this section can again be divided into ten pericopes. After the introduction (**19** 1–8), which contains a cardinal feature of Ex (cf under I, 2 above), nos. 1 and 2 (**19** 9–19.20–25) report the preparation for the conclusion of the Covenant. No. 2 in ver 23 refers expressly to no. 1, but is distinguished from no. 1 through the new addition in ver 20 after ver 18, as also through the express amplified application of the ordinances referring to purifications and the restriction of the prohibition to the priests (cf vs 22.21.24 with vs 10.12). Nos. 3+4 (**20** 1–17. 18–26) contain the Decalogue and the directions for the cultus, together with a description of the impression made by the revelation of the law. Nos. 5+6 (**21** 1—**23** 13 expressly circumscribed by a subscription, **23** 14–19) contain legal ordinances and further directions for the cultus. Nos. 3–6 accordingly contain the laws or the conditions of the Covenant. Now follow in nos. 7+8 the promises of the Covenant (**23** 20–26.27–33), which in vs 20+27, 23+28 and 24+32 f correspond to each other. Nos. 9+10 (**24** 3–8.9–18*a*, combined more closely by vs 1.2) describe the conclusion of the Covenant and the Covenant congregation in different stages. Further, typical numbers at this place also appear in the laws, nos. 3–6. No. 4 (**20** 18 ff) contains five directions (vs 23*a*.23*b*.24.25.26); no. 6 (**23** 14–19) is divided into 2×5 ordinances (cf the anaphoristic addition in vs 14 and 17), viz. vs 14.15*a*.15*b*.16*a*. 16*b*—17.18*a*.18*b*.19*a*.19*b*. No. 3 (**20** 1 ff, the Decalogue) contains, according to **34** 28; Dt **4** 13; **10** 4, "ten words" m, according to the two tables doubtless divided into two groups of five each, no matter how in detail we may divide and number them. In the same way no. 5 (**21** 1—**23** 13) falls into ten sections, separate in form and contents, yet belonging together; and these again are divided into 2×5 groups, as will appear presently. Taken altogether then we have in nos. 3–6 (**20** 1—**23** 19) 17×5 legal ordinances or groups of laws. While in the historical sections the divisions into 5×2 pericopes was made, we here find three times the division into 2×5, although here too the beginning of the last five pericopes in the second and third sections is particularly noticeable (cf **9** 8+**16** 1), and in the same way a new division can be made at **4** 18. No. 5 (**21** 1—**23** 13) is, however, divided as follows: I+II (**21** 2–6.7–11) ordinances for the protection of slaves; III+IV (**21** 12–17.18–27) protection of life, or liberty, of the dignity of parents, and hygienic laws; V (**21** 28—**22** 3) harm to animals; VI (**22** 4–16) to property; VII (**22** 17–26) against witchcraft, against imitating the Canaanites, and lack of mercy; VIII (**22** 27–30) the relation to God; IX+X (**23** 1–5.6–12) ethical and humane law practice. I–IV accordingly contain laws pertaining to persons; V+VI those referring to things; VII–X, those referring to religion, morality, and administration of justice. But the chief line of demarkation is to be made after V; for I–V contain each four ordinances, VI–X each seven, which in the original text in almost each case are in their language separated from each other by particular conjunctions or by the construction. Only in VI (**22** 4–16) one command seems to be lacking; for only **22** 4.5.6 f.9–12.13 f.15 f are distinguished by the "*kī*" in the beginning; but the seventh ordinance is found in ver 8. Here too, in each case, II+I, two and two as a rule are more closely connected, after the manner of the division in the first three sections, **1** 8—**7** 7; **7** 8—**13** 16; **13** 17—**18** 27; at least this is the case in I+II, III+IV—VII+VIII, IX+X.

(*b*) In this section, too, **19** 1—**24** 18*a*, there is no real occasion for a division into sources. It is claimed that P is found only in **19** 1.2*a*; **24** 15–18; but **19** 1.2*a* is indispensable for ver 2*b* on account of the word "there"; and before **24** 15 ff there is an omission, if the preceding verses are to be ascribed to a different source. The duplicates **19** 8.9; **19** 18.20 are best explained by the assumption of a new beginning in ver 9 at ver 20 (cf above); **24** 1.2, which at the same time introduces **24** 9 ff, is placed before ver 3, because in point of time it belongs here. According to the original text, the tr at this place must read: "To Moses he spoke," in contrast to the ordinances which, in **21** 1 ff, are addressed to the congregation of Israel. Certainly **24** 3–8 is purposely formulated to show in almost the same words that ver 3 reports the violation and vs 4 ff the writing of the decision to obey on the part of Israel (vs 3*b* and 7*b*). It is not perfectly clear to the reader where Moses was during the promulgation of the Decalogue, whether upon the mountain or at the foot of the mountain (cf **19** 24 f; **20** 18 ff· but also Dt **5** 5). In view of the importance of the matter itself and the vividness of the narrative and the continual change in the place where Moses abode, it is psychologically easily understood that the clearness of the account has suffered somewhat.

(5) **24** 18*b*—**31** 18: (*a*) During the forty days which Moses tarries with God on the mountain, and

at the conclusion of which he receives the two tables of the law (**31** 18), God converses with him seven times (**25** 1; **30** 11.17.22.34; **31** 1.12). No. 1 (**25** 1—**30** 10) contains directions in reference to the building of the Tabernacle, and laws for the priests serving in it. Nos. 2–6 bring a number of directions supplementing no. 1, namely, no. 2 (**30** 11–16), individual tax; no. 3 (**30** 17–21), copper washing vessels; no. 4 (**30** 22–33), oil for anointing; no. 5 (**30** 34–38), incense; no. 6 (**31** 1–11), the calling of Bezalel and Aholiab to be the master builders; additionally and in conclusion, no. 7 (**31** 12–17), the Sabbath command. It is probably not accidental that the Sabbath idea is touched upon 7 t, namely, in addition to the present passage, also in (*a*) **16** 5 JE (?); vs 23–29 P+R; (*b*) **20** 8–11 E; (*c*) **23** 10–12 E; (*d*) **24** 16 P; (*e*) **34** 21 J; (*f*) **35** 1–3 P, and that as is the case in this present passage, other passages too, such as **24** 16 P; **35** 1–3 P conclude a main section, and **22** 10–22 a subordinate section, with this reference.

The first more complete pericope itself (**25** 1—**30** 10) is, however, divided into 12 pieces (we cannot at this place enter into details in reference to the typical numbers found so often in the measurements of the Tabernacle, but can refer only to the cubical form of the Holy of Holies on the basis of 10 cubits), viz. (1) contributions for the sanctuary (**25** 1–9); (2) the holy ark (**25** 10–22); (3) table of shewbread (**25** 23–30); (4) golden candlesticks (**25** 31–40); (5) tabernacle (**26** 1–37) in which at the same time the articles mentioned from 2 to 4 are placed (cf vs 33 ff); (6) altar for burnt sacrifices (**27** 1–8); (7) court (**27** 9–19) in which this altar stood (cf **40** 29.33); (8) oil for the lights (**27** 20.21); (9) sacred garments for the priests (**28** 1–43); (10) consecration of priests (**29** 1–37); (11) the burnt sacrifices (**29** 38–46); (12) incense altar (**30** 1–10). The five articles included in 8 to 12 are combined into a contrast to the five in 1 to 7 by their express reference to the priests (cf in addition to 9+10 also **27** 21; **29** 44; **30** 7 f.10). With the incense altar, which was of great importance, and of equal importance with the great altar on the Day of Atonement (**30** 10), this section closes (cf [*b*]).

Thus it will under all circumstances be better to search for an explanation for putting oil in the place of the candlesticks and of the incense altar, which at first seems surprising, than in the case of every difficulty to appeal to a redactor's working without system or order. However, the entire portion **24** 18*b*—**31** 18 finds its explanation in the promise of **25** 8 that Jeh will dwell in the midst of Israel (cf **29** 45 f). He is enthroned on the ark, in which the accusing law as the expression of the Divine will is deposited (for this reason called *hā-'ēdhūth*; **25** 16.21; **26** 33.34), but above the atonement lid, the *kappōreth*, at which on the Day of Atonement, the atonement ceremony is carried out (cf **25** 17–22; Lev **16**; see DAY OF ATONEMENT).

(*b*) This whole section, with the exception of **31** 18 E (?) is ascribed to P, although at this place, though without good reasons, different strata are distinguished. In regard to the contradiction claimed to exist in the different persons to be anointed (high priest, or all the priests; cf **29** 7 over against **28** 41; **29** 21), see LEVITICUS. Also the duplicates of the *tāmīdh* sacrifice and of the candlesticks (cf I, 3, above) are not at all the decisive factor in proof of a difference of sources within the parts treating of the priests, providing it can be shown that each passage stands where it belongs. With regard to the candlesticks, see LEVITICUS. In addition cf passages like Mt **10** 39+**16** 25; **10** 22+24.13; **6** 14 ff+**18** 35; **5** 29 f+**18** 8 ff; **19** 30+**20** 16. But as far as attributing certain passages to P in general is concerned, it is self-evident that ordinances referring to the cultus make use of technical terms pertaining to the cultus, without this fact justifying any conclusion as to a particular author or group of authors. On the other hand, it could not at all be understood how P could so often call the Decalogue *ha-'ēdhūth*, without having contained this all-important law itself (cf **25** 16.21 f; **26** 33 f; **34** 29; **38** 21, etc). On the other hand, as is well known, the fourth commandment (Ex **20** 8–11 E) expressly refers back to Gen **2** 2.3, that is, to P; also **23** 15 to **12** 20.

(6) **32** 1—**35** 3: (*a*) God's promise to dwell in the midst of Israel, the turning-point in the fifth section, seems to have become a matter of doubt, through the apostasy of Israel, but is nevertheless realized in consequence of the intercession of Moses and of the grace of God, which, next to His primitive holiness, is emphasized very strongly. This entire sixth section is to be understood from this standpoint. As was the case in the preceding section, the forty days are prominent in this too (cf **34** 28 J with **24** 18 P). We can divide the contents here also into ten pericopes. No. 1 (**32** 1–14) reports that Jeh tells Moses of the idolatry with the golden calf, that He is determined to destroy Israel, but is influenced to change this determination by the intercession of Moses. No. 2 (**32** 15–29) describes the wrath of Moses and the punishment through him. He breaks the tablets into pieces, grinds the golden calf into powder, reproves Aaron, dissolves through the Levites the curse which had for this reason impended over them since Gen **49** 5–7 and causes this to be changed into a blessing: three thousand killed. No. 3 (**32** 30–35) reports that Jeh at the petition of Moses will send some of His angels, but later on will punish the people for their sins. No. 4 (**33** 1–6) reports that Jeh Himself no longer accompanies His people, which, on the one hand, is an act of grace, since the presence of God would even harm the people, but on the other hand is a punishment, and is felt as such by Israel. No. 5 (**33** 7–11) declares that God meets Moses only outside of the camp in a tent, but communes with him face to face. No. 6 introduces the last six pericopes in a natural way, since God's grace is appearing in constantly increasing glory (**33** 12–33). Here we have the petition of Moses to Jeh that He in person should accompany him and show him His glory (Jeh's grace is made esp. prominent in vs 12.13.16.17.19). No. 7 (**34** 1–10) describes the preparation for the new conclusion of the covenant; Jeh appears to Moses as the gracious, merciful, long-suffering kind, and faithful God, so that Moses again appeals to His grace. No. 8 (**34** 11–28) describes the new establishment of the covenant on the basis of the renewal of the Divine and grandiose promises of ordinances pertaining to religion and cultus, and the ten words. No. 9 (**34** 29–35) describes how, in consequence of his close communion with God, Moses' face shines. No. 10 (**35** 1–3) contains the Sabbath command (see [5*a*]). Nos. 9 and 10 give expression to the renewed covenant relationship. If we again in the larger group 1 to 8 take two and two together we find that each of these four groups contains a petition of Moses: **32** 11 ff; **33** 30–32; **33** 12 ff; **38** 8.9. The entire section brings out equally prominently the love and the holiness of God, and does this in such a way that both characteristics find their expression in each group of two of these ten numbers. The progress beyond the third section (leading Israel to Sinai) is noticeable, since the murmuring is in each case followed only by an expression of the love of God; but equally this present section stands in contrast to Nu **11** ff, where, on the occasion of the continuous murmuring of Israel the love of God is not indeed ignored, but it must take a place in the background as compared with His punitive holiness, which is particularly apparent in the story of the return of the spies in Nu **14** 11 ff. Here is at once seen the great similarity with the present section of Nu **14** 12.15. 16.17 ff and with Ex **32** 10.12; **34** 6 f, but at the same time the great difference caused by a divergency of the events (cf Nu **14** 21 ff). In contrast

to this, **32** 34 refers back to Nu **14**, and **32** 35 is a proleptic judgment based on this experience.

(*b*) It is incomprehensible how critics have found in the renewal of the covenant caused by the apostasy of Israel and in the conditions of this renewal, viz. in the Books of the Covenant and in the Decalogue, duplicates, which are distributed between E and J (Ex **20** 1 ff; **21** ff; **24** 8—**34** 1 ff.28; **34** 11-26; **34** 27). But in Ex **34** 11-26 there is no sign of the number ten being used in connection with the ordinances referring to the religion and the cultus. Goethe's attempt to find at this place the original Decalogue, which effort is constantly being repeated, is accordingly without any foundation, even in the use of the number ten. In ver 28*b*, according to ver 1 and tradition (cf Dt **10** 2.4; also Ex **24** 12; **31** 18), Jeh is to be regarded as the subject. Again **33** 4 and 5 ff are not duplicates. In ver 4 the people are described as having laid aside their ornaments a single time as a sign of repentance; according to vs 5.6 the people permanently dispense with these, a state of mind which makes it possible for God again to show His mercy. It is an arbitrary assumption that these ornaments were used in the construction of the Tabernacle, the building of which had been announced beforehand in Ex **25** ff, so that in front of **33** 7 a ‖ account to **35** ff P taken from JE would have been omitted. In **33** 7 ff according to the text the author has in mind a tent already in existence, which up to this time had been standing within the camp and now had to be taken without, because Jeh for the present can no longer dwell in the midst of the people (**32** 34; **33** 3.5), until Moses, through his intercession, again makes this possible (**33** 15-17; **34** 9.10). And the promised tabernacle takes the place of the provisional tent (chs **35** ff), which, as is done by the LXX, is probably to be preferred to Moses' own tent. In P, to whom **34** 29 ff is attributed, such a provisional arrangement is presupposed in ver 35, since already at this place, and before the building of the tabernacle in chs **35** ff, mention is made of the fact that Moses entered for the purpose of receiving the revelation of God. This accordingly presupposes what is reported in **33** 7 ff. Even without the facts mentioned and for other reasons, too, an omission must be accepted before **34** 29 ff; for ver 29 speaks of the tables of the Law, concerning the origin of which P has reported nothing; and in ver 32 concerning the commandments which Moses received on Mt. Sinai and had imparted to the people, which, however, do not refer to the directions that were given in 25 ff, since these, according to **35** 4 ff, are yet to be expressly communicated to the people.

(7) **35** 4—**40** 38: (*a*) The construction of the Tabernacle. This section is divided into four pericopes, each with four subdivisions (cf Structure of Leviticus 16 in Day of Atonement). The same principle of division is found also in the history of Abraham and in Dt **12-26**. No. I (**35** 4—**36** 7) describes the preparation for the construction: (1) **35** 4-19 appeals for contributions for this purpose; (2) **35** 20-29, contributions; (3) **35** 30—**36** 1, characterization of the builders; (4) **36** 2-7, delivering the contributions to the builders. Nos. II and III (**36** 8—**38** 31; **39** 1-31) report the construction of the Tabernacle and the preparation of the priests' garments (cf **39** 32.1); no. II: (1) **36** 8-38, dwelling-place; (2) **37** 1—**38** 9, utensils; (3) **38** 10-20, court; (4) **38** 24-31, cost of 1-3; no. III (1) **39** 2-7, shoulder garment; (2) vs 8-21, pocket; (3) vs 22-26, outer garment; (4) vs 27-31, summary account concerning coats, miter, bonnets, breeches, girdle, diadem. No. IV (**39** 32—**40** 38) reports the completion: (1) **39** 32-43, consecration of these objects; (2) **40** 1-15, command to erect; (3) vs 16-33, carrying out this command; (4) vs 34-38, entrance of the glory of Jeh. In this way the dwelling of Jeh, which had been promised in **25** 8 P, and in chs **32-34** JE had been uncertain, has become a reality. The whole section is closely connected with chs **25-31**, yet is independent in character. The full details found in both groups are completely justified by the importance of the object. It is self-evident that at this place, too, the language of the cultus is demanded by the object itself.

(*b*) The attempts to distribute this section among different authors are a total failure in view of the unity of the structure, which is independent also over against chs **25-31**. Since the numbers given in **38** 26 agree entirely with the numbers gathered later in Nu **2** 32, it is evident that for the latter the lists for the contributions were used, which in itself is very probable because it was practical. In case this section is ascribed to P it is inexplicable how the writer can in **40** 34 ff speak of the pillar of fire as of something well known, since this has not yet been mentioned in the parts ascribed to P, but has been in **13** 21 f JE; **14** 19.24 J.

III. Historical Character.—The fact that extra-Israelitish and esp. Egyp sources that can lay claim to historical value have reported nothing authentic concerning the exodus of Israel need not surprise us when we remember how meager these documents are and how one-sided Egyp history writing is.

1. General Consideration

Whether the expulsion of the lepers and the unclean, who before this had desolated the country and acquired supremacy over it as reported by Manetho and other historians, is an Egyp version of the exodus of Israel, cannot be investigated at this place, but is to the highest degree improbable. If Israel was oppressed by the Egyptians for a long period, then surely the latter would not have invented the fable of a supremacy on the part of Israel; and, on the other hand, it would be incomprehensible that the Israelites should have changed an era of prosperity in their history into a period of servitude. Over against this the remembrance of the exodus out of Egypt not only is re-echoed through the entire lit. of Israel (cf I, 4, above), but the very existence of the people of God forces us imperatively to accept some satisfactory ground for its origin, such as is found in the story of the exodus and only here. In addition, the Book of Ex shows a good acquaintance with the localities and the conditions of Egypt, as also of the desert. It is indeed true that we are still in doubt on a number of local details. But other statements in the book have in such a surprising manner been confirmed by discoveries and geographical researches, that we can have the greatest confidence in regard to the other difficulties: cf e.g. Naville's *The Store-city of Pithom* (Ex **1** 11). In general, the opening chapters of Ex, esp. the narratives of the different plagues, contain so much Egyp coloring, that this could scarcely have resulted from a mere theoretical study of Egypt, esp. since in the narrative everything makes the impression of resulting from recent experience. The fact that Israel from its very origin received ordinances in regard to religion, morality, law and cultus, is explained from the very conditions surrounding this origin and is indispensable for the explanation of the later development of the nation. None of the later books or times claim to offer anything essentially new in this respect; even the prophets appear only as reformers; they know of the election of Israel, and, on the other hand, everywhere presuppose as something self-evident the knowledge of a righteous, well-pleasing relation with God and chide the violation of this relation as apostasy. Ethical monotheism as the normal religion of Israel is reflected in the same way in all the sources of Israel's history, as has been proven in my work ("Die Entwicklung der alttestamentlichen Gottesidee in vorexilischer Zeit," in the May, 1903, issue of *Beiträge zur Förderung christlicher Theologie*). And the idea that an oriental people, esp. if they came out of Egypt, should have had no religious cultus, is in itself unthinkable. If all of these norms, also the direction for the cultus in the Books of Covenant, of the PC, or D, at least in the kernel, do not go back to the Mosaic times, then we have to deal with an insoluble problem (cf my work, *Are the Critics Right?*).

The Book of Ex is as a matter of fact from its first to its last page filled with miraculous stories; but in this characteristic these contents agree perfectly with the whole history of redemption. In this immediate and harmonious activity of God, for the purpose of establishing a chosen people, all these miracles find their purpose and explanation, and this again is only in harmony with other periods of sacred history. The reason is self-explanatory when these miracles are found grouped at the turning-points in this history, as is the case also in the critical age of Elijah and Elisha, and in the experiences and achievements of "Jonah," so significant for the universality of the Bib. religion. Above all is this true in the ministry of Jesus Christ; and also again in His return to judgment. And in the same way, too, we find this at the beginning of Israel as a nation [see my article in Murray's *Dictionary*]. Cf in this respect the rapid numerical growth of the nation, the miracles, the plagues, in the presence of Pharaoh, the passage through the Red Sea, the miraculous preservation of the people in the desert, the many appearances of God to Moses, to the people, to the elders, the protection afforded by the cloud, the providential direction of the people of Israel and of the Egyptians, and of individual persons (Moses and Pharaoh). The fact that the author himself knows that Israel without the special care and protection of God could not have survived in the desert is in complete harmony with his knowledge of the geographical situation already mentioned.

2. The Miraculous Character

If any part of the laws in Ex is to be accepted as Mosaic, it is the Decalogue. It is true that the ten commandments are found in two recensions (Ex **20**; Dt **5**). The original form is naturally found in Ex **20**. Only Moses could regard himself as inwardly so independent of the Decalogue as it had been written by God, that he did not consider himself bound in Dt **5** by its exact wording. The legal ordinances in Ex **21** 1 ff have found an analogy already in CH, more than 500 years older although moving in a lower sphere. As Israel had lived in Goshen, and according to Gen **26** 12 Isaac had even been engaged in agriculture, and Israel could not remain in the desert but was to settle down in permanent abodes again, the fact of the existence of this law of Israel, which in a religious and ethical sense rises infinitely above the CH, is in itself easily understood. And again since the sacred ark of the covenant plays an important rôle also in the other sources of the Pent (Nu **10** 33 ff; **14** 44 JE; Dt **10** 1–8; **31** 9.25) and in the history of Israel (cf Josh **3**; **6** 6–8; **8** 33; Jgs **20** 27; 1 S **6** 2 ff; 2 S **15** 24 f; 1 K **3** 15; **6** 19; 8 1–9), then a suitable tent, such as is announced in Ex **25** ff, and was erected according to Ex **35** ff, was an actual necessity.

3. The Special Legal Parts

As the Paschal sacrifice, according to Ex **12** 3 ff; vs 43 ff P; vs 21 ff JE (?) was to be killed in the houses, and this on the 14th of Nisan in the evening (**12** 6), and as P directs that a festival assembly shall be held on the next day at the sanctuary (cf Lev **23** 6 ff; Nu **28** 17 ff), these are conditions which can be understood only in case Israel is regarded as being in the wilderness. For this reason Dt **16** 5 ff changes this direction, so that from now on the Passover is no longer to be celebrated in the houses but at the central sanctuary. In the same way the direction Ex **22** 29, which ordered that the firstborn of animals should be given to Jeh already on the 8th day, could be carried out only during the wanderings in the desert, and is for this reason changed by Dt **14** 23 ff; **15** 19 ff to meet the conditions of the people definitely settled after this wandering. Cf my work, *Are the Critics Right?* 188–89, 194–95.

As is well known, the average critic handles the Bib. chronology in a very arbitrary manner and is not afraid of changing the chronology of events by hundreds of years. If we leave out of consideration some details that often cause great difficulties, we still have a reliable starting-point in the statements found in 1 K **6** 1 and Ex **12** 40 f. According to the first passage, the time that elapsed between the exodus of the Israelites and the building of the temple in the 4th year of Solomon was 480 years; and according to the second passage, the time of the stay in Egypt was 430 years. A material change in the first-mentioned figures is not permitted by the facts in the Book of Jgs, even if some particular data there mentioned are contemporaneous; and to reduce the 430 years of the stay in Egypt, as might be done after the LXX, which includes also the stay of the patriarchs in Canaan in this period. or to reduce the whole period from the entrance into Egypt to the building of the temple, is contrary to the synchronism of Hammurabi and Abraham (Gen **14**). The first-mentioned could not have lived later than 2100 BC. The 430 years in Ex **12** 40.41 P are also, independently of this passage, expressly supported by the earlier prediction of an oppression of Israel for 400 years from the time of Abraham (Gen **15** 13 J); and the 480 years of 1 K **6** 1 are confirmed by Jgs **11** 26, according to which, at the time of the suppression by the Amorites and of Jephthah as judge, already 30 years must have elapsed since the east Jordan country had been occupied by the Israelites. According to this the exodus must have taken place not long after 1500 BC. And in perfect agreement with this supposition would be the condition of affairs in Pal as we know them from the Am Tab dating about 1450–1400 BC, according to which the different Canaanitish cities had been attacked by the Chabiri in the most threatening manner, as this is reported too in the Book of Josh. As is well known linguistically, too, the identification of the Chabiri with the Hebrews is unobjectionable. Finally, on the well-known Menepthah stele of the 13th cent. BC, Israel is mentioned in connection with Canaan, Ashkelon, Gezer, Y-nu'm (=Janoah, Josh **16** 6.7?), and accordingly is already regarded as settled in Canaan. A date supported in such different ways makes it impossible for me to find in Rameses II the Pharaoh of the oppression, and in Menepthah the Pharaoh of the exodus (both between 1300 and 1200 BC). A conclusive proof that the name and the original building of the city Rameses (Ex **1** 11 JE; **12** 37 P; Nu **33** 3.5 P) necessarily leads back to Rameses II can, at least at the present time, not yet be given (cf on this point also, Köhler, *Lehrbuch der biblischen Geschichte des Alten Testamentes*, I, 238 ff).

4. Chronology

All these attacks on the historical character of this book which originate only in the denial of the possibility of miracles, the Christian theologian can and must ignore. Such attacks do not stand on the ground of history but of dogma. Let us accordingly examine other objections. Thus, it is claimed that the number of men in Israel, which in Ex **12** 37 is said to have been 600,000, is too high, because not only the desert but Goshen also would not have been able to support two million people, and Israel had been too short a time in Egypt to grow into so populous a nation. Yet Israel, beginning with the time of the oppression, which, according to **2** 23; **1** 8 continued many years and hence began before the highest number in population had been reached, had claims for support from the Egyp corn granaries; and the 430 years in **12** 40 certainly cannot be reduced, as has been shown under (4) above. To this must be added that in Ex **1** 7.9 f, 12.20 f the rapid numerical growth of Israel is represented as the result of a

5. Unjustifiable Attacks

Divine blessing. Then, too, in the company of Jacob and his descendants, doubtless servants, male and female, came down to Egypt (cf the 318 servants of Abraham alone in Gen **14**). The figures in Ex **12** 37 P are further confirmed by Nu **11** 21 (according to critics from JE) and by the results of the two enumerations, Nu **1** f (**2** 31; cf Ex **38** 26 [603, 550]) and Nu **26** 51 (601, 730). The attacks made also on the existence of the Tabernacle must be rejected as groundless. According to the Wellhausen school the Tabernacle is only a copy of the temple of Solomon dated back into the Mosaic times; and the fact that there is only one central seat of the cultus is regarded as a demand first made by the Deuteronomistic legislation in the 7th cent. Against this latter claim militates not only the impossibility of placing Dt at this time (cf my work *Are the Critics Right?* 1–55), but also the legislation of the Book of the Covenant, which, in **23** 17.19; **34** 23.24.26 presupposes a sanctuary, and which even in the passages incorrectly analyzed by Wellhausen, **20** 24 (cf again, *Are the Critics Right?* 19, 48, 161 ff, 189 ff) speaks only of a single altar (cf also **21** 14) and not of several existing at the same time. (The matter mentioned here is the building of an altar, according to a theophany, for temporary use.) Against the critical view we can quote the prophetic utterances of Amos, who condemns the cult in the Northern Kingdom (**5** 4 f), but teaches that God speaks out of Zion (**1** 2; cf probably also, **9** 1); those of Isaiah (**1** 12; **2** 2 ff; **4** 5 f; **6**; **8** 18; **18** 7; **30** 29; **33** 20; **14** 32; **28** 16); also the facts of history (cf esp. the central sanctuary in Shiloh, 1 S **1–4**; Jgs **21** 19, which is placed on the same level with Zion in Jer **7** 12 ff; **26** 6; Ps **78** 60–72). To this must be added such statements as 2 S **7** 6; Josh **18** 1; 1 K **3** 4; **8** 4; 1 Ch **16** 39.40; 2 Ch **1** 3. All these facts are not overthrown by certain exceptions to the rule (cf LEVITICUS). But the whole view leads to conclusions that in themselves cannot possibly be accepted. What a foolish fancy that would have been, which would have pictured the Tabernacle in the most insignificant details as to materials, amounts, numbers, colors, objects, which in Nu **4** has determined with exact precision who was to carry the separate parts of the tent, while e.g. for the service of the Tabernacle, so important for later times, only very general directions are given in Nu **18** 2.4.6; **8** 22 ff. This complete picture would be entirely without a purpose and meaningless, since it would have no connection whatever with the tendency ascribed to it by the critics, but rather, in part, would contradict it. Cf my book, *Are the Critics Right?* 72 ff, 87 ff.

That particularly in the post-exilic period it would have been impossible to center the Day of Atonement on the covering of the ark of the covenant, since the restoration of this ark was not expected according to Jer **3** 16, has already been emphasized in DAY OF COVENANT. If God had really determined to give to His people a pledge of the constant presence of His grace, then there can be absolutely no reason for doubting the erection of the Tabernacle, since the necessary artistic ability and the possession of the materials needed for the structure are sufficiently given in the text (cf also Ex **25** 9.40; **26** 30; **27** 8—**31** 2 ff; **35** 30 ff—**12** 35; **3** 21.22; **11** 2 f; Gen **15** 14; Ex **33** 4 ff). The examination of the separate passages in Ex, such as the relation of **20** 24 (see above) to Dt, or the ordinances concerning the Passover and the firstborn (**12** f), and other laws in the different codices, goes beyond the purpose of this article (cf however under 3 above, at the close).

IV. Authorship.—As the Book of Ex is only a part of a large work (cf I, 3 above), the question as to authorship cannot be definitely decided at this place, but we must in substance restrict ourselves to those data which we find in the book itself. In several parts it is expressly claimed that Moses wrote them. He sang the hymn found in Ex **15**, after the passage of the Red Sea, and it breathes the enthusiasm of what the author has himself experienced. Vs 13 ff do not speak against the unity of the hymn, but rather for it, since the perfects here found as prophetic perfects only give expression to the certainty that the Israelites will take possession of the land of promise. In the course of history the nations often acted quite differently from what is here stated and often antagonized Israel (cf Nu **14** 39–45; **20** 18 ff; **21** 4.21–35; **22** 6; Josh **6–12**; also Ex **13** 17). In Ex **15** 13.17 not only Zion is meant, but all Canaan; cf Lev **25** 23; Nu **35** 34; Jer **2** 7; for *har*, "mountain," cf Dt **1** 7.20 ("hill-country"); **3** 25; Ps **78** 54.55. According to Ex **17** 14 Moses writes in a book the promise of Jeh to destroy Amalek from the face of the earth. It is absolutely impossible that only this statement should have been written without any connecting thought and without at least a full description of the situation as given in Ex **17** 8 ff. And as **17** 14 linguistically at least can mean merely 'to write a sheet,' as Nu **5** 23, it yet appears in the light of the connection of a comparison with related passages, such as Josh **24** 26; 1 S **10** 25, much more natural to think of a book in this connection, in which already similar events had been recorded or could at any time be recorded.

1. Connection with Moses

The Ten Words (Ex **20** 1 ff) were written down by God Himself and then handed over to Moses; cf Ex **24** 12; **31** 18; **34** 1 ff.28 (Dt **10** 2.4). The laws and judicial ordinances beginning with Ex **21**, according to **24** 4, were also written down by Moses himself, and the same is true of the ordinances in **34** 11 ff, according to **34** 27.

The proof that formerly had to be furnished, to the effect that the knowledge of the art of writing in the days of Moses was not an anachronism, need not trouble us now, since both in Egypt and Babylon much older written documents have been discovered. But already from the passages quoted we could conclude nothing else than that Moses understood how to make use of different forms of literature—the poetical, the historical and the legal—unless the different statements to this effect by decisive reasons could be shown to be incorrect. In Nu **33**, in the catalogue of stations, there is a portion ascribed to Moses that bears the express characteristics of the PC; and, finally Dt, with its hortatory, pastoral style, claims him as its author. Already in Ex **17** 14 there were reasons to believe that Moses had written not only this statement which is there expressly attributed to him. Thus it becomes a possibility, that in general only in the case of particularly important passages the fact that Moses penned these also was to be made prominent, if it can be shown as probable that he in reality wrote more, as we find in ‖ cases in the writings of the prophets (cf Isa **8** 1; **30** 8; Jer **30** 2; Ezk **43** 11; Hab **2** 2). In addition, we notice in this connection that in the catalogue of stations mentioned above and ascribed to Moses (Nu **33**), the close relation of which to the portions attributed to P is certain, not only this part, but also the other words from JE in the present Bible text from Ex **12–19** (see above) are regarded as self-evident as Mosaic (as is the case also later with the corresponding historical part), and this is an important witness in favor of the Mosaic authorship of the historical parts. But Ex **25–31, 35–40** also claim, at least so far as contents are concerned, to be the product of the Mosaic period. The entire portable sanctuary is built with a view to the wanderings in the desert. Aaron and his sons are as yet the only representatives of the priesthood (**27** 21; **28** 4.12.41–43; **29** 4 ff, etc). In view of the relationship which Nu **33** shows with P, it is clear, if we accept the genuineness of this part, a matter that is in the highest degree probable, that this style was current in Moses' time, and that he had the mastery of it, even if other hands, too, have contributed to the final literary forms of these laws. In favor of the Mosaic authorship of the whole Book of Ex we find a weighty reason in the unity and the literary construction of the work as shown above. This indeed does not preclude the use and adaptation of other sources of historical or legal statements, either from the author's own hands or from others, if such a view should perhaps be suggested or made imperative by the presence of many hard constructions, unconnected transitions, unexpected repetitions, etc. But even on the presupposition of the Mosaic authorship, a difference in style in the different kinds of matters discussed is not impossible, just as little as this is the case with peculiarities of language, since these could arise particularly in the course of vivid narration of the story (cf the anacolouths in Paul's writings). But still more a reason for accepting the Mosaic authorship of Ex is found in the grand and deep conception and reproduction of all the events recorded, which presupposes a congenial prophetic personality; and finally, too, the natural and strong probability that Moses did not leave his people without such a Magna Charta for the future. This Mosaic authorship becomes almost a certainty, in case the Book of Dt is genuine, even if only in its essential parts. For Dt at every step presupposes not only P (cf *Are the Critics Right?* 171 ff), but also the history and the Books of the Covenant (Ex **21** ff; **34** 11 ff) as recorded in Ex.

2. Examination of Objections

Against the Mosaic authorship of Ex the use of the third person should no longer be urged, since Caesar and Xenophon also wrote their works in the third person, and the use of this provision is eminently adapted to the purpose and significance of Ex for all future times. In Isa **20** 1 ff; Ezk **24** 24, we have analogies of this in prophetic lit. The statement (**11** 3) that Moses was so highly regarded by the Egyptians is entirely unobjectionable in the connection in which it is found. That the book was not written for the self-glorification of Moses appears clearly in **4** 10–16; **6** 12. In itself it is possible that some individual passages point to a later date, without thereby overthrowing the Mosaic authorship of the whole (cf also under [1]). In this case we are probably dealing with supplementary material. Ex **16** 35 declares that Israel received manna down to the time when the people came to the borders of Canaan. Whether it was given to them after this time, too, cannot be decided on the basis of this passage (cf however Josh **5** 12). If the entire Book of Ex was composed by Moses, then Ex **16** 35 would be a proof that at least the final editing of the book had been undertaken only a short time before his death. This is suggested also by ver 34*b*, since at the time when the manna was first given the ark of the covenant did not yet exist; and the statement in **32** 35 takes into consideration the later development as found in Nu **13** f. In the same way Ex **16** 36 could be a later explanation, but is not necessarily so, if the *'ōmer* was not a fixed measure, of which nothing further is known, and which probably was not to be found in every Israelitish household, but a customary measure, the average content of which is given in ver 36. If we take Ex alone there is nothing that compels us to go later than the Mosaic period (concerning the father-in-law of Moses, see under II, 2, 1 [**1** 8—**7** 7] at the close). The question as to whether there are contradictions or differences between the different legal ordinances in Ex and in later books cannot be investigated at this place, nor the question whether the connection of Ex with other books in any way modifies the conclusion reached under (1).

Literature.—Books that in some way cover the ground discussed in the article: Against the separation into different sources: Eerdmans, *Alttestamentliche Studien*, III ("Das Buch Exodus"); Orr, *Problem of the OT;* Möller, *Wider den Bann der Quellenscheidung*. In favor of the construction of Ex **21** ff: Merx, *Die Bücher Moses und Josua* ("Religionsgeschichtliche Volksbücher," II, Series, no. 3). For Ex **21** ff in its relation to CH: A. Jeremias, *Das Alte Testament im Lichte des alten Orients;* J. Jeremias, *Moses und Hammurabi* (with fuller lit.); Histories of Israel by Kittel, König, Oettli, Köhler, Klostermann, Hengstenberg; Commentaries of Ryssel, Lange, Keil, Strack; Introductions to the OT by Strack, Baudissin, Driver, Sellin. Against the Wellhausen hypothesis: Möller, *Are the Critics Right?* (with fuller lit.); Orr (see above). Against the evolutionary theory: Orr (see above); Möller, *Die Entwicklung der alttestamentlichen Gottesidee in vorexilischer Zeit* (with fuller lit.). Representatives of other schools: The Introductions of Kuenen and Cornill; the Commentaries of Holzinger and Baentsch; the Histories of Israel by Wellhausen and Stade.

Wilhelm Möller

EXORCISM, ek'sor-siz'm, **EXORCIST**, ek'sor-sist (**'Εξορκιστής**, *Exorkistḗs*, from **ἐξορκίζω**, *exorkízō*, "to adjure" [Mt **26** 63]): One who expels demons by the use of magical formulae.

1. Definition

In the strict etymological sense there is no exorcism in the Bible. The term "exorcists" is used once (Acts **19** 13) in a way to discredit the professional exorcists familiarly known both among Jews and Gentiles.

2. Method of Expelling Demons in the NT

The method of Jesus in dealing with demoniacs was not that of the exorcists. While it is said (Mt **8** 16) that He "cast out the spirits with a word," it is abundantly clear that the word in question was not ritualistic but authoritative.

In Lk **4** 35 we have a typical sentence uttered by Our Lord in the performance of His cures: "Hold thy peace, and come out of him." In Mk **9** 29 we have Christ's own emphasis upon the ethical element in dealing with these mysterious maladies: "This kind can come out by nothing, save by prayer." In Mt **12** 28 Jesus gives His own explanation of the method and power used in His cures: "But if I by the Spirit of God cast out demons, then is the kingdom of God come upon you."

In Lk **9** 1 the terms "authority" and "power" are used in such a way as to show the belief of the evangelists that to cure demon-possession an actual power from God, together with the right to use it, was necessary. This group of passages gives the NT philosophy of this dread mystery and its cure. The demons are personal evil powers afflicting human life in their opposition to God. It is beyond man unaided to obtain deliverance from them. It is the function of Christ as the redeemer of mankind to deliver men from this as well as other ills due to sin. Miraculous cures of the same kind as those performed by Christ Himself were accomplished by His disciples in His name (Mk **16** 17). The power attributed to "His name" supplies us with the opportunity for a most enlightening comparison and contrast.

3. Exorcism in Ethnic and Jewish Writings

Exorcism among ancient and primitive peoples rests largely upon faith in the power of magical formulas, ordinarily compounded of the names of deities and pronounced in connection with exorcistic rites, upon the bodies of the afflicted. The words themselves are supposed to have power over the demons, and the mere recital of the correct list of names is supposed to be efficacious.

Attention should be called again to the incantation texts of the Babylonians and Assyrians (see, for translations and full exposition of texts, Rogers, *Religion of Babylonia and Assyria*, 146 ff). In this direction the absurdities and cruelties of superstition have carried men to extreme lengths. In the case of Jos we are amazed to see how even in the case of an educated man the most abject superstition controls his views of such subjects. In *Ant*, VIII, v, in speaking of the wisdom of Solomon, he says that "God enabled him to learn that skill which expels demons, which is a science useful and sanitative to him." He also describes, in the same connection, a cure which he alleges to have seen, "in the presence of Vespasian and his sons," performed in accordance with methods of incantation ascribed to Solomon. A ring to which was attached a kind of root mentioned by Solomon was placed at the nostrils of the demoniac and the demon was drawn out through the nostrils. The proof that exorcism had actually taken place was given in the overturning of a basin placed nearby.

The absurdities of this narrative are more than equaled by the story of exorcism told in the Book of Tob (see Lange, *Apocrypha*, 151–53) where the liver and heart of a fish, miraculously caught, are burned upon the ashes of incense, and the resulting smoke drives away a demon. This whole story is well worthy of careful reading for the light it throws upon the unrestrained working of the imagination upon such matters.

In the rabbinical writers the very limit of diseased morbidness is reached in the long and repulsive details, which they give of methods used in exorcism (see Whitehouse, *HDB*, art. "Demon," I, 592*b;* cf 593*b;* Edersheim, *Life and Times of Jesus the Messiah*, II, 775–76).

In most striking contrast with this stand the Bib. narratives. The very point of connection which we have noted is also the point of contrast. The mighty and efficacious word with which Jesus rebuked and controlled demons was no exorcistic formula spoken by rote, but His own living word of holy power. "In the name of Jesus" did not mean that the sacred name formally uttered possessed magical power to effectuate a cure. The ancient Sem formula, "in the name of," given a deep ethical meaning in the OT, had a still deeper meaning in the NT. The proper and helpful use of it meant a reliance upon the presence and living power of Christ from whom alone power to do any mighty work comes (Jn **15** 5).

4. Contrasts of NT and Popular Methods with Demons

This fundamental difference between the ideas and methods of Jesus and His disciples and current conceptions and usages becomes the more striking when we remember that the lower range of ideas and practices actually prevailed among the people with whom the Lord and His followers were associated. The famous passage (Mt **12** 24 and ||) in which the Pharisees attribute to demoniacal influence the cures wrought by Jesus upon the demonized, usually studied with reference to Our Lord's word about the unforgivable sin, is also remarkable for the idea concerning demons which it expresses. The idea which evidently underlies the accusation against Jesus was that the natural way to obtain control over demons is by obtaining, through magic, power over the ruler of demons. In reply to this Jesus maintains that since the demons are evil they can be controlled only by opposition to them in the power of God.

It is most suggestive that we have in Acts **19** 13 ff a clear exposition, in connection with exorcism, of just the point here insisted upon. According to this narrative a group of wandering professional Jewish exorcists, witnessing the cures accomplished by Paul, attempted to do the same by the ritualistic use of the name of Jesus. They failed ignominiously because, according to the narrative, they lacked faith in the living Christ by whose power such miracles of healing were wrought, although they were letter-perfect in the use of the formula. This narrative shows clearly what the NT understanding of the expression "in my name" implied in the way of faith and obedience.

Here as elsewhere, the chastened mental restraint under which the NT was composed, the high spiritual and ethical results of the intimacy of the disciples with Jesus, are clearly manifest.

Our Lord and His disciples dealt with the demoniacs as they dealt with all other sufferers from the malign, enslaving and wasting power of sin, with the tenderness of an illimitable sympathy, and the firmness and effectiveness of those to whom were granted in abundant measure the presence and power of God. LOUIS MATTHEWS SWEET

EXPECT, eks-pekt′, **EXPECTATION**, eks-pek-tā′shun: Of the three Gr words, tr[d] in the NT by "expect," *prosdokáō*, meaning to look forward toward what will probably occur, whether in hope or dread (Acts **3** 5; Lk **3** 15), is not as intense as *ekdéchomai* (He **10** 13), meaning to wait for that of the realization of which one is assured ("as the husbandman waits for the processes of Nature [Jas **5** 7], and the patriarchs for the Divine promise," Westcott), or as vivid as the noun *apokaradokía* (Rom **8** 19; Phil **1** 20, "earnest expectation"), which describes the stretching forth of the head toward an object that is anticipated (see Ellicott on Phil **1** 20). In the OT "expectation" always means that which is expected, as Prov **10** 28, "The expectation of the wicked shall perish."

H. E. JACOBS

EXPECTATION, MESSIANIC, mes-i-an′ik. See CHRISTS, FALSE; ESCHATOLOGY OF OT; JESUS CHRIST; MESSIAH.

EXPEDIENT, eks-pē′di-ent (**συμφέρω**, *sumphérō*): The Gr word tr[d] "expedient" (*sumphérō*) means lit. "to bear or bring together"; with a personal reference, "to be well or profitable." In the NT it never means "profitable" or "convenient" as opposed to what is strictly right. It is tr[d] "expedient" (Jn **11** 50, "it is expedient for us," RV "for you"; **16** 7, "It is expedient for you that I go away," i.e. "profitable," "for your good," **18** 14; 1 Cor **6** 12; **10** 23; 2 Cor **8** 10; **12** 1). In Mt **19** 10, instead of "not good to marry," RV has "not expedient." The modern sense of "expediency" as "hastening" or "acceleration," is not found in the NT, any more than its bad sense of "mere convenience." "Nothing but the *right* can ever be expedient" (Whately).

W. L. WALKER

EXPERIENCE, eks-pē′ri-ens: This word is employed 3 t. In Gen **30** 27 AV, Laban says to Jacob, "I have learned by experience [RV "divined"] that Jeh hath blessed me for thy sake." Here it translates the Heb נָחַשׁ, *nāḥash*, "to observe diligently," as when one examines the entrails of a bird or animal for the purpose of divination.

In Eccl **1** 16, the writer says, "I have gotten me great wisdom . . . . ; my heart hath had great *experience* of wisdom and knowledge." Here the Heb (*rā′āh*) means "hath seen abundantly," and the idea seems to be that of a wide outlook combined with actual trial of the things discovered or known.

In Rom **5** 4 AV, the Gr word δοκιμή, *dokimē̂* (ARV more correctly "approvedness"), means the proof or testing of a thing. We rejoice in tribulation because it works out or produces patience, while the latter develops an experience of God, i.e. it brings out as a proved fact His power and love toward us in our preservation in and deliverance from trial.

Thus it is seen the Bible use of the word is not different from the ordinary, which means "the sum of practical wisdom taught by the events and observations of life," or, to go a little farther, the personal and practical acquaintance with what is so taught. He **5** 13 gives a good practical example. AV says, "Every one that useth milk is unskilful [*ápeiros*] in the word of righteousness: for he is a babe," while RV renders "unskilful" by "without experience of." The thought is that he who fails to search out the deep things of the word of God is so lacking in the exercise of his spiritual senses as to be unable really to know truth from error.

JAMES M. GRAY

EXPERIMENT, eks-per'i-ment (**δοκιμή**, *dokimḗ*, "approvedness," "tried character"): "The experiment of this ministration" (2 Cor **9** 13 AV, RV "the proving of you by his ministration"), i.e. the sincerity of their Christian profession was evidenced by their liberal contribution.

EXPIATION, eks-pi-ā'shun: This word represents no Heb or Gr word not rendered also by "atonement." In Nu **8** 7 it is employed in RV to translate *ḥāṭath* and in Dt **32** 43, *kippēr*. This version also employs "expiate" in m of several passages, e.g. Ps **65** 3; **79** 9. Always its use in EV is somewhat more narrow and specific than "atonement" and has especial reference to specific uncleanness or sin. It will be sufficient to refer to ATONEMENT; SACRIFICE; PROPITIATION.

EXPOSURE, eks-pō'zhur, **TO WILD BEASTS.** See PUNISHMENTS.

EXPRESS, eks-pres': In AV of He **1** 3 "express" has the meaning "exactly resembling the original," as the impress of a seal resembles the figure engraved upon the seal. Thus "express image" in the ver referred to is a good tr (Gr χαρακτήρ, *charaktḗr*, lit. "engraving" and hence "impression"); RV "the very image."

EXQUISITE, eks'kwi-sit (**ἀκριβής**, *akribḗs*): The Gr word means "accurate," "searched out," equivalent to *exquisitus* from which "exquisite" is derived. It also means in argument "close," "subtle." In Ecclus **18** 29, we have, "They poured forth exquisite parables," RV "apt proverbs," and **19** 25, AV and RV "There is an exquisite subtility, and the same is unjust."

EXTINCT, eks-tinkt': In Job **17** 1, "My days are extinct" (זָעַךְ, *zā'akh* [in Niphal]) and in Isa **43** 17, "They are extinct" (דָּעַךְ, *dā'akh*), the word "extinct" should be recognized as a form of the participle, equivalent to "extinguished," so that in both passages an action, not merely a state, is indicated.

EXTORTION, eks-tor'shun: This particular word occurs twice in AV: Ezk **22** 12 (עֹשֶׁק, *'ōshek*), and Mt **23** 25 (ἁρπαγή, *harpagḗ*), and indicates that one who is an extortioner is guilty of snatching away from another by strife, greed and oppression that which does not lawfully belong to him. The element of covetousness and usury is involved in the meaning of this word; for it is greedily gotten gain. The publicans were considered as being specially guilty of this sin; this is clear from the Pharisee's deprecatory remark: "I am not . . . . an extortioner . . . . as this publican" (Lk **18** 11). Paul classes extortion (*pleonexía*, lit. "over-reaching") among a category of the grossest crimes known to humanity (1 Cor **5** 10.11); indeed, so grievous is it that it closes the door of heaven in the face of the one guilty of it (**6** 10).

WILLIAM EVANS

EXTREME, eks-trēm', **EXTREMITY**, eks-trem'-i-ti: We have the adj. "extreme" in 2 Esd **5** 14, "extreme fear," RV "trembling"; in Wisd **12** 27, "extreme [*térma*] damnation," RV "the last end of condemnation"; in 2 Macc **7** 42, "extreme [*huperballoúsas*] tortures," RV "exceeding barbarities"; in Ecclus **42** 8 it is used as an advb., "the extreme aged" (*eschatogḗrōs*), RV "of extreme old age."

Extremity: פֶּשַׁע, *pash;* LXX παράπτωμα, *paráptōma*, occurs only in Job **35** 15 AV, RV "arrogance," and ἀκμή, *akmḗ*, in 2 Macc **1** 7.

EYE, ī (עַיִן, *'ayin;* **ὀφθαλμός**, *ophthalmós*):

(1) The physical organ of sight, "the lamp of the body" (Mt **6** 22), one of the chief channels of information for man. A cruel custom therefore sanctioned among heathen nations the putting out of the eyes of an enemy or a rival, because thus his power was most effectually shattered (Jgs **16** 21; 2 K **25** 7; Jer **39** 7). Such blinding or putting out of the "right eye" was also considered a deep humiliation, as it robbed the victim of his beauty, and made him unfit to take his part in war (1 S **11** 2; Zec **11** 17).

The eye, to be useful, was to be "single," i.e. not giving a double or uncertain vision (Mt **6** 22 = Lk **11** 34). Eyes may grow dim with sorrow and tears (Job **17** 7), they may "waste away with griefs" (Ps **6** 7; **31** 9; **88** 9). They may "pour down" (Lam **3** 49), "run down with water" (Lam **1** 16; **3** 48). Eyes may "wink" in derision (Ps **35** 19; Prov **6** 13; **10** 10; cf also Prov **16** 30; **30** 17), and the harlot takes the lustling "with her eyelids" (Prov **6** 25). To 'lift up the eyes' (Gen **13** 10 *et passim*) means to look up or around for information and often for help; to 'turn away the eye' or 'hide the eyes' indicates carelessness and lack of sympathy (Prov **28** 27); to 'cast about the eyes,' so that they "are in the ends of the earth" (Prov **17** 24) is synonymous with the silly curiosity of a fool, and with the lack of attention of him who is everywhere but at his work. In the execution of justice the "eye shall not pity," i.e. not be deflected from the dictates of the law by favorable or unfavorable impressions (Dt **19** 13 *et passim*), nor spare (Ezk **5** 11 *et passim*), and the *lex talionis* demanded "life for life, eye for eye, tooth for tooth, hand for hand, foot for foot" (Ex **21** 24; Dt **19** 21).

(2) **Figurative:** The eye of the heart or mind, the organ of spiritual perception, which may be enlightened or opened (Ps **119** 18). This is done by the law of God (**19** 8) or by the spirit of God (Eph **1** 18), or it may be "darkened" and "holden" (Lk **24** 16; cf Mt **13** 13; 2 Cor **4** 4).

(3) The eye as an index of the mind and disposition of man. The Bible speaks of the "good" m, or "bountiful" eye, i.e. the kindly disposition (Prov **22** 9); of "proud," "haughty," "lofty eyes" (Ps **18** 27; **131** 1; Prov **6** 17); of the 'lowly eyes' of the humble (Job **22** 29 m; cf also Lk **18** 13); of 'adulterous eyes,' "eyes which play the harlot" (Ezk **6** 9, in the sense of idolatrous inclinations; 2 Pet **2** 14). Rage or anger is shown by the "sharpening" of the eyes (Job **16** 9).

(4) The eyes of God, as well as the "seven eyes" of the Lamb (Rev **5** 6) and the 'many eyes' of the four living creatures of the Apocalypse (Rev **4** 6; also Ezk **1** 18; **10** 12) are figurative expressions for the omniscience of God (cf He **4** 13; Ps **139** 16) and of His watchfulness and loving care (Jer **32** 19). As the human eye may, with the slightest glance or motion, give an indication, a command, so

God is able to "guide" or "counsel" His obedient child "with his eye" (Ps **32** 8).

(5) Three Heb expressions are tr^d by **"apple of the eye"**: (*a*) אִישׁוֹן, *'īshōn*, lit. "the little man," which probably means the "pupil of the eye," it being the part of the eye in which the close onlooker may see his image reflected *en miniature*. Several oriental languages have very similar expressions (Dt **32** 10; Ps **17** 8; Prov **7** 2). (*b*) בָּבָה, *bābhāh*, lit. "the gate of the eye" (Zec **2** 8). (*c*) בַּת־עַיִן, *bath-'ayin*, lit. "the daughter of the eye" (Ps **17** 8; Lam **2** 18). All these three phrases seem to indicate the pupil rather than the "apple of the eye," and designate the most sensitive part of the eye, which we protect with the greatest care. Thus the Scriptures declare, for our great comfort, that God will protect and care for those that are His own.

To eye (עָוַן, *'āwan*, "to watch closely," "to look maliciously at"): "Saul eyed David from that day and forward" (1 S **18** 9). See Envy; Evil Eye.

H. L. E. Luering

EYELID, ī'lid: Eyes and eyelids in Heb are sometimes used synonymously, as in the parallelism of Prov **4** 25 (cf **6** 4; **30** 13):

> "Let thine eyes look right on,
> And let thine eyelids look straight before thee."

(Cf Job **41** 18; Ps **11** 4; Jer **9** 18.) The alluring power of the wanton woman is conceived of as centered in her eyes (Prov **6** 25; Isa **3** 16): "Neither let her take thee with her eyelids." **Painting** the eyelids was resorted to to intensify the beauty, antimony (q.v.) being used for darkening the lashes (2 K **9** 30; Jer **4** 30; Ezk **23** 40).

Painted Eyes.

Geo. B. Eager

EYEPAINT, ī'pānt. See Antimony; Eyelid; Keren-happuch.

EYESALVE, ī'säv (κολλούριον, *kolloúrion; collyrium;* Rev **3** 18): A Phrygian powder mentioned by Galen, for which the medical school of Laodicea seems to have been famous (see Ramsay, *The Letters to the Seven Churches of Asia*), but the **figurative** reference is to the restoring of spiritual vision.

EYES, BLINDING, blīnd'ing, **OF THE.** See Eye; Punishments.

EYES, COVERING, kuv'ēr-ing, **OF THE:** In Gen **20** 16, means forgetfulness of the past, a willingness to overlook the wrong to which Sarah had been exposed.

EYES, DISEASES, di-zēz'is, **OF THE:** Blindness, defects of sight and diseases of the eye are frequently mentioned in the Scriptures, but usually in general terms. It is probable that in the period covered by the Bible, ophthalmia was as common in Pal and Egypt as it is now. See Blindness. The commonest of the diseases at present is the purulent conjunctivitis which is a highly infectious malady affecting people of all ages, but esp. children, and whose germs are carried from eye to eye by the flies, which are allowed to walk freely over the diseased eyes. This is one of the most disgusting sights in a Palestine village, but I have been told by mothers that it is esteemed unlucky to drive off the flies. In this manner the disease is propagated. The number of persons in any Palestine village whose eyes are more or less blemished by disease is on this account phenomenally large.

Blindness incapacitated a man from serving in the priesthood (Lev **21** 16.18); even a blemish of the eye was regarded as a disqualification (Lev **21** 20).

The cases in the NT of persons blind from their birth (as Jn **9** 1) were probably the results of this ophthalmia, but may have been due to congenital malformation. The interesting psychological record of the difficulty of interpreting the new visual sensations by the blind man healed by Our Lord (Mk **8** 22) indicates that it was probably not a case of congenital blindness, as the evangelist uses the word *apokatestáthē* ("restored"), but he had been so long blind that he had lost the power of appreciating the sense-impressions. This condition has been often discussed as a psycho-physical problem since the days of Molyneux and Locke (*Essay on the Human Understanding*, II, 9, 8).

The blindness of St. Paul was probably a temporary paralysis of the retina from the shock of a dazzling light accentuated by the intense emotion which accompanied his vision on the road to Damascus. The "scales" mentioned in Acts **9** 18 were not material, but his sight was restored as if (*hōsei*) scales had fallen from his eyes. How far this left his eyes weak we do not know, but from his inability to recognize the high priest (Acts **23** 5) and from his employing an amanuensis for transcribing his epistles (Rom **16** 22), as well as from his writing in characters of large size (*pēlíkos;* Gal **6** 11), it is probable that his vision was defective, and this it has been conjectured was the "thorn in the flesh" of 2 Cor **12** 7.

Senile blindness, the result either of cataract or retinal degeneration, is mentioned in the cases of Isaac (Gen **27** 1), Jacob (Gen **48** 10) and Eli (1 S **4** 15). The frequency of such senile dimness of sight made the case of Moses the more remarkable that at the age of 120 his eye was not dim (Dt **34** 7).

Tobit's blindness, caused by the irritation of the sparrow's dung (Tob **2** 10), was a traumatic conjunctivitis which left an opacity. It is not said that the whiteness was itself sufficiently large to destroy vision. There was with it probably a considerable amount of conjunctival thickening, and it is possible that the remedy might have removed this. It certainly could not remove a cicatricial white spot of the nature of an albugo. The conjecture of a recent commentator that the gall, by coloring the spot, made the eye look as if sight was restored when it really was not, seems ludicrously inept. In any case the historical accuracy of the narrative is so problematical that explanation is unnecessary. See Blindness.

Alex. Macalister

EYESERVICE, ī'sûr-vis (ὀφθαλμοδουλεία, *ophthalmodouleía*): A term coined by Paul to express the conduct of slaves, who work only when they are watched, and whose motive, therefore, is not fidelity to duty, but either to avoid punishment or to gain reward from their masters (Eph **6** 6; Col **3** 22). "A vice which slavery everywhere creates and exhibits. Hence the need for drivers and overseers" (Eadie).

EYES, TENDER. See Blindness.

EZAR, ē'zar. See Ezer.

EZBAI, ez'bā-i, ez'bī (אֶזְבָּי, *'ezbāy*, "shining," "blooming"; Ἀζωβαί, *Azōbaí*): One of David's "mighty men" (1 Ch **11** 37; cf 2 S **23** 35m).

EZBON, ez'bon:

(1) (אֶצְבֹּן, *'eçbōn;* Pesh, אצבעון; LXX Θασοβάν, *Thasobán*): A son of Gad (Gen **46** 16) = Ozni of Nu **26** 16 (see Ozni).

(2) (אֶצְבּוֹן, *'eçbōn;* LXX Ἀσεβών, *Asebṓn*): In 1 Ch **7** 7 is said to be a grandson of Benjamin.

Curtis (*Ch.*, 148) holds that the genealogical table there is that of Zebulun and not Benjamin, and says that Ezbon suggests Ibzan (Jgs **12** 8–10), a minor judge of Bethlehem of Zebulun (Moore, *Judges*, 310).

EZECHIAS, ez-ē-kī'as, **EZECIAS**, ez-ē-sī'as. See Ezekias (3).

EZEKIAS, ez-ē-kī'as (**Ἐζεκίας**, *Ezekias*):

(1) AV Gr form of Hezekiah (thus RV; Mt **1** 9.10). A king of Judah.

(2) AV Ezechiad (1 Esd **9** 14), called Jahzeiah in Ezr **10** 15.

(3) AV Ezecias (1 Esd **9** 43), called Hilkiah in Neh **8** 4.

EZEKIEL, ē-zē'ki-el:

- I. The Prophet and His Book
  - 1. The Person of Ezekiel
    - Name, Captivity and Trials
  - 2. The Book
    - (1) Its Genuineness
    - (2) Its Structure
    - (3) Relation to Jeremiah
    - (4) Fate of the Book and Its Place in the Canon
- II. Significance of Ezekiel in Israel's Religious History
  - 1. Formal Characteristics of Ezekiel
    - (1) Visions
    - (2) Symbolical Acts
    - (3) Allegories
    - (4) Lamentations
  - 2. Ezekiel and the Levitical System
    - (1) Ezk **44** 4 ff: Theory That the Distinction of Priests and Levites Was Introduced by Ezekiel
      - (*a*) The Biblical Facts
      - (*b*) Modern Interpretation of This Passage
      - (*c*) Examination of Theory
        - (α) Not Tenable for Preëxilic Period
        - (β) Not Sustained by Ezk
        - (γ) Not Supported by Development after Ezk
      - (*d*) The True Solution
    - (2) Ezk **40–48**: Priority Claimed for Ezk as against the Priest Codex
      - (*a*) Sketch of the Modern View
      - (*b*) One-Sidedness of This View
      - (*c*) Impossibility That Ezk Preceded P
      - (*d*) Correct Interpretation of Passage
    - (3) Ezekiel's Leviticism
  - 3. Ezk and the Messianic Idea
  - 4. Ezk and Apocalyptic Literature
  - 5. Ezekiel's Conception of God

I. The Prophet and His Book.—The name יְחֶזְקֵאל, *y^eḥezḳē'l*, signifies "God strengthens." The LXX employed the form **Ἰεζεκιήλ**, *Iezekiēl*, from which the Vulg took its "Ezechiel" and Luther "Hesekiel." In **1** 3 the prophet is said to be the son of a certain Buzi, and that he was a priest. This combination of the priestly and prophetic offices is not accidental at a time when the priests began to come more and more into the foreground. Thus, too, Jeremiah (**1** 1) and Zechariah (**1** 1; cf Ezr **5** 1; **6** 14; Neh **12** 4.16, and my art. "Zechariah" in Murray's *Illustrated Bible Dictionary*) were priests and prophets; and in Zec **7** 3 a question in reference to fasting is put to both priests and prophets at the same time. And still more than in the case of Zechariah and Jeremiah, the priestly descent makes itself felt in the case of Ezekiel. We here already draw attention to his Levitical tendencies, which appear particularly prominent in chs **40–46** (see under II, 2 below), and to the high-priestly character of his picture of the Messiah (**21** 25 f; **45** 22; see II, 3 below).

1. The Person of Ezekiel

We find Ezekiel in Tel-abib (**3** 15) at the river Chebar (**1** 1.3; **3** 15) on a Euphrates canal near Nippur, where the American expedition found the archives of a great business house, "Murashu and Sons." The prophet had been taken into exile in 597 BC. This event so deeply affected the fate of the people and his personal relations that Ezekiel dates his prophecies from this event. They begin with the 5th year of this date, in which year through the appearance of the Divine glory (cf II, 1 below) he had been consecrated to the prophetic office (**1** 2) and continued to the 27th year (**29** 17), i.e. from 593 to 571 BC. The book gives us an idea of the external conditions of the exiles. The expressions "prison," "bound," which are applied to the exiles, easily create a false impression, or at any rate a one-sided idea. These terms surely to a great extent are used **figuratively**. Because the Jews had lost their country, their capital city, their temple, their service and their independence as a nation, their condition was under all circumstances lamentable, and could be compared with the fate of prisoners and those in fetters.

The external conditions in themselves, however, seem rather to have been generally tolerable. The people live in their own houses (Jer **29** 5). Ezekiel himself is probably the owner of a house (Ezk **3** 24; **8** 1). They have also retained their organization, for their elders visit the prophet repeatedly (**8** 1; **14** 1; **20** 1). This makes it clear why later comparatively few made use of the permission to return to their country. The inscriptions found in the business house at Nippur contain also a goodly number of Jewish names, which shows how the Jews are becoming settled and taking part in the business life of the country.

Ezekiel was living in most happy wedlock. Now God reveals to him on a certain night that his wife, "the desire of his eye," is to die through a sudden sickness. On the evening of the following day she is already dead. But he is not permitted to weep or lament over her, for he is to serve as a sign that Jerus is to be destroyed without wailing or lamentation (**24** 15 ff). Thus in his case too, as it was with Hosea, the personal fate of the prophet is most impressively interwoven with his official activity.

The question at what age Ezekiel had left Jerus has been answered in different ways. From his intimate acquaintance with the priestly institutions and with the temple service, as this appears particularly in chs **40** to **48**, the conclusion is drawn that he himself must have officiated in the temple. Yet, the knowledge on his part can be amply explained if he only in a general way had been personally acquainted with the temple, with the law and the study of the Torah. We accept that he was already taken into exile at the age of 25 years, and in his 30th year was called to his prophetic office; and in doing this we come close to the statement of Jos, according to which Ezekiel had come to Babylon in his youth. At any rate the remarkable statement in the beginning of his book, "in the 30th year," by the side of which we find the customary dating, "in the 5th year" (**1** 1.2), can still find its best explanation when referred to the age of the prophet. We must also remember that the 30th year had a special significance for the tribe of Levi (Nu **4** 3.23.30.39), and that later on, and surely not accidentally, both Jesus and John the Baptist began their public activity at this age (Lk **3** 23).

It is indeed true that the attempt has been made to interpret this statement of Ezekiel on the basis of an era of Nabopolassar, but there is practically nothing further known of this era; and in addition there would be a disagreement here, since Nabopolassar ruled from 625 on, and his 30th year would not harmonize with the year 593 as determined by Ezk **1** 2. Just as little can be said for explaining these 30 years as so many years after the discovery of the book of the law in 623, in the reign of Josiah (2 K **22** f). For this case too there is not the slightest hint that this event had been made the beginning of a new era, and, in addition, the statement in Ezk **1** 1, without further reference to this event, would be unthinkable.

As in the case of the majority of the prophets, legends have also grown around the person of Ezekiel. He is reported to have been the teacher of Pythagoras, or a servant of Jeremiah, or a martyr, and is said to have been buried in the tomb of Shem and Arphaxad. He indeed did stand in close relationship to Jeremiah (see 2, 3 below). Since the publication of Klostermann's essay in the *Studien und Kritiken*, 1877, it has been customary, on the basis of **3** 14 f.26 f; **4** 4 ff; **24** 27, to regard Ezekiel as subject to catalepsy (cf the belief often entertained that Paul was an epileptic). Even if his condition, in which he lay speechless or motionless, has some similarity with certain forms of catalepsy or kindred diseases, i.e. a temporary suspension of the power of locomotion or of speech; yet in the case of Ezekiel we never find that he is describing a disease, but his unique condition occurs only at the express command of God (**3** 24 ff; **24** 25 ff); and this on account of the stubbornness of the house of Israel (**3** 26). This latter expression which occurs with such frequency (cf **2** 5 ff; **3** 9.27, etc) induces to the consideration of the reception which the prophet met at the hand of his contemporaries.

He lives in the midst of briars and thorns and dwells among scorpions (**2** 6). Israel has a mind harder than a rock, firmer than adamant (**3** 8 f). "Is he not a speaker of parables?" is cast up to him by his contemporaries, and he complains to God on this account (**20** 49); and God in turn sums up the impression which Ezekiel has made on them in the words (**33** 32): "Thou art unto them as a very lovely song of one that hath a pleasant voice, and can play well on an instrument; for they hear thy words, but they do them not." They consequently estimate him according to his aesthetic side (cf II, 1, below), but that is all.

2. The Book

(1) *Its genuineness.*—When compared with almost every other prophetic book, we are particularly favorably situated in dealing with the genuineness of the Book of Ezk (cf my work, *Die messianische Erwartung der vorexilischen Propheten, zugleich ein Protest gegen moderne Textzersplitterung*), as this is practically not at all called into question, and efforts to prove a complicated composition of the book are scarcely made.

Both the efforts of Zunz, made long ago (cf *Zeitschrift der deutsch-morgenländischen Gesellschaft*, 1873, and *Die gottesdienstlichen Vorträge der Juden*), and of Seinecke (*Geschichte des Volkes Israel*, II, 1 ff) to prove a Pers or even a Gr period as the time of the composition of the book; as also the later attempt of Kroetzmann, in his *Comm. on Ezk*, to show that there are two recensions of the book, have found no favor. The claim that chs **40–48** were written by a pupil of Ezekiel was made as a timid suggestion by Volz, but, judging from the tendency of criticism, the origin of these chapters will probably yet become the subject of serious debate. But in general the conviction obtains that the book is characterized by such unity that we can only accept or reject it as a whole, but that for its rejection there is not the least substantial ground. This leads us to the contents.

(2) *Its structure.*—The parts of the book are in general very transparent. First of all the book is divided into halves by the announcement of the fall of Jerus in ch **33**; of which parts the first predominantly deals with punishments and threats; the other with comfort and encouragement. Possibly it is these two parts of the book that Jos has in mind when he says (*Ant*, X) that Ezekiel had written two books. That the introduction of prophecies of redemption after those of threats in other prophetical books also is often a matter of importance, and that the right appreciation of this fact is a significant factor in the struggle against the attacks made on the genuineness of these books has been demonstrated by me in my book, *Die messianische Erwartung der vorexilischen Propheten* (cf 39–40 for the case of Amos; 62 ff, 136 f, for the case of Hosea; 197 ff for Isa **7–12**; 238 ff for Micah; see also my article in Murray's *Illustrated Bible Dictionary*).

Down to the time when Jerus fell, Ezekiel was compelled to antagonize the hopes, which were supported by false prophets, that God would not suffer this calamity. Over against this, Ezekiel persistently and emphatically points to this fact, that the apostasy had been too great for God not to bring about this catastrophe. There is scarcely a violation of a single command—religious, moral or cultural—which the prophet is not compelled to charge against the people in the three sections, **3** 16 ff; **8** 1 ff; **20** 1 ff, until in **24** 1 ff, on the 10th day of the 10th month of the 9th year (589 BC) the destruction of Jerus was symbolized by the vision of the boiling pot with the piece of meat in it, and the unlamented destruction of the city was prefigured by the unmourned and sudden death of his wife (see **1** above). After the five sections of this subdivision I, referring to Israel—each one of which subdivisions is introduced by a new dating, and thereby separated from the others and chronologically arranged (**1** 1 ff, with the consecration of the prophet immediately following it; **3** 16 ff; **8** 1 ff; **20** 1 ff; **24** 1 ff)—there follow as a second subdivision the seven oracles against the Ammonites (**25** 1 ff); the Moabites (**25** 8 ff); the Edomites (**25** 12 ff); the Philis (**25** 15 ff); Tyre (**26** 1 ff); Sidon (**28** 20 ff); Egypt (**29** 1 ff), evidently arranged from a geographical point of view.

The most extensive are those against Tyre and the group of oracles against Egypt, both provided with separate dates (cf **26** 1—**29** 1; **30** 20; **31** 1; **32** 1.17). The supplement in reference to Tyre (**29** 17 ff) is the latest dated oracle of Ezekiel (from the year 571 BC), and is found here, at a suitable place, because it is connected with a threat against Egypt (chs **40–48** date from the year 573 according to ch **40** 1). The number seven evidently does not occur accidentally, since in other threats of this kind a typical number appears to have been purposely chosen, thus: Isa **13–22,** i.e. ten; Jer **46–51,** also ten; which fact again under the circumstances is an important argument in repelling attacks on the genuineness of the book.

Probably the five parts of the first subdivision, and the seven of the second, supplement each other, making a total of twelve (cf the analogous structure of Ex **25** 1—**30** 10 under Exodus, and probably the chiastic structure of Ezk **34–48,** with 7+5 pieces; see below). The oracles against the foreign countries are not only in point of time to be placed between ch **24** and **33** 21, but also, as concerns contents, help splendidly to solve the difficulty suggested by ch **24,** and in this way satisfactorily fill the gap thus made. The arrival of the news of the fall of Jerus, in 586 BC (cf **33** 21 ff), which had already been foretold in ch **24,** introduced by the mighty watchman's cry to repentance (**33** 1 ff), and followed by a reproof of the superficial reception of the prophetic word (see **1** above), concludes the first chief part of the book.

The second part also naturally falls into two subdivisions, of which the first contains the development of the nearer and more remote future, as to its inner character and its historical course (chs **34–39**): (1) the true shepherd of Israel (ch **34**); (2) the future fate of Edom (ch **35**); (3) Israel's deliverance from the disgrace of the shameful treatment by the heathen, which falls back upon the latter again (**36** 1–15); (4) the desecration of the name of

Jeh by Israel and the sanctification by Jeh (**36** 15–38); (5) the revival of the Israelitish nation (**37** 1–14); (6) the reunion of the separated kingdoms, Judah and Israel (**37** 15–28); (7) the overthrow of the terrible gentile power of the north (chs **38** f).

The second subdivision (chs **40–48**) contains the reconstruction of the external affairs of the people in a vision, on the birthday of 573, "in the beginning of the year" (beginning of a jubilee year? [Lev **25** 10]; cf also DAY OF ATONEMENT). After the explanatory introduction (**40** 1–4), there follow five pericopes: (1) directions with reference to the temple (cf the subscription **43** 12) (**40** 5—**43** 12); (2) the altar (**43** 13—**46** 24); (3) the wonderful fountain of the temple, on the banks of which the trees bear fruit every month (**47** 1–12); (4) the boundaries of the land and its division among the twelve tribes of Israel (**47** 13—**48** 29); (5) the size of the holy city and the names of its twelve gates (**48** 30–35).

In (3) to (5) the prominence of the number twelve is clear. Perhaps we can also divide (1) and (2) each into twelve pieces: (1) would be **40** 5 ff.17 ff. 28 ff.39 ff.48 ff; **41** 1 ff.5 ff.12 ff.15 ff; **42** 1 ff.15 ff; **43** 1 ff; for (2) it would be **43** 13 ff.18 ff; **44** 1 ff. 4 ff.15 ff; **45** 1 ff.9 ff.13 ff.18 ff; **46** 1 ff.16 ff.19 ff.

At any rate the entire second chief part, chs **34–48,** contains predictions of deliverance. The people down to 586 were confident, so that Ezekiel was compelled to rebuke them. After the taking of Jerus a change took place in both respects. Now the people are despairing, and this is just the right time for the prophet to preach deliverance. The most important separate prophecies will be mentioned and examined in another connection (II below).

The transparent structure of the whole book suggests the idea that the author did not extend the composition over a long period, but wrote it, so to say, at one stretch, which of course does not make it impossible that the separate prophecies were put into written form immediately after their reception, but rather presupposes this. When the prophet wrote they were only woven together into a single uniform book (cf also EXODUS, IV, 1, 2).

(3) *His relation to Jeremiah.*—As Elijah and Elisha, or Amos and Hosea, or Isaiah and Micah, or Haggai and Zechariah, so too Jeremiah and Ezekiel constitute a prophetic couple (cf **1** above); cf e.g. in later time the sending out of the disciples of Jesus, two by two (Lk **10** 1), the relation of Peter and John in Acts **3** ff; of Paul and Barnabas in Acts **13** ff; of Luther and Melanchthon, Calvin and Zwingli. Both prophets prophesy about the same time; both are of priestly descent (cf **1** above), both witness the overthrow of the Jewish nation, and with their prophecies accompany the fate of the Jewish state down to the catastrophe and beyond that, rebuking, threatening, warning, admonishing, and also comforting and encouraging.

In matters of detail, too, these two prophets often show the greatest similarity, as in the threat against the unfaithful shepherds (Ezk **34** 2 ff; Jer **23** 1 ff); in putting into one class the Northern and the Southern Kingdom and condemning both, although the prediction is also made that they shall eventually be united and pardoned (Ezk **23, 16**; Jer **3** 6 ff; Ezk **37** 15 ff; Jer **3** 14–18; **23** 5 f; **30** f); in the individualizing of religion (cf the fact that both reject the common saying: "The fathers have eaten sour grapes, and the children's teeth are set on edge," Ezk **18** 2; Jer **31** 29); in their inwardness (Ezk **36** 25 ff; Jer **24** 7; **31** 27–34; **32** 39; **33** 8); in their comparisons of the coming judgment with a boiling pot (Ezk **24** 1 ff; Jer **1** 13 ff); and finally, in their representation of the Messiah as the priest-king (see **1** above; viz. in Ezk **21** 25 f; **45** 22; cf Jer **30** 21; **33** 17 ff; see II, 3, and my work *Messianische Erwartung,* 320 ff, 354 ff). Neither is to be considered independently of the other, since the prophetical writings, apparently, received canonical authority soon after and perhaps immediately after they were written (cf the expression "the former prophets" in Zec **1** 4; **7** 7.12, also the constantly increasing number of citations from earlier prophets in the later prophets, and the understanding of the "exact succession of the prophets" down to Artaxerxes in Jos, *CAp,* I, 8), it is possible that Ezekiel, with his *waw consecutivum,* with which the book begins, is to be understood as desiring to connect with the somewhat older Jeremiah (cf a similar relation of Jonah to Obadiah; see my arts. "Canon of the OT" and "Jonah" in Murray's *Illustrated Bible Dictionary*).

(4) *Fate of the book and its place in the Canon.*—With Jeremiah and Ezekiel, many Heb MSS, esp. those of the Ger. and Fr. Jews, begin the series of "later prophets," and thus these books are found before Isa; while the Massorah and the MSS of the Spanish Jews, according to the age and the size of the books, have the order, Isa, Jer, Ezk. The text of the book is, in part, quite corrupt, and in this way the interpretation of the book, not easy in itself, is made considerably more difficult. Jerome, *Ad Paul.,* writes that the beginning and the end of the book contained many dark passages; that these parts, like the beginning of Gen, were not permitted to be read by the Jews before these had reached their 30th year. During the time when the schools of Hillel and Shammai flourished, Ezk belonged to those books which some wanted "to hide," the others being Prov, Eccl, Est and Cant. In these discussions the question at issue was not the reception of the book into the Canon, which was rather presupposed, nor again any effort to exclude them from the Canon again, which thought could not be reconciled with the high estimate in which it is known that Est was held, but it was the exclusion of these books from public reading in the Divine service, which project failed. The reasons for this proposal are not to be sought in any doubt as to their authenticity, but in reference to their contents (cf my art. "Canon of the OT," in Murray's *Illustrated Bible Dictionary*). Possibly, too, one reason was to be found in the desire to avoid the profanation of the most sacred vision in the beginning of the book, as Zunz suggests. There is no doubt, however, that the difference of this book from the Torah was a reason that made it unadvisable to read it in public. It was hoped that these contradictions would be solved by Elijah when he should return. But finally, rabbinical research, after having used up three hundred cans of oil, succeeded in finding the solution. These contradictions, as a matter of fact, have not yet been removed, and have in modern times contributed to the production of a very radical theory in criticism, as will be shown immediately under II, 2.

II. Significance of Ezekiel in Israel's Religious History.—Under the first head we will consider the formal characteristics and significance of the book; and the examination of its contents will form the subject under the next four divisions.

It is not correct to regard Ezekiel merely as a writer, as it is becoming more and more customary to do. Passages like **3** 10 f; **14** 4 ff; **20** 1 ff.27; **24** 18 ff; **43** 10 f show that just as the other prophets did, he too proclaimed by word of mouth the revelations of God he had received. However, he had access only to a portion of the people. It was indeed for him even more important than it had been for the earlier prophets to provide for the wider circulation and permanent influence of his message by putting

1. The Formal Characteristics of Ezekiel

it into written form. We will, at this point, examine his book first of all from its formal and its aesthetic side. To do this it is very difficult, in a short sketch, to give even a general impression of the practically inexhaustible riches of the means at his command for the expression of his thoughts.

(1) *Visions.*—Thus, a number of visions at once attract our attention. In the beginning of his work there appears to him the Divine throne-chariot, which comes from the north as a storm, as a great cloud and a fire rolled together. This chariot is borne by the four living creatures in the form of men, with the countenances of a man, of a lion, of an ox and of an eagle, representing the whole living creation. It will be remembered that these figures have passed over into the Rev of St. John (**4** 7), and later were regarded as the symbols of the four evangelists. In chs **10** f this throne-chariot in the vision leaves the portal of the temple going toward the east, returning again in the prediction of deliverance in ch **43**. Moreover, the entire last nine chapters are to be interpreted as a vision (cf **40** 2). We must not forget, finally, the revivification of the Israelitish nation in ch **37**, represented in the picture of a field full of dead bones, which are again united, covered with skin, and receive new life through the *rūaḥ* (word of two meanings, "wind" and "spirit").

As a rule the visions of Ezekiel, like those of Zechariah (cf my art. "Zechariah" in Murray's *Illustrated Bible Dictionary*), are not regarded as actual experiences, but only as literary forms. When it is given as a reason for this that the number of visions are too great and too complicated, and therefore too difficult of presentation, to be real experiences, we must declare this to be an altogether too unsafe, subjective and irrelevant rule to apply in the matter. However correct the facts mentioned are in themselves they do not compel us to draw this conclusion. Not only is it uncertain how many visions may be experiences (cf e.g. the five visions in Am **7** ff, which are generally regarded as actual experiences), but it is also absolutely impossible to prove such an a priori claim with reference to the impossibility and the unreality of processes which are not accessible to us by our own experience. As these visions, one and all, are, from the religious and ethical sides, up to the standards of OT prophecy, and as, further, they are entirely unique in character, and as, finally, there is nothing to show that they are only literary forms, we must hold to the conviction that the visions are actual experiences.

(2) *Symbolical acts.*—Then we find in Ezk, also, a large number of symbolical acts. According to Divine command Ezekiel sketches the city of Jerus and its siege on a tile (**4** 1 ff); or he lies bound on his left side, as an atonement, 390 days, and 40 days on his right side, according to the number of years of the guilt of Israel and Judah (**4** 4 ff). During the 390 days the condition of the people in exile is symbolized by a small quantity of food daily of the weight of only 20 shekels, and unclean, being baked on human or cattle dung, and a small quantity of water, which serves as food and drink of the prophet (**4** 9 ff).

By means of his beard and the hair of his head, which he shaves off and in part burns, in part strikes with the sword, and in part scatters to the wind, and only the very smallest portion of which he ties together in the hem of his garment, he pictures how the people shall be decimated so that only a small remnant shall remain (**5** 1 ff). In ch **12**, he prepares articles necessary for marching and departs in the darkness. Just so Israel will go into captivity and its king will not see the country into which he goes (cf the blinding of Zedekiah, 2 K **25** 7). In **37** 15 ff, he unites two different sticks into one, with inscriptions referring to the two kingdoms, and these picture the future union of Israel and Judah. It is perhaps an open question whether or not some of these symbolical actions, which would be difficult to carry out in actuality, are not perhaps to be interpreted as visions; thus, e.g. the distributing the wine of wrath to all the nations, in Jer **25** 15, can in all probability not be understood in any other way. But, at any rate, it appears to us that here, too, the acceptance of a mere literary form is both unnecessary and unsatisfactory, and considering the religio-ethical character of Ezk, not permissible.

(3) *Allegories.*—In regard to the numerous allegories, attention need be drawn only to the picture of the two unfaithful sisters, Oholah and Oholibah (i.e. Samaria and Jerus), whose relation to Jeh as well as their infidelity is portrayed in a manner that is actually offensive to over-sensitive minds (ch **23**; cf ch **16**). In ch **17**, Zedekiah is represented under the image of a grapevine, which the great eagle (i.e. the king of Babylon) has appointed, which, however, turns to another great eagle (king of Egypt), and because of this infidelity shall be rooted out, until God, eventually, causes a new tree to grow out of a tender branch.

(4) *Lamentations.*—Of the lamentations, we mention the following: according to ch **19**, a lioness rears young lions, one after the other, but one after the other is caught in a trap and led away by nose-rings. The ones meant are Jehoahaz and certainly Jehoiachin. The lion mother, who before was like a grapevine, is banished (Zedekiah). Another lamentation is spoken over Tyre, which is compared to a proud ship (cf **27** 1 ff); also over the king of Tyre, who is hurled down from the mountain of the gods (**28** 11–19); and over Pharaoh of Egypt, who is pictured as a crocodile in the sea (**32** 1 ff).

That his contemporaries knew how to appreciate the prophet at least from the aesthetic side, we saw above (I, 1). What impression does Ezekiel make upon us today, from this point of view? He is declared to be "too intellectual for a poet"; "fantastic"; "vividness in him finds a substitute in strengthening and repetition"; "he has no poetical talent"; "he is the most monotonous prose writer among the prophets." These and similar opinions are heard. In matters of taste there is no disputing; but there is food for reflection in the story handed down that Frederick von Schiller was accustomed to read Ezk, chiefly on account of his magnificent descriptions, and that he himself wanted to learn Heb in order to be able to enjoy the book in the original. And Herder, with his undeniable and undenied fine appreciation of the poetry of many nations, calls Ezekiel "the Aeschylus and the Shakespeare of the Hebrews" (cf Lange's *Comm. on Ezk*, 519).

2. Ezekiel and the Levitical System

(1) Ezk **44** 4 ff: *The claim that the distinction between priests and Levites was introduced by Ezekiel.*—(*a*) The Bib. facts on the subject: In the vision of the reconstruction of the external relations of the people in the future (chs **40**–**48**), in the second pericope, which treats of the cultus (**43** 13—**46** 24; cf I, 2, 2), it is claimed that Ezekiel, at the command of Jeh, reproaches the Israelites that they engage in their room strangers, uncircumcised in heart and uncircumcised in flesh, to take charge of the service of Jeh in the sanctuary, instead of doing this service themselves, and thus desecrate the temple (**44** 4–8). From now on the Levites, who hitherto have been participating in the service of the idols on the high places and had become for Israel an occasion for guilt, are to attend to this work. They are degraded from the priesthood as a punishment of

their guilt, and are to render the above-mentioned service in the temple (vs 9 ff), while only those Levitical priests, the sons of Zadok, who had been rendering their services in the sanctuary in the proper way, while Israel was going astray, are to be permitted to perform priestly functions (vs 15 ff).

(*b*) The modern interpretation of this passage (Ezk **44** 4 ff) is regarded as one of the most important proofs for the Wellhausen hypothesis. Down to the 7th cent. BC it is claimed that there are no signs that a distinction was made between the persons who had charge of the cultus in Israel, and this is held to be proved by the history of the preceding period and by the Book of Dt, placed by the critics in this time. It is said that Ezekiel is the first to change this, and in this passage introduces the distinction between priests and the lower order of Levites, which difference is then presupposed by the PC. According to this view, the high priest of the PC, too, would not yet be known to Ezekiel, and would not yet exist in his time. More fully expressed, the development would have to be thought as follows: the Book of Dt, which abolished the service on the high places, and had introduced the concentration of the cultus, had in a humane way provided for the deposed priests who had been serving on the high places, and, in **18** 6 ff, had expressly permitted them to perform their work in Jerus, as did all of their brethren of their tribe, and to enjoy the same income as these. While all the other Deuteronomic commands had in principle been recognized, this ordinance alone had met with opposition: for in 2 K **23** 9 we are expressly told that the priests of the high places were not permitted to go up to Jerus. Ezekiel now, according to Wellhausen's statement, "hangs over the logic of the facts a moral mantle," by representing the deposition of the priests of the high places as a punishment for the fact that they were priests of the high places, although they had held this position in the past by virtue of legal right.

It is indeed true, it is said, that these priests did not submit to such a representation of the case and such treatment. The violent contentions which are said to have arisen in consequence are thought to have their outcome expressed in Nu **16** f (the rebellion of Korah, the budding staff of Aaron). The PC, however, continued to adhere to the distinction once it had been introduced, and had become a fact already at the return in 538 BC (cf Ezr **2** 36 ff), even if it was found impossible to limit the priesthood to the Zadokites, and if it was decided to make an honorable office out of the degraded position of the Levites as given by Ezekiel. The fact that, according to Ezr **2** 36–39, in the year 538 BC, already 4,289 priests, but according to ver 40, only 74 Levites, returned, is also regarded as proving how dissatisfied the degraded priests of the high places had been with the new position, created by Ezekiel, to which they had been assigned. With the introduction of the PCodex in 444 BC, which made a distinction between high priest, priests and Levites within the tribe of Levi, this development reached an end for the time being. While Dt speaks of the "Levitical priests," which expression is regarded as confirming the original identity of the priests and the Levites, it is claimed that since the days of Ezekiel, priests and Levites constitute two sharply distinguished classes.

(*c*) Examination of this view: Both the exegesis of Ezk **44** 4 ff and the whole superstructure are in every direction indefensible and cannot be maintained (cf also my work, *Are the Critics Right?* 30 ff, 124 ff, 196 ff).

(*α*) Proof that the hypothesis cannot be maintained for the preëxilic period. The claim that down to the 7th cent. BC there did not exist in Israel any distinction among the persons engaged in the public cultus is in itself an absurdity, but has in addition against it the express testimony of history. In preëxilic times the high priest is expressly mentioned in 2 K **12** 9 ff; **22** 4.8; **23** 4. Accordingly he cannot have been a product of the post-exilic period. The rank of an Eli (1 S **1** ff), Ahimelech (1 S **21** f), Abiathar (1 K **2** 26 f), Zadok (1 K **2** 35), is vastly above that of an ordinary priest. The fact that the expression "high priest" does not happen to occur here is all the less to be pressed, as the term is found even in the PC only in Lev **21** 10; Nu **35** 25–28. From Dt **10** 6; Josh **24** 33; Jgs **20** 28, we learn that the office of high priest was transmitted from Aaron to his son, Eleazar, and then to his son, Phinehas (cf also Nu **25** 11). Before the time of Eli, according to 1 Ch **24** 3, it had passed over to the line of the other surviving son of Aaron, that of Ithamar, but, according to 1 K **2** 26 f.35, at the deposition of Abiathar and the appointment of Zadok, it returned again to the line of Eleazar (cf 1 S **2** 27.28.35 f with 1 Ch **24** 3). Distinctions within the tribe are also expressly presupposed by Jer **20** 1; **29** 25 f.29; **52** 24; 2 K **25** 18. In the same way Levites are expressly mentioned in history (cf Jgs **17** f; **19–21**; 1 S **6** 15; 2 S **15** 24; 1 K **8** 3 ff). This very division of the priestly tribe into three parts possibly suggested the three parts of the temple of Solomon (the holy of holies, the holy place, the forecourt). According to all this, it is not possible that this distinction is not found in Dt, esp. if this book was not written until the 7th cent. BC and throughout took into consideration the actual condition of affairs at that time, as is generally claimed. But this difference is found in Dt, the false dating of which we can here ignore, and is probably suggested by it; for, if this were not the case, then the addition of the words "the whole tribe of Levi" to the words "Levitical priests" in **18** 1 would be tautology. But as it is, both expressions already refer to what follows: viz. vs 3–5 to the priests and vs 6 ff to the rest of the Levites. In the same way, the Levites are in **12** 12.18 f; **14** 27.29; **16** 11.14 the objects of charity, while **18** 3 ff prescribes a fixed and not insignificant income for the priests. Then, finally, such general statements as are found in **10** 8; **18** 2 ff; **33** 8 ff, not only demand such specific directions as are found only in P, but in **10** 9; **18** 2 there is a direct reference to Nu **18** 20.24 (from P). On the other hand, Dt, in harmony with its general tendency of impressing upon Israel in the spirit of pastoral exhortation the chief demands of the law, does not find it necessary, in every instance, to mention the distinctions that existed in the tribe of Levi.

In Nu **18** 7 we have in P even an analogon to Dt **10** 8; **33** 8 ff; since here, too, no distinction is made between priests and high priests separately, but the whole priestly service is mentioned in a summary manner (cf further Lev **6** 22 in comparison with ver 25; Nu **35** in comparison with Josh **21**). That Dt cannot say "Aaron and his sons," as P does, is certainly self-evident, because Aaron was no longer living at the time when the addresses of Dt were delivered. And how the expression "Levitical priests," which Dt uses for the expression found in P, and which was entirely suitable, because under all circumstances the priests were of the tribe of Levi, is to be understood as excluding the subordinate members of the cultus-officers belonging to the same tribe, is altogether incomprehensible (cf the emphasis put on the Levitical priesthood in P itself, as found in Nu **17**; Josh **21** 4.10 ff). So are other passages which originated at a time after the introduction by Ezekiel, or, according to the critics, are claimed to have been introduced then (cf Mal **2** 1 ff.4.8; **3** 3; Jer **33** 18; Isa **66** 21; 2 Ch **5** 5; **23** 18; **29** 4 ff; **30** 27), and even in

Ezk (**44** 15). The claims that Dt is more humane in its treatment of the priests who had engaged in the worship in high places (cf e.g. 2 K **22** f) cannot at all be reconciled with Dt **13**, which directs that death is to be the punishment for such idolatry. If, notwithstanding this, it is still claimed that Dt **18** 6 ff allows the priests of the high places to serve in Jerus, then it is incomprehensible how in 2 K **23** 9 these men did not appeal directly to Dt in vindication of their rights over against all hindrances, since Dt was regarded as the absolute norm in carrying out the cultus tradition.

(*β*) Examination of the hypothesis on the basis of Ezk: No less unfavorable to the view of the critics must the judgment be when we examine it in the light of the contents of Ezk itself. The prophet presupposes a double service in the sanctuary, a lower service which, in the future, the degraded priests of the high places are to perform and which, in the past, had been performed in an unlawful manner by strangers (**44** 6–9), and a higher service, which had been performed by the Zadokites, the priests at the central sanctuary, in the proper way at the time when the other priests had gone astray, which service was for this reason to be intrusted to them alone in the future (cf, also, **40** 45.46; **43** 19). Since in vs 6 ff the sharpest rebukes are cast up to Israel (according to the reading of the LXX, which here uses the second person, even the charge of having broken the covenant), because they had permitted the lower service to be performed by uncircumcised aliens, it is absolutely impossible that Ezekiel should have been the first to introduce the distinction between higher and lower service, but he presupposes this distinction as something well known, and, also, that the lower service has been regulated by Divine ordinances. As we have such ordinances clearly given only in Nu **18** 2 ff (from P) it is in itself natural and almost necessary that Ezekiel has reference to these very ordinances, but these very ordinances direct that the Levites are to have charge of this lower service. This is confirmed by Ezk **48** 12 f, where the designation "Levites" in contradistinction from the priests is a fixed and recognized term for the lower cultus officials. For Ezekiel has not at all said that he would from now on call these temple-servants simply by the name "Levites," but, rather, he simply presupposes the terminology of P as known and makes use of it. He would, too, scarcely have selected this expression to designate a condition of punishment, since the term "Levites" is recognized on all hands to be an honorable title in the sacred Scriptures. And when he, in addition, designates the Zadokites as "Levitical priests" (**44** 15), this only shows anew that Ezekiel in his designation of the lower temple-servants only made use of the terminology introduced by P.

But, on the representation of the critics, the whole attitude ascribed to Ezekiel cannot be upheld. It is maintained that a prophet filled with the highest religious and ethical thoughts has been guilty of an action that, from an ethical point of view, is to be most sharply condemned. The prophet is made to write reproaches against the people of Israel for something they could not help (vs 6 ff), and he is made to degrade and punish the priests of the high places, who also had acted in good faith and were doing what they had a right to do (vs 9 ff; cf "the moral mantle" which, according to Wellhausen, "he threw over the logic of facts"). Ezekiel is accordingly regarded here as a bad man; but at the same time he would also be a stupid man. How could he expect to succeed in such an uncouth and transparent trick? If success had attended the effort to exclude from the service in Jerus the priests of the high places according to 2 K **23** 9, and notwithstanding Dt **18** 6 ff, which according to what has been said under (*a*) is most improbable, then this would through the action of Ezekiel again have been made a matter of uncertainty. Or, was it expected that they would suffer themselves to be upbraided and punished without protesting if they had done no wrong? Finally, too, the prophet would have belonged to that class whose good fortune is greater than their common sense. This leads us to the following:

(*γ*) Examination of the development after the time of Ezekiel: Ezekiel's success is altogether incomprehensible, if now the distinction between priests and Levites has, at once, been introduced and at the return from captivity, in the year 538 (Ezr **2** 36 ff), certainly was a fact. It is true that we at once meet with a host of difficulties. Why do only 74 Levites return according to Ezr **2** **40** if their degradation from the ranks of the priesthood through Ezekiel had not preceded? asks the Wellhausen school. Why did any Levites, at all, return, if they had been so disgraced? is our question. But, how is it at all possible that so many priests could return (4,289 among 42,360 exiles, or more than one-tenth of the whole number; cf Ezr **2** 36–38 with ver 64; but many more than one-tenth if women are included in the 42,360), if, since the times of Ezekiel, there were none other than Zadokite priests? In examining the writers claimed as the authors of P, all those difficulties recur again which are found in the case of Ezekiel himself. That Nu **16** f indicates and reflects the opposition of the degraded is nothing but an unproved assertion; but if they had revolted, which was probable enough, then there would have been no worse and more foolish means than to change the degraded position of the Levites according to Ezk into the honorable position assigned them in P. This would only have made the matter worse. The Levites would again have been able to claim their old rights and they would have acquired the strongest weapons for their opposition. The fact that Ezekiel's restoration of the priesthood to the Zadokites would have been ignored by P, as also the descent of Aaron through Eleazar and Ithamar, according to the account of P, that is, that in reality also others were admitted to the priesthood, would only have the effect of making those who still were excluded all the more rebellious, who could appeal to each case of such an admission as a precedent and accordingly as a violation of the principle. What possible purpose the authors of P could have had in the creation of those products of imagination, Nadab and Abihu, and the portrayal of the terrible fate of these sons of Aaron (Lev **10**) remains incomprehensible (cf the purposeless and constructive imagination in the description of the details of the Ark of the Covenant, which stands in no connection with the tendency of P; see Exodus, III, 5). Nor can it be understood why the creators of the PC would have had assigned other duties to the Levites than Ezekiel had done; the slaying of the burnt offerings and the sacrifices (**44** 11) and the cooking of the latter (**46** 24) is lacking in P, in which document the transportation of the imaginary tabernacle would have exhausted the duties of the priests (Nu **4**), while in other respects, their services would be described only in such general notices as in Nu **8** 23 ff; **18** 2 ff (cf for this reason the very credible account in Ch, which through Ezk **44** 11; **46** 24 only becomes all the more trustworthy, where we are told of the enlargement of the duties of the Levites already by David in **1** Ch **23** 25 ff). In short, the critical views offer one monstrosity after another, and each greater than its predecessor. We will only mention further that, if the critics are right in this matter, then of the directions found in Ezk **40–48** nothing else has ever been carried out in reality, even when these chapters are correctly understood (see 2 [*d*] below), and at first nothing was intended to be carried out, so that it would be all the more surprising if this one feature of the program of Ezekiel had alone been picked out and had been carried out with an inexplicable haste, and that too at a time when the whole cultus was not at all observed (573, according to **40** 1).

(*d*) The solution of the problem: The text as it reads in Ezk **44** 9 ff actually does speak of a degradation. If the matter involved only a mere putting back into the *status quo ante*, of the Levites, who on the high places, contrary to the law, had usurped the prerogatives of the higher priestly offices, as this could easily be understood, then the expression in vs 10. 12, "They shall bear their iniquity," would lose much of its significance. On the other hand, the whole matter finds its explanation if, in the first place, the lower order of Levites did not put a high estimate on their office, so that they transferred their service to aliens (vs 6 ff), and if, in the second place, by those Levites who departed from Jeh, when Israel was going astray, not all the Levites are to be understood, but only a certain group of priests, who by these words were for themselves and their contemporaries clearly enough designated: namely, the descendants of Aaron through Ithamar and Eleazar in so far as they were not Zadokites, that is, had not officiated at the central sanctuary. The non-Zadokite priests had permitted themselves to be misled to officiate in the idolatry in the services of the high places, and for this reason were for the future to be degraded to the already existing lower order of the Levites.

The fact that in the ranks of lower participants in the cultus, already in the days of David, according to Ch, a still further division had taken place (1 Ch **23–26**), so that by the side of the Levites in the most narrow sense of the word, also the singers and the gate watchmen were Levites of a lower rank (Neh **12** 44–47; **13** 10), is again in itself entirely credible, and, in addition, is made very probable by Ezr **2** 40 ff. This too at once increases the small number of Levites who returned from the exile from 74 to 341. In comparison to the number of priests (4,289) the number yet remains a small one, but from Ezk **44** 6 ff we learn further that the Levites also before the days of Ezekiel had not appreciated their office, for then they would not have given it over to aliens. In this way not only does everything become clear and intelligible, but the weapon which was to serve for the defence of the Wellhausen school has in every respect been turned against these critics. The historical order can only be: first, the PC, and after that Ezk; never vice versa.

(2) Ezk **40–48**: *Priority claimed for Ezekiel over against the Priest Codex* (cf *Are the Critics Right?* 114 ff).—(*a*) Sketch of the modern view: The entire vision of what the external condition of affairs would be in the future in chs **40–48**, and not only what is particularly stated in **44** 4 ff, is made a part of Israel's religious development in accordance with the scheme of the Wellhausen school. For this hypothesis, this section is one of the chief arguments, besides the opposition which it claims exists on the part of the prophets against the sacrifices, in addition to the proof taken from the history of the people and from the comparison of the different collections of laws with each other. In Ezk **40–48** many things are different from what they are in the PC, and in Ezk much is lacking that is found in P. How now would a prophet dare to change the legislation in P? Hence P is regarded as later than Ezk. This is, briefly, the logic of the Wellhausen school.

(*b*) The one-sidedness of this view and its dangerous consequences: If we first state the facts in the case and complete the observations of the modern school, the picture will at once assume quite a different form and the conclusions drawn will in their consequences prove very embarrassing. It is a fact that in Ezk the high priest so prominent in P is lacking. No mention is made of the equipment of the holy of holies, and in the holy place the table of the shewbread and the candlesticks, old utensils that are mentioned in the tabernacle of P, and in part play an important rôle there. But the differences in Ezk are not found only in comparison with P, but just as much, too, in features which belong to the legislation of Dt, as also of the Book of the Covenant, accepted at all hands as preëxilic (Ex **21–23**; **34**). Thus there is lacking in Ezk **40–48** not only the tithes of P (Lev **27** 30–33), also the laws with reference to the firstborn from P (vs 26 f; Nu **18** 15 f), the ordinances with reference to the portions of the redemption sacrifice to be given to the priests from P (Lev **7** 31 ff), but equally the ordinance with reference to the tithes, firstborn and sacrificial gifts from Dt (cf **14** 22 ff; **26** 12 ff; **14** 23–26; **15** 19–23; **18** 3). The feast of weeks is wanting, which is demanded not only by P in Lev **23** 15 ff; Nu **28** 26 ff, but also by the older legislation (Ex **23** 16; **34** 22; Dt **16** 9 ff); and in the place of the three ‖ feasts demanded everywhere, only the Passover and the Feast of the Tabernacles are prescribed (Ezk **45** 21). Thus too the direction with regard. e.g. to the Day of Atonement in Ezk **45** 18 ff is different in regard to number, time and ritual from P in Lev **16**, etc (cf Day of Atonement, I, 1), but also the command found in Ex **20** 26 (from E) that it was not permitted to ascend on steps to the altar of Jeh is overthrown by Ezk **43** 17. And, according to what has been described under (1), criticism itself accepts (although without reason) that Ezekiel had changed the commandment of Dt **18** 6 ff, according to which all the Levites in Jerus could perform priestly service, so that he not only forbade this, as did 2 K **23** 9, but that he also degraded these priests of the high places as a punishment and reduced them to a lower service.

As is the case in reference to the law, Ezekiel also disagrees with the facts of history. He changes the dimensions of the Solomonic temple entirely (**40** 5—**42** 20); he gives an entirely different distribution of the Holy Land (**47** 13—**48** 29) from that which was carried out in actual history. What sheer arbitrariness and short-sightedness it would be, to pick out of this condition of affairs only those features in which he differs from P, in order, for this reason, to force the composition of the PC into the post-exilic period, and at the same time to close one's eyes to the necessary conclusion that if this principle of interpretation is correct, then the Book of the Covenant and Dt, the temple and the migration into Canaan must also be post-exilic. "The prophet is not allowed to change P," we are told; but as a matter of fact he has changed P no more than he changed the older laws and history. Hence the claim is false. And then, too, P is not to be regarded as unchangeable. Even the writer of Ch, who writes from the standpoint of P, has changed P; for he narrates in 1 Ch **23** 24.27 that the age of the Levites since the time of David had been reduced from 30 or 25 years (Nu **4** 3.23.30.35; **8** 23 ff) to 20 years (cf also the participation of the Levites in the burnt sacrifices and the Passover under Hezekiah [2 Ch **29** 34; **30** 17.19]), and in P itself, according to Nu **9** 6–12, the observation of the Passover after the regular time was permitted, and in general if such changes and adaptations of the law on the part of Ezk could not be demonstrated elsewhere, the difficulties for the advocates of the Wellhausen hypothesis would be exactly as great as they are for the adherents of the Bib. views, only that the problem would be inverted to explain how the author of P could have ventured to deviate so far from the will of God as this had been revealed to Ezekiel.

(*c*) Impossibility that Ezk preceded P: While the description of the temple in **40** 5 ff and of the future dwelling-places of the people (**47** 13 ff) is comparatively complete, it is the very legislation of the ritual in **43** 13—**46** 24, in which it is maintained that the authors of P followed the precedent of the prophet, that is in itself so full of omissions in Ezk, that it could not possibly have been a first sketch, but must presuppose P, if it is not to be regarded as suspended in the air. Ezk presupposes not only burnt offerings, peace offerings and food offerings, but also sin offerings (**40** 39; **42** 13; **43** 19.21.22.25; **44** 27.29; **46** 20). Ezekiel is indeed the first and the only prophet who mentioned sin offerings, just as the guilt offerings are found outside of Ezk only in Isa **53** 10. But this reference is of such a kind that he presupposes on the part of his readers an acquaintance also with these two kinds of sacrifices; hence it is, in itself, a natural conclusion, that the sacrificial legislation of P, that is, chiefly Lev **1** to **7,** is older, and as the guilt offerings and the sin offerings are prescribed only by P, and in Lev **4** f appear to be emphasized anew, this conclusion becomes a necessity.

If this is not the case then Ezk is without any foundation. In the same way the injunctions with reference to what is clean and unclean are presupposed as known in **44** 23.25 f (cf **22** 26). How long the uncleanness described in ver 26 continued can be seen only from Nu **19** 11 ff. Since in Ezk **22** 26 there is presupposed a definitely fixed Torah or Law, which it is possible to violate, then it is only natural to conclude that such commands existed before the days of Ezekiel, esp. such as are found in Lev **11–15.** In the same way the general character of the ordinances (**44** 30*a*), concerning the tithes due to the cultus officials, demand such further developments as are found especially in Nu **18** in P. The high priests, too, although Ezekiel makes no mention of them, belong to the period earlier than Ezekiel, as was proved under (1). If there had been no high priest before the days of Ezekiel, it would have been a perfect mystery, in addition, how he would be found after 520 BC (Hag **1** 1; Zec **3** 8; **6** 10 ff), without a word having been mentioned of the establishment of such an important institution. In addition, if the office had been created just at this time, this would make it very uncomfortable for the contentions of the Wellhausen school, since the other ordinances of P were introduced only in 444 BC, and should here be regarded as innovating.

That Ezekiel presupposed the ordinances of P in reference to the cultus officials has been demonstrated under (1). Accordingly, there yet remains to be discussed the universally recognized relationship that exists between Ezk and the so-called Law of Holiness (H) in Lev **17–26** (cf Leviticus), which is so great, that for a time Ezekiel was regarded as the author or the editor of this law, a view which, however, has been dropped, because a number of the peculiarities of Ezk do not admit of its acceptance. The more advanced critics then went farther, and claimed that H is later than Ezk, which is the only possible and defensible position. For practical reasons we here examine, in addition to Ezk **40–48,** also the older parts of the book. Especially do we take into consideration, in addition to ch **44,** also chs **18, 20** and **22;** but in the end the contents of H are suggested by the entire Book of Ezk. Esp. Lev **26** has been very fully used by Ezk; cf for the details, Driver's *Intro to the OT;* or, Hoffmann, *Die wichtigsten Instanzen gegen die Graf-Wellhausensche Hypothese.* That Ezk could not be the earlier of the two can be concluded as far as P in general is concerned, and for H in particular, esp. from this, that Ezk is just as closely connected with Dt and Jer, as with P; while, on the other hand, in the passage in question, P is connected only with Ezk, while the expressions which Ezk has in common with Dt and those Ezk has in common with Jer are not found in P (cf the exceedingly interesting and instructive proof in Hoffmann, op. cit.). Equally striking is the proof of Köhler, *Biblische Geschichte,* III, 154 ff, who shows that the contents of the Torah (Law) presupposed and recognized by Jer and Ezk as dating from the Mosaic period, take into consideration not only the Books of the Covenant (Ex **21** ff; **34**) and Dt, but esp. P in general and H in particular. Further, if we place P in a later period, it would be incomprehensible that this body of laws, in which the systematic feature is so important, can differ from the still more systematic ordinances of Ezk, and thus become more unsystematic. Thus the sacrifices on the Passover and the Feast of Tabernacles are in number of the same kind in Ezk **45** 21 ff; but not so in P in Nu **28** 16 ff; **29** 12 ff. In the same way in the food offerings on the feasts as far as oxen, rams, lambs, and the amount of oil to be given are concerned, there is everywhere the proper proportion in **45** 18—**46** 15, while in Nu **28** this is regulated according to a different principle. Then in Ezk are found in the description of the sanctuary (**42** 15–20; **45** 2), of the inner and outer courts (**40** 23.27.47; cf also **40** 19; **48** 16 f), square figures in places where they are not found in the tabernacle according to P. To this must be added that no other ordinances of Ezk would be carried out in actual practice. Even the ordinances in **44** 4 ff, according to the views of the critics, would be changed in P, in so far as the establishment and work of the lower cultus officials and the enlargement of the powers of the higher cultus officials are concerned (cf [1]). The Day of Atonement, whose roots are said to be found in **45** 18 ff, would be materially changed in number, length and ritual (cf Day of Atonement, I, 1 and III, 1). When the Israelites returned from captivity, they did not think at all of building the temple or the tabernacle in accordance with Ezekiel's scheme, or dividing the land according to the directions of his book (both of these subjects have great prominence in Ezk **40–48;** cf **40** 5—**43** 12; **47** 13—**48** 29), or of harmonizing Ezk with P, or of carrying out the latter practically. The Wellhausen hypothesis is then in conflict with all ritual legislation, whether real or constructed by Wellhausen himself.

(*d*) The correct interpretation of Ezk **40–48:** These chapters dare not be made a part of the development of the law in the OT. Ezekiel's was not a program that was under all circumstances to be carried out or even could be carried out, for it presupposes conditions that were beyond the control of Israel. For in **40** 2 ff, a new geographical or geological situation is presupposed, which the country up to this time did not possess (cf the "very high mountain," **40** 2), and the same is true in **47** 1 ff in reference to the miraculous temple fountain with its equally miraculous powers, and in **47** 13 ff in the division of the land. Only after these changes had been effected in the character of the localities by Jeh, and Jeh should again have entered the holy city according to **43** 1 ff, would it be possible to carry out also the other injunctions. It is impossible, either, to interpret these chapters as an allegory. This interpretation is out of the question on account of a large number of directions and measurements. It is, however, true that the whole is an ideal scheme, which portrays to the eye the continuation of the kingdom of God, and represents symbolically the presence of Jeh, which sanctifies all around about it and creates for itself a suitable outward form. This is particularly apparent in the new name which is assigned to Jerus, namely, "Jeh at that place," or the conclusion of this section and at the same time of the entire book. This, finally, leads us to a brief account of the views presented.

(3) *Ezekiel's Leviticism.*—In (1) and (2) above, it has been shown that Ezk was not the starting-point of Leviticism in Israel: it rather represents the extreme development of this tendency. It was in harmony with the elementary stage of the OT to give the thoughts and demands of God, not in a purely abstract form, but to clothe them in objective and external materials, in order to prepare and educate Israel to understand Christianity. (The negative side of Leviticism, which is not to be overlooked by the side of the positive, is discussed in the art. LEVITICUS.) It is a matter of utmost importance for the correct understanding of the OT, that we recognize that the prophets too throughout think Levitically; in their discourses, too, sacred trees, sacrifices, times, persons, tithes, play a most important rôle, notwithstanding all the spiritualization of religion on their part; and where it is thought possible to show an absolute opposition on the part of the prophets to the Levitical system, namely, in the matter of sacrifices, a close consideration, but esp., too, the analogy of the other external institutions, shows that we have in these cases only a relative antithesis (cf *Are the Critics Right?* 99 ff; *Messianische Erwartung der vorexilischen Propheten*, 333 ff). Thus e.g. Jeremiah who, in **6** 20; **7** 21 ff, engages as sharply as possible in polemics against the sacrificial system, and in **31** 31 ff, in the passage treating of the new covenant, spiritualizes religion as much as possible, has assigned to sacrifices a place in his predictions of the future (cf **17** 19 ff.26; **31** 14; **33** 18), just as the abiding-place and the revelation of God for this prophet too, are always found connected with the Holy Land, Jerus or Zion (cf **3** 17; **12** 15; **30** 18; **31** 6.11.12; **32** 36 ff; **33** 9). That in this the ultimate development of the kingdom of God has not yet been reached, but that the entire OT contains only a preliminary stage, cannot be too sharply emphasized. In so far Ezekiel, in whose book Leviticism appears in its most developed state, more than others, shares in the limitations of the OT. But just as little can it be denied that the Levitical system was really one stage, and that, too, an important and indispensable stage in the development of the kingdom of God; and that in this system, the question at issue is not only that of a change of a religion into a stereotyped formalism or externalism, which is the case if this system loses its contents, but the fact that it contained a valuable kernel which ripened in this shell, but would not have ripened if this shell had been prematurely discarded. The external conditions, their harmonious arrangement, the ceremonial ordinances, keeping clean from external pollution, are indeed only forms; but in them valuable contents succeed in finding their expression; through these Israel learned to understand these contents. The kernel could not be given without the shell nor the contents without the form, until in Christianity the time came when the form was to be broken and the shell discarded. This significance of the Levitical system becomes more evident in Ezk than is the case, e.g. in P, where indeed a few passages like Ex **25** 8; **29** 45 ff; **40** 34 ff; Lev **16**; **19** 18; **26** 31.41 clearly show in what sense the entire legislation is to be understood; but the mere fact that there are so few of these passages makes it easy to overlook them; while in Ezk, in addition to the purely Levitical utterances, and in part more closely connected with these, the entire work is saturated with the emphasis put on the highest religious and ethical thoughts, so that both must be in the closest harmony with each other (cf on this subject also Ezekiel's conception of God under 5 below). That Ezk and the Law of Holiness stand in such close relations to each other is not to be explained from this, that Ezekiel is in any way to be connected with the composition of the law in Lev **17–26,** but on the ground of the tendency common to both. The fact that Ezekiel shows a special liking for these chapters in P does not, accordingly, justify the conclusion that Lev **17** ff ever existed as a separate legal codex. We must in this connection not forget the close connection of the prophets with the rest of P mentioned under (2) above (cf LEVITICUS). We close this part of the discussion with the statement that Ezekiel constructed his system on the basis of the Levitical ordinance, but as priest-prophet (cf under **I, 1**) utilized this material independently and freely.

Chs **40–48** treat of the future, and furnish us the transition to another matter, in which Ezk by modern theology has been forced into a wrong light, namely, in regard to the Messianic idea.

3. Ezekiel and the Messianic Idea

After the critics had, as a matter of fact, eliminated from the entire preëxilic prophetical writings nearly all of the passages speaking of the Messiah on the ground that they were not genuine (e.g. Am **9** 8 ff; Hos **1** 10.11; **3** 5; Mic **2** 12 f; **4** f; Isa **4** 2–6; **7** 14; **9** 1–7; **11** 1–10, etc), Marti and Volz have now completed this task. While the former declared as not genuine all the Messianic predictions down to Deutero-Isaiah, the latter has, in his work, *Die vorexilische Jahwe-Prophetie und der Messias*, halted at Ezk, but for this works up the entire material into a uniform fundamental conception with pronounced characteristics. He declares that prophecy and the Messianic idea are two mutually exclusive phenomena, by regarding the Messiah as a purely political and national fact, but the prophetic expectation of the future as something purely religious. Ezekiel he regards as the first prophet with whose views on other matters the Messianic idea indeed did not harmonize, but who, nevertheless, yielded to the tendencies of his times and to the general national feelings, and submitted to the influence of the false prophets, who had created the carnal national expectation of a Messiah and constantly fed this, and accordingly received into his book the Messiah passages in **17** 22–24; **21** 25 f; **34** 23 f; **37** 22. 24.25. But this too is, all in all, simply a monstrous assumption. It is exegetically incorrect to regard the Messiah merely as a political, national and particularistic person, whenever the religious and ethical and universalistic characteristics of the Messiah are portrayed by prophecy; and it is also incorrect to regard prophecy as abstractly religious, when the national and external side of the kingdom of God is ignored. It is impossible to eliminate the different Messianic passages preceding the time of Ezekiel, as these are proved to be genuine by their contents and form, their close connection with the context, the structure of the prophetic writings, and by the mutual relation of these passages to each other. But we must here refer to our book, *Die messianische Erwartung der vorexilischen Propheten*. We draw attention to this only because since the publication of Gressmann's book, *Der Ursprung der israelitisch-jüdischen Eschatologie*, the critics have begun to be a little less skeptical in reference to the genuine character of the Messianic passages in the older prophetical writings. We here point to the fact, that the positive contentions of Volz, which ascribe to Ezk the introduction of the Messianic idea out of the popular faith, are exceedingly inconsiderate. The different passages mentioned above, which in Ezk speak of the Messiah, can scarcely be said to add any new features to the picture of the Messiah as it is found in earlier lit. (of one exception to this we will speak later). If the Messiah was not yet portrayed in the earlier prophetic lit., then Ezekiel had the less occasion to introduce this new feature, if this feature did not harmonize with his other views, as Volz claims. And, if this is only a mistake, it is yet a fact that in Ezk the Messianic idea is not relatively a prominent feature; he, as it were, only recalls the pictures known from the predictions of the earlier prophets; he accepts these pictures as revealed truth, because they, in his conviction, evidently originated in the development of prophecy. Cf for the idea that the Messiah is to come forth from small origins and from a lowly station Ezk **17** 22–24; Isa **10** 33.34; **11** 1; Mic **5** 1 ff. Ezk **21** 32 only hints at the general expectation of a Messiah; Ezk **34** 23 f; **37** 22. 24.25 connect esp. with the promises given to David in 2 S **7**. Then the reunion of the two kingdoms into one scepter is found also in Am **9** 11; Hos **2** 2; **3** 5; Isa **8** 23—**9** 1 ff; **11** 13 f; Mic **5** 2; Jer **3** 18; **23** 5 f; 1 K **11** 39; the blessing of Nature, Isa **11** 6–8; Am **9** 13 ff; Hos **2** 20 ff; **14** 6 ff. At all events the Messianic expectations of Ezekiel exhibit too few peculiar features and are too little prominent in the body of his prophecies to justify the belief that he was the first prophet to have introduced this so important Messianic figure. On the other hand, let us remember too that Ezekiel opposes the national feelings as sharply as possible by representing the entire past history of Israel as an unbroken chain of heathenish abominations (chs **1–24, 33,** esp. **16** and **23**), and remember it was just he who like Jeremiah saw his most bitter opponents in the false prophets (**13** 1 ff; **14** 9; **22** 28), and that in the most pronounced antithesis to these he proclaimed before the fall of Jerus that this fall would and must come. And now it is claimed that he borrowed his Messianic idea from these very people, although this Messianic conception is everywhere represented as being a Divine revelation and not a natural product of the popular consciousness. A greater blunder in theological thought could scarcely be imagined.

In one point, however, we do find in Ezk a further development of the Messianic idea, namely, that in His work, in addition to His characteristics as a king, the Messiah has also those of a high priest, as this is shown at the same period by Jeremiah (see under I, 1, and 2, 3; cf later Zec **3** f, and possibly **6** 9 ff). The *miçnepheth*, which the Messiah bears according to Ezk **21** 26, is in other connections always the mitre of the high priest (cf Ex **28** 4.39; **29** 6; **39** 28.31; see above II, 2, 1*a* and 2*c*). At the Passover feast, at least, the *prince* conducts a purification through a bullock for a sin offering, which, through the fact that this is done for himself and for the entire people of the land, reminds us of the ceremony of the high priest on the day of atonement (Ezk **45** 22; Lev **16** 17.24.33; cf Day of Atonement, I, 1, and *Messianische Erwartung der vorexilischen Propheten*, 356 ff). Over against the current view, we finally emphasize the fact that Ezekiel's expectations of a Messianic feature are not confined to Israel, but like those of Isaiah (**2** 2 ff; **11** 10; Mic **5** 3.6) and of other prophets are universal in their scope (cf Ezk **17** 23; **16** 53.61; **34** 26).

4. Ezekiel and Apocalyptic Literature

Ezekiel is also, finally, regarded as the creator of apocalyptic lit., which in prophetic garment sought to satisfy the curiosity of the people and picture the details of the last times. In this connection the critics have in mind esp. Ezk **38, 39,** that magnificent picture of the final onslaught of the nations under Gog and Magog, which will end with the certain victory of the Divine cause and the terrible overthrow of the enemies of Jeh. On the mountains of Israel the hosts will fall (**39** 4); seven years it will be possible to kindle fires with the weapons of the enemies (**39** 9); it takes seven months to bury the dead (**39** 12); a great feast is prepared for the birds (**39** 17 ff).

In reply to this there are two things to be said. First of all Ezekiel is not the creator of these thoughts. There is a whole list of passages in the Prophets that already before his time picture how matters will be after and beyond the Messianic age (cf Mic **2** 12*b* f; **4** 11 f; **5** 4 f.7.20; Joel **3** 2.12 f; Isa **11** 4; **28** 6; Hos **2** 2). These are, however, all regarded by the critics as not genuine, or as the product of a later period, but they forget in this to observe that Ezekiel in these passages refers to older prophets (**38** 17; **39** 8), and thus they saw off the branch upon which he sits. In regard, however, to painting the fullest details of the picture, Ezekiel is equaled by none of his predecessors. In this matter, too, he represents the highest point of development, in which he is followed by Zec **12; 13** 7 ff; **14** 1 ff, and Dnl, and with direct dependence on Ezk **38** f by the Apocalypse of St. John (ch **19** 17 ff). On the other hand, Ezk is entirely different from the later Jewish apocalyptic lit. The latter borrowed the prophetic form but possesses neither the Divine contents nor the Divine inspiration of the prophet. For this reason the apocalyptic lit. appears anonymously or under a pseudonym. Ezekiel, however, openly places his name over his prophecies. In Ezk the eschatology is a part of his prophetic mission, and as he in his thoughts throughout remains within the bounds of the religious and ethical ideals of prophecy, this feature, too, of his work is to be regarded as a Divine revelation in a form in harmony with the OT stage of the development of the kingdom of God. We are here indeed considering a matter in connection with which it is esp. difficult to determine how much in reality belongs to the eternally valid contents, and how much to the temporary forms. Here too, as is the case in the exegesis of chs **40–48,** Christian theology will vacillate between the extremes of spiritualism and realism, one extreme constantly correcting the other, and in this way constantly approaching the correct middle course, until at some time in the future we will reach the full truth in the matter.

5. Ezekiel's Conception of God

A prophet who, from the aesthetic side, enjoyed the highest appreciation of a Schiller and a Herder (see 1 above), who has brought the Leviticism of the OT to the highest stage of development (cf 2 above), who in his portrait of the Messiah has introduced the high-priestly characteristics (cf 3 above), who in eschatology developed new features and laid the foundation for the development that followed in later times (cf 4 above), can scarcely with any right or reason be termed a "secondary character among the prophets." This fact becomes all the more sure when we now finally examine the conception of God as taught in Ezk. In grandeur and variety of thought, in this respect only, Isaiah and Moses can be compared with Ezekiel. Already in the visions, we are struck by the sublimity of God as there pictured, esp. in the opening vision, where He appears as the absolute ruler of all creation, over which He sits enthroned (cf II, 1, above). He is constantly called "the Lord Jehovah," over against whom the prophet is at all times only "the son of man." More than fifty times it is said that the purpose of the prophecy was that the heathen nations, as well as the Israelites, shall by His judgments and His promises recognize that He is Jehovah.

On this side Ezekiel stands in an esp. close relation to the description of the exodus from Egypt (cf Ex **7** 5.17; **8** 10.22; **9** 14.29.30; **10** 2; **11** 7; **14** 4.18, and see Exodus, II, 2, on **7** 8—**13** 16). Above everything Jeh's honor must be defended (**36** 23.32). Here again there is a place where the evolutionist hypothesis of the development of the idea of God is thoroughly put to shame. For in the preprophetic times it is claimed that God is, in the OT, merely placed by the side of other gods and was regarded only as the God of Israel, with which He was indissolubly connected, because His existence had depended on the existence of the nation. As a proof, reference is made to the defence of His honor; and now we find the same thought in Ezekiel, in whose case it is impossible that any doubt as to his absolute monotheism can any longer arise (cf my *Entwicklung der Gottesidee in vorexilischer Zeit,* 138 ff, 152 ff). The sublimity of this conception of God also appears in its universality. He is declared to be punishing the nations (cf chs **25** ff, **35** f); He uses them for His purposes (cf chs **38** f, **17, 19, 24, 33**); He intends to give them salvation (chs **17, 23; 16** 53.61; **34** 26; cf 3 above).

Most of all, Ezekiel's conception of God, according to the preceding sketch, reminds us of that of Calvin. By the exalted character of God we find also a second feature. On the one side we find the holy God; on the other, sinful man. The entire development of the people is from the beginning a wrong one. Ezekiel's thoughts are to be regarded as those for days of penance when he, on the one hand, emphasizes the great guilt of the people as such (cf chs **16** and **23**), and by the side of this maintains the principle that each one must be punished on account of his own sins (**18** 2), so that the individual cannot excuse himself, and the individual cannot be freed through the guilt of the people as a totality.

But now comes the highest conception. The exalted and holy God comes to be a God of love. What is it but love, that He does not reject His people forever, but promises them a future (cf chs **34–48,** in which also the divided kingdoms are to be reunited, **37** 15 ff)? As Ex finds its culmination point in the indwelling of God among His people, which He promised in Ex **25** ff (**25** 8; **29** 45 f), but seems to have become a matter of doubt again in chs **32** ff through the apostasy of the people, and nevertheless is finally realized in chs **35** ff (**40** 34 ff), thus too in Ezk **10** f, Jeh leaves the city, but in **43** 1 ff He again returns, and now the name of the city is "Jehovah is there" (**48** 35). But as every single member participates in the sin and the punishment of the people, so too he takes part in the deliverance.

Ezekiel is indeed, as little as is Jeremiah, the creator of individualism, which he has often been declared to be. Against this claim, e.g. the character of the patriarchs can be appealed to. But a deeper conception of individualism has actually been brought about by Jeremiah and Ezekiel. The national organization as such was for the present dissolved. Accordingly, these prophets have now to deal more with the individual (cf 1, 2, 3, above). Ezekiel is actually the pastor of those in exile. He has been appointed the watchman of the house of Israel (**3** 16 ff and **33** 1 ff). He can bear the responsibility for the individual souls (cf also ch **18**). The wicked man who dies without having been warned is demanded from his hand by God. Jeh does not wish the death of the sinner, but that he should repent and live.

Here such a clear mirror is given, that before it conscientious Christian preachers must all feel ashamed. Jeh is the gracious God, who does not treat men simply according to the principle of retaliation, else what would become of man? God rather desires to bestow all things out of free grace; he that repents shall live. This is the highest ideal of the prophet, and with it we close.

The Feast of Weeks, the Pentecost of the Israelites, Ezekiel does not mention (cf II, 2, 2*b*, above). This festival has come to be one of higher importance since on Pentecost the Holy Spirit was poured out, and this Spirit Ezekiel knows. Besides, such passages as Jer **32** 15; **44** 1–6; Ps **51** 12 ff; Joel **2** 28 ff; Jer **31** 31 ff, it is Ezk which contains the clearest predictions of Pentecost. It is the Spirit who in ch **37** awakens to new life the dead bones of Israel.

And in **36** 25–28 we read: "And I will sprinkle clean water upon you, and ye shall be clean: from all your filthiness, and from all your idols, will I cleanse you. A new heart also will I give you, and a new spirit will I put within you; and I will take away the stony heart out of your flesh, and I will give you a heart of flesh. And I will put my Spirit within you, and cause you to walk in my statutes, and ye shall keep mine ordinances, and do them. And ye shall dwell in the land that I gave to your fathers; and ye shall be my people, and I will be your God."

Literature.—Comm. of Keil, Hävernick, Hengstenberg, von Orelli, Smend, Bertholet, Kraetzschmar.

For the Messianic Prophecies, the works of von Orelli, Riehm, Delitzsch, Hengstenberg. Compare also Volz, *Die vorexilische Jahwe-Prophetie und der Messias;* Möller, *Die messianische Erwartung der vorexilischen Propheten, zugleich ein Protest gegen moderne Textzersplitterung;* Cornill, *The Prophet Ezekiel;* Klostermann, *Studien und Kritiken*, 1877.

Intro of Kuenen, Strack, Baudissin, König, Cornill, Driver.

Histories of Israel, by Köhler, König, Kittel, Klostermann, Oettli, Stade, Wellhausen.

Bible Lexicons, see under "Ezekiel."

Against the Graf-Wellhausen Hypothesis, Möller, *Are the Critics Right?* In this Encyclopaedia, for further literature compare also the art. Leviticus; Orr, *POT;* Wiener, *Essays in Pentateuchal Criticism*, and *The Origin of the Pent;* Hoffmann, *Die wichtigsten Instanzen gegen die Graf-Wellhausensche Hypothese;* Kegel, *Wilhelm Vatke u. die Graf-Wellhausensche Hypothese;* Zunz, *Die gottesdienstlichen Vorträge der Juden;* Seinecke, *Geschichte des Volkes Israel*, II.

Wilhelm Möller

EZEL, ē′zel (הָאֶזֶל, *hā-'āzel;* LXX **παρὰ τὸ ἐργὰβ ἐκεῖνο,** *pará tó ergáb ekeíno*): As it stands, the narrative in 1 S **20** 19 records the tryst of Jonathan with David at the stone Ezel. The name occurs only here. There is general agreement that the text is corrupt, but there is no agreement as to how it should be restored. The LXX reads "this mound" (RVm), or "yonder cairn"; and in ver 41 instead of "out of a place toward the South" it reads "from beside the mound" or "cairn." Dr. Cheyne suggests "yonder juniper tree" (*EB* s.v.).

EZEM, ē′zem (עֶצֶם, *'eçem,* "bone"; **Βοοσάλ,** *Boosál,* **Βοασόμ,** *Boasóm*): A city in the extreme S. of Judah, assigned to Simeon. Some identify it with Azmon (Josh **15** 29; **19** 3; 1 Ch **4** 29).

EZER, ē′zẽr (עֵזֶר, *'ēzer,* "help"):

(1) A Horite chief (Gen **36** 21; 1 Ch **1** 38).

(2) A Judahite (1 Ch **4** 4).

(3) An Ephraimite, slain by men of Gath (1 Ch **7** 21).

(4) A Gadite who followed David while in exile on account of the wrath of Saul (1 Ch **12** 9).

(5) One of those who under direction of Nehemiah repaired the wall of Jerus (Neh **3** 19).

(6) A musician in one of the great companies appointed by Nehemiah to give thanks at the dedication of the wall of Jerus (Neh **12** 42).

EZERIAS, ez-ē-rī′as (**'Εζερίας,** *Ezerías*): 1 Esd **8** 1 AV, RV "Zechrias," the Azariah of Ezr **7** 1.

EZIAS, ē-zī′as: RV OZIAS (q.v.).

EZION-GEBER, ē-zi-on-gē′bẽr (עֶצְיוֹן גֶּבֶר, *'eçyōn gebher;* **Γασιών Γάβερ,** *Gasiōn Gáber*): Always mentioned along with Elath ("Eziongaber," Nu **33** 35 f AV). When the children of Israel left "the way of the Arabah," having come from the N.W., they seem to have turned to the N.E. from the neighborhood of 'Aḳaba, passing up by *Wādy el-Ithm* toward the eastern desert (Dt **2** 8). Elath and Ezion-geber were evidently not far apart. They are named together again in connection with the maritime enterprises of Solomon and Jehoshaphat (1 K **9** 26, etc). They therefore both lay on the shore of the sea. No trace of Ezion-geber is to be found on the present coast line. It is probable, however, that in ancient times the sea covered a considerable stretch of the mud flats at the S. end of *Wādy el-'Arabah,* and the site of Ezion-geber may be sought near the spring *'Ain el-Ghuḍyān,* about 15 miles N. of the present head of the Gulf of 'Aḳaba. W. Ewing

EZNITE, ez′nīt (עֶצְנִי or עֶצְנוֹ, *'eçnī* or *'eçnō*). See Adino.

EZORA, ē-zō′ra (**'Εζωρά,** *Ezōrá,* AV **Ozora**): He and his six sons "gave their hands to put away their strange wives" (1 Esd **9** 20.34="Machnadebai" of Ezr **10** 40).

EZRA, ez′ra (Aram. or Chaldee, עֶזְרָא, *'ezrā',* "help"; a hypocoristicon, or shortened form of Azariah, "Jeh has helped." The Heb spells the name עֶזְרָה, *'ezrāh,* as in 1 Ch **4** 17, or uses the Aram. spelling of the name, as in Ezr **7** 1. The Gr form is Esdras):

(1) A priest who returned with Zerubbabel from Babylon (Neh **12** 1). In Neh **10** 2, Azariah, the full form of the name, is found.

(2) A descendant of Judah and father of Jethro and other sons (1 Ch **4** 17).

(3) The distinguished priest who is the hero of the Book of Ezr and coworker with Nehemiah.

1. Family

The genealogy of Ezra is given in Ezr **7** 1–6, where it appears that he was the son of Seraiah, the son of Azariah, the son of Hilkiah, the son of Shallum, the son of Ahitub, the son of Amariah, the son of Azariah, the son of Meraioth, the son of Zerahiah, the son of Uzzi, the son of Bukki, the son of Abishua, the son of Phinehas, the son of Eleazar, the son of Aaron, the high priest. Since Seraiah, according to the Book of K, was killed by Nebuchadrezzar at Riblah (2 K **25** 18–21), and since he was the father of Jehozadak, the high priest who was carried into captivity by Nebuchadrezzar (1 Ch **6** 14.15 [Heb **5** 40], etc) in 588 BC, and since the return under Ezra took place in 458 BC, the word "son" must be used in Ezr **7** 2 in the sense of descendant. Since, moreover, Joshua, or Jeshua, the high priest, who returned from Babylon with Zerubbabel, was the son of Jehozadak and the grandson of Seraiah, Ezra was probably the great-grandson or great-great-grandson of Seraiah. Inasmuch as Jehozadak is never mentioned as one of his forefathers, Ezra was probably not descended from Jehozadak, but from a younger brother. He would thus not be a high priest, though he was of high-priestly descent as far as Seraiah. For the sake of shortening the list of names, six names are omitted in Ezr **7** 2–7 between Azariah and Meraioth, and one between Shallum and Ahitub from the corresponding list found in 1 Ch **6** 4–14 (Heb **5** 30–40).

2. Occupation

Being a priest by birth, it is to be supposed that Ezra would have performed the ordinary functions of a member of his order, if he had been born and had lived in Pal. Jos, indeed, says that he was high priest of his brethren in Babylon, a statement that in view of the revelation of the Elephantine papyri may not be without a foundation in fact. According to the Scriptures and Jewish tradition, however, Ezra was preëminently a scribe, and esp. a scribe of the law of Moses. He is called "a ready scribe in the law of Moses," a "scribe of the words of the commandments of Jeh, and of his statutes to Israel," "the scribe of the law of the God of heaven." As early as the time of Jeremiah (cf Jer **8** 8), "scribe" had already attained the meaning of one learned in the Scriptures, one who had made the written law a subject of investigation. Ezra is the first who is called by the title of "the scribe," the title by which Artaxerxes designates him in his letter of instructions in Ezr **7** 6.11.

3. His Commission

In the 7th year of Artaxerxes I (459–458 BC) Ezra requested permission of the king to go up to Jerus; for "Ezra had set his heart to seek the law of Jeh, and to do it, and to teach in Israel statutes and ordinances." Artaxerxes granted his request, and gave him a letter permitting as many of the people of Israel and of the priests and Levites as so desired to accompany him to Jerus, and commissioning him to inquire concerning Judah and Jerus, and to carry a gift of money from the king and his counsellors, and all the money to be found in the province of Babylon, and the freewill offerings of the people and priests, with which to buy offerings to offer upon the altar of the house of God which was in Jerus. He was commissioned also to carry vessels for the service of the house of God, and to do at the expense of the royal treasury whatever was needful for the house of God. The king decreed, moreover, that the treasurers of the king should assist Ezra with a tribute of wheat, wine, oil and salt, and that they should impose no tribute, custom or toll upon any of those employed in the service of the house of God. Moreover, Ezra was authorized to appoint judges to judge the people according to the law of God and the law of the king, and to inflict punishments upon all who would not obey these laws.

Ascribing this marvelous letter of the king to the lovingkindness of his God, and strengthened by this evidence of God's power, Ezra proceeded to gather together out of Israel the chief men and teachers and ministers of the house to go up with him to Jerus. He gathered these men in camp at Casiphia, on the river Ahava. Here he proclaimed a time of fasting and prayer, that God might prosper their journey (Ezr **8** 15–23). Then, having delivered the treasures into the hands of the priests, the assembled company departed for Jerus, where by the help of God they arrived in safety, delivered over the money and gifts by number and weight, offered burnt offerings and sin offerings, delivered the king's commissions and furthered the people and the house of God.

Shortly after Ezra's arrival at Jerus, the princes accused the people, the priests, and the Levites of having intermarried with the peoples of the land, even asserting that the princes and rulers had been leaders in the trespass. Upon hearing this, Ezra was confounded, rent his garments, plucked off his hair, fell upon his knees and prayed a prayer of confession, weeping and casting himself down before the house of God. While he prayed the people assembled and wept, acknowledged their sin and promised to do according to the law. The whole people were then assembled in counsel, and in spite of some opposition the strange wives were put away.

In Neh **8**, Ezra appears again upon the scene at the Feast of Tabernacles as the chief scribe of the law of Moses, the leader of the priests and Levites who read and explained the law to the people. On his advice the people ceased from their mourning and celebrated the festival according to the law of Moses with joy and thanksgiving and giving of gifts, dwelling also in booths in commemoration of the manner of their fathers' sojourning while in the wilderness.

4. Traditions The traditions with regard to Ezra found in Jos and in the Talm are so discrepant that it is impossible to place reliance upon any of their statements which are not found also in the canonical Scriptures.

R. Dick Wilson

EZRA-NEHEMIAH:

1. Name The books of Ezr and Neh, by whomsoever written, are properly so named according to analogy from the principal persons mentioned in them. In the Heb Bibles, the former is headed simply, Ezra, and the latter, Nehemiah. The two books are counted in the Talm, in Jos, and in the Canon of Melito, 171 AD, as one, and are so treated also in the subscription of the MT, which reads: "The totality of the verses of Ezr and Neh is 688, and its sign is 'Remember, Jeh, the reproach of thy servants,' and its two parts [are at the sentence] 'unto the ascent of the corner' [Neh **3** 31] and its chapters (*ṣ^edhārāyw*) are ten, and its sign is 'Upon a high mountain get thee up, O thou that announcest good tidings to Zion.'" In the LXX, Ezr-Neh is called Esdras B, while an apocryphal Book of Ezr is called Esdras A (see below). In the catalogues of the OT writings handed down to us by the Fathers (Origen, Cyril, Melito, Jerome and the Council of Laodicea) our Ezr is called 1 Ezr; Neh, 2 Ezr; the apocryphal Gr Ezr, 3 Ezr; and an apocalyptic book, falsely called a book of Ezr, is denominated 4 Ezr.

2. Object The object of the books is to show that God fulfilled His promise, or prophecy, to restore His exiled people to their inheritance, through the instrumentality on the one hand of the great heathen monarchs, Cyrus, Darius and Artaxerxes, and on the other hand by stirring up the spirit of such great men among the chosen people as Joshua and Zerubbabel, Haggai and Zechariah, and Ezra and Nehemiah, through whom the altar, the temple, the houses and walls of Jerus, and finally the worship and ceremony of the Jewish people were reëstablished, the people being separated from foreign admixtures, customs and idolatry, and their religious observances purified and fixed for all time.

3. Plan The object of the work justifies the selection and arrangement of the material and the plan pursued by the composer, or composers; all matter being stringently excluded which does not bear directly upon the purpose in view. However much we may wish that other historical records had been included, it is not proper to criticize the work because of these omissions, nor is it fair to argue that the writer was ignorant of what he has not seen fit to record.

4. Unity The unity of the combined work is shown by the fact that they have the same common object, the same plan, and a similarity of language and style; that they treat, for the most part, of the same period of time; and that Ezra is one of the most prominent persons in both. It is not fair to deny the essential unity on the ground that the list of priests and others found in Ezr **2** is repeated in Neh **7**; for there is no doubt that Ezra was the compiler of parts at least of the book called after him, and that Nehemiah also was the original writer of parts of the book that bears his name. Whoever was the final editor of the whole work, he has simply retained the two almost identical lists in their appropriate places in the documents which lay before him.

5. Sources The Books of Ezr and Neh are a compilation of genealogical lists, letters and edicts, memoirs and chronicles. We cannot be certain as to who was the composer of either or both books. Many think that Ezra compiled both the books out of preëxisting materials, adding parts of his own composition. Others, suppose that Ezra wrote the book named after him, while Nehemiah composed the Book of Neh. Others, again, are of the opinion that neither Ezra nor Nehemiah, but some other unknown editor, most probably the compiler of the Books of Ch, put together the Books of Ezr and Neh, using largely the memoirs of the two great men who are the principal persons in the records. While there is still much difference of opinion as to who was the final redactor, there is a general agreement as to the composite character of the whole, and that the person who wrote the parts that bind together the original sources was the same as he who wrote the canonical books of Chronicles.

6. Literary Character of the Books The diversified character of the style, languages and other literary peculiarities of the books is accounted for by the large number and the variety of sources. From the style and contents of the first chapter it has been argued with great plausibility that it was written by Daniel; for similar reasons it has been argued that the portion of Ezr from **3** 2 to **4** 22 inclusive was written by Haggai the prophet. All admit that the parts of Ezr and Neh in which the 1st per. is employed were written by Ezra and Nehemiah respectively. As to who it was who added the other connecting portions there is and must always be great doubt arising from the fact that the author is not mentioned. The style points to the same hand as that which composed the Book of Chronicles. Those who believe that Ezra compiled the Book of Ch will believe that he most probably composed also the Books of Ezr and Neh. The principal objection to his authorship arises from the inexplicable change from the 1st to the 3d per. occurring in both Ezr and Neh. Inasmuch as the 3d per. is the proper form to use in the best style of Bib. historical composition; inasmuch as Herodotus, Thucydides and Xenophon often employ it in their histories; inasmuch as some of the Bab monuments mingle the 1st and 3d pers. in the same document; and finally, inasmuch as the prophets and psalmists of Israel likewise interchange the persons in what is for us often an unaccountable manner: this characteristic of the style of Ezr-Neh seems an insufficient reason upon which to base the denial of the claim that Ezra may have been the author.

The facts that there is unevenness in the treatment of the history, and that there are long periods on which the narrator is silent, do not militate against the authorship of Ezra nor do they imply a date long after his age; for the author is perfectly consistent in his purpose to stick to the object and plan which he had in view for himself, that is, to give an account of the reëstablishment of the Israelitish people and of their Divinely given institutions. That he has omitted other matters does not imply that he was ignorant of them.

7. Languages The language of the books is Heb, except Ezr **4** 7—**6** 18 and **7** 12-26, which is written in Aram. The Heb closely resembles that of Dnl, Hag and Ch, much more so than it does that of Ecclus, which was written probably about 180 BC. The Aram. (formerly called Chaldee) is very much like that of the Egyp papyri which are dated in the 5th cent. BC. It closely resembles also the Aram. in Dnl.

Neither language nor style can be assigned as a ground for asserting a date later than the 5th cent. BC as the time of the composition of the book. A much stronger reason against placing the final redaction of the books at so early a time is the mention of a Jaddua among the high priests in Neh **12** 11.22, it being assumed that this is the same Jaddua whom Jos mentions (*Ant*, XI, viii, 4) as having filled the high-priestly office in the time of Alexander the Great. In view of the fact that Jos is the only source of information as to the period between 400 and 300 BC, it seems unfair to accept what he says as to the existence of this Jaddua, while rejecting substantially all the rest of the same chapter in Jos which tells about Sanballat, Manasseh and Alexander's meeting with Jaddua. Inasmuch as the Sachau papyri, written in the 17th year of Darius Nothus, that is, in 410–408 BC, mention the sons of Sanballat the governor of Samaria, the Sanballat who was their father must have lived about 450 BC. The same papyrus mentions Jehohanan (Johanan of Neh **12** 22) as the high priest of the temple at Jerus, and Bagohi (Bagoas) was the Pers governor of Jerus in 410–408 BC. Since, according to Neh **13** 6, Nehemiah was governor in 434–433 BC, the 32d year of Artaxerxes, Bagoas would be perhaps his immediate successor. If we are to put any confidence in the story of Jos, then there must have been at least two Sanballats, and probably two Jadduas, and at two different times a son of a high priest must have married a daughter of a Sanballat. While this is not impossible, it seems better to suppose that Jos has confused matters beyond any possibility of disentanglement, and we might be justified in throwing over entirely his account of a Sanballat, a Manasseh, and a Jaddua as living in the year 330 BC, when Alexander conquered Syria. As far, of course, as the Jaddua of Neh **12** 11.22 is concerned, he may well have been high priest as early as 406 BC, and have continued to serve till 330 BC. On the other hand, another of the same name, probably a grandson, may, for all we know to the contrary, have been high priest in 330 BC. In view of the numerous Oniases, Simons, and Johns who served in that position between 600 and 150 BC, and in view, further, of our almost absolute lack of information as to the history of this period, it will be a bold man who will dare to deny, on the ground of the Jaddua of Jos, that Ezr-Neh might have been written as early as 400 BC.

8. Historicity

The objection against the books having been composed in the Pers period, based upon the use of the titles of the kings of Persia, is fully answered by the fact that the same titles as those used in these books are found to have been used by the Pers kings themselves. (See the arts. of the present writer in the *Presbyterian Reformed Review* for 1905–6.) The "Darius the Persian" of Neh **12** 22 is shown by the Sachau papyri to have been Darius Nothus, as Keil long ago suggested. The author may have called him "the Persian" to distinguish him from Darius the Mede. At any rate, it is best for us to remember that our inability to explain why the author called him by this title does not prove that he did not do so. Of all the Dariuses known to history, any one might have been called "the Persian," except Darius the Mede, because all but he were Persians. The assertion that a king of Persia could only have been called a Persian "after the Pers period was past" involves, on the one hand, the assumption of such thorough knowledge of the possibilities of the *usus loquendi* of that time, and, on the other hand, such real ignorance of the usage of all times in such matters, as well as of the usage of the Pers and Bab monuments of the Pers era, as almost to cause one to believe that it can scarcely have been seriously made. (See the writer's arts. cited above.) Jos, it is true, apparently confuses in his account Darius II and Darius III.

The phrase "the days of Nehemiah" (ver 26) certainly implied that the final redactor "looked back upon them as past." But there is no intimation as to how long they were past. According to Neh **5** 14, Nehemiah returned to Babylon in the 32d year of Artaxerxes, that is, in 434 BC. As Bagoas was already governor of Jerus, and Johanan high priest in 408 BC, a writer living about 400 BC can very well have referred to what happened "in the days of Joiakim . . . . and in the days of Nehemiah the governor, and of Ezra the priest and the scribe" as having occurred "in the days of Zerubbabel, and in the days of Nehemiah" (**12** 47). From all we know it appears that these were the only Jews who were ever governors of Jerus under the Pers domination. Certainly Bagoas is not a Heb name any more than Sanballat, and it looks as if on the death of Nehemiah his place as governor of Jerus had been filled by a native Persian, just as the governorship of Samaria was held by Sanballat, a Cuthean. If we can trust Jos, Bagoas treated the Jews with harshness and even desecrated the temple itself (*Ant*, XI, vii, 1). Already, then, in 405 BC, any patriotic and pious Israelite may have justly looked back upon the days of their native governors with longing and pride, and have written with appropriate eulogy of the days of Zerubbabel, Nehemiah and Ezra—the time of his people's semi-independence and of the glorious and unforgetable restoration of the temple and city, just as we today refer to the time of Bismarck, Victoria, or Lincoln (cf 1 Ch **13** 3). Waiving the discussion of the probability of Ezra's having called himself "a ready scribe in the law of Moses," and one who had prepared his heart to seek the law of the Lord, etc, it certainly cannot be denied that someone writing in 405 BC may have employed the language here used. There is not the slightest proof that any of Ezr-Neh is unhistorical, nor the least indication that all of it may not have been written as early as 405 BC.

The section Ezr **4** 1–6 presents difficulties of date and composition. The section may have been misplaced. It may be episodical. It may be explained, as suggested by Klostermann, as having been inserted here as a sort of résumé which is later expanded. But however explained, it is a literary rather than a historical or linguistic problem which it presents, and may safely be left for solution to those who think that everything in literature whose purpose or meaning they cannot perceive is therefore inexplicable.

In conclusion, we would say in the words of Professor Cornill, that since Ed. Meyer's demonstration of the authenticity of the documents in Ezr **4–7**, the hypercritical reconstruction of the books "has lost all claim to serious consideration, and we may rest assured that in Ezr-Neh we have every reason to recognize an essentially trustworthy recital of the events narrated therein."

9. Text

The most thorough investigation of the text of Ezr-Neh has been made by Professor A. Klostermann, his results being published in the 3d German ed of *RE*. After an examination of the Arab., Syr, Gr and Lat VSS and a comparison of them with the Heb MT, he comes to the conclusion that our Heb text as a whole is of more value than that represented by the VSS. The writer of this art. has noted a wonderful accuracy in the transmission of the Aram. part of Ezr, the spelling or writing of the words resembling in many of the smallest particulars that of the Aram. papyri of Elephantine, which date from the 5th cent. BC.

Literature.—Commentaries and Introductions: A, Introductions: Sayce, *Intro to Ezr, Neh, Est;* Angus-Suen, *The Cyclopedic Hand-Book to the Bible;* Rarnu, *Intro to the OT;* Keil, *OT Intro.* B, Commentaries: Keil, *Ezr, Neh, and Est;* Rawlinson, in the *Speaker's Comm.*, and in the *Pulpit Comm.;* and in *Ezr and Neh* ("Men of the Bible" series); Lange's *Comm.;* Meyer, *Entstehung des Judenthums; OTJC*[2]; *RE*[2].

R. Dick Wilson

EZRAHITE, ez′ra-hīt (אֶזְרָחִי, *'ezrāḥī;* **'Ασεβών,** *Asebṓn*): Found in 1 K **4** 31; Pss **88, 89,** titles; from which it appears that the word is a patronymic for Ethan and Heman. It may be derived from Zerah, instead of Ezrah, seeing that there were an Ethan and a Heman who were descendants of Zerah, head of a Judahite family (1 Ch **2** 6). There were also an Ethan and a Heman who were Levites (1 Ch **15** 17).

EZRI, ez′rī (עֶזְרִי, *'ezrī,* "my help"; **'Εζραί,** *Ezraí,* or **'Εζδρί,** *Ezdrí*): "Ezri, the son of Chelub," appointed by David to be superintendent of agriculture (1 Ch **27** 26).

EZRIL, ez′ril (**'Εζρίλ,** *Ezríl,* AV Esril): One who had married a foreign wife (1 Esd **9** 34); called Azarel in Ezr **10** 41.

F

FABLE, fā′b'l (**μῦθος,** *múthos*):

(1) Primitive man conceives of the objects around him as possessing his own characteristics. Consequently in his stories, beasts, trees, rocks, etc, think, talk and act exactly as if they were human beings. Of course, but little advance in knowledge was needed to put an end to this mode of thought, but the form of story-telling developed by it persisted and is found in the folk-tales of all nations. More particularly, the archaic form of story was used for the purpose of moral instruction, and when so used is termed the *fable.* Modern definitions distinguish it from the parable (*a*) by its use of characters of lower intelligence than man (although reasoning and speaking like men), and (*b*) by its lesson for this life only. But, while these distinctions serve some practical purpose in distinguishing (say) the fables of Aesop from the parables of Christ, they are of little value to the student of folk-lore. For fable, parable, allegory, etc, are all evolutions from a common stock, and they tend to blend with each other. See Allegory; Parable.

(2) The Sem mind is peculiarly prone to allegorical expression, and a modern Arabian story-teller will invent a fable or a parable as readily as he will talk. And we may be entirely certain that the very scanty appearance of fables in the OT is due only to the character of its material and not at all to an absence of fables from the mouths of the Jews of old. Only two examples have reached us. In Jgs **9** 7–15 Jotham mocks the choice of Abimelech as king with the fable of the trees that could find no tree that would accept the trouble of the kingship except the worthless bramble. And in 2 K **14** 9 Jehoash ridicules the pretensions of Amaziah with the story of the thistle that wished to make a royal alliance with the cedar. Yet that the distinction between fable and allegory, etc, is artificial is seen in Isa **5** 1.2, where the vineyard is assumed to possess a deliberate will to be perverse.

(3) In the NT, "fable" is found in 1 Tim **1** 4; **4** 7; 2 Tim **4** 4; Tit **1** 14; 2 Pet **1** 16, as the tr of *muthos* ("myth"). The sense here differs entirely from that discussed above, and "fable" means a (religious) story that has no connection with reality—contrasted with the knowledge of an eyewitness in 2 Pet **1** 16. The exact nature of these "fables" is of course something out of our knowledge, but the mention in connection with them of "endless genealogies" in 1 Tim **1** 4 points with high probability to some form of gnostic speculation that interposed a chain of aeons between God and the world. In some of the gnostic systems that we know, these chains are described with a prolixity so interminable (the *Pistis Sophia* is the best example) as to justify well the phrase "old wives' fables" in 1 Tim **4** 7. But that these passages have gnostic reference need not tell against the Pauline authorship of the Pastorals, as a fairly well developed "Gnosticism" is recognizable in a passage as early as Col **2,** and as the description of the fables as Jewish in Tit **1** 14 (cf **3** 9) is against 2d-cent. references. But for details the commentaries on the Pastoral Epistles must be consulted. It is worth noting that in 2 Tim **4** 4 the adoption of these fables is said to be the result of dabbling in the dubious. This manner of losing one's hold on reality is, unfortunately, something not confined to the apostolic age.

Burton Scott Easton

FACE, fās: In Heb the tr of three expressions: (1) פָּנִים, *pānīm,* (2) עַיִן, *'ayin,* lit. "eye," and (3) אַף, *'aph,* lit. "nose," "nostril," already noted s.v. Countenance, which see. The first and second of these words are used synonymously, even in metaphorical expressions, as, e.g. in the phrase "the face of the earth," where *pānīm* is used (Dt **6** 15 *et passim*) and *'ayin* (Nu **22** 5 *et passim*). The third expression preserves more clearly its original meaning. It is generally used in the phrases "to bow one's self to the earth," "to fall on one's face," where the nose actually touched the ground. Often "my face," "thy face" is mere oriental circumlocution for the personal pronoun "I," "me," "thou," "thee." "In thy face" means "in thy presence," and is often so tr[d]. A very large number of idiomatic Heb expressions have been introduced into our language through the medium of the Bible tr. We notice the most important of these phrases.

"To seek the face" is to seek an audience with a prince or with God, to seek favor (Ps **24** 6; **27** 8 *bis;* **105** 4; Prov **7** 15; Hos **5** 15; cf Prov **29** 26, where RV translates "Many seek the ruler's favor," lit. many seek the face [Heb *pᵉnē*] of a ruler).

If God "hides his face" He withdraws His presence, His favor (Dt **32** 20; Job **34** 29; Ps **13** 1; **30** 7; **143** 7; Isa **54** 8; Jer **33** 5; Ezk **39** 23.24; Mic **3** 4). Such withdrawal of the presence of God is to be understood as a consequence of man's personal disobedience, not as a wrathful denial of God's favor (Isa **59** 2). God is asked to "hide his face," i.e. to disregard or overlook (Ps **51** 9; cf **10** 11). This is also the idea of the prayer: "Cast me not away from thy presence" (lit. "face," Ps **51** 11), and of the promise: "The upright shall dwell in thy presence" (lit. "face," Ps **140** 13). If used of men, "to hide the face" expresses humility and reverence before an exalted presence (Ex **3** 6; Isa **6** 2); similarly Elijah "wrapped his face in his mantle" when God passed by (1 K **19** 13). The "covering of the face" is a sign of mourning (2 S **19** 4=Ezk **12** 6.12); a "face covered with fatness" is synonymous with prosperity and arrogance (Job

15 27); to have one's face covered by another person is a sign of hopeless doom, as if one were already dead. This was done to Haman, when judgment had been pronounced over him (Est **7** 8).

"To turn away one's face" is a sign of insulting indifference or contempt (2 Ch **29** 6; Ezk **14** 6; Sir **4** 4; cf Jer **2** 27; **18** 17; **32** 33); on the part of God an averted face is synonymous with rejection (Ps **13** 1; **27** 9; **88** 14).

"To harden the face" means to harden one's self against any sort of appeal (Prov **21** 29; Isa **50** 7; Jer **5** 3; cf Ezk **3** 9). See also Spit.

In this connection we also mention the phrase "to respect persons," lit. to "recognize the face" (Lev **19** 15, or, slightly different in expression, Dt **1** 17; **16** 19; Prov **24** 23; **28** 21), in the sense of unjustly favoring a person, or requiting him with undue evil. Compare also the Heb *hādhar* (Ex **23** 3 AV), "to countenance" (see s.v.).

The "showbread" meant lit. "bread of the face," "of the presence," Heb *leḥem pānīm;* Gr *ártoi enṓpioi, ártoi tḗs prothéseōs.*

H. L. E. Luering

FACT: Lit. "a deed." The word occurs only in the heading of the chapter, 2 K **10** AV, "Jehu excuseth the fact by the prophecy of Elijah," and in 2 Macc **4** 36, with reference to the murder of Onias, "certain of the Greeks that abhorred the fact [the deed] also" (*summisoponēroúntōn,* lit. "hating wickedness together with [others]," RV "the Greeks also joining with them in hatred of the wickedness."

FADE, fād (נָבֵל, *nābhēl;* **μαραίνω,** *maraínō*): "To fade" is in the OT the tr of *nābhēl,* "to droop or wither," **fig.** "to fade," or "pass way" (Ps **18** 45; Isa **1** 30; **24** 4; **28** 1.4; **40** 7.8); once it is the tr of *bālal,* "to well up," "to overflow"; perhaps from *nābhal* (Isa **64** 6, "We all do fade as a leaf"); in the NT of *marainō,* "to come to wither or to fade away" (Jas **1** 11, "So also shall the rich man fade away in his ways," RV "in his goings"); cf Wisd **2** 8, "Let us crown ourselves with rosebuds, before they be withered" (*marainō*); *amarántinos* (amaranth), "unfading," occurs in 1 Pet **5** 4, "the crown of glory that fadeth not away," and *amárantos* (1 Pet **1** 4), "an inheritance . . . . that fadeth not away"; cf Wisd **6** 12, "Wisdom is glorious [RV "radiant"], and fadeth not away."

For "fade" (Ezk **47** 12), RV has "wither"; for "fall," "falleth," "falling" (Isa **34** 4), "fade," "fadeth," "fading."

W. L. Walker

FAIL, fāl (כָּלָה, *kālāh,* כָּרַת, *kārath;* **ἐκλείπω,** *ekleípō*): "Fail" is both intrans, "to fall short," "be wanting," and trans, "to be wanting to."

Of the many words tr[d] "fail" in the OT, *kālāh* is the most frequent, meaning "to be consumed," "ended" (Job **11** 20; **17** 5; Ps **69** 3; **71** 9, etc; Prov **22** 8; Isa **15** 6, etc; Jer **14** 6; Lam **2** 11; **3** 22; **4** 17); it is the tr of *kārath,* "to be cut off" (2 S **3** 29, of failure in succession; so 1 K **2** 4, etc); *'ādhar,* "to marshal," "to be missed" or "lacking" (Isa **34** 16 AV; **40** 26 AV; **59** 15 AV; Zeph **3** 5); of *rāphāh,* "to become faint" or "to make feeble" (Dt **31** 6.8; "I will not fail thee, nor forsake thee," Josh **1** 5; 1 Ch **28** 20); of *'ābhadh,* "to perish," "be lost" (Ps **142** 4, "Refuge hath failed me"; Ezk **12** 22, "Every vision faileth"). Many other Heb words are tr[d] "fail," "faileth," for the most part in single instances.

In the NT, *ekleipō,* "to leave out" or "off," is thrice rendered "fail" (Lk **16** 9, "when it shall fail"; **22** 32, "that thy faith fail not"; He **1** 12, "Thy years shall not fail"); *ekpíptō,* "to fall off or away" (1 Cor **13** 8, "Charity [RV "love"] never faileth"); *katargéō,* "to make useless" (**13** 8 AV, "Whether prophecies, they shall fail"); *husteréō,* "to be behind," "to lack" (He **12** 15 AV); *apopsúchō,* "to swoon away," "failing" (Lk **21** 26 AV).

RV has "fail," in a new tr of Jer **18** 14, for "fall" (Lam **1** 14, m "stumble"); "his hand fail" for "fallen in decay" (Lev **25** 35); "I will in no wise fail thee" for "I will never leave thee" (He **13** 5; cf Dt **31** 6; Josh **1** 5); "failed to enter" for "entered not" (He **4** 6); "faileth" (ARV) for "ceaseth" (Ps **49** 8), ERV "must be let alone for ever"; "failing" for "was darkened" (Lk **23** 45); for "fail" (Ezr **4** 22), "be slack," "be missing" (Isa **34** 16); "falleth short of" (He **12** 15, m "falleth back from"); for "failed," "was all spent" (Gen **47** 15); "wholly" (Josh **3** 16); "fail [in looking]" (Lam **4** 17); for "faileth," "is lacking" (Isa **40** 26; **59** 15); for "men's hearts failing them" (Lk **21** 26), "men fainting," m "expiring."

W. L. Walker

FAIN, fān (advb.): Occurs twice in EV, in the sense of "gladly": (1) in Job **27** 22 as the rendering of בָּרַח, *bārah,* "to flee with haste" (from anything), "He would fain flee out of his hand," lit. as in m of AV, "in fleeing he would flee"; (2) in Lk **15** 16, as the tr of ἐπιθυμέω, *epithuméō,* "to fix the mind or desire on," "He would fain have filled his belly with the husks which the swine did eat." RV adds two instances: (1) Lk **13** 31, "Herod would fain kill thee"; (2) Acts **26** 28, "Thou wouldest fain make me a Christian." See Almost.

FAINT, fānt (עָיֵף, *'āyēph,* עוּף, *'ūph,* יָעַף, *yā'aph,* עָלַף, *'ālaph,* עָטַף, *'āṭaph,* דַּוָּי, *dawwāy,* יָגֵעַ, *yāghē[a]',* מָסַס, *māṣaṣ,* רָכַךְ, *rākhakh,* פָּגַר, *pāghar,* כָּהָה, *kāhāh;* **ἐκλύω,** *eklúō,* **ἐκκακέω,** *ekkakéō,* **κάμνω,** *kámnō*): The Heb vocabulary for the depressing physical conditions and mental emotions which are rendered in AV by the Eng. words "faint," "faintness," and other compounds of that stem, is, as will be seen above, wide and varied in derivation. The 11 Heb and 3 Gr words and their derivatives are used in 62 passages in AV to express these conditions.

'Āyēph is used to express the exhaustion from fatigue and hunger in the case of Esau (Gen **25** 29.30). This and its variants come from a root which primarily means "to cover or conceal," therefore "to be dark or obscure," and so, **fig.** "to be faint or depressed." Israel's helpless state when harassed by Amalek (Dt **25** 18) and the plight of Gideon's weary force when they sought in vain for help at Succoth (Jgs **8** 4) are described by the same word. Isaiah also uses it to picture the disappointed and unsatisfied appetite of the thirsty man awakening from his dream of refreshment (Isa **29** 8). In 2 S **16** 14, *'āyēphīm* is probably a proper name of a place (RVm).

'Ūph in 1 S **14** 28–31 describes the exhaustion of Saul's host in pursuit of the Philis after the battle of Michmash. The same word expresses the failure of David's strength when in conflict with the same foes, which led to his imminent peril and to the consequent refusal of the commander of his army to allow him to take part personally in the combat (2 S **21** 15).

Yā'aph is used by Ziba when he brought refreshments to David's men on the flight from Absalom (2 S **16** 2); see also its use in Isa **40** 28. Cognate verbal forms occur in Isa **40** 30.31; Jer **2** 24; **51** 58.64; Hab **2** 13, as also in Jgs **8** 15, meaning in all cases the faintness or exhaustion of fatigue or weariness.

'Ālaph expresses the faintness from thirst in Am **8** 13, or from the heat of the sun (Jon **4** 8), and **fig.** the despondency which was the result of the captivity (Isa **51** 20). Ezekiel uses it **allegorically**

as describing the withering of the trees for grief at the death of the Assyr kings (Ezk **31** 15).

'Āṭaph is the weariness of the wanderers in the desert (Ps **107** 5), the faintness from hunger (Lam **2** 19), or the despondency of Jonah dispelled by his remembrance of God's mercies (Jon **2** 7).

Dawwāy, from a root which signifies the sickness produced by exhaustion from loss of blood, is used in Isa **1** 5 for the faintness of heart, the result of remorse for sin, and in Jer **8** 18 for the prophet's sorrow for the sins of Israel. A cognate form expresses his sorrow on account of the judgments of God which were incurred as punishments for the national backsliding (Lam **1** 13.22; **5** 17).

Māṣaṣ, lit. "dissolving or melting," is applied to the contagious fear which the example of a cowardly soldier produces among his comrades (Dt **20** 8, RV "melt"). In the remarkable passage in Isa **10** 18, in which God pronounces the doom of Assyria when his purposes of chastisement on Israel have been fulfilled, the collapse of Assyria is said to be "as when a standard-bearer fainteth." For this RVm substitutes "as when a sick man pineth away," which is probably the correct rendering. The word *māṣaṣ* may mean either a sick man, or else something glittering and seen from afar, such as a standard, but the former sense is more intelligible and suggestive in the context. The rarely used verbal form cognate to *māṣaṣ* is used on account of its assonance.

Yāghēa' (*yāgha'*), which is usually tr[d] "grieved" or "tormented" or "fatigued," is rendered as "fainted" in Jer **45** 3. This passage, "I fainted in my sighing" AV, is in Heb the same as that which reads, "I am weary with my groaning" in Ps **6** 6, and is similarly rendered in RV.

Rākhakh, like *māṣaṣ,* primarily signifies "to melt" or "to become soft," and is used in prophetic exhortations in which the people are encouraged not to be panic-stricken in the presence of enemies (Dt **20** 3, and also Jer **51** 46; Isa **7** 4). Another related word, *mōrekh,* in the sense of despair and utter loss of courage, is used in expressing the consequences of God's wrath against Israel (Lev **26** 36). In its literal sense it signifies "blandness," as of the words of a hypocritical enemy (Ps **55** 21).

Pāghar is the prostration of utter fatigue whereby one is unable to raise himself or to proceed on a journey, as were some of David's little band (1 S **30** 10–21). A cognate word describes the prostration of amazement and incredulity with which Jacob heard of Joseph's condition in Egypt (Gen **45** 26).

Kāhāh, the pining of earnest, longing desire, is tr[d] "fainteth" in Ps **84** 2; **119** 81; elsewhere it is rendered by words expressing wasting or languishing. The panic in Canaan due to famine is expressed (Gen **47** 13) by the word *lāhāh,* which implies a state of frenzy.

The only records of actual fainting are (1) Daniel, in Dnl **8** 27, where the word used is the Niphal of the vb. *hāyāh,* lit. "became," meaning that he became weak; (2) swooning is mentioned in Ad Est **15** 7–15.

In the NT "faint" is used in the sense of physical exhaustion (Mt **9** 36 AV; **15** 32; Mk **8** 3), where it is part of the vb. *ekluō,* "to relax." Otherwise it is used **fig.** of discouragement of spirit. The same vb. is used in Gal **6** 9; He **12** 3.5; but in Lk **18** 1; 2 Cor **4** 1–16; Eph **3** 13 it is part of the vb. *ekkakeō* (according to some authorities *egkakeō,* pronounced *enkakeō,* meaning "to be faint-hearted" or "to be culpably negligent"). In Rev **2** 3 it is κοπιάω, *kopiaō,* lit. "to be tired."

ALEX. MACALISTER

FAIR, fâr: The word tr[d] in AV from 9 Heb and 4 Gr expressions has nowhere in the Bible the modern sense of "blond," "fair-skinned." The tr of Isa **54** 11, "fair colors," refers to the cosmetic use of פּוּךְ, *pūkh,* stibium, antimony powder, with which black margins were painted around the eyelids, so as to make the eyes appear large and dark. The stones of rebuilt Jerus, beautifully laid in their black mortar, are compared with such eyes. We can distinguish the following varieties of meaning: (1) Beautiful, attractive, טוֹב, *ṭōbh,* יָפָה, *yāphāh,* יָפֶה, *yāpheh;* Aram. שַׁפִּיר, *shappīr;* LXX καλός, *kalós;* in the NT ἀστεῖος, *asteíos.* This latter word is in both places where it is found used of Moses (Acts **7** 20; He **11** 23, RV "goodly"), and means lit. town bred (as opposed to boorish), polite, polished in manners, urbane, then nice, pretty. (2) Pure, free of defilement, RV "clean," טְהוֹר, *ṭāhōr* (Zec **3** 5). (3) "Fair speech," plausible, persuasive (לֶקַח, *lekah,* Prov **7** 21; εὔλαλος, *eúlalos,* Sir **6** 5; cf εὐλογία, *eulogía,* Rom **16** 18). (4) Making a fine display (εὐπροσωπεῖν, *euprosōpeín,* Gal **6** 12, "to make a fair show"). (5) Good (of weather) (זָהָב, *zāhābh,* "golden," "clear," Job **37** 22, RV "golden splendor"); εὐδία, *eudía* (Mt **16** 2).

H. L. E. LUERING

FAIR HAVENS, fâr hā'v'nz (**Καλοὶ Λιμένες,** *Kaloí Liménes*): A roadstead on the S. coast of Crete, about 5 miles E. of Cape Matala, the most southerly point of the island. The harbor is formed by a bay, open to the E., and sheltered on the S.W. by two small islands. Here Paul waited for a considerable time (Acts **27** 9); but while it afforded good anchorage and a shelter from N. and N.W. winds, "the haven was not commodious to winter in" (vs 8.12). See CRETE.

FAIRS, fârz: Found only 5 t in AV (Ezk **27** 12. 14.16.19.27), apparently incorrect tr of עִזָּבוֹן, *'izzābhon,* according to modern Hebraists (though Gesenius gives "fair" as one of its meanings). The LXX tr[s] the Heb of the above five passages by two different words, ἀγορά, *agorá,* "market-place" (vs 12.14.16.19), and μισθός, *misthós,* "hire," "pay" (vs 27.33). AV follows the Wyclif version in ver 12 and the Geneva version throughout, although it properly tr[s] "wares" in ver 33. RV gives "wares" (q.v.) throughout.

FAITH, fāth:

1. Etymology
2. Meaning: a Divergency
3. Faith in the Sense of Creed
4. A Leading Passage Explained
5. Remarks
6. Conclusion

In the OT (AV) the word occurs only twice: Dt **32** 20 (אֵמוּן, *'ēmūn*); Hab **2** 4 (אֱמוּנָה, *'ĕmūnāh*). In the latter RV places in m the alternative rendering, "faithfulness." In the NT it is of very frequent occurrence, always representing πίστις, *pístis,* with one exception in AV (not RV), He **10** 23, where it represents ἐλπίς, *elpís,* "hope."

The history of the Eng. word is rather interesting than important; use and contexts, alike for it and its Heb and Gr parallels, are the surest guides to meaning. But we may note that it occurs in the form "feyth," in *Havelok the Dane* (13th cent.); that it is akin to *fides* and this again to the Sanskrit root *bhidh,* "to unite," "to bind." It is worth while to recall this primeval suggestion of the spiritual work of faith, as that which, on man's side, *unites him to God* for salvation.

1. Etymology

Studying the word "faith" in the light of use and contexts, we find a bifurcation of significance in the Bible. We may distinguish the two senses as the passive and the active; on the one side, "fidelity," "trustworthiness"; and "faith," "trust," on the other.

In Gal **5** 22, e.g. context makes it clear that "fidelity" is in view, as a quality congruous with the associated graces. (RV accordingly renders *pistis* there by "faithfulness.")

2. Meaning: a Divergency

Again, Rom **3** 3 AV, "the faith *of God*," by the nature of the case, means His fidelity to promise. But in the overwhelming majority of cases, "faith," as rendering *pistis*, means "reliance," "trust." To illustrate would be to quote many scores of passages. It may be enough here to call attention to the recorded use of the word by Our Lord. Of about twenty passages in the Gospels where *pistis* occurs as coming from His lips, only one (Mt **23** 23) presents it in the apparent sense of "fidelity." All the others conspicuously demand the sense of "reliance," "trust." The same is true of the apostolic writings. In them, with rarest exceptions, the words "reliance," "trust," precisely fit the context as alternatives to "faith."

Another line of meaning is traceable in a very few passages, where *pistis*, "faith," appears in the sense of "creed," the truth, or body of truth, which is trusted, or which justifies trust. The most important of such places is the paragraph Jas **2** 14–26, where an apparent contradiction to some great Pauline *dicta* perplexes many readers. The riddle is solved by observing that the writer uses "faith" in the sense of creed, orthodox "belief." This is clear from ver 19, where the "faith" in question is illustrated: "Thou believest that *God is one*." This is the credal confession of the orthodox Jew (the *sh^ema'*; see Dt **6** 4), taken as a passport to salvation. Briefly, James presses the futility of creed without life, Paul the necessity of reliance in order to receive "life and peace."

3. Faith in the Sense of Creed

It is important to notice that He **11** 1 is no exception to the rule that "faith" normally means "reliance," "trust." There "Faith *is* the substance [or possibly, in the light of recent inquiries into the type of Gr used by NT writers, "the guaranty"] of things hoped for, the evidence [or "convincing proof"] of things not seen." This is sometimes interpreted as if faith, in the writer's view, were, so to speak, a faculty of second sight, a mysterious intuition into the spiritual world. But the chapter amply shows that the faith illustrated, e.g. by Abraham, Moses, Rahab, was simply *reliance* upon a God known to be trustworthy. Such reliance enabled the believer to treat the future as present and the invisible as seen. In short, the phrase here, "faith *is* the evidence," etc, is parallel in form to our familiar saying, "Knowledge *is* power."

4. A Leading Passage Explained

A few detached remarks may be added: (*a*) The history of the use of the Gr *pistis* is instructive. In the LXX it normally, if not always, bears the "passive" sense, "fidelity," "good faith," while in classical Gr it not rarely bears the active sense, "trust." In the *koinē*, the type of Gr universally common at the Christian era, it seems to have adopted the active meaning as the ruling one *only just in time*, so to speak, to provide it for the utterance of Him whose supreme message was "reliance," and who passed that message on to His apostles. Through their lips and pens "faith," in that sense, became the supreme watchword of Christianity. See JUSTIFICATION; UNION WITH CHRIST.

5. Remarks

In conclusion, without trespassing on the ground of other arts., we call the reader's attention, for his Scriptural studies, to the *central place of faith in Christianity*, and its significance. As being, in its true idea, a reliance as simple as possible upon the word, power, love, of Another, it is precisely that which, on man's side, *adjusts him* to the living and merciful presence and action of a trusted God. In its nature, not by any mere arbitrary arrangement, it is his one possible receptive attitude, that in which he brings nothing, so that he may receive all. Thus "faith" is our side of union with Christ. And thus it is our means of possessing all His benefits, pardon, justification, purification, life, peace, glory.

6. Conclusion

As a comment on our exposition of the ruling meaning of "faith" in Scripture, we may note that this precisely corresponds to its meaning in common life, where, for once that the word means anything else, it means "reliance" a hundred times. Such correspondence between religious terms (in Scripture) and the meaning of the same words in common life, will be found to be invariable.

HANDLEY DUNELM

FAITHFUL, fāth′fool, **FAITHFULNESS**, fāth′-fool-nes:

1. Faithfulness of God in the OT
2. Faithfulness of God in the NT

LITERATURE

Faithfulness is a quality or attribute applied in the Scripture to both God and man. This art. is limited to the consideration of the Scripture teaching concerning the meaning of faithfulness in its application to God.

Faithfulness is one of the characteristics of God's ethical nature. It denotes the firmness or constancy of God in His relations with men, especially with His people. It is, accordingly, one aspect of God's truth and of His unchangeableness. God is true not only because He is really God in contrast to all that is not God, and because He realizes the idea of Godhead, but also because He is constant or faithful in keeping His promises, and therefore is worthy of trust (see TRUTH). God, likewise, is unchangeable in His ethical nature. This unchangeableness the Scripture often connects with God's goodness and mercy, and also with His constancy in reference to His covenant promises, and this is what the OT means by the Faithfulness of God (see UNCHANGEABLENESS).

In the OT this attribute is ascribed to God in passages where the Heb words denoting faithfulness do not occur. It is implied in the covenant name Jehovah as unfolded in Ex **3** 13–15, which not only expresses God's self-existence and unchangeableness, but, as the context indicates, puts God's immutability in special relation to His gracious promises, thus denoting God's unchangeable faithfulness which is emphasized in the OT to awaken trust in God (Dt **7** 9; Ps **36** 5 [Heb 6]; Isa **11** 5; Hos **12** 6.9). (For fuller remarks on the name Jehovah in Ex **3** 13–15, see art. UNCHANGEABLENESS.) It is, moreover, God's faithfulness as well as His immutability which is implied in those passages where God is called a rock, as being the secure object of religious trust (Dt **32** 4.15; Ps **18** 2 [Heb 3]; **42** 9 [Heb 10]; Isa **17** 10, etc). This same attribute is also implied where God reveals Himself to Moses and to Israel as the God of Abraham, Isaac and Jacob, and their fathers' God (Ex **3** 6.15.16). The truth concerning God here taught is not simply that He stood in a gracious relation to the Patriarchs, but that He is faithful to His gracious promise to their fathers, and that what He was to them He will continue to be to Moses and to Israel. This is the fundamental idea in the OT concerning the faithfulness of God.

1. Faithfulness of God in the OT

This can be seen also from the Heb words which are used to express this quality of God's nature and activity. These words are *ne'ĕmān*, the Niphal participle of the vb. *'āman* used as an adj.—"faithful"—and the nouns *'ĕmeth* and *'ĕmūnāh*—"faithfulness." The verbal stem *'āman* means "to be secure or firm." In the Ḳal it denotes the firmness of that which supports something, being used in the participle of a nurse who carries a child (Nu **11** 12; 2 S **4** 4; Isa **49** 23). In the Niphal it denotes the firmness of that which is supported, for example, a child which is carried (Isa **60** 4); a well-founded house (1 S **2** 35; **25** 28); a wall which firmly holds a nail (Isa **22** 23.25); a kingdom firmly established (2 S **7** 16); persons secure in political station (Isa **7** 9); a heart which is faithful (Neh **9** 8). Hence in the Niphal the vb. comes to have the meaning of being true in the sense of the agreement of words and assertions with reality; for example, of words and revelations (Gen **42** 20; Hos **5** 9); and of persons (Isa **8** 2; Jer **42** 5). It has also the meaning of being faithful, being applied to men in Nu **12** 7; Ps **101** 6; Neh **13** 13, etc. In this sense the term is applied to the covenant-keeping Jeh to express the truth that He is firm or constant, that is, faithful in regard to His covenant promises, and will surely fulfil them (Dt **7** 9; Isa **49** 7; and possibly Hos **11** 12 [Heb **12** 1]).

A similar use is made of the nouns *'ĕmeth* and *'ĕmūnāh*. Apart from the instances where *'ĕmeth* denotes the idea of truth or the correspondence of words and ideas with reality, and the instances where it denotes the agreement of acts and words with the inner disposition, that is, sincerity, it is also used to denote the idea of faithfulness as above defined. As regards the noun *'ĕmūnāh*, apart from a few passages where it is doubtful whether it means truth or faithfulness, it usually denotes the latter idea. Both these nouns, then, are used to signify the idea of faithfulness, that is, constancy or firmness, esp. in the fulfilment of all obligations. In this sense these words are not only applied to men, but also to God to express the idea that He is always faithful to His covenant promises. It is this attribute of God which the Psalmist declares (Ps **40** 10 [Heb 11]), and the greatness of which he affirms by saying that God's faithfulness reacheth to the clouds (**36** 5 [Heb 6]). It is this which he makes the object of praise (**89** 1.2 [Heb 2.3]; **92** 2 [Heb 3]); and which he says should be praised and reverenced by all men (**89** 5.8 [Heb 6.9]). And even this faithfulness is itself characterized by constancy, if we may so speak, for the Psalmist says that it endures to all generations (**100** 5). Being thus a characteristic of God, it also characterizes His salvation, and becomes the basis of confidence that God will hear prayer (**143** 1). It thus becomes the security of the religious man (**91** 4); and the source of God's help to His people (**31** 5 [Heb 6]). Accordingly in the teaching of prophecy, the salvation of the covenant people rests upon no claim or merit of their own, but solely upon Jeh's mercy, grace and faithfulness. When Israel incurred God's judgments, it might have appeared as if His promise was to fail, but, so far from this being true, as Jehovah He is faithful to His word of promise which stands forever (Isa **40** 8). Even from eternity His counsels are characterized by faithfulness and truth (**25** 1); and this is not because of Israel's faithfulness, but it is for His own sake that Jeh blotteth out their transgressions (**43** 22–25; Mic **7** 18–20). It is, moreover, this same characteristic of Jeh which is asserted in many cases where the Heb words *'ĕmeth* and *'ĕmūnāh* are tr[d] by the word "truth" in AV. In Ex **34** 6 it is God's faithfulness (*'ĕmeth*) which is referred to, since it evidently signifies His constancy from generation to generation; and in Dt **32** 4 it is also God's faithfulness (*'ĕmūnāh*) which is mentioned, since it is contrasted with the faithlessness of Israel. The same is true of *'ĕmeth* in Mic **7** 20; Ps **31** 5 [Heb 6]); **91** 4; **146** 6. This is also true of the numerous instances where God's mercy and truth (*'ĕmeth*) are combined, His mercy being the source of His gracious promises, and His truth the faithfulness with which He certainly fulfils them (Ps **25** 10; **57** 3 [Heb 4]; **61** 7 [Heb 8]; **85** 10 [Heb 11]; **86** 15). And since the covenant-keeping Jehovah is faithful, faithfulness comes also to be a characteristic of the New Covenant which is everlasting (Ps **89** 28 [Heb 29]); cf also for a similar thought, Isa **54** 8 ff; Jer **31** 35 ff; Hos **2** 19 f; Ezk **16** 60 ff.

It is in this connection, moreover, that God's faithfulness is closely related to His righteousness in the OT. In the second half of the prophecy of Isaiah and in many of the psalms, righteousness is ascribed to God because He comes to help and save His people. Thus righteousness as a quality parallel with grace, mercy and faithfulness is ascribed to God (Isa **41** 10; **42** 6; **45** 13.19.21; **63** 1). It appears in these places to widen out from its exclusively judicial or forensic association and to become a quality of God as Saviour of His people. Accordingly this attribute of God is appealed to in the Pss as the basis of hope for salvation and deliverance (Ps **31** 1 [Heb 2]; **35** 24; **71** 2; **143** 11). Hence this attribute is associated with God's mercy and grace (Ps **36** 5 [Heb 6].9 [Heb 10]; **89** 14 [Heb 15]); also with His faithfulness (Zec **8** 8; Ps **36** 6 [Heb 7]); **40** 10 [Heb 11]; **88** 11.12 [Heb 12.13]; **89** 14 [Heb 15]; **96** 13; **119** 137. 142; **143** 1). Accordingly the OT conception of the righteousness of God has been practically identified with His covenant faithfulness, by such writers as Kautzsch, Riehm and Smend, Ritschl's definition of it being very much the same. Moreover, Ritschl, following Diestel, denied that the idea of distributive and retributive justice is ascribed to God in the OT. In regard to this latter point, it should be remarked in passing that this denial that the judicial or forensic idea of righteousness is ascribed to God in the OT breaks down, not only in view of the fact that the OT does ascribe this attribute to God in many ways, but also in view of the fact that in a number of passages the idea of retribution is specifically referred to the righteousness of God (see RIGHTEOUSNESS; cf against Diestel and Ritschl, Dalman, *Die richterliche Gerechtigkeit im Alten Testament*).

That which concerns us, however, in regard to this close relation between righteousness and faithfulness is to observe that this should not be pressed to the extent of the identification of righteousness with covenant faithfulness in these passages in the Pss and the second half of Isa. The idea seems to be that Israel has sinned and has no claim upon Jeh, finding her only hope of deliverance in His mercy and faithfulness. But this very fact that Jeh is merciful and faithful becomes, as it were, Israel's claim, or rather the ground of Israel's hope of deliverance from her enemies. Hence in the recognition of this claim of His people, God is said to be righteous in manifesting His mercy and faithfulness, so that His righteousness, no less than His mercy and faithfulness, becomes the ground of His people's hope. Righteousness is thus closely related in these cases to faithfulness, but it is not identified with it, nor has it in all cases lost entirely its forensic tone. This seems to be, in general, the meaning of righteousness in the Pss and the second half of Isa, with which may also be compared Mic **6** 9; Zec **8** 8.

The emphasis which this attribute of God has in the OT is determined by the fact that throughout the whole of the OT the covenant relation of Jeh to His people is founded solely in God's grace, and not on any merit of theirs. If this covenant relation had been based on any claim of Israel, faithfulness on God's part might have been taken for granted. But since Jeh's covenant relation with Israel and His promises of salvation spring solely from, and depend wholly upon, the grace of God, that which gave firm assurance that the past experience of God's grace would continue in the future was this immutable faithfulness of Jeh. By it the experience of the fathers was given a religious value for Israel from generation to generation. And even as the faithfulness of God bridged over the past and the present, so also it constituted the connecting link between the present and the future, becoming thus the firm basis of Israel's hope; cf Ps **89** which sets forth the faithfulness of God in its greatness, its firmness as the basis of the covenant and the ground it affords of hope for future help from Jeh, and for hope that His covenant shall endure forever. When God's people departed from Him all the more emphasis was put upon His faithfulness, so that the only hope of His wayward people lay not only in His grace and mercy but also in His faithfulness, which stands in marked contrast with the faithlessness and inconstancy of His people. This is probably the meaning of the difficult ver Hos **11** 12 (Heb **12** 1).

2. Faithfulness of God in the NT

In the NT teaching concerning the faithfulness of God the same idea of faithfulness to His gracious promises is emphasized and held up as the object of a confident trust in God. This idea is usually expressed by the adj. *pistós*, and once by the noun *pistis*, which more frequently has the active sense of faith or trust.

An attempt has been made by Wendt (*SK*, 1883, 511 f; *Teaching of Jesus*, ET, I, 259 f) to interpret the words *alḗtheia* and *alēthḗs* in many instances, especially in the Johannine writings, as denoting faithfulness and rectitude, after the analogy of the LXX rendering *éleos kaí alḗtheia* for the Heb phrase "mercy and truth," in which truth is equivalent to faithfulness. But the most that could be inferred from the fact that the LXX uses the word *alḗtheia* to translate the Heb word *'ĕmeth*, and in about one-half the cases where *'ĕmūnāh* occurs, would be that those Gr words might have been prepared for such a use in the NT. But while it is true that there is one usage of these words in John's writings in an ethical sense apparently based on the OT use of *'ĕmeth* and *'ĕmūnāh*, the Gr words do not have this meaning when employed to denote a characteristic of God. Neither is the adj. *alēthinós* so used. See TRUTH.

In the Epp. of Paul the word *alḗtheia* occurs quite frequently to denote the truth revealed by God to man through reason and conscience, and to denote the doctrinal content of the gospel. In two passages, however, the words *alēthḗs* and *alḗtheia* seem to signify the faithfulness of God (Rom **3** 4.7; **15** 8). In the former passage Paul is contrasting the faithfulness of God with the faithlessness of men, the word *alēthḗs*, ver 4, and *alḗtheia*, ver 7, apparently denoting the same Divine characteristic as the word *pistis*, ver 3. In the latter passage (Rom **15** 8), the vindication of God's covenant faithfulness, through the realization of His promises to the fathers, is declared to have been the purpose of the ministry of Jesus Christ to the Jews.

This faithfulness of God to His covenant promises is frequently emphasized by Paul, the words he employs being the noun *pistis* (once) and the adj. *pistos*. The noun *pistis* is used once by Paul in this sense (Rom **3** 3 ff). In this place Paul is arguing that the unbelief of the Jews cannot make void God's faithfulness. Both Jew and Gentile, the apostle had said, are on the same footing as regards justification. Nevertheless the Jews had one great advantage in that they were the people to whom the revelation of God's gracious promises had been committed. These promises will certainly be fulfilled, notwithstanding the fact that some of the Jews were unfaithful, because the fulfilment of these promises depends not on human conduct but on the faithfulness of God, which cannot be made void by human faithlessness and unbelief. And to the supposition that man's faithlessness could make of none effect God's faithfulness, Paul replies 'let God be faithful [*alēthḗs*] and every man a liar' (ver 4), by which Paul means to say that in the fulfilment of God's promises, in spite of the fact that men are faithless, the faithfulness of God will be abundantly vindicated, even though thereby every man should be proven untrue and faithless. And not only so, but human faithlessness will give an opportunity for a manifestation of the faithfulness (*alḗtheia*) of God, abounding to His glory (ver 7). God's faithfulness here is His unchangeable constancy and fidelity to His covenant promises; and it is this fidelity to His promises, or the fact that God's gracious gifts and election are without any change of mind on His part, which gave to Paul the assurance that all Israel should finally be saved (Rom **11** 25–29). Moreover this covenant faithfulness of God is grounded in His very nature, so that Paul's hope of eternal life rests on the fact that God who cannot lie promised it before the world began (Tit **1** 2); and the certainty that God will abide faithful notwithstanding human faithlessness rests on the fact that God cannot deny Himself (2 Tim **2** 13). It is because God is faithful that His promises in Christ are yea and amen (2 Cor **1** 18.20). This attribute of God, moreover, is the basis of Paul's confident assurance that God will preserve the Christian in temptation (1 Cor **10** 13); and establish him and preserve him from evil (2 Thess **3** 3). And since God is faithful and His gracious promises trustworthy, this characteristic attaches to the "faithful sayings" in the Pastoral Epistles which sum up the gospel, making them worthy of trust and acceptance (1 Tim **1** 15; **4** 9; Tit **3** 8).

This faithfulness of God in the sense of fidelity to His promises is set forth as the object of sure trust and hope by the writer of the Epistle to the Hebrews. It was the basis of Sarah's faith that she would bear a child when she was past age (He **11** 11); and it is because God is faithful to His promise in Christ that we can draw nigh to Him with full assurance of faith, holding fast without wavering the profession of hope (He **10** 23).

John also ascribes this attribute to God. Since one of the most precious of God's promises through Christ is the pardon of sin through the "blood of Jesus Christ," John says that God's faithfulness, as well as His righteousness, is manifested in the forgiveness of sin (1 Jn **1** 9).

The faithfulness of God is viewed from a slightly different point by Peter when he tells his readers that those who suffer as Christians and in accordance with God's will should "commit their soul's in well-doing unto a faithful Creator" (1 Pet **4** 19). The quality of faithfulness, which in the Scripture is more frequently ascribed to God in His relation to man as gracious Saviour, and as the ground of hope in His gracious promises, is here applied by Peter to God in His relation to man as his Creator, and is made the ground of comfort under persecution and suffering. The omission of the art. before the words "faithful Creator" makes emphatic that this is a characteristic of God as Creator, and the position of the words in the sentence throws great emphasis on this attribute of God as the basis of comfort under suffering. It is as if Peter would say to suffering Christians, "You suffer not by chance but in accordance with God's will; He, the almighty Creator, made you, and since your suffering is in accordance with His will, you ought to trust yourselves to Him who as your Creator is faithful." It is, of course, Christians who are to derive this comfort, but the faithfulness of God is extended here to cover all His relations to His people, and to pledge all His attributes in their behalf.

This attribute is also ascribed to Christ in the NT. Where Jesus is called a faithful high priest, the idea expressed is His fidelity to His obligations to God and to His saving work (He **2** 17; **3** 2.6). But when in the Book of Revelation Jesus Christ is called the "faithful witness" or absolutely the "Faithful and True," it is clear that the quality of faithfulness, in the most absolute sense in which it is characteristic of God in contrast with human changeableness, is ascribed to Christ (Rev **1** 5; **3** 14; **19** 11). This is esp. clear in the last-named passage. The heavens themselves open to disclose the glorified Christ, and He appears not only as a victorious warrior whose name is faithful and true, but also as the one in whom these attributes have their highest realization, and of whom they are so characteristic as to become the name of the exalted Lord. This clearly implies the Deity of Jesus.

In summing up the Scripture teaching concerning God's faithfulness, three things are noteworthy. In the first place, this characteristic of God is usually connected with His gracious promises of salvation, and is one of those attributes which make God the firm and secure object of religious trust. As is the case with all the Scripture teaching concerning God, it is the religious value of His faithfulness which is made prominent. In the second place, the so-called moral attributes, of which this is one, are essential in order to constitute God the object of religion, along with the so-called incommunicable attributes such as Omnipotence, Omnipresence and Unchangeableness. Take away either class of attributes from God, and He ceases to be God, the object of religious veneration and trust. And in the third place, while these moral attributes, to which faithfulness belongs, have been called "communicable," to distinguish them from the "incommunicable" attributes which distinguish God from all that is finite, it should never be forgotten that, according to the Scripture, God is faithful in such an absolute sense as to contrast Him with men who are faithful only in a relative sense, and who appear as changeable and faithless in comparison with the faithfulness of God. See RIGHTEOUSNESS; TRUTH; UNCHANGEABLENESS.

LITERATURE.—Besides the Commentaries on the appropriate passages, see Oehler, *Theol. of the OT*, ET, 95, 112 f, 505; Dillmann, *Handbuch der alttest. Theol.*, 268–76, 269–70; Schlatter, *Der Glaube im NT*, 21–22, 259–60. In the works on NT theology this subject is treated under the sections on the truthfulness of God.

On the relation of God's truth and faithfulness, see Wendt, *Der Gebrauch der Wörter, ἀλήθεια, ἀληθής und ἀληθινός im NT, SK*, 1883, 511 f; Stanton, art. "Truth," in *HDB*, IV, 816 f; and the above-mentioned work of Schlatter. On the relation of the faithfulness to the righteousness of God, see Diestel, "Die Idee der Gerechtigkeit vorzüglich im AT," *Jahrbücher für deutsche Theologie*, 1860, 173 f; Kautzsch, *Ueber die Derivate des Stammes* צדק *im AT Sprachgebrauch;* Riehm, *AT Theol.*, 271 f; Smend, *Alttest. Religionsgeschichte*, 363 f; Ritschl, *Justification and Reconciliation;* Dalman, *Die richterliche Gerechtigkeit im AT;* and the above-mentioned OT Theologies of Dillmann and Oehler.

CASPAR WISTAR HODGE

FAITHFUL SAYINGS, sā'inz (**πιστὸς ὁ λόγος,** *pistós ho lógos*): "This is a faithful saying and worthy of all acceptation" (AV). These words form a striking formula which is found—with slight variations—only in the Pastoral Epistles, in 1 Tim **1** 15; **3** 1; **4** 9; 2 Tim **2** 11; Tit **3** 8. A similar expression occurs in Rev (**21** 5 and **22** 6 AV), "These sayings are faithful and true."

The Five "Sayings."—Paul's faithful sayings are thus five in number, and "were no doubt rehearsed constantly in the assemblies, till they became well-known watchwords in the various churches scattered over the Mediterranean-washed provinces of the Rom empire" (Ellicott, *NT Comm.* on 1 Tim **1** 15).

1. The First "Saying"

The first of the faithful sayings speaks of the pre-existence of Christ, of His coming into the world, and the purpose why He came is distinctly stated—to save the lost, irrespective of race or nationality, sinners who, apart from Christ, are without God and without hope.

2. The Second "Saying"

The second of the faithful sayings refers to the work of being a minister of the gospel, a work then so full of danger and always full of difficulty. The office in question is honorable and Christlike, and, in those early days, it meant stern and ceaseless work, grave and constant danger. This faithful saying would act as a call to young men to offer themselves for the work of proclaiming the gospel to the world, and of witnessing for Christ.

3. The Third "Saying"

The third saying is that godliness has an influence that is world-wide; it consists, not merely in holiness and in that fellowship and communion with God which is the very life of the soul; it is also an active force which springs from "the love of Christ constraining us," and manifests itself in love toward all our fellow-men, for they are God's creatures. Godliness transfigures every rank and condition of life. It has the promise of the life that now is: to those who seek the kingdom of God first, all other things will be added. And it has the promise of the life that is to come, the rich prospect of eternal blessedness with Christ. Compare with this saying the remarkable words in Tit **1** 2, "in hope of eternal life, which God, who cannot lie, promised before times eternal." Godliness gives all gladness here, and future glory too. This is a faithful saying.

4. The Fourth "Saying"

The fourth of the faithful sayings speaks of the Christian believer's union with Christ, and of the blessedness of that union. The Christian is "dead with Christ," he "suffers with Christ." But the union with Christ is eternal, "We shall also live with him; . . . . we shall also reign with him" in life that is fadeless, endless and full of glory. Surely then, no one will draw back, for "if we deny him," "if we believe not," "he also will deny us," for "he abideth faithful, he cannot deny himself."

5. The Fifth "Saying"

The fifth and last of the faithful sayings speaks of our former unconverted state, "for we also once were foolish, disobedient, deceived, serving divers lusts and pleasures. But . . . . the kindness and love of God . . . . toward man appeared, not by works which we did ourselves, but according to his mercy he saved us." Blessedness is now the Christian's lot, and this is the result not of our works: we owe it all to the tender love of God, to His Divine pity, to His redeeming grace. Yes, this is a faithful saying.

JOHN RUTHERFURD

FAITHLESS, fāth'les: The tr of **ἄπιστος,** *ápistos*, "without faith," having the sense of "unbelieving," "disbelieving." Jesus upbraids the people, "O faithless and perverse generation!" (Mt **17** 17; Mk **9** 19; Lk **9** 41); He says to Thomas, "Be not faithless, but believing" (Jn **20** 27); RV adds, "If we are faithless," instead of "believe not" (2 Tim **2** 13); cf 1 Cor **7** 12–15; **10** 27; **14** 22.24, etc; Tit **1** 15. In Lk **12** 46 *apistos* has the sense of "unfaithful," so RV; perhaps also Rev **21** 8, "unbelieving."

FALCON, fô'k'n, fôl'k'n, fal'kun: The Hebrews did not know the word. Their bird corresponding to our falcon, in all probability, was one of the smaller kestrels covered by the word *nēç*, which seemed to cover all lesser birds of prey that we include in the hawk family. That some of our many divisions of species were known to them is indicated by the phrase "after its kind." The word occurs in RV in Job **28** 7, to tr *'ayyāh*, Gr *γύψ*, *gúps* (cf Lev **11** 14; Dt **14** 13):

> "That path no bird of prey knoweth,
> Neither hath the falcon's eye seen it."

This substitutes "falcon" for "vulture" in AV. The change weakens the force of the lines. All ornithologists know that eagles, vultures and the large hawks have such range of vision that they at once descend from heights at which we cannot see them to take prey on earth or food placed to tempt them. The falcons and sparrow hawks are small members of the family, some of which feed on little birds, some on insects. They are not celebrated for greater range of vision than other birds of the same location and feeding habits. The strength of these lines lay in the fact that if the path to the mine were so well concealed that the piercing eye of the vulture failed to find it, then it was perfectly hidden indeed. GENE STRATTON-PORTER

FALL, fôl (vb.): The idea of falling is most frequently expressed in Heb by נָפַל, *nāphal*, but also by many other words; in Gr by πίπτω, *piptō*, and its compounds. The uses of the word in Scripture are very varied. There is the literal falling by descent; the falling of the countenance in sorrow, shame, anger, etc (Gen **4** 5.6); the falling in battle (**14** 10; Nu **14** 3, etc); the falling into trouble, etc (Prov **24** 16.17); prostration in supplication and reverence (Gen **17** 3; Nu **14** 5, etc); falling of the Spirit of Jeh (Ezk **11** 5; cf **3** 24; **8** 1); of apostasy (2 Thess **2** 3; He **6** 6; Jude ver 24), etc. RV frequently changes "fall" of AV into other words or phrases, as "stumble" (Lev **26** 37; Ps **64** 8; 2 Pet **1** 10, etc), "fade" (Isa **33** 4), etc; in Acts **27**, RV reads "be cast ashore on rocky ground" for "have fallen upon rocks" (ver 29), "perish" for "fall" (ver 34), "lighting upon" for "falling into" (ver 41). W. L. WALKER

FALL, fôl, **THE:**

1. Meaning of Gen 3
2. Gen 3 in the Old and New Testaments
3. The Fall and the Theory of Evolution
4. The Character of the Fall

The question concerning the origin, the age and the written record of the history of the Fall in Gen **3** need not be discussed here. For in the first place, science can never reach to the oldest origins and the ultimate destinies of humanity, and historical and critical inquiry will never be able to prove either the veracity or the unveracity of this history. And in the second place, exactly as it now lies before us, this history has already formed for centuries a portion of holy Scripture, an indispensable element in the organism of the revelation of salvation, and as such has been accepted in faith by the Heb congregation (Jewish people), by Christ, by the apostles, and by the whole Christian church.

1. Meaning of Gen, Ch 3

That Gen **3** gives us an account of the fall of man, of the loss of his primitive innocence and of the misery, particularly death, to which he has since been subjected, cannot reasonably be denied. The opinion of the Ophites, Kant, Schiller, Hegel, etc, that Gen **3** relates the awakening of man to self-consciousness and personality (see ADAM IN OT AND APOC), and therefore does not tell us of a fall, but a marked progression, is controverted by the name which the forbidden tree bears, as indicating to man not merely a tree of knowledge in the ordinary way, but quite specially a tree of knowledge of *good and evil.*

Gen **3** is not in the least meant to relate to us how man obtained the idea of his nakedness and sexual passions, and from a state of childlike innocence changed in this respect to manlike maturity (Eerdman's *De Beteekenis van het Paradijsverhaal, TT,* 1905, 485–511). For according to Gen, man was created full-grown, received a wife immediately as helpmeet, and at the same time saw himself allotted the task of multiplying and replenishing the earth. Moreover, the idea that sexual desire is something sinful and deserves punishment was entirely foreign to ancient Israel.

Finally, the interpretation of Wellhausen (*Geschichte Israels,* 1878, 344) cannot be accepted, that man in Gen **3** should obtain "die intellektuelle Welterkenntniss, die metaphysische Erkenntniss der Dinge in ihrem Zusammenhange, ihrem Werth oder Unwerth, ihrem Nutzen oder Schaden" ("the intellectual knowledge of the world, the metaphysical knowledge of things in their connection, their worth or unworth, their utility or hurtfulness"). For in the first place, according to Gen, this was man's peculiar province from the beginning; he received indeed the vocation to subdue the earth, to keep and till the ground, to give the animals their names. And in the second place, the acquiring of this knowledge among the Israelites, who esteemed practical wisdom so highly, is difficult to represent as a fall, or as a punishment deserved for disobedience.

There is no other explanation possible of Gen **3** than that it is the narration of a fall, which consists in the transgression of an explicit command of God, thus bearing a moral significance, and therefore followed by repentance, shame, fear and punishment. The context of the chapter places this interpretation beyond all doubt, for before his fall man is represented as a creature made after God's image and receiving paradise as a dwelling-place, and after the fall he is sent into a rough world, is condemned to a life of labor and sorrow, and increases more and more in sin until the judgment of the Flood.

2. Gen, Ch 3 in the OT and NT

It is indeed remarkable how very seldom the OT refers to this history of the Fall. This is not a sufficient reason for pronouncing it of later origin, for the same peculiarity presents itself at the time when, according to all criticism, it was recorded in literature. Prophets, Psalms, Proverbs never quote it; at the most, allusions may be found to it in Hos **6** 7 and Eccl **7** 29; and even Jesus and His apostles in the NT very seldom appeal to Gen **3** (Jn **8** 44; Rom **5** 12; 1 Cor **15** 22; 2 Cor **11** 3; 1 Tim **2** 14). But it may be considered that the Prophets, Psalms and Proverbs only mention special facts of the past by way of exception, that the apostles even hardly ever quote the words and deeds of Jesus, and that all lived at a time when revelation itself was still proceeding and did not lie before them as a complete whole. With us it is quite a different matter; we are in a certain sense outside revelation, make it a subject of our study and meditation, try to discover the unity which holds all its parts together, and devote our special interest to Adam as a figure and counterpart of Christ. The creation and fall of man occupy therefore a much broader place in the province of our thoughts than they did among the writers of the books of the Old and New Testaments.

Nevertheless, the Fall is the silent hypothesis of the whole Bib. doctrine of sin and redemption; it does not rest only on a few vague passages, but forms an indispensable element in the revelation of salvation. The whole contemplation of man and humanity, of Nature and history, of ethical and physical evil, of redemption and the way in which to obtain it, is connected in Scripture with a Fall, such as Gen **3** relates to us. Sin, for example, is common to all men (1 K **8** 46; Ps **14** 3; **130** 3; **143** 2), and to every man from his conception (Gen **6** 5; **8** 21; Job **14** 4; Ps **51** 7). It arouses God's anger and deserves all kinds of punishment, not only of an ethical but of a physical nature (Gen **3** 14–19; **4** 14; **6** 7.13; **11** 8; Lev **26** 14 f; Dt **28** 15; Ps **90** 7, etc); the whole of Scripture proceeds from the thought that sin and death are connected in the closest degree, as are also obedience and life.

In the new heaven and new earth all suffering ceases with sin (Rev **21** 4). Therefore redemption is possible only in the way of forgiveness (Ps **32** 1; Isa **43** 25, etc), and circumcision of the heart (Dt **10** 16; **30** 16; Jer **4** 4), and this includes, further, life, joy, peace, salvation. When Paul in Rom **5** 12; 1 Cor **15** 22 indicates Adam as the origin of sin and death, and Christ as the source of righteousness and life, he develops no ideas which are contrary to the organism of revelation or which might be neglected without loss; he merely combines and formulates the data which are explicitly or silently contained in it.

3. The Fall and the Theory of Evolution

Tradition does little toward the confirmation and elucidation of the Bib. narrative of the Fall. The study of mythology is still too little advanced to determine the ideal or historical value which may be contained in the legend of a Golden Age, in many people's obsequious honoring of the serpent, in the equally widespread belief in a tree of life. The Bab representation also (a seal on which a man and woman, seated, are figured as plucking fruit from a tree, while a serpent curls up behind the woman as if whispering in her ear), which G. Smith, Lenormant and Friedrich Delitzsch compare with the Paradise narrative, shows no similarity on nearer view (A. Jeremias, *Das AT im Lichte des alten Orients*[2], Leipzig, 1906, 203). Indirectly, however, a very powerful witness for the fall of man is furnished by the whole empirical condition of the world and humanity. For a world, such as we know it, full of unrighteousness and sorrow, cannot be explained without the acceptance of such a fact. He who holds fast to the witness of Scripture and conscience to sin as sin (as ἀνομία, *anomia*) cannot deduce it from creation, but must accept the conclusion that it began with a transgression of God's command and thus with a deed of the will. Pythagoras, Plato, Kant, Schelling, Baader have all understood and acknowledged this with more or less clearness. He who denies the Fall must explain sin as a necessity which has its origin in the Creation, in the nature of things, and therefore in God Himself; he justifies man but accuses God, misrepresents the character of sin and makes it everlasting and indefeasible. For if there has not been a fall into sin, there is no redemption of sin possible; sin then loses its merely ethical significance, becomes a trait of the nature of man, and is inexterminable.

This comes out, in later years, in the many endeavors to unite the Fall with the doctrine of evolution (cf Tennant, *The Origin and Propagation of Sin*[2], 1905; A. S. Peake, *Christianity: Its Nature and Its Truth*, 1908; W. E. Orchard, *Modern Theories of Sin*, 1909; Francis J. Hall, *Evolution and the Fall*, 1910). All these endeavors lead to setting on one side the objective standard of sin, which is the law of God, and determining the nature and importance of sin subjectively by the feeling of guilt, which in its turn again depends on the knowledge of and the love for the moral ideal, and itself forms an important factor in moral progress. It is true that the strength of all these endeavors is drawn from the theory of the descent of man from the animal. But as to this theory, it is worthy of notice: (1) that it is up to the present day a hypothesis, and is proved by no single observation, whether direct or indirect; (2) that the fossils of prehistoric men, found in Germany, Belgium, France and elsewhere have demonstrated the low degree of culture in which these men have lived, but in no sense their dissimilarity with mankind of today (W. Branca, *Der Stand unserer Kenntnisse vom fossilen Menschen*, Leipzig, 1910); (3) that the uncivilized and prehistoric man may be as little identified with the first man as the unjustly so-called nature-people and children under age; (4) that the oldest history of the human race, which has become known through the discoveries at Babylon in the last century, was not that of a state of barbarism, but of high and rich culture (D. Gath Whitley, "What was the Primitive Condition of Man?" *Princeton Theol. Review*, October, 1906; J. Orr, *God's Image in Man*, 1906); (5) that the acceptance of the theory of descent as a universal and unlimited rule leads to the denial of the unity of the human race, in a physical and also in an intellectual, moral and religious sense. For it may be possible, even in the school of Darwin, to maintain the unity of the human race so long a time as tradition exercises its influence on the habit of mind; but theory itself undermines its foundation and marks it as an arbitrary opinion. From the standpoint of evolution, there is not only no reason to hold to the "of one blood" of Acts **17** 26 AV, but there has never even been a first man; the transition from animal to man was so slow and successive, that the essential distinction fails to be seen. And with the effacing of this boundary, the unity of the moral ideal, of religion, of the laws of thought and of truth, fails also; the theory of evolution expels the absolute everywhere and leads necessarily to psychologism, relativism, pragmatism and even to pluralism, which is literally polytheism in a religious sense. The unity of the human race, on the other hand, as it is taught in holy Scripture, is not an indifferent physical question, but an important intellectual, moral and religious one; it is a "postulate" of the whole history of civilization, and expressly or silently accepted by nearly all historians. And conscience bears witness to it, in so far as all men show the work of the moral law written in their hearts, and their thoughts accuse or excuse one another (Rom **2** 15); it shows back to the Fall as an "Urthatsache der Geschichte."

4. The Character of the Fall

What the condition and history of the human race could hardly lead us to imagine, holy Scripture relates to us as a tragic fact in its first pages. The first man was created by God after His own image, not therefore in brutish unconsciousness or childlike *naïveté*, but in a state of bodily and spiritual maturity, with understanding and reason, with knowledge and speech, with knowledge esp. of God and His law. Then was given to him moreover a command not to eat of the tree of knowledge of good and evil. This command was not contained in the moral law as such; it was not a natural but a positive commandment; it rested entirely and only on God's will and must be obeyed exclusively for this reason. It placed before man the choice, whether he would be faithful and obedient to God's word and would leave to Him alone the decision as to what is good or evil, or whether he would reserve to himself the right arbitrarily to decide what is good or evil. Thus the question was: Shall theonomy or autonomy be the way to happiness? On this account also the tree was called the tree of knowledge of good and evil. It did not bear this name in the sense that man might obtain from it the empirical knowledge of good and evil, for by his transgression he in truth lost the empirical knowledge of good. But the tree was so named, because man, by eating of it and so transgressing God's commandment, arrogated to himself "*die Fähigkeit zur selbständigen Wahl der Mittel, durch die man sein Glück schaffen will*": "the capacity of independent choice of the means by which he would attain his happiness" (Köberle, *Sünde und Gnade im relig. Leben des Volkes Israel bis auf Christentum*, 1905, 64). Theonomy, as obedience to God from free love, includes as such the idea and the possibility of autonomy, therefore that of antinomy also,

But it is the free act and therefore the guilt of man that has changed the possibility into reality. For the mind, there remains here an insoluble problem, as much in the question, why God allowed this Fall to take place, as in the other, how man, created in the likeness of God, could and did fall. There is a great deal of truth in the often-expressed thought, that we can give no account of the origin of sin, because it is not logical, and does not result as a conclusion drawn from two premises. But facts are brutal. What seems logically impossible often exists in reality. The laws of moral life are different from those of thought and from those also of mechanical nature. The narrative in Gen **3**, in any case, is psychologically faithful in the highest degree. For the same way as it appears there in the first man, it repeatedly takes place among ourselves (Jas **1** 14.15). Furthermore we ought to allow God to justify Himself. The course of revelation discovers to faith how, through all the ages, He holds sin in its entire development in His own almighty hands, and works through grace for a consummation in which, in the dispensation of the fulness of times, He will gather together in one all things in Christ (Eph **1** 10). (J. Orr, *Sin as a Problem of Today*, London, 1910.)

HERMAN BAVINCK

FALLING STARS. See ASTRONOMY.

FALLOW, fal'ō (דָּמַם, *dāmam*): *Dāmam* is tr^d^ only once in the sense of "fallow" (Ex **23** 11). The law required that the Israelites allow their ground to lie fallow one year in seven. AV is (Dt **14** 5) נִר, *nir*, and is tr^d^ "fallow" in its more obsolete sense of "tilled ground" in AV (Jer **4** 3; Hos **10** 12).

FALSE, fôls, **CHRISTS.** See CHRISTS, FALSE.

FALSEHOOD, fôls'ho͝od. See LYING.

FALSE PROPHETS. See PROPHESYINGS, FALSE.

FALSE SWEARING, WITNESS. See OATH; PERJURY; CRIMES.

FAME, fām (שֵׁם, *shēm*, שֵׁמַע, *shēma'*; ἀκοή, *akoē*, φήμη, *phēmē*): "Fame" has the twofold meaning, (1) of report or rumor, (2) of renown or reputation (in the OT it is not always easy to distinguish the two senses). "Fame," *shēma'*, "fame," "rumor," "report" (Nu **14** 15; Job **28** 22, RV "rumor") probably means "report"; but in 1 K **10** 1; 2 Ch **9** 1; Isa **66** 19, it is most probably "renown," or "reputation"; *sh^e^mū'āh* (1 K **10** 7; 2 Ch **9** 6) may have either meaning; *shōma'* (Josh **6** 27; **9** 9; Est **9** 4) seems to mean "fame" in the sense of reputation; but in Jer **6** 24 (as ARV) "report"; *shēm*, "name," has the sense of reputation (1 K **4** 31; 1 Ch **14** 17; **22** 5; Zeph **3** 19, RV "name"); *ḳōl*, "voice," is report (Gen **45** 16, ARV "report"). In the NT *akoē*, "hearing," is "report," so RV (Mt **4** 24; **14** 1; Mk **1** 28); *phēmē*, "word," "rumor," is report, fame in this sense (Mt **9** 26; Lk **4** 14); *ēchos*, "a sound," "noise" (Lk **4** 37, RV "rumor"), and *lógos*, "word" (Lk **5** 15, RV "report") have the same meaning; *diaphēmízō*, "to say throughout," "to report publicly" (Mt **9** 31, "they . . . . spread abroad his fame"), seems to imply fame in the sense of reputation.

In 1 Macc **3** 26, we have "fame" in the sense of reputation, "His fame [*ónoma*, RV "name"] came near even to the king"; so **3** 41, "heard the fame of them."

ERV has "fame" for "report" (*shēma'*), Jer **50** 43.

W. L. WALKER

FAMILIAR, fa-mil'yar: Is found as an adj. qualifying "friend" and "spirit."

(1) Used, in a number of OT passages, of spirits which were supposed to come at the call of one who had power over them. אוֹב, *'ōbh*, lit. something "hollow"; cf אוֹב, *'ōbh*, "bottle" (Job **32** 19 AV); because the voice of the spirit might have been supposed to come from the one possessed, as from a bottle, or because of the hollow sound which characterized the utterance, as out of the ground (Isa **29** 4); or, as some have conjectured, akin to אוּב, *'ūbh*, "return" (νεκρόμαντις, *nekrómantis*). Probably called "familiar" because it was regarded as a servant (*famulus*), belonging to the family (*familiaris*), who might be summoned to do the commands of the one possessing it. The practice of consulting familiar spirits was forbidden by the Mosaic law (Lev **19** 31; **20** 6.27; Dt **18** 11). King Saul put this away early in his reign, but consulted the witch of Endor, who "had a familiar spirit" (1 S **28** 3.7. 8.9; 1 Ch **10** 13). King Manasseh fell into the same sin (2 K **21** 6; 2 Ch **33** 6); but Josiah put those who dealt with familiar spirits out of the land (2 K **23** 24).

It seems probable, however, that the practice prevailed more or less among the people till the exile (Isa **8** 19; **19** 3). See "Divination by the 'Ôb" in *Expos T*, IX, 157; ASTROLOGY, 1; COMMUNION WITH DEMONS.

(2) "Familiars," "familiar friend," fr יָדַע, *yādha'*, "to know," hence "acquaintance," one intimately attached (Job **19** 14); but more frequently of *'ĕnōsh shālōm*, "man of [my or thy] peace," that is, one to whom the salutation of peace is given (Ps **41** 9; Jer **20** 10; **38** 22; also in Ob ver 7, rendered "the men that were at peace with thee").

EDWARD BAGBY POLLARD

FAMILY, fam'i-li (מִשְׁפָּחָה, *mishpāḥāh*, בַּיִת, *bayith*; πατριά, *patriá*):

1. The Foundation
2. Monogamy the Ideal Relation
3. Equality of the Sexes
4. Polygamy
5. The Commandments and the Family (5th Commandment)
6. The Commandments and the Family (7th Commandment)
7. The Commandments and the Family (10th Commandment)
8. Primitive Monogamic Ideal
9. Reforms of Ezra and Nehemiah
10. The NT
11. The Teaching of Jesus
12. The Teaching of Paul
13. Modern Dangers

LITERATURE

The Bible is the world's great teacher of monogamy—the union for life of one man and one woman in marriage as the basis of the family.

1. The Foundation

Whatever may be said about the time of the writing of the books of the Bible, or of parts of them, the testimony of the whole is incontrovertibly to the point that marriage springs from the choice of one man and one woman of each other for a permanent family relation. Over and through the whole of the Bible this ideal is dominant. There may be instances shown here and there of violation of this rule. But such cases are to be regarded as contrary to the underlying principle of marriage—known even at the time of their occurrence to be antagonistic to the principle.

There may be times when moral principle is violated in high places and perhaps over wide reaches in society. The Bible shows that there were such times in the history of man. But it is undeniable that its tone toward such lapses of men and of society is not one of condonation but one of regret and disapproval. The disasters consequent are faithfully set forth. The feeling that finds expression in its whole history is that in such cases there had been violation of the ideal of right in the sex relation. The ideal of monogamic relation is put in the forefront of the history of man.

2. Monogamy the Ideal Relation

The race is introduced synthetically as a species in the incoming of life. "And God created man in his own image, in the image of God created he him; male and female created he them" (Gen **1** 27). But with the first particularization of the relation of the sexes to each other the great charter of monogamy was laid down so clearly that Jesus was content to quote it, when with His limitless ethical scrutiny He explained the marriage relation. "And the man said [when the woman was brought to him], This is now bone of my bones, and flesh of my flesh: she shall be called Woman, because she was taken out of Man. Therefore shall a man leave his father and his mother, and shall cleave unto his wife: and they shall be one flesh" (Gen **2** 23.24). It is well to pause and look at the grammatical number of the nouns: "a man," "his wife." The words of the charter hold the sexes to monogamy. The subsequent words make marriage life-lasting. "They twain shall be one flesh." A dualism becomes an individualism. So said Christ: "Wherefore they are no more twain but one flesh" (Mt **19** 6 AV). Nothing but death separates a man from his own flesh. Nothing but life-monogamy can find place in the language of this charter.

There is much in the setting of this charter in the account given in Gen that is suggestive of the fine sentiment which we know has always gone along with love and marriage. That this account should have held the place in history that it has had adds testimony to the fine perception of sentiment and the strong grasp on principle out of which it came.

3. Equality of the Sexes

Eve, "the mother of all living," comes out as distinctly as Adam on the canvas in the portraiture of the first pair. She is the feminine representative—*'ishshāh*—of the race, as Adam is the masculine—*'īsh* (Gen **2** 23). The personality of Eve is as complete as that of Adam. She is a rational and accountable creature, as Adam is. In primitive intellectual and moral transactions she has share on equality with Adam, and is equally involved in their results. Different physical consequences fall on her for "transgression," because she is "woman," "the mother of all living" (Gen **3** 16). But Adam does not escape retribution for sin, and it may be questioned whether its burden did not fall hardest on him (Gen **3** 18.19), for motherhood has its joy as well as its pain, in the companionship of new-born child-life; but the wrestler for subsistence from a reluctant earth must bear his hardship alone. It cannot but be that much of the primitive conjugal love survived the fall.

4. Polygamy

According to the record, monogamy seems long to have survived the departure from Eden. It is not till many generations after that event that we find a case of polygamy —that of Lamech (Gen **4** 19–24). Lamech is said to have had "two wives." The special mention of "two" seems to show that man had not yet wandered far away from monogamy. The indications seem to be that as the race multiplied and went out over the face of the earth they forgot the original kinship and exhibited all manner of barbarities in social relations. Lamech was a polygamist, but he was also a quarrelsome homicide: "I have slain a man for wounding me, and a young man for bruising me" (Gen **4** 23). If such acts and dispositions as are disclosed in the case of Lamech become common, it will certainly not be a long while before the only apt description of the condition of society must be that upon which we come in Gen **6** 5: "And Jeh saw that the wickedness of man was great in the earth, and that every imagination of the thoughts of his heart was only evil continually." Out of such condition will come war and slavery, and polygamy—and come they did. It is a straight road from Gen **6** 5 to "The Koran, tribute or the sword," and the polygamy of Mohammedans.

5. The Commandments and the Family (5th Commandment)

The commandments (Ex **20** 12; Dt **5** 16) are a succinct summary of the supreme moral relations and duties of man. The first four pertain to our relationship to God. The six following concern human relations. Of these six, three have considerations of the family involved in them. Commandments do not come to people ignorant of the subjects to which they relate. A commandment to cover an unknown moral relation is an absurdity. The text of the Fifth Commandment is, "Honor thy father and thy mother." This refers to the relation of children to parents. This commandment could scarcely have arisen when polygamy was a common practice, certainly never from promiscuity. The equality of father and mother is stamped on its face. That idea never could have had strength and solemnity enough, except in a prevailing condition of monogamy, to entitle the command in which it appeared to rank with the important subjects covered by the other commands. Before the gaze of the children to whom this commandment came, the family stood in monogamic honor—the mother a head of the family as well as the father. There is no question about the position of the mother in this commandment. She stands out as clear as Sinai itself. There is no cloud on her majesty. Such honor as goes to the father goes to the mother. She is no chattel, no property, no inferior being, but the mother; no subordinate to the father, but his equal in rank and entitled to equal reverence with him. The commandment would not and could not have so pictured the mother had she been one of the inmates of a harem.

6. The Commandments and the Family (7th Commandment)

The Seventh Commandment (Ex **20** 14; Dt **5** 18) gives the family. It secures the home. It says that whatever children are born to the race shall be born in a home and of the home—shall be family-born. The terms adultery and fornication have now become synonymous. Under the influence of polygamous practices a distinction was made in respect to unlawful sex union as to whether one or both of the parties thereto were married or not, or whether one or both were single. Such distinction will not hold in morals. All or any sex union out of marriage is barred by the family idea. Outside of that all sex union is sin.

While it is true that in the laws of Israel sex sin outside the family relation was treated as a subject by itself, yet when we remember how early in life marriage came in those ancient days, and that betrothal in childhood was deemed as sacred as marriage itself, we see that even then the sweep of the commandment was well-nigh universal and over what a broad range it protected the family. The family is the primal eldest institution of man—the greatest and the holiest. Over this institution this commandment stands sentry. It prevents men from breaking up in complete individual isolation, from reverting to solitary savagery. Think to what a child is born outside of the family relation! Then think of all children being so born, and you have the picture of a low plane of animalism from which all trace of the moral responsibility of fatherhood has disappeared, and where even motherhood will be reduced to simple care during the short period of helpless infancy, to such care as belongs to animal instinct. Put up now the idea that marriage shall be universal and that the children born in marriage shall belong genuinely to it, and you have a new heaven and a new earth in the sex relations of the race of man.

7. The Commandments and the Family (10th Commandment)

The Tenth Commandment seems almost out of place on the list of the commandments. All the others enjoin specific acts. This tenth seems to be a foregleam of the Saviour's method—going to the thoughts and intents of the heart. It is an attempt at regulation *in* man. It goes beyond outward acts and deals with the spirit. Its purpose seems not regulation of man in society but in himself. So far as it has outward relation it seems to apply primarily to the rights of property. We have at common law the expression, "rights of persons; and rights of things," i.e. to property. But the list of things enumerated in the commandment comprises the things most common to family life: house, servants, animals. One is forbidden not only to take but even to desire such things. They are necessary to family life. In this list of things belonging to a neighbor that a man is forbidden to desire occurs the term "wife." To first thought it may seem strange that she should be listed with property in house and chattels. But it may not be very singular. One of woman's greatest blessings to man is helpfulness. Eve, the mother of all living, came as a helpmeet for Adam. Sarah is mistress of domestic operations. A wife quick of thought, accurate in judgment and deft of hand is usually the key to a man's material prosperity. As such help a man's desire might stray to his neighbor's wife as well as to his cattle. Even on this lower plane she is still a constituent element of the family. Here the thought of sex is scarcely discernible. Covetousness unlimited in the accumulation of property is what comes under ban. To treat of that matter would lead too far astray. See COVETOUSNESS.

It is well to remember in taking leave of the commandments that half of those pertaining to human relations hold the family plainly in view. This is as it should be. The race is divided equally between male and female, and their relations to each other, we might expect, would call for half of the directions devoted to the whole.

8. Primitive Monogamic Ideal

The laws against adultery and incest (Lev **20** and the like) may seem barbarously severe. Be it so; that fact would show they were carried along by a people tremendously in earnest about the integrity of the family. Beneath pioneer severity is usually a solemn principle. That the children of Israel had a tough grasp on the primitive monogamic ideal is not only apparent in all their history, but it comes out clear in what they held as history before their own began. Mr. Gladstone said the tenth chapter of Genesis is the best document of ancient ethnography known to man. But it is made up on family lines. It is a record of the settlement of heads of families as they went forth on the face of the earth. The common statement for the sons of Noah as they filed out over the lands of which they took possession is, 'these are the sons of . . . . after their families, after their tongues, in their lands, in their nations.' Mr. Gladstone called attention to the fact that modern philology verifies this classification of the nations which rests on outgrowth from *families*.

9. Reforms of Ezra and Nehemiah

Turning now to a very distant point in history—the return of the Jews from captivity in Babylon—we find in Ezr and Neh the most critical regard for genealogy. The effort to establish "pure blood" was fairly a fanaticism and might even be charged with injustice. Yet this effort was ratified by the people—sufferers in degraded name though many of them must have been. This could never have been done had not the monogamic family idea rested in their hearts as just and right. Nehemiah (**13** 26) unsparingly condemned the mighty Solomon for his polygamy, and Israel approved the censure.

10. The NT

When we come to the times of the NT, contemporaneous polygamy in Jewish society was dead. Wherever NT influences have gone, contemporaneous polygamy has ceased to be.

There has been in the United States by Mormonism a belated attempt to revive that crime against the family. But it has had its bad day, and, if it lives at all, it is under the ban of social sentiment and is a crime by law. Consecutive polygamy still exists in nations that are called Christian by the permission of divorce laws. But the tide of Christian sentiment is setting strongly against it, and it takes no special clearness of vision to see that it must go to extinction along with polygamy contemporaneous.

Jesus reaffirmed the original charter of the monogamic family (Mt **19** 1–12; Mk **10** 2–12). It is to be noticed that He affirmed the indissolubility of the family not only against the parties thereto but against the power of society. See DIVORCE.

11. The Teaching of Jesus

At first sight it seems a little strange that Jesus said so little about the family. But as we reflect on the nature of His mission we shall catch the explanation of His silence. He said, "Think not that I came to destroy the law or the prophets: I came not to destroy, but to fulfil" (Mt **5** 17), that is, to fill out, to expound and expand. He also said, "For the Son of man is come to save that which was lost" (**18** 11 AV), and, "I came not to call the righteous, but sinners" (**9** 13), that is, to rectify what was wrong. To what was right He gave the right of way—let it go on in its own course. When the law was right, He said, not one jot or tittle of it should fail (**5** 18). With regard to the family, He held the old charter written in the heart of man, before it was burned in brick or committed to manuscript, was right. It was comprehensive, would and ought to stand. So He stood by that, and that sufficed His purpose. Christ did not try to regulate the family so much as to regulate the persons who entered into family life. This may explain why we have no utterance from Him in regard to the conduct and duties of children toward parents. Still stood the ancient statute, "Honor thy father and thy mother." He came not to destroy but to fulfil that. That still indicated the right relation of children to parents. If a child had asked about his relation to his parents, Christ would doubtless have referred him to that commandment, as He did other inquirers about duties to the commandments that cover so large a part of the ethical realm.

12. The Teaching of Paul

Paul, who particularizes so much in explanation of duties in all relations, scarcely gets beyond the old commandment, "Honor thy father and thy mother," when he says, "Children, obey your parents in all things, for this is well-pleasing in the Lord." It has always been well-pleasing in the Lord. To be sure there was new inspiration to obedience from the new revelation of duty which came to them in Christ, but the duty was enforced by the Fifth Commandment, and that was copied from the deeper revelation in the heart of man.

13. Modern Dangers

In modern society the two great foes of the family are Divorce and Migration. Families no longer live a continuous life together. We have less family life than the old pastoral nomads. They had to keep together for several generations in order to protect their lives and their flocks and herds. So arose the clan, the tribe and the nation. Family influence can be detected through them. Modern industries are very much localized. We should easily think that families would be under their controlling influence. But they are not; the industries are localized, the workers are becoming rovers. When trouble comes in an industry, a workman's first resort is to try somewhere else. Cheapness of transportation gives him the opportunity he desires. So with a satchel he goes hunting, much as a barbarian roams the forest for game, alone. He may take his family or leave it behind. He may be separated from his family for months or years—possibly abandon it forever. A very common cause of divorce is abandonment of family by its male head.

In fact, those engaged in a great deal of legitimate industry are looking out for a better place quite as much as to develop the capacities of business in their own locations. The signs over places of business are few that carry the same name in town or city for a generation. Moving is perhaps more the order of the day than movement. The families are few that can be found in the same place for a quarter of a century. The wealthy cannot stay in the same house six months at a time. They have a house in the city for the winter and one in the country for the summer, and then forsake both and fly over the sea, perhaps to remain for years—traveling. How can family ties survive under such migratory life? Society supersedes the family.

Even education is subject to this malign influence. At their most impressive age, when they need family influence most around them, children are sent away to prepare for or to enter upon higher courses of education. This fits them for something else than life in the family from which they sprang and they rarely return to it. We may not be able to check this drift, but we ought to see its tendency to degrade the estimate of the value of the family.

Literature.—Wolsey, *Divorce*, Scribners; Publications of the National Divorce Reform League; Reports State and National, *ad rem;* Peabody, *Jesus Christ and the Social Question*, ch iii; Caverno, *Divorce*, Midland Pub. Co., Madison, Wis.; *The Ten Words*, Pilgrim Press, Boston.

C. Caverno

FAMILY RELATIONSHIPS. See Relationships, Family.

FAMINE, fam'in (רָעָב, *rā'ābh;* **λιμός**, *limós*):

1. Natural Causes
2. Famines Mentioned
3. Divine Relations
4. Figurative Uses

The common OT word for "famine" is *rā'ābh; r^e'ābhōn* also occurs (Gen **42** 19.33; Ps **37** 19), and *kāphān* (Job **5** 22; **30** 3), all meaning "hunger" and "famine"; in the NT the word is *limos*, meaning primarily "failure," "want of food."

In early times, esp. in lands dependent on their own productions, famines were not infrequent.

1. Natural Causes

They were generally caused by local irregularities of the rainfall, by destructive hail storms (Ex **9** 23.31.32), by ravages of insects (Ex **10** 15; Joel **1** 4) and by enemies (Dt **28** 51); in a city a famine might be caused by a siege (2 K **6** 25); pestilence often followed in its wake, and the suffering was great.

Famines are recorded in the time of Abraham (Gen **12** 10, etc), of Isaac (**26** 1), of Jacob, when

2. Famines Mentioned

Joseph was in Egypt—seven years of famine even in Egypt after seven of plenty (**41** 54), which also affected Canaan (**42** 1), and, indeed, "was over all the face of the earth" (**41** 56); in the time of the Judges (Ruth **1** 1), of David, for three years (2 S **21** 1), of Ahab and Elijah (1 K **17** 1; **18** 2; Ecclus **48** 2.3), of Elisha (2 K **4** 38), during the siege of Samaria (**6** 25), the seven years foretold by Elisha (**8** 1), in the reign of Zedekiah in Jerus when besieged by Nebuchadnezzar (2 K **25** 3; Jer **52** 6; cf **14** 1), its great severity is referred to (Lam **5** 10; Bar **2** 25); a "dearth" is also mentioned after the return from Captivity (Neh **5** 3); when the city was besieged by Antiochus Eupator (1 Macc **6** 54), after the death of Judas (**9** 24), when Jerus was besieged by Simon (**13** 49), in the time of Claudius (Acts **11** 28, in his reign there were frequent famines, one of which in 45 AD severely affected Pal; Jos, *Ant*, XX, v); Christ predicted "famines . . . . in divers places" as characterizing the end of the age (Mt **24** 7; Mk **13** 8; Lk **21** 11); in the siege of Jerus by Titus a terrible famine raged, the consequences of which to the people have never been surpassed.

Famines are frequently said to be sent as punishments sometimes threatened as such (Lev **26** 19 f;

3. Divine Relations

Dt **28** 49–51; 2 K **8** 1; Ps **105** 16; Isa **14** 30; **51** 19; Jer **14** 12.15; **18** 21, etc; Ezk **5** 16, etc; Am **8** 11; 2 Esd **15** 5.49; **16** 19; Tob **4** 13; Ecclus **39** 29; **40** 9).

The righteous or godly should be preserved by God in time of famine (Job **5** 20, "In famine he will redeem thee from death"; Ps **33** 19, "to keep them alive in famine"; **37** 19, "In the days of famine they shall be satisfied"); this was a special mark of the Divine favor and power.

A famine is used by Amos to indicate the absence of Divine communications as a punishment that

4. Figurative Uses

should come on the people, a "famine . . . . of hearing the words of Jeh" (**8** 11; cf 1 S **3** 1; **28** 6; 2 Ch **15** 3; Ezk **7** 26; Mic **3** 6); by Zephaniah of the destruction of heathen deities (**2** 11).

RV has "dearth" for "famine" (Job **5** 22); "famine" for "dearth" (Gen **41** 54*b;* 2 Ch **6** 28; Acts **7** 11; **11** 28); for "hunger" (Jer **38** 9; Ezk **34** 29; Rev **6** 8); "famines" for "famines and pestilences" (Mt **24** 7), "famines and troubles" (Mk **13** 8), revised texts.

W. L. Walker

FAMISH, fam'ish (רָעֵב, *rā'ēbh*, רָזָה, *rāzāh*): "To famish" as a trans vb. is the tr of *rā'ēbh*, "to hunger" (Gen **41** 55): "All the land of Egypt was famished"; of *rā'ābh*, "hunger" (Isa **5** 13), "Their honorable men are famished," m "Heb their glory are men of famine"; of *rāzāh*, "to make lean," "famish" (Zeph **2** 11), "For he will famish all the gods of the earth"; it is intrans as the tr of *rā'ēbh* (Prov **10** 3), "Jeh will not suffer the soul of the righteous to famish."

FAN, FANNER, fan'ẽr: The word "fan" occurs 3 t only in ARV (Jer **15** 7; Mt **3** 12; Lk **3** 17). In Isa **30** 24 *mizreh* is tr[d] "fork," which is a much better tr if the instrument referred to was shaped like the winnowing fork used by the Syrian farmer today and still so called. In Isa **41** 16; Jer **4** 11; **15** 7, the vb. *zārāh* is rendered "winnow" in ARV. In Jer **51** 2, RV substitutes "strangers" for "fanners."

FANCY, fan'si (**φαντάζω**, *phantázō*, "to cause to appear," "show"): In Ecclus **34** 5, "And the heart fancieth, as a woman's in travail" (cf Wisd **6** 16; He **12** 21).

FAR, fär, **FARTHER**, fär'thẽr: "Far" (adj.), distant, remote; (advb.) widely removed, is most frequently in the OT the tr of רָחוֹק, *rāḥōḳ*, and in the NT of *μακράν*, *makrán*, but also of other Heb and Gr words. The word *ḥālīlāh*, an exclamation of abhorrence or aversion (LXX *mḗ génoito;* see Forbid), is rendered "far from me," "far from thee," etc (Gen **18** 25; 1 S **2** 30; **20** 9; **22** 15; 2 S **20** 20; **23** 17; Job **34** 10). Besides its literal sense, distance in a spiritual sense is expressed by "far," as "Salvation is far from the wicked" (Ps **119** 155; cf Prov **15** 29), "far from righteousness" (Isa **46** 12), "not far from the kingdom of God" (Mk **12** 34), etc. For "far" RV has "aloof" in Job **30** 10; in several places the word in AV is omitted (Jgs **9** 17; Ps **27** 9; Isa **19** 6; **26** 15; Mk **13** 34); "a far country" is changed to "another" (Mt **21** 33; **25** 14; Mk **13** 34), etc. For "God forbid" RV has "far be it," "far be it from me" (Gal **6** 14; in ARV, Gen **44** 7.17; 1 S **12** 23; Job **27** 5, etc).

The comparative "farther" occurs only once in the OT (Eccl **8** 17), and thrice in the NT (Mt **26** 39; Mk **1** 19; **10** 1), and in each case is replaced in RV by another word or phrase. RV, on the other hand, has "its farthest height" for "the height of his border" (Isa **37** 24), and "his farthest lodging-place" for "the lodgings of his borders" (2 K **19** 23).

W. L. WALKER

FAR HOUSE: The marginal explanation in RV of *Beth-merhak* (בֵּית הַמֶּרְחָק, *bēth ha-merḥāḳ*, "house of distance"), which is given in the text of 2 S **15** 17 instead of "a place that was far off." See BETH-MERHAK.

FARE, fâr: Occurs twice in the OT as the tr of two Heb words, שָׁלוֹם, *shālōm*, "peace," "prosperity," "completeness" (1 S **17** 18), found in the section on David's family history omitted by the LXX translators, and שָׂכָר, *sākhār*, "hire," "reward," LXX ναῦλον, *naúlon*, "passage-money," "fare" (Jon **1** 3). In Heb both words are substantives; in Eng. the former is a vb. meaning "to go," or "get on as to circumstances" (*Century Dict.*), the latter, a subst. meaning the price which Jonah paid for a sea-voyage to Tarshish.

In Apoc the Eng. vb. "fare" helps in the tr of three Gr words, κακόω, *kakóō*, "fare evil" (RV "fare ill"), Sir **3** 26; ἐλαττόω, *elattóō*, "fare worse" (RV "suffer loss"), **32** 24; ῥώννυμι, *rhōnnumi*, "be strong," "prosper," in 2 pers. (sing.) imperat. (ἔρρωσο, *érr[h]ōso*) or pl. (ἔρρωσθε, *érr[h]ōsthe*) as a farewell salutation, or at the close of a letter, or to describe the welfare (usually physical or social) of a friend (2 Macc **9** 20; **11** 21.28, etc). Cf Acts **15** 29; **23** 30 m.

In the NT the Eng. vb. "fare," in addition to its occurrence in the word "farewell" (which see), occurs only once (Lk **16** 19), where it is said that the rich man "fared sumptuously every day" (RVm "living in mirth and splendor every day").

The Gr is εὐφραίνομαι, *euphraínomai*, "be merry," and occurs 14 t in the NT, 10 in a good sense (Lk **15** 23.24. 29.32, all referring to the merry-making over the return of the lost son; Acts **2** 26, tr of Heb שָׂמַח, *sāmaḥ*, "be glad"; Rom **15** 10, tr of Heb רָנָה, *rānāh*, "to sing"; 2 Cor **2** 2; Gal **4** 27, tr of Heb רָנָה, *rānāh*, "to sing"; Rev **12** 12; **18** 20); 4 in a bad, or less favorable, sense (Lk **12** 19; **16** 19; Acts **7** 41; Rev **11** 10). The Gr word is variously trd in the NT, "be merry," "make merry," "be glad," "rejoice," "make glad," and only once "fare" (Lk **16** 19). In the last passage it means the general physical and material welfare of the rich man (so the Geneva [1560], the Bishops' and Rhemish Bibles, RV [1881], and not simply partaking of rich food so Vulg, Wyclif, Coverdale, Cranmer, Geneva [1557] and AV). Luther translates Lk **16** 19, "lebte alle Tage herrlich und in Freuden"; Weizsäcker, "genoss sein Leben alle Tage in Glanze"; Ostervald, "se traitoit bien et magnifiquement"; Oltremare, "faisait brillante chère"; Segond, "menait joyeuse et brillante vie"; Weymouth, "enjoyed a splendid banquet every day," all of which virtually agree with the view taken by us as to meaning of "fare." The λαμπρῶς, *lamprō̃s*, "sumptuously," shows that the rich man's manner of living was "brilliant," "magnificent." RV has "fare" for "do" (Acts **15** 36), "fared" for "did" (2 S **11** 7), "hath fared" for "was" (Gen **30** 29).

CHARLES B. WILLIAMS

FAREWELL, fâr-wel′ (χαίρω, *chaírō*), **Fare ye, or thou, well:** Originally a wish at parting for those faring forth (traveling):

(1) As a parting wish at the close of a letter it represents the Gr ἔρρωσο, *érr[h]ōso*, "Be strong," imperat. of ῥώννυμι, *rhōnnumi*, "to make strong" (Acts **15** 29; **23** 30 AV; see RVm; 2 Macc **11** 21); once χαίρετε, *chaírete* (imp. of χαίρω), "Rejoice!" (2 Cor **13** 11, RVm "Rejoice: be perfected").

(2) As equivalent to our saying "good-bye," it represents the Gr ἀποτάσσομαι, *apotássomai*, "to separate one's self," "to take leave," "to bid farewell" (Lk **9** 61, "to bid farewell to them that are at my house"; Acts **18** 21, "bade them farewell," RV "taking his leave of them"). See FARE; GREETING.

W. L. WALKER

FARM, färm: Mt **22** 5 is the only passage where ἀγρός, *agrós*, has been rendered "farm." In the many other passages where the same word occurs it is rendered "field" or "piece of ground." Farms such as the Occidental is accustomed to see, namely, isolated dwellings with their groups of outbuildings, surrounded by walls or hedges and overlooking the planted fields, were probably unknown in Pal. For protection against wild beasts and Arab marauders everyone lived in a village and went out to his fields, located perhaps miles away, only as occasion required.

JAMES A. PATCH

FARTHING, fär′thing: The rendering of two words in the Gr of the NT, ἀσσάριον, *assárion*, and κοδράντης, *kodrántēs*, Lat *quadrans*. The *assarion* was the tenth part of the *denarius*, and hence in value about one penny or two cents. The *quadrans* was the fourth part of the Roman *as*, and worth only about three mills, or less than the Eng. farthing, and is the only term rendered farthing by ARV. It occurs in Mt **5** 26 and Mk **12** 42, while *assarion*, which occurs in Mt **10** 29 and Lk **12** 6, is rendered "penny" by ARV.

FASHION, fash′un (מִשְׁפָּט, *mishpāṭ*; σχῆμα, *schēma*, the make, pattern, shape, manner or appearance of a thing [from Lat *faction-em*, "a making," through Old Fr. *façon, fachon*]): In the OT the noun "fashion" represents 3 Heb words:

(1) *Mishpāṭ*=lit. "judgment," hence judicial sentence, right, custom, manner; usually trd "judgment" (very frequent), but also a few times "sentence," "cause," "charge," and more frequently "manner" (nearly 40 t in AV). In 3 passages it is trd "fashion," in the sense of style, shape, make, in each case of a building or part of a building (Ex **26** 30; 1 K **6** 38; Ezk **42** 11).

(2) *Tekhūnāh*=lit. "arrangement," "adjustment" (cf *tākhan*, "to set right," "adjust," from *kūn*, *hēkhīn*, "to set up," "establish"); Ezk **43** 11, "the form of the house, and the fashion thereof." A cognate word in the preceding verse is trd "pattern" (RVm "sum").

(3) *Demūth*="resemblance" (from *dāmāh*, "to be similar"), generally trd "likeness" in EV, but "fashion" in 2 K **16** 10, where it means pattern or model. The vb. "to fashion" stands for (*a*) *yāçar*, "to form," "fashion" (Ps **33** 15; **139** 16 AV; Isa **22** 11 AV; **44** 12; **45** 9); (*b*) *'āsāh*, "to work," "make," "form" (Job **10** 8); (*c*) *kūn*, "to set up," "establish," "prepare" (Job **31** 15; Ps **119** 73; Ezk **16** 7); (*d*) *çūr*, "to bind up together," "compress" (Ex **32** 4, of Aaron fashioning the golden calf out of the golden rings).

In the NT, the noun represents 5 Gr words:

(1) Of these, the most interesting is *schēma*, "figure," "shape," "fashion" (from σχεῖν, *schein*, aor. of ἔχειν, *échein*, "to have," cf Lat *habitus*, from *habeo*, "I have"). *Schēma* denotes a transient, external semblance or fashion, and so it may be distinguished from its synonym μορφή, *morphḗ*, which denotes the essential intrinsic form of a thing, expressing its real nature. (See Lightfoot, Detached Note on Phil **2**; Trench, *NT Syn.*, 252 ff; Gifford, *Incarnation*, 22 ff. The distinction is rejected by Meyer, on Rom **12** 2, and by others.) In the NT, the noun *schēma* occurs but twice: 1 Cor **7** 31, "The fashion of this world passeth away," where there seems to be an allusion to theatrical scenes, which are in their very nature transitory (cf 2 Macc **4** 13); and Phil **2** 8, "being found in fashion as a man," i.e. having the outward figure and bearing of a man, such marks of human nature as strike the senses (contrast *morphē Theoú*, "form of God," ver 6, and *morphē doúlou*, "form of servant," ver 7, which describe Christ's real inner nature). The word *schēma* is found in compound vbs. in the following passages: Rom **12** 2, "Be not fashioned [*sunschēmatízesthe*] according to this world: but be ye

transformed [*metamorphoústhe*] by the renewing of your mind" (so RV), paraphrased by Sanday and Headlam, "Do not adopt the external and fleeting fashion of this world, but be ye transformed in your inmost nature" (*Comm.* in loc.); 2 Cor **11** 13 f, *metaschēmatízomai*, AV "transformed," better RV "fashioned," the reference being to "the fictitious, illusory transformation whereby evil assumes the mask of good" (Lightfoot, *Comm. on Phil,* 131); 1 Pet **1** 14, "not fashioning yourselves according to your former lusts," paraphrased by Lightfoot, "not falling in with the capricious guidance of the passions" (ib). In Phil **3** 21, the adj. *súmmorphos* is tr[d] "fashioned" in AV, but better "conformed" as in RV.

(2) Εἶδος, *eídos*, lit. "thing seen," "external appearance," "shape," is tr[d] "fashion" in Lk **9** 29, of the glorified appearance of the transfigured Christ.

(3) Πρόσωπον, *prósōpon*, lit. "face," hence look, appearance, Jas **1** 11, "The grace of the fashion of it perisheth."

(4) Τύπος, *túpos*, type, model, tr[d] "fashion" in Acts **7** 44 AV (RV "figure"), the Gr word being taken from the LXX of the quoted passage, Ex **25** 40. The same phrase, *katá tón túpon,* in the ‖ passage, He **8** 5, is tr[d] "according to the pattern."

(5) In one instance the phrase "on this fashion," "in this manner," represents the Gr advb. οὕτως, *hoútōs,* "thus" (Mk **2** 12). D. Miall Edwards

FAST, fast, **FASTING,** fast'ing (צוֹם, *çūm;* עִנָּה נֶפֶשׁ, *'innāh nephesh,* "afflict soul or self," i.e. practise self-denial; **νηστεία,** *nēsteía,* **νηστεύειν,** *nēsteúein*): It is necessary to get rid of some modern notions associated with fasting before we can form a correct idea of its origin and significance in the ancient world. For instance, in the case of many ailments the dieting of the patient is an essential part of the remedy. But we may readily assume that originally fasting was not based on the salutary influence which it exercised on the health of the subject. Considerations of therapeutics played no part in the institution. The theory that fasting, like many other ancient customs, had a religious origin, is in favor with scholars, but we must not assume a religious origin for all practices which in process of time came to be associated with religion.

Many customs, purely secular in their origin, have gradually obtained a religious significance, just as purely religious customs have been dissociated from religion. It is also possible and, in the light of some usages, probable, that different motives operated in the association of fasting, as of some other customs, with religion. Scholars have been too ready to assume that the original significance of fasting was the same in all countries and among all nations. Robertson Smith in his *Religion of the Semites* advanced and defended the theory that fasting was merely a mode of preparation for the tribal meal in which sacrifice originated, and came to be considered at a later stage as part of the sacrificial act. This hypothesis apparently accounts for the otherwise strange fact that both *fasting* and *feasting* are religious acts, but it does not give a satisfactory explanation of the constant association of fasting with the "wearing of sackcloth," the "putting of ashes on the head," and other similar customs. It is obvious that very different motives operated in the institution of fasting and of feasting as religious observances.

It is a matter of common observation and experience that great distress causes loss of appetite and therefore occasions abstinence from food. Hannah, who was greatly distressed on account of her childlessness, "wept, and did not eat" (1 S **1** 7). Violent anger produces the same effect (**20** 34). According to 1 K **21** 4, Ahab, "heavy and displeased" on account of Naboth's refusal to part with his estate, sulked and "would eat no bread." Fasting, originally the natural expression of grief, became the customary mode of proving to others the inner emotion of sorrow. David demonstrated his grief at Abner's death (2 S **3** 35) by fasting, just as the Psalmist indicated his sympathy with his adversaries' sorry plight in the same way (Ps **35** 13). In such passages as Ezr **10** 6; Est **4** 3, it is not clear whether fasting is used in its religious significance or simply as a natural expression of sorrow (cf also Lk **5** 33 and see below). This view explains the association of fasting with the mourning customs of antiquity (cf 1 S **31** 13; 2 S **1** 12). As fasting was a perfectly natural and human expression and evidence of the subject's grief, it readily claimed a place among those religious customs whose main object was the pacification of the anger of God, or the excital of His compassion. Any and every act that would manifest the distressful state of the suppliant would appeal to the Deity and move Him to pity. The interesting incident recorded in 2 S **12** 16–23 suggests the twofold significance of fasting as a religious act or a mode of appealing to the Deity and as a funeral custom. David defends his fasting before and not after the child's death on the ground that while the child was alive David's prayer might be answered. His fasting was intended to make his petition effectual (cf also 1 K **21** 27; Ezr **8** 21; Est **4** 16). Occasionally fasting was proclaimed on a national scale, e.g. in case of war (Jgs **20** 26; 2 Ch **20** 3) or of pestilence (Joel **1** 13 f). Fasting having thus become a recognized mode of seeking Divine favor and protection, it was natural that it should be associated with confession of sin, as indisputable evidence of penitence or sorrow for sin.

Fasting might be partial, i.e. abstinence from certain kinds of food, or total, i.e. abstinence from all food as well as from washing, anointing, sleeping. It might be of shorter or longer duration, e.g. for one day, from sunrise to sunset (Jgs **20** 26; 1 S **14** 24; 2 S **1** 12; **3** 35). In 1 S **31** 13 allusion is made to a seven days' fast, while Daniel abstained from "pleasant bread," flesh, wine and anointing for three weeks (Dnl **10** 3). Moses (Ex **34** 28) and Elijah (1 K **19** 8) fasted for 40 days. It is probable that these last three references presuppose a totally different conception of the significance of fasting. It is obvious that dreams made a deep impression on primitive man. They were communications from the departed members of the family. At a later stage they were looked upon as revelations from God. During sleep there is total abstinence from food. It was easy to draw the inference that fasting might fit the person to receive these communications from the world of spirits (Dnl **10** 2). The close connection between fasting and insight—intellectual and spiritual—between simple living and high thinking is universally recognized. See further under Abstinence; Feasts and Fasts.

Literature.—Nowack, *Hebräische Archäologie;* Benzinger, *Hebräische Archäologie;* Robertson Smith, *Religion of the Semites.*

T. Lewis

FASTS AND FEASTS. See Feasts and Fasts.

FAT (חֵלֶב, *ḥēlebh,* חֵלֶב, *ḥelebh*): The layer of subcutaneous fat and the compact suet surrounding the viscera and imbedded in the entrails, which, like the blood, was forbidden as food in the Mosaic code (Lev **3** 17). It was to be sacrificed to God by being burnt upon the altar (**3** 16; **7** 30). This had to be done on the very day on which a beast had been slaughtered, to remove temptation from the Israelite to use it otherwise (Ex **23** 18). The law was probably a sanitary restriction, for, at an early date, leprosy, scrofula and disfiguring cutaneous diseases were thought to be caused by the use of fat as food. It was, moreover, an important pedagogical provision teaching the idea of self-denial, and the maxim that the richest and best meat of the edible animal belonged to Jeh. See also Fatling; Fowl, Fatted.

The expression "fat" is often used in **figurative** senses, e.g. abundant, exuberant, lusty, fertile, robust, outwardly successful (Dt **32** 15; Ps **92** 14 AV; **119** 70; Prov **11** 25; **13** 4, etc).

H. L. E. Luering

FAT (VAT). Wine, Wine Press, II.

FATHER, fä'thẽr (AS *Fæder;* Ger. *Vater;* Heb אָב, *'ābh,* etymology uncertain, found in many cognate languages; Gr **πατήρ,** *patḗr,* from root *pâ,* "nourisher," "protector," "upholder"):

1. Immediate Male Ancestor

Immediate male ancestor. The father in the Heb family, as in the Rom, had supreme rights over his children, could dispose of his daughter in marriage (Gen **29**), arrange his son's marriage (Gen **24**), sell his children (Ex **21** 7), but not his daughter to a stranger (Neh **5** 5), had power of life and death, as in the case of Isaac (Gen **22**), Jephthah's daughter (Jgs **11** 34 ff), the sacrificing of his children to Molech (Lev **18** 21; **20** 3–5), etc. Respect, reverence and affection for fathers (and equally for mothers) is most tenderly, explicitly and sternly prescribed from the earliest times (Ex **20** 12; Lev **19** 3; Dt **5** 16; Mic **7** 6; Ezk **22** 7, etc). A symmetrical and beautiful picture of the duties and character of the ideal human father may be built up from the OT, with added and enlarged touches from the NT. He loves (Gen **37** 4); commands (Gen **50** 16; Prov **6** 20); instructs (**1** 8, etc); guides, encourages, warns (Jer **3** 4; 1 Thess **2** 11); trains (Hos **11** 3); rebukes (Gen **34** 30); restrains (Eli, by contrast, 1 S **3** 13); punishes (Dt **21** 18); chastens (Prov **3** 12; Dt **8** 5); nourishes (Isa **1** 2); delights in his son (Prov **3** 12), and in his son's wisdom (**10** 1); is deeply pained by his folly (**17** 25); he is considerate of his children's needs and requests (Mt **7** 10); considerate of their burdens, or sins (Mal **3** 17, "As a man spareth his own son"); tenderly familiar (Lk **11** 7, "with me in bed"); considerately self-restrained (Eph **6** 4, "Provoke not your children to wrath"); having in view the highest ends (ib, "Nurture them in the chastening and admonition of the Lord"); pitiful (Ps **103** 13, "as a father pitieth his children"); the last human friend (but one) to desert the child (Ps **27** 10: "When [a thing to the psalmist incredible] my father and my mother forsake me, then Jeh will take me up").

2. Ancestors, Immediate or Remote

(*a*) Ancestor, immediate or remote: Gen **28** 13, "Abraham thy father" (grandfather); 1 K **22** 50, "Jehoshaphat . . . . David his father"; Jer **35** 6, "Jonadab, the son of Rechab, our father"; Dnl **5** 11, "Nebuchadnezzar thy father" (personal or official ancestor); Gen **15** 15, "Go to thy fathers in peace" (and so [in the pl.] in over 500 passages). The expressions "slept with his fathers," "go down to his fathers," "buried with his fathers," "gathered to his fathers," are self-explanatory euphemisms. (*b*) The founders of the (Heb) race, specifically the patriarchs: Rom **9** 5, "whose are the fathers," considered here also as in a sense the religious ancestors of all believers. (*c*) Progenitors of clans, i.e. (RV) "fathers' houses": Ex **6** 14; 1 Ch **27** 1, etc. (*d*) Gods as progenitors of men: Jer **2** 27, "Who say to a stock, thou art my father."

3. Figurative and Derived Uses

Figurative and derived uses: (*a*) A spiritual ancestor, one who has infused his own spirit into others, whether good, as Abraham, the father of the faithful, Rom **4** 11; or bad, as Jn **8** 44, "Ye are of your father the devil." (*b*) Indicating closest resemblance, kinship, affinity: Job **17** 14, "If I have said to corruption, Thou art my father." (*c*) A source: Eph **1** 17, "Father of glory"; Job **38** 28, "Hath the rain a father?" (*d*) Creator: Jas **1** 17, "the Father of lights." (*e*) The inventor or originator of an art or mode of life: Gen **4** 20, "father of such as dwell in tents" (a hint here of hereditary occupations? Probably not). (*f*) One who exhibits the fatherly characteristics: Ps **68** 5, "a father of the fatherless." (*g*) One who occupies a position of counsel, care, or control (frequently applied by sultans to their prime ministers): Gen **45** 8, "a father to Pharaoh"; Jgs **17** 10, "Be unto me a father and a priest." (*h*) A revered or honored superior: 2 K **5** 13, "My father, if the prophet had bid thee"; but esp. applied to prophets: 2 K **2** 12, "My father, my father!" also to elderly and venerable men: 1 Jn **2** 13, "I write unto you, fathers"; hence also, with perhaps an outlook on (2) (*a*), deceased early Christians: 2 Pet **3** 4, "from the day that the fathers fell asleep." (*i*) An ecclesiastical title, condemned (in principle) by Our Lord: Mt **23** 9, "Call no man your father on the earth"; but applied, under the power of the Spirit, to members of the Sanhedrin (probably) by Stephen: Acts **7** 2; and by Paul: **22** 1, but the latter, perhaps also the former, may simply refer to the elderly among his hearers. Christ's condemnation is clearly of the praise-seeking or obsequious spirit, rather than of a particular custom.

"Father," used by Mary of Joseph, in relation to Jesus, equals "putative father," a necessary reserve at a time when the virgin birth could not yet be proclaimed (Lk **2** 49). But note Jesus' answer: "my Father's house."

Philip Wendell Crannell

FATHER, GOD THE: In the Christian religion God is conceived of as "Father," "Our Father . . . . in heaven" (Mt **6** 9.14.26, etc), "the God and Father of the Lord Jesus" (2 Cor **11** 31, etc). The tenderness of relation and wealth of love and grace embraced in this profound designation are peculiar to Christ's gospel. Pagan religions also could speak of God as "Father" (*Zeus Patḗr*), and in the general sense of Creator God has a universal fatherly relation to the world (Acts **17** 24–28). In the OT God was revealed as Father to the chosen nation (Ex **4** 22), and to the special representative of the nation, the king (2 S **7** 14), while fatherly love is declared to be the image of His pity for those who fear Him (Ps **103** 13). In the gospel of Jesus alone is this Fatherhood revealed to be of the very essence of the Godhead, and to have respect to the individual. Here, however, there is need for great discrimination. To reach the heart of the truth of the Divine Fatherhood it is necessary to begin, not with man, but with the Godhead itself, in whose eternal depths is found the spring of that Fatherly love that reveals itself in time. It is first of all in relation to the eternal Son—before all time—that the meaning of Fatherhood in God is made clear (Jn **1** 18). In "God the Father" we have a name pointing to that relation which the first Person in the adorable Trinity sustains to "Son" and "Holy Spirit"—also Divine (Mt **28** 19). From this eternal fountain-head flow the relations of God as Father (1) to the world by creation; (2) to believers by grace. Man as created was designed by affinity of nature for sonship to God. The realization of this—his true creature-destiny—was frustrated by sin, and can now only be restored by redemption. Hence the place of sonship in the gospel, as an unspeakable privilege (1 Jn **3** 1), obtained by grace, through regeneration (Jn **1** 12.13), and adoption (Rom **8** 14.19). In this relation of nearness and privilege to the Father in the kingdom of His Son (Col **1** 13), believers are "sons of God" in a sense true of no others. It is a relation, not of nature, but of grace. Fatherhood is now the determinative fact in God's relation to them (Eph **3** 14 ff). It is an error, nevertheless, to speak of fatherhood as if the whole character of God was therein sufficiently expressed. God is Father, but equally fundamental is His relation to His world as its Moral Ruler and Judge. From eternity to eternity the holy God must pronounce Himself against sin (Rom **1** 18); and His fatherly grace cannot avert judgment where the heart remains hard and impenitent (**2** 1–9). For the fuller discussion of these points see GOD; CHILDREN OF GOD; TRINITY. JAMES ORR

FATHER-IN-LAW, fä'thẽr-in-lô. See RELATIONSHIPS, FAMILY.

FATHERLESS, fä'thẽr-les (יָתוֹם, *yāthōm;* **ὀρφανός,** *orphanós*): The fatherless are frequently mentioned in the OT, generally in association with the widow and the stranger, as typical instances of the unprotected and necessitous, who are specially subject to oppression, and also to God's special protection. Great philanthropic regard is bestowed on this class throughout. In early legislation there is a special clause to guard them against affliction (Ex **22** 22–24). They have a still more prominent place in the Deuteronomic legislation, which gives instructions that a charitable fund be formed out of the tithe, once every three years, for the relief of the destitute (Dt **14** 28.29; **26** 12–14), and that gleanings be left in the cornfield, the olive garden, and the vineyard for the benefit of this class (**24** 19–22; cf Lev **19** 9 f; **23** 22, where, however, the "fatherless" are not specially mentioned). The Deuteronomist declares that God is on their side (**10** 18), and strongly condemns those who would oppress them (**24** 17; **27** 19). The prophets and psalmists are equally emphatic in pleading for mercy and justice to the fatherless, and in declaring that God is their special guardian (Isa **1** 17; Jer **7** 6 f; **22** 3; Hos **14** 3; Zec **7** 10; Ps **10** 14; **68** 5; **82** 3; **146** 9; cf Prov **23** 10). Oppressing the fatherless is frequently mentioned as a typical act of cruelty and injustice (cf Job **6** 27; **22** 9; **24** 3. 9; **29** 12 f; **31** 16.17.21; Ps **94** 6; Isa **1** 23; **10** 2; Jer **5** 28; Ezk **22** 7; Mal **3** 5). Here we have instances of the prophetic passion for righteousness and compassion for the helpless, inspired by a profound sense of the value of human life. Passages in the Apoc reflect the same spirit (2 Esd **2** 20; Ecclus **4** 10).

In the NT the word "fatherless" occurs but once, where James declares, in the spirit of the OT prophets, that true religious ritual consists in visitation of the fatherless and widows and in moral purity (Jas **1** 27). Here the word for "fatherless" is *orphanos* ("bereft," "orphaned"), which is the LXX tr of the OT *yāthōm*. In the NT the Gr word is found besides only in Jn **14** 18, where it means destitute of a teacher or guide (cf Lam **5** 3). D. MIALL EDWARDS

FATHERS' BROTHER. See RELATIONSHIPS, FAMILY.

FATHER'S HOUSE, FATHERS' HOUSE (בֵּית אָב, *bēth 'ābh,* בֵּית אָבוֹת, *bēth 'ābhōth*): Father's house in the OT is (1) a dwelling, the family home (Gen **12** 1; **31** 14.30; **38** 11; 1 S **18** 2); (2) a family or household (Gen **41** 51; **46** 31; Ex **12** 3, RV "fathers' houses"); (3) the group of households, of several of which the "family" or "clan" was constituted, aggregations of which formed the "tribe," generally "fathers' houses" (Nu **1** 18.20 ff; **17** 2; Ezr **2** 59; Neh **10** 34, etc); (4) the "family" (clan), *mishpāḥāh,* "fathers' houses" (Ex **6** 14 f; Nu **3** 20 ff); (5) the tribe, "fathers' house," "houses" (Nu **7** 2; **17** 1–3, etc).

In the NT "father's house" (**οἶκος τοῦ πατρός,** *oíkos toú patrós*) occurs in the sense of dwelling, house (Lk **16** 27; cf **16** 4). Our Lord also uses the phrase (1) of the earthly temple-dwelling of God at Jerus (Jn **2** 16, "Make not my Father's house a house of merchandise"; cf Ps **11** 4; Isa **63** 15); (2) of heaven as the abode of God and His children (Jn **14** 2, "In my Father's house are many mansions," RVm "abiding places," *oikía,* "house," "dwelling," also household, family; cf Ps **33** 13; Isa **63** 15; Mt **6** 9). The phrase occurs also (Acts **7** 20) of Moses, "nourished . . . . in his father's house" (*oikos*).

RV has "father's house" for "principal household" (1 Ch **24** 6), "heads of the fathers' houses" for "chief fathers" (Nu **31** 26; **32** 28; **36** 1; 1 Ch **9** 34, etc); "one prince of a father's house," for "each of" (Josh **22** 14); "the heads of the fathers' [houses]" for "the chief of the fathers," and "the fathers' houses of the chief," for "the principal fathers" (1 Ch **24** 31).

W. L. WALKER

FATHOM, fath'um (**ὀργυιά,** *orguiá*): The lit. meaning is the length of the outstretched arms, and it was regarded as equal to 4 cubits, or about 6 ft. (Acts **27** 28). See WEIGHTS AND MEASURES.

FATLING, FATTED. See CALF.

FATNESS, fat'nes (דֶּשֶׁן, *deshen;* **πιότης,** *piótēs*): The tr of *deshen* (Jgs **9** 9, "But the olive-tree said unto them, Should I leave my fatness?";

1. Literal Job **36** 16 [of food]), "full of fatness"; of *ḥēlebh,* "fat," "the best part," "the marrow" (Job **15** 27; Ps **73** 7; Isa **34** 6.7); of *mishmān,* "fatness," "fertility" (Gen **27** 28, "the fatness of the earth"; Isa **17** 4, "the fatness of his flesh"); of *shemen,* "fatness," "oil" (Ps **109** 24); of *piotēs,* "fat," "fatness" (Rom **11** 17, "partaker . . . . of the root of the fatness of the olive tree").

"Fatness" is used **fig.** for the richness of God's goodness; as such it is the tr of *deshen* ("They shall be abundantly satisfied [m "Heb

2. Figurative watered"] with the fatness of thy house" (Ps **36** 8); "Thy paths drop fatness" (**65** 11; cf Isa **55** 2; Jer **31** 14).

"With fatness" is supplied, Dt **32** 15 AV, "covered with fatness"; RV has "become sleek"; for "The yoke shall be destroyed because of the anointing" (Isa **10** 27) ARV has "by reason of fatness," m "Heb oil"; ERV as AV, with m as ARV; the text is believed to be corrupt; LXX has "from your shoulders."

W. L. WALKER

FAUCHION, fô'shun. See SCIMITAR.

FAULT, fôlt (חָטָא, *ḥāṭā';* **αἰτία,** *aitía,* **μέμφομαι,** *mémphomai*): Implies defect, of less moral weight than crime or sin. It is the tr of *ḥāṭā',* "error," "failure," "sin" (Ex **5** 16); of *ḥēṭ',* same meaning (Gen **41** 9, "I do remember my faults this day"); of *'āwōn,* "perversity," "iniquity" (2 S **3** 8; Ps **59** 4); of *rish'āh,* "wrongness," "wickedness" (Dt **25** 2, RV "wickedness"); of *sh^{e}hath* (Aram.) "corruption" (Dnl **6** 4 *bis*); *m^e'ūmāh,* "anything" (1 S **29** 3, "no fault in him," lit. "not anything"); of *aitia,* "cause," "case," "guilt" (Jn **18** 38; **19** 4.6; Pilate of Jesus, " I find no fault in him," RV "no crime"; the same word is rendered "accusation," i.e. 'legal cause for prosecution,' Mt **27** 37; Mk **15** 26; cf Acts **25** 18.27); of *aítion,* same meaning (Lk **23** 4.14; ver 22, *aition thanátou* "cause of death"); of *hḗttēma,* "a worse condition," "defect" (1 Cor **6** 7, RV "a defect," m "a loss to you"); of *paráptōma,* "a falling aside" (Gal **6** 1, "If a man be overtaken in a fault," RV "in any trespass," m "by"; Jas **5** 16, "Confess your faults one to another," RV "Confess therefore your sins one to another"); *hamartánō,* "to miss," "err," "sin," is tr^d "your faults" (1 Pet **2** 20 RV, "when ye sin"); *memphomai,* "to blame," is tr^d "to find fault" (Mk **7** 2 omitted RV; Rom **9** 19; He **8** 8); *elégchō*, "to convict," "to tell one's fault" (Mt **18** 15, RV "show him his fault"); *ámōmos*, "without blemish," "spotless," is tr[d] "without fault" (Rev **14** 5, RV "without blemish," "faultless"; Jude ver 24, "able to present you faultless," RV "without blemish"); *ámemptos*, "blameless," "without reproach" (He **8** 7, "for if that first covenant had been faultless"). "Faulty" is the tr of *'āshēm*, "guilty" (2 S **14** 13, "as one which is faulty," RV "guilty"); of *'āsham*, "to be or become guilty" (Hos **10** 2, RV "guilty").

W. L. Walker

FAVOR, fā'vẽr (חֵן, *ḥēn*, רָצוֹן, *rāçōn*, with other Heb words; **χάρις**, *cháris*): Means generally good will, acceptance, and the benefits flowing from these; in older usage it meant also the countenance, hence appearance. Alternating in EV with "grace," it is used chiefly of man, but sometimes also of God (Gen **18** 3; **30** 27; **39** 21; Ex **3** 21; 2 S **15** 25, "in the eyes of Jeh," etc). It is used perhaps in the sense of "countenance" in Prov **31** 30, "Favor is deceitful, and beauty is vain" (AV), where for "favor" RV has "grace"; the reference is to external appearance. "Favored" is used in the sense of "appearance" in the phrase "well-favored" (Gen **29** 17; **39** 6; **41** 2.4); conversely, "ill-favored" (Gen **41** 3.4). For "favor" RV has "have pity on" (Ps **109** 12), "good will" (Prov **14** 9), "peace" (Cant **8** 10); ERV "grace" (Ruth **2** 13), ARV "kindness" (Est **2** 17; Dnl **1** 9), etc. In ARV "the acceptable year of the Lord" (Isa **61** 2) is changed into "the year of Jeh's favor"; "Do I now persuade men" (Gal **1** 10) into, "Am I now seeking the favor of men," and there are other RV changes.

W. L. Walker

FAWN, fôn. See Deer.

FEAR, fēr (יִרְאָה, *yir'āh*, יָרֵא, *yārē'*; **φόβος**, *phóbos*, **φοβέω**, *phobéō*): "Fear" is the tr of many words in the OT; the chief are: *yir'āh*, "fear," "terror," "reverence," "awe," most often "the fear of God," "of Jeh" (Gen **20** 11; 2 Ch **19** 9, etc); also of "fear" generally (Job **22** 4; Isa **7** 25; Ezk **30** 13, etc); *yārē'*, "to be afraid," "to fear," "to reverence" (Gen **15** 1; Lev **19** 3.14; Dt **6** 2, etc); *paḥadh*, "fear," "terror," "dread" (Gen **31** 42.53; Dt **11** 25; 1 S **11** 7 AV; Job **4** 14; Isa **2** 10 AV, etc).

Terms, etc

"Fearful" (timid) is the tr of *yārē'* (Dt **20** 8; Jgs **7** 3); "to be feared," *yārē'* (Ex **15** 11; Dt **28** 58; cf Ps **130** 4); in Isa **35** 4, it is the tr of *māhar*, "hasty," "them that are of a fearful heart," m "Heb hasty"; perhaps, ready to flee (for fear).

"Fearfully" (Ps **139** 14): *yārē'*, "I am fearfully [and] wonderfully made," so RV; "and" is not in the text, so that "fearfully" may be equivalent to "extremely," to an awesome degree; cf Ps **65** 5, "by terrible things . . . . in righteousness"; **66** 3, "How terrible are thy works (*yārē'* "fearful"); the LXX, Pesh, Vulg have "Thou art fearfully wonderful."

"Fearfulness" occurs in Ps **55** 5 (*yir'āh*); Isa **21** 4 (*pallāçūth*), RV "horror"; Isa **33** 14 (*re'ādhāh*, "trembling"), "Fearfulness hath surprised the hypocrites," RV "Trembling hath seized the godless ones."

In the NT the chief words are *phobos*, "fear," "terror," "affright" (Mt **14** 26; **28** 4.8; Lk **21** 26; 1 Jn **4** 18, etc), and *phobeō*, "to put in fear" (both used of ordinary fear) (Mt **1** 20; **10** 26; **28** 5; 2 Cor **12** 20, etc); of the fear of God, the noun (Rom **3** 18; 2 Cor **7** 1), the vb. (Lk **18** 4; **23** 40, etc); *deilía*, "timidity," "fear," occurs in 2 Tim **1** 7, "God hath not given us the spirit of fear," RV "a spirit of fearfulness"; *ékphobos*, "frightened out [of one's senses]," "greatly terrified" (He **12** 21; cf Dt **9** 19; Wisd **17** 9 AV); *apó tēs eulabeías* is tr[d] (He **5** 7) "[of Christ] who was heard in that he feared," RV "having been heard for his godly fear"; so all the Gr commentators; *eulábeia*, properly, "caution," "circumspection," is used in the NT for godly fear (He **12** 28, RV "reverence and awe," m as AV); cf *eulabēs* (Lk **2** 25; Acts **2** 5; **8** 2); *eulabéomai*, "to act with caution" (Acts **23** 10). *Deilós*, "fearful," "timid," occurs in Mt **8** 26; Mk **4** 40; Rev **21** 8, "Their part shall be . . . . the second death"; *phoberós*, "fearful," "terrible" (He **10** 27. 31); *phóbētron*, "something fearful," "a terrible sign or portent" (Lk **21** 11, RV "terrors").

Fear is a natural and, in its purpose, beneficent feeling, arising in the presence or anticipation of danger, and moving to its avoidance; it is also awakened in the presence of superiors and of striking manifestations of power, etc, taking the form of awe or reverence. Fear has been said to be the source of religion, but religion can never have originated from fear alone, since men are impelled to draw nigh with expectation to the object of worship.

"Fear" is certainly a prominent element in OT religion; the "fear of God" or of Jeh, "the fear of the Lord," is indeed synonymous with religion itself (Ps **34** 11; Prov **1** 7; Isa **11** 2.3; Jer **2** 19; Eccl **12** 13, "the whole duty of man," RVm "the duty of all men"). But although the element of dread, or of "fear" in its lower sense, is not always absent and is sometimes prominent in the earlier stages especially, though not exclusively (Ex **23** 27, *'ēmāh;* 1 S **11** 7; 2 Ch **20** 29; Ps **119** 120; Isa **2** 10.19.21), it is more the feeling of reverent regard for their God, tempered with awe and fear of the punishment of disobedience. As such it is a sentiment commanded and to be cherished toward Jeh (Ex **20** 20; Dt **6** 13; Josh **4** 24; 1 S **12** 24; Job **6** 14; Ps **33** 8; **34** 9; Prov **23** 17; Eccl **5** 7, etc). It is an essential element in the worship and service of Jeh (2 K **17** often; Ps **2** 11, etc); it is a Divine qualification of the Messiah (Isa **11** 2.3). This "fear of Jeh" is manifested in keeping God's commandments, walking in His ways, doing His will, avoiding sin, etc (Ex **20** 20; Dt **6** 13.24; 2 S **23** 3; Ps **34** 4.9 ‖ Prov **8** 13; **16** 6). It is the true wisdom (Job **28** 28; Ps **25** 14; Prov **1** 7; **15** 33); it gives life (Prov **10** 27, etc), blessedness (Ps **128** 1.4), sufficiency (**34** 9), Divine friendship (**25** 14), protection (**34** 7), deliverance (**85** 9), forgiveness (**130** 4). In Ps **90** 11 AV has "According to thy fear so is thy wrath," RV "and thy wrath according to the fear that is due unto thee"; the meaning probably is "thy wrath is in proportion to thy fear."

The "fear of the Lord" is a frequent phrase in Apoc, and is highly exalted, e.g. Ecclus **1** 11–30; the idea of it became gradually more and more elevated; in **2** 15.16 it is joined with the *love* of God.

"Fear" is the natural consequence of sin (Gen **3** 10; **4** 13.14; Prov **28** 1); it comes as a punishment (Dt **28** 25.28). The fear of man and of evils are dangers to be avoided, from which the fear of God delivers (Nu **14** 9; **21** 34; Ps **23** 4; **31** 14, etc).

"Fear" sometimes stands for the *object* of fear (Prov **10** 24; Isa **66** 4); for the object of worship (Gen **31** 42.53, "the God of Abraham, and the Fear of Isaac," *paḥadh*).

In the NT dread, or fear of God in the lower sense, is removed; He is revealed as the loving and forgiving Father, who gives to men the spirit of sonship (Rom **8** 15; 2 Tim **1** 7; 1 Jn **4** 18); we are invited even to come "with boldness unto the throne of grace," with confidence, assurance (*parrhēsía*), which, however, may have its literal meaning of free "utterance" (He **4** 16; **10** 19); but there remains a filial fear and sense of awe and of the greatness of the issues involved (Rom **11** 20; Eph **5** 21, RV "of Christ"; 1 Tim **5** 20; He **4** 1); all other fears should be dismissed (Mt **8** 26; **10** 26–28.31; Lk **12** 32); in Mt **10** 28; Lk **12** 5, "fear" is used in the sense of "stand in awe of," so perhaps Lk **23** 40; to "fear God" is sometimes used in the NT as equivalent to religion (Lk **18** 4; Acts **10** 2.35; **13** 16.26, used of proselytes); in He **10** 27, it is said that if Christ be wilfully rejected, nothing remains but "a fearful looking for [RV "expectation"] of judgment," and ver 31, "It is a fearful thing to fall into the hands of the living God," in which places "fearful" means "terrible," something well to be feared. RV gives frequently a more literal rendering of the words trd "fear."

W. L. Walker

FEASTS, fēsts, **AND FASTS** (מוֹעֵד, *mō'ēdh*, "an appointed day" or "an assembling," חַג, *ḥagh*, חָגַג, from *ḥāghagh*, "to dance," or possibly "to make a pilgrimage"; צוֹם, *çōm*, "fast," תַּעֲנִית, *ta'ănīth*, "a day of affliction"):

I. Preëxilic
- A) Annual
  1. Passover, 15th–22d Nīṣān } Pilgrimage Festivals
  2. Pentecost, 6th Ṣīwān }
  3. Tabernacles, 15th–22d Tishrī }
  4. *Shemīnī 'Ăçereth*, 23d Tishrī
  5. New Year, Feast of Trumpets, 1st Tishrī
  6. Atonement, 10th Tishrī
- B) Periodic
  1. Weekly Sabbath
  2. New Moon
  3. Sabbath Year
  4. Jubilee Year

II. Post-exilic
1. Feast of Dedication, 25th Kiṣlēw
2. Fast of Esther, 13th 'Ădhār
3. Feast of Purim, 14th 'Ădhār
4. Fast of the Fourth Month, 17th Tammūz
5. Fast of the Fifth Month, 9th 'Ābh
6. Fast of the Seventh Month, 3d Tishrī
7. Fast of the Tenth Month, 10th Tēbheth
8. Feast of Acra, 23d Īyar
9. Feast of Nicanor, 13th 'Ădhār
10. Feast of Woodcarrying, Midsummer Day, 15th 'Ābh
11. New Year for Trees, 15th Shebhaṭ
12. Bi-weekly Fasts, Mondays and Thursdays after Festivals
13. Second Days of Festivals Instituted
14. New Modes of Observing Old Festivals Instituted

The Nature of the Hebrew Festivals

The Hebrews had an abundance of holidays, some based, according to their tradition, on agriculture and the natural changes of times and seasons, some on historical events connected with the national or religious life of Israel, and still others simply on immemorial custom. In most instances two or more of these bases coexist, and the emphasis on the natural, the agricultural, the national, or the religious phase will vary with different writers, different context, or different times. Any classification of these feasts and fasts on the basis of original significance must therefore be imperfect.

We should rather classify them as preëxilic and post-exilic, because the period of the Bab captivity marks a complete change, not only in the kinds of festivals instituted from time to time, but also in the manner of celebrating the old.

I. Preëxilic List.—The preëxilic list includes the three pilgrimage festivals, the Passover week, Pentecost, and the Feast of Tabernacles, together with the Eighth Day of Assembly at the conclusion of the last of these feasts, and New Year and Atonement Days, the weekly Sabbath and the New Moon.

1. Observances Common to All

The preëxilic festivals were "holy convocations" (Lev **23**; Nu **28**). Special sacrifices were offered on them in addition to the daily offerings. These sacrifices, however, varied according to the character of the festival (Nu **28, 29**). On all of them trumpets (*ḥăçōçerōth*) were blown while the burnt offerings and the peace-offerings were being sacrificed (Nu **10** 10). They were all likened to the weekly Sabbath as days of rest, on which there must be complete suspension of all ordinary work (Lev **16** 29; **23** 7.8.21.24.25.28.35.36).

2. Significance of the Festivals

The three pilgrimage festivals were known by that name because on them the Israelites gathered at Jerus to give thanks for their doubly joyful character. They were of agricultural significance as well as commemorative of national events. Thus the Passover is connected with the barley harvest; at the same time it is the *zeman ḥērūth*, recalling the Exodus from Egypt (Ex **12** 6; Lev **23** 5.8; Nu **28** 16–25; Dt **16** 1–8).

Pentecost has an agricultural phase as *ḥagh habikkūrīm*, the celebration of the wheat harvest; it has a religious phase as *zeman mattan Thōrāh* in the Jewish liturgy, based on the rabbinical calculation which makes it the day of the giving of the Law, and this religious side has so completely overshadowed the agricultural that among modern Jews the Pentecost has become "confirmation day" (Ex **34** 26; Lev **23** 10–14; Nu **28** 26–31).

The Feast of Tabernacles is at once the general harvest festival, *ḥagh he-'āṣīph*, and the anniversary of the beginnings of the wanderings in the wilderness (Ex **23** 16; Lev **23** 33 ff; Dt **16** 13–15). The Eighth Day of Assembly immediately following the last day of Tabernacles (Lev **23** 36; Nu **29** 35 ff; Jn **7** 37) and closing the long cycle of Tishrī festivals seems to have been merely a final day of rejoicing before the pilgrims returned to their homes.

New Year (Lev **23** 23–25; Nu **29** 1–6) and the Day of Atonement (Lev **16** 1 ff; **23** 26–32; Nu **29** 7–11) marked the turning of the year; primarily, perhaps, in the natural phenomena of Pal, but also in the inner life of the nation and the individual. Hence the religious significance of these days as days of judgment, penitence and forgiveness soon overshadowed any other significance they may have had. The temple ritual for these days, which is minutely described in the OT and in the Talm, was the most elaborate and impressive of the year. At the same time Atonement Day was socially an important day of rejoicing.

In addition to these annual festivals the preëxilic Hebrews celebrated the Sabbath (Nu **28** 9.10; Lev **23** 1–3) and the New Moon (Nu **10** 10; **28** 11–15). By analogy to the weekly Sabbath, every seventh year was a Sabbath Year (Ex **23** 11; Lev **25** 1–7; Dt **15** 1), and every cycle of seven Sabbath years was closed with a Jubilee Year (Lev **25** 8–18) somewhat after the analogy of the seven weeks counted before Pentecost.

For further details of all of these preëxilic festivals see the separate articles.

II. The Post-exilic List.—In post-exilic times important historical events were made the basis for the institution of new fasts and feasts. When the first temple was destroyed and the people were carried into captivity, "the sacrifice of the body and one's own fat and blood" were substituted for that of animals (see Talm, *Berākhōth* **17***a*). With such a view of their importance, fasts of all sorts were as a matter of course rapidly multiplied. (Note that the Day of Atonement was the only preëxilic fast.) Of these post-exilic fasts and feasts, the Feast of Dedication (1 Macc **4** 52–59; Jn **10** 22; Mish, *Ta'ănīth* **2** 10; *Mō'ēdh Ḳāṭōn* **3** 9; Jos, *Ant*, XII, vii; *CAp*, II, xxxix) and the Feast of Purim (Est **3** 7; **9** 24 ff; 2 Macc **15** 36); and the fasts of the *fourth* (Zec **8** 19; Jer **39, 52**; Mish, *Ta'ănīth* **4** 6), the *fifth* (Zec **7** 3.4; **8** 19; *Ta'ănīth* **4** 6), the *seventh* (Zec **7** 5; **8** 19; Jer **41** 1 ff; 2 K **25** 25; *Ṣēdher 'Ōlām Rabbā'* **26**; *Meghillath Ta'ănīth* c. 12), the *tenth* months (Zec **8** 19; 2 K **25**), and the Fast of Esther (Est **4** 16 f; **9** 31) have been preserved by Jewish tradition to this day. (The Feast of Dedication, the Feast of Purim and the Fast of Esther are described in separate articles.)

The fasts of the fourth, fifth, seventh and tenth months are based on historical incidents connected with one or more national calamities.

Significance In several instances the rabbis have by close figuring been able to connect with the dates of the fasts as well as the feasts other important national events than those for which the days were primarily instituted. Not less than four incidents are connected with the fasts of the fourth month (17th of Tammūz): (*a*) on this day the Israelites made the golden calf; (*b*) Moses broke the tables of law; (*c*) the daily sacrifices ceased for want of cattle when the city was closely besieged prior to the destruction of Jerus; and (*d*) on this day Jerus was stormed by Nebuchadnezzar. The fast of the fifth month (9th day of 'Ābh) receives its significance from the fact that the First Temple was destroyed upon this day by Nebuchadnezzar, and the Second Temple on the same day of the year by Titus. In addition it is said that on this day Jeh decreed that those who left Egypt should not enter the land of promise; the day is also the anniversary of the capture of the city of Bether by the Emperor Hadrian. The fast of the seventh month (the 3d day of Tishrī) commemorates the murder of Gedaliah at Mizpah. That of the tenth month (10th day of Tebheth) commemorates the beginning of the siege of Jerus by Nebuchadnezzar.

Other fasts and feasts no doubt were instituted on similar occasions and received a local or temporary observance, for example, the Feast of Acra (1 Macc **13** 50–52; cf **1** 33), to celebrate the recapture of Acra ("the citadel") on the 23d of 'Iyār 141 BC, and the Feast of Nicanor, in celebration of the victory over Nicanor on the 13th day of 'Ădhār 160 BC (1 Macc **7** 49).

Several other festivals are mentioned in the Talm and other post-Biblical writings which may have been of even greater antiquity. The Feast of Woodcarrying (Midsummer Day: Neh **10** 34; Jos, *BJ*, II, vii, 6; *Meghillath Ta'ănīth* c.v, p. 32, Mish, *Ta'ănīth* **4** 8*a*), for example, is referred to as the greatest day of rejoicing of the Hebrews, ranking with Atonement Day. It was principally a picnic day to which a religious touch was given by making it the woodgatherers' festival for the Temple. A New Year for trees is mentioned in the Talm (*Rō'sh ha-Shānāh* **1** 1). The pious, according both to the Jewish tradition and the NT, observed many private or semi-public fasts, such as the Mondays, Thursdays and following Monday after Nīṣān and Tishrī (the festival months: Lk **18** 12; Mt **9** 14; **6** 16; Mk **2** 18; Lk **5** 33; Acts **10** 30; *Meghillāh* **31***a; Ta'ănīth* **12***a; Bābhā' Ḳamā'* **8** 2). The day before Passover was a fast day for the firstborn (*Ṣōpherīm* **21** 3).

In post-Biblical times the Jews outside of Pal doubled each of the following days: the opening and closing day of Passover and Tabernacles and Pentecost, because of the *ṣāphēḳ*, or doubt as to the proper day to be observed, growing out of the delays in the transmission of the official decree of the *ṣanhedhrīn* in each season. Differences in hours of sunrise and sunset between Pal and other countries may have had something to do at least with the perpetuation of the custom. New Year's Day seems to have been doubled from time immemorial, the forty-eight hours counting as one "long day."

Many new modes of observance appear in post-exilic times in connection with the old established festivals, esp. in the high festival season of Tishrī. Thus the *ṣimḥath bēth ha-shō'ēbhāh*, "water drawing festival," was celebrated during the week of Tabernacles with popular games and dances in which even the elders took part, and the streets were so brilliantly illuminated with torches that scarcely an eye was closed in Jerus during that week (Talm, *Ḥullīn*).

The last day of Tabernacles was known in Talmudic times as *yōm ḥibbuṭ 'ărābhōth*, from the custom of beating willow branches, a custom clearly antedating the various symbolical explanations offered for it. Its festivities were connected with the dismantling of the booth. In later times the day was known as *hōsha' nā' rabbā'*, from the liturgical passages beginning with the word *hōsha'nā'*, recited throughout the feast and "gathered" on that day. The day after Tabernacles has been made *ṣimḥath Tōrāh*, the Feast of the Law, from the custom of ending on that day the cycle of fifty-two weekly portions read in the synagogues.

In general it may be said that although the actual observance has changed from time to time to meet new conditions, the synagogal calendar of today is made up of the same festivals as those observed in NT times. Ella Davis Isaacs

FEASTS, SEASONS FOR, regulated by the sun and moon. See Astronomy, I, 5.

FEATHERS, feth'ẽrz (נֹצָה, *nōçāh*; Lat *penna*): "Gavest thou the goodly wings unto the peacocks? or wings [RV "pinions"] and feathers [ARV "plumage"] unto the ostrich?" (Job **39** 13 AV); "He shall cover thee with his feathers, and under his wings shalt thou trust; his truth shall be thy shield and buckler" (Ps **91** 4 AV). In RV this is again changed to pinions. In Dnl **4** 33 the word "feathers" is left. The wonderful plumage of birds was noted and prized in those days, just as now. Old ostriches were too tough and rank of flesh for food. They were pursued for their feathers, which were used for the headdressing and shield ornaments of desert princes. No one doubts that the ships of Solomon introduced peacocks because of their wonderful feathers. Those of the eagle were held in superstitious reverence as late as the days of Pliny, who was ten years old at the time of the crucifixion of Christ. Pliny wrote that the eagle was so powerful that if its feathers be laid in a box with those of other birds, the eagle feathers would "devour and consume all the rest."

Gene Stratton-Porter

FEEBLE KNEES, fē'b'l nēz: The expression is found in three places (one being a free quotation of another): Job **4** 4, "Thou hast made firm the feeble [כָּרַע, *kāra'*, "bending," "bowing"] knees," and He **12** 12, "Wherefore lift up the hands that hang down, and the palsied [AV "feeble"] knees." The Gr word used here (παραλελυμένα, *paralelumĕna*, "paralyzed," "motionless") implies the loss of junction, interrupted articulation, the cutting off of vital strength; cf Gr χωλός, *chōlós*, "lame," and see Delitzsch in his *Comm. on He*, loc. cit.

Such an affection of the knees may be due to different causes. It is, e.g., a very frequent symptom of the disease known in the Orient as *beriberi*, when the muscles of the lower leg shrink to such a degree as to render voluntary locomotion impossible. It always disables its victim, and is therefore often expressive of general debility, e.g. in Ps **109** 24, where such weakness is described as the outcome of protracted fasting. In Ezk **7** 17 and **21** 7, "All knees shall be weak as water," the expression indicates a complete relaxation of the muscles. Fear effected the same condition in Belshazzar's case, when he saw the writing on the wall (Dnl **5** 6), "The joints of his loins were loosed, and his knees smote one against another" (cf Nah **2** 10).

The "sore boil . . . . in the knees, and in the legs," a disease announced in Dt **28** 35 as a punishment upon

Israel for disobedience, cannot now be fully determined. Driver (in his commentary on the passage) thinks of elephantiasis, which is possible but not probable on account of the additional statement, "whereof thou canst not be healed, from the sole of thy foot unto the crown of thy head" which would be unexplained, as elephantiasis rarely presents a form in which the whole body is sympathetically affected. I rather think of some form of bubonic plague, which causes very high fever all over the body. In ver 27 in the enumeration of plagues mention is made of the "boil of Egypt," and some commentators have explained this as "bubonic plague." There is, however, no doubt that the "boil or botch of Egypt" is identical with the disease known to modern medicine as *bouton du Nil*, Biskra button, Bagdad or Aleppo sore.

H. L. E. Luering

FEEBLE-MINDED, fē'b'l-mīn'ded (**ὀλιγόψυχος,** *oligópsuchos*): Only in 1 Thess **5** 14 AV, in the sense of "fainthearted," as in RV. In LXX it is used as the equivalent of *kōshēl*, the tottering or feeble-kneed in Isa **35** 3; **54** 6; *oligopsuchía* occurs in LXX twice (Ex **6** 9; Ps **54** 7), for "anguish of spirit" and "trouble." The term refers to weakness of will and vacillation of purpose rather than to idiocy or morbid imbecility.

FEELING, fēl'ing: The following varieties of meaning are to be noted:

(1) "To touch," "handle," "grope after" (מָשַׁשׁ, *māshash* (Gen **27** 12.22; Ex **10** 21; מוּשׁ, *mūsh*, Gen **27** 21; Jgs **16** 26; ψηλαφάω, *psēlapháō*, Acts **17** 27).

(2) "To know," "understand," "experience" (בִּין, *bīn*, Ps **58** 9; יָדַע, *yādha'*, Prov **23** 35; γινώσκω, *ginṓskō*, Mk **5** 29).

(3) "To have a fellow feeling," "to place one's self into the position of another," esp. while suffering, "to have compassion" (συμπαθεῖν, *sumpathein*, He **4** 15; cf **10** 34; which is to be carefully distinguished from the similar vb. συμπάσχειν, *sumpáschein*, which means "to share in the same suffering with another," Rom **8** 17; 1 Cor **12** 26). See Delitzsch, *Comm.* on He **4** 15.

(4) "To feel harm," "pain," "grief," "to be sensitive" (πάσχειν, *páschein*, with the roots *path-* and *penth-*, Acts **28** 5); or with the negation: "to have ceased to feel," "to be apathetic," "past feeling," "callous," ἀπηλγηκώς, *apēlgēkōs*, perf. part. of ἀπαλγέω, *apalgéō* (Eph **4** 19) which describes the condition of the sinner, who by hardening his heart against moral influences is left without a sense of his high vocation, without an idea of the awfulness of sin, without reverence to God, without an appreciation of the salvation offered by Him, and without fear of His judgment.

H. L. E. Luering

FEET, WASHING OF. See Foot; Washing of Feet.

FEIGN, fān (בָּדָא, *bādhā'*, נָכַר, *nākhar*; **πλαστός,** *plastós*): Occurs (1) in the sense of "to devise," "invent" as the tr of *bādhā'*, "to form," "to fashion" (Neh **6** 8, "Thou feignest them out of thine own heart"; cf 1 K **12** 33, EV "devised of his own heart"); of *plastos*, "formed," "molded" (2 Pet **2** 3, "with feigned words make merchandise of you"); (2) in the sense of "pretense," *nākhar*, "to be foreign," "strange" (1 K **14** 5, "feign herself to be another woman," ver 6; cf Gen **42** 7; Prov **26** 24); *'ābhal*, "to mourn," "to act as a mourner" (2 S **14** 2); *hālal*, "to make a show," Hithpael, "to be mad," "to feign madness" (of David, 1 S **21** 13; cf Jer **25** 16; **50** 38); *hupokrínomai*, "to give judgment, or act, under a mask" (Lk **20** 20, "who feigned themselves to be righteous"); (3) in the sense of "deceit," "fraud," "insincerity," *mirmāh*, "prayer, that goeth not out of feigned lips" (Ps **17** 1); *sheḳer*, "falsehood," "a lie," "Judah hath not returned unto me with her whole heart, but feignedly" (Jer **3** 10; cf 2 Esd **8** 28); *kāhash*, "to lie," "to feign, or flatter" (2 S **22** 45; Ps **18** 44; **66** 3; **81** 15), where the text of AV and RV, "shall submit themselves," is rendered m, AV and RV, "yield feigned obedience, Heb *lie*." RV has "feign" for "make" (2 S **13** 5), and "feigned" for "made" (ver 6).

W. L. Walker

FELIX, fē'liks, **ANTONIUS,** an-tō'ni-us (**Φῆλιξ,** *Phēlix*, from Lat *felix*, "happy"): A Rom procurator of Judaea, appointed in succession to Cumanus by the emperor Claudius. The event which led to the introduction of Felix into the narrative of Acts was the riot at Jerus (Acts **21** 27). There Paul, being attacked at the instigation of the Asiatic Jews for alleged false teaching and profanation of the temple, was rescued with difficulty by Lysias the chief captain. But Lysias, finding that Paul was a Rom citizen, and that therefore the secret plots against the life of his captive might entail serious consequences upon himself, and finding also that Paul was charged on religious rather than on political grounds, sent him on to Felix at Caesarea for trial (Acts **21** 31—**23** 34). On his arrival, Paul was presented to Felix and was then detained for five days in the judgment hall of Herod, till his accusers should also reach Caesarea (Acts **23** 33–35). The trial was begun, but after hearing the evidence of Tertullus (see Tertullus) and the speech of Paul in his own defence, Felix deferred judgment (Acts **24** 1–22). The excuse he gave for delay was the non-appearance of Lysias, but his real reason was in order to obtain bribes for the release of Paul. He therefore treated his prisoner at first with leniency, and pretended along with Drusilla to take interest in his teaching. But these attempts to induce Paul to purchase his freedom failed ignominiously; Paul sought favor of neither Felix nor Drusilla, and made the frequent interviews which he had with them an opportunity for preaching to them concerning righteousness and temperance and the final judgment. The case dragged on for two years till Felix, upon his retirement, "desiring to gain favor with the Jews . . . . left Paul in bonds" (Acts **24** 27). According to the Bezan text, the continued imprisonment of Paul was due to the desire of Felix to please Drusilla.

Felix was the brother of Pallas, who was the infamous favorite of Claudius, and who, according to Tacitus (*Annals* xiii.14), fell into disgrace in 55 AD. Tacitus implies that Felix was joint procurator of Judaea, along with Cumanus, before being appointed to the sole command, but Jos is silent as to this. Both Tacitus and Jos refer to his succeeding Cumanus, Jos stating that it was at the instigation of Jonathan the high priest. There is some doubt as to the chronology of Felix' tenure of office. Harnack and Blass, following Eusebius and Jerome, place his accession in 51 AD, and the imprisonment of Paul in 54–56 AD; but most modern commentators incline to the dates 52 AD and 56–58 AD. These latter interpret the statement of Paul, "Thou hast been of many years a judge unto this nation" (Acts **24** 10), as referring to some judicial office, not necessarily that of co-procurator (see Tac.), previously held by Felix in the time of Cumanus, and argue that this earlier connection of Felix with Judaea supplied a reason for the advocacy by Jonathan of Felix' claims to the procuratorship on the deposition of Cumanus. The testimony of Acts as to the evil character of Felix is fully corroborated by the writings of Jos (*BJ*, II, xiii). Although he suppressed the robbers and murderers who infested Judaea, and among them the "Egyptian" to whom Lysias refers (Acts **21** 38), yet "he himself was more hurtful than them all." When occasion offered, he did not hesitate to employ the *sicarii* (see Assassins) for his own ends. Trading upon the influence of his brother at court, his cruelty and rapacity knew no bounds, and during his rule revolts became continuous, and marked a distinct stage in that seditious movement which culminated in the outbreak of 70 AD (so Schürer). His leaving Paul in bonds was but a final instance of one who sacrificed duty and justice for the sake of his own unscrupulous selfishness. For more detailed information as to dates, etc, cf Knowling (*Expos Gr Test.*, II, 477 ff). C. M. Kerr

FELLOES, fel′ōz (1 K **7** 33). See Wheel.

FELLOW, fel′ō (חָבֵר, *ḥābhēr*, רֵעַ, *rēa'*; ἑταῖρος, *hetaíros*): Meant originally a "partner," from *fe*, "property," and *lag*, "to lay," then "a companion," "an equal," "a person or individual," "a worthless person."

(1) As "companion" it is the tr of *ḥābhēr*, "associate," "companion," "friend" (also *ḥabbār*, Job **41** 6 [Heb **40** 30], where we have the original sense of partnership, trd "bands" RV, AV "companions"); Ps **45** 7, "God hath anointed thee . . . . above thy fellows"; of *habhrāh* (Eccl **4** 10; Dnl **7** 20); of *rēa'*, "companion," "friend," "another" (Ex **2** 13; Jgs **7** 13.14.22); *rē'āh* (or *ra'yāh*), "a female friend" (Jgs **11** 37, "I and my fellows," RV "companions"; here AV applies "fellow" to a female; cf Bar **6** 43, "She reproacheth her fellow," *hē plēsíon*); in Jgs **11** 38, "companions" is the tr of *'āmīth*, "fellowship"; *'amīth* (Zec **13** 7, "the man that is my fellow," lit. "the man of my fellowship"); *hetairos*, "companion" (Mt **11** 16); *métochos*, "partner"; (cf Lk **5** 7; He **1** 9, quoted from Ps **45** 7, LXX for *ḥābhēr*).

(2) As an individual or person "fellow" is the tr of *'īsh*, "a man," "an individual": "make this fellow return" (1 S **29** 4 AV, RV "the man"); in the same ver "fellow" is supplied instead of "he"; "fellow" in 1611 meant simply "a man," and it is difficult to say in what passages the ideas of "worthless," etc, are meant to be implied; probably, however, in Jgs **18** 25, where the Heb is simply *'ĕnōsh*, "man," and the text is almost the only deviation from the rendering "man," "men," "lest angry [m, RV "bitter of soul"] fellows fall upon you"; also Acts **17** 5, *anḗr*, "a man," "certain lewd fellows of the baser sort," RV "vile fellows"; cf 2 S **6** 20, "vain [*rēḳ*] fellows" (supplied); 1 Macc **10** 61, "contain pestilent fellows" (*anḗr*); Ecclus **8** 15, "a bold fellow" (*tolmērós*), RV "a rash man"; in several places of the OT "fellow" represents *zeh*, "this," and in these instances there seems to be something of worthlessness or contempt implied (1 S **21** 15 *bis;* **25** 21; 1 K **22** 27; 2 K **9** 11, and, as before, 1 S **29** 4 RV); in the NT also "fellow" often represents *hoútos*, "this," and in most of these cases AV seems to intend something depreciatory to be understood; RV gives simply "man" (Mt **12** 24; **26** 61.71; Lk **22** 59; **23** 2; Jn **9** 29; Acts **18** 13); so Ecclus **13** 23, "If the poor man speaks, they say, What fellow is this?" RV "who is this?" 1 Macc **4** 5, "These fellows flee from us," RV "these men." RV has "fellows" for "persons" (Jgs **9** 4), for "men" (**11** 3); "base fellows" for "men the children of Belial" (Dt **13** 13), m, "sons of worthlessness"; ARV "worthless fellow" for "son of Belial" (1 S **25** 17.25), "base fellows" for "sons of Belial" (Jgs **19** 22; **20** 13, etc); RV has also "companions" for "fellows" (Jgs **11** 37, as above; Ezk **37** 19; Dnl **2** 13), "each man his fellow" for "one another" (2 K **3** 23); "fellow by" for "neighbor in" (1 K **20** 35).

Fellow-citizen, Fellow-disciple, Fellow-heirs, Yokefellow, etc. In composition, "fellow" always means partner or companion.

W. L. Walker

FELLOWSHIP, fel′ō-ship. See Communion.

FEMALE, fē′māl: Two Heb words are thus trd:

(1) נְקֵבָה, *nᵉḳēbhāh*, which is merely a physiological description of the sexual characteristic (from נָקַב, *nāḳabh*, "to perforate"), and which corresponds to זָכָר, *zākhār*, "male" (see s.v.).

(2) אִשָּׁה, *'ishshāh*, with the irregular pl. נָשִׁים, *nāshīm* (only Gen **7** 2, in all other places "wife," "woman"), the fem. form of אִישׁ, *'īsh*, "man."

The Gr word is θῆλυς, *thḗlus*, lit. "the nursing one," "the one giving suck" (from θηλάζω, *thēlázō*, "to suckle").

Israelitic law seems frequently guilty of unjust partiality in favor of the male sex, but we have to consider that most of these legal and religious disabilities of women can be explained from the social conditions prevailing at the time of legislation. They are therefore found also in contemporaneous gentile religions. Though traces of this prejudice against the weaker sex are found in the NT, the religious discrimination between the sexes has practically ceased, as is evident from Gal **3** 28: "There can be no male and female; for ye all are one man in Christ Jesus"; cf also 1 Pet **3** 7.

H. L. E. Luering

FENCE, fens (בָּצַר, *bāçar*, מִבְצָר, *mibhçār*): Commonly used in AV in the description of fortified places, as the tr of *bāçar*, "to cut off," "to separate," "to fortify" (and forms) (Dt **3** 5; **9** 1; **28** 52, etc); *mibhçar*, "fenced city," is a fortified place (Nu **32** 17.36; Josh **10** 20; **19** 35, etc); *māçōr*, "fenced cities," means "bulwark," "citadel" (2 Ch **8** 5); *mᵉçūrāh*, "fortification" (2 Ch **11** 23; **12** 4; **14** 6; **21** 3); for "fenced" ARV substitutes "fortified" in all these instances; in Dnl **11** 15, *mibhçar* is "a well-fortified city," m "the fortified cities," ERV "well-fenced"; "fence" is also the tr of *gādhēr*, "a wall" or "fence" (Job **19** 8 ARV, "walled up" [*gādhar*]; Ps **62** 3); *'āzaḳ*, "to loosen" (the ground) as with a mattock (Isa **5** 2, where AV has "fenced" it [the vineyard], ARV "digged it," ERV "made a trench about it," m "digged it"); *sūkh*, "to interweave" or "interlace" (Job **10** 11, RV "clothed"); *mālē'*, "to be or become full" (2 S **23** 7, RV "armed," m "Heb filled").

ERV has "fence" for "wall" (Nu **22** 24; Isa **5** 5; Hos **2** 6; ARV retains "wall"), for "hedge" (Eccl **10** 8; Ezk **13** 5; **22** 30; ARV "wall"); "fenced" for "walled" (Nu **13** 28; Dt **1** 28; ARV "fortified"); cf for "strong" Josh **19** 29; Neh **9** 25; Ps **108** 10 (m Josh **19** 29, "the city of Mibzar-zor, that is, the fortress of Tyre," ERV "fenced"), for "hedged" (Lam **3** 7, ARV "walled"); cf for "defenced," ERV "fenced," ARV "fortified" (Isa **36** 1; **37** 26, etc); "fences" for "hedges" (Ps **80** 12, ARV "walls"); in Jer **49** 3, ERV and ARV have "fences." See also Hedge.

W. L. Walker

FENCED CITIES. See Fortification.

FERRET, fer′et (אֲנָקָה, *'ănāḳāh*, RV GECKO): Occurs only in Lev **11** 30 AV, in the list of animals which are unclean "among the creeping things that creep upon the earth." RV has "gecko" with the marginal note, "Words of uncertain meaning, but probably denoting four kinds of lizards." The list of animals in Lev **11** 29.30 includes (1) *ḥōledh*, EV "weasel"; (2) *'akhbār*, EV "mouse"; (3) *çābh*, AV "tortoise," RV "great lizard"; (4) *'ănāḳāh*, AV "ferret," RV "gecko"; (5) *kōaḥ* AV "chameleon," RV "land crocodile"; (6) *lᵉṭā'āh*, EV "lizard"; (7) *ḥōmeṭ*, AV "snail," RV "sand lizard"; (8) *tinshemeth*, AV "mole," RV "chameleon." It will be noted that while RV makes the first two mammals and the remaining six reptiles, AV makes not only (1) and (2) but also (4) and (8) mammals, and (7) a mollusk. So far as this general classification is concerned AV follows the LXX, except in the case of

(7). It must be borne in mind that all these words except (2) and (8) occur only in this passage, while (2) and (8) occur each in only a few passages where the context throws but uncertain light upon the meaning. Under these circumstances we ought to be content with the rendering of the LXX, unless from philology or tradition we can show good reason for differing. For *'ănāḳāh*, LXX has μυγάλη, *mugálē*, which occurs in Herodotus and Aristotle and may be a shrew mouse or a field mouse. Just as the next word, *kōaḥ*, is found in other passages (see CHAMELEON) with the meaning of "strength," so *'ănāḳāh* occurs in several places signifying "moaning" or "sighing" (Ps **12** 5; **79** 11; **102** 20; Mal **2** 13). It seems to be from the root, *'ānaḳ*, "to choke," "to be in anguish" (cf *'ānāḳ*, "a collar"; *ḥānaḳ*, "to choke"; Arab. *'unḳ*, "neck"; Arab. *khanaḳ*, "to strangle"; Gr ἀνάγκη; Lat *angustus;* Ger. *enge, Nacken;* Eng. "anxious," "neck"). Some creature seems to be meant which utters a low cry or squeak, and neither "ferret" (AV) nor "gecko" (RV) seems to have a better claim than the older LXX rendering of μυγάλη = "shrew mouse" or "field mouse."

ALFRED ELY DAY

FERRY-BOAT, fer'i-bōt (2 S **19** 18). See SHIPS AND BOATS.

FERVENT, fûr'vent (דָּלַק, *dālaḳ;* ἐκτενής, *ektenḗs*, ζέω, *zéō*): "Fervent" (from Lat *fervēre*, "to boil") does not occur in AV of the OT, but RV gives it as the tr of *dālaḳ*, "to burn" (Prov **26** 23), instead of "burning," "fervent lips and a wicked heart." In the NT it is the tr of *ektenḗs*, "stretched out," hence intent, earnest (1 Pet **4** 8, "being fervent in your love among yourselves"); of *zeō*, "to boil," "to be hot" (Rom **12** 11, "fervent in spirit," Acts **18** 25); of *zḗlos*, "zeal," "fervor" (2 Cor **7** 7, RV "zeal"), in Jas **5** 16 AV has: "The effectual fervent prayer of a righteous man availeth much," where the Gr is: *polú ischúei déēsis dikaíou energouménē*, which RV renders, "The supplication of a righteous man availeth much in its working."

"Fervently" is the tr of *agonízomai*, "to strive or struggle" (agonize), Col **4** 12 AV, RV "Epaphras . . . . striving for you in his prayers"; of *ektenṓs*, lit. in an outstretched manner (1 Pet **1** 22, RV "Love one another from the heart fervently"; cf 1 Pet **4** 8, "fervent in your love among yourselves"). Christian love too often lacks this *fervency*, but Christ's love for us was "stretched out" to the uttermost.

RV has "fervently" for "earnestly" (Jas **5** 17, m "with prayer").

W. L. WALKER

FESTIVAL, fes'ti-val. See FEASTS AND FASTS.

FESTUS, fes'tus, **PORCIUS,** pôr'shi-us (Πόρκιος Φῆστος, *Pórkios Phḗstos*): The Rom governor or procurator who succeeded Felix in the province of Judaea (Acts **24** 27), and was thus brought into prominence in the dispute between Paul and the Sanhedrin which continued after the retirement of Felix (chs **25, 26**). Upon the arrival of Festus in Jerus, the official capital of his province, the Jews besought of him to send Paul from Caesarea to Jerus to appear before them, intending to kill him on the way (**25** 3). Festus at first refused their request, and upon his return to Caesarea proceeded himself to examine Paul (ver 6). But on finding that the evidence was conflicting, and reflecting that, as the accused was apparently charged on religious rather than on political grounds, the Sanhedrin was a more suitable court for his case than a Rom tribunal, he asked Paul if he were agreeable to make the journey to Jerus (vs 7–9). But Paul, who knew well the nefarious use that the Jews would make of the pleasure which Festus was willing to grant them, made his appeal unto Caesar (vs 10.11). To this request of a Rom citizen accused on a capital charge (cf ver 16), Festus had perforce to give his consent (ver 12). But the manner of his consent indicated his pique at the apparent distrust shown by Paul. By the words "unto Caesar shalt thou go," Festus implied that the case must now be proceeded with to the end: otherwise, had it been left in his own hands, it might have been quashed at an earlier stage (cf also **26** 32). Meantime King Agrippa and Bernice had arrived in Caesarea, and to these Festus gave a brief explanation of the circumstances (**25** 13–21). The previous audiences of Festus with Paul and his accusers had, however, served only to confuse him as to the exact nature of the charge. Paul was therefore summoned before the regal court, in order both that Agrippa might hear him, and that the governor might obtain more definite information for insertion in the report he was required to send along with the prisoner to Rome (vs 22–27). The audience which followed was brought to an abrupt conclusion by the interruption of Paul's speech (**26** 1–23) by Festus: "Paul, thou art mad; thy much learning is turning thee mad" (ver 24). Yet the meeting was sufficient to convince both Agrippa and Festus that "this man doeth nothing worthy of death or of bonds" (ver 31). While Festus displayed a certain contempt for what he regarded as the empty delusions of a harmless maniac, his conduct throughout the whole proceeding was marked by a strict impartiality; and his straightforward dealing with Paul formed a marked contrast to the dilatoriness of Felix. The praise bestowed upon the latter by Tertullus (**24** 2) might with better reason have been bestowed on Festus, in that he freed the country from many robbers (*Sicarii:* Jos, *Ant*, XX, viii–x; *BJ*, II, xiv, 1); but his procuratorship was too short to undo the harm wrought by his predecessor. The exact date of his accession to office is uncertain, and has been variously placed at 55–61 AD (cf Knowling in *Expos Gr Test.*, II, 488–89; see also FELIX).

C. M. KERR

FETCH, fech (לָקַח, *lāḳaḥ*): Has generally the meaning of "to bring"; it is commonly the tr of Heb *lāḳaḥ*, "to take" or "lay hold of," Hoph. "to be brought, seized or snatched away" (Gen **18** 4, etc; **27** 9, etc; **42** 16; 1 S **4** 3; 1 K **17** 10, etc); twice of *nāsā'*, "to lift up" (2 Ch **12** 11, ARV "bare"; Job **36** 3); of *bō'*, "to come in" (2 Ch **1** 17; Neh **8** 15); of *'ālāh*, "to cause to come up" (1 S **6** 21; **7** 1); of *yāçā'*, "to cause to come out" (Nu **20** 10, ARV "bring forth"; Jer **26** 23), and of a number of other words.

In the NT it is the tr of *exágō*, "to lead out" (Acts **16** 37, "Let them come themselves and fetch us out," RV "bring"); "to fetch a compass" is the tr of *ṣābhabh* (Nu **34** 5; Josh **15** 3, RV "turn," "turned about"; 2 S **5** 23, RV "make a circuit"; 2 K **3** 9, RV "made a circuit"); of *periérchomai* (aor. 2, *periḗlthon*), "to go about," "to wander up and down" (of a ship driven about; Acts **28** 13, RV "made a circuit," m "some ancient authorities read *cast loose*").

RV has "fetch" for "bring" (1 K **3** 24), for "call for" (Acts **10** 5; **11** 13); "fetched" for "called for" (Est **5** 10), for "took out" (Jer **37** 17); "fetched" for "took" (2 Ch **8** 18).

W. L. WALKER

FETTER, fet'ẽr: Found only in the pl. in both OT and NT; fetters of iron (Ps **105** 18; **149** 8; so probably Mk **5** 4; Lk **8** 29) or brass (Jgs **16** 21; 2 K **25** 7) were frequently used for securing prisoners. See CHAIN.

Figurative: of trouble (Job **36** 8).

FEVER, fē'vẽr (קַדַּחַת, *ḳaddaḥath*, דַּלֶּקֶת, *dalleḳeth;* πυρετός, *puretós*, derived from a root signifying "to burn"): A generic term, applied to all diseases characterized by high temperature of body. Several forms of febrile disease are among the commonest of all maladies in Pal today, as they were also in the period covered by the Bible history. Of these the most prevalent is ague or intermittent malarial fever, which is common in all parts but esp. in low-lying districts or places where there are pools or marshes in which mosquitoes breed, these insects being the commonest carriers of the malaria bacillus. These fevers are generally more severe in late summer and autumn, when the mosquitoes are most numerous, and when there is a liability to chill, owing to the sudden drop of temperature at sunset. During the day one uses as light clothing as possible, but immediately after sunset the air becomes chilly and damp, and the physiological resistance to the influence of the parasite is remarkably diminished. On this account travelers in Pal at this season should be particular to avoid exposure to these evening damps, and to use mosquito curtains invariably at night. In most tropical countries now houses are rendered mosquito-proof by close wire netting, and thereby the risk of infection is much diminished. In Pal the marshes of the north about Banias and the Water of Merom, the Shephelah, and the Jordan valley are the most fever-stricken regions of the country. The word *ḳaddaḥath* is tr[d] **burning ague** in Lev **26** 16 AV (RV "fever"), and is coupled with *dalleḳeth*, tr[d] **inflammation** in Dt **28** 22. LXX renders the former word *puretos*, and the latter *rhígos* in this passage, a collocation which is interesting as Galen uses these words together *rhigopúretos* in his description of a fever identical with that common in Pal. In Lev the word in LXX is *íkteros* which lit. means jaundice, a disease otherwise not mentioned in the Bible. In Pal as in other malarious countries the condition of **jaundice** or yellowing of the skin frequently accompanies repeated and protracted attacks of fever which cause organic disease of the liver. On this account Hippocrates describes all fevers as due to a perverted secretion of bile. These fevers begin with severe shivering fits, hence the name *rhigos* which is used by Hippocrates. This is followed by a period of burning dry heat, ending in a period of profuse perspiration. Such attacks may take place daily, a few hours of interval with normal temperature separating the end of one fit from the onset of the next. The commonest type however is that called **tertian,** in which a whole day separates one fit from the next. In some of the severe fevers which are rife in the Jordan valley the temperature never falls to the normal, and while there is a short remission between the attacks with a body heat a little above the normal, there is no intermission. Rarer febrile conditions which have been met with in Pal, such as the **Malta fever,** present the same characteristics and may continue for months. Cases also of genuine **blackwater fever** have been recorded by several authorities. It is probable that in former days these fevers were even worse than they are now, as ancient medicine knew of no certain remedy for them. At present they generally yield at once to treatment by quinine, and in my own experience I believe that the administration of this remedy in large and repeated doses is the most effectual treatment.

Other febrile diseases are rife in certain districts in Pal, and probably existed in Bible times. **Typhoid** is common in some crowded towns and villages, and considering how little protected the wells are from contamination, the wonder is that it is not much more prevalent. It is probable also that **typhus** then, as now, was present as an occasional epidemic in the more crowded cities, but even the physicians of Greece and Rome did not differentiate these diseases. All these fevers seem also to have existed in Egypt to much the same extent as in Pal. The Papyrus Ebers speaks of **"a fever of the gods"** (46) and another called **"a burning of the heart"** (102). Its causation is attributed to the influence of the "god of fever," and the evil sequelae of the disease as it affects the heart, stomach, eyes and other organs are described in terms which remind us of the minatory passages in Lev **26** and Dt **28.** The conditions there mentioned, such as consuming the eyes and causing sorrow of heart or pining away of the soul, graphically describe the state frequently seen affecting those in the Shephelah villages who have suffered from frequent returns of fever, and who in consequence have developed serious local affections of the liver, spleen and other organs. Before the introduction of quinine, cases of this kind must have been much more commonly met with than they are now. It is probable that this state is that called *shaḥepheth*, or **consumption,** in these passages.

Another form of fever, *ḥarḥur*, the **"extreme burning"** of AV or **"fiery heat"** of RV, is coupled with the other forms of fever in Dt **28** 22. This is called in LXX *erethismós* or **irritation,** and may have been a feverish condition with a reddened skin, possibly erysipelas or else one of the eruptive fevers. At present outbreaks of **scarlatina, measles** and **erysipelas** are of fairly frequent occurrence and are often very severe.

In the NT fever is mentioned eight times. The disease which affected Simon's wife's mother is called a "great fever" (Lk **4** 38), and that which nearly proved fatal to the nobleman's son in the same district was also a fever (Jn **4** 52). Cases of the kind are common all round the Sea of Galilee at the present day. ALEX. MACALISTER

FIELD, fēld. See AGRICULTURE.

FIERY HEAT, fī′ĕr-i, fīr′i hēt: In Dt **28** 22, where AV has "an extreme burning." See FEVER.

FIERY SERPENT. See SERPENT.

FIG, FIG-TREE, fig′trē (תְּאֵנָה, *t*ᵉ*'ēnāh*, pl. תְּאֵנִים, *t*ᵉ*'ēnīm*, specially "figs"; פַּגִּים, *paggīm*, "green figs" only in Cant **2** 13; **συκῆ,** *sukḗ*, "fig-tree," **σῦκον,** *súkon*, "fig"):

1. Fig-Trees in the OT

The earliest OT reference to the fig is to the leaves, which Adam and Eve converted into aprons (Gen **3** 7). The promised land was described (Dt **8** 8) as "a land of wheat and barley, and vines and fig-trees and pomegranates," etc. The spies who visited it brought, besides the cluster of grapes, pomegranates and figs (Nu **13** 23). The Israelites complained that the wilderness was "no place of seed, or of figs, or of vines, or of pomegranates" (Nu **20** 5). When Egypt was plagued, the fig-trees were smitten (Ps **105** 33); a similar punishment was threatened to unfaithful Israel (Jer **5** 17; Hos **2** 12; Am **4** 9). It is only necessary to ride a few miles among the mountain villages of Pal, with their extensive fig gardens, to realize what a long-lasting injury would be the destruction of these slow-growing trees. Years of patient labor—such as that briefly hinted at in Lk **13** 7—must pass before a newly planted group of fig-trees can bear profitably. Plenitude of fruitful vines and fig-trees, specially individual ownership, thus came to be emblematical of long-continued peace and prosperity. In the days of Solomon "Judah and Israel dwelt safely, every man under his vine and under his fig-tree" (1 K **4** 25). Cf also 2 K **18** 31; Isa **36** 16; Mic **4** 4; Zec **3** 10; 1 Macc **14** 12. Only a triumphal faith in Jeh could rejoice in Him "though the fig-tree shall not flourish" (Hab **3** 17).

2. Natural History of the Fig-Tree

The *Ficus carica*, which produces the common fig, is a tree belonging to the N.O. *Urticaceae*, the nettle family, which includes also the banyan, the India rubber fig-tree, the sycamore fig and other useful plants. Fig-trees are cultivated all over the Holy Land, esp. in the mountain regions. Wild fig-trees—usually rather shrubs than trees—occur also everywhere; they are usually barren and are described by the *fellahin* as "male" trees; it is generally supposed that their presence is beneficial to the cultivated variety. The immature flowers harbor small insects which convey pollen to the female flowers and by their irritating presence stimulate the growth of the fruit. Artificial fertilization has been understood since ancient times, and there may be a reference to it in Am **7** 14.

Fig-trees are usually of medium height, 10 or 15 ft. for full-grown trees, yet individual specimens sometimes attain as much as 25 ft. The summer foliage is thick and surpasses other trees of its size in its cool and dense shade. In the summer owners of such trees may be seen everywhere sitting in their shadow (Jn **1** 48). Such references as Mic **4** 4; Zec **3** 10, etc, probably are to this custom rather than to the not uncommon one of having a fig-tree overhanging a dwelling.

3. Figs

The fruit of the fig-tree is peculiar. The floral axis, instead of expanding outward, as with most flowers, closes, as the flower develops, upon the small internal flowers, leaving finally but a small opening at the apex; the axis itself becomes succulent and fruit-like. The male flowers lie around the opening, the female flowers deeper in; fertilization is brought about by the presence of small hymenopterous insects.

Fig (*Ficus carica*).

There are many varieties of figs in Pal differing in sweetness, in color and consistence; some are good and some are bad (cf Jer **24** 1.8; **29** 17). In Pal and other warm climates the fig yields two crops annually—an earlier one, ripe about June, growing from the "old wood," i.e. from the midsummer sprouts of the previous year, and a second, more important one, ripe about August, which grows upon the "new wood," i.e. upon the spring shoots.

By December, fig-trees in the mountainous regions of Pal have shed all their leaves, and they remain bare until about the end of March, when they commence putting forth their tender leaf buds (Mt **24** 32; Mk **13** 28.32; Lk **21** 29–33), and *at the same time*, in the leaf axils, appear the tiny figs. They belong to the early signs of spring:

> "The voice of the turtle-dove is heard in our land;
> The fig-tree ripeneth her green figs" (*paggim*)
> —Cant **2** 12.13.

4. Early Figs

These tiny figs develop along with the leaves up to a certain point—to about the size of a small cherry—and then the great majority of them fall to the ground, carried down with every gust of wind. These are the "unripe figs" (*ólunthos*)—tr[d], more appropriately in AV, as "untimely figs"—of Rev **6** 13. Cf also Isa **34** 4 AV—in RV "leaf" has been supplied instead of "fig." These immature figs are known to the *fellahīn* as *taksh*, by whom they are eaten as they fall; they may even sometimes be seen exposed for sale in the markets in Jerus. In the case of many trees the whole of this first crop may thus abort, so that by May no figs at all are to be found on the tree, but with the best varieties of fig-trees a certain proportion of the early crop of figs remains on the tree, and this fruit reaches ripe perfection about June. Such fruit is known in Arab. as *dafūr*, or "early figs," and in Heb as *bikkūrāh*, "the first-ripe" (Isa **28** 4; Jer **24** 2; Hos **9** 10). They are now, as of old, esteemed for their delicate flavor (Mic **7** 1, etc).

5. The Cursing of the Barren Fig-Tree

The miracle of Our Lord (Mt **21** 18–20; Mk **11** 12.13.20.21) which occurred in the Passover season, about April, will be understood (as far as the natural phenomena are concerned) by the account given above of the fruiting of the fig-tree, as repeatedly observed by the present writer in the neighborhood of Jerus. When the young leaves are newly appearing, in April, every fig-tree which is going to bear fruit at all will have some *taksh* ("immature figs") upon it, even though "the time of figs" (Mk **11** 13 AV), i.e. of ordinary edible figs—either early or late crop—"was not yet." This *taksh* is not only eaten today, but it is sure evidence, even when it falls, that the tree bearing it is not barren. This acted parable must be compared with Lk **13** 6.9; *now* the time of judgment was surely coming, the fate of the fruitless Jewish nation was forcibly foretold.

6. Dried Figs

While fresh figs have always been an important article of diet in their season (Neh **13** 15), the dried form is even more used. They are today dried in the sun and threaded on strings (like long necklaces) for convenience of carriage. A "cake of figs" (*d^ebhēlāh*, lit. "pressed together") is mentioned (1 S **30** 12); Abigail gave 200 such cakes of figs to David (**25** 18); the people of N. Israel sent, with other things, "cakes of figs" as a present to the newly crowned David (1 Ch **12** 40). Such masses of figs are much used today—they can be cut into slices with a knife like cheese. Such a mass was used externally for Hezekiah's "boil" (Isa **38** 21; 2 K **20** 7); it was a remedy familiar to early medical writers. E. W. G. Masterman

FIGHT. See War; Games.

FIGURE, fig'ūr, fig'yur (סֶמֶל, סֵמֶל, *ṣemel, ṣēmel*; **τύπος,** *túpos*): The tr of *ṣemel*, or *ṣēmel*, "a likeness or image"; perhaps a transposition of *çelem*, the usual word for likeness; it is elsewhere tr[d] "idol" and "image" (Dt **4** 16, "the similitude of any figure," RV "in the form of any figure"); of *tabhnīth*, "form or likeness" (Isa **44** 13, "shapeth it [the idol] . . . . after the figure of a man"; cf Dt **4** 16); of *miḳla'ath*, "carving," "carved work" (1 K **6** 29: "And he carved all the walls of the house round about with carved figures of cherubim and palm-trees and open flowers, within and without," only here and in ver 32, **7** 31 where the word is tr[d] "carving" and "graving"); in the NT "figure" is the tr of *tupos*, primarily "a mark," "print," "impression," "something made by blows," hence, "figure," "statue," tropically "form," "manner"; a person bearing the form or figure of another, having a certain resemblance, preceding another to come, model, exemplar (Acts **7** 43), "the figures [images] which ye made to worship them"; Rom **5** 14, "who is the figure [RV, "a figure"] of him that was to come," that is, the first Adam was a type of the second Adam, Christ; of *antitupon*, that which corresponds to a type or model (He **9** 24 AV, "Christ is not entered into the holy places made with hands, which are the figures of the true; but into heaven itself"); the meaning is simply the correspondence, or likeness (of the tabernacle to heaven), therefore RV renders "like in pattern to the true" (1 Pet **3** 21, "the like figure whereunto [even] baptism doth also now save us," i.e. baptism is the antitype of the ark "wherein . . . . eight souls were saved [or brought safely] through water," RV "which also after a true likeness [m "in the antitype"] doth now save you, even baptism"); of *parabolḗ*, "a placing alongside," a "comparison," "similitude," hence, image, figure, type (He **9** 9, "which was a figure for the time then present," ARV "which is a figure for the time present," ERV "parable" and "[now] present," viz. the entrance of the high priest into the Holy of Holies was a type of Christ's entrance into heaven; **11** 19, "from whence [from the dead] also he received him in a figure," i.e. Abraham received Isaac back from the dead *as it were*, in the *likeness* of a resurrection, he not being actually dead, ARV "from whence he did also in a figure receive him back," ERV "in a parable"); *metaschēmatízō*, "to change the form or appearance," "to transfer figuratively" (1 Cor **4** 6, "These things, brethren, I have in a figure transferred to myself and Apollos"; the Geneva version reads "I have figuratively described in my own person"). Paul is "substituting himself and Apollos for the teachers most in repute at Corinth that he might thus avoid personality."

"Figure" is supplied in Ecclus **49** 9, with *en ómbrō*, "He made mention of the enemies under the figure of the rain," RV "He remembered the enemies in storm," m "Gr rain."

RV has "a figure" m "an interpretation," for "the interpretation" (Prov **1** 6; the word is *m[e]līçāh*, only here and Hab **2** 6, meaning properly what is involved and needs interpretation; in Hab **2** 6 it is tr[d] "taunting proverb," RVm "riddle"); "figured stone" for "image of stone" (Lev **26** 1); "figured stones" for "pictures" (Nu **33** 52).

W. L. Walker

FILE, fīl: Found only in 1 S **13** 21, but the text here is obscure. The Heb (*p[e]çīrāh phīm*) signifies "bluntness of edge," and is so rendered in RVm. See Tools.

FILLET, fil'et (חוּט, *ḥūṭ*, חָשֻׁק, *ḥāshuḳ*):

(1) *Ḥūṭ*, from a root not used, meaning probably "to sew," therefore a string or a measuring rod or cord, and so a line, tape, thread, fillet. Jer **52** 21 tr[d] "line" (AV "fillet"), measuring 12 cubits long, encircling brass pillars standing 18 cubits high, part of the temple treasure plundered by the Chaldaeans; and many other things "that were in the house of Jeh, did the Chaldeans break in pieces." Tr[d] "thread," used by Rahab, in Josh **2** 18, and "cord," "three fold . . . . is not quickly broken," in Eccl **4** 12.

(2) *Ḥāshuḳ*, from a root meaning "to join" and therefore something joined or attached, and so a rail or rod between pillars, i.e. a fillet. The hangings of the court of the tabernacle were supported by brass pillars set in brass sockets, "The hooks of the pillars and their fillets shall be of silver" (Ex **27** 10.11). The embroidered screen for the door of the Tent was supported by five pillars socketed in brass: "And he overlaid their capitals and their fillets with gold" (Ex **36** 38). The pillars for the court and the gate of the court had fillets of silver (Ex **38** 10 ff). The vb. is used in Ex **27** 17; **38** 17, "All the pillars of the court were *filleted* with silver."

William Edward Raffety

FILTH, filth, **FILTHINESS,** fil'thi-nes, **FILTHY,** fil'thi (צֹאָה, *çō'āh*, טֻמְאָה, *ṭum'āh*; ῥυπόω, *rhupóō*): The word once tr[d] "filth" in the OT is *çō'āh*, "excrement" or "dung," elsewhere tr[d] "dung" (Isa **4** 4, used figuratively of evil doings, sin, "the filth of the daughters of Zion"; cf Prov **30** 12); in the NT we have *perikátharma*, "cleansings," "sweepings," "offscourings" (1 Cor **4** 13, "We are made as the filth of the world," RVm "or refuse"); *rhúpos*, "filth," "dirt," LXX for *çō'āh* in Isa **4** 4 (1 Pet **3** 21, "the filth of the flesh").

"Filthiness" is the tr of *ṭum'āh*, "uncleanness" (ritual, Lev **5** 3; **7** 20, etc), used figuratively of moral impurity, tr[d] "filthiness" (Ezr **6** 21; Lam **1** 9; Ezk **22** 15; **24** 11.13 *bis*; **36** 25); *niddāh*, "impurity" (2 Ch **29** 5); figuratively (Ezr **9** 11); RV has "uncleanness," but "filthiness" for uncleanness at close of verse (*niddāh*); *n[e]ḥōsheth*, "brass," figuratively (for "impurity" or "impudence") (Ezk **16** 36); *aischrótēs*, primarily "ugliness," tropical for unbecomingness, indecency (only Eph **5** 4, "nor filthiness, nor foolish talking"; Alford has "obscenity," Weymouth, "shameful"); *akathártēs*, "uncleanness" (Rev **17** 4 AV), corrected text, *tá akátharta*, "the unclean things," so RV.

"Filthy" is the tr of *'ālaḥ*, "to be turbid," to become foul or corrupt in a *moral* sense (Job **15** 16 AV; Ps **14** 3; **53** 3); *'iddīm*, pl. of *'iddāh*, from *'ādhadh*, "to number or compute [monthly courses]"; Isa **64** 6, "All our righteousnesses are as filthy rags," RV "as a polluted garment"; cf Ezk **36** 17; *aischros*, "ugly," tropical for unbecoming, shameful (Tit **1** 11, "for filthy lucre's sake"; cf ver 7); shameful discourse *aischrologia* (Col **3** 8 AV); *rhupoō*, "filthy," in a moral sense polluted (Rev **22** 11, "He that is filthy, let him be filthy still," RV "let him be made filthy still" [corrected text], m "yet more"; Alford, "Let the filthy [morally polluted] pollute himself still" [in the constant middle sense of passive vbs. when the act depends on the man's self]).

In Apoc we have (Ecclus **22** 1): "A slothful man is compared to a filthy [*ardalóō*] stone," RV "a stone that is defiled," ver 2 "A slothful man is compared to the filth [*bólbiton*] of a dunghill"; **27** 4 "So the filth [*skúbalon*] of a man in his talk [RV "of man in his reasoning"] remaineth." See Uncleanness.

W. L. Walker

FIN. See Fish.

FINE, fīn (adj., from Lat *finire*, "to finish"): Indicates superior quality. Only in a few instances does "fine" represent a separate word: (1) *ṭōbh*, "good," qualifies gold (2 Ch **3** 5.8, "fine gold"; cf Gen **2** 12, "good"); fine gold (Lam **4** 1, AV "most fine gold," RV "most pure gold," lit. "good fine gold"), copper (Ezr **8** 27, RV "fine bright brass"); *ṭabh*, Aram. (Dnl **2** 32, "fine gold"). (2) *pāz*, "refined" (Cant **5** 11, "the most fine gold"). (3) *ḥēlebh*, "fatness," "the best of any kind"; cf Gen **45** 18; Dt **32** 14, etc (Ps **81** 16, "the finest of the wheat," RVm Heb "fat of wheat"). (4) *sārīḳ*, "fine combed" (Isa **19** 9, "fine flax," RV "combed flax").

In other places it expresses a quality of the substantive: *kethem*, "fine gold" (Job **31** 24; Dnl **10**

5, RV "pure gold"); *pāz,* used as a noun for refined gold (Job **28** 17; Ps **19** 10; Prov **8** 19; Isa **13** 12; Lam **4** 2); *ḥārūç,* "fine gold" (Prov **3** 14; cf Ps **68** 13, "yellow gold"); *ṣōleth,* "flour," rendered "fine flour," rolled or crushed small (Lev **2** 1.4.5.7, etc); *semídalis,* "the finest wheaten flour" (Rev **18** 13); *ḳemaḥ ṣōleth,* "fine meal" (Gen **18** 6); *ṣādhīn,* "linen garment" (LXX *sindṓn,* Prov **31** 24 AV; Isa **3** 23); *shēsh,* "white," "fine linen" (Gen **41** 42; Ex **25** 4, etc); in Prov **31** 22 AV has "silk"; *shēshī* (Ezk **16** 13, "fine flour"); *'ēṭūn,* "what is twisted or spun," "yarn" (Prov **7** 16 AV, "fine linen of Egypt," RV "yarn of Egypt"); *būç,* "fine white cloth," "cotton or linen," "fine linen" (1 Ch **4** 21; Ezk **27** 16, etc; 2 Ch **5** 12, AV "white," RV "fine"); *bússos,* "byssus," "linen" from *būç* (LXX for which, 2 Ch **2** 14; **3** 14), deemed very fine and precious, worn only by the rich (Lk **16** 19; Rev **18** 12); *bússinos,* "byssine," made of fine linen, LXX for *būç* (1 Ch **15** 27) (Rev **18** 16, "clothed in fine linen," RV "arrayed," **19** 8.14); *sindōn,* "fine linen" (Mk **15** 46, "He bought fine linen," RV "a linen cloth"; cf Mk **14** 51.52; Mt **27** 59; Lk **23** 53); it was used for wrapping the body at night, also for wrapping round dead bodies; *sindōn* is LXX for *ṣādhīn* (Jgs **14** 12.13; Prov **31** 24); *chalkolíbanon* (Rev **1** 15; **2** 18, AV "fine brass").

The meaning of this word has been much discussed; *chálkos* is "brass" in Gr (with many compounds), and *líbanos* is the LXX for *lebhōnāh,* "frankincense," which word was probably derived from the root *lābhan,* "to burn"; this would give *glowing brass,* "as if they burned in a furnace"; in Dnl **10** 6 it is *neḥōsheth ḳālāl,* AV "polished brass," RV "burnished" (*ḳālal* is "to glow"). Plumptre deemed it a hybrid word composed of the Gr *chalkos,* "brass," and the Heb *lābhān,* "white," a technical word, such as might be familiar to the Ephesians; RV has "burnished brass"; Weymouth, "silver-bronze when it is white-hot in a furnace"; the whiteness being expressed by the second half of the Gr word. See Thayer's *Lexicon* (s.v.).

In Apoc we have "fine linen," *bussinos* (1 Esd **3** 6), "fine bread"; the adj. *katharós,* separate (Jth **10** 5, RVm "pure bread"); "fine flour" (Ecclus **35** 2; **38** 11); *semídalis* (Bel ver 3; 2 Macc **1** 8, RV "meal offering"). W. L. WALKER

FINER, fīn'ẽr, **FINING,** fīn'ing (Prov **25** 4 AV). See REFINER.

FINES, fīnz. See PUNISHMENTS.

FINGER, fiṇ'gẽr (Heb and Aram. אֶצְבַּע, *'eçba';* δάκτυλος, *dáktulos*): The fingers are to the Oriental essential in conversation; their language is frequently very eloquent and expressive. They often show what the mouth does not dare to utter, esp. grave insult and scorn. The scandalous person is thus described in Prov **6** 13 as "teaching" or "making signs with his fingers." Such insulting gestures (compare e.g. the gesture of Shimei in throwing dust or stones at David, 2 S **16** 6) are even now not infrequent in Pal. The same habit is alluded to in Isa **58** 9 by the expression, "putting forth of fingers."

The fingers were decorated with rings of precious metal, which, with other jewelry worn ostentatiously on the body, often formed the only possession of the wearer, and were therefore carefully guarded. In the same way the law of Jeh was to be kept: "Bind them [my commandments] upon thy fingers; write them upon the tablet of thy heart" (Prov **7** 3).

Figurative: In 1 K **12** 10 and 2 Ch **10** 10 Rehoboam gives the remarkable answer to his dissatisfied people, which is, at the same time, an excellent example of the use of figurative language in the Orient: "My little finger is thicker than my father's loins," a figure explained in the next verse: "Whereas my father did lade you with a heavy yoke, I will add to your yoke: my father chastised you with whips, but I will chastise you with scorpions." The Heb word used here for little finger is קֹטֶן, *ḳōṭen,* lit. "pettiness," "unimportant thing."

The "finger of God," like the "hand of God," is synonymous with power, omnipotence, sometimes with the additional meaning of the infallible evidence of Divine authorship visible in all His works (Ps **8** 3; Lk **11** 20), esp. in His law (Ex **8** 19; **31** 18; Dt **9** 10; cf Ex **32** 15.16).

The finger or digit as a linear measure is mentioned in Jer **52** 21 (Gr *daktulos;* Jos, *Ant,* VIII, iii, 4). It is equal to one finger-breadth, ¼ of a hand-breadth (palm) = 18.6 millimeters or .73 in.

H. L. E. LUERING

FINGER, fiṇ'gẽr (אֶצְבַּע, *'eçba'*): The smallest of the Heb linear measures. It was equal to the breadth of the finger, or about ¾ in., four of which made a palm (Jer **52** 21). See WEIGHTS AND MEASURES.

FINISH, fin'ish (כָּלָה, *kālāh;* τελέω, *teléō,* with other Heb and Gr words): The proper sense of "finish" is to end or complete; so for "finish," "finished," in AV, there is sometimes met with in RV the change to "complete" (Lk **14** 28; 2 Cor **8** 6), "accomplish" (Jn **4** 34; **5** 36; **17** 4), "made an end of doing" (2 Ch **4** 11; cf **24** 14), etc. In Jas **1** 15, for "sin, when it is finished," RV reads "sin, when it is full-grown," corresponding to "conceived" of the previous clause. On the other hand, RV has frequently "finished" for other words, as "ended" (Gen **2** 2; Dt **31** 30), "accomplished" (Jn **19** 28), "filled up," "fulfilled" (Rev **15** 1.8), etc. The grandest Scriptural example of the word is the cry upon the cross, "It is finished" (*Tetélestai,* Jn **19** 30). W. L. WALKER

FINISHER, fin'ish-ẽr (τελειωτής, *teleiōtḗs*): This word is applied to Jesus (He **12** 2), and comes from *teleióō,* "to complete," "to make perfect"; hence it means finisher in the sense of completing; AV "the author and finisher of our faith," RV "the author [m "captain"] and perfecter of our faith"; but "our" is supplied, and in the connection in which the passage stands—after the examples which have been adduced of the power of faith—most probably the best rendering is "the Leader [or Captain] and Perfecter of the Faith," that is of the faith which has been illustrated by those mentioned in ch **11,** who are as "a great cloud of witnesses" to the power of faith; but above all "looking to Jesus, our Leader" in whom it was perfected, as is shown in what follows: "who for the joy that was set before him endured the cross," etc. "In His human nature He exhibited Faith in its highest form, from first to last, and placing Himself as it were at the head of the great army of heroes of Faith, He carried Faith, the source of their strength, to its most complete perfection and to its loftiest triumph" (Westcott). W. L. WALKER

FIR, fûr, **FIR-TREE** (RVm "cypress"; בְּרוֹשׁ, *berōsh,* 2 S **6** 5; 1 K **5** 8.10, etc; בְּרוֹתִים, *berōthīm* [pl. only], an Aram. form, Cant **1** 17): This tree was one of the chief trees of Lebanon (Isa **60** 13); one of usefulness (**41** 19; **55** 13); associated with the cedar (2 K **19** 23; Ps **104** 17; Isa **14** 8; Zec **11** 2); its boughs were wide and great (Ezk **31** 8); it was evergreen (Hos **14** 8); it could supply boards and timber for doors (1 K **6** 15.24); beams for roofing the temple (2 Ch **3** 5); planks for shipbuilding (Ezk **27** 5). In 2 S **6** 5 we read: "David and all the house of Israel played before Jeh with all manner of instruments made of

1. OT References

fir-wood," etc. It is practically certain that the reading in the ‖ passage in 1 Ch **13** 8 is more correct: "David and all Israel played before God with all their might, even with songs," etc. This view is supported by the LXX tr (ἐν πάσῃ δυνάμει, *en pásē dunámei*). There is therefore no necessity to suppose that *b^erōsh* was a wood used for musical instruments.

2. The Identity of "Berōsh"

The identity of *berōsh* is uncertain. It was a name applied either to several of the *Coniferae* in common or to one or more outstanding species. If the latter is the case we can only seek for the most suited to OT requirements. The Aleppo pine, *Pinus Halepensis*, is a fine tree which flourishes in the Lebanon, but its wood is not of special excellence and durability. A better tree (or couple of trees) is the *sherbin* of the Syrians; this name includes two distinct varieties in the suborder *Cypressineae*, the fine tall juniper, *Juniperis excelsa* and the cypress, *Cypressus sempervirens*. They both still occur in considerable numbers in the Lebanon and Anti-Lebanon; they are magnificent trees and produce excellent wood—resinous, fragrant, durable. If these trees were not classed locally, as now, under one name, then the cypress is of the two more probably the *berōsh*. The coffins of Egyp mummies were made of cypress; a compact variety of this cypress is cultivated all over the Turkish empire by the Moslems as an ornament in cemeteries. From early times the cypress has been connected with mourning.

In the Apoc there are two definite references to the cypress (κυπάρισσος, *kupárissos*). In Sir **24** 13, Wisdom says:

"I was exalted like a cedar in Libanus,
And as a cypress tree on the mountains of Hermon."

And in Sir **50** 10 the high priest Simon is said to be

"As an olive tree budding forth fruits,
And as a cypress growing high among the clouds."

These passages, esp. the former, certainly favor the idea that *berōsh* was the cypress; the name may, however, have included allied trees.

E. W. G. Masterman

FIRE, fīr (אֵשׁ, *'ēsh;* πῦρ, *púr*): These are the common words for fire, occurring very frequently. *'Ūr*, "light" (Isa **24** 15 AV; cf RV; **31** 9, and see Fires), *nūr* (Aram.) (Dnl **3** 22 ff) are found a few times, also *'eshshāh* (Jer **6** 29), and *be'ērāh* (Ex **22** 6), once each. Acts **28** 2.3 has *purá*, "pyre," and Mk **14** 54; Lk **22** 56, *phôs*, "light," RV "in the light [of the fire]." "To set on fire," *yāçath* (2 S **14** 31), *lāhaṭ* (Dt **32** 22, etc), *phlogízō* (Jas **3** 6).

Fire was regarded by primitive peoples as supernatural in origin and specially Divine. Molech, the fire-god, and other deities were worshipped by certain Canaanitish and other tribes with human sacrifices (Dt **12** 31; 2 K **17** 31; Ps **106** 37), and, although this was specially forbidden to the Israelites (Lev **18** 21; Dt **12** 31; **18** 10), they too often lapsed into the practice (2 K **16** 3; **21** 6; Jer **7** 31; Ezk **20** 26.31). See Molech; Idolatry.

1. Literal Usage

Fire in the OT is specially associated with the Divine presence, e.g. in the making of the Covenant with Abraham (Gen **15** 17), in the burning bush (Ex **3** 2–4), in the pillar of fire (**13** 21), on Sinai (**19** 18), in the flame on the altar (Jgs **13** 20). Jeh was "the God that answereth by fire" (1 K **18** 24.38). In the Law, therefore, sacrifices and offerings (including incense) were to be made by fire (Ex **12** 8.9.10; Lev **1**). Fire from Jeh signified the acceptance of certain special and separate sacrifices (Jgs **6** 21; 1 K **18** 38; 1 Ch **21** 26). In Lev **9** 24 the sacrificial fire "came forth from before Jeh." The altar-fire was to be kept continually burning (**6** 12.13); offering by "strange fire" (other than the sacred altar-fire) was punished by "fire from before Jeh" (**10** 1.2). Fire came from heaven also at the consecration of Solomon's Temple (2 Ch **7** 1).

According to 2 Macc **1** 19–22, at the time of the Captivity priests hid the sacred fire in a well, and Nehemiah found it again, in a miraculous way, for the second Temple. Later, Maccabaeus is said to have restored the fire by "striking stones and taking fire out of them" (**10** 3).

Fire was a frequent instrument of the Divine primitive wrath (Gen **19** 24; Ex **9** 23 [lightning]; Nu **11** 1; **16** 35, etc; Ps **104** 4, ARV "Who maketh . . . . flames of fire his ministers"). Fire shall yet dissolve the world (2 Pet **3** 12). It was frequently used by the Israelites as a means of destruction of idolatrous objects and the cities of their enemies (Dt **7** 5.25; **12** 3; **13** 16; Josh **6** 24; Jgs, frequently); sometimes also of punishment (Lev **20** 14; **21** 9; Josh **7** 25; 2 Macc **7** 5).

The domestic use of fire was, as among other peoples, for heating, cooking, lighting, etc, but according to the Law no fire could be kindled on the Sabbath day (Ex **35** 3). It was employed also for melting (**32** 24), and refining (Nu **31** 23; Mal **3** 2.3, etc). For the sacrificial fire wood was used as fuel (Gen **22** 3.6; Lev **6** 12); for ordinary purposes, also charcoal (Prov **25** 22; Isa **6** 6, RVm "or hot stone"; Hab **3** 5, RV "fiery bolts," m "or burning coals"; Jn **21** 9, "a fire of coals" RVm "Gr, a fire of charcoal"; Rom **12** 20); branches (Nu **15** 32; 1 K **17** 12); thorns (Ps **58** 9; **118** 12; Eccl **7** 6; Isa **33** 12); grass and other herbage (Mt **6** 30; Lk **12** 28).

2. Figurative Use

Fire was an emblem (1) of Jeh in His glory (Dnl **7** 9); (2) in His holiness (Isa **6** 4); (3) in His jealousy for His sole worship (Dt **4** 24; He **12** 29; Ps **79** 5; perhaps also Isa **33** 14); (4) of His protection of His people (2 K **6** 17; Zec **2** 5); (5) of His righteous judgment and purification (Zec **13** 9; Mal **3** 2.3; 1 Cor **3** 13.15); (6) of His wrath against sin and punishment of the wicked (Dt **9** 3; Ps **18** 8; **89** 46; Isa **5** 24; **30** 33, "a Topheth is prepared of old"; Mt **3** 10–12; **5** 22, RV "the hell of fire," m "Gr, Gehenna of fire"; see Isa **30** 33; Jer **7** 31; Mt **13** 40.42; **25** 41, "eternal fire"; Mk **9** 45–49; see Isa **66** 24; 2 Thess **1** 7; He **10** 27; Jude ver 7); (7) of the word of God in its power (Jer **5** 14; **23** 29); (8) of Divine truth (Ps **39** 3; Jer **20** 9; Lk **12** 49); (9) of that which guides men (Isa **50** 10.11); (10) of the Holy Spirit (Acts **2** 3); (11) of the glorified Christ (Rev **1** 14); (12) of kindness in its melting power (Rom **12** 20); (13) of trial and suffering (Ps **66** 12; Isa **43** 2; 1 Pet **1** 7; **4** 12); (14) of evil (Prov **6** 27; **16** 27; Isa **9** 18; **65** 5); lust or desire (Hos **7** 6; Sir **23** 16; 1 Cor **7** 9); greed (Prov **30** 16); (15) of the tongue in its evil aspects (Jas **3** 5.6); (16) of heaven in its purity and glory (Rev **15** 2; see also **21** 22.23).

W. L. Walker

FIRE BAPTISM. See Baptism of Fire; Molech.

FIRE, LAKE OF. See Lake of Fire.

FIRE, STRANGE. See Fire.

FIRE, UNQUENCHABLE. See Unquenchable Fire.

FIREBRAND, fīr′brand (אוּד, *'ūdh*, used for a burning stick taken out of the fire): In Jgs **15** 4.5 describing the "brands" (m "torches") which Samson tied to the foxes' tails, the word is *lappīdh* ("lamp"; see Jgs **7** 16.20 RV, "torches"). Other words are *ziḳḳīm*, "sparks," "flames" (fiery darts; Prov **26** 18), and *zīḳōth* (Isa **50** 11); *'ūdh* is used **figuratively** of angry men (Isa **7** 4), and of those mercifully rescued from destruction (Am **4** 11; Zec **3** 2; RV "brand"). RV gives "firebrand" as tr of *mōḳēdh* (AV "hearth") in Ps **102** 3, "My bones are burned as a firebrand" (m "as a hearth"). See Brand.

W. L. Walker

FIREPAN, fīr′pan (מַחְתָּה, *maḥtāh,* "firepan," "censer," "snuffdish," from חָתָה, *ḥāthāh,* "to snatch up"): A vessel for carrying coals. Brazen firepans were part of the furnishings of the altar of burnt offerings (Ex **27** 3; **38** 3, and in Nu **4** 14, where AV wrongly reads "censers," the context indicating a vessel belonging to the brazen altar).

The same word is trd "snuffdishes" in Ex **25** 38; **37** 23; Nu **4** 9, where it refers to golden firepans which belonged to the golden candlestick or lamp stand, and were used to receive the burnt ends of the wicks. In 1 K **7** 50 and 2 Ch **4** 22, although AV reads "censers," the context points to the firepans belonging to the candlestick; as also in 2 K **25** 15 and Jer **52** 19, trd "firepans" in AV and RV. A similar firepan designated by the same Heb word but trd "censer" was used to carry the burning coals upon which the incense was thrown and burned (Lev **10** 1; **16** 12; Nu **16** 6.17 ff). See CENSER.

The firepan or censer of the Hebrews was doubtless similar to the censer of the Egyptians, pictures of which have been found. It consisted of a pan or pot for the coals, which was held by a straight or slightly curved long handle. The style of censer used in recent centuries, swung by three chains, came into use about the 12th cent. AD.

GEORGE RICE HOVEY

FIRES, fīrz: In Isa **24** 15 AV translates אֻרִים, *'urīm* ("lights," esp. Urim in the phrase "Urim and Thummim") "fires." RV, understanding the word to mean the region of light, translates "east," which satisfies the context far better, and is adopted by many modern scholars. In Ezk **39** 9.10 RV has "fires"; in ver 9 "make fires" is a tr of a vb. of different root; in ver 10 "fires" translates the common sing. noun for fire.

FIRKIN, fûr′kin (μετρητής, *metrētēs*): The liquid measure used in Jn **2** 6 to indicate the capacity of the water-pots mentioned in the narrative of the miracle of turning the water into wine. It is regarded as equivalent to the Heb *bath,* and thus contained about nine gallons. See WEIGHTS AND MEASURES.

FIRMAMENT, fûr′ma-ment. See ASTRONOMY, III, 3.

FIRST, fûrst (אֶחָד, *'eḥādh,* רִאשׁוֹן, *ri'shōn;* **πρῶτον,** *prōton,* **τὸ πρῶτον,** *tó prōton,* **πρῶτος,** *prōtos*): Of these words, which are those most frequently used for "first," *ri'shōn* is from *rōsh,* "the head," and is used for the highest, chief, etc; also of time, the beginning, e.g. Gen **8** 13, "in the first month"; in Isa **44** 6; **48** 12, it is used of Jeh as Eternal and solely Supreme—the First and the Last (cf **41** 4). Special usages are in connection with "firstborn," "first-fruit," etc; *prōton* is used of that which is first in order; but also of that which is first or chief in importance, etc (Mt **6** 33; Jas **3** 17). In 1 Tim **1** 15, Paul says Jesus came "to save sinners; of whom I am chief," lit. "first"; the same word is used by Jesus of the "first" of the commandments (Mk **12** 29); where we read in 1 Cor **15** 3, "I delivered unto you first of all," it is *en prōtois* ("in the foremost place"); "The first and the last" is applied to Christ as Eternal and Supreme (Rev **1** 17; **2** 8; **22** 13); *prōtos* is "the first day" (Mt **26** 17; Mk **16** 9); in Mt **28** 1; Mk **16** 2; Lk **24** 1; Jn **20** 1.19; Acts **20** 7, it is *mia* ("one").

W. L. WALKER

FIRST-BEGOTTEN, fûrst-bē-got″n (**πρωτότοκος,** *prōtótokos*): This Gr word is trd in two passages in AV by "first-begotten" (He **1** 6; Rev **1** 5), but in all other places in AV, and always in RV, by "firstborn." It is used in its natural literal sense of Jesus Christ as Mary's firstborn (Lk **2** 7; Mt **1** 25 AV); it also bears the literal sense of the firstborn of men and animals (He **11** 28). It is not used in the NT or LXX of an only child, which is expressed by *monogenēs* (see below).

Metaphorically, it is used of Jesus Christ to express at once His relation to man and the universe and His difference from them, as both He and they are related to God. The laws and customs of all nations show that to be "firstborn" means, not only priority in time, but a certain superiority in privilege and authority. Israel is Jeh's firstborn among the nations (Ex **4** 22; cf Jer **31** 9). The Messianic King is God's firstborn (LXX *prōtotokos*), "the highest of the kings of the earth" (Ps **89** 27). Philo applies the word to the Logos as the archetypal and governing idea of creation. Similarly Christ, as "the firstborn of all creation" (Col **1** 15), is not only prior to it in time, but above it in power and authority. "All things have been created through him, and unto him" (ver 16). He is "sovereign Lord over all creation by virtue of primo-geniture" (Lightfoot). It denotes His status and character and not His origin; the context does not admit the idea that He is a part of the created universe. So in His incarnation He is brought into the world as "firstborn," and God summons all His angels to worship Him (He **1** 6). In His resurrection He is "firstborn from the dead" (Col **1** 18) or "of the dead" (Rev **1** 5), the origin and prince of life. And finally He is "firstborn among many brethren" in the consummation of God's purpose of grace, when all the elect are gathered home. Not only is He their Lord, but also their pattern, God's ideal Son, and men are "foreordained to be conformed to [his] image" (Rom **8** 29). Therefore the saints themselves, as growing in His likeness, and as possessing all the privileges of eldest sons, including the kingdom and the priesthood, may be called the "church of the firstborn who are enrolled in heaven" (He **12** 23). See also BEGOTTEN, and Lightfoot on Col **1** 15.

T. REES

FIRSTBORN, fûrst′bôrn, **FIRSTLING,** fûrst′ling (בְּכוֹר, *bekhōr;* **πρωτότοκος,** *prōtótokos*): The Heb word denotes the firstborn of human beings as well as of animals (Ex **11** 5), while a word from the same root denotes first-fruits (Ex **23** 16). All the data point to the conclusion that among the ancestors of the Hebrews the sacrifice of the firstborn was practised, just as the firstlings of the flocks and the first-fruits of the produce of the earth were devoted to the deity. The narrative of the Moabite war records the sacrifice of the heir to the throne by Mesha, to Chemosh, the national god (2 K **3** 27). The barbarous custom must have become extinct at an early period in the religion of Israel (Gen **22** 12). It was probably due to the influence of surrounding nations that the cruel practice was revived toward the close of the monarchical period (2 K **16** 3; **17** 17; **21** 6; Jer **7** 31; Ezk **16** 20; **23** 37; Mic **6** 7). Jeremiah denies that the offering of human beings could have been an instruction from Yahweh (**7** 31; **19** 5). The prophetic conception of God had rendered such a doctrine inconceivable. Clear evidence of the spiritualization and humanization of religion among the Israelites is furnished in the replacement, at an early stage, of the actual sacrifice of the firstborn by their dedication to the service of Yahweh. At a later stage the Levites were substituted for the firstborn. Just as the firstlings of unclean animals were redeemed with money (Ex **13** 13; **34** 20), for the dedication of the firstborn was substituted the consecration of the Levites to the service of the sanctuary (Nu **3** 11–13.45). On the 30th day after birth the firstborn was brought to the priest by the father, who paid five shekels for the child's redemption from service in the temple (cf Lk **2** 27; Mish *Bekhōrōth* viii.8). For that service the Levites were accepted in place of the redeemed firstborn (Nu **3** 45). See note. According to Ex **22** 29–31 the firstborn were to be given to Yahweh. (The firstborn of clean animals, if free from spot or blemish, were to be sacrificed after eight days, Nu **18** 16 ff.) This allusion to the sacrifice of the firstborn as part of the religion of Yahweh has been variously explained. Some scholars suspect the text, but in all probability the verse means no more than similar references to the fact that the firstborn belonged to Yahweh (Ex **13** 2; **34** 19). The modifying clause, with regard to the redemption of the firstborn, has been omitted. The firstborn possessed definite privileges which were denied to other members of the family. The Law forbade the disinheriting of the firstborn (Dt **21** 15–17). Such legislation, in polygamous times, was necessary to prevent a favorite wife from exercising undue influence over her husband in distributing his property, as in the case of Jacob (Gen **25** 23). The oldest son's share was twice as large as that of any other son. When Elisha prayed for a double portion of Elijah's spirit, he simply wished to be considered the firstborn, i.e. the successor, of the dying prophet. Israel was Yahweh's firstborn (Ex **4** 22; cf Jer **31** 9 [Ephraim]). Israel, as compared with other nations, was entitled to special privileges. She occupied a unique position in virtue of the special relationship between Yahweh and the nation. In three passages (Rom **8** 29; Col **1** 15; He **1** 6), Jesus Christ is the firstborn—among many brethren (Rom **8** 29); of every creature (Col **1** 16). This application of the term to Jesus Christ may be traced back to Ps **89** 27 where the Davidic ruler, or perhaps the nation, is alluded to as the firstborn of Yahweh. See Child; Circumcision; First-begotten; Plagues of Egypt.

Note.—The custom of redeeming the firstborn son is preserved among the Jews to this day. After thirty days the father invites the "Kohen," i.e. a supposed descendant of Aaron, to the house. The child is brought and shown to the "Kohen," and the father declares the mother of the child to be an Israelite. If she is a "Kohen," redemption is not necessary. The "Kohen" asks the father which he prefers, his child or the five shekels; the father answers that he prefers his son, and pays to the "Kohen" a sum equivalent to five shekels. After receiving the redemption-money, the "Kohen" puts his hands on the child's head and pronounces the Aaronite blessing (Nu **6** 22–27).

T. Lewis

FIRST-FRUITS, fûrst′-froōts (רֵאשִׁית, *rē'shīth*, בִּכּוּרִים, *bikkūrīm;* **ἀπαρχή**, *aparchḗ*. LXX translates *rē'shīth* by *aparchē*, but for *bikkūrīm* it uses the word *prōtogennḗmata;* cf Philo **22** 33): In acknowledgment of the fact that the land and all its products were the gift of Jeh to Israel, and in thankfulness for His bounty, all the first-fruits were offered to Him. These were offered in their natural state (e.g. cereals, tree fruits, grapes), or after preparation (e.g. musk, oil, flour, dough), after which the Israelite was at liberty to use the rest (Ex **23** 19; Nu **15** 20; **18** 12; Dt **26** 2; Neh **10** 35.37). No absolute distinction can be made between *rē'shīth* and *bikkūrīm*, but *rē'shīth* seems generally to mean what is prepared by human labor, and *bikkūrīm* the direct product of Nature. The phrase "the first of the first-fruits" (Ex **23** 19; **34** 26; Ezk **44** 30), Heb *rē'shīth bikkūrē*, Gr *aparchaí tôn prōtogennēmátōn*, is not quite clear. It may mean the first-ripe or the choicest of the first-fruits. The *rē'shīth* offerings were individual, except that a *rē'shīth* of dough was to be offered as a heave offering (Nu **15** 17–21). The priest waved a *rē'shīth* of corn before the Lord on the morrow after the Sabbath in the week of unleavened bread (Lev **23** 9–11). These offerings all fell to the priest (Nu **18** 12). *Bikkūrīm* refers specially to things sown (Ex **23** 16; Lev **2** 14). At the Feast of Weeks, seven weeks after the offering of the sheaf, *bikkūrīm* of corn in the ear, parched with fire and bruised, were brought to the House of the Lord as a meal offering (Ex **34** 22–26; Lev **2** 14–16). The *bikkūrīm* also fell to the priest, except a portion which was burned as a memorial (Lev **2** 8–10.16). The beautiful ceremony of the offering of the *rē'shīth* in the House of God is described in Dt **26** 1–11, and is enlarged upon in the Talm (*Bikkūrīm* **3** 2). According to the Talm (*Terūmōth* **4** 3) a sixtieth part of the first-fruits in a prepared form was the minimum that could be offered; the more generous brought a fortieth part, and even a thirtieth. The fruits of newly planted trees were not to be gathered during the first three years; the fruits of the fourth year were consecrated to Jeh, and from the fifth year the fruits belonged to the owner of the trees (Lev **19** 23–25). According to Mish, *'Orlāh* i.10, even the shells of nuts and pomegranates could not be used during the first three years as coloring matter or for the lighting of fires. It is held by some scholars that the institution of the tithe (see Tithe) is a later development from the first-fruits.

Figurative: In the OT, in Jer **2** 3, Israel is called "the *rē'shīth* of his increase." In the NT *aparchē* is applied fig. to the first convert or converts in a particular place (Rom **16** 5; 1 Cor **16** 15); to the Christians of that age (Jas **1** 18; 2 Thess **2** 13, WHm), and to the 144,000 in heaven (Rev **14** 4); to Christ, as the first who rose from the dead (1 Cor **15** 20.23); also to the blessings which we receive now through the Spirit, the earnest of greater blessings to come (Rom **8** 23).

Paul Levertoff

FIRSTLING. See Firstborn.

FISH (דָּג, *dāgh*, דָּגָה, *dāghāh*, דָּאג, *dā'gh;* **ἰχθύς**, *ichthús*, **ἰχθύδιον**, *ichthúdion*, **ὀψάριον**, *opsárion*):

1. Natural History

Fishes abound in the inland waters of Pal as well as the Mediterranean. They are often mentioned or indirectly referred to both in the OT and in the NT, but it is remarkable that no particular kind is distinguished by name. In Lev **11** 9–12 and Dt **14** 9 f, "whatsoever hath fins and scales in the waters" is declared clean, while all that "have not fins and scales" are forbidden. This excluded not only reptiles and amphibians, but also, among fishes, siluroids and eels, sharks, rays and lampreys. For our knowledge of the inland fishes of Pal we are mainly indebted to Tristram, *NHB* and *Fauna and Flora of Pal;* Lortet, *Poissons et reptiles du Lac de Tibériade;* and Russegger, *Reisen in Europa, Asien, Afrika*, 1835–1841. The most remarkable feature of the fish fauna of the Jordan valley is its relationship to that of the Nile and of E. Central Africa. Two Nile fishes, *Chromis nilotica* Hasselquist, and *Clarias macracanthus* Gunth., are found in the Jordan valley, and a number of other species found only in the Jordan valley belong to genera (*Chromis* and *Hemichromis*) which are otherwise exclusively African. This seems to indicate that at some time, probably in the early Tertiary, there was some connection between the Palestinian and African river systems. No fish can live in the Dead Sea, and many perish through being carried down by the swift currents of the Jordan and other streams. There are, however, several kinds of small fish which live in salt springs on the borders of the Dead Sea, springs which are as salt as the Dead Sea but which, according to Lortet, lack the magnesium chloride which is a constituent of the Dead Sea water and is fatal to the fish. *Capoëta damascina* Cuv. and Val., one of the commonest fishes of Syria and Pal, has been taken by the writer in large numbers in the Arnon and other streams flowing into the Dead Sea. This is surprising in view of the fact that the Dead Sea seems to form an effective barrier between the fishes of the different streams flowing into it. The indiscriminate mention of

Fishes of the Sea of Galilee (*PEF* Drawing).

fishes without reference to the different kinds is well illustrated by the numerous passages in which "the fishes of the sea, the birds of the heavens, and the beasts of the field," or some equivalent expression, is used to denote all living creatures, e.g. Gen **1** 26; **9** 2; Nu **11** 22; Dt **4** 18; 1 K **4** 33; Job **12** 8; Ps **8** 8; Ezk **38** 20; Hos **4** 3; Zeph **1** 3; 1 Cor **15** 39.

2. Jonah's Fish

An unusually large shark might fulfil the conditions of Jonah's fish (*dāgh, dāghāh;* but Mt **12** 40, κῆτος, *kḗtos*, "whale" or "sea monster"). The whale that is found in the Mediterranean (*Balaena australis*) has a narrow throat and could not swallow a man. No natural explanation is possible of Jonah's remaining alive and conscious for three days in the creature's belly. Those who consider the book historical must regard the whole event as miraculous. For those who consider it to be a story with a purpose, no explanation is required.

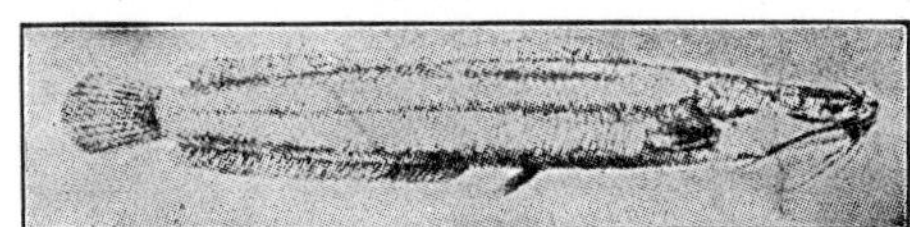

Carp Found in the Sea of Galilee (*PEF* Drawing).

3. Fishing

The present inhabitants of Moab and Edom make no use of the fish that swarm in the Arnon, the Ḥisa and other streams, but fishing is an important industry in Galilee and Western Pal. Now, as formerly, spear hooks and nets are employed. The fish-spear (Job **41** 7) is little used. Most of the OT references to nets have to do with the taking of birds and beasts and not of fishes, and, while in Hab **1** 15 *ḥērem* is rendered "net" and *mikhmereth* "drag," it is not clear that these and the other words rendered "net" refer to particular kinds of nets. In the NT, however, σαγήνη, *sagḗnē* (Mt **13** 47), is clearly the dragnet, and ἀμφίβληστρον, *amphíblēstron* (Mt **4** 18), is clearly the casting net. The word oftenest used is δίκτυον, *díktuon*. Though this word is from *dikeín*, "to throw," or "to cast," the context in several places (e.g. Lk **5** 4; Jn **21** 11) suggests that a dragnet is meant. The dragnet may be several hundred feet long. The upper edge is buoyed and the lower edge is weighted. It is let down from a boat in a line parallel to the shore and is then pulled in by ropes attached to the two ends, several men and boys usually pulling at each end. The use of the casting net requires much skill. It forms a circle of from 10 to 20 feet in diameter with numerous small leaden weights at the circumference. It is lifted by the center and carefully gathered over the right arm. When well thrown it goes to some distance, at the same time spreading out into a wide circle. A cord may be attached to the center, but this is not always the case. When lifted again by the center, the leads come together, dragging over the bottom, and sometimes a large number of fish may be inclosed. The novice has only to try, to realize the dexterity of the practised fishermen.

Figurative: The fact that so many of Our Lord's disciples were fishermen lends a profound interest to their profession. Christ tells Simon and Andrew (Mt **4** 19; Mk **1** 17) that He will make them fishers of men. The Kingdom of Heaven (Mt **13** 47) is likened unto a net that was cast into the sea, and gathered of every kind; which, when it was filled, they drew up on the beach; and they sat down and gathered the good into vessels, but the bad they cast away. Tristram (*NHB*) says that he has seen the fishermen go through their net and throw out into the sea those that were too small for the market or were considered unclean. In Jer **16** 16, we read: "Behold, I will send for many fishers, saith Jeh, and they shall fish them up; and afterward I will send for many hunters, and they shall hunt them from every mountain, and from every hill, and out of the clefts of the rocks." In the vision of Ezekiel (Ezk **47** 9 f), the multitude of fish and the nets spread from *En-gedi* to *En-eglaim* are marks of the marvelous change wrought in the Dead Sea by the stream issuing from the temple. The same sign, i.e. of the spreading of nets (Ezk **26** 5. 14), marks the desolation of Tyre. It is a piece of broiled fish that the risen Lord eats with the Eleven in Jerus (Lk **24** 42), and by the Sea of Galilee (Jn **21** 13) He gives the disciples bread and fish.

Alfred Ely Day

FISHER, fish'ẽr, **FISHERMAN,** fish'ẽr-man (דַּיָּג, *dayyāgh,* דַּוָּג, *dawwāgh;* **ἁλιεύς,** *halieús;* WH *haleeús*): Although but few references to fishermen are made in the Bible, these men and their calling are brought into prominence by Jesus' call to certain Galilee fishermen to become His disciples (Mt **4** 18.19; Mk **1** 16.17). Fishermen, then as now, formed a distinct class. The strenuousness of the work (Lk **5** 2) ruled out the weak and indolent. They were crude in manner, rough in speech and in their treatment of others (Lk **9** 49.54; Jn **18** 10). James and John before they became tempered by Jesus' influence were nicknamed the "sons of thunder" (Mk **3** 17). The fishermen's exposure to all kinds of weather made them hardy and fearless. They were accustomed to bear with patience many trying circumstances. They often toiled for hours without success, and yet were always ready to try once more (Lk **5** 5; Jn **21** 3). Such men, when impelled by the same spirit as filled their Master, became indeed "fishers of men" (Mt **4** 19; Mk **1** 17).

One of the striking instances of the fulfilment of prophecy is the use by the Syrian fishermen today of the site of ancient Tyre as a place for the spreading of their nets (Ezk **26** 5.14).

Figurative: Fish were largely used as food (Hab **1** 16), hence the lamentation of the fishermen, who provided for all, typified general desolation (Isa **19** 8). On the other hand, abundance of fish and many fishermen indicated general abundance (Ezk **47** 10). Our modern expression, "treated like a dog," had its counterpart in the language of the OT writers, when they portrayed the punished people of Judah as being treated like fish. Jeh would send many fishers to fish them up and put sticks or hooks through their cheeks as a fisherman strings his fish (Jer **16** 16; Job **41** 2). Such treatment of the people of Judah is depicted on some of the Assyr monuments.

James A. Patch

FISHER'S COAT, kōt: This expression is found in Jn **21** 7 where RV and ARV have "coat." John here, after representing Peter as "naked" (γυμνός, *gumnós*), pictures him as girding on his "coat" (ἐπενδύτης, *ependútēs*), lit. "upper garment," and not at all specifically a "fisher's coat." See DRESS; UPPER GARMENT, etc.

FISH GATE. See JERUSALEM.

FISHERS MENDING THEIR NETS BY THE SEA OF GALILEE.

FISHHOOK, fish'ho͝ok (סִיר דּוּגָה, *ṣīr dūghāh*, חַכָּה, *ḥakkāh*): The word "fishhooks" occurs but twice in ARV (Job **41** 1; Am **4** 2). In other passages the word "hook" or "angle" is applied to this instrument for fishing (Isa **19** 8; Job **41** 2). The ancient Egyp noblemen used to amuse themselves by fishing from their private fishpools with hook and line. The Egyp monuments show that the hook was quite commonly used for catching fish. The hook is still used in Bible lands, although not as commonly as nets. It is called a *ṣinnârat*, probably from the same root as *çinnāh*, the pl. of which is tr[d] hooks in Am **4** 2. In Mt **17** 27, ἄγκιστρον, *ágkistron* (lit. "fishhook"), is rendered "hook."

JAMES A. PATCH

FISHING, fish'ing (ἁλιεύω, *halieúō*): Several methods of securing fish are resorted to at the present day along the seashores of Pal. Two of these, dynamiting and poisoning with the juice of cyclamen bulbs or other poisonous plants, can be passed over as having no bearing on ancient methods.

(1) With hooks: Some fishing is done with hooks and lines, either on poles when fishing from shore, or on trawls in deep-sea fishing. The fishhooks now used are of European origin, but bronze fishhooks of a very early date have been discovered. That fishing with hooks was known in Jesus' time is indicated by the Master's command to Peter (Mt **17** 27). See FISHHOOK.

(2) With spears: Job **41** 7 probably refers to an instrument much like the barbed spear still used along the Syrian coast. It is used at night by torchlight.

(3) With nets: In the most familiar Bible stories of fisherman life a net was used. Today most of the fishing is done in the same way. These nets are homemade. Frequently one sees the fishermen or members of their families making nets or repairing old ones during the stormy days when fishing is impossible.

Nets are used in three ways: (*a*) A circular net, with small meshes and leaded around the edge, is cast from the shore into the shallow water in such a manner that the leaded edge forms the base of a cone, the apex being formed by the fisherman holding the center of the net in his hand. The cone thus formed incloses such fish as cannot escape the quick throw of the fisher. (*b*) A long net or seine of one or two fathoms depth, leaded on one edge and provided with floats on the other, is payed out from boats in such a way as to surround a school of fish. Long ropes fastened to the two ends are carried ashore many yards apart, and from five to ten men on each rope gradually draw in the net. The fish are then landed from the shallow water with small nets or by hand. This method is commonly practised on the shore of the Sea of Galilee. (*c*) In deeper waters a net similar to that described above, but four or five fathoms deep, is cast from boats and the ends slowly brought together so as to form a circle. Men then dive down and bring one portion of the weighted edge over under the rest, so as to form a bottom. The compass of the net is then narrowed, and the fish are emptied from the net into the boat. Sometimes the net with the fish inclosed is towed into shallow water before drawing. The above method is probably the one the disciples used (Mt **4** 18; Mk **1** 16; Lk **5** 2-10; Jn **21** 3-11). Portions of nets with leads and floats, of early Egyp origin, may be seen in the British Museum. See NET.

The fishermen today usually work with their garments girdled up about their waists. Frequently they wear only a loose outer garment which is wet much of the time. This garment can be quickly removed by pulling it over the head, when occasion requires the fisherman to jump into the sea. If methods have not changed, Peter had probably just climbed back into the boat after adjusting the net for drawing when he learned that it was Jesus who stood on the shore. He was literally naked and pulled on his coat before he went ashore (Jn **21** 7).

JAMES A. PATCH

FISHPOOLS, fish'pōōls: This is a mistranslation. The Heb בְּרֵכוֹת, *berēkhōth* (Cant **7** 4) simply means "pools" (RV); "fish" is quite unwarrantably introduced in AV. In Isa **19** 10, again, instead of "all that make sluices and ponds for fish" (AV), we should certainly read, with RV, "All they that work for hire shall be grieved in soul."

FIT, FITLY, fit'li: The word "fit" (adj. and vb.) occurs a few times, representing nearly as many Heb and Gr words. RV frequently alters, as in Lev **16** 21 (*'ittī*, "timely," "opportune," "ready"), where for "fit" it reads, "in readiness," m "appointed." In 1 Ch **7** 11 RV has "that were able"; in Isa **44** 13, "shapeth"; in Prov **24** 27, "ready," etc. "Fitly" in Prov **25** 11 is in RVm "in due season"; in Cant **5** 12, "fitly set" is in RVm "sitting by full streams." In the NT "fit" is the tr of *eúthetos*, "well placed" (Lk **9** 62; **14** 35), of *kathḗkon*, "suitable" (Acts **22** 22), and of *katartízō*, "to make quite ready" (Rom **9** 22, "vessels of wrath fitted unto destruction"). W. L. WALKER

FITCHES, fich'iz (the Eng. word "fitch" is the same as "vetch"):

(1) קֶצַח, *keçaḥ* (Isa **28** 25.27; RVm has "black cummin" [*Nigella sativa*]). This is the "nutmeg flower," an annual herb (N.O. *Ranunculaceae*), the black seeds of which are sprinkled over some kinds of bread in Pal. They were used as a condiment by the ancient Greeks and Romans. These seeds have a warm aromatic flavor and are carminative in their properties, assisting digestion. They, like all such plants which readily yield their seed, are still beaten out with rods. The contrast between the stouter staff for the "fitches" and the lighter rod for the cummin is all the more noticeable when the great similarity of the two seeds is noticed.

(2) כֻּסְּמִים, *kuṣṣemīm* (pl.) (Ezk **4** 9) RV "spelt" (which see). E. W. G. MASTERMAN

FIVE, fīv (חָמֵשׁ, *ḥāmēsh;* πέντε, *pénte*). See NUMBER.

FLAG: Two Heb words:

(1) סוּף, *ṣūph* (Ex **2** 3.5, "flags"; Isa **19** 6, "flags"; Jon **2** 5, "weeds"). This is apparently a general name which includes both the fresh-water weeds growing along a river bank and "seaweeds." The Red Sea was known as *Yam ṣūph*.

(2) אָחוּ, *'āḥū* (Gen **41** 2.18, AV "meadow," RV "reed-grass"; Job **8** 11, "Can the rush grow up without mire? Can the flag [m "reed-grass"] grow without water?"). Some such general term as "sedges" or "fens" would better meet the requirements.

FLAGON, flag'un: The tr of אֲשִׁישָׁה, *'ăshīshāh*, in AV in 2 S **6** 19; 1 Ch **16** 3; Cant **2** 5; Hos **3** 1. In all these passages RV reads "cake of raisins" or "raisins." It was probably a pressed raisin cake. AV and RV read "flagons," in Isa **22** 24 as a rendering of נְבָלִים, *nebhālīm*, which is elsewhere (1 S **1** 24; **10** 3; 2 S **16** 1, etc) rendered "bottles," RVm "skins." These were the bags or bottles made of the whole skin of a kid, goat or other animal. RV has "flagons" in Ex **25** 29 and **37** 16 as tr of קְשָׂוֹת, *keshāwōth*, a golden jug or jar used in the tabernacle from which the drink offerings were poured out. The same word is trd "cups" in Nu **4** 7. GEORGE RICE HOVEY

FLAKE, flāk (מַפָּל, *mappāl*, a word of uncertain meaning): It is used in the sense of "refuse [husks] of the wheat" in Am **8** 6. With regard to the body we find it used in Job **41** 23 in the description of leviathan (the crocodile): "The flakes of his flesh are joined together: they are firm upon him; they cannot be moved." Baethgen in Kautzsch's tr of the OT translates "*Wampen*," i.e. the collops or lateral folds of flesh and armored skin. A better tr would perhaps be: "the horny epidermic scales" of the body, differentiated from the bony dermal scutes of the back (Heb "channels of shields," "courses of scales"), which are mentioned in ver 15 m. H. L. E. LUERING

FLAME, flām (לַהַב, *lahabh*, and other forms from same root; φλόξ, *phlóx*): In Jgs **13** 20 *bis;* Job **41** 21; Isa **29** 6; Joel **2** 5, the word is *lahabh*. Various other words are trd "flame"; *mas'ēth*, "a lifting or rising up" (Jgs **20** 38.40 AV), RV "cloud" (of smoke); *kālīl*, "completeness" (Jgs **20** 40*b* AVm, "a holocaust, or offering wholly consumed by fire"; cf Lev **6** 15); *shalhebheth* (Job **15** 30; Cant **8** 6; ARV "a very flame of Jeh," m "or, a most vehement flame"; Ezk **20** 47, RV "the flaming flame"); *shābhībh* (Job **18** 5; RVm); *shebhībh*, Aram. (Dnl **3** 22; **7** 9). In Ps **104** 4 ARV has "maketh . . . . flames of fire his ministers"; RV "flame" for "snare" (Prov **29** 8).

Figuratively: "Flame" is used to denote excitement (Prov **29** 8 RV), shame, astonishment, "faces of flame" (Isa **13** 8); in Rev **1** 14, the glorified Christ is described as having eyes "as a flame of fire," signifying their searching purity (cf **2** 18; **19** 12). Flame is also a symbol of God's wrath (Ps **83** 14; Isa **5** 24; **10** 17). See also FIRE.

W. L. WALKER

FLAT NOSE (חָרֻם, *ḥārum;* LXX κολοβόριν, *kolobórin*): Used only in Lev **21** 18 as the name of a deformity which disqualified a member of a priestly family for serving the altar. The root of the word signifies "to cut off" or "to cut flat," and in RVm "slit nose" is substituted. The condition indicated is most probably the depressed, flattened nose which so often accompanies harelip, esp. in its double form. A mere snub-nose can scarcely be regarded as a blemish of sufficient importance to unfit a priest for the service of "offering the bread of God"; but harelip, like blindness or the other congenital malformations or deformities enumerated in this passage, might well render a son of Aaron unfit or unsuitable for public religious duty. ALEX. MACALISTER

FLAX, flaks (פֵּשֶׁת, *pesheth*, also פִּשְׁתָּה, *pishtāh;* **λίνον,** *línon* [Mt **12** 20]): The above Heb words are applied (1) to the plant: "The flax was in bloom" (AV "bolled"; Ex **9** 31); (2) the "stalks of flax," lit. "flax of the tree," put on the roof to dry (Josh **2** 6); (3) to the fine fibers used for lighting: AV "tow," "flax," RV. "A dimly burning wick will

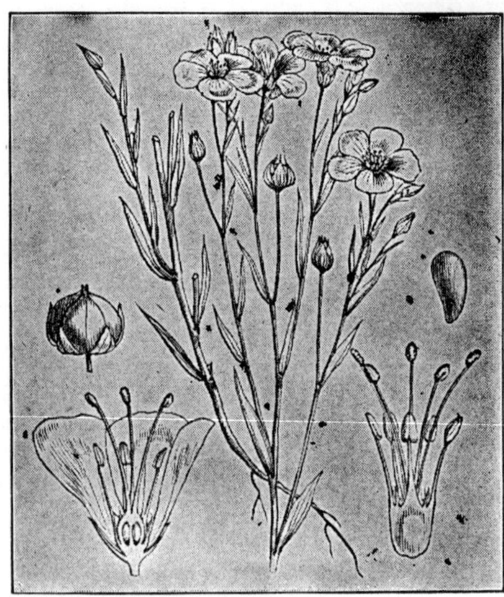

Flax (*Linum usitatissimum*).

he not quench" (Isa **42** 3); "They are quenched as a wick" (Isa **43** 17). The thought is perhaps of a scarcely lighted wick just kindled with difficulty from a spark. (4) In Isa **19** 9 mention is made of "combed flax," i.e. flax hackled ready for spinning (cf Hos **2** 5.9; Prov **31** 13). The reference in Jgs **15** 14 is to flax twisted into cords. (5) In Jgs **16** 9; Isa **1** 31, mention is made of נְעֹרֶת, *ne'ōreth*, "tow," lit. something "shaken off"—as the root implies—from flax. (6) The pl. form *pishtīm* is used in many passages for linen, or linen garments, e.g. Lev **13** 47.48.52.59; Dt **22** 11; Jer **13** 1 ("linen girdle"); Ezk **44** 17 f. Linen was in the earliest historic times a favorite material for clothes. The Jewish priestly garments were of pure linen. Egyp mummies were swathed in linen. Several other Heb words were used for linen garments. See LINEN.

Flax is the product of *Linum usitatissimum*, a herbaceous plant which has been cultivated from the dawn of history. It is perennial and grows to a height of 2 to 3 ft.; it has blue flowers and very fibrous stalks. The tough fibers of the latter, after the decay and removal of the softer woody and gummy material, make up the crude "flax." Linseed, linseed oil and oilcake are useful products of the same plant. E. W. G. MASTERMAN

FLAYING, flā'ing. See PUNISHMENTS.

FLEA, flē (פַּרְעֹשׁ, *par'ōsh;* cf Arab. *barghût*, "flea," and *barghash*, "mosquito" [1 S **24** 14; **26** 20]; כִּנִּים, *kinnīm* [Ex **8** 16], "lice," RVm "sand-flies" or "fleas"; LXX **σκνίφες,** *skníphes*, probably best rendered "gnat"; see GNAT; LICE): In 1 S **24** Saul seeks David in the wilderness of *En-gedi*, and David, after cutting off the skirt of Saul's robe in the cave, calls out to him, "After whom is the king of Israel come out? after whom dost thou pursue? after a dead dog, after a flea" (ver 14). Again in 1 S **26** 20 Saul seeks David in the wilderness of Ziph, and David after taking the spear and cruse from beside Saul while he slept, cries out to him, ". . . . the king of Israel is come out to seek a flea, as when one doth hunt a partridge in the mountains." The flea is here used as a symbol of David's insignificance, coupled perhaps, in the second passage, with a thought of the difficulty that Saul had in laying hands on him. In *EB* Cheyne finds fault with a similar interpretation given in *DB* on the ground that it is absurd that David should refer to hunting "a single flea," and proposes to change *par'ōsh 'eḥādh*, "a flea," to *pere' midhbār*, "wild ass of the desert." The writer will only say that no observant resident of Pal would consider the textual alteration to be called for.

Linnaeus recognized two species of flea, *Pulex irritans*, the common parasite of man, and *Pulex* (*Sarcopsylla*) *penetrans*, the tropical and sub-tropical jigger flea. More than a hundred species are now listed, and the recent discovery that certain fleas are instrumental in the transmission of the plague has given a new impetus to the study of these tiny pests. A flea that is often commoner in houses than *Pulex irritans* is the "dog and cat flea," variously known as *Pulex serraticeps*, *Pulex canis*, *Pulex felis* or *Ctenocephalus canis*.

ALFRED ELY DAY

FLEE, flē. See FLY.

FLEECE, flēs. See GIDEON; SHEEP; WOOL.

FLESH (בָּשָׂר, *bāsār*, שְׁאֵר, *she'ēr*): Used in all senses of the word, the latter, however, most frequently in the sense of kin, family,

1. Etymology

relationship (cf שַׁאֲרָה, *sha'ărāh*, "kinswoman," Lev **18** 17): Lev **18** 6; **25** 49; Prov **11** 17; Jer **51** 35, and probably Ps **73** 26. In all other places *she'ēr* means "flesh"=body (Prov **5** 11) or=food (Ps **78** 20.27; Mic **3** 2.3). טִבְחָה, *ṭibhḥāh*, is "[slaughtered] flesh for food," "butcher's meat" (1 S **25** 11). The word אֶשְׁפָּר, *'eshpār*, found only in two ‖ passages (2 S **6** 19=1 Ch **16** 3), is of very uncertain meaning. The Eng. VSS translate it with "a good piece [portion] of flesh," the Vulg with "a piece of roast meat," others with "a portion of flesh" and "a measure of wine." It probably means simply "a measured portion." לָחֻם, לְחוּם, *laḥūm*, lit. "eaten," then food (cf לֶחֶם, *leḥem*, "bread"), has been rarely specialized as flesh or meat (cf Arab. *laḥm*, "meat," "flesh," so in Zeph **1** 17, where it stands in parallelism with "blood"). The Gr terms are *σάρξ*, *sárx*, and *κρέας*, *kréas*, the latter always meaning "butcher's meat" (Rom **14** 21; 1 Cor **8** 13).

We can distinguish the following varieties of meaning in Bib. language:

2. Ordinary Sense

In a physical sense, the chief substance of the animal body, whether used for food and sacrifice, or not; also the flesh of man (Gen **2** 21; Ex **21** 10 m; Isa **31** 3; Ezk **23** 20; 1 Cor **15** 39; Rev **19** 18.21).

The whole body. This meaning is the extension of the preceding (*pars pro toto*). This is indicated by the LXX, where *bāsār* is often trd by the pl. *αἱ σάρκες*, *hai sárkes* (Gen **40** 19;

Nu **12** 12; Job **33** 25), and occasionally by σῶμα, *sôma*, i.e. "body" (Lev **15** 2; 1 K **21** 27). This meaning is also very clear in passages like the following: Ex **4** 7; Lev **17** 14; Nu **8** 7; 2 K **4** 34; Prov **5** 11, where *bāsār* and *sheʼēr* are combined; and Prov **14** 30; Eccl **12** 12.

3. The Body

Flesh, as the common term for living things, animals and men, esp. the latter (Gen **6** 13.17.19; Nu **16** 22; Jer **12** 12; Mk **13** 20); often in the phrase "all flesh" (Ps **65** 2; Isa **40** 5.6; Jer **25** 31; Ezk **20** 48; Joel **2** 28; Lk **3** 6).

4. The Term "All Flesh"

Flesh as opposed to the spirit, both of which were comprised in the preceding meaning (Gen **6** 3; Ps **16** 9; Lk **24** 39, where "flesh and bones" are combined; Jn **6** 63). Thus we find in Jn **1** 14, "The Word became flesh"; 1 Tim **3** 16, "He who was manifested in the flesh"; 1 Jn **4** 2, and all passages where the incarnation of Christ is spoken of. The word in this sense approaches the meaning of "earthly life," as in Phil **1** 22.24, "to live in the flesh," "to abide in the flesh"; cf Philem ver 16 and perhaps 2 Cor **5** 16. Under this meaning we may enumerate expressions such as "arm of flesh" (2 Ch **32** 8; Jer **17** 5), "eyes of flesh" (Job **10** 4), etc. Frequently the distinction is made to emphasize the weakness or inferiority of the flesh, as opposed to the superiority of the spirit (Isa **31** 3; Mt **26** 41; Mk **14** 38; Rom **6** 19). In this connection we mention also the expression "flesh and blood," a phrase borrowed from rabbinical writings and phraseology (see also Sir **14** 18, "the generation of flesh and blood," and **17** 31, "man whose desire is flesh and blood" AV). The expression does not convey, as some have supposed, the idea of inherent sinfulness of the flesh (a doctrine borrowed by gnostic teachers from oriental sources), but merely the idea of ignorance and frailty in comparison with the possibilities of spiritual nature. The capabilities of our earthly constitution do not suffice to reveal unto us heavenly truths; these must always come to us from above. So St. Peter's first recognition of the Divine sonship of Jesus did not proceed from a logical conviction based upon outward facts acting upon his mind, but was based upon a revelation from God vouchsafed to his inner consciousness. Christ says therefore to him: "Blessed art thou, Simon Bar-Jonah: for flesh and blood hath not revealed it unto thee, but my Father who is in heaven" (Mt **16** 17). Similarly the kingdom of God, being a realm of perfect spiritual submission to God, cannot be inherited by flesh and blood (1 Cor **15** 50), nor was the richly endowed mind a competent tribunal to which St. Paul could refer his heaven-wrought conviction of his great salvation and the high calling to be a witness and apostle of Christ, so he did well that he "conferred not with flesh and blood" (Gal **1** 16). That "flesh and blood" does not imply a sense of inherent sinfulness is moreover shown in all passages where Christ is declared a partaker of such nature (Eph **6** 12; He **2** 14, where, however, we find in the original text the inverted phrase "blood and flesh").

5. As Opposed to the Spirit

Flesh in the sense of carnal nature (σάρκικος, *sárkikos*, "carnal"; AV uses *sarkinós* in Rom **7** 14). Human nature, being inferior to the spiritual, is to be in subjection to it. If man refuses to be under this higher law, and as a free agent permits the lower nature to gain an ascendancy over the spirit, the "flesh" becomes a revolting force (Gen **6** 3.12; Jn **1** 13; Rom **7** 14; 1 Cor **3** 1.3; Col **2** 18; 1 Jn **2** 16). Thus the fleshly or carnal mind, i.e. a mind in subjection to carnal nature, is opposed to the Divine spirit, who alone is a sufficient corrective, Christ having secured for us the power of overcoming (Rom **8** 3), if we manifest a deep desire and an earnest endeavor to overcome (Gal **5** 17.18).

6. Applied to the Carnal Nature

Flesh in the sense of relationship, tribal connection, kith and kin. For examples, see what has been said above on Heb *sheʼēr*. The following passages are a few of those in which *bāsār* is used: Gen **2** 24; **37** 27; Job **2** 5; cf the NT passages: Mt **19** 5.6; Rom **1** 3; **9** 3.5.8. The expressions "bone" and "flesh" are found in combination (Gen **2** 23; **29** 14; Jgs **9** 2; 2 S **5** 1; **19** 12.13; Eph **5** 31, the latter in some MSS only).

7. In the Sense of Relationship

Some other subdivisions of meanings might be added, for example where "flesh" takes almost the place of "person," as in Col **2** 1: "as many as have not seen my face in the flesh," i.e. have not known me personally, or ver 5, "absent in the flesh, yet am I with you in the spirit," etc.

8. Other Meanings

H. L. E. Luering

FLESH AND BLOOD. See Flesh, 5.

FLESH-HOOK, flesh'hŏŏk (מַזְלֵג, *mazlēgh*, and pl. מִזְלָגוֹת, *mizlāghōth*): One of the implements used around the sacrificial altar. According to Divine direction given to Moses (Ex **27** 3; **38** 3), it was to be made of brass, but later David felt impelled by "the Spirit" or "in his spirit" to determine that for use in the magnificent Temple of Solomon it should be made of gold (1 Ch **28** 17). But Huram made it, with other altar articles, of "bright brass" (2 Ch **4** 16). In Samuel's time, it was made with three hook-shaped tines, and was used in taking out the priests' share of the meat offering (1 S **2** 13.14). With the other altar utensils, it was in the special charge of the Kohathites (Nu **4** 14). The hooks mentioned in Ezk **40** 43 were altogether different and for another purpose. See Hook.

Leonard W. Doolan

FLESH-POT, flesh'pot (סִיר הַבָּשָׂר, *ṣīr ha-bāsār*, "pot of the flesh"): One of the six kinds of cooking utensils spoken of as pots or pans or caldrons or basins. Probably usually made of bronze or earthenware. The only mention of flesh-pots, specifically so named, is in Ex **16** 3. See Food.

FLIES, flīz. See Fly.

FLINT, flint (חַלָּמִישׁ, *ḥallāmīsh* [Dt **8** 15; **32** 13; Job **28** 9; Ps **114** 8], צֹר, *çōr* [Ex **4** 25; Ezk **3** 9], צֵר, *çēr* [Isa **5** 28], צוּר, *çūr* [Job **22** 24; Ps **89** 43], צֻרִים, *çurīm* [Josh **5** 2 f]; **κόχλαξ** [=κάχληξ, "pebble"], *kóchlax* [1 Macc **10** 73]): The word *ḥallāmīsh* signifies a hard stone, though not certainly flint, and is used as a **figure** for hardness in Isa **50** 7, "Therefore have I set my face like a flint." A similar use of *çōr* is found in Ezk **3** 9, "As an adamant harder than flint have I made thy forehead," and Isa **5** 28, "Their horses' hoofs shall be accounted as flint"; and of *ṣelaʻ* in Jer **5** 3, "They have made their faces harder than a rock." The same three words are used of the rock from which Moses drew water in the wilderness: *ḥallāmīsh* (Dt **8** 15; Ps **114** 8); *çūr* (Ex **17** 6; Dt **8** 15; Ps **78** 20; Isa **48** 21); *ṣelaʻ* (Nu **20** 8; Neh **9** 15; Ps **78** 16). *Çūr* and *ṣelaʻ* are used oftener than *ḥallāmīsh* for great rocks and cliffs, but *çūr* is used also for flint knives in Ex **4** 25, "Then Zipporah took a flint [AV "sharp stone"], and cut off the foreskin of her son," and in Josh **5** 2 f, "Jeh said unto Joshua, Make thee knives of flint [AV "sharp knives"], and circumcise again the children of Israel the second time." Surgical implements of flint were used by the ancient Egyptians, and numerous flint chippings with occasional flint implements are found associated with the remains of early man in Syria and Pal. Flint and the allied mineral, chert, are found in great abundance in the limestone rocks of Syria, Pal and Egypt. See ROCK.

ALFRED ELY DAY

FLOAT (FLOTE), flōt. See RAFT; SHIPS AND BOATS.

FLOCK. See CATTLE.

FLOOD, flud: In AV not less than 13 words are rendered "flood," though in RV we find in some passages "river," "stream," "tempest," etc. The word is used for: the deluge of Noah, מַבּוּל, *mabbūl* (Gen **6** 17 ff); κατακλυσμός, *kataklusmós* (Mt **24** 38.39; Lk **17** 27); the waters of the Red Sea, נָזַל, *nāzal* (Ex **15** 8); the Euphrates, נָהָר, *nāhār*, "Your fathers dwelt of old time on the other side of the flood" (RV "beyond the River" Josh **24** 2): the Nile, יְאוֹר, *y*ᵉ*'ōr*, "the flood [RV "River"] of Egypt" (Am **8** 8); the Jordan, נָהָר, *nāhār*, "They went through the flood [RV "river"] on foot" (Ps **66** 6); torrent, זֶרֶם, *zerem*, "as a flood [RV "tempest"] of mighty waters" (Isa **28** 2); ποταμός, *potamós*, "The rain descended and the floods came" (Mt **7** 25); πλημμύρα, *plēmmúra*, "When a flood arose, the stream brake against that house" (Lk **6** 48).

Figurative: נַחַל, *naḥal*, "The floods of ungodly men [RV "ungodliness," RVm "Heb Belial"] made me afraid" (2 S **22** 5; Ps **18** 4); also אֹר, *'ōr* (Am **8** 8 [AV]); שִׁבֹּלֶת, *shibbōleth* (Ps **69** 2); שֶׁטֶף, *sheṭeph* (Dnl **11** 22 [AV]); שֵׁטֶף, *shēṭeph* (Ps **32** 6 [AV]); ποταμοφόρητος, *potamophórētos* (Rev **12** 15 [AV]). See DELUGE OF NOAH.

ALFRED ELY DAY

FLOOR, flōr. See HOUSE; THRESHING-FLOOR.

FLOTE (FLOAT). See RAFT; SHIPS AND BOATS.

FLOUR, flour. See BREAD; FOOD.

FLOURISH, flur'ish (פָּרַח, *pāraḥ*, צוּץ, *çūç*; ἀναθάλλω, *anathállō*): The tr of *pāraḥ*, "to break forth" (Ps **72** 7; **92** 12.13; Prov **14** 11; Isa **66** 14; Cant **6** 11; **7** 12; RV "budded"); of *çūç*, "to bloom" (Ps **72** 16; **90** 6; **92** 7; **103** 15; **132** 18); *ra'ănān*, "green," "fresh," is trd "flourishing" in Ps **92** 14, RV "green," and *ra'ănan*, Aram. in Dnl **4** 4; *nūbh*, "to sprout" (Zec **9** 17, AV "cheerful").

In an interesting passage (Eccl **12** 5 AV), the Hiphil fut. of *nā'aç*, meaning properly "to pierce or strike," hence, to slight or reject, is trd "flourish"; it is said of the old man "The almond tree shall flourish," RV "blossom" (so Ewald, Delitzsch, etc); *nā'aç* has nowhere else this meaning; it is frequently rendered "contemn," "despise," etc. Other renderings are, "shall cause loathing" (Gesenius, Knobel, etc), "shall be despised," i.e. the hoary head; "The almond tree shall shake off its flowers," the silvery hairs falling like the fading white flowers of the almond tree; by others it is taken to indicate "sleeplessness," the name of the almond tree (*shāḳēdh*) meaning the watcher or early riser (cf Jer **1** 11, "a rod of an almond-tree," lit. "a wakeful [or early] tree"), the almond being the first of the trees to wake from the sleep of winter. See ALMOND.

"Flourish" appears once only in the NT, in AV, as tr of *anathallō*, "to put forth anew," or "to make put forth anew" (Phil **4** 10): "Your care for me hath flourished again," RV "Ye have revived your thought for me."

W. L. WALKER

FLOWERS, flou'ẽrz (**BLOOM, BLOSSOM, etc**):

(1) גִּבְעֹל, *gibh'ōl*, lit. "a small cup," hence calyx or corolla of a flower (Ex **9** 31, "The flax was in bloom").

(2) נֵץ, *nēç* (Gen **40** 10, נִצָּה, *niççāh*, "a flower" or "blossom"; Job **15** 33; Isa **18** 5). These words are used of the early berries of the vine or olive.

(3) נִצָּן, *niççān*, "a flower"; pl. only, נִצָּנִים, *niççānīm* (Cant **2** 12, "The flowers appear on the earth").

(4) פֶּרַח, *peraḥ*, root to "burst forth" expresses an early stage of flowering; "blossom" (Isa **5** 24; **18** 5); "flower" (Nah **1** 4, "The flower of Lebanon languisheth"). Used of artificial flowers in candlesticks (Ex **25** 31 ff).

(5) צִיץ, *çīç*, "flower" (Isa **40** 6); pl. צִצִּים, *çiççīm*, flowers as architectural ornaments (1 K **6** 18); צִיצָה, *çīçāh*, "the fading flower of his glorious beauty" (Isa **28** 1.4; also Nu **17** 8; Job **14** 2, etc).

(6) ἄνθος, *ánthos*, in LXX equivalent of all the Heb words (Jas **1** 10.11; 1 Pet **1** 24).

The beauty of the profusion of flowers which cover Pal every spring receives but scant reference in the OT; Cant **2** 12 is perhaps the only clear reference. It is noticeable that the native of Syria thinks little of flowers unless it be for their perfume. Our Lord's reference to the flowers ("lilies") is well known (Mt **6** 28; Lk **12** 27). For details of the flowers of modern Pal, see BOTANY. The aptness of the expression "flower of the field" for a type of the evanescence of human life (Job **14** 2; Ps **103** 15; Isa **40** 6; Jas **1** 10) is the more impressive in a land like Pal where the annual display of wild flowers, so glorious for a few short weeks, is followed by such desolation. The fresh and brilliant colors fade into masses of withered leaves (not uncommonly cleared by burning), and then even these are blown away, so that but bare, cracked and baked earth remains for long months where once all was beauty, color and life.

E. W. G. MASTERMAN

FLUE, flōō, **NET** (AVm Hab **1** 15). See FISH; FISHING.

FLUTE, flōōt. See MUSIC.

FLUX, fluks. See BLOODY FLUX; DYSENTERY.

FLY, flī, **FLIES,** flīz (עָרֹב, *'ārōbh* [Ex **8** 21 ff; Ps **78** 45; **105** 31; LXX κυνόμυια, *kunómuia*; "dog-fly"], זְבוּב, *z*ᵉ*bhūbh* [Eccl **10** 1; Isa **7** 18; LXX μυῖαι, *muíai*, "flies"]; cf בַּעַל זְבוּב, *ba'al-z*ᵉ*bhūbh*, "Baal-zebub" [2 K **1** 2 ff], and βεελζεβούλ, *beelzeboúl*, "Beelzebul," or βεελζεβούβ, *beelzeboúb*, "Beelzebub" [Mt **10** 25; **12** 24.27; Lk **11** 15.18.19]; cf Arab. ذُبَاب, *dhubâb*, "fly" or "bee"; N.B. *dh* for Arab. *dhâl*, pronounced like *d* or *z* or like *th* in "the"): The references in Pss as well as in Ex are to the plague of flies, and the word *'ārōbh* is rendered "swarm of flies" throughout, except in Ps **78** 45; **105** 31 AV, where we find "divers sorts of flies" (cf Vulg *omne genus muscarum*). In Ex **8** 21 we read, "I will send swarms of flies upon thee, and upon thy servants, and upon thy people, and into thy houses: and the houses of the Egyptians shall be full of swarms of flies, and also the ground whereon they are"; in Ex **8** 24, ... "the land was corrupted by reason of the swarms of flies"; in Ps **78** 45, "He sent among them swarms of flies, which devoured them." There has been much speculation as to what the insects were, but all the texts cited, including even Ps **78** 45, may apply perfectly well to the common house fly (*Musca* *domestica*). Some species of blue-bottle fly (*Calliphora*) might also suit.

The other word, *zᵉbhūbh*, occurs in Eccl **10** 1, "Dead flies cause the oil of the perfumer to send forth an evil odor; so doth a little folly outweigh wisdom and honor"; and Isa **7** 18, "And it shall come to pass in that day, that Jeh will hiss for the fly that is in the uttermost part of the rivers of Egypt, and for the bee that is in the land of Assyria." The house fly would fit perfectly the reference in each, but that in Isa would seem to suggest rather one of the horse flies (*Tabanidae*) or gad flies (*Oestridae*). Whatever fly may be meant, it is used as a symbol for the military power of Egypt, as the bee for that of Assyria.

Owing to deficiencies in public and private hygiene, and also for other reasons, house flies and others are unusually abundant in Pal and Egypt and are agents in the transmission of cholera, typhoid fever, ophthalmia and anthrax. *Glossina morsitans*, the tsetse fly, which is fatal to many domestic animals, and *Glossina palpalis*, which transmits the sleeping sickness, are abundant in tropical Africa, but do not reach Egypt proper. See PLAGUES.

ALFRED ELY DAY

FLY (vb.; עוּף, *'ūph*; **πετάομαι**, *petáomai*, or, contracted, *ptáomai*): Used in preference to "flee" when great speed is to be indicated. "To fly" is used: (1) Literally, of birds, *'ūph* (Gen **1** 20; Ps **55** 6); *dā'āh* (Dt **28** 49), of sparks (Job **5** 7); of the arrow (Ps **91** 5); of the seraphim (Isa **6** 2.6); of an angel (Dnl **9** 21, *ya'aph*, "to be caused to fly"); of swift action or movement (Ps **18** 10; Jer **48** 40); of people (Isa **11** 14); of a fleet (Isa **60** 8; 1 S **15** 19, *'īṭ;* **14** 32, *'āsāh*, "to do," etc). (2) **Figuratively**, of a dream (Job **20** 8); of man's transitory life (Ps **90** 10); of riches (Prov **23** 5); of national glory (Hos **9** 11).

For "fly" RV has "soar" (Job **39** 26), "fly down" (Isa **11** 14); for "flying" (Isa **31** 5) ARV has "hovering."

W. L. WALKER

FOAL, fōl. See COLT.

FOAM, fōm (קֶצֶף, *ḳeçeph* [Hos **10** 7]; **ἀφρός**, *aphrós* [Lk **9** 39], **ἀφρίζω**, *aphrízō* [Mk **9** 18.20], **ἐπαφρίζω**, *epaphrízō* [Jude ver 13]): *Ḳeçeph* from *ḳāçaph*, "to break to pieces," or "to break forth into anger," "to be angry," occurs often in the sense of "wrath" or "anger" (e.g. Nu **1** 53; Ps **38** 1, etc), and in this passage has been rendered "twigs" or "chips," "As for Samaria, her king is cut off, as foam [RVm "twigs"] upon the water" (Hos **10** 7). The other references are from the NT. In Jude, evil-doers or false teachers are compared to the "wild waves of the sea, foaming out their own shame." In Mk and Lk the references are to the boy with a dumb spirit who foamed at the mouth.

ALFRED ELY DAY

FODDER, fod'ēr. See PROVENDER.

FOLD, fōld, **FOLDING**, fōld'ing (vb.; חָבַק, *ḥābhaḳ*, סָבַךְ, *sābhakh;* **ἑλίσσω**, *helíssō*): The vb. occurs only 3 t in AV, and in each instance represents a different word; we have *ḥābhaḳ* "to clasp" (Eccl **4** 5), "The fool foldeth his hands together" (cf Prov **6** 10); *ṣābhak*, "to interweave" (Nah **1** 10, "folden together as thorns," ERV "like tangled thorns," ARV "entangled like thorns"; see ENTANGLED); *helíssō* "to roll or fold up" (He **1** 12, quoted from Ps **102** 26 [LXX], RV "As a mantle shalt thou roll them up").

Folding occurs as tr of *gālīl*, "turning" or "rolling" (1 K **6** 34 *bis*, folding leaves of door). See also HOUSE.

W. L. WALKER

FOLK, fōk: The tr of עַם, *'am*, עָם, *'ām*, "a people or nation" (Gen **33** 15, "some of the folk that are with me"; Prov **30** 26, "The conies are but a feeble folk"); of לְאֹם, *lᵉ'ōm*, with the same meaning (Jer **51** 58, "the folk in the fire," RV "the nations for the fire"); "sick folk" is the tr of ἄρρωστος, *árrhōstos*, "not strong" (Mk **6** 5); of τῶν ἀσθενούντων, *tōn asthenoúntōn*, part. of ἀσθενέω, *asthenéō*, "to be without strength," "weak," "sick" (Jn **5** 3, RV "them that were sick"); "sick folks," of ἀσθενεῖς, pl. of ἀσθενής, *asthenḗs*, "without strength," RV "sick folk" (Acts **5** 16).

W. L. WALKER

FOLLOW, fol'ō (אַחַר, *'aḥar*, רָדַף, *rādhaph;* **ἀκολουθέω**, *akolouthéō*, **διώκω**, *diṓkō*): Frequently the tr of *'aḥar*, "after," e.g. Nu **14** 24, "hath followed me fully," lit. "fulfilled *after* me" (Nu **32** 11. 12; Dt **1** 36; Am **7** 15); *rādhaph* is "to pursue," and is often so trᵈ; it is trᵈ "follow" (Ps **23** 6; Isa **5** 11, etc); "follow after" (Gen **44** 4; Ex **14** 4); *reghel*, "foot," is several times trᵈ "follow" (lit. "at the foot of"; Ex **11** 8; Jgs **8** 5, etc); *hālakh 'aḥar*, "to go after" (Dt **4** 3; 1 K **14** 8, etc); *yālakh 'aḥar*, "to go on after" (Gen **24** 5; Jgs **2** 19, etc); *dābhēḳ*, "to cause to cleave to" is "follow hard after" (1 S **14** 22; Ps **63** 8, etc).

In the NT, in addition to *akoloutheō* (Mt **4** 20. 22.25, etc) various words and phrases are rendered "follow," e.g. *Deúte opísō mou*, "Come after me" (Mt **4** 19, "Follow me," RV "Come ye after me"); *diōkō*, "to pursue" (Lk **17** 23; 1 Thess **5** 15, RV "follow after," etc); *miméomai*, "to imitate" (He **13** 7, "whose faith follow," RV "imitate their faith"; 2 Thess **3** 7.9; 3 Jn ver 11); compounds of *akoloutheō* with *ex*, *pará*, *sun*, etc (2 Pet **1** 16; Mk **16** 20; Acts **16** 17; Mk **5** 37, etc).

ERV "Follow after faithfulness" makes an important change in Ps **37** 3, where AV has "and verily thou shalt be fed"; but ARV has "feed on his faithfulness," m "feed securely or *verily* thou shalt be fed." For "attained" (1 Tim **4** 6) RV gives "followed until now."

W. L. WALKER

FOLLOWER, fol'ō-ēr (**μιμητής**, *mimētḗs*): "Followers" is in AV the tr of *mimētḗs*, "to imitate" (in the NT in the good sense of becoming imitators, or following an example), rendered by RV "imitators" (1 Cor **4** 16; **11** 1; Eph **5** 1; 1 Thess **1** 6; **2** 14; He **6** 12); *summimētaí*, "joint imitators" (Phil **3** 17); in 1 Pet **3** 13, AV "followers of that which is good," the word, according to a better text, is *zēlōtís*, RV "if ye be zealous of that which is good."

FOLLY, fol'i. See FOOL.

FOOD, fōōd:

I. VEGETABLE FOODS
1. Primitive Habits
2. Cereals
3. Leguminous Plants
4. Food of Trees
II. ANIMAL FOOD
LITERATURE

In a previous art. (see BREAD) it has been shown that in the Bible "bread" usually stands for food in general and how this came to be so. In a complementary article on MEALS the methods of preparing and serving food will be dealt with. This article is devoted specifically to the **foodstuffs** of the Orient, more esp. to articles of food in use among the Hebrews in Bible times. These are divisible into two main classes.

I. Vegetable Foods.—Orientals in general are vegetarians, rather than flesh eaters. There is some reason to believe that primitive man was a vegetarian (see Gen **2** 16; **3** 2.6). It would seem, indeed, from a comparison of Gen **1** 29 f with **9** 3 f that Divine permission to eat the flesh of animals was first given to Noah after the Deluge, and then

1. Primitive Habits

only on condition of drawing off the blood in a prescribed way (cf the kosher [*kāshēr*] meat of the Jews of today).

The chief place among the foodstuffs of Orientals must be accorded to the cereals, included in ARV under the generic term "grain," in AV and ERV "corn." The two most important of these in the nearer East are **wheat** (*ḥiṭṭāh*) and **barley** (*s*e'*ōrīm*). The most primitive way of using the wheat as food was to pluck the fresh ears (Lev **23** 14; 2 K **4** 42), remove the husks by rubbing in the hands (Dt **23** 25; Mt **12** 1), and eat the grains raw. A common practice in all lands and periods, observed by the fellaheen of Syria today, has been to parch or roast the ears and eat the grain unground. This is the **parched corn** (ARV "grain") so often mentioned in the OT, which with bread and vinegar (sour wine) constituted the meal of the reapers to which Boaz invited Ruth (Ruth **2** 14).

2. Cereals

Later it became customary to grind the wheat into flour (*kemaḥ*), and, by bolting it with a fine sieve, to obtain the **"fine flour"** (*ṣōleth*) of our EV, which, of course, was then made into "bread" (which see), either without leaven (*maççāh*) or with (*leḥem ḥāmēç*, Lev **7** 13).

Meal, both of wheat and of barley, was prepared in very early times by means of the primitive rubbing-stones, which excavations at Lachish, Gezer and elsewhere show survived the introduction of the hand-mill (see MILL; cf *PEFS*, 1902, 326). **Barley** (*s*e'*ōrīm*) has always furnished the principal food of the poorer classes, and, like wheat, has been made into bread (Jgs **7** 13; Jn **6** 9.13). Less frequently **millet** (Ezk **4** 9) and **spelt** (*kuṣṣemeth;* see FITCHES) were so used. (For details of baking, bread-making, etc, see BREAD, III, 1,2,3.)

Vegetable foods of the pulse family (*leguminosae*) are represented in the OT chiefly by lentils and beans. The pulse of Dnl **1** 12 (*z*e*rō'īm*) denotes edible "herbs" in general (RVm, cf Isa **61** 11, "things that are sown"). The **lentils** (*'ădhāshīm*) were and are considered very toothsome and nutritious. It was of "red lentils" that Jacob brewed his fateful pottage (Gen **25** 29.34), a stew, probably, in which the lentils were flavored with onions and other ingredients, as we find it done in Syria today. Lentils, beans, cereals, etc, were sometimes ground and mixed and made into bread (Ezk **4 9**). I found them at Gaza roasted also, and eaten with oil and salt, like parched corn.

3. Leguminous Plants

The children of Israel, when in the wilderness, are said to have looked back wistfully on the "cucumbers . . . . melons . . . . leeks . . . . onions, and the garlic" of Egypt (Nu **11** 5). All these things we find later were grown in Pal. In addition, at least four varieties of the bean, the chickpea, various species of chickory and endive, the **bitter herbs** of the Passover ritual (Ex **12** 8), mustard (Mt **13** 31) and many other things available for food, are mentioned in the Mish, our richest source of information on this subject. **Cucumbers** (*ḳishshu'īm*) were then, as now, much used. The oriental variety is much less fibrous and more succulent and digestible than ours, and supplies the thirsty traveler often with a fine substitute for water where water is scarce or bad. The poor in such cities as Cairo, Beirut and Damascus live largely on bread and cucumbers or melons. The cucumbers are eaten raw, with or without salt, between meals, but also often stuffed and cooked and eaten at meal time. **Onions** (*b*e*çālīm*), **garlic** (*shummīm*) and **leeks** (*ḥāçīr*) are still much used in Pal as in Egypt. They are usually eaten raw with bread, though also used for flavoring in cooking, and, like cucumbers, pickled and eaten as a relish with meat (*ZDPV*, IX, 14). Men in utter extremity sometimes "plucked saltwort" (*mallūaḥ*) and ate the leaves, either raw or boiled, and made "the roots of the broom" their food (Job **30** 4).

In Lev **19** 23 f it is implied that, when Israel came into the land to possess it, they should "plant all manner of trees for food." They doubtless found such trees in the goodly land in abundance, but in the natural course of things needed to plant more. Many **olive trees** remain fruitful to extreme old age, as for example those shown the tourist in the garden of Gethsemane, but many more require replanting. Then the olive after planting requires ten or fifteen years to fruit, and trees of a quicker growth, like the fig, are planted beside them and depended on for fruit in the meantime. It is significant that Jotham in his parable makes the olive the first choice of the trees to be their king (Jgs **9** 9), and the olive tree to respond, "Should I leave my fatness, which God and man honor in me, and go to wave to and fro over the trees?" (ARVm). The berries of the olive (*zayith*) were doubtless eaten, then as now, though nowhere in Scripture is it expressly so stated. The chief use of the berries, now as ever, is in furnishing "oil" (q.v.), but they are eaten in the fresh state, as also after being soaked in brine, by rich and poor alike, and are shipped in great quantities. Olive trees are still more or less abundant in Pal, esp. around Bethlehem and Hebron, on the borders of the rich plains of Esdraelon, Phoenicia, Sharon and Philistia, in the vale of Shechem, the plain of Moreh, and in the trans-Jordanic regions of Gilead and Bashan. They are esteemed as among the best possessions of the towns, and the culture of them is being revived around Jerus, in the Jordan valley and elsewhere throughout the land. They are beautiful to behold in all stages of their growth, but esp. in spring. Then they bear an amazing wealth of blossoms, which in the breeze fall in showers like snowflakes, a fact that gives point to Job's words, "He shall cast off his flower as the olive-tree" (**15** 33). The mode of gathering the fruit is still about what it was in ancient times (cf Ex **27** 20).

4. Food of Trees

Next in rank to the olive, according to Jotham's order, though first as an article of food, is the **fig** (in the OT *t*e*'ēnāh*, in the NT *sukē*), whose "sweetness" is praised in the parable (Jgs **9** 11). It is the principal shade and fruit tree of Pal, growing in all parts, in many spontaneously, and is the emblem of peace and prosperity (Dt **8** 8; Jgs **9** 10; 1 K **4** 25; Mic **4** 4; Zec **3** 10; 1 Macc **14** 12). The best fig and olive orchards are carefully plowed, first in the spring when the buds are swelling, sometimes again when the second crop is sprouting, and again after the first rains in the autumn. The "first-ripe fig" (*bikkūrāh*, Isa **28** 4; Jer **24** 2), i.e. the early fig which grows on last year's wood, was and is esteemed as a great delicacy, and is often eaten while it is young and green. The late fig (*t*e*'ēnīm*) is the kind dried in the sun and put up in quantities for use out of season. Among the Greeks and the Romans, as well as among the Hebrews, dried figs were most extensively used. When pressed in a mold they formed the **"cakes of figs"** (*d*e*bhēlāh*) mentioned in the OT (1 S **25** 18; 1 Ch **12** 40), doubtless about such as are found today in Syria and Smyrna, put up for home use and for shipment. It was such a fig-cake that was presented as a poultice (AV "plaster") for Hezekiah's boil (Isa **38** 21; cf 2 K **20** 7). As the fruit-buds of the fig appear before the leaves, a tree full of leaves and without fruit would be counted "barren" (Mk **11** 12 f; cf Isa **28** 4; Jer **24** 2; Hos **9** 10; Nah **3** 12; Mt **21** 19; Lk **13** 7).

Grapes (*'ănābhīm*), often called "the fruit of the

vine" (Mt **26** 29), have always been a much-prized article of food in the Orient. They are closely associated in the Bible with the fig (cf "every man under his vine and under his fig-tree," 1 K **4** 25). Like the olive, the fig, and the date-palm, grapes are indigenous to Syria, the soil and climate being most favorable to their growth and perfection. Southern Pal esp. yields a rich abundance of choice grapes, somewhat as in patriarchal times (Gen **49** 11.12). J. T. Haddad, a native Syrian, for many years in the employment of the Turkish government, tells of a variety in the famous valley of Eshcol near Hebron, a bunch from which has been known to weigh twenty-eight pounds (cf Nu **13** 23). Of the grapevine there is nothing wasted; the young leaves are used as a green vegetable, and the old are fed to sheep and goats. The branches cut off in pruning, as well as the dead trunk, are used to make charcoal, or for firewood. The failure of such a fruit was naturally regarded as a judgment from Jeh (Ps **105** 33; Jer **5** 17; Hos **2** 12; Joel **1** 7). Grapes, like figs, were both enjoyed in their natural state, and by exposure to the sun dried into **raisins** (*çimmūḳīm*), the "dried grapes" of Nu **6** 3. In this form they were esp. well suited to the use of travelers and soldiers (1 S **25** 18; 1 Ch **12** 40). The meaning of the word rendered "raisin-cake," ARV "a cake of raisins" (2 S **6** 19 and elsewhere), is uncertain. In Bible times the bulk of the grape product of the land went to the making of **wine** (q.v.). Some doubt if the Hebrews knew grape-syrup, but the fact that the Aram. *dibs*, corresponding to Heb *d[e]bhash*, is used to denote both the natural and artificial honey (grape-syrup), seems to indicate that they knew the latter (cf Gen **43** 11; Ezk **27** 17; and see HONEY).

Less prominent was the fruit of the mulberry fig-tree (or sycomore) (*shiḳmāh*), of the date-palm (*tāmār*), the dates of which, according to the Mish, were both eaten as they came from the tree, and dried in clusters and pressed into cakes for transport; the pomegranate (*tappū[a]ḥ*), the "apple" of AV (see APPLE), or *quinch*, according to others; the husks (Lk **15** 16), i.e. the pods of the carob tree (κεράτιον), are treated elsewhere. Certain nuts were favorite articles of food—pistachio nuts (*boṭnīm*), almonds (*sh[e]ḳēdhīm*) and walnuts (*'ĕghōz*); and certain spices and vegetables were much used for seasoning: cummin (*kammōn*), anise, dill (AV) (*ḳeçaḥ*), mint (ἡδύοσμον) and mustard (σίναπι), which see. **Salt** (*melaḥ*), of course, played an important part, then as now, in the cooking and in the life of the Orientals. To "eat the salt" of a person was synonymous with eating his bread (Ezr **4** 14), and a "covenant of salt" was held inviolable (Nu **18** 19; 2 Ch **13** 5).

II. Animal Food.—Anciently, even more than now in the East, flesh food was much less used than among western peoples. In the first place, in Israel and among other Sem peoples, it was confined by law to the use of such animals and birds as were regarded as "clean" (see CLEAN; UNCLEANNESS), or speaking according to the categories of Lev **11** 2.3; Dt **14** 4–20, domestic animals and game (see Driver on Dt **14** 4–20). Then the poverty of the peasantry from time immemorial has tended to limit the use of meat to special occasions, such as family festivals (*ḥaggīm*), the entertainment of an honored guest (Gen **18** 7; 2 S **12** 4), and the sacrificial meal at the local sanctuary.

The **goat** (*'ēz*, etc), esp. the "kid of the goats" (Lev **4** 23.28 AV), was more prized for food by the ancient Hebrews than by modern Orientals, by whom goats are kept chiefly for their milk—most of which they supply (cf Prov **27** 27). For this reason they are still among the most valued possessions of rich and poor (cf Gen **30** 33; **32** 14 with 1 S **25** 2). A kid, as less valuable than a lamb, was naturally the readier victim when meat was required (cf Lk **15** 29).

The **sheep** of Pal, as of Egypt, are mainly of the fat-tailed species (*Ovis aries*), the tail of which was forbidden as ordinary food and had to be offered with certain other portions of the fat (Ex **29** 22; Lev **3** 9). To kill a lamb in honor of a guest is one of the highest acts of Bedouin hospitality. As a rule only the lambs are killed for meat, and they only in honor of some guest or festive occasion (cf 1 S **25** 18; 1 K **1** 19). Likewise the "calves of the herd" supplied the daintiest food of the kind, though the flesh of the neat cattle, male and female, was eaten. The "fatted calf" of Lk **15** 23 will be recalled, as also the "fatlings" and the "stalled" (stall-fed) ox of the OT (Prov **15** 17). A sharp contrast suggestive of the growth of luxury in Israel is seen by a comparison of 2 S **17** 28f with 1 K **4** 22f. The food furnished David and his hardy followers at Mahanaim was "wheat, and barley, and meal, and parched grain, and beans, and lentils, and parched pulse, and honey, and butter, and sheep, and cheese of the herd," while the daily provision for Solomon's table was "thirty measures of fine flour, and threescore measures of meal, ten fat oxen, and twenty oxen out of the pastures, and a hundred sheep, besides harts, and gazelles, and roebucks, and fatted fowl." Nehemiah's daily portion is given as "one ox and six choice sheep" (Neh **5** 18).

Milk of large and small animals was a staple article of food (Dt **32** 14; Prov **27** 27). It was usually kept in skins, as among the Syrian peasants it is today (Jgs **4** 19). We find a generic term often used (*ḥem'āh*) which covers also cream, clabber and cheese (Prov **30** 33). The proper designation of **cheese** is *g[e]bhīnāh* (Job **10** 10), but *ḥālābh* also is used both for ordinary milk and for a cheese made directly from sweet milk (cf 1 S **17** 18, *ḥărīçē he-ḥālābh*, and our "cottage cheese"). See MILK.

Honey (*d[e]bhāsh*, *nōpheth ha-çūphīm*), so often mentioned with milk, is ordinary bees' honey (see HONEY). The expression "honey" in the combination *d[e]bhash w[e]ḥālābh*, for which Pal was praised, most likely means *d[e]bhash t[e]mārīm*, i.e. "date-juice." It was much prized and relished (Ps **19** 10; Prov **16** 24), and seems to have been a favorite food for children (Isa **7** 15).

Of **game** seven species are mentioned (Dt **14** 5). The **gazelle** and the **hart** were the typical animals of the chase, much prized for their flesh (Dt **12** 15), and doubtless supplied the **venison** of Esau's "savory meat" (Gen **25** 28; **27** 4).

Of **fish** as food little is said in the OT (see Nu **11** 5; Jer **16** 16; Ezk **47** 10; Eccl **9** 12). No particular species is named, although thirty-six species are said to be found in the waters of the Jordan valley alone. But we may be sure that the fish which the Hebrews enjoyed in Egypt "for nought" (Nu **11** 5) had their successors in Canaan (Kennedy). Trade in cured fish was carried on by Tyrian merchants with Jerus in Nehemiah's day (Neh **13** 16), and there must have been a fish market at or near the fish gate (**3** 3). The Sea of Galilee in later times was the center of a great fish industry, as is made clear by the Gospels and by Jos. In the market of Tiberias today fresh fish are sold in great quantities, and a thriving trade in salt fish is carried on. The "small fishes" of Our Lord's two great miracles of feeding were doubtless of this kind, as at all times they have been a favorite form of provision for a journey in hot countries.

As to the exact price of food in ancient times little is known. From 2 K **7** 1.16 we learn that one *ș[e]'āh* of fine flour, and two of barley, sold for a shekel (cf Mt **10** 29). For **birds** allowed as food see Dt **14** 11 and arts. on CLEAN; UNCLEANNESS.

Pigeons and **turtle doves** find a place in the ritual of various sacrifices, and so are to be reckoned as "clean" for ordinary uses as well. The species of domestic fowl found there today seem to have been introduced during the Pers period (cf 2 Esd **1** 30; Mt **23** 37; **26** 34, etc). It is thought that the **fatted fowl** of Solomon's table (1 K **4** 23) were geese (see Mish). Fatted goose is a favorite food with Jews today, as it was with the ancient Egyptians.

Of game birds used for food (see Neh **5** 18) the **partridge** and the **quail** are prominent, and the humble **sparrow** comes in for his share of mention (Mt **10** 29; Lk **12** 6). Then, as now, the **eggs** of domestic fowls and of all "clean" birds were favorite articles of food (Dt **22** 6; Isa **10** 14; Lk **11** 12).

Edible insects (Lev **11** 22 f) are usually classed with animal foods. In general they are of the **locust** family (see LOCUST). They formed part of the food of John the Baptist (Mt **3** 4, etc), were regarded by the Assyrians as delicacies, and are a favorite food of the Arabs today. They are prepared and served in various ways, the one most common being to remove the head, legs and wings, to drop it in meal, and then fry it in oil or butter. It then tastes a little like fried frogs' legs. In the diet of the Baptist, locusts were associated with **wild honey** (see HONEY).

As to **condiments** (see separate arts. on SALT; CORIANDER, etc) it needs only to be said here that the **caperberry** (Eccl **12** 5 m) was eaten before meals as an appetizer and, strictly speaking, was not a condiment. **Mustard** was valued for the leaves, not for the seed (Mt **13** 31). **Pepper,** though not mentioned in Scripture, is mentioned in the Mish as among the condiments. Before it came into use, spicy seeds like cummin, the coriander, etc, played a more important rôle than since.

The abhorrence of the Hebrews for all food prepared or handled by the heathen (see ABOMINATION) is to be attributed primarily to the intimate association in early times between flesh food and sacrifices to the gods. This finds conspicuous illustration in the case of Daniel (Dnl **1** 8), Judas Maccabaeus (2 Macc **5** 27), Jos (*Vita*, III), and their compatriots (see also Acts **15** 20.29; 1 Cor **8** 1–10; **10** 19.28). As to **sources of food supply** and **traffic in food stuffs,** for primitive usages see Gen **18** 7; **27** 9; 1 K **21** 2. As to articles and customs of commerce adopted when men became dwellers in cities, see Jer **37** 21, where bakers were numerous enough in Jerus to give their name to a street or bazaar, where doubtless, as today, they baked and sold bread to the public (cf Mish, *passim*). Extensive trade in "victuals" in Nehemiah's day is attested by Neh **13** 15 f, and by specific mention of the "fish gate" (**3** 3) and the "sheep gate" (**3** 1), so named evidently because of their nearby markets. In John's Gospel (**4** 8; **13** 29) we have incidental evidence that the disciples were accustomed to buy food as they journeyed through the land. In Jerus, cheese was clearly to be bought in the cheesemakers' valley (Tyropœon), oil of the oil merchants (Mt **25** 9), and so on; and Corinth, we may be sure, was not the only city of Paul's day that had a provision market ("shambles," 1 Cor **10** 25 RV).

LITERATURE.—Mish, *B.M.* i. 1,2 and *passim;* Jos, *Vita* and *BJ;* Robinson's *Researches*, II, 416, etc; and Bib. Dictionaries, arts. on "Food," etc.

GEO. B. EAGER

FOOL, fōōl, **FOLLY** (נָבָל, *nābhāl*, אֱוִיל, *'ĕwīl*, כְּסִיל, *keṣīl*, סָכָל, *ṣākhāl*, and forms; **ἄφρων**, *áphrōn*, **ἀφροσύνη,** *aphrosúnē*, **μωρός,** *mōrós*):

I. In the Old Testament.—Taking the words generally, apart from the Wisdom literature, we find *nābhāl* frequently trd "fool" and *nebhālāh*, "folly"; *nābhāl*, however, denotes a wicked person, an evil character, "shamelessly immoral," equivalent

1. General

to "a son of Belial" (Cheyne), rather than a merely "foolish" person, and *nebhālāh*, "wickedness," "shameless impropriety," rather than simple folly. We have almost a definition of *nābhāl* in Isa **32** 6: "For the fool will speak folly, and his heart will work iniquity, to practise profaneness, and to utter error against Jeh, to make empty the soul of the hungry, and to cause the drink of the thirsty to fail." Abigail described her husband, Nābhāl, as "a son of Belial" (RV "worthless fellow"), "for as his name is, so is he" (1 S **25** 25), and what we read of him bears out this character. Other occurrences of the words support the above meaning; they are generally associated with some form of wickedness, frequently with base and unnatural lewdness (Gen **34** 7; Dt **22** 21; Josh **7** 15; Jgs **19** 23.24; **20** 6.10; 2 S **13** 12). When in Ps **14** 1; **53** 1 it is said, "The fool hath said in his heart, There is no God," it is followed by the statement, "They are corrupt, they have done abominable works," showing that more than "folly" is implied. In Isa **32** 5.6 AV, *nābhāl* is trd "vile person" and *nebhālāh* "villany," RV "fool" and "folly," Jer **29** 23; *hālal*, implying loud boasting is in AV trd "foolish," but it means, rather, "arrogant," which RV adopts (Ps **5** 5; **73** 3; **75** 4, m "fools"); *ṣākhāl*, "a fool," also occurs (Gen **31** 28; 1 S **13** 13, etc) for which word see (4) below; also *yā'al* "to be empty," "to be or become foolish" (Nu **12** 11; Isa **19** 13; Jer **5** 4; **50** 36).

In the *Ḥokhmāh* or Wisdom literature, which, within the Bible, is contained in Job, Prov (esp.),

2. The Wisdom Literature

Eccl, Cant, some Pss and certain portions of the prophetic writings, "fool" and "folly" are frequent and distinctive words. Their significance is best seen in contrast with "Wisdom." This was the outcome of careful observation and long pondering on actual life in the light of religion and the Divine revelation. Wisdom had its seat in God and was imparted to those who "feared" Him ("The fear of Jeh is the beginning [chief part] of knowledge" Prov **1** 7). Such wisdom was the essence of life, and to be without it was to walk in the way of death and destruction. The *fool* was he who was thoughtless, careless, conceited, self-sufficient, indifferent to God and His Will, or who might even oppose and scoff at religion and wise instruction. See WISDOM. Various words are used to designate "the fool" and his "folly."

(1) *nābhāl* (Job **2** 10; **30** 8; Ps **53** 1; Prov **17** 7–21); *nebhālāh* (Job **42** 8; Isa **9** 17) (see above).

(2) *'ĕwīl*, one of the commonest, the idea conveyed by which is that of one who is hasty, impatient, self-sufficient (Prov **12** 15; **15** 5; **16** 22); despising advice and instruction (**1** 7; **14** 9; **24** 7); ready to speak and act without thinking (**10** 14; **12** 16; **20** 3); quick to get angry, quarrel and cause strife (**11** 29; **14** 17 *'iwweleth;* **29** 9); unrestrained in his anger (Job **5** 2; Prov **17** 12); silly, stupid even with brute stupidity (Prov **7** 22; **26** 11; **27** 22; cf Isa **19** 11; Jer **4** 22); he is associated with "transgression" (Ps **107** 17; Prov **13** 15; **17** 18.19), with "sin" (**24** 9), with the "scoffer" (ib); *'iwweleth*, "foolishness" occurs (Ps **38** 5; **69** 5; Prov **13** 16; "folly," **14** 8.24.29, etc).

(3) *keṣīl* is the word most frequent in Prov. It is probably from a root meaning "thickness," "sluggishness," suggesting a slow, self-confident person, but it is used with a wide reference. Self-confidence appears (Prov **14** 16; **28** 26); ignorance (Eccl **2** 14); hate of instruction (Prov **1** 22; **18** 2); thoughtlessness (**10** 23; **17** 24); self-exposure (**14** 33; **15** 2; **18** 7; **29** 11; Eccl **5** 1; **10** 12); anger and contention (Prov **18** 6; **19** 1; Eccl

7 9); rage (Prov **14** 16; **17** 12); indolence and improvidence (Eccl **4** 5; Prov **21** 20); silly merriment (Eccl **7** 4.5.6); brutishness (Prov **26** 11; cf Ps **49** 10; **92** 6); it is associated with slander (Prov **10** 18), with evil (**13** 19).

(4) *ṣākhāl*, *ṣekhel*, *ṣikhlūth*, also occur. These are probably from a root meaning "to be stopped up" (Cheyne), and are generally taken as denoting thickheadedness; but they are used in a stronger sense than mere foolishness (cf 1 S **26** 21; 2 S **24** 10, etc). These words do not occur in Prov, but in Eccl **2** 12; **7** 25; *ṣikhlūth* is associated with "madness" ("Wickedness is folly, and . . . . foolishness is madness").

(5) *p^ethī*, "simple," is only once tr[d] "foolish" (Prov **9** 6 AV).

(6) *ba'ar*, "brutish," is tr[d] "foolish" (Ps **73** 22 AV, RV "brutish").

(7) *tāphēl*, "insipid," "untempered," is tr[d] "foolish" (Lam **2** 14); *tiphlāh*, "insipidity" (Job **1** 22, "foolishly," ERV, "with foolishness"; **24** 12, "folly"; Jer **23** 13, "folly," AVm "unsavoury, *or*, an absurd thing").

(8) *tohŏlāh* (Job **4** 18: "Behold, he putteth no trust in his servants; and his angels he chargeth with folly" [Delitzsch, "imperfection," others, "error"], AVm "nor in his angels in whom he put light").

II. In the Apocrypha.—In the continuation of the Wisdom literature in Wisd and Ecclus, "fool" frequently occurs with a signification similar to that in Prov; in Wisd we have *aphrōn* (**12** 24; **15** 5, etc), in Ecclus *mōros* (**18** 18; **19** 11, etc; **20** 13; **21** 16, etc).

III. In the New Testament.—In the NT we have various words tr[d] "fool," "foolish," "folly," etc, in the ordinary acceptation of these terms; *aphrōn*, "mindless," "witless" (Lk **11** 40; **12** 20; 1 Cor **15** 36); *aphrosunē*, "want of mind or wisdom" (2 Cor **11** 1; Mk **7** 22); *ánoia*, "want of understanding" (2 Tim **3** 9); *mōraínō*, "to make dull," "foolish" (Rom **1** 22; 1 Cor **1** 20); *mōros*, "dull," "stupid" (Mt **7** 26; **23** 17; **25** 2; 1 Cor **1** 25.27); *mōría*, "foolishness" (1 Cor **1** 18, etc); *mōrología*, "foolish talk" (Eph **5** 4).

In Mt **5** 22 Our Lord says: "Whosoever shall say [to his brother], Thou fool [*mōré*], shall be in danger of the hell of fire [the Gehenna of fire]." Two explanations of this word are possible: (1) that it is not the vocative of the Gr *mōros*—a word which was applied by Jesus Himself to the Pharisees (Mt **23** 17.19), but represents the Heb *mōrāh*, "rebel," applied in Nu **20** 10 by Moses to the people, "ye rebels" (for which he was believed to be excluded from the promised land; cf ver 12; hence we have in RVm "or *mōreh*, a Heb expression of condemnation"); or (2) that, as Our Lord spake in the Aram. it is the Gr tr of a word representing the Heb *nābhāl*, "vile, or worthless fellow," atheist, etc (Ps **14** 1; **53** 1). W. L. WALKER

FOOLERY, fōōl'ẽr-i: The pl. "fooleries" occurs Ecclus **22** 13 AV: "Talk not much with a fool . . . . and thou shalt never be defiled with his fooleries." The Gr word is ἐντιναγμός, *entinagmós*, "a striking or throwing in," "an attack," from *entinássō*, "to strike into," "cast at," etc (1 Macc **2** 36; 2 Macc **4** 41; **11** 11). RV renders "Thou shalt not be defiled in his onslaught," m "defiled: in his onslaught turn." The meaning is most probably "with what he throws out," i.e. his foolish or vile speeches, as if it were slaver.

FOOT, fo͝ot (רֶגֶל, *reghel*, קַרְסֹל, *ḳarṣōl* [only twice in ‖ passages: 2 S **22** 37 = Ps **18** 36, where it probably means ankle]; πούς, *poús*): The dusty roads of Pal and other eastern lands make a much greater care of the feet necessary than we are accustomed to bestow upon them. The absence of socks or stockings, the use of sandals and low shoes rather than boots and, to an even greater degree, the frequent habit of walking barefoot make it necessary to wash the feet repeatedly every day. This is always done when entering the house, esp. the better upper rooms which are usually carpeted. It is a common dictate of good manners to perform this duty to a visitor, either personally or through a servant; at least water for washing has to be presented (Gen **18** 4; Lk **7** 44). This has therefore become almost synonymous with the bestowal of hospitality (1 Tim **5** 10). At an early date this service was considered one of the lowest tasks of servants (1 S **25** 41), probably because the youngest and least trained servants were charged with the task, or because of the idea of defilement connected with the foot. It was, for the same reason, if rendered voluntarily, a service which betokened complete devotion. Jesus taught the greatest lesson of humility by performing this humble service to His disciples (Jn **13** 4–15). The undoing of the latchets or leather thongs of the sandals (Mk **1** 7; Lk **3** 16; Jn **1** 27) seems to refer to the same menial duty.

Often the feet and shoes were dusted on the highway, as is being done in the Orient to this day, but if it were done in an ostentatious manner in the presence of a person or a community who had refused hospitality to a stranger, it was understood in the same sense in which the cutting in two of the tablecloth was considered in the days of knighthood: it meant rejection and separation (Mt **10** 14; Acts **13** 51).

The roads of the desert were not only dusty but rough, and the wanderer was almost sure to ruin his ill-made shoes and wound his weary feet. A special providence of God protected the children of Israel from this experience during the long journey through the wilderness. "Thy raiment waxed not old upon thee, neither did thy foot swell, these forty years" (Dt **8** 4; **29** 5).

In the house shoes and sandals were never worn; even the most delicate would put on shoes only when going out (Dt **28** 56). The shoes were left outside of the house or in a vestibule. This was esp. done in the house of God and at the time of prayer, for whenever or wherever that might be, the law was: "Put off thy shoes from off thy feet, for the place whereon thou standest is holy ground" (Ex **3** 5; Josh **5** 15; Acts **7** 33). This custom still prevails among the Moslems of our day. Probably it was the idea of defilement through contact with the common ground which gave rise to its moral application by the Preacher, "Keep thy foot when thou goest to the house of God" (Eccl **5** 1 [Heb **4** 17]).

Nakedness of the feet in public, esp. among the wealthier classes, who used to wear shoes or sandals, was a token of mourning (Ezk **24** 17 and probably also Jer **2** 25 and Isa **20** 2–4). A peculiar ceremony is referred to in Dt **25** 9.10, whereby a brother-in-law, who refused to perform his duty under the Levirate law, was publicly put to shame. "And his name shall be called in Israel, The house of him that hath his shoe loosed." See also Ruth **4** 7.8.

Numerous are the phrases in which the word "foot" or "feet" is used in Bib. language. "To cover the feet" (1 S **24** 3) is synonymous with obeying a call of Nature. "To speak with the feet" is expressive of the eloquence of abusive and obscene gesticulation among oriental people, where hands, eyes and feet are able to express much without the use of words (Prov **6** 13). "To sit at the feet," means to occupy the place of a learner (Dt **33** 3;

Lk **10** 39; Acts **22** 3). Vanquished enemies had to submit to being trodden upon by the conqueror (a ceremony often represented on Egyp monuments; Josh **10** 24; Ps **8** 6; **110** 1; cf Isa **49** 23). St. James warns against an undue humiliation of those

Assyrian King Placing His Foot on the Neck of an Enemy.

who join us in the service of God, even though they be poor or mean-looking, by bidding them to take a lowly place at the feet of the richer members of the congregation (Jas **2** 3). We read of dying Jacob that "he gathered up his feet into the bed," for he had evidently used his bed as a couch, on which he had been seated while delivering his charge to his several sons (Gen **49** 33). "Foot" or "feet" is sometimes used euphemistically for the genitals (Dt **28** 57; Ezk **16** 25). In Dt **11** 10 an interesting reference is made to some Egyp mode of irrigating the fields, 'the watering with the foot,' which mode would be unnecessary in the promised land of Canaan which "drinketh water of the rain of heaven." It is, however, uncertain whether this refers to the water-wheels worked by a treadmill arrangement or whether reference is made to the many tributary channels, which, according to representations on the Egyp monuments, intersected the gardens and fields and which could be stopped or opened by placing or removing a piece of sod at the mouth of the channel. This was usually done with the foot. Frequently we find references to the foot in expressions connected with journeyings and pilgrimages, which formed so large a part in the experiences of Israel, e.g. Ps **91** 12, "lest thou dash thy foot against a stone"; **94** 18, "My foot slippeth"; **121** 3, "He will not suffer thy foot to be moved," and many more. Often the reference is to the "walk," i.e. the moral conduct of life (**73** 2; Job **23** 11; **31** 5).

Figurative: In the metaphorical language of Isa **52** 7 "the feet" are synonymous with "the coming."

H. L. E. Luering

FOOTMAN, fŏŏt′man. See War.

FOOTSTOOL, fŏŏt′stōōl (כֶּבֶשׁ, *kebhes;* **ὑποπόδιον,** *hupopódion,* "trodden on"): The 15 Scripture references to this term may be classified as literal or figurative. Of the former are the two passages: 2 Ch **9** 18 and Jas **2** 3. In these the footstool was a sort of step or support for the feet placed before the throne or any pretentious seat.

Of **figurative** uses, there are the following groups: (1) Of the earth: Isa **66** 1; Mt **5** 35; Acts **7** 49. (2) Of the ark: 1 Ch **28** 2. (3) Of the Temple: Ps **99** 5; **132** 7; Lam **2** 1; cf Isa **60** 13. (4) Of heathen enemies subdued by the Messianic King: Ps **110** 1; Mt **22** 44 AV; Mk **12** 36; Lk **20** 43; Acts **2** 35; He **1** 13; **10** 13. Thus the uses of this term are mainly metaphorical and symbolic of subjection, either to God as universal Lord or to God's Son as King by redemptive right. Cf 1 Cor **15** 25–27, in which all things, including death, are represented as subject to Christ and placed beneath His feet.

Leonard W. Doolan

FOR, fôr (כִּי, *kī* [conj.], לְ, *l*ᵉ, from אֶל, *'el* [prep.], and various other words. In the NT also the words are various, chiefly **γάρ,** *gár,* **καὶ γάρ,** *kaí gár,* **ὅτι,** *hóti* [conjs.]; **ἀντί,** *antí,* **ἀπό,** *apó,* **εἰς,** *eis,* **διά,** *diá* [acc.], **ἐπί,** *epí* [dat. and acc.], **περί,** *perí* [gen.], **πρός,** *prós* [gen. and acc.], **ὑπέρ,** *hupér* [gen.] [preps.]): ERV and ARV give in many cases more literal or more accurate renderings than those in AV.

In the NT the most important preps. from a doctrinal point of view are *anti,* "face to face," "over against," "instead," "on behalf of," *peri,* "around," "about," "concerning," *huper,* "over," "on behalf of." The first has been claimed as stating the substitutionary nature of Christ's sacrifice as contrasted with *huper* and *peri,* more frequently used of it. But, although *anti* in the NT often means "instead of," "answering to," it does not necessarily imply substitution. On the other hand, in classical Gr *huper* is sometimes used in that sense (see Trench, *Synonyms*). "Here as always the root idea of the prep., the root idea of the case, and the context must all be considered" (Robertson, *Grammar,* 124). *Anti* is found in this connection only in Mt **20** 28, and Mk **10** 45. In Mt **26** 28; Mk **14** 24, we have *peri,* also in He **10** 6.8.18.26; 1 Pet **3** 18; 1 Jn **2** 2; **4** 10. Lk **22** 19.20 has *huper,* which is the word commonly used by Paul, as in Rom **5** 6.8; **8** 32; **14** 15; 1 Cor **15** 3, etc, also by John in his Gospel, **6** 51; **10** 11, etc, and 1 Jn **3** 16; also He **2** 9; **10** 12; 1 Pet **2** 21; **3** 18; **4** 1; in Rom **8** 3 it is *peri.*

W. L. Walker

FORAY, for′ā (2 S **3** 22). See War.

FORBEAR, for-bâr′ (חָדַל, *ḥādhal;* **ἀνέχομαι,** *anéchomai*): In the OT *ḥādhal,* "to leave off," is the word most frequently trᵈ "forbear" (Ex **23** 5, etc); *dāmam,* "to be silent," *ḥāsakh,* "to keep back," *māshakh,* "to draw or stretch out," occur once each; RV renders Ezk **24** 17 (*dāmam*), "Sigh, but not aloud," m "Heb be silent"; Prov **24** 11 (*ḥāsakh*), "See that thou hold back," m "*or* forbear thou not to deliver," AV "if thou forbear to deliver"; Neh **9** 30 (*māshakh*), "bear" instead of "forbear"; *'aph* lit. "breathing," the "nose," hence from violent breathing, "anger" (*'erekh,* "long," understood), and *kūl* "to hold," are trᵈ "forbearing" (Prov **25** 15; Jer **20** 9, respectively).

In the NT we have *anechomai,* "to hold self back or up," "with longsuffering, forbearing one another" (Eph **4** 2; Col **3** 13); *aniēmi,* "to send back," AV and RV "forbear threatening" (Eph **6** 9); *pheidomai,* "to spare," "but I forbear" (2 Cor **12** 6); *mḗ ergázesthai,* "not to work," "to forbear working" (1 Cor **9** 6); *stégō,* "to cover," "conceal": "when I could no longer forbear" (1 Thess **3** 1.5).

W. L. Walker

FORBEARANCE, for-bâr′ans (**ἀνοχή,** *anochḗ*): "Forbearance" (*anochē,* "a holding back") is ascribed to God (Rom **2** 4, "the riches of his goodness and forbearance and longsuffering"; **3** 25 RV, "the passing over of the sins done aforetime, in the forbearance of God," AV "remission" [m "passing over"] of sins, that are past, through the forbearance of God"); in Phil **4** 5, *tó epieikés* is trᵈ by RV "forbearance," m "gentleness"; it is a Christian grace in likeness to God. "Forbearing" (AVm) is substituted by RV for "patient" (*anexíkakos,* "holding up under evil") in 2 Tim **2** 24. W. L. Walker

FORBID, for-bid′ (כָּלָא, *kālā′*; κωλύω, *kōlúō*): Occurs very seldom in the OT except as the rendering of *ḥālīlāh* (see below); it is once the tr of *kālā′*, "to restrain" (Nu **11** 28, "Joshua . . . . said, My lord Moses, forbid them"); twice of *çāwāh*, "to command" (Dt **2** 37, "and whereso-ever Jeh our God forbade us"; **4** 23, "Jeh thy God hath forbidden thee," lit. "commanded"); once of *lō′*, "not," RV "commanded not to be done" (Lev **5** 17). In the phrases, "Jeh forbid" (1 S **24** 6; **26** 11; 1 K **21** 3), "God forbid" (Gen **44** 7; Josh **22** 29; **24** 16; 1 S **12** 23; Job **27** 5, etc), "My God forbid it me" (1 Ch **11** 19), the word is *ḥālīlāh*, denoting profanation, or abhorrence (rendered, Gen **18** 25 AV, "that be far from thee"); ERV leaves the expressions unchanged; ARV substitutes "far be it from me," "thee," etc, except in 1 S **14** 45; **20** 2, where it is, "Far from it."

In the NT *kōluō*, "to cut short," "restrain," is the word commonly tr[d] "forbid" (Mt **19** 14, "forbid them not," etc); in Lk **6** 29, RV has "withhold not"; *diakōlúō*, with a similar meaning, occurs in Mt **3** 14, "John forbade him," RV "would have hindered him"; *akōlútōs*, "uncut off" (Acts **28** 31), is tr[d] "none forbidding him." The phrase "God forbid" (*mḗ génoito*, "let it not be," Lk **20** 16; Rom **3** 4, etc) is retained by RV, with m "Be it not so," except in Gal **6** 14, where the text has "Far be it from me"; *mē genoito* is one of the renderings of *ḥālīlāh* in LXX. "God forbid" also appears in Apoc (1 Macc **2** 21, RV "Heaven forbid," m "Gr may he be propitious," **9** 10, RV "Let it not be").

W. L. WALKER

FORCES, fōr′sis (חַיִל, *ḥayil*):

(1) The word is used as a military term, equivalent to army, in 2 K **25** 23.26 (where AV reads "armies"); 2 Ch **17** 2; Jer **40** 7, etc. See ARMY.

(2) In Isa **60** 5.11, it is rendered in RV by "wealth," and in Ob ver 11, by "substance."

Two other Heb words are also tr[d] "forces" in AV, *ma′ămaççīm* (Job **36** 19), and *mā′ōz* (Dnl **11** 38), the latter being rendered in RV "fortresses."

FORD, fōrd (מַעֲבָר, *ma′ăbhār* [Gen **32** 22; "pass" (of Michmash), 1 S **13** 23; "stroke" (RVm "passing"), Isa **30** 32]; מַעְבָּרָה, *ma′bārāh* [Josh **2** 7; Jgs **3** 28; **12** 5.6; Isa **16** 2; "pass" (of Michmash), 1 S **14** 4; "passages" (RVm "fords"), Jer **51** 32]; עֲבָרָה, *′ăbhārāh* [2 S **15** 28; **17** 16; "ferry-boat" (RVm "convoy"), 2 S **19** 18]; from עָבַר, *′ābhar*, "to pass over"; cf Arab. عَبَرَ, *′abar*, "to pass over," and مَعْبَر, *ma′bar*, "a ford"): In the journeyings of the children of Israel, in addition to the miraculous passages of the Red Sea and the Jordan, they had other streams to pass over, esp. the Zered (*Ḥisa′*) and the Arnon (*Maujib*) (Nu **21** 12.13; Dt **2** 24). The Jabbok (*Zarḳa*) is frequently referred to, particularly in connection with Jacob (Gen **32** 22) The most frequent references are to the Jordan which, in time of flood, was impassable (Josh **3** 15). The lower Jordan is about 100 ft. wide, and from 5 to 12 ft. deep, so that in the absence of bridges, the places where it was possible to ford were of great importance. The passage of the Jordan is referred to in connection with Jacob (Gen **32** 10), Gideon (Jgs **8** 4), the children of Ammon (Jgs **10** 9), Abner and his men (2 S **2** 29), David (2 S **10** 17; **17** 22), Absalom (2 S **17** 24), and others. Jesus undoubtedly crossed the Jordan, and John is thought to have baptized at the ford of the Jordan near Jericho. The fords of the Jordan are specifically mentioned in Josh **2** 7 in connection with the pursuit of the spies who were hidden in Rahab's house, and in 2 S **15** 28; **17** 16 in connection with the flight of David. In the last two passages we have *′ăbhārāh*, the same word which, in the account of David's return (2 S **19** 18), is rendered "ferry-boat" (RVm "convoy"). See JORDAN.

ALFRED ELY DAY

FORECAST, fōr-kast′ (vb.) (חָשַׁב, *ḥāshabh*): To forecast is both to plan or scheme beforehand and to consider or see beforehand. It is in the first sense that it is used in Dnl **11** 24.25 (AV) as the tr of *ḥāshabh*, "to think," "meditate," "devise," "plot," "He shall forecast his devices [AVm "Heb think his thoughts"] against the strongholds"; "They shall forecast devices against him," RV "devise his devices"; cf Nah **1** 9, "What do ye devise against Jeh?" In the second sense, the word occurs in Wisd **17** 11 RV, "Wickedness . . . . always forecasteth the worst lot" (*proeílēphen*), m "Most authorities read hath added" (*proseílēphen*).

W. L. WALKER

FOREFATHER, fōr′fä-thẽr:

(1) אָב רִאשׁוֹן, *′ābh rī′shōn*, "first father," "chief father," hence "early ancestor": "turned back to the iniquities of their forefathers" (Jer **11** 10).

(2) πρόγονος, *prógonos*, "born before," "ancestor": "whom I serve from my forefathers" (2 Tim **1** 3). It is tr[d] "parents" (including grandparents) in 1 Tim **5** 4: "and to requite their parents."

FOREFRONT, fōr′frunt (פָּנִים, *pānīm*): For "forefront," "front" is now generally used, since "back-front" has gone out of use. "Forefront" is the tr of *pānīm*, "face" (2 K **16** 14; Ezk **40** 19 *bis;* **47** 1); of *mūl pānīm*, "over against the face" (Ex **26** 9; Lev **8** 9, "And he put the mitre upon his head; also upon the mitre even upon his forefront, did he put the golden plate"; for "upon his forefront" RV has "in front"; 2 S **11** 15, "in the forefront of the hottest battle"); of *rō′sh*, "head" (2 Ch **20** 27); of *shēn*, "tooth" (1 S **14** 5, "The forefront [AVm "Heb tooth"] of the one was situated northward over against Michmash," RV "The one crag rose up on the north in front of Michmash"); in 1 Macc **4** 57 m it is the tr of *prósōpon*, "face": "They decked the forefront of the temple with crowns of gold."

RV has "forefront" for "face" (Ezk **40** 15), "in the forefront of" for "over against" (Josh **22** 11).

W. L. WALKER

FOREGO, fōr-gō′. See FORGO.

FOREHEAD, for′ed (מֵצַח, *mēçaḥ;* μέτωπον, *métōpon*):

(1) In a **literal** sense the word is used frequently in the Scriptures. Aaron and after him every high priest was to wear on the forehead the golden frontlet having the engraved motto, "Holy to Jeh" (Ex **28** 36.38). The condition of the forehead was an important criterion in the diagnosis of leprosy by the priest (Lev **13** 42.43; 2 Ch **26** 20). It was in the forehead that brave young David smote Goliath with the stone from his sling (1 S **17** 49). The faulty tr of AV in Ezk **16** 12 has been corrected in RV, reference being had in the passage to a nose-ring, not to an ornament of the forehead. While the cutting or tattooing of the body was strictly forbidden to the Israelite on account of the heathen associations of the custom (Lev **19** 28), we find frequent mention made of markings on the forehead, which were esp. used to designate slaves (see Philo, *De Monarchia*, I) or devotees of a godhead (Lucian, *De Syria Dea*, 59). In 3 Macc **2** 29 we read that Ptolemy IV Philopator branded some Jews with the sign of an ivy leaf, marking them as devotees of Bacchus-Dionysos. Possibly we may compare herewith the tr of Isa **44** 5 (RVm): "And another

shall write on his hand, Unto Jeh" (or Jeh's *slave*). Very clear is the passage Ezk **9** 4.6 (and perhaps Job **31** 35), where the word used for "mark" is *tāw*, the name of the last letter of the Heb alphabet which in its earliest form has the shape of an upright + (Baal Lebanon Inscr, 11th cent. BC) or of a lying (St Andrew's) cross × (Moabite Inscr, 9th cent. BC), the simplest sign in the old Israelite alphabet, and at the same time the character which in the Gr alphabet represents the X, the initial of Christ. In the NT we find a clear echo of the above-mentioned OT passage, the marking of the foreheads of the righteous (Rev **7** 3; **9** 4; **14** 1; **22** 4). The godless followers of the beast are marked on the (right) hand and on the forehead (**13** 16; **14** 9; **20** 4), and the apocalyptic woman dressed in scarlet and purple has her name written on her forehead (**17** 5).

(2) In a **metaphorical** sense the expression, "a harlot's forehead," is used (Jer **3** 3) to describe the shameless apostasy and faithlessness of Israel. Ezk speaks of the stiff-necked obstinacy and the persistent unwillingness of Israel to hear the message of Jeh: "All the house of Israel are of a hard forehead and of a stiff heart" (**3** 7), and God makes his prophet's "forehead hard . . . . as an adamant harder than flint," whereby an unflinching loyalty to God and a complete disregard of opposition is meant (vs 8.9). Compare the phrase: "to harden the face," s.v. FACE. H. L. E. LUERING

FOREIGN DIVINITIES, for'in di-vin'i-tiz (Acts **17** 18 m). See GOD(s), STRANGE.

FOREIGNER, for'in-ẽr: The tr of נָכְרִי, *nokhrī*, "unknown," "foreign," frequently rendered "stranger" (Dt **15** 3; Ob ver 11); of תּוֹשָׁב, *tōshābh*, "a settler," "an alien resident" (Ex **12** 45; RV "sojourner"; cf Lev **25** 47; Ps **39** 12); of *pároikos*, "dwelling near," "sojourner" (Eph **2** 19, RV sojourners").

RV has "foreigner" for "stranger" (Dt **17** 15; **23** 20; **29** 22; Ruth **2** 10; 2 S **15** 19), for "alien" (Dt **14** 21); "the hand of a foreigner" for "a stranger's hand" (Lev **22** 25). See ALIEN; STRANGER AND SOJOURNER.

FOREKNOW, fōr-nō', **FOREKNOWLEDGE,** fōr-nol'ej:

1. Meaning of the Term
2. Foreknowledge as Prescience
3. Foreknowledge Based on Foreordination
4. Foreknowledge as Equivalent to Foreordination

LITERATURE

1. Meaning of the Term

The word "foreknowledge" has two meanings. It is a term used in theology to denote the prescience or foresight of God, that is, His knowledge of the entire course of events which are future from the human point of view; and it is also used in AV and RV to translate the Gr words *proginṓskein* and *prógnōsis* in the NT, in which instances the word "foreknowledge" approaches closely the idea of foreordination.

2. Foreknowledge as Prescience

In the sense of prescience foreknowledge is an aspect of God's omniscience (see OMNISCIENCE). God's knowledge, according to the Scripture, is perfect, that is, it is omniscience. It is true that the Scripture makes use of anthropomorphic forms of expression as regards the way in which God obtains knowledge (Gen **3** 8), and sometimes even represents Him as if He did not know certain things (Gen **11** 5; **18** 21); nevertheless the constant representation of the Scripture is that God knows everything. This perfect knowledge of God, moreover, is not merely a knowledge which is practically unlimited for all religious purposes, but is omniscience in the strictest sense of the term. In the historical books of the OT the omniscience of God is a constant underlying presupposition when it is said that God watches men's actions, knows their acts and words, and discloses to them the future; while in the Psalms, Prophets and Wisdom literature, this Divine attribute becomes an object of reflection, and finds doctrinal expression. It cannot, however, be said that this attribute of God appears only late in the history of special revelation; it is a characteristic of the Bib. idea of God from the very first, and it is only its didactic expression which comes out with especial clearness in the later books. God's knowledge, then, is represented as perfect. Since He is free from all limits of space, His omniscience is frequently connected with His omnipresence. This is the thought which underlies the anthropomorphic expressions where God is represented as seeing, beholding and having eyes. God's eyes go to and fro throughout the whole earth (2 Ch **16** 9), and are in every place beholding the evil and the good (Prov **15** 3). Even Sheol is naked and open to God's sight (Prov **15** 11; Job **26** 6). The night and darkness are light to Him, and darkness and light for God are both alike (Ps **139** 12). All animals and fowls are His, and so are known by Him (**50** 11), and as their Creator God knows all the hosts of the heavenly bodies (Ps **147** 4; Isa **40** 26). He knows also the heart of man and its thoughts (1 S **16** 7; 1 K **8** 39; Ps **7** 9 [Heb 10]; **94** 11; **139** 2; Jer **11** 20; **17** 9.10; **20** 12; Ezk **11** 5). Furthermore, God knows man entirely in all his ways (Ps **139** 1–5; Prov **5** 21). He looks from heaven and sees all men (Ps **11** 4; **14** 2; **33** 13. 14.15). Evil and sin are also known to God (Gen **3** 11; **6** 5.9.13; 2 S **7** 20; Ps **69** 5 [Heb 6]; Jer **16** 17; **18** 23). In a word, God knows with absolute accuracy all about man (Job **11** 11; **34** 21; Ps **33** 15; Prov **5** 21; Hos **5** 3; Jer **11** 20; **12** 3; **17** 9 f; **18** 23). This perfect knowledge finds its classic expression in Ps **139**.

God is also, according to the OT, free from all limitations of time, so that His consciousness is not in the midst of the stream of the succeeding moments of time, as is the case with the human consciousness. God is not only without beginning or end of days, but with Him a thousand years are as one day. Hence God knows in one eternal intuition that which for the human consciousness is past, present and future. In a strict sense, therefore, there can be no foreknowledge or prescience with God, and the distinction in God's knowledge made by theologians, as knowledge of reminiscence, vision and prescience, is after all an anthropomorphism. Nevertheless this is the only way in which we can conceive of the Divine omniscience in its relation to time, and consequently the Scripture represents the matter as if God's knowledge of future events were a foreknowledge or prescience, and God is represented as knowing the past, present and future.

It is God's knowledge of events which from the human point of view are future that constitutes His foreknowledge in the sense of prescience. God is represented as having a knowledge of the entire course of events before they take place. Such a knowledge belongs to the Scriptural idea of God from the very outset of special revelation. He knows beforehand what Abraham will do, and what will happen to him; He knows beforehand that Pharaoh's heart will be hardened, and that Moses will deliver Israel (Gen **15** 13 ff; Ex **3** 19; **7** 4; **11** 1 ff). The entire history of the patriarchal period of revelation exhibits plainly the foreknowledge of God in this sense. In prophecy this aspect of the Divine knowledge is made the subject of explicit assertion, and its religious significance is brought out. Nothing future is hidden from Jeh (Isa **41** 22 ff; **42** 9; **43** 9–13; **44** 6–8; **46** 10; Dnl **2** 22; Am **3** 7), and this foreknowledge embraces the entire course of man's life (Ps **31** 15 [Heb 16]; **39** 5 [Heb 6]; **139** 4–6.16; Job **14** 5). These passages from Isa show that it is from the occurrence of events in accordance with Jeh's prediction that the Prophet will prove his foreknowledge; and that in contrast with the worshippers of idols which are taken by surprise, Israel is warned of the future by the omniscient Jeh.

In the NT likewise, God's omniscience is explicitly affirmed. Jesus taught that God knows the hidden secrets of man's heart (Lk **16** 15); and this is also the teaching of the apostles (Acts **1** 24; **15** 8; 1 Cor **2** 10; **3** 20; 1 Thess **2** 4; Rev **2** 23). In a word, according to the author of the Epistle to the He, everything is open to God, so that He is literally omniscient (He **4** 13). And as in the OT, so also in the NT, foreknowledge in the sense of prescience is ascribed to God. Jesus asserts a foreknowledge by God of that which is hidden from the Son (Mk **13** 32), and James asserts that all God's works are foreknown by Him (Acts **15** 18). Moreover the many references in the NT to the fulfilment of prophecy all imply that the NT writers ascribed foreknowledge, in this sense of foresight, to God.

Denials of the Divine foreknowledge, in this sense of prescience, have been occasioned, not by exegetical considerations, but by the supposed conflict of this truth with human freedom. It was supposed that in order to be free, an event must be uncertain and contingent as regards the fact of its futurition, and that too in the most absolute sense, that is, from the Divine as well as the human point of view. Hence the Socinians and some Arminians denied the foreknowledge of God. It was supposed either that God voluntarily determines not to foresee the free volitions of man, or else that since God's omniscience is simply the knowledge of all that is knowable, it does not embrace the free acts of man which are by their nature uncertain and so unknowable. And upon this view of freedom, this denial of God's foreknowledge was logically necessary. If the certainty of events with respect to the fact of their futurition is inconsistent with freedom, then human freedom does conflict with God's foreknowledge, since God cannot know future events as certainly future unless they actually are so. Since, therefore, the Divine foreknowledge is quite as inconsistent with this view of freedom as is the Divine foreordination, the view of those who regard God as a mere onlooker on the course of future events which are supposed to be entirely independent of His purpose and control, does not help matters in the least. If God foreknows future events as certain, then they must be certain, and if so, then the certainty of their actually occurring must depend either upon God's decree and providential control, or else upon a fate independent of God. It was to escape these supposed difficulties that the doctrine known as *scientia media* was propounded. It was supposed that God has a knowledge of events as conditionally future, that is, events neither merely possible nor certainly future, but suspended upon conditions undetermined by God. But this hypothesis is of no help and is not true. Besides being contrary to the Scripture in its idea that many events lie outside the decree of God, and that God must wait upon man in His government of the world, there is really no such class of events as this theory asserts. If God foreknows that the conditions on which they are suspended will be fulfilled, then these events belong to the class of events which are certainly future; whereas if God does not know whether or not the conditions will be fulfilled by man, then His foreknowledge is denied, and these events in question belong to the class of those merely possible. Nor do the Scripture passages to which appeal is made, such as Gen **11** 6; Ex **3** 19; Dt **7** 3.4; 1 S **23** 10–13; 2 S **12** 8, etc, afford a basis for this doctrine. The Scripture of course recognizes that God has put all things in relations of mutual dependence, and speaks of what can or cannot happen under such and such conditions; but none of these passages assert or imply that the events are suspended upon conditions which are either unknown or undetermined by God.

3. Foreknowledge Based on Foreordination

God's foreknowledge, according to the Scripture teaching, is based upon His plan or eternal purpose, which embraces everything that comes to pass. God is never represented as a mere onlooker seeing the future course of events, but having no part in it. That God has such a plan is the teaching of the entire Scripture. It is implied in the OT conception of God as an Omnipotent Person governing all things in accordance with His will. This idea is involved in the names of God in the patriarchal revelation, *'Ēl*, *'Ĕlōhīm*, *'Ēl Shadday*, and in the prophetic name Jeh of Hosts. This latter name teaches not only God's infinite power and glory, but also makes Him known as interposing in accordance with His sovereign will and purpose in the affairs of this world, and as having also the spiritual powers of the heavenly world at His disposal for the execution of His eternal purpose. Hence this idea of God comes to signify the omnipotent Ruler of the universe (Ps **24** 10; Isa **6** 3; **51** 5; **54** 5; Jer **10** 16; Am **9** 5; cf Oehler, *Theol. of the OT*, ET, II, 280).

Not only in this conception of God as omnipotent and sovereign Ruler is the thought of His eternal plan evolved; it is explicitly asserted throughout the whole OT. The purpose of God as determining human history in the Book of Gen lies clearly upon the surface of the narrative, as, for example, in the history of Abraham and of Joseph. And where there is no abstract statement of this truth, it is evident that the writer regards every event as but the unfolding of the purpose of God. In the Psalms, Prophets, and Wisdom literature, this truth finds explicit and reiterated assertion. Jeh has an eternal purpose (Ps **33** 11), and this purpose will certainly come to pass (Isa **14** 27; **43** 13). This purpose includes all events and renders certain their occurrence (Isa **14** 24; **40** 10; **46** 9.10; Zec **1** 6). In the Wisdom literature the ethical character of this plan is dwelt upon, as well as its all-embracing character, and the certainty of its fulfilment (Prov **16** 4.33; **19** 21; **20** 24; Job **28** 23). The providential control wherewith Jeh executes this plan includes the heart of man (Prov **21** 1).

The NT likewise regards all history as but the unfolding of God's eternal purpose (Acts **4** 28), which includes man's salvation (Eph **1** 4.5; 2 Tim **1** 9), the provision of Christ as Saviour (1 Pet **1** 20), and the good works of the Christian (Eph **2** 10). See PREDESTINATION.

Now while the writers of the OT and the NT do not write in an abstract or philosophical manner nor enter into metaphysical explanations of the relation between God's foreknowledge and foreordination, it is perfectly evident that they had a clear conception upon this subject. Although anthropomorphisms are used in regard to the manner in which God knows, He is never conceived as if He obtained His knowledge of the future as a mere onlooker gazing down the course of events in time. The idea that the omnipotent Creator and sovereign Ruler of the universe should govern the world and form His plan as contingent and dependent upon a mere foresight of events outside His purpose and control is not only contrary to the entire Scriptural idea of God's sovereignty and omnipotence, but is also contrary to the Scriptural idea of God's foreknowledge which is always conceived as dependent upon His sovereign purpose. According to the Scriptural conception, God foreknows because He has foreordained all things, and because in

His providence He will certainly bring all to pass. His foreknowledge is not a dependent one which must wait upon events, but is simply the knowledge which God has of His own eternal purpose. Dillmann has called this "a productive foreknowledge" (*Handbuch d. attest. Theol.*, 251). This is not exactly correct. The OT does not conceive God's foreknowledge as "producing" or causing events. But when Dillmann says that in the OT there is no hint of an "idle foreknowledge" on God's part, he is giving expression to the truth that in the OT God's foreknowledge is based upon His foreordination and providential control of all things. The Divine foreknowledge, therefore, depends upon the Divine purpose which has determined the world plan (Am **3** 7), and all its details (Job **28** 26.27). Before man is born God knows him and chooses him for his work (Jer **1** 5; Job **23** 13.14), and God's thorough knowledge of man in Ps **139** is made to rest upon the fact that God has determined man's lot beforehand (Ps **139** 14–16).

The same thing is true of the NT teaching on this subject. The Divine foreknowledge is simply God's knowledge of His own eternal purpose. This is esp. clear in those cases where God's eternal purpose of redemption through Christ is represented as a mystery which is known by God and which can be known by man only when it pleases God to reveal it (Eph **1** 9; **3** 4.9).

While, therefore, the foreknowledge of God in the sense of prescience is asserted in the NT, this is not the meaning of the term when used to translate the Gr words *proginōskein* and *prognōsis*. These words which are tr[d] in AV and RV by the word "foreknowledge," and once by the word "foreordain" (1 Pet **1** 20 AV), mean much more than mere intellectual foresight or prescience. Both the vb. and the noun approach the idea of foreordination and are closely connected with that idea in the passages where these words occur. Thus in Peter's speeches in Acts the predestination which finds expression in **4** 28 is practically identified with the term *prognōsis* in **2** 23. Everything which happened to Jesus took place in accordance with "the determinate counsel and foreknowledge of God," so that nothing happened except that which God had foreordained. In this verse the term foreknowledge is an expansion of the idea of God's "counsel" or plan, regarding it as an intelligent prearrangement, the idea of foreknowledge being assimilated to that of foreordination. The same idea is found in 1 Pet **1** 20. Here the apostle speaks of Christ as a lamb "foreordained" by God before the foundation of the world. The Gr vb. *proegnōsménou*, meaning lit. "foreknown" (as in RV) is tr[d] "foreordained" in AV. It is evidently God's foreordination of Jesus as Saviour which Peter has in mind. Also in 1 Pet **1** 2 those to whom the apostle is writing are characterized as "elect according to the foreknowledge [*prognōsis*] of God," where the election is based on the "foreknowledge." By the *prognōsis* or foreknowledge, however, far more is meant than prescience. It has the idea of a purpose which determines the course of the Divine procedure. If it meant simply prevision of faith or love or any quality in the objects of the election, Peter would not only flatly contradict Paul (Rom **9** 11; Eph **1** 3.4; 2 Tim **1** 9); but also such a rendering would conflict with the context of this passage, because the objects of election are chosen "unto obedience and sprinkling of the blood of . . . . Christ," so that their new obedience and relation to Christ are determined by their election by God, which election springs from a "foreknowledge" which therefore cannot mean a mere prescience.

4. Foreknowledge as Equivalent to Foreordination

In view of the fact that there was a classical use of the simple vb. *ginōskein* in the sense of "resolve," and more esp. of the fact that this word is used in the NT to denote an affectionate or loving regard or approbation in accordance with a common use of the Heb *yādha'* (Mt **7** 23; 1 Cor **8** 3; Gal **4** 9; 2 Tim **2** 19), there is nothing arbitrary in giving it this sense when compounded with the preposition *pro* when the context clearly demands it, as it does in the above passage (cf Johnstone, *Comm. on Pet* in loc.; *per contra* Meyer on passages in Acts and Rom). The word *prognōsis* is, however, discriminated from "predestination." It is that loving regard in God from which the Divine election springs, which election Peter evidently regarded as sovereign, since sanctification is only a confirmation of it (2 Pet **1** 10), and stumbling and disobedience are referred to 'appointment to unbelief' (1 Pet **2** 8). Here, then, we have a pregnant use of foreknowledge in which it is assimilated to the idea of purpose, and denotes a sovereign and loving regard.

The word *prognōsis* is also found in this sense in the writings of Paul, in cases where it is manifestly impossible to regard it as a mere intellectual foresight, not only because of Paul's doctrine that election is absolutely sovereign (Eph **1** 3.4; Rom **9** 11; 2 Tim **1** 9), but also because of the contexts in which the term occurs.

In Rom **8** 29.30 the word "foreknow" occurs in immediate connection with God's predestination of the objects of salvation. Those whom God foreknew, He also did predestinate to be conformed to the image of His son. Now the foreknowledge in this case cannot mean a mere prescience or foresight of faith (Meyer, Godet) or love (Weiss) in the subjects of salvation, which faith or love is supposed to determine the Divine predestination. This would not only contradict Paul's view of the absolutely sovereign and gracious character of election, but is diametrically opposed to the context of this passage. These verses form a part of the encouragement which Paul offers his readers for their troubles, including their own inward weakness. The apostle tells them that they may be sure that all things work together for good to them that love God; and these are defined as being those whom God has called in accordance with His purpose. Their love to God is evidently their love as Christians, and is the result of a calling which itself follows from an eternal purpose, so that their Christian love is simply the means by which they may know that they have been the subjects of this call. They have not come within the sphere of God's love by their own choice, but have been "called" into this relationship by God, and that in accordance with an eternal purpose on His part.

What follows, therefore, must have as its motive simply to unfold and ground this assurance of salvation by tracing it all back to the "foreknowledge" of God. To regard this foreknowledge as contingent upon anything in man would thus be in flat contradiction with the entire context of the passage as well as its motive. The word "foreknowledge" here evidently has the pregnant sense which we found it to have in Peter. Hence those whom God predestinates, calls, justifies and glorifies are just those whom He has looked upon with His sovereign love. To assign any other meaning to "foreknowledge" here would be out of accord with the usage of the term elsewhere in the NT when it is put in connection with predestination, and would contradict the purpose for which Paul introduces the passage, that is, to assure his readers that their ultimate salvation depends, not on their weakness, but on God's sovereign love and grace and power.

It is equally impossible to give the word *prognōsis* any other sense in the other passage where Paul uses it. In Rom **11** 2, speaking of the Jews, Paul says that "God did not cast off his people which he foreknew." It is quite impossible to regard this as meaning that God had a foresight or mere prevision of some quality in Israel which determined His choice of them, not only because it is the teaching of the entire Scripture that God's choice of Israel was sovereign and gracious, and not only because of the actual history of Israel, but also because of the context. Paul says that it would be absurd to suppose that God had cast off His people because He foreknew them, His foreknowledge of them being adduced as a ground for His not casting them off. Hence the argument would have no force if anything in Israel, foreseen by God, were supposed to ground an assurance that He had not cast them off, because the context is full of the hardness of heart and unbelief of Israel. The foreknowledge here has evidently the same sense as in the former passage.

Foreknowledge, therefore, in the NT is more than mere prescience. It is practically identical with the Divine decree in two instances, and in the other places where the term occurs it denotes the sovereign loving regard out of which springs God's predestination or election of men to salvation. See OMNISCIENCE; PREDESTINATION.

LITERATURE.—Besides the Comms. on the appropriate passages, esp. those on Isaiah, see Dillmann, *Handbuch d. alttest. Theol.*, 249–52; H. Schultz, *Alttest. Theol.*, 417, 421; H. Cremer, *Die christliche Lehre von den Eigenschaften Gottes, Beiträge zur Förderung christl. Theol.*, I, 93–101; Stewart, art. "Foreknowledge," *HDB*, II, 51–53. Considerable Bib. as well as historical material will be found in works on systematic theology, such as Böhl, *Dogmatik*, 54–59; Bavinck, *Gereformeerde Dogmatik*², I, 182–95. For a history of the discussion of the problem of foreknowledge and freedom see J. Müller, *Die christl. Lehre von der Sünde*, III, 2, 2. See also literature under OMNISCIENCE.

On the relation of foreknowledge and foreordination, and the meaning of *prognōsis*, see K. Müller, *Die göttliche Zuvorsehung und Erwählung*, 37 f, 81 f; Pfleiderer, *Paulinismus*², 268 f; *Urchristentum*, 289; Gennrich, *Studien zur Paulinischen Heilsordnung*, *S. K.*, 1898, 377 f; and on the meaning of προγινώσκειν in Rom **8** 29 see esp. pp. 382–95; also Cremer, *Bibl.-theol. Wörterb.*, 263–65; Beyschlag, *Neutest. Theol.*, II, 109; B. Weiss, *Bib. Theol. of NT*, ET, I, 205 f; II, 6; H. Holtzmann, *Lehrbuch d. neutest. Theol.*, II, 165 f; B. B. Warfield, art. "Predestination," *HDB*, IV, 52–57. See also discussions of the meaning of προγινώσκειν in the Comms. on 1 Pet and Rom, esp. Fritzsche on Rom **8** 29, and Johnstone on 1 Pet **1** 2. See also literature under PREDESTINATION.

CASPAR WISTAR HODGE

FOREORDAIN, fōr-ôr-dān′, **FOREORDINATION,** fōr-ôr-di-nā′shun: The word "foreordain" is uniformly used in RV to render the Gr προορίζω, *proörízō*, in the passages where this vb. occurs (Acts **4** 28; Rom **8** 29.30; 1 Cor **2** 7; Eph **1** 5.11). In the passages in Rom and Eph it takes the place of the AV word "predestinate," a return to the usage of the older Eng. VSS. The word has simply the sense of determining beforehand. It is thus kindred in meaning with a number of other NT words expressing the idea of Divine purpose, as "foreknow" (in pregnant sense, Acts **2** 23; Rom **8** 29, etc); "determine" (Acts **17** 26); "appoint" (1 Pet **2** 8). Foreordination, in the widest sense, is coextensive with the sphere of God's universal providence, being but another name for that Divine plan, purpose or counsel which embraces all things, great and small (Mt **10** 29.30), that happen in Nature, or fall out in human life. Man's free actions are not regarded in Scripture as excluded from it (Acts **2** 28). Foreordination, at the same time, is not to be conceived of as in any way overriding, or doing violence to, human freedom. Man acts freely, as Nature acts necessarily, but it is God who appoints the time, place and circumstances of the free act, permits its happening, and overrules it and its issues for the furthering of His own wise and holy ends. See PROVIDENCE. Foreordination in the sphere of grace has respect to the choice, calling and blessing of those who, through faith, are made partakers of eternal life (Rom **8** 29.30; Eph **1** 5.11). In this, its soteriological aspect, the subject is considered in special articles. See CHOOSE; ELECTION; PREDESTINATION. JAMES ORR

FOREPART, fōr′pärt: The tr of פָּנִים, *pānīm*, "face" (Ex **28** 27; **39** 20; 1 K **6** 20, RV "within"; Ezk **42** 7, RV "before"), and of πρῶρα, *prōra*, the forward part of a ship, the prow (Acts **27** 41, "the forepart stuck fast," RV "the foreship struck").

ARV has "its forepart into" for "with his face towards" (Joel **2** 20 m "with its forepart"); "in the forepart thereof" for "before it" (Ex **28** 25; **39** 18).

FORERUNNER, fōr-run′ẽr (πρόδρομος, *pródromos*): This word occurs but once in the Bible: "Whither as a forerunner Jesus entered for us" (He **6** 20). The word signifies one who comes in advance to a place where the rest are to follow, or one who is sent on before as a scout to take observations. In this sense Christ is our forerunner for He has gone into heaven to prepare a place for His people into which He will eventually lead them. The idea of a forerunner is peculiar to the Christian dispensation. The OT Levitical economy knew nothing of such. The high priest was a representative, not a forerunner: where he led, viz. into the Holy of Holies, the people could not follow. He was not the pioneer of the people; Christ is. Christ goes nowhere but where His people may follow. He is the *file-leader* (cf He **12** 2, "the *author* . . . . of faith"). He goeth before His people to prepare the way for them, to open the gates of heaven by His atoning blood and priestly intercession. The believer is led into full fellowship with God through Jesus Christ. See also JOHN THE BAPTIST; RUNNER. WILLIAM EVANS

FORESAIL, fōr′sāl, fōr′s'l (Acts **27** 40). See SHIPS AND BOATS.

FORESHIP, fōr′ship (Acts **27** 30). See FOREPART; SHIPS AND BOATS.

FORESKIN, fōr′skin (עָרְלָה, *'orlāh;* ἀκροβυστία, *akrobustia*, often euphemistically tr[d] "uncircumcision"):

(1) In the **literal** sense the word is frequently mentioned owing to the rite of circumcision in vogue in Israel since the days of Abraham (Gen **17** 9–14) and among several other peoples of antiquity and modern times. The act of circumcision is represented in the temple of Khonsu, a medical deity, at Karnak. Among the Jews of antiquity circumcision had to be performed by means of a flint or stone knife (Ex **4** 25; Josh **5** 2.3) on the eighth day after birth (Gen **17** 12; **21** 4; Lev **12** 3; Lk **2** 21; Phil **3** 5), even if this day was the Sabbath (Jn **7** 23).

Very early we find the practice one of which the descendants of Abraham became proud (Gen **34** 14), so that we see the uncircumcised despised and scorned (1 S **17** 26), and in the time of oppression under King Antiochus Epiphanes many Israelites suffered martyrdom rather than give up the distinctive sign of their people (1 Macc **1** 48.60.61; 2 Macc **6** 10). Among the Arabs and all Mohammedans the custom of circumcision prevails from pre-Islamic times, for it is nowhere ordered in the Koran, and the appellation "uncircumcised" (غلف, *ghalaf*) is considered the greatest possible insult.

A peculiar martial custom is mentioned in 1 S **18** 25.27 (cf 2 S **3** 14), where Saul is represented as asking "a hundred foreskins of the Philis" as a dowry from David for the hand of Michal. This does not seem to have been an exceptional booty in war, esp. if it meant that no very careful operation was expected to be performed, but the act became practically equivalent to extermination. We find in Egyp history at the time of Ramses III, that an invasion into Egypt had been made by several Libyan tribes (see Dümichen, *Histor. Inschr.*, I, plates I–VI, and II, plates 47 ff). The Egyp army sent against the invaders defeated them and returned with a large number of *karnatha* which is a transcription into hieroglyphics of the Sem word, קְרֵנוֹת, *ḳarenōth*, the word being used euphemistically as is proven by the accompanying determinative sign of a phallus. See Chabas, *Études sur l'antiquité historique d'après les sources égyptiennes*, etc, 234; Bondi, *Hebr.-Phoen. Lehnworte im Egyptischen*, Leipzig, 1886, 72–74.

(2) **Metaphorically** the word is used in a variety of ways: (*a*) In the sense of "unlawful," "forbidden as food," "taboo." The fruit of newly planted trees was not to be eaten (Lev **19** 23–25). (*b*) In the sense of "obstinacy," "opposition to God's law." The rite of circumcision meant submission

under the law. While an outward form could not be identical with an inward attitude toward God, the use of the word "circumcision" was soon extended to that of purity and obedience of the heart (Dt **10** 16; **30** 6; and Col **2** 11, where this circumcision is called a "circumcision not made with hands, ... the circumcision of Christ"). The uselessness of outward circumcision, which does not include obedience and purity, is shown by St. Paul (Rom **2** 25; 1 Cor **7** 18; cf Acts **7** 51). (*c*) In the sense of "Gentiles," "non-Israelites" (Gal **2** 7; Eph **2** 11; Col **3** 11). See CIRCUMCISION; CONCISION. H. L. E. LUERING

FOREST, for'est:

(1) חֹרֶשׁ, *ḥōresh* (cf proper name *Harosheth*), 2 Ch **27** 4. In 1 S **23** 15 ff tr[d] "wood"; in Isa **17** 9, "wood"; in Ezk **31** 3, "forest-like shade." Applied to any thick growth of vegetation but not necessarily so extensive as (3).

(2) פַּרְדֵּס, *pardēṣ*: Neh **2** 8, m "park"; Eccl **2** 5, AV "orchards," RV "parks"; Cant **4** 13, EV "orchard," RVm "paradise." A word of Pers origin signifying probably an inclosure. See PARADISE.

(3) יַעַר, *ya'ar*, from root meaning "rugged"; cf Arab. *wa'ar*, "a rugged, stony region." It is sometimes rendered "forest" and sometimes (but less often in RV) "wood." It is used of certain definite wooded tracts: "the forest in Arabia" (Isa **21** 13, m "thickets"); "the forest of Carmel" (2 K **19** 23 AV, RV "of his fruitful field"); "the forest of Hereth" (1 S **22** 5); "the forest of Lebanon" (1 K **7** 2 f; **10** 17–21; 2 Ch **9** 16–20); "the forest of Ephraim," E. of the Jordan (2 S **18** 6.8.17). The word *ya'ar* appears also in well-known Kiriath-jearim, "the city of forests," and Mt. Jearim (Josh **15** 10). Among numerous other references the following may be cited: Dt **19** 5; Josh **17** 15.18; 1 Ch **16** 33; 2 K **2** 24; Ps **80** 13; **83** 14; **96** 12; **132** 6; Eccl **2** 6; Cant **2** 3; 1 S **7** 2; **14** 25.26; Jer **4** 29; **46** 23; Ezk **34** 29; Mic **3** 12; **7** 14.

(4) סְבָךְ, *ṣ^ebhakh*, from root meaning "to interweave." A "thicket" (Gen **22** 13; Jer **4** 7); "thicket of trees" (Ps **74** 5); "thickets of the forest" (Isa **9** 18; **10** 34).

(5) עָבִים, *'ābhīm*, "thicket" (Jer **4** 29).

From many references it is evident that Pal had in OT times much more extensive forests and woodlands than today. For a discussion of the subject see BOTANY. E. W. G. MASTERMAN

FOREST OF EPHRAIM. See EPHRAIM.

FORETELL, fōr-tel', **FORETOLD,** fōr-tōld': The AV occurrences of these words in the NT represent as many Gr terms, and are in each case rendered differently in RV: (1) Mk **13** 23 (προεῖπον, *proeípon*), RV "told beforehand"; (2) Acts **3** 24 (προκαταγγέλλω, *prokataggéllō*), RV simply "told"; (3) 2 Cor **13** 2 (προλέγω, *prolégō*), RV "said beforehand," m "plainly"; cf 1 Thess **3** 4. The foretelling of future events is claimed in the OT as a prerogative of Jeh (Isa **41** 22.23; **42** 9, etc; cf Dt **18** 22). See PROPHECY.

FORFEIT, fôr'fit (חָרַם, *ḥāram*): "Forfeit" (from *forisfacere*, "to act beyond") implies loss through transgression or non-observance of some law or rule. The word occurs only once as the tr of *ḥāram*, "to shut in," frequently to devote or consecrate a person or thing to God beyond redemption (cf Lev **27** 28.29; Mic **4** 13; Ezr **10** 8, "That whosoever came not within three days, ... all his substance should be forfeited, and himself separated from the assembly of the captivity," AVm, ARVm and RV "devoted"; cf 1 Esd **9** 4, "Their cattle should be seized to the use of the temple" [*anieróō*, "to consecrate," "devote"]; **6** 32, "all his goods seized for the king" [*tá hupárchonta autoú eínai (eis) basiliká*]).

RV has "forfeited" (*ḳādhēsh*, "consecrated," "devoted") for "defiled" (Dt **22** 9), m "Heb consecrated"; "forfeit his life" for "lose his own soul" (*psuchḗ*) (Mt **16** 26; Mk **8** 36); "lose or forfeit his own self" for "lose himself or be cast away" (Lk **9** 25, *heautón dé apolésas ḗ zēmiōtheís*; *zēmióō* is the LXX for *'ānash*, "to be mulcted," or "fined," Ex **21** 22; Dt **22** 19; Prov **17** 26 m; **19** 19; **21** 11; **22** 3); Weymouth renders Lk **9** 25, "to have lost or forfeited his own self" (or "had to pay his own self—his own existence—as a fine"); in the other instances of *zēmioō* (1 Cor **3** 15; Phil **3** 8), AV and RV render "suffer loss," "suffered . . . . loss"; 2 Cor **7** 9 AV, "receive damage." W. L. WALKER

FORGE, fōrj, **FORGER,** fōr'jēr (טָפַל, *ṭāphal*): "Forgers of lies" occurs in Job's reply to his comforters (**13** 4; cf **14** 17); the word is the tr of *ṭāphal*, "to patch," "lay on," "besmear," hence to impute, overcharge, etc; in Ps **119** 69, "forged" occurs with a similar meaning: "The proud have forged a lie against me" (cf Sir **51** 2). "Forger," in the sense of "one who forges, makes, anything," is the RV rendering of *lāṭash*, "to smite," or "hammer," in Gen **4** 22 AV: "Tubal-cain, an instructor of every artificer in brass and iron," RV "the forger of every cutting instrument of brass and iron," m "an instructor of every artificer of copper and iron." W. L. WALKER

FORGET, for-get', **FORGETFUL,** for-get'ful (שָׁכַח, *shākhaḥ*; ἐπιλανθάνομαι, *epilanthánomai*): "Forget" is to fail to hold in mind, and the forgetfulness may be either innocent or blameworthy. In the OT the word is most frequently used as tr of *shākhaḥ* in a blameworthy sense: to forget the covenant, the law, Jeh their God (Dt **4** 9.23.31; **6** 12; Jgs **3** 7; 1 S **12** 9; Ps **44** 20, etc). In an innocent or neutral, sometimes good, sense it is used in Gen **27** 45; Dt **24** 19; Job **9** 27; **11** 16; **24** 20; Ps **102** 4, etc. It is also used of God forgetting or not seeming to care (Ps **9** 12; **10** 11.12; **13** 1; **42** 9; **77** 9; Isa **49** 15, etc). To "forget" sometimes means to forsake (Ps **45** 10; **74** 19, etc).

In the NT *epilanthanomai* is used of simple forgetting (Mt **16** 5; Mk **8** 14, etc; in Lk **12** 6 the sense of care is implied); Phil **3** 13, "forgetting the things which are behind," has the force of leaving behind. "Forgetful" in Jas **1** 25 is *epilēsmonḗ*, RV "a hearer that forgetteth." "Forgetfulness" Ps **88** 12, "the land of forgetfulness," is a synonym for Sheol, where all forget and are forgotten. RV has "forget not" for "be ignorant of" (2 Pet **3** 8; similarly ver 5). W. L. WALKER

FORGIVENESS, for-giv'nes (כָּפַר, *kāphar*, נָשָׂא, *nāsā'*, סָלַח, *ṣālaḥ*; ἀπολύειν, *apolúein*, χαρίζεσθαι, *charízesthai*, ἄφεσις, *áphesis*, πάρεσις, *páresis*):

1. Etymology
2. Pagan and Jewish Ideas
3. The Teaching of Christ
4. Conditions of Forgiveness
5. The Offended Party
6. Divine and Human Forgiveness
7. Forgiveness and Justification
8. OT Teaching
9. Limitations of Forgiveness
10. Christ's Power to Forgive Sins
11. The Need of an Atonement
12. The NT Doctrine of Atonement

Of the seven words, three Heb and four Gr, which are used to express the idea of forgiveness, the last two occur in this sense only once each.

1. Etymology

Apoluein (Lk **6** 37) is used because of the analogy of sin to debt, and denotes the release from it. It has the meaning "forgiveness" in 2 Macc **12** 45 also, in which passage the word for sin is expressed. In Rom **3** 25 Paul uses *paresis* instead of the usual *aphesis*. The former means "putting aside," "disregarding," "pretermission"; the latter, "putting away" completely and unreservedly (Trench, *Synonyms of the NT*, § xxxiii). It does not mean forgiveness in the complete sense, and in AV is incorrectly tr[d] "remission." Nor does it mean that God had temporarily suspended punishment which at some later date He might inflict (Sanday on Rom **3** 25). It was apparent that God had treated sins as though He had forgiven them, though in fact such an attitude on the part of God was without such a foundation as was later supplied by an adequate atonement, and so the apostle avoids saying that God forgave them. This passing over of sins had the tendency of destroying man's conception of God's righteousness, and in order to avert this Christ was set forth as a propitiation and God's disregard of sin (*paresis*) became a real forgiveness (*aphesis*); cf Acts **14** 16; **17** 30. *Charizesthai* is not found outside of the writings of Luke and Paul, and in the sense "to forgive sins" is peculiarly Pauline (2 Cor **2** 7; **12** 13; Eph **4** 32; Col **2** 13; **3** 13). It expresses, as no other of these words does, his conception of the graciousness of God's pardon. *Kāphar* (Dt **21** 8; Ps **78** 38; Jer **18** 23) and *ṣālah* (Nu **30** 5.8.12; 1 K **8** 30.34.36.39. 50, etc) are used only of Divine forgiveness, while *nāsā'* is used in this sense (Ex **32** 32; Nu **14** 19; Josh **24** 19; Ps **25** 18; **32** 1.5; **99** 8; Isa **2** 9), and also of human forgiveness (Gen **50** 17; Ex **10** 17; 1 S **25** 28). Remission (Mt **26** 28; Mk **1** 4; Lk **1** 77; **24** 47; Acts **2** 38; **10** 43; He **9** 22; **10** 18) and blotting out (Ps **51** 1.9; Isa **43** 25; Jer **18** 23; Acts **3** 19) are synonyms of forgiveness, and to understand it fully such words as save, justify, reconcile and atonement should also be considered.

2. Pagan and Jewish Ideas

Forgiveness was not a pagan virtue. The large-souled man might disregard offences in cases where he considered them beneath his notice, but to forgive was weak-spirited (F. W. Robertson on 1 Cor **4** 12). Even in the OT, man's forgiveness of his fellow-man is infrequently mentioned. In every case the one asking forgiveness is in a position of subserviency, and is petitioning for that to which he has no just right (Gen **50** 17; Ex **10** 17; 1 S **15** 25; **25** 28). The Imprecatory Psalms attest the fact that forgiveness of enemies was not esteemed as a virtue by Israel. They could appeal to the law which enjoined upon them to seek neither the peace nor the prosperity of their avowed enemies (Dt **23** 6; cf Ezr **9** 12). Jesus gave the popular summing-up of the law and not its exact words when he said, "Ye have heard that it was said . . . . hate thine enemy" (Mt **5** 43), and this certainly does represent their attitude and their understanding of the teaching of the Scriptures.

3. The Teaching of Christ

Christ taught that forgiveness is a duty. No limit can be set to the extent of forgiveness (Lk **17** 4) and it must be granted without reserve. Jesus will not admit that there is any wrong so gross nor so often repeated that it is beyond forgiveness. To Him an unforgiving spirit is one of the most heinous of sins (Bruce, *Parabolic Teaching*, 376 ff). This is the offence which God will not forgive (Mt **18** 34.35). It is the very essence of the unpardonable sin (Mk **3** 22–30). It was the one blemish of the elder son which marred an otherwise irreproachable life (Lk **15** 28–30). This natural, pagan spirit of implacability Jesus sought to displace by a generous, forgiving spirit. It is so far the essence of His teaching that in popular language "a Christian spirit" is not inappropriately understood to be synonymous with a forgiving disposition. His answer to Peter that one should forgive not merely seven times in a day, but seventy times seven (Mt **18** 21.22), not only shows that He thought of no limit to one's forgiveness, but that the principle could not be reduced to a definite formula.

4. Conditions of Forgiveness

Jesus recognized that there are conditions to be fulfilled before forgiveness can be granted. Forgiveness is part of a mutual relationship; the other part is the repentance of the offender. God does not forgive without repentance, nor is it required of man. The effect of forgiveness is to restore to its former state the relationship which was broken by sin. Such a restoration requires the coöperation of both parties. There must be both a granting and an acceptance of the forgiveness. Sincere, deep-felt sorrow for the wrong which works repentance (2 Cor **7** 10) is the condition of mind which insures the acceptance of the forgiveness. Hence Jesus commands forgiveness when the offender turns again, saying, "I repent" (Lk **17** 3.4). It was this state of mind which led the father joyfully to welcome the Prodigal before he even gave utterance to his newly formed purpose (**15** 21).

5. The Offended Party

It is not to be supposed, however, that failure to repent upon the part of the offender releases the offended from all obligation to extend forgiveness. Without the repentance of the one who has wronged him he can have a forgiving state of mind. This Jesus requires, as is implied by, "if ye forgive not every one his brother from your hearts" (Mt **18** 35). It is also implied by the past tense in the Lord's Prayer: "as we also have forgiven our debtors" (**6** 12). It is this forgiving spirit which conditions God's forgiveness of our sins (Mk **11** 25; Mt **6** 14.15). In such a case the unforgiving spirit is essentially unrepentance (Mt **18** 23–35). "Of all acts, is not, for a man, repentance the most Divine?"

The offended is to go even farther and is to seek to bring the wrongdoer to repentance. This is the purpose of the rebuking commanded in Lk **17** 3. More explicitly Jesus says, "If thy brother sin against thee, go, show him his fault between thee and him alone" (Mt **18** 15–17). He is to carry his pursuit to the point of making every reasonable effort to win the wrongdoer, and only when he has exhausted every effort may he abandon it. The object is the gaining of his brother. Only when this is evidently unattainable is all effort to cease.

The power of binding and loosing, which means forbidding and allowing, was granted to Peter (**16** 19) and to the Christian community (**18** 18; Jn **20** 23). It clearly implies the possession of the power to forgive sins. In the case of Peter's power it was exercised when he used the keys of the kingdom of heaven (Mt **16** 19). This consisted in the proclamation of the gospel and esp. of the conditions upon which men might enter into relationship with God (Acts **2** 38; **10** 34 ff). It was not limited to Peter only, but was shared by the other apostles (Mt **16** 19; **18** 18). Christ left no fixed rules the observance or non-observance of which would determine whether one is or is not in the kingdom of God. He gave to His disciples principles, and in the application of these principles to the problems of life there had to be the exercise of discriminating judgment. The exercise of this judgment was left to the Christian community (2 Cor **2** 10). It is limited by the principles which are the basis of the kingdom, but within these principles the voice of the community is supreme. The forgiveness here implied is not the pronouncing of absolution for the sins of individuals, but the determination of courses of conduct and worship which will be acceptable. In doing this its decisions will be ratified in heaven (Westcott on Jn **20** 23).

That there is a close analogy between human and Divine forgiveness is clearly implied (Mt **5** 23.24; **6** 12; Mk **11** 25; Lk **6** 37; Col **1** 14; **3** 13). God's forgiveness is conditional upon man's forgiveness of the wrongs done him, not because God forgives grudgingly but because forgiveness alone indicates that disposition of mind which will humbly accept the Divine pardon. Repentance is a necessary ingredient of the fully developed forgiveness. There is no essential difference between the human and the Divine pardon, though the latter is necessarily more complete. It results in the complete removal of all estrangement and alienation between God and man. It restores completely the relationship which existed prior to the sin. The total removal of the sin as a result of the Divine forgiveness is variously expressed in the Scriptures: "Thou hast cast all my sins behind thy back" (Isa **38** 17); "Thou wilt cast all their sins into the depths of the sea" (Mic **7** 19); "I will forgive their iniquity, and their sin will I remember no more" (Jer **31** 34); "I, even I, am he that blotteth out thy transgressions" (Isa **43** 25); "As far as the east is from the west, so far hath he removed our transgressions from us" (Ps **103** 12). Ideally this same result is attained in human forgiveness, but actually the memory of the sin remains with both parties as a barrier between them, and even when there is a complete restoration of amity the former state of alienation cannot entirely be removed from memory. When God forgives, however, He restores man to the condition of former favor. Release from punishment is involved, though Divine forgiveness is more than this. In most cases the consequences, which in some instances are spoken of as punishment, are not removed, but they lose all penal character and become disciplinary. Nor does the forgiveness remove from human mind the consciousness of sin and the guilt which that involved, but it does remove the mistrust which was the ground of the alienation. Mistrust is changed into trust, and this produces peace of mind (Ps **32** 5–7; Rom **5** 1); consciousness of the Divine love and mercy (Ps **103** 2 ff); removes fear of punishment (2 S **12** 13); and awakens love to God.

6. Divine and Human Forgiveness

Paul rarely uses the term "forgiveness," but in its place prefers justification. They are to his understanding practically synonymous (Stevens, *Theology of the NT*, 418). He preferred the latter, however, because it was better fitted to express the idea of secure, present and permanent acceptance in the sight of God. It connoted both a complete and a permanent state of grace. In popular thought forgiveness is not so comprehensive, but in the Bib. sense it means no less than this. It removes all of the guilt and cause of alienation from the past; it assures a state of grace for the present; and promises Divine mercy and aid for the future. Its fulness cannot adequately be conveyed by any one term or formula.

7. Forgiveness and Justification

Divine, like human, forgiveness is always contingent upon the fulfilment of conditions. It must be preceded by repentance and a firmly fixed intention not to repeat the offence. In addition to this, one was required to conform to certain legal or formal acts before the assurance of pardon was his. These acts were expressive of the sinner's state of mind. They consisted of certain acts of sacrifice in the pre-Christian times and of baptism during the ministry of John the Baptist (Mk **1** 4; Lk **3** 3) and under Christ (Acts **2** 38; **22** 16). These acts are never regarded as in any sense a *quid pro quo* in return for which the benefit of forgiveness is granted. It is an act of pure grace on God's part, and these acts are required as expressions of the man's attitude toward God. The state of mind required in order to obtain the gift of forgiveness is that to which the Prodigal Son came (Lk **15** 17–19), and that of the sinner who went to his house justified rather than the Pharisee (**18** 9–14), because he realized that forgiveness was to him an act of pure favor.

There was real and actual forgiveness of sins in the OT times as well as since Christ. Certain passages have been construed to teach that the Law provided only for a passing over or rolling back of sins, and that there was not then an actual forgiveness. The sacrifices prescribed by the Law were not adequate atonements, so that there was constant necessity of yearly remembrance of sin (He **10** 3; cf Lev **16** 21). The atonement of Christ is, however, of permanent adequacy, and became retroactive in the sense that it unified in Christ the Divine arrangement for saving mankind in all ages (He **11** 40). "The passing over of the sins done aforetime" (Rom **3** 25) does not imply a partial or apparent forgiveness, but means that they were forgiven, though seemingly without adequate recognition on the part of God of their heinous character. In view of God's righteous character men might naturally have expected punishment, but instead the offenders were spared (cf Acts **14** 16; **17** 30). No expression in the OT suggests any inadequacy of the forgiveness extended to Israel, but on the other hand many passages may be quoted to show how rich and full it was deemed to be (Pss **32, 103;** Mic **7** 19; Isa **38** 17, Jer **31** 34).

8. OT Teaching

Two passages seem to limit God's forgiveness. They are Christ's discussion of the unpardonable sin (Mt **12** 31.32; Mk **3** 28–30; Lk **12** 10), and the one which mentions the sin unto death (1 Jn **5** 16; cf He **6** 4–6). In the former passage there is mentioned a sin which has no forgiveness, and in the latter, one on behalf of which the apostle cannot enjoin prayer that it be forgiven, though he does not prohibit it. In both cases the sin is excluded from the customary forgiveness which is extended to sins of all other classes.

9. Limitations of Forgiveness

The act of the Pharisees which led Jesus to speak of the unpardonable sin was the attributing of a good deed wrought by Him through the Spirit of God (Mt **12** 28) to Beelzebub. No one could do such a thing unless his moral nature was completely warped. To such a person the fundamental distinctions between good and evil were obliterated. No ordinary appeal could reach him, for to him good seemed evil and evil seemed good. The possibility of winning him back is practically gone; hence he is beyond the hope of forgiveness, not because God has set an arbitrary line of sinfulness, beyond which His grace of forgiveness will not reach, but because the man has put himself beyond the possibility of attaining to that state of mind which is the essential condition of Divine forgiveness. It is practically certain that John did not have any particular sinful act in mind when he spoke of the sin which is unto death. See BLASPHEMY.

There is no possible way of determining what specific sin, if any, he refers to. Probably the same principle applies in this case as in that of the unpardonable sin. God's forgiveness is limited solely by the condition that man must accept it in the proper spirit.

There are some passages which seem to imply that forgiveness was the principal Messianic task. This is suggested by the name given to the Messiah during His earthly career (Mt **1** 21), and by the fact that He was the Saviour. The remission of sins was the preparation for the advent of the Messiah (Lk **1** 77), and repentance and remission of sins were the prerequisites to a state of preparation for the kingdom.

It is not surprising, therefore, that we find Jesus laying claim to the power to forgive sins. This provoked a bitter controversy with the Jews, for it was axiomatic with them that no one could forgive sins but God only (Mk **2** 7; Lk **5** 21; **7** 49). This Jesus did not question, but He would have them infer from His power to forgive sins that He was the possessor of Divine power. Jesus asserted His possession of this power on two occasions only, though it has been insufficiently inferred from Jn **5** 14; **8** 11 that He was accustomed to pronounce absolution upon all of those He healed. On one of these occasions He not merely asserted that He possessed the power, but

10. Christ's Power to Forgive Sins

demonstrated it by showing Himself to be the possessor of the Divine gift of healing. The impostor might claim some such intangible power as the authority to forgive sins, but he would never assert the possession of such easily disproved power as the ability to heal the sick. But Jesus claimed both, and based His claim to be the possessor of the former on the demonstration that He possessed the latter. God would not support an impostor, hence his aid in healing the paralytic proved that Jesus could forgive sins. The multitude accepted this logic and "glorified God, who had given such authority unto men" (Mt **9** 2–9; cf Mk **2** 3–12; Lk **5** 18–26).

On the other occasion when His possession of this power was under discussion (Lk **7** 36–50), He offered no other proof than the forgiven woman's deep gratitude and love. One expression that He uses, however, has raised some discussion as to the relative order in time of her love and forgiveness (ver 47). Did she love because she was forgiven, or vice versa? Manifestly the forgiveness precedes the love, in spite of the fact that ver 47 seems to assert the opposite, for this is the bearing of the parable of the Two Debtors (vs 41–43), and the latter part of ver 47 has the same implication. It is clear that she had previously repented and had been accepted, and the anointing of Jesus was an outpouring of her gratitude. The phrase of ver 47, "for she *loved much*," is proof of the greatness of her sin rather than a reason why she was forgiven. In both cases where Jesus forgave sins, He did so because the state of mind of the person forgiven showed worthiness of the blessing. To this as a condition of forgiveness there is no exception. Christ's prayer on the cross (Lk **23** 34) would not avail to secure the pardon of His murderers without their repentance.

11. The Need of an Atonement

Though forgiveness is on God's part an act of pure grace prompted by His love and mercy, and though He forgives freely all those who comply with the condition of repentance and abandonment of sin, yet this does not dispense with the necessity of an atonement. The parable of the Prodigal Son was spoken to teach the freedom of God's forgiveness and acceptance of returning sinners, and the duty of men to assume the same attitude toward them. This much it teaches, but it fails to set forth entirely God's attitude toward sin. With reference to the sinner God is love and mercy, but with reference to sin He is righteous, and this element of God's nature is no less essential to Him than His love, and must be considered in any effort to set forth completely the doctrine of God's forgiveness of sinners. The atonement of Christ and the many atonements of the Law were manifestations of this phase of God's nature.

12. The NT Doctrine of Atonement

The idea of an atonement is fundamental in the teachings of the NT (Rom **5** 10; 2 Cor **5** 18–21; Col **1** 21). It is very clearly implied in such terms as reconciliation and propitiation, and is no less present in pardon, remission and forgiveness. The doctrine of the atonement is not developed by Jesus, but it is strongly hinted at and is unmistakably implied in the language of Mt **20** 28; **26** 28; Mk **10** 45; Lk **24** 46.47. John the Baptist's salute, "Behold, the Lamb of God, that taketh away the sin of the world!" (Jn **1** 29), also implies it. In the writings of the apostles it is repeatedly and clearly affirmed that our forgiveness and reconciliation to God is based upon the death of Christ. "In none other is there salvation" (Acts **4** 12); through Him is the redemption (Rom **3** 24); God set Him forth to be a propitiation (ver 25); through Him "we have now received the reconciliation" (**5** 11); "God was in Christ reconciling the world unto himself" (2 Cor **5** 19); "Him who knew no sin he made to be sin on our behalf" (ver 21); and "Christ redeemed us from the curse of the law, having become a curse for us" (Gal **3** 13). Such citations might be greatly multiplied. That which was so perfectly accomplished by the offering of Christ was in an analagous though imperfect way accomplished by the sacrifices required by the Law. It had "a shadow of the good things to come" (He **10** 1).

The unvarying effect of sin is to produce an estrangement between the injurer and the wronged. The nature of God is such and the relationship between Him and man is of such a character that sin brings about an alienation between them. It is this presupposition of an estrangement between them which renders the atonement necessary before forgiveness can be extended to man. This estrangement must be removed, and the alienation be transformed into a reconciliation. In what then does the alienation consist?

The sin of man produces a changed attitude toward each other on the part of both God and man. God holds no personal pique against man because of his sin. The NT language is very carefully chosen to avoid any statement which would seem to convey such a conception. Yet God's holy righteousness is such that He cannot be indifferent to sin. His wrath must rest upon the disobedient (Jn **3** 36; Rom **1** 18). It is not merely impersonal. It is not enough to say He hates the sin. Man's unrighteousness has not merely alienated him from God, but God also from him. The word "enemies" (*echthroí*) of Rom **5** 10 is passive, and means the object of God's enmity (Sanday, ad loc.). It was because of this fact that God set forth Christ to be a propitiation to show His righteousness because of the passing over of sins done aforetime (**3** 25.26). God's passing over, without inflicting punishment, the sins of pre-Christian times had placed in jeopardy His righteousness; had exposed Him to the implication that He could tolerate sin. God could not be true to Himself while He tolerated such an imputation, and so instead of visiting punishment upon all who sinned—which would have been one way of showing His righteousness—He set forth Christ to death ("in his blood"), and in this way placed Himself beyond the imputation of unrighteousness while it enabled Him to show mercy to sinners. The effect of sin upon man was to estrange him from God, to lead him farther and farther away from his Maker. Each successive sin produced a greater barrier between the two. Now the atonement was designed to remove the cause of this estrangement and restore the former relationship between God and man. This too, it has been observed, is the purpose of forgiveness, so that the atonement finds its completion in forgiveness. It should be noted that the reconciliation originates with God and not with man (Rom **3** 25; 2 Cor **5** 19). God woos man before the latter seeks God. The effect of the atonement on man is to reconcile him, attract him, to God. It shows him God's love for man, and the forgiveness, in that it removes sin completely, takes away the estranging factor between them and so wins man back to God. "We love, because he first loved us." At the same time the atonement is such a complete expression of both the love and the righteousness of God that, while on the one hand it exhibits his yearning for man, on the other it shows that He is not tolerant toward sin. In the atonement of Christ, therefore, is the meeting-place and the reconcilement of God's holy horror of sin and the free bestowal of forgiveness upon penitent believers.

Wm. Chas. Morro

FORGO, for-gō′ (from *for*, negative, and *go*): Occurs in Ecclus **7** 19, as tr of ἀστοχέω, *astochéō*, which means "to miss the mark," "turn or swerve from." "Forgo not a wise and good wife [AV "woman"]; for her grace is above gold," meaning "Turn not away from her"; in **8** 9, the word is rendered "miss not"; cf 1 Tim **1** 6; **6** 21; 2 Tim **2** 18.

FORK, fôrk (שְׁלֹשׁ קִלְּשׁוֹן, *shelōsh ḳillešhōn*): This compound word, meaning strictly "three points" or "three prongs," is found only once (1 S **13** 21), and doubtless there refers to the agricultural tool now known as the pitchfork. It might, however, also be a weapon.

FORM, fôrm (יָצַר, *yāçar*, תֹּאַר, *tō'ar*; **μορφή**, *morphḗ*):

(1) To *form* is "to fashion," "create," "produce." In the OT it is for the most part the tr of *yāçar*, "to form," "to fashion" (Gen **2** 7, etc, "Jeh God formed man of the dust of the ground," etc); also of *ḥūl* and *ḥīl*, "to be twisted," "turned round," "to bring forth [in pain]" (cf Isa **13** 8; Mic **4** 10; Dt **32** 18 AV, "God that formed thee"; Job **26** 13 AV; Ps **90** 2, "or ever thou hadst formed the earth," etc; Prov **26** 10 AV). In the NT we have *morphóō*, "to form" (Gal **4** 19, "until Christ be formed in you"); *plássō*, "to form," "to mold" (Rom **9** 20, "him that formed it"; **1** Tim **2** 13, "Adam was first formed"; 2 Macc **7** 23, "the Creator . . . . who formed the generation of man," RV "fashioned"; ver 22, "that formed the members [*diarrhuthmízō*]," RV "brought into order").

(2) *Form* (noun) is used for (*a*) appearance, *mar'eh*, "sight," "appearance" (Job **4** 16, "I could not discern the form thereof," RV "appearance," with "form" for "image" [*temūnāh*] in next sentence); *çelem*, Aram. "image" (Dnl **3** 19, "The form of his visage was changed"); *rēw*, "form," "likeness" (**2** 31; **3** 25, RV "aspect"); *tō'ar*, "visage," "form" (1 S **28** 14, "What form is he of?"); (*b*) the fixed or characteristic form of anything, *tabhnīth*, "model," "form" (Ezk **8** 3; **10** 8, "the form of a hand"; **8** 10, "every form of creeping things"); *morphḗ*, characteristic form as distinguished from *schēma*, changing fashion (Phil **2** 6, "in the form of God"; ver 7, "the form of a servant"; less distinctly, Mk **16** 12, "in another form"); (*c*) shape, model, pattern, mold, *çūrāh*, "shape," from *çūr*, "to cut or carve" (Ezk **43** 11, *ter*, "the form of the house," etc); *mishpāṭ*, "rule" (2 Ch **4** 7 AV); *túpos*, "type," "impress" (Rom **6** 17, RVm "pattern"); *hupotúpōsis*, "outline," pattern (2 Tim **1** 13, RV "pattern"); *mórphōsis*, "form," "appearance" (Rom **2** 20, "the form of knowledge"); (*d*) orderly arrangement, giving shape or form (Gen **1** 2; Jer **4** 23, the earth was "without form," *tōhū*, RV "waste"; Wisd **11** 17, *ámorphos*); "form of speech" (2 S **14** 20, aspect, *pānīm*, "face," RV "to change the face of the matter"); as giving comeliness or beauty, *tō'ar* (Isa **52** 14; **53** 2, "He hath no form nor comeliness"; cf Gen **29** 17; **39** 6, etc; Wisd **15** 5, "desiring the form [*eídos*] of a dead image," RV "the breathless form"); (*e*) Show, without substance, *morphōsis*, "form" (2 Tim **3** 5, "holding a form of godliness").

ARV has "didst form" for "hast possessed" (Ps **139** 13, so ERVm; both have "formed" for "made" (Ps **104** 26), ARV for "framed" *bis* (Isa **29** 16); both for "formed thee," "gave birth" (Dt **32** 18); "pierced" (Job **26** 13); "woundeth" (Prov **26** 10); "fashioned" (Isa **44** 10); for "are formed from" (Job **26** 5), "tremble"; for "their form" (2 Ch **4** 7), "the ordinance concerning them"; "form" for "similitude" (Nu **12** 8; Dt **4** 12.15); for "size" (1 K **6** 25; **7** 37); for "shape" (Lk **3** 22; Jn **5** 37); "in the form" for "similitude" (Dt **4** 16); for "or the like" (**4** 23.25); ARV "[beholding] thy form" for "thy likeness" (Ps **17** 15, ERVm); "every form" for "all appearance" (1 Thess **5** 22; so ERVm "appearance").

W. L. WALKER

FORMER, fôr′mẽr: The word in the sense of "maker," "framer," occurs only in Jer **51** 19, "He is the former [from *yāçar*, "to form"] of all things." The adj., in the sense of preceding in the order of time, is commonly in Heb the tr of *rī'shōn*, "first," "foremost" (Gen **40** 13; Nu **21** 26; Dt **24** 4, etc); in Gr of *próteros* (Eph **4** 22; He **10** 32; 1 Pet **1** 14); and in two cases (Acts **1** 1; Rev **21** 4) of *prōtos*, where RV has (in Acts in m) "the first." As denoting place or position the word occurs in the OT in Zec **14** 8, "the former sea" as tr of *ḳadhmōnī*, "in front," where RV has "eastern," i.e. the Dead Sea, in contrast with the Mediterranean, or western sea (cf Ezk **47** 18; Joel **2** 20). For "former iniquities" (Ps **79** 8) RV has simply "the iniquities"; other changes may be seen in Nu **6** 12; Isa **65** 7; Ezk **36** 11; Mic **4** 8; Hag **2** 3.

W. L. WALKER

FORNICATION, fôr-ni-kā′shun. See CRIMES.

FORSWEAR, for-swâr′. See CRIMES.

FORTH, fōrth: "Forth," advb. (from "for"), signifies movement (1) forward, (2) out of, (3) beyond a certain boundary. In a few instances in the OT it is the tr of the prep. *'al*, properly "above," "upon" (2 K **11** 15; 2 Ch **23** 14; Am **7** 17 AV), and of *ḥūç*, "without" (Gen **39** 13; Jgs **19** 25). "Forth" is often used as an expletive of various vbs., as "break [forth]," "bring [forth]," "call [forth]," etc. In the Gospel of Jn it is the tr of *éxō*, "without," as "Lazarus, come forth" (**11** 43; so **15** 6; **19** 4 AV, etc; also Acts **5** 34; **9** 40). "Stand forth" in Mk **3** 3 is the tr of *égeire eis tó méson*, m "Arise into the midst." RV has a great many changes, frequently substituting "out," "away," "abroad," etc; "forth from" for "out of" (Job **41** 21; Isa **45** 23); "spread forth" for "stretched out" (Ps **44** 20; **88** 9; **136** 6), etc. In Col **1** 6, for "bringeth forth fruit" RV reads "bearing fruit."

W. L. WALKER

FORTIFICATION, for-ti-fi-kā′shun (including **FORT, FORTIFIED [FENCED] CITIES, FORTRESS**):

Has a number of words representing its various elements and aspects:

(1) מִבְצָר, *mibhçār*, is the term generally rendered "fenced" or "defenced city." In both AV and RV of Isa and Jer we find for the most part the more formal "defenced city." It is found by itself (Isa **17** 3); with *'īr*, "city" (1 S **6** 18; 2 K **3** 19; pl. *'ārē mibhçār*, "fenced [ARV "fortified"] cities," Nu **32** 17); with צֹר, *çōr*, "Tyre" (Josh **19** 29; 2 S **24** 7, where it is rendered "stronghold"). (2) מִשְׂגָּב, *misgābh*, "high fort" (Isa **25** 12; Jer **48** 1 RVm; Ps **9** 9, and many other places in the Pss). (3) מָעוֹז, *mā'ōz*, "fortress," "stronghold" (Jgs **6** 26; Ps **31** 2; Dnl **11** 39). (4) מְצוּדָה, *meçūdhāh*, "fort" AV, "stronghold" RV (2 S **5** 9.17). (5) מְצוּרָה, *meçūrāh*, "fort" (Isa **29** 3 AV; pl. RV "siege works"). (6) מֻצָּב, *muççābh* (Isa **29** 3, "fort" ERV, "mount" AV, "posted troops" ARV). (7) דָּיֵק, *dāyēḳ*, "fort" (for the siege of a city, the wall of circumvallation cast up by the besiegers, 2 K **25** 1; Jer **52** 4; Ezk **4** 2, **17** 17; **21** 22; **26** 8). (8) מָצוֹר, *māçōr*, "fortress" (Jer **10** 17 m, wall of circumvallation; Hab **2** 1, "tower"

AV, "fortress" RVm; Zec **9** 3). (9) בִּירָה, *bīrāh*, "palace" AV, "castle" RV (Neh **2** 8; **7** 2). *Bīrāh* Grecized is βᾶρις, *báris*, which has the double meaning of "palace" and "fortress." Nehemiah's "castle" figures largely in the books of Maccabees and in Jos, and is the Castle of Antonia of the Acts of the Apostles. (10) ὀχύρωμα, *ochúrōma* (2 Cor **10** 4, its only occurrence in the NT though it is the chief equivalent of *mibhçār* in LXX). In this connection it is to be noted that חוֹמָה, *ḥōmāh*, is Heb for "wall," Gr τεῖχος, *teíchos;* חֵל or חֵיל, *ḥēl*, is Heb for the "ditch," or "rampart," or "bastion" of a fortress; מִגְדָּל, *mighdāl*, "tower"; פִּנָּה, pl. פִּנּוֹת, *pinnāh*, *pinnōth*, "corner towers."

Fortified Places

From the very beginning of their history as a nation the Israelites were acquainted with fortified cities. The report of cities "great and fortified up to heaven," inhabited by the sons of Anak, by Amalekites, Hittites, Jebusites, Amorites and Canaanites, struck terror into the hearts of the Israelites in the wilderness, and called forth murmurings from them on their way to Canaan (Nu **13** 28 ff; Dt **1** 28). Not that these cities were at all of the extent or population of modern cities, or of Nineveh, Babylon and Memphis of old. But to a people who were as yet little better than a horde of fugitives accustomed to the simple camp life of the wilderness and unacquainted with appliances for siege and assault, the prospect of scaling the walls and conquering the inhabitants was appalling. The cities of the Canaanites were already old when Joshua led the Israelites to the conquest of the land. Not a little of their history has become known to us, and the character of their defensive works has been disclosed by Palestinian excavation in recent years.

I. In Recent Excavations.—

1. Excavation of Tells

It has been largely to the *tells*, or mounds of buried cities, chiefly in the southwest of the land, that exploration has been directed. The Palestine Exploration Fund, drawing its resources from Great Britain and also from America, was the first, and has all along been the foremost, in the work of excavation. Through the labors of Professor Flinders Petrie at Tell el-Hesy; of Dr. F. J. Bliss, and Professor Stewart Macalister at Tell Zakarîyah, Tell eṣ-Ṣafi, Tell ej-Judeideh, Tell Sandahannah, and more recently of Professor Macalister at Gezer, the Fund has added largely to our knowledge of the fenced cities of Canaan. The work of Sir Charles Warren, Sir Charles W. Wilson, Colonel Conder and other explorers at Jerus under the same auspices has been of great value for illustrating the defensive works of a later time. Germany and Austria have not been behind. The excavation, first, of Tell Ta'anek in the Plain of Esdraelon, and, at the present time (1911), of Jericho by Professor E. Sellin, formerly of Vienna, now of Rostock; and of Tell el-Mutesellim, the ancient Megiddo, by Gottlieb Schumacher, has yielded results of the highest importance. Since 1908 an American expedition from Harvard University, first under Schumacher and now under Dr. Reisner, who had previously excavated at the Pyramids and other places in Egypt, has explored with remarkable results the site of the capital of the Northern Kingdom, Samaria. Excavations have also been conducted by the German Orient Committee at Sinjerli which have thrown a flood of light upon the archaeology of Northern Syria and esp. upon the wonderful Hittite people. The memoirs and reports of these excavations have furnished abundance of material for tracing the evolution and understanding the anatomy of the *tell*. They usefully supplement the Scripture narratives, and confirm them in many particulars.

2. Sites

These cities of the primitive inhabitants of Canaan occupied sites easily capable of defence. They were built either upon a projecting spur of a mountain ridge, like Gezer, Megiddo, Tell eṣ-Ṣafi (believed to be the ancient Gath) and primitive Jerus, or upon an isolated eminence in the plain like Tell el-Hesy (Lachish) or Taanach. Compared with modern cities the area was small—in the case of Gezer about a quarter of a mile square, Lachish 15 acres, Megiddo and Taanach 12 to 13 acres. A sufficient water supply within easy reach was an essential feature. Speaking of Gezer, Professor Macalister says: "Water, the first necessity of life, was in abundance. The three primitive modes of livelihood—hunting, pasturing, and agriculture—could be practised here better than in many places. Further, for defence—another prime necessity in early days—the hill is admirably fitted. It is steep and not easy to climb; and being fairly high it commands a wide prospect, so that the approach of enemies can be seen and prepared for" (*Bible Side-Lights from Gezer*, 25,26).

3. Primitive Character

Their history goes back in most cases to a very remote antiquity. "It cannot have been much later than 3000 BC," says Professor Macalister regarding Gezer, "when a primitive race of men first realized that the bare rocky hill (as it then was) would be a suitable dwelling-place. This tribe was a cave-dwelling race" (as above; and *PEFS*, 1904, 311 ff). The primitive race had occupied the hill perhaps five hundred years when the Canaanites drove them out, as they in turn were driven out by the Israelites. But the nature of their original habitations, the earliest relics of their social life, and what can be gathered of their religious rites all bear witness to a remote antiquity. From the mound of Tell el-Hesy, now almost certainly identified with the site of Lachish, eleven cities, one above the other have been disinterred, the eleventh or highest having nine cities between itself and the first Amorite buildings reared upon the original bluff. This lowest city is believed to go back some 2000 years BC, Professor Flinders Petrie having dated the successive cities by means of the pottery found in the strata of the mound. One of the eleven cities, possibly the fourth from the bottom, was that of Lachish, which fell a prey to Joshua (Josh **10** 32), the walls of which, built of crude brick and 10–12 ft. in thickness, are a witness to its character as a fenced city (Bliss, *A Mound of Many Cities*, ch iv).

4. Walls

While the site of the Can. city was chosen for its natural strength, the first settlers soon felt the need of some fortification. At Sinjerli the excavators have been able to trace the general growth of the site from a group of shepherds' huts into a walled town. The earliest fortification attempted was a rampart of earth following the natural contour of the hill (*PEFS*, 1903, 113). Within some such inclosing wall, houses were built and the inhabitants lived and pursued their avocations safely. The primitive earthbank in the case of Gezer was in course of time replaced first by an inner and then by an outer wall in succession. The outer wall when it was added to strengthen the inner was the *ḥēl*, rendered in the Eng. version "bulwark" (Isa **26** 1) or "rampart" (Nah **3** 8, where the waters of the Nile served the same purpose). Professor Macalister estimates that the inner wall of Gezer had fallen into disuse and ruin by about 1450 BC and that it was the outer that saw the conquest of Canaan by the Israelites. "Even in its present ruined form," says Professor Macalister, "the outer city wall is an imposing structure. In places it still stands to a height of from 10 to 14 ft., and these can hardly be regarded as being much more than the underground foundations. The outer face of the city wall, towering above the hill on which the city was built, may well have seemed impregnable to the messengers of Moses" (*Bible Side-Lights*, 142). The walls of a later time, as we learn from Assyr representations, were provided with battlements, very often crenellated, and "thy pinnacles of rubies" (Isa **54** 12, RV, RVm "windows") may refer to them. For the purpose of strengthening the walls, esp. at the least defensible points, revetments or facings of stone or kiln-burnt bricks were sometimes added. Even these again would be rendered less assailable by a trench (*ḥēl*) serving to cut off a fortress from adjacent level or sloping ground, as may still be seen outside the N. wall of Jerus, and many parts of the walls of Constantinople.

5. Towers

Towers were sometimes built at the corners or at points on the wall where attack was to be apprehended (Zeph **1** 16; 2 Ch **14** 7). Such towers have been disclosed on the crest of the hill at Tell Zakarîyah. At Gezer 30 towers were found round the outer wall. On the walls of Sinjerli there rose no fewer than 800 towers (Garstang, *Land of the Hittites*, 273). On the evidence of the excavations at this ancient Hittite site we gather that the cities about the time of the entrance of the Israelites into Canaan "were already surrounded by masoned walls, supported by numerous external towers, and entered through gateways barred by a pair of double doors and guarded by wing towers on either hand" (*Land of the Hittites,* 367). For illustrations, see CITY.

Boghaz-keui: the Hittite Fortress Called Yenige Kaleh.

6. Acropolis or Castle

Every one of these ancient cities had an inner fortress which would be an internal means of protection, and the last refuge of the defenders in extremity. At Tell Zakarîyah the acropolis wall has been traced, and its shape has been found to be conditioned by the contours of the hill on which it stood. In an old Hittite settlement a fortress has been found rectangular in shape and supported by an outer and lower wall at a distance of 12 to 30 yds. (*Land of the Hittites,* 162). There is evidence that the mound or bluff originally occupied remained the fortress or acropolis of the city when it spread out over a larger area, and this seems to have been the case for some time at least with the Jebusite fort taken by David and made the capital of the kingdom. At Sinjerli, while there was a wall surrounding the whole township, there was an outer as well as an inner defensive wall to the citadel. Upon this citadel were found palaces from which the Assyr king, Tiglath-pileser I, copied the plan of a Hittite palace, called in Assyr *Hilani.*

7. Masonry

The excavations enable us to see the progress of the art of fortification from very primitive beginnings. Crude brick and rough stonework were the materials of the earliest walls. They are usually found of uncoursed masonry in which the large stones are undressed field bowlders. The facings of stone and the joints in walls were often packed with pebbles or with limestone chippings, the stones themselves being more or less roughly trimmed and dressed to shape by a hammer. Corner-stones are found in the towers showing marks of the chisel, but it is not till well on in the Heb period that stones are found with bosses and marginal drafting. At Zakarîyah the walls of the acropolis were of rubble laid in mud, mixed with straw without lime, and they contained some well-worked stones, irregularly intermingled with field stones of various sizes. At a later time mortar was used to cover the walls and give greater strength and support. But the clay used for the purpose was apt to crack unless it was given consistency by treading with the feet and mixing with water. Thus we read of a wall daubed with untempered mortar (Ezk **13** 10–16; **22** 28; cf Nah **3** 14). In the masonry of the Can. period there is no appearance of the use of mortar. In the Hittite fortress (see [6] above) the masonry of the inner wall is rough, dry stonewalling, while the outer is built of stones roughly pentagonal in shape, irregular in size, fitted to one another and laid without mortar, somewhat like the Cyclopean walls of the earliest periods of Gr history. See GEZER.

8. Gates

The gates of the fenced cities of Canaan may not have had the social importance which the city gate came to possess in later times, but they were an important element in the defensive works of a city. They were as few as possible, so as to give only the necessary ingress and egress. The gate of Jericho was shut and secured at nightfall (Josh **2** 5). The gate of Gaza had two leaves which were not hinged to the two gate-posts, but turned on pins moving in sockets in the sill and lintel, the bar stretching between the two posts and let into them to secure the gate (Jgs **16** 3, with Moore's notes). The hundred gates of Babylon, according to Herodotus, were all of brass (i.179); and Jeh promises to Cyrus to break in pieces the doors of brass and to cut in sunder the bars of iron (Isa **45** 2). That the bars were sometimes of wood is clear from what is said of the bars of Nineveh (Nah **3** 13). To protect the gate it was supplied with towers. Uzziah built towers in Jerus at the corner gate and at the valley gate, and fortified them (2 Ch **26** 9). In the inner wall of Gezer, to which reference has been made, a gate of very remarkable structure has been found. The wall is of stone, but the gateway consists of a passage between two solid towers of brick. The passage is 9 ft. wide and 42 ft. long, roughly paved with stones. Stone slabs on each side of the passageway bear traces of fire, and the absence of any wooden barrier may be due to a conflagration at the capture of the city. The towers remain standing and rise to a total height of about 16 ft. In later times watchmen were set on the tower over the the gate to descry the approach of friend or foe or messenger (2 S **18** 24 ff), and the tower had chambers in it which might be occupied by visitors or by a guard. For the more general purposes see GATE.

9. Water Supply

One of the essential requisites of the primitive Can. fortress was a supply of water. At Gezer a copious spring within easy reach was available. Tell el-Hesy commands the only springs in that region (*A Mound of Many Cities,* 16). It is a strong point in favor of the modern theory of the ridge of Ophel being the site of Zion or David's town that the Virgin's Fountain, the only perennial spring in the whole circuit of Jerus, was close to it, and would have been an inducement to the Jebusites to build their fortress there. In the sites that have been excavated, cisterns, sometimes vaulted over and with steps down into them, have been constantly found. Traces have also been observed of concealed passages or tunnels by which access has been obtained to the nearest spring. Some such explanation has been given of the "gutter" (2 S **5** 8 AV, "watercourse" RV), by which Joab obtained access to the fortress of Jebus and enabled David to capture it (1 Ch **11** 6; cf Vincent, *Canaan d'après l'exploration récente,* 26). During an investment of a fortified city by an enemy, it was a point in strategy for the inhabitants to secure the fountain and to divert or conceal the stream flowing from it so that the besiegers might be left without a water supply (2 K **3** 19.25; 2 Ch **32** 3; compare also 2 S **12** 26.27, *Century Bible,* Kennedy's note).

II. In Biblical History.—On the passage of the Jordan the Israelites found in Jericho a walled city of great strength barring their progress. The excavations recently made have disclosed the common features of Can fortresses—an outer wall, surrounding the entire area, 6½ ft. thick, a citadel and protecting walls of hardly less substantial workmanship. Nearby also is the essential spring to furnish the water supply. Within the citadel were found the walls and rooms of Can. houses, and in many cases remains of infants buried in jars under the clay floors (Driver, *Modern Research as Illustrating the Bible,* 91 ff). These examples of "foundation sacrifices" with which the excavations at Gezer have made us familiar give

1. Before the Monarchy

TRIPLE GATE—GERMAN EXCAVATIONS AT NABLUS

point to the account of the resettlement of the city in the days of Ahab, when Hiel the Bethelite rebuilt Jericho, laying the foundation thereof with the loss of Abiram, his firstborn, and setting up the gates thereof with the loss of his youngest son Segub (1 K **16** 34). See CORNER STONE; CANAAN.

In the Book of Jgs we read of the strong tower, or citadel, of Thebez, into which the inhabitants had crowded and to which Abimelech was setting fire when a woman upon the wall hurled a millstone upon him and broke his skull (Jgs **9** 51 f). It does not appear that at this period the Israelites were in possession of the strongholds of the land, for when the Philis overran the country, they had no fortresses to flee to, but "did hide themselves in caves, and in thickets, and in rocks, and in coverts, and in pits" (1 S **13** 6).

When David captured the Jebusite fortress (2 S **5** 6 ff) and transferred his capital from Hebron to Jerus, a new era of independence and even of conquest began. The natural strength of David's town, with such fortification as had been added, made it impregnable to any Phili or Syrian foe, and one of the strongest fortresses in Western Asia.

2. In the Period of the Monarchy

Although Solomon was a man of peace, he included among the great buildings which he executed fortresses and works of defence. He built the wall of Jerus round about. He built Millo (called Akra ["citadel"] in the LXX), and closed the breaches of the city of David, so that there might be no vulnerable point found in the defences of the city (1 K **9** 15). This fortification is represented in LXX, which has here an addition to the MT, as securing the complete subjection of the original inhabitants who remained. Solomon also built Hazor to watch Damascus, Megiddo to guard the plain of Jezreel, and Gezer overlooking the maritime plain, his work being one of refortification rather than of building from the foundation. He fortified also Beth-horon, Upper and Nether, to block the way against Phili invasion. The store cities, and cities to accommodate his chariots and horses, were also part of his military system (1 K **9** 18 ff).

The disruption of the kingdoms, and the jealousy and hostility that followed between Judah and Israel, necessitated fresh undertakings of fortification, on the part of both kingdoms. Rehoboam dwelt in Jerus, and built cities for defence in Judah. He fortified the strongholds and provisioned them and stored arms within them in case of siege (2 Ch **11** 5 ff). One of Jeroboam's first acts on ascending the throne was to build the two fortresses, Shechem to guard Mt. Ephraim, and Penuel to protect Gilead (1 K **12** 25 f). Baasha later pushed his frontier within a few miles of Jerus, fortifying Ramah to overawe Asa in his very capital. The long war which lasted through the reigns of Jeroboam, Nadab, Baasha and Elah, kings of Israel, was largely a war of sieges, one of them, that of Gibbethon, having apparently lasted 27 years (1 K **15** 27, compared with 1 K **16** 15 ff).

With Omri there arose in Israel a powerful ruler whose name is mentioned with respect in the Assyr monuments, which designate the kingdom of Israel *Mât Bît Khumri*, "the land of the house of Omri." He was the builder of Samaria which remained the capital of the Northern Kingdom till its fall in 722 BC. In excavations but recently carried on by the archaeological expedition of Harvard University, the walls of Omri's palace and fortress were laid bare, giving an impression of the great strength of the place.

While Solomon built the wall of Jerus, we read that Uzziah built towers at the corner gate, and at the valley gate, and at the turning of the wall, and fortified them (2 Ch **26** 9). Jotham his son, continued his father's labors in the further fortification of the city (**27** 3.4). Hezekiah had good reason to add still further to the strength of the city, seeing that he had to bear the brunt of Sennacherib's expedition to the west. Sennacherib boasts that of Hezekiah's fortified towns, he captured 46, with innumerable fortresses besides (Schrader, *COT*, I, 286), but he cannot tell that Jerus was among them, for it came through the ordeal unscathed. In the reign of Manasseh Jerus was captured and the king himself carried away to Nineveh, but on his repentance he was restored to the throne and set himself to strengthen the fortifications of the city (2 Ch **33** 14). The city was unable, however, to hold out against Nebuchadrezzar and his captains; for it was taken in 597 BC, and King Jehoiachin and the flower of the population were deported to Babylon. After a siege of two years it was again taken in 586 BC, and temple and city were destroyed, and the walls razed to the ground.

SIEGE OF A CITY (ASSYRIAN SCULPTURE IN THE BRITISH MUSEUM).

The patriotic labor of Nehemiah in the rebuilding of the wall of Jerus belongs properly to the history of the city (see JERUSALEM). In the Maccabean struggle, the Akra (1 Macc **1** 33; **3** 45, etc), the citadel, was long held by a Syrian garrison, and was in the end delivered up to the high priest by Demetrius (**10** 32). Notable also still later was the castle of Antonia (Acts **22** 24) on the site of the earlier castle of Nehemiah's day (Neh **2** 8; **7** 2).

3. In the Period of the Return

III. In the Psalms and the Prophets.—Under the image of a fortress, or mountain fastness, inaccessible to any common foot, where there is perfect safety from enemies and persecutors, the Psalmist delights to express his confidence in God. Jeh, in virtue of His righteous judgments, is a high tower to the downtrodden, a place of refuge and security (*misgābh*) to those who are in trouble (Ps **9** 9). When he exults in the strength of God who has

1. The Psalms

given him deliverance, he multiplies words to utter his confidence: "I love Thee, O Jeh, my strength. Jeh is my rock, and my fortress [m^eçūdhāh], ... my God . . . . my high tower [*misgābh*]" (Ps **18** 1.2). Thirteen times in the Pss we find this word: **9** 9; **18** 2; **46** 7.11; **59** 9.16.17 (where AV translates "defence" and RV "high tower"), etc. Elsewhere *m^eçūdhāh* is employed (Ps **31** 2; lit. "house of fortresses"; **91** 2; **144** 2). If we were at liberty to accept such psalms as Pss **18** and **59** as Davidic, the appropriateness of them to the circumstances of the Shepherd King when persecuted by Saul, taking refuge in the cave of Adullam and enduring the perils and anxieties of an outlaw's life, would at once be apparent.

2. The Prophets

Although Jeremiah has been called the weeping prophet, yet for the fearless fulfilment of his commission to a gainsaying people, God made him "a fortified city ['*īr mibhçār*], and an iron pillar, and brazen walls" (Jer **1** 18; cf **6** 27; **15** 20). Hosea in the Northern Kingdom predicted the destruction of its "fortresses" (*mibhçār*) by the invading Assyrians (**10** 14; cf **8** 14). The prophets in proclaiming God's message to their day addressed themselves not only to Israel and Judah, but also to those great world-powers with which the Heb people had relations. In the oracles of the prophets to the nations—to Egypt, Babylon, Assyria, Syria, Edom, and others—we obtain glimpses of great and fortified cities like No-amon (Thebes), Babylon, Nineveh, Damascus, whose natural defences and added fortifications did not save them from capture and destruction. And the teaching of the prophets for the comfort of Israel and Judah is that Jeh was a better defence to them than the great rivers of Assyria and Egypt were to those nations. When Nineveh was at the height of her pride, fierceness and worldly glory, Nahum asks her: "Art thou better than No-amon [Thebes of Egypt], that was situate among the rivers, that had the waters round about her; whose rampart [*ḥēl*] was the sea [the Nile], and her wall [*ḥōmāh*] was of the sea?" (Nah **3** 8). Of Nineveh itself we know that it was protected, not only by walls and fortresses of great strength, but also by canals and streams drawn round the city. Yet Nahum declares in his sublime apostrophe: "All thy fortresses shall be like fig-trees with the first-ripe figs: if they be shaken, they fall into the mouth of the eater" (ver 12). Babylon had walls whose strength and height, as described by Herodotus and other historians, were fabulous. Its great monarch Nebuchadrezzar was in his day the greatest ruler of the East, and Sir Henry Layard has told that scarcely a brick unearthed in the mounds of the great Bab plain was without his name. Yet when the day of reckoning came, the wall, said to be mountain-high, and 80 ft. thick, with its moat so broad that an arrow could not be shot over it, and all its elaborate works of defence, were as if they had not been; it surrendered to Cyrus without a blow being struck. It is in the visions of the prophets, in the universal peace which is to accompany the restoration of Israel, that we hear of "them that are at rest, that dwell securely, all of them dwelling without walls, and having neither bars nor gates" (Ezk **38** 11). "In that day shall this song be sung in the land of Judah: We have a strong city; salvation will he appoint for walls and bulwarks" (*ḥēl*) (Isa **26** 1). "Violence shall no more be heard in thy land, desolation nor destruction within thy borders; but thou shalt call thy walls Salvation, and thy gates Praise" (**60** 18). Building of fenced cities, with riding upon horses and military preparation, was a note of the false prophet, who urged alliances with foreign powers such as Assyria and Egypt, and relied too much upon the material resources of the nation. The true prophet realized that the strength of the nation lay in God and urged the people to put their trust in Him (Hos **8** 14). "Jerusalem," says Zechariah in the days of the Return, "shall be inhabited as villages without walls, by reason of the multitude of men and cattle therein. For I, saith Jeh, will be unto her a wall of fire round about, and I will be the glory in the midst of her" (**2** 4.5; cf **8** 4.5).

IV. In the New Testament.—In a well-known passage (2 Cor **10** 3–5), St. Paul, as he often does,

1. In St. Paul's Epistles

draws upon his knowledge of Rom methods of warfare, and introduces for the enforcement of great spiritual lessons the pulling down of "strongholds" as the ultimate object of every campaign. The word employed (*ochurōmata*) is the Gr equivalent of the Heb word commonly rendered "fortress" (*mibhçār*). "The 'strongholds' are the rock forts, such as those which once bristled along the coast of his native Cilicia and of which he must often have heard when his father told him how they were 'pulled down' by the Romans in their wars against the pirates. Those 'high things that exalt themselves'—those high eminences of the pride of Nature—occupied in force by hostile troops —had been a familiar experience in many wars throughout Asia Minor, while one of the grandest of all was the Acropolis that towered over Corinth" (Dean Howson, *The Metaphors of St. Paul*, 34 f).

2. In the Acts of the Apostles

From the stairs of the Castle of Antonia, St. Paul, by leave of Claudius Lysias, the commandant of the garrison at Jerus, in whose charge he was, addressed the excited crowd and told the story of his conversion. Antonia was the quarters, then, as it was in the time of Our Lord, of the Rom garrison, which occupied the Jewish capital (Acts **21** 37; Jn **18** 28); and the same site is to this day covered with a Turkish barracks.

Tower of Antonia.

3. In the Gospel History

Although it is not mentioned by name, the gloomy fortress of Machaerus on the E. of the Dead Sea is believed to have been the scene of the imprisonment and murder of John the Baptist. The description of it given by Jos (*BJ*, VII, vi, 1) shows it to have been a place of immense strength. "It was quite necessary that that fortress should be demolished lest it might draw away many into rebellion because of its strength; for the nature of the place was very capable of affording sure hope of safety to those who held it, and delay and fear to those who attacked it. For what was defended by a fort was itself a rocky hill, rising to a very great height, which circumstance alone made it very difficult to capture it. It was also so contrived by Nature that it could not easily be approached; for it is intrenched by ravines on all sides, so deep that the eye cannot reach their bottoms, nor are they easy to cross over, and it is quite impossible to fill them up with earth." Machaerus, like the Herodium, Jotapata, Masada, figured largely in the tragic scenes of the Jewish War so graphically described by Jos. See BETH-SHEAN, KIRIATH-SEPHER.

LITERATURE.—Bliss and Macalister, *Excavations in Pal;* Bliss, *A Mound of Many Cities;* Macalister, *Bible Side-Lights from Mound of Gezer; PEFS* for 1903–6, referring to Gezer; Driver, *Modern Research as Illustrating the Bible;* Vincent, *Canaan d'après l'exploration récente;* Billerbeck, *Der Festungsbau im alten Orient.*

T. NICOL

FORTUNATUS, fôr-tū-nā'tus (**Φορτουνάτος,** *Phortounátos*): A Rom proper name turned into Gr; same as Lat adj. *fortunatus,* meaning "blest," or "fortunate." Found only once in the Bible (1 Cor **16** 17). Fortunatus, with Stephanas and Achaicus, was an amabassador of the Corinthian church, whose presence at Ephesus refreshed the spirit of the apostle Paul.

FORTUNE, fôr'tūn (Gad): A god of Good Luck, possibly the Hyades. See ASTROLOGY, 10.

FORTY, fôr'ti (אַרְבָּעִים, *'arbā'īm;* **τεσσαράκοντα,** *tessarákonta*). See FOUR (5); NUMBER.

FORUM, fō'rum: AV **Appii Forum** (Acts **28** 15), is in RV MARKET OF APPIUS (q.v.).

FORWARD, fôr'wẽrd, **FORWARDNESS,** fôr'wẽrd-nes (הָלְאָה, *hāl*ᵉ*'āh,* נָסַע, *nāṣa';* **σπουδαῖος,** *spoudaíos*): As an advb. "forward" has the meaning of "onward" in space or time, or in the movement of affairs. As an adj. it has the sense of "readiness," "willingness," etc. The advb. only is found in the OT. It is the tr of *hāl*ᵉ*'āh,* "distance," "onward"; in space (Nu **32** 19; 1 S **10** 3); in time (Ezk **39** 22, "from that day and forward"; **43** 27); once of *hālakh,* "to go on" (Gen **26** 13, "went forward," AVm "Heb went going," RV "grew more and more"); twice of *ma'al,* "above," "upward" (1 S **16** 13; **30** 25, "from that day forward"); once of *yā'al,* "to cause to go up," "advance" (Job **30** 13, "They set forward [advance or help on] my calamity"); twice of *l*ᵉ*phānīm,* "to the front" (**Jer 7** 24; Ezk **10** 22, "They went every one straight forward," lit. "on the side of their face"); once of *ḳedhem,* "before" (Job **23** 8, "Behold, I go forward, but he is not there"); once with *nākhāh,* "to smite" (2 K **3** 24); frequently in Nu, and once in Ex, of *nāṣa',* "to lift up," "remove," "journey" (Ex **14** 15, "Speak unto the children of Israel, that they go forward"; Nu **1** 51, "when the tabernacle setteth forward"; **2** 24 AV, "They shall go forward," etc); it is also the tr of *nāçaḥ* (Piel), "to be over," "to take the lead," "to superintend" (1 Ch **23** 4, "to set forward [to carry onward, to advance] the work of the house of the Lord," AVm and text of RV "to oversee"; 2 Ch **34** 12, "to set it forward," RV retains, m, "to preside over it"; Ezr **3** 8 m, "set forward the work"). This word means also "to lead" in music, to precent; hence in the title of many psalms, *la-m*ᵉ*naçē*ᵃ*ḥ,* "For the chief musician." *Proérchomai,* "to go forward," etc, is trᵈ "went forward" (Mk **14** 35); *propémpō,* "to send forward" (3 Jn ver 6, "bring forward," RV "set forward"); *probállō,* "to throw or put forward" (Acts **19** 33, "putting him forward"); as adj. it is the tr of *thélō,* "to wish," "will" (2 Cor **8** 10, "to be forward a year ago"; AVm Gr "willing," RV "to will"); of *spoudaios,* "speedy," "earnest" (2 Cor **8** 17, "being more forward," RV "very earnest"); of *spoudázō,* "to make haste," "to be earnest" (Gal **2** 10, "which I also was forward to do," RV "zealous to do").

"Forward" occurs several times in Apoc, e.g. 1 Esd **1** 27, "The Lord is with me hasting me forward" (*epispeúdō*); 2 Esd **3** 6, "before ever the earth came forward" (*adventaret*), meaning, perhaps, before it was ready for planting.

Forwardness is the tr of *spoudḗ,* "speed," "zeal," etc (2 Cor **8** 8, RV "earnestness"); of *prothumía,* "readiness of mind" (2 Cor **9** 2, "the forwardness of your mind," RV "your readiness"; Wisd **14** 17, "that by their forwardness [*spoudē*] they might flatter," RV "zeal").

For "forward" RV has "forth" (Nu **2** 24; cf 1 Cor **16** 11); for "go forward" (Nu **10** 5), "take their journey"; for "set forward" (**21** 10; **22** 1), "journeyed"; "forward" for "ready" (Dt **1** 41), for "forth" (Prov **25** 6), for "farther" (Mt **26** 39); "put forward" for "appointed" (Acts **1** 23); "set forward according to" for "took" (Nu **10** 12); "set forward" for "went" (Nu **10** 14.34), for "departed" (ver 33); "set me forward" for "bring me" (1 Cor **16** 6).

W. L. WALKER

FOUL, foul (רָפַשׂ, *rāphas;* **ἀκάθαρτος,** *akáthartos*): The vb. "to foul" (defile) occurs as the tr of *rāphas,* "to trample" or "muddle" (streams) (Ezk **32** 2; **34** 18); of *ḥāmar,* "to burn," "to be red" (Job **16** 16, "My face is foul with weeping," ARV and ERVm "red"); of *mirpās,* "a treading" (Ezk **34** 19). The adj. is the tr of *akathartos,* "unclean," "impure," "wicked" (Mk **9** 25; Rev **18** 2, "foul spirit," RV "unclean"), and of *cheimôn,* "winter," "stormy or foul weather" (Mt **16** 3). RV has "The rivers shall become foul" (Isa **19** 6) instead of AV "They shall turn the rivers far away," ERV "The rivers shall stink." W. L. WALKER

FOUNDATION, foun-dā'shun: In Heb the words for "foundation" are mostly derivatives from יָסַד, *yāṣadh,* "to found," and in Gr two words are used: one, *καταβολή, katabolḗ,* of "foundation of the world" (Mt **13** 35; **25** 34; Lk **11** 50; Jn **17** 24, etc); the other, *θεμέλιος, themélios,* of the foundation of a building (Lk **6** 48.49; **14** 29; Acts **16** 26, etc), in which sense it is also used **metaphorically** in various connections (Christ the foundation of the church, 1 Cor **3** 11; or the apostles and prophets the foundation, with Christ as corner-stone, Eph **2** 20; the foundation of repentance, He **6** 1, etc). In Ps **11** 3, "if the foundations be destroyed," the Heb word is *shath.* In Jer **50** 15, RV reads "bulwarks" for "foundations"; conversely in Ps **89** 14; **97** 2, for AV "habitation," RV reads "foundation," and in Isa **6** 4 for AV "posts," reads "foundations." JAMES ORR

FOUNDER, foun'dẽr (from צָרַף, *çāraph*): A worker in molten metal (Jgs **17** 4, etc). The word in AV in Jer **10** 9.14; **51** 17 is rendered in RV "goldsmith," and in **6** 29 by a paraphrase, "They go on refining." See REFINER; GOLDSMITH.

FOUNTAIN, foun'tin, foun'tān: In a country where no rain falls for half of the year, springs assume an importance unknown in more favored lands. In both eastern and western Pal and even in Lebanon there are many villages which depend entirely upon reservoirs or cisterns of rain water. Others are situated along the courses of the few perennial streams. But wherever a spring exists it is very apt to be the nucleus of a village. It may furnish sufficient water to be used in irrigation, in which case the gardens surrounding the village become an oasis in the midst of the parched land. Or there may be a tiny stream which barely suffices for drinking water, about which the village women and girls sit and talk waiting their turns to fill their jars, sometimes until far in the night. The water of the village fountain is often conveyed by a covered conduit for some distance from the source to a convenient spot in the village where an arch is built up, under which the water gushes out. See CISTERN; SPRING; WELL; EN-, and place-names compounded with EN-.

Figurative: (1) of God (Ps **36** 9; Jer **2** 13; **17** 13); (2) of Divine pardon and purification, with an obvious Messianic reference (Zec **13** 1); (3) of wisdom and godliness (Prov **13** 14; **14** 27); (4) of wives (Prov **5** 18); (5) of children (Dt **33** 28; cf Ps **68** 26; Prov **5** 16); (6) of prosperity (Ps **107** 35; **114** 8; Hos **13** 15); (7) of the heart (Eccl **12** 6; see CISTERN); (8) of life everlasting (Rev **7** 17; **21** 6). ALFRED ELY DAY

FOUNTAIN GATE. See JERUSALEM.

FOUR, fōr (אַרְבַּע, *'arba'*; **τέσσαρες**, *téssares*): "Four" (cardinal number) was a sacred and complete number with the Hebrews, as well as with several other peoples. It occurs very frequently in the OT and the NT.

(1) It indicates completeness. We have the four rivers of Paradise (Gen **2** 10); the four winds of heaven (Ezk **37** 9; Dnl **7** 2; **8** 8; **11** 4; Zec **6** 5, RVm "spirits"; 2 Esd **13** 5); "the four winds" (Mt **24** 31; Mk **13** 27); "the four corners of the earth" (Isa **11** 12; Rev **7** 1; **20** 8, AV "quarters"); "the four corners of the house" (Job **1** 19); Jephthah's daughter was bewailed four days a year (Jgs **11** 40); "four cities" are several times mentioned in Josh in the allotment of inheritances (**19** 7; **21** 18, etc); Nehemiah's enemies sent to him "four times" (Neh **6** 4); "four kinds" (RVm "families" of destroyers were threatened, Jer **15** 3); Jeh's "four sore judgments" (Ezk **14** 21); "four generations" were seen by Job (**42** 16).

(2) "Four" is frequent in prophetic visions: Daniel saw "four . . . . beasts" arise, representing four kings (**7** 3.17); "four notable horns" (**8** 8. 22; cf 2 Esd **11** 39); "four gates" (2 Esd **3** 19; four wings, **12** 2 AV); "four horns" were seen by Zechariah, as the powers that had scattered Israel, and "four smiths" (RV) as powers that would cast the four horns down (**1** 18–21); "four chariots and . . . . horses" represented the "four spirits," AV and RVm (better than "winds"), that went "forth from standing before the Lord of all the earth" (**6** 1–5); in the visions of Ezk, "four living creatures," each with four faces, four wings, etc, were the bearers of the throne of God (**1** 5 f.23); so, in the visions of John there were "four living creatures" before and around the throne (Rev **4** 6; **5** 6.8.14; **6** 1; **15** 7; **19** 4); John saw "four angels" of destruction loosed for their work (Rev **9** 14 f).

(3) "Four" occurs frequently in the measurements of the sacred buildings, etc (*a*) of the tabernacle (Ex **25**; **26**; **27**; **28** 17; **36**, etc); (*b*) of Solomon's temple (1 K **7** 2, etc; 1 Ch **9** 24); (*c*) of Ezekiel's temple (Ezk **40** 41; **41** 5; **42** 20; **43** 14, etc).

(4) "Four" is used as an alternative with "three" (Prov **30** 15.18.21.24.29); we have "three or four" (2 Esd **16** 29.31); "the third and . . . . the fourth generation" (Ex **20** 5; **34** 7; Nu **14** 18; Dt **5** 9).

(5) Ten times four, or forty is also a special and sacred number, e.g. forty years did Israel eat manna (Ex **16** 35); forty years in the wilderness (Nu **14** 33; **32** 13); "the land had rest forty years" (Jgs **3** 11; **5** 31); Israel was delivered unto the hands of the Philis for forty years (**13** 1); Eli judged Israel forty years (1 S **4** 18); Moses was forty years old when he visited his brethren (Acts **7** 23); the flood continued for "forty days and forty nights" (Gen **7** 4); Moses was in the Mount "forty days and forty nights" (Ex **24** 18; **34** 28; Dt **9** 9); Jesus fasted in the desert forty days and nights (Mt **4** 2, etc); He remained with His disciples forty days after His resurrection (Acts **1** 3).

(6) Fourscore is also frequent (*sh^emōnīm*) (Ex **7** 7; Jgs **3** 30; Jer **41** 5, etc; *ogdoēkonta*, Lk **2** 37; **16** 7).

(7) Four hundred represents a large number, e.g. the years of the oppression in Egypt (Gen **15** 13); Esau's company (**33** 1); the men with David (1 S **22** 2; **25** 13; **30** 10.17); the prophets of Baal "four hundred and fifty," of Asherah, "four hundred" (1 K **18** 19.22); the prophets of Israel (**22** 6). Four thousand represents a larger number, e.g. the musicians and porters of Solomon's temple (1 Ch **23** 5); the stalls for horses in Solomon's stables (2 Ch **9** 25); the Assassins who made insurrection under an Egyptian (Acts **21** 38); Christ fed "four thousand men, besides women and children" (Mt **15** 38). Four hundred thousand represents a *very* large number, e.g. the congregation of Israel that gathered at Mizpah, "four hundred thousand footmen that drew sword" (Jgs **20** 2.17); Abijah's army (2 Ch **13** 3; Jeroboam's, twice that number).

(8) The fourth part also frequently occurs (Ex **29** 40; Lev **23** 13; Nu **23** 10; Rev **6** 8, etc).

W. L. WALKER

FOUR HUNDRED. See FOUR.

FOUR THOUSAND. See FOUR.

FOURFOLD, fōr′fōld: Occurs but twice in EV: 2 S **12** 6, "He shall restore the lamb fourfold"; and Lk **19** 8 AV, "If I have wrongfully exacted ought . . . . I restore fourfold." From this statement of Zacchaeus we are to understand that fourfold the amount of that which was stolen was the restoration the law required of a thief. This was the extreme penalty the law imposed. In some cases double the amount was to be restored (Ex **22** 4.7); in others, a fifth of its value was added to the thing restored (Lev **6** 5); still again, an amount equal to that taken was to be restored (1 S **12** 3).

FOURSCORE, fōr′skōr. See FOUR; NUMBER.

FOURSQUARE, fōr′skwār (רָבַע, *rābha'*; **τετράγωνος**, *tetrágōnos*): "Foursquare," meaning equal in length and breadth, not round, is the tr of *rābha'* (from obs. *r^ebha'*, "four"); it occurs in the description of the altar of burnt offering (Ex **27** 1; **38** 1); of the altar of incense (**30** 2; **37** 25); of the breastplate of the high priest (**28** 16; **39** 9); of the panels of the gravings upon the mouth of the brazen or molten sea in Solomon's temple (1 K **7** 31); of the inner court of Ezekiel's temple (Ezk **40** 47); of "the holy oblation" of the city of Ezekiel's vision (**48** 20, *r^ebhī'ī*, "fourth"); of the new Jerus of John's vision (Rev **21** 16, *tetragōnos*), and conveys the idea of perfect symmetry. In AVm of 1 K **6** 31, we have "five-square," square being formerly used for equal-sided, as it still is in "three-square file."

W. L. WALKER

FOURTEEN, fōr′tēn. See NUMBER.

FOURTH PART. See FOUR.

FOWL, foul (עוֹף, *'ōph*; **πετεινόν**, *peteinón*): The word is now generally restricted to the larger, esp. the edible birds, but formerly it denoted all flying creatures; in Lev **11** 20 AV we have even, "all fowls that creep, going upon all four," ver 21, "every flying creeping thing that goeth upon all four."

The word most frequently tr^d "fowl" is *'ōph* from *'ūph*, "to cover," hence wing; it is used collectively for birds and fowl in general (Gen **1** 20, etc; **2** 19.20, etc); *'ayiṭ* (from *'ūṭ*, "to rush") means a ravenous beast, or bird of prey, used collectively of ravenous birds (Gen **15** 11 AV; Isa **18** 6 AV "fowls"; Job **28** 7, "a path which no fowl knoweth," RV "no bird of prey"); in Isa **46** 11 it is used as a symbol of a conqueror (cf Jer **12** 9, "bird," "birds of prey"; Ezk **39** 4, "ravenous birds"); *çippōr*, Aram. *çippar* (from *çāphar*, "to twitter or chirp"), "a chirper," denotes a small bird or sparrow (Dt **4** 17 AV; Neh **5** 18; Dnl **4** 14); to give the carcases of men to the fowls (birds) of the air was an image of destruction (Dt **28** 26 AV; 1 S **17** 44.46; Ps **79** 2; Jer **7** 33, etc); *barburīm*, rendered (1 K **4** 23) **"fatted fowl"** (among the provisions for Solomon's table for one day), is probably a mimetic word, like Gr *bárbaros*, Lat *murmuro*, Eng. *babble*, perhaps denoting *geese* from their cackle (Gesenius, from *bārar*, "to cleanse," referring to their white plumage; but other derivations and renderings are given). They might have been ducks or swans. They could have been guineas or pigeons. The young of the ostrich was delicious food, and no doubt when Solomon's ships brought peafowl they also brought word that they were a delicacy for a king's table. The domestic fowl was not common so early in Pal, but it may have been brought by Solomon with other imports from the East; in NT times chickens were common; *ba'al kānāph*, "owner of a wing," is used for a bird of any kind in Prov **1** 17. "In vain is the net spread in the sight of any bird," AVm "Heb, in the eyes of everything that hath a wing."

1. OT Terms and References

In the Levitical law fowls (birds) were distinguished as clean and unclean (Lev **11** 13 f; Dt **14** 11–20; cf Gen **8** 20); the first were allowed to be eaten because they fed on grains, seeds, and vegetables; the second were forbidden because they fed on flesh and carrion.

2. In the Levitical Law

In the NT the common word for "fowl" is *peteinon*, "winged fowl." "The fowls of the air" (RV "the birds of the heaven") are pointed to by Our Lord as examples of the providential care of God (Mt **6** 26; Lk **12** 24); in another connection the "sparrows" (*strouthíon*) sold cheap, probably for food, are so employed (Mt **10** 29, "Are not two sparrows sold for a penny?" Lk **12** 6, "five . . . . for two pence"); their quickly picking up seeds from the ground is made to illustrate the influences which render "the word" powerless (Mt **13** 4); their being sheltered in the branches, the growth of the kingdom (**13** 32, *peteinon*); the hen's (*órnis*) sheltering care for her chickens, His desire to protect and save Jerus (Mt **23** 37; cf 2 Esd **1** 30; Ruth **2** 12); the fowls were shown in vision to Peter as among the things made clean by God (Acts **10** 12; **11** 6); in Rev **18** 2; **19** 17.21, *órneon*, "bird," "fowl," a carnivorous bird (RV "bird"), is the representative of desolation and of destruction.

3. NT References and Illustrative Uses

For "fowls" ARV has "birds" (Gen **6** 7.20; **7** 3; Lev **20** 25*b*; Acts **10** 12; **11** 6; with ERV Mt **6** 26; **13** 4; Mk **4** 4.32; Lk **8** 5; **12** 24; **13** 19); for "every feathered fowl" (Ezk **39** 17), RV has "the birds of every sort"; for "all fowls that creep" (Lev **11** 20) and for "every flying creeping thing" (ver 21), "all winged creeping things."

W. L. Walker

FOWL, FATTED. See preceding article.

FOWLER, foul'ẽr (יָקֹשׁ, *yōḳēsh*): A professional birdcatcher. In the days previous to firearms, birds were captured with nets spread on the ground, in traps and snares. There was a method of taking young birds from a nest, raising them by hand, and when they had become very tame, they were confined in hidden cages so that their voices would call others of their kind to the spot and they could be killed by arrows of concealed bowmen or the use of the throw-stick (Ecclus **11** 30). This was a stick $1\frac{1}{2}$ ft. in length and $\frac{1}{2}$ in. in diameter, hurled with a rotary motion at the legs of the birds and was very effective when thrown into flocks of ground birds, such as partridge or quail, esp. if the birds were running up hill. There was also a practice of sewing a

Egyptian Fowler.

captured bird's eyelids together and confining it so that its cries would call large numbers of birds through curiosity and they could then be taken in the several ways mentioned. The fowlers supplied the demand for doves and other birds used for caged pets, and furnished the market with wild pigeons and doves for sacrifice and such small birds as were used for food. Ps **91** 3:

"For he will deliver thee from the snare of the fowler,
And from the deadly pestilence."

This is David's promise that the Almighty will deliver us from the evil plans laid to ruin us, as a bird sometimes in its struggles slips the hair and escapes from the "snare" (q.v.) set for it. Ps **124** 7:

"Our soul is escaped as a bird out of the snare of the fowlers:
The snare is broken, and we are escaped."

Here is the fulfilment of the former promise in a cry of rejoicing. Sometimes the snare held fast, sometimes it broke; then the joy in the heart of a freed man was like the wild exultation in the heart of the escaping bird. Prov **6** 5:

"Deliver thyself as a roe from the hands of the hunter,
And as a bird from the hand of the fowler."

With methods so primitive as these for taking birds, it must have occurred frequently that a stunned, wounded or entrapped bird slipped even from the hand that held it and made good its escape.

Jer **5** 26: "For among my people are found wicked men: they watch, as fowlers lie in wait; they set a trap, they catch men." Here is the plain comparison strongly drawn between wicked men entrapping their fellows and fowlers taking unsuspecting birds.

The last reference is in Hos **9** 8: "Ephraim was a watchman with my God: as for the prophet, a fowler's snare is in all his ways, and enmity in the house of his God." Wherever he goes, the prophet is in danger of being trapped. Gene Stratton-Porter

FOX (שׁוּעָל, *shū'āl;* cf Arab. ثَعْلَب, *tha'lab* [Jgs **15** 4; Neh **4** 3; Ps **63** 10; Cant **2** 15; Lam **5** 18; Ezk **13** 4]; ἀλώπηξ, *alōpēx* [Mt **8** 20; Lk **9** 58; **13** 32]): The foxes of different parts of Europe and Western Asia differ more or less from each other, and some authors have given the local types distinct specific names. Tristram, for instance, distinguishes the Egyp fox, *Vulpes nilotica*, of Southern Pal, and the tawny fox, *Vulpes flavescens*, of the N. and E. It is possible that the range of the desert fox, *Vulpes leucopus*, of Southwestern Asia may also reach Syria. We have, however, the authority of the *Royal Natural History* for considering all these as merely local races of one species, the

Fox.

common fox, *Vulpes alopex* or *Canis vulpes*. The natives of Syria and Pal do not always distinguish the fox and jackal although the two animals are markedly different. The jackal and wolf also are frequently confounded. See DRAGON; JACKAL.

In Ps **63** 9 f we have, "Those that seek my soul, to destroy it, ... shall be given over to the power of the sword: they shall be a portion for foxes" (*shū'ālīm*). It has been thought that the jackal is meant here (RVm), and that may well be, though it is also true that the fox does not refuse carrion. In RVm, "jackal" is suggested in two other passages, though why is not clear, since the rendering "fox" seems quite appropriate in both. They are Neh **4** 3, ". . . . if a fox go up, he shall break down their stone wall," and Lam **5** 17 f, ". . . . our eyes are dim; for the mountain of Zion which is desolate: the foxes walk upon it." RVm also has "jackals" in Jgs **15** 4 f, where Samson "caught three hundred foxes . . . . and put a firebrand in the midst between every two tails . . . . and let them go into the standing grain of the Philis, and burnt up both the shocks and the standing grain, and also the oliveyards." Jackals are probably more numerous than foxes, but the substitution does not appreciably diminish the difficulties in the way of any natural explanation of the story. In Cant **2** 15 we have a reference to the fondness of the fox for grapes. In Mt **8** 20 and Lk **9** 58 Jesus says in warning to a would-be follower, "The foxes have holes, and the birds of the heaven have nests; but the Son of man hath not where to lay his head." Foxes differ from most of the *Canidae* in burrowing holes for their lairs, unless indeed they take possession of the burrow of another animal, such as the badger. In Lk **13** 32 Jesus compares Herod to a fox. ALFRED ELY DAY

FRAGMENT, frag'ment (**κλάσμα,** *klásma*): "Fragment," a piece broken off, occurs only in the pl., in the accounts of the miracles of the Loaves in the Gospels and references thereto. It is the tr of *klasma* (from *kláō*, "to break"), "a piece broken off" (Mt **14** 20 AV); "broken meat" (**15** 37).

RV has in each instance "broken pieces." The change is important because it shows that the pieces left over were not mere fragments or crumbs left by the people after eating, but some of the original pieces into which it is said in all the synoptic narratives and references Jesus "broke" the "loaves," which, being thin cakes, were usually *broken* before distribution; hence the phrase, "breaking of bread." See *HDB*, s.v. "Fragment"; Weymouth translates "broken portions," viz. "those into which the Lord had broken the loaves; not mere scraps or crumbs." W. L. WALKER

FRAME, frām:

(1) יֵצֶר, *yēçer* (from root *yāçar*, "to knead," mold with the fingers): "For he knoweth our frame; he remembereth that we are dust" (Ps **103** 14).

(2) עֵרֶךְ, *'ērekh* (from root *'ārakh*, "to put in order," "to set in a row," "to arrange"): "goodly frame" (Job **41** 12, AV "goodly proportion").

(3) עֹצֶם, *'ōçem*, "bony frame," "body": "My frame was not hidden from thee, when I was made in secret" (Ps **139** 15), AV "my substance," AVm "my strength, or, my body." See also BONE.

(4) מִבְנֶה, *mibhneh*, "building, frame" (Ezk **40** 2, "frame of a city").

(5) נָתַן, *nāthan*, "to give," "to direct": "They will not frame their doings" (Hos **5** 4, AV and RVm).

(6) **συναρμολογέω,** *sunarmologéō*, "to fit or join closely together" (Eph **2** 21).

(7) **καταρτίζω,** *katartízō*, "to fit out," "make fit," "adjust" (He **11** 3). H. L. E. LUERING

FRANKINCENSE, frank'in-sens (לְבֹנָה, *lᵉbhōnāh*, from root meaning "whiteness," referring to the milky color of the fresh juice: Ex **30** 34; Lev **2** 1 f.15 f; **5** 11; **6** 15; **24** 7; Nu **5** 15; 1 Ch **9** 29; Neh **13** 5.9; Cant **3** 6; **4** 6.14; Isa **43** 23; **60** 6; **66** 3; Jer **6** 20; **17** 26; **41** 5; trd in the last six references "incense" in AV, but correctly in RV; **λίβανος,** *líbanos*: Mt **2** 11; Rev **18** 13. The Eng. word is derived from old Fr. *franc encens*, i.e. "pure incense"): The common frankincense of the pharmacopoeas is a gum derived from the common fir,

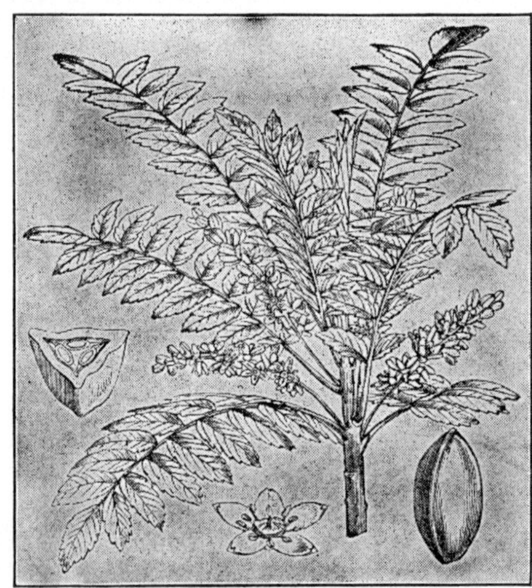

Frankincense (*Boswellia serrata*).

but the frankincense of the Jews, as well as of the Greeks and Romans, is a substance now called *Olibanum* (from the Arab. *el lubān*), a product of certain trees of the genus *Boswellia* (N.O. *Amyridaceae*), growing on the limestone rocks of south Arabia and Somali-land (Isa **60** 6; Jer **6** 20). The most important species are *B. Carteri* and *B. Frereana*. Some of the trees grow to a considerable height and send down their roots to extraordinary depths. The gum is obtained by incising the bark, and is collected in yellowish, semitransparent tears, readily pulverized; it has a nauseous taste. It is used for making incense for burning in churches and in Indian temples, as it was among the Jews (Ex **30** 34). See INCENSE. It is often associated with myrrh (Cant **3** 6; **4** 6) and with it was made an offering to the infant Saviour (Mt **2** 11). A specially "pure" kind, *l^ebhōnāh zakkāh*, was presented with the shewbread (Lev **24** 7).

E. W. G. MASTERMAN

FRANKLY, fraṉk'li (**χαρίζομαι**, *charízomai*): "Frankly" in the sense of "freely," "readily," "graciously," occurs only in the tr of *charizomai*, properly "to gratify," "to do that which is grateful or pleasing," "to forgive" (Lk **7** 42, "He frankly forgave them both," RV has simply "forgave"; the same word is tr[d] in ver 43, AV and RV, "forgave," in ver 21 AV it is "gave," RV "bestowed," granted to see). It occurs in the NT only in Lk and Paul.

FRAY, frā (חָרַד, *ḥāradh*, "to make afraid," "cause to tremble": AV of Dt **28** 26; Jer **7** 33; Zec **1** 21; RV "frighten," "terrify"). See WAR.

FRECKLED, frek''ld, **SPOT** (בֹּהַק, *bōhaḳ*; LXX **ἀλφός**, *alphós*, called in RV "a tetter," and described as a bright shining spot [*b^ehārōth l^ebhēnōth*]): These white eruptions did not render the person so marked ceremonially unclean (Lev **13** 39). This form of skin disease is described by Hippocrates as usually of no great importance and indicative of a sluggishness of body; it is probably some form of local psoriasis. There is a cognate modern Arab. word applied to a facial eczematous eruption. For other references to skin diseases, see LEPROSY.

FREE, FREEDOM. See CHOICE; WILL.

FREEDMAN, frēd'man, **FREEMAN**, frē'man: The term occurs in 1 Cor **7** 22; Col **3** 11, and Rev **6** 15, and represents two slightly different words. In 1 Cor **7** 22 the word is ἀπελεύθερος, *apeleútheros*, "a freeman," one who was born a slave and has received freedom. In this case it refers to spiritual freedom. He that was in bondage to sin has been presented with spiritual freedom by the Lord. In Rev **6** 15 the word is simply ἐλεύθερος, *eleútheros*, "a free man" as opposed to a slave.

FREELY, frē'li (חִנָּם, *ḥinnām*, נְדָבָה, *n^edhābhāh*; **δωρεάν**, *dōreán*, **παῤῥησιάζομαι**, *parrhēsiázomai*): "Freely" occurs in three senses:

(1) Gratis, for nothing (Nu **11** 5, *ḥinnām*, "for nought," "the fish which we did eat in Egypt freely," RV "for nought"); Mt **10** 8, *dōrean*, "Freely ye have received, freely give," RV omits "have"; Rom **3** 24, "being justified freely by his grace"; 2 Cor **11** 7, "I have preached to you the gospel freely," RV "for nought"; Rev **21** 6; **22** 17, "Take the water of life freely"; *charizomai* (Rom **8** 32) is tr[d] "freely give," *tá charisthénta* (1 Cor **2** 12), "the things that are freely given," ARV has "were" for "are."

(2) Willingly, spontaneously: *n^edhābhāh*, "willing offering" (Ps **54** 6, "I will freely sacrifice unto thee," RV "with a freewill-offering"; Hos **14** 4, "I will love them freely"); *nādhabh*, "to give willingly" (Ezr **2** 68, RV "willingly offered"; cf **1** 6); *n^edabh* Aram. (**7** 15; cf vs 13.16).

(3) Without hindrance or restraint, *'ākhal*, "to eat" is rendered in Gen **2** 16, "Thou mayest freely eat," AVm "Heb, eating thou shalt eat"; 1 S **14** 30, "if . . . . the people had eaten freely"; *parrhēsiazomai*, "to speak freely, openly, boldly" (Acts **26** 26, "Unto whom also I speak freely"); *metá parrhēsías*, "with full speech" (**2** 29, "I may say unto you freely").

RV has "have drunk freely" for "well drunk" (Jn **2** 10). The word is *methúskō*, Pass. "to become drunk." Comparison with Lk **12** 45; Eph **5** 18; 1 Thess **5** 7; Rev **17** 2, where the same word is tr[d] AV "made drunk," RV "made drunken" (Mt **24** 49; Acts **2** 15; 1 Cor **11** 21; Rev **17** 6, "drunken"), will show that the meaning is "drunk," which was the rendering of Tyndale and Cranmer; Vulg has *cum inebriati fuerint;* Plummer renders "have become drunk, are drunk."

W. L. WALKER

FREEWILL OFFERING, frē'wil of'ẽr-ing. See SACRIFICE.

FREEWOMAN, frē'wŏŏm-an (**ἐλευθέρα**, *eleuthéra*): Found but 4 t in AV (Gal **4** 22.23.30.31). In the first three passages it refers to Sarah, the freewoman and true wife of Abraham as in contrast with Hagar, the Egyp slave girl who became his concubine (Gen **16** 1 ff). In the last passage a **metaphorical** application of the term is made to the Christians who are the children of promise, of freedom, of the spirit, the children of the freewoman, in contrast with the Jews who are the children of the letter, of bondage, of the bondwoman.

FREQUENT, frē'kwent (**περισσοτέρως**, *perissotérōs*): "Frequent," adj. (from Lat *frequens, frequentis*, "crowded") occurs only once in the text of AV, as the tr of *perissoterōs*, advb. in comparative degree of *perissós*, "abundantly," hence "more abundantly" (cf 2 Cor **1** 12); in 2 Cor **11** 23, "in prisons more frequent," RV "more abundantly"; and once in m of AV (Prov **27** 6) as tr of *'āthar*, "to be abundant," RV in text, "profuse."

ARV has "frequent" for "open" (1 S **3** 1, "The word of Jehovah was precious [m, rare] in those days; there was no frequent vision," m "Heb widely spread" (the word is *pāraç*, "to break forth," "to scatter," etc). ERV retains "open," with "frequent, Heb widely spread" in m. "Frequent" (the vb.) does not occur.

W. L. WALKER

FRESH, adj.: The tr of חָדָשׁ, *ḥādhāsh*, "new," "fresh" (Job **29** 20, "My glory is fresh in me"); of לְשַׁד, *l^eshadh*, "sap," "moisture" (Nu **11** 8, of the manna, "as the taste of fresh oil," RVm "cakes baked with oil"); of רַעֲנָן, *ra'ănān*, "to be fresh and green" (Ps **92** 10, "fresh oil"); of γλυκύς, *glukús*, "sweet" (Jas **3** 12, "salt water and fresh," RV "sweet"). **Fresher** is the tr of רֻטֲפַשׁ, *ruṭăphash*, "to become fresh" (Job **33** 25; "His flesh shall be fresher than a child's").

RV has "fresh" for "green" (Gen **30** 37; Lev **23** 14), for "moist" (Nu **6** 3), for "full" (Lev **2** 14; 2 K **4** 42), for "new" (Jgs **15** 15; Mt **9** 17; Mk **2** 22; Lk **5** 38).

W. L. WALKER

FRET, FRETTING (חָרָה, *ḥārāh*, מָאַר, *mā'ar*): To "fret" is from *for* (prefix) and *etan*, "to eat," "to consume." The word is both trans and intrans in AV: (1) trans as tr of *ḥārāh*, "to burn," Hithpael, "to fret one's self," "to be angry" (Ps **37** 1, "Fret not thyself because of evil-doers"; vs 7.8; Prov **24** 19); of *ḳāçaph*, "to be angry," etc (Isa **8** 21, "They shall fret themselves, and curse," etc); of *rāghaz*, "to be moved" (with anger, etc) (Ezk **16** 43, "Thou hast fretted me in all these things," ARV "raged against me"). For Lev **13** 55, see under **Fretting** below. (2) Intrans, it is the tr of *rā'am*, "to rage," Hiphil, "to provoke to anger" (1 S **1** 6, "Her rival provoked her sore, to make her fret"); of *zā'aph*, "to be sad," "to fret" (Prov **19** 3, "His heart fretteth against Jeh").

Fretting in the sense of eating away, consuming, is used of the leprosy, *mā'ar*, "to be sharp, bitter, painful" (Lev **13** 51.52; **14** 44, "a fretting leprosy"; in ver 55 we have "it [is] fret inward" ("fret" past part.), as the tr of *p^eḥetheth* from *pāḥath*, "to dig" (a pit), the word meaning "a depression," "a hollow or sunken spot in a garment affected by a kind of leprosy," RV "it is a fret."

RV has "fretful" for "angry" (Prov **21** 19), m "vexation." W. L. Walker

FRIED, frīd. See Bread, III, 3, (2); Food, II; Locusts.

FRIEND, frend, **FRIENDSHIP,** frend'ship: In the OT two words, variously tr^d "friend" or "companion": רֵעֶה, *rē'eh*, indicating a mere associate, passing friend, neighbor, or companion; אָהַב, *'āhabh*, indicating affection natural or unnatural. In the NT also two words: ἑταῖρος, *hetaíros*, "a comrade," or "fellow," and φίλος, *phílos*, suggesting a more affectionate relation.

Literature abounds in concrete examples of friendship of either kind noted above, and of profoundly philosophic as well as sentimental and poetic expositions of the idea of friendship. Notable among these are the OT examples. Abraham, because of the intimacy of his relations, was called "the friend of God" (2 Ch **20** 7; Isa **41** 8; Jas **2** 23). "Jeh spake unto Moses face to face, as a man . . . . unto his friend" (Ex **33** 11). The romantic aspect of the friendship of Ruth and Naomi is interesting (Ruth **1** 16–18). The devotion of Hushai, who is repeatedly referred to as David's friend (2 S **15** 37; **16** 16), is a notable illustration of the affection of a subordinate for his superior. The mutual friendship of David and Jonathan (1 S **18** 1), from which the author is made to say, "The soul of Jonathan was knit with the soul of David, and Jonathan loved him as his own soul," is another example. Again in his pathetic lament for Jonathan (2 S **1** 26), David says in highly emotional tones that his love "was wonderful, passing the love of women." Elijah and Elisha form a unique illustration of semi-professional affection (2 K **2**).

In the NT, Jesus and His disciples illustrate the growth of friendship from that of teacher and disciple, lord and servant, to that of friend and friend (Jn **15** 13–15). Paul and Timothy are likewise conspicuous (2 Tim **1** 2).

In general lit. we have the classic incident, recorded by Plutarch, of Damon and Pythias during the rule of Dionysius. Pythias, condemned to death, was about to be executed but desired to see his family. Damon offered himself as a ransom in case he should not return in time for the hour of execution. Returning in time, both were released by the great Dionysius, who asked to be taken into the secret of such friendship. The writings on friendship are many. Plato and Cicero have immortalized themselves by their comments. Cicero held dearly the friendship of Scipio, declaring that of all that Nature or Fortune ever gave him there was nothing which could compare with the friendship of Scipio. Bacon, Emerson, Black, Gladden, King, Hillis, and many others in later days have written extensively concerning friendship. The best illustration of the double use of the word (see above) is that in Prov **18** 24, "He that maketh many friends doeth it to his own destruction; but there is a friend that sticketh closer than a brother." Again, "Iron sharpeneth iron; so a man sharpeneth the countenance of his friend" (**27** 17). The honesty and frankness of genuine friends are set forth in the maxim, "Faithful are the wounds of a friend" (**27** 6). Walter G. Clippinger

FRIENDS, CHIEF FRIENDS (**οἱ φίλοι πρῶτοι,** *hoi phíloi prōtoi*): Expressions used in 1 and 2 Macc to designate the favored courtiers of the Antiochi. Mattathias is promised enrolment among the king's Friends, to tempt him to apostatize (1 Macc **2** 18); Alexander Balas writes Jonathan among his Chief Friends (**10** 65). Cf also 1 Macc **3** 38; **6** 10.14; **10** 60; **11** 26.27; 2 Macc **8** 9.

FRINGES, frin'jis (צִיצִת, *çīçith*, "tassel, lock" [Nu **15** 38.39], גְּדִלִים, *g^edhilīm*, "twisted threads," "festoons" [Dt **22** 12]): Tassels worn by the Israelites on the four corners of their garments as reminders of "all the commandments of Jehovah," in

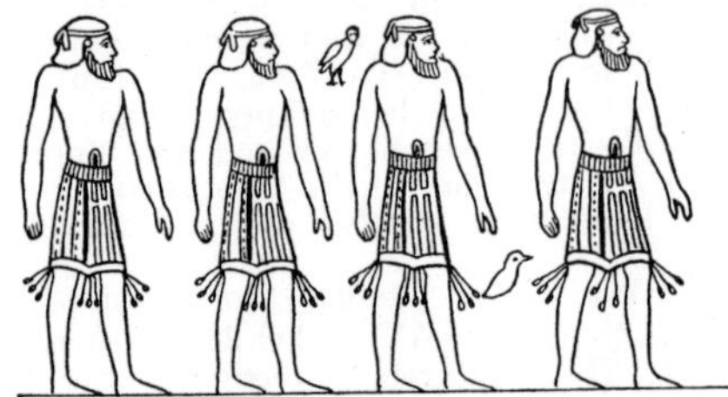

Fringed Skirts from Tomb at Bab-el Melook.

accordance with the law set out in Nu **15** 37–41 and Dt **22** 12. These tassels originally contained a thread of *t^ekhēleth*, "violet." Jewish tradition, however, has failed to retain the *t^ekhēleth*, because of doubt as to the exact meaning of the term, and instead dark blue lines were dyed on the borders of the *ṭallīth* or garment in which the fringes were placed. According to tradition any garment having four corners required the mnemonic fringes, the importance of which was weighed against "all the commandments of the Lord." In NT times such garments were still worn (cf Mt **9** 20; **14** 36; **23** 5). The later Jews, after adopting the garments of the Diaspora, in order to observe the *çīçith* commandment began to use two extra four-cornered fringed garments: the large *ṭallīth* while at prayer, and the small *ṭallīth*, or *'arba' kan^ephōth*, as an undergarment during the day. Their tradition prescribes the exact manner in which each tassel

Assyrian Fringed Garment.

shall be made, and gives a symbolic meaning to the numbers of windings and knots, somewhat after the manner of the string-writing of several early civilizations (cf the Peruvian *quipus*). Thus in the *çīçith* a long cord is wrapped around seven shorter cords first seven times, then eight, then eleven, and finally thirteen, each series being separated from the others by two knots. The numbers seven and eight constituting fifteen together suggest יה, *YH*, and the number eleven, וה, *WH*. Together they make up the holy name *YaHWeH*. The number thirteen stands for אֶחָד, *'eḥādh*, the letters of which taken as numerals equal thirteen. The sentence *Yahweh 'eḥādh* means "Yahweh is one." Many other suggestions, more or less fanciful, have been worked out, all tending to associate the fringes with the Law in the mind of the wearer. See DRESS.

ELLA DAVIS ISAACS

FROCK, frok (שִׂמְלָה, *simlāh;* ὠμόλινον, *hōmólinon*): The hempen frock, mentioned in Ecclus **40** 4 as a mark of the lowly, was a simple garment consisting of a square piece of cloth wrapped around the body. It is the same as the garment (*simlāh*) which we find the poor man using as his only bed covering by night (Ex **22** 26 f); the traveler, as the receptacle for his belongings (cf Ex **12** 34); and the common people of both sexes as their general outer garments, though there was some difference in appearance between the *simlāh* of the man and that of the woman (Dt **22** 5). See DRESS.

ELLA DAVIS ISAACS

FROG (צְפַרְדֵּעַ, *çephardēa';* cf Arab. ضِفْدَع, *ḍafda'* [Ex **8** 2 ff; Ps **78** 45; **105** 30]; **βάτραχος,** *bátrachos* [Rev **16** 13]): The references in Pss, as well as in Ex, are to the plague of frogs. In Rev **16** 13 we have, "And I saw coming out of the mouth of the dragon, and out of the mouth of the beast, and out of the mouth of the false prophet, three unclean spirits, as it were frogs." The word *çephardēa'* probably referred both to frogs and to toads, as does the Arab. *ḍafda'*. In Pal and Syria *Rana esculenta, Bufo viridis* and *Hyla arborea* are common. According to Mr. Michael J. Nicoll, assistant director of the Zoölogical Gardens at *Gîzah*, near Cairo, the commonest Egyp species are *Rana mascariensis* and *Bufo regularis*. *Rana esculenta, Bufo viridis* and *Bufo vittatus* are also found, but are much less common.

ALFRED ELY DAY

FRONTIER, fron'tēr, frun'tēr (קָצֶה, *ḳāçeh*): The word occurs once in pl. in Ezk **25** 9. RVm has "in every quarter."

FRONTLETS, frunt'lets (טוֹטָפוֹת, *ṭōṭāphōth*, fr *ṭūph*, "to bind"): Ornaments worn on the forehead, particularly **phylacteries** (which see), which were worn in this manner and also on the arms (Ex **13** 16; Dt **6** 8; **11** 18; cf also Ex **13** 9).

FROST, frost (כְּפֹר, *kephōr*, "hoar-frost," Ex **16** 14; Job **38** 29; חֲנָמַל, *ḥănāmal*, perh. "the *aphis*," Ps **78** 47; קֶרַח, *ḳeraḥ*, "cold," Gen **31** 40; Job **37** 10 AV; Jer **36** 30):

1. Formation

A temperature of freezing or lower is called frost. Dew forms when the temperature is decreased; and if below freezing, the dew takes the form of a white film or covering over rocks and leaves. This white covering is called hoar-frost. Like dew it is the result of condensation of the moisture of the air on objects which radiate their heat quickly. In order that condensation may take place the atmosphere must be saturated. Frost may be expected on clear, still nights when the radiation is sufficient to reduce the temperature below the freezing-point.

2. In Syria and Palestine

In Syria and Pal frost is a very rare occurrence at sea-level; but on the hills and elevated plains it is usual in winter, beginning with November, and on the highest elevations throughout the year. Late spring frosts in March or early April do great damage to fruit. In clear weather there is often a great variation in the temperature of the day and the night, esp. on the inland plains, so that lit., as Jacob said to Laban, "In the day the drought consumed me, and the frost by night" (Gen **31** 40); "In the day to the heat, and in the night to the frost" (Jer **36** 30; cf **22** 19), a passage which suggests that Jehoiakim's corpse was left unburied.

3. In Egypt

The meaning of *ḥănāmal*, tr[d] "frost" in Ps **78** 47 (see above), "He destroyed .... their sycomore-trees with frost" (m "great hail-stones"), is uncertain. "Frost is unknown in Egypt, and Gesenius suggests 'ants,' comparing it with Arab. *namal*" (Temple, *BD*, s.v.).

4. Figurative Uses

The manna in the wilderness is compared to hoar-frost. "A small round thing, small as the hoar-frost" (Ex **16** 14). Manna is occasionally found in Syria now as a flaky, gelatinous substance formed on bushes and rocks. The elements of Nature are indications of God's power, and are referred to as signs of His might: "By the breath of God frost is given" (Job **37** 10 AV). "The hoary frost of heaven, who hath gendered it?" (Job **38** 29); "He destroyed their vines with hail, and their sycomore-trees with frost" (Ps **78** 47); "He scattereth the hoar-frost like ashes" (Ps **147** 16).

ALFRED H. JOY

FROWARDNESS, frō'wērd-nes: The tr of תַּהְפֻּכוֹת, *tahpukhōth*, the pl. of *tahpūkhāh*, "perversity," "foolishness" (from *hāphakh*, "to turn about") in Prov **2** 14, "delight in the frowardness of the wicked," ARV "the perverseness of evil," m "the evil man" (cf ver 12; some render "deceit"); **6** 14 ARV, "perverseness"; **10** 32, "the mouth of the wicked speaketh frowardness," ARV "speaketh perverseness," m "is."

FRUIT, frōōt. See FOOD; BOTANY, and special arts. on APPLE; FIG; VINE, etc.

FRUSTRATE, frus'trāt (פָּרַר, *pārar;* ἀθετέω, *atheteō*): "Frustrate" (from *frustra*, "vain") is the tr of *pārar*, "to break," "to make void," "to bring to nothing" (Ezr **4** 5), "to frustrate their purpose" (Isa **44** 25, "that frustrateth the signs of the liars"); of *atheteō*, "to displace," "to reject or make void or null": Gal **2** 21, "I do not frustrate the grace of God" (by setting up the righteousness which is "through the law"), RV "make void"; cf 1 Macc **11** 36, "Nothing hereof shall be revoked," RV "annulled" (*atheteō*).

RV has "frustrateth" for "disappointeth" (Job **5** 12, *pārar*).

The adj. appears (2 Esd **10** 34), "frustrate of my hope" (Jth **11** 11, "frustrate of his purpose" [*ápraktos*]).

W. L. WALKER

FRYING-PAN, frī'ing-pan. See BREAD; PAN.

FUEL, fū'el (אָכְלָה, *'okhlāh*, or מַאֲכֹלֶת, *ma'ăkhōleth*, "food"): Is mentioned specifically only in the OT, in Isa **9** 5.19; Ezk **15** 4.6; **21** 32. Its general, lit. meaning in these connections is "food for fire," and might include any sort of combustible material. The common forms of fuel were wood of various sorts (even including thorns, Ps **58** 9; **118** 12; Eccl **7** 6), and dried stalks of flowers or grass (Mt **6** 30), charred wood as charcoal (Lev **16** 12; Isa **44** 19, and frequently), and dried dung (Ezk **4** 12.15). There is no certain indication that our coal was known to the Hebrews as fuel, and their houses, being without chimneys, were not constructed for the extensive use of fuel for warmth.

LEONARD W. DOOLAN

FUGITIVE, fū'ji-tiv (פָּלִיט, *pālīṭ*, from פָּלַט, *pālaṭ*, "to escape"; נָע, *nā'*, from נוּעַ, *nūa'*, "to waver"; נֹפֵל, *nōphēl*, from נָפַל, *nāphal*, "to fall"; בָּרִיחַ, *bārīah*, בְּרִיחַ, *berīah*, and מִבְרָח, *mibhrāh*, from בָּרַח, *bārah*, "to flee"): One who flees from danger (Isa **15** 5; Ezk **17** 21); escapes from bondage (2 Macc **8** 35 [as adj.]); deserts from duty (Jgs **12** 4; 2 K **25** 11 AV; cf Jth **16** 12 AV), or wanders aimlessly (Gen **4** 12.14).

FULFIL, fo͝ol-fil' (מָלֵא, *mālē'*; **πληρόω**, *plēróō*, **τελέω**, *teléō*, with other words): "Fulfil" is used (1) in a sense more or less obsolete, "to fill up," complete (Gen **29** 21.28; Ex **23** 26; Job **36** 17, RV "full," m "filled up"; Mt **3** 15, "to fulfil all righteousness"; Phil **2** 2, "Fulfil ye my joy," ARV "make full"; cf 2 Cor **10** 6); (2) in the sense of "to accomplish," "to carry into effect," as to fulfil the word of Jeh (1 K **2** 27; **8** 15.24; 2 Ch **36** 21, etc); in the NT very frequently used of the fulfilment of prophetic Scripture (Mt **1** 22; **2** 15, etc). Love is declared to be "the fulfilment [*plērōma*, "fulness"] of the law" (Rom **13** 10). For "fulfil" RV has "do" (Rev **17** 17); for "fulfilled" has "performed" (2 S **14** 22), "accomplished" (Ezr **1** 1; Mt **5** 18; **24** 34; Lk **21** 32; Jn **19** 28), with numerous other changes. W. L. WALKER

FULLER, fo͝ol'ẽr (כָּבַס, *kābhaṣ*; lit. "to trample," **γναφεύς**, *gnapheús*): The fuller was usually the dyer, since, before the woven cloth could be properly dyed, it must be freed from the oily and gummy substances naturally found on the raw fiber. Many different substances were anciently used for cleansing. Among them were white clay, putrid urine, and the ashes of certain desert plants (Arab. *ḳali*, Bib. "soap"; Mal **3** 2). The fuller's shop was usually outside the city (2 K **18** 17; Isa **7** 3; **36** 2), first, that he might have sufficient room to spread

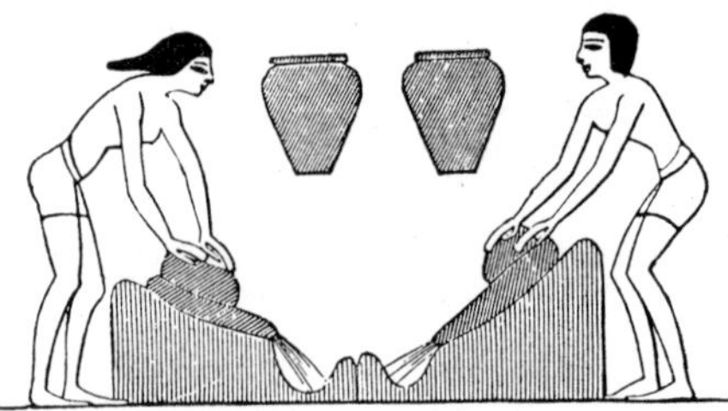

Egyptian Fuller.

out his cloth for drying and sunning, and second, because of the offensive odors sometimes produced by his processes. The Syrian indigo dyer still uses a cleaning process closely allied to that pictured on the Egyp monuments. The unbleached cotton is soaked in water and then sprinkled with the powdered ashes of the *ishnan*, locally called *ḳali*, and then beaten in heaps on a flat stone either with another stone or with a large wooden paddle. The cloth is washed free from the alkali by small boys treading on it in a running stream or in many changes of clean water (cf *En-rogel*, lit. "foot fountain," but tr[d] also "fuller's fountain" because of the fullers' method of washing their cloth). Mark describes Jesus' garments at the time of His transfiguration as being whiter than any fuller on earth could whiten them (Mk **9** 3). JAMES A. PATCH

FULLER'S FIELD, fo͝ol'ẽrs fēld, **THE** (שְׂדֵה כוֹבֵס, *sedhēh khōbhēṣ*): In all references occurs "the conduit of the upper pool, in the highway of the fuller's field"; this must have been a well-known landmark at Jerus in the time of the monarchy. Here stood Rabshakeh in his interview with Eliakim and others on the wall (2 K **18** 17; Isa **36** 2); clearly the highway was within easy earshot of the walls. Here Isaiah met Ahaz and Shear-jashub his son by command of Jeh (Isa **7** 3). An old view placed these events somewhere near the present Jaffa Gate, as here runs an aqueduct from the *Birket Mamilla* outside the walls of the *Birket Hamam el Batrah*, inside the walls; the former was considered the "Upper Pool" and is traditionally called the "Upper Pool" of Gihon. But these pools and this aqueduct are certainly of later date (see JERUSALEM). Another view puts this highway to the N. side of the city, where there are extensive remains of a "conduit" running in from the N. In favor of this is the fact that the N. was the usual side for attack and the probable position for Rabshakeh to gather his army; it also suits the conditions of Isa **7** 3. Further, Jos (*BJ*, V, iv, 2) in his description of the walls places a "Monument of the Fuller" at the N.E. corner, and the name "fuller" survived in connection with the N. wall to the 7th cent., as the pilgrim Arculf mentions a gate W. of the Damascus gate called *Porta Villae Fullonis*. The most probable view, however, is that this conduit was one connected with Gihon, the present "Virgin's Fountain" (see GIHON). This was well known as "the upper spring" (2 Ch **32** 30), and the pool, which, we know, was at the source, would probably be called the "Upper Pool." In this neighborhood—or lower down the valley near *En-rogel*, which is supposed by some to mean "the spring of the fuller"—is the natural place to expect "fulling." Somewhere along the Kidron valley between the Virgin's Fountain and the junction with the Tyropœon was the probable scene of the interview with Rabshakeh; the conversation may quite probably have occurred across the valley, the Assyr general standing on some part of the cliffs now covered by the village of Siloam. E. W. G. MASTERMAN

FULLER'S FOUNTAIN. See EN-ROGEL.

FULNESS, fo͝ol'nes: The tr of πλήρωμα, *plērōma*, which is generally, but not invariably, rendered "fulness" in the NT. Etymologically, *plērōma*—which itself is derived from the vb. *pleróō*, "I fill"—signifies "that which is or has been filled"; it also means "that which fills or with which a thing is filled"; then it signifies "fulness," "a fulfilling."

1. "Fulness" in the Gospels

In the Gospels it occurs as follows: Mt **9** 16 and Mk **2** 21: in both of these passages it means "the fulness," that by which a gap or rent is filled up, when an old garment is repaired by a patch; Mk **6** 43, 'They took up fragments, the fulness of twelve baskets'; **8** 20, 'The fulness of how many baskets of fragments did ye take up?' Jn **1** 16, 'out of his fulness we all received.'

2. Its Use in the Pauline Epistles

Elsewhere in the NT "fulness" is used by Paul alone, who employs it 12 t, in addition to the frequent use he makes of the vb. "to fill." Of these 12, no fewer than 6 are in Eph and Col. The references are these: Rom **11** 12, "If . . . . their loss [is] the riches of the Gentiles; how much more their fulness?" The "fulness" of Israel here refers to their being, as a nation, received by God to a participation in all the benefits of Christ's salvation. Ver 25, "A hardening . . . . hath befallen Israel, until the fulness of the Gentiles be come in." **13** 10, "Love . . . . is the fulfilment [the fulfilling] of the law"; that is, love is not a partial fulfilment, by obedience to this or that commandment, but a complete filling up of what the law enjoins. **15** 29, "I shall come in the fulness of the blessing of Christ." 1 Cor **10** 26, "The earth is the Lord's, and the fulness thereof." Gal **4** 4, "when the fulness of the time came." The fulness of the time is that portion of time by which the longer antecedent period is completed. Eph **1** 10, "unto a dispensation of the fulness of the times." Ver 23, "the church, which is his body, the fulness of him that filleth all in all." The church is the fulness of Christ; the body of believers is filled with the presence, power, agency and riches of Christ. **3** 19, "that ye may be filled unto all the fulness of God"—that ye may be wholly filled with God and with His presence and power and grace. **4** 13, "unto the measure of the stature of the fulness of Christ." Col **1** 19, "In him should all the fulness dwell." **2** 9, "In him dwelleth all the fulness of the Godhead bodily" (cf Lk **2** 40.52; **4** 1).

3. "Fulness" in Eph and Col

"Fulness" in Eph and Col is used to present some of the most prominent thoughts in these epistles, sometimes referring to Christ, sometimes to the church and the individual Christian. Christ is Himself to "fulfil" all things in heaven and on earth (Eph **4** 10 AVm). We cannot separate "the fulness of Christ" in this passage (ver 13) from the statement in **1** 23, that the Christ is being fulfilled, and finds His fulness in the church. When all the saints have come to the unity which is their destined goal, or in other words, to the full-grown man, the Christ will have been fulfilled. Thus they will have together reached "the full measure of the maturity of the fulness of the Christ" (J. Armitage Robinson, *Comm. on Eph*, 183). The church and individual believers have, by faith, the full possession of all that Christ has to impart—the grace and comfort and strength of Christ received by them now. Cf Jn **1** 16; 'In him ye are complete, are made full' (Col **2** 10); that is, the fulness of moral, intellectual and spiritual perfection is communicated by Christ to all who are united to Him. "When as the result of the Holy Spirit's inward strengthening, Christ dwells in the heart, and His knowledge-surpassing love is known, the only limit to spiritual excellence is 'to be filled unto all the fulness of God'!" (*HDB*, 735).

4. Its Use by the False Teachers at Colossae

In the passages from Col, "the fulness" in Christ is contrasted with the mediating aeons or angelic powers or spiritual manifestations supposed to be intermediate between God and the world. The false teachers at Colossae seem to have used "fulness," as a technical or semi-technical term, for the purpose of their philosophical or theosophical teaching, employing it to signify the entire series of angels or aeons, which filled the space or interval between a holy God and a world of matter, which was conceived of as essentially and necessarily evil. Teaching of this sort was entirely derogatory to the person and work of Christ. In opposition, therefore, to the Colossian false teaching in regard to "the fulness," Paul shows what the facts really are, that in Christ dwells all the fulness of the Godhead bodily. The fulness of the Godhead is the totality of the Di-

5. The Fulness in Christ

vine powers and attributes, all the wealth of the being and of the nature of God—eternal, infinite, unchangeable in existence, in knowledge, in wisdom, in power, in holiness, in goodness, in truth, in love. This is the fulness of the nature of God—life, light, love; and this has its permanent, its settled abode in Christ. All that is His own by right is His by His Father's good pleasure also. It was the Father's good pleasure that in Christ should all the fulness dwell.

Any limitation, therefore, of the meaning of "fulness," which would make the indwelling of the fulness of the Godhead in Christ a matter either of the future, or of the past only, is inconsistent with what is said of "the fulness" in Him, in Col **1** 19; **2** 9. The reference in both passages is to the timeless and eternal communication of the fulness of the Godhead from the Father to the Son.

It was in a sense developed along the lines of the Colossian teaching regarding "the fulness," that the Gnostics afterward used the term. See GNOSTICISM.

JOHN RUTHERFURD

FUNERAL, fū'nẽr-al. See BURIAL.

FURLONG, fûr'long (**στάδιον,** *stádion,* "stadium"; Lk **24** 13; Jn **6** 19; **11** 18; Rev **14** 20; **21** 16): A Gr measure of length, being 600 Gr ft., or 100 *orguiai* equal to 606¾ Eng. ft., and thus somewhat less than a furlong, which is 660 ft. See WEIGHTS AND MEASURES.

FURNACE, fûr'nās: The word is used in the OT EV to translate several Heb words:

Kibhshān, in Gen **19** 28, where the smoke of the destruction of the cities of the plain is said to have ascended "as the smoke of a f."; in Ex **9** 8, where Jeh commands to take "handfuls of ashes of the f. and . . . . sprinkle it toward heaven," etc.

Kūr, in Dt **4** 20, where Jeh is represented, when speaking of taking the children of Israel out of Egypt, as taking them "out of the iron furnace."

'Ălīl, in Ps **12** 6, where "the words of Jeh" are said to be "pure," "as silver tried in a f."; cf Prov **17** 3, "f. for gold."

'Attūn, in Dnl **3** 6, where mention is made of "a burning fiery f." into which Daniel and his companions were cast. There is good reason to believe that these words all stand for either a brick-kiln or a smelting furnace.

In the NT a notable **figurative** use is made of the word in the phrase "the f. of fire," ἡ κάμινος τοῦ πυρός, *hē káminos toú purós.* It is found in the parable of the Tares (Mt **13** 42) as part of the remarkable imagery of that parable; while in the companion parable of the Drag-Net (ver 50) it stands as a symbol of the final destiny of the impenitent, a synonym of "hell"; cf Jer **29** 22; Dnl **3** 6.22; Rev **20** 14–15, etc, and "eternal fire" (Mt **25** 41), "unquenchable fire" (**3** 12), "the Gehenna of fire" (**5** 22 m; **18** 9 ∥ Mk **9** 43 m, etc). A fact which modern travelers speak of, that furnaces for punishment have been found in Persia as elsewhere in the East, sheds some light upon this use of the expression "the f. of fire."

GEO. B. EAGER

FURNACES, TOWER OF THE (Neh **3** 11). See JERUSALEM.

FURNISH, fûr'nish (מָלֵא, *mālē';* **πλήθομαι,** *plḗthomai*): To "furnish" is to supply with what is useful or necessary, to fit out, provide, equip. It is the tr of several Heb or Gr words: of *mālē',* "to fill in or up," "to complete" (Isa **65** 11 AV); *nāsā,* "to lift up," "to aid" (1 K **9** 11); *'ānaḳ,* Hiphil, prob. "to lay on the neck," "to encircle" (with a bracelet) (Dt **15** 14), of a slave set at liberty; *'ārakh,* "to arrange in order," "to lay out a table" (Ps **78** 19 AV; Prov **9** 2); *'āsāh kelī,* "to make a vessel for containing things" (Jer **46** 19, "Furnish thyself to go into captivity," RVm "Heb, make thee vessels of captivity"); *plēthomai,* "to be filled" (Mt **22** 10 AV); *strōnnumi,* "to strew," "to spread" (Mk **14** 15; Lk **22** 12); *exartízō,* "to complete fully," "to equip" (2 Tim **3** 17).

In Ecclus **29** 26 we have "furnish a table" (*kosméō*); **44** 6, "furnished with ability" (*chorēgéō*); 1 Macc **14** 34 AV, "He furnished them with all things" (*títhēmi*).

W. L. WALKER

FURNITURE, fûr′ni-ṭūr (כַּר, *kār*, כֵּלִים, *kēlīm;* σκευή, *skeuḗ*): In Gen **31** 34 *kār* is tr[d] "furniture" in AV, but "saddle" in ARV. The latter is decidedly preferable. It was the "camel-basket," or the basket-saddle of the camel, which was a sort of palanquin bound upon the saddle. Upon this saddle-basket Rachel sat with the teraphim hidden beneath, and her wily father did not suspect the presence of his **gods** in such a place. In other places the word *kēlīm* is used, and is generally rendered "vessels," though sometimes "furniture." It may have many other renderings also (see *BDB*). Ex **31** 7; **39** 33 mention the furniture of the Tent, which is specified in other places. Moses is instructed (**25** 9) to make a sanctuary or tabernacle and the furniture thereof according to the pattern showed him in the Mount. The furniture of the Court consisted of the brazen altar and laver (**40** 29.30); that of the Holy Place, of the table of showbread, the golden lampstand and altar of incense (**39** 36; **40** 22–26; He **9** 2); that of the Holy of Holies, of the ark and mercy-seat overshadowed by the cherubim. The tribe of Levi was set apart by Jeh to "keep all the furniture of the tent of meeting" (Nu **3** 8). When David organized the tabernacle-worship in Jerus and assigned the Levites their separate duties, certain men "were appointed over the furniture, and over all the vessels of the sanctuary" (1 Ch **9** 29). In Nah **2** 9 the sing. form of the word *k*ᵉ*lī* is used, and is rendered "furniture." The prophet refers to the abundant, costly, luxurious furniture and raiment, largely the results of their conquests and plunder in many countries.

In Acts **27** 19 the word *skeuē* is tr[d] in AV and RV "tackling," with "furniture" in RVm.

By way of information regarding the general furniture of the house little is said directly in the Scriptures. The chamber built for Elisha upon the wall contained a bed, a table, a seat, and lampstand. This was doubtless the furnishing of most bedrooms when it could be afforded. The prophet Amos had a supreme contempt for the luxurious furniture of the grandees of Samaria (**3** 12; **6** 4). For full particulars see HOUSE; TABERNACLE; TEMPLE.

J. J. REEVE

FURROW, fur′ō (תֶּלֶם, *telem*): The word is tr[d] "furrows" in Job **39** 10; **31** 38; Ps **65** 10; Hos **10** 4; **12** 11 (Ps **65** 10 AV, "ridges"). In these passages the fields are pictured as they were in the springtime or late autumn. When the showers had softened the earth, the seed was sown and the soil turned over with the plow and left in furrows, not harrowed and pulverized as in our modern farming. The Syrian farmer today follows the custom of his ancient predecessors.

Another word, מַעֲנָה, *ma'ănāh*, occurs in two passages, first in the **figurative** sense in Ps **129** 3, and second in an obscure passage in 1 S **14** 14. Three other words, גְּדוּדָה, *g*ᵉ*dhūdhāh*, עֲרוּגָה, *'ărūghāh*, עַיִן, *'ayin*, tr[d] "furrows" in AV, are probably more properly rendered in ARV "ridges" (Ps **65** 10), "beds" (Ezk **17** 7.10), and "transgressions" (Hos **10** 10). See AGRICULTURE; PLOW.

JAMES A. PATCH

FURTHER, fûr′thẽr, **FURTHERANCE,** fûr′thẽr-ans (יָסַף, *yāṣaph;* ἔτι, *éti*, προκοπή, *prokopḗ*): **Further,** advb. and adj., is comparative of "forth," meaning "to a greater distance," "something more," "moreover," etc; the vb. "to further," means "to help forward," "advance," "assist." The vb. occurs (Ezr **8** 36) as the tr of *nāsā'*, "to lift up": "They furthered the people and the house of God" (cf 1 K **9** 11; Ezr **1** 4); of *pūḳ* "to send forth," "carry out" (Ps **140** 8, "Further not his evil device").

Furtherance is the tr of *prokopē*, "a going forward," "advance" (Phil **1** 12, "the furtherance of the gospel," RV "progress," ver 25, "for your furtherance and joy," RV "progress").

Furthermore is the tr of *eíta*, "then," "so then" (He **12** 9); of *tó loipón*, "for the rest," or "as to the rest" (1 Thess **4** 1, RV "finally then").

RV omits "further" (Acts **12** 3); has "further" for "more than right" (Job **34** 23), for "farther thence" (Mk **1** 19, different text); "What further need have we of witnesses?" for "What need we any further witnesses?" (**14** 63); "your fellowship in furtherance of the gospel" (Phil **1** 5; **2** 22); "to the furthest bound" for "all perfection" (Job **28** 3).

W. L. WALKER

FURY, fū′ri (ἀλάστωρ, *alástōr*, "not to forget," "significant of revenge"): Occurs only in 2 Macc **7** 9 AV, "Thou like a fury [RV "Thou, miscreant"] takest us out of this present life." See also WRATH; FIERCENESS; ANGER.

FUTURE, fū′ṭūr, fū′chur. See ESCHATOLOGY.

G

GAAL, gā′al (גַּעַל, *ga'al*, "rejection," or "loathing"; according to Wellhausen, "beetle," *HPN*, 110): A man of whose antecedents nothing is known, except that his father's name was Ebed. He undertook to foment and lead a rebellion on the part of the inhabitants of Shechem against Abimelech, son of Gideon, and his rebellion failed (Jgs **9** 26–45). See also ABIMELECH.

GAASH, gā′ash (גַּעַשׁ, *ga'ash*): First mentioned in connection with the burial place of Joshua "in the border of his inheritance in Timnath-serah, which is in the hill-country of Ephraim, on the north [side] of the mountain of Gaash" (Josh **24** 30; cf Jgs **2** 9); see TIMNATH-HERES. The "brooks," or rather the wadies or "watercourses" of Gaash are mentioned as the native place of Hiddai (2 S **23** 30), or Hurai (1 Ch **11** 32), one of David's heroes. No likely identification has been suggested. See EPHRAIM, MOUNT.

GABA, gā′ba (גָּבַע, *gābha'* [in pause]). See GEBA.

GABAEL, gab′ā-el (Γαβαήλ, *Gabaḗl;* Vulg "Gabelus"):

(1) An ancestor of Tobit (Tob **1** 1).

(2) A poor Jew of Rages, a city of Media, to whom Tobit lent ten talents of silver (**1** 14). The money was restored to Tobit in the time of his distress through his son Tobias, whom the angel Raphael led to Gabael at Rages (**1** 14; **4** 1.20; **5** 6; **6** 9; **10** 2).

GABATHA, gab′a-tha (Γαβαθά, *Gabathá*): A eunuch of Mardocheus (Ad Est **12** 1).

GABBAI, gab′ā-ī (גַּבַּי, *gabbay*, "collector"): One of the chiefs of the Benjamites in Jerus after the return from the Babylonish captivity (Neh **11** 8).

GABBATHA, gab′a-tha: Given (Jn **19** 13) as the name of a special pavement (τὸ λιθόστρωτον, *tó lithóstrōton*), and is probably a transcription in Gr of the Aram. גַּבְּתָא, *gabh*ᵉ*thā'*, meaning "height" or "ridge." Tradition which now locates the Praetorium at the Antonia and associates the triple Rom arch near there with the "Ecce Homo" scene, naturally identifies an extensive area of massive Rom pavement, with blocks 4 ft.×3½ ft. and 2 ft. thick, near the "Ecce Homo Arch," as the Gabbatha. This paved area is in places roughened for a roadway, and in other places is marked with incised designs for Rom games of chance. The site is a lofty one, the ground falling away rapidly to the E. and W., and it must have been close to, or perhaps included in, the Antonia. But apart from the fact that it is quite improbable that the Praetorium was here (see PRAETORIUM), it is almost certain that the *lithostrōton* was a mosaic pavement (cf Est **1** 6), such as was very common in those days, and the site is irretrievably lost. E. W. G. MASTERMAN

GABBE, gab'ē (**Γαββή,** *Gabbḗ;* AV **Gabdes** [1 Esd **5** 20]): Called Geba in Ezr **2** 26.

GABRIAS, gā'bri-as (**Γαβρίας,** *Gabrías*): Brother of GABAEL (q.v.). In Tob **4** 20 he is described as his father. The readings are uncertain.

GABRIEL, gā'bri-el (גַּבְרִיאֵל, *gabhrī'ēl,* "Man of God"; **Γαβριήλ,** *Gabriḗl*): The name of the angel commissioned to explain to Daniel the vision of the ram and the he-goat, and to give the prediction of the 70 weeks (Dnl **8** 16; **9** 21). In the NT he is the angel of the annunciation to Zacharias of the birth of John the Baptist, and to Mary of the birth of Jesus (Lk **1** 19.26). Though commonly spoken of as an archangel, he is not so called in Scripture. He appears in the Book of En (chs **9, 20, 40**) as one of 4 (or 6) chief angels. He is "set over all powers," presents, with the others, the cry of departed souls for vengeance, is "set over the serpents, and over Paradise, and over the cherubim." He is prominent in the Jewish Tgs, etc. See ANGEL.

JAMES ORR

GAD (גָּד, *gādh,* "fortune"; **Γάδ,** *Gád*): The seventh son of Jacob, whose mother was Zilpah (Gen **30** 11), and whose birth was welcomed by Leah with the cry, "Fortunate!" Some have sought to connect the name with that of the heathen deity Gad, of which traces are found in Baal-gad, Migdal-gad, etc. In the blessing of Jacob (**49** 19) there is a play upon the name, as if it meant "troop," or "marauding band." "Gad, a troop shall press upon him; but he shall press upon their heel" (Heb *gādh, gᵉdhūdh, yᵉghūdhennū, wᵉhū yāghūdh 'āḳēbh*). Here there is doubtless a reference to the high spirit and valor that characterized the descendants of Gad. The enemy who attacked them exposed himself to grave peril. In the blessing of Moses again (Dt **33** 20 ff) it is said that Gad "dwelleth as a lioness, and teareth the arm, yea, the crown of the head." Leonine qualities are ascribed to the **Gadites,** mighty men of valor, who joined David (1 Ch **12** 8.14). Their "faces were like the faces of lions, and they were as swift as the roes upon the mountain." Among their captains "he that was least was equal to a hundred, and the greatest to a thousand."

1. The Name

Of the patriarch Gad almost nothing is recorded. Seven sons went down with him into Egypt, when Jacob accepted Joseph's invitation (Gen **46** 16). At the beginning of the desert march Gad numbered 45,650 "from twenty years old and upward, all that were able to go forth to war" (Nu **1** 24). In the plains of Moab the number had fallen to 40,500 (**26** 18). The place of Gad was with the standard of the camp of Reuben on the S. side of the tabernacle (**2** 14). The prince of the tribe was Eliasaph, son of Deuel (**1** 14), or Reuel (**2** 14). Among the spies Gad was represented by Geuel son of Machi (**13** 15). See NUMBERS.

2. The Tribe

From time immemorial the dwellers E. of the Jordan have followed the pastoral life. When Moses had completed the conquest of these lands, the spacious uplands, with their wide pastures, attracted the great flock-masters of Reuben and Gad. In response to their appeal Moses assigned them their tribal portions here: only on condition, however, that their men of war should go over with their brethren, and take their share alike in the hardship and in the glory of the conquest of Western Pal (ch **32**). When the victorious campaigns of Joshua were completed, the warriors of Reuben and Gad returned to their possessions in the E. They halted, however, in the Jordan valley to build the mighty altar of Ed. They feared lest the gorge of the Jordan should in time become all too effective a barrier between them and their brethren on the W. This altar should be for all time a "witness" to their unity in race and faith (Josh **22**). The building of the altar was at first misunderstood by the western tribes, but the explanation given entirely satisfied them.

3. The Tribal Territory

It is impossible to indicate with any certainty the boundaries of the territory of Gad. Reuben lay on the S., and the half-tribe of Manasseh on the N. These three occupied the whole of Eastern Pal. The S. border of Gad is given as the Arnon in Nu **32** 34; but six cities to the N. of the Arnon are assigned in vs 16 ff to Reuben. Again, Josh **13** 26 makes *Wādy Ḥesbān* the southern boundary of Gad. Mesha, however (MS), says that the men of Gad dwelt in Ataroth from old time. This is far S. of *Wādy Ḥesbān.* The writer of Nu **32** may have regarded the Jabbok as the northern frontier of Gad; but Josh **13** 27 extends it to the Sea of Chinnereth, making the Jordan the western boundary. It included Rabbath-ammon in the E. We have not now the information necessary to explain this apparent confusion. There can be no doubt that, as a consequence of strifes with neighboring peoples, the boundaries were often changed (1 Ch **5** 18 f). For the Bib. writers the center of interest was in Western Pal, and the details given regarding the eastern tribes are very meager. We may take it, however, that, roughly, the land of Gilead fell to the tribe of Gad. In Jgs **5** 17 Gilead appears where we should naturally expect Gad, for which it seems to stand. The city of refuge, Ramoth in Gilead, was in the territory of Gad (Josh **20** 8). For description of the country see GILEAD.

4. Boundaries

Reuben and Gad were absent from the muster against Sisera (Jgs **5** 15 ff); but they united with their brethren in taking vengeance on Benjamin, Jabesh-gilead, from which no contingent was sent, being destroyed (**20** f). Jephthah is probably to be reckoned to this tribe, his house, Mizpah (Jgs **11** 34), being apparently within its territory (Josh **13** 26). Gad furnished a refuge for some of the Hebrews during the Philistine oppression (1 S **13** 7). To David, while he avoided Saul at Ziklag, certain Gadites attached themselves (1 Ch **12** 8 ff). A company of them also joined in making him king at Hebron (ver 38). In Gad the adherents of the house of Saul gathered round Ish-bosheth (2 S **2** 8 ff). Hither David came in his flight from Absalom (**17** 24). Gad fell to Jeroboam at the disruption of the kingdom, and Penuel, apparently within its borders, Jeroboam fortified at first (1 K **12** 25). It appears from the Moabite Stone that part of the territory afterward passed into the hands of Moab. Under Omri this was recovered; but Moab again asserted its supremacy. Elijah probably belonged to this

5. History

district; and the brook Cherith must be sought in one of its wild secluded glens.

Gad formed the main theater of the long struggle between Israel and the Syrians. At Ramoth-gilead Ahab received his death wound (ch **22**). Under Jeroboam II, this country was once more an integral part of the land of Israel. In 734 BC, however, Tiglath-pileser appeared, and conquered all Eastern Pal, carrying its inhabitants captive (2 K **15** 29; 1 Ch **5** 26). This seems to have furnished occasion for the children of Ammon to occupy the country (Jer **49** 1). In Ezekiel's ideal picture (**48** 27.34), a place is found for the tribe of Gad. Obadiah seems to have forgotten the tribe, and their territory is assigned to Benjamin (ver 19). Gad, however, has his place among the tribes of Israel in Rev **7**. W. Ewing

GAD (גָּד, *gādh,* "fortunate"): David's seer (*ḥōzeh,* 1 Ch **21** 9; **29** 29; 2 Ch **29** 25), or prophet (*nābhī';* cf 1 S **22** 5; 2 S **24** 11). He appears (1) to advise David while an outlaw fleeing before Saul to return to the land of Judah (1 S **22** 5); (2) to rebuke David and give him his choice of punishments when, in spite of the advice of Joab and the traditional objections (cf Ex **30** 11 ff), he had counted the children of Israel (2 S **24** 11; 1 Ch **21** 9 ff); (3) to instruct David to erect an altar on the threshing-floor of Araunah when the plague that had descended on Israel ceased (2 S **24** 18; 1 Ch **21** 18); and (4) to assist in the arrangement of Levitical music with cymbals, psalteries and harps (cf 2 Ch **29** 25). Of his writings none are known, though he is said to have written a history of a part of David's reign (1 Ch **29** 29). Ella Davis Isaacs

GAD (גָּד, *gadh,* "fortune"): A god of Good Luck, possibly the Hyades. The writer in Isa **65** 11 m pronounces a curse against such as are lured away to idolatry. The warning here, according to Cheyne, is specifically against the Samaritans, whom with their religion the Jews held in especial abhorrence. The charge would, however, apply just as well to superstitious and semi-pagan Jews. "But ye that forsake Jeh, that forget my holy mountain, that prepare a table for Fortune, and that fill up mingled wine unto Destiny; I will destine you to the sword, and ye shall all bow down to the slaughter." There is a play upon words here: "Fill up mingled wine unto Destiny" (מְנִי, *m^enī*) and "I will destine [מָנִיתִי, *mānithī,* i.e. portion out] you for the sword" (vs 11.12). Gad and Meni mentioned here are two Syrian deities (Cheyne, *Book of the Prophet Isaiah,* 198). Schürer (*Gesch. d. jüd. Volkes,* II, 34 n., and bibliography) disputes the reference of the Gr Τύχη (*Túchē*) cult to the Sem Gad, tracing it rather to the Syrian "Astarte" worship. The custom was quite common among heathen peoples of spreading before the gods tables laden with food (cf Herod. i. 181, 183; Smith, *Rel. of Semites,* Lect X).

Nothing is known of a Bab deity named Gad, but there are Aramaean and Arab. equivalents. The origin may have been a personification of fortune and destiny, i.e. equivalent to the Fates. The Nabataean inscriptions give, in pl. form, the name of Meni. Achimenidean coins (Pers) are thought by some to bear the name of Meni. How widely spread these Syrian cults became, may be seen in a number of ways, e.g. an altar from Vaison in Southern France bearing an inscription:

"Belus Fortunae rector, Menisque Magister,"

Belus, signifying the Syrian Bel of Apamaea (Driver). Canaanitish place-names also attest the prevalence of the cult, as Baal-gad, at the foot of Hermon (Josh **11** 17; **12** 7; **13** 5); Migdal-gad, possibly Mejdel near Askalon (Josh **15** 37); Gaddi and Gaddiel (Nu **13** 10 f). In Talmudic lit. the name of Gad is frequently invoked (cf McCurdy in *Jew Enc,* V, 544). Indeed the words of Leah in Gen **30** 11 may refer not to good fortune or luck but to the deity who was esp. regarded as the patron god of Good Fortune (cf Kent, *Student's OT,* I, 111). Similar beliefs were held among the Greeks and Romans, e.g. Hor. *Sat.* ii.8, 61:

". . . Fortuna, quis est crudelior in nos te deus?"

Cic. *N.D.* iii.24, 61:

"Quo in genere vel maxime est Fortuna numeranda."

The question has also an astronomical interest Arab. tradition styled the planet Jupiter the greater fortune, and Venus the lesser fortune. Jewish tradition identified Gad with the planet Jupiter, and it has been conjectured that Meni is to be identified with the planet Venus. See, however, Astrology, 10. W. N. Stearns

GAD (אָזַל, *'āzal,* "to go about"): Used once in Jer **2** 36, "Why gaddest thou about so much to change thy way?" of going after Egypt and Assyria.

GAD, VALLEY OF (נַחַל הַגָּד, *naḥal ha-gādh;* AV **River of Gad**): In 2 S **24** 5 we read that Joab and the captains of the host passed over Jordan and pitched in Aroer, on the right side of the city that is in the midst of the valley of Gad. If we refer to Josh **13** 25 f, this might seem to indicate a valley near Rabbath-ammon. According to a generally accepted emendation suggested by Wellhausen, however, we should read, "They began from Aroer, and from the city that is in the middle of the torrent valley, toward Gad." See Ar. The valley is evidently the Arnon. W. Ewing

GADARA, gad'a-ra (**Γάδαρα,** *Gádara*): This city is not named in Scripture, but the territory belonging to it is spoken of as χώρα τῶν Γαδαρηνῶν, *chōra tōn Gadarēnōn,* "country of the Gadarenes" (Mt **8** 28). In the ‖ passages (Mk **5** 1; Lk **8** 26.37) we read: χώρα τῶν Γερασηνῶν, *chōra tōn Gerasēnōn,* "country of the Gerasenes." There is no good reason, however, to question the accuracy of the text in either case. The city of Gadara is represented today by the ruins of *Umm Ḳeis* on the heights south of *el-Ḥummeh*—the hot springs in the Yarmūk valley—about 6 miles S.E. of the Sea of Galilee. It may be taken as certain that the jurisdiction of Gadara, as the chief city in these regions, extended over the country E. of the sea, including the lands of the subordinate town, Gerasa (q.v.). The figure of a ship frequently appears on its coins: conclusive proof that its territory reached the sea. The place might therefore be called with propriety, either "land of the Gerasenes," with reference to the local center, or "land of the Gadarenes," with reference to the superior city.

1. Country of the Gadarenes

Note.—The *TR* reading, τῶν Γεργεσηνῶν, *tōn Gergesēnōn,* "of the Gergesenes," must be rejected (WH, II, App., 11).

2. History

The name Gadara appears to be Sem. It is still heard in *Jedūr,* which attaches to the ancient rock tombs, with sarcophagi, to the E. of the present ruins. They are closed by carved stone doors, and are used as storehouses for grain, and also as dwellings by the inhabitants. The place is not mentioned till later times. It was taken by Antiochus the Great when in 218 BC he first invaded Pal (Polyb. v.71). Alexander Jannaeus invested the place, and reduced it after a ten months' siege (*Ant,* XIII, iii, 3; *BJ,* I, iv, 2). Pompey is said to have restored it, 63 BC (*Ant,* XIV, iv, 4; *BJ,* I, vii, 7); from which it would appear to have declined in Jewish hands. He gave it a free constitution. From this date the era of the city was reckoned. It was the seat of one of the councils instituted by Gabinius for the government of the Jews (*Ant*, XIV, v, 4; *BJ*, I, viii, 5). It was given by Augustus to Herod the Great in 30 BC (*Ant*, XV, vii, 3; *BJ*, I, xx, 3). The emperor would not listen to the accusations of the inhabitants against Herod for oppressive conduct (*Ant*, XV, x, 2 f). After Herod's death it was joined to the province of Syria, 4 BC (*Ant*, XVII, xi, 4; *BJ*, II, vi, 3). At the beginning of the Jewish revolt the country around Gadara was laid waste (*BJ*, II, xviii, 1). The Gadarenes captured some of the boldest of the Jews, of whom several were put to death, and others imprisoned (ib, 5). A party in the city surrendered it to Vespasian, who placed a garrison there (*BJ*, IV, vii, 3). It continued to be a great and important city, and was long the seat of a bishop (Reland, *Pal*, 776). With the conquest of the Moslems it passed under eclipse, and is now an utter ruin.

3. Identification and Description

Umm Ḳeis answers the description given of Gadara by ancient writers. It was a strong fortress (*Ant*, XIII, iii, 3), near the Hieromax —i.e. *Yarmūk* (Pliny *NH*, xvi)—E. of Tiberias and Scythopolis, on the top of a hill, 3 Rom miles from hot springs and baths called Amatha, on the bank of the Hieromax (*Onom*, s.v.). The narrow ridge on which the ruins lie runs out toward the Jordan from the uplands of Gilead, with the deep gorge of *Wādy Yarmūk*—Hieromax—on the N., and *Wādy el ʻArab* on the S. The hot springs, as noted above, are in the bottom of the valley to the N. The ridge sinks gradually to the E., and falls steeply on the other three sides, so that the position was one of great strength. The ancient walls may be traced in almost their entire circuit of 2 miles. One of the great Rom roads ran eastward to *Ḍerʻah;* and an aqueduct has been traced to the pool of *el Khab*, about 20 miles to the N. of *Ḍerʻah*. The ruins include those of two theaters, a basilica, a temple, and many important buildings, telling of a once great and splendid city. A paved street, with double colonnade, ran from E. to W. The ruts worn in the pavement by the chariot wheels are still to be seen.

That there was a second Gadara seems certain, and it may be intended in some of the passages referred to above. It is probably represented by the modern *Jedūr*, not far from *es-Salṭ* (Buhl, *GAP*, 255; Guthe). Jos gives Pella as the northern boundary of Peraea (*BJ*, III, iii, 3). This would exclude Gadara on the Hieromax. The southern city, therefore, should be understood as "the capital of Peraea" in *BJ*, IV, vii, 3.

Gadara was a member of the DECAPOLIS (q.v.).

W. EWING

GADARENES, gad-a-rēnz′. See preceding article.

GADDI, gad′ī (גַּדִּי, *gaddī*, "my fortune"): One of the twelve spies, son of Susi, and a chief of Manasseh (Nu **13** 11).

GADDIEL, gad′i-el (גַּדִּיאֵל, *gaddī′ēl*, "blest of God"): One of the twelve men sent by Moses from the wilderness of Paran to spy out the land of Canaan. He represented the tribe of Zebulun (Nu **13** 10).

GADDIS, gad′is (A, **Γαδδίς,** *Gaddís;* **Καδδίς,** *Kaddís;* AV **Caddis**): Surname of John, the eldest brother of Judas Maccabaeus (1 Macc **2** 2).

GADI, gā′dī (גָּדִי, *gādhī*, "fortunate"): The father of Menahem, one of the kings of Israel who reached the throne through blood (2 K **15** 14.17).

GADITES, gad′īts: Members of the tribe of Gad (Dt **3** 12, etc).

GAHAM, gā′ham (גַּחַם, *gaḥam*): A son of Nahor, brother of Abraham, by his concubine Reumah (Gen **22** 24).

GAHAR, gā′hār (גַּחַר, *gaḥar*): A family name of the Nethinim who came up with Zerubbabel to Jerus (Ezr **2** 47; Neh **7** 49); in 1 Esd **5** 30 called Geddur.

GAI, gā′ī (גַּיְא, *gay′*): In RV of 1 S **17** 52 for AV "valleys." RVm notes: "The Syr and some editions of the Sept have *Gath*" (thus also Wellhausen, Budde, Driver, etc).

GAIN, gān: In the OT the tr of three Heb substs., בֶּצַע, *beçaʻ*, "unjust gain," "any gain" (Jgs **5** 19; Job **22** 3; Prov **1** 19; **15** 27; Isa **33** 15; **56** 11; Ezk **22** 13.27; Mic **4** 13); מְחִיר, *meḥīr*, "price" for which a thing is sold (Dnl **11** 39, the only place where the Heb word is trd "gain" in AV, though it occurs in other places trd "price"); תְּבוּאָה, *tebhū′āh*, "produce," "profits," "fruit" (Prov **3** 14). It is the tr of one Heb vb., בָּצַע, *bāçaʻ*, "to gain dishonestly" (Job **27** 8); of one Aram. vb., זְבַן, *zebhan*, "to buy," "procure for oneself" (Dnl **2** 8, here used of buying time, i.e. "seeking delay" [Gesenius]).

In the NT, the tr of three Gr substs., ἐργασία, *ergasía*, "gain gotten by work," "profit" (Acts **16** 16.19; **19** 24 [AV]); κέρδος, *kérdos*, "gain," "advantage" (Phil **1** 21; **3** 7, in the former, Paul asserting that to him to die was a personal advantage, because then he would "be with Christ"; in the latter, he counts as "loss" his personal privileges in the flesh, when compared with "the excellency of the knowledge of Christ"); πορισμός, *porismós*, "gain," "a source of gain" (1 Tim **6** 5.6, where the apostle asserts, not "gain" [earthly] is godliness, but godliness is "gain" [real, abiding]). It is the tr of three Gr vbs., κερδαίνω, *kerdaínō*, "to gain," "acquire," in Mt **16** 26, where Jesus teaches that the soul, or life in its highest sense ("his own self," Lk **9** 25), is worth more than the "gaining" of the whole (material) world; Mt **18** 15, concerning the winning of a sinning brother by private interview; **25** 17. 22, the parable of the Talents; Acts **27** 21 AV, injury "gained," sustained, by sailing from Crete; 1 Cor **9** 19.20 *bis*, 21.22, all referring to Paul's life-principle of accommodation to others to "gain," win, them to Christ; in Jas **4** 13 used in a commercial sense; ποιέω, *poiéō*, "to make," "make gain" (Lk **19** 18 AV, the parable of the Pounds); προσεργάζομαι, *prosergázomai*, "to gain by trading" (**19** 16, commercial use, in the same parallel).

CHARLES B. WILLIAMS

GAINSAY, gān-sā′, gān′sā (**ἀντεῖπον,** *anteipon*, **ἀντιλέγω,** *antilégō*, "to say or speak against"): Occurs as *anteipon*, "not . . . . able to withstand or to gainsay" (Lk **21** 15); as *antilegō*, "a disobedient and gainsaying people" (Rom **10** 21); 2 Esd **5** 29, *contradicebant;* Jth **8** 28, *anthístēmi;* **12** 14, *anterō;* Ad Est **13** 9, *antitássō;* 1 Macc **14** 44, *anteipon.*

Gainsayer, *antilegō* (Tit **1** 9, "exhort and convince [RV "convict"] the gainsayers").

Gainsaying, *antilogía* (Jude ver 11, "the gainsaying of Korah"); *antilogia* is LXX for *merībhāh* (Nu **20** 13); *anantirrhētōs*, "without contradiction" (Acts **10** 29, "without gainsaying").

RV has "gainsaid" for "spoken against" (Acts **19** 36); "not gainsaying" for "not answering again" (Tit **2** 9); "gainsaying" for "contradiction" (He **12** 3).

W. L. WALKER

GAIUS, gā'yus (**Γάϊος,** *Gáïos;* WH, *Gaíos*):

(1) The Gaius to whom 3 Jn is addressed. He is spoken of as "the beloved" (3 Jn vs 1.2.5.11), "walking in the truth" (vs 3.4), and doing "a faithful work" "toward them that are brethren and strangers withal" (vs 5.6). He has been identified by some with the Gaius mentioned in the Apos Const (VII, 46), as having been appointed bishop of Pergamum by John.

(2) Gaius of Macedonia, a "companion in travel" of St. Paul (Acts **19** 29). He was one of those who were seized by Demetrius and the other silversmiths in the riot at Ephesus, during St. Paul's third missionary journey.

(3) Gaius of Derbe, who was among those who accompanied St. Paul from Greece "as far as Asia," during his third missionary journey (Acts **20** 4). In the corresponding list given in the "Contendings of St. Paul" (cf Budge, *Contendings of the Twelve Apostles*, II, 592), the name of this Gaius is given as "Gallius."

(4) Gaius, the host of St. Paul when he wrote the Ep. to the Rom, and who joined in sending his salutations (Rom **16** 23). As St. Paul wrote this epistle from Corinth, it is probable that this Gaius is identical with (5).

(5) Gaius, whom St. Paul baptized at Corinth (1 Cor **1** 14). C. M. Kerr

GALAAD, gal'ā-ad (**Γαλαάδ,** *Galaád,* Gr form of Gilead [1 Macc **5** 9.55; Jth **1** 8]).

GALAL, gā'lal (גָּלָל, *gālāl*): The name of two Levites, one mentioned in 1 Ch **9** 15, the other in 1 Ch **9** 16 and Neh **11** 17.

GALATIA, ga-lā'shi-a, ga-lā'sha (**Γαλατία,** *Galatía*):

I. Introductory.—"Galatia" was a name used in two different senses during the 1st cent. after Christ: (1) geographically, to designate a country in the north part of the central plateau of Asia Minor, touching Paphlagonia and Bithynia N., Phrygia W. and S., Cappadocia and Pontus S.E. and E., about the headwaters of the Sangarios and the middle course of the Halys; (2) politically, to designate a large province of the Rom empire, including not merely the country Galatia, but also Paphlagonia and parts of Pontus, Phrygia, Pisidia, Lycaonia and Isauria. The name occurs in 1 Cor **16** 1; Gal **1** 2; 1 Pet **1** 1, and perhaps 2 Tim **4** 10. Some writers assume that Galatia is also mentioned in Acts **16** 6; **18** 23; but the Gr there has the phrase "Galatic region" or "territory," though the EV has "Galatia"; and it must not be assumed without proof that "Galatic region" is synonymous with "Galatia." If e.g. a modern narrative mentioned that a traveler crossed British territory, we know that this means something quite different from crossing Britain. "Galatic region" has a different connotation from "Galatia"; and, even if we should find that geographically it was equivalent, the writer had some reason for using that special form.

1. Two Senses of Name

The questions that have to be answered are: (*a*) In which of the two senses is "Galatia" used by Paul and Peter? (*b*) What did Luke mean by Galatic region or territory? These questions have not merely geographical import; they bear most closely, and exercise determining influence, on many points in the biography, chronology, missionary work and methods of Paul.

2. Questions to Be Answered

II. Origin of the Name "Galatia."—The name was introduced into Asia after 278–277 BC, when a large body of migrating Gauls (*Galátai* in Gr) crossed over from Europe at the invitation of Nikomedes, king of Bithynia; after ravaging a great part of Western Asia Minor they were gradually confined to a district, and boundaries were fixed for them after 232 BC. Thus originated the independent state of Galatia, inhabited by three Gaulish tribes, Tolistobogioi, Tektosages and Trokmoi, with three city-centers, Pessinus, Ankyra and Tavia (Tavion in Strabo), who had brought their wives and families with them, and therefore continued to be a distinct Gaulish race and stock (which would have been impossible if they had come as simple warriors who took wives from the conquered inhabitants). The Gaulish language was apparently imposed on all the old inhabitants, who remained in the country as an inferior caste. The Galatai soon adopted the country religion, alongside of their own; the latter they retained at least as late as the 2d cent. after Christ, but it was politically important for them to maintain and exercise the powers of the old priesthood, as at Pessinus, where the Galatai shared the office with the old priestly families.

1. The Gaulish Kingdom

The Galatian state of the Three Tribes lasted till 25 BC, governed first by a council and by tetrarchs, or chiefs of the twelve divisions (four to each tribe) of the people, then, after 63 BC, by three kings. Of these, Deiotaros succeeded in establishing himself as sole king, by murdering the two other tribal kings; and after his death in 40 BC his power passed to Castor and then to Amyntas, 36–25 BC. Amyntas bequeathed his kingdom to Rome; and it was made a Rom province (Dion Cass. 48, 33, 5; Strabo, 567, omits Castor). Amyntas had ruled also parts of Phrygia, Pisidia, Lycaonia and Isauria. The new province included these parts, and to it were added Paphlagonia 6 BC, part of Pontus 2 BC (called Pontus Galaticus in distinction from Eastern Pontus, which was governed by King Polemon and styled Polemoniacus), and in 64 also Pontus Polemoniacus. Part of Lycaonia was non-Rom and was governed by King Antiochus; from 41 to 72 AD Laranda belonged to this district, which was distinguished as *Antiochiana regio* from the Rom *regio Lycaonia* called *Galatica*.

2. Transference to Rome

This large province was divided into *regiones* for administrative purposes; and the *regiones* coincided roughly with the old national divisions Pisidia, Phrygia (including Antioch, Iconium, Apollonia), Lycaonia (including Derbe, Lystra and a district organized on the village-system), etc. See Calder in *Journal of Rom Studies*, 1912. This province was called by the Romans Galatia, as being the kingdom of Amyntas (just like the province Asia, which also consisted of a number of different countries as diverse and alien as those of province Galatia, and was so called because the Romans popularly and loosely spoke of the kings of that congeries of countries as kings of Asia). The extent of both names, Asia and Galatia, in Rom language, varied with the varying bounds of each province. The name "Galatia" is used to indicate the province, as it was at the moment, by Ptolemy, Pliny v.146, Tacitus *Hist.* ii.9; *Ann.* xiii,

3. The Roman Province

35; later chroniclers, Syncellus, Eutropius, and *Hist. Aug. Max. et Balb.* 7 (who derived it from earlier authorities, and used it in the old sense, not the sense customary in their own time); and in inscriptions *CIL*, III, 254, 272 (*Eph. Ep.* v.51); VI, 1408, 1409, 332; VIII, 11028 (Mommsen rightly, not Schmidt), 18270, etc. It will be observed that these are almost all Rom sources, and (as we shall see) express a purely Rom view. If Paul used the name "Galatia" to indicate the province, this would show that he consistently and naturally took a Rom view, used names in a Rom connotation, and grouped his churches according to Rom provincial divisions; but that is characteristic of the apostle, who looked forward from Asia to Rome (Acts **19** 21), aimed at imperial conquest and marched across the Empire from province to province (Macedonia, Achaia, Asia are always provinces to Paul). On the other hand, in the East and the Graeco-Asiatic world, the tendency was to speak of the province either as the Galatic Eparchia (as at Iconium in 54 AD, *CIG*, 3991), or by enumeration of its *regiones* (or a selection of the *regiones*). The latter method is followed in a number of inscriptions found in the province (*CIL*, III, *passim*). Now let us apply these contemporary facts to the interpretation of the narrative of Luke.

III. The Narrative of Luke.—The evangelization of the province began in Acts **13** 14. The stages are: (1) the audience in the synagogue, vs 42 f; (2) almost the whole city, ver 44; (3) the whole region, i.e. a large district which was affected from the capital (as the whole of Asia was affected from Ephesus **19** 10); (4) Iconium another city of this region: in **13** 51 no boundary is mentioned; (5) a new region Lycaonia with two cities and surrounding district (**14** 6); (6) return journey to organize the churches in (*a*) Lystra, (*b*) Iconium and Antioch (the secondary reading of WH, καὶ εἰς Ἰκόνιον καὶ Ἀντιόχειαν [*kaí eis Ikónion kaí Antiócheian*], is right, distinguishing the two regions [*a*] Lycaonia, [*b*] that of Iconium and Antioch); (7) progress across the region Pisidia, where no churches were founded (Pisidian Antioch is not in this region, which lies between Antioch and Pamphylia).

1. Stages of Evangelization of Province

Again (in **16** 1–6) Paul revisited the two *regiones:* (1) Derbe and Lystra, i.e. *regio Lycaonia Galatica*, (2) the Phrygian and Galatic region, i.e. the region which was racially Phrygian and politically Galatic. Paul traversed both regions, making no new churches but only strengthening the existing disciples and churches. In **18** 23 he again revisited the two *regiones*, and they are briefly enumerated: (1) the Galatic region (so called briefly by a traveler, who had just traversed Antiochiana and distinguished Galatica from it); (2) Phrygia. On this occasion he specially appealed, not to churches as in **16** 6, but to disciples; it was a final visit and intended to reach personally every individual, before Paul went away to Rome and the West. On this occasion the contribution to the poor of Jerus was instituted, and the proceeds later were carried by Timothy and Gaius of Derbe (Acts **20** 4; **24** 17; 1 Cor **16** 1); this was a device to bind the new churches to the original center of the faith.

These four churches are mentioned by Luke always as belonging to two *regiones*, Phrygia and Lycaonia; and each *regio* is in one case described as Galatic, i.e. part of the province Galatia. Luke did not follow the Rom custom, as Paul did; he kept the custom of the Greeks and Asiatic peoples, and styled the province by enumerating its *regiones*, using the expression Galatic (as in Pontus Galaticus and at Iconium, *CIG*, 3991) to indicate the supreme unity of the province. By using this adjective about both *regiones* he marked his point of view that all four churches are included in the provincial unity.

2. The Churches Mentioned by Luke

From Paul's references we gather that he regarded the churches of Galatia as one group, converted together (**4** 13), exposed to the same influences and changing together (**1** 6.8; **3** 1; **4** 9), naturally visited at one time by a traveler (**1** 8; **4** 14). He never thinks of churches of Phrygia or of Lycaonia; only of province Galatia (as of provinces Asia, Macedonia, Achaia). Paul did not include in one class all the churches of one journey: he went direct from Macedonia to Athens and Corinth, but classes the churches of Macedonia separate from those of Achaia. Troas and Laodicea and Colossae he classed with Asia (as Luke did Troas, Acts **20** 4), Philippi with Macedonia, Corinth with Achaia. These classifications are true only of the Rom usage, not of early Gr usage. The custom of classifying according to provinces, universal in the fully formed church of the Christian age, was derived from the usage of the apostles (as Theodore Mopsuestia expressly asserts in his *Comm. on First Timothy* [Swete, II, 121]; Harnack accepts this part of the statement [*Verbreitung*, 2d ed, I, 387; *Expansion*, II, 96]). His churches then belonged to the four provinces, Asia, Galatia, Achaia, Macedonia. There were no other Pauline churches; all united in the gift of money which was carried to Jerus (Acts **20** 4; **24** 17).

IV. St. Paul's Use of "Galatians."—The people of the province of Galatia, consisting of many diverse races, when summed up together, were called Galatai, by Tacitus *Ann.* xv.6; Syncellus, when he says Αὔγουστος Γαλάταις φόρους ἔθετο (*Augoústos Galátais phórous étheto*), follows an older historian describing the imposing of taxes on the province; and an inscription of Apollonia Phrygiae calls the people of the city Galatae (Lebas-Waddington, 1192). If Paul spoke to Philippi or Corinth or Antioch singly, he addressed them as Philippians, Corinthians, Antiochians (Phil **4** 15; 2 Cor **6** 11), not as Macedonians or Achaians; but when he had to address a group of several churches (as Antioch, Iconium, Derbe and Lystra) he could use only the provincial unity, Galatae.

All attempts to find in Paul's letter to the Galatians any allusions that specially suit the character of the Gauls or Galatae have failed. The Gauls were an aristocracy in a land which they had conquered. They clung stubbornly to their own Celtic religion long after the time of Paul, even though they also acknowledged the power of the old goddess of the country. They spoke their own Celtic tongue. They were proud, even boastful, and independent. They kept their native law under the Empire. The "Galatians" to whom Paul wrote had changed very quickly to a new form of religion, not from fickleness, but from a certain proneness to a more oriental form of religion which exacted of them more sacrifice of a ritual type. They needed to be called to freedom; they were submissive rather than arrogant. They spoke Greek. They were accustomed to the Graeco-Asiatic law: the law of adoption and inheritance which Paul mentions in his letter is not Rom, but Graeco-Asiatic, which in these departments was similar, with some differences; on this see the writer's *Historical Commentary on Gal.*

W. M. Ramsay

GALATIANS, ga-lā′shanz. See preceding article.

GALATIANS, EPISTLE TO THE:

When and to whom, precisely, this letter was written, it is difficult to say; its authorship and purpose are unmistakable. One might conceive it addressed by the apostle Paul, in its main tenor, to almost any church of his gentile mission attracted to Judaism, at any point within the years cir 45–60 AD. Some plausibly argue that it was the earliest, others place it among the later, of the Pauline Epistles. This consideration dictates the order of our inquiry, which proceeds from the plainer to the more involved and disputable parts of the subject.

I. The Authorship.—The Tübingen criticism of the last century recognized the four major epistles of Paul as fully authentic, and made them the corner-stone of its construction of NT history. Only Bruno Bauer (*Kritik. d. paulin. Briefe*, 1850–52) attacked them in this sense, while several other critics accused them of serious interpolations; but these attempts made little impression. Subsequently a group of Dutch scholars, beginning with Loman in his *Quaestiones Paulinae* (1882) and represented by Van Manen in the *EB* (art. "Paul"), have denied all the canonical epistles to the genuine Paul. They postulate a gradual development in NT ideas covering the first century and a half after Christ, and treat the existing letters as "catholic adaptations" of fragmentary pieces from the apostle's hand, produced by a school of "Paulinists" who carried their master's principles far beyond his own intentions. On this theory, Gal, with its advanced polemic against the law, approaching the position of Marcion (140 AD), was a work of the early 2d cent. Edwin Johnson in England (*Antiqua Mater*, 1887), and Steck in Germany (*Galaterbrief*, 1888), are the only considerable scholars outside of Holland who have adopted this hypothesis; it is rejected by critics so radical as Scholten and Schmiedel (see the art. of the latter on "Galatians" in *EB*). Knowling has searchingly examined the position of the Dutch school in his *Witness of the Epistles* (1892)—it is altogether too arbitrary and uncontrolled by historical fact to be entertained; see Jülicher's or Zahn's *Introduction to NT* (ET), to the same effect. Attempts to dismember this writing, and to appropriate it for other hands and later times than those of the apostle Paul, are idle in view of its vital coherence and the passionate force with which the author's personality has stamped itself upon his work; the *Paulinum pectus* speaks in every line. The two contentions on which the letter turns—concerning Paul's apostleship, and the circumcision of gentile Christians—belonged to the apostle's lifetime: in the fifth and sixth decades these were burning questions; by the 2d cent. the church had left them far behind.

1. Position of the Dutch School

Early Christianity gives clear and ample testimony to this document. Marcion placed it at the head of his *Apostolikon* (140 AD); Justin Martyr, Athenagoras, Melito, quoted it about the same time. It is echoed by Ignatius (*Philad.*, i) and Polycarp (*Philip.*, iii and v) a generation earlier, and seems to have been used by contemporary gnostic teachers. It stands in line with the other epistles of Paul in the oldest Lat, Syr and Egyp tr^s^, and in the Muratorian (Rom) Canon of the 2d cent. It comes full into view as an integral part of the new Scripture in Irenaeus, Clement of Alexandria and Tertullian at the close of this period. No breath of suspicion as to the authorship, integrity or apostolic authority of the Ep. to the Gal has reached us from ancient times.

2. Early Testimony

II. Matter of the Epistle.—

***A*) Summary of Contents**

A double note of war sounds in the address and greeting (1 1.4). Astonishment replaces the customary thanksgiving (vs 6–10): The Galatians are listening to preachers of "another gospel" (vs 6.7) and traducers of the apostle (vs 8.10), whom he declares "anathema." Paul has therefore two objects in writing—*to vindicate himself, and to clear and reinforce his doctrine.* The first he pursues from **1** 11 to **2** 21; the second from **3** 1 to **5** 12. Appropriate moral exhortations follow in **5** 13—**6** 10. The closing paragraph (**6** 11–17) resumes incisively the purport of the letter. Personal, argumentative, and hortatory matter interchange with the freedom natural in a letter to old friends.

1. Outline

Paul's independent apostleship.—Paul asserts himself for his gospel's sake, by showing that his commission was God-given and complete (vs 11.12). On four decisive moments in his course he dwells for this purpose—as regards the second manifestly (ver 20), as to others probably, in correction of misstatements:

2. Personal History (1:11—2:21 [4:12–20; 6:17])

(1) A thorough-paced Judaist and persecutor (vs 13.14), Paul was supernaturally converted to Christ (ver 15), and received at conversion his charge for the Gentiles, about which he consulted no one (vs 16.17).

(2) Three years later he "made acquaintance with Cephas" in Jerus and saw James besides, but no "other of the apostles" (vs 18.19). For long he was known only by report to "the churches of Judaea" (vs 21–24).

(3) At the end of "fourteen years" he "went up to Jerus," with Barnabas, to confer about the "liberty" of gentile believers, which was endangered by "false brethren" (**2** 1–5). Instead of supporting the demand for the circumcision of the "Greek" Titus (ver 3), the "pillars" there recognized the sufficiency and completeness of Paul's "gospel of the uncircumcision" and the validity of his apostleship (vs 6–8). They gave "right hands of fellowship" to himself and Barnabas on this understanding (vs 9.10). The freedom of gentile Christianity was secured, and Paul had not "run in vain."

(4) At Antioch, however, Paul and Cephas differed (ver 11). Cephas was induced to withdraw from the common church-table, and carried "the rest of the Jews," including Barnabas, with him (vs 12.13). "The truth of the gospel," with Cephas' own sincerity, was compromised by this "separation," which in effect "compelled the Gentiles to Judaize" (vs 13.14). Paul therefore reproved Cephas publicly in the speech reproduced by vs 14–21, the report of which clearly states the evangelical position and the ruinous consequences (vs 18.21) of reëstablishing "the law."

(1) *Thesis.*—The doctrinal polemic was rehearsed in the autobiography (**2** 3–5.11–12). In **2** 16 is laid down the thesis of the epistle: "A man is not justified by the works of law but through faith in Jesus Christ." This proposition is (*a*) demonstrated from experience and history in **3** 1—**4** 7; then (*b*) enforced by **4** 8—**5** 12.

3. Doctrinal Polemic (3:1—5:12)

(2) *Main argument.*—(*a*1) From his own experience (**2** 19–21) Paul passes to that of the readers, who are "bewitched" to forget "Christ cruci-

fied" (**3** 1)! Had their life in "the Spirit" come through "works of the law" or the "hearing of faith"? Will the flesh consummate what the Spirit began (vs 2–5)? (*a*2) Abraham, they are told, is the father of God's people; but 'the men of faith' are Abraham's true heirs (vs 6–9). "The law" curses every transgressor; Scripture promised righteousness through faith for the very reason that justification by legal "doing" is impossible (vs 10–12). "Christ redeemed us from the curse of the law" in dying the death it declared "accursed" (ver 13). Thus He conveyed to the nations "the promise of the Spirit," pledged to them through believing Abraham (vs 7.14). (*a*3) The "testament" God gave to "Abraham and his seed" (a single "seed," observe) is unalterable. The Mosaic law, enacted 430 years later, could not nullify this instrument (vs 15–17 AV). Nullified it would have been, had its fulfilment turned on legal performance instead of Divine "grace" (ver 18). (*a*4) "Why then the law?" Sin required it, pending the accomplishment of "the promise." Its promulgation through intermediaries marks its inferiority (vs 19.20). With no power 'to give life,' it served the part of a jailer guarding us till "faith came," of "the *paedagogus*" training us 'for Christ' (vs 21–25). (*a*5) But now "in Christ," Jew and Greek alike, "ye are all sons of God through faith"; being such, "you are Abraham's seed" and 'heirs in terms of the promise' (vs 26–29). The 'infant' heirs, in tutelage, were 'subject to the elements of the world,' until "God sent forth his Son," placed in the like condition, to "redeem" them (**4** 1–5). Today the "cry" of "the Spirit of his Son" in your "hearts" proves this redemption accomplished (vs 6.7).

The demonstration is complete; **3** 1—**4** 7 forms the core of the epistle. The growth of the Christian consciousness has been traced from its germ in Abraham to its flower in the church of all nations. The Mosaic law formed a disciplinary interlude in the process, which has been all along a life of faith. Paul concludes where he began (**3** 2), by claiming the Spirit as witness to the full salvation of the Gentiles; cf Rom **8** 1–27; 2 Cor **3** 4–18; Eph **1** 13.14. From **4** 8 onward to **5** 12, the argument is pressed home by appeal, illustration and warning.

(3) *Appeal and warning.*—(*b*1) After "knowing God," would the Galatians return to the bondage in which ignorantly they served as gods "the elements" of Nature? (vs 8.9). Their adoption of Jewish "seasons" points to this backsliding (vs 10.11). (*b*2) Paul's anxiety prompts the entreaty of vs 12–20, in which he recalls his fervent reception by his readers, deplores their present alienation, and confesses his perplexity. (*b*3) Observe that Abraham had *two* sons—"after the flesh" and "through promise" (vs 21–23); those who want to be under law are choosing the part of Ishmael: "Hagar" stands for 'the present Jerusalem' in her bondage; 'the Jerusalem above is free—she is our mother!' (vs 24–28.31). The fate of Hagar and Ishmael pictures the issue of legal subjection (vs 29.30): "Stand fast therefore" (**5** 1). (*b*4) The crucial moment comes at **5** 2: the Galatians are half-persuaded (vs 7.8); they will fatally commit themselves, if they consent to 'be circumcised.' This will sever them from Christ, and bind them to complete observance of Moses' law: *law or grace*—by one or the other they must stand (vs 3–5). "Circumcision, uncircumcision"—these "count for nothing in Christ Jesus" (ver 6). Paul will not believe in the defection of those who 'ran' so "well"; "judgment" will fall on their 'disturber' (vs 7–10.12). Persecution marks himself as no circumcisionist (ver 11)!

The ethical application is contained in the phrase of Rom **8** 2, "the law of the Spirit of life in Christ Jesus."

4. The Ethical Application (5:13—6:10)

(1) Love guards Christian liberty from license; it 'fulfils the whole law in a single word' (**5** 13–15). (2) The Spirit, who imparts freedom, guides the free man's "walk." Flesh and spirit are oppugnant principles: deliverance from "the flesh" and its "works" is found in possession by "the Spirit," who bears in those He rules His proper "fruit." 'Crucified with Christ' and 'living in the Spirit,' the Christian man keeps God's law without bondage under it (**5** 16–26). (3) In cases of unwary fall, 'men of the Spirit' will know how to "restore" the lapsed, 'fulfilling Christ's law' and mindful of their own weakness (**6** 1–5). (4) Teachers have a peculiar claim on the taught; to ignore this is to 'mock God.' Men will "reap corruption" or "eternal life," as in such matters they 'sow to the flesh' or 'to the Spirit.' Be patient till the harvest! (vs 6–10).

The autograph conclusion (ver 11) exposes the sinister motive of the circumcisionists, who are ashamed of the cross, the Christian's only boast (vs 12–15).

5. The Epilogue (6:11–18)

Such men are none of "the Israel of God!" (ver 16). "The brand of Jesus" is now on Paul's body; at their peril "henceforth" will men trouble him! (ver 17). The benediction follows (ver 18).

The postscript reveals the inwardness of the legalists' agitation. They advocated circumcision from policy more than from conviction, hoping to conciliate Judaism and atone for accepting the Nazarene—to hide the shame of the cross—by capturing for the Law the gentile churches. They attack Paul because he stands in the way of this attempt. Their policy is treason; it surrenders to the world that cross of Christ, to which the world for its salvation must unconditionally submit.

B) Salient Points

1. The Principles at Stake

The grace of God the one source of salvation (**1** 3; **2** 21; **5** 4), the cross of Christ its sole ground (**1** 4; **2** 19–21; **3** 13; **6** 14), faith in the Good News its all-sufficient means (**2** 16.20; **3** 2.5–9.23–26; **5** 5), the Spirit its effectuating power (**3** 2–5; **4** 6.7; **5** 5.16–25; **6** 8)—hence emancipation from the Jewish law, and the full status of sons of God open to the Gentiles (**2** 4.5.15–19; **3** 10–14; **3** 28—**4** 9.26–31; **5** 18; **6** 15): these connected principles are at stake in the contention; they make up the doctrine of the epistle.

2. Present Stage of the Controversy

Circumcision is now proposed by the Judaists as *a supplement to faith in Christ*, as the qualification for sonship to Abraham and communion with the apostolic church (**3** 7.29). After the Council at Jerus, they no longer say outright, "Except ye be circumcised after the custom of Moses, ye cannot be saved" (Acts **15** 1). Paul's Galatian converts, they admit, "have begun in the Spirit"; they bid them "be perfected" and attain the full Christian status by conforming to Moses—"Christ will profit" them much more, if they add to their faith circumcision (**3** 3; **5** 2; cf Rom **3** 1). This insidious proposal might seem to be in keeping with the findings of the Council; Peter's action at Antioch lent color to it. Such a grading of the Circumcision and Uncircumcision within the church offered a tempting solution of the legalist controversy; for it appeared to reconcile the universal destination of the gospel with the inalienable prerogatives of the sons of Abraham. Paul's reply is, that believing Gentiles are already Abraham's "seed"—nay, sons and heirs of God; instead of adding anything, circumcision would rob them of everything they have won in Christ; instead of going on to perfection by its aid, they would draw back unto perdition.

3. Paul's Depreciation of the Law

Paul carries the war into the enemies' camp, when he argues, (*a*) that the law of Moses brought condemnation, not blessing, on its subjects (**3** 10–24); and (*b*) that instead of completing the work of faith, its part in the Divine economy was subordinate (**3** 19–25). It was a temporary provision, due to man's sinful unripeness for the original covenant (**3** 19.24; **4** 4). The Spirit of sonship, now manifested in the Gentiles, is the infallible sign that the promise made to mankind in Abraham has been fulfilled. The whole position of the legalists is undermined by the use the apostle makes of the Abrahamic covenant.

4. The Personal Question

The religious and the personal questions of the epistle are bound up together; this **5** 2 clearly indicates. The latter naturally emerges first (**1** 1.11 ff). Paul's authority must be overthrown, if his disciples are to be Judaized. Hence the campaign of detraction against him (cf 2 Cor **10–12**). The line of defence indicates the nature of the attack. Paul was said to be a second-hand, second-rate apostle, whose knowledge of Christ and title to preach Him came from Cephas and the mother church. In proof of this, an account was given of his career, which he corrects in **1** 13—**2** 21. "Cephas" was held up (cf 1 Cor **1** 12) as the chief of the apostles, whose primacy Paul had repeatedly acknowledged; and "the pillars" at Jerus were quoted as maintainers of Mosaic rule and authorities for the additions to be made to Paul's imperfect gospel. Paul himself, it was insinuated, "preaches circumcision" where it suits him; he is a plausible time-server (**1** 10; **5** 11; cf Acts **16** 3; 1 Cor **9** 19–21). The apostle's object in his self-defence is not to sketch his own life, nor in particular to recount his visits to Jerus, but to prove his independent apostleship and his consistent maintenance of gentile rights. He states, therefore, what really happened on the critical occasions of his contact with Peter and the Jerus church. To begin with, he received his gospel and apostolic office from Jesus Christ directly, and apart from Peter (**1** 13–20); he was subsequently recognized by "the pillars" as apostle, on equality with Peter (**2** 6–9); he had finally vindicated his doctrine when it was assailed, in spite of Peter (**2** 11–12). The adjustment of Paul's recollections with Luke's narrative is a matter of dispute, in regard both to the conference of **2** 1–10 and the encounter of **2** 11–21; to these points we shall return, iv.3 (4), (5).

C) Characteristics

This is a letter of expostulation. Passion and argument are blended in it. Hot indignation and righteous scorn (**1** 7–9; **4** 17; **5** 10.12; **6** 12.13), tender, wounded affection (**4** 11–20), deep sincerity and manly integrity united with the loftiest consciousness of spiritual authority (**1** 10–12.20; **2** 4–6.14; **5** 2; **6** 17), above all a consuming devotion to the person and cross of the Redeemer, fill these few pages with an incomparable wealth and glow of Christian emotion.

1. Idiosyncrasy of the Epistle

The power of mind the epistle exhibits matches its largeness of heart. Rom indeed carries out the argument with greater breadth and theoretic completeness; but Gal excels in pungency, incisiveness, and debating force. The style is that of Paul at the summit of his powers. Its spiritual elevation, its vigor and resource, its subtlety and irony, poignancy and pathos, the *vis vivida* that animates the whole, have made this letter a classic of religious controversy. The blemishes of Paul's composition, which contribute to his mastery of effect, are conspicuous here—his abrupt turns and apostrophes, and sometimes difficult ellipses (**2** 4–10.20; **4** 16–20; **5** 13), awkward parentheses and entangled periods (**2** 1–10.18; **3** 16.20; **4** 25), and outburst of excessive vehemence (**1** 8.9; **5** 12). The anti-legalist polemic gives a special OT coloring to the epistle; the apostle meets his adversaries on their own ground.

2. Jewish Coloring

In **3** 16.19–20; **4** 21–31, we have examples of the rabbinical exegesis Paul had learned from his Jewish masters. These texts should be read in part as *argumenta ad hominem;* however peculiar in form such Pauline passages may be, they always contain sound reasoning.

III. Relations to Other Epistles.—(1) The connection of Gal with Rom is patent; it is not sufficiently understood how pervasive that connection is and into what manifold detail it extends. The similarity of doctrine and doctrinal vocabulary manifest in Gal **2** 13—**6** 16 and Rom **1** 16—**8** 39 is accounted for by the Judaistic controversy on which Paul was engaged for so long, and by the fact that this discussion touched the heart of his gospel and raised questions in regard to which his mind was made up from the beginning (**1** 15.16), on which he would therefore always express himself in much the same way. Broadly speaking, the difference is that Rom is didactic and abstract, where Gal is personal and polemical; that the former presents a measured and rounded development of conceptions projected rapidly in the latter under the stress of controversy. The emphasis lies in Rom on justification by faith; in Gal on the freedom of the Christian man. The contrast of tone is symptomatic of a calmer mood in the writer—the lull which follows the storm; it suits the different address of the two epistles.

1. Galatians and Romans

Besides the correspondence of purport, there is a verbal resemblance to Rom pervading the tissue of Gal, and traceable in its mannerisms and incidental expressions. Outside of the identical quotations, we find more than 40 Gr locutions, some of them rare in the language, common to these two and occurring in these only of Paul's epistles—including the words rendered "bear" (Rom **11** 18 and Gal **5** 10, etc); "blessing" or "gratulation" (*makarismós*), "divisions" (Rom **16** 17; Gal **5** 20); "fail" or "fall from" (*ekpíptō*); "labour on" or "upon" (of persons), "passions" (*pathḗmata*, in this sense); "set free" or "deliver" (*eleutheróō*); "shut up" or "conclude," and "shut out" or "exclude"; "travail [together]," and such phrases as "die to" (with dative), "hearing of faith," "if possible," "put on [the Lord Jesus] Christ," "those who do such things," "what saith the Scripture?" "where then?" (rhetorical), "why any longer?" The list would be greatly extended by adding expressions distinctive of this pair of letters that occur sporadically elsewhere in Paul. The kinship of Gal-Rom in vocabulary and vein of expression resembles that existing between Col-Eph or 1-2 Thess; it is twice as strong proportionately as that of 1-2 Cor. Not only the same current of thought, but with it, much the same stream of language was running through Paul's mind in writing these two epistles.

The association of Gal with the two Corinthian letters, though less intimate than that of Gal-Rom, is unmistakable.

2. Links with 1 and 2 Corinthians

We count 23 distinct locutions shared by 2 Cor alone (in its 13 chs) with Gal, and 20 such shared with 1 Cor (16 chs)—a larger proportion for the former. Among the Gal-1 Cor peculiarities are the sayings, "A little leaven," etc, "circumcision is nothing," etc, and the phrases, "be not deceived," "it is manifest" (*dḗlon* as predicate to a sentence), "known by God," "profit nothing" and "to be something," "scandal of the cross," "the spiritual" (of persons), "they that are Christ's [of Christ Jesus]." Peculiar to Gal-2 Cor are "another gospel" and "false brethren," "brings into bondage," "devour" and "zealously seek" or "am jealous over" (of persons); "a new creation," "confirm" or "ratify" (*kuróō*); "I am perplexed," the antithesis of "sowing" and "reaping" (fig.); the phrase "on the contrary" or "contrariwise" (*t'ounantíon*), etc. The conception of the "two covenants" (or "testaments") is conspicuous in both epistles (Gal **3** 17–21; **4** 21–31; 2 Cor **3** 8–18), and does not recur in Paul; in each case the ideas of "law" (or "letter"), "bondage," "death," are associated with the one, *diathḗkē*, of "spirit," "freedom," "life," with the other. Gal **3** 13 ("Christ . . . . made a curse for us") is matched by 2 Cor **5** 21 ("made sin for us"); in Gal **2** 19 and **6** 14 we find Paul "crucified to the world" in the cross of his Master and "Christ" alone "living in" him; in 2 Cor **5** 14.15 this experience becomes a universal law for Christians; and where in Gal **6** 17 the apostle appears as 'from henceforth . . . . bearing in' his 'body the brand of Jesus,' in 2 Cor **4** 10 he is "always bearing about in" his "body the dying of Jesus."

These identical or closely congruous trains of thought and turns of phrase, varied and dominant as they are, speak for some near connection between the two writings. By its list of vices in **5** 19.20 Gal curiously, and somewhat intricately, links itself at once with 2 Cor and Rom (see 2 Cor **12** 20; Rom **13** 13; **16** 17). Gal is allied by argument and doctrine with Rom, and by temper and sentiment with 2 Cor. The storm of feeling agitating our epistle blows from the same quarter, reaches the same height, and engages the same emotions with those which animate 2 Cor **10–13**.

3. With the Corinthians-Romans Group

If we add to the 43 locutions confined in the Pauline Epp. to Gal-Rom the 23 such of Gal-2 Cor, the 20 of Gal-1 Cor, the 14 that range over Gal-Rom-2 Cor, the 15 of Gal-Rom-1 Cor, the 7 of Gal-1-2 Cor, and the 11 running through all four, we get a total of 133 words or phrases (apart from OT quotations) specific to Gal in common with one or more of the Cor-Rom group—an average, that is, of close upon 3 for each chapter of those other epistles.

With the other groups of Pauline letters Gal is associated by ties less numerous and strong, yet marked enough to suggest, in conjunction with the general style, a common authorship.

4. With Other Groups of Epistles

The proportion of locutions peculiar to Gal and the 3d group (Col-Philem-Eph-Phil) is 1 to each of their 15 chapters. The more noticeable of these are in Gal-Col: "elements of the world," and the maxim, "There is no Jew nor Greek," etc, associated with the "putting on of Christ" ("the new man"); "fulness of the time" (or "seasons") and "householders of faith [of God]," also "Christ loved me [the church] and gave up himself for me [her]," in Gal-Eph; "he that supplieth [your supplying of, *epichorēgía*] the Spirit," and "vain-glory" (*kenodoxía*), in Gal-Phil; "redeem" (*exagorázō*) and "inheritance" are peculiar to Gal with Col-Eph together; the association of the believer's "inheritance" with "the Spirit" in Gal-Eph is a significant point of doctrinal identity.

The Thess and Tim-Tit (1st and 4th) groups are outliers in relation to Gal, judged by vocabulary. There is little to associate our epistle with either of these combinations, apart from pervasive Cor-Rom phrases and the Pauline complexion. There are 5 such expressions registered for the 8 chapters of 1 and 2 Thess, 7 for the 13 of 1 and 2 Tim and Tit—just over one to two chapters for each group. While the verbal coincidences in these two cases are, proportionately, but one-half so many as those connecting Gal with the 3d group of epistles and one-fifth or one-sixth of those linking it to the 2d group, they are also less characteristic; the most striking is the contrast of "well-doing" (*kalopoiéō*) with "fainting" or "wearying" (*egkakéō*) in Gal **6** 9 and 2 Thess **3** 13.

5. General Comparison

No other writing of Paul reflects the whole man so fully as this—his spiritual, emotional, intellectual, practical, and even physical, idiosyncrasy. We see less of the apostle's tenderness, but more of his strength than in Phil; less of his inner, mystic experiences, more of the critical turns of his career; less of his "fears," more of his "fightings," than in 2 Cor. While the 2d letter to Timothy lifts the curtain from the closing stage of the apostle's ministry, Gal throws a powerful light upon its beginning. The Pauline theology opens to us its heart in this document. The apostle's message of deliverance from sin through faith in the crucified Redeemer, and of the new life in the Spirit growing from this root, lives and speaks; we see it in Gal as a working and fighting theology, while in Rom it peacefully expands into an ordered system. The immediately saving truth of Christianity, the gospel of the Gospel, finds its most trenchant utterance in this epistle; here we learn "the word of the cross" as Paul received it from the living Saviour, and defended it at the crisis of his work.

IV. The Destination and Date.—The question of the people to whom, is bound up with that of the time at which, the Epistle to the Galatians was written. Each goes to determine the other. The expression "the first time" (*tó próteron*) of **4** 13 presumes Paul to have been twice with the readers previously—for the first occasion, see **4** 13–15; for the second, **1** 9; **5** 3. The explanation of Round (*Date of Ep. to Gal*, 1906), that the apostle intended to distinguish his first arrival at the several (S.) Galatian cities from his return *in the course of the same journey* (Acts **14** 21–23), cannot be accepted: Derbe, the limit of the expedition, received Paul and Barnabas but once on that round, and in retracing their steps the missionaries were completing an interrupted work, whereas Gal **4** 13 implies a second, distinct visitation of the churches concerned as a whole; in Acts **15** 36 Paul looks back to the journey of Acts **13** 14—**14** 26 as one event.

1. Place and Time Interdependent

Now the apostle revisited the S. Galatian churches in starting on the 2d missionary tour (Acts **16** 1–5). Consequently, if his "Galatians" were Christians of Pisidian Antioch, Iconium, Lystra and Derbe (the S. Galatian hypothesis), the letter was written in the further course of the 2d tour—from Macedonia or Corinth about the time of 1 and 2 Thess (so Zahn, *Intro to the NT*, I, ET), or from Antioch in the interval between the 2d and 3d journeys (so Ramsay); for on this latter journey (Acts **18** 23) Paul (*ex hyp.*) traversed 'the [S.] Galatian country' a third time. On the other hand, if they were people of Galatia proper, i.e. of N. (Old) Galatia, the epistle cannot be earlier than the occasion of Acts **18** 23, when Paul touched a second time "the Galatian country," which, on this supposition, he had evangelized in traveling from S. Galatia to Troas during the previous tour (Acts **16** 6–8). On the N. Galatian hypothesis, the letter was dispatched from Ephesus during Paul's long residence there (Acts **19**; so most interpreters, ancient and modern), in which case it heads the 2d group of the epistles; or later, from Macedonia or Corinth, and shortly before the writing of the Epistle to the Rom (thus Lightfoot, Salmon, A. L. Williams and others).

Per contra, the earlier date, if proved independently, carries with it the S. Galatian, the later date the N. Galatian theory. The subscription of the TR "written from Rome," rests on inferior MS authority and late Patristic tradition. Clemen, with no suggestion as to *place* of origin, assigns to the writing a date subsequent to the termination of the 3d missionary tour (55 or 57 AD), inasmuch as the epistle reflects the controversy about the Law, which in Rom is comparatively mild, at an acute, and, therefore (he supposes), an advanced stage.

2. Internal Evidence

Lightfoot (ch iii of Intro to *Comm.*) placed Gal in the 2d group of the epistles between 2 Cor and Rom, upon considerations drawn from "the style and character" of the epistle. His argument might be strengthened by a detailed linguistic analysis (see III, 1–3, above). The more minutely one compares Gal with Rom and 1 and 2 Cor, the more these four are seen to form a continuous web, the product of the same experience in the writer's mind and the same situation in the church. This presumption, based on internal evidence, must be tested by examination of the topographical and chronological data.

3. External Data

(1) *Galatia and the Galatians.*—The double sense of these terms obtaining in current use has been shown in the art. on GALATIA; Steinmann sets out the evidence at large in his essay on *Der Leserkreis des Galaterbriefes*, 61–76 (1908); see also A. L. Williams' Intro to Gal in *Cambr. Gr Test.* (1910). Rom authors of the period in using these expressions commonly thought of provincial Galatia,[1] which then embraced in addition to Galatia proper a large tract of Southern Phrygia and Lycaonia, reaching from Pisidian Antioch in the west to Derbe in the east; but writers of Asia Minor leaned to the older local and national usage, according to which "Galatia" signified the north-central highlands of the peninsula, on both sides of the river Halys, in which the invading Galatae had settled long before this time. (On their history see the previous art.) It is asserted that Paul strictly followed the official, as against the popular, *usus loquendi* in these matters—a questionable dictum (see A. L. Williams, op. cit., xix, xx, or Steinmann's *Leserkreis*, 78–104), in view of Gal **1** 21.22 (note the Gr double article), to go no farther. There was nothing in Paul's Rom citizenship to make him a precisian in a point like this. Ramsay has proved that all four cities of Acts **13** 14—**14** 23 were by this time included in provincial Galatia. Their inhabitants might therefore, officially, be styled "Galatians" (*Galatae*); it does not follow that this

[1] Schürer seems to be right, however, in maintaining that "Galatia" was only the abbreviated designation for the province, named *a parte potiori*, and that in more formal description it was styled "Galatia, Pisidia, Phrygia," etc.

was a fit or likely compellation for Paul to use. Jülicher says this would have been a piece of "bad taste" on his part. The attachment of the southern districts (Phrygian, Pisidian, Lycaonian) to Galatia was recent—Derbe had been annexed so late as the year 41—and artificial. Supposing that their Rom "colonial" rank made the designation "Galatians" agreeable to citizens of Antioch or Lystra, there was little in it to appeal to Iconians or Derbeans (cf Schmiedel, in *EB*, col. 1604).

(2) *Prima facie sense of Acts* ***16*** *6*.—The "Galatian country" (*Galatikē chōra*) is mentioned by Luke, with careful repetition, in Acts **16** 6 and **18** 23. Luke at any rate was not tied to imperial usage; he distinguishes "Phrygia" from "Asia" in Acts **2** 9.10, although Phrygia was administratively parceled out between Asia and Galatia. When therefore "Asia" is opposed in **16** 6 to "the Phrygian and Galatian country" (or "Phrygia and Galatian country," Zahn), we presume that the three terms of locality bear alike a non-official sense, so that the "Galatian country" means Old Galatia (or some part of it) lying to the N.E., as "Asia" means the narrower Asia west of "Phrygia." On this presumption we understand that Paul and Silas, after completing their visitation of "the cities" of the former tour (Acts **16** 4.5; cf **15** 36, in conjunction with **13** 14—**14** 23), since they were forbidden to proceed westward and "speak the word in Asia," turned their faces to the region—first Phrygian, then Galatian—that stretched northward into new territory, through which they traveled toward "Mysia" and "Bithynia" (ver 7). Thus ver 6 fills in the space between the S. Galatia covered by vs 4 and 5, and the Mysian-Bithynian border where we find the travelers in ver 7. Upon this, the ordinary construction of Luke's somewhat involved sentence, N. Galatia was entered by Paul on his 2d tour; he retraversed, more completely, "the Galatian region" at the commencement of the 3d tour, when he found "disciples" there (Acts **18** 23) whom he had gathered on the previous visit.

(3) *The grammar of Acts* ***16*** *6*.—In the interpretation of the Lukan passages proposed by Ramsay, ver 16*a*, detached from 16*b*, is read as the completion of vs 1–5 ('And they went through the Phrygian . . . . region. They were forbidden by the Holy Ghost . . . . in Asia, and came over against Mysia,' etc); and "the Phrygian and Galatian region" means the southwestern division of Provincia Galatia, a district at once Phrygian (ethnically) and Galatian (politically). The combination of two local adjs., under a common art., to denote the same country in different respects, if exceptional in Gr idiom (**15** 41 and **27** 5 illustrate the usual force of this collocation), is clearly possible—the one strictly ‖ geographical expression, "the Ituraean and Trachonite country" in Lk **3** 1, unfortunately, is also ambiguous. But the other difficulty of grammar involved in the new rendering of Acts **16** 6 is insuperable: the severance of the participle, "having been forbidden" (*kōluthéntes*), from the introductory vb., "they went through" (*diēlthon*), wrenches the sentence to dislocation; the aorist participle in such connection "must contain, if not something antecedent to 'they went,' at least something synchronous with it, in no case a thing subsequent to it, if all the rules of grammar and all sure understanding of language are not to be given up" (Schmiedel, *EB*, col. 1599; endorsed in Moulton's *Proleg. to Grammar of NT Gr*, 134; see also Chase in *Expos*, IV, viii, 404–11, and ix, 339–42). Acts **10** 29 ("I came . . . . when I was sent for") affords a grammatical ‖ to **16** 6 ('They went through . . . . since they were hindered').

Zahn's position is peculiar (*Intro to NT*, I, 164–202). Rejecting Ramsay's explanation of Acts **16** 6, and of **18** 23 (where R. sees Paul a *third* time crossing S. Galatia), and maintaining that Luke credits the apostle with successful work in N. Galatia, he holds, notwithstanding, the S. Galatian view of the epistle. This involves the paradox that Paul in writing to "the churches of Galatia" ignored those of N. Galatia to whom the title properly belonged—an incongruence which Ramsay escapes by denying that Paul had set foot in Old Galatia. In the 1st ed of the *Einleitung* Zahn had supposed N. and S. Galatia together included in the address; this supposition is contrary to the fact that the readers form a homogeneous body, the fruit of a single mission (**4** 13), and are affected simultaneously by the same disturbance (**1** 6; **5** 7–9). Associating the letter in 2d ed with S. Galatians alone, Zahn suggests that while Paul had labored in N. Galatia and found "disciples" there on his return, these were too few and scattered to form "churches"—an estimate scarcely in keeping with Luke's phrase **5** 7–9 "all the disciples" (**18** 23), and raising a distinction between "disciples" and "churches" foreign to the historian's usage (see Acts **6** 2; **9** 19; **14** 20). We must choose between N. and S. Galatia; and if churches existed among the people of the north at the time of writing, then the northerners claim this title by right of use and wont—and the epistle with it. The reversal of "Galatian and Phrygia[n]" in Acts **18** 23, as compared with **16** 6, implies that the apostle on the 3d tour struck "the Galatian country" first, traveling this time directly N. from Syrian Antioch, and turned westward toward Phrygia when he had reached Old Galatia; whereas his previous route had brought him westward along the highroad traversing S. Galatia, until he turned northward at a point not far distant from Pisidian Antioch, to reach N. Galatia through Phrygia from the southwest. See the Map of Asia Minor.

(4) *Notes of time in the epistle.*—The "3 years" of **1** 18 and the "14 years" of **2** 1 are both seemingly counted from Paul's conversion. (*a*) The synchronism of the conversion with the murder of Stephen and the free action of the high priest against the Nazarenes (Acts **9** 2, etc), and of Saul's visit to Jerus in the 3d year thereafter with Aretas' rule in Damascus (2 Cor **11** 32.33), forbid our placing these two events further back than 36 and 38—at furthest, 35 and 37 AD (see Turner on "Chronology of the NT" in *HDB*, as against the earlier dating). (*b*) This calculation brings us to 48–49 as the year of the conference of Gal **2** 1–10—a date precluding the association of that meeting with the errand to Jerus related in Acts **11** 30 and **12** 25, while it suits the identification of the former with the council of Acts **15**. Other indications converge on this as the critical epoch of Paul's apostleship. The expedition to Cyprus and S. Galatia (Acts **13, 14**) had revealed in Paul 'signs of the apostle' which the chiefs of the Judaean church now recognized (Gal **2** 7–9; cf Acts **15** 12), and gave him the ascendency which he exercised at this crisis; up to the time of Acts **13** 1 "Saul" was known but as an old persecutor turned preacher (Gal **1** 23), one of the band of "prophets and teachers" gathered round Barnabas at Antioch. The previous visit of Barnabas and Saul to Jerusalem (Acts **11, 12**) had no ostensible object beyond that of famine-relief. From Acts **12** we learn that the mother church just then was suffering deadly persecution; Peter certainly was out of the way. There was no opportunity for the negotiation described in Gal **2** 1–10, and it would have been premature for Paul to raise the question of his apostleship at this stage. In all likelihood, he saw few Judaean Christians then beyond "the elders," who received the Antiochene charity (Acts **11** 30). Nothing transpired in connection with this remittance, important as it was from Luke's standpoint, to affect the question of Gal **1, 2**; it would have been idle for Paul to refer to it. On the other hand, no real contradiction exists between Acts **15** and Gal **2**: "The two accounts admirably complete each other" (Pfleiderer; cf *Cambr. Gr Test.*, 145, 146; Steinmann, *Die Abfassungszeit d. Gal.-Briefes*, §7); in matters of complicated dispute involving personal considerations, attempts at a private understanding naturally precede the public settlement. It would be strange indeed if the same question of the circumcision of gentile believers had twice within a few years been raised at Antioch, to be twice carried to Jerus and twice over decided there by the same parties—Barnabas and Paul, Peter and James—and with no reference made in the second discussion (that of Acts, *ex hyp.*) to the previous compact (Gal **2**). Granting the epistle written after the council, as both Ramsay and Zahn suppose, we infer that Paul has given his more intimate account of the crisis, about which the readers were already informed in the sense of Acts **15**, with a view to bring out its essential bearing on the situation.

(*c*) The encounter of Paul and Cephas at Antioch (**2** 11–21) is undated. The time of its occurrence bears on the date of the epistle. As hitherto, the order of narration presumably follows the order of events, the "but" of ver 11 appears to contrast Cephas' present attitude with his action in Jerus just described. Two possible opportunities present themselves for a meeting of Paul and Cephas in Antioch subsequently to the council—the time of

Paul's and Barnabas' sojourn there on their return from Jerus (Acts **15** 35.36), or the occasion of Paul's later visit, occupying "some time," between the 2d and 3d tours (**18** 22.23), when for aught we know Barnabas and Peter may both have been in the Syrian capital.

The former dating assumes that Peter yielded to the Judaizers on the morrow of the council, that "Barnabas too was carried away" while still in colleagueship with Paul and when the cause of gentile freedom, which he had championed, was in the flush of victory. It assumes that the legalists had no sooner been defeated than they opened a new attack on the same ground, and presented themselves as "from James" when James only the other day had repudiated their agitation (Acts **15** 19.24). All this is very unlikely. We must allow the legalists time to recover from their discomfiture and to lay new plans (see II 2, (2), (3), (4). Moreover, Luke's detailed narrative in Acts **15** 30–36, which makes much of the visit of Judas and Silas, gives no hint of any coming of Peter to Antioch at that time, and leaves little room for this; he gives an impression of settled peace and satisfaction following on the Jerus *concordat*, with which the strife of Gal **2** 11 ff would ill accord. Through the course of the 2d missionary tour, so far as the Thessalonian epistles indicate, Paul's mind remained undisturbed by legalistic troubles. "The apostle had quitted Jerus [after his understanding with the pillars] and proceeded to his 2d missionary journey full of satisfaction at the victory he had gained and free from anxiety for the future. . . . . The decisive moment of the crisis necessarily falls between the Thessalonian and Galatian epistles. . . . . A new situation suddenly presents itself to him on his return" to Antioch (A. Sabatier, *The Apostle Paul*, ET, 10, 11, also 124–36).

(5) *Paul's renewed struggle with legalism.*—The new situation arose through the vacillation of Peter; and the "certain from James" who made mischief at Antioch, were the forerunners of "troublers" who agitated the churches far and wide, appearing simultaneously in Corinth and N. Galatia. The attempt to set up a separate church-table for the circumcised at Antioch was the first movement in a crafty and persistent campaign against gentile liberties engineered from Jerus. The Ep. to the Rom signalized Paul's conclusive victory in this struggle, which covered the period of the 3d missionary tour. On his revisitation of the Galatians (**1** 9; **5** 3 ‖ Acts **18** 23), fresh from the contention with Cephas and aware of the wide conspiracy on foot, Paul gave warning of the coming of "another gospel"; it had arrived, fulfilling his worst fears. Upon this view of the course of affairs (see Neander, *Planting and Training of the Christian Church*, III, vii; Godet's *Intro to the NT, Epp. of Paul*, 200–201; Sabatier, as above), the mistake of Peter at Antioch was the proximate antecedent of the trouble in Galatia; hence Gal **2** 11–24 leads up to **3** 1 and the main argument. Now, if the Antiochene collision befell so late as this, then the epistle is subsequent to the date of Acts **18** 22.23; from which it follows, once more, that Gal belongs to the 3d missionary tour and the Cor-Rom group of letters.

(6) *Ephesus or Corinth?*—Chiefly because of the words, "you are removing *so quickly*," in **1** 6, the epistle is by many referred to the earlier part of the above period, the time of Paul's protracted sojourn in Ephesus (Acts **19** 8.10: 54–56 AD); "so quickly," however, signifies not "so soon after my leaving you," but "so suddenly" and "with such slight persuasion" (**5** 7.8). From Ephesus, had the apostle been there when the trouble arose, he might as easily have visited Galatia as he did Corinth under like circumstances (so much is implied in 2 Cor **13** 1): he is longing to go to Galatia, but cannot (Gal **4** 19.20). A more distant situation, such as Macedonia or Corinth (Acts **20** 1–3), where Paul found himself in the last months of this tour (56–57 AD), and where, in churches of some standing, he was surrounded by a body of sympathetic "brethren" (**1** 1) whose support gave weight to his remonstrance with the Galatians, suits the epistle better on every account.

(7) *Paul's first coming to Galatia.*—In **4** 13–15 the apostle recalls, in words surcharged with emotion, his introduction to the readers. His "preaching the good news" to them was due to "weakness of the flesh"—to some sickness, it seems, which arrested his steps and led him to minister in a locality that otherwise he would have "passed over," as he did Mysia a little later (Acts **16** 8). So we understand the obscure language of ver 13. The S. Galatian theorists, in default of any reference to illness as affecting the apostle's movements in Acts **13** 13.14, favor Ramsay's conjecture that Paul fell a victim to malaria on the Pamphylian coast, and that he and Barnabas made for Pisidian Antioch by way of seeking the cooler uplands. The former explanation lies nearer to the apostle's language: he says "I *preached* to you," not "I *came* to you, because of illness." The journey of a hundred miles from Perga to Antioch was one of the least likely to be undertaken by a fever-stricken patient (see the description in Conybeare and Howson's *Life of St. Paul*, or in Ramsay's *Paul the Traveller*). Besides, if this motive had brought Paul to *Antioch*, quite different reasons are stated by Luke for his proceeding to the other S. Galatian towns (see **13** 50.51; **14** 6.19.20). Reading Gal **4** 13–15, one imagines the missionary hastening forward to some further goal (perhaps the important cities of Bithynia, Acts **16** 7), when he is prostrated by a malady the physical effects of which were such as to excite extreme aversion. As strength returns, he begins to offer his gospel in the neighborhood where the unwilling halt has been made. There was much to prejudice the hearers against a preacher addressing them under these conditions; but the Galatians welcomed him as a heaven-sent messenger. Their faith was prompt and eager, their gratitude boundless.

The deification of Barnabas and Paul by the Lycaonians (**14** 11–18) is the one incident of Luke's narrative of which the apostle's description reminds us. To this the latter is thought to be alluding when he writes, "You received me as an angel of God, as Christ Jesus!" But could he speak thus of his reception—hateful at the time—in the character of a heathen god, and of a reception that ended in his stoning? The "welcome" of the messenger implies faith in his message (cf Gal **4** 14; 2 Cor **6** 1; 1 Thess **1** 6; Mt **10** 40.41, where the same Gr vb. is used).

Paul's mishandling at Lystra (Acts **14** 19.20) has suggested a correspondence in the opposite sense between the epistle and the story of the S. Galatian mission. The Lystran stones left their print on Paul's body; in these disfiguring scars one might see "the marks of Jesus" to which he points in Gal **6** 17, were it not for the note of time, "from henceforth," which distinguishes these stigmata as a *fresh* infliction, identifying the servant now more than ever with his Master. The true ‖ to Gal **6** 17 is 2 Cor **4** 10 (see the context in **4** 7—**5** 4, also **1** 8), which we quoted above (III, 2). When he wrote 2 Cor, the apostle was emerging from an experience of crucial anguish, which gave him an aspect imaging the dying Saviour whom he preached; to this new consecration the appeal of our epistle seems to refer.

(8) *Barnabas and the Galatians.*—The references to Barnabas in **2** 1.9.13, at first sight suggest the S. Galatian destination of the letter. For Barnabas and Paul were companions on the first only of the three tours, and Barnabas is named thrice here and but twice in the rest of the epistles. Yet these very references awaken misgiving. Barnabas was Paul's full partner in the S. Galatian mission; he was senior in service, and had introduced Saul to the apostles at Jerus; he was the leader at the outset of this journey (Acts **9** 27; **11** 22–26; **13** 1–3; **15** 25)—Barnabas was taken for "Zeus" by the heathen of Lystra, while the eloquent Paul was identified with "Hermes" (Acts **14** 12). The churches of S. Galatia had *two* founders, and owed allegiance to Barnabas along with Paul. Yet Paul deals with the readers as though he alone were their father in Christ. Referring to Barnabas conspicu-

ously in the letter and as differing from himself on a point affecting the question at issue (**2** 13), Paul was the more bound to give his old comrade his due and to justify his assumption of sole authority, if he were in truth addressing communities which owed their Christianity to the two men in conjunction. On the S. Galatian hypothesis, the apostle appears ungenerously to have elbowed his colleague out of the partnership. The apostle Paul, it is to be noted, was particularly sensitive on matters of this kind (see 1 Cor **4** 15; 2 Cor **10** 13–16). The name of Barnabas was known through the whole church (see 1 Cor **9** 6; Col **4** 10); there is no more difficulty in supposing the N. Galatians to be familiar with it than with the names of James and John (**2** 9). Possibly Paul, as his responsibilities extended, had left the care of S. Galatia to Barnabas, who could readily superintend this district from Antioch in Syria; Paul refers to him in 1 Cor **9** 6, long after the separation of Acts **15** 39, as a fellow-worker. This would account for his making direct for N. Galatia on the 3d tour; see IV, 3 (3).

(9) *The two Antiochs.*—In **2** 11 Paul refers to "Antioch," the famous city on the Orontes. To S. Galatians "Antioch" meant, as in 2 Tim **3** 11, the Pisidian city of that name. Had Paul been addressing S. Galatians, and Antiochenes *imprimis*, he could not without singular inadvertence have failed to make the distinction. The *gaucherie* would have been as marked as if, in writing to a circle of West-of-England towns including Bradford-on-Avon, one should mention "Bradford" without qualification, meaning the Yorkshire Bradford.

The arguments drawn from local difference in legal usage—in the matters of adoption, testament, etc—in favor of the S. Galatian destination (see Schmiedel's examination of Ramsay's views in *EB*, coll. 1608–9), and from the temperament of Paul's "Galatians" in favor of N. Galatia (Lightfoot), are too precarious to build upon.

(10) *Wider bearings of the problem.*—On a broad view of the scope of Paul's missionary work and of the relation of his letters to Acts, there is much to commend the S. Galatian theory. It simplifies the situation by connecting this cardinal writing of Paul with churches of cardinal importance in Luke's narrative. The S. Galatian cities lay along the main route of the apostle's travels, and in the mid-stream of the church's life. The epistle, when associated with the Christian communities of this region, gains a definite setting and a firm point of attachment in NT history; whereas the founding of N. Galatian Christianity is indicated by Luke, if at all, in the most cursory fashion, and it held an obscure place in the early church. How, it is asked, could Paul's intimate friend have been (on the N. Galatian theory) so uninterested in churches by which Paul himself set such store? And how can Paul have ignored, apart from the allusion of 2 Tim **3** 11, the S. Galatians who formed the first-fruits of his wider labors and supplied a vital link in his chain of churches? In reply, we must point out: (1) that for anything we know Paul wrote many letters to S. Galatia; we possess but a selection from his correspondence; the choice of the canonical epistles was not governed by the importance of the parties addressed in them—witness Col and Philem; nor were Paul's concern for his churches, and the *empressement* with which he wrote, determined by their magnitude and position, but by their needs and their hold on his affections (see Gal **1** 6, etc; **4** 12–20). (2) The N. Galatian mission lay off the central line of Paul's journeyings and of the advance of gentile Christianity; this is probably the reason why Luke, who was compelled to a strict economy of space, just ignores this field, though he shows himself aware of its existence. The apostle's confession that he preached to the readers, in the first instance, not from choice but necessity (**4** 13), accords with the neglect of N. Galatia in Acts; the evangelizing of the N. Galatians was an *aside* in Paul's work—an incident beyond the scope of his plans, from which at this period he was compelled again and again to deviate (Acts **16** 6–10).

After all, though less important during the 1st cent. than S. Galatia, N. Galatia was not an unimportant or inaccessible region. It was traversed by the ancient "Royal Road" from the E. to the Hellespont, which the apostle probably followed as far as Phrygia in the journey of Acts **18** 22.23. Planted by Paul in Old Galatia, the gospel would spread to Bithynia and Pontus farther north, as it certainly had done by the time Peter wrote to the churches of Asia Minor (1 Pet **1** 1). It is observable that "Galatia" stands between "Pontus and Cappadocia" in Peter's enumeration of the provinces—an order indicating that Christians of *North* Galatia were particularly in the writer's mind. Had Paul never set foot in N. Galatia, had he not worked along the Royal Road and put his message in the way of reaching the northern provinces of Asia Minor, the claim of Rom **15** 19 is difficult to sustain, that "from Jerusalem, and in a circle as far as Illyricum, he had fulfilled the gospel of Christ." On the whole, we find the external evidence in accord with the testimony given by the internal character and affinities of the epistle: we judge that this epistle was written cir the autumn or winter of 56–57 AD, from Macedonia or Corinth, toward the end of Paul's third missionary tour; that it was addressed to a circle of churches situated in Galatia proper or N. Galatia, probably in the western part of this country contiguous to (or overlapping) Phrygia (Acts **16** 6); and that its place lies between the two Corinthian and the Rom letters among the epistles of the second group.

LITERATURE.—The S. Galatian destination was proposed by the Danish Mynster (*Einltg. in d. Brief an d. Gal*, 1825; M. however included N. Galatia), and adopted by the French Perrot (*De Galatia Provincia Romana*, 1867) and Renan (*S. Paul*); by the German Clemen (*Chronologie d. paulin. Briefe*, 1893; *Die Adressaten d. Gal.-Briefes; Paulus: sein Leben u. Wirken*, 1904), Hausrath (*NT Zeitgeschichte*, 1873, ET), Pfleiderer (*Paulinismus*, 1873, ET; *Paulinismus*[2], much altered; *Urchristenthum*, 1902), Steck (as above), Weizsäcker (*Das apost. Zeitalter*[3], 1902, ET); after Ramsay (see under GALATIA), by Belser (*Beiträge z. Erklärung d. AG*, etc), O. Holtzmann (*Zeitschrift f. KG*, 1894), von Soden (*Hist of Early Christian Lit.*, ET; he includes S. with N. Galatia), Weber (*Die Adressaten d. Gal.-Briefes*), J. Weiss (*RE*[3], art. "Kleinasien"), in Germany; by Askwith (*Ep. to Gal: An Essay on Its Destination and Date*), Bacon (*Expos*, V, vii, 123–36; x, 351–67), Bartlet (*Expos*, V, x, 263–80), Gifford (*Expos*, IV, x, 1–20), Maclean (1-vol *HDB*), Rendall (*Expos*, IV, ix, 254–64; *EGT*, Intro to "Galatians"), Round (as above), Sanday (with hesitation, *Expos*, IV, vii, 491–95), Woodhouse (*EB*, art. "Galatia"). The N. Galatian destination, held by earlier scholars up to Lightfoot and Salmon (*DB*[2], an illuminating discussion), is reasserted, in view of Ramsay's findings, by Chase (*Expos*, IV, viii, 401–19; ix, 331–42), Cheetham (*Class. Review*, 1894), Dods (*HDB*, art. "Galatians"), Williams (*Cambr. Gr Test.*, 1910), in this country; by Sabatier (*L'Apôtre Paul*[2], ET, 1891); by Gheorghiu (*Adressatii ep. c. Galateni*, Cernauti, 1904, praised by Steinmann), and by the German critics Blass (*Acta Apost.*), von Dobschütz (*Die urchr. Gemeinden*, 1902, and *Probleme d. apost. Zeitalters*), Harnack (*Apostelgeschichte*, 1908, 87–90), H. Holtzmann (*Handcomm. z. NT*, "AG"), Jülicher (*NT Intro*, ET), Lipsius (*Handcomm. z. NT*, "Galater") Lietzmann (doubtfully, *Handbuch z. NT*, III, i, "Galaterbrief"), Mommsen (*ZNTW*, 1901, 81–96), Schmiedel (*EB*), Schürer (*Jahrbuch f. prot. Theologie*, XVIII, 460–74), Sieffert (*Meyer's Kommentar*), Steinmann (as above), Zöckler (a full and masterly discussion: *Studien u. Kritiken*, 1895, 51–102). Mommsen's verdict is thus expressed: "To apprehend 'the Galatians' of Paul otherwise than in the strict and narrower sense of the term, is unallowable. The Provinces associated with Galatia under the rule of a single legate, as e.g. Lycaonia certainly was as early as the time of Claudius, were in no way incorporated in that region; the official inscriptions simply set Galatia at the head of the combined regions. Still less could the inhabitants of Iconium and Lystra be named 'Galatians' in common speech."

Apart from the aforesaid controversy, besides the standard Comm. on Paul's Epp., Luther's *Ad Galatas* is of unique historical interest; the interpretations of Usteri (1833), Hilgenfeld (1852), Winer (1859[4]), Holsten (*Das Evangel. d. Paulus*, 1880), Philippi (1884), in German; Baljon (1889), in Dutch; and of B. Jowett, Ellicott, Beet, are specially serviceable, from different points of view; see also *CGT* and *EB*.

George G. Findlay

GALBANUM, gal'ba-num (חֶלְבְּנָה, *ḥelbenāh*; **χαλβάνη,** *chalbánē*): A gum-resin which occurs in small, round, semitranslucent tears or in brownish yellow masses; has a pleasant aromatic odor and a bitter taste; and is today, at any rate, imported from Persia. It is derived from certain umbelliferous plants, *Ferula galbaniflua* and *F. rubricaulis.* It is mentioned in Ex **30** 34 as an ingredient of the holy incense, and also in Sir **24** 15: "a pleasant odour . . . . as galbanum."

GALEED, gal'ē-ed (גַּלְעֵד, *gal'ēdh*): Derived from the Heb *gal*, "a heap of stones," and *'ēdh*, "witness." The meaning therefore is "cairn" or "heap of witness," corresponding to *y^eghar-sāhădhūthā'* in Aram. (Gen **31** 47). It is applied to the cairn raised by Jacob and Laban, beside which they sealed their covenant in a common meal, the memory of which they appealed to the silent cairn to preserve. The ancient custom of associating events with inanimate objects as witnesses is often illustrated in Heb history (Josh **4** 4 ff, etc). There may be in this narrative a suggestion of how the name "Gilead" came to be applied to that country. W. Ewing

GALGALA, gal'gal-a (**Γάλγαλα,** *Gálgala*): Gr equivalent for Gilgal. The word occurs in 1 Macc **9** 2 in connection with Arbela, in Galilee—"The way to Galgala"—but it is doubtful which Gilgal is meant. Cf Jos, *Ant,* XII, xi, 1; and see Gilgal.

GALILEAN, gal-i-lē'an. See Galilee.

GALILEE, gal'i-lē (הַגָּלִיל, הַגְּלִילָה, *ha-gālīl, ha-g^elīlāh*, lit. "the circuit" or "district"; **ἡ Γαλιλαία,** *hē Galilaía*):

1. Galilee of the Nations

Kedesh, the city of refuge, is described as lying in Galilee, in Mt. Naphtali (Josh **20** 7; cf **21** 32). The name seems originally to have referred to the territory of Naphtali. Joshua's victorious campaign in the north (ch **11**), and, subsequently, the triumph of the northern tribes under Deborah and Barak (Jgs **4** f) gave Israel supremacy; yet the tribe of Naphtali was not able to drive out all the former inhabitants of the land (**1** 33). In the time of Solomon the name applied to a much wider region, including the territory of Asher. In this land lay the cities given by Solomon to Hiram (1 K **9** 11). Cabul here named must be identical with that of Josh **19** 27. The Asherites also failed to possess certain cities in their allotted portion, so that the heathen continued to dwell among them. To this state of things, probably, is due the name given in Isa **9** 1 to this region, "Galilee of the nations," i.e. a district occupied by a mixed population of Jews and heathen. It may also be referred to in Josh **12** 23, where possibly we should read "king of the nations of Galilee" (*l^egālīl*), instead of "Gilgal" (*b^egilgāl*). Yet it was within this territory that, according to 2 S **20** 18 (LXX) lay the two cities noted for their preservation of ancient Israelitish religious customs in their purity—Abel-beth-maacah and Dan.

There is nothing to guide us as to the northern boundary of Galilee in the earliest times. On the

2. Ancient Boundaries

E. it was bounded by the upper Jordan and the Sea of Galilee, and on the S. by the plain of *el-Baṭṭauf.* That all within these limits belonged to Galilee we may be sure. Possibly, however, it included Zebulun, which seems to be reckoned to it in Isa **9** 1. In this territory also there were unconquered Canaanite cities (Jgs **1** 30).

At the instigation of Asa, king of Judah, Benhadad, son of Tabrimmon of Damascus, moved against

3. Before the Exile

Israel, and the cities which he smote all lay within the circle of Galilee (1 K **15** 20). Galilee must have been the arena of conflict between Jehoahaz and Hazael, king of Syria. The cities which the latter captured were recovered from his son Benhadad by Joash, who defeated him three times (2 K **10** 32; **13** 22 ff). The affliction of Israel nevertheless continued "very bitter," and God saved them by the hand of Jeroboam son of Joash, the great warrior monarch of the Northern Kingdom, under whom Galilee passed completely into the hands of Israel (2 K **14** 25 ff). But the days of Israel's supremacy in Northern Pal were nearly over. The beginning of the end came with the invasion of Tiglath-pileser III, who took the chief cities in Galilee, and sent their inhabitants captive to Assyria (ver 29). Probably, as in the case of the Southern Kingdom, the poorest of the land were left as husbandmen. At any rate there still remained Israelites in the district (2 Ch **30** 10 f); but the measures taken by the conqueror must have made for the rapid increase of the heathen element.

In post-exilic times Galilee is the name given to the most northerly of the three divisions of Western

4. After the Exile

Pal. The boundaries are indicated by Jos (*BJ*, III, iii, 1). It was divided into Lower and Upper Galilee, and was encompassed by Phoenicia and Syria. It marched with Ptolemais and Mt. Carmel on the W. The mountain, formerly Galilean, now belonged to the Syrians. On the S. it adjoined Samaria and Scythopolis (*Beisān*) as far as the river Jordan. It was bounded on the E. by Hippene, Gadara, Gaulonitis and the borders of the kingdom of Agrippa, while the northern frontier was marked by Tyre and the country of the Tyrians. The northern limit of Samaria was Ginea, the modern *Jenīn*, on the south border of Esdraelon. Lower Galilee, therefore, included the great plain, and stretched northward to the plain of *er-Rāmeh*—Ramah of Josh **19** 36. Jos mentions Bersabe, the modern *Abu-Shebā*, and the Talm, *K^ephar Ḥănanyāh*, the modern *Kefr 'Anan*, as the northern border; the former being about a mile N. of the latter. The plain reaches to the foot of the mountain chain, which, running E. and W., forms a natural line of division. Upper Galilee may have included the land as far as the gorge of the *Liṭāny*, which, again, would have formed a natural boundary to the N. Jos, however, speaks of Kedesh as belonging to the Syrians (*BJ*, II, xviii, 1), situated "between the land of the Tyrians and Galilee" (*Ant*, XIII, v, 6). This gives a point on the northern frontier in his time; but the rest is left indefinite. Guthe, Sanday and others, followed by Cheyne (*EB*, s.v.), on quite inadequate grounds conclude that certain localities on the E. of the Sea of Galilee were reckoned as Galilean.

In the mixed population after the exile the purely Jewish element must have been relatively small.

5. Character of the Galileans

In 165 BC Simon Maccabaeus was able to rescue them from their threatening neighbors by carrying the whole community away to Judaea (1 Macc **5** 14 ff). Jos tells of the conquest by Aristobulus I of Ituraea (*Ant*, XIII, xi, 3). He compelled many of them to adopt Jewish religious customs, and to obey the Jewish law. There can be little doubt that Galilee and its people were treated in the same way. While Jewish in their religion, and in their patriotism too, as subsequent history showed, the population of Galilee was composed of strangely mingled elements—Aramaean, Ituraean, Phoen and Gr. In the circumstances they could not be expected to prove such sticklers for high orthodoxy as the Judaeans. Their mixed origin explains the differences in speech which distinguished them from their brethren in the S., who regarded Galilee and the Galileans with a certain proud contempt (Jn **1** 46; **7** 52). But a fine type of manhood was developed among the peasant farmers of the two Galilees which, according to Jos (*BJ*, III, iii, 2), were "always able to make a strong resistance on all occasions of war; for the Galileans are inured to war from their infancy . . . . nor hath the country ever been destitute of men of courage." Jos, himself a Galilean, knew his countrymen well, and on them he mainly relied in the war with Rome. In Galilee also the Messianic hope was cherished with the deepest intensity. When the Messiah appeared, with His own Galilean upbringing, it was from the north-countrymen that He received the warmest welcome, and among them His appeal elicited the most gratifying response.

6. Later History

In 47 BC, Herod the Great, then a youth of 25, was made military commander of Galilee, and won great applause by the fashion in which he suppressed a band of robbers who had long vexed the country (*Ant*, XIV, ix, 2). When Herod came to the throne, 37 BC, a period of peace and prosperity for Galilee began, which lasted till the banishment of his son Antipas in 40 AD. The tetrarchy of Galilee was given to the latter at his father's death, 4 BC. His reign, therefore, covered the whole life of Jesus, with the exception of His infancy. After the banishment of Antipas, Galilee was added to the dominions of Agrippa I, who ruled it till his death in 44 AD. Then followed a period of Rom administration, after which it was given to Agrippa II, who sided with the Romans in the subsequent wars, and held his position till 100 AD. The patriotic people, however, by no means submitted to his guidance. In their heroic struggle for independence, the command of the two Galilees, with Gamala, was intrusted to Jos, who has left a vivid narrative, well illustrating the splendid courage of his freedom-loving countrymen. But against such an adversary as Rome even their wild bravery could not prevail; and the country soon lay at the feet of the victorious Vespasian, 67 AD. There is no certain knowledge of the part played by Galilee in the rebellion under Hadrian, 132–35 AD.

At the beginning of the Rom period Sepphoris (*Ṣafūriyeh*), about 3 miles N. of Nazareth, took the leading place. Herod Antipas, however, built a new city on the western shore of the Sea of Galilee, which, in honor of the reigning emperor, he called Tiberias. Here he reared his "golden house," and made the city the capital of his tetrarchy. See TIBERIAS. After the fall of Jerus, Galilee, which had formerly been held in contempt, became the home of Jewish learning, and its chief seat was found in Tiberias where the Mish was committed to writing, and the Jerus Talm was composed. Thus a city into which at first no pious Jew would enter, in a province which had long been despised by the leaders of the nation, became the main center of their national and religious life.

7. Cities of Galilee

Among the more notable cities in Galilee were Kedesh Naphtali, the city of refuge, the ruins of which lie on the heights W. of *el-Ḥuleh;* Chorazin, Bethsaida and Capernaum, N. of the Sea of Galilee; Nazareth, the city of the Saviour's youth and young manhood; Jotapata, the scene of Jos' heroic defence against the Romans, which stood at *Tell Jefāt*, N. of the plain of Asochis (*BJ*, III, vii, viii); Cana of Galilee; and Nain, on the northern slope of the mountain now called Little Hermon.

8. General Description

In physical features Galilee is the most richly diversified and picturesque district in Western Pal; while in beauty and fertility it is strongly contrasted with the barren uplands of Judah. Cut off from Mt. Lebanon in the N. by the tremendous gorge of the *Liṭāny*, it forms a broad and high plateau, sinking gradually southward until it approaches *Ṣafed*, when again it rises, culminating in *Jebel Jermuk*, the highest summit on the W. of the Jordan. From *Ṣafed* there is a rapid descent by stony slope and rocky precipice to the shore of the Sea of Galilee. The mountains of which *Jebel Jermuk* is the N.E. outrunner stretch westward across the country, and drop upon the plain of *er-Rameh* to the S. Irregular hills and valleys, with breadths of shady woodlands, lie between this plain and that of Asochis (*el-Baṭṭauf*). The latter is split from the E. by the range of *Jebel Ṭor'ān*. S. of Asochis rise lower hills, in a cup-like hollow among which lies the town of Nazareth. S. of the town they sink steeply into the plain of Esdraelon. The isolated form of Tabor stands out on the E., while Carmel bounds the view on the W. The high plateau in the N. terminates abruptly at the lip of the upper Jordan valley. As the Jordan runs close to the base of the eastern hills, practically all this valley, with its fine rolling downs, is included in Galilee. The plain of Gennesaret runs along the northwestern shore of the Sea of Galilee. From the uplands to the W., stretching from *Ḳurūn Ḥaṭṭīn* (the traditional Mount of Beatitudes) to the neighborhood of Tabor, the land lets itself down in a series of broad and fertile terraces, falling at last almost precipitously on the western shore of the Sea of Galilee. The descent toward the Mediterranean is much more gradual; and the soil gathered in the longer valleys is deep and rich.

The district may be described as comparatively well watered. The Jordan with its mighty springs is, of course, too low for purposes of irrigation. But there are many perennial streams fed by fountains among the hills. The springs at Jenin are the main sources of the river Kishon, but for the greater part of its course through the plain the bed of that river is far below the surface of the adjoining land. The dews that descend from Lebanon and Hermon are also a perpetual source of moisture and refreshment.

9. Products

Galilee was famous in ancient times for its rich and fruitful soil, "full of the plantations of trees of all sorts, insomuch that it invites the most slothful to pains in its cultivation by its fruitfulness; accordingly it is all cultivated by its inhabitants, and no part of it lies idle" (*BJ*, III, iii, 2). See also GENNESARET, LAND OF. The grapes grown in Naphtali were in high repute, as were the pomegranates of Shikmona —the Sykaminos of Jos—which stood on the shore near Mt. Carmel. The silver sheen of the olive meets the eye in almost every valley; and the olive oil produced in Galilee has always been esteemed of the highest excellence. Its wheat fields also yielded an abundant supply, the wheat of Chorazin being proverbial. The great plain of Esdraelon must also have furnished rich provision. It cannot be doubted that Galilee was largely drawn upon for the gifts in kind which Solomon bestowed upon the king of Tyre (2 Ch **2** 10). At a much later day the inhabitants of Tyre and Sidon depended upon the produce of Galilee (Acts **12** 20).

Galilee was in easy touch with the outside world by means of the roads that traversed her valleys, crossed her ridges and ran out eastward, westward and southward. Thus she was connected with the harbors on the Phoen seaboard, with Egypt on the

S., with Damascus on the N.E., and with the markets of the E. by the great caravan routes (see "Roads" under PALESTINE).

10. Contact with the Outside World In the days of Christ the coming and going of the merchantmen, the passing of armies and the movements of the representatives of the Empire, must have made these highways a scene of perpetual activity, touching the dwellers in Galilee with the widening influences of the great world's life.

11. Population The peasant farmers of Galilee, we have seen, were a bold and enterprising race. Encouraged by the fruitfulness of their country, they were industrious cultivators of the soil. Jos estimates the population at 3,000,000. This may be an exaggeration; but here we have all the conditions necessary for the support of a numerous and prosperous people. This helps us to understand the crowds that gathered round and followed Jesus in this district, where the greater part of His public life was spent. The cities, towns and villages in Galilee are frequently referred to in the Gospels. That the Jewish population in the centuries immediately after Christ was numerous and wealthy is sufficiently proved by the remains from those times, esp. the ruins of synagogues, e.g. those at *Tell Ḥūm, Kerāzeh, Irbid, el-Jish, Kefr Birʻim, Meirōn*, etc. Near the last named is shown the tomb of the great Jewish teacher Hillel.

Galilee was not without her own heroic memories. The great battlefields of Megiddo, Gilboa, and the waters of Merom lay within her borders; and among the famous men of the past she could claim Barak, Ibzan, Elon and Tola of the judges; of the prophets, Jonah and Elisha at least; possibly also Hosea who, according to a Jewish tradition, died in Babylon, but was brought to Galilee and buried in *Ṣafed* (Neubauer, *Geog. der Talmud*, 227). When the chief priests and Pharisees said, "Search, and see that out of Galilee ariseth no prophet," it argued strange and inexcusable ignorance on their part (Jn **7** 52). Perhaps, however, in this place we should read ὁ προφήτης, *ho prophḗtēs*, "the prophet," i.e. the Messiah. It is significant that 11 out of the 12 apostles were Galileans.

For detailed description of the country, see ISSACHAR; ASHER; ZEBULUN AND NAPHTALI; see also GALILEE, SEA OF. W. EWING

GALILEE, MOUNTAIN IN: After the resurrection the disciples "went into Galilee, unto the mountain where Jesus had appointed them" (Mt **28** 16). Here Jesus came to them, declared that all authority in heaven and earth had been given to Him, commanded them to go and make disciples of all nations, concluding with the memorable promise: "Lo, I am with you always, even unto the end of the world." Probably it was some well-known height not far from the scenes most frequented during the Galilean ministry. Looking from the western shore at the uplands N. of the lake, it is not easy to imagine a more appropriate spot for this never-to-be-forgotten interview than *Jebel Ḳanʻān*, a bold headland not far to the E. of *Ṣafed*, overlooking the land of Gennesaret and the sea, and commanding from its lofty summit a view of about 80 miles in every direction. Of course, there is no certainty. W. EWING

GALILEE, SEA OF (**ἡ θάλασσα τῆς Γαλιλαίας**, *hē thálassa tḗs Galilaías*):

1. The Name This is the name 5 t given in the NT (Mt **4** 18; **15** 29; Mk **1** 16; **7** 31; Jn **6** 1) to the sheet of water which is elsewhere called "the sea of Tiberias" (Jn **21** 1; cf **6** 1); "the lake of Gennesaret" (Lk **5** 1); "the sea" (Jn **6** 16, etc), and "the lake" (Lk **5** 1, etc). The OT names were "sea of Chinnereth" (יַם־כִּנֶּרֶת, *yam-kinnereth:* Nu **34** 11; Dt **3** 17; Josh **13** 27; **19** 35), and "sea of Chinneroth" (יַם־כִּנְּרוֹת, *yam-kinᵉrōth:* Josh **12** 3; cf **11** 2; 1 K **15** 20). In 1 Macc **11** 67 the sea is called "the water of Gennesar" (RV "Gennesareth"). It had begun to be named from the city so recently built on its western shore even in NT times (Jn **21** 1; **6** 1); and by this name, slightly modified, it is known to this day—*Baḥr Ṭabarīyeh.*

Sea of Galilee.

2. General Description The sea lies in the deep trough of the Jordan valley, almost due E. of the Bay of Acre. The surface is 680 ft. below the level of the Mediterranean. It varies in depth from 130 ft. to 148 ft., being deepest along the course of the Jordan (Barrois, *PEFS*, 1894, 211–20). From the point where the Jordan enters in the N. to its exit in the S. is about 13 miles. The greatest breadth is in the N., from *el-Mejdel* to the mouth of *Wādy Semak* being rather over 7 miles. It gradually narrows toward the S., taking the shape of a gigantic pear, with a decided bulge to the W. The water of the lake is clear and sweet. The natives use it for all purposes, esteeming it light and pleasant. They refuse to drink from the Jordan, alleging that "who drinks Jordan drinks fever." Seen from the mountains the broad sheet appears a beautiful blue; so that, in the season of greenery, it is no exaggeration to describe it as a sapphire in a setting of emerald. It lights up the landscape as the eye does the human face; and it is often spoken of as "the eye of Galilee." To one descending from Mt. Tabor and approaching the edge of the great hollow, on a bright spring day, when the land has already assumed its fairest garments, the view of the sea, as it breaks upon the vision in almost its whole extent, is one never to be forgotten. The mountains on the E. and on the W. rise to about 2,000 ft. The heights of Naphtali, piled up in the N., seem to culminate only in the snowy summit of Great Hermon. If the waters are still, the shining splendors of the mountain may be seen mirrored in the blue depths. Round the greater part of the lake there is a broad pebbly beach, with a sprinkling of small shells. On the sands along the shore from *el-Mejdel* to *ʻAin et-Tīneh* these shells are so numerous as to cause a white glister in the sunlight.

The main formation of the surrounding district is limestone. It is overlaid with lava; and here and there around the lake there are outcrops of basalt through the limestone. At *eṭ-Ṭābgha* in the N., at *ʻAin el Fulīyeh*, S. of *el-Mejdel*, and on the shore, about 2 miles S. of modern Tiberias, there are strong hot springs. These things, together with the frequent, and sometimes terribly destructive, earthquakes, sufficiently attest the volcanic character of the region. The soil on the level parts around the sea is exceedingly fertile. See GENNESARET, LAND OF. Naturally the temperature in the valley is higher than that of the uplands; and here wheat and barley are harvested about a month earlier. Frost is not quite unknown; but no one now alive remembers it to have done more than lay the most delicate fringe of ice around some of the stones on the shore. The fig and the vine are still cultivated with success. Where vegetable gardens are planted they yield plentifully. A few palms are still to be seen. The indigo plant is grown in the plain of Gennesaret. In their season the wild flowers lavish a wealth of lovely colors upon the surrounding slopes; while bright-blossoming oleanders fringe the shore.

Coming westward from the point where the Jordan enters the lake, the mountains approach within a short distance of the sea. On the shore, fully 2 miles from the Jordan, are the ruins of *Tell Ḥūm.* See CAPERNAUM. About 2 miles farther W. are the hot springs of *eṭ-Ṭabgha.* Here a shallow vale breaks northward, bounded on the W. by *Tell 'Areimeh.* This tell is crowned by an ancient Canaanite settlement. It throws out a rocky promontory into the sea, and beyond this are the ruins of *Khān Minyeh,* with *'Ain et-Tīneh* close under the cliff. Important Rom remains have recently been discovered here. From this point the plain of Gennesaret (*el-Ghuweir*) sweeps round to *el-Mejdel,* a distance of about 4 miles. W. of this village opens the tremendous gorge, *Wādy el-Ḥamām,* with the famous robbers' fastnesses in its precipitous sides, and the ruins of Arbela on its southern lip. From the northern parts of the lake the Horns of *Ḥaṭṭīn,* the traditional Mount of Beatitudes, may be seen through the rocky jaws of the gorge. S. of *el-Mejdel* the mountains advance to the shore, and the path is cut in the face of the slope, bringing us to the hot spring, *'Ain el-Fulīyeh,* where is a little valley, with gardens and orange grove. The road then crosses a second promontory, and proceeds along the base of the mountain to Tiberias. Here the mountains recede from the shore, leaving a crescent-shaped plain, largely covered with the ruins of the ancient city. The modern town stands at the northern corner of the plain; while at the southern end are the famous hot baths, the ancient Hammath. A narrow ribbon of plain between the mountain and the shore runs to the S. end of the lake. There the Jordan, issuing from the sea, almost surrounds the mound on which are the ruins of *Kerak,* the Tarichaea of Jos. Crossing the floor of the valley, past *Semakh,* which is now a station on the Haifa-Damascus railway, we find a similar strip of plain along the eastern shore. Nearly opposite Tiberias is the stronghold of *Ḳal'at el-Ḥoṣn,* possibly the ancient Hippos, with the village of *Fīḳ,* the ancient Aphek, on the height to the E. To the N. of this the waters of the sea almost touch the foot of the steep slope. A herd of swine running headlong down the mountain would here inevitably perish in the lake (Mt **8** 32, etc). Next we reach the mouth of *Wādy Semak,* in which lie the ruins of *Kurseh,* probably representing the ancient Gerasa. Northward the plain widens into the marshy breadths of *el-Baṭeiḥah,* and once more we reach the Jordan, flowing smoothly through the flat lands to the sea.

3. Storms

The position of the lake makes it liable to sudden storms, the cool air from the uplands rushing down the gorges with great violence and tossing the waters in tumultuous billows. Such storms are fairly frequent, and as they are attended with danger to small craft, the boatmen are constantly on the alert. Save in very settled conditions they will not venture far from the shore. Occasionally, however, tempests break over the lake, in which a boat could hardly live. Only twice in over 5 years the present writer witnessed such a hurricane. Once it burst from the S. In a few moments the air was thick with mist, through which one could hear the roar of the tortured waters. In about ten minutes the wind fell as suddenly as it had risen. The air cleared, and the wide welter of foam-crested waves attested the fury of the blast. On the second occasion the wind blew from the E., and the phenomena described above were practically repeated.

Fishing on the Sea of Galilee.

4. Fish

The sea contains many varieties of fish in great numbers. The fishing industry was evidently pursued to profit in the days of Christ. Zebedee was able to hire men to assist him (Mk **1** 20). In recent years there has been a considerable revival of this industry. See FISHING. Four of the apostles, and these the chief, had been brought up as fishermen on the Sea of Galilee—Peter and Andrew, James and John.

The towns around the lake named in Scripture are treated in separate articles. Some of these it is impossible to identify. Many are the ruins of great and splendid cities on slope and height of which almost nothing is known today. But from their mute testimony we gather that the lake in the valley which is now so quiet was once the center of a busy and prosperous population. We may assume that the cities named in the Gospels were mainly Jewish. Jesus would naturally avoid those in which Gr influences were strong. In most cases they have gone, leaving not even their names with any certainty behind; but His memory abides forever. The lake and mountains are, in main outline, such as His eyes beheld. This it is that lends its highest charm to "the eye of Galilee."

The advent of the railway has stirred afresh the pulses of life in the valley. A steamer plies on the sea between the station at *Semakh* and Tiberias. Superior buildings are rising outside the ancient walls. Gardens and orchards are being planted. Modern methods of agriculture are being employed in the Jewish colonies, which are rapidly increasing in number. Slowly, perhaps, but surely, the old order is giving place to the new. If freedom and security be enjoyed in reasonable measure, the region will again display its long-hidden treasures of fertility and beauty. W. EWING

GALL, gôl:

(1) רֹאשׁ, *rō'sh,* or רוֹשׁ, *rōsh* (Dt **32** 32 only, "grapes of gall"): Some very bitter plant, the bitterness as in (2) being associated with the idea of poison. Dt **29** 18 m "*rosh,* a poisonous herb"; Lam **3** 5.19; Jer **8** 14; **9** 15; **23** 15, "water of gall," m "poison"; Hos **10** 4, tr[d] "hemlock"; Am **6** 12, "Ye have turned justice into gall"; Job **20** 16, the "poison of asps": here *rōsh* clearly refers

SUNRISE OVER THE SEA OF GALILEE

to a different substance from the other references, the points in common being bitterness and poisonous properties. Hemlock (*Conium maculatum*), colocynth (*Citrullus colocynthus*) and the poppy (*Papaver somniferum*) have all been suggested as the original *rōsh*, the last having most support, but in most references the word may represent any bitter poisonous substance. *Rōsh* is associated with *la'ănāh*, "wormwood" (Dt **29** 18; Lam **3** 19; Am **6** 12).

(2) מְרֵרָה, *m^erērāh* (Job **16** 13), and מְרֹרָה, *m^erōrāh* (**20** 14.25), both derived from a root meaning "to be bitter," are applied to the human gall or "bile," but like (1), *m^erōrāh* is once applied to the venom of serpents (**20** 14). The poison of these animals was supposed to reside in their bile.

(3) χολή, *cholē* (Mt **27** 34), "They gave him wine to drink mingled with gall"; this is clearly a reference to the LXX version of Ps **69** 21: "They gave me also gall [*cholē*, Heb *rōsh*] for my food; and in my thirst they gave me vinegar to drink." In Mk **15** 23, it says, "wine mingled with myrrh." It is well known that the Romans gave wine with frankincense to criminals before their execution to alleviate their sufferings; here the *cholē* or bitter substance used was myrrh (Pliny *Ep.* xx.18; Sen. *Ep.* 83). E. W. G. Masterman

GALLANT, gal'ant: The tr of אַדִּיר, *'addīr*, "bright," "splendid," "mighty" (Isa **33** 21, "Neither shall gallant [*'addīr*] ship pass thereby"); the word is tr^d "mighty" in Ex **15** 10; 1 S **4** 8; Isa **10** 34; Zec **11** 2 AV. In Isa **33** 21, above, it is applied to Jeh, "glorious [*'addīr*] Lord" AV, RV "Jeh . . . in . . . . majesty"; cf also Ps **16** 3, "the excellent." As a noun it is used in m of Nah **2** 5 as alternative for "worthies," RV "nobles"; in Zec **11** 2, for "the mighty," RV "goodly ones," m "glorious"; it is tr^d "nobles" in Jgs **5** 13; 2 Ch **23** 20, etc. See also Ships and Boats.

GALLERY, gal'ēr-i:

(1) (אַתּוּק, *'attūḳ*, K^ethībh; אַתִּיק, *'attīḳ*, used only in Ezk **41** 16; **42** 3.5; etymology and meaning uncertain; among the more probable suggestions are "pillar," "column," "walk with pillars," "colonnades," "passageway," "porches," "galleries" and "terraces." Cornill suggests the substitution of *ḳīrōth*, "walls," to suit the context; others, e.g. Rothstein, would omit it as a dittography or other corruption): A long narrow balcony formed either by pillars or by the receding upper stories of a building. Both kinds are described in Ezekiel's vision of the Temple restored. They surround the three stories of side chambers around the Temple proper, and also the "building before the separate place which was at the back thereof," and the three-story structure containing rows of chambers in the outer court opposite the side-chambers of the Temple. Those around the Temple proper were apparently supported by pillars, and hence they did not take away from the width of the 2d- and 3d-story rooms (cf **41** 7). On the other hand, the galleries of the outer buildings which were not supported by pillars and therefore not on top of each other, but in terraces, did take away from the upper stories more than from the lowest and middlemost: the upper chambers were shortened or "straitened more than the lowest and the middlemost from the ground."

The lower porches of the outer court were cut off from the view of those of the inner court by a low wall, but in the 3d story, gallery looked out to gallery across the "twenty cubits which belonged to the inner court and the pavement which belonged to the outer court." These "galleries," or *'attīḳīm*, are one of the few features that distinguish the temple of Ezekiel's vision from Solomon's temple. The idea and perhaps the word seem to have been borrowed from the more elaborate architecture of the countries of the Exile, which must have impressed the Jews of Ezekiel's time very strongly. The building Ezekiel would place in the outer court with its terraces is a perfect Bab *ziggurat* or stage-tower temple (cf *Enc Brit*, 11th ed, II, 374, *c-d*).

(2) (רַהַט, *rahaṭ*, probably "lock of hair," Cant **7** 5; רָהִיט, *rāhīṭ*, K^erē, רָחִיט, *rāḥīṭ*, K^ethībh, probably "rafters," Cant **11** 7; both words and also the similar word [*r^ehāṭīm*, Gen **30** 38; Ex **2** 16], tr^d "troughs," are probably connected with the Aram. *r^ehaṭ*, "to flow," "to run"): Although AV uses "galleries" in Cant **7** 5 and **1** 17 m, the context in each place clearly points to another meaning. In the former of these passages, "the king is held captive in the tresses thereof," there follows a description of the head. In the latter passage the word in question is in parallelism with *ḳōrōth bātēnū*, "the beams of our house," and "rafters" AV, or possibly "boards," is suggested. Nathan Isaacs

GALLEY, gal'i. See Ships and Boats, II, 2, (2).

GALLIM, gal'im (גַּלִּים, *gallīm*, "heaps"): Probably two distinct places:

(1) A town mentioned among the 11 additional cities of Judah which are in the LXX appended to Josh **15** 59, and have altogether disappeared from the Heb text. It occurs between Karem (*'Ain Kairem*) and Baither (*Bettîr*); it is probably the large and flourishing village of *Beit Jāla*, near Bethlehem.

(2) Gallim is mentioned in Isa **10** 30; not far from Laishah and Anathoth and certainly N. of Jerus. It was the home of Palti the son of Laish (1 S **25** 44), and it is by many authorities identified with the Gilgal on the N. border of Judah (Josh **15** 7), the *G^elīlōth* of the ‖ passage (**18** 17), and the Beth-gilgal of Neh **12** 29. E. W. G. Masterman

GALLIO, gal'i-ō (Γαλλίων, *Galliōn*): The Rom deputy or proconsul of Achaia, before whom Paul was haled by his Jewish accusers on the apostle's first visit to Corinth, during his second missionary journey (Acts **18** 12-17). The trial was not of long duration. Although Gallio extended his protection to the Jewish religion as one of the religions recognized by the state, he contemptuously rejected the claim of the Jews that their law was binding upon all. In the eyes of the proconsul, the only law universally applicable was that of the Rom code and social morality: under neither was the prisoner chargeable; therefore, without even waiting to hear Paul's speech in his own defence, he summarily ordered his lictors to clear the court. Even the subsequent treatment meted out to Sosthenes, the chief ruler of the synagogue, was to him a matter of indifference. The beating of Sosthenes is ascribed by different readings to "Jews" and to "Greeks," but the incident is referred to by the writer of Acts to show that the sympathies of the populace lay with Paul, and that Gallio made no attempt to suppress them. Gallio has often been instanced as typical of one who is careless or indifferent to religion, yet in the account given of him in Acts, he merely displayed an attitude characteristic of the manner in which Rom governors regarded the religious disputes of the time (cf also Lysias; Felix; Festus). Trained by his administrative duties to practical thinking and precision of language, he refused to adjudicate the squabbles of what he regarded as an obscure religious sect, whose law was to him a subtle quibbling with "words and names."

According to extra-canonical references, the original name of Gallio was Marcus Annaeus Novatus, but this was changed on his being adopted by the rhetorician, Lucius Junius Gallio. He was born at Cordova, but came to Rome in the reign of Tiberius. He was the brother of the philosopher Seneca, by whom, as also by Statius, reference is made to the affable nature of his character. As Achaia was reconstituted a proconsular province by Claudius in 44 AD, the accession of Gallio to office must have been subsequent to that date, and has been variously placed at 51–53 AD (cf also Knowling in *Expos Gr Test.*, II, 389–92). C. M. Kerr

GALLOWS, gal'ōz. See Hanging; Punishments.

GAMAEL, gam'ā-el (**Γαμαήλ,** *Gamaēl*): Chief of the family of Ithamar who went up from Babylon with Ezra (1 Esd **8** 29); called Daniel in Ezr **8** 2.

GAMALIEL, ga-mā'li-el (גַּמְלִיאֵל, *gamlī'ēl*, "reward or recompense of God"; **Γαμαλιήλ,** *Gamaliēl*):

(1) The son of Pedahzur, and "prince of the children of Manasseh," chosen to aid in taking the census in the Wilderness (Nu **1** 10; **2** 20; **7** 54.59; **10** 23).

(2) A Pharisee who at the meeting of the "council" succeeded in persuading its members to adopt a more reasonable course when they were incensed at the doctrine of Peter and the rest of the apostles and sought to slay them (Acts **5** 33–40). That he was well qualified for this task is attested by the fact that he was himself a member of the Sanhedrin, a teacher of the law, and held in high honor among all the people. In his speech he pointed out to his fellow-councillors the dire consequences that might ensue upon any precipitous action on their part. While quoting instances, familiar to his hearers, of past insurrections or seditions that had failed, he reminded them at the same time that if this last under Peter "is of God, ye will not be able to overthrow them; lest haply ye be found even to be fighting against God." As a result of his arguments, the apostles, after being beaten and admonished to speak no longer in the name of Jesus, were released. In the speech which he was permitted by Lysias to deliver from the stairs of the palace after the riot in Jerus, Paul referred to Gamaliel as the teacher of his youth, who instructed him rigidly in the Mosaic law (Acts **22** 3).

The toleration and liberality displayed by Gamaliel upon the occasion of his speech before the Sanhedrin were all the more remarkable because of their rarity among the Pharisees of the period. Although the strict observance by the Christians of temple-worship, and their belief in immortality, a point in dispute between Pharisees and Sadducees, may have had influence over him (Knowling), no credence is to be attached to the view that he definitely favored the apostles or to the tradition that he afterward became a Christian. The high place accorded him in Jewish tradition, and the fact that the title of Rabban, higher even than Rabbi or Master, was first bestowed upon him, testify that he remained a Pharisee to the end. His speech is rather indicative of one who knew the deeper truth in the OT of the universal fatherhood of God, and who recognized that the presence of His power was the deciding factor in all human enterprise. His social enactments were permeated by the same broad-minded spirit. Thus his legislation on behalf of the poor was formulated so as to include Gentiles as well as Jews. The authenticity of his speech has been questioned by Wendt and others, chiefly on account of the alleged anachronism in regard to Theudas (see Theudas); but the internal evidence is against this view (cf Knowling in *Expos Gr Test.*, II, 161). It has also been objected by Baur and the Tübingen school that the liberal, peace-loving Gamaliel could not have been the teacher of the fanatical Saul. To this, reply has been made, firstly, that the charges against Stephen of destroying the temple and subverting the laws of Moses were not brought against Peter and the other apostles, and, secondly, that the doctrines of any teacher, however moderate he himself may be, are liable to be carried to extremes by an over-zealous pupil.

Literature.—Conybeare and Howson, *Life and Epp. of St. Paul*, ch ii; Kitto, *Cyclopaedia of Bib. Lit.*, 1866, art. "Gamaliel" (Ginsberg).

C. M. Kerr

GAMES, gāmz:

I. Israelitish Games
  1. Children's Games
     Mimicry
  2. Sports
  3. Games of Chance and Skill
  4. Story-Telling
  5. Dancing
  6. Proverbs
  7. Riddles
II. The Games of Greece and Rome
  1. Historical Introduction
  2. General References
  3. Specific References to Greek Athletics
  4. References to the Theater and the Drama
Literature

About the amusements of the ancient Israelites we know but little, partly on account of the nature of our literary sources, which are almost exclusively religious, partly because the antiquities thus far discovered yield very little information on this topic as compared with those of some other countries, and partly because of the relatively serious character of the people. Games evidently took a less prominent place in Heb life than in that of the Greeks, the Romans and the Egyptians. Still the need for recreation was felt and to a certain extent supplied in ways according with the national temperament. Mere athletics (apart from Gr and Rom influence) were but little cultivated. Simple and natural amusements and exercises, and trials of wit and wisdom, were more to the Heb taste. What is known or probably conjectured may be summed up under the following heads: Games of Children; Sports; Games of Chance and Skill; Story-telling; Dancing; Proverbs; Riddles. The amusements of Greece and Rome, which to some extent influenced later Jewish society and esp. those which are directly or indirectly referred to in the NT, will be the theme of the latter part of the article.

I. Israelitish Games.—There are two general references to the playing of children: Zec **8** 5: "And the streets of the city shall be full of boys and girls playing in the streets thereof"; and Gen **21** 9 m, where we read of Ishmael "playing" (*m^eçaḥēḳ*). The rendering of our Bibles, "mocking," is open to question. Of specific games and pets there is hardly a mention in the OT. Playing with *ball* is alluded to in Isa **22** 18: "He will . . . . toss thee like a ball into a large country," but children need not be thought of as the only players. If the balls used in Pal were like those used by the Egyptians, they were sometimes made of leather or skin stuffed with bran or husks of corn, or of string and rushes covered with leather (cf Wilkinson, *Popular Account*, I, 198–201; *British Museum Guide to the Egyp Collections*, 78). The question of Jeh to Job (**41** 5): "Wilt thou play with him [the crocodile] as with a bird? or wilt thou bind him for thy maidens?" suggests that tame birds were petted by Heb children, esp. by girls. The NT has one reference to children's play, viz. the half-parable about the children in the market-place who would neither dance to the flute as if at *a marriage feast* nor wail as if at *a funeral* (Mt **11** 16 f ‖ Lk **7** 32).

1. Children's Games

Mimicry.—There are interesting accounts in *Les enfants de Nazareth*, by the Abbé Le Camus (60–66; 101–10), of the way in which the children of the modern Nazareth mimic scenes connected with weddings and funerals. That Israelitish children had toys (dolls, models of animals, etc) cannot be doubted in view of the finds in Egypt and elsewhere, but no positive evidence seems to be as yet forthcoming.

2. Sports

Running was no doubt often practised, esp. in the time of the early monarchy. Saul and Jonathan (2 S **1** 23), Asahel (**2** 18), Ahimaaz (**18** 23.27) and some of the Gadites in David's service (1 Ch **12** 8) were renowned for their speed, which can only have been the result of training and exercise. The same may be said of the feats of those who ran before a king or a prince (1 S **8** 11; 2 S **15** 1; 1 K **1** 5; **18** 46). The Psalmist must have watched great runners before he pictured the sun as rejoicing like a strong man to run his course (Ps **19** 5*b;* cf also Eccl **9** 11; Jer **8** 6; **23** 10). For running in the Gr games,see the latter part of this article.

Archery practice is implied in the story of Jonathan's touching interview with David (1 S **20** 20.35–38) and in Job's complaint: "He hath also set me up for his mark. His archers compass me round about" (Job **16** 12 f). Only by long practice could the 700 left-handed Benjamite slingers, every one of whom could sling stones at a hair-breadth and not miss (Jgs **20** 16), and the young David (1 S **17** 49), have attained to the precision of aim for which they are famous.

In Zec **12** 3, "I will make Jerus a burdensome stone," lit. "a stone of burden," Jerome found an allusion to a custom which prevailed widely in Pal in his day, and has been noticed by a recent traveler, of *stone-lifting*, i.e. of testing the strength of young men by means of heavy round stones. Some, he says, could raise one of these stones to the knees, others to the waist, others to the shoulders and the head, and a few could lift it above the head. This interpretation is not quite certain (Wright, *Comm*., 364), but the form of sport described was probably in vogue in Pal in Bib. times.

High leaping or jumping was probably also practised (Ps **18** 29). The "play" referred to in 2 S **2** 14 ff of 12 Benjamites and 12 servants of David was not a sport but a combat like that of the Horatii and the Curiatii.

3. Games of Chance and Skill

Dice were known to the ancient Egyptians, and Assyr dice have been found, made of bronze with points of gold, but there is no trace of them in the OT. Recent research at *Ta'annek* has brought to light many bones which seem to have been used in somewhat the same way as in a game played by the modern Arabs, who call it *ka'ab*, the very word they apply to dice. These bones were "the oldest and most primitive form of dice" (König after Sellin, *RE*[3], XVIII, 634). The use of dice among the later Jews is attested by the condemnation of dice-players in the Mish (*Sanh*., iii. 3). The Syrian soldiers who cast lots for the raiment of Jesus at the cross (Mt **27** 35 ‖ Mk **15** 24; Lk **23** 34; Jn **19** 24) may have used dice, but that can neither be proved nor disproved.

It has been suggested that the *mockery* of Jesus before the Sanhedrin described in Mt **26** 67 f ‖ Mk **14** 65; Lk **22** 63 f may have been connected with a Gr game in which one of the players held the eyes of another while a third gave him a box on the ear. The last was then asked with what hand he had been struck. A somewhat similar game is represented in an Egyp tomb picture (Wilkinson, *Popular Account*, I, 192). This reference, however, though not quite inadmissible, is scarcely probable. Games with boards and men bearing some resemblance to our draughts were in great favor in Egypt (ib, 190–95), but cannot be proved for the Jews even in NT times.

Listening to stories or recitations has long been a favorite amusement of Orientals (cf Lane, *Modern Egyptians*, 359–91: "The Thousand and One Nights"), but there seems to be no reference to it in the Bible. There can be no reasonable doubt, however, that the Hebrews, like their neighbors, had story-tellers or reciters, and heard them with delight. Egyp tales of great antiquity are well known from the two volumes edited by Professor Petrie in 1895; and there are several non-canonical Jewish tales which combine romance and moral teaching: the Books of Tob and Jth and perhaps the Story of Ahikar, the last of which, with the help of the Aram. papyri discovered at Elephantine, can be traced back (in some form) to about 400 BC (Schürer, *GJV*[4], III, 255). There are also many short stories in the Haggadic portions of the Talm and the Midr.

4. Story-Telling

5. Dancing

Dancing, that is, the expression of joy by rhythmical movements of the limbs to musical accompaniment, is scarcely ever mentioned in the Bible as a social amusement, except in a general way (Jgs **16** 25.27[?]; Job **21** 11; Ps **30** 11; Eccl **3** 4; Jer **31** 4.13; Lam **5** 15; Mt **11** 17; Lk **15** 25). There is one exception, the

Egyptian Dance—from Tomb at Thebes.

dancing of Salome, the daughter of Herodias, before Herod Antipas and his court (Mt **14** 6 ‖ Mk **6** 22), which was a solo dance, probably of a pantomimic character affected by Rom influence. The other Bib. references to dancing can be grouped under two heads: the dance of public rejoicing, and the dance which was more or less an act of worship. Of the former we have two striking examples in the OT: the dance accompanied by the tambourine with which the maidens of Israel, led by Jephthah's daughter, met that leader after his victory (Jgs **11** 34), and the dances of the Israelitish women in honor of Saul and David to celebrate the triumph over the Philis (1 S **18** 6; **21** 11; **29** 5).

It was probably usual to welcome a king or general with music and dancing. There is a good illustration in a fine Assyr sculpture in the British Museum which represents a band of 11 instrumentalists taking part in doing homage to a new ruler. Three men at the head of the procession are distinctly dancing (*SBOT*, "Psalms," Eng., 226).

The distinctly religious dance is more frequently mentioned. The clear instances of it in the Bible are the dance of the women of Israel at the Red Sea, headed by Miriam with her tambourine (Ex **15** 20); the dance of the Israelites round the golden calf (**32** 19); the dance of the maidens of Shiloh at an annual feast (Jgs **21** 19 ff); the leaping or limping of the prophets of Baal round their altar on Carmel (1 K **18** 26), and the dancing of David in front of the ark (2 S **6** 14.16 ‖ 1 Ch **15** 29). There are general references in Ps **149** 3: "Let them praise his name in the dance"; **150** 4: "Praise him with timbrel and dance"; and perhaps in **68** 25. The allusions in Cant **6** 13, "the dance of Mahanaim," and in the proper name Abel-meholah, "the meadow of the dance" (1 K **19** 16, etc), are too uncertain to be utilized. The ritual dance was probably widespread in the ancient East. David's performance has Egyp parallels. Seti I, the father of Rameses II, and three other Pharaohs are said to have danced before a deity (Budge, *The Book of the Dead*, I, xxxv), and Asiatic monuments attest the custom elsewhere. About the methods of dancing practised by the ancient Hebrews but little is known. Probably the dancers in some cases joined hands and formed a ring, or part of a ring, as in some heathen representations. The description of David's dance: he "danced before Jeh with all his might . . . . leaping and dancing before Jeh" (2 S **6** 14–16) suggests three features of that particular display and the mode of dancing which it represented: violent exertion, leaping (*mephazzēz*), and whirling round (*mekharkēr*). Perhaps the whirling dance of Islam is a modern parallel to the last. Women seem generally to have danced by themselves, one often leading the rest, both in dancing and antiphonal song; so Miriam and the women of Israel, Jephthah's daughter and her comrades, the women who greeted Saul and David, and, in the Apoc, Judith and her sisters after the death of Holofernes (Jth **15** 12 f). Once the separation of the sexes is perhaps distinctly referred to (Jer **31** 13). In public religious dances they may have occasionally united, as was the case sometimes in the heathen world, but there is no clear evidence to that effect (cf, however, 2 S **6** 20 and Ps **68** 25). Of the social dancing of couples in the modern fashion there is no trace. There seems to be some proof that the religious dance lingered among the Jews until the time of Christ and later.

If the Mish can be trusted (*Sukkāh*, v.4), there was a torch-light dance in the temple in the illuminated court of the women at the Feast of Tabernacles in which men of advanced years and high standing took part. The Gemara to the Jerus Talm adds that a famous dancer on these occasions was Rabbi Simeon or Simon, the son of Gamaliel, who lived in the apostolic age (Jos, *BJ*, IV, iii, 9). According to another passage (*Ta'ănith* **4** 8) the daughters of Jerus used to dance dressed in white in the vineyards on Tishri the 10th and Ab the 15th. Religious dancing in the modern East is illustrated not only by the dances of the dervishes mentioned above, but also by occasional dances led by the sheikh in honor of a saint (Curtiss, *Primitive Semitic Religion To-day*, 169). Among the later Jews dancing was not unusual at wedding feasts. More than one eminent rabbi is said to have danced before the bride (*Kethubbōth* **17***a*). Singing and dancing, with lighted torches, are said to be wedding customs of the modern Arabs.

Literature.—Arts. "Dance" in Smith *DB*[2], *HDB*, *DCG*, *EB*, *Jew Enc* (also "Games"); "Tanz" in *RE*[3] and the German Dictionaries of Winer, Riehm, and Guthe (*Reigen*); Nowack, *HA*, I, 278 f.

6. Proverbs

Proverbs (מָשָׁל, *māshāl*; παροιμία, *paroimía*): Proverbs and proverbial expressions seem to have been, to some extent, a means of amusement as well as instruction for the ancient Oriental who delighted in the short, pointed statement of a moral or religious truth, or a prudential maxim, whether of literary or popular origin. Most of these sayings in the Bible belong to the former class, and are couched in poetic form (see Proverbs; Ecclesiastes; Ecclesiasticus). The others which are shorter and simpler, together with a number of picturesque proverbial phrases, must have recurred continually in daily speech and have added greatly to its vivacity.

The OT supplies the following 10 examples of the popular proverb: (1) "Like Nimrod a mighty hunter before Jeh" (Gen **10** 9); (2) "As the man is, so is his strength" (Jgs **8** 21), only two words in the Heb; (3) "Is Saul also among the prophets?" (1 S **10** 11 f; **19** 24); (4) "Out of the wicked [wicked men] cometh forth wickedness" (1 S **24** 13); (5) "There are the blind and the lame; he cannot come into the house" (2 S **5** 8); (6) "Let not him that girdeth on his armor boast himself as he that putteth it off" (1 K **20** 11); (7) "Skin for skin, yea, all that a man hath will he give for his life" (Job **2** 4); (8) "The days are prolonged, and every vision faileth" (Ezk **12** 22), a scoffing jest rather than a proverb; (9) "As is the mother, so is her daughter" (Ezk **16** 44), two words in the Heb; (10) "The fathers have eaten sour grapes, and the children's teeth are set on edge" (Jer **31** 29; Ezk **18** 2). In the NT we find 10 others: (1) "Physician, heal thyself" (Lk **4** 23); in the *Midhrash Rabbāh* on Gen: "Physician heal thine own wound"; (2) "Can the blind guide the blind? shall they not both fall into a pit?" (**6** 39); (3) "With what measure ye mete, it shall be measured unto you" (Mt **7** 2 ‖ Mk **4** 24; Lk **6** 38), almost identical with a Jewish proverb, "measure for measure" cited several times in the ancient Midrash, the *Mekhiltā'*: (4) "One soweth, and another reapeth" (Jn **4** 37); (5) "A prophet is not without honor, save in his own country" (Mt **13** 57; Lk **4** 24; Jn **4** 44; Logion of Oxyrhynchus); (6) "There are yet four months, and then cometh the harvest" (Jn **4** 35), possibly a kind of proverb; (7) "Wheresoever the carcase is, there will the eagles [m "vultures"] be gathered together" (Mt **24** 28 ‖ Lk **17** 37); perhaps a proverb of which there is a trace also in the reference to the vulture: "Where the slain are, there is she" (Job **39** 30); (8) "It is hard for thee to kick against the goad" (Acts **26** 14), a Gr proverb: for proof cf Wetstein's note; (9) "The dog turning to his own vomit again, and the sow that had washed to wallowing in the mire" (2 Pet **2** 22); Wetstein gives rabbinic parallels for the former half, and Gr for the latter; (10) "Ye . . . . strain out the gnat, and swallow the camel" (Mt **23** 24).

There are also many proverbial phrases which added piquancy to conversation. Exceeding smallness was likened to the eye of a needle (Mt **19** 24 ‖ Mk **10** 25; Lk **18** 25), or to a grain of mustard (Mt **13** 31 ‖ Mk **4** 31; Mt **17** 20 ‖ Lk **17** 6), comparisons both found also in the Talm, the Koran, and modern Arab. sayings. Relative greatness was likened to a camel (Mt **19** 24, etc), in the Talm to a camel or an elephant. Great number was illustrated by reference to "the sand which is upon the sea-shore" (Gen **22** 17 and many other passages); "the dust of the earth" (**13** 16, etc; also an Arabian figure); "the grass of the earth" (Job **5** 25; Ps **72** 16; cf **92** 7), an early Bab figure; a swarm of locusts (Nah **3** 15 and 4 other passages), a similitude used also by Sennacherib (*RP*, n.s. VI, 97), and the stars of heaven (Gen **15** 5 and 10 other passages). When complete security was promised or described it was said that not a hair of the head was or should be injured or perish (1 S **14** 45; 2 S **14** 11; 1 K **1** 52; Dnl **3** 27; Lk **21** 18; Acts **27** 34). Overcoming of difficulties was referred to as the removal of mountains (Mt **17** 20; **21** 21 ‖ Mk **11** 23; 1 Cor **13** 2), an expression which has rabbinic parallels. Other proverbial phrases may perhaps be found in the saying about the mote and the beam (Mt **7** 3–5), jot or tittle (Mt **5** 18 ‖ Lk **16** 17), and the foolish words of Rehoboam and his young advisers (1 K **12** 10 f). Many old proverbs have no doubt perished. Dukes in his *Rabbinische Blumenlese* gives 665 proverbs and proverbial expressions from the Talm and related lit., and modern collections show that proverbial lore is still in great favor in the Bib. Orient. See also Proverbs.

Literature.—In addition to works already mentioned König, *Stilistik*, etc, *DCG* ("Jesus' Use of Proverbs"); Murray, *DB*, art. "Proverbs"; Cohen, *Ancient Jewish Proverbs*, 1911.

7. Riddles

Riddles (חִידָה, *ḥīdhāh*; αἴνιγμα, *aínigma*): Riddle-making and riddle-guessing were in favor in the ancient East, both in educated circles and in comparatively common life. There is a tablet in the British Museum (K 4347: *Guide to Assyr and Bab Antiquities*[2], 53) from the library of Ashur-bani-pal which attests the use of riddles not only by the Assyrians of the 7th cent. BC, but also in a far earlier age, for it contains a Sumer as well as a Sem text. So it is not surprising that we find a remarkable example in early Israelitish history in Samson's famous riddle: "Out of the eater came forth food, and out of the strong came forth sweetness" (Jgs **14** 14). The riddle is couched in poetic form, as is also the solution: "What is sweeter than honey? and what is stronger than a lion?" (ver 18), and the comment: "If ye had not plowed with my heifer, ye had not found out my riddle" (ib). The stipulation of a prize or penalty according to the success or failure of the persons challenged to solve the riddle was a custom met with also among the ancient Greeks and in a later age among the Arabs. In 1 K **10** 1 ‖ 2 Ch **9** 1 the word used of Samson's riddle (*ḥīdhāh*) is employed of the "hard questions" put to Solomon by the queen of Sheba. The LXX seems to have understood the word as "riddle" here also, for it renders "enigmas," and some of the later Jews not only adopted this interpretation, but actually gave riddles said to have been propounded. Of these riddles which, of course, have no direct historic value, but are interesting specimens of riddle lore, one of the best is the following: "Without movement while living, it moves when its head is cut off"; the answer to which is: "a tree" (*Jew Enc*, art. "Riddle"; see also for these riddles

Wünsche, *Die Räthselweisheit bei den Hebräern,* 15–23). If Jos can be trusted, historians of Phoenicia recorded a riddle-contest between Solomon and the Phoen Hiram in which the latter finally won with the help of a Tyrian named Abdemon (*Ant,* VIII, v, 3; *CAp,* 1, 18). In this case, too, defeat involved penalty. The testing of ability by riddles has a striking parallel in the Pers epic, the *Shah Nameh,* in the trial of the hero Sal by the mobeds or wise men (Wünsche, op. cit., 43–47). Solomon's fame as an author of riddles and riddle-like sayings is referred to in Sir **47** 15.17 (Heb): "With song, and proverbs, dark sayings [*ḥīdhāh*] and figures, thou didst greatly move the nations." *Ḥīdhāh* occurs only once in Prov (**1** 6): "the words of the wise, and their dark sayings," but the collection contains several examples of what König calls "the numerical riddle": **6** 16–19; **30** 7 ff.15 f.18 f.21 ff. 24–28.29 ff. In each case the riddle is stated first and then the solution. The saying in Prov **26** 10: "As an archer that woundeth all, so is he that hireth the fool and he that hireth them that pass by," has been cited as a riddle, and it is certainly obscure enough, but the obscurity may be due to textual corruption. There are several passages in the OT in which the word *ḥīdhāh* seems to be used in the general sense of "mysterious utterance": Nu **12** 8; Ps **49** 4; **78** 2; Dnl **5** 12 (the Aram. equivalent of *ḥīdhāh*); **8** 23; Hab **2** 6. In Ezk **17** 1 it describes the parable or allegory of the Two Eagles and the Cedar and the Vine. Sir has several numerical riddles: **23** 16; **25** 1 f.7 f; **26** 5 f; **50** 25 f; and there are similar sayings in *Ab* **5** 1–11.16–21 (Taylor's ed). In the Book of Jer (**25** 26; **51** 41; **51** 1) are two examples of a cryptic or cipher mode of writing which comes very near the riddle. SHē SHaKH, in the first two passages, represented by the three letters *shīn, shīn, kaph,* answering to our *sh, sh, k,* is meant to be read with the substitution for each letter of the letter as near the beginning of the alphabet as it is near the end, the result being *sh=b, sh=b, k=l,* that is, *B b l* or *Babel,* Babylon. In the same way in the last passage the consonants composing the word *Lebkamai l, b, k, m, y,* suggest *k, s, d, y, m,* that is, *Kasdīm* or Chaldees. This cipher or riddle-writing was called by the Jews *'At-bash* (cf Buxtorf, *Lexicon Chaldaicum,* etc, I, 131, 137 f, edited by Fischer; and modern commentaries on Jer). The NT contains no riddle except the numerical puzzle, Rev **13** 18 (cf NUMBER; GEMATRIA), and has the Gr equivalent of *ḥīdhāh* only in 1 Cor **13** 12, "for now we see . . . . *darkly,*" RVm "in a riddle" (Gr *en ainígmati*). There can be little doubt that riddles enlivened marriage festivals, such as that of Cana. Wünsche (op. cit.) gives some interesting specimens of later Jewish riddles, subsequent indeed to Our Lord's time, but such as might have been in circulation then.

LITERATURE.—The most important authority is the above-cited monograph of Wünsche. König has an interesting paragraph in his *Stilistik, Rhetorik, Poetik,* etc, 12 f. Cf also Hamburger, *RE,* II, 966 ff; arts. on "Riddle" in *Jew Enc,* Smith's *DB, HDB,* larger and smaller; Murray's *DB;* German Bible Dictionaries of Winer, Riehm², and Guthe; Rosenmüller, *Das alte und neue Morgenland,* III, 48 f.

II. The Games of Greece and Rome.—This is not the place to give a detailed account of the Greek gymnasia and the elaborate contests for which candidates were prepared in them, or to describe the special forms of sport introduced by the Romans, but these exercises and amusements were so well known in Pal and throughout the Rom Empire in the time of Christ and the apostles that they cannot be passed over in silence. Some acquaintance with them is absolutely necessary for the interpretation of many passages in the NT, esp. in the Epistles. Hellenic athletics found their way into Jewish society through the influence of the Gr kingdom ruled over by the Seleucidae. Early in the reign of Antiochus Epiphanes (cir 176 BC) a gymnasium, "place of exercise," was built in Jerus

1. Historical Introduction

Theater at Gerasa.

(1 Macc **1** 14; 2 Macc **4** 9.12) and frequented by priests (vs 14 f), who are spoken of as "making of no account the honours of their fathers, and thinking the glories of the Greeks best of all." After the success of the Maccabean rising Gr games fell into disrepute among the Jewish population of Pal, and were thenceforth regarded with suspicion by all strict religionists, even the worldly Jos sharing the general feeling (*Ant,* XV, viii, 1). Nevertheless gentile games must have been familiar to most in Jerus and elsewhere during the Herodian rule and the Rom occupation. Herod the Great built a theater and amphitheater in the neighborhood of the city (Jos, ib; for probable sites, see G. A. Smith, *Jerusalem,* II, 493), and instituted in the name of Caesar games which included Rom as well as Hellenic sports, celebrated every 5 years. There was also a hippodrome or race-course for horses and chariots, bearing considerable resemblance to the Rom circus (Jos, *Ant,* XVII, x, 2; *BJ,* II, iii, 1). Jericho, too, was provided with a theater, an amphitheater and a hippodrome. There was a hippodrome also at Tarichaea. In addition there were scattered over Syria many Hellenic and partially Hellenic cities—Schürer (*GJV*⁴, II, 108–221) gives the history of 33—Caesarea Stratonis, Caesarea Philippi, the cities of the Decapolis, Tiberias, etc, which would all have had gymnasia and games. In Tarsus, which must have had a large Gr element in its population, Paul must have heard, and perhaps seen, in his childhood, much of the athletic exercises which were constantly in progress, and in later life he must often have been reminded of them, esp. at Corinth, near which were celebrated biennially the Isthmia or Isthmian Games which drew visitors from all parts of the Empire, at Caesarea which possessed a theater, an amphitheater and a stadium, and at Ephesus. The custom, indeed, seems to have been almost universal. No provincial city of any importance was without it (Schürer, op. cit., 48), esp. after the introduction of games in honor of the Caesars. The early Christians, therefore, whether of Jewish or gentile origin, were able to understand, and the latter at any rate to appreciate, references either to the games in general, or to details of their celebration.

2. General References

The word which described the assembly gathered together at one of the great Grecian games (*agôn*) was also applied to the contests themselves, and then came to be used of any intense effort or conflict. The corresponding vb. (*agōnízomai*) had a similar history. Both these words are used **fig.** in the Pauline Epistles: the noun in Phil **1** 30; Col **2** 1; 1 Thess **2** 2; 1 Tim **6** 12; 2 Tim **4** 7, rendered in RV (except in the second passage), "conflict" or "fight"; the vb. in Col **1** 29; **4** 12; 1 Tim **4** 10; **6** 12; 2 Tim **4** 7, trᵈ "strive," "fight." In

1 Cor **9** 25; 2 Tim **2** 5 (where another word is used) there are literal references. The former passage ERV: "Every man that striveth in the games [*agōnizómenos*] is temperate in all things," also

Fighting with Wild Beasts.

alludes to the rigid self-control enforced by long training which the athlete must practise. The training itself is glanced at in the exhortation: "Exercise thyself [*gúmnaze*] unto godliness" (1 Tim **4** 7), and in the remark which follows: "Bodily exercise [*gumnasía*] is profitable for a little." It is remarkable that the word *gymnasium*, or "place of training," which occurs in the Apoc (2 Macc **4** 9. 12) is not met with in the NT. The necessity for the observance of rules and regulations is referred to in the words: "And if also a man contend in the games, he is not crowned, except he have contended lawfully" (2 Tim **2** 5). In all these passages the games will have been more or less in the apostle's thought (for other possible NT references cf He **5** 14; **10** 32; **12** 1; 2 Pet **2** 14).

In addition to these general references there are many allusions to details, again found mainly in the Pauline Epistles. These may most conveniently be grouped in alphabetical order.

3. Specific References to Greek Athletics

(*a*) *Beast-fight.*—The combats of wild animals with one another and with men, which were so popular at Rome toward the close of the Republic and under the Empire, were not unknown in Pal. Condemned criminals were thrown to wild beasts by Herod the Great in his amphitheater at Jerus, "to afford delight to spectators," a proceeding which Jos (*Ant*, XV, viii, 1) characterizes as impious. After the fall of Jerus in 70 AD many Jewish captives were slain in fighting with wild beasts (*BJ*, VII, ii). This horrible form of sport must have been in the apostle's mind when he wrote: "I fought with beasts [*ethēriomáchēsa*] at Ephesus" (1 Cor **15** 32). The reference is best understood as **figurative,** as in Ignatius on Rom **5** 1, where the same word (*thēriomachéō*) is used, and the soldiers are compared to leopards.

Boxing with the Cestus.
[From Panofka, *Bilder des antiken Lebens.*]

(*b*) *Boxing.*—This form of sport is directly referred to in 1 Cor **9** 26: "So box I [RVm, Gr *pukteúō*], as not beating the air." The allusion is probably continued in ver 27*a:* "but I buffet [RVm "bruise," Gr *hupōpiázō*] my body."

(*c*) *The course.*—Foot-races and other contests took place in an inclosure 606 ft. 9 in. in length, called a stadium. This is once referred to in a passage in the context of that just mentioned, which almost seems based on observation: "They that run in a race-course [RVm, Gr *stádion*] run all" (ver 24).

(*d*) *Discus throwing.*—The throwing of the discus, a round plate of stone or metal 10 or 12 in. in diameter, which was a prominent feature of Gr athletics and is the subject of a famous statue, a copy of which is in the British Museum, is not mentioned in the NT, but is alluded to in 2 Macc **4** 14 as one of the amusements indulged in by Hellenizing priests in the reign of Antiochus Epiphanes.

(*e*) *The foot-race.*—The words for "run" and "race" (Gr *tréchō* and *drómos*) sometimes clearly, and in other cases probably, allude to foot-races at the games. For obvious references cf 1 Cor **9** 24; He **12** 1; 2 Tim **4** 7; for possible references see Acts **13** 25; **20** 24; Rom **9** 16; Gal **2** 2; **5** 7; Phil **2** 16; 2 Thess **3** 1. The second of these

Discus Thrower.

passages (He **12** 1) alludes to the necessity for the greatest possible reduction of weight, and for steady concentration of effort. All the passages would remind the first readers of the single-course and double-course foot-races of the games.

(*f*) *The goal.*—The goal of the foot-race, a square pillar at the end of the stadium opposite the entrance, which the athlete as far as possible kept in view and the sight of which encouraged him to redouble his exertions, is alluded to once: "I press on toward the goal" (Phil **3** 14, Gr *skopós*).

(*g*) *The herald.*—The name and country of each competitor were announced by a herald and also the name, country and father of a victor. There may be an allusion to this custom in 1 Cor **9** 27: "after that I have been a herald [RVm, Gr *kērússō*] to others"; cf also 1 Tim **2** 7; 2 Tim **1** 11, where the Gr for "preacher" is *kḗrux*, "herald."

(*h*) *The prize.*—Successful athletes were rewarded at the great games by a wreath consisting in the apostolic age of wild olive (Olympian), parsley

(Nemean), laurel (Pythian), or pine (Isthmian). This is referred to in a general way in Phil **3** 14, and in 1 Cor **9** 24: "One receiveth the prize" (Gr in both cases *brabeíon;* cf also Col **3** 15: "Let the

Foot-Race.

peace of Christ arbitrate [RVm] in your hearts," where the vb. is *brabeúō*). The wreath (*stéphanos*) is directly alluded to in 1 Cor **9** 25: "They [the athletes] do it to receive a corruptible crown"; 2 Tim **2** 5: "A man . . . . is not crowned, except he have contended lawfully"; and 1 Pet **5** 4: "Ye shall receive the crown of glory that fadeth not away." There may be allusions also in Phil **4** 1; 1 Thess **2** 19; He **2** 7.9; Jas **1** 12; Rev **2** 10; **3** 11. In the palm-bearing multitude of the Apocalypse (Rev **7** 9) there is possibly a reference to the carrying of palm-branches by victors at the games. The judges who sat near the goal and who, at Olympia at any rate, had been carefully prepared for their task, may be glanced at in 2 Tim **4** 8: "The crown . . . . which the Lord, the righteous judge, shall give to me at that day."

(*i*) *Wrestling.*—This form of sport, which was in great favor in Gr society from the age of Homer onward, is alluded to once in the NT: "Our wrestling [Gr *pálē*] is not against flesh and blood," etc (Eph **6** 12). The exercise made great demands on strength, perseverance and dexterity. There is an indirect allusion in the term *palaestra*, which first meant "place for wrestling," and then "place for athletic exercises in general" (2 Macc **4** 14).

Isthmian Crowns.

4. References to the Theater and the Drama

Although there is no direct reference in the NT to the intellectual contests in which the Greeks delighted as much as in athletics, the former cannot be entirely ignored. The word "theater" (Gr *théatron*) occurs 3 t: twice in the sense of "public hall" (Acts **19** 29.31); and once with a clear reference to its use as a place of amusement: "We are made a spectacle" (1 Cor **4** 9). "The drama was strongly discountenanced by the strict Jews of Pal, but was probably encouraged to some extent by some of the Jews of the Diaspora, esp. in Asia Minor and Alexandria. Philo is known to have witnessed the representation of a play of Euripides, and the Jewish colony to which he belonged produced a dramatic poet named Ezekiel, who wrote *inter alia* a play on the Exodus, some fragments of which have been preserved (Schürer, *GJV*[4], II, 60; III, 500 ff). An inscription found not long ago at Miletus shows that part of the theater of that city was reserved for Jews (Deissmann, *Light from the Ancient East*, 446 ff). The readers of the Pauline Epistles, Jews as well as Gentiles, would be generally more or less familiar with the theater and the drama. It has been suggested that there is a glimpse of a degraded form of the drama, the mime or mimic play, which was exceedingly popular in the 1st cent. and afterward, in the mockery of Jesus by the soldiers (Mt **27** 27–30 ‖ Mk **15** 16–19). The "king" seems to have been a favorite character with the comic mime. The mockery of the Jewish king, Agrippa I, by the populace of Alexandria, a few years later, which furnishes a very striking parallel to the incident recorded in the Gospels (Schürer, *GJV*[4], I, 497), is directly connected by Philo with the mimes. The subject is very ably discussed by a German scholar, Hermann Reich, in a learned monograph, *Der König mit der Dornenkrone* (1905). Certainty is, of course, unattainable, but it seems at least fairly probable that the rude Syrian soldiers, who were no doubt in the habit of attending the theater, may have been echoing some mimic play in their mock homage to "the king of the Jews."

LITERATURE.—In addition to works already mentioned see for the whole subject: arts. "Games" in Smith, *DB*[2]; *HDB*, large and small; *EB; Jew Enc;* arts. "Spiele" in Winer, *RWB*, and Riehm[2], and esp. König, "Spiele bei den Hebräern," *RE*[3]. On the games of Greece and Rome see arts. in Smith's *Dict. of Gr and Rom Antiquities*, "Amphitheatrum," "Circus," "Olympia," "Stadium," etc.

WILLIAM TAYLOR SMITH

GAMMADIM, gam′a-dim (גַּמָּדִים, *gammādhīm*): The word occurs only in Ezk **27** 11, in AV in form "Gammadims," in ERV "Gammadim." In ARV, as also in ERVm, it is rendered "valorous men." Some think a proper name is required, but identification is not possible, and the meaning remains doubtful.

GAMUL, gā′mul (גָּמוּל, *gāmūl*, "weaned"): The head of the 22d of the 24 courses of priests inaugurated by David (1 Ch **24** 17).

GANGRENE, gaṇ′grēn (**γάγγραινα,** *gággraina*, pronounced *gáṇ-graina;* AV **canker**): The name was used by the old Gr physicians for an eating ulcer which corrodes the soft parts and, according to Galen, often ends in mortification. St. Paul compares the corrupting influence of profane babbling or levity, in connection with subjects which ought to be treated with reverence, to this disease (2 Tim **2** 17). The old Eng. word "canker" is used by 16th- and 17th-cent. authors as the name of a caterpillar which eats into a bud. In this sense it occurs 18 t in Shakespeare (e.g. *Midsummer Night's Dream*, II, ii, 3). The **canker-worm** mentioned 6 t by Joel and Nahum is probably the young stage of *Acridium peregrinum*, a species of locust. **Cankered** in Jas **5** 3 AV means "rusted" (Gr *katíōtai*), and is so rendered in RV. In Sus ver 52 Coverdale uses the phrase, "O thou old cankered carle," in Daniel's address to the elder, where EV has "waxen old in wickedness." The word is still used in the Scottish dialect and applied to persons who are cross-grained and disagreeable. ALEX. MACALISTER

GAP: The tr of פֶּרֶץ, *pereç*, "a breach" (Ezk **13** 5, "Ye have not gone up into the gaps," RVm "breaches"; **22** 30, "I sought for a man among them, that should build up the wall, and stand in the gap before me for the land"). Said of prophets who failed to stand up for the right and to strengthen and preserve the people.

GAR, gär: AV for Gas (q.v.).

GARDEN, gär′d'n (גַּן, *gan*, גַּנָּה, *gannāh*, גִּנָּה, *ginnāh;* **κῆπος,** *kēpos*): The Arab. *jannah* (dim. *jannainah*), like the Heb *gannāh*, lit. "a covered or hidden place," denotes in the mind of the dweller in the East something more than the ordinary garden. Gardens in Bib. times, such as are frequently referred to in Sem lit., were usually walled inclosures, as the name indicates (Lam **2** 6 ARVm), in which there were paths winding in and out among shade and fruit trees, canals of running water, fountains, sweet-smelling herbs, aromatic blossoms and convenient arbors in which to sit and enjoy the effect. These gardens are mentioned in Gen **2** and **3;** **13** 10; Cant **4** 12–16; Eccl **2** 5.6; Ezk **28** 13; **31** 8.9; **36** 35; Joel **2** 3. Ancient Bab, Assyr and Egyp records show the fondness of the rulers of these countries for gardens laid out on a grand scale and planted with the rarest trees and plants. The drawings made by the ancients of their gardens leave no doubt about their general features and their correspondence with Bib. gardens. The Pers word *pardeṣ* (*παράδεισος*, *parádeisos*) appears in the later Heb writings to denote more extensive gardens or parks. It is tr[d] "orchards" in Eccl **2** 5 AV; Cant **4** 13. See Paradise.

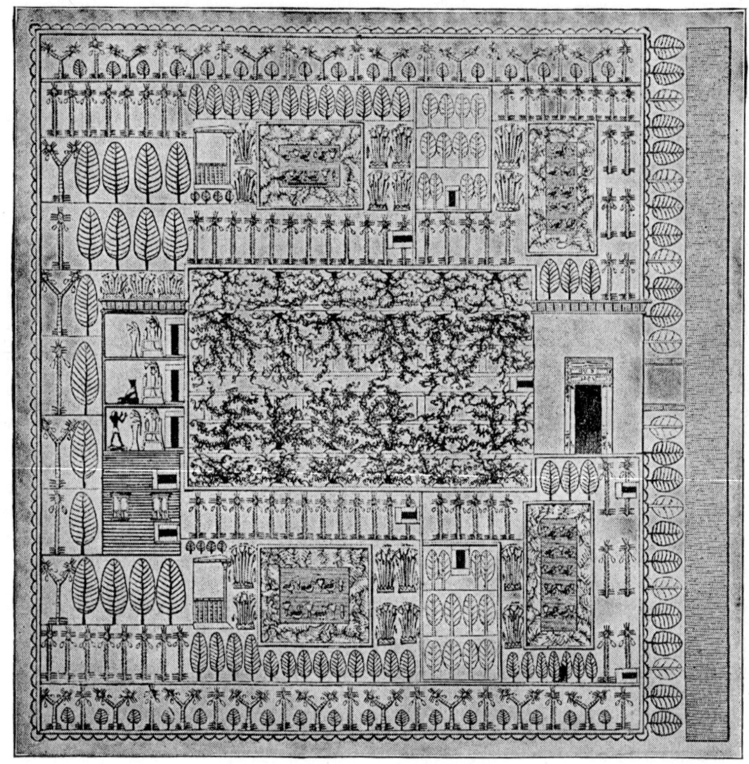

Plan of an Egyptian Garden with House, Temple or Chapel, Vineyard, Tanks of Water or Ponds, and Summer Houses.—*Rosellini.*

Such gardens are still common throughout the Levant. They are usually situated on the outskirts of a city (cf Jn **18** 1.26; **19** 41), except in the case of the more pretentious estates of rich pashas or of the government seats (cf 2 K **21** 18; Est **1** 5; **7** 7.8; Neh **3** 15; 2 K **25** 4; Jer **39** 4; **52** 7). They are inclosed with walls of mud blocks, as in Damascus, or stone walls capped with thorns, or with hedges of thorny bushes (cf Lam **2** 6 ARVm), or prickly pear. In nearly treeless countries, where there is no rain during 4 or 5 months, at least, of the year, the gardens are often the only spots where trees and other vegetation can flourish, and here the existence of vegetation depends upon the water supply, brought in canals from streams, or raised from wells by more or less crude lifting machines (cf Nu **24** 7). Such references as Gen **2** 10; Nu **24** 6; Dt **11** 10; Isa **1** 30; **58** 11; Cant **4** 15 indicate that in ancient times they were as dependent upon irrigation in Bib. lands as at present. The planning of their gardens so as to utilize the water supplies has become instinctive with the inhabitants of Pal and Syria. The writer has seen a group of young Arab boys modeling a garden out of mud and conducting water to irrigate it by channels from a nearby canal, in a manner that a modern engineer would admire. Gardens are cultivated, not only for their fruits and herbs (cf Cant **6** 11; Isa **1** 8; 1 K **21** 2) and shade (cf Cant **6** 11; Lk **13** 19), but they are planned to serve as dwelling-places during the summer time when the houses are hot and stuffy. That this was an ancient practice is indicated by Cant **5** 2; **6** 2; **8** 13. A shaded garden, the air laden with the ethereal perfumes of fruits and flowers, accompanied by the music of running water, a couch on which to sit or recline, suggest a condition of bliss dear to the Oriental. Only one who has traveled for days in a dry, glaring desert country and has come upon a spot like the gardens of such a city as Damascus, can realize how near like paradise these gardens can appear. Mohammed pictured such a place as the future abode of his followers. No doubt the remembrances of his visit to Damascus were fresh in his mind when he wrote. *El-Jannah* is used by the Moslems to signify the "paradise of the faithful."

Gardens were used as places of sacrifice, esp. in heathen worship (Isa **1** 29; **65** 3; **66** 17). They sometimes contained burial places (2 K **21** 18.26; Jn **19** 41).

Figurative: The destruction of gardens typified desolation (Am **4** 9); on the other hand, fruitful gardens figured prosperity (Nu **24** 6; Job **8** 16; Isa **51** 3; **58** 11; **61** 11; Jer **29** 5.28; **31** 12; Am **9** 14). JAMES A. PATCH

GARDEN, THE KING'S: Mention is made of "the king's garden" in 2 K **25** 4; Jer **39** 4; **52** 7 (fundamentally the same passage), in connection with the flight of Zedekiah from Jerus; and again in Neh **3** 15. The last passage shows that the "garden" was at the pool of Siloah (RV "Shelah"), at the mouth of Tyropœon, near the "fountain gate." This would seem to be "the gate between the two walls which was by the king's garden" of the passages in 2 K and Jer (cf 2 Ch **32** 5). On the topography, see JERUSALEM; also Robinson, *Pal*, II, 142. Arnold (in Herzog) thinks the garden is probably identical with "the garden of Uzza" of 2 K **21** 18.26. JAMES ORR

GARDENER, gär'd'n-ẽr (κηπουρός, *kēpouros*): "Gardener" occurs once in the EV (Jn **20** 15), the tr of *kēpos* and *oúros*, "warden" or "keeper." It is likely that the man referred to was the watchman or keeper (Arab. *naṭûr;* Heb *nōçēr*), corresponding to those mentioned in 2 K **17** 9; **18** 8; Job **27** 18, etc, and not one who did the manual labor. It is the common practice in Pal today to set a watchman over a garden during its productive season. See WATCHMAN.

GARDEN-HOUSE (בֵּית הַגָּן, *bēth ha-gān*): A place mentioned in describing the flight of Ahaziah, king of Judah, from Jehu (2 K **9** 27). Probably we ought not to translate the Heb, but take it as a proper name, BETH-HAGGAN (q.v.). If he fled southward, the town might possibly be *Jenīn*, EN-GANNIM, which see.

GAREB, gā'reb (גָּרֵב, *gārēbh*): One of David's "mighty men of the armies" (2 S **23** 38; 1 Ch **11** 40), an "Ithrite," i.e. a member of one of the families of Kiriath-jearim (1 Ch **2** 53). Some, however, read *ha-yattirī* for *ha-yithrī*, thus making him a native of Jattir. See IRA.

GAREB, gā'reb, **THE HILL OF** (גָּרֵב, *gārēbh*): A hill in the neighborhood of Jerus, which was one of the landmarks to which the prophet Jeremiah (**31** 39) foresaw that the city should extend. The site is unknown. Cheyne (*EB*) would connect this with the "mountain that lieth before the valley of Hinnom westward" (Josh **15** 8), but this is too far S.; it is inconceivable that the prophet could have imagined the city extending so far in this direction; most probably the hill was to the N.—the one natural direction for the city's extension—and is now incorporated in the modern suburbs. E. W. G. MASTERMAN

GARIZIM, gar'i-zim. See GERIZIM.

GARLAND, gär'land (στέμμα, *stémma*, "wreath"): Mentioned only in Acts **14** 13, where it is said that the priest of Jupiter brought oxen and garlands unto the gates with which to offer sacrifices unto Barnabas and Paul. The rendering "oxen and garlands," instead of "oxen garlanded," seems to imply that the garlands were for the priests and altar and worshippers themselves, as well as for the victims sacrificed. Only occasionally did the Hebrews use such ornaments for themselves, and that almost altogether in their later history. See CROWN.

GARLIC, gär'lik (שׁוּם, *shūm*, used only in pl. שׁוּמִים, *shūmīm;* cf Arab. ثُوم, *thûm*): One of the delights of Egypt for which the Israelites in the Wilderness longed (Nu **11** 5); we know from other sources that, though originally a product of Central Asia, garlic was known to the ancient Egyptians. It is the bulb of *Allium sativum*, N.O. *Liliaceae*, and is cultivated all over the Orient. It is eaten cooked in stews; its disagreeable penetrating odor is in evidence in the houses and on the breath of most Orientals. A bulb of garlic, hung over a bed or over the door of a house, is a powerful charm against the evil eye and other malign influences. E. W. G. MASTERMAN

GARMENT, gär'ment. See DRESS.

GARMITE, gär'mīt (גַּרְמִי, *garmī*): A gentilic name applied to Keilah in 1 Ch **4** 19. The reason for this is not known.

GARNER, gär'nẽr (מָזוּ, *māzū;* ἀποθήκη, *apothēkē*): "Garners," derived from *zāwāh*, "to gather," occurs in Ps **144** 13; *'ōçār* is similarly tr[d] in Joel **1** 17. In the NT *apothēkē* is twice tr[d] "garner" (Mt **3** 12; Lk **3** 17). The same word is tr[d] "barns" in Mt **6** 26; **13** 30; Lk **12** 18.24.

GARNISH, gär'nish (צִפָּה, *çippāh*, שִׁפְרָה, *shiphrāh;* κοσμέω, *kosméō*): The word is used twice in the OT. In 2 Ch **3** 6, *çippāh* means "to overlay," or "to plate." Thus he "garnished" the house or "overlaid" it, "studded" it, with precious stones, and thus adorned and beautified it. In Job **26** 13, *shiphrāh* is a fem. noun meaning "fairness," "beauty," "brilliancy." "By his Spirit the heavens are garnished," i.e. the clouds are driven off by the wind or breath of Jeh, and the sky made bright and clear.

In the NT (Mt **12** 44; **23** 29) the word *kosmeō* means "set in order," "make ready," "adorn," etc. In Mt **25** 7 it is tr[d] "trimmed," and in Rev **21** 19 "adorned." J. J. REEVE

GARRISON, gar'i-s'n. See WAR.

GAS, gas (Γάς, *Gás*): Named among the "sons of the servants of Solomon" (1 Esd **5** 34); not mentioned in the lists of Ezr and Neh.

GASHMU, gash'mū, gash'mōō (גַּשְׁמוּ, *gashmū*): A form of the name GESHEM (q.v.), found in Neh **6** 6 (cf ver 1), "And Gashmu saith it." According to *BDB* the same termination *-u* is found in Nabataean proper names.

GATAM, gā'tam (גַּעְתָּם, *ga'tām*): An Edomite chief, grandson of Esau (Gen **36** 11.16; 1 Ch **1** 36).

GATE, gāt (Heb normally [over 300 t] שַׁעַר, *sha'ar;* occasionally דֶּלֶת, *deleth*, prop. "gateway" [but cf Dt **3** 5]; elsewhere the gateway is פֶּתַח, *pethaḥ* [cf esp. Gen **19** 6]; Aram. תְּרַע, *t[e]ra';* Gr πυλών, *pulôn*, πύλη, *púlē;* ERV and AV add סַף, *ṣaph*, "threshold," in 1 Ch **9** 19.22; and AV adds דְּלָתַיִם, *d[e]lāthayim*, "double-door," in Isa **45** 1; θύρα, *thúra*, "door," Acts **3** 2):

(1) The usual gateway was provided with double doors, swung on projections that fitted into sockets

in the sill and lintel. Ordinarily the material was wood (Neh **2** 3.17), but greater strength and protection against fire was given by plating with metal (Ps **107** 16; Isa **45** 2). Jos (*BJ*, V, v, 3) speaks of the *solid* metal doors of the Beautiful Gate (Acts **3** 2) as a very exceptional thing. Some doors were solid slabs of stone, from which the imagery of single jewels (Isa **54** 12; Rev **21** 21) was derived. When closed, the doors were secured with a bar (usually of wood, Nah **3** 13, but sometimes of metal, 1 K **4** 13; Ps **107** 16; Isa **45** 2), which fitted into clamps on the doors and sockets in the post, uniting the whole firmly (Jgs **16** 3). Sometimes, perhaps, a portcullis was used, but Ps **24** 7 refers to the enlargement or enrichment of the gates. As the gate was esp. subject to attack (Ezk **21** 15.22), and as to "possess the gate" was to possess the city (Gen **22** 17; **24** 60), it was protected by a tower (2 S **18** 24.33; 2 Ch **14** 7; **26** 9), often, doubtless, overhanging and with flanking projections. Sometimes an inner gate was added (2 S **18** 24). Unfortunately, Pal gives us little monumental detail.

GATE, EAST: The expressions are found in Ezk: "Even the gate that looketh toward the east" (**43** 1); "The gate whose prospect is toward the east" (ver 4); but the idea of a gate on the eastern side as the principal entrance to the court of the sanctuary goes back to the days of the tabernacle (Ex **27** 13–16). In addition to its use as admitting to the sanctuary inclosure, it may be presumed, in analogy with the general mode of the administration of justice, to have been the place where in earlier times cases were tried which were referred to the jurisdiction of the sanctuary (cf Ex **18** 19–22; Dt **17** 8; **19** 16.18; Nu **27** 2.3, etc).

1. The Tabernacle

In Ex **27** 13–16 the "gate" by which the congregation entered the tabernacle is carefully described. An embroidered screen of the three sacred colors (blue, purple and scarlet), 20 cubits in width, hung from 4 pillars (really 5 pillars, 5 cubits apart; on the reckoning see TABERNACLE), in the center of the E. side of the tabernacle court. This is further alluded to in Nu **4** 26, "the screen for the door of the gate of the court."

PERSIAN SATRAP DICTATING TERMS TO GRECIAN CHIEFS AT THE GATE OF A CITY. BAS-RELIEF FROM LYCIAN MONUMENT.—*Brit. Mus.*

(2) As even farm laborers slept in the cities, most of the men passed through the gate every day, and the gate was the place for meeting others (Ruth **4** 1; 2 S **15** 2) and for assemblages. For the latter purpose "broad" or open places (distinguished from the "streets" in Prov **7** 12) were provided (1 K **22** 10; Neh **8** 1), and these were the centers of the public life. Here the markets were held (2 K **7** 1), and the special commodities in these gave names to the gates (Neh **3** 1.3.28). In particular, the "gate" was the place of the legal tribunals (Dt **16** 18; **21** 19; **25** 7, etc), so that a seat "among the elders in the gates" (Prov **31** 23) was a high honor, while "oppression in the gates" was a synonym for judicial corruption (Job **31** 21; Prov **22** 22; Isa **29** 21; Am **5** 10). The king, in especial, held public audiences in the gate (2 S **19** 8; 1 K **22** 10; Jer **38** 7; cf Jer **39** 3), and even yet "Sublime Porte" (the French tr of the Turkish for "high gate") is the title of the Court of Constantinople. To the gates, as the place of throngs, prophets and teachers went with their message (1 K **22** 10; Jer **17** 19; Prov **1** 21; **8** 3; **31** 31), while on the other hand the gates were the resort of the town good-for-nothings (Ps **69** 12).

(3) "Gates" can be used **figuratively** for the glory of a city (Isa **3** 26; **14** 31; Jer **14** 2; Lam **1** 4; contrast Ps **87** 2), but whether the military force, the rulers or the people is in mind cannot be determined. In Mt **16** 18 "gates of Hades" (not "hell") may refer to the hosts (or princes) of Satan, but a more likely tr is 'the gates of the grave [which keep the dead from returning] shall not be stronger than it.' The meaning in Jgs **5** 8.11 is very uncertain, and the text may be corrupt. See CITY; JERUSALEM; TABERNACLE; TEMPLE. BURTON SCOTT EASTON

GATE, CORNER, FOUNTAIN, HORSE, SUR, etc. See JERUSALEM.

2. Solomon's Temple

Nothing is said of the position of gates in connection with Solomon's temple, but there was an "inner" (1 K **6** 36), and also an "outer" or "great" court (2 Ch **4** 9), the latter with doors overlaid with brass, and analogy makes it certain that here also the chief gate (inner or outer court? see COURT) was on the E. side. Provision was made by Solomon in his adjoining palace for the administration of justice in a hall or "porch of judgment" (1 K **7** 7), but graver cases were still, apparently, referred for decision to the sanctuary (Jer **26** 10). The trial in Jeremiah's case, however, took place, not at the E. gate, but at "the entry of the new gate of Jeh's house" (Jer **26** 10; cf **36** 10), probably Jotham's "upper gate" (2 K **15** 35).

3. Ezekiel's Temple

In Ezekiel's ideal temple, "the gate whose prospect was toward the east" was that by which the glory of Jeh went up from the city (**11** 23), and by which the prophet in vision saw it return (**43** 4).

4. Second Temple

Nothing is told of an E. gate in the temple of Zerubbabel, but it may be assumed that there was one as in the other cases.

5. Herod's Temple

The great E. gate of the Herodian temple, which followed those above mentioned, was that "Beautiful Gate of the temple" where the miracle of the healing of the lame man was performed (Acts **3** 1–10). See GATE, THE BEAUTIFUL; HARSITH; SHECANIAH. W. SHAW CALDECOTT

GATE, THE BEAUTIFUL, bū'ti-fŏŏl (**ἡ ὡραία πύλη τοῦ ἱεροῦ**, *hē hōraía púlē toú hieroú*): This gate of Herod's temple is mentioned in the narrative of the healing of the lame man by Peter and John in Acts **3** 2.10. Little dispute exists as to the identification of the Beautiful Gate with the splendid "gate of Nicanor" of the Mish (Mid., i.4), and "Corinthian Gate" of Jos (*BJ*, V, v, 3), but authorities are divided as to whether this gate was situated at the entrance to the women's court on the E., or was the gate reached by 15 steps, dividing that court from the court of the men. The balance of recent opinion inclines strongly to the former view (cf Kennedy, "Problems of Herod's Temple," *Expos T*, XX, 170); others take the opposite view (Waterhouse, in *Sacred Sites of the Gospels*, 110), or leave the question open (thus G. A. Smith, *Jerusalem*, II, 212). See TEMPLE, HEROD'S. The gate itself was of unusual size and splendor. It received the name "Nicanor" from its being the work, or having been constructed at the expense, of an Alexandrian Jew of this name. Lately an ossuary was discovered on Mt. Olivet bearing the Gr inscription: "The bones of Nicanor the Alexandrian, who made the doors." Its other name, "Corinthian," refers to the costly material of which it was constructed—Corinthian bronze. Jos gives many interesting particulars about this gate, which, he tells us, greatly excelled in workmanship and value all the others (*BJ*, V, v, 3). These were plated with gold and silver, but this still more richly and thickly. It was larger than the other gates; was 50 cubits in height (the others 40); its weight was so great that it took 20 men to move it (*BJ*, VI, vi, 3). Its massiveness and magnificence, therefore, well earned for it the name "Beautiful."

W. SHAW CALDECOTT

GATE, VALLEY: In Neh **2** 13 AV, "gate of the valley." See JERUSALEM.

GATH, gath (גַּת, *gath;* LXX **Γέθ,** *Géth*, "wine-press"): One of the five chief cities of the Philis (Josh **13** 3; 1 S **6** 17). It was a walled town (2 Ch **26** 6) and was not taken by Joshua, and, although many conflicts took place between the Israelites and its people, it does not seem to have been captured until the time of David (1 Ch **18** 1). It was rendered famous as the abode of the giant Goliath whom David slew (1 S **17** 4), and other giants of the same race (2 S **21** 18–22). It was to G. that the Ashdodites conveyed the ark when smitten with the plague, and G. was also smitten (1 S **5** 8.9). It was G. where David took refuge twice when persecuted by Saul (**21** 10; **27** 2–4). It seems to have been destroyed after being taken by David, for we find Rehoboam restoring it (2 Ch **11** 8). It was after this reoccupied by the Philis, for we read that Uzziah took it and razed its walls (**26** 6), but it must have been restored again, for we find Hazael of Damascus capturing it (2 K **12** 17). It seems to have been destroyed before the time of Amos (Am **6** 2), and is not further mentioned in the OT or Macc, except in Mic **1** 10, where it is referred to in the proverb, "Tell it not in Gath" (cf 2 S **1** 20). Since its destruction occurred, probably, in the middle of the 8th cent. BC, it is easy to understand why the site has been lost so that it can be fixed only conjecturally. Several sites have been suggested by different explorers and writers, such as: *Tell es Sâfi*, *Beit Jibrîn*, *Khurbet Jeladîyeh*, *Khurbet Abu Geith*, *Jennata* and *Yebna* (see *PEFS*, 1871, 91; 1875, 42, 144, 194; 1880, 170–71, 211–23; 1886, 200–202). Tradition in the early centuries AD fixed it at 5 Rom miles N. of Eleutheropolis (*Beit Jibrîn*, toward Lydda, which would indicate *Tell es Sâfi* as the site, but the Crusaders thought it was at Jamnia (*Yebna*), where they erected the castle of Ibelin, but the consensus of opinion in modern times fixes upon *Tell es Sâfi* as the site, as is to be gathered from the references cited in *PEFS* above. The Bib. notices of G. would indicate a place in the Phili plain or the Shephelah, which was fortified, presumably in a strong position on the border of the Phili country toward the territory of Judah or Dan. *Tell es Sâfi* fits into these conditions fairly well, but without other proof this is not decisive. It is described in *SWP*, II, 240, as a position of strength on a narrow ridge, with precipitous cliffs on the N. and W., connected with the hills by a narrow neck, so that it is thrust out like a bastion, a position easily fortified. In 1144 Fulke of Anjou erected here a castle called Blanchegarde (*Alba Specula*). The writer on "Gath and Its Worthies" in *PEFS*, 1886, 200–204, connects the name *Sâfi* with that of the giant Saph (2 S **21** 18), regarding him as a native of Gath, but the most direct evidence from early tradition connecting *Tell es Sâfi* with Gath is found in a MS said to be in the library of the Patriarchate of Jerus, which informs us that Catherocastrum was situated on a mountain called Telesaphion or Telesaphy, which is clearly *Tell es Sâfi*. Catherocastrum must be the Lat for "camp of Gath" (*PEFS*, 1906, 305).

H. PORTER

GATHER, gath'ēr (אָסַף, *'āṣaph*, קָבַץ, *ḳābhaç;* **συλλέγω,** *sullégō*, **συνάγω,** *sunágō*): "Gather," trans "to bring together," "collect," etc, and intrans "to come together," "assemble," etc, occurs frequently and represents many Heb and Gr words. It is the tr of *'āṣaph*, "to bring together," in Josh **6** 9, AVm "gathering host"; Ps **27** 10, AVm "The Lord will gather me"; cf Nu **12** 14.15; Isa **52** 12 AVm. The phrases "gather thee unto thy fathers," "gathered unto his fathers," "gathered into the grave," etc, are frequently used for "to die" and "death" (Gen **25** 8.17; **49** 29.33; Dt **32** 50; 2 K **22** 20; 2 Ch **34** 28; Job **27** 19; cf Jer **8** 2), etc; *ḳābhaç*, "to take or grasp with the hand," is frequently used of the Divine "gathering" or restoration of Israel (Dt **30** 3.4; Neh **1** 9; Ps **106** 47; Isa **43** 5, etc; Ezk **20** 34, etc; Hos **8** 10; Mic **2** 12; Zeph **3** 19.20; Zec **10** 8.10); **figuratively,** Isa **40** 11, "He shall gather the lambs with [RV "in"] his arm" (cf Ps **27** 10 AVm); sometimes it denotes bringing together for punishment or destruction (Mic **4** 12), "He hath gathered them as the sheaves to the threshing-floor."

In the NT we have *sullegō*, "to lay together," "to collect" (Mt **13** 28.29.30.40.41.48); *sunagō*, "to lead or bring together," "to gather," "to collect" (**25** 26, "seek returns"; Jn **4** 36, "fruit unto life eternal"); *episunágō*, "to lead or bring together" (Mt **23** 37, "even as a hen gathereth her chickens"); *anakephalaióomai*, "to sum up under one head," "to recapitulate" (Eph **1** 10, "that he might gather together in one all things in Christ," RV "to sum up all things in Christ"; cf **2** 14; in Rom **13** 9 the pass. is tr[d] "be briefly comprehended," RV "summed up").

"To gather," in the sense of "to infer," occurs in Acts **16** 10 as the tr of *sumbibázō*, "to bring together" (here, in mind), "assuredly gathering," RV "concluding" (cf **9** 22, "proving").

Gatherer occurs in Am **7** 14 as the tr of *bōlēṣ*, from *bālaṣ*, to cultivate figs or sycomores, "a gatherer of sycamore fruit," RV "a dresser of sycomore-trees" ("a nipper of sycomore figs, i.e. helping to cultivate a sort of figs or mulberries produced by the real sycamore tree" [used only by the poorest], which requires *nipping* in the cultivation, perhaps an occupation of shepherds; Vulg *vellicans sycamnia*).

Gathering is the tr of *episunagōgē*, "leading together unto" (2 Thess **2** 1), "our gathering together unto him"; in 1 Cor **16** 2 we have "gathering" (*logía* from *legō*) in the sense of a collection of many, RV "collection," as AV in ver 1.

"Gather," etc, occurs frequently in Apoc, e.g. "will gather us out of all the nations," *sunagō* (Tob **13** 5); "gather them together" (1 Macc **9** 7; **10** 8); "Gather together our dispersion," *episunágage tēn diasporán hēmōn* (2 Macc **1** 27); "gathered to his fathers" *prosetéthē prós tón laón autoú*, RV "people" (Jth **16** 22; Bel ver 1, *toús patéras;* 1 Macc **2** 69); "gathering up briefly," RV "gather," *suntémnō* (2 Macc **10** 10); a "gathering" in the sense of a *collection* of money (**12** 43), RV "collection."

Among the changes in RV we have "hold firm" for "gather" (Jer **51** 11); "Gather thee together" for "Go one way or other" (Ezk **21** 16 m, "Make thyself one"); for "gather blackness" (Nah **2** 10), "are waxed pale"; for "or gather together" (Job **11** 10), "and call unto judgment," m "Heb call an assembly"; for "even as a hen doth gather her brood" (Lk **13** 34) "gathereth her own brood"; for "as the partridge sitteth on eggs and hatcheth them not," ARV has "that sitteth on eggs which she hath not laid," m "gathereth young which she hath not brought forth," text of ERV and AVm (Jer **17** 11).

W. L. WALKER

GATH-HEPHER, gath-hē′fẽr (גַּת הַחֵפֶר, *gath ha-ḥēpher*, "winepress of the pit"): A town on the boundary of Zebulun (Josh **19** 13; AV in error, "Gittah-hapher"), the birthplace of the prophet Jonah (2 K **14** 25). Jerome (*Comm. on Jon*) speaks of Geth as an inconsiderable village, about 2 miles from Sepphoris on the Tiberias road, where the tomb of Jonah was shown. Benjamin of Tudela says that Jonah the son of Amittai the prophet was buried "in the mountain" near Sepphoris (Bohn, *Early Travels in Pal*, 88). These indications agree with the local tradition which identifies Gath-hepher with *el-Meshhed*, a village with ancient ruins on a height N. of the road as one goes to Tiberias, about 2 miles from Nazareth, and half a mile from *Kefr Kennah*.

W. EWING

GATH-RIMMON, gath-rim′un (גַּת רִמּוֹן, *gath rimmōn*, "winepress of Rimmon"):

(1) A city in the territory of Dan named with Bene-berak and Me-jarkon, in the plain not far from Joppa (Josh **19** 45), assigned to the Kohathite Levites (**21** 24), reckoned to Ephraim in 1 Ch **6** 69. *Onom* locates it 12 miles from Eleutheropolis on the way to Diospolis. This, however, is too far to the S. More probably it is identical with the "Gath" which *Onom* places between Antipatris and Jamnia. It is not identified.

(2) A town in the territory of Manasseh, W. of Jordan, given to the Levites (Josh **21** 25). There is nothing to indicate the position of the place, and there is much confusion in the writing of the name: LXX A, "Baithsa"; B, "Jebatha." In 1 Ch **6** 70 it is replaced by "Bileam," i.e. IBLEAM (q.v.).

W. EWING

GAULONITIS, gôl-on-ī′tis. See GOLAN.

GAULS, gôlz (**Γαλάται**, *Galátai*): Galatia in Asia Minor is literally the *Gallia* of the East; its inhabitants are called *Galli* by Rom writers, just as the inhabitants of ancient France are called *Galatai* by Gr writers. In some MSS in 2 Tim **4** 10, *eis Gallían* is read for *eis Galatían*. The emigration of the Gauls from Europe and their settlement in the central region of the peninsula of Asia Minor are somewhat obscure subjects, but the ancient authorities leave no doubt of the main facts. In 1 Macc **8** 2 it is difficult to say whether Judas Maccabaeus is referring to the Gauls of Europe or the Gauls of Asia Minor. Both became finally subject to the Romans, and about the same time. It was in 191 BC that Gallia Cisalpina was reduced to the form of a Rom province, and in 189 BC occurred the defeat of Antiochus, king of Asia. Mommsen argues that the reference is to the Gauls in the N. of Italy, from the circumstance that they are mentioned as being under tribute to the Romans, and also from their mention in connection with Spain. Not much, however, can be argued from this, as the notice of them is in a manner rhetorical, and the defeat of Antiochus is mentioned practically in the same connection. In 2 Macc **8** 20 the reference is without doubt to the Asiatic Gauls or Galatians, as they are more commonly called. In the Maccabean period they were restless and fond of war, and often hired themselves out as auxiliaries to the Asiatic kings.

J. HUTCHISON

GAZA, gā′za (עַזָּה, *'azzāh*, "strong"; LXX **Γάζα,** *Gáza;* Arab. غَزَّة, *Ghazzeh*): One of the five chief towns of Philistia and probably the oldest, situated near the coast in lat. 31° 30′ and about 40 miles S. of Jaffa. It is on a hill rising 60 to 200 ft. above the plain, with sand dunes between it and the sea, which is about 2½ miles distant. The plain around is fertile and wells abound, and, being on the border of the desert between Syria and Egypt and lying in the track of caravans and armies passing from one to the other, it was anciently a place of importance. The earliest notices of it are found in the records of Egypt. Thothmes III refers to it in the account of his expedition to Syria in 1479 BC, and it occurs again in the records of the expedition

Gaza.

of Seti I in 1313 BC (Breasted, *History of Egypt*, 285, 409). It occurs also in the early catalogue of cities and tribes inhabiting Canaan in the earliest times (Gen **10** 19). Joshua reached it in his conquests but did not take it (Josh **10** 41; **11** 22). Judah captured it (Jgs **1** 18) but did not hold it long, for we find it in the hands of the Philis in the days of Samson, whose exploits have rendered it noteworthy (**16** 1–3.21.30). The hill to which he carried off the gate of the city was probably the one now called *el-Muntar* ("watch-tower"), which lies S.E. of the city and may be referred to in 2 K **18** 8, "from the tower of the watchmen to the fortified city." G., with the other chief towns, sent a trespass offering to Jeh when the ark was returned (1 S **6** 17). Hezekiah defeated and pursued the Philis to G., but does not seem to have captured it. It was taken by Sargon in 720 BC, in his war with Egypt, since Khanun, the king of G., joined the Egyptians and was captured at the battle of Raphia (Rawlinson, *Ancient Monarchies*, II, 142). It was probably destroyed (see Am **1** 7). It was certainly dismantled by Alexander the Great in 332, when it dared to resist him. It was then exceedingly strong, verifying its name, and was most bravely defended, so that it took Alexander two months tc reduce it. He put to death all the men and sold the women and children as slaves (Grote, *History of Greece*, XI, 467 ff). It was restored, however, and we learn that Jonathan forced it to submit to him (Jos, *Ant*, XIII, v, 5; 1 Macc **11** 62), and Alexander Jannaeus took it and massacred the inhabitants who escaped the horrors of the siege (Jos, *Ant*, XIII, xiii, 3). Pompey restored the freedom of G. (ib, XIV, iv, 4), and Gabinius rebuilt it in 57 BC (ib, XIV, v, 3). G. is mentioned only once in the NT (Acts **8** 26), in the account of Philip and the eunuch. In the 2d and 3d cents. AD, it became a center of Gr commerce and culture, and pagan influence was strong, while the church founded there was struggling for existence. Many martyrs there testified to the faith, until finally, under Theodosius, Christianity gained the supremacy (*HGHL*, 12th ed, 188). It fell into the hands of the Arabs in 634 AD, and became and has remained a Moslem city since the days of Saladin, who recovered it from the Crusaders in 1187, after the battle of Hattin. It is now a city of some 20,000 inhabitants, among whom are a few hundred Christians. See also Azzah.

H. Porter

GAZARA, ga-zā'ra (**Γαζάρα,** *Gazára,* **Γαζηρά,** *Gazērá*): A fortress of great strength in Judaea, which figures often in the Maccabean wars. To this place Judas pursued Gorgias (1 Macc **4** 15). It was fortified by the Gr general Bacchides (**9** 52; *Ant,* XIII, i, 3). It was captured by Simon Maccabaeus, who turned out the inhabitants and purified the city. He built here a palace for himself, and appointed his son John commander of his army (1 Macc **13** 43 ff). A different account of this occurrence is given in 2 Macc **10** 32 ff, where the capture is attributed to Judas. The narrative here, however, is inspired by antagonism to Simon because he had assumed the high-priesthood.

The fortress is identical with *Tell Jezer,* the ancient Gezer (q.v.). It is interesting to note that recent excavations have uncovered the ruins of Simon's palace (*PEFS,* 1905, 26). W. Ewing

GAZATHITES, gā'zath-īts (עַזָּתִים, *'azzāthīm*): The inhabitants of Gaza (q.v.) (Josh **13** 3 AV), rendered "Gazites" (Jgs **16** 2).

GAZELLE, ga-zel' (צְבִי, *çebhī,* and fem. צְבִיָּה, *çebhīyāh;* cf **Ταβειθά,** *Tabeithá* [Acts **9** 36], and Arab. ظبي, *ẓabi;* also Arab. غزال, *ghazâl;* **Δορκάς,** *Dorkás* [**9** 36]; modern Gr **ζαρκάδι,** *zarkádi*): The word "gazelle" does not occur in AV, where *çebhī* and *çebhīyāh,* in the 16 passages where they occur, are uniformly trd "roe" or "roebuck." In RV the treatment is not uniform. We find "gazelle" without comment in Dt **12** 15.22; **14** 5; **15** 22; 1 K **4** 23. We find "roe," with marginal note "or gazelle," in Prov **6** 5; Cant **2** 7.9.17; **4** 5; **8** 14;

Gazelle (*Gazella dorcas*).

Isa **13** 14. We find "roe" without comment in 2 S **2** 18; 1 Ch **12** 8; Cant **3** 5; **7** 3. In the last passage cited, Cant **7** 3, while ARV has no note, ERV refers to Cant **4** 5, where "gazelle" is given in the m. In the opinion of the writer, the rendering should be "gazelle" in all of these passages. It must be acknowledged, however, that the gazelle and the roe-deer are of about the same size, and are sometimes confused with each other. The Gr *dorkas* may refer to either, and in Syria the roe-deer is sometimes called *ghazâl* or even *wa'l,* which is the proper name of the Pers wild goat.

The gazelle is an antelope belonging to the bovine family of the even-toed ruminants. There are more than twenty species of gazelle, all belonging to Asia and Africa. The species found in Syria and Pal is the Dorcas gazelle (*Gazella dorcas*). It is 2 ft. high at the shoulders. Both sexes have unbranched, lyrate, ringed horns, which may be a foot long. The general coloration is tawny, but it is creamy white below and on the rump, and has a narrow white line from above the eye to the nostril. Several varieties have been distinguished, but they will not bear elevation to the rank of species, except perhaps *G. merilli,* a form of which a few specimens have been obtained from the Judaean hills, having distinctly different horns from those of the common gazelle. The gazelle is found singly or in small groups on the interior plains and the uplands, but not in the high mountains. It is a marvel of lightness and grace, and a herd, when alarmed, makes off with great rapidity over the roughest country (2 S **2** 18; 1 Ch **12** 8; Prov **6** 5; Cant **8** 14). The beauty of the eyes is proverbial. The skin is used for floor coverings, pouches or shoes, and the flesh is eaten, though not highly esteemed. See Deer; Goat; Zoölogy. Alfred Ely Day

GAZER, gā'zẽr (גָּזֶר, *gāzer* [in pause]). See Gezer.

GAZERA, ga-zē'ra (**Γαζηρά,** *Gazērá*):

(1) A fortress of Judaea (1 Macc **4** 15; **7** 45); in RV always Gazara (q.v.).

(2) Head of a family of temple-servants who returned with Zerubbabel (1 Esd **5** 31) = "Gazzam" in Ezr **2** 48 and Neh **7** 51.

GAZEZ, gā'zez (גָּזֵז, *gāzēz,* "shearer"):

(1) A son of Ephah, Caleb's concubine (1 Ch **2** 46).

(2) A second Gazez is mentioned in the same ver as a son of Haran, another son of Ephah.

GAZING-STOCK, gāz'ing-stok: This obs word occurs twice: (1) in Nah **3** 6, as the tr of רֹאִי, *rŏ'ī,* "a sight" or "spectacle" (from *rā'āh,* "to look," "see," also "to look down upon," "despise"); "I will .... make thee vile, and will set thee as a gazing-stock," as one set up to be gazed at, mocked and despised—a form of punishment in olden times; cf "mocking stock" (2 Macc **7** 7), and "laughing-stock" still in use. The Heb word occurs only here and in Gen **16** 13; 1 S **16** 12; Job **7** 8; **33** 21, in which places it does not have the same bad meaning; for a similar threatening cf Isa **14** 16; Jer **51** 37. (2) In He **10** 33, it is the tr of *theatrízō,* "to bring upon the theater," "to be made a spectacle of," "made a gazing stock both by reproaches and afflictions"; cf 1 Cor **4** 9, *théatron gínomai,* where St. Paul says the apostles were "made a spectacle unto the world," AVm "Gr theatre." The reference in both instances is to the custom of exhibiting criminals, and esp. gladiators, men doomed to death, in the theaters. "In the morning men are exposed to lions and bears; at mid-day to their spectators; those that kill are exposed to one another; the victor is detained for another slaughter; the conclusion of the fight is death" (Seneca, *Ep.* vii, quoted by Dr. A. Clarke on 1 Cor **4** 9). We are apt to forget what the first preachers and professors of Christianity had to endure. W. L. Walker

GAZITES, gāz'īts: Inhabitants of Gaza, who were Philis when the Israelites came into contact with them (Josh **13** 3; Jgs **16** 2), but there was an older stratum of population which occupied the place before the invasion of the Philis, probably of Amorite stock.

GAZZAM, gaz′am (גַּזָּם, *gazzām*, "devouring"): Head of a family of Nethinim who returned from exile (Ezr **2** 48; Neh **7** 51; 1 Esd **5** 31, "Gazera").

GEBA, gē′ba (גֶּבַע, *gebha'*, "hill"):

(1) A town on the N.E. boundary of the territory of Benjamin (Josh **18** 24), given to the Levites (Josh **21** 17; 1 Ch **6** 60). It stood on the northern frontier of the kingdom of Judah, Geba and Beersheba marking respectively the northern and southern limits (2 K **23** 8). In 2 S **5** 25 "Geba" should be altered to "Gibeon," which stands in the corresponding passage, 1 Ch **14** 16. In Jgs **20** 10.33; 1 S **13** 3.16, the Heb reads "Geba," the tr "Gibeah" being due to confusion of the two names. From 1 S **14** 5 we gather that Geba stood to the S. of the great gorge, *Wādy Suweinīt*, commanding the pass at Michmash. This was the scene of Jonathan's daring enterprise against the Philis, when, accompanied by his armor-bearer, he accomplished an apparently impossible feat, climbing the rocky steeps of the gorge to the N. and putting the enemy to flight. There can be no doubt that the modern village of *Jeba'* occupies the ancient site. It stands to the S. of *Wādy Suweinīt*, looking toward Michmash—modern *Mukhmās*—with Seneh, the crag on the southern lip of the gorge, in front of it. The distance from Jerus is about 6 miles. It was fortified by Asa with materials that his enemy Baasha had used to fortify Ramah against him (1 K **15** 22). It is named by Isaiah in his description of the terrifying march of the Assyrians upon Jerus from the N. (**10** 28 ff). It appears among the cities which were reoccupied by Israel after the Exile (Ezr **2** 26, etc; Neh **11** 31).

(2) (Γαιβαί, *Gaibai*): Between a fortress so named and Scythopolis (*Beisān*), Holofernes pitched his camp (Jth **3** 10). On the high road that runs through *Jenīn*, and down the Vale of Jezreel to *Beisān*, about 2 miles to the S. of *Sanūr*, stands the village of *Jeba'*, with which this fortress may be identified. W. Ewing

GEBAL, gē′bal (גְּבַל, *gebhal*, "border"; **Βύβλος**, *Búblos*, and **Βίβλος**, *Bíblos; Byblus*, mod. *Jebeil*):

(1) An ancient Phoen city, situated on a bluff of the foothills of Lebanon, overlooking the Mediterranean. It was one of the principal seaports of Phoenicia, and had a small but good harbor for small ships. It lies in lat. 34° 8′, nearly, and about 4 miles N. of the river Adonis (*Nahr Ibrahîm*). It was regarded as a holy city by the ancients. Philo mentions the tradition that it was founded by Kronos, and was sacred to the worship of Beltis and, later, of Adonis, whose rites were celebrated yearly at the river of the same name and at its source in the mountain, at Apheca (see Tammuz). G. was the center of quite an extensive district, extending from the Eleutherus on the N. to the Tamyras on the S., a distance of 60 or 70 miles along the coast. It is mentioned by Josh (**13** 5) as the land of the **Gebalites** (q.v.) (AV "Giblites"), and the Gebalites are also mentioned in 1 K **5** 18 (Heb 32) as aiding in the construction of Solomon's temple. The "elders" and the "wise men" of G. are among the workmen employed on Tyrian ships (Ezk **27** 9 ARVm). The earliest mention of G. found in history is in the Am Tab, which were composed in the first half of the 14th cent. BC. It had become, in connection with all Phoenicia, a dependency of Egypt in the days of Thothmes III and was under Egyp governors, but, in the reign of Amenhotep IV (Ikhnaton), the Hittites and Amorites from the N. and Khabiri from the S. attacked the territory of G., and its governor wrote letters to Amenhotep, calling for help. There are over 60 of these, describing the desperate condition of the city and of its governor, Ribaddi, who was expelled and took refuge in Beirût, but afterward regained his capital only to be besieged and lose all his dependencies, and finally to fall into the hands of the enemy. G. afterward became independent, as is shown by the records of Ramses IX (1442–1423 BC) and of Ramses XII, for its king retained the emissaries of the former 17 years in captivity, and treated a trusted agent of the latter with scant civility. Its king at this time was Zakkar-Baal, and kings of G. are mentioned in the Assyr records, one paying tribute to Ashurnazir-pal (c 887 BC) and another to Sennacherib (705–680). The latter king was Uru-melek, and kings of G. are mentioned in connection with other Phoen cities under Pers rule. The city submitted to Alexander the Great without opposition, and furnished a fleet to aid him in the siege of Tyre (332). Strabo refers to it as a town of note in the days of Pompey (xvi.2.17), and it is frequently mentioned in Phoen (*CIS*, 1) and Assyr inscriptions in the forms *Gubal* and *Gubli* (*COT*, I, 174).

(2) (גְּבָל, *gebhāl*; **Γοβολῖτις**, *Gobolitis*): A district S.E. of the Dead Sea, which is referred to in Ps **83** 7 (Heb 8) in connection with Moab, Ammon, Amalek and others, as making a covenant together against Israel (cf 1 Macc **5**). Robinson (*BR*, II, 154) found the name *Jebâl* still applied to this region, and Jos (*Ant*, II, i, 2) speaks of a *Gebalitis* as forming part of Idumaea. It is a hilly region, as the modern name signifies, and includes the towns of *Shobek* and *Ṭolfîeh*. H. Porter

GEBALITES, gē′bal-īts (הַגִּבְלִים, *ha-gibhlīm*): Inhabitants of Gebal (q.v.). According to the present text of Josh **13** 5, "the land of the Gebalites" was given to Israel as part of its future territory. But it was never occupied by the Israelites. LXX, however, has a very different reading, indicating an early corruption of the text. Perhaps with many modern scholars it is better to read "to the borders of the Gebalites."

In 1 K **5** 18 AV translates this word "stonesquarers," AVm gives "Giblites," and RV "Gebalites," as workmen who, with the men of Solomon and of Hiram, fashioned the stones for the temple. Here also the text is doubtful, and some by a slight change would read: "and made a border for them" (i.e. for the stones). In Ezk **27** 9 the men of Gebal are described as the "calkers" of the ships of Tyre and Sidon. George Rice Hovey

GEBER, gē′bĕr (גֶּבֶר, *gebher*, "man," "strong one"):

(1) According to 1 K **4** 13 AV the father of one of the 12 officers who provided food for Solomon and his household (but here RV "Ben-geber"). His district lay to the N.E. of Jordan.

(2) Another, and the last in the list of Solomon's commissariat officers (1 K **4** 19). His district was also E. of the Jordan, but probably to the S. of that named in connection with the official of ver 13 (RV "Ben-geber"). According to the rendering of EV, he is said to have been "the only officer that was in the land." Unless the text, which presents some difficulties, is corrupt, as some suppose, it probably means that this large region was assigned to one official because less able than the others to furnish the required supplies. Benjamin Reno Downer

GEBIM, gē′bim (גֵּבִים, *gēbhīm*, "trenches"): A place named only in Isa **10** 31. Some would place it at *Jebīa*, identifying it with the Geba of

Eusebius, 5 Rom miles from Gophna (modern *Jifneh*), on the way to Shechem. Its place, however, in the order of names, after Anathoth, seems to point to some position S. of that village, to the N.E. of Jerus.

GECKO, gek'ō (RV for אֲנָקָה, *'ănāḳāh*, only in Lev **11** 30; LXX μυγάλη, *mugálē*, "shrew mouse" or "field mouse"; AV **ferret**): Probably a shrew or a field mouse. See FERRET; LIZARD; SPIDER.

GEDALIAH, ged-a-lī'a (גְּדַלְיָה, *g^edhalyāh*, except in 1 Ch **25** 3.9 and Jer **38** 1, where it is גְּדַלְיָהוּ, *g^edhalyāhū*, "Yah[u] is great"):

(1) Gedaliah, the son of Ahikam (the friend and protector of Jeremiah) and grandson of Shaphan (the scribe in the reign of Josiah) (2 K **25** 22–25; Jer **39** 14; **40** 5–16; **41** 1–18).

After the destruction of Jerus and the carrying away captive of the Jews to Babylon (586 BC),

1. His Appointment as Governor in Judah

Gedaliah was appointed by Nebuchadnezzar governor over the poor Jews who had been left in the land to be vinedressers and husbandmen (2 K **25** 12.22). To his charge were committed also some royal princesses (Jer **43** 6) and courtiers (**41** 16) who had been allowed to remain as unlikely to cause any trouble. Gedaliah fixed his residence at Mizpah, a few miles N.W. of Jerus. Here he was joined by Jeremiah (**40** 6).

The Jewish soldiers who had escaped capture, having heard that the Chaldaeans had departed, and

2. His Conciliatory Spirit and Wise Rule

that Gedaliah, one of their own nation, had been appointed governor in Judah, came with Ishmael, Johanan and other officers at their head, to Gedaliah at Mizpah (2 K **25** 23.24; Jer **40** 7–10). The governor assured them that they need have no fear of vengeance from their conquerors, and promised them on oath protection and security, if they would remain and cultivate the land and become the peaceful subjects of the king of Babylon. This assurance led to a general gathering around Gedaliah of refugees from all the neighboring countries (Jer **40** 11.12). For two months (some think longer) Gedaliah's beneficent and wise rule did much to consolidate affairs in Judah and to inspire the feeble remnant of his countrymen with heart and hope.

But evil spirits were at work against him. Baalis, king of Ammon, had determined upon his life

3. His Treacherous Assassination

(Jer **40** 13–16). The peaceful and popular rule which was being established by the good governor stood in the way of the accomplishment of any plan of conquest he entertained. Baalis found a ready instrument for his murderous design in Ishmael who, as one of royal birth and in the counsels of the king (**41** 1), was doubtless jealous of the man who had been chosen governor in preference to himself. Gedaliah was informed by Johanan and the other captains of the plot to assassinate him, and Johanan at a private interview expressed to him a strong desire to go himself and slay Ishmael secretly, declaring that the safety of the Jews depended upon the life of the governor. But Gedaliah refused to allow Johanan to anticipate his enemy, believing, in the generosity of his heart, that Ishmael was not capable of such an act of treachery. He soon found, however, that his confidence had been sadly misplaced. Ishmael, with ten of his companions, came on a visit to him to Mizpah, and after they had been hospitably entertained they fell upon their good host and murdered him, along with all the Jewish and the Chaldaean soldiers whom he had with him for order and protection (2 K **25** 25; Jer **41** 1–3). They then cast the bodies of their victims into the cistern which Asa had made (ver 9). Ishmael was pursued and overtaken by Johanan, but he succeeded in effecting his escape to the Ammonites (vs 11–15). Then Johanan and the other captains, afraid lest the Chaldaeans should avenge upon them the murder of the governor (vs 16–18), and against the earnest entreaties of Jeremiah (ch **42**), fled to Egypt, taking the prophet and the Jewish remnant with them (**43** 5–7). In memory of the date of Gedaliah's assassination the Jews kept a fast (which is still retained in the Jewish calendar) on the 3d day of the 7th month, Tishri (Zec **7** 5; **8** 19).

The narratives reveal Gedaliah in a very attractive light, as one who possessed the confidence alike

4. His Noble Character

of his own people and their conquerors; a man of rare wisdom and tact, and of upright, transparent character, whose kindly nature and generous disposition would not allow him to think evil of a brother; a man altogether worthy of the esteem in which he was held by succeeding generations of his fellow-countrymen.

(2) (*g^edhalyāhū*): Son of Jeduthun, and instrumental leader of the 2d of the 24 choirs in the Levitical orchestra (1 Ch **25** 3.9).

(3) A priest of the "sons of Jeshua," in the time of Ezra, who had married a foreign woman (Ezr **10** 18).

(4) (*g^edhalyāhū*): Son of Pashhur (who beat Jeremiah and put him in the stocks, Jer **20** 1–6), and one of the chiefs of Jerus who, with the sanction of the king, Zedekiah, took Jeremiah and let him down with cords into a cistern where he sank in the mud (**38** 1.4–6).

(5) Grandfather of Zephaniah the prophet, and grandson of Hezekiah, probably the king (Zeph **1** 1).

JAMES CRICHTON

GEDDUR, ged'ur (Γεδδούρ, *Geddoúr*): Head of a family of temple-servants (1 Esd **5** 30), corresponding to Gahar of Ezr **2** 47 and Neh **7** 49.

GEDEON, ged'ē-on (He **11** 32 AV). See GIDEON.

GEDER, gē'dẽr (גֶּדֶר, *gedher*): A royal city of the Canaanites taken by Joshua along with Lachish, Eglon, Gezer, Debir and Hormah (Josh **12** 13 f). It may be the city called "Beth-gader" in 1 Ch **2** 51, and the birthplace of Baal-hanan, who had charge of David's olives and sycomores (**27** 28); unidentified.

GEDERAH, ge-dē'ra, **GEDERATHITE,** ge-dē'ra-thīt (הַגְּדֵרָה, *ha-g^edhērāh*, "the inclosed place"): A town in the Shephelah of Judah, named with Socoh, Azekah, Shaaraim and Adithaim (Josh **15** 36). In 1 Ch **4** 23 RV reads, "the inhabitants of Netaim and Gederah," for AV, "those that dwelt among plants and hedges." It is probably represented by *Khirbet Jadīreh*, about 3 miles S.W. of Gezer. "Gederathite," applied to Jozabad (**12** 4), probably meant an inhabitant of this place.

GEDERITE, gē'dẽr-īt, ge-dē'rīt (גְּדֵרִי, *g^edhērī*): Inhabitant of GEDER, which see (1 Ch **27** 28).

GEDEROTH, ged'ē-roth, ge-dē'rōth (גְּדֵרוֹת, *g^edhērōth*): A town in the Shephelah of Judah, named with Kithlish, Beth-dagon, Naamah and Makkedah (Josh **15** 41). It is mentioned along with Beth-shemesh and Aijalon as taken by the Philis in the reign of Ahaz (2 Ch **28** 18). It possibly corresponds with the "Kidron" of 1 Macc **15** 39.41; **16** 9. *Onom* places a very large village named Gedrom 10 Rom miles from Lydda on the road to Eleutheropolis. This points to *Ḳaṭrah*, S.E. of *Yebnah*.

GEDEROTHAIM, ged-ē-rō-thā'im (גְּדֵרֹתַיִם, *gedhērōthayim*, "place of inclosures"): Stands as the 15th in a list which professes to give only the names of 14 cities in the Judaean Shephelah (Josh **15** 36). AVm suggests that we might read "or" for "and" after Gederah, but this is impossible. LXX reads, "and its cattle shelters." Probably, however, the name has arisen by dittography from the preceding GEDERAH (q.v.).

GEDOR, gē'dor (גְּדוֹר, *gedhōr;* B, Γεδδώρ, *Geddōr*, A, Γεδώρ, *Gedōr*):

(1) A town in the mountains of Judah, named with Halhul and Beth-zur (Josh **15** 58). It seems to be referred to by Eusebius as Gadeira (*Onom*, s.v.), which he identifies with Gaidora (Jerome calls it Gadora), a village in the borders of Jerus, near the terebinth. It is probably represented today by *Khirbet Jedūr*, about 7 miles N. of Hebron (*PEF*, III, 313, Sh XXI).

(2) Among the Benjamites who joined David at Ziklag were the sons of Jeroham of Gedor (1 Ch **12** 7). No trace of this name is found in the territory of Benjamin. It may be identical with (1).

(3) The Simeonites are said to have gone to the entering in of Gedor in search of pasture for their flocks. They smote and expelled the Meunim, "and dwelt in their stead" (1 Ch **4** 39 ff). Here LXX reads Gerar, and this is probably correct

(4) A family in Judah (1 Ch **4** 4).

(5) An ancestor of Saul (1 Ch **8** 31).

W. EWING

GE-HARASHIM, gē-ha-rā'shim (גֵּא חֲרָשִׁים, *gē' ḥărāshīm*): In 1 Ch **4** 14, AV renders "valley of Charashim." In Neh **11** 35, EV renders "valley of craftsmen"; here it is named with Lod and Ono. Something of the name perhaps survives in *Khirbet Hirsa*, E. of Lydda.

GEHAZI, gē-hā'zī (גֵּיחֲזִי, *gēḥăzī*, except in 2 K **4** 31; **5** 25; **8** 4.5, where it is גֵּחֲזִי, *gēḥăzī*, perhaps "valley of vision"): The confidential servant of Elisha. Various words are used to denote his relation to his master. He is generally called Elisha's "boy" (נַעַר, *na'ar*), servant or personal attendant; he calls himself (**5** 25) his master's servant or slave (עֶבֶד, *'ebhedh*), and if the reference be to him in **4** 43 RVm, he receives the designation "minister" (מְשָׁרֵת, *meshārēth*), or chief servant of Elisha.

Mention is made of him on three different occasions. He is first brought under notice in the story of the wealthy Shunammite (2 K **4** 8–37) who provided in her house special accommodation for Elisha, which suited his simple tastes, and of which he availed himself as often as he passed that way. By command of his master, Gehazi called the Shunammite, that she might be rewarded by the prophet for her liberal hospitality. Failing to elicit from the lady a desire for any particular favor, and being himself at a loss to know how to repay her kindness, Elisha consulted with his servant, whose quick perception enabled him to indicate to his master the gift that would satisfy the great woman's heart. When on the death of her child the Shunammite sought out the man of God at Carmel, and in the intensity of her grief laid hold of the prophet's feet, "Gehazi came near to thrust her away" (ver 27)—perhaps not so much from want of sympathy with the woman as from a desire to protect his master from what he considered a rude importunity. Then Elisha, who had discovered of himself (ver 27), from what the woman had said (ver 28), the cause of her sorrow, directed Gehazi, as a preliminary measure, to go at once to Shunem and lay his staff upon the face of the dead child. Gehazi did so, but the child was "not awaked."

1. His Ready Service

In this narrative Gehazi appears in a favorable light, as a willing, efficient servant, jealous of his master's honor; a man of quick observation, whose advice was worth asking in practical affairs.

2. His Grievous Sin

Gehazi, however, reveals himself in a different character in connection with the healing of Naaman (2 K **5** 20–27). As soon as the Syrian general had taken his departure with his retinue from the house of Elisha, the covetous spirit of Gehazi, which had been awakened by the sight of the costly presents the prophet had refused, was no longer able to restrain itself. Running after Naaman, Gehazi begged in the prophet's name a talent of silver (£400=$2,000) and two changes of raiment, alleging, as a specious reason for Elisha's change of mind, the arrival at his master's house of two poor scholars of the prophet, who would require help and maintenance. Naaman, glad to have the opportunity he desired of showing his gratitude to Elisha, urged Gehazi to take two talents and sent two servants with him to carry the money and the garments. When they came to the hill in the neighborhood of the prophet's house, Gehazi dismissed the men and concealed the treasure. Thereafter, with a bold front, as if he had been attending to his ordinary duties, he appeared before his master who at once inquired, "Whence, Gehazi?" (Heb). On receiving the ready answer that he had not been anywhere, Elisha, who felt sure that the suspicion he entertained regarding his beloved servant, his very "heart" (ver 26), was well grounded, sternly rebuked him for the dishonor he had brought upon God's cause, and called down upon him and his family forever the loathsome disease of the man whose treasures he had obtained by his shameful lie. "And he went out from his presence a leper as white as snow."

By this narrative confidence in Gehazi is somewhat unexpectedly and rudely shaken. The active, zealous servant stands confessed a liar and a thief. Gehazi's sin branched out in different directions. By his falsehood he deceived Naaman and misrepresented Elisha; he not only told a lie, but told a lie about another man, and that man his master and friend. Further, he brought true religion into disrepute; for it was not a time (ver 26) for a servant of God to allow any commercial idea to be associated with the prophet's work in the mind of the Syrian general to whom God's power had been so strikingly manifested and when many for worldly gain pretended to be prophets. But while Gehazi's sin had its various ramifications, its one root was covetousness, "the love of money [which] is a root of all kinds of evil" (1 Tim **6** 10).

3. His Probable Repentance

Once more Gehazi is mentioned (2 K **8** 1–6) as having been summoned, leper though he was, by King Jehoram to give him an account of all the great things Elisha had done. And when he came to the story of the restoration of the Shunammite's child to life, the woman herself appeared before the king along with her son, craving to be reinstated in her house and land of which she had been dispossessed during her seven years' absence from her native country in a time of famine. Gehazi testified to the identity of both mother and son, with the result that the king at once ordered the restoration not only of all her former possessions, but also of all the profits her land had yielded during her sojourn in Philistia.

The appearance and conduct of Gehazi on this occasion give some ground for the hope that he had repented of his sin and could now be trusted to speak the truth; and the pleasure he seemed to take in rehearsing the wonderful deeds of a master who, though kind and indulgent to a stranger, was hard upon him, may even warrant the belief that in his earlier days there was some good thing in him toward his master's God. If also, as has been indicated above, the word used in **4** 43 (*m^eshārēth*) applies to him—the same as is applied to Elisha (1 K **19** 21)—we may be the more readily inclined to see in the history of Gehazi how one besetting sin may prevent a man from taking his natural place in the succession of God's prophets. Let us hope, however, that though Gehazi became a "lost leader," "just for a handful of silver," he was yet saved by a true repentance from becoming a lost soul.

JAMES CRICHTON

GEHENNA, gē-hen'a (**γεέννα,** *geénna* [see Grimm-Thayer, s.v.]): Gehenna is a transliteration from the Aram. form of the Heb *gē-hinnōm*, "valley of Hinnom." This latter form, however, is rare in the OT, the prevailing name being "the valley of the son of Hinnom." LXX usually translates; where it transliterates the form is different from Gehenna and varies. In the NT the correct form is *Geénna* with the accent on the penult, not *Géenna*. There is no reason to assume that Hinnom is other than a plain patronymic, although it has been proposed to find in it the corruption of the name of an idol (*EB*, II, 2071). In the NT (ARVm) Gehenna occurs in Mt **5** 22.29.30; **10** 28; **18** 9; **23** 15.33; Mk **9** 43.45.47; Lk **12** 5; Jas **3** 6. In all of these it designates the place of eternal punishment of the wicked, generally in connection with the final judgment. It is associated with fire as the source of torment. Both body and soul are cast into it. This is not to be explained on the principle that the NT speaks metaphorically of the state after death in terms of the body; it presupposes the resurrection. In AV and RV Gehenna is rendered by "hell" (see ESCHATOLOGY OF THE NT). That "the valley of Hinnom" became the technical designation for the place of final punishment was due to two causes. In the first place the valley had been the seat of the idolatrous worship of Molech, to whom children were immolated by fire (2 Ch **28** 3; **33** 6). Secondly, on account of these practices the place was defiled by King Josiah (2 K **23** 10), and became in consequence associated in prophecy with the judgment to be visited upon the people (Jer **7** 32). The fact, also, that the city's offal was collected there may have helped to render the name synonymous with extreme defilement. Topographically the identification of the valley of Hinnom is still uncertain. It has been in turn identified with the depression on the western and southern side of Jerus, with the middle valley, and with the valley to the E. Cf *EB*, II, 2071; *DCG*, I, 636; *RE*[3], VI.

GEERHARDUS VOS

GELILOTH, gē-lī'loth (גְּלִילוֹת, *g^elīlōth*): This word is used for "districts" or "circuits," perhaps indicating the different parts subject to the several lords of the Philis (Josh **13** 2, AV "borders," RV "regions"); for the quarter of the Jordan valley where the eastern tribes built the altar of Ed (**22** 10 f; AV "border of," RV "region about," Jordan); and apparently, for the whole of Philistia (Joel **3** 4, AV "coasts of Pal," RV "regions of Philistia"). But in Josh **18** 17, it is clearly used as a place-name. Geliloth lay on the boundary between Judah and Benjamin which passed En-shemesh (probably *'Ain el-Ḥōḍ*, about 2 miles E. of Jerus), "and went out to Geliloth, which is over against the ascent of Adummim." From this point it "went down" toward the plain. The place cannot therefore be identified with Gilgal in the Jordan valley. Some point on the road leading from Jericho to *Tal'at ed-Dumm*, about 6 miles from Jerus, was probably intended, but no identification is possible.

W. EWING

GEM, jem (Prov **26** 8, ERV "a bag of gems"). See STONES, PRECIOUS.

GEMALLI, gē-mal'ī (גְּמַלִּי, *g^emallī*, "camel owner"): Father of the spy Ammiel from the tribe of Dan (Nu **13** 12), who was one of those sent by Moses to spy out the land of Canaan.

GEMARA, ge-mä'rä. See TALMUD.

GEMARIAH, gem-a-rī'a (גְּמַרְיָהוּ, *g^emaryāhū*, גְּמַרְיָה, *g^emaryāh*, "Jeh hath accomplished"):

(1) Son of Shaphan the scribe, one of the princes, from whose chamber Baruch read Jeremiah's prophecies to the people. He, with others, sought to stay Jehoiakim from burning the roll (Jer **36** 10. 11.12.25).

(2) Son of Hilkiah, one of Zedekiah's ambassadors to Babylon, by whom Jeremiah sent his letter to the captives (Jer **29** 3).

GEMATRIA, gē-mā'tri-a. See NUMBERS; GAMES.

GENDER, jen'dẽr (יָלַד, *yāladh*, עָבַר, *'ābhar;* **γεννάω,** *gennáō*): "Gender" is an abbreviation of "engender." In Job **38** 29 *yāladh* (common for "to bear," "to bring forth") is tr[d] "gender" (after Wicliff), RV "The hoary frost of heaven, who hath gendered it?" m "given it birth." In **21** 10 we have *'ābhar* (either the Piel of *'ābhar*, "to pass over," etc, or of a separate word meaning "to bear," "to be fruitful"), tr[d] "gendereth," "Their bull gendereth, and faileth not"; in Lev **19** 19, *rābha'*, "to lie down with," is used of cattle gendering. In Gal **4** 24 AV we have "Mount Sinai, which gendereth [*gennaō*, "to beget"] to bondage," RV "bearing children unto bondage" (like Hagar, Abraham's bondwoman), and in 2 Tim **2** 23, which "gender strifes," i.e. beget them.

W. L. WALKER

GENEALOGY, jē-nē-al'o-ji, jen-ē-al'ō-ji:

1. Definition
2. Biblical References
3. Importance of Genealogies
4. Their Historical Value
5. Principles of Interpretation
6. Principles of Compilation
7. Sources
8. Principal Genealogies and Lists

LITERATURE

1. Definition

The OT tr[s] (once, Neh **7** 5) the noun יַחַשׂ, *yaḥas;* סֵפֶר הַיַּחַשׂ, *ṣēpher ha-yaḥas*, "book of the genealogy"; also tr[s] a denominate vb. in Hithpael, יָחַשׂ, *yāḥas*, "sprout," "grow" (cf family "tree"); הִתְיַחֵשׂ, *hithyaḥēs*, "genealogy"; the idea is conveyed in other phrases, as סֵפֶר תּוֹלְדוֹת, *ṣēpher tōl^edhōth*, "book of the generations," or simply תּוֹלְדוֹת, *tōl^edhōth*, "generations." In the NT it transliterates *γενεαλογία*, *genealogía*, "account of descent," 1 Tim **1** 4; Tit **3** 9. In Mt **1** 1, *βίβλος γενέσεως*, *bíblos genéseōs*, "book of the generation" of Jesus Christ, is rendered in ARVm "the genealogy of Jesus Christ"; a family register, or register of families, as 1 Ch **4** 33, etc; the tracing backward or forward of the line of ancestry of individual, family, tribe, or nation; pedigree. In Tim and Tit it refers probably to the gnostic (or similar) lists of successive emanations from Deity in the development of created existence.

2. Biblical References

According to the OT, the genealogical interest dates back to the beginnings of sacred history. It appears in the early genealogical tables of Gen **5, 10, 46,** etc; in Ex **6** 14–27, where the sons of Reuben, Simeon and esp. Levi, are given; in Nu **1** 2; **26** 2–51, where the poll of fighting men is made on genealogical principles; in Nu **2** 2, where the positions on the march and in camp are determined by tribes and families; in David's division of priests and Levites into courses and companies (1 Ch **6–9**); is referred to in the account of Jeroboam's reign (2 Ch **12** 15 m, "the words of Iddo, after the manner of genealogies"); is made prominent in Hezekiah's reforms when he reckoned the whole nation by genealogies (1 Ch **4** 41; 2 Ch **31** 16–19); is seen in Jotham's reign when the Reubenites and Gadites are reckoned genealogically (1 Ch **5** 17). Zerubbabel took a census, and settled the returning exiles according to their genealogies (1 Ch **3** 19–24; 1 Ch **9**; Ezr **2**; Neh **7, 11, 12**). With the rigid exclusion of all foreign intermixtures by the leaders of the Restoration (Ezr **10**; Neh **10** 30; **13** 23–31), the genealogical interest naturally deepened until it reached its climax, perhaps in the time of Christ and up to the destruction of Jerus. Jos, in the opening of his *Life*, states that his own pedigree was registered in the public records. Many families in Christ's time clearly possessed such lists (Lk **1** 5, etc). The affirmed, reiterated and unquestioned Davidic descent of Christ in the NT, with His explicit genealogies (Mt **1** 1–17; Lk **3** 23–38); Paul's statement of his own descent; Barnabas' Levitical descent, are cases in point. Davididae, descendants of David, are found as late as the Rom period. There is a tradition that Herod I destroyed the genealogical lists at Jerus to strengthen his own seat, but more probably they persisted until the destruction of Jerus.

3. Importance of Genealogies

Genealogical accuracy, always of interest both to primitive and more highly civilized peoples, was made esp. important by the facts that the land was promised to the descendants of Abraham, Isaac, Jacob, that the priesthood was exclusively hereditary, that the royal succession of Judah lay in the Davidic house, that the division and occupation of the land was according to tribes, families and fathers' houses; and for the Davididae, at least, that the Messiah was to be of the house of David. The exile and return, which fixed indelibly in the Jewish mind the ideas of monotheism, and of the selection and sacred mission of Israel, also fixed and deepened the genealogical idea, prominently so in the various assignments by families, and in the rejection in various ways of those who could not prove their genealogies. But it seems extreme to date, as with many modern critics, its real cultivation from this time. In the importance attached to genealogies the Heb resembles many other ancient literatures, notably the Egyp, Gr, and Arab., but also including Romans, Kelts, Saxons, the earliest history naturally being drawn upon genealogical as well as on annalic lines. A modern tendency to overestimate the likeness and underestimate the unlikeness of the Scripture to its undoubtedly cognate literatures finds in the voluminous artificial genealogical material, which grew up in Arabia after the time of the caliph Omar, an almost exact analogue to the genealogical interest at the time of the return. This, however, is on the assumption of the late date of most of the genealogical material in the older NT books, and rests in turn on the assumption that the progress of religious thought and life in Israel was essentially the same as in all other countries; an evolutionary development, practically, if not theoretically, purely naturalistic in its genesis and progress.

4. Their Historical Value

The direct historical value of the Scripture genealogies is variously estimated. The critically reconstructive school finds them chiefly in the late (priestly) strata of the early books, and dates Ch-Ezr-Neh (our fullest sources) about 300 BC, holding it to be a priestly reconstruction of the national history wrought with great freedom by the "Chronicler." Upon this hypothesis the chief value of the genealogies is as a mirror of the mind and ideas of their authors or recorders, a treasury of reflections on the geographical, ethnological and genealogical status as believed in at their time, and a study of the effect of naïve and exaggerative patriotism dealing with the supposed facts of national life, or else, in the extreme instance, a highly interesting example of bold and inventive juggling with facts by men with a theory, in this particular case a priestly one, as with the "Chronicler." To more conservative scholars who accept the OT at its face value, the genealogies are a rich mine of historical, personal and ethnographic, as well as religious, information, whose working, however, is much hindered by the inevitable corruption of the text, and by our lack of correlative explanatory information. Much interesting illustrative matter may be looked for from such archaeological explorations as those at Gezer and elsewhere under the Pal Exploration Society, the names on the pottery throwing light on the name-lists in Ch, and the similar discoveries on the supposed site of Ahab's palace in Samaria, which also illustrate the conflict between Baal and Jeh worship by the proportion of the proper names compounded by "Baal" or "Jah" (see Macalister, *Bible Sidelights from Gezer*, 150 ff; *PEF*, 1905, 243, 328; *Harvard Theological Review*, 1911). In spite of all such illustrative data, however, the genealogies must necessarily continue to present many insoluble problems. A great desideratum is a careful and systematic study of the whole question by some modern conservative scholar endowed with the patience and insight of the late Lord A. C. Hervey, and equipped with the fruits of the latest discoveries. While much curious and suggestive information may be derived from an intensive study of the names and relationships in the genealogies (although here the student needs to watch his theories), their greatest present value lies in the picture they present of the large-hearted cosmopolitanism, or international brotherliness, in the older ones, notably Gen **10**, recognizing so clearly that God hath made of one all nations to dwell on the earth; and, as they progress, in the successive selection and narrowing as their lines converge upon the Messiah.

5. Principles of Interpretation

In the evaluation and interpretation of the genealogies, certain facts and principles must be held in mind. (1) Lists of names necessarily suffer more in transmission than other literature, since there is almost no connectional suggestion as to their real form. Divergences in different versions, or in different stages, of the same genealogy are therefore to be looked for, with many tangles hard to unravel, and it is precisely at this point that analytic and constructive criticism needs to proceed most modestly and restrain any possible tendency unduly to theorize. (2) Frequently in the Scriptural lists names of nations, countries, cities, districts or clans are found mingled with the names of individuals. This is natural, either as the personification of the clan or nation under the name of its chief, or chief progenitor, or as the designation of the individual clan, family or nation, from its location, so common among many nations. Many of the cases where this occurs are so obvious that the rule may not be unsafe to consider all names as probably standing for individuals where the larger geographical or other reference is not unmistakably clear. This is undoubtedly the intent and understanding of those who transmitted and received them. (3) It is not necessary to assume that the ancestors of various tribes or families are eponymous, even though otherwise unknown The Scriptural explanation of the formation of tribes by the expansion and division of families is not improbable, and is entitled to a certain presumption of correctness. Furthermore, it is extremely difficult to establish a stopping-point for the application of the eponymous theory; under its spell the sons of Jacob disappear, and Jacob, Isaac and even Abraham become questionable. (4) The present quite popular similar assumption that personal details in the genealogy stand for details of tribal history, as, for instance, the taking of a concubine means rather an alliance with, or absorption of, an inferior tribe or clan, is a fascinating and far-reaching generalization, but it lacks confirmation, and would make of the Scripture an allegorical enigma in which historical personages and events, personified peoples or countries, and imaginary ancestors are mingled in inextricable confusion. (5) Scriptural genealogies are often given a regular number of generations by omitting various intermediate steps. The genealogies of Jesus, for instance, cover 42 generations, in 3 subdivisions of 14 each. Other instances are found in the OT, where the regularity or symmetry is clearly intentional. Instance Jacob's 70 descendants, and the 70 nations of Gen **10**. This has in modern eyes an artificial look, but by no means necessarily involves violence done to the facts under the genealogist's purview, and is readily and creditably accounted for by his conceptions and purposes. The theory that in some cases the requisite number has been built up by the insertion of imaginary names (vide Curtis, *ICC*, "Chronicles," 135) has another aspect, and does not seem necessary to account for the facts, or to have sufficient facts to sustain it. See **21** 5, (6) below. It involves a view of the mental and moral equipment and point of view of the Chronicler in particular, which would not seem to leave him many shreds of either historical, or "religious" value, and which a sounder criticism will surely very materially modify. (6) Much perplexity and confusion is avoided by remembering that other modes of entrance into the family, clan, tribe or nation obtained than that by birth: capture, adoption, the substitution of one clan for another just become extinct, marriage. Hence "son of," "father of," "begat," have broader technical meanings, indicating adoptive or official connection or "descent," as well as actual consanguinity, nearer or remote, "son" also meaning "grandson," "great-grandson," etc. Instance Caleb, the son of Jephunneh, of the tribe of Judah, styled (1 Ch **2** 18) a descendant of Hezron and son of Hur, but also, in token of his original descent, called the Kenizzite or "son of Kenaz" (Josh **15** 17), etc. Similarly, where in an earlier genealogy a clan or individual is assigned to a certain tribe, and in a later to another, it has been "grafted in." But while these methods of accretion clearly obtained, the nations freely absorbing neighboring or surrounding peoples, families, or persons, families likewise absorbing individuals, as in American Indian, and many other tribes; yet, as in them, the descent and connection by birth constituted the main line, and in any given case has the presumption unless clear facts to the contrary exist. (7) The repetition of the same name in the same genealogy, as in that of the high priests (1 Ch **6** 1–15), rouses "suspicion" in some minds, but unnecessarily. It is very natural, and not uncommon, to find grandfathers and grandsons, esp. among the Hebrews, receiving the same name (Lk **1** 59). This would be esp. to be expected in a hereditary caste or office like the priesthood. (8) The existence of the same name in different genealogies is not uncommon, and neither implies nor should cause confusion. (9) The omission of one or many links in the succession, often clearly caused by the desire for symmetry, is frequent where the cause is unknown, the writers being careful only to indicate the connection more or less generally, without feeling bound to follow every step. Tribes were divided into families, and families into fathers' houses; tribe, family and fathers' house regularly constituting links in a formal genealogy, while between them and the person to be identified any or all links may be omitted. In similar fashion, there is an absence of any care to keep the successive generations absolutely distinct in a formal fashion, son and grandson being designated as alike "son" of the same ancestor. Gen **46** 21, for instance, contains grandsons as well as sons of Benjamin, Bela, Becher, Ashbel, Gera, Naaman, Ehi, etc. This would be esp. true where the son as well as the father became founder of a house. Some confusion is occasionally caused by the lack of rigid attention to precise terminology, a characteristic of the Heb mind. Strictly the tribe, שֵׁבֶט, *shēbheṭ* (in P, מַטֶּה, *maṭṭeh*), is the larger subdivision, then the clan, מִשְׁפָּחָה, *mishpāḥāh*, "family," and then the "house" or "fathers' house," בַּיִת, *bayith*, or בֵּית אָב, *bēth 'ābh*, or בֵּית אָבוֹת, *bēth 'ābhōth;* but sometimes a "fathers' house" is a tribe (Nu **17** 6), or a clan (1 Ch **24** 6). In this connection it is to be remembered again that sequence of generations often has to do with families rather than with individuals, and represents the succession to the inheritance or headship, rather than the actual relationship of father and son. (10) Genealogies are of two forms, the descending, as Gen **10**: "The sons of Japheth: Gomer," etc; "The sons of Gomer: Ashkenaz," etc; and the ascending, Ezr **7** 1 ff: "Ezra, the son of Seraiah, the son of Azariah, the son of Hilkiah," etc. The descending are the usual. (11) Feminine names are occasionally found, where there is anything remarkable about them, as Sarai and Milcah (Gen **11** 29), Rebekah (**22** 23), etc; or where any right or property is transmitted through them, as the daughters of Zelophehad, who claimed and were accorded "a possession among the brethren of [their] father" (Nu **26** 33; **27** 1–11), etc. In such cases as Azubah and Ephrath, successive wives of Caleb (1 Ch **2** 18–20), many modern critics find tribal history enshrined in this case, "Caleb" or "dog" tribe having removed from Azubah, "deserted" to Ephrathah, Bethlehem, in Northern Judah. But the principle is not, and cannot be, carried out consistently. (12) The state of the text is such, esp. in Ch, that it is not easy, or rather not possible, to construct a complete genealogical table after the modern form. Names and words have dropped out, and other names have been changed, so that the connection is often difficult and sometimes impossible to trace. The different genealogies also represent different stages in the history and, at many places, cannot with any knowledge now at our command be completely adjusted to each other, just as geographical notices at different periods must necessarily be inconsistent. (13) In the present state of our knowledge, and of the text, and also considering the large and vague chronological methods of the Hebrews, the genealogies can give us comparatively little chronological assistance. The uncertainty as to the actual length of a generation, and the custom of frequently omitting links in the descent, increases the difficulty; so that unless they possess special marks of completeness, or have outstanding historical relationships which determine or corroborate them, or several parallel genealogies confirm each other, they must be used with great caution. Their interest is historical, biographical, successional or hereditary, rather than chronological.

The principal genealogical material of the OT is found in Gen **5, 10, 11, 22, 25, 29, 30, 35, 36, 46;** Ex **6;** Nu **1, 2, 7, 10, 13, 26, 34;** scattered notices in Josh, Ruth, 1 S; 2 S **3, 5, 23;** 1 K **4;**

1 Ch **1**–**9**, **11**, **12**, **15**, **23**–**27**; 2 Ch **23**, **29**; Ezr **2**, **7**, **10**; Neh **3**, **7**, **10**, **11**, **12**. The genealogies of Our Lord (Mt **1** 1–17; Lk **3** 23–38) are the only NT material. The OT and NT genealogies bring the record down from the creation to the birth of Christ.

6. Principles of Compilation

After tracing the descent from Adam to Jacob, incidentally (Gen **10**) giving the pedigree of the various nations within their purview, the Heb genealogists give the pedigree of the twelve tribes. As was to be expected, those tribes, which in the developing history assumed greater prominence, received the chief attention. Dan is carried down but 1 generation, and credited with but 1 descendant; Zebulun 1 generation, 3 sons; Naphtali 1 generation, 4 sons; Issachar 4 generations, 15 descendants; Manasseh 4 generations, 39 descendants; Asher 7 generations, 40 descendants; Reuben 8 (?) generations, 22 descendants; Gad 10 generations, 28 descendants; Ephraim 14 (?) generations, 25 descendants. Levi, perhaps first as the priestly tribe, Judah next as the royal, Benjamin as most closely associated with the others, and all three as the survivors of the exile (although representatives of other tribes shared in the return) are treated with the greatest fulness.

7. Sources

Ch furnishes us the largest amount of genealogical information, where coincident with the older genealogies, clearly deriving its data from them. Its extra-canonical sources are a matter of considerable difference among critics, many holding that the books cited by the Chronicler as his sources ("The Book of the Kings of Israel and Judah," "The Book of the Kings of Judah and Israel," "The History of Samuel the Seer," "The History of Nathan the Prophet," etc, to the number of perhaps 16) are our canonical books, with the addition of a "Midrashic History of Israel," from which he quotes the most freely. But the citations are made with such fulness, vividness, and particularity of reference, that it is hard to believe that he did not have before him extensive extra-canonical documents. This is the impression he clearly seeks to convey. Torrey (*AJSL*, XXV, 195) considers that he cites this array of authority purely "out of his head," for impressiveness' sake, a theory which leaves the Chronicler no historical value whatever. It is extremely likely that he had before him also oral and written sources that he has not cited, records, private or public lists, pedigrees, etc, freely using them for his later lists and descents. For the post-exilic names and lists, Ezr-Neh also furnish us much material. In this art. no attempt is made at an exhaustive treatment, the aim being rather by a number of characteristic examples to give an idea of the quality, methods and problems of the Bible genealogies.

In the early genealogies the particular strata to which each has been assigned by reconstructive critics is here indicated by J, P, etc. The signs "=" or ":" following individual names indicate sonship.

8. Principal Genealogies and Lists

(**1**) Gen **4** 16–24. *The Cainites* (assigned to P).

Seven generations to Jabal, Jubal and Tubal-cain, explaining the hereditary origin of certain occupations (supposed by many to be a shorter version of ch **5**).

(**2**) Gen **4** 25.26. *The Sethites* (assigned to J).

(**3**) Gen **5** 1–32. *The Book of the Generations of Adam* (assigned to P, except ver 29 J).

Brings the genealogy down to Noah, and gives the chronology to the Flood. The numbers in the Heb MT, the Sam Heb, and the LXX differ, MT aggregating 1,656 years, Sam 1,307 years, and LXX 2,242 years. Some scholars hold this list to be framed upon that of the ten Bab kings given in Berosus, ending with Xisuthrus, the Bab Noah. An original primitive tradition, from which both lists are derived, the Heb being the nearer, is not impossible. Both the "Cainite" list in Gen **4** and this "Sethite" list end with three brothers.

(**4**) Gen **10** 1–32. *The Generations of the Sons of Noah, "The Table of Nations"* (assigned to P, vs 1–7; J, vs 8–19; P, ver 20; J, ver 21; P, ver 22; J, vs 24–30; P, vs 31.32). Found in abridged form in 1 Ch **1** 5–24.

I. **Japheth** = Gomer, Magog, Badai, Javan, Tubal, Meshech, Tiras.
 1. *Gomer* = Ashkenaz, Riphath (1 Ch **1** 6, Diphath), Togarmah.
 2. *Javan* = Elishah, Tarshish, Kittim, Dodanim (Rodanim, 1 Ch **1** 7, is probably correct, a ד, *d*, having been substituted by a copyist for ר, *r*).

II. **Ham** = Cush, Mizraim, Put, Canaan.
 1. *Cush* = Seba, Havilah, Sibtah, Raamah, Sabteca (Nimrod).
 2. *Mizraim* = Ludim, Anamim, Lehabim, Naphtuhim, Pathrusim, Casluhim (whence the Philis), Caphtorim.
 3. *Canaan* = Zidon (Ch Sidon), Heth; the Jebusite, Amorite, Girgashite, Hivite, Arkite, Sinite, Arvadite, Zemarite, Hittite.
 4. *Raamah* (s. Cush) = Sheba, Dedan.

III. **Elam** = Asshur, Arpachshad, Lud, Aram.
 1. *Aram* = Uz, Hul, Gether, Mash (Ch Meshech).
 2. *Arpachshad* = *Shelah* = *Eber* = Peleg, Joktan.
 3. *Joktan* (s. Eber) = Almodad, Sheleph, Hazarmaveth, Jerah, Hadoram, Uzal, Diklah, Obal, Abimael, Sheba, Ophir, Havilah, Jobab.
 4. *Peleg* (s. Eber) = Reu = Serug = Nahor = Terah = Abraham.

Nearly all these names are of peoples, cities or districts. That Noah, Shem, Ham, Japheth, Nahor, Terah, Abraham, Nimrod, and probably Peleg, Reu, Serug, represent actual persons the general tenor of the narrative and the general teaching of Scripture clearly indicate, although many critics consider these also as purely eponymous. The others can mostly be more or less clearly identified ethnographically or geographically. This table represents the nations known to the writer, and in general, although not in all particulars, expresses the ethnographical relationships as far as they are now known to modern research. It follows a partly ethnological, partly geographical scheme, the descendants of Japheth in general representing the Aryan stock settled in Asia Minor, Media, Armenia, Greece, and the islands of the Mediterranean; those of Ham representing the Hamitic races in Ethiopia, Egypt, in Southwest Arabia, and Southern Babylonia. Many modern writers hold that in making "Nimrod" the son of "Cush," the Scripture writer has confused "Cush," the son of Ham, with another "Cush," the Cassei, living near Elam, since the later Babylonians and Assyrians were clearly Sem in language and racial characteristics. Nevertheless the Scripture statement is accordant with early traditions of a Hamitic settlement of the country (Oannes the fish-god coming out of the Red Sea, etc), and perhaps also with the fact that the earliest language of Babylonia was non-Sem. The sons of Canaan represent the nations and peoples found by the Hebrews in Pal, the Phoenicians and the Canaanites. Heth is the great Hittite nation, by language and racial type strikingly non-Sem. Among the sons of Shem, Eber is by many considered eponymous or imaginary, but the hypothesis is not necessary. Most Assyriologists deny the connection of Elam with Shem, the later Elamites being non-Sem; the inscriptions, however, show that the earlier inhabitants up to 2300 BC were Sem. Lud must be the Lydians of Asia Minor, whose manners and older names resemble the Sem. Asia Minor presents a mixture of races as manifold as does Pal. The sons of Joktan are tribes in Western and Southern Arabia. Havilah is given both as a son of Cush, Hamite, and of Joktan, Semite, perhaps because the district was occupied by a mixed race. It would seem, however, that "begat" or "son of" often represents geographical as well as ethnological relations. And where the classification of the Scripture writer does not accord with the present deliverances of archaeology, it must be remembered that at this distance conclusions drawn from ethnology, philology and archaeology, considering the present incomplete state of these sciences, the kaleidoscopic shifting of races, dynasties and tongues through long periods, and our scanty information, are liable to so many sources of error that dogmatism is precarious. The ancient world possessed a much larger amount of international knowledge than was, until recently, supposed. A writer of 300 BC had a closer range and could have had sources of information much more complete than we possess. On the assumption of the Mosaic authorship, that broad, statesmanlike mind, learned in all the knowledge of the Egyptians, and, clearly, profoundly influenced by Bab law and lit., may be credited with considerable breadth of vision and many sources of information. Aside from the question of inspiration, this Table of Nations, for breadth of scope, for inclusiveness (though not touching peoples outside of the life of its writer), for genial broad-mindedness, is one of the most remarkable documents in any literature.

(5) Gen **11** 10–27. *The Generations of Shem* (assigned to P).

From Shem to Abraham. The list is also chronological, but the versions differ, MT making 290 years, from Shem to Abraham, Sam Heb, 940, and LXX 1,070. LXX inserts Cainan, 130 years, otherwise agreeing with Sam to the birth of Abraham. Arpachshad may be rendered "the territory of Chesed," i.e. of the Chasdim, Chaldaeans. Eber therefore is descended from Arpachshad, Abraham, his descendant, coming from Ur-Chasdim.

(6) Gen **11** 23–26; **22** 20–24. *The Children of Nahor* (**11** 23–26 P; **22** 20–24 J).

Uz, Buz, Kemuel, etc. These descendants of Abraham's brother probably represent Aramaean tribes chiefly E. or N.E. of Canaan. Aram may be the ancestor of the Syrians of Damascus. Uz and Buz probably belong to Arabia Petraea, mentioned in Jer **25** 23 with the Arabian tribes Dedan and Thema. Chesed in this list probably stands, not for the Chaldaeans of Babylonia, but for a related tribe of Northern Syria. In Gen **10** 23 (assigned to P) Uz is the son of Aram, and in **10** 22 Aram is a son of Shem. On the purely tribal hypothesis, this is either a contradiction, or the later statements represent other tribal relationships or subdivisions. Probably other individuals or tribes are indicated. Ch does not have this list, it being a side stream.

(7) Gen **16** 15; **21** 1–3; **25** (also 1 Ch **1** 28–33). *The Sons of Abraham by Sarah, Hagar, Keturah* (**16** 15 assigned to P; **21** 1–3 to J, P, J, P; Gen **25** 1–6 J; 7–11 P; 11*b* J; 12–17 P; 18 J; 19.20 P; 21–26*a* J; 26*b* P; 27–34 J).

The descendants of Abraham through Hagar and Ishmael represent the Ishmaelite tribes of Arabia living N. and N.W. of the Joktanidae, who chiefly peopled Arabia. Twelve princes are named, possibly all sons of Ishmael, perhaps some of them grandsons. The number has seemed "suspicious" as balancing too exactly the twelve tribes of Israel. But twelve is an approved Sem number, determining not necessarily the sons born, but the "sons" mentioned. The Arabians generally were frequently given the name Ishmaelites, perhaps because of the greater prominence and closer contact of these northern tribes with the Hebrews. The sons of Keturah seem to have been chiefly Arabian tribes, whose locations are unknown. Midian, of the sons of Keturah, is the well-known and powerful tribe in the Arabian desert near the Aelanitic Gulf, bordered by Edom on the N.W. Sheba and Dedan are also mentioned as Cushites (Gen **10** 7). Very likely the tribes extensively intermarried, and could claim descent from both; or were adopted into one or the other family. Sheba was in Southwestern Arabia. Dedan lived near Edom, where the caravan routes to various parts of Arabia converged. Asshurim are of course not Assyrians, but an Arabian tribe, mentioned by the side of Egypt in Minaean inscriptions. While the two sons of Isaac are to be accepted as real persons, their typical character is also unmistakable, the history of the two nations, Israel and Edom, being prefigured in their relations.

(8) Gen **29** 31—**30** 24; **35** 16–26. *The Children of Jacob* (**29** 31–35 assigned to P; **30** 1–3*a* JE; 4*a* P; 4*b*–24 JE; **35** 16–22 JE; 23–26 P).

The account of the parentage, birth and naming of the founders of the twelve tribes; by Leah: Reuben, Simeon, Levi, Judah, Issachar, Zebulun (d. Dinah); by Bilhah: Dan, Naphtali; by Zilpah: Gad, Asher; by Rachel: Joseph, Benjamin. Much modern criticism agrees that these names are purely those of tribes, some of them perhaps derived from persons or places impossible now to trace, but mostly eponymous. Accordingly, these chapters are to be trd as follows. An Arab tribe, Jacob, wanders in Canaan, quarrels with Edom, migrates to Haran, forms alliances with the Aramaean clans Rachel, Bilhah, Leah, Zilpah. Rachel and Jacob constitute a new tribe, Joseph. The federation takes the name Jacob. The other allied clans divide into sub-clans, or new clans join them, until Leah has six "sons," Reuben, Simeon, etc; Zilpah, two; Bilhah, two. Zilpah and Bilhah are "concubines" because inferior members of the federation, or else have a left-handed connection with it. The formation of the new tribe Benjamin broke up the old tribe Rachel, which (who) accordingly "died." Although such are the original facts imbedded in the documents, they are now set in a framework of personal narrative, and were understood as narrative by the first hearers and readers. The history thus constituted is necessarily "an enigma which it is very hard to solve" (Bennett, *Gen*, 284), and with almost as many answers as students. For critical purposes it presents a rich field for exploration, analysis and conjecture, but its edificatory value is chiefly found in reading the narratives as personal: a serious and reverent religious romance founded on facts or legends, whose real value lies in the sidelights it throws on national character and ethical principles, expressed in a naïve, vivid, lifelike story, full of suggestion and teaching. This present article, however, proceeds on the Scripture representation of these details and incidents as personal.

The explanations of the names illustrate the Heb fondness for assonances, paronomasia, coming from a time when much importance was attached to words and sounds, but need not be considered mere popular etymologies, the Heb individual mother being fully capable of them. Neither do they necessarily represent the original etymology, or reason for the name, but may give the pregnant suggestion occurring to the maternal or other imagination.

Leah, "wild cow," is supposed by many to be so called from the "totem" of the "Leah" tribe. Reuben (*re'ūbhēn*), original meaning unknown, unless Leah's emotional explanation explains the name, rather than is explained by it: *rā'āh be'onyī*, "hath looked upon my affliction." Superficially, it might be *re'ū bēn*, "See, a son," as in ARVm. Others see in the second statement: "My husband will love me," still another etymology, *ye'ĕhābhani*, "will love me." The lover of assonances can find more than one. The tribe is not prominent after Deborah's time. Simeon, considered by some an animal (totem) name, the Arab. *sim'u*, cross between hyena and wolf, suggests to the mother (or is suggested by that) its likeness to *shāma'*, "hear": "Jeh hath heard." It is not much known after the Conquest. Levi, "adhesion, associate": thought by many a gentilic adjective from Leah, the Leah tribe par excellence; the name is adjectival in form. Leah connects it with *yillāweh*, "He will join," 'Now will my husband be joined unto me.' A similar allusion is found in Nu **18** 2.4, there applied to the "joining" of the tribe to Aaron. Judah is associated with the vb. *hādhāh*, "praise": "Now will I praise Jeh." Jacob makes the same suggestion in Gen **49** 8; no other plausible suggestion of the origin of the name can be made. The etymology and origin of Bilhah are unknown. Dan is associated with *dānāh*, "judge": "God hath judged"; no other etymology can be found. Naphtali is derived from *niphtal*, "wrestle": "I have wrestled," the only discoverable etymology. Zilpah, *zilpāh*, perhaps is "dropping," "drop." Gad, *gādh*, "fortunate," according to Leah. Gad was the well-known Syrian god of "fortune"; but there is no necessary connection here. Asher, from *'āshar*, "happy," *'ashshēr*, "call happy"; so Leah; no connection with Asshur, Assyr god. Issachar, from *sākhar*, "hire," "man of hire": "God hath given me mine hire," also because Leah had "hired" Jacob with her son's mandrakes; a similar allusion in Gen **49**, "a servant under taskwork." Wellhausen would read *'īsh-sakhar*, "man of [some deity, unknown]." Zebulun, from *zebhūl*, "habitation, dwelling": Leah gives two explanations, the first assigned by critics to E (probably), connecting the name with a root found in Zebediah, Zabdi, etc, "endow": "God hath endowed me with a good dowry"; the second with *zābhal*, "dwell": "Now will my husband dwell with me." Dinah, like Dan, is from *dān*, "judge." Supposed by some to be an old tribe of Israel, in some way associated with Dan, possibly a twin division. Rachel is "ewe," hence identified with a "ewe" tribe. Joseph has a twofold suggestion: the first (assigned to E) from *āsaph*, "take away": "God hath taken away my reproach"; the second (assigned to J) from *yāsaph*, "add": "Jeh will add to me another son." None of these three cases of double explanation would so far exhaust Heb maternal imagination as to require the hypothesis of two documents, even though in the last "God" is used in the first suggestion and "Jeh" in the second. Benjamin is called by Rachel Benoni, "the son of my sorrow," which is supposed to be an old tribal name, perhaps related to Onan, a clan of Judah, or the Benjamite city, Ono, and possibly to the Egyp On. Benjamin, Jacob's name for him, "son of the right hand," i.e. of happiness, is understood as "son of the south," because originally the southern section of the Joseph tribe. The attempts to trace these names to tribal origins, local allusions, cognate languages, customs and religions have engaged much research and ingenuity, with results exceedingly diverse.

(9) Gen **36**. *The Generations of Esau* (P).

I. The descent of the Edomite chiefs and clans from Esau through his three wives, the Hittite or Canaanite Adah, the Ishmaelite Basemath, and the Horite Oholibamah (vs 1–19).

The wives' names here differ from the other statements:
In **26** 34 and **28** 9: 1. Judith, d. of Beeri the Hittite.
2. Bashemath, d. of Elon, the Hittite.
3. Mahalath, d. of Ishmael, sister of Nebaioth.
In Gen **36**: 1. Oholibamah, d. of Anah, d. of Zibeon, the Hivite.
2. Adah, d. of Elon the Hittite.
3. Bashemath, d. of Ishmael, sister of Nebaioth.

It is not necessary to resort to the hypothesis of different traditions. Bashemath and Adah are clearly identical, Esau perhaps having changed the name; as are Mahalath and the Ishmaelite Basemath, a transcriber's error being probably responsible for the change. As to Judith and Oholibamah, Anah is probably a man, identical with Beeri (ver 24), the son of Zibeon. Both "Hivite" and "Hittite" are apparently errors for "Horite," the difference being in only one consonant. Or "Hittite" may be used as the larger term embracing "Horite." "Edom" (vs 1.8.19) is a personal name; in vs 9.43 (Heb ARVm) it is national, indicating that to the writer Esau was a person, not an eponym. Nowhere are personal characteristics more vividly and unmistakably portrayed than in the accounts of Jacob and Esau. In these Esauite names are but two compounds of "El" (*'ēl*), none of "Jah" (*yāh*).

II. The aboriginal leaders or clans in Edom, partly subdued by, partly allied with, the Esauites (vs 20–30).

These are descendants of "Seir the Horite" in seven branches, and in sub-clans. "Seir" looks like an eponym or a personification of the country, as no personal details have been preserved. Among these names are no "El" (*'ēl*) or "Jah" (*yāh*) compounds, although they are clearly cognate with the Heb. Several close similarities to names in Judah are found, esp. the Hezronite. Many animal names, "Aiah," "bird of prey," "Aran," "wild goat," etc.

III. Eight Edomite "kings" before the Hebrew monarchy (vs 31–39).

One *'ēl* compound, "Mehitabel," one *ba'al* compound. It is to be noted that the "crown" was not hereditary and that the "capital" shifted; the office was elective, or fell into the hands of the local chief who could win it.

IV. A list of Esauite clan chiefs; "dukes" (EV), "chiefs" (ARV); "sheiks" (vs 40–43).

Apparently arranged territorially rather than tribally. The names seem used here as either clans or places and should perhaps be read: "the chief of Teman," etc. The original ancestor may have given his name to the clan or district, or obtained it from the district or town.

In general this genealogy of Esau shows the same symmetry and balance which rouses suspicion in some minds: excluding Amalek, the son of the concubine, the tribes number twelve. Amalek and his descendants clearly separated from the other Edomites early and are found historically about Kadesh-barnea, and later roaming from the border of Egypt to North Central Arabia.

(**10**) Gen **46** 8–27 (in different form, Nu **26** 1–51, and much expanded in parts of 1 Ch **2–8**; cf Ex **6** 14–16). *Jacob's posterity at the descent into Egypt* (considered a late addition to P).

A characteristic genealogy. It includes the ideal number of 70 persons, obtained by adding to the 66 mentioned in Gen **46** 26, Jacob, Joseph, Ephraim and Manasseh, the two latter born in Egypt. LXX, followed by Stephen (Acts **7** 14), reckons 75, adding to Gen **46** 20 the names of three grandsons and two great-grandsons of Joseph, obtained from Nu **26** 29.35 ff. Some may have been omitted to secure the ideal number so fascinating to the Heb mind. It is to be noted that Leah's male descendants are double those of Zilpah, and Rachel's double those of Bilhah, showing the ideal (but not the fictitious) character of the list. The design, also, seems to be to include those descendants of Jacob from whom permanent divisions sprang, even though, like Manasseh and Ephraim and probably Hezron and Hamul, born after the migration, but before Jacob's death. A comparison with the partial parallels also illustrates the corruption of the text, and the difficulty of uniformity in lists of names. The full list follows:

1. *Jacob*.
2. *Leah's* descendants.
   A. *Reuben*=Hanoch, Pallu, Hezron, Carmi.
   B. *Simeon*=Jemuel, Jamin, Ohad, Jachin, Zohar, Shaul.
   C. *Levi*=Gershon, Kohath, Merari.
   D. *Judah*=Er, Onan, Shelah, Perez, Zerah; Perez, Hezron, Hamul.
   E. *Issachar*=Tolah, Puvah, Iob, Shimron.
   F. *Zebulun*=Sered, Elon, Jahleel.
   G. *Dinah*, daughter.
3. *Zilpah's* descendants, 16.
   A. *Gad*=Ziphion, Haggi, Shuni, Ezbon, Eri, Arodi, Areli.
   B. *Asher*=Imnah, Ishvah, Ishvi, Beriah, Serah (daughter); Beriah=Heber, Malchiel.
4. *Rachel's* descendants, 14.
   A. *Joseph*=Manasseh, Ephraim.
   B. *Benjamin*=Bela, Becher, Ashbel, Gera, Naaman, Ehi, Rosh, Muppim, Huppin, Ard.
5. *Bilhah's* descendants, 7.
   A. *Dan*=Hushim.
   B. *Naphtali*=Jahzeel, Guni, Jezer, Shillem.

The list differs in many respects from those in Nu and Ch, and presents some chronological and other problems. Without entering upon an exhaustive study, a number of names may be touched on.

Carmi (2A), like the other names in *i*, might be a gentilic, "the Carmite," like "the Amorite," etc, esp. if these names are those of clans, as they are in Nu, instead of persons, as the Gen narrative states. A town, "Beth-haccherem," is mentioned in Jer **6** 1. But "the vine-dresser" is also a good rendering.

Hezron (2A). Another Hezron is given as a descendant of Judah. This duplication of names is possible in clans; see instances below, but more likely in persons.

Jemuel (2B). Nemuel in Nu **26** 12; 1 Ch **4** 24, an easy error in transcription, י, *yōdh*, and נ, *nūn*, being easily confused. In Nu, Nemuel is also a Reubenite name.

Jamin (or Jachin) (2B) is Jarib in Ch.

Ohad (2B). Not in Nu or Ch.

Zohar (2B) is Zerah in Nu and Ch.

Gershon (2C). In 1 Ch **6** 16 Gershom; identified by some with Gershom, son of Moses, on the theory that the priestly family of Gershom originally traced its descent to Moses, but its later members were reckoned, not as priests, but as Levites, thus becoming identified with Levi; precarious; its principal foundation being similarity of name and tribe.

Hezron and Hamul (2D) rouse chronological or exegetical difficulties. Pharez (Gen **38**) could not have been old enough at the migration to have two sons; but very possibly Gen **38** is introduced episodically, not chronologically, and therefore its events may have occurred before those of Gen **37**. Jacob was 130 years old at the descent, making Judah not 42 but 62, and Pharez old enough for sons. And, as suggested above, the writer may have done with Hezron and Hamul as with Ephraim and Manasseh—included them constructively, they having been born in Egypt, but before Jacob's death, belonging therefore to the generation of the migration and so reckoned, esp. as they founded permanent tribal divisions.

Puvah (2E). Puah in 1 Ch **7** 1. In Jgs **10** 1, centuries later, Puah is father of Tola, an illustration of the descent of fathers' names.

Iob (2E) is Jashub (Nu, Ch), the latter probably correct. LXX has it here. A copyist, no doubt, omitted the "*shīn*," "*sh*."

Dinah (2G) is thought by some to be a later insertion, on account of the "awkward Heb," "with Dinah." Dinah and Serah as unmarried, and no doubt because of other distinguishing facts, now unknown, are the only women descendants mentioned; married women would not be. On the clan theory of the names, the "Dinah" clan must have disappeared in Egypt, not being found in Nu.

Ziphion (3A). Zephon in Nu, perhaps giving its name to the Gadite city of Zaphon (Josh **13** 27).

Ezbon (3A). Ozni (Nu **26** 16). Possibly Ozni, on Ezbon's death, took his place, founding a tribal family, like Hezron and Hamul in Judah. Copyist's error unlikely.

Arodi (3A). In Nu **26** 17 Arod.

Ishvah (3B). Omitted in Nu; perhaps died childless, or his descendants did not constitute a tribal family.

Beriah (3B). Also an Ephraimite (1 Ch **7** 23); a Benjaminite (**8** 13.16); a Levite (**23** 10.11). The repetition of the name indicates individuals rather than clans; but both the Asherite and Benjamite were heads of families.

Serah (3B), שֶׂרַח, *seraḥ*, "abundance," not the same name as that of Abraham's wife, שָׂרָה, *sārāh*, "princess."

Heber (3B), חֶבֶר, *ḥebher;* in 1 Ch **4** 18, a clan of Judah; **8** 17, of Benjamin. Not the same name as Eber, עֵבֶר, *'ēbher* (**5** 13; **8** 22; and Gen **10** 21).

The Sons of Benjamin. The three lists, Gen, Nu, Ch, represent marked divergences, illustrating the corruption of perhaps all three texts. This list illustrates the genealogical method of counting all descendants as sons, though of different generations. It gives Benjamin ten "sons." Nu **26** 38–40 gives five sons, Naaman and Ard being sons of Bela. The LXX of our passage gives only three sons, Bela, Becher, Ashbel. 1 Ch **7** 6 gives three sons, Bela, Becher, Jediael (Ashbel), and Shuppim and Huppim are Bela's grandsons. Becher is omitted in **8** 1, probably through a copyist's error, who took בֶּכֶר וְאַשְׁבֵּל, *bekher we-'ashbēl*, for "Becher and Ashbel," בְּכֹרוֹ אַשְׁבֵּל, *bekhōrō 'ashbēl*, "his first-born, Ashbel." Jediael, both by older and newer scholars, is usually, but not with absolute certainty, identified with Ashbel. He may be a later chief. Another explanation is that **7** 6 is part of a Zebulunite genealogy which has been transformed into a Benjamite list, Jediael being a remaining Zebulunite "pebble."

Naaman (4B) perhaps appears, by a transcriber's error in **8** 2, as *Nōḥah*, נוחה for נעמן. If Nohah is not Naaman, and not (Keil) Shephupham, or a chief who succeeded him, he may have been one who was born after the migration and not needed to make up the seventy.

Gera (4B) in similar fashion may appear in **8** 2 as Rapha. If not, Rapha also may be one born after the migration, and did not found a family.

Ehi (4B) is Ahiram (Nu **26** 38); Aharah (1 Ch **8** 1). Ehi probably arises from some copyist omitting the "ram."

Rosh (4B) is not in Nu or Ch. He founded no family.

Muppim (4B) troubled the scribes greatly. In Nu **26** 39 he is Shephupham, though as compounded in his family name it is Shupham. In 1 Ch **7** 12 he is Shuppim, and it is not made clear whether he is a son, or other descendant, of Benjamin. He is apparently called, with Huppim, a son of Ir (Iri), son of Bela. In **8** 8 he is catalogued as a son of Bela, as Shephuphan. In old Heb *mem* מ (*m*) and *shin* ש (*sh*) closely resemble each other. As the *sh* also appears in the gentilic names, it is probably the correct form. The corrupt state of the Chronicler's text esp. is apparent, and also the fact that "son" may refer to any male descendant.

Huppim (4B) in Nu **26** 39 is Hupham; in 1 Ch **8** 5 is Huram.

Ard (4B) in 1 Ch **8** 3 is a son of Bela, Addar, the copyist having transposed ד, *d*, and ר, *r*, or mistaken one for the other. In LXX at Gen **46** 21 Ard is son of Gera, son of Bela.

Hushim (5A), the same in 1 Ch **7** 12, is Shuham (Nu **26** 42), by transposition of consonants. Another Hushim is a Benjaminite, son of Aher, but Aher may possibly be a corruption of the numeral "one," it being the Chronicler's frequent habit to add numerals. But see under Dan **21** 6, (3), p. 1194.

Jahzeel (5B) is Jahziel in 1 Ch **7** 13.

Guni (5B) in 1 Ch **5** 15 is also a Gadite name.

Shillem (5B), in 1 Ch **7** 13, Shallum, the commoner form.

(11) Ex **6** 14–25 (assigned to P). *Partial list of heads of fathers' houses of Reuben, Simeon and Levi.*

Reuben and Simeon are as in Gen. Levi follows:

1. *Gershon* = Libni, Shimei.
2. *Kohath.*
   A. *Amram* m. Jochebed = Aaron, Moses; Aaron m. Elisheba, d. of Amminadab, sister of Nahshon = Nadab, Abihu, Eleazar, Ithamar; Eleazar m. d. of Putiel = Phinehas.
   B. *Izhar* = Korah, Nepheg, Zichri; Korah, Assir, Elkanah, Abiasaph.
   C. *Hebron.*
   D. *Uzziel* = Mishael, Elzaphan, Sithri.
3. *Merari* = Mahli, Mushi.

The interest of the list is partly chronological, but chiefly to illustrate the genealogical place of Aaron and Moses. It probably exhibits the genealogical practice of omitting links, Amram the father of Moses apparently being several links from Amram the son of Kohath. By Moses' time the Amramites numbered some 2,000 males (Nu **3** 27, etc). Jochebed (2A) is an instance of Jah in compounds before the Exodus. Putiel (2A) has been considered a partly Egyp name, Puti or Poti, "devoted to" -El (*'ēl*); but probably Heb, "afflicted by God." Hebron is often identified with the city. It is also found in 1 Ch **2** 42.43, as Judahite.

(12) Nu **1** 5–54; **2** 3–29; **7** 12 ff; **10** 4 ff. *The heads of houses representing and leading the tribes* (assigned to P).

I. *Reuben:* Elizur, s. of Shedeur.

II. *Simeon:* Shelumiel, s. of Zurishaddai.

Shelumiel found in Jth.

III. *Judah:* Nahshon, s. of Amminadab.

Both found also in Ex **6** 23; Ruth **4** 9–22; 1 Ch **2** 10–12: Mt 1 4: Lk **3** 32 (genealogies of Christ).

IV. *Issachar:* Nethanel, s. of Zuar.

Neth., name of nine persons in Ch, Neh, Ezr, same as Nathaniel.

V. *Zebulun:* Eliab, s. of Helon.

Other Eliabs, Nu **16** 1 (Reubenite); 1 S **16** 6 (Jesse's son, Judah).

VI. *Joseph: Ephraim:* Elishama, s. of Ammihud.

Other Elishamas: 2 S **5** 16 (s. of David); Jer **36** 12; 2 Ch **17** 8. Ammihuds: 2 S **13** 37 m; Nu **34** 20.28; 1 Ch **9** 4 (Judahite).

VII. *Joseph: Manasseh:* Gamaliel, s. of Pedahzur. NT Gamaliel.

VIII. *Benjamin:* Abidan, s. of Gideoni.

IX. *Dan:* Ahiezer, s. of Ammishaddai.

Another, 1 Ch **12** 3 (Benjamite).

X. *Asher:* Pagiel, s. of Ochran.

XI. *Gad:* Eliasaph, s. of Deuel.

Another, Nu **3** 24 (Levite).

XII. *Naphtali:* Ahira, s. of Enan.

Seven of these names, Amminadab, Ammihud, Abidan, Ahirah, Ahiezer, Eliab, Elishama, are concededly early. The 5 compounded in Shaddai or Zur are said to be of a type found only in P; 9 of the 24 are compounded in *'ēl*, said to be a characteristic of late names. The *'Ēl* is postfixed more times, 5, than it is prefixed, 4; also a characteristic of late names. The proportion of compound names is also greater than in the older names; for these and similar reasons (Gray, *ICC*, "Nu," 6; *HPN*, 191–211; *Expos T*, September, 1897, 173–90) it is concluded that though several of the names are, and more may be, early, the list is late. But see *AHT*, 74, 83 ff, 85 ff, 320. The contention rests largely on the late date of P and of Ch. But while fashions in names changed in Heb life as elsewhere, in view of the persistence of things oriental, the dating of any particular names is somewhat precarious. They may be anticipations or late survivals of classes of names principally prevalent at the later or earlier date. Two of the names, otherwise unknown, have come to us through Ruth, and indicate a source now unknown to us, from which all the names could have been drawn. The fondness for names in *'ēl* very likely indicates not a late date but an early one. *'Ēl* is the Divine name appearing in personal names previous to Moses, succeeded by Jah from Moses and Joshua on. The recurrence of *'ēl* in the time of Ezra and later probably indicates the renewed interest in antiquity as well as the at once wider and narrower outlook brought about by the exile and return. Numerous S. Arabian compounds both with the "ilu," "ili" (*'ēl*), affixed and prefixed, occur in monuments about 1000 BC (*AHT*, 81 ff).

(13) Nu **3** 1–37. *The family of Aaron, with the "princes" of Levi.*

Adds nothing to list in Ex **16** 16–25 except the Levite "princes."

I. *Gershonites:* Eliasaph, s. of Lael.

Also a Benjaminite Eliasaph (Nu **1** 14).

II. *Kohathites:* Elizaphan, s. of Uzziel.

A Zebulunite Elizaphan (Nu **34** 25). Five other Uzziels, Benjamite, Levite, Simeonite.

III. *Merarites:* Zuriel, s. of Abihail.

A Gadite Abihail (1 Ch **5** 14); also father of Queen Esther; also two women: wife of Abishur (1 Ch **2** 29); wife of Rehoboam (2 Ch **11** 18). Four *'ēl* suffixes, two prefixes.

(14) Nu **13** 4–16. *The Twelve Spies* (P).

I. *Reuben:* Shammua, s. of Jaccur.

Other Shammuas (2 S **5** 14; 1 Ch **14** 4 [David's son]; Neh **11** 17, Levite; **12** 18, priest). Seven other Zaccurs, Simeonites and Levites.

II. *Simeon:* Shaphat, s. of Hori.

Four other Shaphats, one Gadite, one Judahite; Elisha's father. Hori looks like the national name of the Horites; perhaps Hori or an ancestor had been adopted, through marriage or otherwise.

III. *Judah:* Caleb, s. of Jephunneh, the Kenizzite (Nu **32** 12; Josh **14** 6.14).

Another Caleb, Chelubai, s. of Hezron, brother of Jerahmeel (1 Ch **2** 9). Either as an individual, or as a clan, Caleb seems to be originally of the pre-Israelitish stock in Canaan, absorbed into the tribe of Judah. Perhaps Jephunneh the Kenizzite married a woman of Caleb's (brother of Jerahmeel) household, and to their firstborn was given the name of Caleb, he becoming head of the house and prince of Judah. Another Jephunneh, an Asherite (**7** 38).

IV. *Issachar:* Igal, s. of Joseph.

Other Igals: 2 S **23** 36 (one of David's heroes); 1 Ch **3** 22. Note the name of another tribe given to a man of Issachar—Joseph (Nu **13** 7).

V. *Ephraim:* Hoshea, s. of Nun.

Hoshea, Joshua's early name. Others: 1 Ch **27** 20; King Hoshea, 2 K **15** 30; Neh **10** 23; Heb name of prophet Hosea.

VI. *Benjamin:* Palti, s. of Raphu. See **16** IV.
VII. *Zebulun:* Gaddiel, s. of Sodi.
VIII. *Joseph-Manasseh:* Gaddi, s. of Susi.

A Gaddi is in 1 Macc **2** 2.

IX. *Dan:* Ammiel, s. of Gemalli.

Another Ammiel (2 S **9** 4).

X. *Asher:* Sethur, s. of Michael.

Nine other Michaels, Gadite, Levite, Issacharite, Benjamite, Manassite, Judahite.

XI. *Naphtali:* Nahbi, s. of Vophsi.
XII. *Gad:* Geuel, s. of Machi.

Four names in *'ēl*. Nine ending with *i;* unusual number. The antiquity of the list cannot be readily questioned.

(15) Nu **26** 5–62 (P). *The heads of houses at the second census.*

Related to Nu **1** and **2**, and closely follows Gen **46**. The divergences in individual names have been noted under **(10)**. This list adds to

I. *Reuben:*
   1. Eliab, s. of Pallu (also Nu **16** 1.12).
   2. Dathan, Abiram, Nemuel, ss. of Eliab.

II. *Manasseh:*
   1. Machir; also Gen **50** 23.
   2. Gilead, s. of Machir.
   3. Iezer (abbreviation for Abiezer), Helek (not in Ch), Asriel, Shechem, Shemida, ss. of Gilead.
   4. Zelophehad, s. of Hepher.
   5. Mahlah, Noah, Hoglah, Milcah, Tirzah, d. of Zelophehad.

III. *Ephraim:*
   1. Shuthelah; also 1 Ch **7** 21.
   2. Becher.
   3. Tahan (Tahath, 1 Ch **7** 20).
   4. Eran (Elead, 1 Ch **7** 21).

The names of Manasseh's grandsons and great-grandsons are puzzling. Gilead is the district except in Jgs **11** 1.2, where it is the father of Jephthah. Shechem sounds like the Ephraimite town. Hepher reminds of Gath-Hepher. In Josh **17** 1.2 the six sons of Gilead are described as sons of Manasseh; loosely, it is probable; they are to be understood as descendants. Perhaps the references may be summarized: The family of Machir, the son of Manasseh, conquered Gilead, and took its name therefrom, either as a family or in the person of a son, Gilead, whose six sons founded clans named from or giving names to certain towns or districts.

The daughters of Zelophehad are noted for the interesting case at law they presented, claiming and receiving the inheritance of their father, which by Gray, *ICC*, "Nu," is considered not historical but a fictitious instance, for the purpose of raising the question, these daughters being clans, and not persons.

Among the sons of Ephraim, Becher has perhaps been misplaced from ver 38, and possibly displaces Bered (1 Ch **7** 20) between Shuthelah and Tahath. It is not found here in the LXX. It is possible that an alliance between the Becherites and the Ephraimites caused one portion of the former to be counted with Ephraim and another with Benjamin; or that at different times the clan was allied with the two different tribes. An error in transcription is more probable. Another Shuthelah is found later in the line (1 Ch **7** 21).

(16) Nu **34** 16–28. *Tribal representatives in the allotment.*

Reuben, Gad, half-Manasseh, omitted because their allotments had already been assigned E. of Jordan; Levi, because receiving none. Changing to the order in **(10)**:

I. *Reuben:* None.
II. *Simeon:* Shemuel, s. of Ammihud.

Shemuel is Heb of Samuel. Another S. is of Issachar, 1 Ch **7** 2. Samuel the prophet, a Levite.

III. *Judah:* Caleb, s. of Jephunneh.
IV. *Issachar:* Paltiel, s. of Azzan.

Another Paltiel, otherwise Palti, David's wife Michal's temporary husband (2 S **3** 15). Another Benjamite spy (Nu **13** 9).

V. *Zebulun:* Elizaphan, s. of Parnach.

Another E., Kohathite Levite (Ex **6** 18.22).

VI. *Gad:* None.
VII. *Asher:* Ahihud, s. of Shelomi.

Another Ahihud, Benjamite (1 Ch **8** 7).

VIII. *Joseph-Ephraim:* Kemuel, s. of Shiftan.

Another Kemuel, s. of Nahor, an Aramaean chief (Gen **22** 21); also Levite of David's time (1 Ch **27** 17).

IX. *Joseph-Manasseh:* Hanniel, s. of Ephod.

Hanniel, also an Asherite (1 Ch **7** 39).

X. *Benjamin:* Elidad, s. of Chislon.
XI. *Dan:* Bukki, s. of Jogli.

Bukki, abbreviation of Bukkiah; another, in high-priestly line of Phinehas (1 Ch **6** 5.51).

XII. *Naphtali:* Pedahel, s. of Ammihud.

A Simeonite Ammihud above.
Seven "El" names, only one "Jah."

(17) Ruth **4** 20. *The ancestry of David* (Perez: Hezron: Ram: Amminadab: Nahshon: Salmon [Salmah]: Boaz: Obed: Jesse: David).

Contained unchanged in 1 Ch **2** 9–15; also Mt **1** 1–6; also Lk **3** 32. Some links have been omitted between Obed and Jesse. Salmon might be traced to the ancestor of the Bethlehemite (1 Ch **2** 51.54), who is, however, of Caleb's line, not Ram's; but the lines may mingle.

(18) 2 S **3** 2–5; **5** 14.15. *David's children* (also in 1 Ch **3** 1–9; **14** 4–7).

I. *Born in Hebron:* Amnon, Chileab, Absalom, Adonijah, Shephatiah, Ithream.
II. *Born in Jerus:* Shammua, Shobab, Nathan, Solomon, Ibhar, Elishua, Nepheg, Japhia, Elishama, Eliada, Eliphelet.

Four names in *'ēl*, all prefixed. Two in "Jah." Chileab is Daniel in 1 Ch **3** 1; uncertain which is right, but probably Daniel is a corruption. Ch adds Nogah to the Jerus sons, probably developed in transcription. **3** 6–8 has two Eliphelets; **14** 6 has Elpalet in place of the first; more probable. This gives David 6 sons in Hebron, and, if both Nogah and Elpalet be correct, 12 in Jerus. Eliada is Beeliada in **14** 7, perhaps the original form, a relic of the time before the Hebrews turned against the use of Baal, "lord," as applied to Jeh; in which case Baaliada, "Lord knows," was changed to Eliada, "God knows." **3** 6 reads Elishama for Elishua. Japhia is also the name of a king of Lachish in Joshua's time (Josh **10** 3–7).

(19) 2 S **23** (also 1 Ch **11** 11–41). *David's knights.*

1. Josheb-bashebeth, the Tahchemonite.

In Ch it is Jashobeam, and should read Ishbaal, the writer's religious horror of Baal leading him to substitute the consonants of *bōsheth*, "shame," as in Mephibosheth, Ishbosheth. LXX has 'Ιεσεβαδά (B), 'Ιεσσεβαδάλ, 'Ισβαάμ (A), in Ch, and 'Ιεβόσθε (B), 'Ιεβοσθαί (A) here. In Ch he is a Hachmonite, probably correct. "Adino the Heznite" is probably a corruption for "He wielded his spear" (Ch).

2. Eleazar, s. of Dodai, the Ahohite.

Dodo in Ch; 8 other Eleazars in the OT. Another Dodo is father of Elhanan.

3. Shammah, s. of Agee, a Hararite.

Omitted by Ch. Three other Shammahs, one of them a knight of David. "Harari" may be "mountaineer," or "inhabitant of the village Harar."

4. Abishai, s. of Zeruiah, brother of Joab.

Abshai (1 Ch **18** 12m). Zeruiah perhaps David's half-sister (2 S **17** 25). Father never mentioned.

5. Benaiah, s. of Jehoaida of Kabzeel.

11 other OT Benaiahs, one of them also a knight. This B. succeeded Joab as commander-in-chief, 4 other Jehoiadas, one B.'s grandson, high in David's counsel, unless a scribe has inverted the order in 1 Ch **27** 34, which should then read B., s. of Jehoiada.

6. Asahel, brother of Joab.

Three other Asahels.

7. Elhanan, s. of Dodo of Bethlehem.

Another E., slayer of the brother of Goliath (2 S **21** 19; 1 Ch **20** 5). Perhaps the same.

8. Shammah the Harodite.

Ch, Shammoth. From Harod, near Gideon's well (Jgs **7** 1).

9. Elika the Harodite.

10. Helez the Paltite.

Paltite perhaps local or family name from Pelet, or Palti.

11. Ira, s. of Ikkesh the Tekoite.

Two others, one a knight. Tekoah, Judaite town, home of Amos, etc.

12. Abiezer the Anathothite.

One other, a Manassite (Josh **17** 2). Anathoth an hour N.E. of Jerus, Jeremiah's town.

13. Mebunnai the Hushathite.

Should read, with Ch, Sibbecai.

14. Zalmon the Ahohite.

Z., also name of mountain (Jgs **9** 48). Descendant of Ahoah, Benjamite of Bela's line. See 1 Ch **8** 14.

15. Maharai the Netophathite.

From Netophah, town.

16. Heleb, s. of Baanah.

1 Ch **11** 30, Heled. Three other Baanahs.

17. Ittai, s. of Ribai of Gibeah of the children of Benjamin.

1 Ch **11** 31, Ithai. An Ittai of Gath also followed David.

18. Benaiah a Pirathonite.

Pirathon, Amalekite town in Ephraimite territory.

19. Hiddai of the brooks of Gaash.

Ch, Hurai (ד for ר). *Ga'ash*, a wady in Ephraim.

20. Abi-albon the Arbathite.

Ch, Abiel, perhaps corrupted from Abi-Baal; from Beth-arabah, Judah or Benjamin.

21. Azmaveth the Barhumite.

Three others, and a Judaite town, of the same name. Baharumite, Ch. B., a Benjamite town.

22. Eliahba the Shaalbonite.

S., a Danite town.

23. The sons of Jashen (better, Hashem).

Ch, "the sons of Hashem the Gizonite." "Sons of" looks like a scribal error, or interpolation, perhaps a repetition of "bni" in "Shaalboni" above.

24. Jonathan, s. of Shammah the Hararite.

Ch adds, "the son of Shagee the Hararite." Shagee should perhaps be Agee (2 S **23** 11); but LXX indicates Shammah here; both S and Ch should read "J., s. of Shammah the Ararite."

25. Ahiam, s. of Sharar the Ararite.

Ch, Sacar the Hararite. S is supported by LXX.

26. Eliphelet, s. of Ahasvai, the son of the Maacathite.

Ch has "Eliphal, s. of Ur," and adds "Hepher the Mecherathite." Both texts are corrupt. Ch should perhaps read, "Eliphelet the son of . . . . , the Maacathite, Eliam," etc.

27. Eliham, s. of Ahithophel the Gilonite.

E., possibly father of Bathsheba. Ahithophel, David's counselor. Gilonite, native of Giloh.

27*a*. Ahijah the Pelonite (in Ch but not S).

Seven other Ahijahs. Pelonite uncertain, probably a corruption; perhaps inserted by a scribe who could not decipher his "copy," and means "such and such a one," as in 1 S **21** 2.

28. Hezro (Hezrai) the Carmelite.

Scribe confused ו and י. Carmel, near Hebron.

29. Paarai the Arbite.

Ch, "Naarai, s. of Esbai." Uncertain. Arab., a town of Judah.

30. Igal, s. of Nathan of Zobah.

Ch, Joel, brother of Nathan. Igal less common than Joel, hence more likely to be corrupted; 2 other Igals; 12 other Joels; 5 other Nathans.

30*a*. Mibhar, s. of Hagri (Ch, not S).

Text uncertain as between this and 31.

31. Bani the Gadite (omitted Ch).

Possibly the Gerarite.

32. Zelek the Ammonite.

Ammon E. of Jordan and upper Jabbok.

33. Naharai the Beerothite, armor-bearer to Joab, s. of Zeruiah.

Beeroth, Benjamite town.

34. Ira the Ithrite.

Ithrites, a family of Kiriath-jearim, Judah.

35. Gareb the Ithrite.

Gareb also a hill W. of Jerus.

36. Uriah the Hittite.

Bathsheba's husband; 3 others. From some Hittite town surrounded by Israel at the Conquest.

37. Zabad, s. of Ahlai (perhaps dropped out of S), Ch.

Ch adds 13 others. The filling of vacancies makes the number 37 instead of 30. Two names, perhaps, in *ba'al*, 5 in *yāh*, 7 in *'ēl*. As far as guessable, 5 from Judah, 3 from Benjamin, 2 from Ephraim, 1 from Dan, 1 from Issachar, 1 Ammonite, 1 Hittite, 2 (or 4) Hararites, 2 Harodites, 2 Ithrites.

(20) 1 K **4** 1–19. *Solomon's "princes" and commissaries.*

11 princes, 12 officers. No mention of their tribal connections; assigned only partly by tribal bounds. 7 *yāh* names, 1 *'ēl*; 5 of the officers are prefixed *ben* as if their own names had dropped out.

(21) 1 Ch **1–9**. *Genealogies, with geographical and historical notices.*

By far the largest body of genealogical material, illustrating most fully the problems and difficulties. The estimate of its value depends on the estimate of the Chronicler's date, purpose, equipment, ethical and mental qualities. He uses freely all previous OT matter, and must have had in hand family or tribal songs, traditions; genealogical registers, as mentioned in Ezr **2** 61–69; Neh **7** 63–65; local traditions; official genealogies, such as "the genealogies reckoned in the days of Jotham king of Judah, and . . . . Jeroboam king of Israel" (1 Ch **5** 17); prophetic, historical and other matter now lost, "the words of Shemaiah . . . . after the manner of genealogies" (2 Ch **12** 15), and elsewhere. The results of David's census seem to have been in his hands (1 Ch **27** 24). Curtis (*ICC*, "Chronicles," 528) suggests that his purpose was partly to provide genealogies for contemporary families, implying an accommodating insertion of names "after the manner of genealogies" today. Two main purposes, however, seem clear: the first historical, to give the historical and personal basis and setting to elucidate the Chronicler's main thesis, that national prosperity depended upon, and national character was measured by, fidelity to the law of

God, esp. as it centered upon the worship and services of Jeh's house. To do this it was necessary to trace the descent of the prominent characters, families, tribes. Hence the space given to Judah, Levi, Benjamin, the main line of fidelity, the survival of the fittest. The other purpose was to conserve purity of blood in the restored nation, to include all who were entitled and to exclude all who were not. We may also credit him with such regard for his material that he preserved it all (with certain comprehensible exceptions), even though extremely fragmentary here and there. His materials are of many degrees of age. It is thought by some that the antiquity is indicated by the last stage in the descent, the genealogy of Sheshan, e.g. ending with Hezekiah's time; Heman's and Asaph's (1 Ch **6** 33) in David's. Name-study and historico-literary criticism seeks still other marks of relative age. The text has suffered much, as lists of names will, from scribal errors. Details of his method will be pointed out in the following analysis. As in this whole article, space forbids exhaustive treatment of the endless textual, critical, historical questions arising. A few illustrative cases only are given.

I. Primeval Genealogies (1 Ch **1** 1–54).

To show Israel's place among the nations; follows Gen closely, omitting only the Cainites; boldly, skilfully compressed, as if the omitted facts were well known.

(1) The ten antediluvian Patriarchs, and Noah's three sons (vs 1–4).

Follows Gen **4** 5, giving only the names.

(2) Japheth's descendants (vs 5–7) (Gen **10** 2–4 unchanged).
(3) The Hamites (vs 8–16) (Gen **10** 6–8.13–18*a* unchanged).
(4) The Semites (vs 17–23) (Gen **10** 22–29; only scribal changes).
(5) Abram's descent (vs 24–27) (Gen **11** 10–26 abridged, giving only the Patriarchs).
(6) The sons of Abraham, Keturah, Isaac (vs 28–34).

Gen **25** 1–4.13–16.25.26; **32** 28. Reverses the order of Ishmael's and Keturah's descendants.

(7) Sons of Esau (vs 35–52) (Gen **36** 4–10).
(8) Kings and sheikhs of Edom (vs 43.54) (Gen **36** 31–43). Scribal changes.

II. Descendants of Jacob (1 Ch **2–9**).

The tribes arranged chiefly geographically. Judah, as the royal line, is given 100 verses, Levi, as the priestly, 81 verses, Benjamin 50, the other ten 56, Dan and Zebulun neglected. His purpose practically confines him to the first three; and these were also the best preserved.

(1) *Sons of Israel.*

Follows substantially the order in Gen **35**. Dan is placed before Rachel's sons. 17 different orders of the tribes in Bible lists.

(2) *Genealogies of Judah* (**2** 3—**4** 23).

(*a*) Descent of Jesse's sons from Judah (**2** 3–17).

Largely gleaned from the historical books. The sons of Zerah (vs 6–8) are not found elsewhere. Chelubai is Caleb. Only 7 sons of Jesse are mentioned. Abishai, Joab, Asahel are always designated by their mother's name, Zeruiah.

(*b*) Genealogy of Bezalel (vs 18–20).

The artificer of the tabernacle, hence greatly interests the Chronicler.

(*c*) Other descendants of Hezron (vs 21–24).
(*d*) The Jerahmeelites (vs 25–41).

Concededly a very old list of this important clan not found elsewhere. Sheshan (ver 35), who married his daughter to Jarha, an Egyp servant, illustrates the introduction of a foreigner into the nation and tribe.

(*e*) The Calebites (vs 41–55).

Not elsewhere. The names are largely geographical. A subdivision of the Hezronites. Not Caleb the son of Jephunneh.

(*f*) David's descendants (**3** 1–24).

Gives first the sons and their birthplaces, then the kings to Jeconiah and Zedekiah, then the Davidic line from Jeconiah to Zerubbabel, then the grandsons of Zerubbabel and the descendants of Shecaniah. Two other lists of David's sons (2 S **5** 14–16; 1 Ch **14** 4–17). Eliphelet and Nogah here are thought to have developed in transcription, with some other changes. Johanan's name (s. of Josiah) is given among the kings, though he never reigned. Zedekiah is called son (instead of brother) of Jehoiachin, perhaps a scribal error. "Jah" names extremely numerous. Names of Zerubbabel's sons are highly symbolic: Meshullam, "Recompensed"; Hananiah, "Jah is gracious"; Shelomith, "Peace"; Hashubah, "Consideration"; Ohel, "Tent," i.e. "Dwelling of Jeh"; Berechiah, "Jah blesses"; Hasadiah, "Jah is kind"; Jushab-hesed, "Loving-kindness returns"; characteristic of the Exile.

Vs 19–24, beginning with Zerubbabel's descendants, are obscure, and a battleground of criticism on account of their bearing on the date of Ch. There are three possible interpretations: (1) Following the Heb, Zerubbabel's descendants stop with Pelatiah and Jeshaiah, his grandsons. Then follow three unclassified sets of "sons." No connection is shown between Jeshaiah and these. Then follows Shecaniah's line with four generations. There are several other instances of unrelated names thus being thrown in. This gives *two* generations after Zerubbabel. (2) Still following the Heb, assume that Shecaniah after Obadiah is in Z.'s line. This gives *six* generations after Z. (3) Following LXX, Syr, Vulg (but the two latter are of very small critical weight), read in ver 21, "Rephaiah his son, Arnan his son," etc —a very possible change: *eleven* generations after Z. According to (3), Ch was written at least 253 years (allowing 23 years to a generation; more probable than 30 or 40) after Zerubbabel (515), hence after 262 BC; (2) makes it after 373; (1) makes it 459, during Ezra's life. The book's last recorded event is Cyrus' decree (538), which indicates the earliest date. The NT casts no light here, none of these names appearing in the genealogies in Mt or Lk. If LXX is correct, Keil suggests that it is a later insertion, a critical device too frequently used to nullify inconvenient facts. The passage itself justifies the statement that "there is no shadow of proof that the families enumerated in ver 21, latter part, were descendants of Hananiah the son of Zerubbabel." Against this, and the other indications, the admittedly faulty LXX furnishes an insufficient basis for so far-reaching a conclusion.

(*g*) Fragmentary genealogies of families of Judah (**4** 1–23).

Contains (1) "sons" of Judah, four or five successive generations; (2) sons of Shobal and Hur; (3) sons of Chelub; (4) sons of Caleb, s. of Jephunneh; (5) sons of Jehaleel; (6) sons of Ezra (of course, not the priest-scribe of the return); (7) sons of "Bethiah the daughter of Pharaoh whom Mered took"; (8) sons of Shimon; (9) sons of Ishi; (10) sons of Shelah. It is hard to trace the law of association here; which fact has its bearing on the discussion under (*f*) above. Chelub may be another Caleb. Vs 9–11 give an interesting name-study, where Jabez by prayer transforms into prosperity the omen of his sorrowful name: "Because I bare him with sorrow," a characteristic note. Vs 21–23 speak of the linen-workers and potters. Similar, even identical, names have been found on pot-handles in Southern Pal.

(3) *Genealogy of Simeon* (**4** 24–43).

(*a*) Simeon's sons. Genealogy of Shimei. After Gen **46** 10; Ex **6** 15; Nu **26** 12–14.
(*b*) Dwelling-places of Simeon. After Josh **19** 2–8.
(*c*) Princes and conquests (vs 34–43).

Source unknown, but considered old. Gray, however, thinks the names of late formation. Meshobab, Jamlech, Joshah, Amaziah, Joel, Jehu, Josibiah, Seraiah, Asiel, Elioenai, Jaakobah, Jeshohaiah, Asaiah, Adiel, Jesimiel, Benaiah, Ziza, Shiphi, Allon, Jedaiah, Shimri, Shemaiah, Ishi, Pelatiah, Neariah, Rephaiah, Uzziel; many undoubtedly old ones; 11 in *yāh*, 5 in *'ēl*. Elioenai sounds post-exilic. The section mentions several exploits of Simeon.

(4) *East-Jordanic tribes* (**5** 1–24).

As in Simeon above, the usual order, deviated from in instances, is (1) Introductory: Sons and immediate descendants; (2) Territory; (3) Princes or Chiefs; (4) Incidents.

(*a*) Reuben (vs 1–10).

Partly follows Gen, Nu; but only as to first generation. Very fragmentary and connections obscure.

(*b*) Gad (vs 11–17).

First generation omitted. Chronicler draws from genealogies "in the days of" Jotham and Jeroboam.

(*c*) Half-Manasseh (vs 23.24).

The whole tribe is treated of (**7** 14 ff). Here only the seats and heads of houses.

(5) *Levi* (**6** 1–81).

Illustrates more fully the Chronicler's attitude and methods.

(*a*) High priests from Levi to Jehozadak (the Exile) (vs 1–15).

(α) Levi's sons: Gershon, Kohath, Merari (Gen **46** 11; Ex **6** 16).

(β) Kohath's sons: Amram, Izhar, Hebron, Uzziel (Ex **6** 18).

(γ) Amram's "sons": Aaron, Moses, Miriam (Ex **6** 20.23 [except Miriam]; Nu **26** 59 f).

(δ) High priests from Eleazar. Also (partly) Ezra (**7** 1–5):

1. Eleazar	12. Azariah
2. Phinehas	13. Johanan
3. Abishua	14. Azariah
4. Bukki	15. Amariah
5. Uzzi	16. Ahitub
6. Zerahiah	17. Zadok
7. Meraioth	18. Shallum
8. Amariah	19. Hilkiah
9. Ahitub	20. Azariah
10. Zadok	21. Seraiah
11. Ahimaaz	22. Jehozadak

Noteworthy omissions: Eli's house, Eli, Phinehas, Ahitub, Ahimelech, Abiathar, because set aside for Zadok's in Solomon's time; Bukki to Zadok being their contemporaries; but the list also omits Amariah in the reign of Jehoshaphat (perhaps), Jehoiada, Joash's "power behind the throne," Urijah in Ahaz' day, Azariah in Hezekiah's. It has been thought that this was done in the interests of a chronological scheme of the Chronicler, making 23 generations of 40 years from the Exodus to the Captivity, or 920 years. The Heb generation, however, was as likely to be 30 as 40 years, and as a matter of fact was nearer 20. The apparent number of generations from Aaron to the Captivity, adding the data from the historical books, is 29, making a generation about 24 years. The reasons for the omission here, as for many others, are not apparent. Outside of Ch and Ezr we know nothing of Abishua, Bukki, Uzzi, Zerahiah, Meraioth, the first Amaziah, Johanan, Amariah, Ahitub, Zadok 2, Shallum, Azariah 3. The list touches historical notices in Aaron, Eleazar, Phinehas, Zadok, Ahimaaz, Azariah 2, contemporary of Solomon, perhaps Amariah, contemporary of Jehoshaphat, Azariah, contemporary of Uzziah, Hilkiah, contemporary of Joshua, Seraiah slain by the Chaldaeans, and Jehozadak. The recurrence of similar names in close succession is characteristically Jewish (but compare names of popes and kings). It is seen in the list beginning with Jehozadak: Jeshua, Joiakim, Eliashib, Joiada, Jonathan, Jaddua, Onias, Simon, Eleazar, Manasseh, Onias, Simon, Onias, Joshua. Also about Christ's time: Eleazar, Jesus, Annas, Ismael, Eleazar, Simon, Joseph, Jonathan, Theophilus, Simon, although these latter do not succeed in a genealogical line.

(*b*) The three Levitical clans (vs 16–19). After Ex **6** 17–19; Nu **3** 17–20.

(*c*) Lineal descendants of Gershom: seven, vs 20.21; thirteen, vs 39–43. See also 1 Ch **23** 7.

The two lists (vs 20.21 and vs 39–43) are clearly the same:

Gershom	Gershom
Libni	Jahath
Zimmah	Zimmah
Joah	Ethan
Iddo	Adaiah
Zerah	Zerah
Jeatherai	Ethni
	Malchiah
	Baaseiah
	Michael
	Shimea
	Berachiah
	Asaph

Jahath, Zimmah, Zerah are in both. By slight changes Joah, יואה, is Ethan, איתן; Iddo, עדו, is עדיה, Adaiah; Jeatherai, יאתרי, is Ethni, אתני. Shimei may have dropped from one and Libni from the other. Jahath and Shimei have been transposed. In 1 Ch **23** 7 Libni is Ladan.

(*d*) Pedigrees of Samuel (vs 27.28; 33–35). See also 1 S **1** 1; **8** 2.

We have three pedigrees of Samuel, all suffering in transcription:

(1) 1 Ch 6:22–24.28	(2) 1 Ch 6:33–38	(3) 1 S 1:1; 8:2
Kohath	Kohath	
Amminadab	Izhar	
Korah	Korah	
Assir, Elkanah, Ebiasaph	Ebiasaph	
Assir	Assir	
Tahath	Tahath	
Uriel	Zephaniah	
Uzziah	Azariah	
Shaul	Joel	
Elkanah	Elkanah	
Amasai	Amasai	
Ahimoth	Mahath	
Elkanah	Elkanah	
Zophai	Zuph	Zuph
Nahath	Toah	Tohu
Eliab	Eliel	Elihu
Jeroham	Jeroham	Jeroham
Elkanah	Elkanah	Elkanah
Samuel	Samuel	Samuel
Joel (Vashni) and Abijah	Joel	Joel
	Heman	

The text is obscure. LXX reads (ver 26), "Elkanah his [Ahimoth's] son, Zophai his son." It has Izhar in (1) for Amminadab, as has Heb in Ex **6** 18.21. Uriel for Zephaniah is unexplainable. Uzziah and Azariah are exchangeable. The other variations are transcriptional. Joel has dropped out of the first list, and the following words, now in 1 S **8** 2, and the Syr here: "and the second," *v-sh-n*, have been read "Vashni." 1 S **1** 1 calls Zuph an Ephraimite. The Chronicler's claiming him (and Samuel) seems to some another instance of Levitical bias and acquisitiveness. The genealogy is also found "clearly artificial," Zuph being a territory, and Toah, Tohu, Nahath, a family. But "Ephraimite" is either merely local, the family having been assigned residence there (Josh **21** 5; 1 Ch **6** 66), or (Hengstenberg, Ewald) because, being thus assigned, it has been incorporated into the tribe. Hannah's vow to devote him to Jeh is said (Curtis, Moore, *ICC* in loc.) to show that he was no Levite, in which case no vow was necessary. But Elkanah's Ephraimitish citizenship may have obscured in Hannah's mind the Levitical descent. In the disorganized times of the Judges an Ephraimitish woman may well have been ignorant of, or indifferent to, the Levitical regulation. She, or the author of 1 S **1** 1, must also have forgotten that every male that openeth the womb from any tribe is equally God's property. A mother's vow to devote her first-born son to Jeh, beyond recall or redemption, and to seal his consecration by the significant symbol of the unshorn head, is not hard to imagine in either a Levite or an Ephraimite, and equally "unnecessary" in either case. Heman, ending the pedigree (2), was David's contemporary.

(*e*) Pedigree of Asaiah the Merarite (1 Ch **6** 29.30).

Merari: Mahli: Libni; Shimei: Uzzah: Shimea: Haggiah: Asaiah. Hard to adjust or place. Libni and Shimei are elsewhere Gershonites, but the same name is frequently found in different tribes or clans. Information below Mahli is entirely wanting.

(*f*) Descent of David's three singers, Heman, Asaph, Ethan (vs 33–47).

(α) Heman has been given under (*d*); 20 links.

(β) Asaph: Gershom: Jahath: Shimei: Zimmah: Ethan: Adaiah: Zerah: Ethni (Jeatherai): Malchijah: Baaseiah: Michael: Shimea: Berechiah: Asaph; 15 links.

(γ) Ethan: Merari: Mushi: Mahli: Shemer: Bani: Amzi: Hilkiah: Amaziah: Hashabiah: Malluch: Abdi: Kishi: Ethan; 12 links.

Hardly anywhere is the Chronicler's good faith more questioned than in these lists. Finding in his day the three guilds of singers claiming descent from David's three, and through these from Levi, he fits them out with pedigrees, borrowing names from vs 16–20, and filling out with his favorite names, or those of his own invention, or from current lists. To make Asaph contemporary with David, he adds Malchijah, Maaseiah, Michael, Shimei, Berechiah. He helps out Ethan with Bani, Amzi, Hilkiah, Amaziah, Hashabiah, Malluch, Abdi, Kishi. The names added are very frequent in Ch and Ezr, not frequent in older writings. Aside from the general objection to this thoroughgoing discredit of Ch, and the theory of religious development in Israel on which it is based, it may be said: (1) The Chronicler's failure to give his three families nearly the same number of links is suspicious, but if he took an old list, as it came to him, it is natural. (2) The fact that these added names occur many more times in Ch, Ezr, Neh indicates simply that Levitical names occur frequently in a writer and among a people whose interests are Levitical. No one would look among the Roundheads for either classical or aristocratic names. (3) In no tribe would such names be more likely to recur, naturally or purposely, than in the Levitical. (4) The Chronicler has inserted among his new names 6 in *yāh* and only 1 in *'ēl*, and that far down the list. (5) Of the "added" names Malchijah occurs in Jer **21** 1; Masseiah, in **29** 21.25; **35** 4, in every case priestly or Levitical. Michael occurs in Nu **13** 13. Berechiah is the name of the prophet Zechariah's father. Hilkiah is the name of Joshua's high priest. Amaziah reigned 800 BC. Bani is mentioned in 2 S **23** 36 (though this is thought to be copied from Ch). Shimea is concededly early. Of the 13 "added names" 8 are found elsewhere. Of the others, Amzi, Abdi, Kishi (Kish, Kushaiah) have an early look. Malluch might be late. If Hashabiah is late the author has scattered it well through the history, 1 several generations before David, 3 in David's time, 1 in Josiah's, 1 in Ezra's, 3 in Nehemiah's, in every case a Levite. (7) While these "added" names occur more times in Ch, Ezr, Neh, than elsewhere, and 5 of the 13 occur nowhere else, it is also true that more than 500 other names also occur only in these three books, and that the total names in these, to say nothing of the "P" portions elsewhere, outnumber the names in the other books about three to one. Other things being equal, three mentions of any common name ought to be found in these books to one in the others. Of all names applied to more than four persons the usual proportion in these books by count is four, to one elsewhere.

(*g*) Pedigree of Ahimaaz (vs 50–53).

Parallel with **6** 4–8.

(*h*) Dwelling-places of Levi.

(6) *The six remaining tribes.*

(*a*) Issachar (**7** 1–5).

Ver 1 derived from Gen **46** 13; Nu **26** 23.24. The rest peculiar to Ch. Closes with a record of fighting men, instead of the usual statement of dwelling-places.

(*b*) Benjamin (**7** 6–13).

A very difficult section. It is considered a Zebulunite genealogy which has been Benjaminized, because (1) there is a Benjamite list elsewhere; (2) Benjamin is out of place here, while in 13 out of 17 tribal lists Zebulun comes at this point, and in this list has no other place; (3) the numbers of Benjamin's sons differ from other Benjamite genealogies; (4) the names of Bela's and Becher's sons are different here; (5) many names are not Benjamite; (6) Tarshish, in this list, is a sea-coast name appropriate to Zebulun, but not Benjamin. But (1) it is called Benjamite; (2) doublets are not unknown in Ch; (3) Dan is also neglected; (4) many Benjamite names are found; (5) both the Zebulunite material and the Benjamite material elsewhere is too scanty for safe conclusions.

(*c*) Dan, ver 12, from Gen **46** 23.

Aher ("another") is a copyist's error or substitute for Dan.

(*d*) Naphtali, ver 13, from Gen **46** 24 (transcriptional changes).

(*e*) Manasseh, E. and W. (vs 14–19).

The text of vs 14.15 very corrupt. No other notice is found of the sons in vs 16.17: Peresh, Sheresh, Ulam, Rakem, Bedan.

(*f*) Ephraim to Joshua (vs 20–29).

Contains an interesting personal note in the mourning of Ephraim over his sons Ezer and Elead, and the subsequent birth of Beriah. Interpreted to mean that the clans Ezer and Elead met with disaster, on which the clan Beriah became prominent.

(*g*) The seats of Joseph's sons (vs 28.29).

Hard to say why this has been placed here.

(*h*) Asher (vs 30–40).

The earliest names derived from Gen **46** 17. Gray considers the others ancient.

(*i*) Benjamin (**8** 1–40).

(*α*) Sons of Benjamin. After Gen **46** 21, with variations. See (6) (*b*).

(*β*) Descendants of Ehud (vs 6–28). Text very corrupt, obscure.

(*γ*) The house of Saul (vs 29–38); repeated (**9** 35–44).

In this passage two exceptions to the usual treatment of Baal compounds. Ishbaal and Meribbaal here are Ishbosheth and Mephibosheth in S.

(7) *The inhabitants of Jerusalem* (**9** 1–34).

With variations in Neh **11** 1–13. This passage has been thought an interpolation, but it is the Chronicler's custom to give dwelling-places. Perhaps this and Neh are two independent abridgments of the same document. This probably describes post-exilic conditions. Vs 1 and 2 here, and Neh **11** seem conclusive on this point. Four classes of returning exiles:

(*a*) The children of Judah, Benjamin, Ephraim, Manasseh.

Constituting "the laity," "Israel."

(*b*) The priests.

Agreeing with Neh, but abridged.

(*c*) The Levites. Paralleling Neh, but not exactly.

(*d*) Nethinim or porters. Fuller than Neh, and different.

(8) *The house of Saul* (**9** 35–44, repeating **8** 29–38).

(**22**) *David's knights* (1 Ch **11** 10–47).

Discussed under (19). Adds to the list, Adina, s. of Shiza, Reubenite; Hanan, s. of Maacah, Joshaphat the Mithnite, Uzziah the Ashterathite, Shama and Jeiel the sons of Hotham the Aroerite, Jediael the son of Shimri, and Joah his brother, the Tizite, Eliel the Mahavite, and Jeribai and Joshaviah, the sons of Elnaam, and Ithmah the Moabite, Eliel, and Obed, and Jaasieh the Mezobaite.

(**23**) *David's recruits at Ziklag* (1 Ch **12**–**22**).

Found only here. Contains 23 names from Benjamin (some may be Judahite); 11 from Gad; 8 from Manasseh; nothing to show that the names are not old.

(**24**) *David's musicians and porters at the bringing of the ark* (1 Ch **15** 16–24).

Also **16** 5.6.37–43. Each division of the Levites represented by a chief musician.

(**25**) *David's organization of the kingdom* (1 Ch **23**–**27**).

I. *The Levites* (ch **23**).

(1) The family of Gershon (vs 7–11); 9 houses.

(2) The family of Kohath (vs 12–20); 11 houses.

(3) The family of Merari (vs 21–23); 4 houses.

II. *The priests* (ch **24**).

24 divisions; 16 divided among descendants of Eleazar, headed by Zadok; 8 among those of Ithamar, headed by Ahimelech (perhaps an error for Abiathar); but perhaps Ahimelech's. Abiathar, s. of Ahimelech, was acting for his father.

(1) Eleazar's courses: Jehoiarib, Harim, Malchijah, Hakkoz, Joshua, Eliashib, Huppah, Bilgah, Hezer, Aphses, Pethahiah, Jehezekel, Jachin, Gamul, Delaiah, Maaziah.

(2) Ithamar: Jedaiah, Seorim, Mijamin, Abijah, Shecaniah, Jachim, Joshebeab, Immer.

Jos gives the same names of courses (*Ant*, VII, xiv, 7; *Vita*, 1). Several are mentioned in Apoc, Talm, and the NT. Jehoiarib, Jedaiah, Harim, Malchijah, Mijamin, Abijah, Shecaniah, Bilgah, Maaziah, are found in one or both of Nehemiah's lists.

(3) Supplementary list of Levites (1 Ch **24** 20–31).

Repeats the Levitical families in 1 Ch **23** 6–23, omitting the Gershonites, adding to the Kohathites and Merarites.

III. *The singers* (1 Ch **25**).

(1) Their families, classified under the three great groups, descendants of Asaph, Jeduthun (Ethan), Heman.

A curious problem is suggested by the fact that the names in ver 4, beginning with Hanani, with a few very slight changes, read: "Hanan ('Have mercy') -iah ('O Jehovah'); Hanani ('Have mercy'); Eli-athah ('Thou art my God'); Giddalti ('I have magnified') (and) Romamti ('exalted') (thy) Ezer ('help'); Josh-bekashah ('In the seat of hardness'); Mallothi ('I spake of it'); Hothir ('Gave still'); Mahazioth ('Visions')." How, or why, this came among these names, cannot be said.

(2) The 24 courses of 12 singers each, of which courses nos. 1, 3, 5, 7 fell to Asaph; nos. 2, 4, 8, 10, 12, 14 fell to Jeduthun; nos. 6, 9, 11, 13, 15–24 fell to Heman.

IV. *Gatekeepers and other officers* (1 Ch **26**).

(1) Genealogies and stations of the gatekeepers (vs 1–19).

(2) Those in charge of the temple treasury (vs 20–28).

(3) Those in charge of the "outward business."

Subordinate magistrates, tax-collectors, etc.

V. *The army, and David's officers* (1 Ch **27**).

(1) The army (vs 1–15).

12 officers, each commanding 24,000 men, and in charge for one month; chosen from David's knights.

(2) The tribal princes (vs 16–24).

After the fashion of Nu **1** 2–15. Gad and Asher are omitted. The 12 are made up by including the Levites and the Aaronites.

(3) The king's twelve stewards (vs 25–31).

(4) The king's court officers (vs 32–34).

Counselor and scribe: Jonathan, the king's uncle, otherwise unknown; tutor: Jehiel; counselor: Ahithophel; "the king's friend" (closest confidant?): Hushai. Possibly two priests are next included: Jehoiada the son of Benaiah, and Abiathar, high priest of the Ithamar branch. But perhaps it should read, "Benaiah, the son of Jehoiada." If two priests are intended, it seems strange that Zadok is not one. The list ends with the commander-in-chief, Joab.

This elaborate organization in every part and branch of the kingdom is looked upon as the Chronicler's glowing Utopian dream of what must have been, underrating the organizing power of the great soldier and statesman.

(**26**) Ezr **2** 1–63. *The exiles who returned with Zerubbabel.*

Paralleled in Neh **7** 6–73. 9 "Jah," 4 "El" names in 107.

(1) *The leaders* (ver 2).

(2) *Numbers, according to families* (vs 3–19).

18 of Ezra's numbers differ from Nehemiah's.

(3) *Numbers according to localities* (vs 20–35).

10 towns probably Judahite, 7 Benjamite.

(4) *The priests* (vs 39.42).

Only 4 families, representing 3 Davidic courses.

(5) *The Levites* (vs 43.44).

Among the singers, only Asaphites.

(6) *The porters* (ver 45).

3 old names, 3 new ones.

(7) *The "Nethinim"* (temple-slaves) (vs 46–56).

(8) *The children of Solomon's servants* (slaves) (vs 57–59).

(9) *Those who could not prove their descent.*

(*a*) General population.

Three families, children of Delaiah, Tobiah, Nekoda.

(*b*) Priestly families.

Hobaiah, Hakkoz, Barzillai. Hakkoz, the seventh of the Davidic courses, perhaps succeeded later in establishing their right (Neh **3** 21).

(**27**) Ezr **6** 1–5. *Ezra's genealogy.*

An ascending genealogy: Ezra, s. of Seraiah, s. of Azariah, s. of Hilkiah, s. of Shallum, s. of Zadok, s. of Ahitub, s. of Amaraiah, s. of Azariah, s. of Meraioth, s. of Zerahiah, s. of Uzzi, s. of Bukki, s. of Abishua, s. of Phinehas, s. of Eleazar, s. of Aaron; 16 links. Follows 1 Ch **6** 7–10 down to Zadok, then omits 7 to Shallum, besides the 7 omitted in Ch.

(**28**) Ezr **8** 1–20. *Numbers and leaders of those who returned with Zerubbabel.*

Numbers much smaller than in Zerubbabel's list (Ezr **2** 1–14). Perhaps 3 new families, Shecaniah, Shelomith, Joah; 7 more leaders. A much smaller proportion of Levites; among them a "man of discretion," perhaps a name, "Ishsecel," of the sons of Mahli, therefore a Merarite, with other Merarites, 39 in all.

(**29**) Ezr **10** 18–44. *Jews who had married foreign women.*

(1) *The priests* (vs 18–22).

17 in all; members of the high priest's family, and of the Davidic courses of Immer and Harim, besides the family of Pashhur.

(2) *The Levites* (ver 23); 6 in all.

(3) *Singers and porters* (ver 24); 4 in all.

(4) *"Israel," "the laity"* (vs 25–43).

16 families represented; 86 persons. Out of a total of 163 names, 39 *yāh* compounds, 19 *'ēl* compounds, 8 prefixed.

(**30**) Neh **3** 1–12. *The leaders in the repair of the wall.*

38 leaders; in 30 instances the father's name also given. As far as mentioned, all from Judah and Jerus.

(**31**) Neh **7** 7–63. *Those who returned with Zerubbabel.*

Follows Ezr **2** 1–63, with transcriptional variations in names and numbers.

(**32**) Neh **8** 4–7. *Levites and others who assisted Ezra in proclaiming the law.*

(**33**) Neh **10** 1–27. *The sealers of the Covenant.*

22 priests, 17 Levites, 20 heads of families already mentioned, 24 individuals.

(**34**) Neh **11** 3–36. *Chief dwellers in Jerusalem and vicinity.*

Parallels in 1 Ch **9** 9–22. Some omissions and variations; 5 priestly courses given, Joiarib, course no. 1; Jedaiah, no. 2; Jachin, no. 23; Malchijah, no. 5; Immer, no. 6. 24 "Jah," 6 "El" names out of 82.

(**35**) Neh **12** 1–8. *Priests and Levites who went up with Zerubbabel.*

Compare with priests' lists in Neh **10** 2–8 (33), and with priests under Joiakim (Neh **12** 12–21 [36]). They are names of families. See Neh **12** 12.

(**36**) Neh **12** 10.11. *High priests from Jeshua to Jaddua.*

(1) Jeshua, 538 to 520 BC.

(2) Joiakim.

(3) Eliashib, 446 till after 433.

(4) Joiada, about 420.

(5) Jonathan, Johanan, 405 to 362.

(6) Jaddua, to 323.

This list bears upon the date of Ezr-Neh. Jaddua was high priest when Alexander visited Jerus, 335 BC. If the Darius of ver 22 is Darius Nothus (425 to 405 BC), and Jaddua, a young boy, is mentioned as the heir to the high-priesthood, this passage was written before 400. If Jaddua's actual high-priesthood is meant, and Darius Codomannus (336 to 330 BC) is the Darius here, the date may be about 330. The enumeration of families here is assigned to the time of Joiakim, before 405, and the latest recorded events to the time of the high priest before Jaddua (Neh **12** 23; **13** 28), hence before 362. The hypothesis of an addition by some scribe after 350 is possible, but not necessary.

(**37**) Neh **12** 12–21. *Heads of priestly families.*

(**38**) Neh **12** 22–26. *Levites and porters under high priest Johanan.*

(**39**) Neh **12** 31–42. *Princes and priests at dedication of the wall.*

(**40**) Mt **1** 1–17. *The genealogy of Jesus Christ* (see separate article).

(**41**) Lk **3** 23–38. *The genealogy of Jesus* (see separate article).

Literature.—Comm. in loc., esp. on Gen, Ex, Nu, Ch, Ezr-Neh, esp. C. F. Keil, *Bible Comm.*, 1872; E. Bertheau, in *Kurzgef. exeget. Handb. zum AT*, 1873; *Bible* ("Speaker's") *Comm.* (Browne, Gen; Clark, Ex; Espin, Nu; Rawlinson, Ch, etc); W. B. Barnes, *Cambridge Bible*, Ch; R. Kittel, *Die Bücher der Ch;* Driver, *Westminster Comm.*, Gen; *ICC* (Gray, Nu; Moore, Jgs; Curtis, Ch, etc); *Pulpit Comm.;* W. R. Harvey-Jellie, Ch in *Century Bible;* S. Oettli, *Kgf. Kom.*, 1889; O. Zoeckler, *Lange's Comm.*, etc.

Encyclopaedia arts., esp. *HDB*, E. L. Curtis, "Genealogies"; *SBD*, A. C. Hervey, "Genealogies"; *EB*, S. A. Cook, "Genealogies"; *EB*, 11th ed, S. A. Cook, "Genealogies"; other encyclopaedia arts., under specific books, tribes, names, genealogies.

General works: Gray, *Studies in Heb Proper Names;* Hommel, *The Ancient Heb Tradition;* A. C. Hervey, *The Genealogies of Our Lord;* Sprenger, *Das Leben u. d. Lehre d. Mohammad;* W. R. Smith, *Kinship and Marriage in Early Arabia;* J. Wellhausen, *De Gentibus et Familiis Judaeis;* J. Wellhausen, *Prolegomena*, 1883 (ET), 177–277; McLennan, *Studies in Anc. Hist.*

Magazine arts.: H. W. Hogg, "Genealogy of Benjamin," *JQR*, XI, 1899, 96–133, 329–44; M. Berlin, "Notes on Genealogies of Levi, 1 Ch **23–26**," *JQR*, XII, 1900, 291–98; M. Berlin, "Gershonite and Merarite Genealogies," *JQR*, XII, 1901, 291 ff; H. W. Hogg, "Ephraimite Genealogy," *JQR*, XIII, 1900–1901, 147–54; J. Marquart, "Genealogies of Benjamin," *JQR*, XIV, 1902, 343–51; J. W. Rothstein, *Die Genealogie des Königs Jojachin und seiner Nachkommen in geschichtlicher Beleuchtung*, Berlin: Reuther u. Reichold, 1902; R. S Macalister, "The Royal Potters, 1 Ch **4** 23," *Expos T*, XVI, 1905, 379 ff; R. S. Macalister, "The Craftsmen Guild of the Tribe of Judah," *PEFS*, 1905, 243–53, 328–42; C. C. Torrey, "The Gr VSS of Ch, Ezr, and Neh," *Proceedings of the Society of Bib. Archaeology*, XXV 1903, 139 ff, and many others.

Philip Wendell Crannell

GENEALOGY OF JESUS CHRIST, THE:

I. Introduction.—The genealogy of Jesus as contained in the First and Third Gospels presents three special problems which lie somewhat apart from general questions of NT criticism: (1) the construction and purpose of each list taken separately; (2) the relation of the two lists, in their coincidences and variations, to each other; (3) the relationship of both lists to the statement concerning the virgin birth of Our Lord with which they are directly connected. These questions necessarily involve the conclusion to be arrived at concerning the trustworthiness of the list of names as forming an actual historical connection between Jesus and His ancestors according to the flesh.

1. The Problems Involved

Before these problems are dealt with, it would be well to consider the kind and degree of importance to be attached to the question at issue. As we see it, the only vital point at stake is the balance, sanity and good judgment of the evangelists.

2. The Nature and Importance of the Issue

(1) That Jesus had a line of ancestors by His human birth may be taken for granted. The tradition, universal from the earliest times among believers and granted even by the bitterest opponents, that He was connected with the line of David, may also readily be accepted. The exact line through which that connection is traced is, on general principles, of secondary importance. The fact is that, while natural sonship to David on the part of the Messiah was of vital importance to many Jewish inquirers, it failed of any very enthusiastic endorsement on the part of Jesus Himself (see the truly remarkable interview recorded in Mk **12** 35–37). The expressions of Paul in this connection will be referred to later; at this point it is sufficient to say that physical kinship to David cannot be insisted upon as the only justification for his words.

(2) If, then, the purpose of the evangelists in having recourse to these lists is worth while, the question of their correctness need not even be raised. Unless some vital issue is involved, the supposition of a special inspiration to go behind lists currently accepted is gratuitous. No such issue seems to be presented here. The Davidic kinship of Jesus, in any sense essential to His Messiahship, is independent of the lists which are used to justify it. This is preliminary to the actual discussion and need not prevent us from giving all due credit to lists which could not have been carelessly compiled nor lightly used.

II. The Genealogies Separately.—(1) The construction and incorporation of Joseph's genealogical tree is, in the light of all the facts, the primary consideration.

1. Peculiarities of Mt's Genealogy

(2) The artificial division into three groups of fourteen generations each. The apparent defect in this arrangement as it actually stands (the third group lacks one member) is probably traceable to a defect of the LXX version of 1 Ch **3** 11, which is reproduced in the Gr gospel (see Zahn, *Intro to the NT*, ET, 564, n. 4). This arrangement into groups is the more striking because it makes 14 generations from the captivity to Joseph, where Lk makes 20 or 21, and because the first group of 14 is formed by the omission of three names. It is perfectly clear, therefore, that this artificial grouping is essential to the purpose of the evangelist.

(3) The insertion of the names of brothers, thus following the historical lists and broadening the genealogy by including collateral lines.

(4) The insertion of the names of women—a practice not only foreign but abhorrent to ordinary usage. This peculiarity is the more marked when we notice that these names introduce what would be considered serious blots in the family history of the Davidic house (see vs 5.7).

(5) The principle upon which the division into periods is constructed: (*a*) from Abraham to David, (*b*) from David to the Captivity, (*c*) from the Captivity to Jesus. Attention has repeatedly been called to the fact that this gives a definite *historical* movement to the genealogy. It involves the origin, the rise to power, the decay and downfall of the house of David (see Allen, *ICC*, "Matthew," 2; cf Zahn, *NT*, ET, I, 535).

Of the many theories which have been constructed to explain the foregoing six peculiarities of the genealogy of Mt, altogether the most satisfactory is that of Professor Zahn. His contention is that the list was framed not to prove the *natural* connection of Jesus with the house of David—a fact which no one doubted—but to defend the one vital point where attack had been made, namely, the *legitimacy* of Jesus' connection with David. No one seems to have questioned that Jesus was born of Mary and was closely connected with the royal house. The question was whether He was of legitimate birth. It was charged—and the slander which was very early in origin and circumstantial in character obtained an extraordinary hold upon the hostile Jewish mind—that Jesus was the illegitimate offspring of Mary. The Gospel of Mt meets that slander by giving a bird's-eye view of the movement of the history from Abraham to the Messiah in the form of a genealogy of Joseph, who in the light of all the facts concerning the origin of Jesus marries Mary and gives her the protection

2. Explanation of the Foregoing

of his stainless name and royal lineage. The extraordinary boldness and brilliancy of this apologetic method ought not to be overlooked. The formal charge that Jesus is son of Mary, not of Joseph, is admitted—the slander involved is refuted by bringing Joseph forward as a witness for Mary. Nothing could have been more natural for a man fearless in the confidence of truth; nothing could have been more impossible for one insecure in his hold upon the facts. So far as the genealogy is concerned, just the moment we realize that the purpose is not to prove the natural sonship of Jesus to David, but to epitomize the history, all hesitancy and apprehension concerning the historicity of the successive names disappear. The continuity of blood relationship through these successive generations becomes of no essential importance. Zahn's explanation (the argument in full should be read by every student), simple in itself, explains all the facts, as a key fits a complicated lock. It explains the choice of a genealogy as a method of epitomizing history and that genealogy Joseph's, the artificial grouping at the expense of changing the traditional lists, the inclusion of the names of brothers and of women.

3. Peculiarities of Lk's Genealogy

(1) The choice of Joseph's genealogical tree on the part of one who is so deeply interested in Mary.

(2) The reversal of order in going back from Joseph to his ancestors. Godet emphasizes the fact that, in the nature of the case, a genealogy follows the order of succession, each new individual being added to the roll of his family. Luke's method indicates that his genealogy has been constructed for a special purpose.

(3) The carrying of the line back of the history of the covenant, which begins with Abraham, to Adam, who represents the race in general. This fact, together with another, that the line of Joseph is traced to David through Nathan who was not David's heir, proves that Luke was not concerned with establishing the Davidic standing of Jesus.

(4) The placing of the genealogy, not at the beginning of the Gospel, but at the beginning of the ministry, between the baptism and the temptation.

(5) The omission of the article before the name of Joseph.

4. Explanation of the Foregoing

(1) In his comment upon the fourth peculiarity enumerated above, namely, the placing of the genealogy at the beginning of the ministry, Godet (*Gospel of St. Luke*, Am. ed, 126) has this to say: "In crossing the threshold of this new era, the sacred historian casts a general glance over the period which thus reaches its close, and sums it up in this document, which might be called the mortuary register of the earlier humanity." In other words, in connecting the genealogy directly with the ministry, Luke exhibits the fact that his interest in it is historical rather than antiquarian or, so to say, genealogical. As Matthew summarizes the history of the covenant people from the days of Abraham by means of the genealogical register, modified so as to make it graphic by its uniformity, so Luke has written the story of the humanity Jesus, as the Second Adam, came to save, by the register of names summarizing its entire course in the world.

It has recently been commented upon that genealogical lists such as those of Gen and the NT are not infrequently used to convey ideas not strictly germane to the matter of descent or the cognate notion of chronology. For example, the statements as to the longevity of the patriarchs are of historical interest only—they are not and could never have been of value for chronological purposes (see Warfield, "Antiquity and Unity of Human Race," *Princeton Review*, February, 1911).

(2) In commenting upon the order which Luke adopts, Godet (who has thrown more light upon this portion of the Gospel than anyone else) says: "The ascending form of genealogy can only be that of a private instrument, drawn up from the public document with a view to the particular individual whose name serves as the starting-point of the whole list" (127).

(3) From the fact that the name of Joseph is introduced without an article Godet draws three conclusions: (*a*) that this name belongs rather to the sentence introduced by Lk; (*b*) that the genealogical document which he consulted began with the name of Heli; (*c*) and consequently, that this piece was not originally the genealogy of Jesus or of Joseph, but of Heli (ib, 128).

(4) (*a*) The importance of these considerations is twofold. In the first place it indicates that Luke is bringing together two separate documents, one of which contained a statement of the foster-fatherhood of Joseph, while the other contained the genealogy of Heli, between whom and Joseph there existed a relationship which made Luke desirous of connecting them. (*b*) In addition, the absence of the article serves to call attention to something exceptional in the relationship of Joseph to the rest of this ancestral line which is brought into connection with his name. To this point we shall recur later. We have an explanation for all the suggested problems except one, and that one, in a sense, the most difficult of all, namely, the choice of Joseph's genealogy.

III. The Genealogies Compared.—In order, however, to discuss this question intelligently, we must enter upon the second stage of our inquiry—as to the relationship between the two lists.

1. Divergences

(1) The most notable fact here is of course the wideness of the divergence together with the contrasted and unintelligible fact of minute correspondence. Between Abraham and David the two lists agree. Between David and Joseph there is evident correspondence in two (see Mt **1** 12; Lk **3** 27), and possible correspondence in four names (that is, if Abiud [Mt **1** 13] and Judah [Lk **3** 30] are the same). This initial and greatest difficulty is of material assistance to us because it makes one conclusion certain beyond peradventure. The two lists are not divergent attempts to perform the same task. Whatever difficulties may remain, this difficulty is eliminated at the outset. It is impossible that among a people given to genealogies two lists purporting to give the ancestry of a man in the same line could diverge so widely. There is, therefore, a difference between these lists which includes the purpose for which they were compiled and the meaning which they were intended to convey.

2. Correspondence

(2) Two of the most striking points in the lists as they stand may be brought into connection and made to explain each other. The two lists coincide in the names of Zerubbabel and Shealtiel—they differ as to the name of Joseph's father, who is Jacob according to Mt and Heli according to Lk. As to the second of these two important items this much is clear. Either these two lists are in violent contradiction, or else Joseph was in some sense son of both Jacob and Heli. Now, in connection with this seeming impossibility, turn to the other item. The names of Shealtiel and Zerubbabel belong to the captivity. Their being common to both lists is easily explained by the fact that during that troubled period a number of collateral family branches might be narrowed down to one or two common representatives (see Zahn, op. cit., 535). In the NT genealogies Zerubbabel is the son of Shealtiel—according to 1 Ch **3** 19 he is the *nephew*

of Shealtiel and the son of Pedaiah. He is, therefore, at one and the same time heir and, legally, son of two men and would appear as such on two collateral lists.

Shealtiel himself appears in Mt (**1** 12) as the son of Jechoniah and in Lk (**3** 27) as the son of Neri. In 1 Ch **3** 17 he appears as son of Jechoniah. The name of Neri is peculiar to Lk, so that we cannot check his use of it and discover the actual parentage of Shealtiel. His appearance in two lists with a double reference of parentage is not surprising in view of what we have already seen. Besides this, a reasonable explanation at once appears. In Jer **36** 30 it is asserted that Jehoiakim should have "none to sit upon the throne of David," and of his son (Jehoiachin, Jechoniah, Coniah) it is said (Jer **22** 30), "Write ye this man childless," etc. It has been rightly pointed out (see *HDB*, II, 557) that this means simply legal proscription, not actual childlessness. It suggests, however, that it might be thought necessary to provide in the genealogy an heir not of their blood for the two disgraced and proscribed members of the royal house. In view of these facts the contradictory references as to Joseph's parentage present no difficulty.

Joseph may easily have been and undoubtedly was, legally, son and heir of both Jacob and Heli. Godet's objection to this is based upon the supposition that Heli and Jacob were brothers, which leaves the divergence beyond these two names unexplained. It is evident, however, that the kinship between Jacob and Heli might have been more distant than this supposition calls for.

(3) When we come to explain how it happened that Joseph was connected with both these lines and that Mt chose one list and Lk the other we are necessarily shut up to conjecture. There is one supposition, however, which is worthy of very careful consideration because it solves so many and such difficult problems. The authorities have been divided as to whether Lk's genealogy is Joseph's, as appears, or Mary's. Godet makes a strong showing for the latter, and, after all has been said per contra, some of his representations remain unshaken (cf Godet and Plummer sub loc.). Most of the difficulties are removed at one stroke, and the known facts harmonized, by the simple supposition that Lk has given us the meeting-point of the lineage both of Joseph and Mary who are akin. This explains the apparent choice of Joseph's list; the peculiar position of his name in that list; the reversal of the order; the coincidences and discrepancies with reference to Mt's; the early tradition of Mary's Davidic origin; the strange reference in the Talm (*Ḥăghīghā'* **77** 4) to Mary as the daughter of Heli; the visit of Mary with Joseph to Bethlehem at the time of the registration; the traditional discrepancy of ages between Joseph and Mary, such that (apparently) Joseph disappears from the scene before Jesus reaches maturity. Against this nothing of real weight can be urged (the kinship with Elisabeth is not such: see Edersheim, *LTJM*, I, 149) except that it is too simple and too felicitous. Its simplicity and felicitous adjustment to the whole complex situation is precisely its recommendation. And there we may let the matter rest.

IV. The Genealogies and the Virgin Birth.—We have now to deal with the relationship of the genealogies to the virgin-birth statement which forms the vital center of the infancy narratives and to the general question of the Davidic origin of Jesus. See VIRGIN BIRTH.

The first part of this question may be most directly approached by a brief consideration of the text of Mt **1** 16. The text upon which RV is based reads: "And Jacob begat Joseph the husband of Mary, of whom was born Jesus, who is called Christ." Beside this there are two readings, one contained in the so-called Ferrar group of MSS, and the other in the Sinaitic which, differing among themselves, unite in ascribing the parentage of Jesus to Joseph. This has been seized upon by negative critics (see for list and discussion Machen, *Princeton Review*, January, 1906, 63; cf Bacon, *HDB*, art. "Genealogy of Jesus Christ," *Am. Jour. Theol.*, January, 1911, who long ago gave in his advocacy to the supposition that the evangelists could easily reconcile the supernatural birth with the actual paternity of Joseph) to support the idea of a primitive Christian tradition that Joseph was the father of Jesus. Of this contention Zahn leaves nothing, and concludes his argument with this statement: "The hope of finding indications in old MSS and VSS that the authors of lost Gospels or brief writings which may have been worked over in our Mt and Lk regarded Joseph as the physical father of Jesus, should at last be dismissed. An author who knew how to make even the dry material of a genealogy to its least detail contribute to the purpose of his thought concerning the slandered miracle of the Messiah's birth, cannot at the same time have taken over statements from a genealogy of Joseph or Jesus used by him which directly contradicted his conception of this fact. Any text of Mt which contained such statements would be condemned in advance as one altered against the author's interest" (op. cit., 567). It is interesting to note that Allen (*ICC*, "Matthew," 8), starting from the extreme position that the Sinaitic form of statement, of all extant texts, most nearly represents the original, reaches the same conclusion as Zahn, that Matthew's Gospel from the beginning taught the virgin birth.

1. Text of Mt 1:16

(1) It is clear, therefore, from the general trend as well as from specific statements of both Gospels, that the genealogies and the birth-narratives were not floating traditions which accidentally touched and coalesced in mid-stream, but that they were intended to weld inseparably the two beliefs that Jesus was miraculously conceived and that He was the heir of David. This could be done only on the basis of Joseph's genealogy, for whatever the lineage of Mary, Joseph was the head of the family, and the Davidic connection of Jesus could only be established by acknowledgment of Him as legal son by Joseph. Upon this basis rests the common belief of the apostolic age (see Zahn, ib, 567, note references), and in accordance with it all statements (such as those of Paul, Rom **1** 3; 2 Tim **2** 8) must be interpreted.

2. General Conclusions

(2) For it must be remembered that, back of the problem of reconciling the virgin birth and the Davidic origin of Jesus, lay the far deeper problem—to harmonize the incarnation and the Davidic origin. This problem had been presented in shadow and intimation by Jesus Himself in the question: "David himself calleth him Lord; and whence is he his Son?" It is further to be noticed that in the annunciation (Lk **1** 32) the promised One is called at once Son of God and Son of David, and that He is the Son of God by virtue of His conception by the Spirit—leaving it evident that He is Son of David by virtue of His birth of Mary. With this should be compared the statement of Paul (Rom **1** 3.4): He who was God's Son was "born of the seed of David according to the flesh, and declared to be the Son of God with power, according to the spirit of holiness, by the resurrection from the dead." This is at least most suggestive (see Orr, *Virgin Birth of Christ*, 119, with note, p. 121), for it indicates that as Paul and Luke were in very close sympathy as to the person of Our Lord, so they are in equally close sympathy as to the mystery of His origin. The unanimity of conviction on the part of the early church as to the Davidic origin of Jesus is closely paralleled by its equally firm conviction as to His supernatural derivation. The meeting-

point of these two beliefs and the resolution of the mystery of their relationship is in the genealogies in which two widely diverging lines of human ancestry, representing the whole process of history, converge at the point where the new creation from heaven is introduced.

Literature.—The lit. on this subject is very copious. The works referred to in the text will serve to introduce the reader to more extensive investigations. The whole situation is well summarized by Plummer (*ICC*, "Luke," sub loc.).

Louis Matthews Sweet

GENERAL, jen'ẽr-al, **GENERALLY,** jen'ẽr-al-i (כֻּלָּה, *kullāh;* πανήγυρις, *panēguris*):

(1) **General** is the tr of *sar,* "master," "head," "chief"; used once in AV in the sense of commander-in-chief, "the general of the king's army" (1 Ch **27** 34), usually in this connection trd "captain," RV "the captain of the king's host."

(2) As an adj. "general assembly" is the tr of *panēguris* (whence we have *panegyric*), "an assembly or convocation of the whole people to celebrate any public festival or solemnity, as the public games or sacrifices, hence a high festival, public convocation, joyful assembly" (Robinson); the word occurs in the NT only in He **12** 23, "to the general assembly and church of the firstborn"; *panēguris* is LXX for *mō'ēdh* (Ezk **46** 11; Hos **2** 11), "solemn assembly," and for *'ăçārāh* (Am **5** 21), with the same meaning. The Gr words trd "and to an innumerable company of angels, to the general assembly and church of the firstborn" (AV) have been variously arranged and trd; Robinson gives "and to countless throngs [even] the joyful assembly of angels, i.e. as hymning the praises of God around His throne"; cf Rev **5** 11 f; Ps **148** 2; Dnl **7** 10). From both Heb and Gr analogies, this is probably correct; similarly, Alford, Delitzsch and others have "festival assembly"; Weymouth trd "to countless hosts of angels, to the great festal gathering and church of the first-born."

(3) **Generally,** advb., occurs in Jer **48** 38 AV as the tr of *kullāh* (Pual of *kālāh*), "the whole of it," "There shall be lamentation generally [universally] upon all the housetops of Moab," RV "every where"; in 2 S **17** 11, *'āşaph,* "to be gathered," is trd "to be generally gathered," RV "gathered together."

In Apoc we have "general" in the sense of "common," "universal" (Ad Est **15** 10 m, *koinós;* 2 Macc **3** 18, *pándēmon*); "in general" (2 Esd **8** 15, "man in general"; Ecclus **18** 1, "all things in general," *koinos,* RV "in common").

W. L. Walker

GENERATION, jen-ẽr-ā'shun (Lat *generatio,* from *genero,* "beget"):

(1) The tr (*a*) of דּוֹר, *dōr,* "circle," "generation," hence "age," "period," "cycle": "many generations" (Dt **32** 7); (*b*) the people of any particular period or those born about the same time: "Righteous before me in this generation" (Gen **7** 1); "four generations" (Job **42** 16); (*c*) the people of a particular class or sort, with some implied reference to hereditary quality; the wicked (Dt **32** 5; Prov **30** 11); the righteous (Ps **14** 5; **112** 2).

(2) תּוֹלְדוֹת, *tōledhōth,* "births," hence (*a*) an account of a man and his descendants: "The book of the generations of Adam" (Gen **5** 1); (*b*) successive families: "The families of the sons of Noah, after their generations" (Gen **10** 32); (*c*) genealogical divisions: "The children of Reuben . . . . their generations, by their families" (Nu **1** 20); (*d*) **fig.,** of the origin and early history of created things: "The generations of the heavens and of the earth" (Gen **2** 4).

(3) γενεά, *geneá,* "a begetting," "birth," "nativity," therefore (*a*) the successive members of a genealogy: "All the generations from Abraham unto David" (Mt **1** 17); (*b*) a race, or class, distinguished by common characteristics, always (in the NT) bad: "Faithless and perverse generation" (Mt **17** 17); (*c*) the people of a period: "This generation shall not pass away" (Lk **21** 32); (*d*) an age (the average lifetime, 33 years): "Hid for [Gr "from the"] ages and [from the] generations" (Col **1** 26). The term is also by a **figurative** transference of thought applied to duration in eternity: "Unto all generations for ever and ever" (Eph **3** 21) (Gr "all the generations of the age of the ages").

(4) γένεσις, *génesis,* "source," "origin": "The book of the generation of Jesus Christ" (Mt **1** 1; ARVm "The genealogy of Jesus Christ").

(5) γέννημα, *génnēma,* "offspring," "progeny"; **figurative:** "O generation of vipers" (Lk **3** 7 AV).

(6) γένος, *génos,* "stock," "race," in this case spiritual: "But ye are a chosen generation" (1 Pet **2** 9; ARV "an elect race").

Philip Wendell Crannell

GENESIS, jen'e-sis:

I. General Data
- 1. The Name
- 2. Survey of Contents
- 3. Connection with Succeeding Books

II. Composition of Genesis in General
- 1. Unity of the Biblical Text
  - (1) The *Tōledhōth*
  - (2) Further Indication of Unity
- 2. Rejection of the Documentary Theory
  - (1) In General
    - (*a*) Statement of Theory
    - (*b*) Reasons Assigned for Divisions
    - (*c*) Examination of the Documentary Theory
      - (α) Style and Peculiarities of Language
      - (β) Alleged Connection of Matter
      - (γ) The Biblico-Theological Data
      - (δ) Duplicates
      - (ε) Manner in Which the Sources Are Worked Together
      - (ζ) Criticism Carried to Extremes
  - (2) In View of the Names for God
    - (*a*) Error of Hypothesis in Principle
    - (*b*) False Basis of Hypothesis
    - (*c*) Improbability That Distinction of Divine Names Is without Significance
    - (*d*) Real Purpose in Use of Names for God
      - (α) Decreasing Use of Jehovah
      - (β) Reference to Approach of Man to God, and Departure from Him
      - (γ) Other Reasons
      - (δ) Systematic Use in History of Abraham
    - (*e*) Scantiness of the Materials for Proof
    - (*f*) Self-Disintegration of the Critical Position
    - (*g*) Different Uses in the LXX

III. Structure of the Individual Pericopes
- 1. The Structure of the Prooemium (Gen **1—2** 3)
- 2. Structure of the 10 *Tōledhōth*
  - (1) The Unity of the Biblical Text
  - (2) Rejection of the Division into Sources Under Abraham, Discussion of So-called Duplicates

IV. The Historical Character
- 1. History of the Patriarchs (Gen **12–50**)
  - (1) Unfounded Attacks on the History
    - (*a*) From General Dogmatic Principles
    - (*b*) From Distance of Time
    - (*c*) From Biblical Data
    - (*d*) From Comparison with Religion of Arabia
  - (2) Unsatisfactory Attempts at Explaining the Patriarchal Age
    - (*a*) Explanation Based on High Places
    - (*b*) The Dating Back of Later Events to Earlier Times
    - (*c*) The Patriarchs as *heroes eponymi*
    - (*d*) Different Explanations Combined
  - (3) Positive Reasons for the Historical Character of Genesis
    - Individuality of Patriarchs, etc
- 2. The Primitive History of Gen **1–11**
  - (1) Prominence of the Religious Element
  - (2) Carefulness as Regards Divergent Results of Scientific Research
  - (3) Frequent Confirmation of the Bible by Science
  - (4) Superiority of the Bible over Heathen Mythologies
    - Babylonian and Biblical Stories

V. Origin and Authorship of Genesis
- 1. Connection with Mosaic Times
- 2. Examination of Counter-Arguments

(1) Possibility of Later Additions
(2) "Prophecy after the Event" Idea
(3) Special Passages Alleged to Indicate Later Date
Examination of These

VI. SIGNIFICANCE
1. Lays Foundation for the Whole of Revelation—Creation, Fall, Man in Image of God, Sin, etc
2. Preparation for Redemption—Promises and Covenants

LITERATURE

I. General Data.—The first book of Moses is named by the Jews from the first word, viz. בְּרֵאשִׁית, *b^erē'shīth*, i.e. "in the beginning" (cf the Βρησιθ of Origen). In the LXX it is called Γένεσις, *Génesis*, because it recounts the beginnings of the world and of mankind. This name has passed over into the Vulg (*Liber Genesis*). As a matter of fact the name is based only on the beginning of the book.

1. The Name

The book reports to us the story of the creation of the world and of the first human beings (ch **1**); of paradise and the fall (chs **2** f); of mankind down to the Deluge (chs **4** f; cf ch **4,** Cain and Abel); of the Deluge itself (chs **6–9**); of mankind down to the age of the Patriarchs (**10** 1—**11** 26; cf **11** 1 ff, the building of the tower of Babel); of Abraham and his house (**11** 27—**25** 18); of Isaac and his house (**25** 19—**37** 2); of Jacob and of Joseph (**37** 2—**50** 26). In other words, the Book of Gen treats of the history of the kingdom of God on earth from the time of the creation of the world down to the beginning of Israel's sojourn in Egypt and to the death of Joseph; and it treats of these subjects in such a way that it narrates in the 1st part (**1** 1—**11** 26) the history of mankind; and in the 2d part (**11** 27—**50** 26) the history of families; and this latter part is at the same time the beginning of the history of the chosen people, which history itself begins with Ex **1**. Though the introduction, chs **1–11**, with its universal character, includes all mankind in the promise given at the beginning of the history of Abraham (**12** 1–3), it is from the outset distinctly declared that God, even if He did originally set apart one man and his family (Gen **12–50**), and after that a single nation (Ex **1** ff), nevertheless intends that this particularistic development of the plan of salvation is eventually to include all mankind. The manner in which salvation is developed historically is particularistic, but its purposes are universal.

2. General Survey of Contents

By the statements just made it has already been indicated in what close connection Gen stands with the subsequent books of the sacred Scriptures. The history of the chosen people, which begins with Ex **1** ff, at the very outset and with a clear purpose, refers back to the history as found in Gen (cf Ex **1** 1–6.8 with Gen **46** 27; **50** 24 ff; and see EXODUS, I, 3), although hundreds of years had elasped between these events; which years are ignored, because they were in their details of no importance for the religious history of the people of God. But to Abraham in Gen **12** 1–3 the promise had been given, not only that he was to be the father of a mighty nation that would recognize him as their founder, and the earliest history of which is reported in Ex and the following books of the Pent, but also that the Holy Land had been promised him. In this respect, the Book of Josh, which gives the story of the capture of this land, is also a continuation of the historical development begun in Gen. The blessing of God pronounced over Abraham, however, continued to be efficacious also in the later times among the people who had descended from him. In this way Gen is an introduction to all of the books of the OT that follow it, which in any way have to do with the fate of this people, and originated in its midst as the result of the special relation between God and this people. But in so far as this blessing of God was to extend to all the nations of the earth (**12** 3), the promises given can be entirely fulfilled only in Christ, and can expand only in the work and success of Christian missions and in the blessings that are found within Christianity. Accordingly, this book treats first of beginnings and origins, in which, as in a kernel, the entire development of the kingdom of God down to its consummation is contained (cf VI below).

3. Connection with Succeeding Books

II. The Composition of Genesis in General.—*The tōl^edhōth.*—The fact that Gen is characterized by a far-reaching and uniform scheme has, at least in outline, been already indicated (see I, 2 and 3). This impression is confirmed when we examine matters a little more closely and study the plan and structure of the book. After the grand introitus, which reports the creation of the world (**1** 1—**2** 3) there follows in the form of 10 pericopes the historical unfolding of that which God has created, which pericopes properly in each case bear the name *tōl^edhōth*, or "generations." For this word never signifies creation or generation as an act, but always the history of what has already been created or begotten, the history of generations; so that for this reason, **2** 4*a*, where mention is made of the *tōl^edhōth* of heaven and of earth, cannot possibly be a superscription that has found its way here from **1** 1. It is here, as it is in all cases, the superscription to what follows, and it admirably leads over from the history of creation of the heavens and the earth in ch **1** to the continuation of this subject in the next chapter. The claim of the critics, that the redactor had at this place taken only the superscription from his source P (the priestly narrator, to whom **1—2** 3 is ascribed), but that the section of P to which this superscription originally belonged had been suppressed, is all the more monstrous a supposition as **2** 4*a* throughout suits what follows.

1. Unity of the Biblical Text

(1) Only on the ground of this correct explanation of the term *tōl^edhōth* can the fact be finally and fully explained, that the *tōl^edhōth* of Terah contain also the history of Abraham and of Lot; the *tōl^edhōth* of Isaac contain the history of Jacob and Esau; the *tōl^edhōth* of Jacob contain the history of Joseph and his brethren. The ten *tōl^edhōth* are the following: I, **2** 4—**4** 26, the *tōl^edhōth* of the heavens and the earth; II, **5** 1—**6** 8, the *tōl^edhōth* of Adam; III, **6** 9—**9** 29, the *tōl^edhōth* of Noah; IV, **10** 1—**11** 9, the *tōl^edhōth* of the sons of Noah; V, **11** 10–26, the *tōl^edhōth* of the sons of Shem; VI, **11** 27—**25** 11, the *tōl^edhōth* of Terah; VII, **25** 12–18, the *tōl^edhōth* of Ishmael; VIII, **25** 19—**35** 29, the *tōl^edhōth* of Isaac; IX, **36** 1—**37** 1, the *tōl^edhōth* of Esau (the fact that **36** 9, in addition to the instance in ver 1, contains the word *tōl^edhōth* a second time, is of no importance whatever for our discussion at this stage, as the entire chapter under any circumstances treats in some way of the history of the generations of Esau; see III, **2** 9); X, **37** 2—**50** 26, the *tōl^edhōth* of Jacob. In each instance this superscription covers everything that follows down to the next superscription.

The number 10 is here evidently not an accidental matter. In the arts. EXODUS, LEVITICUS, DAY OF ATONEMENT, also in EZEKIEL, it has been shown what rôle the typical numbers 4, 7, 10 and 12 play in the structure of the whole books and of the individual pericopes. (In the NT we meet with the same phenomenon, particularly in the Apocalypse of St. John; but compare also in Matthew's Gospel the 3×14 generations in **1** 1 ff, the 7 parables in **13** 1 ff, the 7 woes in **23** 13 ff.) In the same way the entire Book of Lev naturally falls into 10 pericopes (cf LEVITICUS, II, 2, 1), and Lev **19** contains 10 groups, each of 4 (possibly also of 5) commandments; cf possibly also **18** 6–18; **20** 9–18; see LEVITICUS, II, 2, 21, VI. Further, the number 10, with a greater or less degree of certainty, can be regarded as the basis for the construction of the pericopes: Ex **1** 8—**7** 7; **7** 8—**13** 16 (10 plagues); **13** 17—**18** 27 (see EXODUS, II, **2** 1–3); the Decalogue (**20** 1 ff); the first Book of the Covenant (**21** 1—**23** 13; **23** 14–19), and the whole pericope **19** 1—**24** 18*a*, as also **32** 1—**35** 3 (see EXODUS, II, **2**, 4, 6). In the Book of Gen itself cf further the 10 members from Shem to Abraham (**11** 11–26), as also the pericopes **25** 19—**35** 29; **37** 2—**50** 26 (see III, **2**, 8, 10 below), and the 10 nations in Gen **15** 19 ff. And just as in the cases cited, in almost every instance, there is to be found a further division into 5×2 or 2×5 (cf, e.g. the two tables of the Decalogue); thus, too, in the Book of Gen in each case, 5 of the 10 pericopes are more closely combined, since I–V (*tōl^edhōth* of Shem inclusive) stand in a more distant, and VI–X (treating of the *tōl^edhōth* of Terah, or the history of Abraham) in a closer connection with the kingdom of God; and in so far, too, as the first series of *tōl^edhōth* bring into the foreground more facts and events, but the second series more individuals and persons. Possibly in this case, we can further unite 2 *tōl^edhōth;* at any rate I+II (the primitive age), III+IV (Noah and his sons), VII+VIII (Ishmael and Isaac), IX+X (Esau and Jacob) can be thus grouped.

(2) *Further indication of unity.*—In addition to the systematic scheme so transparent in the entire Bib. text of the Book of Gen, irrespective of any division into literary sources, it is to be noticed further, that in exactly the same way the history of those generations that were rejected from any connection with the kingdom of God is narrated before the history of those that remained in the kingdom of God and continued its development. Cain's history (**4** 17 ff) in J stands before the history of Seth (**4** 25 f J; **5** 3 ff P); Japheth's and Ham's genealogy (**10** 1 ff P; **10** 8 ff P+J) before that of Shem (**10** 21 ff J+P), although Ham was the youngest of the three sons of Noah (**9** 24); the further history of Lot (**19** 29 ff P+J) and of Ishmael's genealogy (**25** 12 ff P+J) before that of Isaac (**25** 19 ff P+J+E); Esau's descendants (**36** 1 ff R+P) before the *tōl^edhōth* of Jacob (**37** 2 ff P+J+E).

In favor of the unity of the Bib. text we can also mention the fact that the Book of Gen as a whole, irrespective of all sources, and in view of the history that begins with Ex **1** ff, has a unique character, so that e.g. the intimate communion with God, of the kind which is reported in the beginning of this Book of Gen (cf, e.g. **3** 8; **7** 16; **11** 5 J; **17** 1.22; **35** 9.13 P; **18** 1 ff; **32** 31 J), afterward ceases; and that in Ex, on the other hand, many more miracles are reported than in the Book of Gen (see Exodus, III, 2); that Gen contains rather the history of mankind and of families, while Ex contains that of the nation (see I, 2 above); that it is only in Ex that the law is given, while in the history of the period of the patriarchs we find only promises of the Divine grace; that all the different sources ignore the time that elapses between the close of Gen and the beginning of Ex; and further, that nowhere else is found anything like the number of references to the names of persons or things as are contained in Gen (cf, e.g. **2** 23; **3** 20; **4** 1.25, etc, in J; **17** 5.15.17–20, etc, in P; **21** 9.17.31, etc, in E; **21** 6; **27** 36, etc, in J+E; **28** 19, etc, in R; **49** 8.16.19, etc, in the blessing of Jacob); that the changing of the names of Abram and Sarai to Abraham and Sarah from **17** 5.15 goes on through all the sources, while before this it is not found in any source. Finally, we would draw attention to the psychologically finely drawn portraits of Bib. persons in Gen. The fact that the personal pronoun *hū'* and the noun *na'ar* are used of both masc. and fem. genders is characteristic of Gen in common with all the books of the Pent, without any difference in this regard being found in the different documents, which fact, as all those cited by us in number **1** above, militates against the division of this book into different sources. Let us now examine more closely the reason assigned for the division into different sources.

2. Rejection of the Documentary Theory

(1) *In general.*—(*a*) Statement of the theory: OT scholars of the most divergent tendencies are almost unanimous in dividing the Bib. text of Gen into the sources P, J and E, namely Priest Codex, Jahwist, and Elohist. To P are attributed the following greater and connected parts: **1** 1—**2** 4*a;* **5**; a part of the story of the Deluge in chs **6**–**9**; **11** 10 ff; **17**; **23**; **25** 12 ff; **35** 22*b* ff; the most of **36**. As examples of the parts assigned to J we mention **2** 4*b*—**4** 26; the rest of the story of the Deluge in chs **6**–**9**; **11** 1 ff; **12** f; **16**; **18** f, with the exception of a few verses, which are ascribed to P; ch **24** and others. Connected parts belonging to E are claimed to begin with chs **20** and **21** (with the exception of a number of verses which are attributed to P or J or R), and it is thought that, beginning with ch **22**, E is frequently found in the history of Jacob and of Joseph (**25** 19—**50** 26), in part, however, interwoven with J (details will be found under III, in each case under 2). This documentary theory has hitherto been antagonized only by a few individuals, such as Klostermann, Lepsius, Eerdmans, Orr, Wiener, and the author of the present article.

(*b*) Reasons assigned for the customary division into sources: As is well known, the theory of a separation of certain books of the OT into different sources began originally with the Book of Gen. The use made of the two names of God, namely Jehovah and Elohim, caused Astruc to conclude that two principal sources had been used in the composition of the book, although other data were also used in vindication of the theory; and since the days of Ilgen the conviction gained ground that there was a second Elohist (now called E), in contradistinction to the first (now called P, to whom, e.g., Gen **1** is ascribed). This second Elohist, it was claimed, also made use of the name Elohim, as did the first, but in other respects he shows greater similarity to the Jahwist. These sources were eventually traced through the entire Pent and into later books, and for this reason are discussed in detail in the art. Pentateuch. In this article we must confine ourselves to the Book of Gen, and limit the discussion to some leading points. In addition to the names for God (see under 2), it is claimed that certain contradictions and duplicate accounts of the same matters compel us to accept different sources. Among these duplicates are found, e.g., Gen **1** 1—**2** 4*a* P, and **2** 4*b* ff J, containing two stories of creation; Gen **12** 9 ff J; **20** 1 ff E; **26** 1 ff J; with the narrative of how Sarah and Rebekah, the wives of the two patriarchs, were endangered; chs **15** J and **17** P, with a double acccount of how God concluded His covenant with Abraham; **21** 22 ff E and **26** 12 ff J, the stories of Abimelech; chs **16** J and **21** E, the Hagar episodes; **28** 10 ff J+E and **35** 1 ff E+P, the narratives concerning Bethel, and in the history of Joseph the mention made of the Midianites E, and of the Ishmaelites J, who took Joseph to Egypt (**37** 25 ff; **39** 1); the intervention of Reuben E, or Judah J, for Joseph, etc. In addition a peculiar style, as also distinct theological views, is claimed for each of these sources. Thus there is found in P a great deal of statistical and systematic material, as in **5** 1 ff; **11** 10 ff; **25** 12 ff; **36** 6 ff (the genealogies of Adam, Shem, Ishmael, Esau); P is said to show a certain preference for fixed schemes and for repetitions in his narratives. He rejects all sacrifices earlier than the Mosaic period, because according to this source the Lord did not reveal himself as Jeh previous to Ex **6** 1 ff. Again, it is claimed that E describes God as speaking to men from heaven, or through a dream, and through an angel, while according to J Jeh is said to have conversed with mankind personally. In regard to the peculiarities of language used by the different sources, it is impossible in this place to enumerate the different expressions, and we must refer for this subject to the different Introductions to the OT, and to the commentaries and other literature. A few examples are to be found under (*c*) below, in connection with the discussion of the critical hypothesis. Finally, as another reason for the division of Gen into different sources, it is claimed that the different parts of the sources, when taken together, can be united into a smooth and connected story.

The documents, it is said, have in many cases been taken over word for word and have been united and interwoven in an entirely external manner, so that it is still possible to separate them and often to do this even down to parts of a sentence or to the very words.

(c) Examination of the documentary theory: (α) Style and peculiarities of language: It is self-evident that certain expressions will be repeated in historical, in legal, and in other sections similar in content; but this is not enough to prove that there have been different sources. Whenever J brings genealogies or accounts that are no less systematic than those of P (cf **4** 17 ff; **10** 8 ff; **22** 20–24); or accounts and repetitions occur in the story of the Deluge (**7** 2 ff.7 ff; or **7** 4.12.17; **8** 6; or **7** 4; **8** 8.10.12), this is not enough to make the division into sources plausible. In reference to the linguistic peculiarities, it must be noted that the data cited to prove this point seldom agree. Thus, e.g. the vb. *bārā'*, "create," in Gen **1** 1 is used to prove that this was written by P, but the word is found also in **6** 7 in J. The same is the case with the word *r^ekhūsh*, "possession," which in **12** 5; **13** 6; **36** 7 is regarded as characteristic of P, but in **14** 11 f.16.21 is found in an unknown source, and in **15** 14 in J. In **12** 5; **13** 12*a;* **16** 3; **17** 8 it is said that *'ereç k^ena'an*, "land of Canaan," is a proof that this was written by P; but in chs **42, 44** f, **47, 50** we find this expression in J and E, in Nu **32** 32 in J (R); cf also Nu **33** 40 (PR) where Nu **21** 1–3 (JE) is quoted; *shiphḥāh*, "maid servant," is claimed as a characteristic word of J in contrast to E (cf **16** 1 ff); but in **16** 3; **29** 24.29 we find this word not only in P but in **20** 14; **30** 4.7.18; in E *Mīn*, "kind," is counted among the marks of P (cf e.g. **1** 11 ff), but in Dt **14** 13.14.18 we find it in Dt; rather remarkably, too, in the latest find on the Deluge made by Hilprecht and by him ascribed to 2100 BC. Cf on this subject my book, *Wider den Bann der Quellenscheidung*, and Orr, *POT*, ch vii, sec. vi, and ch x, sec. i; perhaps, too, the Concordance of Mandelkern under the different words. Even in the cases when the characteristic peculiarities claimed for the sources are correct, if the problem before us consisted only in the discovery of special words and expressions in the different sources, then by an analogous process, we could dissect and sever almost any modern work of literature. Particularly as far as the pieces are concerned, which are assigned to P, it must be stated that Gen **1** and **23** are, as far as style and language are concerned, different throughout. Gen **1** is entirely unique in the entire OT. Ch **23** has been copied directly from life, which is pictured with exceptional fidelity, and for this reason cannot be claimed for any special source. The fact that the story of the introduction of circumcision in ch **17** in many particulars shows similarities to the terminology of the law is entirely natural. The same is true when the chronological accounts refer one date to another and when they show a certain typical character, as is, e.g., the case also in the chronological parts of any modern history of Israel. On the other hand, the method of P in its narratives, both in matter and in form, becomes similar to that of J and E, just as soon as we have to deal with larger sections; cf **28** 1 ff; **35** 9 ff; **47** 5 ff, and all the more in Ex and Nu.

Against the claim that P had an independent existence, we must mention the fact of the unevenness of the narratives, which, by the side of the fuller accounts in chs **1, 17** and **23,** of the genealogies and the story of the Deluge, would, according to the critics, have reported only a few disrupted notices about the patriarchs; cf for this in the story of Abraham, **11** 27.31 f; **12** 4*b* f; **13** 6*a*.11*b*.12*a;* **16** 1*a*.3.15 f; **19** 29; **21** 1*b*.2*b*–5; **25** 7–11*a;* and in its later parts P would become still more incomprehensible on the assumption of the critics (see III below). No author could have written thus; at any rate he would not have been used by anybody, nor would there have been such care evinced in preserving his writings.

(β) The alleged connection of matter: The claim that the different sources, as they have been separated by critics, constitute a compact and connected whole is absolutely the work of imagination, and is in conflict with the facts in almost every instance. This hypothesis cannot be consistently applied, even in the case of the characteristic examples cited to prove the correctness of the documentary theory, such as the story of the Deluge (see III, **2,** in each case under [2]).

(γ) The biblico-theological data: The different Bib. and theological data, which are said to be characteristic in proof of the separation into sources, are also misleading. Thus God in J communes with mankind only in the beginning (Gen **2** f; **7** 16 ff; **11** 5; **18** f), but not afterward. In the beginning He does this also, according to P, whose conception of God, it is generally claimed, was entirely transcendental (cf **17** 1.22; **35** 9.13). The mediatorship of the Angel of Jeh is found not only in E, (**21** 17, *'Ĕlōhīm*), but also in J (**16** 7.9–11). In **22** 11 in E, the angel of Jeh (not of the *'Ĕlōhīm*) calls from heaven; theophanies in the night or during sleep are found also in J (cf **15** 12 ff; **26** 24; **28** 13–16; **32** 27). In the case of P, the cultus-theory, according to which it is claimed that this source does not mention any sacrifices before Ex **6** 1 ff, is untenable. If it is a fact that the theocracy, as it were, really began only in Ex **6,** then it would be impossible that P would contain anything of the cultus before Ex **6;** but we have in P the introduction of the circumcision in ch **17;** of the Sabbath in **2** 1 ff; and the prohibition against eating blood in **9** 1 ff; and in addition the drink offerings mentioned in **35** 14, which verse stands between vs 13 and 15, and, ascribed to P, is only in the interests of this theory attributed to the redactor. If then the theory here outlined is not tenable as far as P is concerned, it would, on the other hand, be all the more remarkable that in the story of the Deluge the distinction between the clean and the unclean (**7** 2 ff.8) is found in J, as also the savor of the sacrifice, with the term *rē^aḥ ha-nīḥō^aḥ*, which occurs so often in P (cf Gen **8** 21 with Nu **15** 3.7.10.13 f. 24; **18** 17); that the sacrifices are mentioned in **8** 20 ff, and the number 7 in connection with the animals and days in **7** 4; **8** 8.10.12 (cf in P, e.g. Lev **8** 33; **13** 5 f.21.26 f.31.33.50.54; **14** 8 f.38 f; **14** 7.51; **16** 14 f; Nu **28** 11; **29** 8, etc); further, that the emphasis is laid on the 40 days in **7** 4.12.17; **8** 6 (cf in P, Ex **24** 1–8; Lev **12** 2–4; Nu **13** 25; **14** 34), all of which are ascribed, not as we should expect, to the Levitical P, but to the prophetical J. The document P, which, according to a large number of critics, was written during the Exile (see e.g. LEVITICUS, III, 1, or EZEKIEL II, 2) in a most surprising manner, instead of giving prominence to the person of the high priest, would then have declared that kings were to be the greatest blessings to come to the seed of Abraham (**17** 6.16); and while, on the critical assumption, we should have the right to expect the author to favor particularistic tendencies, he, by bringing in the history of all mankind in Gen **1–11,** and in the extension of circumcision to strangers (**17** 12.23), would have displayed a phenomenal universality. The strongest counter-argument against all such minor and incorrect data of a Bib. and a theological character will always be found in the uniform religious and ethical spirit and world of thought that pervade all these sources, as also in the unity in the accounts of the different patriarchs, who are pictured in such a masterly, psychological and consistent manner, and who could never be the result of an accidental working together and interweaving of different and independent sources (see III below).

(δ) Duplicates: In regard to what is to be thought of the different duplicates and contradictions, see below under III, **2,** in each case under (2).

(ε) The manner in which the sources are worked together: But it is also impossible that these sources could have been worked together in the manner in which the critics claim that this was done. The more arbitrarily and carelessly the redactors are thought to have gone to work in many places in removing contradictions, the more incomprehensible it becomes that they at other places report faithfully such contradictions and permit these to stand side by side, or, rather, have placed them thus. And even if they are thought not to have smoothed over the difficulties anywhere, and out of reverence for their sources, not to have omitted or changed any of these reports, we certainly would have a right to think, that even if they would have perchance placed side by side narratives with such enormous contradictions as there are claimed to be, e.g. in the story of the Deluge in P and J, they certainly would not have woven these together. If, notwithstanding, they still did this without harmonizing them, why are we asked to believe that at other places they omitted matters of the greatest importance (see III, **2,** 3)? Further, J and E would have worked their materials together so closely at different places that a separation between the two would be an impossibility, something that is acknowledged as a fact by many OT students; yet, notwithstanding, the contradictions, e.g. in the history of Joseph, have been allowed to stand side by side in consecutive verses, or have even intentionally been placed thus (cf, e.g. **37** 25 ff). Then, too, it is in the nature of things unthinkable that three originally independent sources for the history of Israel should have constituted separate currents down to the period after Moses, and that they could yet be dovetailed, often sentence by sentence, in the manner claimed by the critics. In conclusion, the entire hypothesis suffers shipwreck through those passages which combine the peculiarities of the different sources, as e.g. in **20** 18, which on the one hand constitutes the necessary conclusion to the preceding story from E (cf ver 17), and on the other hand contains the name Jehovah; or in **22** 14 ff, which contains the real purpose of the story of the sacrificing of Isaac from E, but throughout also shows the characteristic marks of J; or in **39** 1, where the so-called private person into whose house Joseph has been brought, according to J, is more exactly described as the chief of the body-guard, as this is done by E, in **40** 2.4. And when the critics in this passage appeal to the help of the redactor, this is evidently only an ill-concealed example of a "begging of the question." In ch **34,** and esp. in ch **14,** we have a considerable number of larger sections that contain the characteristics of two or even all three sources, and which accordingly furnish ample evidence for protesting against the whole documentary theory.

(ζ) Criticism carried to extremes: All the difficulties that have been mentioned grow into enormous proportions when we take into consideration the following facts: To operate with the three sources J, E and P seems to be rather an easy process; but if we accept the principles that underlie this separation into sources, it is an impossibility to limit ourselves to these three sources, as a goodly number of OT scholars would like to do, as Strack, Kittel, Oettli, Dillmann, Driver. The stories of the danger that attended the wives of the Patriarchs, as these are found in Gen **12** 9 ff and in **26** 1 ff, are ascribed to J, and the story as found in Gen **20** 1 ff to E. But evidently two sources are not enough in these cases, seeing that similar stories are always regarded as a proof that there have been different authors. Accordingly, we must claim three authors, unless it should turn out that these three stories have an altogether different signification, in which case they report three actual occurrences and may have been reported by one and the same author. The same use is made of the laughter in connection with the name Isaac in **17** 17; **18** 12; **21** 6, viz. to substantiate the claim for three sources, P and J and E. But since **21** 9 E; **26** 8 J also contain references to this, and as in **21** 6 JE, in addition to the passage cited above, there is also a second reference of this kind, then, in consistency, the critics would be compelled to accept six sources instead of three (Sievers accepts at least 5, Gunkel 4); or all of these references point to one and the same author who took pleasure in repeating such references. As a consequence, in some critical circles scholars have reached the conclusion that there are also such further sources as J^1 and J^2, as also E^1 and E^2 (cf Budde, Baudissin, Cornill, Holzinger, Kautzsch, Kuenen, Sellin). But Sievers has already discovered five subordinate sources of J, six of P, and three of E, making a total of fourteen independent sources that he thinks can yet be separated accurately (not taking into consideration some remnants of J, E and P that can no longer be distinguished from others). Gunkel believes that the narratives in Gen were originally independent and separate stories, which can to a great extent yet be distinguished in their original form. But if J and E and P from this standpoint are no longer authors but are themselves, in fact, reduced to the rank of collectors and editors, then it is absurd to speak any more of distinct linguistic peculiarities, or of certain theological ideas, or of intentional uses made of certain names of God in J and E and P, not to say anything of the connection between these sources, except perhaps in rare cases. Here the foundations of the documentary theory have been undermined by the critics themselves, without Sievers or Gunkel or the other less radical scholars intending to do such a thing. The manner in which these sources are said to have been worked together naturally becomes meaningless in view of such hypotheses. The modern methods of dividing between the sources, if consistently applied, will end in splitting the Bib. text into atoms; and this result, toward which the development of OT criticism is inevitably leading, will some day cause a sane reaction; for through these methods scholars have deprived themselves of the possibility of explaining the blessed influence which these Scriptures, so accidentally compiled according to their view, have achieved through thousands of years. The success of the Bible text, regarded merely from a historical point of view, becomes for the critic a riddle that defies all solutions, even if all dogmatical considerations are ignored.

(2) *Rejection of documentary theory in view of the names for God.*—(*a*) An error of the hypothesis in principle: The names of God, Jehovah and Elohim, constituted for Astruc the starting-point for the division of Gen into different sources (see [1] above). Two chief sources, based on the two names for God, could perhaps as a theory and in themselves be regarded as acceptable. If we add that in Ex **6** 1 ff, in P, we are told that God had not revealed Himself before the days of Moses by the name of Jehovah, but only as "God Almighty," it seems to be the correct thing to separate the text, which

reports concerning the times before Moses and which in parts contains the name Jehovah, into two sources, one with Jehovah and the other with Elohim. But just as soon as we conclude that the use made of the two names of God proves that there were three and not two sources, as is done from Gen **20** on, the conclusive ground for the division falls away. The second Elohist (E), whom Ilgen was the first to propose (see [1] above), in principle and a priori discredits the whole hypothesis. This new source from the very outset covers all the passages that cannot be ascribed to the Jehovah or the Elohist portions; whatever portions contain the name Elohim, as P does, and which nevertheless are prophetical in character after the manner of J, and accordingly cannot be made to fit in either the Jahwistic or the Elohistic source, seek a refuge in this third source. Even before we have done as much as look at the text, we can say that according to this method everything can be proved. And when critics go so far as to divide J and E and P into many subparts, it becomes all the more impossible to make the names for God a basis for this division into sources. Consistently we could perhaps in this case separate a Jehovah source, an Elohim source, a *ha-'Ĕlōhīm* source, an *'Ēl Shadday* source, an *'Ădhōnāy* source, a *Mal'akh Yahweh* source, a *Mal-'akh 'Ĕlōhīm* source, etc, but unfortunately these characteristics of the sources come into conflict in a thousand cases with the others that are claimed to prove that there are different sources in the Book of Gen.

(*b*) The false basis for the hypothesis: But the basis of the whole hypothesis itself, viz. Ex **6** 1 ff P, is falsely regarded as such. If Jehovah had really been unknown before the days of Moses, as Ex **6** 1 ff P is claimed to prove, how could J then, in so important and decisive a point in the history of the religious development of Israel, have told such an entirely different story? Or if, on the other hand, Jehovah was already known before the time of Moses, as we must conclude according to J, how was it possible for P all at once to invent a new view? This is all the more incredible since it is this author and none other who already makes use of the word Jehovah in the composition of the name of the mother of Moses, namely Jochebed (cf Ex **6** 20 and Nu **26** 59). In addition, we do not find at all in Ex **6** 1 ff that God had before this revealed Himself as *'Ĕlōhīm*, but as *'Ēl Shadday*, so that this would be a reason for claiming not an *'Ĕlōhīm* but an *'Ēl Shadday* source for P on the basis of this passage (cf **17** 1; **28** 3; **35** 11; **48** 3 P—**43** 14 E! cf also **49** 25 in the blessing of Jacob). Finally, it is not at all possible to separate Ex **6** 1 ff P from that which immediately precedes, which is taken from JE and employs the name Jehovah; for according to the text of P we do not know who Moses and who Aaron really were, and yet these two are in Ex **6** 1 ff regarded as well-known persons. The new revelation of God in Ex **6** 1 ff (P) by the side of **3** 1 ff (JE and E) is also entirely defensible and rests on a good foundation; for Moses after the failure of Ex **5** needed such a renewed encouragement (see EXODUS II, 2, 1). If this is the case, then the revelation of the name of Jehovah in Ex **6** 1 ff cannot mean that that name had before this not been known at all, but means that it had only been relatively unknown, i.e. that in the fullest and most perfect sense God became known only as Jehovah, while before this He had revealed His character only from certain sides, but esp. as to His Almighty Power.

(*c*) Improbability that the difference in the use of the names for God is without significance: In view of the importance which among oriental nations is assigned to names, it is absolutely unthinkable that the two names Jehovah and Elohim had originally been used without any reference to their different meanings. The almost total omission of the name Jehovah in later times or the substitution of the name Elohim for it in Pss **42**–**83** is doubtless based in part on the reluctance which gradually arose in Israel to use the name at all; but this cannot be shown as probable for older times, in which it is claimed that E was written. In the case of P the rule, according to which the name Elohim is said to have been used for the pre-Mosaic period, and the reason for the omission of Jehovah would have been an entirely different one. Then, too, it would be entirely inexplicable why J should have avoided the use of the name Elohim. The word Elohim is connected with a root that signifies "to fear," and characterizes God from the side of His power, as this is, e.g., seen at once in Gen **1**. Jehovah is splendidly interpreted in Ex **3** 14 ff, and the word is connected with the archaic form *hāwāh* for *hāyāh*, "to be," and the word characterizes God as the being who at all times continues to be the God of the Covenant, and who, according to Gen **2** 4—**3** 24, can manifestly be none other than the Creator of the universe in Gen **1** 1—**2** 3, even if from Gen **12** on He, for the time being, enters into a special relation to Abraham, his family and his people, and by the use of the combined names Jehovah-Elohim is declared to be identical with the God who created the world, as e.g. this is also done in the section Ex **7** 8—**13** 16, where, in the 10 plagues, Jehovah's omnipotent power is revealed (cf EXODUS, II, 2, 2); and in **9** 30 it is charged against Pharaoh and his courtiers, that they did not yet fear Jehovah-Elohim, i.e. the God of the Covenant, who at the same time is the God of the universe (cf also 1 K **18** 21.37.39; Jon **4** 6).

(*d*) Real purpose in the use of the names for God: But now it is further possible to show clearly, in connection with a number of passages, that the different names for God are in Gen selected with a perfect consciousness of the difference in their meanings, and that accordingly the choice of these names does not justify the division of the book into various sources.

(*a*) Decreasing use of name Jehovah: The fact that the *tōlᵉdhōth* of Terah, of Isaac, and of Jacob begin with the name Jehovah but end without this name. In the history of Abraham are to be noted the following passages: **12** 1.4.7.8.17; **13** 4.10.13.14.18; **14** 22; **15** 1.2.8; **16** 2.5–7.9.10.11.13; **17** 1; in the history of Isaac: **25** 21.22.23; **26** 2.12.22.24.25.28.29; and in the *tōlᵉdhōth* of Jacob **38** 7.10; **39** 2.3.5. In these passages the beginnings are regularly made with the name Jehovah, although with decreasing frequency before the name Elohim is used, and notwithstanding that in all these sections certain selections from P and E must also be considered in addition to J. Beginning with Gen **12,** in which the story of the selection of Abraham is narrated, we accordingly find emphasized, at the commencement of the history of each patriarch, this fact that it is Jehovah, the God of the Covenant, who is determining these things. Beginning with Gen **40** and down to about Ex **2** we find the opposite to be the case, although J is strongly represented in this section, and we no longer find the name Jehovah (except in one passage in the blessing of Jacob, which passage has been taken from another source, and hence is of no value for the distinction of the sources J, E and P; this is the remarkable passage Gen **49** 18). In the same way the story of Abraham (**25** 1–11) closes without mention being made of the name of Jehovah, which name is otherwise found in all of these histories, except in ch **23** (see below). The *tōlᵉdhōth* of Isaac, too, use the name Jehovah for the last time in **32** 10;

and from this passage down to **37** 2 the name is not found. It is accordingly clear that in the history of the patriarchs there is a gradual decrease in the number of times in which the name Jehovah occurs, and in each case the decrease is more marked; and this is most noticeable and clearest in the history of Joseph, manifestly in order to make all the more prominent the fact that the revelation of God, beginning with Ex **3** 1 ff, is that of Jehovah. These facts alone make the division of this text into three sources J, E and P impossible.

(β) Selection of the names of God with reference to the approach of man to God and of his departure from God: The fact, further, that the approach of an individual to God or his departure from God could find its expression in the different uses made of the names of God is seen in the following. In connection with Ishmael and Lot the name Jehovah can be used only so long as these men stood in connection with the kingdom of God through their relation to Abraham (cf **16** 7.9.10.11.13 and **13** 10; **19** 13 f.16), but only the name Elohim can be used as soon as they sever this connection (cf **21** 12.17. 19.20 and **19** 29). On the other hand, Elohim is used in the beginning of the history of the Gentile Abimelech (**20** 3.6.11.13.17; **21** 22 f); while afterward, when he has come into closer relations to the patriarchs, the name Jehovah is substituted (**26** 28. 29). A similar progress is found in separate narratives of the patriarchs themselves, since in **22** 1 ff and ch **28** the knowledge of Elohim is changed into that of Jehovah (cf **22** 1.3.9 with **22** 11.14.15.16, and **28** 12 with **28** 13.16).

(γ) Selection of the names for God for other reasons: Elohim can, further, in many cases be explained on the basis of an implied or expressed contrast, generally over against men (cf **22** 8.12; in the second of these two passages the fear of God is placed in contrast to godlessness); **30** 2; **31** 50; **32** 2 f; cf with vs 4 and 8; **32** 29; **35** 5; or on the basis of an accommodation to the standpoint of the person addressed, as in **3** 1–5 (serpent); **20** 3.6. 11.13.17; **23** 6; **39** 9 (Gentiles); or on the basis of grammar, as in **23** 6; **32** 3; **28** 17.22; because the composition with the proper name Jehovah could never express the indefinite article (*a* prince of God, *a* camp of God, *a* Bethel or house of prayer); or finally in consequence of the connection with earlier passages (cf **5** 1 ff with ch **1**; **21** 2.4; **28** 3 ff; **35** 9 ff with ch **17**). A comparison of these passages shows that, of course, different reasons may have induced the author to select the name Elohim, e.g. **23** 6; **28** 12; **32** 12.

(δ) Systematic use of the names of God, particularly in the history of Abraham: That the names for God are systematically used is finally attested by the fact that in the history of Abraham, after the extensive use of the name Jehovah in its beginning (see above under [α]), this name is afterward found combined with a large number of other and different names; so that in each case it is Jehovah of whom all further accounts speak, and yet the name of Jehovah is explained, supplemented and made clear for the consciousness of believers by the new appellations, while the full revelation of His being indeed begins only in Ex **3** and **6** 1 ff, at which place the different rays of His character that appeared in earlier times are combined in one brilliant light. The facts in the case are the following. In the story of Abraham, with which an epoch of fundamental importance in the history of revelation begins, we find Jehovah alone in **12** f. With the exception of ch **23**, where a characteristic appellation of God is not found, and **25** 1–11, where we can claim a decadence in the conception of the Divinity (concerning **23** 6; **25** 11; see above [γ]+[α]), the name of Jehovah is retained in all of these stories, as these have been marked out (III, **2**, 6); but beginning with ch **14** they do not at all use any longer only one name for God. We here cite only those passages where, in each case, for the first time a new name for God is added, viz. **14** 18, *'Ēl 'Elyōn;* **14** 19, Creator of heaven and of earth; **15** 2, *'Ădhōnāy;* **16** 7, the Angel of Jehovah; **16** 13, the God that seeth; **17** 1, *'Ēl Shadday;* **17** 3, *'Ĕlōhīm;* **17** 18, *hā-'Ĕlōhīm;* chs **18** f, special relation to the three men (cf **18** 2 and **19** 1); **18** 25, the Judge of the whole earth; **20** 13, *'Ĕlohim* constructed as a pl.; **21** 17, the Angel of God; **24** 3, the God of heaven and the God of the earth; **24** 12, the God of Abraham.

(*e*) Lack and weakness in the materials needed to prove the case: If we add, finally, that to prove the hypothesis we are limited to the meager materials found in Gen **1** 1—Ex **6** 1 ff; that in this comparatively small number of chapters Gen **40** to Ex **2** cannot be utilized in this discussion (see above under [*d*] [α]); that all those passages, in which J and E are inseparably united must be ignored in this discussion; that all other passages in which J and E are often and rapidly interchanged from the very outset are suspiciously akin to begging the question; that Gen **20** 18, which with its "Jehovah" is ascribed to R, is absolutely needed as the conclusion of the preceding Elohim story; that in **21** 33 with its "Jehovah" in J, on the other hand, the opening Elohim story from E, which is necessary for an explanation of the dwelling of Abraham in the south country, precedes; that the angel of Jehovah (**22** 11) is found in E; that **2** 4—**3** 24 from J has besides Jehovah the name Elohim, and in **3** 1*b*–5 only Elohim (see above); that in **17** 1; **21** 1 P Jehovah is found; that **5** 29, which is ascribed to J, is surrounded by portions of P, and contains the name Jehovah, and would be a torso, but in connection with ch **5** P, in reality is in its proper place, as is the intervening remark (ver 24 P); that, on the other hand, in **4** 25; **6** 2.4; **7** 9; **9** 27; **39** 9 Elohim is found—in view of all these facts it is impossible to see how a greater confusion than this could result from the hypothesis of a division of the sources on the basis of the use made of the names of God. And then, too, it is from the very outset an impossibility, that in the Book of Gen alone such an arbitrary selection of the names for God should have been made and nowhere else.

(*f*) Self-disintegration of the critical position: The modern critics, leaving out of consideration entirely their further dissection of the text, themselves destroy the foundation upon which this hypothesis was originally constructed, when Sievers demands for Gen **1** (from P) an original Jehovah-Elohim in the place of the Elohim now found there; and when others in Gen **18** f J claim an original Elohim; and when in **17** 1—**21** 1 the name Jehovah is said to have been intentionally selected by P.

(*g*) Different uses in the LXX: Naturally it is not possible to discuss all the pertinent passages at this place. Even if, in many cases, it is doubtful what the reasons were for the selection of the names for God, and even if these reasons cannot be determined with our present helps, we must probably, nevertheless, not forget that the LXX in its tr of Gen in 49 passages, according to Eerdman's reckoning, and still more according to Wiener's, departs from the use of the names for God from the Heb original. Accordingly, then, a division of Gen into different sources on the basis of the different names for God cannot be carried out, and the argument from this use, instead of proving the documentary theory, has been utilized against it.

III. The Structure of the Individual Pericopes.—In this division of the article, there is always to be found (under 1) a consideration of the unity of the Bib. text and (under 2) the rejection of the customary division into different sources.

The conviction of the unity of the text of Gen and of the impossibility of dividing it according to different sources is strongly confirmed and strengthened by the examination of the different pericopes. Here, too, we find the division on the basis of the typical numbers 4.7. 10.12. It is true that in certain cases we should be able to divide in a different way; but at times the intention of the author to divide according to these numbers practically compels acceptance on our part, so that it would be almost impossible to ignore this matter without detriment, esp. since we were compelled to accept the same fact in connection with the articles EXODUS (II); LEVITICUS (II, 2); DAY OF ATONEMENT (I, 2, 1), and also EZEKIEL (I, 2, 2). But more important than these numbers, concerning the importance or unimportance of which there could possibly be some controversy, are the fundamental religious and ethical ideas which run through and control the larger pericopes of the *tōl^edhōth* of Terah, Isaac and Jacob in such a way that it is impossible to regard this as merely the work of a redactor, and *we are compelled to consider the book as the product of a single writer.*

1. Structure of the Proœmium

The structure of the proœmium (Gen **1** 1—**2** 3) is generally ascribed to P. Following the introduction (vs 1.2; creation of chaos), we have the creation of the seven days with the Sabbath as a conclusion. The first and the second three days correspond to each other (1st day, the light; 4th day, the lights; 2d day, the air and water by the separation of the waters above and the waters below; 5th day, the animals of the air and of the water; 3d day, the dry land and the vegetation; 6th day, the land animals and man; cf also in this connection that there are two works on each day). We find Ex also divided according to the number seven (see EXODUS, II, 1; cf also Ex **24** 18*b*—**31** 18; see EXODUS, II, 2, 5, where we have also the sevenfold reference to the Sabbath idea in Ex, and that, too, repeatedly at the close of different sections, just as we find this here in Gen); and in Lev cf chs **23**, **25**, **27**; see LEVITICUS, II, 2; the VIII, IX, and appendix; and in Gen **4** 17 ff J; **5** 1-24 P; **6** 9—**9** 29; **36** 1—**37** 1 (see under **2**, 1.2.3.9).

2. Structure of the Ten Tōl^edhōth

The ten *tōl^edhōth* are found in Gen **2** 4—**50** 26.

1. The *tōl^edhōth* of the heavens and the earth (**2** 4—**4** 26):

(1) *The Biblical text.*—(*a*) **2** 4-25, Paradise and the first human beings; (*b*) **3** 1-24, the Fall; (*c*) **4** 1-16, Cain and Abel; (*d*) **4** 17-26, the Cainites, in seven members (see under **1** above) and Seth. The number 4 appears also in **5** 1—**6** 8 (see under 2); **10** 1—**11** 9 (see under 4); and esp. **11** 27—**25** 11 (under 6). Evidently (*a*)+(*b*) and (*c*)+(*d*) are still more closely connected.

(2) *Rejection of the division into sources* (**11**—**2** 4*a* P and **2** 4*b*—**4** 26 J).—Ch **2** does not contain a new account of creation with a different order in the works of creation. This section speaks of animals and plants, not for their own sakes, but only on account of their connection with man. The creation of the woman is only a further development of ch **1**. While formerly the critics divided this section into **2** 4—**4** 26 J, they now cut it up into J[1] and J[2] (see under II, 2, 1 [c] [ζ]), because, they say, the tree of life is mentioned only in **2** 9 and **3** 23, while in **2** 17 and **3** 3 ff the Divine command is restricted to the tree of knowledge of good and evil. But it is impossible to see why there should be a contradiction here, and just as little can we see why the two trees standing in the midst of the garden should not both have had their significance (cf **2** 9; **3** 3). It is further asserted that a division of J is demanded by the fact that the one part of J knows of the Fall (**6** 9 ff), and the other does not know of such a break in the development of mankind (**4** 17 ff). But the civilization attained by the Cainites could certainly have passed over also to the Sethites (see also **6** 2); and through Noah and his sons have been continued after the Deluge. Then, too, the fact that Cain built a city (**4** 17), and the fact that he became a fugitive and a wanderer (**4** 12), are not mutually exclusive; just as the beginnings made with agriculture (**4** 12) are perfectly consistent with the second fact.

2. The *tōl^edhōth* of Adam (**5** 1—**6** 8):

(1) *The Biblical text.*—(*a*) **5** 1-24, seven generations from Adam to Lamech (see under **1**, and Jude ver 14); (*b*) **5** 25-32, four generations from the oldest of men, Methuselah, down to the sons of Noah; (*c*) **6** 1-4, intermingling of the sons of God and the sons of men; (*d*) **6** 5-8, corruption of all mankind. Evidently at this place (*a*)+(*b*) and (*c*)+(*d*) correspond with each other.

(2) *Rejection of the division into sources* (ch **5** P with the exception of ver 29 [see II, 2, 2 (*e*)]; **5** 29; **6** 1-8 J).—**6** 7 J presupposes ch **1** P; as, on the other hand, the fact that the generations that, according to ch **5** P, had in the meanwhile been born, die, presupposes the advent of sin, concerning which only J had reported in ch **3**. In the case of P, however, in **1** 31 it is said that everything was very good.

3. The *tōl^edhōth* of Noah (**6** 9—**9** 29):

(1) *The Biblical text.*—Seven sections (see **1** above) viz: (*a*) **6** 9-22, the building of the ark; (*b*) **7** 1-9, entering the ark; (*c*) **7** 10-24, the increase of the Flood; (*d*) **8** 1-14, the decrease of the Flood; (*e*) **8** 15-19, leaving the ark; (*f*) **8** 22—**9** 17, declaration of a covenant relation between God and Noah; (*g*) **9** 18-29, transfer of the Divine blessing upon Shem.

(2) *Rejection of the division into sources* (**7** 1-5.7-10. 12.16*b*.17.22 f; **8** 2*b*.3*a*.6-12.13*b*.20-22; **9** 20-27 J, the rest from P).—In all the sources are found the ideas that the Deluge was the punishment of God for sin; further, the deliverance of the righteous Noah and his wife and three sons Shem, Ham and Japheth and their wives; the deliverance of the different kinds of animals; the announcement of the covenant relations between God and mankind after the Deluge; the designation of the Deluge with the term *mabbūl* and of the ark with *tēbhāh*. In the Bab account, which without a doubt stands in some connection with the Bib., are found certain measurements of the ark, which in the Bible are only in P, as also the story of the sending out of the birds when the flood was decreasing, and of the sacrifices of those who had been delivered, which in the Bible are said to be found only in J; and these facts are a very powerful argument against the division into sources. Further, P, in case the critics were right, would have contained nothing of the thanks of Noah for his deliverance, although he was a pious man; and in the case of J we should not be informed what kind of an ark it was into which Noah was directed to go (**7** 1 ff); nor how he can already in **8** 20 build an altar, as he has not yet gone out of the ark; and, further, how the determination of Jeh, that He would not again curse the earth but would bless it, can be a comfort to him, since only P has reported concerning the blessing (**9** 1 ff). Even if the distinction is not always clearly made between clean and unclean animals, and different numbers are found in the case of each (**6** 19 f; **7** 14-16 P, over against **7** 2 f in J), yet this is to be regarded merely as a lack of exactness or, perhaps better, rather as a summary method of procedure. The difficulties are not even made any easier through the separation into sources, since in **7** 8 f in J both numbers and the distinction between the two kinds of animals are used indiscriminately. Here, too, in J we find the name Elohim used. The next contradiction that is claimed, namely that the Deluge according to J lasted only 61 days, and is arranged in 40 days (**7** 4.12.17; **8** 6) plus 3×7 =21 days (**8** 8.10.12), while in P it continues for 1 year and 11 days (**7** 11.24; **8** 3-5.14), is really a self-inflicted agony of the critics. The report of the Bible on the subject is perfectly clear. The rain descends for 40 days (**7** 12 J); but as in addition also the fountains of the deep are broken up (**7** 11 P), we find in this fact a reason for believing that they increased still more (**7** 24 P and **7** 17 J). The 40 days in **8** 6 J cannot at all be identified with those mentioned in **7** 17; for if this were the case the raven would have been sent out at a time when the waters had reached their highest stage, and even according to J the Deluge covered the entire world. In general see above, II, 2, 1 (*c*) (γ).

4. The *tōl^edhōth* of the sons of Noah (**10** 1—**11** 9):

(1) *The Biblical text.*—(*a*) **10** 2-5, the Japhethites; (*b*) **10** 6-20, the Hamites; (*c*) **10** 21-32, the Shemites; (*d*) **11** 1-9, the Bab confusion of tongues. Evidently (*a*) to (*c*) is to be regarded as in contrast to (*d*) (cf also **11** 1.9 J in addition to **10** 32 P).

(2) *Rejection of the division into sources* (**10** 1-7.20. 22 f.31 f P, the rest belonging to J).—The distribution of ch **10** between P and J is actually ridiculous, since in this case J does not speak of Japheth at all, and the genealogy of the Hamites would connect directly with P, a phenomenon which must have been repeated in vs 24 ff. The Jewish Midr, in addition, and possibly correctly, counts 70 peoples (cf **46** 27; Ex **1** 5; Nu **11** 16.25; Lk **10** 1).

5. The *tōl^edhōth* of Shem (**11** 10-26): 10 generations (see under II, 1).

6. The *tōl^edhōth* of Terah (**11** 27—**25** 11):

(1) *The Biblical text.*—After the introduction (**11** 27–32), the theme of the history of Abraham is given in **12** 1–4*a* (ver 1, the promise of the holy land; ver 2, promise of many descendants; ver 3, announcement of the double influence of Abraham on the world; ver 4*a*, the obedience of Abraham's faith in his trust upon the Divine promise). In contrast to the first three thoughts which characterize God's relation to Abraham, the fourth is placed, which emphasizes Abraham's relation to God (see under [*d*]). But both thoughts give complete expression to the intimate communion between God and Abraham. On the basis of these representations, which run through the entire story and thus contribute materially to its unification, this section can also be divided, as one of these after the other comes into the foreground. These four parts (**12** 4*b*—**14** 24; **15** 1—**18** 15; **18** 16—**21** 34; **22** 1—**25** 11) can each be divided again into four subdivisions, a scheme of division that is found also in Ex **35** 4—**40** 38; Lev **11–15, 16** (cf Exodus, II, 2, 7; Leviticus, II, 2, 2, III and IV; Day of Atonement, I, 2, 1), and is suggested by Dt **12–26** (cf also my book, *Wider den Bann der Quellenscheidung*, the results of the investigation of which work are there reproduced without entering upon the details of the argument).

(*a*) **12** 4*b*—**14** 24, in which the reference to the promised land is placed in the foreground; see **12** 1, and the passages and statements in parentheses in the following: (α) **12** 4*b*–8, Abraham's journey to Canaan (vs 5 P, 6.7.8 J); (β) **12** 9—**13** 4, descent to Egypt from Canaan, and return (**12** 9.10; **13** 1–4J); (γ) **13** 5–18, separation from Lot (vs 6 P, 7.9 J, 12*a* P, 14 f.17.18 J); (δ) ch **14,** expedition against Chedorlaomer, etc (Abraham is blessed by the priest-king of the country, and receives as homage from the products of the country bread and wine [vs 18 f], while he in return gives tithes [ver 20]). The division of this section (**12** 4*b*—**14** 24) is to be based on the similarity of the closing verses (**12** 8; **13** 4; **13** 18).

(*b*) **15** 1—**18** 15, unfolding of the promise of descendants for Abraham by this announcement that he is to have a son of his own; cf **12** 2 and what is placed in parentheses in the following: (α) ch **15,** Jeh's covenant with Abraham (vs 2.3 JE, 4 J, 5 E, 13.14.16.18 J). The promise is not fulfilled through Eliezer, but only through an actual son (vs 3.4); (β) **16** 1–16, Hagar gives birth to Ishmael as the son of Abraham. Hagar's son, too, namely Ishmael, is not the genuine heir, notwithstanding the connection between **16** 10 and **12** 2 (cf **17** 18–20 P); (γ) ch **17** P, promise of the birth of Isaac given to Abraham (vs 2–17.19.21); (δ) **18** 1–15, Sarah also hears that Isaac is promised (vs 10.12–15).

(*c*) **18** 16—**21** 34, the double influence of Abraham on the world; cf **12** 3 and what is in parentheses in the following: (α) **18** 16—**19** 38, the pericope dealing with Sodom; (i) **18** 16–33, Abraham's petition for the deliverance of Sodom; (ii) **19** 1–11, the sin of the Sodomites, while Lot shows some of the characteristics of Abraham; (iii) **19** 12–28, story of the destruction, in connection with which Lot receives the benefit of his relation to Abraham (vs 16.19.21.22); (iv) Lot ceases to be a part of this history after this destruction; (β) **20** 1–18, Abraham with Abimelech (vs 6.9 E, 18 R, punishment; vs 7.17, intercession); (γ) **21** 1–21, Ishmael ceases to be part of this history (vs 13.18. 20 E); (δ) **21** 22–34, Abraham's agreement with Abimelech (the latter seeks Abraham's friendship and fears his enmity, vs 27.23 E).

(*d*) **22** 1—**25** 11 ff, Abraham's faith at its culminating point; cf **12** 4*a* and what is in parentheses in the following: (α) **22** 1–19, the sacrifice of Isaac (vs 2.12 E, 16.18 R); (β) ch **23,** purchase of the place to bury the dead, which act was the result of his faith in the promised land; (γ) ch **24** is introduced by **22** 20–24, which has no independent character. With the twelve descendants of Nahor cf the twelve sons of Jacob, the twelve of Ishmael (**25** 12 ff; **17** 20), and on the number 12 see Ex **24** 18—**30** 10, under Exodus, II, 2, 5; Lev **1–7** under Leviticus, II, 2, 2, i, and under Ezekiel, I, 2, 2. Ch **24** itself contains the story of how a wife was secured for Isaac from among his relatives (the faith in the success of this plan is transmitted from Abraham to his servant); (δ) **25** 1–11, the sons of the concubine of Abraham (J+R) cease to be a part of this history; transfer of the entire inheritance to the son of promise (J); burial in the ground bought for this purpose (P) (all of these concluding acts stand in close connection with Abraham's faith). In reference to the force of the names of God in connecting Gen **11** 27—**25** 11, see above under II, 2, 2 (*d*).

(2) *Rejection of the division into sources* (**11** 27.31 f; **12** 4*b*.5; **13** 6*a*.11*b*.12*a*; **16** 1*a*.3.15 f; **17; 19** 29; **21** 1*b*. 2*b*–5; **23; 25** 7–11*a* P; **14** from an unknown source; **15** 6; **20** 1–17; **21** 8–32; **22** 1–13.19 E; **15** 1–3; **21** 6 JE; **20** 18; **22** 14–18; **25** 6 R; all else belongs to J).—Through the passages ascribed to P breaks are caused in the text of J in **11** 28 f; **12** 4*a* (Lot); in ch **16,** where the conclusion is lacking; in **18** 1 (the reference of the pronoun); in **24** 67 (Sarah's death); in **25** 1 ff (no mention of Abraham's death). On the other hand P presupposes the text of J in **11** 31 f; **12** 4*b*; **16** 1*b*; **19** 29. In the case of E we need mention only the abrupt break in **20** 1; and, finally, the text of P, leaving out of consideration the larger sections (chs **17** and **23**), is entirely too meager to constitute an independent document.

We will here discuss also the so-called duplicates (see under II, 2, 1, *a*+*c*, δ). The different stories concerning the danger in which the wives of Abraham and Isaac were involved in **12** 9 ff J; **20** 1 ff E; **26** 1 ff J directly presuppose each other. Thus in **20** 13 E Abraham regards it as a fact that such situations are often to be met with, and consequently the possibility of an occurrence of such an event could not have appeared so remarkable to an Oriental as it does to a modern critic; ch **26** 1 suggests the story in **12** 9 ff. The words used here also show that the three stories in question did not originate independently of each other (cf **26** 7; **20** 5; **12** 19—**26** 7; **20** 11; **12** 12—**26** 10; **20** 9; **12** 18—**26** 3; **20** 1; **12** 10 [*gūr*]; see under II, 2, 1, *c*, ζ). The two Ishmael pericopes (chs **16** J+P+**21** E) differ from each other throughout, and, accordingly, are surely not duplicates. The two stories of the conclusion of a covenant in chs **15** J and **17** P are both justified, esp. since in **17** 7 the author speaks of an "establishment" of the covenant which already existed since ch **15.** Ch **17** P+**18** 1 ff J are certainly intended to be pendants, so that it is impossible to ascribe them to different authors; cf the analogous beginning of the theophanies of Jeh in **17** 1 and **18** 1 (even the pronoun referring to Abraham in **18** 1 J, unless taken in connection with ch **17** P, is without any context), also the laughing of Abraham and of Sarah (**17** 17; **18** 12 f; see under II, 2, 1 [*c*] [ζ]), the prominence given to their age (**17** 17; **18** 11 f), and the designation of the time in **17** 11; **18** 10.14.

Nor can we quote in favor of a division into sources the passage **21** 14 f E, on the ground that Ishmael is described here as being so small that he could be laid upon the shoulder of his mother and then be thrown by her under a shrub, while according to the Bib. text he must have been 15 years of age (**16** 16; **21** 5 P). For the original does not say that he was carried on her shoulders; and in Mt **15** 30 it is even said of adults that they were thrown down. On the other hand, also according to E, Ishmael could not have been so small a child, for in **21** 18*b* he is led by the hand, and according to ver 9 he already mocks Isaac, evidently because the latter was the heir of the promise.

Sarah's age, too, according to ch **20** E, does not speak in favor of a division into sources. That she was still a beautiful woman is not claimed here.

Evidently Abimelech was anxious only for a closer connection with the powerful Abraham (cf **21** 23. 27). Then, too, all the sources ascribe an advanced age to Sarah (cf **21** 6 J+E; **18** 12 f J; **17** 17 P).

7. The *tōlᵉdhōth* of Ishmael (**25** 12–18): 12 princes descended from Ishmael (see under 6 [*d*] [γ]).

8. The *tōlᵉdhōth* of Isaac (**25** 19—**35** 29): The correct conception of the fundamental thought can be gained at once in the beginning of this section (**25** 22 f): Jeh's oracle to Rebekah, that the older of the twins, with whom she was pregnant, should serve the younger; also in Rom **9** 10 ff with reference to Mal **1** 2 f; and finally, the constant reference made to Esau in addition to Jacob until the former ceases to be a factor in this history in ch **36**. Accordingly in the end everything is made dependent on the one hand on Jacob's election, notwithstanding his wrongdoings, on the other hand, on Esau's rejection notwithstanding his being the firstborn, or in other words, upon the perfectly free grace of God; and all the different sources alike share in this fundamental thought. But in dividing between the different parts of this section, we must particularly draw attention to this, that in all of these parts both thoughts in some way or other find their expression.

(1) *The Biblical text.*—Containing 10 parts (see under II, 1), namely (*a*) **25** 19–26, the birth of Esau and Jacob; (*b*) **25** 27–34, Esau despises and loses his birthright; (*c*) **26** 1–35, Isaac receives the blessing of Abraham, which afterward is transmitted to Jacob, while Esau, through his marriage with heathen women, prepares the way for his rejection (vs 34 f); (*d*) **27** 1–40, Jacob steals the blessing of the firstborn; (*e*) **27** 41–45, Jacob's flight out of fear of Esau's vengeance; (*f*) **27** 46—**28** 9, Jacob is sent abroad out of fear of his brother's bad example; (*g*) **28** 10—**32** 33, Jacob in a strange land and his fear of Esau, which is overcome in his contest of prayer in Peniel on his return: (α) **28** 10–22, the ladder reaching to heaven in Bethel when he went abroad; (β) **29** 1—**30** 43, twenty years with Laban (see **31** 38); (γ) **31** 1–54, Jacob's departure from Mesopotamia; (δ) **32** 1–33, his return home; (*h*) ch **33**, reconciliation with Esau, who returns to Seir (ver 16; cf **32** 4), while Jacob becomes the owner of property in the Holy Land (vs 19 f); (*i*) **34** 1—**35** 22, Jacob remains in this land, notwithstanding the slaughter made by his sons Simeon and Levi (cf **34** 30; **35** 5); the new appearance of God in Bethel, with a repetition of the story of the changing of Jacob's name, with which the story of Jacob's youth is closed, and which presupposes the episode at Bethel (cf **35** 1.6*b*.9–15 with **28** 10 ff), and which is not in contradiction with the first change in the name of Jacob in ch **32** (cf the twofold naming of Peter in Jn **1** 43 and Mt **16** 18). Esau is yet mentioned in **35** 1.7, where there is a reference made to Jacob's flight before him; (*j*) **35** 23–29, Jacob's 12 sons as the bearers of the promise; while Esau is mentioned only as participating in Isaac's burial, but inwardly he has no longer any part in the history of the kingdom of God, as is seen from ch **36**, and in **32** 4; **33** 16 is already hinted at. In this section, too, evidently there are groups, each of two parts belonging together, namely (*a*)+(*b*) describing the earliest youth; (*c*)+(*d*) in which Isaac plays a prominent part; (*e*)+(*f*) both of which do not exclude but supplement each other in assigning the motives for Jacob's flight; (*g*)+(*h*) Jacob's flight and reconciliation; (*i*)+(*j*) Jacob both according to family and dwelling-place as the recognized heir of the promise.

(2) *Rejection of the division into sources.*—As **25** 29 f. 26*b*; **26** 34 f; **27** 46—**28** 9; **29** 24.29; **31** 18; **35** 6*a*. 9–12.15; **35** 22*b*–29; **36** 6–30.40–43 are ascribed to P, it is clear that these are in part such ridiculously small extracts, that we should be justified in attributing them to a sensible author. The whole sojourn in Mesopotamia is ignored in P, according to the critics, except the brief notices in **29** 24.29; **33** 18. Further, the parts of the rest of the text cannot in many cases be dispensed with; as, e.g. we do not know in **25** 26*b* who was born; nor in **26** 34 f who Esau was; nor in **27** 46 who Jacob was; nor in **29** 24 who Laban was; nor in **29** 24.29 in what connection and for what purposes Leah and Rachel are mentioned. P makes no mention of any promise given to Isaac, which is, however, presupposed in **35** 12 and later in Ex **2** 24. In **28** 1 ff P is most closely connected with J (cf **12** 1–3, the blessing of Abraham, and ch **24**). It is, further, impossible to separate the sources E and J in ch **28** (ladder reaching to heaven); cf **28** 10–12. 17 f.20–22 E, vs 13–16 J, ver 19, and the name of God in ver 21 R, and this proposed division actually becomes absurd in chs **29** f in the story of the birth of Jacob's children, which are said to be divided between the sources J and E.

9. The *tōlᵉdhōth* of Esau (**36** 1—**37** 1): In 7 divisions (see under **1**), namely (*a*) **36** 1–5 R, Esau's family; the different names for Esau's wives, as compared with **26** 34 f; **28** 7–9 P, are doubtless based on the fact that oriental women are apt to change their names when they marry; and the fact that these names are without further remark mentioned by the side of the others is rather an argument against the division into sources than for it; (*b*) **36** 6–8, Esau's change of abode to Seir, which, according to **32** 4; **33** 14.16, already took place before Jacob's return. Only in case that Esau (**35** 29) would have afterward remained for a longer period in Canaan, could we think of a new separation in this connection. It is more probable that at this place all those data which were of importance in connection with this separation are once more given without any reference to their difference in point of time; (*c*) **36** 9–14, Esau as the founder of the Edomites (in ver 9 the word *tōlᵉdhōth* is repeated from ver **1**, while the narrative of the descendants of Esau begins only at this later passage in so far as these were from Seir; cf ver 9 with ver 5, and above, under II, 1); (*d*) **36** 15–19, the leading line of the sons of Esau; (*e*) **36** 20–30, genealogy of the original inhabitants of the country, mentioned because of their connection with Esau (cf ver 25 with ver 2); (*f*) **36** 31–39, the elective kingdoms of Edom; (*g*) **36** 40–43, the Edomites' chief line of descent, arranged according to localities. We have here accordingly geographical accounts, and not historical or genealogical, as in **36** 15 ff. 20 ff (30); cf also vs 40.43, for which reason we find also names of women.

10. The *tōlᵉdhōth* of Jacob (**37** 2—**50** 26):

(1) *The Biblical text.*—The key to the history of Joseph is found in its conclusion, viz. in **50** 14–21, in the confession of Joseph, in the light of his past, namely, that God has ended all things well; and in **50** 22 ff, in his confidence in the fulfilment of the Divine promise in the lives of those God has chosen; cf also Ps **105** 16 ff. According to the two viewpoints in **50** 14–26, and without any reference to the sources, this whole pericope (**37** 2—**50** 15) is divided into two halves, each of five subdivisions, or a total of ten (see under II, 1). In the exact demonstration of this, not only the contents themselves, but also regard for the different names for God will often render good service, which names, with good effect, are found at the close and in harmony with the fundamental thought of the entire section, viz. (*a*) **37** 2—**39** 6*a*, Joseph enters Potiphar's house (4 pieces, see under 6, 1, namely [α] **37** 2–11, the hatred of the brethren, [β] **37** 12–36, selling Joseph, [γ] **38** 1 ff, the Jehovah-displeasing conduct in the house of Judah, cf **38** 7.10, [δ] **39** 1–6, Jeh's pleasure in Joseph, in contrast to [γ]); (*b*) **39** 6*b*–23, Joseph is cast into prison, but Jeh was with him (vs 21.23); (*c*) **40** 1—**41** 52, the exaltation of Joseph, which at the end esp. is shown by the nam-

ing of Ephraim and Manasseh as caused by God, but which for the present passes by the history of his family (4 pieces, viz. [α] **40** 1, interpretation of the dreams of the royal officials, [β] **41** 1–36, interpretation of the two dreams of Pharaoh, [γ] **41** 37–46*a*, the exaltation of Joseph, [δ] **41** 46*b*–52, Joseph's activity for the good of the country); (*d*) **41** 55—**46** 7, Joseph becomes a blessing to his family; cf the promise of God to Jacob in Beersheba to be with him in Egypt in **46** 2 ff with **45** 6–9 (in four pieces, viz. [α] **41** 53–57, the general famine, [β] **42** 1–38, the first journey of the brothers of Joseph, [γ] **43** 14—**4** 34, the second journey [in four subdivisions, (i) **43** 1–14, the departure, (ii) **43** 14–34, the reception by Joseph, (iii) **44** 1–17, final trial of the brethren, (iv) **44** 18–34, the intercession of Judah]; [δ] **45** 1—**46** 7, Joseph makes himself known and persuades Jacob to come to Egypt); (*e*) **46** 8—**47** 26, Joseph continues to be a blessing to his family and to Egypt (in 4 subdivisions, of which the 4th is placed in contrast to the first 3 exactly as this is done in **10** 1—**11** 9 and **11** 27—**25** 11, viz. [α] **46** 8–27, list of the descendants of Jacob, [β] **46** 28–34, meeting with Joseph, [γ] **47** 1–12, Jacob in the presence of Pharaoh, [δ] **47** 13–26, the Egyptians who have sold themselves and their possessions to Pharaoh laud Joseph as the preserver of their lives). From this point on the attention is now drawn to the future: (*f*) **47** 27–31, Jacob causes Joseph to take an oath that he will have him buried in Canaan (cf ver 30 J with ch **23** P); in (*e*)+(*f*) there is also lacking a designation for God; (*g*) ch **48,** Jacob adopts and blesses Ephraim and Manasseh (cf also the emphasis placed on the providential guidance of God in vs 8 f.11.15 f, esp. vs 16 and 20 ff); (*h*) **49** 1–27, Jacob blesses his 12 sons and prophesies their future fate (here, **49** 18, appears the name of Jeh, which had disappeared since ch **40;** see under II, 2, 2 (*d*) (*a*), and other designations for God, vs 24 f); (*i*) **49** 28–33, Jacob's death after he had again expressed the wish, in the presence of all his sons, that he should be buried in Canaan; (*j*) **50** 1–13, the body of Jacob is taken to Canaan. In these 10 pericopes again we can easily find groups of two each, viz. (*a*)+(*b*), Joseph's humiliation (sold, prison); (*c*)+(*d*), Joseph becomes a blessing to Egypt and to his family; (*g*)+(*h*), blessing of the grandchildren and the sons of Jacob; (*i*)+(*j*), Jacob's death and burial; here too the name of God is lacking as in (*e*) and (*f*).

(2) *Rejection of the division into sources.*—Here, too, the separation of P from the rest of the text as a distinct source is untenable, since in the section from **37** 2—**46** 34, after **37** 2, only the following fragments are attributed to this source, viz. **41** 46*a;* **46** 6f (according to some also to ver 27). In the same way P abruptly sets in at **47** 5.27*b;* **49** 28*b*. Further, **48** 3 ff knows nothing of Ephraim or Manasseh, of whom P reports nothing, so that **50** 13 f are the only verses that could naturally connect with the preceding statements of P. In **47** 5 ff P reports entirely in the manner of ordinary narratives, and there is no sign of any systematic arrangement. But the separation between J and E cannot be carried out either. In the first place, when these two sources are actually separated by the critics, innumerable omissions in the story arise, which we cannot at this place catalogue. The contradictions which are claimed to exist here are the products of the critics' imagination. It is claimed that according to J it is Judah who plays a prominent rôle, while according to E it is Reuben; but in **37** 21 Reuben is mentioned by J, and the rôle played by Judah in ch **38** J is anything but creditable. Why cannot both of these brethren have played a prominent rôle, as this was also the case with Simeon (**42** 24.36; **43** 14) and Benjamin (**42** 13.20.32 ff.36.38; **43** 3 ff; **44; 45** 14)? Just as little are the Midianites in **37** 28.36 E and the Ishmaelites of **37** 25.27.28; **39** 1 J mutually exclusive or contradictory, since the Midianites in the Gideon story, too, in Jgs **7** f; **8** 24 are called Ishmaelites (cf in the German the name *Prager* for traveling musicians, whether they are from Prague or not). In J it is further claimed that Joseph's master was a private gentleman (**39** 1 ff), while in E he was the captain of the bodyguard (**40** 3 f). But in this instance the documentary theory can operate only when it calls in the assistance of R in ch **39** 1. The fact that in ch **39** 1 the name of the nationality is added to that of the office, is explained on the ground of the contrast to the Ishmaelites who sold Joseph. Finally, it is claimed to have been caused by the combination of the different sources in such a way that Benjamin in **43** 8.29; **44** 30.31.33 J is described as a boy, but in **46** 21, R or P, as the father of ten children. But evidently the author of ch **46** has in view the number 70 (cf ver 27; see Ex **1** 5; Nu **11** 16.25; Lk **10** 1; Ex **15** 27; Jgs **12** 13; and in Gen **10** above, under 4,2); and for this reason, e.g. in ver 17, he mentions only one granddaughter of Jacob; and for this he mentions all of the descendants of Jacob, even those who were born later in Egypt, but who already, as it were, had come to Egypt in the loins of their fathers, according to the view of the author. It certainly would be remarkable if no more grandchildren had been born to Jacob in Egypt, since Nu **26** does not mention a single son of any of the sons of Jacob later than those reported in Gen **46**. In **46** 27 Joseph's sons, too, who were born in Egypt, are included in the list, entirely in harmony with Dt **10** 22. For such an arrangement and adjustment of a genealogy cf the 3×14 generations in Mt **1**. From this point of view no conclusions, as far as the documentary theory is concerned, can be drawn from the ten sons of Benjamin.

IV. The Historical Character.—(1) *Unfounded attacks upon the historical character.*—(*a*) Proofs from general dogmatic principles: In order to disprove the historical character of the patriarchs, the critics are accustomed to operate largely with general dogmatic principles, such as this, that no nation knows who its original founder was. In answer to this it can be said that the history of Israel is and was from the beginning to the end unique, and cannot be judged by the average principles of historiography. But it is then claimed that Abraham's entire life appears to be only one continuous trial of faith, which was centered on the one promise of the true heir, but that this is in reality a psychological impossibility. Over against this claim we can in reply cite contrary facts from the history of several thousands of years; and that, too, in the experience of those very men who were most prominent in religious development, such as Paul and Luther.

1. History of the Patriarchs: Gen 12–50

(*b*) Argument based on the time that elapsed between these events and their records: Secondly, critics emphasize the long period of time that elapsed between these events themselves and their first records, esp. if these records can be accredited to so late a period as the 9th or the 8th cent. BC. In consequence of this, it is claimed that much of the contents of Gen is myth or fable; and Gunkel even resolves the whole book into a set of unconnected little myths and fables. Over against this claim we can again appeal to the universal feeling in this matter. I do not think that it can be made plausible, that in any race fables and myths came in the course of time more and more to be accepted as actual facts, so that perchance we should now be willing to accept as historical truths the stories of the Nibelungenlied or Red Riding Hood. But this, according to the critics, must have been the case in Israel. Prophets accepted the story of the destruction of the two cities in the Jordan valley, as recorded in Gen **19**, as correct (cf Am **4** 11; Isa **1** 9; **3** 9; Hos **11** 8); also Abraham as a historical person (Isa **29** 22; **41** 8; **51** 1 ff; Mic **7** 20; Jer **33** 26; Ezk **33** 24; and possibly Mal **2** 15); then Isaac (Am **7** 9.16; Jer **33** 26); also Jacob (Hos **12** 3 ff; Am **9** 8; Jer **33** 26); also Joseph (Am **5** 6.15); and these prophets evidently thought that these events and persons were regarded as historical by the people in general. In the NT we can cite, for Abraham, Mt **3** 9; Gal **3; 4** 21 ff; Rom **4** 9 ff; **9** 7 ff; He **7** 1 ff; **11** 8 ff; Jas **2** 21 ff, and esp. the words of Jesus in Mt **8** 11; Lk **16** 22 ff; Jn **8** 52 ff; finally in Mt **22** 31 f, the whole argument for the resurrection of the dead is without a foundation if the patriarchs are not historical personages. Over against this, there was no period in the history of

Israel in which it can be shown that these stories of Gen were regarded only as myths. If these events were actual occurrences, then those things which the patriarchs experienced were so unique that these experiences were not forgotten for a long time. Then, too, we can also refer to the strength of the memory of those nations that were not accustomed to have written records of their history.

(*c*) Proofs from the Bible itself: Finally, the attempt has been made to discover in the Bible itself a pre-Mosaic stage in its ideas of man concerning God, which is claimed to contradict the higher development of Divine ideas in the patriarchs, for which purpose the critics appeal to Ezk **23** 3.8; **20** 7 ff; Josh **24** 14 ff. But at these places it is evident that the idolatry of the people is pictured as apostasy. And when in Ex **6** 2 ff the name of Jeh is as a matter of fact represented as something new, it is nevertheless a fact that in these very passages the revelation given is connected with the history of the patriarchs. The same is true of Ex **3** 1 ff. The whole hypothesis that the religion before the days of Moses was polytheistic has not been derived from the Bible, but is interpreted into it, and ends in doing violence to the facts there recorded (cf my book, *Die Entwicklung der alttestamentlichen Gottesidee in vorexilischer Zeit*).

(*d*) Comparison with the religion of Arabia: The critics further compare the pre-Mosaic religion of Israel with the low grade of religion in Arabia in the 5th cent. after Christ; but in order to do this, they must isolate Israel entirely, since all the surrounding nations at the time of the Am Tab had attained to an altogether different and higher stage of religious development and civilization.

(2) *Unsatisfactory attempts at explaining the patriarchal age.*—(*a*) The explanation based on the "high places": In denying the historical character of the account of the patriarchs in Gen, the critics are forced to contrive some scheme in explanation of the existence of these stories, but in doing this they make some bad breaks. Thus, e.g., they say that the Israelites when they entered Canaan found there the high places of the heathen peoples; and since if they wanted to make use of these in the service of Jeh they must first declare them legitimate places of worship, this was done by inventing the history of the patriarchs, who long before this are said to have already consecrated all these places to the Jeh worship. But how is it possible on this supposition to explain the story of Joseph, which transpired in Egypt? Then, too, the reasons for the origin of the other stories of the patriarchs would be enshrouded in a remarkable mystery and would be of very inferior character. Again, it is nowhere declared in the passages of Gen that here come into consideration that they are reporting the beginnings of a permanent cultus when they give an account of how God appeared to the patriarchs or when they erected altars in His honor. And, finally, while it is indeed true that the cultus localities of the patriarchs are in part identical with those of later times (cf Bethel, Beersheba)—and this is from the outset probable, because certain places, such as hills, trees, water, etc, as it were, of themselves were suitable for purposes of the cultus—yet such an identification of earlier and later localities does not cover all cases. And can we imagine that a prophetical method of writing history would have had any occasion in this manner to declare the worship of calves in Bethel a legitimate service?

(*b*) Explanation based on dating back later events to earlier times: But we are further told that the pre-prophetic condition of affairs in Israel was in general dated back into the primitive period, and this was done in such a way that the character of Abraham was regarded as reproducing ideal Israel, and the character of Jacob the empirical Israel in the past; something that certainly is from the outset an odd speculation of too much learning! If this explanation is correct, what shall we then do with Isaac and Joseph? And why is the whole story of the condition of civilization pictured in Gen so entirely different from that of later times? And is Abraham really a perfect ideal? Is he not rather, notwithstanding his mighty faith, a human being of flesh and blood, who can even doubt (**15** 2 f; **17** 17); who can make use of sinful means to realize the promise (ch **16,** Hagar); who tells a falsehood, although for the best of purposes, viz., to protect his wife (**12** 9 ff), and for this reason must accept the rebuke of the heathen Abimelech (**20** 9 f)? In addition, Abraham is married to his half-sister (**20** 12), which, according to Dt **27** 22; Lev **18** 9. 11; **20** 17, is forbidden with the penalty of death for the transgressor. In the same way Jacob, according to Gen **29** f, has two sisters as wives, which is also declared by Lev **18** 18 to be a crime.

(*c*) The patriarchs as eponymous heroes: In the third place, it is said that the people have in the persons of the patriarchs made for themselves eponymous heroes. But why did they make so many at one time? In addition, Abraham cannot possibly be regarded as such a hero as Jacob or Israel is, and in exceptional cases also Isaac and Joseph (Am **7** 9.16; **5** 6.15). It is not correct to place genealogies like those in Gen **10** 1 ff; **25** 1 ff.13 ff on a level with the stories concerning the patriarchs. In the latter case we are dealing with individualities of pronounced character, who in the experiences of their lives represent great fundamental principles and laws in the kingdom of God—Abraham, the principle of the grace of God, to which faith on the part of man is the counterpart; Jacob, the principle of Divine election; Joseph, that of the providential guidance of life; while Isaac, it is true, when he becomes prominent in the history, evinces no independent character, but merely follows in the footsteps of Abraham (cf **26** 1 ff.3 ff.15.18.24 ff), but is in this very imitative life pictured in an excellent way.

(*d*) Different explanations combined: If we combine two or more of these different and unsatisfactory attempts at an explanation of the history of the patriarchs, we must become all the more distrustful, because the outcome of this combination is such an inharmonious scheme.

(3) *Positive reasons for the historical character of Genesis.*—The individuality of the patriarchs as well as their significance in the entire development of the history of the kingdom of God, and their different missions individually; further, the truthful portraiture of their method of living, which had not yet reached the stage of permanent settlement; and, finally, the fact that the prophets, the NT and above all Jesus Himself regard their historical character as something self-evident (see [1*b*] above), make the conviction a certainty, that we must insist upon their being historical personages; esp., too, because the attacks on this view (see [1] above), as also the efforts to explain these narratives on other grounds (see [2] above), must be pronounced to be failures. To this we must add the following: If Moses were the founder of the religion of Israel, it would scarcely have been possible that a theory would have been invented and have found acceptance that robs Moses of this honor by the invention of the story of the patriarchs. Rather the opposite would be the case. Besides, this older revelation of God is absolutely necessary in order to make Moses' work and success intelligible and possible. For he himself expressly declares that his work is based on the promises of God given to the fathers. Through this connection with the older revelation it was possible for Moses to win the attention and the con-

fidence of the people (cf Ex **2** 24; **3** 6.13 ff; **4** 5; **6** 3.8; **15** 2; **32** 13 f; **33** 1; cf also my book, *Die Entwicklung der alttestamentlichen Gottesidee in vorexilischer Zeit*, 117 ff; and Strack, *Genesis*, 93 ff).

Individuality of patriarchs: In so far as the history of the patriarchs contains miracles, they are in perfect harmony with the entire character of sacred history (cf Exodus, III, 2); and as far as the number of miracles is concerned, there are in fact fewer reported in the days of the patriarchs than in the times of Moses. On the view that the history of the patriarchs, which is earlier than the period of Moses, was an invention and not history, the opposite condition of affairs could be expected. Leaving out of consideration the unsatisfactory instances cited under V, 2, below, there is to be found also in the Book of Gen absolutely no reference to indicate events of a later period, which would throw a doubt on the historical character of what is here reported. In every direction (e.g. in connection with the theophanies and the cultus worship), there is a noticeable progress to be seen in going from Gen to Ex, a fact which again is an important argument for the historical reliability of the contents of both books. Finally, we add the following. Ch **14** (the Chedorlaomer and the Melchizedek episodes) has through recent archaeological researches been brilliantly confirmed as far as the names are concerned, as also in reference to the political conditions of the times, the general historical situation and the chronology. In the same way the religious conditions of Egypt, as described in Gen **12,** and in the entire history of Joseph, are so faithfully pictured that it is absolutely impossible to regard these accounts as the work of imagination. These accounts must be the outcome, on the part of the author, of a personal knowledge of these things and conditions, as they are absolutely correct, even to the details of the coloring.

2. Primitive History of Gen 1–11

(1) *Prominence of the religious element.*—In the primitive history as recorded in the opening chapters of Gen we must yet emphasize, more than is done elsewhere, that the chief interest for the Christian is found in the religious and moral teachings of this account; and that these teachings remain unshaken, even when chronological, historical, archaeological, physical, geographical or philological sciences would tempt us to reach negative conclusions. It is a wise thing, from the outset, not to be too timid in this direction, and to concede considerable liberty in this matter, when we remember that it is not the purpose of the Bible to give us scientific knowledge in scientific forms, but to furnish us with religious and ethical thoughts in a language which a childlike mind, that is open to Divine things, can understand.

(2) *Carefulness as regards divergent results of scientific research.*—On the other hand, it is right over against the so-called "results" of these different sciences to be very critical and skeptical, since in very many cases science retracts today what with a flourish of trumpets it declared yesterday to be a "sure" result of investigations; e.g. as far as the chronology is concerned, the natural and the historical sciences often base their computations on purely arbitrary figures, or on those which are constructed entirely upon conclusions of analogy, and are far from conclusive, if perchance the history of the earth or of mankind has not at all times developed at the same pace, i.e. has moved upward and downward, as e.g. a child in its earlier years will always learn more rapidly than at any later period of its life.

(3) *Frequent confirmations of the Bible by science.*—But finally the Holy Scriptures, the statements of which at this period are often regarded slightingly by the theologians, are regarded much more highly by men of science. This is done, e.g., by such scientists as Reinke and K. E. von Baer, who declare that Moses, because of his story of the creation, was a man of unsurpassed and unsurpassable scientific thought; or when many geological facts point to such an event as the Deluge in the history of the earth. The history of languages, as a whole and in its details, also furnishes many proofs for the correctness of Gen **10,** and that chapter has further been confirmed in a most surprising manner by many other discoveries (cf the existence of Babel at a period earlier than Nineveh, and the colonizing of Assur by Babel). Then facts like the following can be explained only on the presupposition that the reports in Gen are correct, as when a Dutchman in the 17th cent. built an ark after the measurements given in Gen and found the vessel in every particular adapted to its purposes; and when today we again hear specialists who declare that the modern ocean sailing vessel is being more and more constructed according to the relative proportions of the ark.

(4) *The superiority of the Bible over heathen mythologies.*—Finally, the similarity of the Bib. and the Bab accounts of the creation and the Deluge, as these have been discovered by learned research (and we confine ourselves to these two most important reports)—although this similarity has been misinterpreted and declared to be hostile to the historical reliability and the originality of Gen **1** and **6–9**—does not prove what critics claim that it does. Even if we acknowledge that the contents of these stories were extant in Babylon long before the days of Moses, and that these facts have been drawn from this source by Israel, there yet can be no question that the value of these accounts, the fact that they are saturated with a monotheistic and ethical spirit, is found only in Israel and has been breathed into them only by Israel. For the inner value of a story does not depend upon its antiquity, but upon its spirit. But even this conception of the matter, which is shared by most theologians, cannot satisfy us. When we remember how Bab mythology is honeycombed by the grossest superstition and heathenism, and that our ethical feelings are often offended by it in the most terrible manner, it is really not possible to see how such a system could have had any attraction for Israel after the Spirit, and how a man who thought as a prophet could have taken over such stories. If Israel has been a pathfinder in the sphere of religion, as is acknowledged on all hands, why do the critics always talk of their borrowing from others? And then, since similar stories are found also among other nations, and as the natural sciences are anything but a unit in hostility to the Bib. narratives, all these factors can find a satisfactory explanation only on the supposition that there existed an original or primitive revelation, and that in Israel this revelation was transmitted in its greater purity, while among the other nations it was emptied of its contents or was perverted. In this way the universality of these stories can be explained, as also the inferiority in character of similar stories among the other nations.

The particularly close connection that exists between the Bab and the Bib. versions of these stories is in perfect harmony with the fact that it was from Babylon that the dispersion of mankind set in. The purity of the Bib. tradition is further attested by the fact that it reports the actual history of all mankind (see under I, 2), while the mythologies of other nations are restricted nationally and locally, i.e. the beginnings of the history of the individual nations and the beginnings of the history of mankind are identical, and the earliest history is always reported as taking place in the native land of the people reporting it. The fact that in earlier times there prevailed in Babylon too a purer knowledge of God, which, however, steadily degenerated, is proved by many data, and esp. by the recently discovered fragment of a Deluge story, according to which the God who destroyed the world by the Flood and the God who delivered the one family is the same God, which is in perfect agreement with the Bible, but is in contradiction to the later Bab story. That in earlier times a purer conception of God prevailed, seems to be confirmed also by the experiences of the missionaries. Evolutionism, i.e. the development of a higher conception of God out of a lower, is nothing but an unproved theory, which at every step is contrary to actual facts. Cf also my book, *Die Entwicklung der Gottesidee in vorexilischer Zeit*, 129 ff, and Schmidt, *Die babylonische Religion: Gedanken über ihre Entwicklung*, a dissertation in which the fact that religion naturally degenerates is proved also as far as the Greeks, the Egyptians, the East Indians and the Chinese are concerned.

V. Origin and Authorship of Genesis.—That the Book of Gen stands in some kind of literary connection with the succeeding books of the Pent is generally acknowledged. But if this is the case, then the question as to the origin and the time of the composition of this whole body of books can be decided only if we take them all into consideration. In this article we have only to consider those facts which are found in Gen for the solution of this problem. It is self-evident that the conclusion we have reached with reference to the literary unity of the book is of great importance for this question (see under II and III above). The historical character of the book, as demonstrated under IV above, also speaks emphatically for this claim that the literary composition of the book must have taken place when the memory of these events was still trustworthy, and the impression and experiences were still fresh and had not yet faded. Such individualistic and vivid pictures of historical personages as are reported by Gen, such a faithful adherence to the accounts of the civilization in the different countries and districts and at different times, such detailed accounts of foreign customs, conditions and historical events, could scarcely have been possible, if the Mosaic age with its powerful new impressions, the period of the Judges, with its characteristic apostasy, or even the division of Israel into two kingdoms, with its dire effects on the external union of the people, had all passed by before these accounts were actually written down. On the other hand, the highly developed prophetic conception of these events, and the skilful plan of the book demand that the author must have been a religious and ethical personality of the first rank. And as, finally, it is scarcely credible that Moses would have failed to provide for a systematic report of the great past of the people, for which account, before this and as long as only family histories were involved, there was no need felt, and as the subsequent books of the Pent, which are acknowledged in a literary way to be connected with Gen, in many of their parts expressly declare that Moses was their author (cf EXODUS, IV), the Mosaic authorship of this book is as good as proved. This is not to deny that older sources and documents were used in the composition of the book, such as perhaps the genealogical tables or the events recorded in Gen **14**, possibly, too, some referring to the history of the times before the Deluge and before Abraham. This is probable; but as all the parts of the book have been worked together into a literary unity (see under II and III above), and as such sources are not expressly mentioned, it is a hopeless task to try to describe these different sources in detail or even to separate them as independent documents, after the manner refuted under II and III above, as a theory and in its particulars. And for the age of Gen, we can refer to the fact that the personal pronoun here is still used for both genders, masculine and feminine, which is true also of the word *na'ar* ("youth"), a peculiarity which is shared also by the other books of the Pent almost throughout.

1. Connection with Mosaic Times

2. Examination of Counter-Arguments

(1) *Possibility of later additions.*—In itself it would be possible that from time to time some explanatory and interpreting additions could have been made to the original text, in case we find indications of a later period in some statements of the book. But that in this case these additions could not have been made by any unauthorized persons, but only officially, should, in the case of a book like Gen, be regarded as self-evident. But in our times this fact must be emphasized all the more, as in our days the most radical ideas obtain in reference to the way in which sacred books were used in former times. And then it must be said that we cannot prove as an absolute certainty that there is a single passage in Gen that originated in the post-Mosaic period.

(2) *Rejection of the "prophecy-after-the-event" idea.*—It is self-evident also that the fulfilment of a prophecy is not an evidence of a "prophecy after the event" (*vaticinium post eventum*), altogether independently of the fact that in this case Gen **12** 1–3, which is still in process of fulfilment, could not have been written down even today (cf on this matter, perhaps, Noah's prophecy [**9** 25 ff]; or the prediction of the career of Esau [**25** 23; **27** 40]; or of Ishmael [**16** 10 ff; **21** 18]; or Jacob's blessing [Gen **49**]). The last-mentioned case cannot in any way be interpreted as the product of a later time; cf the curse of Levi in vs 5–8 as compared with the honor bestowed on this tribe already in the Mosaic period (Ex **32** 26–29; Dt **33** 8–11), and in the time of the Judges (Jgs **17** 7–13; 1 S **2** 27 f). Zebulun, too, according to **49** 13 is regarded as being settled on the coast, which is not in agreement with historical reality (cf Josh **19** 10–16.27). In the same way the curse on Simeon in **49** 5–7, which declared that his tribe should be distributed among Israel, was not fulfilled in the time when the people entered Canaan (cf Josh **19** 1 and 2 Ch **34** 6). In **49** 10 "Shiloh" cannot refer to the coming of the tabernacle to Shiloh (cf Josh **18** 1); for Shiloh is, on the other hand, to be interpreted personally and Messianically. As long as Shiloh was of any importance (cf **1 S 1** ff), Judah was not in the possession of the scepter; but when this scepter did come into the control of Judah, Shiloh had long since ceased to be of any significance (cf my book, *Die messianische Erwartung der vorexilischen Propheten*, 360 f).

(3) *Special passages alleged to indicate a later date* (Gen **12** 6; **13** 7; **22** 2; **36** 31 ff; **13** 18; **23** 2; **14** 14).—In Gen **12** 6; **13** 7, it is claimed that it is presupposed that at the time of the author there were no longer any Canaanites in the country, so that these verses belong to a much later period than that of Moses. But on this supposition these verses would be altogether superfluous and therefore unintelligible additions. For that in the time of Abraham the Canaanites had not yet been expelled by Israel, was a self-evident matter for every Israelite. As a matter of fact, the statements in both verses can easily be interpreted. Abraham leaves his native country to go into a strange land. When he comes to Canaan, he finds it inhabited by the Canaanites (cf **10** 6.15; **9** 25 ff). This could have made his faith to fail him. God, accordingly, repeats His promise at this very moment and does so with greater exactness (cf ver 7 with ver 1), and Abraham shows that God can trust his faith (vs 7 f). The question whether the Canaanites no longer existed at the time the book was written, has nothing at all to do with the meaning of these verses. The same is true of **13** 7, on account of the presence of the Canaanites and of the Perizzites, which latter tribe had probably come in the meanwhile and is not yet mentioned in Gen **10**, but is mentioned in

15 20, and which makes the separation of Abraham and Lot only all the more necessary.

That in Gen **22** 2 the land of Moriah is mentioned is claimed by the critics to be a proof that this passage was written after the times of David and even of Solomon, because according to 2 Ch **3** 1 the temple stood on Mt. Moriah. But as in this latter passage one particular mountain is called Moriah, but in Abraham's time a whole country was so called, it is scarcely possible that Gen **22** 2 could have been written at so late a period.

Usually, too, the list of 8 Edomite kings, who ruled before there was a king of Israel, according to **36** 31 ff, is cited as a proof that this part was written only after the establishment of the kingdom in Israel, although the time down to the age of Saul would be entirely too long for only eight kings, as already in the Mosaic period there were kings in Edom (Nu **20** 14). Then, too, we find in the days of Solomon a hereditary kingdom in Edom (1 K **11** 14), while in Gen **36** 31 ff we have to deal with an elective kingdom. Also it would be impossible to understand why this list of kings is carried down only so far and no farther, namely down to the time when there were kings in Israel. This statement can properly be interpreted only in the light of **17** 6.16, where the promise is given to Abraham that kings should be found among his descendants (cf also **17** 20 with **25** 16); and in the light of ch **14,** where Abraham is explicitly brought into connection with kings in a number of ways (with the four kings of the East, whom he conquers; with the five kings of the Jordan valley, whom he assists; with the King's Vale [ver 17], which prepared the way for the Melchizedek episode; and with this Priest-King himself, who blesses him and to whom he gives tithes [vs 18 ff]; with the king of Sodom, whom he rebukes [vs 21 ff]). Accordingly, the statement in **36** 31 is not merely a dry historical notice, but is a reference to the blessing of God, which is realized in Israel at a much later time than in the kindred tribe of Esau, and which puts the faith of Israel to a new test. As the death of the last Edomite king is not mentioned (cf **36** 39 in contrast to the preceding passage and to 1 Ch **1** 50 f), but as detailed family data are given, we are doubtless dealing here with living contemporaries of Moses, in whose time already the Edomites possessed a kingdom (Nu **20** 14; Jgs **11** 17), just as this was the case with Amalek (Nu **24** 7), with Moab (**21** 26; **22** 4) and Midian (Nu **31** 8). And why would a later writer have mentioned neither Selah (Petra), so important in later times (cf Isa **16** 1; Jgs **1** 36; 2 K **14** 7), nor Ezion-Geber (1 K **9** 26; 2 Ch **8** 17 f), among the places given in Gen **36** 40 ff? In Moses' time, however, the last-mentioned place was only prairie (Nu **33** 35 f).

Just as little is it an argument against the Mosaic times that Hebron is mentioned in Gen **13** 18; **23** 2, which city, according to Josh **14** 15; **15** 13, is called Kiriath-arba, a name which Gen also is acquainted with (cf **23** 2), and which in its signification of "city of Arba" points to an originally proper name. Hebron is the older name, which was resumed at a later period, after it had in the meanwhile been supplanted by the Canaanitic name, just as the name of Salem, which occurs already in the Am Tab, for a period of time gave way to the name of Jebus, but was afterward resumed. That Hebron was an old city and that it existed at a period earlier than the Arba mentioned in Josh **14** 15; **15** 13, and from whom its later name was derived, can be concluded from Nu **13** 22.

Further, the mention of Dan in **14** 14 does not necessarily favor the view that this chapter did not originate until after Josh **19** 47. Jgs **18** 29, where Leshem or Laish is changed into Dan (2 S **24** 6; cf vs 2 and 15), does make the existence of another Dan probable. Since in Gen **14** 2.3.7.17 so many ancient names are mentioned, and as the author is most fully informed as to the conditions of the political complexion of the old nations of that time (vs 5–7), it would be incomprehensible if he should not have made use of the ancient names Laish and Leshem. However, if this Dan was really meant, we should at most have to deal with a revision, such as that pointed out above. Some other less important arguments against the origin of Gen from the Mosaic times we can here ignore. The most important argument for the Mosaic origin of the book, in addition to those mentioned under 1, will now be discussed.

VI. Significance.—In the history of the creation the most important feature for us is the fact that the world was created out of nothing (cf **1** 1 and the word *bārā'*), which guarantees the absoluteness of God and His perfect control of the entire material world; further, the creation of man, as the crown of all creation, for which all things previously created prepare, and who is to rule over them, but who—most important of all—is created after the image of God (**1** 26 f), and whose body has been created by the hand of God and his soul breathed into him by God (**2** 7). On this fact, too, in the end, is founded the possibility of man's redemption even after the Fall (**5** 1.3; cf Col **3** 9; Eph **4** 24), as also the possibility of the incarnation of Jesus Christ, who also is the image of God (Col **1** 15; 2 Cor **4** 4). Then, too, another all-important factor for us is the unity of the human race, for thereby is made possible and can be understood the fact that all men have become subject to sin and all can be the recipients of grace (Rom **5** 12 ff; 1 Cor **15** 22 f.45 f). Also the need of redemption is brought out strongly in the Book of Gen. Cf, in connection with the Fall, the pains that shall attend the birth of a child, the cursing of the land, death (**3** 15 ff), which finds its first victim in Abel, and the monotonous and emphatic repetition of the formula, "and he died," in Gen **5,** as characterizing the dismal fate of mankind, and which finds its expression in the rapid decrease of the length of life in the genealogies and in the ages of the patriarchs (**5** 1 ff; **11** 10 ff; **25** 7; **35** 28; **47** 28; **50** 26; Ps **90** 10), and in the irresistible and increasing power of death. By the side of this, sin at once assumes its most horrible form (Gen **3,** doubt, pride, fear, boldness of Eve and Adam), and is propagated and increases; cf the murder and the despair of Cain (Gen **4** 1 ff), which is still surpassed by the defiant blasphemy of Lamech (**4** 23 f); and in the same way, death, which is coming more and more rapidly (see above), is a proof for this, that sin is being more and more intimately interwoven with the human race. Cf, further, the corruption of the whole earth, which brings with it as a consequence the judgment of the Deluge (**6** 5 ff), after the period of grace extending over 120 years had fruitlessly passed by; the lack of reverence on the part of Ham (**9** 22); the arrogance in connection with the building of the tower of Babel (**11** 1 ff); the Sodomitic sin in **18** 16—**19** 15; the daughters of Lot (**19** 30 ff). Still worse is it, that the elect also are not without blame. On Abraham, see IV, 1, 2*b;* then concerning Noah (**9** 21) and Lot's fearful drunkenness (**19** 32 ff); Isaac's and Rebekah's preference for Esau or Jacob (**25** 28); Jacob's deceptions of various kinds, his preference for Joseph (**37** 3); the horrible deeds of Simeon and Levi (**34** 25 ff; **49** 5 ff); Reuben's incest (**35** 22; **49** 3 f); the cruelty of the brethren of Joseph toward him and his father (ch **37**); finally, Joseph's pride and his reporting his brethren (**37** 2.5 ff). In short,

1. Foundation for the Whole of Revelation

wherever we look, we see in Gen already a proof for the truth of Rom **3** 23, "All have sinned, and fall short of the glory of God."

2. Preparation for Redemption

By the side of this need of salvation there is to be found also the longing for salvation; cf the name of Noah (**5** 29), and the word of blessing from the lips of Jacob (**49** 18); and, further, the fact that Abraham reaches out after the promised heir in Gen **15–18,** and his desire for the possession of the land (**12–14; 23; 28** 20 ff; **33** 19 f); and esp. from **47** 27 on. And in harmony with this need and this longing for redemption we find above all other things the saving and the promising grace of God. He does not cause the bodily death to follow immediately upon the Fall in Gen **3** (although the beginning of the spiritual death sets in at once with the separation from God); He provides for mankind by Himself making garments for them out of skins (**3** 21); even the expulsion from Paradise is not merely a punishment; God fears that man might live forever if he should eat from the tree of life (**3** 22 ff). He sets enmity between the human race and the seed of the serpent, so that at least the possibility of a moral contest yet exists; He strengthens the good in Cain (**4** 7); He removes the pious Enoch (**5** 24); He saves Noah and his family and makes a covenant with him (**8** 21 ff); He gives His promise to Abraham (**12** 1–3) and makes a covenant with him (chs **15, 17**); He delivers Lot (**19** 13 ff); He is willing even to preserve Sodom at Abraham's prayer, if there are as many as 10 just men in the city (**18** 32); He bestows a blessing on Ishmael also (**16** 10 ff; **17** 20; **21** 13 ff), and permits Isaac to bless Esau (**27** 39 ff); but above all He is with Isaac, Jacob and Joseph. It is indeed true that the thought runs through Gen that not all men are capable of receiving His grace, and that not all are drawn to the Father. Cain's sacrifice is not acceptable before God, as was Abel's; the Cainites with their advance in civilization (**4** 17 ff), to whom Lamech also belonged, are different from Seth (**4** 26; **5** 1 ff), who continues the line of the elect. Finally, the godly, too, permit themselves to be deceived (**6** 1 ff), and Noah stands alone in his piety. After that Ham is cursed in his youngest son, Canaan (**9** 22; cf **10** 6); but Shem is blessed to such a degree that his blessing is to extend to Japheth also; cf, further, the elimination from sacred history of Lot (**19** 29 ff); of Ishmael (**25** 12 ff), and of Esau (**36** 1 ff); of Sodom and Gomorrah (ch **19**); then the choice of Jacob in preference to Esau (**25** 19—**37** 1); the preference of Ephraim over Manasseh (**48** 17 ff); the transmission of the Messianic promises to Judah (**49** 10; cf my book, *Messianische Erwartung,* 360 f), so that at the close of Gen we find already the hope of a personal Messiah expressed, in whom also the word (**3** 15) that was originally spoken to all mankind is to be entirely fulfilled, and in whom also the blessing given to Abraham shall find its significance and realization for the benefit of all mankind (**12** 3, and see above, I, 2 and 3). But in the history of Abraham this fact also becomes clear, that in the end this was all grace on the part of God, and faith on the part of man; and because both grace and faith are in Gen placed and emphasized at the very beginning of the history of mankind, and before the giving of the law (Ex **19** ff); then this grace and faith cannot be abrogated through the latter or made ineffective. Not by works but by faith is man saved (cf Gal **3** 2; Rom **4**; He **11** 8 ff; Jas **2** 21 ff). But the guidance of individuals and of His people by God, the ways which He took with His elect, become clear and intelligible ultimately in the history of Joseph; and all and everything must in the end serve the good of those who are His.

LITERATURE.—Against the separation into documents we mention, of older works: Hävernick, *Specielle Einleitung in den Pent;* Hengstenberg, *Beiträge zur Einleitung,* II, III; Keil, *Einleitung in das AT,* and his *Comm. on Gen;* Ewald, *Die Komposition der Gen.* Of later works: Orr, *Problem of the OT;* Eerdmans, *Die Komposition der Gen;* Möller, *Wider den Bann der Quellenscheidung.* Against the evolutionary theory: Orr, *Problem of the OT;* Wiener, *EPC* and *OP;* Green, *Unity of Book of Gen;* Möller, *Die Entwicklung der alttestamentlichen Gottesidee in vorexilischer Zeit* (here also further lit.). On modern archaeological researches: Orr, *Problem of the OT;* Jeremias, *Das AT im Lichte des alten Orients;* Urquhart, *Die neueren Entdeckungen und die Bibel* (to be used with caution; the work is reliable in the facts but not careful in its conclusions and in its account of OT criticism). Further, cf the histories of Israel by Köhler, König, Kittel, Oettli, Klostermann, Stade, Wellhausen: the Commentaries on Gen by Keil, Delitzsch, Dillmann, Lange, Strack, Gunkel, Holzinger; the Introductions to the OT by Kuenen, Strack, Baudissin, König, Cornill, Driver; the Bib. Theologies by Marti, Smend, Budde, Schulz, Oehler. Finally compare Sievers, *Metrische Studien,* II: "Die hebräische Gen."

WILHELM MÖLLER

GENNAEUS, ge-nē'us, **GENNEUS,** ge-nē'us (**Γενναῖος**, *Gennaíos*): Father of Apollonius, one of the Syrian generals who troubled the Jews while Lysias was governor for Antiochus Eupator (2 Macc **12** 2). The description is added to distinguish the Apollonius here mentioned from several others of the same name. See APOLLONIUS. There is no need with Luther to take the name simply as an adj. "des edlen Apollonius." The name occurs elsewhere as a proper name.

GENNESARET, ge-nes'a-ret, **LAKE OF.** See GALILEE, SEA OF.

GENNESARET, LAND OF, ge-nes'a-ret (**ἡ γῆ Γεννησαρέτ**, *hē gē Gennēsarét*): The first syllable of the

1. The Name

name Gennesaret is evidently the Heb *gan,* "garden"; while the second may be a proper name. Possibly, however, the name may represent the Heb *gannē sārīm,* "princely gardens." It is applied to a district on the N.W. shore of the Sea of Galilee (Mt **14** 34; Mk **6** 53), now known as *el-Ghuweir,* "little Ghōr." It curves round from *el-Mejdel* in the S., to *'Ain et-Tīneh,* or *Khān Minyeh,* in the N., a distance of over 3 miles, with an average breadth from the sea to the foot of the mountains of about a mile. The soil is deep, rich loam, of amazing fertility. In the S. it is watered by the

2. Water

stream from *Wādy el-Ḥamām,* the gorge that opens to the W. of *el-Mejdel.* The middle portion is supplied from *'Ain el-Madawwerah,* a copious fountain near the western edge of the plain, round which a wall has been built, to raise the level of the water; and from the perennial stream, *Wādy er-Rubadīyeh,* which drives a mill before starting on its work of irrigation. Farther N., *Wādy el-'Amūd* brings down much water in the rainy season. The water from *'Ain et-Ṭābgha* was brought round the promontory at *'Ain et-Tīneh* by a conduit cut in the rock. It was used to drive certain mills, and also to refresh the neighboring land. This seems to be the fountain called "Capharnaum" by Jos (*BJ,* III, x, 8). This writer extols the productiveness of the plain. He says the "soil is so fruitful that all sorts of trees can grow upon it." The walnut, the palm, the olive

3. Fertility

and the fig, which usually require diverse conditions, flourish together here. "One may call this place the ambition of nature; . . . . it is a happy contention of the seasons, as if each of them claimed this country; for it not only nourishes different sorts of autumnal fruit beyond men's expectation, but preserves them a great while." He says that it supplies grapes and figs through ten months of the year, and other fruits as they ripen together throughout the year (ib). The fruits of Gennesaret had such high repute among the rabbis that they were not allowed in Jerus at the time of the feasts, lest any might be tempted to come merely for their enjoyment (Neubauer, *Géog. du Talm*, 45 f).

Centuries of neglect made a sad change in the plain. It was largely overgrown with thorn-bushes, and it yielded one of the finest crops of thistles in the country. Cultivation was confined to the S.W. part; and the rest furnished grazing ground for a tribe of nomads. Recently the German Catholics made extensive purchases, including the village of *el-Mejdel*. Considerable portions have also passed into the hands of Jews. The land is almost entirely cleared, and it rewards the toil of the husbandman with all its ancient generosity. W. EWING

GENTILES, jen′tīlz (גּוֹי, *gōy*, pl. גּוֹיִם, *gōyim;* **ἔθνος,** *éthnos*, "people," "nation"): *Goy* (or *Goi*) is rendered "Gentiles" in AV in some 30 passages, but much more frequently "heathen," and oftener still, "nation," which latter is the usual rendering in RV, but it is commonly used for a non-Israelitish people, and thus corresponds to the meaning of "Gentiles." It occurs, however, in passages referring to the Israelites, as in Gen **12** 2; Dt **32** 28; Josh **3** 17; **4** 1; **10** 13; 2 S **7** 23; Isa **1** 4; Zeph **2** 9, but the word *'ām* (עָם) is the term commonly used for the people of God. In the NT *ethnos* is the word corresponding to *gōy* in the OT and is rendered "Gentiles" by both VSS, while *laós* (λαός) is the word which corresponds to *'ām.* AV also renders Ἕλληνες, *Héllēnes*, "Gentiles" in six passages (Jn **7** 35; Rom **2** 9.10; **3** 9; 1 Cor **10** 32; **12** 13), but RV renders "Greeks."

The Gentiles were far less sharply differentiated from the Israelites in OT than in NT times. Under OT regulations they were simply non-Israelites, not from the stock of Abraham, but they were not hated or despised for that reason, and were to be treated almost on a plane of equality, except certain tribes in Canaan with regard to whom there were special regulations of non-intercourse. The Gentile stranger enjoyed the hospitality of the Israelite who was commanded to love him (Dt **10** 19), to sympathize with him, "For ye know the heart of the stranger, seeing ye were strangers in the land of Egypt" (Ex **23** 9 AV). The Kenites were treated almost as brethren, esp. the children of Rechab (Jgs **1** 16; **5** 24; Jer **35**). Uriah the Hittite was a trusted warrior of David (2 S **11**); Ittai the Gittite was captain of David's guard (**18** 2); Araunah the Jebusite was a respected resident of Jerus. The Gentiles had the right of asylum in the cities of refuge, the same as the Israelites (Nu **35** 15). They might even possess Israelitish slaves (Lev **25** 47), and a gentile servant must not be defrauded of his wage (Dt **24** 15). They could inherit in Israel even as late as the exile (Ezk **47** 22.23). They were allowed to offer sacrifices in the temple at Jerus, as is distinctly affirmed by Jos (*BJ*, II, xvii, 2–4; *Ant*, XI, viii, 5; XIII, viii, 2; XVI, ii, 1; XVIII, v, 3; *CAp*, II, 5), and it is implied in the Levitical law (Lev **22** 25). Prayers and sacrifices were to be offered for gentile rulers (Jer **29** 7; Bar **1** 10.11; Ezr **6** 10; 1 Macc **7** 33; Jos, *BJ*, II, x, 4). Gifts might be received from them (2 Macc **5** 16; Jos, *Ant*, XIII, iii, 4; XVI, vi, 4; *BJ*, V, xiii, 6; *CAp*, II, 5). But as we approach the Christian era the attitude of the Jews toward the Gentiles changes, until we find, in NT times, the most extreme aversion, scorn and hatred. They were regarded as unclean, with whom it was unlawful to have any friendly intercourse. They were the enemies of God and His people, to whom the knowledge of God was denied unless they became proselytes, and even then they could not, as in ancient times, be admitted to full fellowship. Jews were forbidden to counsel them, and if they asked about Divine things they were to be cursed. All children born of mixed marriages were bastards. That is what caused the Jews to be so hated by Greeks and Romans, as we have abundant evidence in the writings of Cicero, Seneca and Tacitus. Something of this is reflected in the NT (Jn **18** 28; Acts **10** 28; **11** 3).

If we inquire what the reason of this change was we shall find it in the conditions of the exiled Jews, who suffered the bitterest treatment at the hands of their gentile captors and who, after their return and establishment in Judaea, were in constant conflict with neighboring tribes and esp. with the Gr rulers of Syria. The fierce persecution of Antiochus IV, who attempted to blot out their religion and Hellenize the Jews, and the desperate struggle for independence, created in them a burning patriotism and zeal for their faith which culminated in the rigid exclusiveness we see in later times. H. PORTER

GENTILES, COURT OF THE. See TEMPLE.

GENTILES, ISLES OF THE. See ISLES OF THE GENTILES.

GENTLENESS, jen′t'l-nes (עֲנָה, *'ānāh;* **ἐπιείκεια,** *epieíkeia*, **χρηστότης,** *chrēstótēs*): In 2 S **22** 36 *'ānāh*, "to bend low," "to condescend," is tr[d] "gentleness," "Thy gentleness hath made me great," RVm "or condescension"; so also Ps **18** 35, where the word is *'anwāh*, "humility," "gentleness," or "condescension." In the NT *epieikeia* ("fairness," "moderation," in Acts **24** 4 tr[d] "clemency") is in 2 Cor **10** 1 tr[d] "gentleness," "the meekness and gentleness of Christ" (2 Macc **2** 22 "favour," RV "forbearance"); *chrēstotēs*, "kindness," "usefulness," is tr[d] "gentleness" in Gal **5** 22 AV, RV "kindness"; *chrēstós* is the word tr[d] "kind" (to the unthankful and evil, Lk **6** 35), and *chrēstotēs* seems to carry in it a similar idea of active *kindness.*

Gentle occurs in the OT only in RV of Jer **11** 19, "I was like a gentle lamb" (*kebhes*). In the NT it is the tr of *ēpios*, "mild," "gentle" (1 Thess **2** 7; 2 Tim **2** 24), and of *epieikēs*, "fitting," "proper," etc (1 Tim **3** 3 RV; Tit **3** 2; Jas **3** 17; 1 Pet **2** 18); also, with art., Phil **4** 5 (AV "moderation," RV "forbearance"). In 2 Macc **15** 12 Onias is said (AV) to be "gentle [*práos*] in condition," RV "in manner." W. L. WALKER

GENUBATH, gē-nū′bath (גְּנֻבַת, *g[e]nubhath*, "theft"): Son of Hadad, the fugitive Edomite prince, born and brought up at the court of Egypt, whither Hadad had fled when David conquered Edom (1 K **11** 20). His mother was a sister of Tahpenes, queen of the Pharaoh who ruled Egypt at that time, and who belonged to the notoriously weak and uninfluential 21st dynasty.

GEOGRAPHY, jē-og′ra-fi. See PALESTINE; TABLE OF NATIONS; WORLD.

GEOLOGY, je-ol′o-ji, **OF PALESTINE:** The geology of Pal cannot be discussed intelligently without taking into consideration the surrounding regions. The accompanying map shows, with considerable freedom, the distribution of the superficial strata of Syria, Pal and Sinai, with parts of Asia Minor, Arabia and Egypt. (Data for this map were obtained from the "Geological Map of Egypt" [1:1,000,000] and from the "Carte géologique internationale de l'Europe" [1:1,500,000].) It will be noted that Crystalline, or Archaean, rocks (A) occupy extensive areas in Asia Minor, and that they are found in the S. in Sinai, Western Arabia, and Eastern and Southern Egypt. Relatively small areas of Paleozoic rocks (P) adjoin the Crystalline rocks in Sinai and Arabia and E. of Caesarea in Asia Minor. A notable area of Paleozoic occurs S.E. of the Dead Sea. This is also adjacent to Crystalline rocks, which could not be indicated on the map on account of their slight superficial extent. Bordering either the Crystalline or the Paleozoic rocks in Egypt, Sinai and Arabia are large areas of Nubian Sandstone (N). The Nubian Sandstone in turn is generally bounded by Upper Cretaceous limestone (C), and the last by Tertiary deposits (T). The Quaternary, or Recent, deposits (R) and also the Eruptive rocks (E) sustain no constant relations to any particular ones of the other formations. The Quaternary follows the great rivers and the seacoasts. The Eruptive rocks usually overlie the others. They occupy extensive areas in Asia Minor, Syria and Arabia.

If we concentrate our attention upon the Crystalline, Cretaceous, and Tertiary, which are the most extensive formations, we find that the Crystalline rocks are abundant in the S. and in the N., that the Cretaceous are most widely spread in Pal and Southern Syria, and the Tertiary in Northern Syria and Egypt. We may believe that the Crystalline areas of the N. and S. have been land since the end of the Archaean age, and that what are now Syria, Pal and most of Egypt remained sea for a long time afterward. The Paleozoic areas were lifted above the sea and added to the northern and southern land areas during or at the end of the Paleozoic era. The regions in which we find Nubian Sandstone or Upper Cretaceous limestone became land by the end of the Mesozoic era. Finally the Tertiary areas were lifted out of the sea. During the Quaternary period the Nile and the rivers of Mesopotamia have added large areas to the land surface.

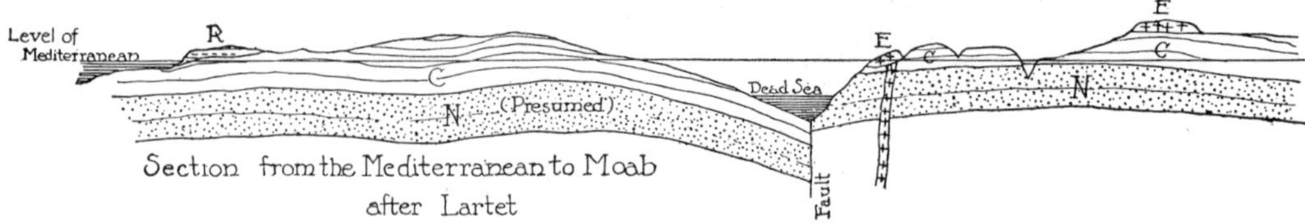

Section from the Mediterranean to Moab after Lartet

1. Crystalline Rocks (A)

The Crystalline rocks consist mainly of granite and crystalline schists, frequently interrupted with dykes of porphyry, diorite and other eruptives. It will be seen by the map that the Crystalline rocks are nowhere adjacent to the Mediterranean, but that they touch the Nile at *Aṣwân*, where the river in pouring over these rocks makes the First Cataract, or rather did before the construction of the great dam. Granite quarried at *Aṣwân* could be loaded on boats and conveyed to any city on the shores of the Mediterranean, and it is the granite of *Aṣwân* of which are composed not only many of the monuments of Egypt, but also the pillars which adorned many temples in Syria and Pal.

2. Paleozoic Rocks (P)

The Paleozoic rocks of Sinai and Arabia are of Carboniferous age, but do not include any beds of coal. Those E. of Caesarea are Devonian. Those S.E. of the Dead Sea are the oldest of all, being of Cambrian age.

3. Triassic and Jurassic Rocks (J)

Several formations which are well developed in the British Islands, are not found in Pal, but a small Triassic area is found near the Gulf of Alexandretta, while Jurassic strata are found in the region of Hermon and in Lebanon and Anti-Lebanon. The small scale of the accompanying map makes it impossible to represent accurately the extent of these rocks.

4. Nubian Sandstone (N)

This name was given by Russegger, who in the middle of the 19th cent. followed and studied this formation from the Sûdân to Syria. Wherever the Nubian Sandstone is found in contact with the Upper Cretaceous limestone it underlies the latter conformably. In Lebanon, Anti-Lebanon and Hermon (but not farther S.) it is conformably underlaid by Jurassic limestone. It follows, therefore, that its upper strata (the only ones found in the N.) must be of Lower or Middle Cretaceous age. In the S., however, the Jurassic limestone is entirely absent. In Western Sinai the Nubian Sandstone rests conformably on Carboniferous limestone, and by the Dead Sea on Cambrian limestone, while at Petra and at many other places it rests unconformably on Crystalline rocks. While the consideration of the age of the Nubian Sandstone presents no difficulty in Lebanon, Anti-Lebanon and Hermon, it is a very different matter in Western Sinai, and by the Dead Sea. Sandstone is generally supposed to be formed more rapidly than most other rocks. It is, therefore, rather staggering to try to conceive of even the 2,000 ft. of sandstone at the S.E. end of the Dead Sea as having been in process of formation from the Cambrian to the Cretaceous. The Nubian Sandstone is commonly brown or reddish, but in places shows great variety of color. The temples and tombs of Petra were all carved in this rock. It is in places very friable, and in others compact and hard. The sands of the Arabian deserts have been in the main derived from it, being carried by the prevailing west winds. Where it is covered by a sheet of eruptive rock (*ḥarrah*), it is protected from erosion, with the result that the land to the E. is not converted into a sandy desert (Hogarth, *Penetration of Arabia*). It frequently includes strata of clay and shale and thin seams of coal or lignite, and must have been deposited in seas which were at the time relatively shallow.

5. Upper Cretaceous Limestone (C)

This is the principal rock of Pal, Lebanon, and Anti-Lebanon. Many of its strata are very fossiliferous, and no doubt exists as to its age. It furnishes the best of building stone and is a source of lime. The soils formed from it are fertile, and the mountain sides have been terraced by the patient labor of centuries.

6. Tertiary Rocks (T)

A notable Tertiary fossil is the Nummulite, which occurs in abundance in the rock of the pyramids of *Gîzeh* and in other places. Relatively small masses of Tertiary strata (not shown on the map) are found on the coast at the mouths of the principal streams of Lebanon, showing that while the mass of Lebanon had risen from the sea by the beginning of the Tertiary, the elevation was not complete. The principal river courses had, however, already been formed, and the streams were already carrying into the sea the scourings of the rocks of early Lebanon, which were being laid down to form these Tertiary strata.

These consist mainly of the superficial deposits of the Nile, the Euphrates and other large streams. At various points along the coast of Syria and Pal are extensive sand dunes. Frequently under the loose sand, or exposed, is found a sandstone which instead of being entirely siliceous, like most sandstones, is partly calcareous, containing from 15 to 25 per cent of calcium-carbonate. This is probably an aeolian formation, i.e. consolidated under the influence of the atmosphere, and not formed under the sea, like most stratified rocks. It is easily worked and is much used for building.

7. Quaternary and Recent Strata (R)

It may be gathered from the foregoing statements that the rocks of Pal are mainly Cretaceous. The Jurassic limestone, which in Lebanon and Anti-Lebanon underlies the Nubian Sandstone, is absent in Pal, but, at least in Eastern Pal, as in Lebanon, we find the Upper Cretaceous limestone to be underlaid by the Nubian Sandstone. A striking feature of the geology of Pal is the Jordan valley fault. At some time, probably at the beginning of the Tertiary period, when Lebanon, Anti-Lebanon, and the Judaean hills were being lifted out of the sea, the earth's crust was rent for at least several hundred miles along a line nearly N. and S., or more exactly from a little W. of S. to a little E. of N. This line runs through the Gulf of 'Aḳabah, the *Wâdi-'Arabah*, the Dead Sea, the Jordan valley, the Sea of Tiberias, the *Ḥûleh*, and the valley between Hermon and Anti-Lebanon on the one hand and Lebanon on the other. The resulting disturbance of the strata is most evident in the region of the Dead Sea. There is no evidence that the two walls of the fissure separated from one another, but the E. wall slipped up and the W. wall down for perhaps 2,000 ft, so that on the E. shore of the Dead Sea and in the valleys entering the Jordan, Dead Sea, and *'Arabah* from the E., the Nubian Sandstone is exposed, underlying the Upper Cretaceous limestone, while on the W. side, even down to the level of the Dead Sea, 1,290 ft. below the Mediterranean, the Nubian Sandstone is nowhere visible, although it may be presumed to exist there also below the upper limestone. (See the acccompanying ideal section, after Lartet, through Judaea, the Dead Sea and Moab.) The great fault and the subsidiary faults which accompany it occasioned the outpourings of igneous rock which are abundant along the line of the fault. The numerous hot springs (e.g. Tiberias, *Wâdi-Yarmûk*, *Wâdi-Zarḳa-Mâ'în* [Callirrhoe], *Wâdi-ul-Ḥisa*) may be due to subterranean streams of water coming in contact with deeply buried and still heated masses of igneous rock.

8. Palestine

ALFRED ELY DAY

GEON, gē'on. See GIHON (Apoc).

GEPHYRUN, ge-fī'run (**Γεφυρούν**, *Gephuroún*): In 2 Macc **12** 13, referring to the capture by Judas of a stronghold E. of Jordan, RV reads, "And he also fell upon a certain city Gephyrun, ... it was named Caspin." There appears to be some confusion in the text. There is nothing to indicate the relation between the two names. AV renders, "He went also about to make a bridge." The name of the city in Jos (*Ant*, XII, viii, 5) is EPHRON (q.v.).

GERA, gē'ra (גֵּרָא, *gērā'*, "grain"): A family name of the tribe of Benjamin, hence not necessarily a separate individual in (3) and (4) below:

(1) A son of Benjamin (Gen **46** 21).

(2) According to 1 Ch **8** 3.5.7, son of Bela and grandson of Benjamin. The name is repeated (ver 5) in the list of Bela's sons.

(3) Father, or ancestor, of the judge Ehud (Jgs **3** 15).

(4) Father, or ancestor, of Shimei, the Benjamite, who cursed David when he fled from Absalom (2 S **16** 5; **19** 16.18; 1 K **2** 8).

GERAH, gē'ra (גֵּרָה, *gērāh*, "grain" or "kernel"): A weight, the 20th part of a shekel (Ex **30** 13; Lev **27** 25; Nu **3** 47; **18** 16; Ezk **45** 12). See WEIGHTS AND MEASURES.

GERAR, gē'rär (גְּרָר, *g^erār*, "circle," "region"; **Γεραρά**, *Gerará*): A town in the Phili plain S. of Gaza (Gen **10** 19), where both Abraham and Isaac sojourned for a time, and where they came into contact with Abimelech, king of G. (Gen **20** and **26**, *passim*). The place has not been fully identified, but the site is probably in one of the branches of *Wady Sheri'a*, at a place called *Um Jerrâr*, near the coast S.W. of Gaza and 9 miles from it (*SWP*, III, 389–90). The site answers fairly well to the statements of Eusebius and Jerome, *Onom*, that it was 25 (Rom) miles S. of Eleutheropolis (*Beit Jibrîn*). It is actually 30 Eng. miles, but distances were not very accurately determined in early times. G. was known in the first 5 cents. AD, when it was the seat of a bishopric, and its bishop, Marcian, attended the Council of Chalcedon 451 AD. It was also the seat of a monastery.

The statements in Gen indicate that G. belonged to the Philis, and we are led to infer that Abimelech was king of that people, but it is quite certain that they did not occupy this region until after the time of Abraham, in fact only a short time before the Exodus. It is probable, however, that the writer of Gen would refer to the country as it was known in his day. The town certainly existed in the Phili period, for it is mentioned in connection with Asa, who defeated the Ethiopian host under Zerar and pursued them in their flight unto G. (2 Ch **14** 13). Sir William Flinders Petrie, in his work at Gerar, 1928, found the Philistine furnaces for smelting iron. The incoming of Israel as shown at Kiriath-sepher was at the beginning of the Iron Age. These furnaces explain the sudden introduction of iron. Kiriath-sepher has a great layer of ashes, below which everything is Canaanite, Bronze Age; above which everything is Israelite, Iron Age. An actual Conquest by Israel is shown and a cultural date clearly indicated. The best opinion of experts puts this 1275 BC. See KIRIATH-SEPHER.

H. PORTER

GERASA, ger'a-sa, **GERASENES**, ger'a-sēnz (**Γέρασα**, *Gérasa*; **Γερασηνῶν**, *Gerasēnōn*):

1. Country of the Gerasenes

(1) The town itself is not named in Scripture, and is referred to only in the expression, "country of the Gerasenes" (Mk **5** 1; Lk **8** 26.37; see WH, App., 11). This describes the district in which Christ met and healed the demoniac from the tombs, where also took place the destruction of the swine. It was on the eastern shore of the Sea of Galilee, and must have been a locality where the steep edges of the Bashan plateau drop close upon the brink of the lake. This condition is fulfilled only by the district immediately S. of *Wādy Semak*, N. of *Ḳal 'at el-Ḥuṣn*. Here the slopes descend swiftly almost into the sea, and animals, once started on the downward run, could not avoid plunging into the depths. Many ancient tombs are to be seen in the face of the hills. Gerasa itself is probably represented by the ruins of *Kurseh* on the S. side of *Wādy Semak*, just where it opens on the seashore. The ruins of the town are not considerable; but there are remains of a strong wall which must have surrounded the place. Traces of ancient buildings in the vicinity show that there must have been a fairly numerous population in the district.

(2) The great and splendid city in the Decapolis is first mentioned as taken after a siege by Alexander Jannaeus, 85 BC (*BJ*, I, iv, 8). Jos names it as marking the eastern limit of Peraea (*BJ*, III, iii, 3). He calls the inhabitants Syrians, when, at the

2. History beginning of the Jewish revolt, the district round Gerasa was laid waste. The Syrians made reprisals, and took many prisoners. With these, however, the Gerasenes dealt mercifully, letting such as wished go free, and escorting them to the border (*BJ*, II, xviii, 1, 5). Lucius Annius, at the instance of Vespasian, sacked

Extremity of the Grand Colonnade at Gerasa.

and burned the city, with much slaughter (*BJ*, IV, ix, 1). From this disaster it appears soon to have recovered, and the period of its greatest prosperity lay, probably, in the 2d and 3d cents. of our era. It became the seat of a bishopric, and one of its bishops attended the Council of Chalcedon. Reland (*Pal*, II, 806) notes certain extant coins of Gerasa, from which it is clear that in the 2d cent. it was a center of the worship of Artemis. It was besieged by Baldwin II, in 1121 AD. Mention is made of the strength of the site and the mighty masonry of its walls. William of Tyre calls the city Jarras, and places it 16 miles E. of Jordan (*Hist*, xii, 16). The distance is about 19 miles from the river. It was conquered by the Moslems in the time of Omar (Guy le Strange, *Pal under the Moslems*, 462). The sultan of Damascus is said to have fortified it; but there is nothing to show that the Moslems occupied it for any length of time.

3. Description Modern *Jerash* lies on both banks of *Wādy Jerash*, about 6 miles from its confluence with *Wādy ez-Zerḳā* (the Jabbok). It is almost 20 miles from *'Ammān* (Philadelphia), and 22 from *Fāhil* (Pella). The ruins are wide and imposing and are better preserved than any others on the E. of Jordan. They include several splendid temples, theaters, basilica, palaces and baths, with hippodrome and naumachia. The triumphal arch to the S. of the city is almost entire. Two paved streets with double colonnades cut through the city at right angles, four massive pedestals still marking the point of intersection. An excellent account of the ruins is given in Thomson's *LB*, III, 558 ff.

There is nothing above ground of older date than the 2d and 3d cents. of our era; but there is no reason to doubt that the Gr city of Gerasa stood on the same site. The presence of a copious spring of sweet water makes it probable that the site has been occupied from olden time; but no trace remains of any ancient city. Some would identify the place with Ramoth-gilead, which see.

The site is now occupied by a colony of Circassians, and there is reason to fear that, unless something is done to preserve them, many valuable remains of antiquity will perish.

W. Ewing

GERGESENES, gûr'ge-sēnz, gûr-ge-sēnz': A false reading of "Gadarenes" retained in AV of Mt **8** 28. See Gadara.

GERIZIM, ger'i-zim, gē-rī'zim, **MOUNT** (הַר גְּרִזִּים, *har g^{e}rizzīm*): Named in the directions for the reading of the law (Dt **11** 29), and

1. Scriptural References in the account of that great ceremony (Dt **27** 12; Josh **8** 33 f). Mts. Ebal and Gerizim stood over against each other, and on their sides the peoples were placed, half upon one and half upon the other, while in the vale which separates the mountains stood the ark, with the Levites. Those who stood on Gerizim responded to the blessings, those on Mt. Ebal to the cursings, as these were spoken "with a loud voice" by the Levites. From a spur of Mt. Gerizim Jotham spoke his taunting parable to the men of Shechem (Jgs **9** 7). Such acoustics at this point are now well attested. In consequence of the dispute which arose over the marriage of Manasseh, who belonged to the high-priestly family, with a daughter of Sanballat the Horonite (Neh **13** 28), a temple was built on Gerizim as a rival to that in Jerus (c 432 BC). This was the beginning of the schism which lasts to the present day (*Ant*, XI, viii, 2, 4). See Samaritans. The temple was destroyed by John Hyrcanus c 110 BC (*Ant*, XIII, ix, 1; *BJ*, I, ii, 6).

2. Description Mt. Gerizim, the modern *Jebel eṭ-Ṭūr*, stands on the S., Mt. Ebal on the N., of the narrow pass which cuts through the mountain range, opening a way from the sea to the Jordan. In the throat of this pass to the W., on the S. of the vale, and close to the foot of Gerizim, lies the town of *Nablūs*, the ancient Shechem. Here copious fountains rise, filling the valley with beauty and fruitfulness. The sides of the mountain are steep and rocky on E. and N.; on the W. the ascent is more gradual, and here, by means of a system of terraces carried almost to the summit, it is cultivated with great care and success. Its height is 2,849 ft. above the level of the sea, 228 ft. lower than its northern companion.

3. Samaritan Traditions Abraham came through the pass and camped near Gerizim at the oak of Moreh (Gen **12** 6). According to Sam tradition it was on this mountain that he prepared to sacrifice Isaac, and at Salem, not far distant, he met Melchizedek (Gen **14** 17 ff). The scene of Jacob's dream is placed at *Khirbet Lauzeh* on the summit (Gen **28** 11 f). In a little hollow W. of the ridge, the Samaritans annually celebrate the Passover in accordance with the directions of the Pent. This is done in the open air, their temple having long since disappeared.

4. Antiquities The most important remains on the mountain today are those of Justinian's fortress, built in 533 AD, to protect the church which had been erected in 475 AD. Near the center of the plateau is a bare piece of rock, on which, tradition says, the altar stood in the Sam temple. A cup-like hollow in it may have been used for libations. In the western wall of *el-Ḳal'ah*, Justinian's castle, there are 12 stones under which, it is said, are the stones which Israel took from the bed of the Jordan (Josh **4** 20).

Mount Gerizim with Shechem.

Gerizim was certainly "this mountain" pointed to by the woman of Samaria in her conversation with Jesus (Jn **4** 20 f); the cliffs of the mountain almost overhanging the Well of Jacob.

For the reason why Gerizim was chosen for the blessing and Ebal for the cursing we are left to conjecture. The directions were fixed by one looking to the E., not, as with us, looking to the N. For one standing in the valley, therefore, Gerizim was on the right hand, "the side of good fortune" (Driver, *Deuteronomy* on **11** 28).

Onom places Ebal and Gerizim much nearer the Jordan valley. This was doubtless to meet the difficulty raised by the long distance from Ai to Shechem. But their nearness to the "oaks of Moreh" (Dt **11** 30) points to this locality, and this is confirmed by Jos, who speaks of Shechem, the metropolis of the Samaritans, as "a city situated at Mt. Gerizim" (*Ant*, XI, viii, 6).

Andronicus, appointed governor of Gerizim by Antiochus Epiphanes, is mentioned in 2 Macc **5** 23 (AV "Garizim"). W. Ewing

GERON, gē'run (**Γέρων,** *Gérōn*): Not much seems to be gained by translating with RVm "Geron, an Athenian," for "an old man of Athens" in 2 Macc **6** 1.

GERRENIANS, ge-rē'ni-anz (**ἕως τῶν Γερρηνῶν,** *héōs tōn Gerrēnōn*): The name indicates the southern limit of the territory assigned by Antiochus Eupator to the government of Judas Maccabaeus when he "left Hegemonides governor from Ptolemaïs even unto the Gerrenians" (2 Macc **13** 24, AV "Gerrhenians"). It is not easy to say exactly who the G. were. They were wrongly associated by Grotius with the town Gerrha, and are with more probability connected with the ancient city of Gerar, S.E. of Gaza. One MS reads Gerarēnōn, which could easily be corrupted into Gerrēnōn, and would place the government of Hegemonides between Ptolemaïs and Gerar.
J. Hutchison

GERSHOM, gûr'shom (גֵּרְשֹׁם, *gērᵉshōm*, from *gārash*, "to cast out"; explained, however, in Ex **2** 22 and **18** 3 as from *gūr*, "For he said, I have been a sojourner in a foreign land"):

(1) Firstborn son of Moses and Zipporah. The only details of his life contained in the Pent are the account of his circumcision (Ex **4** 25), and his remaining under the care of Jethro, while Moses was in Egypt leading the Exodus. His descendants were numbered among the tribes of Levi (1 Ch **23** 14). One of them apparently was the Jonathan who officiated as priest of the idolatrous sanctuary at Dan, and whose descendants held the office until the captivity. The MT inserts a suspended נ, *n*, in the name of Moses (משׁה), causing it to be read מנשׁה, *Manasseh*, for the purpose, according to tradition, of disguising the name out of respect for the revered Lawgiver. Another descendant described as a "son" was Shebuel, a ruler over the treasuries of David.

(2) A son of Levi, so called in 1 Ch **6** 16.17.20.43.62.71 (Heb 1.2.5.28.47.56); **15** 7; elsewhere Gershon (q.v.).

(3) A descendant of Phinehas, the head of a father's house, who journeyed with Ezra from Babylon to Jerus in the reign of Artaxerxes (Ezr **8** 2).
Ella Davis Isaacs

GERSHON, gûr'shon, **GERSHONITES,** gûr'shon-īts (גֵּרְשׁוֹן, *gērᵉshōn*, written also *gērᵉshōm*): Firstborn of the 3 sons of Levi (Ex **6** 16; Nu **3** 17; 1 Ch **6** 1.16 m; **23** 6). He had two sons, Libni, also known as Ladan (1 Ch **23** 7; **26** 21), and Shimei (Ex **6** 17; Nu **3** 18; 1 Ch **6** 17.20), and consequently two groups of descendants, enumerated in the census taken in the Wilderness of Sinai (Nu **3** 21 ff) and that in the Plains of Moab (Nu **26** 57). In the distribution of functions among the Levites, the Gershonites were charged with the carrying of the curtains, coverings, screens, hangings, cords and instruments of the tabernacle and the tent of meeting on the journeys in the wilderness, under the supervision of Ithamar the son of Aaron. Their function was thus more exalted than that of the Merarites, who carried the boards, and less so than that of the Kohathites, who carried the most holy utensils and symbols. The Gershonites were given two wagons with four oxen—half as many as the Merarites, according to their service (Nu **7** 7). Thirteen cities were assigned to the Gershonites in Northern Pal by Eleazar and Joshua (Josh **21** 6.27–33 ‖ 1 Ch **6** 62.71–76).

Among the Gershonites who achieved distinction in later Bib. times was the family of Asaph, the singers from the time of David to the days of the Second Temple (1 Ch **6** 31–47; **25** 1–7; **15** 7.17.19; **16** 5.7; 2 Ch **35** 15; Ezr **2** 41; **3** 10; Neh **11** 17.22; **12** 35; 1 Ch **9** 15). Other Gershonites named are the heads of the fathers' houses in the days of David in connection with the dividing of the Levites into courses (1 Ch **23** 7–11); the superintendents of the treasuries of the house of the Lord of the same time (1 Ch **26** 21.22; **29** 8); and, finally, Gershonites are mentioned among those who cleansed the house of the Lord in the days of Hezekiah (2 Ch **29** 12.13).
Ella Davis Isaacs

GERSON, gûr'sun (**Γηρσών,** *Gērsōn;* 1 Esd **8** 29): Called Gershom in Ezr **8** 2.

GERUTH CHIMHAM, gē'rōōth kim'ham (גֵּרוּת כִּמְהָם, *gērūth kimhām*): If the reading *gērūth* is correct, a "lodging-place" or "khan" on the highway to Egypt, may be meant (Jer **41** 17). It may have been built by Chimham son of Barzillai; or it may have been named from him as owner of the land on which it stood. But probably with Jos we should read *gidhrōth*, "hurdles" or "sheep pens" (*Ant*, X, ix, 5).

GERZITES, gûr'zīts (1 S **27** 8 AVm). See Girzites.

GESHAN, gē'shan (גֵּישָׁן, *gēshān*, "firm," "strong"): A descendant of Judah through Caleb (1 Ch **2** 47). AV has "Gesham," but not in the original 1611 edition.

GESHEM, gē'shem (גֶּשֶׁם, *geshem*, גַּשְׁמוּ, *gashmū;* **Γῆσαμ,** *Gēsam*, "rain storm"): An Arabian, probably chief of an Arabian tribe that had either settled in Southern Pal during the exile in Babylon, or had been settled in or near Samaria by Sargon (Neh **2** 19; **6** 1.2.6). He was a confederate of Sanballat and Tobiah, and strenuously opposed the building of the wall under Nehemiah. He with the others mocked at the first efforts to build the wall, and afterward repeatedly sought to entice Nehemiah to the plains of Ono. The name also occurs in the form *Gashmū*, perhaps an Assyr form of the same name Geshem. J. J. Reeve

GESHUR, gē'shur (גְּשׁוּר, *gᵉshūr*, "bridge"): An Aramaean kingdom (2 S **15** 8) of no great size which lay probably to the S. of Maacah, and formed with it the western boundary of the land of Bashan (Dt **3** 14; Josh **12** 5; **13** 11). The territory of these two probably corresponded roughly with modern *Jaulān*. It may not have reached quite to the Jordan on the W.; in which case the Geshurites lit. dwelt "in the midst" of Israel (Josh **13** 13), since they were not expatriated by the half-tribe of Manasseh, and they retained their independence. David married Maacah, daughter of Talmai, king of Geshur, who became the mother of Absalom and Tamar (2 S **3** 3). To Talmai Absalom fled for safety after the murder of Amnon (**13** 37 f), and thence Joab brought him back to Jerus (**14** 23). The Geshurites and Aram are said to have taken the cities of Jair—i.e. Havvoth-jair—which lay in the land of Gilead (1 Ch **2** 23). It is possible that "Geshurites" should be read, with Vulg, Syr, etc, instead of "Ashurites" in 2 S **2** 9. The only difficulty is that Geshur was an independent kingdom, and there is nothing to show how it was brought under the sway of the son of Saul. In the catalogue of land still to be possessed in Josh **13** 2, AV reads "Geshuri," RV "the Geshurites," referring evidently to a district bordering on the Philis. Both AV and RV render the same word by "Geshurites" in 1 S **27** 8, where apparently the same territory is indicated as invaded by David. In neither passage is the text above suspicion; in 1 S **27** 8 LXX B omits the name. No satisfactory explanation has been suggested. W. Ewing

GESHURITES, gesh'ū-rīts, gē-shōō'rīts (גְּשׁוּרִי, *g^eshūrī*). See preceding article.

GESTURE, jes'ṭur, jes'ṭūr: The Oriental is rich in gestures by which feelings are expressed and force added to words. Of this we have abundant illustration in the Bible. Almost every available part of the body was employed in gesture. In *salutations* the whole body was bowed, sometimes to the ground (Gen **18** 2; **19** 1; **33** 7; **42** 6; **33** 3, 7 t), falling on the face to the ground and bowing to the ground, 3 t (1 S **20** 41; cf Gen **23** 7; 2 S **9** 8; **18** 21; 1 K **2** 19); it was common also to embrace and kiss (Ex **18** 7), etc, weeping for joy. Esau "fell on [Jacob's] neck, and kissed him: and they wept" (Gen **33** 4); cf Joseph and his brethren (**45** 14.15); David and Jonathan (1 S **20** 41), and the father of the prodigal (Lk **15** 20). We have the kiss also in the story of Judas with his Master (Mt **26** 49). Bowing the knee was also in Egypt an act of homage to a superior (Gen **41** 43); bowing the knee and bowing down were common in *prayer* and *worship* (1 K **19** 18; 2 Ch **6** 13; Ezr **9** 5; Isa **45** 23); in prayer the head and whole body were also bowed (Gen **24** 26; 2 K **5** 18; 2 Ch **29** 28 f). The rabbins decreed that in prayer "in bowing down, the back must be bent so low that every vertebra becomes conspicuous," and endless questions arose as to what it was lawful to do during prayer (Edersheim). We read also of prayer offered *standing* (1 S **1** 26; 1 K **8** 22; Mt **6** 5; Mk **11** 25), lifting up and spreading forth *the hands* (1 K **8** 22; 2 Ch **6** 13; Ezr **9** 5; Neh **8** 6; 1 Tim **2** 8); "lifting up the hands" was synonymous with prayer (Ps **77** 2; **141** 2; Lam **2** 19; 1 Tim **2** 8); falling on the knees in pleading (1 K **1** 13). Reverence for the aged was expressed by rising up in their presence (Lev **19** 32, "Thou shalt rise up before the hoary head"; cf Lam **5** 12). The hand was also laid on the mouth in token of respect (Job **29** 9); in token of blessing the right hand was placed on the head (Gen **48** 14; cf **49** 26; Prov **10** 6). The hands were laid on the head of the animal to be sacrificed; on the scapegoat and sin offering as denoting the transference of sin; on the burnt offering, perhaps as representing the offerer (Lev **1** 4; **16** 21). The hands were lifted up in blessing (Lev **9** 22), in solemn swearing (Gen **14** 22; Ex **6** 8 m; Dt **32** 40), in defiance and threatening (2 S **20** 21); extended in pleading (Isa **65** 2). Giving the hand or joining hands as a pledge of friendship and fidelity (2 K **10** 15; Prov **11** 21) was the origin of the widespread custom of "shaking hands"; "striking hands" signified the clenching of a bargain or agreement (Prov **6** 1 RV); as a solemn pledge the hand was placed under the thigh of the person to whom it was given (Gen **24** 2; **47** 29); plucking the hand out of the bosom was a sign of action (Ps **74** 11); clapping the hands, of rejoicing (2 K **11** 12; Ps **47** 1; **98** 8; Isa **55** 12), also of ridicule, contempt and rejoicing over one (Job **27** 23; Lam **2** 15; Nah **3** 19). We read of "beckoning with the hand" (Lk **5** 7; Jn **13** 24), preliminary to speaking (Acts **12** 17; **13** 16; **19** 33; **21** 40; **26** 1, he "stretched forth his hand"); drooping of the hands indicated failure, weakness or distress (He **12** 12; cf Isa **35** 3; Ecclus **25** 23); washing the hands (publicly) was a declaration of innocence, "of freedom from complicity" (Dt **21** 6.7; Mt **27** 24).

Mohammedans Praying in the Mosque at Damascus.

The *head* lifted up was a sign of arrogance or pride (Ps **83** 2); of exaltation, or recovery from trouble, etc (Jgs **8** 28; Ps **27** 6; **110** 7; Zec **1** 21); to cover the head was a symbol of grief or mourning (2 S **15** 30; Est **6** 12; Jer **14** 3), also putting the hand on the head (2 S **13** 19; Jer **2** 37), or ashes, dust or earth (Josh **7** 6; 1 S **4** 12; 2 S **1** 2; **13** 19; Est **4** 1); wagging (or shaking) the head expressed contempt or malicious enjoyment (Job **16** 4; Ps **64** 8; Jer **18** 16; Lam **2** 15; with "hissing," cf Mt **27** 39; Mk **15** 29; cf Ps **22** 7; **44** 14; **109** 25; Jer **48** 27).

Uncovering *the feet* was a sign of grief (2 S **15** 30; Isa **20** 2.4); lifting up the *heel* against one was a symbol of opposition (Ps **41** 9; Jn **13** 18); shaking the dust from the feet, of freeing from responsibility and of complete rejection (Mt **10** 14; Acts **13** 51; at Corinth Paul "shook out his raiment," Acts **18** 6); strong joyous feeling found (as elsewhere) expression in dancing (Jgs **11** 34; **21** 21; 1 S **18** 6; Jer **31** 4.13), before Jeh (Ex **15** 20; 2 S **6** 14.16).

Shooting out *the lip* was an expression of contempt (Ps **22** 7); to incline the *ear* signified attention (Ps **45** 10); rending the garments expressed the sense of horror (as in the presence of disaster, blasphemy, etc) (Nu **14** 6; Josh **7** 6; 1 S **4** 12; 2 S **1** 2; **13** 19; **15** 32; Mt **26** 65; Acts **14** 14); the *smile* indicated favor and gave confidence (Job **29** 24); lifting up the eyelids was a sign of pride (Prov **30** 13); Isaiah speaks also of the "outstretched necks and wanton eyes" of the haughty daughters of Zion, "walking and mincing as they go, and making a tinkling with their feet" (Isa **3** 16). The perverse man "winketh with his eyes . . . . speaketh with his feet . . . . maketh signs with his fingers" (Prov **6** 13).

It is interesting to note the gestures ascribed in the Gospels to Jesus. The expression of His eyes is often referred to; we read how He "lifted up his eyes on his disciples" before pronouncing the Beatitudes, indicating a loving regard for them (Lk **6** 20); how He "looked upon" the young ruler and "loved him," and, with another expressive "look" (round about)—a sad look—said, "How hardly shall they that have riches enter into the kingdom of God" (Mk **10** 21.23); how He "looked up to heaven" before He blessed and brake the loaves (Mt **14** 19; Mk **6** 41; Lk **9** 16); also before healing (Mk **7** 34); how He "looked round" on His adversaries in the synagogue (Lk **6** 10), "with anger, being grieved at the hardening of their heart" (Mk **3** 5); how He "turned and looked upon Peter" so that he remembered his boasting and fall, and went out and wept bitterly (Lk **22** 61); we read also how He took a little child into His arms and held him up as an example to His disciples (Mk **9** 36), and how He "took [little children] in his arms, and blessed them, laying his hands upon them" (Mk **10** 16); how He "stooped down, and with his finger wrote on the ground" when the woman accused of adultery was brought to Him, then "lifted up himself" and spake, again "stooped down, and with his finger wrote on the ground," till the woman's accusers had departed one by one, condemned and ashamed, when He again "lifted up himself" and sent the woman away (Jn **8** 6 ff); how on His way to the tomb of Lazarus, He was agitated, AV and RV "was troubled," m "troubled himself." Meyer has "shuddered." Some tr "shook himself" (Jn **11** 33). See, further, ATTITUDES.

W. L. WALKER

GET, GETTING: A great many Heb words are in the OT tr[d] "get," "got," etc. The word "get" has two meanings: (1) with the idea of movement, "to go," etc; (2) with that of acquisition, "to gain," "obtain," etc. (1) In the first sense the most frequent words are *bō'*, "to come, or go in" (Gen **45** 17; 1 S **22** 5, etc); *yālakh* "to go on" (Gen **12** 1; **22** 2; Ex **5** 4; Jer **5** 5, etc); *yāradh*, "to go down" (Gen **42** 2; Joel **3** 13); *'ālāh*, "to go up" (Gen **44** 17; Isa **40** 9; Jer **49** 31, etc). Other words are *nūdh*, "to move off" (Jer **49** 30 AV; Dnl **4** 14); *nāsā'*, "to remove" (Nu **14** 25); *yāçā'*, "to go out" (Gen **19** 14; **31** 13; Ex **11** 8). (2) In the sense of *acquisition*, the words most frequently tr[d] "get," etc, are *'āsāh*, "to do," "to make" (Gen **12** 5; **31** 1; Dt **8** 17.18); *ḳānāh*, "to get," "obtain" (Gen **4** 1; Prov **4** 5.7; Eccl **2** 7 AV, RV "bought"; Jer **13** 1, RV "buy"); *māçā'* "to find" (Nu **31** 50; 2 S **20** 6); *rākhash*, "to acquire," "gain" (Gen **31** 18; **36** 6 AV, RV "gathered"; **46** 6).

Getting is the tr of *pō'al* (Prov **21** 6), of *ḳinyān* "obtaining" (Gen **31** 18; Prov **4** 7, ERV text and ARV m "all thou hast gotten"). In the NT "get" in the first sense is the tr of *exérchomai*, "to go out or forth" (Lk **13** 31; Acts **7** 3; **22** 18); of *éxeimi*, "to go out or forth" (Acts **27** 43); of *katabaínō*, "to go down" (Acts **10** 20); *hupágō*, "to go away or under," "Get . . . . behind" (Mt **16** 23; Lk **4** 8 AV, "Get . . . . hence"; Mt **4** 10). The only separate word tr[d] "get" in the second sense is *heurískō*, "to begin to find" (usually tr[d] "find") (Lk **9** 12 AV, "that they may go . . . . and get victuals").

For "get" RV has "mount" (Dt **28** 43), "buy" (Prov **17** 16; Jer **13** 1; **19** 1); for "get you down" (Joel **3** 13), "tread ye," m "get you down"; "get" for "possess" (Lk **18** 12); "get them away" for "gather themselves together" (Ps **104** 22); "get us" for "apply" (Ps **90** 12); "let us get grain" for "therefore we take up corn for them," and for "that we might buy corn" (Neh **5** 2.3); "get you no" for "provide neither" (Mt **10** 9); "getteth prudence" for "is prudent," m "dealeth prudently" (Prov **15** 5); "getteth" for "coveteth" (Hab **2** 9).

W. L. WALKER

GETHER, gē'thẽr (גֶּתֶר, *gether*): In Gen **10** 23 named as one of the 4 sons of Aram. In 1 Ch **1** 17 mentioned simply among the sons of Shem.

GETHSEMANE, geth-sem'a-nē (Γεθσημανεί, *Gethsēmaneí* [for other spellings and accents see Thayer, s.v.]; probably from the Aram. גַּת שְׁמָנִים, *gath shemānīm*, "oil press"): Mentioned (Mt **26** 36; Mk **14** 32) as a place (*chōríon*), m "enclosed piece of ground," to which Jesus and the disciples retired

Gethsemane.

after the last supper; in Jn **18** 1 it is described as a "garden" (κῆπος, *kēpos*), while Lk (**22** 40) simply says "place" (τόπος, *tópos*). From Jn **18** 1 it is evident that it was across the Kidron, and from Lk **22** 39, that it was on the Mount of Olives. Very possibly (Lk **21** 37; **22** 39) it was a spot where Jesus habitually lodged when visiting Jerus. The owner—whom conjecture suggests as Mary the mother of Mark—must have given Jesus and His disciples special right of entry to the spot.

Tradition, dating from the 4th cent., has fixed on a place some 50 yds. E. of the bridge across the Kidron as the site. In this walled-in enclosure once of greater extent, now primly laid out with garden beds, by the owners—the Franciscans—are eight old olive trees supposed to date from the time of Our Lord. They are certainly old, they appeared venerable to the traveler Maundrell more than two centuries ago, but that they go back to the time claimed is impossible, for Jos states (*BJ*, VI, i, 1) that Titus cut down all the trees in the neighborhood of Jerus at the time of the siege. Some 100 yds. farther N. is the "Grotto of the Agony," a cave or cistern supposed to be the spot "about a stone's cast" to which Our Lord retired (Lk **22** 41). The Greeks have a rival garden in the neighborhood, and a little higher up the hill is a large Russian church. The traditional site may be somewhere near the correct one, though one would think too near the public road for retirement, but the contours of the hill slopes must have so much changed their forms in the troublous times of the first and second centuries, and the loose stone walls of such enclosures are of so temporary a character, that it is impossible that the site is exact. Sentiment, repelled by the artificiality of the modern garden, tempts the visitor to look for a more suitable and less artificial spot farther up the valley. Yet the sweet simplicity with which the Garden is kept, with its carefully guarded old olive trees and its flower beds, and the kindliness of the monks who have charge of it, make it a most impressive place for meditation.

E. W. G. MASTERMAN

GEUEL, gū'el, gē̆-ū'el (גְּאוּאֵל, *ge'ū'ēl*, "majesty of God"): The spy from the tribe of Gad (Nu **13** 15), sent by Moses to spy out the land of Canaan.

GEZER, gē'zẽr (גֶּזֶר, *gezer*): A city of great military importance in ancient times, the site of which has recently been thoroughly explored. The excavations at this spot are the most thorough and extensive of any in Pal, and have not only done much to confirm the history of the place, as known from Bib. and other sources, but have also thrown a flood of light upon the general history, civilization and religion of Pal in pre-Israelite and Israelitish times.

City Wall at Gezer. [From *Bible Side-Lights from the Mound of Gezer.*]

1. The Discovery and Position of the Site

The long-lost site of Gezer was discovered by M. Clermont-Ganneau in 1873, and his suggestion that the modern name for the place, *Tell Jezer* (or *Tell el Jezereh*) was a survival of the ancient name was confirmed by his further discovery of three bilingual inscriptions, in Heb and Gr, cut on surfaces of rock by a certain Alkios, apparently once the governor of the city; in one of them occurred the expression "the boundary of Gezer."

The natural features and the position of *Tell Jezer* abundantly explain the extreme importance of Gezer in ancient times. The buried remains crown a narrow hill, running from N.W. to S.E., about 1,700 ft. long by 300 to 500 ft. broad. The approach is steep on every side, and in early times, before the accumulation around the sides of the rubbish of some millenniums, must have been much more so. The hill stands, like an outpost, projecting into the great plain, and is connected with the low hills behind it, part of the Shephelah, with but a narrow neck. At the foot of the hill runs a great high road from Egypt to Syria; to the N. lies the Vale of Aijalon, across which runs the modern carriage road to Jerus, and up which ran the great high road, by the Beth-horons, to the plateau N. of Jerus; to the S. lies the Vale of Sorek, where stood Beth-shemesh, and along which went a great highway from the country of the Philis to the hill country of Judah. Today the Jerus-Jaffa railway, after sweeping some miles away in the plain round the whole western and southern sides of the site, passes along this open vale to plunge into the narrow defile—the *Wady Isma'in*, which it follows to Jerus. From the summit of the *Tell*, a vast expanse of country is visible between the long blue line of the Mediterranean to the W., and the abrupt and lofty mountains of Judah to the E. That it has been all through history the scene of military contest is fully understood when its strategic position is appreciated; no military leader even today, if holding the highlands of Pal against invasion, could afford to neglect such an outpost.

2. History of Gezer

Although the excavation of the site shows that it was occupied by a high civilization and a considerable population at an extremely early period, the first historical mention is in the list of the Palestinian cities captured by Tahutmes III (XVIIIth Dynasty, about 1500 BC). From this time it was probably under Egyp governors (the Egyp remains at all periods are considerable), but from the Am Tab, a century or so later, we learn that Egyp influence was then on the wane. Three of these famous clay tablets are dated from Gezer itself and are written in the name of the governor *Yapaḥi;* he was then hard pressed by the Khabiri, and he appealed for help in vain to Egypt. In other letters belonging to this series, there are references to this city. In one, a certain freebooter named Lapaya makes excuses that he had broken into the city. He "has been slandered. Is it an offence that he has entered Gazri and levied the people?" (no. CCXL, Petrie's tr).

In the well-known "Song of Triumph" of Meren-ptah, who is considered by many to be the Pharaoh of the Exodus, occurs the expression "Gezer is taken." (In connection with this it is interesting to notice that an ivory pectoral with the cartouche of Meren-ptah was unearthed at Gezer.)

In the time of Joshua's invasion a certain "king of Gezer" named Horam (הֹרָם, *hōrām*, but in LXX Αἰλάμ, *Ailám*, or Ἐλάμ, *Elám*) came to the assistance of Lachish against the Israelites, but was slain (Josh **10** 33). Gezer was taken, but the Canaanites were not driven out, but remained in servitude (Josh **16** 10; Jgs **1** 29). The city became one of the towns on the southern border of Ephraim (Josh **16** 3), but was assigned to the Kohath clan of the Levites (**21** 21). In 2 S **5** 25 (AV "Gazer") we read that David chased the Philis after their defeat in the valley of Rephaim "from Geba until thou come to Gezer," showing that this was on the frontier of the Phili territory; and in **1** Ch **20** 4 it states, "There arose war at Gezer with the Philis; then Sibbecai the Hushathite slew Sippai, of the sons of the giant; and they were subdued." In the corresponding account in 2 S **21** 18 the scene of this event is said to be Gob, which is probably a copyist's error—גוב for גזר. According to Jos (*Ant*, VIII, vi, 1), at the commencement of Solomon's reign Gezer was in the hands of the Philis, which may explain 1 K **9** 16, where it is stated that a certain Pharaoh, whose daughter Solomon married, captured and burnt Gezer and gave the site to his daughter. Solomon rebuilt it (ver **17**). There are no further references to Gezer during the later Jewish monarchy, but there are several during the Maccabean period. Judas pursued Gorgias to "Gazara and into the plains of Idumaea and Azotis and Jamnia" (1 Macc **4** 15); Bacchides, after his defeat by Jonathan, "fortified also the city of Beth-sura, and Gazara, and the tower, and put forces in them and provision of victuals" (1 Macc **9** 52 AV); a little later Simon "camped against Gazara and besieged it round about; he made also an engine of war, and set it by the city and battered a certain tower, and took it" (1 Macc **13** 43 AV), after which he purified it (vs 47.48). From Jos (*Ant*, XIII, viii, 2) we gather that Antiochus had taken Gezer from the Jews.

The governor, Alkios, who made the bilingual inscriptions, may come in about this time or a little later; the rock inscriptions, of which half a dozen are now known, give no information regarding their date.

In the period of the Crusades this site, under the

name "Mount Gisart," was a crusading fort and gave its name to a family. Here King Baldwin IV gained a victory over Saladin in 1177, and in 1191 the latter monarch camped here while conducting some fruitless negotiations with King Richard Cœur de Lion. In 1495 a skirmish occurred here between the governor of Jerus and certain turbulent Bedouin. The history of Gezer, as known, is thus one of battles and sieges extending over at least 3,000 years; from the archaeological remains we may infer that its history was similar for at least 1,000 years earlier.

3. History of the Excavations

In 1904 the Pal Exploration Fund of England obtained a "permit" for the excavation of *Tell Jezer*. The whole site was the private property of certain Europeans, whose agent, living much of the time on the *Tell* itself, was himself deeply interested in the excavations, so that unusually favorable conditions obtained for the work. Mr. (now Professor) R. A. Stewart Macalister, M.A., was sent out, and for 3 years (1904–7) he instituted an examination of the hidden remains in the mound, after a manner, till then, unexampled in Pal exploration. His ambition was to turn over every cubic foot of soil down to the original rock, so that nothing of importance could be overlooked. As at the expiration of the original "permit" much remained unexplored, application was made to the authorities for a second one, and, at the end of 1907, Mr. Macalister embarked on a further 2 years of digging. Altogether he worked for the greater part of 5 years, except for necessary interruptions of the work due to unfavorable weather. Some two-thirds of the total accumulated débris on the mound was ransacked, and besides this, many hundreds of tombs, caves and other antiquarian remains in the neighborhood were thoroughly explored.

4. Chief Results of the Explorations

It was found that the original bare rock surface of the hill was crowned with buried remains, in some parts 20 and 30 ft. deep, made up of the débris of all the cities which had stood on the site during three or four thousand years; on the part excavated there were no remains so late as the commencement of the Christian era, the Gezer of that time, and the crusading fort, being built on a neighboring site. The earliest inhabitants were Troglodytes living in the many caves which riddled the hill surface; they were apparently a non-Sem race, and there was some evidence that they at least knew of cremation. These, or a race soon after—the earliest Semites—inclosed the hilltop with high earth rampart faced with rough stones —the earliest "walls" going back at least before 3000 BC. At an early period—probably about 3000 BC—a race with a relatively high civilization fortified the whole hilltop with a powerful and remarkably well-built wall, 14 ft. thick, with narrow towers of short projection at intervals of 90 ft. At a point on the S. side of this was unearthed a very remarkable, massive, brick gateway (all the other walls and buildings are of stone), with towers on each side still standing to the height of 16 ft., but evidently once much higher. This gate showed a strong Egyp influence at work long before the first historic reference (XVIIIth Dynasty), for both gateway and wall to which it belonged had been ruined at an early date, the former indeed, after its destruction, was overlaid by the buildings of a city, which from its datable objects—scarabs, etc—must have belonged to the time of Amenhotep III, i.e. as early as 1500 BC.

The later wall, built, we may conclude, soon after the ruin of the former, and therefore about 1500 BC, was also a powerful construction and must have existed considerably over a thousand years, down, indeed, till 100 BC at least, when Gezer disappears from history as a fortified site. These walls inclosed a larger area than either of the previous ones; they show signs of destruction and repairs, and Mr. Macalister is of the opinion that some of the extensive repairs—in one place a gap of 150 ft.—and the 28 inserted towers are the work of Solomon (1 K **9** 17). This wall must have existed in use through all we know of Gezer from Bible sources. When, from the ruined remains, we reconstruct in imagination these mighty ramparts, we need not wonder that the Hebrews, fresh from long wanderings in the wilderness, found it no easy task to capture cities so fortified as was this (Nu **13** 28; Dt **1** 28).

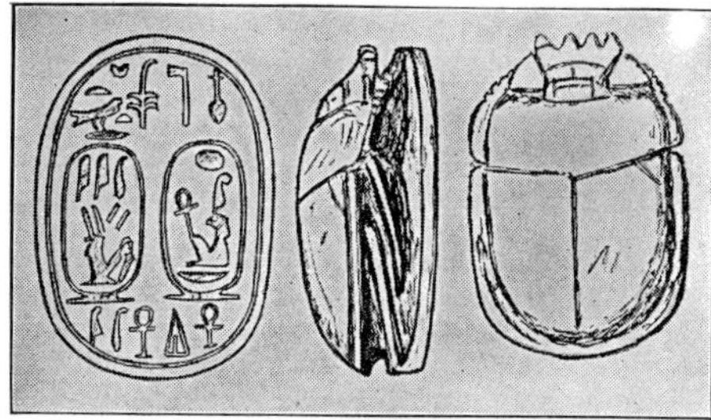

Scarab with Name of Amenhotep III, from Gezer.
[From *Bible Side-Lights from the Mound of Gezer.*]

The foundations of a powerful building, which were found inserted in a gap in the southern walls, turned out conclusively to be the palace of Simon Maccabaeus—who captured the city (1 Macc **13** 43)—a graffito being found upon one of its stones running thus:

Πάμπρα(ς) Σιμῶνος κατεπάγῃ (?) π(ῦρ) βασίλειον
Pámpra(s) Simṓnos katepágē(?) p(úr) basíleion

which seems to mean, "Pamphras, may he bring down [fire] on the palace of Simon."

Within the city walls the foundations of some seven or eight cities of various successive periods were found, superimposed one above the other. The city's best days appear to have been shortly before the time of Joshua; the next, perhaps, at the time of the Judges. With the period to which we should probably assign the arrival of the Hebrews, there is a great increase in the population, the hitherto inviolate environs of the "temple" being encroached upon by private dwellings: an interesting commentary on Josh **16** 10.

The great "High Place" which was uncovered is one of unique interest, and its discovery has thrown a flood of light upon the religion of the early Canaanites, that religion—"the worship of Baal and Ashteroth"—which was the great rival of the purer religion of Israel. This Ba'al temple, or *bāmōth*, consisted of a row of 8 *maççēbhōth* or rude stone pillars ranging in height from 5 ft. 5 in. to 10 ft. 9 in. (see High Place; Pillar), together with a curious trough which may have been a socket for the *'Ăshērāh* (see Asherah), or some kind of altar. The area around these pillars had a kind of rough floor of consolidated earth under which were found a number of large jars containing infant bones, considered to be the remains of infant sacrifice. In close proximity to this "temple" was a double cave, the construction of which strongly suggested that it had been arranged for the giving of oracles. This high place had been used for very many centuries; the *maççēbhōth* were not all of one period but had gradually been increased from one to seven, and an eighth of a more definitely sculptured form—a *simulacrum priapi*—had been added some time later. In the accumulated rubbish around these pillars were found enormous numbers of small stone phallic images, together with pottery plaques of Astarte, made with rude exaggeration of the sexual organs (see BAAL; ASHTEROTH).

Sacrificed Infant Buried in a Jar at Gezer. [From *Bible Side-Lights from the Mound of Gezer.*]

Another monument of great interest—and high antiquity—was the great rock-cut tunnel. It is about 23 ft. high, and 13 ft. wide, and descends by 80 steps, 94½ ft. through the solid rock, to a cave in which there is a spring. It is very similar to the great tunnel known as "Warren's tunnel and shaft" which was clearly constructed by the early Jebusites to reach from within the city's walls to the fountain of Gihon (see SILOAM; ZION). This Gezer tunnel must date at least to 2000 BC; it is evident from the nature of the accumulated débris which blocked its mouth that it was actually abandoned about 1400 BC. Its antiquity is confirmed by the fact that it was evidently excavated with flint knives.

At a much later period in history, in that of the Maccabees, the water supply of the city, in time of siege, at any rate, was largely dependent on an enormous open cistern which Mr. Macalister cleared of earth and found capable of containing 2,000,000 gallons of water. Among the smaller "finds" which throw light upon the Bible history may be mentioned two much broken, cuneiform tablets, both referring to land contracts, which, from the names of the eponyms, can be dated to 651 and 649 BC respectively. They therefore belong to the time of the last, and one of the greatest, of the Assyr monarchs, Ashurbanipal, the "noble Osnappar" of Ezr **4** 10, and they show that he was not only a great conqueror, but that in Pal he had an organized government and that legal civil business was transacted in the language of Assyria.

The illumination of OT history which the excavations of Gezer have afforded can here be only hinted at, but references to it will occur in many of the articles in other parts of this Encyclopaedia.

LITERATURE.—In *Bible Side-Lights from the Mound of Gezer* Professor R. A. S. Macalister has described in a popular form with illustrations some of his most remarkable discoveries; while in the *Memoirs of the Excavations at Gezer* (1912), published by the Palestine Exploration Fund, Professor Macalister deals with the subject exhaustively.

E. W. G. MASTERMAN

GEZRITES, gez′rīts. See GIRZITES.

GHOST, gōst (נֶפֶשׁ, *nephesh;* **πνεῦμα**, *pneúma*): "Ghost," the middle-Eng. word for "breath," "spirit," appears in AV as the tr of *nephesh* ("breath," "the breath of life," animal soul or spirit, the vital principle, hence "life"), in two places of the OT, viz. Job **11** 20, "the giving up of the ghost" (so RV), and Jer **15** 9, "She hath given up the ghost"; *gāwa‘*, "to gasp out," "expire" (die), is also several times so tr^d (Gen **25** 8.17; **35** 29; **49** 33; Job **3** 11; **10** 18; **13** 19; **14** 10; Lam **1** 19). In Apoc (Tob **14** 11) *psuchḗ* is tr^d in the same way as *nephesh* in the OT, and in 2 Macc **3** 31, *en eschátē pnoḗ* is rendered "give up the ghost," RV "quite at the last gasp."

In the NT "to give up the ghost" is the tr of *ekpnéō*, "to breathe out" (Mk **15** 37.39; Lk **23** 46; so RV); of *ekpsúchō*, "to breathe out," "expire" (Acts **5** 5.10; **12** 23); in Mt **27** 50, *aphḗken tó pneúma*, and in Jn **19** 30, *parédōken tó pneúma*, are rendered respectively, "yielded" and "gave up the ghost," RV "yielded up his spirit," "gave up his spirit."

"The Holy Ghost" is also frequent in AV; in ARV it is invariably changed to "Holy Spirit," in ERV sometimes only, chiefly in the Gospels. See HOLY SPIRIT; SPIRIT. W. L. WALKER

GHOST, HOLY. See HOLY SPIRIT.

GIAH, gī′a (גִּיחַ, *gīaḥ*): An unidentified place on the route followed by Abner in his flight, pursued by Joab (2 S **2** 24). LXX renders *Gaí*, corresponding to the Heb *gē*, "valley." The form *gīaḥ* may be due to corruption of the text.

GIANTS, jī′ants: The word appears in AV as the tr of the Heb words נְפִילִים, *nephīlīm* (Gen **6** 4; Nu **13** 33); רְפָאִים, *rephā'īm* (Dt **2** 11.20; **3** 11.13; Josh **12** 4, etc); רָפָא, *rāphā'* (1 Ch **20** 4.6.8), or רָפָה, *rāphāh* (2 S **21** 16.18.20.22); in one instance of גִּבּוֹר, *gibbōr*, lit. "mighty one" (Job **16** 14).

In the first two cases RV changes "giants" into the Heb words "Nephilim," *nephīlīm*, and "Rephaim," *rephā'īm*, respectively (see these words). The "Nephilim" of Gen **6** 4 are not to be confounded with the "mighty men" subsequently described as the offspring of the unlawful marriages of "the sons of God" and "the daughters of men." It is told that they overspread the earth prior to these unhallowed unions. That the word, whatever its etymology, bears the sense of men of immense stature is evident from the later passages, Nu **13** 33. The same is true of the "Rephaim," as shown by the instance of Og (Dt **3** 11; Josh **12** 4). There is no doubt about the meaning of the word in the case of the giants mentioned in 2 S **21** and 1 Ch **20**. See also ANTEDILUVIANS.

JAMES ORR

GIANTS, VALLEY OF THE. See REPHAIM, VALLEY OF.

GIBBAR, gib′är (גִּבָּר, *gibbār*, "hero"): In Ezr **2** 20 the "children of Gibbar" are mentioned among those who returned with Zerubbabel. The ‖ passage (Neh **7** 25) has "children of Gibeon."

GIBBETHON, gib′e-thon (גִּבְּתוֹן, *gibbethōn*): A city in the territory of Dan in the plain named with Eltekeh and Baalath (Josh **19** 44), and assigned to the Kohathite Levites (**21** 23). Later we find it in the hands of the Philis; and it was while besieging the city that Nadab was slain by Baasha (1 K **15** 27). After 25 years Omri, the general of Baasha, was here made king of the army when news reached them of Zimri's regicide (1 K **16** 15 ff). It may possibly be identified with *Kibbiah*, which lies about 16 miles S.E. of Jaffa; but no certain identification is possible. W. EWING

GIBEA, gib′ē-a (גִּבְעָא, *gibh‘ā'*, "hill"): A grandson of Caleb (1 Ch **2** 49). His father was Sheva, whose mother was Maacah, Caleb's concubine (ver 48).

GIBEAH, gib'ē-a (גִּבְעָה, *gibh'āh,* "hill"): The Heb word denotes generally an eminence or hill, in distinction from *har,* which is used for mountain, or mountain range. It occurs, however, in two instances, as a place-name. Under Geba (q.v.) we have seen that Geba, Gibeah, and Gibeon are liable to be confused. This arises from their resemblance in form and meaning.

(1) An unidentified city in the territory of Judah (Josh **15** 57). It is named in the group containing Carmel, Ziph and Kain; it is therefore probably to be sought to the S.E. of Hebron. It may be one of the two villages mentioned by *Onom* (s.v. "Gabathōn"), Gabaa and Gabatha, in the E. of the Daroma. It is probably identical with Gibeah mentioned in 2 Ch **13** 2.

1. History

(2) A city described as belonging to Benjamin (Josh **18** 28; Jgs **19** 14), Gibeah of Benjamin (1 S **13** 2.15; **14** 16), Gibeah of the children of Benjamin (2 S **23** 29), Gibeah of Saul (1 S **11** 4; Isa **10** 29), and possibly, also, Gibeah of God (1 S **10** 5 m); see Gibeath, 4. The narrative in which it first appears is one of extraordinary and tragic interest, casting priceless light on the conditions prevailing in those days when "there was no king in Israel" (Jgs **19** ff). A Levite sojourning on the farther side of Mt. Ephraim was deserted by his concubine who returned to her father's house in Beth-lehem-judah. Thither he went to persuade her to return. Hospitably entertained by her father, he tarried till the afternoon of the fifth day. The evening was nigh when they came over against Jebus—Jerusalem—but, rejecting his servant's suggestion that they should lodge in this "city of a stranger"—i.e. the Jebusite—the Levite pressed on, and when they were near to Gibeah the sun set. They entered the city and sat down in the street. The laws of hospitality today do not compel the entertainment of strangers who arrive after sunset. But it may have been through disregard of all law that they were left unbefriended. An old man from Mt. Ephraim took pity on them, invited them to his house, and made himself responsible for their necessities. Then follows the horrible story of outrage upon the Levite's concubine; the way in which he made known his wrongs to Israel; and the terrible revenge exacted from the Benjamites, who would not give up to justice the miscreants of Gibeah.

Gibeah was the home of Saul, the first king of Israel, and thither he returned after his election at Mizpah (1 S **10** 26). From Gibeah he summoned Israel to assemble for the relief of Jabesh-gilead, which was threatened by Nahash the Ammonite (1 S **11** 4 ff). In the wars of Saul with the Philis, Gibeah seems to have played a conspicuous part (1 S **13** 15). Here were exposed the bodies of the seven sons of Saul, slain by David's orders, to appease the Gibeonites, furnishing the occasion for Rizpah's pathetic vigil (2 S **21** 1 ff). Gibeah is mentioned in the description of the Assyr advance on Jerus (Isa **10** 29).

2. Identification

The site now generally accepted as that of Gibeah is on *Teleil el-Fūl,* an artificial mound about 4 miles N. of Jerus, a short distance E. of the high road to Shechem. A little way N. of *Teleil el-Fūl,* the high road bifurcates, one branch turning eastward to *Jeba',* i.e. Geba (which should be read instead of "Gibeah" in Jgs **20** 31); the other continuing northward to Bethel. Not far from the parting of the ways, on the road to *Jeba'* lies *er-Rām,* corresponding to Ramah (Jgs **19** 13). At Gibeah, about 30 furlongs from Jerus, Titus encamped for the night on his advance against the city from the N. *Teleil el-Fūl* quite satisfactorily suits all the data here indicated.

The words in Jgs **20** 33 rendered by AV "the meadows of Gibeah," RV "Maareh-geba"—simply transliterating—and RVm "the meadow of Geba" (or Gibeah), by a slight emendation of the text, read "from the west of Gibeah," which is certainly correct. W. Ewing

GIBEATH, gib'ē-ath (גִּבְעַת, *gibh'ath*): This is the *status constructus* of the foregoing (Gibeah). It is found in several compound place-names.

(1) *Gibeath-ha-araloth* (גִּבְעַת הָעֲרָלוֹת, *gibh'ath hā'ărālōth*). EV tr^s lit. "hill of the foreskins"; but the margins suggest the proper name. Here the Israelites were circumcised after the passage of the Jordan (Josh **5** 3). The place was therefore between that river and Jericho.

(2) *Gibeath Phinehas* (גִּבְעַת פִּינְחָס, *gibh'ath pīn^e ḥāṣ*), the burial place of Eleazar the son of Aaron in Mt. Ephraim (Josh **24** 33 AV "a hill that pertained to Phinehas," RV "the hill of Phinehas," RVm "Gibeah of Phinehas"). Conder would identify it with *'Awertah* in the plain of Makhneh, not far from *Nablūs,* where "the Samaritans show the tombs of Phinehas and Eleazar, Abishuah and Ithamar" (*Tent Work,* 41 f). The "tomb of Eleazar" is 18 ft. long, plastered all over and shaded by a splendid terebinth." Guérin places it at *Jībia,* 3 miles N. of *Ḳaryat el-'Anab* (*Judée,* III, 37 f; *Samarie,* 106 ff). There is no certainty.

(3) *Gibeath hammoreh* (גִּבְעַת הַמּוֹרֶה, *gibh'ath hamōreh*), a hill on the N. side of the valley from the camp of Gideon, beside which lay the Midianites (Jgs **7** 1, EV "the hill of Moreh"; the Heb is lit. "hill of the teacher"). It is probably identical with *Jebel Duḥy,* which rises on the N. of the Vale of Jezreel. Moore (*Judges,* 200) mistakenly calls the mountain *Nabī Daḥī.* This is, of course, the name of the "prophet" whose shrine crowns the hill. See Moreh.

(4) *Gibeath ha-Elohim* (גִּבְעַת הָאֱלֹהִים, *gibh-'ath hā-'ĕlōhīm*), the place where Saul, after leaving Samuel, met the company of prophets, and prophesied with them (1 S **10** 5.10). It is defined as the place "where is the garrison [or pillar] of the Philis." This may be intended to distinguish it from Gibeah (2), with which it is often identified. In this case it may be represented by the modern *Ramallah,* about 10 miles N. of Jerus. See also Tabor.

(5) *Gibeath ha-Hachilah* (1 S **23** 19; **26** 1) is identical with Hachilah (q.v.).

(6) *Gibeath Ammah* (2 S **2** 24) is identical with Ammah (q.v.).

(7) *Gibeath Gareb* (Jer **31** 39) is identical with Gareb (q.v.). W. Ewing

GIBEATH (Josh **18** 28). See Gibeah (2).

GIBEATHITE, gib'ē-ath-īt. See Shemaah.

GIBEON, gib'ē-un (גִּבְעוֹן, *gibh'ōn*): One of the royal cities of the Hivites (Josh **9** 7). It was a greater city than Ai; and its inhabitants were reputed mighty men (**10** 2). It fell within the territory allotted to Benjamin (**18** 25), and was one of the cities given to the Levites (**21** 17).

1. The Gibeonites

By a stratagem the Gibeonites secured for themselves and their allies in Chephirah, Beeroth and Kiriath-jearim immunity from attack by the Israelites. Terrified by the fate of Jericho and Ai, a company disguised as ambassadors from a far country, their garments and shoes worn, and their provisions moldy as from the length of their journey, went to Joshua at Gilgal, and persuaded him and the princes of Israel to make a covenant with them Three days later the deception was discovered and the wrath of the congregation of Israel aroused. In virtue of the covenant their lives were secured; but for their duplicity Joshua cursed them, and condemned them to be bondmen, "hewers of wood and drawers of water for the house of my God" (Josh **9** 23), "for the congregation and for the altar of the Lord" (ver 27 AV). This points to their employment in the sanctuary; and possibly may shed some light on the massacre of the Gibeonites by Saul (2 S **21** 1 f). The rest of the Canaanites resented the defection of the Hivites which so greatly weakened the forces for defence, and, headed by Adoni-zedek of Jerus, they assembled to wreak vengeance on Gibeon. The threatened city appealed to Joshua, who made a swift night march, fell suddenly upon the confederates, routed them, and "chased them by the way of the ascent of Beth-horon, and smote them to Azekah, and unto Makkedah" (Josh **10** 1 ff).

A three years' famine in the days of David was attributed to God's anger at the unexpiated crime of Saul in slaying the Gibeonites. He did this "in his zeal for . . . . Israel and Judah," who may have fretted at the inconvenience of having the Gibeonites among them. The latter believed that Saul's desire was to destroy them utterly. When David tried to arrange matters with them they stood upon their ancient rights, claiming life for life. They would take no blood money: they demanded blood from the family of the slayer of their people. This demand David could not resist, and handed over to them seven sons of Saul (2 S **21** 1 ff).

The army of Ishbosheth under Abner, and that of David under Joab, met at the pool of Gibeon.

2. The Champions

An attempt to settle the quarrel, by means of 12 champions on either side, failed, as each man slew his fellow, and the 24 perished side by side. A "sore battle" ensued in which Abner was beaten; he was pursued by the fleet-footed Asahel, brother of Joab, whom he slew. See Helkath-hazzurim.

Possibly we should read "Gibeon" instead of "Geba" in 2 S **5** 25, as in the ‖ passage, 1 Ch **14** 16 (*HDB*, s.v.) From Baal-perazim David was to make a circuit and fall upon the Philis who were encamped in the plain of Rephaim W. of Jerus. Perhaps, however, we should read "Gibeah" in both places. Cheyne (*EB*, s.v.) thinks the hill town of Baal-perazim may be intended.

When, after the death of Absalom and the suppression of his rebellion, Bichri raised the standard

3. Murder of Amasa

of revolt, Amasa was sent to call out the men of Judah against him. Tarrying longer than the time appointed, there was danger lest Bichri might have opportunity to strengthen his position; so David dispatched Abishai and the troops that were with him to attack Bichri at once. Joab went with this expedition. Obviously he could never be content with a second place. The force of Amasa was met at "the great stone of Gibeon." There Joab treacherously slew that unsuspecting general, and, himself assuming command, stamped out the rebellion with his accustomed thoroughness (2 S **20** 4 ff). "The great stone" appears to have been well known, and may have possessed some religious character.

Gibeon was the seat of an ancient sanctuary, called in 1 K **3** 4 "the great high place." Here,

4. The Sanctuary

according to 2 Ch **1** 3, was the tabernacle made in the wilderness—but see 1 K **8** 4. It was the scene of Solomon's great sacrifice after which he slept in the sanctuary and dreamed his famous dream (1 K **3** 4 ff; **9** 2; 2 Ch **1** 3.13, etc).

By "the great waters that are in Gibeon" Johanan overtook Ishmael the son of Nethaniah, and freed the captives he had taken from Mizpah (Jer **41** 11 ff). Among those who returned with Zerubbabel were 95 "children of Gibeon" (Neh **7** 25; cf **3** 7). At Gibeon Cestius Gallus encamped when marching against Jerus from Antipatris (*BJ*, II, xix, 1).

The ancient city is represented by the modern village *el-Jīb*. It is fully 5 miles N.W. of Jerus, and

5. Identification and Description

about a mile N. of *Neby Samwīl*, on a double knoll, with terraced slopes, but rocky and precipitous to the E. The village stands amid striking remains of antiquity. About a hundred paces from the village to the E. is a large reservoir with a spring. Lower down, among the olives, are the remains of another and larger reservoir, which collected the overflow from the first. This is probably the "pool" of 2 S **2** 13, and "the great waters" of Jer **41** 12. *El-Jīb* stands in the midst of a rich upland plain not far S. of the great pass which goes down by way of the Beth-horons into the vale of Aijalon.

W. Ewing

GIBEONITES, gib'ē-un-īts. Inhabitants of Gibeon (q.v.).

GIBLITES, gib'līts. See Gebalites.

GIDDALTI, gi-dal'tī (גִּדַּלְתִּי, *giddaltī*, "I magnify [God]"): A son of Heman (1 Ch **25** 4.29), one of David's musicians.

GIDDEL, gid'el (גִּדֵּל, *giddēl*, "very great," "stout"):

(1) The name of the head of a family of Nethinim (Ezr **2** 47=Neh **7** 49=1 Esd **5** 30 [here as Cathua]).

(2) The name of the head of a family of Solomon's servants (Ezr **2** 56=Neh **7** 58=1 Esd **5** 33 [here Isdael]).

GIDEON, gid'ē-un (גִּדְעוֹן, *gidh'ōn*, "cutter down," "feller" or "hewer"): Also named Jerubbaal (Jgs **6** 32) and Jerubbesheth (2

1. His Family and Home

S **11** 21), youngest son of Joash, of the clan of Abiezer in the tribe of Manasseh. His home was at Ophrah, and his family an obscure one. He became the chief leader of Manasseh and the fifth recorded judge of Israel. The record of his life is found in Jgs **6**–**8**.

Joash was an idolater, and sacrifices to Baal were common among the entire clan. Gideon seems to have held this worship in contempt, and to have pondered deeply the causes of Israel's reverses and the injuries wrought upon his own family by the hand of the Midianites.

The Midianites under Zebah and Zalmunna, their two greatest chiefs, accompanied by other wild

2. The Midianite Oppression

tribes of the eastern desert, had gradually encroached on the territory of Israel in Central Pal. They came first as marauders and pillagers at the time of the harvests, but later they forcibly took possession of lands, and thus inflicted permanent injury and loss, esp. upon Manasseh and Ephraim. The conflicts became so numerous, the appropriation of land so flagrant, that the matter of sustenance became a serious problem (**6** 4). The multitude of these desert hordes and the cruelty of their depredation rendered defence difficult, and, lacking in the spirit of national unity, the Israelites were driven to dens, caves and rocky strongholds for safety (**6** 2). After seven years of such invasion and suffering Gideon comes upon the scene.

It is probable that Gideon had already distinguished himself in resistance to the Midianites

3. The Call of Gideon

(**6** 12), but he now receives Divine commission to assume the leadership. Having taken his own little harvest to a secret place for threshing, that it might escape the greed of the Midianites, he is surprised while at work by a visit from the Lord in the form of an angel. However this scene (**6** 11 ff) and its miraculous incidents may be interpreted, there can be no question of the divineness of Gideon's call or that the voice which spoke to him was the voice of God. Neither the brooding over the death of his brothers at Tabor (**8** 18) nor the patriotic impulses dwelling within him can account for his assumption of leadership. Nor did he become leader at the demand of the people. He evidently had scarcely thought of himself as his country's deliverer. The call not only came to him as a surprise, but found him distrustful both of himself (**6** 15) and of his people (ver 13). It found him too without inclination for the task, and only his conviction that the command was of God persuaded him to assume leadership. This gives the note of accuracy to the essential facts of the story. Gideon's demand for a sign (ver 17) being answered, the food offered the messenger having been consumed by fire at the touch of his staff, Gideon acknowledged the Divine commission of his visitor, and at the place of visitation built an altar to Jeh (vs 19 ff).

4. His First Commission

The call and first commission of Gideon are closely joined. He is at once commanded to destroy the altars of Baal set up by his father at Ophrah, to build an altar to Jeh at the same place and thereon to offer one of his father's bullocks as a sacrifice (vs 25 f). There is no reason to look on this as a second version of Gideon's call. It is rather the beginning of instruction, and is deeply significant of the accuracy of the story, in that it follows the line of all revelation to God's prophets and reformers to begin their work at home. Taking ten men, under the cover of darkness, Gideon does as commanded (ver 27). The morning revealed his work and visited upon him the wrath of the people of Ophrah. They demand of Joash that he put his son to death. The answer of Joash is an ironical but valid defence of Gideon. Why should the people plead for Baal? A god should be able to plead his own cause (vs 28 ff). This defence gained for Gideon the name Jerubbaal (*y^erubba'al*, i.e. *yārebh bō ha-ba'al*, "Let Baal plead," **6** 32 AV).

The time intervening between this home scene and the actual campaign against the Midianites cannot definitely be named. It is probable that it took months for Gideon even to rally the people of his own clan. The fact is that all the subsequent events of the story are somewhat confused by what looks like a double narrative in which there are apparent but not vital differences. Without ignoring this fact it is still possible to get a connected account of what actually transpired.

5. Gideon's Army

When the allied invaders were in camp on the plain of Jezreel, we find Gideon, having recruited the Abiezrites and sent messengers to the various tribes of Israel (**6** 34 f), pitching his camp near the Midianites. The location of the various camps of Gideon is difficult, as is the method of the recruiting of the tribes. For instance, **6** 35 seems to be in direct contradiction to **7** 23, and both are considered of doubtful origin. There was evidently, however, a preliminary encampment at the place of rallying. While waiting here, Gideon further tested his commission by the dry and wet fleece (**6** 37 ff) and, convinced of God's purpose to save Israel by his leadership, he moves his camp to the S.E. edge of the plain of Jezreel nearby the spring of Harod. From his point of vantage here he could look down on the tents of Midian. The account of the reduction of his large army from 32,000 to 300 (**7** 2 ff) is generally accepted as belonging to a later tradition. Neither of the tests, however, is unnatural, and the first was not unusual. According to the account, Gideon at the Lord's command first excused all the fearful. This left him with 10,000 men. This number was reduced to 300 by a test of their method of drinking. This test can easily be seen to evidence the eagerness and courage of men for battle (Jos).

6. The Midianites' Discomfiture and Flight

Having thus reduced the army and having the assurance that the Lord would deliver to him and his little band the forces of Midian, Gideon, with a servant, went by night to the edge of the camp of his enemy, and there heard the telling and interpretation of a dream which greatly encouraged him and led him to strike an immediate blow (**7** 9 ff). Again we find a conflict of statement between **7** 20 and **7** 22, but the conflict is as to detail only. Dividing his men into three equal bands, Gideon arranges that with trumpets, and lights concealed in pitchers, and with the cry, "The sword of Jeh and of Gideon!" they shall descend and charge the Midianites simultaneously from three sides. This stratagem for concealing his numbers and for terrifying the enemy succeeds, and the Midianites and their allies flee in disorder toward the Jordan (**7** 18 ff). The rout was complete, and the victory was intensified by the fact that in the darkness the enemy turned their swords against one another. Admitting that we have two narratives (cf **7** 24; **8** 3 with **8** 4 ff) and that there is some difference between them in the details of the attack and the progress of the conflict, there is no need for confusion in the main line of events. One part of the fleeing enemy evidently crossed the Jordan at Succoth, being led by Zebah and Zalmunna. The superior force followed the river farther south, toward the ford of Bethbarah. Gideon sent messengers to the men of Ephraim (**7** 24), probably before the first attack, asking them to intercept the Midianites, should they attempt to escape by the fords in their territory.

7. Death of Oreb and Zeeb

This they did, defeating the enemy at Beth-barah and slaying the princes Oreb and Zeeb ("the Raven" and "the Wolf"). As proof of their victory and valor they brought the heads of the princes to Gideon and accused him of having discounted their bravery by not calling them earlier into the fight. But Gideon was a master of diplomacy, as well as of strategy, and won the friendship of Ephraim by magnifying their accomplishment in comparison with his own (**8** 1 ff).

Gideon now pursues Zebah and Zalmunna on the E. side of the river. The people on that side are still in great fear of the Midianites and refuse even to feed his army. At Succoth they say to him, "Are the hands of Zebah and Zalmunna now in thy hand, that we should give bread unto thine army?" (**8** 6). At Penuel he meets with the same refusal (**8** 8). Promising to deal with Succoth and Penuel as they deserve when he is through with his present task, Gideon pushes on with his half-famished but courageous men, overtakes the Midianites, defeats them, captures Zebah and Zalmunna, and, returning, punishes, according to his promise, both Succoth and Penuel (**8** 7.9.13 ff).

8. Death of Zebah and Zalmunna

Thus was the power of the Midianites and the desert hordes broken in Canaan and a forty years' peace came to Israel. But the two kings of Midian must now meet their fate as defeated warriors. They had led their forces at Tabor when the brothers of Gideon perished. So Gideon commands his young son Jether to slay them as though they were not worthy of death at a warrior's hand (**8** 20). The youth fearing the task, Gideon himself put them to death (**8** 21).

The people clamored to make Gideon king. He refused, being moved possibly by a desire to maintain the theocracy. To this end he asks only the jewelry taken as spoil in the battles (**8** 24 ff), and with it makes an ephod, probably an image of Jeh, and places it in a house of the Lord at Ophrah. By this act it was later thought that Gideon contributed to a future idolatry of Israel. The narrative properly closes with **8** 28. The remaining verses containing the account of Gideon's family and death (**8** 30 ff) and the record of events immediately subsequent to Gideon's death (**8** 33 ff) come from other sources than the original narrators.

9. Gideon's Ephod

10. His Death

C. E. Schenk

GIDEONI, gid-ē-ō′nī (גִּדְעֹנִי, *gidh'ōnī*): The father of Abidan who was prince of Benjamin, mentioned only in connection with the son (Nu **1** 11; **2** 22; **7** 60.65; **10** 24).

GIDOM, gī′dom (גִּדְעֹם, *gidh'ōm*): The limit eastward, from Gibeah toward the wilderness, of the pursuit of Benjamin by Israel (Jgs **20** 45). No name suggesting this has yet been recovered. It is not mentioned elsewhere.

GIER-EAGLE, jēr′-ē-g'l (רָחָם, *rāhām;* **κύκνος,** *kúknos,* in Lev, **πορφυρίων,** *porphuríōn,* in Dt): The name applied to one of the commonest of the vultures, and not an eagle at all. The word is derived from a Heb root, meaning "to love," and was applied to the birds because mated pairs seldom separated. These were smaller birds and inferior to the largest members of the family. They nested on a solid base, lived in pairs, and not only flocked over carrion as larger species permitted, but also ate the vilest offal of all sorts, for which reason they were protected by a death penalty by one of the Pharaohs.

Gier-Eagle (*Neophron percnopterus*).

Because of this the birds became so frequent and daring around camps, among tent-dwellers, and in cities, that they were commonly called "Pharaoh's chickens." They are mentioned in the Bible in the lists of abominations found in Lev **11** 13 and Dt **14** 12 (AV "ossifrage"); **14** 17 AV (RV "vulture").

Gene Stratton-Porter

GIFT, gift (מַתָּנָה, *mattānāh,* מִנְחָה, *minhāh,* שֹׁחַד, *shōhadh;* **δῶρον,** *dōron,* **δωρεά,** *dōreá,* **χάρισμα,** *chárisma*): In Gen **25** 6; Ex **28** 38; Nu **18** 6.7.29; Ezk **20** 26, etc, *mattānāh,* "a gift," is so rendered; *minhāh,* an offering or present, used esp. of the "meat offerings," is tr^d "gift" (2 S **8** 2.6 AV; 2 Ch **26** 8), in which passages "tribute" is meant, as RV; **32** 23; Ps **45** 12. A few other words occur singly, e.g. *'eshkar,* "a reward" (Ps **72** 10); *mas'ēth,* "lifting up" (Est **2** 18); *nāthūn* is tr^d "gifts" (Nu **8** 19; RVm "Heb *n^ethūnīm,* given"); *nēdheh, nādhān,* "impure gifts" (Ezk **16** 33); *nissē'th,* "a thing lifted up" (2 S **19** 42); *shōhadh* means "a bribe" (Ex **23** 8; Dt **16** 19; 2 Ch **19** 7; Prov **6** 35; **17** 8.23; Isa **1** 23; Ezk **22** 12); in each instance ARV has "bribe" except Prov **6** 35, "gifts"; *t^erūmāh,* "a present" (Prov **29** 4), may also mean a bribe, AV "he that receiveth gifts," RV "he that exacteth gifts," m "imposeth tribute, Heb a man of offerings."

In the NT *dōron,* "a present," "gift" (from *dídōmi,* "to give"), is tr^d "gift" (Mt **2** 11; **5** 23.24 *bis;* Mk **7** 11 AV; He **5** 1; Rev **11** 10, etc, referring chiefly to gifts or offerings to God); *dōrea,* "a free gift" (Jn **4** 10; Acts **2** 38; Rom **5** 15.17; 2 Cor **9** 15; He **6** 4, etc, referring to the gifts of God); *dṓrēma,* "a free gift" (Rom **5** 16; Jas **1** 17, ERV "boon"); *dósis,* "a giving" (Jas **1** 17, "every good gift," RVm "giving"); *charisma,* "grace," "favor," a benefit or good conferred, is also used of Divine gifts and favors, esp. of the supernatural gifts imparted by the Holy Spirit (*charismata*) enumerated in Rom **12;** 1 Cor **12;** the word occurs tr^d "gift, gifts" (Rom **1** 11), "some spiritual gift" (**5** 15.16, "free gift"; **6** 23, "The gift of God is eternal life," RV "free gift"; **11** 29; 1 Cor **1** 7; **7** 7; 2 Cor **1** 11; 1 Tim **4** 14; 2 Tim **1** 6; 1 Pet **4** 10); *cháris,* "grace," "favor" (2 Cor **8** 4, RV "grace"); *merismós,* "distribution," "parting" (He **2** 4, RVm "distributions"); *anáthēma,* "a thing devoted to God," is once (Lk **21** 5) used of "the goodly gifts" (RV "offerings") which adorned the Temple at Jerus.

In RV "gift" is substituted in the text of Gen **33** 11 for blessing, m "Heb blessing"; "boasteth himself of his gifts falsely" (Prov **25** 14) for "boasteth himself of a false gift," m "Heb in a gift of falsehood"; "a parting gift" for "presents" (Mic **1** 14); "Given to God" for "a gift" (Mk **7** 11).

W. L. Walker

GIFT OF TONGUES. See Tongues, Gift of.

GIFTS OF HEALING. See Healing.

GIFTS, SPIRITUAL. See Spiritual Gifts.

GIHON, gī′hon (גִּיחוֹן, *gīhōn;* **Γηών,** *Gēōn*): One of the four rivers of Eden (Gen **2** 13). It is said to compass the whole land of Cush (Ethiopia), probably a province E. of the Tigris. The Gihon is thought by Sayce to be the Kerkha, coming down from Luristan through the province known in the cuneiform texts as Kassi, probably the Cush of the Bible. See Eden.

Used **fig.** of wisdom in Sir **24** 27, "as Gihon [AV Geon] in the days of vintage."

GIHON (גִּיחוֹן, *gīhōn,* גִּחוֹן, *gihōn* [in 1 K], from root גִּיחַ, "to burst forth"):

(1) See preceding article.

(2) The Nile in Jer **2** 18 LXX (Γηῶν, *Gēōn*); in Heb שִׁחוֹר, *shihōr* (see Shihor).

(3) A spring in Jerus, evidently sacred, and, for that reason, selected as the scene of Solomon's coronation (1 K **1** 38). It is without doubt the spring known to the Moslems as *'Ain Umm ed deraj* ("the spring of the steps") and to the Christians as *'Ain Sitti Miriam* ("the spring of the lady Mary"), or commonly as the "Virgin's Fount." It is the one true spring of Jerus, the original source of attraction to the site of the early settlers; it is sit-

uated in the Kidron valley on the E. side of "Ophel," and due S. of the temple area. See JERUSALEM. The water in the present day is brackish and impregnated with sewage. The spring is intermittent in character, "bursting up" at intervals: this feature may account for the name Gihon and for its sacred characters. In NT times it was, as it is today, credited with healing virtues. See BETHESDA. Its position is clearly defined in the OT. Manasseh "built an outer wall to the city of David, on the W. side of Gihon, in the valley" (=Nahal, i.e. the Kidron; 2 Ch **33** 14). From Gihon Hezekiah made his aqueduct (2 Ch **32** 30), now the Siloam tunnel. See SILOAM.

The Virgin's Fount.

The spring is approached by a steep descent down 30 steps, the water rising deep underground; the condition is due to the vast accumulation of rubbish—the result of the many destructions of the city—which now fills the valley bed. Originally the water ran down the open valley. The water rises from a long deep crack in the rock, partly under the lowest of the steps and to a lesser extent in the mouth of a small cave, 11½ ft. long by 5 ft. wide, into which all the water pours. The village women of Siloam obtain the water at the mouth of the cave, but when the supply is scanty they actually go under the lowest step—where there is a kind of chamber—and fill their vessels there. At the farther end of this cave is the opening leading into the aqueduct down which the water flows to emerge after many windings at the pool of Siloam. The first part of this aqueduct is older than the time of Hezekiah and led originally to the perpendicular shaft, connected with "Warren's tunnel" described elsewhere (see SILOAM; ZION).

The preëminent position of importance which Gihon held in the eyes of the earlier inhabitants of Jerus is shown by the extraordinary number of passages, rock cuttings, walls and aqueducts which exist all about the spring. Walls have been made at different periods to bank up the waters and direct them into the channels provided for them. Of aqueducts, besides the "Siloam aqueduct," two others have been formed. One running from the source at a considerable lower level than that of Hezekiah was followed by the present writer (see *PEFS*, 1902, 35–38) for 176 ft. It was very winding, following apparently the W. side of the Kidron valley. It was a well-cemented channel, about 1½ ft. wide and on an average of 4½ ft. high, roofed in with well-cut stones. There are no certain indications of age, but in the writer's opinion it is a much later construction than Hezekiah's aqueduct, though the rock-cut part near the source may be older. It was discovered by the Siloam *fellahin*, because, through a fault in the dam, all the water of the "Virgin's Fount" was disappearing down this channel. A third aqueduct has recently been discovered running off at a higher level than the other two. It is a channel deeply cut in the rock with curious trough-like stones all along its floor. It appears to be made for water, but one branch of it actually slopes upward toward its end. The pottery, which is early Hebrew, shows that it is very ancient. The whole accumulated débris around the source is full of pre-Israelite and early Israelite pottery.

E. W. G. MASTERMAN

GILALAI, gil'a-lī, gi-lā'lī (גִּלֲלַי, *gilălay*): A musician in the procession at the dedication of the wall, son of a priest (Neh **12** 36).

GILBOA, gil-bō'a, **MOUNT** (הַר הַגִּלְבֹּעַ, *har ha-gilbōaʿ*, "Mount of the Gilboa"): Unless we should read "Gilboa" for "Gilead" in Jgs **7** 3 (see GILEAD, 2) this mountain is mentioned in Scripture only in connection with the last conflict of Saul with the Philis, and his disastrous defeat (1 S **28** 4; **31** 1.8; 2 S **1** 6.21; **21** 12; 1 Ch **10** 1.8). If *Zerʿīn* be identical with Jezreel—a point upon which Professor R. A. S. Macalister has recently cast some doubt—Saul must have occupied the slopes on the N.W. side of the mountain, near "the fountain which is in Jezreel" (1 S **29** 1). The Philis attacked from the plain, and the battle went sore against the men of Israel, who broke and fled; and in the flight Jonathan, Abinadab and Malchi-shua, sons of Saul, were slain. Rather than be taken by his lifelong foes, Saul fell upon his sword and died (1 S **31** 1 ff).

The modern name of the mountain is *Jebel Faḳuʿa*. It rises on the eastern edge of the plain of Esdraelon, and, running from *Zerʿīn* to the S.E., it then sweeps southward to join the Samarian uplands. It presents an imposing appearance from the plain, but the highest point, *Sheikh Burḳān*, is not more than 1,696 ft. above sea level. In the higher reaches the range is rugged and barren; but vegetation is plentiful on the lower slopes, esp. to the W. The Kishon takes its rise on the mountain. Under the northern cliffs rises *ʿAin Jalūd*, possibly identical with HAROD, WELL OF, which see. In *Jelbūn*, a village on the western declivity, there is perhaps an echo of the old name.

W. EWING

GILEAD, gil'ē-ad (הַגִּלְעָד, *ha-gilʿādh*, "the Gilead"): The name is explained in Gen **31** 46 ff.51, as derived from Heb *gal*, "a cairn," and *ʿēdh*, "witness," agreeing in meaning with the Aram. *yᵉghar-sāhădhūthā'*. The Arab. *jilʿād* means "rough," "rugged."

(1) A city named in Hos **6** 8; **12** 11, possibly to be identified with Gilead near to Mizpah (Jgs **10** 17). If this is correct, the ancient city may be represented by the modern *Jilʿād*, a ruin about 5 miles N. of *es-Salṭ*.

(2) A mountain named in Jgs **7** 3. Gideon, ordered to reduce the number of men who were with him, commanded all who were "fearful and trembling" to "return and depart from Mt. Gilead." RVm reads "return and go round about from Mt. Gilead." Gideon and his army lay to the S. of the plain of Jezreel on the lower slopes of Gilboa. It has been suggested (Studer, *Comm.*, ad loc.) that, as the Midianites lay between the men of the northern tribes and their homes, they were told to cross the Jordan, make a détour through Gilead, and thus avoid the enemy. Possibly, however, we should read Gilboa for Gilead; or part of the mountain may have borne the name of Gilead. The last suggestion is favored by the presence of a strong spring under the northern declivity of Gilboa, nearly 2 miles from *Zerʿīn*, possibly to be identified with the Well of Harod. In the modern name, *ʿAin Jalūd*, there may be an echo of the ancient Gilead.

(3) The name is applied generally to the mountain mass lying between the *Yarmūk* on the N., and *Wādy Hesbān* on the S.; the Jordan being the boundary on the W., while on the E. it marched with the desert.

1. The Land of Gilead

Mount Gilead—lit. "Mount of the Gilead"—may refer to some particular height which we have now no means of identifying (Gen **31** 23). The name *Jebel Jil'ād* is still, indeed, applied to a mountain S. of *Nahr ez-Zerḳā* and N. of *es-Salṭ;* but this does not meet the necessities of the passage as it stands. The same expression in Dt **3** 12 obviously stands for the whole country. This is probably true also in Cant **4** 1. The name Gilead is sometimes used to denote the whole country E. of the Jordan (Gen **37** 25; Josh **22** 9; 2 S **2** 9, etc). Again, along with Bashan, it indicates the land E. of Jordan, as distinguished from the Moab plateau (Dt **3** 10; Josh **13** 11; 2 K **10** 33). In the N. Gilead bordered upon Geshur and Maacah (Josh **13** 11.13); and here the natural boundary would be formed by the deep gorge of the *Yarmūk* and *Wādy esh-Shellāleh.* In pre-Israelite times the Jabbok (*Nahr ez-Zerḳā*), which cuts the country in two, divided the kingdom of Sihon from that of Og (Dt **3** 16; Josh **12** 2). The frontiers between the tribes of Reuben, Gad and Manasseh cannot be indicated with any certainty. Probably they varied at different times (cf Josh **13** 24 ff; 1 Ch **5** 8.9.11.16). It greatly increases the difficulty that so many of the cities named are still unidentified. But in any case it is clear that the bulk of Gilead fell to Gad, so that Gilead might stand for Gad (Jgs **5** 17). Havvoth-jair (which see), "the villages of Jair," lay in Gilead (Jgs **10** 4). The modern division of the country follows the natural features. From the *Yarmūk* to *Nahr ez-Zerḳā* is the district of *'Ajlūn;* and from the *Zerḳā* to the Arnon is *el-Belḳā.*

2. Bashan

The geological formation is the same as that of Western Pal, but the underlying sandstone, which does not appear W. of the Jordan, forms the base slopes of the chain of Moab and Gilead, and is traceable as far as the Jabbok. It is covered in part by the more recent white marls which form the curious peaks of the foothills immediately above the Jordan valley; but reaches above them to an elevation of 1,000 ft. above the Mediterranean on the S., and forms the bed of the *Buḳei'a* basin farther E., and 1,000 ft. higher. Above this lies the hard, impervious dolomite limestone which appears in the rugged hills round the Jabbok and in *Jebel 'Ajlūn,* rising on an average 1,500 ft. above the sandstone and forming the bed of the copious springs. It also dips toward the Jordan valley, and the water from the surface of the plateau, sinking down to the surface of their formation, bursts out of the hill slopes on the W. in perennial brooks. It was from the ruggedness of this hard limestone that Gilead obtained its name. Above this again is the white chalk of the desert plateau, the same as that found in Samaria and Lower Galilee, with bands of flint or chert in contorted layers, or strewn in pebbles on the surface. Where this formation is deep the country is bare and arid, supplied by cisterns and deep wells. Thus the plateau becomes desert, while the hill slopes abound in streams and springs; and for this reason Western Gilead is a fertile country, and Eastern Gilead is a wilderness (Conder, *DB*, s.v.).

3. Geology

The uplands of Gilead may be described as the crumpling of the edge of the great eastern plateau ere it plunges into the *Ghōr.* The average height of the range is about 4,000 ft. above the Jordan valley, or 3,000 ft. above the Mediterranean. The greatest height is toward the S., where it culminates in *Jebel Osh'a* (3,597 ft.), to the N. of *es-Salṭ.* This mountain commands a most spacious view. To the E. of it lies the hollow (an old lake bottom) of *el-Buḳei'a,* fully 1,500 ft. lower. In the N. we have *Jebel Hakart* (3,408 ft.), W. of *Reimūn.* Almost as high (3,430 ft.) is *Jebel Kafkafah,* about 12 miles to the N.E. A striking point (2,700 ft.) fully 2 miles N.W. of *'Ajlūn,* is crowned by *Ḳal'at er-Rabad,* whence again a view of extraordinary extent is gained.

4. Mountains

The *Yarmūk* and the *Zerḳā*—see Jabbok—are the main streams, but almost every valley has its perennial brook. While not so rich as the volcanic loam in the N. and in the S., the soil of Gilead amply repays the labor of the husbandman. Of flowers the most plentiful are the phlox, the cistus and the narcissus. Hawthorn, mastic and arbutus abound, while many a glen and slope is shady with shaggy oak woods, and, in the higher reaches, with pines. The streams are fringed with oleander. The monotony of the stony plateau is broken by clumps of the hardy white broom. In the lower ground are found the tamarisk and the lotus, with many a waving cane-brake. The scenery is more beautiful and picturesque than that of any other district of Pal. The soil is not now cultivated to any great extent; but it furnishes ample pasture for many flocks and herds (Cant **6** 5).

5. Streams and Products

The Ishmaelites from Gilead (Gen **37** 25) were carrying "spicery and balm and myrrh." From old time Gilead was famed for its Balm (q.v.). The *lōṭ,* tr[d] "myrrh" in the above passage, was probably the gum produced by the *Cistus ladaniferus,* a flower which still abounds in Gilead.

After the conquest, as we have seen, Gilead passed mainly into the hands of Gad. An Ammonite attack was repulsed by the prowess of Jephthah (Jgs **11** 1 ff); and the spite of the Ephraimites was terribly punished (**12** 1 ff). Gilead at first favored the cause of Ishbosheth (2 S **2** 9), but after the murder of that prince the Gileadites came with the rest of Israel to David (**5** 1). By the conquest of the fortress Rabbah, which the Ammonites had continued to hold, the land passed finally under the power of David (**12** 26 ff). David fled to Mahanaim from Absalom, and that rebel prince perished in one of the forests of Gilead (2 S **17** 24; **18** 6 ff). Joab's census included Gilead (**24** 6). Solomon had two commissariat districts in Gilead (1 K **4** 13 f.19). Before Ramoth-gilead, which he sought to win back from the Syrians who had captured it, Ahab received his death wound (**22** 1 ff). The Syrians asserted their supremacy in Gilead (2 K **10** 32 f) where Moab and Israel had contended with varying fortune (M S). At length Tiglath-pileser overran the country and transported many of the inhabitants (2 K **15** 29). This seems to have led to a reconquest of the land by heathenism, and return to Gilead was promised to Israel (Zec **10** 10).

6. History

At a later time the Jewish residents in Gilead were exposed to danger from their heathen neighbors. On their behalf Judas Maccabaeus invaded the country and met with striking success (1 Macc **5** 9 ff). Alexander Jannaeus, who had subdued Gilead, was forced to yield it again to the king of Arabia (*Ant,* XIII, xiv, 2; *BJ,* I, iv, 3). During the Roman period, esp. in the 2d and 3d cents. AD, the land enjoyed great prosperity. Then were built such cities as Gadara and Gerasa, which are still imposing, even in ruins. The appearance of the Moslem armies was the signal for its decay. Attempts were made to recover it for Christianity by Baldwin I (1118 AD) and Baldwin II (1121 AD); and the Crusaders left their mark in such strongholds as *Kal'at er-Rabad,* and the castle at *es-Salt.* With the reassertion of Moslem supremacy a curtain falls over the history of the district; and only in comparatively recent times has it again become known to travelers. The surveys directed by the Pal Exploration Fund, in so far as they have been carried out, are invaluable. N. of the Jabbok are many villages, and a fair amount of cultivation. *Es Salt* is the only village of any importance in the S. It is famous for its raisins. Its spacious uplands, its wooded and well-watered valleys have been for centuries the pasture-land of the nomads.

LITERATURE.—Useful information will be found in Merrill, *East of the Jordan;* Oliphant, *Land of Gilead;* Thomson, *LB;* and esp. in Conder, *Heth and Moab,* and in *Memoirs of the Survey of Eastern Pal.*

W. EWING

GILEAD (גִּלְעָד, *gil'ādh*):

(1) A son of Machir, grandson of Manasseh (Nu **26** 29.30).

(2) The father of Jephthah (Jgs **11** 1.2).

(3) A Gadite, the son of Michael (1 Ch **5** 14).

GILEAD, BALM OF. See BALM OF GILEAD.

GILEAD, MOUNT. See GILEAD (2).

GILEADITES, gil'ē-ad-īts:

(1) A branch of the tribe of Manasseh (Nu **26** 29).

(2) Natives of the district of Gilead (Jgs **10** 3; **11** 1, etc).

GILGAL, gil'gal (גִּלְגָּל, *gilgāl,* "circle"; **Γάλγαλα,** *Gálgala*): The art. is always with the name except in Josh **5** 9. There are three places to which the name is attached:

(1) The first camp of Israel after crossing the Jordan (Josh **4** 19; **5** 9.10; **9** 6; **10** 7; **14** 6; **15** 7; Dt **11** 30). According to Josh **15** 7 it lay to the N. of the valley of Achor, which formed the border between Judah and Benjamin. Here 12 memorial stones taken from the bed of the river were set up by Joshua, after the miraculous crossing of the Jordan; and here (Josh **5** 5 ff) the people were circumcised preparatory to their possession of the land, when it is said in Josh, with a play upon the word, "This day have I rolled away the reproach of Egypt from off you." Whereupon the Passover was celebrated (ver 10) and the manna ceased (ver 12). To Gilgal the ark returned every day after having compassed the city of Jericho during its siege (**6** 11). Hither the Gibeonites came to make their treaty (**9** 3 ff), and again (**10** 6) to ask aid against the Amorites. Gilgal was still the headquarters of the Israelites after the battle with the Amorites (ver 15); again after Joshua's extensive victorious campaign in the hill country of Judaea extending to Kadesh-barnea and Gaza (**10** 15 ff); and still later upon his return from the great battle at the Waters of Merom (**14** 6). At the conclusion of the conquest (**18** 1), the headquarters were transferred to Shiloh on the summit of the mountain ridge to the W.

Gilgal reappears frequently in subsequent history. Samuel (1 S **7** 16) made it one of the three places where he annually held circuit court, the other places being Bethel and Mizpah. The LXX text adds that these were holy places. The place continued as one of special resort for sacrifices (**10** 8; **13** 8.9.10; **15** 21), while it was here that Samuel hewed Agag to pieces before the Lord (**15** 33), and that Saul was both crowned (**11** 14.15) and rejected as king. It was at Gilgal, also (2 S **19** 15), that the people assembled to welcome David as he returned from his exile beyond Jordan during Absalom's rebellion. The early prophets refer to Gilgal as a center of idolatry in their day (Hos **4** 15; **9** 15; **12** 11; Am **4** 4; **5** 5). Micah (**6** 5) represents Gilgal as at the other end of the Dead Sea from Shittim.

In 1874 Conder recognized the name Gilgal as surviving in *Birket Jiljûlieh,* a pool beside a tamarisk tree 3 miles E. of old Jericho. The pool measures 100 ft. by 84, and is surrounded with a wall of roughly hewn stones. N. of the pool Bliss discovered lines of masonry 300 yds. long, representing probably the foundations of an ancient monastery. S. of the pool there are numerous mounds scattered over an area of one-third of a sq. mile, the largest being 50 ft. in diameter, and 10 in height. On excavation some pottery and glass were found. These ruins are probably those of early Christian occupation, and according to Conder there is nothing against their marking the original site. Up to the Middle Ages the 12 stones of Joshua were referred to by tradition.

(2) According to 2 K **2** 1; **4** 38, Elisha for a time made his headquarters at Gilgal, a place in the mountains not far from Bethel identified by Conder as *Jiljilia,* standing on a high hill on the N. side of the *Wādy el-Jib.* It is lower than Bethel, but the phrase in 2 K **2** 2, "they went down to Beth-el," may refer to their initial descent into the *wādy.* It could not have been said that they went *down* from Gilgal to Bethel in the Jordan valley. The place seems to be referred to in Neh **12** 29 as Beth-gilgal.

(3) Gilgal of the nations: In Josh **12** 23 Gilgal is mentioned as a royal city associated with Dor, evidently upon the maritime plain. Dor is identified with *Tantura,* while Conder identifies this Gilgal with *Jiljûlieh,* 30 miles S. of Dor and 4 miles N. of Anti-patris. GEORGE FREDERICK WRIGHT

GILOH, gī'lō (גִּלֹה, *gilōh*): A town in the hill country of Judah mentioned along with Jattir, Socoh, Debir, Eshtemoa, etc (Josh **15** 51). Ahithophel came from here (2 S **15** 12) and is called the Gilonite (2 S **23** 34). Driver infers from this last that the original form was Gilon, not Giloh. Probably the ruins *Kh. Jālā,* in the hills 3 miles N.W. of *Hulhūl,* mark the site (*PEF,* III, 313, Sh XXI).

GILONITE, gī'lō-nīt. See preceding article.

GIMEL, gē'mel, gim'el (ג, גּ): The 3d letter of the Heb alphabet, and used as such to designate the 3d part of Ps **119**; transliterated in this Encyclopaedia with the dagesh as *g,* and without as *gh* (aspirated *g*). It came also to be used for the number three (3), and with the dieresis for 3,000. For name, etc, see ALPHABET.

GIMZO, gim'zō (גִּמְזוֹ, *gimzō;* **Γαμζώ,** *Gamzṓ*): A town of Judah on the border of the Phili plain, captured by the Philis in the days of Ahaz (2 Ch **28** 18). It is the modern *Jimzu,* a small mud village about 3½ miles S.E. of Ludd (Lydda), on the old mule road from there to Jerus (Robinson, *BR,* II, 248–49; *SWP,* II, 297).

GIN, jin (מוֹקֵשׁ, *mōḳēsh,* פַּח, *paḥ*): A noose of hair or wire for snaring wild birds alive. There are over half a dozen traps and net devices indicated by different terms in the Bible. The gin was of horse-hair for small birds and wire for larger ones. It is mentioned in Am **3** 5: "Can a bird fall in a snare upon the earth, where no gin is set for him? shall a snare spring up from the ground, and have taken nothing at all?" Job writing in mental and physical discomfort on the ash heap included **all** methods mentioned in one outburst:

"For he is cast into a *net* by his own feet,
And he walketh upon the *toils*.
A *gin* shall take him by the heel,
And a *snare* shall lay hold on him,
A *noose* is hid for him in the ground,
And a *trap* for him in the way" (Job **18** 8 ff).

GENE STRATTON-PORTER

GINATH, gī'nath (גִּינַת, *gīnath*): Father of Tibni, the unsuccessful rival of Omri (1 K **16** 21. 22).

GINNETHOI, gin-ē-thō'ī (AV **Ginnetho**), **GINNETHON,** gin'ē-thon (גִּנְּתוֹי, *ginnᵉthōy*, and גִּנְּתוֹן, *ginnᵉthōn*): The head of a priestly family. Ginnethoi (Ginnetho) is found in Neh **12** 4, and Ginnethon in **10** 6; **12** 16.

GIRDLE, gûr'd'l. See ARMOR; DRESS.

GIRGASHITE, gûr'ga-shīt (גִּרְגָּשִׁי, *girgāshī;* **Γεργεσαῖος,** *Gergesaíos;* also punctuated [?] Girgasite [Gen **10** 16 AV]): A son of (the land of) Canaan (Gen **10** 16), and accordingly enumerated along with the Canaanite in the list of tribes or nationalities inhabiting that country (Gen **15** 21; Dt **7** 1; Josh **3** 10; **24** 11; Neh **9** 8). It has been supposed that the name survived in that of "the Gergesenes," AV (RV "the Gadarenes"), of Mt **8** 28, on the E. side of the Sea of Galilee; Jos (*Ant,* I, vi, 2), however, states that nothing was known about it. The inscriptions of the Egyp king, Ramses II, mention the Qarqish who sent help to the Hittites in their war with Egypt; but Qarqish was more probably in Asia Minor than in Syria. Pinches (*The OT in the Light of the Historical Records,* 324) would identify the Girgashites with the Kirkishati of an Assyr tablet; the latter people, however, seem to have lived to the E. of the Tigris, and it may be that, as in the case of the Hittites, a colony of the Qarqish, from Asia Minor, was established in Pal. A. H. SAYCE

GIRL, gûrl: Twice in the OT as the rendering of יַלְדָּה, *yaldāh* (Joel **3** 3; Zec **8** 5), in both cases in association with boys. Same word rendered "damsel" in Gen **34** 4. See DAUGHTER; MAID, MAIDEN.

GIRZITES, gûr'zīts. See GIZRITES.

GISHPA, gish'pa (AV **Gišpa;** גִּשְׁפָּא, *gishpā'*): An officer of the Nethinim (Neh **11** 21). A comparison with Ezr **2** 43 makes it probable that he is to be identified with Hasupha, and quite possible that this word is a corruption of Hasupha.

GITTAH-HEPHER, git-ä-hē'fẽr (גִּתָּה חֵפֶר, *gittāh ḥēpher*): AV (Josh **19** 13) for Gath-hepher. Gittah is correctly Gath with *hē* (ה) locale, meaning "toward Gath."

GITTAIM, git'ā-im (גִּתַּיִם, *gittayim*): The town to which the Beerothites fled, and where they lived as *gērīm,* or protected strangers (2 S **4** 3). The place need not have been beyond the boundaries of Benjamin, so it may be identical with Gittaim of Neh **11** 33, which was occupied by Benjamites after the exile. It is named with Hazor and Ramah; but so far the site has not been discovered.

GITTITES, git'īts (גִּתִּים ,גִּתִּי, *gittīm,* pl. of *gittī*): The inhabitants of Gath. They are mentioned along with the inhabitants of the other chief Phili cities in Josh **13** 3. It would seem that numbers of them emigrated to Judah, for we find 600 of them acting as a bodyguard to David with Ittai at their head (2 S **15** 18 ff; **18** 2). Obed-edom, to whom David intrusted the ark when he was frustrated in bringing it into the city of David, was a Gittite (2 S **6** 11 f; 1 Ch **13** 13). The Gittites seem to have been remarkable for their great stature (2 S **21** 19; 1 Ch **20** 5 ff).

GITTITH, git'ith. See MUSIC; PSALMS.

GIVE (נָתַן, *nāthan,* יָהַב, *yāhabh,* שׂוּם, *sūm;* **δίδωμι,** *dídōmi*): "Give" is a very common word in the OT. It is most frequently the tr of *nāthan,* "to give" (Gen **1** 29; **3** 6; Ex **2** 9; Dt **1** 8.20, etc, over 800 instances); *nāthan* is also trd "to give up" (Dt **23** 14; Isa **43** 6; Hos **11** 8); of *yāhabh,* "to give" (Gen **30** 1; 1 Ch **16** 28 AV). In Ps **55** 22 we have the perfect with suffix, "Cast thy burden upon Jeh," m "what he hath given thee"; elsewhere it is the imperative "Give!" (AV in Gen, "Go to"); *sūm,* "to put," "place" (Nu **6** 26; Prov **8** 29); *rūm,* "to lift up," "exalt" (2 Ch **30** 24 *bis;* **35** 7.8.9, "to give to"); *shūbh,* "to cause to turn back" (Lev **25** 51.52; 2 K **17** 3, "to give again"); various other words are in single instances trd "give."

In the NT, the common word is *didōmi,* "to give" (Mt **4** 9; Jn **1** 12; Rev **1** 1; **21** 6, etc); we have also *apodídōmi,* "to give away [from one's self]" (Mt **12** 36; Lk **16** 2; Acts **4** 33; **19** 40; Rev **22** 12); *diadídōmi,* "to give throughout" (Rev **17** 13); *epidídōmi,* "to give upon or besides" (Mt **7** 9.10; Jn **13** 26); *metadídōmi,* "to give a share" (Rom **12** 8); *paradídōmi,* "to give over to" (Rom **1** 28; 1 Cor **13** 3; Gal **2** 20, etc); *prodídōmi,* "to give forth or foremost" (Rom **11** 35); *aponémō,* "to apportion" (1 Pet **3** 7); *dōréomai,* "to give as a gift" (Mk **15** 45, RV "granted"; 2 Pet **1** 3.4 AV); *marturéō,* "to give testimony or witness" (1 Jn **5** 10); *pareisphérō,* "to bring forward therewith" (2 Pet **1** 5); *paréchō,* "to hold near by" (Col **4** 1; 1 Tim **6** 17); *kataphérō,* "to bear against or down" (Acts **26** 10); *charízomai,* "to grant as a favor" (Lk **7** 21; Acts **27** 24; Rom **8** 32; Gal **3** 18; Phil **2** 9; Philem ver 22 AV). A few other words mostly occurring singly are trd "give."

Of the many changes in RV, the following are among the most important: for "Thou hast also given me the necks of mine enemies," "Thou hast also made mine enemies turn their backs unto me" (2 S **22** 41; Ps **18** 40); for "He that made him can make his sword to approach *unto him*" (Job **40** 19), ARV has "He *only* that made him giveth him his sword," ERVm "furnished"; for "hasten after another god" (Ps **16** 4), ARV has "give gifts for" (ERVm); for "give" (Ps **29** 1.2, etc), ARV has "ascribe"; for "give myself unto wine" (Eccl **2** 3), "cheer my flesh with wine"; for "giveth his life" (Jn **10** 11), "layeth down"; "given" is supplied (Acts **19** 2), where we read instead of "We have not so much as heard whether there be any Holy Ghost," "We did not so much as hear whether the Holy Spirit was *given,*" m "there is a Holy Spirit"; for "Christ shall give thee light" (Eph **5** 14), "Christ shall shine upon thee"; for "give in charge" (1 Tim **5** 7), "command"; for "not given to wine" (1 Tim **3** 3; Tit **1** 7), "no brawler," m "not quarrelsome over wine"; for "she that liveth in pleasure" (1 Tim **5** 6), "giveth herself to"; for "All scripture is given by inspiration of God" (2 Tim **3** 16), "Every scripture inspired of God," m "Every scripture is inspired of God"; for "given to filthy lucre" (Tit **1** 7), "greedy of"; in He **2** 16, ARV has "For verily not to angels doth he give help," m "For verily not of angels doth he take hold, but he taketh hold," etc (cf Isa **41** 9; Ecclus **4** 11; **8** 9 [in the Gr] ERV, "not of angels doth he take hold") (the idea is that of taking hold of to lift up or help); in **13** 15 for "giving thanks to his name," RV reads "make confession to his name"; for "giving all diligence" (2 Pet **1** 5), "adding."

The prominence of "give" in the Bible reminds us that God is the great Giver (Jas **1** 5), and of the words of the Lord Jesus, "It is more blessed to give than to receive" (Acts **20** 35), "Freely ye received, freely give" (Mt **10** 8). W. L. WALKER

GIZONITE, gī'zon-īt: This gentilic name in 1 Ch **11** 34, "Hashem the Gizonite," is probably an error for "Gunite" (cf Nu **26** 48), and the passage should be corrected, after 2 S **23** 32, into "Jashen the Gunite."

GIZRITES, giz'rīts (גִּזְרִי, *gizrī* [Kᵉthībh]; AV **Gezrites**): Inhabitants of GEZER (q.v.). Ḳᵉrē reads גִּרְזִי, *girzī*, Girzites (1 S **27** 8).

GLAD TIDINGS, tī'dingz (εὐαγγελίζω, *euaggelízō*): "Glad-tidings" occurs in AV in the tr of the vb. *euaggelizō*, "to tell good news" (Lk **1** 19; **8** 1; Acts **13** 32; Rom **10** 15); in each instance, except the last, RV trˢ "good tidings." The vb. is also very frequently trᵈ in AV "to preach *the gospel*," the original meaning of which word (god-spell) is "good news or tidings" (Mt **11** 5; Lk **4** 18; **7** 22; **9** 6; **20** 1); in the first two passages RV substitutes "good tidings," m "the gospel"; in the last two instances "the gospel" is retained, ARVm "good tidings"—the gospel or good tidings being the announcement of the near approach of the promised, long-looked-for salvation and kingdom of God; in Rom **1** 15; **15** 20; 1 Cor **1** 17, etc, AV has "the gospel," viz. that of God's reconciliation of the world to Himself in Christ; RV in some passages substitutes "good tidings," or gives this in the margin; but "glad tidings" stands only in Rom **10** 15. W. L. WALKER

GLASS, glas (זְכוּכִית, *zᵉkhūkhīth;* ὕαλος, *húalos*): Glass is of great antiquity. The story of its discovery by accident, as related by Pliny (*NH*, xxxvi.65), is apocryphal, but it was natural for the Greeks and Romans to ascribe it to the Phoenicians, since they were the producers of the article as known to them. The Egyp monuments have revealed to us the manufacture in a time so remote that it must have preceded that of the Phoenicians. A representation of glass-blowing on monuments of the Old Empire, as formerly supposed, is now regarded as doubtful, but undoubted examples of glazed pottery of that age exist. A fragment of blue glass has been found inscribed with the name of Antef III, of the XIth

1. History

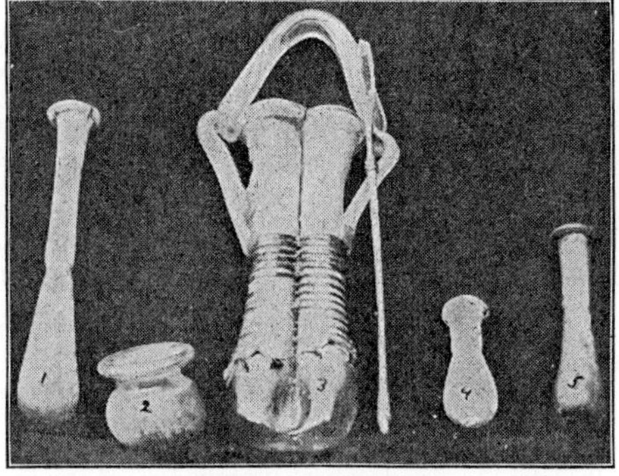

Glass Bottles.

Dynasty, dating from 2000 or more BC (Davis, *Ancient Egypt*, 324). The oldest dated bottle, or vase, is one bearing the name of Thothmes III, 1500 or more BC, and numerous examples occur of later date. The close connection between Egypt and Syria from the time of Thothmes on must have made glass known in the latter country, and the Phoenicians, so apt in all lines of trade and manufacture, naturally seized on glass-making as a most profitable art and they became very proficient in it. The earliest glass was not very transparent, since they

Glass Vases.

did not know how to free the materials used from impurities. It had a greenish or purplish tinge, and a large part of the examples we have of Phoen glass exhibit this. But we have many examples of blue, red and yellow varieties which were purposely colored, and others quite opaque and of a whitish color, resembling porcelain (Perrot and Chipiez, *Art in Ancient Phoenicia and Its Dependencies*). But both they and the Egyptians made excellent transparent glass also, and decorated it with brilliant coloring on the surface (ib; Beni Hasan, *Archeol. Survey of Egypt*, Pt IV). Layard (*Nineveh and Babylon*) mentions a vase of transparent glass bearing the name of Sargon (522–505 BC), and glass was early known to the Babylonians.

Phoenicia was the great center, and the quantities found in tombs of Syria and Pal go to confirm the statement that this was one of the great industries of this people, to which ancient authors testify (Strabo, *Geog.;* Pliny, *NH*). Jos refers to the sand of the Belus as that from which glass was made (*BJ*, II, x, 2). It seems to have been esp. adapted for the purpose, but there are other places on the coast where plenty of suitable sand could be obtained. The potash required was obtained by burning certain marine and other plants, and saltpetre, or nitre, was also employed. The manufacture began centuries BC on this coast, and in the 12th cent. AD a factory is mentioned as still being worked at Tyre, and the manufacture was later carried on at Hebron, even down to recent times (Perrot and Chipiez).

2. Manufacture

Both the Egyptians and Phoenicians gained such proficiency in making transparent and colored glass that they imitated precious stones with such skill as to deceive the unwary. Necklaces are found composed of a mixture of real brilliants and glass imitations. Cut glass was manufactured in Egypt as early as the XVIIIth Dynasty, and diamonds were made use of in the art. Glass composed of different colors in the same piece was made by placing layers of glass wire, of different colors, one above the other and then fusing them so that they became united in a solid mass without intermingling. Colored designs on the surface were produced by tracing the patterns, while the glass was still warm and plastic, deep enough to receive the threads of colored glass which were imbedded in them. The whole was heated again sufficiently to fuse the threads and attach them to the body. The surface was then made even by polishing. By this process vessels and ornaments of very beautiful design were produced. Many of the specimens, as found, are covered by an exquisite iridescence which is due wholly to the decomposition of the surface by chemical action, from lying buried for centuries in the soil which thus acts upon it. This is often lost in handling by the scaling off of the outer surface.

Glass, in the strict sense, is rarely mentioned in Scripture, but it was certainly known to the Hebrews, and occurs in Job **28** 17 (tr[d] "crystal" in AV). Bottles, cups and other vessels in glass must have been in use to some extent. The wine cup of Prov **23** 31 and the bottle for tears mentioned in Ps **56** 8 were most likely of glass. Tear bottles are found in great quantities in the tombs throughout the land and were undoubtedly connected with funeral rites, the mourners collecting their tears and placing them in these bottles to be buried with the dead. As mourners were hired for the purpose, the number of these bottles would indicate the extent to which the deceased was honored. These were, of course, small, some quite diminutive (see illustration), as also were the vials or pots to contain the ointment for the eyebrows and eyelashes, used to heighten the beauty of the women, which was probably a custom among the Hebrews as well as their neighbors. Rings, bracelets and anklets of glass are very common and were doubtless worn by the Heb women (see Isa **3** 18 f). In the NT the Gr *hualos* occurs in Rev **21** 18.21, and the adj. derived from it (*huálinos*) in **4** 6 and **15** 2. In the other passages, where in AV "glass" occurs, the reference is to **"looking-glass,"** or mirror, which was not made of glass, but of bronze, and polished so as to reflect the light similar to glass. The Heb word for this is גִּלָּיוֹן, *gillāyōn* (Isa **3** 23), or מַרְאָה, *mar'āh* (Ex **38** 8), and the Gr ἔσοπτρον, *ésoptron* (1 Cor **13** 12; Jas **1** 23; cf Wisd **7** 26; Sir **12** 11).

The composition of the Phoen glass varies considerably. The analysis shows that, besides the ordinary constituents of silica, lime, lead, potash or soda, other elements are found, some being used for the purpose of coloring, such as manganese to give the purplish or violet hue, cobalt for blue, copper for red, etc. The articles illustrated above are of ordinary transparent glass with an iridescent surface, caused by decomposition, as mentioned above, indicated by the scaly appearance. Nos. 1, 4 and

Mirror of Polished Bronze.

5 are tear bottles, no. 4 being only 1¾ in. in height; nos. 2 and 3 are ointment vases which were used for the ointment with which ladies were accustomed to color their eyebrows and eyelashes to enhance their beauty. This custom still prevails in the East. The small ladle by the side of the larger vase is of bronze, used in applying the ointment. This vase is double and 6¾ in. high, ornamented with glass wire wound upon it while plastic. The larger vases (nos. 6 and 7) are about 6 in. in height. The hand-mirror ("looking-glass" AV) is bronze, and had originally a polished surface, but is now corroded.

H. Porter

GLASS, SEA OF (**θάλασσα ὑαλίνη,** *thálassa hualínē;* Rev **4** 6; **15** 2): In the vision of heaven in these two apocalyptic passages a "glassy sea" is seen before the throne of God. The pure translucency of the sea is indicated in the former reference by the words, "like unto crystal"; and the fiery element that may symbolize the energy of the Divine holiness is suggested in the latter passage by the trait, "mingled with fire." On the margin of this sea—on the inner side—stood the victorious saints, with harps, singing the song of Moses and of the Lamb (**15** 2–4). The imagery here points to a relation with the triumphal song in Ex **15,** after the deliverance from Pharaoh at the Red Sea. It is not easy to define the symbolism precisely. The sea, reflecting in its crystalline depths the purity and holiness of the Divine character and administration, speaks at the same time of difficulties surmounted, victory obtained and safety assured, the after-glow of the Divine judgments by which this result has been secured still illuminating the glassy expanse that has been crossed. James Orr

GLEANING, glēn'ing (לָקַט, *lāḳaṭ,* עָלַל, *'ālal*): The custom of allowing the poor to follow the reapers in the field and glean the fallen spears of grain is strikingly illustrated in the story of Ruth (Ruth **2** 2–23). This custom had back of it one of the early agricultural laws of the Hebrews (Lev **19** 9; **23** 22; Dt **24** 19–21). Breaking this law was a punishable offence. The generosity of the master of the crop determined the value of the gleanings, as the story of Ruth well illustrates (Ruth **2** 16). A reaper could easily impose upon the master by leaving too much for the gleaners, who might be his own children. The old Levitical law no longer holds in the land, but the custom of allowing the poor to glean in the grain fields and vineyards is still practised by generous landlords in Syria. The writer has seen the reapers, even when they exercised considerable care, drop from their hands frequent spears of wheat. When the reapers have been hirelings they have carelessly left bunches of wheat standing behind rocks or near the boundary walls. The owner usually sends one of his boy or girl helpers to glean these. If he is of a generous disposition, he allows some needy woman to follow after the reapers and benefit by their carelessness. It is the custom in some districts, after the main crop of grapes has been gathered, to remove the watchman and allow free access to the vineyards for gleaning the last grapes.

Gideon touched the local pride of the men of Ephraim when he declared that the glory of their conquest surpassed his, as the gleanings of their vineyards did the whole crop of Abiezer (Jgs **8** 2). **Gleaned** is used of a captured enemy in Jgs **20** 45.

Figurative: Israel, because of her wickedness, will be utterly destroyed, even to a thorough gleaning and destruction of those who first escape (Jer **6** 9). The same picture of complete annihilation is given in Jer **49** 9.10. James A. Patch

GLEDE, glēd (רָאָה, *rā'āh;* **γύψ,** *gúps*): A member of the hawk species. It is given among the list of abominations in Dt **14** 13, but not in the Lev list (Lev **11** 14). The kite is substituted. The Arabs might have called one of the buzzards the glede. In England, where specimens of most of these birds appear in migration, the glede is synonymous with kite, and was given the name from glide, to emphasize a gliding motion in flight. See illustration, p. 1235.

GLISTERING, glis'tẽr-ing (פּוּךְ, *pūkh,* "dye" [spec. "stibium"], "fair colors"; **στίλβοντα,** *stílbonta*): "'Glistering stones' (1 Ch **29** 2) is better than the 'inlaid' of RV; for some kind of colored, brilliant stone seems meant" (*HDB*, II, 182); cf Isa **54** 11 RVm. The term is employed in Mk **9** 3 to denote the white, lustrous appearance of Christ's garments at the transfiguration. It occurs nowhere else in the NT. For once the Divine effulgence shone through the veil of the humiliation (cf Jn **1** 14).

Glede (*Buteo ferox*).

GLITTER, glit'ẽr, **GLITTERING,** glit'ẽr-ing (בָּרָק, *bārāḳ*, "lightning"): The word is used in sense of "glittering" in the OT with "sword," "spear" (Dt **32** 41; Job **20** 25; Ezk **21** 10.28; Nah **3** 3; Hab **3** 11). In Ezk **21** 10 RV changes "glitter" to "as lightning," and in Dt **32** 41 RVm gives, "the lightning of my sword." In Job **39** 23, where the word is different (*lahabh*), RV has "flashing."

GLORIFY, glō'ri-fī: The Eng. word is the equivalent of a number of Heb and Gr words whose essential significance is discussed more fully under the word Glory (q.v.). The word "glorious" in the phrases "make or render glorious" is used most frequently as a tr of vbs. in the original, rather than of genuine adjs. In dealing with the vb. it will be sufficient to indicate the following most important uses.

(1) Men may glorify God, that is, give to Him the worship and reverence which are His due (Isa **24** 15; **25** 3; Ps **22** 23; Dnl **5** 23; Sir **43** 30; Mt **5** 16, and generally in the Synoptic Gospels and in some other passages of the NT).

(2) God, Yahweh (Jehovah), glorifies His people, His house, and in the NT, His Son, manifesting His approval of them and His interest in them, by His interposition on their behalf (Isa **55** 5; Jer **30** 19; Wisd **18** 8; Sir **45** 3; Jn **7** 39, and often in the Fourth Gospel).

(3) By a usage which is practically confined to the OT, Jeh glorifies Himself, that is, secures the recognition of His honor and majesty, by His direction of the course of history, or by His interposition in history, either the history of His own people or of the world at large (Lev **10** 3; Isa **26** 15; Ezk **28** 22; Hag **1** 8). Walter R. Betteridge

GLORIOUS, glō'ri-us: The adj. "glorious" is used in the majority of cases as the tr of one of the nouns which are fully discussed in the article Glory, and the general meaning is the same, for the glorious objects or persons have the quality which is described by the word "glory," that is, they are honorable, dignified, powerful, distinguished, splendid, beautiful or radiant. It is worthy of note that in many passages in the NT where AV has "glorious," RV has the noun "glory." So among others in Rom **8** 21, AV has "glorious liberty," RV "liberty of the glory of the sons of God." The obsolete use of the word glorious in the sense of "boastful," "vain-glorious," "eager for glory," as it is used in Wycliffe, Tindale and Bacon, and once or twice in Shakespeare, as in *Cymbeline*, I, 7, in the first speech of Imogen, "Most miserable is the desire that's glorious," and in Gower's *Prologue to Pericles*, 1.9, "The purchase of it is to make men glorious" occurs at least once in the apocryphal books, Ad Est **16** 4 AV, "but also lifted up with the glorious words of lewd persons." Walter R. Betteridge

GLORY, glō'ri (subst.):

I. Method of Treatment.—In this art. we deal, *first*, with a group of words, tr[d] "glory" in the EV, and in which the ideas of size, rarity, beauty and adornment are prominent, the emphasis being laid in the first instance in each case upon some external physical characteristic which attracts the attention, and makes the object described by the word significant or prominent.

These are *'addereth* (אַדֶּרֶת), perhaps to be connected with the Assyr root *'adaru*, meaning "wide," "great"; *hādhar*, *hădhārāh* (הָדָר, הֲדָרָה), perhaps with root-meaning of "brightness"; *hōdh* (הוֹד), with essentially the same meaning of "brightness," "light"; *t*[e]*hār* (טְהָר), Ps **89** 44, tr[d] "glory" in AV, in RV rendered "brightness"; *y*[e]*ḳārā'* (יְקָרָא), an Aram. root meaning "rare"; *tiph'ārāh* (תִּפְאָרָה), with the root-meaning of "beauty"; and finally *ç*[e]*bhī* (צְבִי), perhaps on the basis of the Assyr *ṣabu*, meaning "desire," "desirable."

Secondly, this art. will discuss the most common and characteristic word for "glory" in the OT, the Heb *kābhōdh* (כָּבֹד) including the special phrase "the glory of God" or "the glory of Jeh." In dealing with the OT usage, attention will also be called to the original Heb of the Book of Ecclus or Wisdom of Jesus the Son of Sirach, cited in this art. as Sir. *Thirdly*, with the Gr word *dóxa* (δόξα) in the Apoc and in the NT. The nouns *kaúchēma*, *kaúchēsis*, tr[d] "glory" or "glorying" in the NT, will be dealt with in the concluding paragraphs in which the use of the word glory as a vb. will briefly be discussed. It will be possible within the limits of this art. to give only the main outlines of the subject as illustrated by a few of the most significant references. The lexicons and the commentaries must be consulted for the details.

II. General Use of the Term.—In the first group, as has already been stated, the ideas of beauty, majesty and splendor are prominent.

1. As Applied to External Things

And these qualities are predicated first of all, of things. David determines to make the temple which Solomon is to build "a house of fame and of glory" (1 Ch **22** 5). Then, and more commonly, glory belongs to men, and esp. to men of prominence, like kings. This glory may consist in wealth, power, position, or even in the inherent majesty and dignity of character of its possessor. The reference is most frequently, however, to the external manifestations. Physical power is suggested in Dt **33** 17, where "glory" of AV is replaced by "majesty" in RV. The king's glory consists in the multitude of his people (Prov **14** 28). The glory and the pomp of the rebellious people shall descend into Sheol (Isa **5** 14). Here the reference is clearly to those external things upon which the people depend, and the possession of which is the ground of their confidence.

But chiefly glory is the possession and characteristic of Jeh, and is given by Him to His people or to anything which is connected with Him.

2. As Applied to Jehovah

In Isa **60** 7 the Lord promises to glorify the house of His glory, and the meaning is clearly that He will impart to His house something of the beauty and majesty which belong to Him. Glory is one of the qualities which are distinctive of Jeh (1 Ch **29** 11); and Isaiah, in one of his earliest utterances, uses the word "glory" to describe Jeh's self-manifestation in judgment to bring to naught the pride and power of men (Isa **2** 10.19.21). The use of the word in Ps **78** 61 is not quite certain. The most natural interpretation would perhaps be to refer it to the ark as the symbol of the presence of Jeh, but in view of the ‖ word "strength," it is perhaps better to interpret glory as meaning power, and to suppose that the Psalmist means that Jeh allowed His power to be temporarily obscured, and Himself to be seemingly humiliated on account of the sin of His people.

III. The Uses of Kābhōdh.—The use and significance of *kābhōdh* in the OT and in Sir: The fundamental idea of this root seems to be "weight," "heaviness," and hence in its primary uses it conveys the idea of some external, physical manifestation of dignity, preëminence or majesty. At least three uses may be distinguished: (1) It defines the wealth or other material possessions which give honor or distinction to a person; (2) the majesty, dignity, splendor or honor of a person; (3) most important of all, it describes the form in which Jehovah (Yahweh) reveals Himself, or is the sign and manifestation of His presence.

1. Material Wealth

In Gen **31** 1 (m "wealth") it describes the flocks and herds which Jacob has acquired; in Ps **49** 16 f, as the parallelism indicates, it refers to the wealth of the sinner; and in Isa **10** 3 it is said that in the day of desolation the heartless plunderers of the poor shall not know where to leave their ill-gotten gain. This idea is also probably to be found in Hag **2** 7, where the parallelism seems to indicate that the glory with which Jeh will fill the house is the treasure which He will bring into it. See also Sir **9** 11, where the glory of the sinner which is not to be envied is probably his wealth.

2. Human Dignity and Majesty

It describes the majesty and dignity or honor of men due to their adornment or to their position. In Gen **45** 13, Joseph bids his brethren tell their father of his glory in Egypt; according to Ex **28** 40, the priestly garments are intended for the glorification of their wearers; in 1 S **4** 21 f, the loss of the ark means, for Israel, the loss of her glory, that which gave her distinction from, and preëminence over, her neighbors; in Isa **22** 23 it is said that Eliakim is to be a throne of glory, i.e. the source and manifestation of the splendor and dignity of his father's house; in Job **19** 9 the complaint that God has stripped him of his glory must be taken to refer to his dignity and honor. Reference may also be made to the numerous passages in which the glory of Israel and other nations describes their dignity, majesty or distinction; so we hear of the glory of Ephraim (Hos **9** 11), of Moab (Isa **16** 14), of Kedar (Isa **21** 16). This use is quite common in Sir. Sir **3** 10 f states that the glory of man comes from the honor of his father; the possessor of wisdom shall inherit glory (**4** 13; **37** 26); note also **4** 21 with its reference to "a shame that is glory and grace," and **49** 5 where the forfeited independence of Judah is described by the terms "power" and "glory."

Closely related to this use of *kābhōdh* to describe the majesty of men is the group of passages in which the phrase "my glory," in paral-

3. "My Soul": the Self

lelism with *nephesh* (נֶפֶשׁ), "soul," "self," or some similar expression, means the man himself in his most characteristic nature. In the blessing of Jacob (Gen **49** 6) we read, "Unto their assembly, my glory, be not thou united." Other passages are Ps **4** 2; **7** 5; **16** 9; **30** 12; **57** 8; **108** 1 and perhaps Job **29** 20. Some recent interpreters, partly because of the LXX rendering in Gen **49** 6 (*tá hḗpatá mou*), "my liver," and partly because of the Assyr root, *kabittu*, meaning "temper" or "heart" (see Delitzsch, *Assyrisches Handwörterbuch*, 317*a*), would read in all these passages *kābhēdh*, lit. "liver," as in Lam **2** 11, and interpret the figure as referring to the emotions as the expression of the self. The arguments in favor of the change are not without weight. Of course on either interpretation the language is highly figurative. It hardly seems necessary to change the reading, esp. as the LXX renders the passages in the Pss and in Job by *doxa*, the ordinary Gr rendering for *kābhōdh*, and it does not seem improbable that in poetry the word *kābhōdh* might be used to describe the man himself, indicating that man as such is honorable and glorious, possibly because as in Ps **8** 1, he is thought of as having been crowned by his Creator with glory and honor.

Before leaving this use of *kābhōdh* it is necessary to call attention to the fact that in a few cases it is used to describe things, perhaps because these things are thought of as practically personified. The "glory of the forest" (Isa **10** 18) is clearly a personification, referring to the majestic force of the Assyrians. We may probably assume a personification also in the case of the glory of Lebanon in Isa **35** 2; **60** 13, and the nature of the parable in Ezk **31** makes it probable that personification is intended in ver 18.

But unquestionably the most important use of the word *kābhōdh* is its employment either with the following gen. God or Jeh, or ab-

4. Self-manifestation of God (Jehovah)

solutely, to describe the method or the circumstances of the self-manifestation of God. In discussing this subject we shall deal first of all with the use of the term as connected with actual or historical manifestations of the Deity, and then with its use to describe the characteristic features of the ideal state of the future, or, otherwise stated, the Messianic kingdom.

(1) *Ex 23 18 ff.*—The significance of the phrase in its earliest occurrence is by no means clear. Notwithstanding the uncertainty as to the exact docu-

mentary connection of the famous passage in Ex **33** 18 ff, it seems quite certain that we may claim that this is the earliest historical reference that the OT contains to the glory of Jeh. "And he [Moses] said, Show me, I pray thee, thy glory. And he [Jeh] said Thou canst not see my face; . . . . and it shall come to pass, while my glory passeth by, that I will put thee in a cleft of the rock, and will cover thee with my hand until I have passed by: and I will take away my hand, and thou shalt see my back; but my face shall not be seen." The passage in its present form bears unmistakable evidences of the editorial hand, due perhaps, as Baentsch (*Handkommentar zum AT*, "Ex-Lev-Nu," 279) suggests, to a desire to transform the primitive, concrete, physical theophany into a revelation of the ethical glory of God, but in its basis it belongs to J and is therefore the earliest literary reference to the glory of God in the OT. The glory of Jeh is clearly a physical manifestation, a form with hands and rear parts, of which Moses is permitted to catch only a passing glimpse, but the implication is clear that he actually does see Jeh with his physical eyes.

It seems not improbable that in its original form it was related that Moses saw the glory, i.e., the form of Jeh, and thus that we are to find in this narrative the source for the statement in Nu **12** 8, that he (Moses) will behold (or perhaps better rendering the tense as a frequentative), beholds the form of Jeh (see also the description in Ex **24** 9–11). The mention of the cloud (Ex **34** 5) as the accompaniment of the manifestation of Jeh suggests that the form of Jeh was thought of as being outlined in cloud and flame, and that Jeh was originally thought of as manifesting Himself in connection with meteorological or more probably volcanic phenomena.

(2) *Isa **6**.*—Later the glory of Jeh and the form of Jeh are no longer identical terms, but the glory is still the physical manifestation of the Divine presence. This is clear from Isaiah's account of his great inaugural vision. The prophet sees the enthroned Jeh with His skirts filling the temple. There is no indication of what it was that he saw or how he recognized that it was Jeh. The attendant seraphim in addition to the solemn "Holy, Holy, Holy" declare that "the whole earth is full of his glory."

Unquestionably His glory is here regarded as something visible, something, a part of which at least, Isaiah sees. The glory as such has no ethical significance except in so far as it is the method of manifestation of one who is undoubtedly an ethical being. The phraseology suggests that the skirts which fill the temple and the glory which fills the whole earth refer to the phenomena of fire and smoke. Some think that the smoke is caused by the clouds of incense that would fill the temple in connection with the sacrificial observances. But in view of Isaiah's horror of these observances, this interpretation is very questionable. A more probable interpretation connects the clouds and gloom with the phenomena of a great storm, and even possibly of an earthquake, for it seems highly plausible that the call of Isaiah in the year of the death of King Uzziah coincided with the great earthquake in the days of Uzziah referred to in Zec **14** 5. (It seems at least probable that the references to the darkness and light in Zec **14** 6 f may have their origin in the phenomena attendant upon this earthquake. It is probable that the earthquake by which the prophecy of Amos is dated [Am **1** 1] is also this same historic earthquake.) The clouds and fire attendant upon this storm or earthquake become the media by which the glory of Jeh is made known to the youthful prophet, and this glory partly reveals and partly conceals the presence of Jeh of which, through and in part by means of, these phenomena, Isaiah is made so vividly conscious.

(3) *Ps **19** 1.*—This conception of Isaiah that the glory of Jeh fills the earth is closely related to the thought of Ps **19** 1 that "the heavens declare the glory of God; and the firmament showeth his handiwork," the difference being that in the psalm Jeh's glory is manifested in the ordinary rather than in the extraordinary phenomena. Parallel thoughts may be found in Ps **8** 1; **57** 5; **108** 5; **113** 4. In Ps **29** 1.2.3.9, as in Isaiah, the glory of Jeh is revealed in the extraordinary physical phenomena which the psalm describes. Glory here is a purely external, meteorological thing and is the manifestation of the presence of Jeh, no matter whether the psalm is regarded, as it usually is, as a description of a thunderstorm, or whether with von Gall and others it is taken as a description of the phenomena which accompany the inauguration of the Messianic kingdom (see Joel **2** 30 f ERV).

(4) *Sinai and the Temple.*—Dt **5** 24 indicates that in the theophany at the time of the giving of the law, the glory and the greatness of Jeh consisted in the fire and thick darkness which enveloped the mountain, and out of which Jeh spoke to the people. Essentially the same idea is expressed in the account of the dedication of Solomon's temple (1 K **8** 10 f; 2 Ch **5** 14). The cloud which filled the house of Jeh, preventing the priests from ministering, is identified with the glory of Jeh which filled the house. It is noteworthy that in 2 Ch **7** 1–3 the glory of Jeh which fills the house manifests itself in the form of the cloud of smoke from the sacrifices which were consumed by the fire coming down from heaven.

(5) *Ezekiel's visions.*—Perhaps the most elaborate description of the glory of Jeh to be found in the OT is that given by Ezekiel in the various accounts of his visions. It is not easy to interpret his conception, but it seems clear that he does not identify the glory with the stormy clouds, the fire, the cherubim and the chariots. "The appearance of the likeness of the glory of Jeh" (Ezk **1** 28) is not applied to all the phenomena which have been described in the preceding verses, but only to the likeness of form which looked like a man above the sapphire throne (ver 26). The same idea is indicated in **9** 3 which states that "the glory of the God of Israel was gone up from the cherub, whereupon it was"; that is, the glory is something peculiar to Jeh, and is not quite identical with the phenomena which accompany it. This is true of all his visions. The glory of Jeh manifests itself with all the accompaniments which he describes with such richness of imagery, but the accompaniments are not the glory. For other descriptions of the glory of Jeh in Ezekiel, see **3** 12.23; **8** 4; **10** 4.18 ff; **11** 22 f.

Very similar to this conception of Ezekiel is that given in those passages of the Pent which are usually assigned to the PC. When the children of Israel murmured against Moses and Aaron on account of the lack of food, the glory of Jeh appeared in the cloud as they "looked toward the wilderness" (Ex **16** 7.10; cf Ex **24** 16 f). And just as in Ezk, the glory is distinguished from its attendant circumstances; for after the completion of the Tent of Meeting, the cloud covers the tent, and the glory of Jeh fills the tabernacle (Ex **40** 34 f; see also Lev **9** 6.23; Nu **14** 21 f; **16** 19.42; **20** 6). The same thought is suggested in the references in Sir **17** 13; **45** 3.

(6) *Messianic ideal.*—These passages just cited stand on the border between the historical and the ideal descriptions of the glory of Jeh, for whatever may be one's views as to the historical worth of P's account of the Exodus and the wilderness sojourn, all must agree in seeing in it really the program or constitution for the ideal state of the future. And in this state the distinguishing characteristic is to be the manifest presence of Jeh in His sanctuary, and this manifestation is the glory. This is the view of Ezekiel, for whom the essential action in the establishment of the new community is the return of the glory of Jeh to the house of Jeh (Ezk **43** 2.4.5; **44** 4). The same thought is expressed very clearly in Isa **4** 5 f, which may be rendered on the basis of a slight rearrangement and regrouping of the original, 'And Jeh will create over . . . . Mt. Zion

. . . . , a cloud and smoke by day, and the shining of a flaming fire by night; for over everything the glory [of Yahweh] shall be a canopy and a pavilion, and it shall serve as a shelter from the heat, and a refuge and a covert from the storm and the rain.' This tr has the advantage that it furnishes an intelligible and characteristic conclusion to the description of the Messianic age which the chapter contains. Isa **11** 10, reading with RVm, "and his resting-place shall be glory," has the same thought, for it is clearly the glory of Jeh that is manifested in the resting-place of the root of Jesse, and this resting-place can be none other than Mt. Zion (cf also Isa **24** 23).

The Pss and Deutero-Isa have many passages in which this phase of the thought is brought out. For both books the restoration of the people from captivity is to be accompanied by, or, perhaps better, itself is, a revelation of the glory of Jeh (Isa **40** 5). The children of Israel have been created for the glory of Jeh, and hence they must be restored that His glory may be made manifest (**43** 7). The light of the restored community is to be the glory of Jeh (**60** 1 f). The presence of Jeh brings grace and glory (Ps **84** 11), and His salvation of those that fear Him causes glory to dwell in the land (Ps **85** 9). To these and many similar passages in Isa and the Pss may also be added Sir **36** 14, which refers probably to the manifestation of God in glory in the Messianic kingdom.

(7) *Its ethical content.*—But these passages make it quite evident that "glory" is not always used in the external, lit. or fig. physical sense. It comes to have an ethical significance, and this because, like the holiness with which it is associated in Isa **6**, it is connected with Jeh, who is more and more exclusively viewed as an ethical being. As holiness gradually loses its physical sense of aloofness, apartness, and comes to describe moral purity, so glory, because it is an attribute or expression of Jeh, comes to have a moral sense. This transformation, as we have seen, is already being made in the present text of Ex **33** 18.20, and the connection with holiness in Isa **6** makes it almost certain that Isaiah gave the word an ethical connotation. So the God of glory of Ps **29** 3 suggests a moral quality because Jeh is a moral being. All doubt on this matter disappears when we find the word "glory" used as the term for the essential nature of Jeh, as we have already found it to be used of man. In Isa **42** 8, "I am Jeh, that is my name; and my glory will I not give to another," the meaning would seem to be, my essential character and power, that is, my glory, I will not share with other gods (cf also Isa **48** 11). And in Isa **58** 8 the glory must be taken in a figurative sense and refer to Jeh Himself in His saving grace, who attends His people in advance and in the rear. It hardly seems possible to deny the ethical sense in Ezk **39** 21, where the manifestation of the glory of Jeh comes as a result of the execution of His purposes of justice and righteousness upon His people. And in Hab **2** 14, the glory of Jeh which is to be known throughout the earth cannot be limited to any physical, external thing. It is equivalent to the righteous and just will of Jeh. These passages are sufficient to prove the ethical significance of the word *kābhōdh*, but it may be worth while to quote one more passage and this time from Ps **97** with its wonderful description of the blessings of the righteous rule of Jeh. It is stated in ver 6 that "the heavens declare his righteousness, and all the peoples have seen his glory." His righteousness may include, as Kirkpatrick suggests, "His faithfulness to His people and His sovereign justice in the punishment of all," or it may refer only to the former of these qualities; but in any case, it is a moral act, and by it the peoples recognize the glory of Jeh as the supreme moral ruler.

IV. In Apoc and NT.—"Glory" in the apocryphal books and in the NT is almost exclusively the tr of the Gr noun *doxa*. In all these writings the OT usage seems to be the most important, and it seems to be the fact, if one may judge from the LXX and from the original Heb of Sir, that the Gr noun *doxa*, in the great majority of cases, represents the Heb *kābhōdh*, so that the underlying thought is Heb, even though the words may be Gr.

1. In the Apoc

(1) *As applied to external things.*—It will be perhaps a little more convenient to deal with the usage of the Apoc separately, following essentially the order that has been adopted for the OT discussion of *kābhōdh*, and bearing in mind that the usage of Sir has been discussed under the OT. The use of the word "glory" to describe the honor, reputation and splendor which belong to men is quite common. In this sense 1 Esd **1** 33 refers to the glory of Josiah, while in Wisd **10** 14 the perpetual glory given by Wisd to Joseph must be interpreted in the same way. In 2 Macc **5** 16.20 glory refers to the beautification and adornment of the temple in a sense like that of *tiph'ārāh* in Isa **60** 7. In Jth **15** 9 "glory" is the tr of the Gr *gaurίama*, and indicates that Judith is the pride of Israel.

(2) *As applied to God.*—But the most significant use of *doxa* in the Apocrypha is that in which it refers to the light and splendor which are regarded as the invariable accompaniments of God. The reference may be to the historic manifestation of God in glory at Mt. Sinai, as in 2 Esd **3** 19, or to the manifestation of God in Israel, which is to be the especial characteristic of the Messianic kingdom. In 1 Esd **5** 61 songs sung to the praise of the Lord, "because his goodness and his glory are forever in all Israel," are based upon the hope that Jeh is about to establish the Messianic kingdom among the people who have bound themselves to obey His law. In several passages in 2 Esd the reference seems to be not to the Messianic kingdom in the historical sense, but rather to that kingdom of God which the saints are to inherit after death. This is clearly the thought in 2 Esd **2** 36 and in **7** 52; also in **8** 51 where the context shows clearly that the reference is to the glory of Paradise, which is the heritage of all those who are like Ezra in their devotion to Jeh (cf also **10** 50).

But most frequently in the Apoc, in a sense which approximates that of the NT, the word "glory" refers to the blaze of light and splendor which is the essential expression of the holy majesty of Jeh. The prayer of Manasseh refers to the unbearable majesty of the glory of Jeh; while 2 Esd **8** 30, trusting in Jeh's glory is equivalent to trusting in Jeh Himself; and in **16** 53 the oath "before God and his glory" is simply before the Lord God Himself. The same thought is expressed in Tob **12** 15; **13** 14; Wisd **7** 25. In the Three, vs 31.33, the glory of Jeh refers to His self-manifestation in His heavenly kingdom, and this is undoubtedly the significance in the frequently recurring doxologies, "Thine is the glory forever."

2. In the NT

(1) *As applied to men.*—In the NT, much the same variety of usage is to be noted as in the OT and the Apoc, and it is not easy to trace the exact relationship and order of the various meanings. The ordinary classical use of the word in the sense of "opinion," "judgment," "view," occurs in Hellenistic Gr only in 4 Macc **5** 17 (18) on the authority of Thayer.

It is perhaps as convenient to follow generally the order adopted in the preceding discussion. In some places the word refers to the manifestations and insignia of rank and power, as in the familiar phrase, "Solomon in all his glory" (Mt **6** 29), or the glory of the kingdoms of the world (**4** 8), or the glory of the kings and nations of the earth which shall be brought into the heavenly city (Rev **21** 24.26). *Doxa* also defines the praise, honor and dignity of men. This is the meaning in Jn **5** 41.44, where Christ distinguishes between His accusers and Himself in that He receives not glory from men, while they receive glory one of another (cf also Jn **7** 18). In Eph **3** 13, Paul declares that his tribulations for those to whom he is writing are a glory or distinction to them, while in 1 Thess **2** 20 he declares that the Thessalonian Christians are his glory and joy.

(2) *As applied to God.*—Closely related to this usage is the employment of the word to ascribe honor

and praise to God; see Lk **17** 18, where only the stranger returned to give glory to God; or Jn **9** 24, where the man who had been born blind is bidden to give glory to God; or the phrase "to the glory of God" in Rom **15** 7, where the meaning is to secure the honor and praise of God among men. Similar is the use in the frequently recurring doxologies such as, "Glory to God in the highest," "to him," that is, to God, "be glory," etc.

While the foregoing meanings are frequently illustrated in the NT, it is undoubtedly true that the characteristic use of the word *doxa* in the NT is in the sense of brightness, brilliance, splendor; and first of all, in the literal sense, referring to the brightness of the heavenly bodies, as in 1 Cor **15** 40 f, or to the supernatural brightness which overcame Saul of Tarsus on the road to Damascus (Acts **22** 11).

(3) *As applied to the saints.*—But the most common use of the word is to describe the brilliance which is the characteristic of all persons who share in the heavenly glory. Moses, Elijah and Jesus Himself have this glory on the Mt. of Transfiguration (Lk **9** 31 f). It was the same glory which gave the angel who came out of heaven power to lighten the earth (Rev **18** 1), and also which shone about the shepherds when the angel appeared unto them (Lk **2** 9). Paul refers to this glory, when he speaks of the face of Moses as it appeared after God had spoken with him (2 Cor **3** 7 f). And as in the case of Moses, so here, the source of this glory is God Himself, who is the God of glory (Acts **7** 2, and frequently).

(4) *As applied to the Messianic kingdom.*—It is also used to describe the ideal Messianic kingdom of the future. It is applied to Christ to describe His royal majesty when He comes to set up His kingdom. So James and John ask to sit, one on His right hand and one on His left in His glory (Mk **10** 37). Christ is to appear in glory with the angels (Mt **16** 27 and often), for His condition in the coming age as it was before the incarnation is a condition of glory (Lk **24** 26; Jn **17** 5.22.24). But not merely the Messiah, but also all His followers shall share in the glory of the Messianic kingdom. This use is so common that it is scarcely necessary to illustrate it by reference. This glory is to be revealed to all Christians in the future (Rom **8** 18. 21; **9** 23; cf also 1 Cor **2** 7; 2 Cor **4** 17).

In all these cases it has a distinctly ethical signification, for it is the term which is used to describe the essential nature, the perfection of the Deity, and is shared by others because they are made partakers of the Divine nature. So Paul refers to "the glory of the incorruptible God" (Rom **1** 23; cf also Eph **1** 17 f, and often). And the essential nature of Christ comes to be described in the same way. He has glory as of the only begotten of the Father (Jn **1** 14); he shows His glory in the performance of miracles (Jn **2** 11); and like the Father, He is the Lord of glory (1 Cor **2** 8).

3. Its Ethical Significance

As a vb. in the OT the most common signification of the word "glory" is, to make one's boast in or of anything, usually of the pious glorying in Yahweh (Jeh), but occasionally with some other reference, as in Jer **9** 23 of man glorying in his riches, might or wisdom. In all these cases it represents the Heb *hith-hallēl*. In Ex **8** 9 the phrase, "Have thou this glory over me," is the tr of the Heb *hith-pā'ēr*, and means take to thyself the honor or distinction as regards me. In 2 K **14** 10 it translates the Heb *hik-kābhēdh*, "honor thyself," i.e. be satisfied with the home which you have already attained.

In the apocryphal books it means either "glorify thyself," the middle voice of the vb. *doxázō*, as in Sir **3** 10, where the original Heb has *hith-kabbēdh*, or "to exult," "boast over," as in Jth **9** 7, where it represents the Gr *gauróomai;* or "to boast," "take pride in," where it represents, as it does usually in the NT, the Gr *kaucháomai* (Sir **17** 9; **24** 1; **38** 25; **39** 8; **48** 4, in the second and fourth of which cases it represents the Heb *hith-pā'ēr*).

In the NT the vb. is used 3 t in Jas, and several times in the Epp. of Paul, and everywhere is used to translate the vb. *kaucháomai*, or, in two cases in Jas, the same vb. is compounded with the preposition *katá*. In all these cases the meaning is "to take pride in," "to congratulate oneself," upon anything.

In this connection attention may be called to the use of the noun "glorying," once or twice rendered "to glory," where the meaning is either the occasion or ground of glorying, or sometimes the act of glorying. The original has *kauchēma* or *kauchēsis*. This usage occurs in Jas **4** 16; He **3** 6, and several times in the Epp. of Paul.

Literature.—In addition to the commentaries and works on Bib. theology among which, Briggs, *ICC* on the Pss, Scribner, N.Y., 1906, esp. the note in I, 66, 67; and Weiss, *Bib. Theology of the NT*, ET, T. & S. Clark, Edinburgh, 1882–83, may be mentioned esp., the chief works on the subject are von Gall, *Die Herrlichkeit Gottes*, Giessen, 1900; and Caspari, *Die Bedeutungen der Wortsippe* כבד *im Hebraeischen*, Leipzig, 1908. The discussions by G. B. Gray and J. Massie in *HDB*, II, are valuable, and also the brief but significant article by Zenos in the *Standard Bible Dict.*, Funk & Wagnalls, N.Y., 1909.

Walter R. Betteridge

GLOWING, glō'ing, SAND (Isa **35** 11). See Mirage.

GLUTTON, glut''n, GLUTTONOUS, glut''n-us (זָלַל, *zālal*, "to be lavish"; φάγος, *phágos*): "Glutton" (from *glut*, to swallow greedily) is the tr of *zōlēl* from *zālal*, "to shake or pour out," "to be lavish, a squanderer." In Dt **21** 20, "This our son . . . . is a glutton, and a drunkard," the word may mean a squanderer or prodigal; ERV has "a riotous liver." In Prov **23** 21, "For the drunkard and the glutton shall come to poverty" (following *zōlē bhāsār*, "squanderers of flesh," RV "gluttonous eaters of flesh"), "glutton" in the usual sense is intended; "a man gluttonous," "a gluttonous man" (RV) (*phagos*, "an eater," "a glutton") was a term applied to Christ in His freedom from asceticism (Mt **11** 19; Lk **7** 34).

RV has "idle gluttons" (m Gr, "bellies") for "slow bellies" (Tit **1** 12); "gluttonous" "gluttons," for "riotous" (Prov **23** 20; **28** 7).

W. L. Walker

GNASH, nash (חָרַק, *ḥārak;* βρυγμός, *brugmós*): "Gnash" is used of grinding or striking together the teeth in rage, pain or misery of disappointment. In the OT it is the tr of *ḥārak*, a mimetic word, and represents for the most part rage, anger, hatred (Job **16** 9, "He gnasheth upon me with his teeth," RV "hath gnashed upon me"; Ps **35** 16; **37** 12; **112** 10, grief; Lam **2** 16, contempt or derision); *brúchō*, "to gnash the teeth in rage," indicates anger, rage, LXX for *ḥārak* (Acts **7** 54, of Stephen, "They gnashed on him with their teeth"). The several instances of *brugmos*, "gnashing," in the Gospels seem to express disappointment rather than anger (Mt **8** 12, "There shall be wailing and gnashing of teeth," RV "the weeping and the gnashing of teeth"; **13** 42.50; **22** 13; **24** 51; **25** 30; Lk **13** 28—a vivid representation of the misery of disappointed expectations; cf Ecclus **30** 10, "lest thou shalt gnash thy teeth in the end," *gomphiázō*, "to have the teeth set on edge"); *trízō* (Mk **9** 18), which means "to give out a creaking, grating sound," "to screak," is used in the NT (in the above instance only) to mean "to grate or gnash with the teeth," indicating the effect of a paroxysm, RV "grindeth his teeth."

W. L. Walker

GNAT, nat (in EV, only in Mt **23** 24, **κώνωψ,** *kṓnōps*. In Ex **8** 16, for EV "lice," one of the plagues of Egypt, כִּנִּם, *kinnim*, כִּנִּים, *kinnīm*, or כִּנָּם, *kinnām*, we find in RVm "sand flies" or "fleas" [Gesenius "gnat"; Mandelkern "culex"]. For *k^emō kēn* [Isa **51** 6], EV "in like manner," LXX **ὥσπερ ταῦτα,** *hṓsper taúta*, Vulg *sicut haec*, RVm has "like gnats," since כֵּן, *kēn*, elsewhere "thus," may here be taken to be a sing. of the form כִּנִּים, *kinnīm*, which occurs in Ex **8**): In the NT passage, the difference between AV and RV should be noted. "Strain at a gnat, and swallow a camel" is changed to "strain out the gnat and swallow the camel," the reference being to the inconsistency of the Jewish religious leaders in taking extraordinary pains in some things, as in the preparation of food, while leaving weightier matters unattended to.

In Isa **51** 6, the suggestion of RVm, "They that dwell therein shall die like gnats," seems a decided improvement on the "shall die in like manner" of EV, esp. as *kēn*, "thus" (see *supra*), is a repetition of *k^emō*, whose meaning is practically the same, "in like manner" being the rendering in EV of *k^emō kēn*.

As to the creatures, *kinnīm*, of the Egyp plague, there is little choice between "lice" of EV and the others suggested, except as we may be influenced by the LXX rendering, *skníphes*, which may mean "gnats" or "mosquitoes." See FLEA; LICE.

ALFRED ELY DAY

GNOSTICISM, nos'ti-siz'm:

I. GENERAL DEFINITION
II. SOURCES OF GNOSTICISM
  1. Alexandrian Philosophy
  2. Zoroastrianism
III. NATURE OF GNOSTICISM
  Chief Points
IV. GNOSTICISM IN THE CHRISTIAN CHURCH
  1. Colossians
  2. 1 Cor: "Knowledge" at Corinth
  3. Pastoral Epistles
  4. 1 John
    (1) Gnostic Claims
    (2) Its Loveless Nature
    (3) Docetism
    (4) The Antichrist
    (5) Its Antinomian Side
  5. "To Know the Depths," Rev
V. THE CHRISTIAN ANTITHESIS
  1. God and the World
    How Did the World Originate?
  2. Evil
    (1) Christian Doctrine of Sin
    (2) Sin and the Moral Law
  3. Christ and Redemption
  4. Asceticism and Antinomianism
VI. HARNACK'S VIEW OF GNOSTICISM
VII. INFLUENCE AND DEVELOPMENT OF GNOSTICISM
  1. Not a Heresy of the Humbler Classes
  2. Cerinthus: His Teaching
  3. The Gospel of John
  4. Various Sects
    (1) The Ophites
    (2) Valentinus
    (3) Basilides
    (4) Saturninus
    (5) Marcion
  5. Relation to the OT
  6. The Christian Verities
  7. Influence on Theology
  8. Truth Underlying Docetism
VIII. MODERN GNOSTICISM
LITERATURE

Gnosticism—except perhaps in 1 Tim **6** 20, where St. Paul warns Timothy against "the *gnôsis*, which is falsely so called"—is not directly alluded to in the NT. Nevertheless its leaven was actually working, as will immediately be seen, and constituted a most serious peril in the apostolic church. "That strange, obscure movement, partly intellectual, partly fanatical . . . . in the 2d cent. spread with the swiftness of an epidemic over the church from Syria to Gaul" (Law, *The Tests of Life*, 26). It is therefore of high importance to gain a right conception of the nature of this potent anti-Christian influence. This is not easy. The difficulty in dealing with Gnosticism is that it was not a homogeneous system of either religion or philosophy, but embraced many widely diversified sects holding opinions drawn from a great variety of sources "The infinitely varied shapes assumed by the systems render it almost impossible to classify them, or even to give an account of their leading ideas, which shall not be open to objection. We might as well try to classify the products of a tropical jungle, or the shapes and hues of the sunset clouds, which change under our view as we look at them" (Orr, *The Progress of Dogma*, 58).

I. General Definition.—On the general definition of Gnosticism a few authorities may be cited. "Gnosticism," says Dr. Gwatkin, "may be provisionally described as a number of schools of philosophy, oriental in general character, but taking in the idea of a redemption through Christ, and further modified in different sects by a third element, which may be Judaism, Hellenism, or Christianity . . . . the Gnostics took over only the idea of a redemption through Christ, not the full Christian doctrine, for they made it rather a redemption of the philosophers from matter, than a redemption of mankind from sin" (*Early Church History to AD 313*, II, 20).

Dr. Orr writes, "Gnosticism may be described generally as the fantastic product of the blending of certain Christian ideas—particularly that of redemption through Christ—with speculations and imaginings derived from a medley of sources (Gr, Jewish, Parsic; philosophies, religions, theosophies, mysteries) in a period when the human mind was in a kind of ferment, and when opinions of every sort were jumbled together in an unimaginable welter. It involves, as the name denotes, a claim to *'knowledge,'* knowledge of a kind of which the ordinary believer was incapable, and in the possession of which 'salvation' in the full sense consisted. This knowledge of which the Gnostic boasted, related to the subjects ordinarily treated of in religious philosophy; Gnosticism was a species of *religious philosophy*" (*The Early Church*, 71).

Neander has described Gnosticism as "the first notable attempt to introduce into Christianity the existing elements of mental culture, and to render it more complete on the hitherto rather neglected side of theoretical knowledge; it was an attempt of the mind of the ancient world in its yearning after knowledge, and in its dissatisfaction with the present, to bring within its grasp and to appropriate the treasures of this kind which Christianity presented" (*Antignostikus*, Intro, 199).

Gnosticism accordingly comprehends in itself many previously existing tendencies; it is an amalgam into which quite a number of different elements have been fused. A heretical system of thought, at once subtle, speculative and elaborate, it endeavored to introduce into Christianity a so-called higher knowledge, which was grounded partly on the philosophic creed in which Greeks and Romans had taken refuge consequent on the gradual decay and breaking-up of their own religions, partly, as will be shown, on the philosophies of Plato and of Philo, and still more on the philosophies and theosophies and religions of the East, especially those of Persia and of India.

"For a long time the pagan beliefs had ceased to be taken seriously by thoughtful men and had been displaced by various creeds derived from philosophical speculation. These in themselves were abstract and unsatisfying, but had been partly vitalized by union with the theosophies of the East. An attempt was made on the part of this philosophical religion to effect an alliance with Christianity. A section of the church was dissatisfied with the simplicity of the gospel, and sought to advance to something higher by adopting the current speculations. . . . . The late books of the NT are all occupied, more or less, with this movement, which was the more dangerous as it threatened the church from within" (Professor E. Scott, *The Apologetic of the NT*, 14).

Gnosticism, though usually regarded as a heresy, was not really such: it was not the perverting of Christian truth; it came, rather, from outside. Having worked its way into the Christian church, it was then heretical. "Although it became a corrupting influence within the church, it was an alien by birth. While the church yet sojourned within the pale of Judaism, it enjoyed immunity from this plague; but as soon as it broke through these narrow bounds, it found itself in a world where the decaying religions and philosophies of the West were in acute fermentation under the influence of a new and powerful leaven from the East; while the infusion of Christianity itself into this fermenting mass only added to the bewildering multiplicity of gnostic sects and systems it brought forth" (Law, *The Tests of Life*, 26).

II. Sources of Gnosticism.—Mansel (in his work on *The Gnostic Heresies*, 32) sums up the principal sources of Gnosticism in these three, Platonism, the Pers religion, and the Buddhism of India. To Platonism it owed much of its philosophical form and tendencies. From the Dualism of the Pers religion it derived its speculations regarding the origin of evil, and much of what it taught about emanations. To Buddhism, he thinks, it owed the doctrine of the antagonism between matter and spirit, and the unreality of derived existence—the germ of Docetism. Mansel also holds that there is the possibility that Gnosticism derived certain of its features from the Kabbala (*ḳabbālāh*), or secret teaching of the Jews in the two books, the *Ṣēpher yeçīrāh*, or Book of Creation, and the *Zōhar*, or Book of Light. An influence of Buddhism on Gnosticism, however, may safely be doubted, as there is no reason to believe that the knowledge of Buddhist doctrine had so early penetrated into the West. The Jewish works named by Mansel are really products of the Middle Ages (Westcott, *Intro to the Study of the Gospels*, 144–45). The other sources named were really influential. We notice two—the Alexandrian philosophy and the Parsic dualism.

1. Alexandrian Philosophy

Alexandrian philosophy endeavored to unite Gr philosophy and Heb religion. Philo, the great Jewish commentator of Alexandria, had tried to interpret the ancient Jewish Scriptures by the aid of the Gr philosophy, to expound the OT in terms of Plato's thought and to discover allegorical meanings where none were intended. In Philo's teaching there is a sharp line drawn between God and the material world: with him God cannot exert any action upon the world of matter, except through intermediate agency, the Jewish angels and the heathen demons. Philo has much to say in regard to the Logos. His utterances on this subject may be compared with what is said of the attributes of "Wisdom" in ch **8** of the Book of Prov, and also with the Logos or "Word" of the Gospel of John. With Philo, the Logos is the power of God, or the Divine reason endowed with energy, and embracing within itself all subordinate powers. The Logos is impersonal in its relations to God; and herein is one huge difference between Philo's conception and that in the gospel. Philo teaches that the Logos is the only firstborn of God, the chief of the angels, the viceroy of God, and representative of man. See LOGOS.

According to Philo the creation of the universe was a gradual molding out of matter; hence arises evil. He also teaches the preëxistence of the soul, which is now imprisoned in the flesh. The wise man, therefore, will break the thraldom of the flesh, and will rise by a sort of ecstasy to the immediate vision of God. It will be seen how much of this teaching was assimilated by the various gnostic sects.

2. Zoroastrianism

The Zoroastrian or Pers system was based on the assumption that there existed two original and independent powers of good and evil, of light and darkness, Ormuzd (Ahura-Mazda), the wise Lord, and Ahriman (Angra-Mainyu), the wicked spirit. These powers were believed to be equal, and each supreme in his own domain. The earth, which was created by Ormuzd, became the battlefield of the two powers. Ahriman led away the first man and woman from their allegiance to Ormuzd, and so all evils result to mankind.

"In oriental (Pers) dualism," says Professor Bousset, "it is within this material world that the good and the evil powers are at war, and this world beneath the stars is by no means conceived as entirely subject to evil. Gnosticism has combined the two, the Gr opposition between spirit and matter, and the sharp Zoroastrian dualism, which, where the Gr mind conceived of a higher and a lower world, saw instead two hostile worlds standing in contrast to each other like light and darkness. And out of the combination of these two dualisms arose the teaching of Gnosticism with its thoroughgoing pessimism and its fundamental asceticism" ("Gnosticism," in *Enc Brit*, 11th ed, XII, 154).

III. Nature of Gnosticism.—"Gnosticism," says Dr. Gwatkin, "is Christianity perverted by learning and speculation" (*Early Church History*, 73). The intellectual pride of the Gnostics refined away the gospel into a philosophy. The clue to the understanding of Gnosticism is given in the word from which it is derived—*gnōsis*, "knowledge." Gnosticism puts knowledge in the place which can only rightly be occupied by Christian faith. To the Gnostic the great question was not the intensely practical one, "What must I do to be saved from sin?" but "What is the origin of evil?" "How is the primitive order of the universe to be restored?" In the knowledge of these and of similar questions, and in the answers given to these questions, there was redemption, as the Gnostic understood it.

"These little gnostic sects and groups all lived in the conviction that they possessed a secret and mysterious knowledge, in no way accessible to those outside, which was not to be proved or propagated, but believed in by the initiated, and anxiously guarded as a secret. This knowledge of theirs was not based on reflection or scientific inquiry and proof, but on revelation. It was derived directly from the times of primitive Christianity, from the Saviour Himself and His disciples and friends, with whom they claimed to be connected by a secret tradition, or else from later prophets, of whom many sects boasted. It was laid down in wonderful mystic writings, which were in the possession of the various circles.

"In short, Gnosticism in all its various sections, its form and its character, falls under the category of mystic religions, which were so characteristic of the religious life of decadent antiquity. In Gnosticism, as in the other mystic religions, we find the same contrast of the initiated and the uninitiated, the same loose organization, the same kind of petty sectarianism and mystery-mongering. All alike boast a mystic revelation and a deeply veiled wisdom" (Bousset, op. cit., 153).

Chief Points in Gnosticism

The questions, therefore, with which Gnosticism concerned itself were those of the relation of the finite and the infinite, the origin of the world and of evil, the cause, meaning, purpose and destiny of all things, the reason of the difference in the capacities and in the lot in life of individual men, the method of salvation. The following may be regarded as the chief points in the characteristics of the gnostic systems: (1) A claim on the part of the initiated to a special knowledge of the truth, a tendency to regard knowledge as superior to faith, and as the special possession of the more enlightened, for ordinary Christians did not possess this secret and higher doctrine. (2) The essential separation of matter and spirit, the former of these being essentially evil, and the source from which all evil has arisen. (3) An attempt at the solution of the problems of creation and of the origin of evil by the conception of a Demiurge, i.e. a Creator or Artificer of the world as distinct from the Supreme Deity, and also by means of emanations extending between God and the visible universe. It should be observed that this conception merely concealed the difficulties of the problem, and did not solve them. (4) A denial of the true humanity of Christ, a docetic Christology, which looked upon the earthly life of Christ and esp. on His sufferings on the cross as unreal. (5) The denial of the personality of the Supreme God, and the denial also of the free will of man. (6) The teaching, on the one hand, of asceticism as the means of attaining to spiritual communion with God, and, on the other hand, of an indifference which led directly to licentiousness. (7) A syncretistic tendency which combined certain more or less misunderstood Christian doctrines, various elements from oriental and Jewish and other sources. (8) The Scriptures of the OT were ascribed to the Demiurge or inferior Creator of the world, who was the God of the Jews, but not the true God. Some of these characteristic ideas are more obvious in one, and some of them in others of the gnostic systems. The relation of these ideas to Christian facts and doctrines is dealt with more particularly below.

IV. Gnosticism in the Christian Church.—(1) *In the NT and the Apostolic Age.*—The germ of Gnosticism in the Christian church made its appearance in the apostolic age, and is referred to by St. Paul in several of his epistles, notably in that to the Colossians and in the Pastoral Epistles. It is also referred to by the apostles Peter and Jude; references to it are found, besides, in the Apocalypse, the First Epistle of John and the Gospel of John.

1. Colossians

In Col a great deal is said regarding a false teaching, an insidious theosophist doctrine, the teachers of which were alienating the Christians in Colossae from the gospel, and were disseminating their speculations, which led to the worship of angels in contrast to the worship of Christ, to esoteric exclusiveness wholly opposed to the universality of the gospel, and to an asceticism injurious to Christian freedom, and derogatory to the human body as indwelt by the Holy Ghost. These tenets are identical with the more fully developed Gnosticism of the generation succeeding that of the apostles; and at the root of the Colossian false teaching there lay the same error which the gnostic mind had no way of meeting, viz. that there could be no connection between the highest spiritual agency, that is God, and gross corporeal matter.

From this theoretical basis arose another error—that as sin is inherent in the material substance of the body, therefore the only way by which perfection can be reached is to punish the body by asceticism, so that through the infliction of pain and the mortification of the flesh the region of pure spirit may be reached, and thus man may be etherealized and become like God. This ascetic tendency is wonderfully widespread; it reappears century after century, and shows itself in many forms of religion, not merely in distorted forms of Christianity, but in the Hindu religions, in Buddhism and elsewhere. In the Epistle to the Col, accordingly, there are definite references to ascetic practices which were inculcated by the false teachers at Colossae. The very terms which they employed have been preserved, "Touch not," "Taste not," "Handle not." It was in this way that these teachers had "at their own hand" invented a worship different from that of the Christian faith, which endeavored to attain the deliverance of the soul by "the neglecting of the body" (Col **2** 21.23 AV). These gnostic teachers showed these tendencies still more boldly when Paul wrote his First Epistle to Tim (see below), for he describes them as "forbidding to marry, and commanding to abstain from meats" (1 Tim **4** 3). These ascetic practices were afterward taught by various gnostic sects, the Encratites, the followers of Saturninus, and others.

These tendencies in the Colossian church St. Paul set himself to correct in his epistle. The method which he adopts is not so much to demolish error, as to establish the contrary truth, setting before the Colossians the person and work of Christ, Christ the Creator, Christ in whom there dwells not merely some or even much of the fulness of God, but all the fulness of the Godhead bodily; Christ the God of providence, the Upholder of all things, in whom matter and all creatures and all events "consist" and have their being; Christ the Reconciler who has reconciled us unto God through the blood of the cross. In view of truths like these, Colossian error and all other forms of Gnosticism crumble into decay and vanish. See COLOSSIANS, EPISTLE TO THE.

2. 1 Cor: "Knowledge" at Corinth

The Epistle to the Col is the first of the Pauline Epistles in which distinctively gnostic teaching is found in its attack upon the Christian faith. But from incidental notices in epistles of Paul written at an earlier period, it can be seen how congenial was the soil into which gnostic teaching was about to fall. For even in Corinth when Paul wrote his First Epistle to the church there, there had been a claim on the part of some that they possessed "knowledge," as if others were destitute of it, a claim which the apostle refuses to admit, and meets with stern resistance. They thought themselves "wise," they were given to disputing, they professed that they "all had knowledge" (1 Cor **8** 1), nay, they could "know all mysteries and all knowledge" (**13** 2); but this knowledge did not edify them, did not build them up, it only puffed them up (**8** 1); it did not make them sympathetic or tender-hearted toward the weak (**8** 7-11).

3. Pastoral Epistles

In 1 Tim **6** 20.21 Paul speaks of the "knowledge [the *gnōsis*] which is falsely so called; which some professing have erred concerning the faith." In other places in that epistle reference is made to tenets which are exactly those of Gnosticism. In **1** 4 the apostle speaks of "fables and endless genealogies, which minister questionings, rather than a dispensation of God which is in faith." Philo had given a great impetus to an allegorizing interpretation of the OT. His writings were well known and were popular in many of the Jewish schools. These fanciful interpretations would hinder the growth of the Christian church; and this allegorizing of Scripture, joined to the teaching of the genealogies of the aeons, would leave no place for a Redeemer. In **4** 3, as already noted, Paul describes ascetic practices which were regarded by their votaries as most meritorious. To abstain from marriage and from various kinds of food was the teaching of the Essenes and also of the Gnostics. This ascetic teaching was unnatural, as contrary to the constitution of the world, as that has been arranged by a holy and wise Creator, and it is also subversive of Christian liberty. Nothing can be esteemed common or unclean without throwing a reproach upon the Creator.

Antinomian development.—But another and contrary result also followed from the principles of the sinfulness of matter, and of redemption as deliverance from the flesh, viz. that there was an easier way of relief, by treating the soul and the body as separate entities which have nothing in common. Let the soul go its way on the wings of spiritual thought, while the body may indulge its fleshly desires. For, so it was held, as body and soul are entirely distinct in their nature, the spiritual cannot be defiled by anything, however carnal and gross, that the body can do. This was the antinomian development of Gnosticism. Many traces of this are apparent in the Pastoral Epistles and in 2 Pet and Jude. The Gnostics, against whom Paul warns Timothy, were "lovers of self, lovers of money, boastful, haughty, railers, disobedient to parents, unthankful, unholy, without natural affection, implacable, slanderers, without self-control, fierce, no lovers of good, traitors, headstrong, puffed-up, lovers of pleasure rather than lovers of God; holding a form of godliness, but having denied the power thereof" (2 Tim **3** 2.3.4). Such, too, is the testimony borne regarding them by Ignatius (Law, *The Tests of Life*, 30): "They give no heed to love, caring not for the widow, the orphan or the afflicted, neither for those who are in bonds, nor for those who are released from bonds, neither for the hungry nor the thirsty." Such persons professed that they knew God, but by their works they denied Him; they were "abominable, and disobedient, and unto every good work reprobate" (Tit **1** 16). They enticed others into sins of impurity (2 Tim **3** 5.6). They allured others through the lusts of the flesh; and the means by which they succeeded in doing this was that they spoke great swelling words of vanity, and the end was that in their destroying of others they themselves also were surely destroyed (2 Pet **2** 12.18). They were ungodly men, turning the grace of God into lasciviousness and denying our only Master and Lord, Jesus Christ; they gave themselves up to the sins of the flesh, and ran riotously after error in hope of a gain in money; they were sensual men, not having the Spirit (Jude vs 4.8.11.19). The entire Ep. of Jude is directed against this antinomian and licentious development of Gnosticism, and against its terrible permission of an unholy life (see below on Book of Rev).

4. 1 John

In the First Epistle of John there is a distinct polemical purpose. There is no book of the NT which is more purposeful in its attack of error. There is "the spirit of error" (1 Jn **4** 6), opposing the Spirit of truth. "Many false prophets are gone out into the world" (**4** 1), and this from the church itself, "They went out from us, but they were not of us" (**2** 19); and these false prophets are distinctly named "the antichrist" (**2** 22) and "the liar" (ib), and "the deceiver and the antichrist" (2 Jn ver 7). This peril, against which the apostle writes, and from which he seeks to defend the church, was Gnosticism, as is proved by what is said again and again in the epistle of the characteristics of this insidious and deadly teaching.

(1) *Gnostic claims.*—The gnostic claim to knowledge throws light upon many passages in this epistle. St. John refers to his opponents' using such phrases as "I know God," "I abide in Christ," "I am in the light." These lofty claims were made by persons who did not love their brethren on earth, who did not walk in Christ's footsteps, and who were destitute of love. The apostle therefore describes these lofty claims as false, because those who made them possessed neither love nor obedience.

In contrast to these gnostic claims—for those who made them were no other than the early Gnostics—St. John shows how the Christ of history is the Christ of experience: for those to whom he is writing know Christ, who is from the beginning, and they know the Father. "We know him that is true, and we are in him that is true, even in his Son Jesus Christ. This is the true God, and eternal life" (**5** 20). This knowledge of God and communion with Him are attained, not by gnostic speculation, but by the obedience of faith, the outcome of which is brotherly love and a life in which the Christian walks even as Christ did (**2** 6). And thus also obedience and brotherly love are the test of the profession which any man may make that he knows God. "Every one also that doeth righteousness is begotten of him" (**2** 29); "Whosoever doeth not righteousness is not of God, neither he that loveth not his brother" (**3** 10).

(2) *Its loveless nature.*—Gnosticism was distinguished by an unethical, loveless intellectualism. This seems to be the explanation of the false teaching against which this epistle is directed. The apostle describes the dry head-knowledge which left the heart and life untouched by love, and which led men, while they professed to love God, nevertheless to remain destitute of love to their fellow-men. They did not fold their human brethren to their hearts, they were dead to the fact that where pity dwells, the love of God dwells also. In Gnosticism knowledge was in itself the supreme end and purpose of life, the sum of highest good to which a man could attain, the crown of life. The system was loveless to the core.

(3) *Docetism.*—Now, when the attempt was made to amalgamate these gnostic ideas with the Christian faith, the inevitable result was Docetism. Just because God cannot have any immediate contact with matter, therefore the incarnation of Almighty God in the person of the Lord Jesus Christ is inconceivable. From this position it is, of course, only a step to deny that the incarnation and the true human life of Christ ever took place at all.

(4) *The Antichrist.*—The Antichrist of the First Epistle of John is docetic Gnosticism. The soul of the apostle rushes onward, with glowing zeal for the honor of his Master whom Gnosticism dishonored, to identify personally the historical Jesus with the Divine Being, "the Son of God," "the Word of Life," "the Christ." "Who is the liar but he that denieth that Jesus is the Christ? This is the antichrist, even he that denieth the Father and the Son. Whosoever denieth the Son, the same hath not the Father: he that confesseth the Son hath the Father also" (**2** 22.23). It should be noted that the last clause in ver 23, which is printed in italics in AV, is restored in RV to its rightful position in the original text. "Every spirit that confesseth that Jesus Christ is come in the flesh is of God: and every spirit that confesseth not Jesus is not of God: and this is the spirit of the antichrist, whereof ye have heard that it cometh; and now it is in the world already" (**4** 2.3).

(5) *Its antinomian side.*—The antinomian side of Gnosticism is not so directly referred to in the First Epistle of John as Docetism is; but evidences are manifest that the apostle had it clearly before him. "Little children," he writes, "let no man lead you astray: he that doeth righteousness is righteous, even as he is righteous: he that doeth sin is of the devil" (**3** 7.8). And these were the methods by which those deceivers endeavored to lead the members of the church astray. They alleged that sin was a thing indifferent in itself. It made no difference to the spiritual man whether he sinned with his body or not. It is for this reason that the apostle, in opposing those teachers, insists that "sin is lawlessness" (**3** 4); "All unrighteousness is sin" (**5** 17); "Whosoever is begotten of God doeth no sin" (**3** 9); "In this the children of God are manifest, and the children of the devil: whosoever doeth not righteousness is not of God, neither he that loveth not his brother" (**3** 10). The whole passage presupposes, as familiar to its readers, a doctrine of moral indifferentism, according to which the status of the 'spiritual' man is not to be tested by the commonplace facts of moral conduct" (*The Tests of Life*, 34). See John, First Epistle of.

5. "To Know the Depths": Rev

As time advanced, and the later books of the NT were written, Gnosticism assumed more of its distinctive peculiarities. "Those who had knowledge" regarded themselves as a superior order of believers. One of their phrases was "to know the depths" (Rev **2** 24 AV), and this was valued far more highly than love and obedience. "From this language, we may, I think, infer the existence of an Ophite sect, boasting of its peculiar *gnōsis*, before the date of the Apocalypse" (Mansel, *The Gnostic Heresies*, 105). The claim of the Ophites was that they alone knew "the depths." "Yes," is the apostle's reply to claims of this kind, "yes, the depths, but not of God, the depths of Satan"; for such is a just description of a teaching which ascribed the origin and the working of evil to God. It is in the light of gnostic teaching of this sort that the meaning can be seen of the same apostle's language in his First Epistle, "And this is the message which we have heard from him and announce unto you, that God is light, and in him is no darkness at all" (1 Jn **1** 5).

The Nicolaitans.—In the Epistles to the Seven Churches in the Apocalypse there are other references to Gnosticism. Who the Nicolaitans were (**2** 6.15) is not absolutely certain; but it is not unlikely that they were so called because of their having assumed the name of "Nicolaüs, a proselyte of Antioch" (Acts **6** 5). The first step to the reception of gentile believers into the Christian church on an equal footing with the Jews may have been the appointment of Nicolaüs as one of the first deacons, for the facts that he was a native of Antioch and a proselyte, show that he had been a heathen by birth. And it is noteworthy to find such a person appointed to office in the church at so very early a period, even before the conversion of the apostle Paul. The Nicolaitans therefore may have distorted in an antinomian sense the doctrine taught by Nicolaüs, who in all probability proclaimed the liberty of the gospel, as his fellow-deacon, Stephen, did (Acts **7** throughout). But the liberty claimed by the Nicolaitans was liberty to sin. They are mentioned in the Epistle to Ephesus, and their deeds are characterized as deeds which

Christ hates (Rev **2** 6). Their name occurs again in the Epistle to Pergamum, and there also their doctrine is described as a doctrine which the Lord hates (ver 15). Their teaching was one of licentiousness—eating things sacrificed to idols, and committing fornication (ver 14). Again in the Epistle to Thyatira, the Gnostics are spoken of as practising the same evil courses, and as holding a doctrine of "the depths of Satan" (vs 20.21.24 AV)—see above. The persons mentioned in the Epistle to Philadelphia were also evidently Gnostics. They are described as being "of the synagogue of Satan" (**3** 9).

"In the language of St. Jude, as in that of St. Peter, which it closely imitates, we may clearly discern a reference to the gnostic sect of the Nicolaitans mentioned by name in Rev. The comparison in all these passages, of the error condemned with that of Balaam, is decisive as to the identity of the persons intended. The other characteristics noted by St. Peter are also repeated by St. Jude—their denial of the Lord, their profligate lives, their contempt of government, and evil speaking of dignities and of things that they know not, their pollution of the feasts of charity, their great swelling words. The antinomian, no less than the ascetic side of Gnosticism, seems by this time to have fully manifested itself" (Mansel, *The Gnostic Heresies*, 71).

V. The Christian Antithesis.—The principal points of contrast between Gnosticism and Christian teaching in regard to leading doctrines will now be apparent, and can be briefly summarized.

1. God and the World

According to the Gnostics, God is thought of as the ultimate, nameless, unknowable Being, of whom they speak as the "Abyss." He is perfect, but the material world is alien to the Divine nature. How then does it come to exist at all? What is the source of its imperfections and evils?

How did the world originate?—The Gnostic answer is that the *plērōma* or fulness of the Deity (see FULNESS) could flow out in no other way than in emanations or aeons or angels, all of which are necessarily imperfect, the highest of these emanations or aeons or angels being more spiritual than the grade immediately below it. Of these aeons there is a gradation so numerous, that at length the lowest of them is almost wholly corporeal, the spiritual element having been gradually diminished or eliminated, until at last the world of man and of matter is reached, the abode of evil. In this way the gulf is bridged between God and the world of mankind. The highest aeons approximate closely to the Divine nature, so spiritual are they and so nearly free from matter. These form the highest hierarchy of angels, and these as well as many other grades of the angelic host are to be worshipped.

In opposition to this view, Christian faith worships God as the free self-sufficient Creator, infinitely good and wise and powerful and holy, the Author of all things, and affirms creation as an incomprehensible fact revealed to faith, and which rises above the grasp of the understanding. "By faith we understand that the worlds have been framed by the word of God, so that what is seen hath not been made out of things which do appear" (He **11** 3 AV).

The doctrine of evil follows directly from the above account of the relation of God to the world.

2. Evil

According to Gnosticism the manifestation of God is possible only through self-limitation on His part, for in His essence God is the unfathomable Abyss. Through this Divine self-limitation are evolved, first, the Divine powers or attributes, which previously were hidden in the Abyss of His being. These Divine powers (the *plērōma*) become the principles of all further developments of life. Life continues to be unfolded in such a way that its successive grades sink farther and farther from the purity of God, the life is feebler the nearer they come to matter, with which, at length, they blend. Such, according to Gnosticism, is the origin of evil.

Whenever men are not content with acknowledging evil to be the act of their own free will, which has chosen to forsake its absolute dependence upon God; whenever they go beyond this and seek for another origin of evil, then one of two results follows. They either limit the holiness of God, and find the cause of evil in God Himself, thus annihilating all distinction between good and evil—which is Pantheism; or they limit the power of God by granting the existence of an eternal evil power beyond the control of God—which is Dualism. In avoiding Pantheism, Gnosticism accepted the dualistic solution, ascribing to evil an eternal self-subsistent nature, which is to make it absolute as God Himself is. As absolute self-subsistence can be affirmed of none but God, the eternally self-subsistent evil of Dualism must be God, which it cannot possibly be, because it is not good. Here is the self-contradiction on which Gnosticism was wrecked.

(1) *The Christian doctrine of sin.*—Directly contrary to this is the Christian doctrine, according to which evil is the refusal of the creature-will to lean absolutely and utterly on God, upon His care and love and upholding grace. Sin is that which ought not to be; it has no right to exist at all; it is defiance of God; it is moral transgression; its magnitude cannot be exaggerated. If it could, it would dethrone God. It has defied His righteousness and wisdom and holiness and even His grace. Sin therefore is dealt with by God in two ways, either by direct punishment or by redemption, in which provision is made for its removal by its being borne by the Lamb of God who taketh away the sin of the world.

The gnostic idea of the origin of evil follows at once from, and is inseparably involved in, their dualistic interpretation of nature. The question "What is sin?" is no mere academic or philosophical discussion, in which one opinion may be as good as another. "Everything in Christianity is connected more or less directly with the great facts of Sin and Redemption; and the plan of Redemption, which is the essence of Christianity, cannot be rightly understood until the doctrine of Sin be adequately recognized and established. Here, certainly, if anywhere, Christian theology must fight *pro aris et focis*" (Julius Müller, quoted in Dr. Orr's *Sin as a Problem of Today*, 6).

(2) *Sin and the moral law.*—The universality of sin, its persistence, its gravity, its power to destroy and to deprave—these are facts which can hardly be exaggerated. To view sin aright, it is impossible to leave out of sight its relation to moral law, to God, and to His kingdom. Sin is the transgression of moral law; it is transgression also against a holy God, of whose character and will moral law is a transcript or reflection. "Sin is transgression against God, the substitution of the creature-will for the will of the Creator; revolt of the creature-will from God" (*Sin as a Problem of Today*, 7). It is the resolve of the will to make itself independent of God and to renounce His authority. Sin is self-will, false independence, freedom which ends in bondage and misery.

But in Gnosticism sin is something quite different; it is not the act and the disposition of the human will in rebellion against God; it is only a physical fact or quality inherent in the body and in matter everywhere. Redemption therefore does not consist in the work of Christ for us on the cross, and the applying of the benefits of that work by the Holy Spirit of God in the renewal of the moral nature of man. Redemption is simply each man's efforts to secure emancipation from the flesh—from physical evil.

It is easily seen that a system of this kind had no need of Christ and leaves no place for redemption in the Christian sense of that term.

3. Christ and Redemption

Redemption in this scheme of thought is not deliverance from sin, it is not removal of guilt and renewing of the mind. It is something quite different, and consists in the restoration of the cosmic order and illumination of the mind of the select few through knowledge. Christ is not the Saviour who saves His people from their sins, and who gives them unceasingly, through union with Himself, deliverance from the power of sin. He is only one of the aeons, the highest of them. He is an originated being, and not God. There is thus no place in Gnosticism either for the creation of the universe by God, or for the incarnation and work of Christ. Once grant that matter is essentially evil, and there is excluded the possibility of Christ's having assumed a true human nature, simply for the one reason that the world and human nature are originally and necessarily evil. Thus, as already seen, we are landed in Docetism.

The Christology of the Gnostics accordingly assumed one of two types. "One class of early Gnostics separated the spiritual being Christ from the man Jesus; they supposed that the Christ entered Jesus at the time of His baptism, and left Him at the moment of His crucifixion. Thus the Christ was neither born as a man nor suffered as a man. In this way they obviated the difficulty, insuperable to the gnostic mind, of conceiving the connection between the highest spiritual agency and gross corporeal matter, which was involved in the Catholic doctrine of the Incarnation and Passion, and which Gnostics of another type more effectually set aside by the doctrine of Docetism, i.e. by assuming that the human body of Our Lord was only a phantom body, and not real flesh and blood. Irenaeus represents the former class as teaching that 'Jesus was the receptacle of the Christ,' and that the Christ 'descended upon Him from heaven in the form of a dove, and after He had declared to mankind the nameless Father, entered again into the *plērōma* imperceptibly and invisibly.' Here no names are given. But in another passage he ascribes precisely the same doctrine, without however naming the *plērōma*, to Cerinthus" (Lightfoot, *Col*, 264). How strenuously this doctrine was combated in apostolic circles has already been shown in speaking of St. John's First Epistle.

The necessary consequence of the gnostic theory in an ascetic morality which passed over by sure steps into antinomian license has likewise been fully illustrated in the foregoing, and need not be further enlarged on.

4. Asceticism and Antinomianism

The whole has its root in a false intellectualism, to which the gospel in its inculcation of humility, faith and dependence upon God's Spirit for guidance into truth is, in its inmost principle, opposed.

VI. Harnack's View of Gnosticism.—Harnack's view of Gnosticism differs from that now given in laying the chief emphasis on its Judaeo-Hellenistic side. He describes well how, when Christianity appeared, an extensive spiritualizing or allegorizing of the OT had already taken place. "This spiritualizing was the result of a philosophic view of religion, and this philosophic view was the outcome of a lasting influence of Gr philosophy, and of the Gr spirit generally, upon Judaism. In consequence of this view, all facts and sayings of the OT in which one could not find his way, were allegorized. Nothing was what it seemed, but was only the symbol of something invisible. The history of the OT was here sublimated to a history of the emancipation of reason from passion" (*History of Dogma*, I, 223). This allegorical interpretation disclosed to the mature mind a wealth of relations, of hints and of intuitions from the OT, which to the uninitiated was only a dry record of fact. This view of the OT gave its readers a strange interest, which proceeded to transfer their ancient Jewish hopes into the world of Gr philosophy, and transformed the result into a metaphysic. When these thinkers entered the Christian church, Christian hopes and terms were added to the already existing Judaic-Gr-Alexandrian compound, and such was Gnosticism. It represented the acute secularizing or Hellenizing of Christianity. The Gnostics "are therefore those Christians, who, in a swift advance, attempted to capture Christianity for Hellenic culture, and Hellenic culture for Christianity, and who gave up the OT in order to facilitate the conclusion of the covenant between the two powers and make it possible to assert the absoluteness of Christianity" (p. 227).

Harnack indeed grants that there were other elements in Gnosticism, but he strongly asserts that the Gr element was the predominating one. In this he seems to us to be in error. Laying the chief emphasis on Hellenism, he fails to give the due and preponderating place to eastern dualism. As already seen, an eastern dualistic theosophy is the chief element in Gnosticism. This eastern source is also acknowledged by Harnack, but only as if it were subsidiary to Hellenism. As he regards it, "Gnosticism was an acute Hellenizing of Christianity" (p. 230).

In regard to the fundamental philosophic doctrines of Gnosticism, the indefinable nature of the Divine primeval Being, the sinfulness of matter, the fulness of God in aeons, the Demiurge, etc, Harnack agrees generally with other writers, and adds, "All these are ideas for which we find the way prepared in the philosophy of the time, anticipated by Philo, and represented in neo-Platonism as the great final result of Gr philosophy" (p. 233).

VII. Influence and Development of Gnosticism.—Gnosticism is peculiarly the heresy of the 2d cent., and in itself a proof of the extent to which a knowledge of the Christian faith had, at that early period, penetrated in literary and philosophical circles. Though it is true that Christianity at first influenced chiefly the humbler classes, yet it was not among these persons that the various gnostic heresies arose.

1. Gnosticism Not a Heresy of the Humbler Classes

Gnosticism "was a product which did not spring up spontaneously in the minds of the mechanics and slaves and women and children, whom most, like Celsus, suppose to have formed the bulk of the Christian communities, but could only have taken its rise in minds of a more cultured and speculative cast. This, indeed, was its claim—to be a religion of '*gnōsis*' or knowledge, for the more highly trained or *élite*. It could only exist at all, therefore, as the result of a Christian ferment which had entered these speculative circles, and was there powerfully at work. Baur rightly appreciates the situation, when he says: 'Gnosticism gives the clearest proof that Christianity had now come to be one of the most important factors in the history of the time, and it shows esp. what a mighty power of attraction the new Christian principles possessed for the highest intellectual life then to be found either in the pagan or in the Jewish world.' Above all, these systems are a striking witness to the impression produced on the heathen mind by the great Christian idea of redemption. 'When the gnostic systems,' says Neander, 'describe the movement which was produced in the kingdom of the Demiurge by the appearance of Christ as the manifestation of a new and mighty principle which had entered the precincts of this lower world, they give us to understand how powerful was the impression which the contemplation of the life of Christ and His influence on humanity, had left on the minds of the founders of these systems, making all earlier institutions seem to them as nothing in comparison with Christianity.' We must beware, therefore, of underestimating either the extent or the intensity of this great intellectual ferment set up by the gospel in the heart of heathenism" (Orr, *Neglected Factors*, etc, 196).

The earliest of the Gnostics known to us by name is Cerinthus, the antagonist of the apostle John.

2. Cerinthus: His Teaching

It seems to be beyond reasonable doubt that these two encountered each other at Ephesus. Irenaeus relates on the authority of those who heard the story from Polycarp how the apostle and Cerinthus met in the public baths in that city. When St. John discovered that Cerinthus was in the same building with him, he instantly left, exclaiming that he could not remain while Cerinthus, the enemy of God and of man, was there. From the accounts which have been preserved of Cerinthus and of his teaching, it can be gathered that he taught that the world was created not by the Supreme God, but by an inferior power, and that he also taught a docetic theory of the Incarnation. Caius of Rome, a disciple of Irenaeus, records that Cerinthus held that there would be a millennium of unrestrained sensuality. Dionysius of Alexandria (c 260 AD) more than confirms this. "Thus so far as they go, the historical data harmonize with the internal evidence of the Epistle [of John] itself, in giving the impression that the different tendencies it combats are such as were naturally combined in one consistently developed gnostic system, and that the object of its polemic is, throughout, one and the same" (*The Tests of Life*, 37).

As regards the Gospel of John there is the testimony of Irenaeus, that it was written to oppose that form of Gnosticism which was taught by Cerinthus, and, before him, by the Nicolaitans. The nature of that heresy may be stated in the words of Irenaeus himself:

"A certain Cerinthus," he says, "in Asia, taught that the world was not made by the Supreme God, but by some power altogether separate and distinct from that Sovereign Power which is over the universe, and one ignorant of the God who is over all things. He taught, moreover, that Jesus was not born of a virgin (for this seemed to him to be impossible), but was the son of Joseph and Mary, born after the manner of other men; though preëminent above other men in justice and prudence and wisdom; and that after His baptism the Christ, in the form of a dove, descended upon Him from that Sovereign Power which is over all things; and that He then announced the unknown Father and wrought miracles; but that, at the end, the Christ departed again from Jesus, and that Jesus suffered and was raised from the dead, while the Christ continued impassible, as a spiritual being" (Mansel, *The Gnostic Heresies*, 74).

Such a passage as Jn **19** 34.35 seems to refer to docetic Gnosticism, and to be a personal protest

3. The Gospel of John

against it. After describing the piercing of Christ's side by the soldier's spear, and how "straightway there came out blood and water," the apostle adds, "And he that hath seen hath borne witness, and his witness is true: and he knoweth that he saith true, that ye also may believe." There are many other passages which seem to be directed against Docetism, e.g. "The Word became flesh, and dwelt among us (and we beheld his glory)" (**1** 14); "Jesus therefore, being wearied with his journey, sat thus by the well" (**4** 6); "Reach hither thy finger, and see my hands; and reach hither thy hand, and put it into my side: and be not faithless, but believing" (**20** 27).

Cerinthus seems to have taught that the religion of Christ was identical with undiluted Mosaism, including even circumcision and the earthly kingdom of the future. The Cerinthian theory, however, was held under various forms by its adherents, some teachers holding that the God of the OT was, at the best, a subordinate angel of limited power, wisdom and goodness, and that the creation of the world was very imperfect. Others went so far as to identify the God of the OT with Satan. The ethic of systems such as these was antinomian, sometimes even going the length of libertinism.

Generally, the forms under which Gnosticism appeared varied greatly in different periods. Some went farther than others from the Christian faith. Some communities, such as the Encratites, laid the greatest stress on the necessity for asceticism; other

4. Various Sects

communities were wholly docetic; the Carpocratians taught the philosophy and communism of Plato. One of these teachers, Epiphanes, was honored as a god, and this sect crowned the image of Jesus along with those of Pythagoras, Plato and Aristotle. Further, there were impostors of all varieties: magicians, soothsayers, jugglers, deceivers and hypocrites, "who appeared using mighty words with a host of unintelligible formulae and taking up with scandalous ceremonies in order to rob men of their money" (Harnack, op. cit., 239), and even for viler purposes.

(1) *The Ophites.*—Gnosticism, before reaching its full development, is chiefly represented by the ophite sects or systems. These were so named from the word *óphis*, "serpent," to which they paid honor as the symbol of intelligence. They held that the Creator of the world was an ignorant and imperfect being, Ialdaboth, the Son of Chaos; and that it was a meritorious act when the serpent persuaded Adam and Eve to disobey him. There were several of the ophite sects, such as the Cainites, who reversed all the standards of moral judgment, choosing as their heroes the persons whom the Bible condemned, such as Cain, the men of Sodom, Esau and Korah.

(2) *Valentinus.*—By the time of Justin Martyr (c 150 AD), Gnosticism had become divided into a variety of sects and schools, Valentinians, Basilideans, Saturninians and Marcionites. In the Valentinian system, Christ and the Holy Spirit were two aeons. The Valentinians granted that ordinary Christians were better than the heathen, and that they might look forward to a kind of salvation; even now ordinary Christians occupied a middle position, better than the "hylic" or "psychic," but inferior to the "pneumatic" or "spiritual," as the Gnostics termed themselves.

(3) *Basilides.*—The Basilideans take their name from Basilides of Alexandria, a man of powerful intellect. He and his son Isidore taught this system, which was afterward considerably modified for the purpose of popular apprehension. The world is continuously evolved from a *pansperma* or "seed of the world," in which all things were originally potentially contained. It is ruled by two great Archons, who yet subserve the designs of the Supreme. There are no aeons, but the highest "light" descends through the successive spheres till it rests on Jesus of Nazareth. The process is complete when the Divine element ("sonship") is all drawn out and restored to God; oblivion then falls on lower intelligences. Many fine sayings are attributed to Basilides, e.g. "I will say anything rather than doubt the goodness of Providence" (Orr, *The Early Church*, 75).

(4) *Saturninus.*—The Saturninians were so called from Saturninus, said to be a disciple of Menander, who in turn is said to have been a disciple of Simon Magus. The system of Saturninus is marked both by a strong dualism and by a gloomy asceticism. He is also reported to have been one of the founders of the Encratite heresy, which condemned marriage. Tatian, Justin Martyr's disciple, became a member of this gnostic sect, holding, it is alleged, the usual theory of aeons, and that there was a Demiurge, who was not the Supreme God.

(5) *Marcion.*—Marcion, a native of Pontus, taught in Rome c 140–55 AD. His system differs much from ordinary gnostic theories, except that he absolutely distinguished between the God of the OT, who is regarded as merely great, harsh, rigorous, and the good God of the NT, who is wholly love. He also held to the usual gnostic dualism and

docetism. Marcion's system has been described as an overstrained Paulinism, as he lays the stress on faith, not on knowledge. Marcion was the author of a book called the *Anthitheses*, which contrasted the OT with the NT. He also drew up a canon of Scripture, which contained only one gospel, viz. Lk in a mutilated state, and ten Epp. of Paul. Marcion was a rigorous ascetic. In the Lord's Supper he allowed only water to be used instead of wine. The Marcionites refused baptism to married persons. This sect or "church" endured for several centuries.

5. Relation to the OT

"All the gnostic systems had one feature in common, viz. that they regarded the OT and the NT as revelations of two different Gods, and considered the mission of Christ to proceed from a higher power than the God of the Jewish religion, who was identified with the Demiurge, or Maker of the world. But under this common assumption there was room for two very opposite estimates of the older revelation and of the God whom it reveals. Some of the gnostic sects regarded the Demiurge as being altogether alien from and opposed to the Supreme God; others considered him merely as a subordinate power, inferior but not hostile to the Supreme God, and acting before the coming of a more perfect revelation, as his unconscious organ" (Mansel, *The Gnostic Heresies*, 45). "There can be no doubt that the gnostic propaganda was seriously hindered by the inability to organize and discipline churches, which is characteristic of all philosophic systems of religion" (Harnack, *History of Dogma*, I, 252). "From about 210 they ceased to be a factor of the historical development, though the church of Constantine and Theodosius was alone really able to suppress them" (ib, 251).

6. The Christian Verities

In contrast to Gnosticism the Christian church held fast to these great facts, that Jesus Christ is the Son of God, preëxistent before the Incarnation, and manifest in the flesh and crucified for us men and for our salvation; that He rose from the dead; that the OT is a true revelation of the one supreme and holy God, the Creator of all things. Dualism, the eternity of matter and its inherent evil, as well as Docetism and oriental mythologies were accordingly rejected as contrary to the Christian faith.

7. Influence on Theology

During the period of the prevalence of Gnosticism there took place the earlier developments of Christian theology. Gnosticism gave a powerful impetus to the formation of a NT canon of Scripture, and to the shaping of the earliest creed. See Apostles' Creed.

8. Truth Underlying Docetism

In the revulsion from Gnosticism and Docetism it should not be forgotten that there is truth to be found even amid the errors of these systems. Docetism was an overstatement of a great truth, an overstatement so large as to destroy the true humanity of Our Lord. But the truth in Docetism is that the eternal Christ touches and appeals to and has a definite relationship to and actually influences every human heart; and also, that, to the Christian believer, Christ is more and does more than this; Christ dwells in the believer's heart by faith, "Christ in you, the hope of glory" (Col **1** 27). "Docetism was not all folly. Rather we may regard it as one primitive form of the assertion of that mystical element which has never been wanting to Christianity from the first days until now, and we may be sure, never will be wanting to it" (Sanday, *Christologies Ancient and Modern*, 9).

VIII. Modern Gnosticism.—Gnosticism in its ancient form has passed away, but it is interesting to observe how its spirit reappears from time to time in modern days. Gnosticism, as already seen, is not one aspect of thought alone, but many. And in one form or another it is seen again and again. For example, the modern denial of the virgin birth of Our Lord is that form of Gnosticism which taught that the man Jesus became Christ only at His baptism, when the Holy Ghost descended upon Him from heaven.

Phases of gnostic teaching are reproduced in modern pantheistic philosophies and other forms of religious doctrine, which hold that there has been no objective atonement and no resurrection of Christ from the dead. "Basilides with his powerful speculative grasp and all-embracing evolutionary process might be termed the Hegel of the movement; Valentinus with his robe of fantasy and triple fall and redemption was its Schelling; Marcion with his severe practical bent, his doctrine of faith, and his antitheses of the just God and the good, might without straining be termed its Ritschl" (Orr, *The Progress of Dogma*, 59).

"Fichte said, 'There were no external realities at all, they were the mere objectivity of the subject or creations of the inward eye'; after Fichte came Schelling, and Schelling said, 'Then this creating eye is God's own eye'; and after Schelling came Hegel, and Hegel said that 'God and man are one, and God all men, and all men God, and the whole universe God eternally thinking in the process of development,' and that or something like it is Hegelianism. I feel in studying this philosophy, as Baron Humboldt says he felt, when he experienced the first shock of an earthquake. I feel a dreadful sense of restlessness and insecurity. The ground seems to give way beneath, and the earth and the heaven to dissolve, the universe becomes a dream, a myth" (W. B. Robertson, D.D., *Martin Luther, German Student Life*, etc, 138).

"Philosophy," says Mansel, "striving after a first principle which shall be one and simple and unconditioned and incapable of all further analysis in thought, is naturally tempted to soar above that complex combination of attributes which is implied in our conception of personality, and in endeavoring to simplify and purify our representation of the Divine nature, ends by depriving it of every attribute which can make God the object of any religious feeling or the source of any moral obligation" (*The Gnostic Heresies*, 11). God is no longer the author and source of goodness and truth and moral law, but the mind is occupied with the metaphysical relation between God and the world, as absolute and relative, cause and effect, principle and consequence, and God becomes identical with the world.

It is easily seen how teaching of this sort strikes at the root of all religion and morality. The personality of God, the personality and free will of man, the existence of moral evil, the incarnation of our Lord Jesus Christ, the redemption which He accomplished for the world, His resurrection, the whole significance of His person and His work—all is denied. This is the spirit and the meaning of Gnosticism.

Dr. Gwatkin sums up the matter thus: "Gnosticism undermined Christian monotheism by its distinction of the Creator from the Supreme, Christian morals by its opposition of the philosopher to the unlearned, Christian practice by its separation of knowledge from action; and it cut away the very basis of the gospel whenever it explained away its history. In every case it had got hold of truth on one side—the reality of evil in the world, the function of knowledge in religion, the difference between the letter and the spirit; but fragments of truth are not enough for a gospel, which is false if all truth is not summed up in Christ. Therefore there could be no peace between the gnostic *illuminati* and the Christian churches" (*Early Church History*, II, 68).

LITERATURE.—Uhlhorn, *The Conflict of Christianity with Heathenism;* Neander, *Church History, Antignostikus;* Reuss, *History of Christian Theology in the Apostolic Age;* Lightfoot, *Notes on Epistles of St. Paul, Col, Phil;* Gwatkin, *Early Church History to 313 AD*, II; W. Bousset, art. "Gnosticism," *Enc Brit*, 11th ed; Harnack, *History of Dogma*, I (ET); Orr, *Neglected Factors in the Study of the Early Progress of Christianity, Sin as a Problem of Today, The Progress of Dogma, The Early Church;* Mansel, *The Gnostic Heresies;* Robert Law, B.D., *The Tests of Life.*

JOHN RUTHERFURD

GO (הָלַךְ, *hālakh*, יָלַךְ, *yālakh*, בּוֹא, *bō'*, יָצָא, *yāçā'*; **ἄγω**, *ágō*, **ὑπάγω**, *hupágō*, **ἀναβαίνω**, *anabaínō*, **ἔρχομαι**, *érchomai*, **ἀπέρχομαι**, *apérchomai*, **πορεύομαι**, *poreúomai*): "Go" ("went," etc) occurs very frequently in the Eng. Bible, and is the tr of a great many different Heb and Gr terms. As the word implies *movement* of all kinds, physical and mental, it has naturally many applications.

1. In the OT

In the OT *hālakh* and *yālakh* are among the commonest words, meaning "to go" in its original sense of "to walk," but also in the most varied senses, according to the verbal conjugations, etc, the prep. attached, and the words in connection with which the terms stand; *hālakh* and *yālakh* are often used **figuratively** (trd "to walk," etc) for *to live*, to pursue a way of life, e.g. "to walk ever in his ways" (Dt **19** 9; cf Ps **15** 2; **89** 30; 1 K **2** 3 f; **3** 3, etc); *to die*, "He departed [Heb "went"] without being desired" (2 Ch **21** 20); *bō'*, properly "to go in," "to enter" (e.g. Gen **7** 9), is very common, and *yāçā'*, "to go or come out," also occurs frequently; *yāçā'* has frequently the meaning "to go forth," e.g. Gen **8** 7, "He sent forth a raven, and it went forth." Other frequent words are *yāradh*, "to go down" (Gen **11** 7, etc); *'ālah*, "to go or come up" (Gen **2** 6, etc; Isa **15** 5, "go it up," AV); used also **figuratively**, e.g. "to rise up or excel," "Thou excellest them all" (Prov **31** 29), "to come up on the heart," to be remembered, "The former things shall not be remembered, nor come into mind" (Isa **65** 17; cf Jer **3** 16); *'ābhar*, "to go or pass over," "to cross" (Gen **41** 46, etc), also used **figuratively** "to pass away," e.g. "as chaff that passeth away" (Isa **29** 5), 'passeth by transgression' (Mic **7** 18); *shūbh*, "to go again" (Gen **43** 2, etc); *sāṭāh* and *ṣūr*, "to go aside," occur several times with the meaning of wrongdoing (e.g. Nu **5** 12; Dt **28** 14, RV "turn aside"); *nāsā'*, "to remove" (Ex **14** 15), "Speak unto the children of Israel that they *go forward*" (ver 19 "removed"; Nu **2** 24, etc); *'ăzal* (Aram.), "to go away or about" (Ezr **4** 23; Dnl **2** 17, etc). Many other words occur only once or twice, e.g. *'āraḥ*, "to travel" (Job **34** 8); *'āshar*, "to go straight or right" (Prov **4** 14; **9** 6, RV "walk"); *dārakh*, "to tread" (Isa **59** 8); *dādhāh*, "to go softly" (Ps **42** 4; Isa **38** 15, RVm "as in solemn procession"); *rāghal*, "to stir," "to move," "I taught Ephraim to go" (Hos **11** 3, RV "to walk").

The obsolete expression "go to" (derived from Tindale) is the tr of *yāhabh* in Gen **11** 3.4.7; **38** 16; Ex **1** 10, "come on," RV "come"; of *bō'* (2 K **5** 5 RV), "go now"; *nā'* (Jgs **7** 3; Isa **5** 5; Jer **18** 11, omitted in RV).

2. In the NT

In the NT *anabainō* is "to go up" (Mt **3** 16; **5** 1, etc); *erchomai*, "to go on" (Mt **12** 9, etc); *aperchomai*, "to go off or away" (Mt **2** 22; **4** 24, etc); *poreuomai*, "to go or pass on" (Mt **2** 8.20, etc); *hupagō*, "to go away" (Mt **5** 41; **8** 32, etc). We have also other combinations with different shades of meaning, e.g. *huperbainō*, "to go over or beyond" (1 Thess **4** 6); *eisérchomai*, "to go into" (Mt **7** 13; **15** 11, etc); *proporeúomai*, "to go before" (Lk **1** 76; Acts **7** 40), and other forms; *agō* (*ágōmen*), "Let us go" (Mt **26** 46; Jn **14** 31, etc); *áge* is rendered "go to" (Jas **4** 13; **5** 1), RV "come."

"Go about [to]" AV is the tr of *zētéō*, "to seek," in Jn **7** 19, "Why go ye about to kill me?" RV "Why seek ye?" and Rom **10** 3; of *peirázō*, "to try," "attempt" (Acts **24** 6, RV "assayed"), and of *peiráomai* (**26** 21, RV "assayed"), of *epicheiréō* "to lay hands on" (Acts **9** 29), which remains in ERV unchanged, ARV "seeking"; "to let go" is the tr of *apolúō*, "to loose off" or "away" (Lk **14** 4, etc), "to go astray," of *planáō* (Mt **18** 12, etc).

Various other words occurring singly are trd by forms of "go," e.g. *phérō*, "to bear on," AV "Let us go on unto perfection" (He **6** 1, see below); *epidúō*, "to go in upon," "Let not the sun go down upon your wrath" (Eph **4** 26).

Among the many changes in RV are the following: For "go," Ex **4** 26, "alone"; Lev **9** 7, "draw near"; Nu **2** 31, "set forth"; **16** 46, "carry it"; Isa **11** 15; **27** 4, "march"; Mt **11** 4; Jn **8** 11, "Go your way"; Lk **17** 7, "Come straightway"; **18** 25, "enter in"; Jn **21** 3*b*, "come." "Go" is substituted for "pass" (Ex **12** 12), "came" (**13** 4), "away" (**19** 24), "be put" (Lev **6** 12), "enter" (Job **34** 23), "return" (Eccl **1** 7), "come" (Mic **4** 2; cf Zec **14** 18*b*.19), "should be cast" (Mt **5** 30); "if I go up" for "I will come up" (Ex **33** 5); "make to go forth" for "bring forth" (Ps **37** 6); "let them go" for "gave them up" (Ps **81** 12). For the phrase, "go a whoring," ARV has "play the harlot" (Ex **34** 15 f, etc, "commit fornication"); for "go about even now" (Dt **31** 21, ARV), "frame this day"; for "go well" (Prov **30** 29), "are stately in their march"; for "suffer us to go" (Mt **8** 31), "send us" (a different text); for "not to think of men above that which is written" (1 Cor **4** 6), "not [to go] beyond the things which are written"; for "that no man go beyond" (1 Thess **4** 6), "transgress," m "overreach"; for "Let us go on unto perfection" (Heb **6** 1), ERV "and press," ARV "Let us press on unto perfection."

W. L. WALKER

GOAD, gōd (דָּרְבָן, *dōrebhān*, מַלְמָד, *malmādh*, **κέντρον**, *kéntron*): The goad used by the Syrian farmer is usually a straight branch of oak or other strong wood from which the bark has been stripped, and which has at one end a pointed spike and at the other a flat, chisel-shaped iron. The pointed end is to prod the oxen while plowing. The flattened iron at the other end is to scrape off the earth which clogs the ploughshare. The ancient goad was probably similar to this instrument. It could do villainous work in the hands of an experienced fighter (Jgs **3** 31). If 1 S **13** 21 is correctly trd, the goads were kept sharpened by files.

Figurative: "The words of the wise are as goads" (Eccl **12** 11). The only reference to goads in the NT is the familiar passage, "It is hard for thee to kick against the goad" (Acts **26** 14). It was as useless for Saul to keep on in the wrong way as for a fractious ox to attempt to leave the furrow. He would surely be brought back with a prick of the goad.

JAMES A. PATCH

GOAH, gō'a (גֹּעָה, *gō'āh;* AV **GOATH**, gō'ath; LXX reads **ἐξ ἐκλεκτῶν λίθων**, *ex eklektōn líthōn*): A place named in describing the boundaries of Jerus as restored in the "days to come" (Jer **31** 39). If Gareb is the N.E. hill, then probably Goah is to be identified with the N.W. hill, which is called by Jos "the camp of the Assyrians" (*BJ*, V, vii, 3; xii, 2). See JERUSALEM.

GOAT, gōt: The common generic word for "goat" is עֵז, *'ēz* (cf Arab. عَنْز, *'anz*, "she-goat"; **αἴξ**,

1. Names

aíx), used often for "she-goat" (Gen **15** 9; Nu **15** 27), also with גְּדִי, *gedhī*, "kid," as גְּדִי עִזִּים, *gedhī 'izzīm*, "kid of the goats" (Gen **38** 17), also with שָׂעִיר, *sā'īr*, "he-goat," as שְׂעִיר עִזִּים, *se'īr 'izzīm*, "kid of the goats" or "he-goat," or trd simply "kids," as in 1 K **20** 27, "The children of Israel encamped before them like two little flocks of kids." Next frequently used is שָׂעִיר, *sā'īr*, lit. "hairy" (cf Arab. شَعْر, *sha'r*, "hair"; χήρ, *chḗr*, "hedgehog"; Lat *hircus*, "goat"; *hirtus*, "hairy"; also Ger. *Haar;* Eng. "hair"), like *'ēz* and *'attūdh* used of goats for offerings. The goat which is sent into the wilderness bearing the sins of the people is *sā'īr* (Lev **16** 7–22). The same name is used of devils (Lev **17** 7; 2 Ch **11** 15, RV "he-goats") and of satyrs (Isa **13** 21; **34** 14, RVm "he-goats," ARV "wild goats"). Cf also שְׂעִירַת עִזִּים, *s^e'īrath 'izzīm*, "a female from the flock" (Lev **4** 28; **5** 6). The male or leader of the flock is עַתּוּד, *'attūdh;* Arab. *'atûd*, "yearling he-goat"; **fig.** "chief ones" (Isa **14** 9; cf Jer **50** 8). A later word for "he-goat," used also **figuratively,** is צָפִיר, *çāphīr* (2 Ch **29** 21; Ezr **8** 35; Dnl **8** 5.8.21). In Prov **30** 31, one of the four things "which are stately in going" is the he-goat, תַּיִשׁ, *tayish* (Arab. تَيْس, *tais*, "he-goat"), also mentioned in Gen **30** 35; **32** 14 among the possessions of Laban and Jacob, and in 2 Ch **17** 11 among the animals given as tribute by the Arabians to Jehoshaphat. In He **9** 12.13.19; **10** 4, we have τράγος, *trágos*, the ordinary Gr word for "goat"; in Mt **25** 32.33, ἔριφος, *ériphos*, and its dim. ἐρίφιον, *erı́phion;* in He **11** 37 δέρμα αἴγειον, *dérma aígeion*, "goatskin," from *aix* (see *supra*). "Kid" is גְּדִי, *g^edhī* (cf En-gedi [1 S **23** 29], etc), fem. גְּדִיָּה, *g^edhīyāh* (Cant **1** 8), but also *'ēz*, *g^edhī 'izzīm*, *s^e'īr 'izzīm*, *s^e'īrath 'izzīm*, *b^enē 'izzīm*, and *ériphos*. There remain יָעֵל, *yā'ēl* (1 S **24** 2; Job **39** 1; Ps **104** 18), EV "wild goat"; יַעֲלָה, *ya'ălāh* (Prov **5** 19), AV "roe," RV "doe"; אַקּוֹ, *'akkō* (Dt **14** 5), EV "wild goat"; and זֶמֶר, *zemer* (Dt **14** 5), EV "chamois."

2. Wild Goats

The original of our domestic goats is believed to be the Pers wild goat or pasang, *Capra aegagrus*, which inhabits some of the Gr islands, Asia Minor, Syria, Mesopotamia, Persia, Afghanistan, and Northwestern India. It is called *wa'l* (cf Heb *yā'ēl*) by the Arabs, who in the N. apply the same name to its near relative, the Sinaitic ibex, *Capra beden*. The last, doubtless the "wild goat" (*yā'ēl*) of the Bible, inhabits Southern Pal, Arabia, Sinai, and Eastern Egypt, and within its range is uniformly called *beden* by the Arabs. It is thought by the writer that the "chamois" (*zemer*) of Dt **14** 5 may be the Pers wild goat. The word occurs only in this passage in the list of clean animals. See CHAMOIS; DEER; ZOÖLOGY. Wild goats are found only in Southern Europe, Southwestern Asia, and Northeastern Africa. They include the well-known, but now nearly extinct, Alpine ibex, steinbok, or bouquetin, the markhor, and the Himalayan ibex, which has enormous horns. The so-called Rocky Mountain goat is not properly a goat, but is an animal intermediate between goats and antelopes.

Wild Goat of Sinai.

3. Domestic Goats

Domestic goats differ greatly among themselves in the color and length of their hair, in the size and shape of their ears, and in the size and shape of their horns, which are usually larger in the males, but in some breeds may be absent in both sexes. A very constant feature in both wild and domestic goats is the bearded chin of the male. The goats of Pal and Syria are usually black (Cant **4** 1), though sometimes partly or entirely white or brown. Their hair is usually long, hanging down from their bodies. The horns are commonly curved outward and backward, but in one very handsome breed they extend nearly outward with slight but graceful curves, sometimes attaining a span of 2 ft. or more in the old males. The profile of the face is distinctly convex. They are herded in the largest numbers in the mountainous or hilly districts, and vie with their wild congeners in climbing into apparently impossible places. They feed not only on herbs, but also on shrubs and small trees, to which they are most destructive. They are largely responsible for the deforested condition of Judaea and Lebanon. They reach up the trees to the height of a man, holding themselves nearly or quite erect, and even walk out on low branches.

4. Economy

Apart from the ancient use in sacrifice, which still survives among Moslems, goats are most valuable animals. Their flesh is eaten, and may be had when neither mutton nor beef can be found. Their milk is drunk and made into cheese and *semn*, a sort of clarified butter much used in cooking. Their hair is woven into tents (Cant **1** 5), carpets, cloaks, sacks, slings, and various camel, horse and mule trappings. Their skins are made into bottles (*nō'dh;* Gr *askós;* Arab. *ḳirbeh*) for water, oil, *semn*, and other liquids (cf also He **11** 37).

5. Religious and Figurative

Just as the kid was often slaughtered for an honored guest (Jgs **6** 19; **13** 19), so the kid or goat was frequently taken for sacrifice (Lev **4** 23; **9** 15; **16** 7; Nu **15** 24; Ezr **8** 35; Ezk **45** 23; He **9** 12). A goat was one of the clean animals (*sēh 'izzīm*, Dt **14** 4). In Dnl, the powerful king out of the W. is typified as a goat with a single horn (**8** 5). One of the older goats is the leader of the flock. In some parts of the country the goatherd makes different ones leaders by turns, the leader being trained to keep near the goatherd and not to eat so long as he wears the bell. In Isa **14** 9, ". . . . stirreth up the dead for thee, even all the chief ones of the earth," the word tr^d "chief ones" is *'attūdh*, "he-goat." Again, in Jer **50** 8, we have "Go forth out of the land of the Chaldeans, and be as the he-goats before the flocks." In Mt **25** 32, in the scene of the last judgment, we find "He shall separate them one from another, as the shepherd separateth the sheep from the goats." It is not infrequent to find a flock including both goats and sheep grazing over the mountains, but they are usually folded separately.

ALFRED ELY DAY

GOATSKINS, gōt'skinz (ἐν αἰγείοις δέρμασιν, *en aigeíois dérmasin*): Such skins are mentioned only once (He **11** 37), where the wearing of goatskins, indicating extreme poverty, is referred to, by implication, as the possible lot of the faithful Christian, even as it had been of others. Ascetics of different religions, esp. of the Moslem sects, are frequently seen going about Syria and Pal today, clad in sheepskins or goatskins, a sign of their renunciation of all things worldly.

GOATS' HAIR (עֵז, *'ēz*): The word for she-goat is used elliptically to mean goats' hair, which was used in the tabernacle furnishings in the form of curtains (Ex **26** 7; **36** 14). Goats' hair was probably used in the Midianite and Israelitish camps in much the same way as in the Bedouin camps today (cf Nu **31** 20). The tents, tent ropes and rugs are made of spun goats' hair. The provision sacks which hold wheat, rice, etc, and the saddlebags are made of the same material. A strip of the cloth rolled up furnishes a bolster for the head while sleeping (cf 1 S **19** 15.16). Goats' hair cloth is admirably suited to stand the hard usage of a frequently shifting encampment. The children of Israel appreciated its utility, even for the tabernacle, where to the modern critical eye it would have looked out of place, matched against scarlet and fine linen (Ex **25** 4; **35** 6.26). The fact that goats' hair was used is good indication of the comparative crudeness of the tabernacle, when contrasted with present-day furnishings. See also Hair; Weaving. James A. Patch

GOB, gob (גֹּב, גּוֹב, *gōbh*): A place mentioned in 2 S **21** 18 f as the scene of two of David's battles with the Philis. The name appears here only. In the ‖ passage, 1 Ch **20** 4, it is called Gezer (cf *Ant*, VII, xii, 2). Certain texts read "Nob" for "Gob," while Syr and LXX read "Gath." The latter is probably correct.

GOBLET, gob'let (אַגָּן, *'aggān*): A bowl or basin (Cant **7** 2), the only place where the word is used. *'Aggān* is used in the pl. in Ex **24** 6 and Isa **22** 24, and is tr[d] "basins" and "cups." These "basins" were used to hold the blood of the sacrifices and must have been of moderate size. The "cups" were bowl-shaped vessels and belonged evidently to the smaller class of vessels used in a house.

GOD, god (אֱלֹהִים, *'ĕlōhīm*, אֵל, *'ēl*, עֶלְיוֹן, *'elyōn*, שַׁדַּי, *shaddāy*, יַהְוֶה, *yahweh*; θεός, *theós*):

I. Introduction to the General Idea
 1. The Idea in Experience and in Thought
 2. Definition of the Idea
 3. The Knowledge of God
 4. Ethnic Ideas of God
  (1) Animism
  (2) Fetichism
  (3) Idolatry
  (4) Polytheism
  (5) Henotheism
  (6) Pantheism
  (7) Deism
  (8) Semitic Monolatry
  (9) Monotheism
II. The Idea of God in the OT
 1. The Course of Its Development
 2. Forms of Its Manifestation
  (1) The Face or Countenance of God
  (2) The Voice and Word of God
  (3) The Glory of God
  (4) The Angel of God
  (5) The Spirit of God
  (6) The Name of God
  (7) Occasional Forms
 3. The Names of God
  (1) Generic
  (2) Attributive
  (3) Jehovah
 4. Pre-prophetic Conceptions of God
  (1) Jeh Alone the God of Israel
   (*a*) His Early Worship
   (*b*) Popular Religion
   (*c*) Polytheistic Tendencies
    (i) Coördination
    (ii) Assimilation
    (iii) Disintegration
   (*d*) No Hebrew Goddesses
   (*e*) Human Sacrifices
  (2) Nature and Character of Jeh
   (*a*) A God of War
   (*b*) His Relation to Nature
  (3) Most Distinctive Characteristics of Jeh
   (*a*) Personality
   (*b*) Law and Judgment
 5. The Idea of God in the Prophetic Period
  (1) Righteousness
  (2) Holiness
  (3) Universality
  (4) Unity
  (5) Creator and Lord
  (6) Compassion and Love
 6. The Idea of God in Post-exilic Judaism
  (1) New Conditions
  (2) Divine Attributes
  (3) Surviving Limitations
   (*a*) Disappearing Anthropomorphism
   (*b*) Localization
   (*c*) Favoritism
   (*d*) Ceremonial Legalism
  (4) Tendencies to Abstractness
   (*a*) Transcendence
   (*b*) Skepticism
   (*c*) Immanence
  (5) Logos, Memra and Angels
III. The Idea of God in the NT
 1. Dependence on the OT
 2. Gentile Influence
 3. Absence of Theistic Proofs
 4. Fatherhood of God
  (1) In the Teaching of Jesus Christ
   (*a*) Its Relation to Himself
   (*b*) To Believers
   (*c*) To All Men
  (2) In Apostolic Teaching
   (*a*) Father of Jesus Christ
   (*b*) Our Father
   (*c*) Universal Father
 5. God Is King
  (1) The Kingdom of God
  (2) Its King
   (*a*) God
   (*b*) Christ
   (*c*) Their Relation
  (3) Apostolic Teaching
 6. Moral Attributes
  (1) Personality
  (2) Love
  (3) Righteousness and Holiness
 7. Metaphysical Attributes
 8. The Unity of God
  (1) The Divinity of Christ
  (2) The Holy Spirit
  (3) The Church's Problem
Literature

I. Introduction to the General Idea.—Religion gives the idea of God, theology construes and organizes its content, and philosophy establishes its relation to the whole of man's experience. The logical order of treating it might appear to be, first, to establish its truth by philosophical proofs; secondly, to develop its content into theological propositions; and finally, to observe its development and action in religion. Such has been the more usual order of treatment. But the actual history of the idea has been quite the reverse. Men had the idea of God, and it had proved a creative factor in history, long before reflection upon it issued in its systematic expression as a doctrine. Moreover, men had enunciated the doctrine before they attempted or even felt any need to define its relation to reality. And the logic of history is the truer philosophy. To arrive at the truth of any idea, man must begin with some portion of experience, define its content, relate it to the whole of experience, and so determine its degree of reality.

1. The Idea in Experience and in Thought

Religion is as universal as man, and every religion involves some idea of God. Of the various philosophical ideas of God, each has its counterpart and antecedent in some actual religion. Pantheism is the philosophy of the religious consciousness of India. Deism had prevailed for centuries as an actual attitude of men to God, in China, in Judaism and in Islam, before it found expression as a rational theory in the philosophy of the 18th cent. Theism is but the attempt to define in general terms the Christian conception of God, and of His relation to the world. If Pluralism claims a place among the systems of philosophy, it can appeal to the religious consciousness of that large portion of mankind that has hitherto adhered to Polytheism.

But all religions do not issue in speculative reconstructions of their content. It is true in a sense that all religion is an unconscious philosophy, because it is the reaction of the whole mind, including the intellect, upon the world of its experience, and, therefore, every idea of God involves some kind of an explanation of the world. But conscious reflection upon their own content emerges only in a few of the more highly developed religions. Brahmanism, Buddhism, Judaism, Islam and Christianity are the only religions that have produced great systems of thought, exhibiting their content in a speculative and rational form. The religions of Greece and

Rome were unable to survive the reflective period. They produced no theology which could ally itself to a philosophy, and Gr philosophy was from the beginning to a great extent the denial and supersession of Gr religion.

Bib. lit. nearly all represents the spontaneous experience of religion, and contains comparatively little reflection upon that experience. In the OT it is only in Isa **40–66,** in the Wisdom literature and in a few Pss that the human mind may be seen turning back upon itself to ask the meaning of its practical feelings and beliefs. Even here nothing appears of the nature of a philosophy of Theism or of religion, no theology, no organic definition and no ideal reconstruction of the idea of God. It never occurred to any OT writer to offer a proof of the existence of God, or that anyone should need it. Their concern was to bring men to a right relation with God, and they propounded right views of God only in so far as it was necessary for their practical purpose. Even the fool who "hath said in his heart, There is no God" (Ps **14** 1; **53** 1), and the wicked nations "that forget God" (Ps **9** 17) are no theoretical atheists, but wicked and corrupt men, who, in conduct and life, neglect or reject the presence of God.

The NT contains more theology, more reflection upon the inward content of the idea of God, and upon its cosmic significance; but here also, no system appears, no coherent and rounded-off doctrine, still less any philosophical construction of the idea on the basis of experience as a whole. The task of exhibiting the Bib. idea of God is, therefore, not that of setting together a number of texts, or of writing the history of a theology, but rather of interpreting the central factor in the life of the Heb and Christian communities.

Logically and historically the Bib. idea stands related to a number of other ideas. Attempts have been made to find a definition of so general a nature as to comprehend them all. The older theologians assumed the Christian standpoint, and put into their definitions the conclusions of Christian doctrine and philosophy. Thus Melanchthon: "God is a spiritual essence, intelligent, eternal, true, good, pure, just, merciful, most free and of infinite power and wisdom." Thomasius more briefly defines God as "the absolute personality." These definitions take no account of the existence of lower religions and ideas of God, nor do they convey much of the concreteness and nearness of God revealed in Christ. A similar recent definition, put forward, however, avowedly of the Christian conception, is that of Professor W. N. Clarke: "God is the personal Spirit, perfectly good, who in holy love creates, sustains and orders all" (*Outline of Christian Theology,* 66). The rise of comparative religion has shown that "while all religions involve a conscious relation to a being called God, the Divine Being is in different religions conceived in the most different ways; as one and as many, as natural and as spiritual, as like to and manifested in almost every object in the heavens above or earth beneath, in mountains and trees, in animals and men; or, on the contrary, as being incapable of being represented by any finite image whatsoever; and, again, as the God of a family, of a nation, or of humanity" (E. Caird, *Evolution of Religion,* I, 62). Attempts have therefore been made to find a new kind of definition, such as would include under one category all the ideas of God possessed by the human race. A typical instance of this kind of definition is that of Professor W. Adams Brown: "A god in the religious sense is an unseen being, real or supposed, to whom an individual or a social group is united by voluntary ties of reverence and service" (*Christian Theology in Outline,* 30). Many similar definitions are given: "A supersensible being or beings" (Lotze, A. M. Fairbairn); "a higher power" (Allan Menzies); "spiritual beings" (E. B. Tylor); "a power not ourselves making for righteousness" (Matthew Arnold). This class of definition suffers from a twofold defect. It says too much to include the ideas of the lower religions, and too little to suggest those of the higher. It is not all gods that are "unseen" or "supersensible," or "making for righteousness," but all these qualities may be shared by other beings than gods, and they do not connote that which is essential in the higher ideas of God. Dr. E. Caird, looking for a definition in a germinative principle of the genesis of religion, defines God "as the unity which is presupposed in the difference of the self and not-self, and within which they act and re-act on each other" (op. cit., I, 40, 64). This principle admittedly finds its full realization only in the highest religion, and it may be doubted whether it does justice to the transcendent personality and the love of God as revealed in Jesus Christ. In the lower religions it appears only in fragmentary forms, and it can only be detected in them at all after it has been revealed in the absolute religion. Although this definition may be neither adequate nor true, its method recognizes that there can be only one true idea and definition of God, and yet that all other ideas are more or less true elements of it and approximations to it. The Bib. idea does not stand alone like an island in mid-ocean, but is rather the center of light which radiates out in other religions with varying degrees of purity.

2. Definition of the Idea of God

It is not the purpose of this article to deal with the problem of the philosophy of religion, but to give an account of the idea of God at certain stages of its development, and within a limited area of thought. The absence of a final definition will present no practical difficulty, because the denotation of the term God is clear enough; it includes everything that is or has been an object of worship; it is its connotation that remains a problem for speculation.

A third class of definition demands some attention, because it raises a new question, that of the knowledge or truth of any idea whatsoever. Herbert Spencer's definition may be taken as representative: God is the unknown and unknowable cause of the universe, "an inscrutable power manifested to us through all phenomena" (*First Principles,* V, 31). This means that there can be no definition of the idea of God, because we can have no idea of Him, no knowledge "in the strict sense of knowing." For the present purpose it might suffice for an answer that ideas of God actually exist; that they can be defined and are more definable, because fuller and more complex, the higher they rise in the scale of religions; that they can be gathered from the folklore and traditions of the lower races, and from the sacred books and creeds of the higher religions. But Spencer's view means that, in so far as the ideas are definable, they are not true. The more we define, the more fictitious becomes our subject-matter. While nothing is more certain than that God exists, His being is to human thought utterly mysterious and inscrutable. The variety of ideas might seem to support this view. But variety of ideas has been held of every subject that is known, as witness the progress of science. The variety proves nothing.

3. The Knowledge of God

And the complete abstraction of thought from existence cannot be maintained. Spencer himself does not succeed in doing it. He says a great many things about the "unknowable" which implies an extensive knowledge of Him. The traditional proofs of the "existence" of God have misled the Agnostics. But existence is meaningless except for thought, and a noumenon or first cause that lies hidden in impenetrable mystery behind phenomena cannot be conceived even as a fiction. Spencer's idea of the Infinite and Absolute are contradictory and unthinkable. An Infinite that stood outside all that is known would not be infinite, and an Absolute out of all relation could not even be imagined. If there is any truth at all in the idea of the Absolute, it must be true to human experience and thought; and the true Infinite must include within itself every possible and actual perfection. In truth, every idea of God that has lived in religion refutes Agnosticism, because they all qualify and interpret experience, and the only question is as to the degree of their adequacy and truth.

A brief enumeration of the leading ideas of God that have lived in religion will serve to place the Bib. idea in its true perspective.

4. Ethnic Ideas of God

(1) *Animism* is the name of a theory which explains the lowest (and perhaps the earliest) forms of religion, and also the principle of all religion, as the belief in the universal presence of spiritual beings which "are held to affect or control the events of the material world, and man's life here and hereafter; and, it being considered that they hold intercourse with men, and receive pleasure or displeasure from human actions, the belief in their existence leads naturally, and, it might almost be said, inevitably, sooner or later, to active reverence and propitiation" (E. B. Tylor, *Primitive Culture*, I, 426–27). According to this view, the world is full of disembodied spirits, regarded as similar to man's soul, and any or all of these may be treated as gods.

(2) *Fetichism* is sometimes used in a general sense for "the view that the fruits of the earth and things in general are divine, or animated by powerful spirits" (J. G. Frazer, *Adonis, Attis, Osiris*, 234); or it may be used in a more particular sense of the belief that spirits "take up their abode, either temporarily or permanently, in some object, ... and this object, as endowed with higher power, is then worshipped" (Tiele, *Outlines of the History of Religion*, 9).

(3) *Idolatry* is a term of still more definite significance. It means that the object is at least selected, as being the permanent habitation or symbol of the deity; and, generally, it is marked by some degree of human workmanship, designed to enable it the more adequately to represent the deity. It is not to be supposed that men ever worship *mere* "stocks and stones," but they address their worship to objects, whether fetiches or idols, as being the abodes or images of their god. It is a natural and common idea that the spirit has a form similar to the visible object in which it dwells. Paul reflected the heathen idea accurately when he said, "We ought not to think that the Godhead is *like unto* gold, or silver, or stone, graven by art and device of man" (Acts **17** 29).

(4) *Polytheism*.—The belief in many gods, and the worship of them, is an attitude of soul compatible with Animism, Fetichism and Idolatry, or it may be independent of them all. The term Polytheism is more usually employed to designate the worship of a limited number of well-defined deities, whether regarded as pure disembodied spirits, or as residing in the greater objects of Nature, such as planets or mountains, or as symbolized by images "graven by art and device of man." In ancient Greece or modern India the great gods are well defined, named and numerable, and it is clearly understood that, though they may be symbolized by images, they dwell apart in a spiritual realm above the rest of the world.

(5) *Henotheism*.—There is, however, a tendency, both in individuals and in communities, even where many gods are believed to exist, to set one god above the others, and consequently to confine worship to that god alone. "The monotheistic tendency exists among all peoples, after they have reached a certain level of culture. There is a difference in the degree in which this tendency is emphasized, but whether we turn to Babylonia, Egypt, India, China, or Greece, there are distinct traces of a trend toward concentrating the varied manifestations of Divine powers in a single source" (Jastrow, *The Study of Religion*, 76). This attitude of mind has been called Henotheism or Monolatry—the worship of one God combined with the belief in the existence of many. This tendency may be governed by metaphysical, or by ethical and personal motives, either by the monistic demands of reason, or by personal attachment to one political or moral rule.

(6) *Pantheism*.—Where the former principle predominates, Polytheism merges into Pantheism, as is the case in India, where Brahma is not only the supreme, but the sole, being, and all other gods are but forms of his manifestation. But, in India, the vanquished gods have had a very complete revenge upon their vanquisher, for Brahma has become so abstract and remote that worship is mainly given to the other gods, who are forms of his manifestation. Monolatry has been reversed, and modern Hinduism were better described as the belief in one God accompanied by the worship of many.

(7) *Deism*.—The monistic tendency, by a less thorough application of it, may take the opposite turn toward Deism, and yet produce similar religious conditions. The Supreme Being, who is the ultimate reality and power of the universe, may be conceived in so vague and abstract a manner, may be so remote from the world, that it becomes a practical necessity to interpose between Him and men a number of subordinate and nearer beings as objects of worship. In ancient Greece, Necessity, in China, Tien or Heaven, were the Supreme Beings; but a multiplicity of lower gods were the actual objects of worship. The angels of Zoroastrianism, Judaism and Islam and the saints of Romanism illustrate the same tendency. Pantheism and Deism, though they have had considerable vogue as philosophical theories, have proved unstable and impossible as religions, for they have invariably reverted to some kind of polytheism and idolatry, which seems to indicate that they are false processes of the monistic tendency.

(8) *Semitic monolatry*.—The monistic tendency of reason may enlist in its aid many minor causes, such as tribal isolation or national aggrandizement. It is held that many Sem tribes were monolatrists for either or both of these reasons; but the exigencies of intertribal relations in war and commerce soon neutralized their effects, and merged the tribal gods into a territorial pantheon.

(9) *Monotheism*, ethical and personal: One further principle may combine with Monism so as to bring about a stable Monotheism, that is the conception of God as standing in moral relations with man. Whenever man reflects upon conduct as moral, he recognizes that there can be only one moral standard and authority, and when God is identified with that moral authority, He inevitably comes to be recognized as supreme and unique. The belief in the existence of other beings called gods may survive for a while; but they are divested of all the attributes of deity when they are seen to be inferior or opposed to the God who rules in conscience. Not only are they not worshipped, but their worship by others comes to be regarded as immoral and wicked. The ethical factor in the monistic conception of God safeguards it from diverging into Pantheism or Deism and thus reverting into Polytheism. For the ethical idea of God necessarily involves His personality, His transcendence as distinct from the world and above it, and also His intimate and permanent relation with man. If He rules in conscience, He can neither be merged in dead nature or abstract being, nor be removed beyond the heavens and the angel host. A thoroughly moralized conception of God emerges first in the OT where it is the prevailing type of thought.

II. The Idea of God in the OT.

—Any attempt to write the whole history of the idea of God in the OT would require a preliminary study of the literary and historical character of the documents, which lies beyond the scope of this article and the province of the writer.

1. Course of Its Development

Yet the OT contains no systematic statement of the doctrine of God, or even a series of statements that need only to be collected into a consistent conception. The OT is the record of a rich and varied life, extending over more than a thousand years, and the ideas that ruled and inspired that life must be largely inferred from the deeds and institutions in which it was realized; nor was it stationary or all at one level. Nothing is more obvious than that revelation in the OT has been progressive, and that the idea of God it conveys has undergone a development. Certain well-marked stages of the development can be easily recognized, without entering upon any detailed criticism. There can be no serious question that the age of the Exodus, as centering around the personality of Moses, witnessed an important new departure in Heb religion. The most ancient traditions declare (perhaps not unanimously) that God was then first known to Israel under the personal name Jehovah (*Yahweh* [*YHWH*] is the correct form of the word, Jehovah being composite of the consonants of Yahweh and the vowels of *'ădhōnāy*, or lord. Jeh is retained here as the more familiar form). The Heb people came to regard Him as their Deliverer from Egypt, as their war god who assured them the conquest of Canaan, and He, therefore, became their king, who ruled over their destinies in their new heritage. But the settlement of Jeh in Canaan, like that of His people, was challenged by the native gods and their peoples. In the 9th cent. we see the war against Jeh carried into His own camp, and Baal-worship attempting to set itself up within Israel. His prophets therefore assert the sole right of Jeh to the worship of His people, and the great prophets of the 8th cent. base that right upon His moral transcendence. Thus they at once reveal new depths of His moral nature, and set His uniqueness and supremacy on higher grounds. During the exile and afterward, Israel's outlook broadens by contact with the greater world, and it draws out the logical implications of ethical monotheism into a theology at once more universalistic and abstract. Three fairly well-defined periods thus emerge, corresponding to three stages in the development of the OT idea of God: the pre-prophetic period governed by the Mosaic conception, the prophetic period during which ethical monotheism is firmly established, and the post-exilic period with the rise of abstract monotheism. But even in taking these large and obvious divisions, it is necessary to bear in mind the philosopher's maxim, that "things are not cut off with a hatchet." The most characteristic ideas of each period may be described within their period; but it should not be assumed that they are altogether absent from other periods; and, in particular, it should not be supposed that ideas, and the life they represent, did not exist before they emerged in the clear witness of history. Mosaism had undoubtedly its antecedents in the life of Israel; but any attempt to define them leads straight into a very morass of conjectures and hypotheses, archaeological, critical and philosophical; and any results that are thus obtained are contributions to comparative religion rather than to theology.

2. Forms of the Manifestation of God

Religious experience must always have had an inward and subjective aspect, but it is a long and difficult process to translate the objective language of ordinary life for the uses of subjective experience. "Men look outward before they look inward." Hence we find that men express their consciousness of God in the earliest periods in language borrowed from the visible and objective world. It does not follow that they thought of God in a sensuous way, because they speak of Him in the language of the senses, which alone was available for them. On the other hand, thought is never entirely independent of language, and the degree in which men using sensuous language may think of spiritual facts varies with different persons.

(1) *The face or countenance* (*pānīm*) *of God* is a natural expression for His presence. The place where God is seen is called Peniel, the face of God (Gen **32** 30). The face of Jeh is His people's blessing (Nu **6** 25). With His face (RV "presence") He brought Israel out of Egypt, and His face (RV "presence") goes with them to Canaan (Ex **33** 14). To be alienated from God is to be hid from His face (Gen **4** 14), or God hides His face (Dt **31** 17.18; **32** 20). In contrast with this idea it is said elsewhere that man cannot see the face of God and live (Ex **33** 20; cf Dt **5** 24; Jgs **6** 22; **13** 22). In these later passages, "face" stands for the entire being of God, as distinguished from what man may know of Him. This phrase and its cognates enshrine also that fear of God, which shrinks from His majesty even while approaching Him, which enters into all worship.

(2) *The voice* (*ḳōl*) *and word* (*dābhār*) *of God* are forms under which His communion with man is conceived from the earliest days to the latest. The idea ranges from that of inarticulate utterance (1 K **19** 12) to the declaration of the entire law of conduct (Dt **5** 22–24), to the message of the prophet (Isa **2** 1; Jer **1** 2), and the personification of the whole counsel and action of God (Ps **105** 19; **147** 18.19; Hos **6** 5; Isa **40** 8).

(3) *The glory* (*kābhōdh*) *of God* is both a peculiar physical phenomenon and the manifestation of God in His works and providence. In certain passages in Ex, ascribed to the PC, the glory is a bright light, "like devouring fire" (**24** 17); it fills and consecrates the tabernacle (**29** 43; **40** 34.35); and it is reflected as beams of light in the face of Moses (**34** 29). In Ezk, it is a frequent term for the prophet's vision, a brightness like the appearance of a rainbow (**1** 28; **10** 4; **43** 2). In another place, it is identified with all the manifested goodness of God, and is accompanied with the proclamation of His name (Ex **33** 17–23). Two passages in Isa seem to combine under this term the idea of a physical manifestation with that of God's effectual presence in the world (**3** 8; **6** 3). God's presence in creation and history is often expressed in the Pss as His glory (**19** 1; **57** 5.11; **63** 2; **97** 6). Many scholars hold that the idea is found in Isa in its earliest form, and that the physical meaning is quite late. It would, however, be contrary to all analogy, if such phenomena as rainbow and lightning had not first impressed the primitive mind as manifestations of God. See GLORY.

(4) *The angel* (*mal'ākh*) *of God* or of Jeh is a frequent mode of God's manifestation of Himself in human form, and for occasional purposes. It is a primitive conception, and its exact relation to God, or its likeness to man, is nowhere fixed. In many passages, it is assumed that God and His angel are the same being, and the names are used synonymously (as in Gen **16** 7 ff; **22** 15.16; Ex **3** 2.4; Jgs **2** 4.5); in other passages the idea blurs into varying degrees of differentiation (Gen **18**; **24** 40; Ex **23** 21; **33** 2.3; Jgs **13** 8.9). But everywhere, it fully represents God as speaking or acting for the time being; and it is to be distinguished from the subordinate and intermediate beings of later angelology. Its identification with the Messiah and the Logos is only true in the sense that these later terms are more definite expressions of the idea of revelation, which the angel represented for primitive thought.

(5) *The spirit* (*rūᵃḥ*) *of God* in the earlier period is a form of His activity, as it moves warrior and prophet to act and to speak (Jgs **6** 34; **13** 25; 1 S **10** 10), and it is in the prophetic period that it becomes the organ of the communication of God's thoughts to men. See HOLY SPIRIT.

(6) *The name* (*shēm*) *of God* is the most comprehensive and frequent expression in the OT for His self-manifestation, for His person as it may be known to men. The name is something visible or audible which represents God to men, and which, therefore, may be said to do His deeds, and to stand in His place, in relation to men. God reveals Himself by making known or proclaiming His name (Ex **6** 3; **33** 19; **34** 5.6). His servants derive their authority from His name (Ex **3** 13.15; 1 S **17** 45). To worship God is to call upon His name (Gen **12** 8; **13** 4; **21** 33; **26** 25; 1 K **18** 24–26), to fear it (Dt **28** 58), to praise it (2 S **22** 50; Ps **7** 17; **54** 6), to glorify it (Ps **86** 9). It is wickedness to take God's name in vain (Ex **20** 7), or to profane and blaspheme it (Lev **8** 21; **24** 16). God's dwelling-place is the place where He chooses "to cause his name to dwell" (2 S **7** 13; 1 K **3** 2; **5** 3.5; **8** 16–19; **18** 32; Dt **12** 11.21). God's name defends His people (Ps **20** 1; Isa **30** 27). For His name's sake He will not forsake them (1 S **12** 22), and if they perish, His name cannot remain (Josh **7** 9). God is known by different names, as express-

ing various forms of His self-manifestation (Gen **16** 13; **17** 1; Ex **3** 6; **34** 6). The name even confers its revelation-value upon the angel (Ex **23** 20–23). All God's names are, therefore, significant for the revelation of His being.

(7) *Occasional forms.*—In addition to these more or less fixed forms, God also appears in a variety of exceptional or occasional forms. In Nu **12** 6–8, it is said that Moses, unlike others, used to see the form (*t^emūnāh*) of Jeh. Fire, smoke and cloud are frequent forms or symbols of God's presence (e.g. Gen **15** 17; Ex **3** 2–4; **19** 18; **24** 17), and notably "the pillar of cloud by day, and the pillar of fire by night" (Ex **13** 21f). According to later ideas, the cloud rested upon the tabernacle (Ex **40** 34), and in it God appeared upon the ark (Lev **16** 2). Extraordinary occurrences or miracles are, in the early period, frequent signs of the power of God (Ex **7** ff; 1 K **17** ff).

The questions of the objectivity of any or all of these forms, and of their relation to the whole Divine essence raise large problems. OT thought had advanced beyond the naïve identification of God with natural phenomena, but we should not read into its figurative language the metaphysical distinctions of a Gr-Christian theology.

3. The Names of God

All the names of God were originally significant of His character, but the derivations, and therefore the original meanings, of several have been lost, and new meanings have been sought for them.

(1) *Generic names.*—One of the oldest and most widely distributed terms for Deity known to the human race is *'Ēl*, with its derivations *'Ēlīm*, *'Ĕlōhīm* and *'Ĕlō^ah*. Like *theos*, *Deus* and *God*, it is a generic term, including every member of the class deity. It may even denote a position of honor and authority among men. Moses was *'Ĕlōhīm* to Pharaoh (Ex **7** 1) and to Aaron (Ex **4** 16; cf Jgs **5** 8; 1 S **2** 25; Ex **21** 5.6; **22** 7ff; Ps **58** 11; **82** 1). It is, therefore, a general term expressing majesty and authority, and it only came to be used as a proper name for Israel's God in the later period of abstract monotheism when the old proper name Jeh was held to be too sacred to be uttered. The meaning of the root *'Ēl*, and the exact relation to it, and to one another, of *'Ĕlōhīm* and *'Ĕlō^ah*, lie in complete obscurity. By far the most frequent form used by OT writers is the pl. *'Ĕlōhīm*, but they use it regularly with sing. vbs. and adjs. to denote a singular idea. Several explanations have been offered of this usage of a pl. term to denote a sing. idea—that it expresses the fulness and manifoldness of the Divine nature, or that it is a pl. of majesty used in the manner of royal persons, or even that it is an early intimation of the Trinity; other cognate expressions are found in Gen **1** 26; **3** 22; 1 K **22** 19f; Isa **6** 8. These theories are, perhaps, too ingenious to have occurred to the early Heb mind, and a more likely explanation is, that they are survivals in language of a polytheistic stage of thought. In the OT they signify only the general notion of Deity.

(2) *Attributive names.*—To distinguish the God of Israel as supreme from others of the class *'Ĕlōhīm*, certain qualifying appellations are often added. *'Ēl 'Elyōn* designates the God of Israel as the highest, the most high, among the *'Ĕlōhīm* (Gen **14** 18–20); so do *Jeh 'Elyōn* (Ps **7** 17) and *'Elyōn* alone, often in Pss and in Isa **14** 14.

'Ēl Shaddāy, or *Shaddāy* alone, is a similar term which on the strength of some tradition is tr^d "God Almighty"; but its derivation and meaning are quite unknown. According to Ex **6** 3 it was the usual name for God in patriarchal times, but other traditions in the Pent seem to have no knowledge of this.

Another way of designating God was by His relation to His worshippers, as God of Abraham, Isaac and Jacob (Gen **24** 12; Ex **3** 6), of Shem (Gen **9** 26), of the Hebrews (Ex **3** 18), and of Israel (Gen **33** 20).

Other names used to express the power and majesty of God are *çūr*, "Rock" (Dt **32** 18; Isa **30** 29), *'ăbhīr* (cstr fr *'ābhīr*), "the Strong One" (Gen **49** 24; Isa **1** 24; Ps **132** 2); *melekh*, "King"; *'ādhōn*, "lord," and *'ădhōnāy*, "my lord" (Ex **23** 17; Isa **10** 16.33; Gen **18** 27; Isa **6** 1). Also *ba'al*, "proprietor" or "master," may be inferred as a designation once in use, from its appearance in such Heb proper names as Jerubbaal and Ish-baal. The last three names describe God as a Master to whom man stands in the relation of a servant, and they tended to fall into disuse as the necessity arose to differentiate the worship of Jeh from that of the gods of surrounding nations.

A term of uncertain meaning is *Yahweh* or *'Ĕlōhīm ç^ebhā'ōth*, "Jeh" or "God of hosts." In Heb usage "host" might mean an army of men, or the stars and the angels—which, apart or in conjunction, made up the host of heaven. God of Hosts in early times meant the war god who led the armies of Israel (1 S **4** 4; 2 S **7** 8). In 1 S **17** 45 this title stands in parallelism with "the God of the armies of Israel." So all Israel is called the host of Jeh (Ex **12** 41). In the Prophets, where the term has become a regular appellation, it stands in relation to every form of the power and majesty, physical and moral, of God (e.g. Isa **2** 12; **6** 3.5; **10** 23.33). It stands in parallelism with Isaiah's peculiar title, the Holy One of Israel (Isa **5** 16.24). It has, therefore, been thought that it refers to the host of heaven. In the Prophets it is practically a proper name. Its original meaning may well have been forgotten or dropped, but it does not follow that a new special significance was attached to the word "hosts." The general meaning of the whole term is well expressed by the LXX tr, *kúrios pantokrátōr*, "Lord Omnipotent."

(3) *Jehovah* (*Yahweh*).—This is the personal proper name *par excellence* of Israel's God, even as Chemosh was that of the god of Moab, and Dagon that of the god of the Philis. The original meaning and derivation of the word are unknown. The variety of modern theories shows that, etymologically, several derivations are possible, but that the meanings attached to any one of them have to be imported and imposed upon the word. They add nothing to our knowledge. The Hebrews themselves connected the word with *hāyāh*, "to be." In Ex **3** 14 Jeh is explained as equivalent to *'ehyeh*, which is a short form of *'ehyeh 'ăsher 'ehyeh*, tr^d in RV "I am that I am." This has been supposed to mean "self-existence," and to represent God as the Absolute. Such an idea, however, would be a metaphysical abstraction, not only impossible to the time at which the name originated, but alien to the Heb mind at any time. And the imperfect *'ehyeh* is more accurately tr^d "I will be what I will be," a Sem idiom meaning, "I will be all that is necessary as the occasion will arise," a familiar OT idea (cf Isa **7** 4.9; Ps **23**).

This name was in use from the earliest historical times till after the exile. It is found in the most ancient lit. According to Ex **3** 13f, and esp. **6** 2.3, it was first introduced by Moses, and was the medium of a new revelation of the God of their fathers to the children of Israel. But in parts of Gen it is represented as being in use from the earliest times. Theories that derive it from Egypt or Assyria, or that would connect it etymologically with Jove or Zeus, are supported by no evidence. We have to be content either to say that Jeh was the tribal God of Israel from time immemorial, or to accept a theory that is practically identical with that of Ex—that it was adopted through Moses from the Midianite tribe into which he married. The Kenites, the tribe of Midianites related to Moses, dwelt in the neighborhood of Sinai, and attached themselves to Israel (Jgs **1** 16; **4** 11). A few passages suggest that Sinai was the original home of Jeh (Jgs **5** 4.5; Dt **33** 2). But there is no direct evidence bearing upon the origin of the worship of Jeh: to us He is known only as the God of Israel.

4. Pre-prophetic Conceptions of Jeh

(1) *Jeh alone was the God of Israel.*—Heb theology consists essentially of the doctrine of Jeh and its implications. The teachers and leaders of the people at all times worship and enjoin the worship of Jeh alone. "It stands out as a prominent and incontrovertible fact, that down to the reign of Ahab . . . . no prominent man in Israel, with the doubtful exception of Solomon, known by name and held up for condemnation, worshipped any other god but Yahveh. In every national and tribal crisis, in all times of danger and of war, it is Yahveh and Yahveh alone who is invoked to give victory and deliverance" (Montefiore, *Hibbert Lectures*[3], 21). This is more evident in what is, without doubt, very early lit., even than in later writings (e.g. Jgs **5**; Dt **33**; 1 S **4–6**). The isolation of the desert was more favorable to the integrity of Jeh's sole worship than the neighborhood of powerful peoples who worshipped many other gods. Yet that early religion of Jeh can be called monotheistic only in the light of the end it realized, for in the course of its development it had to overcome many limitations.

(*a*) The early worship of Jeh did not exclude belief in the existence of other gods. As other nations believed in the existence of Jeh (1 S **4** 8; 2 K **17** 27), so Israel did not doubt the reality of other gods (Jgs **11** 24; Nu **21** 29; Mic **4** 5). This limitation involved two others: Jeh is the God of Israel only; with them alone He makes a COVENANT (q.v.) (Gen **15** 18; Ex **6** 4.5; 2 K **17** 34.35), and their worship only He seeks (Dt **4** 32–37; **32** 9; Am **3** 2). Therefore He works, and can be worshipped only within a certain geographical area. He may have been associated with His original home in Sinai long after the settlement in Canaan (Jgs **5** 4; Dt **33** 2; 1 K **19** 8.9), but gradually His home and that of His people became identical (1 S **26** 19; Hos **9** 3; Isa **14** 2.25). Even after the deportation of the ten tribes, Canaan remains Jeh's land (2 K **17** 24–28). Early Israelites are, therefore, more properly described as Monolatrists or Henotheists than as Monotheists. It is characteristic of the religion of Israel (in contrast with, e.g. Gr thought) that it arrived at absolute Monotheism along the line of moral and religious experience, rather than that of rational inference. Even while they shared the common Sem belief in the reality of other gods, Jeh alone had for them "the value of God."

(*b*) It is necessary to distinguish between the teaching of the religious leaders and the belief and practice of the people generally. The presence of a higher religion never wholly excludes superstitious practices. The use of Teraphim (Gen **31** 30; 1 S **19** 13.16; Hos **3** 4), Ephod (Jgs **18** 17–20; 1 S **23** 6.9; **30** 7), Urim and Thummim (1 S **28** 6; **14** 40, LXX), for the purposes of magic and divination, to obtain oracles from Jeh, was quite common in Israel. Necromancy was practised early and late (1 S **28** 7 ff; Isa **8** 19; Dt **18** 10. 11). Sorcery and witchcraft were not unknown, but were condemned by the religious leaders (1 S **28** 3). The burial places of ancestors were held in great veneration (Gen **35** 20; **50** 13; Josh **24** 30). But these facts do not prove that Heb religion was animistic and polytheistic, any more than similar phenomena in Christian lands would justify such an inference about Christianity.

(*c*) Yet the worship of Jeh maintained and developed its monotheistic principle only by overcoming several hostile tendencies. The Baal-worship of the Canaanites and the cults of other neighboring tribes proved a strong attraction to the mass of Israelites (Jgs **2** 13; **3** 7; **8** 33; **10** 10; 1 S **8** 8; **12** 10; 1 K **11** 5.33; Hos **2** 5.17; Ezk **20**; Ex **20** 5; **22** 20; **34** 16.17). Under the conditions of life in Canaan, the sole worship of Jeh was in danger of modification by three tendencies, coördination, assimilation and disintegration.

(i) When the people had settled down in peaceful relations with their neighbors, and began to have commercial and diplomatic transactions with them, it was inevitable that they should render their neighbor's gods some degree of reverence and worship. Courtesy and friendship demanded as much (cf 2 K **5** 18). When Solomon had contracted many foreign alliances by marriage, he was also bound to admit foreign worship into Jerus (1 K **11** 5). But Ahab was the first king who tried to set up the worship of Baal, side by side with that of Jeh, as the national religion (1 K **18** 19). Elijah's stand and Jehu's revolution gave its death blow to Baal-worship and vindicated the sole right of Jeh to Israel's allegiance. The prophet was defending the old religion and Ahab was the innovator; but the conflict and its issue brought the monotheistic principle to a new and higher level. The supreme temptation and the choice transformed what had been a natural monolatry into a conscious and moral adherence to Jeh alone (1 K **18** 21.39).

(ii) But to repudiate the name of Baal was not necessarily to be rid of the influence of Baal-worship. The ideas of the heathen religions survived in a more subtle way in the worship of Jeh Himself. The change from the nomad life of the desert to the agricultural conditions of Canaan involved some change in religion. Jeh, the God of flocks and wars, must now be recognized as the God of the vintage and the harvest. That this development occurred is manifest in the character of the great religious festivals. "Three times thou shalt keep a feast unto me in the year. The feast of unleavened bread shalt thou keep . . . . and the feast of harvest, the first-fruits of thy labors, which thou sowest in the field: and the feast of ingathering, at the end of the year, when thou gatherest in thy labors out of the field" (Ex **23** 14–16). The second and the third obviously, and the first probably, were agricultural feasts, which could have no meaning in the desert. Israel and Jeh together took possession of Canaan. To doubt that would be to admit the claims of the Baal-worship; but to assert it also involved some danger, because it was to assert certain similarities between Jeh and the Baalim. When those similarities were embodied in the national festivals, they loomed very large in the eyes and minds of the mass of the people (W. R. Smith, *Prophets of Israel*, 49–57). The danger was that Israel should regard Jeh, like the Baals of the country, as a Nature-god, and, by local necessity, a national god, who gave His people the produce of the land and protected them from their enemies, and in return received from them such gifts and sacrifices as corresponded to His nature. From the appearance in Israel, and among Jeh worshippers, of such names as Jerub-baal, Esh-baal (son of Saul) and Beeliada (son of David, 1 Ch **14** 7), it has been inferred that Jeh was called Baal, and there is ample evidence that His worship was assimilated to that of the Canaanite Baalim. The bulls raised by Jeroboam (1 K **12** 26 ff) were symbols of Jeh, and in Judah the Canaanite worship was imitated down to the time of Asa (1 K **14** 22–24; **15** 12.13). Against this tendency above all, the great prophets of the 8th cent. contended. Israel worshipped Jeh as if He were one of the Baalim, and Hosea calls it Baal-worship (Hos **2** 8.12.13; cf Am **2** 8; Isa **1** 10–15).

(iii) And where Jeh was conceived as one of the Baalim or Masters of the land, He became, like them, subject to disintegration into a number of local deities. This was probably the gravamen of Jeroboam's sin in the eyes of the "Deuteronomic" historian. In setting up separate sanctuaries, he divided the worship, and, in effect, the godhead of Jeh. The localization and naturalization of Jeh, as well as His assimilation to the Baals, all went together, so that we read that even in Judah the number of gods was according to its cities (Jer **2** 28; **11** 13). The vindication of Jeh's moral supremacy and spiritual unity demanded, among other things, the unification of His worship in Jerus (2 K **23**).

(*d*) In one respect the religion of Jeh successfully resisted the influence of the heathen cults. At no time was Jeh associated with a goddess. Although the corrupt sensual practices that formed a large part of heathen worship also entered into Israel's worship (see ASHERAH), it never penetrated so far as to modify in this respect the idea of Jeh.

(*e*) It is a difficult question how far human sacrifices at any time found place in the worship of Jeh. The outstanding instance is that of Jephthah's daughter, which, though not condemned, is certainly regarded as exceptional (Jgs **11** 30–40). Perhaps it is rightly regarded as a unique "survival." Then the story of the sacrifice of Isaac, while reminiscent of an older practice, represents a more advanced view. Human sacrifice, though not demanded, is not abhorrent to Jeh (Gen **22**). A further stage is represented where Ahaz' sacrifice of his son is condemned as an "abomination of the nations" (2 K **16** 3). The sacrifice of children is emphatically condemned by the prophets as a late and foreign innovation which Jeh had not commanded (Jer **7** 31; Ezk **16** 20). Other cases, such as the execution of the chiefs of Shittim (Nu **25** 4), and of Saul's sons "before Jeh" (2 S **21** 9), and the *ḥērem* or ban, by which whole communities were devoted to destruction (Jgs **21** 10; 1 S **15**), while they show a very inadequate idea of the sacredness of human life, are not sacrifices, nor were they demanded by Jeh's worship. They were survivals of savage customs connected with tribal unity, which the higher morality of Jeh's religion had not yet abolished.

(2) *The nature and character of Jeh* are manifested in His activities. The OT makes no statements about the essence of God; we are left to infer it from His action in Nature and history and from His dealing with man.

(*a*) In this period, His activity is predominantly martial. As Israel's Deliverer from Egypt, "Jeh is a man of war" (Ex **15** 3). An ancient account of Israel's journey to Canaan is called "the book of the Wars of Jeh" (Nu **21** 14). By conquest in war He gave His people their land (Jgs **5**; 2 S **5** 24; Dt **33** 27). He is, therefore, more concerned with men and nations, with the moral, than with the physical world.

(*b*) Even His activity in Nature is first connected with His martial character. Earth, stars and rivers come to His battle (Jgs **5** 4.20.21). The forces of Nature do the bidding of Israel's Deliverer from Egypt (Ex **8–10**; **14** 21). He causes sun and moon to stand while He delivers up the Amorites (Josh **10** 12). Later, He employs the forces of Nature to chastise His people for infidelity and sin (2 S **24** 15; 1 K **17** 1). Amos declares that His moral rule extends to other nations and that it determines their destinies. In harmony with this idea, great catastrophes like the Deluge (Gen **7**) and the overthrow of the Cities of the Plain (Gen **19**) are ascribed to His moral will. In the same pragmatic manner the oldest creation narrative describes Him creating man, and as much of the world as He needed (Gen **2**), but as yet the idea of a universal cause had not emerged, because the idea of a universe had not been formed. He acts as one of great, but limited, power and knowledge (Gen **11** 5–8; **18** 20). The more universal conception of Gen **1** belongs to the same stratum of thought as Second Isa. At every stage of the OT the metaphysical perfections of Jeh follow as an inference from His ethical preëminence.

(3) *The most distinctive characteristic of Jeh*, which finally rendered Him and His religion absolutely unique, was the moral factor. In saying that Jeh was a moral God, it is meant that He acted by free choice, in conformity with ends which He set to Himself, and which He also imposed upon His worshippers as their law of conduct.

(*a*) The most essential condition of a moral nature is found in His vivid personality, which at every stage of His self-revelation shines forth with an intensity that might be called aggressive. Divine personality and spirituality are never expressly asserted or defined in the OT; but nowhere in the history of religion are they more clearly asserted. The modes of their expression are, however, qualified by anthropomorphisms, by limitations, moral and physical. Jeh's jealousy (Ex **20** 5; Dt **5** 9; **6** 15), His wrath and anger (Ex **32** 10–12; Dt **7** 4) and His inviolable holiness (Ex **19** 21.22; 1 S **6** 19; 2 S **6** 7) appear sometimes to be irrational and immoral; but they are the assertion of His individual nature, of His self-consciousness as He distinguishes Himself from all else, in the moral language of the time, and are the conditions of His having any moral nature whatsoever. Likewise, He dwells in a place and moves from it (Jgs **5** 5); men may see Him in visible form (Ex **24** 10; Nu **12** 8); He is always represented as having organs like those of the human body, arms, hands, feet, mouth, eyes and ears. By such sensuous and figurative language alone was it possible for a personal God to make Himself known to men.

(*b*) The content of Jeh's moral nature as revealed in the OT developed with the growth of moral ideas. Though His activity is most prominently martial, it is most permanently judicial, and is exercised through judges, priests and prophets. *Tōrāh* and *mishpāṭ*, "law" and "judgment," from the time of Moses onward, stand, the one for a body of customs that should determine men's relations to one another, and the other for the decision of individual cases in accordance with those customs, and both were regarded as issuing from Jeh. The people came to Moses "to inquire of God" when they had a matter in dispute, and he "judged between a man and his neighbor, and made them know the statutes of God, and his laws" (Ex **18** 15.16). The judges appear mostly as leaders in war; but it is clear, as their name indicates, that they also gave judgments as between the people (Jgs **3** 10; **4** 4; **10** 2.3; 1 S **7** 16). The earliest literary prophets assume the existence of a law which priest and prophet had neglected to administer rightly (Hos **4** 6; **8** 1.12; Am **2** 4). This implied that Jeh was thought of as actuated and acting by a consistent moral principle, which He also imposed on His people. Their morality may have varied much at different periods, but there is no reason to doubt that the Decalogue, and the moral teaching it involved, emanated substantially from Moses. "He taught them that Yahveh, if a stern, and often wrathful, Deity, was also a God of justice and purity. Linking the moral life to the religious idea, he may have taught them too that murder and theft, adultery and false witness, were abhorred and forbidden by their God" (Montefiore, *Hibbert Lectures*[3], 49). The moral teaching of the OT effected the transition from the national and collective to the individual and personal relation with Jeh. The most fundamental defect of Heb morality was that its application was confined within Israel itself and did little to determine the relation of the Israelites to people of other nations; and this limitation was bound up with Henotheism, the idea that Jeh was God of Israel alone. "The consequence of this national conception of Jeh was that there was no religious and moral bond regulating the conduct of the Hebrews with men of other nations. Conduct which between fellow-Hebrews was offensive in Jeh's eyes was inoffensive when practised by a Hebrew toward one who was not a Hebrew (Dt **23** 19 f). . . . . In the latter case they were governed purely by considerations of expediency. This ethical limitation is the real explanation of the 'spoiling of the Egyptians'" (Ex **11** 2.3) (G. Buchanan Gray, *The Divine Discipline of Israel*, 46, 48).

The first line of advance in the teaching of the prophets was to expand and deepen the moral demands of Jeh. So they removed at once the ethical and the theological limitations of the earlier view. But they were conscious that they were only developing elements already latent in the character and law of Jeh.

5. The Idea of God in the Prophetic Period

Two conditions called forth and determined the message of the 8th-cent. prophets—the degradation of morality and religion at home and the growing danger to Israel and Judah from the all-victorious Assyrian. With one voice the prophets declare and condemn the moral and social iniquity of Israel and Judah (Hos **4** 1; Am **4** 1; Isa **1** 21–23). The worship of Jeh had been assimilated to the heathen religions around (Am **2** 8; Hos **3** 1; Isa **30** 22). A time of prosperity had produced luxury, license and an easy security, depending upon the external bonds and ceremonies of religion. In the threatening attitude of Assyria, the prophets see the complement of Israel's unfaithfulness and sin, this the cause and that the instruments of Jeh's anger (Isa **10** 5.6).

(1) *Righteousness.*—These circumstances forced into first prominence the righteousness of Jeh. It was an original attribute that had appeared even in His most martial acts (Jgs **5** 4; 1 S **12** 7). But the prophet's interpretation of Israel's history revealed its content on a larger scale. Jeh was not like the gods of the heathen, bound to the purposes and fortunes of His people. Their relation was not a natural bond, but a covenant of grace which He freely bestowed upon them, and He demanded as its condition, loyalty to Himself and obedience to His law. Impending calamities were not, as the naturalistic conception implied, due to the impotence of Jeh against the Assyr gods (Isa **31** 1), but the judgment of God, whereby He applied impartially to the conduct of His people a standard of righteousness, which He both had in Himself and declared in judgment upon them. The prophets did not at first so much transform the idea of righteousness, as assert its application as between the people and Jeh. But in doing that they also rejected the external views of its realization. It consists not in unlimited gifts or in the costliest oblations. "What doth Jeh require of thee, but to do justly, and to love kindness, and to walk humbly with thy God?" (Mic **6** 8). And it tends to become of universal application. Jeh will deal as a righteous judge with all nations, including Israel, and Israel as the covenant people bears the greater responsibility (Am **1–3**). And a righteous judge that metes out even justice to all nations will deal similarly with individuals. The ministry of the prophets produced a vivid consciousness of the personal and individual relation of men to God. The prophets themselves were not members of a class, no order or school or profession, but men impelled by an inner and individual call of God, often against their inclination, to proclaim an unpopular message (Am **7** 14.15; Isa **6**; Jer **1** 6–9; Ezk **3** 14). Jeremiah and Ezekiel in terms denounced the old idea of collective responsibility (Jer **31** 29 ff; Ezk **18**). Thus in the prophets' application of the idea of righteousness to their time, two of the limitations adhering to the idea of God, at least in popular religion hitherto, were transcended. Jeh's rule is no longer limited to Israel, nor concerned only with the nation as a collective whole, but He deals impartially with every individual and nation alike. Other limitations also disappear. His anger and wrath, that once appeared irrational and unjust, now become the intensity of His righteousness. Nor is it merely forensic and retributive righteousness. It is rather a moral end, a chief good, which He may realize by loving-kindness and mercy and forgiveness as much as by punishment. Heb thought knows no opposition between God's righteousness and His goodness, between justice and mercy. The covenant of righteousness is like the relation of husband to wife, of father to child, one of loving-kindness and everlasting love (Hos **3** 1; **11** 4; Isa **1** 18; **30** 18; Mic **7** 18; Isa **43** 4; **54** 8; Jer **31** 3 ff.34; **9** 24). The stirring events which showed Jeh's independence of Israel revealed the fulness of grace that was always latent in His relation to His people (Gen **33** 11; 2 S **24** 14). It was enshrined in the Decalogue (Ex **20** 6), and proclaimed with incomparable grandeur in what may be the most ancient Mosaic tradition: "Jeh, Jeh, a God merciful and gracious, slow to anger and abundant in lovingkindness and truth; keeping lovingkindness for thousands, forgiving iniquity and transgression and sin" (Ex **34** 6.7).

(2) *The holiness of Jeh* in the Prophets came to have a meaning closely akin to His righteousness. As an idea more distinctly religious and more exclusively applied to God, it was subject to greater changes of meaning with the development or degradation of religion. It was applied to anything withdrawn from common use to the service of religion—utensils, places, seasons, animals and men. Originally it was so far from the moral meaning it now has that it was used of the "sacred" prostitutes who ministered to the licentiousness of Canaanitish worship (Dt **23** 18). Whether or not the root-idea of the word was "separateness," there is no doubt that it is applied to Jeh in the OT to express his separateness from men and his sublimity above them. It was not always a moral quality in Jeh; for He might be unapproachable because of His mere power and terror (1 S **6** 20; Isa **8** 13). But in the Prophets, and esp. in Isa, it acquires a distinctly moral meaning. In his vision, Isaiah hears Jeh proclaimed as "holy, holy, holy," and he is filled with the sense of his own sin and of that of Israel (Isa **6**; cf **1** 4; Am **2** 7). But even here the term conveys more than moral perfection. Jeh is already "the high and lofty One that inhabiteth eternity, whose name is Holy" (Isa **57** 15). It expresses the full Divinity of Jeh in His uniqueness and self-existence (1 S **2** 2; Am **4** 2; Hos **11** 9). It would therefore seem to stand in antithesis to righteousness, as expressing those qualities of God, metaphysical and moral, by which He is distinguished and separated from men, while righteousness involves those moral activities and relations which man may share with God. But in the Prophets, God's entire being

is moral and His whole activity is righteous. The meanings of the terms, though not identical, coincide; God's holiness is realized in righteousness. "God the Holy One is sanctified in righteousness" (Isa **5** 16). So Isaiah's peculiar phrase, "the Holy One of Israel," brings God in His most exalted being into a relation of knowledge and moral reciprocity with Israel.

(3) *The moralizing of righteousness and holiness universalized Deity.*—From Amos downward Jeh's moral rule, and therefore His absolute power, were recognized as extending over all the nations surrounding Israel, and the great world-power of Assyria is but the rod of His anger and the instrument of His righteousness (Am **1–2;** Isa **10** 5; **13** 5 ff; **19** 1 ff). Idolatrous and polytheistic worship of all kinds are condemned. The full inference of Monotheism was only a gradual process, even with the prophets. It is not clear that the 8th-cent. prophets all denied the existence of other gods, though Isaiah's term for them, *'ĕlīlīm* ("things of nought," "no-gods"), points in that direction. At least the monotheistic process had set in. And Jeh's control over other nations was not exercised merely from Israel's point of view. The issue of the judgment upon the two great powers of Egypt and Assyria was to be their conversion to the religion of Jeh (Isa **19** 24.25; cf **2** 2–4=Mic **4** 1–3). Yet Heb universalism never went beyond the idea that all nations should find their share in Jeh through Israel (Zec **8** 23). The nations from the ends of the earth shall come to Jeh and declare that their fathers' gods were "lies, even vanity and things wherein there is no profit" (Jer **16** 19). It is stated categorically that "Jeh he is God in heaven above and upon the earth beneath; there is none else" (Dt **4** 39).

(4) *The unity of God* was the leading idea of Josiah's reformation. Jerus was cleansed of every accretion of Baal-worship and of other heathen religions that had established themselves by the side of the worship of Jeh (2 K **23** 4–8.10–14). The semi-heathen worship of Jeh in many local shrines, which tended to disintegrate His unity, was swept away (2 K **23** 8.9). The reform was extended to the Northern Kingdom (2 K **23** 15–20), so that Jerus should be the sole habitation of Jeh on earth, and His worship there alone should be the symbol of unity to the whole Heb race.

But the monotheistic doctrine is first fully and consciously stated in Isa **40–66.** There is no God but Jeh: other gods are merely graven images, and their worshippers commit the absurdity of worshipping the work of their own hands (Isa **42** 8; **44** 8–20). Jeh manifests His deity in His absolute *sovereignty* of the world, both of Nature and history. The prophet had seen the rise and fall of Assyria, the coming of Cyrus, the deportation and return of Judah's exiles, as incidents in the training of Israel for her world-mission to be "a light of the Gentiles" and Jeh's "salvation unto the end of the earth" (**42** 1–7; **49** 1–6). Israel's world-mission, and the ordering of historical movements to the grand final purpose of universal salvation (**45** 23), is the philosophy of history complementary to the doctrine of God's unity and universal sovereignty.

(5) *Creator and Lord.*—A further inference is that He is Creator and Lord of the physical universe. Israel's call and mission is from Jeh who "created the heavens, and stretched them forth; he that spread abroad the earth and that which cometh out of it; he that giveth breath unto the people upon it, and spirit to them that walk therein" (**42** 5; cf **40** 12.26; **44** 24; **45** 18; Gen **1**). All the essential factors of Monotheism are here at last exhibited, not in abstract metaphysical terms, but as practical motives of religious life. His counsel and action are His own (Isa **40** 13) Nothing is hid from Him; and the future like the past is known to Him (**40** 27; **42** 9; **44** 8; **48** 6). Notwithstanding His special association with the temple in Jerus, He is "the high and lofty One that inhabiteth eternity"; the heaven is His throne, and no house or place can contain Him (**57** 15; **66** 1). No force of history or Nature can withstand His purpose (**41** 17–20; **42** 13; **43** 13). He is "the First and the Last," an "Everlasting God" (**40** 28; **41** 4; **48** 12). Nothing can be likened to Him or compared with Him (**46** 5). As the heavens are higher than the earth, so His thoughts and ways transcend those of men (**55** 8.9). But anthropomorphic and anthropopathic expressions still abound. Eyes, mouth, ears, nostrils, hands, arms and face are His; He is a man of war (**42** 13; **63** 1 ff); He cries like a travailing woman (**42** 14), and feeds His flock like a shepherd (**40** 11). Thus alone could the prophet express His full concrete Divinity.

(6) *His compassion and love* are expressed in a variety of ways that lead up directly to the NT doctrine of Divine Fatherhood. He folds Israel in His arms as a shepherd his lambs (**40** 11). Her scattered children are His sons and daughters whom He redeems and restores (**43** 5–7). In wrath for a moment He hides His face, but His mercy and kindness are everlasting (**54** 8). Greater than a mother's tenderness is Jeh's love for Israel (**49** 15; **66** 13). "It would be easy to find in the prophet proof-texts for everything which theology asserts regarding God, with the exception perhaps that He is a spirit, by which is meant that He is a particular kind of substance" (A. B. Davidson in Skinner, *Isa,* II, xxix). But in truth the spirituality and personality of God are more adequately expressed in the living human language of the prophet than in the dead abstractions of metaphysics.

6. Idea of God in Post-exilic Judaism

Monotheism appears in this period as established beyond question, and in the double sense that Jeh the God of Israel is one Being, and that beside Him there is no other God. He alone is God of all the earth, and all other beings stand at an infinite distance from Him (Ps **18** 31; **24** 1 ff; **115** 3 ff). The generic name God is frequently applied to Him, and the tendency appears to avoid the particular and proper name Jeh (see esp. Pss **73–89;** Job; Eccl).

(1) *New conditions.*—Nothing essentially new appears, but the teaching of the prophets is developed under new influences. And what then was enforced by the few has now become the creed of the many. The teaching of the prophets had been enforced by the experiences of the exile. Israel had been punished for her sins of idolatry, and the faithful among the exiles had learned that Jeh's rule extended over many lands and nations. The foreign influences had been more favorable to Monotheism. The gods of Canaan and even of Assyria and Babylonia had been overthrown, and their peoples had given place to the Persians, who, in the religion of Zarathushtra, had advanced nearer to a pure Monotheism than any gentile race had done; for although they posited two principles of being, the Good and the Evil, they worshipped only Ahura-Mazda, the Good. When Persia gave way to Greece, the more cultured Greek, the Greek who had ideas to disseminate, and who established schools at Antioch or Alexandria, was a pure Monotheist.

(2) *Divine attributes.*—Although we do not yet find anything like a dogmatic account of God's attributes, the larger outlook upon the universe and the deeper reflection upon man's individual experience have produced more comprehensive and far-reaching ideas of God's being and activity. (*a*) Faith rests upon His eternity and unchangeableness (Ps

90 1.2; **102** 27). His omniscience and omnipresence are expressed with every possible fulness (Ps **139**; Job **26** 6). His almighty power is at once the confidence of piety, and the rebuke of blasphemy or frowardness (Ps **74** 12–17; **104** *et passim;* Job **36**; **37** *et passim;* Ecclus **16** 17 ff). (*b*) His most exalted and comprehensive attribute is His holiness; by it He swears as by Himself (Ps **89** 35); it expresses His majesty (Ps **99** 3.5.9) and His supreme power (Ps **60** 6 ff). (*c*) His righteousness marks all His acts in relation to Israel and the nations around her (Ps **119** 137–144; **129** 4). (*d*) That both holiness and righteousness were conceived as moral qualities is reflected in the profound sense of sin which the pious knew (Ps **51**) and revealed in the moral demands associated with them; truth, honesty and fidelity are the qualities of those who shall dwell in God's holy hill (Ps **15**); purity, diligence, kindliness, honesty, humility and wisdom are the marks of the righteous man (Prov **10–11**). (*e*) In Job and Prov wisdom stands forth as the preeminent quality of the ideal man, combining in itself all moral and intellectual excellences, and wisdom comes from God (Prov **2** 6); it is a quality of His nature (Prov **8** 22) and a mode of His activity (Prov **3** 19; Ps **104** 24). In the Hellenistic circles of Alexandria, wisdom was transformed into a philosophical conception, which is at once the principle of God's self-revelation and of His creative activity. Philo identifies it with His master-conception, the Logos. "Both Logos and Wisdom mean for Him the reason and mind of God, His image impressed upon the universe, His agent of creation and providence, the mediator through which He communicates Himself to man and the world, and His law imposed upon both the moral and physical universe" (*Mansfield Essays*, 296). In Book of Wisd it is represented as proceeding from God, "a breath of the power of God, and a clear effulgence of the glory of the Almighty . . . . an unspotted mirror of the working of God, and an image of his goodness" (**7** 25.26). In man, it is the author of knowledge, virtue and piety, and in the world it has been the guide and arbiter of its destiny from the beginning (chs **10–12**). (*f*) But in the more purely Heb lit. of this period, the moral attribute of God that comes into greatest prominence is His *beneficence*. Goodness and mercy, faithfulness and loving-kindness, forgiveness and redemption are His willing gifts to Israel. "Like as a father pitieth his children, so Jeh pitieth them that fear him" (Ps **103** 13; **145** 8; **103** 8; Ecclus **2** 11). To say that God is loving and like a father goes far on the way to the doctrine that He is Love and Father, but not the whole way; for as yet His mercy and grace are manifested only in individual acts, and they are not the natural and necessary outflow of His nature. All these ideas of God meant less for the Jewish than for the Christian mind, because they were yet held subject to several limitations.

(3) *Survival of limitations.*—(*a*) We have evidence of a changed attitude toward anthropomorphisms. God no longer walks on earth, or works under human limitation. Where His eyes or ears or face or hands are spoken of, they are clearly **figurative** expressions. His activities are universal and invisible, and He dwells on high forevermore. Yet anthropomorphic limitations are not wholly overcome. The idea that He sleeps, though not to be taken literally, implies a defect of His power (Ps **44** 23).

(*b*) In the metaphysical attributes, the chief limitation was the idea that God's dwelling-place on earth was on Mt. Zion in Jerus. He was no longer confined within Pal; His throne is in heaven (Ps **11** 4; **103** 19), and His glory above the heavens (**113** 4); but

"In Judah is God known:
His name is great in Israel.
In Salem also is his tabernacle,
And his dwelling-place in Zion"
(Ps **76** 1.2; **110** 2; cf Ecclus **24** 8 ff).

That these are no figures of speech is manifested in the yearning of the pious for the temple, and their despair in separation from it (Pss **42, 43**; cf **122**).

(*c*) This involved a moral limitation, the sense of God's favoritism toward Israel, which sometimes developed into an easy self-righteousness that had no moral basis. God's action in the world was determined by His favor toward Israel, and His loving acts were confined within the bounds of a narrow nationalism. Other nations are wicked and sinners, adversaries and oppressors, upon whom God is called to execute savage vengeance (Ps **109**; **137** 7–9). Yet Israel did not wholly forget that it was the servant of Jeh to proclaim His name among the nations (Ps **96** 2.3; **117**). Jeh is good to all, and His tender mercies are over all His works (Ps **145** 9; Ecclus **18** 13; cf Ps **104** 14; Zec **14** 16, and the Book of Jonah, which is a rebuke to Jewish particularism).

(*d*) God's holiness in the hands of the priests tended to become a material and formal quality, which fulfilled itself in established ceremonial, and His righteousness in the hands of the scribes tended to become an external law whose demands were satisfied by a mechanical obedience of works. This external conception of righteousness reacted upon the conception of God's government of the world. From the earliest times the Heb mind had associated suffering with the punishment of sin, and blessedness with the reward of virtue. In the post-exilic age the relation came to be thought of as one of strict correspondence between righteousness and reward and between sin and punishment. Righteousness, both in man and God, was not so much a moral state as a measurable sum of acts, in the one case, of obedience, and in the other, of reward or retribution. Conversely, every calamity and evil that befell men came to be regarded as the direct and equivalent penalty of a sin they had committed. The Book of Job is a somewhat inconclusive protest against this prevalent view.

These were the tendencies that ultimately matured into the narrow externalism of the scribes and Pharisees of Our Lord's time, which had substituted for the personal knowledge and service of God a system of mechanical acts of worship and conduct.

(4) *Tendencies to abstractness.*—Behind these defective ideas of God's attributes stood a more radical defect of the whole religious conception. The purification of the religion of Israel from Polytheism and idolatry, the affirmation of the unity of God and of His spirituality, required His complete separation from the manifoldness of visible existence. It was the only way, until the more adequate idea of a personal or spiritual unity, that embraced the manifold in itself, was developed. But it was an unstable conception, which tended on the one hand to empty the unity of all reality, and on the other to replace it by a new multiplicity which was not a unity. Both tendencies appear in post-exilic Judaism.

(*a*) The first effect of distinguishing too sharply between God and all created being was to set Him above and apart from all the world. This tendency had already appeared in Ezk, whose visions were rather symbols of God's presence than actual experiences of God. In Dnl even the visions appear only in dreams. The growth of the Canon of sacred lit. as the final record of the law of God, and the rise of the scribes as its professional interpreters, signified that God need not, and would not, speak face to face with man again; and the stricter organization of the priesthood and its sacrificial acts in Jerus tended to shut men generally out from access to God, and to reduce worship into a mechanical performance. A symptom of this fact was the disuse of the personal name Jeh and the substitution for it of more general and abstract terms like God and Lord.

(*b*) Not only an exaggerated awe, but also an element of skepticism, entered into the disuse of the proper name, a sense of the inadequacy of any name. In the Wisdom literature, God's incomprehensibility and remoteness appear for the first time as a conscious search after Him and a difficulty to find Him (Job **16** 18–21; **23** 3.8.9; Prov **30** 2–4). Even the doctrine of immortality developed with the sense of God's present remoteness and the hope of His future nearness (Ps **17** 15; Job **19** 25). But Jewish theology was no cold Epicureanism or rationalistic Deism. Men's religious experiences apprehended God more intimately than their theology professed.

(*c*) By a "happy inconsistency" (Montefiore) they affirmed His immanence both in Nature (Ps **104**; Wisd **8** 1; **12** 1.2) and in man's inner experience (Prov **15** 3.11; 1 Ch **28** 9; **29** 17.18). Yet that transcendence was the dominating thought is manifest, most of all, in the formulation of a number of mediating conceptions, which, while they connected God and the world, also revealed the gulf that separated them.

(5) *Logos, memra* (*mēm*[e]*rā'*) *and angels*.—This process of abstraction had gone farthest in Alexandria, where Jewish thought had so far assimilated Platonic philosophy, that Philo and Wisd conceive God as pure being who could not Himself come into any contact with the material and created world. His action and revelation are therefore mediated by His Powers, His Logos and His Wisdom, which, as personified or hypostatized attributes, become His vicegerents on earth. But in Pal, too, many mediating agencies grew up between God and man. The *memra*, or word of God, was not unlike Philo's Logos. The deified law partly corresponded to Alexandrian Wisdom. The Messiah had already appeared in the Prophets, and now in some circles He was expected as the mediator of God's special favor to Israel. The most important and significant innovation in this connection was the doctrine of angels. It was not entirely new, and Bab and Pers influences may have contributed to its development; but its chief cause lay in the general scheme of thought. Angels became intermediaries of revelation (Zec **1** 9.12.19; **3** 1 ff), the instruments of God's help (Dnl **3** 28; 2 Macc **11** 6), and of His punishment (Apoc Bar **21** 23). The ancient gods of the nations became their patron angels (Dnl **10** 13–20); but Israel's hatred of their gentile enemies often led to their transforming the latter's deities into demons. Incidentally a temporary solution of the problem of evil was thus found, by shifting all responsibility for evil from Jeh to the demons. The unity and supremacy of God were maintained by the doubtful method of delegating His manifold, and esp. His contradictory, activities to subordinate and partially to hostile spirits, which involved a new Polytheism. The problem of the One and the Many in ultimate reality cannot be solved by merely separating them. Heb Monotheism was unstable; it maintained its own truth even partially by affirming contradictories, and it contained in itself the demand for a further development. The few pluralistic phrases in the OT (as Gen **1** 26; **3** 22; **11** 7; Isa **6** 8, and *'Ĕlōhīm*) are not adumbrations of the Trinity, but only philological survivals. But the Messianic hope was an open confession of the incompleteness of the OT revelation of God.

III. The Idea of God in the NT.—The whole of the NT presupposes and rests upon the OT. Jesus Christ and His disciples inherited the idea of God revealed in the OT, as it survived in the purer strata of Jewish religion. So much was it to them and their contemporaries a matter of course, that it never occurred to them to proclaim or enforce the idea of God. Nor did they consciously feel the need of amending or changing it. They sought to correct some fallacious deductions made by later Judaism, and, unconsciously, they dropped the cruder anthropomorphisms and limitations of the OT idea. But their point of departure was always the higher teaching of the prophets and Pss, and their conscious endeavor in presenting God to men was to fulfil the Law and the Prophets (Mt **5** 17). All the worthier ideas concerning God evolved in the OT reappear in the NT. He is One, supreme, living, personal and spiritual, holy, righteous and merciful. His power and knowledge are all-sufficient, and He is not limited in time or place. Nor can it be said that any distinctly new attributes are ascribed to God in the NT. Yet there is a difference. The conception and all its factors are placed in a new relation to man and the universe, whereby their meaning is transformed, enhanced and enriched. The last trace of particularism, with its tendency to Polytheism, disappears. God can no longer bear a proper name to associate Him with Israel, or to distinguish Him from other gods, for He is the God of all the earth, who is no respecter of persons or nations. Two new elements entered men's religious thought and gradually lifted its whole content to a new plane—Jesus Christ's experience and manifestation of the Divine Fatherhood, and the growing conviction of the church that Christ Himself was God and the full and final revelation of God.

1. Dependence on OT

Gr thought may also have influenced NT thought, but in a comparatively insignificant and subordinate way. Its content was not taken over bodily as was that of Heb thought, and it did not influence the fountain head of NT ideas. It did not color the mind and teaching of Jesus Christ. It affected the form rather than matter of NT teaching. It appears in the clear-cut distinction between flesh and spirit, mind and body, which emerges in Paul's Epp., and so it helped to define more accurately the spirituality of God. The idea of the Logos in John, and the kindred idea of Christ as the image of God in Paul and He, owe something to the influence of the Platonic and Stoic schools. As this is the constructive concept employed in the NT to define the religious significance of Christ and His essential relation to God, it modifies the idea of God itself, by introducing a distinction within the unity into its innermost meaning.

2. Gentile Influence

Philosophy never appears in the NT on its own account, but only as subservient to Christian experience. In the NT as in the OT, the existence of God is taken for granted as the universal basis of all life and thought. Only in three passages of Paul's, addressed to heathen audiences, do we find anything approaching a natural theology, and these are concerned rather with defining the nature of God, than with proving His existence. When the people of Lystra would have worshipped Paul and Barnabas as heathen gods, the apostle protests that God is not like men, and bases His majesty upon His creatorship of all things (Acts **14** 15). He urges the same argument at Athens, and appeals for its confirmation to the evidences of man's need of God which he had found in Athens itself (Acts **17** 23–31). The same natural witness of the soul, face to face with the universe, is again in Rom made the ground of universal responsibility to God (**1** 18–21). No formal proof of God's existence is offered in the NT. Nor are the metaphysical attributes of God, His infinity,

3. No Theistic Proofs in the NT

omnipotence and omniscience, as defined in systematic theology, at all set forth in the NT. The ground for these deductions is provided in the religious experience that finds God in Christ all-sufficient.

The fundamental and central idea about God in NT teaching is His Fatherhood, and it determines all that follows. In some sense the idea was not unknown to heathen religions. Greeks and Romans acknowledged Father Zeus or Jupiter as the creator and preserver of Nature, and as standing in some special relation to men. In the OT the idea appears frequently, and has a richer content. Not only is God the creator and preserver of Israel, but He deals with her as a father with his child. "Like as a father pitieth his children, so Jeh pitieth them that fear Him" (Ps **103** 13; cf Dt **1** 31; **32** 6; Jer **3** 4.19; **31** 20; Isa **63** 16; Hos **11** 1; Mal **3** 17). Even His chastisements are "as a man chasteneth his son" (Dt **8** 5; Isa **64** 8). The same idea is expressed under the figure of a mother's tender care (Isa **49** 15; **66** 13; Ps **27** 10), and it is embedded in the covenant relation. But in the OT the idea does not occupy the central and determinative position it has in NT, and it is always limited to Israel.

4. Divine Fatherhood

(1) *In the teaching of Jesus Christ*—God is pre-eminently the Father. It is his customary term for the Supreme Being, and it is noteworthy that Jesus' usage has never been quite naturalized. We still say "God" where Jesus would have said "the Father." He meant that the essential nature of God, and His relation to men, is best expressed by the attitude and relation of a father to his children; but God is Father in an infinitely higher and more perfect degree than any man. He is "good" and "perfect," the heavenly Father, in contrast with men, who, even as fathers, are evil (Mt **5** 48; **7** 11). What in them is an ideal imperfectly and intermittently realized, is in Him completely fulfilled. Christ thought not of the physical relation of origin and derivation, but of the personal relation of love and care which a father bestows upon his children. The former relation is indeed implied, for the Father is ever working in the world (Jn **5** 17), and all things lie in His power (Lk **22** 42). By His preserving power, the least as well as the greatest creature lives (Mt **6** 26; **10** 29). But it is not the fact of God's creative, preserving and governing power, so much as the manner of it, that Christ emphasizes. He is absolutely good in all His actions and relations (Mt **7** 11; Mk **10** 18). To Him men and beasts turn for all they need, and in Him they find safety, rest and peace (Mt **6** 26.32; **7** 11). His goodness goes forth spontaneously and alights upon all living things, even upon the unjust and His enemies (Mt **5** 45). He rewards the obedient (Mt **6** 1; **7** 21), forgives the disobedient (Mt **6** 14; cf **18** 35) and restores the prodigal (Lk **15** 11 ff). "Fatherhood is love, original and underived, anticipating and undeserved, forgiving and educating, communicating and drawing to his heart" (Beyschlag, *NT Theol*, I, 82). To the Father, therefore, should men pray for all good things (Mt **6** 9), and He is the ideal of all perfection, to which they should seek to attain (Mt **5** 48). Such is the general character of God as expressed in His Fatherhood, but it is realized in different ways by those who stand to Him in different relations.

(*a*) Jesus Christ knows the Father as no one else does, and is related to Him in a unique manner. The idea is central in His teaching, because the fact is fundamental in His experience. On His first personal appearance in history He declares that He must be about His Father's business (Lk **2** 49), and at the last He commends His spirit into His Father's hands. Throughout His life, His filial consciousness is perfect and unbroken. "I and the Father are one" (Jn **10** 30). As He knows the Father, so the Father knows and acknowledges Him. At the opening of His ministry, and again at its climax in the transfiguration, the Father bears witness to His perfect sonship (Mk **1** 11; **9** 7). It was a relation of mutual love and confidence, unalloyed and infinite. "The Father loveth the Son, and hath given all things into his hand" (Jn **3** 35; **5** 20). The Father sent the Son into the world, and intrusted Him with his message and power (Mt **11** 27). He gave Him those who believed in Him, to receive His word (Jn **6** 37.44.45; **17** 6.8). He does the works and speaks the words of the Father who sent Him (Jn **5** 36; **8** 18.29; **14** 24). His dependence upon the Father, and His trust in Him are equally complete (Jn **11** 41; **12** 27 f; **17**). In this perfect union of Christ with God, unclouded by sin, unbroken by infidelity, God first became for a human life on earth all that He could and would become. Christ's filial consciousness was in fact and experience the full and final revelation of God. "No one knoweth the Son, save the Father; neither doth any know the Father, save the Son, and he to whomsoever the Son willeth to reveal him" (Mt **11** 27). Not only can we see in Christ what perfect sonship is, but in His filial consciousness the Father Himself is so completely reflected that we may know the perfect Father also. "He that hath seen me hath seen the Father" (Jn **14** 9; cf **8** 19). Nay, it is more than a reflection: so completely is the mind and will of Christ identified with that of the Father, that they interpenetrate, and the words and works of the Father shine out through Christ. "The words that I say unto you I speak not from myself: but the Father abiding in me doeth his works. Believe me that I am in the Father, and the Father in me" (Jn **14** 10.11). As the Father, so is the Son, for men to honor or to hate (**5** 23; **15** 23). In the last day, when He comes to execute the judgment which the Father has intrusted to Him, He shall come in the glory of the Father (Mt **16** 27; Mk **8** 38; Lk **9** 26). In all this Jesus is aware that His relation to the Father is unique. What in Him is original and realized, in others can only be an ideal to be gradually realized by His communication. "I am the way, and the truth, and the life: no one cometh unto the Father, but by me" (Jn **14** 6). He is, therefore, rightly called the "only begotten son" (**3** 16), and His contemporaries believed that He made Himself equal to God (**5** 18).

(*b*) Through Christ, His disciples and hearers, too, may know God as their Father. He speaks of "your Father," "your heavenly Father." To them as individuals, it means a personal relation; He is "thy Father" (Mt **6** 4.18). Their whole conduct should be determined by the consciousness of the Father's intimate presence (**6** 1.4). To do His will is the ideal of life (**7** 21; **12** 50). More explicitly, it is to act as He does, to love and forgive as He loves and forgives (**5** 45); and, finally, to be perfect as He is perfect (**5** 48). Thus do men become sons of their Father who is in heaven. Their peace and safety lay in their knowledge of His constant and all-sufficient care (**6** 26.32). The ultimate goal of men's relation to Christ is that through Him they should come to a relation with the Father like His relation both to the Father and to them, wherein Father, Son, and believers form a social unity (Jn **14** 21; **17** 23; cf ver 21).

(*c*) While God's fatherhood is thus realized and revealed, originally and fully in Christ, derivatively and partially in believers, it also has significance for all men. Every man is born a child of God and heir of His kingdom (Lk **18** 16). During childhood, all men are objects of His fatherly love and care (Mt **18** 10), and it is not His will that one of them should perish (**18** 14). Even if they become His enemies, He still bestows His beneficence upon the evil and the unjust (Mt **5** 44.45; Lk **6** 35). The prodigal son may become unworthy to be called a son, but the father always remains a father. Men may become so far unfaithful that in them the fatherhood is no longer manifest and that their inner spirits own not God, but the devil, as their father (Jn **8** 42–44). So their filial relation to God may be broken, but His nature and attitude are not changed. He is *the* Father absolutely, and as Father is He perfect (Mt **5** 48). The essential and universal Divine Fatherhood finds its eternal and continual object in the only begotten Son who is in the bosom of the Father. As a relation with men, it is qualified by their attitude to God; while some by faithlessness make it of no avail, others by obedience become in the reality of their experience sons of their Father in heaven. See CHILDREN OF GOD.

(2) *In the apostolic teaching*, although the Fatherhood of God is not so prominently or so abundantly exhibited as it was by Jesus Christ, it lies at the root of the whole system of salvation there presented. Paul's central doctrine of justification by faith is but the scholastic form of the parable of the Prodigal Son. John's one idea, that God is love, is but an abstract statement of His fatherhood. In complete accord with Christ's teaching, that only through Himself men know the Father and come to Him, the whole apostolic system of grace is mediated through Christ the Son of God, sent because "God so loved the world" (Jn **3** 16), that through His death men might be reconciled to God (Rom **5** 10; **8** 3). He speaks to men through the Son who is the effulgence of His glory, and the very image of His substance (He **1** 2.3). The central position assigned to Christ involves the central position of the Fatherhood.

As in the teaching of Jesus, so in that of the apostles, we distinguish three different relationships in which the fatherhood is realized in varying degrees: (*a*) Primarily He is the God and Father of Our Lord Jesus Christ (Rom **15** 6; 2 Cor **1** 3). As such He is the source of every spiritual blessing in the heavenly places in Christ (Eph **1** 3). Through Christ we have access unto the Father (Eph **2** 18). (*b*) He is, therefore, God our Father (Rom **1** 7; 1 Cor **1** 3). Believers are sons of God through faith in Christ Jesus (Gal **3** 26). "For as many as are led by the Spirit of God, these are sons of God" (Rom **8** 14). These receive the spirit of adoption whereby they cry, Abba, Father (Rom **8** 15; Gal **4** 6). The figure of adoption has sometimes been understood as implying the denial of man's natural sonship and God's essential Fatherhood, but that would be pressing the figure beyond Paul's purpose. (*c*) The apostles' teaching, like Christ's, is that man in sin cannot possess the filial consciousness or know God as Father; but God, in His attitude to man, is always and essentially Father. In the sense of creaturehood and dependence, man in any condition is a son of God (Acts **17** 28). And to speak of any other natural sonship which is not also morally realized is meaningless. From God's standpoint, man even in his sin is a possible son, in the personal and moral sense; and the whole process and power of his awakening to the realization of his sonship issues from the fatherly love of God, who sent His Son and gave the Spirit (Rom **5** 5.8). He is "the Father" absolutely, "one God and Father of all, who is over all, and through all, and in all. But unto each one of us was the grace given according to the measure of the gift of Christ" (Eph **4** 6.7).

5. God is King

After the Divine Fatherhood, the kingdom of God (Mk and Lk) or of heaven (Mt) is the next ruling conception in the teaching of Jesus. As the doctrine of the Fatherhood sets forth the individual relation of men to God, that of the kingdom defines their collective and social condition, as determined by the rule of the Father.

(1) *The kingdom of God.*—Christ adopted and transformed the OT idea of Jeh's rule into an inner and spiritual principle of His gospel, without, however, quite detaching it from the external and apocalyptic thought of His time. He adopts the Jewish idea in so far as it involves the enforcing of God's rule; and in the immediate future He anticipates such a reorganization of social conditions in the manifestation of God's reign over men and Nature, as will ultimately amount to a regeneration of all things in accordance with the will of God (Mk **9** 1; **13** 30; Mt **16** 28; **19** 28). But He eliminated the particularism and favoritism toward the Jews, as well as the non-moral, easy optimism as to their destiny in the kingdom, which obtained in contemporary thought. The blessings of the kingdom are moral and spiritual in their nature, and the conditions of entrance into it are moral too (Mt **8** 11; **21** 31.43; **23** 37.38; Lk **13** 29). They are humility, hunger and thirst after righteousness, and the love of mercy, purity and peace (Mt **5** 3–10; **18** 1.3; cf Mt **20** 26–28; **25** 34; **7** 21; Jn **3** 3; Lk **17** 20.21). The king of such a kingdom is, therefore, righteous, loving and gracious toward all men; He governs by the inner communion of spirit with spirit and by the loving coördination of the will of His subjects with his own will.

(2) *Its king.*—But who is the king? (*a*) Generally in Mk and Lk, and sometimes in Mt, it is called the kingdom of God. In several parables, the Father takes the place of king, and it is the Father that gives the kingdom (Lk **12** 32). God the Father is therefore the King, and we are entitled to argue from Jesus' teaching concerning the kingdom to His idea of God. The will of God is the law of the kingdom, and the ideal of the kingdom is, therefore, the character of God. (*b*) But in some passages Christ reveals the consciousness of his own Kingship. He approves Peter's confession of his Messiahship, which involves Kingship (Mt **16** 16). He speaks of a time in the immediate future when men shall see "the Son of man coming in his kingdom" (Mt **16** 28). As judge of all men, He designates Himself king (Mt **25** 34; Lk **19** 38). He accepts the title king from Pilate (Mt **27** 11.12; Mk **15** 2; Lk **23** 3; Jn **18** 37), and claims a kingdom which is not of this world (Jn **18** 36). His disciples look to Him for the restoration of the kingdom (Acts **1** 6). His kingdom, like that of God, is inner, moral and spiritual. (*c*) But there can be only one moral kingdom, and only one supreme authority in the spiritual realm. The coördination of the two kingships must be found in their relation to the Fatherhood. The two ideas are not antithetical or even independent. They may have been separate and even opposed as Christ found them, but He used them as two points of apperception in the minds of His hearers, by which He communicated to them His one idea of God, as the Father who ruled a spiritual kingdom by love and righteousness, and ordered Nature and history to fulfil His purpose of grace. Men's prayer should be that the Father's kingdom may come (Mt **6** 9.10). They enter the kingdom by doing the Father's will (Mt **7** 21). It is their Father's good pleasure to give them the kingdom (Lk **12** 32). The Fatherhood is primary, but it carries with it authority, government, law and order, care and provision, to set up and organize a kingdom reflecting a Father's love and expressing His will.

And as Christ is the revealer and mediator of the Fatherhood, He also is the messenger and bearer of the kingdom. In his person, preaching and works, the kingdom is present to men (Mt **4** 17.23; **12** 28), and as its king He claims men's allegiance and obedience (Mt **11** 28.29). His sonship constitutes His relation to the kingdom. As son He obeys the Father, depends upon Him, represents Him to men, and is one with Him. And in virtue of this relation, He is the messenger of the kingdom and its principle, and at the same time He shares with the Father its authority and Kingship.

(3) *Apostolic teaching.*—In the apostolic writings, the emphasis upon the elements of kingship, authority, law and righteousness is greater than in the gospels. The kingdom is related to God (Gal **5** 21; Col **4** 11; 1 Thess **2** 12; 2 Thess **1** 5), and to Christ (Col **1** 13; 2 Tim **4** 1.18; 2 Pet **1** 11), and to both together (Eph **5** 5; cf 1 Cor **15** 24). The phrase "the kingdom of the Son of his love" sums up the idea of the joint kingship, based upon the relation of Father and Son.

6. Moral Attributes

The nature and character of God are summed up in the twofold relation of Father and King in which He stands to men, and any abstract statements that may be made about Him, any attributes that may be ascribed to Him, are deductions from His royal Fatherhood.

(1) *Personality.*—That a father and king is a *person* needs not to be argued, and it is almost tautology to say that a person is a *spirit*. Christ relates directly the spirituality of God to His Fatherhood. "The true worshippers shall worship the Father in spirit and truth: for such doth the Father seek to be his worshippers. God is Spirit" (Jn **4** 23.24 m). **Figurative** expressions denoting the same truth are the Johannine phrases, 'God is life' (1 Jn **5** 20), and "God is light" (1 Jn **1** 5).

(2) *Love* is the most characteristic attribute of Fatherhood. It is the abstract term that most fully expresses the concrete character of God as Father. In John's theology, it is used to sum up all God's perfections in one general formula. God is love, and where no love is, there can be no knowledge of God and no realization of Him (1 Jn **4** 8.16). With one exception (Lk **11** 42), the phrase "the love of God" appears in the teaching of Jesus only as it is represented in the Fourth Gospel. There it expresses the bond of union and communion, issuing from God, that holds together the whole spiritual society, God, Christ and believers (Jn **15** 10; **14** 21). Christ's mission was that of revelation, rather than of interpretation, and what in person and act He represents before men as the living Father, the apostles describe as almighty and universal love. They saw and realized this love first in the Son, and esp. in His sacrificial death. It is "the love of God, which is in Christ Jesus our Lord" (Rom **8** 39). "God commendeth his own love toward us, in that, while we were yet sinners, Christ died for us" (Rom **5** 8; cf Eph **2** 4). Love was fully made known in Christ's death (1 Jn **3** 16). The whole process of the incarnation and death of Christ was also a sacrifice of God's and the one supreme manifestation of His nature as love (1 Jn **4** 9.10; cf Jn **3** 16). The love of God is His fatherly relation to Christ extended to men through Christ. By the Father's love bestowed upon us, we are called children of God (1 Jn **3** 1). Love is not only an emotion of tenderness and beneficence which bestows on men the greatest gifts, but a relation to God which constitutes their entire law of life. It imposes upon men the highest moral demands, and communicates to them the moral energy by which alone they can be met. It is law and grace combined. The love of God is perfected only in those who keep the word of Jesus Christ the Righteous (1 Jn **2** 5). "For this is the love of God, that we keep his commandments" (1 Jn **5** 3). It is manifested esp. in brotherly love (1 Jn **4** 12.20). It cannot dwell with worldliness (1 Jn **2** 15) or callous selfishness (**3** 17). Man derives it from God as he is made the son of God, begotten of Him (**4** 7).

(3) *Righteousness and holiness* were familiar ideas to Jesus and His disciples, as elements in the Divine character. They were current in the thought of their time, and they stood foremost in the OT conception. They were therefore adopted in their entirety in the NT, but they stand in a different context. They are coördinated with, and even subordinated to, the idea of love. As kingship stands to fatherhood, so righteouness and holiness stand to love.

(*a*) Once we find the phrase "Holy Father" spoken by Jesus (Jn **17** 11; cf 1 Pet **1** 15.16). But generally the idea of holiness is associated with God in His activity through the Holy Spirit, which renews, enlightens, purifies and cleanses the lives of men. Every vestige of artificial, ceremonial, non-moral meaning disappears from the idea of holiness in the NT. The sense of separation remains only as separation from sin. So Christ as high priest is "holy, guileless, undefiled, separated from sinners" (He **7** 26). Where it dwells, no uncleanness must be (1 Cor **6** 19). Holiness is not a legal or abstract morality, but a life made pure and noble by the love of God shed abroad in men's hearts (Rom **5** 5). "The kingdom of God is . . . . righteousness and peace and joy in the Holy Spirit" (Rom **14** 17).

(*b*) Righteousness as a quality of character is practically identical with holiness in the NT. It is opposed to sin (Rom **6** 13.20) and iniquity (2 Cor **6** 14). It is coupled with goodness and truth as the fruit of the light (Eph **5** 9; cf 1 Tim **6** 11; 2 Tim **2** 22). It implies a rule or standard of conduct, which in effect is one with the life of love and holiness. It is brought home to men by the conviction of the Holy Spirit (Jn **16** 8). In its origin it is the righteousness of God (Mt **6** 33; cf Jn **17** 25). In Paul's theology, "the righteousness of God through faith in Jesus Christ unto all them that believe" (Rom **3** 22) is the act of God, out of free grace, declaring and treating the sinner as righteous, that he thereby may become righteous, even as "we love, because he first loved us" (1 Jn **4** 19). The whole character of God, then, whether we call it love, holiness or righteousness, is revealed in His work of salvation, wherein He goes forth to men in love and mercy, that they may be made citizens of His kingdom, heirs of His righteousness, and participators in His love.

7. Metaphysical Attributes

The abstract being of God and His metaphysical attributes are implied, but not defined, in the NT. His infinity, omnipotence and omniscience are not enunciated in terms, but they are postulated in the whole scheme of salvation which He is carrying to completion. He is Lord of heaven and earth (Mt **11** 25). The forces of Nature are at His command (Mt **5** 45; **6** 30). He can answer every prayer and satisfy every need (Mt **7** 7-12). All things are possible to Him (Mk **10** 27; **14** 36). He created all things (Eph **3** 9). All earthly powers are derived from Him (Rom **13** 1). By His power, He raised Christ from the dead and subjected to Him "all rule, and authority, and power, and dominion" in heaven and on earth (Eph **1** 20.21; cf Mt **28** 18). Every power and condition of existence are subordinated to the might of His love unto His saints (Rom **8** 38.39). Neither time nor place can limit Him: He is the eternal God (Rom **16** 26). His knowledge is as infinite as

His power; He knows what the Son and the angels know not (Mk **13** 32). He knows the hearts of men (Lk **16** 15) and all their needs (Mt **6** 8.32). His knowledge is esp. manifested in His wisdom by which He works out His purpose of salvation, "the manifold wisdom of God, according to the eternal purpose which he purposed in Christ Jesus our Lord" (Eph **3** 10.11). The teaching of the NT implies that all perfections of power, condition and being cohere in God, and are revealed in His love. They are not developed or established on metaphysical grounds, but they flow out of His perfect fatherhood. Earthly fathers do what good they can for their children, but the Heavenly Father does all things for the best for His children—"to them that love God all things work together for good"—because He is restricted by no limits of power, will or wisdom (Mt **7** 11; Rom **8** 28).

8. The Unity of God

It is both assumed through the NT and stated categorically that God is one (Mk **12** 29; Rom **3** 30; Eph **4** 6). No truth had sunk more deeply into the Heb mind by this time than the unity of God.

(1) *The divinity of Christ.*—Yet it is obvious from what has been written, that Jesus Christ claimed a power, authority and position so unique that they can only be adequately described by calling Him God; and the apostolic church both in worship and in doctrine accorded Him that honor. All that they knew of God as now fully and finally revealed was summed up in His person, "for in him dwelleth all the fulness of the Godhead bodily" (Col **2** 9). If they did not call Him God, they recognized and named Him everything that God meant for them.

(2) *The Holy Spirit.*—Moreover, the Holy Spirit is a third term that represents a Divine person in the experience, thought and language of Christ and His disciples. In the Johannine account of Christ's teaching, it is probable that the Holy Spirit is identified with the risen Lord Himself (Jn **14** 16.17; cf ver 18), and Paul seems also to identify them in at least one passage: "the Lord is the Spirit" (2 Cor **3** 17). But in other places the three names are ranged side by side as representing three distinct persons (Mt **28** 19; 2 Cor **13** 14; Eph **4** 4–6).

(3) *The church's problem.*—But how does the unity of God cohere with the Divine status of the Son and the distinct subsistence of the Holy Spirit? Jesus Christ affirmed a unity between Himself and the Father (Jn **10** 30), a unity, too, which might be realized in a wider sphere, where the Father, the Son and believers should form one society (**17** 21. 23), but He reveals no category which would construe the unity of the Godhead in a manifoldness of manifestation. The experience of the first Christians as a rule found Christ so entirely sufficient to all their religious needs, so filled with all the fulness of God, that the tremendous problem which had arisen for thought did not trouble them. Paul expresses his conception of the relation of Christ to God under the figure of the image. Christ "is the image of the invisible God, the firstborn of all creation" (Col **1** 15; 2 Cor **4** 4). Another writer employs a similar metaphor. Christ is "the effulgence of [God's] glory, and the very image of his substance" (He **1** 3). But these figures do not carry us beyond the fact, abundantly evident elsewhere, that Christ in all things represented God because He participated in His being. In the prologue to the Fourth Gospel, the doctrine of the Word is developed for the same purpose. The eternal Reason of God who was ever with Him, and of Him, issues forth as revealed thought, or spoken word, in the person of Jesus Christ, who therefore is the eternal Word of God incarnate. So far and no farther the NT goes. Jesus Christ is God revealed; we know nothing of God, but that which is manifest in Him. His love, holiness, righteousness and purpose of grace, ordering and guiding all things to realize the ends of His fatherly love, all this we know in and through Jesus Christ. The Holy Spirit takes of Christ's and declares it to men (Jn **16** 14). The problems of the coördination of the One with the Three, of personality with the plurality of consciousness, of the Infinite with the finite, and of the Eternal God with the Word made flesh, were left over for the church to solve. The Holy Spirit was given to teach it all things and guide it into all the truth (Jn **16** 13). "And lo, I am with you always, even unto the end of the world" (Mt **28** 20).

See Jesus Christ; Holy Spirit; Trinity.

Literature.—Harris, *The Philosophical Basis of Theism; God the Creator and Lord of All;* Flint, *Theism;* Orr, *The Christian View of God and the World;* E. Caird, *The Evolution of Religion;* James Ward, *The Realm of Ends;* Fairbairn, *The Philosophy of the Christian Religion;* W. N. Clarke, *The Christian Doctrine of God;* Adeney, *The Christian Conception of God;* Rocholl, *Der Christliche Gottesbegriff;* O. Holtzmann, *Der Christliche Gottesglaube, seine Vorgeschichte und Urgeschichte;* G. Wobbernim, *Der Christliche Gottesglaube in seinem Verhältnis zur heutigen Philosophie und Naturwissenschaft;* Köstlin, art. "Gott" in *RE;* R. S. Candlish, Crawford and Scott-Lidgett, books on *The Fatherhood of God:* OT Theologies by Oehler, Schultz and Davidson; NT Theologies by Schmid, B. Weiss, Beyschlag, Holtzmann and Stevens; Wendt, *The Teaching of Jesus;* sections in systems of Christian Doctrine by Schleiermacher, Darner, Nitzsch, Martensen, Thomasius, Hodge, etc.

T. Rees

GOD, CHILDREN OF. See Children of God.

GOD, IMAGE OF: In Gen **1** 26.27, the truth is declared that God created man in His own "image" (*çelem*), after His "likeness" (*d^e^mûth*). The two ideas denote the same thing—*resemblance* to God. The like conception of man, tacit or avowed, underlies all revelation. It is given in Gen **9** 6 as the ground of the prohibition of the shedding of man's blood; is echoed in Ps **8**; is reiterated frequently in the NT (1 Cor **11** 7; Eph **4** 24; Col **3** 10; Isa **3** 9). The nature of this image of God in man is discussed in other arts.—see esp. Anthropology. It lies in the nature of the case that the "image" does not consist in bodily form; it can only reside in spiritual qualities, in man's mental and moral attributes as a self-conscious, rational, personal agent, capable of self-determination and obedience to moral law. This gives man his position of lordship in creation, and invests his being with the sanctity of personality. The image of God, defaced, but not entirely lost through sin, is restored in yet more perfect form in the redemption of Christ. See the full discussion in the writer's work, *God's Image in Man and Its Defacement*; see also Dr. J. Laidlaw, *The Bible Doctrine of Man.*

James Orr

GOD, NAMES OF:

I. Introductory
  1. The Phrase "His Name"
  2. Classification.
II. Personal Names of God in the OT
  1. *'Ĕlōhīm*
  2. *'Ēl*
  3. *'Ĕlō^a^h*
  4. *'Ādhōn, 'Ădhōnāy*
  5. *Yahweh* (Jehovah)
  6. *Çūr* (Rock)
  7. *Ḳādhōsh*
  8. *Shadday*
III. Descriptive Names of God in the OT
  1. *'Ăbhīr*
  2. *'Ēl-'Ĕlōhē-Yisrā'el*
  3. *'Elyōn*
  4. *Gibbōr*
  5. *'Ēl-rŏ'ī*
  6. *Çaddīḳ*
  7. *Ḳannā'*
  8. *Yahweh Çebhā'ōth*
  9. "I Am That I Am"

I. Introduction.—To an extent beyond the appreciation of modern and western minds the people of Bib. times and lands valued the name of the person. They always gave to it symbolical or character meaning.

While our modern names are almost exclusively designatory, and intended merely for identification, the Bib. names were also descriptive, and often prophetic. Religious significance nearly always inhered in the name, a parent relating his child to the Deity, or declaring its consecration to the Deity, by joining the name of the Deity with the service which the child should render, or perhaps commemorating in a name the favor of God in the gracious gift of the child, e.g. Nathanael ("gift of God"); Samuel ("heard of God"); Adonijah ("Jeh is my Lord"), etc. It seems to us strange that at its birth, the life and character of a child should be forecast by its parents in a name; and this unique custom has been regarded by an unsympathetic criticism as evidence of the origin of such names and their attendant narratives long subsequent to the completed life itself; such names, for example, as Abraham, Sarah, etc. But that this was actually done, and that it was regarded as a matter of course, is proved by the name given to Our Lord at His birth: "Thou shalt call his name Jesus; for it is he that shall save his people" (Mt **1** 21). It is not unlikely that the giving of a character name represented the parents' purpose and fidelity in the child's training, resulting necessarily in giving to the child's life that very direction, which the name indicated. A child's name, therefore, became both a prayer and a consecration, and its realization in character became often a necessary psychological effect. Great honor or dishonor was attached to a name. The OT writings contain many and varied instances of this. Sometimes contempt for certain reprobate men would be most expressively indicated by a change of name, e.g. the change of Esh-baal, "man of Baal," to Ish-bosheth, "man of shame" (2 S **2** 8 ff), and the omission of Jeh from the name of the apostate king, Ahaz (2 K **15** 38, etc). The name of the last king of Judah was most expressively changed by Nebuchadnezzar from Mattaniah to Zedekiah, to assure his fidelity to his overlord who made him king (2 K **24** 17). See Names, Proper.

1. The Phrase "His Name"

Since the Scriptures of the OT and NT are essentially for purposes of revelation, and since the Hebrews laid such store by names, we should confidently expect them to make the Divine name a medium of revelation of the first importance. People accustomed by long usage to significant character indications in their own names, necessarily would regard the names of the Deity as expressive of His nature. The very phrase "name of Jeh," or "His name," as applied to the Deity in Bib. usage, is most interesting and suggestive, sometimes expressing comprehensively His revelation in Nature (Ps **8** 1; cf **138** 2); or marking the place of His worship, where men will call upon His name (Dt **12** 5); or used as a synonym of His various attributes, e.g. faithfulness (Isa **48** 9), grace (Ps **23** 3), His honor (Ps **79** 9), etc. "Accordingly, since the name of God denotes this God Himself as He is revealed, and as He desires to be known by His creatures, when it is said that God will *make a name* for Himself by His mighty deeds, or that the new world of the future shall be unto Him for a name, we can easily understand that the *name of God* is often synonymous with the *glory of God*, and that the expressions for both are combined in the utmost variety of ways, or used alternately" (Schultz, *OT Theology*, ET, I, 124–25; cf Ps **72** 19; Isa **63** 14; also Davidson, *OT Theol.*, 37–38).

2. Classification of the Subject

From the important place which the Divine name occupies in revelation, we would expect frequency of occurrence and diversity of form; and this is just that which we find to be true. The many forms or varieties of the name will be considered under the following heads: (1) Absolute or Personal Names, (2) Attributive, or Qualifying Names, and (3) Names of God in the NT. Naturally and in course of time attributive names tend to crystallize into personal names through frequent use and devotional regard into personal names; e.g. the attributive adj. *ḳadhōsh*, "holy," becomes the personal, transcendental name for Deity in Job and Isa. For fuller details of each name reference may be made to separate articles.

II. Absolute or Personal Names.—The first form of the Divine name in the Bible is אֱלֹהִים, *'Ĕlōhīm*,

1. 'Ĕlōhīm, "God"

ordinarily tr[d] "God" (Gen **1** 1). This is the most frequently used name in the OT, as its equivalent θεός, *theós*, is in the NT, occurring in Gen alone approximately 200 t. It is one of a group of kindred words, to which belong also *'Ēl* and *'Ĕlōah*. (1) Its *form* is pl., but the construction is uniformly sing., i.e. it governs a sing. vb. or adj., unless used of heathen divinities (Ps **96** 5; **97** 7). It is characteristic of Heb that extension, magnitude and dignity, as well as actual multiplicity, are expressed by the pl. It is not reasonable, therefore, to assume that plurality of form indicates primitive Sem polytheism. On the contrary, historic Heb is unquestionably and uniformly monotheistic.

(2) The *derivation* is quite uncertain. Gesenius, Ewald and others find its origin in אוּל, *'ūl*, "to be strong," from which also are derived *'ayil*, "ram," and *'ēlāh*, "terebinth"; it is then an expanded pl. form of *'ēl*; others trace it to אָלָה, *'ālah*, "to terrify," and the sing. form is found in the infrequent אֱלוֹהַּ, *'ĕlōah*, which occurs chiefly in poetical books; *BDB* inclines to the derivation from אָלָה, *'ālāh*, "to be strong," as the root of the three forms, *'Ēl*, *'Ĕlōah* and *'Ĕlōhīm*, although admitting that the whole question is involved in uncertainty (for full statement see *BDB*, s.v. אלה); a somewhat fanciful suggestion is the Arab. root *'ûl*, "to be in front," from which comes the meaning "leader"; and still more fanciful is the suggested connection with the prep. אֶל, *'el*, signifying God as the "goal" of man's life and aspiration. The origin must always lie in doubt, since the derivation is prehistoric, and the name, with its kindred words *'Ēl* and *'Ĕlōah*, is common to Sem languages and religions and beyond the range of Heb records.

(3) It is the reasonable conclusion that the meaning is "might" or "power"; that it is common to Sem language; that the form is pl. to express majesty or "all-mightiness," and that it is a generic, rather than a specific personal, name for Deity, as is indicated by its application to those who represent the Deity (Jgs **5** 8; Ps **82** 1) or who are in His presence (1 S **28** 13).

2. 'Ĕlōah

The sing. form of the preceding name, אֱלוֹהַּ, *'Ĕlōah*, is confined in its use almost exclusively to poetry, or to poetic expression, being characteristic of the Book of Job, occurring oftener in that book than in all other parts of the OT. It is, in fact, found in Job oftener than the elsewhere more ordinary pl. *'Ĕlōhīm*. For derivation and meaning see above under **1** (2). Cf also the Aram. form, אֱלָהּ, *'ĕlāh*, found frequently in Ezr and Dnl.

3. 'Ēl

In the group of Sem languages, the most common word for Deity is El (אֵל, *'ēl*), represented by the Bab *ilu* and the Arab. *'Allah*. It is found throughout the OT, but oftener in Job and Pss than in all the other books. It occurs seldom in the historical books, and not at all in Lev. The same variety of derivations is attributed to it as to Elohim (q.v.), most probable of which is אוּל, *'ūl*, "to be strong." *BDB* interprets *'ūl* as meaning "to be in front," from which came *'ayil*, "ram," the one in front of the flock, and *'ēlāh*, the prominent "terebinth," deriving El from *'ālāh*, "to be strong." It occurs in many of the more ancient names; and, like Elohim, it is used of pagan gods. It is frequently combined with nouns or adjectives to express the Divine name with reference to particular attributes or phases of His being, as *'Ēl 'Elyōn, 'Ēl-Rō'ī*, etc (see below under III, "Attributive Names").

An attributive name, which in prehistoric Heb had already passed over into a generic name of God, is אָדוֹן, *'Ādhōn,* אֲדֹנָי, *'Ădhōnāy,* the latter formed from the former, being the const. pl., *'ădhōnē,* with the 1st pers. ending *ay,* which has been lengthened to *āy* and so retained as characteristic of the proper name and distinguishing it from the possessive "my Lord." AV does not distinguish, but renders both as possessive, "my Lord" (Jgs **6** 15; **13** 8), and as personal name (Ps **2** 4); RV also, in Ps **16** 2, is in doubt, giving "my Lord," possessive, in text and "the Lord" in m. *'Ădhōnāy,* as a name of Deity, emphasizes His sovereignty (Ps **2** 4; Isa **7** 7), and corresponds closely to *Kúrios* of the NT. It is frequently combined with Jeh (Gen **15** 8; Isa **7** 7, etc) and with *'Ĕlōhīm* (Ps **86** 12). Its most significant service in MT is the use of its vowels to point the unpronounceable tetragrammaton יהוה, indicating that the word *'Ădhōnāy* should be spoken instead of *Yahweh.* This combination of vowels and consonants gives the transliteration "Jehovah," adopted by ARV, while the other EV, since Coverdale, represents the combination by the capitals LORD. LXX represents by *Kurios.*

4. 'Ādhōn, 'Ădhōnāy

The name most distinctive of God as the God of Israel is Jehovah (יְהוָה, a combination of the tetragrammaton with the vowels of *'Ădhōnāy,* transliterated *Y^ehōwāh,* but read by the Hebrews *'ădhōnāy*). While both derivation and meaning are lost to us in the uncertainties of its ante-Bib. origin, the following inferences seem to be justified by the facts: (1) This name was common to religions other than Israel's, according to Friedr. Delitzsch, Hommel, Winckler, and Guthe (*EB*, s.v.), having been found in Bab inscriptions. Ammonite, Arab. and Egyp names appear also to contain it (cf Davidson, *OT Theol.*, 52 f); but while, like Elohim, it was common to primitive Sem religion, it became Israel's distinctive name for the Deity. (2) It was, therefore, not first made known at the call of Moses (Ex **3** 13–16; **6** 2–8), but, being already known, was at that time given a larger revelation and interpretation: God, to be known to Israel henceforth under the name "Jehovah" and in its fuller significance, was the One sending Moses to deliver Israel; "when I shall say unto them, The God of your fathers hath sent me unto you; and they shall say to me, What is his name? what shall I say unto them? And God said . . . . I WILL BE THAT I WILL BE . . . . say . . . . I WILL BE hath sent me" (Ex **3** 13.14 m). The name is assumed as known in the narrative of Gen; it also occurs in pre-Mosaic names (Ex **6** 20; 1 Ch **2** 25; **7** 8). (3) The *derivation* is from the archaic הוה, *hāwāh,* "to be," better "to become," in Bib. Heb *hāyāh;* this archaic use of *w* for *y* appears also in derivatives of the similar חָיָה, *ḥāyāh,* "to live," e.g. *ḥawwāh* in Gen **3** 20. (4) It is evident from the interpretative passages (Ex **3**; **6**) that the *form* is the fut. of the simple stem (Ḳal) and not fut. of the causative (Hiph'īl) stem in the sense "giver of life"—an idea not borne out by any of the occurrences of the word. The fanciful theory that the word is a combination of the fut., pres. and perfect tenses of the vb., signifying "the One who will be, is, and was," is not to be taken seriously (Stier, etc, in Oehler's *OT Theol.*, in loc.). (5) The *meaning* may with some confidence be inferred from Origen's transliteration, *Iaō,* the form in Sam, *Iabe,* the form as combined in OT names, and the evident signification in Ex **3** and other passages, to be that of the simple fut., יַהְוֶה, *yahweh,* "he will be." It does not express causation, nor *existence* in a metaphysical sense, but the covenant promise of the Divine presence, both at the immediate time and in the Messianic age of the future. And thus it became bound up with the Messianic hope, as in the phrase, "the Day of Jehovah," and consequently both it and the LXX tr *Kurios* were applied by the NT as titles of Christ. (6) It is the *personal* name of God, as distinguished from such generic or essential names as *'Ēl, 'Ĕlōhīm, Shadday,* etc. Characteristic of the OT is its insistence on the possible knowledge of God as a person; and Jehovah is His name as a person. It is illogical, certainly, that the later Hebrews should have shrunk from its pronunciation, in view of the appropriateness of the name and of the OT insistence on the personality of God, who as a person has this name. ARV quite correctly adopts the transliteration "Jehovah" to emphasize its significance and purpose as a personal name of God revealed.

5. "Jehovah"

Five t in the "Song" of Moses (Dt **32** 4.15.18. 30.31) the word צוּר, *çūr,* "Rock," is used as a title of God. It occurs also in the Pss, Isa and poetical passages of other books, and also in proper names, Elizur, Zuriel, etc. Once in AV (Isa **44** 8) it is tr^d "God," but "Rock" in ARV and ARVm. The effort to interpret this title as indicating the animistic origin of OT religion is unnecessary and a pure product of the imagination. It is customary for both OT and NT writers to use descriptive names of God: "rock," "fortress," "shield," "light," "bread," etc, and is in harmony with all the rich figurativeness of the Scriptures; the use of the article in many of the cases cited further corroborates the view that the word is intended to be a descriptive title, not the name of a Nature-deity. It presents the idea of God as stedfast: "The appellation of God as *çūr,* 'rock,' 'safe retreat,' in Dt refers to this" (Oehler, *OT Theol.*). It often occurs, in a most striking figure, with the pers. suffix as "my rock," "their rock," to express confidence (Ps **28** 1).

6. "Rock" (Çūr)

The name (קָדוֹשׁ, *ḳādhōsh,* "holy") is found frequently in Isa and Pss, and occasionally in the other prophets. It is characteristic of Isa, being found 32 t in that book. It occurs often in the phrase קְדוֹשׁ יִשְׂרָאֵל, *ḳ^edhōsh yisrā'ēl,* "Holy One of Israel." The derivation and meaning remain in doubt, but the customary and most probable derivation is from *ḳādhash,* "to be separate," which best explains its use both of man and of the Deity. When used of God it signifies: (1) His transcendence, His separateness above all other beings, His aloneness as compared to other gods; (2) His peculiar relation to His people Israel unto whom He separated Himself, as He did not unto other nations. In the former sense Isaiah used it of His sole deity (**40** 25), in the latter of His peculiar and unchanging covenant-relation to Israel (**43** 3; **48** 17), strikingly expressed in the phrase "Holy One of Israel." *Ḳādhōsh* was rather attributive than personal, but became personal in the use of such absolute theists as Job and Isaiah. It expresses essential Deity, rather than personal revelation.

7. Kādhōsh, "Holy One"

In the patriarchal lit., and in Job particularly, where it is put into the mouths of the patriarchs, this name appears sometimes in the compound אֵל שַׁדַּי, *'ēl shadday,* sometimes alone. While its root meaning also is uncertain, the suggested derivation from שָׁדַד, *shādhadh,* "to destroy," "to terrify,"

8. Shadday, "Almighty"

seems most probable, signifying the God who is manifested by the terribleness of His mighty acts. "The Storm God," from שָׁדָא, *shādhā'*, "to pour out," has been suggested, but is improbable; and even more so the fanciful שֶׁ, *she*, and דַּי, *day*, meaning "who is sufficient." Its use in patriarchal days marks an advance over looser Sem conceptions to the stricter monotheistic idea of almightiness, and is in accord with the early consciousness of Deity in race or individual as a God of awe, or even terror. Its monotheistic character is in harmony with its use in the Abrahamic times, and is further corroborated by its ‖ in LXX and NT, παντοκράτωρ, *pantokrátōr*, "all-powerful."

III. Attributive, or Qualifying Names.—It is often difficult to distinguish between the personal and the attributive names of God, the two divisions necessarily shading into each other. Some of the preceding are really attributive, made personal by usage. The following are the most prominent descriptive or attributive names.

1. 'Ābhīr, "Mighty One"

This name (אֲבִיר, *'ābhīr*), trd in EV "Mighty One," is always combined with Israel or Jacob; its root is אָבַר, *'ābhar*, "to be strong," from which is derived the word אֵבֶר, *'ēbher*, "pinion," used of the strong wing of the eagle (Isa **40** 31), fig. of God in Dt **32** 11. It occurs in Jacob's blessing (Gen **49** 24), in a prayer for the sanctuary (Ps **132** 2.5), and in Isa (**1** 24; **49** 26; **60** 16), to express the assurance of the Divine strength in behalf of the oppressed in Israel (Isa **1** 24), or in behalf of Israel against his oppressors; it is interesting to note that this name was first used by Jacob himself.

2. 'Ēl-'Ĕlōhē-Israel

The name *'Ēl* is combined with a number of descriptive adjs. to represent God in His various attributes; and these by usage have become names or titles of God. For the remarkable phrase 'Ēl-'Ĕlōhē-Israel (Gen **33** 20), see separate art.

3. 'Elyōn, "Most High"

This name (עֶלְיוֹן, *'elyōn*, "highest") is a derivative of עָלָה, *'ālāh*, "to go up." It is used of persons or things to indicate their elevation or exaltation: of Israel, favored above other nations (Dt **26** 19), of the aqueduct of "the upper pool" (Isa **7** 3), etc. This indicates that its meaning when applied to God is the "Exalted One," who is lifted far above all gods and men. It occurs alone (Dt **32** 8; Ps **18** 13), or in combination with other names of God, most frequently with El (Gen **14** 18; Ps **78** 35), but also with Jeh (Ps **7** 17; **97** 9), or with Elohim (Ps **56** 2 AV; **78** 56). Its early use (Gen **14** 18 f) points to a high conception of Deity, an unquestioned monotheism in the beginnings of Heb history.

4. Gibbōr, "Mighty [One]"

The ancient Hebrews were in constant struggle for their land and their liberties, a struggle most intense and patriotic in the heroic days of Saul and David, and in which there was developed a band of men whose great deeds entitled them to the honorable title "mighty men" of valor (גִּבּוֹרִים, *gibbōrīm*). These were the knights of David's "Round Table." In like manner the Hebrew thought of his God as fighting for him, and easily then this title was applied to God as the Mighty Man of war, occurring in David's psalm of the Ark's Triumphant Entry (Ps **24** 8), in the allegory of the Messiah-King (**45** 3), either alone or combined with El (Isa **9** 6; Jer **32** 18), and sometimes with Jeh (Isa **42** 13).

5. 'Ēl-Rō'ī

When Hagar was fleeing from Sarah's persecutions, Jeh spoke to her in the wilderness of Shur, words of promise and cheer. Whereupon "she called the name of Jeh that spake unto her, Thou art El roi" (Gen **16** 13 m). In the text the word רֳאִי, *rō'ī*, deriv. of *rā'āh*, "to see," is trd "that seeth," lit. "of sight." This is the only occurrence of this title in the OT.

6. Çaddīḳ, "Righteous"

One of the covenant attributes of God, His righteousness, is spoken of so often that it passes from adj. to subst., from attribute to name, and He is called "Righteous" (צַדִּיק, *çaddīḳ*), or "the Righteous One." The word is never transliterated but always trd in EV, although it might just as properly be considered a Divine name as 'Elyōn or Ḳādhōsh. The root צָדַק, *çādhaḳ*, "to be straight" or "right," signifies fidelity to a standard, and is used of God's fidelity to His own nature and to His covenant-promise (Isa **41** 10; **42** 6; cf Hos **2** 19); it occurs alone (Ps **34** 17), with El (Dt **32** 4), with Elohim (Ezr **9** 15; Ps **7** 9; **116** 5), but most frequently with Jeh (Ps **129** 4, etc). In Ex **9** 27 Pharaoh, in acknowledging his sin against Jeh, calls Him 'Jeh the Righteous,' using the article. The suggestive combination, "Jeh our Righteousness," is the name given to David's "righteous Branch" (Jer **23** 6) and properly should be taken as a proper noun—the name of the Messiah-King.

7. Ḳannā, "Jealous"

Frequently in the Pent, oftenest in the 3 VSS of the Commandments (Ex **20** 5; **34** 14; Dt **5** 9), God is given the title "Jealous" (קַנָּא, *ḳannā'*), most specifically in the phrase "Jeh, whose name is Jealous" (Ex **34** 14). This word, however, did not bear the evil meaning now associated with it in our usage, but rather signified "righteous zeal," Jeh's zeal for His own name or glory (cf Isa **9** 7, "the zeal of Jeh," קִנְאָה, *ḳin'āh;* also Zec **1** 14; **8** 2).

8. Çebha'oth, "Lord of Hosts"

Connected with the personal and covenant name Jeh, there is found frequently the word Sabaoth (צְבָאוֹת, *çebhā'ōth*, "hosts"). Invariably in the OT it is trd "hosts" (Isa **1** 9; Ps **46** 7.11, etc), but in the NT it is transliterated twice, both in the Gr and Eng. (Rom **9** 29; Jas **5** 4). The passage in Rom is a quotation from Isa **1** 9 through LXX, which does not translate, but transliterates the Heb. Origin and meaning are uncertain. It is used of heavenly bodies and earthly forces (Gen **2** 1); of the army of Israel (2 S **8** 16); of the Heavenly beings (Ps **103** 21; **148** 2; Dnl **4** 35). It is probable that the title is intended to include *all* created agencies and beings, of which Jeh is maker and leader.

9. "I am That I am"

When God appeared to Moses at Sinai, commissioning him to deliver Israel; Moses, being well aware of the difficulty of impressing the people, asked by what name of God he should speak to them: "They shall say to me, What is his name?" Then "God said unto Moses, I AM THAT I AM . . . . say . . . . I AM hath sent me unto you" (Ex **3** 14). The name of the Deity given here is similar to Jeh (*yahweh*) except that the form is not 3d pers. fut., as in the usual form, but the 1st pers. (*'ehyeh*), since God is here speaking of Himself. The optional reading in ARVm is much to be preferred: "I WILL BE THAT I WILL BE," indicating His covenant pledge to be with and for Israel in all the ages to follow. For further explanation see above, II, 5.

IV. NT Names of God.—The variety of names which characterizes the OT is lacking in the NT, where we are all but limited to two names, each of which corresponds to several in the OT. The most frequent is the name "God" (Θεός, *Theós*) occurring over 1,000 t, and corresponding to El, Elohim, etc, of the OT. It may, as Elohim, be used by accommodation of heathen gods; but in its true sense it expresses essential Deity, and as expressive of such it is applied to Christ as to the Father (Jn **20** 28; Rom **9** 5).

1. Theos, "God"

Five t "Lord" is a tr of δεσπότης, *despótēs* (Lk **2** 29; Acts **4** 24; 2 Pet **2** 1 AV; Jude ver 4; Rev **6** 10 AV). In each case there is evident emphasis on sovereignty and correspondence to the 'Ādhōn of the OT. The most common Gr word for Lord is Κύριος, *Kúrios*, representing both Jeh and 'Adhonai of the OT, and occurring upwards of 600 t. Its use for Jeh was in the spirit of both the Heb scribes, who pointed the consonants of the covenant name with the vowels of Adhonay, the title of dominion, and of the LXX, which rendered this combination as *Kurios*. Consequently quotations from the OT in which Jeh occurs are rendered by *Kurios*. It is applied to Christ equally with the Father and the Spirit, showing that the Messianic hopes conveyed by the name Jeh were for NT writers fulfilled in Jesus Christ; and that in Him the long hoped-for appearance of Jeh was realized.

2. Kurios, "Lord"

As in the OT, so in the NT various attributive, descriptive or fig. names are found, often corresponding to those in the OT. Some of these are: The "Highest" or "Most High" (ὕψιστος, *húpsistos*), found in this sense only in Lk (**1** 32.35.76; **2** 14, etc), and equivalent to Elyon (see III, 3, above); "Almighty," Παντοκράτωρ, *Pantokrátōr* (2 Cor **6** 18; Rev **1** 8, etc), corresponding to Shadday (see II, 8 above; see also ALMIGHTY); "Father," as in the Lord's Prayer, and elsewhere (Mt **6** 9; **11** 25; Jn **17** 25; 2 Cor **6** 18); "King" (1 Tim **1** 17); "King of kings" (1 Tim **6** 15); "King of kings," "Lord of lords" (Rev **17** 14; **19** 16); "Potentate" (1 Tim **6** 15); "Master" (*kurios*, Eph **6** 9; 2 Pet **2** 1; Rev **6** 10); "Shepherd," "Bishop" (1 Pet **2** 25).

3. Descriptive and Figurative Names

LITERATURE.—*Theology of OT* by various authors: Oehler, Schultz, Davidson; Delitzsch, *Psychology of the OT;* H. P. Smith, "Theophorous Names of OT" in *OT and Sem Studies;* Gray, *HPN;* "God" in *HDB* and *EB*.

EDWARD MACK

GOD, SON (SONS) OF. See SONS OF GOD (OT); SONS OF GOD (NT).

GOD, THE FATHER. See FATHER, GOD THE.

GOD, THE UNKNOWN. See UNKNOWN.

GODDESS, god'es (אֱלֹהִים, *'ĕlōhīm*, θεά, *theá*): There is no separate word for "goddess" in the OT. In the only instance in which the word occurs in EV (1 K **11** 5.33), the gender is determined by the noun—"Ashtoreth, the god [goddess] of the Sidonians." In the NT the term is applied to Diana of Ephesus (Acts **19** 27.35.37).

GODHEAD, god'hed: The word "Godhead" is a simple doublet of the less frequently occurring "Godhood." Both forms stand side by side in the *Ancren Riwle* (about 1225 AD), and both have survived until today, though not in equally common use. They are representatives of a large class of abstract substs., formed with the suffix -head or -hood, most of which formerly occurred in both forms almost indifferently, though the majority of them survive only, or very preponderatingly (except in Scottish speech), in the form -hood. The two suffixes appear in Middle Eng. as *-hêde* and *-hôd*, and presuppose in the Anglo-Saxon which lies behind them a fem. *haêda* (which is not actually known) by the side of the masc. *hád*. The Anglo-Saxon word "was originally a distinct subst., meaning 'person, personality, sex, condition, quality, rank'" (Bradley, in *A New Eng. Dict. on a Historical Basis*, s.v. "-hood"), but its use as a suffix early superseded its separate employment. At first *-hêde* appears to have been appropriated to adjs., *-hôd* to substs.; but, this distinction breaking down and the forms coming into indiscriminate use, *-hêde* grew obsolete, and remains in common use only in one or two special forms, such as "Godhead," "maidenhead" (Bradley, as cited, s.v. "-head").

The general elimination of the forms in -head has been followed by a fading consciousness, in the case of the few surviving instances in this form, of the qualitative sense inherent in the suffix. The words accordingly show a tendency to become simple denotatives. Thus "the Godhead" is frequently employed merely as a somewhat strong synonym of "God," although usually with more or less emphasis upon that in God which makes Him God. One of its established usages is to denote the Divine essence as such, in distinction from the three "hypostases" or "persons" which share its common possession in the doctrine of the Trinity. This usage is old: Bradley (op. cit.) is able to adduce instances from the 13th cent. In this usage the word has long held the rank of a technical term, e.g. the Thirty-Nine Articles of the Church of England, 1571, Art. I: "And in the unitie of this Godhead, there be three persons" (cf the Irish Articles of 1615, and the Westminster Confession, II, 3); Westminster Shorter Catechism, Q. 6: "There are three persons in the Godhead." Pursuant to the fading of the qualitative sense of the word, there has arisen a tendency, when the qualitative consciousness is vivid, to revive the obsolescent "Godhood," to take its place; and this tendency naturally shows itself esp. when the contrast with humanity is expressed. Carlyle, for example (*French Revolution*, III, Book vi, ch iv, § 1), speaking of the posthumous reaction against Marat, writes: "Shorter godhood had no divine man"; and Phillips Brooks (*Sermons*, XIII, 237) speaks of Christ bridging the gulf "between the Godhood and the manhood." "Godhood" seems, indeed, always to have had a tendency to appear in such contrasts, as if the qualitative consciousness were more active in it than in "Godhead." Thus it seems formerly to have suggested itself almost as inevitably to designate the Divine nature of Christ, as "Godhead" did to designate the common Divine essence of the Trinity. Bradley cites instances from 1563 down.

The fundamental meaning of "Godhead" is, nevertheless, no less than that of "Godhood," the state, dignity, condition, quality, of a god, or, as monotheists would say, of God. As manhood is that which makes a man a man, and childhood that which makes a child a child, so Godhead is that which makes God, God. When we ascribe Godhead to a being, therefore, we affirm that all that enters into the idea of God belongs to Him. "Godhead" is thus the Saxon equivalent of the Lat "Divinity," or, as it is now becoming more usual to say, "Deity." Like these terms it is rendered concrete by prefixing the article to it. As "the Divinity," "the Deity," so also "the Godhead" is only another way of saying "God," except that when we say "the Divinity," "the Deity," "the Godhead," we are saying "God" more abstractly and more qualitatively, that is with more emphasis, or at least with a more lively consciousness, of the constitutive qualities which make God the kind of being we call "God."

The word "Godhead" occurs in AV only 3 t (Acts **17** 29; Rom **1** 20; Col **2** 9), and oddly enough it translates in these 3 passages, 3 different, though closely related, Gr words, *tó theion* (τὸ θεῖον), *theiótēs* (θειότης), *theótēs* (θεότης).

To theion means "that which is Divine," concretely, or, shortly, "the Deity." Among the Greeks it was in constant use in the sense of "the Divine Being," and particularly as a general term to designate the Deity apart from reference to a particular god. It is used by Paul (Acts **17** 29) in an address made to a heathen audience, and is inserted into a context in which it is flanked by the simple term "God" (*ho theós*, ὁ θεός) on both sides. It is obviously deliberately chosen in order to throw up into emphasis the qualitative idea of God; and this emphasis is still further heightened by the direct contrast into which it is brought with the term "man." "Being, then, the offspring of God, we ought not to think that it is to gold or silver or stone graven by art and device of *man* that the *Godhead* is like." In an effort to bring out this qualitative emphasis, RVm suggests that we might substitute for "the Godhead" here the periphrastic rendering, "that which is Divine." But this seems both clumsy and ineffective for its purpose. From the philological standpoint, "the Godhead" is a very fair equivalent for *to theion*, differing as it does from the simple "God" precisely by its qualitative emphasis. It may be doubted, however, whether in the partial loss by "Godhead" of its qualitative force in its current usage, one of its synonyms, "the Divinity" (which is the rendering here of the Rhemish version) or "the Deity," would not better convey Paul's emphasis to modern readers.

Neither of these terms, "Divinity," "Deity," occurs anywhere in AV, and "Deity" does not occur in RV either; but RV (following the Rhemish version) substitutes "Divinity" for "Godhead" in Rom **1** 20. Of the two, "Divinity" was originally of the broader connotation; in the days of heathendom it was applicable to all grades of Divine beings. "Deity" was introduced by the Christian Fathers for the express purpose of providing a stronger word by means of which the uniqueness of the Christians' God should be emphasized. Perhaps "Divinity" retains even in its Eng. usage something of its traditional weaker connotation, although, of course, in a monotheistic consciousness the two terms coalesce in meaning. There exists a tendency to insist, therefore, on the "Deity" of Christ, rather than his mere "Divinity," in the feeling that "Divinity" might lend itself to the notion that Christ possessed but a secondary or reduced grade of Divine quality. In Acts **17** 29 Paul is not discriminating between grades of Divinity, but is preaching monotheism. In this context, then, *to theion* does not lump together "all that is called God or is worshipped," and declare that all that is in any sense Divine should be esteemed beyond the power of material things worthily to represent. Paul has the idea of God at its height before his mind, and having quickened his hearers' sense of God's exaltation by his elevated description of Him, he demands of them whether this Deity can be fitly represented by any art of man working in dead stuff. He uses the term *to theion*, rather than *ho theos*, not merely in courteous adoption of his hearers' own language, but because of its qualitative emphasis. On the whole, the best Eng. tr of it would probably be "the Deity." "The Godhead" has ceased to be sufficiently qualitative: "the Godhood" is not sufficiently current: "the Divine" is not sufficiently personal: "the Divinity" is perhaps not sufficiently strong: "Deity" without the article loses too much of its personal reference to compensate for the gain in qualitativeness: "the Deity" alone seems fairly to reproduce the apostle's thought.

The Gr term in Rom **1** 20 is *theiotēs*, which again, as a term of quality, is not unfairly rendered by "Godhead." What Paul says here is that "the everlasting power and Godhead" of God "are clearly perceived by means of His works." By "Godhead" he clearly means the whole of that by which God is constituted what we mean by "God." By coupling the word with "power," Paul no doubt intimates that his mind is resting esp. upon those qualities which enter most intimately into and constitute the exaltation of God; but we must beware of limiting the connotation of the term—all of God's attributes are glorious. The context shows that the thought of the apostle was moving on much the same lines as in Acts **17** 29; here, too, the contrast which determines the emphasis is with "corruptible man," and along with him, with the lower creatures in general (ver 23). How could man think of the Godhead under such similitudes—the *Godhead*, so clearly manifested in its glory by its works! The substitution for "Godhead" here of its synonym "Divinity" by RV is doubtless due in part to a desire to give distinctive renderings to distinct terms, and in part to a wish to emphasize, more strongly than "Godhead" in its modern usage emphasizes, the qualitative implication which is so strong in *theiotēs*. Perhaps, however, the substitution is not altogether felicitous. "Divinity," in its contrast with "Deity," may have a certain weakness of connotation clinging to it, which would unsuit it to represent *theiotēs* here. It is quite true that the two terms, "Divinity" and "Deity," are the representatives in Lat Patristic writers respectively of the Gr *theiotēs* and *theotēs*. Augustine (*The City of God*, VII, **1**; cf X, 1) tells us that "Deity" was coined by Christian writers as a more accurate rendering of the Gr *theotēs* than the current "Divinity." But it does not follow that because "Deity" more accurately renders *theotēs*, therefore "Divinity" is always the best rendering of *theiotēs*. The stress laid by the Gr Fathers on the employment of *theotēs* to express the "Deity" of the Persons of the Trinity was in sequence to attempts which were being made to ascribe to the Son and the Spirit a reduced "Divinity"; and it was the need the Lat Fathers felt in the same interests which led them to coin "Deity" as a more accurate rendering, as they say, of *theotēs*. Meanwhile *theiotēs* and "Divinity" had done service in the two languages, the former as practically, and the latter as absolutely, the only term in use to express the idea of "Deity." *Theotēs* is very rare in classical Gr, "Deity" non-existent in classical Lat. To represent *theiotēs* uniformly by "Divinity," if any reduced connotation at all clings to "Divinity," would therefore be to represent it often very inadequately. And that is the case in the present passage. What Paul says is clearly made known by God's works, is His everlasting power and all the other everlasting attributes which form His Godhead and constitute His glory.

It is *theotēs* which occurs in Col **2** 9. Here Paul declares that "all the fulness of the Godhead" dwells in Christ "bodily." The phrase "fulness of the Godhead" is an esp. emphatic one. It means everything without exception which goes to make up the Godhead, the totality of all that enters into the conception of Godhood. All this, says Paul, dwells in Christ "bodily," that is after such a fashion as to be manifested in connection with a bodily organism. This is the distinction of Christ: in the Father and in the Spirit the whole plenitude of the Godhead dwells also, but not "bodily"; in them it is not manifested in connection with a bodily life. It is the incarnation which Paul has in mind; and he tells us that in the incarnate Son, the fulness of the Godhead dwells. The term chosen to express the Godhead here is the strongest and the most unambiguously decisive which the language affords.

Theiotēs may mean all that *theotēs* can mean; on monotheistic lips it does mean just what *theotēs* means; but *theotēs* must mean the utmost that either term can mean. The distinction is, not that *theotēs* refers to the essence and *theiotēs* to the attributes; we cannot separate the essence and the attributes. Where the essence is, there the attributes are; they are merely the determinants of the essence. And where the attributes are, there the essence is; it is merely the thing, of the kind of which they are the determinants. The distinction is that *theotēs* emphasizes that it is the highest stretch of Divinity which is in question, while *theiotēs* might possibly be taken as referring to Deity at a lower level. It it not merely such divinity as is shared by all the gods many and lords many of the heathen world, to which "heroes" might aspire, and "demons" attain, all the plenitude of which dwells in Christ as incarnate; but that Deity which is peculiar to the high gods, or, since Paul is writing out of a monotheistic consciousness, that Deity which is the Supreme God alone. All the fulness of supreme Deity dwells in Christ bodily. There is nothing in the God who is over all which is not in Christ. Probably no better rendering of this idea is afforded by our modern Eng. than the term "Godhead," in which the qualitative notion still lurks, though somewhat obscured behind the individualizing implication, and which in any event emphasizes precisely what Paul wishes here to assert—that all that enters into the conception of God, and makes God what we mean by the term "God," dwells in Christ, and is manifested in Him in connection with a bodily organism. BENJAMIN B. WARFIELD

GODLESS, god'les: This word is not found in the text of AV. It is found, however, in Apoc (2 Macc **7** 34, "O godless [RV "unholy"] man"). RV substitutes the word "godless" for the word "hypocrite" in the following passages: Job **8** 13; **13** 16; **15** 34; **17** 8; **20** 5; **27** 8; **34** 30; **36** 13; Prov **11** 9; Isa **33** 14. RV does not seem to be consistent in carrying out the idea of "godless" for "hypocrite," for in Isa **9** 17; **10** 6; Ps **35** 16 this same Heb word *ḥānēph* is tr[d] "profane." The principal idea lying at the root of the word is that of pollution and profanity; a condition of not merely being without God but assuming an attitude of open and blatant opposition toward God. The godless man is not merely the atheistic, unbelieving or even irreligious, but the openly impious, wicked and profane man. Indeed it can hardly be rightly claimed that the idea of hypocrisy is involved in the meaning of the word, for the "godless" man is not the one who professes one thing and lives another, but the one who openly avows not only his disbelief in, but his open opposition to, God. Doubtless the idea of pollution and defilement is also to be included in the definition of this word; see Jer **3** 9; Nu **35** 33; Dnl **11** 31. WILLIAM EVANS

GODLINESS, god'li-nes, **GODLY,** god'li (**εὐσέβεια,** *eusébeia,* **εὐσεβής, -ῶς,** *eusebḗs, -ōs*): In the OT the word rendered "godly" in Ps **4** 3; **32** 6 (חָסִיד, *ḥāṣīdh*) is lit. "kind," then "pious" (RVm renders it in the former passage, "one that he favoreth"). Sometimes in both the OT and the NT a periphrasis is employed, "of God," "according to God" (e.g. "godly sorrow," 2 Cor **7** 10). Godliness, as denoting character and conduct determined by the principle of love or fear of God in the heart, is the summing up of genuine religion. There can be no true religion without it: only a dead "form" (2 Tim **3** 5). The term is a favorite one in the Pastoral Epistles. The incarnation is "the mystery of godliness" (1 Tim **3** 16).

JAMES ORR

GODS (אֱלֹהִים, *'ĕlōhīm;* **θεοί,** *theoí*):

The Heb pl. *'ĕlōhīm* is generally known as the pl. of "majesty" and is the ordinary name for God. The meaning of the pl. seems to be "plenitude of powers." It denotes the fulness of those attributes of power which belonged to the Divine Being. Thus it is usually tr[d] in the sing., "God," when referring to the God of Israel. When reference is made to the gods of the other nations the word is tr[d] in the pl., "gods." The heathen nations usually had a plurality of gods. Among the Semites it was customary for one nation or tribe to have its own particular god. Often there were many tribes, or families, or communities, in one nation, each having a particular god. Thus even among Semites a nation may have many gods and be polytheistic. Among the other nations, Iranian, Hamitic, etc, there were always a number of deities, sometimes a multitude. There are many references to these in the OT. In a few cases where the pl. is used, the sing. would be better, e.g. Gen **3** 5 AV; Ex **32** 4.8.23; Ruth **1** 15 AV; Jgs **17** 5; **18** 24; 1 S **17** 43. This, however, might be disputed.

I. In the OT.—The following are the more important usages of the word in the OT: The tr of Ps **8** 5 is disputed. LXX and AV translate it "angels," RV and ARV, "God," with "angels" in the margin. The Epistle to the He has the word "angels." This seems to be more in keeping with the OT ideas of the relation between God, men and angels. Gen **1** 26 has the pl. "us," but it is not certain to whom it refers, most probably to the angels or mighty ones which surrounded the throne of God as servants or counsellors; cf Job **38** 7, and see SONS OF GOD. In Ps **97** 7 the expression "worship him, all ye gods," may possibly refer to the gods of the nations, but more probably to the angels or mighty ones.

1. Superhuman Beings Including God and Angels

Judges, rulers, are regarded "either as Divine representatives at sacred places, or as reflecting Divine majesty and power" (see *BDB,* s.v.). Ex **21** 6 might better be tr[d] as in the margin, "the judges." These were men appointed to represent God and adjudicate on important matters of law. LXX has "Criterion of God." In Ex **22** 8 the word is used in the same sense, and ver 9 would also be better tr[d] "the judges"; ver 28 likewise. See also 1 S **2** 25; Ps **82** 1.6, where the reference is to those who act as judges.

2. Judges, Rulers

(1) The ancestors of Israel "beyond the River" had their gods (Josh **24** 14 f). While there is no mention of idolatry before the Deluge, the ancestors and kindred of Abraham were idolaters. Ur of the Chaldees was the center for the worship of Sin, the Moon-god. Many others were worshipped in the various cities of Babylon. See BABYLONIA.

3. Gods of the Nations as Objects of Worship

(2) The gods of Laban and his family (Gen **31** 30.32; **35** 2.4) were household gods or *t^erāphīm,* and were stolen by Rachel and carried off in her flight with Jacob. See TERAPHIM.

(3) Gods of Egypt: For many centuries before the time of Abraham there had been numerous objects of worship in Egypt. Many of these were animals, birds and natural objects. Horus, the

hawk, was one of the earliest of all. The cat, the bull, etc, were worshipped at times. The plagues of Egypt were specially directed against these wretched deities (Nu **33** 4; Ex **12** 12). Jeh took vengeance on all the gods of Egypt. These terrible events showed that "Jeh is greater than all gods" (**18** 11). He redeemed His people from the nations and its gods (2 S **7** 23). Jeremiah predicted the time when Jeh should destroy the gods of Egypt (Jer **43** 12 f; **46** 25).

(4) Of the gods of the Amorites (Jgs **6** 10) no names are given, but they probably were the same as the gods of the Canaanites.

(5) The gods of the Canaanites were Nature-gods, and their worship was that of the productive and chiefly reproductive powers of Nature. Their service was perhaps the most immoral and degrading of all. The high places and altars of the different Baals, Ashtoreths, etc, were numerous throughout Canaan. These deities were always represented by images and Moses makes frequent reference to them with warnings against this seductive worship (Dt **7** 25; **12** 3.30.31; **13** 7; **20** 18; **29** 18; **32** 16, etc). See also IDOLATRY; BAAL; ASHTORETH; ASHERAH, etc.

(6) Gods of the Philis: The champion Goliath cursed David by his gods (1 S **17** 43). Perhaps it would be better rendered "god." Saul's and his son's armor was put into the house of their gods (1 Ch **10** 10). See also DAGON; BAALZEBUB.

(7) The two golden calves erected by Jeroboam at Dan and Bethel to keep the people from going to Jerus to worship are called gods (1 K **12** 28; 2 Ch **13** 8 f). See CALF, GOLDEN.

(8) The gods of Damascus: Ben-hadad was accustomed to worship in the house of the god Rimmon (2 K **5** 18). No other names are mentioned, but from 2 Ch **28** 23 it is clear that there were many gods in Syria. See RIMMON.

(9) Solomon's many wives worshipped their own gods, and he provided the means for their worship. Chief among these were Chemosh of Moab and Molech of Ammon (1 K **11** 2.4.8). See CHEMOSH; MOLECH.

(10) The mixed peoples transplanted into Samaria by Sargon had their various gods and mingled their service with that of Jeh, after being taught by a priest of Jeh. The names of some of these gods were Succoth-benoth, Nergal, Ashima, Nibhaz, Tartak, Adrammelech (2 K **17** 29.30.31.33). See separate articles.

(11) Of the gods of Seir, which were brought to Jerus by Amaziah, the names are not given (2 Ch **25** 14).

(12) The gods of the nations conquered by Sennacherib and his fathers, viz. Hamoth, Arpad, Sepharvaim, Hena, Ivvah (2 K **18** 33–35; **19** 13). Also those conquered by Sennacherib's fathers, Gozan, Haran, Rezeph, Eden or Telassar (2 K **19** 12; Isa **36** 18.19.20; 2 Ch **32** 13 f).

(13) Gods of Moab are mentioned in Ruth **1** 15; 1 K **11** 1.7. Possibly Ruth **1** 15 should be tr[d] "god." See CHEMOSH.

(14) Gods of Babylon: The graven images of her gods referred to in Isa **21** 9; **42** 17; Bel and Nebo mentioned in Isa **46** 1; other gods of silver and gold (Ezr **1** 7; Dnl **4** 8.9.18; **5** 4.11.14.23).

(15) Nineveh's gods are merely referred to in Nah **1** 14. Sennacherib was worshipping in the house of Nisroch his god when slain by his sons (2 K **19** 37).

(16) The coastlands or borders and peninsulas of the Aegean Sea had numerous idol gods, shrines and devotees. Isaiah challenges them to prove that they are gods (Isa **41** 22 f).

4. The Superiority of Jehovah to Other Gods

Jeh was "greater than all gods" (Ex **15** 11; **18** 11); "God of gods, and Lord of lords" (Dt **10** 14. 17); "The Mighty One" (Josh **22** 22); "to be feared above all gods" (1 Ch **16** 25; 2 Ch **2** 5; Ps **96** 4 f); "King above all gods" (Ps **95** 3; **97** 7.9; **86** 8; **135** 5; **136** 2; **138** 1; Jer **10** 11; Zeph **2** 11; Dnl **2** 18.47). Jeremiah advances so far toward a pure and well-defined monotheism that he speaks of all other gods as "not gods." They have no existence to him (Jer **2** 11; **5** 7; **16** 20). A similar position is taken in Isa **41, 43,** etc.

5. Regulations Regarding the Gods of the Nations

The laws of Moses give no uncertain sound concerning them. The Decalogue begins: "Thou shalt have no other gods before me." Whatever may be the exact meaning of this, it is perfectly clear that Israel was to have nothing to do with any God but Jeh (Ex **20** 3; Dt **5** 7). No images shall be made of them (Ex **20** 4.23; **34** 17; Lev **19** 4; Dt **5** 8 f). No mention shall be made of them (Ex **23** 13; Josh **23** 7). They are not to be worshipped but destroyed (Ex **23** 24). They are to make no covenant with the people or their gods would be a snare to them (Ex **23** 32; Dt **6** 14; **7** 4.25). A curse will follow any defection from Jeh to them (Dt **11** 28; **28** 14 ff; **12** 3.30; **13** 7; **20** 18; **29** 17). These gods are an abomination to Jeh (Dt **12** 31; **20** 18; **29** 17; **32** 37; Ezk **7** 20; 1 K **11** 5; 2 K **23** 13). They are to be as foreign gods to Israel (1 S **7** 3 f; Josh **24** 20.23; Jgs **10** 16; 2 Ch **14** 3; **33** 15).

6. Israel's Tendency to Go after Other Gods

The constant tendency of Israel to go after other gods was first made manifest at Sinai (Ex **32** 1.4.8. 23.31; **34** 15). Hosea says (**11** 2), "The more the prophets called them, the more they went from them." Ezekiel declares (**16** 3), "The Amorite was thy father, and thy mother was a Hittite," referring doubtless to the idolatrous taint in the blood of Israel. The tendency manifested itself also at Baal-peor where Israel was led into the licentious rites of the Moabites (Nu **25** 2 f). Moses saw the taint in the blood, foresaw the danger and repeatedly warned them (Dt **17** 3; **18** 20; **29** 26; **30** 17; **31** 18). Perhaps the most striking passages in Dt are chs **13, 28, 30,** where are pictured the consequences of going after other gods. Joshua also warns them (**23** 7), and the history of the period of the Judges is the story of their periodical defection from Jeh and the punishment resulting therefrom (Jgs **2** 12.17.19; **5** 8; **10** 6 f; 1 S **8** 8). Solomon himself gave an impetus in that direction (1 K **11** 5–8). After the disruption, the religion of the Northern Kingdom became very corrupt (1 K **14** 9; 2 Ch **13** 8 f). The golden calves of Jeroboam opened the door for an inrush of idols and other gods. Ahab's marriage to Jezebel threatened to wipe out Jeh-worship and substitute Baal-worship, and, but for the powerful ministry of Elijah and Elisha, might have effected such a result. Partly checked for a time, the evil broke out in other forms, and even the preaching of Amos and Hosea failed to turn the tide of idolatry. The result was the destruction of the kingdom (2 K **17** 7 ff; Jer **3** 6–8; 1 Ch **5** 25). The Southern Kingdom fared better. Other gods were countenanced by Rehoboam, Abijah, Athaliah, Jehoram, Ahaz, Amon, Manasseh, Jehoiakim, etc. Reform movements were attempted by Asa, Jehoshaphat, Hezekiah and Josiah, but did not wholly avail. In the reign of Manasseh the nation plunged into the worship of other gods. The ministries of Isaiah, Jeremiah, etc, availed not to stop the tide (2 Ch **34** 25; Jer **11** 13; **5** 19; 2 K **22** 17; Jer **1** 16; **19** 4; **7** 6; **13** 10; **16** 11; **44** 5.8). The nation was carried into exile because of its going after other gods (2 K **22** 17; Dt **29** 25 f). The captivity had its desired effect. The Israel that returned and perpetuated the nation never again lapsed into the worship of other gods.

II. In the Apocrypha.—The Apoc reiterates much of the OT teaching: the defection of Israel (2 Esd **1** 6); the gods of the nations (Jth **3** 8; **8** 18); the gods which their fathers worshipped (**5** 7 f); the sin of Israel (Ad Est **14** 7). The Book of Wisd refers to the "creatures which they supposed to be gods" (**12** 27; **13** 2.3.10; **15** 15). Mention is made of the gods of Babylon (Bar **1** 22; **6** 6–57 *passim;* Bel **1** 27).

III. In the NT.—The expression "gods" occurs in six places in the NT: (1) Jesus, in reply to the Pharisees, who questioned His right to call Himself the son of God, quoted Ps **82** 6: "I said, Ye are gods." He argues from this that if God Himself called them gods to whom the word of God came, i.e. the judges who acted as representatives of God in a judicial capacity, could not He who had been sanctified and sent into the world justly call Himself the Son of God? It was an *argumentum ad hominem* (Jn **10** 34–37). (2) When Paul and Barnabas preached the gospel in Lystra they healed a certain man who had been a cripple from birth. The Lycaonians, seeing the miracle, cried out in their own dialect, "The gods are come down to us in the likeness of men. And they called Barnabas, Jupiter; and Paul, Mercury" (Acts **14** 11 f). Their ascription of deity to the apostles in such times shows their familiarity with the Gr pantheon. (3) As Paul preached Jesus and the resurrection at Athens the people said he seemed to be a setter forth of strange gods. The conception of only one God seemed to be wholly foreign to them (Acts **17** 18). (4) In 1 Cor **8** 5 Paul speaks of "gods many, and lords many," but the context shows that he did not believe in the existence of any god but one; "We know that no idol is anything in the world." (5) While at Ephesus, Paul was said to have "persuaded and turned away much people, saying that they are no gods, that are made with hands" (Acts **19** 26). (6) The Galatians had been "in bondage to them that by nature are no gods" (Gal **4** 8). Indirect references are also found in Acts **17** 16, where Paul observed the city full of idols. Likewise in Rom **1** 22 f.25 ff. Paul refers to the numerous gods of the heathen world. These were idols, birds, four-footed beasts and creeping things. The results of this degrading worship are shown in the ver following. See also IDOLATRY; GOD, NAMES OF.

J. J. REEVE

GOD(S), STRANGE, strānj: The word "strange," as used in this connection in the OT, refers to the fact that the god or gods do not belong to Israel, but are the gods which are worshipped by other families or nations. In several cases a more exact tr would give us the "gods of the stranger" or foreigner. So in Gen **35** 2.4; Josh **24** 2; Jgs **10** 16; Dt **31** 16; **32** 12, etc. In a few passages like Dt **32** 16; Ps **44** 20; **81** 9; Isa **43** 12, the word is an adj., but the idea is the same: the gods are those which are worshipped by other peoples and hence are forbidden to Israel, which is under obligation to worship Yahweh alone (cf 2 Esd **1** 6).

In the NT the phrase occurs only once, in the account of Paul's experiences in Athens (Acts **17** 18), when some of his auditors said, "He seemeth to be a setter forth of strange gods" (ξένα δαιμόνια, *xéna daimónia*). Here the thought is clearly that by his preaching of Jesus he was regarded as introducing a new divinity, that is one who was strange or foreign to the Athenians and of whom they had never heard before. Like the Romans of this period the Athenians were doubtless interested in, and more or less favorable to, the numerous new cults which were coming to their attention as the result of the constant intercourse with the Orient. See preceding article.

WALTER R. BETTERIDGE

GODSPEED, god'spēd (χαίρω, *chaírō*): "Godspeed" occurs only in 2 Jn vs 10.11 AV as the tr of *chaírein*, the infin. of *chairō*, and is rendered in RV "greeting." It means "rejoice," "be of good cheer," "be it well with thee"; *chaíre, chaírete, chaírein*, were common forms of greeting, expressive of good-will and desire for the person's prosperity, tr[d] in the Gospels, "Hail!" "All Hail!" (Mt **26** 49; **27** 29; **28** 9, etc); *chaírein* is the LXX for *shālōm* (Isa **48** 22; **57** 21; cf 2 Macc **1** 10). "Godspeed" first appears in Tindale's version; Wyclif had "heil!" Rheims, "God save you."

In the passage cited Christians are forbidden thus to salute false teachers who might come to them. The injunction does not imply any breach of charity, since it would not be right to wish anyone success in advocating what was believed to be false and harmful. We should be sincere in our greetings; formal courtesy must yield to truth, still courteously, however, and in the spirit of love.

W. L. WALKER

GOEL, gō'el (גֹּאֵל, *gō'ēl*, "redeemer"): Goel is the participle of the Heb word *gā'al* ("to deliver," "to redeem") which aside from its common usage is frequently employed in connection with Heb law, where it is the technical term applied to a person who as the nearest relative of another is placed under certain obligations to him. (1) If a Jew because of poverty had been obliged to sell himself to a wealthy "stranger or sojourner," it became the duty of his relatives to redeem him. Cf Lev **25** 47 ff and the art. JUBILEE. (2) The same duty fell upon the nearest kinsman, if his brother, being poor, had been forced to sell some of his property. Cf Lev **25** 23 ff; Ruth **4** 4 ff, and the art. JUBILEE. (3) It also devolved upon the nearest relative to marry the childless widow of his brother (Ruth **3** 13; Tob **3** 17). (4) In Nu **5** 5 ff a law is stated which demands that restitution be made to the nearest relative, and after him to the priest, if the injured party has died (Lev **6** 1 ff). (5) The law of blood-revenge (*Blut-Rache*) made it the sacred duty of the nearest relative to avenge the blood of his kinsman. He was called the *gō'ēl ha-dām* (גֹּאֵל הַדָּם), "the avenger of blood." This law was based upon the command given in Gen **9** 5 f: "Whoso sheddeth man's blood, by man shall his blood be shed," and was carried out even if an animal had killed a man; in this case, however, the payment of a ransom was permitted (Ex **21** 28 ff). A clear distinction was made between an accidental and a deliberate murder. In both cases the murderer could find refuge at the altar of the sanctuary; if, however, the investigation revealed presumptuous manslaughter, he was taken from the altar to be put to death (Ex **21** 12 ff; **1** K **1** 50; **2** 28). In Nu **35** 9 ff definite regulations as to the duties of the Goel are given. Six cities were to be appointed as "cities of refuge," three on each side of the Jordan. The congregation has judgment over the murderer. There must be more than one witness to convict a man. If he is found guilty, he is delivered to the Goel; if murder was committed by accident he is permitted to live within the border of the city of refuge; in case the manslayer leaves this city before the death of the high priest, the avenger of blood has a right to slay him. After the death of the high priest the murderer may return to his own city. Ransom cannot be given for the life of a murderer; no expiation can be made for a murder but by the blood of the murderer (Dt **19** 4 ff; Josh **20**; 2 S **14** 6 ff). According to the law the children of a murderer could not be held responsible for the crime of their father (Dt **24** 16; 2 K **14** 6), but see 2 S **21** 1 ff. The order in which the nearest relative was considered the Goel is given in Lev **25** 48 f: first a brother, then an uncle or an uncle's son, and after them any other near relative. This order was observed in connection with (1) above, but probably also in the other cases except (4).

For the **figurative** use of Goel ("redeemer") see Ps **119** 154; Prov **23** 11; Job **19** 25; Isa **41** **14b**. See also AVENGE; MURDER; REFUGE, CITIES OF.

ARTHUR L. BRESLICH

GOG, gog (גּוֹג, *gōgh;* **Γούγ,** *Goúg*):

(1) A son of Joel, and descendant of the tribe of Reuben (1 Ch **5** 4).

(2) The prince of Rosh, Meshech and Tubal (Ezk **38** 2 f; **39** 1–16). His territory was known as the land of Magog, and he was the chief of those northern hordes who were to make a final onslaught upon Israel while enjoying the blessings of the Messianic age. He has been identified with Gagi, ruler of Sakhi, mentioned by Asshurbanipal, but Professor Sayce thinks the Heb name corresponds more closely to Gyges, the Lydian king, the Gugu of the cuneiform inscriptions. According to Ezekiel's account Gog's army included in its numbers Persia, Cush, Put, Gomer or the Cimmerians, and Togarmah, from the extreme N. They are represented as a vast mixed horde from the far-off parts of the N., the limits of the horizon, completely armed and equipped for war. They were to come upon the mountains of Israel and cover the land like a cloud. Their purpose is plunder, for the people of Israel are rich and dwell in towns and villages without walls. His coming, which had been prophesied by the seers of Israel, shall be accompanied by a theophany and great convulsions in Nature. A panic shall seize the hosts of Gog, rain, hailstones, pestilence, fire and brimstone shall consume them. Their bodies shall be food for the birds, their weapons shall serve as firewood for seven years and their bones shall be buried E. of the Jordan in Hamon-gog and thus not defile the holy land. The fulfilment of this strange prophecy can never be literal. In general it seems to refer to the last and desperate attempts of a dying heathenism to overturn the true religion of Jeh, or make capital out of it, profiting by its great advantages.

(3) In Rev **20** 7 Satan is let loose and goes to the four corners of the earth, Gog and Magog, to muster his hosts for the final struggle against God. In Ezk the invasion of Gog occurs during the Messianic age, while in Rev it occurs just at the close of the millennium. In Ezk Gog and Magog are gathered by Jeh for their destruction; in Rev they are gathered by Satan. In both cases the number is vast, the destruction is by supernatural means, and is complete and final. See MAGOG.

J. J. REEVE

GOIIM, gōi'yim (גּוֹיִם, *gōyim*): This word, rendered in AV "nations," "heathen," "Gentiles," is commonly tr[d] simply "nations" in RV. In Gen **14** 1 where AV has "Tidal, king of nations," RV retains in the text the Heb "Goiim" as a proper name. Some identify with Gutium. The Heb word is similarly retained in Josh **12** 23.

GOING, gō'ing, **GOINGS,** gō'ingz: Besides, occasionally, forms of the common words for "go" (see GO), for "going" and "goings," the Heb has אַשֻּׁר, *'ashshur* (*'ăshūr, 'āshūr*), "step," מוֹצָא, *mōçā'*, תּוֹצָאוֹת, *tōçā'ōth*, "goings out," "outgoings." The word "goings" is sometimes used lit., as in Nu **33** 2, "Moses wrote their goings out" (Heb *mōçā'*). "Going up," *ma'ăleh*, is in many passages rendered in RV (as in Nu **34** 4; 2 S **15** 30 AV) "ascent," as e.g. Josh **15** 7; Jgs **1** 36; Neh **12** 37 (ARV only). In Ezk **44** 5, ARV substitutes "egress" (way out or place of exit) for "going forth." "The goings out [place of exit; hence, boundary] of it" (Nu **34** 4.5.9.12 AV) occurs frequently. The verbal forms *bō'*, *mābhō'*, also *mē'āl* (Dnl **6** 14), are used of the sunset, "the going down of the sun." Thus Josh **8** 29 RV, AV "as soon as the sun was down."

In the NT, RV substitutes "going out" for "gone out" (*sbénnumi*) (Mt **25** 8); "going up" for "ascending" (Lk **19** 28); "going in" for "coming in" (Acts **9** 28); "going about" for "wandering" (1 Tim **5** 13); "seeking" for "going about" (Rom **10** 3).

Metaphorically: "Goings" is used for a man's ways or conduct (Ps **17** 5, RV "steps"; **40** 2; Prov **14** 15, etc). In Ps **17** 5 "Hold up my goings in thy paths, that my footsteps slip not" becomes in RV "My steps have held fast to thy paths, my feet have not slipped"; Prov **5** 21, "He pondereth all his goings," is in RV "He maketh level all his paths," m "weigheth carefully"; conversely, in Ps **37** 23, RV has "goings" for "steps"; in Jas **1** 11 "goings" for "ways." In the important prophetic passage, Mic **5** 2, it is said of the Ruler from Bethlehem, "whose goings forth have been from of old, from everlasting," RV "are from of old, from everlasting," m "from ancient days." Of God it is said in Hab **3** 6 "His ways are everlasting," RV "His goings were as of old," m "His ways are everlasting."

W. L. WALKER

GOLAN, gō'lan (גּוֹלָן, *gōlān*), **GAULONITIS** (**Γαυλανῖτις,** *Gaulanítis*): Golan was a city in the territory allotted to Manasseh in Bashan, the most northerly of the three cities of refuge E. of the Jordan (Dt **4** 43; Josh **20** 8); assigned with its "suburbs" to the Gershonite Levites (Josh **21** 27; 1 Ch **6** 71). It must have been a great and important city in its day; but the site cannot now be determined with any certainty. It was known to Jos (*Ant*, XIII, xv, 3). Near Golan Alexander was ambushed by Obodas, king of the Arabians; and his army, crowded together in a narrow and deep valley, was broken in pieces by the multitude of camels (*BJ*, I, iv, 4). This incident is located at Gadara in *Ant*, XIII, xiii, 5. Later, Golan was destroyed by Alexander. It had already given its name to a large district, Gaulonitis (*BJ*, III, iii, 1, 5; IV, i, 1). It formed the eastern boundary of Galilee. It was part of the tetrarchy of Philip (*Ant*, XVII, viii, 1; XVIII, iv, 6). The city was known to Eusebius as "a large village," giving its name to the surrounding country (*Onom*, s.v. Γαυλών, *Gaulōn*). This country must have corresponded roughly with the modern *Jaulān*, in which the ancient name is preserved. The boundaries of the province today are Mt. Hermon on the N., Jordan and the Sea of Galilee on the W., *Wādy Yarmūk* on the S., and *Nahr 'Allān* on the E. This plateau, which in the N. is about 3,000 ft. high, slopes gradually southward to a height of about 1,000 ft. It is entirely volcanic, and there are many cone-like peaks of extinct volcanoes, esp. toward the N. It affords good pasturage, and has long been a favorite summer grazing-ground of the nomads. Traces of ancient forests remain, but for the most part today it is treeless. To the E. of the Sea of Galilee the soil is deep and rich. Splendid crops of wheat are grown here, and olives flourish in the hollows. The country is furrowed by deep valleys that carry the water southwestward into the Sea of Galilee. This region has not yet been subjected to thorough examination, but many important ruins have been found, which tell of a plentiful and prosperous population in times long past. The best description of these, and of the region generally, will be found in Schumacher's *The Jaulān*, and *Across the Jordan*. To him also we owe the excellent maps which carry us eastward to the province of *el-Ḥaurān*.

Schumacher inclines to the belief that the ancient Golan may be represented by *Sahm el-Jaulān*, a large village fully 4 miles E. of *Nahr 'Allān*, and 4 miles S.E. of *Tsīl*. The extensive ruins probably date from early in the Christian era. The buildings are of stone, many of them of spacious dimensions, while the streets are wide and straight. The inhabitants number not more than 280. The surrounding soil is rich and well watered, bearing excellent crops. The present writer, after personal examination, corroborates Dr. Schumacher's description. Standing in the open country, it would be seen from afar; and it was easily accessible from all directions.

W. EWING

GOLD, gōld (זָהָב, *zāhābh;* χρυσός, *chrusós*): No metal has been more frequently mentioned in OT writings than gold, and none has had more terms applied to it. Among these terms the one most used is *zāhābh*. The Arab. equivalent, *dhahab*, is still the common name for gold throughout Pal, Syria and Egypt. With *zāhābh* frequently occur other words which, tr^d^, mean "pure" (Ex **25** 11), "refined" (1 Ch **28** 18), "finest" (1 K **10** 18), "beaten" (1 K **10** 17), "Ophir" (Ps **45** 9).

1. Terms

Other terms occurring are: פָּז, *pāz*, "fine gold" (Job **28** 17; Ps **19** 10; **21** 3; **119** 127; Prov **8** 19; Cant **5** 11.15; Isa **13** 12; Lam **4** 2); חָרוּץ, *ḥārūç* (Ps **68** 13; Prov **3** 14; **8** 10.19; **16** 16; Zec **9** 3); כֶּתֶם, *kethem*, lit. "carved out" (Job **28** 16.19; **31** 24; Prov **25** 12; Lam **4** 1; Dnl **10** 5); סָגוּר, *ṣeghōr* (1 K **6** 20; **7** 50; Job **28** 15); בֶּצֶר, *beçer* (in AV only: Job **22** 24; RV "treasure").

2. Sources

Sources definitely mentioned in the OT are: Havilah (Gen **2** 11.12); Ophir (1 K **9** 28; **10** 11; **22** 48; 1 Ch **29** 4; 2 Ch **8** 18; **9** 10; Job **22** 24; **28** 16; Ps **45** 9; Isa **13** 12); Sheba (1 K **10** 2.10; 2 Ch **9** 1.9; Ps **72** 15; Isa **60** 6; Ezk **27** 22; **38** 13); Arabia (2 Ch **9** 14). We are not justified in locating any of these places too definitely. They probably all refer to some region of Arabia.

The late origin of the geological formation of Pal and Syria precludes the possibility of gold being found in any quantities (see METALS), so that the large quantities of gold used by the children of Israel in constructing their holy places was not the product of mines in the country, but was from the spoil taken from the inhabitants of the land (Nu **31** 52), or brought with them from Egypt (Ex **3** 22). This gold was probably mined in Egypt or India (possibly Arabia), and brought by the great caravan routes through Arabia to Syria, or by sea in the ships of Tyre (1 K **10** 11.22; Ezk **27** 21. 22). There is no doubt about the Egyp sources. The old workings in the gold-bearing veins of the Egyp desert and the ruins of the buildings connected with the mining and refining of the precious metal still remain. This region is being reopened with the prospect of its becoming a source of part of the world's supply. It might be inferred from the extensive spoils in gold taken from the Midianites (£100,000 *HDB*, s.v.) that their country (Northwestern Arabia) produced gold. It is more likely that the Midianites had, in turn, captured most of it from other weaker nations. The tradition that Northwestern Arabia is rich in gold still persists. Every year Moslem pilgrims, returning from Mecca by the Damascus route, bring with them specimens of what is supposed to be gold ore. They secure it from the Arabs at the stopping-places along the route. Samples analyzed by the writer have been iron pyrites only. No gold-bearing rock has yet appeared. Whether these specimens come from the mines mentioned by Burton (*The Land of Midian Revisited*) is a question.

3. Forms

Gold formed a part of every household treasure (Gen **13** 2; **24** 35; Dt **8** 13; **17** 17; Josh **22** 8; Ezk **28** 4). It was probably treasured (*a*) in the form of nuggets (Job **28** 6 RVm), (*b*) in regularly or irregularly shaped slabs or bars (Nu **7** 14.20.84.86; Josh **7** 21.24; 2 K **5** 5), and (*c*) in the form of dust (Job **28** 6). A specimen of yellow dust, which the owner claimed to have taken from an ancient jar, unearthed in the vicinity of the Hauran, was once brought to the writer's laboratory. On examination it was found to contain iron pyrites and metallic gold in finely divided state. It was probably part of an ancient household treasure. A common practice was to make gold into jewelry with the dual purpose of ornamentation and of treasuring it. This custom still prevails, esp. among the Moslems, who do not let out their money at interest. A poor woman will save her small coins until she has enough to buy a gold bracelet. This she will wear or put away against the day of need (cf Gen **24** 22.53). It was weight and not beauty which was noted in the jewels (Ex **3** 22; **11** 2; **12** 35). Gold coinage was unknown in the early OT times.

4. Uses

(1) The use of gold as the most convenient way of treasuring wealth is mentioned above. (2) Jewelry took many forms: armlets (Nu **31** 50), bracelets (Gen **24** 22), chains (Gen **41** 42), crescents (Jgs **8** 26), crowns (2 S **12** 30; 1 Ch **20** 2), earrings (Ex **32** 2.3; Nu **31** 50; Jgs **8** 24.26), rings (Gen **24** 22; **41** 42; Jas **2** 2). (3) Making and decorating objects in connection with places of worship: In the description of the building of the ark and the tabernacle in Ex **25** ff, we read of the lavish use of gold in overlaying wood and metals, and in shaping candlesticks, dishes, spoons, flagons, bowls, snuffers, curtain clasps, hooks, etc (one estimate of the value of gold used is £90,000; see *HDB*). In 1 K **6** ff; 1 Ch **28** f; 2 Ch **1** ff are records of still more extensive use of gold in building the temple. (4) Idols were made of gold (Ex **20** 23; **32** 4; Dt **7** 25; **29** 17; 1 K **12** 28; Ps **115** 4; **135** 15; Isa **30** 22; Rev **9** 20). (5) Gold was used for lavish display. Among the fabulous luxuries of Solomon's court were his gold drinking-vessels (1 K **10** 21), a throne of ivory overlaid with gold (1 K **10** 18), and golden chariot trimmings (1 Ch **28** 18). Sacred treasure saved from votive offerings or portions dedicated from booty were principally gold (Ex **25** 36; Nu **7** 14.20.84.86; **31** 50.52.54; Josh **6** 19.24; 1 S **6** 8.11.15; 2 S **8** 11; 1 Ch **18** 7.10.11; **22** 14. 16; Mt **23** 17). This treasure was the spoil most sought after by the enemy. It was paid to them as tribute (1 K **15** 15; 2 K **12** 18; **14** 14; **16** 8; **18** 14–16; **23** 33.35), or taken as plunder (2 K **24** 13; **25** 15).

5. Figurative

Gold is used to symbolize earthly riches (Job **3** 15; **22** 24; Isa **2** 7; Mt **10** 9; Acts **3** 6; **20** 33; Rev **18** 12). Finer than gold, which, physically speaking, is considered nonperishable, typifies incorruptibility (Acts **17** 29; 1 Pet **1** 7.18; **3** 3; Jas **5** 3). Refining of gold is a figure for great purity or a test of stedfastness (Job **23** 10; Prov **17** 3; Isa **1** 25; Mal **3** 2; 1 Pet **1** 7; Rev **3** 18). Gold was the most valuable of metals. It stood for anything of great value (Prov **3** 14; **8** 10.19; **16** 16. 22; **25** 12), hence was most worthy for use in worshipping Jeh (Ex **25** ff; Rev **1** 12.13.20, etc), and the adornment of angels (Rev **15** 6) or saints (Ps **45** 13). The head was called golden as being the most precious part of the body (Cant **5** 11; Dnl **2** 38; cf "the golden bowl," Eccl **12** 6). "The golden city" meant Babylon (Isa **14** 4), as did also "the golden cup," sensuality (Jer **51** 7). A crown of gold was synonymous with royal honor (Est **2** 17; **6** 8; Job **19** 9; Rev **4** 4; **14** 14). Wearing of gold typified lavish adornment and worldly luxury (Jer **4** 30; **10** 4; 1 Tim **2** 9; 1 Pet **3** 3; Rev **17** 4). Comparing men to gold suggested their nobility (Lam **4** 1.2; 2 Tim **2** 20).

JAMES A. PATCH

GOLDEN, gōld″n, **CALF:** Probably a representation of the sun in *Taurus.* See Astrology, 7; Calf, Golden.

GOLDEN, gōld″n, **CITY:** The tr "golden city" (Isa **14** 4) is an attempt to render the received text (מַדְהֵבָה, *madhhēbhāh*), but can hardly be justified. Almost all the ancient VSS read מַרְהֵבָה (*marhēbhāh*), a word which connotes unrest and insolence, fitting the context well.

GOLDEN NUMBER, gōld″n num′bẽr: Used in the regulation of the ecclesiastical calendar, in the "Metonic cycle" of 19 years, which almost exactly reconciles the natural month and the solar year. See Astronomy, I, 5.

GOLDSMITH, gōld′smith (צוֹרֵף, *çōrēph*): Goldsmiths are first mentioned in connection with the building of the tabernacle (Ex **31** 4; **36** 1). Later, goldsmiths' guilds are mentioned (Neh **3** 8.32). The art of refining gold and shaping it into objects was probably introduced into Pal from Phoenicia (see Crafts). Examples of gold work from the earliest Egyp periods are so numerous in the museums of the world that we do not have to draw on our imaginations to appreciate the wonderful skill of the ancient goldsmiths. Probably their designs and methods were those later used by the Jews. The goldsmiths' art was divided into (1) the refining of the impure gold (Job **28** 1; Prov **17** 3; **25** 4; **27** 21; Isa **1** 25; Mal **3** 3); (2) shaping of objects, (*a*) casting idols (Nu **33** 52; Hos **13** 2), (*b*) making graven images (2 Ch **34** 3.4; Jer **10** 14; Nah **1** 14), (*c*) the making of beaten or turned work (Ex **25** 18), (*d*) plating or overlaying (Ex **25** 11; 1 K **6** 20), (*e*) soldering (Isa **41** 7), (*f*) making of wire (Ex **28** 6; **39** 3). Most of these processes are carried on in Bible lands today. In Damascus there is a goldsmiths' quarter where the refining, casting and beating of gold are still carried on, probably in much the same way as in Solomon's time. Jews are found among the goldsmiths. In Beirût, it is a Jew who is esp. skilled in making refiners' pots. Daily, one can see the gold being refined, cast into lumps, beaten on an anvil, rolled between rollers into thin sheets, cut into narrow strips (wire), and wound on bobbins ready for the weaver. There are houses in Damascus and Aleppo still possessing beautiful gold overlaid work on wooden walls and ceilings, the work of goldsmiths of several centuries ago. James A. Patch

GOLGOTHA, gol′gō-tha (**Γολγοθᾶ**, *Golgothá*, from Aram. גָּלְגַּלְתָּא, *gulgaltā′*, "a skull"): In three references (Mt **27** 33; Mk **15** 22; Jn **19** 17) it is interpreted to mean κρανίου τόπος, *kraníou tópos*, "the place of a skull." In Lk **23** 33 AV it is called "Calvary," but in RV simply "The skull." From the NT we may gather that it was outside the city (He **13** 12), but close to it (Jn **19** 20), apparently near some public thoroughfare (Mt **27** 39), coming from the country (Mk **15** 21). It was a spot visible, from some points, from afar (Mk **15** 40; Lk **23** 49).

1. The Name

Four reasons have been suggested for the name Golgotha or "skull": (1) That it was a spot where skulls were to be found lying about and probably, therefore, a public place of execution. This tradition apparently originates with Jerome (346–420 AD), who refers to (3), to condemn it, and says that "outside the city and without the gate there are places wherein the heads of condemned criminals are cut off and which have obtained the name of Calvary—that is, of the beheaded." This view has been adopted by several later writers. Against it may be urged that there is no shadow of evidence that there was any special place for Jewish executions in the 1st cent., and that, if there were, the corpses could have been allowed burial (Mt **27** 58; Jn **19** 38), in conformity with Jewish law (Dt **21** 23) and with normal custom (Jos, *BJ*, IV, v, 2). (2) That the name was due to the skull-like shape of the hill—a modern popular view. No early Lat or Gr writer suggests such an idea, and there is no evidence from the Gospels that the Crucifixion occurred on a raised place at all. Indeed Epiphanius (4th cent.) expressly says: "There is nothing to be seen on the place resembling this name; for it is not situated upon a height that it should be called [the place] of a skull, answering to the place of the head in the human body." It is true that the tradition embodied in the name *Mons Calvary* appears as early as the 4th cent., and is materialized in the traditional site of the Crucifixion in the church of the Holy Sepulcher, but that the hill was skull-like in form is quite a modern idea. Guthe combines (2) and (3) and considers that a natural skull-like elevation came to be considered, by some folklore ideas, to be the skull of the first man. One of the strangest ideas is that of the late General Gordon, who thought that the resemblance to a skull lay in the contours of the ground as laid down in the ordinance survey map of Jerus. (3) That the name is due to an ancient pre-Christian tradition that the skull of Adam was found there. The first mention of this is by Origen (185–253 AD), who himself lived in Jerus 20 years. He writes: "I have received a tradition to the effect that the body of Adam, the first man, was buried upon the spot where Christ was crucified," etc. This tradition was afterward referred to by Athanasius, Epiphanius, Basil of Caesarea, Chrysostom and other later writers. The tomb and skull of Adam, still pointed out in an excavated chamber below the traditional Calvary, marks the survival of this tradition on the spot. This is by far the most ancient explanation of the name Golgotha and, in spite of the absurdity of the original tradition about Adam, is probably the true one.

(4) The highly improbable theory that the *Capitolium* of Ælia Capitolina (the name given by Hadrian to his new Jerus) stood where the Church of the Holy Sepulcher now is, and gave rise to the name Golgotha, is one which involves the idea that the site first received the name Golgotha in the 2d cent., and that all the references in the Gospels were inserted then. This is only mentioned to be dismissed as incompatible with history and common sense.

2. The Site

With regard to the position of the site of the Crucifixion (with which is bound up the site of the Tomb) the NT gives us no indication whatever; indeed, by those who abandon tradition, sites have been suggested on all sides of the city—N., S., E., and W. Two views hold the field today: (1) that the site of the Crucifixion, or at any rate that of the Tomb itself, is included within the precincts of the Church of the Holy Sepulcher; and (2) that a prominent, rounded, grassy hill above the so-called "Grotto of Jeremiah," N.E. of the Modern Damascus Gate, has at least a very high probability of being the true site. It is impossible here to go into the whole question, which requires minute and long elaboration, but excellent review of the whole evidence may be consulted in "Golgotha and the Holy Sepulcher," by the late Sir Charles W. Wilson, of *PEF*. Here only a few points can be touched upon. (1) For the traditional view it may be said that it seems highly improbable that so sacred a spot as this, particularly the empty tomb, could have been entirely forgotten. Although it is true that Jews and Heb Christians were driven out of Jerus after the second great revolt (130–33 AD), yet gentile Christians were free to return, and there was no break long enough to account for a site like this being entirely lost. Indeed there are traditions that this site was deliberately defiled by pagan buildings to annoy the Christians. Eusebius, at the time of Constantine, writes as if it were well known that a Temple of Aphrodite lay over the tomb.

Grotto of Jeremiah—"Gordon's Calvary."

He gives an account of the discovery of the spots still venerated as the Golgotha and the Tomb, and of the erection of churches in connection with them (*Life of Constantine*, III, 25–40). From the time of Constantine there has been no break in the reverence paid to these places. Of the earlier evidence Sir C. Wilson admits (loc. cit.) that "the tradition is so precarious and the evidence is undoubtedly so unsatisfactory as to raise serious doubts."

The topographical difficulties are dealt with in the art. JERUSALEM. It is difficult for the visitor to Jerus sufficiently to realize that the center of gravity of the city has much changed; once it was on the Hill Ophel, and the southern slopes, now bare, were in Christ's time crammed with houses; in later times, from the 4th cent., it was the Church of the Holy Sepulcher round which the city tended to center. There is no insurmountable difficulty in believing that the site of the Crucifixion may be where tradition points out. As Sir C. Wilson says at the end of his book, "No objection urged against the sites [i.e. Golgotha and the Tomb] is of such a convincing nature that it need disturb the minds of those who accept, in all good faith, the authenticity of the places which are hallowed by the prayers of countless pilgrims since the days of Constantine" (loc. cit.).

(2) The so-called "Skull Hill" or "Green Hill" appears to have appealed first to Otto Thenius (1842), but has received its greatest support through the advocacy of the late Col. Conder and of the late Dr. Selah Merrill, U.S.A. consul at Jerus. The arguments for this site are mainly: (*a*) its conspicuous and elevated position—a position which must impress every reverent pilgrim as strikingly suitable for an imaginary reconstruction of the scene. The very greenness of the hill—it is the first green spot in the neighborhood of the city—may influence the subconsciousness of those who have been brought up from childhood to think of the "green hill far away," as the popular hymn puts it. When, however, we consider the question historically, there is not the slightest reason to expect that the crucifixion of Jesus, one of many hundreds, should have been dramatically located in a setting so consonant with the importance with which the world has since learned to regard the event. There is no evidence whatever that the crucifixion was on a hill, much less on such a conspicuous place. (*b*) The supposed resemblance to a human skull strikes many people, but it may be stated without hesitation that the most arresting points of the resemblance, the "eyeholes" and the rounded top, are not ancient; the former are due to artificial excavations going back perhaps a couple of centuries. Probably the whole formation of the hill, the sharp scarp to the S. and the 10 or more feet of earth accumulated on the summit are both entirely new conditions since NT times. (*c*) The nearness of the city walls and the great N. road which make the site so appropriate today are quite different conditions from those in NT times. It is only if the present N. wall can be proved to be on the line of the *second* wall that the argument holds good. On this see JERUSALEM. (*d*) An argument has been based upon a supposed tradition that this spot was the Jewish place of stoning. This so-called tradition is worthless, and not a trace of it can be found outside interested circles, and even if it were the "place of stoning," it would be no argument for its being "Golgotha." To the Oriental, with his great respect for traditional sites, the church of the Holy Sepulcher, covering at once the Tomb, the Calvary, and other sacred spots, will probably always appeal as the appropriate spot: to the western tourist who wishes to visualize in the environs of Jerus in an appropriate setting the great world's tragedy, such a site as this "Skull Hill" must always make the greater appeal to his imagination, and both may find religious satisfaction in their ideas; but cold reason, reviewing the pros and cons, is obliged to say "not proven" to both, with perhaps an admission of the stronger case for the traditional spot.

E. W. G. MASTERMAN

GOLIATH, gō̆-lī′ath (גָּלְיָת, *golyāth;* **Γολιάθ**, *Goliáth*):

(1) The giant of Gath, and champion of the Phili army (1 S **17** 4–23; **21** 9; **22** 10; 2 S **21** 19; 1 Ch **20** 5 ff). He defied the armies of Israel, challenging anyone to meet him in single combat while the two armies faced each other at Ephes-dammim. He was slain by the youthful David. Goliath was almost certainly not of Phili blood, but belonged to one of the races of giants, or aboriginal tribes, such as the Anakim, Avvim, Rephaim, etc. The Avvim had lived at Philistia, and most probably the giant was of that race. His size was most extraordinary. If a cubit was about 21 in., he was over 11 ft. in height; if about 18 in., he was over 9 ft. in height. The enormous weight of his armor would seem to require the larger cubit. This height probably included his full length in armor, helmet and all. In either case he is the largest man known to history. His sword was wielded by David to slay him and afterward carried about in his wanderings, so it could not have been excessively heavy. The story of his encounter with David is graphic, and the boasts of the two champions were perfectly in keeping with single combats in the Orient.

(2) The Goliath of 2 S **21** 19 is another person, and quite probably a son of the first Goliath. He was slain by Elhanan, one of David's mighty men. The person mentioned in 1 Ch **20** 5 is called Laḥmi, but this is almost certainly due to a corruption of the text. "The brother of Goliath" is the younger Goliath and probably a son of the greater Goliath, who had four sons, giants, one of them having 24 fingers and toes. See ELHANAN; LAHMI.

J. J. REEVE

GOMER, gō′mẽr (גֹּמֶר, *gōmer*): Given in Gen **10** 2 f; 1 Ch **1** 5 f as a son of Japheth. The name evidently designates the people called Gimirrâ by the Assyrians, Kimmerians by the Greeks. They were a barbaric horde of Aryans who in the 7th cent. BC left their abode in what is now Southern Russia and poured through the Caucasus into Western Asia, causing serious trouble to the Assyrians and other nations. One division moved eastward toward Media, another westward, where they conquered Cappadocia and made it their special abode. They fought also in other parts of Asia Minor, conquering some portions. The Armenian name for Cappadocia, Gamir, has come from this people. In Ezk **38** 6 Gomer is mentioned as one of the northern nations.

GEORGE RICKER BERRY

GOMER, gō′mẽr (גֹּמֶר, *gōmer;* **Γαμέρ**, *Gamér*): Wife of Hosea. Hosea married Gomer according to Divine appointment, and this was the beginning of God's word to him (Hos **1** 3; **3** 1–4). She was to be a wife of whoredom and they were to have children of whoredom. This need not mean that at the time of marriage she was thus depraved, but she had the evil taint in her blood, had inherited immoral instincts. These soon manifested themselves, and the unfaithful, depraved wife of the prophet went deeper into sin. She seems to have left him and become the slave of her paramour (**3** 1). Hosea is now commanded by Jeh to buy her back, paying the price of the ordinary slave. The prophet keeps her in confinement and without a husband for some time. This experience of the prophet was typical of Israel's unfaithfulness, of Israel's exile, and of God bringing her back after the punishment of the exile. See HOSEA. J. J. REEVE

GOMORRAH, gō̆-mor′a (עֲמֹרָה, *‛ămōrāh;* LXX and NT **Γομόρρα**, *Gomórra*, or **Γόμορρα**, *Gómorra;* Arab. *Ghamara,* "to overwhelm with water"): One of the CITIES OF THE PLAIN (q.v.) destroyed by fire from heaven in the time of Abraham and Lot (Gen **19** 23–29). It was located probably in the plain S. of the Dead Sea, now covered with water. See ARABAH; CITIES OF THE PLAIN; DEAD SEA. De Saulcy, however, with others who place the Cities of the Plain at the N. end of the Dead Sea, fixes upon *Khumran* (or *Gumran*), marked on the Survey Map of Pal N. of *Ras Feshkeh,* where there are ruins about a mile from the Dead Sea. But there is nothing to support this view except the faint resemblance of the name and the inconclusive arguments placing the Cities of the Plain at that end of the sea. GEORGE FREDERICK WRIGHT

GOOD, gŏŏd (טוֹב, *ṭōbh,* טוּב, *ṭūbh,* יָטַב, *yāṭabh;* **ἀγαθός**, *agathós,* **ἀγαθόν**, *agathón,* **καλός**, *kalós,* **καλόν**, *kalón*): In Eng. "good" is used in various senses, most of which are represented in the Bible.

(1) In the OT the commonest word is *ṭōbh,* occurring very frequently and tr[d] in a great variety of ways. Of the different shades of meaning, which frequently run into each other, the following may be distinguished: (*a*) *Possessing desirable qualities, beneficial, agreeable,* e.g. "good for food" (Gen **2** 9); "We will do thee good" (Nu **10** 29); "Who will show us any good?" (Ps **4** 6); "good tidings of good" (Isa **52** 7). (*b*) *Moral excellence, piety:* "to know good and evil" (Gen **3** 22); "that which is right and good" (Dt **6** 18*a;* 1 S **12** 23); "good and bad" (1 K **3** 9, RV "evil"); "Depart from evil and do good" (Ps **37** 27); "a good man" (Prov **12** 2); cf Isa **5** 20; Mic **6** 8, etc. (*c*) *Kind, benevolent:* "The men were very good unto us" (1 S **25** 15); "Give thanks unto Jeh; for he is good" (1 Ch **16** 34); "the good Jeh" (2 Ch **30** 18); "God is good to Israel" (Ps **73** 1); "Jeh is good to all" (Ps **145** 9), etc. (*d*) *Serviceable, adequate, sufficient:* "saw the light that it was good" (Gen **1** 4; so vs 10.12, etc); "not good that the man should be alone" (**2** 18); in the frequent phrase, "if it seem good" (1 Ch **13** 2; Est **5** 4, etc), sometimes rendered, "if it please" (Neh **2** 5. 7; Est **1** 19, etc). (*e*) *Not small* or *deficient* (full, complete): "a good old age" (Gen **15** 15; **25** 8); "a good dowry" (**30** 20); "good ears," "years," "kine" (**41** 24.26.35); "good understanding" (1 S **25** 3); "good trees"—"land" (2 K **3** 19.25), etc. (*f*) *Not blemished, fair, honorable:* "tender and good" (Gen **18** 7); "good kids" (**27** 9); "good report" (1 S **2** 24; cf 2 K **20** 3; Jer **24** 2); and the renderings "fair" (Gen **26** 7, etc), "beautiful" (2 S **11** 2), "pleasant" (2 K **2** 19), etc. (*g*) *Pleasure-giving, happy:* "glad of heart" (1 K **8** 66; Est **5** 9); sometimes in AV and RV tr[d] "merry" (Jgs **16** 25; 1 S **25** 36; 2 S **13** 28; Prov **15** 15, RV "cheerful"), etc.

Changes that may be noted in RV are such as, "good" for "ready" (Isa **41** 7); "I have no good beyond thee" for "My goodness extendeth not to thee" (Ps **16** 2); "goodly" for "good" (**45** 1); "good" for "goodness" (**107** 9); "good" for "well" (Zec **8** 15).

Ṭūbh means *something good,* e.g. "the good of the land" (Gen **45** 18.20; Dt **6** 11; Job **21** 16, RV "prosperity").

Yāṭabh, "to do good," occurs several times, as, "I will surely do thee good" (Gen **32** 12); "to do good" (Lev **5** 4); "Make your ways and your doings good," RV "amend" (Jer **18** 11; Zeph **1** 12, etc).

Numerous other Heb words are rendered "good" in various verbal connections and otherwise, as "to bring good tidings" (2 S **4** 10; Isa **40** 9, etc); "take good heed" (Dt **2** 4; **4** 15; Josh **23** 11); "make good" (Ex **21** 34), etc; "good will" (*raçōn,* Dt **33** 16; Mal **2** 13); "what good?" RV "what advantages?" (*kishrōn,* Eccl **5** 11); "good for nothing," RV "profitable" (*çālēaḥ,* Jer **13** 10), etc. In Jer **18** 4, "as seemed good to the potter," the word is *yāshār,* which means lit. "right."

(2) In the NT the words most frequently tr[d] "good" are *agathos* and *kalos.* The former, *agathos,* denotes good as a *quality,* physical or moral. Thus, "He maketh his sun to rise on the evil and the good" (Mt **5** 45); "good gifts" (**7** 11); "Good Master [RV "Teacher"] . . . . Why callest thou me good? none is good save one" (Mk **10** 17 f; Lk **18** 18 f; cf Mt **19** 16 f); "they that have done good" (Jn **5** 29). Sometimes it is equivalent to "kind" (thus Tit **2** 5 RV); *to agathon* is "that which is good" (Lk **6** 45; Rom **7** 13; 1 Thess **5** 15; 1 Pet **3** 13), etc; "that which is honest," RV "honorable" (2 Cor **13** 7); "meet" (Mt **15** 26; Mk **7** 27); "worthy," RV "honorable" (Jas **2** 7); *agathon* is "a good thing," as "good things to them that ask him" (Mt **7** 11); "Can any good thing come out of Nazareth?" (Jn **1** 46), etc; *agathoergéō* (1 Tim **6** 18), and *agathopoiéō* (Mk **3** 4; Acts **14** 17), etc, "to do good."

Kalos is properly, "beautiful," "pleasing," "useful," "noble," "worthy" in a moral sense, e.g. "that they may see your good works" (Mt **5** 16); "She hath wrought a good work on me" (Mt **26** 10; Mk **14** 6); "the good shepherd" (Jn **10** 11.14); "Many good works have I showed you" (**10** 32); "good and acceptable before God" (1 Tim **5** 4; RV omits "good"); "the good fight" (2 Tim **4** 7); "good works" (Tit **2** 7); "the good word of God" (He **6** 5). But it is often practically equivalent to *agathos,* e.g. "good fruit" (Mt **3** 10); "good ground" (**13** 23); "good seed" (**13** 24); but the idea of *useful* may underlie such expressions; *to kalon* is properly "that which is beautiful." It occurs in Rom **7** 18.21; 1 Thess **5** 21, "Hold fast that which is good." In Rom **7** it seems to be used interchangeably with *to agathon.* In Rom **5** 7, "the good man" (*ho agathos*) is distinguished from "a righteous man" (*díkaios*): "For the good man some one would even dare to die" (cf Rom **7** 16; He **5** 14; Jas **4** 17); *kalōs,* "well," "pleasantly," is tr[d] "good" (Lk **6** 27; Jas **2** 3); *kalodidáskalos* (Tit **2** 3), "teachers of good things," RV "of that which is good."

"Good" occurs in the rendering of many other Gr words and phrases, as *eudokía,* "good pleasure" (Eph **1** 9); "good will" (Lk **2** 14; Phil **1** 15); *sumphérō,* "to bear together," "not good to marry" (Mt **19** 10), RV "expedient"; *philágathos,* "a lover of good" (Tit **1** 8); *chrēstología,* "good words" (Rom **16** 18, RV "smooth speech," etc).

The following changes in RV may be noted. In Lk **2** 14 for "men of good will" (*eudokia*) RV reads "in whom he is well pleased," m "good pleasure among men, Gr men of good pleasure." The meaning is "men to whom God is drawing nigh in goodwill or acceptance"; cf Lk **4** 19, "the acceptable year of the Lord"; **4** 43, "Preach the good tidings of the kingdom of God." In Mt **11** 5; Lk **4** 43; **7** 22; 1 Pet **1** 25 and (ARV) Rev **14** 6 "the gospel" is changed into "good tidings." In Mt **18** 8 f; Mk **9** 43.45.47; Lk **5** 39, "good" is substituted for "better"; on the last passage in notes "Many authorities read 'better' "; in 1 Cor **9** 15, "good . . . . rather" for "better"; "good" is substituted in Lk **1** 19; **8** 1 and Acts **13** 32 for "glad"; in Acts **6** 3 for "honest"; in He **13** 9 for "a good thing." In 2 Thess **1** 11, "all the good pleasure of his goodness" becomes "every desire of goodness" (m "Gr good pleasure of goodness"); in 1 Tim **3** 2, "good" (*kósmios*) becomes "orderly." There are many other instances of like changes. See GOODNESS; GOOD, CHIEF. W. L. WALKER

GOOD, CHIEF: What this consisted in was greatly discussed in ancient philosophy. Varro enumerated 288 answers to the question. By Plato "the good" was identified with God.

In the OT while the "good" of the nation consisted in earthly well-being or prosperity (Dt **28** etc), that of the individual was to be found only in God Himself (Ps **16** 2 RV, "I have no good beyond thee"; **42** 1–5; **43** 5; **73** 25–28; Jer **31** 33 f; Hab **3** 17–19). This implied godly conduct (Mic **6** 8, etc), and led to the experience described as "blessedness" (Ps **1**, etc; Jer **17** 7, etc). It is the "Wisdom" extolled in Prov **1** 20; **8** 1 f (cf Ecclus **1** 1 f; **5** 1 f), elsewhere described as "the fear of Jeh." That God alone can be the true "good" of man is implied in the fact that man was created in the image of God (Gen **1** 27).

In the NT the true "good" is placed by Jesus in "the kingdom of God" (Mt **6** 33; **13** 44 f, etc). This means nothing earthly merely (Mt **6** 19), but heavenly and eternal. It implies the OT conception that God is the true "good"; for to seek the Kingdom supremely means whole-hearted devotion to God as our heavenly Father and to His righteousness. It was also spoken of by Jesus, as sonship to the heavenly Father (Mt **5** 45, etc). This "good" is not something merely to be *given* to men, but must be sought after and won through taking up a right attitude toward God and our fellows, cherishing the Love that God is, and acting it out in kindness and righteousness, in resemblance to our God and Father (Mt **5** 43–48; here Gen **1** 27 is implied).

In some of the epistles Christ is represented as the true "good" (Phil **3** 8 f; Col **3** 1–4.11). This is because in Him God was manifested in His Truth and Grace; in Him "the Kingdom" was present; through His cross the world is so reconciled to God that men can find acceptance and rest in Him as their "good"; Christ Himself in the Spirit is our Life; in Him we have "God with us." Having God as our "good," nothing but good, in the truest and highest sense, can come to us. Even the most seemingly adverse things are turned into good "to them that love God" (Rom **8** 28).

Our true "good" is found thus in God even in this present life; but its fulness can be realized only in the eternal life beyond. Placing our "good" in God leads to such life in devotion to the "good" that God is, as tends to bring all that is best to this present world. It is men's failure to do this that is the source of our misery (Jer **2** 13, etc). The ultimate ideal is that God shall be "all in all" (1 Cor **15** 28).

W. L. WALKER

GOODLINESS, good'li-nes: This word is found in Isa **40** 6 as the tr of חֶסֶד, *ḥeṣedh*, commonly trd "mercy," "kindness," etc: "All flesh is grass, and all the goodliness [beauty, charm, comeliness] thereof is as the flower of the field." The rendering is retained by ERV and ARV as appropriate in this place; *ḥeṣedh* is frequently trd "goodness." In Isa **40** 6 LXX has *dóxa*, "glory" (so also 1 Pet **1** 24), which also fitly expresses the idea of the passage.

GOODLY, good'li (טוֹב, *ṭōbh;* **καλός,** *kalós,* **λαμπρός,** *lamprós*): In the OT various words are trd "goodly," the most of them occurring only once; *ṭōbh* (the common word for "good") is several times trd "goodly," chiefly in the sense of *form* or *appearance*, e.g. "a goodly child" (Ex **2** 2); "that goodly mountain" (Dt **3** 25); *yāpheh* ("fair") is similarly trd in Gen **39** 6, RV "comely," and *mar'eh* in 2 S **23** 21. Other words, such as *'addīr* imply excellence, honor, etc, e.g. Ezk **17** 23, "bear fruit, and be a goodly cedar"; *hōdh,* "his goodly horse" (Zec **10** 3); others imply beauty, ornament, such as *pe'ēr*, "goodly bonnets," RV "headtires" (Ex **39** 28); *shāphar* ("bright," "fair"), "a goodly heritage" (Ps **16** 6); once *'Ēl* ("God of might") is employed, RV "cedars of God," m "goodly cedars" (Ps **80** 10); *renānīm* ("joyous soundings or shoutings") is trd in Job **39** 13, "goodly wings," probably from the *sound* made in flying or flapping; ERV has "The wing of the ostrich rejoiceth," ARV (wings) "wave proudly." For "goodly castles" (Nu **31** 10) RV has "encampments"; "goodly vessels" (2 Ch **32** 27) for "pleasant jewels"; "goodly" is substituted for "good" (Ps **45** 1; Cant **1** 3); "goodly things" for "all the goods" (Gen **24** 10); "goodly frame," ARV for "comely proportion" (Job **41** 12).

In the NT *kalos* ("beautiful") is trd "goodly" in Mt **13** 45, "goodly pearls" and Lk **21** 5 "goodly stones"; *lampros* ("bright") in Jas **2** 2, "goodly apparel," RV "fine clothing," and Rev **18** 14, "dainty and goodly," RV "dainty and sumptuous." In He **11** 23, RV substitutes "goodly" for "proper."

"Goodly" occurs in Apoc, 1 Esd **4** 18; Jth **8** 7 (*hōraíos*); 2 Macc **9** 16, "goodly gifts," *kállistos*, RV "goodliest." W. L. WALKER

GOODLY TREES (פְּרִי עֵץ הָדָר, *perī 'ēç hādhār*, "the fruit [AV "boughs"] of goodly [=beautiful or noble] trees"): One of the four species of plants used in the Feast of Tabernacles (Lev **23** 40). In the Talm (*Ṣukkāh* **35***a*) this is explained to be the citron

Citron (*Citrus medica*).

(*Citrus medica*) known in Heb as *'ethrōgh*. This tradition is ancient, at least as old as the Maccabees. Jos (*Ant*, XIII, xiii, 5) records that Alexander Jannaeus, while serving at the altar during this feast, was pelted by the infuriated Jews with citrons. This fruit also figures on coins of this period. It is probable that the citron tree (*Malum Persica*) was imported from Babylon by Jews returning from the captivity. A citron is now carried in the synagogue by every orthodox Jew in one hand, and the *lūlābh* (of myrtle, willow, and palm branch) in the other, on each day of the Feast of Tabernacles.

Originally the "goodly trees" had a much more generic sense, and the term is so interpreted by the LXX and Vulg. See Feasts and Fasts; Booth.

E. W. G. Masterman

GOODMAN, go͝od'man (אִישׁ, *'īsh;* **οἰκοδεσπότης,** *oikodespótēs*): The word occurs once in the OT and is a tr of the ordinary word for "man," *'īsh* (Prov **7** 19). "The goodman is not at home," so AV and RV, but ARV, more correctly, "The man is not at home"; i.e. the husband is not at home; the Geneva and Douay VSS have "My husband is not at home": so Wycliffe; while the Vulg has "There is not a man in her house." In the NT "goodman" is a tr of *oikodespotēs*. This word occurs 12 t in the Synoptists, and nowhere else. AV and RV have 3 translations of the word, ARV 2. In 4 places AV has "goodman" while ARV has "householder" or "master of the house" (Mt **20** 11; **24** 43; Lk **12** 39; **22** 11). In all the other places it is trd "householder" or "master of the house." RV retains "goodman" in Mk **14** 14 and Lk **22** 11. The word lit. means "master of the house," or "husband." The adj. is a mark of respect, and is used somewhat as our word "Mr.," an appellative of respect or civility. Relationship by marriage was distinguished by this epithet, as "good-father," "good-sister," both in England and Scotland. Later the adj. lost its distinguishing force and was swallowed up in the word.

J. J. Reeve

GOODNESS, go͝od'nes: This word in the OT is the tr of *ṭōbh* (Ex **18** 9; Ps **16** 2, RV "good"; **23** 6), etc; of *ṭūbh* (Ex **33** 19; Ps **31** 19; Jer **31** 14; Hos **3** 5), etc; of *ḥeṣedh* (Ex **34** 6), "abundant in g.," ERV "plenteous in mercy," ARV "abundant in loving kindness"; "The g. of God endureth continually," RV "mercy," ARV "loving kindness" (Ps **52** 1), etc.

In the NT it is the tr of *chrēstótēs* ("usefulness," benignity); "the riches of his g." (Rom **2** 4; **11** 22, *thrice*); of *chrēstós* ("useful," "benign," "kind," as in Lk **6** 35); "The g. of God leadeth thee to repentance" (Rom **2** 4); of *agathōsúnē* (found only in the NT and LXX and writings based thereon), "full of g." (Rom **15** 14); "gentleness, goodness, faith" (Gal **5** 22); "in all g. and righteousness and truth" (Eph **5** 9); "all the good pleasure of his g.," RV "every desire of g." (2 Thess **1** 11).

The thought of God as good and the prominence given to "good" and "goodness" are distinctive features of the Bible. In the passage quoted above from Gal **5** 22, "goodness" is one of the fruits of the indwelling Spirit of God, and in that from Eph **5** 9 it is described as being, along with righteousness and truth, "the fruit of the light" which Christians had been "made" in Christ. Here, as elsewhere, we are reminded that the Christian life in its truth is likeness to God, the source and perfection of all good. 2 Thess **1** 11 regards God Himself as expressing His goodness in and through us. See Good; Good, Chief.

W. L. Walker

GOODS, go͝odz (רְכוּשׁ, *rekhūsh,* טוּב, *ṭūbh;* **τὰ ὑπάρχοντα,** *tá hupárchonta*): In the OT *rekhūsh* ("substance") is most frequently trd "goods," as in Gen **14** 11.12.16.21, etc; *ṭūbh* is also 3 t so trd in AV (Gen **24** 10, RV "goodly things," m "all the goods"; Neh **9** 25, RV "good things"; Job **20** 21, RV "prosperity"). Other words are *'ōn* (Job **20** 10, RV "wealth"); *ḥayil* ("force," Nu **31** 9; Zeph **1** 13, RV "wealth"); *ṭōbh* (Dt **28** 11, RV "for good"; Eccl **5** 11); *melā'khāh* ("work," Ex **22** 8.11); *nikhṣīn* (Aram. "riches," Ezr **6** 8; **7** 26); *ḳinyān*, "getting" (Ezk **38** 12 f). We have *ta huparchonta* (lit. "the things existing") in Mt **24** 47, "ruler over all his goods," RV "all that he hath," etc. *Agathós* is trd "goods" in Lk **12** 18 f; *skeúos* ("instrument") in Mt **12** 29; Mk **3** 27; *tá sá* ("the things belonging to thee") in Lk **6** 30; *ousía* ("substance") in Lk **15** 12, RV "substance"; *húparxis* ("existence," "substance") in Acts **2** 45; *ploutéō* ("to be rich") in Rev **3** 17, RV "have gotten riches." In RV "goods" stands instead of "carriage" (Jgs **18** 21), of "stuff" (Lk **17** 31), of "good" (1 Jn **3** 17). "Goods" was used in the sense of "possessions" generally; frequently in this sense in Apoc (1 Esd **6** 32); *ta huparchonta* (Tob **1** 20); Ecclus **5** 1, "Set not thy heart upon thy goods" (*chrḗma*), etc.

W. L. Walker

GOPHER WOOD, gō'fẽr wo͝od (עֲצֵי גֹפֶר, *'ăçē ghōpher*): The wood from which Noah's ark was made (Gen **6** 14). Gopher is a word unknown elsewhere in Heb or allied languages. Lagarde considered that it was connected with גָּפְרִית, *gophrīth*, meaning "brimstone," or "pitch," while others connect it with כֹּפֶר, *kōphēr*, also meaning "pitch"; hence, along both lines, we reach the probability of some resinous wood, and pine, cedar, and cypress have all had their supporters. A more probable explanation is that which connects *gōpher* with the modern Arab. *kufa*, a name given to the boats made of interwoven willow branches and palm leaves with a coating of bitumen outside, used today on the rivers and canals of Mesopotamia. In the Gilgameš story of the flood it is specially mentioned that Noah daubed his ark both inside and out with a kind of bitumen. See Deluge of Noah.

E. W. G. Masterman

GORE, gōr (נָגַח, *nāghaḥ*): "Gore" occurs only three times in AV, viz. Ex **21** 28.31 *bis*, "if an ox gore a man or a woman," etc; in vs 29.32.36, AV has "push" (with his horn), RV "gore." The same vb. in Piel and Hithpael is elsewhere trd "push" and "pushing" (Dt **33** 17, "He shall push the peoples," RVm "gore"; 1 K **22** 11; Ps **44** 5; Ezk **34** 21; Dnl **8** 4; **11** 40, RV "contend," m "Heb push at," as an ox pushes with his horns so should the king fight—a fitting description of warfare).

GORGEOUS, gôr'jus, **GORGEOUSLY,** gôr'jus-li (מִכְלוֹל, *mikhlōl;* **λαμπρός,** *lamprós*): *Mikhlōl* occurs twice in the OT, trd in AV and RV "most gorgeously" (Ezk **23** 12); in Ezk **38** 4, AV translates "all sorts" (of armor), RV "clothed in full armor." *Lampros* ("shining," "bright"), is only once trd "gorgeous" (Lk **23** 11); "Herod . . . . arrayed him in a gorgeous robe," RV "gorgeous apparel." We have also in Lk **7** 25, "They that are gorgeously apparelled [*éndoxos*, "splendid," "glorious"] . . . . are in kings' courts." They were scarcely to be looked for among the prophets, or in the new community of Jesus.

W. L. Walker

GORGET, gôr'jet: Appears only once in AV (1 S **17** 6), being placed in the margin as an alternative to "target [of brass]" in the description of the armor worn by Goliath of Gath. The Heb word thus trd (כִּידוֹן, *kīdhōn*) really means a "javelin," and is so rendered in RV and ARV here and in 1 S **17** 45 ("Thou comest to me with a sword, and with a spear, and with a *javelin*"). See Armor, I, 4, (3). Gorget, though so rarely used in Scripture and now displaced in our revised versions, occurs not infrequently and in various senses in Eng. lit. In the meaning of "a piece of armor for the gorge or throat" which seems to have been in the mind of King James's translators, it is found in early Eng.

writers and down to recent times. Spenser has it in *Faerie Queene,* IV, iii, 12:

"His weasand-pipe it through his gorget cleft";

Scott, *Marmion,* V, ii:

"Their brigantines and gorgets light";

and Prescott, *Ferdinand and Isabella,* III, 47: "The gorget gave way and the sword entered his throat."

T. Nicol

GORGIAS, gôr′ji-as (**Γοργίας,** *Gorgías*): A general in the service of Antiochus Epiphanes (1 Macc **3** 38; 2 Macc **8** 9). Lysias, who had been left as regent during the absence of Antiochus in Persia, appointed Gorgias to take the command against Judaea in 166 BC. In 1 Macc **4** 1–24 is recorded a night attack by Gorgias with 5,000 foot and 1,000 horse upon the camp of Judas Maccabaeus in the neighborhood of Emmaus, in which Judas was completely victorious. The victory was all the more striking as the force of Judas was considerably smaller in number and had "not armor nor swords to their minds" (1 Macc **4** 6). Later on (164 BC) he held a garrison in Jamnia, and gained a victory over the forces of Joseph and Azarias who, envying the glory of Judas and Jonathan, in direct disobedience to the orders of Judas, attacked Gorgias and were defeated.

Jamnia as given in Jos, *Ant,* XII, viii, 6, is probably the correct reading for Idumaea in 2 Macc **12** 32. The doings of Gorgias in 2 Macc are recorded with some confusion. He was regarded with special hostility by the Jews. In 2 Macc **12** 35 he is described as "the accursed man." J. Hutchison

GORTYNA, gor-tī′na (**Γορτύναι,** *Gortúnai*): A city in Crete, next in importance to Gnossus. It is mentioned in 1 Macc **15** 23. See Crete.

GOSHEN, gō′shen (גֹּשֶׁן, *gōshen;* **Γεσέμ,** *Gesém*): The region where the Hebrews dwelt in Egypt. If the LXX reading *Gesem* be correct, the word, which in its Heb form has no known meaning, may mean "cultivated"—comparing the Arab. root *jashima,* "to labor." Egyptologists have suggested a connection with the Egyp word *ḳās,* meaning "inundated land" because Goshen was apparently the same region, called by the Greeks the "Arabian nome," which had its capital at Phakousa representing the Egyp *Pa-ḳas* (Brugsch, *Geog.,* I, 298), the name of a town, with the determinative for "pouring forth." Van der Hardt, indeed, more than a century ago (see Sayce, *Higher Criticism,* 235), supposed the two words to be connected. Dr. Naville in 1887 found the word as denoting the vicinity of Pi-sopt (now *Saft el Henneh),* 6 miles E. of Zagazig—in the form *Ḳ-s-m.* He concludes that this was the site of Phakousa, but the latter is usually placed at *Tell el Faḳûs,* about 15 miles S. of Zoan (q.v.), and this appears to be the situation of the "City of Arabia" which St. Silvia, about 385 AD, identifies with Gesse or Goshen; for she reached it in her journey from Heroöpolis, through Goshen to Tathnis or Taphnis (Daphnai), and to Pelusium.

1. Meaning of Name

It is generally agreed that Goshen was the region E. of the Bubastic branch of the Nile; and in Ps **78** 12.43, it seems to be clearly identified with the "field [or pastoral plain] of Zoan," which was probably also the "land of Rameses" mentioned (Gen **47** 11) as possessed by Jacob's family (see Raamses; Zoan). Where first mentioned (Gen **45** 10), Goshen is promised by Joseph to Jacob as a land fit for flocks, and the LXX here reads, "Gesem of Arabia," probably referring to the Arabian nome which took its name from the "desert" which defended the E. border of Egypt. In the second notice (Gen **46** 28 f), the boundary of the land of Goshen, where Joseph met his father, is called in the LXX *Hērōō(n)-polis,* and also (ver 28) "the land of Ramesse(s)"; so that in the 3d cent. BC Goshen seems to have been identified with

2. Situation

Corn and Palm Trees in Goshen.

the whole region of the Arabian nome, as far S. as Heroöpolis which (see Pithom) lay in *Wâdy Tumeilât.* Goshen included pastoral lands (Gen **46** 34; **47** 1.4.6.27; **50** 8) and was still inhabited by the Hebrews at the time of the Exodus (Ex **8** 22; **9** 26), after which it is unnoticed in the OT. The name, however, applied to other places which were probably "cultivated" lands, including a region in the S. of Pal (Josh **10** 41; **11** 16), "all the country of Goshen [LXX *Gosóm*], even unto Gibeon," and a city of Judah (Josh **15** 51) in the mountains near Beersheba. These notices seem to show that the word is not of Egyp origin.

3. Description

The region thus very clearly indicated was not of any great extent, having an area of only about 900 sq. miles, including two very different districts. The western half, immediately E. of the Bubastic branch of the Nile, stretches from Zoan to Bubastis (at both of which cities records of the Hyksos ruler Apepi have been found), or a distance of about 35 miles N. and S. This region is an irrigated plain which is still considered to include some of the best land in Egypt. The description of the land of Rameses (see Raamses), in the 14th cent. BC, shows its fertility; and St. Silvia says that the land of Goshen was 16 miles from Heroöpolis, and that she traveled for two days in it "through vineyards, and balsam plantations, and orchards, and tilled fields, and gardens." The region narrows from about 15 miles near the seashore to about 10 miles between *Zagazig* and *Tell el Kebîr* on the S. E. of this, a sandy and gravelly desert lies between the Nile plain and the Suez Canal, broadening southward from near Daphnai (*Tell Defeneh*) to *Wâdy Tumeilât,* where it is 40 miles across E. and W. S. of this valley an equally waterless desert stretches to Suez, and from the Bitter Lakes on the E. to the vicinity of Heliopolis (S.E. of Cairo) on the W. Thus *Wâdy Tumeilât,* which is fertilized by the Nile waters (see Pi-Hahiroth), and contains villages and corn fields, is the only natural route for a people driving with their flocks and herds by which the vicinity of the Red Sea can be reached, the road leading from the S. end of the "field of Zoan" near Bubastis, and 40 miles eastward to the "edge of the wilderness" (see ETHAM) and the head of the Bitter Lakes. This physical conformation is important in relation to the route of the Israelites (see EXODUS); and *Wâdy Tumeilât* may very possibly be intended to be included in Goshen, as the LXX translators supposed.

C. R. CONDER

GOSHEN, gō'shen (גֹּשֶׁן, *gōshen*):

(1) Mentioned as a country (אֶרֶץ, *'ereç*) in the S. of Judah distinct from the "hill country," the Negeb and the Shephelah (Josh **10** 41; **11** 16). Unidentified.

(2) A town in the S.W. part of the hill country of Judah (Josh **15** 51), very probably connected in some way with the district (1).

(3) See preceding article.

GOSPEL, gos'pel (**τὸ εὐαγγέλιον**, *tó euaggélion*): The word "gospel" is derived from the AS word which meant "the story concerning God." In the NT the Gr word *euaggelion*, means "good news." It proclaims tidings of deliverance. The word sometimes stands for the record of the life of Our Lord (Mk **1** 1), embracing all His teachings, as in Acts **20** 24. But the word "gospel" now has a peculiar use, and describes primarily the message which Christianity announces. "Good news" is its significance. It means a gift from God. It is the proclamation of the forgiveness of sins and sonship with God restored through Christ. It means remission of sins and reconciliation with God. The gospel is not only a message of salvation, but also the instrument through which the Holy Spirit works (Rom **1** 16).

The gospel differs from the law in being known entirely from revelation. It is proclaimed in all its fulness in the revelation given in the NT. It is also found, although obscurely, in the OT. It begins with the prophecy concerning the 'seed of the woman' (Gen **3** 15), and the promise concerning Abraham, in whom all the nations should be blessed (Gen **12** 3; **15** 5) and is also indicated in Acts **10** 43 and in the argument in Rom **4**.

In the NT the gospel never means simply a book, but rather the message which Christ and His apostles announced. In some places it is called "the gospel of God," as, for example, Rom **1** 1; 1 Thess **2** 2.9; 1 Tim **1** 11. In others it is called "the gospel of Christ" (Mk **1** 1; Rom **1** 16; **15** 19; 1 Cor **9** 12.18; Gal **1** 7). In another it is called "the gospel of the grace of God" (Acts **20** 24); in another "the gospel of peace" (Eph **6** 15); in another "the gospel of your salvation" (Eph **1** 13); and in yet another "the glorious gospel" (2 Cor **4** 4 AV). The gospel is Christ: He is the subject of it, the object of it, and the life of it. It was preached by Him (Mt **4** 23; **11** 5; Mk **1** 14; Lk **4** 18 m), by the apostles (Acts **16** 10; Rom **1** 15; **2** 16; 1 Cor **9** 16) and by the evangelists (Acts **8** 25).

We must note the clear antithesis between the law and the gospel. The distinction between the two is important because, as Luther indicates, it contains the substance of all Christian doctrine. "By the law," says he, "nothing else is meant than God's word and command, directing what to do and what to leave undone, and requiring of us obedience of works. But the gospel is such doctrine of the word of God that neither requires our works nor commands us to do anything, but announces the offered grace of the forgiveness of sin and eternal salvation. Here we do nothing, but only receive what is offered through the word." The gospel, then, is the message of God, the teaching of Christianity, the redemption in and by Jesus Christ, the only begotten Son of God, offered to all mankind. And as the gospel is bound up in the life of Christ, His biography and the record of His works, and the proclamation of what He has to offer, are all gathered into this single word, of which no better definition can be given than that of Melanchthon: "The gospel is the gratuitous promise of the remission of sins for Christ's sake." To hold tenaciously that in this gospel we have a supernatural revelation is in perfect consistency with the spirit of scientific inquiry. The gospel, as the whole message and doctrine of salvation, and as chiefly efficacious for contrition, faith, justification, renewal and sanctification, deals with facts of revelation and experience.

DAVID H. BAUSLIN

GOSPEL ACCORDING TO THE HEBREWS. See APOCRYPHAL GOSPELS.

GOSPELS OF THE CHILDHOOD, chīld'hŏŏd. See APOCRYPHAL GOSPELS.

GOSPELS, SPURIOUS, spū'ri-us. See APOCRYPHAL GOSPELS.

GOSPELS, THE SYNOPTIC, si-nop'tik:

I. Introductory.—The present art. is confined to the consideration of the relations and general features of the first 3 Gospels (Mt, Mk, Lk)—ordinarily named "the Synoptic Gospels," because, in contrast with the Fourth Gospel, they present, as embodying a common tradition, the same general view of the life and teaching of Jesus during His earthly ministry, and of His death and resurrection. The Fourth Gospel, in itself and in its relation to the Synoptics, with the Johannine literature and theology generally, are treated in special articles. See JOHN, GOSPEL OF; JOHANNINE THEOLOGY, etc.

1. Scope of Article

The place of the Gospels in church tradition is secure. Eusebius places the 4 Gospels among the books that were never controverted in the church (*HE*, III, 25). It is acknowledged that by the end of the 2d cent. these 4 Gospels, and none else, ascribed to the authors whose names they bear, were in universal circulation and undisputed use throughout the church, stood at the head of church catalogues and of all VSS, were freely used, not only by the Fathers of the church (Irenaeus, Tertullian, Clement, Origen, etc), but by pagans and heretics, and by these also were ascribed to the disciples of Christ as their authors. Justin Martyr, in the middle of the century, freely quotes from "Memoirs of the Apostles," "which are

2. The Gospels in Church Tradition

called Gospels," "composed by the apostles and those that followed them" (1 *Apol.* 66–67; *Dial. with Trypho,* 10, 100, 103). What these Gospels were is made apparent by the *Diatessaron,* or Harmony of Four, of his disciple Tatian (c 170), constructed from the 4 Gospels we possess. The first to mention Mt and Mk by name is Papias of Hierapolis (c 120–30; in Euseb., *HE,* III, 39). Dr. Sanday is disposed to carry back the extracts from Papias to about 100 AD (*Fourth Gospel,* 151); Dr. Moffatt likewise says, "These explanations of Mt and Mk must have been in circulation by the end of the 1st cent." (*Intro to Lit. of NT,* 187). The gist of the testimony of Papias is: "Mark, having become the interpreter of Peter, wrote down accurately, though he did not record in order, that which was either said or done by Christ"; "Matthew composed the Oracles [*Logia*] in Heb [Aram.], and each one interpreted them as he was able." Eusebius evidently took what he quotes about Mt and Mk from Papias to refer to our present Gospels, but a problem arises as to the relation of the Aram. "Logia" said to be composed by Matthew to our canonical Gr Gospel, which was the only Gospel of Mt known to the early Fathers. There is no ground for the supposition that the Jewish-Christian GOSPEL ACC. TO THE HE (q.v.) was the original of the Greek Mt; it was on the other hand derived from it. The Gnostic Marcion used a mutilated Lk. Cf, further, below on dating, and for details see special arts. on the respective Gospels; also BIBLE; CANON OF THE NT.

II. The Synoptic Problem.—Arising from their peculiar nature, there has always been a Synoptic problem, ever since the 3 Gospels appeared together in the Canon of the NT. No one could read these Gospels consecutively with attention, without being aware of the resemblances and differences in their contents. Each writer sets forth his own account without reference to the other two, and, with the partial exception of Luke (**1** 1–4), does not tell his readers anything about the sources of his Gospel. A problem thus arose as to the relations of the three to one another, and the problem, though it approaches a solution, is not yet solved. A history of the Synoptic problem will be found in outline in many recent works; the most elaborate and best is in Zahn's *Intro,* III. In it Zahn briefly indicates what the problem was as it presented itself to the church in the earlier centuries, and gives in detail the history of the discussion from the time of Lessing (1778) to the present day. It is not possible within the limits of this art. to refer otherwise than briefly to these discussions, but it may be remarked that, as the discussion went on, large issues were raised; every attempt at solution seemed only to add to the difficulty of finding an adequate one; and at length it was seen that no more complex problem was ever set to literary criticism than that presented by the similarities and differences of the Synoptic Gospels.

1. Nature of Problem

Of the hypotheses which seek to account for these resemblances and differences, the following are the most important. (1) The hypothesis of *oral tradition:* This theory has rather fallen into disfavor among recent critics. Dr. Stanton, e.g., says, "The relations between the first 3 Gospels cannot be adequately explained simply by the influence of oral tradition" (*Gospels as Hist. Documents,* II, 17; similarly Moffatt, op. cit. 180 ff). Briefly stated, the theory is this. It assumes that each of the evangelists wrote independently of the others, and derived the substance of his writing, not from written sources, but from oral narratives of sayings and doings of Jesus, which, through dint of repetition, had assumed a relatively fixed form. The teaching of the apostles, first given in Jerus, repeated in the catechetical schools (cf Lk **1** 4, RV), and intrusted to the trained memories of the Christian converts, is held to be sufficient to account for the phenomena of the 3 Gospels. The oral Gospel took its essential form in Pal, and written editions of it would by and by appear in more or less complete form (Lk **1** 1). The first distinguished advocate of the oral hypothesis was Gieseler (1818). It was upheld in Britain by Alford and Westcott, and is today advocated, with modifications, by Dr. A. Wright in his *Synopsis of the Gospels in Gr* (2d ed, 1908).

2. Proposed Solutions

(2) The *mutual use* hypothesis: As old as Augustine, this hypothesis, which assumes the use of one of the Gospels by the other two, has been frequently advocated by scholars of repute in the history of criticism. There have been many variations of the theory. Each of the 3 Gospels has been put first, each second, and each third, and each in turn has been regarded as the source of the others. In fact, all possible permutations (6 in number) have been exhausted. As the hypothesis has few advocates at the present day, it is not necessary to give a minute account of these permutations and combinations. Two of them which may be regarded as finally excluded are (*a*) those which put Lk first; and (*b*) those which put Mk last (the view of Augustine; in modern times, of F. Baur and the Tübingen school).

(3) The hypothesis of *sources:* This is the theory which may be said to hold the field at the present time. The tendency in criticism is toward the acceptance of *two* main sources for the Synoptic Gospels. (*a*) One source is a Gospel like, if not identical with, the canonical Gospel of Mk. As regards this 2d Gospel there is a consensus of opinion that it is prior to the other two, and the view that the 2d and 3d used it as a source is described as the one solid result of literary criticism. Eminent critics of various schools of thought are agreed on this point (cf W. C. Allen, *St. Matthew,* Pref. vii; F. C. Burkitt, *Gospel History and Its Transmission,* 37). It has been shown that most of the contents of Mk have been embodied in the other two, that the order of events in Mk has been largely followed by Mt and Lk, and that the departures from the style of Mk can be accounted for by the hypothesis of editorial amendment. (*b*) The other source (now commonly named Q) is found first by an examination of the matter not contained in the 2d Gospel, which is common to Mt and Lk. While there are differences as to the extent and character of the 2d source, there is something like general agreement as to its existence. It is not agreed as to whether this source contained narratives of events, as well as sayings, or whether it was a book of sayings alone (the former is thought to be the more probable view), nor is it agreed as to whether it contained an account of the Passion week (on the differing views of the extent of Q, see Moffatt, op. cit., 197 ff); but while disagreement exists as to these and other points, the tendency, as said, is to accept a "two-source" theory in some form as the only sufficient account of the phenomena of the Gospels.

(4) *Other sources:* To make the source-theory probable, some account must be taken of other sources beyond the two enumerated above. Both the 1st and the 3d Gospels contain material not borrowed from these sources. There is the fore-history of Mt **1 2**, which belongs to that Gospel alone, with other things likewise recorded by Mt only (**9** 27–34; **12** 22; **14** 28–33; **17** 24 ff, etc). Then not only has Lk a fore-history (chs **1, 2**), but a large part of his Gospel consists of material found nowhere else (e.g. **7** 11–16.36–50; **10** 25 ff; parables

in chs **15**, **16**, **18** 1–14, etc). This *Sondergut* of Mt and Lk will be more appropriately treated in the arts. which deal with these Gospels respectively. Here it is sufficient to point out that the criticism of the Synoptic Gospels is not complete till it has found a probable source (*a*) for what is common to them all, (*b*) for what is common to any two of them, and (*c*) for what is peculiar to each. The literature on the subject is so voluminous that only a few references can be given. In addition to those named, the following works may suffice to set forth the present condition of the Synoptic problem: B. Weiss, *Intro to NT*, and other works; Harnack, *Luke the Physician*, *The Sayings of Jesus*, *The Acts of the Apostles*, *Date of the Acts of the Apostles and of the Synoptic Gospels* (ETs); Wellhausen, *Einleitung in die drei ersten Evangelien*, and works on each of the Synoptic Gospels, esp. *Studies in the Synoptic Problem*, edited by Dr. Sanday.

III. Literary Analysis and Oral Tradition.—Looked at merely as a problem of literary analysis, it is scarcely possible to advance farther than has been done in the works of Harnack, of Sanday and his coadjutors, and of Stanton, referred to above. The work done has been of the most patient and persevering kind. No clue has been neglected, no labor has been spared, and the interrelations of the three Gospels have been almost exhaustively explored. Yet the problem remains unsolved. For it must not be forgotten that the materials of the Synoptic Gospels were in existence before they assumed a written form. Literary analysis is apt to forget this obvious fact, and to proceed by literary comparison alone. The Gospel was confessedly at first and for some years a spoken Gospel, and this fact has to be taken into account in any adequate attempt to understand the phenomena. It is not enough to say with Dr. Stanton that "the relations of the first three Gospels cannot be adequately explained simply by the influence of oral tradition"; for the question arises, Can the relations between the first three Gospels be explained simply by the results of literary analysis, be it as exhaustive and thorough as it may? Let it be granted that literary analysis has accomplished a great deal; that it has almost compelled assent to the two-source hypothesis; that it has finally made good the priority of Mk; that it has made out a probable source consisting mainly of sayings of Jesus, yet many problems remain which literary analysis cannot touch, at least has not touched. There is the problem of the order of events in the Gospels, which is so far followed by all three. How are we to account for that sequence? Is it sufficient to say, as some do, that Mk set the style of the Gospel narrative, and that the others so far followed that style? All Gospels must follow the method set by Mk, so it is affirmed. But if that is the case, how did Mt and Lk depart from that copy by writing a fore-history? Why did they compile a genealogy? Why did they give so large a space to the sayings of Jesus, and add so much not contained in the Gospel which, on the hypothesis, set the pattern of what a Gospel ought to be? These questions cannot be answered on the hypothesis that the others simply followed a fashion set by Mk. Sometimes the 2d Gospel is described as if it were suddenly launched on the Christian world; as if no one had ever heard of the story contained in it before Mk wrote it. From the nature of the case, it is obvious that the church had knowledge of many of the facts in the life of Christ, and was in possession of much of His teaching before any of the Gospels were written. So much is plain from the Epistles of St. Paul. How many facts about Jesus, and how much of His teaching may be gathered from these epistles, we do not inquire at present. But we do learn much from St. Paul about the historical Jesus.

1. The Problem Not Solely a Literary One

The Christian church in its earlier form arose out of the teaching, example and influence of the apostles at Jerus. It was based on apostolic testimony as to the life, character, teaching, death and resurrection of Jesus Christ. That testimony told the church what Jesus had done, what He had taught, and of the belief of the apostles as to what He was, and what He continued to be. We read that the early church "continued stedfastly in the apostles' teaching and fellowship" (Acts **2** 42). The "teaching" consisted of reminiscences of the Lord, of interpretations of the facts about Jesus and of agreements between these and the OT. The first instruction given to the church was oral. Of this fact there can be no doubt. How long oral teaching continued we may not say, but it is likely that it continued as long as the apostles dwelt together at Jerus. To them an appeal could constantly be made. There was also the strictly catechetical teaching given to the converts, and this teaching would be given after the manner to which they had been accustomed in their earlier education. It consisted mainly in committing accurately to memory, and in repetition from memory (see CATECHIST; CATECHUMEN). There would thus be a stricter tradition, as it was taught in the catechetical classes, and a looser tradition which consisted of as much as the people could carry with them from the preaching of the apostles at the weekly assemblies. Those, besides, who were present at the day of Pentecost, and others present at the feasts at Jerus, who had passed under Christian influence, would carry with them on their return to their homes some knowledge of the life and death, resurrection and ascension of Jesus. It may have been a meager Gospel that these carried with them to Antioch, to Rome, or to other cities in which the *diaspora* dwelt. But that they did carry a Gospel with them is plain, for from their testimony arose the church at Antioch, where the Christians had without question a knowledge of the Gospel, which informed their faith and guided their action.

2. Influence of Oral Instruction

IV. Order of Events and Time of Happenings in the Synoptic Gospels.—It is known from Acts that the main topic of the preaching of the apostles was the resurrection of the Lord. "With great power gave the apostles their witness of the resurrection of the Lord Jesus" (Acts **4** 33). It is evident, however, that the apostolic witness would not be *limited* to the events of the Passion week, or to the fact of the resurrection. There would arise a thirst for information regarding the life of Jesus, what He had done, what He had said, what manner of life He had lived, and what teaching He had given. Accounts of Him and of His work would be given by the apostles, and once these accounts were given, they would continue to be given in the same form. Tell a story to a child and he will demand that it be always given in the form in which he first knew it. Hearers of a story are impatient of variations in the subsequent telling of it. Memory is very tenacious and very conservative.

1. Range of Apostolic Witness

It is clear that the first lessons of the apostles were accounts of the Passion week, and of the resurrection. But it went backward to events and incidents in the life of Jesus, and as we read the Synoptic Gospels, we soon see that the order was dictated by the events themselves. They are grouped together for no other reason than that they happened so. Most of the incidents are hung on a geographical thread. In the 2d Gospel, which seems to preserve

2. Bearing on Order

most faithfully the traditional order, this is obvious to every attentive reader; but in all the 3 Gospels many of the narratives go in well-established cycles. To take only one illustration, where many might be instanced, the healing of the woman with the issue of blood is represented as occurring in the course of the walk to the house of Jairus (Mk **5** 21 ff). The only explanation is that this was the actual mode of its happening. Events happened, incidents arose, in the course of the journeys of Jesus and His disciples, words were also spoken, and in the memories of the disciples, when the journey was recalled, there arose also what had happened in the course of the journey. In fact, as we follow the journey through Galilee, to the coasts of Tyre and Sidon, through Samaria, down the valley of the Jordan, through Jericho to Jerus, we find that the grouping of the material of the Gospels is determined by the facts. Most of what is recorded happened in the course of the journeys, and was borne in the memories of the disciples in the order of its happening. The order, then, is not arbitrary, nor is it the product of reflection; it is the outcome of the facts. It is true that in pursuance of their several plans, Lk sometimes, Mt frequently, deserts the order of Mk, but it is noteworthy that they never do so together. As Professor Burkitt says, "Mt and Lk never agree against Mk in transposing a narrative. Lk sometimes deserts the order of Mk, and Mt often does so; but in these cases Mk is always supported by the remaining Gospel" (op. cit., 36). In Mt, after **19** 1, the events follow each other quite as in Mk.

3. Time of Happenings

When one studies the rather kaleidoscopic political geography of Pal in the first 40 years of our era, he will find many confirmations of the historic situation in the Synoptic Gospels. The birth of Jesus was in the time of Herod the Great, when the whole of Pal was under one government. After the death of Herod, Pal was under several rulers. Archelaus had possession of Judaea until the year 9 AD. Galilee was under Herod Antipas until the year 37, and the tetrarchy of Philip had a distinct government of its own. About the year 40 Pal was again under one government under Herod Agrippa. Now it is clear that the events of the Gospels happened while Herod Antipas ruled in Galilee and Peraea, and while Pilate was procurator in Judaea (see CHRONOLOGY OF NT, and JESUS CHRIST). Nor is the significance of this environment exhausted by the reference to the time. As Professor Burkitt has shown (op. cit., in his chapter entitled "Jesus in Exile"), in the itinerary recorded in Mk **5**, the parts avoided are the dominions of Herod Antipas. It is said in Mk **3** 6, "And the Pharisees went out, and straightway with the Herodians took counsel against him, how they might destroy him." The significance of this alliance between the Pharisees and the Herodians is well drawn out by Professor Burkitt in the work cited above. It is simply noted by Mk, and on it the evangelist makes no remark. But the conspiracy had a great effect on the work of Jesus. A little later we find Jesus no more in any of the synagogues. He devotes Himself to the training of the Twelve, and is outside of the dominions of Herod Antipas. It is not to be forgotten that during these months Jesus is an exile from His own land, and it was during that period of exile that the issue of His work became clear to Him, and from the time of the great confession at Caesarea-Philippi He began to tell His disciples of the decease He should accomplish at Jerus (Mt **16** 13 ff ‖).

V. Dating of the Synoptic Gospels.—The question as to the dates at which the Synoptic Gospels appear in a published form may more suitably be dealt with in connection with the arts. on the separate Gospels. It need only be observed here that opinion is tending toward much earlier dates than were common till lately.

1. Return to Earlier Dating

By all but extreme writers it is now admitted that the first 3 Gospels fall well within the limits of the apostolic age. In the Preface to his work on Luke (1906), Harnack reminded his readers that 10 years before he had told them that "in the criticism of the sources of the oldest Christianity we are in a movement backward to tradition." The dates he formerly favored were, for Mk between 65 and 70 AD, for Mt between 70 and 75, for Lk between 78 and 93. Harnack's more recent pronouncement as to the date of Acts, which he states with all the emphasis of italics, "It seems now to be established beyond question that both books of this great historical work were written while St. Paul was yet alive" (*Date of the Acts and the Synoptic Gospels*, 124, ET), must have a determining influence on critical opinion. If Acts were written during the lifetime of St. Paul (cf Acts **28** 30 f), then the 3d Gospel must have been written earlier. It is likely that Lk had all his material in hand during the imprisonment of St. Paul at Caesarea. If he made use of the 2d Gospel, then Mk must have had a still earlier date, and the whole problem of the dating of the Gospels is revolutionized. The essential thing is that the 3 Gospels were probably written and published before the destruction of Jerus (70 AD). There is nothing in their contents that makes this view untenable.

2. The Material Still Older

It is still to be remembered, however, that the materials of which the Gospels are composed existed before they were put into a written form. Every discussion must take note of that fact. The lit. of the NT presupposes just such accounts of the life of Jesus as we find in the Synoptic Gospels, and readers of the Gospels have a right to rest on their veracity and sufficiency as accounts of Jesus, of what He was, what He said, and what He did. They are their own best witnesses.

VI. The Messianic Idea in Its Bearings on Historicity of the Gospels.—In a striking passage in his *Das Evangelium Marci* (65, 66), Wellhausen vividly sets forth the significant contrast between the Jewish and the Christian conceptions of the Messiah.

1. The Jewish and the Christian Messiah

We quote the words, notwithstanding the fact that Wellhausen does not regard the passage, Mk **8** 31 ff, as historical. With him what is set forth there is not the figure of the historical Jesus, but a picture of the persecuted church.

"The confession of Peter, 'Thou art the Messiah,' affords," he says, "the occasion for the setting forth of what up to this time was latent. He has elicited the confession and accepted it. Nevertheless He accepts it with a correction; a correction that follows as a matter of course. He is not the Messiah who will restore the kingdom of Israel, but another Messiah altogether. Not to set up the kingdom does He go to Jerus, but He goes in order to be crucified. Through sorrow and death He goes into glory, and only by this way can others also enter. The kingdom of God is no Judaistic kingdom; the kingdom is destined only for some chosen individuals, for disciples. The thought of the possibility of a *metanoia* of the people has wholly disappeared. Into the place of a command to repent addressed to all steps the command to follow, and that can be obeyed only by a very few. The conception of following loses now its proper forces and takes a higher meaning. It does not mean what it meant up to this time, viz. to accompany and to follow Him during His lifetime; it overflows that meaning; one is to follow Him even unto death. The following is an *imitatio* possible only after His death, and this is to be attained only by a very few. One must bear his cross after Him. . . . The situation of the oldest congregation and its tone is here foreshadowed by Jesus as He goes to meet his fate."

A similar passage occurs in the *Einleitung*, which ends with the significant sentence, "All these are noteworthy signs of the time in which He takes His standpoint" (81).

Elsewhere Wellhausen admits that the sections of the Gospels following the scene at Caesarea-Philippi contain what was known as the distinctive Gospel of the apostolic church. But this Gospel owed its origin to the apostolic church itself. It is a question of the highest importance, and the answer cannot be determined by mere literary criticism: Is the Christian conception of the Messiah due to Jesus? or is it due to the reflection of the church? Which is the more probable? It is agreed, Wellhausen being witness, that the Christian conception was subversive of the Jewish, that the two were in contradiction in many ways. One can understand the Christian conception, and its triumph over the Jewish among the Christian people, if it had been set forth by the Master; but it is unintelligible as a something which originated in the congregation itself. The conception of a crucified Messiah, of a suffering Saviour, was a conception which was, during the years of His earthly ministry, in the mind of Jesus alone. It was not in the minds of the disciples, until He had risen from the dead. And it was not in the minds of His contemporaries. But it was the ruling conception in the Jerus church as it is in the Epistles of St. Paul. No: the conception of the suffering Saviour was not the invention of the church, nor did it rise from her thought of her own needs; it was a gift to her from the suffering and risen Lord. Not without a great impulse, nor without a strong source of persuasion, do men displace notions which they have cherished for generations, and substitute notions which are contradictory and subversive of those fiercely and firmly held.

2. Originality of the Christian Conception

We take these chapters therefore as historical, and as descriptive of the historical Jesus. If we can do so, then the matter is intelligible, not otherwise. It is also to be observed in this relation that the needs of the church are new needs. There is no provision in the NT for the needs of the natural man. The critical view often puts the cart before the horse, and this is one illustration of the fact. The needs of the church are the creation of Christ. They are new needs, or needs only imperfectly felt by humanity before Jesus came.

3. The Messianic Hope

Be the needs of the church as great as they may, they are not creative; they are only responsive to the higher call. Nor is it a possible hypothesis that lies at the basis of the criticism of Wellhausen and of many others. Since the time of Baur it has often been said or assumed that it was the Messianic hope that gave concreteness to Christianity; that through the prevalence of the Messianic hope, Christianity was enabled to enter on its career of victory. This is another case of the *hysteron proteron*. It is the historical Jesus that has given concreteness and definiteness to the Messianic conceptions which were current in His time. Because at the heart of the Christian conception there was this concrete gracious figure, and because of the commanding influence of Jesus Christ, this form of Messianism entered into human life, flourished and endured, and is with us today. Other forms of Messianism have only an antiquarian value. They may be discussed as of literary interest, but their practical significance is as nothing. No doubt Messianic categories were ransacked by the church to see if they could be used in order more fully to set forth the significance of Jesus Christ. But the essence of the matter did not lie in them but in Him, whom they had known, loved and served. It is time that a newer critical assumption should be found than the obsolete, worn-out one that the church invented the Christ. We know a little of the early church, and we know its immaturity and its limitations. We have learned something, too, of the Jews at the time of Our Lord, and we note that in the Gospels their limitations have been transcended, their immaturity has been overcome, and how? By the fact of Christ. He is so great that He must be real.

VII. The OT in Its Bearing on the Synoptic Gospels.—It is always to be remembered that the OT was the Bible of the early Christians. They accepted it as the Word of God, and as authoritative for the guidance of life and conduct. It is one thing to admit and assert this; it is another thing to say that the story of the OT molded and directed the story of Jesus as it is in the Synoptic Gospels. This has been widely asserted, but without adequate proof. As a matter of fact Christianity, when it accepted the OT as the word of God, interpreted it in a fashion which had not been accepted before. It interpreted it in the light of Jesus Christ. Tendencies, facts, meanings, which had been in the OT came into light, and the Bible of the Christians was a Bible which testified of Christ. That on which the Jews laid stress passed into the background, and that which they had neglected came into prominence. This view is set forth by St. Paul: "Unto this day, whensoever Moses is read, a veil lieth upon their heart" (2 Cor **3** 15). Or as it is put in Lk, "O foolish men, and slow of heart to believe in all that the prophets have spoken! Behooved it not the Christ to suffer these things, and to enter into his glory?" (**24** 25 f). In the Christian interpretation stress was laid on meanings which Jewish readers had neglected, and so the church read the OT in the new light, and things formerly hidden leaped into view. So the suffering servant of Jeh became for them the keystone of the OT, and the ritual sacrifices and ceremonies of the OT obtained a new meaning. The story of Israel and of its patriarchs, lawgivers, priests, kings and prophets, became full of significance for the new religion, and its psalms and prophecies were searched because they testified of Christ. This is not the place to inquire into the truth of the Christian interpretation, but the fact is undeniable. The inference is that the OT did not, as it was understood by the Jews, influence the conceptions which the church had of Christ; rather the influence of Christ, His commanding personality, and His history gave a new meaning to the OT, a meaning undreamt of before. The Epistle to the Hebrews might have as an alternative title, "How to find Christ in the OT." So powerful was the impression made on the disciples by the personality of Jesus, by His whole demeanor, by His teaching, His life, death and resurrection, that they saw all things in the light of it. The difficulty we have in justifying the references to prophecy, in the light of historical criticism, is a testimony to the fact that the prophecy did not dictate the fact; it was the fact that dictated the accommodation of the prophecy. In this relation also, the supreme fact is the personality of Jesus.

VIII. The Jesus of the Gospels as Thinker.—

1. Ethics of Jesus

Turning from the conception of the suffering Saviour in the Synoptics, we come to the aspect of Jesus as teacher and thinker, and here also we find abundant evidence of the historical character of the Gospel presentation. As the ethics of Jesus are treated in another art., it is sufficient to say here that the conception of the ethical man and His conduct set forth in His teaching is of unusual breadth, and when worked out in detail, yields an ideal of man in himself, and in relation to others, which transcends all other ethical teaching known to mankind. This, too, we must trace to His unique personality, and not to the reflection of the church.

2. Jesus as Thinker

A glance may be taken at Jesus under His more general aspect as thinker. As thinker, Jesus stands alone. He speaks with authority, and whoever understands must obey. The Synoptic Gospels, in this respect, are unique. There is nothing like them in literature. Not even in the Bible is there anything to compare with them. Even in the other books of the NT we do not find anything like the attitude of Jesus to the common things of life. The world's literature shows no parallel to the parables of the Gospels. Here, at any rate, we are on safe ground in saying that these are not due to the reflection of the church. They have an individual stamp which accredits them as the product of one mind. But a great deal more may be said on the characteristic features of the thinking of Jesus. He is the only thinker who goes straight from the common things of daily life and daily experience into the deepest mysteries of life. The deepest thoughts which man can think are suggested to Him by what everybody sees or does. It is not easy within reasonable limits to do justice to this feature of the Synoptic Gospels. Jesus is at home amid the common things and common occupations of life, because He discerns the Father's presence in them all. What a series of pictures of the world, and of occupations of men, could be gathered from these Gospels! This feature of them was neglected until men under the teaching of poets and painters returned into sympathy with external Nature. We are only beginning to see what wealth, from this point of view, is in the Gospels. Poetic sympathy with Nature is a comparatively modern attainment, yet it is in the Gospels. Wind and weather, mountain and valley, seedtime and harvest, summer and winter, sowing and reaping, buying and selling, all are there, transfigured into higher meanings, and made vocal of the mysteries of the kingdom of heaven. Other thinkers rise gradually, and by many steps, from common experience, into what they have to describe of the higher thought and wider generalizations through which they seek to interpret the mystery of life and of the universe. But this thinker needs no middle terms. He sees, e.g., a woman preparing bread for the use of the family, and in this process perceives the mystery of the kingdom of heaven. Whenever He touches on these common things, immediately they are transfigured. They become luminous with the presence of the spiritual world, and earth becomes full of heaven, and every bush is aflame with God.

We note these things because they have a close bearing on the origin and character of the Synoptic Gospels. They bear the stamp of a unique, a creative personality. Be the processes through which the materials of the Gospels have passed what they may, yet these have not obliterated nor blurred the essential characteristics of that unique personality. When the comparisons of the similarities and differences of the Gospels have been exhausted, the problem of their origin remains, and that problem can be solved only by the recognition of a creative personality who alike by word and work was unlike any other that the world has ever seen.

IX. The Problem of the Gospels.—The Jesus of the Gospels is the Son of God. Stated in its highest form, the problem which the evangelists had in hand was how to represent a Divine being under human conditions, and to set Him forth in such a way that in that presentation there should be nothing unworthy of the Divine, and nothing inconsistent with the human conditions under which He worked and lived. This was the greatest problem ever set to literature, and how the evangelists presented and solved it is found in the Gospels. There it has been solved. Even a writer like Bousset admits: "Already for Mk is Jesus not only the Messiah of the Jewish people, but the miraculous eternal Son of God, whose glory shone in the world. . . . . For the faith of the community, which the oldest evangelist already shares, Jesus is the miraculous Son of God, in whom men believe, whom men put wholly on the side of God" (*Was wissen wir von Jesus?* 54, 57). The contrast between the Jesus of the Synoptics and the Pauline and Johannine Christ, so often emphasized, thus begins to disappear. The purpose of the Synoptics, as of Jn, is to lead men to "believe that Jesus is the Christ, the Son of God," that, believing, they "may have life in his name" (Jn **20** 31).

LITERATURE.—Besides the works mentioned in the art., reference may be made to the following: E. A. Abbott, art. "Gospels" in *Enc Brit*, ed 9 (with Rushbrooke), *Common Tradition of the Synoptic Gospels*, and other works; Sanday, *Gospels in the 2d Cent.*, *The Life of Christ in Recent Criticism;* Sir John Hawkins, *Horae Synopticae;* G. Salmon, *Intro to NT;* H. Chase, "The Gospels in the Light of Historical Criticism," Essay X in *Cambridge Bib. Essays*, edited by Dr. Swete (1905); H. L. Jackson, "The Present State of the Synoptic Problem," Essay XIII in *Cambridge Bib. Essays*, edited by Dr. Swete (1909); Peake, *Intro to NT;* A. Loisy, *Les évangiles synoptiques* (1907–8); J. M. Thomson, *The Synoptic Gospels, Arranged in Parallel Cols.* (1910; this scholarly work does for EV what such works as Greswell's *Harmonia Evangelica*, Rushbrooke's *Synopticon* and Wright's *Synopsis* have done for the Gr texts); A. A. Hobson, *The Diatessaron of Tatian and the Synoptic Problem* (The University of Chicago Press, 1904).

JAMES IVERACH

GOTHIC, goth'ik, **VERSION.** See VERSIONS.

GOTHOLIAS, goth-ō-lī'as (**Γοθολίας**, *Gotholías*): Father of Josias, one of the sons of Elam who returned from Babylon with Ezra (1 Esd **8** 33). The name corresponds to Athaliah, the Gr *G* being substituted for the Heb guttural *'ayin*, as in Gomorrha, Gaza, etc. Taken with 2 K **11** 1, the name would seem to have been used for both men and women.

GOTHONIEL, gō-thō'ni-el (**Γοθονιήλ**, *Gothoniēl*): The same as Othniel, father of Chabris who was one of the governors of the city of Bethulia (Jth **6** 15).

GOURD, gōrd, gŏŏrd (קִיקָיוֹן, *ḳīḳāyōn*): The Vulg has *hedera* ("ivy"), which is impossible. Philologically *ḳīḳāyōn* appears to be connected with κίκι (*kiki*), which was the Egyp name for the castor oil plant (*Ricinus communis*). This grows plentifully all over the Orient, and under favorable conditions may reach a height of 10 to 15 ft.; its larger leaves afford a grateful shade. The requirements of the narrative in Jon **4** 6 ff are, however, much more suitably met by the "bottle gourd" (*Cucurbita lagenaria*), the Arab. *ḳar'ah*. This is a creeping, vinelike plant which may frequently be seen trained over the rough temporary sun-shelters erected in fields or by the roadside in Pal and Mesopotamia.

E. W. G. MASTERMAN

GOURD, WILD, wīld (פַּקֻּעֹת שָׂדֶה, *paḳḳu'ōth sādheh*, 2 K **4** 39): The √ פָּקַע, *pāḳa'*, means "to split" or "burst open," and on this ground these "wild gourds" have been identified with the fruit of the squirting cucumber (*Ecballium elaterium*). This little gourd, $1\frac{1}{2}$ to 2 in. long, when fully ripe falls suddenly when touched or shaken, the bitter, irritating juice is squirted to a considerable distance, and the seeds are thrown all around. It is exceedingly common in Pal, and its familiar poisonous properties, as a drastic cathartic, made it unlikely that under any circumstances its fruit could be mistaken for any edible gourd; it is, too, in no way vinelike ("wild vine," 2 K **4** 39) in appearance; the stem is stiff and upright, and there are no tendrils. The traditional plant, *Cucumis prophetarum*, which grows in the desert, and has very small "gourds," has nothing really to recommend it. By far the most probable plant is the Colocynth (*Citrullus colocynthis*), belonging like the last two to N.O. *Cucurbitaceae*. This view has the support of the

Colocynth (*Citrullus colocynthis*).

LXX and Vulg. It is a vinelike plant which spreads over the ground or attaches itself by its spiral tendrils to other plants. The rounded "gourds" are 3 in. or more in diameter, and contain a pulp intensely bitter and, in any but minute quantities, extremely poisonous.

E. W. G. MASTERMAN

GOVERNMENT, guv'ērn-ment: The government of the Hebrews varied at different periods, of which we may distinguish seven: (1) the nomadic period, from the Exodus to the entrance into Pal; (2) the period of transition from nomadic to civil life; (3) the monarchy; (4) the period of subjection to other oriental nations; (5) the period from Ezra to the Greeks; (6) Greek rule; (7) Roman rule.

1. The Nomadic Period

The government of the primitive period is that proper to nomadic tribes composed of families and clans, in no wise peculiar to the Hebrews, but shared in its essential features by the most diverse peoples at a corresponding stage of civilization. Though we might draw illustrations from many sources, the government of the Bedouins, Sem nomads inhabiting the steppes of Arabia, affords the most instructive parallel. In the patriarchal state the family is the household (including slaves and concubines) of the father, who is its head, having power of life and death over his children (Gen **22**; Jgs **11** 31 ff). A clan is a collection of families under a common chieftain, chosen for his personal qualifications, such as prowess and generous hospitality. The composition of the clan was essentially shifting, subject, according to circumstances, to the loss or accession of individuals and families. Although the possession of the same grazing-grounds doubtless played a large part in determining the complexion of the clan, the fiction of descent from a common ancestor was maintained, even when kinship was established by the blood covenant. In all probability community of worship, which cemented the tribe, served as the most effective bond of union also in the clan. Vestiges of such clan cults are still to be detected (1 S **20** 5 ff; Jgs **18** 19). The familiar tradition of the twelve tribes must not be allowed to blind us to the evidence that the tribe also was not constant. Mention of the Kenites (Jgs **1** 16) and the list of tribes in the Song of Deborah (Jgs **5**) remind us that such organizations vanished. In the readjustment incident to the change from the pastoral life of the nomad to that of the settled agricultural population of Pal, many units were doubtless shifted from one tribe to another, and the same result may be assumed as following from the endless strife between the tribes before and during the period of the kings. The large and powerful tribe of Judah seems to have originated comparatively late. The union of the tribes under the leadership of Moses was essentially similar to the formation of a new tribe out of a group of clans actuated by a desire to accomplish a common end. Many such temporary aggregations must have originated, only to succumb to the centrifugal forces of jealousy and conflicting interests. Even after the entrance of the Hebrews into Pal, their history for long is that of kindred tribes, rather than that of a nation. The leadership of Moses rested on personal, not on constitutional, authority, and was rendered precarious by the claims of family and of clan, as in the case of Korah, Dathan, and Abiram (Nu **16**). The authority of Moses naturally extended to the administration of justice, as well as to matters pertaining to war and religion. He appointed officers to assist him in this judicial function (Ex **18** 21 ff), but the laws according to which they rendered judgment were those of custom and usage, not those of a written code. As among the tribal chieftains, important matters were referred to the leader, who, in cases of doubt or in default of recognized custom, resorted to the lot or to the oracle.

2. The Period of Transition

When the nomad tribes settled in Pal to become an agricultural people, there ensued a period of unrest due to the necessity for readjustment to changed conditions. The old tribal organization, admirably adapted to the former, ill suited the new requirements. These may be summed up in the demand for the substitution of local organization, based on the rights of individuals, for the tribal government, which had regard solely to the interests of family, clan and tribe. Such readjustment did not, of course, at once ensue, but came piecemeal in answer to the gradually realized wants of the community. Nor was the development entirely from within, but was unquestionably in large measure influenced by the institutions existing among the Canaanite population, only a part of which had been expelled by the invaders. Although the tribes still clung to the notion of descent from a common ancestor, which was embodied in the accepted genealogies with their filiation of clans into tribes and of tribes into a nation, that which henceforth passed as a "tribe" was less an aggregation of kindred units than a geographical unit or group of units. The times were turbulent, disturbed by contending elements within and by foes without the tribes. Then it was that there arose a class of chieftains of strongly marked character, called by a new name. The "judge" (שֹׁפֵט, *shōphēt*) was not the ruler of a nation, but the chieftain of a tribe, winning and maintaining his authority by virtue of his personal prowess. The cases of Gideon and Abimelech (Jgs **8, 9**) show that the authority of the "judge" was not hereditary. Agreeably to the generally changed conditions, the "elders" (זְקֵנִים, *zᵉḳēnīm*), who were formerly heads of families or kindreds, now came, possibly under the influence of the Canaanites, to be constituted an aristocratic upper class, with certain functions as administrative officers and councilors. Cities also grew and acquired importance, so that the adjacent hamlets were subordinated to them, probably even ruled from them as executive centers. In all this there is a certain similarity to the process by which, in the period just preceding the beginning of real history, Athens became the metropolis of Attica, and conventional tribes supplanted those based on kinship, while the rise of the purely local organization of the demos led speedily to the appearance of the "tyrants." The high places of clans and tribes continued to be frequented, and certain "seers" (1 S **9** 6 ff) enjoyed considerable prestige by virtue of their peculiar relation to the tribal god.

3. The Monarchy

While the succession of tribal chieftains and of the "judges" depended on fitness and call of God, the principle of heredity is essential to the institution of monarchy, which originated in the desire to regulate the succession with a view to having an assured authoritative leadership. This principle could not, of course, be invoked in the appointment of Saul, the first king (מֶלֶךְ, *melekh*), who won this distinction in virtue of his personal prowess, supported by the influence of Samuel directed of God. His son Ishbosheth ruled two years over Israel, but lost his throne through the disaffection of his subjects (2 S **2**-**4**). The accession of David, king of Judah, to the throne of all Israel was likewise exceptional, owing as much to the character of the heir presumptive, as to his own qualifications. Solomon promised of God and his father David succeeded by right of heredity with the support of the military and religious leaders. In the Southern Kingdom of Judah, heredity was henceforth observed because of its homogeneity and the consequent absence of internal discord; whereas the principle often failed in the turbulent Northern Kingdom of Israel, which was distracted by tribal jealousies. But even when not effectually operative, heredity was recognized as constituting a claim to the succession, although the popular voice, which had been supreme in the institution of the monarchy, was a power always to be reckoned with.

(1) *Royal prerogatives.*—The history and functions of monarchy defined the prerogatives and duties of the king. Just as the head of the family, or the chieftain of a tribe, functioned as representative of those subject to him in matters of religion, war, and the administration of justice, so also was it with the king. In all these spheres he was supreme, exercising his authority either personally or through representatives who thus became part of the royal establishment. It is to be noted that the sacerdotal or sacral character of the king, which was merely an extension of his privileges as individual and head of a household, was not emphasized among the Hebrews to a like extent as among other oriental peoples; and the priests whom he appointed were perhaps in the first instance court chaplains, though in time they came to assume greater authority. The responsibility of the king for the public safety carried with it the obligation to guard the state treasures, to which the treasures of the temples were felt to belong; and it was his privilege to use them when necessary for defence. The levying of taxes, also, and the collection and use of revenues from various sources likewise fell of necessity to the king and his representatives.

(2) *Officers.*—In regard to the constitution of the king's court under Saul and David we learn comparatively little; even touching that of Solomon we are not fully informed, although we know that it must have been far removed from the original simplicity. We may classify the known officers as follows: (*a*) religious: priests (2 S **8** 17; **20** 23 ff); (*b*) household: cupbearer (1 K **10** 5); master of the vestry (2 K **10** 22); master of the household (1 K **4** 6), who probably was a eunuch (1 K **22** 9 m; 2 K **8** 6 m; **9** 32); (*c*) state: scribe or clerk (2 S **8** 17; **20** 25, etc); recorder, or prompter (1 K **4** 3); king's counselor (2 S **15** 12); and, perhaps, the king's friend (2 S **15** 37; **16** 16); overseer of taskwork (2 S **20** 24); (*d*) military: commander-in-chief of the army (2 S **8** 16); commander of the king's guards (?) (2 S **8** 18; **20** 23).

(3) *Fiscal institutions.*—The simplicity of Saul's rule was such as to make slight demands upon the resources of the people. He lived in the manner of a tribal chieftain on his ancestral estate, receiving from his subjects voluntary gifts (1 S **10** 27; **16** 20), and also, without doubt, his due share of the booty. Whether he instituted a regular tax (cf 1 S **17** 25) is not certain. With the growth and prosperity of the nation, David changed the character of the court, imitating in a measure the state of other oriental potentates. It is not clear whether he levied a regular tax, although it may be surmised that he had it in view, together with the regulation of taskwork, in ordaining the census taken in his time (2 S **24** 1 ff). We know that he received his portion of the booty (2 S **8** 11; **12** 30). The increasing luxury of Solomon's court required the imposition of additional taxes. It is probable that some income was derived from the enforced cultivation of crown lands (1 S **8** 12), although the taskwork, which became extremely burdensome and subsequently provoked the secession of the Northern Kingdom, was chiefly applied to public works. The tribute of subject peoples (1 K **4** 21) was considerable (1 K **10** 14). We now for the first time hear of taxes upon caravans and merchants, although it was in all probability a source of income even in the time of the nomad chieftains; there was also revenue from the carrying trade of his merchant fleet (1 K **10** 11.22) and from the trade in horses and chariots carried on with Egypt (1 K **10** 28 ff). Solomon also divided his kingdom into twelve provinces commanded by prefects, who should provide victuals for the king and his household: each prefect had to make provision for a month in the year (1 K **4** 7 ff). It does not appear whether Judah, which is not included in the list of provinces, was as a mark of special favor exempted from this tax, or whether the omission is to be otherwise explained. The seizure of the vineyard of Naboth by Ahab (1 K **21**) makes it seem not improbable that the property of persons condemned on certain charges was confiscate to the king.

(4) *Administration of justice.*—The king, like the tribal chieftain of the steppes, still sat in judgment, but chiefly in matters of moment; less important cases were decided by the prefects of provinces and other officers. Under the earlier kings there was no code except the Book of the Covenant (Ex **20**-**23**), but judgment was rendered on the basis of the law of custom or usage, the function of the judge being essentially that of an arbiter. For the later code see DEUTERONOMY.

(5) *Religion.*—The king was regarded as the natural representative of his people before God; but while he did exercise certain sacerdotal functions in person, such offices were generally performed by the priest whom he had appointed.

(6) *Secular administration.*—The authority of the king in matters of state was exercised partly by him in person, partly through his ministers, the "princes" (1 K **4** 2 ff). Among these functions are to be classed the communication with subject and foreign princes and the direction of the taskwork, which was employed for public improvements, partly military, as in the fortification of cities, partly religious, as in the building of the temple. Local affairs had always been left largely to the tribes and their subdivisions, but, with the gradual increase of royal authority, the king sought to exercise it more and more in the conduct of the village communities.

Conversely, the "elders of the people," as the (albeit aristocratic) representatives of the communes, occasionally had a voice even in larger matters of state.

The principle of local autonomy was widely observed in the oriental states, which concerned themselves chiefly about political and military organization and about the collection of revenues. Hence there is no occasion for surprise on finding that the Jews enjoyed a large measure of autonomy during the period of their subjection to other oriental powers and that even during the exile they resorted, in matters of dispute, to their own representatives for judgment. Under Pers rule Pal formed part of the satrapy lying W. of the Euphrates and had, for a time, its own governor.

4. Israel under Oriental Potentates

Ezra and Nehemiah endeavored to introduce a new code, which, after a period of perhaps two centuries, established a dual form of government subject to the supreme authority of the suzerain power. By the new code the secular officers were subordinated to the high priest, who thus virtually assumed the position of a constitutional prince, ruling under the Law. The "prince," however, as the representative of the tribes, and the "elders of the people," as the representatives of the communes, continued to exercise a certain limited authority.

5. After the Restoration

Under the Gr rulers of Egypt and Syria the Jews continued to enjoy a large measure of autonomy, still maintaining in general the type of internal government formulated under Ezra and Nehemiah. We now hear of a council of "elders" presided over by the high priest. The latter, appointed by the kings, was recognized as ethnarch by both Ptolemies and Seleucids and held accountable for the payment of the tribute, for the exaction of which he was, of course, empowered to levy taxes. The brief period of political independence under the Hasmoneans (see ASMONEANS) did not materially alter the character of the government, except that the high priest, who had long been a prince in everything but in name, now openly so styled himself. The council of the "elders" survived, although with slightly diminished authority. In other respects the influence of Gr institutions made itself felt.

6. The Greeks

When Pompey terminated the reign of the Hasmoneans, the government still continued with little essential change. Following the example of the Gr kings, the Romans at first appointed the high priest to the "leadership of the nation." He was soon, however, shorn for a time of his political dignity, the country being divided into five districts, each governed by its "synod"; but Caesar once more elevated the high priest to the office of ethnarch. Under Herod, the high priest and the synedrium (Sanhedrin), appointed or deposed at will as his interests seemed to require, lost much of their former prestige and power. After the death of Herod the land was again divided, and a procurator, subordinate to the governor of Syria, ruled in Judaea, having practical independence in his sphere. In their internal affairs the Jews now, as under former masters, enjoyed a large measure of freedom. The high priest no longer exercising any political authority, the synedrium, of which he was a member, now gained in influence, being in fact an aristocratic council in many respects not unlike the Rom senate. It combined judicial and administrative functions, limited in the exercises of its authority only by the provision that its decisions might be reviewed by the procurator. (See GOVERNOR.) Naturally the outlying jurisdictions were organized on the same model, each with its synedrium competent in local matters. The synedrium at Jerus served also as a governing board for the city.

7. The Romans

WILLIAM ARTHUR HEIDEL

GOVERNOR, guv'ẽr-nẽr: The word "governor" is employed in EV in rendering a great variety of Heb and Gr words. In certain cases strict consistency is neither observed nor possible.

In the rendering of Heb terms account has naturally been taken of the tr[s] offered in LXX, which, being the work of different hands, is both uneven in quality and inconsistent. But there are inherent difficulties which can never be entirely overcome. First and most important, there is the difficulty arising from our ignorance of many details of the government of the oriental nations to which the terms apply. Hardly less is the embarrassment occasioned by the vague employment of words in indiscriminate reference to persons of superior rank and somehow exercising authority. There is consequently much confusion in the use of titles such as "deputy," "duke," "judge," "lawgiver," "overseer," "prince," "ruler," etc, for which the student may consult the special articles.

1. In the OT

(1) אַלּוּף or אַלֻּף, *'allūph*, "governor" (RV "chieftain") in Judah (Zec **9** 7; **12** 5 f).

(2) חוֹקֵק, *ḥōḳēḳ* (Jgs **5** 9; **5** 14, AVm "or lawgivers"). The word is variously rendered with "ruler" or "lawgiver" in EV of Gen **49** 10; Dt **33** 21; Isa **33** 22.

(3) מֹשֵׁל, *mōshēl*, part. of מָשַׁל, *māshal*, "to be master," "to rule" (Gen **45** 26, RV "ruler").

(4) נָשִׂיא, *nāsī'* (2 Ch **1** 2, RV "prince").

(5) סָגָן, *ṣāghān* (Dnl **3** 2 f; Jer **51** 23, RVm "or lieutenants"; vs 28.57; Ezk **23** 6.12.23). The same word is rendered "rulers" or "deputies" (Isa **41** 25; Ezr **9** 2; Neh **2** 16; **5** 7; **7** 5; **12** 40).

(6) פֶּחָה, *peḥāh*, is variously used: (*a*) of the military governor of a province among the Assyrians (Isa **36** 9); (*b*) among the Chaldees (Ezk **23** 6.23; Jer **51** 23.28.57); (*c*) among the Persians (Est **3** 12; **8** 9; **9** 3); (*d*) of the governor-general of the province beyond the River (Euphrates) (Ezr **8** 36; Neh **2** 7.9); (*e*) of Nehemiah as subordinate "governor in the land of Judah" under him (Neh **5** 14 ff); (*f*) of Zerubbabel as "governor of Judah" (Hag **1** 1.14; **2** 2.21); (*g*) of Solomon's governors (1 K **10** 15; **20** 24 [in Syria]).

(7) פָּקִיד, *pāḳīdh* (Jer **20** 1, RV "chief officer"). Elsewhere it is rendered "overseer" or "officer" (cf Gen **41** 34; 2 K **25** 19; Neh **11** 9.22).

(8) שַׂר, *sar*, "governor of the city" (1 K **22** 26). Elsewhere commonly rendered "prince."

(9) שַׁלִּיט, *shallīṭ* (Gen **42** 6). Elsewhere rendered "ruler" or "captain."

(10) תִּרְשָׁתָא, *tirshāthā'*; RV "the governor," AV "the Tirshatha" (Ezr **2** 63; Neh **7** 70). See TIRSHATHA.

The word "governor" in EV represents an almost equal variety of Gr words. Here again the usage is for the most part lax and untechnical; but since reference is chiefly had to officers of the Rom imperial administration, concerning which we possess ample information, no embarrassment is thereby occasioned. The words chiefly in use for "governor" are derived from √*ag*, "drive," "lead":

2. In the NT

(1) ἡγέομαι, *hēgéomai*, "lead" (Mt **2** 6; of Joseph as grand vizier of Egypt, Acts **7** 10).

(2) ἡγεμών, *hēgemṓn*, "leader" (Mt **10** 18; 1 Pet **2** 14; of Pilate, Mt **27** 2.11.14.15.21.27; of Felix, Acts **23** 24.26.33; of Festus, Acts **24** 1.10; **26** 30).

(3) ἡγεμονεύω, *hēgemoneúō*, "function as leader" (Lk **2** 2; of Pilate, Lk **3** 1).

To these are added terms of more specific meaning:

(4) ἐθνάρχης, *ethnárchēs*, "ethnarch" or "ruler of a nation" (2 Cor **11** 32). See GOVERNMENT, 6, 7.

(5) εὐθύνω, *euthúnō*, "direct," "guide" (Jas **3** 4). Here RV properly renders "steersman."

(6) ἀρχιτρίκλινος, *architríclinos*, "president of a banquet" (Jn **2** 8 f, ARV "ruler of the feast").

(7) οἰκονόμος, *oikonómos*, "steward," "manager of a household or estate" (Gal **4** 2, RV "stewards").

It is thus seen that in the NT "governor" in the political sense occurs chiefly in reference to the Rom procurators of Judaea—Pilate, Felix, and Festus. See PILATE; FELIX; FESTUS. It remains for us here to speak briefly of the government of Rom provinces.

Lat *provincia* signifies a magistrate's sphere of duty or authority, either (*a*) judicially or legally, defining the scope of his competence, or (*b*) geographically, designating the territorial limits within which he may exercise authority. It is in the latter sense that we are now considering the word. When, in the 3d cent. BC, Rome began to rule conquered lands outside Italy, each territory was set under the authority of a single magistrate, and hence came to be called a "province." Conquered territories left under the rule of native princes or kings were not so designated, although their government was practically directed by Rome. At first provinces were governed by proconsuls or propraetors (i.e. ex-consuls or ex-praetors); but with the steady multiplication of provinces various expedients became necessary in order to provide governors of suitable rank and dignity. Thus the number of praetors was largely augmented, and the term of possible service as governor was extended. Under Augustus the provinces were parceled out between the emperor and the senate, the former reserving for himself such as seemed to require the maintenance of a considerable armed force. In these the emperor was himself proconsul. Early in the Empire imperial provinces of a different type appear, in which the emperor, regarded as sovereign proprietor, governs by a viceroy (*praefectus*) or steward (*procurator*). In some of these, tributary kings or princes ruled with the emperor's representative—a *legatus* or a *procurator*—by their side, much as England now rules Egypt. Among the provinces so ruled were Egypt and Judaea, partly, no doubt, because of their strategic position, partly because of the temper of their inhabitants. WILLIAM ARTHUR HEIDEL

GOYIM, goi'yim. See GOIIM.

GOZAN, gō'zan (גּוֹזָן, *gōzān*; **Γωζάν**, *Gōzán*, B, *Gōzár* in 2 K **17** 6, *Chōzár* in 1 Ch **5** 26): A place in Assyria to which Israelites were deported on the fall of Samaria (2 K **17** 6; **18** 11; 1 Ch **5** 26). It is also mentioned in a letter of Sennacherib to Hezekiah (2 K **19** 12; Isa **37** 12). The district is that named Guzana by the Assyrians, and Gauzanitis by Ptolemy, W. of Nisibis, with which, in the Assyr geographical list (*WAI*, II, 53, l. 43), it is mentioned as the name of a city (*âlu Guzana; âlu Nasibina*). It became an Assyr province, and rebelled in 759 BC, but was again reduced to subjection. See HABOR; HALAH. JAMES ORR

GRABA, grā'ba. See AGGABA.

GRACE, grās: In the Eng. NT the word "grace" is always a tr of χάρις (*cháris*), a word that occurs in the Gr text something over 170t (the reading is uncertain in places). In secular Gr of all periods it is also a very common word, and in both Bib. and secular Gr it is used with far more meanings than can be represented by any one term in Eng.

1. The Word *Cháris*

Primarily (*a*) the word seems to denote pleasant external appearance, "gracefulness," "loveliness"; cf the personification in "the Graces." Such a use is found in Lk **4** 22, where 'wondered at the charm of his words' is a good tr; and similarly in Col **4** 6. (*b*) Objectively, *charis* may denote the impression produced by "gracefulness," as in 3 Jn ver 4 'greater *gratification* have I none than this' (but many MSS read *chará*, "joy," here). (*c*) As a mental attribute *charis* may be tr[d] by "graciousness," or, when directed toward a particular person or persons, by "favor." So in Lk **2** 52, "Jesus advanced . . . . in favor with God and men." (*d*) As the complement to this, *charis* denotes the emotion awakened in the recipient of such favor, i.e. "gratitude." So Lk **17** 9 reads lit. 'Has he gratitude to that servant?' In a slightly transferred sense *charis* designates the words or emotion in which gratitude is expressed, and so becomes "thanks" (some 10t, Rom **6** 17, etc). (*e*) Concretely, *charis* may mean the *act* by which graciousness is expressed, as in 1 Cor **16** 3, where AV translates by "liberality," and RV by "bounty." These various meanings naturally tend to blend into each other, and in certain cases it is difficult to fix the precise meaning that the writer meant the word to convey, a confusion that is common to both NT and secular Gr. And in secular Gr the word has a still larger variety of meanings that scarcely concern the theologian.

Naturally, the various meanings of the word were simply taken over from ordinary language by the NT writers. And so it is quite illegitimate to try to construct on the basis of all the occurrences of the word a single doctrine that will account for all the various usages.

2. Grace as Power

That one word could express both "charm of speech" and "thankfulness for blessings" was doubtless felt to be a mere accident, if it was thought of at all. But, none the less, the very elasticity of the word enabled it to receive still another—new and technically Christian—meaning. This seems to have originated in part by fusing together two of the ordinary significances. In the first place, as in (*e*) above, *charis* may mean "a gift." In 1 Cor **16** 3; 2 Cor **8** 19 it is the money given by the Corinthians to the Jerusalemites. In 2 Cor **9** 8 it is the increase of worldly goods that God grants for charitable purposes. In 2 Cor **1** 15 it is the benefit received by the Corinthians from a visit by St. Paul. In a more spiritual sense *charis* is the endowment for an office in the church (Eph **4** 7), more particularly for the apostolate (Rom **1** 5; **12** 3; **15** 15; 1 Cor **3** 10; Eph **3** 2.7). So in 1 Cor **1** 4–7 m *charis* is expanded into "word and all knowledge," endowments with which the Corinthians were esp. favored. In 1 Pet **1** 13 *charis* is the future heavenly blessedness that Christians are to receive; in **3** 7 it is the present gift of "life." In the second place, *charis* is the word for God's *favor*, a sense of the term that is esp. refined by St. Paul (see below). But God's favor differs from man's in that it cannot be conceived of as inactive. A favorable "thought" of God's about a man involves of necessity the reception of some blessing by that man, and "to look with favor" is one of the commonest Bib. paraphrases for "bestow a blessing." Between "God's favor" and "God's favors" there exists a relation of active power, and as *charis* denoted both the favor and the favors, it was the natural word for the power that connected them. This use is very clear in 1 Cor **15** 10, where St. Paul says, "not I, but the grace of God which was with me" labored more abundantly than they all: grace is something that *labors*. So in 2 Cor **12** 9, "My grace is sufficient for thee: for my power is made perfect in weakness"; cf 2 Tim **2** 1, "strengthened in the grace," and 1 Pet **4** 10, "stewards of the manifold grace." Evidently in this sense "grace" is almost a synonym for the Spirit (see HOLY SPIRIT), and there is little real difference between "full of the Holy Spirit" and "full of grace and power" in Acts **6** 5.8, while there is a very striking ‖ between Eph **4** 7–13 and 1 Cor

12 4–11, with "gifts of grace" in the one passage, and "gifts of the Spirit" in the other. And this connection between grace and the Spirit is found definitely in the formula "Spirit of grace" in He **10** 29 (cf Zec **12** 10). And, as is well known, it is from this sense of the word that the Catholic doctrine of grace developed.

This meaning of *charis* was obtained by expanding and combining other meanings. By the opposite process of narrowly restricting one of the meanings of the word, it came again into Christian theology as a technical term, but this time in a sense quite distinct from that just discussed. The formation of this special sense seems to have been the work of St. Paul. When *charis* is used with the meaning "favor," nothing at all is implied as to whether or not the favor is deserved. So, for instance, in the NT, when in Lk **2** 52 it is said that "Jesus advanced . . . . in favor with God and men," the last possible thought is that Our Lord did not *deserve* this favor. Cf also Lk **2** 40 and Acts **2** 47 and, as less clear cases, Lk **1** 30; Acts **7** 46; He **4** 16; **12** 15.28. But the word has abundant use in secular Gr in the sense of unmerited favor, and St. Paul seized on this meaning of the word to express a fundamental characteristic of Christianity. The basic passage is Rom **11** 5.6, where as a definition is given, "If it is by grace, it is no more of works: otherwise grace is no more grace." That the word is used in other senses could have caused no 1st-cent. reader to miss the meaning, which, indeed, is unmistakable. "Grace" in this sense is an attitude on God's part that proceeds entirely from within Himself, and that is conditioned in no way by anything in the objects of His favor. So in Rom **4** 4. If salvation is given on the basis of what a man has done, then salvation is given by God as the payment of a debt. But when faith is reckoned for what it is not, i.e. righteousness, there is no claim on man's part, and he receives as a pure gift something that he has not earned. (It is quite true that faith involves moral effort, and so may be thought of as a sort of a "work"; it is quite true that faith does something as a preparation for receiving God's further gifts. But it simply clouds the exegetical issue to bring in these ideas here, as they certainly were not present in St. Paul's mind when the verses were being written.) "Grace," then, in this sense is the antinomy to "works" or to "law"; it has a special relation to the guilt of sin (Rom **5** 20; **6** 1), and has almost exactly the same sense as "mercy." Indeed, "grace" here differs from "mercy" chiefly in connoting eager love as the source of the act. See JUSTIFICATION. Of course it is this sense of grace that dominates Rom **3–6**, esp. in the thesis **3** 24, while the same use is found in Gal **2** 21; Eph **2** 5.8; 2 Tim **1** 9. The same strict sense underlies Gal **1** 6 and is found, less sharply formulated, in Tit **3** 5–7. (Gal **5** 4 is perhaps different.) Outside of St. Paul's writings, his definition of the word seems to be adopted in Jn **1** 17; Acts **15** 11; He **13** 9, while a perversion of this definition in the direction of antinomianism is the subject of the invective in Jude ver 4. And, of course, it is from the word in this technical Pauline sense that an elaborate Protestant doctrine of grace has been developed.

3. Grace in Justification

A few special uses of the word may be noted. That the special blessing of God on a particular undertaking (Acts **14** 26; **15** 40) should be called a "grace" needs no explanation. In Lk **6** 32–34, and 1 Pet **2** 19.20, *charis* seems to be used in the sense of "that which deserves the thanks of God," i.e. a specifically Christian act as distinguished from an act of "natural morality." "Grace for grace" in Jn **1** 16 is a difficult phrase, but an almost exact ‖ in Philo (*Poster. Cain*, 43) may fix the sense as "benefit on benefit." But the tendency of the NT writers is to combine the various meanings the word can have, something that is particularly well illustrated in 2 Cor **8, 9**. In these two chapters the word occurs 10 t, but in so many different senses as to suggest that St. Paul is consciously playing with the term. *Charis* is the money given to the Jerusalemites by the Corinthians (**8** 19), it is the increase of goods that God will grant the Corinthians (**9** 8), it is the disposition of the givers (**8** 6), it is the power of God that has wrought this disposition (**8** 1; **9** 14), it is the act of Christ in the Incarnation (**8** 9; contrast the distinction between "God's grace" and "Christ's act" in He **2** 9), it is the thanks that St. Paul renders (2 Cor **9** 15). That all a Christian is and all that he has is God's gift could have been stated of course without the use of any special term at all. But in these two chapters St. Paul has taught this truth by using for the various ideas always the same term and by referring this term to God at the beginning and the end of the section. That is, to the multiplicity of concepts there is given a unity of terminology, corresponding to the unity given the multiple aspects of life by the thought of entire dependence on God. So *charis*, "grace," becomes almost an equivalent for "Christianity," viewed as the religion of dependence on God through Christ. As one may think of entering Christianity, abiding in it, or falling from it, so one may speak of entering into (Rom **5** 2), abiding in (Acts **13** 43), or falling from (Gal **5** 4) grace; cf 1 Pet **5** 12. So the teaching of Christianity may be summed up as the word or gospel of grace (Acts **14** 3; **20** 24.32). So "grace be with you" closes the Epistles as a sufficient summary of all the blessings that can be wished Christian readers. At the beginning of the Epistles the words "and peace" are usually added, but this is due only to the influence of the Jewish greeting "peace be with you" (Lk **10** 5, etc), and not to any reflection on "grace" and "peace" as separate things. (It is possible that the Gr use of *chairein*, "rejoice," as an epistolary salutation [so in Jas **1** 1] influenced the Christian use of *charis*. But that "grace and peace" was *consciously* regarded as a universalistic combination of Jewish and gentile custom is altogether unlikely.) The further expansion of the introductory formula by the introduction of "mercy" in 1 and 2 Tim is quite without theological significance.

4. Special Uses

In the Gr Gospels, *charis* is used in the words of Christ only in Lk **6** 32–34; **17** 9. As Christ spoke in Aram., the choice of this word is due to St. Luke, probably under the influence of its common Christian use in his own day. And there is no word in Our Lord's recorded sayings that suggests that He employed habitually any especial term to denote grace in any of its senses. But the ideas are unambiguously present. That the pardon of sins is a free act on God's part may be described as an essential in Christ's teaching, and the lesson is taught in all manner of ways. The prodigal knowing only his own wretchedness (Lk **15** 20), the publican without merit to urge (Lk **18** 13), the sick who need a physician (Mk **2** 17), they who hunger and thirst after righteousness (Mt **5** 6), these are the ones for whom God's pardon is inexhaustible. And positive blessings, be they temporal or spiritual, are to be looked for from God, with perfect trust in Him who clothes the lilies and knows how to give good gifts to His children (Mt **7** 11; here Lk **11** 13 has "Holy Spirit" for "gifts," doubtless a Lukan interpretation, but certainly a correct one). Indeed, it is not too much to say that Christ knows but one unpar-

5. Teaching of Christ

donable sin, the sin of spiritual self-satisfaction—"That which is exalted among men is an abomination in the sight of God" (Lk **16** 15; cf Lk **17** 7–10; Mt **20** 1–16).

6. In the OT

There is no word in Heb that can represent all the meanings of *charis*, and in the LXX *charis* itself is used, practically, only as a tr of the Heb *ḥēn* (חֵן), "favor," this restriction of meaning being due to the desire to represent the same Heb word by the same Gr word as far as possible. And *ḥēn*, in turn, is used chiefly only in the phrase "find favor" (Gen **6** 8, etc), whether the reference is to God or men, and without theological importance. Much nearer St. Paul's use of *charis* is *rāçōn* (רָצוֹן), "acceptance," in such passages as Isa **60** 10, "In my favor have I had mercy on thee"; Ps **44** 3, "not . . . . by their own sword . . . . but . . . . because thou wast favorable unto them." Perhaps still closer parallels can be detected in the use of *ḥeṣedh* (חֶסֶד), "kindness," "mercy," as in Ex **20** 6, etc. But, of course, a limitation of the sources for the doctrine to passages containing only certain words would be altogether unjust. The main lines seem to be these: (1) Technically, salvation by grace in the NT is opposed to an OT doctrine of salvation by works (Rom **4** 4; **11** 6), or, what is the same thing, by law (Rom **6** 14; Jn **1** 17); i.e. men and God are thought of as parties to a contract, to be fulfilled by each independently. Most of the legislation seems to presuppose some idea of man as a quantity quite outside of God, while Dt **30** 11–14 states explicitly that the law is not too hard nor too far off for man. (2) Yet even this legalism is not without important modifications. The keeping of the law is man's work, but that man has the law to keep is something for which God only is to be thanked. Ps **119** is the essence of legalism, but the writer feels overwhelmed throughout by the greatness of the mercy that disclosed such statutes to men. After all, the initial (and vital!) act is God's not man's. This is stated most sharply in Ezk **23** 1–4—Oholibah and her sister became God's, not because of any virtue in them, but in spite of most revolting conduct. Cf Dt **7** 7, etc. (3) But even in the most legalistic passages, an absolute literal keeping of the law is never (not even in such a passage as Nu **15** 30.31) made a condition of salvation. The thought of transgression is at all times tempered with the thought of God's pardon. The whole sacrificial system, in so far as it is expiatory, rests on God's gracious acceptance of something in place of legal obedience, while the passages that offer God's mercy without demanding even a sacrifice (Isa **1** 18; Mic **7** 18–20, etc) are countless. Indeed, in Ezk **16, 20, 23,** mercy is promised to a nation that is spoken of as hardly even desiring it, a most extreme instance. (4) But a mere negative granting of pardon is a most deficient definition of the OT idea of God's mercy, which delights in conferring positive benefits. The gift to Abraham of the land of Canaan, liberation from Egypt, food in the wilderness, salvation from enemies, deliverance from exile—all of Israel's history can be felt to be the record of what God did for His people through no duty or compulsion, grateful thanksgiving for such unmerited blessings filling, for instance, much of the Psalter. The hearts of men are in God's keeping, to receive from Him the impulse toward what is right (1 Ch **29** 18, etc). And the promise is made that the God who has manifested Himself as a forgiving Father will in due time take hold of His children to work in them actual righteousness (Isa **1** 26; **4** 3.4; **32** 1–8; **33** 24; Jer **31** 33.34; Ezk **36** 25.26; Zec **8**; Dnl **9** 24; Ps **51** 10–12) With this promise—for the OT always a matter of the future—the OT teaching passes into that of the NT.

7. Summary

Most of the discussions of the Bib. doctrine of grace have been faulty in narrowing the meaning of "grace" to some special sense, and then endeavoring to force this special sense on all the Bib. passages. For instance, Roman Catholic scholars, starting with the meaning of the word in (say) 2 Cor **12** 9, have made Rom **3** 24 state that men are justified by the infusion of Divine holiness into them, an interpretation that utterly ruins St. Paul's argument. On the other hand, Protestant extremists have tried to reverse the process and have argued that grace cannot mean anything except favor as an attitude, with results that are equally disastrous from the exegetical standpoint. And a confusion has resulted that has prevented men from seeing that most of the controversies about grace are at cross-purposes. A rigid definition is hardly possible, but still a single conception is actually present in almost every case where "grace" is found—the conception that all a Christian has or is, is centered exclusively in God and Christ, and depends utterly on God through Christ. The kingdom of heaven is reserved for those who become as little children, for those who look to their Father in loving confidence for every benefit, whether it be for the pardon so freely given, or for the strength that comes from Him who works in them both to will and to do.

Literature.—All the Bib. theologies contain full discussions of the subject; for the NT the closest definitions are given by Bernard Weiss. But for the meaning of "grace" in any particular place the commentaries must be consulted, although the student may be warned against discussions that argue too closely from what may seem to be ∥ passages.

Burton Scott Easton

GRACIOUS, grā'shus (חָנַן, *ḥānan;* χάρις, *cháris*): In general, the word means "to favor," "to show kindness" to an inferior and "to be compassionate." All OT passages are derived from the same root, and yet there are two evident shades of meaning derived from it. (1) As above, "favorable" or, causative, "to cause to be g.," as "Jeh make his face to shine upon thee, and be g. unto thee" (Nu **6** 25); "And the Lord was g. unto them" (2 K **13** 23 AV); "The Lord is g. and full of compassion" (Ps **145** 8 AV). (2) In a modified sense, "graceful," "winsome" or "attractive," as applied particularly to persons and things. Used thus 3t in the OT and once in the NT. "A g. woman retaineth honor" (Prov **11** 16 AV; cf Eccl **10** 12 and Lk **4** 22).

The word is used once in the NT from root of Gr word χρηστός, *chrēstós*, meaning "useful" as a benefit: "if ye have tasted that the Lord is g." (1 Pet **2** 3).

In the main, however, the adj. is applied in the OT to Jeh, as indicative of His favor and mercy, His long-suffering and general inclination of favor and kindness. Walter G. Clippinger

GRAECIA, grē'sha. See Greece.

GRAFT, graft (ἐγκεντρίζω, *egkentrízo;* RV GRAFT; AV **Graff**): The word occurs 6 t in Rom **11**. Paul assumed that those living about Rome were familiar with the process of grafting olive trees, for olive culture had been adopted by the Greeks and Romans in Paul's time. The wild olive trees (Arab. colloquial, *zeitûn berri*) are cut back, slits made on the freshly sawed branch ends, and two or three grafts from a cultivated olive (Arab. colloquial, *zeitûn jouwi*) are inserted in such a way that the bark of the scion and of the branch coincide. The exposed ends are smeared with mud made from clay, and then bound with cloth or date straw, which is held by thongs made from the bark of young mulberry branches. The fruit thus obtained is good. Wild olives cannot be made cultivated olives by ingrafting, as Paul implies (ver 24), but a wild olive branch thus grafted would thrive. So Gentiles would flourish spiritually when grafted into the fulness of God's mercy, first revealed to the world through Israel. JAMES A. PATCH

GRAIN, grān. See AGRICULTURE; GARNER.

GRANARY, gran'a-ri. See GARNER; STOREHOUSES.

GRAPES, grāps. See VINE.

GRAPES, WILD (בְּאֻשִׁים, *be'ushīm*, Isa **5** 2.4): A word closely allied to בָּאְשָׁה, *bo'shāh*, Job **31** 40, tr[d] "cockle" (which see). It implies something noisome or worthless, but no particular fruit.

GRASP, grasp: The word ἁρπαγμός, *harpagmós* (Phil **2** 6), is rendered by AV "robbery," by RV "a prize," and by ARV "a thing to be grasped." By derivation the term may denote either an act of seizing or the aim or result of the action. In the context Paul is discussing, not Christ's opinion of His equality with God, but His amazing self-sacrifice in laying aside His equality for our sakes. He treated it not as a treasure to be held for Himself, but laid it aside for us. It is better to render with RV "a prize."

GRASS, gras:

(1) חָצִיר, *ḥāçīr*, from a root meaning "greenness"; cf Arab. *Khudra*, which includes grasses and green vegetables (1 K **18** 5; 2 K **19** 26; Job **40** 15; Ps **104** 14, etc). Isa **15** 6 is tr[d] in AV "hay," RV "grass"; Prov **27** 25, EV "hay," m "Heb grass"; Nu **11** 5 EV translates "leeks." It is a term for herbage in general.

(2) דֶּשֶׁא, *deshe'*, from root meaning "to sprout abundantly." Generally tr[d] "tender grass" (Gen **1** 11 f; 2 S **23** 4; Job **6** 5; Isa **15** 6; **66** 14; Jer **14** 5, etc); tr[d] "grass" (Job **6** 5; Jer **14** 5); tr[d] "herb" (2 K **19** 26; Ps **27** 2; Isa **37** 27; **66** 14). In Jer **50** 11 we have "heifer at grass" (*deshe'*) in AV and RVm, but in RV "heifer that treadeth out the grain." דִּתְאָ, *dethe'*, the Aram. form, occurs in Dnl **4** 15.23, and is tr[d] "tender grass."

(3) חֲשַׁשׁ, *ḥăshash*, probably "dry" or "cut grass"; cf Arab. حَشِيش, *ḥashesh*, "dry fodder" or "cut grass" (Isa **5** 24, AV "chaff," RV "dry grass"; **33** 11, EV "chaff").

(4) לֶקֶשׁ, *leḳesh*, from root meaning "to come late," hence used in Am **7** 1 for the "latter growth" of grass after mowing.

(5) יֶרֶק, *yereḳ*, lit. "green thing" (Nu **22** 4, elsewhere tr[d] "herb").

(6) עֵשֶׂב, *'ēsebh* (Dt **11** 15, etc), generally tr[d] "herb" (for [5] and [6] see HERB).

(7) χόρτος, *chórtos* (Mt **6** 30; **14** 19; Mk **6** 39; Lk **12** 28; Jn **6** 10; Jas **1** 10.11; 1 Pet **1** 24; Rev **8** 7; **9** 4); tr[d] "blade" (Mt **13** 26; Mk **4** 28); tr[d] "hay" (1 Cor **3** 12).

There are 243 species of true grasses (N.O. *Gramineae*) in Pal, but Heb, like modern Arab., does not discriminate between these and other herbs which together make up herbage. Actual turf is practically unknown in Pal, and grass seed is not artificially sown; young green barley is used in the neighborhood of towns as fresh fodder for horses and cattle. It is not the native custom to cut herbage for hay, though the writer has seen many carloads of sweet-smelling hay being carried from the land by Circassian settlers, E. of the Jordan.

The "grass upon the house tops" (Ps **129** 6; Isa **37** 27), the growth which springs from the seeds mingled with the mud of which the roof is made, springs up quickly with the rains, but as quickly dries up before it reaches half its normal height—or not infrequently is set on fire.

Dew, rain or showers upon the grass are mentioned (Dt **32** 6; Prov **19** 12; Mic **5** 7; Ps **72** 6, "rain upon the mown grass," i.e. the grass eaten short by cattle). E. W. G. MASTERMAN

GRASSHOPPER, gras'hop-ẽr. See LOCUST.

GRATE, grāt, **GRATING**, grāt'ing (מִכְבָּר, *mikhbār*, רֶשֶׁת, *resheth;* AV **Grate**): This "grating of network of brass" (Ex **27** 4; **38** 4), called also "the net" (**27** 4 f), and "grating of brass" (**38** 4), was that reticulated casting or wrought work of bronze which, in the tabernacle system, formed an element of the altar of sacrifice. Its position is well defined: "Thou shalt put it under the ledge round the altar beneath, that the net may reach halfway up the altar" (**27** 5; cf **38** 4). The altar being a hollow box—"hollow with planks" (**27** 8)—3 cubits high, overlaid with brass, and presumably filled with stones, there appears to have been a ledge round about it halfway from the base, from which depended vertically this grating of bronze. On the grating were four rings through which the staves were passed by which the altar was borne (**27** 4.7). If the ledge was for the priests to stand on while handling the sacrifices on the altar, the grating need be thought of only as an ornamental support for the ledge. Others ascribe to it different uses. W. SHAW CALDECOTT

GRAVE, grāv. See BURIAL.

GRAVE (adj.). See GRAVITY.

GRAVE, GRAVING, grāv'ing. See CRAFTS; ENGRAVING.

GRAVEL, grav'el (חָצָץ, *ḥāçāç*, from root חָצַץ, *ḥāçaç*, "to divide." Kindred roots have the meaning of "to cut," "to hew," "to sharpen," hence חֵץ, *ḥēç*, "arrow" [2 K **13** 17; Ps **64** 7 and often]; cf Arab. حَصَّ, *ḥaṣṣa*, "to fall to the lot of," حِصَّة, *ḥiṣṣah*, "portion"): In Prov **20** 17, we have:

> "Bread of falsehood is sweet to a man;
> But afterwards his mouth shall be filled with gravel."

And in Lam **3** 16:

> "He hath also broken my teeth with gravel stones; he hath covered me with ashes."

The only other occurrence of the word is in Ps **77** 17, where it is the equivalent of *ḥēç*, "arrow" (see *supra*):

> "The clouds poured out water;
> The skies sent out a sound:
> Thine arrows also went abroad."

Prov **20** 17 and Lam **3** 16 both suggest the frequent occurrence of grit in the coarse bread, the source of the grit being not necessarily the grindstone, but possibly even small stones originally mingled with the wheat and never properly separated from it. ALFRED ELY DAY

GRAVITY, grav'i-ti (σεμνότης, *semnótēs*): The word, meaning properly "venerableness," "sanctity," is used in 2 Macc **3** 12 of the "sanctity" of the temple. In 1 Tim **3** 4 the writer declares that a characteristic of a bishop should be that he has "his children in subjection with all g." Titus is enjoined (**2** 7 f) in his "doctrine" (teaching) to show "uncorruptness, g., sound speech [RV], that cannot be condemned" (cf 1 Tim **3** 8). In 1 Tim **2** 2 the same word is tr[d] "honesty" (RV "gravity"), "that we may lead a tranquil and quiet life in all godliness and g." A better rendering of *semnotēs* might be "dignity" or "dignified seriousness" (Olshausen), which quality is necessary, both on the part of parents in relation to their children, if they are to be properly trained, and on the part of preachers and teachers, if their "doctrine" is to be worthily represented. All mere lightness of demeanor (the opposite of gravity) tells against the great trusts committed to both parents and teachers (cf 1 Tim **3** 11; Tit **2** 2). Such "gravity" or "dignified seriousness" ought indeed to characterize Christian demeanor in general, as in 1 Tim **2** 2 above. W. L. Walker

GRAY, grā. See Colors; Hoary.

GREASE, grēs (חֵלֶב, *ḥēlebh*, "fat," "suet"): The word occurs once in the **metaphorical** sense "prosperous," then dull, gross, brutal: "Their heart is as fat as grease" (Ps **119** 70; cf Isa **6** 10, and see Fat).

GREAT, grāt, **GREATNESS,** grāt′nes: "Great" occurs very often in Scripture. The chief words so tr[d] are גָּדוֹל, *gādhōl*, רַב, *rabh*; **μέγας,** *mégas*, **πολύς,** *polús*.

(1) In the OT many other terms are employed: (*a*) *gādhōl* is used to express greatness in various senses, chiefly of *magnitude*, including *excellence*, e.g. "great lights" (Gen **1** 16); "the great city" (**10** 12); "a great nation" (**12** 2); "a great sight" (Ex **3** 3); "Moses was very great" (**11** 3); "the great God" (Dt **10** 17; Neh **1** 5); "great is Jeh" (Ps **48** 1). It is sometimes tr[d] by "mighty" (Dt **4** 37; **7** 21, "a mighty God," RV "great"). It is also used to designate the high priest (lit. "great," Lev **21** 10; Zec **3** 1, etc); also to express the "elder" of a family, e.g. Gen **27** 1, "Esau his eldest son," RV "elder"; probably also of great stature: "a great man among the Anakims," RV "the greatest" (Josh **14** 15). (*b*) *rabh* denotes, rather, *quantity, number*, therefore, often, "many" (Gen **21** 34, etc; Ex **2** 23 RV, etc); "abundant" (Ex **34** 6, ERV "plenteous"), and similar terms; thus we have "a great people" (Josh **17** 14); "His mercies are great," RVm "many" (2 S **24** 14; 1 Ch **21** 13); "Great was the company," RV "a great host" (Ps **68** 11); "great reward" (Ps **19** 11); "Mine iniquity . . . . is great" (**25** 11); "exceedingly" (Ps **123** 3). In the LXX *rabh* is, for the most part, tr[d] by *polus*. But it is used for "great" in other senses, e.g. "the great [God]" (Prov **26** 10), RV "as an archer," m "master worker; Heb text obscure"; "a saviour, and a great one," RV "defender," m "or a mighty one" (Isa **19** 20); "Great shall be the peace" (Isa **54** 13), etc. It is sometimes tr[d] "mighty" (Ps **89** 50, RVm "many"; Isa **63** 1). (*c*) Other words thus tr[d] are *kābhēdh*, "heavy," e.g. "so great a people," RV "thy great people," m "heavy" (1 K **3** 9); *m*[e]*'ōdh*, implying *force, might*, e.g. "with all his might" (2 K **23** 25). *'Ēl and 'Ĕlōhīm* are sometimes used to express greatness. In Ps **36** 6, we have "Thy righteousness is like the great [*'Ēl*] mountains," RV "mountains of God"; in Gen **30** 8, "with great [*'Ĕlōhīm*] wrestlings," RV "mighty," m "wrestlings of God"; and in 1 S **14** 15 "a very great [*'Ĕlōhīm*] trembling," RV "exceeding great," m "a trembling of God."

(2) (*a*) *Megas* denotes *magnitude*, in its various aspects, physical, moral, etc, e.g. "great joy" (Mt **2** 10); "a great light" (**4** 16); "the great King" (**5** 35); "great in the kingdom" (**5** 19, etc); "Great is thy faith" (**15** 28); "The greatest is charity" (love), RVm "greater" (1 Cor **13** 13); "a great high priest" (He **4** 14); "the great shepherd" (**13** 20); "a great voice" (Rev **1** 10); in Rev *megas* is very frequent. (*b*) *Polus* denotes properly *number, multitude*, e.g. "great multitudes" (Mt **4** 25); "a great company" (Lk **5** 29, RV "a great multitude"; frequent in the Gospels); "great possessions" (Mk **10** 22). But also "great" in the sense of magnitude, e.g. "great plainness of speech," RV "boldness" (2 Cor **3** 12; **7** 4); "a great trial of affliction," RV "much proof" (**8** 2); "great love" (Eph **2** 4). (*c*) Among other terms we have *tēlikoútos*, "so great" (in degree), "so great a salvation" (He **2** 3); *tosoútos*, "so great" (in quantity), "so great faith" (Mt **8** 10; Lk **7** 9); "so great a cloud of witnesses" (He **12** 1); *hósos*, "how great" (in quantity) (Mk **3** 8; **5** 19 f); *hēlíkos*, "how great" (in degree) (Col **2** 1; Jas **3** 5, "how great a matter," RV "how much wood," m "how great a forest"); *pēlíkos*, "how great" (in degree) (He **7** 4); *pósos*, "how great" (in quantity) (Mt **6** 23), etc.

(3) In His person and teaching, Jesus introduced into the world a new conception of **greatness**. It was to be found in humility and self-forgetting service: "Whosoever would become great among you shall be your minister [RVm "servant"]; and whosoever would be first among you shall be your servant [RVm "Gr bond-servant"]: even as the Son of man came not to be ministered unto, but to minister, and to give his life a ransom for many" (Mt **20** 26–28; cf also Mt **18** 1–4; **23** 11; Phil **2** 5–11). W. L. Walker

GREAVES, grēvz. See Armor, Arms, IV, 4.

GRECIANS, grē′shanz, **GREEKS,** grēks: In the OT the word "Grecians" occurs but once (Joel **3** [**4**] 6). For references to Greece in the OT see Javan. In AV of the OT Apoc "Grecians" and "Greeks" are used without distinction, e.g. 1 Macc **1** 10; **6** 2; **8** 9; 2 Macc **4** 15.36. Thus in 1 Macc **1** 1, Alexander the Great is spoken of as king of Greece, and in 1 Macc **1** 10 the Macedonian empire is called "the kingdom of the Greeks" (βασιλεία Ἑλλήνων, *basileía Hellḗnōn*). In 2 Macc **13** 2 the army of Antiochus, king of Syria, is called "Grecian" (δύναμις Ἑλληνική, *dúnamis Hellēnikḗ*), and in 2 Macc **6** 8 the "Greek cities" (πόλεις Ἑλληνίδες, *póleis Hellēnídes*) are Macedonian colonies. Reference is made in 2 Macc **6** 1 to an aged Athenian who was sent by Antiochus the king charged with the duty of Hellenizing the Jews; in 2 Macc **9** 15 Antiochus vows that he will make the Jews equal to the Athenians; in 1 Macc **12–14** reference is made to negotiations of Jonathan, the high priest, with the Spartans, whom he calls brethren, seeking the renewal of a treaty of alliance and amity against the Syrians. With the spread of Gr power and influence, everything not specifically Jewish was called Gr; thus in 2 Macc **4** 36; **11** 2; 3 Macc **3** 3.8 the "Greeks" contrasted with the Jews are simply non-Jews, so called because of the prevalence of Gr institutions and culture, and "Greek" even came to be used in the sense of "anti-Jewish" (2 Macc **4** 10.15; **6** 9; **11** 24).

In Isa **9** 12 the LXX reads τοὺς Ἕλληνας, *toús Héllēnas*, for פְּלִשְׁתִּים (*p*[e]*lishtīm*), "Philistines"; but we are not therefore justified in assuming a racial connection between the Philis and the Greeks. Further light on the ethnography of the Mediterranean basin may in time show that there was actually such a connection; but the rendering in question proves nothing, since "the oppressing sword" of Jer **46** 16 and **50** 16 is likewise rendered in the LXX with "the sword of the Greeks" (μάχαιρα Ἑλληνική, *máchaira Hellēnikḗ*). In all these cases the translators were influenced by the conditions existing in their own day, and were certainly not disclosing obscure relations long forgotten and newly discovered.

In the NT, EV attempts to distinguish between Ἕλληνες (*Héllēnes*), which is rendered "Greeks," and Ἑλληνισταί (*Hellēnistai*), which is rendered "Grecians" or "Grecian Jews," or in RVm "Hellenists," e.g. Acts **6** 1; **9** 29. These latter were Jews of the Dispersion, who spoke Greek (see HELLENISM; HELLENIST), as distinguished from Palestinian Jews; but since many of the latter also spoke Gr by preference, the distinction could in no sense be absolute. Indeed in Jn **7** 35, "the Dispersion among [RVm "Gr of"] the Greeks," can hardly refer to any but "Grecian Jews" (*Hellēnistai*), although *Hellēnes* is used, and in Jn **12** 20 the "Greeks" (*Hellēnes*) who went up to worship at the feast of the Passover were almost certainly "Grecian Jews" (*Hellēnistai*). Thus, while EV consistently renders *Hellēnes* with "Greeks," we are not by that rendering apprised of the real character of the people so designated. This difficulty is aggravated by the fact, already noted in connection with the OT Apoc, that, in consequence of the spread of Hellenism, the term *Hellēnes* was applied not only to such as were of Hellenic descent, but also to all those who had appropriated the language of Greece, as the universal means of communication, and the ideals and customs collectively known as Hellenism. The latter were thus in the strict sense Hellenists, differing from the "Grecians" of EV only in that they were not of Jewish descent. In other words, *Hellēnes* (except perhaps in Jn **7** 35 and **12** 20, as noted above) is, in general, equivalent to *tá éthnē*, "Gentiles" (see GENTILES). The various readings of the MSS (and hence the difference between AV and RV) in 1 Cor **1** 23 well illustrate this. There is consequently much confusion, which it is quite impossible, with our limited knowledge of the facts in particular cases, to clear up. In general, it would seem probable that where "Greeks" are comprehensively contrasted with "Jews," the reference is to "Gentiles," as in Acts **14** 1; **17** 4; **18** 4; **19** 10.17; **20** 21; Rom **1** 16; **10** 12; 1 Cor **1** 22–24 (RV "Gentiles," representing ἔθνεσιν, *éthnesin*); Gal **3** 28; Col **3** 11. In Mk **7** 26 the woman of Tyre, called "a Greek [RVm "Gentile"], a Syrophoenician," was clearly not of Hellenic descent. Whether Titus (Gal **2** 3) and the father of Timothy (Acts **16** 1.3) were in the strict sense "Greeks," we have no means of knowing. In Rom **1** 14, "I am debtor both to Greeks and to Barbarians," there is an undoubted reference to Greeks strictly so called; possibly, though by no means certainly, the "Greeks" of Acts **21** 28, alluding to Trophimus the Ephesian (Acts **21** 29), are to be taken in the same sense. References to the Gr language occur in Jn **19** 20 (Lk **23** 38 is properly omitted in RV); Acts **21** 37; Rev **9** 11.

In Acts **11** 20 the MSS vary between Ἑλληνιστάς, *Hellēnistás*, and Ἕλληνας, *Héllēnas* (AV "Grecians," RV "Greeks"), with the preponderance of authority in favor of the former; but even if one adopts the latter, it is not clear whether true Greeks or Gentiles are intended. WILLIAM ARTHUR HEIDEL

GREECE, grēs, **GRAECIA,** grē'sha: In the earliest times there was no single name universally and exclusively in use either of the people or of the land of Greece. In Homer, three appellations, Ἀχαιοί (*Achaioí*), Δαναοί (*Danaoí*), Ἀργεῖοι (*Argeíoi*), were with no apparent discrimination applied to all the Greeks. By the Orientals they were called Ionians. See JAVAN. The name Ἕλληνες (*Héllēnes*), which in historical times came into general use as a collective appellation, was applied in Homer to a small tribe in Thessaly. But the corresponding name Ἑλλάς (*Hellás*) was not primarily a geographical term, but designated the abode of the Hellenes wherever they had their own states or cities. In the 4th cent. BC many felt, as did Isocrates, that even "Hellene" stood not so much for a distinction in race, as for preëminence of culture, in contrast to the despised "Barbarian." Hence there was much dispute as touching certain peoples, as, e.g. the Epirotes, Macedonians, and even the Thessalians, whether they should be accounted Hellenes and as included in Hellas. The word Γραικοί (*Graikoí*, Lat *Graeci*) occurs in Aristotle, who says that it was an older name for those who were later called Hellenes. The meaning and truth of this statement are alike in doubt; but he probably refers only to the tribe inhabiting the vicinity of Dodona, in Epirus. At any rate, *Graeci* and *Graecia* owed their introduction practically to the Romans after their contact with the Greeks in the war with Pyrrhus, and in consequence they included (what "Hellenes" and "Hellas" did not) Epirus and Macedonia.

1. Name

"Hellas," as the land of the Hellenes, is used in a broad sense to include not only Greece proper, but also the islands of the Ionian and Aegean seas, the seaboard of the Hellespont, of the Pontus, and of Asia Minor, the flourishing colonial regions of Magna Graecia and Sicily, Crete, and occasionally Cyprus, Cyrene, and the scattered colonies dotting the shore of the Mediterranean, almost to the Pillars of Hercules. "Graecia," however, was used in a more restricted sense as applying to "Continuous" (or continental) Greece, which forms the southern extremity of the Balkan peninsula. While the Romans included Macedonia and Epirus, it will be well for us to limit Greece to the territory lying roughly below 40°, and extending almost to 36° N. lat., and ranging between 17° and 23° E. long. If, as is proper, we include the immediately adjacent islands, its greatest length, from Mt. Olympus in the N. to Cythera in the S., is about 280 miles; its greatest breadth, from Cephallenia in the W. to Euboea in the E., is about 240 miles. The area, however, owing to the great irregularity of its contour, is far less than one might expect, amounting to about 30,000 sq. miles. With an area, therefore, considerably less than that of Portugal, Greece has a coastline exceeding in length that of Spain and Portugal combined. In Greece the ratio of coastline to area is 1:3¼, whereas that of the Iberian peninsula is 1:25.

2. Location and Area

The northern boundary of Greece is formed by an irregular series of mountain chains, beginning on the W. with the Acroceraunian range and ending in Mt. Olympus (now, *Elymbos*, 9,790 ft.) on the E. Intersecting this line, the lofty Pindus range, forming the backbone of Northern Greece, extends southward to Mt. Tymphrestus (now, *Velouchi*, 7, 610 ft.) in Aetolia, at which point spurs radiate through Central Greece. The highest peaks are Mt. Corax (now, *Vardusia*, 8,180 ft.) in Aetolia, Mt. Oeta (7,060 ft.), Parnassus (now, *Lyakoura*, 8,070 ft.), Helicon (now, *Paléo Vouno*, 5,740 ft.), Cithaeron (now, *Elatias*, 4,630 ft.), lying on the boundary between Boeotia and Attica, Mt. Geranea (now, *Makri Plaghi*, 4,500 ft.), N. of the Isthmus, and, in Attica, Parnes (now, *Ozea*, 4,640 ft.), Pentelicon (now, *Mendeli*, 3,640 ft.) and Hymettus (now,

3. Mountain Structure

Trelovouni, 3,370 ft.). Along the eastern coast extends a broken range of mountains, the highest peaks of which are Ossa (now, *Kissavos*, 6,400 ft.), Pelion (now, *Plessidi*, 5,310 ft.); and, in Euboea, which virtually belongs to this range, Dirphys (now, *Delphi*, 5,730 ft.) and Ocha (now, *St. Elias*, 4,610 ft.). Southern Greece, or the Peloponnesus, is united to Central Greece only by a narrow isthmus (now cut by a canal 4 miles long), with a minimum altitude of about 250 ft. In the northern portion, a confused mass of mountains rises to great heights in Cyllene (now, *Ziria*, 7,790 ft.), Erymanthus (now, *Olonos*, 7,300 ft), Maenalus (now, *Apano Chrepa*, 6,500 ft.), all in Arcadia, Panachaïcus (now, *Voïdia*, 6,320 ft.), in Achaea; and, running southward through Laconia, the two important ranges called Taÿgetus (now, *Pentedaktylo*, 7,900 ft.) and Parnon (now, *Malevo*, 6,430 ft.). Minor ranges jut seaward in Argolis, Laconia and Messenia.

4. Rivers and Lakes

The rainfall in Greece is not abundant and is confined largely to late autumn and winter. Whether the present rainfall differs much in amount from that of antiquity is a matter in dispute, although it seems reasonable to assume that the progressive denudation of the mountains since the 5th cent. AD has entailed a corresponding loss in humidity. Even in antiquity, however, the rivers of Greece were much like the *arroyos* of the S.W. portion of the U.S.A., which are in winter raging mountain torrents, and in summer dry channels. Owing to the proximity of the sea to all points in Greece, the rivers are short, and the scarcity of springs makes them dependent upon the direct and immediate rainfall. Among the more considerable rivers may be enumerated, in Northern Greece, the Peneius, with its tributaries, in Thessaly; Central Greece, the Achelous and the Evenus, in Aetolia; the Spercheius, flowing between Oeta and Othrys into the Maliac Gulf; the storied, but actually insignificant, Ilyssus and Cephissus, of the Attic plain; in Southern Greece, the Alpheius, rising in Arcadia and flowing westward through Elis, and the Eurotas, which drains Laconia. Eastern Greece consists of a series of somewhat considerable basins, which become lakes in winter and are pestilent marshes in summer, except where Nature or man has afforded an outlet. The former is the case with the Peneius, which has cut a channel through the celebrated Vale of Tempe. Lake Copais, in Boeotia, affords an example of man's activity. The Minyae, in prehistoric times, are credited with enlarging the natural outlets, and so draining the basin for a time; in recent times the same undertaking has again been brought to a successful issue. Similar basins occur at Lake Boebeis, in Thessaly, and at Lake Stymphalus, in Arcadia, besides others of less importance. Western Greece has relatively few such basins, as at Lake Pambotis, in Epirus, and at Lake Trichonis, in Aetolia. In many cases, where there is no surface outlet to these basins, subterranean channels (called by the Greeks *Katavothrae*) are formed in the calcareous rock, through which the waters are drained and occasionally again brought to the surface at a lower level.

5. Climate

The climate of Greece was probably much the same in ancient times as it is today, except that it may have been more salubrious when the land was more thickly populated and better cultivated. Herodotus says that of all countries, Greece possessed the most happily tempered seasons; and Hippocrates and Aristotle commend it for the absence of extremes of heat and cold, as favorable for intelligence and energy. But owing to the inequalities of its surface, to the height of its mountains and the depth of its valleys, the climate varies greatly in different districts. In the highlands of the interior the winter is often cold and severe, the snow lying on the ground until late in the spring, while in the lowlands near the sea there is rarely any severe weather, and snow is almost unknown. The following data for Athens may be taken as a basis for comparison: humidity 41 per cent, rainfall 13.2 in., distributed over 100 days; mean temperature, Jan. 48.2° F., July 80.6° F. Greece lies open to the northern winds which, during certain seasons, prevail and give a bracing quality to the air not always present in places of the same latitude.

6. Geology

The western half of Greece, in which the mountain ranges run generally from N. to S., consists of a formation of greyish and yellowish-white compact limestone, while the eastern half — Macedonia, Thessaly, Euboea, Cyllene, and the mountains from Artemision to Cape Malea and Taÿgetus—together with the greater part of Attica and of the Cyclades, consists of mica-schist and crystalline-granular limestone (marble). Tertiary formations occur in narrow strips on the N. and N.W. slopes of the ranges in the Peloponnesus and in the valley of the Eurotas, in Boeotia and Euboea. Volcanic action is evidenced both in the parallel elevations of similar or contemporary formation, and in the earthquakes frequent in all ages, esp. in Southern and Central Greece, and in the islands of the Aegean. Perennially active volcanoes are nowhere found in Greece, but new formations due to volcanic action are most clearly seen on the island of Thera among the Cyclades, where they have occurred within the last half-century. The solfatara between Megara and Corinth, and the abundant hot springs at widely scattered points in Greece also bear witness to the volcanic character of the region. Many an ancient site, venerated for its sanctity in antiquity, like those of Delphi and Olympia, in their ruined temples offer mute testimony to the violence of the earthquakes; and history records repeated instances of cities engulfed by tidal waves of appalling height.

7. Topography

Mention has already been made of the sinuous coastline of Greece, and the land has been spoken of as consisting of three divisions. Northern Greece, to which Epirus and Thessaly belong, is marked off from Central Greece by the deep indentations of the Ambracian Gulf on the W. and the Maliac Gulf on the E. The Pegasaean Gulf, virtually continued by Lake Boebeis, reaches far into Thessaly, and divides it from Magnesia, which lies to the eastward. The land of the Dolopians really belongs to Northern Greece. Central Greece consists of Acarnania and Aetolia on the W., and of Phocis, Boeotia and Attica (with the adjacent island of Euboea) on the E., separated by a group of lesser states, Aenis, Oetaea, Doris, Locris and Phocis. Southern Greece is separated from Central Greece by the Corinthian and Saronic Gulfs, which almost meet at the Isthmus of Corinth, and are now, after repeated efforts, dating from the time of Julius Caesar, united by a sea-level canal. Megaris, which, by its position, belongs to Central Greece, is here, in accordance with its political affinities and predilections, classed with Corinth, the keeper of the isthmus, as belonging to Southern Greece. Facing the Corinthian Gulf, Achaea forms the northern division of the Peloponnesus, touching Elis, Arcadia and Argolis, which belt the peninsula in this order from W. to E. Arcadia is the only political division which does not have access to the sea, occupying as it does the great central plateau intersected by lesser ranges of varying height. The southernmost divisions, Messenia and Laconia, are deeply indented by the Messeniac and Laconic Gulfs, and Laconia is separated from the peninsula of Argolis by the Argolic Gulf, all of which head somewhat W. of N. Of the subjacent islands, which a reasonable view must include in the boundaries of Greece, Euboea has already been mentioned; but we should add the group of great islands lying in the Ionian Sea, viz. Corcyra (now, *Corfu*), Leukas, Ithaca, Cephallenia (now, *Cephalonia*), Zacynthus (now, *Zante*), and Cythera (now, *Cerigo*), at the mouth of the Laconic Gulf, as well as Salamis and Aegina in the Saronic Gulf.

Greece was never, in ancient times, a united state, but consisted of a large number of separate states. These were essentially of two types, (*a*) city-states, in which a city dominated the adjacent territory whose free population constituted its citizenship, or (*b*) confederacies, in which neighboring cities or districts combined into political organizations which we may call federal states. These matters cannot, however, be discussed except in connection with the history of Greece, for which the reader must consult the standard works. It may be advisable here, however, to name the principal cities of Greece. Northern Greece had no great cities which developed as commercial centers. Aegina was the first to attain to special importance, then Corinth and Athens; Chalcis and Eretria, in Euboea, were for a time rich and prosperous, and Megara, in Megarid, and Argos, in Argolis, became formidable rivals of Athens. Sparta, though never a commercial center, early won and long maintained the hegemony of Greece, for a while disputed by Athens, in virtue of her power as the home of the militant Dorian aristocracy, which was disastrously defeated by the Boeotians under Epaminondas, when Thebes, for a time, assumed great importance. Megalopolis, in Arcadia, enjoyed a brief prominence at the time of the Achaean League, and Corcyra flourished in the 5th and 4th cents. BC. We should also not fail to mention three great centers of Gr religion: Olympia, in Elis, as the chief sanctuary of Zeus; Delphi, in Phocis, as the oracular seat of Apollo; and Eleusis, in Attica, as the pilgrim-shrine to which all Greeks resorted who would be initiated in the mysteries of Demeter and Cora. Argos also possessed a far-famed shrine of Hera, and Thermopylae and Calauria were the centers at which met the councils of influential amphictyonies. Epidaurus was famous for her sanctuary of Asclepius. Delos, a little island in mid-Aegean, celebrated as a sanctuary of Apollo and as the meeting-place of a most influential amphictyony, falls without the limits of Greece proper; but Dodona, in Southern Epirus, should be mentioned as the most ancient and venerable abode of the oracle of Zeus. The Greeks, incorrigibly particularistic in politics, because of the almost insuperable barriers erected by Nature between neighboring peoples in the lofty mountain ranges, were in a measure united by their religion which, like the sea, another element making for intercourse and union, touched them at nearly every point.

For Greece in the OT, see JAVAN. In the NT "Greece" occurs but once—Acts **20** 2—where it is distinguished from Macedonia.

WILLIAM ARTHUR HEIDEL

GREECE, RELIGION IN ANCIENT:

I. The Greek Gods.—The gods of ancient Greece are well known to our western civilization through the myths which have found so large a place in our literature. In Greece itself, fancy had free play in dealing with these divine beings, and the myths were the main treasure-house from which the poet drew; the same myths and the same gods, under different names, reappear in Rome; and Rome passed them on, a splendid heritage of imagination, to the literatures of later Europe. It is characteristic of myths that they deal with persons, not so different from men in their nature, but with more than human powers. Gods, nymphs and satyrs, noble "heroes" or evil spirits have superhuman powers in varying degree, but they remain persons with a human interest because of their human type. And, further, as men are organized in families, cities and states, so there is a tendency to organize the beings of myth into social groups, and even to bring men, heroes and gods together into one large social organism, the universe of persons.

1. Greek Myths

Coin of Elis—Zeus of Pheidias.

These Gr myths, the story of Athena's birth full-armed from the brain of Zeus, of Circe's magic

Zeus from Mylasa.

potion, of Poseidon's chariot on the waves, and of Apollo's shafts are familiar to us from childhood. To regard them as expressing the content of Gr religion is as natural as it is false. Very few myths have any religious meaning at all, in spite of the large part the gods play in them. A little comparison with the facts of worship serves to show that here the gods are quite different from the gods of story. Some of the gods hardly appear in myths, and some of the beings of myth are not worshipped; in worship, each god is for the time being the only god thought of, not a member of the hierarchy established in myth; moreover in myth the gods are treated as universal, while the gods of worship are most closely attached, each to one shrine. Along with these external differences goes the one essential difference between a being of story and an object of worship. The failure to recognize the deep meaning of Gr religion results from the superficial assumption that myths constitute a peculiar kind of theology, when in reality they teach but little, and that, indirectly, about religion proper.

2. Mythology Distinguished from Religion

The essential fact about the gods of Gr religion is that each god was worshipped in a unique form at one or another particular shrine by a group of worshippers more or less definite. The group might include the state, the dwellers in one locality or simply the family; whatever its limits, it included those connected with the god by a social-religious tie, and the fundamental purpose of the worship was to strengthen this tie. In a city like Athens there were hundreds of such shrines, varying in importance, each the place where one particular phase of a god was worshipped at specified times. The particular form of the god was ordinarily indicated by an epithet attached to his name, Zeus Olympios, Dionysus Eleutherios, Athena Nike. This epithet might refer to the locality of the worship (Aphrodite of the Gardens), to the center from which the worship was brought (Artemis Brauronia), to some local spirit identified with the greater god (Poseidon Erechtheus), or to the nature of the god himself (Apollo Patroos). Each of the many shrines in Athens had thus its unique god, its group of worshippers connected with the god, its particular form of worship and times of worship, its own officials. While the state exercised general supervision over all the shrines, they were not organized in a hierarchy under any distinctly religious officials, but remained as independent units. Religious worship in a given city meant the aggregation of independent worships at the different local shrines.

3. Local Shrines

Athena Promachos.

Aphrodite.

4. Epithets of the Gods

The god of worship, then, was the god of a local shrine whose blessing and favor were sought at certain times by those who had the right to worship there. As in myth the gods were drawn after human types, that is, with human virtues and human frailties, and bodies almost human, except that they were not made to die; so in worship the gods were persons not unlike men in their nature. Worship proceeds on the assumption that gods are like human rulers, in that men honor the gods by games and processions, seek to please them by gifts, and ask them to share banquets made in their honor. Only the humanness of the gods in worship is something more subtle, more intimate than in myth. No stress is laid on human form or the vagaries of human character in the gods of worship; in form they remain spirits more or less vague, but spirits who care for men, who may be approached as a man approaches his ruler, spirits bound to man by close social ties which it is his duty and pleasure to strengthen. Zeus is father of gods and men, a father not untouched by the needs of his children; Athena cares for the city of Athens as her special pride; each family worships gods which are all but akin to the family; in the gymnasium, Apollo or Hermes is represented as the patron and ideal of the youths who exercise there; the drama is part of the service of Dionysus; in a word each form of human activity, be it work or pleasure, was a point of contact with the gods. The real forces at work in the world were *first* men, and *secondly* beings with a

5. Nature of the Gods of Worship

nature like man's, but with powers superior to man's; worship was the attempt to ally the gods more closely to man by social-religious ties, in order that as both worked together the ends of life might be successfully attained. This conception of the gods as higher members of society is the keynote of Gr religion. In some ethnic religions the gods seem to be evil beings whose desire for mischief man must overcome; in others they are beings to be avoided as much as possible; or again they are rulers who delight in man's abject servitude; or again by cultivating the friendship of one god, man may hope to win blessing and avoid harm from the others. In Greece all the gods of worship were essentially friendly to man, because they were akin to him and a part of the society in which he lived.

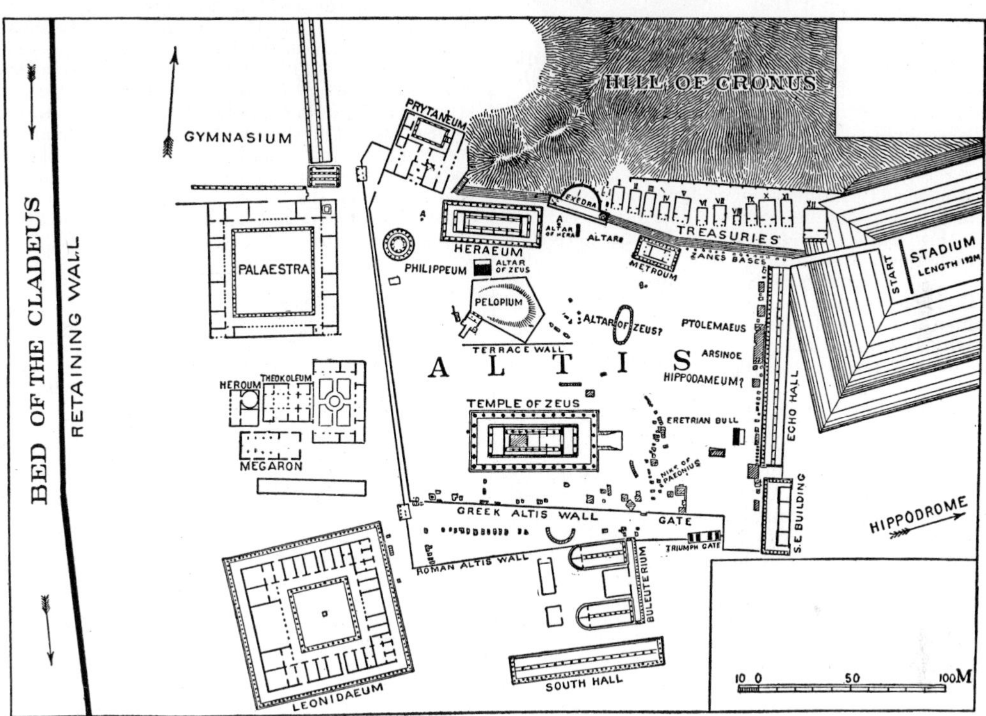

Ground Plan of Olympia.

6. Relation of Greek Gods to Nature

The relation of the gods to Nature is not so simple as might at first appear. Within certain limits the forces of Nature were subject to the will of the gods. From the Gr point of view, however, the relation is much more intimate, in that the forces in the world, at least in so far as they affect man, are personal activities, activities that express the will of divine beings. We say that Poseidon personifies the sea, Gaia the earth, Helios the sun; and the origin of religion has been sought in man's awe before the forces of Nature. The truer statement is that the Gr world, including the physical world, was made up of spiritual beings, not of physical forces. "The fire, as useful as it is treacherous, is the province of Hephaestus; all the dangers and changeableness of the sea are reflected in Poseidon and his followers; an Artemis is there to guide the hunter, a Demeter to make the grain sprout, a Hermes or Apollo to watch over the herds; Athena is the spirit of wisdom, Hermes of shrewdness, Ares of tumultuous war. . . . . In a word the Gr gods are *in* the world, not above the world, superior beings who embody in personal form all the forces that enter into human life." The contrast between such a personal point of view and the mechanical view of modern science is as marked as the contrast between it and the Heb conception of a universe brought into being and controlled by a God quite distinct from the physical world.

7. The Greater Gods of Greece

Of the particular gods, little need be said. The five greater gods, Zeus, Hera, Athena, Apollo and Artemis, are not closely connected with any one phenomenon of Nature or human life, though Zeus has to do with the sky, and Apollo and Artemis acquire a connection with the sun and moon. The most important worship of Zeus was at Olympia, where the pan-Hellenic games were held in his honor. Elsewhere he was worshipped mainly in connection with the weather and the changing seasons. Apparently much of his preëminence in Gr thought was due to myth. Hera was worshipped with Zeus on mountain tops, but her special place in worship was as the goddess of marriage. Athena, the maiden goddess of war and of handicrafts, was worshipped esp. in Northern Greece. War dances found a place in her worship, and she was rarely represented without aegis, spear and helmet. All the arts, agriculture, handicrafts, even the art of government, were under her care. Apollo was worshipped widely as the protector of the crops, and of the shepherd's flocks. In this aspect his festivals included purifications and rites to ward off dangers. He was also the god of music and of prophecy. At Delphi his prophetic powers won great renown, but the Pythian games with their contests in music, in rhythmic dancing, and in athletic sports were hardly less important. Artemis, in myth the chaste sister of Apollo, was worshipped as the queen of wild creatures and the mother of life in plants as well as in animals. She was the patron and the ideal of young women, as was Apollo of young men.

The gods most closely associated with Nature were not so important for religion. Gaia, mother earth, received sacrifices occasionally as the abode of the dead. Rhea in Crete, Cybele in Asia Minor, also in origin forms of the earth mother, received more real worship; this had to do primarily with the birth of vegetation in the spring, and again with its destruction by drought and heat. Rivers were honored in many places as gods of fertility, and springs as nymphs that blessed the land and those who cultivated it. Poseidon was worshipped that he might bless fishing and trade by sea; inland he was sometimes recognized as the "father of waters," and a god of fertility; and where horses were raised, it was under the patronage of Poseidon. The heavenly bodies marked the seasons of worship, but were rarely themselves worshipped. In general, the phenomena of Nature seem to have been too concrete to rouse sentiments of worship in Greece.

8. Nature Gods

River-God (Represented as a Human-headed Bull).

A third class of gods, gods of human activities and emotions, were far more important for religion. Demeter, once no doubt a form of the original earth-goddess, was the goddess of the grain, worshipped widely and at many seasons by an agricultural people. Dionysus, god of souls, of the inner life, and of inspiration by divine power, was worshipped by all who cultivated the vine or drank wine. The Attic drama was the most important development of his worship. Hermes was quite generally honored as the god of shepherds and the god of roads. As the herald, and the god of trade and gain, he found a place in the cities. Aphrodite was perhaps first the goddess of the returning life of the spring; in Greece proper she was rather the goddess of human love, of marriage and the family, the special patron of women. Ares, the Thracian god of war, was occasionally worshipped in Greece, but more commonly the god of each state was worshipped to give success in battle to his people. Hephaestus, pictured as himself a lame blacksmith working at the art which was under his protection, was worshipped now as the fire, now as the patron of cunning work in metal. Asclepius received men's prayers for relief from disease.

9. Gods of Human Activity and Emotions

II. Revelation: Inspiration.—For the Greeks revelation was a knowledge of the divine will in special circumstances, and inspiration was evinced by the power to foresee the divine purpose in a particular case. There is no such thing as the revelation of the divine nature, nor any question of universal truth coming to men through an inspired teacher; men knew a god through his acts, not through any seer or prophet. But some warning in danger or some clue to the right choice in perplexity might be expected from gods so close to human need as were the Gr gods. The Homeric poems depicted the gods as appearing to men to check them, to encourage them or to direct them. In Homer also men might be guided by signs; while in later times divine guidance came either from signs or from men who were so close to the gods as to foresee something of the divine purpose.

Head of the Bearded Dionysus.

The simplest class of signs were those that occurred in Nature. In the *Iliad* the thunderbolt marked the presence of Zeus to favor his friends or check those whose advance he chose to stop. The Athenian assembly adjourned when rain began to fall. Portents in Nature—meteors, comets, eclipses, etc—claimed the attention of the superstitious; but there was no science of astrology, and superstition had no great hold on the Greeks. In the Homeric poems, birds frequently denoted the will of the gods, perhaps because their place was in the sky beyond any human control, perhaps because certain birds were associated with particular gods. The presence of an eagle on the right hand (toward the E.) was favorable, esp. when it came in answer to prayer. At times, the act of the bird is significant, as when the eagle of Zeus kills the geese eating grain in Odysseus' hall—portent of the death of the suitors. In later Gr history there are but few references to signs from birds. The theory of these signs in Nature is very simple: all Nature but expresses the will of the gods, and when the gods wish to give men some vague hint of the future, it is necessary only to cause some event not easily explained to attract man's attention.

1. Omens

Bird Sign; Above a Four-Horse Chariot, Driven by a Goddess, Appears an Eagle Flying.

From the 5th cent. on, divination by means of sacrificial victims took the place ordinarily of signs such as have just been described. In the presence of the enemy or before some important undertaking, animals were sacrificed to the gods. If they came willingly to the altar, if the inward parts, esp. the liver, were sound and well shaped and of good color, if the sacrifice burned freely and without disturbing the arrangement on the altar, success might be expected. The theory was very simple: if the gods were pleased and accepted the sacrifice, their favor was assured; but if the sacrifice deviated in any way from the normal, it would not please the gods. Thus any sacrifice might have prophetic significance, while sacrifices offered before important undertakings had special meaning. The practice arose of repeating sacrifices before a battle until a favorable one was obtained, and at length, as religion began to lose its hold, the time came when a general might disregard them completely.

2. Divination by Sacrifice

An important means of learning the will of the gods was through dreams, when the ordinary channels of perception were closed and the mind was free to receive impressions from the gods. The treacherousness of dreams was fully recognized, even in the Homeric poem; students of natural science came to recognize that dreams arose from natural causes; none the less they were generally regarded as a source of knowledge about the future, and gradually a science

3. Dreams

for interpreting dreams was evolved. For Pindar and for Plato the soul was more free when the body slept, and because the soul was the divine part of man's nature it could exercise the power of divination in sleep. Many of the recorded dreams are signs which came to the mind in sleep, like the dreams of Joseph and of Pharaoh, signs that needed later interpretation. See DIVINATION; DREAMS.

Prophets and seers were not as important in Greece as among many peoples. The blind Teiresias belongs to the realm of myth, though there were great families of seers, like the Iamidae at Olympia, who were specially gifted to interpret dreams, or signs from sacrifices. Ordinarily it was the "chresmologist," the man with a collection of ancient sayings to be applied to present events, whose advice was sought in time of need; or else men turned to the great oracles of Greece.

The most important oracle was that of Apollo at Delphi. Hither came envoys of nations
4. Oracles as well as individuals, and none went away without some answer to their questions. After preliminary sacrifices, the priestess purified herself and mounted the tripod in the temple; the question was propounded to her by a temple official, and it was his function also to put her wild ravings into hexameter verse for the person consulting the oracle. A considerable number of these answers remain to us, all, of course, somewhat vague, many of them containing shrewd advice on the question that was brought to the oracle. The honor paid to the oracle and its influence, on the whole an influence making for high ethical standards and wise statesmanship, must be recognized. The early Christian Fathers held that the Pythian priestess was inspired by an evil spirit; later critics have treated the whole institution as a clever device to deceive the people; but in view of the respect paid to the oracle through so many generations, it is hard to believe that its officials were not honest in their effort to discover and make known the will of the god they served.

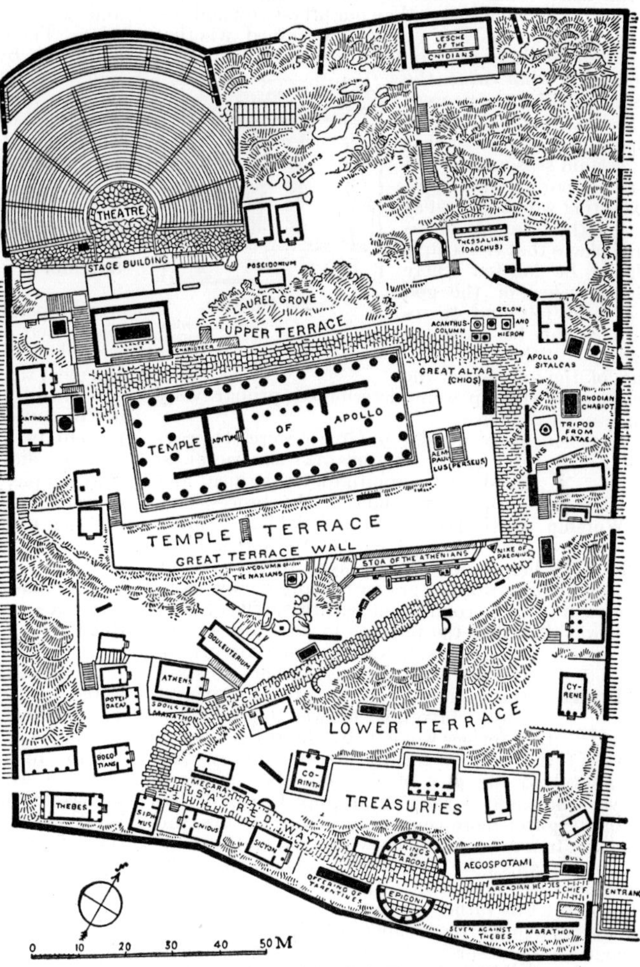

Plan of the Precincts of Apollo's Temple at Delphi.

III. Forms of Worship.—It has already been pointed out that Gr religion centered about local shrines. While in early times the
1. Shrines shrine consisted of an altar with perhaps a sacred grove, and later it might be no more than a block of stone on which offerings were laid, the more important shrines consisted of a plot of land sacred to the god, a temple or home for the god, and an altar for sacrifices. The plot of land, esp. in the case of shrines outside a city, might be very large, in which case it often was used as a source of income to the shrine, being cultivated by the priests or leased under restrictions to private persons. In this precinct stood the temple, facing toward the E., so that the morning sun
2. Temples would flood its interior when it was opened on a festival day. With one or two exceptions, the temple was not a place of assembly for worship, but a home for the god. It contained some symbol of his presence, after the 5th cent. BC ordinarily an image of the god; it served as the treasure-house for gifts brought to the god; worship might be offered in it by the priests, while the people gathered at the sacrifice outside. And as a home for the god, it was adorned with all the beauty and magnificence that could be commanded. The images of the gods, the noblest creation of sculpture in the 5th and 4th cents., were not exactly "idols"; that is, the images were not themselves worshipped, even though they were thought to embody the god in some semblance to his true form. In Greece men worshipped the gods themselves, grateful as they were to artists who showed them in what beautiful form to think of their deities.

Each of these shrines was directly in the hands of one or more officials, whose duty it was to care for the shrine and to keep up its worship
3. Priests in due form. Occasionally the priesthood was hereditary and the office was held for life; quite as often priests were chosen for a year or a term of years; but it was exceptional when the duties of the office prevented a man from engaging in other occupations. In distinction from the priests of many other forms of religion, the Gr priest was not a sacred man set apart for the service of the gods; the office may be called sacred, but the office was distinct from the man. The result was important, in that the priests in Greece could never form a caste by themselves, nor could they claim any other powers than were conferred on them by

the ritual of the shrine. Thus Gr religion remained in the possession of the people, and developed no esoteric side either in dogma or in worship.

4. Seasons of Worship: Festivals

The seasons of worship varied with each particular shrine. While the state observed no recurring sabbath, it recognized a certain number of religious festivals as public holidays; thus at Athens the number of religious holidays in the year was somewhat larger than our fifty-two Sundays. The tradition of each shrine determined whether worship should be offered daily or monthly or yearly, and also what were the more important seasons of worship. The principle of the sacred days was that at certain seasons the god was present in his temple expecting worship; just as it was the principle of sacred places that the temple should be located where the presence of the god had been felt and therefore might be expected again. Neither the location of the temple nor the seasons of worship were determined primarily by human convenience.

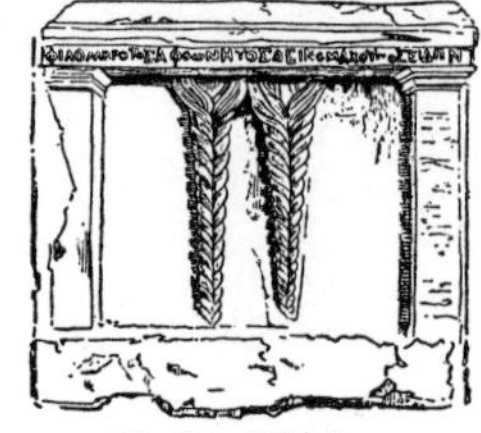

Votive Offering.

Two braids of hair hang in a niche below the inscription "Philombrotus, Apthonetus, (sons) of Deinomachus, (to) Poseidon."

5. Elements of Worship

The elements of worship in Greece were (1) prayers, hymns, and votive offerings, (2) the sacrificial meal, (3) propitiatory sacrifice and purification, and (4) the processions, musical contests and athletic games, which formed part of the larger festivals. The heroes of Homer prayed to the gods at all times, now a word of prayer in danger, now more formal prayers in connection with a sacrifice; and such was doubtless the practice in later times. In the more formal prayers, it was customary to invoke

6. Prayer

the god with various epithets, to state the petition, and to give the reason why a favorable answer might be expected—either former worship by the petitioner, or vows of future gifts, or former answers to prayer, or an appeal to the pity of the god. Sometimes a prayer reads as if it were an attempt to win divine favor by gifts; more commonly, if not always, the appeal is to a relationship between man and his god, in which man's gifts play a very subordinate part. Thanksgiving finds small place in prayer or in sacrifice, but it was rather expressed in votive offerings. In every temple these abounded, as in certain Roman Catholic shrines today; and as is the case today they might be of value in themselves, they might have some special reference to the god, or they might refer to the human need in which the giver had found help. So far as the great public festivals are concerned, the prayer seems to have been merged with the hymn of praise in which the element of petition found a small place.

Black-figured Vase Painting (Brit. Mus.).

A procession headed by a priestess with tray of offerings, and a man playing the double flute is conducting a bull to the altar of Athena; behind the altar is a statue of Athena and a serpent.

7. Burnt Offering or Sacrificial Meal

The most common form of worship consisted of the sacrificial meal, like the meat offering or meal offering of the Hebrews. The sacrifice consisted of a domestic animal, selected in accordance with the ritual of the shrine where it was to be offered. First the animal was led to the altar, consecrated with special rites and killed by the offerer or the priest while hymns and cries of worship were uttered by the worshippers. Then some of the inward parts were roasted and eaten by priests and worshippers. Finally the remainder of the creature was prepared, the thigh bones wrapped in fat and meat to be burned for the god, the balance of the meat to be roasted for the worshippers; and with libations of wine the whole was consumed. The religious meaning of the act is evidently found in the analogy of a meal prepared

8. Meaning of the Sacrifice

for an honored guest. The animal, an object valuable in itself, is devoted to this religious service; the god and his worshippers share alike this common meal; and the god is attached to his worshippers by a closer social bond, because they show their desire to honor and commune with him, while he condescends to accept the gift and to share the meal they have prepared. (Possibly the animal was once thought to have been made divine by the act of consecration, or the god was believed to be present in his flesh, but there is no evidence that such a belief existed in the 5th cent. BC, or later.) The simple, rational character of this worship is characteristic of Gr religion.

9. Propitiatory Sacrifice

When men felt that the gods were displeased or in circumstances where for any reason their favor was doubtful, a different form of sacrifice was performed. A black animal was selected, and brought to a low altar of earth; the sacrifice was offered toward evening or at night, and the whole animal was consumed by fire. While in general this type of sacrifice may be called propitiatory, its form, if not its meaning, varied greatly. It might be worship to spirits of the earth whose anger was to be feared; it might be offered when an army was going into battle, or when the crops were in danger of blight, or of drought; or again it was the normal form of worship in seasons of pestilence or other trouble. Sometimes the emphasis seems to be laid on the propitiation of anger by an animal wholly devoted to the god, while at other times there is the suggestion that some evil substance is removed by the rite. The later conception is

Purification.

The three daughters of Melampus (?) are being purified from their insanity by a bearded priest who holds above them a young pig and a branch for sprinkling; at the right is a young attendant and at the left possibly Artemis.

10. Purification

clearer in rites of purification, where, by washing, by fire, or by the blood of an animal slain for the purpose, some form of defilement is removed. In the sacrifice of a pig to Demeter for this purpose, or of a dog to Hecate, some mystic element may exist, since these animals were sacred to the respective goddesses.

These various elements of worship were combined in varying degree in the great religious festivals. These lasted from a day to a fortnight. After purification of the worshippers, which might be simple or elaborate, and some preliminary sacrifice, there was often a splendid procession followed by a great public sacrifice. In the greater festivals, this was followed by athletic games and horse races in honor of the god, and sometimes by contests in music and choral dancing, or, in the festivals of Dionysus at Athens, by the performance of tragedy and comedy in the theater. In all this, the religious element seems to retreat into the background, though analogies may be found in the history of Christianity. The religious mystery plays were the origin of our own drama; and as for the horse races, one may still see them performed as a religious function, for example, at Siena. The horse races and the athletic games were performed for the gods as for some visiting potentate, a means of affording them pleasure and doing them honor. The theatrical performances apparently originated in ceremonies more essentially religious, in which men acted some divine drama depicting the experiences attributed to the gods themselves. This

11. The Great Religious Festivals

last feature is most evident in the mysteries at Eleusis, where the experiences of Demeter and Persephone were enacted by the people with the purpose of bringing the worshippers into some more intimate connection with these goddesses, such that their blessing was assured not only for this world, but for the life after death.

12. Mysteries at Eleusis

In all the forms of Gr worship perhaps the most striking feature was the absence of magic or superstition, almost the absence of mystery. Men approached the gods as they would approach superior men, bringing them petitions and gifts, making great banquets for their entertainment, and performing races and games for their pleasure, although this was by no means the whole of Gr religion, a phase of religion far more highly developed in the rational atmosphere of Gr thought than among other races. As the Gr gods were superior members of the social universe, so Gr worship was for the most part social, even human, in its character.

13. Absence of Magic and Mystery

Ruins of Eleusis.

IV. The Future Life.—Gr thought of the life after death was made up of three elements which developed successively, while the earlier ones never quite lost their hold on the people in the presence of the later. The oldest and most permanent thought of the future found its expression in the worship of ancestors. Whether the body of the dead was buried or burned, the spirit was believed to survive, an unsubstantial shadowy being in the likeness of the living man. And rites were performed for these shades to lay them to rest and to prevent them from injuring their survivors, if not to secure their positive blessing. As at other points in Gr religion, the rites are fairly well known, while the belief must be inferred from the rites. The rites consisted first of an elaborate funeral, including sometimes animal sacrifices and even athletic games, and secondly of gifts recurring at stated intervals, gifts of water for bathing, of wine and food, and

1. Funeral Rites

Mourners about a Couch on Which Rests the Body of the Dead.

of wreaths and flowers. The human wants and satisfaction of the spirit are thus indicated. And the purpose is perhaps to keep the spirit alive, certainly to keep it in good humor so that it will not injure the survivors and bring on them defilement which would mean the wrath of the gods. At the same time, any contact with death demands purification before one can approach the gods in worship.

The second element in Gr thought of the future life appears in the Homeric poems, and through the epic exerted a wide influence on later periods. Here the separateness of the souls of the dead from the human life is emphasized. Once the bodies of the dead are burned, the souls go to the realm of Hades, whence there is no return even in dreams, and where (according to one view) not even consciousness remains to them. It would seem that the highly rational view of the world in the epic, a point of view which laid stress on the greater Olympian gods, banished the belief in souls as akin to the belief in sinister and magic influences. We might almost say that the thought of the greater gods as personal rulers tended to drive out the thought of lesser and more mystic spiritual influences, and made a place for souls only as shades in the realm of Hades. Certainly the result for Gr religion was to render far less vivid any idea of a real life after death.

2. Future Life in the Homeric Poems

The third element was associated with the worship of the gods of the lower world, and in particular Demeter and Persephone. In this worship, particularly at Eleusis, the fact of life after death was assumed, a fact that the Greeks never had denied; but the reality of the future life, the persistence of human relationship after death, and the kindly rule of Persephone as Queen of Souls were vividly impressed on the worshippers. In part through the influence of the Orphic sect, the actual divinity of the soul was believed by many thinkers, a doctrine which was formulated by Plato in a manner which profoundly affected early Christian thought. If the epic emphasis on the greater gods made the souls mere shades in Hades, it was again a religious movement, namely the worship of gods like Persephone and Dionysus, which taught to some Greeks the divine reality of the soul and its hope for a blessed life in communion with the gods.

3. Later Beliefs in Immortality

This development in Greece is the more interesting because there are indications of the same thing in Heb history. In the OT there are found traces of an old worship of souls, practised by races akin to the Hebrews if not by the Hebrews themselves; this worship was brought to an end under the clarifying power of the worship of Jeh; and finally the later prophets perceived the truth that while souls were not to be worshipped, the dead who died in the Lord did not become mere shades, but continued to live as the objects of His Divine love.

V. Sin, Expiation, and the Religious Life.—The ancient Heb religion made much of sin, and of the remedy for sin which God, in loving mercy to His people, had provided; in Greece the thought of sin found no such place in the religious life, though of course it was not absent altogether. If sin is defined as that which causes divine displeasure and wrath, it appears in Gr thought in three forms: (1) as the transgression of moral law, (2) as neglect of the gods and consequent presumption, and (3) as pollution. The cause of sin is traced to human folly, either some passion like envy or anger or desire for gain, or to undue self-reliance which develops into presumption; and once a man has started in the wrong direction, his sin so affects judgment and will that he is all but inevitably led on into further sin. According to the simple Gr theodicy, the transgression of moral law brings its penalty, nor can any sacrifice induce the gods to intervene on behalf of the transgressor. All that expiation can accomplish is to set right the spirit of the transgressor so that he will not be led into further sin. Neglect of the gods—the second type of sin—brings its penalty in the results of divine wrath, but in this case, prompt repentance and submission to the gods may appease the wrath and therefore change its results. Pollution, the third cause of divine displeasure, often cannot be called sin; the failure to remove pollution, however, esp. before one approaches the gods, is a just cause of divine anger. In general the Gr thought of sin centers about the idea of undue self-reliance and presumption, ὕβρις (*húbris*), which is the opposite of the characteristic Gr virtue, σωφροσύνη (*sōphrosúnē*), namely that temperate mode of life in which everything is viewed in right proportion. Inasmuch as the Gr gods are righteous rulers, the nature of sin lies in its opposition to divine justice, not in unholiness or in the rejection of divine love.

1. Greek Idea of Sin

Orestes Pursued by Two Erinyes.

The demands of the religious life in Greece were relatively simple. To avoid acts of impiety such as are mentioned above, to perform the ordinary acts of worship regularly and punctiliously, were all that was required, though the religious man might find many opportunities for worship beyond what was expected of everyone. Little is said of the spirit of worship which underlay the outward acts. Nor does the command, "Be ye therefore holy, even as I am holy," find an echo in Greece. At the same time the fact that the gods so definitely represented human ideals of life, must have meant that in a way men aimed to make their lives conform to divine ideals. The essential feature of the religious life was the true recognition of human dependence on the gods, a dependence which showed itself in obedience to the divine rule, in trustful confidence that the gods would bless their worshippers, in resignation when misfortune came, and particularly in the belief in the loving care and protection of the divine rulers. In Greece, the religious man looked to the gods not so much for salvation from evil, as for positive blessings.

2. Religious Ideals

VI. The Influence of Greek Religion on Christianity.—This is not the place to speak of the decadence of Gr religion, of its ameliorating influence on the Alexandrian world, or of the control it exercised over the Rom state. Its most permanent effect is found rather in Christianity. And here its shaping influence is first noted in Christian theology beginning with Paul and the Apostle John. For although Gr religion was more free from dogma or anything that could be called theology than are most religions, it furnished the religious content to the greatest philosophical systems we know; and all through the centuries the leaders of Christian thought have been trained in the religious philosophy of Plato and of Aristotle. Our Christian conceptions of the nature of God and the soul, of the relation of God to the physical universe, and of God's government of the world, have been worked out along the lines laid down by these Gr thinkers. And while the debt is primarily to Gr philosophy, it should never be forgotten that Gr philosophy formulated these conceptions out of the material which Gr religion furnished; indeed one may believe that it was the religious conceptions formulated by centuries of thoughtful worshippers which found final expression in the Gr philosophic systems.

1. Greek Philosophy and Christian Theology

Again, the organization of the early Christian church and its form of government was quite as much Gr as it was Heb in origin. Here the influence of Gr religion as such was less marked; still it must be remembered that every form of Gr organization had its religious side, be it family, or school, or state; and further, that some phases of religion in Greece were quite thoroughly organized in a manner that was adapted without much difficulty to the conditions of the new religion. Moreover the thought of the Gr priest as not a sacred man, but a man appointed by the community to a sacred office, was naturally adopted by the nascent Christian communities. Even in the organization of worship, in the prayers and hymns and liturgy which gradually developed from the simplest beginnings, it is not difficult to trace the influence of what the Gr converts to Christianity had been brought up to regard as worship of the gods.

2. Greek Influence on Christian Liturgy

The most striking case of the effect of the old religion on the new is found in the method of celebrating the Christian sacraments. In the 2d cent. AD, the baptismal bath took place after a brief period of instruction, and at the common meal the bread and wine were blessed in commemoration of the Master. Three centuries passed and this simplicity had given way to splendid ceremony. Baptism ordinarily was performed only on the "mystic night," the night before Easter. Almost magic rites with fasting had exorcised evil from the candidate; ungirded, with loose hair and bare feet, he went down into the water, and later was anointed with oil to signify the gift of the Holy Spirit; then the candidates, dressed in white, wearing crowns, and carrying torches, proceeded to their first communion in which a mixture of honey and milk might take the place of

3. Greek Influence on the Sacraments

wine. The whole ceremony had been assimilated to what Gr religion knew as an *initiation*, in which the baptized underwent some essential change of nature. They were said to have "put on the dress of immortality."

The Lord's Supper was carefully limited to those who had been through this initiation, and even among these, at length, degrees of privilege arose. The ceremony came to be known as a mystery, the table as an altar, the officiating priest as a "hierarch," and the result as a blessed "vision" of sacred things by which the resurrection life was imparted. In its formal character and the interpretation of its meaning, as well as in the terms used to describe it, the effect of the Gr mysteries may be seen.

Yet during these three centuries Christianity had been waging a life-and-death struggle with the old religion. It is indeed impossible to believe that converts to Christianity should intentionally copy the forms of a worship which they had often at much cost to themselves rejected as false. The process must have been slow and quite unconscious. As the language of heathen philosophy was used in forming a Christian theology, so the conceptions and practices which had developed in Gr religion found their way into the developing Christian ritual. Much of this ritual which had no essential place in Christianity was later rejected; some still remains, the contribution of the religious life of Greece to the forms of worship in our world religion.

LITERATURE.—O. Gruppe, "Griechische Mythologie und Religionsgeschichte" in I. von Müller's *Handbuch*, 1897–1906; Preller-Robert, *Griechische Mythologie*, I, 1894; W. H. Roscher, *Ausführliches Lexikon der griechischen und römischen Mythologie*, 1884–; L. R. Farnell, *The Cults of the Greek States*, 1896–1910; L. Campbell, *Religion in Greek Literature*, 1898; J. Adam, *The Religious Teachers of Greece*, 1908; P. Stengel, "Die griechischen Kultusaltertümer," in I. von Müller's *Handbuch*, 2d ed, 1898; B. I. Wheeler, *Dionysus and Immortality*, 1899; E. Hatch, *Greek Ideas and Usages, Their Influence upon the Christian Church*, 1890; G. Anrich, *Das antike Mysterienwesen in seinem Einfluss auf das Christentum*, 1894; E. E. G., *The Makers of Hellas: A Critical Inquiry into the Philosophy and Religion of Ancient Greece*, 1903; E. Caird, *Evolution of Theology in Greek Philosophers*, 1904; E. A. Gardner, *Religion and Art in Ancient Greece*, 1910; A. Fairbanks, *Handbook of Greek Religion*, 1910.

ARTHUR FAIRBANKS

GREECE, SONS OF: "I will stir up thy sons, O Zion, against thy sons, O Greece, and will make thee as the sword of a mighty man" (Zec **9** 13). The passage doubtless refers to the captive Hebrews who are held by the Greeks. The exhortation is to insurrection against the Greeks. Although bearing a striking similarity to the passage in Joel **3** 6, there is evidently no connection between the two. In the first, there was conflict between the nations; in the second, simply a reflection upon Tyre and Sidon for having sold into Greece certain Jewish captives. From a Jewish standpoint the Maccabean wars were really between Jews and Greeks. See JAVAN; ASMONEANS.

GREEK LANGUAGE. See LANGUAGE OF NT.

GREEK VERSIONS. See SEPTUAGINT; VERSIONS.

GREEKS. See GRECIANS.

GREEN, grēn, **GREENISH.** See COLOR.

GREETING, grēt′ing (שָׁאַל, *shā'al*; **χαίρω**, *chairō*, **ἀσπασμός**, *aspasmós*, **ἀσπάζομαι**, *aspázomai*):

(1) *Shā'al* means "to ask," "to inquire of anyone respecting welfare," hence "to greet." In the OT the word "greet" occurs only once in AV or RV, viz. in 1 S **25** 5, "Go to Nabal, and greet him in my name." But it is implied in other places where *shālōm* ("well," "prosperity," "peace"), the common Heb greeting, is used; e.g. in Gen **37** 4, it is said of Joseph that "his brethren could not speak peaceably unto him," i.e. could not give him the common friendly greeting of "Peace!" "Peace be to thee!" So, in Gen **43** 27, RV "He asked them of their welfare" (AVm "peace"); Ex **18** 7, "They asked each other of their welfare" (AVm "peace"); 2 S **11** 7, "how Joab did, and how the people did" (RV "fared," AVm "of the peace of"); Joab said to Amasa (2 S **20** 9), RV "Is it well with thee, my brother?" (Heb "Art thou in peace, my brother?"); Boaz greeted his reapers with "Jeh be with you," and they answered, "Jeh bless thee" (Ruth **2** 4; cf Ps **129** 8, "The blessing of Jeh be upon you; we bless you in the name of Jeh"). For the king, we have, AV and ERV, "God save the king" (m "Let the king live," ARV "[Long] live the king") (1 S **10** 24, etc); "Let my lord king David live for ever" (1 K **1** 31; see also Neh **2** 3; Dnl **2** 4, etc). In Ecclus **6** 5 it is said "a fair-speaking tongue will increase kind greetings," RV "multiply courtesies" (*euprosḗgora*).

(2) When Jesus sent forth His disciples to proclaim the kingdom, they were to "salute" the house they came to (Mt **10** 12), saying (Lk **10** 5), "Peace [*eirḗne*] be to this house!"; if it was not worthy, the blessing should return to themselves. After His resurrection He greeted His disciples saying, "Peace be unto you" (Lk **24** 36; Jn **20** 19.21.26); He left His "peace" with them as His parting blessing (Jn **14** 27)—"not as the world giveth," in a formal way. A frequent form of greeting in the NT is *chairō* ("to rejoice," imp. and inf., *chaire*, *chairete*, "Joy to thee," "Joy to you," tr[d] "Hail!" and "All hail!" Mt **26** 49; **27** 29; **28** 9; Mk **15** 18; Lk **1** 28; Jn **19** 3), "Rejoice!" (Phil **3** 1; ERVm "farewell"). Another word for greeting is *aspasmos*, "greetings in the markets" (AV Mt **23** 7; Mk **12** 38, "salutations"; Lk **11** 43, "greetings," Lk **20** 46; also Lk **1** 29.41.44; 1 Cor **16** 21; Col **4** 18; 2 Thess **3** 17; in all these places RV has "salutation").

(3) Of *epistolary greetings* we have examples in Ezr **4** 17, "Peace" (*shelām*), etc; **5** 7; Dnl **4** 1; **6** 25. These are frequent in the Apoc: 1 Esd **6** 7, "to King Darius greeting" (*chairō*); **8** 9; 1 Macc **10** 18, etc; 2 Macc **1** 10, "greeting, health," etc. We have the same form in Acts **15** 23; **23** 26. In 3 Jn ver 14 it is, "Peace [be] unto thee. The friends salute thee." Paul opens most of his epistles with the special Christian greeting, "Grace to you and peace from God our Father and the Lord Jesus Christ" (Rom **1** 7; 1 Cor **1** 3, etc). Also at the close, "The grace of the Lord Jesus Christ be with you" (1 Cor **16** 23; 2 Cor **13** 14, etc). He directs greetings to be given to various persons, and sends greetings from those who are with him (Rom **16** 5–23; 1 Cor **16** 19 f; 2 Cor **13** 13; Phil **4** 21 f; Col **4** 10, etc). In those cases the word is *aspazomai*, and RV tr[s] "salute," etc (cf Jas **1** 1; 1 Pet **1** 2; **5** 14; 2 Pet **1** 2; 2 Jn vs 3.13; Jude ver 2). See GODSPEED; KISS.

W. L. WALKER

GREYHOUND, grā′hound. See DOG.

GRIEF, grēf, **GRIEVE,** grēv: There are some 20 Heb words tr[d] in AV by "grief," "grieve," "to be grieved," etc. Among the chief are חָלָה, *ḥālāh*, חֳלִי, *ḥŏlī*, יָגוֹן, *yāghōn*, כַּעַס, *ka'aṣ*, עָצַב, *'āçabh*. They differ, partly, in their physical origin, and partly, in the nature and cause of the feeling expressed. RV in several instances gives effect to this.

(1) *Ḥālāh*, *ḥŏlī* express the sense of weakness, sickness, pain (e.g. Samson, in Jgs **16** 7.11.17, "Then shall I become weak [*ḥālāh*], and be as another man"); Isa **17** 11 AV, "a heap in the day of grief"; **53** 3.4, "a man of sorrows, and acquainted

with grief," "He hath borne our griefs" (*ḥŏlī*), RVm "Heb sickness, sicknesses"; ver 10, "He hath put him to grief," RVm "made him sick" (*ḥālāh*) (trd by Dillmann and others, "to crush him incurably"; cf Mic **6** 13; Nah **3** 19); *yāghōn*, perhaps from the pain and weariness of toil (Ps **31** 10), "For my life is spent with grief," RV "sorrow"; "The Lord added grief to my sorrow," RV "sorrow to my pain" (Jer **45** 3); *ka'aṣ* implies provocation, anger, irritation; thus Hannah said to Eli (AV), "Out of the abundance of my complaint and my grief [RV "provocation"] have I spoken" (1 S **1** 16). Ps **6** 7; **31** 9, "grief"; Prov **17** 25, "A foolish son is a grief to his father" (i.e. source of provocation; the same word is rendered "wrath" in **12** 16, AV "a fool's wrath," RV "vexation"; so also **27** 3); Job **6** 2, "Oh that my grief were thoroughly weighed," RV "Oh that my vexation were but weighed" (in **5** 2 AV the same word is trd "wrath," RV "vexation"); *ke'ēbh*, is "sorrow," "pain," properly "to hurt." It occurs in Job **2** 13, "His grief [RVm "or pain"] was very great"; also **16** 6 RV, "grief"; *makh'ōbh* "sorrows," "pain," "suffering" (2 Ch **6** 29, RV "sorrow"; Ps **69** 26, RVm "or pain"; Isa **53** 3, "a man of sorrows"; ver 4, "Surely he hath carried our sorrows"); *mārāh* and *mārar* indicate "bitterness" (Gen **26** 35; **49** 23; 1 S **30** 6; Ruth **1** 13; Prov **14** 10, "The heart knoweth its own bitterness," *mārāh*); *pūḳāh* implies staggering, or stumbling, only in 1 S **25** 31, "This shall be no grief unto thee," RVm "Heb cause of staggering"; *ra'* (a common word for "evil") denotes an evil, a calamity, only once in AV trd "grief," viz. of Jonah's gourd, "to deliver him from his grief," RV "from his evil case" (Jon **4** 6); *yāra'*, "to be evil," Dt **15** 10, RV "Thy heart shall not be grieved when thou givest unto him" (also 1 S **1** 8; Neh **2** 10; **13** 8; several times trd "grievous"); *ḥārāh*, "to burn," "to be wroth" (e.g. Gen **4** 6, "Why art thou wroth?"), is trd "grieved" in Gen **45** 5, and 1 S **15** 11 AV (RV "Samuel was wroth"); the same word is often used of the *kindling* of anger; *lā'āh*, "to be weary," "tired," "faint" (Prov **26** 15), AV "The slothful hideth his hand in his bosom, it grieveth him to bring it again to his mouth," RV "wearieth"; also Job **4** 2; *'āçabh*, "to grieve," "to be vexed," occurs in Gen **6** 6; **34** 7; **45** 5, etc; Ps **78** 40, "How oft did they . . . . grieve him in the desert." Of other words sometimes trd "grief" may be mentioned *ḳūṭ*, "to weary of," "to loathe" (Ps **95** 10), "Forty long years was I grieved with that generation"; in **119** 158; **139** 21, RVm "loathe"; *ḥāmēç*, implying to be bitterly or violently moved, sour (often trd "leavened"), only in Ps **73** 21, RV "For my soul was grieved," m "Heb was in a ferment."

(2) In the NT "grief," "grieve," etc, are infrequent. The commonest words are *lúpē* (1 Pet **2** 19), RV "griefs," elsewhere trd "sorrow"; *lupéō*, "to grieve," "afflict" (Mk **10** 22, RV "sorrowful"; Jn **21** 17, "Peter was grieved"; Rom **14** 15; 2 Cor **2** 4, RV "made sorry"; ver 5, "caused sorrow"; Eph **4** 30, "Grieve not the Holy Spirit of God"); *diaponéomai*, lit. "to labor through," "to grieve self," occurs twice (Acts **4** 2; **16** 18, RV "sore troubled"); *stenázō*, "to groan, or sigh," once only trd "grief" (He **13** 17), RVm "groaning"; *prosochthízō*, "to be indignant," etc, twice (He **3** 10.17, RV "displeased"). The reference is to Ps **95** 10, where the LXX by this Gr word trs *ḳūṭ* (see above).

The less frequency in the NT of words denoting "grief" is significant. Christ came "to comfort all that mourn—to give a garland for ashes, the oil of joy for mourning, the garment of praise for the spirit of heaviness." Christians, however, cannot but feel sorrow and be moved by grief, and it is to be noted that in both the OT and NT, God Himself is said to be susceptible to grief. W. L. WALKER

GRIEVANCE, grēv'ans (עָמָל, *'āmāl*): Occurs only in AV as a tr of Hab **1** 3, "Why dost thou show me iniquity, and cause me to behold grievance?" (RV "look upon perverseness"); *'āmāl* is also trd "perverseness" by AV and RV in Nu **23** 21, "perverseness in Israel"; Isa **10** 1, AV "grievousness," RV "perverseness." In Hab **1** 13, AV trs the same word "iniquity" (m "grievance"), "Thou art of purer eyes than to behold evil and canst not look on iniquity" (m "grievance"), RV "perverseness." The word means originally "toil," "labor" with sorrow, misery, etc, as the consequence, and is often so trd. It is the word in Isa **53** 11, "He shall see of the *travail* of his soul, and shall be satisfied." W. L. WALKER

GRIEVOUS, grēv'us, **GRIEVOUSLY**, grēv'us-li, **GRIEVOUSNESS**, grēv'us-nes: In addition to several of the words mentioned under GRIEF (q.v.), we have *kābhēdh* ("heavy") 8 t, e.g. Gen **12** 10, "The famine was grievous in the land," RV "sore"; *māraç* ("powerful"), "a grievous curse" (1 K **2** 8); *ṣūr*, "to turn aside" (Jer **6** 28), "grievous revolters"; *ḳāsheh*, "to make sharp" (1 K **12** 4; 2 Ch **10** 4); *taḥălu'īm* (Jer **16** 4), "They shall die grievous deaths," RVm "deaths of sicknesses"; *'āthāḳ* (Ps **31** 18), "which speak grievous things proudly," RV "against the righteous insolently"; *ḥēṭ*, "sin" (Lam **1** 8), "Jerus hath grievously sinned" (lit. "hath sinned a sin"); *mā'al*, "trespass" (Ezk **14** 13), "trespassing grievously" (lit. "trespassing a trespass"), RV "committing a trespass"; *kōbhedh*, "weight" (Isa **21** 15), "grievousness"; *barús*, "heavy," "grievous wolves" (Acts **20** 29), "grievous charges" (**25** 7), "His commandments are not grievous" (1 Jn **5** 3); *oknērós*, RV "irksome" (Phil **3** 1); *ponērós*, "evil" (Rev **16** 2), "a grievous sore"; *dusbástaktos*, "grievous to be borne" (Mt **23** 4; Lk **11** 46); *deinós*, "greatly," "grievously tormented" (Mt **8** 6); *kakôs*, "badly," "grievously vexed" (Mt **15** 22). W. L. WALKER

GRINDER, grīn'dēr. See MILL.

GRINDING, grīnd'ing. See CRAFTS.

GRISLED, griz''ld, **GRIZZLED**. See COLORS.

GROAN, grōn (נָאַק, *nā'aḳ*, אָנַק, *'ānaḳ*; **στενάζω**, *stenázō*, **ἐμβριμάομαι**, *embrimáomai*): The Eng. word, noun and vb., is an attempt to imitate the vocal sound which is expressive of severe pain or distress, physical or mental. It is cognate with the Scottish dialect word *girn*, and with *grin* in its original obsolete sense, as used in the Anglican Prayer-book version of Ps **59** 6.14, "grin like a dog and go about the city"; here "grin" is a tr of *hāmāh*, and means the sound of the nightly howling of the pariah dogs in Jerus and other oriental cities. It is used in the OT:

(1) To denote the expression accompanying physical suffering, as in the case of the Israelites in Egypt oppressed by Pharaoh's taskmasters (Ex **2** 24; **6** 5), or in Pal under the yoke of the Canaanites (Jgs **2** 18, *neḳāḳāh*). It is also used in Job's description of the sufferings and wretchedness of the poor (**24** 12), as well as in his complaint concerning his own suffering when smitten by the hand of God (**23** 2). The Psalmist speaks of groaning when fever-stricken and remorseful, AV and RV "roaring all the day long" (Ps **32** 3; **38** 9; **102** 5; **22** 1).

(2) The expression of suffering on the part of beasts, hungry and thirsty in drought (Joel **1** 18).

(3) The manifestation of mental and spiritual distress as in Ps **6** 6; **102** 20 (RV "sighing").

(4) **Metaphorically** groaning is the despairing note of Egypt in the prophecy of her overthrow by

Babylon, the sound being that uttered by a deadly wounded man (Ezk **30** 24; similarly in the prophecy of the Pers conquest the misery of Babylon is thus represented by Jer **51** 52); and the misery of Tyre when taken by Babylon is similarly described (Ezk **26** 15, AV "cry").

The word for "sigh" (*'ănāḥāh*) is closely allied, and the meanings are sufficiently akin, so that the terms seem interchangeable. A sigh is physically a sign of respiratory distress due to depressed action of the heart; sighing is consequently the indication of physical weakness or mental disquietude, as Ps **12** 5; **31** 10; **79** 11; Isa **21** 2; **24** 7; **35** 10; Jer **45** 3.

Nā'aḳ is the crying of persons dying or starving, as in Ezk **30** 24; Job **24** 12. A somewhat similar word, *hāghāh*, means the complaining sound like that of the cooing of doves (Isa **59** 11; Nah **2** 7). *Nehī* is the sound of lamentation of the dead (Jer **9** 10; **31** 15; Am **5** 16).

In the NT "groaning" is used for the expression of mental distress. In Jn **11** 33.35 the word used is part of the vb. *embrimaomai*, which conveys the idea of deep and earnest emotion. The same word in two other passages is tr[d] "strictly charged," and indicates the emphasis of the charge (Mt **9** 30; Mk **1** 43). Elsewhere "sighing" and "groaning" are renderings of words derived from the vb. *stenazō*, as in Rom **8** 23; 2 Cor **5** 2.4; Mk **7** 34; **8** 12. Stephen calls the groaning of Israel in Egypt *stenagmós* (Acts **7** 34), and the united wail of the travailing creation is expressed by St. Paul by the word *sunstenázei* (Rom **8** 22). The sigh is a characteristic sign of woe in Isa **21** 2; **24** 7; Jer **45** 3; Lam **1** 4.8.11.12; Ezk **9** 4; **21** 6 f.

ALEX. MACALISTER

GROSS, grōs (עֲרָפֶל, *'ărāphel*): Used twice with "darkness" in Isa **60** 2; Jer **13** 16. In the NT the vb. παχύνω, *pachúnō*, "to make fat," is applied twice to "making gross" the heart (Mt **13** 15; Acts **28** 27). See GREASE.

GROUND, ground, **GROUNDED**, ground'ed (אֲדָמָה, *'ădhāmāh*, אֶרֶץ, *'ereç*; γῆ, *gē*):

(1) "Ground" is in AV the tr of *'ădhāmāh*, "the soil," the ground so called from its red color, frequently also tr[d] "earth" and "land" (Gen **2** 5 f, etc; Ex **3** 5; **8** 21, etc); it is more often the tr of *'ereç*, which means rather *the earth*, oftenest tr[d] "earth" and "land" (Gen **18** 2; Ps **74** 7; Isa **3** 26, etc); other words are *ḥelḳāh*, "portion," "field" (2 S **23** 12, RV "plot"); *ḥārīsh*, "ploughing" (1 S **8** 12); *sādheh*, "a plain," "a field" (1 Ch **11** 13, RV "plot of ground"); for other special words see DRY; FALLOW; PARCHED.

(2) In the NT the common word for "ground" is *gē*, "earth," "soil," "land" (Mt **13** 8; Acts **7** 33, "holy ground," etc); other words are *ágros*, "field" (Lk **14** 18, "I have bought a piece of ground," RV "field"); *chōríon*, "spot," "place" (Jn **4** 5, "parcel of ground").

(3) As past part. of "to grind," "ground" appears as the tr of *rīphōth*, pounded corn (2 S **17** 19, RV "bruised"); "ground" is also the tr of *ṭāḥan* (Ex **32** 20; Nu **11** 8; Dt **9** 21, RV "grinding").

(4) "Ground," as the basis or foundation of anything, occurs in 1 Tim **3** 15 as the tr of *hedraíōma* (from *édaphos*), "the pillar and ground of the truth," RVm "stay."

"Grounded" is used in the sense of *founded, based, fixed in* (Isa **30** 32), "and in every place where the grounded staff shall pass, which the Lord shall lay upon him," AVm "Heb every passing of the rod founded," RV "and every stroke [m "Heb passing"] of the appointed staff [m "Or staff of doom (Heb foundation)"], which Jeh shall lay upon him"; following, ver 31, "with his rod will he [Jeh] smite him"; Delitzsch, "every stroke of the rod of destiny which Jeh causes to fall upon Asshur"; the word is *mūṣādhāh*, from *yāṣadh*, "to place," "to found," "to appoint," "to ordain," hence "appointed rod [of punishment]," seems the simplest rendering.

In Eph **3** 17 we have "rooted and grounded in love," and in Col **1** 23, "if ye continue in the faith, grounded and settled," RV "steadfast," both *themelióō*, "to lay a foundation." In Ecclus **18** 6 "ground" is used for the "bottom of things," but RV has "to track them out" (*exichneúō*), "to trace out."

(5) **Figurative** uses of "ground" are as representing *the heart* in relation to its reception of words of truth and righteousness (Jer **4** 3; Hos **10** 12, "Break up your fallow ground"); to the word of the kingdom as preached by Christ (Mt **13** 8.23); dry, parched, thirsty ground stands for a poor condition (Ps **107** 33.35; Isa **35** 7; **44** 3; **53** 2; Ezk **19** 13).

W. L. WALKER

GROVE, grōv: (1) אֲשֵׁרָה, *'ăshērāh*. See ASHERAH. (2) אֵשֶׁל, *'ēshel* (Gen **21** 33 AV, RV "a tamarisk tree"). See TAMARISK.

GRUDGE, gruj (נָטַר, *nāṭar*; στενάζω, *stenázō*, γογγυσμός, *goggusmós*): "Grudge" (perhaps a mimetic word, cf Gr *grú*) is "to grumble" or "murmur" at any person or thing, to entertain an envious or covetous feeling, to do or give anything unwillingly, etc. It occurs in AV as the tr of *nāṭar*, "to keep [anger]" (Lev **19** 18, "Thou shalt not . . . . bear any grudge against the children of thy people"); in Ps **59** 15, as the tr, in text, of Heb *lūn* or *līn*, "to pass the night," "to tarry," Niphal, "to show oneself obstinate," "to murmur or complain" (of the enemies who were hunting David like dogs), "Let them wander up and down for meat, and *grudge* if they be not satisfied," m "If they be not satisfied then will they stay all night," RV "And tarry all night if they be not satisfied"; but see Ex **15** 24; **16** 2; Nu **14** 2; Josh **9** 18, etc, where the tr is "murmur"; may not the meaning be "and growl [or howl] if they be not satisfied"? "Grudge" formerly implied open expression of discontent, etc, e.g. Wyclif has in Lk **15** 2, "The farisies and scribis grucchiden seiynge," etc.

In Jas **5** 9, *stenazō*, "to groan," "to complain" (from affliction or from impatience or ill-humor), is tr[d] "grudge," "Grudge not one against another, brethren," RV "murmur not"; *goggusmos*, "a murmuring" (cf Jn **7** 12 f; Acts **6** 1), is rendered "grudging" (1 Pet **4** 9), "Use hospitality one to another without grudging," RV "murmuring"; cf Phil **2** 14; *mē ek lúpēs*, "not out of grief," is "without grudging" (2 Cor **9** 7, RV "not grudgingly," m "Gr of sorrow"); in Ecclus **10** 25 we have "will not grudge" (*goggúzō*), RV "murmur."

"Grudge" was frequent in the earlier VSS, but is changed in AV for the most part into "murmur"; RV completes the change, except Lev **19** 18, and text of 2 Cor **9** 7.

W. L. WALKER

GUARD, gärd: (1) שַׂר הַטַּבָּחִים, *sar ha-ṭabbāḥīm*, "captain of the guard," lit. "slaughterers" (Gen **37** 36; **39** 1; **40** 3.4; **41** 10.12); רַב־טַבָּחִים, *rabh ṭabbāḥīm* (2 K **25** 8.11.20; Jer **39** 9, etc); רַב טַבָּחַיָּה, *rabh tabbāḥayyāh* (Dnl **2** 14); רָצִים, *rāçīm*, "guard," AV "footmen" (1 S **22** 17); *sārē hā-rāçīm*, "chief of the guard," AV "captains of the guard" (1 K **14** 27); *tā' hā-rāçīm*, "guard-chamber" (1 K **14** 28; cf Ezk **40** 21, etc, where "lodges" are "guardrooms"; see A. B. Davidson ad loc.). (2) מִשְׁמָר, *mishmār*, "guard," a defence to a point of danger (Neh **4** 22 f; Ezk **38** 7). (3) מִשְׁמַעַת, *mishma'ath*, "guard" (2 S **23** 23, where ARVm and RVm have "council," the body over which Benaiah was set by David and whose functions were perhaps those of consultation). (4) Σπεκουλάτωρ, *spekouláto̅r*, "guard" (Mk **6** 27, "a man of Herod's guard," where, as in one or two other cases, St. Mark, writing for Romans, simply transliterates the Lat *speculator* "a scout," "an executioner," as in loc.). (5) Στρατοπεδάρχης, *stratopedárche̅s*, "captain of the guard" AV, "captain of the praetorian guard" RVm, Acts **28** 16. See CAPTAIN. (6) Κουστωδία, *kousto̅día*, "watch" AV, "guard" ARV and RV (Mt **27** 65.66; **28** 11).

1. Royal Body-Guard

An oriental monarch's body-guard consisted of picked men attached to his person and ready to fulfil his pleasure in important and confidential concerns. At the courts of Egypt and Babylon the members of the guard were known as "slaughterers," "executioners" (Gen **37** 36 AVm, ARVm and RVm, where Potiphar is called their captain); 2 K **25** 8, where Nebuzaradan is called their captain (AVm "chief marshal"). Whether it had ever been the function of the body-guard to kill meat for the royal table there is little directly to show; that they acted as executioners can be well understood. In Israel they were known as "the footmen" (1 S **22** 17 AV, ARVm and RVm "runners") who acted as royal messengers or couriers from the time of Saul onward (2 K **10** 25; **11** 6); and this designation connects them with the couriers of the kings of Persia (Est **3** 13.15; **8** 14, where our VSS render "posts," though the Heb is *rāçīm*).

2. Composed of Foreigners

The men of the royal body-guard were usually foreigners like the janissaries of oriental monarchs down to modern times, who prefer to have around their persons warriors uninfluenced by family connection with the people of the land. Rameses II had such a body-guard whose commanders ranked with the great officers of the crown (Maspero, *Struggle of the Nations*, 766). David's body-guard of 600, known also as the *gibbōrīm* or "mighty men," consisted of Cherethites, Pelethites, and Gittites (2 S **15** 18; **20** 23), and we read of Carites (2 K **11** 19), who may have been Carians or Cretans, as forming part of the guard at the coronation of King Jehoash.

3. Connection with the Temple

That this guard had duties in connection with the temple as well as the king's house seems clear. That they were employed as slaughterers of the sacrifices before the Levites were intrusted with the office is unlikely, inasmuch as this guard is not said to have been composed of "slaughterers" but of "runners." But they accompanied King Rehoboam when he visited the temple (1 K **14** 28), and to their captains were committed the shields of brass which took the place of the shields of gold which Solomon had hung up in the temple; Jehoiada employed their captains to put Athaliah to death and to exterminate the worshippers of Baal who had fled to the temple precincts (2 K **11** 4 ff); the temple gate leading to the palace was called "the gate of the guard" (2 K **11** 19). At this time, and for this occasion, at least, the royal body-guard were the temple guards; and when Ezekiel drew up his plans for the temple which he conceived to replace the temple destroyed by Nebuchadrezzar, the "lodges" or "little chambers" were rooms for the accommodation of the temple guard (Ezk **40** 7.10.21.33, etc).

LITERATURE.—Robertson Smith, *OTJC*, 262, and note.

T. NICOL

GUARDIAN, gär'di-an. See FAMILY; ANGEL.

GUDGODAH, gud-gō'da (גֻּדְגֹּדָה, *gudhgōdhāh*): A place in the wilderness journeyings (Dt **10** 7), corresponding to Hor-haggidgad in Nu **33** 32. LXX in each case renders Γαδγάδ, *Gadgád*. The site cannot now be identified; but there may be an echo of the ancient name in that of *Wādy Guḍāghiḍ*, a confluent of *Wādy Jerāfeh*, which comes down from *et Tīh* into the *'Arabah* nearly due W. of Petra. There are difficulties, however, as the consonants do not correspond.

GUEST, gest (קָרָא, *ḳārā'*; **ἀνάκειμαι,** *anákeimai*): Oriental customs growing out of a nomadic life demand a greater abandon and freedom with respect to the relation of host and guest than are permitted by the conventionalities of western life. A householder is expected to entertain a traveler, and in turn the traveler may accept with perfect ease the hospitality shown without any obligation to pay. See HOSPITALITY. The significance of the word is that of one who is called or invited. A certain sacredness, unknown to modern western society, was attached to the guest, so that a special apartment was set aside for the guests. See GUEST-CHAMBER. In the OT only 3 t is the word itself used, with reference to the guests of Adonijah (1 K **1** 41.49), of the foolish woman (Prov **9** 18), and of Jeh (Zeph **1** 7). In the NT, 3 t (Mt **22** 10 f; Lk **19** 7 AV, RV "to lodge"). Though but few actual uses of the word occur, there are abounding illustrations of the guest relation in both OT and NT. Esp. is this manifest in the striking social attitudes of Jesus on occasions. Notable among these are the hospitality of Matthew (Lk **5** 29 ff); Jesus' relation to Martha and Mary (**10** 38 ff), and His entrance into the home of Zacchaeus (Lk **19** 1 ff). Likewise Jesus spoke frequently of the relation which should exist between the guest and his host (see Lk **7** 44–46; Mt **25** 35; **10** 40).

WALTER G. CLIPPINGER

GUEST-CHAMBER, gest'chām-bẽr: The tr of (1) לִשְׁכָּה, *lishkāh* (1 S **9** 22, AV "parlor"), and (2) κατάλυμα, *katáluma* (Mk **14** 14 ‖ Lk **22** 11). The *lishkāh* was probably a room in which the sacrificial feasts were held. *Kataluma* is derived from *katalúō*, which means "to slacken," i.e. the ropes of the beasts of burden, and hence "to lodge." *Kataluma* has accordingly often the sense of "inn," but as used in Mk and Lk it has the narrower meaning of a room in which to eat.

GUIDE, gīd (אַלּוּף, *'allūph*, נָהַל, *nāhal*, נָחָה, *nāḥāh*; **ὁδηγός,** *hodēgós*, **ὁδηγέω,** *hodēgéō*): "Guide" (noun) is the tr of *'allūph*, "an intimate," "a friend," the leader of a family or tribe: Ps **55** 13, "a man mine equal, my guide," RV "my companion"; Prov **2** 17, "the guide of her youth," RV "friend," m "or guide"; Jer **3** 4, "My father, thou [art] the guide of my youth," RVm "companion"; Mic **7** 5, "Put ye not confidence in a guide," ARV "in a friend," m "confidant" (which the context shows to be the meaning), ERV "guide," m "familiar friend"; once of *ḳāçīn*, "a judge," "a military leader or commander" (cf Josh **10** 24; Dnl **11** 18); Prov **6** 7, RV "chief," m "judge"; once *nāhagh*, "to lead," is tr[d] "guide" (Ps **48** 14). In the NT *hodēgos*, "a way-leader," is tr[d] "guide" (Mt **23** 16, "ye blind guides"; **23** 24; Acts **1** 16; Rom **2** 19); "to guide" is the tr of *nāḥāh*, "to lead forth" (Job **38** 32; Ps **73** 24); once of *'āshar*, Piel, "to guide" or "lead straight" (Prov **23** 19); of *yā'aç*, "to command," "to give counsel" ("I will guide thee with mine eye," RV "I will counsel thee with mine eye upon thee," Ps **32** 8); of *kūl*, "to contain," "to sustain" (Ps **112** 5, "He will guide his affairs with discretion," RV "He shall maintain his cause in judgment"); of *nāhagh*, "to drive," "to lead" (Ps **78** 52); of *hodēgeō*, "to show the way," "guide" (Jn **16** 13, "He shall guide you into all truth," RV "the truth";

Acts **8** 31); *oikodespotéō* is tr[d] "to guide the house," RV "rule the household" (1 Tim **5** 14); the word means lit. to be a *house-master* (the head of the house).

RV has "guide" for "lead" (Ps **25** 5; Mt **15** 14; Lk **6** 39; Rev **7** 17); "a guide to" for "more excellent than" (Prov **12** 26); "guided" for "brought in" (Ps **78** 26); "guideth" for "maketh" (2 S **22** 33), for "leadeth" (Ps **23** 3); "my heart yet guiding me," m "holding its course," for "yet acquainting mine heart" (Eccl **2** 3). "Guide-posts" is substituted for "high heaps" (Jer **31** 21).

W. L. Walker

GUILE, gīl (מִרְמָה, *mirmāh;* δόλος, *dólos*): "Guile" is twice the tr of *mirmāh,* "fraud," "deceit" (Ps **34** 13, "Keep . . . . thy lips from speaking guile"; **55** 11, "deceit and guile," RV "oppression [m "fraud"] and guile"); once of *'ormāh,* "craftiness," "guile" (Ex **21** 14); once of *r^emīyāh,* "deception," "fraud" (Ps **32** 2, "in whose spirit there is no guile"); in the NT of *dolos,* "bait," hence generally, "fraud," "guile," "deceit"; LXX for *mirmāh* (Isa **53** 9, EV "deceit") and for *r^emīyāh* (Job **13** 7, EV "deceitfully"; Jn **1** 47; 2 Cor **12** 16, "Being crafty, I caught you with guile"; 1 Thess **2** 3; 1 Pet **2** 1; **2** 22; **3** 10, quoted from Ps **34** 13; Rev **14** 5, "In their mouth was found no guile," RV after corrected text, "no lie").

St. Paul's words in 2 Cor **12** 16 have sometimes been quoted in justification of "guile" in religious work, etc; but he is not describing his actual procedure; but that which the Corinthians *might* have attributed to him; the lips of the Christian must be kept free from all guile (Ps **34** 13; 1 Pet **2** 1, etc; Wisd **1** 5, "A holy spirit of discipline will flee deceit" [*dolos*], RV "A holy spirit"). "Guile" does not appear in Apoc; *dolos* is frequently rendered "deceit."

RV has "guile" for "subtilty" (Gen **27** 35; Acts **13** 10); "cover itself with guile" for "is covered by deceit" (Prov **26** 26); "with guile" for "deceitfully" (Gen **34** 13); "spiritual milk which is without guile" for "sincere milk of the word," ERVm "reasonable," ARVm "Gr belonging to the reason" (cf Rom **12** 1; 1 Pet **2** 2); "guileless" for "harmless" (He **7** 26). W. L. Walker

GUILT, gilt: The Christian idea of guilt involves three elements: responsibility (Gr *aitía,* "cause," depending upon a man's real freedom), blameworthiness (Lat *reatus culpae,* depending upon a man's knowledge and purpose) and the obligation to make good through punishment or compensation (Lat *reatus poenae;* cf Gr *opheílēma,* "debt," Mt **6** 12). In other words, in thinking of guilt we ask the questions of cause, motive and consequence, the central idea being that of the personal blameworthiness of the sinner.

I. In the OT.—Not all of this is found at once in the OT. The idea of guilt corresponds to that of righteousness or holiness. When these are ritual and legal, instead of ethical and spiritual, they will determine similarly the idea of guilt. This legalistic and ritualistic conception of guilt may first be noted. Personal blameworthiness does not need to be present. "If any one sin, and do any of the things which Jeh hath commanded not to be done; though he knew it not, yet is he guilty, and shall bear his iniquity" (Lev **5** 17). The man is guilty, not because he might or should have known; he may merely have touched unwittingly the body of an unclean beast (Lev **5** 2.3). The guilt is here because the law has been transgressed and must be made good (cf Lev **5** 15.16; **4** 2.3.13.22.27; see also **5** 2.3.4.17).

1. The Ritualistic and Legalistic Conception

Moreover, the element of personal responsibility is sometimes lacking where guilt is assigned. The priest may sin "so as to bring guilt on the people" (Lev **4** 3). One man's wrongdoing may "cause the land to sin" (Dt **24** 4). Israel has sinned in Achan's greed and therefore suffers. Even when the guilty man is found, his children and his very cattle must bear the guilt and punishment with him, though there is no suggestion of their participation or even knowledge (Josh **7**; cf 2 S **24**). Here the full moral idea of sin and guilt is wanting because the idea of personality and personal responsibility has not come to its own. The individual is still merged here in the clan or nation.

The central idea in all this is not that of the individual, his responsiblity, his motive, his blame. It is that of a rule and the transgression of it, which must be made good. For this reason we see the ideas of sin and guilt and punishment constantly passing over into each other. This may be seen by noting the use of the words whose common root is *'shm,* the distinctive Heb term for guilt. In Lev **5** to **7** in the adj. form it is rendered "guilty," in the noun as "trespass offering." In Hos **5** 15 it seems to mean punishment (see m, "have borne their guilt," and cf Ezk **6** 6), while in Nu **5** 7.8 the idea is that of compensation (rendered "restitution for guilt").

With the prophets, the ideas of sin and righteousness come out more clearly as ethical and personal, and so we mark a similar advance in the conception of guilt. It is not ritual correctness that counts with God, incense and sacrifices and new moons and Sabbaths, but to cease to do evil, to learn to do well (Isa **1**). Thus the motive and the inner spirit come in (Mic **6** 8; Isa **57** 15; **58** 1–12), and guilt gains a new depth and quality. At the same time the idea of personal responsibility comes. A man is to bear his own sins. The children's teeth are not to be set on edge because the fathers have eaten sour grapes (Jer **31** 29.30; Ezk **18** 29–32; 2 K **14** 6; cf 2 S **24** 17).

2. Prophetic Teaching

II. In the NT.—Here as elsewhere Jesus came to fulfil. With Him it is the inner attitude of the soul that decides. It is the penitent publican who goes down justified, not the Pharisee with his long credit account (Lk **18** 9–14). That is why His attitude is so kindly toward some notorious sinners and so stern toward some religious leaders. The Pharisees are outwardly correct, but their spirit of bigotry and pride prevents their entering the kingdom of heaven, while the penitent harlots and publicans take it by storm.

1. With Jesus

Because it is not primarily a matter of the outward deed but of the inner spirit, Jesus marks different degrees of guilt as depending upon a man's knowledge and motive (Lk **11** 29–32; **12** 47.48; **23** 34). And yet Jesus does not lighten the sense of guilt but rather deepens it. The strength of the OT thought lay in this, that it viewed all transgression as a sin against God, since all law came from Him. This religious emphasis remains with Jesus (Lk **15** 21; cf Ps **51** 4). But with Jesus God is far more than a giver of rules. He gives Himself. And so the guilt is the deeper because the sin is against this love and mercy and fellowship which God offers us. Jesus shows us the final depth of evil in sin. Here comes the NT interpretation of the cross, which shows it on the one hand as the measure of God's love in the free gift of His Son, and on the other as the measure of man's guilt whose sin wrought this and made it necessary.

Paul also recognizes differences of degree in guilt, the quality of blameworthiness which is not simply determined by looking at the outward transgression (Acts **17** 30; Eph **4** 18; Rom **2** 9; **3** 26; **5** 13; **7** 13). He, too, looks within to decide the question of guilt (Rom **14** 23). But sin is not a matter of

2. With Paul

single acts or choices with Paul. He sees it as a power that comes to rule a man's life and that rules in the race. The question therefore arises, Does Paul think of guilt also as native, as belonging to man because man is a part of the race? Here it can merely be pointed out that Rom **5** 12–21 does not necessarily involve this. Paul is not discussing whether all men committed sin in Adam's fall, or whether all are guilty by virtue of their very place in a race that is sinful. It is not the question of guilt in fact or degree, but merely the fact that through one man men are now made righteous as before through one sin came upon them all. This no more involves native guilt as a non-ethical conception than it does the idea that the righteousness through Christ is merely forensic and non-ethical. Paul is simply passing over the other elements to assert one fact. Rom **1** suggests how Paul looked at universal sin as involving guilt because universal knowledge and choice entered in. See also SIN.

LITERATURE.—Mueller, *Christian Doctrine of Sin*, I, 193–267; Schultz, *OT Theology;* Kaehler, art. "Schuld," *PRE*[4].

HARRIS FRANKLIN RALL

GUILT OFFERING. See SACRIFICE.

GUILTLESS, gilt'les: The primary meaning of the Heb word is "to be clean." Sometimes the meaning is "freedom from blame," at other times to be "free from punishment," these two ideas running over into each other as with the word "guilt." The latter meaning seems to predominate in Ex **20** 7; Dt **5** 11; 2 S **14** 9; 1 K **2** 9. The other meaning holds in Nu **32** 22; Josh **2** 19; 2 S **3** 28; Mt **12** 5.7.

GUILTY, gil'ti: In addition to the general discussion under GUILT (q.v.), several NT passages demand special notice because the word "guilty" is not used in the principal sense of blameworthy, but with one of the two lesser meanings noted above which go to make up the complete idea. In 3 of these passages AV renders "guilty" and RV gives another rendering. In Mt **26** 66 AV, Jesus' foes declare he is "guilty of death" (ἔνοχος, *énochos*, "liable to"). Here "guilty" simply means the one who is legally held, and the reference is not to the blame but to the consequence. This is a true use of the word in the lower and legal sense. It does not correspond with our higher usage, and so we have it in RV "worthy of death." So in Rom **3** 19, "guilty" is changed to "under the judgment," and in Mt **23** 18, to "debtor."

In Jas **2** 10 and 1 Cor **11** 27, the word "guilty" is also used in the lesser or more primitive sense, not primarily as involving blame but as involving the sinner's authorship or responsibility. This is the first element suggested in the definition of guilt given above, just as the preceding passages illustrate the third element. The man who stumbles in one point is "guilty" of the whole law. James does not refer here to the degree of blameworthiness. "Guilty of" means transgressor of, and he has transgressed the whole because the law is one. So in 1 Cor **11** 27, those "guilty of the body and the blood of the Lord" are those who have transgressed in the matter of the body and the blood of the Lord.

HARRIS FRANKLIN RALL

GULF (**χάσμα**, *chásma*, "a chasm," "vent," "a gaping opening"—a great interval; from **χαίνω**, *chaínō*, "to gape" or "yawn"): Occurs only in Lk **16** 26, "Between us and you there is a great gulf fixed" (cf "afar off" in ver 23). This is very different from, though it probably reflects, the rabbinical conception of the separation between the two compartments of Hades (Sheol) by "a hand's breadth," "a wall," or even, later, "a chasm," as the parable can be given here only a **figurative** significance, and is of purely ethical import. The fundamental difference between the Rich Man and Lazarus lies not in their conditions but in their characters. For "besides all this" (ver 26) RVm gives "in all these things," thus implying that the moral distinctions which exist in this life (ver 25) become more pronounced ("fixed") in the next world, and the "gulf" is impassable in the sense that a change of condition will not necessarily produce a change of soul. See also ABRAHAM'S BOSOM; HADES.

M. O. EVANS

GUNI, gū'nī, **GUNITES,** gū'nīts (גּוּנִי, *gūnī*): (1) The name of a Naphtalite clan (Gen **46** 24; Nu **26** 48; 1 Ch **7** 13). In Nu **26** 48 the gentilic "Gunites" is also found, having in Heb the same form, with the article.

(2) The head of a Gadite family (1 Ch **5** 15).

GUR, gûr, **THE ASCENT,** a-sent', **OF** (מַעֲלֵה־גוּר, *ma'ălēh ghūr*): The place where the servants of Jehu mortally wounded Ahaziah, king of Judah (2 K **9** 27). The ascent (AV "going up") was hard by Ibleam, the site of which is identified about ½ mile S. of *Jenin*.

GUR-BAAL, gûr-bā'al (גּוּר־בַּעַל, *gūr ba'al*): The residence of certain Arabs against whom God helped Uzziah, king of Judah (2 Ch **26** 7). Its mention immediately after the Philis may have suggested the "Gerar" of the Tg. Association with the Meunim points to the E. It may be taken as certain that *Jebel Neby Hārūn*, near Petra, has always been crowned by a sanctuary. This may have been "the dwelling place of Baal"; or, accepting Kittel's emendation (*ṭūr ba'al*), "the rock" or "mountain of Baal." The Arabs probably dwelt in the region before the days of Petra (*EB*, s.v.)

W. EWING

GUTTER, gut'ẽr. See HOUSE.

GYMNASIUM, jim-nā'zi-um. See GAMES; PALAESTRA.

H

HA, hä (הֶאָח, *he'āḥ*): In Job **39** 25, RV "Aha," of the battle-horse. See AH, AHA.

HAAHASHTARI, hā-a-hash'ta-rī (הָאֲחַשְׁתָּרִי, *hā-'ăḥashtārī*, possibly a corruption of הָאַשְׁחוּרִי, *hā-'ashḥūrī*): A descendant of Judah (1 Ch **4** 6). The name is probably corrupt. If the emendation suggested above is accepted, it means the Ashhurites, and is a description of the preceding names.

HABAIAH, ha-bā'ya, **HOBAIAH** (חֲבָיָה, *ḥăbhāyāh*, חֳבַיָּה, *ḥŏbhāyāh*): A post-exilic priestly family which was unable to establish its pedigree. "Habaiah" is the form in Ezr **2** 61; in the ‖ passage (Neh **7** 63), AV has "Habaiah," and RV "Hobaiah"; in the ‖ passage in 1 Esd **5** 38, the form is *Obdiá* (Ὀβδιά), B, *Obbeiá*.

HABAKKUK, ha-bak'uk, hab'a-kuk:

- I. THE AUTHOR
  - 1. Name
  - 2. Life
- II. THE BOOK
  - 1. Interpretation of Chs 1 and 2
  - 2. Contents
  - 3. Style
  - 4. Integrity
- III. THE TIME
  - 1. Date
  - 2. Occasion
- IV. ITS TEACHING
  - 1. Universal Supremacy of Jeh
  - 2. Faithfulness the Guarantee of Permanency
- LITERATURE

I. The Author.—Habakkuk (חֲבַקּוּק, *ḥăbhakkūḳ*) means "embrace," or "ardent embrace." Some of the ancient rabbis, connecting the name with 2 K **4** 16, "Thou shalt embrace a son," imagined that the prophet was the son of the Shunammite woman. The LXX form of the name, *Hambakoúm*, Theod. *Hambakouk*, presupposes the Heb *ḥabbaḳūḳ*. A similar word occurs in Assyr as the name of a garden plant.

1. Name

Practically nothing is known of Habakkuk. The book bearing his name throws little light upon his life, and the rest of the OT is silent concerning him; but numerous legends have grown up around his name. The identification of the prophet with the son of the Shunammite woman is one. Another, connecting Isa **21** 6 with Hab **2** 1, makes Habakkuk the watchman set by Isaiah to watch for the fall of Babylon. One of the recensions of the LXX text of Bel declares that the story was taken "from the prophecy of Habakkuk, the son of Jesus of the tribe of Levi." This must refer to an unknown apocryphal book ascribed to our prophet. What authority there may be for calling his father Jesus we do not know. The claim that he was of the tribe of Levi may be based upon the presence of the musical note at the end of the third chapter. According to the *Lives of the Prophets*, ascribed, though perhaps erroneously, to Epiphanius, bishop of Salamis in Cyprus during the latter part of the 4th cent. AD, he belonged to *Bēthçōhar*, of the tribe of Simeon. A very interesting story is found in Bel (33–39), according to which Habakkuk, while on his way to the field with a bowl of pottage, was taken by an angel, carried to Babylon and placed in the lions' den, where Daniel ate the pottage, when Habakkuk was returned to his own place. According to the *Lives*, Habakkuk died two years before the return of the exiles from Babylon. All these legends have little or no historical value.

2. Life

II. The Book.—It is necessary to consider the interpretation of chs **1** and **2** before giving the contents of the book, as a statement of the contents of these chapters will be determined by their interpretation. The different interpretations advocated may be grouped under three heads: (1) According to the first view: **1** 2–4: The corruption of Judah; the oppression of the righteous Jews by the wicked Jews, which calls for the Divine manifestation in judgment against the oppressors. **1** 5–11: Jeh announces that He is about to send the Chaldaeans to execute judgment. **1** 12–17: The prophet is perplexed. He cannot understand how a righteous God can use these barbarians to execute judgment upon a people more righteous than they. He considers even the wicked among the Jews better than the Chaldaeans. **2** 1–4: Jeh solves the perplexing problem by announcing that the exaltation of the Chaldaeans will be but temporary; in the end they will meet their doom, while the righteous will live. **2** 5–20: Woes against the Chaldaeans.

1. Interpretation of Chs 1 and 2

(2) The second view finds it necessary to change the present arrangement of the verses **1** 5–11; in their present position, they will not fit into the interpretation. For this reason Wellhausen and others omit these verses as a later addition; on the other hand, Giesebrecht would place them before **1** 2, as the opening verses of the prophecy. The transposition would require a few other minor changes, so as to make the verses a suitable beginning and establish a smooth transition from ver 11 to ver 2. Omitting the troublesome verses, the following outline of the two chapters may be given: **1** 2–4: The oppression of the righteous Jews by the wicked Chaldaeans. **1** 12–17: Appeal to Jeh on behalf of the Jews against their oppressors. **2** 1–4: Jeh promises deliverance (see above). **2** 5–20: Woes against the Chaldaeans.

(3) The third view also finds it necessary to alter the present order of verses. Again **1** 5–11, in the present position, interferes with the theory; therefore, these verses are given a more suitable place after **2** 4. According to this interpretation the outline is as follows: **1** 2–4: Oppression of the righteous Jews by the wicked Assyrians (Budde) or Egyptians (G. A. Smith). **1** 12–17: Appeal to Jeh on behalf of the oppressed against the oppressor. **2** 1–4: Jeh promises deliverance (see above). **1** 5–11: The Chaldaeans will be the instrument to execute judgment upon the oppressors and to bring deliverance to the Jews. **2** 5–20: Woes against the Assyrians or Egyptians.

A full discussion of these views is not possible in this article (see Eiselen, *Minor Prophets*, 466–68). It may be sufficient to say that on the whole the first interpretation, which requires no omission or transposition, seems to satisfy most completely the facts in the case.

The contents of chs **1** and **2** are indicated in the preceding paragraph. Ch **3** contains a lyrical passage called in the title "Prayer." The petitioner speaks for himself and the community. He remembers the mighty works of Jeh for His people; the thought of them causes him to tremble; nevertheless, he calls for a repetition of the ancient manifestations (ver 2). In majestic pictures the poet describes the wonderful appearances of Jeh in the past (vs 3–11) for His chosen people (vs 12–15). The remembrance of these manifestations fills the Psalmist with fear and trembling, but also with joy and confidence in the God of his salvation (vs 16–19).

2. Contents

Only the Heb student can get an adequate idea of the literary excellence of the Book of Hab. "The literary power of Habakkuk," says Driver, "is considerable. Though his book is a brief one, it is full of force; his descriptions are graphic and powerful; thought and expression are alike poetic; he is still a master of the old classical style, terse, parallelistic, pregnant; there is no trace of the often prosaic diffusiveness which manifests itself in the writings of Jeremiah and Ezekiel. And if ch **3** be his, he is, moreover, a lyric poet of high order; the grand imagery and the rhythmic flow of this ode will bear comparison with some of the finest productions of the Heb muse."

3. Style

More than half of the book, including **1** 5–11; **2** 9–20, and ch **3** entire, has been denied to the prophet Habakkuk. If the prophecy is rightly interpreted (see above), no valid reason for rejecting **1** 5–11 can be found. Vs 9–20 of ch **2** are denied to Habakkuk chiefly on two grounds: (1) The "woes" are said to be in part, at least, unsuitable, if supposed to be addressed to the Chaldaean king. This difficulty vanishes when it is borne in mind that the king is not addressed as an individual, but as representing the policy of the nation, as a personification of the nation. (2) Some parts, esp. vs 12–14, "consist largely of citations and reminiscences of other passages, including some late ones" (cf ver 12 with Mic **3** 10; ver 13 with Jer **51** 58; ver 14 with Isa **11** 9; ver 16*b* with Jer **25** 15.16; vs 18–20 with Isa **44** 9 ff; **46** 6.7; Jer **10** 1–16). Aside from the fact that the argument from literary parallels is always precarious, in this case the resemblances are few in number and of such general character that they do not necessarily presuppose literary dependence. Ch **3** is denied to the prophet even more persistently, but the arguments are by no means conclusive. The fact that the chapter belongs to the psalm literature does not prove a late date unless it is assumed, without good reasons, that no psalms originated in the preëxilic period. Nor do the historical allusions, which are altogether vague, the style, the relation to other writers, and the character of the religious ideas expressed, point necessarily to a late date. The only doubtful verses are 16 ff, which seem to allude to a calamity other than the invasion of the Chaldaeans; and Driver says, not without reason, "Had the poet been writing under the pressure of a hostile invasion, the invasion itself would naturally have been expected to form a prominent feature in this picture." Hence, while it may be impossible to prove that Habakkuk is the author of the prayer, it is equally impossible to prove the contrary; and while there are a few indications which seem to point to a situation different from that of Habakkuk, they are by no means definite enough to exclude the possibility of Habakkuk's authorship.

4. Integrity

III. The Time.—The question of date is closely bound up with that of interpretation. Budde, on the theory that the oppressors, threatened with destruction, are the Assyrians (see above, 3), dates the prophecy 621 to 615 BC. Granting that the Assyrians are in the mind of the prophet, the date suggested by Betteridge (*AJT*, 1903, 674 ff), c 701 BC, is to be preferred; but if the Assyrians are not the oppressors, then with the Assyrians fall the dates proposed by Budde and Betteridge. If the prophecy is directed against Egypt, we are shut up to a very definite period, between 608 and 604 BC, for the Egyp supremacy in Judah continued during these years only. If the Egyptians are not the oppressors, another date will have to be sought. If the Chaldaeans are the oppressors of Judah, the prophecy must be assigned to a date subsequent to the battle of Carchemish in 605–604, for only after the defeat of the Egyptians could the Chaldaeans carry out a policy of world conquest; and it was some years after that event that the Chaldaeans first came into direct contact with Judah. But on this theory, **1** 2–4.12 ff; **2** 8 ff, presupposes the lapse of a considerable period of conquest, the subduing of many nations, the cruel oppression of Judah for some length of time; therefore, Nowack is undoubtedly correct, on this theory, in bringing the prophecy down to a period subsequent to the first exile in 597, or, as he says, "in round numbers about 590 BC."

1. Date

A different date must be sought if **1** 2–4 is interpreted as referring to the oppression of Jews by Jews, and **1** 5 ff, as a threat that Jeh will raise up the Chaldaeans, already known as a nation thirsting for blood, to punish the wickedness of Judah. These verses would seem to indicate (1) that the Chaldaeans had not yet come into direct contact with Judah, and (2) that they had already given exhibitions of the cruel character of their warfare. Nebuchadnezzar advanced against Judah about 600 BC; but the years since the fall of Nineveh, in 607–606, and the battle of Carchemish, in 605–604, had given abundant opportunity to the Chaldaeans to reveal their true character, and to the prophet and his contemporaries to become acquainted with this cruel successor of Nineveh. On this theory, therefore, the prophetic activity of Habakkuk must be assigned to shortly before 600 BC.

If Habakkuk prophesied about 600 BC, he lived under King Jehoiakim. The pious and well-meaning Josiah had been slain in an attempt to stop the advance of Egypt against Assyria. With his death the brief era of reform came to an end. After a reign of three months Jehoahaz was deposed by Pharaoh-necoh, who placed Jehoiakim on the throne. The latter was selfish, tyrannical and godless. In a short time the deplorable conditions of Manasseh's reign returned. It was this situation that caused the prophet's first perplexity: "O Jeh, how long shall I cry, and thou wilt not hear? I cry out unto thee of violence, and thou wilt not save" (**1** 2).

2. Occasion

IV. Its Teaching.—In the Book of Hab a new type of prophecy appears. The prophets were primarily preachers and teachers of religion and ethics. They addressed themselves to their fellow-countrymen in an attempt to win them back to Jeh and a righteous life. Not so Habakkuk. He addresses himself to Jeh, questioning the justice or even the reality of the Divine Providence. He makes complaint to God and expostulates with Him. The prophet Habakkuk, therefore, is a forerunner of the author of the Book of Job. "As a whole, his book is the fruit of religious reflection. It exhibits the communings and questionings of his soul—representative, no doubt, of many other pious spirits of the time—with God; and records the answers which the Spirit of God taught him for his own sake and for the sake of tried souls in every age."

Habakkuk has been called the prophet of faith. He possessed a strong, living faith in Jeh; but he, like many other pious souls, was troubled and perplexed by the apparent inequalities of life. He found it difficult to reconcile these with his lofty conception of Jeh. Nevertheless, he does not sulk. Boldly he presents his perplexities to Jeh, who points the way to a solution, and the prophet comes forth from his trouble with a faith stronger and more intense than ever. It is in connection with his attempts to solve the perplexing problems raised by the unpunished sins of his countrymen and the unlimited success of the Chaldaeans that Habakkuk gives utterance to two sublime truths:

1. The Universal Supremacy of Jeh

(1) Jeh is interested not only in Israel. Though Habakkuk, like the other prophets, believes in a special Divine Providence over Israel, he is equally convinced that Jeh's rule embraces the whole earth; the destinies of all the nations are in His hand. The Chaldaeans are punished not merely for their sins against Judah, but for the oppression of other nations as well. Being the only God, He cannot permit the worship of other deities. Temporarily the Chaldaeans may worship idols, or make might their god, they may "sacrifice unto their net," and burn incense "unto their drag," because by them "their portion is fat and their food plenteous"; but Jeh is from everlasting, the Holy One, and He will attest His supremacy by utterly destroying the boastful conqueror with his idols.

2. Faithfulness the Guarantee of Permanency

(2) The second important truth is expressed in **2** 4: "The righteous shall live by his faith" (ARVm "faithfulness"). Faithfulness assures permanency. The thought expressed by the prophet is not identical with that expressed by the apostle who quotes the words (Gal **3** 11); nevertheless, the former also gives expression to a truth of profound significance. "Faithfulness" is with the prophet an external thing; it signifies integrity, fidelity, stedfastness under all provocations; but this implies, in a real sense, the NT conception of faith as an active principle of right conduct. A living faith determines conduct; religion and ethics go hand in hand, and esp. in the hour of adversity a belief in Jeh and unflinching reliance upon Him are the strongest preservers of fidelity and integrity. Faith without works is dead; faith expresses itself in life. Habakkuk places chief emphasis upon the expressions of faith, and he does so rightly; but in doing this he also calls attention, by implication at least, to the motive power behind the external manifestations. As an expression of living faith, **3** 17–19 is not surpassed in the OT.

LITERATURE.—Commentaries on the Minor Prophets by Ewald, Pusey, Keil, Orelli, G. A. Smith (*Expositor's Bible*), Driver (*New Century Bible*), Eiselen; A. B. Davidson, *Comm. on* "Nah," "Hab," "Zeph" (*Cambridge Bible*); A. F. Kirkpatrick, *Doctrine of the Prophets;* F. C. Eiselen, *Prophecy and the Prophets;* F. W. Farrar, *Minor Prophets* ("Men of the Bible"); Driver, *LOT; HDB*, art. "Habakkuk"; *EB*, art. "Habakkuk."

FREDERICK CARL EISELEN

HABAKKUK, THE PRAYER OF. See BETH-HORON, BATTLE OF.

HABAZINIAH (חֲבַצִּנְיָה, *ḥăbhaççinyāh*. Thus in AV, but more correctly as in RV HABAZZINIAH, hab-a-zi-nī'a [Jer **35** 3]): The grandfather of Jaazaniah, who was the leader of the Rechabites who were tested by Jeremiah as to their obedience to their ancestor's command with reference to wine. Their loyalty to the commands of Jonadab was effectively used by Jeremiah in an appeal to the people of Judah to obey the words of Jeh.

HABERGEON, hab'ẽr-jun, ha-bûr'jun, AV (תַּחֲרָא, *taḥărā'*): In RV, Ex **28** 32; **39** 23, etc, "coat of mail"; in Job **41** 26, "pointed shaft," m "coat of mail." See ARMS, ARMOR.

HABITATION, hab-i-tā'shun: Properly a place of sojourn or dwelling. The term in AV representing some 16 Heb words (*mōshābh, mā'ōn, mishkān, nāweh*, etc), and 5 Gr words, is variously changed in certain passages in RV, as Gen **49** 5, "swords"; Lev **13** 46, "dwelling"; Job **5** 24; Jer **25** 30*b*. 37, "fold"; Ps **89** 14; **97** 2, etc, "foundation"; Ps **132** 5, "tabernacle"; Lk **16** 9, "tabernacles," etc. Conversely, "habitation" appears in RV for AV "dwelling place" in 2 Ch **30** 27; Ps **79** 7, "house"; Ps **83** 12; 2 Cor **5** 2, "tabernacle," Acts **7** 46, etc. See HOUSE. JAMES ORR

HABOR, hā'bor (חָבוֹר, *ḥābhōr;* **'Αβώρ,** *Habṓr*, **'Αβιώρ,** *Habiṓr;* Isidor of Charax, *Aburas* ['**Αβουράς**], Zosias, *Aboras*):

1. Its Position and Course

Is described in 2 K **17** 6; **18** 11 (cf 1 Ch **5** 26) as "the river of Gozan." It is the Arab. *Khabur*, and flows in a southerly direction from several sources in the mountains of *Karaj Dāgh* (*Mons Masius*), which, in the 37th parallel, flanks the valley of the Tigris on the W. The river ultimately joins the Euphrates after receiving its chief tributary, the *Jaghjagha Su* (*Mygdonius*), at Circesium (*Kirkisiyeh*).

2. Etymologies of Habor

The meaning of its name is doubtful, but Delitzsch has suggested a Sumerian etymology, namely, *ḥabur*, "the fish-waterway," or it may be connected with "mother Ḫubur," a descriptive title of Tiāmat (see MERODACH; RAHAB).

3. Historical References

Layard found several interesting Assyrian remains in the district, including man-headed bulls bearing the name of Mušeš-Ninip, possibly an Assyr governor. Tiglath-pileser I (c 1120 BC) boasts of having killed 10 mighty elephants in Haran and on the banks of the Habor; and Aššur-naṣir-apli (c 880 BC), after conquering Ḫaršit (Ḫarrit, Ḫarmiš), subjugated the tract around *piate ša nâr Ḫabur*, "the mouths of the Habor." According to 2 K and 1 Ch, Shalmaneser IV and Sargon transported the exiled Israelites thither. Philological considerations exclude the identification of the Chebar of Ezk **1** 3, etc, with the Habor.

T. G. PINCHES

HACALIAH, hak-a-lī'a (חֲכַלְיָה, *ḥăkhalyāh*, meaning doubtful, perhaps "wait for Jeh"; AV **Hachaliah**): Father of Nehemiah (Neh **1** 1; **10** 1).

HACHILAH, ha-kī'la, hak'i-la, **HILL OF** (חֲכִילָה, *ḥăkhīlāh*): A hill in the wilderness of Judah, associated with the wanderings of David. It is stated (1 S **23** 19) to be "on the S. of the desert" (or Jeshimon), and (1 S **26** 1) to be "before [on the front (i.e. edge) of] the desert." It was near Ziph and Maon. The only plausible hypothesis is that it is represented by the ridge *Dhahreṭ el-Kōlāh* in the wilderness of Ziph, toward the desert of En-gedi (*PEF*, III, 313, Sh XXI).

HACHMONI, hak-mō'nī, hak'mō-nī, or probably **HACHMONITE** (חַכְמוֹנִי, *ḥakhmōnī*, "wise"): The same word is rendered "Hachmoni," a proper name, in 1 Ch **27** 32 and "a Hachmonite" in 1 Ch **11** 11. The form of the Heb word suggests that the latter tr should be adopted in both passages, and that it describes the warrior in one case, and the companion or tutor of David's sons in the other, as a member of a certain family—a Hachmonite of which nothing further is known. 2 S **23** 8, "Josheb-basshebeth a Tahchemonite," bears the marks of a corrupt text, and should be ‖ with 1 Ch **11** 11 so far as the name goes, reading "Jashobeam the Hachmonite." So Klostermann, Driver, Wellhausen, Budde, etc. GEORGE RICE HOVEY

HADAD, hā'dad:

(1) (חֲדַד, *ḥădhadh*, "sharpness"): One of the twelve sons of Ishmael (Gen **25** 15, where AV, following a mistake in Heb text, has "Hadar"; but "Hadad" is found in ‖ passage 1 Ch **1** 30; RV reads "Hadad" in both places).

(2) (הֲדַד, *hădhadh*): A king of Edom, son of Bedad (Gen **36** 35.36 ‖ 1 Ch **1** 46.47), "who smote Midian in the field of Moab," and whose "city was Avith."

(3) Another king of Edom, written "Hadar" in Gen **36** 39 by a copyist's mistake, but "Hadad" in the ‖ passage 1 Ch **1** 50.51. His city was Pau or Pai.

(4) A member of the royal family of Edom in David's time, who as a child escaped Joab's slaughter of the Edomites, and fled to Egypt. On David's death he returned to Edom, where he made trouble for Solomon by stirring up the Edomites against the rule of Israel (1 K **11** 14–22.25).

(5) The supreme god of Syria, whose name is found in Scripture in the names of Syrian kings, Benhadad, Hadadezer. The god Hadad (=perhaps, "maker of loud noise") is mentioned in Assyr inscriptions, and called on the monolith of Shalmaneser "the god of Aleppo." In the Assyr inscriptions he is identified with the air-god Rammon or Rimmon. The union of the two names in Zec **12** 11 suggests this identity, though the reference is uncertain, some regarding Hadadrimmon as the name of a place, others as the name of the god—"Hadad [is] Rimmon." The name "Hadad" is found in various other forms: Adad, Dadu, and Dadda. See A. H. Sayce in *HDB* s.v. "Hadad."

George Rice Hovey

HADADEZER, had-ad-ē'zẽr (הֲדַדְעֶזֶר, *hădhadh'ezer;* so 2 S **8**; 1 K **11** 23, but הֲדַרְעֶזֶר, *hădhar'ezer*, 2 S **10**; 1 Ch **18**): Mentioned in connection with David's wars of conquest (2 S **8** 3 ff; 2 S **10** 1–19; 1 Ch **18** 3 ff); was king of Zobah in Syria. The exact position and size of this Syrian principality are uncertain, but it seems to have extended in David's time southward toward Ammon and eastward to the Euphrates. When the Ammonites had put themselves in the wrong with David by the insult done to his ambassadors (2 S **10** 1–5) they summoned to their aid against the incensed king of Israel the Syrians of various adjoining principalities, among them the Syrians of Zobah under Hadadezer, the son of Rehob. The strategy of Joab, who set the force under command of Abishai his brother in array against the Ammonites, and himself attacked the Syrian allies, won for Israel a decisive victory. Not content with this result, Hadadezer gathered together another Syrian force, summoning this time also "the Syrians that were beyond the River" (2 S **10** 16), with Shobach the captain of his host at their head. On this occasion David himself took command of the Israelitish forces, and again defeated them near Helam, Shobach being left dead on the field. Hadadezer and his Syrian vassals, finding resistance hopeless, "made peace with Israel, and served them" (2 S **10** 19). For the name Hadad- or Hadarezer, see Benhadad.

Literature.—Winckler, *Geschichte Israels,* I, 137 ff; McCurdy, *HPM*, 204; Maspèro, *The Struggle of the Nations,* 731.

T. Nicol

HADADRIMMON, hā-dad-rim'on, had-ad-rim'on (הֲדַד רִמּוֹן, *hădhadh rimmōn*): A name which occurs, along with Megiddon, in Zec **12** 11. It was long thought that this was a place in the plain of Megiddo, and that the mourning referred to was that for Josiah, slain in battle with Pharaoh-necoh (2 K **23** 29). This last, however, was certainly at Jerus. Jerome (*Comm. on Zec*) identifies Hadadrimmon with Maximianopolis, a village near Jezreel, probably Legio, the ancient Megiddo. Possibly, however, the form "Hadadrimmon" has arisen through the combination of two divine names; and the weeping may be that for Tammuz (Ezk **8** 14), with whom the old Sem deity had become confused in the popular mind.

W. Ewing

HADAR, hā'dar (Gen **36** 39). See Hadad (3).

HADAREZER, had-ar-ē'zẽr. See Hadadezer.

HADASHAH, ha-dā'sha, had'a-sha (חֲדָשָׁה, *ḥădhāshāh*, "new"): A town in the Shephelah of Judah, named with Zenan and Migdal-gad (Josh **15** 37). According to the Mish (*'Ērūbhīn,* v. 6), it was the smallest town in Judah. It is not identified.

HADASSAH, ha-das'a (הֲדַסָּה, *hădhaṣṣāh*, "myrtle"): The Heb name (Est **2** 7) formerly borne by Esther (q.v.).

HADATTAH, ha-dat'a (חֲדַתָּה, *ḥădhattāh*, "new"): See Hazor.

HADES, hā'dēz (Ἅιδης, *Haídēs*, ᾅδης, *haídēs*, "not to be seen"): Hades, Gr originally *Haídou*, in genitive, "the house of Hades," then, as nominative, designation of the abode of the dead itself. The word occurs in the NT in Mt **11** 23 (‖ Lk **10** 15); **16** 18; Lk **16** 23; Acts **2** 27.31; Rev **1** 18; **6** 8; **20** 13 f. It is also found in *TR* 1 Cor **15** 55, but here the correct reading (Tischendorf, WH, RV) is probably *Thánate*, "O Death," instead of *Háidē*, "O Hades." AV renders "Hades" by "hell" in all instances except 1 Cor **15** 55, where it puts "grave" (m "hell") in dependence on Hos **13** 14. RV everywhere has "Hades."

1. In OT: Sheol

In the LXX Hades is the standing equivalent for Sheol, but also translates other terms associated with death and the state after it. The Gr conception of Hades was that of a locality receiving into itself all the dead, but divided into two regions, one a place of torment, the other of blessedness. This conception should not be rashly transferred to the NT, for the latter stands not under the influence of Gr pagan belief, but gives a teaching and reflects a belief which model their idea of Hades upon the OT through the LXX. The OT Sheol, while formally resembling the Gr Hades in that it is the common receptacle of all the dead, differs from it, on the one hand, by the absence of a clearly defined division into two parts, and, on the other hand, by the emphasis placed on its association with death and the grave as abnormal facts following in the wake of sin. The OT thus concentrates the partial light it throws on the state after death on the negative, undesirable side of the prospect apart from redemption. When in the progress of OT revelation the state after death begins to assume more definite features, and becomes more sharply differentiated in dependence on the religious and moral issue of the present life, this is not accomplished in the canonical writings (otherwise in the apocalyptic literature) by dividing Sheol into two compartments, but by holding forth to the righteous the promise of deliverance from Sheol, so that the latter becomes more definitely outlined as a place of evil and punishment.

2. In NT: Hades

The NT passages mark a distinct stage in this process, and there is, accordingly, a true basis in Scripture for the identification in a certain aspect of Sheol—Hades—with hell as reflected in AV. The theory according to which Hades is still in the NT the undifferentiated provisional abode of all the dead until the day of judgment, with the possibility of ultimate salvation even for those of its inmates who have not been saved in this life, is neither in harmony with the above development nor borne out by the facts of NT usage. That dead believers abide in a local Hades cannot be proven from 1 Thess **4** 16; 1 Cor **15** 23, for these passages refer to the grave and the body, not to a gathering-place of the dead. On the other hand Lk **23** 43; 2 Cor **5** 6–8; Phil **1** 23; Rev **6** 9; **7** 9 ff; **15** 2 ff teach that the abode of believers immediately after death is with Christ and God.

3. Acts 2:27.31

It is, of course, a different matter, when Hades, as not unfrequently already the OT Sheol, designates not the *place* of the dead but the *state* of death or disembodied existence. In this sense even the soul of Jesus was in Hades according to Peter's statement (Acts **2** 27.31—on the basis of Ps **16** 10). Here the abstract sense is determined by the parallel expression, "to see corruption." None the less from a comparatively early date this passage has been quoted in support of the doctrine of a local descent of Christ into Hades.

4. Rev 20:13; 6:8; 1:18

The same abstract meaning is indicated for Rev **20** 13. Death and Hades are here represented as delivering up the dead on the eve of the final judgment. If this is more than a poetic duplication of terms, Hades will stand for the personified state of death, Death for the personified cause of this state. The personification appears plainly from ver 14: "Death and Hades were cast into the lake of fire." In the number of these "dead" delivered up by Hades, believers are included, because, even on the chiliastic interpretation of vs 4–6, not all the saints share in the first resurrection, but only those "beheaded for the testimony of Jesus, and for the word of God," i.e. the martyrs. A similar personifying combination of Death and Hades occurs in Rev **6** 8 ("a pale horse: and he that sat upon him, his name was Death; and Hades followed with him"). In Rev **1** 18, on the other hand, Death and Hades are represented as prisons from which Christ, in virtue of His own resurrection, has the power to deliver, a representation which again implies that in some, not necessarily local, sense believers also are kept in Hades.

5. Lk 16:23

In distinction from these passages when the abstract meaning prevails and the local conception is in abeyance, the remaining references are more or less locally conceived. Of these Lk **16** 23 is the only one which might seem to teach that recipients of salvation enter after death into Hades as a place of abode. It has been held that Hades is here the comprehensive designation of the locality where the dead reside, and is divided into two regions, "the bosom of Abraham" and the place of torment, a representation for which Jewish parallels can be quoted, aside from its resemblance to the Gr bisection of Hades. Against this view, however, it may be urged, that if "the bosom of Abraham" were conceived as one of the two divisions of Hades, the other division would have been named with equal concreteness in connection with Dives. In point of fact, the distinction is not between "the bosom of Abraham" and another place, as both included in Hades, but between "the bosom of Abraham" and Hades as antithetical and exclusive. The very form of the description of the experience of Dives: "In Hades he lifted up his eyes, being in torments," leads us to associate Hades as such with pain and punishment. The passage, therefore, does not prove that the saved are after death in Hades. In further estimating its bearing upon the problem of the local conditions of the disembodied life after death, the parabolic character of the representation must be taken into account. The parable is certainly not intended to give us topographical information about the realm of the dead, although it presupposes that there is a distinct place of abode for the righteous and wicked respectively.

6. Mt 11:23

The two other passages where Hades occurs in the teaching of Our Lord (Mt **11** 23 ‖ Lk **10** 15; and Mt **16** 18) make a metaphorical use of the conception, which, however, is based on the local sense. In the former utterance it is predicted of Capernaum that it shall in punishment for its unbelief "go down unto Hades." As in the OT Sheol is a **figure** for the greatest depths known (Dt **32** 22; Isa **7** 11; **57** 9; Job **11** 8; **26** 6), this seems to be a **figure** for the extreme of humiliation to which that city was to be reduced in the course of history. It is true, ver 24, with its mention of the day of judgment, might seem to favor an eschatological reference to the ultimate doom of the unbelieving inhabitants, but the usual restriction of Hades to the punishment of the intermediate state (see below) is against this.

7. Mt 16:18

In the other passage, Mt **16** 18, Jesus declares that the gates of Hades shall not *katischúein* the church He intends to build. The vb. *katischuein* may be rendered, "to overpower" or "to surpass." If the former be adopted, the **figure** implied is that of Hades as a stronghold of the power of evil or death from which warriors stream forth to assail the church as the realm of life. On the other rendering there is no reference to any conflict between Hades and the church, the point of comparison being merely the strength of the church, the gates of Hades, i.e. the realm of death, serving in common parlance as a **figure** of the greatest conceivable strength, because they never allow to escape what has once entered through them.

The above survey of the passages tends to show that Hades, where it is locally conceived, is not a provisional receptacle for all the dead, but plainly associated with the punishment of the wicked. Where it comes under consideration for the righteous there is nothing to indicate a local sense. On 1 Pet **3** 19; **4** 6 (where, however, the word "Hades" does not occur), see arts. ESCHATOLOGY OF THE NT; SPIRITS IN PRISON.

8. Not a Final State

The element of truth in the theory of the provisional character of Hades lies in this, that the NT never employs it in connection with the final state of punishment, as subsequent to the last judgment. For this GEHENNA (q.v.) and other terms are used. Dives is represented as being in Hades immediately after his death and while his brethren are still in this present life. Whether the implied differentiation between stages of punishment, depending obviously on the difference between the disembodied and reëmbodied state of the lost, also carries with itself a distinction between two places of punishment, in other words whether Hades and Gehenna are locally distinct, the evidence is scarcely sufficient to determine. The NT places the emphasis on the eschatological developments at the end, and leaves many things connected with the intermediate state in darkness.

GEERHARDUS VOS

HADID, hā'did (חָדִיד, *ḥādhīdh*): A city in Benjamin (Neh **11** 33 f) named with Lod and Ono (Ezr **2** 33; Neh **7** 37), probably identical with Adida (LXX 'Αδιδά, *Hadidá*) of 1 Macc **12** 38; **13** 13, "over against the plain," which was fortified by Simon Maccabaeus. It is represented by the modern *el-Ḥadītheh*, about 3 miles N.E. of Lydda.

HADLAI, had'lī, had'lā-ī (חַדְלָי, *ḥadhlāy*, "resting"): An Ephraimite (2 Ch **28** 12), father of Amasa, who was one of the heads of the tribe in the time of Pekah, king of Israel.

HADORAM, ha-dō'ram (הֲדוֹרָם, *hădhōrām*): (1) Son of Joktan and apparently 6th in descent from Noah (Gen **10** 27 ‖ 1 Ch **1** 21).

(2) Son of Tou, king of Hamath, sent by his father with presents to King David (1 Ch **18** 10). In 2 S **8** 9.10, written probably incorrectly "Joram," "son of Toi."

(3) Rehoboam's superintendent of the forced labor department (2 Ch **10** 18), called Adoram 1 K **12** 18, a contraction of Adoniram (which see). He was sent by Rehoboam as messenger to Israel at the time of the revolt of the ten tribes and was stoned to death by them. George Rice Hovey

HADRACH, hā'drak, had'rak (חַדְרָךְ, *ḥadhrākh*): "The land of Hadrach" is mentioned only once in Scripture (Zec **9** 1), and there it is grouped with Damascus, Hamath, Tyre and Sidon. It may be safely identified with the "Hatarikka" of the Assyr inscriptions, against which Assur-dan III made expeditions in his 1st (772 BC), 8th and 18th years. It also appears in inscriptions of Tiglath-pileser III. They place it in the N. of Lebanon.

HAGAB, hā'gab (חָגָב, *ḥāghābh*, "locust"): Ancestor of some of the Nethinim who returned from the Bab captivity with Zerubbabel and Nehemiah. The name occurs second after Hagabah in Ezr **2** 46, but is omitted entirely from the ‖ list of Neh **7** 48.

HAGABA, ha-gā'ba, hag'a-bä (חֲגָבָא, *ḥăghābhā'*): Same as the following (Neh **7** 48).

HAGABAH, ha-gā'ba, hag'a-bä (חֲגָבָה, *ḥăghābhāh*, "locust"): Like Hagab, an ancestor of some of the Nethinim who returned from Babylon with Zerubbabel (Ezr **2** 45); spelled Hagaba in the ‖ passage (Neh **7** 48).

HAGAR, hā'gar (הָגָר, *hāghār*, "emigration," "flight"; Ἁγάρ, *Hagár*, Ἄγαρ, *Ágar*): An Egyp woman, the handmaid or slave of Sarai; a present, perhaps, from Pharaoh when Abram dissembled to him in Egypt (Gen **12** 16). Mention is made of her in two passages (Gen **16**; **21** 8–21).

In the first narrative (Gen **16**) it is related that Sarai, despairing at her age of having children, gave Hagar to Abram as a concubine.

1. The Scornful Handmaid and Her Flight

As Hagar was not an ordinary household slave but the peculiar property of her mistress (cf **29** 24.29), any offspring which she might bear to Abram would be reckoned as Sarai's (cf **30** 3–9). In the prospect of becoming a mother, Hagar, forgetting her position, seems to have assumed an insolent bearing toward her childless mistress. Sarai felt keenly the contempt shown her by her handmaid, and in angry tones brought her conduct before Abram. Now that her plan was not working out smoothly, she unfairly blamed her husband for what originated with herself, and appealed to Heaven to redress her grievance. Abram refused to interfere in the domestic quarrel, and renouncing his rights over his concubine, and her claims on him, put her entirely at Sarai's disposal. Under the harsh treatment of her mistress Hagar's life became intolerable, and she fled into the wilderness, turning her steps naturally toward Egypt, her native land.

But the angel of Jeh (who is here introduced for the first time as the medium of the theophany) appeared to her as she was resting by

2. Her Vision and Return

a spring and commanded her to return and submit herself to her mistress, promising her an innumerable seed through her unborn son, concerning whom he uttered a striking prediction (see Ishmael). To the angel (who is now said to be Jeh Himself) Hagar gave the name "Thou art a God of seeing" (RV "that seeth"), for she said, "Have I even here [in the desert where God, whose manifestations were supposed to be confined to particular places, might not be expected to reveal Himself] looked after him that seeth me?"—the meaning being that while God saw her, it was only while the all-seeing God in the person of His angel was departing that she became conscious of His presence. The spring where the angel met with her was called in Heb tradition *Bᵉ'ēr-laḥay-rō'ī*, "the well of the living one who seeth me" (RVm).

Obedient to the heavenly vision Hagar returned, as the narrative implies, to her mistress and gave birth to Ishmael, Abram being then eighty-six years old.

The idea in ver 13 is not very clearly expressed. The word tr^d^ "here" generally means "hither," and there is no explanation of the "living one" in the name of the well. It has therefore been proposed to emend the Heb text and read "Have I even seen God, and lived after my seeing?"—an allusion to the belief that no one could "see God and live" (cf Gen **32** 30; Ex **33** 20). But there are difficulties in the way of accepting this emendation. The name of God, "a God of seeing," would require to be interpreted in an objective sense as "a God who is seen," and the consequent name of the well, "He that seeth me liveth," would make God, not Hagar, as in ver 13, the speaker.

The other narrative (Gen **21** 8–21) relates what occurred in connection with the weaning of Isaac.

3. Her Harsh Expulsion and Divine Help

The presence and conduct of Ishmael during the family feast held on the occasion roused the anger and jealousy of Sarah who, fearing that Ishmael would share the inheritance with Isaac, peremptorily demanded the expulsion of the slave-mother and her son. But the instincts of Abraham's fatherly heart recoiled from such a cruel course, and it was only after the revelation was made to him that the ejection of Hagar and her son would be in the line of the Divine purpose—for Isaac was his real seed, while Ishmael would be made a nation too—that he was led to forego his natural feelings and accede to Sarah's demand. So next morning the bondwoman and her son were sent forth with the bare provision of bread and a skin of water into the wilderness of Beersheba. When the water was spent, Hagar, unable to bear the sight of her boy dying from thirst, laid him under a shrub and withdrew the distance of a bowshot to weep out her sorrow. But the angel of God, calling to her out of heaven, comforted her with the assurance that God had heard the voice of the lad and that there was a great future before him. Then her eyes were opened to discover a well of water from which she filled the skin and gave her son to drink. With God's blessing the lad grew up amid the desert's hardships, distinguished for his skill with the bow. He made his home in the wilderness of Paran, and his mother took a wife for him out of her own country.

The life and experience of Hagar teach, among other truths, the temptations incident to a new position;

4. Practical Lessons from the History

the foolishness of hasty action in times of trial and difficulty; the care exercised over the lonely by the all-seeing God; the Divine purpose in the life of everyone, however obscure and friendless; how God works out His gracious purposes by seemingly harsh methods; and the strength, comfort and encouragement that ever accompany the hardest experiences of His children.

Ch **16** belongs to J (except vs 1*a*.3.15 f which are from P), and **21** 8–21 to E. From the nature of the variations in the narratives many critics hold that we have here two different accounts of the same incident. But the narratives as they stand seem to be quite distinct, the one referring to Hagar's flight before the birth of Ishmael, and the other to her expulsion at the weaning of Isaac. It is said, however, that E represents Ishmael as a child "playing" (RVm, LXX παίζοντα, *paízonta*) with Isaac at the weaning festival, and young enough to be carried by his mother and "cast" under a shrub; while according to P (**16** 16; **21** 5), as a child was weaned at the age of two or three years, he would be a lad of sixteen at that time. The argument for the double narrative here does not seem conclusive. The word *meçaḥēḳ* (ver 9) does not necessarily mean "playing" when used absolutely; it is so used in ch **19** 14, evidently in the sense of "mocking" or "jesting," and Delitzsch gives it that meaning there. Then as to ver 14, the MT does not state that the child was put on her shoulder, although the LXX does; nor does "cast" (ver 15) so "clearly imply" that Ishmael was an infant carried by his mother (cf Mt **15** 30). It may be added that the words *yeledh* and *na'ar*, trd "child" and "lad" respectively, determine nothing as to age, as they are each used elsewhere in both senses.

5. Critical Points in the Documents

In Gal **4** 21 ff St. Paul makes an allegorical use of this episode in the history of Ishmael and Isaac to support his argument for the transitory character of the Jewish ritual and the final triumph of Christian freedom over all Judaizing tendencies. In elaborating his reference, the apostle institutes a series of contrasts. Hagar, the bondwoman, represents the old covenant which was given from Mt. Sinai; and as Ishmael was Abraham's son after the flesh, so the Judaizing Christians, who wish to remain in bondage to the law, are Hagar's children. On the other hand, Sarah, the freewoman, represents the new covenant instituted by Christ; and as Isaac was born to Abraham in virtue of the promise, so the Christians who have freed themselves entirely from the law of carnal ordinances and live by faith are Sarah's children. Thus Hagar corresponds to "the Jerus that now is," that is, the Jewish state which is in spiritual bondage with her children; while Sarah represents "the Jerus that is above," "our mother" (RV), the mother of us Christians, that free spiritual city to which Christians even now belong (Phil **3** 20). By this allegory the apostle would warn the Galatian Christians of the danger which beset them from their Judaizing brethren, of their subjection to the covenant of works and their ultimate expulsion from the household of faith.

6. Allegorical Use of the Story by St. Paul

To us St. Paul's reference does not appeal with the same force as it would do to those to whom he was writing. The incident taken by itself, indeed, does not contain any suggestion of such a hidden meaning. Yet the history of the Heb nation is but typical of the history of the church in all ages, and the apostle's familiarity with rabbinical modes of interpretation may have led him to adopt this method of confirming the truth which he had already proved from the law itself.

For a discussion of the text and interpretation of Gal **4** 25*a*, "Now this Hagar is mount Sinai in Arabia," and an account of Philo's allegory of Hagar and Sarah, see Lightfoot's notes at the end of ch iv in his *Comm. on Gal.* JAMES CRICHTON

HAGARENES, hā'gar-ēnz, **HAGARITES,** hă'-gar-īts. See HAGRITES.

HAGERITE, hā'gēr-īt (הַגְרִי, *haghrī*). See HAGRITES.

HAGGADA, ha-gä'dä. See TALMUD.

HAGGAI, hag'a-ī, hag'ă-i (חַגַּי, *ḥaggay*, an adj. formed from חַג, *ḥagh*, "feast"): The word "Haggai" may mean "festal," the prophet having been born perhaps on a festival day; cf the Rom name "Festus." Heb proper names were sometimes formed in this manner, e.g. Barzillai, "a man of iron," from *barzel*, "iron." Haggai may, however, be a shortened form of Haggiah (1 Ch **6** 30), meaning "festival of Jeh," as Mattenai is an abbreviation of Mattaniah (Ezr **10** 33.26). In Gr Ἀγγαῖος, *Haggaíos*, in Lat, *Aggaeus* or *Aggeus*, sometimes *Haggaeus*. Haggai is the 10th in the order of the Twelve Prophets.

1. Name

Little is really known of his personal history. But we do know that he lived soon after the captivity, being the first of the prophets of the Restoration. From **2** 3 of his prophecies it is inferred by many that he had seen the first temple, which, as we know, was destroyed in 586 BC. If so, he must have prophesied when a comparatively old man, for we know the exact date of his prophecies, 520 BC. According to Ezr **5** 1; **6** 14, he was a contemporary of Zechariah, and was associated with him in the work of rebuilding the temple; besides, in the Gr and Lat and Syr VSS, his name stands with Zechariah's at the head of certain pss, e.g. Ps **111** (**112**), in the Vulg alone; Pss **125, 126,** in the Pesh alone; Ps **137,** in the LXX alone; Pss **146, 147, 148,** in LXX and Pesh; and Ps **145,** in LXX, Pesh and Vulg; perhaps these pss were introduced into the temple-service on their recommendation. He was a prophet of great faith (cf **2** 1–5); it is possible that he was a priest also (cf **2** 10–19). Like Malachi he bears the name of "Jeh's messenger" (**1** 13; cf Mal **3** 1). According to Jewish tradition, he was a member of the Great Synagogue.

2. Personal History

Haggai's work was intensely practical and important. Jeh employed him to awaken the conscience and stimulate the enthusiasm of his compatriots in the rebuilding of the temple. "No prophet ever appeared at a more critical juncture in the history of the people, and, it may be added, no prophet was more successful" (Marcus Dods). Zechariah assisted him (cf Hag **1** 1; Zec **1** 1).

3. Work

Haggai's prophecies, like Ezekiel's, are dated "in the second year of Darius" (**1** 1; **2** 10), i.e. 520 BC. The Jews, 42,360 strong (Ezr **2** 64), had returned from Babylon 16 years before (536 BC), under the leadership of Zerubbabel, the civil head of the community, and Joshua, the ecclesiastical. The generous edict of Cyrus had made return possible (cf Ezr **1** 1–4). The new colonists had settled in Jerus and in the neighboring towns of Bethlehem, Bethel, Anathoth, Gibeon, Kiriath-jearim, and others adjacent (Ezr **2** 20 ff). Eager to reëstablish the public worship of the sanctuary, they set about at once to erect the altar of burnt offering upon its old site (Ezr **3** 2.3; cf Hag **2** 14). Plans were also made for the immediate rebuilding of the temple, and the foundation stone was actually laid in the 2d month of the 2d year of the return (Ezr **3** 8–10), but the work was suddenly interrupted by the jealous, half-caste, semi-pagan Samaritans, descendants of the foreign colonists introduced into Samaria in 722 BC (cf 2 K **17** 24–41), whose offer to coöperate had been refused (Ezr **4** 1–5.24). For 16 years thereafter nothing was done toward rearing the superstructure (Ezr **4** 5.24; **5** 16); indeed, the Jews became indifferent, and began to build for themselves "ceiled houses" (Hag **1** 4). (W. H. Kosters has attempted to show that there was no return under Cyrus, and that Haggai and Zechariah, who never allude to any return, but rather look upon the return as still in the future [cf Zec **2** 6.7], preached to the Jews who remained in Jerus, never having been carried by Neb-

4. Period and Circumstances

uchadnezzar into captivity in 586 BC. But this theory is opposed by too many converging lines of Scriptural statement to warrant serious credence.) With the accession of Darius Hystaspes (i.e. Darius, the son of Hystaspes), the tide turned. Darius was a true successor to Cyrus, and favored religious freedom. Through the influence of the prophets Haggai and Zechariah, the people were roused from their lethargy, and the work of rebuilding was resumed with energy in 520 BC (Hag **1** 14.15). The foundations were relaid (Hag **2** 18). Four years later, in the 6th year of Darius, the whole structure was completed and dedicated (Ezr **6** 15). Meanwhile important events were taking place in the Pers empire. On the death of Cambyses in 522 BC, the throne had been seized by a usurper, the so-called Pseudo-Smerdis, who held it, however, for some 7 months only. He was murdered by Darius, and the latter was elevated to the throne. But this gave other ambitious pretenders cause to rebel, and many provinces revolted, among them Susiana, Media, Assyria, Armenia, Parthia, and others (cf the famous Behistun inscription). Altogether Darius fought 19 battles in putting down his rivals, and did not succeed in vanquishing all of his foes till the year after Haggai prophesied. This accounts for the prophet's repeated allusions to Jeh's "shaking" the nations (**2** 6.7.21.22). Haggai seems to regard the "shaking" of the nations as the precursor of the Messianic age. It was, therefore, important from the prophet's point of view, that Jeh's temple should be made ready for the Messiah's advent, that it might become the religious center of the world (cf Isa **2** 2–4). The exact date of Haggai's preaching was from September to December, 520 BC.

5. Analysis

Haggai's prophecies are dated and therefore easily analyzed. They are composed of four distinct discourses, all four being delivered within 4 months' time in the year 520 BC: (1) Ch **1**, delivered on the 1st day of the 6th month (September), in which the prophet reproaches the people for their indifference to the work of rebuilding the temple, and warns them to consider their ways; assuring them that their procrastination was not due to want of means (**1** 4), and that God on account of their apathy was withholding the produce of the field (**1** 10). The effect of this appeal was that 24 days later, all the people, including Zerubbabel and Joshua, began the work of reconstruction (**1** 14.15). (2) **2** 1–9, delivered on the 21st day of the 7th month (October), which was about one month after the work had been resumed, and containing a note of encouragement to those who felt that the new structure was destined to be so much inferior to Solomon's temple. The prophet, on the contrary, assures them that the latter glory of the new house shall eclipse that of Solomon's magnificent temple, for soon a great "shaking" on Jeh's part among the nations will usher in the Messianic age, and the precious things of all nations will flow in to beautify it (cf He **12** 26–28). (3) **2** 10–19, delivered on the 24th day of the 9th month (December) which was exactly 3 months after the building had been resumed, and containing, like the first discourse, a rebuke to the people because of their indifference and inertia. The discourse is couched in the form of a parable (vs 11–14), by means of which the prophet explains why the prayers of the people go unanswered. It is because they have so long postponed the completion of the temple; a taint of guilt vitiates everything they do, and blasting and mildew and hail, and consequently unfruitful seasons, are the result. On the other hand, if they will but press forward with the work, Jeh will again bless them, and fruitful seasons will follow their revived zeal (**2** 19; cf Zec **8** 9–12). (4) **2** 20–23, delivered on the 24th day of the 9th month, the very same day as that on which the discourse in **2** 10–19 was delivered. The sequence is immediate. For when Jeh "shakes" the nations, He will establish Zerubbabel, the representative of the Davidic dynasty and the object of patriotic hopes. When the heathen powers are overthrown, Zerubbabel will stand unshaken as Jeh's honored and trusted vicegerent, and as the precious signet on Jeh's hand (cf Jer **22** 24; Cant **8** 6).

6. Message

The most striking feature in Haggai's message is its repeated claim of Divine origin: 5 t in the 38 verses of his prophecies, he tells us that "the word of Jeh came" unto him (**1** 1.3; **2** 1.10.20); 4 t, also, he used the formula, "Thus saith Jeh of hosts" (**1** 2. 5.7; **2** 11); 5 t "saith Jeh of hosts" (**1** 9; **2** 6.7. 9.23); and 4 t simply "saith Jeh" (**1** 13; **2** 4.14.17). Altogether he uses the exalted phrase "Jeh of hosts" 14 t, besides 19 repetitions of the single but ineffable name "Jeh." The most striking sentence in all his prophecies is probably that found in **1** 13, "Then spake Haggai, Jeh's messenger in Jeh's message unto the people." His single purpose, as we have above seen, was to encourage the building of the temple. This he seems to have regarded as essential to the purity of Israel's religion. His key-exhortation is, "Consider your ways" (**1** 5 7; cf **2** 15.18). His prophecies reflect the conditions of his age. He points to judgments as a proof of the Divine displeasure (**1** 9.10; **2** 15–19). Unlike the earlier prophets, he does not denounce idolatry; but like his contemporary, Zechariah, and his successor, Malachi, he does lay stress on the external side of religion. Chief interest centers in the somewhat unusual parable contained in **2** 10–19, which teaches that holiness is not contagious, but that evil is. "The faint aroma of sanctity coming from their altar and sacrifices was too feeble to pervade the secular atmosphere of their life" (A. B. Davidson, *Exile and Restoration*, 82). Haggai argues that Israel's sacrifices for 16 years had been unclean in God's sight, and had brought them no blessing, because they had left the temple in ruins; and, that while a healthy man cannot give his health to another by touching him, a sick man may easily spread contagion among all those about him. The thought is suggestive. Haggai may or may not have been a priest, "but in so short a prophecy this elaborate allusion to ritual is very significant." Another very striking thought in Haggai's book is his reference to Zerubbabel as Jeh's "servant" and "signet," whom Jeh has "chosen" (**2** 23). Wellhausen regards these words as an equivalent to making Zerubbabel the Messiah; but it is enough to think that the prophet is attempting only to restore him to the honorable position from which his grandfather, Jehoiachin, in Jer **22** 24, had been degraded. Thus would the prophet link Zerubbabel, the political hope of the post-exilic congregation, to the royal line of Judah. Isaiah speaks of Cyrus in similar terms without any Messianic implication (Isa **44** 28; **45** 1). On the other hand, the implicit Messianic import of **2** 7.8 is recognized on all sides.

7. Style

Haggai's style is suited to the contents of his prophecies. While he is less poetical than his predecessors, yet parallelism is not altogether wanting in his sentence (**2** 8). Compared with the greater books of prophecy, his brief message has been declared "plain and unadorned," "tame and prosaic", yet it must be acknowledged that he is not wanting in pathos when he reproves, or in force when he exhorts. Though he labors under a poverty of terms, and frequently repeats the same formulae, yet he was profoundly in earnest, and became the most successful in his purpose of all his class. He was esp. fond of interrogation. At best we have only a summary, probably, of what he actually preached.

The critical questions involved in Haggai's case are not serious: **2** 5*a*, for example, is wanting in the LXX; to **2** 14 the LXX adds from Am **5** 10; **2** 17 is very similar to, and seems dependent on, Am **4** 9; **1** 7*b* and 13, are rejected by some as later interpolations; while Klostermann and Marti hold that the book as a whole was not written by Haggai at all, but rather *about* his prophetic activity, a perfectly gratuitous assumption without any substantial proof in its favor.

8. Criticism

LITERATURE.—Driver, *New Century Bible,* "The Minor Prophets," II, 1906; *LOT,* 1909; G. A. Smith, *Expositor's Bible,* "The Twelve Prophets," II, 1898; E. B. Pusey, *The Minor Prophets,* II, 1878; M. Dods, "Handbooks for Bible Classes," *Hag, Zec, Mal;* J. Wellhausen, *Die kleinen Propheten übersetzt u. erklärt,* 1898; W. Nowack, *Die kleinen Propheten übersetzt u. erklärt,* 1905; K. Marti, *Dodekapropheton erklärt,* 1904; H. G. Mitchell, *ICC,* 1912.

GEORGE L. ROBINSON

HAGGERI, hag'ē-rī. See HAGRI.

HAGGI, hag'ī (חַגִּי, *ḥaggī,* "festive"): The second son of Gad (Gen **46** 16; Nu **26** 15). The latter refers to his descendants as Haggites, of whom nothing else is known.

HAGGIAH, ha-gī'a (חַגִּיָּה, *ḥaggīyāh,* "feast of Jeh"): Named in 1 Ch **6** 30 as among the descendants of Levi.

HAGGITES, hag'īts. See HAGGI.

HAGGITH, hag'ith (חַגִּית, *ḥaggīth,* "festal"): According to 2 S **3** 4; 1 K **1** 5.11; **2** 13; 1 Ch **3** 2, the fifth wife of David and the mother of his fourth son, Adonijah. The latter was born in Hebron while David's capital was there (2 S **3** 4.5).

HAGIA, hā'gi-a. See AGIA.

HAGIOGRAPHA, hag-i-og'ra-fa. See BIBLE; CANON OF OT.

HAGRI, hag'rī (הַגְרִי, *haghrī,* "wanderer"; AV **Haggeri**): The father of Mibhar, one of the "mighty men" who rallied round David during his foreign wars. Mentioned only in 1 Ch **11** 38, whose ‖ passage, 2 S **23** 36, gives, instead, the name "Bani the Gadite."

HAGRITES, hag'rīts (הַגְרִיאִים, *haghrī'īm*): An Arab tribe, or confederation of tribes (1 Ch **5** 10.19.20 AV "Hagarites"; **27** 31 AV "Hagerite"; Ps **83** 6 "Hagarenes"), against which the Reubenites fought in the days of Saul. In Gen **25** 12–18 are recorded the descendants, "generations," of Ishmael, "whom Hagar the Egyp, Sarah's handmaid, bare unto Abraham." Two, and possibly three, of these tribes, Jetur, Naphish and Kedemah (ver 15), appear to be identical with the 3 tribes whom the Reubenites and the other Israelitish tribes E. of the Jordan conquered and dispossessed (1 Ch **5**). The correspondence of names in Gen and 1 Ch leaves little doubt that "Hagrite" is a generic term roughly synonymous with "Ishmaelite," designating the irregular and shifting line of desert tribes stretching along the E. and S. of Pal. Those "E. of Gilead," "Jetur, Naphish and Nodah," were overcome by Reuben: "The Hagrites were delivered into their hand, and all that were with them. . . . . And they took away their cattle . . . . they dwelt in their stead until the captivity" (1 Ch **5** 20–22).

These along with other Arab tribes are mentioned in the inscriptions of Tiglath-pileser III (745–727 BC). Jetur gave his name to the Ituraeans of Rom times, who were famed soldiers dwelling in Anti-Libanus. Cf Curtis, *Comm. on Ch;* Skinner, "Gen," *ICC,* in loc.

EDWARD MACK

HA-HIROTH, ha-hī'roth. See PI-HAHIROTH.

HAI, hā'ī (הָעַי, *hā-'ay,* "the heap"): Gen **12** 8; **13** 3 AV; RV AI (which see).

HAIL, hāl (בָּרָד, *bārādh;* χάλαζα, *chálaza*): Hail usually falls in the spring or summer during severe thunder storms. Hailstones are made up of alternate layers of ice and snow, and sometimes reach considerable size, causing great damage by their fall. Upward currents of air carry up raindrops already formed to the colder regions above, where they freeze, and as they again pass through layers of cloud, their bulk increases until, too heavy to be carried by the current, they fall to the ground. Hailstorms, like thunder storms, occur in narrow belts a few miles in breadth and are of short duration. Almost without exception they occur in the daytime. If they take place before the time of harvest they do great damage to grain and fruit, and in extreme cases have injured property and endangered life.

1. Its Occurrence

Hailstorms, while by no means common in Syria and Pal, are not unusual and are of great severity. They occasionally take place in Egypt. Within a few years hailstones of unusual size fell in Port Said, breaking thousands of windows.

2. In Syria

(1) The plague of hail (Ex **9** 23–24; Ps **78** 47), which was a local storm, as they usually are, falling on the Egyptians and not striking the children of Israel in Goshen. It was of great severity. "There was hail, and fire mingled with the hail, very grievous, such as had not been in all the land of Egypt since it became a nation" (Ex **9** 24). It took place in January, for the barley "was in the ear, and the flax was in bloom" (ver 31), and caused great damage. (2) After the battle with the Amorites at Gibeon, "Jeh cast down great stones from heaven upon them unto Azekah, and they died: they were more who died with the hailstones than they whom the children of Israel slew with the sword" (Josh **10** 11).

3. Biblical Instances

Hail is often spoken of as a means of punishing the wicked: "As a tempest of hail . . . . will he cast down" (Isa **28** 2); "The hail shall sweep away the refuge of lies" (ver 17); and as symbols of God's anger: "I will rain . . . . great hailstones, fire, and brimstone" (Ezk **38** 22); "There shall be . . . . great hailstones in wrath to consume it" (Ezk **13** 13; cf Isa **30** 30; Hag **2** 17; Rev **8** 7; **11** 19; **16** 21).

4. As Punishment

Jeh's power and wisdom are shown in controlling the hail: "Hast thou seen the treasuries of the hail?" (Job **38** 22); "Fire and hail, snow and vapor . . . . fulfilling his word" (Ps **148** 8).

5. God's Power

ALFRED H. JOY

HAIL, hāl: Interjection, found only in the Gospels as the tr of χαῖρε, *chaíre,* χαίρετε, *chaírete,* imp. of χαίρω, *chaírō,* "to rejoice," is used as a greeting or salutation. The word "Hail" is OE and was formerly an adj., used with the vb. to be, meaning "well," "sound," "hale," e.g. "Hale be thou." Wiclif has "heil" without the vb., followed by other Eng. VSS, except that the Geneva has "God save thee," in Mt **26** 49; **28** 9. The word occurs in Mt **26** 49; **27** 29; **28** 9, "all hail!"; Mk **15** 18; Lk **1** 28; Jn **19** 3. See GODSPEED; GREETING.

HAIR, hâr (שֵׂעָר, *sē'ār*, שַׂעַר, *sa'ar*, Aram. שְׂעַר, *s*e*'ar*, and their derivatives; θρίξ, *thríx*, gen. case τριχός, *trichós*, κόμη, *kómē*):

1. Hair Fashions

Hair was worn in different fashions by the Orientals of Bib. times, and not always in the same way among the same people in different epochs. We know this clearly from Egyp lit. and monuments, as well as from the writings of Gr authors (esp. Herodotus), that the dwellers on the Nile had their heads shaved in early youth, leaving but a side lock until maturity was attained, when this mark of childhood was taken away. Priests and warriors kept their heads closely shaved; nothing but the exigencies of arduous warfare were allowed to interfere with this custom. On the other hand, the Heb people, like their Bab neighbors (Herod. i.195), affected long and well-cared-for, bushy curls of hair as emblems of manly beauty. Proofs thereof are not infrequent in the Scriptures and elsewhere. Samson's (Jgs **16** 13.19) and Absalom's (2 S **14** 26) long luxuriant hair is specially mentioned, and the Shulammite sings of the locks of her beloved which are "bushy [RVm "curling"], and black as a raven" (Cant **5** 11). Jos (*Ant*, VIII, vii, 3 [185]) reports that Solomon's body-guard was distinguished by youthful beauty and "luxuriant heads of hair." In the history of Samson we read of "the seven locks of his head" (Jgs **16** 19). It is likely that the expression signifies the plaits of hair which are even now often worn by the young Bedâwin warrior of the desert.

Assyrian Manner of Wearing Hair.
(From sculpture in Brit. Mus.)

2. Hair in Idol-Worship

It is well known that among the surrounding heathen nations the hair of childhood or youth was often shaved and consecrated at idolatrous shrines (cf Herod. ii.65 for Egypt). Frequently this custom marked an initiatory rite into the service of a divinity (e.g. that of Orotal [Bacchus] in Arabia, Herod. iii.8). It was therefore an abomination of the Gentiles in the eyes of the Jew, which is referred to in Lev **19** 27; Jer **9** 26; **25** 23; **49** 32. The Syr version of the latter passage renders, "Ye shall not let your hair grow long" (i.e. in order to cut it as a religious rite in honor of an idol). It is, however, probable that among the Jews, as now among many classes of Mohammedans, the periodical cropping of the hair, when it had become too cumbersome, was connected with some small festivity, when the weight of the hair was ascertained, and its weight in silver was given in charity to the poor. At least, the weighing of Absalom's hair (2 S **14** 26) may be referred to some such custom, which is not unparalleled in other countries. The use of balances in connection with the shaving-off of the hair in Ezk **5** 1 is certainly out of the common. See illustration, "Votive Offering," on p. 1302.

Egyptian Manner of Wearing Hair.
(From statues of an officer of rank and his wife or sister, XIXth Dynasty, Brit. Mus.)

3. The Nazirite Vow

We may also compare the shaving of the head of the Nazirite to these heathen practices, though the resemblance is merely superficial. The man who made a vow to God was responsible to Him with his whole body and being. Not even a hair was to be injured wilfully during the whole period of the vow, for all belonged to God. The conclusion of the Nazirite vow was marked by sacrifices and the shaving of the head at the door of the sanctuary (Nu **6** 1–21), indicative of a new beginning of life. The long untouched hair was therefore considered as the emblem of personal devotion (or devotedness) to the God of all strength. Thus it was an easy step to the thought that in the hair was the seat of strength of a Samson (Jgs **16** 17.20). God has numbered the very hairs of the head (Mt **10** 30; Lk **12** 7), which to human beings conveys the idea of the innumerableness (Ps **40** 12; **69** 4). What God can number, He can also protect, so that not even a hair of the head might "fall to the earth" or "perish." These phrases express complete safety (1 S **14** 45; 2 S **14** 11; 1 K **1** 52; Lk **21** 18; Acts **27** 34).

4. Later Fashions

In NT times, esp. in the Diaspora, the Jews frequently adopted the fashion of the Romans in cropping the hair closely (1 Cor **11** 14); still the fear of being tainted by the idolatrous practice of the heathen, which is specially forbidden in Lev **21** 5, was so great that the side locks remained untouched and were permitted to grow *ad libitum*. This is still the custom among the Jews of Eastern Europe and the Orient. See also HEAD.

5. Woman's Hair

If Heb men paid much attention to their hair, it was even more so among Heb women. Long black tresses were the pride of the Jewish maiden and matron (Cant **7** 5; Jn **11** 2; 1 Cor **11** 5.6.15), but many of the expressions used in connection with the "coiffures" of women do not convey to us more than a vague idea. The "locks" of AV in Cant **4** 1.3; **6** 7; Isa **47** 2 (צַמָּה, *çammāh*) probably do not refer to the hair, but should be tr[d] (as does RV, which follows the LXX) by "veil." דַּלָּה, *dallāh* (Cant **7** 5), signifies the slender threads which represent the unfinished web in the loom (cf Isa **38** 12), and thence the flowing hair of women (RV "hair"). רְהָטִים, *r*e*hāṭīm* (RV "tresses"), in the same ver of the Song of Songs means lit. the "gutters" at which the flocks were watered (cf Gen **30** 38.41), and thus the long plaits of the maiden with which the lover toys and in which he is held captive. The braiding or dressing of woman's hair is expressed in 2 K **9** 30 and Jth **10** 3. In NT times Christian women are warned against following the fashionable world in elaborate hairdressing (1 Tim **2** 9; 1 Pet **3** 3).

6. Barbers

The care of the hair, esp. the periodical cutting of the same, early necessitated the trade of the barber. The Heb word גַּלָּב, *gallābh*, is found in Ezk **5** 1, and the pl. form of the same word occurs in an inscription at Citium (Cyprus) (*CIS*, 1586), where the persons thus described clearly belonged to the priests or servants of a temple. See BARBER.

7. Ointments

Numerous were the cosmetics and ointments applied to the hair (Eccl **9** 8; Mt **6** 17; perhaps Ruth **3** 3), but some, reserved for sacramental purposes, were prohibited for profane use (Ex **30** 32; Ps **133** 2). Such distinction we find also in Egypt, where the walls of temple laboratories were inscribed with extensive recipes of such holy oils,

Modern Jew of Jericho with Long Side Locks.

while the medical papyri (see esp. Papyrus Ebers, plates 64–67) contain numerous ointments for the hair, the composition of some of which is ascribed to a renowned queen of antiquity. Even Gr and Rom medical authors have transmitted to us the knowledge of some such prescriptions compounded, it is said, by Queen Cleopatra VI of Egypt, the frivolous friend of Caesar and Antony (see my dissertation, *Die über die medicinischen Kenntnisse der alten Aegypter berichtenden Papyri*, etc, Leipzig, 1888, 121–32). We know from Jos (*Ant*, XVI, viii, 1 [233]), that Herod the Great, in his old age, dyed his hair black, a custom, however, which does not appear to be specifically Jewish, as hair-dyes as well as means for bleaching the hair were well known in Greece and Rome. It is certain that the passage Mt **5** 36 would not have been spoken, had this been a common custom in the days of the Lord. A special luxury is mentioned by Jos (*Ant*, VIII, vii, 3 [185]), who states that the young men who formed the body-guard of King Solomon were in the habit, on festive occasions, of sprinkling their long hair with gold-dust (*ψῆγμα χρυσοῦ, psḗgma chrusoú*).

For the Jews the anointing of the head was synonymous with joy and prosperity (cf Ps **23** 5; **92** 10; He **1** 9; cf also "oil of joy," Isa **61** 3, and "oil of gladness," Ps **45** 7). It was also, like the washing of feet, a token of hospitality (Ps **23** 5; Lk **7** 46).

On the contrary, it was the custom in times of personal or national affliction and mourning to wear the hair unanointed and disheveled, or to cover the head with dust and ashes (2 S **14** 2; Josh **7** 6; Job **2** 12), or to tear the hair or to cut it off (Ezr **9** 3; Neh **13** 25; Jer **7** 29).

8. Symbolical Use of Word

We have referred to the thickness of hair which supplied the Heb with a suitable expression for the conception "innumerable." Hair is also expressive of minuteness; thus the 700 left-handed men of Benjamin were able to "sling stones at a hairbreadth, and not miss" (Jgs **20** 16). Gray hairs and the hoary white of old age were highly honored by the Jews (Prov **16** 31; **20** 29; 2 Macc **6** 23). Besides expressing old age (Isa **46** 4), they stand for wisdom (Wisd **4** 9 [10]). Sometimes white hair is the emblem of a glorious, if not Divine, presence (Dnl **7** 9; 2 Macc **15** 13; Rev **1** 14). Calamity befalling the gray-headed was doubly terrible (Gen **42** 38; **44** 29). The "hair of the flesh" is said to "stand up" (Job **4** 15; Sir **27** 14) when sudden terror or fear takes hold of a person. The symbolical language of Isa **7** 20 uses the "hair of the feet" (see FEET) and "the beard" as synonymous with "the humble" and "the "mighty of the people."

Camel's hair (Mt **3** 4; Mk **1** 6) is mentioned in connection with the description of John the Baptist's raiment. It represents, according to Jerome, a rough shirt worn under the coat or wrapper, though a rather soft fabric is produced in Arabia from the finer wool of the camel.

Goat's hair was the material of a cloth used for wearing apparel and for a more or less waterproof covering of tents and bundles. It is the 'black tent-cloth of Kedar' (Cant **1** 5; Ex **26** 7; **36** 14). In NT times it was the special product of St. Paul's native province, Cilicia, whence its name *cilicium*, and its manufacture formed the apostle's own trade (Acts **18** 3). It is also mentioned as a material for stuffing pillows (1 S **19** 13). See also WEAVING.

H. L. E. LUERING

HAIR, PLUCKING OF THE. See PUNISHMENTS.

HA-JEHUDIJAH, ha-jĕ-hū-dī′ja (הַיְּהֻדִיָּה, *ha-yᵉhudhīyāh*): Named in the genealogical list (1 Ch **4** 18). Possibly a proper name (RVm), but probably "the Jewess" (RV). May be so given in order to distinguish from the Egyp named in this verse. AV translates "Jehudijah."

HAKKATAN, hak′a-tan (הַקָּטָן, *ha-ḳāṭān*, "the little one"): The father of Johanan, who returned with Ezra to Jerus (Ezr **8** 12=Akatan, 1 Esd **8** 38).

HAKKOZ, hak′oz (הַקּוֹץ, *haḳḳōç*, or *ha-ḳōç*, "the nimble"):

(1) A priest and chief of the 7th course of Aaron's sons selected by David (1 Ch **24** 10). According to Ezr **2** 61; Neh **3** 4.21; **7** 63, his descendants returned with Zerubbabel from the captivity. But AV considers the name in Ezr and Neh as having the art. prefixed, hence renders "Koz."

(2) One of Judah's descendants (1 Ch **4** 8).

HAKUPHA, ha-kū′fa (חֲקוּפָא, *ḥăḳūphā'*, "incitement"). A family name of some of the Nethinim who returned with Zerubbabel from Babylon (Ezr **2** 51; Neh **7** 53).

HALAH, hā′la (חֲלַח, *ḥălaḥ;* **Ἁλάε,** *Haláe*, **Ἁλλάε,** *Halláe*, **Χαάχ,** *Chaách*, for **Χαλάχ,** *Chalách*, **Χαλά,** *Chalá;* Vulg *Hala*): Mentioned in

1. Many Identifications

2 K **17** 6; **18** 11; 1 Ch **5** 26, as one of the places to which the kings of Assyria sent the exiled Israelites (see GOZAN; HABOR). Various identifications have been proposed, all of them except the last more or less improbable for philological reasons: (1) the Assyr *Kalaḫ* (*Nimrūd*, the Calah of Gen **10** 11); (2) the Assyr *Ḫilakku* (Cilicia);

(3) Chalkitis in Mesopotamia (Ptol. v.18, 4), adjoining Gauzanitis (Gozan)—a good position otherwise; (4) the Calachene of Strabo, in the N. of Assyria. Equally unsuitable, also, is (5) the Chalonitis of Pliny and Strabo, N.E. of Assyria, notwithstanding that this was apparently called *Halah* by the Syrians. An attractive identification was (6) with the river Balīkh (by change of H into B)—cf LXX "in Halae and in Habor, *rivers* of Gozan"—but even this has to be abandoned in favor of (7) the Assyr *Ḫalaḫḫu*, which (except the doubling and the case-ending) is the same, letter for letter. It is mentioned in the *W. Asia Inscr*, II, pl. 53, l. 35, between *Arrapḫa* (Arrapachitis) and *Raṣappu* (Reseph).

2. The Most Probable of Them

According to the tablet K. 123, where it is called *mat Ḫalaḫḫi*, "the land of Ḫalaḫḫu," it apparently included the towns Še-bisê, Še-îrriši, Lu-ammu[ti ?], and Še-Akkulani, apparently four grain-producing centers for the Assyr government. The first quotation implies that Halah was near or in Gauzanitis, and had a chief town of the same name. Of the 8 personal names in K. 123, 5 are Assyr, the remainder being Syrian rather than Israelitish.

T. G. Pinches

HALAK, hā'lak, **MOUNT** (הָהָר הֶחָלָק, *hā-hār he-ḥālāḳ*): A mountain that marked the southern limit of the conquests of Joshua (Josh **11** 17; **12** 7). It is spoken of as the "mount Halak [lit. "the bare" or "smooth mountain"] that goeth up to Seir." The latter passage locates it on the W. of the Arabah. The southern boundary of the land is defined by the ascent of Akrabbim (Nu **34** 4; Josh **15** 3). This may with some certainty be identified with the pass known today as *naḳb eṣ-Ṣafā*, "pass of the smooth rock," through which runs the road from the S. to Hebron. To the S.W. opens *Wādy Maderah*, a continuation of *Wādy el-Fiḳrah*, in which there rises a conspicuous hill, *Jebel Maderah*, composed of limestone, answering well the description of a bare or smooth mountain. It is a striking feature of the landscape viewed from all sides, and may well be the mount here referred to. See also Hor, Mount.

W. Ewing

HALAKHA, ha-lä'ka. See Talmud.

HALE, hāl, vb., **HALING,** hāl'ing (OE *halen*): "To pull" or "drag," the AV tr of σύρω, *súrō*, "to draw or drag" (Acts **8** 3, "haling men and women," ARV "dragging"), and of κατασύρω, *katasúrō*, "to drag down" or "force along" (Lk **12** 58, "lest he hale thee to the judge," ARV "lest haply he *drag* thee unto the judge"). A more frequent modern form is "haul."

HALF, häf. See Number.

HALHUL, hal'hul (חַלְחוּל, *ḥalḥūl*): A city in the hill country of Judah (Josh **15** 58), "Halhul, Beth-zur and Gedor." It is without doubt the modern *Ḥalḥūl*, a village on a hill, surrounded by fine fields and vineyards, some 4 miles N. of Hebron and less than a mile to the E. of the modern carriage road. It is conspicuous from a considerable distance on account of its ancient mosque, *Wely Nebi Yûnas*, the "shrine of the Prophet Jonah"—a tradition going back at least to the 14th cent. The mosque, which has a minaret or tower, is built upon a rock platform artificially leveled. In the 14th cent. it was stated by Isaac Chilo (a Jewish pilgrim) that the tomb of Gad the Seer (1 S **22** 5; 2 S **24** 11 f) was situated in this town. Beth-zur (*Beit Sûr*) and Gedor (*Jedûr*) are both near. In Jos (*BJ*, IV, ix, 6) we read of an Alurus (where the Idumaeans assembled), and in Jerome (*OS* **119** 7) of a village Alula near Hebron, which both probably refer to the same place (*PEF*, III, 305; Sh XXI).

E. W. G. Masterman

HALI, hā'lī (חֲלִי, *ḥălī*): A town named with Helkath, Beten and Achshaph on the border of Asher (Josh **19** 25). No certain identification is possible; but it may be represented by the modern *Khirbet 'Alia*, c 13 miles N.E. of Acre.

HALICARNASSUS, hal-i-kär-nas'us (Ἁλικαρνασσός, *Halikarnassós*): The largest and strongest city of the ancient country of Caria in Asia Minor, situated on the shore of a bay, 15 miles from the island of Cos. Its site was beautiful; its climate temperate and even; the soil of the surrounding country was unusually fertile and noted for its abundance of fig, orange, lemon, olive and almond trees. When the ancient country fell into the possession of the Persians, the kings of Caria were still permitted to rule. One of the rulers was the famous queen Artemisia who fought at the battle of Salamis. The most famous of the kings, however, was Maussollos (Mausōlus), who ruled from 373 to 353 BC, and the tomb in which he was buried was long considered one of the wonders of the ancient world. Pliny describes the tomb as a circular structure, 140 ft. high, 411 ft. in circumference, and surrounded by 36 columns; it was covered with a pyramidal dome. The ancient writer Vitruvius, in his description of the city, says that the agora was along the shore; back of it was the mausoleum, and still farther away was the temple of Mars. To the right of the agora were the temples of Venus and Mercury, and to the left was the palace of Maussollos. Alexander the Great destroyed the city only after a long siege, but he was unable to take the acropolis. The city never quite recovered, yet it was later distinguished as the supposed birthplace of Herodotus and Dionysius. That a number of Jews lived there is evident from the fact, according to 1 Macc **15** 23, that in the year 139 BC, a letter was written by the Rom Senate in their behalf. In the 1st cent. BC, a decree was issued granting to the Jews in Halicarnassus liberty to worship "according to the Jewish laws, and to make their *proseuchē* at the sea-side, according to the customs of their forefathers" (Jos, *Ant*, XIV, x, 23).

The modern town of *Budrun*, which represents the ancient Halicarnassus and covers a part of its site, stands a little to the W. of the castle of St. Peter. This castle was erected by the Knights of Rhodes in 1404 AD, partly from the ruins of the mausoleum. Lord Redcliffe, who explored the ruins in 1846, sent many of the sculptured slabs from the castle to the British Museum where they may now be seen. Sir C. Newton conducted excavations there in 1857–58, adding other sculptures to the collection in the British Museum. He discovered the foundation of the Ionic temple of Aphrodite, and the greenstone foundation of the mausoleum upon which modern Turkish houses had been built. He also opened several tombs which were outside the ancient city. The city walls, built by Maussollos about 360 BC, and defining the borders of the ancient city, are still preserved; but the ancient harbor which was protected by a mole, has now disappeared. The ruins may best be reached by boat from the island of Cos.

E. J. Banks

HALL, hôl (Lk **22** 55 AV). See House.

HALL, JUDGMENT. See Judgment Hall; Praetorium.

HALLEL, ha-lāl', hal'el: In the fifth book of the Pss (**107–50**) there are several groups of Hallelujah Psalms: **104–6; 111–13; 115–17; 135; 146–50.** In the worship of the synagogue Pss **135–136** and **146–50** were used in the daily morning service. Pss **113–18** were called the "Egyp Hallel," and were sung at the feasts of the Passover, Pentecost, Tabernacles and Dedication. At the Passover, Pss **113** and **114** (according to the school of Shammai only Ps **113**) were sung before the feast, and Pss **115–18** after drinking the last cup. The song used by Our Lord and the disciples on the night of the betrayal (Mt **26** 30), just before the departure for the Mount of Olives, probably included Pss **115–18**.

John Richard Sampey

HALLELUJAH, hal-ē-lōō'ya (הַלְלוּ־יָהּ, *halelū-yāh*, "praise ye Jeh"; **ἀλληλουιά,** *allēlouiá*): The word is not a compound, like many of the Heb words which are composed of the abbreviated form of "Jehovah" and some other word, but has become a compound word in the Gr and other languages. Even if the Jews perhaps had become accustomed to use it as a compound, it is never written as such in the text. In some Pss, H. is an integral part of the song (Ps **135** 3), while in others it simply serves as a liturgical interjection found either at the beginning (Ps **111**) or at the close (Ps **104**) of the psalms or both (Ps **146**). The H. Pss are found in three groups: **104–6; 111–13; 146–50.** In the first group H. is found at the close of the psalm as a lit. interjection (**106** 1 is an integral part of the psalm). In the second group H. is found at the beginning (**113** 9 is an integral part of the psalm depending on the adj. "joyful"). In the third group H. is found both at the close and at the beginning of the psalms. In all other cases (Pss **115, 116, 117**) H. seems to be an integral part of the psalms. These three groups were probably taken from an older collection of psalms like the group Pss **120–34**. In the NT H. is found as part of the song of the heavenly host (Rev **19** 1 ff). The word is preserved as a liturgical interjection by the Christian church generally.

A. L. Breslich

HALLOHESH, ha-lō'hesh (הַלּוֹחֵשׁ, *ha-lōḥēsh*, "the whisperer," "the slanderer"): A post-exilic chief whose son Shallum assisted in repairing the walls of Jerus (Neh **3** 12, AV "Halohesh"). He was also one of the leaders who signed the national covenant (**10** 24 [Heb 25]).

HALLOW, hal'ō, **HALLOWED,** hal'ōd, hal'ō-ed ("to render or treat as holy," AS *hālgian*, from *hālig*, "holy"): It translates several forms of קָדַשׁ, *ḳādhash*, "set apart," "devote," "consecrate," frequently rendered in AV, RV, ARV "consecrate," "dedicate," "holy," and esp. "sanctify," closely synonymous, "hallow" perhaps containing more of the thought of reverence, sacredness, holiness. It embraces the idea of marked separateness. It is applied to persons, as the priest (Lev **22** 2.3); to places or buildings, as the middle of the temple court (1 K **8** 64); the tabernacle (Ex **40** 9); to things, like the portion of the sacrifice set apart for the priests (Nu **18** 8); to times and seasons, as the Sabbath (Jer **17** 22; Ezk **20** 20) and the Jubilee year (Lev **25** 10); to God Himself (Lev **22** 32). Its underlying idea of the separateness of holy nature or holy use works out into several often overlapping senses: (1) To set apart, dedicate, offer, reserve, for the worship or service of God: Ex **28** 38, "The holy things, which the children of Israel shall hallow in all their holy gifts"; also Lev **22** 3; Nu **18** 29, etc; 2 K **12** 4, "All the money of the hallowed things" (AV "dedicated"), etc. (2) To make holy, by selecting, setting apart, claiming, or acknowledging as His own: Gen **2** 3, "God blessed the seventh day, and hallowed it" (AV "sanctified"); but Ex **20** 11 (AV, ERV, ARV), "hallowed." So of the temple (1 K **9** 7); of the firstborn, spared in Egypt (Nu **3** 13). (3) To dedicate or consecrate by formal ceremonial, with the accompanying idea of cleansing from sin and uncleanness: Ex **29** 1, "This is the thing that thou shalt do unto them [Aaron and his sons] to hallow them, to minister unto me in the priest's office." The whole chapter is devoted to the elaborate ceremonial, consisting of ablutions, enduement in priestly robes and paraphernalia, anointing with oil, the offering of a bullock for a sin offering, and of a ram, the placing of the blood of another ram upon the right ear, right thumb, right great toe of each, the wave offering, the anointing of the holy garments, and the eating of the consecrated food, all this lasting seven days, and indicating the completeness with which they were set apart, the deep necessity of purification, and the solemnity and sacredness of the office. The tabernacle and its furniture were similarly "hallowed" by a simpler ceremony, using the anointing oil. (4) To render ritually fit for religious service, worship, or use: Lev **16** 19, "Hallow it [the altar with the sprinkled blood] from the uncleannesses of the children of Israel"; Nu **6** 11, "The priest shall .... make atonement for him, for that he sinned by reason of the dead, and shall hallow his head that same day." (5) To hold sacred, reverence, keep holy: Jer **17** 22, "But hallow ye the Sabbath day," by keeping it distinct and separate, esp. (Jer **17** 24.27) by refraining from unnecessary work, from burden-bearing, travel, or traffic (Neh **13** 16). See Ex **20** 8–11 (the Sabbath Commandment). (6) To revere, hold in awe, and reverence as holy and "separated from sinners" in majesty, power, sacredness: Lev **22** 32, "And ye shall not profane my holy name; but I will be hallowed among the children of Israel." *Ḳādhash* is elsewhere tr[d] "sanctify" in this connection, meaning "to be manifested in awe-producing majesty, power, or grace": Ezk **38** 23, "And I will .... sanctify myself, and I will make myself known in the eyes of many nations; and they shall know that I am Jeh"; cf Ezk **28** 22.23, etc.

In the NT "hallow" occurs only in the "Lord's Prayer," there rendering ἁγιάζω, *hagiázō*, the LXX word for *ḳādhash:* Mt **6** 9; Lk **11** 2, "Hallowed be thy name." *Hagiazō* is quite frequent in the NT, and is always (ARV) rendered "sanctify," except here, and in Rev **22** 11, "He that is holy, let him be made holy still." To "hallow the name" includes not only the inward attitude and outward action of profound reverence and active praise, but also that personal godliness, loving obedience and aggressive Christlikeness, which reveal the presence of God in the life, which is His true earthly glory.

Philip Wendell Crannell

HALT, hôlt (צָלַע, *çāla'*, "to limp"; **χωλός,** *chōlós*, "lame," "crippled"): ARV in Gen **32** 31 prefers "limped"; in Mic **4** 6.7; Zeph **3** 19, "is [or was] lame"; in Lk **14** 21, ARV and ERV have "lame." In 1 K **18** 21 a different word (*pāṣaḥ*) is used in EV of moral indecision: "How long halt ye between two opinions?" ARV renders, "How long go ye limping between the two sides?"

HAM, ham (חָם, *ḥām;* **Χάμ,** *Chám*):

The youngest son of Noah, from whom sprang the western and southwestern nations known to the Hebrews.

1. The Youngest Son of Noah

His name first occurs in Gen **5** 32, where, as in **6** 10 and elsewhere, it occupies the second place. In Gen **9** 18 Ham is described as "the father of Canaan," to prepare the reader for vs 25–27, where Noah, cursing Ham for having told Shem and Japheth of his nakedness, refers to him as Canaan. On account of this, it has been suggested that "Canaan" stood originally in all the passages where the three brothers are spoken of, and that this was later changed to "Ham," except in the verses containing the curse. It seems more likely, however, that the name "Canaan" is inserted prophetically, as Noah would not desire to curse his son, but only one branch of that son's descendants, who were later the principal adversaries of the Hebrews.

2. Ham as a Nationality

The name given, in Ps **105** 23.27; **106** 22 (cf **78** 51), to Egypt as a descendant of Ham, son of Noah. As Shem means "dusky," or the like, and Japheth "fair," it has been supposed that Ham meant, as is not improbable, "black." This is supported by the evidence of Heb and Arab., in which the word *ḥāmam* means "to be hot" and "to be black," the latter signification being derived from the former.

3. Meaning of the Word

That Ham is connected with the native name of Egypt, *Kem*, or, in full *pa ta' en Kem*, "the land of Egypt," in Bashmurian Coptic *Kheme*, is unlikely, as this form is probably of a much later date than the composition of Gen, and, moreover, as the Arab. shows, the guttural is not a true *kh*, but the hard breathing *h*, which are both represented by the Heb *ḥēth*.

4. The Nations Descending from Ham

Of the nationalities regarded as descending from Ham, none can be described as really black. First on the list, as being the darkest, is Cush or Ethiopia (Gen **10** 6), after which comes *Miçrayim*, or Egypt, then *Puṭ* or Libyia, and Canaan last. The sons or descendants of each of these are then taken in turn, and it is noteworthy that some of them, like the Ethiopians and the Canaanites, spoke Sem, and not Hamitic, languages—Seba (if connected with the Sabaeans), Havilah (Yemen), and Sheba, whose queen visited Solomon. Professor Sayce, moreover, has pointed out that Caphtor is the original home of the Phoenicians, who spoke a Sem language. The explanation of this probably is that other tongues were forced upon these nationalities in consequence of their migrations, or because they fell under the dominion of nationalities alien to them. The non-Sem Babylonians, described as descendants of Nimrod (Merodach), as is well known, spoke Sumerian, and adopted Sem Bab only on account of mingling with the Semites whom they found there. Another explanation is that the nationalities described as Hamitic—a parallel to those of the Sem section—were so called because they fell under Egyp dominion. This would make the original Hamitic race to have been Egyp, and account for Ham as a (poetical) designation of that nationality. Professor F. L. Griffith has pointed out that the Egyp Priapic god of Panopolis (*Akhmim*), sometimes called Menu, but also apparently known as Khem, may have been identified with the ancestor of the Hamitic race—he was worshipped from the coast of the Red Sea to Coptos, and must have been well known to Egypt's eastern neighbors. He regards the characteristics of Menu as being in accord with the shamelessness of Ham as recorded in Gen **9** 20 ff. See JAPHETH; SHEM; TABLE OF NATIONS.

T. G. PINCHES

HAM (הָם, *hām*):

(1) A place E. of the Jordan named between Ashteroth-karnaim and Shaveh-kiriathaim, in which Chedorlaomer smote the Zu-zim (Gen **14** 5). No name resembling this has been recovered. LXX reads *bāhem*, "with them," instead of *bᵉhām*, "in Ham." Some have thought that "Ham" may be a corruption from "Ammon"; or that it may be the ancient name of Rabbath-ammon itself.

(2) A poetical appellation of Egypt: "the land of Ham" (Ps **105** 23, etc) is the land of Jacob's sojourning, i.e. Egypt; "the tents of Ham" (Ps **78** 51) are the dwellings of the Egyptians. It may be derived from the native name of Egypt, *Kēmi*, or *Khēmi*. See MIZRAIM; SHEM.

W. EWING

HAMAN, hā'man (הָמָן, *hāmān*; Ἀμάν, *Hamán*): A Pers noble and vizier of the empire under Xerxes. He was the enemy of Mordecai, the cousin of Esther. Mordecai, being a Jew, was unable to prostrate himself before the great official and to render to him the adoration which was due to him in accordance with Pers custom. Haman's wrath was so inflamed that one man's life seemed too mean a sacrifice, and he resolved that Mordecai's nation should perish with him. This was the cause of Haman's downfall and death. A ridiculous notion, which, though widely accepted, has no better foundation than a rabbinic suggestion or guess, represents him as a descendant of Agag, the king of Amalek, who was slain by Samuel. But the language of Scripture (1 S **15** 33) indicates that when Agag fell, he was the last of his house. Besides, why should his descendants, if any existed, be called Agagites and not Amalekites? Saul's posterity are in no case termed Saulites, but Benjamites or Israelites. But the basis of this theory has been swept away by recent discovery. Agag was a territory adjacent to that of Media. In an inscription found at Khorsabad, Sargon, the father of Sennacherib, says: "Thirty-four districts of Media I conquered and I added them to the domain of Assyria: I imposed upon them an annual tribute of horses. The country of Agazi [Agag] . . . . I ravaged, I wasted, I burned." It may be added that the name of Haman is not Heb, neither is that of Hammedatha his father. "The name of Haman," writes M. Oppert, the distinguished Assyriologist, "as well as that of his father, belongs to the Medo-Persian."

JOHN URQUHART

HAMATH, hā'math (חֲמָת, *ḥămāth*; Ἡμάθ, *Hēmáth*, Αἱμάθ, *Haimáth*; Swete also has *Hemath*): The word signifies a defence or citadel, and such designation was very suitable for this chief royal city of the Hittites, situated between their northern and southern capitals, Carchemish and Kadesh, on a gigantic mound beside the Orontes. In Am **6** 2 it is named Great Hamath, but not necessarily to distinguish it from other places of the same name.

The Hamathite is mentioned in Gen **10** 18 among the sons of Canaan, but in historic times the

1. Early History

population, as the personal names testify, seems to have been for the most part Sem. The ideal boundary of Israel reached the territory, but not the city of Hamath (Nu **34** 8; Josh **13** 5; Ezk **47** 13–21). David entered into friendly relations with Toi, its king (2 S **8** 9 ff), and Solomon erected store cities in the land of Hamath (2 Ch **8** 4). In the days of Ahab we meet with it on the cuneiform inscriptions, under the name *mat hamatti*, and its king Irhuleni was a party to the alliance of the Hittites with Ben-hadad of Damascus and Ahab of Israel against Shalmaneser II; but this was broken up by the battle of Qarqar in 854 BC, and Hamath became subject to Assyria. Jeroboam II attacked, partially destroyed, and held it for a short time (2 K **14** 28; Am **6** 2). In 730 BC, its king Eni-ilu paid tribute to Tiglath-pileser, but he divided its lands among his generals, and transported 1,223 of its inhabitants to Sura on the Tigris. In 720, Sargon "rooted out the land of Hamath and dyed the skin of Ilubi'idi [or Jau-bi'idi] its king, like wool," and colonized the country with 4,300 Assyrians, among whom was Deioces the Mede. A few years later Sennacherib also claims to have taken it (2 K **18** 34; **19** 13; 1 Ch **36** 19; **37** 13). In Isa **11** 11, mention is made of Israelites in captivity at Hamath, and Hamathites were among the colonists settled in Samaria (2 K **17** 24) by Esarhaddon in 675 BC. Their special object of worship was Ashima, which, notwithstanding various conjectures, has not been identified.

2. Later History

The Hamathite country is mentioned in 1 Macc **12** 25 in connection with the movements of Demetrius and Jonathan. The Seleucidae renamed it Epiphaneia (Jos, *Ant*, I, vi, 2), and by this name it was known to the Greeks and the Romans, even appearing as Paphunya in Midr *B*ᵉ*r Rab* ch **37**. Locally, however, the ancient name never disappeared, and since the Moslem conquest it has been known as Hama. Saladin's family ruled it for a century and a half, but after the death of Abul-fida in 1331 it sank into decay.

3. Modern Condition

The position of Hama in a fruitful plain to the E. of the Nusairiyeh Mountains, on the most frequented highway between Mesopotamia and Egypt, and on the new railway, gives it again, as in ancient times, a singular significance, and it is once more rising in importance. The modern town is built in four quarters around the ancient citadel-mound, and it has a population of at least 80,000. It is now noted for its gigantic irrigating wheels. Here, too, the Hittite inscriptions were first found and designated Hamathite.

4. Entering in of Hamath

In connection with the northern boundary of Israel, "the entering in of Hamath" is frequently mentioned (Nu **13** 21; 1 K **8** 65, etc, ARV "entrance"). It has been sought in the Orontes valley, between Antioch and Seleucia, and also at *Wādy Nahr el-Bārid*, leading down from Homs to the Mediterranean to the N. of Tripoli. But from the point of view of Pal, it must mean some part of the great valley of Coele-Syria (*Biqa'a*). It seems that instead of translating, we should read here a place-name—"Libo of Hamath"—and the presence of the ancient site of Libo (mod. *Leboué*) 14 miles N.N.E. of Baalbek, at the head-waters of the Orontes, commanding the strategical point where the plain broadens out to the N. and to the S., confirms us in this conjecture.

W. M. CHRISTIE

HAMATH-ZOBAH, hā'math-zō'ba (חֲמַת צוֹבָה, *ḥămath çōbhāh;* Βαισωβά, *Baisōbá*): Mentioned only in 2 Ch **8** 3. Apart from Great Hamath no site answering to this name is known. It does not seem to be implied that Solomon took possession of Hamath itself, but rather that he "confirmed" his dominion over parts of the kingdom of Zobah, which on its fall may have been annexed by Hamath. LXX cod. B suggests a reading—Beth-zobah—omitting all reference to Hamath. On the other hand, the geographical distinctions between Zobah and Hamath having passed away long before Ch was written, the double name may have been used to indicate generally the extent of Solomon's conquests, as also to avoid confusion with the Zobah in the Hauran (2 S **23** 36).

W. M. CHRISTIE

HAMMATH, ham'ath (חַמַּת, *ḥammāth*, "hot spring"):

(1) "The father of the house of Rechab" (1 Ch **2** 55).

(2) One of the fenced cities of Naphtali, named with Zer, Rakkath and Chinnereth (Josh **19** 35). It is doubtless identical with Emmaus mentioned by Jos (*Ant*, XVIII, ii, 3; *BJ*, IV, i, 3) as near Tiberias, on the shore of the lake of Gennesareth. It is represented by the modern *el-Ḥammām*, nearly 2 miles S. of Tiberias. It was, of course, much nearer the ancient Tiberias, which lay S. of the present city. The hot baths here, "useful for healing," in the time of Jos, have maintained their reputation. In recent years, indeed, there has been a marked increase in the number of sick persons from all parts who visit the baths. The waters are esteemed specially valuable for rheumatism and skin troubles. In the large public bath the water has a temperature of over 140° Fahr. Parts of the ancient fortification still cling to the mountain side above the baths; and the remains of an aqueduct which brought fresh water from sources in the S.W. may be traced along the face of the slopes. Hammath is identical with **Hammon** (1 Ch **6** 76); and probably also with **Hammoth-dor** (Josh **21** 32).

W. EWING

HAMMEAH, ha-mē'a, ham'ē-a, **THE TOWER OF** (הַמֵּאָה, *ha-mē'āh* [Neh **3** 1]; AV **Meah**): The origin of the name is obscure; in m the meaning is given "Tower of the hundred"; it has been suggested that it may have been 100 cubits high or had 100 steps. It was the most important point on the walls of Jerus in going W. from the Sheep Gate, and is mentioned along with the T. of HANANEL (q.v.) (Neh **3** 1), and was therefore near the N.E. corner, and probably stood where the Baris and Antonia afterward were, near the N.W. corner of the *ḥaram* where are today the Turkish barracks. See JERUSALEM.

E. W. G. MASTERMAN

HAMMEDATHA, ham-ē-dā'tha (הַמְּדָתָא, *ham-m*ᵉ*dhāthā'*): The father of Haman (Est **3** 1). He is generally termed the "Agagite"; the name is of Pers etymology, signifying "given by the moon."

HAMMELECH, ham'ē-lek (הַמֶּלֶךְ, *ha-melekh*, "the king"): Wrongly trᵈ as a proper name in AV. It should be rendered "the king," as in ARV (Jer **36** 26; **38** 6).

HAMMER, ham'ēr: The Heb מַקֶּבֶת, *maḳḳebheth*, occurs in Jgs **4** 21, where it refers to the mallet (probably wooden) used to drive tent-pins into the ground. The same word occurs in 1 K **6** 7; Isa **44** 12; Jer **10** 4 as applied to a workman's hammer. פַּטִּישׁ, *paṭṭīsh* (cf Arab. *faṭīs*), occurs in Isa **41** 7; Jer **23** 29; **50** 23. It was probably a blacksmith's hammer or heavy hammer used for breaking rock. There is doubt about the rendering of Jgs **5** 26, where the word, הַלְמוּת, *halmūth*, occurs. From the context, the instrument mentioned was probably not a hammer. In Ps **74** 6, כֵּילַף, *kēlāph*, is better trᵈ "axes," not "hammers." See TOOLS.

JAMES A. PATCH

HAMMIPHKAD, ha-mif'kad, **GATE OF** (שַׁעַר הַמִּפְקָד, *sha'ar ha-miphḳādh*, "Gate of the Muster"): One of the gates of Jerus (Neh **3** 31) not mentioned elsewhere; probably situated near the N.E. corner of the Temple area.

HAMMOLECHETH, ha-mol'ē-keth (הַמֹּלֶכֶת, *ha-mōlekheth*, "the queen"; LXX Μαλέχεθ, *Malécheth;* AV **Hammoleketh**): The daughter of Machir and sister of Gilead (1 Ch **7** 18).

HAMMON, ham'on (חַמּוֹן, *ḥammōn*, "glowing"):

(1) A place on the seaward frontier of Asher, named with Rehob and Kanah (Josh **19** 28), to be sought, therefore, not far from Tyre. The most probable identification so far suggested is with *Umm el'Amūd*, "motner of the column" (or *'Awāmīd*, "columns"), at the mouth of *Wādy Ḥāmūl*, on the shore, about 10 miles S. of Tyre. An inscription found by Renan shows that the place was

associated with the worship of Ba'al Ḥammān (*CIS*, I, 8).

(2) A city in Naphtali, given to the Gershonite Levites (1 Ch **6** 76). It is identical with Hammath (Josh **19** 35), and probably also with Hammoth-dor (Josh **21** 32). W. EWING

HAMMOTH-DOR, ham-oth-dôr′ (חַמֹּת דֹּאר, *ḥammōth dō'r;* **'Εμαθδώρ**, *Emathdōr*, as also several corrupt forms): A fenced, Levitical city of Naphtali (Josh **19** 35; **21** 32); also named Hammon (1 Ch **6** 61 Heb). Probably the *hammatu* of the Karnak lists, and the *hamatam* of *WAI*, II, 53; certainly the Emmaus of Jos, *Ant*, XVIII, ii, 3; *BJ*, IV, i, 3; Hamata of *'Erūbhīn* v. 5; *Meghillāh* **2***b*, and the modern *el-Hammām*, 1½ miles S. of Tiberias. The name signifies "hot springs," and these, 4 in number, still exist. They have a temperature of 144° F., are salt and bitter in taste and sulphurous in smell. Considered invaluable for rheumatism, they are crowded in June and July. This health-giving reputation is of ancient date. It is mentioned in Jos, *BJ*, IV, i, 3; and a coin of Tiberias of the reign of Trajan depicts Hygeia sitting on a rock beside the springs, feeding the serpent of Aesculapius. Being used for pleasure also, they were permitted to the Jew on the Sabbath, whereas had they been used only medicinally, they would have been forbidden (Talm Bab, *Shab* **109***a;* cf Mt **12** 10). W. M. CHRISTIE

HAMMUEL, ham′ū-el (חַמּוּאֵל, *ḥammū'ēl*, "wrath of God"): A son of Mishma, a Simeonite, of the family of Shaul (1 Ch **4** 26).

ḤAMMURABI, ḥam-ōō-rä′bē:

1. Etymology of His Name, with Reference to Amraphel. His Dynasty
2. The Years Following His Accession
3. Military Operations and Further Pious Works. Inauguration of His Image
4. The Capture of Rîm-Sin
5. Various Works, and an Expedition to Mesopotamia
6. His Final Years
7. No Record of His Expedition to Palestine
8. The Period When It May Have Taken Place
9. Ḫammurabi's Greatness as a Ruler

The name of the celebrated warrior, builder and lawgiver, who ruled over Babylonia about 2000 BC.

1. Etymology of His Name with Reference to Amraphel. His Dynasty

In accordance with the suggestion of the late Professor Eb. Schrader, he is almost universally identified with the AMRAPHEL of Gen **14** 1, etc (q.v.). Ḫammurabi was apparently not of Bab origin, the so-called "Dynasty of Babylon," to which he belonged, having probably come from the W. The commonest form of the name is as above, but Ḫamu(m)-rabi (with mimmation) is also found. The reading with initial *b* in the second element is confirmed by the Bab rendering of the name as *Kîmta-rapaštum*, "my family is widespread," or the like, showing that *rabi* was regarded as coming from *rabû*, "to be great." A late letter-tablet, however (see *PSBA*, May, 1901, p. 191), gives the form *Ammurapi*, showing that the initial is not really *kh*, and that the *b* of the second element had changed to *p* (cf Tiglath-pil-eser for Tukulti-abil-ešar, etc). Amraphel (for *Amrapel, Amrabel, Amrabe*) would therefore seem to be due to Assyr influence, but the final *l* is difficult to explain. Professor F. Hommel has pointed out, that the Bab rendering, "my family is widespread," is simply due to the scribes, the first element being the name of the Arab. deity *'Am*, making *'Ammu-rabi*, "Am is great." Admitting this, it would seem to be certain that Ḫammurabi's dynasty was that designated Arabian by Berosus. Its founder was apparently Sumu-âbi, and Ḫammurabi was the fifth in descent from him. Ḫammurabi's father, Sin-mubaliṭ, and his grandfather, Abil-Sin, are the only rulers of the dynasty which have Bab names, all the others being apparently Arabic.

Concerning Ḫammurabi's early life nothing is recorded, but as he reigned at least 43 years, he

2. The Years Following His Accession

must have been young when he came to the throne. His accession was apparently marked by some improvement in the administration of the laws, wherein, as the date-list says, he "established righteousness." After this, the earlier years of his reign were devoted to such peaceful pursuits as constructing the shrines and images of the gods, and in his 6th year he built the wall of the city of Laz. In his 7th year he took Unug (Erech) and Isin—two of the principal cities of Babylonia, implying that the Dynasty of Babylon had not held sway in all the states.

While interesting himself in the all-important work of digging canals, he found time to turn his

3. Military Operations and Further Pious Works. Inauguration of His Image

attention to the land of Yamutbālu (8th year), and in his 10th he possibly conquered, or received the homage of, the city and people (or the army) of Malgia or Malgâ. Next year the city Rabiku was taken by a certain Ibik-Iškur, and also, seemingly, a place called Šalibu. The inauguration of the throne of Zēr-panitum, and the setting up, seemingly, of some kind of royal monument, followed, and was succeeded by other religious duties—indeed, work of this nature would seem to have occupied him every year until his 21st, when he built the fortress or fortification of the city Bazu. His 22d year is described as that of his own image as king of righteousness; and the question naturally arises, whether this was the date when he erected the great stele found at Susa in Elam, inscribed with his Code of Laws, which is now in the Louvre. Next year he seems to have fortified the city of Sippar, where, it is supposed, this monument was originally erected.

Pious works again occupied him until his 30th year, when the army of Elam is referred to, possibly

4. The Capture of Rîm-Sin

indicating warlike operations, which paved the way for the great campaign of his 31st year, when, "with the help of Anu and Enlil," he captured Yamutbālu and King Rîm-Sin, the well-known ruler of Larsa. In his 32d year he destroyed the army of Ašnunna or Ešnunnak.

After these victories, Ḫammurabi would seem to have been at peace, and in his 33d year he dug the

5. Various Works and an Expedition to Mesopotamia

canal *Ḫammurabi-nuhuš-niši*, "Ḫammurabi the abundance of the people," bringing to the fields of his subjects fertility, "according to the wish of Enlila." The restoration of the great temple at Erech came next, and was followed by the erection of a fortress, "high like a mountain," on the banks of the Tigris. He also built the fortification of Rabiku on the bank of the Tigris, implying preparations for hostilities, and it was possibly on account of this that the next year he made supplication to Tašmêtum, the spouse of Nebo. The year following (his 37th), "by the command of Anu and Enlila," the fortifications of Maur and Malka were destroyed, after which the country enjoyed a twelve-month of peace. In all probability, however, this was to prepare for the expedition of his 39th year, when he subjugated Turukku, Kagmû and Subartu, a part of Mesopotamia. The length of this year-date implies that the expedition was regarded as being of importance.

Untroubled by foreign affairs, the chief work of Ḫammurabi during his 40th year was the digging of the canal Tišit-Enlila, at Sippar, following this up by the restoration of the temple Ê-mete-ursag and a splendid temple-tower dedicated to Zagaga and Ištar. The defences of his country were apparently his last thought, for his 43d year, which seemingly terminated his reign and his life, was devoted to strengthening the fortifications of Sippar, a work recorded at greater length in several cylinder-inscriptions found on the site.

6. His Final Years

Unfortunately none of the documents referring to his reign makes mention of his attack, in company with the armies of Chedorlaomer, Tidal and Arioch, upon the rebel-kings of Sodom and Gomorrah. This naturally throws doubt on the identification of Ḫammurabi with the Amraphel of Gen **14** 1 ff. It must be remembered, however, that we do not possess a complete history either of his life or his rule. That he was a contemporary of Arioch seems undoubted, and if this be the case, Chedorlaomer and Tidal were contemporaries too. Various reasons might be adduced for the absence of references to the campaign in question—his pride may have precluded him from having a year named after an expedition—no matter how satisfactory it may have been—carried out for another power—his suzerain; or the allied armies may have suffered so severely from attacks similar to that delivered by Abraham, that the campaign became an altogether unsuitable one to date by.

7. No Record of an Expedition to Palestine

If Eri-Aku was, as Thureau-Dangin has suggested, the brother of Rîm-Sin, king of Larsa (Elassar), he must have preceded him on the throne, and, in that case, the expedition against the kings of the Plain took place before Ḫammurabi's 30th year, when he claims to have defeated Rîm-Sin. As the date of Rîm-Sin's accession is doubtful, the date of Eri-Aku's (Arioch's) death is equally so, but it possibly took place about 5 years before Rîm-Sin's defeat. The expedition in question must therefore have been undertaken during the first 25 years of Ḫammurabi's reign. As Amraphel is called *king* of Shinar (Babylonia), the period preceding Ḫammurabi's accession ought probably to be excluded.

8. Period When It May Have Taken Place

Of all the kings of early Babylonia so far known, Ḫammurabi would seem to have been one of the greatest, and the country made good progress under his rule. His conflicts with Elam suggest that Babylonia had become strong enough to resist that warlike state, and his title of *adda* or "father" of Martu (=Amurrū, the Amorites) and of Yamutbālu on the E. implies not only that he maintained the country's influence, but also that, during his reign, it was no longer subject to Elam. Rîm-Sin and the state of Larsa, however, were not conquered until the time of Samsu-iluna, Ḫammurabi's son. It is noteworthy that his Code of Laws (see 3, above) not only determined legal rights and responsibilities, but also fixed the rates of wages, thus obviating many difficulties. See Amraphel; Arioch; Chedorlaomer; Tidal, etc.

9. Ḫammurabi's Greatness as a Ruler

T. G. Pinches

HAMMURABI, THE CODE, kōd, OF:

I. Historical
  1. Discovery of the Code
  2. Editions of the Code
  3. Description of the Stone
  4. History of the Stone
  5 Origin and Later History of the Code

II. Contents of the Code
  1. The Principles of Legal Process
  2. Theft, Burglary, Robbery
  3. Laws concerning Vassalage
  4. Immovables
  5. Trader and Agent
  6. Taverns
  7. Deposits
  8. Family
  9. Concerning Wounding, etc
  10. Building of Houses and Ships
  11. Hiring in General, etc
  12. Slaves

III. The Significance of the Code
  1. Hammurabi and Moses
  2. The Code and Other Legal Systems

Literature

I. Historical.—When Professor Meissner published, in 1898, some fragments of cuneiform tablets from the library of the Assyr king Ashurbanipal (668–628 BC), he also then suggested that these pieces were parts of a copy of an old Book of Law from the time of the so-called First Bab Dynasty, one of the kings of which was Hammurabi (more exactly Ḫammurapi, c 2100 BC). A few years later this suggestion was fully established. In December, 1901, and January, 1902, a French expedition under the leadership of M. J. de Morgan, the chief aim of which was the exploration of the old royal city Susa, found there a diorite stone, 2.25 m. high and almost 2 m. in circumference. This stone had a relief (see below) and 44 columns of ancient Bab cuneiform writing graven upon it. Professor V. Scheil, O.P., the Assyriological member of the expedition, recognized at once that this stele contains the collection of laws of King Hammurabi, and published this characteristic discovery as early as 1902 in the official report of the expedition: *Délégation en Perse* (Tome IV, Paris).

1. Discovery of the Code

At the same time Scheil gave the first tr of the text. Since then the text has several times been published, tr[d] and commented upon; cf esp.: H. Winckler, *Die Gesetze Hammurabis* (=*Der alte Orient*, IV, Leipzig; 1st ed, 1903; 4th ed, 1906); H. Winckler, *Die Gesetze Hammurabis in Umschrift und Übersetzung*, Leipzig, 1904; D. H. Müller, *Die Gesetze Hammurabis und die Mosaische Gesetzgebung*, Vienna, 1903; R. F. Harper, *The Code of Ḫammurabi*, Chicago, 1904; C. H. W. Johns, *Babylonian and Assyrian Laws, Contracts, Letters*, Edinburgh, 1904, 44 ff; T. G. Pinches, *The OT in the Light of the Historical Records and Legends of Assyria and Babylonia*, London, 1908, 487; A. Ungnad, *Altorientalische Texte und Bilder zum Alten Testament*, Tübingen, 1909, I, 140 ff; A. Ungnad, *Keilschrifttexte der Gesetze Ḫammurapis*, Leipzig, 1909; J. Kohler, F. Peiser and A. Ungnad, *Hammurabis Gesetz*, 5 vols, Leipzig, 1904–11.

2. Editions, etc, of the Code

The stone has the form of a column the cross-section of which is approximately an ellipse. The upper part of the face has a relief (see illustration). We see the king in supplicating attitude standing before the sun-god who sits upon a throne and is characterized by sun rays which stream out from his shoulders. As the king traced back the derivation of the Code to an inspiration of this god, we may suppose that the relief represents the moment when the king received the laws from the mouth of the god. Lower on the face of the stone are 16 columns of text, which read from top to bottom; 7 other columns were erased some time later than Hammurabi in order to make room for a new inscription. The reverse side contains 28 columns of text.

3. Description of the Stone

The stone was set up by the king, toward the end of his reign of 43 years, in the temple Esagila at Babylon, the capital of his dominion (c 2100 BC). It was probably stolen from there by the Elamitic king Shutruk-Nakhunte, in the 12th cent. BC, at the time of the plundering of Babylon, and set up as a trophy of war in the Elamitic capital Susa. The same king had, it would seem, the 7 columns from the face side erased in order to engrave there an account of his own deeds, but through some unknown circumstance this latter was not accomplished. After the discovery of the stele it was brought to Paris where it now forms one of the most important possessions of the Louvre.

4. History of the Stone

Hammurabi Receiving the Laws.

If, however, Hammurabi was not the first legislator of Babylonia, still he was, as far as we can see, the first one who used the language of the people, i.e. the Sem idiom. We know that nearly 1,000 years earlier a king, Urukagina, promulgated laws in Babylonia which have been lost; an ancestor of Hammurabi, Sumulaël, appears also to have given laws. As we are able to recognize from the actual practice of Bab social life, the legislation of Hammurabi signifies nothing essentially new. Even before his time laws after the same principles were administered. His service lies before all in that he gathered together the extant laws and set them up in the Sem language. The laws were promulgated already in the 2d year of his reign, but the stele known to us was set up in the temple at Babylon about 30 years later. Moreover, the laws were set up in more than one copy, for in Susa fragments of another copy were found. How long the laws were in actual use it is impossible to determine. In any case, as late as the time of Ashurbanipal (see above), they used to be copied; indeed we even possess copies in neo-Bab characters which are later than the 7th cent. BC. Fortunately the duplicates contain several passages which are destroyed on the large stele in consequence of the erasure of the seven columns. Thus we are able, in spite of the gaps in the large stele, almost completely to determine the contents of the Code.

5. Origin and Later History of the Code

II. The Contents of the Code.—The laws themselves are preceded by an introduction which was added later, after the law had already been published about 30 years. The introduction states in the first place that already in the primeval age, when Marduk the god of Babylon was elected king of the gods, Hammurabi was predestined by the gods "to cause justice to radiate over the land, to surrender sinners and evildoers to destruction, and to take care that the strong should not oppress the weak." Hammurabi's Code is, indeed, conceived from this standpoint.

Farther on, the king lauds his services to the principal cities of Babylonia, their temples and cults. He appears as a true server of the gods, as a protector of his people and a gracious prince to those who at first would not acknowledge his supremacy. To be sure, this introduction is not entirely free from presumption; for the king describes himself as "god of the kings" and "sun-god of Babylon"! The hopes of a Saviour, which heathen antiquity also knew, he regards as realized in his own person.

The Code itself may be divided into 12 divisions. It manifests, in no way, a very definite logical system; the sequence is often interrupted, and one recognizes that it is not so much a systematic and exhaustive work as a collection of the legal standards accumulated in the course of time. Much that we would expect to find in a Code is not even mentioned.

The first five paragraphs treat of some principles of legal process. In the first place false accusation is considered. The unprovable charge of sorcery is dealt with in an especially interesting manner (§2). The accused in this case has to submit to an ordeal at the hands of the River-god; nevertheless nothing is said concerning the details of this ordeal. If he is convicted by the god as guilty, the accuser receives his house; in the opposite case, the accuser is condemned to death and the accused receives his house. The law also proceeds rigorously against false witnesses: in a process in which life is at stake, conscious perjury is punished with death (§3). Finally the king strives also for an uncorrupt body of judges; a judge who has not carried out the judgment of the court correctly has not only to pay twelve times the sum at issue, but he is also dismissed with disgrace from his office.

1. The Principles of Legal Process

The next sections (§§6–25) occupy themselves with serious theft, burglary, robbery and other crimes of a like nature. Theft from palace or temple, or the receiving and concealing of stolen property, is punished with death or a heavy fine according to the nature of what is stolen (§§6, 8). As it was a custom in Babylonia to effect every purchase in the presence of witnesses or with a written deed of sale, one understands the regulation that, in certain cases in which witnesses were not forthcoming, or a deed could not be shown, theft was assumed: the guilty person suffered death (§7). A careful procedure is prescribed for the case in which lost goods are found in the hands of another: he who, in the investigation, cannot prove his legitimate right, suffers death, just as a deceiver who tries to enrich himself through making a false accusation (§§9 ff). Kidnapping of a free child or carrying away and concealing a slave from the palace is punished with death (§§14 ff). As slavery had the greatest economic significance in Babylonia, detailed regulations concerning the seizing of runaway slaves and similar matters were given (§§17ff). Burglary, as also robbery, is punished with death (§§21 ff). If a robber is not caught, the persons or corporations responsible for the safety of the land had to make compensation (§§ 22 ff). Whoever attempts to enrich himself from a building in conflagration is thrown into the fire (§ 25).

2. Theft, Burglary, Robbery

The next paragraphs (§§ 26–41) control vassalage, particularly in reference to rights and duties of a military kind, concerning which we are not yet quite clear. Here also Hammurabi's care for those of a meaner position is exhibited, since he issues rigid regulations against misuse of the power of office and punishes certain offences of this kind even with death (§ 34). The crown had, in every case, authority in reference to estates in fee which a vassal could not sell, exchange or transmit to his wife or daughters (§§ 36 ff, 41); as a rule the sons took over the estates after the death of the father together with the accompanying rights and duties. The same was the case if, in the service of the king, the father had been lost sight of (§§ 28 f). The estates in fee of what we may call "lay-priestesses" (concerning whom we shall have to speak later) take a special position (§ 40).

3. Laws concerning Vassalage

not the means to do this could be sold with his family into slavery (§§ 53 ff). Special regulations protect the landowner from unlicensed grazing on his fields of crops (§§ 57 f).

The regulations concerning horticulture (§§ 59–66) are similar; here also the relation of the proprietor to the gardener who had to plant or to cultivate the garden is carefully considered; the same is true with respect to the business liabilities of the owner. These regulations concerning horticulture are not entirely preserved upon the stele, but, through the above-mentioned duplicates, we can restore them completely.

Our knowledge concerning the legal relations between house-owners and tenants (§§ 67 ff) is less, because the parts dealing with these on the stele are entirely lost and can only be partially restored from

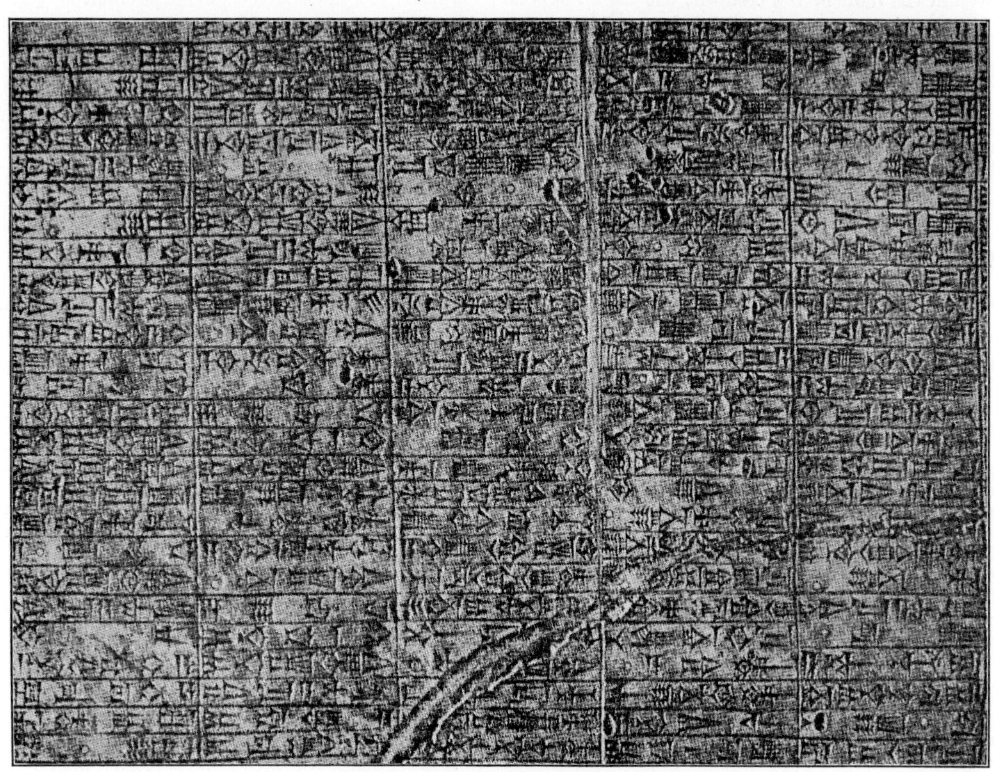

Text of the Code of Hammurabi.

A longer section (§§ 41 ff) is given to immovables (field, garden, house); for the economic life of the ancient Babylonians depended first of all upon the cultivation of grain and date-palms; the legal relations of the land tenants are exactly explained (§§ 42 ff): neglect of his work does not liberate the tenant from his duties to his overlord. On the other hand, in cases of losses through the weather, he is so far released from his duties that of the rent not yet paid he has to pay only an amount corresponding to the quantity of the product of his tenancy (§§ 45 f). Also the landowner with liabilities, who suffers through failure of crops and inundation, enjoys far-reaching protection (§ 48), and his business relations generally are adequately regulated (§§ 49 ff). As the regular irrigation of the fields was the chief condition for profitable husbandry in a land lacking rain, strong laws are made in reference to this: damage resulting from neglect has to be compensated for; indeed, whoever had

4. Immovables

duplicates. Reference is once more made to vassalage (§ 71). The relations between neighbors are also regulated, but we cannot ascertain how in detail (§§ 72 ff). Concerning the precise rights of tenants and landlords we are also but slightly informed (§ 78).

On account of the gaps, we are not able to determine how far the regulations concerning immovables extended. In the gaps there seem to have been still other laws concerning business liabilities. The number of missing paragraphs can only approximately be determined, so that our further enumeration of the paragraphs cannot be regarded as absolutely correct.

The text begins again with the treatment of the legal relations between the trader and his agents (§§ 100–107); these agents are a kind of officials for the trader whose business they look after. While the Code discusses their responsibilities and duties to their masters, it also protects them from unjust and deceitful ones.

5. Trader and Agent

6. Taverns

The taverns of Babylonia (§§ 108–11) seem very often to have been the resort of criminals. As a rule they were in the hands of proprietresses who were made responsible for what took place on their premises (§ 109). Priestesses were forbidden to visit these houses under penalty of being burned (§ 110).

7. Deposits

The next division (§§ 112–26) deals esp. with deposits, although some of its regulations are only indirectly therewith connected. Deceptive messengers are to be punished (§ 112). The debtor is protected from violent encroachments of the creditor (§ 113). Detailed regulations are given concerning imprisonment for debt (§§ 114 ff). The creditor must guard himself from mistreating a person imprisoned for debt, in his house; if a child of the debtor dies through the fault of the creditor, the *jus talionis* is resorted to: a child of the creditor is killed (§ 116). The members of a family imprisoned for debt have to be released after three years (§ 117). If anyone desires to give something to another to be saved for him, he must do it in the presence of witnesses or draw up a statement of the transaction; otherwise later claims cannot be substantiated (§§ 122 ff). Whoever accepts the objects is responsible for them (§ 125), but is also protected from unjustified claims of his client (§ 126).

8. Family

The sections occupied with the rights of the family are very extensive (§§ 127–95). Matrimony rests upon a contract (§ 128) and presupposes the persistent fidelity of the wife (§§ 129 ff), while the husband is not bound, in this respect, by regulations of any kind. An unfaithful wife may be thrown into the water, but the partner of her sin may also, under certain circumstances, suffer the penalty of death. Long unpreventable absence of the husband justifies the wife to marry again only when she lacks the means of support (§§ 133 ff). On the part of the husband, there are no hindrances to divorce, so long as he settles any matters with his wife concerning her property, provides for the upbringing of the children and, in certain cases, gives a divorce-sum as compensation (§§ 137 ff). Disorderly conduct of the wife is sufficient for the annulling of the marriage; in this case the husband may reduce the wife to the state of a slave (§ 141). The wife may only annul the marriage if her husband grossly neglects his duties toward her (§ 142). If a wife desires the annulling of the marriage for any other reason, she is drowned (§ 143).

As a rule polygamy is not allowed. If a barren wife gives to her husband a slave girl who bears children to him, then he may not marry another wife (§ 144); otherwise he might do so (§ 145). The slave given to the husband is bound to show due deference to her mistress; if she does not do this she loses her privileged position, but she may not be sold if she has borne a child to the husband (§§ 146 f). Incurable disease of the wife is a ground for the marriage of another wife (§§ 148 f).

Gifts of the husband to the wife may not be touched by the children at the death of the husband, but nevertheless property has to remain in the family (§ 150). Debts contracted before the marriage by one side or the other are not binding for the other, if an agreement has been made to that effect (§ 151 f).

Rigid laws are made against abuses in sexual life. The wife who kills her husband for the sake of a lover is impaled upon a stake (§ 153). Incest is punished, according to the circumstances, with exile or death (§§ 154 ff).

Breach of promise by the man without sufficient reason entails to him the loss of all presents made for the betrothed. If the father of the betrothed annuls the engagement, he must give back to the man twice the value of the presents (§§ 159 ff); esp. the sum paid for the wife to her father (Bab *terḫâtu*).

Matters concerning inheritance are carefully dealt with (§§ 162 ff). The dowry of a wife belongs, after her death, to her children (§ 162). Presents made during the lifetime are not reckoned in the dividing of the inheritance (§ 165), apart from the outlay which a father has to make in the case of each of his sons, the chief portion of which is the money for a wife (§ 166). Children borne from different mothers share the paternal inheritance equally (§ 167).

Disinheritance of a child is permitted only in the case of serious offences after a previous warning (§§ 168 f). Illegitimate children borne from slaves have part in the inheritance only if the father has expressly acknowledged them as his children (§ 170); otherwise, at the death of the father, they are released (§ 171).

The chief wife, whose future needs had not been secured during the lifetime of her husband, receives from the property of the deceased husband a portion equal to that received by each child, but she has only the use of it (§ 172). A widow may marry again, but then she loses all claim on the property of her first husband, in favor of his children (§§ 172, 177); the children of both her marriages share her own property equally (§§ 173 f).

The children from free women married to slaves are free (§ 175). The master of the slave has only a claim to half of the property of the slave which he has acquired during such a marriage (§§ 176 f).

Unmarried daughters mostly became priestesses or entered a religious foundation (Bab *malgû*); they also received, very often, a sort of dowry, which, however, remained under the control of their brothers and which, on the death of the former, fell to the brothers and sisters, if their fathers had not expressly given them a free hand in this matter (§§ 178 f). In cases where the father did not give such a dowry, the daughter received, from the property left, a share equal to that of the others, but only for use; those dedicated to a goddess obtained only a third of such an amount (§ 180 f). The lay-priestesses of the god Marduk of Babylon enjoyed special privileges in that they had full control over any property thus acquired (§ 182).

As a rule, adopted children could not be dismissed again (§§ 185 ff). Parents who had given their child to a master, who had adopted it and taught it handwork, could not claim it again (§§ 188 f). Gross insubordination of certain adopted children of a lower class is severely punished by the cutting off of the tongue (§ 192) or the tearing out of an eye (§ 193). Deceitful wet-nurses are also severely punished (§ 194). The last paragraph of this section (§ 195) states the punishment for children who strike their father as the cutting off of the hand.

9. Concerning Wounding, etc

The next division (§§ 196–227) occupies itself with wounding of all kinds, in the first place with the *jus talionis:* an eye for an eye, a bone for a bone, a tooth for a tooth. Persons lower in the social grade usually accepted money instead (§§ 196 ff). A box on the ears inflicted by a free man upon a free man cost the former 60 shekels (§ 203); in the case of one half-free, 10 shekels (§ 204); but if a slave so strikes a free man, his ear is to be cut off (§ 205). Unintentional wounding of the body, which proves to be fatal, is covered by a fine (§§ 207 f). Anyone who strikes a pregnant free woman, so as to cause a miscarriage and the death of the woman, is punished by having his daughter killed (§ 210); in the case of a half-free woman or a slave, a money compensation was sufficient (§§ 212 ff).

The surgeon is responsible for certain operations; if they succeed, he receives a legally determined high reward; if they fail, under certain circumstances his hand might be cut off (§§ 215 ff). Certainly this law was an effective preventive against quacks! Farther on come regulations concerning the fees of surgeons (§§ 221 ff) and veterinary surgeons; to a certain degree the latter are responsible for the killing of an animal under their charge (§§ 224 f).

10. Building of Houses and Ships

Later, the building of houses and ships is treated of (§§ 228–40). The builder is responsible for the stability of the house built by him; if it falls down and kills the master of the house, the builder is killed; if it kills a child of the house, a child of the builder is killed (§§ 229 f). For any other damages incurred, the builder is likewise responsible (§§ 231 ff). The regulations for the builders of ships are similar (§§ 234 ff). The man who hires a ship is answerable to the proprietor (§§ 236 ff). With the busy shipping trade on the canals, special attention had to be given to prevent accidents (§ 240).

11. Hiring in General, etc

Already in earlier sections there were regulations concerning hiring (rent) and wages. This eleventh division (§§ 241–77) deals with the matter more in detail, but it also brings many things forward which are only slightly related thereto. It states tariffs for working animals (§§ 242 f), and in conclusion to this makes equally clear to what extent the hirer of such an animal is responsible for harm to the animal (§§ 244 ff). Special attention must be given an ox addicted to goring (§§ 250 ff; see below). Care is taken that unfaithful stewards do not escape their punishment: in gross cases of breach of confidence they are punished with the cutting off of the hand or by being torn (in the manner of being tortured on a rack) by oxen (§§ 253 ff). The wages for agricultural laborers are determined (§§ 257 f), and in connection with this, lesser cases of theft of field-utensils are considered and covered by a money fine (§§ 259 f). The wages of a shepherd and his duties form the subject of some other paragraphs (§§ 261 ff). Finally, matters having to do with hiring are mentioned: the hiring of animals for threshing (§§ 268 ff), of carriages (§ 271), wages of laborers (§ 273) and handworkers (§ 274), and the hire of ships (§§ 276 f).

12. Slaves

The last division (§§ 278–82) treats of slaves in so far as they are not already mentioned. The seller is responsible to the buyer that the slave does not suffer from epilepsy (§ 278), and that nobody else has a claim upon him (§ 279). Slaves of Bab origin, bought in a foreign land, must be released, if they are brought back to Babylonia and recognized by their former master (§ 280). If a slave did not acknowledge his master, his ear could be cut off (§ 282).

Here the laws come to an end. In spite of many regulations which seem to us cruel, they show keen sense of justice and impartiality. Thus the king, in an epilogue, rightly extols himself as a shepherd of salvation, as a helper of the oppressed, as an adviser of widows and orphans, in short, as the father of his people. In conclusion, future rulers are admonished to respect his laws, and the blessings of the gods are promised to those who do so. But upon those who might attempt to abolish the Code he calls down the curse of all the great gods, individually and collectively. With that the stele ends.

III. The Significance of the Code has been recognized ever since its discovery; for, indeed, it is the most ancient collection of laws which we know. For judgment concerning the ancient Bab civilization, for the history of slavery, for the position of woman and many other questions the Code offers the most important material. The fact that law and religion are nearly always distinctly separated is worthy of special attention.

1. Hammurabi and Moses

It is not to be wondered at that a monument of such importance demands comparison with similar monuments. In this reference the most important question is as to the relation in which the Code stands to the Law of Moses. Hammurabi was not only king of Babylonia but also of Amurru (= "land of the Amorites"), called later Pal and Western Syria. As his successors also retained the dominion over Amurru, it is quite possible that, for a considerable time, the laws of Hammurabi were in force here also, even if perhaps in a modified form. In the time of Abraham, for example, one may consider the narratives of Sarah and Hagar (Gen **16** 1 ff), and Rachel and Bilhah (Gen **30** 1 ff), which show the same juridical principles as the Code (cf §§ 144 ff; see above). Other narratives of the OT indicate the same customs as the Code does for Babylonia; cf Gen **24** 53, where the bridal gifts to Rebekah correspond to the Bab *terḫâtu* (§ 159); similarly Gen **31** 14 f.

Between the Code and the Law of Moses, esp. in the so-called Book of the Covenant (Ex **20** 22—**23** 33), there are indeed extraordinary parallels. We might mention here the following examples:

Ex **21** 2: "If thou buy a Heb servant, six years he shall serve: and in the seventh he shall go out free for nothing." Similarly, CH, § 117: "If a man become involved in debt, and give his wife, his son or his daughter for silver or for labor, they shall serve three years in the house of their purchaser or bondmaster: in the fourth year they shall regain their freedom."

Ex **21** 15: "And he that smiteth his father, or his mother, shall be surely put to death." Cf CH, § 195: "If a son strike his father, his hand shall be cut off."

Ex **21** 18 f: "And if men contend, and one smite the other with a stone, or with his fist, and he die not, but keep his bed; if he rise again, and walk abroad upon his staff, then shall he that smote him be quit: only he shall pay for the loss of his time, and shall cause him to be thoroughly healed." Cf CH, § 206: "If a man strike another man in a noisy dispute and wound him, that man shall swear, 'I did not strike him knowingly'; and he shall pay for the physician."

Ex **21** 22: "If men strive together, and hurt a woman with child, so that her fruit depart, and yet no harm follow; he shall surely be fined, according as the woman's husband shall lay upon him; and he shall pay as the judges determine." Cf CH, § 209: "If a man strike a free woman and cause her fruit to depart, he shall pay ten shekels of silver for her fruit."

Ex **21** 24: "Eye for eye, tooth for tooth, hand for hand, foot for foot." Cf CH, § 196: "If a man destroy the eye of a free man, his eye shall be destroyed." § 197: "If he break the bone of a free man, his bone shall be broken." § 200: "If a man knock out the teeth of a man of the same rank, his teeth shall be knocked out."

Ex **21** 28–32: "If an ox gore a man or a woman to death, the ox shall be surely stoned, and its flesh shall not be eaten; but the owner of the ox shall be quit. But if the ox was wont to gore in time past, and it hath been testified to its owner, and he hath not kept it in, but it hath killed a man or a woman; the ox shall be stoned, and its owner also shall be put to death. . . . . If the ox gore a man-servant or a maid-servant, there shall be given unto their master 30 shekels of silver, and the ox shall be stoned." Cf CH, §§ 250 ff: "If an ox, while going along the street, gore a man and cause his death, no claims of any kind can be made. If a man's ox be addicted to goring and have manifested to him his failing, that it is addicted to goring, and, nevertheless, he have neither blunted his horns, nor fastened up his ox; then if his ox gore a free man and cause his death, he shall give 30 shekels of silver. If it be a man's slave, he shall give 20 shekels of silver."

Ex **22** 7 ff reminds one of CH, §§ 124 ff; Ex **22** 10 ff of CH, §§ 244 ff and 266 f.

The resemblances between the other parts of the Pent and the Code are not so striking as those between the Code and the Book of the Covenant; nevertheless one may compare Lev **19** 35 f with CH, § 5; Lev **20** 10 with CH, § 129; Lev **24** 19 f with CH, §§ 196 ff; Lev **25** 39 ff with CH, § 117; Dt **19** 16 ff with CH, §§ 3 f; Dt **22** 22 with CH, § 129; Dt **24** 1 with CH, §§ 137 ff and §§ 148 f; Dt **24** 7 with CH, § 14; esp. Dt **21** 15 ff.18 ff, with CH, §§ 167, 168 f, where, in both cases, there is a transition from regulations concerning the property left by a man, married several times, to provisions referring to the punishment of a disobedient son, certainly a remarkable agreement in sequence.

One can hardly assert that the parallels quoted are accidental, but just as little could one say that they are directly taken from the Code; for they bear quite a definite impression due to the Israelitish culture, and numerous marked divergences also exist. As we have already mentioned, the land Amurru was for a time Bab territory, so that Bab law must have found entrance there. When the Israelites came into contact with Bab culture, on taking possession of the land of Canaan (a part of the old Amurru), it was natural that they should employ the results of that culture as far as they found them of use for themselves. Under no circumstances may one suppose here direct quotation. Single parts of the Laws of Moses, esp. the Decalogue (Ex **20**), with its particularly pointed conciseness, have no ‖ in CH.

It has also been attempted to establish relations between the Code and other legal systems. In the

2. The Code and Other Legal Systems

Talm, esp. in the fourth order of the *Mishnāh* called *n^ezīḳīn* (i.e. "damages"), there are many regulations which remind one of the Code. But one must bear in mind that the Jews during the exile could hardly have known the Code in detail; if there happen to be similarities, these are to be explained by the fact that many of the regulations of the Code were still retained in the later Bab law, and the Talm drew upon this later Bab law for many regulations which seemed useful for its purposes. The connection is therefore an indirect one.

The similarities with the remains of old Arabian laws and the so-called Syrio-Rom Lawbook (5th cent. AD) have to be considered in the same way, though some of these agreements may have only come about accidentally.

That the similarities between Rom and Gr legal usages and the Code are only of an accidental nature may be taken as assured. This seems all the more probable, in that between the Code and other legal systems there are quite striking similarities in individual points, even though we cannot find any historical connection, e.g. the Salic law, the lawbook of the Salic Franks, compiled about 500 AD, and which is the oldest preserved Germanic legal code.

Until a whole number of lost codes, as the Old Amoritish and the neo-Bab, are known to us in detail, one must guard well against hasty conclusions. In any case it is rash to speak of direct borrowings where there may be a whole series of mediating factors.

Literature.—Concerning the questions treated of in the last paragraphs refer esp. to: S. A. Cook, *The Laws of Moses and Code of Hammurabi*, London, 1903; J. Jeremias, *Moses and Hammurabi*, Leipzig, 1903; S. Oettli, *Das Gesetz Hammurabis und die Thora Israels*, Leipzig, 1903; H. Grimme, *Das Gesetz Chammurabis und Moses*, Köln, 1903; H. Fehr, *Ḫammurapi und das Salische Recht*, Bonn, 1910.

Arthur Ungnad

HAMONAH, ha-mō'na (הֲמוֹנָה, *hămōnāh*): The name of a city which stood apparently near Hamon-gog (q.v.) (Ezk **39** 16).

HAMON-GOG, hā'mon-gog (הֲמוֹן־גּוֹג, *hămōn-gōgh*, "the multitude of Gog"): The name of the place where "Gog and all his multitude" are to be buried (Ezk **39** 11.15). By a change in the pointing of ver 11, *hā-'ăbhārīm* for *hā-'ōbh^{e}rīm*, we should read "valley of Abarim" for "valley of them that pass through." In that case it would seem that the prophet thought of some ravine in the mountains E. of the Dead Sea.

HAMOR, hā'mor (חֲמוֹר, *ḥămōr*, "an ass"; **'Εμμώρ,** *Emmôr*): Hamor was the father of Shechem from whom Jacob bought a piece of ground on his return from Paddan-aram for one hundred pieces of silver (Gen **33** 19), and the burial place of Joseph when his body was removed from Egypt to Canaan (Josh **24** 32). "The men of Hamor" were inhabitants of Shechem, and suffered a great loss under Abimelech, a prince over Israel (Jgs **9** 22–49). Dinah, Jacob's daughter, was criminally treated by Hamor, who requested her to be given to him in marriage, in which plan he had the coöperation of his father, Shechem. The sons of Jacob rejected their proposition and laid a scheme by which the inhabitants of the city were circumcised, and in the hour of helplessness slew all the males, thus wreaking special vengeance upon Hamor and his father Shechem. It is mere conjecture to claim that Hamor and Dinah were personifications of early central Palestinian clans in sharp antagonism, and that the course of Simeon and Levi was really the treachery of primitive tribes. Because the word Hamor means "an ass" and Shechem "a shoulder," there is no reason for rejecting the terms as designations of individuals and considering the titles as mere tribal appellations. Byron H. DeMent

HAMRAN, ham'ran. See Hemdan.

HAMUEL, ham'ū-el, ha-mū'el. See Hammuel.

HAMUL, hā'mul (חָמוּל, *ḥāmūl*, "pitied," "spared"): A son of Perez, and head of one of the clans of Judah (Gen **46** 12; 1 Ch **2** 5; Nu **26** 21). His descendants were called Hamulites.

HAMUTAL, ha-mū'tal (חֲמוּטַל, *ḥămūṭal*, "father-in-law" or "kinsman of the dew"): A daughter of Jeremiah of Libnah, and wife of King Josiah, and mother of Jehoahaz and Zedekiah (2 K **23** 31; **24** 18; Jer **52** 1). In the last two references and in the LXX the name appears as "Hamital." Swete gives a number of variants, e.g. 2 K **24** 18: B, Μιτάτ, *Mitát*, A, 'Αμιτάθ, *Amitáth;* Jer **52** 1: B, 'Αμειταάλ, *Hameitaál*, א A 'Αμιταάλ, *Hamitaál*, Q, 'Αμιτάλ, *Hamitál*.

HANAMEL, han'a-mel (חֲנַמְאֵל, *hănam'ēl;* AV **Hanameel,** ha-nam'ē-el): The son of Shallum, Jeremiah's uncle, of whom the prophet, while in prison, during the time when Jerus was besieged by the Chaldaeans, bought a field with due formalities, in token that a time would come when house and vineyards would once more be bought in the land (Jer **32** 6–15).

HANAN, hā′nan (חָנָן, *ḥānān*, "gracious"):

(1) A chief of the tribe of Benjamin (1 Ch **8** 23).

(2) The youngest son of Azel, a descendant of Saul (1 Ch **8** 38; **9** 44).

(3) One of David's mighty men of valor (1 Ch **11** 43).

(4) The head of a family of the Nethinim who returned with Zerubbabel (Ezr **2** 46; Neh **7** 49).

(5) An assistant of Ezra in expounding the law (Neh **8** 7). Possibly the same person is referred to in Neh **10** 10 (11).

(6) One of the four treasurers put in charge of the tithes by Nehemiah (Neh **13** 13).

(7, 8) Two who "sealed the covenant" on the eve of the restoration (Neh **10** 22 [23].26 [27]).

(9) A son of Igdaliah, "the man of God," whose sons had a chamber in the temple at Jerus (Jer **35** 4).

Byron H. DeMent

HANANEL, han′an-el, **THE TOWER OF** (חֲנַנְאֵל, *ḥănan'ēl*, "'*ēl* is gracious"; AV **Hananeel,** ha-nan′ē-el): A tower in the walls of Jerus adjoining (Neh **3** 1; **12** 39) the tower of Hammeah (q.v.). The company of Levites coming from the W. passed "by the fish gate, and the tower of Hananel, and the tower of Hammeah, even unto the sheep gate" (Neh **12** 39). In Jer **31** 38 it is foretold "that the city shall be built to Jeh from the tower of Hananel unto the gate of the corner"—apparently the whole stretch of N. wall. In Zec **14** 10 it says Jerus "shall dwell in her place, from Benjamin's gate unto the place of the first gate, unto the corner gate, and from the tower of Hananel unto the king's winepresses." These last were probably near Siloam, and the distance "from the tower of Hananel unto the king's winepresses" describes the greatest length of the city from N. to S. All the indications point to a tower, close to the tower of Hammeah, near the N.E. corner, a point of the city always requiring special fortification and later the sites successively of the Baris and of the Antonia. See Jerusalem.

E. W. G. Masterman

HANANI, ha-nā′nī (חֲנָנִי, *ḥănānī*, "gracious"):

(1) A musician and son of Heman, David's seer, and head of one of the courses of the temple service (1 Ch **25** 4.25).

(2) A seer, the father of Jehu. He was cast into prison for his courage in rebuking Asa for relying on Syria (1 K **16** 1.7; 2 Ch **19** 2; **20** 34).

(3) A priest, of the sons of Immer, who had married a foreign wife (Ezr **10** 20).

(4) A brother or kinsman of Nehemiah who carried news of the condition of the Jews in Pal to Susa and became one of the governors of Jerus (Neh **1** 2; **7** 2).

(5) A priest and chief musician who took part in the dedication of the walls of Jerus (Neh **12** 36).

Byron H. DeMent

HANANIAH, han-a-nī′a (חֲנַנְיָהוּ, *ḥănanyāhū*, חֲנַנְיָה, *ḥănanyāh;* Ἀνανίας, *Ananías;* also with aspirate, "Jeh hath been gracious"): This was a common name in Israel for many centuries.

(1) A Benjamite (1 Ch **8** 24).

(2) A captain of Uzziah's army (2 Ch **26** 11).

(3) Father of one of the princes under Jehoiakim (Jer **36** 12).

(4) One of the sons of Heman and leader of the 16th division of David's musicians (1 Ch **25** 4.23).

(5) Grandfather of the officer of the guard which apprehended Jeremiah on a charge of desertion (Jer **37** 13).

(6) A false prophet of Gibeon, son of Azzur, who opposed Jeremiah, predicting that the yoke of Babylon would be broken in two years, and that the king, the people and the vessels of the temple would be brought back to Jerus. Jeremiah would be glad if it should be so, nevertheless it would not be. The question then arose, Which is right, Jeremiah or Hananiah? Jeremiah claimed that he was right because he was in accordance with all the great prophets of the past who prophesied evil and their words came true. Therefore his words are more likely to be true. The prophet of good, however, must wait to have his prophecy fulfilled before he can be accredited. Hananiah took off the yoke from Jeremiah and broke it in pieces, symbolic of the breaking of the power of Babylon. Jeremiah was seemingly beaten, retired and received a message from Jeh that the bar of wood would become a bar of iron, and that Hananiah would die during the year because he had spoken rebellion against Jeh (Jer **28** *passim*).

(7) One of Daniel's companions in Babylon whose name was changed to Shadrach (Dnl **1** 7.11.19).

(8) A son of Zerubbabel (1 Ch **3** 19.21).

(9) A Levite, one of the sons of Bebai, one of those who married foreign wives (Ezr **10** 28; 1 Esd **9** 29).

(10) One of the perfumers (AV "apothecaries") who wrought in rebuilding the wall under Nehemiah (Neh **3** 8).

(11) One who helped to repair the wall above the horse gate (Neh **3** 30). This may be the same person as no. 10.

(12) A governor of the castle, i.e. the *bīrāh* or fortress, and by Nehemiah placed in charge of the whole city of Jerus, because "he was a faithful man, and feared God above many" (Neh **7** 2).

(13) One of those who sealed the covenant under Nehemiah (Neh **10** 23); a Levite.

(14) A priest who was present at the dedication of the walls of Jerus (Neh **12** 12.41).

J. J. Reeve

HAND (יָד, *yādh*, "hand"; כַּף, *kaph*, "the hollow hand," "palm"; יָמִין, *yāmīn*, "the right hand"; שְׂמֹאל, *semō'l*, "the left hand"; χείρ, *cheír*, "hand"; δεξιά, *dexiá*, "the right hand"; ἀριστερά, *aristerá*, "the left hand" [only Lk **23** 33; 2 Cor **6** 7], or euphemistically [for evil omens come from the left hand; cf Lat *sinister*, Ger. *linkisch*, etc]; εὐώνυμος, *euōnumos*, lit. "having a good name"): The Heb words are used in a large variety of idiomatic expressions, part of which have passed into the Gr (through the LXX) and into modern European languages (through the translations of the Bible; see *Oxford Heb Lex.*, s.v. "*yādh*"). We group what has to be said about the word under the following heads:

The human hand (considered physically) and, anthropopathically, the hand of God (Gen **3** 22; Ps **145** 16): The hand included the wrist, as will be seen from all passages in which bracelets are mentioned as ornaments of the hand, e.g. Gen **24** 22.30.47; Ezk **16** 11; **23** 42, or where the Bible speaks of fetters on the hands (Jgs **15** 14, etc).

1. The Human Hand: Various Uses

On the other hand, it cannot seem strange that occasionally the expression "hand" may be used for a part, e.g. the fingers, as in Gen **41** 42, etc. According to the *lex talionis*, justice demanded "hand for hand" (Ex **21** 24; Dt **19** 21). We enumerate the following phrases without claiming to present a complete list: "To fill the hand" (Ex **32** 29 m; 1 Ch **29** 5 m) means to consecrate, evidently from the filling of hands with sacrificial portions for the altar. Cf also Lev **7** 37; **8** 22.28.29.31.33, where the sacrifice, the ram, the basket of consecration are mentioned. "To put or set the hand unto" (Dt **15** 10;

23 20; **28** 8.20), to commence to do; "to put forth the hand" (Gen **3** 22; **8** 9); "to stretch out the hand" (Ezk **25** 13.16; Zeph **2** 13); "to shake or wag the hand upon" (Isa **10** 32; Zeph **2** 15; Zec **2** 9), to defy. "To lay the hand upon the head" (2 S **13** 19) is an expression of sadness and mourning, as we see from Egyp representations of scenes of mourning. Both in joy and in anger hands are "smitten together" (Nu **24** 10), and people "clap their hands" at a person or over a person in spiteful triumph (Job **27** 23; Lam **2** 15; Nah **3** 19). "To put one's life into one's hand" is to risk one's life (1 S **19** 5; **28** 21). "To lay hands upon" is used in the sense of blessing (Mt **19** 13), or is symbolical in the act of miraculous healing (Mt **9** 18; Mk **8** 23; Acts **28** 8), or an emblem of the gift of the Holy Spirit and His endowments (Acts **8** 17–19; **13** 3; 1 Tim **4** 14; 2 Tim **1** 6); but it also designates the infliction of cruelty and punishment (Gen **37** 22; Lev **24** 14), the imposition of responsibility (Nu **8** 10; Dt **34** 9). Thus also the sins of the people were symbolically transferred upon the goat which was to be sent into the wilderness (Lev **16** 21). This act, rabbinical writings declare, was not so much a laying on of hands, as a vigorous pressing. "Lifting up the hand" was a gesture accompanying an oath (Dt **32** 40) or a blessing pronounced over a multitude (Lev **9** 22; Lk **24** 50), a prayer (Ps **119** 48). "To put the hands to the mouth" is indicative of (compulsory) silence (Job **21** 5; **40** 4; Prov **30** 32; Mic **7** 16). To "slack one's hand" is synonymous with negligence and neglect (Josh **10** 6), and "to hide or bury the hand in the dish" is descriptive of the slothful, who is tired even at meals (Prov **19** 24; **26** 15).

2. The Hand as Power

The hand in the sense of power and authority: (cf Assyr *îdu*, "strength"); Josh **8** 20 m, "They had no hands [RV "power"] to flee this way or that way"; Jgs **1** 35, "The hand of the house of Joseph prevailed"; Ps **76** 5, "None of the men of might have found their hands"; Ps **89** 48 m, "shall deliver his soul from the hand [RV "power"] of Sheol"; 2 K **3** 15, "The hand of Jeh came upon him"; Ex **14** 31 m, "Israel saw the great hand [RV "work"] which Jeh did upon the Egyptians"; Dt **34** 12, "in all the mighty hand . . . . which Moses wrought in the sight of all Israel."

3. The Hand for the Person

The hand used (*pars pro toto*) for the person: "His hand shall be against every man" (Gen **16** 12). "Slay the priests of Jeh; because their hand also is with David" (1 S **22** 17). "Jonathan went to David into the wood and strengthened his hand in God" (1 S **23** 16). In this sense penalty is exacted "from the hand" or "at the hand" of the transgressor (Gen **9** 5; Ezk **33** 8).

4. Hand, Meaning Side

The hand in the sense of side: "All the side [Heb "hand"] of the river Jabbok" (Dt **2** 37); "by the wayside" (Heb "by the hand of the way," 1 S **4** 13). The MSS have here the error יַךְ, *yakh*, for יַד, *yādh;* cf the Heb of Ps **140** 5[6] (לְיַד־מַעְגָּל, *l^eyādh ma'gāl*); "On the side [Heb "hand"] of their oppressors there was power" (Eccl **4** 1); "I was by the side [Heb "hand"] of the great river" (Dnl **10** 4).

5. English Idiom

Mention must also be made here of the Eng. idiom, "at hand," frequently found in our VSS of the Scriptures. In Heb and Gr there is no reference to the word "hand," but words designating nearness of time or place are used. The usual word in Heb is קָרַב, *ḳārabh*, "to be near," and קָרוֹב, *ḳārōbh*, "near"; in Gr ἐγγύς, *eggús*, "near," and the vb. ἐγγίζω, *eggízō*, "to come near." Rarely other words are used, as ἐνέστηκεν, *enéstēken*, "has come," ERV "is now present" (2 Thess **2** 2), and ἐφέστηκεν, *ephéstēken*, "is come" (2 Tim **4** 6).

Frequently the words refer to the "day" or "coming of the Lord"; still it must not be forgotten that it may often refer to the nearness of God in a local sense, as in Jer **23** 23, "Am I a God at hand, saith Jeh, and not a God afar off?" and probably in Phil **4** 5, "The Lord is at hand," though many, perhaps most, commentators regard the expression as a version of the Aram. μαρὰν ἀθά, *marán athá* (1 Cor **16** 22). Passages such as Ps **31** 20; **119** 151; Mt **28** 20 would, however, speak for an interpretation which lays the ictus on the abiding presence of the Lord with the believer.

NOTE.—The ancients made a careful distinction of the respective values of the two hands. This is perhaps best seen from Gen **48** 13–19, where the imposition of the hands of aged Israel upon the heads of Joseph's sons seems unfair to their father, because the left hand is being placed upon the elder, the right hand upon the younger son. The very word *euōnumos* proves the same from the Gr point of view. This word is a euphemistic synonym of *aristera*, and is used to avoid the unlucky omen the common word may have for the person spoken to. Thus the goats, i.e. the godless, are placed at the left hand of the great Judge, while the righteous appear at His right (Mt **25** 33). We read in Eccl **10** 2, "A wise man's heart is at his right hand; but a fool's heart at his left," i.e. is inclined to evil. As the Jews orientated themselves by looking toward the rising of the sun (Lat *oriens*, the east), the left hand represented the north, and the right hand the south (1 S **23** 19.24; 2 S **24** 5). The right hand was considered the more honorable (1 K **2** 19; Ps **45** 9); therefore it was given in attestation of a contract, a federation or fellowship (Gal **2** 9) It is the more valuable in battle; a friend or protector will therefore take his place at the right to guard it (Ps **16** 8; **73** 23; **109** 31; **110** 5; **121** 5), but the enemy will, for the same reason, try to assail it (Job **30** 12; Ps **109** 6; Zec **3** 1). It was also the unprotected side, because the shield was carried on the left arm: hence the point of danger and honor. The right hand is also the side of power and strength (Ps **60** 5; **63** 8; **108** 6; **118** 15.16; **110** 1; Mt **22** 44; Mt **20** 21.23). Both hands are mentioned together in the sense of close proximity, intimate association, in Mk **10** 37.

H. L. E. LUERING

HANDBREADTH, hand'bredth (טֶפַח, *ṭephaḥ*, טֹפַח, *ṭōphaḥ*, 1 K **7** 26; 2 Ch **4** 5; Ps **39** 5; Ex **25** 25; **37** 12; Ezk **40** 5.43; **43** 13): A Heb linear measure containing 4 fingers, or digits, and equal to about 3 in. See WEIGHTS AND MEASURES.

HANDFUL, hand'fo͝ol: There are five words in Heb used to indicate what may be held in the hand, either closed or open.

(1) חֹפֶן, *ḥōphen*, חָפְנַיִם, *ḥophnayim*. The *fist* or *closed* hand occurs in the dual in Ex **9** 8, where it signifies what can be taken in the two hands conjoined, a *double* handful.

(2) כַּף, *kaph*, "hollow of the hand," the palm; an open handful (Lev **9** 17; 1 K **17** 12; Eccl **4** 6).

(3) עָמִיר, *'āmīr*, "sheaf or bundle." It signifies the quantity of grain a gleaner may gather in his hand (Jer **9** 22 [Heb 21]).

(4) קֹמֶץ, *ḳōmeç*, "the *closed* handful" (Gen **41** 47; Lev **2** 2; **5** 12; **6** 15 [Heb **6** 8]; Nu **5** 26).

(5) שֹׁעַל, *shō'al*, "the hollow of the hand," or what can be held in it (1 K **20** 10; Ezk **13** 19). In Isa **40** 12 it signifies "measure."

(6) פִּסָּה, *piṣṣāh* (Ps **72** 16) is rendered "handful" by AV, but is properly "abundance" as in RV.

H. PORTER

HANDICRAFT, han'di-kraft. See CRAFTS.

HANDKERCHIEF, haṇ'kẽr-chif (σουδάριον, *soudárion*): A loan-word from the Lat *sudarium*, found in pl. in Acts **19** 12, *soudária;* cf *sudor*, "perspiration"; lit. "a cloth used to wipe off perspiration." Elsewhere it is rendered "napkin" (Lk **19** 20; Jn **11** 44; **20** 7), for which see DRESS; NAPKIN.

HANDLE, han'd'l (כַּף, *kaph*): The noun occurs once in Cant **5** 5, "handles of the bolt" (AV "lock"). The vb. "handle" represents several Heb (*'āḥaz, māshakh, tāphas*, etc) and Gr (θιγγάνω, *thiggánō*, Col **2** 21; ψηλαφάω, *psēlapháō*, Lk **24** 39; 1 Jn **1** 1) words in AV, but is also sometimes substituted in RV for other renderings in AV, as in Cant **3** 8 for "hold"; in Lk **20** 11, "handled shamefully," for "entreated shamefully"; in 2 Tim **2** 15, "handling aright," for "rightly dividing," etc.

HANDMAID, hand'mād: Which appears often in the OT, but seldom in the NT, like bondmaid, is used to translate two Heb words (שִׁפְחָה, *shiphḥāh*, and אָמָה, *'āmāh*), both of which normally mean a female slave. It is used to translate the former word in the ordinary sense of female slave in Gen **16** 1; **25** 12; **29** 24.29; Prov **30** 23; Jer **34** 11. 16; Joel **2** 29; to translate the latter word in Ex **23** 12; Jgs **19** 19; 2 S **6** 20. It is used as a term of humility and respectful self-depreciation in the presence of great men, prophets and kings, to translate the former word in Ruth **2** 13; 1 S **1** 18; **28** 21; 2 S **14** 6; 2 K **4** 2.16; it translates the latter word in the same sense in Ruth **3** 9; 1 S **1** 16; **25** 24.28.31.41; 2 S **20** 17; 1 K **1** 13.17; **3** 20. It is also used to express a sense of religious humility in translating the latter word only, and appears in this sense in but three passages, 1 S **1** 11; Ps **86** 16; **116** 16.

In the NT it occurs 3 t, in a religious sense, as the tr of δούλη, *doúlē*, "a female slave" (Lk **1** 38.48; Acts **2** 18), and twice (Gal **4** 22.23) as the tr of παιδίσκη, *paidískē*, AV "bondmaid."

WILLIAM JOSEPH MCGLOTHLIN

HANDS, IMPOSITION, im-pō-zish'un **(LAYING ON), OF** (**ἐπίθεσις χειρῶν**, *epíthesis cheirōn*, Acts **8** 18; 1 Tim **4** 14; 2 Tim **1** 6; He **6** 2): The act or ceremony of the imposition of hands appears in the OT in various connections: in the act of blessing (Gen **48** 14 ff); in the ritual of sacrifice (hands of the offerer laid on head of victim, Ex **29** 10.15.19; Lev **1** 4; **3** 2.8.13; **4** 4.24.29; **8** 14; **16** 21); in witness-bearing in capital offences (Lev **24** 14). The tribe of Levi was set apart by solemn imposition of hands (Nu **8** 10); Moses appointed Joshua to be his successor by a similar act (Nu **27** 18.23; Dt **34** 9). The idea in these cases varies with the purpose of the act. The primary idea seems to be that of conveyance or transference (cf Lev **16** 21), but, conjoined with this, in certain instances, are the ideas of identification and of devotion to God.

In the NT Jesus laid hands on the little children (Mt **19** 13.15 ‖ Mk **10** 16) and on the sick (Mt **9** 18; Mk **6** 5, etc), and the apostles laid hands on those whom they baptized that they might receive the Holy Spirit (Acts **8** 17.19; **19** 6), and in healing (Acts **12** 17). Specially the imposition of hands was used in the setting apart of persons to a particular office or work in the church. This is noticed as taking place in the appointment of the Seven (Acts **6** 6), in the sending out of Barnabas and Saul (Acts **13** 3), at the ordination of Timothy (1 Tim **4** 14; 2 Tim **1** 6), but though not directly mentioned, it seems likely that it accompanied all acts of ordination of presbyters and deacons (cf **1** Tim **5** 22; He **6** 2). The presbyters could hardly convey what they had not themselves received (1 Tim **1** 14). Here again the fundamental idea is communication. The act of laying on of hands was accompanied by prayer (Acts **6** 6; **8** 15; **13** 3), and the blessing sought was imparted by God Himself. No ground is afforded by this symbolical action for a sacrament of "Orders." See SACRIFICE; MINISTRY; ORDINATION.

JAMES ORR

HANDSTAFF, hand'staf (מַקֵּל יָד, *maḳḳēl yādh*): In pl. in Ezk **39** 9, among weapons of war. See STAFF.

HAND WEAPON, hand'wep'un (Nu **35** 18 AV). See ARMOR.

HANDWRITING, hand'rīt-ing. See WRITING; MANUSCRIPTS.

HANES, hā'nēz (חָנֵס, *ḥānēṣ*): Occurs only in Isa **30** 4. The one question of importance concerning this place is its location. It has never been certainly identified. It was probably an Egyp city, though even that is not certain. Pharaoh, in his selfish haste to make league with the kingdom of Judah, may have sent his ambassadors far beyond the frontier. The language of Isa, "Their ambassadors came to H.," certainly seems to indicate a place in the direction of Jerus from Tanis. This indication is also the sum of all the evidence yet available. There is no real knowledge concerning the exact location of H. Opinions on the subject are little more than clever guesses. They rest almost entirely upon etymological grounds, a very precarious foundation when not supported by historical evidence. The LXX has, "For there are in Tanis princes, wicked messengers." Evidently knowing no such place, they tried to translate the name. The Aram. version gives "Tahpanhes" for H., which may have been founded upon exact knowledge, as we shall see.

H. has been thought by some commentators to be Heracleopolis Magna, Egyp *Hunensuten*, abridged to *Hunensu*, Copt *Ahnes*, Heb *Ḥānēṣ*, Arab. *Ahneysa*, the capital of the XXth Nome, or province, of ancient Egypt. It was a large city on an island between the Nile and the Bahr Yuseph, opposite the modern town of *Beni Suef*. The Greeks identified the ram-headed god of the place with Heracles, hence, "Heracleopolis." The most important historical notes in Egypt and the best philological arguments point to this city as H. But the plain meaning of Isa **30** 4 points more positively to a city somewhere in the delta nearer to Jerus than Tanis (cf Naville's cogent argument, "Ahnas el Medineh," 3–4). Dumichen considered the hieroglyphic name of Tahpanhes to be Hens. Knowledge of this as a fact may have influenced the Aram. rendering, but does not warrant the arbitrary altering of the Heb text.

M. G. KYLE

HANGING, hang'ing (תָּלָה, *tālāh*, "to hang up," "suspend," 2 S **21** 12; Dt **28** 66; Job **26** 7; Ps **137** 2; Cant **4** 4; Hos **11** 7): Generally, where the word is used in connection with punishments, it appears to have reference to the hanging of the corpse after execution. We find but two clear instances of death by hanging, i.e. strangulation—those of Ahithophel and Judas ((2 S **17** 23; Mt **27** 5), and both these were cases of suicide, not of execution. The foregoing Heb word is clearly used for "hanging" as a mode of execution in Est **5** 14; **6** 4; **7** 9 ff; **8** 7; **9** 13.14.25; but probably the "gallows" or "tree" (עֵץ, *'ēç*) was a stake for the purpose of impaling the victim. It could be lowered for this purpose, then raised "fifty cubits high" to arrest the public gaze. The Gr word used in Mt **27** 5 is ἀπάγχεσθαι, *apágchesthai*, "to strangle oneself." See *HDB*, art. "Hanging," for an exhaustive discussion.

FRANK E. HIRSCH

HANGINGS, hang'ingz:

(1) In EV this word in the pl. represents the Heb קְלָעִים, *ḳelā'īm*, the curtains of "fine twined linen" with which the court of the tabernacle was inclosed.

These were five cubits in height, and of lengths corresponding to the sides of the inclosure and the space on either side of the entrance in front, and were suspended from hooks fastened to the pillars of the court. They are described at length in Ex **27** 9–15; **38** 9–18. See, besides, Ex **35** 17; **39** 40; Nu **3** 26; **4** 26.

(2) In AV another word, *māṣākh* (RV uniformly "screen"), is distinguished from the preceding only by the singular, "hanging" (Ex **35** 17; **38** 18, etc). It is used of the screen or portière, embroidered in colors, that closed the entrance of the court (Ex **27** 16; **35** 17; **38** 18; **39** 40; **40** 8.33; Nu **3** 26; **4** 26); of the screen of similar workmanship at the entrance of the tabernacle (Ex **26** 36.37; **35** 15; **36** 37; **39** 38; **40** 5.28; Nu **3** 25; **4** 25); and once (Nu **3** 31) of the tapestry veil, adorned with cherubim, at the entrance of the Holy of Holies (elsewhere, *pārōkheth*, "veil," Ex **26** 31–33, etc, or *pārōkheth ha-māṣākh*, "veil of the screen," Ex **35** 12, etc). In Nu **3** 26, AV renders *māṣākh* "curtain," and in Ex **35** 12; **39** 34; **40** 21 (cf also Nu **4** 5), "covering."

(3) In 2 K **23** 7 we read of "hangings" (Heb "houses") which the women wove for the Asherah. If the text is correct we are to think perhaps of *tent shrines* for the image of the goddess. Lucian's reading (*stolás*, "robes") is preferred by some, which would have reference to the custom of bringing offerings of clothing for the images of the gods. In 1 K **7** 29 RV, "wreaths of hanging work" refers to a kind of ornamentation on the bases of the lavers. In Est **1** 6, "hangings" is supplied by the translators. Benjamin Reno Downer

HANIEL, han′i-el. See Hanniel.

HANNAH, han′a (חַנָּה, *ḥannāh*, "grace," "favor"; Ἄννα, *Hánna*): One of the two wives of Elkanah, an Ephraimite who lived at Ramathaim-zophim. Hannah visited Shiloh yearly with her husband to offer sacrifices, for there the tabernacle was located. She was greatly distressed because they had no children. She therefore prayed earnestly for a male child whom she promised to dedicate to the Lord from his birth. The prayer was heard, and she called her son's name Samuel ("God hears"). When he was weaned he was carried to Shiloh to be trained by Eli, the priest (1 S **1**). Hannah became the mother of five other children, three sons and two daughters (**2** 2). Her devotion in sending Samuel a little robe every year is one of the tenderest recorded instances of maternal love (**2** 19). She was a prophetess of no ordinary talent, as is evident from her elevated poetic deliverance elicited by God's answer to her prayer (**2** 1–10). Byron H. DeMent

HANNATHON, han′a-thon (חַנָּתֹן, *hannāthōn*): A city on the northern boundary of Zebulun (Josh **19** 14). It is probably identical with Kefar Hananyah, which the Mish gives as marking the northern limit of lower Galilee (Neubauer, *Géog. du Talm*, 179). It is represented by the modern *Kefr ʿAnān*, about 3 miles S.E. of *er-Rāmeh*.

HANNIEL, han′i-el (חַנִּיאֵל, *ḥannī′ēl*, "grace of God"):

(1) The son of Ephod and a prince of Manasseh who assisted in dividing Canaan among the tribes (Nu **34** 23).

(2) A son of Ulla and a prince and hero of the tribe of Asher (1 Ch **7** 39); AV "Haniel."

HANOCH, hā′nok, **HANOCHITES,** hā′nok-īts (חֲנוֹךְ, *ḥănōkh*, "initiation," "dedication"):

(1) A grandson of Abraham by Keturah, and an ancestral head of a clan of Midian (Gen **25** 4; 1 Ch **1** 33, AV "Henoch").

(2) The eldest son of Reuben (Gen **46** 9; Ex **6** 14; 1 Ch **5** 3).

The descendants of Hanoch were known as **Hanochites** (Nu **26** 5).

HANUN, hā′nun (חָנוּן, *ḥānūn*, "favored," "pitied"):

(1) A son and successor of Nahash, king of Ammon. Upon the death of Nahash, David sent sympathetic communications to Hanun, which were misinterpreted and the messengers dishonored. Because of this indignity, David waged a war against him, which caused the Ammonites to lose their independence (2 S **10** 1 ff; 1 Ch **19** 1 ff).

(2) One of the six sons of Zalaph who assisted in repairing the E. wall of Jerus (Neh **3** 30).

(3) One of the inhabitants of Zanoah who repaired the Valley Gate in the wall of Jerus (Neh **3** 13). Byron H. DeMent

HAP, hap, **HAPLY,** hap′li (מִקְרֶה, *miḳreh*, לוּ, *lū*; μήποτε, *mēpote*):

Hap (a Saxon word for "luck, chance") is the tr of *miḳreh*, "a fortuitous chance," "a lot" (Ruth **2** 3, AV "Her hap was to light on a part of the field belonging unto Boaz"); in **1 S 6** 9, the same word is tr[d] "chance" (that happened); "event," in Eccl **9** 2.3, with "happeneth," in **2** 14.

Haply (from "hap") is the tr of *lū*, "if that" (1 S **14** 30, "if haply the people had eaten freely"); of *ei ára*, "if then" (Mk **11** 13, "if haply he might find anything thereon"); of *ei árage* (Acts **17** 27, "if haply they might feel after him"); of *mēpote*, "lest ever," "lest perhaps," etc (Lk **14** 29; Acts **5** 39); of *mē pōs*, "lest in any way" (2 Cor **9** 4 AV, "lest haply," RV "lest by any means").

RV has "haply" for "at any time" (Mt **4** 6; **5** 25; **13** 15; Mk **4** 12; Lk **4** 11; **21** 34; He **2** 1); introduces "haply" (Mt **7** 6; **13** 29; **15** 32; **27** 64; Mk **14** 2; Lk **3** 15; **12** 58; **14** 8.12; Acts **27** 29; He **4** 1); has "haply there shall be," for "lest there be" (He **3** 12). W. L. Walker

HAPHARAIM, haf-a-rā′im (חֲפָרַיִם, *ḥăphārayim*; AV **Haphraim,** haf-rā′im, possibly "place of a moat"): A town in the territory of Issachar, named with Shunem and Anaharath (Josh **19** 19). *Onom* identifies it with "Affarea," and places it 6 miles N. of Legio-Megiddo. This position corresponds with that of the modern *el-Ferrīyeh*, an ancient site with remarkable tombs N.W. of *el-Lejjūn*.

HAPPEN, hap′'n (קָרָה, *ḳārāh*; συμβαίνω, *sumbainō*): "Happen" (from "hap"), "to fall out," "befall," etc, "come to anyone," is the tr of *ḳārāh*, "to meet," etc (1 S **28** 10, "There shall no punishment happen to thee," RVm "guilt come upon thee"; 2 S **1** 6; Est **4** 7; Eccl **2** 14.15; **9** 11 Isa **41** 22); of *ḳārā′*, "to meet," "cause to happen," etc (2 S **20** 1); of *hāyāh*, "to be" (1 S **6** 9, "It was a chance that happened to us"); of *nāghaʿ*, "to touch," "to come to" (Eccl **8** 14 *bis*). In the NT it is in several instances the tr of *sumbainō*, "to go" or "come up together," "to happen" (Mk **10** 32; Lk **24** 14; Acts **3** 10; 1 Cor **10** 11; 1 Pet **4** 12; 2 Pet **2** 22); once of *ginomai*, "to become," "to happen" (Rom **11** 25, RV "befallen"). "Happeneth" occurs (Eccl **2** 15, "as it happeneth to the fool" [*miḳreh*]; 2 Esd **10** 6; Bar **3** 10 [*tí estin*]). RV supplies "that happened" for "were done" (Lk **24** 35). See also Chance. W. L. Walker

HAPPINESS, hap′i-nes. See Blessedness.

HAPPIZZEZ, hap′i-zez (הַפִּצֵּץ, *ha-piççēç*; AV **Aphses**): A priest on whom fell the lot for the 18th of the 24 courses which David appointed for the temple service (1 Ch **24** 15).

HARA, hā'ra (הָרָא, *hārā';* LXX omits): A place named in 1 Ch **5** 26 along with Halah, Habor and the river of Gozan, whither the Reubenites, the Gadites and the half-tribe of Manasseh were carried by Tiglath-pileser. In 2 K **17** 6; **18** 11, Hara is omitted, and in both, "and in the cities of the Medes" is added. LXX renders ὄρη Μήδων, *órē Mḗdōn,* "the mountains of the Medes," which may represent Heb הָרֵי מָדַי, *hārē mādhay,* "mountains of Media," or, עָרֵי מָדַי, *'ārē mādhay,* "cities of Media." The text seems to be corrupt. The second word may have fallen out in 1 Ch **5** 26, *hārē* being changed to *hārā'*. W. Ewing

HARADAH, ha-rā'da, har'a-dä (חֲרָדָה, *ḥărādhāh,* "fearful"): A desert station of the Israelites between Mt. Shepher and Makheloth (Nu **33** 24 25). See Wanderings of Israel.

HARAN, hā'ran (הָרָן, *hārān*):

(1) Son of Terah, younger brother of Abraham and Nahor, and father of Lot (Gen **11** 27). He had two daughters, Milcah and Iscah (ver 29).

(2) A Gershonite, of the family of Shimei (1 Ch **23** 9).

HARAN, hā'ran (חָרָן, *ḥārān;* Χαῤῥάν, *Charhrán*): The city where Terah settled on his departure from Ur (Gen **11** 31 f); whence Abram set out on his pilgrimage of faith to Canaan (**12** 1 ff). It was probably "the city of Nahor" to which Abraham's servant came to find a wife for Isaac (**24** 10 ff). Hither came Jacob when he fled from Esau's anger (**27** 43). Here he met his bride (**29** 4), and in the neighboring pastures he tended the flocks of Laban. It is one of the cities named by Rabshakeh as destroyed by the king of Assyria (2 K **19** 12; Isa **37** 12). Ezekiel speaks of the merchants of Haran as trading with Tyre (**27** 23).

The name appears in Assyro-Bab as *Ḥarran,* which means "road"; possibly because here the trade route from Damascus joined that from Nineveh to Carchemish. It is mentioned in the prism inscription of Tiglath-pileser I. It was a seat of the worship of Sin, the moon-god, from very ancient times. A temple was built by Shalmaneser II. Haran seems to have shared in the rebellion of Assur (763 BC, the year of the solar eclipse, June 15). The privileges then lost were restored by Sargon II. The temple, which had been destroyed, was rebuilt by Ashurbanipal, who was here crowned with the crown of Sin. Haran and the temple suffered much damage in the invasion of the Umman-Manda (the Medes). Nabuna'id restored temple and city, adorning them on a lavish scale. Near Haran the Parthians defeated and slew Crassus (53 BC), and here Caracalla was assassinated (217 AD). In the 4th cent. it was the seat of a bishopric; but the cult of the moon persisted far into the Christian centuries. The chief temple was the scene of heathen worship until the 11th cent., and was destroyed by the Mongols in the 13th.

The ancient city is represented by the modern *Ḥarrān* to the S.E. of Edessa, on the river Belias, an affluent of the Euphrates. The ruins lie on both sides of the stream, and include those of a very ancient castle, built of great basaltic blocks, with square columns, 8 ft. thick, which support an arched roof some 30 ft. in height. Remains of the old cathedral are also conspicuous. No inscriptions have yet been found here, but a fragment of an Assyr lion has been uncovered. A well nearby is identified as that where Eliezer met Rebekah.

In Acts **7** 2.4, AV gives the name as Charran.
W. Ewing

HARARITE, hā'ra-rīt (הַהֲרָרִי, *ha-hărārī,* or הָאֲרָרִי, *hā-'ărārī*): Lit. "mountaineer," more particularly an inhabitant of the hill country of Judah. Thus used of two heroes:

(1) Shammah, the son of Agee (2 S **23** 11.33). The ‖ passage, 1 Ch **11** 34, has "Shage" in place of "Shammah."

(2) Ahiam, the son of Sharar the Ararite (2 S **23** 33). In 1 Ch **11** 35, "Sacar" for Sharar as here.

HARBONA, HARBONAH, här-bō'na (חַרְבוֹנָא, *ḥar^ebhōnā',* חַרְבוֹנָה, *ḥar^ebhōnāh*): One of the seven eunuchs who served Ahasuerus and to whom was given the command to bring Queen Esther before the king (Est **1** 10). It was he who suggested that Haman be hanged upon the self-same gallows that he had erected for Mordecai (**7** 9). Jewish tradition has it that Harbona had originally been a confederate of Haman, but, upon noting the failure of the latter's plans, abandoned him. The Pers equivalent of the name means "donkey-driver."

HARBOUR, här'bẽr. Used **figuratively** of God in Joel **3** 16 AVm, "Heb, place of repair. *or,* harbour" (AV "hope," RV "refuge"). See Haven; Ships and Boats, I, II, (1), II, 3.

HARD, härd, **HARDINESS,** här'di-nes, **HARDNESS,** härd'nes, **HARDLY,** härd'li (קָשֶׁה, *ḳāsheh,* פָּלָא, *pālā';* σκληρός, *sklērós*): The senses in which **hard** is used may be distinguished as:

(1) "Firm," "stiff," opposite to soft: Job **41** 24, *yāçaḳ,* "to be firm," "his heart . . . . as hard as a piece of the nether millstone," RV "firm"; Ezk **3** 7, *ḳāsheh,* "sharp," "hard of heart"; *ḥāzāḳ,* "firm," "As an adamant harder than flint have I made thy forehead"; Jer **5** 3, "They have made their faces harder than a rock"; Prov **21** 29, *'āzaz,* "to make strong," "hard," "impudent," "a wicked man hardeneth his face"; Prov **13** 15 probably belongs here also where *'ēthān* is tr[d] "hard": "The way of the transgressor is hard," ERV "The way of the treacherous is rugged"; the Heb word means, "lasting," "firm," poet. "rocks" (the earth's foundations, Mic **6** 2), and the meaning seems to be, not that the way (path) of transgressors, or the treacherous (Delitzsch has "uncultivated"), is hard (rocky) to them, but that *their* way, or mode of acting, is *hard,* unsympathetic, unkind, "destitute of feeling in things which, as we say, would soften a stone" (Delitzsch on passage); also Mt **25** 24, *sklēros,* "stiff," "thou art a hard man"; Wisd **11** 4, *sklēros,* "hard stone," RV "flinty rock," m "the steep rock."

(2) "Sore," "trying," "painful," *ḳāsheh* (Ex **1** 14, "hard service"; Dt **26** 6; 2 S **3** 39; Ps **60** 3; Isa **14** 3); *ḳāshāh,* "to have it hard" (Gen **35** 16.17; Dt **15** 18); *'āthāḳ,* "stiff" (Ps **94** 4 AV, "They utter and speak hard things"); *sklēros* (Jn **6** 60, "This is a hard saying"—hard to accept, hard in its nature; Acts **9** 5 AV; **26** 14; Jude ver 15, "hard speeches"; Wisd **19** 13).

(3) "Heavy," "pressing hard," *kābhēdh,* "weighty" (Ezk **3** 5.6, "a people of a strange speech and of a hard language," RVm "Heb deep of lip and heavy of tongue"); *ṣāmakh,* "to lay" (Ps **88** 7, "Thy wrath lieth hard upon me").

(4) "Difficult," "hard to do," "know," etc, *pālā',* "difficult to be done" (Gen **18** 14, "Is anything too hard for Jeh?"; Jer **32** 17.27; Dt **17** 8; 2 S **13** 2); *ḳāsheh* (Ex **18** 26, "hard causes"); *ḳāshāh* (Dt **1** 17; 2 K **2** 10); *ḥīdhāh,* "something twisted,"

"involved," "an enigma"; cf Jgs **14** 14 (1 K **10** 1; 2 Ch **9** 1, "to prove Solomon with hard questions"); *'ăḥīdhān*, Aram. (Dnl **5** 12); *dúskolos*, lit. "difficult about food," "hard to please," hence "difficult to accomplish" (Mk **10** 24, "How hard is it for them that trust in riches to enter into the kingdom of God"); *dusnóētos*, "hard to be understood" (He **5** 11; 2 Pet **3** 16; cf Ecclus **3** 21, "things too hard for thee," *chalepós*).

(5) "Close," or "near to" (hard by), *nāghash*, "to come nigh" (Jgs **9** 52, ARV "near"); *dābhāḳ* and *dābhēḳ*, "to follow hard after" (Jgs **20** 45; Ps **63** 8, etc); *'ēçel*, "near" (1 K **21** 1); *le'ummath*, "over against" (Lev **3** 9); *'adh*, "to" "even to" (1 Ch **19** 4, AV "hard by," RV "even to").

Hardiness occurs in Jth **16** 10 (*thrásos*), RV "boldness."

Hardness is the tr of *mūçāḳ*, "something poured out," "dust wetted," "running into clods" (Job **38** 38), RV "runneth into a mass"; "hardness of heart" occurs in the Gospels; in Mk **3** 5, it is *pṓrōsis*, "hardness," "callousness"; Mt **19** 8; Mk **10** 5; **16** 14, *sklērokardía*, "dryness," "stiffness of heart"; cf Ecclus **16** 10; in Rom **2** 5, it is *sklērótēs;* in 2 Tim **2** 3 AV we have, "Endure hardness, as a good soldier of Jesus Christ," RV "Suffer hardship with me" (corrected text), m "Take thy part in suffering hardship" (*kakopathéō*, "to suffer evil").

Hardly occurs in the OT (Ex **13** 15), "Pharaoh would hardly let us go," *ḳāshāh*, lit. "hardened to let us go," RVm "hardened himself against letting us go"; "hardly bestead" (Isa **8** 21) is the tr of *ḳāshāh*, ARV "sore distressed." In the NT "hardly" is the tr of *duskólōs*, "hard to please," "difficult," meaning not *scarcely* or *barely*, but *with difficulty* (Mt **19** 23, "A rich man shall hardly enter into the kingdom of heaven," RV "it is hard for"; Mk **10** 23; Lk **18** 24, "how hardly" ["with what difficulty"]); of *mógis*, "with labor," "pain," "trouble" (Lk **9** 39, "hardly departeth from him" ["painfully"]); of *mólis* "with toil and fatigue" (Acts **27** 8, RV "with difficulty"; Wisd **9** 16, "Hardly do we guess aright at things that are upon earth"; Ecclus **26** 29, "A merchant shall hardly keep himself from wrong doing"; **29** 6, "He shall hardly receive the half," in each instance the word is *molis*, but in the last two instances we seem to see the transition to "scarcely"; cf also Ex **13** 15).

RV has "too hard" for "hidden" (Dt **30** 11, m "wonderful"); "hardness" for "boldness" (of face) (Eccl **8** 1); for "sorrow" (Lam **3** 65); "deal hardly with me" for "make yourselves strong to me" (Job **19** 3); omits "It is hard for thee to kick against the pricks" (Acts **9** 5, corrected text); "hardship" for "trouble" (2 Tim **2** 9).

W. L. WALKER

HARDEN, här'd'n (חָזַק, *ḥāzaḳ*, קָשָׁה, *ḳāshāh;* **σκληρύνω**, *sklērúnō*):

(1) "Harden" occurs most frequently in the phrase "to harden the heart," or "the neck." This hardening of men's hearts is attributed both to God and to men themselves, e.g. with reference to the hearts of Pharaoh and the Egyptians; the Hiphil of *ḥāzaḳ*, "to make strong," is frequently used in this connection (Ex **4** 21, "I will harden his heart," RVm "Heb make strong"; **7** 13, "And he hardened P.'s heart," RV "was hardened," m "Heb was strong"; **7** 22; **8** 19; **9** 12; **10** 20.27, etc; **14** 17, "I will harden the hearts of the Egyptians," RVm "Heb make strong"; cf Josh **11** 20); *ḳāshāh*, "to be heavy," "to make hard" (Ex **7** 3); *kābhēdh*, "heavy," "slow," "hard," not easily moved (Ex **10** 1, RVm "Heb made heavy"). When the hardening is attributed to man's own act *kābhēdh* is generally used (Ex **8** 15, "He hardened his heart, and hearkened not," RVm "Heb made heavy"; **8** 32, "Pharaoh hardened his heart" [RVm as before]; **9** 7.34; 1 S **6** 6 *bis*). The "hardening" of men's hearts by God is in the way of punishment, but it is always a consequence of their own self-hardening. In Pharaoh's case we read that "he hardened his heart" against the appeal to free the Israelites; so hardening himself, he became always more confirmed in his obstinacy, till he brought the final doom upon himself. This is how sin is made to become its own punishment. It was not confined to Pharaoh and the Egyptians, nor does it belong to the past only. As St. Paul says (Rom **9** 18), "Whom he will he hardeneth" (*sklērunō*); **11** 7, "The election obtained it, and the rest were hardened" (RV and AVm, *pōróō*, "to make hard" or "callous"); ver 25, a "Hardening in part hath befallen Israel" (*pṓrōsis*); cf Jn **12** 40 (from Isa **6** 10), "He hath blinded their eyes, and he hardened their heart"; Isa **63** 17, "O Jeh, why dost thou make us to err from thy ways, and hardenest our heart from thy fear?" (*ḳāshaḥ*, "to harden"); cf on the other side, as expressing the human blameworthiness, Job **9** 4, "Who hath hardened himself against him, and prospered?" Mk **3** 5, "being grieved at the hardening of their heart"; **6** 52, "Their heart was hardened"; Rom **2** 5, "after thy hardness and impenitent heart." In Heb religious thought everything was directly attributed to God, and the hardening *is* God's work, in His physical and ethical constitution and laws of man's nature; but it is always the consequence of human action out of harmony therewith. Other instances of *sklērunō* are in Acts **19** 9; He **3** 8.13. 15; **4** 7.

(2) "Harden" in the sense of "to fortify one's self" (make one's self hard) is the tr of *ṣāladh*, "to leap," "exult" (Job **6** 10 AV, "I would harden myself in sorrow," RV "Let me exult in pain," m "harden myself").

(3) In Prov **21** 29 "harden" has the meaning of "boldness," "defiance" or "shamelessness" (brazen-faced); *'āzaz*, Hiphil, "to strengthen one's countenance," "A wicked man hardeneth his face"; Delitzsch, "A godless man showeth boldness in his mien"; cf **7** 13; Eccl **8** 1; see also HARD.

For "harden" RV has "stubborn" (Ex **7** 14; **9** 7, m "heavy"); "hardenest" (Isa **63** 17); "made stiff" (Jer **7** 26; **19** 15); for "is hardened" (Job **39** 16, ARV "dealeth hardly," and ERVm); "at the hardening" instead of "for the hardness" (Mk **3** 5); "hardening" for "blindness" (Eph **4** 18).

W. L. WALKER

HARDLY, HARDNESS. See HARD.

HARD SAYINGS, sā'ingz; **HARD SENTENCES,** sen'ten-siz: In Dnl **5** 12 AV (Aram. אֲחִידָן, *'ăḥīdhān*), RV "dark sentences," of enigmatic utterances which preternatural wisdom was needed to interpret; in Jn **6** 60 (σκληρός . . . . ὁ λόγος, *sklērós* . . . . *ho lógos*), of sayings (Christ's words at Capernaum about eating His flesh and drinking His blood) difficult for the natural mind to understand (cf ver 52).

HARE, hâr (אַרְנֶבֶת, *'arnebheth* [Lev **11** 6; Dt **14** 7]; cf Arab. أَرْنَب, *'arnab*, "hare"): This animal is mentioned only in the lists of unclean animals in Lev and Dt, where it occurs along with the camel, the coney and the swine. The camel, the hare and the coney are unclean, 'because they chew the cud but part not the hoof,' the swine, "because he parteth the hoof . . . . but cheweth not the cud." The hare and the coney are not ruminants, but might be supposed to be from their habit of almost continually moving their jaws. Both are freely eaten by the Arabs. Although *'arnebheth* occurs only in the two places cited, there is no doubt that it is the hare. LXX has δασύποδα, *dasúpous*, "rough-footed," which, while not the commonest Gr word (λαγῶς, *lagōs*), refers to the remarkable fact that in hares and rabbits the soles of the feet are densely covered with hair. *'Arnab*, which is the common Arab. word for "hare," is from the same root as the Heb *'arnebheth*.

Lev **11** 4–7: ver 4, EV "camel"; LXX τὸν κάμηλον, *tón kámēlon;* Vulg *camelus;* Heb הַגָּמָל, *ha-gāmāl*. Ver 5, EV "coney"; LXX τὸν δασύποδα, *tón dasúpoda;* Vulg *choerogryllus;* Heb הַשָּׁפָן, *ha-shāphān*. Ver 6, EV "hare"; LXX τὸν χοιρογρύλλιον, *tón choirogrúllion;* Vulg *lepus;* Heb הָאַרְנֶבֶת, *ha-'arnebheth*. Ver 7, EV "swine"; LXX τὸν ὗν, *tón hún;* Vulg *sus;* Heb הַחֲזִיר, *ha-ḥăzīr*.

Dt **14** 7: EV "camel"; LXX τὸν κάμηλον; Vulg *camelum;* Heb הַגָּמָל; EV "hare"; LXX δασύποδα; Vulg *leporem;* Heb הָאַרְנֶבֶת; EV "coney"; LXX χοιρογρύλλιον; Vulg *choerogryllum;* Heb הַשָּׁפָן.

Dt **14** 8: EV "swine"; LXX τὸν ὗν; Vulg *sus;* Heb הַחֲזִיר.

It is evident from the above and from the meanings of δασύπους and χοιρογρύλλιος as given in Liddell and Scott, that the order of LXX in Lev **11** 5.6 does not follow the Heb, but has apparently assimilated the order of that of Dt **14** 7.8. In Ps **104** 18, LXX has χοιρογρύλλιος for שָׁפָן; also in Prov **30** 26.

As the word "coney," which properly means "rabbit," has been applied to the hyrax, so, in America at least, the word "rabbit" is widely used for various species of hare, e.g. the gray rabbit and the jack-rabbit, both of which are hares. Hares have longer legs and ears and are swifter than rabbits. Their young are hairy and have their eyes open, while rabbits are born naked and blind. Hares are widely distributed in the Northern Hemisphere, and there is one species in South America. Rabbits are apparently native to the Western Mediterranean countries, although they have been distributed by man all over the world.

Lepus syriacus, the common hare of Syria and Pal, differs somewhat from the European hare. *Lepus judeae* is cited by Tristram from Northeastern Pal, and he also notes three other species from the extreme south. ALFRED ELY DAY

HAREPH, hā'ref (חָרֵף, *ḥārēph*, "scornful"): A chief of Judah, one of the sons of Caleb and father of Beth-gader (1 Ch **2** 51). A quite similar name, Hariph, occurs in Neh **7** 24; **10** 19, but it is probably that of another individual.

HARETH, hā'reth (חָרֶת, *ḥāreth*, in pause). See HERETH.

HARHAIAH, här-hā'ya (חַרְהֲיָה, *ḥarhăyāh*, "Jeh protects"): A goldsmith, whose son, Uzziel, helped to repair the walls of Jerus under Zerubbabel (Neh **3** 8).

HARHAS, här'has (חַרְחַס, *ḥarḥaṣ*, "splendor"): Grandfather of Shallum, husband of Huldah (2 K **22** 14). Name given as "Hasrah" in ‖ passage (2 Ch **34** 22).

HARHUR, här'hur (חַרְחוּר, *ḥarḥur*, "free-born" or "fever"; Ἁσουρ, *Hásour*): One of the Nethinim whose descendants came from Babylon with Zerubbabel (Ezr **2** 51; Neh **7** 53; 1 Esd **5** 31).

HARIM, hā'rim (חָרִם, *ḥārim*): A family name. (1) A non-priestly family that returned from captivity with Zerubbabel (Ezr **2** 32; Neh **7** 35); mentioned among those who married foreign wives (Ezr **10** 31); also mentioned among those who renewed the covenant (Neh **10** 27).

(2) A priestly family returning with Zerubbabel (Ezr **2** 39; Neh **7** 42; **12** 3.15 [see REHUM]); members of this family covenanted to put away their foreign wives (Ezr **10** 21; Neh **10** 5). A family of this name appears as the third of the priestly courses in the days of David and Solomon (1 Ch **24** 8).

(3) In Neh **3** 11 is mentioned Malchijah, son of Harim, one of the wall-builders. Which family is here designated is uncertain. W. N. STEARNS

HARIPH, hā'rif (חָרִיף, *ḥarīph*, חָרִף, *ḥariph*): One of those who returned from exile under Zerubbabel and helped to seal the covenant under Nehemiah and Ezra (Neh **7** 24; **10** 19 [20]). Ezr **2** 18 has "Jorah."

HARLOT, här'lot: This name replaces in RV "whore" of AV. It stands for several words and phrases used to designate or describe the unchaste woman, married or unmarried, e.g. זוֹנָה, *zōnāh*, אִשָּׁה נָכְרִיָּה, *'ishshāh nokhrīyāh*, קְדֵשָׁה, *ḳedhēshāh;* LXX and NT πόρνη, *pórnē*. πορνεία, *porneía* is used chiefly of prenuptial immorality, but the married woman guilty of sexual immorality is said to be guilty of *porneia* (Mt **5** 32; **19** 9; cf Am **7** 17 LXX). These and cognate words are applied esp. in the OT to those devoted to immoral service in idol sanctuaries, or given over to a dissolute life for gain. Such a class existed among all ancient peoples, and may be traced in the history of Israel. Evidence of its existence in very early times is found (Gen **38**). It grew out of conditions, sexual and social, which were universal. After the corrupting foreign influxes and influences of Solomon's day, it developed to even fuller shamelessness, and its voluptuous songs (Isa **23** 16), seductive arts (Prov **6** 24), and blighting influence are vividly pictured and denounced by the prophets (Prov **7** 10; **29** 3; Isa **23** 16; Jer **3** 3; **5** 7; Ezk **16** 25; cf Dt **23** 17). Money was lavished upon women of this class, and the weak and unwary were taken captive by them, so that it became one of the chief concerns of the devout father in Israel to "keep [his son] from the evil woman," who "hunteth for the precious life" (Prov **6** 24.26). From the title given her in Prov, a "foreign woman" (**23** 27), and the warnings against "the flattery of the foreigner's tongue" (**6** 24; cf 1 K **11** 1; Ezr **10** 2), we may infer that in later times this class was chiefly made up of strangers from without. The whole subject must be viewed in the setting of the times. Even in Israel, then, apart from breaches of marriage vows, immoral relations between the sexes were deemed venial (Dt **22** 28 f). A man was forbidden to compel his daughter to sin (Lev **19** 29), to "profane [her] and make her a harlot," but she was apparently left free to take that way herself (cf Gen **38**). The children of the harlot, though, were outlawed (Dt **23** 2), and later the harlot is found under the sternest social ban (Mt **21** 31.32).

The subject takes on even a darker hue when viewed in the light of the hideous conditions that prevailed in ancient Syria affecting this practice. The harlot represented more than a social peril and problem. She was a *ḳedhēshāh*, one of a consecrated class, and as such was the concrete expression and agent of the most insidious and powerful influence and system menacing the purity and permanence of the religion of Jeh. This system deified the reproductive organs and forces of Nature and its devotees worshipped their idol symbols in grossly licentious rites and orgies. The temple prostitute was invested with sanctity as a member of the religious caste, as she is today in India. Men and women thus prostituted themselves in the service of their gods. The Canaanite sanctuaries were gigantic brothels, legalized under the sanctions of religion. For a time, therefore, the supreme religious question was whether such a cult should be established and allowed to naturalize itself in Israel, as it had done in Babylon (Herod. i.199) and in Greece (Strabo viii.6). That the appeal thus made to the baser passions of the Israelites was all too successful is sadly clear (Am **2** 7; Hos **4** 13 ff). The prophets give vivid pictures of the syncretizing of the worship of Baal and Astarte with that of Jeh and the extent to which the local sanctuaries were given over to this form of corruption. They denounced it as the height of impiety and as sure to provoke Divine judgments. Asa and Jehoshaphat undertook to purge the land of such vile abominations (1 K **14** 24; **15** 12; **22** 46). The Dt code required that all such "paramours" be banished, and forbade the use of their unholy gains as temple revenue (Dt **23** 17.18, Driver's note). The Lev law forbade a priest to take a harlot to wife (Lev **21** 7), and commanded that the daughter of a priest who played the harlot should be burned (**21** 9). See Ashtoreth; Images; Idolatry.

It is grimly significant that the prophets denounce spiritual apostasy as "harlotry" (AV "whoredom"). But it would seem that the true ethical attitude toward prostitution was unattainable so long as marriage was in the low, transitional stage mirrored in the OT; though the religion of Jeh was in a measure delivered from the threatened peril by the fiery discipline of the exile.

In NT times, a kindred danger beset the followers of Christ, esp. in Greece and Asia Minor (Acts **15** 20.29; Rom **1** 24 ff; 1 Cor **6** 9 ff; Gal **5** 19). That lax views of sexual morality were widely prevalent in the generation in which Christ lived is evident both from His casual references to the subject and from His specific teaching in answer to questions concerning adultery and divorce (cf Jos, *Ant*, IV, viii, 23; *Vita*, § 76; Sir **7** 26; **25** 26; **42** 9, and the Talm). The ideas of the times were debased by the prevalent polygamous customs, "it being of old permitted to the Jews to marry many wives" (Jos, *BJ*, I, xxiv, 2; cf *Ant*, XVII, i, 2). The teaching of Jesus was in sharp contrast with the low ideals and the rabbinical teaching of the times. The controversy on this question waxed hot between the two famous rival rabbinical schools. Hillel reduced adultery to the level of the minor faults. Shammai opposed his teaching as immoral in tendency. Κατὰ πᾶσαν αἰτίαν, *katá pásan aitían* (Mt **19** 3), gives incidental evidence of the nature of the controversy. It was characteristic of the teaching of Jesus that He went to the root of the matter, making this sin to consist in "looking on a woman to lust after her." Nor did He confine Himself to the case of the married. The general character of the terms in Mt **5** 28, πᾶς ὁ βλέπων, *pás ho blépōn*, forbids the idea that γυναῖκα, *gunaíka*, and ἐμοίχευσεν, *emoícheusen*, are to be limited to post-nuptial sin with a married woman. On the other hand it is a characteristic part of the work of Jesus to rescue the erring woman from the merciless clutches of the Pharisaic tribunal, and to bring her within the pale of mercy and redemption (Mt **21** 31.32). He everywhere leaned to the side of mercy in dealing with such cases, as is indicated by the traditional and doubtless true narrative found in the accepted text of the Fourth Gospel (Jn **7** 53—**8** 11). Geo. B. Eager

HARLOTRY, här'lot-ri. See Crimes.

HAR-MAGEDON, här-ma-ged'on (**Ἁρμαγεδών,** *Harmagedṓn* from Heb *har meghiddō*, "Mount of Megiddo"; AV **Armageddon**): This name is found only in Rev **16** 16. It is described as the rallying-place of the kings of the whole world who, led by the unclean spirits issuing from the mouth of the dragon, the beast and the false prophet, assemble here for "the war of the great day of God, the Almighty." Various explanations have been suggested; but, as Nestle says (*HDB*, s.v), "Upon the whole, to find an allusion here to Megiddo is still the most probable explanation." In the history of Israel it had been the scene of never-to-be-forgotten battles. Here took place the fatal struggle between Josiah and Pharaoh-necoh (2 K **23** 29; 2 Ch **35** 22). Long before, the hosts of Israel had won glory here, in the splendid victory over Sisera and his host (Jgs **5** 19). These low hills around Megiddo, with their outlook over the plain of Esdraelon, have witnessed perhaps a greater number of bloody encounters than have ever stained a like area of the world's surface. There was, therefore, a peculiar appropriateness in the choice of this as the arena of the last mighty struggle between the powers of good and evil. The choice of the hill as the battlefield has been criticized, as it is less suitable for military operations than the plain. But the thought of Gilboa and Tabor and the uplands beyond Jordan might have reminded the critics that Israel was not unaccustomed to mountain warfare. Megiddo itself was a hill-town, and the district was in part mountainous (cf Mt. Tabor, Jgs **4** 6.12; "the high places of the field," **5** 18). It will be remembered that this is apocalypse. Har-Magedon may stand for the battlefield without indicating any particular locality. The attempt of certain scholars to connect the name with "the mount of congregation" in Isa **14** 13 (Hommel, Genkel, etc), and with Bab mythology, cannot be pronounced successful. Ewald (*Die Johan. Schrift*, II, 204) found that the Heb forms of "Har-Magedon" and "the great Rome" have the same numerical value—304. The historical persons alluded to in the passage do not concern us here. W. Ewing

HARNEPHER, här'nē-fēr, här-nē'fēr (חַרְנֶפֶר, *ḥarnepher*): A member of the tribe of Asher (1 Ch **7** 36).

HARNESS, här'nes: A word of Celtic origin meaning "armour" in AV; it is the tr of *shiryān*, "a coat of mail" (1 K **22** 34; 2 Ch **18** 33); of *neshek*, "arms," "weapons" (2 Ch **9** 24, RV "armor"); of *'āṣar* "to bind" (Jer **46** 4), "harness the horses," probably here, "yoke the horses"; cf 1 S **6** 7, "tie the kine to the cart" (bind them), Gen **46** 29; another rendering is "put on their accoutrements"; cf 1 Macc **6** 43, "one of the beasts armed with royal harness" (θώραξ, *thṓrax*), RV "breastplates"; cf 1 Macc **3** 3, "warlike harness"; **6** 41 (ὅπλα, *hópla*), RV "arms"; 2 Macc **3** 25, etc; **harnessed** represents *ḥămushīm*, "armed," "girded" (Ex **13** 18, "The children of Israel went up harnessed," RV "armed"). Tindale, Cranmer, Geneva have "harnes" in Lk **11** 22, Wiclif "armer."

W. L. Walker

HAROD, hā'rod, **WELL OF** (עֵין חֲרֹד, *'ēn ḥărōdh*, "fountain of trembling"): The fountain beside which (probably above it) Gideon and his army were encamped (Jgs **7** 1). Moore (*Judges*, in loc.) argues, inconclusively, that the hill Moreh must be sought near Shechem, and that the well of Harod must be some spring in the neighborhood of that city. There is no good reason to question the accuracy of the common view which places this spring at *'Ain Jalūd*, on the edge of the vale of Jezreel, about 2 miles E. of *Zer'īn*, and just under the northern cliffs of Gilboa. A copious spring of clear cold water rises in a rocky cave and flows out into a large pool, whence it drains off, in *Nahr Jalūd*, down the vale past *Beisān* to the Jordan. This is probably also to be identified with the spring "which is in Jezreel," i.e. in the district, near which Saul encamped before the battle of Gilboa (1 S **29** 1). *'Ain el-Meiyiteh*, just below *Zer'īn* on the N., is hardly of sufficient size and importance to be a rival to *'Ain Jalūd*. See Esdraelon.

W. Ewing

HARODITE, hā'rod-īt (חֲרֹדִי, *ḥărōdhī*): Two of David's heroes, Shamma and Elika, are so called (2 S **23** 25). LXX omits the second name. In 1 Ch **11** 27, the first is called "Shammoth the Harorite," while the second is omitted. "Harorite" is a clerical error for "Harodite," ד being taken for

ר. Possibly Harodite may be connected with the well of Harod (q.v.).

HAROEH, ha-rō′e (הָרֹאֶה, *hā-rō'eh,* "the seer"): A Judahite (1 Ch **2** 52).

HARORITE, hā′rō-rīt. See Harodite.

HAROSHETH, ha-rō′sheth, **OF THE GENTILES,** or **OF THE NATIONS** (חֲרֹשֶׁת הַגּוֹיִם, *ḥărōsheth ha-gōyīm*): There is now no means of discovering what is meant by the phrase "of the nations." This is the place whence Sisera led his hosts to the Kishon against Deborah and Barak (Jgs **4** 13), to which the discomfited and leaderless army fled after their defeat (ver 16). No site seems so well to meet the requirements of the narrative as *el Ḥarithīyeh.* There are still the remains of an ancient stronghold on this great double mound, which rises on the N. bank of the Kishon, in the throat of the pass leading by the base of Carmel, from the coast to Esdraelon. It effectually commands the road which here climbs the slope, and winds through the oak forest to the plain; Megiddo being some 16 miles distant. The modern also preserves a reminiscence of the ancient name. By emending the text, Cheyne would here find the name "Kadshon," to be identified with Kedesh in Galilee (*EB,* s.v.). On any reasonable reading of the narrative this is unnecessary. W. Ewing

HARP, härp. See Music.

HARROW, har′ō (שִׂדֵּד, *sādhadh*): *Sādhadh* occurs in 3 passages (Job **39** 10; Isa **28** 24; Hos **10** 11). In the first 2 it is tr[d] "harrow," in the last "break the clods." That this was a separate operation from plowing, and that it was performed with an instrument drawn by animals, seems certain. As to whether it corresponded to our modern harrowing is a question. The reasons for this uncertainty are: (1) the ancient Egyptians have left no records of its use; (2) at the present time, in those parts of Pal and Syria where foreign methods have not been introduced, harrowing is not commonly known, although the writer has been told that in some districts the ground is leveled after plowing with the threshing-sledge or a log drawn by oxen. Cross-plowing is resorted to for breaking up the lumpy soil, esp. where the ground has been baked during the long rainless summer. Lumps not reduced in this way are further broken up with a hoe or pick. Seed is always sown before plowing, so that harrowing to cover the seed is unnecessary. See Agriculture. **Fig.** used of affliction, discipline, etc (Isa **28** 24). James A. Patch

HARROWS, har′ōz (חָרִיץ, *ḥārīç*): *Ḥārīç* has no connection with the vb. tr[d] "harrows." The context seems to indicate some form of pointed instrument (2 S **12** 31; 1 Ch **20** 3; see esp. RVm).

HARSHA, här′sha (חַרְשָׁא, *ḥarshā'*): Head of one of the families of the Nethinim (Ezr **2** 52; Neh **7** 54); 1 Esd **5** 32, "Charea."

HARSITH, här′sith (חַרְסִית, *ḥarṣīth*): One of the gates of Jerus (Jer **19** 2 RV); m suggests "gate of the potsherds"; AV has "east gate" and AVm "sun gate," both deriving the name from חֶרֶס, *ḥereṣ,* "sun." The gate opened into the valley of Hinnom. See Jerusalem; Potsherd.

HART, härt. See Deer.

HARUM, hā′rum, hâr′um (הָרֻם, *ḥārum*): A Judahite (1 Ch **4** 8).

HARUMAPH, ha-rōō′maf (חֲרוּמַף, *ḥărūmaph*): Father of Jedaiah who assisted in repairing the walls of Jerus under Nehemiah (Neh **3** 10).

HARUPHITE, ha-rōō′fīt (חֲרוּפִי, *ḥărūphī,* or חֲרִיפִי, *ḥărīphī*); In 1 Ch **12** 5 Shephatiah, one of the companions of David, is called a Haruphite (K) or Hariphite (Q). If the latter be the correct reading, it is connected with Hariph or perhaps Hareph (q.v.).

HARUZ, hā′ruz (חָרוּץ, *ḥārūç*): Father of Meshullemeth, the mother of Amon, king of Judah (2 K **21** 19).

HARVEST, här′vest (קָצִיר, *ķāçīr;* θερισμός, *therismós*): To many of us, harvest time is of little concern, because in our complex life we are far removed from the actual production of our food supplies, but for the Heb people, as for those in any agricultural district today, the harvest was a most important season (Gen **8** 22; **45** 6). Events were reckoned from harvests (Gen **30** 14; Josh **3** 15; Jgs **15** 1; Ruth **1** 22; **2** 23; 1 S **6** 13; 2 S **21** 9; **23** 13). The three principal feasts of the Jews corresponded to the three harvest seasons (Ex **23** 16; **34** 21.22); (1) the feast of the Passover in April at the time of the barley harvest (cf Ruth **1** 22); (2) the feast of Pentecost (7 weeks later) at the wheat harvest (Ex **34** 22), and (3) the feast of Tabernacles at the end of the year (October) during the fruit harvest. The seasons have not changed since that time. Between the reaping of the barley in April and the wheat in June, most of the other cereals are reaped. The grapes begin to ripen in August, but the gathering in for making wine and molasses (*dibs*), and the storing of the dried figs and raisins, is at the end of September. Between the barley harvest in April and the wheat harvest, only a few showers fall, which are welcomed because they increase the yield of wheat (cf Am **4** 7). Samuel made use of the unusual occurrence of rain during the wheat harvest to strike fear into the hearts of the people (1 S **12** 17). Such an unusual storm of excessive violence visited Syria in 1912, and did much damage to the harvests, bringing fear to the superstitious farmers, who thought some greater disaster awaited them. From the wheat harvest until the fruit harvest no rain falls (2 S **21** 10; Jer **5** 24; cf Prov **26** 1). The harvesters long for cool weather during the reaping season (cf Prov **25** 13).

Many definite laws were instituted regarding the harvest. Gleaning was forbidden (Lev **19** 9; **23** 22; Dt **24** 19) (see Gleaning). The first-fruits were required to be presented to Jeh (Lev **23** 10). In Syria the Christians still celebrate *'id er-rubb* ("feast of the Lord"), at which time the owners of the vineyards bring their first bunches of grapes to the church. The children of Israel were enjoined to reap no harvest for which they had not labored (Lev **25** 5). In Prov the ants' harvesting is mentioned as a lesson for the sluggard (Prov **6** 8; **10** 5; **20** 4).

Figurative: A destroyed harvest typified devastation or affliction (Job **5** 5; Isa **16** 9; **17** 11; Jer **5** 17; **50** 16). The "time of harvest," in the OT frequently meant the day of destruction (Jer **51** 33; Hos **6** 11; Joel **3** 13). "Joy in harvest" typified great joy (Isa **9** 3); "harvest of the Nile," an abundant harvest (Isa **23** 3). "The harvest is past" meant that the appointed time was gone (Jer **8** 20). Jeh chose the most promising time to cut off the wicked, namely, "when there is a cloud of dew in the heat of harvest" (Isa **18** 4.5). This occurrence of hot misty days just before the ripening of the grapes is still common. They are welcome because they are supposed to hasten the harvest. The Syrian farmers in some districts call it *et-tabbakh el 'ainib wa tîn* ("the fireplace of the grapes and figs").

In the Gospels, Jesus frequently refers to the harvest of souls (Mt **9** 37.38 *bis;* **13** 30 *bis*.39; Mk **4** 29; Jn **4** 35 *bis*). In explaining the parable of the Tares he said, "The harvest is the end of the world" (Mt **13** 39; cf Rev **14** 15). See also AGRICULTURE. JAMES A. PATCH

HASADIAH, has-a-dī'a (חֲסַדְיָה, *ḥăṣadhyāh,* "Jeh is kind"): A son of Zerubbabel (1 Ch **3** 20). In Bar **1** 1 the Gr is *Asadías.*

HASENUAH, has-e-nū'a (הַסְּנֻאָה, *haṣṣ^e nu'āh*): In AV (1 Ch **9** 7) for HASSENUAH (q.v.).

HASHABIAH, hash-a-bī'a (חֲשַׁבְיָה, *ḥăshabhyāh*):

(1) Two Levites of the family of Merari (1 Ch **6** 45; **9** 14).

(2) A Levite who dwelt in Jerus at the time of Nehemiah (Neh **11** 15).

(3) A son of Jeduthun (1 Ch **25** 3).

(4) A Hebronite, chief of a clan of warriors who had charge of West Jordan in the interests of Jeh and the king of Israel (1 Ch **26** 30).

(5) A Levite who was a "ruler" (1 Ch **27** 17).

(6) One of the Levite chiefs in the time of Josiah, who gave liberally toward the sacrifices (2 Ch **35** 9). In 1 Esd **1** 9 it is "Sabias."

(7) A Levite whom Ezra induced to return from exile with him (Ezr **8** 19). 1 Esd **8** 48 has "Asebias."

(8) One of the twelve priests set apart by Ezra to take care of the gold, the silver, and the vessels of the temple on their return from exile (Ezr **8** 24; 1 Esd **8** 54, "Assamias").

(9) Ruler of half of the district of "Keilah," who helped to repair the walls under Nehemiah (Neh **3** 17), and also helped to seal the covenant (Neh **10** 11; **12** 24).

(10) A Levite (Neh **11** 22).

(11) A priest (Neh **12** 21). J. J. REEVE

HASHABNAH, ha-shab'na (חֲשַׁבְנָה, *ḥăshabhnāh*): One who helped to seal the covenant under Nehemiah (Neh **10** 25).

HASHABNEIAH, hash-ab-nē-ī'a (חֲשַׁבְנְיָה, *ḥăshabhn^e yāh;* AV **Hashabniah,** hash-ab-nī'a).

(1) Father of one of the builders of the wall (Neh **3** 10).

(2) A Levite mentioned in connection with the prayer preceding the signing of the covenant (Neh **9** 5); possibly identical with the Hashabiah (*ḥăshabhyāh*) of Ezr **8** 19.24; Neh **10** 11; **11** 22; **12** 24, or one of these.

HASHBADANA, hash-ba-dā'na, **HASHBADDANA,** hash-bad'a-na (חַשְׁבַּדָּנָה, *ḥashbaddānāh*): Probably a Levite. He was one of those who stood at Ezra's left hand when he read the law, and helped the people to understand the meaning (Neh **8** 4). 1 Esd **9** 44 has "Nabarias" (Ναβαρείας, *Nabareías*).

HASHEM, hā'shem (הָשֵׁם, *hāshēm*): The "sons of Hashem" are mentioned (1 Ch **11** 34) among David's mighty men. The ‖ passage (2 S **23** 32) has "sons of Jashen."

HASHMONAH, hash'mō-na (חַשְׁמֹנָה, *ḥashmōnāh,* "fatness"): A desert camp of the Israelites between Mithkah and Moseroth (Nu **33** 29.30). See WANDERINGS OF ISRAEL.

HASHUB, hā'shub, hash'ub. See HASSHUB.

HASHUBAH, ha-shōō'ba (חֲשֻׁבָה, *ḥăshubhāh,* "consideration"): One of the sons of Zerubbabel (1 Ch **3** 20).

HASHUM, hā'shum (חָשֻׁם, *ḥāshum*):

(1) In Ezr **2** 19; Neh **7** 22, "children of Hashum" are mentioned among the returning exiles. In Ezr **10** 33 (cf 1 Esd **9** 33, "Asom"), members of the same family are named among those who married foreign wives.

(2) One of those who stood on Ezra's left at the reading of the law (Neh **8** 4; 1 Esd **9** 44, "Lothasubus"). The signer of the covenant (Neh **10** 18) is possibly the same.

HASIDAEANS, has-i-dē'anz (Ἀσιδαῖοι, *Hasidaíoi,* a transliteration of *ḥăṣīdhīm,* "the pious," "Puritans"): A name assumed by the orthodox Jews (1 Macc **2** 42; **7** 13) to distinguish them from the Hellenizing faction described in the Maccabean books as the "impious," the "lawless," the "transgressors." They held perhaps narrow but strict and seriously honest views in religion, and recognized Judas Maccabaeus as their leader (2 Macc **14** 6). They existed as a party before the days of the Maccabees, standing on the ancient ways, caring little for politics, and having small sympathy with merely national aspirations, except when affecting religion (1 Macc **1** 63; 2 Macc **6** 18 ff; Jth **12** 2; *Ant,* XIV, iv, 3). Their coöperation with Judas went only to the length of securing the right to follow their own religious practices. When Bacchides came against Jerus, they were quite willing to make peace because Alcimus, "a priest of the seed of Aaron," was in his company. Him they accepted as high priest, though sixty of them soon fell by his treachery (1 Macc **7** 13). Their desertion of Judas was largely the cause of his downfall. J. HUTCHISON

HASMONEANS. See ASMONEANS.

HASRAH, haz'ra, has'ra (חַסְרָה, *ḥaṣrāh*): Grandfather of Shallum, who was the husband of Huldah the prophetess (2 Ch **34** 22). In 2 K **22** 14, HARHAS (q.v.).

HASSENAAH, has-ē-nā'a (הַסְּנָאָה, *haṣṣ^e nā'āh*): In Neh **3** 3 the "sons of Hassenaah" are mentioned among the builders of the wall. Probably the same as Senaah (Ezr **2** 35; Neh **7** 38) with the definite article, i.e. has-Senaah. The latter, from the connection, would appear to be a place-name. See also HASSENUAH.

HASSENUAH, has-e-nū'a (הַסְּנֻאָה, הַסְּנוּאָה, *haṣṣ^e nū'āh*): A family name in the two lists of Benjamite inhabitants of Jerus (1 Ch **9** 7, AV "Hasenuah"; Neh **11** 9, "Senuah"). The name is possibly the same as HASSENAAH (q.v.), yet the occurrence of the singular ("son of H.") does not so well accord with the idea of a place-name.

HASSHUB, hash'ub (חַשּׁוּב, *ḥashshūbh,* "considerate"; AV everywhere **Hashub** except 1 Ch **9** 14):

(1) A builder of the wall (Neh **3** 11).

(2) Another builder of the same name (Neh **3** 23).

(3) One of the signers of the covenant (Neh **10** 23).

(4) A Levite chief (Neh **11** 15; 1 Ch **9** 14). *BDB* makes (1) and (3) identical.

HASSOPHERETH, has-o-fē'reth. See SOPHERETH.

HASTE, hāst (חָפַז, *ḥāphaz*, חוּשׁ, *ḥūsh*, מָהַר, *māhar;* σπεύδω, *speúdō*): "Haste" (from a root meaning "to pursue") implies "celerity of motion."

(1) The noun occurs as tr of *māhar*, "to hasten," etc (Ex **10** 16; **12** 33, "in haste"); of *ḥāphaz*, "to make haste" (2 K **7** 15; Ps **31** 22; **116** 11, "I said in my haste [RVm "alarm"], All men are liars"); of *ḥippāzōn*, a "hasty flight" (Ex **12** 11; Dt **16** 3; Isa **52** 12); of *nāḥaç*, "to be urgent" (1 S **21** 8, "The king's business required haste").

(2) "Haste" as a vb. is trans and intrans; instances of the transitive use are, *'ūç*, "to hasten," "press" (Ex **5** 13, "And the taskmasters hasted them," RV "were urgent"); *ḥūsh*, "to make haste" (Isa **5** 19); *māhar* (2 Ch **24** 5 *bis*); *shāḳadh*, "to watch," "to fix one's attention" on anything (Jer **1** 12 AV, "I will hasten my word"); *māhīr*, "hasting" (Isa **16** 5, "hasting righteousness," RV "swift to do"). The intransitive use is more frequent and represents many different words.

Hasty also occurs in several instances (Prov **21** 5; **29** 20, *'ūç*, etc); in Isa **28** 4, *bikkūr*, "first-fruit," is trd "hasty fruit," RV "first-ripe fig."

RV has "Haste ye" for "assemble yourselves" (Joel **3** 11 m, as AV); "make haste" for "speedily" (Ps **143** 7); "and hasted to catch whether it were his mind" (for 1 K **20** 33 AV); "and it hasteth toward the end," m "Heb panteth," for "but at the end it shall speak" (Hab **2** 3); "hastily" for "suddenly" (1 Tim **5** 22); for "and for this I make haste" (Job **20** 2), "even by reason of my haste that is in me," m "and by reason of this my haste is within me"; for "hasten after another god" (Ps **16** 4), ARV has "that give gifts for another god," ERV "exchange the Lord for"; for "hasten hereunto" (Eccl **2** 25), "have enjoyment"; for "hasten hither" (1 K **22** 9), "fetch quickly"; for "and gather" (Ex **9** 19), "hasten in"; for "hasteneth that he may" (Isa **51** 14), "shall speedily"; for "hasteth to" (Job **9** 26), "swoopeth on"; for "and hasteth" (**40** 23), "he trembleth"; for "hasty" (Dnl **2** 15), "urgent."

W. L. Walker

HASUPHA, ha-sū'fa (חֲשׂוּפָא, חֲשֻׂפָא, *ḥăsūphā'*): Head of a family of Nethinim among the returning exiles (Ezr **2** 43; Neh **7** 46). Neh **7** 46 AV has "Hashupha," and 1 Esd **5** 29, "Asipha."

HAT: The original word (כַּרְבְּלָא, *karbelā'*, Aram.) rendered "hat" in Dnl **3** 21 AV is very rare, appearing only here in the OT. There is acknowledged difficulty in translating it, as well as the other words of the passage. "Hat" of AV certainly fails to give its exact meaning. The hat as we know it, i.e. headgear distinguished from the cap or bonnet by a circular brim, was unknown to the ancient East. The nearest thing to the modern hat among the ancients was the *petasus* worn by the Romans when on a journey, though something like it was used on like occasions by the early Greeks. In the earlier Heb writings there is little concerning the headgear worn by the people. In 1 K **20** 31 we find mention of "ropes" upon the head in connection with "sackcloth" on the loins. On Egyp monuments are found pictures of Syrians likewise with cords tied about their flowing hair. The custom, however, did not survive, or was modified, clearly because the cord alone would afford no protection against the sun, to which peasants and travelers were perilously exposed. It is likely, therefore, that for kindred reasons the later Israelites used a head-covering similar to that of the modern Bedouin. This consists of a rectangular piece of cloth called *keffîyeh*, which is usually folded into triangular form and placed over the head so as to let the middle part hang down over the back of the neck and protect it from the sun, while the two ends are drawn as needed under the chin and tied, or thrown back over the shoulders. A cord of wool is then used to secure it at the top. It became customary still later for Israelites to use a head-covering more like the "turban" worn by the fellaheen today. It consists in detail of a piece of cotton cloth worked into the form of a cap (*takîyeh*), and so worn as to protect the other headgear from being soiled by the perspiration. A felt cap, or, as among the Turks, a fez or red tarbush, is worn over this. On the top of these is wound a long piece of cotton cloth with red stripes and fringes, a flowered kerchief, or a striped *keffîyeh*. This protects the head from the sun, serves as a sort of purse by day, and often as a pillow by night. Some such headgear is probably meant by the "diadem" of Job **29** 14 and the "hood" of Isa **3** 23, Heb *çānīph*, from *çānaph*, "to roll up like a coil" (cf Isa **22** 18).

Geo. B. Eager

HATACH, hā'tak. See Hathach.

HATCHET, hach'et (כַּשִּׁיל, *kashshīl*): Ps **74** 6 RV, "hatchet," AV "axes." See Ax.

HATE, hāt, **HATRED,** hā'tred (vb., שָׂנֵא, *sānē'*, "oftenest," שָׂטַם, *sāṭam*, Gen **27** 41, etc; noun, שִׂנְאָה, *sin'āh;* μισέω, *miséō*): A feeling of strong antagonism and dislike, generally malevolent and prompting to injury (the opposite of love); sometimes born of moral resentment. Alike in the OT and NT, hate of the malevolent sort is unsparingly condemned (Nu **35** 20; Ps **109** 5; Prov **10** 12; Tit **3** 3; 1 Jn **3** 15), but in the OT hatred of evil and evil-doers, purged of personal malice, is commended (Ps **97** 10; **101** 3; **139** 21.22, etc). The NT law softens this feeling as regards persons, bringing it under the higher law of love (Mt **5** 43.44; cf Rom **12** 17–21), while intensifying the hatred of evil (Jude ver 23; Rev **2** 6). God himself is hated by the wicked (Ex **20** 5; Ps **139** 21; cf Rom **8** 7). Sometimes, however, the word "hate" is used hyperbolically in a relative sense to express only the strong preference of one to another. God loved Jacob, but hated Esau (Mal **1** 3; Rom **9** 13); father and mother are to be hated in comparison with Christ (Lk **14** 26; cf Mt **10** 37). See Enmity.

James Orr

HATHACH, hā'thak (הֲתָךְ, *hăthākh;* LXX Ἀχραθαῖος, *Hachrathaíos*): One of the chamberlains of Ahasuerus, appointed to attend on Esther (Est **4** 5.6.9.10, AV "Hatach"), through whom she learned from Mordecai of Haman's plot.

HATHATH, hā'thath (חֲתַת, *ḥăthath*, "terror"): Son of Othniel and grandson of Kenaz (1 Ch **4** 13).

HATIPHA, ha-tī'fa, hat'i-fa (חֲטִיפָא, *ḥăṭīphā'*, "taken," "captive" [?]): The ancestral head of a family of Nethinim that returned from Babylon (Ezr **2** 54; Neh **7** 56 = "Atipha," 1 Esd **5** 32).

HATITA, ha-tī'ta, hat'i-ta (חֲטִיטָא, *ḥăṭīṭā'*): Head of a family among the "children of the porters" who returned from exile (Ezr **2** 42; Neh **7** 45; 1 Esd **5** 28, "Ateta").

HATSI-HAMMENUCHOTH, hat-si-ham-en-ū'koth: A marginal reading in 1 Ch **2** 52 AV. It disappears in RV, which reads in text, "half of the Menuhoth" (q.v.) (Heb *ḥăçī ha-menuḥōth*).

HATTIL, hat'il (חַטִּיל, *ḥaṭṭīl*): A company of servants of Solomon appearing in the post-exilic literature (Ezr **2** 57; Neh **7** 59). Same called "Agia" in 1 Esd **5** 34.

HATTUSH, hat'ush (חַטּוּשׁ, *ḥaṭṭūsh*):

(1) Son of Shemaiah, a descendant of the kings of Judah, in the 5th generation from Zerubbabel (1 Ch **3** 22). He returned with Zerubbabel and

Ezra from Babylon to Jerus (Ezr **8** 2; Neh **12** 2). (There is some doubt as to whether the Hattush of the lineage of David and the priest of the same name, mentioned in Neh **10** 4 and **12** 2, are one and the same.) He was one of those who signed the covenant with Nehemiah (Neh **10** 4).

(2) Son of Hashabneiah; aided Nehemiah to repair the walls of Jerus (Neh **3** 10).

HORACE J. WOLF

HAUNT, hônt, hänt: The vb. in OE was simply "to resort to," "frequent"; a place of dwelling or of business was a *haunt.* The noun occurs in 1 S **23** 22 as the tr of *reghel,* "foot," "See his place where his haunt is," RVm "Heb 'foot' "; the vb. is the tr of *yāshabh,* "to sit down," "to dwell" (Ezk **26** 17, "on all that haunt it," RV "dwelt there," m "inhabited her"), and of *hālakh,* "to go," or "live" (1 S **30** 31, "all the places where David himself and his men were wont to haunt").

HAURAN, hō'ran (חַוְרָן, *ḥawrān;* LXX **Αὐρανῖτις,** *Auranitis,* also with aspirate): A province of Eastern Pal which, in Ezk **47** 16.18, stretched from Dan in the N. to Gilead in the S., including all that lay between the Jordan and the desert. It thus covered the districts now known as *el-Jēdūr, el-Jaulān,* and *el-Ḥaurān.* It corresponded roughly with the jurisdiction of the modern Turkish governor of Hauran. The Auranites of later times answered more closely to the Hauran of today.

1. Extent of Province in Ancient Times

The name *Ḥaurān* probably means "hollow land." Between *Jebel ed-Druze* (see BASHAN, MOUNT OF) on the E., and *Jēdūa* and *Jaulān* (see GOLAN) on the W., runs a broad vale, from *Jebel el 'Aswad* in the N., to the *Yarmuk* in the S.W., and the open desert in the S.E. It is from 1,500 to 2,000 ft. above sea-level, and almost 50 miles in length, by 45 in breadth. *Ḥaurān* aptly describes it. To the modern *Ḥaurān* are reckoned 3 districts, clearly distinguished in local speech: (1) *En-Nuḳrah,* "the cavity." This district touches the desert in the S.E., the low range of *ez Zumleh* on the S.W., *Jaulān* on the W., *el-Lejā'* on the N. and, *Jebel ed-Druze* on the E. The soil, composed of volcanic detritus, is extraordinarily rich. Here and there may be found a bank of vines; but the country is practically treeless: the characteristic product is wheat, and in its cultivation the village population is almost wholly occupied. (2) *El-Lejā',* "the asylum." This is a rocky tract lying to the N. of *en-Nuḳrah.* It is entirely volcanic, and takes, roughly, the form of a triangle, with apex in the N. at *el Burak,* and a base of almost 20 miles in the S. For the general characteristics of this district, see TRACHONITIS. Its sharply marked border, where the rocky edges fall into the surrounding plain, have suggested to some the thought that here we have *ḥebhel 'argōbh,* "the measured lot of Argob." See, however, ARGOB. There is little land capable of cultivation, and the Arabs who occupy the greater part have an evil reputation. As a refuge for the hunted and for fugitives from justice it well deserves its name. (3) *El-Jebel,* "the mountain." This is the great volcanic range which stands on the edge of the desert, protecting the fertile reaches of *el-Ḥaurān* from encroachment by the sand, known at different times as Mons Asaldamus, *Jebel Ḥaurān,* and *Jebel ed-Druze.* This last is the name it bears today in consequence of the settlement of Druzes here, after the massacre in Mt. Lebanon in 1860. Those free-spirited people have been a thorn in the side of the Turks ever since: and whether or not the recent operations against them (January, 1911) will result in their entire subjugation, remains to be seen. The western slopes of the mountain are well cultivated, and very fruitful; vineyards abound; and there are large reaches of shady woodlands. *Ṣalkhad,* marking the eastern boundary of the land of Israel, stands on the ridge of the mountain to the S. *Jebel el-Kuleib* in which the range culminates, reaches a height of 5,730 ft. *Jebel Ḥaurān* is named in the Mish (*Rōsh ha-shānāh,* ii.4) as one of the heights from which fire-signals were flashed, announcing the advent of the new year. For its history see BASHAN. The ruins which are so plentiful in the country date for the most part from the early Christian centuries; and probably nothing above ground is older than the Rom period. The substructions, however, and the subterranean dwellings found in different parts, e.g. at *Ḍer'ah,* may be very ancient. The latest mention of a Christian building is in an inscription found by the present writer at *el-Kufr,* which tells of the foundation of a church in 720 AD (*PEFS,* July, 1895, p. 275, Inscr no. 150). A good account of Hauran and its cities is given in *HGHL,* XXIX, 611.

2. Modern Hauran

3. En-Nuḳrah

4. El-Lejā'

5. El-Jebel

W. EWING

HAVE, hav: "To have" is to own or possess; its various uses may be resolved into this, its proper meaning.

A few of the many changes in RV are, for "a man that hath friends" (Prov **18** 24), "maketh many friends," m "Heb a man of friends"; for "all that I have" (Lk **15** 31), "all that is mine"; for "we have peace with God" (Rom **5** 1) ERV has "let us have," m "some authorities read we have," ARV as AVm "many ancient authorities read let us have"; for "what great conflict I have" (Col **2** 1), "how greatly I strive"; for "will have" (Mt **9** 13; **12** 7), "desire"; **27** 43, "desireth"; for "would have" (Mk **6** 19; Acts **10** 10), "desired"; **16** 27, "was about"; **19** 30, "was minded to"; **23** 28, "desiring"; He **12** 17, "desired to"; for "ye have" (He **10** 34), ERV has "ye yourselves have," m "ye have your own-selves," ARV "ye have for yourselves," m "many ancient authorities read, ye have your own selves for a better possession" (cf Lk **9** 25; **21** 19); "having heard" for "after that ye heard" (Eph **1** 13); "having suffered before," for "even after that we had suffered" (1 Thess **2** 2); "and thus, having," for "so after he had" (He **6** 15).

W. L. WALKER

HAVEN, hā'v'n ([1] חוֹף, *ḥōph* [Gen **49** 13, RVm "beach"; Jgs **5** 17, RVm "shore," AV "seashore," AVm "port"]; elsewhere "sea-shore" [Dt **1** 7; Josh **9** 1; Jer **47** 7] or "sea coast" [Ezk **25** 16]; from root חָפַף, *ḥāphaph,* "to wash" or "to lave"; cf Arab. حَفَّ, *ḥaffa,* "to rub"; and حَفَّة, *ḥaffat,* "border"; حُفُوف, *Ḥufûf,* in Eastern Arabia; [2] מָחוֹז, *māḥōz* [Ps **107** 30]; [3] **λιμήν,** *limēn* [Acts **27** 12 *bis*]; also Fair Havens, **καλοὶ λιμένες,** *kaloí liménes* [Acts **27** 8]): While the Gr *limēn* is "harbor," the Heb *ḥōph* is primarily "shore." There is no harbor worthy of the name on the shore of Pal S. of Ḥaifa. Indeed there is no good natural harbor on the whole coast of Syria and Pal. The promontories of Carmel, Beirût and Tripolis afford shelter from the prevalent southwest wind, but offer no refuge from the fury of a northern gale. On rocky shores there are inlets which will protect sail boats at most times, but the ships of the ancients were beached in rough weather, and small craft are so treated at the present time. See illustration under BITHYNIA, p. 483.

ALFRED ELY DAY

HAVENS, hā'v'nz, **FAIR.** See FAIR HAVENS.

HAVILAH, hav′i-lä (חֲוִילָה, *ḥăwīlāh;* **Εὐιλά,** *Heuilá*):

(1) Son of Cush (Gen **10** 7; 1 Ch **1** 9).

(2) Son of Yoktan, descendant of Shem (Gen **10** 29; 1 Ch **1** 23).

(3) Mentioned with Shur as one of the limits of the territory of the Ishmaelites (Gen **25** 18); cf the same limits of the land of the Amalekites (1 S **15** 7), where, however, the text is doubtful. It is described (Gen **2** 11.12) as bounded by the river Pishon and as being rich in gold, bdellium and "shoham-stone" (EV "onyx"). The shoham-stone was perhaps the Assyr *samtu,* probably the malachite or turquoise. The mention of a Cushite Havilah is explained by the fact that the Arabian tribes at an early time migrated to the coast of Africa. The context of Gen **10 7** thus favors a situation on the Ethiopian shore, and the name is perhaps preserved in the *kolpos Aualites* and in the tribe *Abalitai* on the S. side of the straits of *Bab-el-Mandeb.* Or possibly a trace of the name appears in the classical Aualis, now *Zeila'* in Somaliland. But its occurrence among the Yoktanite Arabs (Gen **10** 29) suggests a location in Arabia. South Arabian inscriptions mention a district of Khaulan (*Ḥaulan*), and a place of this name is found both in Tihama and S.E. of *San'ā'.* Again Strabo's *Chaulotaioi* and *Ḥuwaila* in Bahrein point to a district on the Arabian shore of the Pers Gulf. No exact identification has yet been made.

A. S. Fulton

HAVOC, hav′ok: "Devastation," "to make havoc of" is the tr of λυμαίνομαι, *lumaínomai,* "to stain," "to disgrace"; in the NT "to injure," "destroy" (Acts **8** 3, "As for Saul he made havoc of the church," RV "laid waste"; 1 Macc **7** 7, "what havoc," RV "all the havock," *exolóthreusis,* "utter destruction").

RV has "made havoc of" (*porthéō*) for "destroyed" (Acts **9** 21; Gal **1** 23), for "wasted" (Gal **1** 13).

HAVVAH, hav′a (חַוָּה, *ḥawwāh*): Heb spelling, rendered Eve, "mother of all living," Gen **3** 20 RVm. See Eve.

HAVVOTH-JAIR, hav-oth-jā′ir (חַוֹּת יָאִיר, *ḥawwōth yā'īr,* "the encampments" or "tent villages of Jair"; AV **Havoth-Jair,** hā-voth-jā′ir): The word *ḥawwōth* occurs only in this combination (Nu **32** 41; Dt **3** 14; Jgs **10** 4), and is a legacy from the nomadic stage of Heb life. Jair had thirty sons who possessed thirty "cities," and these are identified with Havvoth-jair in Jgs **10** 3 ff. The district was in Gilead (ver 5; Nu **32** 41). In Dt **3** 13 f, it is identified with Bashan and Argob; but in 1 K **4** 13, "the towns of Jair" are said to be in Gilead; while to him also "pertained the region of Argob, which is in Bashan, threescore great cities with walls and brazen bars." There is evident confusion here. If we follow Jgs **10** 3 ff, we may find a useful clue in ver 5. Kamon is named as the burial place of Jair. This probably corresponds to Kamun taken by Antiochus III, on his march from Pella to Gephrun (Polyb. v.70, 12). Schumacher (*Northern 'Ajlūn,* 137) found two places to the W. of Irbid with the names *Ḳamm* and *Ḳumeim* (the latter a diminutive of the former) with ancient ruins. *Ḳamm* probably represents the Heb *Ḳāmōn,* so that Havvoth-jair should most likely be sought in this district, i.e. in North Gilead, between the Jordan valley and *Jebel ez-Zumleh.*

W. Ewing

HAWK, hôk (נֵץ, *nēç;* **ἱέραξ,** *hiérax,* and **γλαῦξ,** *glaúx;* Lat *Accipiter nisus*): A bird of prey of the genus *accipiter.* Large hawks were numerous in Pal. The largest were 2 ft. long, have flat heads, hooked beaks, strong talons and eyes appearing the keenest and most comprehensive of any bird. They can sail the length or breadth of the Holy Land many times a day. It is a fact worth knowing that mist and clouds interfere with the vision of birds and they hide, and hungry and

Kestrel (*Tinnunculus alaudarius*).

silent wait for fair weather, so you will see them sailing and soaring on clear days only. These large hawks and the glede are of eagle-like nature, nesting on Carmel and on the hills of Galilee, in large trees and on mountain crags. They flock near Beersheba, and live in untold numbers in the wilderness of the Dead Sea. They build a crude nest of sticks and twigs and carry most of the food alive to their young. Of course they were among the birds of prey that swarm over the fresh offal from slaughter and sacrifice. No bird steers with its tail in flight in a more pronounced manner than the hawk. These large birds are all-the-year residents, for which reason no doubt the people distinguished them from smaller families that migrated. They knew the kite that Isaiah mentioned in predicting the fall of Edom. With them the smaller, brighter-colored kestrels, that flocked over the rocky shores of the Dead Sea and over the ruins of deserted cities, seemed to be closest in appearance to the birds we include in the general term "falcon." They ate mice, insects and small birds, but not carrion. The abomination lists of Lev **11** 16 and Dt **14** 15 each include hawks in a general term and specify several species as unfit for food. Job **39** 26 reads:

"Is it by thy wisdom that the hawk soareth,
And stretcheth her wings toward the south?"

Aside from calling attention to the miraculous flight, this might refer to migration, or to the wonderful soaring exhibitions of these birds. See Glede; Kite; Night Hawk; Falcon.

Gene Stratton-Porter

HAY, hā. See Grass.

HAZAEL, ha-zā′el, hā′za-el, haz′a-el (חֲזָאֵל and חֲזָהאֵל, *ḥăzā'ēl* and *ḥăzāh'ēl;* **'Αζαήλ,** *Hazaḗl;* Assyr *haza'ilu*): Comes first into Bib. history as a high officer in the service of Ben-hadad II, king of Syria (2 K **8** 7 ff; cf 1 K **19** 15 ff). He had been sent by his sick sovereign to inquire of the prophet

Elisha, who was then in Damascus, whether he should recover of his sickness or not. He took

1. In Biblical History

with him a present "even of every good thing of Damascus, forty camels' burden," and stood before the man of God with his master's question of life or death. To it Elisha made the oracular response, "Go, say unto him, Thou shalt surely recover; howbeit Jeh hath showed me that he shall surely die." Elisha looked stedfastly at Hazael and wept, explaining to the incredulous officer that he was to be the perpetrator of horrible cruelties against the children of Israel: "Their strongholds wilt thou set on fire, and their young men wilt thou slay with the sword, and wilt dash in pieces their little ones, and rip up their women with child" (2 K **8** 12). Hazael protested against the very thought of such things, but Elisha assured him that Jeh had shown him that he was to be king of Syria. No sooner had Hazael delivered to his master the answer of the man of God than the treacherous purpose took shape in his heart to hasten Ben-hadad's end, and "He took the coverlet, and dipped it in water, and spread it on his face, so that he died: and Hazael reigned in his stead" (2 K **8** 15). The reign which opened under such sinister auspices proved long and successful, and brought the kingdom of Syria to the zenith of its power. Hazael soon found occasion to invade Israel. It was at Ramoth-gilead, which had already been the scene of a fierce conflict between Israel and Syria when Ahab met his death, that Hazael encountered Joram, the king of Israel, with whom his kinsman, Ahaziah, king of Judah, had joined forces to retain that important fortress which had been recovered from the Syrians (2 K **9** 14.15). The final issue of the battle is not recorded, but Joram received wounds which obliged him to return across the Jordan to Jezreel, leaving the forces of Israel in command of Jehu, whose anointing by Elisha's deputy at Ramoth-gilead, usurpation of the throne of Israel, slaughter of Joram, Ahaziah and Jezebel, and vengeance upon the whole house of Ahab are told in rapid and tragic succession by the sacred historian (2 K **9, 10**).

Whatever was the issue of this attack upon Ramoth-gilead, it was not long before Hazael laid waste the whole country E. of the Jordan—"all the land of Gilead, the Gadites, and the Reubenites, and the Manassites, from Aroer, which is by the valley of the Arnon, even Gilead and Bashan" (2 K **10** 33; cf Am **1** 3). Nor did Judah escape the heavy hand of the Syrian oppressor. Marching southward through the plain of Esdraelon, and following a route along the maritime plain taken by many conquerors before and since, Hazael fought against Gath and took it, and then "set his face to go up to Jerus" (2 K **12** 17). As other kings of Judah had to do with other conquerors, Jehoash, who was now on the throne, bought off the invader with the gold and the treasures of temple and palace, and Hazael withdrew his forces from Jerus.

Israel, however, still suffered at the hands of Hazael and Ben-hadad, his son, and the sacred historian mentions that Hazael oppressed Israel all the days of Jehoahaz, the son of Jehu. So grievous was the oppression of the Syrians that Hazael "left not to Jehoahaz of the people save fifty horsemen, and ten chariots, and ten thousand footmen; for the king of Syria destroyed them, and made them like the dust in threshing" (2 K **13** 1–7). Forty or fifty years later Amos, in the opening of his prophecy, recalled those Syrian campaigns against Israel when he predicted vengeance that was to come upon Damascus. "Thus saith Jeh . . . . I will send a fire into the house of Hazael, and it shall devour the palaces of Ben-hadad" (Am **1** 3.4).

Already however, the power of Syria had passed its meridian and had begun to decline. Events of which

2. In the Monuments

there is no express record in the Bib. narrative were proceeding which, ere long, made it possible for the son of Jehoahaz, Joash or Jehoash, to retrieve the honor of Israel and recover the cities that had been lost (2 K **13** 25). For the full record of these events we must turn to the Assyr annals preserved in the monuments. We do read in the sacred history that Jeh gave Israel "a saviour, so that they went out from under the hand of the Syrians" (2 K **13** 5). The annals of the Assyr kings give us clearly and distinctly the interpretation of this enigmatic saying. The relief that came to Israel was due to the crippling of the power of Syria by the aggression of Assyria upon the lands of the West. From the Black Obelisk in the British Museum, on which Shalmaneser II (860–825 BC) has inscribed the story of the campaign he carried on during his long reign, there are instructive notices of this period of Israelitish history. In the 18th year of his reign (842 BC), Shalmaneser made war against Hazael. On the Obelisk the record is short, but a longer account is given on one of the pavement slabs from Nimroud, the ancient Kalab. It is as follows: "In the 18th year of my reign for the 16th time I crossed the Euphrates. Hazael of Damascus trusted to the strength of his armies and mustered his troops in full force. Senir [Hermon], a mountain summit which is in front of Lebanon, he made his stronghold. I fought with him; his defeat I accomplished; 600 of his soldiers with weapons I laid low; 1,121 of his chariots, 470 of his horses, with his camp I took from him. To save his life, he retreated; I pursued him; in Damascus, his royal city, I shut him up. His plantations I cut down. As far as the mountains of the Hauran I marched. Cities without number I wrecked, razed, and burnt with fire. Their spoil beyond count I carried away. As far as the mountains of Baal-Rosh, which is a headland of the sea [at the mouth of the *Nahr el-Kelb*, Dog River], I marched; my royal likeness I there set up. At that time I received the tribute of the Syrians and Sidonians and of Yahua [Jehu] the son of Khumri [Omri]" (Ball, *Light from the East*, 166; Schrader, *COT*, 200 f). From this inscription we gather that Shalmaneser did not succeed in the capture of Damascus. But it still remained an object of ambition to Assyria, and Ramman-nirari III, the grandson of Shalmaneser, succeeded in capturing it, and reduced it to subjection. It was this monarch who was "the saviour" whom God raised up to deliver Israel from the hand of Syria. Then it became possible for Israel under Jehoash to recover the cities he had lost, but by this time Hazael had died and Ben-hadad, his son, Ben-hadad III, called Mari on the monuments, had become king in his stead (2 K **13** 24.25).

Literature.—Schrader, *COT*, 197–208; McCurdy, *HPM*, I, 282 ff.

T. Nicol

HAZAIAH, ha-zā'ya (חֲזָיָה, *ḥăzāyāh*, "Jah sees"): Among the inhabitants of Jerus mentioned in the list of Judahites in Neh **11** 5.

HAZAR, hā'zär (חֲצַר, *ḥăçar*, constr. of חָצֵר, *ḥāçēr*, "an inclosure," "settlement," or "village"): Is frequently the first element in Heb place-names.

Hazar-addar (Heb *ḥăçar 'addār*), a place on the southern boundary of Judah (Nu **34** 4), is prob-

1. Hazar-addar

ably identical with Hazron (Josh **15** 3), which, in this case, however, is separated from Addar (AV "Adar"). It seems to have lain somewhere to the S.W. of Kadesh-barnea.

Hazar-enan (Heb *ḥăçar 'ēnān*, "village of springs": *'ēnān* is Aram.; once [Ezk **47** 17] it is

2. Hazar-enan

called Enon), a place, unidentified, at the junction of the northern and eastern frontiers of the land promised to Israel (Nu **34** 9 f; cf Ezk **47** 17; **48** 1). To identify it with the sources of the Orontes seems to leave too great a gap between this and the places named to the S. Buhl (*GAP*, 66 f) would draw the northern boundary from *Nahr el-Ḳāsimīyeh* to the foot of Hermon, and would locate Hazar-enan at *Bāniās*. The springs there lend fitness to the name; a condition absent from *el-Ḥāḍr*, farther east, suggested by von Kesteren. But there is no certainty.

Hazar-gaddah (Heb *hăçar-gaddāh*), a place in the territory of Judah "toward the border of Edom in the South" (Josh **15** 21.27).
3. Hazar-gaddah *Onom* (s.v. "Gadda") places it in the uttermost parts of the Daroma, overlooking the Dead Sea. This might point to the site of Masada, or to the remarkable ruins of *Umm Bajjaḳ* farther south (*GAP*, 185).

Hazar-hatticon (RV HAZER-HATTICON; Heb *ḥăçēr ha-tīkhōn*, "the middle village"), a place named on the ideal border of Israel
4. Hazar-hatticon (Ezk **47** 16). The context shows that it is identical with Hazar-enan, for which this is apparently another name. Possibly, however, it is due to a scribal error.

Hazarmaveth (Heb *ḥăçarmāweth*), the name of a son of Joktan attached to a clan or district in South Arabia (Gen **10** 26; 1 Ch **1**
5. Hazar-maveth 20). It is represented by the modern *Ḥaḍramaut*, a broad and fruitful valley running nearly parallel with the coast for about 100 miles, north of *el-Yemen*. The ruins and inscriptions found by Glaser show that it was once the home of a great civilization, the capital being Sabata (Gen **10** 7) (Glaser, *Skizze*, II, 20, 423 ff).

Hazar-shual (Heb *ḥăçar shū'āl*), a place in the S. of Judah (Josh **15** 28) assigned to Simeon (Josh **19** 3; 1 Ch **4** 28). It was re-
6. Hazar-shual occupied after the exile (Neh **11** 27). *Sa'weh* on a hill E. of Beersheba has been suggested; but there is no certainty.

Hazar-susah (Heb *ḥăçar ṣūṣāh*, Josh **19** 5), **Hazar-susim** (Heb *ḥăçar ṣūṣīm*, 1 Ch **4** 31). As it stands, the name means "station of a
7. Hazar-susah mare" or "of horses," and it occurs along with Beth-marcaboth, "place of chariots," which might suggest depots for trade in chariots and horses. The sites have not been identified. W. EWING

HAZAR-ADDAR, ad'är; **-ENAN,** ē'nan; **-GADDAH,** gad'a; **-HATTICON,** hat'i-kon; **-MAVETH,** mā'veth; **-SHUAL,** shōō'al; **-SUSA,** sū'sa; **-SUSIM,** sū'sim. See HAZAR.

HAZAZON-TAMAR, haz'a-zan-tā'mar (חַצְצֹן תָּמָר, *haçăçōn tāmār;* AV **Hazezon Tamar**): "Hazazon of the palm trees," mentioned (Gen **14** 7) as a place of the Amorites, conquered, together with En-mishpat and the country of the Amalekites, by Chedorlaomer; in 2 Ch **20** 2 it is identified with EN-GEDI (q.v.); and if so, it must have been its older name. If this identification be accepted, then Hazazon may survive in the name *Wādy Husāsah*, N.W. of *'Ain Jidy*. Another suggestion, which certainly meets the needs of the narrative better, is that Hazazon-tamar is the Thamara of *OS* (**85** 3; **210** 86), the Θαμαρω, *Thamarō*, of Ptol. xvi.3. The ruin *Kurnub*, 20 miles W.S.W. of the S. end of the Dead Sea—on the road from Hebron to Elath—is supposed to mark this site.

E. W. G. MASTERMAN

HAZEL, hā'z'l (Gen **30** 37 AV). See ALMOND.

HAZELELPONI, haz-el-el-pō'nī. See HAZZELELPONI.

HAZER-HATTICON, hā'zēr-hat'i-kon, **HAZAR-HATTICON.** See HAZAR.

HAZERIM, ha-zē'rim, haz'ēr-im (חֲצֵרִים, *ḥăçērīm*): Is rendered in AV (Dt **2** 23) as the name of a place in the S.W. of Pal, in which dwelt the Avvim, ancient inhabitants of the land. The word means "villages," and ought to be tr[d] as in RV. The sentence means that the Avvim dwelt in villages—not in fortified towns—before the coming of the Caphtorim, the Philis, who destroyed them.

HAZEROTH, ha-zē'rōth, haz'ēr-oth (חֲצֵרוֹת, *ḥăçērōth*, "inclosures"): A camp of the Israelites, the 3d from Sinai (Nu **11** 35; **12** 16; **33** 17; Dt **1** 1). It is identified with *'Ain Ḥaḍrah* ("spring of the inclosure"), 30 miles N.E. of *Jebel Musa*, on the way to the 'Arābāh. See WANDERINGS OF ISRAEL.

HAZEZON-TAMAR, haz'ē-zon-tā'mar (חַצְצֹן תָּמָר, *haçăçōn tāmār*, Gen **14** 7 AV; חַצְצֹן תָּמָר, *ḥaççōn tāmār*, 2 Ch **20** 2). See HAZAZON-TAMAR.

HAZIEL, hā'zi-el (חֲזִיאֵל, *ḥăzī'ēl*, "God sees"): A Levite of the sons of Shimei, of David's time (1 Ch **23** 9).

HAZO, hā'zō (חֲזוֹ, *ḥăzō*, fifth son of Nahor [Gen **22** 22]): Possibly the eponym of a Nahorite family or clan.

HAZOR, hā'zor (חָצוֹר, *ḥāçōr;* **Νασώρ,** *Nasōr*, **א, 'Ασώρ,** *Asōr*, 1 Macc **11** 67):

(1) The royal city of Jabin (Josh **11** 1), which, before the Israelite conquest, seems to have been the seat of a wide authority (ver 11). It was taken by Joshua, who exterminated the inhabitants, and it was the only city in that region which he destroyed by fire (vs 11–13). At a later time the Jabin Dynasty appears to have recovered power and restored the city (Jgs **4** 2). The heavy defeat of their army at the hands of Deborah and Barak led to their final downfall (vs 23 ff). It was in the territory allotted to Naphtali (Josh **19** 36). Hazor was one of the cities for the fortification of which Solomon raised a levy (1 K **9** 15). Along with other cities in Galilee, it was taken by Tiglath-pileser III (2 K **15** 29). In the plain of Hazor, Jonathan the Maccabee gained a great victory over Demetrius (1 Macc **11** 67 ff). In Tob **1** 2 it is called "Asher" (LXX Ασήρ, *Asēr*), and Kedesh is said to be "above" it. Jos (*Ant*, V, v, 1) says that Hazor was situated over the lake, Semechonitis, which he evidently identifies with the Waters of Merom (Jos **11** 13). For Hazor before time was the head of all these kingdoms (Jos **11**). The Tell el-Amarna tablets, including the new one brought out by Thureau-Dangin discovered five years ago, confirm this statement. The long-lost city was discovered by Garstang, 1926, since confirmed by Vincent and Albright. It is at *Tell el-Qedaḥ* 4 miles west of the southern end of Lake Ḥuleh. It measured 900 by 450 m., much larger than the great fortress of Megiddo (*Annals of Anthropology and Archaeology*, XIV, 35 ff). The statements of Josh are thus fully confirmed (*Bull. American Schools of Oriental Research*, Feb. 1928). This whole upper Jordan valley has yielded to the researches of Vincent, Albright, and Garstang a wonderful revelation concerning the early civilization of Palestine which extended to the Cities of the Plain.

(2) A town, unidentified, in the S. of Judah (Josh **15** 23).

(3) A town in the S. of Judah (Josh **15** 25). See KERIOTH-HEZRON.

(4) A town in Benjamin (Neh **11** 33) now represented by *Khirbet Ḥazzūr*, not far to the E. of *Neby Samwīl*.

(5) An unidentified place in Arabia, smitten by Nebuchadnezzar (Jer **49** 28.33). W. EWING

HAZOR-HADATTAH, hā'zor-ha-dat'a (Aram. חָצוֹר חֲדַתָּה, *ḥāçōr ḥădhattāh*, "New Hazor"): "An Aram. adj., however, in this region is so strange that the reading must be questioned" (Di). One of the "uttermost cities . . . . of Judah toward the border of Edom" (Josh **15** 25). Eusebius and Jerome describe a "New Hazor" to the E. of Ascalon, but this is too far N.

HAZZELELPONI, haz-e-lel-pō'nī (הַצְּלֶלְפּוֹנִי, *haççelelpōnī*): A feminine name occurring in the list of the genealogy of Judah (1 Ch **4** 3); probably representing a clan.

HE, hā (ה): The fifth letter of the Heb alphabet; transliterated in this Encyclopaedia as *h*. It came also to be used for the number 5. For name, etc, see ALPHABET.

HEAD, hed (רֹאשׁ, *rō'sh*, Aram. רֵאשׁ, *rē'sh*, and in special sense גֻּלְגֹּלֶת, *gulgōleth*, lit. "skull," "cut-off head" [1 Ch **10** 10], whence Golgotha [Mt **27** 33; Mk **15** 22; Jn **19** 17]; מְרַאֲשָׁה, *m*e*ra'ăshāh*, lit. "head-rest," "pillow," "bolster" [1 K **19** 6]; קָדְקֹד, *ḳodhḳōdh*, lit. crown of the head [Dt **28** 35; **33** 16.20; 2 S **14** 25; Isa **3** 17; Jer **48** 45]; בַּרְזֶל, *barzel*, "the head of an axe" [Dt **19** 5, RVm "iron"; 2 K **6** 5]; לֶהָבָה, *lehābhāh*, לַהֶבֶת, *lahebheth*, "the head of a spear" [1 S **17** 7]; κεφαλή, *kephalḗ*): The first-mentioned Heb word and its Aram. form are found frequently in their literal as well as metaphorical sense. We may distinguish the following meanings:

1. Used of Men

By a slight extension of meaning, "head" occasionally stands for the person itself. This is the case in all passages where evil is said to return or to be requited upon the head of a person (see below).

2. Used of Animals

The word is also used in connection with the serpent's head (Gen **3** 15), the head of the sacrificial ram, bullock and goat (Ex **29** 10.15.19; Lev **4** 4.24), the head of leviathan (Job **41** 7 [Heb **40** 31]).

3. The Head-Piece

It is used also as representing the top or summit of a thing, as the capital of a column or pillar (Ex **36** 38; **38** 28; 2 Ch **3** 15); of mountains (Ex **19** 20; Nu **21** 20; Jgs **9** 7; Am **1** 2; **9** 3); of a scepter (Est **5** 2); of a ladder (Gen **28** 12); of a tower (Gen **11** 4).

4. Beginning, Source, Origin

As a fourth meaning the word occurs (Prov **8** 23; Eccl **3** 11; Isa **41** 4) in the sense of beginning of months (Ex **12** 2), of rivers (Gen **2** 10), of streets or roads (Isa **51** 20; Ezk **16** 25; **21** 21).

5. Leader, Prince

As a leader, prince, chief, chieftain, captain (or as an adj., with the meaning of foremost, uppermost), originally: "he that stands at the head"; cf "God is with us at our head" (2 Ch **13** 12); "Knowest thou that Jeh will take away thy master from thy head?" (2 K **2** 3); "headstone," RV "top stone," i.e. the uppermost stone (Zec **4** 7). Israel is called the head of nations (Dt **28** 13); "The head [capital] of Syria is Damascus, and the head [prince] of Damascus is Rezin" (Isa **7** 8); "heads of their fathers' houses," i.e. elders of the clans (Ex **6** 14); cf "heads of tribes" (Dt **1** 15), also "captain," lit. head (Nu **14** 4; Dt **1** 15; 1 Ch **11** 42; Neh **9** 17). The phrase "head and tail" (Isa **9** 14; **19** 15) is explained by the rabbis as meaning the nobles and the commons among the people; cf "palm-branch and rush" (**9** 14), "hair of the feet . . . . and beard" (**7** 20), but cf also Isa **9** 15. In the NT we find the remarkable statement of Christ being "the head of the church" (Eph **1** 22; **5** 23), "head of every man" (1 Cor **11** 3), "head of all principality and power" (Col **2** 10), "head of the body, the church" (Col **1** 18; cf Eph **4** 15). The context of 1 Cor **11** 3 is very instructive to a true understanding of this expression: "I would have you know, that the head of every man is Christ; and the head of the woman is the man; and the head of Christ is God" (cf Eph **5** 23). Here, clearly, reference is had to the lordship of Christ over His church, not to the oneness of Christ and His church, while in Eph **4** 16 the dependence of the church upon Christ is spoken of. These passages should not therefore be pressed to include the idea of Christ being the intellectual center, the brain of His people, from whence the members are passively governed, for to the Jewish mind the heart was the seat of the intellect, not the head. See HEART.

6. Various Uses

As the head is the most essential part of physical man, calamity and blessing are said to come upon the head of a person (Gen **49** 26; Dt **33** 16; Jgs **9** 57; 1 S **25** 39; 2 Ch **6** 23; Ezk **9** 10; **11** 21; **16** 43; **22** 31). For this reason hands are placed upon the head of a person on which blessings are being invoked (Gen **48** 14.17.18; Mt **19** 15) and upon the sacrificial animal upon which sins are laid (Ex **29** 15; Lev **1** 4; **4** 29.33). Responsibility for a deed is also said to rest on the head of the doer (2 S **1** 16; **3** 29; 1 K **8** 32; Ps **7** 16; Acts **18** 6). The Bible teaches us to return good for evil (Mt **5** 44), or in the very idiomatic Heb style, to "heap coals of fire upon [the] head" of the adversary (Prov **25** 22; Rom **12** 20). This phrase is dark as to its origin, but quite clear as to its meaning and application (cf Rom **12** 17.19.21). The Jew was inclined to swear by his head (Mt **5** 36), as the modern Oriental swears by his beard. The head is said to be under a vow (Nu **6** 18.19; Acts **18** 18; **21** 23), because the Nazirite vow could readily be recognized by the head.

There are numerous idiomatic expressions connected with the head, of which we enumerate the following: "the hoary head" designates old age (see HAIR); "to round the corners of the head," etc (Lev **19** 27; cf also Dt **14** 1; Am **8** 10), probably refers to the shaving of the side locks or the whole scalp among heathen nations, which was often done in idolatrous shrines or in token of initiation into the service of an idol. It was therefore forbidden to Israel, and its rigid observance gave rise to the peculiar Jewish custom of wearing long side locks (see HAIR). "Anointing the head" (Ps **23** 5; **92** 10; He **1** 9) was a sign of joy and hospitality, while the "covering of the head" (2 S **15** 30; Est **6** 12; Jer **14** 3), "putting the hand upon the head" (2 S **13** 19) and putting earth, dust or ashes upon it (Josh **7** 6; 1 S **4** 12; 2 S **1** 2; **13** 19; Lam **2** 10; cf Am **2** 7) were expressive of sadness, grief, deep shame and mourning. In Est **7** 8 Haman's face is covered as a condemned criminal, or as one who has been utterly put to shame, and who has nothing more to say for his life.

In this connection the Pauline injunction as to the veiling of women in the public gatherings of the Christians (1 Cor **11** 5), while men were instructed to appear bareheaded, must be mentioned. This is diametrically opposed to the Jewish custom, according to which men wore the head covered by the *ṭallīth* or prayer shawl, while women were considered sufficiently covered by their long hair (1 Cor **11** 15). The apostle here simply commends a Gr custom for the congregation residing among Gr populations; in other words, he recommends obedience to local standards of decency and good order.

"To bruise the head" (Gen **3** 15) means to injure gravely; "to smite through the head" (Ps **68**

21) is synonymous with complete destruction. "To shake or wag the head" (Ps **22** 7; **44** 14; **64** 8; Jer **18** 16; **48** 27; Lam **2** 15; Mt **27** 39; Mk **15** 29) conveys the meaning of open derision and contempt. "To bow down the head" (Isa **58** 5) indicates humility, sadness and mourning, but it may also be a mere pretense for piety (Sir **19** 26).

H. L. E. LUERING

HEADBAND, hed'band. See DRESS.

HEADDRESS, hed'dres. See DRESS.

HEADSTONE, hed'stōn. See CORNER-STONE.

HEADSTRONG, hed'strong. See HEADY.

HEADTIRE, hed'tīr. See BONNET; DRESS.

HEADY, hed'i: The tr in AV of προπετής, *propetḗs*, "falling forward," trop. "prone," "ready to do anything," "precipitate," "headlong" (2 Tim **3** 4, "heady, high-minded," etc, RV "headstrong"; in Acts **19** 36, the only other place in the NT where *propetēs* occurs, AV has "rashly," RV "rash"). "*Headstrong* signifies strong in the head or the mind, and *heady*, full of one's own head" (Crabb, *Eng. Synonymes*). "*Heady* confidence promises victory without contest" (Johnson).

HEAL, hēl (רָפָא, *rāphā'*; θεραπεύω, *therapeúō*, ἰάομαι, *iáomai*, διασῴζω, *diasṓzō*): The Eng. word is connected with the AS *hælan*, and is used in several senses: (1) Lit., in its meaning of making whole or well, as in Eccl **3** 3. In this way it occurs in prayers for restoration to health (Nu **12** 13; Ps **6** 2; Jer **17** 14); and also in declarations as to God's power to restore to health (Dt **32** 39; 2 K **20** 5–8). (2) **Metaphorically** it is applied to the restoration of the soul to spiritual health and to the repair of the injuries caused by sin (Ps **41** 4; Jer **30** 17). (3) The restoration and deliverance of the afflicted land is expressed by it in 2 Ch **7** 14; Isa **19** 22. (4) It is applied to the forgiveness of sin (Jer **3** 22).

In the NT, *therapeuō* is used 10 t in describing Our Lord's miracles, and is trd "heal." *Iaomai* is used to express spiritual healing (Mt **13** 15; Lk **5** 17; Jn **12** 40), and also of curing bodily disease (Jn **4** 47). *Diasōzō*, meaning "to heal thoroughly," is used in Lk **7** 3 AV where RV renders it "save." The act of healing is called *íasis* twice, in Acts **4** 22.30; *sṓzō*, to save or deliver, is trd "made whole" by RV in Mk **5** 23; Lk **8** 36; Acts **14** 9, but is "healed" in AV. Conversely "made whole" AV in Mt **15** 28 is replaced by "healed" in RV.

Healed is used 33 t in the OT as the rendering of the same Heb word, and in the same variety of senses. It is also used of purification for an offence or breach of the ceremonial law (2 Ch **30** 20); and to express the purification of water which had caused disease (2 K **2** 21.22). **Figuratively** the expression "healed slightly" (ERV "lightly") is used to describe the futile efforts of the false prophets and priests to remedy the backsliding of Israel (Jer **6** 14; **8** 11); here the word for "slightly" is the contemptuous term, *ḳālal*, which means despicably or insignificantly. In Ezk **30** 21, the word "healed" is the rendering of the feminine passive part., *rephū'āh* and is better trd in RV "apply healing medicines." In the NT "healed" usually occurs in connection with the miracles of Our Lord and the apostles. Here it is worthy of note that St. Luke more frequently uses the vb. *iaomai* than *therapeuō*, in the proportion of 17:4, while in Mt and Mk the proportion is 4:8.

Healer (חָבַשׁ, *ḥābhash*) occurs once in Isa **3** 7; the word lit. means a "wrapper up" or "bandager."

ALEX. MACALISTER

HEALING, hēl'ing (מַרְפֵּא, *marpē'*, תְּעָלָה, *te'ālāh*, כֵּהָה, *kēhāh*): In the OT this word is always used in its **figurative** sense; *marpē'*, which lit. means "a cure," is used in Jer **14** 19 twice, and in Mal **4** 2; *te'ālāh*, which lit. means "an irrigation canal," here means something applied externally, as a plaster, in which sense it is used metaphorically in Jer **30** 13; *kēhāh* occurs only in Nah **3** 19 AV and is trd "assuagings" in RV.

In the NT 5 t the vb. is *therapeúō*; once (Acts **10** 38) *iáomai*; in the other passages it is either *íama*, as in 1 Cor **12** 9–30, or *íasis*, as in Acts **4** 22, derivatives from this vb.

HEALING, GIFTS OF (χαρίσματα ἰαμάτων, *charísmata iamátōn*): Among the "spiritual gifts" enumerated in 1 Cor **12** 4–11.28 are included "gifts of healings." See SPIRITUAL GIFTS. The subject has risen into much prominence of recent years, and so calls for separate treatment. The points to be considered are: (1) the NT facts, (2) the nature of the gifts, (3) their permanence in the church.

1. The NT Facts

The Gospels abundantly show that the ministry of Christ Himself was one of healing no less than of teaching (cf Mk **1** 14 f with vs 32–34). When He sent forth the Twelve (Mk **6** 7.13) and the Seventy (Lk **10** 1.9), it was not only to preach the Kingdom of God but to heal the sick. The unauthentic conclusion of Mark's Gospel, if it does not preserve words actually used by Christ Himself, bears witness at all events to the traditional belief of the early church that after His departure from the world His disciples would still possess the gift of healing. The Book of Acts furnishes plentiful evidence of the exercise of this gift by apostles and other prominent men in the primitive church (Acts **3** 7 f; **5** 12–16; **8** 7; **19** 12; **28** 8 f), and the Ep. of Jas refers to a ministry of healing carried on by the elders of a local church acting in their collective capacity (Jas **5** 14 f). But Paul in this passage speaks of "gifts of healings" (the pl. "healings" apparently refers to the variety of ailments that were cured) as being distributed along with other spiritual gifts among the ordinary members of the church. There were men, it would seem, who occupied no official position in the community, and who might not otherwise be distinguished among their fellow-members, on whom this special *chárisma* of healing had been bestowed.

On this subject the NT furnishes no direct information, but it supplies evidence from which conclusions may be drawn.

2. The Nature of the Gifts

We notice that the exercise of the gift is ordinarily conditional on the faith of the recipient of the blessing (Mk **6** 5.6; **10** 52; Acts **14** 9)—faith not only in God but in the human agent (Acts **3** 4 ff; **5** 15; **9** 17). The healer himself is a person of great faith (Mt **17** 19 f), while his power of inspiring the patient with confidence points to the possession of a strong, magnetic personality. The diseases cured appear for the most part to have been not organic but functional; and many of them would now be classed as nervous disorders. The conclusion from these data is that the gifts of healing to which Paul alludes were not miraculous endowments, but natural therapeutic faculties raised to their highest power by Christian faith.

Modern psychology, by its revelation of the marvels of the subliminal self or subconscious mind and the power of "suggestion," shows how it is possible for one man to lay his hand on the very springs of personal life in another, and so discloses the *psychical* basis of the gift of healing. The medical science of our time, by its recognition of the dependence of the physical upon the spiritual, of the control of the bodily functions by the subconscious self, and of the physician's ability by means of suggestion, whether waking or hypnotic, to influence the subconscious soul and set free the healing powers of Nature, provides the *physiological* basis. And may we not add that many incontestable cases of Christian faith-cure (take as a type the well-known instance in which Luther at Weimar "tore Melanchthon," as the latter put it, "out of the very jaws of death"; see *RE*, XII, 520) furnish the religious basis, and prove that faith in God, working through the soul upon the body, is the mightiest of all healing influences, and that one who by his own faith and sympathy and force of personality can stir up faith in others may exercise by God's blessing the power of healing diseases?

There is abundant evidence that in the early centuries the gifts of healing were still claimed and practised within the church (Justin, *Apol.* ii.6; Irenaeus, *Adv. Haer.* ii. 32, 4; Tertullian, *Apol.* xxiii; Origen, *Contra Celsum*, vii.4). The free exercise of these gifts gradually ceased, partly, no doubt, through loss of the early faith and spirituality, but partly through the growth of an ascetic temper which ignored Christ's gospel for the body and tended to the view that pain and sickness are the indispensable ministers of His gospel for the soul. All down the history of the church, however, there have been notable personalities (e.g. Francis of Assisi, Luther, Wesley) and little societies of earnest Christians (e.g. the Waldenses, the early Moravians and Quakers) who have reasserted Christ's gospel on its physical side as a gospel for sickness no less than for sin, and claimed for the gift of healing the place Paul assigned to it among the gifts of the Spirit. In recent years the subject of Christian healing has risen into importance outside of the regularly organized churches through the activity of various faith-healing movements. That the leaders of these movements have laid hold of a truth at once Scriptural and scientific there can be little doubt, though they have usually combined it with what we regard as a mistaken hostility to the ordinary practice of medicine. It is worth remembering that with all his faith in the spiritual gift of healing and personal experience of its power, Paul chose Luke the physician as the companion of his later journeys; and worth noticing that Luke shared with the apostle the honors showered upon the missionaries by the people of Melita whom they had cured of their diseases (Acts **28** 10). Upon the modern church there seems to lie the duty of reaffirming the reality and permanence of the primitive gift of healing, while relating it to the scientific practice of medicine as another power ordained of God, and its natural ally in the task of diffusing the Christian gospel of health.

3. Permanence of Healing Gifts in the Church

LITERATURE.—Hort, *Christian Ecclesia*, ch x; A. T. Schofield, *Force of Mind, Unconscious Therapeutics;* E. Worcester and others, *Religion and Medicine; HJ*, IV, 3, p. 606; *Expos T*, XVII, 349, 417.

J. C. LAMBERT

HEALTH, helth (שָׁלֹם, *shālōm*, יְשׁוּעָה, *yeshū'āh*, רִפְאוּת, *riph'ūth*, אֲרוּכָה, *'ărūkhāh;* **σωτηρία,** *sōtēría,* **ὑγιαίνω,** *hugiainō*): *Shālōm* is part of the formal salutation still common in Pal. In this sense it is used in Gen **43** 28; 2 S **20** 9; the stem word means "peace," and is used in many varieties of expression relating to security, success and good bodily health. *Yeshū'āh*, which specifically means deliverance or help, occurs in the refrain of Ps **42** 11; **43** 5, as well as in Ps **67** 2; in ARV it is rendered "help." *Riph'ūth* is lit. "healing," and is found only in Prov **3** 8. *Marpē'* also means healing of the body, but is used in a **figurative** sense as of promoting soundness of mind and moral character in Prov **4** 22; **12** 18; **13** 17; **16** 24, as also in Jer **8** 15, where RV renders it "healing." *'Ărūkhāh* is also used in the same **figurative** sense in Isa **58** 8; Jer **8** 22; **30** 17; **33** 6; lit. means "repairing or restoring"; it is the word used of the repair of the wall of Jerus by Nehemiah (ch **4**).

The word "health" occurs twice in the NT: in Paul's appeal to his shipmates to take food (Acts **27** 34), he says it is for their *sotēria*, lit. "safety"; so ARV, AV "health." The vb. *hugiainō* is used in 3 Jn ver 2, in the apostle's salutation to Gaius.

ALEX. MACALISTER

HEAP, hēp (עֲרֵמָה, *'ărēmāh*, גַּל, *gal*, נֵד, *nēdh*, תֵּל, *tēl*): "Heap" appears (1) in the simple sense of a gathering or pile, as the tr of *'ărēmāh*, a "heap," in Ruth **3** 7 of grain; Neh **4** 2 of stones; in 2 Ch **31** 6, etc, of the tithes, etc; of *ḥōmer* (boiling up), a "heap"; in Ex **8** 14 of frogs; of *gal*, a "heap"; in Job **8** 17 of stones. (2) As indicating "ruin," "waste," *gal* (2 K **19** 25; Job **15** 28; Isa **25** 2; **37** 26; Jer **9** 11; **51** 37); *me'ī* (Isa **17** 1); *'ī* (Ps **79** 1; Jer **26** 18; Mic **1** 6; **3** 12); *tēl*, "mound," "hillock," "heap" (Dt **13** 16; Josh **8** 28; Jer **30** 18 AV; **49** 2). (3) Of waters, *nēdh*, "heap," "pile" (Ex **15** 8; Josh **3** 13.16; Ps **33** 7; **78** 13); *ḥōmer* (Hab **3** 15, "the heap of mighty waters," RVm "surge"). (4) A cairn, or heap of stones (*a*) over the dead body of a dishonored person, *gal* (Josh **7** 26; **8** 29; 2 S **18** 17); (*b*) as a witness or boundary-heap (Gen **31** 46 f, *Gal'ēdh* [Galeed] in Heb, also *miçpāh*, "watch tower," *Yeghar-Sāhădhūthā'* [Jegar-sahadutha] in Aram., both words meaning "the heap of witness"; see Gen **31** 47.49 RV). (5) As a way mark, *tamrūrīm*, from *tāmar*, "to stand erect" (Jer **31** 21 AV, "Set thee up waymarks, make thee high heaps," RV "guide-posts," a more likely tr).

"To heap" represents various single words: *ḥāthāh*, "to take," "to take hold of," with one exception, applied to fire or burning coals (Prov **25** 22, "Thou wilt heap coals of fire upon his head," "Thou wilt take coals of fire [and heap them] on his head"); *ṣāphāh*, "to add" (Dt **32** 23); *çābhar*, "to heap up" (Hab **1** 10); *kābhaç*, "to press together" (with the fingers or hand) (Hab **2** 5); *rābhāh*, "to multiply" (Ezk **24** 10); *episōreúō*, "to heap up upon" (2 Tim **4** 3, they "will heap to themselves teachers after their own lusts"); *sōreúō*, "to heap up" (Rom **12** 20, "Thou shalt heap coals of fire upon his head"); *thēsaurízō*, "to lay up" (as treasure) (Jas **5** 3 AV, "Ye have heaped treasure together," RV "laid up"); *çābhar*, "to heap up," "to heap" or "store up" (Job **27** 16, "silver"; Ps **39** 6, "riches"; Zec **9** 3, "silver"); *sūm*, *sīm* "to place," "set," "put" (Job **36** 13 AV, "The hypocrites in heart heap up wrath," RV "They that are godless in heart lay up anger"). In Jgs **15** 16 we have *ḥămōr, ḥămōrothāyim*, "with the jawbone of an ass, heaps upon heaps," RVm "heap, two heaps"; one of Samson's sayings; *ḥămōr* means "an ass," *ḥōmer* "a heap."

For "heap up words" (Job **16** 4), RV has "join together"; for "shall be a heap" (Isa **17** 11), "fleeth away," m "shall be a heap"; "heap" for "number" (Nah **3** 3); ERV "heap of stones" for "sling," m as AV and ARV (Prov **26** 8); "in one heap" for "upon a heap" (Josh **3** 16); "he heapeth up [dust]" for "they shall heap" (Hab **1** 10).

W. L. WALKER

HEART, härt (לֵב, *lēbh*, לֵבָב, *lēbhābh;* **καρδία,** *kardía*): The different senses in which the word occurs in the OT and the NT may be grouped under the following heads:

It represents in the first place the *bodily organ*, and by easy transition those experiences which affect or are affected by the body. Fear, love, courage, anger, joy, sorrow, hatred are always ascribed to the heart—esp. in the OT; thus courage for which usually *rūaḥ* is used (Ps **27** 14); joy (Ps **4** 7); anger (Dt **19** 6, "while his heart is hot," *lēbhābh*); fear (1 S **25** 37); sorrow (Ps **13** 2), etc.

1. Various Meanings

Hence naturally it came to stand for the *man himself* (Dt **7** 17; "say in thine heart," Isa **14** 13).

As representing the man himself, it was considered to be the seat of the emotions and passions and appetites (Gen **18** 5; Lev **19** 17; Ps **104** 15), and embraced likewise the intellectual and moral faculties—though these are necessarily ascribed to the "soul" as well. This distinction is not always observed.

2. Heart and Personality

"Soul" in Heb can never be rendered by "heart"; nor can "heart" be considered as a synonym for "soul." Cremer has well observed: "The Heb *nephesh* ("soul") is never tr[d] *kardia* ("heart"). . . . . The range of the Heb *nephesh*, to which the Gr *psuchḗ* alone corresponds, differs so widely from the ideas connected with *psuchē*, that utter confusion would have ensued had *psuchē* been employed in an unlimited degree for *lēbh* ("heart"). The Bib. *lēbh* never, like *psuchē*, denotes the personal subject, nor could it do so. That which in classical Gr is ascribed to *psuchē* [a good soul, a just soul, etc] is in the Bible ascribed to the *heart* alone and cannot be otherwise" (Cremer, *Lexicon*, art. "Kardia," 437 ff, German ed).

3. Soul and Heart

In the heart *vital action* is centered (1 K **21** 7). "Heart," except as a bodily organ, is never ascribed to animals, as is the case sometimes with *nephesh* and *rūaḥ* (Lev **17** 11, *nephesh;* Gen **2** 19; Nu **16** 22; Gen **7** 22, *rūaḥ*). "Heart" is thus often used interchangeably with these two (Gen **41** 8; Ps **86** 4; **119** 20); but "it never denotes the personal subject, always the personal organ."

4. Center of Vital Action

As the central organ in the body, forming a focus for its vital action, it has come to stand for the center of its moral, spiritual, intellectual life. "In particular the heart is the place in which the process of self-consciousness is carried out, in which the soul is at home with itself, and is conscious of all its doing and suffering as its own" (Oehler). Hence it is that men of "courage" are called "men of the heart"; that the Lord is said to speak "in his heart" (Gen **8** 21); that men "know in their own heart" (Dt **8** 5); that "no one considereth in his heart' (Isa **44** 19 AV). "Heart" in this connection is sometimes rendered "mind," as in Nu **16** 28 ("of mine own mind," Vulg *ex proprio corde*, LXX *ap' emautoú*); the foolish "is void of understanding," i.e. "heart" (Prov **6** 32, where the LXX renders *phrenôn*, Vulg *cordis*, Luther "der ist ein Narr"). God is represented as "searching the heart" and "trying the reins" (Jer **17** 10 AV). Thus "heart" comes to stand for "conscience," for which there is no word in Heb, as in Job **27** 6, "My heart shall not reproach me," or in 1 S **24** 5, "David's heart smote him"; cf 1 S **25** 31. From this it appears, in the words of Owen: "The heart in Scripture is variously used, sometimes for the mind and understanding, sometimes for the will, sometimes for the affections, sometimes for the conscience, sometimes for the whole soul. Generally, it denotes the whole soul of man and all the faculties of it, not absolutely, but as they are all one principle of moral operations, as they all concur in our doing of good and evil."

5. Heart and Mind

The radical corruption of human nature is clearly taught in Scripture and brought into connection with the heart. It is "uncircumcised" (Jer **9** 26; Ezk **44** 7; cf Acts **7** 51); and "hardened" (Ex **4** 21); "wicked" (Prov **26** 23); "perverse" (Prov **11** 20); "godless" (Job **36** 13); "deceitful and desperately wicked" (Jer **17** 9 AV). It defiles the whole man (Mt **15** 19.20); resists, as in the case of Pharaoh, the repeated call of God (Ex **7** 13). There, however, the law of God is written (Rom **2** 15); there the work of grace is wrought (Acts **15** 9), for the "heart" may be "renewed" by grace (Ezk **36** 26), because the "heart" is the seat of sin (Gen **6** 5; **8** 21).

6. Figurative Senses

This process of heart-renewal is indicated in various ways. It is the removal of a "stony heart" (Ezk **11** 19). The heart becomes "clean" (Ps **51** 10); "fixed" (Ps **112** 7) through "the fear" of the Lord (ver 1); "With the heart man believeth" (Rom **10** 10); on the "heart" the power of God is exercised for renewal (Jer **31** 33). To God the bereaved apostles pray as a knower of the heart (Acts **1** 24—a word not known to classical writers, found only here in the NT and in Acts **15** 8, *kardiognôstēs*). In the "heart" God's Spirit dwells with might (Eph **3** 16, *eis tón ésō ánthrōpon*); in the "heart" God's love is poured forth (Rom **5** 5). The Spirit of His son has been "sent forth into the heart" (Gal **4** 6); the "earnest of the Spirit" has been given "in the heart" (2 Cor **1** 22). In the work of grace, therefore, the heart occupies a position almost unique.

7. Process of Heart Renewal

We might also refer here to the command, on which both the OT and NT revelation of love is based: "Thou shalt love Jeh thy God with all thy heart, and with all thy soul, and with all thy might" (Dt **6** 5); where "heart" always takes the first place, and is the term which in the NT rendering remains unchanged (cf Mt **22** 37; Mk **12** 30. 33; Lk **10** 27, where "heart" always takes precedence).

8. The Heart First

A bare reference may be made to the employment of the term for that which is innermost, hidden, deepest in anything (Ex **15** 8; Jon **2** 3), the very center of things. This we find in all languages. Cf Eph **3** 16.17, "in the inward man," as above. J. I. MARAIS

9. A Term for "Deepest"

HEARTH, härth: Occurs 7 t in AV: Gen **18** 6; Ps **102** 3; Isa **30** 14; Jer **36** 22.23 *bis;* Zec **12** 6; 4 t in RV: Lev **6** 9; Isa **30** 14; Ezk **43** 15.16 ("altar hearth"); cf also Isa **29** 1 RVm. It will be noted that the renderings of the two VSS agree in only one passage (Isa **30** 14).

(1) The hearth in case of a tent was nothing more than a depression in the ground in which fire was kindled for cooking or for warmth. Cakes were baked, after the fashion of Gen **18** 6, in the ashes or upon hot stones. In this passage, however, there is nothing in the Heb corresponding to AV "on the hearth." In the poorer class of houses also the hearth consisted of such a depression, of varying dimensions, in the middle or in one corner of the room. There was no chimney for the smoke, which escaped as it could, or through a latticed opening for the purpose (the "chimney" of Hos **13** 3). While the nature of the hearth is thus clear enough, more or less uncertainty attaches to specific terms used in the Heb. In Isa **30** 14 the expression means simply "that which is kindled," referring to the bed of live coals. From this same vb. (*yāḳadh*, "be kindled") are formed the nouns *mōḳēdh* (Ps **102** 3 [Heb 4]) and *mōḳᵉdhāh* (Lev **6** 9 [Heb 2]), which might, according to their formation, mean either the *material* kindled or the *place* where a fire is kindled. Hence the various renderings, "firebrand," "hearth," etc. Moreover in Lev **6** 9[2] the termination *-āh* of *mōḳᵉdhāh* may be taken as the pronominal suffix, "its"; hence RVm "on its firewood."

(2) Two other terms have reference to heating in the better class of houses. In Jer **36** 22.23 the word (*'āḥ*) means a "brazier" of burning coals, with

which Jehoiakim's "winter house" was heated. The same purpose was served by the "pan [*kiyyōr*] of fire" of Zec **12** 6 RV, apparently a wide, shallow vessel otherwise used for cooking (1 S **2** 14, EV "pan"), or as a wash basin (cf Ex **30** 18; 1 K **7** 38, etc, "laver").

(3) Another class of passages is referred to the signification "altar hearth," which seems to have been a term applied to the top of the altar of burnt offering. The *mōkᵉdhāh* of Lev **6** 9 [2], though related by derivation to the words discussed under (1) above, belongs here (cf also Ecclus **50** 12, "by the hearth of the altar," *παρ' ἐσχάρᾳ βωμοῦ, par' eschára bōmoú*). Again in Ezekiel's description of the altar of the restored temple (**43** 15.16), he designates the top of the altar by a special term (RVm *ariel*), which is by most understood to mean "altar hearth" (so RV). With this may be compared the symbolical name given to Jerus (Isa **29** 1), and variously explained as "lion [or lioness] of God," or "hearth of God."

Benjamin Reno Downer

HEARTILY, här'ti-li: Occurs (Col **3** 23) as the tr of ἐκ ψυχῆς, *ek psuchḗs*, "out of the soul," "Whatsoever ye do, do it heartily as unto the Lord [who sees the heart and recompenses "whatsoever good thing a man does"] and not unto men" (however they, your masters according to the flesh, may regard it); RV "work heartily," m "Gr from the soul."

In 2 Macc **4** 37, we have "Antiochus was heartily sorry," *psuchikōs* ("from the soul").

HEAT, hēt (חֹם, *ḥōm*, חֹרֶב, *hōrebh*, "drought," Job **30** 30; Isa **4** 6; **25** 4; Jer **36** 30; שָׁרָב, *shārābh*, Isa **49** 10, tr[d] in RVm "mirage"; ζεστός, *zestós*, "fervent," Rev **3** 15, θέρμη, *thérmē*, Acts **28** 3, καῦμα, *kaúma*, Rev **7** 16, καύσων, *kaúsōn*, Mt **20** 12; see Mirage): The heat of the summer is greatly dreaded in Pal, and as a rule the people rest under cover during the middle of the day, when the sun is hottest. There is no rain from May to October, and scarcely a cloud in the sky to cool the air or to screen off the burning vertical rays of the sun. The first word of advice given to visitors to the country is to protect themselves from the sun. Even on the mountains, where the temperature of the air is lower, the sun is perhaps more fierce, owing to the lesser density of the atmosphere.

1. Dreaded in Pal

This continuous summer heat often causes sunstroke, and the glare causes diseases of the eye which affect a large percentage of the people of Pal and Egypt.

2. Causes Disease

It is to be expected that in these times of heat and drought the ideal pleasure has come to be to sit in the shade by some cool flowing fountain. In the mountains the village which has the coolest spring of water is the most desired. These considerations give renewed meaning to the passages: "as cold waters to a thirsty soul" (Prov **25** 25); "He maketh me to lie down in green pastures; he leadeth me beside still waters" (Ps **23** 2). What a blessing to be "under the shadow of the Almighty" (Ps **91** 1), where "the sun shall not strike upon them, nor any heat" (Rev **7** 16)!

3. Relief Sought

The middle of the day is often referred to as the "heat of the day" (1 S **11** 11). It made a great difference to the army whether it could win the battle before the midday heat. Saladin won the great battle at Hattin by taking advantage of this fact. It was a particular time of the day when it was the custom to rest. "They came about the heat of the day to the house of Ish-bosheth, as he took his rest at noon" (2 S **4** 5). Jeh appeared to Abraham as "he sat in the tent door in the heat of the day" (Gen **18** 1). The hardship of working throughout the day is expressed in Mt **20** 12, "who have borne the burden of the day and scorching heat." Sometimes just after sunrise the contrast of the cold of night and the heat of the sun is esp. noticeable. "The sun ariseth with the scorching wind" (Jas **1** 11).

4. Midday Heat

In summer the wind is usually from the S.W., but in case it is from the S. it is sure to be hot. "When ye see a south wind blowing, ye say, There will be a scorching heat" (Lk **12** 55). The heat on a damp, sultry day, when the atmosphere is full of dust haze is esp. oppressive, and is referred to in Isa **25** 5 as "the heat by the shade of a cloud." The heat of summer melts the snow on the mountains and causes all vegetation to dry up and wither. Ice and snow vanish in the heat thereof (Job **6** 17), "Drought and heat consume the snow waters" (Job **24** 19). But the "tree planted by the waters, that spreadeth out its roots by the river . . . . shall not fear when heat cometh, but its leaf shall be green" (Jer **17** 8).

5. Summer Heat

The word is used often in connection with anger in the Scriptures: "hot anger" (Ex **11** 8); "hot displeasure" (Dt **9** 19); "anger of the Lord was hot against Israel" (Jgs **2** 14 AV); "thine anger from waxing hot" (Ps **85** 3 AVm); "I know thy works, that thou art neither cold nor hot" (Rev **3** 15).

6. Figurative Uses

Alfred H. Joy

HEATH, hēth. See Tamarisk.

HEATHEN, hē'th'n, hē'then. See Gentiles.

HEAVE OFFERING, hēv of'ẽr-ing. See Sacrifice.

HEAVEN, hev''n. See Astronomy.

HEAVEN, HOST OF. See Astronomy, I, 1.

HEAVEN, ORDINANCES OF. See Astronomy, I, 1; II, 13.

HEAVEN, WINDOWS OF. See Astronomy, III, 4.

HEAVENLY, hev''n-li (οὐράνιος, *ouránios*, ἐπουράνιος, *epouránios*): Pertaining to heaven or the heavens. See Heavens. The phrase *tá epouránia*, tr[d] "heavenly things" in Jn **3** 12; He **8** 5; **9** 23, but in Eph "heavenly places" (**1** 3.20; **2** 6; **3** 10; **6** 12), has shades of meaning defined by the context. In Jn **3** 12, in contrast with "earthly things" (i.e. such as can be brought to the test of experience), it denotes truths known only through revelation (God's love in salvation). In He the sense is local. In Eph it denotes the sphere of spiritual privilege in Christ, save in **6** 12, where it stands for the unseen spiritual world, in which both good and evil forces operate. It is always the sphere of the super-earthly. James Orr

HEAVENS, hev''nz (שָׁמַיִם, *shāmayīm;* οὐρανοί, *ouranoí*): On the physical heavens see Astronomy; World. Above these, in popular conception, were the celestial heavens, the abode of God and of the hosts of angels (Ps **11** 4; **103** 19–21; Isa **66** 1; Rev **4** 2; **5** 11; cf Dnl **7** 10), though it was recognized that Jeh's presence was not confined to any region (1 K **8** 27). Later Judaism reckoned seven heavens. The apostle Paul speaks of himself as caught up into "the third heaven," which he evidently identifies with Paradise (2 Cor **12** 2). See Heavenly.

HEAVENS, NEW (AND EARTH, NEW):

1. Eschatological Idea

The formal conception of new heavens and a new earth occurs in Isa **65** 17; **66** 22; 2 Pet **3** 13; Rev **21** 1 (where "heaven," singular). The idea in substance is also found in Isa **51** 16; Mt **19** 28; 2 Cor **5** 17; He **12** 26–28. In each case the reference is eschatological, indeed the adj. "new" seems to have acquired in this and other connections a semi-technical eschatological sense. It must be remembered that the OT has no single word for "universe," and that the phrase "heaven and earth" serves to supply the deficiency. The promise of a new heavens and a new earth is therefore equivalent to a promise of world renewal.

2. Earliest National Type

It is a debated question how old in the history of revelation this promise is. Isaiah is the prophet with whom the idea first occurs in explicit form, and that in passages which many critics would assign to the post-exilic period (the so-called Trito-Isaiah). In general, until recently, the trend of criticism has been to represent the universalistic-cosmic type of eschatology as developed out of the particularistic-national type by a gradual process of widening of the horizon of prophecy, a view which would put the emergence of the former at a comparatively late date. More recently, however, Gressmann (*Der Ursprung der israelitisch-jüdischen Eschatologie*, 1905) and others have endeavored to show that often even prophecies belonging to the latter type embody material and employ means of expression which presuppose acquaintance with the idea of a world-catastrophe at the end. On this view the world-eschatology would have, from ancient times, existed alongside of the more narrowly confined outlook, and would be even older than the latter. These writers further assume that the cosmic eschatology was not indigenous among the Hebrews, but of oriental (Bab) origin, a theory which they apply not only to the more developed system of the later apocalyptic writings, but also to its preformations in the OT. The cosmic eschatology is not believed to have been the distinctive property of the great ethical prophets, but rather a commonly current mythological belief to which the prophets refer without formally endorsing it. Its central thought is said to have been the belief that the end of the world-process must correspond to the beginning, that consequently the original condition of things, when heaven and earth were new, must repeat itself at some future point, and the state of paradise with its concomitants return, a belief supposed to have rested on certain astronomical observations.

3. Different from Mythological Theory

4. Antiquity of Cosmical Conception

While this theory in the form presented is unproven and unacceptable, it deserves credit for having focused attention on certain phenomena in the OT which clearly show that Messianic prophecy, and particularly the world-embracing scope which it assumes in some predictions, is far older than modern criticism had been willing to concede. The OT from the beginning has an eschatology and puts the eschatological promise on the broadest racial basis (Gen **3**). It does not first ascend from Israel to the new humanity, but at the very outset takes its point of departure in the race and from this descends to the election of Israel, always keeping the universalistic goal in clear view. Also in the earliest accounts, already elements of a cosmical universalism find their place side by side with those of a racial kind, as when Nature is represented as sharing in the consequences of the fall of man.

5. The Cosmical Dependent on the Ethico-Religious

As regards the antiquity of the universalistic and cosmical eschatology, therefore, the conclusions of these writers may be registered as a gain, while on the two other points of the pagan origin and the unethical character of the expectation involved, dissent from them should be expressed. According to the OT, the whole idea of world-renewal is of strictly supernatural origin, and in it the cosmical follows the ethical hope. The cosmical eschatology is simply the correlate of the fundamental Bib. principle that the issues of the world-process depend on the ethico-religious developments in the history of man (cf 2 Pet **3** 13).

6. The End Correspondent to the Beginning

But the end correspondent to the beginning is likewise a true Scriptural principle, which the theory in question has helped to reëmphasize, although there is this difference, that Scripture does not look forward to a repetition of the same process, but to a restoration of the primeval harmony on a higher plane such as precludes all further disturbance. In the passages above cited, there are clear reminiscences of the account of creation (Isa **51** 16, "that I may plant the heavens, and *lay the foundations* of the earth"; **65** 17, "I *create* new heavens and a new earth"; 2 Pet **3** 13 compared with vs 4–6; Rev **21** 1 compared with the imagery of paradise throughout the chapter). Besides this, where the thought of the renewal of earth is met with in older prophecy, this is depicted in colors of the state of paradise (Isa **11** 6–9; Hos **2** 18–21). The "regeneration" (*palingenesía*) of Mt **19** 28 also points back to the first genesis of the world. The 'inhabited earth to come' (*oikouménē méllousa*) of He **2** 5 occurs at the opening of a context throughout which the account of Gen **1–3** evidently stood before the writer's mind.

7. The Cosmical Heavens: He 12: 26–29

In the combination "new heavens and a new earth," the term "heavens" must therefore be taken in the sense imposed upon it by the story of creation, where "heavens" designates not the celestial habitation of God, but the cosmical heavens, the region of the supernal waters, sun moon and stars. The Bible nowhere suggests that there is anything abnormal or requiring renewal in God's dwelling-place (He **9** 23 is of a different import). In Rev **21,** where "the new heaven and the new earth" appear, it is at the same time stated that the new Jerus comes down from God out of heaven (cf vs 1.2.10). In He **12** 26–28 also the implication is that only the lower heavens are subject to renewal. The "shaking" that accompanies the new covenant and corresponds to the shaking of the law-giving at Sinai, is a shaking of "not the earth only, but also the heaven." This shaking, in its reference to heaven as well as to earth, signifies a removal of the things shaken. But from the things thus shaken and removed (including heaven), the writer distinguishes "those things which are not shaken," which are destined to remain, and these are identified with the kingdom of God. The kingdom of God, however, according to the general trend of the teaching of the epistle, has its center in the heavenly world. The words "that have been made," in ver 27, do not assign their created character as the reason why heaven and earth can be shaken, an exegesis which would involve us in the difficulty that among that which remains there is something uncreated besides God; the true construction and correct paraphrase are: "as of things that were made with the thought in the mind of God that those things which cannot be shaken may remain," i.e. already at creation God contemplated an unchangeable universe as the ultimate, higher state of things.

In Mt **19** 28 the term *palingenesia* marks the world-renewing as the renewal of an abnormal state of things. The Scripture teaching, therefore, is that around the center of God's heaven, which is not subject to deterioration or renewal, a new cosmical heaven and a new earth will be established to be the dwelling-place of the eschatological humanity. The light in which the promise thus appears reminds us that the renewed kosmos, earth as well as cosmical heavens, is destined to play a permanent (not merely provisional, on the principle of chiliasm) part in the future life of the people of God. This is in entire harmony with the prevailing Bib. representation, not only in the OT but likewise in the NT (cf Mt **5** 5; He **2** 5), although in the Fourth Gospel and in the Pauline Epp. the emphasis is to such an extent thrown on the heaven-centered character of the future life that the rôle to be played in it by the renewed earth recedes into the background. Rev, on the other hand, recognizes this element in its imagery of "the new Jerus" coming down from God out of heaven upon earth.

8. Palingenesis: Mt 19:28

That the new heavens and the new earth are represented as the result of a "creation" does not necessarily involve a production *ex nihilo*. The terms employed in 2 Pet **3** 6–13 seem rather to imply that the renewal will out of the old produce a purified universe, whence also the catastrophe is compared to that of the Deluge. As then the old world perished by water and the present world arose out of the flood, so in the end-crisis "the heavens shall be dissolved by fire and the elements melt with fervent heat," to give rise to the new heaven and the new earth in which righteousness dwells. The term *palingenesia* (Mt **19** 28) points to renewal, not to creation *de novo*. The Talm also teaches that the world will pass through a process of purification, although at the same time it seems to break up the continuity between this and the coming world by the phantastic assumption that the new heavens and the new earth of Isa **65** 17 were created at the close of the Hexemeron of Gen **1**. This was inferred from the occurrence of the article in Isa **66** 22, "*the* new heavens and *the* new earth."

9. A Purified Universe

GEERHARDUS VOS

HEAVY, hev'i, **HEAVINESS**, hev'i-nes (כָּבֵד, *kābhēdh*, דְּאָגָה, *de'āghāh*; λύπη, *lúpē*):

Heavy (heave, to lift) is used lit. with respect to material things, as the tr of *kōbhēdh*, "heaviness" (Prov **27** 3, "a stone is heavy"); of *kābhēdh*, "to be weighty" (1 S **4** 18; 2 S **14** 26; Lam **3** 7); of *'āmaṣ*, "to load" (Isa **46** 1 AV; cf Mt **26** 43; Mk **14** 40; Lk **9** 32, "Their eyes were heavy"); *baréomai*, "to be weighed down."

1. Literal

It is used (1) for what is hard to bear, oppressive, *kābhēdh* (Ex **18** 18; Nu **11** 14; 1 S **5** 6.11; Ps **38** 4; Isa **24** 20); *mōṭāh*, a "yoke" (Isa **58** 6, RV "bands of the yoke"); *ḳāsheh*, "sharp," "hard" (1 K **14** 6, "heavy tidings"); *barús*, "heavy" (Mt **23** 4); (2) for sad, sorrowful (weighed down), *mar*, "bitter" (Prov **31** 6, RV "bitter"); *ra'*, "evil" (Prov **25** 20); *adēmonéō*, lit. "to be sated," "wearied," then, "to be very heavy," "dejected" (Mt **26** 37, of Our Lord in Gethsemane, "[he] began to be sorrowful and very heavy," RV "sore troubled"); "*adēmonein* denotes a kind of stupefaction and bewilderment, the intellectual powers reeling and staggering under the pressure of the ideas presented to them" (Mason, *The Conditions of Our Lord's Life on Earth*); cf Mk **14** 33; (3) morose, sulky, as well as sad, *ṣar*, "sullen," "sour," "angry" (1 K **20** 43; **21** 4, "heavy and displeased"); (4) dull, *kābhēdh* (Isa **6** 10, "make their ears heavy"; **59** 1, "neither [is] his ear heavy"); (5) "tired" seems to be the meaning in Ex **17** 12, "Moses' hands were heavy" (*kābhēdh*); cf Mt **26** 43 and ‖s above.

2. Figuratively

Heavily is the tr of *kebhēdhuth*, "heaviness" (Ex **14** 25), meaning "with difficulty"; of *ḳādhar*, "to be black," "to be a mourner" (Ps **35** 14 AV, RV "I bowed down mourning"); of *kābhēdh* (Isa **47** 6).

Heaviness has always the sense of anxiety, sorrow, grief, etc; *de'āghāh*, "fear," "dread," "anxious care" (Prov **12** 25, "Heaviness in the heart of a man maketh it stoop," RVm "or care"); *kēhāh*, "to be feeble," "weak" (Isa **61** 3, "the spirit of heaviness"); *pānīm*, "face," "aspect" (Job **9** 27 AV, "I will leave off my heaviness," RV "[sad] countenance"; cf 2 Esd **5** 16; Wisd **17** 4; Ecclus **25** 23); *ta'ănīyāh*, from *'ānāh*, "to groan," "to sigh" (Isa **29** 2, RV "mourning and lamentation"); *tūghāh*, "sadness," "sorrow" (Ps **119** 28; Prov **10** 1; **14** 13); *ta'ănīth*, "affliction of one's self," "fasting" (Ezr **9** 5, RV "humiliation," m "fasting"); *katḗpheia*, "dejection," "sorrow" (lit. "of the eyes") (Jas **4** 9, "your joy [turned] to heaviness"); *lupē*, "grief" (Rom **9** 2, RV "great sorrow"; 2 Cor **2** 1, RV "sorrow"); *lupéomai* (1 Pet **1** 6, RV "put to grief"); for *nūsh*, "to be sick," "feeble" (Ps **69** 20, RVm "sore sick"), and *adēmoneō* (Phil **2** 26 RV "sore troubled"), AV has "full of heaviness." "Heaviness," in the sense of sorrow, sadness, occurs in 2 Esd **10** 7. 8.24; Tob **2** 5; *lupē* (Ecclus **22** 4, RV "grief"; **30** 21, "Give not thy soul to heaviness," RV "sorrow"; 1 Macc **6** 4); *lupeō* (Ecclus **30** 9, RV "will grieve thee"); *pénthos* (1 Macc **3** 51, etc).

RV has "heavier work" for "more work" (Ex **5** 9); "heavy upon men" for "common among men" (Eccl **6** 1); for "were heavy loaden" (Isa **46** 1), "are made a load"; for "the burden thereof is heavy" (Isa **30** 27), "in thick rising smoke."

W. L. WALKER

HEBER, hē'bẽr (חֶבֶר, *ḥebher*, "associate" or, possibly, "enchanter"; Ἔβερ, *Éber*): A name occurring several times in the OT as the name of an individual or of a clan.

(1) A member of the tribe of Asher and son of Beraiah (Gen **46** 17; Nu **26** 45; 1 Ch **7** 31 f).

(2) A Kenite, husband of Jael, who deceptively slew Sisera, captain of the army of Jabin, a Canaanite king (Jgs **4** 17; **5** 24). He had separated himself from the main body of the Kenites, which accounts for his tent being near Kedesh, the place of Sisera's disastrous battle (Jgs **4** 11).

(3) Head of a clan of Judah, and son of Mered by his Jewish, as distinguished from an Egyp, wife. He was father, or founder, of Soco (1 Ch **4** 18).

(4) A Benjamite, or clan or family of Elpaal belonging to Benjamin (1 Ch **8** 17).

(5) Heber, of Our Lord's genealogy (Lk **3** 35 AV), better, Eber.

So, the name "Eber," עֵבֶר, *'ēbher*, in 1 Ch **5** 13; **8** 22, is not to be confused with Heber, חֶבֶר, *ḥebher*, as in the foregoing passages.

EDWARD BAGBY POLLARD

HEBERITES, hē'bẽr-īts (הַחֶבְרִי, *ha-ḥebhrī*): Descendants of Heber, a prominent clan of Asher, (Nu **26** 45). Supposed by some to be connected with the Ḥabiri of the Am Tab.

HEBREW, hē′brōō, **HEBREWESS,** hē′brōō-es (עִבְרִי, *'ibhrī*, fem. עִבְרִיָּה, *'ibhrīyāh;* **Ἑβραῖος,** *Hebraíos*): The earliest name for Abraham (Gen **14** 13) and his descendants (Joseph, Gen **39** 14.17; **40** 15; **41** 12; **43** 32; Israelites in Egypt, Ex **1** 15; **2** 6.11.13; **3** 18; in laws, Ex **21** 2; Dt **15** 12; in history, 1 S **4** 6.9; **13** 7.19, etc; later, Jer **34** 9, "Hebrewess," 14; Jon **1** 9; in the NT, Acts **6** 1; 2 Cor **11** 22; Phil **3** 5). The etymology of the word is disputed. It may be derived from Eber (Gen **10** 21.24.25, etc), or, as some think, from the vb. עָבַר, *'ābhar*, "to cross over" (people from across the Euphrates; cf Josh **24** 2). A connection is sought by some with the *apri* or *epri* of the Egyp monuments, and again with the Habiri of the Am Tab. In Acts **6** 1, the "Hebrews" are contrasted with "Hellenists," or Gr-speaking Jews. By the "Heb" tongue in the NT (*Hebraïstí*, Jn **5** 2; **19** 13.17.20; **20** 16) is meant ARAMAIC (q.v.), but also in Rev **9** 11; **16** 16, Heb proper.

JAMES ORR

HEBREW LANGUAGE. See LANGUAGES OF THE OT; ARAMAIC.

HEBREWS, hē′brōōz, **EPISTLE TO THE:**

I. Title.—In AV and ERV the title of this book describes it as "the Epistle of Paul the Apostle to the Hebrews." Modern scholarship has disputed the applicability of every word of this title. Neither does it appear in the oldest MSS, where we find simply "to Hebrews" (*prós Hebraíous*). This, too, seems to have been prefixed to the original writing by a collector or copyist. It is too vague and general for the author to have used it. And there is nothing in the body of the book which affirms any part of either title. Even the shorter title was an inference from the general character of the writing. Nowhere is criticism less hampered by problems of authenticity and inspiration. No question arises, at least directly, of pseudonymity either of author or of readers, for both are anonymous. For the purpose of tracing the history and interpreting the meaning of the book, the absence of a title, or of any definite historical data, is a disadvantage. We are left to infer its historical context from a few fragments of uncertain tradition, and from such general references to historical conditions as the document itself contains. Where no date, name or well-known event is fixed, it becomes impossible to decide, among many possibilities, what known historical conditions, if any, are presupposed. Yet this very fact, of the book's detachment from personal and historical incidents, renders it more self-contained, and its exegesis less dependent upon understanding the exact historical situation. But its general relation to the thought of its time must be taken into account if we are to understand it at all.

II. Literary Form.—The writer was evidently a man of culture, who had a masterly command of the Gr language.

1. The Author's Culture and Style

The theory of Clement of Alexandria, that the work was a tr from Heb, was merely an inference from the supposition that it was first addressed to Heb-speaking Christians. It bears none of the marks of a tr. It is written in pure idiomatic Gr. The writer had an intimate knowledge of the LXX, and was familiar with Jewish life. He was well-read in Hellenic lit. (e.g. Wisd), and had probably made a careful study of Philo (see VI below). His argument proceeds continuously and methodically, in general, though not strict, accord with the rules of Gr rhetoric, and without the interruptions and digressions which render Paul's arguments so hard to follow. "Where the literary skill of the author comes out is in the deft adjustment of the argumentative to the hortatory sections" (Moffatt, *Intro*, 424 f). He has been classed with Lk as the most "cultured" of the early Christian writers.

It has been questioned whether He is rightly called a letter at all. Unlike all Paul's letters, it opens without any personal note of address or salutation; and at the outset it sets forth, in rounded periods and in philosophical language, the central theme which is developed throughout.

2. Letter, Epistle or Treatise?

In this respect it resembles the Johannine writings alone in the NT. But as the argument proceeds, the personal note of application, exhortation and expostulation emerges more clearly (**2** 1; **3** 1–12; **4** 1.14; **5** 11; **6** 9; **10** 9; **13** 7); and it ends with greetings and salutations (**13** 18 ff). The writer calls it "a word of exhortation." The vb. *epésteila* (RV "I have written") is the usual expression for writing a letter (**13** 22). Hebrews begins like an essay, proceeds like a sermon, and ends as a letter.

Deissmann, who distinguishes between a "true letter," the genuine personal message of one man to another, and an "epistle," or a treatise written in imitation of the form of a letter, but with an eye on the reading public, puts He in the latter class; nor would he "consider it anything but a literary oration—hence not as an epistle at all—if the *epesteila*, and the greetings at the close, did not permit of the supposition that it had at one time opened with something of the nature of an address as well" (*Bible Studies*, 49–50). There is no textual or historical evidence of any opening address having ever stood as part of the text; nor does the opening section bear any mark or suggestion of fragmentariness, as if it had once followed such an address.

Yet the supposition that a greeting once stood at the beginning of our document is not so impossible as Zahn thinks (*Intro to the NT*, II, 313 f), as a comparison with Jas or 1 Pet will show.

So unusual is the phenomenon of a letter without a greeting, that among the ancients, Pantaenus had offered the explanation that Paul, out of modesty, had refrained from putting his name to a letter addressed to the Hebrews, because the Lord Himself had been apostle to them.

In recent times, Jülicher and Harnack have conjectured that the author intentionally suppressed the greeting, either from motives of prudence at a time of persecution, or because it was unnecessary, since the bearer of the letter would communicate the name of the sender to the recipients.

Fr. Overbeck advanced the more revolutionary hypothesis that the letter once opened with a greeting, but from someone other than Paul; that in order to satisfy the general conditions of canonization, the non-apostolic greeting was struck out by the Alexandrians, and the personal references in **13** 22–25 added, in order to represent it as Pauline.

3. A Unity or a Composite Writing?

W. Wrede, starting from this theory, rejects the first part of it and adopts the second. He does not base his hypothesis on the conditions of canonization, but on an examination of the writing itself. He adopts Deissmann's rejected alternative, and argues that the main part of the book was originally not an epistle at all, but a general doctrinal treatise. Then ch **13,** and esp. vs 18 ff, were added by a later hand, in order to represent the whole as a Pauline letter, and the book in its final form was made, after all, pseudonymous. The latter supposition is based upon an assumed reference to imprisonment in **13** 19 (cf Philem ver 22) and upon the reference to Timothy in **13** 23 (cf Phil **2** 19); and the proof that these professed Pauline phrases are not really Pauline is found in a supposed contradiction between **13** 19 and **13** 23. But ver 19 does not necessarily refer to imprisonment exclusively or even at all, and therefore it stands in no contradiction with ver 23 (cf Rom **1** 9–13). And Timothy must have associated with many Christian leaders besides Paul. But why should anybody who wanted to represent the letter as Pauline and who scrupled not to add to it for that purpose, refrain from the obvious device of prefixing a Pauline greeting? Moreover, it is only by the most forced special pleading that it can be maintained that chs **1–12** are a mere doctrinal treatise, devoid of all evidences of a personal relation to a circumscribed circle of readers. The period and manner of the readers' conversion are defined (**2** 3 f). Their present spiritual condition is described in terms of such anxiety and hope as betoken a very intimate personal relation (**5** 11 f; **6** 9–11). Their past conflicts, temptations, endurance and triumph are recalled for their encouragement under present trials, and both past and present are defined in particular terms that point to concrete situations well known to writer and readers (**10** 32–36). There is, it is true, not in He the same intense and all-pervading personal note as appears in the earlier Pauline letters; the writer often loses sight of his particular audience and develops his argument in detached and abstract form. But it cannot be assumed that nothing is a letter which does not conform to the Pauline model. And the presence of long, abstract arguments does not justify the excision or explaining away of undoubted personal passages. Neither the language nor the logic of the book either demands or permits the separation of doctrinal and personal passages from one another, so as to leave for residuum a mere doctrinal treatise. Doctrinal statements lead up to personal exhortations, and personal exhortations form the transition to new arguments; they are indissolubly involved in one another; and ch **13** presents no such exceptional features as to justify its separation from the whole work. There is really no reason, but the unwarrantable assumption that an ancient writer must have conformed with a certain convention of letter-writing, to forbid the acceptance of He for what it appears to be—a defence of Christianity written for the benefit of definite readers, growing more intimate and personal as the writer gathers his argument into a practical appeal to the hearts and consciences of his readers.

III. The Author.—Certain coincidences of language and thought between this epistle and that of

1. Tradition

Clement of Rome to the Corinthians justify the inference that He was known in Rome toward the end of the 1st cent. AD (cf He **11** 7.31 and **1** 3 ff with Clem ad Cor 9.12.36). Clement makes no explicit reference to the book or its author: the quotations are unacknowledged. But they show that He already had some authority in Rome. The same inference is supported by similarities of expression found also in the Shepherd of Hermas. The possible marks of its influence in Polycarp and Justin Martyr are too uncertain and indefinite to justify any inference. Its name does not appear in the list of NT writings compiled and acknowledged by Marcion, nor in that of the Muratorian Fragment. The latter definitely assigns letters by Paul to only seven churches, and so inferentially excludes He.

When the book emerges into the clear light of history toward the end of the 2d cent., the tradition as to its authorship is seen to divide into three different streams.

(1) In Alexandria, it was regarded as in some sense the work of Paul. Clement tells how his teacher, apparently Pantaenus, explained why Paul does not in this letter, as in others, address his readers under his name. Out of reverence for the Lord (II, 2, above) and to avoid suspicion and prejudice, he as apostle of the Gentiles refrains from addressing himself to the Hebrews as their apostle. Clement accepts this explanation, and adds to it that the original Heb of Paul's epistle had been tr[d] into Gr by Luke. That Paul wrote in Heb was assumed from the tradition or inference that the letter was addressed to Aram.-speaking Hebrews. Clement also had noticed the dissimilarity of its Gr from that of Paul's epistles, and thought he found a resemblance to that of Acts.

Origen starts with the same tradition, but he knew, moreover, that other churches did not accept the Alexandrian view, and that they even criticized Alexandria for admitting He into the Canon. And he feels, more than Clement, that not only the language, but the forms of thought are different from those of Paul's epp. This he tries to explain by the hypothesis that while the ideas were Paul's, they had been formulated and written down by some other disciple. He found traditions that named Luke and Clement of Rome, but who the actual writer was, Origen declares that "God alone knows."

The Pauline tradition persisted in Alexandria, and by the 4th cent. it was accepted without any of the qualifications made by Clement and Origen. It had also in the same period spread over the other eastern churches, both Gr and Syrian. But the Pauline tradition, where it is nearest the fountainhead of history, in Clement and Origen, only ascribes He to Paul in a secondary sense.

(2) In the West, the Pauline tradition failed to assert itself till the 4th cent., and was not generally accepted till the 5th cent. In Africa, another tradition prevailed, namely, that Barnabas was the author. This was the only other definite tradition of authorship that prevailed in antiquity. Tertullian, introducing a quotation of He **6** 1.4–6, writes: "There is also an Ep. to the Hebrews under the name of Barnabas . . . . and the Ep. of Barnabas is more generally received among the churches than that apocryphal 'Shepherd' of adulterers" (*De Pudicitia*, 20). Tertullian is not expressing his mere personal opinion, but quoting a tradition which had so far established itself as to appear in the title of the epistle in the MS, and he betrays no consciousness of the existence of any other tradition. Zahn infers that this view prevailed in Montanist churches and may have origi-

nated in Asia. Moffatt thinks that it had also behind it "some Rom tradition" (*Intro*, 437). If it was originally, or at any time, the tradition of the African churches, it gave way there to the Alexandrian view in the course of the 4th cent. A Council of Hippo in 393 reckons "thirteen epp. of the apostle Paul, and one by the same to the Hebrews." A council of Carthage in 419 reckons "fourteen epp. of the apostle Paul." By such gradual stages did the Pauline tradition establish itself.

(3) All the evidence tends to show that in Rome and the remaining churches of the West, the epistle was originally anonymous. No tradition of authorship appears before the 4th cent. And Stephen Gobarus, writing in 600, says that both Irenaeus and Hippolytus denied the Pauline authorship. Photius repeats this statement as regards Hippolytus. Neither he nor Gobarus mentions any alternative view (Zahn, *Intro*, II, 310). The epistle was known in Rome (to Clement) toward the end of the 1st cent., and if Paul's name, or any other, had been associated with it from the beginning, it is impossible that it could have been forgotten by the time of Hippolytus. The western churches had no reason for refusing to admit He into the Pauline and canonical list of books, except only that they did not believe it to be the work of Paul, or of any other apostle.

It seems therefore certain that the epistle first became generally known as an anonymous writing. Even the Alexandrian tradition implies as much, for it appears first as an explanation by Pantaenus why Paul concealed his name. The idea that Paul was the author was therefore an Alexandrian inference. The religious value of the epistle was naturally first recognized in Alexandria, and the name of Paul, the chief letter-writer of the church, at once occurred to those in search for its author. Two facts account for the ultimate acceptance of that view by the whole church. The spiritual value and authority of the book were seen to be too great to relegate it into the same class as the Shepherd or the Ep. of Barnabas. And the conception of the Canon developed into the hard-and-fast rule of apostolicity. No writing could be admitted into the Canon unless it had an apostle for its author; and when He could no longer be excluded, it followed that its apostolic authorship must be affirmed. The tradition already existing in Alexandria supplied the demand, and who but Paul, among the apostles, could have written it?

The Pauline theory prevailed together with the scheme of thought that made it necessary, from the 5th to the 16th cent. The Humanists and the Reformers rejected it. But it was again revived in the 17th and 18th cents., along with the recrudescence of scholastic ideas. It is clear, however, that tradition and history shed no light upon the question of the authorship of He. They neither prove nor disprove the Pauline, or any other theory.

We are therefore thrown back, in our search for the author, on such evidence as the epistle itself affords, and that is wholly inferential.

2. The Witness of the Epistle Itself

It seems probable that the author was a Hellenist, a Gr-speaking Jew. He was familiar with the Scriptures of the OT and with the religious ideas and worship of the Jews. He claims the inheritance of their sacred history, traditions and institutions (**1** 1), and dwells on them with an intimate knowledge and enthusiasm that would be improbable, though not impossible, in a proselyte, and still more in a Christian convert from heathenism. But he knew the OT only in the LXX tr, which he follows even where it deviates from the Heb. He writes Gr with a purity of style and vocabulary to which the writings of Lk alone in the NT can be compared. His mind is imbued with that combination of Heb and Gr thought which is best known in the writings of Philo. His general typological mode of thinking, his use of the allegorical method, as well as the adoption of many terms that are most familiar in Alexandrian thought, all reveal the Hellenistic mind. Yet his fundamental conceptions are in full accord with the teaching of Paul and of the Johannine writings.

The central position assigned to Christ, the high estimate of His person, the saving significance of His death, the general trend of the ethical teaching, the writer's opposition to asceticism and his esteem for the rulers and teachers of the church, all bear out the inference that he belonged to a Christian circle dominated by Pauline ideas. The author and his readers alike were not personal disciples of Jesus, but had received the gospel from those who had heard the Lord (**2** 3) and who were no longer living (**13** 7). He had lived among his readers, and had probably been their teacher and leader; he is now separated from them but he hopes soon to return to them again (**13** 18 f).

Is it possible to give a name to this person?

(1) Although the Pauline tradition itself proves nothing, the internal evidence is conclusive against it. We know enough about Paul to be certain that he could not have written He, and that is all that can be said with confidence on the question of authorship. The style and language, the categories of thought and the method of argument, all differ widely from those of any writings ascribed to Paul. The latter quotes the OT from the Heb and LXX, but He only from LXX. Paul's formula of quotation is, "It is written" or "The scripture saith"; that of He, "God," or "The Holy Spirit," or "One somewhere saith." For Paul the OT is law, and stands in antithesis to the NT, but in He the OT is covenant, and is the "shadow" of the New Covenant. Paul's characteristic terms, "Christ Jesus," and "Our Lord Jesus Christ," are never found in He; and "Jesus Christ" only 3 t (**10** 10; **13** 8), and "the Lord" (for Christ) only twice (**2** 3; **7** 14)—phrases used by Paul over 600 t (Zahn). Paul's Christology turns around the death, resurrection and living presence of Christ in the church, that of He around His high-priestly function in heaven. Their conceptions of God differ accordingly. In He it is Judaistic-Platonistic, or (in later terminology) Deistic. The revelation of the Divine Fatherhood and the consequent immanence of God in history and in the world had not possessed the author's mind as it had Paul's. Since the present world is conceived in He as a world of "shadows," God could only intervene in it by mediators.

The experience and conception of salvation are also different in these two writers. There is no evidence in He of inward conflict and conversion and of constant personal relation with Christ, which constituted the entire spiritual life of Paul. The apostle's central doctrine, that of justification by faith, does not appear in He. Faith is less the personal, mystical relation with Christ, that it is for Paul, than a general hope which lays hold of the future to overcome the present; and salvation is accomplished by cleansing, sanctification and perfection, not by justification. While Paul's mind was not uninfluenced by Hellenistic thought, as we find it in Alexandria (as, e.g. in Col and Eph), it nowhere appears in his epp. so clearly and prominently as it does in He. Moreover, the author of He was probably a member of the community to which he writes (**13** 18 f), but Paul never stood in quite the relation supposed here to any church. Finally, Paul could not have written He **2** 3, for he emphatically declares that he did not receive his gospel from the older disciples (Gal **1** 12; **2** 6). The general Christian ideas on which He was in agreement with Paul were part of the heritage which the apostle had left to all the churches. The few more particular affinities of He with certain Pauline writings (e.g. He **2** 2 ‖ Gal **3** 19; He **12** 22; **3** 14 ‖ Gal **4** 25; He **2** 10 ‖ Rom **11** 36; also with Eph; see von Soden, *Hand-Commentar*, 3) are easily explicable either as due to the author's reading of Paul's Epp. or as reminiscences of Pauline phrases that were current in the churches. But they are too few and slender to rest upon them any presumption against the arguments which disprove the Pauline tradition.

(2) The passage that is most conclusive against the Pauline authorship (**2** 3) is equally conclusive against any other apostle being the author. But almost every prominent name among the Christians of the second generation has been suggested. The epistle itself excludes Timothy (**13** 23), and Titus awaits his turn. Otherwise Luke, Clement of Rome, Barnabas, Silas, Apollos, Priscilla and Aquila, Philip the Deacon, and Aristion have all had their champions.

(*a*) The first two, Luke and Clement, were brought in through their connection with Paul. Where it was recognized that a direct Pauline authorship could not be maintained, the Pauline tradition might still be retained, if the epistle could be assigned to one of the apostle's disciples. These two were fixed upon as being well-known writers. But this very fact reveals the improbability of the theory. Similar arguments from language and thought to those derived from the comparison of He with the Pauline writings avail also in the comparison of He with the writings of Lk and Clement. Both these disciples of the apostle adhere much closer to his system of thought than He does, and they reveal none of the influences of Alexandrian thought, which is predominant in He.

(*b*) Of all the other persons suggested, so little is known that it is impossible to establish, with any convincing force, an argument for or against their authorship.

(α) Barnabas was a Levite of Cyprus (Acts **4** 36), and once a companion of Paul (Acts **13** 2 ff). Another ancient writing is called "the Epistle of Barnabas," but it has no affinity with He. The coincidence of the occurrence of the word "consolation" in Barnabas' name (Acts **4** 36) and in the writer's description of He (**13** 22) is quite irrelevant. Tertullian's tradition is the only positive argument in favor of the Barnabas theory. It has been argued against it that Barnabas, being a Levite, could not have shown the opposition to the Levitical system, and the unfamiliarity with it (He **7** 27; **9** 4), which is supposed to mark our epistle. But the author's Levitical system was derived, not from the Heb OT, nor from the Jerus temple, but from Jewish tradition; and the supposed inaccuracies as to the daily sin offering (**7** 27), and the position of the golden altar of incense (**9** 4) have been traced to Jewish tradition (see Moffatt, *Intro*, 438). And the writer's hostility to the Levitical system is not nearly as intense as that of Paul to Pharisaism. There is nothing that renders it intrinsically impossible that Barnabas was the author, nor is anything known of him that makes it probable; and if he was, it is a mystery why the tradition was confined to Africa.

(β) Harnack has argued the probability of a joint authorship by Priscilla and Aquila. The interchange of "I" and "we" he explains as due to a dual authorship by persons intimately related, but such an interchange of the personal "I" and the epistolary "we" can be paralleled in the Epp. of Paul (e.g. Rom) where no question of joint authorship arises. The probable relation of the author to a church in Rome may suit Priscilla and Aquila (cf Rom **16** 5 with He **13** 22–24), but even if this interpretation of the aforementioned passages were correct, it is possible and probable that Luke, Barnabas, Apollos, and certainly Clement, stood in a similar relation to a Rom church. Harnack, on this theory, explains the disappearance of the author's name as due to prejudice against women teachers. This is the only novel point in favor of this theory as compared with several others; and it does not explain why Aquila's name should not have been retained with the address. The evidences adduced of a feminine mind behind the epistle are highly disputable. On the other hand, a female disciple of Paul's circle would scarcely assume such authority in the church as the author of He does (**13** 17 f; cf 1 Cor **14** 34 f). And nothing that is known of Priscilla and Aquila would suggest the culture and the familiarity with Alexandrian thought possessed by this writer. Acts **18** 26 does not prove that they were expert and cultured teachers, but only that they knew and could repeat the salient points of Paul's early preaching. So unusual a phenomenon as this theory supposes demands more evidence to make it even probable. (But see Rendel Harris, *Sidelights on NT Research*, 148–76.)

(γ) Philip the Deacon and Aristion, "a disciple of the Lord" mentioned by Papias, are little more than names to us. No positive knowledge of either survives on which any theory can be built. It is probable that both were personal disciples of the Lord, and they could not therefore have written He **2** 3.

(δ) Apollos has found favor with many scholars from Luther downward. No ancient tradition supports this theory, a fact which tells heavily against it, but not conclusively, for someone must have written the letter, and his name was actually lost to early tradition, unless it were Barnabas, and that tradition too was unknown to the vast majority of the early churches. All that is known of Apollos suits the author of He. He may have learnt the gospel from "them that heard" (**2** 3); he was a Jew, "an Alexandrian by race, a learned [or eloquent] man," "mighty in the Scriptures," "he powerfully confuted the Jews" (Acts **18** 24 ff), and he belonged to the same Pauline circle as Timothy and Titus (1 Cor **16** 10–12; Tit **3** 13; cf He **13** 23). The Alexandrian type of thought, the affinities with Philo, the arguments from Jewish tradition and ceremonial, the fluent style, may all have issued from "an eloquent Jew of Alexandria." But it does not follow that Apollos was the only person of this type. The author may have been a Gentile, as the purity of his Gr language and style suggests; and the combination of Gr and Heb thought, which the epistle reflects, and even Philo's terms, may have had a wide currency outside Alexandria, as for instance in the great cosmopolitan cities of Asia. All that can be said is that the author of He was someone generally like what is known of Apollos, but who he actually was, we must confess with Origen, "God alone knows."

IV. Destination.—The identity of the first readers of He is, if possible, more obscure than that of the author. It was written to Christians, and to a specific body or group of Christians (see I above). The title "to Hebrews" might mean properly Palestinian Jews who spoke the Heb language, but the fact that the epistle was written in Gr excludes that supposition. It therefore meant Christians of Jewish origin, and gives no indication of their place of residence. The title represents an early inference drawn from the contents of the document, and the tradition it embodies was unanimously accepted from the 2d cent. down to the early part of the last cent. Now, however, a considerable body of critics hold that the original readers were Gentiles. The question is entirely one of inference from the contents of the epistle itself.

1. General Character of the Readers

The readers, like the writer, received the gospel first from "them that heard" (**2** 3), from the personal disciples of the Lord, but they were not of their number. They had witnessed "signs and wonders" and "manifold powers" and "gifts of the Holy Spirit" (**2** 4). Their conversion had been thorough, and their faith and Christian life had been of a high order. They had a sound knowledge of the first principles of Christ (**6** 1 ff). They had become "partakers of Christ," and had need only to "hold fast the beginning of [their] confidence firm unto the end" (**3** 14). They had been fruitful in good works, ministering unto the saints (**6** 10), enduring suffering and persecution, and sympathizing with whose who were imprisoned (**10** 32–34). All this had been in former days which appeared now remote. Their rulers and ministers of those days are now dead (**13** 7). And they themselves have undergone a great change. While they should have been teachers, they have become dull of hearing, and have need again to be taught the rudiments of the first principles of the gospel (**5** 12), and they are in danger of a great apostasy from the faith. They need warning against "an evil heart of unbelief, in falling away from the living God" (**3** 12). They are become sluggish (**6** 12), profane like Esau (**12** 16), worldly-minded (**13** 5). Perhaps their religion was tending toward a false asceticism and outward works (**13** 4.9). And now that this moral dulness and spiritual indifference had fallen upon them, they are being subjected to a new test by persecution from outside (**10** 36; **12** 4), which renders the danger of their falling away from the faith all the more imminent. The author apparently bases his claim to warn them on the fact that he had been a teacher among them, and hoped soon to return to them (**13** 18 f). The same might be said perhaps of Timothy (**13** 23). Both author and readers had friends in Italy (**13** 24) who were with the author when he wrote, either in Italy saluting the readers outside, or outside, saluting the readers in Italy. In all this there is little or nothing to help to fix the destination of the letter, for it might be true at some time or other of any church.

2. Jews or Gentiles?

The old tradition that the readers were Jews claims some more definite support from the epistle itself. The writer assumes an intimate knowledge of the OT and of Jewish ceremonial on their part. The fathers of the Heb race are also their fathers (**1** 1; **3** 9). The humanity that Christ assumed and redeemed is called "the seed of Abraham" (**2** 16). All this, however, might stand in reference to a gentile church, for the early Christians, without distinction of race, regarded themselves as the true Israel and heirs of the Heb revelation, and of all that related to it (1 Cor **10** 1; Gal **3** 7 ff; **4** 21 ff; Rom **4** 11–18). Still there is force in Zahn's argument that "Hebrews does not contain a single sentence in which it is so much as intimated that the readers *became* members of God's people who descended from Abraham, and heirs of the promise given to them and their forefathers, and how they became such" (*Intro to NT*, II, 323). Zahn further finds a direct proof in **13** 13 that "both the readers and the author belong to the Jewish people," which he interprets as "meaning that the readers were to renounce fellowship with the Jewish people who had rejected Jesus, to confess the crucified Jesus, and to take upon themselves all the ignominy that Jesus met at the hands of his countrymen" (ib, 324–25). But that is too large an inference to draw from a figurative expression which need not, and probably does not, mean more than an exhortation to rely on the sacrifice of Christ, rather than upon any external rules and ceremonies. Nor were the "divers and strange teachings" about marriage and meats (**13** 4.9) necessarily Jewish doctrines. They might be the doctrines of an incipient Gnosticism which spread widely throughout the Christian churches, both Jewish and gentile, toward the end of the 1st cent. There is otherwise no evidence that the apostasy, of which the readers stood in danger, was into Judaism, but it was rather a general unbelief and "falling away from the living God" (**3** 12).

It is the whole argument of the epistle, rather than any special references, that produced the tradition, and supports the view, that the readers were Jews. The entire message of the epistle, the dominant claims of Christ and of the Christian faith, rests upon the supposition that the readers held Moses, Aaron, the Jewish priesthood, the old Covenant and the Levitical ritual, in the highest esteem. The author's argument is: You will grant the Divine authority and greatness of Moses, Aaron and the Jewish institutions: Christ is greater than they; therefore you ought to be faithful to Him. He assumes an exclusively Jewish point of view in the minds of his readers as his major premise. He could scarcely do that, if they had been Gentiles. Paul, when writing to the mixed church at Rome, relates his philosophy of the Christian revelation to both Jewish and gentile pre-Christian revelation. Gentile Christians adopted the Jewish tradition as their own in consequence of, and secondary to, their attachment to Christianity. Even Judaizing gentile Christians, such as may be supposed to have belonged to the Galatian and Corinthian churches, adopted some parts of the Jewish law only as a supplement to Christianity, but not as its basis.

Von Soden and others have argued with much reason that these Christians were not in danger of falling back into Judaism from Christianity, but rather of falling away from all faith into unbelief and materialism, like the Israelites in the wilderness (**3** 7 ff), or Esau (**12** 16). With all its references to OT sacrifice and ceremonial, the letter contains not a single warning against reviving them, nor any indications that the readers were in danger of so doing (*Hand-Commentar*, 12–16). But it has been too readily assumed that these facts prove that the readers were not Jews. The pressure of social influence and persecution rendered Jews and Jewish Christians, as well as gentile Christians, liable to apostatize to heathenism or irreligion (Wisd **2** 10.20; 2 Macc **4, 6, 7**; Philo, *De Migratione Abrahami*, XVI; Mt **24** 10.12; Acts **20** 30; 1 Cor **10** 7.14; 2 Thess **2** 4; 1 Jn **2** 18; **5** 21; Pliny Ep. X, 96). Von Soden's argument really cuts the other way. If the writer had been dealing with gentile Christians who were in danger of relapsing into heathenism or of falling into religious indifference, his argument from the shadowy and temporary glories of Judaism to the perfect salvation in Christ would avail nothing, because, for such, his premises would depend upon his conclusion. But if they were Jewish Christians, even though leaning toward heathenism, his argument is well calculated to call up on its side all the dormant force of their early religious training. He is not arguing them out of a "subtle Judaism" quickened by the zeal of a propaganda (Moffatt, *Intro*, 449–50), but from "drifting away" (**2** 1), from "neglect" (**2** 3), from "an evil heart of unbelief, in falling away from the living God" (**3** 12), from "disobedience" (**4** 11), from "a dulness of hearing" (**5** 11), but into "diligence . . . . that ye be not sluggish" (**6** 11 f), into "boldness and patience" (**10** 35 f), and to "lift up the hands that hang down, and the palsied knees" (**12** 12); and this he might well do by his appeal to their whole religious experience, both Jewish and Christian, and to the whole religious history of their race.

3. The Locality of the Readers

The question of the locality of these "Hebrews" remains a matter for mere conjecture. Jerus, Alexandria, Rome, Antioch, Colossae, Ephesus, Berea, Ravenna and other places have been suggested. Tradition, since Clement of Alexandria, fixed on Jerus, but on the untenable ground that the letter was written to Aram.-speaking Jews. The undisputed fact that it was written in Gr tells against Jerus. So does the absence of all reference to the temple ritual, and the mention of almsgiving as the chief grace of the "Hebrews" (**6** 10). Jerus received rather than gave alms. Nor is it likely that all the personal disciples of the Lord would have died out in Jerus (**2** 3). And it could not be charged against the mother church that it had produced no teachers (**5** 12). These points also tell with almost equal force against any Palestinian locality.

Alexandria was suggested as an alternative to Jerus, on the supposition that those references to Jewish ritual which did not correspond with the Jerus ritual (**7** 27; **9** 4; **10** 11) might refer to the temple at Leontopolis. But the ritual system of the epistle is that of the tabernacle and of tradition, and not of any temple. The Alexandrian character of the letter has bearing on the identity of the author, but not so much on that of his readers. The erroneous idea that Paul was the author arose in Alexandria, but it would have been least likely to arise where the letter was originally sent.

Rome has lately found much favor. We first learn of the existence of the letter at Rome. The phrase "they of Italy salute you" (**13** 24) implies that either the writer or his readers were in Italy. It may be more natural to think of the writer, with a small group of Italian friends away from home, sending greetings to Italy, than to suppose that a greeting from Italy generally was sent to a church at a distance. It is probable that a body of Jewish Christians existed in Rome, as in other large cities of the Empire. But this view does not, as von Soden thinks, explain any coincidences between He and Rom. A Rom origin might. It could explain the use of He by Clement. But the letter might also have come to Rome by Clement's time, even though it was originally sent elsewhere. The slender arguments in favor of Rome find favor chiefly because no arguments can be adduced in favor of any other place.

V. Date.—The latest date for the composition of He is clearly fixed as earlier than 96 AD by reason of its use by Clement of Rome about that time. There is no justification for the view that He shows dependence on Jos. The earliest date cannot be so definitely fixed. The apparent dependence of He on Paul's Epp., Gal, 1 Cor and Rom, brings it beyond 50 AD.

1. Terminal Dates

But we have data in the epistle itself which require a date considerably later. The readers had been converted by personal disciples of the Lord (**2** 3). They did not, therefore, belong to the earliest group of Christians. But it is not necessary to suppose a long interval between the Lord's ascension and their conversion. The disciples were scattered widely from Jerus by the persecution that followed the death of Stephen (Acts **8** 1). "We may well believe that the vigorous preaching of St. Stephen would set a wave in motion which would be felt even at Rome" (Sanday, *Romans*, xxviii). They are not, therefore, necessarily to be described as Christians of the 2d generation in the strict chronological sense. But the letter was written a considerable time after their conversion. They have had time for great development (**5** 12). They have forgotten the former days after their conversion (**10** 32). Their early leaders are now dead (**13** 7). Yet the majority of the church still consists of the first converts (**2** 3; **10** 32). And although no argument can be based upon the mention of 40 years (**3** 9), for it is only an incidental phrase in a quotation, yet no longer interval could lie between the founding of the church and the writing of the letter. It might be shorter. And the church may have been founded at any time from 32 to 70 AD.

2. Conversion and History of Readers

The doctrinal development represented in He stands midway between the system of the later Pauline Epp. (Phil, Col, Eph) and that of the Johannine writings. The divers and strange teachings mentioned include only such ascetic tendencies about meat and marriage (**13** 4.9) as are reflected in Paul's Epp. early and late. There is no sign of the appearance of the full-blown heresies of the Ebionites, Docetists, and Gnostics, which became prevalent before the end of the 1st cent. On the other hand the Logos-doctrine as the interpretation of the person of Christ (**1** 1–4) is more fully thought out than in Paul, but less explicit, and less assimilated with the purpose of Christianity, than in the Fourth Gospel.

3. Doctrinal Development

It has been argued that the letter must have been written before the fall of Jerus in 70 AD, because in writing to a Jewish community, and esp. in dealing with Jewish ritual, the writer would have referred to that event, if it had happened. This point would be relevant, if the letter had been addressed to Jerus, which is highly improbable. But, at a distance, an author so utterly unconcerned with contemporary history could easily have omitted mention of even so important a fact. For in fact the author never mentions the temple or its ritual. His system is that of the tabernacle of the OT and of Jewish tradition. The writer's interest is not in historical Judaism, and his omission to mention the great catastrophe does not prove that it had not occurred. The use of the present tense of the ritual does not imply its present continuance. "The present expresses the fact that so it is enjoined in the law, the past that with the founding of the New Covenant the old had been abolished" (Peake, *Hebrews*, 39).

4. The Fall of Jerusalem

A point of contact with contemporary history is found in the fact that Timothy was still living and active when He was written (**13** 23), but it does not carry us far. Timothy was a young man and already a disciple, when Paul visited Galatia on his 2d journey about 46 AD (Acts **16** 1). And he may have lived to the end of the century or near to it. It cannot be safely argued from the mere mention of his name alone, that Paul and his other companions were dead.

5. Timothy

Two incidents in the history of the readers are mentioned which afford further ground for a somewhat late date. Immediately after their conversion, they suffered persecution, "a great conflict of sufferings; partly, being made a gazingstock both by reproaches and afflictions; and partly, becoming partakers with them that were so used" (He **10** 32 f). And now again, when the letter is written, they are entering upon another time of similar trial, in which they "have need of

6. Two Persecutions

patience" (**10** 36), though they "have not yet resisted unto blood" (**12** 4). Their leaders, at least, it would appear, the writer and Timothy, have also been in prison, but one is at liberty and the other expects to be soon (**13** 19.23). It has been conjectured that the first persecution was that under Nero in 64 AD, and the second, that in the reign of Domitian, after 81 AD. But when it is remembered that in some part of the Empire Christians were almost always under persecution, and that the *locale* of these readers is very uncertain, these last criteria do not justify any dogmatizing. It is certain that the letter was written in the second half of the 1st cent. Certain general impressions, the probability that the first apostles and leaders of the church were dead, the absence of any mention of Paul, the development of Paul's theological ideas in a new medium, the disappearance of the early enthusiasm, the many and great changes that had come over the community, point strongly to the last quarter of the century. The opinions of scholars at present seem to converge about the year 80 AD or a little later.

VI. Contents and Teaching.—

1. Summary of Contents

I. The Revelation of God in His Son (**1**–**2**).
  1. Christ the completion of revelation (**1** 1–3).
  2. Christ's superiority over the angels (**1** 4 ff).
    (1) Because He is a Son (**1** 4–6).
    (2) Because His reign is eternal (**1** 7 ff).
  3. The dangers of neglecting salvation through the Son (**2** 1–4).
  4. The Son and humanity (**2** 5 ff).
    (1) The lowliness and dignity of man (**2** 5–8).
    (2) Necessity for the Incarnation (**2** 9 ff).
      (*a*) To fulfil God's gracious purpose (**2** 9 f).
      (*b*) That the Saviour and saved might be one (**2** 11–15).
      (*c*) That the Saviour may sympathize with the saved (**2** 16 ff).

II. The Prince of Salvation (**3** 1—**4** 13).
  1. Christ as Son superior to Moses as servant (**3** 1–6).
  2. Consequences of Israel's unbelief (**3** 7–11).
  3. Warning the "Hebrews" against similar unbelief (**3** 12 ff).
  4. Exhortations to faithfulness (**4** 1–13).
    (1) Because a rest remains for the people of God (**4** 1–11).
    (2) Because the omniscient God is judge (**4** 12 f).

III. The Great High Priest (**4** 14—**10** 18).
  1. Christ's priesthood the Christian's confidence (**4** 14–16).
  2. Christ has the essential qualifications for priesthood (**5** 1–10).
    (1) Sympathy with men (**5** 1–3).
    (2) God's appointment (**5** 4–10).
  3. The spiritual dulness of the Hebrews (**5** 11—**6** 12).
    (1) Their lack of growth in knowledge (**5** 11 ff).
    (2) "Press on unto perfection" (**6** 1–3).
    (3) The danger of falling away from Christ (**6** 4–8).
    (4) Their past history a ground for hoping better things (**6** 9–12).
  4. God's oath the ground of Christ's priesthood and of the believer's hope (**6** 13 ff).
  5. Christ a priest after the order of Melchizedek (**7** 1 ff).
    (1) The history of Melchizedek (**7** 1–3).
    (2) The superiority of his order over that of Aaron (**7** 4–10).
    (3) Supersession of the Aaronic priesthood (**7** 11–19).
    (4) Superiority of Christ's priesthood (**7** 20–24).
    (5) Christ a priest befitting us (**7** 24 ff).
  6. Christ the true high priest (**8** 1—**10** 18).
    (1) Because He entered the true sanctuary (**8** 1–5).
    (2) Because He is priest of the New Covenant (**8** 6 ff).
    (3) A description of the old tabernacle and its services (**9** 1–7).
    (4) Ineffectiveness of its sacrifices (**9** 8–10).
    (5) Superiority of Christ's sacrifice (**9** 11–14).
    (6) The Mediator of the New Covenant through His own blood (**9** 15 ff).
    (7) Weakness of the sacrifices of the law (**10** 1–5).
    (8) Incarnation for the sake of sacrifice (**10** 6–9).
    (9) The one satisfactory sacrifice (**10** 10–18).

IV. Practical Exhortations (**10** 19—**13** 25).
  1. Draw near to God and hold fast the faith (**10** 19–23).
  2. The responsibility of Christians and the judgment of God (**10** 24–31).
  3. Past faithfulness a ground for present confidence (**10** 32 ff).
  4. The household of faith (**11** 1 ff).
    (1) What is faith? (**11** 1–3).
    (2) The examples of faith (**11** 4–32).
    (3) The triumphs of faith (**11** 33 ff).
  5. Run the race looking unto Jesus (**12** 1–3).
  6. Sufferings as discipline from the Father (**12** 4–11).
  7. The duty of helping and loving the brethren (**12** 12–17).
  8. Comparison of the trials and privileges of Christians with those of the Israelites (**12** 18 ff).
  9. Various duties (**13** 1–17).
    (1) Moral and social relations (**13** 1–6).
    (2) Loyalty to leaders (**13** 7 f).
    (3) Beware of Jewish heresies (**13** 9–14).
    (4) Ecclesiastical worship and order (**13** 15–17).
  10. Personal affairs and greetings (**13** 18 ff).
    (1) A request for the prayers of the church (**13** 18 f).
    (2) A prayer for the church (**13** 20 f).
    (3) "Bear with the word of exhortation" (**13** 22).
    (4) "Our brother Timothy" (**13** 23).
    (5) Greetings (**13** 24).
    (6) Grace (**13** 25).

2. The Main Theme

The theme of the epistle is the absoluteness of the Christian religion, as based upon the preëminence of Jesus Christ, the one and only mediator of salvation. The essence of Christ's preëminence is that He fully realizes in His own person the principles of revelation and reconciliation. It is made manifest in His superiority over the Jewish system of salvation, which He therefore at once supersedes and fulfils. The author's working concept is the Logos-doctrine of Philo; and the empirical data to which it is related is the religious history of Israel, as it culminates in Christianity. He makes no attempt to prove either his ideal first principles or his historical premises, and his philosophy of religion takes no account of the heathen world. The inner method of his argument is to fit Judaism and Christianity into the Logos-concept; but his actual is related to the ideal in the way of Plato's antithesis, of shadow and reality, of pattern and original, rather than in Aristotle's way of development, although the influence of the latter method may often be traced, as in the history of faith, which is carried back to the beginnings of history, but is made perfect only in the Christian consummation (**11** 40). In a number of other ideas the teleological movement may be seen cutting across the categories of shadow and reality (**1** 3; **1** 10; **4** 8 f; **5** 8 f; **9** 12; **10** 12; **12** 22).

3. Alexandrian Influences

The form of the argument may be described as either rabbinical or Alexandrian. The writer, after laying down his proposition, proceeds to prove it by quotations from the OT, taken out of their context and historical connection, adapted and even changed to suit his present purpose. This practice was common to Palestinian and Alexandrian writers; as was also the use of allegory, which plays a large part in He (e.g. **3** 7—**4** 11; **13** 11 f). But the writer's allegorical method differs from that of the rabbis in that it is like Philo's, part of a conscious philosophy, according to which the whole of the past and present history of the world is only a shadow of the true realities which are laid up in heaven (**8** 5; **9** 23 f; **10** 1). His interest in historical facts, in OT writers, in Jewish institutions and even in the historical life of Jesus, is quite subordinate to his prepossession with the eternal and heavenly realities which they, in more or less shadowy fashion, represent. That the affinities of He are Alexandrian rather than Palestinian is further proved by many philological and literary correspondences with Wisd and Philo. Most of the characteristic terms and phrases of the epistle are also found in these earlier writers. It has been argued that He and Wisd came from the same hand, and it seems certain that the author of He was familiar with both Wisd and the writings of Philo (Plumptre in *Expos*, I, 329 ff, 409 ff; von Soden in *Hand-Commentar*, 5–6). In Philo the dualism of appearance and reality finds its ultimate synthesis in his master-conception of the Logos, and although this term does not appear in He in Philo's sense, the doctrine is set forth in Philonic phraseology in the opening verses (**1** 1–4). As Logos, Christ excels the prophets as revealer of God, is superior to the angels who were the mediators of the old Covenant, and is more glorious than Moses as the builder of God's true tabernacle, His eternal house; He is a greater Saviour than Joshua, for He brings his own to final rest; and He supersedes the Aaronic priesthood, for while they ministered in a "holy place made with hands, like in pattern to the true," under a "law having a shadow of the good things to come, not the very image of the things" (**9** 24; **10** 1), He "having come a high priest of the good things to come, through the greater and more perfect tabernacle, not made with hands . . . . nor yet through the blood of goats and calves, but through his own blood, entered in once for all into the holy place, having obtained eternal redemption" (**9** 11 f).

Yet it is possible to exaggerate the dependence of He on Alexandrian thought. Deeper than the allegorical interpretation of passages culled from the LXX, deeper than the Logos-philosophy which formed the framework of his thought, is the writer's experience and idea of the personal Christ. His central interest lies, not in the theoretical scheme which he adopts, but in the living person who, while He is the eternal reality behind all shadows, and the very image of God's essence, is also our brother who lived and suffered on earth, the author of our salvation, our "forerunner within the veil," who "is able to save to the uttermost them that draw near unto God through him, seeing he ever liveth to make intercession for them" (**1** 1–4; **2** 14 ff; **2** 10; **5** 7–9; **4** 14–15; **6** 20; **7** 25). As in Paul and Jn, so in He, the historical and ever-living Christ comes in as an original and creative element, which transforms the abstract philosophy of Hellenistic thought into a living system of salvation. Because of His essential and personal preëminence over the institutions and personalities of the old Covenant, Christ has founded a new Covenant, given a new revelation and proclaimed a new gospel. The writer never loses sight of the present bearing of these eternal realities on the lives of his readers. They are for their warning against apostasy, for their encouragement in the face of persecution, and for their undying hope while they 'run the race that is set before [them], looking unto Jesus the author and perfecter of . . . . faith' (**2** 3; **3** 12 ff; **4** 1 ff; **10** 28 ff; **12** 1 f.22 ff).

4. The Christian Factor

LITERATURE.—(1) Comm. by A. S. Peake, *Century Bible;* A. B. Davidson, *Bible Handbooks;* Marcus Dods, *Expositor's Gr Test.;* T. C. Edwards, *Expositor's Bible;* F. Rendall (London, 1888); Westcott[3] (1903); von Soden, *Hand-Commentar;* Hollmann, *Die Schriften des NT*.
(2) Introductions by Moffatt, *Introduction to the Lit. of the NT;* A. B. Bruce in *HDB;* von Soden in *EB;* Zahn, *Intro to the NT;* H.H.B Ayles, *Destination, Date, and Authorship of the Ep. to the He;* Harnack, "Probabilia über die Addresse und den Verfasser des Hebräerbriefes," *ZNTW*, I (1900); W. Wrede, *Das literarische Rätsel des Hebräerbriefes* (1906).
(3) Theology: Bruce, *The Ep. to the He;* Milligan, *The Theology of the Ep. to the He;* Ménégoz, *La théologie de l'épitre aux Hébreux*. For fuller list, see Moffatt, op. cit.

T. REES

HEBREWS, GOSPEL ACCORDING TO THE

(Εὐαγγέλιον καθ' Ἑβραίους, *Euaggélion kath' Hebraíous*, τὸ Ἑβραϊκόν, *tó Hebraïkón*, τὸ Ἰουδαϊκόν, *tó Ioudaïkón; Evangelium Hebraeorum, Judaeorum*):

"The Gospel according to the Hebrews" was a work of early Christian literature to which reference is frequently made by the church Fathers in the first five centuries, and of which some twenty or more fragments, preserved in their writings, have come down to us. The book itself has long disappeared. It has, however, been the subject of many critical surmises and discussions in the course of the last century. It has been regarded as the original record of the life of Jesus, the Archimedes-point of the whole gospel history. From it Justin Martyr has been represented as deriving his knowledge of the works and words of Christ, and to it have been referred the gospel quotations found in Justin and other early writers when these deviate in any measure from the text of the canonical gospels. Recent discussions have thrown considerable light upon the problems connected with this Gospel, and a large literature has grown up around it of which the most important works will be noted below.

1. References in Early Church History

Speaking of *Papias* Eusebius mentions that he has related the story of a woman who was accused of many sins before the Lord, which is contained in the "Gospel according to the Hebrews." This does not prove that Papias was acquainted with this Gospel, for he might have obtained the story, which cannot any longer be regarded as part of St. John's Gospel, from oral tradition. But there is a certain significance in Eusebius' mentioning it in this connection (Euseb., *HE*, III, xxxix, 16). Eusebius, speaking of *Ignatius* and his epp., takes notice of a saying of Jesus which he quotes (*Ep. ad Smyrn*, iii; cf Lk **24** 39), "Take, handle me, and see that I am not an incorporeal spirit." The saying differs materially from the saying in St. Luke's Gospel, and Eusebius says he has no knowledge whence it had been taken by Ignatius. Jerome, however, twice over attributes the saying to the "Gospel according to the Hebrews," and Origen quotes it from the "Teaching of Peter." Ignatius may have got the saying from oral tradition, and we cannot, therefore, be sure that he knew this Gospel.

The first early Christian writer who is mentioned as having actually used the "Gospel according to the Hebrews" is *Hegesippus*, who flourished in the second half of the 2d cent. Eusebius, to whom we owe the reference, tells us that Hegesippus in his *Memoirs* quotes passages from "the Syriac Gospel according to the Hebrews" (*HE*, IV, xxii, 7).

Irenaeus, in the last quarter of the 2d cent., says the Ebionites use only the "Gospel according to Matthew" and reject the apostle Paul, calling him an apostate from the law (*Adv. Haer.*, i. 26, 2). There is reason to believe that there is some confusion in this statement of Irenaeus, for we have the testimony of Eusebius, Jerome and Epiphanius that it was the "Gospel according to the Hebrews" that was used by the Ebionites. With this qualification we may accept Irenaeus as a witness to this Gospel.

Clement of Alexandria early in the 3d cent. quotes from it an apocryphal saying with the same formula as he employs for quotation of Holy Scripture (*Strom.*, ii.9). Origen, Clement's successor at

Alexandria, has one very striking quotation from the "Gospel according to the Hebrews" (*Comm. in Joann*, ii), and Jerome says this Gospel is often used by Origen.

Eusebius, in the first half of the 4th cent., mentions that the Ebionites use only the "Gospel according to the Hebrews" and take small account of the others (*HE*, III, xxvii, 4). He has, besides, other references to it, and in his widely known classification of Christian Scriptures into "acknowledged" "disputed," and "rejected," he mentions this Gospel which he says some have placed in the last category, although those of the Hebrews who have accepted Christ are delighted with it (*HE*, III, xxv, 5). Eusebius had himself in all probability seen and handled the book in the library of his friend Pamphilus at Caesarea, where Jerome, half a century later, found it and tr[d] it.

Epiphanius, who lived largely in Pal, and wrote his treatise on heresies in the latter half of the 4th cent., has much to say of the Ebionites, and the Nazarenes. Speaking of the Ebionites, he says they receive the "Gospel according to Matthew" to the exclusion of the others, mentioning that it alone of the NT books is in Heb speech and Heb characters, and is called the "Gospel according to the Hebrews" (*Haer.*, xxx.3). He goes on to say, that their "Gospel according to Matthew," as it is named, is not complete but falsified and mutilated, "and they call it the Heb Gospel" (*Haer.*, xxx.13). The quotations which Epiphanius proceeds to make show that this Gospel diverges considerably from the canonical Gospel of Mt and may well be that according to the Hebrews. It is more likely that "the Gospel according to Matthew, very full, in Hebrew," of which Epiphanius speaks, when telling about the Nazarene, is the Heb "Gospel of Matthew" attested by Papias, Irenaeus, and a widespread early tradition. But as Epiphanius confesses he does not know whether it has the genealogies, it is clear he was not himself acquainted with the book.

Jerome, toward the end of the 4th cent., is our chief authority for the circulation and use of the "Gospel according to the Hebrews," although his later statements on the subject do not always agree with the earlier. He was proud of being "trilinguis," acquainted with Heb as well as with Lat and Gr. "There is a Gospel," he says, "which the Nazarenes and Ebionites use, which I lately tr[d] from the Heb tongue into Gr and which is called by many the authentic Gospel of Matthew" (*Comm.* on Mt **12** 13). The fact here mentioned, that he tr[d] the work, seems to imply that this Gospel was really something different from the canonical Mt which he had in his hands. In another place, however, he writes: "Matthew . . . . first of all composed the Gospel of Christ in Heb letters and words, in Judaea, for behoof of those of the circumcision who had believed, and it is not quite certain who afterward tr[d] it into Gr. But the very Heb is preserved to this day in the Caesarean library, which Pamphilus the Martyr, with such care, collected. I myself was allowed the opportunity of copying it by the Nazarenes in Berea who use this volume. In which it is to be observed that the evangelist, when he uses the testimonies of the OT, either in his own person, or in that of the Lord and Saviour, does not follow the authority of the LXX translators, but the Heb. Of those, the following are two examples: 'Out of Egypt have I called my Son' (Mt **2** 15 AV); and 'He shall be called a Nazarene' (Mt **2** 23)" (*De Vir. Ill.*, iii). It certainly looks as if in the former instance Jerome meant the Gospel according to the Hebrews, and in the latter the well-authenticated Heb Gospel of St. Matthew. At a later time, however, Jerome appears to withdraw this and to introduce a confusing or even contradictory note. His words are: "In the Gospel according to the Hebrews, which was written indeed in the Chaldee-Syr (Aram.) language, but in Heb characters, which the Nazarenes use as the 'Gospel of the Apostles,' or as most people think 'according to Matthew,' which also is contained in the library at Caesarea, the narrative says" (*Adv. Pelag.*, iii.2). As he proceeds, he quotes passages which are not in the canonical Mt. He also says: "That Gospel which is called the Gospel of the Hebrews which was latedly tr[d] by me into Gr and Lat, and was used frequently by Origen" (*Catal. Script. Eccl.*, "Jacobus"). Jerome's notices of the actual Gospel were frequent, detailed and unequivocal.

Nicephorus at the beginning of the 9th cent. puts the Gospel according to the Hebrews in his list of disputed books of the NT along with the Apocalypse of St. John, the Apocalypse of Peter, and the Ep. of Barnabas. This list is believed to rest upon an authority of about the year 500 AD, and, in the stichometry attached, this Gospel is estimated to have occupied 2,200 lines, while the canonical Mt occupied 2,500.

Codex Λ of the 9th cent., discovered by Tischendorf, and now in the Bodleian Library at Oxford, has marginal notes affixed to four passages of Mt giving the readings of *to Ioudaïkon*, the lost Gospel according to the Hebrews (Scrivener, *Textual Criticism*, I[4], 160; see also Plate XI, 30, p. 131).

All that survives, and all that we are told, of this work, show that it was of the nature of a Gospel, and that it was written in the manner of the Synoptic Gospels. But it seems not to have acquired at any time ecclesiastical standing outside the very limited circles of Jewish Christians who preferred it. And it never attained canonical authority. The Muratorian Fragment has no reference to it. Irenaeus knew that the Ebionites used only the Gospel according to Matthew in Heb, although, as we have seen, this may be really the Gospel according to the Hebrews; but his fourfold Gospel comprises the Gospels of Mt, Mk, Lk and Jn, which we know. There is no reason to believe that it was the source of the quotations made by Justin from the *Apomnemoneumata*, or of quotations made anonymously by others of the early Fathers.

2. Its Character and Contents

Like the Synoptic Gospels, however, it contained narratives of events as well as sayings and discourses. It had an account of John the Baptist's ministry, of the baptism of Jesus, of the call of the apostles, of the woman taken in adultery, of the Last Supper, of the denial of Peter, of appearances of Jesus after the resurrection; and it contained the Lord's Prayer, and sayings of Jesus, like the forgiveness of injuries seventy times seven, the counsel to the rich young ruler, and others. One or two sayings have a gnostic tinge, as when Jesus calls the Holy Spirit His mother, and is made to express His unwillingness to eat the flesh of the Passover Lamb. There are apocryphal additions, even where incidents and sayings are narrated belonging to the canonical Gospels, and there are sayings and incidents wholly apocryphal in the fragments of the Gospel which have survived. But these superfluities do not imply any serious deviation from Catholic doctrine; they only prove, as Professor Zahn says, "the earnestness of the redactor of the Gospel according to the Hebrews to enrich the only Gospel which Jewish Christians possessed up to that time from the still unexhausted source of private oral tradition" (*GK*, II, 717).

The very title of the work suggests that it circulated among Jewish Christians. Those Christians of Pal to whom Jerus was the ecclesiastical center betook themselves, after the troubles which befell the Holy City, to the less frequented regions beyond the Jordan, and were thus cut off from the main stream of catholic Christianity.

3. Its Circulation and Language

It was accordingly easier for the spirit of exclusiveness to assert itself among them and also for heretical tendencies to develop. The Ebionites went farthest in this direction. They denied the supernatural birth of Our Lord, and insisted upon the binding character of the Law for all Christians. The Nazarenes, as all Jewish Christians were called at first, observed the ceremonial law themselves, but did not impose it upon gentile Christians. And they accepted the catholic doctrine of the person of Christ. It was among a community of these Nazarenes at Berea, the modern Aleppo, that Jerome, during a temporary residence at Chalcis in Northern Syria, found the Gospel according to the Hebrews in circulation. No fewer than 9 t does he mention that this Gospel is their one Gospel, and only once does he connect the Ebionites with them in the use of it. Epiphanius draws a clear line of distinction between the Ebionites and the Nazarenes; and we can scarcely suppose that a Gospel which satisfied the one would be wholly acceptable to the other. There is reason to believe that the Heb Gospel of St. Matthew was most to the mind of the Heb Christians, and that it took different forms in the hands of the sects into which the Jewish Christian church became divided. Thus the Gospel of the Nazarenes was the Gospel according to the Hebrews, which in all probability had some affinity with the Heb Gospel of St. Matthew. The Gospel of the Ebionites, which seems to have been the same as the Gospel of the Twelve Apostles, was something of a more divergent doctrinal tendency suited to the exclusive and heretical views of that sect. But it is not easy to reconcile the statements of Epiphanius with those of Eusebius and Jerome.

That the Heb tongue in which Papias says St. Matthew composed his Logia was the Aram. of Pal is generally accepted. This Aram. was closely akin to the Syr spoken between the Mediterranean and the Tigris. It was the same as the Chaldee of the books of Ezr, Neh, and Dnl, of which examples have so recently been found in the Aram. papyri from Elephantine at Assouan. Eusebius and Jerome are emphatic and precise in recording the fact that the Gospel according to the Hebrews was not only Heb or Aram. in composition, but written in the square Heb characters, so different from the Old Heb of the Moabite Stone and the Siloam inscription. That there was a Gr tr before the time of Jerome of the Gospel according to the Hebrews, which was used by Origen, Clement of Alexandria, and others, is strenuously affirmed by Professor Harnack (*Altchristliche Literatur*, I, 6 ff) and as strenuously denied by Professor Zahn (*GK*, II, 648 ff). One reason why the book never attained to any ecclesiastical authority was no doubt its limited circulation in a tongue familiar, outside the circle of Jewish Christians, to only a learned few. For this reason also it is unlikely that it will ever be found, as the Epistle of Barnabas, the Shepherd, and other works have been.

4. Relation to St. Matthew

It is natural to seek for traces of special relationship between the Gospel according to the Hebrews, circulating among communities of Jewish Christians, and the Gospel according to St. Matthew which grew up on the soil of Pal, and which was originally composed in the interest of Jewish Christians, and circulated at a very early period in a Heb recension, soon superseded by the canonical Gospel of Mt and now altogether lost. We have already seen that Irenaeus in all likelihood confused the "Gospel according to the Hebrews" with the Heb Gospel of St. Matthew; and that Jerome says the Gospel used by the Nazarenes was called by many the authentic Gospel of St. Matthew. Moreover, among the fragments that have survived, there are more which resemble St. Matthew's record than either of the other Synoptics. E. B. Nicholson, after a full and scholarly examination of the fragments and of the references, puts forward the hypothesis that "St. Matthew wrote *at different times* the canonical Gospel and the Gospel according to the Hebrews, or, at least, that large part of the latter which runs ∥ to the former" (*The Gospel according to the Hebrews*, 104). The possibility of two editions of the same Gospel-writing coming from the same hand has recently received illustration from Professor Blass's theory of two recensions of the Acts and of St. Luke's Gospel to explain the textual peculiarities of these books in Codex D. This theory has received the adhesion of eminent scholars, but Nicholson has more serious differences to explain, and it cannot be said that his able argument and admirably marshaled learning have carried conviction to the minds of NT scholars.

5. Time of Composition

If we could be sure that Ignatius in his Ep. to the Smyrneans derived the striking saying attributed to Our Lord, "Take, handle me, and see that I am not an incorporeal spirit," from the Gospel according to the Hebrews, we should be able to fix its composition as at any rate within the 1st cent. The obscurity of its origin, the primitive cast of its contents, and the respect accorded to it down into the 5th cent., have disposed some scholars to assign it an origin not later than our Synoptic Gospels, and to regard it as continuing the Aram. tradition of the earliest preaching and teaching regarding Christ. The manifestly secondary character of some of its contents seems to be against such an early origin. Professor Zahn is rather disposed to place it not earlier than 130, when, during the insurrection of Bar-cochba, the gulf that had grown up between Jews and Jewish Christians was greatly deepened, and with an exclusively gentile church in Jerus, the Jewish Christians had lost their center and broken off into sects. The whole situation seems to him to point to a date somewhere between 130–50 AD. The data for any precise determination of the question are wanting.

6. Uncanonical Sayings and Incidents

There is a saying which Clement of Alexandria quotes from it as Scripture: "He that wonders shall reign and he that reigns shall rest" (*Strom.*, ii.9). Origen quotes from it a saying of Jesus, reminding us somewhat of Ezk (**8** 3): "Just now My Mother the Holy Spirit took me by one of my hairs, and bore me away to the great mountain Thabor" (Orig., *In Joann.*, ii; it is quoted several times both by Origen and Jerome). Jerome more than once quotes from it a saying of the Lord to His disciples: "Never be joyful except when ye look on your brother in love" (Hieron. *in Eph* **5** 4; *in Ezk* **18** 7). In his comm. on Mt (**6** 11) Jerome mentions that he found in the third petition of the Lord's prayer for the difficult and unique Gr word ἐπιούσιος, *epioúsios*, which he tr[s] *supersubstantialis*, the Aram. word *māḥār*, *crastinus*, so that the sense would be, "Tomorrow's bread give us today." Of unrecorded incidents the most notable is that of the appearance of the Risen Lord to James: "And when the Lord had given His linen cloth to the servant of the priest, He went to James and appeared to him. For James had sworn that he would not eat bread from that hour wherein he had drunk the cup of the Lord until he saw Him rising from the dead. Again a little afterward the Lord says, Bring a table and bread. Immediately it is added: He took bread and blessed and brake, and afterward gave it to James the Just and said to him, My brother, eat thy bread for the Son of Man has risen from them that sleep" (Hieron., *De Vir. Illustr.*, "Jacobus").

Jerome also tells that in the Gospel according to the Hebrews, there is the following passage: "Lo the mother of the Lord and His brethren said unto Him: John the Baptist is baptizing for the remission of sins; let us go and be baptized by him. But He said to them: What sin have I committed that I should go and be baptized by him? Unless perchance this very word which I have spoken is a sin of ignorance" (Hieron., *Adv. Pelag.*, iii.2).

Mosque over the Cave of Machpelah at Hebron.

7. Conclusion

This Gospel is not to be classed with heretical Gospels like that of Marcion, nor with apocryphal Gospels like that of James or Nicodemus. It differed from the former in that it did not deviate from any essential of catholic truth in its representation of Our Lord. It differed from the latter in that it narrated particulars mostly relating to Our Lord's public ministry, while they occupy themselves with matters of curiosity left unrecorded in the canonical Gospels. It differs from the canonical Gospels only in that it is more florid in style, more diffuse in the relation of incidents, and more inclined to sectional views of doctrine. Its uncanonical sayings and incidents may have come from oral tradition, and they do lend a certain interest and picturesqueness to the narrative. Its language confined it to a very limited sphere, and its sectional character prevented it from ever professing Scriptural authority or attaining to canonical rank. See also Apocryphal Gospels.

Literature.—E. B. Nicholson, *The Gospel according to the Hebrews* (1879); R. Handmann, *Das Hebräer-Evangelium: Texte u. Untersuchungen*, Band V (1889); Zahn, *GK*, II, 642–723 (1890); Harnack, *Geschichte der altchristlichen Literatur*, I, 6 ff; II, 1, 625–51 (1897); *Neutestamentliche Apocryphen* (Hennecke), I, 11–21 (1904).

T. Nicol

HEBREWS, RELIGION OF THE. See Israel, Religion of.

HEBRON, hē′brun (חֶבְרוֹן, *ḥebhrōn*, "league" or "confederacy"; **Χεβρών**, *Chebrōn*): One of the most ancient and important cities in Southern Pal, now known to the Moslems as *el Khalîl* (i.e. *Khalîl er Rahmān*, "the friend of the Merciful," i.e. of God, a favorite name for Abraham; cf Jas **2** 23). The city is some 20 miles S. of Jerus, situated in an open valley, 3,040 ft. above sea-level.

I. History of the City.—Hebron is said to have been founded before Zoan (i.e. *Tanis*) in Egypt (Nu **13** 22); its ancient name was Kiriath-arba, probably meaning the "Four Cities," perhaps because divided at one time into four quarters, but according to Jewish writers so called because four patriarchs, Abraham, Isaac, Jacob and Adam were buried there. According to Josh **15** 13 it was so called after Arba, the father of Anak.

1. Patriarchal Period

Abram came and dwelt by the oaks of Mamre (q.v.), "which are in Hebron" (Gen **13** 18); from here he went to the rescue of Lot and brought him back after the defeat of Chedorlaomer (**14** 13 f); here his name was changed to Abraham (**17** 5); to this place came the three angels with the promise of a son (**18** 1 f); Sarah died here (**23** 2), and for her sepulcher Abraham bought the cave of Machpelah (**23** 17); here Isaac and Jacob spent much of their lives (**35** 27; **37** 14); from here Jacob sent Joseph to seek his brethren (**37** 14), and hence Jacob and his sons went down to Egypt (**46** 1). In the cave of Machpelah all the patriarchs and their wives, except Rachel, were buried (**49** 30 f; **50** 13).

2. Times of Joshua and Judges

The spies visited Hebron and near there cut the cluster of grapes (Nu **13** 22 f). Hoham (q.v.), king of Hebron, was one of the five kings defeated by Joshua at Beth-horon and slain at Makkedah (Josh **10** 3 f). Caleb drove out from Hebron the "three sons of Anak" (**14** 12; **15** 14); it became one of the cities of Judah (**15** 54), but was set apart for the Kohathite Levites (**21** 10 f), and became a city of refuge (**20** 7). One of Samson's exploits was the carrying of the gate of Gaza "to the top of the mountain that is before Hebron" (Jgs **16** 3).

David, when a fugitive, received kindness from the people of this city (1 S **30** 31); here Abner was treacherously slain by Joab at the gate (2 S **3** 27), and the sons of Rimmon, after their hands and feet had been cut off, were hanged "beside the pool" (**4** 12). After the death of Saul, David was here

3. The Days of the Monarchy

anointed king (**5** 3) and reigned here 7½ years, until he captured Jerus and made that his capital (**5** 5); while here, six sons were born to him (**3** 2). In this city Absalom found a center for his disaffection, and repairing there under pretense of performing a vow to Jeh, he raised the standard of revolt (**15** 7 f). Jos mistakenly places here the dream of Solomon (*Ant*, VIII, ii, 1) which occurred at Gibeon (1 K **3** 4). Hebron was fortified by Rehoboam (2 Ch **11** 10).

Abraham's Oak.

4. Later History

Probably during the captivity Hebron came into the hands of Edom, though it appears to have been colonized by returning Jews (Neh **11** 25); it was recovered from Edom by Simon Maccabaeus (1 Macc **5** 65; Jos, *Ant*, XII, viii, 6). In the first great revolt against Rome, Simon bar-Gioras captured the city (*BJ*, IV, ix, 7), but it was retaken, for Vespasian, by his general Cerealis who carried it by storm, slaughtered the inhabitants and burnt it (ib, 9).

During the Muslim period Hebron has retained its importance on account of veneration to the patriarchs, esp. Abraham; for the same reason it was respected by the Crusaders who called it *Castellum ad Sanctum Abraham*. In 1165 it became the see of a Lat bishop, but 20 years later it fell to the victorious arms of Saladin, and it has ever since remained a fanatic Moslem center, although regarded as a holy city, alike by Moslem, Jew and Christian.

II. The Ancient Site.—Modern Hebron is a straggling town clustered round the *Haram* or sacred enclosure built above the traditional cave of Machpelah (q.v.); it is this sacred spot which has determined the present position of the town all through the Christian era, but it is quite evident that an exposed and indefensible situation, running along a valley, like this, could not have been that of earlier and less settled times. From many of the pilgrim narratives, we can gather that for long there had been a tradition that the original site was some distance from the modern town, and, as analogy might suggest, upon a hill. There can be little doubt that the site of the Hebron of OT history is a lofty, olive-covered hill, lying to the W. of the present town, known as *er Rumeidy*. Upon its summit are cyclopian walls and other traces of ancient occupation. In the midst are the ruins of a mediaeval building known as *Dêr el-Arbaʿin*, the "monastery of the forty" (martyrs) about whom the Hebronites have an interesting folklore tale. In the building are shown the so-called tombs of Jesse and Ruth. Near the foot of the hill are several fine old tombs, while to the N. is a large and very ancient Jewish cemetery, the graves of which are each covered with a massive monolith, 5 and 6 ft. long. At the eastern foot of the hill is a perennial spring, *ʿAin el Judeideh;* the water rises in a vault, roofed by masonry and reached by steps. The environs of this hill are full of folklore associations; the summit would well repay a thorough excavation.

A mile or more to the N.W. of Hebron is the famous oak of Mamre (q.v.), or "Abraham's oak," near which the Russians have erected a hospice. It is a fine specimen of the Holm oak (*Quercus coccifera*), but is gradually dying. The present site appears to have been pointed out as that of Abraham's tent since the 12th cent.; the earlier traditional site was at *Rāmet el Khalîl*. See Mamre.

III. Modern Hebron.—Modern Hebron is a city of some 20,000 inhabitants, 85 per cent of whom are Moslems and the remainder mostly Jews. The city is divided into seven quarters, one of which is known as that of the "glass blowers" and another as that of the "water-skin makers." These industries, with the manufacture of pottery, are the main sources of trade. The most conspicuous building is the *Haram* (see Machpelah). In the town are two large open reservoirs the *Birket el Ḳassasîn*, the "pool of the glass blowers" and *Birket es Sultan*, "the pool of the Sultan." This latter, which is the larger, is by tradition the site of the execution of the murderers of Ishbosheth (2 S **4** 12). The Moslem inhabitants are noted for their fanatical exclusiveness and conservatism, but this has been greatly modified in recent years through the patient and beneficent work of Dr. Paterson, of the U. F. Ch. of S. Med. Mission. The Jews, who number about 1,500, are mostly confined to a special ghetto; they have four synagogues, two Sephardic and two Ashkenazic; they are a poor and unprogressive community.

For **Hebron** (Josh **19** 28) see Ebron.

E. W. G. Masterman

HEBRON (חֶבְרוֹן, *ḥebhrōn*, "league," "association"):

(1) The third son of Kohath, son of Levi (Ex **6** 18; Nu **3** 19.27; 1 Ch **6** 2.18; **23** 12.19).

(2) A son of Mareshah and descendant of Caleb (1 Ch **2** 42.43). See also Korah.

HEBRONITES, hē′brun-īts (חֶבְרוֹנִי, חֶבְרֹנִי, *ḥebhrōnī*): A family of Levites, descendants of Hebron, third son of Kohath (Nu **3** 27; **26** 58, etc).

HEDGE, hej:

(1) מְסוּכָה, *m*e*ṣūkhāh*, "a thorn hedge," only in Mic **7** 4; מְשֻׂכָּה, *m*e*sukkāh*, "a hedge" (Isa **5** 5); מְשֻׂכַת חָדֶק, *m*e*sukhath ḥādheḳ*, "a hedge of thorns" (Prov **15** 19).

(2) גָּדֵר, *gādhēr*, and גְּדֵרָה, *g*e*dhērāh*, trd "hedges" in RV only in Ps **89** 40, elsewhere "fence." Gederah (q.v.) in RVm is trd "hedges" (1 Ch **4** 23).

(3) נַעֲצוּץ, *naʿăçūç*, "thorn-hedges" (Isa **7** 19).

(4) φραγμός, *phragmós*, trd "hedge" (Mt **21** 33; Mk **12** 1; Lk **14** 23); "partition" in Eph **2** 14, which is its literal meaning. In the LXX it is the usual equivalent of the above Heb words.

Loose stone walls without mortar are the usual "fences" around fields in Pal, and this is what *gādher* and *gᵉdhērāh* signify in most passages. Hedges made of cut thorn branches or thorny bushes are very common in the plains and particularly in the Jordan valley.

E. W. G. Masterman

HEDGEHOG, hej'hog (LXX **ἐχῖνος,** *echīnos,* "hedgehog," for קִפֹּד, *ḳippōdh,* in Isa **14** 23; **34** 11; Zeph **2** 14, and for קִפּוֹז, *ḳippōz,* in Isa **34** 15). See Porcupine; Bittern; Owl; Serpent.

HEED, hēd: This word, in the sense of giving careful attention ("take heed," "give heed," etc), represents several Heb and Gr words; chief among them שָׁמַר, *shāmar,* "to watch"; *βλέπω, blépō,* "to look," *ὁράω, horáō,* "to see." As opposed to thoughtlessness, disregard of God's words, of the counsels of wisdom, of care for one's ways, it is constantly inculcated as a duty of supreme importance in the moral and spiritual life (Dt **4** 9.15.23; **27** 9 AV, etc; Josh **22** 5; **23** 11; Ps **39** 1; Mt **16** 6; Mk **4** 24; **13** 33; Lk **12** 15; 1 Cor **3** 10; **8** 9; **10** 12; Col **4** 17, etc). James Orr

HEEL, hēl (עָקֵב, *'āḳēbh*): "The iniquity of my heels" (Ps **49** 5 AV) is a literal tr, and might be understood to indicate the Psalmist's "false steps," errors or sins, but that meaning is very doubtful here. RV gives "iniquity at my heels." RVm gives a still better sense, "When the iniquity of them that would supplant me compasseth me about, even of them that trust in . . . . riches"—treacherous enemies ever on the watch to trip up a man's heels (cf Hos **12** 3). Of Judah it was said, "Thy heels [shall] suffer violence" (Jer **13** 22) through being "made bare" (AV), and thus subject to the roughness of the road as she was led captive.

Figurative: (1) Of the partial victory of the evil power over humanity, "Thou shalt bruise [m "lie in wait for"] his heel" (Gen **3** 15), through constant, insidious suggestion of the satisfaction of the lower desires. Or if we regard this statement as a part of the Protevangelium, the earliest proclamation of Christ's final and complete victory over sin, the destruction of "the serpent" ("He shall bruise thy head"), then the reference is evidently to Christ's sufferings and death, even to all that He endured in His human nature. (2) Of the stealthy tactics of the tribe of Dan in war, "An adder in the path, that biteth the horse's heels" (Gen **49** 17), by which it triumphed over foes of superior strength. (3) Of violence and brutality, "Who . . . . hath lifted up his heel against me" (Ps **41** 9; Jn **13** 18), i.e. lifted up his foot to trample upon me (cf Josh **10** 24). M. O. Evans

HEGAI, hē'gā-ī, **HEGE,** hē'ge (הֵגַי, *hēghay;* **Γαΐ,** *Gaí* [Est **2** 8.15], and הֵגֶא, *hēghē',* Hege [Est **2** 3]): One of the officers of the Pers king Ahasuerus; a chamberlain or eunuch (keeper of women), into whose custody the "fair young virgins" were delivered from whom the king intended to choose his queen in the place of the discredited Vashti.

HEGEMONIDES, heg-e-mon'i-dēz, hej-e-mō-nī'-dēz (**Ἡγεμονίδης,** *Hēgemonídēs*): The Syrian officer placed in command of the district extending from Ptolemaïs to the Gerrenians (2 Macc **13** 24). It is not easy to see how in AV and even in Swete's revised text the word can be taken as a mere appellative along with *stratēgón,* the two being rendered "principal officer": one of the two could certainly be omitted (Swete, 3d ed, 1905, capitalizes *Hegemonidēs*). In RV the word is taken as the name of some person otherwise unknown.

HEIFER, hef'ēr (פָּרָה, *pārāh,* in Nu **19** [see following art.] and Hos **4** 16; עֶגְלָה, *'eghlāh,* elsewhere in the OT; **δάμαλις,** *dámalis,* in He **9** 13): For the "heifer of three years old" in AV, RVm of Isa **15** 5; Jer **48** 34, see Eglath-Shelishiyah. A young cow (contrast Bullock). The *'eghlāh* figures specifically in religious rites only in the ceremony of Dt **21** 1–9 for the cleansing of the land, where an unexpiated murder had been committed. This was not a sacrificial rite—the priests are witnesses only, and the animal was slain by breaking the neck —but sacrificial purity was required for the heifer. Indeed, it is commonly supposed that the rite as it now stands is a rededication of one that formerly had been sacrificial. In the sacrifices proper the heifer could be used for a peace offering (Lev **3** 1), but was forbidden for the burnt (Lev **1** 3) or sin (**4** 3.14) offerings. Hence the sacrifice of 1 S **16** 2 was a peace offering. In Gen **15** 9 the ceremony of the ratification of the covenant by God makes use of a heifer and a she-goat, but the reason for the use of the females is altogether obscure. Cf following article.

Figuratively: The heifer appears as representing sleekness combined with helplessness in Jer **46** 20 (cf the comparison of the soldiers to 'stalled calves' in the next verse). In Jer **50** 11; Hos **10** 11, the heifer is pictured as engaged in threshing. This was particularly light work, coupled with unusually abundant food (Dt **25** 4), so that the threshing heifer served esp. well for a picture of contentment. ("Wanton" in Jer **50** 11, however, is an unfortunate tr in RV.) Hosea, in contrast, predicts that the "heifers" shall be set to the hard work of ploughing and breaking the sods. In Jgs **14** 18, Samson uses "heifer" in his riddle to refer to his wife. This, however, was not meant to convey the impression of licentiousness that it gives the modern reader. Burton Scott Easton

HEIFER, RED. In Nu **19** a rite is described in which the ashes of a "red heifer" and of certain objects are mixed with running water to obtain the so-called "water for impurity." (Such is the correct tr of ARV in Nu **19** 9.13.20.21; **31** 23. In these passages, AV and ERV, through a misunderstanding of a rather difficult Heb term, have "water of separation"; LXX and the Vulg have "water of sprinkling." ERVm, "water of impurity," is right, but ambiguous.) This water was employed in the removal of the uncleanness of a person or thing that had been in contact with a dead body, and also in removing ritual defilement from booty taken in war.

The general origin of the rite is clear enough, as is the fact that this origin lies back of the official sacrificial system of Israel.

1. Origin and Significance of the Rite

For the removal of impurity, ritual as well as physical, water, preferably running water (ver 17; cf Lev **14** 5 ff; **15** 13), is the natural means, and is employed universally. But where the impurity was unusually great, mere water was not felt to be adequate, and various substances were mixed with it in order to increase its efficacy. So (among other things) blood is used in Lev **14** 6.7, and dust in Nu **5** 17 (see Water of Bitterness). The use, however, of ashes in Nu **19** 17 is unique in the OT, although parallels from elsewhere can be adduced. So e.g. in Ovid *Fasti,* iv.639–40, 725, 733, in the last of these references, "The blood of a horse shall be a purification, and the ashes of calves," is remarkably close to the OT. The ashes were obtained by burning the heifer completely, "her skin, and her flesh, and her blood, with her dung" (the contents of the entrails) (ver 5; cf Ex **29** 14). Here only in the OT is blood burned for a ceremonial purpose, and here only is burning a *preliminary;* elsewhere it is either a chief act or serves to consume the remnants of a finished sacrifice—Lev **4** 12 and Nu **19** 3 are altogether different.

The heifer is a *female.* For the regular sin offering for the congregation, only the male was permitted (Lev **4** 14), but the female was used in the purificatory ceremony of Dt **21** 3 (a rite that has several points of similarity to that of Nu **19**). An individual sin offering by one of the common people, however, required a female (Lev **4** 28), but probably only in order to give greater prominence to the more solemn sacrifices for which the male was reserved. A female is required again in the cases enumerated in Lev **5** 1–6, most of which are ritual defilements needing purification; a female was required at the purification of a leper (in addition to two males, Lev **14** 10), and a female, with one male, was offered when a Nazirite terminated his vows (Nu **6** 14). Some connection between purification and the sacrifice of a female may be established by this list, for even in the case of the Nazirite the idea may be removal of the state of consecration. But the reason for such a connection is anything but obvious, and the various explanations that have been offered are hardly more than guesses. The most likely is that purificatory rites originated in a very primitive stage when the female was thought to be the more sacred animal on account of its greater usefulness. Of the other requirements for the heifer she must be "red," i.e. reddish brown (Nu **19** 2). Likeness in color to blood is at first sight the most natural explanation, but likeness in color to ripe grain is almost equally plausible. It may be noted that certain Egyp sacrifices also required red cattle as victims (Plutarch, *De Isid.* 31). The heifer is to be "without spot" ("faultless"), "wherein is no blemish," the ordinary requirement for sacrifices. (The Jewish exegetes misread this "perfectly red, wherein is no blemish," with extraordinary results; see below.) But an advance on sacrificial requirements is that she shall be one "upon which never came yoke." This requirement is found elsewhere only in Dt **21** 3 and in 1 S **6** 7 (that the animals in this last case were finally sacrificed is, however, not in point). But in other religions this requirement was very common (cf *Iliad* x.293; Vergil, *Georg.* iv.550–51; Ovid, *Fasti* iv.336).

2. Use of Cedar and Hyssop

While the heifer was being burned, "cedar-wood, and hyssop, and scarlet" (i.e. scarlet wool or thread) were cast into the flames. The same combination of objects (although differently employed) is found at the cleansing of a leper (Lev **14** 4), but their meaning is entirely unknown. The explanations offered are almost countless. It is quite clear that hyssop was esp. prized in purifications (Ps **51** 7), but the use of hyssop as a sprinkler and the use of ashes of hyssop may be quite unrelated. Hyssop and cedar were supposed to have medicinal properties (see CEDAR; HYSSOP). Or the point may be the use of aromatic woods. For a mixture of cedar and other substances in water as a purificatory medium cf Fossey, *Magie Assyrienne,* 285. The scarlet wool offers still greater difficulties, apart from the color, but it may be noted that scarlet wool plays a part in some of the Bab conjurations (*Assyr. Bibl.,* XII, 31). But, obviously, none of this leads very far and it may all be in the wrong direction. All that can be said definitely is that Lev **14** 4 and Nu **19** 6 show that the combination of objects was deemed to have a high purificatory value.

3. Application and Sacredness of the Ashes

The ashes, when obtained, were used in removing the greatest of impurities. Consequently, they themselves were deemed to have an extraordinarily "consecrated" character, and they were not to be handled carelessly. Their consecration extended to the rite by which they were produced, so that every person engaged in it was rendered unclean (Nu **19** 7.8.10), an excellent example of how in primitive religious thought the ideas of "holiness" and "uncleanness" blend. It was necessary to perform the whole ceremony "without the camp" (ver 3), and the ashes, when prepared, were also kept without the camp (ver 9), probably in order to guard against their touch defiling anyone (as well as to keep them from being defiled). When used they were mixed with running water, and the mixture was sprinkled with hyssop on the person or object to be cleansed (vs 17–19). The same water was used to purify booty (**31** 23), and it *may* also be meant by the "water of expiation" in **8** 7.

4. Of Non-Priestly and Non-Israelitish Origin

In addition to the similarities already pointed out between Nu **19** and Dt **21** 1–9, the rites resemble each other also in the fact that, in both, laymen are the chief functionaries and that the priests have little to do (in Dt **21** 1–9 they are mere passive witnesses). This suggests a non-priestly origin. The title "sin-offering" in Nu **19** 9.17 (unless used in a unique sense) points to an original sacrificial meaning, although in Nu **19** the heifer is carefully kept away from the altar. Again, the correspondences with rites in other religions indicate a non-Israelitish origin. Such a ceremony may well have passed among the Israelites and have become prized by them. It contained nothing objectionable and seemed to have much of deep worth, and a few slight additions—chiefly the sprinkling (ver 4; cf Lev **4** 6.17)—made it fit for adoption into the highest system. Some older features may have been eliminated also, but as to this, of course, there is no information. But, in any case, the ceremony is formed of separate rites that are exceedingly old and that are found in a great diversity of religions, so that any elaborate symbolic interpretation of the details would seem to be without justification. The same result can be reached by comparing the countless symbolic interpretations that have been attempted in the past, for they differ hopelessly. As a matter of fact, the immense advance that has been gained in the understanding of the meaning of the OT rites through the comparative study of religions has shown the futility of much that has been written on symbolism. That a certain rite is widely practised may merely mean that it rests on a true instinct. To be sure, the symbolism of the future will be written on broader lines and will be less pretentious in its claims, but for these very reasons it will rest on a more solid basis. At present, however, the chief task is the collection of material and its correct historical interpretation.

5. Obscurity of Later History

The later history of the rite is altogether obscure. As no provision was made in Nu **19** for sending the ashes to different points, the purification could have been practised only by those living near the sanctuary. Rabbinical casuistry still further complicated matters by providing that two black or white hairs from the same follicle would disqualify the heifer (see above), and that one on whom even a cloth had been laid could not be used. In consequence, it became virtually or altogether impossible to secure a proper animal, and the Mishnic statement that only nine had ever been found (*Pārāh,* iii.5) probably means that the rite had been obsolete long before NT times. Still, the existence of the tractate, *Pārāh,* and the mention in He **9** 13 show that the provisions were well remembered. See also SACRIFICE.

LITERATURE.—Baentsch (1903), Holzinger (1903), and (especially) Grey (1903) on Nu; Kennedy in *HDB;* Edersheim, *Temple and Ministry,* ch xviii (rabbinic traditions. Edersheim gives the best of the "typological" explanations).

BURTON SCOTT EASTON

HEIGHT, hīt, **HEIGHTS:** The Eng. terms represent a large number of Heb words (*gōbhah, mārōm, ḳōmāh, rūm,* etc). A chief thing to notice is that in RV "height" and "heights" are frequently substituted for other words in AV, as "coast" (Josh **12** 23), "region" (1 K **4** 11), "borders" (Josh **11** 2), "countries" (Josh **17** 11), "strength" (Ps **95** 4), "high places" (Isa **41** 18; Jer **3** 2.21; **7** 29; **12** 12; **14** 6), "high palaces" (Ps **78** 69). On the other hand, for "height" in AV, RV has "stature" (Ezk **31** 5.10), "raised basement" (Ezk **41** 8), etc. In the NT we have *húpsōma,* prop. of space (Rom **8** 39), and *húpsos* of measure (Eph **3** 18; Rev **21** 16).

JAMES ORR

HEIR, âr: In the NT "heir" is the invariable tr of **κληρόνομος,** *klērónomos* (15 t), the technical equivalent in Gr, and of the compound **συνκληρόνομος,** *sunklērónomos,* "coheir," in Rom **8** 17; Eph **3** 6; He **11** 9; 1 Pet **3** 7 (in Gal **4** 30; He **1** 14, contrast AV and RV). In the OT "heir" and "to be heir" both represent some form of the common vb. יָרַשׁ, *yārash,* "possess," and the particular rendition of the vb. as "to be heir" is given only by the context (cf e.g. AV and RV in Jer **49** 2; Mic **1** 15). Exactly the same is true of the words trd "inherit," "inheritance," which in by far the great majority of cases would have been represented better by "possess," "possession" (see INHERITANCE and *OHL* on נחל). Consequently, when God is said, for instance, to have given Palestine to Israel as an 'inheritance' (Lev **20** 24, etc), nothing more need be meant than 'given as a possession.' The LXX, however, for the sake of variety in its rendition of Heb words, used *klēronoméō* in many such cases (esp. Gen **15** 7.8; **22** 17), and thereby fixed on 'heir' the sense of 'recipient of a gift from God.' And so the word passed in this sense into NT Gr—Rom **4** 13.14; Gal **3** 29; Tit **3** 7; He **6** 17; **11** 7; Jas **2** 5; cf Eph **3** 6; He **11** 9; 1 Pet **3** 7. On the other hand, the literal meaning of the word is found in Mk **12** 7 (and ||s) and Gal **4** 1—in the latter case being suggested by the transferred meaning in **3** 29—while in Rom **8** 17; Gal **4** 7, the literal and transferred meanings are blended. This blending has produced the phrase "heirs of God," which, literally, is meaningless and which doubtless was formed without much deliberation, although it is perfectly clear. A similar blending has applied "heir" to Christ in He **1** 2 (cf Rom **8** 17 and perhaps Mk **12** 7) as the recipient of all things in their totality. But apart from these "blended" passages, it would be a mistake to think that sonship is always consciously thought of where "heir" is mentioned, and hence too much theological implication should not be assigned the latter word.

1. The Word "Heir"

The heirs of property in the OT were normally the sons and, chief among these, the firstborn.

2. Heir in OT Law

(1) Dt **21** 15–17 provides that the firstborn shall inherit a "double portion," whence it would appear that all the other sons shared equally. (It should be noted that in this law the firstborn is the eldest son of the *father,* not of the mother as in Ex **13** 2.) Uncertain, however, is what Dt **21** 15–17 means by "wife," and the practice must have varied. In Gen **21** 10 the son of the handmaid was not to be heir with Isaac, but in Gen **30** 1–13 the sons of Bilhah and Zilpah are reckoned as legitimate children of Jacob. See MARRIAGE. Nor is it clear that Dt **21** 15–17 forbids setting aside the eldest son because of his *own* sin—cf the case of Reuben (Gen **49** 3.4; 1 Ch **5** 1), although the son of a regular wife (Gen **29** 32). The very existence of Dt **21** 15–17, moreover, shows that in spite of the absence of formal wills, a man could control to some extent the disposition of his property after his death and that the right of the firstborn could be set aside by the father (1 Ch **26** 10). That the royal dignity went by primogeniture is asserted only (in a particular case) in 2 Ch **21** 3, and both David (1 K **1** 11–13) and Rehoboam (2 Ch **11** 21–23) chose younger sons as their successors. A single payment in the father's lifetime could be given in lieu of heritage (Gen **25** 6; Lk **15** 12), and it was possible for two brothers to make a bargain as to the disposition of the property after the father's death (Gen **25** 31–34).

(2) When there were sons alive, the daughters had no right of inheritance, and married daughters had no such right in any case. (Job **42** 15 describes an altogether exceptional procedure.) Probably unmarried daughters passed under the charge of the firstborn, as the new head of the family, and he took the responsibility of finding them husbands. Nu **27** 1–11; **36** 1–12 treat of the case where there were no sons—the daughters inherited the estate, but they could marry only within the tribe, lest the tribal possessions be confused. This right of the daughters, however, is definitely stated to be a new thing, and in earlier times the property probably passed to the nearest male relatives, to whom it went in later times if there were no daughters. In extreme cases, where no other heirs could be found, the property went to the slaves (Gen **15** 3; Prov **30** 23, noting that the meaning of the latter ver is uncertain), but this could have happened only at the rarest intervals. A curious instance is that of 1 Ch **2** 34.35, where property is preserved in the family by marrying the daughter to an Egyp slave belonging to the father; perhaps some adoption-idea underlies this.

(3) The wife had no claim on the inheritance, though the disposition made of her dowry is not explained, and it may have been returned to her. If she was childless she resorted to the Levirate marriage (Dt **25** 5–10). If this was impracticable or was without issue she returned to her own family and might marry another husband (Gen **38** 11; Lev **22** 13; Ruth **1** 8). The inferior wives (concubines) were part of the estate and went to the heir; indeed, possession of the father's concubines was proof of possession of his dignities (2 S **16** 21.22; 1 K **2** 13–25). At least, such was the custom in the time of David and Solomon, but at a later period nothing is heard of the practice.

(4) The disposition of land is a very obscure question. Nu **36** 4 states explicitly that each heir had a share, but the continual splitting up of an estate through successive generations would have produced an impossible state of affairs. Possibly the land went to the eldest born as part of his portion, possibly in some cases it was held in common by the members of the family, possibly some member bought the shares of the others, possibly the practice differed at different times. But our ignorance of the facts is complete.

NOTE.—The dates assigned by different scholars to the passages cited have an important bearing on the discussion.

BURTON SCOTT EASTON

HELAH, hē'lä (חֶלְאָה, *ḥel'āh*): A wife of Ashhur, father of Tekoa (1 Ch **4** 5.7).

HELAM, hē′lam (חֵילָם, *ḥēlām,* 2 S **10** 16 f; in ver 17 with ה *locale;* LXX **Αἰλάμ,** *Hailám*): A place near which David is said to have defeated the Aramaean world under Hadarezer (2 S **10** 16 ff). Its site is unknown. Cornill and others introduce it into the text of Ezk **47** 16 from the LXX (Ἡλιάμ, *Hēliám*). This would place it between the territories of Damascus and Hamath, which is not unreasonable. Some scholars identify it with Aleppo, which seems too far north.

HELBAH, hel′ba (חֶלְבָּה, *ḥelbāh*): A place in the territory assigned to Asher (Jgs **1** 31). It may be identical with Mahalliba of Sennacherib's prism inscription. The site, however, has not been recovered.

HELBON, hel′bon (חֶלְבּוֹן, *ḥelbōn;* **Χελβών,** *Chelbôn,* **Χεβρών,** *Chebrôn*): A district from which Tyre received supplies of wine through the Damascus market (Ezk **27** 18); universally admitted to be the modern *Halbun,* a village at the head of a fruitful valley of the same name among the chalk slopes on the eastern side of Anti-Lebanon, 13 miles N.N.W of Damascus, where traces of ancient vineyard terracing still exist. Records contemporary with Ezk mention *mat helbunim* or the land of Helbon, whence Nebuchadnezzar received wine for sacrificial purposes (Belinno Cylinder, I, 23), while *karan hulbunu,* or Helbonian wine, is named in *WAI,* II, 44. Strabo (xv.735) also tells that the kings of Persia esteemed it highly. The district is still famous for its grapes—the best in the country—but these are mostly made into raisins, since the population is now Moslem. Helbon must not be confounded with Chalybon (Ptol. v.15, 17), the Gr-Rom province of Haleb or Aleppo.

W. M. Christie

HELCHIAH, hel-kī′a. See Helkias.

HELDAI, hel′dā-ī (חֶלְדַּי, *ḥelday*):

(1) A captain of the temple-service, appointed for the 12th month (1 Ch **27** 15). Same as Heled (חֵלֶד, *ḥēledh*) in ‖ list (cf 1 Ch **11** 30), and is probably also to be identified with Heleb, son of Baanah the Metophathite, one of David's heroic leaders (2 S **23** 29).

(2) One of a company of Jews who brought gifts of gold and silver from Babylon to assist the exiles under Zerubbabel (Zec **6** 10).

HELEB, hē′leb (חֵלֶב, *ḥēlebh,* 2 S **23** 29). See Heldai.

HELED, hē′led (חֵלֶד, *ḥēledh,* 1 Ch **11** 30). See Heldai.

HELEK, hē′lek (חֵלֶק, *ḥēlekh*): Son of Gilead the Manassite (Nu **26** 30; Josh **17** 2). Patronymic, **Helekites** (Nu **26** 30).

HELEM, hē′lem:

(1) הֵלֶם, *hēlem;* LXX B, **Βαλαάμ,** *Balaám,* omitting "son," A, **υἱός Ἐλάμ,** *huiós Elám,* "son of Elam" (1 Ch **7** 35). A great-grandson of Asher, called Hotham in ver 32. The form "Elam" appears as the name of a Levite in 1 Esd **8** 33.

(2) חֵלֶם, *ḥēlem,* "strength," regarded by LXX as a common noun (Zec **6** 14). One of the ambassadors from the Jews of the exile to Jerus; probably the person called Heldai in ver 10 is meant.

HELEPH, hē′lef (חֵלֶף, *ḥeleph*): A place on the southern border of Naphtali (Josh **19** 33); unidentified.

HELEZ, hē′lez (חֶלֶץ, *ḥeleç,* "vigor"; LXX **Σέλλης,** *Séllēs,* **Χέλλης,** *Chéllēs*):

(1) 2 S **23** 26; 1 Ch **11** 27; **27** 10. One of David's mighty men; according to 1 Ch **27 10,** he belonged to the sons of Ephraim and was at the head of the 7th course in David's organization of the kingdom.

(2) LXX *Chellēs,* 1 Ch **2** 39. A man of Judah of the clan of the Jerahmeelites.

HELI, hē′lī (**Ἡλεί,** *Hēlei* for עֵלִי, *'ēlī*):

(1) The father of Joseph, the husband of Mary, in St. Luke's account of the genealogy of Jesus (Lk **3** 23).

(2) An ancestor of Ezra (2 Esd **1** 2).

HELIODORUS, hē-li-ō-dō′rus (**Ἡλιόδωρος,** *Hēliódōros*): Treasurer of the Syrian king Seleucus IV, Philopator (187–175 BC), the immediate predecessor of Antiochus Epiphanes who carried out to its utmost extremity the Hellenizing policy begun by Seleucus and the "sons of Tobias." Greatly in want of money to pay the tribute due to the Romans as one of the results of the victory of Scipio over Antiochus the Great at Magnesia (190 BC), Seleucus learned from Apollonius, governor of Coele-Syria (Pal) and Phoenicia, of the wealth which was reported to be stored up in the Temple at Jerus and commissioned H. (2 Macc **3**) to plunder the temple and to bring its contents to him. On the wealth collected in the Temple at this time, Jos (*Ant,* IV, vii, 2) may be consulted. The Temple seems to have served the purposes of a bank in which the private deposits of widows and orphans were kept for greater security, and in 2 Macc **3** 15–21 is narrated the panic at Jerus which took place when H. came with an armed guard to seize the contents of the Temple (see Stanley, *Lectures on the History of the Jewish Church,* III, 287). In spite of the protest of Onias, the high priest, H. was proceeding to carry out his commission when, "through the Lord of Spirits and the Prince of all power," a great apparition appeared which caused him to fall down "compassed with great darkness" and speechless. When "quite at the last gasp" he was by the intercession of Onias restored to life and strength and "testified to all men the works of the great God which he had beheld with his eyes." The narrative given in 2 Macc **3** is not mentioned by any other historian, though 4 Macc refers to the plundering of the Temple and assigns the deed to Apollonius. Raffaelle used the incident in depicting, on the walls of the Vatican, the triumph of Pope Julius II over the enemies of the Pontificate.

J. Hutchison

HELIOPOLIS, hē-li-op′ō-lis. See On.

HELKAI, hel′kā-ī, hel′kī, hel-kā′ī (חֶלְקָי, *ḥelḳāy,* perhaps an abbreviation for Helkiah, "Jeh is my portion." Not in LXX B; LXX L, Χελκίας, *Chelkías* [Neh **12** 15]): The head of a priestly house in the days of Joiakim.

HELKATH, hel′kath (חֶלְקַת, *ḥelḳath* [Josh **19** 25]; *ḥelḳāth* [**21** 31]; by a scribal error *ḥūḳōḳ* [1 Ch **6** 75]): A town or district on the border of Asher, assigned to the Levites; unidentified.

HELKATH-HAZZURIM, hel′kath-haz′ū-rim, -ha-zū′rim (חֶלְקַת הַצֻּרִים, *ḥelḳath ha-çurīm;* **Μερὶς τῶν ἐπιβουλῶν,** *Merís tôn epiboulôn*): The name as it stands means "field of the sword edges," and is applied to the scene of the conflict in which twelve champions each from the army of Joab and that of Abner perished together, each slaying **his**

fellow (2 S **2** 16). Some, following LXX, would read חֶלְקַת הַצֹּדִים, *ḥelḳath ha-çōdhīm*, "field of the crafty," i.e. "of the ambush." Thenius suggested ח׳ הַצָּרִים, *ḥelḳath ha-çārīm*, "field of the adversaries" (see also H. P. Smith, *ICC*, "Samuel," 271). Probably, however, the text as it stands is correct.

W. Ewing

HELKIAS, hel-kī'as (חִלְקִיָּה, *ḥilḳīyāh;* **Χελκίας,** *Chelkías;* AV **Chelcias**):

(1) Father of Susanna (Sus vs 2.29.63). According to tradition he was brother of Jeremiah, and he is identified with the priest who found the Book of the Law in the time of Josiah (2 K **22** 8).

(2) Ancestor of Baruch (Bar **1** 1).

(3) Father of Joiakim the high priest (Bar **1** 7). The name represents Hilkiah (q.v.).

HELL, hel (see Sheol; Hades; Gehenna): The Eng. word, from a Teutonic root meaning "to hide" or "cover," had originally the significance of the world of the dead generally, and in this sense is used by Chaucer, Spenser, etc, and in the Creed ("He descended into hell"); cf ERV Preface. Now the word has come to mean almost exclusively the place of punishment of the lost or finally impenitent; the place of torment of the wicked. In AV of the Scriptures, it is the rendering adopted in many places in the OT for the Heb word *sh*ᵉ'*ōl* (in 31 out of 65 occurrences of that word it is so tr[d]), and in all places, save one (1 Cor **15** 55) in the NT, for the Gr word *Hades* (this word occurs 11 t; in 10 of these it is tr[d] "hell"; 1 Cor **15** 55 reads "grave," with "hell" in m). In these cases the word has its older general meaning, though in Lk **16** 23 (parable of Rich Man and Lazarus) it is specially connected with a place of "torment," in contrast with the "Abraham's bosom" to which Lazarus is taken (ver 22).

1. The Word in AV

In the above cases RV has introduced changes, replacing "hell" by "Sheol" in the passages in the OT (ERV retains "hell" in Isa **14** 9.15; ARV makes no exception), and by "Hades" in the passages in the NT (see under these words).

2. The Word in RV

Besides the above uses, and more in accordance with the modern meaning, the word "hell" is used in the NT in AV as the equivalent of Gehenna (12 t; Mt **5** 22.29; **10** 28, etc). RV in these cases puts "Gehenna" in m. Originally the Valley of Hinnom, near Jerus, Gehenna became among the Jews the synonym for the place of torment in the future life (the "Gehenna of fire," Mt **5** 22, etc; see Gehenna).

3. Gehenna

In yet one other passage in the NT (2 Pet **2** 4), "to cast down to hell" is used (AV and RV) to represent the Gr *tartaróō*, ("to send into Tartarus"). Here it stands for the place of punishment of the fallen angels: "spared not angels when they sinned, but cast them down to hell, and committed them to pits [or chains] of darkness" (cf Jude ver 6; but also Mt **25** 41). Similar ideas are found in certain of the Jewish apocalyptic books (Book of En, Book of Jub, Apoc Bar, with apparent reference to Gen **6** 1-4; cf Eschatology of the OT).

4. Tartarus

On the theological aspect, see Punishment, Everlasting. For literature, see references in above-named arts., and cf art. "Hell" by Dr. D. S. Salmond in *HDB*.

James Orr

HELLENISM, hel'en-iz'm, **HELLENIST,** hel'en-ist: Hellenism is the name we give to the manifold achievements of the Greeks in social and political institutions, in the various arts, in science and philosophy, in morals and religion. It is customary to distinguish two main periods, between which stands the striking figure of Alexander the Great, and to apply to the earlier period the adj. "Hellenic," that of "Hellenistic" to the latter. While there is abundant reason for making this distinction, it must not be considered as resting upon fortuitous changes occasioned by foreign influences. The Hellenistic age is rather the sudden unfolding of a flower whose bud was forming and maturing for centuries.

1. The Expansion of the Greek Peoples

Before the coming of the Hellenic peoples into what we now call Greece, there existed in those lands a flourishing civilization to which we may give the name "Aegean." The explorations of archaeologists during the last few decades have brought it to light in many places on the continent, as well as on the islands of the Aegean and notably in Crete. When the Hellenic peoples came, it was not as a united nation, nor even as homogeneous tribes of a common race; though without doubt predominantly of kindred origin, it was the common possession of an Aryan speech and of similar customs and religion that marked them off from the peoples among whom they settled. When their southward movement from Illyria occurred, and by what causes it was brought about, we do not know; but it can hardly have long antedated the continuance of this migration which led to the settlement of the coast districts of Asia Minor and the islands of the Aegean from about the 13th to the 10th cents. BC. In the colonization of these new territories the Hellenic peoples became conscious of their kinship, partly because the several colonies received contingents from various regions of the motherland, partly because they were in common brought into striking contrast to the alien "Barbarians" who spoke other unintelligible languages. As the older communities on the mainland and on the islands began to flourish, they felt the need, arising from various causes, for further colonization. Among these causes we may mention the poverty of the soil in Greece proper, the restricting pressure of the strong tribes of Asia Minor who prevented expansion inland, a growing disaffection with the aristocratic régime in almost all Gr states and with the operation of the law of primogeniture in land tenure, and lastly the combined lure of adventure and the prospect of trade. Thus it came about that in the 8th and 7th cents. BC, two great movements of colonial expansion set in, one toward the Hellespont and to the shores of the Pontus, or Black Sea, beyond, the other westward toward Southern Italy, Sicily, and beyond as far as Gades in Spain. To the 7th cent. belongs also the colonization of Naucratis in Egypt and of Cyrene in Libya. Then followed a period of relative inactivity during the 5th cent., which was marked by the desperate conflict of the Greeks with Persia in the E. and with Carthage in the W., succeeded by even more disastrous conflicts among themselves. With the enforced internal peace imposed by Macedonia came the resumption of colonial and military expansion in a measure before undreamed of. In a few years the empire of Alexander embraced Thrace, Asia Minor, Egypt, and Asia eastward beyond the Indus. The easternmost regions soon fell away, but Asia Minor, Syria and Egypt long continued under Gr rule, until Rome in the 1st cent. BC made good her claims to sovereignty in those lands.

Throughout this course of development and expansion we speak of the people as Greeks, although it is evident that even such racial homogeneity as they may have had on coming into Greece must have been greatly modified by the absorption of conquered peoples. But the strong individuality of the Hellenic population manifested itself everywhere in its civilization. In the evolution from the Homeric kingship (supported by the nobles in council, from which the commonalty was excluded, or where it was supposed at most to express assent or dissent to proposals laid before it) through oligarchic or aristocratic rule and the usurped authority of the tyrants, to the establishment of democratic government, there is nothing surprising to the man of today. That is because Gr civilization has become typical of all western civilization. In the earlier stages of this process, moreover, there is nothing strikingly at variance with the institutions of the Hebrews, at least so far as concerns the outward forms. But there existed throughout a subtle difference of spirit which made it possible, even inevitable, for the Greeks to attain to democratic institutions, whereas to the Hebrews such a development was impossible, if not unthinkable. It is difficult to define this spirit, but one may say that it was marked from the first by an inclination to permit the free development and expression of individuality subordinated to the common good; by a corresponding recognition of human limitations over against one's fellow-man as over against Deity; by an instinctive dread of excess as inhuman and provoking the just punishment of the gods; and lastly by a sane refusal to take oneself too seriously, displaying itself in a certain good-humored irony even among men who, like Socrates and Epicurus, regarded themselves as charged with a sublime mission, in striking contrast with the Heb prophets who voiced the thunders of Sinai, but never by any chance smiled at their own earnestness. Even the Macedonians did not attempt to rule Greece with despotic sway, leaving the states in general in the enjoyment of their liberties; and in the Orient, Alexander and his successors, Rom as well as Gr, secured their power and extended civilization by the foundation and encouragement of Hellenic cities in extraordinary numbers. The city-state, often confederated with other city-states, displaced the organization of tribe or clan, thus substituting a new unit and a new interest for the old; and the centers thus created radiated Hellenic influence and made for order and good government everywhere. But in accordance with the new conditions the state took on a somewhat different form. While the city preserved local autonomy, the state became monarchical; and the oriental deification of the king reinforced by the Hellenic tendency to deify the benefactors of mankind, eventuated in modes of speech and thought which powerfully influenced the Messianic hopes of the Jews.

2. The Hellenic State

The life of the Greeks, essentially urban and dominated by political interests fostered in states in which the individual counted for much, was of a type wholly different from the oriental. Although the fiction of consanguinity was cultivated by the Hellenic city-state as by the Sem tribe, it was more transparent in the former, particularly in the newer communities formed in historical times. There was thus a powerful stimulus to mutual tolerance and concession which, supported as it was by the strong love of personal independence and the cultivation of individuality, led to the development of liberty and the recognition of the rights of man. A healthy social life was the result for those who shared the privileges of citizenship, and also, in hardly less degree, for those resident aliens who received the protection of the state. Women also, though not so free as men, enjoyed, even at Athens where they were most limited, liberties unknown to the Orientals. In the Hellenistic age they attained a position essentially similar to that of modern Europe. There were slaves belonging both to individuals and the state, but their lot was mitigated in general by a steadily growing humanity. The amenities of life were many, and were cultivated no less in the name of religion than of art, literature, and science.

3. Hellenic Life

As in every phase of Gr civilization, the development of art and letters was free. Indeed their supreme excellence must be attributed to the happy circumstances which suffered them to grow spontaneously from the life of the people without artificial constraints imposed from within, or overpowering influences coming from without: a fortune which no other great movement in art or letters can boast. Gr art was largely developed in the service of religion; but owing to the circumstance that both grew side by side, springing from the heart of man, their reactions were mutual, art contributing to religion quite as much as it received. The creative genius of the Hellenic people expressed itself with singular directness and simplicity in forms clearly visualized and subject to the conditions of psychologically effective grouping in space or time. Their art is marked by the observance of a just proportion and by a certain natural restraint due to the preponderance of the intellectual element over the purely sensuous. Its most characteristic product is the ideal type in which only enough individuality enters to give to the typical the concreteness of life. What has been said of art in the narrower sense applies equally to artistic letters. The types thus created, whether in sculpture, architecture, music, drama, history, or oratory, though not regarded with superstitious reverence, commended themselves by the sheer force of inherent truth and beauty to succeeding generations, thus steadying the course of development and restraining the exuberant originality and the tendency to individualism. In the Hellenistic age, individualism gradually preponderated where the lessening power of creative genius did not lead to simple imitation.

4. Hellenic Art and Letters

The traditional views of the Hellenic peoples touching Nature and conduct, which did not differ widely from those of other peoples in a corresponding stage of culture, maintained themselves down to the 7th cent. BC with comparatively little change. Along with and following the colonial expansion of Hellenism there came the awakening intellectual curiosity, or rather the shock of surprise necessary to convert attention into question. The mythology of the Greeks had contained a vague theology, without authority indeed, but satisfactory because adequate to express the national thought. Ethics there was none, morality being customary. But the extending horizon of Hellenic thought discovered that customs differed widely in various lands; indeed, it is altogether likely that the collection of strange and shocking customs which filled the quivers of the militant Sophists in the 5th cent. had its inception in the 6th and possibly the 7th cent. At any rate it furnished the fiery darts of the adversary until ethics was founded in reason by the quest of Socrates for the universal, not in conduct, but in judgment. As ethics arose out of the irreconcilable contradictions of conduct, so natural philosophy sprung from the contradictions of mythical theology and in opposition to it. There were in fact two strata of conceptions touching supernatural beings; one, growing out of a primitive animism, regarded their operations essentially from the point of view of magic, which refuses to be surprised at any result, be it never so ill-proportioned to the means em-

5. Philosophy of Nature and of Conduct

ployed, so long as the mysterious word was spoken or the requisite act performed; the other, sprung from a worship of Nature in her most striking phenomena, recognized an order, akin to the moral order, in her operations. When natural philosophy arose in the 6th cent., it instinctively at first, then consciously, divested Nature of personality by stripping off the disguise of myth and substituting a plain and reasoned tale founded on mechanical principles. This is the spirit which pervades pre-Socratic science and philosophy. The quest of Socrates for universally valid judgments on conduct directed thought to the laws of mind, which are teleological, in contradistinction to the laws of matter, which are mechanical; and thus in effect dethroned Nature, regarded as material, by giving primacy to mind. Henceforth Gr philosophy was destined, with relatively few and unimportant exceptions, to devote itself to the study of human conduct and to be essentially idealistic, even where the foundation, as with the Stoics, was ostensibly materialistic. More and more it became true of the Gr philosophers that they sought God, "if haply they might feel after him and find him," conscious of the essential unity of the Divine and the human, and defining philosophy as the endeavor to assimilate the soul to God.

6. Hellenic and Hellenistic Religion

The Homeric poems present a picture of Gr life as seen by a highly cultivated aristocratic society having no sympathy with the commonalty. Hence we are not to regard Homeric religion as the religion of the Hellenic peoples in the Homeric age. Our first clear view of the Hellenic commoner is presented by Hesiod in the 8th cent. Here we find, alongside of the worship of the Olympians, evidences of chthonian cults and abundant hints of human needs not satisfied by the well-regulated religion of the several city-states. The conventionalized monarchy of Zeus ruling over his fellow-Olympians is known to be a fiction of the poets, having just as much—no more—foundation, in fact, as the mythical overlordship of Agamemnon over the assembled princes of the Achaeans; while it caught the imagination of the Greeks and dominated their literature, each city-state possessed its own shrines sacred to its own gods, who might or might not be called by the names of Olympians. Yet the great shrines which attracted Greeks from every state, such as those of Zeus at Dodona (chiefly in the period before the 7th cent.) and Olympia, of Apollo at Delos and Delphi, and of Hera at Argos, were the favored abodes of Olympians. Only one other should be mentioned: that of Demeter at Eleusis. Her worship was of a different character, and the great repute of her shrine dates from the 5th cent. If the Zeus of Olympia was predominantly the benign god of the sky, to whom men came in joyous mood to delight him with pomp and festive gatherings, performing feats of manly prowess in the Olympic games, the Zeus of Dodona, and the Delphian Apollo, as oracular deities, were visited in times of doubt and distress. The 7th and 6th cents. mark the advent—or the coming into prominence—of deities whose appeal was to the deepest human emotions, of ecstatic enthusiasm, of fear, and of hope. Among them we must mention Dionysus, the god of teeming Nature (see DIONYSUS), and Orpheus. With their advent comes an awakening of the individual soul, whose aspiration to commune with Deity found little satisfaction in the general worship of the states. Private organizations and quasi-monastic orders, like those of the Orphics and Pythagoreans, arose and won countless adherents. Their deities found admission into older shrines, chiefly those of chthonian divinities, like that of Demeter at Eleusis, and wrought a change in the spirit and to a certain extent in the ritual of the "mysteries" practised there. It was in these "mysteries" that the Christian Fathers, according to the mood or the need, polemic or apologetic, of the moment, saw now the propaedeutic type, now the diabolically instituted counterfeit, of the sacraments and ordinances of the church. The spirit and even the details of the observances of the "mysteries" are difficult to determine; but one must beware of accepting the hostile judgments of Christian writers who were in fact retorting upon the Greeks criticisms leveled at the church: both were blinded by partisanship and so misread the symbols.

If we thus find a true *praeparatio evangelica* in the Hellenistic developments of earlier Hellenic religion, there are parallel developments in the other religions which were adopted in the Hellenistic age. The older national religions of Persia and Egypt underwent a similar change, giving rise respectively to the worship of Mithra and of Isis, both destined, along with the chthonian mysteries of the Greeks, to be dangerous rivals for the conquest of the world of Christianity, itself a younger son in this prolific family of new religions. Space is wanting here for a consideration of these religious movements, the family resemblance of which with Christianity is becoming every day more apparent; but so much at least should be said, that while every candid student must admit the superiority of Christianity in moral content and adaptation to the religious nature of man, the difference in these respects was not at first sight so obvious that the successful rival might at the beginning of the contest have been confidently predicted. See GREECE, RELIGION OF.

As with other manifestations of the Hellenic spirit, so, too, in matters of religion, it was the free development of living institutions that most strikingly distinguishes the Greeks from the Hebrews. They had priests, but were never ruled by them; they possessed a literature regarded with veneration, and in certain shrines treasured sacred writings containing directions for the practice and ritual of the cults, but they were neither intended nor suffered to fix for all time the interpretation of the symbols. In the 5th and 4th cents. the leaders of Gr thought rebuked the activity of certain priests, and it was not before the period of Rom dominion that priests succeeded even in a small measure in usurping power, and sacred writings began to exercise an authority remotely comparable to that recognized among the Jews.

A most interesting question is that concerning the extent to which Gr civilization and thought had penetrated and influenced Judaism. During three centuries before the advent of Jesus, Hellenism had been a power in Syria and Judaea. The earliest writings of the Hebrews showing this influence are Dnl and the OT Apoc. Several books of the Apoc were originally written in Gr, and show strong influence of Gr thought. The LXX, made for the Jews of the Dispersion, early won its way to authority even in Pal, where Aram. had displaced Heb, which thus became a dead language known only to a few. NT quotations of the OT are almost without exception taken from the LXX. Thus the sacred literature of the Jews was for practical purposes Gr. Though Jesus spoke Aram., He unquestionably knew some Gr. Yet there is no clear evidence of specifically Gr influence on this thought, the presuppositions of which are Jewish or generally those of the Hellenistic age. All the writings of the NT were originally composed in Gr, though their authors differed widely in the degree of proficiency in the use of the language and in acquaintance with Hellenic thought. Their debt to these sources can be profitably considered only in connection with the individual writers; but one who is acquainted with the Heb and Gr literature instinctively feels in reading the NT that the national character of the Jews, as reflected in the OT, has all but vanished, remaining only as a subtle tone of moral earnestness and as an imaginative coloring, except in the simple story of the Synoptic Gospels. But for the bitterness aroused by the destruction of Jerus, it is probable that the Jews would have yielded completely to Hellenic influences.

William Arthur Heidel

HELM, helm. See Ships.

HELMET, hel'met. See Arms, Armor.

HELON, hē'lon (חֵלֹן, *ḥēlōn*, "valorous"; LXX B, **Χαιλών**, *Chailōn*): The father of Eliab, the prince of the tribe of Zebulun (Nu **1** 9; **2** 7; **7** 24. 29; **10** 16).

HELP: With the sense of that which brings aid, support, or deliverance, "help" (noun and vb.) represents a large variety of words in Heb and Gr (noun 7, vb. 16). A principal Heb word is עָזַר, *'āzar*, "to help," with the corresponding nouns עֵזֶר, *'ēzer*, עֶזְרָה, *'ezrāh;* a chief Gr word is *βοηθέω*, *boēthéō* (Mt **15** 25; Mk **9** 22.24, etc). True help is to be sought for in Jeh, in whom, in the OT, the believer is constantly exhorted to trust, with the renouncing of all other confidences (Ps **20** 2; **33** 20; **42** 5; **46** 1; **115** 9.10.11; **121** 2; Isa **41** 10. 13.14, etc). In Rom **8** 26 it is said, "the Spirit also helpeth our infirmity," the vb. here (*sunantilambánetai*) having the striking meaning of to "take hold along with one." In the story of Eden, Eve is spoken of as "a help meet" for Adam (Gen **2** 18.20). The idea in "meet" is not so much "suitability," though that is implied, as likeness, correspondence in nature (Vulg *similem sibi*). One like himself, as taken from him, the woman would be an aid and companion to the man in his tasks.

James Orr

HELPMEET, help'mēt. See Help.

HELPS (**ἀντιλήμψεις**, *antilēmpseis*, 1 Cor **12** 28): In classical Gr the word *antilēmpsis* means "remuneration," the hold one has on something, then perception, apprehension. But in Bib. Gr it has an altruistic meaning. Thus it is used in the LXX, both in the OT Scriptures and in the Apocrypha (Ps **22** 19; **89** 19; 1 Esd **8** 27; 2 Macc **15** 7). Thus we obtain a clue to its meaning in our text, where it has been usually understood as referring to the *deacons*, the following word *kubernēseis*, tr[d] "governments," being explained as referring to the presbyters.

Henry E. Dosker

HELPS (**βοήθειαι**, *boētheiai*, Acts **27** 17). See Ships and Boats, III, 2.

HELVE, helv (עֵץ, *'ēç*, "wood," "tree"): The handle or wooden part of an ax. "The head [m "iron"] slippeth from the helve" (m "tree," Dt **19** 5). The marginal reading suggests that "the ax is supposed to glance off the tree it is working on."

HEM (**κράσπεδον**, *kráspedon*): The classic instance of the use of "hem" in the NT is Mt **9** 20 AV (cf **14** 36), where the woman "touched the hem of his [Christ's] garment." The reference is to the fringe or tassel with its traditional blue thread which the faithful Israelite was directed to wear on the corners of the outer garment (Nu **15** 37 ff; Dt **22** 12). Great importance came to be attached to it, the ostentatious Pharisees making it very broad or large (Mt **23** 5). Here the woman clearly thought there might be peculiar virtue in touching the tassel or fringe of Jesus' garment. Elsewhere the word is rendered Border (q.v.). See also Dress; Fringe.

Geo. B. Eager

HEMAM, hē'mam (Gen **36** 22 AV and ERV). See Heman; Homam.

HEMAN, hē'man (הֵימָן, *hēmān*, "faithful"): The name of two men in the OT.

(1) A musician and seer, a Levite, son of Joel and grandson of the prophet Samuel; of the family of the Kohathites (1 Ch **6** 33), appointed by David as one of the leaders of the temple-singing (1 Ch **15** 17; 2 Ch **5** 12). He had 14 sons (and 3 daughters) who assisted their father in the chorus. Heman seems also to have been a man of spiritual power; is called "the king's seer in matters of God" (1 Ch **25** 5; 2 Ch **35** 15).

(2) One of the noted wise men prior to, or about, the time of Solomon. He was one of the three sons of Mahol (1 K **4** 31 [Heb **5** 11]); also called a son of Zerah (1 Ch **2** 6).

Ps **88** is inscribed to Heman the Ezrahite, who is probably to be identified with the second son of Zerah.

Edward Babgy Pollard

HEMATH, hē'math. See Hammath (1 Ch **2** 55).

HEMDAN, hem'dan (חֶמְדָּן, *ḥemdān*, "pleasant"): A descendant of Seir, the Horite (Gen **36** 26). Wrongly tr[d] "Amram" by AV in 1 Ch **1** 41 (RV "Hamran"), where the transcribers made an error in one vowel and one consonant, writing *ḥamrān* (חַמְרָן), instead of *ḥemdān* (חֶמְדָּן).

HEMLOCK, hem'lock. See Gall.

HEN, hen (חֵן, *ḥēn*, "favor"). In Zec **6** 14, EV reads, "And the crowns shall be to Helem . . . . and to Hen the son of Zephaniah." But as this person is called Josiah in ver 10, RVm "and for the kindness of the son of Zephaniah" is probably right, but the text is uncertain. See Josiah.

HEN (**ὄρνις**, *órnis*): Mentioned in the accounts of the different disciples in describing the work of Jesus (Mt **23** 37; Lk **13** 34).

HENA, hē'na (הֵנַע, *hēna'*; **'Ανά**, *Aná*): Named in 2 K **19** 13, as one of the cities destroyed by Sennacherib along with Sepharvaim. It does not appear in a similar connection in **17** 24. The text is probably corrupt. No reasonable identification has been proposed. Cheyne (*EB*, s.v.) says of the phrase "Hena and Ivah" that "underlying this is a witty editorial suggestion that the existence of cities called הנע and עוה respectively has passed out of mind (cf Ps **9** 6[7]), for הֵנַע וְעִוָּה, *hēna' w^e'iwwāh*, clearly means 'he has driven away and overturned' (so Tg, Sym)." He would drop out הנע. Hommel (*Expos T*, IX, 330) thinks that here we have divine names; Hena standing for the Arab. star-name *al-han'a*, and Ivvah for *al-'awwā'u*. See Ivah.

W. Ewing

HENADAD, hen'a-dad (חֵנָדָד, *ḥēnādhādh*, "favor of Hadad"; LXX **'Ηναάδ**, *Hēnaád;* **'Ηναδάδ**, *Hēnadád;* **'Ηναδάβ**, *Hēnadáb;* **'Ηναλάβ**, *Hēnaláb* [Ezr **3** 9; Neh **3** 18.24; **10** 9]): One of the heads of the Levites in the post-exilic community.

HENNA, hen'a (Cant **1** 14; **4** 13): An aromatic plant.

HENOCH, hē'nok (חֲנֹךְ, *ḥănōkh;* **'Ενώχ**, *Henōch;* in 1 Ch **1** 3 AV RV, "Enoch"; in Gen **25** 4, AV and RV "Hanoch"; 1 Ch **1** 33, AV "Henoch," RV "Hanoch"): The name of a Midianite, a descendant of Abram.

HEPHER, hē'fēr, **HEPHERITES,** hē'fēr-īts (חֵפֶר, *ḥēpher*, חֶפְרִי, *ḥephrī*):

(1) LXX Ὄφερ, *Hópher* (Nu **26** 32 f; **27** 1; Josh **17** 2 f), the head of a family or clan of the tribe of Manasseh. The clan is called the **Hepherites** in Nu **26** 32.

(2) LXX Ἡφάλ, *Hēphál* (1 Ch **4** 6), a man of Judah.

(3) LXX Ὄφερ, *Hópher* (1 Ch **11** 36), one of David's heroes.

HEPHER (חֵפֶר, *ḥēpher*):

(1) LXX Ὄφερ, *Hópher* (Josh **12** 17), a Canaanitish town mentioned between Tappuah and Aphek, unidentified.

(2) In 1 K **4** 10 a district connected with Socoh, and placed by Solomon under the direction of Ben-hesed of Arubboth, unidentified.

HEPHZIBAH, hef'zi-ba (חֶפְצִי־בָהּ, *ḥephçī-bhāh*, "my delight is in her"):

(1) LXX Ὀψειβά, *Hopseibá*, Ἀψειβά, *Hapseibá*, Ὀφσιβά, *Hophsibá*, the mother of Manasseh (2 K **21** 1).

(2) The new name of Zion (Isa **62** 4); LXX translates Θέλημα ἐμόν, *Thélēma emón*, "my delight."

HERAKLES, her'a-klēz (Ἡρακλῆς, *Hēraklḗs*). See HERCULES.

HERALD, her'ald: The word occurs once (Dnl **3** 4) as the tr of the Aram. word כָּרוֹז, *kārōz* (cf κήρυξ, *kḗrux*): "Then the herald cried aloud." See also GAMES.

HERB, hûrb, ûrb:

(1) יָרָק, *yārāḳ*, "green thing" (Ex **10** 15; Isa **15** 6); "a garden of herbs" (Dt **11** 10; 1 K **21** 2); "[a dinner, m portion of] herbs" (Prov **15** 17).

(2) עֵשֶׂב, *'ēsebh;* cf Arab. *'ushb*, "herbage," "grass," etc; "herbs yielding seed" (Gen **1** 11); "herbage" for food (Gen **1** 30; Jer **14** 6); trd "grass" (Dt **11** 15; Am **7** 2); "herbs" (Prov **27** 25, etc).

(3) דֶּשֶׁא, *deshe'*, trd "herb" (2 K **19** 26; Prov **27** 25; Isa **37** 27; **66** 14 AV), but generally GRASS (q.v.).

(4) חָצִיר, *ḥāçīr*, vegetation generally, but trd GRASS (q.v.).

(5) אֹרֹת, אוֹרוֹת, *'ōrōth* (pl. only), "green plants" or "herbs." In 2 K **4** 39 the Talm interprets it to mean "colewort," but it may mean any edible herbs which had survived the drought. In Isa **26** 19 the expression "dew of herbs" is in m trd "dew of light" which is more probable (see DEW), and the tr "heat upon herbs" (Isa **18** 4 AV) is in RV trd "clear heat in sunshine."

(6) βοτάνη, *botánē* (He **6** 7).

(7) λάχανα, *láchana*=*yārāḳ* (Mt **13** 32). See also BITTER HERBS. E. W. G. MASTERMAN

HERCULES, hûr'kū-lēz (Ἡρακλῆς, *Hēraklḗs*): The process of Hellenizing the Jews which began at an earlier date was greatly promoted under Antiochus Epiphanes (175–164 BC). Jason, who supplanted his brother Onias in the office of high priest by promising Antiochus an increase of tribute, aided the movement by setting up under the king's authority a Gr *palaestra* for the training of youth in Gr exercises, and by registering the inhabitants of Jerus as citizens of Antioch (2 Macc **4** 8 f). Certain of these Antiochians of Jerus Jason sent to Tyre, where games were held every five years in honor of Hercules, that is, the national Tyrian deity Melcart, identified with Baal of OT history. According to Jos (*Ant*, VII, v, 3) Hiram, king of Tyre in the days of Solomon, built the temple of Hercules and also of Astarte. Jason's deputies carried 300 drachmas of silver for the sacrifice of Hercules, but they were so ashamed of their commission that they "thought it not right to use the money for any sacrifice," and "on account of present circumstances it went to the equipment of the galleys" (2 Macc **4** 18–20). J. HUTCHISON

HERD, hûrd. See CATTLE.

HERDSMAN, hûrdz'man (בּוֹקֵר, *bōḳer;* AV, ERV "herdman"): A cowherd (Am **7** 14). The same word is used in Syria today. רֹעֶה, *rō'eh*, has its equivalent in the language of Syria and Pal (Arab. *ra'i*), and is a general term for any kind of a herdsman (Gen **13** 7.8; **26** 20; 1 S **21** 7). נֹקֵד, *nōḳēdh*, occurs in one passage (Am **1** 1); lit. it means one who spots or marks the sheep, hence a herdsman. Spotting the wool with different dyes is still the method of distinguishing between the sheep of different flocks. The herdsman is seldom the owner of the sheep, but a hireling. See SHEEP; SHEEP TENDING. JAMES A. PATCH

HERE, hēr, in composition:

Hereafter, hēr-aft'ēr (here [this present] and after) represents Heb *'āḥar*, "hinder part," "end" (Isa **41** 23), "the things that are to come hereafter" (*'āḥōr* after, behind the present), with *dēn*, "this," *'aḥărē dhēn*, Aram. (Dnl **2** 29.45), *'aḥar*, "after," "behind," "last" (Ezk **20** 39), Gr *ap' árti*, "from now" (Mt **26** 64), "Hereafter ye shall see the Son of man sitting on the right hand of power, and coming in the clouds of heaven," which does not mean "at a future time," according to the more modern usage of "hereafter," but (as the Gr) "from now," RV "henceforth"; Tindale and the chief VSS after him have "hereafter," but Wiclif has "fro hennes forth." Jn **1** 51, "Hereafter ye shall see the heaven opened," etc, where "hereafter" has the same meaning; it is omitted by RV after a corrected text (Wiclif also omits); *éti*, "yet," "still," "any more," "any longer" (Jn **14** 30, RV "I will no more speak much with you," Wiclif, "now I schal not"); *mēkéti*, "no more," "no longer" (Mk **11** 14, "no man eat fruit of thee hereafter," RV "henceforward"); *apó toú nún*, "from now" (Lk **22** 69, RV "From henceforth shall the Son of man be seated at the right hand of the power of God," Wiclif "aftir this tyme"); *metá taúta* (Jn **13** 7, "Thou shalt know [RV "understand"] hereafter," Wiclif "aftirward").

Hereby, hēr-bī', represents *beẓō'th*, "in or by this" (Gen **42** 15, "Hereby ye shall be proved"); *ek toútou*, "out of this" (1 Jn **4** 6, RV "by this"); *en toútō*, "in this," "by this means" (1 Cor **4** 4; 1 Jn **2** 3.5; **3** 16.19.24; **4** 2.13).

Herein, hēr-in', Heb *beẓō'th*, "in" or "by this" (Gen **34** 22, RV "on this condition"); *en toútō* (Jn **4** 37; **9** 30; **15** 8; Acts **24** 16; 2 Cor **8** 10; 1 Jn **4** 10.17).

Hereof, hēr-ov', Gr *haútē*, "this" (Mt **9** 26); *hoútos*, "this" (He **5** 3, RV "thereof").

Heretofore, hēr-tōō-fōr', Heb *temōl*, "yesterday," "neither heretofore, nor since" (Ex **4** 10; cf **5** 7.8. 14; Josh **3** 4; Ruth **2** 11); *'ethmōl shilshōm*, "yesterday," "third day" (1 S **4** 7, "There hath not been such a thing heretofore."

Hereunto, hēr-un-tōō', Gr *eis toúto*, "unto," "with a view to this" (1 Pet **2** 21, "For hereunto were ye called"): "hereunto" is supplied (Eccl **2**

25, "Who else can hasten hereunto more than I," RV "who can have enjoyment," m "hasten thereto").

Herewith, hēr-with′, Heb *bā-zō'th*, *b^{e}zō'th*, "in," "by," or "with this" (Ezk **16** 29; Mal **3** 10, "Prove me now herewith, saith Jeh").

RV has "herein" for "to do this" (Ezr **4** 22); for "in these things" (Rom **14** 18); "of them that have sinned heretofore" for "which have sinned already" (2 Cor **12** 21); "hereunto" for "thereunto" (1 Pet **3** 9); "herewith" for "thus" (Lev **16** 3).

W. L. Walker

HEREDITY, hē-red′i-ti: Heredity, in modern language, is the law by which living beings tend to repeat their characteristics, physiological and psychical, in their offspring, a law familiar in some form to even the most uncultured peoples. The references to it in the Bible are of various kinds.

1. Physiological Heredity

Curiously enough, little mention is made of physiological heredity, even in so simple a form as the resemblance of a son to his father, but there are a few references, such as, e.g., those to giants with giants for sons (2 S **21** 18–22; 1 Ch **20** 4–8; cf Gen **6** 4; Nu **13** 33; Dt **1** 28, etc). Moreover Dt **28** 59–61 may contain a thought of hereditary diseases (cf 2 K **5** 27). On the psychical side the data are almost equally scanty. That a son and his father may differ entirely is taken for granted and mentioned repeatedly (esp. in Ezk **18** 5–20). Even in the case of the king, the frequent changes of dynasty prevented such a phrase as "the seed royal" (2 K **11** 1; Jer **41** 1) from being taken very seriously. Yet, perhaps, the inheritance of mechanical dexterity is hinted at in Gen **4** 20–22, if "father" means anything more than "teacher." But, in any case, the fact that "father" could have this metaphorical sense, together with the corresponding use of "son" in such phrases as "son of Belial" (Jgs **19** 22 AV), "son of wickedness" (Ps **89** 22), "sons of the prophets" (Am **7** 14 m, etc), "son of the wise, ... of ancient kings" (Isa **19** 11; this last phrase may be meant literally), shows that the inheritance of characteristics was a very familiar fact. See Son.

2. Hebrew Conception of Heredity

The question, however, is considerably complicated by the intense solidarity that the Hebrews ascribed to the family. The individual was felt to be only a link in the chain, his "personality" (very vaguely conceived) somehow continuing that of his ancestors and being continued in that of his descendants. After death the happiness (or even existence; see Death) of this shade in the other world depended on the preservation of a posterity in this. Hence slaying the sons of a dead man was thought to affect him directly, and it would be a great mistake to suppose that an act such as that of 2 S **21** 1–9, etc, was simply to prevent a blood-feud. Nor was it at all in point that the children might repeat the qualities of the father, however much this may have been realized in other connections. Consequently, it is impossible to tell in many cases just how much of a modern heredity idea is present.

The most important example is the conception of the position of the nations. These are traced back to single ancestors, and in various cases the qualities of the nation are explained by those of the ancestor (Gen **9** 22–27; **21** 20.21; **49**, etc). The influences that determine national characteristics are evidently thought to be hereditary, and yet not all of them are hereditary in our sense; e.g. in Gen **27**, the condition of the descendants of Jacob and Esau is conceived to have been fixed by the nature of the blessings (mistakenly) pronounced by Isaac. On the other hand, Ezra (**9** 11.12) thinks of the danger of intermarrying with the children of a degenerate people in an entirely modern style, but in Dt **23** 3–6 the case is not so clear. There a curse pronounced on the nations for their active hostility is more in point than moral degeneracy (however much this may be spoken of elsewhere, Nu **25** 1–3, etc), and it is on account of the curse that the taint takes ten generations to work itself out, while, in the case of Edomite or Egyp blood, purity was attained in three. Hence it is hard to tell just how Ex **20** 5.6 was interpreted. The modern conception of the effect of heredity was surely present in part, but there must have been also ideas of the extension of the curse-bearing individuality that we should find hard to understand.

3. Abraham's Children

The chiefest question is that of the Israelites. Primarily they are viewed as the descendants of Abraham, blessed because he was blessed (Gen **22** 15–18, etc). This was taken by many with the utmost literalness, and physical descent from Abraham was thought to be sufficient (esp. Mt **3** 9; Jn **8** 31–44; Rom **9** 6–13), or at least necessary (esp. Ezr **2** 59; **9** 2; Neh **7** 61), for salvation. Occasionally this descent is stated to give superior qualities in other regards (Est **6** 13). But a distinction between natural inheritance of Abraham's qualities and the blessing bestowed by God's unbounded favor and decree on his descendants must have been thoroughly recognized, otherwise the practice of proselytizing would have been impossible.

4. Heredity and the NT

In the NT the doctrine of original sin, held already by a certain school among the Jews (2 Esd **7** 48), alone raises much question regarding heredity (cf 1 Cor **7** 14). Otherwise the OT concepts are simply reversed: where likeness of nature appears, there is (spiritual) descent (Rom **4** 12; Gal **3** 7, etc). None the less, that the Israel "after the flesh" has a real spiritual privilege is stated explicitly (Rom **3** 1.2; **11** 26; Rev **11** 13). See Blessing; Curse; Family; Salvation; Sin; Tradition.

Burton Scott Easton

HERES, hē′rēz, hē′res:

(1) הַר־חֶרֶס, *har-ḥereṣ*, "Mount Heres" (Jgs **1** 34 f), a district from which the Amorites were not expelled; it is mentioned along with Aijalon and Shaalbim. In Josh **19** 41 f we have then two towns in association with Ir-shemesh and many authorities consider that as *ḥereṣ*=*shemesh*, i.e. the sun, and הַר, *har*, being perhaps a copyist's error for עִיר, *'ir*, "city," we have in Jgs **1** 34 a reference to Beth-shemesh, the modern *'Ain Shems*. Conder thinks that *Batn Harâsheh*, N.E. of Aijalon, a prominent hill, may be the place referred to. Budde thinks Har-heres may be identified with the Bit-Ninib (Ninib being the fierce morning sun) of the Am Tab; this place was in the district of Jerus.

(2) מַעֲלֵה הֶחָרֶס, *ma'ălēh he-ḥāreṣ*, "the ascent of Heres" (Jgs **8** 13, AV "before the sun *was up*"), the place from which Gideon returned to Succoth after his defeat of Zebah and Zalmunna. RV is probably a great improvement on AV, but both the text and the topography are uncertain.

(3) עִיר הַחֶרֶס, *'īr ha-ḥereṣ*, "City of Heres" EVm, "City of Destruction" (חֶרֶם, *ḥerem*) EV, or "City of the sun" (חֶרֶס, *ḥereṣ*) EVm. This is the name of one of the "five cities in the land of Egypt that speak the language of Canaan, and swear to Jeh of hosts" (Isa **19** 18). See Ir-ha-heres.

E. W. G. Masterman

HERESH, hē′resh (חֶרֶשׁ, *ḥeresh*; LXX B, Ῥαραιήλ, *Rharaiēl*, A, Ἀρές, *Harés*): A Levite (1 Ch **9** 15).